THE PHILOSOPHER'S INDEX

1990 CUMULATIVE EDITION

Special Editions

The Philosopher's Index: A Retrospective Index to U.S. Publications from 1940 includes approximately 15,000 articles from U.S. journals published during 1940 – 1966, and approximately 5,000 books published during 1940–1976. Supported by NEH Grant RT-23984-76-375.

Published in April 1978. 1619 pages. Hardbound in three volumes. $295 (Individuals: $130). ISBN 0-912632-09-7.

The Philosopher's Index: A Retrospective Index to Non-U.S. English Language Publications from 1940 includes approximately 12,000 articles published during 1940 – 1966, and approximately 5,000 philosophy books published during 1940 – 1978. Supported by NEH Grant RT-27265-77-1360.

Published in April 1980. 1265 pages. Hardbound in three volumes. $280 (Individuals: $120). ISBN 0-912632-12-7.

THE PHILOSOPHER'S INDEX

*An International Index
To Philosophical Periodicals and Books*

1990 CUMULATIVE EDITION
VOLUME XXIV

PHILOSOPHY
DOCUMENTATION
CENTER

BOWLING GREEN STATE UNIVERSITY, Bowling Green, **OH. 43403-0189, U.S.A.**

PHILOSOPHY DOCUMENTATION CENTER

The mission of the Philosophy Documentation Center is to serve philosophers, students, and others by providing them with reliable information, quality products and needed services.

Director

Richard H. Lineback

Editorial Board

Peter Caws
George Washington University
Vere Chappell
University of Massachusetts
Richard De George
University of Kansas
Alan Donagan
California Institute of Technology
Jude P. Dougherty
Catholic University of America
Allan Gotthelf
Trenton State College
Adolf Grünbaum
University of Pittsburgh

Jaakko Hintikka
Boston University
David Hoekema
University of Delaware
Jerome Shaffer
University of Connecticut
Patrick Suppes
Stanford University
Robert G. Turnbull
Ohio State University
Gilbert Varet
University of Besançon
Christian Wenin
University of Louvain

Advisory Board

From the faculty of Bowling Green State University

Thomas Attig
Professor of Philosophy
Joseph L. Gray III
Professor of German
Boleslav Povsic
Professor of Latin

V. Frederick Rickey
Professor of Mathematics
René Ruiz
Professor of Romance Languages

The Philosopher's Index

The Philosopher's Index (ISSN 0031-7993), a publication of the Philosophy Documentation Center, is a subject and author index with abstracts. Major philosophy journals in English, French, German, Spanish, and Italian are indexed, along with selected journals in other languages and related interdisciplinary publications. English language books and some books in other languages are also indexed. This periodical is published quarterly as a service to the philosophical community. Suggestions for improving this service are solicited and should be sent to the Editor.

Policies: Each number of the *Index* indexes the articles of journals and the books that are received in the months prior to its publication. The dates on the journals indexed vary due to dissimilar publishing schedules and to delays encountered in overseas mailing.

The following factors are weighed in selecting journals to be indexed: 1) the purpose of the journal, 2) its circulation, and 3) recommendations from members of the philosophic community. Articles in interdisciplinary journals are indexed only if they are related to philosophy.

Most of the journal articles and books cited in *The Philosopher's Index* can be obtained from the Bowling Green State University library, through the Inter-Library Loan Department. The library, though, requests that you first try to locate the articles and books through your local or regional library facilities.

Subscriptions should be mailed to *The Philosopher's Index*, Bowling Green State University, Bowling Green, Ohio 43403-0189. The 1991 subscription price (4 numbers) is $138 (Individuals $39). The price of single numbers, including back issues, is $38 (Individuals $12). An annual Cumulative Edition of *The Philosopher's Index* is published in the spring following the volume year.

THE PHILOSOPHER'S INDEX

Editor

Richard H. Lineback

Editorial Staff

Thomas Attig, Assistant Editor
  Bowling Green State University
Mark Christensen, Assistant Editor
  Bowling Green State University
Douglas D. Daye, Assistant Editor
  Bowling Green State University
Robert Goodwin, Assistant Editor
  Bowling Green State University

Brenda Jubin, Assistant Editor
  Yale University
Fred Miller, Assistant Editor
  Bowling Green State University
René Ruiz, Assistant Editor
  Bowling Green State University
Robert Wolf, Assistant Editor
  Southern Illinois University

Production Staff

Tina Amos, Production Specialist
Carolyn Lineback, Proofreader
Michael Novotny, Printing Technician
Cindy Richards, Editorial Secretary

Steve Shurts, Systems Analyst
Kathleen Tweney, Production Specialist
Janet Wilhelm, Subscription Manager

Table of Contents

Abbreviations of Periodicals Indexed

(*Journal is no longer indexed and/or published. However, the abbreviation is included here for use in conjunction with DIALOG.)

Abraxas*	Abraxas
Acta Phil Fennica	Acta Philosophica Fennica
Agora*	Agora
Agr Human Values	Agriculture and Human Values
Aitia	Aitia
Ajatus*	Ajatus
Aletheia*	Aletheia
Alg Log*	Algebra and Logic
Alg Ned Tijdschr Wijs	Algemeen Nederlands Tijdschrift voor Wijsbegeerte
Amer J Philo	American Journal of Philology
Amer J Theol Phil	American Journal of Theology & Philosophy
Amer Phil Quart	American Philosophical Quarterly
An Cated Suarez*	Anales de la Catedra Francisco Suarez
An Seminar Metaf	Anales del Seminario de Metafisica
Analisis Filosof	Analisis Filosofico
Analysis	Analysis
Ancient Phil	Ancient Philosophy
Ann Esth*	Annales D'Esthétique
Ann Fac Lett Filosof	Annali della Facolta di Lettere e Filosofia
Ann Univ Mariae Curie-Phil	Annales Universitatis Mariae Curie-Skłodowska, Sectio I/Philosophia-Sociologia
Annals Math Log	Annals of Mathematical Logic (see Annals Pure Applied Log)
Annals Pure Applied Log	Annals of Pure and Applied Logic (formerly Annals of Mathematical Logic)
Antioch Rev	Antioch Review
Anu Filosof	Anuario Filosofico
Apeiron	Apeiron
Applied Phil	Applied Philosophy (see Int J Applied Phil)
Aquinas	Aquinas
Arch Begriff*	Archiv für Begriffsgeschichte
Arch Filosof*	Archivio di Filosofia
Arch Gesch Phil	Archiv für Geschichte der Philosophie
Arch Math Log*	Archiv für Mathematische Logik und Grundlagen Forschung
Arch Phil	Archives de Philosophie
Arch Rechts Soz	Archiv für Rechts und Sozialphilosophie
Arch Stor Cult	Archivio di Storia della Cultura
Argumentation	Argumentation
Aris Soc	The Aristotelian Society: Supplementary Volume
Asian J Phil	The Asian Journal of Philosophy
Augustin Stud	Augustinian Studies
Augustinus	Augustinus
Auslegung	Auslegung
Austl J Phil	Australasian Journal of Philosophy
Behavior Phil	Behavior and Philosophy (formerly Behaviorism)
Behaviorism	Behaviorism (see Behavior Phil)
Berkeley News	Berkeley Newsletter
Between Species	Between the Species
Bigaku	Bigaku
Bijdragen	Bijdragen, Tijdschrift voor Filosofie en Theologie
Bioethics	Bioethics
Bioethics Quart	Bioethics Quarterly (see J Med Human)
Biol Phil	Biology & Philosophy
Boll Centro Stud Vichiani	Bollettino del Centro di Studi Vichiani
Boston Col Stud Phil*	Boston College Studies in Philosophy
Brahmavadin*	Brahmavadin
Bridges	Bridges: An Interdisciplinary Journal of Theology, Philosophy, History, and Science
Brit J Aes	The British Journal of Aesthetics
Brit J Phil Sci	British Journal for the Philosophy of Science
Bull Hegel Soc Gt Brit	Bulletin of the Hegel Society of Great Britain
Bull Santayana Soc	Overheard in Seville: Bulletin of the Santayana Society
Bull Sect Log	Bulletin of the Section of Logic
Bull Soc Fr Phil	Bulletin de la Société Française de Philosophie
Bus Prof Ethics J	Business & Professional Ethics Journal
Cad Hist Filosof Cie	Cadernos de História e Filosofia da Ciéncia
Can J Phil	Canadian Journal of Philosophy
Can J Theol*	Canadian Journal of Theology
Can Phil Rev	Canadian Philosophical Reviews
Chin Stud Hist Phil	Chinese Studies in History and Philosophy (see Chin Stud Phil)
Chin Stud Phil	Chinese Studies in Philosophy (formerly Chin Stud Hist Phil)
Cirpho*	Cirpho Review
Cl Quart*	The Classical Quarterly

Key to Abbreviations

List of Periodicals Indexed

Acta Philosophica Fennica. ISSN 0355-1792. (irr) Academic Bookstore, Keskuskatu 1, 00100 Helsinki, Finland

Agriculture and Human Values. ISSN 0889-048X. (q) Managing Editor, 370 ASB, University of Florida, Gainesville, FL 32611, USA

Aitia: Philosophy-Humanities Magazine. ISSN 0731-5880. (3 times a yr) Knapp Hall 15, SUNY at Farmingdale, Farmingdale, NY 11735, USA

Algemeen Nederlands Tijdschrift voor Wijsbegeerte. ISSN 0002-5275. (q) Van Gorcum, Postbus 43, 9400 AA Assen, The Netherlands

American Journal of Philology. ISSN 0002-9475. (q) The Johns Hopkins University Press, 701 West 40th Street, Suite 275, Baltimore, MD 21211, USA

American Journal of Theology & Philosophy. ISSN 0194-3448. (3 times a yr) W. Creighton Peden, Editor, Department of Philosophy, Augusta College, Augusta, GA 30910, USA

American Philosophical Quarterly. ISSN 0003-0481. (q) Philosophy Documentation Center, Bowling Green State University, Bowling Green, OH 43403-0189, USA

Anales del Seminario de Metafísicá. ISSN 0580-8650. (ann) Editor, Universidad Complutense, Noviciado 3, 28015 Madrid, Spain

Analisis Filosofico. ISSN 0326-1301. (semi-ann) Bulnes 642, 1176 Buenos Aires, Argentina

Analysis. ISSN 0003-2638. (q) Basil Blackwell, 108 Cowley Road, Oxford OX41JF, England (or 3 Cambridge Center, Cambridge, MA 02142, USA)

Ancient Philosophy. ISSN 0740-2007. (semi-ann) Prof. Ronald Polansky, Duquesne University, Pittsburgh, PA 15282, USA

Annales Universitatis Mariae Curie-Skłodowskiej, Sectio 1/Philosophia-Sociologia. ISSN 0137-2025. (ann) Biuro Wydawnictw, Uniwersytet Marii Curie-Skłodowskiej, Pl. Marii Curie-Skłodowskiej 5, 20-031 Lublin, Poland

Annali della Facolta di Lettere e Filosofia. Pubblicazioni dell'Università di Studi di Bari, Palazzo Ateneo, 70100 Bari, Italy

Annals of Pure and Applied Logic. ISSN 0168-0072. Elsevier Science Publishers, Box 211, 1000 AE Amsterdam, The Netherlands

Antioch Review. ISSN 0003-5769. (q) P.O. Box 148, Yellow Springs, OH 45387, USA

Anuario Filosofico. ISSN 0066-5215. Service de Publicaciones de la Universidad de Navarra, S.A. Edificio Bibliotecas, Campus Universitario, 31080 Pamplona, Spain

Apeiron: A Journal of Ancient Philosophy and Science. ISSN 0003-6390. (q) Academic Printing and Publishing, P.O. Box 4834, Edmonton, Alberta, Canada T6E 5G7

Aquinas. ISSN 0003-7362. (3 times a yr) Pontificia Universita Lateranense, Piazza S. Giovanni in Laterano 4, 00120 Città del Vaticano, Vatican City State

Archiv für Geschichte der Philosophie. ISSN 0003-9101. (3 times a yr) Walter de Gruyter, Genthiner Str. 13, 1000 Berlin 30, Germany

Archiv für Rechts und Sozialphilosophie. ISSN 0001-2343. (q) Franz Steiner Verlag Wiesbaden GmbH, P.O.B. 101526, D-7000 Stuttgart, Germany

Archives de Philosophie. ISSN 0003-9632. 72 rue des Saints-Pères, 75007 Paris, France

Archivio di Storia della Cultura. (ann) Morano Editore S.P.A., Vico S. Domenico Maggiore, 9-80134 Naples, Italy

Argumentation. ISSN 0920-427X. (q) Kluwer Academic Publishers, P.O. Box 358, Accord-Station, Hingham, MA 02018-0358, USA

The Aristotelian Society: Supplementary Volume. ISSN 0309-7013. (ann) Members: The Aristotelian Society, Department of Philosophy, Birkbeck College, University of London, Malet Street, London WC1E 7HX, England. Non-members: Basil Blackwell, 108 Cowley Road, Oxford OX4 1JF, England (or 3 Cambridge Center, Cambridge, MA 02142, USA)

The Asian Journal of Philosophy. (semi-ann) Prof. Tran Van Doan, Department of Philosophy, National Taiwan University, Roosevelt Road, Sec. 4, 10764 Taipei, Taiwan, Republic of China

Augustinian Studies. ISSN 0094-5323. (ann) Tolentine Hall, P.O. Box 98, Villanova University, Villanova, PA 19085, USA

Augustinus. ISSN 0004-802X. (q) P. José Oroz Reta, General Dávila 5, Madrid 28003, Spain

Auslegung: A Journal of Philosophy. ISSN 0733-4311. (semi-ann) Editors, Department of Philosophy, University of Kansas, Lawrence, KS 66045, USA

Australasian Journal of Philosophy. ISSN 0004-8402. (q) Robert Young, Editor, Department of Philosophy, La Trobe University, Bundoora, Victoria 3083, Australia

Behavior and Philosophy. (semi-ann) Boyd Printing, 49 Sheridan Avenue, Albany, NY 12210, USA

Berkeley Newsletter. ISSN 0332-026X. (ann) The Editor, Department of Philosophy, Trinity College, Dublin 2, Ireland

Between the Species: A Journal of Ethics. (q) Schweitzer Center, San Francisco Bay Institute, P.O. Box 254, Berkeley, CA 94701, USA

Bigaku. ISSN 0520-0962. (q) The Japanese Society for Aesthetics, c/o Faculty of Letters, University of Tokyo, Bunkyo-Ku, Tokyo, Japan

Bijdragen, Tijdschrift voor Filosofie en Theologie. ISSN 0006-2278. (q) Administratie Bijdragen, Krips Repro B.V., Postbus 106, 7940 AC Meppel, The Netherlands

Bioethics. ISSN 0269-9702. (q) Basil Blackwell, 108 Cowley Road, Oxford OX41JF, United Kingdom (or 3 Cambridge Center, Cambridge, MA 02142, USA)

Biology & Philosophy. ISSN 0169-3867. (q) Kluwer Academic Publishers, 101 Philip Drive, Norwell, MA 02061, USA

Bollettino del Centro di Studi Vichiani. ISSN 0392-7334. (ann) Bibliopolis, Edizioni di Filosofia e Scienze, SpA, Via Arangio Ruiz 83, 80122 Naples, Italy

Bridges: An Interdisciplinary Journal of Theology, Philosophy, History, and Science. ISSN 1042-2234. (semi-ann) Robert S. Frey, Editor, 5702 Yellow Rose Court, Columbia, MD 21045, USA

The British Journal of Aesthetics. ISSN 0007-0904. (q) Oxford University Press, Pinkhill House, Southfield Road, Eynsham, Oxford OX8 1JJ, England

British Journal for the Philosophy of Science. ISSN 0007-0882. (q) Oxford University Press, Pinkhill House, Southfield Road, Eynsham, Oxford OX8 1JJ, England

Bulletin de la Société Française de Philosophie. ISSN 0037-9352. (q) 12 rue Colbert, 75002 Paris, France

Bulletin of the Hegel Society of Great Britain. ISSN 0263-5232. (bi-ann) H. Williams, Department of International Politics, University College of Wales, Penglais Aberystwyth, Dyfed SY23 3DB, Great Britain

Bulletin of the Section of Logic.(q) Managing Editor, Grzegorz Malinowski, 8 Marca 8, 90-365 Lòdź, Poland

Business & Professional Ethics Journal. ISSN 0277-2027. (q) Center for Applied Philosophy, 243 Dauer Hall, University of Florida, Gainesville, FL 32611, USA

Cadernos de História e Filosofia da Ciéncia. ISSN 0101-3424. (semi-ann) Editor, Centro de Lógica-Unicamp, C.P. 6133, 13.081 Campinas, São Paulo, Brazil

Canadian Journal of Philosophy. ISSN 0045-5091. (q) University of Calgary Press, 2500 University Drive NW, Calgary, Alberta, Canada T2N 1N4

Canadian Philosophical Reviews. ISSN 0228-491X. (m) Academic Printing and Publishing, Box 4834, Edmonton, Alberta, Canada T6E 5G7

Chinese Studies in Philosophy. ISSN 0023-8627. (q) M.E. Sharpe, 80 Business Park Drive, Armonk, NY 10504, USA

Clio. ISSN 0884-2043. (q) Indiana University-Purdue University, Fort Wayne, IN 46805, USA

Cogito. ISSN 0950-8864. (3 times a yr) Carfax Publishing Company, P.O. Box 25, Abingdon, Oxfordshire OX14 3UE, England

Cognition: International Journal of Cognitive Science. ISSN 0010-0277. (m) Elsevier Science Publishers, P.O. Box 211, 1000 AE Amsterdam, The Netherlands

Communication and Cognition. ISSN 0378-0880. (q) Blandijnberg 2, B-9000 Gent, Belgium

Conceptus: Zeitschrift für Philosophie. ISSN 0010-5155. (3 times a yr) Verband der Wissenschaftlichen Gesellschaften, Oesterreichs, Lindengasse 37, A-1070 Vienna, Austria

Criminal Justice Ethics. ISSN 0731-129X. (semi-ann) The Institute for Criminal Justice Ethics, CUNY, John Jay College of Criminal Justice, 899 Tenth Avenue, New York, NY 10019, USA

Crítica: Revista Hispanoamericana de Filosofía. ISSN 0011-1503. (3 times a yr) Apartado 70-447, 04510 Mexico, DF, Mexico

Critical Inquiry. ISSN 0093-1896. (q) The University of Chicago, Wieboldt Hall 202, 1050 East 59th Street, Chicago, IL 60637, USA

Critical Review: An Interdisciplinary Journal. ISSN 0891-3811. (q) P.O. Box 14528, Dept. 26A, Chicago, IL 60614, USA

Critical Texts: A Review of Theory and Criticism. ISSN 0730-2304. (3 times a yr) Department of English and Comparative Literature, 602 Philosophy Hall, Columbia University, New York, NY 10027, USA

Cuadernos de Filosofía. ISSN 0590-1901. (semi-ann) Prof. Margarita Costa, Editor, Instituto de Filosofía, 25 de Mayo 217, 1002 Buenos Aires, Argentina

Darshan-Manjari: The Burdwan University Journal of Philosophy. (ann) Aminul Haque, Gopal Ch. Khan, Editors, Department of Philosophy, The University of Burdwan, Golabag, Burdwan 713104, India

De Philosophia. ISSN 0228-412X. Editor, Department of Philosophy, University of Ottawa, Ottawa, Ontario, Canada K1N 6N5

Deutsche Zeitschrift für Philosophie. ISSN 0012-1045. (m) VEB Deutscher Verlag der Wissenschaften, DDR-1080 Berlin, Germany

Dialectica: Revue Internationale de Philosophie de la Connaissance. ISSN 0012-2017. (q) P.O. Box 1081, CH-2501 Bienne, Switzerland

Dialectics and Humanism. ISSN 0324-8275. (q) Foreign Trade Enterprise, Ars Polona, Krakowskie Przedmieście 7, 00-068 Warsaw, Poland

Dialogo Filosofico. ISSN 0213-1196. (3 times a yr) Apartado 121, 28770 Colmenar Viejo, Madrid, Spain

Diálogos. ISSN 0012-2122 (semi-ann) Box 21572, UPR Station, Río Piedras, PR 00931, USA

Dialogue. ISSN 0012-2246. (semi-ann) Phi Sigma Tau, Department of Philosophy, Marquette University, Milwaukee, WI 53233, USA

Dialogue: Canadian Philosophical Review-Revue Canadienne de Philosophie. ISSN 0012-2173. (q) Prof. Steven Davis, Editor, Department of Philosophy, Simon Fraser University, Burnaby, British Columbia, Canada V5A 1S6

Diánoia. ISSN 0185-2450. (ann) Instituto de Investigaciones Filosóficas, Dirección del Anuario de Filosofía, Circuito Mtro. Mario de la Cueva, Ciudad de la Investigación en Humanidades, Coyoacán 04510, Mexico, DF, Mexico

Diogenes. ISSN 0392-1921. (q) Casalini Libri, 50014 Fiesole, Florence, Italy

Dionysius. ISSN 0705-1085. (ann) Department of Classics, Dalhousie University, Halifax, Nova Scotia, Canada B3H 3J5

Diotima. (ann) Hellenic Society for Philosophical Studies, 40 Hypsilantou Street, Athens 11521, Greece

Economics and Philosophy. ISSN 0266-2671. (semi-ann) Cambridge University Press, 40 West 20th Street, New York, NY 10011, USA (or The Edinburgh Building, Shaftesbury Road, Cambridge CB2 2RU, England)

Educação e Filosofia. ISSN 0102-6801. (semi-ann) Revista "Educação e Filosofia", Universidade Federal de Uberlândia, Av. Universitaria, 155 C.P. 593, Campus Santa Monica, 38.400 Uberlândia MG, Brazil

Educational Philosophy and Theory. ISSN 0013-1857. (semi-ann) D.N. Aspin, Editor, Faculty of Education, Monash University, Clayton, Victoria 3168, Australia

Educational Studies. ISSN 0013-1946. (q) Richard LaBrecque, Editor, 131 Taylor Education Building, University of Kentucky, Lexington, KY 40506-0001, USA

Educational Theory. ISSN 0013-2004. (q) Education Building, University of Illinois, 1310 South 6th Street, Champaign, IL 61820, USA

Eidos: The Canadian Graduate Journal of Philosophy. ISSN 0707-2287. (semi-ann) Editors, Department of Philosophy, University of Waterloo, Waterloo, Ontario, Canada N2L 3G1

Environmental Ethics: An Interdisciplinary Journal Dedicated to the Philosophical Aspects of Environmental Problems. ISSN 0163-4275. (q) Department of Philosophy, The University of North Texas, P.O. Box 13496, Denton, TX 76203-3496, USA

Epistemologia: An Italian Journal for the Philosophy of Science. (semi-ann) Tilgher-Genova s.a.s., via Assarotti 52, 16122 Genova, Italy

Erkenntnis: An International Journal of Analytic Philosophy. ISSN 0165-0106. Kluwer Academic Publishers, 101 Philip Drive, Norwell, MA 02061, USA

Espíritu. ISSN 0014-0716. (ann) Durán y Bas Nr 9, Apartado 1382, 08080 Barcelona, Spain

Estetika. ISSN 0014-1291. (q) Kubon & Sagner GmbH, Hess-Str 39/41, Postfach 34 01 08, D-8 München 34, Germany

Ethics: An International Journal of Social, Political, and Legal Philosophy. ISSN 0014-1704. (q) University of Chicago Press, P.O. Box 37005, Chicago, IL 60637, USA

Ethics and Medicine: A Christian Perspective on Issues in Bioethics. (3 times a yr) Rutherford House Periodicals, 127 Woodland Road, Wyncot, PA 19095, USA

Etudes. ISSN 0014-2263. (m) Jean-Yves Calvez, Rédacteur en chef, 14 rue d'Assas, 75006 Paris, France

Etyka. (semi-ann) Zaklad Etyki, Instytut Filozofii UW, Krakowskie Przedmescie 3, 00-326, Warsaw 64, Poland

Explorations in Knowledge. ISSN 0261-1376. (semi-ann) David Lamb, Sombourne Press, 294 Leigh Road, Chandlers Ford, Eastleigh, Hants SO5 3AU, Great Britain

Faith and Philosophy. ISSN 0739-7046. (q) Michael Peterson, Managing Editor, Asbury College, Wilmore, KY 40390, USA

Feminist Studies. ISSN 0046-3663. (3 times a yr) Claire G. Moses, Women's Studies Program, University of Maryland, College Park, MD 20742, USA

Filosofia. ISSN 0015-1823. (q) Piazzo Statuto 26, 10144 Turin, Italy

Filozoficky Casopis CSAV. ISSN 0015-1831. (bi-m) Kubon & Sagner GmbH, Hess-Str 39/41, Postfach 34 01 08, D-8 München 34, Germany

Filozofska Istraživanja. ISSN 0351-4706. Editor, Filozofski Fakultet, D. Salaja 3, p.p. 171, 41000 Zagreb, Yugoslavia

Franciscan Studies. ISSN 0080-5459. (ann) St. Bonaventure University, St. Bonaventure, NY 14778, USA

Free Inquiry. ISSN 0272-0701. (q) Paul Kurtz, Editor, Box 5, Central Park Station, Buffalo, NY 14215, USA

Freiburger Zeitschrift für Philosophie und Theologie. ISSN 0016-0725. (semi-ann) Editions St.-Paul, Perolles 42, CH-1700 Fribourg, Switzerland

Giornale Critico della Filosofia Italiana. ISSN 0017-0089. (q) LICOSA, SpA, Subscription Department, Via B. Fortini 120/10, 50125 Florence, Italy

Giornale di Metafisica. (3 times a yr) Tilgher-Genova s.a.s., via Assarotti 52, 16122 Genova, Italy

Gnosis: A Journal of Philosophic Interest. ISSN 0316-618X. (ann) Editor, Department of Philosophy, Concordia University, 1455 de Maisonneuve Boulevard West, Montreal, Quebec, Canada H3G 1M8

Graduate Faculty Philosophy Journal. ISSN 0093-4240. (semi-ann) Editor, Department of Philosophy, New School for Social Research, 65 Fifth Avenue, New York, NY 10003, USA

Grazer Philosophische Studien. ISSN 0165-9227. (ann) Humanities Press International, Atlantic Highlands, NJ 07716, USA

Gregorianum. ISSN 0017-4114. (q) 4 Piazza della Pilotta, 1-00187 Rome, Italy

Hastings Center Report. ISSN 0093-0334. (bi-m) The Hastings Center, 255 Elm Road, Briarcliff Manor, NY 10510, USA

Heidegger Studies. (ann) Duncker & Humblot GmbH, Postfach 41 03 29, 1000 Berlin 41, Germany

Hermathena: A Dublin University Review. ISSN 0018-0750. (semi-ann) The Editor, Trinity College, Dublin 2, Ireland

The Heythrop Journal. ISSN 0018-1196. (q) The Manager, 11 Cavendish Square, London W1M 0AN, England

History and Philosophy of Logic. ISSN 0144-5340. (semi-ann) Taylor & Francis, 4 John Street, London WC1N 2ET, England

History and Philosophy of the Life Sciences. ISSN 0391-9114. (semi-ann) Taylor & Francis, 1900 Frost Road, Suite 101, Bristol, PA 19007, USA (or Rankine Road, Basingstoke, Hants RG24 0PR, England)

History and Theory: Studies in the Philosophy of History. ISSN 0018-2656. (q) Julia Perkins, History and Theory, Wesleyan Station, Middletown, CT 06457, USA

History of European Ideas. ISSN 0191-6599. (bi-m) Pergamon Press, Headington Hill Hall, Oxford OX3 0BW, England

History of Philosophy Quarterly. ISSN 0740-0675. (q) Philosophy Documentation Center, Bowling Green State University, Bowling Green, OH 43403-0189, USA

History of Political Thought. ISSN 0143-781X. (q) Imprint Academic, 32 Haldon Road, Exeter EX4 4DZ, England

Hobbes Studies. (ann) Van Gorcum, P.O. Box 43, 9400 AA Assen, The Netherlands

Horizons Philosophiques. ISSN 0709-4469. (semi-ann) Service de l'Edition, College Edouard-Montpetit, 945 chemin Chambly, Longueuil, Quebec, Canada J4H 3M6

Human Studies: A Journal for Philosophy and the Social Sciences. ISSN 0163-8548. (q) Martinus Nijhoff Publishers, P.O. Box 322, 3300 AH Dordrecht, The Netherlands

The Humanist. ISSN 0018-7399. (bi-m) Lloyd L. Morain, Editor, American Humanist Assocation, 7 Harwood Drive, P.O. Box 146, Amherst, NY 14226-0146, USA

Hume Studies. ISSN 0319-7336. (semi-ann) Editor, Department of Philosophy, University of Western Ontario, London, Ontario, Canada N6A 3K7

Husserl Studies. ISSN 0167-9848. (q) Kluwer Academic Publishers, P.O. Box 322, 3300 AA Dordrecht, The Netherlands (or 101 Philip Drive, Norwell, MA 02061, USA)

Hypatia: A Journal of Feminist Philosophy. ISSN 0887-5367. (3 times a yr) Linda Lopez McAlister, Editor, University of South Florida, SOC 107, Tampa, FL 33620-8100, USA

Idealistic Studies: An International Philosophical Journal. ISSN 0046-8541. (3 times a yr) Walter Wright, Editor, Department of Philosophy, Clark University, Worcester, MA 01610, USA

Il Protagora. (semi-ann) via A. Gidiuli 19, 73100 Lecce, Italy

The Independent Journal of Philosophy. ISSN 0378-4789. (irr) George Elliott Tucker, Editor, 47 Van Winkle Street, Boston, MA 02124, USA

Indian Philosophical Quarterly. ISSN 0376-415X. The Editor, Department of Philosophy, University of Poona, Pune 411 007, India

Informal Logic. ISSN 0824-2577. (3 times a yr) Assistant to the Editors, Department of Philosophy, University of Windsor, Windsor, Ontario, Canada N9B 3P4

Inquiry: An Interdisciplinary Journal of Philosophy. ISSN 0020-174X. (q) Universitetsforlaget, P.O. Box 2959, Tøyen, 0608 Oslo 6, Norway

International Journal for Philosophy of Religion. ISSN 0020-7047. (q) Kluwer Academic Publishers, Distribution Centre, P.O. Box 322, 3300 AH Dordrecht, The Netherlands

International Journal of Applied Philosophy. ISSN 0739-098X. (semi-ann) Indian River Community College, Fort Pierce, FL 34981-5599, USA

International Journal of Moral and Social Studies. ISSN 0267-9655. (3 times a yr) Journals, One Harewood Row, London NW1 6SE, United Kingdom

International Logic Review. (semi-ann) Editor, via Belmeloro 3, 40126 Bologna, Italy

International Philosophical Quarterly. ISSN 0019-0365. (q) Vincent Potter, S.J., Fordham University, Bronx, NY 10458, USA

International Studies in Philosophy. ISSN 0270-5664. (3 times a yr) Scholars Press, P.O. Box 15288, Atlanta, GA 30333, USA

International Studies in the Philosophy of Science. ISSN 0269-8595. (3 times a yr) Carfax Publishing Company, P.O. Box 25, Abingdon, Oxfordshire OX14 3UE, England

Interpretation: A Journal of Political Philosophy. ISSN 0020-9635. (3 times a yr) Hilail Gildin, Editor-in-Chief, King Hall 101, Queens College, Flushing, NY 11367-0904, USA

Irish Philosophical Journal. ISSN 0266-9080. (semi-ann) Dr. Bernard Cullen, Editor, Department of Scholastic Philosophy, Queen's University, Belfast BT7 1NN, Northern Ireland

Iyyun: The Jerusalem Philosophical Quarterly. ISSN 0021-3306. (q) Manager, S.H. Bergman Centre for Philosophical Studies, Hebrew University of Jerusalem, Jerusalem 91905, Israel

Journal for the Theory of Social Behavior. ISSN 0021-8308. (q) Basil Blackwell, 108 Cowley Road, Oxford OX4 1JF, England (or 3 Cambridge Center, Cambridge, MA 02142, USA)

The Journal of Aesthetic Education. ISSN 0021-8510. (q) University of Illinois Press, 54 East Gregory Drive, Champaign, IL 61820, USA

The Journal of Aesthetics and Art Criticism. ISSN 0021-8529. (q) Donald W. Crawford, Editor, University of Wisconsin-Madision, 5145 H.C. White Hall, 600 North Park Street, Madison, WI 53706, USA

Journal of Agricultural Ethics. ISSN 0893-4282. (bi-ann) Room 039, MacKinnon Building, University of Guelph, Guelph, Ontario, Canada N1G 2W1

Journal of Applied Philosophy. ISSN 0264-3758. (bi-ann) Carfax Publishing Company, P.O. Box 25, Abingdon, Oxfordshire OX14 3UE, England

Journal of Business Ethics. ISSN 0167-4544. Kluwer Academic Publishers, 101 Philip Drive, Norwell, MA 02061, USA

Journal of Chinese Philosophy. ISSN 0301-8121. (q) Dialogue Publishing Company, P.O. Box 11071, Honolulu, HI 96828, USA

The Journal of Critical Analysis. ISSN 0022-0213. (q) The National Council for Critical Analysis, Shirley Schievella, P.O. Box 137, Port Jefferson, NY 11777, USA

Journal of Dharma. ISSN 0253-7222. (q) Center for the Study of World Religions, Dharmaram College, Bangalore 560029, India

The Journal of Hellenic Studies. ISSN 0075-4269. (ann) Secretary, The Hellenic Society, 31-34 Gordon Square, London WC1H 0PP, England

Journal of Indian Council of Philosophical Research. ISSN 0970-7794. (3 times a yr) Subscription Department, Motilal Banarsidass, Bungalow Road, Jawahar Nagar, Delhi 110007, India

Journal of Indian Philosophy. ISSN 0022-1791. Kluwer Academic Publishers, 101 Philip Drive, Norwell, MA 02061, USA

The Journal of Libertarian Studies. ISSN 0363-2873. (q) Center for Libertarian Studies, P.O. Box 4091, Burlingame, CA 94011, USA

Journal of Medical Ethics: The Journal of the Institute of Medical Ethics. ISSN 0306-6800. (q) Subscription Manager, Professional and Scientific Publications (JME), Tavistock House East, Tavistock Square, London WC1H 9JR, England (or Professional and Scientific Publications, 1172 Commonwealth Avenue, Boston, MA 02134, USA)

The Journal of Medical Humanities. ISSN 1041-3545. (q) Human Sciences Press, 233 Spring Street, New York, NY 10013, USA

The Journal of Medicine and Philosophy. ISSN 0360-5310. Kluwer Academic Publishers, 101 Philip Drive, Norwell, MA 02061, USA

The Journal of Mind and Behavior. ISSN 0271-0137. (q) Circulation Department, P.O. Box 522, Village Station, New York, NY 10014, USA

Journal of Moral Education. ISSN 0305-7240. (3 times a yr) Carfax Publishing Company, P.O. Box 25, Abingdon, Oxfordshire OX14 3UE, England

The Journal of Non-Classical Logic. (bi-ann) Centro de Lógica-Unicamp, C.P. 6133, 13.081 Campinas, São Paulo, Brazil

Journal of Philosophical Logic. ISSN 0022-3611. Kluwer Academic Publishers, 101 Philip Drive, Norwell, MA 02061, USA

Journal of Philosophical Research. ISSN 1053-8364. (ann) Philosophy Documentation Center, Bowling Green State University, Bowling Green, OH 43403-0189, USA

The Journal of Philosophy. ISSN 0022-362X. (m) 709 Philosophy Hall, Columbia University, New York, NY 10027, USA

Journal of Philosophy of Education. ISSN 0309-8249. (semi-ann) Carfax Publishing Company, P.O. Box 25, Abingdon, Oxfordshire OX14 3UE, England

Journal of Pragmatics. ISSN 0378-2166. (bi-m) Elsevier Science Publishers, P.O. Box 211, 1000 AE Amsterdam, The Netherlands

The Journal of Religious Ethics. ISSN 0384-9694. (semi-ann) Scholars Press, P.O. Box 15288, Atlanta, GA 30333, USA

Journal of Semantics. ISSN 0167-5133. (q) Oxford University Press, Pinkhill House, Southfield Road, Eynsham, Oxford OX8 1JJ, England

Journal of Social Philosophy. ISSN 0047-2786. (3 times a yr) Dr. Peter French, Editor, Trinity University, San Antonio, TX 78212, USA

The Journal of Speculative Philosophy. ISSN 0891-625X. (q) Pennsylvania State University Press, Suite C, 820 North University Drive, University Park, PA 16802, USA

The Journal of Symbolic Logic. ISSN 0022-4812. Association for Symbolic Logic, Department of Mathematics, University of Illinois, 1409 West Green Street, Urbana, IL 61801, USA

The Journal of the British Society for Phenomenology. ISSN 007-1773. (3 times a yr) Haigh & Hochland, JBSP Department, Precinct Centre, Manchester M13 9QA, England

Journal of the History of Ideas. ISSN 0022-5037. (q) Donald R. Kelley, Executive Editor, 442 Rush Rhees Library, University of Rochester, Rochester, NY 14627, USA

Journal of the History of Philosophy. ISSN 0022-5053. (q) Business Office, Department of Philosophy, Washington University, St. Louis, MO 63130, USA

Journal of the Philosophy of Sport. ISSN 0094-8705. (ann) Human Kinetics Publishers, Box 5076, Champaign, IL 61820-9971, USA

Journal of Thought. ISSN 0022-5231. (q) Dr. Robert M. Lang, Editor, College of Education, Leadership, and Educational Policy Studies, Northern Illinois University, Dekalb, IL 60115, USA

The Journal of Value Inquiry. ISSN 0022-5363. (q) Martinus Nijhoff Publishers, Spuiboulevard 50, 311 GR Dordrecht, The Netherlands

Kant-Studien: Philosophische Zeitschrift der Kant-Gesellschaft. ISSN 0022-8877. (q) Walter de Gruyter, Genthiner Str. 13, 1000 Berlin 30, Germany

Kennis en Methode: Tijdschrift voor Wetenschapsfilosofie en Methodologie. ISSN 0165-1773. (q) Boompers, Box 58, 7940 AB Meppel, The Netherlands

Kinesis: Graduate Journal in Philosophy. ISSN 0023-1568. (semi-ann) Department of Philosophy, Southern Illinois University, Carbondale, IL 62901, USA

Kriterion: Revista de Filosofia. (bi-ann) Faculdade de Filosofia e Ciências Humanas, Rua Carangola, 288-sala 817, C.P. 253, 30350 Belo Horizonte, Brazil

Laval Théologique et Philosophique. ISSN 0023-9054. (3 times a yr) Service de Revues, Les Presses de l'Université Laval, C.P. 2447, Quebec, Canada G1K 7R4

Law and Philosophy: An International Journal for Jurisprudence and Legal Philosophy. ISSN 0167-5249. Kluwer Academic Publishers, 101 Philip Drive, Norwell, MA 02061, USA

Linguistics and Philosophy. ISSN 0165-0157. Kluwer Academic Publishers, 101 Philip Drive, Norwell, MA 02061, USA

Listening: Journal of Religion and Culture. ISSN 0024-4414. (3 times a yr) P.O. Box 1108, Route 53, Romeoville, IL 60441-2298, USA

The Locke Newsletter. ISSN 0307-2606. (ann) Roland Hall, Department of Philosophy, University of York, York, England

Logique et Analyse. ISSN 0024-5836. (q) Editions E. Nauwelaerts, 17 Kolonel Begaultlaan, B-3010 Leuven, Belgium

Logos: Philosophic Issues in Christian Perspective. ISSN 0276-5667. (ann) Department of Philosophy, Santa Clara University, Santa Clara, CA 95053, USA

Logos: Revista de Filosofía. ISSN 0185-6375. (3 times a yr) Apartado Postal 18-907, Colonia Tacubaya, Delegación Miguel Hidalgo, C.P. 11800, Mexico, DF, Mexico

Magyar Filozófiai Szemle. ISSN 0025-0090. (bi-m) Kultura, P.O. Box 149, H-1389 Budapest 62, Hungary

Man and Nature/L'homme et la Nature. (ann) Academic Printing and Publishing, P.O. Box 4834, South Edmonton, Alberta, Canada T6E 5G7

Man and World: An International Philosophical Review. ISSN 0025-1534. Martinus Nijhoff Publishers, P.O. Box 322, 3300 AH Dordrecht, The Netherlands

Manuscrito: Revista Internacional de Filosofia. ISSN 0100-6045. (bi-ann) Circulation Department, Centro de Lógica, Unicamp C.P. 6133, 13.081 Campinas, São Paulo, Brazil

Mediaeval Studies. ISSN 0076-5872. (ann) Dr. Ron B. Thomson, Director of Publications, Pontifical Institute of Mediaeval Studies, 59 Queen's Park Crescent East, Toronto, Ontario, Canada M5S 2C4

Medical Humanities Review. ISSN 0892-2772. (bi-ann) Institute for the Medical Humanities, University of Texas Medical Branch, Galveston, TX 77550, USA

Metaphilosophy. ISSN 0026-1068. Basil Blackwell, 108 Cowley Road, Oxford OX4 1JF, England (or 3 Cambridge Center, Cambridge, MA 02142, USA)

Method: Journal of Lonergan Studies. ISSN 0736-7392. (semi-ann) Manager, Department of Philosophy, Loyola Marymount University, Loyola Boulevard at West 80th Street, Los Angeles, CA 90045, USA

Methodology and Science. ISSN 0543-6095. (q) Dr. P.H. Esser, Secretary and Editor, Beelslaan 20, 2012 PK Haarlem, The Netherlands

Midwest Studies in Philosophy. (ann) Editor, Dr. Theodore E. Uehling, Jr., Division of the Humanities, University of Minnesota, 112 Humanities Building, Morris, MN 56267, USA

Mind: A Quarterly Review of Philosophy. ISSN 0026-4423. (q) Oxford University Press, Pinkhill House, Southfield Road, Eynsham, Oxford OX8 1JJ, England

Mind & Language. ISSN 0268-1064. (q) Basil Blackwell, 108 Cowley Road, Oxford OX4 1JF, England (or 3 Cambridge Center, Cambridge, MA 02142, USA)

The Modern Schoolman: A Quarterly Journal of Philosophy. ISSN 0026-8402. (q) William C. Charron, Editor, Department of Philosophy, St. Louis University, St. Louis, MO 63103, USA

Modern Theology. ISSN 0266-7177. (q) Basil Blackwell, 108 Cowley Road, Oxford OX4 1JF, United Kingdom (or 3 Cambridge Center, Cambridge, MA 02142, USA)

The Monist: An International Quarterly Journal of General Philosophic Inquiry. ISSN 0026-9662. (q) P.O. Box 600, La Salle, IL 61301, USA

NAO Revista de la Cultura del Mediterráeo. (3 times a yr) Mansilla 3344, 1° C, 1425 Capital Federal, Argentina

National Forum: Phi Kappa Phi Journal. ISSN 0162-1831. (q) Subscription Department, 129 Quad Center, Auburn University, Auburn University, AL 36849, USA

Neue Hefte für Philosophie. ISSN H085-3917. (irr/ann) Vandenhoeck & Ruprecht, Postfach 3753, D-3400 Göttingen, Germany

The New Scholasticism. ISSN 0028-6621. (q) Treasurer, The American Catholic Philosophical Association, Catholic University of America, Washington, DC 20064, USA

New Vico Studies. ISSN 0733-9542. (ann) Institute for Vico Studies, 69 Fifth Avenue, New York, NY 10003, USA (or Humanities Press International, 171 First Avenue, Atlantic Highlands, NJ 07716, USA)

Notre Dame Journal of Formal Logic. ISSN 0029-4527. (q) Business Manager, University of Notre Dame, Box 5, Notre Dame, IN 46556, USA

Notre Dame Journal of Law, Ethics & Public Policy. (semi-ann) Zigad I. Naccasha, Managing Editor, University of Notre Dame, Notre Dame, IN 46556, USA

Noûs. ISSN 0029-4624. (q) Department of Philosophy, 126 Sycamore Hall, Indiana University, Bloomington, IN 47405, USA

Nouvelles de la République des Lettres. ISSN 0392-2332. (bi-ann) C.C. 1794767/01, Banca Commerciale Italiana, AG3 Naples, Italy

The Owl of Minerva. ISSN 0030-7580. (semi-ann) Department of Philosophy, Villanova University, Villanova, PA 19085, USA

Pacific Philosophical Quarterly. ISSN 0279-0750. (q) Expediters of the Printed Word, 515 Madison Avenue, New York, NY 10022, USA

Patristica et Mediaevalia. ISSN 0235-2280. (ann) Editor, Miembros del Centro de Estudios de Filosofía Medieval, 25 de Mayo 217, 2° Piso, 1002 Buenos Aires, Argentina

Pensamiento. ISSN 0031-4749. (q) Administración, Pablo Aranda 3, 28006 Madrid, Spain

The Personalist Forum. ISSN 0889-065X. Editor, Department of Philosophy, Furman University, Greenville, SC 29613, USA

Philosophia. ISSN 0031-8000. (ann) Editorial Office-Distribution, Research Center for Greek Philosophy, Academy of Athens, 14 Anagnostopoulou Street, Athens 106 73, Greece

Philosophia: Philosophical Quarterly of Israel. ISSN 0048-3893. (q) Bar-Ilan University, Subscriptions, Department of Philosophy, Ramat-Gan 52100, Israel

Philosophia Mathematica. ISSN 0031-8019. (semi-ann) J. Fang, Philosophia Mathematica, Box 206, Wood Crossroad, VA 23190, USA

Philosophia Naturalis. ISSN 0031-8027. (bi-ann) Vittorio Klostermann GmbH, Postfach 90 06 01, Frauenlobstrasse 22, 6000 Frankfurt AM Main 90, Germany

Philosophia Reformata. ISSN 0031-8035. (q) Centrum voor Reformatorische Wijsbegeerte, P.O. Box 368, 3500 AJ Utrecht, The Netherlands

Philosophic Exchange: Annual Proceedings. ISSN 0193-5046. (ann) Center for Philosophic Exchange, SUNY at Brockport, Brockport, NY 14420, USA

Philosophica. ISSN 0379-8402. (semi-ann) Rozier 44, B-9000 Gent, Belgium

Philosophica. (q) 38A/10 Belgachia Road, Calcutta 700037, India

Philosophica: Zborník Univerzity Komenského. (ann) Dr. Miroslav Marcelli, Editor-in-Chief, Študijné a informačné stredisko Spoločenskovedných pracovísk Univerzity Komenského, Šafarikovo nám estie 6, 808 01 Bratislava, Czechoslovakia

Philosophical Books. ISSN 0031-8051. (q) Basil Blackwell, 108 Cowley Road, Oxford OX4 1JF, England (or 3 Cambridge Center, Cambridge, MA 02142, USA)

The Philosophical Forum. ISSN 0031-806X. (q) CUNY, Baruch College, Box 239, 17 Lexington Avenue, New York, NY 10010, USA

Philosophical Inquiry: An International Philosophical Quarterly. (q) Prof. D.Z. Andriopoulos, Editor, Department of Philosophy, Adelphi University, Garden City, Long Island, NY 11530, USA (or P.O. Box 3825, C.P. Athens, Greece)

Philosophical Investigations. ISSN 0190-0536. (q) Basil Blackwell, 108 Cowley Road, Oxford OX4 1JF, England (or 3 Cambridge Center, Cambridge, MA 02142, USA)

Philosophical Papers. ISSN 0556-8641. (3 times a yr) Department of Philosophy, Rhodes University, P.O. Box 94, Grahamstown 6140, South Africa

Philosophical Psychology. ISSN 0951-5089. (3 times a yr) Carfax Publishing Company, P.O. Box 25, Abingdon, Oxfordshire OX14 3UE, United Kingdom

Philosophical Quarterly. ISSN 0031-8094. (q) Basil Blackwell, 108 Cowley Road, Oxford OX4 1JF, England (or 3 Cambridge Center, Cambridge, MA 02142, USA)

Philosophical Review. (ann) Editor-in-Chief, Department of Philosophy, National Taiwan University, Taipei 10764, Taiwan, Republic of China

The Philosophical Review. ISSN 0031-8103. (q) 327 Goldwin Smith Hall, Cornell University, Ithaca, NY 14853, USA

Philosophical Studies. ISSN 0554-0739. (ann) Prof. Dermot Moran, Editor, Department of Philosophy, University College Dublin, Dublin 4, Ireland

Philosophical Studies: An International Journal for Philosophy in the Analytic Tradition. ISSN 0031-8116. Kluwer Academic Publishers, 101 Philip Drive, Norwell, MA 02061, USA

Philosophical Studies in Education: Proceedings of the Annual Meeting of the Ohio Valley Philosophy of Education Society. ISSN 0160-7561. (ann) Terence O'Connor, Indiana State University, Terre Haute, IN 47809, USA

Philosophical Topics. ISSN 0276-2080. (semi-ann) Christopher S. Hill, Editor, Department of Philosophy, University of Arkansas, Fayetteville, AR 72701, USA

Philosophie et Logique. ISSN 0035-4031. (q) Editura Academiei Republicii Socialiste Romania, Str. Gutenberg 3 bis, Sector 6, Bucaresti, Romania

Philosophiques. ISSN 0316-2923. (semi-ann) Les Editions Bellarmin, 165 rue Deslauriers, Saint-Laurent, Quebec, Canada H4N 2S4

Philosophische Rundschau: Zeitschrift für Philosophische Kritik. ISSN 0031-8159. (q) J.C.B. Mohr (Paul Siebeck), Postfach 2040, 7400 Tübingen, Germany

Philosophy. ISSN 0031-8191. (q plus 2 supps). Cambridge University Press, Edinburgh Building, Shaftesbury Road, Cambridge, CB2 2RU, England, (or 40 West 20th Street, New York, NY 10011, USA)

Philosophy and Literature. ISSN 0190-0013. (semi-ann) The Johns Hopkins University Press, 701 West 40th Street, Suite 275, Baltimore, MD 21211-2190, USA

Philosophy and Phenomenological Research. ISSN 0031-8205. (q) Brown University, Box 1947, Providence, RI 02912, USA

Philosophy and Public Affairs. ISSN 0048-3915. (q) The Johns Hopkins University Press, 701 West 40th Street, Suite 275, Baltimore, MD 21211-2190, USA

Philosophy and Rhetoric. ISSN 0031-8213. (q) Department of Philosophy, The Pennsylvania State University, University Park, PA 16802, USA

Philosophy and Social Action. ISSN 0377-2772. (q) Business Editor, M-120 Greater Kailash-I, New Delhi 110048, India

Philosophy and Social Criticism. ISSN 0191-4537. (q) David M. Rasmussen, Editor, P.O. Box 368, Lawrence, KS 66044, USA

Philosophy and Theology: Marquette University Quarterly. ISSN 0-87462-559-9. (q) A. Tallon, Department of Philosophy and Theology, Marquette University, Milwaukee, WI 53233, USA

Philosophy East and West. ISSN 0031-8221. (q) The University of Hawaii Press, 2840 Kolowalu Street, Honolulu, HI 96822, USA

Philosophy in Context. ISSN 0742-2733. (ann) Department of Philosophy, Cleveland State University, Cleveland, OH 44115, USA

Philosophy in Science. ISSN 0277-2434. (ann) Pachart Publishing House, 1130 San Lucas Circle, Tucson, AZ 85704, USA

Philosophy of Education: Proceedings of the Philosophy of Education Society. ISSN 8756-6575. (ann) Dr. Thomas W. Nelson, Managing Editor, Illinois State University, Normal, IL 61761, USA

Philosophy of Science. ISSN 0031-8248. (q) Executive Secretary, Philosophy of Science Association, Department of Philosophy, 114 Morrill Hall, Michigan State University, East Lansing, MI 48824-1036, USA

Philosophy of the Social Sciences. ISSN 0048-3931. (q) Sage Publications, 2455 Teller Road, Newbury Park, CA 91320, USA

Philosophy Today. ISSN 0031-8256. (q) DePaul University, 802 West Belden Avenue, Chicago, IL 60614, USA

Phoenix. ISSN 0031-8299. (q) J. Schutz, Editorial Assistant, Trinity College, Larkin 339, University of Toronto, Toronto, Ontario, Canada M5S 1H8

Phronesis: A Journal for Ancient Philosophy. ISSN 0031-8868. (3 times a yr) Van Gorcum, P.O. Box 43, 9400 AA Assen, The Netherlands

Polis. (semi-ann) P. P. Nicholson, Department of Politics, University of York, York YO1 5DD, United Kingdom (or Prof. Kent F. Moors, Department of Political Science, Duquesne University, Pittsburgh, PA 15282-0001, USA)

Political Theory. ISSN 0090-5917. (q) Sage Publications, 2455 Teller Road, Newbury Park, CA 91320, USA

Praxis International. ISSN 0260-8448. Basil Blackwell, 108 Cowley Road, Oxford OX4 1JF, England (or 3 Cambridge Center, Cambridge, MA 02142, USA)

Proceedings and Addresses of the American Philosophical Association. ISSN 0065-972X. (7 times a yr) The American Philosophical Association, University of Delaware, Newark, DE 19716, USA

Proceedings of the American Catholic Philosophical Association. ISSN 0065-7638. (ann) Treasurer, The American Catholic Philosophical Association, Catholic University of America, Washington, DC 20064, USA

Proceedings of the Aristotelian Society. ISSN 0066-7374. Basil Blackwell, 108 Cowley Road, Oxford OX4 1JF, England (distributes to institutions). The Aristotelian Society, Department of Philosophy, Birkbeck College, London WC1E 7HX, United Kingdom

Proceedings of the Boston Area Colloquium in Ancient Philosophy. (ann) Co-publishing Program, University Press of America, 4720 Boston Way, Lanham, MD 20706, USA

Proceedings of the South Atlantic Philosophy of Education Society. (ann) Warren Strandberg, School of Education, Virginia Commonwealth University, Richmond, VA 23284-2020, USA

Process Studies. ISSN 0360-6503. (q) Center for Process Studies, 1325 North College Avenue, Claremont, CA 91711, USA

Public Affairs Quarterly. ISSN 0887-0373. (q) Philosophy Documentation Center, Bowling Green State University, Bowling Green, OH 43403-0189, USA

Quest: Philosophical Discussions. ISSN 1011-226X. (bi-ann) Circulation Manager, P.O. Box 9114, 9703 LC Groningen, The Netherlands

Radical Philosophy. (3 times a yr) Howard Feather, Thurrock Technical College, Woodview, Grays, Essex RM16 4YR, England

Ratio. ISSN 0034-0066. (semi-ann) Basil Blackwell, 108 Cowley Road, Oxford OX4 1JF, England (or 3 Cambridge Center, Cambridge, MA 02142, USA)

Ratio Juris: An International Journal of Jurisprudence and Philosophy of Law. ISSN 0952-1919. (3 times a year) Basil Blackwell, 3 Cambridge Center, Cambridge, MA 02142 USA

Reason Papers: A Journal of Interdisciplinary Normative Studies. ISSN 0363-1893. (ann) Department of Philosophy, Auburn University, Auburn University, AL 36849, USA

Religious Humanism. ISSN 0034-4095. (q) Fellowship of Religious Humanists, P.O. Box 278, Yellow Springs, OH 45387, USA

Religious Studies. ISSN 0034-4125. (q) Cambridge University Press, Edinburgh Building, Shaftesbury Road, Cambridge, CB2 2RU, United Kingdom (or 40 West 20th Street, New York, NY 10011, USA)

Reports on Mathematical Logic. ISSN 0137-2904. (ann) Centrala Handlu Zagranicznego "Ars Polona," ul. Krakowskie Przedmiescie 7, 00-068 Warsaw, Poland

Reports on Philosophy. ISSN 0324-8712. Elzbieta Paczkowska-Lagowska, Editor-in-Chief, Instytut Filozofii, ul. Grodzka 52, 31-044 Krakow, Poland

Research in Phenomenology. ISSN 0085-5553. (ann) Humanities Press International, Atlantic Highlands, NJ 07716, USA

Review of Existential Psychology & Psychiatry. ISSN 0361-1531. (3 times a yr) Keith Hoeller, Editor, Box 23220, Seattle, WA 98102, USA

The Review of Metaphysics. ISSN 0034-6632. (q) Catholic University of America, Washington, DC 20064, USA

Revista de Filosofía. ISSN 0185-3481. (3 times a yr) Universidad Iberoamericana, Prolongaciuon Paseo de la Reforma No. 880, Lomas de Santa Fe, 01210 Mexico, DF, Mexico

Revista de Filosofía. (semi-ann) Centro de Estidios Filosóhicos, Edificio Viyaluz piso 8, Apartado 526, Maracaibo, Venezuela

Revista de Filosofia: Publicatión de la Asociatión de Estudios Filosóficos. ISSN 0326-8160. (semi-ann) Marcelo Diego Boeri, ADEF C.C. 3758 Correo Central, 1000 Capital Federal, Argentina

Revista de Filosofía de la Universidad de Costa Rica. ISSN 0034-8252. (semi-ann) Editor, Universidad de Costa Rica, Apartado 75-2060, San José, Costa Rica

Revista de Filosofie. ISSN 0034-8260. (bi-m) Rompresfilatelia, Calea Victoriei 125, 79717 Bucharest, Romania

Revista Latinoamericana de Filosofía. ISSN 0325-0725. (3 times a yr) Box 1192, Birmingham, AL 35201, USA (or Casilla de Correo 5379, Correo Central, 1000 Buenos Aires, Argentina)

Revista Portuguesa de Filosofia. ISSN 0035-0400. (q) Faculdade de Filosofia, UCP, 4719 Braga , Portugal

Revista Venezolana de Filosofía. (semi-ann) Departamento de Filosofía, Apartado 80659, Caracas, Venezuela

Revue de Métaphysique et de Morale. ISSN 0035-1571. (q) 156 Avenue Parmentier, 75010 Paris, France

Revue de Théologie et de Philosophie. ISSN 0035-1784. (q) 7 ch. des Cèdres, CH-1004 Lausanne, Switzerland

Revue des Sciences Philosophiques et Théologiques. ISSN 0035-2209. (q) J. Vrin, 6 Place de la Sorbonne, 75005 Paris, France

Revue Internationale de Philosophie. ISSN 0048-8143. 2.000 FB. (q) Imprimérie Universa, rue Hoender 24, B-9230 Wetteren, Belgium

Revue Philosophique de la France et de L'etranger. ISSN 0035-3833. (q) Redaction de la Revue Philosophique, 12 rue Jean-de-Beauvais, 75005 Paris, France

Revue Philosophique de Louvain. ISSN 0035-3841. (q) Editions Peeters, B.P. 41, B-3000 Leuven, Belgium

Revue Thomiste: Revue Doctrinale de Théologie et de Philosophie. ISSN 0035-4295. (q) Ecole de Théologie, Avenue Lacordaire, Cedex, 31078 Toulouse, France

Rivista di Filosofia. ISSN 0035-6239. (q) Societa Editrice Il Mulino, Strada Maggiore 37, 40125 Bologna, Italy

Rivista di Filosofia Neo-Scolastica. ISSN 0035-6247. (q) Pubblicazioni dell'Universita Cattolica del Sacro Cuore, Vita e Pensiero, Largo A. Gemelli, 20123 Milan, Italy

Rivista di Studi Crociani. ISSN 0035-659X. (q) Presso la Societa di Storia Partia, Piazza Municipio, Maschio Angiolino, 80133 Naples, Italy

Rivista Internazionale di Filosofia del Diritto. (q) Casa Editrice Dott. A. Giuffre, via Busto Arsizio 40, 20151 Milan, Italy

Russell: Journal of the Bertrand Russell Archives. ISSN 0036-0163. (q) McMaster University Library Press, McMaster University, Hamilton, Ontario, Canada L8S 4L6

Sapientia. ISSN 0036-4703. (q) Bartolome Mitre 1869, 1039 Buenos Aires, Argentina

Sapienza. ISSN 0036-4711. (q) Vicoletto S. Pietro a Maiella, 4-80134 Naples, Italy

Schopenhauer-Jahrbuch. ISSN 0080-6935. (ann) Verlag Kramer, Bornheimer Landwehr 57a, Postfach 600445, 6000 Frankfurt 60, Germany

Science, Technology, and Human Values. ISSN 0162-2439. (q) Sage Publications, 2455 Teller Road, Newbury Park, CA 91320, USA

Scientia: An International Review of Scientific Synthesis. ISSN 0036-8687. (3 times a yr) via F. Ili Bronzetti 20, 20129 Milan, Italy

Social Epistemology: A Journal of Knowledge, Culture, and Policy. ISSN 0269-1728. (q) Taylor and Francis, 1900 Frost Road, Suite 101, Bristol, PA 19007, USA (or Rankine Road, Basingstoke, Hants RG24 0PR, United Kingdom)

Social Indicators Research: An International and Interdisciplinary Journal for Quality-of-Life Measurement. ISSN 0303-8300. Kluwer Academic Publishers, 101 Philip Drive, Norwell, MA 02061, USA

Social Philosophy and Policy. ISSN 0265-0525. (semi-ann) Basil Blackwell, 108 Cowley Road, Oxford OX4 1JF, England (or 3 Cambridge Center, Cambridge, MA 02142, USA)

Social Theory and Practice. ISSN 0037-802X. (3 times a yr) Department of Philosophy R-36C, 203 Dodd Hall, The Florida State University, Tallahassee, FL 32306-1054, USA

Sophia. ISSN 0038-1527. (3 times a yr) School of Humanities, Deakin University, Victoria 3217, Australia

South African Journal of Philosophy. ISSN 0258-0136. (q) Bureau for Scientific Publications, P.O. Box 1758, Pretoria 0001, South Africa

The Southern Journal of Philosophy. ISSN 0038-4283. (q) Editor, Department of Philosophy, Memphis State University, Memphis, TN 38152, USA

Southwest Philosophical Studies. ISSN 0885-9310. (3 times a yr) Jack Weir, Co-Editor, Department of Philosophy, Hardin-Simmons University, Abilene, TX 79698, USA (or Joseph D. Stamey, Co-Editor, Department of Philosophy, McMurry University, Abilene, TX 79697, USA)

Southwest Philosophy Review. ISSN 0897-2346. (semi-ann) Department of Philosophy, University of Central Arkansas, Conway, AR 72302, USA

Soviet Studies in Philosophy. ISSN 0038-5883. (q) M.E. Sharpe, 80 Business Park Drive, Armonk, NY 10504, USA

Stromata. ISSN 0049-2353. (q) Universidad del Salvador, C.C. 10, 1663 San Miguel, Argentina

Studia Leibnitiana. ISSN 0039-3185. (semi-ann) Franz Steiner Verlag Wiesbaden GmbH, Postfach 101526, 7000 Stuttgart, Germany

Studia Logica. ISSN 0039-3215. Kluwer Academic Publishers, 101 Philip Drive, Norwell, MA 02061, USA

Studia Philosophiae Christiane. ISSN 0585-5470. (semi-ann) ATK, ul. Dewajtis 5, 01-653 Warsaw, Poland

Studia Philosophica. (ann) Helmut Holzhey and Jean-Pierre Leyvraz, Editors, Verlag Paul Haupt, Falkenplatz 11/14, CH-3001 Berne, Switzerland

Studia Spinozana. ISSN 0179-3896. (ann) Douglas J. Den Uyl, Bellarmine College, Newburg Road, Louisville, KY 40205, USA

Studies in History and Philosophy of Science. ISSN 0039-3681. (q) Pergamon Press, Maxwell House, Fairview Park, Elmsford, NY 10523, USA

Studies in Philosophy and Education. ISSN 0039-3746. (q) Kluwer Academic Publishers, P.O. Box 358, Accord Station, Hingham, MA 02018-0358, USA

Studies in Philosophy and the History of Philosophy. (irr) Catholic University of America Press, Washington, DC 20064, USA

Studies in Soviet Thought. ISSN 0039-3797. Kluwer Academic Publishers, 101 Philip Drive, Norwell, MA 02061, USA

Synthese: An International Journal for Epistemology, Methodology, and Philosophy of Science. ISSN 0039-7857. Kluwer Academic Publishers, 101 Philip Drive, Norwell, MA 02061, USA

Teaching Philosophy. ISSN 0145-5788. (q) Philosophy Documentation Center, Bowling Green State University, Bowling Green, OH 43403-0189, USA

Teorema. ISSN 0210-1602. (q) Apartado 61, 159, 28080 Madrid, Spain

Teoria: Rivista di Filosofia. (bi-ann) E.T.S., C.C.P. 12157566, Piazza Torricelli 4, 56100 Pisa, Italy

Theoretical Medicine: An International Journal for the Philosophy and Methodology of Medical Research and Practice. ISSN 0167-9902. Kluwer Academic Publishers, 101 Philip Drive, Norwell, MA 02061, USA

Theoria. ISSN 0495-4548. (3 times a yr) Plaza de Pio XII, 1, 6°, 1ª, Apartado 1.594, 20.080 San Sebastian, Spain

Theoria: A Swedish Journal of Philosophy. ISSN 0046-5825. (3 times a yr) Filosofiska Institution, Kungshuset i Lundagard, S-223 50 Lund, Sweden

Theory and Decision: An International Journal for Philosophy and Methodology of the Social Sciences. ISSN 0040-5833. Kluwer Academic Publishers, 101 Philip Drive, Norwell, MA 02061, USA

Thinking: The Journal of Philosophy for Children. ISSN 0190-3330. (q) The Institute for the Advancement of Philosophy for Children, Montclair State College, Upper Montclair, NJ 07043, USA

The Thomist. ISSN 0040-6325. (q) The Thomist Press, 487 Michigan Avenue NE, Washington, DC 20017, USA

Thought: A Review of Culture and Idea. ISSN 0040-6457. (q) Fordham University Press, Fordham University, Bronx, NY 10458, USA

Tijdschrift voor de Studie van de Verlichting en van Het Vrije Denken. ISSN 0774-1847. (q) Centrum voor de Studie van de Verlichting en van Het Vrije Denken, Vrije Universiteit Brussel, Pleinlaan 2-B416, 1050 Brussels, Belgium

Tijdschrift voor Filosofie. ISSN 0040-750X. (q) Kardinaal Merciorploin 2, B-3000 Leuven, Belgium

Topoi: An International Review of Philosophy. ISSN 0167-7411. Kluwer Academic Publishers, 101 Philip Drive, Norwell, MA 02061, USA

Trans/Form/Ação. ISSN 0101-3173. (ann) Biblioteca Central da UNESP, Av. Vicente Ferreira, 1278 C.P. 603, 17500 Marilia, SP, Brazil

Transactions of the Charles S. Peirce Society: A Quarterly Journal in American Philosophy. ISSN 0009-1774. (q) Editor, Department of Philosophy, Baldy Hall, SUNY at Buffalo, Buffalo, NY 14260, USA

Tulane Studies in Philosophy. ISSN 0082-6776. (ann) Department of Philosophy, Tulane University, New Orleans, LA 70118, USA

Ultimate Reality and Meaning: Interdisciplinary Studies in the Philosophy of Understanding. ISSN 0709-549X. (q) University of Toronto Press, 5201 Dufferin Street, Downsview, Ontario, Canada M3H 5T8

Universitas Philosophica. (semi-ann) Facultad de Filosofía, Univeridad Javeriana, Carrera 7, No. 39-08, Bogota D.E. 2, Colombia

Utilitas: A Journal of Utilitarian Studies. (semi-ann) Oxford University Press, Pinkhill House, Southfield Road, Eynsham, Oxford OX8 1JJ, England

Vera Lex. (semi-ann) Prof. Virginia Black, Editor, Department of Philosophy and Religious Studies, Pace University, Pleasantville, NY 10570, USA

Vivarium: An International Journal for the Philosophy and Intellectual Life of the Middle Ages and Renaissance. ISSN 0042-7543. (semi-ann) E.J. Brill, Plantijnstr. 2, Postbus 9000, 2300 PA Leiden, The Netherlands

Zeitschrift für Mathematische Logik und Grundlagen der Mathematik. ISSN 0044-3050. (bi-m) Deutscher Verlag der Wissenschaften GmbH, Johannes-Dieckmann-Str 10, 1080 Berlin, Germany

Zeitschrift für Philosophische Forschung. ISSN 0044-3301. (q) Vittorio Klostermann GmbH, Postfach 90 06 01, 6000 Frankfurt AM Main 90, Germany

Zygon: Journal of Religion and Science. ISSN 0591-2385. (q) Karl E. Peters, Editor, Rollins College, Winter Park, FL 32789, USA

Guidance on the Use of the Subject Index

The Subject Index lists in alphabetical order the significant subject descriptors and proper names that describe the content of the articles and books indexed. Since titles are frequently misleading, the editors read each article and book to determine which subject headings accurately describe it. Each entry under a subject heading includes the complete title of the book or article and the author's name.

Subject entries fall into the following classes:

1) proper names, such as Quine, Kant, and Hegel;
2) nationalities, such as American and Soviet;
3) historical periods, which are: ancient, medieval, renaissance, modern, nineteenth-century, and twentieth century;
4) major fields of philosophy, which are: aesthetics, axiology, education, epistemology, ethics, history, language, logic, metaphysics, philosophical anthropology, philosophy, political philosophy, religion, science, and social philosophy;
5) subdivisions of the major fields of philosophy, such as: utilitarianism, induction, realism, and nominalism;
6) other specific topics, such as grue, pain, paradox, and Turing-machine;
7) bibliographies, which are listed under "bibliographies," the person or subject, and the appropriate historical period.

The Subject Index is used like the index found in the back of a textbook. Scan the alphabetical listing of significant words until the desired subject is found. If the title confirms your interest, then locate the author's name, which occurs after the title, in the section entitled "Author Index with Abstracts." The title, in addition to suggesting the content of the article or book, indicates the language in which the document is written.

Although every effort was made to standardize subject headings, complete uniformity was impossible. Hence, check for various spellings of subject headings, particularly of proper names. Due consideration should be given to subject headings that sometimes are written with a space, a hyphen, or an umlaut. The following example illustrates some possibilities:

DE MORGAN
DE-MORGAN
DEMORGAN

Not only does the computer treat the above subject headings as different, but it may file other subject headings between them.

Generally, only the last names of famous philosophers are used as subject headings. Last names and first initials usually are used for other philosophers. The following list indicates who of two or more philosophers with the same last name is designated by last name only.

Alexander (Samuel)
Austin (J L)
Bacon (Francis)
Bradley (Francis H)
Brown (Thomas)
Butler (Joseph)
Collins (Anthony)
Darwin (Charles)
Eckhart (Meister)
Edwards (Jonathan)
Green (Thomas H)
Hartmann (Edward von)
Huxley (T H)

James (William)
Jung (Carl G)
Lewis (C I)
Mill (John Stuart)
Moore (G E)
Niebuhr (Reinhold)
Paul (Saint)
Price (Richard)
Russell (Bertrand)
Schiller (Friedrich)
Toynbee (Arnold)
Wolff (Christian)

A POSTERIORI
Hume and the Problem of Miracles: A Solution. LEVINE, Michael P.
Identity Statements and the Necessary A Posteriori. STEWARD, Helen.
Kant's Conception of Empirical Law—I. GUYER, Paul.
Kant's Conception of Empirical Law—II. WALKER, Ralph.

A PRIORI
El a priori histórico (la historia y sus hechos). SAMPEDRO, Ceferino.
Hume and the Problem of Miracles: A Solution. LEVINE, Michael P.
Philosophical Works. KALOYEROPOULOS, N A.
The *A Priori* from Kant to Schelling. LAWRENCE, Joseph P (trans) and GRONDIN, Jean.
The *A Priori* Method and the *Actio* Concept Revised. RANEA, Alberto Guillermo.
The Abyssal Categories of Blaga's Apriorism. RAMBU, Nicolae.
Contingencia a priori. VALDÉS, Margarita.
Kant's Conception of Empirical Law—I. GUYER, Paul.
Kant's Conception of Empirical Law—II. WALKER, Ralph.
On the Kantian Background of Neopositivism. SAUER, Werner.
Transcendental Thomism and the Thomistic Texts. KNASAS, John F X.

ABBOT, F
The Abbot-Royce Controversy. PEDEN, Creighton.

ABDUCTION
Hypothesis and the Spiral of Reflection. WEISSMAN, David.
Peirce's Abductive Argument and the Enthymeme. SABRE, Ru Michael.

ABELARD
Fiat Voluntas Tua! Vício e Pecado na ética de Abelardo. ESTEVÁO, J C.

ABILITY(-TIES)
Action and Ability. BROWN, Mark A.
Rawls and the Collective Ownership of Natural Abilities. KERNOHAN, Andrew.
A Sketch for a Theory of Health. NORDENFELT, Lennart.
Young Children Generate Philosophical Ideas. MC CALL, Catherine.

ABOLITION
"After Chernobyl: The Ethics of Risk-Taking" in *Ethics and the Environmental Responsibility*, SHAW, D.
"Having It Both Ways: The Gradual Wrong in American Strategy" in *Nuclear Deterrence and Moral Restraint*, SHUE, Henry.

ABORTION
Health Care Ethics: Principles and Problems. GARRETT, Thomas M (ed).
Medical Ethics: Essays on Abortion and Euthanasia. BARRY, Robert L.
Preventing Birth: Contemporary Methods and Related Moral Controversies. CALLAHAN, Joan C.
Splitting the Difference: Compromise and Integrity in Ethics and Politics. BENJAMIN, Martin.
Abortion and Feminism. MARKOWITZ, Sally.
Abortion Rights. EDWARDS, Rem B.
The Abortion Struggle in America. WARREN, Mary Anne.
Abortion: The Right to an Argument. MEILAENDER, Gilbert.
Die psychologischen Probleme der Frau vor dem Schwangerschaftsabbruch (in Polish). OSTROWSKA, Krystyna.
Does a Fetus Already Have a Future-like-ours?. MC INERNEY, Peter K.
The Economic Efficiency and Equity of Abortion. MEEKS, Thomas J.
Four-One-Four. ANNAS, George J.
The Future of Abortion. FLYNN, Tom.
Killing, Abortion, and Contraception: A Reply to Marquis. NORCROSS, Alastair.
Metaphysical Accounts of the Zygote as a Person and the Veto Power of Facts. BOLE III, Thomas J.
Moral Conflict in Public Policy. GORDVITZ, Samuel.
The Moral Significance of Birth. WARREN, Mary Anne.
Nature as Demonic in Thomson's Defense of Abortion. WILCOX, John T.
On Transplanting Human Fetal Tissue: Presumptive Duties and the Task of Casuistry. MILLER, Richard B.
Operation Rescue: Domestic Terrorism or Legitimate Civil Rights Protest?. NATHANSON, Bernard.
The Price of Abortion Sixteen Years Later. CHOPKO, Mark E and HARRIS, Phillip and ALVARÉ, Helen M.
Pro-Choice: A New Militancy. DAVIS, Susan E.
Selective Termination of Pregnancy and Women's Reproductive Autonomy. OVERALL, Christine.
Sensationalized Philosophy: A Reply to Marquis's "Why Abortion is Immoral". CUDD, Ann E.
Viewing Fetuses as Scarce Natural Resources. SCHEDLER, George.
We Must Rescue Them. LEBER, Gary.
When Becoming Pregnant Is a Crime. PALTROW, Lynn M.

ABOUTNESS
Aboutness and Substitutivity. MARTI, Genoveva.

ABRAHAM
Kierkegaard's Fear and Trembling. GELLMAN, Jerome I.

ABSOLUTE
see also God
Absolute Becoming and Absolute Necessity. SMALL, Robin.
Absolute Truth Theories for Modal Languages as Theories of Interpretation. LE PORE, Ernest and LOEWER, Barry.
The Absolute, Community, and Time. WILLIAMS, Robert R.
Bradley e Spinoza: L'iper-spinozismo di F H Bradley (I). DEREGIBUS, Arturo.
From Absolute Idealism to Instrumentalism: The Problem of Dewey's Early Philosophy. WELCHMAN, Jennifer.
Hegel's Conception of Absolute Knowing. LUDWIG, Walter D.
La philosophie de Hegel (in Greek). KANELLOPOULOS, P.
On Relativizing Kolmogorov's Absolute Probability Functions. LEBLANC, Hugues and ROEPER, Peter.
La philosophie et l'absolu. TILLIETTE, Xavier.
Reply to Professor Robin Small's "Absolute Becoming and Absolute Necessity". RICHARDSON, John.
Victor Cousin: Commonsense and the Absolute. MANNS, James W and MADDEN, Edward H.
Was Hegel a Panlogicist?. EISENBERG, Paul.

ABSOLUTENESS
"Existenz zwischen Unbedingheit und Endlichkeit" in *Agora: Zu Ehren von Rudolph Berlinger*, WEIER, Winfried.
On Absoluteness. HABART, Karol.

ABSOLUTES
Moral Absolutes: An Essay on the Nature and Rationale of Morality. RESCHER, Nicholas.
Hegel über die Rede vom Absoluten—Teil I: Urteil, Satz und Spekulativer Gehalt. GRAESER, Andreas.

ABSOLUTISM
"In Defense of Ethical Absolutism" in *Inquiries into Values: The Inaugural Session of the International Society for Value Inquiry*, FOWLER, Corbin.
Absolutism, Individuality and Politics: Hobbes and a Little Beyond. FLATHMAN, Richard E.
Response to Professor Feinberg's Presidential Address: A Role for Philosophy of Education in Intercultural Research. GOLDSTONE, Peter.
A Role for Philosophy of Education in Intercultural Research: Reexamination of the Relativism-Absolutism Debate. FEINBERG, Walter.
A Skeptical Appreciation of Natural Law Theory. GINSBERG, Robert.

ABSTRACT
Who Thinks in an Abstract Manner? M Sobokta: Commentary (in Czechoslovakian). HEGEL, G W F.

ABSTRACT ENTITY(-TIES)
God and Abstract Entities. LEFTOW, Brian.

ABSTRACT IDEA(S)
Abstract General Ideas in Hume. PAPPAS, George S.

ABSTRACTION(S)
Nature's Capacities and their Measurement. CARTWRIGHT, Nancy.
"Abstraktion, Begriffsanalyse, und Urteilskraft in Schopenhauers Erkenntnislehre" in *Schopenhauer: New Essays in Honor of His 200th Birthday*, MALTER, Rudolf.
"Capacities and Abstractions" in *Scientific Explanation (Minnesota Studies in the Philosophy of Science, Volume XIII)*, CARTWRIGHT, Nancy.
"Locke's Ideas, Abstraction, and Substance" in *Cause, Mind, and Reality: Essays Honoring C B Martin*, HINCKFUSS, Ian.
Aristotle on the Difference between Mathematics and Physics and First Philosophy. MODRAK, D K W.
Naturaleza del conocimiento humano: El significado de la abstracción en Santo Tomás (III). DERISI, Octavio N.

ABSTRACTIONISM
A Philosophical (Hermeneutical) Survey of Modern Abstract Art (in Czechoslovakian). PINKAVA, J.

ABSURDITY
Is Life Absurd?. WESTPHAL, Jonathan and CHERRY, Christopher.
Universalism as a Metaphilosophy of the New Peace Movement. KUCZYNSKI, Janusz and PETROWICZ, Lech (trans) and RODZINSKA, Aleksandra (trans).

ACADEMIA
The Antithesis. BAUER, Henry.
Metaphysics in the Philosophy of Education. HALDANE, John.
The Schoolman's Advocate: In Defence of the Academic Pursuit of

AESTHETICS

"Schopenhauer and Platonic Ideas: A Groundwork for an Aesthetic Metaphysics" in *Schopenhauer: New Essays in Honor of His 200th Birthday*, CHANSKY, James D.

"Schopenhauer, Art, and the Dark Origin" in *Schopenhauer: New Essays in Honor of His 200th Birthday*, DESMOND, William.

"Signification des modifications morphologiques de la coupole: LE TEMPS et *le temps*" in *Cultural Hermeneutics of Modern Art: Essays in Honor of Jan Aler*, BRION-GUERRY, Liliane.

"Style As the Man: From Aesthetics to Speculative Philosophy" in *Analytic Aesthetics*, ALTIERI, Charles.

"The Work of Making a Work of Music" in *What is Music?*, WOLTERSTORFF, Nicholas.

"*Condurre tutte le metafore ad absurdum*": Riflessioni filosofiche attorno alla poetica di Celan. SAMONÀ, Leonardo.

"Ein paar Seiten Schopenhauer"—überlegungen zu Rilkes Schopenhauer—Lektüre und deren Folgen (2 Teil). STAHL, August.

A Philosophical (Hermeneutical) Survey of Modern Abstract Art (in Czechoslovakian). PINKAVA, J.

A proposito di Jean-Paul Sartre. TOGNONATO, Claudio.

Adorno After Adorno (in Japanese). YOSHIOKA, Hiroshi.

Aesthetic Consciousness and Aesthetic Non-Differentiation: Gadamer, Schiller, and Lukács. PIZER, John.

Aesthetic Education: A Small Manifesto. ABBS, Peter.

Aesthetic Qualities and Aesthetic Value. GOLDMAN, Alan H.

Aesthetic Theories Concerning the Picturesque: Gilpin, Price and Knight (in Japanese). ANZAI, Shin-ichi.

Aesthetic Thinking of Karel Capek (in Czechoslovakian). HLAVACEK, Lubos.

Aesthetic Valuing of Design (in Czechoslovakian). VASICEK, Milan.

Aesthetic Versus Moral Evaluations. GOLDMAN, Alan H.

The Aesthetic-Artistic Domain, Criticism, and Teaching. CHAMBERS, John H.

Aestheticism, Feminism, and the Dynamics of Reversal. NEWMAN, Amy.

Aesthetics and the Insularity of Arts Educators. MC ADOO, Nick.

Aesthetics in Discipline-Based Art Education. CRAWFORD, Donald W.

Aesthetics in Science and in Art. ENGLER, Gideon.

La alegria del arte: Hegel y Heidegger. CONSTANTE, Alberto.

Annotated Bibliography on Feminist Aesthetics in the Visual Arts. KRUMHOLZ, Linda and LAUTER, Estella.

Architecture, Philosophy and the Public World. HALDANE, John.

Are Kant's "Aesthetic Judgment" and "Judgment of Tase" Synonymous?. GRACYK, Theodore A.

The Arousal and Expression of Emotion by Music. ALLEN, R T.

Art and Art Criticism: A Definition of Art. DAUER, Francis.

Art and Morality: Critical Theory About the Conflict and Harmony between Art and Morality. KORTHALS, Michiel.

Art and the Joycean Artist. SCHIRALLI, Martin.

Art and the Rhetoric of Allusion. NUYEN, A T.

Art as an Axiology of Man. MOUTSOPOULOS, E.

Art as Understanding. PERKINS, D N.

Art, Education, and Life-Issues. MC FEE, Graham.

El arte y el mal. GRIMALDI, Nicolás.

Artist and Audience. PERRICONE, Christopher.

Artist—Work—Audience: Musings on Barthes and Tolstoy. KRUKOWSKI, Lucian.

Artistic and Aesthetic Value. ORAMO, Ilkka.

Artistic Convention and the Issue of Truth in Art. MARSHALL, Ernest C.

Artistic Intention and Mental Image. HAGBERG, Garry.

Ästhetischer Subjektivismus. PAWLOWSKI, Tadeusz.

Authors Without Paradox. POLLARD, D E B.

Autonomie der Kunst in der *Ästhetischen Theorie* Adornos (in Japanese). IMURA, Akira.

Autonomy and the Death of the Arts. COVEOS, Costis M.

Bach as a Paradigm in Aesthetic Discourse. ZIMMERMANN, Jörg.

Beardsley's Aesthetic Instrumentalism. BAILEY, George.

Beauty as the Transition from Nature to Freedom in Kant's Critique of Judgement. DÜSING, Klaus.

Beauty in Design and Pictures: Idealism and Aesthetic Education. STANKIEWICZ, Mary Ann.

Beethoven's Symphonic Style and Temporality in Music. DAHLHAUS, Carl.

Belongings. LLEWELYN, John.

Between the Philosophy of Art and Microaesthetics. GOLASZEWSKA, Maria.

Beyond Truth: Santayana on the Functional Relations of Art, Myth, and Religion. CONNER, Frederick W.

Blame, Fictional Characters, and Morality. SANKOWSKI, Edward.

The Boundaries of Art. STECKER, Robert.

Can Aesthetic Value Be Explained?. GASKIN, Richard M.

The Changing Image of Art Education: Theoretical Antecedents of Discipline-Based Art Education. SMITH, Ralph A.

Chinese Theories of Appreciation—with Particular Attention to Painting (in Japanese). KÔNO, Michifusa.

The Claims of Tragedy: An Essay in Moral Psychology and Aesthetics Theory. SCHIER, Flint.

The Cognitive in Aesthetic Activity. DAVEY, Earl.

Collingwood on Art and Fantasy. LEWIS, Peter.

Colourization Ill-Defended. LEVINSON, Jerrold.

Composers' Texts as Objects of Musicological Study. HEINIÖ, Mikko.

A Consideration of Criticism. BARRETT, Terry.

Contemporary Aesthetic Issue: The Colorization Controversy. SAITO, Yuriko.

Contemporary Consciousness and Originary Thinking in a Nietzschean Joke. SCHEIER, Claus-Artur.

Contexts of Dance. SPARSHOTT, Francis.

Contextualism and Autonomy in Aesthetics. KRUKOWSKI, Lucian.

Creating, Experiencing, Sense-Making: Art Worlds in Schools. GREENE, Maxine.

Creativity and Routine. PERRY, Leslie R.

Democracy and Excellence. SHAW, Roy.

The Development of Aesthetic Judgment: Analysis of a Genetic-Structuralist Approach. DE MUL, Jos.

Dialects of Aestheticism (in Dutch). KUIPER, M.

Different Readings: A Reply to Magnus, Solomon, and Conway. NEHAMAS, Alexander.

Dionysian Classicism, or Nietzsche's Appropriation of an Aesthetic Norm. DEL CARO, Adrian.

Dirac and the Aesthetic Evaluation of Theories. MC ALLISTER, James W.

Dynamism of Meaningful Unification of Work and Coherence of Text (in Czechoslovakian). CERVENKA, Miroslav.

The Eclipse of Truth in the Rise of Aesthetics. KORSMEYER, Carolyn.

The Education of Taste. GOLDMAN, Alan H.

An Emendation in Kant's Theory of Taste. COHEN, Ted.

Emerson, Whitman, and Conceptual Art. LEONARD, George J.

The End of Aesthetic Theory. NEGRIN, Llewellyn.

Energeia and "The Work Itself". HICKS, Michael.

Ethos, techne y kalon en Platón. LOMBA FUENTES, Joaquín.

Etica y estética en la literatura. SPANG, Kurt.

Exemplification Reconsidered. ARRELL, Douglas.

Experiencia y comprensión: Estudio a través del arte como lenguaje. MARTINEZ, Juana M.

Expression as Hands-on Construction. HOWARD, V A.

The Female Voice: Sexual Aesthetics Revisited. GATES, Eugene.

Feminine Perspectives and Narrative Points of View. BARWELL, Ismay.

Feminist Film Aesthetics: A Contextual Approach. SHRAGE, Laurie.

Feminist Literary Criticism and the Author. WALKER, Cheryl.

Fiction, Self-Deception, Contemplation (in Dutch). BURMS, A.

Fictional Emotion, Quasi-Desire and Background Relief. BORUAH, Bijoy H.

Fin de Siècle, End of the "Globe Style"? The Concept of Object in Contemporary Art. POR, Peter and WALKER, R Scott (trans).

Fish Fingered: Anatomy of a Deconstructionist. MEYNELL, Hugo A.

Forma y contenido del arte. BOROBIO, Luis.

Freud, Racine, and the Epistemology of Tragedy. BRODY, Jules.

From Stubborn Structure to Double Mirror: The Evolution of Northrop Frye's Theory of Poetic Creation and Response. BOGDAN, Deanne.

Golden Rules and Golden Bowls. RIGHTER, William.

Grazia e dignità dell'estetica schilleriana. DOLORES FOLLIERO, Granzia.

A Gynecentric Aesthetic. COX, Renée.

Das Hässliche und die "Kritik der ästhetischen Urteilskraft". STRUB, Christian.

Having Bad Taste. GRACYK, Theodore A.

The Heart's Education: Why We Need Poetry. SWANGER, David.

Hegel y Marcuse: *El Ideal* o la Forma Estética. FACIO, Tatiana.

Heidegger on Hermeneutics and Music Today. CHARLES, Daniel.

How Did We Get From Simulation To Symbol?. BROOK, Donald.

Hume on Virtue, Beauty, Composites, and Secondary Qualities. BAXTER, Donald L M.

Husserl's Concept of Inner Temporal Consciousness and Aesthetics (in Czechoslovakian). ZUSKA, Vlastimil.

Husserl—Bolzano I (in Czechoslovakian). BAYEROVA, Marie.

The Idea of Music in India and the Ancient West. ROWELL, Lewis.

The Ideal Aesthetic Observer Revisited. TALIAFERRO, Charles.

La imagen del hombre en la teoría kantiana del genio. LABRADA, Maria Antonia.

The Influence of Traditional Japanese Aesthetics on the Film Theory of Sergei Eisenstein. ODIN, Steve.

AESTHETICS

La teoria dello spazio immaginario in Leopardi. LO BUE, Salvatore.

The Horizon of Aesthetics (in Czechoslovakian). SINDELAR, Dusan.

The Logical Structure of Aesthetic Value Judgements: An Outline of a Popperian Aesthetics (in Hebrew). KULKA, Tomas.

The Pain of Simulation on Heidegger's Philosophy of Art (in Dutch). DE SCHUTTER, Dirk.

The Questions of Contemporary Aesthetics (in Czechoslovakian). SINDELAR, Dusan.

Theater as Art. SHPET, G.

Theory of Novel and Historical Poetics (in Czechoslovakian). SVATON, Vladimir.

Thinking Eye of Karl Capek (in Czechoslovakian). HLAVACEK, Lubos.

To the Program of Aesthetic Evolution for the Whole Society (in Czechoslovakian). CHYBA, Milos.

Tonal Harmony as a Formal System. PYLKKÖ, Pauli.

Towards an Histrionic Aesthetics: Diderot's *Paradoxes* as Pre-Text for Romantic Irony. SPENCER, Judith.

Towards—and Away from—an Aesthetic of Popular Culture. DOHERTY, Thomas.

Tragédia: uma alegoria da alienação. BOLOGNESI, Mário Fernando.

Translation, Art, and Culture. PERRICONE, Christopher.

Troubles with Fiction. POLLARD, Denis E B.

Ugly Duckling, Funny Butterfly: Bette Davis and *Now, Voyager*. CAVELL, Stanley.

Understanding Music: Remarks on the Relevance of Theory. TORMEY, Alan.

La unidad perdida del proyecto arquitectónico. ELÍCEGUI, Juan M O.

Universality and Difference: O'Keeffe and McClintock. MACCOLL, San.

Unknown Masterpiece. HELLER, Agnes.

Validation by Touch in Kandinsky's Early Abstract Art. OLIN, Margaret.

Variations sur Schopenhauer et la musique. LEYVRAZ, Jean-Pierre.

Variations upon Variation, or Picasso Back to Bach. GOODMAN, Nelson.

Vom Ursprung des Kunstwerks: Erste Ausarbeitung. HEIDEGGER, Martin.

Wang Yuyang's Natural Thought on Art. TIAOGONG, Wu.

Weaving Chaos into Order: A Radically Pragmatic Aesthetic. SEIGFRIED, Charlene Haddock.

What Music Is. SERAFINE, Mary Louise.

Why Dewey Now?. SHUSTERMAN, Richard.

The Woman in White: On the Reception of Hegel's *Antigone*. DONOUGHO, Martin.

Young's Critique of Authenticity in Musical Performance. THOM, Paul.

Zwei Arten der Malerei: Von der Umwandelung der Interpretation der Kunst bei Hegel (in Japanese). IWAKI, Ken-ichi.

AETIUS

Chrysippus and the *Placita*. MANSFELD, Jaap.

Xenophanes on the Moon: A *Doxographicum* in Aëtius. RUNIA, David T.

AFFECTION(S)

La giustizia nella dottrina della volontà di Giovanni Duns Scoto. PIZZO, Giovanni.

AFFIRMATION

Of Particles. GALLIE, Roger D.

Ricerca ed affermazione. RIGOBELLO, Armando.

AFFIRMATIVE ACTION

Affirmative Action and the Doctrine of Double Effect. COONEY, William.

Affirmative Action as a Form of Restitution. GROARKE, Leo.

What is Wrong With Reverse Discrimination?. HETTINGER, Edwin C.

AFRICAN

Paths Toward a Clearing: Radical Empiricism and Ethnographic Inquiry. JACKSON, Michael.

African Cosmology and Ontology. DUKOR, Maduabu.

African Philosophy: Paulin J Hountondji—His Dilemma and Contributions. OTAKPOR, Nkeonye.

Bedingungen für die Aneignung und Verbreitung des Marxismus-Leninismus in afrikanischen ländern. BASTOS, Feliciano Moreira.

Critique of Technological Policy in Africa. FORJE, John W.

Ethnophilosophy in the Philosophical Discourse in Africa: A Critical Note. NEUGEBAUER, Christian.

God and Godlings in African Ontology. DUKOR, Maduabuchi.

Narrative in African Philosophy. BELL, Richard H.

Options in African Philosophy. SOGOLO, G S.

Philosophie, Ideologie et Acteurs Economique en Afrique. KIBAMBE-KIA-NKIMA, Kapongola.

The Question of Relevance in Current Nigerian Philosophy. KIMMERLE, Heinz.

Reading Africa Through Foucault: V Y Mudimbe's Re-affirmation of the Subject. DIAWARA, Manthia.

AFTERLIFE

Bodily Continuity, Personal Identity and Life After Death. WEI, Tan Tai.

Chthonic Themes in Plato's *Republic*. MOORS, Kent F.

Why We Need Immortality. TALIAFERRO, Charles.

AGENCY

Natural Agency: An Essay on the Casual Theory of Action. BISHOP, John.

Self-Direction and Political Legitimacy: Rousseau and Herder. BARNARD, F M.

Virtue and Self-Knowledge. JACOBS, Jonathan A.

"Doers and their Deeds: Schopenhauer on Human Agency" in *Schopenhauer: New Essays in Honor of His 200th Birthday*, ATWELL, John E.

Agency, Human Nature and Character in Kantian Theory. RUMSEY, Jean P.

Can God Forgive Us Our Trespasses?. BRIEN, Andrew.

Dewey's Conception of Growth Reconsidered. PEKARSKY, Daniel.

Ethical Perspectives on the Foreign Direct Investment Decision. STANLEY, Marjorie T.

Kant's Third Antinomy: Agency and Causal Explanation. GREENWOOD, John D.

The Moral Importance of Free Action. BENSON, Paul.

Personal Identity, the Temporality of Agency and Moral Responsibility. LEE, Win-Chiat.

Ranken on Disharmony and Business Ethics. GIBSON, Kevin.

A Research Strategy for Studying Telic Human Behavior. HOWARD, George S and YOUNGS, William H.

Self-Conscious Agency and the Eternal Consciousness: Ultimate Reality in Thomas Hill Green. CROSSLEY, David.

Social Power and Human Agency. KERNOHAN, Andrew.

The Vulnerability of Action. ELLIS, Robert.

Which Beings are Exemplary? Comments on Charles Guignon's "Truth as Disclosure: Art, Language, History". NENON, Thomas J.

AGENT(S)

"Adams on the Mind: Mind as Meaning and as Agent" in *Mind, Value and Culture: Essays in Honor of E M Adams*, HALL, R.

"The Ideology of Representation and the Role of the Agent" in *Dismantling Truth: Reality in the Post-Modern World*, WOOLGAR, Steve.

Deontology and the Agent: A Reply to Jonathan Bennett. SCHEFFLER, Samuel.

Disparate Conceptions of Moral Theory. HUGHES, Paul.

Limited Paternalism and the Pontius Pilate Plight. WALTERS, Kerry S.

A Note on Some Puzzling Phrases in Aquinas. VANDER WEEL, Richard L.

Pain and the Quantum Leap to Agent-Neutral Value. CARLSON, George R.

Talking About Actions. SEGERBERG, Krister.

AGGRESSION

Sociobiology, Sex, and Aggression. FLAGEL, David.

AGING

The Biomedical Model and Just Health Care: Reply to Jecker. DANIELS, Norman.

What Children Owe Parents: Ethics in an Aging Society. POST, Stephen G.

AGNOSTICISM

Agnosticism and Atheism. BRINTON, Alan.

A Dialogue with God. JAMBOR, Mishka.

Le origini dell'ateismo antico (terza parte). ZEPPI, Stelio.

AGREEMENT(S)

Reason and Agreement in Social Contract Views. FREEMAN, Samuel.

AGRICOLA, R

Lorenzo Valla and Rudolph Agricola. MONFASANI, John.

AGRICULTURE

Agrarianism and the American Philosophical Tradition. THOMPSON, Paul B.

Agricultural Technology, Wealth, and Responsibility. WUNDERLICH, Gene.

Agriculture: A War on Nature?. SURGEY, John.

Does Metaphysics Rest on an Agrarian Foundation? A Deweyan Answer and Critique. MARSOOBIAN, Armen.

Emerson and the Agricultural Midworld. CORRINGTON, Robert S.

Irony, Tragedy, and Temporality in Agricultural Systems, or, How Values and Systems are Related. BUSCH, Lawrence.

Media Ethics and Agriculture: Advertiser Demands Challenge Farm Press's Ethical Practices. REISNER, Anne E and HAYS, Robert G.

The Metaphysical Transition in Farming: From the Newtonian-Mechanical to the Eltonian Ecological. CALLICOTT, J Baird.

Multi-Party Responses to Environmental Problems: A Case of Contaminated Dairy Cattle. MORREN JR, George E B.

Personhood and the Land. CAMPBELL, James.

A Rationale for the Support of the Medium-Sized Family Farm. DANIELS,

ALTRUISM
Love and Friendship in Plato and Aristotle. PRICE, A W.
Dutch Objections to Evolutionary Ethics. RICHARDS, Robert J.
Humanism and Altruism. MADIGAN, Tim.
Integralism and the Reconstruction of Society: The Idea of Ultimate Reality and Meaning in the World of P A Sorokin. JOHNSTON, Barry V.
A Problem about Higher Order Desires. MOORE, F C T.
The Thee Generation. REGAN, Tom.

AMBIGUITY
Philosophy without Ambiguity: A Logico-Linguistic Essay. ATLAS, Jay David.
Truth Theoretical Semantics and Ambiguity. GILLON, Brendan S.

AMERICAN
see also Latin American
The American Evasion of Philosophy: A Genealogy of Pragmatism. WEST, Cornel.
Ethics in America: Study Guide. NEWTON, Lisa H.
Political Writings: Thomas Paine. KUKLICK, Bruce (ed).
The Unvarnished Doctrine: Locke, Liberalism, and the American Revolution DWORETZ, Steven M.
William James, Public Philosopher. COTKIN, George.
"Human Rights and the Founding Fathers" in *Moral Reasoning and Statecraft: Essays Presented to Kenneth W Thompson,* LANG, Daniel G.
"The Naturalists" in *Reading Philosophy for the Twenty-First Century,* KURTZ, Paul.
"The Pragmatists" in *Reading Philosophy for the Twenty-First Century,* MC DERMOTT, John J.
Agrarianism and the American Philosophical Tradition. THOMPSON, Paul B.
The American Founders and Classical Political Thought. ZVESPER, John.
Backing Into Vico: Recent Trends in American Philosophy. LILLA, Mark.
Edmund Burke and the American Constitution. FRISCH, Morton J.
Het experiment als bron van artefacten. VAN GINNEKEN, Jaap.
From Liberalism to Radicalism: Tom Paine's Rights of Man. KATES, Gary.
The Hypervisual Meaning of the American West. MEYER, William E H.
Individualism, Community, and Education: An Exchange of Views. GRIFFIN, Robert S and NASH, Robert J.
Leo Strauss as Citizen and Jew. DANNHAUSER, Werner J.
New Documents on Josiah Royce. CLENDENNING, John and OPPENHEIM, Frank M.
Philosophy in the United States (A Dialogue of Laurent Stern and Márta Fehér) (in Hungarian). STERN, Laurent and FEHÉR, Márta.
Teaching American Philosophy. CAMPBELL, James.
Was Tocqueville a Philosopher?. LAWLER, Peter A.

AMORAL
La Prétention amoraliste. CLOUTIER, Yvan.
The Rational Status of A-Moral Choices (in Hebrew). YONAH, Yossi.

AMPHIBOLY
The Many Faces of Amphiboly. ENGEL, S Morris.

ANABAPTIST
Evangelical Ethics and the Anabaptist-Reformed Dialogue. MOUW, Richard J and YODER, John H.

ANACHRONISM
"Posthumous Anachronisms in the Work of Sartre" in *Inquiries into Values: The Inaugural Session of the International Society for Value Inquiry,* CAWS, Peter.

ANALOGICAL ARGUMENT(S)
La verità come inganno—L'Arte di Gorgia. VITALE, Vincenzo.

ANALOGY(-GIES)
Analogical Arguings and Explainings. JOHNSON, Fred.
Analogies and Missing Premises. GOVIER, Trudy.
Analogy and Interpretation (in Polish). LUBANSKI, Mieczyslaw.
Beardsley's Theory of Analogy. BARKER, Evelyn M.
By Parity of Reasoning. WOODS, John and HUDAK, Brent.
The Cognitive Effect of Metaphor. GERHART, Mary and RUSSELL, Allan Melvin.
Reasoning by Analogy in Hume's Dialogues. BARKER, Stephen F.
Two Traditions of Analogy. BROWN, William R.

ANALYSIS
see also Linguistic Analysis
The Growth of Knowledge: An Inquiry into the Kuhnian Theory. VERRONEN, Veli.
An Introduction to Philosophical Analysis (Third Edition). HOSPERS, John.
Social Theory and the Crisis of Marxism. MC CARNEY, Joseph.
"Comment: Positivism and the Foundations of Legal Authority" in *Issues in Contemporary Legal Philosophy: The Influence of H L A Hart,* FINNIS, John.
An Argumentation-Analysis of a Central Part of Lenin's Political Logic. SMIT, P A.
Causes, Enablers, and the Counterfactual Analysis. LOMBARD, Lawrence Brian.
Disciplining Qualitative Decision Exercises: Aspects of a Transempirical Protocol, I. SUTHERLAND, John W.
Fixed Point Theory in Weak Second-Order Arithmetic. SHIOJI, Naoki and TANAKA, Kazuyuki.
In Defense of '⊃'. THOMSON, James F.
Insider Trading: An Ethical Appraisal. IRVINE, William B.
The Means of Analysis and the Future of Liberalism: A Response to Hariman. STOESZ, David.
Money: A Speech Act Analysis. HADREAS, Peter.
A New Model for Intuitionistic Analysis. SCOWCROFT, Philip.
Prima e terza persona: Un recente contributo alla "Philosophy of Mind". MARRONE, Pierpaolo.
Seeming to See Red. BAKER, Lynne Rudder.
Some Aspects of the Methodology of Comparative Research in Politics WIATR, Jerzy J.
Why Did Kant Bother About 'Nothing'?. VAN KIRK, Carol A.
Wittgenstein on Grammar and Analytic Philosophy of Education. RIZVI, Fazal.

ANALYTIC
Analytic Aesthetics. SHUSTERMAN, Richard (ed).
Looser Ends: The Practice of Philosophy. BENCIVENGA, Ermanno.
The Rehabilitation of Whitehead: An Analytic and Historical Assessment of Process Philosophy. LUCAS JR, George R.
"The Analysts" in *Reading Philosophy for the Twenty-First Century,* URMSON, John O.
"Analytic Implication: Its History, Justification and Varieties" in *Directions in Relevant Logic,* PARRY, William T.
"Analytic Philosophy and the Meaning of Music" in *Analytic Aesthetics,* SCRUTON, Roger.
"Analytic/Dialectic" in *Reading Kant,* BRANDT, Reinhard.
"The Eclipse and Recovery of Analytic Aesthetics" in *Analytic Aesthetics,* MARGOLIS, Joseph.
"The Inevitability of Pluralism: Philosophical Practice and Philosophical Excellence" in *The Institution of Philosophy: A Discipline in Crisis?,* MANDT, A J.
"Introduction: Analysing Analytic Aesthetics" in *Analytic Aesthetics,* SHUSTERMAN, Richard.
"Philosophy of Art After Analysis and Romanticism" in *Analytic Aesthetics,* WOLTERSTORFF, Nicholas.
"Why is a Philosopher?" in *The Institution of Philosophy: A Discipline in Crisis?,* PUTNAM, Hilary.
The Analytic Turn: An Institutional Account. SARTWELL, Crispin.
Analytical Marxism and Marx's Systematic Dialectical Theory. SMITH, Tony.
How Marxism Became Analytic. MARTIN, Bill.
The Identity of American Neo-Pragmatism; or, Why Vico Now?. MEGILL, Allan.
Is Critical Thinking Guilty of Unwarranted Reductionism. HATCHER, Donald.
New Trends in Literary Aesthetics: An Overview. TAYLOR, Paul.
On Analytic Filters and Prefilters. ZAFRANY, Samy.
Selbst das Selbst ist nicht Selbst. ESSLER, Wilhelm K.
A Sociobiological Explanation of Strategies of Reading and Writing Philosophy. GILMAN, Roger William.
The Use of Symbols in Religion from the Perspective of Analytical Psychology. MC GLASHAN, A R.
The Vienna Roundabout: On the Significance of Philosophical Reaction. HRACHOVEC, Herbert.
Zur Analytizität hypothetischer Imperative. BURRI, Alex and FREUDIGER, Jürg.

ANALYTICITY
Necessity, Essence, and Individuation: A Defense of Conventionalism. SIDELLE, Alan.
Questions of Form: Logic and the Analytic Proposition from Kant to Carnap. PROUST, Joëlle.
Analyticity, Indeterminacy and Semantic Theory: Some Comments on "The Domino Theory". GREENWOOD, John D.
Analytico-Referentiality and Legitimation in Modern Mathematics. ROUSSOPOULOS, George.
Lesniewski's Strategy and Modal Logic. KEARNS, John T.

ANAPHORA
Descriptions. NEALE, Stephen.
Anaphoric Attitudes. CRESSWELL, M J.
Descriptive Pronouns and Donkey Anaphora. NEALE, Stephen.

ANAPHORA
E-Type Pronouns and Donkey Anaphora. HEIM, Irene.
Modal Subordination and Pronominal Anaphora in Discourse. ROBERTS, Craige.

ANARCHISM
"Politics and Feyerabend's Anarchist" in *Knowledge and Politics*, HANNAY, Alastair.
Is Post-Structuralist Political Theory Anarchist?. MAY, Todd.

ANARCHY
"Reflections on Hobbes: Anarchy and Human Nature" in *The Causes of Quarrel: Essays on Peace, War, and Thomas Hobbes*, LANDESMAN, Charles.
Beyond Aestheticism: Derrida's Responsible Anarchy. CAPUTO, John D.
Entre positivisme et anarchie? Trois voies de recherche dans la construction des theories en science litteraire. DECREUS, F.
Il radicalismo negli Stati Uniti degli anni '80: l'anarco-ecologismo di Murray Bookchin. DONNO, A.

ANATOMY
Preventing Birth: Contemporary Methods and Related Moral Controversies. CALLAHAN, Joan C.

ANAXAGORAS
Nous, the Concept of Ultimate Reality and Meaning in Anaxagoras. SILVESTRE, Maria Luisa.

ANAXIMANDER
"Ἀρχή γ ἐναντίωσις: su nexo en el pensamiento preparmenideo". MELENDO, Tomás.
Thales, Anaximander, and Infinity. DANCY, R M.
Vom epischen zum logischen sprechen: der spruch des Anaximander. RIEDEL, M.

ANCESTRAL RELATION(S)
Searching for Ancestors. O'HAGAN, Timothy.

ANCIENT
see also Greek
The "Meditations" of Marcus Aurelius: A Study. RUTHERFORD, R B.
"The Son of Apollo": Themes of Plato. WOODBRIDGE, Frederick J E.
Aisthesis: Grundzüge und Perspektiven der Aristotelischen Sinneslehre. WELSCH, Wolfgang.
Aristotle on Substance: The Paradox of Unity. GILL, Mary Louise.
Aristotle's Concept of the Universal. BRAKAS, George.
Aristotle's Poetics. APOSTLE, Hippocrates G (trans).
Beauty and Holiness: The Dialogue between Aesthetics and Religion. MARTIN JR, James Alfred.
Cicero's Knowledge of the Peripatos. FORTENBAUGH, William W (ed).
El individuo y la feminidad. PEREZ ESTEVEZ, Antonio.
Epistemology (Companions to Ancient Thought: 1). EVERSON, Stephen (ed).
The Ethics of Geometry: A Genealogy of Modernity. LACHTERMAN, David R.
Il Giogo: Alle origini della ragione: Eschilo. SEVERINO, Emanuele.
Greek Scepticism: Anti-Realist Trends in Ancient Thought. GROARKE, Leo.
Love and Friendship in Plato and Aristotle. PRICE, A W.
The Nature of Man in Early Stoic Philosophy. REESOR, Margaret E.
Paul and the Popular Philosophers. MALHERBE, Abraham J.
Philosophia Togata: Essays on Philosophy and Roman Society. GRIFFIN, Miriam (ed).
Pythagoras Revived: Mathematics and Philosophy in Late Antiquity. O'MEARA, Dominic J.
Pythagoras: An Annotated Bibliography. NAVIA, Luis E.
Socrates in the Apology: An Essay on Plato's Apology of Socrates. REEVE, C D C.
Socrates on Trial. BRICKHOUSE, Thomas C.
Understanding Plato. MELLING, David J.
Wesen, Freiheit und Bildung des Menschen. HAGER, Fritz-Peter.
"Beobachtungen zu Ciceros philosophischem Standpunkt" in *Cicero's Knowledge of the Peripatos*, STEINMETZ, Peter.
"Gibt es Spuren von Theophrasts *Phys op* bei Cicero?" in *Cicero's Knowledge of the Peripatos*, MANSFELD, Jaap.
"Theophrast in Cicero's *De finibus*" in *Cicero's Knowledge of the Peripatos*, GIGON, Olof.
"Ἀρχή γ ἐναντίωσις: su nexo en el pensamiento preparmenideo". MELENDO, Tomás.
"Questions Philosophers Ask": Response to Michael Baur. NALEZINSKI, Alix.
The 'Theology' of the Hippocratic Treatise On the Sacred Disease. VAN DER EIJK, P J.

1987 Controversy Over the Evaluations of Confucius. DINGBO, Wu.
The Ancient Sceptic's Way of Life. MORRISON, Donald.
The *Apology* and the *Crito*: A Misplaced Inconsistency. WARD, Andrew.
The Argument Against a Dramatic Date for Plato's *Republic*. MOORS, Kent F.
Aristotle on 'Time' and 'A Time'. WHITE, Michael J.
Aristotle's Crowning Virtue. COOPER, Neil.
Aristotle's Four Types of Definition. DESLAURIERS, Marguerite.
Aristotle's God and the Authenticity of *De mundo*: An Early Modern Controversy. KRAYE, Jill.
The Biographies of Siddhasena: A Study in the Texture of Allusion and the Weaving of a Group-Image (Part I). GRANOFF, Phyllis.
Carneades' Distinction Between Assent and Approval. BETT, Richard.
Chrysippus and the *Placita*. MANSFELD, Jaap.
Coins and Classical Philosophy. BRUMBAUGH, Robert.
A Comparative Study of Natural Philosophy in Pre-Qin China and Ancient Greece. SHAOJUN, Weng.
The Concerns of Odysseus: An Introduction to the *Odyssey*. BOLOTIN, David.
Cornelia de Vogel fra vecchio e nuovo paradigma ermeneutico nell'interpretazione di Platone. PEROLI, Enrico.
Democritus and the Impossibility of Collision. GODFREY, Raymond.
Dialectic and Deliberation in Aristotle's Practical Philosophy. BAYNES, Kenneth.
The Enigma of *Categories* 1a20ff and Why It Matters. MATTHEWS, Gareth B.
The Ergon Inference. GOMEZ-LOBO, Alfonso.
Forms of Life and Forms of Discourse in Ancient Philosophy. HADOT, Pierre and DAVIDSON, Arnold (trans) and WISSING, Paula (trans).
Gab es eine Dialektische Schule?. DÖRING, Klaus.
Geometry and Medicine: Mathematics in the Thought of Galen of Pergamum. GRANT, Hardy.
Hannah Arendt and Leo Strauss: The Uncommenced Dialogue. BEINER, Ronald.
The Hedonic Calculus in the *Protagoras* and the *Phaedo*: A Reply. GOSLING, J C B.
The Hellenistic Version of Aristotle's Ethics. ANNAS, Julia.
Heraclito de efeso entre la experiencia y la razon. ANDRADE, Ciro Schmidt.
The Idea of Music in India and the Ancient West. ROWELL, Lewis.
Is There a History of Sexuality?. HALPERIN, David M.
Joan Kung's Reading of Plato's *Timaeus*. MUELLER, Ian.
Love and Beauty in Plato's *Symposium*. WHITE, F C.
Il luogo dell'ultima stera nei commenti tardo-antichi e medievali a "Physica" IV:5. TRIFOGLI, Cecilia.
Measurement, Pleasure, and Practical Science in Plato's *Protagoras*. RICHARDSON, Henry S.
More on Plato, *Meno* 82 c 2-3. SHARPLES, R W.
Mortal Immortals: Lucretius on Death and the Voice of Nature. NUSSBAUM, Martha C.
The *Munus* of Transmitting Human Life: A New Approach to *Humanae Vitae*. SMITH, Janet E.
New Light on Antiphon. BARNES, Jonathan.
On the Skeptical Influence of Gorgias's *On Non-Being*. HAYS, Steve.
Le origini dell'ateismo antico (quarta parte). ZEPPI, Stelio.
The Origins of Political Theory. WRIGHT, R M.
Parmenides 142b5-144e7: The "Unity is Many" Arguments. CURD, Patricia Kenig.
Perceptual and Objective Properties in Plato. WHITE, Nicholas P.
Philosophy and Rhetoric in the *Menexenus*. COVENTRY, Lucinda.
Plato and Totalitarianism. HALL, Robert W.
Plato's Aporetic Style. RUDEBUSCH, George.
Plato's *Euthyphro*. MORRIS, T F.
Plato's *Lysis*: An Introduction to Philosophic Friendship. TESSITORE, Aristide.
Platón filósofo-educador: valor "alusivo" de la escritura. BONAGURA, Patricia.
Political Animals in the *Nicomachean Ethics*. ROBERTS, Jean.
The Practical Element in Ancient Exact Sciences. KNORR, Wilbur R.
Praxis and Poesis in Aristotle's Practical Philosophy. BALABAN, Oded.
Problems in the Argument of Plato's *Crito*. KAHN, Charles H.
A Rejoinder to Professors Gosling and Taylor. WEISS, Roslyn.
A Response to A A Long's "The Stoics on World-Conflagration and Everlasting Recurrence". HUDSON, Hud.
The Rhetoric of Socrates. ROSSETTI, Livio.
Seeing Justice Done: Aeschylus' *Oresteia*. FLAUMENHAFT, Mera J.
The Sophists and Relativism. BETT, Richard.
Sul concetto di filosofia nel *Fedro* platonico. ALBERT, Karl.

ANCIENT
The Symmetry Argument: Lucretius Against the Fear of Death. ROSENBAUM, Stephen E.
Thales, Anaximander, and Infinity. DANCY, R M.
Two Ideals of Friendship. O'CONNOR, David K.
Unto the Mountain: Toward a Paradigm for Early Chinese Thought. DOERINGER, Franklin M.
Victor Cousin: frammenti socratici. RAGGHIANTI, Renzo.
Vida y evolución en la filosofía griega. CAPPELLETTI, Angel J.
The Whole as Setting for Man: On Plato's *Timaeus*. CROPSEY, Joseph.
Wo beginnt der Weg der Doxa?. EBERT, Theodor.
Xenophanes on the Moon: A *Doxographicum* in Aëtius. RUNIA, David T.

ANDERSSON, G
Der Mythos des Rahmens am Pranger: Anderssons Antwort auf die wissenschaftsgeschichtliche Herausforderung. ALBERT, Hans.

ANDREW OF NOVO CASTRO
Andrew of Novo Castro, OFM, and the Moral Law. KENNEDY, Leonard A.

ANDROGYNY
Androgyny and Leadership Style. KORABIK, Karen.
Cinquante-six conceptions de l'androgynie. BOUCHARD, Guy.

ANGEL(S)
Angelic Interiority. CASEY, Gerard N.
Angelology, Metaphysics, and Intersubjectivity: A Reply to G N Casey. KAINZ, Howard P.

ANGER
The Wrath of God. OAKES, Robert.

ANGLICANISM
Philosophie et théologie chez Austin Farrer. HENDERSON, Edward H.

ANIMAL EXPERIMENTATION
Animal Rights and Human Obligations (Second Edition). REGAN, Tom.
Bibliography of Bioethics, Volume 15. WALTERS, LeRoy (ed).
Animal Models in 'Exemplary' Medical Research: Diabetes as a Case Study. NELSON, James Lindemann.
Animals in the Research Laboratory: Science or Pseudoscience?. CATALANO, George D.
Animals, Science, and Ethics. DONNELLEY, Strachan (ed) and NOLAN, Kathleen (ed).
Comment on James Nelson's "Animals in 'Exemplary' Medical Research: Diabetes as a Case Study". FINSEN, Lawrence.
The Ethics Crunch: Can Medical Science Advance Without the Use of Animals?. KOWALSKI, Gary.
A New Approach to Regulating the Use of Animals in Science. ANDERSON, Warwick.
The Responsible Use of Animals in Biomedical Research. HETTINGER, Edwin Converse.

ANIMAL RIGHTS
Animal Rights and Human Obligations (Second Edition). REGAN, Tom.
Ethics and the Environmental Responsibility. DOWER, Nigel (ed).
Keyguide to Information Sources on Animal Rights. MAGEL, Charles R.
"Animal Rights and Human Wrongs" in *Ethics and the Environmental Responsibility*, LA FOLLETTE, Hugh.
The "Values" of Sentient Beings. FOX, Michael W.
Akrasia and Animal Rights: Philosophy in the British Primary School. COSTELLO, Patrick J M.
Environmental Ethics and the Locus of Value. SAPONTZIS, Steve F.
The Ethics Crunch: Can Medical Science Advance Without the Use of Animals?. KOWALSKI, Gary.
The Fiery Fight for Animal Rights. JACKSON, Christine M.
Grassroots Opposition to Animal Exploitation. SIEGEL, Steve.
Hartshorne and the Metaphysics of Animal Rights. BARAD, Judith.
Nonsense, Fate, and Policy Analysis: The Case of Animal Rights and Experimentation. ROE, Emery M.
Practical Solutions. MIDGLEY, Mary.
Realism and Respect. BALDNER, Kent.
Rejoinder to Sapontzis's "Environmental Ethics and the Locus of Value". BALDNER, Kent.
The Responsible Use of Animals in Biomedical Research. HETTINGER, Edwin Converse.
To Do or Not to Do?. SINGER, Peter.
Treating Animals Naturally?. ROLSTON III, Holmes.

ANIMAL(S)
"Persons, Animals, and Ourselves" in *The Person and the Human Mind: Issues in Ancient and Modern Philosophy*, SNOWDON, P F.
Alberto Magno y los últimos unicornios. DE ASUA, M J C.
The Death of the Animal: Ontological Vulnerability. SHAPIRO, Kenneth Joel.

Ethical Similarities in Human and Animal Social Structures. ELLOS, William J.
Kant on Descartes and the Brutes. NARAGON, Steve.
Metaphysics. WEININGER, Otto and BURNS, S A M (trans).
The Morality of Animals. GHOSH-DASTIDAR, Koyeli.
Nonhuman Experience: A Whiteheadian Analysis. ARMSTRONG-BUCK, Susan.
Self-Consciousness in Chimps and Pigeons. DAVIS, Lawrence H.
Tragedy and Nonhumans. PUTMAN, Daniel.

ANIMISM
Fools, Young Children, Animism, and the Scientific World-Picture. KENNEDY, David.

ANNAS, J
Platon, Arcésilas, Carnéade: Réponse à J Annas. LÉVY, Carlos.

ANOMIE
The Theme of Civilization and its Discontents in Durkheim's *Division of Labor*. MESTROVIC, Stjepan G.

ANONYMITY
Anonymous Writings of David Hume. RAPHAEL, D D and SAKAMOTO, Tatsuya.

ANSCOMBE, G
Actions and Other Events: The Unifier-Multiplier Controversy. PFEIFER, Karl.
Anscombe on Justifying Claims to Know One's Bodily Position. LOTT, Tommy L.
Essential Aims and Unavoidable Responsibilities: A Response to Anscombe. COUGHLAN, Michael J.
Neurophilosophy and the Logic-Causation Argument. KIAMIE, Kimberly A.

ANSELM
Anselm's Proof. STONE, Jim.
Individual and Attribute in the Ontological Argument. LEFTOW, Brian.
Lenguaje y misterio en Anselmo de Canterbury. BRIANCESCO, Eduardo.
La libertad en S Anselmo. GARAY SUÁREZ-LLANOS, Jesús.
Libertad y necesidad en el "cur Deus homo" de San Anselmo de Canterbury. CORTI, E C.
La metafisica della Prima Persona *(Ego Sum Qui Sum)*: Parte prima. ARATA, Carlo.
Reference in Anselm's Ontological Proof. WERTZ, S K.
Saint Anselm of Canterbury on Ultimate Reality and Meaning. DECORTE, Jos.

ANSWER(S)
Collingwood's Logic of Question and Answer. SOMERVILLE, James.

ANTECEDENCE
The Changing Image of Art Education: Theoretical Antecedents of Discipline-Based Art Education. SMITH, Ralph A.

ANTECEDENT(S)
Double Conditionals. MORTON, Adam.

ANTHROPOCENTRISM
"The Metaphysics of Environmentalism" in *Ethics and the Environmental Responsibility*, MATTHEWS, Eric.
Anti-Anthropocentrism as a Value in Science. PIATEK, Zdzislawa.
Descartes' Legacy and Deep Ecology. MILLER, Peter.
Realism and Respect. BALDNER, Kent.
Rejoinder to Sapontzis's "Environmental Ethics and the Locus of Value". BALDNER, Kent.

ANTHROPOLOGY
Body, Soul, and Life Everlasting: Biblical Anthropology and the Monism-Dualism Debate. COOPER, John W.
Demokrit: Texte seiner Philosophie. LOBL, Rudolf.
Evolution of the Brain: Creation of the Self. ECCLES, John C.
Moral Absolutes: An Essay on the Nature and Rationale of Morality. RESCHER, Nicholas.
Paths Toward a Clearing: Radical Empiricism and Ethnographic Inquiry. JACKSON, Michael.
Whitehead's Metaphysics of Creativity. RAPP, Friedrich (ed).
"Whitehead's Cosmology of Feeling Between Ontology and Anthropology" in *Whitehead's Metaphysics of Creativity*, WIEHL, Reiner.
Anthropologische Prolegomena zur Metaphysik. HENRICI, Peter.
The Anthropology of 'Semantic Levels' in Music. KARBUSICKY, Vladimir.
Anthropology of Peace. MAZUREK, Franciszek Janusz and LECKI, Maciej (trans).
Anthropology on the Boundary and the Boundary in Anthropology. MARTIN, Dan.
Le cas Lévy-Bruhl. MERLLIÉ, Dominique.
Dialectics of a Dialogical Ideal: Studying Down, Studying Sideways and

ANTHROPOLOGY

Studying Up. SCHRIJVERS, Joke.

The National Axiological Anthropological Atlas: A "Chart" of the Premiss Values of the Romanian People's Culture (I). CARAMELEA, Vasile V (and others).

The Small-Republic Argument in Modern Micronesia. PETERSEN, Glenn.

Die soziobiologische Obsoletierung des "Reichs der Zwecke". DORSCHEL, Andreas.

The Latest Philosophical Anthropology of Max Scheler (in Dutch). VEDDER, Ben.

ANTHROPOMORPHISM

Analogy Sans Portrait: God-Talk as Literal But Non-Anthropomorphic. MILLER, Barry.

Animals, Science, and Ethics. DONNELLEY, Strachan (ed) and NOLAN, Kathleen (ed).

Anthropomorphic Concepts of God. SCHOEN, Edward.

Judging God By "Human" Standards: Reflections on William James' Varieties of Religious Experience. TUMULTY, Peter.

Theological Empiricism: Aspects of Johann Georg Hamann's Reception of Hume. GRAUBNER, Hans.

ANTI-SEMITISM

Heidegger and Nazism. MARGOLIS, Joseph (ed).

On Heidegger's Silence. KOVACS, George.

ANTILOGISM(S)

Directions in Relevant Logic. NORMAN, Jean (ed).

"Introduction: Routes in Relevant Logic" in Directions in Relevant Logic, NORMAN, Jean and SYLVAN, Richard.

ANTINOMY(-MIES)

Antinomies and Paradoxes and their Solutions. WEINGARTNER, Paul.

How Can Theology Be Moral?. O'DONOVAN, Oliver.

Kant's Third Antinomy: Agency and Causal Explanation. GREENWOOD, John D.

Die kosmologischen Antinomien in der Kritik der reinen Vernunft und die moderne physikalische Kosmologie. MITTELSTAEDT, Peter and STROHMEYER, Ingeborg.

ANTIOCHUS OF ASCALON

"Antiochus of Ascalon" in Philosophia Togata: Essays on Philosophy and Roman Society, BARNES, Jonathan.

ANTIPHON

New Light on Antiphon. BARNES, Jonathan.

ANTIREALISM

Greek Scepticism: Anti-Realist Trends in Ancient Thought. GROARKE, Leo.

Anti-Realism in the Philosophy of Probability: Bruno de Finetti's Subjectivism. GALAVOTTI, Maria Carla.

Anti-Realism Under Mind?. KHLENTZOS, Drew.

Antirealism and Holes in the World. HAND, Michael.

Extragalactic Reality: The Case of Gravitational Lensing. HACKING, Ian.

Idealized Laws, Antirealism, and Applied Science: A Case in Hydrogeology. SHRADER-FRECHETTE, K S.

Misconstruals Made Manifest: A Response to Simon Blackburn. WRIGHT, Crispin.

NOA's Ark—Fine for Realism. MUSGRAVE, Alan.

Realism versus Antirealism: The Venue of the Linguistic Consensus. POLS, Edward.

Supervaluational Anti-Realism and Logic. RASMUSSEN, Stig Alstrup.

Two Incomplete Anti-Realist Modal Epistemic Logics. WILLIAMSON, Timothy.

ANXIETY

"Hermeneutics and Its Anxieties" in Reading Philosophy for the Twenty-First Century, BERNSTEIN, Richard J.

Does Anxiety Explain Original Sin?. QUINN, Philip L.

The Echo of Narcissus: Anxiety, Language and Reflexivity in "Envois". JOHNSON, Cyraina E.

Scepticism and Angst: The Case of David Hume. COHEN, Avner.

APARTHEID

"Abolishing Apartheid: The Importance of Sanctions" in Inquiries into Values: The Inaugural Session of the International Society for Value Inquiry, AUXTER, Thomas.

On Being Ethical in Unethical Places: The Dilemmas of South African Clinical Psychologists. STEERE, Jane and DOWDALL, Terence.

Responsibility and Complicity. ARONSON, Ronald.

APE(S)

How to Learn a Language Like a Chimpanzee. GAUKER, Christopher.

Language as a Cause-Effect Communication System. SAVAGE-RUMBAUGH, E S.

APEL, K

Il dibattito sulla razionalità oggi: un ritorno a Kant? Interviste a K O Apel & J Petitot. QUARANTA, M.

Discourse Ethics and the Legitimacy of Law. TUORI, Kaarlo.

Scepticism, Certain Grounds and the Method of Reflexivity (in Dutch). VAN WOUDENBERG, R.

De transcendentale grondlegging van de ethiek van Karl-Otto Apel. VAN WOUDENBERG, R.

APHORISM(S)

Le Tractatus de Wittgenstein: Considérations sur le système numérique et la forme aphoristique. HESS, Gérald.

APOCALYPSE

The Self-Embodiment of God. ALTIZER, Thomas J J.

Is the End of the World Nigh?. LESLIE, John.

APOLOGETICS

Unapologetic Theology: A Christian Voice in a Pluralistic Conversation. PLACHER, William C.

A Stakeholder Apologetic for Management. SHARPLIN, Arthur and PHELPS, Lonnie D.

APOLOGY(-GIES)

Socrates in the Apology: An Essay on Plato's Apology of Socrates. REEVE, C D C.

Philosophical Apology in the Theaetetus. HEMMENWAY, Scott R.

APPEARANCE(S)

The Critique of Thought: A Re-Examination of Hegel's Science of Logic. JOHNSON, Paul Owen.

The Doctoral Dissertation of Karl Marx. TEEPLE, G.

Dressing Down Dressing Up—The Philosophic Fear of Fashion. HANSON, Karen.

Kant's Account of Sensation. FALKENSTEIN, Lorne.

APPERCEPTION

The Categorial Satisfaction of Self-Reflexive Reason. PINKARD, Terry.

The Role of Apperception in Kant's Transcendental Deduction of the Categories. CASTAÑEDA, Héctor-Neri.

APPLE, M

Capitalist Schools: Explanation and Ethics in Radical Studies of Schooling. LISTON, Daniel P.

APPLICATION(S)

The Fabric of This World: Inquiries into Calling, Career Choice, and the Design of Human Work. HARDY, Lee.

Issues in Evolutionary Epistemology. HAHLWEG, Kai (ed).

The Born-Einstein Debate: Where Application and Explanation Separate. CARTWRIGHT, Nancy.

Critical Thinking as Applied Epistemology: Relocating Critical Thinking in the Philosophical Landscape. BATTERSBY, Mark E.

Idealized Laws, Antirealism, and Applied Science: A Case in Hydrogeology. SHRADER-FRECHETTE, K S.

Impartial Application of Moral and Legal Norms: A Contribution to Discourse Ethics. GÜNTHER, Klaus.

Moral Understandings: Alternative "Epistemology" for a Feminist Ethics. WALKER, Margaret Urban.

Some Applications of Process and Reality I and II to Educational Practice. BRUMBAUGH, Robert S.

What Is and What Is Not Practical Reason?. HELLER, Agnes.

APPLIED ETHICS

Foundations of Environmental Ethics. HARGROVE, Eugene C.

Moral Reasoning: A Philosophic Approach to Applied Ethics. FOX, Richard M.

"Toward an Adequate Theory of Applied Ethics". DE MARCO, Joseph P.

Bioengineering, Scientific Activism, and Philosophical Bridges. DURBIN, Paul T.

The Limited Relevance of Analytical Ethics to the Problems of Bioethics. HOLMES, Robert L.

Method in Bioethics: A Troubled Assessment. GREEN, Ronald M.

Philosophers and the Public Policy Process: Inside, Outside, or Nowhere at All?. MOMEYER, Richard W.

The Role of Applied Ethics in Philosophy. MARQUIS, D.

Sociobiology, Sex, and Aggression. FLAGEL, David.

What Is Applied About "Applied" Philosophy?. KOPELMAN, Loretta M.

APPLIED PHILOSOPHY

"Vaticinal Visions and Pedagogical Prescriptions" in Mind, Value and Culture: Essays in Honor of E M Adams, HOOKER, Michael.

Against Theory, or: Applied Philosophy—A Cautionary Tale. FULLINWIDER,

ARCHITECTURE

Tears. TAYLOR, Mark C.
The Architecture of Science and the Idea of a University. FORGAN, Sophie.
Architecture, Philosophy and the Public World. HALDANE, John.
Aufbau/Bauhaus: Logical Positivism and Architectural Modernism. GALISON, Peter.
El bien en arquitectura. SAGARDOY, María A F.
Building for Democracy: Organic Architecture in Relation to Progressive Education. ROCHE, John F.
The Language of Architecture. DONOUGHO, Martin.
A Point of Reconciliation Between Schopenhauer and Hegel. KORAB-KARPOWICZ, W J.
La unidad perdida del proyecto arquitectónico. ELÍCEGUI, Juan M O.

ARENDT, H

Hannah Arendt: Lectures on Kant's Political Philosophy. BEINER, Ronald (ed).
Agency, Identity, and Culture: Hannah Arendt's Conception of Citizenship. D'ENTRÈVES, Maurizio Passerin.
Arendt's Politics: The Elusive Search for Substance. SCHWARTZ, Joseph M.
Arendt, Camus, and Postmodern Politics. ISSAC, Jeffrey C.
Arendt, Republicanism and Patriarchalism. SPRINGBORG, Patricia.
Freedom, Plurality, Solidarity: Hannah Arendt's Theory of Action. D'ENTRÈVES, Maurizio Passerin.
Hannah Arendt and Leo Strauss: The Uncommenced Dialogue. BEINER, Ronald.
Hannah Arendt on Judgment, Philosophy and Praxis. KNAUER, James T.
Thinking Politics without a Philosophy of History: Arendt and Merleau-Ponty. ROMAN, Joël and MICHELMAN, Stephen (trans).

ARGUMENT(S)

Coleridge, Shelley, and Transcendental Inquiry: Rhetoric, Argument, Metapsychology. HODGSON, John A.
Critical Thinking: Evaluating Claims and Arguments in Everyday Life—Second Edition. MOORE, Brook Noel.
David Hume's Argument Against Miracles: A Critical Analysis. BECKWITH, Francis.
The Evidential Force of Religious Experience. DAVIS, Caroline Franks.
If "P", then "Q": Conditionals and the Foundations of Reasoning. SANFORD, David H.
Informal Logic: A Handbook for Critical Argumentation. WALTON, Douglas N.
Introduction to Logic and Critical Thinking (Second Edition). SALMON, Merrilee H.
A Logical Introduction to Philosophy. PURTILL, Richard L.
Philosophical Rhetoric: The Function of Indirection in Philosophical Writing. MASON, Jeff.
Practical Reasoning. WRIGHT, Larry.
Schaum's Outline of Theory and Problems of Logic. NOLT, John Eric.
Sense and Certainty: A Dissolution of Scepticism. MC GINN, Marie.
"The Figure and the Argument" in *From Metaphysics to Rhetoric,* REBOUL, Olivier.
"To Reason While Speaking" in *From Metaphysics to Rhetoric,* GRIZE, Jean-Blaise.
Analogical Arguings and Explainings. JOHNSON, Fred.
Analogies and Missing Premises. GOVIER, Trudy.
Anselm's Proof. STONE, Jim.
Argumentos no son razones. FEILING, Carlos.
Arguments for the Existence of God. SWINBURNE, Richard.
Beardsley's Theory of Analogy. BARKER, Evelyn M.
By Parity of Reasoning. WOODS, John and HUDAK, Brent.
A Case Study in *Ad Hominem* Arguments: Fichte's *Science of Knowledge.* SUBER, Peter.
Comment on Shrader-Frechette's "Parfit and Mistakes in Moral Mathematics". GRACELY, Edward J.
A Critique of Philosophical Conversation. WALZER, Michael.
Fetishism, Argument, and Judgment in *Capital.* FINOCCHIARO, Maurice A.
Frank Jackson's Knowledge Argument Against Materialism. FURASH, Gary.
How to Argue about Practical Reason. WALLACE, R Jay.
Interpreting Arguments and Judging Issues. DAVSON-GALLE, Peter.
The Intuitionist Argument. SIMON, Caroline J.
Liar Syllogisms. DRANGE, Theodore M.
Light from Darkness, From Ignorance Knowledge. WREEN, Michael.
The Only Game in Town. ACHINSTEIN, Peter.
Parmenides 142b5-144e7: The "Unity is Many" Arguments. CURD, Patricia Kenig.
Practical Arguments and Situational Appreciation in Teaching. PENDLEBURY, Shirley.
La priorità ontologica e gnoseologica dell'esistenza di Dio in Spinoza.

NICOLOSI, Salvatore.
Properly Unargued Belief in God. LANGTRY, Bruce.
Rawls, Habermas, and Real Talk: A Reply to Walzer. WARNKE, Georgia.
The Refutation of the Ontological Argument. MC GRATH, P J.
Speech Acts and Arguments. JACOBS, Scott.
Two Traditions of Analogy. BROWN, William R.
Virtue Ethics and Anti-Theory. LOUDEN, Robert B.

ARGUMENTATION

From Metaphysics to Rhetoric. MEYER, Michel (ed).
Rhetoriques. PERELMAN, Chaïm.
"Argumentativity and Informativity" in *From Metaphysics to Rhetoric,* ANSCOMBRE, Jean-Claude and DUCROT, Oswald.
"Formal Logic and Informal Logic" in *From Metaphysics to Rhetoric,* PERELMAN, Chaïm.
"Logic and Argumentation" in *From Metaphysics to Rhetoric,* LADRIERE, Jean.
"Organization and Articulation of Verbal Exchanges" in *From Metaphysics to Rhetoric,* OLERON, Pierre.
An Argumentation-Analysis of a Central Part of Lenin's Political Logic. SMIT, P A.
Argumentos no son razones. FEILING, Carlos.
Buridano e le consequenze. BERTAGNA, Mario.
Conversation, Relevance, and Argumentation. HAFT-VAN REES, M Agnes.
Deconstructionist Metaphysics and the Interpretation of Saussure. FREUNDLIEB, Dieter.
Favorable Relevance and Arguments. BOWLES, George.
Persuasive Argumentation in Negotiation. SYCARA, Katia P.
Principles and Moral Argumentation. WREN, Thomas.
Problems in the Use of Expert Opinion in Argumentation. WALTON, Douglas N.
The Schoolman's Advocate: In Defence of the Academic Pursuit of Philosophy. THOMAS, J L H.
Self-Application in Philosophical Argumentation. JOHNSTONE JR, Henry W.
Speech Act Conditions as Tools for Reconstructing Argumentative Discourse. VAN EEMEREN, Frans H and GROOTENDORST, Rob.
Suppositions in Argumentation. FISHER, Alec.
Sur la structure particulière du dialogue argumentatif. MIHAI, Gheorghe.
Teoria della argomentazione e filosofia della scienza. BARROTTA, Pierluigi.
Teoría lógica y argumentación. NAISHTAT, Francisco.
What Is Reasoning? What Is an Argument?. WALTON, Doug.

ARIOSTO

The Origins of Post-Modernism: The Ariosto-Tasso Debate. MC KINNEY, Ronald H.

ARISTARCHUS

Aristarchus of Samos on Thales' Theory of Eclipses. LEBEDEV, Andrei V.

ARISTOCRACY

Nietzsche and the Politics of Aristocratic Radicalism. DETWILER, Bruce.

ARISTOTELIANISM

Eros, Agape and Philia: Readings in the Philosophy of Love. SOBLE, Alan (ed).
El aristotelismo de Juan de Secheville. RODRÍGUEZ, Juan Acosta.
La conception stoïcienne et la conception aristotélicienne du bonheur. IRWIN, T H.
A Contribution to the Gadamer-Lonergan Discussion. BAUR, Michael.
Crick, Hampshire and MacIntyre or Does an English-Speaking Neo-Aristotelianism Exist?. GIORGINI, Giovanni.
Deux propositions aristotéliciennes sur le droit naturel chez les continentaux d'Amérique. BODÉÜS, Richard.
La finalidad en el mundo natural según san Agustín. MAGNAVACCA, Silvia.
Lectures on the I Ching (in Serbo-Croatian). CHUNG, Albert C.
Philosophie antique et byzantine: à propos de deux nouvelles collections. O'MEARA, Dominic J.
El Pseudo-Justino en la historia del aristotelismo. MARTÍN, José Pablo.
El status lógico de los *topoi* aristotélicos. CHICHI, Graciela.

ARISTOTELIANS

El Concepto de Materia al Comienzo de la Escuela Franciscana de Paris. PEREZ ESTEVEZ, Antonio.
The Anthropology of Incommensurability. BIAGIOLI, Mario.
On the Scholastic or Aristotelian Roots of "Intentionality" in Brentano. RUNGGALDIER, Edmund.

ARISTOTLE

Aisthesis: Grundzüge und Perspektiven der Aristotelischen Sinneslehre. WELSCH, Wolfgang.
Aristotle on Substance: The Paradox of Unity. GILL, Mary Louise.

ARISTOTLE

Aristotle's Concept of the Universal. BRAKAS, George.

Aristotle's Poetics. APOSTLE, Hippocrates G (trans).

Cartesian Logic: An Essay on Descartes's Conception of Inference. GAUKROGER, Stephen.

Cicero's Knowledge of the Peripatos. FORTENBAUGH, William W (ed).

Democracy and Dictatorship. BOBBIO, Norberto.

Demokrit: Texte seiner Philosophie. LOBL, Rudolf.

The Ethics of Geometry: A Genealogy of Modernity. LACHTERMAN, David R.

First Principles, Final Ends and Contemporary Philosophical Issues. MAC INTYRE, Alasdair.

The Infinite. MOORE, A W.

Interpreting Education. EDEL, Abraham.

The Language of Imagination. WHITE, Alan R.

Love and Friendship in Plato and Aristotle. PRICE, A W.

Rhetorica I—Reden mit Vernunft: Aristoteles, Cicero, Augustinus. MAINBERGER, Gonsalv K.

Rhetorica II—Spiegelungen des Geistes: Sprachfiguren bei Vico und L Strauss. MAINBERGER, Gonsalv K.

Suicide and Euthanasia. BRODY, Baruch A (ed).

Time, Freedom, and the Common Good: An Essay in Public Philosophy. SHEROVER, Charles M.

Treatise on Basic Philosophy, Volume 8—Ethics: The Good and the Right. BUNGE, Mario.

Ursprung und Thema von Ersten Wissenschaft. KÖNIGSHAUSEN, Johann-Heinrich.

""Naturrecht" bei Aristoteles und bei Cicero (*De legibus*): Ein Vergleich" in *Cicero's Knowledge of the Peripatos,* GIRARDET, Klaus M.

"Aristotelian Material in Cicero's *De natura deorum*" in *Cicero's Knowledge of the Peripatos,* FURLEY, David J.

"Aristotle and Theophrastus Conjoined in the Writings of Cicero" in *Cicero's Knowledge of the Peripatos,* RUNIA, David T.

"Aristotle's Epistemology" in *Epistemology (Companions to Ancient Thought: 1),* TAYLOR, C C W.

"Aristotle" in *Ethics in the History of Western Philosophy,* GOMEZ-LOBO, Alfonso.

"Averroes and the West: The First Encounter/Nonencounter" in *A Straight Path: Studies in Medieval Philosophy and Culture,* IVRY, Alfred L.

"Cicero and the Aristotelian Theory of Divination by Dreams" in *Cicero's Knowledge of the Peripatos,* KANY-TURPIN, José and PELLEGRIN, Pierre.

"Cicero und die 'Schule des Aristoteles'" in *Cicero's Knowledge of the Peripatos,* GÖRLER, Woldemar.

"Cicero's Knowledge of the Rhetorical Treatises of Aristotle and Theophrastus" in *Cicero's Knowledge of the Peripatos,* FORTENBAUGH, William W.

"Dialectic, Rhetoric and Critique in Aristotle" in *From Metaphysics to Rhetoric,* COULOUBARITSIS, Lambros.

"Foreword—The Modernity of Rhetoric" in *From Metaphysics to Rhetoric,* MEYER, Michel.

"The Goals of Natural Science" in *Scientific Knowledge Socialized,* MC MULLIN, Ernan.

"Maimonides on Aristotle and Scientific Method" in *Moses Maimonides and His Time,* KRAEMER, Joel L.

"The Political Animal's Knowledge According to Aristotle" in *Knowledge and Politics,* LABARRIÈRE, Jean-Louis.

"Toward an Anthropology of Rhetoric" in *From Metaphysics to Rhetoric,* MEYER, Michel.

"What is it to be Moral?" in *Inquiries into Values: The Inaugural Session of the International Society for Value Inquiry,* ANDERSON, Lyle V.

"Wisdom, Faith and Reason" in *The Wisdom of Faith: Essays in Honor of Dr Sebastian Alexander Matczak,* JAMES, Theodore E.

"Bedeutung", "Idee" und "Begriff": Zur Behandlung einiger bedeutungstheorietischer Paradoxien durch Leibniz. ROS, Arno.

"Denn das Sein oder Nichstein ist kein Merkmal der Sache". SONDEREGGER, Erwin.

"Kunst der Überlistung" oder "Reden mit Vernuft"? Zu Philosophischen Aspekten der Rhetorik. NIEHUES-PRÖBSTING, Heinrich.

"Sub ratione ardui": Paura e speranza nella filosofia. FRANCHI, Alfredo.

"Vivere" e "vivere bene": Note sul concetto aristotelico di πρᾶξιζ. CHIEREGHIN, Franco.

The 'Imaginative Syllogism' in Arabic Philosophy: A Medieval Contribution to the Philosophical Study of Metaphor. BLACK, Deborah L.

Acquiring Ethical Ends. DE MOSS, David J.

El acto de ser: Un don. GILBERT, Paul.

Alternative Interpretations of Aristotle on Exchange and Reciprocity. MC NEILL, Desmond.

Ambition. DOMBROWSKI, Daniel A.

Ancient Non-Beings: Speusippus and Others. DANCY, R M.

Appréciation de l'oeuvre théologico-philosophique de Thomas d'Aquin au tournant des XIIIe-XIVe ss (in Polish). MORAWIEC, Edmund.

Are There Categories in Chinese Philosophy? (in Serbo-Croatian). CHALIER, Agnes.

Arendt, Republicanism and Patriarchalism. SPRINGBORG, Patricia.

Aristotele, Platone e l'IBM. PARISI, Giorgio.

El Aristóteles de Hegel. SACCHI, Mario E.

Aristóteles en *El Nombre de la Rosa.* GIRALT, María de los Angeles.

The Aristotelian Character of Schiller's Ethical Ideal. CORDNER, Christopher.

An Aristotelian Theory of Moral Development. TOBIN, Bernadette M.

Aristotle and Pleasure. STEWART, Robert Scott.

Aristotle and the Classical Greek Concept of Despotism. RICHTER, Melvin.

Aristotle and the Functionalist Debate. GRANGER, Herbert.

Aristotle and the Mind-Body Problem. HEINAMAN, Robert.

Aristotle and the Value of Political Participation. MULGAN, Richard.

Aristotle on 'Time' and 'A Time'. WHITE, Michael J.

Aristotle on Heat, Cold, and Teleological Explanation. COHEN, Sheldon M.

Aristotle on Inferences from Signs (*Rhetoric* I 2, 1357 b 1-25). WEIDEMANN, Hermann.

Aristotle on Responsibility for Action and Character. ROBERTS, Jean.

Aristotle on the Difference between Mathematics and Physics and First Philosophy. MODRAK, D K W.

Aristotle on the Mechanics of Thought. WEDIN, M V.

Aristotle The First Cognitivist?. MODRAK, D K W.

Aristotle's Compatibilism in the *Nicomachean Ethics.* EVERSON, Stephen.

Aristotle's Conception of the Science of Being. LUDWIG, Walter D.

Aristotle's Criticism of Plato's Form of the Good: Ethics Without Metaphysics?. SANTAS, Gerasimos.

Aristotle's Crowning Virtue. COOPER, Neil.

Aristotle's Four Types of Definition. DESLAURIERS, Marguerite.

Aristotle's God and the Authenticity of *De mundo*: An Early Modern Controversy. KRAYE, Jill.

Aristotle's *Horror Vacui.* THORP, John.

Aristotle's Political Naturalism. MILLER JR, Fred D.

Aristotle's Theory of Time and Entropy. HUGHEN, Richard E.

Aristotle, Demonstration, and Teaching. WIANS, William.

Le caractère aporétique de la *Métaphysique* d'Aristote. IRWIN, T H.

Categorías aristotélicas y categorías intensionales. STAHL, Gérold.

Color and Color-Perception in Aristotle's *De anima.* SILVERMAN, Allan.

La conception stoïcienne et la conception aristotélicienne du bonheur. IRWIN, T H.

El concepto aristotélico de violencia. QUEVEDO, Amalia.

The Contribution of *Nicomachean Ethics iii 5* to Aristotle's Theory of Responsibility. CURREN, Randall.

Conversion Principles and the Basis of Aristotle's Modal Logic. PATTERSON, Richard.

Cosa è pensare: Saggio sulle "Categorie" di Aristotele. CALEO, Marcello.

Cremonini e le origini del libertinismo. BOSCO, Domenico.

La crítica aristotélica al Bien platónico. LA CROCE, Ernesto.

Das Eudaimonie-Problem und seine aristotelische Lösung (in Greek). PAPADIS, D.

De l'explication causale dans la biologie d'Aristote. PELLEGRIN, Pierre.

La deliberación en Hobbes. COSTA, Margarita.

Descartes and Some Predecessors on the Divine Conservation of Motion. MENN, Stephen.

Un desliz en la *Summa Logicae* de Guillermo de Ockham?. ROTELLA, Oscar.

Dialectic and Deliberation in Aristotle's Practical Philosophy. BAYNES, Kenneth.

Dialectical Contradiction and the Aristotelian Principle of Non-Contradiction (in Czechoslovakian). ZELENY, J.

Dialectical, Rhetorical, and Aristotelian Rhetoric. CONSIGNY, Scott.

Die ethischen Schriften des Aristoteles (in Greek). KESSIDIS, T.

Dwellers in an Unfortified City: Death and Political Philosophy. SCHALL, James V.

Educational Theories: Ideas of Things to Do. CHAMBLISS, J J.

Elementos y esencias. ANSCOMBE, G E M.

The Enigma of *Categories* 1a20ff and Why It Matters. MATTHEWS, Gareth B.

Ente Natural y Artefacto en Guillermo de Ockham. LARRE, Olga L.

Equality of Opportunity and the Problem of Nature. BLITS, Jan H.

The Ergon Inference. GOMEZ-LOBO, Alfonso.

A Fact About the Virtues. RAY, A Chadwick.

El filosofar y el lenguaje. PIEPER, Josep.

ART

The Horizon of Aesthetics (in Czechoslovakian). SINDELAR, Dusan.
The Pain of Simulation on Heidegger's Philosophy of Art (in Dutch). DE SCHUTTER, Dirk.
Theater as Art. SHPET, G.
To the Program of Aesthetic Evolution for the Whole Society (in Czechoslovakian). CHYBA, Milos.
Towards More Effective Arts Education. GARDNER, Howard.
Truth as Disclosure: Art, Language, History. GUIGNON, Charles.
Universality and Difference: O'Keeffe and McClintock. MACCOLL, San.
Variations upon Variation, or Picasso Back to Bach. GOODMAN, Nelson.
The Violence of Public Art: *Do the Right Thing*. MITCHELL, W J T.
Vom Ursprung des Kunstwerks: Erste Ausarbeitung. HEIDEGGER, Martin.
Wang Yuyang's Natural Thought on Art. TIAOGONG, Wu.
What Music Is. SERAFINE, Mary Louise.

ART CRITICISM

Esthetics Contemporary—Revised Edition. KOSTELANETZ, Richard (ed).
Evaluating Art. DICKIE, George.
Art and Art Criticism: A Definition of Art. DAUER, Francis.
Art and the Rhetoric of Allusion. NUYEN, A T.
Interpretation in Aesthetics: Theories and Practices. MC CORMICK, Peter.
Storied Bodies, or Nana at Last Unveil'd. BROOKS, Peter.
Validation by Touch in Kandinsky's Early Abstract Art. OLIN, Margaret.

ART EDUCATION

Aesthetics and the Insularity of Arts Educators. MC ADOO, Nick.
Aesthetics in Discipline-Based Art Education. CRAWFORD, Donald W.
The Changing Image of Art Education: Theoretical Antecedents of Discipline-Based Art Education. SMITH, Ralph A.
Creativity and Routine. PERRY, Leslie R.

ART OBJECT(S)

Colourization Ill-Defended. LEVINSON, Jerrold.
Emerson, Whitman, and Conceptual Art. LEONARD, George J.
Interpretation and Its Art Objects: Two Views. KRAUSZ, Michael.
Note on Colourization. DANIELS, Charles B.
Preserving, Restoring, Repairing. GODLOVITCH, Stan.
Unknown Masterpiece. HELLER, Agnes.

ARTIFACT(S)

Ente Natural y Artefacto en Guillermo de Ockham. LARRE, Olga L.
The Nature of Artifacts. LOSONSKY, Michael.
Realism, Naturalism and Culturally Generated Kinds. ELDER, Crawford L.
Self-Ownership. DAY, J P.

ARTIFICIAL INSEMINATION

Ethical Issues in the New Reproductive Technologies. HULL, Richard T (ed).
Control and Compensation: Laws Governing Extracorporeal Generative Materials. ANDREWS, Lori B.

ARTIFICIAL INTELLIGENCE

Artificial Intelligence in Psychology: Interdisciplinary Essays. BODEN, Margaret A.
Automated Deduction in Nonclassical Logics. WALLEN, Lincoln A.
Lawless Mind. ABELSON, Raziel.
The Mundane Matter of the Mental Language. MALONEY, J Christopher.
The Philosopher's Habitat: Introduction to Investigations in, and Applications of, Modern Philosophy. GOLDSTEIN, Laurence.
Philosophical Logic and Artificial Intelligence. THOMASON, Richmond H (ed).
Probabilistic Reasoning in Intelligent Systems: Networks of Plausible Inference. PEARL, Judea.
"The Analysis of Nominal Compounds" in *Meaning and Mental Representation*, LEHNERT, Wendy G.
"Reference and Its Role in Computational Models of Mental Representations" in *Meaning and Mental Representation*, WILKS, Yorick.
Against Positing Central Systems in the Mind. ROSS, Don.
AI, as an Action Science, as an Utopia or as a Scapegoat. VANDAMME, Fernand.
Application on the Relevance of AI Assumptions for Social Practitioners. MURPHY, John.
Artificial Intelligence and Law: How To Get There From Here. MC CARTY, L Thorne.
Can Semantics Be Syntactic?. JAHREN, Neal.
Deontic Logic and Legal Knowledge Representation. JONES, Andrew J I.
Des fondements théoriques pour l'intelligence artificielle et la philosophie de l'esprit. MARCHAL, Bruno.
Does Artificial Intelligence Require Artificial Ego? A Critique of Haugeland. EDELSON, Thomas.
The Early Work of Husserl and Artificial Intelligence. MÜNCH, Dieter.

Form and Content in Semantics. WILKS, Yorick.
Gödel, Escher, Bach and Dooyeweerd. VERKERK, M J.
Induction, Conceptual Spaces, and AI. GÄRDENFORS, Peter.
Information Processing: From a Mechanistic to a Natural Systems Approach. VAN CAMP, Ingrid.
Intelligence artificielle et mentalité primitive. JORION, Paul.
Intelligence artificielle et signification: À propos des limites et des possibilités des sciences cognitives. MENDONÇA, W P.
Is kennis belichaamd?. SCHOPMAN, Joop.
Kunstmatige intelligentie: Een voortzetting van de filosofie met andere middelen. VAN BENTHEM, Johan.
The Logic of Time in Law and Legal Expert Systems. MACKAAY, Ejan (and others).
Une Machine spéculative (informatique, intelligence artificielle et recherche cognitive). BORILLO, Mario.
Moral Dilemmas Concerning the Ultra Intelligent Machine. DE GARIS, Hugo.
Philosophy and Machine Learning. THAGARD, Paul.
Quelle est la place de l'intelligence artificielle dans l'étude de la cognition?. ANDLER, Daniel.
Radical Interpretation and the Gunderson Game. WARD, Andrew.
The Reflexivity of Self-Consciousness: Sameness/Identity, Data for Artificial Intelligence. CASTAÑEDA, Hector-Neri.
Representations without Rules. HORGAN, Terence and TIENSON, John.
Robots that Learn: A Test of Intelligence. SUPPES, Patrick and CRANGLE, Colleen.
Searle on Strong AI. CAM, Philip.
Een vergelijking van inductief-statistisch redeneren en default logica. TAN, Yao-Hua.

ARTIST(S)

Art and the Joycean Artist. SCHIRALLI, Martin.
Artist and Audience. PERRICONE, Christopher.
Artist—Work—Audience: Musings on Barthes and Tolstoy. KRUKOWSKI, Lucian.
Artistic Learning: What and Where Is It?. WOLF, Dennie.
Colourization Ill-Defended. LEVINSON, Jerrold.
Expression as Hands-on Construction. HOWARD, V A.
Note on Colourization. DANIELS, Charles B.
The Subjective Thinker as Artist. WALSH, Sylvia I.

ARTISTIC

"The Historical Genesis of a Pure Aesthetic" in *Analytic Aesthetics*, BOURDIEU, Pierre.
Artistic and Aesthetic Value. ORAMO, Ilkka.
Artistic Intention and Mental Image. HAGBERG, Garry.
Personality and Artistic Creativity. JARRETT, James L.
The Recurring Postmodern: Notes on the Constitution of Musical Artworks. UUSITALO, Jyrki.

ARTISTIC TRUTH

Mondo sociale, mimesi e violenza in R Girard. BOTTANI, Livio.

ARTS

Annotated Bibliography on Feminist Aesthetics in the Visual Arts. KRUMHOLZ, Linda and LAUTER, Estella.
From Salomon's House to the Land-Grant College: Practical Arts Education and the Utopian Vision of Progress. WATEROUS, Frank B.
Le talent. WALD, Henri.

ASCETICISM

Recent Interpretations of Early Christian Asceticism. YOUNG, Robin Darling.

ASCRIPTION(S)

Propositional Attitudes: An Essay on Thoughts and How We Ascribe Them. RICHARD, Mark.
How I Say What You Think. RICHARD, Mark.
Individuation and Intentional Ascriptions. OKRENT, Mark.

ASEITY

Aseity as Relational Problematic. PRATT, Douglas.

ASIAN

see also Oriental
Nature in Asian Tradition of Thought: Essays in Environmental Philosophy. CALLICOTT, J Baird (ed).
"'Conceptual Resources' in South Asia for 'Environmental Ethics'" in *Nature in Asian Tradition of Thought: Essays in Environmental Philosophy*, LARSON, Gerald James.
"The Asian Traditions as a Conceptual Resource for Environmental Philosophy" in *Nature in Asian Tradition of Thought: Essays in Environmental Philosophy*, CALLICOTT, J Baird and AMES, Roger T.
"Epilogue: On the Relation of Idea and Action" in *Nature in Asian Tradition*

BETTI, E

Emilio Betti's Debt to Vico. NOAKES, Susan.

L'herméneutique comme science rigoureuse selon Emilio Betti (1890-1968). GRONDIN, Jean.

BETTING

Scotching the Dutch Book Argument. MILNE, Peter.

Subjective Probabilities and Betting Quotients. HOWSON, Colin.

BHARTRHARI

Derrida and Bhartrhari's Vākyapadīya on the Origin of Language. COWARD, Harold.

BIAS(ES)

Bias, Controversy, and Abuse in the Study of the Scientific Publication System. MAHONEY, Michael J.

Confirmational Response Bias Among Social Work Journals. EPSTEIN, William M.

Cultural and Ideological Bias in Pornography Research. CHRISTENSEN, Ferrel M.

Gender Is an Organon. KEHOE, Alice B.

Improving the Quality of Social Welfare Scholarship: Response to "Confirmational Response Bias". SCHUERMAN, John R.

Reflections on "Confirmational Response Bias Among Social Work Journals". HOPPS, June Gary.

BIBLE

Bible and Ethics in the Christian Life. BIRCH, Bruce C.

Biblical Narrative in the Philosophy of Paul Ricoeur: A Study in Hermeneutics and Theology. VANHOOZER, Kevin J.

The Bitterness of Job: A Philosophical Reading. WILCOX, John T.

The Melody of Theology: A Philosophical Dictionary. PELIKAN, Jaroslav.

"The Bible's First Sentence in Gregory of Nyssa's View" in A Straight Path: Studies in Medieval Philosophy and Culture, VERBEKE, G.

"The Fear of the Lord is the Beginning of Wisdom" in The Wisdom of Faith: Essays in Honor of Dr Sebastian Alexander Matczak, THOMPSON, Henry O.

"Everything Depends on the Type of the Concepts that the Interpretation is Made to Convey". COMSTOCK, Gary L.

Le "Letture dai Vangeli" di Antonio Maddalena. PAREYSON, Luigi.

Le "suaire" johannique: Réponse a quelques questions. ROBERT, René.

Accepting the Authority of the Bible: Is It Rationally Justified?. KELLER, James A.

Crisi ecologica e concezione cristiana di Dio. SALVATI, Giuseppe M.

God, the Bible and Circularity. COLWELL, Gary.

Interpretation and the Bible: The Dialectic of Concept and Content in Interpretive Reading. POLKA, Brayton.

Literality. BARR, James.

Narrative Accounts of Biblical Authority: The Need for a Doctrine of Revelation. SYKES, John.

The Politics of Interpretation: Spinoza's Modernist Turn. LANG, Berel.

Postmodern Biblicism: The Challenge of René Girard for Contemporary Theology. WALLACE, Mark I.

Revelation and the Bible. MAVRODES, George I.

Visits to the Sepulcher and Biblical Exegesis. STUMP, Eleonore S.

BIBLIOGRAPHY

Bibliography of Bioethics, Volume 15. WALTERS, LeRoy (ed).

Index to Theses on German Philosophy Accepted by Universities of Great Britain & Ireland, 1900-1985. GABEL, Gernot U.

Johann Gottfried Herder: A Bibliographical Survey, 1977-1987. MARKWORTH, Tino.

Keyguide to Information Sources in Animal Rights. MAGEL, Charles R.

Pythagoras: An Annotated Bibliography. NAVIA, Luis E.

A Bibliographical Survey on Confucian Studies in Western Languages: Retrospect and Prospect (in Serbo-Croatian). KANG, Thomas H.

Annotated Bibliography on Feminist Aesthetics in the Visual Arts. KRUMHOLZ, Linda and LAUTER, Estella.

Bibliographie de Claude Bruaire. GÉLY, Raphaël.

Bibliographie der bis zum 8 Mai 1989 veröffentlichten Schriften Edmund Husserls. SCHMITZ, Manfred.

Las cuitas de Zarathustra: Algunas publicaciones recientes sobre Friedrich Nietzsche. KERKHOFF, Manfred.

Teaching Business Ethics: The Use of Films and Videotapes. HOSMER, LaRue Tone and STENECK, Nicholas H.

BIEMEL, W

En torno a Heidegger. BIMEL, Walter.

BILOW, S

Response to Bilow: Future Persons and the Justification of Education. SCHRAG, Francis.

BINET, A

Thinking Skill Programs: An Analysis. MAYS, Wolfe and SHARP, Ann Margaret.

BIOENGINEERING

The Bioengineered Competitor?. MURRAY, Thomas H.

Liabilities and Realities Faced in Biomedical Engineering. MORSE, M Steven.

BIOETHICS

see also Medical Ethics

Alpha and Omega: Ethics at the Frontiers of Life and Death. YOUNG, Ernlé W D.

Animal Rights and Human Obligations (Second Edition). REGAN, Tom.

Bibliography of Bioethics, Volume 15. WALTERS, LeRoy (ed).

Contemporary Issues in Bioethics (Third Edition). BEAUCHAMP, Tom L (ed).

Ethical Issues in Modern Medicine (Third Edition). ARRAS, John.

Final Choices: Autonomy in Health Care Decisions. SMITH, George P.

Surrogate Motherhood: The Ethics of Using Human Beings. SHANNON, Thomas A.

Taking Sides: Clashing Views on Controversial Bioethical Issues (Third Edition). LEVINE, Carole (ed).

Animals, Science, and Ethics. DONNELLEY, Strachan (ed) and NOLAN, Kathleen (ed).

Appréciation morale des ingerences biomédiques dans le processusde de transmision (in Polish). KOWALSKI, Edmund.

Bioengineering, Scientific Activism, and Philosophical Bridges. DURBIN, Paul T.

Bioethics and the Contemporary Jewish Community. NOVAK, David.

Bioethics as Civic Discourse. JENNINGS, Bruce.

Bioethics Discovers the Bill of Rights. VEATCH, Robert M.

Biomedicine and Technocratic Power. FINKELSTEIN, Joanne L.

Brain Death and Brain Life: Rethinking the Connection. DOWNIE, Jocelyn.

Brain Death and the Anencephalic Newborns. TRUOG, Robert D.

The Burden of Decision. CAPRON, Alexander Morgan.

Can Bioethics Be Evangelical?. HOLLINGER, Dennis.

Can Theology Have a Role in "Public" Bioethical Discourse?. CAHILL, Lisa Sowle.

China: Moral Puzzles. TIAN-MIN, Xu.

Commentary: Live Sperm, Dead Bodies. ROSS, Judith Wilson.

Commentary: Live Sperm, Dead Bodies. ROTHMAN, Cappy Miles.

Consciousness, the Brain and What Matters. GILLETT, Grant R.

A Critique of Principlism. CLOUSER, K Danner and GERT, Bernard.

Death, Democracy and Public Ethical Choice. CUSHMAN, Reid and HOLM, Soren.

Ethics Committees. COHEN, Cynthia B (ed).

Ethics in Bioengineering. MITCHAM, Carl.

La fondation de la bioéthique: une perspective épistémologique. TOURNIER, F.

Fooling with Mother Nature. GAYLIN, Willard.

Genetic Control. FLETCHER, Joseph.

Interpretive Bioethics: The Way of Discernment. CARSON, Ronald A.

Liabilities and Realities Faced in Biomedical Engineering. MORSE, M Steven.

The Limited Relevance of Analytical Ethics to the Problems of Bioethics. HOLMES, Robert L.

Method in Bioethics: A Troubled Assessment. GREEN, Ronald M.

Militant Morality: Civil Disobedience and Bioethics. COHEN, Carl.

The Philippines: A Public Awakening. DE CASTRO, Leonardo D.

Philosophers and the Public Policy Process: Inside, Outside, or Nowhere at All?. MOMEYER, Richard W.

Philosophical Integrity and Policy Development in Bioethics. BENJAMIN, Martin.

The Place of Autonomy in Bioethics. CHILDRESS, James F.

Public Philosophy: Distinction Without Authority. MENZEL, Paul T.

Quality of Scholarship in Bioethics. BRODY, Baruch A.

Regulating AIDS Research on Infants and Children: The Moral Task of Institutional Review Boards. CARTER, Michele and WICHMAN, Alison and MC CARTHY, Charles R.

Religion and Moral Meaning in Bioethics. CAMPBELL, Courtney S.

Religion and the Secularization of Bioethics. CALLAHAN, Daniel.

Resolving Disputes Over Frozen Embryos. ROBERTSON, John A.

Studies in the Explanation of Issues in Biomedical Ethics: (II) On "On Play[ing] God", Etc.. ERDE, Edmund L.

Talking of God—But with Whom?. VERHEY, Allen D.

Thailand: Refining Cultural Values. RATANAKUL, Pinit.

To Rectify an Amoral Design. COMNINOU, Maria.

What Can Religion Offer Bioethics?. WIND, James P.

Whither the Genome Project?. SINSHEIMER, Robert L.

BIOETHICS
Zur ethischen Problematik der Keimbahn-Gentherapie am Menschen. WIMMER, Reiner.

BIOGRAPHY
Chu Hsi: New Studies. CHAN, Wing-Tsit.
Heidegger and Nazism. MARGOLIS, Joseph (ed).
Hume. PHILLIPSON, N T.
Kierkegaard, Godly Deceiver: The Nature and Meaning of His Pseudonymous Writings. HARTSHORNE, M Holmes.
Schopenhauer and the Wild Years of Philosophy. SAFRANSKI, Rüdiger.
"Cyril Loukaris: A Protestant Patriarch or a Pioneer Orthodox Ecumenist?" in *The Wisdom of Faith: Essays in Honor of Dr Sebastian Alexander Matczak,* TSIRPANLIS, Constantine N.
"Engaged Reflection: The Life and Work of E Maynard Adams" in *Mind, Value and Culture: Essays in Honor of E M Adams,* WEISSBORD, David.
The Biographies of Siddhasena: A Study in the Texture of Allusion and the Weaving of a Group-Image (Part I). GRANOFF, Phyllis.
A Drama of Love and Death: Michael Pedersen Kierkegaard and Regine Olsen Revisited. PATTISON, George.
Francesco Venini: Un philosophe a Parma (1764-1772). MAMIANI, Maurizio.
George Santayana and the Genteel Tradition. AARON, Daniel.
George Santayana. LACHS, John.
Martin Buber—A Jew from Galicia. GÓRNIAK-KOCIKOWSKA, Krystyna.
Persons and Places. LYON, Richard C.
Spinoza's Earliest Philosophical Years, 1655-61. POPKIN, Richard H.
The Young Heidegger: Rumor of a Hidden King (1919-1926). VAN BUREN, Edward J.

BIOLOGY
see also Darwinism, Ecology, Evolution, Life
Historical Roots of Cognitive Science. MEYERING, Theo C.
Mental Content. MC GINN, Colin.
The Metaphysics of Evolution. HULL, David L.
Philosophy of Biology Today. RUSE, Michael.
The Rational and the Social. BROWN, James Robert.
The Structure of Biological Theories. THOMPSON, Paul.
"Biology as a Cosmological Science" in *Nature in Asian Tradition of Thought: Essays in Environmental Philosophy,* MOROWITZ, Harold J.
"An Evolutionary Perspective on the Re-Emergence of Cell Biology" in *Issues in Evolutionary Epistemology,* BECHTEL, William.
"From Physics to Biology: Rationality in Popper's Conception" in *Issues in Evolutionary Epistemology,* STOKES, Geoff.
Alberto Magno y los últimos unicornios. DE ASUA, M J C.
Biological Functions and Biological Interests. VARNER, Gary E.
Biologie en Teleologie. SOONTIENS, Frans.
Biologische constructies en sociale feiten: Obstakels in het onderzoek naar gezondheidsproblemen van vrouwen. HORSTMAN, Klasien.
Biology and Representation. MAC DONALD, Graham.
Complementarity and the Description of Nature in Biological Science. FOLSE JR, Henry J.
De l'explication causale dans la biologie d'Aristote. PELLEGRIN, Pierre.
Del valore: Chi crea l'informazione?. MARCHETTI, Cesare.
Evolutie, teleologie en toeval. SOONTIËNS, Frans.
Evolutionäre Erkenntnistheorie und erkenntnistheoretischer Realismus. WENDEL, Hans Jürgen.
Evolutionary Anti-Reductionism: Historical Reflections. BEATTY, John.
Evolutionary Biology and Naturalism. MASTERS, Roger D.
Finality and Intelligibility in Biological Evolution. MORENO, Antonio.
Freud's Phylogenetic Fantasy: An Essay Review. PARISI, Thomas.
Fundamenten, achtergronden of bondgenootschappen?. VAN DER WEELE, Cor.
Gedrag: wat zit er achter?. VAN DER STEEN, Wim.
How Evolutionary Biology Challenges the Classical Theory of Rational Choice. COOPER, W S.
Intensionality and Perception: A Reply to Rosenberg. MATTHEN, Mohan.
Kleine epistemologie van de kikvors-retina. GOUDSMIT, Arno L.
Modeling in the Museum: On the Role of Remnant Models in the Work of Joseph Grinnell. GRIESEMER, James R.
New Notes from Underground. ELLERMAN, Carl Paul.
Niet vrouw, niet man; wat dan? De rol van biomedische kennis bij de behandeling van pseudohermafrodieten. VAN DEN WIJNGAARD, Marianne and HUYTS, Ini.
Ontogenesi della forma e informazione. FASOLO, Aldo.
Rosenberg's Rebellion. WATERS, C Kenneth.
The Uniqueness of Human Being (in Czechoslovakian). OIZERMAN, T I.
Varieties of Ecological Dialectics. SIMON, Thomas W.
What the Philosophy of Biology Is and Should Be (in Polish). SLAGA,

Szczepan W.
Zur ethischen Problematik der Keimbahn-Gentherapie am Menschen. WIMMER, Reiner.

BIOSPHERE
Green Reason: Communicative Ethics for the Biosphere. DRYZEK, John S.

BIRTH
Impermanence is Buddha-nature: Dōgen's Understanding of Temporality. STAMBAUGH, Joan.
The Moral Significance of Birth. WARREN, Mary Anne.

BIRTH CONTROL
Preventing Birth: Contemporary Methods and Related Moral Controversies. CALLAHAN, Joan C.
The *Munus* of Transmitting Human Life: A New Approach to *Humanae Vitae.* SMITH, Janet E.

BIVALENCE
Purtill on Fatalism and Truth. CRAIG, William Lane.

BLACK STUDIES
"I've Known Rivers": Black Theology's Response to Process Theology. THANDEKA.
Alien Gods in Black Experience. SMITH JR, Archie.
Hartshorne's Neoclassical Theism and Black Theology. WALKER JR, Theodore.

BLACK, M
Philosophical Introduction to Set Theory. POLLARD, Stephen.

BLACK, V
Is and Ought: The "Open Question Argument". FLEW, Antony.

BLACKBURN, S
Blackburn's Projectivism—An Objection. BRIGHOUSE, M H.
Misconstruals Made Manifest: A Response to Simon Blackburn. WRIGHT, Crispin.

BLACKMAIL
The Paradox of Blackmail. FEINBERG, Joel.
Why Blackmail Should be Banned. EVANS, Hugh.

BLACKS
The Lacuna Between Philosophy and History. HARRIS, Leonard.
Process Theology and Black Liberation: Testing the Whiteheadian Metaphysical Foundations. YOUNG, Henry James.
The Question of Black Philosophy. JEFFERSON, Paul.

BLACKSTONE
Bentham and Blackstone: A Lifetime's Dialectic. BURNS, J H.

BLAGA, L
The Abyssal Categories of Blaga's Apriorism. RAMBU, Nicolae.
Un mythe ouvert dans "Zamolxis" de Lucian Blaga (in Romanian). DADARLAT, Camil Marius.

BLAME
Determinism, Blameworthiness and Deprivation. KLEIN, Martha.
Blame, Fictional Characters, and Morality. SANKOWSKI, Edward.
Internal Reasons and the Obscurity of Blame. WILLIAMS, Bernard.

BLANCHOT, M
Difficult Friendship. DAVIES, Paul.

BLANSHARD, B
"Reply to Blanshard's "Harris on Internal Relations"" in *Dialectic and Contemporary Science,* HARRIS, Errol E.

BLASPHEMY
More on Blasphemy. HOFFMAN, Frank J.

BLINDNESS
Having Ideas and Having the Concept. CRIMMINS, Mark.

BLOCH, E
Ernst Bloch: Trame della speranza. BOELLA, Laura.
Forme estetiche e possibilità utopica in Ernst Bloch. STILE, Alessandro.

BLONDEL, M
Actualidad y fecundidad de la filosofía blondeliana. ISASI, Juan M.
Blondel on the Origin of Philosophy. LONG, Fiachra.

BLOOM, A
The Closing of the Professorial Mind: A Meditation on Plato and Allan Bloom. SILLIMAN, Matt.

BLOOM, B
An Application of Bloom's Taxonomy to the Teaching of Business Ethics. REEVES, M Francis.

BLOOR, D
Chomsky, Wittgenstein, Bloor: Zum Problem einer wissenssoziologischen

BLOOR, D
Metatheorie der Linguistik. KERTÉSZ, András.

BLUM, A
On the Appearance of Contingency: A Rejoinder to Blum. BAYNE, Steven R.

BLUM, L
Particularity, Gilligan, and the Two-Levels View: A Reply. ADLER, Jonathan E.

BLUMENBERG, H
Blumenberg and the Philosophical Grounds of Historiography. INGRAM, David.

BLUMENFELD, D
God and Concept Empiricism. BEATY, Michael and TALIAFERRO, Charles.

BOBBIO, N
Difficoltà della filosofia pubblica (Riflessioni sul pensiero di Norberto Bobbio). POSSENTI, Vittorio.

BODUNRIN, P
Narrative in African Philosophy. BELL, Richard H.

BODY(-DIES)
see also Matter, Minds, Substance(s)
Body, Soul, and Life Everlasting: Biblical Anthropology and the Monism-Dualism Debate. COOPER, John W.
Connections to the World: The Basic Concepts of Philosophy. DANTO, Arthur C.
Embodiments of Mind. MC CULLOCH, Warren S.
Gender Trouble: Feminism and the Subversion of Identity. BUTLER, Judith.
Human Posture: The Nature of Inquiry. SCHUMACHER, John A.
Looking Into Mind: How to Recognize Who You Are and How You Know. DAMIANI, Anthony.
Mind-Body Identity Theories. MACDONALD, Cynthia.
"The Mind-Body Problem: Some Neurobiological Reflections" in Reductionism and Systems Theory in the Life Sciences: Some Problems and Perspectives, LÖWENHARD, Percy.
"Philosophy and its History" in The Institution of Philosophy: A Discipline in Crisis?, ROSENTHAL, David M.
Consciousness in Quantum Physics and The Mind-Body Problem. GOSWAMI, Amit.
Corps et subjectivité chez Claude Bruaire. MARQUET, Jean-François.
Culture or Nature: The Functions of the Term 'Body' in the Work in the Work of Michel Foucault. MC WHORTER, Ladelle.
Descartes's Dualism and the Philosophy of Mind. ALANEN, Lilli.
Establishing the Moral Basis of Medicine: Edmund D Pellegrino's Philosophy of Medicine. THOMASMA, David C.
F H Bradley y E E Harris: acerca de la relación mente-cuerpo. GARCIA, Pablo S.
Flesh and Blood: A Proposed Supplement to Merleau-Ponty. LEDER, Drew.
Foucault and the Paradox of Bodily Inscriptions. BUTLER, Judith.
Kriterien für eine Theorie zur Lösung des Leib-Seele-Problems. METZINGER, Thomas.
Maine de Biran and the Body-Subject. GAINES, Jeffrey J.
The Market for Bodily Parts: Kant and Duties to Oneself. CHADWICK, Ruth F.
McGinn on the Mind-Body Problem. WHITELEY, C H.
Mind and Body. WILKES, K V.
Mind-Body and the Future of Psychiatry. WALLACE IV, Edwin R.
Sport Abjection: Steroids and the Uglification of the Athlete. FAIRCHILD, David L.
Storied Bodies, or Nana at Last Unveil'd. BROOKS, Peter.
Transcendentalism and Its Discontents. WHITE, Stephen L.
Weak Externalism and Mind-Body Identity. MACDONALD, Cynthia.

BOER, S
The Free-Will Defence and Worlds Without Moral Evil. DILLEY, Frank B.

BOESKY, I
The Poverty of Opulence. KOLENDA, Konstantin.

BOETHIUS
Boethius on Eternity. LEFTOW, Brian.
Eternity. WÖRNER, Markus H.

BOFF, C
Clodovis Boff on the Discipline of Theology. CUNNINGHAM, David S.

BOGDAN, D
Engaging the New Literacy: A "Way In" to Philosophy of Education. KOHLI, Wendy.

BOGHOSSIAN, P
Colouring in the World. BIGELOW, John and COLLINS, John and PARGETTER, Robert.

BOHM, D
Human Posture: The Nature of Inquiry. SCHUMACHER, John A.
Relating the Physics and Religion of David Bohm. SHARPE, Kevin J.

BOHR, N
Quantum Probability—Quantum Logic. PITOWSKY, Itamar.
Thematic Origins of Scientific Thought: Kepler to Einstein—Revised Edition. HOLTON, Gerald.
"Bohr on Bell" in Philosophical Consequences of Quantum Theory: Reflections on Bell's Theorem, FOLSE JR, Henry J.
Bohr, Einstein and Realism. DANIEL, Wojciech.
Complementarity and the Description of Nature in Biological Science. FOLSE JR, Henry J.
The Theory of Complimentarity and Mind-Body Dualism: A Critique. CHAKRABARTY, Alpana.

BOLZANO
Questions of Form: Logic and the Analytic Proposition from Kant to Carnap. PROUST, Joëlle.
Husserl—Bolzano I (in Czechoslovakian). BAYEROVA, Marie.

BONAVENTURE
Aelred of Rievaulx and the "Lignum Vitae" of Bonaventure: A Reappraisal. O'CONNELL, Patrick F.
Reason in Mystery. KRETZMANN, Norman.

BONJOUR, L
The Current State of the Coherence Theory. BENDER, John W (ed).
"BonJour's Anti-Foundationalist Argument" in The Current State of the Coherence Theory, STEUP, Matthias.
"BonJour's Coherence Theory of Justification" in The Current State of the Coherence Theory, SWAIN, Marshall.
"BonJour's Coherentism" in The Current State of the Coherence Theory, GOLDMAN, Alan H.
"BonJour's The Structure of Empirical Knowledge" in The Current State of the Coherence Theory, GOLDMAN, Alvin I.
"Circularity, Non-Linear Justification and Holistic Coherentism" in The Current State of the Coherence Theory, DAY, Timothy Joseph.
"Coherence, Observation, and the Justification of Empirical Belief" in The Current State of the Coherence Theory, SILVERS, Stuart.
"Foundations" in The Current State of the Coherence Theory, BLACK, Carolyn.
"The Saint Elizabethan World" in The Current State of the Coherence Theory, TOLLIVER, Joseph Thomas.
Apriority and Metajustification in BonJour's "Structure of Empirical Knowledge". SOLOMON, Miriam.
Bonjour's Objection to Traditional Foundationalism. RAPPAPORT, Steve.

BOOKCHIN, M
Il radicalismo negli Stati Uniti degli anni '80: l'anarco-ecologismo di Murray Bookchin. DONNO, A.

BOOLEAN ALGEBRA
The Boolean Spectrum of an o-Minimal Theory. STEINHORN, Charles and TOFFALORI, Carlo.
Complexity-Theoretic Algebra II: Boolean Algebras. NERODE, A and REMMEL, J B.
Minimal Collapsing Extensions of Models of ZFC. BUKOVSKY, Lev and COPLÁKOVA-HARTOVÁ, E.
On Relativizing Kolmogorov's Absolute Probability Functions. LEBLANC, Hugues and ROEPER, Peter.
Pseudo-Boolean Valued Prolog. FITTING, Melvin.
Strong Negative Partition Above the Continuum. SHELAH, Saharon.

BOON, L
De oppervlakkigheid van de empirisch gewende wetenschapstheorie. RIP, Arie.

BORGES, J
Borges' Proof for the Existence of God. JACQUETTE, Dale.
Spinoza in Borges' Looking-Glass. ABADI, Marcelo.

BOS, A
Dooyeweerd, Bos and the Grondmotief of Greek Culture. RUNIA, D T.

BOSANQUET
The Political Philosophy of the British Idealists: Selected Studies. NICHOLSON, Peter P.

BOSHU, Z
Marxism and Human Sociobiology: A Reply to Zhang Boshu. KEITA, Lansana.

BUSINESS

Systems. TAYLOR, G Stephen.

Justifying Moral Initiative by Business, with Rejoinders to Bill Shaw and Richard Nunan. MULLIGAN, Thomas M.

A Note on the Teaching of Ethics in the MBA Macroeconomics Course. ABELL, John D.

Préoccupations éthiques aux Etats-Unis: la "Business Ethics". GRUSON, Pascale.

Social Contracts and Corporations: A Reply to Hodapp. DONALDSON, Thomas.

Socio-Economic Evolution of Women Business Owners in Quebec (1987). COLLERETTE, P and AUBRY, P.

Trust in Business Relations: Directions for Empirical Research. HUSTED, Bryan W.

Unfree Enterprise. ESTILL, Lyle.

BUSINESS ETHICS

Business Ethics: Where Profits Meet Value Systems. ROBIN, Donald P.

Ethics and Social Concern. SERAFINI, Anthony.

Ethics in Practice: Managing the Moral Corporation. ANDREWS, Kenneth R (ed).

Fundamental Concepts and Problems in Business Ethics. BUCHHOLZ, Rogene A.

Papers on the Ethics of Administration. WRIGHT, N Dale (ed).

The "Modified Vendetta Sanction" as a Method of Corporate-Collective Punishment. CORLETT, J Angelo.

Adam Smith's "Theory" of Justice: Business Ethics Themes in *The Wealth of Nations.* DE VRIES, Paul H.

Affirmative Action as a Form of Restitution. GROARKE, Leo.

An Application of Bloom's Taxonomy to the Teaching of Business Ethics. REEVES, M Francis.

Avoiding the Tragedy of Whistleblowing. DAVIS, Michael.

Bribery and the United States Foreign Corrupt Practices Act. ENGLISH, Parker.

Business and Benevolence. MC CARTY, Richard.

Business Curriculum and Ethics: Student Attitudes and Behavior. GLENN JR, James R.

Business Ethics and the International Trade in Hazardous Wastes. SINGH, Jang B and LAKHAN, V C.

Business Ethics in Banking. GREEN, C F.

Business Ethics in Italy: The State of the Art. UNNIA, Mario.

Business Ethics, Corporate Good Citizenship and the Corporate Social Policy Process: A View from the US. EPSTEIN, Edwin M.

Business Ethics, Fetal Protection Policies, and Discrimination Against Women in the Workplace. QUINN, John F.

Business Ethics: A Literature Review with a Focus on Marketing Ethics. TSALIKIS, John and FRITZSCHE, David J.

Business Ethics: Defining the Twilight Zone. NEL, Deon and PITT, Leyland.

Business Ethics: Diversity and Integration. FLEMING, John E.

Business Regulation, Business Ethics and the Professional Employee. MACKIE, Karl J.

Can Business Ethics Be Taught? Empirical Evidence. JONES, Thomas M.

Christ and Business: A Typology for Christian Business Ethics. VAN WENSVEEN SIKER, Louke.

Collaborative Collective Bargaining: Toward an Ethically Defensible Approach to Labor Negotiations. POST, Frederick R.

A Comparison of the Ethical Values of Business Faculty and Students: How Different Are They?. HARRIS, James R.

Corporate Morality Called in Question: The Case of Cabora Bassa. SCHREYÖGG, Georg and STEINMANN, Horst.

Corporate Responsibility: Morality Without Consciousness. SKIDD, David R A.

The Corporation and Its Employees: A Case Story. DAHL, Tor.

Corruption and Business in Present Day Venezuela. PERDOMO, Rogelio Perez.

The Course in Business Ethics: Can It Work?. PAMENTAL, George L.

Crucial Issues in Successful European Business. VAN LUIJK, Henk.

The Developmental Self-Valuing Theory: A Practical Approach for Business Ethics. JENSEN, Larry C and WYGANT, Steven A.

Ecological Marketing Strategy for Toni Yogurts in Switzerland. DYLLICK, Thomas.

Economic Constraints and Ethical Decisions in the Context of European Ventures. VIGNON, Jerome.

An Empirical Examination of Three Machiavellian Concepts: Advertisers Versus the General Public. FRAEDRICH, John and FERRELL, O C.

An Enterprise/Organization Ethic. DI NORCIA, Vincent.

Ethical and Conceptual Issues in Charitable Investments, Cause Related Marketing, and Advertising. DIENHART, John W and FODERICK, Saundra I.

Ethical Beliefs' Differences of Males and Females. TSALIKIS, John and ORTIZ-BUONAFINA, M.

Ethical Dilemmas for Accountants: A United Kingdom Perspective. LIKIERMAN, Andrew.

Ethical Issues in International Lending. SNOY, Bernard.

Ethical Problems in Competitive Bidding: The Paradyne Case. DAVIS, J Steve.

Ethical Theory in Business Ethics: A Critical Assessment. DERRY, Robbin and GREEN, Ronald M.

Ethics in Bioengineering. MITCHAM, Carl.

The Ethics of Insider Trading. WERHANE, Patricia H.

The Ethics of Smoking Policies. NIXON, Judy C and WEST, Judy F.

A Game-Theoretic Analysis of Professional Rights and Responsibilities. GAA, James C.

Give Goodrich a Break. FIELDER, John H.

Government Spending and the Budget Deficit. PEITCHINIS, Stephen G.

Helping Subordinates with Their Personal Problems: A Moral Dilemma for Managers. MOBERG, Dennis J.

Honesty in Marketing. JACKSON, Jennifer.

The Individual Investor in Securities Markets: An Ethical Analysis. FREDERICK, Robert E and HOFFMAN, W Michael.

Integrating Social Responsibility and Ethics into the Strategic Planning Process. ROBIN, Donald P and REIDENBACH, R Eric.

An Integrative Model for Understanding and Managing Ethical Behavior in Business Organizations. STEAD, W Edward and WORRELL, Dan L and STEAD, Jean Garner.

International Codes of Conduct: An Analysis of Ethical Reasoning. GETZ, Kathleen A.

An International Look at Business Ethics: Britain. MAHONEY, Jack.

Is a Moral Organization Possible?. KLEIN, Sherwin.

Issues Management and Organizational Accounts: An Analysis of Corporate Responses to Accusation of Unethical Business. GARRETT, Dennis E and BRADFORD, Jeffrey L and MEYERS, Renee A and BECKER, Joy.

Issues Surrounding the Theories of Negligent Hiring and Failure to Fire. EXTEJT, Marian M and BOCKANIC, William N.

The Leverage of Foreigners: Multinationals in South Africa. DI NORCIA, Vincent.

Marketing/Business Ethics: A Review of the Empirical Research. FRITSCHE, David J.

MBAs' Changing Attitudes Toward Marketing Dilemmas: 1981-1987. ZINKHAN, George M.

Measuring the Impact of Teaching Ethics to Future Managers: A Review, Assessment, and Recommendations. WEBER, James.

Methodology in Business Ethics Research: A Review and Critical Assessment. RANDALL, D M and GIBSON, A M.

Moral Theory and Defective Tobacco Advertising and Warnings (The Business Ethics of *Cipollone versus Liggett Group*). QUINN, John F.

Norman Bowie and Richard Rorty on Multinationals: Does Business Ethics Need 'Metaphysical Comfort?'. WICKS, Andrew C.

On the Antecedents of Corporate Severance Agreements: An Empirical Assessment. DALTON, Dan R and RECHNER, Paula L.

Organization of Work in the Company and Family Rights of the Employees. MELÉE, Domènec.

Perceptual Differences of Sales Practitioners and Students Concerning Ethical Behavior. DE CONINCK, J B and GOOD, D J.

Plant Closing Ethics Root in American Law. MILLSPAUGH, Peter E.

Platonic Virtue Theory and Business Ethics. KLEIN, Sherwin.

Préoccupations éthiques aux Etats-Unis: la "Business Ethics". GRUSON, Pascale.

Punishing Corporations: A Proposal. RISSER, David T.

Ranken on Disharmony and Business Ethics. GIBSON, Kevin.

Realism in the Practice of Accounting Ethics. COTTELL JR, Philip G.

Recent Developments in European Business Ethics. VAN LUIJK, Henk J L.

The Relationship Between Ethics and Job Satisfaction: An Empirical Investigation. VITELL, Scott J and DAVIS, D L.

The Role of Ethics in Global Corporate Culture. DOBSON, John.

The Sales Process and the Paradoxes of Trust. OAKES, G.

The Salesperson: Clerk, Con Man or Professional?. MORDEN, Michael J.

A Simple Quantitative Test of Financial Ethics. NORTON, Edgar.

The Social Conscience of Business. REILLY, Bernard J and KYJ, Myroslaw J.

The Special Role of Professions in Business Ethics. DAVIS, Michael.

A Stakeholder Apologetic for Management. SHARPLIN, Arthur and PHELPS, Lonnie D.

Student Views on "Ethical" Issues: A Situational Analysis. JONES JR, William A.

Taking Stock: Can the Theory of Reasoned Action Explain Unethical

CATEGORICITY

Classifying $\aleph_0$-Categorical Theories. WEAVER, George.

Counterexamples to a Conjecture on Relative Categoricity. EVANS, D M.

Omega-Categoricity, Relative Categoricity and Coordinatisation. HODGES, Wilfrid and HODKINSON, I M and MACPHERSON, Dugald.

Uncountable Theories that are Categorical in a Higher Power. LASKOWSKI, Michael Chris.

CATEGORY THEORY

Hegel and Category Theory. PIPPIN, Robert B.

CATEGORY(-RIES)

Aristotle's Concept of the Universal. BRAKAS, George.

Ontological Investigations: Inquiry Into the Categories of Nature, Man, Society. JOHANSSON, Ingvar.

Thought and Language. MORAVCSIK, J M.

"Conceptual Semantics" in *Meaning and Mental Representation*, JACKENDOFF, Ray.

The Abyssal Categories of Blaga's Apriorism. RAMBU, Nicolae.

Alpha-Conversion, Conditions on Variables and Categorical Logic. CURIEN, Pierre-Louis.

Die Anschauungsformen und das Schematismuskapitel. MUDROCH, Vilem.

Are There Categories in Chinese Philosophy? (in Serbo-Croatian). CHALIER, Agnes.

Categorías aristotélicas y categorías intensionales. STAHL, Gérold.

Categorías puras y categorías esquematizadas. VON BILDERLING, Beatriz.

Categorical and Algebraic Aspects of Martin-Löf Type Theory. OBTUŁOWICZ, A.

Catégories et raison chez C S Peirce. THIBAUD, Pierre.

Coherence in Cartesian Closed Categories and the Generality of Proofs. SZABO, M E.

Combinators and Categorial Grammar. SIMONS, Peter.

A Comparison Between Lambek Syntactic Calculus and Intuitionistic Linear Propositional Logic. ABRUSCI, V Michele.

Concepts, Categories, and Epistemology. LIVINGSTON, Kenneth R.

Cosa è pensare: Saggio sulle "Categorie" di Aristotele. CALEO, Marcello.

Exemplification Reconsidered. ARRELL, Douglas.

How Kantian Was Hegel?. PINKARD, Terry.

The Inconsistency of Higher Order Extensions of Martin-Löf's Type Theory. JACOBS, Bart.

Kant and the Possibility of Uncategorized Experience. KAIN, Philip J.

Kant's Conception of Empirical Law—I. GUYER, Paul.

Kategoriai and the Unity of Being. MALPAS, J E.

Manufacturing a Cartesian Closed Category with Exactly Two Objects Out of a *C*-Monoid. RODENBURG, P H.

Monoidal Categories With Natural Numbers Object. PARÉ, Robert and ROMÁN, Leopoldo.

A Note on Natural Numbers Objects in Monoidal Categories. JAY, C Barry.

A Note on Russell's Paradox in Locally Cartesian Closed Categories. PITTS, Andrew M and TAYLOR, Paul.

The Notion of Independence in Categories of Algebraic Structures, Part III: Equational Classes. SROUR, Gabriel.

On Lifting of ω-Operations From the Category of Sets to the Category of Enumerated Sets. ORLICKI, Andrzej.

On Some Connections Between Logic and Category Theory. LAMBEK, J.

Peirce's Early Method of Finding the Categories. DE TIENNE, André.

Philosophical Trifles (in Serbo-Croatian). LÁSZLÓ, Bulcsú.

The Prayers of Childhood: T S Eliot's Manuscripts on Kant. HABIB, M A R.

Purpose as Historical Category (in Dutch). DREYER, P S.

The Role of Apperception in Kant's Transcendental Deduction of the Categories. CASTANEDA, Héctor-Neri.

Santayana's Neo-Platonism. KUNTZ, Paul G.

Semisimple Stable and Superstable Groups. BALDWIN, J T and PILLAY, A.

Specimens of Natural Kinds and the Apparent Inconsistency of *Metaphysics Zeta*. SPELLMAN, Lynne.

Spirituality in Santayana. TEJERA, V.

A Theorem on Barr-Exact Categories, with an Infinitary Generalization. MAKKAI, Michael.

Zur teleologischen Grundlage der transzendentalen Deduktion der Kategorien. ROSALES, Alberto.

CATHOLIC

Medical Ethics: Essays on Abortion and Euthanasia. BARRY, Robert L.

Chesterton's Philosophy of Education. HALDANE, John.

Controversies and Discussions about the Post-Council Aspect of Catholic Philosophy. BORGOSZ, Jozef and PACZYNSKA, Maria (trans).

The Ideology of Social Justice in Economic Justice For All. MURNION, William E.

Speculations Regarding the History of *Donum Vitae*. HARVEY, John Collins.

Thomism and Contemporary Philosophical Pluralism. CLARKE, W Norris.

CATHOLICISM

"Cyril Loukaris: A Protestant Patriarch or a Pioneer Orthodox Ecumenist?" in *The Wisdom of Faith: Essays in Honor of Dr Sebastian Alexander Matczak*, TSIRPANLIS, Constantine N.

"The Postmodern Paradigm and Contemporary Catholicism" in *Varieties of Postmodern Theology*, HOLLAND, Joe.

Catholicism and Socialism: The Problems of Political Understanding. OPARA, Stefan and PROTALINSKI, Grzegorz (trans).

The Dialogue of Grand Theories for Peace. PLUZANSKI, Tadeusz and KISIEL, Krystyna (trans) and KISIEL, Chester (trans).

Die Verantwortung des Menschen für seine natürliche Umwelt (in Polish). ROSINSKI, F M and LATAWIEC, A M.

Donum Vitae on Homologous Interventions: Is IVF-ET a Less Acceptable Gift than "Gift"?. CARLSON, John W.

Francisco Suárez on Natural Law. CVEK, Peter P.

L'homme en tant qu'autocréateur; fondements anthropologiques du rejet de l'encyclique (in Polish). SZOSTEK, Andrzej.

La person e en tant que don dans l'enseignement de Jean-Paul II (in Polish). GALKOWSKI, Jerzy W.

Miracles, the Supernatural, and the Problem of Extrinsicism. NICHOLS, Terence L.

The *Munus* of Transmitting Human Life: A New Approach to *Humanae Vitae*. SMITH, Janet E.

The State's Line: On the Change of Paradigm of Austrian Philosophy within Maria-Theresian Reform-Catholicism. GIMPL, Georg.

Wert und Würde der Arbeit in *Laborem Exercens* (in Polish). JUROS, Helmut.

CAUCHY, V

Intervention: Entretien avec Monsieur Venant Cauchy. CHRÉTIEN, Émile and CAUCHY, Venant.

CAUSAL EXPLANATION

"The Causal Mechanical Model of Explanation" in *Scientific Explanation (Minnesota Studies in the Philosophy of Science, Volume XIII)*, WOODWARD, James.

"The Concept of Structure in *The Analysis of Matter*" in *Rereading Russell: Essays on Bertrand Russell's Metaphysics and Epistemology*, DEMOPOULOS, William and FRIEDMAN, Michael.

A Causal Theory of Intending. SHOPE, Robert K.

Genetic Traits. GIFFORD, Fred.

In Defense of the Causal Representative Theory of Perception. FROST, Thomas B.

Kant's Third Antinomy: Agency and Causal Explanation. GREENWOOD, John D.

A Natural Explanation of the Existence and Laws of Our Universe. SMITH, Quentin.

The Objects of Perceptual Experience—I. SNOWDON, Paul.

The Objects of Perceptual Experience—II. ROBINSON, Howard.

One Causal Mechanism in Evolution: One Unit of Selection. KARY, Carla E.

Program Explanation: A General Perspective. JACKSON, Frank and PETTIT, Philip.

CAUSAL LAW(S)

"Capacities and Abstractions" in *Scientific Explanation (Minnesota Studies in the Philosophy of Science, Volume XIII)*, CARTWRIGHT, Nancy.

CAUSALITY

Actions and Other Events: The Unifier-Multiplier Controversy. PFEIFER, Karl.

Beyond the Atom: The Philosophical Thought of Wolfgang Pauli. LAURIKAINEN, K V.

Four Decades of Scientific Explanation. SALMON, Wesley C.

God, Foreknowledge, and Freedom. FISCHER, John Martin (ed).

Lawless Mind. ABELSON, Raziel.

Mind-Body Identity Theories. MACDONALD, Cynthia.

Nietzsche's Philosophy of Nature and Cosmology. MOLES, Alistair.

Ontological Investigations: Inquiry Into the Categories of Nature, Man, Society. JOHANSSON, Ingvar.

Our Philosophy: Allāma Muhammad Bāqir As-Sadr. INATI, Shams C (trans).

Philosophical Consequences of Quantum Theory: Reflections on Bell's Theorem. CUSHING, James T (ed).

The Philosophy of F P Ramsey. SAHLIN, Nils-Eric.

The Philosophy of Quantum Mechanics: An Interactive Interpretation. HEALEY, Richard.

Readings in the Philosophy of Science (Second Edition). BRODY, Baruch A.

Self-Direction and Political Legitimacy: Rousseau and Herder. BARNARD, F M.

Thomas Reid and 'The Way of Ideas'. GALLIE, Roger D.

"C B Martin, A Biographical Sketch" in *Cause, Mind, and Reality: Essays*

CAUSALITY

Honoring C B Martin, SMART, J J C.

"C B Martin, Counterfactuals, Causality, and Conditionals" in *Cause, Mind, and Reality: Essays Honoring C B Martin*, ARMSTRONG, D M.

"Can You Help Your Team Tonight by Watching on TV? More Experimental Metaphysics from Einstein, Podolsky, and Rosen" in *Philosophical Consequences of Quantum Theory: Reflections on Bell's Theorem*, MERMIN, N David.

"The Charybdis of Realism: Epistemological Implications of Bell's Inequality" in *Philosophical Consequences of Quantum Theory: Reflections on Bell's Theorem*, VAN FRAASSEN, Bas C.

"Explanatory Unification and the Causal Structure of the World" in *Scientific Explanation (Minnesota Studies in the Philosophy of Science, Volume XIII)*, KITCHER, Philip.

"Nonfactorizability, Stochastic Causality, and Passion-at-a-Distance" in *Philosophical Consequences of Quantum Theory: Reflections on Bell's Theorem*, REDHEAD, Michael L G.

"Remembering 'Remembering'" in *Cause, Mind, and Reality: Essays Honoring C B Martin*, DEUTSCHER, Max.

Bergson et l'idée de causalité. ÉTIENNE, Jacques.

Causal Hermits. ROGERSON, Kenneth F.

Causalist Internalism. AUDI, Robert.

Creator and Causality: A Critique of Pre-Critical Objections. BEARDS, Andrew.

La crítica aristotélica al Bien platónico. LA CROCE, Ernesto.

De l'explication causale dans la biologie d'Aristote. PELLEGRIN, Pierre.

Descartes on Time and Causality. SECADA, J E K.

Goodman's "New Riddle"—A Realist's Reprise. ELDER, Crawford L.

Hartshorne on the Ultimate Issue in Metaphysics. GILROY JR, John D.

Hermann von Helmholtz: The Problem of Kantian Influence. FULLINWIDER, S P.

Hume and Tetens. KUEHN, Manfred.

Hume's *Tu Quoque*: Newtonianism and the Rationality of the Causal Principle. HAYNES, Michael.

Is Causal Relation Asymmetrical. DEWASHI, Mahadev.

Kant's Challenge: The Second Analogy as a Response to Hume. DELANEY, C.

Making Mind Matter More. FODOR, Jerry A.

Miracles, the Supernatural, and the Problem of Extrinsicism. NICHOLS, Terence L.

More on Making Mind Matter. LE PORE, Ernest and LOEWER, Barry.

Naturaleza y causalidad en Aristóteles: *Física* II 1. BOERI, Marcelo D.

Naturnotwendigkeit und Freiheit: Zu Kants Theorie der Kausalität als Antwort auf Hume. RANG, Bernhard.

On Tooley on Salmon. DOWE, Phil.

Les origines de la notion de cause. FREDE, Michael (trans) and BRUNSCHWIG, J (trans).

Prospective Realism. BROWN, Harold I.

Regarding Rich's "Compatibilism Argument" and the 'Ought'-Implies-'Can' Argument. FAWKES, Don.

A Response to A A Long's "The Stoics on World-Conflagration and Everlasting Recurrence". HUDSON, Hud.

Sense, Reason and Causality in Hume and Kant. NUYEN, A T.

St Thomas et la métaphysique du "liber de causis". ELDERS, Lédon.

Struggling with Causality: Schrödinger's Case. BEN-MENAHEM, Yemima.

Supernatural Acts and Supervenient Explanations. WHITTAKER, John H.

A Taste for Hume. DE MARTELAERE, Patricia.

Techne: dai Greci ai moderni e ritorno. POSSENTI, Vittorio.

Temporal Versus Manipulability Theory of Causal Asymmetry. DEWASHI, Mahadev.

Tertiary Waywardness Tamed. ADAMS, Frederick.

CAUSATION

Connections to the World: The Basic Concepts of Philosophy. DANTO, Arthur C.

Heritage and Challenge: The History and Theory of History. CONKIN, Paul K.

Hume and the Problem of Miracles: A Solution. LEVINE, Michael P.

Natural Agency: An Essay on the Casual Theory of Action. BISHOP, John.

"Pure, Mixed, and Spurious Probabilities and Their Significance for a Reductionist Theory of Causation" in *Scientific Explanation (Minnesota Studies in the Philosophy of Science, Volume XIII)*, PAPINEAU, David.

The Causalist Program: Rational or Irrational Persistence?. FLICHMAN, Eduardo H.

Causation and Perception in Reid. PAPPAS, George S.

Causation, Transitivity, and Causal Relata. HOLT, Dale Lynn.

Causes, Enablers, and the Counterfactual Analysis. LOMBARD, Lawrence Brian.

Hume on Character, Action, and Causal Necessity. JOHNSON, Clarence

Sholé.

The Humean Tradition. CARROLL, John.

Individuation and Causation in Psychology. BURGE, Tyler.

Metaphysics of Causation. BIGELOW, John and PARGETTER, Robert.

Must Intentional States Be IntenSional?. EMMETT, Kathleen.

Neurophilosophy and the Logic-Causation Argument. KIAMIE, Kimberly A.

A New Plausible Exposition of Sānkhya-Kārikā-9. WADHWANI-SHAH, Yashodhara.

One More Time. MOLANDER, Bengt.

Les origines de la notion de cause. FREDE, Michael (trans) and BRUNSCHWIG, J (trans).

Philosophical Functionalism. WARD, Andrew.

Poder causal, experiencia y conceptos *a priori*. CASSINI, Alejandro.

Probabilistic Causation and Causal Processes: A Critique of Lewis. MENZIES, Peter.

Recklessness, Omission, and Responsibility: Some Reflections on the Moral Significance of Causation. SMITH, Patricia G.

There is No Question of Physicalism. CRANE, Tim.

The Trapped Infinity: Cartesian Volition as Conceptual Nightmare. REED, Edward S.

What is Psychological Egoism?. SOBER, Elliott.

CAUSE(S)

Abstract Particulars. CAMPBELL, Keith.

Cause, Mind, and Reality: Essays Honoring C B Martin. HEIL, John (ed).

Nature's Capacities and their Measurement. CARTWRIGHT, Nancy.

On Action. GINET, Carl.

The Past Within Us: An Empirical Approach to Philosophy of History. MARTIN, Raymond.

"Cause in the Later Russell" in *Rereading Russell: Essays on Bertrand Russell's Metaphysics and Epistemology*, EAMES, Elizabeth R.

"Scientific Explanation: The Causes, Some of the Causes, and Nothing But the Causes" in *Scientific Explanation (Minnesota Studies in the Philosophy of Science, Volume XIII)*, HUMPHREYS, Paul W.

'Would Cause'. NEEDHAM, Paul.

Causas y razones en la filosofía de Wittgenstein. CABANCHIK, Samuel.

Cause as an Implication. SYLVAN, Richard and DA COSTA, Newton.

Deus, causa sui *en Descartes*. AGUADO, Javier Fernández.

The Four Causes in Aristotle's Embryology. MATTHEN, Mohan.

How to Learn a Language Like a Chimpanzee. GAUKER, Christopher.

Justification: It Need not Cause but it Must be Accessible. GINET, Carl.

Language as a Cause-Effect Communication System. SAVAGE-RUMBAUGH, E S.

La metafisica della Prima Persona *(Ego Sum Qui Sum)*: Parte prima. ARATA, Carlo.

Observaciones sobre la noción de causa en el opúsculo sobre el movimiento de Berkeley. ABAD, Juan Vázquez.

Philo's Final Conclusion in Hume's *Dialogues*. VINK, A G.

Recent Developments in European Business Ethics. VAN LUIJK, Henk J L.

CAVAILLES, J

Jean Cavaillès' aanloop tot de wetenschapstheorie. CORTOIS, P.

CAVELL, S

Stanley Cavell and Literary Skepticism. FISCHER, Michael.

CEAUSESCU, N

Le développement de la science et le progrès de la société (in Romanian). MARIS, Nicolae.

CELAN, P

"Condurre tutte le metafore *ad absurdum*": Riflessioni filosofiche attorno alla poetica di Celan. SAMONÀ, Leonardo.

CELESTIAL BODY(-DIES)

Copernicus, the Orbs, and the Equant. BARKER, Peter.

CELIBACY

The Distinctiveness of Early Christian Sexual Ethics. PRICE, Richard M.

CENSORSHIP

Censorship and the Displacement of Irreligion. BERMAN, David.

Feminist Moralism, "Pornography," and Censorship. DORITY, Barbara.

Reading Vico Three Times. SUMBERG, Theodore A.

CENTRALIZATION

John Stuart Mill on Democratic Representation and Centralization. KURER, Oskar.

CERTAINTY

Wittgenstein's Later Philosophy. HANFLING, Oswald.

Certeza, duda escéptica y saber. CABANCHIK, Samuel M.

Dewey and Wittgenstein on the Idea of Certainty. EODICE, Alexander R.

La hiérarchie des systèmes—à la frontière de l'intuition et de la certitude. STANCIULESCU, Traian-Dinorel.

CERTITUDE
Della scommessa legislativa sulla discrezionalità dei giudici. MARINI, Gaetano.

CH'ENG
Ch'eng I—The Pattern of Heaven-and-Earth (in Serbo-Croatian). SMITH, Kidder.

CHALLENGE(S)
Heritage and Challenge: The History and Theory of History. CONKIN, Paul K.

CHALMERS, A
Chalmers on Unrepresentative Realism and Objectivism. SIEVERS, K H.

CHALOUPKA, W
John Dewey and Environmental Thought. TAYLOR, Bob Pepperman.

CHAMBLISS, J
Rereading Aristotle and Dewey on Educational Theory: A Deconstruction. PALERMO, James.

CHANCE
see also Probability
Evolutie, teleologie en toeval. SOONTIËNS, Frans.
God's Lottery. MC CALL, Storrs and ARMSTRONG, D M.
Le origini dell'ateismo antico (quarta parte). ZEPPI, Stelio.
The Notion of Chance and the Metaphysics of P Kanellopoulos (in Greek). MARKAKIS, M.

CHANGE
see also Social Change
Holism—A Philosophy for Today: Anticipating the Twenty First Century. SETTANNI, Harry.
"Democracy and Environmental Change" in *Ethics and the Environmental Responsibility*, WENZ, Peter.
"Motion and Change of Distance" in *Cause, Mind, and Reality: Essays Honoring C B Martin*, NERLICH, Graham.
Applied Philosophy in the Post-Modern Age: An Augury. ENGELHARDT JR, H Tristram.
Aristotle and the Mind-Body Problem. HEINAMAN, Robert.
The Changing Image of Art Education: Theoretical Antecedents of Discipline-Based Art Education. SMITH, Ralph A.
Creativity and Routine. PERRY, Leslie R.
God's Unchanging Knowledge of the World. BROWN, Graham.
Lectures on the I Ching (in Serbo-Croatian). CHUNG, Albert C.
New Problems with Repeatable Properties and with Change. FORREST, Peter.
Recent Classical/Process Dialogue on God and Change. CLAYTON, Philip.
Renormalizing Epistemology. LEPLIN, Jarrett.
St Thomas Aquinas on the Halfway State of Sensible Being. HOFFMAN, Paul.
The State at Dusk. MAC GREGOR, David.
A Sweet and Sour Victory in Eastern Europe. SZAKOLCZAI, Árpád and HORVÁTH, Ágnes.
Technology versus Science: The Cognitive Fallacy. DI NUCCI PEARCE, M Rosaria and PEARCE, David.
A Theory of Reference Transmission and Reference Change. BERGER, Alan.

CHAOS
The Time-Like Nature of Mind: On Mind Functions as Temporal Patterns of the Neural Network. FISCHER, Roland.

CHARACTER DEVELOPMENT
Education, Movement and the Curriculum: A Philosophic Enquiry. ARNOLD, Peter J.
"Aesthetics in the Context of Historicity, Moral Education and Character Development" in *The Social Context and Values: Perspectives of the Americas*, LOPEZ, Raul.
Freedom and Virtue in Politics: Some Aspects of Character, Circumstances and Utility from Helvétius to J S Mill. SMITH, G W.
The Morality of Nuclear Deterrence and the Corruption of Character. LOVE JR, Charles E.
Nuclear Deterrence, Character, and Moral Education. KLEIN, J Theodore.
Sport, Character, and Virtue. FEEZELL, Randolph.

CHARACTER TRAIT(S)
Character and Circumstance. WALKER, A D M.
Teaching Virtues and Vices. WILLIAMS, Clifford.

CHARACTER(S)
Agency, Human Nature and Character in Kantian Theory. RUMSEY, Jean P.
The Ancient Sceptic's Way of Life. MORRISON, Donald.
Aristotle on Responsibility for Action and Character. ROBERTS, Jean.

Character, Choice, and Moral Agency: The Relevance of Character to our Moral Culpability Judgments. ARENELLA, Peter.
Character: A Humean Account. MC INTYRE, Jane L.
Characters and Fixed Points in Provability Logic. GLEIT, Zachary and GOLDFARB, Warren.
Choice, Character, and Excuse. MOORE, Michael.
Hume on Character, Action, and Causal Necessity. JOHNSON, Clarence Sholé.
Hypocrisy. TURNER, D.
Porous Vessels: A Critique of the Nation, Nationalism and National Character as Analytical Concepts. FARRAR JR, L L.
Rousseau on Reading "Jean-Jacques": *The Dialogues*. KELLY, Christopher and MASTERS, Roger D.
Stories of Sublimely Good Character. CALLEN, Donald.
Virtues and Character. WALKER, A D M.
Ways of Wrong-Doing, the Vices, and Cruelty. MC KINNON, Christine.

CHARACTERISTICS
The Philosophy of Horror 'or' Paradoxes of the Heart. CARROLL, Noël.
Attitudes Towards Corporate Social Responsibility and Perceived Importance of Social Responsibility Information. TEOH, Hai Yap and SHIU, Godwin Y.
Individual and Organizational Characteristics of Women in Managerial Leadership. ROWNEY, J I A and CAHOON, A R.
Integrative Thinking Is the Essential Characteristic of Creative Thinking. SONGXING, Su and GUOZHENG, Lin.
Philosophy as Critical Thinking. FINOCCHIARO, Maurice A.
What is Wrong With Reverse Discrimination?. HETTINGER, Edwin C.

CHARACTERIZING
On the Control-Theoretic Characterization of the Self. JONES, Andrew J I.

CHARITY
Religion, Interpretation, and Diversity of Belief. GODLOVE, Terry F.
L'amour-propre: Un tema secentesco tra morale e antropologia. BOSCO, Domenico.
Charity and Ideology: The Field Linguist as Social Critic. RAMBERG, Bjorn T.
An Empirical Basis for Charity in Interpretation. HENDERSON, David K.
Flew on Russell on Nozick: Uncharitable Interpretations of Justice and Unjust Views of Charity. SKILLEN, Tony.
Minds Divided. HEIL, John.

CHASTAIN, C
"Why Perception is not Singular Reference" in *Cause, Mind, and Reality: Essays Honoring C B Martin*, MC LAUGHLIN, Brian P.

CHAUVINISM
Chauvinism and Science: Another Reply to Shanon. HENLEY, Tracy B.

CHEATING
God, the Devil and the Perfect Pizza: Ten Philosophical Questions. GOVIER, Trudy.

CHEMISTRY
Reading the Mind of God: In Search of the Principle of Universality. TREFIL, James.
The Conceptual Structure of the Chemical Revolution. THAGARD, Paul.
Kants Theorie der Materie und ihre Wirkung auf die zeitgenössische Chemie. CARRIER, Martin.
Phanerochemistry and Semiotic. TURSMAN, Richard.

CHESTERTON, G
Chesterton's Philosophy of Education. HALDANE, John.

CHESTOV, L
El no al 2x2=4 de León Chestov. MARTÍNEZ, Luis.

CHILD CENTERED
Subject-Centred Versus Child-Centred Education—A False Dualism. PRING, Richard.

CHILDHOOD
Neoteny and the Virtues of Childhood. MILLER, Richard B.

CHILDREN
Essays in Philosophy and Education. STOTT, Laurence J.
"Morality, Parents, and Children" in *Person to Person*, RACHELS, James.
"Some Factors Influencing the Success of Philosophical Discussion in the Classroom. WHALLEY, Michael.
Against Skills. HART, W.
An Appeal for Total Intellectual Openness. AVIRAM, Roni.
The Apprenticeship Model: What We Can Learn from Gareth Matthews. SHEFFER, Susannah.
A Bold Adventure. GUIN, Philip.
Can Parents and Children Be Friends?. KUPFER, Joseph.

CHILDREN

The Child as Craftsman. FELDMAN, David Henry.

The Child-As-Philosopher: A Critique of the Presuppositions of Piagetian Theory. LEVINE, Shellie-helane.

Children's Philosophy—Or: Is Motivation for Doing Philosophy a Pseudo-Problem?. MARTENS, Ekkehard.

Comprehension and Production in Early Lexical Development: A Comment on Stemmer. HARRIS, Margaret.

Controlling the Classroom Clamor: A Few Techniques to Facilitate Philosophical Discourse. SILVER, Ruth E.

Critical Children: Philosophy for the Young. COLES, Martin.

A Critique of Critical Thinking. HATCHER, Donald.

Das Verhältnis von Verbrecherinnen zu ihren Familien (in Polish). ROSINSKI, F M.

Developing the Idea of Intentionality: Children's Theories of Mind. GOPNIK, Alison.

Doing Philosophy with Children. ALLEN, Terry.

Educational Reform Through Philosophy for Children. SPLITTER, Laurance J.

The Effect of the *Pixie* Program on Logical and Moral Reasoning. SCHLEIFER, Michael and LEBUIS, Pierre and CARON, Anita.

An Elementary Conception of Time. AULT JR, Charles R.

Evaluation of a Philosophy for Children Project in Hawaii. MEEHAN, Kenneth A.

Fools, Young Children and Philosophy. KENNEDY, David.

Fools, Young Children, Animism, and the Scientific World-Picture. KENNEDY, David.

Gratitude and the Duties of Grown Children Towards Their Aging Parents. GERBER, Rona M.

The Historical Epistemology of Gaston Bachelard and its Relevance to Science Education. SOUQUE, Jean-Pascal.

How Does the Child Benefit from "Philosophy for Children"?. GUARDA, Victor and SOMMERMEIER, Rolf (trans).

How Does the Child Benefit from "Philosophy for Children"?. CAMHY, Daniela G and SOMMERMEIER, Rolf (trans).

Insight and Reason: The Role of Ratio in Education. BOHM, David.

Intimations of Philosophy in Early Childhood. EDMAN, Irwin.

Is it Possible to Teach Socratically?. SHERMAN, Rosalyn S.

Is There Really Development? An Alternative Interpretation. BECK, Clive.

Johnny Head-In-The-Air and Thales. CHARPA, Ulrich.

Kio and Gus Teach Henrik to Read. NORHOLM, Ingrid.

Looking Backward at Education Reform. HAWLEY, Willis D.

Managing Philosophical Discussions. KYLE, Judy A.

The Mother-Child Relationship. HOLM, Soren.

Nature and Philosophy for Children. RYAN, Mary Melville.

A Note on the Legal Liberties of Children as Distinguished from Adults. VETTERLING-BRAGGIN, Mary.

On Being a Meaning-Maker: Young Children's Experiences of Reading. POLAKOW, Valerie.

On the Relation Between Logic and Thinking. HENLE, Mary.

On Thinking for Yourself. SPLITTER, Laurance J.

On Victor Guarda's "How Does the Child Benefit from 'Philosophy for Children'?". SCHREIER, Helmut.

On What Isn't Learned in School. BRANDON, E P.

Parents Rights and Educational Policy. FORSTER, Kathie.

Parrots Into Owls: The Metamorphosis of a Philosophy for Children Program. VALLONE, Gerard.

Paternalism and the Rationality of the Child. EKMAN, Rosalind.

A Philosopher's Stone in the Hands of Children: Using Classical Philosophy to Teach Children Mathematical Concepts. DRABMAN, Randy.

A Philosophic Fairytale. RICKMAN, H P.

Philosophizing with Children in the Glocksee School in Hanover, Germany. HORSTER, Detlev and ALEXANDER, John V I (trans).

Philosophy and Foolishness. HEINEGG, James.

Philosophy and the Education of the Community. MULVANEY, Robert.

Philosophy for Children and Aesthetic Education. HAMRICK, William S.

Philosophy for Children and Critical Thinking. LIPMAN, Matthew.

Philosophy for Children and the Modernization of Chinese Education. MULVANEY, Robert J.

Philosophy for Children and the Piagetian Framework. GAZZARD, Ann.

Philosophy for Children in its Historical Context. MULVANEY, Robert.

Philosophy for Children: A Traditional Subject in a Novel Format. LIPMAN, Matthew and SHARP, Ann Margaret.

Philosophy for Children: An Example of the Public Dimension in Philosophy of Education. PORTELLI, John P.

Philosophy for Children: An Important Curriculum Innovation. SPLITTER, Laurance J.

The Practice of Philosophy for Children in Austria: How Can Children Think Philosophically?. CAMHY, Daniela G.

The Practice of Philosophy in the Elementary School Classroom. WHALLEY, Michael J.

The Price of Abortion Sixteen Years Later. CHOPKO, Mark E and HARRIS, Phillip and ALVARÉ, Helen M.

Pushing Thoughts With Claire. OSCANYAN, Frederick S.

A Real-Life Brain. HAMRICK, William S.

Reasoning Skills: An Overview. CANNON, Dale and WEINSTEIN, Mark.

Regulating AIDS Research on Infants and Children: The Moral Task of Institutional Review Boards. CARTER, Michele and WICHMAN, Alison and MC CARTHY, Charles R.

Remarks On Teaching "Barefoot" Philosophy. LOECK, Gisela.

Response to Bilow: Future Persons and the Justification of Education. SCHRAG, Francis.

Science Begins with Everyday Thinking. ROYER, Ron.

Socrates In a New Package Helps Kids Learn to Think. BERRIAN, Annette.

The Socratic Method and Philosophy for Children. PORTELLI, John P.

Some Concrete Approaches to Nature in *Kio and Gus*. HAMRICK, William S.

Step by Step in Children's Philosophy. MOSTERT, Pieter.

Teaching as Translation: The Philosophical Dimension. JOHNSON, Tony W.

Teaching Reasoning With Computers. FURLONG, John and CARROLL, William.

Thinking Skill Programs: An Analysis. MAYS, Wolfe and SHARP, Ann Margaret.

Thinking Skills in Science and Philosophy for Children. GAZZARD, Ann.

Thinking, Mind, the Existence of God...Transcript of a Classroom Dialogue with First-and-Second Graders in Montreal. DANIEL, Marie-France.

We Discover That Thinking Is Fun: Doing Philosophy With First Graders. BRÜNING, Barbara.

What Children Owe Parents: Ethics in an Aging Society. POST, Stephen G.

What Kind of Girl is Pippi Longstocking, Anyway?. BRÜNING, Barbara.

Wittgenstein and Philosophy for Children. CURTIS, Barry.

The Words 'Same' and 'Different'. CRAWSHAY-WILLIAMS, Rupert.

Working with Philosophy for Children in Catalonia. CULLELL, Josep.

CHILDRESS, J

Medical Ethics: Principles, Persons, and Problems. FRAME, John M.

Who Lives? Who Dies?: Ethical Criteria in Patient Selection. KILNER, John F.

CHINESE

see also Buddhism, Confucianism, Taoism

Chu Hsi: New Studies. CHAN, Wing-Tsit.

The Confucian Creation of Heaven: Philosophy and the Defense of Ritual Mastery. ENO, Robert.

Disputers of the TAO: Philosophical Argument in Ancient China. GRAHAM, A C.

Man and Nature in the Philosophical Thought of Wang-Fu-Chih. BLACK, Alison Harley.

Man and Nature: The Chinese Tradition and the Future. TANG, Yi-Jie (ed).

The Thought of Mao Tse-Tung. SCHRAM, Stuart.

Xunzi: A Translation and Study of the Complete Works, Volume II—Books 7-16. KNOBLOCK, John (trans).

"On the Unity of Man and Heaven" in *Man and Nature: The Chinese Tradition and the Future*, YI-JIE, Tang.

"Theories Concerning Man and Nature in Classical Chinese Philosophy" in *Man and Nature: The Chinese Tradition and the Future*, DAI-NIAN, Zhang.

"Western and Chinese Philosophy on Man and Nature" in *Man and Nature: The Chinese Tradition and the Future*, DE GEORGE, Richard T.

The "Self" Begins to Awake: On the Philosophical Thought of Gong Zizhen. QI, Feng.

1987 Controversy Over the Evaluations of Confucius. DINGBO, Wu.

Are There Categories in Chinese Philosophy? (in Serbo-Croatian). CHALIER, Agnes.

Changes in the Attitude of Chinese Philosophical Circles Towards Pragmatism. XUFANG, Zhan.

China and Modernization: Past and Present. SOO, Francis.

China: Moral Puzzles. TIAN-MIN, Xu.

Chinese Axial Age in the Light of Kohlberg's Developmental Logic of Moral Consciousness (in Serbo-Croatian). ROETZ, Heiner.

Chinese Theories of Appreciation—with Particular Attention to Painting (in Japanese). KÔNO, Michifusa.

Christian Wolff and China: The Autonomy of Morality (in Serbo-Croatian). CHING, Julia.

Comment on Chad Hansen's "Language Utilitarianism". BRANDT, Richard B.

CHRISTOLOGY

Christological Grounds for Liberation Praxis. PREGEANT, Russell.

The Logic of God Incarnate. HICK, John.

Toward a Process-Relational Christian Soteriology. WHEELER, David L.

CHRYSIPPUS

Chrysippus and the *Placita*. MANSFELD, Jaap.

CHU HSI

Chu Hsi: New Studies. CHAN, Wing-Tsit.

Dai Zhen: The Unity of the Moral Nature (in Serbo-Croatian). EWELL JR, John W.

Mencius: The Mind-Inherence of Morality (in Serbo-Croatian). SHUN, Kwong-loi.

CHUANG TZU

"Theft's Way": A Comparative Study of Chuang Tzu's Tao and Derridean Trace. CHIEN, Chi-Hui.

Radical Concrete Particularity: Heidegger, Lao Tzu and Chuang Tzu. OWENS, Wayne D.

CHURCH

Gramsci, Mariàtegui e la teologia della liberazione. PROTO, M.

Socialism and Atheism. SZCZEPANSKI, Jan and LECKI, Maciej (trans).

Struttura dell'azione e compito pubblico del cristianesimo. POSSENTI, Vittorio.

Towards a Theology of Peace—The Peace Doctrine of John Paul II. RAJECKI, Robert and LECKI, Maciej (trans).

Why is the Bishops' Letter on the US Economy So Unconvincing?. REECE, William S.

CHURCH'S THESIS

The Physical Church Thesis and Physical Computational Complexity. PITOWSKY, Itamar.

Second Thoughts about Church's Thesis and Mathematical Proofs. MENDELSON, Elliott.

Some Notes on Church's Thesis and the Theory of Games. ANDERLINI, Luca.

CHURCHLAND, P

The Absolute Network Theory of Language and Traditional Epistemology. PHILIPSE, Herman.

Disappearance and Knowledge. CLING, Andrew D.

Experience and the Justification of Belief. MILLAR, Alan.

Neurophilosophy and the Logic-Causation Argument. KIAMIE, Kimberly A.

CICERO

Cicero's Knowledge of the Peripatos. FORTENBAUGH, William W (ed).

Rhetorica I—Reden mit Vernunft: Aristoteles, Cicero, Augustinus. MAINBERGER, Gonsalv K.

""Naturrecht" bei Aristoteles und bei Cicero (*De legibus*): Ein Vergleich" in *Cicero's Knowledge of the Peripatos*, GIRARDET, Klaus M.

"Antiochus of Ascalon" in *Philosophia Togata: Essays on Philosophy and Roman Society*, BARNES, Jonathan.

"Aristotelian Material in Cicero's *De natura deorum*" in *Cicero's Knowledge of the Peripatos*, FURLEY, David J.

"Aristotle and Theophrastus Conjoined in the Writings of Cicero" in *Cicero's Knowledge of the Peripatos*, RUNIA, David T.

"Beobachtungen zu Ciceros philosophischem Standpunkt" in *Cicero's Knowledge of the Peripatos*, STEINMETZ, Peter.

"Cicero and the Aristotelian Theory of Divination by Dreams" in *Cicero's Knowledge of the Peripatos*, KANY-TURPIN, José and PELLEGRIN, Pierre.

"Cicero on Stoic Moral Philosophy and Private Property" in *Philosophia Togata: Essays on Philosophy and Roman Society*, ANNAS, Julia.

"Cicero und die 'Schule des Aristoteles'" in *Cicero's Knowledge of the Peripatos*, GÖRLER, Woldemar.

"Cicero's Knowledge of the Rhetorical Treatises of Aristotle and Theophrastus" in *Cicero's Knowledge of the Peripatos*, FORTENBAUGH, William W.

"Cicero's *Topics* and Its Peripatetic Sources" in *Cicero's Knowledge of the Peripatos*, HUBY, Pamela M.

"Constitution and Citizenship: Peripatetic Influence on Cicero's Political Conception in the *De re publica*" in *Cicero's Knowledge of the Peripatos*, FREDE, Dorothea.

"Gibt es Spuren von Theophrasts *Phys op* bei Cicero?" in *Cicero's Knowledge of the Peripatos*, MANSFELD, Jaap.

"Die Peripatetiker in Cicero's *Tuskulanen*" in *Cicero's Knowledge of the Peripatos*, CLASSEN, C Joachim.

"Das Problem Theorie-Praxis in der Peripatos-Rezeption von Ciceros Staatsschrift" in *Cicero's Knowledge of the Peripatos*, MÜLLER, Reimar.

"Theophrast in Cicero's *De finibus*" in *Cicero's Knowledge of the Peripatos*, GIGON, Olof.

Epicurus on Pleasure and the Complete Life. ROSENBAUM, Stephen E.

Machiavel, lecteur des Anciens. ALLARD, Gérald.

CIRCULARITY

The Abyss and the Circle: A Cyclo-Analysis of *Being and Time*. MARTINOT, Steve.

Circolarità di condizione in L'homme et le langage di Jean Brun. GONZI, Andrea.

Definiciones impredicativas. MOLINA, Jorge.

God, the Bible and Circularity. COLWELL, Gary.

CIRCUMSTANCE(S)

Character and Circumstance. WALKER, A D M.

Moral Obligation, Circumstances, and Deontic Foci (A Rejoinder to Fred Feldman). CASTANEDA, Hector-Neri.

CITIZEN(S)

The Citizen Philosopher: Rousseau's Dedicatory Letter to the *Discourse on Inequality*. PALMER, Michael.

Teaching and Learning for Democratic Empowerment: A Critical Evaluation. BROSIO, Richard A.

CITIZENSHIP

Political Innovation and Conceptual Change. BALL, Terence.

Time, Freedom, and the Common Good: An Essay in Public Philosophy. SHEROVER, Charles M.

"Constitution and Citizenship: Peripatetic Influence on Cicero's Political Conception in the *De re publica*" in *Cicero's Knowledge of the Peripatos*, FREDE, Dorothea.

"Two Hundred Years of Reactionary Rhetoric: The Case of the Perverse Effect" in *The Tanner Lectures on Human Values, Volume X*, HIRSCHMAN, Albert O.

Aristotle and the Value of Political Participation. MULGAN, Richard.

Business Ethics, Corporate Good Citizenship and the Corporate Social Policy Process: A View from the US. EPSTEIN, Edwin M.

Leo Strauss as Citizen and Jew. DANNHAUSER, Werner J.

CITY(-TIES)

L'individuo nella città. VERNANT, Jean Pierre.

CIVIL

The Consolations of Philosophy: Hobbes's Secret; Spinoza's Way. ROSENTHAL, Abigail L (ed).

The Civil Revolution and Historical Materialism (in Serbo-Croatian). NOERR, Gunzelin Schmid.

CIVIL DISOBEDIENCE

Civil Disobedience. HARRIS, Paul (ed).

AIDS and Civil Disobedience. SPIERS, Herbert R.

Civil Disobedience in Times of AIDS. NOVICK, Alvin.

The Fiery Fight for Animal Rights. JACKSON, Christine M.

Grassroots Opposition to Animal Exploitation. SIEGEL, Steve.

The Interpretation of Plato's *Crito*. BOSTOCK, David.

Militant Morality: Civil Disobedience and Bioethics. COHEN, Carl.

The Myth of Civil Disobedience. VAN DER BURG, Wibren.

Operation Rescue: Domestic Terrorism or Legitimate Civil Rights Protest?. NATHANSON, Bernard.

Pro-Choice: A New Militancy. DAVIS, Susan E.

To Do or Not to Do?. SINGER, Peter.

We Must Rescue Them. LEBER, Gary.

CIVIL LAW(S)

"Zur Philosophie des Zivilprozessrechts, insbesondere zum Prinzip der Fairness" in *Agora: Zu Ehren von Rudolph Berlinger*, HABSCHEID, Walter J.

Donum Vitae: Civil Law and Moral Values. BYK, Christian.

Physician Investment and Self-Referral: Philosophical Analysis of a Contentious Debate. MORREIM, E Haavi.

Utilitarianism and Distributive Justice: The Civil Law and the Foundations of Bentham's Economic Thought. KELLY, P J.

CIVIL SOCIETY

Art of Judgement. CAYGILL, Howard.

Democracy and Dictatorship. BOBBIO, Norberto.

Hobbes's Persuasive Civil Science. SORELL, Tom.

CIVILIZATION(S)

The Social and Political Thought of R G Collingwood. BOUCHER, David.

The Death Penalty, Civilization, and Inhumaneness. DAVIS, Michael.

The Theme of Civilization and its Discontents in Durkheim's *Division of Labor*. MESTROVIC, Stjepan G.

Wittgenstein on Culture and Civilization. LURIE, Yuval.

CLAIM(S)

The Artificial Inflation of Natural Rights. FLEW, Antony.

Value Judgments and Normative Claims. SINGER, Marcus G.

CLARITY
Klarheit und Methode: Felix Kaufmanns Wissenschaftstheorie. ZILIAN, H G.

CLARK, A
Is This Any Way to be a Realist?. TIENSON, John L.

CLARKE
La prova a priori dell'esistenza di Dio nel Settecento inglese: da Cudworth a Hume. SCRIBANO, Emanuela.

CLASS INTEREST(S)
Class—A Simple View. GRAHAM, Keith.

CLASS STRUGGLE
Paul Tillich on Creativity. KEGLEY, Jacquelyn Ann K (ed).

CLASS THEORY
Class—A Simple View. GRAHAM, Keith.

CLASS(ES)
see also Set(s)
Bivalenza e trascendenza. COZZO, Cesare.
Class—A Simple View. GRAHAM, Keith.
The Classification of Excellent Classes. GROSSBERG, R.
Determination and Consciousness in Marx. MILLS, Charles W.
Identification et analyse des classes d'équivalence de la logique modale par des invariants numériques. SANCHEZ-MAZAS, Miguel.
Inductive Full Satisfaction Classes. KOTLARSKI, Henryk and RATAJCZYK, Zygmunt.
The Notion of Independence in Categories of Algebraic Structures, Part III: Equational Classes. SROUR, Gabriel.
On Analytic Filters and Prefilters. ZAFRANY, Samy.
On the Mathematical Content of the Theory of Classes KM. JANSANA, Ramón.
The Primal Framework I. BALDWIN, J T and SHELAH, S.
Reification, Class and 'New Social Movements'. BROWNE, Paul.

CLASSICISM
"The Classical Philosophers" in Reading Philosophy for the Twenty-First Century, NEMETZ, Anthony.
Classicism and Revolution (in Serbo-Croatian). CACINOVIC-PHUOVSKI, Nadezda.
Dionysian Classicism, or Nietzsche's Appropriation of an Aesthetic Norm. DEL CARO, Adrian.

CLASSICS
El Concepto de Materia al Comienzo de la Escuela Franciscana de Paris. PEREZ ESTEVEZ, Antonio.
Post-Structuralist Classics. BENJAMIN, Andrew (ed).
"Concealing Revealing: A Perspective on Greek Tragedy" in Post-Structuralist Classics, HALLIBURTON, David.

CLASSIFICATION
Christopher Clavius and the Classification of the Sciences. ARIEW, Roger.
The Classification of Excellent Classes. GROSSBERG, R.
Classifying $\aleph_0$-Categorical Theories. WEAVER, George.
Does Kierkegaard Think Beliefs Can Be Directly Willed?. EVANS, C Stephen.
Genetic Traits. GIFFORD, Fred.
Pierre Duhem's Conception of Natural Classification. LUGG, Andrew.
The Primal Framework I. BALDWIN, J T and SHELAH, S.

CLAUDIAN, A
Alexandru Claudian et la conscience de l'unité de l'esprit et de l'âme (in Romanian). GRIGORAS, Ioan.

CLAVIUS, C
Christopher Clavius and the Classification of the Sciences. ARIEW, Roger.

CLIFFORD, W
The End of the Absolute: A Nineteenth-Century Contribution to General Relativity. FARWELL, Ruth and KNEE, Christopher.

CLIMATE
The False Ontology of School Climate Effects. MILLER, Steven I and FREDERICKS, Janet.

CLINICAL PSYCHOLOGY
A Hermeneutic Account of Clinical Psychology: Strengths and Limits. SILVERN, Louise E.
On Being Ethical in Unethical Places: The Dilemmas of South African Clinical Psychologists. STEERE, Jane and DOWDALL, Terence.

CLOSURE
The Classification of Small Weakly Minimal Sets, II. BUECHLER, Steven.
Existentially Closed Algebras and Boolean Products. RIEDEL, Herbert H J.
Resplicing Properties in the Supervenience Base. ODDIE, Graham and TICHY, Pavel.
Supervenience and Closure. VAN CLEVE, James.
Van Cleve versus Closure. BACON, John.

COALITION(S)
Call to Coalition: A Response to Selman and Ross. MC CLELLAN, James E.

CODE OF CONDUCT
International Codes of Conduct: An Analysis of Ethical Reasoning. GETZ, Kathleen A.

CODE(S)
Coding Over a Measurable Cardinal. FRIEDMAN, Sy D.
Toward a Code of Ethics for Business Ethicists. MADSEN, Peter.
Towards a Communication-Concept of Rational Collective Will-Formation: A Thought-Experiment. HABERMAS, Jürgen.

COERCION
Surrogate Motherhood: The Ethics of Using Human Beings. SHANNON, Thomas A.
Are Workers Forced to Work?. EHRING, Douglas.
Coercion and Exploitation: Self-Transposal and the Moral Life. HAMRICK, William S.
Ethical Monotheism and the Whitehead Ethic. HOLMES, Arthur F.
The Power Principle: "Inherent Defects" Reconsidered. TOMASI, John.
Rationally Justifying Political Coercion. HARDIN, Russell.
Robert Stevens on Offers. SWANTON, Christine.

COGITO
The Conflict of Interpretations: Essays in Hermeneutics—Paul Ricoeur. IHDE, Don (ed).
"Degrés de réalité" et "degrés de perfection" dans les Principes de la philosophie de Descartes de Spinoza. RAMOND, Charles.
The Cartesian Cogito, Epistemic Logic, and Neuroscience: Some Surprising Interrelations. HINTIKKA, Jaakko.
Madness and the Cogito: Derrida's Critique of Folie et déraison. COOK, Deborah.
Merleau-Ponty's Tacit Cogito. WILLIAMS, Linda L.
El problema del cogito en san Agustin. FORMENT, Eudaldo.

COGNITION
see also Knowing, Thinking
In and Out of the Black Box: On the Philosophy of Cognition. HAMLYN, D W.
Thought and Language. MORAVCSIK, J M.
"'What Can We Know and When Can We Know It': On the Active Intelligence and Human Cognition" in Moses Maimonides and His Time, KOGAN, Barry S.
"Cognitive Semantics" in Meaning and Mental Representation, LAKOFF, George.
"Value, Cognition, and Cognitive Sciences: Three Questions about Psychological Accounts" in Inquiries into Values: The Inaugural Session of the International Society for Value Inquiry, MARTIN, James E.
An Agenda for Subjectivism. VICKERS, John M.
Alvin I Goldman's Epistemology and Cognition: An Introduction. LEVINE, Michael P.
Belief, Opinion and Consciousness. CLARK, Andy.
The Child as Craftsman. FELDMAN, David Henry.
Computationalism. DIETRICH, Eric.
Content and Self-Knowledge. BOGHOSSIAN, Paul A.
Critique of Structural Analysis in Modeling Cognition: A Case Study of Jackendoff's Theory. BILLMAN, Dorrit and PETERSON, Justin.
The Early Work of Husserl and Artificial Intelligence. MÜNCH, Dieter.
Francisco Sanchez's Theory of Cognition and Vico's verum/factum. FAUR, José.
Gibson's Theory of Direct Perception and the Problem of Cultural Relativism. COSTALL, Alan and STILL, Arthur.
Goldman on Epistemic Justification. ALSTON, William P.
The Human Brain and Human Destiny: A Pattern for Old Brain Empathy With the Emergence of Mind. ASHBROOK, James B.
Husserl, Intentionality, and Cognitive Architecture. BROWN, Charles S.
Kunstmatige intelligentie: Een voortzetting van de filosofie met andere middelen. VAN BENTHEM, Johan.
Language of Cognition—Cognition of Language (in Serbo-Croatian). MARVAN, George J.
Lonergan's Negative Dialectic. KIDDER, Paul.
The Narrative Reconstruction of Science. ROUSE, Joseph.
The Novelty of Marx's Theory of Praxis. MARGOLIS, Joseph.
Philosophical Problems of Mathematics in the Light of Evolutionary Epistemology. RAV, Yehuda.
Das philosophische Menschenbild: Eine konfuzianische Sicht. DOW, Tsung-I.
Quelle est la place de l'intelligence artificielle dans l'étude de la cognition?.

COMMON SENSE

The Absolute Network Theory of Language and Traditional Epistemology. PHILIPSE, Herman.

Critical Common-Sensism and Rational Self-Control. HOOKWAY, Christopher.

The Explanatory Role of Belief Ascriptions. PATTERSON, Sarah.

Feder und Kant. BRANDT, Reinhard.

Flexibele begrippen in kennistheorie en kunstmatige intelligentie. VISSER, H.

Implications of a Self-Effacing Consequentialism. LANGENFUS, William L.

The Import of the Problem of Rationality. AGASSI, Joseph.

Spanish Common Sense Philosophy. CLARK, Kelly James.

COMMONWEALTH

Robertus Britannus, 'On the Best Form of Commonwealth': A Dialogue between Pierre du Chastel and Aymar Ranconet. DYSON, R W (ed & trans) and TUDOR, H (ed & trans).

COMMUNICATION

Civil Disobedience. HARRIS, Paul (ed).

Ecological Communication. LUHMANN, Niklas.

Limited Inc. DERRIDA, Jacques.

The Listening Self: Personal Growth, Social Change and Closure of Metaphysics. LEVIN, David Michael.

Moral Consciousness and Communicative Action. HABERMAS, Jürgen.

Philosophical Logic and Artificial Intelligence. THOMASON, Richmond H (ed).

The Philosophy of Rhetoric (Revised Edition). CAMPBELL, George.

Speech, Crime, and the Uses of Language. GREENAWALT, Kent.

"On the Semiotics of Music" in What is Music?, MARGOLIS, Joseph.

'Communicatief handelen' als theoretisch grondbegrip. COBBEN, Paul.

Begriffe im kommunikativen Handeln: Linguistische Begriffsanalyse als Rekonstruktion von Handlungsmustern. BICKES, Hans.

Buchler on Habermas on Modernity. CAHOONE, Lawrence E.

Communication, Grice, and Languageless Creatures. CARR, Indira Mahalingam.

Das Gestell and L'écriture: The Discourse of Expropriation in Heidegger and Derrida. RADLOFF, Bernhard.

Dialogue, Distanciation, and Engagement: Toward a Logic of Televisual Communication. LANGSDORF, Lenore.

Ecologische communicatie door disciplinering van de moraal. STUY, Johan.

An Explanatory Theory of Communicative Intentions. KURODA, S Y.

Green Reason: Communicative Ethics for the Biosphere. DRYZEK, John S.

Habermas und das Problem der Individualität. GRONDIN, Jean.

Handlungstypen und Kriterien: Zu Habermas' "Theorie des kommunikativen Handelns". DORSCHEL, Andreas.

Kierkegaard and Indirect Communication. LÜBCKE, Poul.

Language as a Cause-Effect Communication System. SAVAGE-RUMBAUGH, E S.

Language of Cognition—Cognition of Language (in Serbo-Croatian). MARVAN, George J.

Literary Communication: The Author, the Reader, the Text. HARKER, W John.

Montaigne, Encoder and Decoder, in Propria Persona. JONES, Robert F.

Niklas Luhmann over ecologische communicatie. BALLIU, Julien.

Non replica, chiarimento. MORPURGO-TAGLIABUE, Guido.

Semantica, Pragmatica, Atti linguistici: note in margine a una polemica. SBISÀ, Marina.

Sur la structure particulière du dialogue argumentatif. MIHAI, Gheorghe.

The Voices of the Medical Record. POIRIER, Suzanne and BRAUNER, Daniel J.

Whose Language Is It Anyway? Some Notes on Idiolects. GEORGE, Alexander.

COMMUNISM

see also Historical Materialism, Leninism, Marxism

Our Philosophy: Allāma Muhammad Bāqir As-Sadr. INATI, Shams C (trans).

Selections from Political Writings, 1910-1920: Antonio Gramsci. GRAMSCI, Antonio.

Selections from Political Writings, 1921-1926: Antonio Gramsci. GRAMSCI, Antonio.

"Wie Müntzers Religionsphilosophie an den Atheismus, so streifte sein politisches Programm an den Kommunismus". HÖPPNER, Joachim.

"Wonderful Vision of a Truly Human World" (On Lukács' Conception of Communism in 1919) (in Hungarian). PERECZ, László.

Un ample programme d'action révolutionnaire et de perfectionnement (in Romanian). IONEL, Nicolae.

Anmerkungen zum Real Existierenden Totalitarismus und zu seinen Apologeten unter uns. MARKO, Kurt.

Beyond Capitalism and Communism: Roberto Unger's Superliberal Political Theory. BELLIOTTI, Raymond.

The Metaphysics of Communism. LURIE, Yuval.

Self-Ownership, Communism and Equality—I. COHEN, G A.

Self-Ownership, Communism and Equality—II. GRAHAM, Keith.

The Specter of Communism. KRAMER, Matthew.

A Sweet and Sour Victory in Eastern Europe. SZAKOLCZAI, Arpád and HORVÁTH, Ágnes.

Zum Philosophieverständnis bedeutender Persönlichkeiten der II. Internationale. WRONA, Vera.

COMMUNITARIANISM

De afkeer van het individualisme bij Alisdair MacIntyre en de soevereiniteit van het individu. KAL, Victor.

Arendt's Politics: The Elusive Search for Substance. SCHWARTZ, Joseph M.

Beyond Liberalism and Communitarianism: Towards a Critical Theory of Social Justice. DOPPELT, G.

Communitarian and Liberal Theories of the Good. PAUL, Jeffrey and MILLER JR, Fred D.

The Communitarian Critique of Liberalism. WALZER, Michael.

Communitarian Politics, the Supreme Court, and Privacy: The Continuing Need for Liberal Boundaries. LUND, William R.

Friedrich Schleiermacher's Theory of the Limited Communitarian State. HOOVER, Jeffrey.

Individualism, Community, and Education: An Exchange of Views. GRIFFIN, Robert S and NASH, Robert J.

Our Vantage Points: Not a View from Nowhere. LEACH, Mary.

Respect for Persons, Autonomy and Equality. NORMAN, Richard.

Sandel and the Limits of Community. ENSLIN, Penny.

Universalisms: Procedural, Contextualist and Prudential. FERRARA, Alessandro.

COMMUNITY LIVING

Crisis Moral Communities: An Essay in Moral Philosophy. FISHER, David.

COMMUNITY(-TIES)

Ethics and Community. DUSSEL, Enrique D.

Faith on Earth: An Inquiry into the Structure of Human Faith. NIEBUHR, Richard R (ed).

The Idea of Political Theory: Reflections on the Self in Political Time and Place. STRONG, Tracy B.

Seductive Reasoning: Pluralism as the Problematic of Contemporary Literary Theory. ROONEY, Ellen.

Wise Choices, Apt Feelings: A Theory of Normative Judgment. GIBBARD, Allan.

The Absolute, Community, and Time. WILLIAMS, Robert R.

Agency, Identity, and Culture: Hannah Arendt's Conception of Citizenship. D'ENTRÈVES, Maurizio Passerin.

Communities of Judgment. GIBBARD, Allan.

Community and Civil Strife. GILBERT, Paul.

Community as Inquiry. TINDER, Glenn.

The Division of Cognitive Labor. KITCHER, Philip.

The Expert and the Public: Local Values and National Choice. GOLDSTEIN, Alfred.

From Cultural Synthesis to Communicative Action: The Kingdom of God and Ethical Theology. SCHWEIKER, William.

Obligations, Communities, and Suffering: Problems of Community Seen in a New Light. LOEWY, Erich H.

Philosophy and the Education of the Community. MULVANEY, Robert.

Rawls on Political Community and Principles of Justice. NICKEL, James W.

Rawlsian Justice and Community Planning. MARLIN, Randal.

The Retreat of the Political in the Modern Age: Jean-Luc Nancy on Totalitarianism and Community. INGRAM, David.

Simmons and the Concept of Consent: Commentary on "Consent and Fairness in Planning Land Use". FOTION, Nicholas.

Strategy, Social Responsibility and Implementation. KRAFT, Kenneth L and HAGE, Jerald.

COMPACTNESS

Compactness in Finite Probabilistic Inference. VICKERS, John M.

A Non-Compactness Phenomenon in Logics with Hyperintensional Predication. BONOTTO, Cinzia.

A Proofless Proof of the Barwise Compactness Theorem. HOWARD, Mark.

Some Compactness Results for Modal Logic. SCHUMM, George F.

COMPARABILITY

Equiprobability. WATT, David.

COMPARATIVE PHILOSOPHY

"Comparative Axiology: Western, Indian and Chinese Theory Compared" in Inquiries into Values: The Inaugural Session of the International Society for Value Inquiry, BAHM, Archie J.

A Comparative Study of Natural Philosophy in Pre-Qin China and Ancient Greece. SHAOJUN, Weng.

COMPARATIVE PHILOSOPHY

Descartes in the Hegelian Perspective. BATTA, Nirmala Devi.

Reply to Richard Bosley's "Virtues and Vices: East and West". TANG, Paul C L.

Virtues and Vices: East and West. BOSLEY, Richard.

COMPARATIVE RELIGION

The Wisdom of Faith: Essays in Honor of Dr Sebastian Alexander Matczak. THOMPSON, Henry O (ed).

COMPARATIVE(S)

Comparative Philosophy and the Philosophy of Scholarship. TUCK, Andrew P.

COMPARISON(S)

Metaphors and the Symmetry/Asymmetry (in Hebrew). SHEN, Yeshayahu.

The Classical vs the PDP Model in Describing the Tic-Tac-Toe Game (in Hebrew). SHAGRIR, Oron.

COMPASSION

Max Scheler's Criticism of Schopenhauer's Account of Morality and Compassion. MAIDAN, Michael.

Medicine and Dialogue. ZANER, Richard M.

COMPATIBILISM

Determinism, Blameworthiness and Deprivation. KLEIN, Martha.

Aristotle's Compatibilism in the Nicomachean Ethics. EVERSON, Stephen.

Free Will, Self-Causation, and Strange Loops. MORDEN, Michael.

How to Mind One's Ethics: A Reply to Van Inwagen. WHITE, V Alan.

Soft Determinism and How We Become Responsible for the Past. TÄNNSJÖ, Torbjörn.

Zur Frage der Vereinbarkeit von Freiheit und Determinismus. RHEINWALD, Rosemarie.

COMPENSATION

Hypolepsis und Kompensation—Odo Marquards philosophischer Beitrag zur Diagnose und Bewältigung der Gegenwart. KERSTING, Wolfgang.

COMPETENCE

About Competence. TIENSON, John L.

COMPETITION

The Metaphysics of Evolution. HULL, David L.

Are Markets Morally Free Zones?. HAUSMAN, Daniel M.

Competitive Equality of Opportunity: A Defense. GREEN, S J D.

Ethical Problems in Competitive Bidding: The Paradyne Case. DAVIS, J Steve.

COMPLEMENTARITY

Complementarity and the Description of Nature in Biological Science. FOLSE JR, Henry J.

The Theory of Complimentarity and Mind-Body Dualism: A Critique. CHAKRABARTY, Alpana.

COMPLETENESS

see also Incompleteness

The Concept of Logical Consequence. ETCHEMENDY, John.

The Semantic Foundations of Logic, Volume 1: Propositional Logics. EPSTEIN, Richard L.

Systems of Logic. MARTIN, Norman M.

Action and Ability. BROWN, Mark A.

Arithmetical Completeness Versus Relative Completeness. GRABOWSKI, Michal.

Completeness and Conservative Extension Results for Some Boolean Relevant Logics. GIAMBRONE, Steve and MEYER, Robert K.

Completeness for Systems Including Real Numbers. BALZER, W.

Completeness Proofs for Propositional Logic with Polynomial-Time Connectives. CROSSLEY, J N and SCOTT, P J.

Hyperidentities of Dyadic Algebras. DENECKE, Klaus.

A Modal Version of Free Logic. BARBA, Juan L.

Model Completeness and Direct Power. TAGHVA, Kazem.

Modularity and Relevant Logic. GARSON, James.

Nondeterministic ω-Computations and the Analytical Hierarchy. CASTRO, J.

Presuppositional Completeness. BUSZKOWSKI, Wojciech.

Quantifiers Determined by Partial Orderings. KRYNICKI, Michal.

Recursively Enumerable Sets Modulo Iterated Jumps and Extensions of Arslanov's Completeness Criterion. JOCKUSCH JR, C G (and others).

Rosser Orderings in Bimodal Logics. CARBONE, Alessandra and MONTAGNA, F.

Simple Completeness Proof of Lemmon's SO:5. KONDO, Michiro.

A Simplification of the Completeness Proofs for Guaspari and Solovay's R. VOORBRAAK, Frans.

Teoría de la recursión y lógica. DIAS, M F and PORTELA FILHO, R N A.

A Theorem on Barr-Exact Categories, with an Infinitary Generalization. MAKKAI, Michael.

COMPLEX NUMBER(S)

Cardano: "Arithmetic Subtlety" and Impossible Solutions. KENNEY, Emelie.

COMPLEXITY

Ecological Communication. LUHMANN, Niklas.

Algorithmic Information Theory. VAN LAMBALGEN, Michiel.

Complexity-Theoretic Algebra II: Boolean Algebras. NERODE, A and REMMEL, J B.

Negativity and Complexity: Some Logical Considerations. HIRSCH, Eli.

On the Complexity of Finding the Chromatic Number of a Recursive Graph I: The Bounded Case. BEIGEL, Richard and GASARCH, W I.

On the Complexity of Finding the Chromatic Number of a Recursive Graph II: The Unbounded Case. BEIGEL, R and GASARCH, W I.

Varieties of Complex Algebras. GOLDBLATT, Robert.

COMPLIANCE

Affirming the Reality of Rule-Following. PETTIT, Philip.

On Taking the Rabbit of Rule-Following out of the Hat of Representation: Response to 'The Reality of Rule-Following'. SUMMERFIELD, Donna M.

Rationalising Conventions. MILLER, Seumas.

COMPLICITY

"Comment: A Theory of Complicity" in Issues in Contemporary Legal Philosophy: The Influence of H L A Hart, GUR-ARYE, Miriam.

COMPOSER(S)

Composers' Texts as Objects of Musicological Study. HEINIÖ, Mikko.

COMPOSITION

"Music and Form" in What is Music?, CONE, Edward T.

"Musical De-Composition" in What is Music?, BERLEANT, Arnold.

"The Work of Making a Work of Music" in What is Music?, WOLTERSTORFF, Nicholas.

Against Compositionality: The Case of Adjectives. LAHAV, Ran.

Compositionality, Implicational Logics, and Theories of Grammar. MORRILL, Glyn and CARPENTER, Bob.

Negative Composition. HANRAHAN, Nancy Weiss.

Raising as Function Composition. JACOBSON, Pauline.

COMPOUND(S)

Reportage as Compound Suggestion. MAY, John D.

COMPREHENSION

An Axiom Schema of Comprehension of Zermelo-Fraenkel-Skolem Set Theory. HEIDEMA, Johannes.

La compréhension en herméneutique: Un héritage de Bultmann. STUCKI, Pierre-André.

The Consistency Problem for Positive Comprehension Principles. FORTI, M and HINNION, R.

Experiencia y comprensión: Estudio a través del arte como lenguaje. MARTINEZ, Juana M.

Non-in-difference in the Thought of Emmanuel Levinas and Franz Rosenzweig. COHEN, Richard.

COMPROMISE(S)

Splitting the Difference: Compromise and Integrity in Ethics and Politics. BENJAMIN, Martin.

Compromise. DAY, J P.

COMPUTABILITY

Computability and Logic (Third Edition). BOOLOS, George S.

Turing L-Machines and Recursive Computability for L-Maps. GERLA, Giangiacomo.

COMPUTATION

An Overview of Paraconsistent Logic in the 80s. DA COSTA, Newton C A and MARCONI, Diego.

COMPUTATIONAL COMPLEXITY

The Physical Church Thesis and Physical Computational Complexity. PITOWSKY, Itamar.

Reachability is Harder for Directed than for Undirected Finite Graphs. AJTAI, Miklos.

A Uniform Method for Proving Lower Bounds on the Computational Complexity of Logical Theories. COMPTON, Kevin J and HENSON, C Ward.

COMPUTATIONAL MODEL(S)

The Physical Church Thesis and Physical Computational Complexity. PITOWSKY, Itamar.

COMPUTATIONALISM

Computationalism. DIETRICH, Eric.

Response to Dietrich's "Computationalism". BALOGH, Imre.

COMPUTATIONALISM

Response to Dietrich's "Computationalism". BEAKLEY, Brian.
Response to Dietrich's "Computationalism". CHURCHLAND, Paul.
Response to Dietrich's "Computationalism". GORMAN, Michael.
Response to Dietrich's "Computationalism". HARNAD, Stevan.
Response to Dietrich's "Computationalism". MERTZ, David.
Response to Dietrich's "Computationalism". PATTEE, H H.
Response to Dietrich's "Computationalism". RAMSEY, W.
Response to Dietrich's "Computationalism". RINGEN, Jon.
Response to Dietrich's "Computationalism". SCHWARZ, Georg.
Response to Dietrich's "Computationalism". SLATOR, Brian.
Response to Dietrich's "Computationalism". STRUDLER, Alan.
Response to Dietrich's "Computationalism". WALLIS, Charles.

COMPUTER SCIENCE

Logic for Computer Scientists. SCHÖNING, Uwe.
Philosophical Logic and Artificial Intelligence. THOMASON, Richmond H (ed).
Une Machine spéculative (informatique, intelligence artificielle et recherche cognitive). BORILLO, Mario.
Programas e Promessas: Sobre o (Ab-)Uso do Jargão Computacional em Teorias Cognitivas da Mente. MENDONÇA, W P.
Robots that Learn: A Test of Intelligence. SUPPES, Patrick and CRANGLE, Colleen.
The Role of Error in Computer Science. JASON, Gary.

COMPUTER(S)

see also Artificial Intelligence
God, the Devil and the Perfect Pizza: Ten Philosophical Questions. GOVIER, Trudy.
The Philosopher's Habitat: Introduction to Investigations in, and Applications of, Modern Philosophy. GOLDSTEIN, Laurence.
"Deus ex machina" redivivus: The "Synthetic A Priori" in the Computer Age. FANG, J.
Aristotele, Platone e l'IBM. PARISI, Giorgio.
Common Knowledge of the Second Kind. BELLA, David and KING, Jonathan.
Computer Programming As a Vehicle for Teaching Thinking Skills. NICKERSON, Raymond S.
The Effect of Computer Intervention and Task Structure on Bargaining Outcome. JONES, Beth H and JELASSI, M Tawfik.
The Impact of Information and Computer Based Training on Negotiators' Performance. GAUVIN, Stéphane and LILIEN, Gary L and CHATTERJEE, Kalyan.
Individual Privacy and Computer-Based Human Resource Information Systems. TAYLOR, G Stephen.
The Physical Church Thesis and Physical Computational Complexity. PITOWSKY, Itamar.
The Possibility of Computers Becoming Persons. DOLBY, R G A.
Reply—The Possibility of Computers Becoming Persons: A Response to Dolby. CHERRY, Christopher.
La sociedad en la perspectiva informática o existe una sociología de los computadores?. GUTIÉRREZ, Claudio.
The Syntheticity of Time: Comments on Fang's Critique of Divine Computers. PALMQUIST, Stephen R.
Teaching Reasoning With Computers. FURLONG, John and CARROLL, William.
Three Generations of Computerized Systems for Public Administration and Implications for Legal Decision-Making. BING, Jon.
Unfree Enterprise. ESTILL, Lyle.
The Use of Logical Models in Legal Problem Solving. KOWALSKI, Robert and SERGOT, Marek.

COMTE

Ce qui est vivant, ce qui est mort dans la philosophie d'Auguste Comte (1935). LÉVY-BRUHL, Lucien.
Lagrange's Analytical Mathematics, Its Cartesian Origins and Reception in Comte's Positive Philosophy. FRASER, Craig G.
Mill's Misreading of Comte on 'Interior Observation'. SCHARFF, Robert C.
Positivism, Philosophy of Science, and Self-Understanding in Comte and Mill. SCHARFF, Robert C.

CONCEPT(S)

see also Idea(s)
Aristotle's Concept of the Universal. BRAKAS, George.
The Philosopher's Habitat: Introduction to Investigations in, and Applications of, Modern Philosophy. GOLDSTEIN, Laurence.
"The Analysts" in Reading Philosophy for the Twenty-First Century, URMSON, John O.
"Man versus Nature and Natural Man" in Man and Nature: The Chinese Tradition and the Future, KUIDE, Chen.
Are There Inalienable Rights?. NELSON, John O.
Begriffe im kommunikativen Handeln: Linguistische Begriffsanalyse als Rekonstruktion von Handlungsmustern. BICKES, Hans.
Beyond the Exclusively Propositional Era. BECHTEL, William and ABRAHAMSEN, Adele A.
Concepto y libertad. VÁSQUEZ, Eduardo.
Concepts and Conceptual Change. THAGARD, Paul.
Concepts, Categories, and Epistemology. LIVINGSTON, Kenneth R.
Concepts, Judgments, and Unity in Kant's Metaphysical Deduction of the Relational Categories. NUSSBAUM, Charles.
La definición como significado textual. NÚÑEZ LADEVÉZE, Luis.
Family Resemblances and the Problem of the Under-Determination of Extension. BELLAIMEY, James E.
Frege's Objects of a Quine Special Kind. SCHIRN, Matthias.
Having Ideas and Having the Concept. CRIMMINS, Mark.
Identity, Survival, and Sortal Concepts. BAILLIE, James.
Interpretation and the Bible: The Dialectic of Concept and Content in Interpretive Reading. POLKA, Brayton.
Is the Ideal of the Overman Possible? (in Hebrew). AVIRAM, Ronni.
Lesniewski's Strategy and Modal Logic. KEARNS, John T.
Methods of Conceptual Change in Science: Imagistic and Analogical Reasoning. NERSESSIAN, Nancy J.
On Explaining Political Disagreement: The Notion of an Essentially Contested Concept. MASON, Andrew.
I presupposti assiologici del riconoscimento nello Hegel prejenese. RIZZI, Lino.
The Primacy of the Virtuous. GARCIA, Jorge.
Schleiermacher's Critique of Ethical Reason: Toward a Systematic Ethics. WALLHAUSSER, John.
Self-Consuming Concepts. MAGNUS, Bernd.
Sobre la noción fregeana "extensión de un concepto". DEL PALACIO, Alfonso Avila.
Supervenience as a Philosophical Concept. KIM, Jaegwon.
What are Concepts?. PEACOCKE, Christopher.

CONCEPTION

Thomas Reid. LEHRER, Keith.
A Fortnight of My Life is Missing: A Discussion of the Status of the Human 'Pre-Embryo'. HOLLAND, Allan.
Liberalism and Liberty: the Fragility of a Tradition. GRAHAM, Keith.
Models of Freedom in the Modern World. WELLMER, Albrecht.
The Zygote: To Be Or Not Be A Person. BEDATE, Carlos A and CEFALO, Robert C.

CONCEPTUAL ANALYSIS

Tharp and Conceptual Logic. WANG, Hao.

CONCEPTUAL SCHEME(S)

Conceptual Schemes and Linguistic Relativism in Relation to Chinese (in Serbo-Croatian). GRAHAM, A C.
The Conceptual Structure of the Chemical Revolution. THAGARD, Paul.
Inconmensurabilidad y criterios de identidad de esquemas conceptuales. HIDALGO, Cecilia.
Putnam on Davidson on Conceptual Schemes. BRENNER-GOLOMB, N and VAN BRAKEL, J.
Semantics, Conceptual Spaces and the Dimensions of Music. GÄRDENFORS, Peter.
Talking Lions and Lion Talk: Davidson on Conceptual Schemes. CRUMLEY, Jack S.
Transcendental Arguments and Conceptual Schemes: A Reconsideration of Körner's Uniqueness Argument. MALPAS, J E.

CONCEPTUALISM

Myth and Mathematics: A Conceptualistic Philosophy of Mathematics. THARP, Leslie.
Tharp's 'Myth and Mathematics'. CHIHARA, Charles.
The Conceptual Structure of Marxist Thought: Some Critical Reflections (in Serbo-Croatian). KRISHNA, Daya.

CONCEPTUALIZATION

The Philosophical Imaginary. LE DOEUFF, Michèle.
"Knowledge Representation in People and Machines" in Meaning and Mental Representation, SCHANK, Roger and KASS, Alex.
"Stephen Toulmin's Theory of Conceptual Evolution" in Issues in Evolutionary Epistemology, JACOBS, Struan.
Epistemological and Ethical Considerations in Conceptualizing and Implementing Human Resource Management. DACHLER, H Peter and ENDERLE, Georges.
Professionalization and the Moral Jeopardy of Teaching. BOYD, Dwight.

CONFUCIUS

1987 Controversy Over the Evaluations of Confucius. DINGBO, Wu.

Confucian Justice: Achieving a Humane Society. PEERENBOOM, Randall P.

Confucius—China's Dethroned Sage? (in Serbo-Croatian). KRAMERS, Robert P.

Learning to be Human: Confucian Resources for Person-Centered Education. CONROY, Fran.

Das philosophische Menschenbild: Eine konfuzianische Sicht. DOW, Tsung-I.

CONFUSION

Die Philosophie und ihre Missbildungen. ESTRELLA, Jorge.

CONGRUENCE(S)

The Status of Epistemic Principles. CHISHOLM, Roderick M.

CONJECTURING

L'idea di "Storia teoretica o congetturale" negli scritti filosofici e sul linguaggio di Adam Smith. IACONO, Alfonso M.

CONJUNCTION(S)

Systems of Logic. MARTIN, Norman M.

"Conjunctive Containment" in Directions in Relevant Logic, BELNAP JR, Nuel D.

CONNECTIONISM

Beyond Eliminativism. CLARK, Andy.

Beyond the Exclusively Propositional Era. BECHTEL, William and ABRAHAMSEN, Adele A.

Connectionism and Epistemology: Goldman on Winner-Take-All Networks. THAGARD, Paul.

Connectionism and the Semantic Content of Internal Representation. GOSCHKE, Thomas and KOPPELBERG, Dirk.

Connectionism and Three Levels of Nativism. RAMSEY, William and STICH, Stephen.

Information Processing: From a Mechanistic to a Natural Systems Approach. VAN CAMP, Ingrid.

Philosophy and Machine Learning. THAGARD, Paul.

Representations without Rules. HORGAN, Terence and TIENSON, John.

CONNECTIVE(S)

Completeness Proofs for Propositional Logic with Polynomial-Time Connectives. CROSSLEY, J N and SCOTT, P J.

CONNEXIVE LOGIC

A Routley-Meyer Affixing Style Semantics for Logics Containing Aristotle's Thesis. BRADY, Ross T.

CONSCIENCE

Burning Conscience: The Guilt of Hiroshima. ANDERS, Gunther.

Conscience and the Reality of God: An Essay on the Experiential Foundations of Religious Knowledge. STATEN, John C.

Conscience. ROSMINI, Antonio.

Ethics in Practice: Managing the Moral Corporation. ANDREWS, Kenneth R (ed).

Conscience et forme dans la pensée critique de Georges Poulet. MARTIN, Mircea.

Conscience, contempolation, wisdom (in Polish). GOGCZC, Mieczyslaw.

Conscience, Sympathy, and Love: Ethical Strategies toward Confirmation of Metaphysical Assertions in Schopenhauer. CYZYK, Mark.

Consequentialism in Search of a Conscience. LANGENFUS, William L.

Eigentlichkeit, Gewissen und Schuld in Heideggers "Sein und Zeit". FEHÉR, István.

Gewissen als Eine Freiheitsnorm (in Polish). ROSIK, Seweryn.

Sobre la privacidad de los estados de conciencia. LARRETA, Juan Rodriguez and DORFMAN, Beatriz.

Le strutture trascendentali della coscienza nel primo Sartre: ipotesi di lettura. COMOLLI, Fabrizio.

CONSCIOUS

On the Inter-relatedness of Theory and Measurement in the Study of Unconscious Processes. REINGOLD, Eyal M and MERIKLE, Philip M.

CONSCIOUSNESS

Autobiographical Reflections—Eric Voegelin. SANDOZ, Ellis (ed).

Color and Consciousness: An Essay in Metaphysics. LANDESMAN, Charles.

Hegel's Concept of Experience. HEIDEGGER, Martin.

Looking Into Mind: How to Recognize Who You Are and How You Know. DAMIANI, Anthony.

Margins of Reality: The Role of Consciousness in the Physical World. JAHN, Robert G.

Mind, Brain and the Quantum: The Compound 'I'. LOCKWOOD, Michael.

The Mundane Matter of the Mental Language. MALONEY, J Christopher.

The Perverted Consciousness: Sexuality and Sartre. LEAK, Andrew N.

Philosophical Problems (Consciousness, Reality and I). VERSTER, Ulrich.

The Problem of the Ideal. DUBROVSKY, David.

Subject and Consciousness: A Philosophical Inquiry Into Self-Consciousness. BALABAN, Oded.

Wittgenstein's Philosophy of Psychology. BUDD, Malcolm.

"Homo conscius sui" in Agora: Zu Ehren von Rudolph Berlinger, FUNKE, Gerhard.

"Nietzsche's New Experience of World" in Nietzsche's New Seas: Explorations in Philosophy, Aesthetics, and Politics, GILLESPIE, Michael Allen (trans) and FINK, Eugen.

"Wittgenstein and the Problem of Machine Consciousness" in Wittgenstein in Focus—Im Brennpunkt: Wittgenstein, NYIRI, J C.

The Abyss and the Circle: A Cyclo-Analysis of Being and Time. MARTINOT, Steve.

Aesthetic Consciousness and Aesthetic Non-Differentiation: Gadamer, Schiller, and Lukács. PIZER, John.

Algunas consideraciones sobre la Refutación del Idealismo. JAUREGUI, Claudia and VIGO, Alejandro G.

Bad Faith. HYMERS, Michael.

Brentano on 'Unconscious Consciousness'. KRANTZ, Susan.

Concerning the Problems Surrounding "Theoretical Consciousness" (in Czechoslovakian). KROH, M.

Consciousness and History. MOULAKIS, Athanasios.

Consciousness in Quantum Physics and The Mind-Body Problem. GOSWAMI, Amit.

Consciousness, Brain and the Physical World. VELMANS, Max.

Consciousness, the Brain and What Matters. GILLETT, Grant R.

Consciousness, Unconsciousness, and Intentionality. SEARLE, John R.

Consciousness. SHANON, Benny.

Contemporary Models of Consciousness: Part I. BURNS, Jean E.

Corporate Responsibility: Morality Without Consciousness. SKIDD, David R A.

Critique of Structural Analysis in Modeling Cognition: A Case Study of Jackendoff's Theory. BILLMAN, Dorrit and PETERSON, Justin.

Determination and Consciousness in Marx. MILLS, Charles W.

Eccentric Subjects: Feminist Theory and Historical Consiousness. DE LAURETIS, Teresa.

Glasnostalgia. LLEWELYN, J.

Husserl Versus Derrida. EDIE, James M.

Husserl's Concept of Inner Temporal Consciousness and Aesthetics (in Czechoslovakian). ZUSKA, Vlastimil.

Kant on Descartes and the Brutes. NARAGON, Steve.

Merleau-Ponty's Indirect Ontology. SMITH, Dale E.

Nonhuman Experience: A Whiteheadian Analysis. ARMSTRONG-BUCK, Susan.

On the Nature and Cognitive Function of Phenomenal Content—Part I. FOX, Ivan.

Overtones of Solipsism in Thomas Nagel's "What is it Like to Be a Bat?" and The View From Nowhere. WIDER, Kathleen.

The Primacy of Perception in Husserl's Theory of Imagining. DROST, Mark P.

The Problem of Consciousness and the Philosopher's Calling. MAMARDASHVILI, M K and STEWART, Philip D (trans).

Reflexive Ideas in Spinoza. RICE, Lee C.

The Role of the Sophists in Histories of Consciousness. JARRATT, Susan C.

El tema principal de la fenomenología de Husserl. WALTON, Roberto J.

What Difference Does Consciousness Make?. VAN GULICK, Robert.

William James on the Human Ways of Being. DOOLEY, Patrick.

CONSENSUS

Pareto Unanimity and Consensus. LEVI, Isaac.

Rawls on Political Community and Principles of Justice. NICKEL, James W.

CONSENT

The Calculus of Consent. SCOFIELD, Giles.

Consent and Fairness in Planning Land Use. SIMMONS, A John.

Date-Rape: A Feminist Analysis. PINEAU, Lois.

Immediate Legitimacy? Problems of Legitimacy in a Consensually Oriented Application of Law. MÄENPÄÄ, Olli.

Made by Contrivance and the Consent of Men. DEN HARTOGH, Govert.

Simmons and the Concept of Consent: Commentary on "Consent and Fairness in Planning Land Use". FOTION, Nicholas.

CONSEQUENCE(S)

The Concept of logical Consequence. ETCHEMENDY, John.

Dilemmas: A Christian Approach to Moral Decision Making. HIGGINSON, Richard.

Treatise on Basic Philosophy, Volume 8—Ethics: The Good and the Right.

CONSEQUENCE(S)

BUNGE, Mario.

Actions, Intentions, and Consequences: The Doctrine of Double Effect. QUINN, Warren S.

Actual Versus Probable Utilitarianism. STRASSER, Mark.

Buridano e le consequenze. BERTAGNA, Mario.

Cultural and Ideological Bias in Pornography Research. CHRISTENSEN, Ferrel M.

Deductive Justification. CANARY, Catherine and ODEGARD, Douglas.

Deontic Logic and Consequence Operations. WOLENSKI, Jan.

Free Will as Psychological Capacity and the Justification of Consequences. SCHOPP, Robert.

Philosophical-Methodological Aspects of Relevant Logic. WOISHVILLO, E K.

Quantified Propositional Calculi and Fragments of Bounded Arithmetic. KRAJICEK, Jan and PUDLAK, Pavel.

A Syntactical Characterization of Structural Completeness for Implicational Logics. WOJTYLAK, Piotr.

A Theorem on Cocongruence of Rings. ROMANO, Daniel A.

CONSEQUENTIALISM

"Moore to Stevenson" in Ethics in the History of Western Philosophy, DARWALL, Stephen.

Autonomy or Integrity: A Reply to Slote. WALKER, Margaret Urban.

Consequentialism and History. GOMBERG, Paul.

Consequentialism in Search of a Conscience. LANGENFUS, William L.

Consequentialism, Egoism, and the Moral Law. CUMMISKEY, David.

The Divestiture Puzzle Dissolved. SHINER, Roger A.

Implications of a Self-Effacing Consequentialism. LANGENFUS, William L.

In Defense of Outcomes-Based Conceptions of Equal Educational Opportunity. HOWE, Kenneth R.

Internalism and Externalism in Moral Epistemology. AUDI, Robert.

Justice in Health Care: The Contribution of Edmund Pellegrino. VEATCH, Robert M.

Parfit's Moral Arithmetic and the Obligation to Obey the Law. KLOSKO, George.

Paternalism and Respect for Autonomy. SCOCCIA, Danny.

Two Departures from Consequentialism. BENNETT, Jonathan.

Two Kinds of Satisficing. HURKA, Thomas.

What Should We Do About Future Generations? Impossibility of Parfit's Theory X. NG, Yew-Kwang.

CONSERVATION

More Heat than Light: Economics as Social Physics, Physics as Nature's Economics. MIROWSKI, Philip.

The Incarceration of Wildness: Wilderness Areas as Prisons. BIRCH, Thomas H.

CONSERVATION LAWS

Descartes and Some Predecessors on the Divine Conservation of Motion. MENN, Stephen.

CONSERVATISM

Skepticism and Modern Enmity: Before and After Eliot. PERL, Jeffrey M.

Conservatism, Radicalism and Democratic Practice. SIMPSON, Evan.

Dilemma of M Oakeshott: Oakeshott's Treatment of Equality of Opportunity in Education and His Political Philosophy. WILLIAMS, Kevin.

Intuitionism and Conservatism. NELSON, Mark T.

Radicals, Conservatives and Moderates in Early Modern Political Thought: A Case of Sandwich Islands Syndrome?. CONDREN, C.

What is Conservatism?. WADLEIGH, Julian.

CONSISTENCY

Conceptual Relevance. GRÜNFELD, Joseph.

Moral Dilemmas. SINNOTT-ARMSTRONG, Walter.

Systems of Logic. MARTIN, Norman M.

The Consistency Problem for Positive Comprehension Principles. FORTI, M and HINNION, R.

The Essential Tension. FEHÉR, Marta.

The Fate of One Forgotten Idea: N A Vasiliev and His Imaginary Logic. BAZHANOV, Valentine A.

Hilbert's Program Relativized: Proof-Theoretical and Foundational Reductions. FEFERMAN, Solomon.

The Machinery of Consistency Proofs. YASUGI, Mariko.

Near Coherence of Filters III: A Simplified Consistency Proof. BLASS, Andreas and SHELAH, Saharon.

The Number of Pairwise Non-Elementarily-Embeddable Models. SHELAH, Saharon.

On Dialectical Consistency. ZELENY, Jindrich.

Paraconsistency. URBAS, Igor.

Partial Realizations of Hilbert's Program. SIMPSON, Stephen G.

Peano's Smart Children: A Provability Logical Study of Systems with Built-In Consistency. VISSER, Albert.

Practical Rationality: Some Kantian Reflections. MC CANN, Hugh J.

Reflexive Consistency Proofs and Gödel's Second Theorem. SAGAL, Paul.

CONSTANT(S)

El a priori histórico (la historia y sus hechos). SAMPEDRO, Ceferino.

On Absoluteness. HABART, Karol.

CONSTITUTION(S)

Civil Disobedience. HARRIS, Paul (ed).

Political Innovation and Conceptual Change. BALL, Terence.

Speech, Crime, and the Uses of Language. GREENAWALT, Kent.

Wie kann man sagen, was nicht ist-Zur Logik des Utopischen. SCHMITZ, Heinz-Gerd.

"The Pseudodemocratization of the American Presidency" in The Tanner Lectures on Human Values, Volume X, DAHL, Robert A.

Bioethics Discovers the Bill of Rights. VEATCH, Robert M.

Constitutional Privacy, Judicial Interpretation, and Bowers versus Hardwick. WAGNER DE CEW, Judith.

Edmund Burke and the American Constitution. FRISCH, Morton J.

Ethics Instruction and the Constitution. HERNDON, James F.

The Fundamental Constitutions of Carolina as a Tool for Lockean Scholarship. MC GUINNESS, Celia.

The Price of Abortion Sixteen Years Later. CHOPKO, Mark E and HARRIS, Phillip and ALVARÉ, Helen M.

The Social Constitution of Action: Objectivity and Explanation. GREENWOOD, John D.

Sulla validità della costituzione dal punto di vista del positivismo giuridico. GUASTINI, Riccardo.

What is Conservatism?. WADLEIGH, Julian.

CONSTITUTIONALISM

American Experience and the Israeli Dilemma. JACOBSOHN, Gary J.

Conciliarism and Constitutionalism: Jean Gerson and Medieval Political Thought. NEDERMAN, Cary J.

The Constitutional Process and the Higher Law. SHANKER, George.

The Liberal Constitution: Rational Design or Evolution?. BARRY, Norman P.

The Strains of Virtue and Constitutionalism. RICHARDS, David A J.

CONSTRAINT(S)

The Limits of Morality. KAGAN, Shelly.

A Definition of Negative Liberty. PETTIT, Philip.

Scientific Problems and the Conduct of Research. HAIG, Brian.

CONSTRUCTION(S)

Pairs of Recursive Structures. ASH, C J and KNIGHT, J F.

A Piagetian Perspective on Mathematical Construction. ARBIB, Michael A.

CONSTRUCTIONALISM

Factual Constraints on Interpreting. STERN, Laurent.

Interpretation and Its Art Objects: Two Views. KRAUSZ, Michael.

CONSTRUCTIVENESS

Varieties of Postmodern Theology. GRIFFIN, David Ray (ed).

CONSTRUCTIVISM

Constructions of Reason: Explorations of Kant's Practical Philosophy. O'NEILL, Onora.

Constructivism and Science: Essays in Recent German Philosophy. BUTTS, Robert E (ed).

Biologische constructies en sociale feiten: Obstakels in het onderzoek naar gezondheidsproblemen van vrouwen. HORSTMAN, Klasien.

Erkenntnistheoretischer Konstruktionismus, Minimalrealismus, empirischer Realismus. ENGELS, Eve-Marie.

Feiten en waarden: de constructie van een onderscheid. PELS, Dick and DE VRIES, G.

A General Constructive Intermediate Value Theorem. BRIDGES, Douglas S.

Kleine epistemologie van de kikvors-retina. GOUDSMIT, Arno L.

Mathematics as Natural Science. GOODMAN, Nicolas D.

De nieuwe zekerheden van het hedendaags wetenschapsonderzoek. AMSTERDAMSKA, Olga and HAGENDIJK, R.

Nonstandard Analysis and Constructivism?. WATTENBERG, Frank.

Resolution in Constructivism. AKAMA, Seiki.

Some Results on Intermediate Constructive Logics. MIGLIOLI, Pierangelo (and others).

A Theorem on Cocongruence of Rings. ROMANO, Daniel A.

Topological Models of Epistemic Set Theory. GOODMAN, Nicolas D.

Toward a Unified Model for Social Problems Theory. JONES, Brian J and MC FALLS JR, Joseph and GALLAGHER III, Bernard J.

CONSTRUCTIVITY

The Strains of Virtue and Constitutionalism. RICHARDS, David A J.

CONSULTATION

An Analysis of Ethics Consultation in the Clinical Setting. SKEEL, Joy D and SELF, Donnie J.

CRISIS(ES)

Crisis and Programs of Identity (Notes to Debate Popular-Urban) (in Hungarian). VARDY, Péter.

Crisis Moral Communities: An Essay in Moral Philosophy. FISHER, David.

La inersorabilità della "nuda inteligencia" in Zubiri. INCARDONA, Nunzio.

On Reading Postmodern Philosophy: Hiley, Redner and the End of Philosophy. COHEN, Avner.

Uso y abuso de las nociones de "crisis" y "modelo" en Ciencias Sociales en Costa Rica. CAMACHO, Luis A.

CRITERIA

"The Problem of the Criterion" in *Epistemology (Companions to Ancient Thought: 1)*, STRIKER, Gisela.

Coherence and the Problem of Criterion. LEHE, Robert T.

Criteria for Theories of Practical Rationality: Reflections on Brandt's Theory. POSTOW, B C.

Dharmakirti on Criteria of Knowledge. CHINCHORE, Mangala R.

Free Will. SCHEER, Richard.

Health Care as a Right: Fairness and Medical Resources. HÄYRY, Matti and HÄYRY, Heta.

Human Natures. LACHS, John.

On Being a Dewey Teacher Today. PRAKASH, Madhu Suri.

Paradoxical Consequences of Balzer's and Gähde's Criteria of Theoreticity. SCHURZ, Gerhard.

Rational Common Ground in the Sociology of Knowledge. KATZ, Jonathan.

Recursively Enumerable Sets Modulo Iterated Jumps and Extensions of Arslanov's Completeness Criterion. JOCKUSCH JR, C G (and others).

CRITERIOLOGY

Epistemologia e neocriticismo in un dibattito degli anni 1912-1914 fra Cassirer e Heidegger. HENRY, Barbara.

CRITIC(S)

A Consideration of Criticism. BARRETT, Terry.

Feminist Literary Criticism and the Author. WALKER, Cheryl.

CRITICAL

Capitalist Schools: Explanation and Ethics in Radical Studies of Schooling. LISTON, Daniel P.

The Philosophical Imaginary. LE DOEUFF, Michèle.

Grundprinzipien einer kritischen Dialektik zwischen Kant und Hegel. IDALOVICHI, Israel.

Kritische Ontologie als Philosophie der Freiheit (in Serbo-Croatian). PREVE, Costanzo.

CRITICAL LEGAL STUDIES

Domination, Legitimation and Law: Introducing Critical Legal Studies. PEIRCE, Michael.

CRITICAL PHILOSOPHY

Contemporary Trends in the Interpretation of Kant's Critical Philosophy. ZAHN, M.

Socratic Dialogue. HECKMANN, Gustav.

Wittgenstein and the Critical Tradition. GARVER, Newton.

CRITICAL RATIONALISM

Critical Rationalism: The Problem of Method in Social Sciences and Law. ALBERT, Hans.

Der Mythos des Rahmens am Pranger: Anderssons Antwort auf die wissenschaftsgeschichtliche Herausforderung. ALBERT, Hans.

Die Situationsanalyse. WERLEN, Benno.

CRITICAL REALISM

Critical Realism?. FAY, Brian.

Realismo crítico y conocimiento en Carlos Popper. DARÓS, W R.

Truth, Relativism, and Crossword Puzzles. MURPHY, Nancey.

CRITICAL THEORY

Critical Theory and Poststructuralism: In Search of a Context. POSTER, Mark.

Critical Theory and Society: A Reader. BRONNER, Stephen Eric (ed).

Jürgen Habermas on Society and Politics: A Reader. SEIDMAN, Steven (ed).

Art and Morality: Critical Theory About the Conflict and Harmony between Art and Morality. KORTHALS, Michiel.

Belief, Doubt and Critical Thinking: Reconciling the Contraries: Response to Garrison and Phelan. BAILIN, Sharon.

Beyond Liberalism and Communitarianism: Towards a Critical Theory of Social Justice. DOPPELT, G.

Critical Theory as Metaphilosophy. BOHMAN, James.

Cultural Critique and Cultural Presuppositions: The Hermeneutical Undercurrent in Critical Theory. ARNASON, Johann P.

The Generalized Others and the Concrete Other: A Response of Marie Fleming. NIELSEN, Kai.

Os Sentidos da "Crítica". BORGES, Bento Itamar.

Universalisms: Procedural, Contextualist and Prudential. FERRARA, Alessandro.

Zur sozialphilosophischen Bedeutung des Sprachbegriffs Wilhelm von Humboldts. SCHILLER, Hans-Ernst.

CRITICAL THINKING

Critical Thinking: Consider the Verdict. WALLER, Bruce N.

Critical Thinking: Evaluating Claims and Arguments in Everyday Life—Second Edition. MOORE, Brook Noel.

Introduction to Logic and Critical Thinking (Second Edition). SALMON, Merrilee H.

Critical Thinking and Moral Education. WEINSTEIN, Mark.

Critical Thinking as Applied Epistemology: Relocating Critical Thinking in the Philosophical Landscape. BATTERSBY, Mark E.

Critical Thinking as Transfer: Reconstructive Integration of Otherwise Discrete Interpretations of Experience. BRELL JR, Carl D.

A Critique of Critical Thinking. HATCHER, Donald.

The Educational Theory of Mary Sheldon Barnes: Inquiry Learning as Indoctrination in History Education. MC ANINCH, Stuart A.

Evaluation of a Philosophy for Children Project in Hawaii. MEEHAN, Kenneth A.

The Human Image System and Thinking Critically in the Strong Sense. FREEMAN, James B.

Is Critical Thinking Guilty of Unwarranted Reductionism. HATCHER, Donald.

Logic in the International Elementary School. SLADE, Christine.

Mind and Brain on Bergen Street. SILVER, Ruth.

Moral Education and a Critical Thinking: The Humanist Perspective. MADIGAN, Tim.

On World Views, Commitment and Critical Thinking. WALTERS, Kerry S.

Parrots Into Owls: The Metamorphosis of a Philosophy for Children Program. VALLONE, Gerard.

Philosophy as Critical Thinking. FINOCCHIARO, Maurice A.

Philosophy for Children and Critical Thinking. LIPMAN, Matthew.

The Rationality of Rationality: Why Think Critically? Response to Siegel. ENNIS, Robert H.

Siegel on Critical Thinking. FINOCCHIARO, Maurice A.

Toward a Feminist Poetic of Critical Thinking. GARRISON, James W and PHELAN, Anne.

Toward a History of Recent Vico Scholarship in English, Part II: 1969-1973. TAGLIACOZZO, Giorgio.

Why Be Rational? On Thinking Critically About Critical Thinking. SIEGEL, Harvey.

CRITICISM

see also Literary Criticism, Textual Criticism

Aesthetic Objects and Works of Art. TOWNSEND, Dabney.

Descriptions. NEALE, Stephen.

Emerging from Meditation: Nakamoto Tominaga. PYE, Michael (trans).

Issues in Evolutionary Epistemology. HAHLWEG, Kai (ed).

The Logic of Sense—Gilles Deleuze. DELEUZE, Gilles.

The Aesthetic-Artistic Domain, Criticism, and Teaching. CHAMBERS, John H.

Against Mentalism in Teleology. BEDAU, Mark.

Arendt's Politics: The Elusive Search for Substance. SCHWARTZ, Joseph M.

Art and the Joycean Artist. SCHIRALLI, Martin.

Blame, Fictional Characters, and Morality. SANKOWSKI, Edward.

Can Emotivism Sustain a Social Ethic?. UNWIN, Nicholas.

Can Kant's Ethics Survive the Feminist Critique?. SEDGWICK, Sally S.

The Communitarian Critique of Liberalism. WALZER, Michael.

A Consideration of Criticism. BARRETT, Terry.

The Critique of Impure Reason: Foucault and the Frankfurt School. MC CARTHY, Thomas.

Darwinism as a Prohibition of Criticism: A Commentary on Friedrich August von Hayek's Theory of Moral Evolution. DORSCHEL, A.

Empiricist Versus Prototype Theories of Language Acquisition. STEMMER, Nathan.

Factual Constraints on Interpreting. STERN, Laurent.

Feminist Critique of Epistemology. RUSSELL, Denise.

Freud's Critique of Philosophy. BERTHOLD-BOND, Daniel.

Kant's Key to the Critique of Taste. BURGESS, Craig.

Knowledge, Criticism, and Coherence. KUYS, Thieu.

Literary Relativism. CARNEY, James D.

Literature, Criticism, and Factual Reporting. COLLETT, Alan.

Montaigne, Encoder and Decoder, in Propria Persona. JONES, Robert F.

A New Music Criticism?. KIVY, Peter.

Objectividade científica: noção e questionamentos. CUPANI, Alberto.

On the Critique of Values. LUNTLEY, Michael.

Plato's Critique of the Poets and the Misunderstanding of his Epistemological Argumentation. WIEGMANN, Hermann.

The Possibility of Film Criticism. POAGUE, Leland and CADBURY, William.

CULTURE(S)

Morality and Culture: A Note on Kant. ROTENSTREICH, Nathan.

The National Axiological Anthropological Atlas: A "Chart" of the Premiss Values of the Romanian People's Culture (I). CARAMELEA, Vasile V (and others).

National Formation and the 'Rise of the Cultural'. JAMES, Paul.

On Ethnomathematics. D'AMBROSIO, Ubiratan.

Options in African Philosophy. SOGOLO, G S.

The Politics of Interpretation: Spinoza's Modernist Turn. LANG, Berel.

Protestant Reconciliation as a Challenge for Today's Culture. HUMMEL, Gert.

The Question of Relevance in Current Nigerian Philosophy. KIMMERLE, Heinz.

Re-enfranchising Art: Feminist Interventions in the Theory of Art. LAUTER, Estella.

A Role for Philosophy of Education in Intercultural Research: Reexamination of the Relativism-Absolutism Debate. FEINBERG, Walter.

Scienze della cultura e storiografia filosofica in Ernst Cassirer. MARTIRANO, Maurizio.

Some Basic Problems in the Development of the Human Sciences in China Today. YOUZHENG, Li.

Storia della cultura e storia sociale. VILLANI, Pasquale.

Le temps de la préhistoire et la venue de l'homme et des cultures sur la terre. MERCIER, A.

The Problems of Czech and Slovak Culture-Political Thinking Between Both World Wars (in Czechoslovakian). BERANOVA, Vera.

The Three Pedagogical Dimensions of Nietzsche's Philosophy. ALONI, Nimrod.

Die traditionelle chinesische Kultur und das Gegenwärtige Rechtssystem Chinas. JIAN, Mi.

Translation, Art, and Culture. PERRICONE, Christopher.

Treating Animals Naturally?. ROLSTON III, Holmes.

Understanding Other Cultures: Studies in the Philosophical Problems of Cross-Cultural Interpretation. SANDBACKA, Carola.

The Vichian Elements in Susanne Langer's Thought. BLACK, David W.

Vico's Significance for the New Cultural History. HUTTON, Patrick H.

Waste and Culture. TIBERG, Nils.

Wittgenstein on Culture and Civilization. LURIE, Yuval.

CUPITT, D

From Kierkegaard to Cupitt: Subjectivity, the Body and Eternal Life. PATTISON, George.

CURRICULUM

Education, Movement and the Curriculum: A Philosophic Enquiry. ARNOLD, Peter J.

Interpreting Education. EDEL, Abraham.

Philosophical Issues in Education. HAMM, Cornel M.

Reading Curriculum Theory: The Development of a New Hermeneutic. REYNOLDS, William M.

"Ethics in America". SCHERER, Donald.

Aesthetic Education: A Small Manifesto. ABBS, Peter.

Democracy and Pragmatism in Curriculum Development. WALKER, J C.

Educating for Democracy: Charles W Eliot and the Differentiated Curriculum. PRESKILL, Stephen.

Logic in the Classroom. SLADE, Christina.

Philosophy for Children: An Important Curriculum Innovation. SPLITTER, Laurance J.

The Study of Teaching and Curriculum. MALANGA, Joseph.

Teaching "Ethics in America". ROSENBAUM, Alan S.

Teaching American Philosophy. CAMPBELL, James.

CURRIE, G

Currie on Fictional Names. LAMB, Roger.

CUSTOM(S)

Nature, Custom, and Stipulation in Law and Jurisprudence. MURPHY, James Bernard.

O grande experimento: sobre a oposição entre eticidade (*Sittlichkeit*) e autonomia em Nietzsche. GIACOIA JUNIOR, Oswaldo.

CUT ELIMINATION

The Gentzenization and Decidability of RW. BRADY, Ross T.

A Note on Sequent Calculi Intermediate Between *LJ* and *LK*. BORICIC, Branislav R.

Sequent-Systems and Groupoid Models, I. DOSEN, Kosta.

CYBERNETICS

Georg Klaus über Kybernetik und Information. STOCK, Wolfgang G.

The New World Synthesis. POPE, N Vivian.

CYCLE(S)

The Shape of Time. CIORANESCU, Alexandre.

CYLINDRIC ALGEBRAS

Isomorphic But Not Lower Base-Isomorphic Cylindric Algebras of Finite Dimension. BIRÓ, Balázs.

CYNICISM

Paul and the Popular Philosophers. MALHERBE, Abraham J.

The Cynicism of Sartre's "Bad Faith". SANTONI, Ronald E.

D'COSTA, G

Straightening the Record: Some Responses to Critics. HICK, John.

D'ENTREVES, A

Why is There a Problem About Political Obligation?. NIELSEN, Kai.

DA COSTA, N

Paraconsistency and the C-Systems of DaCosta. URBAS, Igor.

DAI ZHEN

Dai Zhen: The Unity of the Moral Nature (in Serbo-Croatian). EWELL JR, John W.

DAIMON

"Reason as *Daimōn*" in *The Person and the Human Mind: Issues in Ancient and Modern Philosophy*, CLARK, Stephen R L.

Daimon Life, Nearness and Abyss: An Introduction to Za-ology. KRELL, David Farrell.

DALRYMPLE, J

Stair on Natural Law and Promises. MAC CORMACK, Geoffrey.

DAMIANI, P

Petrus Damiani—ein Freund der Logik?. BUCHER, Theodor G.

DANCE

Contexts of Dance. SPARSHOTT, Francis.

DANIELS, N

Who Lives? Who Dies?: Ethical Criteria in Patient Selection. KILNER, John F.

Just Health Care (II): Is Equality Too Much?. FLECK, Leonard M.

Justice Between Age-Groups: A Comment on Norman Daniels. MC KERLIE, Dennis.

Should We Ration Health Care?. JECKER, Nancy S.

Towards a Theory of Age-Group Justice. JECKER, Nancy S.

DANISH

Death, Democracy and Public Ethical Choice. CUSHMAN, Reid and HOLM, Soren.

The Importance of Knowledge and Trust in the Definition of Death. RIX, Bo Andreassen.

DANTO, A

Art and the Rhetoric of Allusion. NUYEN, A T.

Danto, Dewey and the Historical End of Art. MITCHELL, Jeff.

Interpretation in Aesthetics: Theories and Practices. MC CORMICK, Peter.

Knowledge or Control as the End of Art. CEBIK, L B.

Nesting: The Ontology of Interpretation. ZEMACH, Eddy.

Once Is Not Enough?. WREEN, Michael.

Philosophy, Literature, and the Death of Art. ROSS, Stephanie.

Resurrecting Hegel to Bury Art. BROWN, Lee.

Why the Problem of the Existence of the External Worlds is a Pseudo-Problem: A Revision of Putnam and Danto. SHIRLEY, Edward S.

DAODEJING

Hegel and Daodejing (in Serbo-Croatian). LESJAK, Gregor.

DARWIN

Darwin in Russian Thought. VUCINICH, Alexander.

"Why Darwin is Important for Ethics" in *Mind, Value and Culture: Essays in Honor of E M Adams*, RACHELS, James.

Between Beanbag Genetics and Natural Selection. FALK, Raphael.

Yoga-Sūtra IV, 2-3 and Vivekānanda's Interpretation of Evolution. KILLINGLEY, D H.

DARWINISM

Darwin in Russian Thought. VUCINICH, Alexander.

The Metaphysics of Evolution. HULL, David L.

Philosophy of Biology Today. RUSE, Michael.

The Structure of Biological Theories. THOMPSON, Paul.

A Useful Inheritance: Evolutionary Aspects of the Theory of Knowledge. RESCHER, Nicholas.

"Somatic Evolution and Cultural Form" in *Issues in Evolutionary Epistemology*, BALDUS, Bernd.

"Taking Darwin Even More Seriously" in *Issues in Evolutionary Epistemology*, MUNZ, Peter.

DARWINISM

Darwinism as a Prohibition of Criticism: A Commentary on Friedrich August von Hayek's Theory of Moral Evolution. DORSCHEL, A.

Evolution in Thermodynamic Perspective: An Ecological Approach. WEBER, Bruce H (and others).

The Non-Existence of a Principle of Natural Selection. SHIMONY, Abner.

Pietro Siciliani o del virtuoso darwinismo. SAVORELLI, Alessandro.

Really Taking Darwin Seriously: An Alternative to Michael Ruse's Darwinian Metaethics. ROTTSCHAEFER, William A and MARTINSEN, David.

The Significance of Darwinian Theory for Marx and Engels. TAYLOR, Angus.

DASCAL, M

Significado literal: entre la profunda necesidad de una construcción y la mera nostalgia. CABRERA, Julio.

DASEIN

"Strangers in the Dark: On the Limitations of the Limits of *Praxis* in the Early Heidegger". SCHMIDT, Dennis J.

"The Double Concept of Philosophy" and the Place of Ethics in *Being and Time*. BERNASCONI, Robert L.

Anabase—Acheminement vers l'amont de la "présupposition"—Le chemin de *Sein und Zeit*. GUEST, Gérard.

Dasein's Disclosedness. HAUGELAND, John.

Heidegger als fragender Denker und als Denker der Frage. HAEFFNER, Gerd.

Heidegger and Cognitive Science. GLOBUS, Gordon G.

Heidegger and Davidson (on Haugeland). OKRENT, Mark.

Heidegger and the Question of Ethics. SCOTT, Charles E.

Heidegger and the Question of Humanism. MILES, Murray.

Truth as Disclosure: Art, Language, History. GUIGNON, Charles.

Twisting Free: Being to an Extent Sensible. SALLIS, John.

Which Beings are Exemplary? Comments on Charles Guignon's "Truth as Disclosure: Art, Language, History". NENON, Thomas J.

DATA

The Murky Borderland Between Scientific Intuition and Fraud. SEGERSTRALE, Ullica.

Stability of Weak Second-Order Semantics. CSIRMAZ, László.

Theory Discovery from Data with Mixed Quantifiers. KELLY, Kevin T and GLYMOUR, Clark.

DATABASE(S)

Listenaires: Thoughts on a Database. GILES, Gordon J.

DAVIDSON, D

Actions and Other Events: The Unifier-Multiplier Controversy. PFEIFER, Karl.

Donald Davidson's Philosophy of Language: An Introduction. RAMBERG, Bjorn T.

Rationality and Relativity: The Quest for Objective Knowledge. O'GORMAN, Francis.

Translation and the Nature of Philosophy: A New Theory of Words. BENJAMIN, Andrew.

"Reading Donald Davidson: Truth, Meaning and Right Interpretation" in *Analytic Aesthetics*, NORRIS, Christopher.

Charity and Ideology: The Field Linguist as Social Critic. RAMBERG, Bjorn T.

Coherence, Truth and the 'Omniscient Interpreter'. DALMIYA, Vrinda.

Davidson and Hare on Evaluations. SPITZLEY, Thomas and CRAIG, Edward (trans).

Davidson's Omniscient Interpreter. JANSSENS, C J A M and VAN BRAKEL, J.

Davidson's Semantic and Computational Understanding of Language (in Serbo-Croatian). BOJADZIEV, Damjan.

Davidson, Irrationality, and Weakness of Will. LAVELLE, Kevin C.

Emociones y creencias. HANSBERG, Olbeth.

Experience and the Justification of Belief. MILLAR, Alan.

Heidegger and Davidson (on Haugeland). OKRENT, Mark.

Human Noises. STEWART, Donald.

Hume and Davidson on Pride. ÁRDAL, Páll S.

Impredicative Identity Criteria and Davidson's Criterion of Event Identity. LOWE, E J.

In Defence of Untranslatability. SANKEY, Howard.

In Defense of Davidson's Identity Thesis Regarding Action Individuation. WIDERKER, David.

Judgment, Self-Consciousness, and Object Independence. CHURCH, Jennifer.

Minds Divided. HEIL, John.

The Moral Atmosphere: Language and Value in Davidson. MARTIN, Bill.

On Davidson and Interpretation. BURDICK, Howard.

Putnam on Davidson on Conceptual Schemes. BRENNER-GOLOMB, N and VAN BRAKEL, J.

Realismo II: Donald Davidson. VILLANUEVA, Enrique.

Seeing and Believing: Metaphor, Image, and Force. MORAN, Richard.

Skepticism and Davidson's Omniscient Interpreter Argument. WARD, Andrew.

Subjectivity and Environmentalism. LE PORE, Ernest.

Talking Lions and Lion Talk: Davidson on Conceptual Schemes. CRUMLEY, Jack S.

Truth and Meaning in the Works of Tugendhat and Davidson (in Serbo-Croation). WYLLER, Truls.

Truth, Interpretation and Convention T. PRADHAN, R C.

Verständnis für Unvernünftige. BITTNER, Rüdiger.

Ward on Davidson's Refutation of Scepticism. HURTADO, Guillermo.

DAVIES, M

Descriptions. NEALE, Stephen.

DAVIS, M

Auctions, Lotteries, and the Punishment of Attempts. DUFF, R A.

The Death Penalty, Deterrence, and Horribleness: Reply to Michael Davis. REIMAN, Jeffrey.

DAVIS, S

Response to Davis's "Doubting the Resurrection". KELLER, James A.

DAVIS, W

A Causal Theory of Intending. SHOPE, Robert K.

DE ANQUIN, N

Ser, nada y creación en el pensamiento de Nimio de Anquín. PEREZ, J R.

DE BEAUVOIR

The Thinking Muse: Feminism and Modern French Philosophy. ALLEN, Jeffner (ed).

Sexism and the Philosophical Canon: On Reading Beauvoir's *The Second Sex*. SIMONS, Margaret A.

DE BONO, E

Thinking Skill Programs: An Analysis. MAYS, Wolfe and SHARP, Ann Margaret.

DE FINETTI, B

An Agenda for Subjectivism. VICKERS, John M.

Anti-Realism in the Philosophy of Probability: Bruno de Finetti's Subjectivism. GALAVOTTI, Maria Carla.

Conditions on Upper and Lower Probabilities to Imply Probabilities. SUPPES, Patrick and ZANOTTI, Mario.

De Finetti's Earliest Works on the Foundations of Probability. VON PLATO, Jan.

Possibility and Probability. LEVI, Isaac.

Reading *Probabilismo*. JEFFREY, Richard.

DE GEORGE, R

Is a Moral Organization Possible?. KLEIN, Sherwin.

Tuning in to Whistle Blowing. GOLDBERG, David Theo.

Whistleblowing and Management Accounting: An Approach. LOEB, Stephen E and CORY, Suzanne N.

DE MAN, P

"The *Différance* Between Derrida and de Man" in *The Textual Sublime: Deconstruction and Its Differences*, HARVEY, Irene E.

"On Mere Sight: A Response to Paul de Man" in *The Textual Sublime: Deconstruction and Its Differences*, GASCHÉ, Rodolphe.

"Paul de Man and the Subject of Literary History" in *The Textual Sublime: Deconstruction and Its Differences*, JAY, Gregory S.

"Recovering the Figure of J L Austin in Paul de Man's *Allegories of Reading*" in *The Textual Sublime: Deconstruction and Its Differences*, CARAHER, Brian G.

From Rhetoric to Corporate Populism: A Romantic Critique of the Academy in an Age of High Gossip. CHRISTENSEN, Jerome.

Philosophy and Literature: Their Relationship in the Works of Paul de Man. MICHIELSEN, Peter.

DE MARCO, J

Gauthier's Ethics and Extra-Rational Values: A Comment on DeMarco. CURTIS, Robert A.

DE MARTINO, E

Mondo, persona e storia in E De Martino: Tra Croce e Cassirer. IMBRUGLIA, Girolamo.

DE PAEPE

Intergenerational Justice and Productive Resources; A Nineteenth Century Socialist Debate. CUNLIFFE, John.

DE VOGEL, C

Cornelia de Vogel fra vecchio e nuovo paradigma ermeneutico nell'interpretazione di Platone. PEROLI, Enrico.

DEAD

Callahan on Harming the Dead. SERAFINI, Anthony.

DEATH

"The Son of Apollo": Themes of Plato. WOODBRIDGE, Frederick J E.

Alpha and Omega: Ethics at the Frontiers of Life and Death. YOUNG, Ernlé W D.

Final Choices: Autonomy in Health Care Decisions. SMITH, George P.

Health Care Ethics: Principles and Problems. GARRETT, Thomas M (ed).

Impermanence is Buddha-nature: Dōgen's Understanding of Temporality. STAMBAUGH, Joan.

Patterns of Transcendence: Religion, Death, and Dying. CHIDESTER, David.

Reincarnation: A Philosophical and Practical Analysis. PREUSS, Peter.

The Sanctity-of-Life Doctrine in Medicine: A Critique. KUHSE, Helga.

"Banter and Banquets for Heroic Death" in *Post-Structuralist Classics*, PUCCI, Pietro.

"Do the Numbers Count: A Value-Theoretic Response" in *Inquiries into Values: The Inaugural Session of the International Society for Value Inquiry*, GARCIA, Jorge.

"Schopenhauer on Suffering, Death, Guilt, and the Consolation of Metaphysics" in *Schopenhauer: New Essays in Honor of His 200th Birthday*, CARTWRIGHT, David E.

The AIDS Crisis: Unethical Marketing Leads to Negligent Homicide. KROHN, Franklin B and MILNER, Laura M.

Death and Well-Being. BIGELOW, John and CAMPBELL, John and PARGETTER, Robert.

Death, Democracy and Public Ethical Choice. CUSHMAN, Reid and HOLM, Soren.

A Drama of Love and Death: Michael Pedersen Kierkegaard and Regine Olsen Revisited. PATTISON, George.

Dwellers in an Unfortified City: Death and Political Philosophy. SCHALL, James V.

F M Kamm and the Mirror of Time. FELDMAN, Fred.

The Importance of Knowledge and Trust in the Definition of Death. RIX, Bo Andreassen.

Kierkegaard's View of Death. WATKIN, Julia.

L'innocence de l'être-pour la mort. PORÉE, Jérôme.

Letting and Making Death Happen—Withholding and Withdrawing Life Support: Morally Irrelevant Distinctions. GRATTON, Claude.

Letting and Making Death Happen: Is There Really No Difference? The Problem of Moral Linkage. DAGI, T F.

The Life of Ivan Il'ich. PATTERSON, David.

A Matter of Life and Death in Socratic Philosophy. BRICKHOUSE, Thomas C and SMITH, Nicholas D.

Mortal Immortals: Lucretius on Death and the Voice of Nature. NUSSBAUM, Martha C.

The Nonduality of Life and Death: A Buddhist View of Repression. LOY, David.

On Dying as a Process. FELDMAN, Fred.

Philosophy for an 'Age of Death': The Critique of Science and Technology in Heidegger and Nishitani. HEINE, Steven.

Relearning the World: On the Phenomenology of Grieving. ATTIG, Thomas.

Some Heideggerian Reflections on Euthanasia. NUYEN, A T.

The Symmetry Argument: Lucretius Against the Fear of Death. ROSENBAUM, Stephen E.

Tragedy and Nonhumans. PUTMAN, Daniel.

La volontà di oblio: Per un'ermeneutica della morte. STRUMMIELLO, Giuseppina.

DEATH PENALTY

Justifying Legal Punishment. PRIMORATZ, Igor.

A Case for Capital Punishment. COOPER, W E and KING-FARLOW, John.

The Death Penalty, Civilization, and Inhumaneness. DAVIS, Michael.

The Death Penalty, Deterrence, and Horribleness: Reply to Michael Davis. REIMAN, Jeffrey.

From Hemlock to Lethal Injection: The Case for Self-Execution. WALLER, Bruce N.

Medical Ethics and the Death Penalty. BONNIE, Richard J.

DEATH WISH

La volontà di oblio: Per un'ermeneutica della morte. STRUMMIELLO, Giuseppina.

DEBATE(S)

"Organization and Articulation of Verbal Exchanges" in *From Metaphysics to Rhetoric*, OLERON, Pierre.

An Analysis of Monologues and Dialogues in Political Debates. EVERTS, Diederik.

The French Revolution Debate and British Political Thought. CLAEYS, Gregory.

DEBT(S)

Ethical Issues in International Lending. SNOY, Bernard.

DECEPTION

Essays in Philosophy and Education. STOTT, Laurence J.

"Kunst der Überlistung" oder "Reden mit Vernuft"? Zu Philosophischen Aspekten der Rhetorik. NIEHUES-PRÖBSTING, Heinrich.

Demons, Demonologists and Descartes. SCARRE, Geoffrey.

Ethical Problems in Competitive Bidding: The Paradyne Case. DAVIS, J Steve.

Hypocrisy. TURNER, D.

Openness. MC MAHON, Christopher.

When Do We Deceive Others?. BARNES, Annette.

DECIDABILITY

Complete Local Rings as Domains. STOLTENBERG-HANSEN, V and TUCKER, J V.

Decidable Discrete Linear Orders. MOSES, M.

The Gentzenization and Decidability of RW. BRADY, Ross T.

A New Criterion of Decidability for Intermediate Logics. SKURA, Tomasz.

DECISION ELEMENT(S)

Attitudes Towards Corporate Social Responsibility and Perceived Importance of Social Responsibility Information. TEOH, Hai Yap and SHIU, Godwin Y.

DECISION PROCEDURE(S)

'Utilitarianism Incorporating Justice'—A Decentralised Model of Ethical Decision Making. TRAPP, Rainer W.

Background Rights and Judicial Decision. SCHRADER, David E.

The Elderly and High Technology Medicine: A Case for Individualized, Autonomous Allocation. MOTT, Peter D.

DECISION THEORY

Axioms of Cooperative Decision Making. MOULIN, Hervé.

The Philosophy of F P Ramsey. SAHLIN, Nils-Eric.

Rationality and Dynamic Choice: Foundational Explorations. MC CLENNEN, Edward F.

Commodities, Language, and Desire. BACHARACH, Michael.

Decision Problems Under Uncertainty Based on Entropy Functionals. GOTTINGER, Hans W.

Decision-Theoretic Epistemology. WEINTRAUB, Ruth.

Decisione e origine: Appunti su Schmitt e Heidegger. SCALONE, A.

Disciplining Qualitative Decision Exercises: Aspects of a Transempirical Protocol, I. SUTHERLAND, John W.

Disciplining Qualitative Decision Exercises: Aspects of a Transempirical Protocol, II. SUTHERLAND, John W.

How Evolutionary Biology Challenges the Classical Theory of Rational Choice. COOPER, W S.

Knowing and Believing in the Original Position. CORLETT, J A.

Levi's Decision Theory. LEEDS, Stephen.

Misunderstandings of Epistemic TIT for TAT: Reply to John Woods. BLAIS, Michel J.

The Popcorn Problem: Sobel on Evidential Decision Theory and Deliberation-Probability Dynamics. EELLS, Ellery.

Stable and Retrievable Options. RABINOWICZ, Woldzimierz.

Under Stochastic Dominance Choquet-Expected Utility and Anticipated Utility Are Identical. WAKKER, Peter.

DECISION(S)

Dilemmas: A Christian Approach to Moral Decision Making. HIGGINSON, Richard.

Moral Issues in Military Decision Making. HARTLE, Anthony E.

Rules, Norms, and Decisions: On the Conditions of Practical and Legal Reasoning. KRATOCHWIL, Friedrich V.

"Interpreting Proxy Directives" in *Advance Directives in Medicine*, JUENGST, Eric T and WEIL, Carol J.

Commentary on "Hamlethics in Planning". BALKIS, Kozmas.

Commentary on "Hamlethics in Planning". HARE, R M.

Commentary on "The Expert and the Public". KRIEGER, Martin H.

Commentary on "The Worm and the Juggernaut". BAYLES, Michael D.

Computationalism. DIETRICH, Eric.

A Decision Support System for the Graph Model of Conflicts. KILGOUR, D Marc and FANG, Liping and HIPEL, Keith W.

Ethics in Health Care and Medical Technologies. TAYLOR, Carol.

The Expert and the Public: Local Values and National Choice. GOLDSTEIN, Alfred.

Group Decision and Negotiation Support in Evolving, Nonshared Information Contexts. SHAKUN, Melvin F.

Hamlethics in Planning: To Do or Not To Do. KAUFMAN, Jerome L.

Justificación normativa y pertenencia. CARACCIOLO, Ricardo.

DESCARTES

Elements of Modern Philosophy: Descartes through Kant. BRENNER, William H.

The Ethics of Geometry: A Genealogy of Modernity. LACHTERMAN, David R.

The Fourth Way: A Theory of Knowledge. GROSSMAN, Reinhardt.

Historical Roots of Cognitive Science. MEYERING, Theo C.

Husserl's Phenomenology and the Foundations of Natural Science. HARVEY, Charles W.

The Imitation of Nature. HYMAN, John.

The Possible Influence of Montaigne's "Essais" on Descartes' "Treatise on the Passions". PAULSON, Michael G.

"Derrida and Descartes: Economizing Thought" in *Derrida and Deconstruction*, JUDOVITZ, Dalia.

"Hobbes and Descartes" in *Perspectives on Thomas Hobbes*, TUCK, Richard.

"Toward an Anthropology of Rhetoric" in *From Metaphysics to Rhetoric*, MEYER, Michel.

"...Quod circulum non commiserim..." *Quartae Responsiones.* MOYAL, Georges J D.

"Degrés de réalite" et "degrés de perfection" dans les *Principes de la philosophie de Descartes* de Spinoza. RAMOND, Charles.

The Cartesian Circle: Hegelian Logic to the Rescue. LUFT, Eric V D.

The Cartesian *Cogito*, Epistemic Logic, and Neuroscience: Some Surprising Interrelations. HINTIKKA, Jaakko.

Concerning the Freedom and Limits of the Will. FRANKFURT, Harry G.

Deduction, Confirmation, and the Laws of Nature in Descartes's *Principia Philosophiae.* NADLER, Steven M.

Demons, Demonologists and Descartes. SCARRE, Geoffrey.

Descartes and Some Predecessors on the Divine Conservation of Motion. MENN, Stephen.

Descartes et l'esprit cartésien (1922). LÉVY-BRUHL, Lucien.

Descartes in the Hegelian Perspective. BATTA, Nirmala Devi.

Descartes in the History of Being: Another Bad Novel?. BERNASCONI, Robert L.

Descartes on Freedom of the Will. BEYSSADE, Jean-Marie.

Descartes on Time and Causality. SECADA, J E K.

Descartes' Doctrine of Volitional Infinity. CRESS, Donald A.

Descartes' Legacy and Deep Ecology. MILLER, Peter.

Descartes' Logic of Magnitudes. LOECK, Gisela.

Descartes's Dualism and the Philosophy of Mind. ALANEN, Lilli.

Descartes's *Meditations* and Devotional Meditations. RUBIDGE, Bradley.

Descartes, Skepticism, and Husserl's Hermeneutic Practice. BURKEY, John.

Descartes: um naturalista?. SILVEIRA, Lígia Fraga.

Desire and Love in Descartes' Late Philosophy. BEAVERS, Anthony F.

Deus, causa sui *en Descartes*. AGUADO, Javier Fernández.

Dieu, le roi et les sujets. GUENANCIA, Pierre.

La doble significación científica y filosófica de la evolución del concepto de fuerza de Descartes a Euler. ARANA, Juan.

Essential Truths and the Ontological Argument. SIEVERT, Donald.

La fondation de l'autonomie chez Descartes: Lecture entre Brunschvicg et Derrida. MAESSCHALCK, Marc.

Husserl and Heidegger on the Cartesian Legacy. TRIPATHY, Laxman Kumar.

Kant on Descartes and the Brutes. NARAGON, Steve.

Kant's Metaphysics of the Subject and Modern Society. FRIGERIO, C.

L'esprit cartésien et l'histoire (1936). LÉVY-BRUHL, Lucien.

Liberté et égalité chez Descartes. RODIS-LEWIS, Geneviève.

Mathematics, Physics, and Corporeal Substance in Descartes. BROWN, Gregory.

Merleau-Ponty's Tacit *Cogito*. WILLIAMS, Linda L.

Natural Theology and the Concept of Perfection in Descartes, Spinoza and Leibniz. WEBB, Mark O.

Notes et documents sur "Le Descartes de L Lévy-Bruhl". CAVAILLÉ, Jean-Pierre.

Die Notizen Eugen Finks zur Umarbeitung von Edmund Husserls "Cartesianischen Meditationen". BRUZINA, Ronald.

Objective Reality of Ideas in Descartes, Caterus, and Suárez. WELLS, Norman J.

Of Primary and Secondary Qualities. SMITH, A D.

Pascal: scienza, filosofia, religione. DEREGIBUS, Arturo.

Politique-(s) de Descartes?. BARRET-KRIEGEL, Blandine.

La priorità ontologica e gnoseologica dell'esistenza di Dio in Spinoza. NICOLOSI, Salvatore.

The Priority of Reason in Descartes. LOEB, Louis E.

The Problem of the External World. HAMLYN, D W.

A propos du Cartésianisme Gris de Marion. LOPARIC, Zeljko.

Recent Work on Foundationalism. TRIPLETT, Timm.

Reexamining Berkeley's Notion of Suggestion. BEN-ZEEV, Aaron.

Religion et philosophie chez Descartes et Malebranche. GRIMALDI, Nicolas.

René Descartes n'est pas l'auteur de *La naissance de la paix*. WATSON, Richard A.

Reply to Roth: Locke Is Not a Cartesian with Respect to Knowledge of our Own Existence. HEYD, Thomas.

The Role of Self-Knowledge in the *Critique of Pure Reason*. POLT, Richard F H.

Schopenhauer y la psicología. PINILLOS, José Luis.

A Segurança em Descartes. MACEDO, Leosino Bizinoto.

Stroud and Williams on Dreaming and Scepticism. REIN, Andrew.

System and Training in Descartes' *Meditations*. BEYSSADE, Michelle.

Techne: dai Greci ai moderni e ritorno. POSSENTI, Vittorio.

Le *Traité des passions* de Descartes et les théories modernes de l'émotion. NEUBERG, M.

The Trapped Infinity: Cartesian Volition as Conceptual Nightmare. REED, Edward S.

Trois lectures cartésiennes de la théorie du gouvernement-liage de N Chomsky. POPARDA, Oana.

Why Is the Ontological Proof in Descartes' Fifth Meditation?. WERTZ, S K.

DESCRIPTION(S)

Descriptions. NEALE, Stephen.

"Russell on Indexicals and Scientific Knowledge" in *Rereading Russell: Essays on Bertrand Russell's Metaphysics and Epistemology*, SMITH, Janet Farrell.

"Russelling Causal Theories of Reference" in *Rereading Russell: Essays on Bertrand Russell's Metaphysics and Epistemology*, FUMERTON, Richard.

Acquaintance, Knowledge and Description in Russell. BAR-ELLI, Gilead.

Beyond Eliminativism. CLARK, Andy.

MacIntyre on Traditions. ANNAS, Julia.

The Origins of Russell's Theory of Descriptions. RODRÍGUEZ-CONSUEGRA, Francisco.

DESCRIPTIVE ETHICS

Is Hume a Moral Skeptic?. FIESER, James.

DESCRIPTIVE MEANING

Mental Imagery: On the Limits of Cognitive Science. ROLLINS, Mark.

Geach on 'Good'. PIGDEN, Charles R.

Tesi di Hume e sistemi di logica deontica. GALVAN, Sergio.

DESCRIPTIVE SET THEORY

Descriptive Set Theory Over Hyperfinite Sets. KEISLER, H Jerome (and others).

Some Applications of Positive Formulas in Descriptive Set Theory and Logic. DYCK, Stephen.

DESCRIPTIVES

Metaphysics, Mind, and Mental Science. GOLDMAN, Alvin I.

DESCRIPTIVISM

"Normative and Descriptive Issues in the Analysis of Medical Language" in *Scientific Knowledge Socialized*, MOULIN, Anne-Marie.

DESERT(S)

The Better Endowed and the Difference Principle. MC MAHON, Christopher.

Deserved Punishment. GARCIA, J L A.

Uneven Starts and Just Deserts. WALLER, Bruce N.

DESIGN

Aesthetic Valuing of Design (in Czechoslovakian). VASICEK, Milan.

Re-Visioning Clinical Research—Gender and the Ethics of Experimental Design. ROSSER, Sue V.

DESIGN ARGUMENT

Taylor's Defenses of Two Traditional Arguments for the Existence of God. GARAVASO, Pieranna.

DESIGNATION

"The Revival of 'Fido'-Fido" in *Cause, Mind, and Reality: Essays Honoring C B Martin*, DEVITT, Michael.

Frege's Objects of a Quine Special Kind. SCHIRN, Matthias.

DESIRE(S)

The Idea of a Reason for Acting: A Philosophical Argument. SCHUELER, George Frederick.

An Introductory Guide to Post-Structuralism and Postmodernism. SARUP, Madan.

Lawless Mind. ABELSON, Raziel.

The Perverted Consciousness: Sexuality and Sartre. LEAK, Andrew N.

Scarcity and Modernity. XENOS, Nicholas.

"Desire and the Figure of Fun: Glossing Theocritus 11" in *Post-Structuralist*

DESIRE(S)

Classics. GOLDHILL, Simon.

"Intention" in *Cause, Mind, and Reality: Essays Honoring C B Martin,* CHARLES, David.

Bare Functional Desire. PETTIT, Philip and PRICE, Huw.

Commodities, Language, and Desire. BACHARACH, Michael.

Dennett's Little Grains of Salt. MC CULLOCH, Gregory.

Desire and Emotion in the Virtue Tradition. HARTZ, Glenn A.

Desire and Love in Descartes' Late Philosophy. BEAVERS, Anthony F.

Desire for All/Love of One: Tomas's Tale in *The Unbearable Lightness of Being.* DILLON, Martin C.

Desire's Desire for Moral Realism: A Phenomenological Objection to Non-Cognitivism. NELSON, James Lindemann.

Desire: Direct and Imitative. COHN, Robert Greer.

Desires as Reasons—Discussion Notes on Fred Dretske's "Explaining Behavior: Reasons in a World of Causes". STAMPE, Dennis W.

Dretske's Desires. BRATMAN, Michael E.

Fictional Emotion, Quasi-Desire and Background Relief. BORUAH, Bijoy H.

In Defence of Folk Psychology. JACKSON, Frank and PETTIT, Philip.

The Intentionality of Animal Action. HEYES, Cecilia and DICKINSON, Anthony.

Irresistible Desires. MELE, Alfred R.

L'homme du désir. LAFON, Guy.

Love Delights in Praises: A Reading of *The Two Gentlemen of Verona.* GIRARD, René.

La metafísica de la esperanza y del deseo en Gabriel Marcel. O'CALLAGHAN, Paul.

The Metaphysics of Leisure. COOPER, Wesley E.

Narrative and Theories of Desire. CLAYTON, Jay.

An Objection to Wright's Treatment of Intention. MILLER, Alexander.

On a New Argument for the Existence of God. MARTIN, Michael.

On Desire and its Discontents. SOLL, Ivan.

A Problem about Higher Order Desires. MOORE, F C T.

A Reflection on Lonergan's Notion of the Pure Desire to Know. MORELLI, Elizabeth A.

The Reward Event and Motivation. MORILLO, Carolyn R.

Shame and Desire in the Myths of Origins. HANS, James S.

Some Pleasures of Plato, *Republic IX.* STOKES, Michael.

Where the Traditional Accounts of Practical Reason Go Wrong. HURLEY, Paul.

DESIRING

L'homme du désir. LAFON, Guy.

DESPAIR

Kierkegaard on Despair and the Eternal. MORRIS, T.

DESPOTISM

Aristotle and the Classical Greek Concept of Despotism. RICHTER, Melvin.

DESTINY

Xunzi: A Translation and Study of the Complete Works, Volume II—Books 7-16. KNOBLOCK, John (trans).

DESTRUCTION

Nuclear Deterrence and Moral Restraint. SHUE, Henry (ed).

Justifying Wrongful Employee Behavior: The Role of Personality in Organizational Sabotage. GIACALONE, Robert A and KNOUSE, Stephen B.

DETACHMENT

Principal Type-Schemes and Condensed Detachment. HINDLEY, J Roger.

DETENTE

"Detente, Human Rights and Soviet Behavior" in *Moral Reasoning and Statecraft: Essays Presented to Kenneth W Thompson,* PETRO, Nicolai N.

DETERMINATION

Time and Change: Short But Differing Philosophies. CHACALOS, Elias Harry.

Determination and Consciousness in Marx. MILLS, Charles W.

L'indétermination, la détermination et la relation: Les trois essences de l'être. GUILLAMAUD, Patrice.

DETERMINISM

Accountability in Education: A Philosophical Inquiry. WAGNER, Robert B.

Determinism, Blameworthiness and Deprivation. KLEIN, Martha.

Lawless Mind. ABELSON, Raziel.

On Action. GINET, Carl.

Philosophical Consequences of Quantum Theory: Reflections on Bell's Theorem. CUSHING, James T (ed).

Religious Issues in Contemporary Philosophy. SLAATTE, Howard A.

William James, Public Philosopher. COTKIN, George.

Wisdom and Humanness in Psychology: Prospects for a Christian

Approach. EVANS, C Stephen.

"Freedom and Determinism in Maimonides' Philosophy" in *Moses Maimonides and His Time,* GELLMAN, Jerome I.

'Morality and Determinism': A Reply to Flew. WASSERMANN, Gerhard D.

Alston on Plantinga and Soft Theological Determinism. PIKE, Nelson.

Aristotle's Compatibilism in the *Nicomachean Ethics.* EVERSON, Stephen.

De Finetti's Earliest Works on the Foundations of Probability. VON PLATO, Jan.

An Elementary Proof for Some Semantic Characterizations of Nondeterministic Floyd-Hoare Logic. SAIN, Ildikó.

The Ethical Impulse in Schleiermacher's Early Ethics. CROSSLEY JR, John P.

Free Will, Self-Causation, and Strange Loops. MORDEN, Michael.

Morality and Bad Luck. THOMSON, Judith Jarvis.

Regarding Rich's "Compatibilism Argument" and the 'Ought'-Implies-'Can' Argument. FAWKES, Don.

Soft Determinism and How We Become Responsible for the Past. TÄNNSJÖ, Torbjörn.

Die soziobiologische Obsoletierung des "Reichs der Zwecke". DORSCHEL, Andreas.

Spinoza and Finnish Literature. ELOVAARA, Raili.

Talking Sense About Freedom. WARD, Andrew.

The Notion of Chance and the Metaphysics of P Kanellopoulos (in Greek). MARKAKIS, M.

Two Kinds of Incompatibilism. KANE, Robert.

Zur Frage der Vereinbarkeit von Freiheit und Determinismus. RHEINWALD, Rosemarie.

DETERRENCE

"Finite Deterrence" in *Nuclear Deterrence and Moral Restraint,* FEIVESON, Harold A.

The Death Penalty, Deterrence, and Horribleness: Reply to Michael Davis. REIMAN, Jeffrey.

The Justification of Deterrent Violence. FARRELL, Daniel M.

Kant's Theory of Punishment: Deterrence in its Threat, Retribution in its Execution. BYRD, B Sharon.

Positive Retributivism. TEN, C L.

DEVARAJA, N

Discussion: Professor Devaraja on the Emergence of Facts. PRASAD, Rajendra.

DEVELOPMENT(S)

Man, Science, Humanism: A New Synthesis. FROLOV, Ivan T.

Admonitions to Poland. SZCZEPANSKI, Jan and BYLINA, Maryna.

Business Ethics in Italy: The State of the Art. UNNIA, Mario.

Chinese Axial Age in the Light of Kohlberg's Developmental Logic of Moral Consciousness (in Serbo-Croatian). ROETZ, Heiner.

The Development of Aesthetic Judgment: Analysis of a Genetic-Structuralist Approach. DE MUL, Jos.

Different Conceptions of Stage in Theories of Cognitive and Moral Development. BOOM, Jan.

An International Look at Business Ethics: Britain. MAHONEY, Jack.

La naturaleza y la práctica de una ética del desarrollo. CROCKER, David A.

Neoteny and the Virtues of Childhood. MILLER, Richard B.

Ontogenesi della forma e informazione. FASOLO, Aldo.

Quel développement et pour qui?. PESTIEAU, J.

Recent Developments in European Business Ethics. VAN LUIJK, Henk J L.

Stop or Go: Reflections of Women Managers on Factors Influencing their Career Development. ANDREW, C and CODERRE, C and DENIS, A.

Utilitarianism and Reform: Social Theory and Social Change, 1750-1800. BURNS, J H.

Zum Verhältnis von Entwicklung und Unterentwicklung. HOPFMANN, Arndt.

DEVEREUX, G

Paths Toward a Clearing: Radical Empiricism and Ethnographic Inquiry. JACKSON, Michael.

DEVIANT LOGIC

Neue Entwicklungen im Wahrheitsbegriff. SEUREN, Pieter A M.

DEVLIN, P

Does the Threat of AIDS Create Difficulties for Lord Devlin's Critics?. SCHEDLER, George.

DEWEY

The American Evasion of Philosophy: A Genealogy of Pragmatism. WEST, Cornel.

Classical American Philosophy: Essential Readings and Interpretative Essays. STUHR, John J.

Higher Education: An Arena of Conflicting Philosophies. SPEES, Emil Ray.

Interpreting Education. EDEL, Abraham.

DEWEY

"Dewey" in *Ethics in the History of Western Philosophy*, GOUINLOCK, James.

"An Everyday Aesthetic Impulse: Dewey Revisited" in *Inquiries into Values: The Inaugural Session of the International Society for Value Inquiry*, ZUNIGA, J A.

Danto, Dewey and the Historical End of Art. MITCHELL, Jeff.

Democracy and Schooling: An Essentially Contested Relationship. PEPPERELL, Keith C.

Dewey and Wittgenstein on the Idea of Certainty. EODICE, Alexander R.

Dewey on Religion and History. AUXIER, Randall E.

Dewey's Conception of Growth Reconsidered. PEKARSKY, Daniel.

Does Metaphysics Rest on an Agrarian Foundation? A Deweyan Answer and Critique. MARSOOBIAN, Armen.

Experience and Nature: Teacher as Story Teller. SIMMONS JR, Michael.

From Absolute Idealism to Instrumentalism: The Problem of Dewey's Early Philosophy. WELCHMAN, Jennifer.

The Greatest Metaphysics Ever Told?. ARCILLA, René V.

Greene's Dialectics of Freedom and Dewey's Naturalistic Existential Metaphysics. GARRISON, James W.

John Dewey and Environmental Thought. TAYLOR, Bob Pepperman.

John Dewey, the "Trial" of Leon Trotsky and the Search for Historical Truth. SPITZER, Alan B.

Judgments of Value in John Dewey's Theory of Ethics. CASPARY, William R.

Knowledge as Active, Aesthetic, and Hypothetical. FRISINA, Warren G.

Logic, Language and Dewey: A Student-Teacher Dialectic. PALERMO, James and D'ERASMO, Kate.

Moral Education and a Critical Thinking: The Humanist Perspective. MADIGAN, Tim.

On Being a Dewey Teacher Today. PRAKASH, Madhu Suri.

On Personalism and Education. HART, Richard E.

Philosophy as (Vocational) Education. GARRISON, James W.

Pragmatic Inquiry and Social Conflict: A Critical Reconstruction of Dewey's Model of Democracy. SMILEY, Marion.

Recipes, Cooking, and Conflict: A Response to Heldke's Recipes for Theory. KOCH, Donald F.

The Relation of Dewey's Aesthetics to His Overall Philosophy. BURNETT, Joe R.

Rereading Aristotle and Dewey on Educational Theory: A Deconstruction. PALERMO, James.

Some Remarks on What Happened to John Dewey. FISHER, John.

The Structure and Content of Truth. DAVIDSON, Donald.

What Is the Legacy of Instrumentalism? Rorty's Interpretation of Dewey. GOUINLOCK, James.

Why Dewey Now?. SHUSTERMAN, Richard.

DHARMAKIRTI

Dharmakirti on Criteria of Knowledge. CHINCHORE, Mangala R.

On *Sapaksa*. TILLEMANS, Tom J F.

Post-Udayana Nyaya Reactions to Dharmakirti's Vadanyaya: An Evaluation. CHINCHORE, M.

DIAGNOSIS

Dangerous Diagnostics. NELKIN, Dorothy.

The Little Woman Meets Son of DSM-III. RITCHIE, Karen.

DIAGONAL ARGUMENT

The Diagonal Argument and the Liar. SIMMONS, Keith.

DIAGRAM(S)

An Euler Test for Syllogisms. ARMSTRONG, Robert L and HOWE, Lawrence W.

DIALECTIC

The Dialectic in Journalism: Toward a Responsible Use of Press Freedom. MERRILL, John Calhoun.

The Dialectics of Seeing: Walter Benjamin and the Arcades Project. BUCK-MORSS, Susan.

Hegel, Heraclitus, and Marx's Dialectic. WILLIAMS, Howard.

Husserl und Cohn: Widerspruch, Reflexion, und Telos in Phanomenologie und Dialektik. KLOCKENBUSCH, Reinald.

Impermanence is Buddha-nature: Dōgen's Understanding of Temporality. STAMBAUGH, Joan.

Inwardness and Existence: Subjectivity in/and Hegel, Heidegger, Marx, and Freud. DAVIS, Walter A.

Reclaiming Reality: A Critical Introduction to Contemporary Philosophy. BHASKAR, Roy.

"Analytic/Dialectic" in *Reading Kant*, BRANDT, Reinhard.

"Demonstrative, Dialectical and Sophistic Arguments in the Philosophy of Moses Maimonides" in *Moses Maimonides and His Time*, HYMAN, Arthur.

"Dialectic, Rhetoric and Critique in Aristotle" in *From Metaphysics to Rhetoric*, COULOUBARITSIS, Lambros.

"Dialectical Ethics: A First Look at Sartre's Unpublished Rome Lecture Notes" in *Inquiries into Values: The Inaugural Session of the International Society for Value Inquiry*, BOWMAN, Elizabeth A and STONE, Robert V.

"History as Fact and as Value: The Posthumous Sartre" in *Inquiries into Values: The Inaugural Session of the International Society for Value Inquiry*, FLYNN, Thomas.

"Thomas Aquinas on Dialectics and Rhetoric" in *A Straight Path: Studies in Medieval Philosophy and Culture*, WALLACE, William A.

Acceleration and Restructuring: Dialectics and Problems. LAPIN, Nikolai I.

Actualidad y fecundidad de la filosofía blondeliana. ISASI, Juan M.

Analytical Marxism and Marx's Systematic Dialectical Theory. SMITH, Tony.

Le caractère aporétique de la *Métaphysique* d'Aristote. IRWIN, T H.

A Commentary on Derrida's Reading of Hegel in *Glas*. CRITCHLEY, Simon.

Concerning the Problems Surrounding "Theoretical Consciousness" (in Czechoslovakian). KROH, M.

The Debate Regarding Dialectical Logic in Marx's Economic Writings. SMITH, Tony.

Dialectic and Deliberation in Aristotle's Practical Philosophy. BAYNES, Kenneth.

Dialectic and Inconsistency in Knowledge Acquisition. HAVAS, Katalin G.

The Dialectic of Freedom in Nikolai Berdjaev. IGNATOW, Assen.

Dialectical Contradiction and the Aristotelian Principle of Non-Contradiction (in Czechoslovakian). ZELENY, J.

Dialectical, Rhetorical, and Aristotelian Rhetoric. CONSIGNY, Scott.

Dialectics of a Dialogical Ideal: Studying Down, Studying Sideways and Studying Up. SCHRIJVERS, Joke.

The Dialectics of Peace Education. RAPOPORT, Anatol.

Different Concepts of Dialectics: Methods and Views. KUÇURADI, Ioanna.

Du dialogue référentiel au dialogisme transcendantal: L'itinéraire philosophique de Francis Jacques. GREISCH, Jean.

El empleo del paradigma en Platón, *Politico* 277d-283a. VIGO, Alejandro G.

Gab es eine Dialektische Schule?. DÖRING, Klaus.

Grundprinzipien einer kritischen Dialektik zwischen Kant und Hegel. IDALOVICHI, Israel.

The Historical-Philosophical Change of an Involution Dialectics. IRIMIE, Ioan.

Hobbes's UnAristotelian Political Rhetoric. SORELL, Tom.

Lonergan's Negative Dialectic. KIDDER, Paul.

Lukács, Adorno en de machteloze kritiek. SALMAN, Ton.

Motion and the Dialectical View of the World: On Two Soviet Interpretations of Zeno's Paradoxes. SZÉKELY, Laszlô.

On Dialectical Consistency. ZELENY, Jindrich.

Paraconsistency. URBAS, Igor.

Petrus Damiani—ein Freund der Logik?. BUCHER, Theodor G.

Probleme der Dialektik der sozialistischen Produktionsweise. HEIDLER, Angelika.

Schelling's Critique of Hegel and the Beginnings of Marxian Dialectics. LAWRENCE, Joseph P (trans) and FRANK, Manfred.

Science, Technology, and Society: Considerations of Method. BECKWITH, Guy V.

Some Aspects of Medical Hermeneutics: The Role of Dialectic and Narrative. LOCK, James D.

The Dialectics of the Unity of Linearity and Non-linearity of Physical Processes (in Czechoslovakian). GOTT, V S.

Varieties of Ecological Dialectics. SIMON, Thomas W.

Ways Leading to Bergson's Notion of the "Perpetual Present". KEBEDE, Messay.

Wirtschaftslehre als Heilslehre. ALEKSANDROWICZ, Dariusz.

DIALECTICAL MATERIALISM

see also Historical Materialism

Dialectical Materialism and Logical Pragmatism: On J E McClellan's "Logical Pragmatism and Dialectical Materialism". PANOVA, Elena.

Ergebnisse und Probleme der Entwicklung des historischen Materialismus. STIEHLER, Gottfried.

Filosofi e filosofia nell'URSS della perestrojka. MASTROIANNI, Giovanni.

Materialist Dialectic and Critique of Philosophical Irrationalism (in Czechoslovakian). JANKOV, M.

Philosophical Questions of Mathematics in *Anti-Dühring*. PANFILOV, V A.

Philosophie und Lehre. HAGER, Nina.

Der Widerspruch zwischen Materiellem und Ideellem und der dialektische Materiebegriff. GEBHARDT, Birgit.

DIALOGUE(S)

Informal Logic: A Handbook for Critical Argumentation. WALTON, Douglas N.

DIRECTION
Feminist Directions in Medical Ethics. WARREN, Virginia L.

DIRECTIVE(S)
Advance Directives in Medicine. HACKLER, Chris (ed).

DISABILITY
Toward a Feminist Theory of Disability. WENDELL, Susan.

DISAGREEMENT(S)
Could Ideal Observers Disagree?: A Reply to Taliaferro. CARSON, Thomas L.

DISCIPLINE(S)
"On the Emergence of Scientific Disciplines" in *Scientific Knowledge Socialized,* LAITKO, Hubert.
Aesthetics in Discipline-Based Art Education. CRAWFORD, Donald W.
An Alternative View of Professionalization. SMITH, Timothy H.
The Antithesis. BAUER, Henry.
The Changing Image of Art Education: Theoretical Antecedents of Discipline-Based Art Education. SMITH, Ralph A.
Clodovis Boff on the Discipline of Theology. CUNNINGHAM, David S.
Philosophy of Mathematics as a Theoretical and Applied Discipline. BARABASHEV, A G.
Recent Interpretations of Early Christian Asceticism. YOUNG, Robin Darling.
The Synthesis: A Sociopolitical Critique of the Liberal Professions. ROSSIDES, Daniel.
The Thesis. MINDER, Thomas.

DISCLOSURE(S)
Dasein's Disclosedness. HAUGELAND, John.
The Familiar and the Strange: On the Limits of *Praxis* in the Early Heidegger. FELL, Joseph P.
Poetic Saying as Beckoning: The Opening of Hölderlin's *Germanien.* MALY, Kenneth and EMAD, Parvis.

DISCOURSE
Margins of Political Discourse. DALLMAYR, Fred R.
Philosophical Issues in Education. HAMM, Cornel M.
Towards a Critique of Foucault. GANE, Mike (ed).
Unruly Practices: Power, Discourse and Gender in Contemporary Social Theory. FRASER, Nancy.
"Beyond Aporia" in *Post-Structuralist Classics,* KOFMAN, Sarah.
"Unlearning to Not Speak". PAGET, M A.
Bach as a Paradigm in Aesthetic Discourse. ZIMMERMANN, Jörg.
Bioethics as Civic Discourse. JENNINGS, Bruce.
Das Gestell and *L'écriture*: The Discourse of Expropriation in Heidegger and Derrida. RADLOFF, Bernhard.
Discorso meta-forico e discorso meta-fisico: Heidegger. PELLECCHIA, Pasquale.
Discourse Ethics and Civil Society. COHEN, Jean.
Economic Participation: The Discourse of Work. CHMIELEWSKI, Philip J.
Fallacies are Common. JASON, Gary.
The Gadamer-Habermas Debate Revisited: The Question of Ethics. KELLY, Michael.
Human Noises. STEWART, Donald.
Impartial Application of Moral and Legal Norms: A Contribution to Discourse Ethics. GÜNTHER, Klaus.
In Heidegger's Wake: Belonging to the Discourse of the "Turn". SCHMIDT, Dennis J.
Intuición práctica y ejemplo retórico. SCHOLLMEIER, Paul and FEMENÍAS, María Luisa.
Modal Subordination and Pronominal Anaphora in Discourse. ROBERTS, Craige.
On Explaining Political Disagreement: The Notion of an Essentially Contested Concept. MASON, Andrew.
La parole du philosophe éthicien est-elle crédible?. LEGAULT, Georges A.
Political Theory as an Object of Discourse. WHITE, Roger.
Postmodern Conditions: Rethinking Public Education. KIZILTAN, Mustafa Ü and BAIN, William J and CANIZARES, Anita.
Le problème du discours sur l'indicible chez Plotin. O'MEARA, Dominic J.
Reading Africa Through Foucault: V Y Mudimbe's Re-affirmation of the Subject. DIAWARA, Manthia.
Rorty and Nietzsche: Some Elective Affinities. SHAW, Daniel.

DISCOVERY
Differences in Style as a Way of Probing the Context of Discovery. GAVROGLU, Kostas.
Discovery as the Context of Any Scientific Justification. VAN PEURSEN, C A.
Discovery Logics. NICKLES, Thomas.
Hypothetical and Inductive Heuristics. KLEINER, Scott A.

Methods of Conceptual Change in Science: Imagistic and Analogical Reasoning. NERSESSIAN, Nancy J.
Serendipity as a Source of Evolutionary Progress in Science. KANTOROVICH, Aharon and NE'EMAN, Yuval.

DISCRETION
Della scommessa legislativa sulla discrezionalità dei giudici. MARINI, Gaetano.

DISCRIMINATION
AIDS and the Good Society. ILLINGWORTH, Patricia.
Affirmative Action and the Doctrine of Double Effect. COONEY, William.
Business Ethics, Fetal Protection Policies, and Discrimination Against Women in the Workplace. QUINN, John F.
Discrimination Against Pregnant Employees: An Analysis of Arbitration and Human Rights Tribunal Decisions in Canada. ANDIAPPAN, P and REAVLEY, M.
Opening the Door to Moral Education. MC GOVERN, Edythe M.
What is Wrong With Reverse Discrimination?. HETTINGER, Edwin C.

DISCURSIVE
Narrative Experiments: The Discursive Authority of Science and Technology. ORMISTON, Gayle L.
"Aesthetic discursivity" in *Cultural Hermeneutics of Modern Art: Essays in Honor of Jan Aler,* WILLEMS, Eldert.

DISCURSIVE LOGIC
An Overview of Paraconsistent Logic in the 80s. DA COSTA, Newton C A and MARCONI, Diego.

DISCUSSION(S)
Limited Inc. DERRIDA, Jacques.
Managing Philosophical Discussions. KYLE, Judy A.
Mind and Brain on Bergen Street. SILVER, Ruth.

DISEASE
The 'Theology' of the Hippocratic Treatise On the Sacred Disease. VAN DER EIJK, P J.
Human Gene Therapy: Why Draw a Line?. ANDERSON, W French.
The Little Woman Meets Son of DSM-III. RITCHIE, Karen.

DISJUNCTION
Systems of Logic. MARTIN, Norman M.
The Equivalence of the Disjunction and Existence Properties for Modal Arithmetic. FRIEDMAN, Harvey.
The Property (HD) in Intermediate Logics: A Partial Solution of a Problem of H Ono. MINARI, Pierluigi.

DISORDER(S)
"St Augustine" in *Ethics in the History of Western Philosophy,* LOSONCY, Thomas.
Bipolar Disorders: The Unifying Possibilities of Friendship and Feminist Theory. ALSTON, Kal.

DISPOSITION(S)
The Nature of Man in Early Stoic Philosophy. REESOR, Margaret E.
Are Physical Properties Dispositions?. AVERILL, Edward Wilson.
Are Virtues No More Than Dispositions to Obey Moral Rules?. SCHALLER, Walter E.
Filling in Space. BLACKBURN, Simon.
On Traits as Dispositions: An Alleged Truism. VAN HEERDEN, Jaap and SMOLENAARS, Anton J.

DISPUTATION
Are There Really Perennial Philosophical Disputes?. SMITH, Joseph Wayne.

DISPUTE(S)
Ethical Dilemmas and the Disputing Process: Organizations and Societies. MATHEWS, M Cash.
On Explaining Political Disagreement: The Notion of an Essentially Contested Concept. MASON, Andrew.

DISSENT
"The Alternative of Dissent" in *The Tanner Lectures on Human Values, Volume X,* MUGUERZA, Javier.

DISSERTATIONS
Kant: An Index to Theses and Dissertations Accepted by Universities in Canada and the US, 1879-1985. GABEL, Gernot U.
The Doctoral Dissertation of Karl Marx. TEEPLE, G.

DISSONANCE
Cognitive Dissonance and Scepticism. HOLCOMB III, Harmon R.

DISTANCE
"Motion and Change of Distance" in *Cause, Mind, and Reality: Essays Honoring C B Martin,* NERLICH, Graham.

DURKHEIM

Emile Durkheim and Provinces of Ethics. CLADIS, Mark S.

Lévy-Bruhl et Durkheim: Notes biographiques en marge d'une correspondance—Lettres à L Lévy-Bruhl (1894-1915). MERLLIÉ, Dominique and DURKHEIM, Emile.

The Theme of Civilization and its Discontents in Durkheim's *Division of Labor.* MESTROVIC, Stjepan G.

DUTCH

Effecten en gevolgen van wetenschapsbeleid voor de filosofiebeoefening aan de Nederlandse universiteiten. VAN DER MEULEN, Barend and LEYDESDORFF, Loet.

Het gewicht van de geschiedenis: Over het waardenprobleem in de geschiedwetenschap. LORENZ, Chris.

On the Early Dutch Reception of the *Tractatus-Theologico Politicus.* VAN BUNGE, Wiep.

The Dutch Words *'besef'* and *'beseffen'* (in Dutch). VERHOEVEN, C.

Verburg over Dooyeweerd. STELLINGWERFF, J.

DUTTON, M

Aelred of Rievaulx and the "Lignum Vitae" of Bonaventure: A Reappraisal. O'CONNELL, Patrick F.

DUTY(-TIES)

see also Obligation(s)

The Foundations of Morality. HAZLITT, Henry.

"Duties and Excusing Conditions" in *Inquiries into Values: The Inaugural Session of the International Society for Value Inquiry,* SUTTLE, Bruce.

"Duty or Virtue?" as a Metaethical Question. BRONIAK, Christopher.

Are There Inalienable Rights?. NELSON, John O.

Caring for Frail Elderly Parents: Past Parental Sacrifices and the Obligations of Adult Children. WICCLAIR, Mark.

The Divestiture Puzzle Dissolved. SHINER, Roger A.

The Duty to Rescue and the Slippery Slope Problem. SMITH, Patricia.

Equal Opportunity. WELLMAN, Carl.

Ethik als Grundwissenschaft: Handeln aus Klugheit, Neigung, Pflicht, Ehrfurcht, Mitleid?. FUNKEE, Gerhard.

Das Gesetz oder das Gute? II, Teil: Alleiniges Prinzip des sittlich guten Willens. SALA, Giovanni B.

Gratitude and the Duties of Grown Children Towards Their Aging Parents. GERBER, Rona M.

Kantian Ethics Today. FRANKENA, William K.

Kantian Strict Duties of Benevolence. EGGERMAN, Richard W.

Moral Rights and Duties in Wicked Legal Systems. TEN, C L.

The *Munus* of Transmitting Human Life: A New Approach to *Humanae Vitae.* SMITH, Janet E.

Practical Solutions. MIDGLEY, Mary.

A Reconsideration of Kant's Treatment of Duties to Oneself. PATON, Margaret.

Rights, Justice, and Duties to Provide Assistance: A Critique of Regan's Theory of Rights. JAMIESON, Dale.

Struttura dell'azione e compito pubblico del cristianesimo. POSSENTI, Vittorio.

The View from Above and Below. TALIAFERRO, Charles.

Virtues, Rules and the Foundations of Ethics. CLOWNEY, David.

When is Lying Morally Permissible? Casuistical Reflections on the Game Analogy, Self-Defense, Social Contract Ethics. VAN WYK, Robert N.

DWORKIN, A

Pornography as Representation: Aesthetic Considerations. GRACYK, Theodore A.

DWORKIN, R

"Comment: Legal Theory and the Problem of Sense" in *Issues in Contemporary Legal Philosophy: The Influence of H L A Hart,* GAVISON, Ruth.

"Comment: Legal Theory and the Problem of Sense" in *Issues in Contemporary Legal Philosophy: The Influence of H L A Hart,* HART, H L A.

A *Coup d'État* in Law's Empire: Dworkin's Hercules Meets Atlas. PEERENBOOM, Randall P.

Individual Rights, Collective Interests, Public Law, and American Politics. GEORGE, Robert P.

The Inequality of Markets. ROGERSON, Kenneth F.

Integrity and Judicial Discretion. KASHIYAMA, Paul.

Judges Taken Too Seriously: Professor Dworkin's Views on Jurisprudence. TROPER, Michel.

Liberalism, Distributive Subjectivism, and Equal Opportunity for Welfare. ARNESON, Richard J.

Liberalism, Liberty, and Neutrality. DE MARNEFFE, Peter.

Pragmatism and Precedent: A Response to Dworkin. SULLIVAN, Michael.

Statutory Interpretation and the Counterfactual Test for Legislative Intention. LEE, Win-Chiat.

DYING

see also Death

Autobiographical Reflections—Eric Voegelin. SANDOZ, Ellis (ed).

Medical Ethics: Essays on Abortion and Euthanasia. BARRY, Robert L.

Patterns of Transcendence: Religion, Death, and Dying. CHIDESTER, David.

"Advance Directives and the Denial of Death: Should the Conflict be Resolved?" in *Advance Directives in Medicine,* YOUNGNER, Stuart J.

On Dying as a Process. FELDMAN, Fred.

DYNAMIC LOGIC

Arithmetical Completeness Versus Relative Completeness. GRABOWSKI, Michal.

A Finite Model Theorem for the Propositional μ-Calculus. KOZEN, Dexter.

Interpretation of Dynamic Logic in the Relational Calculus. ORLOWSKA, Ewa.

DYNAMICS

Aesthetic Function and Dynamics of Meaningful Unification (in Czechoslovakian). JANKOVIC, Milan.

Fatalism and Time. BERNSTEIN, Mark.

DYNAMISM

Kants Theorie der Materie und ihre Wirkung auf die zeitgenössische Chemie. CARRIER, Martin.

EARLE, W

"Reply to Earle's "The Evanescent Authority of Philosophy"" in *Dialectic and Contemporary Science,* HARRIS, Errol E.

EARTH

Reading the Mind of God: In Search of the Principle of Universality. TREFIL, James.

EAST EUROPEAN

A Sweet and Sour Victory in Eastern Europe. SZAKOLCZAI, Arpád and HORVÁTH, Ágnes.

EBELING, G

Conscience and the Reality of God: An Essay on the Experiential Foundations of Religious Knowledge. STATEN, John C.

ECKERSLEY, R

Recovering Evolution: A Reply to Eckersley and Fox. BOOKCHIN, Murray.

ECKHART

"Mysticism and Transgression: Derrida and Meister Eckhart" in *Derrida and Deconstruction,* CAPUTO, John D.

ECLECTICISM

Research Perspectives and the Anomalous Status of Modern Ecology. HAGEN, Joel B.

ECO, U

Orden-desorden, a propósito de *Il nome della rosa.* CASTRO, Edgardo.

Philosophical Laughter: Vichian Remarks on Umberto Eco's *The Name of the Rose.* VERENE, Donald Phillip.

Searle ed Eco sulla metafora. BURKHARDT, Armin.

ECOLOGY

Ecological Communication. LUHMANN, Niklas.

Foundations of Environmental Ethics. HARGROVE, Eugene C.

Nature in Asian Tradition of Thought: Essays in Environmental Philosophy. CALLICOTT, J Baird (ed).

Social Philosophy and Ecological Scarcity. LEE, Keekok.

"The Asian Traditions as a Conceptual Resource for Environmental Philosophy" in *Nature in Asian Tradition of Thought: Essays in Environmental Philosophy,* CALLICOTT, J Baird and AMES, Roger T.

"Epilogue: On the Relation of Idea and Action" in *Nature in Asian Tradition of Thought: Essays in Environmental Philosophy,* CALLICOTT, J Baird and AMES, Roger T.

"Marxism and Ecology" in *Inquiries into Values: The Inaugural Session of the International Society for Value Inquiry,* FISCHER, Norman.

"The Metaphysical Implications of Ecology" in *Nature in Asian Tradition of Thought: Essays in Environmental Philosophy,* CALLICOTT, J Baird.

A Game-Theoretical Analysis of Ecological Problems (in Hungarian). VAN ASPEREN, Gertrud M.

Agricultural Technology, Wealth, and Responsibility. WUNDERLICH, Gene.

Body-Vessel-Matrix: Co-creative Images of Synergetic Universe. CARTER, Nancy Corson.

La conciencia ecológica como conciencia moral. SOSA, Nicolás M.

Crisi ecologica e concezione cristiana di Dio. SALVATI, Giuseppe M.

Descartes' Legacy and Deep Ecology. MILLER, Peter.

Ecological Marketing Strategy for Toni Yogurts in Switzerland. DYLLICK, Thomas.

ECOLOGY

Ecologische communicatie door disciplinering van de moraal. STUY, Johan.

Entropy and Information in Evolving Biological Systems. BROOKS, Daniel R (and others).

Human Ecology. JUNGEN, Britta and EGNEUS, Hans.

Is Ecology Transcending Both Marxism and Christianity?. SKOLIMOWSKI, Henryk.

Marxism, the Ecological Crisis and a Master's Attitude to Nature (in Czechoslovakian). ZNOJ, M.

Marxist Critical Theory, Contradictions, and Ecological Succession. CATTON, Philip.

Mens en aarde: Het ecofilosofisch dilemma in het werk van Ludwig Klages. WITZORECK, Kris.

Metaphysical Implications from Physics and Ecology. WITTBECKER, Alan E.

The Metaphysical Transition in Farming: From the Newtonian-Mechanical to the Eltonian Ecological. CALLICOTT, J Baird.

Niklas Luhmann over ecologische communicatie. BALLIU, Julien.

On the Connection Between Ethology and Ecology (in Czechoslovakian). KAMARYT, J and STEINDL, R.

Philosophy and the Devastation of the Earth (in Czechoslovakian). KOLARSKY, R and SMAJS, J.

Philosophy of Regional Cooperation in the Solution of Global Ecological Problems (in Czechoslovakian). MEZRICKY, V.

The Power and the Promise of Ecological Feminism. WARREN, Karen J.

Il radicalismo negli Stati Uniti degli anni '80: l'anarco-ecologismo di Murray Bookchin. DONNO, A.

The Relevance of Deep Ecology to the Third World. JOHNS, David M.

Research Perspectives and the Anomalous Status of Modern Ecology. HAGEN, Joel B.

Scarcity and the Turn from Economics to Ecology. BENDER, Frederic L.

Sport Hunting: Moral or Immoral?. VITALI, Theodore R.

The Concept of "Oikiá" in Classic Greek Philosophy (in Czechoslovakian). MRAZ, M.

The Need of Philosophy and Current Ecological Crisis (in Czechoslovakian). KOLARSKY, R.

The Uniqueness and Value of Terrestrial Nature (in Czechoslovakian). SMAJS, J.

Varieties of Ecological Dialectics. SIMON, Thomas W.

ECONOMETRICS

Nature's Capacities and their Measurement. CARTWRIGHT, Nancy.

ECONOMICS

Axioms of Cooperative Decision Making. MOULIN, Hervé.

Collected Works, Volume 30, Marx: 1861-1863. MARX, Karl.

Collected Works, Volume 31, Marx: 1861-1863. MARX, Karl.

Foundations of Environmental Ethics. HARGROVE, Eugene C.

Lectures on Game Theory. AUMANN, Robert J.

Liberty and Culture: Essays on the Idea of a Free Society. MACHAN, Tibor R.

More Heat than Light: Economics as Social Physics, Physics as Nature's Economics. MIROWSKI, Philip.

Philosophy of Economics: On the Scope of Reason in Economic Inquiry. ROY, Subroto.

Property, Power, and Public Choice: An Inquiry into Law and Economics—Second Ed. SCHMID, A Allan.

Readings from Karl Marx. SAYER, Derek (ed).

Scarcity and Modernity. XENOS, Nicholas.

"The Conflation of Productivity and Efficiency in Economics and Economic History": A Comment. NYE, John Vincent.

Acceleration and Restructuring: Dialectics and Problems. LAPIN, Nikolai I.

Adam Smith's "Theory" of Justice: Business Ethics Themes in The Wealth of Nations. DE VRIES, Paul H.

Adam Smith's Concept of the Social System. COKER, Edward W.

Cooter and Rappoport on the Normative. DAVIS, John B.

La critique marxienne de la religion. TOSEL, André.

The Debate Regarding Dialectical Logic in Marx's Economic Writings. SMITH, Tony.

The Economic Efficiency and Equity of Abortion. MEEKS, Thomas J.

An Economic Newcomb Problem. BROOME, John.

Economic Participation: The Discourse of Work. CHMIELEWSKI, Philip J.

Economic Relations and their Reflection in Working People's Consciousness under Socialism (in Czechoslovakian). HELLER, J.

Economics and Hermeneutics. BERGER, Lawrence A.

Economics and Psychology: Estranged Bedfellows or Fellow Travellers? A Critical Synthesis. SASSOWER, Raphael.

Efficiency, Effectiveness and Legitimation: Criteria for the Evaluation of Norms. UUSITALO, Liisa.

The Eminently Practical Mr Hume or Still Relevant After All These Years.

DAVLANTES, Nancy.

Euthanasia, Ethics and Economics. HÄYRY, Heta and HÄYRY, Matti.

The Future of Psychiatry. MICHELS, Robert and MARKOWITZ, John C.

Hayek and the Interpretive TUrn. MADISON, G B.

The Ideology of Social Justice in Economic Justice For All. MURNION, William E.

The Inefficiency of Some Efficiency Comparisons: A Reply to Nye. SARAYDAR, Edward.

A Legal and Economic Analysis of Insider Trading: Establishing an Appropriate Sphere of Regulation. SALBU, Steven R.

Madison's Party Press Essays. SHEEHAN, Colleen A.

Man in the System of Socioeconomic Values. DUGIN, V N.

The Modal View of Economic Models. RAPPAPORT, Steven.

Moral Conflict in Public Policy. GORDVITZ, Samuel.

The New Economics of Medicine: Special Challenges for Psychiatry. MORREIM, E Haavi.

A Note on the Teaching of Ethics in the MBA Macroeconomics Course. ABELL, John D.

Nozick on Self-Esteem. MASON, Andrew.

Ökonomische Soziologie in Nowosibirst (Literaturbericht). SEGERT, Astrid.

El pensamiento económico de Hegel: Escritos recientes. CORDUA, Carla.

The Poverty of Opulence. KOLENDA, Konstantin.

Private and Public Preferences. KURAN, Timur.

A Rationale for the Support of the Medium-Sized Family Farm. DANIELS, Thomas L.

Resource X: Sirkin and Smith on a Neglected Economic Staple. DE VRIES, Paul H.

Scarcity and the Turn from Economics to Ecology. BENDER, Frederic L.

Schumpeters Theorie der Wirtschaftsentwicklung in philosophischer Sicht. RUBEN, Peter.

Soziale Sicherheit—Triebkraft ökonomischen Wachstums bei der Gestaltung der entwickelten sozialistischen Gesellschaft. HAHN, Toni and WINKLER, Gunnar.

Spinoza et les problèmes d'une théorie de la societé commerçante. BLOM, Hans W.

Wert und Würde der Arbeit in Laborem Exercens (in Polish). JUROS, Helmut.

What Restoring Leninism Means. DAHM, Helmut and SWIDERSKI, E M (trans).

ECONOMY

The Moral Case for the Free Market Economy: A Philosophical Argument. MACHAN, Tibor R.

The Inequality of Markets. ROGERSON, Kenneth F.

Philosophy Cannot Be Implemented in Socialism and Its Economy (in Czechoslovakian). NIKOLIC, P D.

Scarcity and Setting the Boundaries of Political Economy. SASSOWER, Raphael.

The Seventieth Anniversary of the October Revolution. SZCZEPANSKI, Jan and PETROWICZ, Lech (trans).

Why is the Bishops' Letter on the US Economy So Unconvincing?. REECE, William S.

Wirtschaftslehre als Heilslehre. ALEKSANDROWICZ, Dariusz.

ECOSYSTEM(S)

Ecological Communication. LUHMANN, Niklas.

Ecosystem Moral Considerability: A Reply to Cahen. SALTHE, Stanley N and SALTHE, Barbara M.

ECTOGENESIS

Is Pregnancy Necessary: Feminist Concerns About Ectogenesis. MURPHY, Julien S.

ECUMENISM

"Krise des Fortschritts—Umkehr zur Zukunft": Zu einigen Aspekten religiöser Welt-und Fortschrittssicht. HEGENBARTH, Siegfried.

EDUCATION

see also Moral Education

"The Son of Apollo": Themes of Plato. WOODBRIDGE, Frederick J E.

Accountability in Education: A Philosophical Inquiry. WAGNER, Robert B.

Capitalist Schools: Explanation and Ethics in Radical Studies of Schooling. LISTON, Daniel P.

Education, Movement and the Curriculum: A Philosophic Enquiry. ARNOLD, Peter J.

El Concepto de Materia al Comienzo de la Escuela Franciscana de Paris. PEREZ ESTEVEZ, Antonio.

Essays in Philosophy and Education. STOTT, Laurence J.

Good Lives and Moral Education. SIMPSON, Evan.

Interpreting Education. EDEL, Abraham.

The Nature of Social and Educational Inquiry: Empiricism versus Interpretation. SMITH, John K.

EDUCATION

Philosophical Issues in Education. HAMM, Cornel M.

A Philosophy of Music Education (Second Edition). REIMER, Bennett.

Reading Curriculum Theory: The Development of a New Hermeneutic. REYNOLDS, William M.

Rousseau: Selections. CRANSTON, Maurice (ed).

The Voice of Liberal Learning: Michael Oakeshott on Education. FULLER, Timothy (ed).

Wesen, Freiheit und Bildung des Menschen. HAGER, Fritz-Peter.

"The Humanities and the Modern Mind" in *Mind, Value and Culture: Essays in Honor of E M Adams,* NORD, Warren.

"The Teaching of Values in Higher Education" in *Inquiries into Values: The Inaugural Session of the International Society for Value Inquiry,* GINSBERG, Robert.

"Technicism, Education, and Living a Human Life" in *Inquiries into Values: The Inaugural Session of the International Society for Value Inquiry,* TAYLOR, Michael.

"Vaticinal Visions and Pedagogical Prescriptions" in *Mind, Value and Culture: Essays in Honor of E M Adams,* HOOKER, Michael.

The "Evils" of a Technologized Psychology in Teacher Education. ORTON, Robert E.

"Some Factors Influencing the Success of Philosophical Discussion in the Classroom. WHALLEY, Michael.

"What is an Adventure?". REMBERT, Ron.

"What's Real": A Dialogue. BIELFELDT, Dennis.

Achieving the Right Distance. TAUBMAN, Peter M.

The Acquisition of the Ostensive Lexicon: A Reply to Professor Place. STEMMER, Nathan.

The Adolescent's Rights to Freedom, Care and Enlightenment. BANDMAN, Bertram.

Aesthetic Education: A Small Manifesto. ABBS, Peter.

The Aesthetic-Artistic Domain, Criticism, and Teaching. CHAMBERS, John H.

Against Skills. HART, W.

Akrasia and Animal Rights: Philosophy in the British Primary School. COSTELLO, Patrick J M.

La alegoría de la caverna y su sentido. PEREZ RUIZ, F.

An Alternative View of Professionalization. SMITH, Timothy H.

Anna Maria van Schurman's verhouding tot de wetenschap. ROOTHAAN, Angela and VAN ECK, Caroline.

An Appeal for Total Intellectual Openness. AVIRAM, Roni.

An Application of Bloom's Taxonomy to the Teaching of Business Ethics. REEVES, M Francis.

The Apprenticeship Model: What We Can Learn from Gareth Matthews. SHEFFER, Susannah.

An Aristotelian Theory of Moral Development. TOBIN, Bernadette M.

Art, Education, and Life-Issues. MC FEE, Graham.

Artistic Learning: What and Where Is It?. WOLF, Dennie.

Atomic Energy and Moral Glue. HOLLIS, Martin.

Beauty in Design and Pictures: Idealism and Aesthetic Education. STANKIEWICZ, Mary Ann.

Benne's Plato and the Theater of Ideas: Response to Benne. OWEN, David.

Bipolar Disorders: The Unifying Possibilities of Friendship and Feminist Theory. ALSTON, Kal.

Building for Democracy: Organic Architecture in Relation to Progressive Education. ROCHE, John F.

Business Ethics and Business Education: A Report from a Regional State University. CASTRO, Barry.

Call to Coalition: A Response to Selman and Ross. MC CLELLAN, James E.

Can a Political Theory of Education Be Objective?. BAK, Nelleke.

Chesterton's Philosophy of Education. HALDANE, John.

The Child as Craftsman. FELDMAN, David Henry.

The Child-As-Philosopher: A Critique of the Presuppositions of Piagetian Theory. LEVINE, Shellie-helane.

Childhood's End: The Age of Responsibility. FRIQUEGNON, Marie-Loui.

Children's Philosophy—Or: Is Motivation for Doing Philosophy a Pseudo-Problem?. MARTENS, Ekkehard.

The Closing of the Professorial Mind: A Meditation on Plato and Allan Bloom. SILLIMAN, Matt.

Cognitive Apprenticeship Teaching the Craft of Reading, Writing and Mathematics. COLLINS, Allan and BROWN, John Seeley and NEWMAN, Susan E.

A Comparison of the Ethical Values of Business Faculty and Students: How Different Are They?. HARRIS, James R.

Computer Programming As a Vehicle for Teaching Thinking Skills. NICKERSON, Raymond S.

Concept Acquisition and Ostensive Learning: A Response to Professor Stemmer. PLACE, Ullin T.

Contexts and Essences: Indoctrination Revisited. SNOOK, Ivan.

Controlling the Classroom Clamor: A Few Techniques to Facilitate Philosophical Discourse. SILVER, Ruth E.

Couples, Canons, and the Uncouth: Spenser-and-Milton in Educational Theory. PATTERSON, Annabel.

Creating, Experiencing, Sense-Making: Art Worlds in Schools. GREENE, Maxine.

Critical Children: Philosophy for the Young. COLES, Martin.

Critical Thinking and Moral Education. WEINSTEIN, Mark.

Critical Thinking as Transfer: Reconstructive Integration of Otherwise Discrete Interpretations of Experience. BRELL JR, Carl D.

A Critique of Critical Thinking. HATCHER, Donald.

A Critique of the Deconstructionist Account of Gender Equity and Education. PIETIG, Jeanne.

Crossing the Boundaries: Educational Thought and Gender Equity. LEACH, Mary and DAVIES, Bronwyn.

The Dangers of Over-Philosophication—Reply to Arcilla and Nicholson. RORTY, Richard.

Das Problem der Psychologischen Hinführung zur Bildung der reifen und religiösen Persönlichkeit (in Polish). BAZYLAK, Jozef and BIELECKI, Jan.

Democracy and Pragmatism in Curriculum Development. WALKER, J C.

Democracy and Schooling: An Essentially Contested Relationship. PEPPERELL, Keith C.

Democracy and Technology. MARGONIS, Frank.

Democracy, Education, and Sport. ARNOLD, Peter J.

Dewey's Conception of Growth Reconsidered. PEKARSKY, Daniel.

The Dialectics of Peace Education. RAPOPORT, Anatol.

Different Conceptions of Stage in Theories of Cognitive and Moral Development. BOOM, Jan.

The Dilemma of "Relevance" in the Philosophy of Education. BURBULES, Nicholas C.

Dilemma of M Oakeshott: Oakeshott's Treatment of Equality of Opportunity in Education and His Political Philosophy. WILLIAMS, Kevin.

Directive Teaching, Indoctrination, and the Values Education of Children. PHILLIPS, D C.

Doing Philosophy with Children. ALLEN, Terry.

Edification, Conversation, and Narrative: Rortyan Motifs for Philosophy of Education. ARCILLA, René V.

Edith Stein as Educator. OBEN, Freda M.

La educación ética: una asignatura pendiente. LAGO BORNSTEIN, Juan Carlos.

Educating for Democracy: Charles W Eliot and the Differentiated Curriculum. PRESKILL, Stephen.

Education and Philosophy. WOODBRIDGE, Frederick J E.

Education and Wittgenstein's Philosophy. HAMLYN, D W.

Education for Sexism: A Theoretical Analysis of the Sex/Gender Bias in Education. DAVIES, Bronwyn.

The Education of Taste. GOLDMAN, Alan H.

Educational Reform Through Philosophy for Children. SPLITTER, Laurance J.

Educational Theories: Ideas of Things to Do. CHAMBLISS, J J.

The Educational Theory of Mary Sheldon Barnes: Inquiry Learning as Indoctrination in History Education. MC ANINCH, Stuart A.

The Effect of the *Pixie* Program on Logical and Moral Reasoning. SCHLEIFER, Michael and LEBUIS, Pierre and CARON, Anita.

Effecten en gevolgen van wetenschapsbeleid voor de filosofiebeoefening aan de Nederlandse universiteiten. VAN DER MEULEN, Barend and LEYDESDORFF, Loet.

An Elementary Conception of Time. AULT JR, Charles R.

Emerson, Whitman, and Conceptual Art. LEONARD, George J.

Engaging the New Literacy: A "Way In" to Philosophy of Education. KOHLI, Wendy.

Equal Opportunity *Is* Equal Education (within Limits). HOWE, Kenneth R.

Equal Opportunity or Equal Education?. BURBULES, Nicholas C.

Equality of Educational Opportunity as Equality of Educational Outcomes. HOWE, Kenneth R.

Equality of Opportunity as the Noble Lie. ANDREW, Edward.

Ethics in Education: A Comparative Study. LANE, Michael S and SCHAUPP, Dietrich.

Ethics Instruction and the Constitution. HERNDON, James F.

The Ethics of Teaching Ethics. WAITHE, Mary Ellen and OZAR, David T.

Evaluation of a Philosophy for Children Project in Hawaii. MEEHAN, Kenneth A.

Excellence and the Pursuit of Ideas. BRANN, Eva.

Experience and Nature: Teacher as Story Teller. SIMMONS JR, Michael.

Explaining the Persistence of Irrelevance. MC ANINCH, Amy.

The False Ontology of School Climate Effects. MILLER, Steven I and FREDERICKS, Janet.

EDUCATION

Philosophy, Children and Teaching Philosophy. HART, Richard E.

Philosophy: A Key to the Deaf Mind. GEISSER, Maura J.

Physicalism, Realism and Education: A Functionalist Approach. RAINER, Valina.

Plato's Divided Line: A Dramatistic Interpretation. BENNE, Kenneth D.

Plato, Inquiry, and Painting. MORGAN, Michael L.

Platonic Education. REDFIELD, James M.

Postmodern Conditions: Rethinking Public Education. KIZILTAN, Mustafa Ü and BAIN, William J and CAÑIZARES, Anita.

Practical Arguments and Situational Appreciation in Teaching. PENDLEBURY, Shirley.

The Practice of Philosophy for Children in Austria: How Can Children Think Philosophically?. CAMHY, Daniela G.

The Practice of Philosophy in the Elementary School Classroom. WHALLEY, Michael J.

Preparation for Life in Peace—Future Perspectives. SUCHODOLSKI, Bogdan.

Professionalization and the Moral Jeopardy of Teaching. BOYD, Dwight.

Psychoeducational Assessment Practices for the Learning Disabled: A *Philosophical Analysis*. DURAN, Jane.

Qué hacer con los textos. CASTAÑARES, Wenceslao.

A Question of Ethics: Developing Information System Ethics. COHEN, Eli.

A Questionable Resurrection. HESLEP, Robert D.

The Rational Woman. SIMONS, Martin.

Rationality and Artistry in Teaching. BEYER, Landon E.

Rationality, Self-Esteem and Autonomy through Collaborative Enquiry. LANE, Neil R.

Reading and the Process of Reading. WINCH, Christopher.

A Real-Life Brain. HAMRICK, William S.

Religious Upbringing and Rational Autonomy. LAURA, Ronald S and LEAHY, Michael.

Remarks On Teaching "Barefoot" Philosophy. LOECK, Gisela.

Reply to Ward's "Philosophical Functionalism". DOUBLE, Richard.

Rereading Aristotle and Dewey on Educational Theory: A Deconstruction. PALERMO, James.

Research, Myths and Expectations: New Challenges for Management Educators. GRONDIN, Deirdre.

Response to Bilow: Future Persons and the Justification of Education. SCHRAG, Francis.

Response to Feinberg's "Foundationalism and Recent Critiques of Education". SCHRAG, Francis.

Response to Francis Schrag's "Response to Feinberg's 'Foundationalism and Recent Critiques of Education'". FEINBERG, Walter.

Response to Professor Feinberg's Presidential Address: A Role for Philosophy of Education in Intercultural Research. GOLDSTONE, Peter.

Revival of Reasoning in the Modern Age by Developing a Classroom Community of Inquiry Within College Students. SOFO, Frank.

Rhetoric as Instruction: A Response to Vickers on Rhetoric in the *Laws*. YUNIS, Harvey.

The Right to Education: An Inquiry Into Its Foundations. CURLEY, Thomas V.

A Role for Philosophy of Education in Intercultural Research: Reexamination of the Relativism-Absolutism Debate. FEINBERG, Walter.

The Role of Logic in Education. MILL, John Stuart.

Sandel and the Limits of Community. ENSLIN, Penny.

Science Begins with Everyday Thinking. ROYER, Ron.

The Search for Theory in Process-Product Research: Response to Chambers. MACMILLAN, C J B.

Seeking Out Alternatives. CALANDRA, A.

Self-Knowledge and the Modern Mode of Learning. BLITS, Jan H.

Semantic Physiology: Wittgenstein on Pedagogy. MC CARTY, Luise Prior and MC CARTY, Charles.

Sexual Discrimination and the Equal Opportunities Commission: Ought Schools to Eradicate Sex Stereotyping?. SHAW, Beverley.

The Single-Issue Introduction to Philosophy. WHITE, V Alan.

Socrates In a New Package Helps Kids Learn to Think. BERRIAN, Annette.

Socratic Dialogue. HECKMANN, Gustav.

The Socratic Method and Philosophy for Children. PORTELLI, John P.

Socratic Teaching?. JORDAN JR, James A.

Some Applications of *Process and Reality I and II* to Educational Practice. BRUMBAUGH, Robert S.

Some Concrete Approaches to Nature in *Kio and Gus*. HAMRICK, William S.

Some Reflections on Intelligence and the Nature—Nurture Issue. YAPP, Brian.

The Speakerly Teacher: Socrates and Writing. KALLICK, David.

Specific Content Knowledge is Not Necessary for Good Reading. PHILLIPS, Linda M.

Standing Alone: Dependence, Independence and Interdependence in the Practice of Education. GRIFFITHS, Morwenna and SMITH, Richard.

Step by Step in Children's Philosophy. MOSTERT, Pieter.

Strong Democracy, The Ethic of Caring and Civil Education. PRESKILL, Stephen.

The Study of Teaching and Curriculum. MALANGA, Joseph.

Subject-Centred Versus Child-Centred Education—A False Dualism. PRING, Richard.

Teaching and Learning for Democratic Empowerment: A Critical Evaluation. BROSIO, Richard A.

Teaching and Mother Love. KLEIN, J Theodore.

Teaching and Rhetoric. MC EWAN, Hunter.

Teaching as Translation: The Philosophical Dimension. JOHNSON, Tony W.

Teaching *Elfie*. HAMRICK, William S.

Teaching Reading and Educating Persons. RAITZ, Keith L and EDWARDS, Jack.

Teaching Reasoning With Computers. FURLONG, John and CARROLL, William.

Teaching, Learning and Ontological Dependence. PEARSON, Allen T.

There is Relevance in the Classroom: Analysis of Present Methods of Teaching Business Ethics. STRONG, V K and HOFFMAN, A N.

Thinking Skill Programs: An Analysis. MAYS, Wolfe and SHARP, Ann Margaret.

Thinking, Knowing, Doing. EBLE, Kenneth.

Thinking, Mind, the Existence of God...Transcript of a Classroom Dialogue with First-and-Second Graders in Montreal. DANIEL, Marie-France.

Thomas Aquinas and the Reform of Christian Education. FORTIN, Ernest L.

The Three Pedagogical Dimensions of Nietzsche's Philosophy. ALONI, Nimrod.

Towards More Effective Arts Education. GARDNER, Howard.

Training and Women: Some Thoughts from the Grassroots. JOYCE, Glenis.

Le travail de la contradiction dans le Livre I de l'*Emile*. IMBERT, Francis.

The Treadway Commission Recommendations for Education: Professor's Opinions. DONNELLY, William J and MILLER, Gary A.

Truth and Pragmatism in Higher Education. DEVINE, Phillip E.

Two "Representative" Approaches to the Learning Problem. ORTON, Robert E.

The Two Cultures. BROUDY, Harry S.

Unacceptable Notions of Science Held by Process-Product Researchers. CHAMBERS, John H.

We Discover That Thinking Is Fun: Doing Philosophy With First Graders. BRÜNING, Barbara.

What Is Reasoning? What Is an Argument?. WALTON, Doug.

What Kind of Girl is Pippi Longstocking, Anyway?. BRÜNING, Barbara.

What Music Is. SERAFINE, Mary Louise.

What Other Worlds Have to Say About Ontological Dependence: Is There Life in the Logical Thesis?. MC EWAN, Hunter.

Whitehead and a Committee. BRUMBAUGH, Robert S.

Who Can Teach Workplace Ethics?. DAVIS, Michael.

Who is Harry Stottlemeier and What Did He Discover?. JOHNSON, Tony.

Who Is the Enemy? Reflections on the Threat of Managerial Techno-Reason to the Humanities. NORDENHAUG, Theodore D.

Why Be Rational? On Thinking Critically About Critical Thinking. SIEGEL, Harvey.

Why Can't a Man Be More Like a Woman? (A Note on John Locke's Educational Thought). SIMONS, Martin.

Why I Teach Philosophy. TORGERSON, Jon N.

Why Philosophers Should Involve Themselves with Teaching Reasoning in the Schools. SILVERS, Anita.

Why Teachers Need Philosophy. CLARK, Charles.

With Justice for All Beings: Educating as if Nature Matters. COHEN, Michael J.

Wittgenstein and Philosophy for Children. CURTIS, Barry.

Wittgenstein on Grammar and Analytic Philosophy of Education. RIZVI, Fazal.

The Women of Silence. FRANKE, Carrie.

The Words 'Same' and 'Different'. CRAWSHAY-WILLIAMS, Rupert.

Working with Philosophy for Children in Catalonia. CULLELL, Josep.

Young Children Generate Philosophical Ideas. MC CALL, Catherine.

Der Zwang zur "geschlossenen Gesellschaft"—Ein perennes Dilemma der Utopie?. KLARER, Mario.

EDUCATIONAL THEORY(-RIES)

Capitalist Schools: Explanation and Ethics in Radical Studies of Schooling. LISTON, Daniel P.

Liberal Justice and the Marxist Critique of Education: A Study of Conflicting

EDUCATIONAL THEORY(-RIES)
Research Programs. STRIKE, Kenneth A.
Benne's Plato and the Theater of Ideas: Response to Benne. OWEN, David.
Plato's Divided Line: A Dramatistic Interpretation. BENNE, Kenneth D.

EDWARDS
Jonathan Edwards and the Sense of the Heart. WAINWRIGHT, William.
On Trusting One's Own Heart: Scepticism in Jonathan Edwards and Soren Kierkegaard. BELL, Richard H.

EDWARDS, J
The Moral Aspects of Reading: Response to Raitz and Edwards. NORRIS, Stephen P.

EFFECT(S)
The Ethics of Psychoactive Ads. HYMAN, Michael R and TANSEY, Richard.
The False Ontology of School Climate Effects. MILLER, Steven I and FREDERICKS, Janet.
How to Learn a Language Like a Chimpanzee. GAUKER, Christopher.
Language as a Cause-Effect Communication System. SAVAGE-RUMBAUGH, E S.

EFFECTIVENESS
The Effectiveness of a Complaint-Based Ethics Enforcement System: Evidence from the Accounting Profession. BEETS, S Douglas and KILLOUGH, Larry N.
The Problem of Psychotherapeutic Effectiveness. BARTLETT, Steven J.

EFFICIENCY
"The Conflation of Productivity and Efficiency in Economics and Economic History": A Comment. NYE, John Vincent.
The Economic Efficiency and Equity of Abortion. MEEKS, Thomas J.
The Inefficiency of Some Efficiency Comparisons: A Reply to Nye. SARAYDAR, Edward.

EGALITARIANISM
Égalité et justice: une idée de l'homme. LAFRANCE, Guy.
Functions of Egalitarianism in Yugoslav Society. BERNIK, Ivan.
Liberal and Socialist Egalitarianism. NIELSEN, Kai.
Liberal and Socialist Egalitarianism. NIELSEN, Kai.
Liberal Egalitarianism and World Resource Distribution: Two Views. ARNESON, Richard J.
Taking Talents Seriously. GREEN, Simon.
Was Marx an Egalitarian: Skeptical Remarks on Miller's Marx. NIELSEN, Kai.

EGO
see also Self(-ves)
A Note on the Arabic Term 'Anniyyah/'Aniyyah/'Inniyyah (in Hebrew). HARVEY, Warren Zev and HARVEY, Steven.
Does Artificial Intelligence Require Artificial Ego? A Critique of Haugeland. EDELSON, Thomas.
The Ego Revisited. DAUENHAUER, Bernard J.
Maine de Biran and the Body-Subject. GAINES, Jeffrey J.

EGOCENTRISM
Egocentric Phenomenalism and Conservation in Piaget. MATTHEWS, Gareth B.
Environmental Ethics and Political Conflict: A View from California. MERCHANT, Carolyn.

EGOISM
Ethical Theory: Classical and Contemporary Readings. POJMAN, Louis P (ed).
Love and Friendship in Plato and Aristotle. PRICE, A W.
Self and Others: A Study of Ethical Egoism. ÖSTERBERG, Jan.
Social Philosophy and Ecological Scarcity. LEE, Keekok.
Consequentialism, Egoism, and the Moral Law. CUMMISKEY, David.
Doing Justice to Egoism. THOMAS, Laurence.
Egoism and Morality. MULHOLLAND, Leslie.
Egoism and Personal Identity. MAIDAN, Michael.
Hobbes and 'The Beautiful Axiom'. COADY, C A J.
Is Socialism a Psychological Misunderstanding?. REYKOWSKI, Janusz.
Die Möglichkeit der Kooperation unter Egoisten: Neuere Ergebnisse spieltheoretischer Analysen. SCHÜSSLER, Rudolf.

EINSTEIN
The Philosophy of Quantum Mechanics: An Interactive Interpretation. HEALEY, Richard.
Thematic Origins of Scientific Thought: Kepler to Einstein—Revised Edition. HOLTON, Gerald.
Bohr, Einstein and Realism. DANIEL, Wojciech.
The Born-Einstein Debate: Where Application and Explanation Separate. CARTWRIGHT, Nancy.
Einstein and Duhem. HOWARD, Don.

Einstein: el ideal de una ciencia sin sujeto. RIOJA, Ana.
Mādhyamika Buddhism and Quantum Mechanics: Beginning a Dialogue. MANSFIELD, Victor.
Simultaneity and Einstein's *Gedankenexperiment*. COHEN, Michael.
The Newtonian Concept of Space and Time (in Polish). MAZIERSKI, Stanislaw.

EISENSTEIN, S
The Influence of Traditional Japanese Aesthetics on the Film Theory of Sergei Eisenstein. ODIN, Steve.

ELDERLY
"Advance Directives and Health Care for the Elderly" in *Advance Directives in Medicine*, THOMASMA, David C.
Caring for Frail Elderly Parents: Past Parental Sacrifices and the Obligations of Adult Children. WICCLAIR, Mark.
The Elderly and High Technology Medicine: A Case for Individualized, Autonomous Allocation. MOTT, Peter D.
The Ethics of Home Care: Autonomy and Accommodation. COLLOPY, Bart and DUBLER, Nancy and ZUCKERMAN, Connie.
Towards a Theory of Age-Group Justice. JECKER, Nancy S.
Women and Elderly Parents: Moral Controversy in an Aging Society. POST, Stephen G.

ELEMENT(S)
Aristotle on Substance: The Paradox of Unity. GILL, Mary Louise.
Elementos y esencias. ANSCOMBE, G E M.
La estructura matemática de la materia en el *Timeo* de Platón. BOERI, Marcelo D.

ELEMENTARY
Logic in the International Elementary School. SLADE, Christine.

ELIADE, M
Eliade's Vichianism: The Regeneration of Time and the Terror of History. VERENE, Donald Phillip.
Mito y filosofía: En torno a Mircea Eliade. AGÍS, Marcelino.
The Shape of Time. CIORANESCU, Alexandre.

ELIMINATION
Quantifier Elimination in Separably Closed Fields of Finite Imperfectness Degree. HARAN, Dan.

ELIMINATIVISM
Beyond Eliminativism. CLARK, Andy.
Eliminative Materialism: The Reality of the Mental, and Folk Psychology—A Reply to O'Gorman. MILLS, Stephen.
Eliminativism and Methodological Individualism. KINCAID, Harold.
Mentalism-Cum-Physicalism vs Eliminative Materialism. O'GORMAN, P F.
Truth, Eliminativism and Disquotationalism. DAVID, Marian A.

ELIOT, C
Educating for Democracy: Charles W Eliot and the Differentiated Curriculum. PRESKILL, Stephen.

ELIOT, G
Plato, George Eliot, and Moral Narcissism. GOULD, Carol S.

ELIOT, T
Skepticism and Modern Enmity: Before and After Eliot. PERL, Jeffrey M.
Literary Communication: The Author, the Reader, the Text. HARKER, W John.
The Prayers of Childhood: T S Eliot's Manuscripts on Kant. HABIB, M A R.
Towards—and Away from—an Aesthetic of Popular Culture. DOHERTY, Thomas.

ELITISM
Left-Wing Elitism: Adorno on Popular Culture. BAUGH, Bruce.

ELIZABETHANISM
Of the Laws of Ecclesiastical Polity (Preface, Book I, Book VIII), Richard Hooker. MC GRADE, Arthur Stephen (ed).

ELLIN, J
A Reply to Ellin's "Streminger: 'Religion a Threat to Morality'". STREMINGER, Gerhard.

ELLIPSIS
Elliptical Sense. NANCY, Jean-Luc.

ELLIS, A
Logic, Rationality and Counseling. COHEN, Elliot D.

ELLUL, J
La critique de l'utopie et de la technique chez J Ellul et H Jonas. WEYEMBERGH, Maurice.

ELSTER, J
Humanwissenschaft mit oder ohne Subjekt? oder Zur Kritik der Inentionalität. PRABITZ, Gerald.

EMANCIPATION

The French Revolution and the Education of the Young Marx. RUBEL, Maximilien and WALKER, R Scott (trans).

The Laborious and Painful Process of Emancipation (in Serbo-Croatian). JUNQING, Yi.

EMBRYO(S)

Ethical Analyses in the Development of Congressional Public Policy. WHITE, Gladys B.

A Fortnight of My Life is Missing: A Discussion of the Status of the Human 'Pre-Embryo'. HOLLAND, Allan.

New Reproductive Technologies in the Treatment of Human Infertility and Genetic Disease. SILVER, Lee M.

The Philosopher as Insider and Outsider. KAMM, Frances M.

Philosophical Integrity and Policy Development in Bioethics. BENJAMIN, Martin.

Resolving Disputes Over Frozen Embryos. ROBERTSON, John A.

Status Arguments and Genetic Research with Human Embryos. HICKMAN, Larry.

The Zygote: To Be Or Not Be A Person. BEDATE, Carlos A and CEFALO, Robert C.

EMBRYOLOGY

The Four Causes in Aristotle's Embryology. MATTHEN, Mohan.

EMERGENCE

"On the Emergence of Scientific Disciplines" in Scientific Knowledge Socialized, LAITKO, Hubert.

EMERSON

The American Evasion of Philosophy: A Genealogy of Pragmatism. WEST, Cornel.

"Voyage to Syracuse: Adams—Schiller—Emerson" in Mind, Value and Culture: Essays in Honor of E M Adams, SMYTH, Richard.

The Constitutional Process and the Higher Law. SHANKER, George.

Emerson and the Agricultural Midworld. CORRINGTON, Robert S.

EMINESCU, M

Leibniz's Nachklänge im Denken und in der Dichtung von Mihai Eminescu. BOBOC, Alexandru.

EMOTION(S)

see also Feeling(s)

Good Lives and Moral Education. SIMPSON, Evan.

Love: Emotion, Myth, and Metaphor. SOLOMON, Robert C.

Wise Choices, Apt Feelings: A Theory of Normative Judgment. GIBBARD, Allan.

The Arousal and Expression of Emotion by Music. ALLEN, R T.

Conscience, Sympathy, and Love: Ethical Strategies toward Confirmation of Metaphysical Assertions in Schopenhauer. CYZYK, Mark.

The Degeneration of the Cognitive Theory of Emotions. GRIFFITHS, P E.

Desire and Emotion in the Virtue Tradition. HARTZ, Glenn A.

Embarrassment and Self-Esteem. SZABADOS, Béla.

Emociones reactivas. HANSBERG, Olbeth.

Emociones y creencias. HANSBERG, Olbeth.

Emotional Origins of Morality—A Sketch. THOMSON, Anne.

The Ethics of Psychoactive Ads. HYMAN, Michael R and TANSEY, Richard.

Expression as Hands-on Construction. HOWARD, V A.

Fictional Emotion, Quasi-Desire and Background Relief. BORUAH, Bijoy H.

Jealousy. WREEN, Michael.

Listenaires: Thoughts on a Database. GILES, Gordon J.

Melancholic Epistemology. GRAHAM, George.

Modularity, and the Psychoevolutionary Theory of Emotion. GRIFFITHS, P E.

Music and the Expression of Emotion. BUDD, Malcolm.

Nelson Goodman on Emotions in Music. LAMMENRANTA, Markus.

The Rationality of Emotions and of Emotional Behaviour. MC CULLAGH, C Behan.

The Rejection of Ethical Rationalism. KAPUR, Neera Badhwar.

Self-Deception, Human Emotion, and Moral Responsibility: Toward a Pluralistic Conceptual Scheme. WHISNER, William.

A Social Constructionist Critique of The Naturalistic Theory of Emotion. RATNER, Carl.

Le Traité des passions de Descartes et les théories modernes de l'émotion. NEUBERG, M.

Warrant, Emotion, and Value. LEMOS, Noah M.

EMOTIVE

Artistic Convention and the Issue of Truth in Art. MARSHALL, Ernest C.

EMOTIVISM

"How Music Moves" in What is Music?, KIVY, Peter.

Blackburn's Projectivism—An Objection. BRIGHOUSE, M H.

Can Emotivism Sustain a Social Ethic?. UNWIN, Nicholas.

G E Moore and the Revolution in Ethics: A Reappraisal. WELCHMAN, Jennifer.

Vico and MacIntyre. COERS, Kathy Frashure.

EMPATHY

"Empathy as an Objective Value" in Inquiries into Values: The Inaugural Session of the International Society for Value Inquiry, ABBARNO, John M.

EMPIRICAL

The Fourth Way: A Theory of Knowledge. GROSSMAN, Reinhardt.

The Growth of Knowledge: An Inquiry into the Kuhnian Theory. VERRONEN, Veli.

The Past Within Us: An Empirical Approach to Philosophy of History. MARTIN, Raymond.

Can Business Ethics Be Taught? Empirical Evidence. JONES, Thomas M.

An Empirical Study of Moral Reasoning Among Managers. DERRY, Robbin.

The Hierarchical Structure of Testing Theories. KUOKKANEN, Martti.

Measuring the Impact of Teaching Ethics to Future Managers: A Review, Assessment, and Recommendations. WEBER, James.

Methodological Problems in Empirical Logic. FINOCCHIARO, Maurice A.

On Innertheoretical Conditions for Theoretical Terms. GÄHDE, Ulrich.

Trust in Business Relations: Directions for Empirical Research. HUSTED, Bryan W.

EMPIRICAL KNOWLEDGE

Hegel's Epistemological Realism: A Study of the Aim and Method of Hegel's Phenomenology of Spirit. WESTPHAL, Kenneth R.

"Coherence, Observation, and the Justification of Empirical Belief" in The Current State of the Coherence Theory, SILVERS, Stuart.

Apriority and Metajustification in BonJour's "Structure of Empirical Knowledge". SOLOMON, Miriam.

Empirical and Epistemological Issues in Scientists' Explanations of Scientific Stances: A Critical Synthesis. BRANTE, Thomas.

Kant's Conception of Empirical Law—I. GUYER, Paul.

Kant's Conception of Empirical Law—II. WALKER, Ralph.

Putnam on "Empirical Objects". STEINHOFF, Gordon.

Reply to Solomon's "Apriority and Metajustification in BonJour's 'Structure of Empirical Knowledge'". BONJOUR, Laurence.

EMPIRICISM

see also Pragmatism

Fact and Meaning. HEAL, Jane.

Feyerabend's Critique of Foundationalism. COUVALIS, George.

Intimations of Divinity. PLATT, David.

John Stuart Mill. SKORUPSKI, John.

Man and Nature in the Philosophical Thought of Wang-Fu-Chih. BLACK, Alison Harley.

The Metaphysics of Epistemology: Lectures by Wilfrid Sellars. AMARAL, Pedro (ed).

The Nature of Social and Educational Inquiry: Empiricism versus Interpretation. SMITH, John K.

Necessity, Essence, and Individuation: A Defense of Conventionalism. SIDELLE, Alan.

The Philosophy of Rhetoric (Revised Edition). CAMPBELL, George.

Reclaiming Reality: A Critical Introduction to Contemporary Philosophy. BHASKAR, Roy.

Scientific Explanation (Minnesota Studies in the Philosophy of Science, Volume XIII). KITCHER, Philip (ed).

Who Knows: From Quine to a Feminist Empiricism. NELSON, Lynn Hankinson.

"Cause in the Later Russell" in Rereading Russell: Essays on Bertrand Russell's Metaphysics and Epistemology, EAMES, Elizabeth R.

"An Empiricist View of Knowledge: Memorism" in Epistemology (Companions to Ancient Thought: 1), FREDE, Michael.

"Otto Neurath: From Authoritarian Liberalism to Empiricism" in Knowledge and Politics, FREUDENTHAL, Gideon.

"The Physical Manifestation of Empirical Knowledge" in Issues in Evolutionary Epistemology, HATTIANGADI, J N.

"Radical Philosophy and Radical History" in The Institution of Philosophy: A Discipline in Crisis?, MARGOLIS, Joseph.

"Whitehead and the Dichotomy of Rationalism and Empiricism" in Whitehead's Metaphysics of Creativity, LECLERC, Ivor.

Against Feminist Science: Harding and the Science Question in Feminism. LAKOMSKI, Gabriele.

Bonjour's Objection to Traditional Foundationalism. RAPPAPORT, Steve.

Bradley e Spinoza: L'iper-spinozismo di F H Bradley (seconda parte). DEREGIBUS, Arturo.

Can Abstractions Be Causes?. JOHNSON, David M.

The Critique of Equalitarian Society in Malthus's Essay. GILBERT, Geoffrey.

Empirical Versus Epistemological Considerations: A Comment on Stemmer.

EMPIRICISM

MORRIS, Michael.

Empiricist Versus Prototype Theories of Language Acquisition. STEMMER, Nathan.

Epistemologia e neocriticismo in un dibattito degli anni 1912-1914 fra Cassirer e Heidegger. HENRY, Barbara.

Explanation and Justification in Ethics. COPP, David.

Freud, Mooij en de empiristische boeman. DERKSEN, A A.

Il guidizio di Sant'Agostino sulla Nuova Accademia tra scetticismo ed esoterismo. FERRETTI, Silvia.

Henri Poincaré's Philosophy of Science. STUMP, David.

Idealization and Projection in the Empirical Sciences: Husserl versus Heidegger. KOCKELMANS, Joseph J.

Leibniz and the Problem of Induction. WESTPHAL, Jonathan.

Mathematical Skepticism: Are We Brains in a Countable Vat?. TYMOCZKO, Thomas.

The Myth of Jones and the Mirror of Nature: Reflections on Introspection. GARFIELD, Jay L.

Observation in Constructive Empiricism: Arbitrary or Incoherent?. CORDERO, Alberto.

Observation, Instrumentalism, and Constructive Empiricism. GRAYBOSCH, Anthony.

De oppervlakkigheid van de empirisch gewende wetenschapstheorie. RIP, Arie.

A Peircean Response to the Realist-Empiricist Debate. FRENCH, Steven.

Pierre Duhem's *The Aim and Structure of Physical Theory*: A Book Against Conventionalism. MAIOCCHI, Roberto.

Primäre und sekundäre Qualitatäten bei John Locke. KIENZLE, Bertram.

Reading *Probabilismo*. JEFFREY, Richard.

Rondom realisme. RADDER, Hans.

The Science of Man and Wide Reflective Equilibrium. BRANDT, R B.

T H Morgan, Neither an Epistemological Empiricist nor a "Methodological" Empiricist. VICEDO, Marga.

Tacit Metaphysical Premises of Modern Empiricism. NAHLIK, Krzysztof J.

Theological Empiricism: Aspects of Johann Georg Hamann's Reception of Hume. GRAUBNER, Hans.

What Is Empiricism?—I. CARRUTHERS, Peter.

What Is Empiricism?—II, Nativism, Naturalism, and Evolutionary Theory. MACDONALD, Cynthia.

Wittgenstein and Obscurantism. CIOFFI, Frank.

EMPLOYEE(S)

Corporate Loyalty, Does It Have a Future?. GROSMAN, Brian A.

Discrimination Against Pregnant Employees: An Analysis of Arbitration and Human Rights Tribunal Decisions in Canada. ANDIAPPAN, P and REAVLEY, M.

Drug Testing in Employment. DES JARDINS, Joseph and DUSKA, Ronald.

Helping Subordinates with Their Personal Problems: A Moral Dilemma for Managers. MOBERG, Dennis J.

An Integrative Model for Understanding and Managing Ethical Behavior in Business Organizations. STEAD, W Edward and WORRELL, Dan L and STEAD, Jean Garner.

Justifying Wrongful Employee Behavior: The Role of Personality in Organizational Sabotage. GIACALONE, Robert A and KNOUSE, Stephen B.

Managerial Authority. MC MAHON, Christopher.

Organizio of Work in the Company and Family Rights of the Employees. MELÉE, Domènec.

Something Akin to a Property Right: Protections for Job Security. LEE, Barbara A.

EMPLOYER(S)

Corporate Loyalty, Does It Have a Future?. GROSMAN, Brian A.

EMPTINESS

Epoche and Sūnyatā: Skepticism East and West. GARFIELD, J. L.

Sunyatā and Ajāti: Absolutism and the Philosophies of Nagarjuna and Gaudapada. KING, Richard.

What is Non-Existent and What is Remanent in Sunyata. DARGYAY, Lobsang.

ENCYCLOPEDIA(S)

Handlexikon zur Wissenschaftstheorie. SEIFFERT, Helmut.

Enzyklopädie als Aktionswissen?. HÖRZ, Herbert.

END(S)

see also Teleology

Acquiring Ethical Ends. DE MOSS, David J.

Danto, Dewey and the Historical End of Art. MITCHELL, Jeff.

The Four Causes in Aristotle's Embryology. MATTHEN, Mohan.

Knowledge or Control as the End of Art. CEBIK, L B.

Nemesis. BURGER, Ronna.

A Note on Some Puzzling Phrases in Aquinas. VANDER WEEL, Richard L.

Objective Value, Realism, and the End of Metaphysics. POST, John F.

Praxis and *Poesis* in Aristotle's Practical Philosophy. BALABAN, Oded.

ENERGY

Mind, Brain and the Quantum: The Compound 'I'. LOCKWOOD, Michael.

Fisica e storia della scienza nell'opera di Pierre Duhem. RAMONI, Marco.

On the Critique of Energetism and Neoenergetism (in Czechoslovakian). ZEMAN, J.

ENFORCEMENT

The Effectiveness of a Complaint-Based Ethics Enforcement System: Evidence from the Accounting Profession. BEETS, S Douglas and KILLOUGH, Larry N.

Equal Respect and the Enforcement of Morality. DWORKIN, Gerald.

ENGELS

Collected Works, Volume 31, Marx: 1861-1863. MARX, Karl.

Collected Works, Volume 32, Marx: 1861-1863. MARX, Karl.

Collected Works, Volume 44, Marx and Engels: 1870-1873. MARX, Karl.

"'Ideology' in Marx and Engels": A Reply. MC CARNEY, James.

La filosofía política marxista y la revolución. COLBERT, James.

Philosophical Questions of Mathematics in *Anti-Dühring*. PANFILOV, V A.

ENGELS, E

Evolutionäre Erkenntnistheorie und erkenntnistheoretischer Realismus. WENDEL, Hans Jürgen.

ENGINEERING

Applied Liberal Education for Engineers. LUGENBIEHL, Heinz C.

Applying Idealized Scientific Theories to Engineering. LAYMON, Ronald.

Ethics in Bioengineering. MITCHAM, Carl.

La ética ingenieril norteamericana: problems y promesas. MICHAM, Carl.

Science- and Engineering-Related Ethics and Value Studies: Characteristics of an Emerging Field of Research. HOLLANDER, Rachelle D and STENECK, Nicholas H.

ENGLISH

see also British

Hume. PHILLIPSON, N T.

Intercultural Rhetorical Differences in Meaning Construction. FOLMAN, Shoshana and SARIG, Gissi.

ENLIGHTENMENT

see also Modern

Return to Reason: Critique of Enlightenment Evidentialism and a Defense of Reason and Belief in God. CLARK, Kelly James.

The Spirit of the Laws: Charles Montesquieu. COHLER, Anne M (trans).

Wesen, Freiheit und Bildung des Menschen. HAGER, Fritz-Peter.

"The Public Grounds of Truth": The Critical Theory of G B Vico. MALI, Joseph.

Edification, Conversation, and Narrative: Rortyan Motifs for Philosophy of Education. ARCILLA, René V.

Existentialism at the End of Modernity: Questioning the I's Eyes. LEVIN, David Michael.

Imaginative Freedom and the German Enlightenment. KNELLER, Jane.

Natural Law and the Scottish Enlightenment. HAAKONSSEN, Knud.

La première crise de la raison. THÉRIAULT, J Yvon.

ENMITY

Skepticism and Modern Enmity: Before and After Eliot. PERL, Jeffrey M.

ENTAILMENT

"Deducibility, Entailment and Analytic Containment" in *Directions in Relevant Logic*, ANGELL, R B.

"Which Entailments Entail Which Entailments?" in *Directions in Relevant Logic*, BELNAP JR, Nuel D.

'Would Cause'. NEEDHAM, Paul.

Raising as Function Composition. JACOBSON, Pauline.

ENTHYMEME(S)

Peirce's Abductive Argument and the Enthymeme. SABRE, Ru Michael.

ENTITLEMENT

Flew on Entitlements and Justice. PEÑA, L.

ENTITY(-TIES)

Reference, Intentionality, and Nonexistent Entities. ROSENKRANTZ, Gary.

ENTREPRENEURSHIP

Are Women Owner-Managers Challenging Our Definitions of Entrepreneurship? An In-Depth Survey. LEE-GOSSELIN, H and GRISÉ, J.

An Examination of Present Research on the Female Entrepreneur-Suggested Strategies for the 1990's. MOORE, Dorothy P.

A Family Portrait of Canada's Most Successful Female Entrepreneurs. BELCOURT, Monica.

ENTREPRENEURSHIP

Some Methodological Problems Associated with Researching Women Entrepreneurs. STEVENSON, Lois.

ENTROPY

Aristotle's Theory of Time and Entropy. HUGHEN, Richard E.

Decision Problems Under Uncertainty Based on Entropy Functionals. GOTTINGER, Hans W.

Entropy and Information in Evolving Biological Systems. BROOKS, Daniel R (and others).

The Historical-Philosophical Change of an Involution Dialectics. IRIMIE, Ioan.

ENVIRONMENT(S)

Social Philosophy and Ecological Scarcity. LEE, Keekok.

"Environmental Problematics" in Nature in Asian Tradition of Thought: Essays in Environmental Philosophy, INADA, Kenneth K.

"On Seeking a Change of Environment" in Nature in Asian Tradition of Thought: Essays in Environmental Philosophy, HALL, David L.

"Units of Change—Units of Value" in Nature in Asian Tradition of Thought: Essays in Environmental Philosophy, NEVILLE, Robert C.

"Respect", "Dignity" and "Integrity": An Environmental Proposal for Ethics. WESTRA, Laura.

Agriculture: A War on Nature?. SURGEY, John.

Die Verantwortung des Menschen für seine natürliche Umwelt (in Polish). ROSINSKI, F M and LATAWIEC, A M.

Ecologic-Economic Jurisprudence—The Next Step?. LEIDIG, Guido.

On the Future of the Man-Nature Relationship (in Czechoslovakian). MUZIK, J.

Philosophy and the Devastation of the Earth (in Czechoslovakian). KOLARSKY, R and SMAJS, J.

The Ethics Dimension of Human Attitude to the Living Environment (in Czechoslovakian). BURES, R.

ENVIRONMENTAL ETHICS

Essays on Political Morality. HARE, R M.

Ethics and the Environmental Responsibility. DOWER, Nigel (ed).

Foundations of Environmental Ethics. HARGROVE, Eugene C.

Nature in Asian Tradition of Thought: Essays in Environmental Philosophy. CALLICOTT, J Baird (ed).

"'Conceptual Resources' in South Asia for 'Environmental Ethics'" in Nature in Asian Tradition of Thought: Essays in Environmental Philosophy, LARSON, Gerald James.

"The Asian Traditions as a Conceptual Resource for Environmental Philosophy" in Nature in Asian Tradition of Thought: Essays in Environmental Philosophy, CALLICOTT, J Baird and AMES, Roger T.

"Democracy and Environmental Change" in Ethics and the Environmental Responsibility, WENZ, Peter.

"Epilogue: On the Relation of Idea and Action" in Nature in Asian Tradition of Thought: Essays in Environmental Philosophy, CALLICOTT, J Baird and AMES, Roger T.

"What is Environmental Ethics?" in Ethics and the Environmental Responsibility, DOWER, Nigel.

Bioregionalism: Science or Sensibility?. ALEXANDER, Donald.

The Case Against Moral Pluralism. CALLICOTT, J Baird.

The Chainsaws of Greed: The Case of Pacific Lumber. NEWTON, Lisa H.

Concentric Circle Pluralism: A Response to Rolston. WENZ, Peter S.

Concerning the Issue of Points of Departure of Environmental Ethics (in Czechoslovakian). HUBIK, S.

Dilemmas of Disclosure: Ethical Issues in Environmental Auditing. BLUMENFELD, Karen.

Environmental Ethics and Political Conflict: A View from California. MERCHANT, Carolyn.

Environmental Justice. ROLSTON III, Holmes.

Green Reason: Communicative Ethics for the Biosphere. DRYZEK, John S.

John Dewey and Environmental Thought. TAYLOR, Bob Pepperman.

Man Apart and Deep Ecology: A Reply to Reed. NAESS, Arne.

Mens en aarde: Het ecofilosofisch dilemma in het werk van Ludwig Klages. WITZORECK, Kris.

Philosophy and Environmental Issues. HALDANE, J J.

The Power and the Promise of Ecological Feminism. WARREN, Karen J.

A Refutation of Environmental Ethics. THOMPSON, Janna.

The Relevance of Deep Ecology to the Third World. JOHNS, David M.

De rol van het begrip intrinsieke waarde in milieu-ethische argumentaties. MERKS, K W.

Ties that Bind: Native American Beliefs as a Foundation for Environmental Consciousness. BOOTH, Annie L and JACOBS, Harvey L.

Toward a New Relation between Humanity and Nature: Reconstructing T'ien-jen-ho-i. LIU, Shu-hsien.

With Justice for All Beings: Educating as if Nature Matters. COHEN, Michael J.

ENVIRONMENTALISM

Ethics and the Environmental Responsibility. DOWER, Nigel (ed).

"Do Future Generations Matter?" in Ethics and the Environmental Responsibility, CAMERON, J R.

"The Metaphysics of Environmentalism" in Ethics and the Environmental Responsibility, MATTHEWS, Eric.

The Neo-Stoicism of Radical Environmentalism. CHENEY, Jim.

Subjectivity and Environmentalism. LE PORE, Ernest.

Ties that Bind: Native American Beliefs as a Foundation for Environmental Consciousness. BOOTH, Annie L and JACOBS, Harvey L.

ENVY

"Of Jealousy and Envy" in Person to Person, FARRELL, Daniel M.

EPIC

Vom epischen zum logischen sprechen: der spruch des Anaximander. RIEDEL, M.

EPICTETUS

The "Meditations" of Marcus Aurelius: A Study. RUTHERFORD, R B.

EPICUREANS

Paul and the Popular Philosophers. MALHERBE, Abraham J.

EPICURUS

"Epicurus on the Truth of the Senses" in Epistemology (Companions to Ancient Thought: 1), EVERSON, Stephen.

Epicurus and Friendship. STERN-GILLET, Suzanne.

Epicurus on Pleasure and the Complete Life. ROSENBAUM, Stephen E.

The Hermeneutics of the Young Marx: According to Marx's Approach to the Philosophy of Democritus and Epicurus. BALABAN, Oded.

EPIPHENOMENALISM

"Popper, Natural Selection and Epiphenomenalism" in Issues in Evolutionary Epistemology, SHAW, Daniel.

Making Mind Matter More. FODOR, Jerry A.

EPISTEMIC

"Social Change and Epistemic Thought" in Scientific Knowledge Socialized, KROHN, Wolfgang.

Lavoisier, Priestley, and the Philosophes: Epistemic and Linguistic Dimensions to the Chemical Revolution. MC EVOY, John G.

EPISTEMIC LOGIC

The Cartesian Cogito, Epistemic Logic, and Neuroscience: Some Surprising Interrelations. HINTIKKA, Jaakko.

Fitch and Intuitionistic Knowability. PERCIVAL, Philip.

Topological Models of Epistemic Set Theory. GOODMAN, Nicolas D.

Two Incomplete Anti-Realist Modal Epistemic Logics. WILLIAMSON, Timothy.

EPISTEMOLOGY

see also Action(s), Empiricism, Idealism, Imagination, Knowledge, Memory, Perception, Rationalism, Realism, Scepticism, Truth(s)

Arnauld and the Cartesian Philosophy of Ideas. NADLER, Steven M.

Bergson. LACEY, A R.

Common Sense. FORGUSON, Lynd.

The Crisis of Philosophy. MC CARTHY, Michael.

The Current State of the Coherence Theory. BENDER, John W (ed).

Elements of Modern Philosophy: Descartes through Kant. BRENNER, William H.

Epistemic Justification: Essays in the Theory of Knowledge. ALSTON, William P.

Epistemology (Companions to Ancient Thought: 1). EVERSON, Stephen (ed).

Fact and Meaning. HEAL, Jane.

Feyerabend's Critique of Foundationalism. COUVALIS, George.

The Fourth Way: A Theory of Knowledge. GROSSMAN, Reinhardt.

Greek Scepticism: Anti-Realist Trends in Ancient Thought. GROARKE, Leo.

Hegel's Epistemological Realism: A Study of the Aim and Method of Hegel's Phenomenology of Spirit. WESTPHAL, Kenneth R.

Historical Roots of Cognitive Science. MEYERING, Theo C.

History and Anti-History in Philosophy. LAVINE, T Z (ed).

Intentionality and Extension. MATJAZ, Potrc.

Introducing Philosophy: A Text with Integrated Readings (Fourth Edition). SOLOMON, Robert C.

Issues in Evolutionary Epistemology. HAHLWEG, Kai (ed).

John of the Cross and the Cognitive Value of Mysticism. PAYNE, Steven.

Kants Theorie des Verstandes. SEEBOHM, Thomas M (ed).

Knowledge and Evidence. MOSER, Paul K.

Knowledge and Politics. DASCAL, Marcelo (ed).

EPISTEMOLOGY

Laws and Symmetry. VAN FRAASSEN, Bas C.

The Metaphysics of Epistemology: Lectures by Wilfrid Sellars. AMARAL, Pedro (ed).

Natural Signs: A Theory of Intentionality. ADDIS, Laird.

The Nature of Man in Early Stoic Philosophy. REESOR, Margaret E.

Notion and Object: Aspects of Late Medieval Epistemology. BROADIE, Alexander.

Ontological Investigations: Inquiry Into the Categories of Nature, Man, Society. JOHANSSON, Ingvar.

A Philosopher's Harvest: The Philosophical Papers of Isaac Franck. GERBER, William (ed).

The Philosophical Imaginary. LE DOEUFF, Michèle.

Philosophical Works. KALOYEROPOULOS, N A.

Philosophy of Biology Today. RUSE, Michael.

Philosophy of Perception. MACLACHLAN, D L C.

The Philosophy of Thomas Reid. DALGARNO, Melvin (ed).

Pursuit of Truth. QUINE, W V.

Rationality and Relativity: The Quest for Objective Knowledge. O'GORMAN, Francis.

Reclaiming Reality: A Critical Introduction to Contemporary Philosophy. BHASKAR, Roy.

Religion, Interpretation, and Diversity of Belief. GODLOVE, Terry F.

Rereading Russell: Essays on Bertrand Russell's Metaphysics and Epistemology. SAVAGE, C Wade (ed).

Rhetorica I—Reden mit Vernunft: Aristoteles, Cicero, Augustinus. MAINBERGER, Gonsalv K.

Scientific Explanation (Minnesota Studies in the Philosophy of Science, Volume XIII). KITCHER, Philip (ed).

Sense and Certainty: A Dissolution of Scepticism. MC GINN, Marie.

The Sophismata of Richard Kilvington. KRETZMANN, Norman.

A Theory of Content and Other Essays. FODOR, Jerry A.

Theory of Knowledge (Third Edition). CHISHOLM, Roderick M.

Theory of Knowledge. LEHRER, Keith.

Theory of Scientific Method—William Whewell. BUTTS, Robert E (ed).

Thomas Reid and 'The Way of Ideas'. GALLIE, Roger D.

Thought Probes: Philosophy Through Science Fiction Literature (Second Edition). MILLER JR, Fred D.

Truth and Objectivity. ELLIS, Brian.

A Useful Inheritance: Evolutionary Aspects of the Theory of Knowledge. RESCHER, Nicholas.

Vico Revisited: Orthodoxy, Naturalism and Science in the Scienca Nuova. BEDANI, Gino.

Who Knows: From Quine to a Feminist Empiricism. NELSON, Lynn Hankinson.

Wittgenstein's Later Philosophy. HANFLING, Oswald.

"'What Can We Know and When Can We Know It': On the Active Intelligence and Human Cognition" in *Moses Maimonides and His Time*, KOGAN, Barry S.

"Aristotle's Epistemology" in *Epistemology (Companions to Ancient Thought: 1)*, TAYLOR, C C W.

"The Charybdis of Realism: Epistemological Implications of Bell's Inequality" in *Philosophical Consequences of Quantum Theory: Reflections on Bell's Theorem*, VAN FRAASSEN, Bas C.

"Condorcet's Epistemology and His Politics" in *Knowledge and Politics*, POPKIN, Richard H.

"The Crisis of Knowledge and Understanding the Holocaust: Some Epistemological Remarks" in *Inquiries into Values: The Inaugural Session of the International Society for Value Inquiry*, ROSENBERG, Alan.

"David Hume: Crusading Empiricist, Skeptical Liberal" in *Knowledge and Politics*, HERZOG, Don.

"Derrida's Epistemology" in *The Textual Sublime: Deconstruction and Its Differences*, EASTHOPE, Antony.

"Epistemological Reductionism in Biology" in *Reductionism and Systems Theory in the Life Sciences: Some Problems and Perspectives*, HOYNINGEN-HUENE, Paul.

"Epistemology Naturalized vs Epistemology Socialized" in *Scientific Knowledge Socialized*, FEHÉR, Márta.

"Evolution, Epistemology and Visual Science" in *Issues in Evolutionary Epistemology*, SMITH, C U M.

"Evolutionary Explanation and the Justification of Belief" in *Issues in Evolutionary Epistemology*, CLENDINNEN, F John.

"For Whom is the Real Existence of Values a Problem: Or, An Attempt to Show that the Obvious is Plausible" in *Mind, Value and Culture: Essays in Honor of E M Adams*, POTEAT, William H.

"Ideas of Representation" in *Mind, Value and Culture: Essays in Honor of E M Adams*, LYCAN, William G.

"Intentional Parallelism and the Two-Level Structure of Evolutionary Theory" in *Issues in Evolutionary Epistemology*, MATTHEN, Mohan.

"The Interpretive Turn from Kant to Derrida: A Critique" in *History and Anti-History in Philosophy*, LAVINE, T Z.

"Kant's Transcendental Arguments" in *Reading Kant*, BIRD, Graham.

"Lying on the Couch" in *Dismantling Truth: Reality in the Post-Modern World*, FORRESTER, John.

"A Model of End-Directedness" in *Issues in Evolutionary Epistemology*, WARD, Patrick J.

"On Induction and Russell's Postulates" in *Rereading Russell: Essays on Bertrand Russell's Metaphysics and Epistemology*, SAINSBURY, R M.

"The Physical Manifestation of Empirical Knowledge" in *Issues in Evolutionary Epistemology*, HATTIANGADI, J N.

"A Plea for an Interactionist Epistemology" in *Scientific Knowledge Socialized*, LELAS, Srdjan.

"The *Pons Asinorum* in Philosophy" in *Dialectic and Contemporary Science*, MULLER, Philippe.

"Quantum Nonlocality and the Description of Nature" in *Philosophical Consequences of Quantum Theory: Reflections on Bell's Theorem*, STAPP, Henry P.

"Reply to Muller's "The *Pons Asinorum* in Philosophy" in *Dialectic and Contemporary Science*, HARRIS, Errol E.

"Science as Part of Nature" in *Issues in Evolutionary Epistemology*, MUNEVAR, Gonzalo.

"Socializing Epistemology" in *Scientific Knowledge Socialized*, HESSE, Mary.

"Stoic Epistemology" in *Epistemology (Companions to Ancient Thought: 1)*, ANNAS, Julia.

"The Trials and Tribulations of Selectionist Explanations" in *Issues in Evolutionary Epistemology*, AMUNDSON, Ron.

"The Way the World Isn't: What the Bell Theorems Force Us to Give Up" in *Philosophical Consequences of Quantum Theory: Reflections on Bell's Theorem*, WESSELS, Linda.

"El aire es elástico". CAIMI, Mario P M.

"Questions Philosophers Ask": Response to Michael Baur. NALEZINSKI, Alix.

The A Priori from Kant to Schelling. LAWRENCE, Joseph P (trans) and GRONDIN, Jean.

The Absolute Network Theory of Language and Traditional Epistemology. PHILIPSE, Herman.

Abstract General Ideas in Hume. PAPPAS, George S.

Acontecimientos y leyes en la explicación histórica. CORNBLIT, Oscar.

Acquaintance, Knowledge and Description in Russell. BAR-ELLI, Gilead.

Affirming the Reality of Rule-Following. PETTIT, Philip.

Against Feminist Science: Harding and the Science Question in Feminism. LAKOMSKI, Gabriele.

Against Relativism. RADNITZKY, Gerard.

Agnosticism and Atheism. BRINTON, Alan.

AI, as an Action Science, as an Utopia or as a Scapegoat. VANDAMME, Fernand.

Aim-Less Epistemology?. LAUDAN, L.

Alberto Magno y los últimos unicornios. DE ASUA, M J C.

Alvin I Goldman's Epistemology and Cognition: An Introduction. LEVINE, Michael P.

Analyticity, Indeterminacy and Semantic Theory: Some Comments on "The Domino Theory". GREENWOOD, John D.

Der Andere als Zukunft und Gegenwart. RÖMPP, Georg.

Die Anschauungsformen und das Schematismuskapitel. MUDROCH, Vilem.

Anscombe on Justifying Claims to Know One's Bodily Position. LOTT, Tommy L.

Anti-Realism in the Philosophy of Probability: Bruno de Finetti's Subjectivism. GALAVOTTI, Maria Carla.

Anti-Realism Under Mind?. KHLENTZOS, Drew.

Antinomies and Paradoxes and their Solutions. WEINGARTNER, Paul.

Application on the Relevance of AI Assumptions for Social Practitioners. MURPHY, John.

Apriority and Metajustification in BonJour's "Structure of Empirical Knowledge". SOLOMON, Miriam.

Are Salmon's 'Guises' Disguised Fregean Senses?. BRANQUINHO, João.

Aristotele, Platone e l'IBM. PARISI, Giorgio.

Aristóteles en *El Nombre de la Rosa*. GIRALT, María de los Angeles.

Aristotle on the Difference between Mathematics and Physics and First Philosophy. MODRAK, D K W.

Aristotle on the Mechanics of Thought. WEDIN, M V.

Barwise and Etchemendy's Theory of Truth. AOYAMA, Hiroshi.

The Basic Notion of Justification. KVANVIG, Jonathan L and MENZEL, Christopher.

Belief, Acceptance and Belief Reports. ASHER, Nicholas.

EPISTEMOLOGY

Frank Jackson's Knowledge Argument Against Materialism. FURASH, Gary.

Frege's Objects of a Quine Special Kind. SCHIRN, Matthias.

Freud, Racine, and the Epistemology of Tragedy. BRODY, Jules.

From Absolute Idealism to Instrumentalism: The Problem of Dewey's Early Philosophy. WELCHMAN, Jennifer.

From Coffee to Carmelites. PHILLIPS, D Z.

From Extroverted Realism to Correspondence: A Modest Proposal. BIGELOW, John and PARGETTER, Robert.

From Facts to Theory: The Emergence of the Feudal Relics Debate within Chinese Marxism (in Serbo-Croatian). DUTTON, Michael.

Fumerton's Puzzle. FOLEY, Richard.

Functionalism and Inverted Spectra. COLE, David.

Generalizaciones y explicación de la historiografía. PINCIONE, Guido M.

Gilligan's Two Voices: An Epistemological Overview. DURAN, Jane.

Goldman on Epistemic Justification. ALSTON, William P.

Goldman on Epistemology and Cognitive Science. FELDMAN, Richard.

Grundprinzipien einer kritischen Dialektik zwischen Kant und Hegel. IDALOVICHI, Israel.

Il guidizio di Sant'Agostino sulla Nuova Accademia tra scetticismo ed esoterismo. FERRETTI, Silvia.

Having Ideas and Having the Concept. CRIMMINS, Mark.

Hegel über die Rede vom Absoluten—Teil I: Urteil, Satz und Spekulativer Gehalt. GRAESER, Andreas.

Heidegger and Peirce: Beyond "Realism or Idealism". BOURGEOIS, Patrick L and ROSENTHAL, Sandra B.

Heidegger e la sua intuizione di fondo. ZAPPONE, Giuseppe.

Heidegger y la noción tomista de verdad. FILIPPI, Silvana.

A Hermeneutic Account of Clinical Psychology: Strengths and Limits. SILVERN, Louise E.

Hermeneutics and Apodicticity in Phenomenological Method. REEDER, Harry P.

The Hermeneutics of the Young Marx: According to Marx's Approach to the Philosophy of Democritus and Epicurus. BALABAN, Oded.

Heuristic Appraisal: A Proposal. NICKLES, Thomas.

The Historical Epistemology of Gaston Bachelard and its Relevance to Science Education. SOUQUE, Jean-Pascal.

Hobbes's Psychology of Thought: Endeavours, Purpose and Curiosity. BARNOUW, Jeffrey.

How Epistemology Can Be a System. LEE, Donald.

How to Believe the Impossible. BROWN, Curtis.

Human Natures. LACHS, John.

Human Understanding. ZEMACH, Eddy M.

Hume on Virtue, Beauty, Composites, and Secondary Qualities. BAXTER, Donald L M.

Hume's Missing Shade of Blue Re-viewed. NELSON, John O.

Hume's Philosophical Schizophrenia. ERES, Gloria H.

Husserl's Phenomenology as Critique of Epistemic Ideology. HARVEY, Charles W.

Husserl, Intentionality, and Cognitive Architecture. BROWN, Charles S.

Identity Statements and the Necessary A Posteriori. STEWARD, Helen.

Idéologie e conoscenza scientifica: La fondazione delle scienze umane nella gnoseologia sensita idéologique. PELLEREY, Roberto.

Ideology and Epistemology: A Discussion of Mc Carney and Mills. SUSHINSKY, Mary Ann.

Immanent Truth. RESNIK, Michael D.

In and Out of Peirce's Percepts. HAUSMAN, Carl R.

The Inconsistency of Putnam's Internal Realism. POLAKOW, Avron.

Incontinent Belief. MC LAUGHLIN, Brian P.

Indefinitely Repeated Games: A Response to Carroll. BECKER, Neal C and CUDD, Ann E.

Induction, Conceptual Spaces, and AI. GÄRDENFORS, Peter.

Inductive Scepticism and Experimental Reasoning in Moral Subjects in Hume's Philosophy. JACOBSON, Anne Jaap.

Information Processing: From a Mechanistic to a Natural Systems Approach. VAN CAMP, Ingrid.

La ingeniería social como método de testeo. COMESAÑA, Manuel E.

Inspecting Images: A Reply to Smythies. WRIGHT, Edmond.

Integrative Thinking Is the Essential Characteristic of Creative Thinking. SONGXING, Su and GUOZHENG, Lin.

Intensionality and Perception: A Reply to Rosenberg. MATTHEN, Mohan.

The Intentionality of Animal Action. HEYES, Cecilia and DICKINSON, Anthony.

Internalism and Externalism in Moral Epistemology. AUDI, Robert.

Interpretation and the Bible: The Dialectic of Concept and Content in Interpretive Reading. POLKA, Brayton.

Interprétation et mentalité prélogique. ENGEL, Pascal.

Introspection and Misdirection. KORNBLITH, Hilary.

Irresistibility, Epistemic Warrant and Religious Belief. LINTS, Richard.

Is kennis belichaamd?. SCHOPMAN, Joop.

Is the 'Socratic Fallacy' Socratic?. VLASTOS, Gregory.

It's Hard to Believe. MALONEY, J Christopher.

It's Not that Easy Being Grue. MARTIN, Robert M.

A J Ayer: An Appreciation. SPRIGGE, T L S.

John Stuart Mill: su concepción de la Lógica. CAÑÓN, Camino.

Justificación epistémica. LEGRIS, Javier.

Justification des normes: transcendantale ou pragmatique?. GRÜNEWALD, Bernward.

Justification, Reliability and Knowledge. SHOPE, Robert K.

Kant e o ceticismo. LOPARIC, Zeljko.

Kant's Account of Sensation. FALKENSTEIN, Lorne.

Kant's *Analogies* and the Structure of Objective Time. HUGHES, R I G.

Kant's Argument for the Non-Spatiotemporality of Things in Themselves. FALKENSTEIN, Lorne.

Kant's Conception of Empirical Law—I. GUYER, Paul.

Kant's Conception of Empirical Law—II. WALKER, Ralph.

Kantian and Platonic Conceptions of Order. STOLL, Donald.

Kent Bach on Good Arguments. SOBEL, Jordan Howard.

Kierkegaard, a Kind of Epistemologist. PERKINS, Robert L.

Kleine epistemologie van de kikvors-retina. GOUDSMIT, Arno L.

Eine kleine Überraschung für Gehirne im Tank: Eine skeptische Notiz zu einem antiskeptischen Argument. METSCHL, Ulrich.

Knowledge and the Regularity Theory of Information. MORRIS, William Edward.

Knowledge and Truth. LEPAGE, François.

Knowledge as Active, Aesthetic, and Hypothetical. FRISINA, Warren G.

Knowledge, Criticism, and Coherence. KUYS, Thieu.

Die Kommunikation zwischen der Philosophie Chinas und Europas um die Wende zum 20 Jahrhundert. YAO, Jiehou.

La rationnalité interrogative (in Romanian). GRECU, Constantin.

Language and Thought in Kant's Theory of Knowledge (in Hebrew). DASCAL, Marcelo and SENDEROWICZ, Yaron.

Levi's Decision Theory. LEEDS, Stephen.

The Limits of Thought: Rosenzweig, Schelling, and Cohen. GIBBS, Robert.

Literature as a Way of Knowing: An Epistemological Justification for Literary Studies. KASPRISIN, Lorraine.

La logica nella conoscenza. VENTURA, Antonino.

Lógicas divergentes y principios lógicos: Un análisis crítico de algunas tesis de Susan Haack. PALAU, Gladys.

Mach's "Critique of Knowledge" and the Physiology of Senses (in Czechoslovakian). JANKO, Jan.

Más allá del escepticismo, a nuestro leal saber y entender. SOSA, Ernesto.

Materialità del testo e pratica interpretativa: la semanlisi di Julia Kristeva. BRUNO, G.

Maximization, stability of Decision, and Actions in Accordance with Reason. SOBEL, Jordan Howard.

Melancholic Epistemology. GRAHAM, George.

Merleau-Ponty's nieuwe filosofie van de perceptie, de natuur en de logos. KWANT, R C.

Merleau-Ponty: una crítica a la teoría realista de la percepción. GARCIA, Pablo Sebastian.

Metafisica e metaforica. BOTTANI, Livio.

Metafisica e teologia della parola. SAINATI, Vittorio.

Metafisica Todavia? (cont). SANABRIA, José Rubén.

Method and the Authority of Science. TILES, Mary E.

El metodo filosofico segun 'Sapientiale' de Tomas de York. LÉRTORA MENDOZA, Celina A.

La metodología falsacionista y su ecología. RADNITZKY, Gerard.

Mill's Epistemology in Practice in his Liberal Feminism. TULLOCH, Gail.

Minds Divided. HEIL, John.

Miracles and the Uniformity of Nature. ROOT, Michael.

Miseria o valore della metafisica?. TURCO, Giovanni.

Modal Fictionalism. ROSEN, Gideon.

Models of Rationality. VAN STRAATEN, Zak.

Moral Epistemology: Historical Lessons and Contemporary Concerns. JECKER, Nancy S.

Moral Understandings: Alternative "Epistemology" for a Feminist Ethics. WALKER, Margaret Urban.

Mystical Experience and Non-Basically Justified Belief. LEVINE, Michael P.

The Myth of Jones and the Mirror of Nature: Reflections on Introspection. GARFIELD, Jay L.

La natura sprecona, i codici e lo struscio. ECO, Umberto.

Naturaleza del conocimiento humano: El significado de la abstracción en Santo Tomás (III). DERISI, Octavio N.

Naturalism and the Normativity of Epistemology. MAFFIE, James.

EPISTEMOLOGY

Naturalismo prescriptivo: epistemología. MUNÉVAR, Gonzalo.

Nel labirinto dell'informazione: i sistemi complessi. MORCHIO, Renzo.

Il neorealismo epistemologico dell' "Académie Internationale de philosophie des sciences". CASTELLANA, M.

Neue Entwicklungen im Wahrheitsbegriff. SEUREN, Pieter A M.

New Representationalism. WRIGHT, Edmond.

A New Verdict on the 'Jury Passage': *Theaetetus* 201A-C. STRAMEL, James S.

Nietzsche's Politics. THIELE, Leslie Paul.

NOA's Ark—Fine for Realism. MUSGRAVE, Alan.

The Non-Epistemic Explanation of Religious Belief. YANDELL, Keith E.

Die Notizen Eugen Finks zur Umarbeitung von Edmund Husserls "Cartesianischen Meditationen". BRUZINA, Ronald.

Nozick and the Sceptic: The Thumbnail Version. CRAIG, Edward.

L'obiettivazione della vita soggettiva nelle scienze storico-sociali e la fenomenologia trascendentale di Husserl. MASSIMILLA, Edoardo.

Object-Dependent Thoughts. BOËR, Steven E.

Objectividade científica: noção e quiestionamentos. CUPANI, Alberto.

The Objects of Perceptual Experience—I. SNOWDON, Paul.

The Objects of Perceptual Experience—II. ROBINSON, Howard.

Objetos, identidad y mismidad. CASTAÑEDA, Héctor-Neri.

Observation in Constructive Empiricism: Arbitrary or Incoherent?. CORDERO, Alberto.

Observation, Instrumentalism, and Constructive Empiricism. GRAYBOSCH, Anthony.

Odors and Private Language: Observations on the Phenomenology of Scent. ALMAGOR, Uri.

On Dialectical Consistency. ZELENY, Jindrich.

On Equitable Cake-Cutting, or: Caring More about Caring. HAYNES, Felicity.

On Gettier's Notion of Knowledge and Justification. MUKHOPADHYAY, Debabrata.

On Legal Proof. BIRMINGHAM, Robert L.

On Meaning and Understanding. PAVILIONIS, Rolandas.

On *Sapaksa*. TILLEMANS, Tom J F.

On Taking the Rabbit of Rule-Following out of the Hat of Representation: Response to 'The Reality of Rule-Following'. SUMMERFIELD, Donna M.

On the Definition of Risk Aversion. MONTESANO, Aldo.

On the Development of Knowledge. VOISVILO, E K.

On the Inter-relatedness of Theory and Measurement in the Study of Unconscious Processes. REINGOLD, Eyal M and MERIKLE, Philip M.

On the Question of the Active Role of Reflection in Marxist-Leninist Epistemology (in Czechoslovakian). HOGENOVA, A and SAFAR, Z.

On the Typology of Modes of Thought. LI, Cheng.

Ontogenesi della forma e informazione. FASOLO, Aldo.

An Operational Approach to the Dynamics of Science: Kant's Concept of Architectonic. GIUCULESCU, Alexandru.

Our Perception of the External World. TILES, J E.

Pappas on the Role of Sensations in Reid's Theory of Perception. CUMMINS, Phillip D.

El Paradigma de Sistemas: Posibilidades Para Una Práctica Social Emancipadora: Reevaluación Crítica (Primera Part). RODRÍGUEZ HÖLKEMEYER, Patricia.

Paramārtha and Modern Constructivists on Mysticism: Epistemological Monomorphism versus Duomorphism. FORMAN, Robert K C.

Paramnésie et katamnèse. VINSON, Alain.

La parole du philosophe éthicien est-elle crédible?. LEGAULT, Georges A.

Pascal's Theory of Scientific Knowledge. ARNOLD, Keith.

Paul Ricoeur's Methodological Parallelism. FLEMING, Patricia Ann.

Peirce on the Progress and Authority of Science. FORSTER, Paul D.

Peirce's Concept of Knowledge in 1868. SMYTH, Richard.

Peirce's Early Method of Finding the Categories. DE TIENNE, André.

Peirce's Interpretant. LISZKA, James Jakob.

A Peircean Response to the Realist-Empiricist Debate. FRENCH, Steven.

Peircean Scientific Realism. ALMEDER, Robert.

La pensée et la nouveauté de pensée. SCHLANGER, Judith.

Perception: Belief and Experience. PITSON, Anthony.

Phänomenale Realität und naturalistische Philosophie. POHLENZ, Gerd.

Phenomenological Skepticism in Hume. LOPTSON, Peter.

Philosophical Apology in the *Theaetetus*. HEMMENWAY, Scott R.

Die Philosophie und ihre Missbildungen. ESTRELLA, Jorge.

Philosophische Wahrheit aus intuitivem Urdenken. MOLLOWITZ, Gerhard.

Philosophy and Machine Learning. THAGARD, Paul.

Plato's Critique of the Poets and the Misunderstanding of his Epistemological Argumentation. WIEGMANN, Hermann.

Plato's Forms: A Text That Self-Destructs to Shed Its Light. BERRY, John M.

Platon le sceptique. ANNAS, Julia.

Platon, Arcésilas, Carnéade: Réponse à J Annas. LÉVY, Carlos.

Platonische Idee und die anschauliche Welt bei Schopenhauer. KAMATA, Yasuo.

Poder causal, experiencia y conceptos *a priori*. CASSINI, Alejandro.

Poetic Invention and Scientific Observation: James's Model of "Sympathetic Concrete Observation". SEIGFRIED, Charlene Haddock.

The Politics of Epistemology. WHITE, Morton.

Post-Modernism is Not a Scepticism. FUCHS, Wolfgang W.

Practical Knowing: Finnis and Aquinas. SIMPSON, Peter.

Presupposizione e verità: Il problema critico della conoscenza filosofica. MOLINARO, Aniceto.

The Price of Possibility. HART, W D.

The Primacy of Narrative in Historical Understanding. JACQUES, T Carlos.

Primäre und sekundäre Qualitatäten bei John Locke. KIENZLE, Bertram.

The Prince and the Phone Booth: Reporting Puzzling Beliefs. CRIMMINS, Mark and PERRY, John.

The Priority of Reason in Descartes. LOEB, Louis E.

Probabilism. DE FINETTI, Bruno.

Probabilistic Causation and Causal Processes: A Critique of Lewis. MENZIES, Peter.

The Problem of Going *from*: Science Policy and 'Human Factors' in the Experience of Developing Countries. IGNATYEV, A A.

The Problem of Going *To*: Between Epistemology and the Sociology of Knowledge. MOKRZYCKI, Edmund.

The Problem of Knowledge and Phenomenology. PIETERSMA, Henry.

The Problem of the External World. HAMLYN, D W.

The Problem with the *Fragments*: Kierkegaard on Subjectivity and Truth. PIETY, Marilyn.

Psicologia e scienze della natura in Wilhelm Wundt. CAVALLO, Giuliana.

Putnam on "Empirical Objects". STEINHOFF, Gordon.

Putnam's Brains in a Vat and Bouwsma's Flowers. SHIRLEY, Edward S.

The Puzzle of the Self-Torturer. QUINN, Warren S.

Pyrrhonean Scepticism and the Self-Refutation Argument. BAILEY, Alan.

Quelques repères de l'épistémologie contemporaine (in Romanian). ISAC, Ionut.

Radical Interpretation and the Gunderson Game. WARD, Andrew.

Ragione debole e metafisica: Spunti tra vecchia e nuova apologetica. TODISCO, Orlando.

The Rationality of Rationality: Why Think Critically? Response to Siegel. ENNIS, Robert H.

La razón en su uso regulativo y el a priori del "sistema" en la primera Crítica. DOTTI, Jorge E.

Reading *Probabilismo*. JEFFREY, Richard.

Realism and Reality: Some Realistic Reconsiderations. ISAAC, Jeffrey C.

Realism, Reference and Theory. HARRÉ, Rom.

Realismo II: Donald Davidson. VILLANUEVA, Enrique.

Realismus heute. INEICHEN, Hans.

Reasons, Values, and Rational Action. MOSER, Paul K.

Recent Work in the Philosophy of Religion. ZAGZEBSKI, Linda.

Recent Work on Foundationalism. TRIPLETT, Timm.

Reexamining Berkeley's Notion of Suggestion. BEN-ZEEV, Aaron.

Reflexive Epistemology and Social Complexity: *The Philosophical Legacy of Otto Neurath*. ZOLO, Danilo.

Reformed Epistemology and Religious Fundamentalism: How Basic Are Our Basic Beliefs?. TILLEY, Terrence W.

Reliabilism and Relevant Worlds. MOSER, Paul K.

Reliability and Goldman's Theory of Justification. ALMEDER, Robert and HOFF, Franklin J.

Renormalizing Epistemology. LEPLIN, Jarrett.

Replies to the Commentators. GOLDMAN, Alvin I.

Reply to Scheer's "What if Something Really Unheard-of Happened?". MALCOLM, Norman.

Reply to Solomon's "Apriority and Metajustification in BonJour's 'Structure of Empirical Knowledge'". BONJOUR, Laurence.

Representation and Repetition. SARTWELL, Crispin.

Representation in the Eighteenth Brumaire of Karl Marx. REDNER, Harry.

A Representational Account of Mutual Belief. KOONS, Robert C.

Response to Huang Siu-chi's Review of *Knowledge Painfully Acquired*, by Lo Ch'in-shun and Translated by Irene Bloom. BLOOM, Irene.

La revolución científica y las revoluciones filosóficas. ARANA, Juan.

Riflessioni epistemologiche sull'errore. BALDINI, Massimo.

Scattered Sociology: A Response to Bash. FUHRMAN, Ellsworth.

Scepticism about Knowledge of Content. BRUECKNER, Anthony.

Scepticism and *Angst*: The Case of David Hume. COHEN, Avner.

Scepticism and Madness. BELSHAW, Christopher.

Scepticism and Rational Belief. WEDGWOOD, Ralph.

Scepticism, Evidentialism and the Parity Argument: A Pascalian Perspective. HOLYER, Robert.

EPISTEMOLOGY

Schizophrenia and Indeterminacy: The Problem of Validity. HUNT, Geoffrey.

Science and Hermeneutics. RICKMAN, H P.

Selbstreferenz und Zeit: Die dynamische Stabilität des Bewusstseins. BERGMANN, Werner and HOFFMANN, G.

Self Enforceable Paths in Extensive Form Games. PONSSARD, Jean-Pierre.

Sensation, Perception and Immediacy: Mead and Merleau-Ponty. ROSENTHAL, Sandra B and BOURGEOIS, Patrick L.

El sentido de la teoría humeana del tiempo como relación filosófica. MUDROVCIC, María Inés.

Os Sentidos da "Crítica". BORGES, Bento Itamar.

Sich-Wissen als Argument: Zum Problem der Theoretizität des Selbstbewusstseins. RÖMPP, Georg.

The Singularity of Christian Ethics. MEILAENDER, Gilbert.

Six Aspects of Santayana's Philosophy. KERR-LAWSON, Angus.

Skepticism and Davidson's Omniscient Interpreter Argument. WARD, Andrew.

Skepticism and Naturalized Epistemology. WINBLAD, Douglas G.

The So-Called Semantic Concept of Truth. STENIUS, Erik.

The Splitting of the Logos: Some Remarks on Vico and Rabbinic Tradition. FAUR, José.

Stable and Retrievable Options. RABINOWICZ, Woldzimierz.

The Status of Epistemic Principles. CHISHOLM, Roderick M.

Stroud and Williams on Dreaming and Scepticism. REIN, Andrew.

The Structure and Content of Truth. DAVIDSON, Donald.

Subjective Justification. DE PIERRIS, Graciela.

Supervaluational Anti-Realism and Logic. RASMUSSEN, Stig Alstrup.

T H Morgan, Neither an Epistemological Empiricist nor a "Methodological" Empiricist. VICEDO, Marga.

Talking 'Bout a Revolution: Feminism, Historicism, and Liberal Moral Theory. ARNAULT, Lynne.

A Taste for Hume. DE MARTELAERE, Patricia.

Técnica o imagen del mundo?. HÖVELMANN, Gerd H.

La teoría de los objetos en Alexius Meinong. VELARDE MAYOL, V.

Teoría y praxis: evolución de estos conceptos. PONFERRADA, Gustavo Eloy.

The Dialectics of the Unity of Linearity and Non-linearity of Physical Processes (in Czechoslovakian). GOTT, V S.

There Is Nothing Magical about Possible Worlds. MILLER, Richard B.

Thinking with the Weight of the Earth: Feminist Contributions to an Epistemology of Concreteness. HOLLER, Linda.

Thomas Hobbes: La razón-cálculo. PRADO, José Julián.

Through Thick and Thin: Moral Knowledge in Skeptical Times. LOUDEN, Robert B.

Towards a Rationalization of Biological Psychiatry: A Study in Psychobiological Epistemology. RUDNICK, Abraham.

Towards a Typology of Experimental Errors: An Epistemological View. HON, Giora.

Tra intenzionalismo e antirelativismo: l'interpretazione di teorie filosofiche come traduzione. VARNIER, Giuseppe.

Transcendental Arguments and Conceptual Schemes: A Reconsideration of Körner's Uniqueness Argument. MALPAS, J E.

The Truth about Neptune and the Seamlessness of Truth. SANFORD, David H.

Truth in Thomas Aquinas (I). WIPPEL, John F.

Truth, Eliminativism and Disquotationalism. DAVID, Marian A.

Truth, Interpretation and Convention T. PRADHAN, R C.

Truthmongering: An Exercise. KNEZEVICH, Lily.

Truthmongering: Less is True. FINE, Arthur.

Two Concepts of the Given in C I Lewis: Realism and Foundationalism. GOWANS, Christopher W.

Two Fallacious Objections to Adam's Soft/Hard Distinction. WIDERKER, David.

Two Uses of 'Know'. CLARKE JR, D S.

Under Stochastic Dominance Choquet-Expected Utility and Anticipated Utility Are Identical. WAKKER, Peter.

Varieties of Pragmatism. KRAUT, Robert.

The Verification Principle: Another Puncture—Another Patch. WRIGHT, Crispin.

Vérisimilarité et méthodologie poppérienne. LAFLEUR, Gérald.

La verità come inganno—L'Arte di Gorgia. VITALE, Vincenzo.

Verständnis für Unvernünftige. BITTNER, Rüdiger.

Vico and Bakhtin: A Prolegomenon to Any Future Comparison. JUNG, Hwa Yol.

Victor Cousin: Commonsense and the Absolute. MANNS, James W and MADDEN, Edward H.

The Wall and the Shield: K-K Reconsidered. ROTH, Michael.

Watkins and the Pragmatic Problem of Induction. BAMFORD, Greg.

What if Something Really Unheard-of Happened?. SCHEER, R K.

What Is Empiricism?—I. CARRUTHERS, Peter.

What Is Empiricism?—II, Nativism, Naturalism, and Evolutionary Theory. MACDONALD, Cynthia.

When Do We Deceive Others?. BARNES, Annette.

Why Be Rational? On Thinking Critically About Critical Thinking. SIEGEL, Harvey.

Why Did Kant Bother About 'Nothing'?. VAN KIRK, Carol A.

Why is Belief Involuntary?. BENNETT, Jonathan.

Why the Theory of Knowledge Isn't the Same as Epistemology, and What It Might Be Instead. ROSENBERG, Jay F.

William James, Dieu et la possibilité actuelle. GAVIN, William J.

Wittgenstein and Obscurantism. CIOFFI, Frank.

Zetesis. DE OLASO, Ezequiel.

Zur teleologischen Grundlage der transzendentalen Deduktion der Kategorien. ROSALES, Alberto.

EPOCHE

The Ancient Sceptic's Way of Life. MORRISON, Donald.

EPSTEIN, J

Ambition. DOMBROWSKI, Daniel A.

EQUAL OPPORTUNITY

"Can There Be Equal Opportunity Without a Merit Principle" in Inquiries into Values: The Inaugural Session of the International Society for Value Inquiry, KAMPE, Cornelius.

Dilemma of M Oakeshott: Oakeshott's Treatment of Equality of Opportunity in Education and His Political Philosophy. WILLIAMS, Kevin.

Equal Opportunity Is Equal Education (within Limits). HOWE, Kenneth R.

Equal Opportunity or Equal Education?. BURBULES, Nicholas C.

Equal Opportunity. WELLMAN, Carl.

Equality of Educational Opportunity as Equality of Educational Outcomes. HOWE, Kenneth R.

Equality of Opportunity as the Noble Lie. ANDREW, Edward.

In Defense of Outcomes-Based Conceptions of Equal Educational Opportunity. HOWE, Kenneth R.

A Questionable Resurrection. HESLEP, Robert D.

Sexual Discrimination and the Equal Opportunities Commission: Ought Schools to Eradicate Sex Stereotyping?. SHAW, Beverley.

EQUALITY

see also Egalitarianism

Eguaglianza interesse unanimità: La politica di Rousseau. BURGIO, Alberto.

Essays on Political Morality. HARE, R M.

The Good Life: Personal and Public Choices. LOUZECKY, David.

Liberal Justice and the Marxist Critique of Education: A Study of Conflicting Research Programs. STRIKE, Kenneth A.

Time, Freedom, and the Common Good: An Essay in Public Philosophy. SHEROVER, Charles M.

Violence and Equality: Inquiries in Political Philosophy. HONDERICH, Ted.

Who Lives? Who Dies?: Ethical Criteria in Patient Selection. KILNER, John F.

Arithmetic Based on the Church Numerals in Illative Combinatory Logic. BUNDER, M W.

Civil Religion in Tocqueville's Democracy in America. KORITANSKY, John C.

Competitive Equality of Opportunity: A Defense. GREEN, S J D.

The Critique of Equalitarian Society in Malthus's Essay. GILBERT, Geoffrey.

Debating Difference: Feminism, Pregnancy, and the Workplace. VOGEL, Lise.

Dilemmas of Plant Closing Policy in Liberal Society: Equality, Rights, Justice. LEVIN-WALDMAN, Oren M.

Eguaglianza formale ed eguaglianza sostanziale dopo la rivoluzione francese. MATHIEU, Vittorio.

Equal Respect and the Enforcement of Morality. DWORKIN, Gerald.

Equality of Opportunity and the Problem of Nature. BLITS, Jan H.

Equality of Opportunity. YOUNG, Robert.

Equality, Political Order and Ethics: Hobbes and the Systematics of Democratic Rationality. ZIMMERMANN, Rolf.

Equiprobability. WATT, David.

Feminist Ethics: Some Issues for the Nineties. JAGGAR, Alison M.

Is Socialism a Psychological Misunderstanding?. REYKOWSKI, Janusz.

Justice Between Age-Groups: A Comment on Norman Daniels. MC KERLIE, Dennis.

L'égalité au dix'huitième siècle: l'importance de l'aequanimitas. MARCIL-LACOSTE, Louise.

Liberalism and Natural End Ethics. RASMUSSEN, Douglas B.

EQUALITY

Liberté et égalité chez Descartes. RODIS-LEWIS, Geneviève.
Market Equality and Social Freedom. HOLLIS, Martin.
The Right of Self-Determination in International Law. LANGLEY, Winston.
Self-Ownership, Communism and Equality—I. COHEN, G A.
Self-Ownership, Communism and Equality—II. GRAHAM, Keith.
The Theory of Democracy and the Ethics of Equality in the French Revolution (in Serbo-Croatian). REGUERA, Eduardo Bello.
Utilitarian Ethics and Democratic Government. RILEY, Jonathan.
Utilitarianism, Rights, and Equality. CROSSLEY, David J.

EQUATION(S)

Finitary Algebraic Logic. MADDUX, Roger D.
Near-Equational and Equational Systems of Logic for Partial Functions, II. CRAIG, William.
The Notion of Independence in Categories of Algebraic Structures, Part III: Equational Classes. SROUR, Gabriel.

EQUILIBRIUM

The Meaning of General Theoretical Sociology: Tradition and Formalization. FARARO, Thomas J.
Correlated Equilibria and the Dynamics of Rational Deliberation. SKYRMS, Brian.
Far-Sighted Equilibria in 2 x 2, Non-Cooperative, Repeated Games. AAFTINK, Jan.
Indefinitely Repeated Games: A Response to Carroll. BECKER, Neal C and CUDD, Ann E.

EQUIPOLLENCE

Brouwer's Equipotence and Denumerability Predicates. FRANCHELLA, Miriam.

EQUITY

A Critique of the Deconstructionist Account of Gender Equity and Education. PIETIG, Jeanne.
Crossing the Boundaries: Educational Thought and Gender Equity. LEACH, Mary and DAVIES, Bronwyn.
The Economic Efficiency and Equity of Abortion. MEEKS, Thomas J.
The Gandhian Approach to Swadeshi or Appropriate Technology. BAKKER, J I (Hans).
Symbolic Orders and Discursive Practices. WALKER, J C.
Theorizing Gender: How Much of It Do We Need. HOUSTON, Barbara.
Toward the Development of a Multidimensional Scale for Improving Evaluations of Business Ethics. REIDENBACH, R E and ROBIN, D P.

EQUIVALENCE

A General Treatment of Equivalent Modalities. BELLISSIMA, Fabio.
Identification et analyse des classes d'équivalence de la logique modale par des invariants numériques. SANCHEZ-MAZAS, Miguel.
Infinite Sets of Nonequivalent Modalities. BELLISSIMA, Fabio.
The Notion of Independence in Categories of Algebraic Structures, Part III: Equational Classes. SROUR, Gabriel.
On Ehrenfeucht-Fraïssé Equivalence of Linear Orderings. OIKKONEN, Juha.
Paraconsistency and the C-Systems of DaCosta. URBAS, Igor.
Sequences in Countable Nonstandard Models of the Natural Numbers. LETH, Steven C.

ERASMUS

Ought-Implies-Can: Erasmus Luther and R M Hare. PIGDEN, Charles R.
Rhetoric and the Erasmian Defence of Religious Toleration. REMER, Gary.

ERHARD, J

Reason, Revolution and Religion: Johann Benjamin Erhard's Concept of Enlightened Revolution. MARTINSON, Steven D.

EROS

Eros, Agape and Philia: Readings in the Philosophy of Love. SOBLE, Alan (ed).

EROTETIC LOGIC

Presuppositional Completeness. BUSZKOWSKI, Wojciech.

EROTICISM

The Thinking Muse: Feminism and Modern French Philosophy. ALLEN, Jeffner (ed).
Kierkegaard on Despair and the Eternal. MORRIS, T.
Notes on a Great Erotic. MC GHEE, Michael.

ERROR(S)

Religion, Interpretation, and Diversity of Belief. GODLOVE, Terry F.
Augustine's Pretence: Another Reading of Wittgenstein's Philosophical Investigations 1. WALKER, Margaret Urban.
Descartes' Doctrine of Volitional Infinity. CRESS, Donald A.
Error in Action and Belief. NEWTON, Natika.
Error Theory: Logic, Rhetoric, and Philosophy. GLOUBERMAN, M.

Moral Style. AXINN, Sidney.
Riflessioni epistemologiche sull'errore. BALDINI, Massimo.
The Role of Error in Computer Science. JASON, Gary.
Towards a Typology of Experimental Errors: An Epistemological View. HON, Giora.

ESCHATOLOGY

From Phenomenology to Liberation: The Displacement of History and Theology in Levinas's Totality and Infinity. MESKIN, Jacob.

ESOTERISM

Two-Tier Moral Codes. SMITH, Holly M.

ESSE

La esencia y la existencia en Tomas de Aquino. BEUCHOT, Mauricio.

ESSENCE(S)

see also Form(s)
The Critique of Thought: A Re-Examination of Hegel's Science of Logic. JOHNSON, Paul Owen.
Mind-Body Identity Theories. MACDONALD, Cynthia.
Necessity, Essence, and Individuation: A Defense of Conventionalism. SIDELLE, Alan.
"The Flower of the Mouth": Hölderlin's Hint for Heidegger's Thinking of the Essence of Language. VON HERRMANN, Friedrich-Wilhelm.
Aristotle's Conception of the Science of Being. LUDWIG, Walter D.
Artifacts, Essence and Reference. CHAUDHURY, Mahasweta.
Eigentlichkeit, Gewissen und Schuld in Heideggers "Sein und Zeit". FEHÉR, István.
Elementos y esencias. ANSCOMBE, G E M.
La esencia y la existencia en Tomas de Aquino. BEUCHOT, Mauricio.
Existence (wujūd) and Quiddity (māhiyyah) in Islamic Philosophy. NASR, Seyyed Hossein.
Santayana's Neglect of Hartshorne's Alternative. WHITTEMORE, Robert C.
La struttura metafisica dell'esistente. ALESSI, Adriano.

ESSENTIAL TRUTH(S)

Essential Truths and the Ontological Argument. SIEVERT, Donald.

ESSENTIALISM

Changing the Minimal Subject. CARTER, William.
Essentialisme et logique modale (in Romanian). DUMITRU, Mircea.
Identity Statements and the Necessary A Posteriori. STEWARD, Helen.
Interpretation at Risk. MARGOLIS, Joseph.
Supervenience, Essentialism and Aesthetic Properties. CURRIE, Gregory.

ETCHEMENDY, J

Barwise and Etchemendy's Theory of Truth. AOYAMA, Hiroshi.

ETERNAL

Body, Soul, and Life Everlasting: Biblical Anthropology and the Monism-Dualism Debate. COOPER, John W.
Kelly on the Logic of Eternal Knowledge. TAYLOR, James E.
Kierkegaard on Despair and the Eternal. MORRIS, T.
Non Posse Peccare. VAN DEN BELD, Antonie.

ETERNAL RECURRENCE

Nietzschean Narratives. SHAPIRO, Gary.
"Irony and Affirmation in Nietzsche's Thus Spoke Zarathustra" in Nietzsche's New Seas: Explorations in Philosophy, Aesthetics, and Politics, PIPPIN, Robert.
Apokatastasis en herhaling: Nietzsches eeuwigheidsbegrip. VERRYCKEN, K.
Different Readings: A Reply to Magnus, Solomon, and Conway. NEHAMAS, Alexander.
Nietzsche's Eternal Recurrence as Riemannian Cosmology. MOLES, Alistair.
Riemann's Geometry and Eternal Recurrence as Cosmological Hypothesis: A Reply. STACK, George J.
Self-Consuming Concepts. MAGNUS, Bernd.

ETERNITY

Amor y eternidad: La filosofía idealista de McTaggart. GEACH, Peter.
Apocalyptic Anticipations. KIVINEN, S Albert.
Boethius on Eternity. LEFTOW, Brian.
Edith Stein et la philosophie chrétienne: A propos d'Être fini et Être éternel. TILLIETTE, Xavier.
Einige Bemerkungen zur Bedeutung von Ewigkeit und Dauer in Spinozas Ethik. KOPPER, Joachim.
Eternity. WÖRNER, Markus H.
God and Time: Towards a New Doctrine of Divine Timeless Eternity. PADGETT, Alan G.

ETHICAL

From Nietzsche to Wittgenstein: The Problem of Truth and Nihilism in the Modern World. MARTIN, Glen T.

ETHICS

ETHICS

Aus den Überlegungen über die Moralsprachaspekte (in Polish). RODZINSKI, A.

The Authority of Moral Rules. MOREH, J.

Autonomist Internalism and the Justification of Morals. DARWALL, Stephen L.

Autonomy or Integrity: A Reply to Slote. WALKER, Margaret Urban.

Autonomy Without Indeterminism: A Reconstruction of Kant's *Groundwork*, Chapter Three. TERZIS, George N.

Avoiding the Tragedy of Whistleblowing. DAVIS, Michael.

Back to Sainthood. DOMBROWSKI, Daniel A.

Bentham in a Box. JONSEN, Albert R.

Bernard Williams and the Nature of Moral Reflection. CRAGG, A W.

Bernard Williams on Practical Necessity. GAY, Robert J.

Beyond Aestheticism: Derrida's Responsible Anarchy. CAPUTO, John D.

Beyond Good-Evil: A Plea for a Hermeneutic Ethics. OPHIR, Adi.

Beyond Revolt: A Horizon for Feminist Ethics. LINDGREN, Ralph.

Bhopal, India and Union Carbide: The Second Tragedy. TROTTER, R Clayton and DAY, Susan G and LOVE, Amy E.

El bien del arte en Etienne Gilson. HERRERA UBICO, Silvia.

El bien en arquitectura. SAGARDOY, María A F.

The Bioengineered Competitor?. MURRAY, Thomas H.

Bioethics and the Contemporary Jewish Community. NOVAK, David.

Bioethics as Civic Discourse. JENNINGS, Bruce.

Bioethics Discovers the Bill of Rights. VEATCH, Robert M.

Biomedical Ethics: Some Lessons for Social Philosophy. BROCK, Dan W.

The Biomedical Model and Just Health Care: Reply to Jecker. DANIELS, Norman.

Bioregionalism: Science or Sensibility?. ALEXANDER, Donald.

Blackburn's Projectivism—An Objection. BRIGHOUSE, M H.

Blood is Thicker Than Water: Don't Forsake the Family Jewels. BELLIOTTI, Raymond A.

A Bold Adventure. GUIN, Philip.

Buddhist Process Ethics: Dissolving the Dilemmas of Substantialist Metaphysics. PEERENBOOM, R P.

Business and Benevolence. MC CARTY, Richard.

The Business and Society Course: Does It Change Student Attitudes?. WYND, William R and MAGER, John.

Business Curriculum and Ethics: Student Attitudes and Behavior. GLENN JR, James R.

Business Ethics and Business Education: A Report from a Regional State University. CASTRO, Barry.

Business Ethics in Banking. GREEN, C F.

Business Ethics in Italy: The State of the Art. UNNIA, Mario.

Business Ethics, Corporate Good Citizenship and the Corporate Social Policy Process: A View from the US. EPSTEIN, Edwin M.

Business Ethics: A Literature Review with a Focus on Marketing Ethics. TSALIKIS, John and FRITZSCHE, David J.

Business Ethics: Defining the Twilight Zone. NEL, Deon and PITT, Leyland.

Business Ethics: Diversity and Integration. FLEMING, John E.

Business Regulation, Business Ethics and the Professional Employee. MACKIE, Karl J.

The Cake Problem. HART, W D.

The Calculus of Consent. SCOFIELD, Giles.

A Call to Heal Medicine. HOLMES, Helen Bequaert.

Can a Partisan be a Moralist?. GOMBERG, Paul.

Can Business Ethics Be Taught? Empirical Evidence. JONES, Thomas M.

Can Clinical Research Be Both 'Ethical' and 'Scientific'? A Commentary Inspired by Rosser and Marquis. HOLMES, Helen Bequaert.

Can Emotivism Sustain a Social Ethic?. UNWIN, Nicholas.

Can Ethics Take Pluralism Seriously?. ENGELHARDT JR, H Tristram.

Can Kant's Ethics Survive the Feminist Critique?. SEDGWICK, Sally S.

Can Others Exercise an Incapacitated Patient's Right to Die?. ELLMAN, Ira Mark.

Can Theology Have a Role in "Public" Bioethical Discourse?. CAHILL, Lisa Sowle.

Caring for Frail Elderly Parents: Past Parental Sacrifices and the Obligations of Adult Children. WICCLAIR, Mark.

Carneades' Distinction Between Assent and Approval. BETT, Richard.

The Case Against Moral Pluralism. CALLICOTT, J Baird.

The Categorical Imperative and Kant's Conception of Practical Rationality. REATH, Andrews.

Ch'eng I—The Pattern of Heaven-and-Earth (in Serbo-Croatian). SMITH, Kidder.

The Chainsaws of Greed: The Case of Pacific Lumber. NEWTON, Lisa H.

Character and Circumstance. WALKER, A D M.

Character Versus Codes: Models for Research Ethics. LOMBARDI, Louis G.

China: Moral Puzzles. TIAN-MIN, Xu.

Chinese Axial Age in the Light of Kohlberg's Developmental Logic of Moral Consciousness (in Serbo-Croatian). ROETZ, Heiner.

Choosing Death for Nancy Cruzan. BOPP, JR, James.

Christ and Business: A Typology for Christian Business Ethics. VAN WENSVEEN SIKER, Louke.

Christian Wolff and China: The Autonomy of Morality (in Serbo-Croatian). CHING, Julia.

Civil Disobedience in Times of AIDS. NOVICK, Alvin.

Comment on Chad Hansen's "Language Utilitarianism". BRANDT, Richard B.

A Comment on Coughlan's "Using People". ANSCOMBE, G E M.

Comment on Shrader-Frechette's "Parfit and Mistakes in Moral Mathematics". GRACELY, Edward J.

Commentary on "An Empirical Study of Moral Reasoning Among Managers". KELLY, Michaeleen.

Commentary: C-Section for Organ Donation. MATHIEU, Deborah R.

Commentary: C-Section for Organ Donation. NEWMAN, Louis E and BERKOWITZ, Sheldon T.

Commentary: Live Sperm, Dead Bodies. ROSS, Judith Wilson.

Commentary: Live Sperm, Dead Bodies. ROTHMAN, Cappy Miles.

Commentary: Prehospital DNR Orders. ISERSON, Kenneth V.

Commentary: Prehospital DNR Orders. ROUSE, Fenella.

Common Knowledge of the Second Kind. BELLA, David and KING, Jonathan.

Communitarian and Liberal Theories of the Good. PAUL, Jeffrey and MILLER JR, Fred D.

A Comparison of the Ethical Values of Business Faculty and Students: How Different Are They?. HARRIS, James R.

Competitive Equality of Opportunity: A Defense. GREEN, S J D.

Concentric Circle Pluralism: A Response to Rolston. WENZ, Peter S.

La conception stoïcienne et la conception aristotélicienne du bonheur. IRWIN, T H.

Concerning the Paradox of Moral Reparation and Other Matters. FELDMAN, Fred.

La conciencia ecológica como conciencia moral. SOSA, Nicolás M.

Confucian Justice: Achieving a Humane Society. PEERENBOOM, Randall P.

Conscience, contemplation, wisdom (in Polish). GOGZCZ, Mieczyslaw.

Consciousness, the Brain and What Matters. GILLETT, Grant R.

Consequentialism and History. GOMBERG, Paul.

Consequentialism in Search of a Conscience. LANGENFUS, William L.

Consequentialism, Egoism, and the Moral Law. CUMMISKEY, David.

The Contingent Person and the Existential Choice. HELLER, Agnes.

Contrasting Consequences: Bringing Charges of Sexual Harrassment Compared with Other Cases of Whistleblowing. DANDEKAR, Natalie.

The Contribution of *Nicomachean Ethics iii 5* to Aristotle's Theory of Responsibility. CURREN, Randall.

Control and Compensation: Laws Governing Extracorporeal Generative Materials. ANDREWS, Lori B.

Corporate Agency and Reduction. WELCH, John R.

Corporate and Individual Moral Responsibility: A Reply to Jan Garrett. WERHANE, Patricia H.

Corporate Goal Structures and Business Students: A Comparative Study of Values. BEGGS, Joyce M and LANE, Michael S.

Corporate Loyalty, Does It Have a Future?. GROSMAN, Brian A.

Corporate Morality Called in Question: The Case of Cabora Bassa. SCHREYÖGG, Georg and STEINMANN, Horst.

Corporate Punishment: A Proposal. RAFALKO, Robert J.

Corporate Responsibility: Morality Without Consciousness. SKIDD, David R A.

Corporate Social Monitoring in South Africa: A Decade of Achievement, An Uncertain Future. PAUL, Karen.

The Corporation and Its Employees: A Case Story. DAHL, Tor.

Corruption and Business in Present Day Venezuela. PERDOMO, Rogelio Perez.

Could Ideal Observers Disagree?: A Reply to Taliaferro. CARSON, Thomas L.

Could There Be a Rationally Grounded Morality?. BOND, E J.

Courage, Relativism and Practical Reasoning. WALTON, Douglas N.

The Course in Business Ethics: Can It Work?. PAMENTAL, George L.

The Crime of Punishment. BLUME, Robert and BLUME, Delorys.

Crisis Moral Communities: An Essay in Moral Philosophy. FISHER, David.

Critics of Science and Research Ethics in Sweden. GUSTAFSSON, Bengt and TIBELL, Gunnar.

A Critique of Principlism. CLOUSER, K Danner and GERT, Bernard.

Crucial Issues in Successful European Business. VAN LUIJK, Henk.

Dai Zhen: The Unity of the Moral Nature (in Serbo-Croatian). EWELL JR, John W.

ETHICS

ETHICS

Euthanasia, the Ultimate Abandonment. MARKER, Rita L.

Evangelical and Feminist Ethics: Complex Solidarities. BRULAND, Esther Byle.

Evangelical Ethics and the Anabaptist-Reformed Dialogue. MOUW, Richard J and YODER, John H.

Evil. ANDERSON, Susan Leigh.

Explanation and Justification in Ethics. COPP, David.

Expliquer et comprendre: La théorie de l'action de G H von Wright. NEUBERG, Marc.

A Fact About the Virtues. RAY, A Chadwick.

Faith and Ethical Reasoning in the Mystical Theology of St John of the Cross. SANDERLIN, David.

Feminist and Medical Ethics: Two Different Approaches to Contextual Ethics. SHERWIN, Susan.

Feminist Directions in Medical Ethics. WARREN, Virginia L.

A Feminist Ethic and the New Romanticism—Mothering as a Model of Moral Relations. LAURITZEN, Paul.

Feminist Ethics: Some Issues for the Nineties. JAGGAR, Alison M.

Feminist Moralism, "Pornography," and Censorship. DORITY, Barbara.

Feminists Healing Ethics. PURDY, Laura M.

Fiat Voluntas Tua! Vício e Pecado na ética de Abelardo. ESTEVÁO, J C.

The Fiery Fight for Animal Rights. JACKSON, Christine M.

Filosofia dell'educazione e filosofia morale. DUCCI, Edda.

Finitezza ed eticità nel pensiero storico di J G Droysen. CAIANIELLO, Silvia.

Flew on Russell on Nozick: Uncharitable Interpretations of Justice and Unjust Views of Charity. SKILLEN, Tony.

La fondation de la bioéthique: une perspective épistémologique. TOURNIER, F.

Fooling with Mother Nature. GAYLIN, Willard.

Forgetting about Auschwitz? Remembrance as a Difficult Task of Moral Education. SCHWEITZER, Friederich.

Forgiveness. MC GARY, Howard.

Friedenshandlungen und die ethischen Stellungen (in Polish). GRZEGORCZYK, Andrzej.

From Cultural Synthesis to Communicative Action: The Kingdom of God and Ethical Theology. SCHWEIKER, William.

From Militancy to Ethics: On Some Forms and Problems of Militant Action in the Western World. FELDMAN, Jacqueline.

Fundamentación ontológica del sujeto en Kierkegaard. RIGOL, Montserrat Negre.

Further Notes on Feminist Ethics and Pluralism: A Reply to Lindgren. WALKER, Margaret Urban.

G E Moore and the Revolution in Ethics: A Reappraisal. WELCHMAN, Jennifer.

The Gadamer-Habermas Debate Revisited: The Question of Ethics. KELLY, Michael.

A Game-Theoretical Companion to Chisholm's Ethics of Requirement. ÅQVIST, Lennart.

Gauthier's Ethics and Extra-Rational Values: A Comment on DeMarco. CURTIS, Robert A.

Geach on 'Good'. PIGDEN, Charles R.

Generating a Normative System. RANTALA, Veikko.

Genetic Control. FLETCHER, Joseph.

Genetics and Human Malleability. ANDERSON, W French.

Das Gesetz oder das Gute? II, Teil: Alleiniges Prinzip des sittlich guten Willens. SALA, Giovanni B.

Das Gesetz oder das Gute? Zum Ursprung und Sinn des Formalismus in der Ethik Kants. SALA, Giovanni B.

Gesù e la morale (rilettura di un saggio di F Costa). TARTER, Sandro.

Gilligan's Conception of Moral Maturity. MASON, Andrew.

Give Goodrich a Break. FIELDER, John H.

A God By Any Other Name.... STEGLICH, David.

Government Spending and the Budget Deficit. PEITCHINIS, Stephen G.

Grassroots Opposition to Animal Exploitation. SIEGEL, Steve.

Gratitude and the Duties of Grown Children Towards Their Aging Parents. GERBER, Rona M.

Green Reason: Communicative Ethics for the Biosphere. DRYZEK, John S.

Groundwork for a Subjective Theory of Ethics. SAPONTZIS, Steve F.

The Hard Problem of Management is Freedom, Not the Commons. DI NORCIA, Vincent.

Harming Future People. HANSER, Matthew.

Harming Some to Save Others. KAMM, F M.

Hartshorne and the Metaphysics of Animal Rights. BARAD, Judith.

The Hedonic Calculus in the Protagoras and the Phaedo. WEISS, Roslyn.

Hedonism in the Protagoras and the Sophist's Guarantee. WEISS, Roslyn.

Heidegger and the Difficulties of a Postmodern Ethics and Politics. WHITE, Stephen K.

Heidegger and the Question of Ethics. SCOTT, Charles E.

The Hellenistic Version of Aristotle's Ethics. ANNAS, Julia.

Helping Subordinates with Their Personal Problems: A Moral Dilemma for Managers. MOBERG, Dennis J.

Herbert Spiegelberg's Ethics: Accident and Obligation. WIGGINS, Osborne.

High Technology Health Care. LAMM, Richard D.

Histories, Herstories, and Moral Traditions. MEAGHER, Sharon.

History and Decadence: Spengler's Cultural Pessimism Today. SUNIC, Tomislav.

HIV and Pregnancy. ALMOND, Brenda and ULANOWSKY, Carole.

Hobbes and 'The Beautiful Axiom'. COADY, C A J.

Hope in a Secular Ethic. BAKER, Robert E.

Hospital Ethics Committees: One of the Many Centers of Responsibility. GLASER, John W.

How Can Theology Be Moral?. O'DONOVAN, Oliver.

How to Mind One's Ethics: A Reply to Van Inwagen. WHITE, V Alan.

How to Reason About Value Judgments. CLARK, Stephen R L.

Human Gene Therapy: Why Draw a Line?. ANDERSON, W French.

Hume on Character, Action, and Causal Necessity. JOHNSON, Clarence Sholé.

Hypocrisy. TURNER, D.

Hypolepsis und Kompensation—Odo Marquards philosophischer Beitrag zur Diagnose und Bewältigung der Gegenwart. KERSTING, Wolfgang.

The Ideal Aesthetic Observer Revisited. TALIAFERRO, Charles.

Ideal Moral Codes. MAC INTOSH, Duncan.

The Ideology of Social Justice in Economic Justice For All. MURNION, William E.

Illegal Products and the Question of Consumer Redress. BORNA, Shaheen.

The Impact of Trust on Business, International Security and the Quality of Life. MICHALOS, Alex C.

Impartial Application of Moral and Legal Norms: A Contribution to Discourse Ethics. GÜNTHER, Klaus.

Implications of a Self-Effacing Consequentialism. LANGENFUS, William L.

La importancia de la Poética para entender la Etica aristotélica. MC INERNY, Ralph.

The Impracticality of Impartiality. FRIEDMAN, Marilyn.

In Memoriam: Medicine's Confrontation with Evil. SEIDELMAN, William E.

In the Shadow of Aristotle and Hegel: Communicative Ethics and Current Controversies in Practical Philosophy. BENHABIB, Seyla.

The Incommensurability of Moral Argument. SELKIRK, John.

The Individual Investor in Securities Markets: An Ethical Analysis. FREDERICK, Robert E and HOFFMAN, W Michael.

Individual Privacy and Computer-Based Human Resource Information Systems. TAYLOR, G Stephen.

Individuo, tradizioni e pluralismo dei valori. GIAMMUSSO, Salvatore.

Insider Trading: An Ethical Appraisal. IRVINE, William B.

An Instrument to Measure Adherence to the Protestant Ethic and Contemporary Work Values. WAYNE, F Stanford.

Integrating Medical Ethics with Normative Theory: Patient Advocacy and Social Responsibility. JECKER, Nancy.

Integrating Social Responsibility and Ethics into the Strategic Planning Process. ROBIN, Donald P and REIDENBACH, R Eric.

An Integrative Model for Understanding and Managing Ethical Behavior in Business Organizations. STEAD, W Edward and WORRELL, Dan L and STEAD, Jean Garner.

Intencionalidad, responsabilidad y solidaridad: Los nuevos àmbitos del compromiso ético. SEIBOLD, J R.

Interacting with Other Worlds: A Review of Books from the Park Ridge Center. POST, Stephen G.

Internal Reasons and the Obscurity of Blame. WILLIAMS, Bernard.

International Codes of Conduct: An Analysis of Ethical Reasoning. GETZ, Kathleen A.

An International Look at Business Ethics: Britain. MAHONEY, Jack.

Interview with Jürgen Habermas: Ethics, Politics and History. FERRY, Jean-Marc and HABERMAS, Jürgen.

Intimacy and Confidentiality in Psychotherapeutic Relationships. LIPKIN, Robert.

Intuitionism and Conservatism. NELSON, Mark T.

The Intuitionist Argument. SIMON, Caroline J.

Irony, Tragedy, and Temporality in Agricultural Systems, or, How Values and Systems are Related. BUSCH, Lawrence.

Is a Moral Organization Possible?. KLEIN, Sherwin.

Is a Post-Hegelian Ethics Possible?. MC CUMBER, John.

Is and Ought: The "Open Question Argument". FLEW, Antony.

Is Hume a Moral Skeptic?. FIESER, James.

Is Natural Law Ethics Obsolete?. MACHAN, Tibor R.

ETHICS

ETHICS

Realism and Redistribution. NARDIN, Terry.

Realism and Respect. BALDNER, Kent.

Realism in the Practice of Accounting Ethics. COTTELL JR, Philip G.

Really Taking Darwin Seriously: An Alternative to Michael Ruse's Darwinian Metaethics. ROTTSCHAEFER, William A and MARTINSEN, David.

Reason and Passion in Plato's *Republic*. PETERS, James Robert.

Recent Developments in European Business Ethics. VAN LUIJK, Henk J L.

Recent Work in the Philosophy of Religion. ZAGZEBSKI, Linda.

Recklessness, Omission, and Responsibility: Some Reflections on the Moral Significance of Causation. SMITH, Patricia G.

A Reconsideration of Kant's Treatment of Duties to Oneself. PATON, Margaret.

A Refutation of Environmental Ethics. THOMPSON, Janna.

Regarding Rich's "Compatibilism Argument" and the 'Ought'-Implies-'Can' Argument. FAWKES, Don.

The Rejection of Ethical Rationalism. KAPUR, Neera Badhwar.

Rejoinder to Sapontzis's "Environmental Ethics and the Locus of Value". BALDNER, Kent.

The Relationship Between Ethics and Job Satisfaction: An Empirical Investigation. VITELL, Scott J and DAVIS, D L.

Religion and Moral Meaning in Bioethics. CAMPBELL, Courtney S.

Religion and the Secularization of Bioethics. CALLAHAN, Daniel.

Reply to Richard Bosley's "Virtues and Vices: East and West". TANG, Paul C L.

Reply: Flew's "Is and Ought: The 'Open-Question Argument'". BLACK, Virginia.

Resolving Disputes Over Frozen Embryos. ROBERTSON, John A.

Resource X: Sirkin and Smith on a Neglected Economic Staple. DE VRIES, Paul H.

The Responsibility of Socrates. STALLEY, R F.

Revolutionary Horror: Nietzsche and Kristeva on the Politics of Poetry. OLIVER, Kelly.

Reweaving the "One Thread" of the *Analects*. IVANHOE, Philip J.

Rhetoric and Philosophy in Vichian Inquiry. STRUEVER, Nancy S.

A Rhetoric of Motives: Thomas on Obligation as Rational Persuasion. HIBBS, Thomas S.

The Right and the Good. LARMORE, Charles.

Rights in the Workplace: A Nozickian Argument. MAITLAND, Ian.

The Rights of Future People. ELLIOT, Robert.

Rights to Liberty in Purely Private Matters: Part I. RILEY, Jonathan.

Rights, Indirect Utilitarianism, and Contractarianism. HAMLIN, Alan P.

Rights, Justice, and Duties to Provide Assistance: A Critique of Regan's Theory of Rights. JAMIESON, Dale.

Risiko und Entscheidung aus ethischer Sicht. RÖMER, Joachim.

Ritschl's Critique of Schleiermacher's Theological Ethics. BRANDT, James M.

The Role of Caring in a Theory of Nursing Ethics. FRY, Sara T.

The Role of Ethics in Global Corporate Culture. DOBSON, John.

The Role of the *Ergon* Argument in Aristotle's *Nicomachean Ethics*. ACHTENBERG, Deborah.

The Role of Virtues in Alternatives to Kantian and Utilitarian Ethics. MORAVCSIK, Julius M.

Rousseau and Recognition. SHAVER, Robert.

The Salesperson: Clerk, Con Man or Professional?. MORDEN, Michael J.

Sartre y la ética: De la mala fe a la conversión moral. VIDIELLA, Graciela.

Sayre-McCord on Evaluative Facts. DOUBLE, Richard.

Schleiermacher's "Über den Unterschied zwischen Naturgesetz und Sittengesetz". BOYD, George N.

Schleiermacher's Critique of Ethical Reason: Toward a Systematic Ethics. WALLHAUSSER, John.

Schopenhauer as Moral Philosopher—Towards the Actuality of his Ethics. CARTWRIGHT, David.

The Science of Man and Wide Reflective Equilibrium. BRANDT, R B.

Science- and Engineering-Related Ethics and Value Studies: Characteristics of an Emerging Field of Research. HOLLANDER, Rachelle D and STENECK, Nicholas H.

Searching for Ancestors. O'HAGAN, Timothy.

Self-Deception, Human Emotion, and Moral Responsibility: Toward a Pluralistic Conceptual Scheme. WHISNER, William.

The Self-Interest Based Contractarian Response to the Why-Be-Moral Skeptic. SUPERSON, Anita M.

Sensationalized Philosophy: A Reply to Marquis's "Why Abortion is Immoral". CUDD, Ann E.

Seven Moral Myths. ALMOND, Brenda.

Shapiro, Genealogy, and Ethics. COLES, Romand.

Should Competence Be Coerced?: Commentary. REAMER, Frederic G.

Should Competence Be Coerced?: Commentary. KELLY, Michael J.

A Simple Quantitative Test of Financial Ethics. NORTON, Edgar.

The Singularity of Christian Ethics. MEILAENDER, Gilbert.

Sobre Dios como orden moral del universo: Fichte y el golpe de gracia a la teología dogmática. LÓPEZ DOMÍNGUEZ, Virginia E.

The Social Conscience of Business. REILLY, Bernard J and KYJ, Myroslaw J.

Social Contracts and Corporations: A Reply to Hodapp. DONALDSON, Thomas.

Sociobiology and Concern for the Future. JOHNSON, Andrew.

Sociobiology, Sex, and Aggression. FLAGEL, David.

Socrates and Judge Wilhelm: A Case of Kierkegaardian Ethics. MARTINEZ, Roy.

Some Pleasures of Plato, *Republic IX*. STOKES, Michael.

Something Substantial About Natural Law. FRANCIS, Richard P.

Son Ser y Bien realmente convertibles? Una Investigación Fenomenológica. CROSBY, John F and DE LEANIZ CAPRILE, Ignacio García (trans).

The Special Role of Professions in Business Ethics. DAVIS, Michael.

Speculations Regarding the History of *Donum Vitae*. HARVEY, John Collins.

Spinoza: de la alegría. BELTRAN, M.

Sport Hunting: Moral or Immoral?. VITALI, Theodore R.

Sport, Character, and Virtue. FEEZELL, Randolph.

The Status of Principles in Confucian Ethics. CUA, A S.

Student Views on "Ethical" Issues: A Situational Analysis. JONES JR, William A.

Students, Ethics and Surveys. HOFF, J Whitman.

Studies in the Explanation of Issues in Biomedical Ethics: (II) On "On Play[ing] God", Etc.. ERDE, Edmund L.

Substitution: Marcel and Levinas. GIBBS, Robert B.

Suffering, Moral Worth, and Medical Ethics: A New Beginning. LOEWY, Erich H.

Suicide: Its Nature and Moral Evaluation. KUPFER, Joseph.

Sul problema della valutazione morale: A proposito della "Filosofia pratica" di Guiliano Pontara. JELLAMO, Anna.

Taking the Train to a World of Strangers: Health Care Marketing and Ethics. NELSON, Lawrence J and CLARK, H Westley and GOLDMAN, Robert L and SCHORE, Jean E.

Talking of God—But with Whom?. VERHEY, Allen D.

Talking Sense About Freedom. WARD, Andrew.

Teaching "Ethics in America". ROSENBAUM, Alan S.

Teaching Business Ethics: Questioning the Assumptions, Seeking New Directions. FURMAN, Frida Kerner.

Teaching Business Ethics: The Use of Films and Videotapes. HOSMER, LaRue Tone and STENECK, Nicholas H.

Teaching Virtues and Vices. WILLIAMS, Clifford.

Teaching with a Different Ear: Teaching Ethics after Reading Carol Gilligan. SLICER, Deborah.

Teaching Workplace Ethics. DAVIS, Michael.

Testing as a Selection Tool: Another Old and Sticky Managerial Human Rights Issue. MUNCHUS, George.

Thailand: Refining Cultural Values. RATANAKUL, Pinit.

The Ethics Dimension of Human Attitude to the Living Environment (in Czechoslovakian). BURES, R.

The Rational Status of A-Moral Choices (in Hebrew). YONAH, Yossi.

The Theory of Democracy and the Ethics of Equality in the French Revolution (in Serbo-Croatian). REGUERA, Eduardo Bello.

Thomas Aquinas and Contemporary Ethics of Virtue. STALEY, Kevin M.

Thomson and the Trolley Problem. GORR, Michael.

Through Thick and Thin: Moral Knowledge in Skeptical Times. LOUDEN, Robert B.

To Do or Not to Do?. SINGER, Peter.

To Philosophize with Socrates (A Chapter from a Prepared Monography on J Patocka) (in Czechoslovakian). PALOUS, Martin.

To Rectify an Amoral Design. COMNINOU, Maria.

To Welcome the Other: Totality and Theory in Levinas and Adorno. FLOYD, Wayne W.

Toward a Code of Ethics for Business Ethicists. MADSEN, Peter.

Toward a Feminist Theory of Disability. WENDELL, Susan.

Toward a New Relation between Humanity and Nature: Reconstructing *T'ien-jen-ho-i*. LIU, Shu-hsien.

Toward the Development of a Multidimensional Scale for Improving Evaluations of Business Ethics. REIDENBACH, R E and ROBIN, D P.

Towards a Relational Theory of Intergenerational Ethics. AGIUS, Emmanuel.

Towards a Theory of Age-Group Justice. JECKER, Nancy S.

Towards the Integration of Individual and Moral Agencies. MC DONALD, Ross A and VICTOR, Bart.

Tradition and Reason in the History of Ethics. IRWIN, T H.

Tradition, Self-Direction, and Good Life. KOLENDA, Konstantin.

Tragedy and Nonhumans. PUTMAN, Daniel.

De transcendentale grondlegging van de ethiek van Karl-Otto Apel. VAN WOUDENBERG, R.

EUROPEAN

Crucial Issues in Successful European Business. VAN LUIJK, Henk.

Dispute over Democracy at the 17th International Philosophy Congress in Prague in 1934 (in Hungarian). ZNOJ, Milan (and others).

Ecological Marketing Strategy for Toni Yogurts in Switzerland. DYLLICK, Thomas.

Economic Constraints and Ethical Decisions in the Context of European Ventures. VIGNON, Jerome.

Edith Stein as Educator. OBEN, Freda M.

The Jurisprudence of the European Court of Human Rights: Towards an Alternative Foundation of Human Rights. DURÁN Y LALAGUNA, Paloma.

Die Kommunikation zwischen der Philosophie Chinas und Europas um die Wende zum 20 Jahrhundert. YAO, Jiehou.

Philosophy of Regional Cooperation in the Solution of Global Ecological Problems (in Czechoslovakian). MEZRICKY, V.

Recent Developments in European Business Ethics. VAN LUIJK, Henk J L.

EUTHANASIA

Euthanasia: The Moral Issues. BAIRD, Robert M (ed)

Final Choices: Autonomy in Health Care Decisions. SMITH, George P.

Medical Ethics: Essays on Abortion and Euthanasia. BARRY, Robert L.

The Sanctity-of-Life Doctrine in Medicine: A Critique. KUHSE, Helga.

Suicide and Euthanasia. BRODY, Baruch A (ed).

"Death by Free Choice: Modern Variations on an Antique Theme" in Suicide and Euthanasia, ENGELHARDT JR, H Tristram.

"Greek Philosophers on Euthanasia and Suicide" in Suicide and Euthanasia, COOPER, John M.

"A Historical Introduction to Jewish Casuistry on Suicide and Euthanasia" in Suicide and Euthanasia, BRODY, Baruch A.

The Calculus of Consent. SCOFIELD, Giles.

Choosing Death for Nancy Cruzan. BOPP, JR, James.

Euthanasia, Ethics and Economics. HÄYRY, Heta and HÄYRY, Matti.

Euthanasia, the Ultimate Abandonment. MARKER, Rita L.

Nancy Beth Cruzan: In No Voice At All. WOLF, Susan M.

Some Heideggerian Reflections on Euthanasia. NUYEN, A T.

EVALUATION(S)

Evaluating Art. DICKIE, George.

"The Evaluation of Music" in What is Music?, DAVIES, Stephen.

"The Evaluation of Works of Art" in Cultural Hermeneutics of Modern Art: Essays in Honor of Jan Aler, DIFFEY, T J.

"The Riddle of Bacon" in Early Modern Philosophy II, AGASSI, Joseph.

"Towards Evaluating Theories of Practical Rationality" in Inquiries into Values: The Inaugural Session of the International Society for Value Inquiry, POSTOW, Betsy C.

Aesthetic Versus Moral Evaluations. GOLDMAN, Alan H.

Davidson and Hare on Evaluations. SPITZLEY, Thomas and CRAIG, Edward (trans).

Dirac and the Aesthetic Evaluation of Theories. MC ALLISTER, James W.

The Education of Taste. GOLDMAN, Alan H.

L'Évaluation des théories éthiques. BLACKBURN, Pierre.

Moral Education, Liberal Education, and Model Building. FRENCH, Peter A.

Understanding Music: Remarks on the Relevance of Theory. TORMEY, Alan.

EVALUATIVE

Heidegger and Nietzsche on "Thinking in Values". DETMER, David.

Sayre-McCord on Evaluative Facts. DOUBLE, Richard.

EVANGELICALISM

Can Bioethics Be Evangelical?. HOLLINGER, Dennis.

Evangelical and Feminist Ethics: Complex Solidarities. BRULAND, Esther Byle.

Evangelical Ethics and the Anabaptist-Reformed Dialogue. MOUW, Richard J and YODER, John H.

EVANS, G

Descriptions. NEALE, Stephen.

How 'Russellian' Was Frege?. BELL, David.

Peacocke and Evans on Demonstrative Content. MC DOWELL, John.

EVDOKIMOV, P

Gender Roles in the History of Salvation: Man and Woman in the Thought of Paul Evdokimov. PHAN, Peter C.

EVENT(S)

El a priori histórico (la historia y sus hechos). SAMPEDRO, Ceferino.

Actions and Other Events: The Unifier-Multiplier Controversy. PFEIFER, Karl.

Thought and Language. MORAVCSIK, J M.

What is Identity?. WILLIAMS, C J F.

Causes, Enablers, and the Counterfactual Analysis. LOMBARD, Lawrence Brian.

Energy-Events and Fields. BRACKEN, Joseph A.

Events Without Times An Essay On Ontology. CHISHOLM, Roderick M.

Impredicative Identity Criteria and Davidson's Criterion of Event Identity. LOWE, E J.

Musical Work and Possible Events. RANTALA, Veikko.

Passage and the Presence of Experience. HESTEVOLD, H Scott.

Property Exemplification and Proliferation. ROWLANDS, Mark N J.

EVERETT, H

The Philosophy of Quantum Mechanics: An Interactive Interpretation. HEALEY, Richard.

EVIDENCE

David Hume's Argument Against Miracles: A Critical Analysis. BECKWITH, Francis.

The Evidential Force of Religious Experience. DAVIS, Caroline Franks.

Pursuit of Truth. QUINE, W V.

Classifying Conditionals. JACKSON, Frank.

Defending the Hearsay Rule. KADISH, Mortimer R and DAVIS, Michael.

Epistemics and the Total Evidence Requirement. ADLER, Jonathan E.

Evidence, Entitled Belief, and the Gospels. WOLTERSTORFF, Nicholas.

Evidenza della fede?. VIGNA, Carmelo.

Hermeneutics and Apodicticity in Phenomenological Method. REEDER, Harry P.

James's Religious Hypothesis Reinterpreted. JONES, Royce.

Old Evidence, New Theories: Two Unresolved Problems in Bayesian Confirmation Theory. EARMAN, John.

Pseudo-Boolean Valued Prolog. FITTING, Melvin.

Scientific and Legal Standards of Statistical Evidence in Toxic Tort and Discrimination Suits. CRANOR, Carl and NUTTING, Kurt.

Why the Theory of Knowledge Isn't the Same as Epistemology, and What It Might Be Instead. ROSENBERG, Jay F.

EVIDENTIALISM

Return to Reason: Critique of Enlightenment Evidentialism and a Defense of Reason and Belief in God. CLARK, Kelly James.

Properly Unargued Belief in God. LANGTRY, Bruce.

Scepticism, Evidentialism and the Parity Argument: A Pascalian Perspective. HOLYER, Robert.

Theologically Unfashionable Philosophy. STUMP, Eleonore S and KRETZMANN, Norman.

EVIL

Atheism: A Philosophical Justification. MARTIN, Michael.

Beyond the Atom: The Philosophical Thought of Wolfgang Pauli. LAURIKAINEN, K V.

The Bitterness of Job: A Philosophical Reading. WILCOX, John T.

Folly and Intelligence in Political Thought. KLUBACK, William.

God and the Burden of Proof: Plantinga, Swinburne, and the Analytic Defense of Theism. PARSONS, Keith M.

Intimations of Divinity. PLATT, David.

Jewish Philosophy in a Secular Age. SEESKIN, Kenneth.

Known from the Things that Are: Fundamental Theory of the Moral Life. O'KEEFE, Martin D.

New Perspectives on Old-Time Religion. SCHLESINGER, George N.

Philosophy of Religion: Selected Readings (Second Edition). ROWE, William L.

Primordial Truth and Postmodern Theology. GRIFFIN, David Ray.

Religious Issues in Contemporary Philosophy. SLAATTE, Howard A.

Return to Reason: Critique of Enlightenment Evidentialism and a Defense of Reason and Belief in God. CLARK, Kelly James.

Universes. LESLIE, John.

"MacKinnon and the Problem of Evil" in Christ, Ethics and Tragedy: Essays in Honour of Donald MacKinnon, HEBBLETHWAITE, Brian.

"The Problem of Evil" in Dialectic and Contemporary Science, HEPBURN, Ronald.

"Reply to Hepburn's "The Problem of Evil"" in Dialectic and Contemporary Science, HARRIS, Errol E.

Beyond Good-Evil: A Plea for a Hermeneutic Ethics. OPHIR, Adi.

Christian Pacificism and Theodicy: The Free Will Defense in the Thought of John H Yoder. PINCHES, Charles.

The Concept of a Strong Theodicy. SCHUURMAN, Henry.

Evil—A Religious Mystery: A Plea for a More Inclusive Model of Theodicy. DUPRÉ, Louis.

The Free-Will Defence and Worlds Without Moral Evil. DILLEY, Frank B.

God, the Demon, and the Status of Theodicies. STEIN, Edward.

In Memoriam: Medicine's Confrontation with Evil. SEIDELMAN, William E.

La justificación del mal y el nacimiento de la Estética: Leibniz y Baumgarten. ORTIZ IBARZ, José M.

The Limitations of Heidegger's Ontological Aestheticism. ZIMMERMAN, Michael E.

EVIL

La metafora dei "due labirinti" e le sue implicazioni nel pensiero di Leibniz. POMA, Andrea.

Moral Regeneration and Divine Aid in Kant. MICHALSON JR, Gordon E.

The Nature of Immorality. HAMPTON, Jean.

On Failing to Resolve Theism-Versus-Atheism Empirically. O'CONNOR, David.

On the Problem of Evil's Still Not Being What It Seems. O'CONNOR, David.

The Problem of Evil and the Attributes of God. KELLER, James A.

The Problem of Evil: The Unanswered Questions Argument. BEATY, Michael.

Provvidenza: una proposta di intelligibilità del mondo. BACCARI, Luciano.

Schopenhauer as Moral Philosopher—Towards the Actuality of his Ethics. CARTWRIGHT, David.

Surplus Evil. SNYDER, Daniel T.

EVIL(S)

Evil. ANDERSON, Susan Leigh.

L'innocence de l'être-pour la mort. PORÉE, Jérôme.

Le origini dell'ateismo antico (quarta parte). ZEPPI, Stelio.

EVOLUTION

see also Darwinism

Evolution of the Brain: Creation of the Self. ECCLES, John C.

The Metaphysics of Evolution. HULL, David L.

Philosophy of Biology Today. RUSE, Michael.

The Philosophy of Quantum Mechanics: An Interactive Interpretation. HEALEY, Richard.

The Structure of Biological Theories. THOMPSON, Paul.

Treatise on Basic Philosophy, Volume 8—Ethics: The Good and the Right. BUNGE, Mario.

Truth and Objectivity. ELLIS, Brian.

A Useful Inheritance: Evolutionary Aspects of the Theory of Knowledge. RESCHER, Nicholas.

"Determinants of Science Evolution in the 19th and 20th Centuries" in Scientific Knowledge Socialized, HÖRZ, Herbert.

"The Evolution of Approaches to Philosophy" in Reading Philosophy for the Twenty-First Century, MC LEAN, George F.

"Somatic Evolution and Cultural Form" in Issues in Evolutionary Epistemology, BALDUS, Bernd.

"Stephen Toulmin's Theory of Conceptual Evolution" in Issues in Evolutionary Epistemology, JACOBS, Struan.

"The Variance Allocation Hypothesis of Stasis" in Reductionism and Systems Theory in the Life Sciences: Some Problems and Perspectives, WAGNER, Günter P.

Antropología y evolucionismo. CASTRO, Edgardo.

Between Beanbag Genetics and Natural Selection. FALK, Raphael.

Biologie en Teleologie. SOONTIENS, Frans.

The Birth of Modern Science out of the 'European Miracle'. RADNITZKY, Gerard.

La certeza de la evolución (Reflexiones crítico-filosóficas). SEEBER, Federico Mihura.

Developmental Decomposition and the Future of Human Behavioral Ecology. KITCHER, Philip.

Does Evolutionary Biology Contribute to Ethics?. BATESON, Patrick.

Entropy and Information in Evolving Biological Systems. BROOKS, Daniel R (and others).

Erkenntnistheorietischer Konstruktionismus, Minimalrealismus, empirischer Realismus. ENGELS, Eve-Marie.

Evolutie, teleologie en toeval. SOONTIËNS, Frans.

Evolution and Skepticism. COBURN, Robert C.

Evolution in Nature—Development in Society. LASZLO, Ervin.

Evolution, Knowledge and Faith: Gerd Theissen and the Credibility of Theology. VAN HUYSSTEEN, Wentzel.

Evolution, Phenotypic Selection, and the Units of Selection. SHANAHAN, Timothy.

Evolution, Rationality, and Testability. FETZER, James H.

Evolutionäre Erkenntnistheorie und erkenntnistheoretischer Realismus. WENDEL, Hans Jürgen.

Evolutionary Anti-Reductionism: Historical Reflections. BEATTY, John.

Evolutionary Biology and Naturalism. MASTERS, Roger D.

The Evolutionary Risks of Democracy. ZOLO, Danilo.

Evolving Probability. KUKLA, André.

Finality and Intelligibility in Biological Evolution. MORENO, Antonio.

Gedrag: wat zit er achter?. VAN DER STEEN, Wim.

The Historical-Philosophical Change of an Involution Dialectics. IRIMIE, Ioan.

How Evolutionary Biology Challenges the Classical Theory of Rational Choice. COOPER, W S.

The Human Brain and Human Destiny: A Pattern for Old Brain Empathy With the Emergence of Mind. ASHBROOK, James B.

Humanity in Nature: Conserving Yet Creating. PETERS, Karl E.

Modularity, and the Psychoevolutionary Theory of Emotion. GRIFFITHS, P E.

New Notes from Underground. ELLERMAN, Carl Paul.

The Non-Existence of a Principle of Natural Selection. SHIMONY, Abner.

On Adaptation: A Reduction of the Kauffman-Levin Model to a Problem in Graph Theory and Its Consequences. SARKAR, Sahotra.

One Causal Mechanism in Evolution: One Unit of Selection. KARY, Carla E.

Philosophy of Biology Under Attack: Stent Versus Rosenberg. THOMPSON, Paul.

Pietro Siciliani o del virtuoso darwinismo. SAVORELLI, Alessandro.

Raising Darwin's Consciousness: Females and Evolutionary Theory. HRDY, Sarah Blaffer.

Really Taking Darwin Seriously: An Alternative to Michael Ruse's Darwinian Metaethics. ROTTSCHAEFER, William A and MARTINSEN, David.

Recovering Evolution: A Reply to Eckersley and Fox. BOOKCHIN, Murray.

The Social Dynamics Between Evolution and Progress. MURESAN, Valentin.

Sociobiology and Concern for the Future. JOHNSON, Andrew.

Vida y evolución en la filosofía griega. CAPPELLETTI, Angel J.

Yoga-Sūtra IV, 2-3 and Vivekānanda's Interpretation of Evolution. KILLINGLEY, D H.

EVOLUTIONARY EPISTEMOLOGY

Issues in Evolutionary Epistemology. HAHLWEG, Kai (ed).

A Useful Inheritance: Evolutionary Aspects of the Theory of Knowledge. RESCHER, Nicholas.

"Evolution of the Knowledge of Knowledge" in Issues in Evolutionary Epistemology, WOJCIECHOWSKI, Jerzy A.

"Evolution of the Steam Engine" in Issues in Evolutionary Epistemology, CRAGG, C Brian.

"Evolutionary Epistemology and Philosophy of Science" in Issues in Evolutionary Epistemology, HAHLWEG, Kai and HOOKER, C A.

"Evolutionary Epistemology as Naturalized Epistemology" in Issues in Evolutionary Epistemology, BRADIE, Michael.

"An Evolutionary Perspective on the Re-Emergence of Cell Biology" in Issues in Evolutionary Epistemology, BECHTEL, William.

"Self-Organization: A New Approach to Evolutionary Epistemology" in Issues in Evolutionary Epistemology, KROHN, Wolfgang and KÜPPERS, Günter.

"The View from Somewhere: A Critical Defense of Evolutionary Epistemology" in Issues in Evolutionary Epistemology, RUSE, Michael.

Philosophical Problems of Mathematics in the Light of Evolutionary Epistemology. RAV, Yehuda.

Species of Thought: A Comment on Evolutionary Epistemology. WILSON, David Sloan.

What Is Empiricism?—II, Nativism, Naturalism, and Evolutionary Theory. MACDONALD, Cynthia.

EVOLUTIONARY ETHICS

Dutch Objections to Evolutionary Ethics. RICHARDS, Robert J.

The Price of Silence: Commentary. SALZANO, Francisco M.

EVOLUTIONISM

Die Kommunikation zwischen der Philosophie Chinas und Europas um die Wende zum 20 Jahrhundert. YAO, Jiehou.

EXCELLENCE

Democracy and Excellence. SHAW, Roy.

Excellence and the Pursuit of Ideas. BRANN, Eva.

On Taste and Excellence. HALDANE, John.

EXCEPTION(S)

Philosophical Logic and Artificial Intelligence. THOMASON, Richmond H (ed).

EXCHANGE(S)

Alternative Interpretations of Aristotle on Exchange and Reciprocity. MC NEILL, Desmond.

The Salesperson: Clerk, Con Man or Professional?. MORDEN, Michael J.

EXCLUDED MIDDLE

Excluding the Middle. SLATER, B H.

Neue Entwicklungen im Wahrheitsbegriff. SEUREN, Pieter A M.

Normalization and Excluded Middle, I. SELDIN, Jonathan P.

EXCUSES

J L Austin. WARNOCK, G J.

Choice, Character, and Excuse. MOORE, Michael.

EXEGESIS

More on Plato, Meno 82 c 2-3. SHARPLES, R W.

Visits to the Sepulcher and Biblical Exegesis. STUMP, Eleonore S.

Wo beginnt der Weg der Doxa?. EBERT, Theodor.

EXEMPLIFICATION

Exemplification Reconsidered. ARRELL, Douglas.

Property Exemplification and Proliferation. ROWLANDS, Mark N J.

EXISTENCE

see also Being, Dasein, Ontology, Reality

Aristotle's Concept of the Universal. BRAKAS, George.

God, Scepticism and Modernity. NIELSEN, Kai.

God, the Devil and the Perfect Pizza: Ten Philosophical Questions. GOVIER, Trudy.

Inwardness and Existence: Subjectivity in/and Hegel, Heidegger, Marx, and Freud. DAVIS, Walter A.

Making the Body Heard: The Body's Way Toward Existence. APPELBAUM, David.

The Nature of Existence, Volume I. MC TAGGART, John McTaggart Ellis.

Philosophy of Religion: Selected Readings (Second Edition). ROWE, William L.

The World We Found: The Limits of Ontological Talk. SACKS, Mark.

"Existenz zwischen Unbedingheit und Endlichkeit" in Agora: Zu Ehren von Rudolph Berlinger, WEIER, Winfried.

"For Whom is the Real Existence of Values a Problem: Or, An Attempt to Show that the Obvious is Plausible" in Mind, Value and Culture: Essays in Honor of E M Adams, POTEAT, William H.

"Richard Fishacre's Way to God" in A Straight Path: Studies in Medieval Philosophy and Culture, LONG, R James.

"Tense and Existence" in Cause, Mind, and Reality: Essays Honoring C B Martin, CARGILE, James.

"...Quod circulum non commiserim..." Quartae Responsiones. MOYAL, Georges J D.

Algunas consideraciones sobre la Refutación del Idealismo. JAUREGUI, Claudia and VIGO, Alejandro G.

Apocalyptic Anticipations. KIVINEN, S Albert.

Arguments for the Existence of God. SWINBURNE, Richard.

Aseity as Relational Problematic. PRATT, Douglas.

Der Begriff als "nicht wirklich existierende" Einheit vieler "wirklich existerender" Individuen. KAUFMANN, Matthias.

Borges' Proof for the Existence of God. JACQUETTE, Dale.

Bruce Wilshire and the Dilemma of Nontheistic Existentialism. SMITH, Quentin.

Cofinalities of Countable Ultraproducts: The Existence Theorem. CANJAR, R Michael.

Collingwood's Claim that Metaphysics is a Historical Discipline. MARTIN, Rex.

The Concept of Alienation in Janusz Korczak's Works. ROSEN, Henryk and SWIDERSKA, Ewa (trans).

Creator and Causality: A Critique of Pre-Critical Objections. BEARDS, Andrew.

Diverse Orderings of Dionysius's Triplex via by Saint Thomas Aquinas. EWBANK, Michael B.

Does God Create Existence?. DAVIES, Brian.

The Equivalence of the Disjunction and Existence Properties for Modal Arithmetic. FRIEDMAN, Harvey.

Existence (wujūd) and Quiddity (māhiyyah) in Islamic Philosophy. NASR, Seyyed Hossein.

Existence and Reality: The Case for Pseudo-Objects. JOBE, Evan K.

Fear and Trembling and Joyful Wisdom—The Same Book; a Look at Metaphoric Communication. ZELECHOW, Bernard.

God and Abstract Entities. LEFTOW, Brian.

Heidegger's Quest for Being. EDWARDS, Paul.

The Hiddenness of God. MC KIM, Robert.

In Defence of Folk Psychology. JACKSON, Frank and PETTIT, Philip.

Knowledge as Active, Aesthetic, and Hypothetical. FRISINA, Warren G.

A Logic Characterized by the Class of Connected Models with Nested Domain. CORSI, Giovanna.

Lungo i sentieri dell'essere: L'eredità di Heidegger a cento anni dalla nascita. RUSSO, Francesco.

Metaphysical Boundaries: A Question of Independence. CARTER, William R.

The Mode of Existence of Mathematical Objects. ROZOV, M A.

La noción de existencia en la ontología de Berkeley. IBAÑEZ, Alejandro Herrera.

A Note on the Existence Property for Intuitionistic Logic with Function Symbols. DOORMAN, L M.

Note sur la définition wolffienne de la philosophie. ÉCOLE, Jean.

Objects and Existence: Reflections on Free Logic. MENDELSOHN, Richard L.

On an Unsound Proof of the Existence of Possible Worlds. MENZEL, Christopher.

La priorità ontologica e gnoseologica dell'esistenza di Dio in Spinoza. NICOLOSI, Salvatore.

The Problem of the External World. HAMLYN, D W.

Reply to Heyd's Reply to "Locke Is Not a Cartesian with Respect to Knowledge of our Own Existence". ROTH, Robert J.

Reply to Roth: Locke Is Not a Cartesian with Respect to Knowledge of our Own Existence. HEYD, Thomas.

Ross and Scotus on the Existence of God. MAYES, G Randolph.

Sobre la identidad, la existencia y la constitución de las personas y otros seres. ZIRIÓN, Antonio (trans) and SOSA, Ernesto.

La struttura metafisica dell'esistente. ALESSI, Adriano.

Surplus Evil. SNYDER, Daniel T.

Unicidad y categoricidad de teorías. LUNGARZO, Carlos A.

Why the Problem of the Existence of the External Worlds is a Pseudo-Problem: A Revision of Putnam and Danto. SHIRLEY, Edward S.

EXISTENTIAL

Existentially Closed Algebras and Boolean Products. RIEDEL, Herbert H J.

Greene's Dialectics of Freedom and Dewey's Naturalistic Existential Metaphysics. GARRISON, James W.

EXISTENTIAL IMPORT

Free from What?. BENCIVENGA, Ermanno.

Ricerca ed affermazione. RIGOBELLO, Armando.

EXISTENTIAL(S)

E-Type Pronouns and Donkey Anaphora. HEIM, Irene.

EXISTENTIALISM

see also Alienation, Being, Death, Essence(s), Existence, Nihilism

Existentially Speaking: Essays on the Philosophy of Literature. WILSON, Colin.

Holism—A Philosophy for Today: Anticipating the Twenty First Century. SETTANNI, Harry.

Inwardness and Existence: Subjectivity in/and Hegel, Heidegger, Marx, and Freud. DAVIS, Walter A.

The Thinking Muse: Feminism and Modern French Philosophy. ALLEN, Jeffner (ed).

"Authenticity and Historicity: On the Dialectical Ethics of Sartre" in Inquiries into Values: The Inaugural Session of the International Society for Value Inquiry, ZIMMERMAN, R E.

"The Existentialists" in Reading Philosophy for the Twenty-First Century, WILD, John.

"Finite Counterforce" in Nuclear Deterrence and Moral Restraint, LEWIS, David.

"Sartre's Annihilation of Morality" in Inquiries into Values: The Inaugural Session of the International Society for Value Inquiry, REIMAN, Jeffrey.

Beyond Capitalism and Communism: Roberto Unger's Superliberal Political Theory. BELLIOTTI, Raymond.

Bruce Wilshire and the Dilemma of Nontheistic Existentialism. SMITH, Quentin.

Completing the Recovery of Language as an Existential Project. DAVIS, Duane H.

Dialogo sobre humanismo y existencialismo (tercera parte). CAMARENA, Juan M S.

Dialogo sobre humanismo y existencialismo (cuarta y última parte). SILVA CAMARENA, Juan Manuel.

The Ethos of Humanity in Karl Jaspers's Political Philosophy. SALAMUN, Kurt.

Existentialism at the End of Modernity: Questioning the I's Eyes. LEVIN, David Michael.

Die Idee einer existentialontologischen Wendung der Rhetorik in M Heideggers "Sein und Zeit". OESTERREICH, Peter L.

Kierkegaard's Concept of Education (in Hebrew). ROSENOW, Eliyahu.

The Limits of Thought: Rosenzweig, Schelling, and Cohen. GIBBS, Robert.

El no al 2x2=4 de León Chestov. MARTÍNEZ, Luis.

Sartre y la ética: De la mala fe a la conversión moral. VIDIELLA, Graciela.

Selbst das Selbst ist nicht Selbst. ESSLER, Wilhelm K.

Some Notes on the Existentialist Concept of Human Freedom (in Czechoslovakian). CERNOHORSKY, I.

Whitehead and Existential Phenomenology: Is a Synthesis Possible?. RICE, Daryl H.

EXPECTATION(S)

Contemplating Failure: The Importance of Unconscious Omission. SMITH, Patricia G.

EXPENDITURE(S)

Government Spending and the Budget Deficit. PEITCHINIS, Stephen G.

EXPERIENCE(S)

see also Aesthetic Experience(s)

Dietro il paesaggio: Saggio su Simmel. BOELLA, Laura.

EXPLANATION

"Explanatory Unification and the Causal Structure of the World" in *Scientific Explanation (Minnesota Studies in the Philosophy of Science, Volume XIII)*, KITCHER, Philip.

"Four Decades of Scientific Explanation" in *Scientific Explanation (Minnesota Studies in the Philosophy of Science, Volume XIII)*, SALMON, Wesley C.

"Scientific Explanation: The Causes, Some of the Causes, and Nothing But the Causes" in *Scientific Explanation (Minnesota Studies in the Philosophy of Science, Volume XIII)*, HUMPHREYS, Paul W.

Acontecimientos y leyes en la explicación histórica. CORNBLIT, Oscar.

Analogical Arguings and Explainings. JOHNSON, Fred.

Are Reason-Explanations Explanations by Means of Structuring Causes?. TUOMELA, Raimo.

Beyond the *Erklären-Verstehen* Dichotomy. VAN NIEKERK, A A.

Bold Hypotheses: The Bolder the Better?. CLEVELAND, Timothy and SAGAL, Paul T.

The Born-Einstein Debate: Where Application and Explanation Separate. CARTWRIGHT, Nancy.

Can Aesthetic Value Be Explained?. GASKIN, Richard M.

Contingency, Meaning and History. BLOM, Tannelie and NIJHUIS, Ton.

David Owens on Levels of Explanation. NEANDER, Karen and MENZIES, Peter.

Defending Laws in the Social Sciences. KINCAID, Harold.

Empirical and Epistemological Issues in Scientists' Explanations of Scientific Stances: A Critical Synthesis. BRANTE, Thomas.

Explaining the Inexplicable: The Hypotheses of the Faculty of Reflective Judgement in Kant's Third Critique. FRICKE, Christel.

Explaining Wrongdoing. DAVIS, Michael.

Explanation and Justification in Ethics. COPP, David.

Explanation and the Language of Thought. BRADDON-MITCHELL, David and FITZPATRICK, John.

An Explanatory Theory of Communicative Intentions. KURODA, S Y.

G H von Wright on Explanation and Understanding: An Appraisal. MARTIN, Rex.

Geschiedenis en contingentie: Een nieuw perspectief op historisch verklaren. BLOM, Tannelie and NIJHUIS, Ton.

Methodological Individualism and Explanation. TUOMELA, Raimo.

Mind and Body. WILKES, K V.

Miracles and Natural Explanations: A Rejoinder. LARMER, Robert A.

The Non-Epistemic Explanation of Religious Belief. YANDELL, Keith E.

The Practical Element in Ancient Exact Sciences. KNORR, Wilbur R.

Rational Reconstruction and Social Criticism: Habermas's Model of Interpretive Social Science. BAYNES, Kenneth.

Scientific Explanation, Necessity and Contingency. WEBER, Erik.

Technology versus Science: The Cognitive Fallacy. DI NUCCI PEARCE, M Rosaria and PEARCE, David.

Wittgenstein and Obscurantism. CIOFFI, Frank.

EXPLOITATION

'Self-Exploitation' and Workers' Co-Operatives—Or How the British Left Get Their Concepts Wrong. CARTER, Alan.

Coercion and Exploitation: Self-Transposal and the Moral Life. HAMRICK, William S.

An Empirical Examination of Three Machiavellian Concepts: Advertisers Versus the General Public. FRAEDRICH, John and FERRELL, O C.

The Fiery Fight for Animal Rights. JACKSON, Christine M.

Grassroots Opposition to Animal Exploitation. SIEGEL, Steve.

Philosophie, Ideologie et Acteurs Economique en Afrique. KIBAMBE-KIA-NKIMA, Kapongola.

Practical Solutions. MIDGLEY, Mary.

Prostitution, Exploitation and Taboo. GREEN, Karen.

To Do or Not to Do?. SINGER, Peter.

The Unethical Exploitation of Shareholders in Management Buyout Transactions. SCHADLER, F P and KARNS, J E.

Why Worry about How Exploitation Is Defined? Reply to John Roemer. REIMAN, Jeffrey.

EXPRESSION(S)

Croce e i Vociani. COLONNELLO, Pio.

Artistic Learning: What and Where Is It?. WOLF, Dennie.

Expression as Hands-on Construction. HOWARD, V A.

Music and the Expression of Emotion. BUDD, Malcolm.

Musical Expression: Some Remarks on Goodman's Theory. PEARCE, David.

Nelson Goodman on Emotions in Music. LAMMENRANTA, Markus.

Le talent. WALD, Henri.

EXPRESSIVE

Life, Liberty and Exploitation. RYAN, Cheyney.

The Metaphysics of Leisure. COOPER, Wesley E.

EXPRESSIVENESS

The Arousal and Expression of Emotion by Music. ALLEN, R T.

Personal Expressiveness: Philosophical and Psychological Foundations. WATERMAN, Alan S.

EXTENSION

Intentionality and Extension. MATJAZ, Potrc.

Algebraic Extensions in Nonstandard Models and Hilbert's Irreducibility Theorem. YASUMOTO, Masahiro.

Berkeley y los *minima*. ROBLES, José A.

Domain Extension and the Philosophy of Mathematics. MANDERS, Kenneth.

The Domino Theory. KATZ, Jerrold J.

Family Resemblances and the Problem of the Under-Determination of Extension. BELLAIMEY, James E.

Minimal Collapsing Extensions of Models of ZFC. BUKOVSKY, Lev and COPLÁKOVÁ-HARTOVÁ, E.

Moles in Motu: Principles of Spinoza's Physics. KLEVER, W N A.

On the End Extension Problem for Δ_0-PA(S). KOTLARSKI, Henryk.

Sobre la noción fregeana "extensión de un concepto". DEL PALACIO, Alfonso Avila.

Los Wertverläufe de Frege y la teoría de conjuntos. ORAYEN, Raúl.

EXTENSIONALITY

Keith Campbell and the Trope View of Predication. MORELAND, J P.

On Reversal of Temporality of Human Cognition and Dialectical Self. MO, Suchoon S.

EXTERNAL WORLD

Thomas Reid and 'The Way of Ideas'. GALLIE, Roger D.

Our Perception of the External World. TILES, J E.

The Problem of the External World. HAMLYN, D W.

Putnam's Brains in a Vat and Bouwsma's Flowers. SHIRLEY, Edward S.

Why the Problem of the Existence of the External Worlds is a Pseudo-Problem: A Revision of Putnam and Danto. SHIRLEY, Edward S.

EXTERNALISM

Epistemic Justification: Essays in the Theory of Knowledge. ALSTON, William P.

Intentionality and Extension. MATJAZ, Potrc.

Mental Content. MC GINN, Colin.

Theory of Knowledge. LEHRER, Keith.

Internalism and Externalism in Moral Epistemology. AUDI, Robert.

Scepticism about Knowledge of Content. BRUECKNER, Anthony.

Weak Externalism and Mind-Body Identity. MACDONALD, Cynthia.

EXTRINSIC

Personal Identity and Extrinsicness. GARRETT, Brian.

FACT(S)

Fact and Meaning. HEAL, Jane.

Facts and the Function of Truth. PRICE, Huw.

The Nature of Social and Educational Inquiry: Empiricism versus Interpretation. SMITH, John K.

De 'natuurlijke saamhorigheid' van feiten en waarden. PELS, Dick.

'Nice Soft Facts': Fischer on Foreknowledge. CRAIG, William L.

Another Look at Novel Facts. MURPHY, Nancey.

Biologische constructies en sociale feiten: Obstakels in het onderzoek naar gezondheidsproblemen van vrouwen. HORSTMAN, Klasien.

Discussion: Professor Devaraja on the Emergence of Facts. PRASAD, Rajendra.

Duquette, Hegel, and Political Freedom. BIEN, Joseph.

Feitelijk expansionisme, een restrictionistische visie: praktische wetenschappen en waardevrijheid. DE VRIES, Gerard.

Feiten en waarden: de constructie van een onderscheid. PELS, Dick and DE VRIES, G.

From Facts to Theory: The Emergence of the Feudal Relics Debate within Chinese Marxism (in Serbo-Croatian). DUTTON, Michael.

L'idea di "Storia teoretica o congetturale" negli scritti filosofici e sul linguaggio di Adam Smith. IACONO, Alfonso M.

Literature, Criticism, and Factual Reporting. COLLETT, Alan.

Metaphysical Accounts of the Zygote as a Person and the Veto Power of Facts. BOLE III, Thomas J.

Ricerca ed affermazione. RIGOBELLO, Armando.

Sayre-McCord on Evaluative Facts. DOUBLE, Richard.

The Science of Man and Wide Reflective Equilibrium. BRANDT, R B.

Talking About Actions. SEGERBERG, Krister.

Two Fallacious Objections to Adam's Soft/Hard Distinction. WIDERKER, David.

Uncertainty in Moral Theory: An Epistemic Defense of Rule-Utilitarian Liberties. BALL, Stephen W.

FARRELL, M
La justificación de la democracia: entre la negación de la justificación y la restricción de la democracia. NINO, Carlos Santiago.

FARRER, A
The Personalism of Austin Farrer. CONTI, Charles.
Philosophie et théologie chez Austin Farrer. HENDERSON, Edward H.

FASCISM
Dispute over Democracy at the 17th International Philosophy Congress in Prague in 1934 (in Hungarian). ZNOJ, Milan (and others).

FASHION
Time and Change: Short But Differing Philosophies. CHACALOS, Elias Harry.
"Desire and the Figure of Fun: Glossing Theocritus 11" in Post-Structuralist Classics, GOLDHILL, Simon.
Dressing Down Dressing Up—The Philosophic Fear of Fashion. HANSON, Karen.

FATALISM
The Future. An Essay on God, Temporality, and Truth. LUCAS, J R.
God, Foreknowledge, and Freedom. FISCHER, John Martin (ed).
Aquinas on God's Knowledge of Future Contingents. CRAIG, William Lane.
Fatalism and Time. BERNSTEIN, Mark.
Fatalism Revisited. BERNSTEIN, Mark.
The Fate of Thomas Hobbes. HUNTER, Graeme.
Purtill on Fatalism and Truth. CRAIG, William Lane.

FATE
"The Development of the Principle of Subjectivity in Western Philosophy and of the Theory of Man in Chinese Philosophy" in Man and Nature: The Chinese Tradition and the Future, SHI-YING, Zhang.
The Philosophy of Fate as the Basis of Education for Peace. GRZEGORCZYK, Andrzej and PETROWICZ, Lech (trans).

FAULT(S)
Understanding and Justifying Self-Defence. SMART, B J.

FEAR
The Philosophy of Horror 'or' Paradoxes of the Heart. CARROLL, Noël.
"Sub ratione ardui": Paura e speranza nella filosofia. FRANCHI, Alfredo.
Existentialism at the End of Modernity: Questioning the I's Eyes. LEVIN, David Michael.
Fear and the Limits of Human Subjectivity. CACKOWSKI, Zdzislaw and BLAIM, Artur (trans).
The Importance of Reverence. DAVIS, Lawrence H.
The Symmetry Argument: Lucretius Against the Fear of Death. ROSENBAUM, Stephen E.

FECUNDITY
Actualidad y fecundidad de la filosofía blondeliana. ISASI, Juan M.

FEDER, J
Feder und Kant. BRANDT, Reinhard.

FEDERALISM
"Radical Federalism: Responsiveness, Conflict, and Efficiency" in Politics and Process, OSTERFELD, David.

FEELING(S)
see also Emotion(s)
Love: Emotion, Myth, and Metaphor. SOLOMON, Robert C.
Mind: An Essay on Human Feeling. LANGER, Susanne Katherina.
Wittgenstein's Philosophy of Psychology. BUDD, Malcolm.
"What is an Adventure?". REMBERT, Ron.
Akratic Feelings. MELE, Alfred R.
Mill on Moral Wrong. LUNDBERG, Randolph.
The Pluralistic Approach to the Nature of Feelings. NATSOULAS, Thomas.

FEIGL, H
Phänomenale Realität und naturalistische Philosophie. POHLENZ, Gerd.
Sobre la privacidad de los estados de conciencia. LARRETA, Juan Rodriguez and DORFMAN, Beatriz.

FEINBERG, J
Some Problems About One Liberal Conception of Autonomy. SANKOWSKI, E.

FEINBERG, W
Response to Feinberg's "Foundationalism and Recent Critiques of Education". SCHRAG, Francis.
Response to Professor Feinberg's Presidential Address: A Role for Philosophy of Education in Intercultural Research. GOLDSTONE, Peter.

FELDMAN, F
Moral Obligation, Circumstances, and Deontic Foci (A Rejoinder to Fred Feldman). CASTAÑEDA, Hector-Neri.
Paradoxes of Moral Reparation: Deontic Foci versus Circumstances. CASTAÑEDA, Hector-Neri.

FELDMAN, R
The Wall and the Shield: K-K Reconsidered. ROTH, Michael.

FELL, J
"Strangers in the Dark: On the Limitations of the Limits of Praxis in the Early Heidegger". SCHMIDT, Dennis J.

FEMALE(S)
see also Feminism
An Examination of Present Research on the Female Entrepreneur-Suggested Strategies for the 1990's. MOORE, Dorothy P.
The Female Voice: Sexual Aesthetics Revisited. GATES, Eugene.
Logic in the Classroom. SLADE, Christina.
Raising Darwin's Consciousness: Females and Evolutionary Theory. HRDY, Sarah Blaffer.
Why Can't a Man Be More Like a Woman? (A Note on John Locke's Educational Thought). SIMONS, Martin.

FEMINISM
see also Woman, Women
El individuo y la feminidad. PEREZ ESTEVEZ, Antonio.
Feminist Thought: A Comprehensive Introduction. TONG, Rosemarie.
Gender Trouble: Feminism and the Subversion of Identity. BUTLER, Judith.
Maternal Thinking: Toward a Politics of Peace. RUDDICK, Sara.
The Philosophical Imaginary. LE DOEUFF, Michèle.
The Question of the Other: Essays in Contemporary Continental Philosophy. DALLERY, Arleen B (ed).
Thinking Fragments: Psychoanalysis, Feminism, and Postmodernism in the Contemporary West. FLAX, Jane.
The Thinking Muse: Feminism and Modern French Philosophy. ALLEN, Jeffner (ed).
Unruly Practices: Power, Discourse and Gender in Contemporary Social Theory. FRASER, Nancy.
Who Cares: Theory, Research and Educational Implications of the Ethic of Care. BRABECK, Mary M (ed).
Who Knows: From Quine to a Feminist Empiricism. NELSON, Lynn Hankinson.
"Defusing the Canon: Feminist Rereading and Textual Politics" in The Question of the Other: Essays in Contemporary Continental Philosophy, SINGER, Linda.
"Philosophers Against the Family" in Person to Person, SOMMERS, Christina Hoff.
"Social Criticism Without Philosophy" in The Institution of Philosophy: A Discipline in Crisis?, FRASER, Nancy and NICHOLSON, Linda.
Abortion and Feminism. MARKOWITZ, Sally.
Aestheticism, Feminism, and the Dynamics of Reversal. NEWMAN, Amy.
Against Feminist Science: Harding and the Science Question in Feminism. LAKOMSKI, Gabriele.
Analogy as Destiny: Cartesian Man and the Woman Reader. CANTRELL, Carol H.
Annotated Bibliography on Feminist Aesthetics in the Visual Arts. KRUMHOLZ, Linda and LAUTER, Estella.
The Argument for Unlimited Procreative Liberty: A Feminist Critique. RYAN, Maura A.
Beyond Revolt: A Horizon for Feminist Ethics. LINDGREN, Ralph.
Bipolar Disorders: The Unifying Possibilities of Friendship and Feminist Theory. ALSTON, Kal.
A Call to Heal Medicine. HOLMES, Helen Bequaert.
Can Clinical Research Be Both 'Ethical' and 'Scientific'? A Commentary Inspired by Rosser and Marquis. HOLMES, Helen Bequaert.
Can Kant's Ethics Survive the Feminist Critique?. SEDGWICK, Sally S.
Choice, Gift, or Patriarchal Bargain? Women's Consent to In Vitro Fertilization in Male Infertility. LORBER, Judith.
Cinquante-six conceptions de l'androgynie. BOUCHARD, Guy.
Commodification or Compensation: A Reply to Ketchum. MALM, H M.
Crossing the Boundaries: Educational Thought and Gender Equity. LEACH, Mary and DAVIES, Bronwyn.
Cutting Motherhood in Two: Some Suspicions Concerning Surrogacy. NELSON, Hilde and NELSON, James Lindemann.
Date-Rape: A Feminist Analysis. PINEAU, Lois.
Debating Difference: Feminism, Pregnancy, and the Workplace. VOGEL, Lise.
A Dialogue with God. JAMBOR, Mishka.
Dressing Down Dressing Up—The Philosophic Fear of Fashion. HANSON, Karen.
Eccentric Subjects: Feminist Theory and Historical Consiousness. DE LAURETIS, Teresa.

FIRST ORDER THEORY(-RIES)

The Non-Definability Notion and First Order Logic. KRYNICKI, Michal.
Platonismo, unicidad y metateoría. CASANAVE, Abel Lassalle.

FIRST PRINCIPLE(S)

First Principles, Final Ends and Contemporary Philosophical Issues. MAC INTYRE, Alasdair.

FISCHER, J

'Nice Soft Facts': Fischer on Foreknowledge. CRAIG, William L.
Two Fallacious Objections to Adam's Soft/Hard Distinction. WIDERKER, David.

FISH, S

Fish Fingered: Anatomy of a Deconstructionist. MEYNELL, Hugo A.
Literary Relativism. CARNEY, James D.
The Paranoia of Postmodernism. BYWATER, William.
The Use and Abuse of Legal Theory: A Reply to Fish. BARASH, Carol Isaacson.

FISHACRE, R

"Richard Fishacre on the Need for "Philosophy"" in *A Straight Path: Studies in Medieval Philosophy and Culture*, BROWN, Stephen F.
"Richard Fishacre's Way to God" in *A Straight Path: Studies in Medieval Philosophy and Culture*, LONG, R James.

FISHKIN, J

Liberal Neutrality: A Reply to James Fishkin. LARMORE, Charles.

FITCH, F

Fitch and Intuitionistic Knowability. PERCIVAL, Philip.

FIXED POINT(S)

Characters and Fixed Points in Provability Logic. GLEIT, Zachary and GOLDFARB, Warren.
Fixed Point Theory in Weak Second-Order Arithmetic. SHIOJI, Naoki and TANAKA, Kazuyuki.
A New Proof of the Fixed-Point Theorem of Provability Logic. REIDHAAR-OLSON, Lisa.
A Note on Russell's Paradox in Locally Cartesian Closed Categories. PITTS, Andrew M and TAYLOR, Paul.

FLAUBERT

The Perverted Consciousness: Sexuality and Sartre. LEAK, Andrew N.
El Flaubert de Sartre. ZAMORA, Alvaro.

FLEMING, M

The Generalized Others and the Concrete Other: A Response of Marie Fleming. NIELSEN, Kai.

FLEW, A

David Hume's Argument Against Miracles: A Critical Analysis. BECKWITH, Francis.
God and the Burden of Proof: Plantinga, Swinburne, and the Analytic Defense of Theism. PARSONS, Keith M.
'Morality and Determinism': A Reply to Flew. WASSERMANN, Gerhard D.
Flew on Entitlements and Justice. PEÑA, L.
Flew on Russell on Nozick: Uncharitable Interpretations of Justice and Unjust Views of Charity. SKILLEN, Tony.
Reply: Flew's "Is and Ought: The 'Open-Question Argument'". BLACK, Virginia.
What Hume Actually Said About Miracles. FOGELIN, Robert J.

FLORENSKII, P

P A Florenskii's Review of His Work. FLORENSKII, P V and POLOVINKIN, S M.
Preface to the Publication of "P A Florenskii's Review of His Work". ABRAMOV, A I.

FODOR, J

A Theory of Content and Other Essays. FODOR, Jerry A.
Against Positing Central Systems in the Mind. ROSS, Don.
Cognitiewetenschap zonder functionalisme. MEIJSING, Monica.
Explanation and the Language of Thought. BRADDON-MITCHELL, David and FITZPATRICK, John.
Individuation and Causation in Psychology. BURGE, Tyler.

FOLEY, R

How to Believe the Impossible. BROWN, Curtis.

FOOD

Multi-Party Responses to Environmental Problems: A Case of Contaminated Dairy Cattle. MORREN JR, George E B.

FOOT, P

The Strains of Virtue and Constitutionalism. RICHARDS, David A J.
The Virtues of Utilitarianism. STRASSER, Mark.
Virtues, Rules and the Foundations of Ethics. CLOWNEY, David.

FORBES, G

Are Salmon's 'Guises' Disguised Fregean Senses?. BRANQUINHO, João.
Unsuccessful Revisions of CCT. RAMACHANDRAN, Murali.

FORCE(S)

"Force and Fraud" in Hobbes: War Among Nations, WEILER, Gershon.
Defensive Force as an Act of Rescue. FLETCHER, George P.
La doble significación científica y filosófica de la evolución del concepto de fuerza de Descartes a Euler. ARANA, Juan.
Plato on Force: Conflict Between his Psychology and Sociology and his Definition of Temperance in the *Republic*. RICE, Daryl H.
Seeing and Believing: Metaphor, Image, and Force. MORAN, Richard.

FORCING

Near Coherence of Filters III: A Simplified Consistency Proof. BLASS, Andreas and SHELAH, Saharon.
A Proofless Proof of the Barwise Compactness Theorem. HOWARD, Mark.
$\Sigma 1/2$ Sets of Reals. IHODA, Jaime I.
Some Filters of Partitions. MATET, Pierre.
Strong Measure Zero Sets and Rapid Filters. IHODA, Jaime I.
Towers in $[\omega]^\omega$ and $^\omega\omega$. DORDAL, P L.
UFA Fails in the Bell-Kunen Model. MERRILL, John W L.
Where MA First Fails. KUNEN, Kenneth.

FOREIGN

The Leverage of Foreigners: Multinationals in South Africa. DI NORCIA, Vincent.

FOREIGN POLICY

Liberty and Culture: Essays on the Idea of a Free Society. MACHAN, Tibor R.

FOREKNOWLEDGE

The Future: An Essay on God, Temporality, and Truth. LUCAS, J R.
God, Foreknowledge, and Freedom. FISCHER, John Martin (ed).
'Nice Soft Facts': Fischer on Foreknowledge. CRAIG, William L.
Alston on Plantinga and Soft Theological Determinism. PIKE, Nelson.
Aquinas on God's Knowledge of Future Contingents. CRAIG, William Lane.
Does Omniscience Imply Foreknowledge? Craig on Hartshorne. VINEY, Donald Wayne.
Foreknowledge and the Vulnerability of God. LUCAS, J R.
Middle Knowledge: The "Foreknowledge Defense". HUNT, David Paul.
Troubles with Ockhamism. WIDERKER, David.

FORGIVENESS

Can God Forgive Us Our Trespasses?. BRIEN, Andrew.
Forgiveness. MC GARY, Howard.

FORM(S)

see also Essence(s), Idea(s)
Aristotle on Substance: The Paradox of Unity. GILL, Mary Louise.
Parmenides, Plato, and the Semantics of Not-Being. PELLETIER, Francis Jeffry.
Questions of Form: Logic and the Analytic Proposition from Kant to Carnap. PROUST, Joëlle.
Understanding Plato. MELLING, David J.
"Music and Form" in *What is Music?*, CONE, Edward T.
"The Novelist and the Camera Eye" in *Cultural Hermeneutics of Modern Art: Essays in Honor of Jan Aler*, PETERS, Jan.
Aristotle's Criticism of Plato's Form of the Good: Ethics Without Metaphysics?. SANTAS, Gerasimos.
Common Functional Pathways for Texture and Form Vision. VAINA, Lucia M.
Conscience et forme dans la pensée critique de Georges Poulet. MARTIN, Mircea.
A Farewell to Forms of Life. THOMPKINS, E F.
Forms of Life. EMMETT, Kathleen.
Hegel y Marcuse: El Ideal o la Forma Estética. FACIO, Tatiana.
Hylomorphism in Aristotle. WITT, Charlotte.
Joan Kung's Reading of Plato's *Timaeus*. MUELLER, Ian.
The Logic of the Dilemma of Participation and of the Third Man Argument. SCALTSAS, Theodore.
Mental Content in Linguistic Form. LYCAN, William G.
Perceptual and Objective Properties in Plato. WHITE, Nicholas P.
Plato's Forms: A Text That Self-Destructs to Shed Its Light. BERRY, John M.
Robertus Britannus, 'On the Best Form of Commonwealth': A Dialogue between Pierre du Chastel and Aymar Ranconet. DYSON, R W (ed & trans) and TUDOR, H (ed & trans).

FORMAL LANGUAGE(S)

Informal Lectures on Formal Semantics. BACH, Emmon W.
Mathematical Methods in Linguistics. PARTEE, Barbara H.

FORMAL LOGIC

Computability and Logic (Third Edition). BOOLOS, George S.

FORMAL LOGIC
Schaum's Outline of Theory and Problems of Logic. NOLT, John Eric.
"Formal Logic and Informal Logic" in From Metaphysics to Rhetoric, PERELMAN, Chaïm.
"Relevance Principles and Formal Deducibility" in Directions in Relevant Logic, MAKSIMOVA, Larisa.
"To Reason While Speaking" in From Metaphysics to Rhetoric, GRIZE, Jean-Blaise.

FORMALISM
Boundaries Versus Binaries: Bakhtin In/Against the History of Ideas. PECHEY, Graham.
Domination, Legitimation and Law: Introducing Critical Legal Studies. PEIRCE, Michael.
Forman and Semantic Aspects of Tibetan Buddhist Debate Logic. TILLEMANS, Tom J F.
On Quantitative Relationist Theories. MUNDY, Brent.
Pragmatism and the Revolt Against Formalism: Revising Some Doctrines of William James. WHITE, Morton.
The Roots of Contemporary Platonism. MADDY, Penelope.

FORMALIZATION
On the Formalization of Semantic Conventions. WILLIAMS, James G.

FORMATION
En pensamiento político en sociedades sin estado dentro del marco de un nuevo concepto de historia. MORALES, Julian.

FORMENT, E
La utopía de lo supremo y el conocimiento metafísico de Dios. DEL BARCO, Jose Luis.

FORMULA(S)
Some Applications of Positive Formulas in Descriptive Set Theory and Logic. DYCK, Stephen.

FORTAS, A
Civil Disobedience. HARRIS, Paul (ed).

FORTUNE
The Human Origins of Fortuna in Machiavelli's Thought. BALABAN, Oded.

FOUCAULT, M
Critical Theory and Poststructuralism: In Search of a Context. POSTER, Mark.
Existentially Speaking: Essays on the Philosophy of Literature. WILSON, Colin.
French Philosophy of the Sixties: An Essay on Antihumanism. CATTANI, Mary Schnackenberg (trans).
Human Posture: The Nature of Inquiry. SCHUMACHER, John A.
An Introductory Guide to Post-Structuralism and Postmodernism. SARUP, Madan.
Jean Baudrillard: From Marxism to Postmodernism. KELLNER, Douglas.
Michel Foucault's Archaeology of Scientific Reason. GUTTING, Gary.
Thinking Fragments: Psychoanalysis, Feminism, and Postmodernism in the Contemporary West. FLAX, Jane.
Towards a Critique of Foucault. GANE, Mike (ed).
"Derrida and Foucault: Madness and Writing" in Derrida and Deconstruction, FLYNN, Bernard.
"Foucault and Theory: Genealogical Critiques of the Subject" in The Question of the Other: Essays in Contemporary Continental Philosophy, GRUBER, David F.
"Foucault's Move beyond the Theoretical" in The Question of the Other: Essays in Contemporary Continental Philosophy, MC WHORTER, Ladelle.
"The Infernal Recurrence of the Same: Nietzsche and Foucault on Knowledge and Power" in Knowledge and Politics, REDNER, Harry.
"Local Theory" in The Question of the Other: Essays in Contemporary Continental Philosophy, BIRMINGHAM, Peg.
A ética do poder na História da sexualidade de Michel Foucault. VIDEIRA, Antonio A P and PINHEIRO, Ulysses.
Avoiding the Subject: A Foucaultian Itinerary. SEIGEL, Jerrold.
Biomedicine and Technocratic Power. FINKELSTEIN, Joanne L.
The Body Politic: The Embodiment of Praxis in Foucault and Habermas. LEVIN, David.
La Brujería: un Invento Moderno. DÍAZ, Esther.
Carnivals of Atrocity: Foucault, Nietzsche, Cruelty. MILLER, James.
Le cercle et le doublet: Note sur Sartre et Foucault. KNEE, Philip.
Comments on "On the Ordering of Things: Being and Power in Heidegger and Foucault" by Hubert Dreyfus. BRUZINA, Ron.
The Critique of Impure Reason: Foucault and the Frankfurt School. MC CARTHY, Thomas.
Culture or Nature: The Functions of the Term 'Body' in the Work in the Work of Michel Foucault. MC WHORTER, Ladelle.
Dialects of Aestheticism (in Dutch). KUIPER, M.

Duas observações sobre a gramática filosófica. MORENO, Arley R.
Explanatory Grounds: Marx versus Foucault. GOULD, James A.
Le fou stoïcien. BRAGUE, Rémi.
Foucault and the Paradox of Bodily Inscriptions. BUTLER, Judith.
Foucault's Critique of the Liberal Individual. GRUBER, David F.
The Genealogy of Justice and the Justice of Genealogy. WEISS, Harold.
Immanent Critique. TURETZKY, Philip.
Is There a History of Sexuality?. HALPERIN, David M.
Knowledge, Power, Ethics. HIRSCH, Eli.
Madness and the Cogito: Derrida's Critique of Folie et déraison. COOK, Deborah.
Nietzsche, Foucault and the Prospects of Postmodern Political Philosophy. BOTWINICK, Aryeh.
On Knowlegde, Power and Michel Foucault. MEYNELL, Hugo.
On the Ordering of Things: Being and Power in Heidegger and Foucault. DREYFUS, Hubert L.
Power and Resistance. KRIPS, Henry.
Reading Africa Through Foucault: V Y Mudimbe's Re-affirmation of the Subject. DIAWARA, Manthia.
Remapping Modernity. COOK, Deborah.
Self-Recognition and Countermemory. STEINHART, Eric.
The Semiotics of Power: Reading Michel Foucault's Discipline and Punish. OPHIR, Adi.
Shapiro, Genealogy, and Ethics. COLES, Romand.
Social Context and Historical Emergence: The Underlying Dimension of Medical Ethics. PORTO, Eugenia M.
System and Training in Descartes' Meditations. BEYSSADE, Michelle.
Vico, Foucault, and the Strategy of Intimate Investigation. STRUEVER, Nancy S.
What's Left: Marx, Foucault and Contemporary Problems of Social Change. WAPNER, Paul.

FOUNDATION(S)
The Foundations of Morality. HAZLITT, Henry.
The Moral Foundation of Rights. SUMNER, L W.
Acerca de la fundamentación de la ética. SCHULZ, Walter.
Analytico-Referentiality and Legitimation in Modern Mathematics. ROUSSOPOULOS, George.
Concettualità del fondamento: Concetto e fondamento tra riflessione e speculazione. SAMONÀ, Leonardo.
The Dynamics of Belief Systems: Foundations versus Coherence Theories. GÄRDENFORS, P.
Ethik als Grundwissenschaft: Handeln aus Klugheit, Neigung, Pflicht, Ehrfurcht, Mitleid?. FUNKEE, Gerhard.
Les fondements du savoir dans la pensée moraliste des Lumières. MYDLARSKI, Henri.
Husserl and the Origin of Geometry. GRIEDER, Alfons.
The Law of the One and the Law of Contraries in Parmenides. SCHÜRMANN, Reiner.
Presupposition and Foundational Asymmetry in Metaphysics and Logic. JACQUETTE, Dale.
Schleiermacher's Critique of Ethical Reason: Toward a Systematic Ethics. WALLHAUSSER, John.
Second-order Logic, Foundations, and Rules. SHAPIRO, Stewart.

FOUNDATIONALISM
Epistemic Justification: Essays in the Theory of Knowledge. ALSTON, William P.
Feyerabend's Critique of Foundationalism. COUVALIS, George.
Knowledge and Evidence. MOSER, Paul K.
Theory of Knowledge. LEHRER, Keith.
"BonJour's Anti-Foundationalist Argument" in The Current State of the Coherence Theory, STEUP, Matthias.
"Foundations" in The Current State of the Coherence Theory, BLACK, Carolyn.
Bonjour's Objection to Traditional Foundationalism. RAPPAPORT, Steve.
Epistemology as Hermeneutics: Antifoundationalist Relativism. ROCKMORE, Tom.
Foundationalism and Hegelian Logic. ROCKMORE, Tom.
Mystical Experience and Non-Basically Justified Belief. LEVINE, Michael P.
Pragmatism and the Theory of the Reader. MC CALLUM, John.
Recent Work on Foundationalism. TRIPLETT, Timm.
Rorty and Nietzsche: Some Elective Affinities. SHAW, Daniel.
Spanish Common Sense Philosophy. CLARK, Kelly James.
Two Concepts of the Given in C I Lewis: Realism and Foundationalism. GOWANS, Christopher W.

FOURIER, F
Fourier: La Passione dell'Utopia. COLOMBO, Arrigo (ed).

FOX, W

Recovering Evolution: A Reply to Eckersley and Fox. BOOKCHIN, Murray.

FRAME(S)

Framing the Frame Problem. LORMAND, Eric.

FRAMEWORK(S)

A Methodological Assessment of Multiple Utility Frameworks. BRENNAN, Timothy J.

FRANKFURT SCHOOL

Social Theory and the Crisis of Marxism. MC CARNEY, Joseph.

The Critique of Impure Reason: Foucault and the Frankfurt School. MC CARTHY, Thomas.

On Justice and Legitimation: A Critique of Jürgen Habermas' Concept of "Historical Reconstructivism". BALABAN, Oded.

Working Class and Proletariat—On the Relation of Andries Sternheim to the Frankfurt School. MULDER, Bertus and NAUTA, Lolle.

FRANKFURT, H

Determinism, Blameworthiness and Deprivation. KLEIN, Martha.

Lawless Mind. ABELSON, Raziel.

Free Will as Psychological Capacity and the Justification of Consequences. SCHOPP, Robert.

FRAUD

The Murky Borderland Between Scientific Intuition and Fraud. SEGERSTRALE, Ullica.

FREE

Decision Problem for Relatively Free Brouwerian Semilattices. IDZIAK, Pawl M.

The Moral Importance of Free Action. BENSON, Paul.

Technology in a Free Society: The New Frankenstein. BALESTRA, Dominic J.

FREE CHOICE

"Death by Free Choice: Modern Variations on an Antique Theme" in *Suicide and Euthanasia,* ENGELHARDT JR, H Tristram.

FREE LOGIC

First Order Logic with Empty Structures. AMER, Mohamed A.

Free from What?. BENCIVENGA, Ermanno.

A Modal Version of Free Logic. BARBA, Juan L.

Objects and Existence: Reflections on Free Logic. MENDELSOHN, Richard L.

FREE MARKET(S)

The Moral Case for the Free Market Economy: A Philosophical Argument. MACHAN, Tibor R.

Are Markets Morally Free Zones?. HAUSMAN, Daniel M.

The Inequality of Markets. ROGERSON, Kenneth F.

Marxism and Human Sociobiology: A Reply to Zhang Boshu. KEITA, Lansana.

The Role of Self-Interest in Adam Smith's *Wealth of Nations.* WERHANE, Patricia H.

FREE RIDER(S)

Social Contract, Free Ride: A Study of the Public Goods Problem. DE JASAY, Anthony.

FREE SPEECH

Speech, Crime, and the Uses of Language. GREENAWALT, Kent.

FREE THOUGHT

Malebranche et le libertin. MALBREIL, G.

On Thinking for Yourself. SPLITTER, Laurance J.

La paradoja de la libertad de expresión. MADANES, Leiser.

Scepticism and Intellectual Freedom: The Philosophical Foundations of Kant's Politics of Publicity. LAURSEN, John C.

FREE WILL

see also Determinism

Atheism: A Philosophical Justification. MARTIN, Michael.

Bergson. LACEY, A R.

Determinism, Blameworthiness and Deprivation. KLEIN, Martha.

God, the Devil and the Perfect Pizza: Ten Philosophical Questions. GOVIER, Trudy.

The Inner Citadel: Essays on Individual Autonomy. CHRISTMAN, John (ed).

On Action. GINET, Carl.

Return to Reason: Critique of Enlightenment Evidentialism and a Defense of Reason and Belief in God. CLARK, Kelly James.

Vico Revisited: Orthodoxy, Naturalism and Science in the Scienca Nuova. BEDANI, Gino.

William James, Public Philosopher. COTKIN, George.

"Willing Freely According to Thomas Aquinas" in *A Straight Path: Studies in*

Medieval Philosophy and Culture, CLARK, Mary T.

Alston on Plantinga and Soft Theological Determinism. PIKE, Nelson.

Free Will as Psychological Capacity and the Justification of Consequences. SCHOPP, Robert.

Free Will, Self-Causation, and Strange Loops. MORDEN, Michael.

Free Will. SCHEER, Richard.

The Free-Will Defence and Worlds Without Moral Evil. DILLEY, Frank B.

How to *Mind* One's *Ethics:* A Reply to Van Inwagen. WHITE, V Alan.

Innere Autonomie oder Zurechnungsfähigkeit?. SCHÖNRICH, Gerhard.

Is Free Will Incompatible with Something or Other?. GRIFFITHS, A Phillips.

Is Libertarian Free Will Worth Wanting?. SMILANSKY, Saul.

La metafora dei "due labirinti" e le sue implicazioni nel pensiero di Leibniz. POMA, Andrea.

Responsibility and 'Free Will'. VESEY, Godfrey.

Sociobiology and Concern for the Future. JOHNSON, Andrew.

Die soziobiologische Obsoletierung des "Reichs der Zwecke". DORSCHEL, Andreas.

Troubles with Ockhamism. WIDERKER, David.

Wills, Purposes and Actions. HOLMSTRÖM, Ghita.

FREEDOM

see also Liberty

Discourses on the Meaning of History. KLUBACK, William.

An Essay on Moral Responsibility. ZIMMERMAN, Michael J.

Folly and Intelligence in Political Thought. KLUBACK, William.

Freedom and the End of Reason: On the Moral Foundation of Kant's Critical Philosophy. VELKLEY, Richard L.

Freedom. BAUMAN, Zygmunt.

God, Foreknowledge, and Freedom. FISCHER, John Martin (ed).

God, Immortality, Ethics: A Concise Introduction to Philosophy. LACKEY, Douglas P.

The Good Life: Personal and Public Choices. LOUZECKY, David.

The Natural Goodness of Man: On the Systems of Rousseau's Thought. MELZER, Arthur M.

A Philosopher's Harvest: The Philosophical Papers of Isaac Franck. GERBER, William (ed).

Philosophical Works. KALOYEROPOULOS, N A.

Philosophy and the Human Condition (Second Edition). BEAUCHAMP, Tom L (ed).

Philosophy of Economics: On the Scope of Reason in Economic Inquiry. ROY, Subroto.

Rousseau. DENT, N J H.

Time, Freedom, and the Common Good: An Essay in Public Philosophy. SHEROVER, Charles M.

Wesen, Freiheit und Bildung des Menschen. HAGER, Fritz-Peter.

Wisdom and Humanness in Psychology: Prospects for a Christian Approach. EVANS, C Stephen.

"Advance Directives: Beyond Respect for Freedom" in *Advance Directives in Medicine,* CHURCHILL, John.

"Freedom and Indeterminism" in *Cause, Mind, and Reality: Essays Honoring C B Martin,* SHAW, Daniel.

"Freedom as a Skill" in *Culture et Politique/Culture and Politics,* MINOGUE, Kenneth.

"Freedom, Religion and Socio-Logic" in *The Wisdom of Faith: Essays in Honor of Dr Sebastian Alexander Matczak,* AAGAARD-MOGENSEN, L.

"The Obligation to Will the Freedom of Others, According to Jean-Paul Sartre" in *The Question of the Other: Essays in Contemporary Continental Philosophy,* ANDERSON, Thomas C.

"Our Illusory Chains: Rousseau's Images of Bondage and Freedom" in *Culture et Politique/Culture and Politics,* WOKLER, Robert.

"Sartre" in *Ethics in the History of Western Philosophy,* BARNES, Hazel E.

Activity-Work-Culture (in Czechoslovakian). ZLOBIN, N S.

The Adolescent's Rights to Freedom, Care and Enlightenment. BANDMAN, Bertram.

Ateismo e libertà. MONDIN, B.

Atomism and Ethical Life: On Hegel's Critique of the French Revolution. HONNETH, Axel.

Beauty as the Transition from Nature to Freedom in Kant's Critique of Judgement. DÜSING, Klaus.

Capitalism, Freedom and Rhetorical Argumentation. MACHAN, Tibor R.

Capitalism, State Bureaucratic Socialism and Freedom. NIELSEN, Kai.

Civil and Political Freedom in Hegel. DUQUETTE, David A.

Civil Association and the Idea of Contingency. MAPEL, David R.

Comments on Michel Haar's Paper, "The Question of Human Freedom in the Later Heidegger". WRIGHT, Kathleen.

El concepto de libertad en Humano, demasiado humano de Nietzsche. MONTOYA, Rocío Basurto.

Concepto y libertad. VÁSQUEZ, Eduardo.

FREUD

Thinking Fragments: Psychoanalysis, Feminism, and Postmodernism in the Contemporary West. FLAX, Jane.

The Thinking Muse: Feminism and Modern French Philosophy. ALLEN, Jeffner (ed).

Traditions, Tyranny, and Utopias: Essays in the Politics of Awareness. NANDY, Ashis.

Translation and the Nature of Philosophy: A New Theory of Words. BENJAMIN, Andrew.

Typography: Mimesis, Philosophy, Politics. FYNSK, Christopher (ed).

"'Ça cloche'" in *Derrida and Deconstruction*, KOFMAN, Sarah and KAPLAN, Caren (trans).

"Plato and Freud" in *The Person and the Human Mind: Issues in Ancient and Modern Philosophy*, PRICE, A W.

Factual Constraints on Interpreting. STERN, Laurent.

Freud's Critique of Philosophy. BERTHOLD-BOND, Daniel.

Freud's Phylogenetic Fantasy: An Essay Review. PARISI, Thomas.

Freud, Mooij en de empiristische boeman. DERKSEN, A A.

Freud, Racine, and the Epistemology of Tragedy. BRODY, Jules.

Freud-a-til vraiment renié le pouvoir thérapeutique de la psychanalyse?. VACHON, Gérard.

Généalogie ou archéologie de la psychanalyse?. SOULEZ, Philippe.

Husserl and Freud: Time, Memory and the Unconscious. MISHARA, Aaron L.

Inconscient et savoir de la folie: Freud dans le champ psychiatrique. BERCHERIE, Paul.

L'événement freudien: L'objet métapsychologique. ASSOUN, Paul-Laurent.

L'observation: Freud et la scénographie clinique. LACOSTE, Patrick.

Lieux de l'identité freudienne: Judaïsme et Kultur. PFRIMMER, Theo.

Marxism and Psychoanalysis: An Exchange. CRAIB, Ian and KOVEL, Joel.

Marxismus—Subjektwissenschaft—Psychoanalyse. BRAUN, Karl-Heinz.

Psychoanalyse: pseudo-wetenschap of geesteswetenschap?. MOOIJ, A W M.

The Question of the Relation of Philosophy and Psychoanalysis: The Case of Kant and Freud. PETTIGREW, David E.

Wittgenstein, Religion, Freud, and Ireland. HAYES, John.

FREUDIANISM

French Philosophy of the Sixties: An Essay on Antihumanism. CATTANI, Mary Schnackenberg (trans).

FRIEDMAN, M

Justifying Moral Initiative by Business, with Rejoinders to Bill Shaw and Richard Nunan. MULLIGAN, Thomas M.

FRIEDRICH, C

Plato and Totalitarianism. HALL, Robert W.

FRIENDSHIP

Eros, Agape and Philia: Readings in the Philosophy of Love. SOBLE, Alan (ed).

Love and Friendship in Plato and Aristotle. PRICE, A W.

Person to Person. GRAHAM, George (ed).

"Adult Friendships" in *Person to Person*, MC CARTHY, Barry.

"Friends and Lovers" in *Person to Person*, THOMAS, Laurence.

"Paternalism Toward Friends" in *Person to Person*, RICHARDS, Norvin.

Bipolar Disorders: The Unifying Possibilities of Friendship and Feminist Theory. ALSTON, Kal.

Can Parents and Children Be Friends?. KUPFER, Joseph.

Difficult Friendship. DAVIES, Paul.

Epicurus and Friendship. STERN-GILLET, Suzanne.

Friendship and Moral Character: Feminist Implications for Moral Education. THOMPSON, Audrey.

Love Delights in Praises: A Reading of The Two Gentlemen of Verona. GIRARD, René.

Plato's Lysis: An Introduction to Philosophic Friendship. TESSITORE, Aristide.

The Rejection of Ethical Rationalism. KAPUR, Neera Badhwar.

Two Ideals of Friendship. O'CONNOR, David K.

FRYE, N

From Stubborn Structure to Double Mirror: The Evolution of Northrop Frye's Theory of Poetic Creation and Response. BOGDAN, Deanne.

Interpretation, History and Narrative. CARROLL, Noël.

Vico and Frye: A Note. BAHTI, Timothy.

FUKUYAMA, F

The End of History, and the Return of History. GRIER, Philip T.

The New Consensus: The Fukuyama Thesis. FRIEDMAN, Jeffrey.

FULFILLMENT

Paradoxes of Fulfillment. BONEVAC, Daniel.

FULLER, L

Violence, Law, and the Limits of Morality. CRAGG, A W.

FULLER, R

Body-Vessel-Matrix: Co-creative Images of Synergetic Universe. CARTER, Nancy Corson.

FUMERTON, R

Fumerton's Puzzle. FOLEY, Richard.

FUNCTION(S)

see also Recursive Function(s)

Facts and the Function of Truth. PRICE, Huw.

Aesthetic Function and Dynamics of Meaningful Unification (in Czechoslovakian). JANKOVIC, Milan.

Biological Functions and Biological Interests. VARNER, Gary E.

The Boundaries of Art. STECKER, Robert.

Consciousness. SHANON, Benny.

Definability in Terms of the Successor Function and the Coprimeness Predicate in the Set of Arbitrary Integers. RICHARD, Denis.

Des belles paires aux beaux uples. BOUSCAREN, Elisabeth and POIZAT, Bruno.

Descriptive Set Theory Over Hyperfinite Sets. KEISLER, H Jerome (and others).

The Ergon Inference. GOMEZ-LOBO, Alfonso.

Fixed Point Theory in Weak Second-Order Arithmetic. SHIOJI, Naoki and TANAKA, Kazuyuki.

The Formal Language of Recursion. MOSCHOVAKIS, Yiannis N.

The Function of the Press in a Free and Democratic Society. AUDI, Robert.

A General Constructive Intermediate Value Theorem. BRIDGES, Douglas S.

Generalizations of the Kruskal-Friedman Theorems. GORDEEV, L.

A Logic for Distributed Processes. STARK, W Richard.

Misinformation. GODFREY-SMITH, Peter.

Near-Equational and Equational Systems of Logic for Partial Functions, II. CRAIG, William.

Nonstandard Analysis and Constructivism?. WATTENBERG, Frank.

On Relativizing Kolmogorov's Absolute Probability Functions. LEBLANC, Hugues and ROEPER, Peter.

On the Mathematical Content of the Theory of Classes KM. JANSANA, Ramón.

Parametrization Over Inductive Relations of a Bounded Number of Variables. MC COLM, Gregory L.

Poetry as the Naming of the Gods. ZAGANO, Phyllis.

Positive Definite Functions Over Regular f-Rings and Representations as Sums of Squares. MAC CAULL, W A.

The Rank Function and Hilbert's Second E-Theorem. FERRARI, Pier Luigi.

Sobre una presunta inconsecuencia acerca de la noción de función en la doctrina de Frege. GAETA, Rodolfo.

Some Principles Related to Chang's Conjecture. DONDER, Hans-Dieter and LEVINSKI, J P.

Turinici's Fixed Point Theorem and the Axiom of Choice. MANKA, Roman.

What Do Language Games Measure?. LORENZ, Kuno.

FUNCTIONAL ANALYSIS

Ecological Communication. LUHMANN, Niklas.

FUNCTIONALISM

"Two Uses of Functional Explanation" in *Scientific Knowledge Socialized*, DAJKA, Balázs.

Aristotle and the Functionalist Debate. GRANGER, Herbert.

Cognitiewetenschap zonder functionalisme. MEIJSING, Monica.

Empirical Functionalism and Conceivability Arguments. JACOBY, Henry.

Functionalism and Inverted Spectra. COLE, David.

Philosophical Functionalism. WARD, Andrew.

Physicalism, Realism and Education: A Functionalist Approach. RAINER, Valina.

Reply to Ward's "Philosophical Functionalism". DOUBLE, Richard.

Two "Representative" Approaches to the Learning Problem. ORTON, Robert E.

Was Aristotle a Functionalist?. NELSON, John O.

FUNCTOR(S)

Predication in the Logic of Terms. SOMMERS, Fred.

FUNDAMENTALISM

Judging God By "Human" Standards: Reflections on William James' Varieties of Religious Experience. TUMULTY, Peter.

Reformed Epistemology and Religious Fundamentalism: How Basic Are Our Basic Beliefs?. TILLEY, Terrence W.

FUNDING

Funding the Department of Education's TRIO Programs. EKSTEROWICZ, Anthony J and GARTNER, James D.

FUTURE

The Future: An Essay on God, Temporality, and Truth. LUCAS, J R.
The Quarrel over Future Contingents (Louvain 1465-1475). BAUDRY, Leon.
"L'esthétique de demain" in *Cultural Hermeneutics of Modern Art: Essays in Honor of Jan Aler,* DAMNJANOVIC, Milan.
Adams on Actualism and Presentism. KVANVIG, Jonathan L.
Does a Fetus Already Have a Future-like-ours?. MC INERNEY, Peter K.
Fatalism and Time. BERNSTEIN, Mark.
Fatalism Revisited. BERNSTEIN, Mark.
The Future of Psychiatry. MICHELS, Robert and MARKOWITZ, John C.
Future Persons and the Justification of Education. BILOW, Scott H.
Human Existence and Prospective Knowledge. PANA, Laura.
Mind-Body and the Future of Psychiatry. WALLACE IV, Edwin R.
Pensar despues de Heidegger. ALBIZU, Edgardo.
Reply to Kvanvig: "Adams on Actualism and Presentism". ADAMS, Robert Merrihew.
The Rights of Future People. ELLIOT, Robert.
The Social Dynamics Between Evolution and Progress. MURESAN, Valentin.
Vive la Révolution. DUDMAN, V H.
What is Happening to the History of Ideas?. KELLEY, Donald R.

FUTURE GENERATION(S)

"Do Future Generations Matter?" in *Ethics and the Environmental Responsibility,* CAMERON, J R.
Harming Future People. HANSER, Matthew.
The Neo-Stoicism of Radical Environmentalism. CHENEY, Jim.
What Should We Do About Future Generations? Impossibility of Parfit's Theory X. NG, Yew-Kwang.

FUZZY LOGIC

Fuzzy Natural Deduction. GERLA, Giangiacomo and TORTORA, Roberto.
Turing *L*-Machines and Recursive Computability for *L*-Maps. GERLA, Giangiacomo.

GABIROL, S

Salomon Ibn Gabirol's Doctrine of Intelligible Matter. DILLON, John.

GADAMER, H

Hermeneutics: Interpretation Theory in Schleiermacher, Dilthey, Heidegger, and Gadamer. PALMER, Richard E.
"A World of Hope and Optimism Despite Present Difficulties": Gadamer's Critique of Perspectivism. DAVEY, Nicholas.
Aesthetic Consciousness and Aesthetic Non-Differentiation: Gadamer, Schiller, and Lukács. PIZER, John.
Art and the Rhetoric of Allusion. NUYEN, A T.
Concettualità del fondamento: Concetto e fondamento tra riflessione e speculazione. SAMONÀ, Leonardo.
A Contribution to the Gadamer-Lonergan Discussion. BAUR, Michael.
A Conversation with Hans-Georg Gadamer. BAUR, Michael.
Epistemology as Hermeneutics: Antifoundationalist Relativism. ROCKMORE, Tom.
The Ethical Dimension of Gadamer's Hermeneutical Theory. SMITH, P Christopher.
Feminist Social Theory and Hermeneutics: An Empowering Dialectic?. BUKER, Eloise A.
Gadamer, Objectivity, and the Ontology of Belonging. GUEN, Carroll.
The Gadamer-Habermas Debate Revisited: The Question of Ethics. KELLY, Michael.
Hermeneutical Interpretation and Pragmatic Interpretation. DASCAL, Marcelo.
Interpretation at Risk. MARGOLIS, Joseph.
Interpretation in Aesthetics: Theories and Practices. MC CORMICK, Peter.
On the Tragedy of Hermeneutical Experience. BRUNS, Gerald L.
An Orthodox Historicism?. BONSOR, Jack A.
Revelation and Foundationalism: Towards Hermeneutical and Ontological Appropriateness. GUARINO, Thomas.
Sensus Communis in Vico and Gadamer. SCHAEFFER, John D.
Vantage Points of H G Gadamer's Philosophical Thinking (Plato, Herder, Goethe, Hegel) (in Czechoslovakian). HROCH, Jaroslav.

GAHDE, U

Paradoxical Consequences of Balzer's and Gähde's Criteria of Theoreticity. SCHURZ, Gerhard.

GALAN, P

Hegel nel pensiero giuridico-politico spagnolo: Cenni storici della recezione della "Filosofia del diritto". AMENGUAL, Gabriel.

GALEN

Geometry and Medicine: Mathematics in the Thought of Galen of Pergamum. GRANT, Hardy.

GALILEO

Husserl's Phenomenology and the Foundations of Natural Science. HARVEY, Charles W.
The Confirmation of the Superposition Principle: The Role of a Constructive Thought Experiment in Galileo's *Discorsi.* PRUDOVSKY, Gad.
La radice filosofica della rivoluzione scientifica moderna. CRESCINI, Angelo.

GALLIE, W

Style, Politics and the Future of Philosophy. JANIK, Allan.

GALSTON, W

Liberal Goods. GEISE, J P.

GAME THEORY

Axioms of Cooperative Decision Making. MOULIN, Hervé.
Lectures on Game Theory. AUMANN, Robert J.
A Game-Theoretical Analysis of Ecological Problems (in Hungarian). VAN ASPEREN, Gertrud M.
Far-Sighted Equilibria in 2 x 2, Non-Cooperative, Repeated Games. AAFTINK, Jan.
A Game-Theoretic Analysis of Professional Rights and Responsibilities. GAA, James C.
A Game-Theoretical Companion to Chisholm's Ethics of Requirement. ÅQVIST, Lennart.
Indefinitely Repeated Games: A Response to Carroll. BECKER, Neal C and CUDD, Ann E.
Models of Rationality. VAN STRAATEN, Zak.
Die Möglichkeit der Kooperation unter Egoisten: Neuere Ergebnisse spieltheoretischer Analysen. SCHÜSSLER, Rudolf.
Moves and Motives in the Games We Play. HOLLIS, Martin.
Self Enforceable Paths in Extensive Form Games. PONSSARD, Jean-Pierre.
Some Notes on Church's Thesis and the Theory of Games. ANDERLINI, Luca.
When is Lying Morally Permissible? Casuistical Reflections on the Game Analogy, Self-Defense, Social Contract Ethics. VAN WYK, Robert N.

GAME(S)

see also Language Game(s)
Counterfactuals and Backward Induction. BICCHIERI, Christina.
Monadic Π_1^1-Theories of Π_1^1-Properties. DOETS, Kees.
Moves and Motives in the Games We Play. HOLLIS, Martin.
On Beautiful Games. KRETCHMAR, R Scott.
On Ehrenfeucht-Fraïssé Equivalence of Linear Orderings. OIKKONEN, Juha.
Performance Prestidigitation. MEIER, Klaus V.
Some Filters of Partitions. MATET, Pierre.
Some Principles Related to Chang's Conjecture. DONDER, Hans-Dieter and LEVINSKI, J P.
The Trick of the Disappearing Goal. SUITS, Bernard.

GANDHI

The Gandhian Approach to *Swadeshi* or Appropriate Technology. BAKKER, J I (Hans).
Militancy, Violence and Democratic Rights: Indian Experience. BANERJEE, Sumanta.
Non-Violence, Gandhi and Our Times. SINGH, R Raj.
Non-Violence, the Core of Religious Experience in Gandhi. KUTTIANICKAL, Joseph.

GANS, E

La réception du Saint-Simonisme dans l'école hégélienne: l'exemple d'Eduard Gans. WASZEK, Norbert.

GARRISON, J

Belief, Doubt and Critical Thinking: Reconciling the Contraries: Response to Garrison and Phelan. BAILIN, Sharon.

GASSENDI

The Theory of Ideas in Gassendi and Locke. MICHAEL, Fred S and MICHAEL, Emily.

GAUKER, C

Language as a Cause-Effect Communication System. SAVAGE-RUMBAUGH, E S.

GAUTHIER, D

The Libertarian Idea. NARVESON, Jan.
Are Markets Morally Free Zones?. HAUSMAN, Daniel M.
Gauthier on Cooperating in Prisoner's Dilemmas. RAINBOLT, George W.
Gauthier's Ethics and Extra-Rational Values: A Comment on DeMarco. CURTIS, Robert A.
Justice as Reciprocity versus Subject-Centered Justice. BUCHANAN, Allen.
The Problems of Preference Based Morality: A Critique of "Morals by Agreement". DE MARCO, Joseph P.

GAUTHIER, D

Rationality, Coordination, and Convention. GILBERT, Margaret.
Rationality, Reasonableness and Morality. PASKE, Gerald H.
Reason and Agreement in Social Contract Views. FREEMAN, Samuel.
The Rejection of Ethical Rationalism. KAPUR, Neera Badhwar.
The Resurgence of the Foole. ZENZINGER, Theodore S.
The Self-Interest Based Contractarian Response to the Why-Be-Moral Skeptic. SUPERSON, Anita M.

GEACH, P

What is Identity?. WILLIAMS, C J F.
A Fact About the Virtues. RAY, A Chadwick.
Geach on 'Good'. PIGDEN, Charles R.

GEFFRE, C

Le champ herméneutique de la révélation d'après Claude Geffré. RICHARD, Jean.

GEHLEN, A

Antropología y evolucionismo. CASTRO, Edgardo.

GEIST

Of Spirit: Heidegger and the Question. DERRIDA, Jacques.

GENDER

Feminist Thought: A Comprehensive Introduction. TONG, Rosemarie.
Gender Trouble: Feminism and the Subversion of Identity. BUTLER, Judith.
The Perverted Consciousness: Sexuality and Sartre. LEAK, Andrew N.
Thinking Fragments: Psychoanalysis, Feminism, and Postmodernism in the Contemporary West. FLAX, Jane.
Unruly Practices: Power, Discourse and Gender in Contemporary Social Theory. FRASER, Nancy.
Are Women Different and Why are Women Thought to be Different? Theoretical and Methodological Perspectives. GREGORY, Ann.
At the Heart of Women in Management Research: Theoretical and Methodological Approaches and Their Biases. FAGENSON, Ellen A.
The Construction, Deconstruction, and Reconstruction of Difference. ROTHENBERG, Paula.
A Critique of the Deconstructionist Account of Gender Equity and Education. PIETIG, Jeanne.
Cross-Sex Relationships at Work and the Impact of Gender Stereotypes. DEVINE, I and MARKIEWICZ, D.
Crossing the Boundaries: Educational Thought and Gender Equity. LEACH, Mary and DAVIES, Bronwyn.
Education for Sexism: A Theoretical Analysis of the Sex/Gender Bias in Education. DAVIES, Bronwyn.
Ethical Beliefs' Differences of Males and Females. TSALIKIS, John and ORTIZ-BUONAFINA, M.
Feminist and Medical Ethics: Two Different Approaches to Contextual Ethics. SHERWIN, Susan.
Gender Is an Organon. KEHOE, Alice B.
The Gender Question in Criminal Law. SCHULHOFER, Stephen J.
Gender Roles in the History of Salvation: Man and Woman in the Thought of Paul Evdokimov. PHAN, Peter C.
Gender Socialisation and the Nature/Culture Controversy: The Dualist's Dilemma. JONATHAN, Ruth.
Gilligan's Two Voices: An Epistemological Overview. DURAN, Jane.
Just the Facts Ma'am: Informal Logic, Gender and Pedagogy. ORR, Deborah.
Managers, Values, and Executive Decisions. BARNETT, John H and KARSON, Marvin J.
Niet vrouw, niet man; wat dan? De rol van biomedische kennis bij de behandeling van pseudohermafrodieten. VAN DEN WIJNGAARD, Marianne and HUYTS, Ini.
Reviewing the "Subject(s)". LEACH, Mary S.
Symbolic Orders and Discursive Practices. WALKER, J C.
Theorizing Gender: How Much of It Do We Need. HOUSTON, Barbara.

GENE(S)

The Metaphysics of Evolution. HULL, David L.
The Nature of Man—Games that Genes Play?. GÄRDENFORS, Peter.

GENEALOGY

Nietzsche and the Politics of Aristocratic Radicalism. DETWILER, Bruce.
Genealogies as the Language of Time: A Structural Approach—Anthropological Implications. FROUSSART, Bernard.
The Genealogy of Justice and the Justice of Genealogy. WEISS, Harold.
Immanent Critique. TURETZKY, Philip.
Nietzsche: The Subject of Morality. POOLE, Ross.

GENERAL TERM(S)

Abstract General Ideas in Hume. PAPPAS, George S.

GENERAL WELFARE

Why Should We Care About the General Happiness?. EGGERMAN, Richard W.

GENERAL WILL

The Natural Goodness of Man: On the Systems of Rousseau's Thought. MELZER, Arthur M.
The Political Philosophy of the British Idealists: Selected Studies. NICHOLSON, Peter P.

GENERALITY

Coherence in Cartesian Closed Categories and the Generality of Proofs. SZABO, M E.
Critical Thinking as Transfer: Reconstructive Integration of Otherwise Discrete Interpretations of Experience. BRELL JR, Carl D.
The Formal Distinction. SWINDLER, J K.

GENERALIZATION(S)

see also Induction
Disjunctive Laws. OWENS, David.
Intuitionism as Generalization. RICHMAN, Fred.

GENERATION(S)

The Thee Generation. REGAN, Tom.

GENEROSITY

Politics and Generosity. MACHAN, Tibor R.

GENET, J

The Incarceration of Wildness: Wilderness Areas as Prisons. BIRCH, Thomas H.

GENETIC COUNSELING

The Price of Silence: Commentary. CZEIZEL, Andrew.

GENETIC ENGINEERING

Biomedicine and Technocratic Power. FINKELSTEIN, Joanne L.
El dilema argumentativo de la resistencia a las perspectivas técnicas de la biología moderna. VAN DEN DAELE, Wolfgang.
Genetic Control. FLETCHER, Joseph.
Human Gene Therapy: Why Draw a Line?. ANDERSON, W French.
The Limits of Public Participation in Science Revealed. YOXEN, Edward.
New Reproductive Technologies in the Treatment of Human Infertility and Genetic Disease. SILVER, Lee M.
A Scientific Dilemma: The Human Genome Project. CAVALIERI, Liebe F.
Status Arguments and Genetic Research with Human Embryos. HICKMAN, Larry.
Whither the Genome Project?. SINSHEIMER, Robert L.
Zur ethischen Problematik der Keimbahn-Gentherapie am Menschen. WIMMER, Reiner.

GENETIC SCREENING

The Price of Silence: Commentary. CZEIZEL, Andrew.

GENETICS

Philosophy of Biology Today. RUSE, Michael.
"The Variance Allocation Hypothesis of Stasis" in Reductionism and Systems Theory in the Life Sciences: Some Problems and Perspectives, WAGNER, Günter P.
'Morality and Determinism': A Reply to Flew. WASSERMANN, Gerhard D.
Are Genes Units of Inheritance?. FOGLE, Thomas.
Between Beanbag Genetics and Natural Selection. FALK, Raphael.
The Challenge of the New Genetics. ROTHSTEIN, Mark A.
The Crucial Experiment of Wilhelm Johannsen. ROLL-HANSEN, Nils.
Dangerous Diagnostics. NELKIN, Dorothy.
Genetic Traits. GIFFORD, Fred.
Genetics and Human Malleability. ANDERSON, W French.
The Price of Silence: Commentary. LYNCH, Abbyann.
The Real Objective of Mendel's Paper. MONAGHAN, Floyd V and CORCOS, Alain F.
A Scientific Dilemma: The Human Genome Project. CAVALIERI, Liebe F.
T H Morgan, Neither an Epistemological Empiricist nor a "Methodological" Empiricist. VICEDO, Marga.
Zur ethischen Problematik der Keimbahn-Gentherapie am Menschen. WIMMER, Reiner.
The Zygote: To Be Or Not Be A Person. BEDATE, Carlos A and CEFALO, Robert C.

GENIUS

La imagen del hombre en la teoría kantiana del genio. LABRADA, Maria Antonia.
Wittgenstein's Genius. LEWIS, Peter.

GENRE

Beauty and Truth: A Study of Hegel's Aesthetics. BUNGAY, Stephen.

GENTILE
Il neoidelismo italiano e la meccanica quantistica. MAIOCCHI, Roberto.

GENTZ, F
Das Konzept einer "wahren" Politik des Friedrich Gentz. DIETRICH, Therese.

GENTZEN CALCULUS
The Gentzenization and Decidability of RW. BRADY, Ross T.
A Note on Sequent Calculi Intermediate Between *LJ* and *LK*. BORICIC, Branislav R.
Sequent-Systems and Groupoid Models, I. DOSEN, Kosta.

GENTZEN, G
"Gentzen's Cut and Ackermann's Gamma" in *Directions in Relevant Logic*, DUNN, J Michael and MEYER, Robert K.

GEOGRAPHY
Die Situationsanalyse. WERLEN, Benno.
The Vienna Roundabout: On the Significance of Philosophical Reaction. HRACHOVEC, Herbert.

GEOLOGY
Reading the Mind of God: In Search of the Principle of Universality. TREFIL, James.

GEOMETRY
The Ethics of Geometry: A Genealogy of Modernity. LACHTERMAN, David R.
The Philosophy of Set Theory: An Historical Introduction to Cantor's Paradise. TILES, Mary E.
Die "platonische körper": Geometrische, physische, historische und epistemologische aspekte. SOFONEA, Liviu and BENKÖ, Iosif.
EUCLID: Rhetoric in Mathematics. LOOMIS, David E.
Geometria em fragmentos: Forma e conteúdo no contexto wittgensteiniano. THEMUDO, Marina Ramos.
Geometrical Semantics for Spatial Prepositions. SUPPES, Patrick and CRANGLE, Colleen.
Geometry and Medicine: Mathematics in the Thought of Galen of Pergamum. GRANT, Hardy.
Husserl and the Origin of Geometry. GRIEDER, Alfons.
Kant on Euclid: Geometry in Perspective. PALMQUIST, Stephen R.
Le mathématicien et ses images. DELESSERT, André.
More on Plato, *Meno* 82 c 2-3. SHARPLES, R W.
Noch einmal: Zur Rolle der Anschauung in formalen Beweisen. BENDER, Peter.
Strange Attraction, Curious Liaison: Clio Meets Chaos. DYKE, C.

GEORGE, R
Logical and Extralogical Constants. SMOOK, Roger.
El lugar de los sofismas en la Lógica. GAMBRA, José Miguel.

GEORGE, S
Nietzsche und George: Anmerkungen zu einem Buch von Heinz Raschel. WEBER, Frank.

GERMAN
Constructivism and Science: Essays in Recent German Philosophy. BUTTS, Robert E (ed).
Hegel und Das Deutsche Erbe: Philosophie und nationale Frage zwischen Revolution und Reaktion. LOSURDO, Domenico.
Index to Theses on German Philosophy Accepted by Universities of Great Britain & Ireland, 1900-1985. GABEL, Gernot U.
40 Jahre Philosophie in der DDR. WITTICH, Dieter.
Georg Klaus über Kybernetik und Information. STOCK, Wolfgang G.
Schelling: A New Beginning. LAWRENCE, Joseph P.
Sozialistische Gesellschaft und sozialistische Nation in der DDR. KOSING, Alfred.
Two Theories of Ownership in German Classical Philosophy (in Czechoslovakian). SOBOTKA, Milan.
Type Concept Revisited: A Survey of German Idealistic Morphology in the First Half of the Twentieth Century. TRIENES, Rudie.

GERSON, J
Conciliarism and Constitutionalism: Jean Gerson and Medieval Political Thought. NEDERMAN, Cary J.

GERSONIDES, L
"Problems of "Plenitude" in Maimonides and Gersonides" in *A Straight Path: Studies in Medieval Philosophy and Culture*, MANEKIN, Charles H.

GESTALT
Ontological Investigations: Inquiry Into the Categories of Nature, Man, Society. JOHANSSON, Ingvar.
"The Gestalt Model of Scientific Progress" in *Scientific Knowledge Socialized*, DILWORTH, Craig.
"Visible and Audible 'Art Nouveau': The Limits of Comparison" in *Cultural*

Hermeneutics of Modern Art: Essays in Honor of Jan Aler, NOSKE, Frits.

GESTURE(S)
Pictures and Gestures. LÜDEKING, Karlheinz.

GETTIER, E
"When Can What You Don't Know Hurt You?" in *The Current State of the Coherence Theory*, RUSSELL, Bruce.
On Gettier's Notion of Knowledge and Justification. MUKHOPADHYAY, Debabrata.

GHAZALI
"Ghazali and the Avicennan Proof from Personal Identity for an Immaterial Self" in *A Straight Path: Studies in Medieval Philosophy and Culture*, MARMURA, Michael E.
Piety and the Proofs. CLAYTON, John.

GHISELIN, M
Can Abstractions Be Causes?. JOHNSON, David M.

GIBBARD, A
Rights to Liberty in Purely Private Matters: Part II. RILEY, Jonathan.

GIBBON, E
"Hume and Gibbon: The Origin of Naturalistic Study of Religion" in *Early Modern Philosophy II*, WEBER, Andreas.

GIBBS, J
Gibbs' Paradox and Non-Uniform Convergence. DENBIGH, K G and REDHEAD, M L G.

GIBBS, R
Significado literal: entre la profunda necesidad de una construcción y la mera nostalgia. CABRERA, Julio.

GIBSON, J
Gibson, Skinner and Perceptual Responses. GUERIN, Bernard.

GIERE, R
Philosophy of Science Naturalized? Some Problems with Giere's Naturalism. SIEGEL, Harvey.

GILES OF ORLEANS
Gilles d'Orléans était-il averroïste?. KUKSEWICZ, Zdzislaw.

GILLIGAN, C
"Ethical Caring: Pros, Cons, and Possibilities" in *Inquiries into Values: The Inaugural Session of the International Society for Value Inquiry*, PUKA, William.
Gilligan's Conception of Moral Maturity. MASON, Andrew.
Gilligan's Two Voices: An Epistemological Overview. DURAN, Jane.
Histories, Herstories, and Moral Traditions. MEAGHER, Sharon.
The Liberation of Caring: A Different Voice for Gilligan's "Different Voice". PUKA, Bill.
Particularity, Gilligan, and the Two-Levels View: A Reply. ADLER, Jonathan E.
Teaching with a Different Ear: Teaching Ethics after Reading Carol Gilligan. SLICER, Deborah.

GILLIS, C
Straightening the Record: Some Responses to Critics. HICK, John.

GILSON
El bien del arte en Etienne Gilson. HERRERA UBICO, Silvia.
Etienne Gilson ante las falsas interpretaciones del pensamiento de Santo Tomás de Aquino. OBRADORS, Pedro J M.
La noción de ser en Tomás de Sutton. ECHAURI, Raúl.

GINSBERG, M
Sul problema della valutazione morale: A proposito della "Filosofia pratica" di Guiliano Pontara. JELLAMO, Anna.

GINTIS, H
Capitalist Schools: Explanation and Ethics in Radical Studies of Schooling. LISTON, Daniel P.

GINZBERG, R
Comments on Ruth Ginzberg's Paper "Uncovering Gynocentric Science". JAHREN, Neal.

GIRARD, J
Linear Logic Display. BELNAP JR, Nuel D.

GIRARD, R
"Concealing Revealing: A Perspective on Greek Tragedy" in *Post-Structuralist Classics*, HALLIBURTON, David.
Desire: Direct and Imitative. COHN, Robert Greer.
Mondo sociale, mimesi e violenza in R Girard. BOTTANI, Livio.
Postmodern Biblicism: The Challenge of René Girard for Contemporary Theology. WALLACE, Mark I.

GIROUX, H

Capitalist Schools: Explanation and Ethics in Radical Studies of Schooling. LISTON, Daniel P.

GIULIANI, R

Client Taint: The Embarrassment of Rudolph Giuliani. UVILLER, H Richard.

GLOBAL

Holism—A Philosophy for Today: Anticipating the Twenty First Century. SETTANNI, Harry.

Man, Science, Humanism: A New Synthesis. FROLOV, Ivan T.

Margins of Political Discourse. DALLMAYR, Fred R.

The World We Found: The Limits of Ontological Talk. SACKS, Mark.

Adam Schaff and the Club of Rome. KING, Alexander.

Humanity in the World of Life. ZHANG, Hwe Ik.

GLORY

"Hobbes on World Government and the World Cup" in Hobbes: War Among Nations, RIPSTEIN, Arthur.

"Hobbesian Reflections on Glory as a Cause of Conflict" in The Causes of Quarrel: Essays on Peace, War, and Thomas Hobbes, HAMPTON, Jean.

"Mutually Acceptable Glory: Rating among Nations in Hobbes" in The Causes of Quarrel: Essays on Peace, War, and Thomas Hobbes, SACKSTEDER, William.

GNOSTICISM

En torno al modalismo de Marción. ORBE, Antonio.

La reflexión gnoseológica de Francisco Canals Vidal. CORTINA, Juan Luis.

GOAL(S)

Corporate Goal Structures and Business Students: A Comparative Study of Values. BEGGS, Joyce M and LANE, Michael S.

Performance Prestidigitation. MEIER, Klaus V.

A Philosophical Education. REDDIFORD, Gordon.

The Trick of the Disappearing Goal. SUITS, Bernard.

What are Goals and Joint Goals?. TUOMELA, Raimo.

GOD

see also Absolute, Atheism, Ontological Proof

Allāh Transcendent. NETTON, Ian Richard.

The Anthropological Character of Theology: Conditioning Theological Understanding. PAILIN, David A.

Atheism: A Philosophical Justification. MARTIN, Michael.

Benevolent Living: Tracing the Roots of Motivation to God. TURNER, Dean.

The Bitterness of Job: A Philosophical Reading. WILCOX, John T.

Conscience and the Reality of God: An Essay on the Experiential Foundations of Religious Knowledge. STATEN, John C.

The Consolations of Philosophy: Hobbes's Secret; Spinoza's Way. ROSENTHAL, Abigail L (ed).

Divine Nature and Human Language: Essays in Philosophical Theology. ALSTON, William P.

Eros, Agape and Philia: Readings in the Philosophy of Love. SOBLE, Alan (ed).

Folly and Intelligence in Political Thought. KLUBACK, William.

The Future: An Essay on God, Temporality, and Truth. LUCAS, J R.

God and the Burden of Proof: Plantinga, Swinburne, and the Analytic Defense of Theism. PARSONS, Keith M.

God, Foreknowledge, and Freedom. FISCHER, John Martin (ed).

God, Immortality, Ethics: A Concise Introduction to Philosophy. LACKEY, Douglas P.

God, Scepticism and Modernity. NIELSEN, Kai.

God, the Devil and the Perfect Pizza: Ten Philosophical Questions. GOVIER, Trudy.

An Interpretation of Religion: Human Responses to the Transcendent. HICK, John.

Intimations of Divinity. PLATT, David.

Jewish Philosophy in a Secular Age. SEESKIN, Kenneth.

John of the Cross and the Cognitive Value of Mysticism. PAYNE, Steven.

Kant and the Philosophy of History. YOVEL, Yirmiyahu.

Known from the Things that Are: Fundamental Theory of the Moral Life. O'KEEFE, Martin D.

The Light Shineth in Darkness. FRANK, S L.

Looking Into Mind: How to Recognize Who You Are and How You Know. DAMIANI, Anthony.

The Nature of Necessity. PLANTINGA, Alvin.

New Perspectives on Old-Time Religion. SCHLESINGER, George N.

Our Philosophy: Allāma Muhammad Bāqir As-Sadr. INATI, Shams C (trans).

Paul Tillich on Creativity. KEGLEY, Jacquelyn Ann K (ed).

A Philosopher's Harvest: The Philosophical Papers of Isaac Franck. GERBER, William (ed).

Philosophy and the Human Condition (Second Edition). BEAUCHAMP, Tom L (ed).

Philosophy of Religion: Selected Readings (Second Edition). ROWE, William L.

Primordial Truth and Postmodern Theology. GRIFFIN, David Ray.

Religione e Umanità. FICHERA, Giuseppe.

Return to Reason: Critique of Enlightenment Evidentialism and a Defense of Reason and Belief in God. CLARK, Kelly James.

The Self-Embodiment of God. ALTIZER, Thomas J J.

Speaking from the Depths. FRANKLIN, Stephen T.

Universes. LESLIE, John.

Zwischen Revolution und Orthodoxie?. JACOBS, Wilhelm G.

"Hobbes and the Problem of God" in Perspectives on Thomas Hobbes, PACCHI, Arrigo.

"Matter and Form as Attributes of God in Maimonides' Philosophy" in A Straight Path: Studies in Medieval Philosophy and Culture, GOODMAN, L E.

"Modes of Representation and Likeness to God" in Christ, Ethics and Tragedy: Essays in Honour of Donald MacKinnon, SHERRY, Patrick.

"The Problem of Evil" in Dialectic and Contemporary Science, HEPBURN, Ronald.

"Richard Fishacre's Way to God" in A Straight Path: Studies in Medieval Philosophy and Culture, LONG, R James.

"...Quod circulum non commiserim..." Quartae Responsiones. MOYAL, Georges J D.

"A Whirlwind at My Back...": Spinozistic Themes in Bernard Malamud's "The Fixer". COOK, Thomas.

"Malita" e "odium Dei" nella dottrina della volontà di Giovanni Duns Scoto. PIZZO, Giovanni.

"Nature," "Substance," and "God" as Mass Terms in Spinoza's Theologico-Political Treatise. MADANES, Leiser.

"The Source" Spinoza in the Writings of Gabriel Scott. FLOISTAD, Guttorm.

About the Question on God's Government of the World (in Dutch). DE GRIJS, Ferdinand.

Action, Uncertainty, and Divine Impotence. KAPITAN, Tomis.

Analogy Sans Portrait: God-Talk as Literal But Non-Anthropomorphic. MILLER, Barry.

Andrew of Novo Castro, OFM, and the Moral Law. KENNEDY, Leonard A.

Angelic Interiority. CASEY, Gerard N.

Anthropomorphic Concepts of God. SCHOEN, Edward.

Apokatastasis en herhaling: Nietzsches eeuwigheidsbegrip. VERRYCKEN, K.

Aquinas on God's Knowledge of Future Contingents. CRAIG, William Lane.

Arguments for the Existence of God. SWINBURNE, Richard.

Aristotelian Predication, Augustine and the Trinity. RUDEBUSCH, George.

Aristotle's God and the Authenticity of De mundo: An Early Modern Controversy. KRAYE, Jill.

Aseity as Relational Problematic. PRATT, Douglas.

Ateismo e libertà. MONDIN, B.

Attributes of Action in Maimonides. BUIJS, Joseph A.

Augustine's Philosophy of Being. STEAD, Christopher.

Berkeley Kicking His Own Stones. MC GOWAN, William H.

Berkeley's Ideas and the Primary/Secondary Distinction. NADLER, Steven.

Berkeley's Theory of Time. HESTEVOLD, H Scott.

Bérulle, Malebranche et l'amour de Dieu. BEAUDE, Joseph.

The Birth of God. ANEESH.

Borges' Proof for the Existence of God. JACQUETTE, Dale.

Bradley e Spinoza: L'iper-spinozismo di F H Bradley (I). DEREGIBUS, Arturo.

Bruce Wilshire and the Dilemma of Nontheistic Existentialism. SMITH, Quentin.

C S Peirce and the Philosophy of Religion. PARKER, Kelly.

Can God Forgive Us Our Trespasses?. BRIEN, Andrew.

The Cartesian Circle: Hegelian Logic to the Rescue. LUFT, Eric V D.

Coherence and Warranted Theistic Belief. WARD, Andrew.

The Concept of a Strong Theodicy. SCHUURMAN, Henry.

Could God Become Man?. SWINBURNE, Richard.

Creator and Causality: A Critique of Pre-Critical Objections. BEARDS, Andrew.

The Creator's Boundless Palace: William Bartram's Philosophy of Nature. WALTERS, Kerry S.

La cuestion de dios en el pensar de Heidegger. FORNET-BETANCOURT, Raúl.

Cum Deus Calculat—God's Evaluation of Possible Worlds and Logical Calculus. RONCAGLIA, Gino.

Das Vollkommenheitsprinzip bei Leibniz als Grund der Kontingenz. ROLDÁN PANADERO, Concha.

Le désir de Dieu dans L'affirmation de Dieu de Claude Bruaire. CUGNO, Alain.

Le dieu de Claude Bruaire. KAPLAN, Francis.

GOD

GREEK

see also Ancient

Epistemology (Companions to Ancient Thought: 1). EVERSON, Stephen (ed).

Greek Scepticism: Anti-Realist Trends in Ancient Thought. GROARKE, Leo.

"Greek Philosophers on Euthanasia and Suicide" in *Suicide and Euthanasia,* COOPER, John M.

"Plutarch: Roman Heroes and Greek Culture" in *Philosophia Togata: Essays on Philosophy and Roman Society,* PELLING, Christopher.

"The Problem of the Criterion" in *Epistemology (Companions to Ancient Thought: 1),* STRIKER, Gisela.

"Ἀρχή γ ἐναντίωσις: su nexo en el pensamiento preparmenideo". MELENDO, Tomás.

Ataraxia: Happiness as Tranquillity. STRIKER, Gisela.

Athènes, Jérusalem, La Mecque: L'interprétation "musulmane" de la philosophie grecque chez Leo Strauss. BRAGUE, Rémi.

Certain Fundamental Problems and Trends of Thought in Mathematics. STRAUSS, D F M.

Christianity and Politics in Montesquieu's *Greatness and Decline of the Romans.* MYERS, Richard.

Coins and Classical Philosophy. BRUMBAUGH, Robert.

A Comparative Study of Natural Philosophy in Pre-Qin China and Ancient Greece. SHAOJUN, Weng.

Dooyeweerd, Bos and the *Grondmotief* of Greek Culture. RUNIA, D T.

Dreimal keine höflichkeit. INGENKAMP, Heinz Gerd.

Entretiens avec Panayotis Kanellopoulos de *L'Archive de Philosophie et de Théorie des Sciences* (in Greek). KELESSIDOU, A.

EUCLID: Rhetoric in Mathematics. LOOMIS, David E.

New Light on Antiphon. BARNES, Jonathan.

A Philosopher's Stone in the Hands of Children. Using Classical Philosophy to Teach Children Mathematical Concepts. DRABMAN, Randy.

Thales (in Greek). POTAGA, A.

Theosebeia in Plethon's Work: A Concept in Transition. ARGYROPOULOS, R.

Vida y evolución en la filosofía griega. CAPPELLETTI, Angel J.

GREEN

The Political Philosophy of the British Idealists: Selected Studies. NICHOLSON, Peter P.

Self-Conscious Agency and the Eternal Consciousness: Ultimate Reality in Thomas Hill Green. CROSSLEY, David.

T H Green's Theory of the Morally Justified Society. SIMHONY, Avital.

GREENE, M

Greene's Dialectics of Freedom and Dewey's Naturalistic Existential Metaphysics. GARRISON, James W.

GREGORY OF NYSSA

"The Bible's First Sentence in Gregory of Nyssa's View" in *A Straight Path: Studies in Medieval Philosophy and Culture,* VERBEKE, G.

GRICE, H

Communication, Grice, and Languageless Creatures. CARR, Indira Mahalingam.

How to Generalize Grice's Theory of Conversation. ROLF, Eckard.

Meaning N and Meaning NN—An Exposition of the Unformed Gricean Intention. LENKA, Laxminarayan.

The Metaphysical Construction of Value. BAKER, Judith.

On Grandy on Grice. STALNAKER, Robert.

On Grice and Language. GRANDY, Richard E.

Reply to Baker and Grandy. WARNER, Richard.

GRIEF

Relearning the World: On the Phenomenology of Grieving. ATTIG, Thomas.

GRIFFIOEN, S

The Problem of Progress. ROWE, William V.

GRINNELL, J

Modeling in the Museum: On the Role of Remnant Models in the Work of Joseph Grinnell. GRIESEMER, James R.

GROTIUS

Natural Law and the Scottish Enlightenment. HAAKONSSEN, Knud.

Reading Vico Three Times. SUMBERG, Theodore A.

GROUND(S)

Blumenberg and the Philosophical Grounds of Historiography. INGRAM, David.

Heidegger e la sua intuizione di fondo. ZAPPONE, Giuseppe.

GROUP(S)

Adequate Representations of Condorcet Profiles. VISSER, Henk.

Almost Orthogonal Regular Types. HRUSHOVSKI, E.

Collective Inaction and Shared Responsibility. MAY, Larry.

Communities of Judgment. GIBBARD, Allan.

Counterexamples to a Conjecture on Relative Categoricity. EVANS, D M.

Group Decision and Negotiation Support in Evolving, Nonshared Information Contexts. SHAKUN, Melvin F.

Group Rights. MC DONALD, Ian.

Group Rights. SHAPARD, Leslie R.

Groups With Identities. POINT, F.

Groups, I. LANDMAN, Fred.

Groups, II. LANDMAN, Fred.

An Isomorphism Between Rings and Groups. ISKANDER, Awad A.

On Models of the Elementary Theory of $(Z,+,1)$. NADEL, Mark and STAVI, Jonathan.

Porous Vessels: A Critique of the Nation, Nationalism and National Character as Analytical Concepts. FARRAR JR, L L.

Semisimple Stable and Superstable Groups. BALDWIN, J T and PILLAY, A.

Sequent-Systems and Groupoid Models, II. DOSEN, Kosta.

Subgroups of Stable Groups. WAGNER, Frank.

Supporting Individuals in Group-Decision Making. KORHONEN, P and WALLENIUS, J.

GROVER, S

Is the Best Really Necessary?. KRAEMER, E R.

GROWTH

Dewey's Conception of Growth Reconsidered. PEKARSKY, Daniel.

Evolution in Nature—Development in Society. LASZLO, Ervin.

Karl Popper's Philosophy of Scientific Knowledge. NARAYAN, S Shankar.

Philosophy Outside of Schools. SHEFFER, Susannah.

Thinking, Mind, the Existence of God…Transcript of a Classroom Dialogue with First-and-Second Graders in Montreal. DANIEL, Marie-France.

GROZIO, U

Machiavelli, Tacito, Grozio: un nesso "ideale" tra libertinismo e previchismo. SCARCELLA, Cosimo.

GRUE

It's Not that Easy Being Grue. MARTIN, Robert M.

On Grue and Bleen. KERR-LAWSON, Angus.

GRUENBAUM, A

Grünbaum and Psychoanalysis. NASH, Margaret.

Psychoanalyse: pseudo-wetenschap of geesteswetenschap?. MOOIJ, A W M.

GUEROULT, M

Lectio Difficilior: le système dans la théorie platonicienne de l'âme selon interprétation de Gueroult. GAUDIN, Claude.

GUERRE, M

The Martin Guerre Story: A Non-Persian Source for Persian Letter CXLI. GOODMAN, Dena.

GUIGNON, C

The Abyss and the Circle: A Cyclo-Analysis of *Being and Time.* MARTINOT, Steve.

GUILT

Burning Conscience: The Guilt of Hiroshima. ANDERS, Gunther.

Conscience. ROSMINI, Antonio.

"Schopenhauer on Suffering, Death, Guilt, and the Consolation of Metaphysics" in *Schopenhauer: New Essays in Honor of His 200th Birthday,* CARTWRIGHT, David E.

Eigentlichkeit, Gewissen und Schuld in Heideggers "Sein und Zeit". FEHÉR, István.

On the Common Saying that it is Better that Ten Guilty Persons Escape than that One Innocent Suffer: Pro and Con. REIMAN, Jeffrey and VAN DEN HAAG, Ernest.

GUNDERSON, K

Radical Interpretation and the Gunderson Game. WARD, Andrew.

HAACK, S

Lógicas divergentes y principios lógicos: Un análisis crítico de algunas tesis de Susan Haack. PALAU, Gladys.

HAAR, M

Comments on Michel Haar's Paper, "The Question of Human Freedom in the Later Heidegger". WRIGHT, Kathleen.

HABERMAS, J

Critical Theory and Poststructuralism: In Search of a Context. POSTER, Mark.

Habermas on Historical Materialism. ROCKMORE, Tom.

"Participating in Enlightenment" in *Knowledge and Politics,* BOHMAN, James F.

"Interpretation and Solidarity"—An Interview with Richard Bernstein. MELCIC, Dunja.

HABERMAS, J

"System" and "Lifeworld": Habermas and the Problem of Holism. BOHMAN, James.

'Communicatief handelen' als theoretisch grondbegrip. COBBEN, Paul.

The Body Politic: The Embodiment of Praxis in Foucault and Habermas. LEVIN, David.

Buchler on Habermas on Modernity. CAHOONE, Lawrence E.

Discourse Ethics and Civil Society. COHEN, Jean.

Discourse Ethics and the Legitimacy of Law. TUORI, Kaarlo.

The Endorsements of Interpretation. DOEPKE, Frederick.

The Enlightenment's Talking Cure: Habermas, *Legitimation Crisis*, and the Recent Political Landscape. MARTIN, Bill.

The Gadamer-Habermas Debate Revisited: The Question of Ethics. KELLY, Michael.

The Generalized Others and the Concrete Other: A Response of Marie Fleming. NIELSEN, Kai.

Habermas interprète de Schelling. MAESSCHALCK, Marc.

Habermas und das Problem der Individualität. GRONDIN, Jean.

Habermas' Early Lifeworld Appropriation: A Critical Assessment. GEIMAN, Kevin Paul.

Handlungstypen und Kriterien: Zu Habermas' "Theorie des kommunikativen Handelns". DORSCHEL, Andreas.

Intersubjectivity and the Monadic Core of the Psyche: Habermas and Castoriadis on the Unconscious. WHITEBOOK, Joel.

Interview with Jürgen Habermas: Ethics, Politics and History. FERRY, Jean-Marc and HABERMAS, Jürgen.

Is the Moral Point of View Monological or Dialogical? The Kantian Background of Habermas' Discourse Ethics. CLEMENT, Grace.

Liberal Constitutionalism as Ideology: Marx and Habermas. WARREN, Mark.

The Liberal/Communitarian Controversy and Communicative Ethics. BAYNES, K.

Life-World and System at Habermas (in Hungarian). BERGER, Henrik H.

MacIntyre, Habermas, and Philosophical Ethics. KELLY, Michael.

Modern Normativity and the Politics of Deregulation. TREY, George A.

On Justice and Legitimation: A Critique of Jürgen Habermas' Concept of "Historical Reconstructivism". BALABAN, Oded.

On the Use and Abuse of Memory: Habermas, "Anamnestic Solidarity," and the *Historikerstreit*. PENSKY, Max.

Rational Reconstruction and Social Criticism: Habermas's Model of Interpretive Social Science. BAYNES, Kenneth.

Rawls, Habermas, and Real Talk: A Reply to Walzer. WARNKE, Georgia.

Remapping Modernity. COOK, Deborah.

Os Sentidos da "Crítica". BORGES, Bento Itamar.

Zur sozialphilosophischen Bedeutung des Sprachbegriffs Wilhelm von Humboldts. SCHILLER, Hans-Ernst.

HABIT(S)

Creativity and Routine. PERRY, Leslie R.

Hegel on Habit. MC CUMBER, John.

HALL, R

Locke's Simple Ideas, the Blooming, Buzzing Confusion, and Quasi-Photographic Perception. HEYD, Thomas.

HALLDEN-COMPLETENESS

On Halldén-Completeness of Intermediate and Modal Logics. CHAGROV, A V and ZAKHARYASHCHEV, M V.

HALLETT, G

Love, Moral Values and Proportionalism: A Response to Garth Hallett. POPE, Stephen J.

HAMANN

Metakritik und Sprache: Zu Johann Georg Hamanns Kant-Verständnis und seinen metakritischen Implikationen. MAJETSCHAK, Stefan.

Theological Empiricism: Aspects of Johann Georg Hamann's Reception of Hume. GRAUBNER, Hans.

HAMPSHIRE, S

Crick, Hampshire and MacIntyre or Does an English-Speaking Neo-Aristotelianism Exist?. GIORGINI, Giovanni.

HANDICAPPED

Psychoeducational Assessment Practices for the Learning Disabled: A Philosophical Analysis. DURAN, Jane.

HANSEN, C

Comment on Chad Hansen's "Language Utilitarianism". BRANDT, Richard B.

HAPPINESS

see also Pleasure(s)

Benevolent Living: Tracing the Roots of Motivation to God. TURNER, Dean.

Treatise on Basic Philosophy, Volume 8—Ethics: The Good and the Right. BUNGE, Mario.

Apprehending Our Happiness: *Antilepsis* and the Middle Soul in Plotinus, *Ennead* I 4.10. SCHIBLI, H S.

Ataraxia: Happiness as Tranquillity. STRIKER, Gisela.

Das Eudaimonie-Problem und seine aristotelische Lösung (in Greek). PAPADIS, D.

Die ethischen Schriften des Aristoteles (in Greek). KESSIDIS, T.

Hume's Essays on Happiness. IMMERWAHR, John.

Mutual Benevolence and the Theory of Happiness. ESTLUND, David M.

Political Animals in the *Nicomachean Ethics*. ROBERTS, Jean.

Skepticism and Happiness. KOHL, Marvin.

Le socialisme et le conditionnement social du bonheur. BAZAC, Ana.

Why Should We Care About the General Happiness?. EGGERMAN, Richard W.

HARASSMENT

Contrasting Consequences: Bringing Charges of Sexual Harrassment Compared with Other Cases of Whistleblowing. DANDEKAR, Natalie.

HARDING, S

Against Feminist Science: Harding and the Science Question in Feminism. LAKOMSKI, Gabriele.

HARDY, T

"Schopenhauer's Influence on Hardy's *Jude the Obscure*" in *Schopenhauer: New Essays in Honor of His 200th Birthday*, KELLY, Mary Ann.

HARE, R

Davidson and Hare on Evaluations. SPITZLEY, Thomas and CRAIG, Edward (trans).

The Impracticality of Impartiality. FRIEDMAN, Marilyn.

Una nota sobre universalizabilidad. SPECTOR, Horacio.

Ought-Implies-Can: Erasmus Luther and R M Hare. PIGDEN, Charles R.

Rationality, Reasonableness and Morality. PASKE, Gerald H.

Reaching Moral Conclusions on Purely Logical Grounds. VAN WILLIGENBURG, Theo.

Talking 'Bout a Revolution: Feminism, Historicism, and Liberal Moral Theory. ARNAULT, Lynne.

Universal Prescriptivism and Practical Skepticism. MC GRAY, James W.

Utilitarian Ethics and Democratic Government. RILEY, Jonathan.

Zur Methodologie und Logik von "Goldene'Regel"-Argumenten: Eine Gegenposition zu Hoches Hare-Exhaustion. KESE, Ralf.

HARIMAN, R

The Means of Analysis and the Future of Liberalism: A Response to Hariman. STOESZ, David.

HARM(S)

AIDS and the Good Society. ILLINGWORTH, Patricia.

The Limits of Morality. KAGAN, Shelly.

"Autonomy, Toleration, and the Harm Principle" in *Issues in Contemporary Legal Philosophy: The Influence of H L A Hart*, RAZ, Joseph.

"Comment: Autonomy, Toleration, and the Harm Principle" in *Issues in Contemporary Legal Philosophy: The Influence of H L A Hart*, TEN, C L.

Bhopal, India and Union Carbide: The Second Tragedy. TROTTER, R Clayton and DAY, Susan G and LOVE, Amy E.

Callahan on Harming the Dead. SERAFINI, Anthony.

Ecosystem Moral Considerability: A Reply to Cahen. SALTHE, Stanley N and SALTHE, Barbara M.

The Ethics of Dwarf-Tossing. BABER, H E.

The Ethics of Smoking Policies. NIXON, Judy C and WEST, Judy F.

Evil. ANDERSON, Susan Leigh.

Exile and PVS. SCHNEIDERMAN, Lawrence J.

Harming Future People. HANSER, Matthew.

Harming Some to Save Others. KAMM, F M.

Morality: Ought or Naught?. FOLDVARY, Fred E.

Pregnancy, Drugs, and the Perils of Prosecution. MARINER, Wendy K and GLANTZ, Leonard H and ANNAS, George J.

Prenatal Harm and Privacy Rights. BAYLES, Michael D.

The Price of Silence: Commentary. LYNCH, Abbyann.

When Loyalty No Harm Meant. ALLEN, R T.

Why Blackmail Should be Banned. EVANS, Hugh.

HARMONY

Taoist Cultural Reality: The Harmony of Aesthetic Order. THOMPSON, Kirill O.

Tonal Harmony as a Formal System. PYLKKÖ, Pauli.

HARRIS, E

Dialectic and Contemporary Science. GRIER, Philip T (ed).

"The Evanescent Authority of Philosophy" in *Dialectic and Contemporary Science*, EARLE, William.

HEGEL

Kierkegaard and/or Philosophy. BERTMAN, Martin A.

L'itinéraire philosophique de Claude Bruaire: de Hegel à la métaphysique. CHAPELLE, A.

La philosophie de Hegel (in Greek). KANELLOPOULOS, P.

Levinas and Hegel on the Woman as Home: A Comparison (in Dutch). BRÜGGEMAN-KRUIJFF, Atie T.

Lévy-Bruhl et Hegel. BOURGOIS, Bernard.

La libertad y el concepto de lo político. DE ZAN, Julio.

La logica di Hegel come testo filosofico (I). COSTA, Filippo.

The Marcuse-Dunayevskaya Dialogue, 1954-1979. ANDERSON, Kevin.

Metafisica e teologia della parola. SAINATI, Vittorio.

The October Revolution and Spiritual Renewal of Society. NOVIKOVA, Lidia I.

On Desire and its Discontents. SOLL, Ivan.

On the Relation Between Rational Autonomy and Ethical Community: Hegel's Critique of Kantian Morality. STERN, Paul.

On the Use and Abuse of Memory: Habermas, "Anamnestic Solidarity," and the *Historikerstreit*. PENSKY, Max.

The Ontological Argument Reconsidered. BALABAN, Oded and AVSHALOM, Asnat.

Le parcours Hégélien de la révolution Française. D'HONDT, M Jacques.

El pensamiento económico de Hegel: Escritos recientes. CORDUA, Carla.

La periodización hegeliana de la historia, vértice del conflicto interno del pensamiento hegeliano. MAYOS, Gonçal.

Philosophie der Philosophiegeschichte von Hegel bis Hartmann. CEKIC, Miodrag.

Philosophie et religion selon Hegel. PLANTY-BONJOUR, M Guy (and others).

Pippin on Hegel. STERN, Robert.

The Play of Difference/Différance in Hegel and Derrida. MARSH, James L.

A Point of Reconciliation Between Schopenhauer and Hegel. KORAB-KARPOWICZ, W J.

The Politics of the Book: The French Revolution and the Demise of Natural Rights Theory. WARNER, Stuart D.

Présence de Hegel en France: G Fessard et Claude Bruaire. CHAPELLE, A.

I presupposti assiologici del riconoscimento nello Hegel prejenese. RIZZI, Lino.

The Problem of Kant. HARRIS, H S.

Le problème de la fondation de l'éthique: Kant, Hegel. KERVEGAN, Jean-Francois.

Le problème du commencement dans la philosophie de Hegel. ROSEN, Menahem.

Het projet van de Verlichting in het licht van Hegels rechtsfilosofie. COBBEN, Paul.

Reading Horkheimer Reading Vico: An Introduction. DALLMAYR, Fred.

Recenti studi sullo Hegel politico. BONACINA, Giovanni.

Resurrecting Hegel to Bury Art. BROWN, Lee.

Schelling's Critique of Hegel and the Beginnings of Marxian Dialectics. LAWRENCE, Joseph P (trans) and FRANK, Manfred.

Schelling: A New Beginning. LAWRENCE, Joseph P.

Self-Knowledge of the World. ROTENSTREICH, Nathan.

Os Sentidos da "Crítica". BORGES, Bento Itamar.

La spéculation hégélienne. BOURGEOIS, Bernard.

The State at Dusk. MAC GREGOR, David.

The Need of Philosophy and Current Ecological Crisis (in Czechoslovakian). KOLARSKY, R.

The Young Hegel—After 50 Years (in Hungarian). KONCZ, Ilona.

The Theological-Political Tension in Liberalism. FULLER, Timothy.

Two Theories of Ownership in German Classical Philosophy (in Czechoslovakian). SOBOTKA, Milan.

La volonté en Dieu: Thomas d'Aquin et Hegel. BRITO, Emilio.

Was Hegel a Panlogicist?. EISENBERG, Paul.

Whitehead et Hegel: Réalisme, idéalisme et philosophie spéculative. ROCKMORE, Tom.

Who Thinks in an Abstract Manner? M Sobokta: Commentary (in Czechoslovakian). HEGEL, G W F.

Why Hegel? Heidegger and Speculative Philosophy. SCHALOW, Frank.

The Woman in White: On the Reception of Hegel's *Antigone*. DONOUGHO, Martin.

Zwei Arten der Malerei: Von der Umwandelung der Interpretation der Kunst bei Hegel (in Japanese). IWAKI, Ken-ichi.

HEGELIANISM

Absolute Spirit and Universal Self-Consciousness: Bruno Bauer's Revolutionary Subjectivism. MOGGACH, Douglas.

Elaborazione di temi hegeliani in Gramsci. MARINI, Giuliano.

The Gifford Lectures and the Glasgow Hegelians. LONG, Eugene T.

Hegelianism as the Metaphysics of Revolution. ALEKSANDROWICZ, Dariusz.

Lectures on the I Ching (in Serbo-Croatian). CHUNG, Albert C.

Marx's Use of Religious Metaphors. JEANNOT, Thomas M.

La réception du Saint-Simonisme dans l'école hégélienne: l'exemple d'Eduard Gans. WASZEK, Norbert.

HEGEMONY

Bergson and the Hegemony of Language. LAHAV, Ran.

HEIDEGGER

After the Future: Postmodern Times and Places. SHAPIRO, Gary (ed).

The Authority of Language: Heidegger, Wittgenstein, and the Threat of Philosophical Nihilism. EDWARDS, James C.

A Commentary on Heidegger's "Being and Time". GELVEN, Michael.

Conscience and the Reality of God: An Essay on the Experiential Foundations of Religious Knowledge. STATEN, John C.

Dionysus Reborn: Play and the Aesthetic Dimension in Modern Philosophical and Scientific Discourse. SPARIOSU, Mihai I.

Heidegger and Modernity. PHILIP, Franklin (trans).

Heidegger and Nazism. MARGOLIS, Joseph (ed).

Heidegger Interprete di Kant. COLONNELLO, Pio.

Hermeneutics: Interpretation Theory in Schleiermacher, Dilthey, Heidegger, and Gadamer. PALMER, Richard E.

Inwardness and Existence: Subjectivity in/and Hegel, Heidegger, Marx, and Freud. DAVIS, Walter A.

Of Spirit: Heidegger and the Question. DERRIDA, Jacques.

Post-Structuralist Classics. BENJAMIN, Andrew (ed).

Lo storicismo di W Dilthey (Il problema di dio nei grandi pensatori, Volume Quinto). MANNO, Ambrogio Giacomo.

Style, Politics and the Future of Philosophy. JANIK, Allan.

Translation and the Nature of Philosophy: A New Theory of Words. BENJAMIN, Andrew.

Typography: Mimesis, Philosophy, Politics. FYNSK, Christopher (ed).

"Derrida and Heidegger: The Interlacing of Texts" in The Textual Sublime: Deconstruction and Its Differences, CHANTER, Tina.

"Derrida, Heidegger, and the Time of the Line" in Derrida and Deconstruction, SILVERMAN, Hugh J.

"Disseminating Originary Ethics and the Ethics of Dissemination" in The Question of the Other: Essays in Contemporary Continental Philosophy, CAPUTO, John D.

"Ending/Closure: On Derrida's Margining of Heidegger" in The Textual Sublime: Deconstruction and Its Differences, DONATO, Eugenio.

"Fundamental Ontology and Political Interlude: Heidegger as Rector of the University of Freiburg" in Knowledge and Politics, FEHÉR, István M.

"Heideggers Kehren" in Agora: Zu Ehren von Rudolph Berlinger, BRÖCKER, Walter.

"Hermeneutics and Modern Art" in Cultural Hermeneutics of Modern Art: Essays in Honor of Jan Aler, KOCKELMANS, Joseph J.

"On the Saying that Philosophy Begins in Thaumazein" in Post-Structuralist Classics, LLEWELYN, John.

"Strangers in the Dark: On the Limitations of the Limits of Praxis in the Early Heidegger". SCHMIDT, Dennis J.

"The Double Concept of Philosophy" and the Place of Ethics in Being and Time. BERNASCONI, Robert L.

"The Flower of the Mouth": Hölderlin's Hint for Heidegger's Thinking of the Essence of Language. VON HERRMANN, Friedrich-Wilhelm.

"Voix" et "Phénomène" dans l'Ontologie fondamentale de Heidegger. TAMINIAUX, Jacques.

The Abyss and the Circle: A Cyclo-Analysis of Being and Time. MARTINOT, Steve.

Acerca de la pregunta por la determinante de la cosa del pensar. ZUBIRÍA, Martín (trans) and HEIDEGGER, Martin.

El acto de ser: Un don. GILBERT, Paul.

Adorno, Heidegger and Postmodernity. BRUNKHORST, H.

La alegria del arte: Hegel y Heidegger. CONSTANTE, Alberto.

Anabase—Acheminement vers l'amont de la "présupposition"—Le chemin de Sein und Zeit. GUEST, Gérard.

Arte y Ontología en Martin Heidegger (2a parte). BERCIANO VILLALIBRE, Modesto.

Belongings. LLEWELYN, John.

Can Philosophy Perish? (in Czechoslovakian). PATOCKA, Jan.

The Co-Enactment of Heidegger's Being and Time: F W von Herrmann's Elucidation of its "Introduction". LOSCERBO, John.

Comments on "On the Ordering of Things: Being and Power in Heidegger and Foucault" by Hubert Dreyfus. BRUZINA, Ron.

Comments on Michel Haar's Paper, "The Question of Human Freedom in the Later Heidegger". WRIGHT, Kathleen.

Concettualità del fondamento: Concetto e fondamento tra riflessione e

HILBERT, D

Hilbert's Program Relativized: Proof-Theoretical and Foundational Reductions. FEFERMAN, Solomon.

Hilbert's Program Sixty Years Later. SIEG, Wilfried.

Partial Realizations of Hilbert's Program. SIMPSON, Stephen G.

HILDEBRAND, D

El amor al prójimo en la ética fenomenológica de los valores. OLMO, Javier.

Son Ser y Bien realmente convertibles? Una Investigación Fenomenológica. CROSBY, John F and DE LEANIZ CAPRILE, Ignacio García (trans).

HILEY, D

On Reading Postmodern Philosophy: Hiley, Redner and the End of Philosophy. COHEN, Avner.

HINDU

Patterns of Transcendence: Religion, Death, and Dying. CHIDESTER, David.

Radhakrishnan and the Ways of Oneness of East and West. ORGAN, Troy Wilson.

HINDUISM

An Interpretation of Religion: Human Responses to the Transcendent. HICK, John.

Cosmology and Hindu Thought. BALSLEV, Anindita Niyobi.

Reality—Realization through Self-Discipline. VEMPENY, Alice.

Smarta-Varnasrama and the Law of Welfare. SWAIN, Braja Kishore.

Soteriology from a Christian and Hindu Perspective. JENSEN, Debra J.

Sūnyata and Ajāti: Absolutism and the Philosophies of Nāgārjuna and Gaudapāda. KING, Richard.

The Value of the World as the Mystery of God in Advaita Vedanta. RAMBACHAN, Anantanand.

HINTIKKA, J

Certeza, duda escéptica y saber. CABANCHIK, Samuel M.

Hintikka and Vico: An Update on Contemporary Logic. STEINKE, Horst.

Hintikka on Kant and Logic. RUSSELL, Christopher.

HIRING

Issues Surrounding the Theories of Negligent Hiring and Failure to Fire. EXTEJT, Marian M and BOCKANIC, William N.

HIRSCH, E

E D Hirsch's Misreading of Saul Kripke. SPIKES, Michael.

HIRST, P

Metaphysics in Education. ALLEN, R T.

HISTORIAN(S)

"Posidonius as Philosopher-Historian" in *Philosophia Togata: Essays on Philosophy and Roman Society,* KIDD, I G.

Maigret's Method. JACKSON, M W.

HISTORICAL MATERIALISM

see also Dialectical Materialism

Jürgen Habermas on Society and Politics: A Reader. SEIDMAN, Steven (ed).

"Problems of Value in Marxist Philosophy" in *Inquiries into Values: The Inaugural Session of the International Society for Value Inquiry,* MARCZUK, Stanislaw.

The Dialogue of Grand Theories for Peace. PLUZANSKI, Tadeusz and KISIEL, Krystyna (trans) and KISIEL, Chester (trans).

Ergebnisse und Probleme der Entwicklung des historischen Materialismus. STIEHLER, Gottfried.

Fortschritt und Rückschritt. SCHMIDT, Hartwig.

Marxism and Conceptual Scholasticism. KOZYR-KOWALSKI, Stanislaw and OSZKODAR, Zbigniew (trans).

Philosophie und Lehre. HAGER, Nina.

The Civil Revolution and Historical Materialism (in Serbo-Croatian). NOERR, Gunzelin Schmid.

HISTORICAL REALISM

Re-enactment in Retrospect. WEINRYB, Elazar.

HISTORICISM

Lo storicismo di W Dilthey (Il problema di dio nei grandi pensatori, Volume Quinto). MANNO, Ambrogio Giacomo.

"Historicism and Rationalism" in *Scientific Knowledge Socialized,* KELEMEN, János.

"Music and History" in *What is Music?,* DONOUGHO, Martin.

La "fucina del mondo". ADDANTE, Pietro.

Feiten en waarden: de constructie van een onderscheid. PELS, Dick and DE VRIES, G.

Higher Education and the Crisis of Historicism. ZANARDI, William.

Meinecke e Dilthey. DI COSTANZO, Giuseppe.

An Orthodox Historicism?. BONSOR, Jack A.

The Politician and the Philosopher (Some Lessons from Machiavelli).

DOLGOV, Konstantin M and JARKOWSKI, Jan (trans).

HISTORICITY

"Aesthetics in the Context of Historicity, Moral Education and Character Development" in *The Social Context and Values: Perspectives of the Americas,* LOPEZ, Raul.

"Ethics and Historicity" in *The Social Context and Values: Perspectives of the Americas,* PEGORARO, Olinto.

"Hermeneutics, Historicity and Values" in *The Social Context and Values: Perspectives of the Americas,* MC LEAN, George F.

"The Person: Experience of Transcendence Through Immanence" in *The Social Context and Values: Perspectives of the Americas,* DIAZ, Ruben.

"Values in an Historical, Socio-Cultural Context" in *The Social Context and Values: Perspectives of the Americas,* FERRAND DE PIAZZA, Hortensia.

L'esperienza filosofica di Enzo Paci. QUARTA, A.

L'idea di "Storia teoretica o congetturale" negli scritti filosofici e sul linguaggio di Adam Smith. IACONO, Alfonso M.

Philosophy as Exile from Life: Lukacs' 'Soul and Form'. BROWNE, Paul.

The Problem of the Historicity of Values. PEROV, I V.

HISTORIOGRAPHY

El a priori histórico (la historia y sus hechos). SAMPEDRO, Ceferino.

History and Anti-History in Philosophy. LAVINE, T Z (ed).

"Introduction: On the Nature of Philosophic Historiography" in *History and Anti-History in Philosophy,* TEJERA, V.

"The Philosophical Historiography of J H Randall" in *History and Anti-History in Philosophy,* TEJERA, V.

"The Public Grounds of Truth": The Critical Theory of G B Vico. MALI, Joseph.

Blumenberg and the Philosophical Grounds of Historiography. INGRAM, David.

Ciencia e historia en Leibniz. RACIONERO, Quitín.

Generalizaciones y explicación de la historiografía. PINCIONE, Guido M.

Meinecke e Dilthey. DI COSTANZO, Giuseppe.

On the Use and Abuse of Memory: Habermas, "Anamnestic Solidarity," and the *Historikerstreit.* PENSKY, Max.

Past Looking. HOLLY, Michael Ann.

Per una storia della cultura. TESSITORE, Fulvio.

Pietro Siciliani o del virtuoso darwinismo. SAVORELLI, Alessandro.

Recent Developments in Soviet Historiography of Philosophy. VAN DER ZWEERDE, Evert.

Scienze della cultura e storiografia filosofica in Ernst Cassirer. MARTIRANO, Maurizio.

Storia della cultura e storia sociale. VILLANI, Pasquale.

HISTORY

El a priori histórico (la historia y sus hechos). SAMPEDRO, Ceferino.

Aesthetic Objects and Works of Art. TOWNSEND, Dabney.

Discourses on the Meaning of History. KLUBACK, William.

Ethics in the History of Western Philosophy. CAVALIER, Robert J (ed).

Expérience et culture: Fondement d'une théorie générale de l'expérience. REALE, Miguel.

The Fabric of This World: Inquiries into Calling, Career Choice, and the Design of Human Work. HARDY, Lee.

Folly and Intelligence in Political Thought. KLUBACK, William.

Heritage and Challenge: The History and Theory of History. CONKIN, Paul K.

History and Anti-History in Philosophy. LAVINE, T Z (ed).

Hume. PHILLIPSON, N T.

If "P", then "Q": Conditionals and the Foundations of Reasoning. SANFORD, David H.

Innocence and Experience. HAMPSHIRE, Stuart.

Inquiries into Values: The Inaugural Session of the International Society for Value Inquiry. LEE, Sander H.

Kant and the Philosophy of History. YOVEL, Yirmiyahu.

The Main Trends in Philosophy. OIZERMAN, T I.

The Natures of Science. MC MORRIS, Neville.

Ortega y Gasset: Aurore de la Raison Historique. LORVELLEC, Y (trans).

The Past Within Us: An Empirical Approach to Philosophy of History. MARTIN, Raymond.

The Philosophy of Horror 'or' Paradoxes of the Heart. CARROLL, Noël.

Il Potere e l'Ipotesi: Tappe di una filosofia delle Funzioni. FRANCHINI, Raffaello.

The Rational and the Social. BROWN, James Robert.

Readings from Karl Marx. SAYER, Derek (ed).

The Social and Political Thought of R G Collingwood. BOUCHER, David.

Lo storicismo di W Dilthey (Il problema di dio nei grandi pensatori, Volume Quinto). MANNO, Ambrogio Giacomo.

Texts without Referents: Reconciling Science and Narrative. MARGOLIS, Joseph.

HOLDERLIN

"The Flower of the Mouth": Hölderlin's Hint for Heidegger's Thinking of the Essence of Language. VON HERRMANN, Friedrich-Wilhelm.

Dialéctica de la Revolución: Hegel, Schelling y Hölderlin ante la Revolución Francesa. INNERARITY, Daniel.

Heidegger and Hölderlin: The Over-Usage of "Poets in an Impoverished Time". GETHMANN-SIEFERT, Annemarie.

Heidegger and the God of Hölderlin. HAAR, Michel.

Heidegger: Preparing to Read Hölderlin's *Germanien*. GRUGAN, Arthur A.

Noise at the Threshold. FYNSK, Christopher.

Ontological Responsibility and the Poetics of Nature. LLEWELYN, John.

Poetic Saying as Beckoning: The Opening of Hölderlin's *Germanien*. MALY, Kenneth and EMAD, Parvis.

Textuality, Totalization, and the Question of Origin in Heidegger's Elucidation of *Andenken*. FÓTI, Véronique.

The Moment of the Foundation (in Serbo-Croatian). RAULET, Gérard.

The Undiscoverable Fraternity (in Serbo-Croatian). LEFEBVRE, Jean Pierre.

HOLINESS

Beauty and Holiness: The Dialogue between Aesthetics and Religion. MARTIN JR, James Alfred.

HOLISM

Holism—A Philosophy for Today: Anticipating the Twenty First Century. SETTANNI, Harry.

Religion, Interpretation, and Diversity of Belief. GODLOVE, Terry F.

A Theory of Content and Other Essays. FODOR, Jerry A.

"Harris on Internal Relations" in *Dialectic and Contemporary Science*, BLANSHARD, Brand.

"Holism, Separability, and the Metaphysical Implications of the Bell Experiments" in *Philosophical Consequences of Quantum Theory: Reflections on Bell's Theorem*, HOWARD, Don.

"Is the Program of Molecular Biology Reductionistic?" in *Reductionism and Systems Theory in the Life Sciences: Some Problems and Perspectives*, MOHR, Hans.

"Organisms, Vital Forces, and Machines" in *Reductionism and Systems Theory in the Life Sciences: Some Problems and Perspectives*, WUKETITS, Franz M.

"Reply to Blanshard's "Harris on Internal Relations"" in *Dialectic and Contemporary Science*, HARRIS, Errol E.

"System" and "Lifeworld": Habermas and the Problem of Holism. BOHMAN, James.

Beneath Interpretation: Against Hermeneutic Holism. SHUSTERMAN, Richard.

Einstein and Duhem. HOWARD, Don.

Holism a Century Ago: The Elaboration of Duhem's Thesis. BRENNER, Anastasios A.

Juventology: A Holistic Approach to Youth. MAHLER, Fred.

Maiocchi on Duhem, Howard on Duhem and Einstein: Historiographical Comments. BURIAN, Richard M.

Meaning Holism and Intentional Psychology. KUKLA, André and KUKLA, Rebecca.

On Ethnomathematics. D'AMBROSIO, Ubiratan.

Research Perspectives and the Anomalous Status of Modern Ecology. HAGEN, Joel B.

Semantic Holism Without Semantic Socialism: Twin Earths, Thinking, Language, Bodies, and the World. CASTAÑEDA, Hector-Neri.

Truth, Interpretation and Convention T. PRADHAN, R C.

HOLLIS, M

Hollis on Roles and Reason. WILKERSON, T E.

HOLOCAUST

"The Crisis of Knowledge and Understanding the Holocaust: Some Epistemological Remarks" in *Inquiries into Values: The Inaugural Session of the International Society for Value Inquiry*, ROSENBERG, Alan.

"Holocaust and Resistance" in *Inquiries into Values: The Inaugural Session of the International Society for Value Inquiry*, BAR ON, Bat-Ami.

"The Holocaust's Ideological Perversion of Value" in *Inquiries into Values: The Inaugural Session of the International Society for Value Inquiry*, FRANCIS, Richard.

"The Significance of Human Life after Auschwitz" in *Inquiries into Values: The Inaugural Session of the International Society for Value Inquiry*, ROTH, John.

Responsibility and Complicity. ARONSON, Ronald.

Survival Through the Generosity of Strangers. CARGAS, Harry James.

HOLY

Heidegger and the God of Hölderlin. HAAR, Michel.

HOME

The Ethics of Home Care: Autonomy and Accommodation. COLLOPY, Bart and DUBLER, Nancy and ZUCKERMAN, Connie.

HOMER

"The Beginnings of Epistemology: From Homer to Philolaus" in *Epistemology (Companions to Ancient Thought: 1)*, HUSSEY, Edward.

The Concerns of Odysseus: An Introduction to the *Odyssey*. BOLOTIN, David.

Homer, Literacy, and Education. GOLDMAN, Louis.

The Origins of Political Theory. WRIGHT, R M.

The Concept of "Oikiá" in Classic Greek Philosophy (in Czechoslovakian). MRAZ, M.

HOMOGENEITY

Totalitarianism, Homogeneity of Power, Depth: Towards a Socio-Political Ontology. STEINBOCK, A J.

HOMOLOGY

Between Infinity and Community: Notes on Materialism in Spinoza and Leopardi. NEGRI, Antonio.

HOMOSEXUALITY

AIDS and the Good Society. ILLINGWORTH, Patricia.

The AIDS Crisis: Unethical Marketing Leads to Negligent Homicide. KROHN, Franklin B and MILNER, Laura M.

Professor Gould and the "Natural". DALCOURT, Gerard J.

Reproductive Controls and Sexual Destiny. MURPHY, Timothy F.

HONDERICH, T

Honderich on the Indispensability of the Mental. MC CULLOCH, Gregory.

HONESTY

"Honesty and Intimacy" in *Person to Person*, GRAHAM, George and LA FOLLETTE, Hugh.

Honesty in Marketing. JACKSON, Jennifer.

A Simple Quantitative Test of Financial Ethics. NORTON, Edgar.

HOOKER, R

Radicals, Conservatives and Moderates in Early Modern Political Thought: A Case of Sandwich Islands Syndrome?. CONDREN, C.

HOPE

Ernst Bloch: Trame della speranza. BOELLA, Laura.

"Sub ratione ardui": Paura e speranza nella filosofia. FRANCHI, Alfredo.

Hope in a Secular Ethic. BAKER, Robert E.

Hope. SUTHERLAND, Stewart.

La metafísica de la esperanza y del deseo en Gabriel Marcel. O'CALLAGHAN, Paul.

Of Vision, Hope, and Courage. SKOLIMOWSKI, Henryk.

HORKHEIMER, M

Reading Horkheimer Reading Vico: An Introduction. DALLMAYR, Fred.

El tardío pesimismo metafísico de Horkheimer. MOLINUEVO, José Luis.

HORNSBY, J

On the Location of Actions and Tryings: Criticism of an Internalist View. GJELSVIK, Olav.

HORROR

The Philosophy of Horror 'or' Paradoxes of the Heart. CARROLL, Noël.

HORX, M

Individualisierung als Emanzipationsprojekt?. TEICHMANN, Werner.

HOSPERS, J

Aesthetics in Discipline-Based Art Education. CRAWFORD, Donald W.

The Ideal Aesthetic Observer Revisited. TALIAFERRO, Charles.

Sobre la privacidad de los estados de conciencia. LARRETA, Juan Rodriguez and DORFMAN, Beatriz.

HOSPITAL(S)

Ethics Committees. COHEN, Cynthia B (ed) & others.

Private Hospitals in Public Health Systems. HOLM, Soren.

Taking the Train to a World of Strangers: Health Care Marketing and Ethics. NELSON, Lawrence J and CLARK, H Westley and GOLDMAN, Robert L and SCHORE, Jean E.

HOSTAGE(S)

"Agreements with Hostage-Takers" in *Hobbes: War Among Nations*, GOLDING, Martin P.

HOUNTONDJI, P

African Philosophy: Paulin J Hountondji—His Dilemma and Contributions. OTAKPOR, Nkeonye.

HOUSEN, A

The Development of Aesthetic Judgment: Analysis of a Genetic-Structuralist Approach. DE MUL, Jos.

HOWE, K
Equal Opportunity or Equal Education?. BURBULES, Nicholas C.
A Questionable Resurrection. HESLEP, Robert D.

HSUN TZU
Disputers of the TAO: Philosophical Argument in Ancient China. GRAHAM, A C.
Xunzi: A Translation and Study of the Complete Works, Volume II—Books 7-16. KNOBLOCK, John (trans).

HUANG, S
Response to Huang Siu-chi's Review of Knowledge Painfully Acquired, by Lo Ch'in-shun and Translated by Irene Bloom. BLOOM, Irene.

HULL, C
Models, Mechanisms, and Explanation in Behavior Theory: The Case of Hull Versus Spence. SMITH, Laurence D.

HUMAN CONDITION
El deseo de ser. RODRÍGUEZ, Virgilio Ruiz.
El enigma del animal fantastico: Bases para una antropologia y etica de la tecnica. SANCHO, Jesús Conill.
Sartre y la ética: De la mala fe a la conversión moral. VIDIELLA, Graciela.

HUMAN CONSCIOUSNESS
Metaphysics. WEININGER, Otto and BURNS, S A M (trans).

HUMAN DEVELOPMENT
Good Lives and Moral Education. SIMPSON, Evan.
Filosofia dell'educazione e filosofia morale. DUCCI, Edda.
The Use of Symbols in Religion from the Perspective of Analytical Psychology. MC GLASHAN, A R.

HUMAN EXISTENCE
The Fabric of This World: Inquiries into Calling, Career Choice, and the Design of Human Work. HARDY, Lee.
"Nietzsche's New Experience of World" in Nietzsche's New Seas: Explorations in Philosophy, Aesthetics, and Politics, GILLESPIE, Michael Allen (trans) and FINK, Eugen.
Human Existence and Prospective Knowledge. PANA, Laura.
J Patocka: L'esistenza umana come "vita nella verità". DI MARCO, Chiara.
Place de l'homme dans l'univers. MALDAMÉ, Jean-Michel.

HUMAN NATURE
The Logic of Political Belief: A Philosophical Analysis of Ideology. ADAMS, Ian S.
Philosophical Essays in Pragmatic Naturalism. KURTZ, Paul.
Religious Issues in Contemporary Philosophy. SLAATTE, Howard A.
The Tanner Lectures on Human Values, Volume X. PETERSON, Grethe B (ed).
Wesen, Freiheit und Bildung des Menschen. HAGER, Fritz-Peter.
"The Essence of Human Experience in David Lynch's Blue Velvet" in Inquiries into Values: The Inaugural Session of the International Society for Value Inquiry, LEE, Sander H.
"Human Nature and Folk Psychology" in The Person and the Human Mind: Issues in Ancient and Modern Philosophy, BOTTERILL, George.
"Hume" in Ethics in the History of Western Philosophy, NORTON, David Fate.
"The Study of Human Nature and the Subjectivity of Value" in The Tanner Lectures on Human Values, Volume X, STROUD, Barry.
Agency, Human Nature and Character in Kantian Theory. RUMSEY, Jean P.
Aristotle's Political Naturalism. MILLER JR, Fred D.
Ch'eng I—The Pattern of Heaven-and-Earth (in Serbo-Croatian). SMITH, Kidder.
Change So As to Preserve Oneself and One's Nature: On a New Conception of Man. PECHENEV, V.
El concepto de naturaleza. GARCIA MORIYON, Félix.
El enigma de la naturaleza humana. MURILLO, Ildefonso.
Grazia e dignità dell'estetica schilleriana. DOLORES FOLLIERO, Granzia.
Human Nature and Its Cosmic Roots in Huang-Lao Taoism. JAN, Yun-Hua.
Human Natures. LACHS, John.
Le principe constitutif des valeurs morales dans l'éthique de S Thomas d'Aquin (in Polish). BEDNARSKI, F W.
Leo Strauss, Hobbes et la nature humaine. MALHERBE, Michel.
Maimonides on Prophecy and Human Nature: A Problem in Philosophical Interpretation. TRELOAR, John L.
Man Cannot Change His Nature. TSIPKO, A.
Mondo sociale, mimesi e violenza in R Girard. BOTTANI, Livio.
The Nature of Human Nature and its Bearing on Public Health Policy: An Application. KAPLAN, Mark.
The Nature of Man—Games that Genes Play?. GÄRDENFORS, Peter.
New Thinking about the "New Man": Developments in Soviet Moral Theory. FELDMAN, Jan.
Obligation and Human Nature in Hume's Philosophy. COHEN, Mendel F.

Philosophie et religion selon Hegel. PLANTY-BONJOUR, M Guy (and others).
Das philosophische Menschenbild: Eine konfuzianische Sicht. DOW, Tsung-I.
Rationality, Human Nature, and Lists. GERT, Bernard.
Re-Tracing the Human-Nature versus World-Nature Dichotemy: Lao Tzu's Hermeneutics for World-Building. LUSTHAUS, Dan.
A Systematic Exploration of the Marxist Theory of Human Nature. QUANFU, Liu and ZUORONG, He.
Transient Natures at the Edges of Life: A Thomistic Exploration. SMITH, Philip.
Die Unbestimmtheit von Theorien über die menschliche Natur im chinesischen Denken. TANG, Paul C L.
Vico e Joyce attraverso Michelet. VERRI, A.
Virtue under Attack (in Serbo-Croatian). PAS, Julian F.

HUMAN RELATIONS
Human Ecology. JUNGEN, Britta and EGNEUS, Hans.
Values of Knowledge and Values of Action in Human Conduct Structuring. PANA, Laura.

HUMAN RIGHTS
Liberty and Culture: Essays on the Idea of a Free Society. MACHAN, Tibor R.
Moral Reasoning and Statecraft: Essays Presented to Kenneth W Thompson. DAVIS, Reed M (ed).
"The Buddhist Outlook on Poverty and Human Rights" in The Wisdom of Faith: Essays in Honor of Dr Sebastian Alexander Matczak, PUTUWAR, Bhikkhu Sunanda.
"Detente, Human Rights and Soviet Behavior" in Moral Reasoning and Statecraft: Essays Presented to Kenneth W Thompson, PETRO, Nicolai N.
"Human Rights and the Founding Fathers" in Moral Reasoning and Statecraft: Essays Presented to Kenneth W Thompson, LANG, Daniel G.
Are There Inalienable Rights?. NELSON, John O.
Evolución de los derechos humanos en Spinoza y en Leibniz. VERGES, S.
Hobbes: Derechos naturales, sociedad y derechos humanos. RABOSSI, Eduardo.
The Jurisprudence of the European Court of Human Rights: Towards an Alternative Foundation of Human Rights. DURÁN Y LALAGUNA, Paloma.
Der Kapitalismus verletzt die Menschenrechte. KÜNZLI, Arnold.
The Law of Nature, the Uppsala School and the Ius Docendi Affair. SUNDBERG, Jacob.
Marx, Lukes, and Human Rights. BAXTER, David.
On Realization of Human Rights. KANGER, Stig.
Politics and Generosity. MACHAN, Tibor R.
The Right to Education: An Inquiry Into Its Foundations. CURLEY, Thomas V.
A Skeptical Appreciation of Natural Law Theory. GINSBERG, Robert.

HUMAN SCIENCES
The Normal and the Pathological. CANGUILHEM, Georges.
Texts without Referents: Reconciling Science and Narrative. MARGOLIS, Joseph.
Towards a Critique of Foucault. GANE, Mike (ed).
Du moraliste classique au moraliste des Lumières où la naissance des sciences humaines. MYDLARSKI, H.
Idéologie e conoscenza scientifica: La fondazione delle scienze umane nella gnoseologia sensita idéologique. PELLEREY, Roberto.
Paul Ricoeur's Methodological Parallelism. FLEMING, Patricia Ann.
Some Basic Problems in the Development of the Human Sciences in China Today. YOUZHENG, Li.

HUMAN SUBJECT(S)
Distinguishing Medical Practice and Research: The Special Case of IVF. GAZE, Beth and DAWSON, Karen.
The Ethical Assessment of Innovative Therapies: Liver Transplantation Using Living Donors. SINGER, Peter (and others).

HUMAN(S)
see also Man, Person(s)
Biblical Narrative in the Philosophy of Paul Ricoeur: A Study in Hermeneutics and Theology. VANHOOZER, Kevin J.
Divine Nature and Human Language: Essays in Philosophical Theology. ALSTON, William P.
Human Posture: The Nature of Inquiry. SCHUMACHER, John A.
The Philosopher's Habitat: Introduction to Investigations in, and Applications of, Modern Philosophy. GOLDSTEIN, Laurence.
Surrogate Motherhood: The Ethics of Using Human Beings. SHANNON, Thomas A.
Wittgenstein and Moral Philosophy. JOHNSTON, Paul.
"Homo conscius sui" in Agora: Zu Ehren von Rudolph Berlinger, FUNKE, Gerhard.

HUMAN(S)

"The Human Being as an Ethical Norm" in *The Person and the Human Mind: Issues in Ancient and Modern Philosophy*, GILL, Christopher.

"Human Persons" in *The Person and the Human Mind: Issues in Ancient and Modern Philosophy*, SMITH, Peter.

"Human/Nature in Nietzsche and Taoism" in *Nature in Asian Tradition of Thought: Essays in Environmental Philosophy*, PARKES, Graham.

"Philosophy, Love, and Madness" in *The Person and the Human Mind: Issues in Ancient and Modern Philosophy*, ROWE, Christopher.

Consciousness. SHANON, Benny.

The Death of the Animal: Ontological Vulnerability. SHAPIRO, Kenneth Joel.

Dewey's Conception of Growth Reconsidered. PEKARSKY, Daniel.

Éléments de l'histoire (humains et non humains) (in Greek). DESPOTOPOULOS, K I.

Ethical Similarities in Human and Animal Social Structures. ELLOS, William J.

Fear and the Limits of Human Subjectivity. CACKOWSKI, Zdzislaw and BLAIM, Artur (trans).

A Fortnight of My Life is Missing: A Discussion of the Status of the Human 'Pre-Embryo'. HOLLAND, Allan.

From Coffee to Carmelites. PHILLIPS, D Z.

Genetics and Human Malleability. ANDERSON, W French.

Grundprämisse der humanistischen Anthropologie (in Polish). OLEJNIK, Stanislaw.

The Human Being as Subject Matter of the Philosophy of Science. BOTEZ, Angela.

The Human Factor in the Revolution and Perestroika. MINKEVICIUS, Jokubas V.

Human Knowledge and Divine Knowledge in Medieval Philosophy (in Hebrew). SCHWARTZ, Dov.

Humanity in the World of Life. ZHANG, Hwe Ik.

Is Natural Law Ethics Obsolete?. MACHAN, Tibor R.

L'homme en tant qu'autocréateur; fondements anthropologiques du rejet de l'encyclique (in Polish). SZOSTEK, Andrzej.

Language and the Origin of the Human Imagination: A Vichian Perspective. DANESI, Marcel.

Learning to be Human: Confucian Resources for Person-Centered Education. CONROY, Fran.

Menschenbilder in pädagogiknahen Sozialwissenschaften. HUG, Theo.

New Notes from Underground. ELLERMAN, Carl Paul.

Notes on the Underground. CLARK, Stephen R L.

Popper and Historicist Necessities. FLEW, Antony.

The Problem of the Historicity of Values. PEROV, I V.

The Question of Human Freedom in the Later Heidegger. HAAR, Michel.

Schelling's "On the Essence of Human Freedom": An Interpretation of the First Main Points (in Hungarian). HEIDEGGER, Martin.

The Social Constitution of Action: *Objectivity and Explanation*. GREENWOOD, John D.

Technics and the Ontology of the Human Being Nowadays. BOBOC, Alexandru.

The Moment of Ideology and the Human Factor in Lukác's Late Work (in Hungarian). SZABÓ, Tibor.

Using People. COUGHLAN, Michael J.

Whistleblowing: An Ethical Issue in Organizational and Human Behavior. HEACOCK, Marian V and MC GEE, Gail W.

William James on the Human Ways of Being. DOOLEY, Patrick.

HUMANENESS

The Death Penalty, Civilization, and Inhumaneness. DAVIS, Michael.

The Death Penalty, Deterrence, and Horribleness: Reply to Michael Davis. REIMAN, Jeffrey.

HUMANISM

French Philosophy of the Sixties: An Essay on Antihumanism. CATTANI, Mary Schnackenberg (trans).

Heidegger and Modernity. PHILIP, Franklin (trans).

Humanisme de la liberté et philosophie de la justice, Tome II. TRIGEAUD, Jean-Marc.

Man, Science, Humanism: A New Synthesis. FROLOV, Ivan T.

Religious Issues in Contemporary Philosophy. SLAATTE, Howard A.

La "fucina del mondo". ADDANTE, Pietro.

Ars Medicina et Conditio Humana Edmund D Pellegrino, MD, on His 70th Birthday. SPICKER, Stuart F and RATZAN, Richard M.

Beyond Our Species' Potentials: Charles Hartshorne on Humanism. RUSSELL, John M.

Building Bridges to the Right: Libertarians, Conservatives, and Humanists. HUDGINS, Edward.

Christianity and Humanism. LONG, Eugene T.

Considerations on Preparation of Societies for Life in Peace. SHIBATA, Shingo.

Defining—and Implementing—Eupraxophy. FLYNN, T.

Dialogo sobre humanismo y existencialismo (tercera parte). CAMARENA, Juan M S.

Dialogo sobre humanismo y existencialismo (cuarta y última parte). SILVA CAMARENA, Juan Manuel.

A Eupraxopher's Agenda: Humanism and Religion. HOFFMANN, R Joseph.

Feminism, Humanism and Postmodernism. SOPER, Kate.

The Future of Abortion. FLYNN, Tom.

Grassi's Experiment: The Renaissance through Phenomenology. HEIM, Michael.

Grundprämisse der humanistischen Anthropologie (in Polish). OLEJNIK, Stanislaw.

Hartshorne on Humanism: A Comment. SHIELL, Timothy C.

Heidegger and the Question of Humanism. MILES, Murray.

Heidegger, Kant and the 'Humanism' of Science. SCHALOW, Frank.

Humanism and Altruism. MADIGAN, Tim.

Humanism and Political Economy. MACHAN, Tibor R.

Humanism and Socialism. SCHMITT, Richard.

Humanism. FALK, W D.

Investigating the Case of Religion and Humanism. ONWURAH, Emeka.

Learning to be Human: Confucian Resources for Person-Centered Education. CONROY, Fran.

Libertarianism Versus Secular Humanism?. GORDON, David.

Liberty and Democracy, or Socialism?. FLEW, Antony.

Lorenzo Valla and Rudolph Agricola. MONFASANI, John.

Maigret's Method. JACKSON, M W.

Making a Case for Socialism. NIELSEN, Kai.

Marx's Promethean Humanism. ABRAHAM, Kuruvilla C.

Metaphorical Language, Rhetoric, and *Comprehensio*: J L Vives and M Nizolio. HIDALGO-SERNA, Emilio and PINTON, Giorgio (trans).

Militant Atheism Versus Freedom of Conscience. KURTZ, Paul.

Moral Education: Homo Sapiens or Homo Religious?. WATTERS, Wendell W.

The Moral Stance of Theism Without the Transcent God: Wieman and Heidegger. SHAW, Marvin C.

Opening the Door to Moral Education. MC GOVERN, Edythe M.

Parlando di segni, di Hjelmslev e di filosofia del linguaggio. CAPUTO, C.

Pessimismo e umanesimo in Thomas Mann: Una riflessione etica su "Humanität" e "Humanismus". PERNECHELE, Gabriella.

Philosophical Premises of Levinas' Conception of Judaism. LORENC, Iwona and PETROWICZ, Lech (trans).

Positivismo ed umanismo. BÜTTEMEYER, Wilhelm.

The Poverty of Opulence. KOLENDA, Konstantin.

The Social Humanism of Adam Schaff. JAGUARIBE, Helio.

Socialism is Incompatible with Humanism. SHEAFFER, Robert.

The Laborious and Painful Process of Emancipation (in Serbo-Croatian). JUNQING, Yi.

Thomas Aquinas's Complete Guide to Heaven and Hell. LINDSAY, Ronald A.

Thomas Muntzer—Humanist, Reformator, Revolutionär. HERLITZIUS, Erwin and RUDOLPH, Günther.

Tradizione medievale e innovazione umanistica. ALES BELLO, Angela.

Vantage Points of H G Gadamer's Philosophical Thinking (Plato, Herder, Goethe, Hegel) (in Czechoslovakian). HROCH, Jaroslav.

HUMANITIES

Narrative Experiments: The Discursive Authority of Science and Technology. ORMISTON, Gayle L.

"The Humanities and the Modern Mind" in *Mind, Value and Culture: Essays in Honor of E M Adams*, NORD, Warren.

"The Trouble with Confucianism" in *The Tanner Lectures on Human Values*, Volume X, DE BARY, William Theodore.

Applied Liberal Education for Engineers. LUGENBIEHL, Heinz C.

The Birth of the Medical Humanities and the Rebirth of the Philosophy of Medicine: The Vision of Edmund D Pellegrino. ENGELHARDT JR, H Tristram.

Critical Attitudes Inside Social Science and the Humanities—A Swedish Perspective. LIEDMAN, Sven-Eric.

Harde noten om te kraken: de zachte wetenschappen. IBSCH, Elrud.

Humanities in Medical Education: Some Contributions. CLOUSER, K Danner.

More on Knowledge and the Humanities. EDEL, Abraham.

Toward a History of Recent Vico Scholarship in English, Part II: 1969-1973. TAGLIACOZZO, Giorgio.

Toward a History of Recent Vico Scholarship in English, Part IV: The Vico/Venezia Conference 1978, and Its Aftermath. TAGLIACOZZO, Giorgio.

HUMANITIES

Toward a History of Recent Vico Scholarship in English, Part V: After Vico/Venezia (1978-1987) and Appendix. TAGLIACOZZO, Giorgio.

Toward a History of Recent Vico Scholarship in English, Part III: 1974-1977. TAGLIACOZZO, Giorgio.

The Two Cultures. BROUDY, Harry S.

Who Is the Enemy? Reflections on the Threat of Managerial Techno-Reason to the Humanities. NORDENHAUG, Theodore D.

HUMANITY

Religione e Umanità. FICHERA, Giuseppe.

"The Significance of Human Life after Auschwitz" in Inquiries into Values: The Inaugural Session of the International Society for Value Inquiry, ROTH, John.

"Technicism, Education, and Living a Human Life" in Inquiries into Values: The Inaugural Session of the International Society for Value Inquiry, TAYLOR, Michael.

Ce qui est vivant, ce qui est mort dans la philosophie d'Auguste Comte (1935). LÉVY-BRUHL, Lucien.

Dominance of the Thought on Domestication: Threat for Humanum in Our Time (in Hungarian). DUPRÉ, Wilhelm.

The Ethos of Humanity in Karl Jaspers's Political Philosophy. SALAMUN, Kurt.

Humanity in Nature: Conserving Yet Creating. PETERS, Karl E.

Is the End of the World Nigh?. LESLIE, John.

San Agustín y K Rahner: El amor a Dios y el amor al prójimo. GALINDO RODRIGO, José Antonio.

Toward a New Relation between Humanity and Nature: Reconstructing T'ien-jen-ho-i. LIU, Shu-hsien.

Utilitarianism and Respect for Human Life. SPRIGGE, T L S.

HUMANNESS

Idéologie e conoscenza scientifica: La fondazione delle scienze umane nella gnoseologia sensita idéologique. PELLEREY, Roberto.

Man's Yearnings (in Dutch). OBERHOLZER, C K.

Root of Man: A Note. BANDYOPADHYAY, Tirthanath.

The Uniqueness of Human Being (in Czechoslovakian). OIZERMAN, T I.

HUMBOLDT

Zur sozialphilosophischen Bedeutung des Sprachbegriffs Wilhelm von Humboldts. SCHILLER, Hans-Ernst.

HUME

A Combinatorial Theory of Possibility. ARMSTRONG, D M.

Common Sense. FORGUSON, Lynd.

David Hume's Argument Against Miracles: A Critical Analysis. BECKWITH, Francis.

Early Modern Philosophy II. TWEYMAN, Stanley (ed).

Elements of Modern Philosophy: Descartes through Kant. BRENNER, William H.

Hume and the Problem of Miracles: A Solution. LEVINE, Michael P.

Hume. PHILLIPSON, N T.

Husserl's Phenomenology and the Foundations of Natural Science. HARVEY, Charles W.

The Idea of a Reason for Acting: A Philosophical Argument. SCHUELER, George Frederick.

Innocence and Experience. HAMPSHIRE, Stuart.

The Language of Imagination. WHITE, Alan R.

Philosophy of Economics: On the Scope of Reason in Economic Inquiry. ROY, Subroto.

Scarcity and Modernity. XENOS, Nicholas.

Thomas Reid. LEHRER, Keith.

Wie kann man sagen, was nicht ist-Zur Logik des Utopischen. SCHMITZ, Heinz-Gerd.

"Alternative Readings: Hume and His Commentators" in Early Modern Philosophy II, NOXON, James.

"Banter and Banquets for Heroic Death" in Post-Structuralist Classics, PUCCI, Pietro.

"David Hume: Crusading Empiricist, Skeptical Liberal" in Knowledge and Politics, HERZOG, Don.

"Hume and Gibbon: The Origin of Naturalistic Study of Religion" in Early Modern Philosophy II, WEBER, Andreas.

"Hume" in Ethics in the History of Western Philosophy, NORTON, David Fate.

"Skepticism and the Senses in Hume's 'Treatise'" in Early Modern Philosophy II, PAVKOVIC, Aleksandar.

"Suicide in the Age of Reason" in Suicide and Euthanasia, BEAUCHAMP, Tom L.

'Utility' and the 'Utility Principle': Hume, Smith, Bentham, Mill. LONG, Douglas G.

Abstract General Ideas in Hume. PAPPAS, George S.

Anonymous Writings of David Hume. RAPHAEL, D D and SAKAMOTO, Tatsuya.

Berkeley ou le sceptique malgré lui. LEBRUN, Gérard.

Character: A Humean Account. MC INTYRE, Jane L.

Concepts of Justice in the Scottish Enlightenment. MACKINNON, K A B.

David Hume and the Probability of Miracles. GOWER, Barry.

David Hume on Personal Identity and the Indirect Passions. HENDERSON, Robert S.

David Hume's Doctrine of Moral Judgment. JIDA, Yan.

Different Religions and the Difference They Make: Hume on the Political Effects of Religious Ideology. FOSTER, Stephen Paul.

The Eminently Practical Mr Hume or Still Relevant After All These Years. DAVLANTES, Nancy.

A Hobbist Tory: Johnson on Hume. RUSSELL, Paul.

Hume and Davidson on Pride. ÁRDAL, Páll S.

Hume and Tetens. KUEHN, Manfred.

Hume on Character, Action, and Causal Necessity. JOHNSON, Clarence Sholé.

Hume on Virtue, Beauty, Composites, and Secondary Qualities. BAXTER, Donald L M.

Hume y la incurable ineficacia de la filosofía contra la superstición. BADÍA CABRERA, Miguel A.

Hume's Essays on Happiness. IMMERWAHR, John.

Hume's Missing Shade of Blue Re-viewed. NELSON, John O.

Hume's Philosophical Schizophrenia. ERES, Gloria H.

Hume's Tu Quoque: Newtonianism and the Rationality of the Causal Principle. HAYNES, Michael.

Hume, Probability, Lotteries and Miracles. LANGTRY, Bruce.

Hume, Strict Identity, and Time's Vacuum. COSTA, Michael J.

Hume: Justice as Property. BRETT, Nathan.

The Humean Tradition. CARROLL, John.

Inductive Scepticism and Experimental Reasoning in Moral Subjects in Hume's Philosophy. JACOBSON, Anne Jaap.

Interpreting Hume's Dialogues. COLEMAN, Dorothy P.

Is Hume a Moral Skeptic?. FIESER, James.

Kant's Challenge: The Second Analogy as a Response to Hume. DELANEY, C.

Leibniz and the Problem of Induction. WESTPHAL, Jonathan.

The Logic of Probabilities in Hume's Argument against Miracles. WILSON, Fred.

Miracles and the Uniformity of Nature. ROOT, Michael.

Naturnotwendigkeit und Freiheit: Zu Kants Theorie der Kausalität als Antwort auf Hume. RANG, Bernhard.

O ceticismo naturalista de David Hume. SMITH, Plínio Junqueira.

The Objectivity of Taste: Hume and Kant. KULENKAMPFF, Jens.

Obligation and Human Nature in Hume's Philosophy. COHEN, Mendel F.

Personal Identity and the Passions. MC INTYRE, Jane L.

Phenomenological Skepticism in Hume. LOPTSON, Peter.

Philo's Final Conclusion in Hume's Dialogues. VINK, A G.

Poder causal, experiencia y conceptos a priori. CASSINI, Alejandro.

Positivismo ed umanismo. BÜTTEMEYER, Wilhelm.

La prova a priori dell'esistenza di Dio nel Settecento inglese: da Cudworth a Hume. SCRIBANO, Emanuela.

Reason, Inductive Inference, and True Religion in Hume. JANZ, Bruce.

Reasoning by Analogy in Hume's Dialogues. BARKER, Stephen F.

Reconceiving Miracles. GILMAN, James E.

Reid and the Rights of Man. DALGARNO, Melvin.

Religion a Threat to Morality: An Attempt to Throw Some New Light on Hume's Philosophy of Religion. STREMINGER, Gerhard.

A Reply to Ellin's "Streminger: 'Religion a Threat to Morality'". STREMINGER, Gerhard.

The Role of Self-Knowledge in the Critique of Pure Reason. POLT, Richard F H.

Scepticism and Angst: The Case of David Hume. COHEN, Avner.

Scepticism and Madness. BELSHAW, Christopher.

Sense, Reason and Causality in Hume and Kant. NUYEN, A T.

El sentido de la teoría humeana del tiempo como relación filosófica. MUDROVCIC, María Inés.

Some Sources for Hume's Opening Remarks to Treatise I IV III. SOLOMON, Graham.

Some Uses of Imagination in the British Empiricists: A Preliminary Investigation of Locke, as Contrasted with Hume. HALL, Roland.

Streminger: "Religion a Threat to Morality". ELLIN, Joseph.

A Taste for Hume. DE MARTELAERE, Patricia.

Tesi di Hume e sistemi di logica deontica. GALVAN, Sergio.

Theological Empiricism: Aspects of Johann Georg Hamann's Reception of Hume. GRAUBNER, Hans.

What Hume Actually Said About Miracles. FOGELIN, Robert J.

HUME

Where the Traditional Accounts of Practical Reason Go Wrong. HURLEY, Paul.

Zur Frage der Vereinbarkeit von Freiheit und Determinismus. RHEINWALD, Rosemarie.

HUMILITY

"Humility as a Virtue: A Maimonidean Critique of Aristotle's Ethics" in *Moses Maimonides and His Time*, FRANK, Daniel H.

On the Humility of Mathematical Language. JARDINE, David W.

HUMOR

Sense of Humor as a Christian Virtue. ROBERTS, Robert C.

The Incongruity of Incongruity Theories of Humour (in Hebrew). KULKA, Tomas.

HUNGER

"Policies for Hunger Relief: Moral Considerations" in *Inquiries into Values: The Inaugural Session of the International Society for Value Inquiry*, LUCIER, Ruth.

HUNTING

On the Morality of Hunting. CAUSEY, Ann S.

Sport Hunting: Moral or Immoral?. VITALI, Theodore R.

HUSSERL

The Crisis of Philosophy. MC CARTHY, Michael.

Edith Stein: Filosofia E Senso Dell'Essere. LAMACCHIA, Ada.

Expérience et culture: Fondement d'une théorie générale de l'expérience. REALE, Miguel.

Husserl und Cohn: Widerspruch, Reflexion, und Telos in Phanomenologie und Dialektik. KLOCKENBUSCH, Reinald.

Husserl's Phenomenology and the Foundations of Natural Science. HARVEY, Charles W.

Kants Theorie des Verstandes. SEEBOHM, Thomas M (ed).

"Absolute Positivity and Ultrapositivity: Husserl and Levinas" in *The Question of the Other: Essays in Contemporary Continental Philosophy*, COHEN, Richard A.

"On Derrida's 'Introduction' to Husserl's *Origin of Geometry*" in *Derrida and Deconstruction*, BERNET, Rudolf.

Afferent-Efferent Connections and Neutrality-Modifications in Perceptual and Imaginative Consciousness. ELLIS, Ralph D.

After Experiment: Realism and Research. HEELAN, Patrick A.

Der Andere als Zukunft und Gegenwart. RÖMPP, Georg.

Bibliographie der bis zum 8 Mai 1989 veröffentlichten Schriften Edmund Husserls. SCHMITZ, Manfred.

Cancellations: Notes on Merleau-Ponty's Standing between Hegel and Husserl. WATSON, Stephen.

Categorial Modelling of Husserl's Intentionality. BARUSS, Imants.

Constitution and Reference in Husserl's Phenomenology of Phenomenology. HART, James G.

The Contexts of Phenomenology as Theory. LARRABEE, Mary Jeanne.

Descartes, Skepticism, and Husserl's Hermeneutic Practice. BURKEY, John.

Discorso meta-fisico e discorso meta-forico: Derrida. PELLECCHIA, Pasquale.

The Early Work of Husserl and Artificial Intelligence. MÜNCH, Dieter.

Edmund Husserl and Russian Philosophy (in Czechoslovakian). MATHAUSER, Zdenek.

La fenomenología de Husserl y la filosofía de Santo Tomás de Aquino. STEIN, Edith.

La fenomenología. SAN MARTÍN, Javier.

Habermas' Early Lifeworld Appropriation: A Critical Assessment. GEIMAN, Kevin Paul.

Hermeneutics and Apodicticity in Phenomenological Method. REEDER, Harry P.

Husserl and Freud: Time, Memory and the Unconscious. MISHARA, Aaron L.

Husserl and Heidegger on Intentionality and Being. BERNET, Rudolf.

Husserl and Heidegger on the Cartesian Legacy. TRIPATHY, Laxman Kumar.

Husserl and the Origin of Geometry. GRIEDER, Alfons.

Husserl Versus Derrida. EDIE, James M.

Husserl's Account of Phenomenological Reflection and Four Paradoxes of Reflexivity. HOPKINS, Burt C.

Husserl's Concept of Inner Temporal Consciousness and Aesthetics (in Czechoslovakian). ZUSKA, Vlastimil.

Husserl's Paradox. KIDDER, Paul.

Husserl's Phenomenology as Critique of Epistemic Ideology. HARVEY, Charles W.

Husserl's Theory of Parts and Wholes: The Dynamic of Individuating and Contextualizing Interpretation. LAMPERT, Jay.

Husserl, Heidegger, and Transcendental Philosophy: Another Look at the

Encyclopaedia Britannica Article. CROWELL, Steven Galt.

Husserl, Intentionality, and Cognitive Architecture. BROWN, Charles S.

Husserl—Bolzano I (in Czechoslovakian). BAYROVA, Marie.

Husserlian Ontology of Cultural Objects. MONTES, Raúl Iturrino.

Idealization and Projection in the Empirical Sciences: Husserl versus Heidegger. KOCKELMANS, Joseph J.

Immanent Critique. TURETZKY, Philip.

Indexikalität, Wahrnehmung und Bedeutung bei Husserl. BECKER, Wolfgang.

l'Être et le sensible: Edmund Husserl et Thomas D'Aquin. WINANCE, éleuthère.

Linee dell'attività filosofico-teologica della Beata Edith Stein. FABRO, Cornelio.

Die Notizen Eugen Finks zur Umarbeitung von Edmund Husserls "Cartesianischen Meditationen". BRUZINA, Ronald.

L'obiettivazione della vita soggettiva nelle scienze storico-sociali e la fenomenologia trascendentale di Husserl. MASSIMILLA, Edoardo.

Phenomenological Deconstruction: Husserl's Method of *Abbau*. EVANS, J Claude.

The Pluralistic Approach to the Nature of Feelings. NATSOULAS, Thomas.

Postmodern Philosophy?. MADISON, G B.

The Primacy of Perception in Husserl's Theory of Imagining. DROST, Mark P.

The Problem of Knowledge and Phenomenology. PIETERSMA, Henry.

Prospettive teologiche nella filosofia di Husserl. MELCHIORRE, V.

Ein Protokoll aus Husserls Logikseminar vom Winter 1925. REINER, Hans and SCHUHMANN, Karl.

Reflections on Charles S Brown's "Husserl, Intentionality, and Cognitive Architecture". HARVEY, Charles W.

Selbstreferenz und Zeit: Die dynamische Stabilität des Bewusstseins. BERGMANN, Werner and HOFFMANN, G.

El tema principal de la fenomenología de Husserl. WALTON, Roberto J.

Towards a Real Phenomenology of Logic. PERUZZI, Alberto.

The Young Heidegger and Phenomenology. VAN BUREN, John.

HUXLEY

The Metaphysics of Evolution. HULL, David L.

HUYGENS

La doble significación científica y filosófica de la evolución del concepto de fuerza de Descartes a Euler. ARANA, Juan.

HYLOMORPHISM

Hylomorphism in Aristotle. WITT, Charlotte.

HYPOCRISY

"The Necessary Moral Hypocrisy of the Slide into Mutual Assured Destruction" in *Nuclear Deterrence and Moral Restraint*, QUESTER, George H.

Hypocrisy. TURNER, D.

HYPOTHESIS(-SES)

Hypothesis and the Spiral of Reflection. WEISSMAN, David.

"Conjunctive Containment" in *Directions in Relevant Logic*, BELNAP JR, Nuel D.

Bold Hypotheses: The Bolder the Better?. CLEVELAND, Timothy and SAGAL, Paul T.

Hypothèses sur Platon et sur Nietzsche. IOANNIDI, H.

On Advancing Simple Hypotheses. OSHERSON, Daniel N and WEINSTEIN, Scott.

The Only Game in Town. ACHINSTEIN, Peter.

The Simplest Hypothesis. HARMAN, Gilbert.

HYPOTHETICAL IMPERATIVE

Kant's Theory of Practical Reason. HILL JR, Thomas E.

Zur Analytizität hypothetischer Imperative. BURRI, Alex and FREUDIGER, Jürg.

HYPOTHETICO-DEDUCTIVE

Hypothetical and Inductive Heuristics. KLEINER, Scott A.

I

Philosophical Problems (Consciousness, Reality and I). VERSTER, Ulrich.

ICON(S)

Verbal and Pictorial Signification (in Serbo-Croatian). BOZICEVIC, Vanda.

IDEA(S)

see also Concept(s)

Arnauld and the Cartesian Philosophy of Ideas. NADLER, Steven M.

Hobbes's System of Ideas. WATKINS, John W N.

The Idea of Political Theory: Reflections on the Self in Political Time and Place. STRONG, Tracy B.

The Language of Imagination. WHITE, Alan R.

Relevant Logic: A Philosophical Examination of Inference. READ, Stephen.

IDEA(S)

Understanding Plato. MELLING, David J.

Voegelin on the Idea of Race: An Analysis of Modern European Racism. HEILKE, Thomas W.

"Abstraktion, Begriffsanalyse, und Urteilskraft in Schopenhauers Erkenntnislehre" in *Schopenhauer: New Essays in Honor of His 200th Birthday*, MALTER, Rudolf.

"Ideas and Perception in Malebranche" in *Early Modern Philosophy II*, NADLER, Steven M.

"Locke's Ideas, Abstraction, and Substance" in *Cause, Mind, and Reality: Essays Honoring C B Martin*, HINCKFUSS, Ian.

"Propositions and Philosophical Ideas" in *Cause, Mind, and Reality: Essays Honoring C B Martin*, HINTON, J M.

"Bedeutung", "Idee" und "Begriff": Zur Behandlung einiger bedeutungstheoretischer Paradoxien durch Leibniz. ROS, Arno.

Civil Association and the Idea of Contingency. MAPEL, David R.

Doubt and Belief in the *Tractatus De Intellectus Emendatione*. BEAVERS, Anthony F and RICE, Lee C.

Excollonco and the Pursuit of Ideas. BRANN, Eva.

The Folklore of Computers and the True Art of Thinking. ROSZAK, Theodore.

Having Ideas and Having the Concept. CRIMMINS, Mark.

Hume's Missing Shade of Blue Re-viewed. NELSON, John O.

The Idea of Music in India and the Ancient West. ROWELL, Lewis.

Locke on the Making of Complex Ideas. LOSONSKY, Michael.

Locke's Simple Ideas, the Blooming, Buzzing Confusion, and Quasi-Photographic Perception. HEYD, Thomas.

Notion et idée de science chez Eric Weil. BREUVART, Jean-Marie.

Objective Reality of Ideas in Descartes, Caterus, and Suárez. WELLS, Norman J.

Reflexive Ideas in Spinoza. RICE, Lee C.

Schleiermacher's Critique of Ethical Reason: Toward a Systematic Ethics. WALLHAUSSER, John.

The Theory of Ideas in Gassendi and Locke. MICHAEL, Fred S and MICHAEL, Emily.

Virtue and Ignorance. FLANAGAN, Owen.

Young Children Generate Philosophical Ideas. MC CALL, Catherine.

IDEAL OBSERVER

Could Ideal Observers Disagree?: A Reply to Taliaferro. CARSON, Thomas L.

The Ideal Aesthetic Observer Revisited. TALIAFERRO, Charles.

IDEAL(S)

The Problem of the Ideal. DUBROVSKY, David.

The Aristotelian Character of Schiller's Ethical Ideal. CORDNER, Christopher.

Complexity-Theoretic Algebra II: Boolean Algebras. NERODE, A and REMMEL, J B.

Ideal Moral Codes. MAC INTOSH, Duncan.

Machiavelli, Tacito, Grozio: un nesso "ideale" tra libertinismo e previchismo. SCARCELLA, Cosimo.

Moral Ideals and Social Values: The Dialectics of Legitimization. AVINERI, Shlomo.

Platonische Idee und die anschauliche Welt bei Schopenhauer. KAMATA, Yasuo.

The Role of Virtues in Alternatives to Kantian and Utilitarian Ethics. MORAVCSIK, Julius M.

Two Ideals of Friendship. O'CONNOR, David K.

IDEALISM

The Crisis of Philosophy. MC CARTHY, Michael.

Freedom and the End of Reason: On the Moral Foundation of Kant's Critical Philosophy. VELKLEY, Richard L.

Hegel's Epistemological Realism: A Study of the Aim and Method of Hegel's Phenomenology of Spirit. WESTPHAL, Kenneth R.

Holism—A Philosophy for Today: Anticipating the Twenty First Century. SETTANNI, Harry.

The Nature of Existence, Volume I. MC TAGGART, John McTaggart Ellis.

The Nature of Existence, Volume II. MC TAGGART, John McTaggart Ellis.

Nietzsche Contra Nietzsche: Creativity and the Anti-Romantic. DEL CARO, Adrian.

Il Potere e l'Ipotesi: Tappe di una filosofia delle Funzioni. FRANCHINI, Raffaello.

Reading Kant. SCHAPER, Eva (ed).

The World We Found: The Limits of Ontological Talk. SACKS, Mark.

"Idealism and Realism: An Old Controversy Dissolved" in *Christ, Ethics and Tragedy: Essays in Honour of Donald MacKinnon*, KERR, Fergus.

"'Ideology' in Marx and Engels": A Reply. MC CARNEY, J.

The A Priori from Kant to Schelling. LAWRENCE, Joseph P (trans) and GRONDIN, Jean.

Against Technocratic Hubris and Positivistic Idealism: Anti-Naturalistic and Anti-Realistic Fallacies, (Part One). LENK, Hans.

Algunas consideraciones sobre la Refutación del Idealismo. JAUREGUI, Claudia and VIGO, Alejandro G.

Beauty in Design and Pictures: Idealism and Aesthetic Education. STANKIEWICZ, Mary Ann.

Berkeley's Theory of Time. HESTEVOLD, H Scott.

Berkeley's Unstable Ontology. CUMMINS, Phillip D.

Bruno "Iulliano' nell'idealismo italiano dell'Ottocento (con un inedito di Bertrando Spaventa). SAVORELLI, Alessandro.

Emil Lask and the Crisis of Neo-Kantianism: The Rediscovery of the Primordial World. MOTZKIN, Gabriel.

La estructura de la mente según la escuela idealista budista (Yogachara). TOLA, Fernando and DRAGONETTI, Carmen.

Feder und Kant. BRANDT, Reinhard.

From Absolute Idealism to Instrumentalism: The Problem of Dewey's Early Philosophy. WELCHMAN, Jennifer.

G E Moore and the Revolution in Ethics: A Reappraisal. WELCHMAN, Jennifer.

The Gifford Lectures and the Glasgow Hegelians. LONG, Eugene T.

Hegel vor dem Forum der Wissenschaftslehre Fichtes: Reinhard Lauths Untersuchungen zum Frühidealismus. ZAHN, Manfred.

Hegel's Idealism: Prospects. PIPPIN, Robert.

Heidegger and Peirce: Beyond "Realism or Idealism". BOURGEOIS, Patrick L and ROSENTHAL, Sandra B.

The Historical Tasks of Philosophy. SOLOV'EV, V S.

Idealism and Quantum Mechanics. MOHANTY, J N.

Idealist Elements in Thomas Kuhn's Philosophy of Science. HOYNINGEN-HUENE, Paul.

The Idealistic Implications of Bell's Theorem. SCHICK JR, Theodore W.

J G Droysen: Storia universale e Kulturgeschichte. CANTILLO, Giuseppe.

Il neoidelismo italiano e la meccanica quantistica. MAIOCCHI, Roberto.

On Schelling's Philosophy of Nature. JÄHNIG, Dieter and SOLBAKKEN, Elisabeth (trans).

Preface to the Publication of "P A Florenskii's Review of His Work". ABRAMOV, A I.

Realismo crítico y conocimiento en Carlos Popper. DARÓS, W R.

La relación Krause/krausismo como problema hermenéutico. GARCIA MATEO, R.

The Role of the Unconscious in Schelling's System of Transcendental Idealism. SNOW, Dale.

Santayana and Panpsychism. SPRIGGE, Timothy.

Schelling: A New Beginning. LAWRENCE, Joseph P.

Sich-Wissen als Argument: Zum Problem der Theoretizität des Selbstbewusstseins. RÖMPP, Georg.

Type Concept Revisited: A Survey of German Idealistic Morphology in the First Half of the Twentieth Century. TRIENES, Rudie.

Vladimir Solov'ev on the Fate and Purpose of Philosophy. RASHKOVSKII, E B.

Was Hegel a Panlogicist?. EISENBERG, Paul.

Der Widerspruch zwischen Materiellem und Ideellem und der dialektische Materiebegriff. GEBHARDT, Birgit.

Witchcraft and Winchcraft. WILLIAMSON, Colwyn.

IDEALIZATION

Applying Idealized Scientific Theories to Engineering. LAYMON, Ronald.

Idealization and Projection in the Empirical Sciences: Husserl versus Heidegger. KOCKELMANS, Joseph J.

Idealized Laws, Antirealism, and Applied Science: A Case in Hydrogeology. SHRADER-FRECHETTE, K S.

IDENTIFICATION

Interpretation at Risk. MARGOLIS, Joseph.

A Reason for Theoretical Terms. GAIFMAN, Haim and OSHERSON, Daniel N and WEINSTEIN, Scott.

IDENTITY

see also Personal Identity

Abstract Particulars. CAMPBELL, Keith.

Actions and Other Events: The Unifier-Multiplier Controversy. PFEIFER, Karl.

Gender Trouble: Feminism and the Subversion of Identity. BUTLER, Judith.

Lawless Mind. ABELSON, Raziel.

What is Identity?. WILLIAMS, C J F.

"Identity in Intensional Logic: Subjective Semantics" in *Meaning and Mental Representation*, VAN FRAASSEN, Bas.

"The Identity of Thought and Being in Harris's Interpretation of Hegel's Logic" in *Dialectic and Contemporary Science*, RINALDI, Giacomo.

"Quantification, Identity, and Opacity in Relevant Logic" in *Directions in Relevant Logic*, FREEMAN, James B.

ILLUSTRATION(S)
A Pragmatic Method of Reading Confused Philosophic Texts: The Case of Peirce's "Illustrations". OCHS, Peter.

IMAGE(S)
The Dialectics of Seeing: Walter Benjamin and the Arcades Project. BUCK-MORSS, Susan.
The Language of Imagination. WHITE, Alan R.
The Philosophical Imaginary. LE DOEUFF, Michèle.
Colouring in the World. BIGELOW, John and COLLINS, John and PARGETTER, Robert.
The Human Image System and Thinking Critically in the Strong Sense. FREEMAN, James B.
Inspecting Images: A Reply to Smythies. WRIGHT, Edmond.
Is a Work of Art Symbol of Feeling or an Image of Experience?. KAR, Gitangshu.
Le mathématicien et ses images. DELESSERT, André.
Seeing and Believing: Metaphor, Image, and Force. MORAN, Richard.

IMAGERY
Mental Imagery: On the Limits of Cognitive Science. ROLLINS, Mark.
The Philosophy of Horror 'or' Paradoxes of the Heart. CARROLL, Noël.

IMAGINARY
The Philosophical Imaginary. LE DOEUFF, Michèle.

IMAGINATION
Heidegger Interprete di Kant. COLONNELLO, Pio.
The Kantian Sublime: From Morality to Art. CROWTHER, Paul.
The Language of Imagination. WHITE, Alan R.
Morality and Imagination: Paradoxes of Progress. TUAN, Yi-Fu.
The Poetic Structure of the World: Copernicus and Kepler. HALLYN, Fernand.
The 'Imaginative Syllogism' in Arabic Philosophy: A Medieval Contribution to the Philosophical Study of Metaphor. BLACK, Deborah L.
Aristotle The First Cognitivist?. MODRAK, D K W.
Education and Philosophy. WOODBRIDGE, Frederick J E.
Imagination, Totality, and Transcendence. SCHALOW, F.
Imaginative Freedom and the German Enlightenment. KNELLER, Jane.
Immaginazione produttiva e struttura dell'immaginario nelle Rêveries du promeneur solitaire di Jean-Jacques Rousseau. PANELLA, Giuseppe.
Language and the Origin of the Human Imagination: A Vichian Perspective. DANESI, Marcel.
Leading Out Into the World: Vico's New Education. ENGELL, James.
Literature, Philosophy, and the Imagination. LEVI, Albert William.
Music and Understanding: The Concept of Understanding Applied to Listening to Music. MUNRO, Joan.
Pragmatic Imagination. ALEXANDER, Thomas M.
Remarks on the Logic of Imagination. NIINILUOTO, Ilkka.
Some Remarks on Bhartrhari's Concept of Pratibhā. TOLA, Fernando and DRAGONETTI, Carmen.
Some Uses of Imagination in the British Empiricists: A Preliminary Investigation of Locke, as Contrasted with Hume. HALL, Roland.
The Vichian Elements in Susanne Langer's Thought. BLACK, David W.

IMAGINING
Imagining Oneself to be Another. REYNOLDS, Steven L.
The Primacy of Perception in Husserl's Theory of Imagining. DROST, Mark P.

IMITATION
Desire: Direct and Imitative. COHN, Robert Greer.
Love Delights in Praises: A Reading of The Two Gentlemen of Verona. GIRARD, René.
Mondo sociale, mimesi e violenza in R Girard. BOTTANI, Livio.

IMMANENCE
L'autre et l'immanence. GUILLAMAUD, Patrice.

IMMANENTISM
Immanent Critique. TURETZKY, Philip.
Immanent Truth. RESNIK, Michael D.

IMMATERIALISM
Berkeley's Manifest Qualities Thesis. CUMMINS, Phillip D.
Berkeley's Unstable Ontology. CUMMINS, Phillip D.
Divine Ideas: The Cure-All for Berkeley's Immateralism?. STUBENBERG, Leopold.

IMMEDIACY
Immediate Legitimacy? Problems of Legitimacy in a Consensually Oriented Application of Law. MÄENPÄÄ, Olli.
The Play of Difference/Différance in Hegel and Derrida. MARSH, James L.
Sensation, Perception and Immediacy: Mead and Merleau-Ponty.

ROSENTHAL, Sandra B and BOURGEOIS, Patrick L.

IMMORALITY
"Escaping from the Bomb: Immoral Deterrence and the Problem of Extrication" in Nuclear Deterrence and Moral Restraint, COADY, C A J.
The Immorality of Nuclear Deterrence. ARDAGH, David.
The Nature of Immorality. HAMPTON, Jean.

IMMORTALITY
God, Immortality, Ethics: A Concise Introduction to Philosophy. LACKEY, Douglas P.
Pomponazzi's Critique of Aquinas' Arguments for the Immortality of the Soul. TRELOAR, John L.
The Tripartite Soul in the Timaeus. ROBINSON, James V.
Why We Need Immortality. TALIAFERRO, Charles.

IMPARTIALITY
see also Objectivity
Could Ideal Observers Disagree?: A Reply to Taliaferro. CARSON, Thomas L.
The Impracticality of Impartiality. FRIEDMAN, Marilyn.
Morally Privileged Relationships. DONALDSON, Thomas.
Nietzschean Perspectivism: "How Could Such a Philosophy—Dominate?". FOWLER, Mark.
A Normative Conception of Coherence for a Discursive Theory of Legal Justification. GÜNTHER, Klaus.

IMPERATIVES
see also Command(s)
Declaratives Are Not Enough. BELNAP JR, Nuel D.
The Elemental Imperative. LINGIS, Alphonso.

IMPERIALISM
William James, Public Philosopher. COTKIN, George.
Remembering and Re-Creating the Classing. CASANOVA, Pablo González.

IMPERMANENCE
Impermanence is Buddha-nature: Dōgen's Understanding of Temporality. STAMBAUGH, Joan.

IMPLEMENTATION
Epistemological and Ethical Considerations in Conceptualizing and Implementing Human Resource Management. DACHLER, H Peter and ENDERLE, Georges.
Strategy, Social Responsibility and Implementation. KRAFT, Kenneth L and HAGE, Jerald.

IMPLICATION
"Analytic Implication: Its History, Justification and Varieties" in Directions in Relevant Logic, PARRY, William T.
"Real Implication" in Directions in Relevant Logic, MYHILL, John.
"Relevant Implication and Leibnizian Necessity" in Directions in Relevant Logic, PARKS, Zane and BYRD, Michael.
"What is Relevant Implication?" in Directions in Relevant Logic, URQUHART, Alasdair.
Cause as an Implication. SYLVAN, Richard and DA COSTA, Newton.
The Ethical Implications of Corporate Records Management Practices and Some Suggested Ethical Values for Decisions. RUHNKA, John C and WELLER, Steven.
Extra-Logical Inferences. LÓPEZ-ESCOBAR, E G K.
Principal Type-Schemes and Condensed Detachment. HINDLEY, J Roger.
The Property (HD) in Intermediate Logics: A Partial Solution of a Problem of H Ono. MINARI, Pierluigi.
A Syntactical Characterization of Structural Completeness for Implicational Logics. WOJTYLAK, Piotr.

IMPOSSIBILITY
Wie kann man sagen, was nicht ist-Zur Logik des Utopischen. SCHMITZ, Heinz-Gerd.
Democritus and the Impossibility of Collision. GODFREY, Raymond.
How to Believe the Impossible. BROWN, Curtis.

IMPREDICATIVE
"Russell's Paradox, Russellian Relations, and the Problems of Predication and Impredicativity" in Rereading Russell: Essays on Bertrand Russell's Metaphysics and Epistemology, HOCHBERG, Herbert.

IMPRESSION(S)
Hume's Missing Shade of Blue Re-viewed. NELSON, John O.

IMPUTATION
Known from the Things that Are: Fundamental Theory of the Moral Life. O'KEEFE, Martin D.

IN VITRO FERTILIZATION
Ethical Issues in the New Reproductive Technologies. HULL, Richard T (ed).

IN VIRTO FERTILIZATION

Choice, Gift, or Patriarchal Bargain? Women's Consent to *In Vitro* Fertilization in Male Infertility. LORBER, Judith.

Distinguishing Medical Practice and Research: The Special Case of IVF. GAZE, Beth and DAWSON, Karen.

New Reproductive Technologies in the Treatment of Human Infertility and Genetic Disease. SILVER, Lee M.

Resolving Disputes Over Frozen Embryos. ROBERTSON, John A.

INADA, K

Reply to Kenneth K Inada. PILGRIM, Richard.

INALIENABLE RIGHT(S)

Are There Inalienable Rights?. NELSON, John O.

INCARNATION

The Self-Embodiment of God. ALTIZER, Thomas J J.

"Some Aspects of the 'Grammar' of 'Incarnation' and 'Kenosis'" in *Christ, Ethics and Tragedy: Essays in Honour of Donald MacKinnon,* SURIN, Kenneth.

Could God Become Man?. SWINBURNE, Richard.

Incarnation and Timelessness. SENOR, Thomas D.

The Logic of God Incarnate. HICK, John.

INCEST

Does Evolutionary Biology Contribute to Ethics?. BATESON, Patrick.

INCOME

Dual-Career and Dual-Income Families: Do They Have Different Needs?. FALKENBERG, L and MONACHELLO, M.

INCOMMENSURABILITY

Donald Davidson's Philosophy of Language: An Introduction. RAMBERG, Bjorn T.

The Growth of Knowledge: An Inquiry into the Kuhnian Theory. VERRONEN, Veli.

"Incommensurability, Scientific Realism and Rationalism" in *Scientific Knowledge Socialized,* PORUS, N L.

"The Problem of Incommensurability: A Critique of Two Instrumentalist Approaches" in *Scientific Knowledge Socialized,* PEARCE, David.

'If a Lion Could Talk'. CHURCHILL, John.

The Anthropology of Incommensurability. BIAGIOLI, Mario.

The Incommensurability of Moral Argument. SELKIRK, John.

Incommensurability, Intratextuality, and Fideism. TILLEY, Terrence W.

Incommensurability: The Scaling of Mind-Body Theories as a Counter Example. RAKOVER, Sam S.

Inconmensurabilidad y criterios de identidad de esquemas conceptuales. HIDALGO, Cecilia.

Prospective Realism. BROWN, Harold I.

Significado, referencia e inconmensurabilidad. GAETA, Rodolfo.

INCOMPATIBILISM

Determinism, Blameworthiness and Deprivation. KLEIN, Martha.

Two Kinds of Incompatibilism. KANE, Robert.

INCOMPATIBILITY

The Growth of Knowledge: An Inquiry into the Kuhnian Theory. VERRONEN, Veli.

Is Free Will Incompatible with Something or Other?. GRIFFITHS, A Phillips.

INCOMPLETENESS

see also Completeness

"Bell's Theorem: A Guide to the Implications" in *Philosophical Consequences of Quantum Theory: Reflections on Bell's Theorem,* JARRETT, Jon P.

"Incompleteness for Quantified Relevance Logics" in *Directions in Relevant Logic,* FINE, Kit.

Algorithmic Information Theory. VAN LAMBALGEN, Michiel.

Herbrand's Theorem and the Incompleteness of Arithmetic. GOLDFARB, Warren.

On the "Incompleteness" of a Musical Work. GOSWAMI, Roshmi.

Two Incomplete Anti-Realist Modal Epistemic Logics. WILLIAMSON, Timothy.

INCONGRUITY

The Incongruity of Incongruity Theories of Humour (in Hebrew). KULKA, Tomas.

INCONSISTENCY

The Apology and the *Crito*: A Misplaced Inconsistency. WARD, Andrew.

Dialectic and Inconsistency in Knowledge Acquisition. HAVAS, Katalin G.

How to be Realistic About Inconsistency in Science. BROWN, Bryson.

The Inconsistency of Higher Order Extensions of Martin-Löf's Type Theory. JACOBS, Bart.

Injecting Inconsistencies Into Models of PA. SOLOVAY, Robert M.

The Logic of Inconsistency. BUNDER, M W.

Moral Dilemmas: Why They Are Hard To Solve. LEBUS, Bruce.

On Putnam's Argument for the Inconsistency of Relativism. SOLOMON, Miriam.

INCONTINENCE

Incontinent Belief. MC LAUGHLIN, Brian P.

INDEFINITE TERM(S)

Vague Objects and Indefinite Identity. BURGESS, J A.

INDEPENDENCE

Absolutely Independent Axiomatizations for Countable Sets in Classical Logic. GRYGIEL, Joanna.

Aesthetic Protectionism. GODLOVITCH, S.

The Autonomy of Mathematics. STEINER, Mark.

Independent Axiomatizability of Sets of Sentences. WOJTYLAK, Piotr.

Mercy: An Independent, Imperfect Virtue. RAINBOLT, George W.

On Thinking for Yourself. SPLITTER, Laurance J.

Standing Alone: Dependence, Independence and Interdependence in the Practice of Education. GRIFFITHS, Morwenna and SMITH, Richard.

Wittgenstein and Sense-Independence of Truth. PUHL, Klaus.

INDETERMINACY

Analyticity, Indeterminacy and Semantic Theory: Some Comments on "The Domino Theory". GREENWOOD, John D.

Derrida and the Indeterminacy of Meaning. MILLER, Seumas.

L'indétermination, la détermination et la relation: Les trois essences de l'être. GUILLAMAUD, Patrice.

Physicalism, Indeterminacy and Interpretive Science. FELEPPA, Robert.

Quine's Indeterminacy Thesis. LARSON, David.

Schizophrenia and Indeterminacy: The Problem of Validity. HUNT, Geoffrey.

INDETERMINISM

"Freedom and Indeterminism" in *Cause, Mind, and Reality: Essays Honoring C B Martin,* SHAW, Daniel.

Autonomy Without Indeterminism: A Reconstruction of Kant's *Groundwork,* Chapter Three. TERZIS, George N.

Modality, Mechanism and Translational Indeterminacy. MAC INTOSH, Duncan.

INDEX(ES)

Kant: An Index to Theses and Dissertations Accepted by Universities in Canada and the US, 1879-1985. GABEL, Gernot U.

INDEXICAL SENTENCE(S)

Indexikalität, Wahrnehmung und Bedeutung bei Husserl. BECKER, Wolfgang.

INDEXICAL(S)

What Is Said: A Theory of Indirect Speech Reports. BERTOLET, Rod.

"Russell on Indexicals and Scientific Knowledge" in *Rereading Russell: Essays on Bertrand Russell's Metaphysics and Epistemology,* SMITH, Janet Farrell.

Lewis' Indexical Argument for World-Relative Actuality. GALE, Richard M.

Temporal Indexicals. SMITH, Quentin.

INDEXICALITY

From a Normative Point of View. LANCE, Mark and HAWTHORNE, John.

INDIAN

see also Buddhism, Hinduism

A Concise Dictionary of Indian Philosophy: Sanskrit Terms Defined in English. GRIMES, John A.

Jurisculture, Volume II: India. DORSEY, Gray L.

Writings on India (Collected Works of John Stuart Mill, Volume 30). ROBSON, John M (ed).

"Man and Nature in the Indian Context" in *Man and Nature: The Chinese Tradition and the Future,* CHATTERJEE, Margaret.

Āyāranga 2, 16 and Sūyagada 1, 16. BOLLEE, W.

The Biographies of Siddhasena: A Study in the Texture of Allusion and the Weaving of a Group-Image (Part I). GRANOFF, Phyllis.

Cut the Syllogism to its Size! Some Reflections on Indian Syllogism. AGERA, Cassian R.

Forman and Semantic Aspects of Tibetan Buddhist Debate Logic. TILLEMANS, Tom J F.

The Gandhian Approach to *Swadeshi* or Appropriate Technology. BAKKER, J I (Hans).

Groundwork for an Indian Christian Theology. MOOKENTHOTTAM, Antony.

Is Jayarasi a Materialist?. MOHANTA, Dilipkumar.

Laugāksi Bhāskara on Inference: Problems of Generalizing Ideation in Comparative Light. GRADINAROV, Plamen.

The Mīmāmsā Theory of Self-Recognition. TABER, John A.

INDIAN

A New Plausible Exposition of Sānkhya-Kārikā-9. WADHWANI-SHAH, Yashodhara.

On *Sapaksa*. TILLEMANS, Tom J F.

Philosophy of Reservation. AGARWALA, Binod Kumar.

Post-Udayana Nyaya Reactions to Dharmakirti's Vadanyaya: An Evaluation. CHINCHORE, M.

Some Features of the Technical Language of Navya-Nyāya. BHATTACHARYYA, Sibajiban.

The Conceptual Structure of Marxist Thought: Some Critical Reflections (in Serbo-Croatian). KRISHNA, Daya.

The Theory of the Sentence in Pūrva Mīmāmsā and Western Philosophy. TABER, John A.

INDICATOR(S)

Reply to Reviewers of "Explaining Behavior: Reasons in a World of Causes". DRETSKE, Fred.

INDIFFERENCE

L'indifférence religieuse: un aboutissement. PIÉTRI, Gaston.

Non-in-difference in the Thought of Emmanuel Levinas and Franz Rosenzweig. COHEN, Richard.

Stoic Values. WHITE, Nicholas P.

INDIRECT DISCOURSE

Philosophical Rhetoric: The Function of Indirection in Philosophical Writing. MASON, Jeff.

Wittgenstein and Kierkegaard: Religion, Individuality, and Philosophical Method. CREEGAN, Charles L.

Indirection et interaction conversationnelle. ROVENTA-FRUMUSANI, Daniela.

Kierkegaard and Indirect Communication. LÜBCKE, Poul.

INDISCERNIBLES

Large Resplendent Models Generated by Indiscernibles. SCHMERL, James H.

INDIVIDUAL(S)

see also Person(s)

Ethics and Community. DUSSEL, Enrique D.

The Good Life: Personal and Public Choices. LOUZECKY, David.

The Inner Citadel: Essays on Individual Autonomy. CHRISTMAN, John (ed).

Morality and Imagination: Paradoxes of Progress. TUAN, Yi-Fu.

"The Essence of Personal Relationships and Their Value for the Individual" in *Person to Person*, WRIGHT, Paul H.

"Understanding Individuals" in *Reading Kant*, VOSSENKUHL, Wilhelm.

Agency, Identity, and Culture: Hannah Arendt's Conception of Citizenship. D'ENTRÈVES, Maurizio Passerin.

Alasdair MacIntyre: The Virtue of Tradition. ALMOND, Brenda.

Der Begriff als "nicht wirklich existierende" Einheit vieler "wirklich existerender" Individuen. KAUFMANN, Matthias.

Community as Inquiry. TINDER, Glenn.

The Contingent Person and the Existential Choice. HELLER, Agnes.

Corporate and Individual Moral Responsibility: A Reply to Jan Garrett. WERHANE, Patricia H.

Des présages a l'entendement: Notes sur les présages, l'imagination et l'amour dans la lettre à P Balling. SANCHEZ-ESTOP, Juan Dominguez.

Foucault's Critique of the Liberal Individual. GRUBER, David F.

Group Rights. MC DONALD, Ian.

Group Rights. SHAPARD, Leslie R.

The Individual and the General Will: Rousseau Reconsidered. HILEY, David R.

Individual Rights, Collective Interests, Public Law, and American Politics. GEORGE, Robert P.

Is a Post-Hegelian Ethics Possible?. MC CUMBER, John.

Kierkegaard's Concept of Education (in Hebrew). ROSENOW, Eliyahu.

The Lack of an Overarching Conception in Psychology. SARASON, Seymour B.

Liberalism and Liberty: the Fragility of a Tradition. GRAHAM, Keith.

The Nature of Immorality. HAMPTON, Jean.

Of Paradigms, Saints and Individuals: The Question of Authenticity. HADEN, N Karl.

Paternalism and Democracy. SMILEY, Marion.

La risposta di Leroux a Lamennais: Il concetto di Trinità come soluzione del problema sociale. FIORENTINO, Fernando.

Sulla teoria e metodica della storia. MEYER, Eduard.

Towards the Integration of Individual and Moral Agencies. MC DONALD, Ross A and VICTOR, Bart.

Two-Tier Moral Codes. SMITH, Holly M.

Which One Is the Real One?. GRAYBOSCH, Anthony J.

Why Individual Identity Matters. BROWN, Mark T.

Zur methodologischen Bedeutung des Leninschen Prinzips der "Zurückführung des Individuellen auf das Soziale". DANYEL, Jürgen.

INDIVIDUALISM

Freedom. BAUMAN, Zygmunt.

The Moral Case for the Free Market Economy: A Philosophical Argument. MACHAN, Tibor R.

Nietzsche and the Politics of Aristocratic Radicalism. DETWILER, Bruce.

Who Knows: From Quine to a Feminist Empiricism. NELSON, Lynn Hankinson.

William James, Public Philosopher. COTKIN, George.

"Hobbes and Individualism" in *Perspectives on Thomas Hobbes*, RYAN, Alan.

"L'individualisme dans ses rapports avec la culture et la politique" in *Culture et Politique/Culture and Politics*, CHANTEUR, Janine.

"Marxism and Individualism" in *Knowledge and Politics*, ELSTER, Jon.

De afkeer van het individualisme bij Alisdair MacIntyre en de soevereiniteit van het individu. KAL, Victor.

Collingwood's Epistemological Individualism. CODE, Lorraine.

Humanism and Political Economy. MACHAN, Tibor R.

Individualisierung als Emanzipationsprojekt?. TEICHMANN, Werner.

Individualism, Community, and Education: An Exchange of Views. GRIFFIN, Robert S and NASH, Robert J.

Moral Individualism: Agent-Relativity and Deontic Restraints. MACK, Eric.

Nietzsche's Politics. THIELE, Leslie Paul.

On Individualism, Collectivism and Interrelationism. CARTER, Alan.

Quelques aspects psychiques de la conscience morale individuelle (in Romanian). VIDAM, Teodor.

The Individuum and the Context of Individual (in Czechoslovakian). TOMEK, V.

INDIVIDUALITY

The Consolations of Philosophy: Hobbes's Secret; Spinoza's Way. ROSENTHAL, Abigail L (ed).

Innocence and Experience. HAMPSHIRE, Stuart.

Wittgenstein and Kierkegaard: Religion, Individuality, and Philosophical Method. CREEGAN, Charles L.

"Culture, Individuality, and Deference" in *Culture et Politique/Culture and Politics*, LETWIN, Shirley Robin.

Absolutism, Individuality and Politics: Hobbes and a Little Beyond. FLATHMAN, Richard E.

Autonomy and the Death of the Arts. COVEOS, Costis M.

Friedrich Schleiermacher's Theory of the Limited Communitarian State. HOOVER, Jeffrey.

Habermas und das Problem der Individualität. GRONDIN, Jean.

Identity and Individuality in Classical and Quantum Physics. FRENCH, Steven.

L'individuo nella città. VERNANT, Jean Pierre.

La missione filosofica del diritto nella Napoli del giovane Mancini. OLDRINI, Guido.

Momenti della teoria leibniziana della sostanza nel carteggio con Arnauld. DELCÓ, Alessandro.

Naissance de l'auteur—Une Histoire de l'esthétique moderne autour de son alibi (in Japanese). SASAKI, Ken-ichi.

La persona nell'esperienza morale e giuridica. BAGOLINI, Luigi.

I presupposti assiologici del riconoscimento nello Hegel prejenese. RIZZI, Lino.

The Social Humanism of Adam Schaff. JAGUARIBE, Helio.

INDIVIDUATION

Necessity, Essence, and Individuation: A Defense of Conventionalism. SIDELLE, Alan.

Crisi dello storicismo e "bisogno" di "Kulturgeschichte": Il caso Lamprecht. CACCIATORE, Giuseppe.

The Explanatory Role of Belief Ascriptions. PATTERSON, Sarah.

Husserl's Theory of Parts and Wholes: The Dynamic of Individuating and Contextualizing Interpretation. LAMPERT, Jay.

L'identità del diverso. MATHIEU, Vittorio.

Individuation and Causation in Psychology. BURGE, Tyler.

Individuation and Intentional Ascriptions. OKRENT, Mark.

Nom propre et individuation chez Peirce. THIBAUD, P.

On the Location of Actions and Tryings: Criticism of an Internalist View. GJELSVIK, Olav.

The Problem of Individuation for Scotus: A Principle of Indivisibility or a Principle of Distinction. PARK, Woosuk.

INDIVISIBILITY

The Problem of Individuation for Scotus: A Principle of Indivisibility or a Principle of Distinction. PARK, Woosuk.

INFINITARY LOGIC

DYCK, Stephen.
A Theorem on Barr-Exact Categories, with an Infinitary Generalization. MAKKAI, Michael.

INFINITE

The Infinite. MOORE, A W.
Finite Arithmetic with Infinite Descent. GAUTHIER, Yvon.
Infinite Sets of Nonequivalent Modalities. BELLISSIMA, Fabio.
On Infinite Series of Infinite Isols. BARBACK, Joseph.
Solitary Souls and Infinite Help: Kierkegaard and Wittgenstein. HANNAY, Alastair.

INFINITESIMAL(S)

Transfer Theorems for π-Monads. CUTLAND, Nigel J.

INFINITY

Mathematical Methods in Linguistics. PARTEE, Barbara H.
The Philosophy of Set Theory: An Historical Introduction to Cantor's Paradise. TILES, Mary E.
Certain Fundamental Problems and Trends of Thought in Mathematics. STRAUSS, D F M.
Descartes' Doctrine of Volitional Infinity. CRESS, Donald A.
Infini et subjectivité dans la pensée classique. CHÉDIN, Jean-Louis.
Infinité et omniprésence divines: Thomas d'Aquin et Hegel. BRITO, Emilio.
La metafora dei "due labirinti" e le sue implicazioni nel pensiero di Leibniz. POMA, Andrea.
Momenti della teoria leibniziana della sostanza nel carteggio con Arnauld. DELCÓ, Alessandro.
Nietzsche, Dühring, and Time. SMALL, Robin.
The Sensory Presentation of Divine Infinity. SCHOEN, Edward L.
Thales, Anaximander, and Infinity. DANCY, R M.

INFLUENCE(S)

El a priori histórico (la historia y sus hechos). SAMPEDRO, Ceferino.
Nietzsche in Italy. HARRISON, Thomas (ed).
The Possible Influence of Montaigne's "Essais" on Descartes' "Treatise on the Passions". PAULSON, Michael G.
"Antiochus of Ascalon" in *Philosophia Togata: Essays on Philosophy and Roman Society*, BARNES, Jonathan.
"Hobbes's Hidden Influence" in *Perspectives on Thomas Hobbes*, ROGERS, G A J.

INFORMAL FALLACY(-CIES)

Informal Logic: A Handbook for Critical Argumentation. WALTON, Douglas N.
Problems in the Use of Expert Opinion in Argumentation. WALTON, Douglas N.

INFORMAL LOGIC

Critical Thinking: Evaluating Claims and Arguments in Everyday Life—Second Edition. MOORE, Brook Noel.
Informal Logic: A Handbook for Critical Argumentation. WALTON, Douglas N.
"Formal Logic and Informal Logic" in *From Metaphysics to Rhetoric*, PERELMAN, Chaïm.
"To Reason While Speaking" in *From Metaphysics to Rhetoric*, GRIZE, Jean-Blaise.
Analogical Arguings and Explainings. JOHNSON, Fred.
Analogies and Missing Premises. GOVIER, Trudy.
Beardsley's Theory of Analogy. BARKER, Evelyn M.
By Parity of Reasoning. WOODS, John and HUDAK, Brent.
Dialogue, Distanciation, and Engagement: Toward a Logic of Televisual Communication. LANGSDORF, Lenore.
Hedging as a Fallacy of Language. JASON, Gary.
Just the Facts Ma'am: Informal Logic, Gender and Pedagogy. ORR, Deborah.
Logical and Extralogical Constants. SMOOK, Roger.
Massey on Fallacy and Informal Logic: A Reply. JOHNSON, Ralph H.
Reportage as Compound Suggestion. MAY, John D.
Two Traditions of Analogy. BROWN, William R.
The Unspeakable: Understanding the System of Fallacy in the Media. MC MURTRY, John.
Who *Needs* a Theory of Informal Logic?. DOSS, Seale.

INFORMATION

Critical Theory and Poststructuralism: In Search of a Context. POSTER, Mark.
In and Out of the Black Box: On the Philosophy of Cognition. HAMLYN, D W.
Philosophical Logic and Artificial Intelligence. THOMASON, Richmond H (ed).
"Argumentativity and Informativity" in *From Metaphysics to Rhetoric*, ANSCOMBRE, Jean-Claude and DUCROT, Oswald.
Algorithmic Information Theory. VAN LAMBALGEN, Michiel.
Aristotele, Platone e l'IBM. PARISI, Giorgio.
Confidentiality and Patient-Access to Records. SHORT, David S.
Decision Problems Under Uncertainty Based on Entropy Functionals. GOTTINGER, Hans W.
Del valore: Chi crea l'informazione?. MARCHETTI, Cesare.
Entropy and Information in Evolving Biological Systems. BROOKS, Daniel R (and others).
False Reports: Misperceptions, Self Deceptions or Lies?. DAVENPORT, Manuel.
The Folklore of Computers and the True Art of Thinking. ROSZAK, Theodore.
Georg Klaus über Kybernetik und Information. STOCK, Wolfgang G.
Group Decision and Negotiation Support in Evolving, Nonshared Information Contexts. SHAKUN, Melvin F.
The Impact of Information and Computer Based Training on Negotiators' Performance. GAUVIN, Stéphane and LILIEN, Gary L and CHATTERJEE, Kalyan.
Individual Privacy and Computer-Based Human Resource Information Systems. TAYLOR, G Stephen.
Information Processing: From a Mechanistic to a Natural Systems Approach. VAN CAMP, Ingrid.
Institutions, Arrangements and Practical Information. MAC CORMICK, Neil.
Justice: Means versus Freedoms. SEN, Amartya.
Knowledge and the Regularity Theory of Information. MORRIS, William Edward.
Misinformation. GODFREY-SMITH, Peter.
La natura sprecona, i codici e lo struscio. ECO, Umberto.
The New World Synthesis. POPE, N Vivian.
Patents and Free Scientific Information in Biotechnology: Making Monoclonal Antibodies Proprietary. MACKENZIE, Michael and KEATING, Peter.
A Question of Ethics: Developing Information System Ethics. COHEN, Eli.
What is Really Unethical About Insider Trading?. MOORE, Jennifer.

INFORMATION THEORY

La creazione dell'informazione. BARBIERI, Marcello.

INFORMED CONSENT

Health Care Ethics: Principles and Problems. GARRETT, Thomas M (ed).
"From Patient to Agent: On the Implication of the Values Shift in Informed Consent" in *Inquiries into Values: The Inaugural Session of the International Society for Value Inquiry*, COY, Janet.
Control and Compensation: Laws Governing Extracorporeal Generative Materials. ANDREWS, Lori B.
Justifying a Principle of Informed Consent: A Case Study in Autonomy-Based Ethics. GUNDERSON, Martin.
Should Competence Be Coerced?: Commentary. REAMER, Frederic G.
Should Competence Be Coerced?: Commentary. KELLY, Michael J.
Transparency: Informed Consent in Primary Care. BRODY, Howard.
Women in Labor: Some Issues About Informed Consent. LADD, Rosalind Ekman.

INGARDEN, R

Ingarden and the End of Phenomenological Aesthetics. MURRAY, Michael.

INHERITANCE

"Europa und sein Erbe: Skizze zu einer Geschichtsphilosophie" in *Agora: Zu Ehren von Rudolph Berlinger*, PATOCKA, Jan.
"The Fear of the Lord is the Beginning of Wisdom" in *The Wisdom of Faith: Essays in Honor of Dr Sebastian Alexander Matczak*, THOMPSON, Henry O.
Intergenerational Justice and Productive Resources; A Nineteenth Century Socialist Debate. CUNLIFFE, John.

INITIATIVE

Admonitions to Poland. SZCZEPANSKI, Jan and BYLINA, Maryna.
Justifying Moral Initiative by Business, with Rejoinders to Bill Shaw and Richard Nunan. MULLIGAN, Thomas M.
The Talloires Network—A Constructive Move in a Destructive World. RYDEN, Lars and WALLENSTEEN, Peter.

INJURY

Injury as Alienation in Sport. THOMAS, Carolyn E and RINTALA, Janet A.

INJUSTICE

see also Justice
Civil Disobedience. HARRIS, Paul (ed).
"Plato and the Structures of Injustice" in *Inquiries into Values: The Inaugural Session of the International Society for Value Inquiry*, ROCHE, Mark W.
Mill on Moral Wrong. LUNDBERG, Randolph.
Platonic Justice and the *Republic*. HALL, Robert W.

INTERDISCIPLINARY

"Interdisciplinarity as Value" in *Inquiries into Values: The Inaugural Session of the International Society for Value Inquiry*, HETZLER, Florence.

Barriers Against Interdisciplinarity: Implications for Studies of Science, Technology, and Society (STS). BAUER, Henry H.

Psychological Underpinnings of Philosophy. BARTLETT, Steven J.

INTEREST(S)

Eguaglianza interesse unanimità: La politica di Rousseau. BURGIO, Alberto.

Kant and the Philosophy of History. YOVEL, Yirmiyahu.

The Limits of Morality. KAGAN, Shelly.

Biological Functions and Biological Interests. VARNER, Gary E.

Consequentialism and History. GOMBERG, Paul.

Epicurus and Friendship. STERN-GILLET, Suzanne.

Die konfuzianischen Begriffe von Rechtlichkeit und Interesse und ihr Wert im Modernen China. WANG, Rui Shen.

L'Emergence de la notion d'intérêt dans l'esthétique des Lumières. MOSER-VERREY, Monique.

Morality and Interest. HARRISON, Bernard.

Social Power and Human Agency. KERNOHAN, Andrew.

Sources of Value. BARDEN, Garrett.

Zur Diskussion um die Einheit und Vielfalt der Interessen im Sozialismus. ROTHE, Barbara and STEININGER, H.

INTERIORITY

Angelic Interiority. CASEY, Gerard N.

Comparaison des doctrines de Brunschvicg et de Pradines. FOREST, Aimé.

INTERMEDIATE LOGICS

An Algebraic Approach to Intuitionistic Modal Logics in Connection with Intermediate Predicate Logics. SUZUKI, Nobu-Yuki.

Axiomatization of the First-Order Intermediate Logics of Bounded Kripkean Heights I. YOKOTA, Shin'ichi.

A Cut-Free Calculus for Dummett's LC Quantified. CORSI, Giovanna.

Finite and Finitely Separable Intermediate Propositional Logics. BELLISSIMA, Fabio.

A New Criterion of Decidability for Intermediate Logics. SKURA, Tomasz.

A Note on Sequent Calculi Intermediate Between *LJ* and *LK*. BORICIC, Branislav R.

On Axiomatizability of Some Intermediate Predicate Logics (Summary). SKVORTSOV, D P.

On Finite Linear Intermediate Predicate Logics. ONO, Hiroakira.

On Halldén-Completeness of Intermediate and Modal Logics. CHAGROV, A V and ZAKHARYASHCHEV, M V.

The Property (HD) in Intermediate Logics: A Partial Solution of a Problem of H Ono. MINARI, Pierluigi.

Relations Between Intuitionistic Modal Logics and Intermediate Predicate Logics. ONO, Hiroakira and SUZUKI, Nobu-Yuki.

The Simple Substitution Property of the Intermediate Propositional Logics. SASAKI, Katsumi.

Some Results on Intermediate Constructive Logics. MIGLIOLI, Pierangelo (and others).

INTERNAL

Connectionism and the Semantic Content of Internal Representation. GOSCHKE, Thomas and KOPPELBERG, Dirk.

A Dilemma for Internal Realism. MOSER, Paul K.

Internal Reasons and the Obscurity of Blame. WILLIAMS, Bernard.

Philo's Final Conclusion in Hume's *Dialogues*. VINK, A G.

The Self and First Person Metaphysics. ALBERTS, Kelly T.

INTERNAL RELATION(S)

"Harris on Internal Relations" in *Dialectic and Contemporary Science*, BLANSHARD, Brand.

"Reply to Blanshard's "Harris on Internal Relations"" in *Dialectic and Contemporary Science*, HARRIS, Errol E.

INTERNALISM

Epistemic Justification: Essays in the Theory of Knowledge. ALSTON, William P.

Mental Content. MC GINN, Colin.

Theory of Knowledge. LEHRER, Keith.

Apriority and Metajustification in BonJour's "Structure of Empirical Knowledge". SOLOMON, Miriam.

Autonomist Internalism and the Justification of Morals. DARWALL, Stephen L.

Causalist Internalism. AUDI, Robert.

Internalism and Externalism in Moral Epistemology. AUDI, Robert.

Moral Internalism and Moral Relativism. TILLEY, John.

Motivational Internalism: The Powers and Limits of Practical Reasoning. MELE, Alfred R.

On the Location of Actions and Tryings: Criticism of an Internalist View.

GJELSVIK, Olav.

INTERNATIONAL

The Ethics of War and Peace. LACKEY, Douglas P.

Business Ethics and the International Trade in Hazardous Wastes. SINGH, Jang B and LAKHAN, V C.

Corporate Morality Called in Question: The Case of Cabora Bassa. SCHREYÖGG, Georg and STEINMANN, Horst.

International Codes of Conduct: An Analysis of Ethical Reasoning. GETZ, Kathleen A.

Logic in the International Elementary School. SLADE, Christine.

Management Training for Women: International Experiences and Lessons for Canada. LAM, M Natalie.

INTERNATIONAL LAW

Arms and Judgment: Law, Morality, and the Conduct of War in the 20th Century. COHEN, Sheldon M.

Rules, Norms, and Decisions: On the Conditions of Practical and Legal Reasoning. KRATOCHWIL, Friedrich V.

"Hobbes and the Concept of International Law" in *Hobbes: War Among Nations,* GROVER, Robinson A.

"The Hobbesian Structure of International Legal Discourse" in *Hobbes: War Among Nations,* KOSKENNIEMI, Martti.

Is International Law Part of Natural Law?. D'AMATO, Anthony.

National Self-determination. MARGALIT, Avishai.

Nuclearism and International Law. STEGENGA, James A.

The Right of Self-Determination in International Law. LANGLEY, Winston.

INTERNATIONAL RELATION(S)

The Causes of Quarrel: Essays on Peace, War, and Thomas Hobbes. CAWS, Peter (ed).

Moral Reasoning and Statecraft: Essays Presented to Kenneth W Thompson. DAVIS, Reed M (ed).

Rules, Norms, and Decisions: On the Conditions of Practical and Legal Reasoning. KRATOCHWIL, Friedrich V.

"Christianity and Statecraft in International Relations" in *Moral Reasoning and Statecraft: Essays Presented to Kenneth W Thompson,* COLL, Alberto R.

"Hobbes and International Relations" in *The Causes of Quarrel: Essays on Peace, War, and Thomas Hobbes,* FARRELL, Daniel M.

"Hobbes on International Relations" in *Hobbes: War Among Nations,* LOTT, Tommy L.

"Hobbes on World Government and the World Cup" in *Hobbes: War Among Nations,* RIPSTEIN, Arthur.

"The Physicist and the Politicians: Niels Bohr and the International Control of Atomic Weapons" in *Moral Reasoning and Statecraft: Essays Presented to Kenneth W Thompson,* GRAIG, Ian.

"Pride and International Relations" in *Christ, Ethics and Tragedy: Essays in Honour of Donald MacKinnon,* PASKINS, Barrie.

Ethical Issues in International Lending. SNOY, Bernard.

The Impact of Trust on Business, International Security and the Quality of Life. MICHALOS, Alex C.

Messy Morality and the Art of the Possible—I. COADY, C A J.

The Role of Ethics in Global Corporate Culture. DOBSON, John.

The World United. KOLENDA, Konstantin.

INTERPERSONAL

Interpersonal Knowledge According to John Macmurray. ROY, Louis.

A Real-Life Brain. HAMRICK, William S.

INTERPERSONAL RELATION(S)

Il dialogo cristiano-marxista a Budapest. SKALICKY, Carlo.

INTERPERSONALITY

Truth and Interpersonality: An Inquiry into the Argumentative Structure of Heidegger's *Being and Time.* RÖMPP, Georg.

INTERPOLATION

Interpolation in Fragments of Intuitionistic Propositional Logic. RENARDEL DE LAVALETTE, Gerald R.

Uniqueness, Definability and Interpolation. DOSEN, Kosta and SCHROEDER-HEISTER, Peter.

INTERPRETANT(S)

Peirce's Interpretant. LISZKA, James Jakob.

Peirce's Ultimate Logical Interpretant and Dynamical Object: A Pragmatic Perspective. ROSENTHAL, Sandra B.

INTERPRETATION

see also Hermeneutics

Comparative Philosophy and the Philosophy of Scholarship. TUCK, Andrew P.

Fact and Meaning. HEAL, Jane.

Hermeneutics: Interpretation Theory in Schleiermacher, Dilthey, Heidegger,

INTERPRETATION

and Gadamer. PALMER, Richard E.

Kierkegaard, Godly Deceiver: The Nature and Meaning of His Pseudonymous Writings. HARTSHORNE, M Holmes.

Mental Imagery: On the Limits of Cognitive Science. ROLLINS, Mark.

Metaphor. COOPER, David E.

The Nature of Social and Educational Inquiry: Empiricism versus Interpretation. SMITH, John K.

The Past Within Us: An Empirical Approach to Philosophy of History. MARTIN, Raymond.

Recovery of the Measure: Interpretation and Nature. NEVILLE, Robert Cummings.

Rethinking Religion: Connecting Cognition and Culture. LAWSON, E Thomas.

Texts without Referents: Reconciling Science and Narrative. MARGOLIS, Joseph.

Transforming the Hermeneutic Context: From Nietzsche to Nancy. ORMISTON, Gayle L (ed).

"'Knowledge is Remembrance': Diotima's Instruction at *Symposium* 207c 8 - 208b 6" in *Post-Structuralist Classics*, KRELL, David Farrell.

"Hermeneutics and Its Anxieties" in *Reading Philosophy for the Twenty-First Century*, BERNSTEIN, Richard J.

"Reading Donald Davidson: Truth, Meaning and Right Interpretation" in *Analytic Aesthetics*, NORRIS, Christopher.

"Time and Interpretation in Heraclitus" in *Post-Structuralist Classics*, BENJAMIN, Andrew.

Analogy and Interpretation (in Polish). LUBANSKI, Mieczyslaw.

Antwoorden op open interview-vragen als lezingen. NIJHOF, Gerhard.

Beneath Interpretation: Against Hermeneutic Holism. SHUSTERMAN, Richard.

Clinical Interpretation: The Hermeneutics of Medicine. LEDER, Drew.

The Co-Enactment of Heidegger's *Being and Time*: F W von Herrmann's Elucidation of its "Introduction". LOSCERBO, John.

A Comparative Study of the Representational Paradigms Between Liberalism and Socialism. KE, Gang.

Cornelia de Vogel fra vecchio e nuovo paradigma ermeneutico nell'interpretazione di Platone. PEROLI, Enrico.

The Debate Regarding Dialectical Logic in Marx's Economic Writings. SMITH, Tony.

Die Hermeneutik der schriftlichen, mündlichen und innerlichen Rede bei Platon (in Greek). MICHAELIDES, K.

Different Readings: A Reply to Magnus, Solomon, and Conway. NEHAMAS, Alexander.

Domain Interpretations of Martin-Löf's Partial Type Theory. PALMGREN, Erik and STOLTENBERG-HANSEN, Viggo.

The Education of Taste. GOLDMAN, Alan H.

The Endorsements of Interpretation. DOEPKE, Frederick.

Factual Constraints on Interpreting. STERN, Laurent.

Habermas interprète de Schelling. MAESSCHALCK, Marc.

Heidegger and the Problem of Style in Interpretation. HARRIES, Karsten.

Hermeneutical Interpretation and Pragmatic Interpretation. DASCAL, Marcelo.

Hermeneutics in Science and Medicine: A Thesis Understated. CHURCHILL, Larry R.

Immediacy and the Text: Friedrich Schleiermacher's Theory of Style and Interpretation. PFAU, Thomas.

In Defence of Untranslatability. SANKEY, Howard.

Interpretation and Its Art Objects: Two Views. KRAUSZ, Michael.

Interpretation and the Bible: The Dialectic of Concept and Content in Interpretive Reading. POLKA, Brayton.

Interpretation at Risk. MARGOLIS, Joseph.

Interpretation in Aesthetics: Theories and Practices. MC CORMICK, Peter.

Interpretation in Medicine: An Introduction. DANIEL, Stephen L.

Interpretation of Dynamic Logic in the Relational Calculus. ORLOWSKA, Ewa.

Interpretation Psychologized. GOLDMAN, Alvin I.

Interpreting Hume's *Dialogues*. COLEMAN, Dorothy P.

Is Translation Possible?. HARRIS, R Thomas.

Kant and the Interpretation of Nature and History. MAKKREEL, Rudolf.

Kierkegaard on Doctrine: A Post-Modern Interpretation. EMMANUEL, Steven M.

L'equivoque du temps chez Aristote. BAEKERS, Stephan F.

Lectio Difficilior: le système dans la théorie platonicienne de l'âme selon interprétation de Gueroult. GAUDIN, Claude.

Literality. BARR, James.

Les mutations de l'historiographie Révolutionnaire. FURET, M François.

The Narrative Reconstruction of Science. ROUSE, Joseph.

Nature and Semiosis. KRUSE, Felicia.

Nesting: The Ontology of Interpretation. ZEMACH, Eddy.

A New Music Criticism?. KIVY, Peter.

Nietzsche e il "mito" di Nietzsche: In margine a un libro su Nietzsche e il nazismo. ALFIERI, Luigi.

The Non-Definability Notion and First Order Logic. KRYNICKI, Michal.

On Davidson and Interpretation. BURDICK, Howard.

On the Interpretation of Laws. FRIEDMAN, Lawrence M.

Peano's Smart Children: A Provability Logical Study of Systems with Built-In Consistency. VISSER, Albert.

Perspectivism and Postmodern Criticism. GILMOUR, John C.

The Politics of Interpretation: Spinoza's Modernist Turn. LANG, Berel.

The Problem with the *Fragments*: Kierkegaard on Subjectivity and Truth. PIETY, Marilyn.

Psychoanalyse: pseudo-wetenschap of geesteswetenschap?. MOOIJ, A W M.

Radical Interpretation and the Gunderson Game. WARD, Andrew.

The Sense/Intellect Continuum in Early Modern Philosophy: A Critique of Analytic Interpretation. GLOUBERMAN, M.

Social Interpretation and Political Theory: Walzer and His Critics. WARNKE, Georgia.

Socrates' Charitable Treatment of Poetry. PAPPAS, Nickolas.

St Augustine's Idea of Aesthetic Interpretation. PERRICONE, Christopher.

Texts and Their Interpretation. GRACIA, Jorge J E.

Tolerância e interpretação. DASCAL, Marcelo.

Transparency and Doubt: Understanding and Interpretation in Pragmatics and in Law. DASCAL, M and WROBLEWSKI, Jerzy.

Troubles with Popper (in Serbo-Croatian). VUJIC, Antum.

What Could Be the Meaning of the Idea that Morality Depends on Religion? (in Hebrew). SAGI, Avi and STATMAN, Daniel.

INTERPRETATIVE

"Explanation in the Social Sciences" in *Scientific Explanation (Minnesota Studies in the Philosophy of Science, Volume XIII)*, SALMON, Merrilee H.

Interpretation, History and Narrative. CARROLL, Noël.

Life After Difference: The Positions of the Interpreter and the Positionings of the Interpreted. ALTIERI, Charles.

Physicalism, Indeterminacy and Interpretive Science. FELEPPA, Robert.

INTERPRETER(S)

Davidson's Omniscient Interpreter. JANSSENS, C J A M and VAN BRAKEL, J.

Ward on Davidson's Refutation of Scepticism. HURTADO, Guillermo.

INTERRELATEDNESS

On Individualism, Collectivism and Interrelationism. CARTER, Alan.

INTERSUBJECTIVITY

see also Other Minds

John of the Cross and the Cognitive Value of Mysticism. PAYNE, Steven.

Angelology, Metaphysics, and Intersubjectivity: A Reply to G N Casey. KAINZ, Howard P.

Discussion: Professor Devaraja on the Emergence of Facts. PRASAD, Rajendra.

The Person and *The Little Prince* of St Exupéry, Part I. HETZLER, Florence M.

Unknown Masterpiece. HELLER, Agnes.

INTERVAL(S)

Intervals and Sublattices of the RE Weak Truth Table Degrees, Part II: Nonbounding. DOWNEY, R G.

Pointless Metric Spaces. GERLA, Giangiacomo.

INTERVENTION

Intervencionismo y paternalismo. GARZÓN VALDÉS, Ernesto.

John Stuart Mill on Government Intervention. KURER, O.

INTERVIEW(S)

Antwoorden op open interview-vragen als lezingen. NIJHOF, Gerhard.

Conversation between Justus Buchler and Robert S Corrington. CORRINGTON, Robert S.

A Conversation with Hans-Georg Gadamer. BAUR, Michael.

Noam Chomsky: An Interview. CHOMSKY, Noam and EDGLEY, Roy and OSBORNE, Peter and RÉE, Jonathan and WILSON, Deirdre.

A Post-Philosophical Politics? An Interview by Danny Postel. RORTY, Richard.

INTIMACY

Person to Person. GRAHAM, George (ed).

"Honesty and Intimacy" in *Person to Person*, GRAHAM, George and LA FOLLETTE, Hugh.

"Trusting Ex-intimates" in *Person to Person*, BAIER, Annette.

Intimacy and Confidentiality in Psychotherapeutic Relationships. LIPKIN, Robert.

IRRATIONALITY

Delusions, Irrationality and Cognitive Science. RUST, John.
La filosofia del Novecento: dalla razionalità all'irrazionalità. DEL VECCHIO, Dante.
Minds Divided. HEIL, John.
Verständnis für Unvernünftige. BITTNER, Rüdiger.
Wissenschaft, Vorurteil und Wahn. LOH, Werner.

IRREVERSIBILITY

Two Faces of Maxwell's Demon Reveal the Nature of Irreversibility. COLLIER, John D.

IS

"Is and Ought" as a Linguistic Problem. BOUKEMA, H J M.
Is and Ought: A Gap or a Continuity?. BLACK, Virginia.
Of Particles. GALLIE, Roger D.

ISAAC, J

Critical Realism?. FAY, Brian.

ISAYE, G

Being and the Sciences: The Philosophy of Gaston Isaye. LECLERC, Marc.

ISLAM

An Interpretation of Religion: Human Responses to the Transcendent. HICK, John.
Our Philosophy: Allāma Muhammad Bāqir As-Sadr. INATI, Shams C (trans).
Existence (wujūd) and Quiddity (māhiyyah) in Islamic Philosophy. NASR, Seyyed Hossein.
Utopia and Islamic Political Thought. AL-AZMEH, Aziz.

ISLAMIC

Allāh Transcendent. NETTON, Ian Richard.
"The Ideal State of the Philosophers and Prophetic Laws" in A Straight Path: Studies in Medieval Philosophy and Culture, BERMAN, Lawrence V.

ISOCRATES

"Kunst der Überlistung" oder "Reden mit Vernuft"? Zu Philosophischen Aspekten der Rhetorik. NIEHUES-PRÖBSTING, Heinrich.

ISOLS

On Hyper-Torre Isols. DOWNEY, Rod.
On Infinite Series of Infinite Isols. BARBACK, Joseph.

ISOMORPHISM

The Fraenkel-Mostowski Method, Revisited. BRUNNER, Norbert.
Isomorphic But Not Lower Base-Isomorphic Cylindric Algebras of Finite Dimension. BIRÓ, Balázs.
An Isomorphism Between Rings and Groups. ISKANDER, Awad A.
Relatively Point Regular Quasivarieties. CZELAKOWSKI, Janusz.

ISRAEL

"Some Conceptions of the Land of Israel in Medieval Jewish Thought" in A Straight Path: Studies in Medieval Philosophy and Culture, IDEL, Moshe.

ISVARAKRSHANA

A New Plausible Exposition of Sānkhya-Kārikā-9. WADHWANI-SHAH, Yashodhara.

ITALIAN

Nietzsche in Italy. HARRISON, Thomas (ed).
Selections from Political Writings, 1921-1926: Antonio Gramsci. GRAMSCI, Antonio.
Business Ethics in Italy: The State of the Art. UNNIA, Mario.
Les métamorphoses de l'humanisme dans le philosophie marxiste italienne (in Romanian). GHITA, Simion.
Vincenzo Lilla nella filosofia italiana dell' Ottocento. SAVA, G.

ITERATION

The Iterative Hierarchy of Sets. TAIT, William.

JACKSON, F

Frank Jackson's Knowledge Argument Against Materialism. FURASH, Gary.
Temptation and the Will. BIGELOW, John.

JACQUES, F

Du dialogue référentiel au dialogisme transcendantal: L'itinéraire philosophique de Francis Jacques. GREISCH, Jean.

JAHREN, N

Reply to Jahren's "Comments on Ruth Ginzberg's Paper". GINZBERG, Ruth.

JAINISM

The Biographies of Siddhasena: A Study in the Texture of Allusion and the Weaving of a Group-Image (Part I). GRANOFF, Phyllis.

JAMES

The American Evasion of Philosophy: A Genealogy of Pragmatism. WEST, Cornel.
Classical American Philosophy: Essential Readings and Interpretative

Essays. STUHR, John J.
William James, Public Philosopher. COTKIN, George.
James's Faith-Ladder. WERNHAM, James C S.
James's Religious Hypothesis Reinterpreted. JONES, Royce.
Judging God By "Human" Standards: Reflections on William James' Varieties of Religious Experience. TUMULTY, Peter.
Mysticism and Experience. JANTZEN, Grace M.
The Pluralistic Approach to the Nature of Feelings. NATSOULAS, Thomas.
Poetic Invention and Scientific Observation: James's Model of "Sympathetic Concrete Observation". SEIGFRIED, Charlene Haddock.
Pragmatism and the Revolt Against Formalism: Revising Some Doctrines of William James. WHITE, Morton.
Recipes, Cooking, and Conflict: A Response to Heldke's Recipes for Theory. KOCH, Donald F.
Weaving Chaos into Order: A Radically Pragmatic Aesthetic. SEIGFRIED, Charlene Haddock.
William James on the Human Ways of Being. DOOLEY, Patrick.
William James, Dieu et la possibilité actuelle. GAVIN, William J.

JAMES, D

Some Uses of Imagination in the British Empiricists: A Preliminary Investigation of Locke, as Contrasted with Hume. HALL, Roland.

JAMES, H

Knowledge and Silence: The Golden Bowl and Moral Philosophy. BRUDNEY, Daniel.
Stories of Sublimely Good Character. CALLEN, Donald.

JANACEK, L

New Hypothesis on the Theme of Janacek's "Russian" Opera (in Czechoslovakian). BAJER, Jiri.

JANTZEN, G

Why We Need Immortality. TALIAFERRO, Charles.

JAPANESE

see also Buddhism
Emerging from Meditation: Nakamoto Tominaga. PYE, Michael (trans).
Derrida and the Decentered Universe of Ch'an Buddhism. ODIN, Steve.
The Influence of Traditional Japanese Aesthetics on the Film Theory of Sergei Eisenstein. ODIN, Steve.
The Philosophy of History in the "Later" Nishida: A Philosophic Turn. HUH, Woo-Sung.
Translating Nishida. MARALDO, John C.

JAQUELOT, I

La trattazione dell'argomento ontologico nel carteggio Leibniz-Jaquelot (1702-1704). TORTOLONE, Gian Michele.

JASPERS

Folly and Intelligence in Political Thought. KLUBACK, William.
Dialogo sobre humanismo y existencialismo (cuarta y última parte). SILVA CAMARENA, Juan Manuel.
The Ethos of Humanity in Karl Jaspers's Political Philosophy. SALAMUN, Kurt.
Mito e demittizzazione: polemica di Jaspers con Bultmann. PENZO, Giorgio.

JAYARASIBHATTA

Is Jayarasi a Materialist?. MOHANTA, Dilipkumar.

JEALOUSY

"Of Jealousy and Envy" in Person to Person, FARRELL, Daniel M.
Jealousy. WREEN, Michael.

JECKER, N

The Biomedical Model and Just Health Care: Reply to Jecker. DANIELS, Norman.

JEFFERSON

Agrarianism and the American Philosophical Tradition. THOMPSON, Paul B.

JEFFREY, R

Levi's Decision Theory. LEEDS, Stephen.
Temptation and the Will. BIGELOW, John.

JESUITS

Duhem and Koyré on Domingo de Soto. WALLACE, William.
Science, Philosophy and Religion in the Seventeenth Century Encounter Between China and the West (in Serbo-Croatian). STANDAERT, Nicolas.

JESUS

see also Christ
"Suicide and Early Christian Values" in Suicide and Euthanasia, AMUNDSEN, Darrel W.
Jesus and Interpretation: Sheehan's Hermeneutic Radicalism, QUIRK, Michael J.
On Doubts about the Resurrection. CRAIG, William Lane.

JEVONS, W
More Heat than Light: Economics as Social Physics, Physics as Nature's Economics. MIROWSKI, Philip.

JEWISH
see also Judaism
Baruch or Benedict: On Some Jewish Aspects of Spinoza's Philosophy. LEVY, Ze'ev.
Jewish Philosophy in a Secular Age. SEESKIN, Kenneth.
"A Historical Introduction to Jewish Casuistry on Suicide and Euthanasia" in *Suicide and Euthanasia*, BRODY, Baruch A.
"Holocaust and Resistance" in *Inquiries into Values: The Inaugural Session of the International Society for Value Inquiry*, BAR ON, Bat-Ami.
"The Holocaust's Ideological Perversion of Value" in *Inquiries into Values: The Inaugural Session of the International Society for Value Inquiry*, FRANCIS, Richard.
"The Jews in Spain at the Time of Maimonides" in *Moses Maimonides and His Time*, ROTH, Norman.
"The Problem of Creation in Late Medieval Jewish Philosophy" in *A Straight Path: Studies in Medieval Philosophy and Culture*, KOGAN, Barry S.
"Saadya's Goal in his *Commentary on Sefer Yezira*" in *A Straight Path: Studies in Medieval Philosophy and Culture*, BEN-SHAMMAI, Haggai.
"Some Conceptions of the Land of Israel in Medieval Jewish Thought" in *A Straight Path: Studies in Medieval Philosophy and Culture*, IDEL, Moshe.
Beyond Aestheticism: Derrida's Responsible Anarchy. CAPUTO, John D.
Bioethics and the Contemporary Jewish Community. NOVAK, David.
Jews as a Metaphysical Species. LURIE, Yuval.
Leo Strauss as Citizen and Jew. DANNHAUSER, Werner J.
Martin Buber—A Jew from Galicia. GÓRNIAK-KOCIKOWSKA, Krystyna.
Punishment and Self-Defense. FLETCHER, George P.
Representation, Conversion, and Literary Form: Harrington and the Novel of Jewish Identity. RAGUSSIS, Michael.
Skeptizismus und Judentum, mit einer Einleitung und Anmerkungen von Frederick Betz und Jörg Thunecke. MAUTHNER, Fritz.
Speaking for My Self. KOSINSKI, Jerzy.
The Splitting of the Logos: Some Remarks on Vico and Rabbinic Tradition. FAUR, José.

JI KANG
On Ji Kang's "Aestheticist" Aesthetic Thought. JINSHAN, Liu.

JOB
The Bitterness of Job: A Philosophical Reading. WILCOX, John T.
God and the Silencing of Job. TILLEY, Terrence W.

JOB(S)
The Relationship Between Ethics and Job Satisfaction: An Empirical Investigation. VITELL, Scott J and DAVIS, D L.
Something Akin to a Property Right: Protections for Job Security. LEE, Barbara A.

JOHANNSEN, W
The Crucial Experiment of Wilhelm Johannsen. ROLL-HANSEN, Nils.

JOHN OF HOLLAND
Sobre las "Obligationes" de Juan de Holanda. D'ORS, Angel.

JOHN OF SALISBURY
Knowledge, Virtue and the Path to Wisdom: The Unexamined Aristotelianism of John of Salisbury's Metalogicon. NEDERMAN, Cary J.

JOHN OF THE CROSS
John of the Cross and the Cognitive Value of Mysticism. PAYNE, Steven.
Faith and Ethical Reasoning in the Mystical Theology of St John of the Cross. SANDERLIN, David.

JOHN PAUL II
La person e en tant que don dans l'enseignement de Jean-Paul II (in Polish). GALKOWSKI, Jerzy W.

JOHNSON, O
Fingarette and Johnson on Retributive Punishment. STEPHENSON, Wendel.

JOHNSON, S
Berkeley Kicking His Own Stones. MC GOWAN, William H.
A Hobbist Tory: Johnson on Hume. RUSSELL, Paul.

JONAS, H
La critique de l'utopie et de la technique chez J Ellul et H Jonas. WEYEMBERGH, Maurice.

JOURNAL(S)
The "Notes on the Government and Population of the Kingdom of Naples" and Berkeley's Probable Route to Sicily. ALFONSO, Louis.
Bias, Controversy, and Abuse in the Study of the Scientific Publication System. MAHONEY, Michael J.

Entretiens avec Panayotis Kanellopoulos de L'Archive de Philosophie et de Théorie des Sciences (in Greek). KELESSIDOU, A.
Journals Have Obligations, Too: Commentary on "Confirmational Response Bias". HOLLANDER, Rachelle D.

JOURNALISM
The Dialectic in Journalism: Toward a Responsible Use of Press Freedom. MERRILL, John Calhoun.
Ethics and Social Concern. SERAFINI, Anthony.
The Function of the Press in a Free and Democratic Society. AUDI, Robert.
Journalists: A Moral Law Unto Themselves?. HARRIS, Nigel G E.
Media Ethics and Agriculture: Advertiser Demands Challenge Farm Press's Ethical Practices. REISNER, Anne E and HAYS, Robert G.
Reportage as Compound Suggestion. MAY, John D.

JOY
Spinoza: de la alegría. BELTRAN, M.

JOYCE
Art and the Joycean Artist. SCHIRALLI, Martin.
Vico e Joyce attraverso Michelet. VERRI, A.

JUDAISM
Baruch or Benedict: On Some Jewish Aspects of Spinoza's Philosophy. LEVY, Ze'ev.
Hegel and Judaism: A Reassessment. LUFT, Eric V D.
Lieux de l'identité freudienne: Judaïsme et Kultur. PFRIMMER, Theo.
Pardes: l'écriture de la puissance. AGAMBEN, Giorgio.
Philosophical Premises of Levinas' Conception of Judaism. LORENC, Iwona and PETROWICZ, Lech (trans).
Remarques sur Le Livre de la connaissance de Maïmonide. STRAUSS, Leo.
Sibboleth ou de la Lettre. GRANEL, Gérard.

JUDGE(S)
Judges Taken Too Seriously: Professor Dworkin's Views on Jurisprudence. TROPER, Michel.
Socrates and Judge Wilhelm: A Case of Kierkegaardian Ethics. MARTINEZ, Roy.

JUDGING
The Burden of Decision. CAPRON, Alexander Morgan.
How We Refer to Things. CHISHOLM, Roderick M.
Integrity and Judicial Discretion. KASHIYAMA, Paul.
Interpreting Arguments and Judging Issues. DAVSON-GALLE, Peter.

JUDGMENT(S)
see also Aesthetic Judgment, Moral Judgment(s)
Art of Judgement. CAYGILL, Howard.
Hannah Arendt: Lectures on Kant's Political Philosophy. BEINER, Ronald (ed).
The Idea of a Reason for Acting: A Philosophical Argument. SCHUELER, George Frederick.
Kant: Selections. BECK, Lewis White (ed).
The Kantian Sublime: From Morality to Art. CROWTHER, Paul.
The Self-Embodiment of God. ALTIZER, Thomas J J.
Splitting the Difference: Compromise and Integrity in Ethics and Politics. BENJAMIN, Martin.
Wise Choices, Apt Feelings: A Theory of Normative Judgment. GIBBARD, Allan.
"Understanding Individuals" in *Reading Kant*, VOSSENKUHL, Wilhelm.
"What One Thinks: Singular Propositions and the Content of Judgements" in *Whitehead's Metaphysics of Creativity*, KÜNNE, Wolfgang.
Communities of Judgment. GIBBARD, Allan.
Concepts, Judgments, and Unity in Kant's Metaphysical Deduction of the Relational Categories. NUSSBAUM, Charles.
The Development of Aesthetic Judgment: Analysis of a Genetic-Structuralist Approach. DE MUL, Jos.
Disciplining Qualitative Decision Exercises: Aspects of a Transempirical Protocol, II. SUTHERLAND, John W.
An Emendation in Kant's Theory of Taste. COHEN, Ted.
Errant Self-Control and the Self-Controlled Person. MELE, Alfred R.
Explaining the Inexplicable: The Hypotheses of the Faculty of Reflective Judgement in Kant's Third Critique. FRICKE, Christel.
Fetishism, Argument, and Judgment in Capital. FINOCCHIARO, Maurice A.
Hannah Arendt on Judgment, Philosophy and Praxis. KNAUER, James T.
Harry 17: Judgment, Perspective and Philosophy. LINDOP, Clive.
Having Bad Taste. GRACYK, Theodore A.
Hegel über die Rede vom Absoluten—Teil I: Urteil, Satz und Spekulativer Gehalt. GRAESER, Andreas.
In and Out of Peirce's Percepts. HAUSMAN, Carl R.
The Influence of Newman's Doctrine of Assent on the Thought of Bernard Lonergan. HAMMOND, David M.

JUSTICE

On Justice and Legitimation: A Critique of Jürgen Habermas' Concept of "Historical Reconstructivism". BALABAN, Oded.

Plato and Social Justice. DENT, N J H.

Platonic Justice and the *Republic*. HALL, Robert W.

Punishment and Self-Defense. FLETCHER, George P.

Rawls and the Minimum Demands of Justice. MC KENNA, Edward and WADE, Maurice and ZANNONI, Diane.

Rawls on Political Community and Principles of Justice. NICKEL, James W.

Rawlsian Justice and Community Planning. MARLIN, Randal.

Rights, Justice, and Duties to Provide Assistance: A Critique of Regan's Theory of Rights. JAMIESON, Dale.

Saving Grace. BRIEN, Andrew.

Seeing Justice Done: Aeschylus' *Oresteia*. FLAUMENHAFT, Mera J.

Social Justice. WILLIAMS, Bernard.

The Social Relativity of Justice and Rights Thesis. HUND, John.

Socrates' Encounter with Polus in Plato's *Gorgias*. JOHNSON, Curtis N.

Eine Theorie der politischen Gerechtigkeit. KERSTING, Wolfgang.

Towards a Theology of Peace—The Peace Doctrine of John Paul II. RAJECKI, Robert and LECKI, Maciej (trans).

Virtuous Lives and Just Societies. O'NEILL, Onora.

With Justice for All Beings: Educating as if Nature Matters. COHEN, Michael J.

The Worm and the Juggernaut: Justice and the Public Interest. LUCAS, J R.

JUSTIFIABILITY

Justifying a Principle of Informed Consent: A Case Study in Autonomy-Based Ethics. GUNDERSON, Martin.

Melancholic Epistemology. GRAHAM, George.

JUSTIFICATION

Civil Disobedience. HARRIS, Paul (ed).

Contemporary Ethics: Selected Readings. STERBA, James P.

Epistemic Justification: Essays in the Theory of Knowledge. ALSTON, William P.

The Evidential Force of Religious Experience. DAVIS, Caroline Franks.

Knowledge and Evidence. MOSER, Paul K.

Nuclear Deterrence, Morality and Realism. FINNIS, John.

Sense and Certainty: A Dissolution of Scepticism. MC GINN, Marie.

Theory of Knowledge (Third Edition). CHISHOLM, Roderick M.

Theory of Knowledge. LEHRER, Keith.

Wise Choices, Apt Feelings: A Theory of Normative Judgment. GIBBARD, Allan.

"BonJour's Coherence Theory of Justification" in *The Current State of the Coherence Theory*, SWAIN, Marshall.

"BonJour's *The Structure of Empirical Knowledge*" in *The Current State of the Coherence Theory*, GOLDMAN, Alvin I.

"Coherence, Justification, and Knowledge: The Current Debate" in *The Current State of the Coherence Theory*, BENDER, John W.

"Comment: The Middle Way in the Philosophy of Punishment" in *Issues in Contemporary Legal Philosophy: The Influence of H L A Hart*, SCHACHAR, Yoram.

"Epistemic Priority and Coherence" in *The Current State of the Coherence Theory*, LEMOS, Noah M.

"Epistemically Justified Opinion" in *The Current State of the Coherence Theory*, AUNE, Bruce.

"Ethics, Subjective and Secular" in *Inquiries into Values: The Inaugural Session of the International Society for Value Inquiry*, SAPONTZIS, Steve F.

"Evolutionary Explanation and the Justification of Belief" in *Issues in Evolutionary Epistemology*, CLENDINNEN, F John.

"The Illegality of Philosophy" in *The Institution of Philosophy: A Discipline in Crisis?*, ROMANO, Carlin.

"Lehrer's Coherence Theory of Knowledge" in *The Current State of the Coherence Theory*, FELDMAN, Richard.

"Lehrer's Coherentism and the Isolation Objection" in *The Current State of the Coherence Theory*, MOSER, Paul K.

"The Multiple Faces of Knowing: The Hierarchies of Epistemic Species" in *The Current State of the Coherence Theory*, CASTANEDA, Hector-Neri.

"When Can What You Don't Know Hurt You?" in *The Current State of the Coherence Theory*, RUSSELL, Bruce.

Accepting the Authority of the Bible: Is It Rationally Justified?. KELLER, James A.

Aim-Less Epistemology?. LAUDAN, L.

Alvin I Goldman's Epistemology and Cognition: An Introduction. LEVINE, Michael P.

Apriority and Metajustification in BonJour's "Structure of Empirical Knowledge". SOLOMON, Miriam.

Autonomist Internalism and the Justification of Morals. DARWALL, Stephen L.

The Basic Notion of Justification. KVANVIG, Jonathan L and MENZEL, Christopher.

Can a Partisan be a Moralist?. COMBERG, Paul.

Concepts, Categories, and Epistemology. LIVINGSTON, Kenneth R.

Connectionism and Epistemology: Goldman on Winner-Take-All Networks. THAGARD, Paul.

Deductive Justification. CANARY, Catherine and ODEGARD, Douglas.

The Demand for Justification in Ethics. BUTCHVAROV, Panayot.

Discovery as the Context of Any Scientific Justification. VAN PEURSEN, C A.

Explanation and Justification in Ethics. COPP, David.

From Nothing to Sociology. WOLFF, Kurt H.

Goldman on Epistemic Justification. ALSTON, William P.

Goldman on Epistemology and Cognitive Science. FELDMAN, Richard.

How to Define Terrorism. TEICHMAN, Jenny.

In Defense of Good Reasons. BERKSON, William.

La ingeniería social como método de testeo. COMESAÑA, Manuel E.

Introspection and Misdirection. KORNBLITH, Hilary.

Justificación epistémica. LEGRIS, Javier.

The Justification of Deterrent Violence. FARRELL, Daniel M.

Justification of Faith (in Dutch). VANDENBULCKE, J.

Justification, Reliability and Knowledge. SHOPE, Robert K.

Justification: It Need not Cause but it Must be Accessible. GINET, Carl.

Justifying Punishment and the Problem of the Innocent. MARTIN, Rex.

Justifying Tolerance. KING, Preston.

Justifying Wrongful Employee Behavior: The Role of Personality in Organizational Sabotage. GIACALONE, Robert A and KNOUSE, Stephen B.

Literature as a Way of Knowing: An Epistemological Justification for Literary Studies. KASPRISIN, Lorraine.

Más allá del escepticismo, a nuestro leal saber y entender. SOSA, Ernesto.

The Metaphysical Construction of Value. BAKER, Judith.

The Metaphysics of Communism. LURIE, Yuval.

Methodology Is Pragmatic: A Reponse to Miller. BERKSON, William.

Naturalism and Philosophy of Education. EVERS, Colin W.

Nietzsche's Radical Experimentalism. SEIGFRIED, Hans.

A Normative Conception of Coherence for a Discursive Theory of Legal Justification. GÜNTHER, Klaus.

On Gettier's Notion of Knowledge and Justification. MUKHOPADHYAY, Debabrata.

Paternalism Defined. ARCHARD, David.

The Politics of Justification. MACEDO, Stephen.

Professor Kasachkoff on Explaining and Justifying. BOWLES, George.

Pyrrhonean Scepticism and the Self-Refutation Argument. BAILEY, Alan.

Rejoinder to Berkson's "In Defense of Good Reasons". MILLER, David.

Reliabilism and Relevant Worlds. MOSER, Paul K.

Reliability and Goldman's Theory of Justification. ALMEDER, Robert and HOFF, Franklin J.

Religion and Truth (in Dutch). DE DIJN, H.

Replies to the Commentators. GOLDMAN, Alvin I.

Reply to Solomon's "Apriority and Metajustification in BonJour's 'Structure of Empirical Knowledge'". BONJOUR, Laurence.

Responsibility and 'Free Will'. VESEY, Godfrey.

Scepticism and Madness. BELSHAW, Christopher.

Scepticism and Rational Belief. WEDGWOOD, Ralph.

Subjective Justification. DE PIERRIS, Graciela.

Suicide: Its Nature and Moral Evaluation. KUPFER, Joseph.

Teleology and Scientific Method in Kant's Critique of Judgement. BUTTS, Robert E.

Thomson and the Trolley Problem. POSTOW, B C.

Three Approaches to Locke and the Slave Trade. GLAUSSER, Wayne.

The Wall and the Shield: K-K Reconsidered. ROTH, Michael.

Why Be Rational? On Thinking Critically About Critical Thinking. SIEGEL, Harvey.

K'ANG YU-WEI

In Search of an Image of the World: Kang Youwei and Yan Fu (in Serbo-Croatian). RADONIC, Nikola.

KABBALA

"The *Guide* and the *Gate*: The Dialectical Influence of Maimonides on Isaac ibn Latif and Early Spanish Kabbalah" in *A Straight Path: Studies in Medieval Philosophy and Culture*, WILENSKY, Sara Heller.

KADANE, J

Pareto Unanimity and Consensus. LEVI, Isaac.

KADISH, S

"Comment: A Theory of Complicity" in *Issues in Contemporary Legal Philosophy: The Influence of H L A Hart*, GUR-ARYE, Miriam.

KADUSHIN, M

"Everything Depends on the *Type* of the Concepts that the Interpretation is Made to Convey". COMSTOCK, Gary L.

KAHNEMAN, D

Are Theories of Rationality Empirically Testable?. SMOKLER, Howard.

KALUPAHANA, D

Kalupahana on *Nirvāna*. ANDERSON, Tyson.

KAMM, F

F M Kamm and the Mirror of Time. FELDMAN, Fred.

KANDINSKY, W

Validation by Touch in Kandinsky's Early Abstract Art. OLIN, Margaret.

KANELLOPOULOS, P

Entretiens avec Panayotis Kanellopoulos de *L'Archive de Philosophie et de Théorie des Sciences* (in Greek). KELESSIDOU, A.

The Notion of Chance and the Metaphysics of P Kanellopoulos (in Greek). MARKAKIS, M.

KANT

Art of Judgement. CAYGILL, Howard.

Constructions of Reason: Explorations of Kant's Practical Philosophy. O'NEILL, Onora.

Constructivism and Science: Essays in Recent German Philosophy. BUTTS, Robert E (ed).

Dionysus Reborn: Play and the Aesthetic Dimension in Modern Philosophical and Scientific Discourse. SPARIOSU, Mihai I.

Discourses on the Meaning of History. KLUBACK, William.

Early Modern Philosophy II. TWEYMAN, Stanley (ed).

Elements of Modern Philosophy: Descartes through Kant. BRENNER, William H.

Ernst Bloch: Trame della speranza. BOELLA, Laura.

The Ethics of Geometry: A Genealogy of Modernity. LACHTERMAN, David R.

Expérience et culture: Fondement d'une théorie générale de l'expérience. REALE, Miguel.

The Fourth Way: A Theory of Knowledge. GROSSMAN, Reinhardt.

Freedom and the End of Reason: On the Moral Foundation of Kant's Critical Philosophy. VELKLEY, Richard L.

Hannah Arendt: Lectures on Kant's Political Philosophy. BEINER, Ronald (ed).

Hegel und Das Deutsche Erbe: Philosophie und nationale Frage zwischen Revolution und Reaktion. LOSURDO, Domenico.

Hegel, Heraclitus, and Marx's Dialectic. WILLIAMS, Howard.

Heidegger Interprete di Kant. COLONNELLO, Pio.

Historical Roots of Cognitive Science. MEYERING, Theo C.

Humanisme de la liberté et philosophie de la justice, Tome II. TRIGEAUD, Jean-Marc.

Husserl's Phenomenology and the Foundations of Natural Science. HARVEY, Charles W.

Jewish Philosophy in a Secular Age. SEESKIN, Kenneth.

Kant and the Philosophy of History. YOVEL, Yirmiyahu.

Kant: An Index to Theses and Dissertations Accepted by Universities in Canada and the US, 1879-1985. GABEL, Gernot U.

Kant: Selections. BECK, Lewis White (ed).

The Kantian Sublime: From Morality to Art. CROWTHER, Paul.

Kants Theorie des Verstandes. SEEBOHM, Thomas M (ed).

A Moral Military. AXINN, Sidney.

Questions of Form: Logic and the Analytic Proposition from Kant to Carnap. PROUST, Joëlle.

Reading Kant. SCHAPER, Eva (ed).

Religion, Interpretation, and Diversity of Belief. GODLOVE, Terry F.

Schopenhauer and the Wild Years of Philosophy. SAFRANSKI, Rüdiger.

Lo storicismo di W Dilthey (Il problema di dio nei grandi pensatori, Volume Quinto). MANNO, Ambrogio Giacomo.

A Theory of Property. MUNZER, Stephen R.

Treatise on Basic Philosophy, Volume 8—Ethics: The Good and the Right. BUNGE, Mario.

Why You Should: The Pragmatics of Deontic Speech. FORRESTER, James W.

Wie kann man sagen, was nicht ist-Zur Logik des Utopischen. SCHMITZ, Heinz-Gerd.

Zwischen Revolution und Orthodoxie?. JACOBS, Wilhelm G.

"'Between Purgation and Illumination': A Critique of the Theology of Right" in *Christ, Ethics and Tragedy: Essays in Honour of Donald MacKinnon,* MILBANK, John.

"Analytic/Dialectic" in *Reading Kant,* BRANDT, Reinhard.

"Atemporal Necessities of Thought: or, How Not to Bury Philosophy by

History" in *Reading Kant,* HARRISON, Ross.

"Derrida, Kant, and the Performance of Paregonality" in *Derrida and Deconstruction,* HARVEY, Irene E.

"Hegel on Morality" in *Dialectic and Contemporary Science,* WALSH, W H.

"How Are Transcendental Arguments Possible?" in *Reading Kant,* FÖRSTER, Eckart.

"The Identity of the Subject in the Transcendental Deduction" in *Reading Kant,* HENRICH, Dieter.

"Kant on the Modalities of Space" in *Reading Kant,* GREENWOOD, Terry.

"Kant's Transcendental Arguments" in *Reading Kant,* BIRD, Graham.

"Kant" in *Ethics in the History of Western Philosophy,* KORSGAARD, Christine.

"A Metaphysical Grounding for Natural Reverence: East-West" in *Nature in Asian Tradition of Thought: Essays in Environmental Philosophy,* DEUTSCH, Eliot.

"Participating in Enlightenment" in *Knowledge and Politics,* BOHMAN, James F.

"Phenomenality and Materiality in Kant" in *The Textual Sublime: Deconstruction and Its Differences,* DE MAN, Paul.

"The *Pons Asinorum* in Philosophy" in *Dialectic and Contemporary Science,* MULLER, Philippe.

"Realism and Realization in a Kantian Light" in *Reading Kant,* BUCHDAHL, Gerd.

"The Rehabilitation of Transcendental Idealism?" in *Reading Kant,* GUYER, Paul.

"Reply to Muller's "The *Pons Asinorum* in Philosophy" in *Dialectic and Contemporary Science,* HARRIS, Errol E.

"Reply to Walsh's "Hegel on Morality"" in *Dialectic and Contemporary Science,* HARRIS, Errol E.

"Schopenhauers Kritik des kategorischen Imperativs" in *Schopenhauer: New Essays in Honor of His 200th Birthday,* BECKER, Werner.

"Smith and Kant Respond to Mandeville" in *Early Modern Philosophy II,* LEVY, David.

"Suicide in the Age of Reason" in *Suicide and Euthanasia,* BEAUCHAMP, Tom L.

"Transcendental Arguments and Scepticism" in *Reading Kant,* WALKER, Ralph C S.

"Transcendental Idealism and the Representation of Space" in *Reading Kant,* HORSTMANN, Rolf Peter.

"Understanding Individuals" in *Reading Kant,* VOSSENKUHL, Wilhelm.

"Denn das Sein oder Nichtsein ist kein Merkmal der Sache". SONDEREGGER, Erwin.

"Deus ex machina" redivivus: The "Synthetic A Priori" in the Computer Age. FANG, J.

"El aire es elástico". CAIMI, Mario P M.

La "parte pura" de las ciencias de la naturaleza: Observaciones sobre el fundamentalismo kantiano. PACHO GARCÍA, Julián.

"The Right of a State" in Immanuel Kant's *Doctrine of Right.* LUDWIG, Bernd.

'Communicatief handelen' als theoretisch grondbegrip. COBBEN, Paul.

The A Priori from Kant to Schelling. LAWRENCE, Joseph P (trans) and GRONDIN, Jean.

The Abyssal Categories of Blaga's Apriorism. RAMBU, Nicolae.

Agency, Human Nature and Character in Kantian Theory. RUMSEY, Jean P.

Die Anschauungsformen und das Schematismuskapitel. MUDROCH, Vilem.

Are Kant's "Aesthetic Judgment" and "Judgment of Tase" Synonymous?. GRACYK, Theodore A.

The Aristotelian Character of Schiller's Ethical Ideal. CORDNER, Christopher.

Aspects et perspectives du problème de la limite dans la philosophie théorique de Kant. THEIS, R.

Autonomy Without Indeterminism: A Reconstruction of Kant's *Groundwork,* Chapter Three. TERZIS, George N.

Beauty as the Transition from Nature to Freedom in Kant's Critique of Judgement. DÜSING, Klaus.

Between Succession and Duration. ROTENSTREICH, Nathan.

Can Kant's Ethics Survive the Feminist Critique?. SEDGWICK, Sally S.

Categorías puras y categorías esquematizadas. VON BILDERLING, Beatriz.

The Categorical Imperative and Kant's Conception of Practical Rationality. REATH, Andrews.

Ceticismo versus condições de verdade. ROHDEN, Valério.

Commentaire de la Critique de la Raison pure de Kant (1907). COHEN, Hermann.

Concepts, Judgments, and Unity in Kant's Metaphysical Deduction of the Relational Categories. NUSSBAUM, Charles.

La conclusion de la Critique de la raison pure. GRONDIN, Jean.

Consequentialism, Egoism, and the Moral Law. CUMMISKEY, David.

Contemporary Trends in the Interpretation of Kant's Critical Philosophy. ZAHN, M.

KANT

Il dibattito sulla razionalità oggi: un ritorno a Kant? Interviste a K O Apel & J Petitot. QUARANTA, M.

Does Anxiety Explain Original Sin?. QUINN, Philip L.

Double Representation of the 'Paralogisms of Pure Reason' in the Two Editions of Critique of Pure Reason (in German). KOPPER, Joachim.

The Elemental Imperative. LINGIS, Alphonso.

An Emendation in Kant's Theory of Taste. COHEN, Ted.

Emmanuel Kant: La liberté comme droit de l'homme et l'"Idée" de république. PONTON, Lionel.

The Emptiness of the Moral Will. WOOD, Allen W.

Die Ethik—"der Schlussstein von dem ganzen Gebäude der spekulativen Vernunft". BUHR, Manfred.

Explaining the Inexplicable: The Hypotheses of the Faculty of Reflective Judgement in Kant's Third Critique. FRICKE, Christel.

Feder und Kant. BRANDT, Reinhard.

Fin y valor de la acción: recorrido histórico-sistemático. FERRER, Urbano.

Forgetting Abdera (in Serbo-Croatian). ROGOGINSKI, Jacob.

Das Gesetz oder das Gute? Zum Ursprung und Sinn des Formalismus in der Ethik Kants. SALA, Giovanni B.

God, Morality, and Prudence: A Reply to Bernard Williams. TSANG, Lap-Chuen.

Grundprinzipien einer kritischen Dialektik zwischen Kant und Hegel. IDALOVICHI, Israel.

Das Hässliche und die "Kritik der ästhetischen Urteilskraft". STRUB, Christian.

Hegel's Idealism: Prospects. PIPPIN, Robert.

Heidegger, Kant and the 'Humanism' of Science. SCHALOW, Frank.

Hermann von Helmholtz: The Problem of Kantian Influence. FULLINWIDER, S P.

Hintikka on Kant and Logic. RUSSELL, Christopher.

How Kantian Was Hegel?. PINKARD, Terry.

La imagen del hombre en la teoría kantiana del genio. LABRADA, Maria Antonia.

Imaginative Freedom and the German Enlightenment. KNELLER, Jane.

Intervencionismo y paternalismo. GARZÓN VALDÉS, Ernesto.

Is a Post-Hegelian Ethics Possible?. MC CUMBER, John.

Is the Moral Point of View Monological or Dialogical? The Kantian Background of Habermas' Discourse Ethics. CLEMENT, Grace.

Kant and Moral Integrity. JENSEN, Henning.

Kant and the Interpretation of Nature and History. MAKKREEL, Rudolf.

Kant and the Possibility of Uncategorized Experience. KAIN, Philip J.

Kant ante la verdad como hija del tiempo. ROVIRA, Rogelio.

Kant e o ceticismo. LOPARIC, Zeljko.

Kant on Descartes and the Brutes. NARAGON, Steve.

Kant on Euclid: Geometry in Perspective. PALMQUIST, Stephen R.

Kant on Property Rights and the Social Contract. BAYNES, Kenneth.

Kant over Midden, Middel en Doel (I). VAN DER HOEVEN, J.

Kant over midden, middel en doel II. VAN DER HOEVEN, J.

Kant's Account of Sensation. FALKENSTEIN, Lorne.

Kant's Analogies and the Structure of Objective Time. HUGHES, R I G.

Kant's Analysis of Obligation: The Argument of Foundationsl. KORSGAARD, Christine M.

Kant's Argument for the Non-Spatiotemporality of Things in Themselves. FALKENSTEIN, Lorne.

Kant's Challenge: The Second Analogy as a Response to Hume. DELANEY, C.

Kant's Conception of Empirical Law—I. GUYER, Paul.

Kant's Conception of Empirical Law—II. WALKER, Ralph.

Kant's Conception of Rational Action. BASU, Tora.

Kant's Key to the Critique of Taste. BURGESS, Craig.

Kant's Metaphysics of the Subject and Modern Society. FRIGERIO, C.

Kant's Political Theory and Philosophy of History. KAIN, Philip J.

Kant's Theory of Moral Sensibility: Respect for the Moral Law and the Influence of Inclination. REATH, A.

Kant's Theory of Political Authority. CARR, Craig L.

Kant's Theory of Practical Reason. HILL JR, Thomas E.

Kant's Theory of Punishment: Deterrence in its Threat, Retribution in its Execution. BYRD, B Sharon.

Kant's Theory of the Autonomy of Reflective Judgement as an Ethics of Experiential Thinking. PILOT, Harald.

Kant's Third Antinomy: Agency and Causal Explanation. GREENWOOD, John D.

Kant, Naturphilosophie, and Oersted's Discovery of Electromagnetism: A Reassessment. SHANAHAN, Timothy.

Kantian and Platonic Conceptions of Order. STOLL, Donald.

Kantian Strict Duties of Benevolence. EGGERMAN, Richard W.

Kants Theorie der Materie und ihre Wirkung auf die zeitgenössische Chemie. CARRIER, Martin.

Die kosmologischen Antinomien in der Kritik der reinen Vernunft und die moderne physikalische Kosmologie. MITTELSTAEDT, Peter and STROHMEYER, Ingeborg.

Language and Thought in Kant's Theory of Knowledge (in Hebrew). DASCAL, Marcelo and SENDEROWICZ, Yaron.

Lorand and Kant on Free and Dependent Beauty. STECKER, Robert.

The Market for Bodily Parts: Kant and Duties to Oneself. CHADWICK, Ruth F.

Meditaciones sobre la nada. COLOMBRES, Carlos A Iturralde.

Metakritik und Sprache: Zu Johann Georg Hamanns Kant-Verständnis und seinen metakritischen Implikationen. MAJETSCHAK, Stefan.

Metaphors and the Transcendental. BENCIVENGA, Ermanno.

Moral Regeneration and Divine Aid in Kant. MICHALSON JR, Gordon E.

Morality and Culture: A Note on Kant. ROTENSTREICH, Nathan.

Morality and Justice in Kant. KLEIN, Martha.

Moves and Motives in the Games We Play. HOLLIS, Martin.

Murder and Mayhem: Violence and Kantian Casuistry. HERMAN, Barbara.

Naturhermeneutik und Ethik im Denken Heideggers. RIEDEL, Manfred.

Naturnotwendigkeit und Freiheit: Zu Kants Theorie der Kausalität als Antwort auf Hume. RANG, Bernhard.

La nocion de verdad en el ser y el tiempo (cont). VÉLEZ, Francisco Galán.

An Objection to Kantian Ethical Rationalism. TERZIS, George N.

The Objectivity of Taste: Hume and Kant. KULENKAMPFF, Jens.

On Dialectical Consistency. ZELENY, Jindrich.

On Goodness: Human and Divine. LINVILLE, Mark D.

On the Kantian Background of Neopositivism. SAUER, Werner.

On the Relation Between Rational Autonomy and Ethical Community: Hegel's Critique of Kantian Morality. STERN, Paul.

The Ontological Argument Reconsidered. BALABAN, Oded and AVSHALOM, Asnat.

An Operational Approach to the Dynamics of Science: Kant's Concept of Architectonic. GIUCULESCU, Alexandru.

Peirce's Concept of Knowledge in 1868. SMYTH, Richard.

Political Liberalism. LARMORE, Charles.

Postmodern Conditions: Rethinking Public Education. KIZILTAN, Mustafa Ü and BAIN, William J and CAÑIZARES, Anita.

The Prayers of Childhood: T S Eliot's Manuscripts on Kant. HABIB, M A R.

I presupposti assiologici del riconoscimento nello Hegel prejenese. RIZZI, Lino.

El principio de universalización y la razón práctica (1a parte). GUARIGLIA, Osvaldo.

The Problem of Kant. HARRIS, H S.

Le problème de la fondation de l'éthique: Kant, Hegel. KERVEGAN, Jean-Francois.

Psychology in the First Critique. BIRD, G H.

Quelques considérations sur la signification de l'agnosticism Kantien (in Romanian). RAMBU, Nicolae.

The Question of the Relation of Philosophy and Psychoanalysis: The Case of Kant and Freud. PETTIGREW, David E.

Racionalismo ético kantiano y amor puro. BULNES, Maria Elton.

La razón en su uso regulativo y el a priori del "sistema" en la primera Crítica. DOTTI, Jorge E.

Reason and Reflective Judgement: Kant on the Significance of Systematicity. GUYER, Paul.

Reason, Revolution and Religion: Johann Benjamin Erhard's Concept of Enlightened Revolution. MARTINSON, Steven D.

Reasons and Reason. ROTENSTREICH, Nathan.

A Reconsideration of Kant's Treatment of Duties to Oneself. PATON, Margaret.

Reflective Judgement and Taste. GINSBORG, Hannah.

The Rejection of Ethical Rationalism. KAPUR, Neera Badhwar.

The Right and the Good. LARMORE, Charles.

The Role of Apperception in Kant's Transcendental Deduction of the Categories. CASTANEDA, Héctor-Neri.

The Role of Self-Knowledge in the Critique of Pure Reason. POLT, Richard F H.

The Role of Virtues in Alternatives to Kantian and Utilitarian Ethics. MORAVCSIK, Julius M.

Scepticism and Intellectual Freedom: The Philosophical Foundations of Kant's Politics of Publicity. LAURSEN, John C.

Schopenhauer's Account of Aesthetic Experience. DIFFEY, T J.

The Self and First Person Metaphysics. ALBERTS, Kelly T.

Sense, Reason and Causality in Hume and Kant. NUYEN, A T.

The Sensible Foundation for Mathematics: A Defense of Kant's View. RISJORD, Mark.

Os Sentidos da "Crítica". BORGES, Bento Itamar.

KILVINGTON, R
The Sophismata of Richard Kilvington. KRETZMANN, Norman.

KIM, J
Mind-Body Identity Theories. MACDONALD, Cynthia.
Property Exemplification and Proliferation. ROWLANDS, Mark N J.
Supervenience and Closure. VAN CLEVE, James.
Van Cleve versus Closure. BACON, John.

KINCAID, H
Methodological Individualism and Explanation. TUOMELA, Raimo.

KIND(S)
Some Pleasures of Plato, Republic IX. STOKES, Michael.

KING(S)
Forming of an Honorable Man in Classical China: The Junzi's Education (in Serbo-Croatian). DIDIER, Michel.

KING, M
Civil Disobedience. HARRIS, Paul (ed).

KIPLING, R
Civil Peace and Sacred Order: Limits and Renewals I. CLARK, Stephen R L.

KITCHER, P
The Poverty of Pluralism: A Reply to Sterelny and Kitcher. SOBER, Elliott.

KLAGES, L
Mens en aarde: Het ecofilosofisch dilemma in het werk van Ludwig Klages. WITZORECK, Kris.

KLAUS, G
Georg Klaus über Kybernetik und Information. STOCK, Wolfgang G.

KLEIST, H
The Moment of the Foundation (in Serbo-Croatian). RAULET, Gérard.

KLEVER, W
"Reply to Klever's "The Properties of the Intellect"" in Dialectic and Contemporary Science, HARRIS, Errol E.

KLOSKO, G
Obligations of Gratitude and Political Obligation. WALKER, A D M.

KNEALE, M
Negation and Quantification in Aristotle. WEDIN, Michael V.

KNEZEVICH, L
Truthmongering: Less is True. FINE, Arthur.

KNOWING
Faith on Earth: An Inquiry into the Structure of Human Faith. NIEBUHR, Richard R (ed).
Interpreting Education. EDEL, Abraham.
"Saying and Knowing" in From Metaphysics to Rhetoric, SCHLANGER, Judith.
Knowing God and Knowing the Cosmos: Augustine's Legacy of Tension. O'LOUGHLIN, Thomas.
Literature as a Way of Knowing: An Epistemological Justification for Literary Studies. KASPRISIN, Lorraine.
Practical Knowing: Finnis and Aquinas. SIMPSON, Peter.
The Dutch Words 'besef' and 'beseffen' (in Dutch). VERHOEVEN, C.

KNOWLEDGE
see also Epistemology
Beyond the Atom: The Philosophical Thought of Wolfgang Pauli. LAURIKAINEN, K V.
Connections to the World: The Basic Concepts of Philosophy. DANTO, Arthur C.
Conscience and the Reality of God: An Essay on the Experiential Foundations of Religious Knowledge. STATEN, John C.
Embodiments of Mind. MC CULLOCH, Warren S.
Epistemic Justification: Essays in the Theory of Knowledge. ALSTON, William P.
Epistemology (Companions to Ancient Thought: 1). EVERSON, Stephen (ed).
Expérience et culture: Fondement d'une théorie générale de l'expérience. REALE, Miguel.
The Fourth Way: A Theory of Knowledge. GROSSMAN, Reinhardt.
Good Lives and Moral Education. SIMPSON, Evan.
The Growth of Knowledge: An Inquiry into the Kuhnian Theory. VERRONEN, Veli.
Hegel's Concept of Experience. HEIDEGGER, Martin.
Hegel's Epistemological Realism: A Study of the Aim and Method of Hegel's Phenomenology of Spirit. WESTPHAL, Kenneth R.
J L Austin. WARNOCK, G J.
Kants Theorie des Verstandes. SEEBOHM, Thomas M (ed).

Knowledge and Evidence. MOSER, Paul K.
Knowledge and Politics. DASCAL, Marcelo (ed).
The Knowledge of Values: A Methodological Introduction. LÓPEZ QUINTÁS, Alfonso (ed).
Logic and Knowledge: Bertrand Russell, Essays 1901-1950. MARSH, Robert Charles (ed).
Man and Nature in the Philosophical Thought of Wang-Fu-Chih. BLACK, Alison Harley.
The Metaphysics of Epistemology: Lectures by Wilfrid Sellars. AMARAL, Pedro (ed).
The Natures of Science. MC MORRIS, Neville.
Our Philosophy: Allāma Muhammad Bāqir As-Sadr. INATI, Shams C (trans).
Paths Toward a Clearing: Radical Empiricism and Ethnographic Inquiry. JACKSON, Michael.
A Philosopher's Harvest: The Philosophical Papers of Isaac Franck. GERBER, William (ed).
Philosophical Logic and Artificial Intelligence. THOMASON, Richmond H (ed).
Philosophical Works. KALOYEROPOULOS, N A.
Philosophy and the Human Condition (Second Edition). BEAUCHAMP, Tom L (ed).
Philosophy of Economics: On the Scope of Reason in Economic Inquiry. ROY, Subroto.
Philosophy of Perception. MACLACHLAN, D L C.
The Philosophy of Quantum Mechanics: An Interactive Interpretation. HEALEY, Richard.
The Philosophy of Thomas Reid. DALGARNO, Melvin (ed).
The Possible Universe. TALLET, J A.
Pursuit of Truth. QUINE, W V.
Rationality and Relativity: The Quest for Objective Knowledge. O'GORMAN, Francis.
Rhetorica I—Reden mit Vernunft: Aristoteles, Cicero, Augustinus. MAINBERGER, Gonsalv K.
Rhetoriques. PERELMAN, Chaïm.
Science and Its Fabrication. CHALMERS, Alan.
Scientific Knowledge Socialized. HRONSZKY, Imre (ed).
Sense and Certainty: A Dissolution of Scepticism. MC GINN, Marie.
Socrates in the Apology: An Essay on Plato's Apology of Socrates. REEVE, C D C.
Theory of Knowledge (Third Edition). CHISHOLM, Roderick M.
Theory of Knowledge. LEHRER, Keith.
Understanding Plato. MELLING, David J.
Ursprung und Thema von Ersten Wissenschaft. KÖNIGSHAUSEN, Johann-Heinrich.
Wittgenstein's Later Philosophy. HANFLING, Oswald.
"The Beginnings of Epistemology: From Homer to Philolaus" in Epistemology (Companions to Ancient Thought: 1), HUSSEY, Edward.
"BonJour's The Structure of Empirical Knowledge" in The Current State of the Coherence Theory, GOLDMAN, Alvin I.
"Coherence, Justification, and Knowledge: The Current Debate" in The Current State of the Coherence Theory, BENDER, John W.
"Crescas versus Maimonides on Knowledge and Pleasure" in A Straight Path: Studies in Medieval Philosophy and Culture, HARVEY, Warren Zev.
"An Empiricist View of Knowledge: Memorism" in Epistemology (Companions to Ancient Thought: 1), FREDE, Michael.
"Epistemically Justified Opinion" in The Current State of the Coherence Theory, AUNE, Bruce.
"Evolution of the Knowledge of Knowledge" in Issues in Evolutionary Epistemology, WOJCIECHOWSKI, Jerzy A.
"The Externalization of Observation: An Example from Modern Physics" in Scientific Knowledge Socialized, PINCH, Trevor J.
"Hobbes's Science of Moral Philosophy" in Knowledge and Politics, HAMPTON, Jean.
"The Infernal Recurrence of the Same: Nietzsche and Foucault on Knowledge and Power" in Knowledge and Politics, REDNER, Harry.
"Knowledge and Belief in Republic V-VII" in Epistemology (Companions to Ancient Thought: 1), FINE, Gail.
"The Multiple Faces of Knowing: The Hierarchies of Epistemic Species" in The Current State of the Coherence Theory, CASTANEDA, Hector-Neri.
"Plato's Early Theory of Knowledge" in Epistemology (Companions to Ancient Thought: 1), WOODRUFF, Paul.
"The Political Animal's Knowledge According to Aristotle" in Knowledge and Politics, LABARRIÈRE, Jean-Louis.
"The Problem of the Criterion" in Epistemology (Companions to Ancient Thought: 1), STRIKER, Gisela.
"Relevance Logic and Inferential Knowledge" in Directions in Relevant Logic, BARKER, John.
"Russell's 1913 Theory of Knowledge Manuscript" in Rereading Russell:

LANGUAGE

Mental Representation, SCHANK, Roger and KASS, Alex.

"The Metaphilosophical Consequences of Pragmatism" in *The Institution of Philosophy: A Discipline in Crisis?*, OKRENT, Mark.

"On the Saying that Philosophy Begins in *Thaumazein*" in *Post-Structuralist Classics*, LLEWELYN, John.

"On Truth: A Fiction" in *Meaning and Mental Representation*, ECO, Umberto.

"Die Polyglottie als Stilfigur: *Der Fall Doderer*" in *Cultural Hermeneutics of Modern Art: Essays in Honor of Jan Aler*, BIER, Jean Paul.

"A Reflection on Naturalistic Accounts of Language" in *Inquiries into Values: The Inaugural Session of the International Society for Value Inquiry*, BURLINGAME, Charles E.

"Schopenhauer and Wittgenstein on Lonely Languages and Criterialess Claims" in *Schopenhauer: New Essays in Honor of His 200th Birthday*, CLEGG, Jerry S.

"The Subjectivity of the Speaker" in *The Question of the Other: Essays in Contemporary Continental Philosophy*, KUYKENDALL, Eleanor H.

"Tense and Existence" in *Cause, Mind, and Reality: Essays Honoring C B Martin*, CARGILE, James.

"Bedeutung", "Idee" und "Begriff": Zur Behandlung einiger bedeutungstheorietischer Paradoxien durch Leibniz. ROS, Arno.

"Denn das Sein oder Nichstsein ist kein Merkmal der Sache". SONDEREGGER, Erwin.

"Interpretation and Solidarity"—An Interview with Richard Bernstein. MELCIC, Dunja.

"Kunst der Überlistung" oder "Reden mit Vernuft"? Zu Philosophischen Aspekten der Rhetorik. NIEHUES-PRÖBSTING, Heinrich.

"The Flower of the Mouth": Hölderlin's Hint for Heidegger's Thinking of the Essence of Language. VON HERRMANN, Friedrich Wilhelm.

"Unlearning to Not Speak". PAGET, M A.

"Voix" et "Phénomène" dans l'Ontologie fondamentale de Heidegger. TAMINIAUX, Jacques.

'Communicatief handelen' als theoretisch grondbegrip. COBBEN, Paul.

'God-Talk' and 'Tacit' Theo-Logic. SCHWEIZER-BJELIC, Shelley and BJELIC, Dusan I.

'If a Lion Could Talk'. CHURCHILL, John.

'Saturated' and 'Unsaturated': Frege and the Nyāya. SHAW, J L.

A coup de dé(s). MAJOR, René.

A Note on the Arabic Term 'Anniyyah/'Aniyyah/'Inniyyah (in Hebrew). HARVEY, Warren Zev and HARVEY, Steven.

About Competence. TIENSON, John L.

Aboutness and Substitutivity. MARTI, Genoveva.

The Absolute Network Theory of Language and Traditional Epistemology. PHILIPSE, Herman.

Absolute Truth Theories for Modal Languages as Theories of Interpretation. LE PORE, Ernest and LOEWER, Barry.

Against Compositionality: The Case of Adjectives. LAHAV, Ran.

Against Direct Reference. DEVITT, Michael.

Against Global Paraconsistency. BATENS, Diderik.

Análisis semántico de los enunciados de creencia. D'ALESSIO, Juan Carlos.

Analyse critique de quelques modèles sémiotiques de l'idéologie (prémière partie). TREMBLAY, Robert.

The Anthropology of 'Semantic Levels' in Music. KARBUSICKY, Vladimir.

Artifacts, Essence and Reference. CHAUDHURY, Mahasweta.

Augustine's Pretence: Another Reading of Wittgenstein's *Philosophical Investigations* 1. WALKER, Margaret Urban.

Aus den Überlegungen über die Moralsprachaspekte (in Polish). RODZINSKI, A.

Avowals in the "Philosophical Investigations": Expression, Reliability, Description. VON SAVIGNY, Eike.

Belief and the Identity of Reference. DONNELLAN, Keith S.

Bergson and the Hegemony of Language. LAHAV, Ran.

The Brain, the Mental Apparatus and the Text: A Post-Structural Neuropsychology. CILLIERS, F P.

Brentano's Criticism of the Correspondence Conception of Truth and Tarski's Semantic Theory. WOLENSKI, Jan.

Bringing It About. SEGERBERG, Krister.

The Cartesian Anxiety in Epistemic Rhetoric: An Assessment of the Literature. BINEHAM, Jeffery L.

Causal Hermits. ROGERSON, Kenneth F.

Ceticismo semântico. DE SOUZA FILHO, Danilo Marcondes.

Changing the Minimal Subject. CARTER, William.

Charity and Ideology: The Field Linguist as Social Critic. RAMBERG, Bjorn T.

Chomsky, Wittgenstein, Bloor: Zum Problem einer wissenssoziologischen Metatheorie der Linguistik. KERTÉSZ, András.

Cinquante-six conceptions de l'androgynie. BOUCHARD, Guy.

Circolarità di condizione in L'homme et le langage di Jean Brun. GONZI, Andrea.

The Co-Reporting Theory of Tensed and Tenseless Sentences. SMITH, Quentin.

The Cognitive Effect of Metaphor. GERHART, Mary and RUSSELL, Allan Melvin.

Commodities, Language, and Desire. BACHARACH, Michael.

Communication, Grice, and Languageless Creatures. CARR, Indira Mahalingam.

Completing the Recovery of Language as an Existential Project. DAVIS, Duane H.

Compositionality, Implicational Logics, and Theories of Grammar. MORRILL, Glyn and CARPENTER, Bob.

Comprehension and Production in Early Lexical Development: A Comment on Stemmer. HARRIS, Margaret.

Concept Acquisition and Ostensive Learning: A Response to Professor Stemmer. PLACE, Ullin T.

The Concept of Phrase Structure. MANASTER-RAMER, Alexis and KAC, Michael B.

Conceptos y propiedades o Predicación y cópula. STRAWSON, P F.

Conceptual Dependency as the Language of Thought. DUNLOP, Charles E M.

Conceptual Schemes and Linguistic Relativism in Relation to Chinese (in Serbo-Croatian). GRAHAM, A C.

Les conditions proto-logiques des langues naturelles. GRANGER, G G.

Connectionism and Three Levels of Nativism. RAMSEY, William and STICH, Stephen.

Conoscenza e semantica. VENTURA, Antonino.

Considerations on Preparation of Societies for Life in Peace. SHIBATA, Shingo.

Content, Thoughts and Definite Descriptions—I. MILLICAN, Peter.

Content, Thoughts and Definite Descriptions—II, The Object of Definite Descriptions. OVER, David.

Contradictory Belief and Cognitive Access. OWENS, Joseph I.

Conversation, Relevance, and Argumentation. HAFT-VAN REES, M Agnes.

Crossroads of Skepticism: Wittgenstein, Derrida, and Ostensive Definition. MC DONALD, Henry.

Cultural History and Cultural Materialism. BERMAN, Ronald.

Currie on Fictional Names. LAMB, Roger.

Da indiferenciação do dizer ao *autómaton* do falar. DO CARMO SILVA, Carlos Henrique.

Das Gestell and *L'écriture*: The Discourse of Expropriation in Heidegger and Derrida. RADLOFF, Bernhard.

Davidson's Omniscient Interpreter. JANSSENS, C J A M and VAN BRAKEL, J.

Davidson's Semantic and Computational Understanding of Language (in Serbo-Croatian). BOJADZIEV, Damjan.

Declaratives Are Not Enough. BELNAP JR, Nuel D.

Demons, Vats and the Cosmos. LESLIE, John.

Derrida and Bhartrhari's Vākyapadīya on the Origin of Language. COWARD, Harold.

Derrida and the Decentered World of K'ou-Chuan: The Deconstruction of Taoist Semiotics. SASO, Michael.

Derrida and the Indeterminacy of Meaning. MILLER, Seumas.

Derrida et la voix de son maitre. BERNET, Rudolf.

Descriptive Pronouns and Donkey Anaphora. NEALE, Stephen.

Les deux sources de l'herméneutique. STEVENS, Bernard.

Dialects of Aestheticism (in Dutch). KUIPER, M.

Did Hobbes Have a Semantic Theory of Truth?. DE JONG, Willem R.

Die Hermeneutik der schriftlichen, mündlichen und innerlichen Rede bei Platon (in Greek). MICHAELIDES, K.

Difficult Friendship. DAVIES, Paul.

Discorso meta-fisico e discorso meta-forico: Derrida. PELLECCHIA, Pasquale.

Discorso meta-forico e discorso meta-fisico: Ricoeur. PELLECCHIA, Pasquale.

Divided Reference. KVART, Igal.

Does Plato Think False Speech is Speech?. RUDEBUSCH, George.

Dos teorías de la referencia en el *Cratilo*. VALDÉS, Margarita M.

Doublures. SALLIS, John and BARET, Françoise (trans).

Du dialogue référentiel au dialogisme transcendantal: L'itinéraire philosophique de Francis Jacques. GREISCH, Jean.

Duas observações sobre a gramática filosófica. MORENO, Arley R.

Dummett's Criteria for Singular Terms. WETZEL, Linda.

E D Hirsch's Misreading of Saul Kripke. SPIKES, Michael.

E-Type Pronouns and Donkey Anaphora. HEIM, Irene.

The Echo of Narcissus: Anxiety, Language and Reflexivity in "Envois". JOHNSON, Cyraina E.

LANGUAGE

Education and Wittgenstein's Philosophy. HAMLYN, D W.

Emilio Betti's Debt to Vico. NOAKES, Susan.

Empirical Versus Epistemological Considerations: A Comment on Stemmer. MORRIS, Michael.

Empiricist Versus Prototype Theories of Language Acquisition. STEMMER, Nathan.

Entre positivisme et anarchie? Trois voies de recherche dans la construction des theories en science litteraire. DECREUS, F.

Épreuves d'écriture—Notes du traducteur. LYOTARD, Jean-François and DERRIDA, Jacques.

Equal Opportunity. WELLMAN, Carl.

Espacialidad de la metáfora. OLIVERAS, Elena.

Ethical Similarities in Human and Animal Social Structures. ELLOS, William J.

Explanation and the Language of Thought. BRADDON-MITCHELL, David and FITZPATRICK, John.

The Explanatory Role of Belief Ascriptions. PATTERSON, Sarah.

An Explanatory Theory of Communicative Intentions. KURODA, S Y.

La expresión de la falsedad y del error en el vocabulario agustiniano de la mentira. SÁNCHEZ MANZANO, M A.

Family Resemblances and the Problem of the Under-Determination of Extension. BELLAIMEY, James E.

A Farewell to Forms of Life. THOMPKINS, E F.

Filosofar abierto. ESSLER, Wilhelm and RIVADULLA, Andrés (trans).

El filosofar y el lenguaje. PIEPER, Josep.

Form and Content in Semantics. WILKS, Yorick.

Forms of Life. EMMETT, Kathleen.

Free Will. SCHEER, Richard.

Frege on the Purpose and Fruitfulness of Definitions. SCHIRN, Matthias.

Frege's Objects of a Quine Special Kind. SCHIRN, Matthias.

From a Normative Point of View. LANCE, Mark and HAWTHORNE, John.

From Stubborn Structure to Double Mirror: The Evolution of Northrop Frye's Theory of Poetic Creation and Response. BOGDAN, Deanne.

Gebrauchssprache und Logik: Eine Philosophiehistorische Notiz zu Frege und Lotze. SCHMIT, Roger.

Genealogies as the Language of Time: A Structural Approach—Anthropological Implications. FROUSSART, Bernard.

Genetic Traits. GIFFORD, Fred.

Glasnostalgia. LLEWELYN, J.

Golden Rules and Golden Bowls. RIGHTER, William.

Groups, I. LANDMAN, Fred.

Groups, II. LANDMAN, Fred.

Gruesome Arithmetic: Kripke's Sceptic Replies. ALLEN, Barry.

Harvey Sacks—Lectures 1964-1965. JEFFERSON, Gail (ed).

Hedging as a Fallacy of Language. JASON, Gary.

Hegel and the Speech of Reconcilation. STOLL, Donald.

Heidegger after Derrida. WOOD, David.

Heidegger and the Problem of Style in Interpretation. HARRIES, Karsten.

Heidegger: Preparing to Read Hölderlin's Germanien. GRUGAN, Arthur A.

How 'Russellian' Was Frege?. BELL, David.

How a Note Denotes. KURKELA, Kari.

How Did We Get From Simulation To Symbol?. BROOK, Donald.

How I Say What You Think. RICHARD, Mark.

How Marxism Became Analytic. MARTIN, Bill.

How Performatives Work. SEARLE, John R.

How to Generalize Grice's Theory of Conversation. ROLF, Eckard.

How to Learn a Language Like a Chimpanzee. GAUKER, Christopher.

How We Refer to Things. CHISHOLM, Roderick M.

Human Noises. STEWART, Donald.

I Think, Therefore I Can: Attribution and Philosophy for Children. ALLEN, Terry.

L'idea di "Storia teoretica o congetturale" negli scritti filosofici e sul linguaggio di Adam Smith. IACONO, Alfonso M.

Die Idee einer existentialontologischen Wendung der Rhetorik in M Heideggers "Sein und Zeit". OESTERREICH, Peter L.

In Defence of Untranslatability. SANKEY, Howard.

Inconmensurabilidad y criterios de identidad de esquemas conceptuales. HIDALGO, Cecilia.

Indexikalität, Wahrnehmung und Bedeutung bei Husserl. BECKER, Wolfgang.

Indirection et interaction conversationnelle. ROVENTA-FRUMUSANI, Daniela.

Intelligence artificielle et signification: À propos des limites et des possibilités des sciences cognitives. MENDONÇA, W P.

Intercultural Rhetorical Differences in Meaning Construction. FOLMAN, Shoshana and SARIG, Gissi.

Interpretation at Risk. MARGOLIS, Joseph.

Interprétation et mentalité prélogique. ENGEL, Pascal.

Interview with Emmanuel Levinas: December 31, 1982. WYSCHOGROD, Edith.

Intrinsic Reference and the New Theory. ADDIS, Laird.

An Investigation of the Lumps of Thought. KRATZER, Angelika.

Is This Any Way to be a Realist?. TIENSON, John L.

Is Translation Possible?. HARRIS, R Thomas.

Jacques Derrida. PETITDEMANGE, Guy.

Kierkegaard and Indirect Communication. LÜBCKE, Poul.

Knowledge and Silence: The Golden Bowl and Moral Philosophy. BRUDNEY, Daniel.

Kripke e le intenzioni di riferimento. VOLTOLINI, Alberto.

L'"infaillibilité" de l'introspection: Autour de Dennett et de Wittgenstein. BOUVERESSE, Jacques.

L'herméneutique comme science rigoureuse selon Emilio Betti (1890-1968). GRONDIN, Jean.

L'unité de l'oeuvre philosophique de Paul Ricoeur. MUKENGEBANTU, Paul.

La méthodologie et l'éthique herméneutiques (in Romanian). MARGA, Andrei.

Langage et raison: Philosophie, linguistique et ce qui leur ressemble. NICOLET, Daniel.

Language Acquisition: Growth or Learning?. SAMPSON, Geoffrey.

Language and the Origin of the Human Imagination: A Vichian Perspective. DANESI, Marcel.

Language and the Problems of Knowledge (in Serbo-Croatian). CHOMSKY, Noam.

Language and Thought in Kant's Theory of Knowledge (in Hebrew). DASCAL, Marcelo and SENDEROWICZ, Yaron.

Language and World View in Ancient China. BAO, Zhiming.

Language as a Cause-Effect Communication System. SAVAGE-RUMBAUGH, E S.

The Language of Architecture. DONOUGHO, Martin.

Language of Cognition—Cognition of Language (in Serbo-Croatian). MARVAN, George J.

Language, Literature, and Art. SIMPSON, Alan.

Le plus pur des batards (l'affirmation sans issue). KRELL, David Farrell and BARET, Françoise (trans).

Leading Out Into the World: Vico's New Education. ENGELL, James.

El lenguaje y la palabra en Tomas de Aquino. LOBATO, Abelardo.

Lenguaje y misterio en Anselmo de Canterbury. BRIANCESCO, Eduardo.

Levinas's Phenomenology of the Other and Language as the Other of Phenomenology. KLEMM, David E.

Lewis' Indexical Argument for World-Relative Actuality. GALE, Richard M.

Life After Difference: The Positions of the Interpreter and the Positionings of the Interpreted. ALTIERI, Charles.

Lingua degli angli e lingua dei bruti. DE MONTICELLI, Roberta and DI FRANCESCO, Michele.

Linguists of All Countries—On Gramsci's Premise of Coherence. HELSLOOT, Niels.

The Logic of Unification in Grammar. KASPER, Robert T and ROUNDS, William C.

La logica di Hegel come testo filosofico (I). COSTA, Filippo.

Logical Atomism in Plato's Theaetetus. RYLE, G.

Logical Form. MAURY, André.

Ludwig Looks at the Necker Cube: The Problem of "Seeing As" as a Clue to Wittgenstein's Philosophy. HINTIKKA, Jaakko and HINTIKKA, Merrill B.

Ludwig Wittgenstein: Personality and Philosophy (in Czechoslovakian). STERN, Joseph P.

Luther, Metaphor, and Theological Language. BIELFELDT, Dennis.

Malcolm on Language and Rules. BAKER, G P and HACKER, P M S.

Meaning N and Meaning NN—An Exposition of the Unformed Gricean Intention. LENKA, Laxminarayan.

Mémoires gauches. STIEGLER, Bernard.

Mental Content and Linguistic Form. STALNAKER, Robert.

Mental Content in Linguistic Form. LYCAN, William G.

Metafisica e teologia della parola. SAINATI, Vittorio.

Metakritik und Sprache: Zu Johann Georg Hamanns Kant-Verständnis und seinen metakritischen Implikationen. MAJETSCHAK, Stefan.

La métaphore sans métaphore: A propos de l' "Orestie". LORAUX, Nicole.

Metaphorical Language, Rhetoric, and Comprehensio: J L Vives and M Nizolio. HIDALGO-SERNA, Emilio and PINTON, Giorgio (trans).

Metaphors and the Symmetry/Asymmetry (in Hebrew). SHEN, Yeshayahu.

Metaphors, Counterfactuals and Music. GRUND, Cynthia.

Metaphysics through Paradox in Eliot's Four Quartets. WIGHT, Doris T.

Might. WILWERDING, Jonathan.

Mikhail Bakhtin's Body Politic: A Phenomenological Dialogics. JUNG, Hwa Yol.

LANGUAGE

Mo-Tzu: Language Utilitarianism. HANSEN, Chad.

Modal Definability in Enriched Languages. GORANKO, Valentin.

Modal Subordination and Pronominal Anaphora in Discourse. ROBERTS, Craige.

Modality, Mechanism and Translational Indeterminacy. MAC INTOSH, Duncan.

Monads, Nonexistent Individuals and Possible Worlds: Reply to Rosenkrantz. CHISHOLM, Roderick M.

Montaigne, Encoder and Decoder, in Propria Persona. JONES, Robert F.

The Moral Atmosphere: Language and Value in Davidson. MARTIN, Bill.

Morris Lazerowitz and Metaphilosophy. REESE, William L.

Le motif de la déconstruction et ses portées politiques. LISSE, M.

Musical Work and Possible Events. RANTALA, Veikko.

Must Rational Preferences Be Transitive?. PHILIPS, Michael.

Narration and Totality. CASCARDI, Anthony J.

Naturalism and the Normativity of Epistemology. MAFFIE, James.

The New Tenseless Theory of Time: A Reply to Smith. OAKLANDER, L Nathan.

Noise at the Threshold. FYNSK, Christopher.

Nom propre et individuation chez Peirce. THIBAUD, P.

Non replica, chiarimento. MORPURGO-TAGLIABUE, Guido.

Nondeterministic ω-Computations and the Analytical Hierarchy. CASTRO, J.

A Note on 'Languages and Language'. HAWTHORNE, John.

A Note on Thomas Hayne and His Relation to Leibniz and Vico. PERCIVAL, W Keith.

Het objectieve waarheidsbegrip in Waarder. KUIPERS, Theo A F.

Of Particles. GALLIE, Roger D.

On *Begriffsgeschichte* Again. RAYNER, Jeremy.

On Davidson and Interpretation. BURDICK, Howard.

On Grice and Language. GRANDY, Richard E.

On Justification Conditional Models of Linguistic Competence. STERN, Cindy D.

On Synonymy and Ontic Modalities. ZABLUDOWSKI, Andrzej.

On the Humility of Mathematical Language. JARDINE, David W.

On the Modalities and Narrativity in Music. TARASTI, Eero.

One Commends Something By Attributing the Property of Goodness To It (Penultimate Word). GOLDSTICK, D.

Orden-desorden, a propósito de *Il nome della rosa*. CASTRO, Edgardo.

P F Strawson and the Social Context in Language (in Serbo-Croatian). VIDANOVIC, Dorde.

Les paradoxes et le langage. SEUREN, Pieter A M.

Parlando di segni, di Hjelmslev e di filosofia del linguaggio. CAPUTO, C.

Parmenides on What There Is. KETCHUM, Richard J.

La parole du philosophe éthicien est-elle crédible?. LEGAULT, Georges A.

Past Looking. HOLLY, Michael Ann.

Phenomenological Deconstruction: Husserl's Method of *Abbau*. EVANS, J Claude.

Philosophy and Literature: Their Relationship in the Works of Paul de Man. MICHIELSEN, Peter.

Philosophy and Style: Wittgenstein and Russell. HUGHES, John.

Plural Noun Phrases and Their Readings: A Reply to Lasersohn. GILLON, Brendan S.

Poetry as the Naming of the Gods. ZAGANO, Phyllis.

Points of View and their Logical Analysis. HAUTAMAKI, Antti.

The Possibility of Film Criticism. POAGUE, Leland and CADBURY, William.

Postscript (1989): To Whom It May Concern. CAVELL, Stanley.

The Pragmatics of What is Said. RECANATI, François.

Préliminaires à une théorie logique des méthodes pratiques (in Romanian). POPA, Cornel.

Prima e terza persona: Un recente contributo alla "Philosophy of Mind". MARRONE, Pierpaolo.

The Principle of Contextual *Bedeutung* and Triadic Semantics with Frege. CANDIESCU, Calin.

Private Irony and Public Decency: Richard Rorty's New Pragmatism. MC CARTHY, Thomas.

The Problem of Normativity Solved or Spinoza's Stand in the Analogy/Anomaly Controversy. KLIJNSMIT, Anthony J.

Quando ser sujeito não é sujeitar-se. SUMARES, Manuel.

Questions sur le langage poétique à partir de Roman Jakobson. MAESSCHALCK, Marc.

Quine's Indeterminacy Thesis. LARSON, David.

Radicals, Conservatives and Moderates in Early Modern Political Thought: A Case of Sandwich Islands Syndrome?. CONDREN, C.

Raising as Function Composition. JACOBSON, Pauline.

Le rationalisme et l'analyse linguistique. AUROUX, Sylvain.

Reading Africa Through Foucault: V Y Mudimbe's Re-affirmation of the Subject. DIAWARA, Manthia.

Reading and the Process of Reading. WINCH, Christopher.

The Real Objective of Mendel's Paper. MONAGHAN, Floyd V and CORCOS, Alain F.

Reference, Intentionality, and Nonexistent Entities. ROSENKRANTZ, Gary.

Règles et langage privé chez Wittgenstein: deux interprétations. SAUVÉ, Denis.

La relation de réfléchissement pensée/langage. ROVENTA-FRUMUSANI, Daniela.

Remarks on the Concept of "Universal Grammar". CORNILESCU, Alexandra.

Remarks on the Concept of Norm. PAULSON, Stanley L.

Remnants of Meaning by Stephen Schiffer. FODOR, Jerry.

Representation, Truth and the Languages of the Arts. HERMERÉN, Göran.

Republic and Politics in Machiavelli and Rousseau. VIROLI, Maurizio.

The Rhetoric of Grammar: Understanding Wittgenstein's Method. BARNETT, William E.

The Rule-Following Considerations. BOGHOSSIAN, Paul A.

Rules, Communities and Judgements. ZALABARDO, José L.

S'entendre parler. LAPORTE, Roger.

Sambandha and Abhisambandha. AKLUJKAR, Ashok.

Searle ed Eco sulla metafora. BURKHARDT, Armin.

Second-order Logic, Foundations, and Rules. SHAPIRO, Stewart.

Seeming to See Red. BAKER, Lynne Rudder.

Semantic Holism Without Semantic Socialism: Twin Earths, Thinking, Language, Bodies, and the World. CASTAÑEDA, Hector-Neri.

Semantic Physiology: Wittgenstein on Pedagogy. MC CARTY, Luise Prior and MC CARTY, Charles.

Semantica, Pragmatica, Atti linguistici: note in margine a una polemica. SBISÀ, Marina.

Semantics for Nonstandard Languages. MURAWSKI, Roman.

Semantics of Proximity: Language and the Other in the Philosophy of Emmanual Levinas. ZIAREK, Krysztof.

Semantics, Conceptual Spaces and the Dimensions of Music. GÄRDENFORS, Peter.

Sens elliptique. NANCY, Jean-Luc.

Sense and Schmidentity. RAMACHANDRAN, Murali.

Sensus Communis in Vico and Gadamer. SCHAEFFER, John D.

Sibboleth ou de la Lettre. GRANEL, Gérard.

Sign and Knowledge. VASILIU, Emanuel.

Significado literal: entre la profunda necesidad de una construcción y la mera nostalgia. CABRERA, Julio.

The Simplicity of the *Tractatus*. ANSCOMBE, Elizabeth.

Skeptizismus und Judentum, mit einer Einleitung und Anmerkungen von Frederick Betz und Jörg Thunecke. MAUTHNER, Fritz.

Socialism, Feminism and Men. MIDDLETON, Peter.

Socrates' Charitable Treatment of Poetry. PAPPAS, Nickolas.

Some Remarks on Bhartrhari's Concept of Pratibhā. TOLA, Fernando and DRAGONETTI, Carmen.

A Speech Act Analysis of Irony. HAVERKATE, Henk.

Speech Act Conditions as Tools for Reconstructing Argumentative Discourse. VAN EEMEREN, Frans H and GROOTENDORST, Rob.

Speech Acts and Arguments. JACOBS, Scott.

Stroud's Defense of Cartesian Scepticism: A 'Linguistic' Response. GLOCK, Hans-Johann.

The Structure and Content of Truth. DAVIDSON, Donald.

Subject as the Intersect Between Semiotics and Symbol (in Serbo-Croation). SPÖRK, Ingrid.

La superacion del analisis logico del lenguaje por medio de la metafisica. SILVA CAMARENA, Juan Manuel.

Suppositions in Argumentation. FISHER, Alec.

Sur la signification logique et linguistique de la négation (in Romanian). BERCEANU, Barbu B.

Sur la structure particulière du dialogue argumentatif. MIHAI, Gheorghe.

Sur le status théorique de la philosophie moderne du langage (in Romanian). COLTESCU, Viorel.

Sur les Wege zur Aussprache *de Heidegger*. DAVID, Pascal.

Syntactic Metaphor: Frege, Wittgenstein and the Limits of a Theory of Meaning. SCHNEIDER, Hans Julius.

Talking Lions and Lion Talk: Davidson on Conceptual Schemes. CRUMLEY, Jack S.

Tempo e linguaggio nel pensiero di Derrida e Lyotard. MAZZARA, Giuseppe.

Tensed Facts. SWINBURNE, Richard.

The Dutch Words 'besef' and 'beseffen' (in Dutch). VERHOEVEN, C.

The Hermeneutical Ways of the Successful Translation (in Hungarian). PAEPCKE, Fritz.

LANGUAGE

The Philosophy of Language in Scholasticism (in Serbo-Croatian). GOMBOCZ, Wolfgang L.

Theological Empiricism: Aspects of Johann Georg Hamann's Reception of Hume. GRAUBNER, Hans.

Theory Discovery from Data with Mixed Quantifiers. KELLY, Kevin T and GLYMOUR, Clark.

A Theory of Command Relations. BARKER, Chris and PULLUM, Geoffrey K.

A Theory of Reference Transmission and Reference Change. BERGER, Alan.

Theory of Speech Acts (in Serbo-Croatian). IVANETIC, Nada.

The Theory of the Sentence in Pūrva Mīmāmsā and Western Philosophy. TABER, John A.

Thoughts and Their Subject: A Study of Wittgenstein's *Tractatus*. KANNISTO, Heikki.

Threats and Illocutions. NICOLOFF, Franck.

Tolerância e interpretação. DASCAL, Marcelo.

Le *Tractatus* de Wittgenstein: Considérations sur le système numérique et la forme aphoristique. HESS, Gérald.

Translation, Art, and Culture. PERRICONE, Christopher.

Transparency and Doubt: Understanding and Interpretation in Pragmatics and in Law. DASCAL, M and WROBLEWSKI, Jerzy.

Trois lectures cartésiennes de la théorie du gouvernement-liage de N Chomsky. POPARDA, Oana.

Truth and Meaning in the Works of Tugendhat and Davidson (in Serbo-Croation). WYLLER, Truls.

Truth as Disclosure: Art, Language, History. GUIGNON, Charles.

Truth Rules, Hoverflies, and the Kripke-Wittgenstein Paradox. MILLIKAN, Ruth Garrett.

Two Consequences of Hinting. TSOHATZIDIS, Savas L.

Understanding Other Cultures: Studies in the Philosophical Problems of Cross-Cultural Interpretation. SANDBACKA, Carola.

Understanding the Language of Thought. POLLOCK, John L.

Uniqueness. KADMON, Nirit.

Vagueness and Incoherence: A Reply to Burns. SCHWARTZ, Stephen P.

Vagueness Implies Cognitivism. SORENSEN, Roy A.

Varieties of Pragmatism. KRAUT, Robert.

Verbal and Pictorial Signification (in Serbo-Croatian). BOZICEVIC, Vanda.

Vico and Bakhtin: A Prolegomenon to Any Future Comparison. JUNG, Hwa Yol.

Vico and Frye: A Note. BAHTI, Timothy.

Vico on Mythic Figuration as Prerequisite for Philosophic Literacy. DANIEL, Stephen H.

Vive la Révolution. DUDMAN, V H.

The Voices of the Medical Record. POIRIER, Suzanne and BRAUNER, Daniel J.

Vom epischen zum logischen sprechen: der spruch des Anaximander. RIEDEL, M.

Ward on Davidson's Refutation of Scepticism. HURTADO, Guillermo.

Les *Weltalter* de Schelling: Un essai de philosophie narrative. MAESSCHALCK, M.

What Do Language Games Measure?. LORENZ, Kuno.

What is a Question?. COHEN, Felix S.

What Is It To Understand a Directive Speech Act?. DORSCHEL, Andreas.

What is Representation? A Reply to Smythe. LLOYD, Dan.

What Should a Theory of Meaning Do?. PLATTS, Mark.

What the Philosophy of Biology Is and Should Be (in Polish). SLAGA, Szczepan W.

What Water Is or Back to Thales. STROLL, Avrum.

What Wittgenstein Wasn't. GILL, Jerry H.

Whose Language Is It Anyway? Some Notes on Idiolects. GEORGE, Alexander.

Why 'Not'?. PRICE, Huw.

Wittgenstein and Kripke on the Nature of Meaning. HORWICH, Paul.

Wittgenstein and Physicalism. HALLER, Rudolf.

Wittgenstein and Sense-Independence of Truth. PUHL, Klaus.

Wittgenstein et la philosophie. COMETTI, Jean-Pierre.

Wittgenstein on Grammar and Analytic Philosophy of Education. RIZVI, Fazal.

Wittgenstein's Genius. LEWIS, Peter.

Wittgenstein, Bodies and Meaning. NEIMAN, Alven M.

Words. KAPLAN, David.

You Can Say *That* Again. LE PORE, Ernest and LOEWER, Barry.

Zur sozialphilosophischen Bedeutung des Sprachbegriffs Wilhelm von Humboldts. SCHILLER, Hans-Ernst.

LANGUAGE ACT(S)

'If a Lion Could Talk'. CHURCHILL, John.

LANGUAGE GAME(S)

The Authority of Language: Heidegger, Wittgenstein, and the Threat of Philosophical Nihilism. EDWARDS, James C.

Quando ser sujeito não é sujeitar-se. SUMARES, Manuel.

The Rhetoric of Grammar: Understanding Wittgenstein's Method. BARNETT, William E.

What Do Language Games Measure?. LORENZ, Kuno.

What if Something Really Unheard-of Happened?. SCHEER, R K.

LAO TZU

Disputers of the TAO: Philosophical Argument in Ancient China. GRAHAM, A C.

Radical Concrete Particularity: Heidegger, Lao Tzu and Chuang Tzu. OWENS, Wayne D.

Taoist Cultural Reality: The Harmony of Aesthetic Order. THOMPSON, Kirill O.

LAO ZI

Lao Zi and the Xia Culture. BO, Wang.

LAPLACE

The Rule of Succession. ZABELL, Sandy L.

LARGE CARDINALS

Believing the Axioms, I. MADDY, Penelope.

Coding Over a Measurable Cardinal. FRIEDMAN, Sy D.

LARMER, R

Miracles as Evidence for Theism. BASINGER, David.

LARMORE, C

Liberalism and Neo-Aristotelianism. PADEN, Roger.

LARRETA, J

La justificación de la democracia: entre la negación de la justificación y la restricción de la democracia. NINO, Carlos Santiago.

LASK, E

Emil Lask and the Crisis of Neo-Kantianism: The Rediscovery of the Primordial World. MOTZKIN, Gabriel.

LATIN

"Averrois Tractatus de Animae Beatitudine" in *A Straight Path: Studies in Medieval Philosophy and Culture*, DAVIDSON, Herbert A.

The *Munus* of Transmitting Human Life: A New Approach to *Humanae Vitae*. SMITH, Janet E.

LATIN AMERICAN

Aspectos rescatables de la cultura premoderna. MANSILLA, H C F.

Las críticas de Leopoldo Zea a Augusto Salazar Bondy. SOBREVILLA, David.

La pregunta por la "filosofia Latinoamericana" como problema filosofico. FORNET-BETANCOURT, Raúl.

LATTICE(S)

Classical Subtheories and Intuitionism. SZYMANEK, Krzysztof.

Decision Problem for Relatively Free Brouwerian Semilattices. IDZIAK, Pawl M.

Hyperidentities of Dyadic Algebras. DENECKE, Klaus.

On Atomic Join-Semilattices. WOLNIEWICZ, Boguslaw.

Quantales and (Noncommutative) Linear Logic. YETTER, David N.

Some Highly Undecidable Lattices. MAGIDOR, M and ROSENTHAL, J W and RUBIN, M and SROUR, G.

LAUDAN, L

Laudan's Normative Naturalism. SIEGEL, Harvey.

The Naturalist Conception of Methodological Standards in Science. DOPPELT, Gerald.

Normative Naturalism and the Role of Philosophy. ROSENBERG, Alexander.

Renormalizing Epistemology. LEPLIN, Jarrett.

Some Remarks on Laudan's Theory of Scientific Rationality. VON ECKARDT, Barbara.

LAUGHTER

"Ist das Lachen philosophisch? Bruchstücke einer Metaphysik des Lachens" in *Agora: Zu Ehren von Rudolph Berlinger*, BLONDEL, Eric.

LAVATER, J

Philosophical Laughter: Vichian Remarks on Umberto Eco's *The Name of the Rose*. VERENE, Donald Phillip.

LAVELLE, L

The Knowledge of Values: A Methodological Introduction. LÓPEZ QUINTÁS, Alfonso (ed).

Louis Lavelle: l'expérience de l'être comme acte. SCHÖNBERGER, Rolf.

LAVOISIER

The Conceptual Structure of the Chemical Revolution. THAGARD, Paul.

LAVOISIER

Lavoisier, Priestley, and the *Philosophes*: Epistemic and Linguistic Dimensions to the Chemical Revolution. MC EVOY, John G.

LAW

see also Jurisprudence, Justice, Property(-ties), Punishment, Right(s)

Agora: Zu Ehren von Rudolph Berlinger. BERLINGER, Rudolph (and other eds).

Arms and Judgment: Law, Morality, and the Conduct of War in the 20th Century. COHEN, Sheldon M.

At the Intersection of Legality and Morality: Hartian Law as Natural Law. SKUBIK, Daniel W.

Civil Disobedience. HARRIS, Paul (ed).

Hobbes: War Among Nations. AIRAKSINEN, Timo (ed).

The Inner Citadel: Essays on Individual Autonomy. CHRISTMAN, John (ed).

Issues in Contemporary Legal Philosophy: The Influence of H L A Hart. GAVISON, Ruth (ed).

Jurisculture, Volume II: India. DORSEY, Gray L.

Justice and Modern Moral Philosophy. REIMAN, Jeffrey.

Liberty and Culture: Essays on the Idea of a Free Society. MACHAN, Tibor R.

Liberty and Justice. DAY, J P.

Medical Ethics: Essays on Abortion and Euthanasia. BARRY, Robert L.

Miscellaneous Writings (Collected Works of John Stuart Mill, Volume 31). ROBSON, John M (ed).

A Moral Military. AXINN, Sidney.

Natural Right and Natural Law: A Critical Introduction (Second Edition). HERVADA, Javier.

Rules, Norms, and Decisions: On the Conditions of Practical and Legal Reasoning. KRATOCHWIL, Friedrich V.

Self-Direction and Political Legitimacy: Rousseau and Herder. BARNARD, F M.

Speech, Crime, and the Uses of Language. GREENAWALT, Kent.

Vico Revisited: Orthodoxy, Naturalism and Science in the Scienca Nuova. BEDANI, Gino.

"Comment: Legal Theory and the Problem of Sense" in *Issues in Contemporary Legal Philosophy: The Influence of H L A Hart,* HART, H L A.

"Comment: The Normativity of Law" in *Issues in Contemporary Legal Philosophy: The Influence of H L A Hart,* MAC CORMICK, Neil.

"Comment: The Normativity of Law" in *Issues in Contemporary Legal Philosophy: The Influence of H L A Hart,* LYONS, David.

"Comment: The Obligation to Obey the Law" in *Issues in Contemporary Legal Philosophy: The Influence of H L A Hart,* GREENAWALT, Kent.

"Comment: The Obligation to Obey the Law" in *Issues in Contemporary Legal Philosophy: The Influence of H L A Hart,* GANS, Chaim.

"Hobbes's Logic of Law" in *Hobbes: War Among Nations,* LAGERSPETZ, Eerik.

"The Morality of Democracy and the Rule of Law" in *Politics and Process,* LETWIN, Shirley Robin.

"The Normativity of Law" in *Issues in Contemporary Legal Philosophy: The Influence of H L A Hart,* POSTEMA, Gerald J.

"Das Versprechen—problemgeschichtliche Aspekte eines rechtsphänomenologischen Paradigmas" in *Agora: Zu Ehren von Rudolph Berlinger,* WILLOWEIT, Dietmar and WILLOWEIT, Hildegard.

"The Right of a State" in Immanuel Kant's *Doctrine of Right.* LUDWIG, Bernd.

American Experience and the Israeli Dilemma. JACOBSOHN, Gary J.

Artificial Intelligence and Law: How To Get There From Here. MC CARTY, L Thorne.

The Assumption of Risk Argument. KATZ, Leo.

Bentham on the Public Character of Law. POSTEMA, Gerald J.

Choice, Character, and Excuse. MOORE, Michael.

Chthonic Themes in Plato's *Republic.* MOORS, Kent F.

Client Taint: The Embarrassment of Rudolph Giuliani. UVILLER, H Richard.

A *Coup d'État* in Law's Empire: Dworkin's Hercules Meets Atlas. PEERENBOOM, Randall P.

Critical Rationalism: The Problem of Method in Social Sciences and Law. ALBERT, Hans.

Defending the Hearsay Rule. KADISH, Mortimer R and DAVIS, Michael.

Defensive Force as an Act of Rescue. FLETCHER, George P.

Della scommessa legislativa sulla discrezionalità dei giudici. MARINI, Gaetano.

Discourse Ethics and the Legitimacy of Law. TUORI, Kaarlo.

An Empowerment Theory of Legal Norms. PAULSON, Stanley L.

Friedrich Hayek's Moral Science. FULLER, Timothy.

Das Gesetz oder das Gute? II, Teil: Alleiniges Prinzip des sittlich guten Willens. SALA, Giovanni B.

Das Gesetz oder das Gute? Zum Ursprung und Sinn des Formalismus in der Ethik Kants. SALA, Giovanni B.

Hart's Rule of Recognition and the United States. GREENAWALT, Kent.

Immediate Legitimacy? Problems of Legitimacy in a Consensually Oriented Application of Law. MÄENPÄÄ, Olli.

The Importance of Knowledge and Trust in the Definition of Death. RIX, Bo Andreassen.

Institutions, Arrangements and Practical Information. MAC CORMICK, Neil.

Kant's Theory of Moral Sensibility: Respect for the Moral Law and the Influence of Inclination. REATH, A.

Law and Morality. BICKENBACH, Jerome E.

Law as a Bridge between Is and Ought. BODENHEIMER, Edgar.

Law as Co-ordination. FINNIS, John M.

Law as Convention. REYNOLDS, Noel B.

The Logic of Time in Law and Legal Expert Systems. MACKAAY, Ejan (and others).

Mens Rea. HAMPTON, Jean.

Morality and Law. LETWIN, Shirley Robin.

Natural Law Elements in Pound's Philosophy of Law?. MC LEAN, Edward B.

Nature, Custom, and Stipulation in Law and Juriprudence. MURPHY, James Bernard.

Neues zum Thema Gerechtigkeit?. STRANZINGER, Rudolf.

Oakeshott on the Authority of Law. FRIEDMAN, Richard B.

On the Common Saying that it is Better that Ten Guilty Persons Escape than that One Innocent Suffer: Pro and Con. REIMAN, Jeffrey and VAN DEN HAAG, Ernest.

On the Legitimacy of Law: A Conceptual Point of View. AARNIO, Aulis.

On the Relationship Between Law and Morality. COLEMAN, Jules.

The Paradox of Blackmail. FEINBERG, Joel.

Philosophy of Law and the Theory of Speech Acts. AMSELEK, Paul.

Plant Closing Ethics Root in American Law. MILLSPAUGH, Peter E.

Pornography as Representation: Aesthetic Considerations. GRACYK, Theodore A.

Pragmatism and Precedent: A Response to Dworkin. SULLIVAN, Michael.

Problems in the Argument of Plato's *Crito.* KAHN, Charles H.

Reason in Law. BOBBIO, Norberto.

Rechtsstaalichkeit als Moment demokratischer politischer Machtausübung. WILL, Rosemarie.

Remarks on the Concept of Norm. PAULSON, Stanley L.

The Rule of Law in the Russian Intellectual Tradition: Pre-Revolutionary Russia, the Soviet Union and Perestroika. WALICKI, Andrzej.

Scientific and Legal Standards of Statistical Evidence in Toxic Tort and Discrimination Suits. CRANOR, Carl and NUTTING, Kurt.

Statutory Interpretation and the Counterfactual Test for Legislative Intention. LEE, Win-Chiat.

Synthesizing Related Rules from Statutes and Cases for Legal Expert Systems. ALLEN, Layman E and PAYTON, Sallyanne and SAXON, Charles S.

Eine Theorie der politischen Gerechtigkeit. KERSTING, Wolfgang.

Thomas Aquinas and Contemporary Ethics of Virtue. STALEY, Kevin M.

Towards a Communication-Concept of Rational Collective Will-Formation: A Thought-Experiment. HABERMAS, Jürgen.

Transparency and Doubt: Understanding and Interpretation in Pragmatics and in Law. DASCAL, M and WROBLEWSKI, Jerzy.

Violence, Law, and the Limits of Morality. CRAGG, A W.

Wittgenstein, Realism, and CLS: Undermining Rule Scepticism. LANDERS, Scott.

LAWLESSNESS

AIDS and Civil Disobedience. SPIERS, Herbert R.

Civil Disobedience in Times of AIDS. NOVICK, Alvin.

Militant Morality: Civil Disobedience and Bioethics. COHEN, Carl.

LAWS

see also Natural Law(s)

Four Decades of Scientific Explanation. SALMON, Wesley C.

Hume and the Problem of Miracles: A Solution. LEVINE, Michael P.

Laws and Symmetry. VAN FRAASSEN, Bas C.

Of the Laws of Ecclesiastical Polity (Preface, Book I, Book VIII), Richard Hooker. MC GRADE, Arthur Stephen (ed).

The Spirit of the Laws: Charles Montesquieu. COHLER, Anne M (trans).

"Living Will Statutes: Good Public Policy?" in *Advance Directives in Medicine,* WHITE, W D.

The Abortion Struggle in America. WARREN, Mary Anne.

AIDS, Society and Morality—A Philosophical Survey. HÄYRY, Heta and HÄYRY, Matti.

Defending Laws in the Social Sciences. KINCAID, Harold.

Disjunctive Laws. OWENS, David.

Do We Need a Restriction of the Law of Contradiction?. MATERNA, Pavel.

The Duty to Rescue and the Slippery Slope Problem. SMITH, Patricia.

Ethical Dilemmas and the Disputing Process: Organizations and Societies. MATHEWS, M Cash.

LAWS

Idealized Laws, Antirealism, and Applied Science: A Case in Hydrogeology. SHRADER-FRECHETTE, K S.

A Natural Explanation of the Existence and Laws of Our Universe. SMITH, Quentin.

On Necessary Relations Between Law and Morality. ALEXY, Robert.

On the Interpretation of Laws. FRIEDMAN, Lawrence M.

Ontique et deontique. KALINOWSKI, Georges.

Reconceiving Miracles. GILMAN, James E.

Recreational Drugs and Paternalism. HUSAK, Douglas N.

Variations on a Given Theme. KERR-LAWSON, Angus.

LAWYER(S)

Business Regulation, Business Ethics and the Professional Employee. MACKIE, Karl J.

Client Taint: The Embarrassment of Rudolph Giuliani. UVILLER, H Richard.

Should Lawyers Listen to Philosophers about Legal Ethics?. SMITH, M B E.

LAZEROWITZ, M

Morris Lazerowitz and Metaphilosophy. REESE, William L.

LEADERSHIP

Ethics in Practice: Managing the Moral Corporation. ANDREWS, Kenneth R (ed).

Androgyny and Leadership Style. KORABIK, Karen.

Individual and Organizational Characteristics of Women in Managerial Leadership. ROWNEY, J I A and CAHOON, A R.

LEARNING

Understanding Plato. MELLING, David J.

The Voice of Liberal Learning: Michael Oakeshott on Education. FULLER, Timothy (ed).

'God-Talk' and 'Tacit' Theo-Logic. SCHWEIZER-BJELIC, Shelley and BJELIC, Dusan I.

Artistic Learning: What and Where Is It?. WOLF, Dennie.

Concept Acquisition and Ostensive Learning: A Response to Professor Stemmer. PLACE, Ullin T.

Learning and Pleasure: Early American Perspectives. CASEMENT, William.

Psychoeducational Assessment Practices for the Learning Disabled: A Philosophical Analysis. DURAN, Jane.

Robots that Learn: A Test of Intelligence. SUPPES, Patrick and CRANGLE, Colleen.

Teaching, Learning and Ontological Dependence. PEARSON, Allen T.

Two "Representative" Approaches to the Learning Problem. ORTON, Robert E.

LEARNING THEORY

Managing Philosophical Discussions. KYLE, Judy A.

Moral Conventions and Moral Lessons. FULLINWIDER, Robert K.

Philosophy and Machine Learning. THAGARD, Paul.

Self-Knowledge and the Modern Mode of Learning. BLITS, Jan H.

LEBACQZ, K

Organized Religion: New Target for Professional Ethics?. BATTIN, Margaret P.

LEDER, D

Medical Hermeneutics: Where is the "Text" We are Interpreting. BARON, Richard J.

LEE, J

Causation, Transitivity, and Causal Relata. HOLT, Dale Lynn.

LEFT

Left-Wing Elitism: Adorno on Popular Culture. BAUGH, Bruce.

LEGAL

Issues in Contemporary Legal Philosophy: The Influence of H L A Hart. GAVISON, Ruth (ed).

Justifying Legal Punishment. PRIMORATZ, Igor.

"Comment: A Theory of Complicity" in Issues in Contemporary Legal Philosophy: The Influence of H L A Hart, GUR-ARYE, Miriam.

"Comment: Intentions and Mens Rea" in Issues in Contemporary Legal Philosophy: The Influence of H L A Hart, HEYD, David.

"Comment: Legal Theory and the Problem of Sense" in Issues in Contemporary Legal Philosophy: The Influence of H L A Hart, GAVISON, Ruth.

"Legal Theory and the Problem of Sense" in Issues in Contemporary Legal Philosophy: The Influence of H L A Hart, DWORKIN, Ronald.

"The Middle Way in the Philosophy of Punishment" in Issues in Contemporary Legal Philosophy: The Influence of H L A Hart, PRIMORATZ, Igor.

"Positivism and the Foundations of Legal Authority" in Issues in Contemporary Legal Philosophy: The Influence of H L A Hart, SARTORIUS, Rolf.

AIDS and Bowers versus Hardwick. PIERCE, Christine.

Deontic Logic and Legal Knowledge Representation. JONES, Andrew J I.

Does the Threat of AIDS Create Difficulties for Lord Devlin's Critics?. SCHEDLER, George.

Insider Trading: An Ethical Appraisal. IRVINE, William B.

Justice and the Legal Profession. GRCIC, Joseph.

A Legal and Economic Analysis of Insider Trading: Establishing an Appropriate Sphere of Regulation. SALBU, Steven R.

Three Generations of Computerized Systems for Public Administration and Implications for Legal Decision-Making. BING, Jon.

The Use and Abuse of Legal Theory: A Reply to Fish. BARASH, Carol Isaacson.

Why We Mean What We Say: The History and Use of 'Corporate Social Responsibility'. HETZNER, Candace.

LEGAL ETHICS

Should Lawyers Listen to Philosophers about Legal Ethics?. SMITH, M B E.

LEGAL POSITIVISM

At the Intersection of Legality and Morality: Hartian Law as Natural Law. SKUBIK, Daniel W.

Judges Taken Too Seriously: Professor Dworkin's Views on Jurisprudence. TROPER, Michel.

Law and Morality. BICKENBACH, Jerome E.

Law as a Bridge between Is and Ought. BODENHEIMER, Edgar.

On Necessary Relations Between Law and Morality. ALEXY, Robert.

On the Relationship Between Law and Morality. COLEMAN, Jules.

Raz and Legal Positivism. DARE, Tim.

The Varieties and Limitations of Legal Positivism. OTT, Walter.

LEGAL REASONING

Artificial Intelligence and Law: How To Get There From Here. MC CARTY, L Thorne.

The Burden of Decision. CAPRON, Alexander Morgan.

Domination, Legitimation and Law: Introducing Critical Legal Studies. PEIRCE, Michael.

The Fundamental Features of Legal Rationality. GARDIES, Jean-Louis.

Institutions, Arrangements and Practical Information. MAC CORMICK, Neil.

Legal Concepts in a Natural Language Based Expert System. LEHMANN, Hubert.

Legal Reasoning as a Special Case of Moral Reasoning. PECZENIK, Aleksander.

On Legal Proof. BIRMINGHAM, Robert L.

Reason in Law. BOBBIO, Norberto.

The Use of Logical Models in Legal Problem Solving. KOWALSKI, Robert and SERGOT, Marek.

LEGAL RESPONSIBILITY(-TIES)

The Contribution of Nicomachean Ethics iii 5 to Aristotle's Theory of Responsibility. CURREN, Randall.

LEGAL RIGHT(S)

The Moral Foundation of Rights. SUMNER, L W.

A Note on the Legal Liberties of Children as Distinguished from Adults. VETTERLING-BRAGGIN, Mary.

LEGAL SYSTEM(S)

Artificial Intelligence and Law: How To Get There From Here. MC CARTY, L Thorne.

The Ideal Socio-Legal Order: Its "Rule of Law" Dimension. SUMMERS, Robert S.

Moral Rights and Duties in Wicked Legal Systems. TEN, C L.

On the Interpretation of Laws. FRIEDMAN, Lawrence M.

A Pragmatic Version of Natural Law. WALTER, Edward.

The Traditionality of Statutes. KRYGIER, Martin.

LEGALISM

The Ethics of Legalism. MAC CORMICK, Neil.

La filosofia penale di Ippodamo e la cultura giuridica dei sofisti. ROSSETTI, Livio.

Natural Law in the Huang-Lao Boshu. PEERENBOOM, R P.

To Discover Again Marriage. HERVADA, Javier.

LEGALITY

Final Choices: Autonomy in Health Care Decisions. SMITH, George P.

Reducing Legal Realism to Natural Law. MILLER, Myron M.

LEGISLATION

Art of Judgement. CAYGILL, Howard.

Character Versus Codes: Models for Research Ethics. LOMBARDI, Louis G.

The Use of Logical Models in Legal Problem Solving. KOWALSKI, Robert and SERGOT, Marek.

LEGITIMACY

Self-Direction and Political Legitimacy: Rousseau and Herder. BARNARD, F M.

Discourse Ethics and the Legitimacy of Law. TUORI, Kaarlo.

LEGITIMACY

The Enlightenment's Talking Cure: Habermas, *Legitimation Crisis*, and the Recent Political Landscape. MARTIN, Bill.

Immediate Legitimacy? Problems of Legitimacy in a Consensually Oriented Application of Law. MÄENPÄÄ, Olli.

La légitimité. GOYARD-FABRE, Simone.

Made by Contrivance and the Consent of Men. DEN HARTOGH, Govert.

On the Legitimacy of Law: A Conceptual Point of View. AARNIO, Aulis.

The State and Legitimacy. BARRY, Norman.

Towards a New Social Contract. FISHKIN, James S.

LEGITIMATION

Derrida's Deconstruction of the Ideal of Legitimation. CUTROFELLO, Andrew.

On Justice and Legitimation: A Critique of Jürgen Habermas' Concept of "Historical Reconstructivism". BALABAN, Oded.

LEHRER, K

The Current State of the Coherence Theory. BENDER, John W (ed).

"Fundamental Troubles with the Coherence Theory" in *The Current State of the Coherence Theory*, DAVIS, Wayne A and BENDER, John W.

"How Reasonable is Lehrer's Coherence Theory? Beats Me" in *The Current State of the Coherence Theory*, PETERSON, Philip.

"Lehrer's Coherence Theory of Knowledge" in *The Current State of the Coherence Theory*, FELDMAN, Richard.

"Lehrer's Coherentism and the Isolation Objection" in *The Current State of the Coherence Theory*, MOSER, Paul K.

"Personal Coherence, Objectivity, and Reliability" in *The Current State of the Coherence Theory*, MATTEY, G J.

Más allá del escepticismo, a nuestro leal saber y entender. SOSA, Ernesto.

LEIBNIZ

Cartesian Logic: An Essay on Descartes's Conception of Inference. GAUKROGER, Stephen.

A Critical Exposition of the Philosophy of Leibniz. RUSSELL, Bertrand.

Elements of Modern Philosophy: Descartes through Kant. BRENNER, William H.

Kants Theorie des Verstandes. SEEBOHM, Thomas M (ed).

"The 'Universal Thinking Machine', or on the Genesis of Schematized Reasoning in the 17th Century" in *Scientific Knowledge Socialized*, KRÄMER-FRIEDRICH, Sybille.

"Bedeutung", "Idee" und "Begriff": Zur Behandlung einiger bedeutungstheorietischer Paradoxien durch Leibniz. ROS, Arno.

The *A Priori* Method and the *Actio* Concept Revised. RANEA, Alberto Guillermo.

Are There Corporeal Substances for Leibnitz? A Reaction to Stuart Brown. SILVA DE CHOUDENS, José R.

Ars inveniendi et théorie des modèles. BENIS-SINACEUR, Hourya.

Bernard Nieuwentijt and the Leibnizian Calculus. VERMIJ, R H.

Ciencia e historia en Leibniz. RACIONERO, Quitín.

Contingencia y Analiticidad en Leibniz. ZÜRCHER, Joyce M.

Cum Deus Calculat—God's Evaluation of Possible Worlds and Logical Calculus. RONCAGLIA, Gino.

Das Vollkommenheitsprinzip bei Leibniz als Grund der Kontingenz. ROLDÁN PANADERO, Concha.

La doble significación científica y filosófica de la evolución del concepto de fuerza de Descartes a Euler. ARANA, Juan.

Evolución de los derechos humanos en Spinoza y en Leibniz. VERGES, S.

La justificación del mal y el nacimiento de la Estética: Leibniz y Baumgarten. ORTIZ IBARZ, José M.

Leibniz and the Problem of Induction. WESTPHAL, Jonathan.

Leibniz on Locke on Weakness of Will. VAILATI, Ezio.

Leibniz und Ortega y Gasset. DE SALAS ORTUETA, Jaime.

Leibniz's Complete Propositional Logic. CASTAÑEDA, Hector-Neri.

Leibniz's Nachklänge im Denken und in der Dichtung von Mihai Eminescu. BOBOC, Alexandru.

Leibniz, Transubstantiation and the Relation between Pure and Applied Philosophy. ARMOUR, Leslie.

A Leibnizian Cosmological Argument. LEFTOW, Brian.

Mereology in Leibniz's Logic and Philosophy. BURKHARDT, Hans and DEGEN, Wolfgang.

La metafora dei "due labirinti" e le sue implicazioni nel pensiero di Leibniz. POMA, Andrea.

Momenti della teoria leibniziana della sostanza nel carteggio con Arnauld. DELCÓ, Alessandro.

Natural Theology and the Concept of Perfection in Descartes, Spinoza and Leibniz. WEBB, Mark O.

A Note on Thomas Hayne and His Relation to Leibniz and Vico. PERCIVAL, W Keith.

Occasional Identity. GALLOIS, André.

On Leibniz's Essay *Mathesis rationis*. LENZEN, Wolfgang.

Relations and Reduction in Leibniz. COVER, J A.

Some Misconceptions about Leibniz and the Calculi of 1679. VAN RIJEN, Jeroen.

A Systematical Approach to Leibniz's Theory of Relations and Relational Sentences. MUGNAI, Massimo.

La trattazione dell'argomento ontologico nel carteggio Leibniz-Jaquelot (1702-1704). TORTOLONE, Gian Michele.

LEIBNIZ'S LAW

Unsuccessful Revisions of CCT. RAMACHANDRAN, Murali.

LEISURE

The Metaphysics of Leisure. COOPER, Wesley E.

LEMMON, E

A General Logic. SLANEY, John.

LENIN

An Argumentation-Analysis of a Central Part of Lenin's Political Logic. SMIT, P A.

Bedingungen für die Aneignung und Verbreitung des Marxismus-Leninismus in afrikanischen ländern. BASTOS, Feliciano Moreira.

Marxism and Conceptual Scholasticism. KOZYR-KOWALSKI, Stanislaw and OSZKODAR, Zbigniew (trans).

On the Contemporary Theory of Socialism (The October Revolution and Perestroika). SHEVCHENKO, V N.

Theoretische und methodologische Probleme der Erforschung und Propagierung der Geschichte. KNAPPE, Ulrich.

Der Weg eines Mitstreiters und Kampfgefährten Lenins zum Marxismus. HEDELER, Wladislaw.

What Restoring Leninism Means. DAHM, Helmut and SWIDERSKI, E M (trans).

Zum Philosophieverständnis bedeutender Persönlichkeiten der II, Internationale. WRONA, Vera.

Zur methodologischen Bedeutung des Leninschen Prinzips der "Zurückführung des Individuellen auf das Soziale". DANYEL, Jürgen.

LENINISM

The Thought of Mao Tse-Tung. SCHRAM, Stuart.

Leninismo y Marxismo en *Historia y Conciencia de Clases*. GIGLIOLI, Giovanna.

Wirtschaftslehre als Heilslehre. ALEKSANDROWICZ, Dariusz.

LEONARDESCU, C

La morale dans le contexte des sciences de l'homme chez Constantin Leonardescu (in Romanian). COBIANU, Elena.

LEOPARDI, G

Between Infinity and Community: Notes on Materialism in Spinoza and Leopardi. NEGRI, Antonio.

Leopardi e il nichilismo. CARACCIOLO, Alberto.

La teoria dello spazio immaginario in Leopardi. LO BUE, Salvatore.

LEOPOLD, A

Environmental Ethics and Political Conflict: A View from California. MERCHANT, Carolyn.

The Metaphysical Transition in Farming: From the Newtonian-Mechanical to the Eltonian Ecological. CALLICOTT, J Baird.

LEPLIN, J

Normative Naturalism. LAUDAN, Larry.

LEROUX, P

La risposta di Leroux a Lamennais: Il concetto di Trinità come soluzione del problema sociale. FIORENTINO, Fernando.

LESBIAN

Lesbian Angels and Other Matters. ZITA, Jacquelyn.

More Dyke Methods. TREBILCOT, Joyce.

LESNIEWSKI, S

Lesniewski's Strategy and Modal Logic. KEARNS, John T.

LESSING

Kierkegaard's Debt to Lessing: Response to Whisenant. MICHALSON JR, Gordon E.

Kierkegaard's Use of Lessing. WHISENANT, James.

LETTER(S)

Per una storia dell'estetica nel Settecento: Le idee divulgate dal periodico "Il Caffè". SCILIRONI, Carlo.

LEVEL(S)

The Anthropology of 'Semantic Levels' in Music. KARBUSICKY, Vladimir.

David Owens on Levels of Explanation. NEANDER, Karen and MENZIES, Peter.

LEVI, E

Analogical Arguings and Explainings. JOHNSON, Fred.

LEVI, I

Are Theories of Rationality Empirically Testable?. SMOKLER, Howard.

Levi's Decision Theory. LEEDS, Stephen.

Reflective Modalities and Theory Change. FUHRMANN, André.

LEVI-STRAUSS, C

Paths Toward a Clearing: Radical Empiricism and Ethnographic Inquiry. JACKSON, Michael.

Rhetorica II—Spiegelungen des Geistes: Sprachfiguren bei Vico und L Strauss. MAINBERGER, Gonsalv K.

Anthropology on the Boundary and the Boundary in Anthropology. MARTIN, Dan.

LEVIN, M

Contractarianism without Foundations. SCHMIDTZ, David.

LEVINAS, E

"Absolute Positivity and Ultrapositivity: Husserl and Levinas" in The Question of the Other: Essays in Contemporary Continental Philosophy, COHEN, Richard A.

"Derrida, Levinas and Violence" in Derrida and Deconstruction, WYSCHOGROD, Edith.

"From Intentionality to Responsibility: On Levinas's Philosophy of Language" in The Question of the Other: Essays in Contemporary Continental Philosophy, PEPERZAK, Adriaan.

"Rereading Totality and Infinity" in The Question of the Other: Essays in Contemporary Continental Philosophy, BERNASCONI, Robert L.

Der Andere als Zukunft und Gegenwart. RÖMPP, Georg.

Difficult Friendship. DAVIES, Paul.

From Phenomenology to Liberation: The Displacement of History and Theology in Levinas's Totality and Infinity. MESKIN, Jacob.

L'idea di creazione ex nihilo e la libertà nel pensiero di e Levinas. SIGNORINI, Alberto.

Interview with Emmanuel Levinas: December 31, 1982. WYSCHOGROD, Edith.

L'autre et l'immanence. GUILLAMAUD, Patrice.

Levinas and Hegel on the Woman as Home: A Comparison (in Dutch). BRÜGGEMAN-KRUIJFF, Atie T.

Levinas's Phenomenology of the Other and Language as the Other of Phenomenology. KLEMM, David E.

Non-in-difference in the Thought of Emmanuel Levinas and Franz Rosenzweig. COHEN, Richard.

Ontological Responsibility and the Poetics of Nature. LLEWELYN, John.

Philosophical Premises of Levinas' Conception of Judaism. LORENC, Iwona and PETROWICZ, Lech (trans).

Semantics of Proximity: Language and the Other in the Philosophy of Emmanual Levinas. ZIAREK, Krysztof.

Substitution: Marcel and Levinas. GIBBS, Robert B.

Tempo e linguaggio nel pensiero di Derrida e Lyotard. MAZZARA, Giuseppe.

To Welcome the Other: Totality and Theory in Levinas and Adorno. FLOYD, Wayne W.

Visage Versus Visages. BAUM, Mylène.

LEVINE, A

Capitalism, State Bureaucratic Socialism and Freedom. NIELSEN, Kai.

LEVY-BRUHL, L

Le cas Lévy-Bruhl. MERLLIÉ, Dominique.

La correspondance Bergson/Lévy-Bruhl—Lettres à L Lévy-Bruhl (1889-1932). SOULEZ, Philippe and BERGSON, Henri.

Extrait d'une lettre à L Lévy-Bruhl (1904). MARITAIN, J.

Intelligence artificielle et mentalité primitive. JORION, Paul.

Interprétation et mentalité prélogique. ENGEL, Pascal.

Lévy-Bruhl et Durkheim: Notes biographiques en marge d'une correspondance—Lettres à L Lévy-Bruhl (1894-1915). MERLLIÉ, Dominique and DURKHEIM, Emile.

Lévy-Bruhl et Hegel. BOURGOIS, Bernard.

Notes et documents sur "Le Descartes de L Lévy-Bruhl". CAVAILLÉ, Jean-Pierre.

LEWIS

Two Concepts of the Given in C I Lewis: Realism and Foundationalism. GOWANS, Christopher W.

LEWIS, C

Anges et hobbits: le sens des mondes possibles. LACOSTE, Jean-Yves.

Neurophilosophy and the Logic-Causation Argument. KIAMIE, Kimberly A.

LEWIS, D

A Combinatorial Theory of Possibility. ARMSTRONG, D M.

Laws and Symmetry. VAN FRAASSEN, Bas C.

Mind-Body Identity Theories. MACDONALD, Cynthia.

Auctions, Lotteries, and the Punishment of Attempts. DUFF, R A.

Contingent Identity in Counterpart Theory. RAMACHANDRAN, Murali.

Counterfactuals for Free. CREATH, Richard.

Deontic Paradox and Conditional Obligation. TOMBERLIN, James E.

The Humean Tradition. CARROLL, John.

Lewis' Indexical Argument for World-Relative Actuality. GALE, Richard M.

Matter, Motion and Humean Supervenience. ROBINSON, Denis.

A Note on 'Languages and Language'. HAWTHORNE, John.

Probabilistic Causation and Causal Processes: A Critique of Lewis. MENZIES, Peter.

Rationality and Salience. GILBERT, Margaret.

Rationality, Coordination, and Convention. GILBERT, Margaret.

The Verification Principle: Another Puncture—Another Patch. WRIGHT, Crispin.

LEXICON(S)

Handlexikon zur Wissenschaftstheorie. SEIFFERT, Helmut.

LIABILITY

An Essay on Moral Responsibility. ZIMMERMAN, Michael J.

The Contribution of Nicomachean Ethics iii 5 to Aristotle's Theory of Responsibility. CURREN, Randall.

Drugs in the Womb: The Newest Battlefield in the War on Drugs. LOGLI, Paul A.

Protecting Fetuses from Prenatal Hazards: Whose Crimes? What Punishment?. NOLAN, Kathleen.

Reconsidering the Relationship among Voluntary Acts, Strict Liability, and Negligence in Criminal Law. ALEXANDER, Larry.

LIANG QICHAO

Liang Qichao and the Problematic of Social Change (in Serbo-Croatian). PFISTER, Lauren.

LIAR

Liar Syllogisms. DRANGE, Theodore M.

LIAR'S PARADOX

Charles Parsons on the Liar Paradox. SCHMIDTZ, David.

The Diagonal Argument and the Liar. SIMMONS, Keith.

A Representational Account of Mutual Belief. KOONS, Robert C.

LIBERAL EDUCATION

The Voice of Liberal Learning: Michael Oakeshott on Education. FULLER, Timothy (ed).

Applied Liberal Education for Engineers. LUGENBIEHL, Heinz C.

Moral Education, Liberal Education, and Model Building. FRENCH, Peter A.

LIBERALISM

Liberal Justice and the Marxist Critique of Education: A Study of Conflicting Research Programs. STRIKE, Kenneth A.

Unapologetic Theology: A Christian Voice in a Pluralistic Conversation. PLACHER, William C.

The Unvarnished Doctrine: Locke, Liberalism, and the American Revolution. DWORETZ, Steven M.

"David Hume: Crusading Empiricist, Skeptical Liberal" in Knowledge and Politics, HERZOG, Don.

"Liberalism and Moral Education" in Inquiries into Values: The Inaugural Session of the International Society for Value Inquiry, VAN WYK, Robert.

"Otto Neurath: From Authoritarian Liberalism to Empiricism" in Knowledge and Politics, FREUDENTHAL, Gideon.

"Patriotism and Liberal Morality" in Mind, Value and Culture: Essays in Honor of E M Adams, BARON, Marcia.

Alasdair MacIntyre: The Virtue of Tradition. ALMOND, Brenda.

Arendt's Politics: The Elusive Search for Substance. SCHWARTZ, Joseph M.

Beyond Liberalism and Communitarianism: Towards a Critical Theory of Social Justice. DOPPELT, G.

Classical Liberalism and its Crisis of Identity. VINCENT, Andrew.

Communitarian and Liberal Theories of the Good. PAUL, Jeffrey and MILLER JR, Fred D.

The Communitarian Critique of Liberalism. WALZER, Michael.

A Comparative Study of the Representational Paradigms Between Liberalism and Socialism. KE, Gang.

The Complexities of Spontaneous Order. DOBUZINSKIS, Laurent.

Cremonini e le origini del libertinismo. BOSCO, Domenico.

A Definition of Negative Liberty. PETTIT, Philip.

Dilemmas of Plant Closing Policy in Liberal Society: Equality, Rights, Justice. LEVIN-WALDMAN, Oren M.

The End of History, and the Return of History. GRIER, Philip T.

The Epistemology of Pluralism: the Basis of Liberal Philosophy. SMART, Ninian.

LIBERALISM

F A Hayek, ce pourfendeur des droits sociaux. GIROUX, France.
Facing Diversity: The Case of Epistemic Abstinence. RAZ, Joseph.
Foucault's Critique of the Liberal Individual. GRUBER, David F.
Friedrich Hayek's Moral Science. FULLER, Timothy.
Group Rights. MC DONALD, Ian.
Hegel, die Französische Revolution und die liberale Tradition. LOSURDO, Domenico.
The Impossibility of a Paretian Loyalist. GÄRDENFORS, Peter and PETTIT, Philip.
Knowing and Believing in the Original Position. CORLETT, J A.
Liberal and Socialist Egalitarianism. NIELSEN, Kai.
Liberal and Socialist Egalitarianism. NIELSEN, Kai.
Liberal Autonomy. LOMASKY, Loren E.
The Liberal Constitution: Rational Design or Evolution?. BARRY, Norman P.
Liberal Goods. GEISE, J P.
Liberal Neutrality: A Reply to James Fishkin. LARMORE, Charles.
Liberal Values vs Liberal Social Philosophy. CAPALDI, Nicholas.
The Liberal/Communitarian Controversy and Communicative Ethics. BAYNES, K.
Liberalism and Liberty: the Fragility of a Tradition. GRAHAM, Keith.
Liberalism and Natural End Ethics. RASMUSSEN, Douglas B.
Liberalism and Neo-Aristotelianism. PADEN, Roger.
Liberalism and Post-Modern Hermeneutics. NEAMAN, Elliot Yale.
Liberalism, Liberty, and Neutrality. DE MARNEFFE, Peter.
Life, Liberty and Exploitation. RYAN, Cheyney.
The Means of Analysis and the Future of Liberalism: A Response to Hariman. STOESZ, David.
Michael Oakeshott as Liberal Theorist. FRANCO, Paul.
Mill's and Other Liberalisms. GRAY, John.
Morality without Moral Judgment. PRZELECKI, Marian.
Natural Rights Liberalism. MACHAN, Tibor R.
Neutrality and Utility. ARNESON, Richard J.
Op zoek naar een pragmatisch ethos. HOUTEPEN, Rob.
Ortsbestimmungen des Politischen: Neuere Literatur zu Thomas Hobbes. ANGEHRN, Emil.
Paternalism and Democracy. SMILEY, Marion.
Paternalism, Utility and Fairness. ARNESON, Richard J.
Political Liberalism. LARMORE, Charles.
The Politics of Justification. MACEDO, Stephen.
Recenti studi sullo Hegel politico. BONACINA, Giovanni.
The Retreat of the Political in the Modern Age: Jean-Luc Nancy on Totalitarianism and Community. INGRAM, David.
The Rule of Law in Contemporary Liberal Theory. WALDRON, Jeremy.
Spinoza jenseits von Hobbes und Rousseau. GEISMANN, Georg.
Strong Democracy, The Ethic of Caring and Civil Education. PRESKILL, Stephen.
Taking Drugs Seriously (Liberal Paternalism and the Rationality of Preferences). CUDD, Ann E.
The Theological-Political Tension in Liberalism. FULLER, Timothy.
Timely Meditations. RÉE, Jonathan.
Towards a Theory of Age-Group Justice. JECKER, Nancy S.
Whitehead and the New Liberals on Social Progress. MORRIS, Randall C.

LIBERATION

Traditions, Tyranny, and Utopias: Essays in the Politics of Awareness. NANDY, Ashis.
"Liberation and Values" in *The Social Context and Values: Perspectives of the Americas*, DY JR, Manuel B.
"Liberation as Autonomy and Responsibility" in *The Social Context and Values: Perspectives of the Americas*, LOIACONO, James.
Alien Gods in Black Experience. SMITH JR, Archie.
La deliberación en Hobbes. COSTA, Margarita.
Dialéctica de la Revolución: Hegel, Schelling y Hölderlin ante la Revolución Francesa. INNERARITY, Daniel.
Gramsci, Mariàtegui e la teologia della liberazione. PROTO, M.

LIBERATION THEOLOGY

Ethics and Community. DUSSEL, Enrique D.
The Political Theory of Liberation Theology: Toward a Reconvergence of Social Value and Science. POTTENGER, John R.
"Cornel West's Postmodern Theology" in *Varieties of Postmodern Theology*, BEARDSLEE, William A.
"Liberation Theology and Postmodern Philosophy: A Response to Cornel West" in *Varieties of Postmodern Theology*, GRIFFIN, David Ray.
Christological Grounds for Liberation Praxis. PREGEANT, Russell.
From Phenomenology to Liberation: The Displacement of History and Theology in Levinas's Totality and Infinity. MESKIN, Jacob.
Process Theology and Black Liberation: Testing the Whiteheadian

Metaphysical Foundations. YOUNG, Henry James.

LIBERTARIANISM

The Libertarian Idea. NARVESON, Jan.
The Moral Case for the Free Market Economy: A Philosophical Argument. MACHAN, Tibor R.
Building Bridges to the Right: Libertarians, Conservatives, and Humanists. HUDGINS, Edward.
Is Libertarian Free Will Worth Wanting?. SMILANSKY, Saul.
The Libertarian Utopia: Robert Nozick and Aleksander Swietochowski. MIKLASZEWSKA, Justyna.
Libertarianism Versus Secular Humanism?. GORDON, David.
The New Consensus: The Fukuyama Thesis. FRIEDMAN, Jeffrey.
New Gods for Old: In Defense of Libertarianism. BRADFORD, R W.
Van Inwagen on the 'Obviousness' of Libertarian Moral Responsibility. SMILANSKY, Saul.

LIBERTY

Contre nous de la tyrannie: Des relations idéologiques entre Lumières et Révolution. BOULAD-AYOUB, Josiane.
Essays on Political Morality. HARE, R M.
Humanisme de la liberté et philosophie de la justice, Tome II. TRIGEAUD, Jean-Marc.
The Inner Citadel: Essays on Individual Autonomy. CHRISTMAN, John (ed).
John Stuart Mill. SKORUPSKI, John.
The Libertarian Idea. NARVESON, Jan.
Liberty and Culture: Essays on the Idea of a Free Society. MACHAN, Tibor R.
Liberty and Justice. DAY, J P.
Il Potere e l'Ipotesi: Tappe di una filosofia delle Funzioni. FRANCHINI, Raffaello.
Reflective Wisdom: Richard Taylor on Issues That Matter. DONNELLY, John (ed).
The Spirit of the Laws: Charles Montesquieu. COHLER, Anne M (trans).
"John Locke, David Fordyce, and Jean-Jacques Rousseau: On Liberty" in *Early Modern Philosophy II*, TATTON, Susan.
Le "Considèrations" di Montesquieu a 250 anni dalla pubblicazione. LOCHE, Annamaria.
Costituzione e realità attuale: A proposito di un convegno tenuto a Lecce. LIPPOLIS, Laura.
A Definition of Negative Liberty. PETTIT, Philip.
Future Persons and the Justification of Education. BILOW, Scott H.
Hayek on Bentham. DUBE, Allison.
How to Combine Pareto Optimality with Liberty Considerations. VALLENTYNE, Peter.
Liberal Autonomy. LOMASKY, Loren E.
Libertad como gracia y elegancia. CRUZ CRUZ, Juan.
La libertad en S Anselmo. GARAY SUÁREZ-LLANOS, Jesús.
La libertad y el concepto de lo político. DE ZAN, Julio.
Mill's and Other Liberalisms. GRAY, John.
More on Self-Enslavement and Paternalism in Mill. BROWN, D G.
Neues zum Thema Gerechtigkeit?. STRANZINGER, Rudolf.
Recenti studi sullo Hegel politico. BONACINA, Giovanni.
Rights to Liberty in Purely Private Matters: Part I. RILEY, Jonathan.
Rights to Liberty in Purely Private Matters: Part II. RILEY, Jonathan.
Two Visions of Liberty—Berlin and Hayek. POLANOWSKA-SYGULSKA, Beata.

LICHTENBERG

Style, Politics and the Future of Philosophy. JANIK, Allan.

LIE(S)

Aus den Überlegungen über die Moralsprachaspekte (in Polish). RODZINSKI, A.
Equality of Opportunity as the Noble Lie. ANDREW, Edward.
La expresión de la falsedad y del error en el vocabulario agustiniano de la mentira. SÁNCHEZ MANZANO, M A.

LIFE

Alpha and Omega: Ethics at the Frontiers of Life and Death. YOUNG, Ernlé W D.
Body, Soul, and Life Everlasting: Biblical Anthropology and the Monism-Dualism Debate. COOPER, John W.
Demokrit: Texte seiner Philosophie. LOBL, Rudolf.
Dietro il paesaggio: Saggio su Simmel. BOELLA, Laura.
Perspectives on Thomas Hobbes. ROGERS, G A J (ed).
Reincarnation: A Philosophical and Practical Analysis. PREUSS, Peter.
The Sanctity-of-Life Doctrine in Medicine: A Critique. KUHSE, Helga.
Lo storicismo di W Dilthey (Il problema di dio nei grandi pensatori, Volume Quinto). MANNO, Ambrogio Giacomo.
Universes. LESLIE, John.

LIFE

Who Lives? Who Dies?: Ethical Criteria in Patient Selection. KILNER, John F.

The *"Notes on the Government and Population of the Kingdom of Naples"* and Berkeley's Probable Route to Sicily. ALFONSO, Louis.

The Ancient Sceptic's Way of Life. MORRISON, Donald.

Appréciation morale des ingerences biomédiques dans le processusde de transmission (in Polish). KOWALSKI, Edmund.

Art, Education, and Life-Issues. MC FEE, Graham.

Brain Death and Brain Life: Rethinking the Connection. DOWNIE, Jocelyn.

Daimon Life, Nearness and Abyss: An Introduction to Za-ology. KRELL, David Farrell.

El Problema del Origen de la Vida. DE ASUA, Miguel J C.

Exile and PVS. SCHNEIDERMAN, Lawrence J.

A Farewell to Forms of Life. THOMPKINS, E F.

Forms of Life. EMMETT, Kathleen.

Humanity in the World of Life. ZHANG, Hwe Ik.

Is Life Absurd?. WESTPHAL, Jonathan and CHERRY, Christopher.

l'homme en tant qu'autocréateur: fondements anthropologiques du rejet de l'encyclique (in Polish). SZOSTEK, Andrzej.

Die Lebensgeschichte als Versöhnungsgeschichte: Eine paradigmatische Thematik spiritueller Moraltheologie. DEMMER, Klaus.

The Life of Ivan Il'ich. PATTERSON, David.

The Life Principle: A (Metaethical) Rejection. PASKE, Gerald H.

A Matter of Life and Death in Socratic Philosophy. BRICKHOUSE, Thomas C and SMITH, Nicholas D.

Non Posse Peccare. VAN DEN BELD, Antonie.

The Nonduality of Life and Death: A Buddhist View of Repression. LOY, David.

Oscar Wilde and Poststructuralism. WILLOUGHBY, Guy.

The Philosophy of Fate as the Basis of Education for Peace. GRZEGORCZYK, Andrzej and PETROWICZ, Lech (trans).

Platonism and Forms of Life. GASKIN, Richard M.

Preparation for Life in Peace—Future Perspectives. SUCHODOLSKI, Bogdan.

La *Regula recepta* agustiniana, germen de vida religiosa renovada. ANOZ, José.

Socrates and Judge Wilhelm: A Case of Kierkegaardian Ethics. MARTINEZ, Roy.

Speculations Regarding the History of *Donum Vitae.* HARVEY, John Collins.

Tragödie des Lebens und Kunst bei Georg Simmel (in Japanese). OMORI, Atsushi.

Unknown Masterpiece. HELLER, Agnes.

Vida y evolución en la filosofía griega. CAPPELLETTI, Angel J.

LIFE SCIENCE(S)

Reductionism and Systems Theory in the Life Sciences: Some Problems and Perspectives. HOYNINGEN-HUENE, Paul (ed).

LIFE WORLD

"System" and "Lifeworld": Habermas and the Problem of Holism. BOHMAN, James.

Life-World and System at Habermas (in Hungarian). BERGER, Henrik H.

LIGHT

The Light Shineth in Darkness. FRANK, S L.

Proclus on Space as Light. SCHRENK, Lawrence P.

LILLA, V

Vincenzo Lilla nella filosofia italiana dell' Ottocento. SAVA, G.

LIMITS

Civil Peace and Sacred Order: Limits and Renewals I. CLARK, Stephen R L.

Limits of Philosophy: (Limits of Reality?). VERSTER, Ulrich.

Natural Agency: An Essay on the Casual Theory of Action. BISHOP, John.

Anthropology on the Boundary and the Boundary in Anthropology. MARTIN, Dan.

Aspects et perspectives du problème de la limite dans la philosophie théorique de Kant. THEIS, R.

The Boundaries of Art. STECKER, Robert.

Circolarità di condizione in L'homme et le langage di Jean Brun. GONZI, Andrea.

Ecologic-Economic Jurisprudence—The Next Step?. LEIDIG, Guido.

Practical George and Aesthete Jerome Meet the Aesthetic Object. LEDDY, Thomas.

LINDGREN, J

Further Notes on Feminist Ethics and Pluralism: A Reply to Lindgren. WALKER, Margaret Urban.

LINEAR

A Comparison Between Lambek Syntactic Calculus and Intuitionistic Linear Propositional Logic. ABRUSCI, V Michele.

Decidable Discrete Linear Orders. MOSES, M.

Every Recursive Linear Ordering has a Copy in DTIME-SPACE$(n, \log(n))$. GRIGORIEFF, Serge.

Finite Condensations of Recursive Linear Orders. ROY, Dev K and WATNICK, Richard.

L'axiome de normalité pour les espaces totalement ordonnés. HADDAD, Labib and MORILLON, Marianne.

Linear Logic Display. BELNAP JR, Nuel D.

A Linear Parsing Algorithm for Parenthesis Terms. FELSCHER, Walter.

On Ehrenfeucht-Fraïssé Equivalence of Linear Orderings. OIKKONEN, Juha.

On Finite Linear Intermediate Predicate Logics. ONO, Hiroakira.

Quantales and (Noncommutative) Linear Logic. YETTER, David N.

The Dialectics of the Unity of Linearity and Non-linearity of Physical Processes (in Czechoslovakian). GOTT, V S.

LINGUISTIC ANALYSIS

Philosophy without Ambiguity: A Logico-Linguistic Essay. ATLAS, Jay David.

Thought and Language. MORAVCSIK, J M.

"Commentary: Toward a New Logic—Singing the Sirens' Song" in *Nietzsche's New Seas: Explorations in Philosophy, Aesthetics, and Politics,* STRONG, Tracy B (trans) and REY, Jean-Michel.

"On the Circumstantial Relation between Meaning and Content" in *Meaning and Mental Representation,* BARWISE, Jon.

Groups, II. LANDMAN, Fred.

How Performatives Work. SEARLE, John R.

The Logic of Time in Law and Legal Expert Systems. MACKAAY, Ejan (and others).

One Commends Something By Attributing the Property of Goodness To It (Penultimate Word). GOLDSTICK, D.

Le rationalisme et l'analyse linguistique. AUROUX, Sylvain.

A Speech Act Analysis of Irony. HAVERKATE, Henk.

LINGUISTIC CONVENTION(S)

Realism versus Antirealism: The Venue of the Linguistic Consensus. POLS, Edward.

LINGUISTIC RULE(S)

The Theory of the Sentence in Pūrva Mīmāmsā and Western Philosophy. TABER, John A.

LINGUISTICS

The Crisis of Philosophy. MC CARTHY, Michael.

Evolution of the Brain: Creation of the Self. ECCLES, John C.

Informal Lectures on Formal Semantics. BACH, Emmon W.

Landmarks in Linguistic Thought: The Western Tradition from Socrates to Saussure. HARRIS, Roy.

Mathematical Methods in Linguistics. PARTEE, Barbara H.

Saussure, Derrida, and the Metaphysics of Subjectivity. STROZIER, Robert M.

"The Analysis of Nominal Compounds" in *Meaning and Mental Representation,* LEHNERT, Wendy G.

"The Existentialists" in *Reading Philosophy for the Twenty-First Century,* WILD, John.

"Is and Ought" as a Linguistic Problem. BOUKEMA, H J M.

About Competence. TIENSON, John L.

Can One Promise to Love Another?. WILSON, John.

Chomsky, Wittgenstein, Bloor: Zum Problem einer wissenssoziologischen Metatheorie der Linguistik. KERTÉSZ, András.

Counterfactual Analysis: Can the Metalinguistic Theory Be Revitalized?. HALPIN, John F.

Essere è percepire una struttura linguistica: Il pensiero di George Berkeley quale presupposto filosofico. REBAGLIA, Alberta.

An Explanatory Theory of Communicative Intentions. KURODA, S Y.

Immediacy and the Text: Friedrich Schleiermacher's Theory of Style and Interpretation. PFAU, Thomas.

Langage et raison: Philosophie, linguistique et ce qui leur ressemble. NICOLET, Daniel.

Language Acquisition: Growth or Learning?. SAMPSON, Geoffrey.

Language of Cognition—Cognition of Language (in Serbo-Croatian). MARVAN, George J.

Lavoisier, Priestley, and the *Philosophes*: Epistemic and Linguistic Dimensions to the Chemical Revolution. MC EVOY, John G.

Ludwig Wittgenstein: Personality and Philosophy (in Czechoslovakian). STERN, Joseph P.

Modal Subordination and Pronominal Anaphora in Discourse. ROBERTS, Craige.

Noam Chomsky: An Interview. CHOMSKY, Noam and EDGLEY, Roy and OSBORNE, Peter and RÉE, Jonathan and WILSON, Deirdre.

On Justification Conditional Models of Linguistic Competence. STERN,

LINGUISTICS

Cindy D.

La relation de réfléchissement pensée/langage. ROVENTA-FRUMUSANI, Daniela.

Remarks on the Concept of "Universal Grammar". CORNILESCU, Alexandra.

A Sociobiological Explanation of Strategies of Reading and Writing Philosophy. GILMAN, Roger William.

Sur la signification logique et linguistique de la négation (in Romanian). BERCEANU, Barbu B.

Sur la structure particulière du dialogue argumentatif. MIHAI, Gheorghe.

Sur le status théorique de la philosophie moderne du langage (in Romanian). COLTESCU, Viorel.

A Theory of Command Relations. BARKER, Chris and PULLUM, Geoffrey K.

Theory of Speech Acts (in Serbo-Croatian). IVANETIC, Nada.

Le *Tractatus* de Wittgenstein: Considérations sur le système numérique et la forme aphoristique. HESS, Gérald.

Ways of Branching Quantifiers. SHER, Gila.

LINK, G

Groups, I. LANDMAN, Fred.

Groups, II. LANDMAN, Fred.

LIPKIN, R

The Psychiatrist as Moral Advisor. REDMON, Robert B.

LIPMAN, M

Rationality, Self-Esteem and Autonomy through Collaborative Enquiry. LANE, Neil R.

LIPPMANN, W

The Human Image System and Thinking Critically in the Strong Sense. FREEMAN, James B.

LISTENING

The Listening Self: Personal Growth, Social Change and Closure of Metaphysics. LEVIN, David Michael.

The Women of Silence. FRANKE, Carrie.

LITERACY

Contexts of Dance. SPARSHOTT, Francis.

Engaging the New Literacy: A "Way In" to Philosophy of Education. KOHLI, Wendy.

Homer, Literacy, and Education. GOLDMAN, Louis.

Joyce, Dorothy, and Willie: Literary Literacy as Engaged Reflection. BOGDAN, Deanne.

Literate Thinking and Schooling. LANGER, Judith.

On Being a Meaning-Maker: Young Children's Experiences of Reading. POLAKOW, Valerie.

LITERAL

"Literal Relevance" in *Directions in Relevant Logic*, PARKS-CLIFFORD, John.

Literality. BARR, James.

Significado literal: entre la profunda necesidad de una construcción y la mera nostalgia. CABRERA, Julio.

LITERARY

"Paul de Man and the Subject of Literary History" in *The Textual Sublime: Deconstruction and Its Differences*, JAY, Gregory S.

Interpreting Hume's *Dialogues*. COLEMAN, Dorothy P.

Literary Communication: The Author, the Reader, the Text. HARKER, W John.

Literary Relativism. CARNEY, James D.

Mikhail Bakhtin's Body Politic: A Phenomenological Dialogics. JUNG, Hwa Yol.

Variations on a Given Theme. KERR-LAWSON, Angus.

LITERARY CRITICISM

Against Deconstruction. ELLIS, John M.

Existentially Speaking: Essays on the Philosophy of Literature. WILSON, Colin.

Harde noten om te kraken: de zachte wetenschappen. IBSCH, Elrud.

Interpretation in Aesthetics: Theories and Practices. MC CORMICK, Peter.

Is There a Feminist Aesthetic?. FRENCH, Marilyn.

Narrative and Theories of Desire. CLAYTON, Jay.

Philosophy and Literature. PALMER, Anthony.

Totality, Realism, and the Type: Lukács' Later Literary Criticism as Political Theory. SHAW, Brian J.

Vico and Frye: A Note. BAHTI, Timothy.

LITERARY FORM(S)

Irony, Tragedy, and Temporality in Agricultural Systems, or, How Values and Systems are Related. BUSCH, Lawrence.

Representation, Conversion, and Literary Form: *Harrington* and the Novel of Jewish Identity. RAGUSSIS, Michael.

LITERARY THEORY

Philosophical Rhetoric: The Function of Indirection in Philosophical Writing. MASON, Jeff.

Stanley Cavell and Literary Skepticism. FISCHER, Michael.

The Claims of Tragedy: An Essay in Moral Psychology and Aesthetics Theory. SCHIER, Flint.

Contemporary Consciousness and Originary Thinking in a Nietzschean Joke. SCHEIER, Claus-Artur.

Ingarden and the End of Phenomenological Aesthetics. MURRAY, Michael.

Irony and 'The Essence of Writing'. COOPER, David E.

Iterating Revolution: Speech Acts in Literary Theory. PETREY, Sandy.

The Make-Up of Literature. TAYLOR, Paul.

Narrative Theory: Ancient or Modern?. SAVILE, Anthony.

New Trends in Literary Aesthetics: An Overview. TAYLOR, Paul.

Pragmatism and the Theory of the Reader. MC CALLUM, John.

LITERATURE

see also Fiction(s)

Existentially Speaking: Essays on the Philosophy of Literature. WILSON, Colin.

In Quest of the Ordinary: Lines of Skepticism and Romanticism. CAVELL, Stanley.

Postmodernist Culture: An Introduction to Theories of the Contemporary. CONNOR, Steven.

Primal Scenes: Literature, Philosophy, Psychoanalysis. LUKACHER, Ned.

Religious Aesthetics: A Theological Study of Making and Meaning. BURCH BROWN, Frank.

Stanley Cavell and Literary Skepticism. FISCHER, Michael.

Tears. TAYLOR, Mark C.

The Textual Sublime: Deconstruction and Its Differences. SILVERMAN, Hugh J (ed).

"Der alte Schopenhauer schlohweiss—ich und geschichte in Günter Grass' Romanen"" in *Schopenhauer: New Essays in Honor of His 200th Birthday*, FRIZEN, Werner.

"Banter and Banquets for Heroic Death" in *Post-Structuralist Classics*, PUCCI, Pietro.

"Concealing Revealing: A Perspective on Greek Tragedy" in *Post-Structuralist Classics*, HALLIBURTON, David.

"Entertaining Arguments: Terence *Adelphoe*" in *Post-Structuralist Classics*, HENDERSON, John.

"Entfremdung und Verfremdung in der russischen Literatur und Literaturtheorie" in *Agora: Zu Ehren von Rudolph Berlinger*, TROST, Klaus.

"Die hermeneutische Funktion des Literaturmuseums" in *Cultural Hermeneutics of Modern Art: Essays in Honor of Jan Aler*, GÖRES, Jörn.

"Is Deconstruction an Alternative?" in *The Textual Sublime: Deconstruction and Its Differences*, KINCZEWSKI, Kathryn.

"Literatur und Religion zu Dostjevskijs Erzählkunst" in *Agora: Zu Ehren von Rudolph Berlinger*, LETTENBAUER, Wilhelm.

"The Place of Schopenhauer in the Philosophical Education of Leo Tolstoi" in *Schopenhauer: New Essays in Honor of His 200th Birthday*, WALSH, Harry.

"The Possibility of Literary Deconstruction: A Reply to Donato" in *The Textual Sublime: Deconstruction and Its Differences*, WOOD, David.

"Recovering the Figure of J L Austin in Paul de Man's *Allegories of Reading*" in *The Textual Sublime: Deconstruction and Its Differences*, CARAHER, Brian G.

"Rhetoric and Literature" in *From Metaphysics to Rhetoric*, BEAUJOUR, Michel.

Art and the Joycean Artist. SCHIRALLI, Martin.

Business Ethics: A Literature Review with a Focus on Marketing Ethics. TSALIKIS, John and FRITZSCHE, David J.

Contextualism and Autonomy in Aesthetics. KRUKOWSKI, Lucian.

Cultural History and Cultural Materialism. BERMAN, Ronald.

Derrida, a Kind of Philosophy: A Discussion of Recent Literature. CAPUTO, John D.

Desire: Direct and Imitative. COHN, Robert Greer.

La enseñanza de la ética a través de la literatura. LÓPEZ QUINTÁS, Alfonso.

Entre positivisme et anarchie? Trois voies de recherche dans la construction des theories en science litteraire. DECREUS, F.

Etica y estética en la literatura. SPANG, Kurt.

Fish Fingered: Anatomy of a Deconstructionist. MEYNELL, Hugo A.

Forms of Life and Forms of Discourse in Ancient Philosophy. HADOT, Pierre and DAVIDSON, Arnold (trans) and WISSING, Paula (trans).

From Rhetoric to Corporate Populism: A Romantic Critique of the Academy in an Age of High Gossip. CHRISTENSEN, Jerome.

Golden Rules and Golden Bowls. RIGHTER, William.

Idées esthétiques et morales dans le contexte aristique et scientifique de

LITERATURE

l'oeuvre d'A Odobescu (in Romanian). DRAGOMIRESCU, Lucian.
Knowledge and Silence: *The Golden Bowl* and Moral Philosophy. BRUDNEY, Daniel.
Language, Literature, and Art. SIMPSON, Alan.
The Life of Ivan Il'ich. PATTERSON, David.
Literature as a Way of Knowing: An Epistemological Justification for Literary Studies. KASPRISIN, Lorraine.
Literature as Life: Nietzsche's Positive Morality. CONWAY, Daniel W.
Literature, Criticism, and Factual Reporting. COLLETT, Alan.
Literature, Fiction and Autobiography. COLLETT, Alan.
Literature, Philosophy and Nonsense. TILGHMAN, B R.
Literature, Philosophy, and the Imagination. LEVI, Albert William.
Literatuur als bron voor historisch en sociologisch onderzoek. MASO, Benjo.
Love Delights in Praises: A Reading of *The Two Gentlemen of Verona*. GIRARD, René.
Nietzsche and Nehamas's Nietzsche. SOLOMON, Robert C.
Nietzsche's Radical Experimentalism. SEIGFRIED, Hans.
On the Essential Difference between Science, Art and Philosophy, or Philosophy as the Literature of Necessity. BOULLART, Karel.
The Person and *The Little Prince* of St Exupéry, Part I. HETZLER, Florence M.
A Philosophic Fairytale. RICKMAN, H P.
Philosophy and Fiction. RICKMAN, H P.
Philosophy and Literature. PALMER, Anthony.
Philosophy and Literature: Their Relationship in the Works of Paul de Man. MICHIELSEN, Peter.
Philosophy as Exile from Life: Lukacs' 'Soul and Form'. BROWNE, Paul.
Plato, George Eliot, and Moral Narcissism. GOULD, Carol S.
Portia's Suitors. KUHNS, Richard and TOVEY, Barbara.
Santayana's Idea of the Tragic. MC CORMICK, John E.
Spinoza in der schönen Literatur: Bilder aus der Zeit zwischen Vormärz und Weimarer Republik. HELMES, Günther.
Eine Spinoza-Reminizens in Elias Canettis autobiografischer Erzählung "Das Augenspiel". BOLLACHER, Martin.
Stories of Sublimely Good Character. CALLEN, Donald.
A Theory of Command Relations. BARKER, Chris and PULLUM, Geoffrey K.
To the Lighthouse and the Feminist Path to Postmodernity. MARTIN, Bill.
Translation, Art, and Culture. PERRICONE, Christopher.
Troubles with Fiction. POLLARD, Denis E B.
What is Happening to the History of Ideas?. KELLEY, Donald R.
Wittgenstein, Religion, Freud, and Ireland. HAYES, John.

LIU YUXI

"Liu Zongyuan's and Liu Yuxi's Theories of Heaven and Man" in *Man and Nature: The Chinese Tradition and the Future*, LI-TIAN, Fang.

LIU ZONGYUAN

"Liu Zongyuan's and Liu Yuxi's Theories of Heaven and Man" in *Man and Nature: The Chinese Tradition and the Future*, LI-TIAN, Fang.

LIVING

Moral Theory: Thinking, Doing, and Living. CALLAHAN, Daniel.

LIVING WILL(S)

"Do Living Will Statutes Embody a Claim Right or a Mere Privilege to Refuse Life-Prolonging Treatment?" in *Advance Directives in Medicine*, SODERBERG, William.
"Living Will Statutes: Good Public Policy?" in *Advance Directives in Medicine*, WHITE, W D.

LOCKE

Color and Consciousness: An Essay in Metaphysics. LANDESMAN, Charles.
Common Sense. FORGUSON, Lynd.
Early Modern Philosophy II. TWEYMAN, Stanley (ed).
Elements of Modern Philosophy: Descartes through Kant. BRENNER, William H.
The Libertarian Idea. NARVESON, Jan.
Liberty and Justice. DAY, J P.
Social Philosophy and Ecological Scarcity. LEE, Keekok.
Thomas Reid. LEHRER, Keith.
The Unvarnished Doctrine: Locke, Liberalism, and the American Revolution. DWORETZ, Steven M.
"John Locke, David Fordyce, and Jean-Jacques Rousseau: On Liberty" in *Early Modern Philosophy II*, TATTON, Susan.
"Locke's Ideas, Abstraction, and Substance" in *Cause, Mind, and Reality: Essays Honoring C B Martin*, HINCKFUSS, Ian.
"Whitehead's Interpretation of Locke in *Process and Reality*" in *Whitehead's Metaphysics of Creativity*, SPECHT, Rainer.
"Bedeutung", "Idee" und "Begriff": Zur Behandlung einiger bedeutungstheorietischer Paradoxien durch Leibniz. ROS, Arno.

Berkeley's Ideas and the Primary/Secondary Distinction. NADLER, Steven.
Can Abstractions Be Causes?. JOHNSON, David M.
Difference, Diversity, and the Limits of Toleration. MC CLURE, Kirstie M.
The *Fundamental Constitutions of Carolina* as a Tool for Lockean Scholarship. MC GUINNESS, Celia.
A Hobbesian Welfare State?. MORRIS, Christopher W.
John Locke: sobre la justificación del gobierno. AMOR, Claudio O.
Justifying Tolerance. KING, Preston.
Leibniz on Locke on Weakness of Will. VAILATI, Ezio.
Locke on Disagreement Over the Uses of Moral and Political Terms. MASON, Andrew.
Locke on the Making of Complex Ideas. LOSONSKY, Michael.
Locke's Simple Ideas, the Blooming, Buzzing Confusion, and Quasi-Photographic Perception. HEYD, Thomas.
Made by Contrivance and the Consent of Men. DEN HARTOGH, Govert.
Of Particles. GALLIE, Roger D.
The Politics of Epistemology. WHITE, Morton.
Primäre und sekundäre Qualitatäten bei John Locke. KIENZLE, Bertram.
Reply to Heyd's Reply to "Locke Is Not a Cartesian with Respect to Knowledge of our Own Existence". ROTH, Robert J.
Reply to Roth: Locke Is Not a Cartesian with Respect to Knowledge of our Own Existence. HEYD, Thomas.
The Right to Subsistence in a "Lockean" State of Nature. SHEARMUR, Jeremy.
Self-Ownership. DAY, J P.
Some Uses of *Imagination* in the British Empiricists: A Preliminary Investigation of Locke, as Contrasted with Hume. HALL, Roland.
The Theory of Ideas in Gassendi and Locke. MICHAEL, Fred S and MICHAEL, Emily.
Three Approaches to Locke and the Slave Trade. GLAUSSER, Wayne.
Why Can't a Man Be More Like a Woman? (A Note on John Locke's Educational Thought). SIMONS, Martin.

LOCUTIONARY ACT(S)

Semantica, Pragmatica, Atti linguistici: note in margine a una polemica. SBISÀ, Marina.

LOGIC

see also Deontic Logic, Infinitary Logic, Informal Logic, Intuitionistic Logic, Many-Valued Logics, Modal Logic, Predicate Logic, Proof(s), Propositional Logic, Relevant Logics, Tense Logic
Automated Deduction in Nonclassical logics. WALLEN, Lincoln A.
Axioms of Cooperative Decision Making. MOULIN, Hervé.
Being in Time: The Nature of Time in Light of McTaggart's Paradox. FARMER, David J.
Cartesian Logic: An Essay on Descartes's Conception of Inference. GAUKROGER, Stephen.
A Combinatorial Theory of Possibility. ARMSTRONG, D M.
Computability and Logic (Third Edition). BOOLOS, George S.
The Concept of Logical Consequence. ETCHEMENDY, John.
Constructivism and Science: Essays in Recent German Philosophy. BUTTS, Robert E (ed).
The Crisis of Philosophy. MC CARTHY, Michael.
Critical Thinking: Consider the Verdict. WALLER, Bruce N.
Critical Thinking: Evaluating Claims and Arguments in Everyday Life—Second Edition. MOORE, Brook Noel.
The Critique of Thought: A Re-Examination of Hegel's Science of Logic. JOHNSON, Paul Owen.
Descriptions. NEALE, Stephen.
Directions in Relevant Logic. NORMAN, Jean (ed).
The Ethics of Geometry: A Genealogy of Modernity. LACHTERMAN, David R.
If "P", then "Q": Conditionals and the Foundations of Reasoning. SANFORD, David H.
Informal Logic: A Handbook for Critical Argumentation. WALTON, Douglas N.
Introduction to Logic and Critical Thinking (Second Edition). SALMON, Merrilee H.
John Stuart Mill. SKORUPSKI, John.
Lectures on Game Theory. AUMANN, Robert J.
Logic and Knowledge: Bertrand Russell, Essays 1901-1950. MARSH, Robert Charles (ed).
Logic and Philosophy in the Lvov-Warsaw School. WOLÉNSKI, Jan.
Logic for Computer Scientists. SCHÖNING, Uwe.
The Logic of Mind (Second Edition). NELSON, R J.
The Logic of Political Belief: A Philosophical Analysis of Ideology. ADAMS, Ian S.
The Logic of Sense—Gilles Deleuze. DELEUZE, Gilles.
Logic: Analyzing and Appraising Arguments. GENSLER, Harry J.

LOGIC

A Logical Introduction to Philosophy. PURTILL, Richard L.

Looser Ends: The Practice of Philosophy. BENCIVENGA, Ermanno.

Mathematical Methods in Linguistics. PARTEE, Barbara H.

Meaning and Grammar: An Introduction to Semantics. CHIERCHIA, Gennaro.

A Modern Formal Logic Primer, Volume I and II. TELLER, Paul.

The Philosopher's Habitat: Introduction to Investigations in, and Applications of, Modern Philosophy. GOLDSTEIN, Laurence.

Philosophical Introduction to Set Theory. POLLARD, Stephen.

Philosophical Logic and Artificial Intelligence. THOMASON, Richmond H (ed).

The Philosophy of F P Ramsey. SAHLIN, Nils-Eric.

The Philosophy of Set Theory: An Historical Introduction to Cantor's Paradise. TILES, Mary E.

The Possible Universe. TALLET, J A.

Practical Reasoning. WRIGHT, Larry.

Probabilistic Reasoning in Intelligent Systems: Networks of Plausible Inference. PEARL, Judea.

Quantum Probability—Quantum Logic. PITOWSKY, Itamar.

Questions of Form: Logic and the Analytic Proposition from Kant to Carnap. PROUST, Joëlle.

Rationality and Dynamic Choice: Foundational Explorations. MC CLENNEN, Edward F.

Realism, Mathematics and Modality. FIELD, Hartry.

Relevant Logic: A Philosophical Examination of Inference. READ, Stephen.

Rereading Russell: Essays on Bertrand Russell's Metaphysics and Epistemology. SAVAGE, C Wade (ed).

Rhetoriques. PERELMAN, Chaïm.

Schaum's Outline of Theory and Problems of Logic. NOLT, John Eric.

The Semantic Foundations of Logic, Volume 1: Propositional Logics. EPSTEIN, Richard L.

The Sophismata of Richard Kilvington. KRETZMANN, Norman.

Systems of Logic. MARTIN, Norman M.

Understanding Symbolic Logic (Second Edition). KLENK, Virginia.

Writings of Charles S Peirce: A Chronological Edition, Volume 4, 1879-1884. KLOESEL, Christian J W (ed).

"Harris's Commentary on Hegel's Logic" in *Dialectic and Contemporary Science*, SMITH, John E.

"Identity in Intensional Logic: Subjective Semantics" in *Meaning and Mental Representation*, VAN FRAASSEN, Bas.

"Influences on the Conception of Logic and Mind" in *Scientific Knowledge Socialized*, GELLATLY, Angus R H.

"Introduction: On the Nature of Philosophic Historiography" in *History and Anti-History in Philosophy*, TEJERA, V.

"Logic and Argumentation" in *From Metaphysics to Rhetoric*, LADRIERE, Jean.

"On the Scope of Maimonides' Logic, Or, What Joseph Knew" in *A Straight Path: Studies in Medieval Philosophy and Culture*, WEISS, Raymond L.

"Reply to Smith's "Harris's Commentary on Hegel's Logic"" in *Dialectic and Contemporary Science*, HARRIS, Errol E.

"Russell's Reasons for Ramification" in *Rereading Russell: Essays on Bertrand Russell's Metaphysics and Epistemology*, GOLDFARB, Warren.

"Russell's Theory of Logical Types and the Atomistic Hierarchy of Sentences" in *Rereading Russell: Essays on Bertrand Russell's Metaphysics and Epistemology*, COCCHIARELLA, Nino B.

"Deus ex machina" redivivus: The "Synthetic A Priori" in the Computer Age. FANG, J.

'Actually'. TEICHMANN, Roger.

'Ich habe mich wohl gehütet, alle Patronen auf einmal zu zerschiessen': Ernest Zermelo in Göttingen. PECKHAUS, Volker.

Absolute Truth Theories for Modal Languages as Theories of Interpretation. LE PORE, Ernest and LOEWER, Barry.

Absolutely Independent Axiomatizations for Countable Sets in Classical Logic. GRYGIEL, Joanna.

An Account of Peirce's Proof of Pragmatism. MC CARTHY, Jeremiah.

Action and Ability. BROWN, Mark A.

Actuality in Hegel's Logic. LONGUENESSE, Béatrice and WAXMAN, Wayne (trans).

Addendum to "The Truth is Never Simple". BURGESS, John P.

Against Global Paraconsistency. BATENS, Diderik.

An Agenda for Subjectivism. VICKERS, John M.

Albertus Magnus and the Notion of Syllogistic Middle Term. HUBBARD, J M.

Alfred Tarski i la teoria de conjunts. PLA I CARRERA, Josep.

An Algebraic Approach to Intuitionistic Modal Logics in Connection with Intermediate Predicate Logics. SUZUKI, Nobu-Yuki.

Algebraic Extensions in Nonstandard Models and Hilbert's Irreducibility Theorem. YASUMOTO, Masahiro.

Algorithmic Information Theory. VAN LAMBALGEN, Michiel.

Algorithms for Sentences Over Integral Domains. TUNG, Shih Ping.

Almost Orthogonal Regular Types. HRUSHOVSKI, E.

Alpha-Conversion, Conditions on Variables and Categorical Logic. CURIEN, Pierre-Louis.

Analogical Arguings and Explainings. JOHNSON, Fred.

Analogies and Missing Premises. GOVIER, Trudy.

Analytico-Referentiality and Legitimation in Modern Mathematics. ROUSSOPOULOS, George.

Anaphoric Attitudes. CRESSWELL, M J.

Antinomies and Paradoxes and their Solutions. WEINGARTNER, Paul.

Apocalyptic Anticipations. KIVINEN, S Albert.

Apuntes sobre el pensamiento matemático de Ramón Llull. WELCH, John R and PALOS, Ana María.

Are Theories of Rationality Empirically Testable?. SMOKLER, Howard.

An Argumentation-Analysis of a Central Part of Lenin's Political Logic. SMIT, P A.

Argumentos no son razones. FEILING, Carlos.

Aristotle on Inferences from Signs (*Rhetoric* I 2, 1357 b 1-25). WEIDEMANN, Hermann.

Arithmetic Based on the Church Numerals in Illative Combinatory Logic. BUNDER, M W.

Arithmetical Completeness Versus Relative Completeness. GRABOWSKI, Michal.

Ars inveniendi et théorie des modèles. BENIS-SINACEUR, Hourya.

Atomic Realism, Intuitionist Logic and Tarskian Truth. EDWARDS, Jim.

The Autonomy of Mathematics. STEINER, Mark.

An Axiom Schema of Comprehension of Zermelo-Fraenkel-Skolem Set Theory. HEIDEMA, Johannes.

Axiomatization of the First-Order Intermediate Logics of Bounded Kripkean Heights I. YOKOTA, Shin'ichi.

Bar-Hillel: The Man and his Philosophy of Mathematics. MARGALIT, Avishai.

Beardsley's Theory of Analogy. BARKER, Evelyn M.

Belief and Contradiction. DA COSTA, Newton C A and FRENCH, Steven.

Believing the Axioms, I. MADDY, Penelope.

Bertrand Russell 1895-1899: Una filosofía prelogicista de la geometría. RODRIGUEZ-CONSUEGRA, Francisco A.

Bivalenza e trascendenza. COZZO, Cesare.

Boolean Negation and All That. PRIEST, Graham.

The Boolean Spectrum of an o-Minimal Theory. STEINHORN, Charles and TOFFALORI, Carlo.

Bringing It About. SEGERBERG, Krister.

The Brothers James and John Bernoulli on the Parallelism between Logic and Algebra. BOSWELL, Terry.

Brouwer's Equipotence and Denumerability Predicates. FRANCHELLA, Miriam.

Buridano e le consequenze. BERTAGNA, Mario.

By Parity of Reasoning. WOODS, John and HUDAK, Brent.

C S Peirce et le projet d'une "logique du vague". ENGEL-TIERCELIN, Claudine.

Can Knowledge Be Acquired Through Contradiction?. AGAZZI, Evandro.

Can There Be a Proof That Some Unprovable Arithmetic Sentence Is True?. HUGLY, Philip and SAYWARD, Charles.

Cardano: "Arithmetic Subtlety" and Impossible Solutions. KENNEY, Emelie.

Categorial Grammar and Type Theory. VAN BENTHEM, Johan.

Categorías aristotélicas y categorías intensionales. STAHL, Gérold.

Categorical and Algebraic Aspects of Martin-Löf Type Theory. OBTUŁOWICZ, A.

Categoricity of Theories in $L_{\kappa\omega}$ with κ a Compact Cardinal. SHELAH, Saharon and MAKKAI, M.

Causas y razones en la filosofía de Wittgenstein. CABANCHIK, Samuel.

Cause as an Implication. SYLVAN, Richard and DA COSTA, Newton.

Certain Fundamental Problems and Trends of Thought in Mathematics. STRAUSS, D F M.

Certeza, duda escéptica y saber. CABANCHIK, Samuel M.

Ceticismo versus condições de verdade. ROHDEN, Valério.

Characters and Fixed Points in Provability Logic. GLEIT, Zachary and GOLDFARB, Warren.

Der Charakter der Mathematik zwischen Philosophie und Wissenschaft. OTTE, Michael.

Charles Parsons on the Liar Paradox. SCHMIDTZ, David.

Charles Sanders Peirce: ciência enquanto semiótica. SILVEIRA, L F B da.

Chez Fermat A.D. 1637. MAULA, Erkka and KASANEN, Eero.

Classical Subtheories and Intuitionism. SZYMANEK, Krzysztof.

The Classification of Excellent Classes. GROSSBERG, R.

The Classification of Small Weakly Minimal Sets, II. BUECHLER, Steven.

Classifying $\aleph_0$-Categorical Theories. WEAVER, George.

LOGIC

LOGIC

On the Positive Parts of the J-Systems of Arruda and Da Costa. URBAS, Igor.

On the Possibility of Mathematical Revolutions. KENNEY, Emelie.

On the Relation Between Logic and Thinking. HENLE, Mary.

On World Views, Commitment and Critical Thinking. WALTERS, Kerry S.

The Origins of Russell's Theory of Descriptions. RODRÍGUEZ-CONSUEGRA, Francisco.

Overlapping Types in Higher Order Predicate Calculus Based on Combinatory Logic. BUNDER, M W.

An Overview of Paraconsistent Logic in the 80s. DA COSTA, Newton C A and MARCONI, Diego.

Pairs of Recursive Structures. ASH, C J and KNIGHT, J F.

Paraconsistency and the C-Systems of DaCosta. URBAS, Igor.

Paraconsistency. URBAS, Igor.

Paraconsistent Foundations for Logic Programming. BLAIR, Howard A and SUBRAHMANIAN, V S.

A Paraconsistent Many-Valued Propositional Logic. D'OTTAVIANO, Itala M L and EPSTEIN, Richard L.

Paradigms of Measurement. SWISTAK, Piotr.

Les paradoxes et le langage. SEUREN, Pieter A M.

Paradoxes of Fulfillment. BONEVAC, Daniel.

Paradoxes of Moral Reparation: Deontic Foci versus Circumstances. CASTAÑEDA, Hector-Neri.

Paradoxical Tasks. RAY, Christopher.

Parallogic: As Mind Meets Context. HANSON, Barbara Gail.

Parameter-Free Universal Induction. KAYE, Richard.

Parametrization Over Inductive Relations of a Bounded Number of Variables. MC COLM, Gregory L.

Pareto Unanimity and Consensus. LEVI, Isaac.

Parmenides on What There Is. KETCHUM, Richard J.

Partial Realizations of Hilbert's Program. SIMPSON, Stephen G.

Partial Truth, Fringes, and Motion: Three Applications of a Contradictorial Logic. PEÑA, Lorenzo.

Partition Properties and Well-Ordered Sequences. JACKSON, Steve.

Partitions with no Coarsenings of Higher Degree. BRACKIN, Stephen H.

Peano's Smart Children: A Provability Logical Study of Systems with Built-In Consistency. VISSER, Albert.

Peirce's Abductive Argument and the Enthymeme. SABRE, Ru Michael.

Petrus Damiani—ein Freund der Logik?. BUCHER, Theodor G.

Philosophical Investigations 201: A Wittgensteinian Reply to Kripke. SUMMERFIELD, Donna M.

Philosophical Problems of Mathematics in the Light of Evolutionary Epistemology. RAV, Yehuda.

Philosophical Questions of Mathematics in *Anti-Dühring*. PANFILOV, V A.

Philosophical-Methodological Aspects of Relevant Logic. WOISHVILLO, E K.

Philosophy of Mathematics as a Theoretical and Applied Discipline. BARABASHEV, A G.

The Physical Church Thesis and Physical Computational Complexity. PITOWSKY, Itamar.

A Piagetian Perspective on Mathematical Construction. ARBIB, Michael A.

Platonismo, unicidad y metateoría. CASANAVE, Abel Lassalle.

Pointless Metric Spaces. GERLA, Giangiacomo.

Points of View and their Logical Analysis. HAUTAMAKI, Antti.

The Popcorn Problem: Sobel on Evidential Decision Theory and Deliberation-Probability Dynamics. EELLS, Ellery.

Positive Definite Functions Over Regular f-Rings and Representations as Sums of Squares. MAC CAULL, W A.

Possibility and Probability. LEVI, Isaac.

Post Complete and 0-Axiomatizable Modal Logics. BELLISSIMA, Fabio.

Post-Udayana Nyaya Reactions to Dharmakirti's Vadanyaya: An Evaluation. CHINCHORE, M.

A Pragmatic Analysis of Mathematical Realism and Intuitionism. BLAIS, Michel J.

The Pragmatic Problem of Induction: Reply to Gower and Bamford. WATKINS, John.

Predication in the Logic of Terms. SOMMERS, Fred.

Preference-Based Deontic Logic (PDL). HANSSON, Sven Ove.

Préliminaires à une théorie logique des méthodes pratiques (in Romanian). POPA, Cornel.

Presupposition and Foundational Asymmetry in Metaphysics and Logic. JACQUETTE, Dale.

Presuppositional Completeness. BUSZKOWSKI, Wojciech.

The Primal Framework I. BALDWIN, J T and SHELAH, S.

Principal Type-Schemes and Condensed Detachment. HINDLEY, J Roger.

Probabilities of Conditionals—Revisited. HÁJEK, Alan.

A Problem about the Meaning of Intuitionist Negation. HOSSACK, Keith G.

Problems in the Use of Expert Opinion in Argumentation. WALTON, Douglas

N.

Professor Kasachkoff on Explaining and Justifying. BOWLES, George.

A Proof of Morley's Conjecture. HART, Bradd.

A Proofless Proof of the Barwise Compactness Theorem. HOWARD, Mark.

The Property (HD) in Intermediate Logics: A Partial Solution of a Problem of H Ono. MINARI, Pierluigi.

The Propositional Objects of Mental Attitudes. DANIELS, Charles B.

Prospects for Decent Relevant Factorisation Logics. URBAS, Igor and SYLVAN, Richard.

Ein Protokoll aus Husserls Logikseminar vom Winter 1925. REINER, Hans and SCHUHMANN, Karl.

Pseudo-Boolean Valued Prolog. FITTING, Melvin.

Quantales and (Noncommutative) Linear Logic. YETTER, David N.

Quantified Modal Logic and the Plural *De Re*. BRICKER, Phillip.

Quantified Propositional Calculi and Fragments of Bounded Arithmetic. KRAJICEK, Jan and PUDLAK, Pavel.

Quantifier Elimination in Separably Closed Fields of Finite Imperfectness Degree. HARAN, Dan.

Quantifiers Determined by Partial Orderings. KRYNICKI, Michal.

Quantum Logics and Hilbert Spaces. GIUNTINI, Roberto.

R-Algebras and *R*-Model Structures as Power Constructs. BRINK, Chris.

The Rank Function and Hilbert's Second E-Theorem. FERRARI, Pier Luigi.

Reachability is Harder for Directed than for Undirected Finite Graphs. AJTAI, Miklos.

Reason, Inductive Inference, and True Religion in Hume. JANZ, Bruce.

Reasoning by Analogy in Hume's *Dialogues*. BARKER, Stephen F.

Recent Work in the Philosophy of Religion. ZAGZEBSKI, Linda.

Recursive Solvability of Problems with Matrices. KROM, Melven and KROM, Myren.

The Recursively Enumerable Degrees have Infinitely Many One-Types. AMBOS-SPIES, Klaus and SOARE, R I.

Recursively Enumerable Sets Modulo Iterated Jumps and Extensions of Arslanov's Completeness Criterion. JOCKUSCH JR, C G (and others).

Redundancia: Notas para su análisis. NAVARRO, Pablo E.

Référence et identité. SEYMOUR, Michel.

Reflections on Kurt Gödel by Hao Wang. YOURGRAU, Palle.

Reflective Modalities and Theory Change. FUHRMANN, André.

Reflexive Consistency Proofs and Gödel's Second Theorem. SAGAL, Paul.

A Refutation of Jagat Pal's Defence of Aristotelian Square of Opposition. BASU, S and KASEM, A.

A Rejoinder to Hansson. JONES, Andrew J I and PÖRN, Ingmar.

Relations Between Intuitionistic Modal Logics and Intermediate Predicate Logics. ONO, Hiroakira and SUZUKI, Nobu-Yuki.

Relatively Point Regular Quasivarieties. CZELAKOWSKI, Janusz.

Relevant Predication: Grammatical Characterizations. KREMER, Philip.

Remarks on the Church-Rosser Property. LÓPEZ-ESCOBAR, E G K.

Remarks on the Logic of Imagination. NIINILUOTO, Ilkka.

Reportage as Compound Suggestion. MAY, John D.

A Representation Theorem for Languages with Generalized Quantifiers Through Back-and-Forth Methods. PEDROSA, Renato H L and SETTE, Antonio M A.

Resolution in Constructivism. AKAMA, Seiki.

Resplicing Properties in the Supervenience Base. ODDIE, Graham and TICHY, Pavel.

La revolución semántica de Guillermo de Ockham. GUERIN, Ignasi Miralbell.

Ricerca ed affermazione. RIGOBELLO, Armando.

Rigorous Proof and the History of Mathematics: Comments on Crowe. JESSEPH, Douglas.

The Role of Logic in Education. MILL, John Stuart.

The Roots of Contemporary Platonism. MADDY, Penelope.

The Roots of Mathematics Education in Russia in the Age of Peter the Great. ANELLIS, Irving H.

Rosser Orderings in Bimodal Logics. CARBONE, Alessandra and MONTAGNA, F.

A Routley-Meyer Affixing Style Semantics for Logics Containing Aristotle's Thesis. BRADY, Ross T.

The Rule of Succession. ZABELL, Sandy L.

Σ1/2 Sets of Reals. IHODA, Jaime I.

Second Thoughts about Church's Thesis and Mathematical Proofs. MENDELSON, Elliott.

Second-order Logic, Foundations, and Rules. SHAPIRO, Stewart.

Semantics for Nonstandard Languages. MURAWSKI, Roman.

Semisimple Stable and Superstable Groups. BALDWIN, J T and PILLAY, A.

Sense Perceptual Intuition, Mathematical Existence, and Logical Imagination. TRAGESSER, Robert S.

The Sensible Foundation for Mathematics: A Defense of Kant's View. RISJORD, Mark.

LOGIC

Sequences in Countable Nonstandard Models of the Natural Numbers. LETH, Steven C.

Sequent-Systems and Groupoid Models, I. DOSEN, Kosta.

Sequent-Systems and Groupoid Models, II. DOSEN, Kosta.

Set Mappings on Dedekind Sets. BRUNNER, Norbert.

Sets as Singularities in the Intensional Universe. DAYNES, Keith.

Siegel on Critical Thinking. FINOCCHIARO, Maurice A.

A Simple and General Method of Solving the Finite Axiomatizability Problems for Lambek's Syntactic Calculi. ZIELONKA, Wojciech.

Simple Completeness Proof of Lemmon's SO:5. KONDO, Michiro.

The Simple Substitution Property of the Intermediate Propositional Logics. SASAKI, Katsumi.

The Simplest Hypothesis. HARMAN, Gilbert.

The Simplicity of the *Tractatus*. ANSCOMBE, Elizabeth.

A Simplification of the Completeness Proofs for Guaspari and Solovay's R. VOORBRAAK, Frans.

Sobre la identidad, la existencia y la constitución de las personas y otros seres. ZIRIÓN, Antonio (trans) and SOSA, Ernesto.

Sobre las "Obligationes" de Juan de Holanda. D'ORS, Angel.

Sobre preórdenes y operadores de consecuencias de Tarski. CASTRO, Juan Luis and TRILLAS, Enric.

Sobre una presunta inconsecuencia acerca de la noción de función en la doctrina de Frege. GAETA, Rodolfo.

Some Applications of Positive Formulas in Descriptive Set Theory and Logic. DYCK, Stephen.

Some Combinatorial Principles Equivalent to Restrictions of Transfinite Induction Up to Γ_0. KURATA, Reijiro and SHIMODA, M.

Some Compactness Results for Modal Logic. SCHUMM, George F.

Some Features of the Technical Language of Navya-Nyāya. BHATTACHARYYA, Sibajiban.

Some Filters of Partitions. MATET, Pierre.

Some Highly Undecidable Lattices. MAGIDOR, M and ROSENTHAL, J W and RUBIN, M and SROUR, G.

Some Misconceptions about Leibniz and the Calculi of 1679. VAN RIJEN, Jeroen.

Some Modal Propositional Logics Containing CO:8. YOKOTA, Shin-ichi.

Some Nonstandard Methods in Combinatorial Number Theory. LETH, Steven C.

Some Notes on Church's Thesis and the Theory of Games. ANDERLINI, Luca.

Some Principles Related to Chang's Conjecture. DONDER, Hans-Dieter and LEVINSKI, J P.

Some Restrictions on Simple Fixed Points of the Integers. MC COLM, Gregory L.

Some Results in Some Subsystems and In an Extension of C_n. BUNDER, M W.

Some Results on Intermediate Constructive Logics. MIGLIOLI, Pierangelo (and others).

Some Uses of Dilators in Combinatorial Problems, II. ABRUSCI, V Michele and GIRARD, Jean-Yves and VAN DE WIELE, Jacques.

Splitting $P_\kappa \lambda$ into Stationary Subsets. MATSUBARA, Yo.

Stability of Weak Second-Order Semantics. CSIRMAZ, László.

El status lógico de los *topoi* aristotélicos. CHICHI, Graciela.

Stove on Inductive Scepticism. GOWER, Barry.

Strong Measure Zero Sets and Rapid Filters. IHODA, Jaime I.

Strong Negative Partition Above the Continuum. SHELAH, Saharon.

Subformula Semantics for Strong Negation Systems. AKAMA, Seiki.

Subgroups of Stable Groups. WAGNER, Frank.

Subjective Probabilities and Betting Quotients. HOWSON, Colin.

Success Semantics. WHYTE, J T.

La superacion del analisis logico del lenguaje por medio de la metafisica. SILVA CAMARENA, Juan Manuel.

Supervaluational Anti-Realism and Logic. RASMUSSEN, Stig Alstrup.

Supervenience and Closure. VAN CLEVE, James.

Sur la signification logique et linguistique de la négation (in Romanian). BERCEANU, Barbu B.

Sur la structure particulière du dialogue argumentatif. MIHAI, Gheorghe.

Synonymy in Sentential Languages: A Pragmatic View. TOKARZ, Marek.

A Syntactical Characterization of Structural Completeness for Implicational Logics. WOJTYLAK, Piotr.

The Syntheticity of Time: Comments on Fang's Critique of Divine Computers. PALMQUIST, Stephen R.

A Systematical Approach to Leibniz's Theory of Relations and Relational Sentences. MUGNAI, Massimo.

Talking About Actions. SEGERBERG, Krister.

Teoría de la recursión y lógica. DIAS, M F and PORTELA FILHO, R N A.

Teoría lógica y argumentación. NAISHTAT, Francisco.

Tertiary Waywardness Tamed. ADAMS, Frederick.

Tesi di Hume e sistemi di logica deontica. GALVAN, Sergio.

Tharp and Conceptual Logic. WANG, Hao.

Tharp's 'Myth and Mathematics'. CHIHARA, Charles.

A Theorem on Barr-Exact Categories, with an Infinitary Generalization. MAKKAI, Michael.

A Theorem on Cocongruence of Rings. ROMANO, Daniel A.

Théories complètes de paires de corps valués henseliens. LELOUP, Gérard.

Theory Discovery from Data with Mixed Quantifiers. KELLY, Kevin T and GLYMOUR, Clark.

A Theory of Formal Truth Arithmetically Equivalent to ID_1. CANTINI, Andrea.

There Is Nothing Magical about Possible Worlds. MILLER, Richard B.

Three Theorems of Metaphysics. THARP, Leslie.

Tienen significado las contradicciones?. GÓMEZ, Astrid C and GUIBOURG, Ricardo A.

Topological Models of Epistemic Set Theory. GOODMAN, Nicolas D.

Towards a Real Phenomenology of Logic. PERUZZI, Alberto.

Towers in $[\omega]^\omega$ and $^\omega\omega$. DORDAL, P L.

Tractatus 6.2-6.22. HUGLY, Philip and SAYWARD, Charles.

Transfer Theorems for π-Monads. CUTLAND, Nigel J.

Truth and Convention. AZZOUNI, Jody.

Truth Theoretical Semantics and Ambiguity. GILLON, Brendan S.

Truth-Logics. VON WRIGHT, Georg Henrik.

Turing *L*-Machines and Recursive Computability for *L*-Maps. GERLA, Giangiacomo.

Turinici's Fixed Point Theorem and the Axiom of Choice. MANKA, Roman.

Turning Tricks with Convention T: Lessons Tarski Taught Me. RICE, Martin A.

Two Incomplete Anti-Realist Modal Epistemic Logics. WILLIAMSON, Timothy.

Two Traditions of Analogy. BROWN, William R.

Über die Stärke der Aristotelischen Modallogik. NORTMANN, Ulrich.

UFA Fails in the Bell-Kunen Model. MERRILL, John W L.

Uncountable Theories that are Categorical in a Higher Power. LASKOWSKI, Michael Chris.

Une méthode arithmétique de décision pour le système modal S5. SÁNCHEZ-MAZAS, Miguel.

A Uniform Method for Proving Lower Bounds on the Computational Complexity of Logical Theories. COMPTON, Kevin J and HENSON, C Ward.

Unique Nontransitive Measurement on Finite Sets. FISHBURN, Peter C.

The Uniqueness of the Natural Numbers. PARSONS, Charles.

Uniqueness, Definability and Interpolation. DOSEN, Kosta and SCHROEDER-HEISTER, Peter.

Uniqueness. KADMON, Nirit.

The Unspeakable: Understanding the System of Fallacy in the Media. MC MURTRY, John.

Unsuccessful Revisions of CCT. RAMACHANDRAN, Murali.

Urquhart's *C* with Minimal Negation. MÉNDEZ, José M.

The Use of Logical Models in Legal Problem Solving. KOWALSKI, Robert and SERGOT, Marek.

Vague Identity Yet Again. NOONAN, Harold W.

Vagueness and Meaning in Lukács' Ontology. MEZEI, György Iván.

Van Cleve versus Closure. BACON, John.

A Variation on a Paradox. HAZEN, Allen.

Varieties of Complex Algebras. GOLDBLATT, Robert.

Een vergelijking van inductief-statistisch redeneren en default logica. TAN, Yao-Hua.

Vérisimilarité et méthodologie poppérienne. LAFLEUR, Gérald.

La verità come inganno—L'Arte di Gorgia. VITALE, Vincenzo.

Vom epischen zum logischen sprechen: der spruch des Anaximander. RIEDEL, M.

Ways of Branching Quantifiers. SHER, Gila.

Weak Comparability of Well Orderings and Reverse Mathematics. FRIEDMAN, Harvey M and HIRST, J L.

Weakly Minimal Formulas: A Global Approach. NEWELSKI, L.

What are Goals and Joint Goals?. TUOMELA, Raimo.

What Became of Russell's "Relation-Arithmetic"?. SOLOMON, Graham.

What Can the History of Mathematics Learn from Philosophy?. HOVIS, R Corby.

What is a Question?. COHEN, Felix S.

What is Chinese Philosophy? (in Serbo-Croatian). CHENG, Anne.

What Is Reasoning? What Is an Argument?. WALTON, Doug.

Where MA First Fails. KUNEN, Kenneth.

Who *Needs* a Theory of Informal Logic?. DOSS, Seale.

Why 'Not'?. PRICE, Huw.

LOGICAL ANALYSIS
Meaning and Mental Representation. ECO, Umberto (ed).

LOGICAL ATOMISM
Logical Atomism in Plato's *Theaetetus.* RYLE, G.

LOGICAL CONNECTION
Peirce's Concept of Knowledge in 1868. SMYTH, Richard.

LOGICAL CONSTANT(S)
Linear Logic Display. BELNAP JR, Nuel D.
Logical and Extralogical Constants. SMOOK, Roger.
Logical Competence in the Context of Propositional Attitudes. ASTROH, Michael.
An Overview of Paraconsistent Logic in the 80s. DA COSTA, Newton C A and MARCONI, Diego.

LOGICAL EMPIRICISM
see also Logical Positivism
Positivism, Philosophy of Science, and Self-Understanding in Comte and Mill. SCHARFF, Robert C.

LOGICAL FORM
Logical Form. MAURY, André.
Reaching Moral Conclusions on Purely Logical Grounds. VAN WILLIGENBURG, Theo.

LOGICAL POSITIVISM
Holism—A Philosophy for Today: Anticipating the Twenty First Century. SETTANNI, Harry.
Aufbau/Bauhaus: Logical Positivism and Architectural Modernism. GALISON, Peter.
Een vergelijking van inductief-statistisch redeneren en default logica. TAN, Yao-I Iua.

LOGICAL POSSIBILITY
The Logical Limits of Science. SMITH, Joseph Wayne.

LOGICAL THEORY
Philosophy without Ambiguity: A Logico-Linguistic Essay. ATLAS, Jay David.
Teoría lógica y argumentación. NAISHTAT, Francisco.

LOGICAL TRUTH(S)
see also Analytic
A New Meaning in the History of Science: From the Logical Truth Towards the Ethical Truth. ISAC, Victor.

LOGICISM
The Critique of Logocentrism, or (Else) Derrida's Dead Line. DILWORTH, David A.

LOGOS
From Metaphysics to Rhetoric. MEYER, Michel (ed).
The Nature of Man in Early Stoic Philosophy. REESOR, Margaret E.
Logos and Trinity: Patterns of Platonist Influence on Early Christianity. DILLON, John.
Merleau-Ponty's nieuwe filosofie van de perceptie, de natuur en de logos. KWANT, R C.
The Splitting of the *Logos*: Some Remarks on Vico and Rabbinic Tradition. FAUR, José.

LOKERT, G
Notion and Object: Aspects of Late Medieval Epistemology. BROADIE, Alexander.

LOMAX, A
A Gynecentric Aesthetic. COX, Renée.

LONELINESS
Eternal Loneliness: Art and Religion in Kierkegaard and Zen. PATTISON, George.

LONERGAN, B
A Contribution to the Gadamer-Lonergan Discussion. BAUR, Michael.
A Conversation with Hans-Georg Gadamer. BAUR, Michael.
The Influence of Newman's Doctrine of Assent on the Thought of Bernard Lonergan. HAMMOND, David M.
Lonergan's Analysis of Error: An Experiment. TEKIPPE, Terry J.
Lonergan's Negative Dialectic. KIDDER, Paul.
The Notion of the Transcultural in Bernard Lonergan's Theology. LAMB, Matthew.
A Reflection on Lonergan's Notion of the Pure Desire to Know. MORELLI, Elizabeth A.
Ricoeur, Lonergan and the Intelligibility of Cosmic Time. PAMBRUN, James R.
Sources of Value. BARDEN, Garrett.

LONG, A
A Response to A A Long's "The Stoics on World-Conflagration and Everlasting Recurrence". HUDSON, Hud.

LORAND, R
Lorand and Kant on Free and Dependent Beauty. STECKER, Robert.

LORENZEN, P
Constructivism and Science: Essays in Recent German Philosophy. BUTTS, Robert E (ed).

LOSEV, A
Aleksei Fedorovich Losev. TAKHO-GODI, A.

LOTZE
Gebrauchssprache und Logik: Eine Philosophiehistorische Notiz zu Frege und Lotze. SCHMIT, Roger.

LOUKARIS, C
"Cyril Loukaris: A Protestant Patriarch or a Pioneer Orthodox Ecumenist?" in *The Wisdom of Faith: Essays in Honor of Dr Sebastian Alexander Matczak,* TSIRPANLIS, Constantine N.

LOVE
see also Eros
"The Son of Apollo": Themes of Plato. WOODBRIDGE, Frederick J E.
Eros, Agape and Philia: Readings in the Philosophy of Love. SOBLE, Alan (ed).
Love and Friendship in Plato and Aristotle. PRICE, A W.
Love: Emotion, Myth, and Metaphor. SOLOMON, Robert C.
Person to Person. GRAHAM, George (ed).
Reflective Wisdom: Richard Taylor on Issues That Matter. DONNELLY, John (ed).
"'Sunt aliquid manes': Personalities, Personae and Ghosts in Augustan Poetry" in *Post-Structuralist Classics,* COTTERILL, Rowland.
"Love's Way" in *Person to Person,* GARRETT, Richard.
"St Augustine" in *Ethics in the History of Western Philosophy,* LOSONCY, Thomas.
Amor y eternidad: La filosofía idealista de McTaggart. GEACH, Peter.
L'amour-propre: Un tema secentesco tra morale e antropologia. BOSCO, Domenico.
La autofundamentación de la conciencia y la liberación del espíritu. ELTON, Maria.
Can One Promise to Love Another?. WILSON, John.
Desire and Love in Descartes' Late Philosophy. BEAVERS, Anthony F.
Desire for All/Love of One: Tomas's Tale in *The Unbearable Lightness of Being.* DILLON, Martin C.
A Drama of Love and Death: Michael Pedersen Kierkegaard and Regine Olsen Revisited. PATTISON, George.
The Importance of Reverence. DAVIS, Lawrence H.
Love and Beauty in Plato's *Symposium.* WHITE, F C.
Love and the Natural Law. MC DERMOTT, John M.
Love, Beauty, and Death in Venice. WHITE, Richard.
Love, Moral Values and Proportionalism: A Response to Garth Hallett. POPE, Stephen J.
Racionalismo ético kantiano y amor puro. BULNES, Maria Elton.
San Agustín y K Rahner: El amor a Dios y el amor al prójimo. GALINDO RODRIGO, José Antonio.
Santayana's Philosophy of Love. SINGER, Irving.
The Subject of Love. NYE, Andrea.
Teaching and Mother Love. KLEIN, J Theodore.
Universalism Versus Love with Distinctions: An Ancient Debate Revived. WONG, David B.
Which One Is the Real One?. GRAYBOSCH, Anthony J.

LOVE, C
Nuclear Deterrence, Character, and Moral Education. KLEIN, J Theodore.

LOWE, V
The Philosophical Writings of Victor A Lowe (1907-1988). MC HENRY, Leemon B.

LOWENHEIM-SKOLEM THEOREM
Le rôle des théorèmes du type Löwenheim-Skolem dans la logique des prédicats du premier ordre (in Romanian). MIROIU, Adrian.

LOWITH, K
Ermeneutica e storia nel pensiero di Karl Löwith. PIEVATOLO, M Chiara.

LOYALTY
Corporate Loyalty, Does It Have a Future?. GROSMAN, Brian A.
Leo Strauss as Citizen and Jew. DANNHAUSER, Werner J.
On Deciding Whether a Nation Deserves Our Loyalty. NATHANSON, Stephen.
Porous Vessels: A Critique of the Nation, Nationalism and National

LOYALTY

Character as Analytical Concepts. FARRAR JR, L L.
When Loyalty No Harm Meant. ALLEN, R T.

LUCAS, G

"Reply to Lucas's "Science and Teleological Explanations"" in *Dialectic and Contemporary Science*, HARRIS, Errol E.

LUCAS, J

Commentary on "The Worm and the Juggernaut". BAYLES, Michael D.

LUCK

La conception stoïcienne et la conception aristotélicienne du bonheur. IRWIN, T H.
Morality and Bad Luck. THOMSON, Judith Jarvis.

LUCRETIUS

"Lucretius and Politics" in *Philosophia Togata: Essays on Philosophy and Roman Society*, FOWLER, D P.
F M Kamm and the Mirror of Time. FELDMAN, Fred.
Fra Plutone e Lucrezio: primo linea di una storia degli studi di filosofia antica nell'ottocento italiano. SASSI, Maria Michela.
Mortal Immortals: Lucretius on Death and the Voice of Nature. NUSSBAUM, Martha C.
The Symmetry Argument: Lucretius Against the Fear of Death. ROSENBAUM, Stephen E.

LUHMANN, N

Anmerkungen zur Autopoiesis. MOCEK, Reinhard.
L'autoreferenzialità luhmanniana: A proposito di normalizzazione dell'improbabile e improbabilità. AMATO MANGIAMELI, Agata C.
Ecologische communicatie door disciplinering van de moraal. STUY, Johan.
Niklas Luhmann over ecologische communicatie. BALLIU, Julien.

LUKACS, G

Ernst Bloch: Trame della speranza. BOELLA, Laura.
"Wonderful Vision of a Truly Human World" (On Lukács' Conception of Communism in 1919) (in Hungarian). PERECZ, László.
The Ethics of Struggle. DENYER, Tom.
Georg Lukács and the Ideological Fronts 1946-1949 (in Hungarian). RIPP, Zoltán.
Kritische Ontologie als Philosophie der Freiheit (in Serbo-Croatian). PREVE, Costanzo.
Leninismo y Marxismo en *Historia y Conciencia de Clases*. GIGLIOLI, Giovanna.
Lukács, Adorno en de machteloze kritiek. SALMAN, Ton.
Marxist Literary Theory: A Critique. LISMAN, C David.
On the Relationship of Lukács *Ontology* and the Theory of Social Formations (in Hungarian). KARIKÓ, Sándor.
Philosophy as Exile from Life: Lukacs' 'Soul and Form'. BROWNE, Paul.
The Moment of Ideology and the Human Factor in Lukác's Late Work (in Hungarian). SZABÓ, Tibor.
Totality, Realism, and the Type: Lukács' Later Literary Criticism as Political Theory. SHAW, Brian J.
Unknown Masterpiece. HELLER, Agnes.
Vagueness and Meaning in Lukács' Ontology. MEZEI, György Iván.

LUKASIEWICZ

Logic and Philosophy in the Lvov-Warsaw School. WOLÉNSKI, Jan.
La logica polivalente *in Statu Nascendi*. ÖFFENBERGER, Niels.

LUKES, S

Marx, Lukes, and Human Rights. BAXTER, David.

LULL

Apuntes sobre el pensamiento matemático de Ramón Llull. WELCH, John R and PALOS, Ana María.

LUTHER

Luther, Metaphor, and Theological Language. BIELFELDT, Dennis.
Müntzer contra Luther: Der philosophische Gehalt des theologischen Konflikts. GRÜNING, Thomas.
Ought-Implies-Can: Erasmus Luther and R M Hare. PIGDEN, Charles R.

LYCAN, W

Changing the Minimal Subject. CARTER, William.

LYING

Does Plato Think False Speech is Speech?. RUDEBUSCH, George.
Openness. MC MAHON, Christopher.
Successfully Lying to Oneself: A Sartrean Perspective. CATALANO, Joseph S.
When is Lying Morally Permissible? Casuistical Reflections on the Game Analogy, Self-Defense, Social Contract Ethics. VAN WYK, Robert N.

LYOTARD, J

Postmodern Social Analysis and Criticism. MURPHY, John W.
"Christ in the Postmodern Age: Reflections Inspired by Jean-François Lyotard" in *Varieties of Postmodern Theology*, BEARDSLEE, William A.
Discourse and Metaphysics. RUTHROF, Horst.
J F Lyotard's *The Postmodern Condition* and G B Vico's *De nostri temporis studiorum ratione*. KIERNAN, Suzanne.
Leviathan and the Post-Modern. WILLMS, Bernard.
Lyotard's Paralogy and Rorty's Pluralism: Their Differences and Pedagogical Implications. FRITZMAN, J M.
Postmodern Conditions: Rethinking Public Education. KIZILTAN, Mustafa Ü and BAIN, William J and CANIZARES, Anita.

MABILLON

Metafisica e teoria dei saperi da Mabillon a Dom Deschamps. QUILICI, Leana.

MACCOLL, H

Nature as a Source in the History of Logic, 1870-1910. CHRISTIE, Thony.

MACH

Mach's "Critique of Knowledge" and the Physiology of Senses (in Czechoslovakian). JANKO, Jan.

MACHIAVELLI

Democracy and Dictatorship. BOBBIO, Norberto.
Innocence and Experience. HAMPSHIRE, Stuart.
The Human Origins of *Fortuna* in Machiavelli's Thought. BALABAN, Oded.
Machiavel et la question de la Nature. EDMOND, Michel-Pierre.
Machiavel, lecteur des Anciens. ALLARD, Gérald.
Machiavelli, Tacito, Grozio: un nesso "ideale" tra libertinismo e previchismo. SCARCELLA, Cosimo.
Messy Morality and the Art of the Possible—I. COADY, C A J.
Morality, Politics and the Revolutions of 1989. O'NEILL, Onora.
The Politician and the Philosopher (Some Lessons from Machiavelli). DOLGOV, Konstantin M and JARKOWSKI, Jan (trans).
Republic and Politics in Machiavelli and Rousseau. VIROLI, Maurizio.
Virtud e interés: Fundamentos de la polis clásica y de la sociedad civil moderna. DEL BARCO, José Luis.

MACHINE(S)

"Wittgenstein and the Problem of Machine Consciousness" in *Wittgenstein in Focus—Im Brennpunkt: Wittgenstein*, NYIRI, J C.
Une Machine spéculative (informatique, intelligence artificielle et recherche cognitive). BORILLO, Mario.
Moral Dilemmas Concerning the Ultra Intelligent Machine. DE GARIS, Hugo.

MACINTYRE, A

God, Scepticism and Modernity. NIELSEN, Kai.
De afkeer van het individualisme bij Alisdair MacIntyre en de soevereiniteit van het individu. KAL, Victor.
After MacIntyre: Natural Law Theory, Virtue Ethics, and Eudaimonia. HITTINGER, Russell.
Alasdair MacIntyre on the Good Life and the 'Narrative Model'. BRADLEY, James.
Alasdair MacIntyre: The Virtue of Tradition. ALMOND, Brenda.
Can Emotivism Sustain a Social Ethic?. UNWIN, Nicholas.
Communitarian and Liberal Theories of the Good. PAUL, Jeffrey and MILLER JR, Fred D.
Crick, Hampshire and MacIntyre or Does an English-Speaking Neo-Aristotelianism Exist?. GIORGINI, Giovanni.
Epicurus and Friendship. STERN-GILLET, Suzanne.
Histories, Herstories, and Moral Traditions. MEAGHER, Sharon.
The Incommensurability of Moral Argument. SELKIRK, John.
MacIntyre on Traditions. ANNAS, Julia.
MacIntyre's Republic. SWINDLER, J K.
MacIntyre, Habermas, and Philosophical Ethics. KELLY, Michael.
Searching for Ancestors. O'HAGAN, Timothy.
Sport, Character, and Virtue. FEEZELL, Randolph.
Tradition and Reason in the History of Ethics. IRWIN, T H.
Vico and MacIntyre. COERS, Kathy Frashure.

MACKIE, J

God and the Burden of Proof: Plantinga, Swinburne, and the Analytic Defense of Theism. PARSONS, Keith M.

MACKINNON, C

Pornography as Representation: Aesthetic Considerations. GRACYK, Theodore A.

MACKINNON, D

Christ, Ethics and Tragedy: Essays in Honour of Donald MacKinnon. SURIN, Kenneth (ed).

MACKINNON, D

"'Between Purgation and Illumination': A Critique of the Theology of Right" in *Christ, Ethics and Tragedy: Essays in Honour of Donald MacKinnon*, MILBANK, John.

"Idealism and Realism: An Old Controversy Dissolved" in *Christ, Ethics and Tragedy: Essays in Honour of Donald MacKinnon*, KERR, Fergus.

"MacKinnon and the Parables" in *Christ, Ethics and Tragedy: Essays in Honour of Donald MacKinnon*, WHITE, Roger.

"MacKinnon and the Problem of Evil" in *Christ, Ethics and Tragedy: Essays in Honour of Donald MacKinnon*, HEBBLETHWAITE, Brian.

"Modes of Representation and Likeness to God" in *Christ, Ethics and Tragedy: Essays in Honour of Donald MacKinnon*, SHERRY, Patrick.

"On Being 'Placed' by John Milbank: A Response" in *Christ, Ethics and Tragedy: Essays in Honour of Donald MacKinnon*, HAUERWAS, Stanley.

"Pride and International Relations" in *Christ, Ethics and Tragedy: Essays in Honour of Donald MacKinnon*, PASKINS, Barrie.

"Some Aspects of the 'Grammar' of 'Incarnation' and 'Kenosis'" in *Christ, Ethics and Tragedy: Essays in Honour of Donald MacKinnon*, SURIN, Kenneth.

"Theological Rhetoric and Moral Passion in the Light of MacKinnon's 'Barth'" in *Christ, Ethics and Tragedy: Essays in Honour of Donald MacKinnon*, ROBERTS, Richard.

"Tragedy and Atonement" in *Christ, Ethics and Tragedy: Essays in Honour of Donald MacKinnon*, FORD, David F.

"Trinity and Ontology" in *Christ, Ethics and Tragedy: Essays in Honour of Donald MacKinnon*, WILLIAMS, Rowan.

MACMURRAY, J

Interpersonal Knowledge According to John Macmurray. ROY, Louis.
La persona nell'esperienza morale e giuridica. BAGOLINI, Luigi.

MADDALENA, A

Le "Letture dai Vangeli" di Antonio Maddalena. PAREYSON, Luigi.

MADHYAMIKA

Mādhyamika Buddhism and Quantum Mechanics: Beginning a Dialogue. MANSFIELD, Victor.
Relativity in Mādhyamika Buddhism and Modern Physics. MANSFIELD, Victor.

MADISON

Madison's Party Press Essays. SHEEHAN, Colleen A.

MADNESS

Michel Foucault's Archaeology of Scientific Reason. GUTTING, Gary.
Le fou stoïcien. BRAGUE, Rémi.
Madness and the Cogito: Derrida's Critique of *Folie et déraison*. COOK, Deborah.

MAGIC

John Dee's Natural Philosophy: Between Science and Religion. CLULEE, Nicholas H.

MAGNITUDE(S)

Descartes' Logic of Magnitudes. LOECK, Gisela.

MAHAYANA

Relativity in Mādhyamika Buddhism and Modern Physics. MANSFIELD, Victor.
Sūnyata and Ajāti: Absolutism and the Philosophies of Nāgārjuna and Gaudapāda. KING, Richard.

MAHLER, G

"O Mensch—Gib Acht": Friedrich Nietzsches Bedeutung Für Gustav Mahler. NIKKELS, Eveline.

MAIMONIDES

Baruch or Benedict: On Some Jewish Aspects of Spinoza's Philosophy. LEVY, Ze'ev.
Jewish Philosophy in a Secular Age. SEESKIN, Kenneth.
Moses Maimonides and His Time. ORMSBY, Eric L (ed).
A Philosopher's Harvest: The Philosophical Papers of Isaac Franck. GERBER, William (ed).
A Straight Path: Studies in Medieval Philosophy and Culture. LINK-SALINGER, Ruth (ed).
"'What Can We Know and When Can We Know It': On the Active Intelligence and Human Cognition" in *Moses Maimonides and His Time*, KOGAN, Barry S.
"Aquinas's Debt to Maimonides" in *A Straight Path: Studies in Medieval Philosophy and Culture*, BURRELL, David B.
"Crescas versus Maimonides on Knowledge and Pleasure" in *A Straight Path: Studies in Medieval Philosophy and Culture*, HARVEY, Warren Zev.
"Demonstrative, Dialectical and Sophistic Arguments in the Philosophy of Moses Maimonides" in *Moses Maimonides and His Time*, HYMAN,

Arthur.
"Freedom and Determinism in Maimonides' Philosophy" in *Moses Maimonides and His Time*, GELLMAN, Jerome I.
"The *Guide* and the *Gate*: The Dialectical Influence of Maimonides on Isaac ibn Latif and Early Spanish Kabbalah" in *A Straight Path: Studies in Medieval Philosophy and Culture*, WILENSKY, Sara Heller.
"Humility as a Virtue: A Maimonidean Critique of Aristotle's Ethics" in *Moses Maimonides and His Time*, FRANK, Daniel H.
"The Ideal State of the Philosophers and Prophetic Laws" in *A Straight Path: Studies in Medieval Philosophy and Culture*, BERMAN, Lawrence V.
"The Jews in Spain at the Time of Maimonides" in *Moses Maimonides and His Time*, ROTH, Norman.
"Maimonides and Aquinas on the Study of Metaphysics" in *A Straight Path: Studies in Medieval Philosophy and Culture*, MAURER, Armand A.
"Maimonides on Aristotle and Scientific Method" in *Moses Maimonides and His Time*, KRAEMER, Joel L.
"Maimonides' Egypt" in *Moses Maimonides and His Time*, COHEN, Mark R.
"Maimonides' Not-So-Secret Position on Creation" in *Moses Maimonides and His Time*, DUNPHY, William.
"Matter and Form as Attributes of God in Maimonides' Philosophy" in *A Straight Path: Studies in Medieval Philosophy and Culture*, GOODMAN, L E.
"Medieval Biblical Commentary and Philosophical Inquiry" in *Moses Maimonides and His Time*, DOBBS-WEINSTEIN, Idit.
"Newton and Maimonides" in *A Straight Path: Studies in Medieval Philosophy and Culture*, POPKIN, Richard H.
"On the Scope of Maimonides' *Logic*, Or, What Joseph Knew" in *A Straight Path: Studies in Medieval Philosophy and Culture*, WEISS, Raymond L.
"Problems of "Plenitude" in Maimonides and Gersonides" in *A Straight Path: Studies in Medieval Philosophy and Culture*, MANEKIN, Charles H.
A Note on the Arabic Term 'Anniyyah/'Aniyyah/'Inniyyah (in Hebrew). HARVEY, Warren Zev and HARVEY, Steven.
Attributes of Action in Maimonides. BUIJS, Joseph A.
Logical Syntax as a Key to a Secret of the *Guide of the Perplexed* (in Hebrew). STERN, Josef.
Maimonides on Prophecy and Human Nature: A Problem in Philosophical Interpretation. TRELOAR, John L.
Naming God: Moses Maimonides and Thomas Aquinas. STUBBENS, Neil A.
Remarques sur *Le Livre de la connaissance* de Maïmonide. STRAUSS, Leo.
The Problem of "Good" in the Philosophy of Maimonides (in Hebrew). KREISEL, Howard.

MAIORESCU, T

L'idée d'unité et d'autonomie des formes de la culture dans la conception de Titu Maiorescu. ROSCA, I N.

MAJORITY RULE

Public Choice II: A Revised Edition of "Public Choice". MUELLER, Dennis C.
John Locke: sobre la justificación del gobierno. AMOR, Claudio O.

MAKIN, S

Perfection and Necessity. LEFTOW, Brian.

MALCOLM, N

Malcolm on Language and Rules. BAKER, G P and HACKER, P M S.
What if Something Really Unheard-of Happened?. SCHEER, R K.

MALE(S)

Why Can't a Man Be More Like a Woman? (A Note on John Locke's Educational Thought). SIMONS, Martin.

MALEBRANCHE

Arnauld and the Cartesian Philosophy of Ideas. NADLER, Steven M.
"Ideas and Perception in Malebranche" in *Early Modern Philosophy II*, NADLER, Steven M.
Bérulle, Malebranche et l'amour de Dieu. BEAUDE, Joseph.
Malebranche et le libertin. MALBREIL, G.
Méditation malebranchiste sur le problème de l'illusion. VIEILLARD-BARON, Jean-Louis.
Philosophes européens et confucianisme au tournant dex XVIIe siècles. RODIS-LEWIS, Geneviève.
Religion et philosophie chez Descartes et Malebranche. GRIMALDI, Nicolas.

MALICE

"Glory, Respect, and Violent Conflict" in *The Causes of Quarrel: Essays on Peace, War, and Thomas Hobbes*, ALTMAN, Andrew.
"Malita" e "odium Dei" nella dottrina della volontà di Giovanni Duns Scoto. PIZZO, Giovanni.

MALIECKAL, L

A Response to the Paper "Theology of Religions and Sacrifice". FRANCIS, B Joseph.

MALTHUS

The Critique of Equalitarian Society in Malthus's *Essay*. GILBERT, Geoffrey.

The Eleventh Commandment: Sex and Spirit in Wollstonecraft and Malthus. NICHOLSON, Mervyn.

Malthus and Utilitarianism with Special Reference to the *Essay on Population*. HOLLANDER, Samuel.

MAN

see also Human(s), Individual(s), Person(s), Philosophical Anthropology

Man and Nature in the Philosophical Thought of Wang-Fu-Chih. BLACK, Alison Harley.

Man and Nature: The Chinese Tradition and the Future. TANG, Yi-Jie (ed).

The Nature of Man in Early Stoic Philosophy. REESOR, Margaret E.

"Liu Zongyuan's and Liu Yuxi's Theories of Heaven and Man" in *Man and Nature: The Chinese Tradition and the Future*, LI-TIAN, Fang.

"Man and Nature in the Indian Context" in *Man and Nature: The Chinese Tradition and the Future*, CHATTERJEE, Margaret.

"Man versus Nature and Natural Man" in *Man and Nature: The Chinese Tradition and the Future*, KUIDE, Chen.

"On the Relationship Between Man and Nature" in *Man and Nature: The Chinese Tradition and the Future*, NAN-SHENG, Huang and GUANGWU, Zhao.

"On the Unity of Man and Heaven" in *Man and Nature: The Chinese Tradition and the Future*, YI-JIE, Tang.

"Slave—Master—Friend, Philosophical Reflections Upon Man and Nature" in *Man and Nature: The Chinese Tradition and the Future*, ZHEN, Li.

"Theories Concerning Man and Nature in Classical Chinese Philosophy" in *Man and Nature: The Chinese Tradition and the Future*, DAI-NIAN, Zhang.

El acceso del hombre a la realidad según Xavier Zubiri. SIMONPIETRI MONEFELDT, Fannie A.

Anthropology of Peace. MAZUREK, Franciszek Janusz and LECKI, Maciej (trans).

The Areopagus of Values. SOFONEA, Liviu.

Art as an Axiology of Man. MOUTSOPOULOS, E.

Changes in the View on Man in Our Age (in Hungarian). NYÍRI, Tamás.

The Concepts of Man and Nature in Marxism. SARKER, Sunil Kumar.

Considerações Lógicas em torno de uma Definição do Homem. CHAVES-TANNÚS, Márcio.

Il dialogo cristiano-marxista a Budapest. SKALICKY, Carlo.

The Human Dimension of Christian Culture—The Common Heritage of the Nations of Europe. RODZINSKA, Aleksandra (trans) and KRAPIEC, Mieczyslaw A.

La inersorabilità della "nuda inteligencia" in Zubiri. INCARDONA, Nunzio.

Kant's Metaphysics of the Subject and Modern Society. FRIGERIO, C.

Man in the System of Socioeconomic Values. DUGIN, V N.

Man's Yearnings (in Dutch). OBERHOLZER, C K.

Das Menschenbild in der Psychotherapie. TOMAN, Walter.

Nature and Revolution in Paine's *Common Sense*. FRUCHTMAN, Jack.

New Connections of Man to the Nature (in Czechoslovakian). JIRIK, Vlastimil.

Pensar despues de Heidegger. ALBIZU, Edgardo.

Reid and the Rights of Man. DALGARNO, Melvin.

Le temps de la préhistoire et la venue de l'homme et des cultures sur la terre. MERCIER, A.

MANAGEMENT

Ethics in Practice: Managing the Moral Corporation. ANDREWS, Kenneth R (ed).

Papers on the Ethics of Administration. WRIGHT, N Dale (ed).

"The Concentric Circles of Management Thought" in *Papers on the Ethics of Administration*, SCOTT, William G.

"Ethics and Responsibility" in *Papers on the Ethics of Administration*, WALTERS, Kenneth D.

"Introduction" in *Papers on the Ethics of Administration*, WRIGHT, N Dale and MC KONKIE, Stanford S.

"The Paradox of Profit" in *Papers on the Ethics of Administration*, BOWIE, Norman E.

"The Sympathetic Organization" in *Papers on the Ethics of Administration*, HART, David K.

Are Women Different and Why are Women Thought to be Different? Theoretical and Methodological Perspectives. GREGORY, Ann.

Are Women Owner-Managers Challenging Our Definitions of Entrepreneurship? An In-Depth Survey. LEE-GOSSELIN, H and GRISÉ, J.

At the Heart of Women in Management Research: Theoretical and Methodological Approaches and Their Biases. FAGENSON, Ellen A.

Attending to Ethics in Management. WATERS, James A and BIRD, Frederick.

Business Ethics: Defining the Twilight Zone. NEL, Deon and PITT, Leyland.

Career Barriers: Do We Need More Research?. CULLEN, Dallas.

Commentary on "An Empirical Study of Moral Reasoning Among Managers". KELLY, Michaeleen.

An Empirical Study of Moral Reasoning Among Managers. DERRY, Robbin.

An Enterprise/Organization Ethic. DI NORCIA, Vincent.

Epistemological and Ethical Considerations in Conceptualizing and Implementing Human Resource Management. DACHLER, H Peter and ENDERLE, Georges.

The Ethical Implications of Corporate Records Management Practices and Some Suggested Ethical Values for Decisions. RUHNKA, John C and WELLER, Steven.

Formal and Informal Management Training Programs for Women in Canada: Who Seems to Be Doing a Good Job?. LAVOIE, Dina.

Frontiers and New Vistas in Women in Management Research. SEKARAN, Uma.

Funding the Department of Education's TRIO Programs. EKSTEROWICZ, Anthony J and GARTNER, James D.

The Hard Problem of Management is Freedom, Not the Commons. DI NORCIA, Vincent.

Individual and Organizational Characteristics of Women in Managerial Leadership. ROWNEY, J I A and CAHOON, A R.

An Integrative Model for Understanding and Managing Ethical Behavior in Business Organizations. STEAD, W Edward and WORRELL, Dan L and STEAD, Jean Garner.

Management Training for Women: International Experiences and Lessons for Canada. LAM, M Natalie.

Managerial Authority. MC MAHON, Christopher.

Managers, Values, and Executive Decisions. BARNETT, John H and KARSON, Marvin J.

No Bosses Here: Management in Worker Co-Operatives. CONN, Melanie.

Research, Myths and Expectations: New Challenges for Management Educators. GRONDIN, Deirdre.

A Stakeholder Apologetic for Management. SHARPLIN, Arthur and PHELPS, Lonnie D.

Stop or Go: Reflections of Women Managers on Factors Influencing their Career Development. ANDREW, C and CODERRE, C and DENIS, A.

Student Views on "Ethical" Issues: A Situational Analysis. JONES JR, William A.

Testing as a Selection Tool: Another Old and Sticky Managerial Human Rights Issue. MUNCHUS, George.

Training and Women: Some Thoughts from the Grassroots. JOYCE, Glenis.

Value Congruence: The Interplay of Individual and Organizational Value Systems. LIEDTKA, Jeanne M.

The Women in Management Research Program at the National Centre for Management Research and Development. BURKE, R J and MIKALACHKI, D.

MANCINI, P

La missione filosofica del diritto nella Napoli del giovane Mancini. OLDRINI, Guido.

MANDELBAUM, M

Realism and Structurism in Historical Theory: A Discussion of the Thought of Maurice Mandelbaum. LLOYD, Christopher.

MANDEVILLE

"Smith and Kant Respond to Mandeville" in *Early Modern Philosophy II*, LEVY, David.

MANICHEISM

Manichaean Responses to Zoroastrianism. SCOTT, David.

MANIPULATION

An Empirical Examination of Three Machiavellian Concepts: Advertisers Versus the General Public. FRAEDRICH, John and FERRELL, O C.

Goffman's Revisions. MANNING, Phil.

MANKIND

see also Humanity

"Postmortem Thought and the End of Man" in *The Question of the Other: Essays in Contemporary Continental Philosophy*, CLIFFORD, Michael.

Universalism: A New Way of Thinking. KUCZYNSKI, Janusz and PETROWICZ, Lech (trans) and GOLEBIOWSKI, Marek (trans).

MANN, T

Love, Beauty, and Death in Venice. WHITE, Richard.

Pessimismo e umanesimo in Thomas Mann: Una riflessione etica su "Humanität" e "Humanismus". PERNECHELE, Gabriella.

MANNERISM
The Poetic Structure of the World: Copernicus and Kepler. HALLYN, Fernand.

MANNHEIM, K
Sociognoseología y objectividad. MORALES, Julián.

MANUSCRIPT(S)
Berkeley's Introduction Draft. STEWART, M A.
Un manoscritto inedito delle 'Adnotationes' al *Tractatus Theologico-Politicus* di Spinoza. TOTARO, Giuseppina.
Sources for the *Ladies' Library.* HOLLINGSHEAD, Greg.

MANY
see also Pluralism
Parmenides 142b5-144e7: The "Unity is Many" Arguments. CURD, Patricia Kenig.
La síntesis de lo uno y lo múltiple. HARRIS, Errol E.

MANY-VALUED LOGICS
The Semantic Foundations of Logic, Volume 1: Propositional Logics. EPSTEIN, Richard L.
Bivalenza e trascendenza. COZZO, Cesare.
La logica polivalente *in Statu Nascendi.* ÖFFENBERGER, Niels.
Motivation and Demotivation of a Four-Valued Logic. FOX, John.
A Paraconsistent Many-Valued Propositional Logic. D'OTTAVIANO, Itala M L and EPSTEIN, Richard L.
Urquhart's *C* with Minimal Negation. MÉNDEZ, José M.

MAO
The Thought of Mao Tse-Tung. SCHRAM, Stuart.
Tolerância e interpretação. DASCAL, Marcelo.

MAPPING
Set Mappings on Dedekind Sets. BRUNNER, Norbert.

MARCEL
Dialogo sobre humanismo y existencialismo (cuarta y última parte). SILVA CAMARENA, Juan Manuel.
La metafísica de la esperanza y del deseo en Gabriel Marcel. O'CALLAGHAN, Paul.
Some Concrete Approaches to Nature in *Kio and Gus.* HAMRICK, William S.
Substitution: Marcel and Levinas. GIBBS, Robert B.
Tres niveles de conocimiento en la filosofía de Gabriel Marcel. CAÑAS, José Luis.
When Loyalty No Harm Meant. ALLEN, R T.

MARCION
En torno al modalismo de Marción. ORBE, Antonio.

MARCOVICI, S
L'illuministe Simeon Marcovici—un remarquable journaliste et pensuer (in Romanian). ISAR, N.

MARCUS AURELIUS
The "Meditations" of Marcus Aurelius: A Study. RUTHERFORD, R B.

MARCUSE, H
Social Theory and the Crisis of Marxism. MC CARNEY, Joseph.
Hegel y Marcuse: *El Ideal o la Forma Estética.* FACIO, Tatiana.
The Marcuse-Dunayevskaya Dialogue, 1954-1979. ANDERSON, Kevin.
Zur sozialphilosophischen Bedeutung des Sprachbegriffs Wilhelm von Humboldts. SCHILLER, Hans-Ernst.

MARGOLIS, J
Philosophical Aesthetics and the Education of Teachers. REDFERN, H B.

MARITAIN
Intuición estética e intuición ética en Jacques Maritain. CHALMETA, Gabriel.
L'esthétique de l'intuition chez Jacques Maritain (in Japanese). KAMIKURA, Tsuneyuki.

MARKET(S)
The Ethics of Insider Trading. WERHANE, Patricia H.
Market Equality and Social Freedom. HOLLIS, Martin.
Marxist Critical Theory, Contradictions, and Ecological Succession. CATTON, Philip.
Mergers, Acquisitions and the Market for Corporate Control. WERHANE, Patricia H.

MARKETING
The AIDS Crisis: Unethical Marketing Leads to Negligent Homicide. KROHN, Franklin B and MILNER, Laura M.
Attitudes of Marketing Professionals Toward Ethics in Marketing Research: A Cross-National Comparison. AKAAH, Ishmael P.
Business Ethics: A Literature Review with a Focus on Marketing Ethics.

TSALIKIS, John and FRITZSCHE, David J.
Ecological Marketing Strategy for Toni Yogurts in Switzerland. DYLLICK, Thomas.
Ethical and Conceptual Issues in Charitable Investments, Cause Related Marketing, and Advertising. DIENHART, John W and FODERICK, Saundra I.
Ethical Behavior Among Marketing Researchers: An Assessment of Selected Demographic Characteristics. KELLEY, S W and FERRELL, O C and SKINNER, S J.
Honesty in Marketing. JACKSON, Jennifer.
Marketing/Business Ethics: A Review of the Empirical Research. FRITSCHE, David J.
MBAs' Changing Attitudes Toward Marketing Dilemmas: 1981-1987. ZINKHAN, George M.
Perceived Common Myths and Unethical Practices Among Direct Marketing Professionals. STORHOLM, Gordon.
Taking the Train to a World of Strangers: Health Care Marketing and Ethics. NELSON, Lawrence J and CLARK, H Westley and GOLDMAN, Robert L and SCHORE, Jean E.

MARQUARD, O
Hypolepsis und Kompensation—Odo Marquards philosophischer Beitrag zur Diagnose und Bewältigung der Gegenwart. KERSTING, Wolfgang.

MARQUIS, D
Does a Fetus Already Have a Future-like-ours?. MC INERNEY, Peter K.
Killing, Abortion, and Contraception: A Reply to Marquis. NORCROSS, Alastair.
Sensationalized Philosophy: A Reply to Marquis's "Why Abortion is Immoral". CUDD, Ann E.

MARRIAGE
Rational Sex Ethics (Second Edition). ARD, Ben Neal.
"Commitment and the Value of Marriage" in *Person to Person,* GRAHAM, Gordon.
The Distinctiveness of Early Christian Sexual Ethics. PRICE, Richard M.
To Discover Again Marriage. HERVADA, Javier.

MARTIN, C
Cause, Mind, and Reality: Essays Honoring C B Martin. HEIL, John (ed).
"C B Martin, A Biographical Sketch" in *Cause, Mind, and Reality: Essays Honoring C B Martin,* SMART, J J C.
"C B Martin, Counterfactuals, Causality, and Conditionals" in *Cause, Mind, and Reality: Essays Honoring C B Martin,* ARMSTRONG, D M.
"Low Claim Assertions" in *Cause, Mind, and Reality: Essays Honoring C B Martin,* PLACE, Ullin T.
"Verificationism" in *Cause, Mind, and Reality: Essays Honoring C B Martin,* SMART, J J C.

MARTIN, M
Explaining Wrongdoing. DAVIS, Michael.

MARTIN-LOF, P
Categorical and Algebraic Aspects of Martin-Löf Type Theory. OBTULOWICZ, A.
Domain Interpretations of Martin-Löf's Partial Type Theory. PALMGREN, Erik and STOLTENBERG-HANSEN, Viggo.
The Inconsistency of Higher Order Extensions of Martin-Löf's Type Theory. JACOBS, Bart.
A Note on Russell's Paradox in Locally Cartesian Closed Categories. PITTS, Andrew M and TAYLOR, Paul.

MARX
The American Evasion of Philosophy: A Genealogy of Pragmatism. WEST, Cornel.
Collected Works, Volume 31, Marx: 1861-1863. MARX, Karl.
Collected Works, Volume 32, Marx: 1861-1863. MARX, Karl.
Collected Works, Volume 44, Marx and Engels: 1870-1873. MARX, Karl.
Critical Theory and Poststructuralism: In Search of a Context. POSTER, Mark.
The Dialectics of Seeing: Walter Benjamin and the Arcades Project. BUCK-MORSS, Susan.
Fourier: La Passione dell'Utopia. COLOMBO, Arrigo (ed).
Habermas on Historical Materialism. ROCKMORE, Tom.
Hegel, Heraclitus, and Marx's Dialectic. WILLIAMS, Howard.
Heritage and Challenge: The History and Theory of History. CONKIN, Paul K.
An Introductory Guide to Post-Structuralism and Postmodernism. SARUP, Madan.
Inwardness and Existence: Subjectivity in/and Hegel, Heidegger, Marx, and Freud. DAVIS, Walter A.
Liberal Justice and the Marxist Critique of Education: A Study of Conflicting Research Programs. STRIKE, Kenneth A.

MARX

More Heat than Light: Economics as Social Physics, Physics as Nature's Economics. MIROWSKI, Philip.

Readings from Karl Marx. SAYER, Derek (ed).

Social Philosophy and Ecological Scarcity. LEE, Keekok.

Social Theory and the Crisis of Marxism. MC CARNEY, Joseph.

Subject and Consciousness: A Philosophical Inquiry Into Self-Consciousness. BALABAN, Oded.

A Theory of Property. MUNZER, Stephen R.

"Absolute Fruit and Abstract Labor" in *Knowledge and Politics,* WOLFF, Robert Paul.

"Marxism and Individualism" in *Knowledge and Politics,* ELSTER, Jon.

"On Recent Problems of the Sociology of Science in the Context of Karl Marx's Ideas" in *Scientific Knowledge Socialized,* MARKOVA, Ludmilla A.

"On the Relationship Between Man and Nature" in *Man and Nature: The Chinese Tradition and the Future,* NAN-SHENG, Huang and GUANGWU, Zhao.

"'Ideology' in Marx and Engels": A Reply. MC CARNEY, J.

'Communicatief handelen' als theoretisch grondbegrip. COBBEN, Paul.

Alternative Interpretations of Aristotle on Exchange and Reciprocity. MC NEILL, Desmond.

Analytical Marxism and Marx's Systematic Dialectical Theory. SMITH, Tony.

Arendt, Republicanism and Patriarchalism. SPRINGBORG, Patricia.

Ateismo e libertà. MONDIN, B.

The Availability of a Marxian Critique of Technology. KULKARNI, S G.

Can Philosophy Perish? (in Czechoslovakian). PATOCKA, Jan.

Class—A Simple View. GRAHAM, Keith.

The Communitarian Critique of Liberalism. WALZER, Michael.

Critical Theory as Metaphilosophy. BOHMAN, James.

La critique marxienne de la religion. TOSEL, André.

The Debate Regarding Dialectical Logic in Marx's Economic Writings. SMITH, Tony.

Determination and Consciousness in Marx. MILLS, Charles W.

The Dialectics of Peace Education. RAPOPORT, Anatol.

The Doctoral Dissertation of Karl Marx. TEEPLE, G.

Duquette, Hegel, and Political Freedom. BIEN, Joseph.

Économie de la violence, violence de l'économie: Derrida et Marx. MALABOU, Catherine.

Explanatory Grounds: Marx versus Foucault. GOULD, James A.

Fetishism, Argument, and Judgment in *Capital.* FINOCCHIARO, Maurice A.

La filosofia del Novecento: dalla razionalità all'irrazionalità. DEL VECCHIO, Dante.

La filosofía política marxista y la revolución. COLBERT, James.

The French Revolution and the Education of the Young Marx. RUBEL, Maximilien and WALKER, R Scott (trans).

Hegel, Marx and the Cunning of Reason. PARKINSON, G H R.

Heidegger und das Problem der Metaphysik. GERLACH, Hans-Martin.

The Hermeneutics of the Young Marx: According to Marx's Approach to the Philosophy of Democritus and Epicurus. BALABAN, Oded.

How Marxism Became Analytic. MARTIN, Bill.

Intergenerational Justice and Productive Resources; A Nineteenth Century Socialist Debate. CUNLIFFE, John.

Liberal Constitutionalism as Ideology: Marx and Habermas. WARREN, Mark.

Marx et le destin historique de la morale (in Romanian). NITA, Petre.

Marx on Freedom and Necessity. BEEHLER, Rodger.

Marx's Promethean Humanism. ABRAHAM, Kuruvilla C.

Marx's Use of Religious Metaphors. JEANNOT, Thomas M.

Marx, Lukes, and Human Rights. BAXTER, David.

Marxist Critical Theory, Contradictions, and Ecological Succession. CATTON, Philip.

The Metaphysics of Communism. LURIE, Yuval.

Les mutations de l'historiographie Révolutionnaire. FURET, M François.

The Novelty of Marx's Theory of *Praxis.* MARGOLIS, Joseph.

Per una storia della cultura. TESSITORE, Fulvio.

The Problem of the Historicity of Values. PEROV, I V.

Quelques réflexions sur une thèse marxiste (in Romanian). BOTIS, Gheorghe.

Remembering and Re-Creating the Classing. CASANOVA, Pablo González.

Representation in the Eighteenth Brumaire of Karl Marx. REDNER, Harry.

Scarcity and Setting the Boundaries of Political Economy. SASSOWER, Raphael.

The Significance of Darwinian Theory for Marx and Engels. TAYLOR, Angus.

Social Philosophy: The Agenda for the 'Nineties. WOLFF, Robert Paul.

The Critique and Utopia of the Subject (in Serbo-Croatian). SCHILLER, Hans-Ernst.

Was Marx an Egalitarian: Skeptical Remarks on Miller's Marx. NIELSEN, Kai.

Western Marxism: A Fictionalist Deconstruction. GRAY, John.

What's Left: Marx, Foucault and Contemporary Problems of Social Change. WAPNER, Paul.

Zum Philosophieverständnis bedeutender Persönlichkeiten der II, Internationale. WRONA, Vera.

Zur Problematik von Entwicklung und Fortschritt im soziologischen Werk Max Webers. WITTICH, Dietmar.

MARXISM

Darwin in Russian Thought. VUCINICH, Alexander.

French Philosophy of the Sixties: An Essay on Antihumanism. CATTANI, Mary Schnackenberg (trans).

Habermas on Historical Materialism. ROCKMORE, Tom.

Jean Baudrillard: From Marxism to Postmodernism. KELLNER, Douglas.

Liberal Justice and the Marxist Critique of Education: A Study of Conflicting Research Programs. STRIKE, Kenneth A.

Liberty and Culture: Essays on the Idea of a Free Society. MACHAN, Tibor R.

Man, Science, Humanism: A New Synthesis. FROLOV, Ivan T.

Marxism and Morality. LUKES, Steven.

Our Philosophy: Allāma Muhammad Bāqir As-Sadr. INATI, Shams C (trans).

The Political Theory of Liberation Theology: Toward a Reconvergence of Social Value and Science. POTTENGER, John R.

Reclaiming Reality: A Critical Introduction to Contemporary Philosophy. BHASKAR, Roy.

Selections from Political Writings, 1921-1926: Antonio Gramsci. GRAMSCI, Antonio.

Social Theory and the Crisis of Marxism. MC CARNEY, Joseph.

The State and Justice: An Essay in Political Theory. FISK, Milton.

The Thought of Mao Tse-Tung. SCHRAM, Stuart.

Traditions, Tyranny, and Utopias: Essays in the Politics of Awareness. NANDY, Ashis.

"Marxism and Ecology" in *Inquiries into Values: The Inaugural Session of the International Society for Value Inquiry,* FISCHER, Norman.

"The Marxists" in *Reading Philosophy for the Twenty-First Century,* DE GEORGE, Richard T.

"Posthumous Anachronisms in the Work of Sartre" in *Inquiries into Values: The Inaugural Session of the International Society for Value Inquiry,* CAWS, Peter.

"Problems of Value in Marxist Philosophy" in *Inquiries into Values: The Inaugural Session of the International Society for Value Inquiry,* MARCZUK, Stanislaw.

"Themes in Marxism" in *Reading Philosophy for the Twenty-First Century,* SOMERVILLE, John.

"Krise des Fortschritts—Umkehr zur Zukunft": Zu einigen Aspekten religiöser Welt-und Fortschrittssicht. HEGENBARTH, Siegfried.

40 Jahre Philosophie in der DDR. WITTICH, Dieter.

A Philosophical (Hermeneutical) Survey of Modern Abstract Art (in Czechoslovakian). PINKAVA, J.

Analytical Marxism and Marx's Systematic Dialectical Theory. SMITH, Tony.

Anmerkungen zum Real Existierenden Totalitarismus und zu seinen Apologeten unter uns. MARKO, Kurt.

The Availability of a Marxian Critique of Technology. KULKARNI, S G.

Bedingungen für die Aneignung und Verbreitung des Marxismus-Leninismus in afrikanischen ländern. BASTOS, Feliciano Moreira.

Bemerkungen zum Begriff "Austromarxismus". KLEIN, Horst.

Brauchen wir eine Kategorie Persönlichkeit?. RONNEBERG, Heinz.

Catholicism and Socialism: The Problems of Political Understanding. OPARA, Stefan and PROTALINSKI, Grzegorz (trans).

Christianity and Marxism: Confrontation, Dialogue, Universalism. KUCZYNSKI, Janusz.

The Concepts of Man and Nature in Marxism. SARKER, Sunil Kumar.

Concerning the Problems Surrounding "Theoretical Consciousness" (in Czechoslovakian). KROH, M.

Confucius—China's Dethroned Sage? (in Serbo-Croatian). KRAMERS, Robert P.

The Crisis of Marxism and Some of Its Implications. WAMBA-DIA-WAMBA, Ernest.

Dialectical Materialism and Logical Pragmatism: On J E McClellan's "Logical Pragmatism and Dialectical Materialism". PANOVA, Elena.

Il dialogo cristiano-marxista a Budapest. SKALICKY, Carlo.

The Dialogue of Grand Theories for Peace. PLUZANSKI, Tadeusz and KISIEL, Krystyna (trans) and KISIEL, Chester (trans).

Engagement ou néantisation? (in Greek). DÉLIVOYATZIS, S.

Ergebnisse und Probleme der Entwicklung des historischen Materialismus. STIEHLER, Gottfried.

MATERIALISM

Society. JOHANSSON, Ingvar.

Our Philosophy: Allāma Muhammad Bāqir As-Sadr. INATI, Shams C (trans).

The Problem of the Ideal. DUBROVSKY, David.

Reclaiming Reality: A Critical Introduction to Contemporary Philosophy. BHASKAR, Roy.

"Low Claim Assertions" in *Cause, Mind, and Reality: Essays Honoring C B Martin,* PLACE, Ullin T.

"On Formulating Materialism and Dualism" in *Cause, Mind, and Reality: Essays Honoring C B Martin,* SNOWDON, P F.

Between Infinity and Community: Notes on Materialism in Spinoza and Leopardi. NEGRI, Antonio.

The Birth of Nietzsche Out of the Spirit of Lange. WILCOX, John T.

Cultural History and Cultural Materialism. BERMAN, Ronald.

Eliminative Materialism: The Reality of the Mental, and Folk Psychology—A Reply to O'Gorman. MILLS, Stephen.

Emil Lask and the Crisis of Neo-Kantianism: The Rediscovery of the Primordial World. MOTZKIN, Gabriel.

Empirical Functionalism and Conceivability Arguments. JACOBY, Henry

Frank Jackson's Knowledge Argument Against Materialism. FURASH, Gary.

From Lange to Nietzsche: A Response to a Troika of Critics. STACK, George J.

Hermes the Interpreter. SAATKAMP JR, Herman J.

Hobbes's Mortalism. JOHNSTON, David.

Is Jayarasi a Materialist?. MOHANTA, Dilipkumar.

John Paul II vis-à-vis Atheism and Materialism: Remarks on the Encyclical Dominum et vivificantem. TANALSKI, Dionizy and RODZINSKA, Aleksandra (trans).

Lange, Nietzsche, and Stack: The Question of "Influence". BREAZEALE, Daniel.

Matérialisme, métaphysique, éthique (in Polish). FRITZHAND, Marek.

Materialismo Presocrático. SEGURA, Eugenio.

Materialità del testo e pratica interpretativa: la semanlisi di Julia Kristeva. BRUNO, G.

Mentalism-Cum-Physicalism vs Eliminative Materialism. O'GORMAN, P F.

Opposing Science with Art, Again? Nietzsche's Project According to Stack. SEIGFRIED, Hans.

Santayana and Democritus—Two Mutually Interpreting Philosophical Poets. DILWORTH, David A.

Santayana's Autobiography and the Development of his Philosophy. SAATKAMP JR, Herman J.

Santayana's Non-Reductive Naturalism. KERR-LAWSON, Angus.

Santayana's Philosophy of Love. SINGER, Irving.

Thomas Reid's Critique of Joseph Priestley: Context and Chronology. WOOD, Paul B.

Towards a "Materialist" Critique of "Religious Pluralism". SURIN, Kenneth.

MATERIALITY

"Phenomenality and Materiality in Kant" in *The Textual Sublime: Deconstruction and Its Differences,* DE MAN, Paul.

MATHEMATICS

see also Algebra, Geometry

Axioms of Cooperative Decision Making. MOULIN, Hervé.

A Combinatorial Theory of Possibility. ARMSTRONG, D M.

Conceptual Relevance. GRÜNFELD, Joseph.

Constructivism and Science: Essays in Recent German Philosophy. BUTTS, Robert E (ed).

The Ethics of Geometry: A Genealogy of Modernity. LACHTERMAN, David R.

The Fourth Way: A Theory of Knowledge. GROSSMAN, Reinhardt.

The Infinite. MOORE, A W.

John Dee's Natural Philosophy: Between Science and Religion. CLULEE, Nicholas H.

Logic and Knowledge: Bertrand Russell, Essays 1901-1950. MARSH, Robert Charles (ed).

Logic and Philosophy in the Lvov-Warsaw School. WOLÉNSKI, Jan.

Mathematical Methods in Linguistics. PARTEE, Barbara H.

Philosophical Introduction to Set Theory. POLLARD, Stephen.

Philosophische Bemerkungen. KURTH, Rudolf.

The Philosophy of F P Ramsey. SAHLIN, Nils-Eric.

The Philosophy of Set Theory: An Historical Introduction to Cantor's Paradise. TILES, Mary E.

Pythagoras Revived: Mathematics and Philosophy in Late Antiquity. O'MEARA, Dominic J.

Realism, Mathematics and Modality. FIELD, Hartry.

Writings of Charles S Peirce: A Chronological Edition, Volume 4, 1879-1884. KLOESEL, Christian J W (ed).

"Deus ex machina" redivivus: The "Synthetic A Priori" in the Computer Age.

FANG, J.

Le "Pari" de Pascal. BONHOEFFER, Thomas.

Analytico-Referentiality and Legitimation in Modern Mathematics. ROUSSOPOULOS, George.

The Anthropology of Incommensurability. BIAGIOLI, Mario.

Apuntes sobre el pensamiento matemático de Ramón Llull. WELCH, John R and PALOS, Ana María.

Aristotle on the Difference between Mathematics and Physics and First Philosophy. MODRAK, D K W.

Ars inveniendi et théorie des modèles. BENIS-SINACEUR, Hourya.

The Autonomy of Mathematics. STEINER, Mark.

Bar-Hillel: The Man and his Philosophy of Mathematics. MARGALIT, Avishai.

Bernard Nieuwentijt and the Leibnizian Calculus. VERMIJ, R H.

Can Philosophy Be Mathematized?—Probabilistic Theory of Meanings and Semantic Architectonics of Personality. NALIMOV, V V.

Certain Fundamental Problems and Trends of Thought in Mathematics. STRAUSS, D F M.

Der Charakter der Mathematik zwischen Philosophie und Wissenschaft. OTTE, Michael.

Chez Fermat A.D. 1637. MAULA, Erkka and KASANEN, Eero.

Comment on Shrader-Frechette's "Parfit and Mistakes in Moral Mathematics". GRACELY, Edward J.

Definiciones impredicativas. MOLINA, Jorge.

Depolarizing Mathematics and Religion. VOSS, Sarah.

Distortions and Discontinuities of Mathematical Progress: A Matter of Luck, A Matter of Time, ... A Matter of Fact. ANELLIS, Irving H.

Domain Extension and the Philosophy of Mathematics. MANDERS, Kenneth.

Duhem and the History and Philosophy of Mathematics. CROWE, Michael J.

The End of the Absolute: A Nineteenth-Century Contribution to General Relativity. FARWELL, Ruth and KNEE, Christopher.

EUCLID: Rhetoric in Mathematics. LOOMIS, David E.

Fermat's Last Theorem, a General Dimensional Analysis Problem. STAICU, Constantin I.

A Filosofia da Matemática em Wittgenstein. DE SOUSA ALVES, Vitorino.

Foundations of Mathematics or Mathematical Practice: Is One Forced To Choose?. VAN BENDEGEM, Jean Paul.

Frege on the Statement of Number. SULLIVAN, David.

Geometry and Medicine: Mathematics in the Thought of Galen of Pergamum. GRANT, Hardy.

God's Lottery. MC CALL, Storrs and ARMSTRONG, D M.

Hay una filosofía de la ciencia en el último Wittgenstein?. MOULINES, C Ulises.

The Hierarchical Structure of Testing Theories. KUOKKANEN, Martti.

Hilbert's Program Relativized: Proof-Theoretical and Foundational Reductions. FEFERMAN, Solomon.

Hilbert's Program Sixty Years Later. SIEG, Wilfried.

Hintikka on Kant and Logic. RUSSELL, Christopher.

Innovation and Understanding in Mathematics. KITCHER, Philip.

Inquiry Into Meaning and Truth. THOMAS, R S D.

Introduction to 'Three Theorems of Metaphysics'. SKYRMS, Brian.

Is Philosophy, As Is, "Bunk"?. FANG, J.

The Iterative Hierarchy of Sets. TAIT, William.

Lagrange's Analytical Mathematics, Its Cartesian Origins and Reception in Comte's Positive Philosophy. FRASER, Craig G.

La matemática y el ámbito conceptual. DE LORENZO, Javier.

Mathematical Necessity and Reality. FRANKLIN, James.

The Mathematical Philosophy of Contact. HAZEN, A P.

Mathematical Skepticism: Are We Brains in a Countable Vat?. TYMOCZKO, Thomas.

Le mathématicien et ses images. DELESSERT, André.

Mathematics as Natural Science. GOODMAN, Nicolas D.

Mathematics, Physics, and Corporeal Substance in Descartes. BROWN, Gregory.

The Mode of Existence of Mathematical Objects. ROZOV, M A.

The Model-Theoretic Approach in the Philosophy of Science. DA COSTA, Newton C A and FRENCH, Steven.

Myth and Mathematics: A Conceptualistic Philosophy of Mathematics. THARP, Leslie.

A Naturalized Epistemology for a Platonist Mathematical Ontology. RESNIK, Michael D.

A Number is the Exponent of an Operation. HAND, Michael.

On Ethnomathematics. D'AMBROSIO, Ubiratan.

On Historical Reconstruction of Mathematics. GABRIELIAN, O A.

On Hyper-Torre Isols. DOWNEY, Rod.

On Plato's Philosophy of Numbers and its Mathematical and Philosophical Significance. HÖSLE, Vittorio and ADLER, Pierre (trans) and HUMPHREY, Fred (trans).

MEANING

Donald Davidson's Philosophy of Language: An Introduction. RAMBERG, Bjorn T.

Edith Stein: Filosofia E Senso Dell'Essere. LAMACCHIA, Ada.

Fact and Meaning. HEAL, Jane.

Jurisculture, Volume II: India. DORSEY, Gray L.

Meaning and Mental Representation. ECO, Umberto (ed).

Metaphor. COOPER, David E.

The Metaphysics of Epistemology: Lectures by Wilfrid Sellars. AMARAL, Pedro (ed).

The Natural Goodness of Man: On the Systems of Rousseau's Thought. MELZER, Arthur M.

Parmenides, Plato, and the Semantics of Not-Being. PELLETIER, Francis Jeffry.

Philosophy without Ambiguity: A Logico-Linguistic Essay. ATLAS, Jay David.

Philosophy—A Book. VERSTER, Ulrich.

Pursuit of Truth. QUINE, W V.

The Rational and the Social. BROWN, James Robert.

A Theory of Content and Other Essays. FODOR, Jerry A.

Transforming the Hermeneutic Context: From Nietzsche to Nancy. ORMISTON, Gayle L (ed).

What Is Said: A Theory of Indirect Speech Reports. BERTOLET, Rod.

Wisdom and Humanness in Psychology: Prospects for a Christian Approach. EVANS, C Stephen.

Wittgenstein's Later Philosophy. HANFLING, Oswald.

"Adams on the Mind: Mind as Meaning and as Agent" in *Mind, Value and Culture: Essays in Honor of E M Adams,* HALL, R.

"Analytic Philosophy and the Meaning of Music" in *Analytic Aesthetics,* SCRUTON, Roger.

"The Challenge of Contemporary Music" in *What is Music?,* SUBOTNIK, Rose Rosengard.

"Hermeneutic Modes, Ancient and Modern" in *History and Anti-History in Philosophy,* WATSON, W.

"How is Meaning Mentally Represented?" in *Meaning and Mental Representation,* JOHNSON-LAIRD, Philip N.

"On the Circumstantial Relation between Meaning and Content" in *Meaning and Mental Representation,* BARWISE, Jon.

"Philosophical 'Ins' and 'Outs'" in *Mind, Value and Culture: Essays in Honor of E M Adams,* ALDRICH, Virgil.

"Quantification, Roles and Domains" in *Meaning and Mental Representation,* FAUCONNIER, Gilles.

"Relevance, Truth and Meaning" in *Directions in Relevant Logic,* PRIEST, Graham and CROSTHWAITE, Jan.

"Wittgenstein on Meaning" in *Wittgenstein in Focus—Im Brennpunkt: Wittgenstein,* ZEMACH, Eddy.

"Bedeutung", "Idee" und "Begriff": Zur Behandlung einiger bedeutungstheorietischer Paradoxien durch Leibniz. ROS, Arno.

Artifacts, Essence and Reference. CHAUDHURY, Mahasweta.

Autonomy and the Death of the Arts. COVEOS, Costis M.

Between Reference and Meaning. MORAVCSIK, Julius M.

Can Philosophy Be Mathematized?—Probabilistic Theory of Meanings and Semantic Architectonics of Personality. NALIMOV, V V.

The Cognitive Effect of Metaphor. GERHART, Mary and RUSSELL, Allan Melvin.

Collingwood's Logic of Question and Answer. SOMERVILLE, James.

Communication, Grice, and Languageless Creatures. CARR, Indira Mahalingam.

Contingency, Meaning and History. BLOM, Tannelie and NIJHUIS, Ton.

Derrida and the Indeterminacy of Meaning. MILLER, Seumas.

Les deux sources de l'herméneutique. STEVENS, Bernard.

Doing Philosophy with Children. ALLEN, Terry.

E D Hirsch's Misreading of Saul Kripke. SPIKES, Michael.

Elliptical Sense. NANCY, Jean-Luc.

Erich Przywara on Ultimate Reality and Meaning: *Deus Semper Major* 'God Ever Greater'. ZEITZ, James V.

Forms of Life and Forms of Discourse in Ancient Philosophy. HADOT, Pierre and DAVIDSON, Arnold (trans) and WISSING, Paula (trans).

Freedom and Rule-Following in Wittgenstein and Sartre. DWYER, Philip.

From a Normative Point of View. LANCE, Mark and HAWTHORNE, John.

Human Understanding. ZEMACH, Eddy M.

Inquiry Into Meaning and Truth. THOMAS, R S D.

Intercultural Rhetorical Differences in Meaning Construction. FOLMAN, Shoshana and SARIG, Gissi.

Is Translation Possible?. HARRIS, R Thomas.

Lingua degli angli e lingua dei bruti. DE MONTICELLI, Roberta and DI FRANCESCO, Michele.

Logical Atomism in Plato's *Theaetetus.* RYLE, G.

Meaning N and Meaning NN—An Exposition of the Unformed Gricean Intention. LENKA, Laxminarayan.

A Model for the Evaluation of Moral Education. MOREHOUSE, Richard.

Nel labirinto dell'informazione: i sistemi complessi. MORCHIO, Renzo.

Neuropsychology and Meaning in Psychiatry. GILLETT, Grant R.

Non replica, chiarimento. MORPURGO-TAGLIABUE, Guido.

Nous, the Concept of Ultimate Reality and Meaning in Anaxagoras. SILVESTRE, Maria Luisa.

On Meaning and Understanding. PAVILIONIS, Rolandas.

One Commends Something By Attributing the Property of Goodness To It (Penultimate Word). GOLDSTICK, D.

Peirce's Interpretant. LISZKA, James Jakob.

Peirce's Ultimate Logical Interpretant and Dynamical Object: A Pragmatic Perspective. ROSENTHAL, Sandra B.

Philosophy after Wittgenstein and Heidegger. GUIGNON, Charles.

Pictures and Gestures. LÜDEKING, Karlheinz.

The Pragmatics of What is Said. RECANATI, François.

The Principle of Contextual *Bedeutung* and Triadic Semantics with Frege. CANDIESCU, Calin.

A Problem about the Meaning of Intuitionist Negation. HOSSACK, Keith G.

Remnants of Meaning by Stephen Schiffer. FODOR, Jerry.

Saint Anselm of Canterbury on Ultimate Reality and Meaning. DECORTE, Jos.

Science and Hermeneutics. RICKMAN, H P.

Sign and Knowledge. VASILIU, Emanuel.

Significado literal: entre la profunda necesidad de una construcción y la mera nostalgia. CABRERA, Julio.

Some Remarks on Bhartrhari's Concept of Pratibhā. TOLA, Fernando and DRAGONETTI, Carmen.

Synonymy in Sentential Languages: A Pragmatic View. TOKARZ, Marek.

Truth and Meaning in the Works of Tugendhat and Davidson (in Serbo-Croatian). WYLLER, Truls.

Universalism as a Metaphilosophy of the New Peace Movement. KUCZYNSKI, Janusz and PETROWICZ, Lech (trans) and RODZINSKA, Aleksandra (trans).

Vagueness and Meaning in Lukács' Ontology. MEZEI, György Iván.

Values and Meaning: Max Weber's Approach to the Idea of Ultimate Reality and Meaning. CUNEO, Michael W.

Wesshalb implizite Definitionen nicht genug sind. BARTELS, Andreas.

What Should a Theory of Meaning Do?. PLATTS, Mark.

Wittgenstein and Kripke on the Nature of Meaning. HORWICH, Paul.

Wittgenstein, Bodies and Meaning. NEIMAN, Alven M.

You Can Say *That* Again. LE PORE, Ernest and LOEWER, Barry.

MEANING OF LIFE

Philosophy and the Human Condition (Second Edition). BEAUCHAMP, Tom L (ed).

Levine on Hare on Camus' Assumption. O'CONNOR, David.

Literature, Philosophy and Nonsense. TILGHMAN, B R.

Religion and Moral Meaning in Bioethics. CAMPBELL, Courtney S.

MEASURE

The Critique of Thought: A Re-Examination of Hegel's Science of Logic. JOHNSON, Paul Owen.

Recovery of the Measure: Interpretation and Nature. NEVILLE, Robert Cummings.

Coding Over a Measurable Cardinal. FRIEDMAN, Sy D.

Strong Measure Zero Sets and Rapid Filters. IHODA, Jaime I.

MEASUREMENT

Nature's Capacities and their Measurement. CARTWRIGHT, Nancy.

The Philosophy of Quantum Mechanics: An Interactive Interpretation. HEALEY, Richard.

The Language Dependence of Accuracy. BARNES, Eric.

Measurement, Pleasure, and Practical Science in Plato's *Protagoras.* RICHARDSON, Henry S.

Paradigms of Measurement. SWISTAK, Piotr.

Unique Nontransitive Measurement on Finite Sets. FISHBURN, Peter C.

MECHANICS

see also Quantum Mechanics

"Towards a Social History of Newtonian Mechanics: Boris Hessen and Henryk Grossmann Revisited" in *Scientific Knowledge Socialized,* FREUDENTHAL, Gideon.

MECHANISM

The Logic of Mind (Second Edition). NELSON, R J.

Universes. LESLIE, John.

"Organisms, Vital Forces, and Machines" in *Reductionism and Systems Theory in the Life Sciences: Some Problems and Perspectives,* WUKETITS, Franz M.

Democratizing Science: A Humble Proposal. TURNER, Joseph.

MECHANISM

The Fate of Thomas Hobbes. HUNTER, Graeme.

Kant on Descartes and the Brutes. NARAGON, Steve.

Modality, Mechanism and Translational Indeterminacy. MAC INTOSH, Duncan.

Il neoidelismo italiano e la meccanica quantistica. MAIOCCHI, Roberto.

The Real Objective of Mendel's Paper. MONAGHAN, Floyd V and CORCOS, Alain F.

A Social Constructionist Critique of The Naturalistic Theory of Emotion. RATNER, Carl.

MEDIA

Jean Baudrillard: From Marxism to Postmodernism. KELLNER, Douglas.

The Unspeakable: Understanding the System of Fallacy in the Media. MC MURTRY, John.

MEDIATION

Kant over midden, middel en doel II. VAN DER HOEVEN, J.

MEDICAL ETHICS

see also Abortion, Bioethics, Euthanasia

AIDS and the Good Society. ILLINGWORTH, Patricia.

Alpha and Omega: Ethics at the Frontiers of Life and Death. YOUNG, Ernlé W D.

A Casebook of Medical Ethics. ACKERMAN, Terrence F.

Classic Cases in Medical Ethics: Accounts of the Cases That Have Shaped Medical Ethics. PENCE, Gregory E.

Contemporary Issues in Bioethics (Third Edition). BEAUCHAMP, Tom L (ed).

Ethical Issues in Modern Medicine (Third Edition). ARRAS, John.

Ethics and Social Concern. SERAFINI, Anthony.

Euthanasia: The Moral Issues. BAIRD, Robert M (ed).

Final Choices: Autonomy in Health Care Decisions. SMITH, George P.

Health Care Ethics: Principles and Problems. GARRETT, Thomas M (ed).

Medical Ethics (The Encyclopedia of Health: Medical Issues). FINN, Jeffrey.

Medical Ethics: Essays on Abortion and Euthanasia. BARRY, Robert L.

Medical Ethics: Principles, Persons, and Problems. FRAME, John M.

The Sanctity-of-Life Doctrine in Medicine: A Critique. KUHSE, Helga.

Taking Sides: Clashing Views on Controversial Bioethical Issues (Third Edition). LEVINE, Carole (ed).

Who Lives? Who Dies?: Ethical Criteria in Patient Selection. KILNER, John F.

AIDS, Society and Morality—A Philosophical Survey. HÄYRY, Heta and HÄYRY, Matti.

An Analysis of Ethics Consultation in the Clinical Setting. SKEEL, Joy D and SELF, Donnie J.

Animal Models in 'Exemplary' Medical Research: Diabetes as a Case Study. NELSON, James Lindemann.

Appréciation morale des ingerences biomédiques dans le processusde de transmission (in Polish). KOWALSKI, Edmund.

Ars Medicina et Conditio Humana Edmund D Pellegrino, MD, on His 70th Birthday. SPICKER, Stuart F and RATZAN, Richard M.

Biomedical Ethics: Some Lessons for Social Philosophy. BROCK, Dan W.

Brain Death and the Anencephalic Newborns. TRUOG, Robert D.

A Call to Heal Medicine. HOLMES, Helen Bequaert.

Can Clinical Research Be Both 'Ethical' and 'Scientific'? A Commentary Inspired by Rosser and Marquis. HOLMES, Helen Bequaert.

Caring for Frail Elderly Parents: Post Parental Sacrifices and the Obligations of Adult Children. WICCLAIR, Mark.

The Challenge of the New Genetics. ROTHSTEIN, Mark A.

Choice, Gift, or Patriarchal Bargain? Women's Consent to *In Vitro* Fertilization in Male Infertility. LORBER, Judith.

Comment on James Nelson's "Animals in 'Exemplary' Medical Research: Diabetes as a Case Study". FINSEN, Lawrence.

Confidentiality and Patient-Access to Records. SHORT, David S.

Confidentiality and Young People. GILLICK, Victoria.

Confidentiality and Young People: A G.P.'s Response. MORGAN, Huw.

A Critique of Principlism. CLOUSER, K Danner and GERT, Bernard.

Cutting Motherhood in Two: Some Suspicions Concerning Surrogacy. NELSON, Hilde and NELSON, James Lindemann.

Dangerous Diagnostics. NELKIN, Dorothy.

The Doctor's Ethics. POWELL, D E B.

The Elderly and High Technology Medicine: A Case for Individualized, Autonomous Allocation. MOTT, Peter D.

Establishing the Moral Basis of Medicine: Edmund D Pellegrino's Philosophy of Medicine. THOMASMA, David C.

The Ethical Assessment of Innovative Therapies: Liver Transplantation Using Living Donors. SINGER, Peter (and others).

Ethical Principles and Medical Practices. MACKLIN, Ruth.

An Ethical Problem Concerning Recent Therapeutic Research on Breast

Cancer. MARQUIS, Don.

Ethics and Technology in Medicine: An Introduction. SORENSON, John H.

Ethics in Health Care and Medical Technologies. TAYLOR, Carol.

Ethics of Caring and the Institutional Ethics Committee. SICHEL, Betty A.

Euthanasia, Ethics and Economics. HÄYRY, Heta and HÄYRY, Matti.

Euthanasia, the Ultimate Abandonment. MARKER, Rita L.

Exile and PVS. SCHNEIDERMAN, Lawrence J.

Feminist and Medical Ethics: Two Different Approaches to Contextual Ethics. SHERWIN, Susan.

Feminist Directions in Medical Ethics. WARREN, Virginia L.

The Growing Feminist Debate Over the New Reproductive Technologies. DONCHIN, Anne.

Health Care as a Right: Fairness and Medical Resources. HÄYRY, Matti and HÄYRY, Heta.

Hospital Ethics Committees: One of the Many Centers of Responsibility. GLASER, John W.

Integrating Medical Ethics with Normative Theory: Patient Advocacy and Social Responsibility. JECKER, Nancy.

Interacting with Other Worlds: A Review of Books from the Park Ridge Center. POST, Stephen G.

Is Pregnancy Necessary: Feminist Concerns About Ectogenesis. MURPHY, Julien S.

Justice, HMOs, and the Invisible Rationing of Health Care Resources. FLECK, Leonard M.

Letting and Making Death Happen—Withholding and Withdrawing Life Support: Morally Irrelevant Distinctions. GRATTON, Claude.

Letting and Making Death Happen: Is There Really No Difference? The Problem of Moral Linkage. DAGI, T F.

Limiting the Role of the Family in Discontinuation of Life Sustaining Treatment. PURI, Vinod K and WEBER, Leonard J.

The Medical Dilemma. SELBY, G Raymond.

Medical Ethics and the Death Penalty. BONNIE, Richard J.

Medical Joint-Venturing: An Ethical Perspective. GREEN, Ronald M.

Medical Screening: AIDS, Rights, and Health Care Costs. ROTHSTEIN, Mark A.

Method in Bioethics: A Troubled Assessment. GREEN, Ronald M.

Misunderstanding Death on a Respirator. TOMLINSON, Tom.

Moral Discourse About Medicine: A Variety of Forms. GUSTAFSON, James M.

Morphine Use for Terminal Cancer Patients. BEABOUT, Greg.

The New Economics of Medicine: Special Challenges for Psychiatry. MORREIM, E Haavi.

New Reproductive Technologies in the Treatment of Human Infertility and Genetic Disease. SILVER, Lee M.

The Offensive-Defensive Distinction in Military Biological Research. FRISINA, Michael E.

Organ Transplanation: A Paradigm of Medical Progress. BAILEY, Leonard L.

Persuading Pagans. POTTS, S G.

The Philosopher as Insider and Outsider. KAMM, Frances M.

A Plea for the Heart. EVANS, Martyn.

Practicing Ethics: Where's the Action?. KASS, Leon R.

The Price of Silence: Commentary. BERG, Kåre.

The Psychiatrist as Moral Advisor. REDMON, Robert B.

Rapiers and the Religio Medici. CAREY, Jonathan Sinclair.

Re-Visioning Clinical Research—Gender and the Ethics of Experimental Design. ROSSER, Sue V.

The Role of Caring in a Theory of Nursing Ethics. FRY, Sara T.

Should Competence Be Coerced?: Commentary. REAMER, Frederic G.

Should Competence Be Coerced?: Commentary. KELLY, Michael J.

Social Context and Historical Emergence: The Underlying Dimension of Medical Ethics. PORTO, Eugenia M.

Suffering, Moral Worth, and Medical Ethics: A New Beginning. LOEWY, Erich H.

Toward a Feminist Theory of Disability. WENDELL, Susan.

Transplantation du cerveau—une chance pour l'humanité ou bien une menace? (in Polish). LATAWIEC, Anna.

Treatment and Non-Treatment of Defective Newborns. SZAWARSKI, Zbigniew.

The Use of Nazi Medical Experimentation Data: Memorial or Betrayal?. ROSENBAUM, Alan S.

Women in Labor: Some Issues About Informed Consent. LADD, Rosalind Ekman.

MEDICINE

Advance Directives in Medicine. HACKLER, Chris (ed).

Alpha and Omega: Ethics at the Frontiers of Life and Death. YOUNG, Ernlé W D.

Ethical Issues in Modern Medicine (Third Edition). ARRAS, John.

METAPHYSICS

METAPHYSICS

METAPHYSICS

Idealism and Quantum Mechanics. MOHANTY, J N.

L'identità del diverso. MATHIEU, Vittorio.

Identity as Necessity: Nozick's Objection-Kripke Replies. CHAUDHURY, Mahasweta.

Identity, Survival, and Sortal Concepts. BAILLIE, James.

The Imagery of Lampadedromia in Heraclitus. LEBEDEV, A.

Imagination, Totality, and Transcendence. SCHALOW, F.

Imaginative Universals and Historical Falsification: A Rejoinder to Professor Verene. MAC INTYRE, Alasdair.

Imaginative Universals and Narrative Truth. VERENE, Donald Phillip.

Imagining Oneself to be Another. REYNOLDS, Steven L.

Impredicative Identity Criteria and Davidson's Criterion of Event Identity. LOWE, E J.

In Defence of Folk Psychology. JACKSON, Frank and PETTIT, Philip.

In Defense of a Different Taxonomy: A Reply to Owens. WALKER, Valerie.

In Defense of Davidson's Identity Thesis Regarding Action Individuation. WIDERKER, David.

In Defense of Putnam's Brains. TYMOCZKO, Thomas.

In Defense of the Causal Representative Theory of Perception. FROST, Thomas B.

In Heidegger's Wake: Belonging to the Discourse of the "Turn". SCHMIDT, Dennis J.

In the Beginning Was the Contradiction: Problems of the Philosophy of Subject and Object. BOLTUC, Piotr and KMIECIK, Witold (trans).

Incommensurability: The Scaling of Mind-Body Theories as a Counter Example. RAKOVER, Sam S.

Individual and Attribute in the Ontological Argument. LEFTOW, Brian.

Individuation and Causation in Psychology. BURGE, Tyler.

Individuation and Intentional Ascriptions. OKRENT, Mark.

La inersorabilità della "nuda inteligencia" in Zubiri. INCARDONA, Nunzio.

Infini et subjectivité dans la pensée classique. CHÉDIN, Jean-Louis.

Innere Autonomie oder Zurechnungsfähigkeit?. SCHÖNRICH, Gerhard.

Intending and Motivation. MENDOLA, Joseph.

Intending and Motivation: A Rejoinder. MELE, Alfred R.

Intention, Reason, and Action. FARRELL, Daniel M.

Intentional and Physical Relations. HOROWITZ, Amir.

Intentionality and Stich's Theory of Brain Sentence Syntax. JACQUETTE, Dale.

Intentionality, IntenSionality and Representation. ROSENBERG, Alexander.

Interpretation and Its Art Objects: Two Views. KRAUSZ, Michael.

Interpretation Psychologized. GOLDMAN, Alvin I.

Intersubjectivity and the Monadic Core of the Psyche: Habermas and Castoriadis on the Unconscious. WHITEBOOK, Joel.

Introduction to 'Three Theorems of Metaphysics'. SKYRMS, Brian.

Intuición práctica y ejemplo retórico. SCHOLLMEIER, Paul and FEMENÍAS, María Luisa.

Iosif Brucar—penseur rationaliste et historien de la philosophie roumaine (in Romanian). BECLEANU-IANCU, Adela.

Irresistible Desires. MELE, Alfred R.

Is Causal Relation Asymmetrical. DEWASHI, Mahadev.

Is Critical Thinking Guilty of Unwarranted Reductionism. HATCHER, Donald.

Is Free Will Incompatible with Something or Other?. GRIFFITHS, A Phillips.

Is God an Abstract Object?. LEFTOW, Brian.

Is Jayarasi a Materialist?. MOHANTA, Dilipkumar.

Is Ontology Fundamental?. ATTERTON, Peter (trans) and LEVINAS, Emmanuel.

Is the Best Really Necessary?. KRAEMER, E R.

Is the End of the World Nigh?. LESLIE, John.

Is This Any Way to be a Realist?. TIENSON, John L.

A J Ayer: An Appreciation. SPRIGGE, T L S.

Jacques Derrida. PETITDEMANGE, Guy.

Jealousy. WREEN, Michael.

Jews as a Metaphysical Species. LURIE, Yuval.

Judgment, Self-Consciousness, and Object Independence. CHURCH, Jennifer.

Justice as Fairness: Political or Metaphysical?. NEAL, Patrick.

Justification: It Need not Cause but it Must be Accessible. GINET, Carl.

Kant ante la verdad como hija del tiempo. ROVIRA, Rogelio.

Kant on Descartes and the Brutes. NARAGON, Steve.

Kant over Midden, Middel en Doel (I). VAN DER HOEVEN, J.

Kant's Challenge: The Second Analogy as a Response to Hume. DELANEY, C.

Kant's Metaphysics of the Subject and Modern Society. FRIGERIO, C.

Kant's Third Antinomy: Agency and Causal Explanation. GREENWOOD, John D.

Kategoriai and the Unity of Being. MALPAS, J E.

Keith Campbell and the Trope View of Predication. MORELAND, J P.

Kierkegaard's Alternative Metaphysical Theology. HEYWOOD THOMAS, John.

Kierkegaard's View of Death. WATKIN, Julia.

Knowledge and Being in Merleau-Ponty. PIETERSMA, H.

Knowledge as Active, Aesthetic, and Hypothetical. FRISINA, Warren G.

Die konfuzianischen Begriffe von Rechtlichkeit und Interesse und ihr Wert im Modernen China. WANG, Rui Shen.

Die kosmologischen Antinomien in der Kritik der reinen Vernunft und die moderne physikalische Kosmologie. MITTELSTAEDT, Peter and STROHMEYER, Ingeborg.

Kriterien für eine Theorie zur Lösung des Leib-Seele-Problems. METZINGER, Thomas.

Kritische Ontologie als Philosophie der Freiheit (in Serbo-Croatian). PREVE, Costanzo.

L'analyse phénoménologique et la sémantique des mondes possibles (in Romanian). UNGUREANU, Manuela.

L'autre et l'immanence. GUILLAMAUD, Patrice.

L'equivoque du temps chez Aristote. BAEKERS, Stephan F.

L'étant, l'essence et l'être. ANTONIOTTI, Louise-Marie.

l'Être et le sensible: Edmund Husserl et Thomas D'Aquin. WINANCE, éleuthère.

L'indétermination, la détermination et la relation: Les trois essences de l'être. GUILLAMAUD, Patrice.

L'innocence de l'être-pour la mort. PORÉE, Jérôme.

L'intentionalité de dicto, l'intentionalité de re, l'intentionalité de se. CAYLA, Fabien.

L'itinéraire philosophique de Claude Bruaire: de Hegel à la métaphysique. CHAPELLE, A.

La Cosmodicée ou Etica repetita (in Romanian). BRUCAR, Iosif.

La philosophie de Hegel (in Greek). KANELLOPOULOS, P.

La place de Fichte dans l'ouverture de la perspective ontologique sur l'éthique (in Romanian). BELLU, Niculae.

The Lack of an Overarching Conception in Psychology. SARASON, Seymour B.

Lectio Difficilior: le système dans la théorie platonicienne de l'âme selon interprétation de Gueroult. GAUDIN, Claude.

Leibniz on Locke on Weakness of Will. VAILATI, Ezio.

Leibniz und Ortega y Gasset. DE SALAS ORTUETA, Jaime.

Leibniz, Transubstantiation and the Relation between Pure and Applied Philosophy. ARMOUR, Leslie.

A Leibnizian Cosmological Argument. LEFTOW, Brian.

Levinas and Hegel on the Woman as Home: A Comparison (in Dutch). BRÜGGEMAN-KRUIJFF, Atie T.

Levinas's Phenomenology of the Other and Language as the Other of Phenomenology. KLEMM, David E.

Libertad y necesidad en el "cur Deus homo" de San Anselmo de Canterbury. CORTI, E C.

Liberté et égalité chez Descartes. RODIS-LEWIS, Geneviève.

La liberté pour Aristote et les stoïciens. GAUTHIER, Pierre.

The Life of Ivan Il'ich. PATTERSON, David.

Locke on the Making of Complex Ideas. LOSONSKY, Michael.

Locke's Simple Ideas, the Blooming, Buzzing Confusion, and Quasi-Photographic Perception. HEYD, Thomas.

The Logic of God Incarnate. HICK, John.

The Logic of Probabilities in Hume's Argument against Miracles. WILSON, Fred.

The Logic of the Dilemma of Participation and of the Third Man Argument. SCALTSAS, Theodore.

Lonergan's Negative Dialectic. KIDDER, Paul.

Louis Lavelle: l'expérience de l'être comme acte. SCHÖNBERGER, Rolf.

Maine de Biran and the Body-Subject. GAINES, Jeffrey J.

Making Mind Matter More. FODOR, Jerry A.

Man's Yearnings (in Dutch). OBERHOLZER, C K.

Manifesting Realism. BLACKBURN, Simon.

The Marcuse-Dunayevskaya Dialogue, 1954-1979. ANDERSON, Kevin.

Marxist Challenges to Heidegger on Alienation and Authenticity. BALLARD, B W.

La materia prima es conocida por analogía. MC INERNY, Ralph.

Matérialisme, métaphysique, éthique (in Polish). FRITZHAND, Marek.

Materialismo Presocrático. SEGURA, Eugenio.

The Mathematical Philosophy of Contact. HAZEN, A P.

Mathematics, Physics, and Corporeal Substance in Descartes. BROWN, Gregory.

Matter, Motion and Humean Supervenience. ROBINSON, Denis.

Max Scheler's Criticism of Schopenhauer's Account of Morality and Compassion. MAIDAN, Michael.

McGinn on the Mind-Body Problem. WHITELEY, C H.

METAPHYSICS

Meaning Holism and Intentional Psychology. KUKLA, André and KUKLA, Rebecca.

The Mechanics of Rationality. LEON, Mark.

Meditaciones sobre la nada. COLOMBRES, Carlos A Iturralde.

Méditation malebranchiste sur le problème de l'illusion. VIEILLARD-BARON, Jean-Louis.

Das Menschenbild in der Psychotherapie. TOMAN, Walter.

Mental Representations and Intentional Behavior. WARD, Andrew.

Mentalism-Cum-Physicalism vs Eliminative Materialism. O'GORMAN, P F.

Mereology in Leibniz's Logic and Philosophy. BURKHARDT, Hans and DEGEN, Wolfgang.

Merleau-Ponty on Sensations. PLOMER, Aurora.

Merleau-Ponty's Indirect Ontology. SMITH, Dale E.

Merleau-Ponty's Tacit *Cogito*. WILLIAMS, Linda L.

Merleau-Ponty, Metaphor, and Philosophy. GILL, Jerry H.

La metafísica de la esperanza y del deseo en Gabriel Marcel. O'CALLAGHAN, Paul.

Metafísica del yo y hermenéutica diltheyana de la vida. ARREGUI, Jorge Vicente.

Metafisica e metaforica. BOTTANI, Livio.

Metafisica e teologia della parola. SAINATI, Vittorio.

Metafisica todavia? (cont). SANABRIA, José Rubén.

Metafisica Todavia? (cont). SANABRIA, José Rubén.

Metafisica todavia? Heidegger y la metafisica (cont). SANABRIA, José Rubén.

La metafora dei "due labirinti" e le sue implicazioni nel pensiero di Leibniz. POMA, Andrea.

Metafora e concetto: sulla metafora dello specchio in Schelling e nel giovane Hegel. TAGLIAPIETRA, Andrea.

Metamorphosis of the Undecidable. JANICAUD, Dominique.

Metaphysical Accounts of the Zygote as a Person and the Veto Power of Facts. BOLE III, Thomas J.

Metaphysical Boundaries: A Question of Independence. CARTER, William R.

The Metaphysical Construction of Value. BAKER, Judith.

Metaphysical Implications from Physics and Ecology. WITTBECKER, Alan E.

The Metaphysical Transition in Farming: From the Newtonian-Mechanical to the Eltonian Ecological. CALLICOTT, J Baird.

Metaphysics in Education. ALLEN, R T.

Metaphysics in the Philosophy of Education. HALDANE, John.

Metaphysics of Causation. BIGELOW, John and PARGETTER, Robert.

The Metaphysics of Communism. LURIE, Yuval.

The Metaphysics of Leisure. COOPER, Wesley E.

Metaphysics through Paradox in Eliot's *Four Quartets*. WIGHT, Doris T.

Metaphysics, Mind, and Mental Science. GOLDMAN, Alvin I.

Metaphysics. WEININGER, Otto and BURNS, S A M (trans).

Method and Metaphysics: The *Via Resolutionis* in Thomas Aquinas. AERTSEN, Jan A.

Might. WILWERDING, Jonathan.

Mihai Sora and the Traditions of Romanian Philosophy. NEMOIANU, Virgil.

Mill's Misreading of Comte on 'Interior Observation'. SCHARFF, Robert C.

The Mīmāmsā Theory of Self-Recognition. TABER, John A.

Mind and Body. WILKES, K V.

Mind-Body and the Future of Psychiatry. WALLACE IV, Edwin R.

Miracles as Evidence for Theism. BASINGER, David.

Misconstruals Made Manifest: A Response to Simon Blackburn. WRIGHT, Crispin.

Une mise à l'épreuve d'Aristote à partir de Heidegger. DESTRÉE, Pierre.

Miseria o valore della metafisica?. TURCO, Giovanni.

Misinformation. GODFREY-SMITH, Peter.

Mito y filosofía: En torno a Mircea Eliade. AGÍS, Marcelino.

Models, Mechanisms, and Explanation in Behavior Theory: The Case of Hull Versus Spence. SMITH, Laurence D.

Momenti della teoria leibniziana della sostanza nel carteggio con Arnauld. DELCÓ, Alessandro.

Mondo sociale, mimesi e violenza in R Girard. BOTTANI, Livio.

Morality and Culture: A Note on Kant. ROTENSTREICH, Nathan.

More on Making Mind Matter. LE PORE, Ernest and LOEWER, Barry.

Mortal Immortals: Lucretius on Death and the Voice of Nature. NUSSBAUM, Martha C.

Motivational Internalism: The Powers and Limits of Practical Reasoning. MELE, Alfred R.

Must Intentional States Be IntenSional?. EMMETT, Kathleen.

Naturaleza y causalidad en Aristóteles: *Fisica* II 1. BOERI, Marcelo D.

Naturalism and Generality in Buchler and Santayana. SINGER, Beth J.

Nature and Semiosis. KRUSE, Felicia.

The Nature of Artifacts. LOSONSKY, Michael.

The Nature of Ultimate Understanding. KOVACS, George.

Naturnotwendigkeit und Freiheit: Zu Kants Theorie der Kausalität als Antwort auf Hume. RANG, Bernhard.

Negativity and Complexity: Some Logical Considerations. HIRSCH, Eli.

Nesting: The Ontology of Interpretation. ZEMACH, Eddy.

Neurophilosophy and the Logic-Causation Argument. KIAMIE, Kimberly A.

A New Old Meaning of "Ideology". MILLS, Charles W and GOLDSTICK, Danny.

A New Plausible Exposition of Sānkhya-Kārikā-9. WADHWANI-SHAH, Yashodhara.

New Problems with Repeatable Properties and with Change. FORREST, Peter.

Nietzsche's Eternal Recurrence as Riemannian Cosmology. MOLES, Alistair.

Nietzsche's Radical Experimentalism. SEIGFRIED, Hans.

Nietzsche, Dühring, and Time. SMALL, Robin.

La noción de Dios en las "Confesiones". SÁNCHEZ NAVARRO, Luis.

La noción de existencia en la ontología de Berkeley. IBAÑEZ, Alejandro Herrera.

La noción de ser en Tomás de Sutton. ECHAURI, Raúl.

La nocion de verdad en el ser y el tiempo (cont). VÉLEZ, Francisco Galán.

La nocion de verdad en el ser y el tiempo (cont). VÉLEZ, Francisco Galán.

Non-in-difference in the Thought of Emmanuel Levinas and Franz Rosenzweig. COHEN, Richard.

Nonhuman Experience: A Whiteheadian Analysis. ARMSTRONG-BUCK, Susan.

A Note on Some Puzzling Phrases in Aquinas. VANDER WEEL, Richard L.

Note sur la définition wolffienne de la philosophie. ÉCOLE, Jean.

Notes et documents sur "Le Descartes de L Lévy-Bruhl". CAVAILLÉ, Jean-Pierre.

The Notion of the Transcultural in Bernard Lonergan's Theology. LAMB, Matthew.

Nous, the Concept of Ultimate Reality and Meaning in Anaxagoras. SILVESTRE, Maria Luisa.

Object Relations Theory, Buddhism, and the Self: Synthesis of Eastern and Western Approaches. MUZIKA, Edward G.

An Objection to Wright's Treatment of Intention. MILLER, Alexander.

Objective Reality of Ideas in Descartes, Caterus, and Suárez. WELLS, Norman J.

Objective Value, Realism, and the End of Metaphysics. POST, John F.

Observaciones sobre la noción de causa en el opúsculo sobre el movimiento de Berkeley. ABAD, Juan Vázquez.

Occasional Identity. GALLOIS, André.

Of Primary and Secondary Qualities. SMITH, A D.

On Dying as a Process. FELDMAN, Fred.

On Grandy on Grice. STALNAKER, Robert.

On Grice and Language. GRANDY, Richard E.

On Individualism, Collectivism and Interrelationism. CARTER, Alan.

On Knowlegde, Power and Michel Foucault. MEYNELL, Hugo.

On Mentalism, Privacy, and Behaviorism. MOORE, Jay.

On Physical Multiple Realization. ENDICOTT, Ronald P.

On Putnam's Argument for the Inconsistency of Relativism. SOLOMON, Miriam.

On Reversal of Temporality of Human Cognition and Dialectical Self. MO, Suchoon S.

On the Appearance of Contingency: A Rejoinder to Blum. BAYNE, Steven R.

On the Continuing Relevance of Whitehead. CODE, Murray.

On the Control-Theoretic Characterization of the Self. JONES, Andrew J I.

On the Critique of Energetism and Neoenergetism (in Czechoslovakian). ZEMAN, J.

On the Location of Actions and Tryings: Criticism of an Internalist View. GJELSVIK, Olav.

On the Nature and Cognitive Function of Phenomenal Content—Part I. FOX, Ivan.

On the Ordering of Things: Being and Power in Heidegger and Foucault. DREYFUS, Hubert L.

On the Question of Semantics in the Logic of Action: Some Remarks on Pörn's Logic of Action. SEGERBERG, Krister.

On the Social and Political Implications of Cognitive Psychology. PRILLELTENSKY, Isaac.

On the Tragedy of Hermeneutical Experience. BRUNS, Gerald L.

On Tooley on Salmon. DOWE, Phil.

On Traits as Dispositions: An Alleged Truism. VAN HEERDEN, Jaap and SMOLENAARS, Anton J.

On Vallicella's Critique of Heidegger. ZIMMERMAN, Michael E.

On Viewing Pain as a Secondary Quality. NEWTON, Natika.

One More Time. MOLANDER, Bengt.

METAPHYSICS

One Self: The Logic of Experience. ZUBOFF, Arnold.

The Ontological Argument Reconsidered. BALABAN, Oded and AVSHALOM, Asnat.

The Ontological Difference and the Pre-Metaphysical Status of the Being of Beings in Plato. HUDAC, Michael C.

The Ontological Foundation of Russell's Theory of Modality. DEJNOZKA, Jan.

Ontological Responsibility and the Poetics of Nature. LLEWELYN, John.

Ontologie et sagesse. TROTIGNON, P.

Ontologie ohne Ethik? Zur Klärung der Heidegger-Kontroverse. RAPP, Friedrich.

El origen de la energeia en Aristóteles. YEPES, Ricardo.

Origen: The Source of Augustine's Theory of Time. TZAMALIKOS, P.

Les origines de la notion de cause. FREDE, Michael (trans) and BRUNSCHWIG, J (trans).

Ought-Implies-Can: Erasmus Luther and R M Hare. PIGDEN, Charles R.

Our Modern Identity: The Formation of Self. DAVIS, Charles.

Overcoming the übermensch: Nietzsche's Revaluation of Values. CONWAY, Daniel W.

Overtones of Solipsism in Thomas Nagel's "What is it Like to Be a Bat?" and The View From Nowhere. WIDER, Kathleen.

Das Paradox der Zeit und die Dimensionszahl der Temporalität. FRANCK, Georg.

Parfit and the Russians. BECK, Simon.

Parmenides on What There Is. KETCHUM, Richard J.

Passage and the Presence of Experience. HESTEVOLD, H Scott.

Peacocke and Evans on Demonstrative Content. MC DOWELL, John.

Peirce's Ultimate Logical Interpretant and Dynamical Object: A Pragmatic Perspective. ROSENTHAL, Sandra B.

Perceptual and Objective Properties in Plato. WHITE, Nicholas P.

Perceptual Space Is Monadic. CASULLO, Albert.

La persona nell'esperienza morale e giuridica. BAGOLINI, Luigi.

Personal and Impersonal Identity: A Reply to Oderberg. SPRIGGE, T L S.

Personal Identity and Extrinsicness. GARRETT, Brian.

Personal Identity and the Passions. MC INTYRE, Jane L.

Personal Identity, the Temporality of Agency and Moral Responsibility. LEE, Win-Chiat.

Personhood and Moral Responsibility. LOCKE, Lawrence A.

Personhood and Personal Identity. SCHECHTMAN, Marya.

Personhood and the Land. CAMPBELL, James.

El pesimismo de Schopenhauer: sobre la differencia entre voluntad y cosa en sí. SPIERLING, Volker.

Phenomenological Deconstruction: Husserl's Method of Abbau. EVANS, J Claude.

Philosophical Functionalism. WARD, Andrew.

Philosophie antique et byzantine: à propos de deux nouvelles collections. O'MEARA, Dominic J.

La philosophie et l'absolu. TILLIETTE, Xavier.

Philosophie fondamentale. MC EVOY, James.

Das philosophische Menschenbild: Eine konfuzianische Sicht. DOW, Tsung-I.

The Philosophy of the Act and the Phenomenology of Perception: Mead and Merleau-Ponty. ROSENTHAL, Sandra B and BOURGEOIS, Patrick L.

Physiologie und Transzendentalphilosophie bei Schopenhauer. SCHMIDT, Alfred.

Place de l'homme dans l'univers. MALDAMÉ, Jean-Michel.

Plantinga's Defence of Serious Actualism. HINCHLIFF, Mark.

Plato's Forms: A Text That Self-Destructs to Shed Its Light. BERRY, John M.

Platonism and Forms of Life. GASKIN, Richard M.

The Play of Difference/Différance in Hegel and Derrida. MARSH, James L.

The Pluralistic Approach to the Nature of Feelings. NATSOULAS, Thomas.

Poetic Saying as Beckoning: The Opening of Hölderlin's Germanien. MALY, Kenneth and EMAD, Parvis.

Poiesis and Praxis in Fundamental Ontology. TAMINIAUX, Jacques.

A Point of Reconciliation Between Schopenhauer and Hegel. KORAB-KARPOWICZ, W J.

La polémica sobre el ser en el Avicena y Averroes latinos. GARCÍA MARQUÉS, Alfonso.

Possibilia and Possible Worlds. MARCUS, Ruth Barcan.

Potency, Space and Time: Three Modern Theories. CENTORE, F F.

Potentia et Potestas dans les premiers écrits de B Spinoza. FERNANDEZ, Eugenio.

Power and Resistance. KRIPS, Henry.

Practical Rationality: A Response. BRANDT, R B.

A Pragmatic Version of Natural Law. WALTER, Edward.

Praxeologia della costizuione del potere. CAPOZZI, Gino.

Preface to the Publication of "P A Florenskii's Review of His Work". ABRAMOV, A I.

Présence de Hegel en France: G Fessard et Claude Bruaire. CHAPELLE, A.

Presupposition and Foundational Asymmetry in Metaphysics and Logic. JACQUETTE, Dale.

The Price of Possibility. HART, W D.

Prima e terza persona: Un recente contributo alla "Philosophy of Mind". MARRONE, Pierpaolo.

The Primacy of Perception in Husserl's Theory of Imagining. DROST, Mark P.

Primo cadit ens. CALDERA, Rafael Tomas.

The Privileging of Experience in Chinese Practical Reasoning. BLOOM, Alfred H.

The Problem of Individuation for Scotus: A Principle of Indivisibility or a Principle of Distinction. PARK, Woosuk.

The Problem of Weakness of Will. WALKER, Arthur F.

El problema del "alma mala" en la última filosofia de Platón (Leyes X, 896d ss). CARONE, Gabriela Roxana.

El problema del cogito en san Agustin. FORMENT, Eudaldo.

El problema del realismo semántico y nuestro concepto de persona. TIRADO, Alvaro Rodriguez.

La problemática de la libertad en San Agustín. WEISMANN, F J.

Le problème du temps chez Paul Ricoeur. MARCONDES CESAR, C.

Process Theology: Guardian of the Oppressor or Goad to the Oppressed—An Interim Assessment. JONES, William R.

Proclus on Space as Light. SCHRENK, Lawrence P.

Program Explanation: A General Perspective. JACKSON, Frank and PETTIT, Philip.

Het projet van de Verlichting in het licht van Hegels rechtsfilosofie. COBBEN, Paul.

Property Exemplification and Proliferation. ROWLANDS, Mark N J.

Prospective Realism. BROWN, Harold I.

El Pseudo-Justino en la historia del aristotelismo. MARTÍN, José Pablo.

The Pseudo-Problem of Creation in Physical Cosmology. GRÜNBAUM, Adolf.

Psychology in the First Critique. BIRD, G H.

Putnam on Davidson on Conceptual Schemes. BRENNER-GOLOMB, N and VAN BRAKEL, J.

A Puzzle about Necessary Being. PEARL, Leon.

Qualitative Identity and Uniformity. SCHLESINGER, George N.

Quantum Paradoxes and New Realism. FENNER, David E.

Quantum Realism. FENNER, David E W.

Quasi-Quasi-Realism. ZANGWILL, Nick.

Quelques considérations sur la signification de l'agnosticism Kantien (in Romanian). RAMBU, Nicolae.

The Question of Being. SOKOLOWSKI, Robert.

The Question of Human Freedom in the Later Heidegger. HAAR, Michel.

Radical Concrete Particularity: Heidegger, Lao Tzu and Chuang Tzu. OWENS, Wayne D.

Ragione debole e metafisica: Spunti tra vecchia e nuova apologetica. TODISCO, Orlando.

Rationality and Salience. GILBERT, Margaret.

The Rationality of Emotions and of Emotional Behaviour. MC CULLAGH, C Behan.

Re-Tracing the Human-Nature versus World-Nature Dichotemy: Lao Tzu's Hermeneutics for World-Building. LUSTHAUS, Dan.

Realism versus Antirealism: The Venue of the Linguistic Consensus. POLS, Edward.

Realism, Naturalism and Culturally Generated Kinds. ELDER, Crawford L.

Realismo crítico y conocimiento en Carlos Popper. DARÓS, W R.

Reasons and Reason. ROTENSTREICH, Nathan.

Recent Work in the Philosophy of Religion. ZAGZEBSKI, Linda.

Recusación del atomismo ontológico. GARCÍA-BARÓ, Miguel.

Reference in Anselm's Ontological Proof. WERTZ, S K.

A Reflection on Lonergan's Notion of the Pure Desire to Know. MORELLI, Elizabeth A.

Reflections on Charles S Brown's "Husserl, Intentionality, and Cognitive Architecture". HARVEY, Charles W.

Reflections on One Idea of Collingwood's Aesthetics. COHEN, Ted.

La reflexión gnoseológica de Francisco Canals Vidal. CORTINA, Juan Luis.

Reflexive Ideas in Spinoza. RICE, Lee C.

The Reflexivity of Self-Consciousness: Sameness/Identity, Data for Artificial Intelligence. CASTAÑEDA, Hector-Neri.

Reincarnation and Relativized Identity. MAC INTOSH, J J.

Relations and Reduction in Leibniz. COVER, J A.

Relativity in Mādhyamika Buddhism and Modern Physics. MANSFIELD, Victor.

Relearning the World: On the Phenomenology of Grieving. ATTIG, Thomas.

METAPHYSICS

Remarks on General Neo-Thomistic Metaphysics: The Contribution of Christian Revelation to Philosophy. BLANDINO, Giovanni.

Remarks on the Logic of Imagination. NIINILUOTO, Ilkka.

Reply to Baker and Grandy. WARNER, Richard.

Reply to Heyd's Reply to "Locke Is Not a Cartesian with Respect to Knowledge of our Own Existence". ROTH, Robert J.

Reply to Kenneth K Inada. PILGRIM, Richard.

Reply to Kvanvig: "Adams on Actualism and Presentism". ADAMS, Robert Merrihew.

Reply to Professor Robin Small's "Absolute Becoming and Absolute Necessity". RICHARDSON, John.

Reply to Reviewers of "Explaining Behavior: Reasons in a World of Causes". DRETSKE, Fred.

Reply to Richard Bosley's "Virtues and Vices: East and West". TANG, Paul C L.

Reply to Roth: Locke Is Not a Cartesian with Respect to Knowledge of our Own Existence. HEYD, Thomas.

Reply to Ward's "Philosophical Functionalism". DOUBLE, Richard.

Reply to Zimmerman: Heidegger and the Problem of Being. VALLICELLA, William F.

Representations without Rules. HORGAN, Terence and TIENSON, John.

Response to Dietrich's "Computationalism". BALOGH, Imre.

Response to Dietrich's "Computationalism". BEAKLEY, Brian.

Response to Dietrich's "Computationalism". CHURCHLAND, Paul.

Response to Dietrich's "Computationalism". GORMAN, Michael.

Response to Dietrich's "Computationalism". HARNAD, Stevan.

Response to Dietrich's "Computationalism". MERTZ, David.

Response to Dietrich's "Computationalism". PATTEE, H H.

Response to Dietrich's "Computationalism". RAMSEY, W.

Response to Dietrich's "Computationalism". RINGEN, Jon.

Response to Dietrich's "Computationalism". SCHWARZ, Georg.

Response to Dietrich's "Computationalism". SLATOR, Brian.

Response to Dietrich's "Computationalism". STRUDLER, Alan.

Response to Dietrich's "Computationalism". WALLIS, Charles.

Response to Huang Siu-chi's Review of Knowledge Painfully Acquired, by Lo Ch'in-shun and Translated by Irene Bloom. BLOOM, Irene.

Response to Papers. SPIEGELBERG, Herbert.

Response to Richard Pilgrim's Review of The Logic of Unity, by Hosaku Matsuo and Translated by Kenneth K Inada. INADA, Kenneth K.

A Response to Robert Bernasconi's "Heidegger's Destruction of Phronesis". BROGAN, Walter.

Responsibility and 'Free Will'. VESEY, Godfrey.

A Return to Plato in the Philosophy of Substance. ZYCINSKI, Joseph.

The Reward Event and Motivation. MORILLO, Carolyn R.

Ricoeur, Lonergan and the Intelligibility of Cosmic Time. PAMBRUN, James R.

Riemann's Geometry and Eternal Recurrence as Cosmological Hypothesis: A Reply. STACK, George J.

The Role of Apperception in Kant's Transcendental Deduction of the Categories. CASTANEDA, Héctor-Neri.

The Role of Intention in Intentional Action. ADAMS, Frederick.

The Role of Self-Knowledge in the Critique of Pure Reason. POLT, Richard F H.

The Role of the Unconscious in Schelling's System of Transcendental Idealism. SNOW, Dale.

Rorty's Pragmatism and the Pursuit of Truth. BONTEKOE, Ron.

Salomon Ibn Gabirol's Doctrine of Intelligible Matter. DILLON, John.

Santayana and Democritus—Two Mutually Interpreting Philosophical Poets. DILWORTH, David A.

Santayana and Panpsychism. SPRIGGE, Timothy.

Santayana's Neglect of Hartshorne's Alternative. WHITTEMORE, Robert C.

Santayana's Neo-Platonism. KUNTZ, Paul G.

Santayana's Non-Reductive Naturalism. KERR-LAWSON, Angus.

Santayana's Ontology and the Nicene Creed. KERR-LAWSON, Angus.

Santayana's Philosophy of Love. SINGER, Irving.

Santayana's Pragmatism and the Comic Sense of Life. LEVINSON, Henry Samuel.

Sartre y la ética: De la mala fe a la conversión moral. VIDIELLA, Graciela.

Schelling's "On the Essence of Human Freedom": An Interpretation of the First Main Points (in Hungarian). HEIDEGGER, Martin.

Searle on Minds and Brains. SAGAL, Paul T.

Searle on Strong AI. CAM, Philip.

Searle's Narrow Content. VAUGHAN, Rachel.

Seismograph Readings for "Explaining Behavior". MILLIKAN, Ruth Garrett.

Selbst das Selbst ist nicht Selbst. ESSLER, Wilhelm K.

The Self and First Person Metaphysics. ALBERTS, Kelly T.

The Self in Deep Sleep According to Advaita and Visistādvaita. COMANS, Michael.

Self-Conscious Agency and the Eternal Consciousness: Ultimate Reality in Thomas Hill Green. CROSSLEY, David.

Self-Consciousness in Chimps and Pigeons. DAVIS, Lawrence H.

Self-Consuming Concepts. MAGNUS, Bernd.

Self-Knowledge of the World. ROTENSTREICH, Nathan.

Semantic Holism Without Semantic Socialism: Twin Earths, Thinking, Language, Bodies, and the World. CASTAÑEDA, Hector-Neri.

Semantics of Proximity: Language and the Other in the Philosophy of Emmanual Levinas. ZIAREK, Krzysztof.

Sense Experiences and their Contents: A Defence of the Propositional Account. PENDLEBURY, Michael.

Sense, Reason and Causality in Hume and Kant. NUYEN, A T.

The Sensory Presentation of Divine Infinity. SCHOEN, Edward L.

El sentido de la teoría humeana del tiempo como relación filosófica. MUDROVCIC, María Inés.

Ser, nada y creación en el pensamiento de Nimio de Anquín. PEREZ, J R.

Simultaneity and Einstein's Gedankenexperiment. COHEN, Michael.

La síntesis de lo uno y lo múltiple. HARRIS, Errol E.

Six Aspects of Santayana's Philosophy. KERR-LAWSON, Angus.

Sobre la objeción de Orayen a la semántica de Meinong. MORETTI, Alberto.

Sobre objetos posibles y Meinong: una respuesta a Moretti. ORAYEN, Raúl.

The Social Constitution of Action: Objectivity and Explanation. GREENWOOD, John D.

A Social Constructionist Critique of The Naturalistic Theory of Emotion. RATNER, Carl.

Socratic Ignorance—Socratic Wisdom. EVANS, J Claude.

Soft Determinism and How We Become Responsible for the Past. TÄNNSJÖ, Torbjörn.

Solitary Souls and Infinite Help: Kierkegaard and Wittgenstein. HANNAY, Alastair.

Some Heideggerian Reflections on Euthanasia. NUYEN, A T.

Some Notes on the Existentialist Concept of Human Freedom (in Czechoslovakian). CERNOHORSKY, I.

Some Sources for Hume's Opening Remarks to Treatise I IV III. SOLOMON, Graham.

Some Uses of Imagination in the British Empiricists: A Preliminary Investigation of Locke, as Contrasted with Hume. HALL, Roland.

Specimens of Natural Kinds and the Apparent Inconsistency of Metaphysics Zeta. SPELLMAN, Lynne.

La spéculation hégélienne. BOURGEOIS, Bernard.

Speech and Thought, Symbol and Likeness: Aristotle's De Interpretatione 16a3-9. POLANSKY, Ronald and KUCZEWSKI, Mark.

Spirit's Primary Nature is to be Secondary. KERR-LAWSON, Angus.

Spirituality in Santayana. TEJERA, V.

St Thomas et la métaphysique du "liber de causis". ELDERS, Lédon.

The Status of Content. BOGHOSSIAN, Paul A.

La struttura metafisica dell'esistente. ALESSI, Adriano.

Le strutture trascendentali della coscienza nel primo Sartre: ipotesi di lettura. COMOLLI, Fabrizio.

Subjectivity and Environmentalism. LE PORE, Ernest.

Sujeto y tiempo en la "Crítica de la Razón pura". ALARCÓN, Enrique.

Sūnyatā and Ajāti: Absolutism and the Philosophies of Nāgārjuna and Gaudapāda. KING, Richard.

La superacion del analisis logico del lenguaje por medio de la metafisica. SILVA CAMARENA, Juan Manuel.

Supervenience as a Philosophical Concept. KIM, Jaegwon.

Supervenience, Essentialism and Aesthetic Properties. CURRIE, Gregory.

Surviving Matters. SOSA, Ernest.

The Symmetry Argument: Lucretius Against the Fear of Death. ROSENBAUM, Stephen E.

System and Training in Descartes' Meditations. BEYSSADE, Michelle.

Tacit Metaphysical Premises of Modern Empiricism. NAHLIK, Krzysztof J.

Talking Lions and Lion Talk: Davidson on Conceptual Schemes. CRUMLEY, Jack S.

A Taoist Interpretation of 'Differance' in Derrida. CHENG, Chung-Ying.

El tardío pesimismo metafisico de Horkheimer. MOLINUEVO, José Luis.

Tasan's "Practical Learning". SETTON, Mark.

Taylor's Defenses of Two Traditional Arguments for the Existence of God. GARAVASO, Pieranna.

Technics and the Ontology of the Human Being Nowadays. BOBOC, Alexandru.

Teleology and Spontaneous Generation in Aristotle: A Discussion. GOTTHELF, Allan.

El tema principal de la fenomenología de Husserl. WALTON, Roberto J.

Tempo e linguaggio nel pensiero di Derrida e Lyotard. MAZZARA, Giuseppe.

METAPHYSICS

Tempo e spazio negli scritti inediti di Guilio Cesare Ferrari. QUARANTA, M.

Temporal Indexicals. SMITH, Quentin.

Temporal Versus Manipulability Theory of Causal Asymmetry. DEWASHI, Mahadev.

Temptation and the Will. BIGELOW, John.

Textuality, Totalization, and the Question of Origin in Heidegger's Elucidation of *Andenken*. FÓTI, Véronique.

Thales (in Greek). POTAGA, A.

The Dialectics of the Unity of Linearity and Non-linearity of Physical Processes (in Czechoslovakian). GOTT, V S.

The Individuum and the Context of Individual (in Czechoslovakian). TOMEK, V.

The Notion of Chance and the Metaphysics of P Kanellopoulos (in Greek). MARKAKIS, M.

The Subject of Historic Transformations in the Present Era (in Czechoslovakian). HAHN, E.

The Uniqueness of Human Being (in Czechoslovakian). OIZERMAN, T I.

The Theory of Complimentarity and Mind-Body Dualism: A Critique. CHAKRABARTY, Alpana.

The Theory of Ideas in Gassendi and Locke. MICHAEL, Fred S and MICHAEL, Emily.

There is No Question of Physicalism. CRANE, Tim.

Thinking, Poetry and Pain. CAPUTO, John D.

Thomas and the Universe. JAKI, Stanley L.

Thomas Reid's Critique of Joseph Priestley: Context and Chronology. WOOD, Paul B.

Thomism and Contemporary Philosophical Pluralism. CLARKE, W Norris.

Thoughts and Their Subject: A Study of Wittgenstein's *Tractatus*. KANNISTO, Heikki.

Three Theorems of Metaphysics. THARP, Leslie.

Tiempo e Instante. ROJAS, Jorge Ramos.

Time and Value. LIEB, Irwin C.

The Time-Like Nature of Mind: On Mind Functions as Temporal Patterns of the Neural Network. FISCHER, Roland.

To Philosophize with Socrates (A Chapter from a Prepared Monography on J Patocka) (in Czechoslovakian). PALOUS, Martin.

Tomás de Aquino: la aprehensión del "acto de ser". GONZALEZ, Orestes J.

Tractatus 2:063. BLUM, Alex.

A Tragic Idealist: Jacob Ostens (1630-1678). VAN BUNGE, Wiep.

Le *Traité des passions* de Descartes et les théories modernes de l'émotion. NEUBERG, M.

Transcendentalism and Its Discontents. WHITE, Stephen L.

Transient Natures at the Edges of Life: A Thomistic Exploration. SMITH, Philip.

The Trapped Infinity: Cartesian Volition as Conceptual Nightmare. REED, Edward S.

Un tratado de teología natural de Octavio N Derisi. MONDIN, Battista.

Tres niveles de conocimiento en la filosofía de Gabriel Marcel. CAÑAS, José Luis.

The Tripartite Soul in the *Timaeus*. ROBINSON, James V.

Troubles with Ockhamism. WIDERKER, David.

Truth and Interpersonality: An Inquiry into the Argumentative Structure of Heidegger's *Being and Time*. RÖMPP, Georg.

Truth as Disclosure: Art, Language, History. GUIGNON, Charles.

Truth in Thomas Aquinas, (II). WIPPEL, John F.

Truth, Definite Truth, and Paradox. YABLO, Stephen.

Twisting Free: Being to an Extent Sensible. SALLIS, John.

Two Consequences of Hinting. TSOHATZIDIS, Savas L.

Two Kinds of Incompatibilism. KANE, Robert.

Die Unbestimmtheit von Theorien über die menschliche Natur im chinesischen Denken. TANG, Paul C L.

The Underlying Thing, the Underlying Nature and Matter: Aristotle's Analogy in Physics I 7. COOK, Kathleen C.

La utopía de lo supremo y el conocimiento metafísico de Dios. DEL BARCO, Jose Luis.

Vague Objects and Indefinite Identity. BURGESS, J A.

A Vagueness Paradox and Its Solution. ACKERMAN, Felicia.

Vico e Joyce attraverso Michelet. VERRI, A.

Vico on Mythic Figuration as Prerequisite for Philosophic Literacy. DANIEL, Stephen H.

Victor Cousin: Commonsense and the Absolute. MANNS, James W and MADDEN, Edward H.

Virtues and Vices: East and West. BOSLEY, Richard.

La volontà di oblio: Per un'ermeneutica della morte. STRUMMIELLO, Giuseppina.

La volonté en Dieu: Thomas d'Aquin et Hegel. BRITO, Emilio.

Vom epischen zum logischen sprechen: der spruch des Anaximander. RIEDEL, M.

Was Aristotle a Functionalist?. NELSON, John O.

Was Hegel a Panlogicist?. EISENBERG, Paul.

Ways Leading to Bergson's Notion of "Perpetual Present". KEBEDE, Messay.

Ways Leading to Bergson's Notion of the "Perpetual Present". KEBEDE, Messay.

Weak Externalism and Mind-Body Identity. MACDONALD, Cynthia.

Weak Strategy Proofness: The Case of Nonbinary Social Choice Functions. BANDYOPADHYAY, Taradas.

What are Concepts?. PEACOCKE, Christopher.

What Difference Does Consciousness Make?. VAN GULICK, Robert.

What Hume Actually Said About Miracles. FOGELIN, Robert J.

What is Non-Existent and What is Remanent in Sūnyatā. DARGYAY, Lobsang.

What is Psychological Egoism?. SOBER, Elliott.

What is Representation? A Reply to Smythe. LLOYD, Dan.

What Water Is or Back to Thales. STROLL, Avrum.

What's Wrong with Impossible Objects?. PERSZYK, Kenneth J.

What's Wrong with the Syntactic Theory of Mind. EGAN, M Frances.

Which Beings are Exemplary? Comments on Charles Guignon's "Truth as Disclosure: Art, Language, History". NENON, Thomas J.

Which One Is the Real One?. GRAYBOSCH, Anthony J.

Whitehead and Existential Phenomenology: Is a Synthesis Possible?. RICE, Daryl H.

Whitehead et Hegel: Réalisme, idéalisme et philosophie spéculative. ROCKMORE, Tom.

Whitehead's "Theory" of Propositions. STEINBOCK, Anthony J

The Whole as Setting for Man: On Plato's *Timaeus*. CROPSEY, Joseph.

Why are Italians More Reasonable than Australians?. DALE, A J.

Why Individual Identity Matters. BROWN, Mark T.

Why Proper Names are Rigid Designators. PENDLEBURY, Michael.

Why Supervenience?. PAPINEAU, David.

Why the Problem of the Existence of the External Worlds is a Pseudo-Problem: A Revision of Putnam and Danto. SHIRLEY, Edward S.

Why Three Dimensions?. BENCIVENGA, Ermanno.

Wills, Purposes and Actions. HOLMSTRÖM, Ghita.

Wittgenstein and Murdock on the 'Net' in a Taoist Framework. TOMINAGA, Thomas T.

Wittgenstein Never Was a Phenomenologist. REEDER, Harry P.

Wittgenstein's Later Philosophy of Mind: Sensation, Privacy, and Intention. WRIGHT, Crispin.

Wittgenstein, Kant and the "Metaphysics of Experience". WILLIAMS, Meredith.

Wittgenstein, Mind, and Scientism. GOLDFARB, Warren.

Wordsworth and the Zen Void. RUDY, John G.

Yoga-Sūtra IV, 2-3 and Vivekānanda's Interpretation of Evolution. KILLINGLEY, D H.

The Young Heidegger and Phenomenology. VAN BUREN, John.

The Young Heidegger: Rumor of a Hidden King (1919-1926). VAN BUREN, Edward J.

Zarathustra's Dancing Dialectic. NEWELL, Waller R.

Zur Frage der Vereinbarkeit von Freiheit und Determinismus. RHEINWALD, Rosemarie.

Zur Kognitionstheorie Humberto Maturanas. WEIDHAS, Roija.

Zur ontologischen Differenz: Plotin und Heidegger. KREMER, Klaus.

METAPSYCHOLOGY

Le concept d'analyse généralisée ou de "non-analyse". LARUELLE, François.

L'événement freudien: L'objet métapsychologique. ASSOUN, Paul-Laurent.

METASCIENCE

Otto Neurath: Marxist Member of the Vienna Circle. JACOBS, Sturan and OTTO, Karl-Heinz.

METATHEORY

A Modern Formal Logic Primer, Volume I and II. TELLER, Paul.

Incommensurability: The Scaling of Mind-Body Theories as a Counter Example. RAKOVER, Sam S.

METHOD(S)

see also Scientific Method

Klarheit und Methode: Felix Kaufmanns Wissenschaftstheorie. ZILIAN, H G.

Ursprung und Thema von Ersten Wissenschaft. KÖNIGSHAUSEN, Johann-Heinrich.

Wittgenstein and Kierkegaard: Religion, Individuality, and Philosophical Method. CREEGAN, Charles L.

"The Methods of Aesthetics" in *Analytic Aesthetics*, URMSON, J O.

METHOD(S)

Being and the Sciences: The Philosophy of Gaston Isaye. LECLERC, Marc.
A Critical Perspective in the Physical Sciences. ERIKSSON, Karl-Erik.
Effecten en gevolgen van wetenschapsbeleid voor de filosofiebeoefening aan de Nederlandse universiteiten. VAN DER MEULEN, Barend and LEYDESDORFF, Loet.
Ethical Behavior Among Marketing Researchers: An Assessment of Selected Demographic Characteristics. KELLEY, S W and FERRELL, O C and SKINNER, S J.
Ethische theorieën en de ontwikkeling van medische technologie. DE VRIES, Gerard.
Feminist Critique of Epistemology. RUSSELL, Denise.
Foundations of Mathematics or Mathematical Practice: Is One Forced To Choose?. VAN BENDEGEM, Jean Paul.
Getting the Science Right is the Problem, Not the Solution: A Matter of Priority. MIXON, Don.
Looking Backward at Education Reform. HAWLEY, Willis D.
Mathematical Skepticism: Are We Brains in a Countable Vat?. TYMOCZKO, Thomas.
Merleau-Ponty, Metaphor, and Philosophy. GILL, Jerry H.
Method and the Authority of Science. TILES, Mary E.
Method in Bioethics: A Troubled Assessment. GREEN, Ronald M.
El metodo filosofico segun 'Sapientiale' de Tomas de York. LÉRTORA MENDOZA, Celina A.
Pascal's Great Experiment. ARNOLD, Keith.
Peirce's Early Method of Finding the Categories. DE TIENNE, André.
Philosophie der Philosophiegeschichte von Hegel bis Hartmann. CEKIC, Miodrag.
Scientific Problems and the Conduct of Research. HAIG, Brian.
Some Aspects of the Methodology of Comparative Research in Politics. WIATR, Jerzy J.
The Structure-Nominative Reconstruction of Scientific Knowledge. BURGIN, M S.
There is Relevance in the Classroom: Analysis of Present Methods of Teaching Business Ethics. STRONG, V K and HOFFMAN, A N.

METHODOLOGICAL INDIVIDUALISM

Eliminativism and Methodological Individualism. KINCAID, Harold.
Methodological Individualism and Explanation. TUOMELA, Raimo.
Methodological Individualism. TÄNNSJÖ, Torbjörn.

METHODOLOGY

Christianity and the Nature of Science: A Philosophical Investigation. MORELAND, James Porter.
The Knowledge of Values: A Methodological Introduction. LÓPEZ QUINTÁS, Alfonso (ed).
The Natures of Science. MC MORRIS, Neville.
The Rational and the Social. BROWN, James Robert.
Saussure, Derrida, and the Metaphysics of Subjectivity. STROZIER, Robert M.
Science and Its Fabrication. CHALMERS, Alan.
"Comment: The Middle Way in the Philosophy of Punishment" in Issues in Contemporary Legal Philosophy: The Influence of H L A Hart, MORAWETZ, Thomas.
Bemerkungen zur methodologischen Einheit der Wissenschaften. BÜHLER, Axel.
Collingwood's Claim that Metaphysics is a Historical Discipline. MARTIN, Rex.
Descartes in the Hegelian Perspective. BATTA, Nirmala Devi.
Development of Collingwood's Conception of Historical Object. DAS, P S.
Economics and Hermeneutics. BERGER, Lawrence A.
The Essential Tension. FEHÉR, Marta.
Holism a Century Ago: The Elaboration of Duhem's Thesis. BRENNER, Anastasios A.
Is kennis belichaamd?. SCHOPMAN, Joop.
Method and Metaphysics: The Via Resolutionis in Thomas Aquinas. AERTSEN, Jan A.
The Method of "Grounded Theory" in the Age-Old Debate about Induction. RODRIGUEZ, Vincent.
Methodology in Business Ethics Research: A Review and Critical Assessment. RANDALL, D M and GIBSON, A M.
Naturalism and Prescriptivity. RAILTON, Peter.
The Naturalist Conception of Methodological Standards in Science. DOPPELT, Gerald.
Neutrality in Religious Studies. DONOVAN, Peter.
Normative Naturalism and the Role of Philosophy. ROSENBERG, Alexander.
Normative Naturalism. LAUDAN, Larry.
Preference Derived from Urgency. LINDAHL, Lars.
Psychological Underpinnings of Philosophy. BARTLETT, Steven J.

La revisión antihistoricista de la Revolución Francesa. SAZBÓN, José.
The Rhetoric of Grammar: Understanding Wittgenstein's Method. BARNETT, William E.
The Single-Issue Introduction to Philosophy. WHITE, V Alan.
Some Methodological Problems Associated with Researching Women Entrepreneurs. STEVENSON, Lois.
Sulla teoria e metodica della storia. MEYER, Eduard.
T H Morgan, Neither an Epistemological Empiricist nor a "Methodological" Empiricist. VICEDO, Marga.
Tacit Metaphysical Premises of Modern Empiricism. NAHLIK, Krzysztof J.
Teaching Business Ethics: Questioning the Assumptions, Seeking New Directions. FURMAN, Frida Kerner.
Technic Aesthetics as Science (in Czechoslovakian). KLIVAR, Miroslav.
Tra intenzionalismo e antirelativismo: l'interpretazione di teorie filosofiche come traduzione. VARNIER, Giuseppe.
Über eine unzulängliche Auffassung der methodologischen Einheit der Wissenschaft und unbefriedigende Verteidigung. JAKOWLJEWITSCH, Dragan.
Über einen neuen Versuch der Argumentation für die methodologische Einheit der Wissenschaften. JAKOWLJEWITSCH, Dragan.
What the Philosophy of Biology Is and Should Be (in Polish). SLAGA, Szczepan W.
Zur Methodologie und Logik von "Goldene'Regel"-Argumenten: Eine Gegenposition zu Hoches Hare-Exhaustion. KESE, Ralf.

METRICS

Pointless Metric Spaces. GERLA, Giangiacomo.

MEYER, L

Sens et Vérité: Philosophie et théologie chez L Meyer et Spinoza. LAGREE, Jacqueline.

MICRONESIAN

The Small-Republic Argument in Modern Micronesia. PETERSEN, Glenn.

MIDGLEY, M

Fundamenten, achtergronden of bondgenootschappen?. VAN DER WEELE, Cor.

MIGHT

Might. WILWERDING, Jonathan.

MILBANK, J

"On Being 'Placed' by John Milbank: A Response" in Christ, Ethics and Tragedy: Essays in Honour of Donald MacKinnon, HAUERWAS, Stanley.

MILITANCY

From Militancy to Ethics: On Some Forms and Problems of Militant Action in the Western World. FELDMAN, Jacqueline.
Militancy, Violence and Democratic Rights: Indian Experience. BANERJEE, Sumanta.

MILITARISM

Whither the Way?. WOHL, Andrzej and GOLEBIOWSKI, Marek (trans).

MILITARY

Moral Issues in Military Decision Making. HARTLE, Anthony E.
A Moral Military. AXINN, Sidney.
False Reports: Misperceptions, Self Deceptions or Lies?. DAVENPORT, Manuel.
A Historic Chance for Military-Technical Dealienation and the Building of a World Without War. BORGOSZ, Jozef and PETROWICZ, Lech (trans).
Obedience to Superior Orders. STUART, J M.
The Offensive-Defensive Distinction in Military Biological Research. FRISINA, Michael E.

MILL

John Stuart Mill. SKORUPSKI, John.
Miscellaneous Writings (Collected Works of John Stuart Mill, Volume 31). ROBSON, John M (ed).
The Political Philosophy of the British Idealists: Selected Studies. NICHOLSON, Peter P.
Writings on India (Collected Works of John Stuart Mill, Volume 30). ROBSON, John M (ed).
"John Stuart Mill: Fallibilism, Expertise, and the Politics-Science Analogy" in Knowledge and Politics, HOLMES, Stephen.
"Mill" in Ethics in the History of Western Philosophy, LACHS, John.
'Utility' and the 'Utility Principle': Hume, Smith, Bentham, Mill. LONG, Douglas G.
Freedom and Virtue in Politics: Some Aspects of Character, Circumstances and Utility from Helvétius to J S Mill. SMITH, G W.
Intervencionismo y paternalismo. GARZÓN VALDÉS, Ernesto.
J S Mill and Political Violence. WILLIAMS, Geraint.
J S Mill y la prueba del principio de utilidad: Una defensa de Utilitarianism IV, (3). RABOSSI, Eduardo.

MILL

John Stuart Mill on Democratic Representation and Centralization. KURER, Oskar.

John Stuart Mill on Government Intervention. KURER, O.

John Stuart Mill, La falacia de composición y la naturaleza humana. SIMPSON, Thomas M.

John Stuart Mill: su concepción de la Lógica. CAÑÓN, Camino.

Mill in Parliament: The View from the Comic Papers. ROBSON, John M.

Mill on Moral Wrong. LUNDBERG, Randolph.

Mill's and Other Liberalisms. GRAY, John.

Mill's Epistemology in Practice in his Liberal Feminism. TULLOCH, Gail.

Mill's Misreading of Comte on 'Interior Observation'. SCHARFF, Robert C.

More on Self-Enslavement and Paternalism in Mill. BROWN, D G.

No Laughing Matter: John Stuart Mill's Establishment of Women's Sufferage as a Parliamentary Question. ROBSON, John M.

Paternalism, Utility and Fairness. ARNESON, Richard J.

Political Liberalism. LARMORE, Charles.

The Politics of Epistemology. WHITE, Morton.

Positivism, Philosophy of Science, and Self-Understanding in Comte and Mill. SCHARFF, Robert C.

Qualitative Identity and Uniformity. SCHLESINGER, George N.

Rights to Liberty in Purely Private Matters: Part I. RILEY, Jonathan.

Self-Reform as Political Reform in the Writings of John Stuart Mill. EISENACH, Eldon J.

Sympathy and Self-Interest: The Crisis in Mill's Mental History. GREEN, Michele.

MILLER, D

The Language Dependence of Accuracy. BARNES, Eric.

On a Recent Objection to Popper and Miller's "Disproof" of Probabilistic Induction. HOWSON, Colin.

When Probabilistic Support is Inductive. MURA, Alberto.

MILLER, R

Was Marx an Egalitarian: Skeptical Remarks on Miller's Marx. NIELSEN, Kai.

MILLS, C

Ideology and Epistemology: A Discussion of Mc Carney and Mills. SUSHINSKY, Mary Ann.

Mills and Mc Carney on "Ideology" in Marx and Engels. COSTELLO, Dan.

MIMAMSA

The Mīmāṃsā Theory of Self-Recognition. TABER, John A.

The Theory of the Sentence in Pūrva Mīmāṃsā and Western Philosophy. TABER, John A.

MIMESIS

Typography: Mimesis, Philosophy, Politics. FYNSK, Christopher (ed).

"An Ironic Mimesis" in The Question of the Other: Essays in Contemporary Continental Philosophy, MEHURON, Kate.

MIND

see also Soul(s), Spirit(s)

Abstract Particulars. CAMPBELL, Keith.

Artificial Intelligence in Psychology: Interdisciplinary Essays. BODEN, Margaret A.

Bergson. LACEY, A R.

Cause, Mind, and Reality: Essays Honoring C B Martin. HEIL, John (ed).

Connections to the World: The Basic Concepts of Philosophy. DANTO, Arthur C.

Facts and the Function of Truth. PRICE, Huw.

The Fourth Way: A Theory of Knowledge. GROSSMAN, Reinhardt.

Hegels "Sinnliche Gewissheit": Diskursanalytischer Kommentar. KETTNER, Matthias.

Hypothesis and the Spiral of Reflection. WEISSMAN, David.

Lawless Mind. ABELSON, Raziel.

The Logic of Mind (Second Edition). NELSON, R J.

Looking Into Mind: How to Recognize Who You Are and How You Know. DAMIANI, Anthony.

Mental Content. MC GINN, Colin.

Mental Imagery: On the Limits of Cognitive Science. ROLLINS, Mark.

Mind, Brain and the Quantum: The Compound 'I'. LOCKWOOD, Michael.

Mind, Value and Culture: Essays in Honor of E M Adams. WEISSBORD, David (ed).

Mind-Body Identity Theories. MACDONALD, Cynthia.

Mind: An Essay on Human Feeling. LANGER, Susanne Katherina.

Miscellaneous Writings (Collected Works of John Stuart Mill, Volume 31). ROBSON, John M (ed).

The Mundane Matter of the Mental Language. MALONEY, J Christopher.

On Action. GINET, Carl.

The Person and the Human Mind: Issues in Ancient and Modern Philosophy. GILL, Christopher (ed).

The Philosopher's Habitat: Introduction to Investigations in, and Applications of, Modern Philosophy. GOLDSTEIN, Laurence.

The Philosophy of Thomas Reid. DALGARNO, Melvin (ed).

The Problem of the Ideal. DUBROVSKY, David.

Propositional Attitudes: An Essay on Thoughts and How We Ascribe Them. RICHARD, Mark.

Lo storicismo di W Dilthey (Il problema di dio nei grandi pensatori, Volume Quinto). MANNO, Ambrogio Giacomo.

A Theory of Content and Other Essays. FODOR, Jerry A.

Thinking Fragments: Psychoanalysis, Feminism, and Postmodernism in the Contemporary West. FLAX, Jane.

Thomas Reid. LEHRER, Keith.

Wittgenstein's Philosophy of Psychology. BUDD, Malcolm.

"Adams on the Mind: Mind as Meaning and as Agent" in Mind, Value and Culture: Essays in Honor of E M Adams, HALL, R.

"Are We Losing Our Minds?" in Mind, Value and Culture: Essays in Honor of E M Adams, HALL, Ronald L.

"Influences on the Conception of Logic and Mind" in Scientific Knowledge Socialized, GELLATLY, Angus R H.

"The Mind-Body Problem: Some Neurobiological Reflections" in Reductionism and Systems Theory in the Life Sciences: Some Problems and Perspectives, LÖWENHARD, Percy.

"Presocratic Minds" in The Person and the Human Mind: Issues in Ancient and Modern Philosophy, WRIGHT, M R.

"Where I Stand: Response to the Essays" in Mind, Value and Culture: Essays in Honor of E M Adams, ADAMS, E Maynard.

"Why There is No Concept of a Person" in The Person and the Human Mind: Issues in Ancient and Modern Philosophy, MORTON, Adam.

Against Positing Central Systems in the Mind. ROSS, Don.

Are Knowledge and Action Really One Thing—A Study of Wang Yang-ming's Doctrine of Mind. FRISINA, Warren G.

Aristotle The First Cognitivist?. MODRAK, D K W.

Conceptual Dependency as the Language of Thought. DUNLOP, Charles E M.

Consciousness in Quantum Physics and The Mind-Body Problem. GOSWAMI, Amit.

Consciousness, Unconsciousness, and Intentionality. SEARLE, John R.

Content and Self-Knowledge. BOGHOSSIAN, Paul A.

Dai Zhen: The Unity of the Moral Nature (in Serbo-Croatian). EWELL JR, John W.

Des fondements théoriques pour l'intelligence artificielle et la philosophie de l'esprit. MARCHAL, Bruno.

Descartes's Dualism and the Philosophy of Mind. ALANEN, Lilli.

Developing the Idea of Intentionality: Children's Theories of Mind. GOPNIK, Alison.

La estructura de la mente según la escuela idealista budista (Yogachara). TOLA, Fernando and DRAGONETTI, Carmen.

F H Bradley y E E Harris: acerca de la relación mente-cuerpo. GARCIA, Pablo S.

Freud's Critique of Philosophy. BERTHOLD-BOND, Daniel.

Incommensurability: The Scaling of Mind-Body Theories as a Counter Example. RAKOVER, Sam S.

Intentionality and Stich's Theory of Brain Sentence Syntax. JACQUETTE, Dale.

Interpretation Psychologized. GOLDMAN, Alvin I.

Intersubjectivity and the Monadic Core of the Psyche: Habermas and Castoriadis on the Unconscious. WHITEBOOK, Joel.

Kriterien für eine Theorie zur Lösung des Leib-Seele-Problems. METZINGER, Thomas.

Language and the Problems of Knowledge (in Serbo-Croatian). CHOMSKY, Noam.

Maine de Biran and the Body-Subject. GAINES, Jeffrey J.

Making Mind Matter More. FODOR, Jerry A.

McGinn on the Mind-Body Problem. WHITELEY, C H.

Mencius: The Mind-Inherence of Morality (in Serbo-Croatian). SHUN, Kwong-loi.

Mental Representations and Intentional Behavior. WARD, Andrew.

Metaphysics, Mind, and Mental Science. GOLDMAN, Alvin I.

Mind and Body. WILKES, K V.

Mind-Body and the Future of Psychiatry. WALLACE IV, Edwin R.

More on Making Mind Matter. LE PORE, Ernest and LOEWER, Barry.

The Myth of Jones and the Mirror of Nature: Reflections on Introspection. GARFIELD, Jay L.

On the Nature and Cognitive Function of Phenomenal Content—Part I. FOX, Ivan.

Overtones of Solipsism in Thomas Nagel's "What is it Like to Be a Bat?" and The View From Nowhere. WIDER, Kathleen.

MIND

Parallogic: As Mind Meets Context. HANSON, Barbara Gail.

Programas e Promessas: Sobre o (Ab-)Uso do Jargão Computacional em Teorias Cognitivas da Mente. MENDONÇA, W P.

Psychology in the First *Critique*. BIRD, G H.

Searle on Minds and Brains. SAGAL, Paul T.

The Theory of Complimentarity and Mind-Body Dualism: A Critique. CHAKRABARTY, Alpana.

The Time-Like Nature of Mind: On Mind Functions as Temporal Patterns of the Neural Network. FISCHER, Roland.

Transcendentalism and Its Discontents. WHITE, Stephen L.

Tres niveles de conocimiento en la filosofía de Gabriel Marcel. CAÑAS, José Luis.

Truth in Thomas Aquinas, (II). WIPPEL, John F.

Was Aristotle a Functionalist?. NELSON, John O.

Weak Externalism and Mind-Body Identity. MACDONALD, Cynthia.

What Difference Does Consciousness Make?. VAN GULICK, Robert.

What Is Empiricism?—I. CARRUTHERS, Peter.

What's Wrong with the Syntactic Theory of Mind. EGAN, M Frances.

Wittgenstein's Later Philosophy of Mind: Sensation, Privacy, and Intention. WRIGHT, Crispin.

Wittgenstein, Mind, and Scientism. GOLDFARB, Warren.

Wordsworth and the Zen Void. RUDY, John G.

MINDS

see also Other Minds

Embodiments of Mind. MC CULLOCH, Warren S.

Philosophy, Psychiatry and Neuroscience: Three Approaches to the Mind. HUNDERT, Edward M.

"E M Adams and the Modern Mind" in *Mind, Value and Culture: Essays in Honor of E M Adams*, ROSENBERG, Jay F.

"Philosophy and its History" in *The Institution of Philosophy: A Discipline in Crisis?*, ROSENTHAL, David M.

Demons, Vats and the Cosmos. LESLIE, John.

Hobbes on our Minds. ZAGORIN, Perez.

Minds Divided. HEIL, John.

MINK, L

The Primacy of Narrative in Historical Understanding. JACQUES, T Carlos.

MIRACLE(S)

David Hume's Argument Against Miracles: A Critical Analysis. BECKWITH, Francis.

Hume and the Problem of Miracles: A Solution. LEVINE, Michael P.

New Perspectives on Old-Time Religion. SCHLESINGER, George N.

Philosophy of Religion: Selected Readings (Second Edition). ROWE, William L.

David Hume and the Probability of Miracles. GOWER, Barry.

Filosofia e scienza della natura del "Lucidarius" medioaltotedesco. STURLESE, Loris.

Hume, Probability, Lotteries and Miracles. LANGTRY, Bruce.

The Logic of Probabilities in Hume's Argument against Miracles. WILSON, Fred.

Miracles and Natural Explanations: A Rejoinder. LARMER, Robert A.

Miracles and the Uniformity of Nature. ROOT, Michael.

Miracles as Evidence for Theism. BASINGER, David.

Miracles, the Supernatural, and the Problem of Extrinsicism. NICHOLS, Terence L.

Reconceiving Miracles. GILMAN, James E.

Revelation and the Bible. MAVRODES, George I.

What Hume Actually Said About Miracles. FOGELIN, Robert J.

MISGELD, D

Reflective Equilibrium and the Transformation of Philosophy. NIELSEN, Kai.

MISHKIN, M

Complementarity and the Relation Between Psychological and Neurophysiological Phenomena. SNYDER, Douglas M.

MITCHELL, S

One Causal Mechanism in Evolution: One Unit of Selection. KARY, Carla E.

MO TZU

Disputers of the TAO: Philosophical Argument in Ancient China. GRAHAM, A C.

Comment on Chad Hansen's "Language Utilitarianism". BRANDT, Richard B.

Mo-Tzu: Language Utilitarianism. HANSEN, Chad.

Reply to Richard Bosley's "Virtues and Vices: East and West". TANG, Paul C L.

Universalism Versus Love with Distinctions: An Ancient Debate Revived.

WONG, David B.

MODAL LOGIC

Automated Deduction in Nonclassical logics. WALLEN, Lincoln A.

The Future: An Essay on God, Temporality, and Truth. LUCAS, J R.

logic: Analyzing and Appraising Arguments. GENSLER, Harry J.

The Semantic Foundations of logic, Volume 1: Propositional logics. EPSTEIN, Richard L.

'Actually'. TEICHMANN, Roger.

Action and Ability. BROWN, Mark A.

An Algebraic Approach to Intuitionistic Modal Logics in Connection with Intermediate Predicate Logics. SUZUKI, Nobu-Yuki.

Characters and Fixed Points in Provability Logic. GLEIT, Zachary and GOLDFARB, Warren.

Conversion Principles and the Basis of Aristotle's Modal Logic. PATTERSON, Richard.

Duality Between Modal Algebras and Neighbourhood Frames. DOSEN, Kosta.

The Equivalence of the Disjunction and Existence Properties for Modal Arithmetic. FRIEDMAN, Harvey.

Essentialisme et logique modale (in Romanian). DUMITRU, Mircea.

A General Logic. SLANEY, John.

A General Treatment of Equivalent Modalities. BELLISSIMA, Fabio.

Graded Modalities, III. FATTOROSI-BARNABA, M and CERRATO, C.

Identification et analyse des classes d'équivalence de la logique modale par des invariants numériques. SANCHEZ-MAZAS, Miguel.

Infinite Sets of Nonequivalent Modalities. BELLISSIMA, Fabio.

Lesniewski's Strategy and Modal Logic. KEARNS, John T.

La logica polivalente *in Statu Nascendi*. ÖFFENBERGER, Niels.

Misuse of Inference—OR—Why Sherlock Holmes is a Fake. THOMAS, Max W.

Modal Definability in Enriched Languages. GORANKO, Valentin.

A Modal Version of Free Logic. BARBA, Juan L.

Much Shorter Proofs: A Bimodal Investigation. CARBONE, Alessandra and MONTAGNA, Franco.

Multiply Modal Extensions of Da Costa's C_n, Logical Relativism, and the Imaginary. LOKHORST, Gert-Jan C.

Necessity and Contingency. CRESSWELL, M J.

A New Proof of the Fixed-Point Theorem of Provability Logic. REIDHAAR-OLSON, Lisa.

On Halldén-Completeness of Intermediate and Modal Logics. CHAGROV, A V and ZAKHARYASHCHEV, M V.

The Ontological Foundation of Russell's Theory of Modality. DEJNOZKA, Jan.

Peano's Smart Children: A Provability Logical Study of Systems with Built-In Consistency. VISSER, Albert.

Possibilia and Possible Worlds. MARCUS, Ruth Barcan.

Post Complete and 0-Axiomatizable Modal Logics. BELLISSIMA, Fabio.

Quantified Modal Logic and the Plural *De Re*. BRICKER, Phillip.

Relations Between Intuitionistic Modal Logics and Intermediate Predicate Logics. ONO, Hiroakira and SUZUKI, Nobu-Yuki.

Rosser Orderings in Bimodal Logics. CARBONE, Alessandra and MONTAGNA, F.

Simple Completeness Proof of Lemmon's SO:5. KONDO, Michiro.

A Simplification of the Completeness Proofs for Guaspari and Solovay's R. VOORBRAAK, Frans.

Some Compactness Results for Modal Logic. SCHUMM, George F.

Some Modal Propositional Logics Containing CO:8. YOKOTA, Shin-ichi.

Two Incomplete Anti-Realist Modal Epistemic Logics. WILLIAMSON, Timothy.

Über die Stärke der Aristotelischen Modallogik. NORTMANN, Ulrich.

Une méthode arithmétique de décision pour le système modal S5. SÁNCHEZ-MAZAS, Miguel.

Varieties of Complex Algebras. GOLDBLATT, Robert.

MODAL PROOFS

Anselm's Proof. STONE, Jim.

MODAL REALISM

Dog Bites Man: A Defence of Modal Realism. MILLER, Richard B.

MODAL SYLLOGISMS

Models for Modal Syllogisms. JOHNSON, Fred.

Über die Stärke der Aristotelischen Modallogik. NORTMANN, Ulrich.

MODAL THEORY

Absolute Truth Theories for Modal Languages as Theories of Interpretation. LE PORE, Ernest and LOEWER, Barry.

The Crash of Modal Metaphysics. ROSS, James F.

MODALITY

The Nature of Necessity. PLANTINGA, Alvin.

MODALITY

Necessity, Essence, and Individuation: A Defense of Conventionalism. SIDELLE, Alan.

The Possible Universe. TALLET, J A.

Realism, Mathematics and Modality. FIELD, Hartry.

The Crash of Modal Metaphysics. ROSS, James F.

A General Treatment of Equivalent Modalities. BELLISSIMA, Fabio.

Graded Modalities, III. FATTOROSI-BARNABA, M and CERRATO, C.

Infinite Sets of Nonequivalent Modalities. BELLISSIMA, Fabio.

A Logic of *Good, Should, and Would*: Part I. GOBLE, Lou.

Modal Fictionalism. ROSEN, Gideon.

Modal Subordination and Pronominal Anaphora in Discourse. ROBERTS, Craige.

The Modal View of Economic Models. RAPPAPORT, Steven.

Modality, Mechanism and Translational Indeterminacy. MAC INTOSH, Duncan.

On Synonymy and Ontic Modalities. ZABLUDOWSKI, Andrzej.

On the Modalities and Narrativity in Music. TARASTI, Eero.

The Ontological Foundation of Russell's Theory of Modality. DEJNOZKA, Jan.

The Price of Possibility. HART, W D.

Reflective Modalities and Theory Change. FUHRMANN, André.

Scientific Explanation, Necessity and Contingency. WEBER, Erik.

Vague Identity Yet Again. NOONAN, Harold W.

What's Wrong with Impossible Objects?. PERSZYK, Kenneth J.

MODEL THEORY

Informal Lectures on Formal Semantics. BACH, Emmon W.

Mathematical Methods in Linguistics. PARTEE, Barbara H.

Systems of Logic. MARTIN, Norman M.

The Model-Theoretic Approach in the Philosophy of Science. DA COSTA, Newton C A and FRENCH, Steven.

Nonstandard Combinatorics. HIRSHFELD, Joram.

Unicidad y categoricidad de teorías. LUNGARZO, Carlos A.

MODEL(S)

Artificial Intelligence in Psychology: Interdisciplinary Essays. BODEN, Margaret A.

Love: Emotion, Myth, and Metaphor. SOLOMON, Robert C.

"The Causal Mechanical Model of Explanation" in *Scientific Explanation (Minnesota Studies in the Philosophy of Science, Volume XIII)*, WOODWARD, James.

"Explanation: In Search of the Rationale" in *Scientific Explanation (Minnesota Studies in the Philosophy of Science, Volume XIII)*, SINTONEN, Matti.

"Four Decades of Scientific Explanation" in *Scientific Explanation (Minnesota Studies in the Philosophy of Science, Volume XIII)*, SALMON, Wesley C.

Action and Ability. BROWN, Mark A.

Almost Orthogonal Regular Types. HRUSHOVSKI, E.

Analogy and Interpretation (in Polish). LUBANSKI, Mieczyslaw.

Ars inveniendi et théorie des modèles. BENIS-SINACEUR, Hourya.

The Boolean Spectrum of an o-Minimal Theory. STEINHORN, Charles and TOFFALORI, Carlo.

Bootstrapping While Barefoot (Crime Models versus Theoretical Models in the Hunt for Serial Killers). NORDBY, Jon J.

Categoricity of Theories in $L_{\kappa\omega}$ with κ a Compact Cardinal. SHELAH, Saharon and MAKKAI, M.

China and Modernization: Past and Present. SOO, Francis.

The Classification of Excellent Classes. GROSSBERG, R.

Computer Science Temporal Logics Need their Clocks. SAIN, Ildikó.

A Consistent Higher-Order Theory Without a (Higher-Order) Model. FORSTER, Thomas.

Contemporary Models of Consciousness: Part I. BURNS, Jean E.

Critique of Structural Analysis in Modeling Cognition: A Case Study of Jackendoff's Theory. BILLMAN, Dorrit and PETERSON, Justin.

Des belles paires aux beaux uples. BOUSCAREN, Elisabeth and POIZAT, Bruno.

A Dichotomy Theorem for Regular Types. HRUSHOVSKI, E and SHELAH, S.

Dimension of Definable Sets, Algebraic Boundedness and Henselian Fields. VAN DEN DRIES, L.

Elementary Pairs of Models. BOUSCAREN, E.

Extensions Séparées et immédiates des corps valués. DELON, Fançoise.

Far-Sighted Equilibria in 2 x 2, Non-Cooperative, Repeated Games. AAFTINK, Jan.

First Order Logic with Empty Structures. AMER, Mohamed A.

The Fraenkel-Mostowski Method, Revisited. BRUNNER, Norbert.

A General Treatment of Equivalent Modalities. BELLISSIMA, Fabio.

Graded Modalities, III. FATTOROSI-BARNABA, M and CERRATO, C.

Groups With Identities. POINT, F.

Hyperhypersimple Sets and Δ_2 Systems. CHONG, C T.

Injecting Inconsistencies Into Models of PA. SOLOVAY, Robert M.

An Integrative Model for Understanding and Managing Ethical Behavior in Business Organizations. STEAD, W Edward and WORRELL, Dan L and STEAD, Jean Garner.

An Introduction to γ-Recursion Theory (Or What to Do in KP-Foundation). LUBARSKY, Robert S.

An Isomorphism Between Rings and Groups. ISKANDER, Awad A.

Large Resplendent Models Generated by Indiscernibles. SCHMERL, James H.

A Logic Characterized by the Class of Connected Models with Nested Domain. CORSI, Giovanna.

Mathematics of Totalities: An Alternative to Mathematics of Sets. DISHKANT, Herman.

Minimal Collapsing Extensions of Models of ZFC. BUKOVSKY, Lev and COPLÁKOVÁ-HARTOVÁ, E.

The Modal View of Economic Models. RAPPAPORT, Steven.

Model Completeness and Direct Power. TAGHVA, Kazem.

The Model-Theoretic Approach in the Philosophy of Science. DA COSTA, Newton C A and FRENCH, Steven.

Models for Modal Syllogisms. JOHNSON, Fred.

Models of Freedom in the Modern World. WELLMER, Albrecht.

Models of Rationality. VAN STRAATEN, Zak.

Models of Reason, Types of Principles and Reasoning: Historical Comments and Theoretical Outlines. PATTARO, Enrico.

Moral Education, Liberal Education, and Model Building. FRENCH, Peter A.

Much Shorter Proofs: A Bimodal Investigation. CARBONE, Alessandra and MONTAGNA, Franco.

A New Model for Intuitionistic Analysis. SCOWCROFT, Philip.

The Non-Definability Notion and First Order Logic. KRYNICKI, Michal.

Notes on Conditional Logic. SEGERBERG, Krister.

The Number of Pairwise Non-Elementarily-Embeddable Models. SHELAH, Saharon.

Omega-Categoricity, Relative Categoricity and Coordinatisation. HODGES, Wilfrid and HODKINSON, I M and MACPHERSON, Dugald.

On a Subtheory of the Bernays-Gödel Set Theory. MANAKOS, Jannis.

On Absoluteness. HABART, Karol.

On Adaptation: A Reduction of the Kauffman-Levin Model to a Problem in Graph Theory and Its Consequences. SARKAR, Sahotra.

On Finite Models of Regular Identities. DUDEK, Józef and KISIELEWICZ, Andrzej.

On Justification Conditional Models of Linguistic Competence. STERN, Cindy D.

On Models of the Elementary Theory of (Z,+,1). NADEL, Mark and STAVI, Jonathan.

On the Existence of Regular Types. SHELAH, S and BUECHLER, S.

On the Generator Problem. SZWAST, Wieslaw.

On the Mathematical Content of the Theory of Classes KM. JANSANA, Ramón.

Paraconsistent Foundations for Logic Programming. BLAIR, Howard A and SUBRAHMANIAN, V S.

Paradigms of Measurement. SWISTAK, Piotr.

Parameter-Free Universal Induction. KAYE, Richard.

The Primal Framework I. BALDWIN, J T and SHELAH, S.

Probabilities of Conditionals—Revisited. HÁJEK, Alan.

A Proof of Morley's Conjecture. HART, Bradd.

Quantales and (Noncommutative) Linear Logic. YETTER, David N.

Quantifiers Determined by Partial Orderings. KRYNICKI, Michal.

R-Algebras and R-Model Structures as Power Constructs. BRINK, Chris.

Semisimple Stable and Superstable Groups. BALDWIN, J T and PILLAY, A.

Sequent-Systems and Groupoid Models, II. DOSEN, Kosta.

Some Compactness Results for Modal Logic. SCHUMM, George F.

Stability of Weak Second-Order Semantics. CSIRMAZ, László.

The Structure-Nominative Reconstruction of Scientific Knowledge. BURGIN, M S.

A Theorem on Barr-Exact Categories, with an Infinitary Generalization. MAKKAI, Michael.

Théories complètes de paires de corps valués henseliens. LELOUP, Gérard.

Topological Models of Epistemic Set Theory. GOODMAN, Nicolas D.

Towers in $[\omega]^\omega$ and $^\omega\omega$. DORDAL, P L.

Two Incomplete Anti-Realist Modal Epistemic Logics. WILLIAMSON, Timothy.

UFA Fails in the Bell-Kunen Model. MERRILL, John W L.

Uncountable Theories that are Categorical in a Higher Power. LASKOWSKI, Michael Chris.

MODEL(S)

A Uniform Method for Proving Lower Bounds on the Computational Complexity of Logical Theories. COMPTON, Kevin J and HENSON, C Ward.

Urquhart's C with Minimal Negation. MÉNDEZ, José M.

What Is Utility?. HASLETT, D W.

MODELING

A Decision Support System for the Graph Model of Conflicts. KILGOUR, D Marc and FANG, Liping and HIPEL, Keith W.

Forme simili, forme autosimilari. TURCHETTI, Giorgio.

Minimal Representation of a Semiorder. PIRLOT, Marc.

Modeling in the Museum: On the Role of Remnant Models in the Work of Joseph Grinnell. GRIESEMER, James R.

Persuasive Argumentation in Negotiation. SYCARA, Katia P.

Structuring and Simulating Negotiation: An Approach and an Example. KERSTEN, G E and BADCOCK, L and IGLEWSKI, M and MALLORY, G R.

Supporting Individuals in Group-Decision Making. KORHONEN, P and WALLENIUS, J.

MODERN

Arnauld and the Cartesian Philosophy of Ideas. NADLER, Steven M.

A Critical Exposition of the Philosophy of Leibniz. RUSSELL, Bertrand.

David Hume's Argument Against Miracles: A Critical Analysis. BECKWITH, Francis.

Early Modern Philosophy II. TWEYMAN, Stanley (ed).

El individuo y la feminidad. PEREZ ESTEVEZ, Antonio.

Elements of Modern Philosophy: Descartes through Kant. BRENNER, William H.

Freedom and the End of Reason: On the Moral Foundation of Kant's Critical Philosophy. VELKLEY, Richard L.

Greek Scepticism: Anti-Realist Trends in Ancient Thought. GROARKE, Leo.

Heritage and Challenge: The History and Theory of History. CONKIN, Paul K.

Hobbes's System of Ideas. WATKINS, John W N.

Johann Gottfried Herder: A Bibliographical Survey, 1977-1987. MARKWORTH, Tino.

Kant and the Philosophy of History. YOVEL, Yirmiyahu.

Kant: An Index to Theses and Dissertations Accepted by Universities in Canada and the US, 1879-1985. GABEL, Gernot U.

Kant: Selections. BECK, Lewis White (ed).

Perspectives on Thomas Hobbes. ROGERS, G A J (ed).

The Philosophy of Rhetoric (Revised Edition). CAMPBELL, George.

The Philosophy of Thomas Reid. DALGARNO, Melvin (ed).

Political Writings: Thomas Paine. KUKLICK, Bruce (ed).

The Possible Influence of Montaigne's "Essais" on Descartes' "Treatise on the Passions". PAULSON, Michael G.

The Question of Jean-Jacques Rousseau—Ernest Cassirer (Second Edition). GAY, Peter (ed & trans).

Reading Kant. SCHAPER, Eva (ed).

Rousseau, Judge of Jean-Jacques: Dialogues—The Collected Writings of Rousseau, Volume I. MASTERS, Roger D (ed & trans).

Rousseau. DENT, N J H.

Rousseau: Selections. CRANSTON, Maurice (ed).

Skepticism and Modern Enmity: Before and After Eliot. PERL, Jeffrey M.

Thomas Reid. LEHRER, Keith.

The Unvarnished Doctrine: Locke, Liberalism, and the American Revolution. DWORETZ, Steven M.

Vico Revisited: Orthodoxy, Naturalism and Science in the Scienca Nuova. BEDANI, Gino.

"The Eighteenth Century Assumptions of Analytic Aesthetics" in History and Anti-History in Philosophy, BERLEANT, Arnold.

"The Modern Religion of Art" in Cultural Hermeneutics of Modern Art: Essays in Honor of Jan Aler, DETHIER, Hubert.

The "Notes on the Government and Population of the Kingdom of Naples" and Berkeley's Probable Route to Sicily. ALFONSO, Louis.

"Questions Philosophers Ask": Response to Michael Baur. NALEZINSKI, Alix.

Il "Satyricon" di Petronio e la datazione della Grammatica Ebraica Spinoziana. PROIETTI, Omero.

The American Founders and Classical Political Thought. ZVESPER, John.

Anonymous Writings of David Hume. RAPHAEL, D D and SAKAMOTO, Tatsuya.

Berkeley's Introduction Draft. STEWART, M A.

Bruno 'lulliano' nell'idealismo italiano dell'Ottocento (con un inedito di Bertrando Spaventa). SAVORELLI, Alessandro.

A Case Study in Ad Hominem Arguments: Fichte's Science of Knowledge. SUBER, Peter.

Categorías puras y categorías esquematizadas. VON BILDERLING, Beatriz.

The Citizen Philosopher: Rousseau's Dedicatory Letter to the Discourse on Inequality. PALMER, Michael.

Deduction, Confirmation, and the Laws of Nature in Descartes's Principia Philosophiae. NADLER, Steven M.

Descartes' Logic of Magnitudes. LOECK, Gisela.

Distinguishing Modern and Postmodern Theologies. MURPHY, Nancey and MC CLENDON JR, James W.

Du moraliste classique au moraliste des Lumières où la naissance des sciences humaines. MYDLARSKI, H.

Edmund Burke and the American Constitution. FRISCH, Morton J.

The Eminently Practical Mr Hume or Still Relevant After All These Years. DAVLANTES, Nancy.

Essere è percepire una struttura linguistica: Il pensiero di George Berkeley quale presupposto filosofico. REBAGLIA, Alberta.

Étienne Dumont: Genevan Apostle of Utility. BLAMIRES, Cyprian.

Les fondements du savoir dans la pensée moraliste des Lumières. MYDLARSKI, Henri.

Fra Platone e Lucrezio: prime linee di una storia degli studi di filosofia antica nell'ottocento italiano. SASSI, Maria Michela.

Francesco Venini: Un philosophe a Parma (1764-1772). MAMIANI, Maurizio.

Francisco Sanchez's Theory of Cognition and Vico's verum/factum. FAUR, José.

Hobbes alle prese con lo "stolto": La confutazione di Leviathan I. REALE, Mario.

Hobbes come Giano: un pensatore sulla soglia dello Stato moderno. LAMI, Gian Franco.

Hume's Tu Quoque: Newtonianism and the Rationality of the Causal Principle. HAYNES, Michael.

Hume: Justice as Property. BRETT, Nathan.

Immaginazione produttiva e struttura dell'immaginario nelle Rêveries du promeneur solitaire di Jean-Jacques Rousseau. PANELLA, Giuseppe.

Kant and the Possibility of Uncategorized Experience. KAIN, Philip J.

L'égalité au dix'huitième siècle: l'importance de l'aequanimitas. MARCIL-LACOSTE, Louise.

L'Emergence de la notion d'intérêt dans l'esthétique des Lumières. MOSER-VERREY, Monique.

Lavoisier, Priestley, and the Philosophes: Epistemic and Linguistic Dimensions to the Chemical Revolution. MC EVOY, John G.

Un manoscritto inedito delle 'Adnotationes' al Tractatus Theologico-Politicus di Spinoza. TOTARO, Giuseppina.

Melville and Spinoza. HART, Alan.

Modern Normativity and the Politics of Deregulation. TREY, George A.

Natural Law and the Scottish Enlightenment. HAAKONSSEN, Knud.

O ceticismo naturalista de David Hume. SMITH, Plínio Junqueira.

On the Early Dutch Reception of the Tractatus-Theologico Politicus. VAN BUNGE, Wiep.

Our Modern Identity: The Formation of Self. DAVIS, Charles.

Per una nuova edizione del Tractatus De Intellectus Emendatione. MIGNINI, Filippo.

Philosophes européens et confucianisme au tournant dex XVIIᵉ siècles. RODIS-LEWIS, Geneviève.

The Politics of Interpretation: Spinoza's Modernist Turn. LANG, Berel.

A propos du Cartésianisme Gris de Marion. LOPARIC, Zeljko.

Reid and the Rights of Man. DALGARNO, Melvin.

René Descartes n'est pas l'auteur de La naissance de la paix. WATSON, Richard A.

The Role of Self-Interest in Adam Smith's Wealth of Nations. WERHANE, Patricia H.

The Roots of Mathematics Education in Russia in the Age of Peter the Great. ANELLIS, Irving H.

Rousseau on Reading "Jean-Jacques": The Dialogues. KELLY, Christopher and MASTERS, Roger D.

Science, Philosophy and Religion in the Seventeenth Century Encounter Between China and the West (in Serbo-Croatian). STANDAERT, Nicolas.

A Segurança em Descartes. MACEDO, Leosino Bizinoto.

Self-Knowledge and the Modern Mode of Learning. BLITS, Jan H.

Sensus Communis in Vico and Gadamer. SCHAEFFER, John D.

Sources for the Ladies' Library. HOLLINGSHEAD, Greg.

Spinoza and Finnish Literature. ELOVAARA, Raili.

Spinoza in Borges' Looking-Glass. ABADI, Marcelo.

Spinoza in der schönen Literatur: Bilder aus der Zeit zwischen Vormärz und Weimarer Republik. HELMES, Günther.

Spinoza in Poetry. KLEVER, Wim.

Spinoza's Earliest Philosophical Years, 1655-61. POPKIN, Richard H.

Eine Spinoza-Reminizens in Elias Canettis autobiografischer Erzählung "Das Augenspiel". BOLLACHER, Martin.

MODERN

The Undiscoverable Fraternity (in Serbo-Croatian). LEFEBVRE, Jean Pierre.

Thomas Reid's Critique of Joseph Priestley: Context and Chronology. WOOD, Paul B.

Towards an Histrionic Aesthetics: Diderot's *Paradoxes* as Pre-Text for Romantic Irony. SPENCER, Judith.

A Vichian Footnote to Nietzsche's View on the Cognitive Primacy of Metaphor: An Addendum to Schrift. DANESI, Marcel.

Was Tocqueville a Philosopher?. LAWLER, Peter A.

Wittgenstein on Culture and Civilization. LURIE, Yuval.

MODERN ART

"Hermeneutics and Modern Art" in *Cultural Hermeneutics of Modern Art: Essays in Honor of Jan Aler*, KOCKELMANS, Joseph J.

"La polyphonie des herméneutiques dans l'art contemporain" in *Cultural Hermeneutics of Modern Art: Essays in Honor of Jan Aler*, MOURÉLOS, Georges.

MODERNISM

Moral Consciousness and Communicative Action. HABERMAS, Jürgen.

"Schopenhauer, Modernism, and the Rejection of History" in *Schopenhauer: New Essays in Honor of His 200th Birthday*, WILLEY, T E.

"System" and "Lifeworld": Habermas and the Problem of Holism. BOHMAN, James.

Aufbau/Bauhaus: Logical Positivism and Architectural Modernism. GALISON, Peter.

Confessional Postmodernism and the Process-Relational Vision. MURAY, Leslie A.

Ethics: Modern and Postmodern (in Dutch). DE WACHTER, F.

Hauerwas Represented: A Response to Muray. PINCHES, Charles.

Leviathan and the Post-Modern. WILLMS, Bernard.

The Origins of Post-Modernism: The Ariosto-Tasso Debate. MC KINNEY, Ronald H.

Sublime Politics: On the Uses of an Aesthetics of Terror. CRESAP, Steven.

The Self-Understanding of Political Modernism and the Idea of the Revolution (in Serbo-Croatian). JIMÉNEZ, Manuel.

MODERNITY

Heidegger and Modernity. PHILIP, Franklin (trans).

Margins of Political Discourse. DALLMAYR, Fred R.

Postmodern Social Analysis and Criticism. MURPHY, John W.

Il Potere e l'Ipotesi: Tappe di una filosofia delle Funzioni. FRANCHINI, Raffaello.

Scarcity and Modernity. XENOS, Nicholas.

"Reflections on the 'Crisis of Modernity'" in *The Institution of Philosophy: A Discipline in Crisis?*, DASCAL, Marcelo.

Buchler on Habermas on Modernity. CAHOONE, Lawrence E.

Existentialism at the End of Modernity: Questioning the I's Eyes. LEVIN, David Michael.

Hannah Arendt and Leo Strauss: The Uncommenced Dialogue. BEINER, Ronald.

In the Shadow of Aristotle and Hegel: Communicative Ethics and Current Controversies in Practical Philosophy. BENHABIB, Seyla.

Modernidad y filosofía de la historia. UREÑA, Enrique M.

Modernidad y postmodernidad. INNERARITY, Daniel.

Nietzsche: A Radical Challenge to Political Theory?. ANSELL-PEARSON, Keith.

Les séquelles de la crise moderniste. MONTAGNES, Bernard.

MODERNIZATION

China and Modernization: Past and Present. SOO, Francis.

Some Basic Problems in the Development of the Human Sciences in China Today. YOUZHENG, Li.

State, Class, and Technology in Tobacco Production. GREEN, Gary P.

MODIFIER(S)

Los modificadores de predicado y su lógica. OLLER, Carlos A.

MODULARITY

"What" and "Where" in the Human Visual System: Two Hierarchies of Visual Modules. VAINA, Lucia M.

Modularity and Relevant Logic. GARSON, James.

Modularity, and the Psychoevolutionary Theory of Emotion. GRIFFITHS, P E.

MODUS TOLLENS

A Defence of Modus Tollens. SINNOTT-ARMSTRONG, Walter and MOOR, James and FOGELIN, Robert.

MOKSHA

Swāmī Vivekānanda's Use of Science as an Analogy for the Attainment of *Moksa*. RAMBACHAN, Anantanand.

MOLECULE(S)

"Is the Program of Molecular Biology Reductionistic?" in *Reductionism and*

Systems Theory in the Life Sciences: Some Problems and Perspectives, MOHR, Hans.

MOLINA

Is Molinism as Bad as Calvinism?. WALLS, Jerry L.

MOMENT(S)

Santayana and Panpsychism. SPRIGGE, Timothy.

MONADIC

Perceptual Space Is Monadic. CASULLO, Albert.

Relations and Reduction in Leibniz. COVER, J A.

MONADOLOGY

Kants Theorie der Materie und ihre Wirkung auf die zeitgenössische Chemie. CARRIER, Martin.

MONADS

A Critical Exposition of the Philosophy of Leibniz. RUSSELL, Bertrand.

Involutions Defined By Monadic Terms. LEWIN, Renato A.

Monads, Nonexistent Individuals and Possible Worlds: Reply to Rosenkrantz. CHISHOLM, Roderick M.

A Systematical Approach to Leibniz's Theory of Relations and Relational Sentences. MUGNAI, Massimo.

Transfer Theorems for π-Monads. CUTLAND, Nigel J.

MONEY

Money: A Speech Act Analysis. HADREAS, Peter.

MONISM

Body, Soul, and Life Everlasting: Biblical Anthropology and the Monism-Dualism Debate. COOPER, John W.

'Where Two Are to Become One': Mysticism and Monism. JANTZEN, Grace.

MONOD, J

Anti-Anthropocentrism as a Value in Science. PIATEK, Zdzislawa.

MONOLOGUE

An Analysis of Monologues and Dialogues in Political Debates. EVERTS, Diederik.

MONOTHEISM

Ethical Monotheism and the Whitehead Ethic. HOLMES, Arthur F.

L'idea di creazione *ex nihilo* e la libertà nel pensiero di e Levinas. SIGNORINI, Alberto.

MONTAGUE, R

Informal Lectures on Formal Semantics. BACH, Emmon W.

MONTAIGNE

The Possible Influence of Montaigne's "Essais" on Descartes' "Treatise on the Passions". PAULSON, Michael G.

Montaigne, Encoder and Decoder, in Propria Persona. JONES, Robert F.

MONTESQUIEU

Le "Considèrations" di Montesquieu a 250 anni dalla pubblicazione. LOCHE, Annamaria.

Christianity and Politics in Montesquieu's *Greatness and Decline of the Romans.* MYERS, Richard.

MOOIJ, A

Freud, Mooij en de empiristische boeman. DERKSEN, A A.

MOONEY, M

Rhetoric and Philosophy in Vichian Inquiry. STRUEVER, Nancy S.

MOORE

Common Sense. FORGUSON, Lynd.

Sense and Certainty: A Dissolution of Scepticism. MC GINN, Marie.

"Moore to Stevenson" in *Ethics in the History of Western Philosophy*, DARWALL, Stephen.

"Moore's Attack on Naturalism" in *Inquiries into Values: The Inaugural Session of the International Society for Value Inquiry*, MAGNELL, Thomas.

Certeza, duda escéptica y saber. CABANCHIK, Samuel M.

G E Moore and the Revolution in Ethics: A Reappraisal. WELCHMAN, Jennifer.

J S Mill y la prueba del principio de utilidad: Una defensa de *Utilitarianism* IV, (3). RABOSSI, Eduardo.

Zur Frage der Vereinbarkeit von Freiheit und Determinismus. RHEINWALD, Rosemarie.

MOORE, M

"Comment: Intentions and *Mens Rea*" in *Issues in Contemporary Legal Philosophy: The Influence of H L A Hart*, HEYD, David.

"Comment: Intentions and *Mens Rea*" in *Issues in Contemporary Legal Philosophy: The Influence of H L A Hart*, KREMNITZER, Mordechai.

MORAL

The Consolations of Philosophy: Hobbes's Secret; Spinoza's Way.

MORAL JUDGMENT(S)

Mill on Moral Wrong. LUNDBERG, Randolph.

Morality without Moral Judgment. PRZELECKI, Marian.

Sul problema della valutazione morale: A proposito della "Filosofia pratica" di Guiliano Pontara. JELLAMO, Anna.

MORAL LAWS

Andrew of Novo Castro, OFM, and the Moral Law. KENNEDY, Leonard A.

Journalists: A Moral Law Unto Themselves?. HARRIS, Nigel G E.

Schleiermacher's "Über den Unterschied zwischen Naturgesetz und Sittengesetz". BOYD, George N.

MORAL PRINCIPLE(S)

"The Paradox of Profit" in Papers on the Ethics of Administration, BOWIE, Norman E.

"The Sympathetic Organization" in Papers on the Ethics of Administration, HART, David K.

La decisión moral: principios universales, reglas generales y casos particulares. GUTIÉRREZ, Gilberto.

Descartes: um naturalista?. SILVEIRA, Lígia Fraga.

En busca de la voluntad de Dios. FARRELL, Martín D.

La justificación de la democracia: entre la negación de la justificación y la restricción de la democracia. NINO, Carlos Santiago.

The Morality of Software Piracy: A Cross-Cultural Analysis. SWINYARD, W R and RINNE, H and KENG KAU, A.

Openness. MC MAHON, Christopher.

Should Lawyers Listen to Philosophers about Legal Ethics?. SMITH, M B E.

MORAL PSYCHOLOGY

The Claims of Tragedy: An Essay in Moral Psychology and Aesthetics Theory. SCHIER, Flint.

Kant's Theory of Moral Sensibility: Respect for the Moral Law and the Influence of Inclination. REATH, A.

Mutual Benevolence and the Theory of Happiness. ESTLUND, David M.

Utilitarianism, Sociobiology, and the Limits of Benevolence. SCOCCIA, Danny.

MORAL REASONING

Moral Dilemmas. SINNOTT-ARMSTRONG, Walter.

Moral Reasoning: A Philosophic Approach to Applied Ethics. FOX, Richard M.

Who Cares: Theory, Research and Educational Implications of the Ethic of Care. BRABECK, Mary M (ed).

"Constraints on The Expanding Circle: A Critique of Singer" in Inquiries into Values: The Inaugural Session of the International Society for Value Inquiry, SCHONSHECK, Jonathan.

"Moral Reasoning in the Bishops' Pastoral Letter on War and Peace" in Moral Reasoning and Statecraft: Essays Presented to Kenneth W Thompson, KLUNK, Brian E.

Commentary on "An Empirical Study of Moral Reasoning Among Managers". KELLY, Michaeleen.

An Empirical Study of Moral Reasoning Among Managers. DERRY, Robbin.

L'origine de la connaissance morale, traduit par M B de Launay. BRENTANO, Franz and LAUNAY, Marc B (trans).

Legal Reasoning as a Special Case of Moral Reasoning. PECZENIK, Aleksander.

A Model for the Evaluation of Moral Education. MOREHOUSE, Richard.

Reaching Moral Conclusions on Purely Logical Grounds. VAN WILLIGENBURG, Theo.

MORAL RESPONSIBILITY(-TIES)

The Contribution of Nicomachean Ethics iii 5 to Aristotle's Theory of Responsibility. CURREN, Randall.

MORAL SENSE

Freedom and the End of Reason: On the Moral Foundation of Kant's Critical Philosophy. VELKLEY, Richard L.

MORAL SENTIMENT(S)

"Theological Rhetoric and Moral Passion in the Light of MacKinnon's 'Barth'" in Christ, Ethics and Tragedy: Essays in Honour of Donald MacKinnon, ROBERTS, Richard.

MORAL THEORY(-RIES)

see also Ethical Theory(-ries)

Known from the Things that Are: Fundamental Theory of the Moral Life. O'KEEFE, Martin D.

Moral Consciousness and Communicative Action. HABERMAS, Jürgen.

Wittgenstein and Moral Philosophy. JOHNSTON, Paul.

Blackburn's Projectivism—An Objection. BRIGHOUSE, M H.

Character: A Humean Account. MC INTYRE, Jane L.

Christian Wolff and China: The Autonomy of Morality (in Serbo-Croatian). CHING, Julia.

A Critique of Principlism. CLOUSER, K Danner and GERT, Bernard.

Disparate Conceptions of Moral Theory. HUGHES, Paul.

Ethics and Stochastic Processes. HARDIN, Russell.

Histories, Herstories, and Moral Traditions. MEAGHER, Sharon.

The Impracticality of Impartiality. FRIEDMAN, Marilyn.

In the Shadow of Aristotle and Hegel: Communicative Ethics and Current Controversies in Practical Philosophy. BENHABIB, Seyla.

Knowledge and Silence: The Golden Bowl and Moral Philosophy. BRUDNEY, Daniel.

MacIntyre, Habermas, and Philosophical Ethics. KELLY, Michael.

Moral Theory and Defective Tobacco Advertising and Warnings (The Business Ethics of Cipollone versus Liggett Group). QUINN, John F.

Moral Theory: Thinking, Doing, and Living. CALLAHAN, Daniel.

The No Good Reason Thesis. THOMSON, Judith Jarvis.

Political Animals in the Nicomachean Ethics. ROBERTS, Jean.

The Problems of Preference Based Morality: A Critique of "Morals by Agreement". DE MARCO, Joseph P.

Reflections on Hobbes: Recent Work on His Moral and Political Philosophy. CURLEY, Edwin.

Reflective Equilibrium and the Transformation of Philosophy. NIELSEN, Kai.

Seven Moral Myths. ALMOND, Brenda.

Soft Determinism and How We Become Responsible for the Past. TÄNNSJÖ, Torbjörn.

Talking 'Bout a Revolution: Feminism, Historicism, and Liberal Moral Theory. ARNAULT, Lynne.

Through Thick and Thin: Moral Knowledge in Skeptical Times. LOUDEN, Robert B.

MORAL(S)

Issues in Contemporary Legal Philosophy: The Influence of H L A Hart. GAVISON, Ruth (ed).

Man and Nature in the Philosophical Thought of Wang-Fu-Chih. BLACK, Alison Harley.

Marxism and Morality. LUKES, Steven.

Thomas Reid. LEHRER, Keith.

"Comment: Positivism and the Foundations of Legal Authority" in Issues in Contemporary Legal Philosophy: The Influence of H L A Hart, FINNIS, John.

'Ought' Implies 'Can' and the Scope of Moral Requirements. MC CONNELL, Terrance.

Back to Sainthood. DOMBROWSKI, Daniel A.

Can Business Ethics Be Taught? Empirical Evidence. JONES, Thomas M.

Corporate and Individual Moral Responsibility: A Reply to Jan Garrett. WERHANE, Patricia H.

Deontic Logic and the Possibility of Moral Conflict. ALMEIDA, Michael J.

Detailed Analysis of the Philosophia Harmonistica (Introduced and Notes by Zoltán Z Szabó) (in Hungarian). HETÉNYI, János.

The Developmental Self-Valuing Theory: A Practical Approach for Business Ethics. JENSEN, Larry C and WYGANT, Steven A.

Donum Vitae: Civil Law and Moral Values. BYK, Christian.

Emile Durkheim and Provinces of Ethics. CLADIS, Mark S.

The Ethics of Legalism. MAC CORMICK, Neil.

Intuitionism and Conservatism. NELSON, Mark T.

The Intuitionist Argument. SIMON, Caroline J.

Is Hume a Moral Skeptic?. FIESER, James.

Kant's Conception of Rational Action. BASU, Tora.

L'égalité au dix'huitième siècle: l'importance de l'aequanimitas. MARCIL-LACOSTE, Louise.

Liberalism and Neo-Aristotelianism. PADEN, Roger.

The Life Principle: A (Metaethical) Rejection. PASKE, Gerald H.

Michael Oakeshott as Liberal Theorist. FRANCO, Paul.

Moral Individualism: Agent-Relativity and Deontic Restraints. MACK, Eric.

Moral Reasons in Confucian Ethics. SHUN, Kwong-Loi.

Moral Rights and Duties in Wicked Legal Systems. TEN, C L.

Moral Scepticism. SHAIDA, S A.

Moral Style. AXINN, Sidney.

Morality: Ought or Naught?. FOLDVARY, Fred E.

On Cultivating Moral Character: Comments on "Moral Reasons in Confucian Ethics". TRIANOSKY, Gregory W.

On Goodness: Human and Divine. LINVILLE, Mark D.

Plato, George Eliot, and Moral Narcissism. GOULD, Carol S.

The Reconstruction of Political Concepts. MASON, A.

Schopenhauer as Moral Philosopher—Towards the Actuality of his Ethics. CARTWRIGHT, David.

Studies in the Explanation of Issues in Biomedical Ethics: (II) On "On Play[ing] God", Etc.. ERDE, Edmund L.

Van Inwagen on the 'Obviousness' of Libertarian Moral Responsibility. SMILANSKY, Saul.

MORAL(S)

What Is and What Is Not Practical Reason?. HELLER, Agnes.

When is Lying Morally Permissible? Casuistical Reflections on the Game Analogy, Self-Defense, Social Contract Ethics. VAN WYK, Robert N.

MORALISM

AIDS and *Bowers versus Hardwick*. PIERCE, Christine.

Does the Threat of AIDS Create Difficulties for Lord Devlin's Critics?. SCHEDLER, George.

Motive and Obligation in the British Moralists. DARWALL, Stephen L.

MORALITY

Arms and Judgment: Law, Morality, and the Conduct of War in the 20th Century. COHEN, Sheldon M.

At the Intersection of Legality and Morality: Hartian Law as Natural Law. SKUBIK, Daniel W.

Benevolent Living: Tracing the Roots of Motivation to God. TURNER, Dean.

Bergson. LACEY, A R.

Business Ethics: Where Profits Meet Value Systems. ROBIN, Donald P.

Conscience. ROSMINI, Antonio.

Essays on Political Morality. HARE, R M.

Ethics and Community. DUSSEL, Enrique D.

Ethics and Strategic Defense: American Philosophers Debate Star Wars and Nuclear Deterrence. LACKEY, Douglas P (ed).

The Fieldston Ethics Reader. WEINSTEIN, Mark (ed).

The Foundations of Morality. HAZLITT, Henry.

From Warism to Pacifism: A Moral Continuum. CADY, Duane L.

The Inner Citadel: Essays on Individual Autonomy. CHRISTMAN, John (ed).

Innocence and Experience. HAMPSHIRE, Stuart.

Jewish Philosophy in a Secular Age. SEESKIN, Kenneth.

Justice and Modern Moral Philosophy. REIMAN, Jeffrey.

Kant and the Philosophy of History. YOVEL, Yirmiyahu.

The Kantian Sublime: From Morality to Art. CROWTHER, Paul.

Known from the Things that Are: Fundamental Theory of the Moral Life. O'KEEFE, Martin D.

The Libertarian Idea. NARVESON, Jan.

The Limits of Morality. KAGAN, Shelly.

Moral Absolutes: An Essay on the Nature and Rationale of Morality. RESCHER, Nicholas.

The Moral Case for the Free Market Economy: A Philosophical Argument. MACHAN, Tibor R.

A Moral Military. AXINN, Sidney.

Morality and Imagination: Paradoxes of Progress. TUAN, Yi-Fu.

Natural Agency: An Essay on the Casual Theory of Action. BISHOP, John.

New Perspectives on Old-Time Religion. SCHLESINGER, George N.

Nuclear Deterrence, Morality and Realism. FINNIS, John.

On War and Morality. HOLMES, Robert L.

Posterity and Strategic Policy: A Moral Assessment of Nuclear Policy Options. BAILEY, Alison.

Il Potere e l'Ipotesi: Tappe di una filosofia delle Funzioni. FRANCHINI, Raffaello.

Realizing Rawls. POGGE, Thomas W.

Self and Others: A Study of Ethical Egoism. ÖSTERBERG, Jan.

Splitting the Difference: Compromise and Integrity in Ethics and Politics. BENJAMIN, Martin.

The Tanner Lectures on Human Values, Volume X. PETERSON, Grethe B (ed).

What Reason Demands. BITTNER, Rüdiger.

William James, Public Philosopher. COTKIN, George.

Wise Choices, Apt Feelings: A Theory of Normative Judgment. GIBBARD, Allan.

Xunzi: A Translation and Study of the Complete Works, Volume II—Books 7-16. KNOBLOCK, John (trans).

"The Alternative of Dissent" in The Tanner Lectures on Human Values, Volume X, MUGUERZA, Javier.

"Deterrence and the Moral Use of Nuclear Weapons" in Nuclear Deterrence and Moral Restraint, FOELBER, Robert E.

"Dialectical Ethics: A First Look at Sartre's Unpublished Rome Lecture Notes" in Inquiries into Values: The Inaugural Session of the International Society for Value Inquiry, BOWMAN, Elizabeth A and STONE, Robert V.

"Ethical Relativity and Empirical Evaluation of Normative Propositions" in Inquiries into Values: The Inaugural Session of the International Society for Value Inquiry, GOOSSENS, Charles.

"From Freedom to Need: Sartre's First Two Moralities" in Inquiries into Values: The Inaugural Session of the International Society for Value Inquiry, ANDERSON, Thomas C.

"Goethe's Moral Thinking" in Inquiries into Values: The Inaugural Session of the International Society for Value Inquiry, LARKIN, Edward T.

"Hegel on Morality" in Dialectic and Contemporary Science, WALSH, W H.

"Morality and Personal Relations" in Person to Person, DEIGH, John.

"Morality, Parents, and Children" in Person to Person, RACHELS, James.

"Morality, the SDI, and Limited Nuclear War" in Nuclear Deterrence and Moral Restraint, LEE, Steven.

"Nietzsche" in Ethics in the History of Western Philosophy, SCHACHT, Richard.

"Patriotism and Liberal Morality" in Mind, Value and Culture: Essays in Honor of E M Adams, BARON, Marcia.

"Reason of State as Political Morality: A Benign View" in Papers on the Ethics of Administration, ROHR, John A.

"Reply to Walsh's "Hegel on Morality"" in Dialectic and Contemporary Science, HARRIS, Errol E.

"Sanctity of Life and Suicide: Tensions and Developments Within Common Morality" in Suicide and Euthanasia, BOYLE, Joseph.

"Smith and Kant Respond to Mandeville" in Early Modern Philosophy II, LEVY, David.

"The Varieties of Value" in The Tanner Lectures on Human Values, Volume X, QUINTON, Anthony.

"Vivere" e "vivere bene": Note sul concetto aristotelico di πρᾶξιζ. CHIEREGHIN, Franco.

'Morality and Determinism': A Reply to Flew. WASSERMANN, Gerhard D.

AIDS, Society and Morality—A Philosophical Survey. HÄYRY, Heta and HÄYRY, Matti.

Art and Morality: Critical Theory About the Conflict and Harmony between Art and Morality. KORTHALS, Michiel.

The Authority of Moral Rules. MOREH, J.

Autonomist Internalism and the Justification of Morals. DARWALL, Stephen L.

Bernard Williams and the Nature of Moral Reflection. CRAGG, A W.

Bernard Williams on Practical Necessity. GAY, Robert J.

Beyond Revolt: A Horizon for Feminist Ethics. LINDGREN, Ralph.

Blame, Fictional Characters, and Morality. SANKOWSKI, Edward.

Can a Partisan be a Moralist?. GOMBERG, Paul.

Can Ethics Take Pluralism Seriously?. ENGELHARDT JR, H Tristram.

Can God Forgive Us Our Trespasses?. BRIEN, Andrew.

Can There Be a Social Contract with Business?. HODAPP, Paul F.

Le cercle et le doublet: Note sur Sartre et Foucault. KNEE, Philip.

Ch'eng I—The Pattern of Heaven-and-Earth (in Serbo-Croatian). SMITH, Kidder.

Chinese Axial Age in the Light of Kohlberg's Developmental Logic of Moral Consciousness (in Serbo-Croatian). ROETZ, Heiner.

Comment on Shrader-Frechette's "Parfit and Mistakes in Moral Mathematics". GRACELY, Edward J.

Consequentialism in Search of a Conscience. LANGENFUS, William L.

Corporate Morality Called in Question: The Case of Cabora Bassa. SCHREYÖGG, Georg and STEINMANN, Horst.

Could There Be a Rationally Grounded Morality?. BOND, E J.

Crisis Moral Communities: An Essay in Moral Philosophy. FISHER, David.

Dai Zhen: The Unity of the Moral Nature (in Serbo-Croatian). EWELL JR, John W.

Dialectic and Deliberation in Aristotle's Practical Philosophy. BAYNES, Kenneth.

Le droit à la jouissance, la jouissance des droits. TZITZIS, S.

Du moraliste classique au moraliste des Lumières où la naissance des sciences humaines. MYDLARSKI, H.

Ecologische communicatie door disciplinering van de moraal. STUY, Johan.

Equal Respect and the Enforcement of Morality. DWORKIN, Gerald.

Ethical Analyses in the Development of Congressional Public Policy. WHITE, Gladys B.

A Eupraxopher's Agenda: Humanism and Religion. HOFFMANN, R Joseph.

Evolutionary Biology and Naturalism. MASTERS, Roger D.

Les fondements du savoir dans la pensée moraliste des Lumières. MYDLARSKI, Henri.

Friedrich Hayek's Moral Science. FULLER, Timothy.

God, Morality, and Prudence: A Reply to Bernard Williams. TSANG, Lap-Chuen.

Golden Rules and Golden Bowls. RIGHTER, William.

Groundwork for a Subjective Theory of Ethics. SAPONTZIS, Steve F.

Hannah Arendt on Judgment, Philosophy and Praxis. KNAUER, James T.

Hobbes and 'The Beautiful Axiom'. COADY, C A J.

How Can Theology Be Moral?. O'DONOVAN, Oliver.

Hume's Essays on Happiness. IMMERWAHR, John.

Individuo, tradizioni e pluralismo dei valori. GIAMMUSSO, Salvatore.

Is a Post-Hegelian Ethics Possible?. MC CUMBER, John.

Is and Ought: The "Open Question Argument". FLEW, Antony.

Is the Moral Point of View Monological or Dialogical? The Kantian Background of Habermas' Discourse Ethics. CLEMENT, Grace.

The Justification of Deterrent Violence. FARRELL, Daniel M.

Kant's Political Theory and Philosophy of History. KAIN, Philip J.

MORALITY

L'origine de la connaissance morale, traduit par M B de Launay. BRENTANO, Franz and LAUNAY, Marc B (trans).

La morale dans le contexte des sciences de l'homme chez Constantin Leonardescu (in Romanian). COBIANU, Elena.

La Prétention amoraliste. CLOUTIER, Yvan.

Law and Morality. BICKENBACH, Jerome E.

Law and Objectivity: How People are Treated. GREENAWALT, Kent.

Literature as Life: Nietzsche's Positive Morality. CONWAY, Daniel W.

Marx et le destin historique de la morale (in Romanian). NITA, Petre.

Max Scheler's Criticism of Schopenhauer's Account of Morality and Compassion. MAIDAN, Michael.

Mencius: The Mind-Inherence of Morality (in Serbo-Croatian). SHUN, Kwong-loi.

Messy Morality and the Art of the Possible—I. COADY, C A J.

Moral Dilemmas Concerning the Ultra Intelligent Machine. DE GARIS, Hugo.

Moral Ideals and Social Values: The Dialectics of Legitimization. AVINERI, Shlomo.

Moral Internalism and Moral Relativism. TILLEY, John.

The Moral Significance of Birth. WARREN, Mary Anne.

Moral Understandings: Alternative "Epistemology" for a Feminist Ethics. WALKER, Margaret Urban.

Morality and Bad Luck. THOMSON, Judith Jarvis.

Morality and Culture: A Note on Kant. ROTENSTREICH, Nathan.

Morality and Interest. HARRISON, Bernard.

Morality and Justice in Kant. KLEIN, Martha.

Morality and Law. LETWIN, Shirley Robin.

Morality and Nuclear Weapons Policy. LEE, Steven.

The Morality of Refusing to Treat HIV-Positive Patients. SILVER, Mitchell.

Morality without Moral Judgment. PRZELECKI, Marian.

Morality, Politics and the Revolutions of 1989. O'NEILL, Onora.

A New Old Meaning of "Ideology". MILLS, Charles W and GOLDSTICK, Danny.

The New World of Research Ethics: A Preliminary Map. DAVIS, Michael.

Nietzsche and Nehamas's Nietzsche. SOLOMON, Robert C.

Nietzsche: The Subject of Morality. POOLE, Ross.

On Deciding Whether a Nation Deserves Our Loyalty. NATHANSON, Stephen.

On Necessary Relations Between Law and Morality. ALEXY, Robert.

On the Moral Status of Weakness of the Will. DAHL, Norman O.

On the Relationship Between Law and Morality. COLEMAN, Jules.

Opening the Door to Moral Education. MC GOVERN, Edythe M.

Overview of the Reports of the Ethics Committee of the American Fertility Society. SPICKER, Stuart F.

Particularity, Gilligan, and the Two-Levels View: A Reply. ADLER, Jonathan E.

The Power Principle: "Inherent Defects" Reconsidered. TOMASI, John.

Le problème de la fondation de l'éthique: Kant, Hegel. KERVEGAN, Jean-Francois.

The Problems of Preference Based Morality: A Critique of "Morals by Agreement". DE MARCO, Joseph P.

Quelques aspects psychiques de la conscience morale individuelle (in Romanian). VIDAM, Teodor.

Racism and Rationality: *The Need for a New Critique*. GOLDBERG, David Theo.

Rationality, Human Nature, and Lists. GERT, Bernard.

Rationality, Reasonableness and Morality. PASKE, Gerald H.

Religion a Threat to Morality: An Attempt to Throw Some New Light on Hume's Philosophy of Religion. STREMINGER, Gerhard.

Religion and Morality: A Conceptual Understanding. BEHERA, Satrughna.

A Reply to Ellin's "Streminger: 'Religion a Threat to Morality'". STREMINGER, Gerhard.

Reply: Flew's "Is and Ought: The 'Open-Question Argument'". BLACK, Virginia.

Sayre-McCord on Evaluative Facts. DOUBLE, Richard.

Searching for Ancestors. O'HAGAN, Timothy.

Sensationalized Philosophy: A Reply to Marquis's "Why Abortion is Immoral". CUDD, Ann E.

Seven Moral Myths. ALMOND, Brenda.

Sexuality, Rationality, and Spirituality. TOMM, Winnifred A.

Sport Hunting: Moral or Immoral?. VITALI, Theodore R.

St Paul and Moral Responsibility. STOHL, Johan.

Strauss et Nietzsche. MANENT, Pierre.

Streminger: "Religion a Threat to Morality". ELLIN, Joseph.

Supervenience as a Philosophical Concept. KIM, Jaegwon.

Two Departures from Consequentialism. BENNETT, Jonathan.

Universal Prescriptivism and Practical Skepticism. MC GRAY, James W.

The Use of Nazi Medical Experimentation Data: Memorial or Betrayal?. ROSENBAUM, Alan S.

Values and Meaning: Max Weber's Approach to the Idea of Ultimate Reality and Meaning. CUNEO, Michael W.

Vico and MacIntyre. COERS, Kathy Frashure.

Violence, Law, and the Limits of Morality. CRAGG, A W.

Ways of Wrong-Doing, the Vices, and Cruelty. MC KINNON, Christine.

What Could Be the Meaning of the Idea that Morality Depends on Religion? (in Hebrew). SAGI, Avi and STATMAN, Daniel.

What is Morality All About?. HUDSON, Stephen D.

Woman, Morality, and Fiction. ROBINSON, Jenefer and ROSS, Stephanie.

MORGAN, T

T H Morgan, Neither an Epistemological Empiricist nor a "Methodological" Empiricist. VICEDO, Marga.

MORITZ, K

"Ob das ächte Schöne erkannt werden könne?" in *Agora: Zu Ehren von Rudolph Berlinger*, BÖHM, Peter.

MORPHOLOGY

"Signification des modifications morphologiques de la coupole: LE TEMPS et *le temps*" in *Cultural Hermeneutics of Modern Art: Essays in Honor of Jan Aler*, BRION-GUERRY, Liliane.

Type Concept Revisited: A Survey of German Idealistic Morphology in the First Half of the Twentieth Century. TRIENES, Rudie.

MORRIS, T

God and Abstract Entities. LEFTOW, Brian.

The Logic of God Incarnate. HICK, John.

MORTALITY

Hobbes's Mortalism. JOHNSTON, David.

Modernizing Mortality: Medical Progress and the Good Society. CALLAHAN, Daniel.

MOTHERHOOD

Maternal Thinking: Toward a Politics of Peace. RUDDICK, Sara.

A Feminist Ethic and the New Romanticism—Mothering as a Model of Moral Relations. LAURITZEN, Paul.

Mary of Nazareth, Feminism and the Tradition. CADEGAN, Una M and HEFT, James L.

The Mother-Child Relationship. HOLM, Soren.

The Radical Feminist View of Motherhood: Epistemological Issues and Political Implications. SCHEDLER, George.

Teaching and Mother Love. KLEIN, J Theodore.

MOTION(S)

Bergson. LACEY, A R.

"Motion and Change of Distance" in *Cause, Mind, and Reality: Essays Honoring C B Martin*, NERLICH, Graham.

Aristotle on 'Time' and 'A Time'. WHITE, Michael J.

Atomism Between Orthodoxy and Heterodoxy. CHERCHI, Gavina.

The Confirmation of the Superposition Principle: The Role of a Constructive Thought Experiment in Galileo's *Discorsi*. PRUDOVSKY, Gad.

Descartes and Some Predecessors on the Divine Conservation of Motion. MENN, Stephen.

Gravity (in Dutch). KLEVER, W N A.

Hobbesian Dualism: Hobbes's Theory of Motion. BLITS, Jan H.

Matter, Motion and Humean Supervenience. ROBINSON, Denis.

MOTIVATION(S)

Benevolent Living: Tracing the Roots of Motivation to God. TURNER, Dean.

The Limits of Morality. KAGAN, Shelly.

"The Objectivity of Agent Relative Values" in *Inquiries into Values: The Inaugural Session of the International Society for Value Inquiry*, ROBINS, Michael H.

Children's Philosophy—Or: Is Motivation for Doing Philosophy a Pseudo-Problem?. MARTENS, Ekkehard.

Consequentialism in Search of a Conscience. LANGENFUS, William L.

Doing Justice to Egoism. THOMAS, Laurence.

Exciting Intentions. MELE, Alfred R.

Handlungstypen und Kriterien: Zu Habermas' "Theorie des kommunikativen Handelns". DORSCHEL, Andreas.

How to Argue about Practical Reason. WALLACE, R Jay.

The Importance of Motivation, Precision and Presence in Teaching. BRUMBAUGH, Robert S.

Intending and Motivation. MENDOLA, Joseph.

Intending and Motivation: A Rejoinder. MELE, Alfred R.

Internal Reasons and the Obscurity of Blame. WILLIAMS, Bernard.

Kant's Analysis of Obligation: The Argument of *Foundationsl*. KORSGAARD, Christine M.

MOTIVATION(S)

Motivational Internalism: The Powers and Limits of Practical Reasoning. MELE, Alfred R.

The Reward Event and Motivation. MORILLO, Carolyn R.

Rousseau and Recognition. SHAVER, Robert.

Why Did Psammenitus Not Pity His Son?. BEN-ZEEV, Aaron.

MOTIVE(S)

Bentham on Peace and War. CONWAY, Stephen.

Do Motives Matter?. GOODIN, Robert E.

Kant and Moral Integrity. JENSEN, Henning.

Motive and Obligation in the British Moralists. DARWALL, Stephen L.

MOUNCE, H

From Coffee to Carmelites. PHILLIPS, D Z.

MOUNIER, E

El talante intelectual de la obra de Emmanuel Mounier. REY TATO, J.

MOVEMENT(S)

Education, Movement and the Curriculum: A Philosophic Enquiry. ARNOLD, Peter J.

Human Posture: The Nature of Inquiry. SCHUMACHER, John A.

"The Anxity of American Deconstruction" in The Textual Sublime: Deconstruction and Its Differences, FELPERIN, Howard.

El movimiento accidental en Aristóteles. QUEVEDO, Amalia.

Ricoeur, Lonergan and the Intelligibility of Cosmic Time. PAMBRUN, James R.

MULLER, P

"Reply to Muller's "The Pons Asinorum in Philosophy" in Dialectic and Contemporary Science, HARRIS, Errol E.

MULTINATIONAL CORPORATION(S)

Bhopal, India and Union Carbide: The Second Tragedy. TROTTER, R Clayton and DAY, Susan G and LOVE, Amy E.

Ethical Perspectives on the Foreign Direct Investment Decision. STANLEY, Marjorie T.

The Leverage of Foreigners: Multinationals in South Africa. DI NORCIA, Vincent.

Norman Bowie and Richard Rorty on Multinationals: Does Business Ethics Need 'Metaphysical Comfort?'. WICKS, Andrew C.

MULTIPLICATION

Some Restrictions on Simple Fixed Points of the Integers. MC COLM, Gregory L.

MULTIPLICITY

A Cast of Many: Nietzsche and Depth-Psychological Pluralism. PARKES, Graham.

La struttura metafisica dell'esistente. ALESSI, Adriano.

MUNTZER, T

"Wie Müntzers Religionsphilosophie an den Atheiusmus, so streifte sein politisches Programm an den Kommunismus". HÖPPNER, Joachim.

Müntzer contra Luther: Der philosophische Gehalt des theologischen Konflikts. GRÜNING, Thomas.

Thomas Muntzer—Humanist, Reformator, Revolutionär. HERLITZIUS, Erwin and RUDOLPH, Günther.

Zu Problemen der revolutionären Theologie Thomas Müntzers. KOLESNYK, Alexander.

MURDER

A Case for Capital Punishment. COOPER, W E and KING-FARLOW, John.

MURDOCH, I

Wittgenstein and Murdock on the 'Net' in a Taoist Framework. TOMINAGA, Thomas T.

MURPHY, J

Forgiveness. MC GARY, Howard.

Saving Grace. BRIEN, Andrew.

MURRAY, J

Murray, Niebuhr, and the Problem of the Neutral State. HUNT, Robert P.

Public Philosophy and Contemporary Pluralism. DOUGLASS, R Bruce.

MUSES

"Hesiod's Mimetic Muses and the Strategies of Deconstruction" in Post-Structuralist Classics, FERRARI, Giovanni.

MUSEUM(S)

The MOMA and the ICA: A Common Philosophy of Modern Art. THISTLEWOOD, David.

MUSIC

"O Mensch—Gib Acht": Friedrich Nietzsches Bedeutung Für Gustav Mahler. NIKKELS, Eveline.

Analytic Aesthetics. SHUSTERMAN, Richard (ed).

A Philosophy of Music Education (Second Edition). REIMER, Bennett.

Religious Aesthetics: A Theological Study of Making and Meaning. BURCH BROWN, Frank.

What is Music?. ALPERSON, Philip A.

"Aesthetics of Music: Limits and Grounds" in What is Music?, SPARSHOTT, Francis.

"Analytic Philosophy and the Meaning of Music" in Analytic Aesthetics, SCRUTON, Roger.

"The Challenge of Contemporary Music" in What is Music?, SUBOTNIK, Rose Rosengard.

"The Evaluation of Music" in What is Music?, DAVIES, Stephen.

"The Form-Content Problem in Nietzsche's Conception of Music" in Nietzsche's New Seas: Explorations in Philosophy, Aesthetics, and Politics, HEILKE, Thomas W (trans) and JANZ, Curt Paul.

"How Music Moves" in What is Music?, KIVY, Peter.

"Introduction: The Philosophy of Music" in What is Music?, ALPERSON, Philip.

"Music and Form" in What is Music?, CONE, Edward T.

"Music and History" in What is Music?, DONOUGHO, Martin.

"Music as a Representational Art" in What is Music?, ROBINSON, Jenefer.

"Music as Philosophy" in What is Music?, ALPERSON, Philip.

"Musical De-Composition" in What is Music?, BERLEANT, Arnold.

"Musical Understanding and Musical Culture" in What is Music?, SCRUTON, Roger.

"Nietzsche's Musical Politics" in Nietzsche's New Seas: Explorations in Philosophy, Aesthetics, and Politics, GILLESPIE, Michael Allen.

"On the Semiotics of Music" in What is Music?, MARGOLIS, Joseph.

"Performance and Obligation" in What is Music?, GROSSMAN, Morris.

"Song and Music Drama" in What is Music?, LEVINSON, Jerrold.

"The Work of Making a Work of Music" in What is Music?, WOLTERSTORFF, Nicholas.

Aesthetics and the Insularity of Arts Educators. MC ADOO, Nick.

The Anthropology of 'Semantic Levels' in Music. KARBUSICKY, Vladimir.

The Arousal and Expression of Emotion by Music. ALLEN, R T.

Bach as a Paradigm in Aesthetic Discourse. ZIMMERMANN, Jörg.

Beethoven's Symphonic Style and Temporality in Music. DAHLHAUS, Carl.

Beyond Music Minus Memory?. OLIVIER, G.

Composers' Texts as Objects of Musicological Study. HEINIÖ, Mikko.

Energeia and "The Work Itself". HICKS, Michael.

Ethos, techne y kalon en Platón. LOMBA FUENTES, Joaquín.

Heidegger on Hermeneutics and Music Today. CHARLES, Daniel.

How a Note Denotes. KURKELA, Kari.

The Idea of Music in India and the Ancient West. ROWELL, Lewis.

Listenaires: Thoughts on a Database. GILES, Gordon J.

Metaphors, Counterfactuals and Music. GRUND, Cynthia.

Music and the Expression of Emotion. BUDD, Malcolm.

Music and the Living Brain. BERGSTRÖM, Matti.

Music and Understanding: The Concept of Understanding Applied to Listening to Music. MUNRO, Joan.

Musical Expression: Some Remarks on Goodman's Theory. PEARCE, David.

Musical Work and Possible Events. RANTALA, Veikko.

Negative Composition. HANRAHAN, Nancy Weiss.

Nelson Goodman on Emotions in Music. LAMMENRANTA, Markus.

A New Music Criticism?. KIVY, Peter.

Newton on the Number of Colours in the Spectrum. TOPPER, David.

On Ji Kang's "Aestheticist" Aesthetic Thought. JINSHAN, Liu.

On the "Incompleteness" of a Musical Work. GOSWAMI, Roshmi.

On the Aesthetic Significance of Wang Fuzhi's Theory of the Unity of Poetry and Music, with Criticisms of Certain Biases. JIEMO, Zhang.

Philosophie et Musique selon Schopenhauer. PICLIN, Michel.

Quelques repésentants de l'Esthétique musicale Roumaine (in Romanian). MARIAN, Marin.

The Recurring Postmodern: Notes on the Constitution of Musical Artworks. UUSITALO, Jyrki.

Semantics, Conceptual Spaces and the Dimensions of Music. GÄRDENFORS, Peter.

So Called Nonmusicality of Before Hussitic and Hussitic Reformation (in Czechoslovakian). UHLIR, Zdenek.

Some Distinctions on the Role of Metaphor in Music. PUTMAN, Daniel.

Tonal Harmony as a Formal System. PYLKKÖ, Pauli.

Understanding Music: Remarks on the Relevance of Theory. TORMEY, Alan.

Variations sur Schopenhauer et la musique. LEYVRAZ, Jean-Pierre.

Variations upon Variation, or Picasso Back to Bach. GOODMAN, Nelson.

What Music Is. SERAFINE, Mary Louise.

The Women of Silence. FRANKE, Carrie.

Young's Critique of Authenticity in Musical Performance. THOM, Paul.

MUSIC EDUCATION
A Philosophy of Music Education (Second Edition). REIMER, Bennett.

MUSICOLOGY
Composers' Texts as Objects of Musicological Study. HEINIÖ, Mikko.
On the Modalities and Narrativity in Music. TARASTI, Eero.

MUTABILITY
Incarnation and Timelessness. SENOR, Thomas D.

MUTUALITY
A Representational Account of Mutual Belief. KOONS, Robert C.

MYSTERY(-RIES)
In the Onthic Human Centre: Solitariness Overcome by Solitude. AGERA, Cassian R.
Reason in Mystery. KRETZMANN, Norman.
The Value of the World as the Mystery of God in Advaita Vedanta. RAMBACHAN, Anantanand.

MYSTIC(S)
Autobiographical Reflections—Eric Voegelin. SANDOZ, Ellis (ed).
Lo místico como síntesis entre bien y belleza. ELTON, María.

MYSTICISM
John of the Cross and the Cognitive Value of Mysticism. PAYNE, Steven.
Philosophy of Religion: Selected Readings (Second Edition). ROWE, William L.
"Saadya's Goal in his Commentary on Sefer Yezira" in A Straight Path: Studies in Medieval Philosophy and Culture, BEN-SHAMMAI, Haggai.
"The Wisdom of Islam in Sufism" in The Wisdom of Faith: Essays in Honor of Dr Sebastian Alexander Matczak, OZTURK, Yasar Nuri.
"Wisdom, Mysticism and Near-Death Experiences" in The Wisdom of Faith: Essays in Honor of Dr Sebastian Alexander Matczak, CLARK, Walter Houston.
'Where Two Are to Become One': Mysticism and Monism. JANTZEN, Grace.
Could There Be a Mystical Core of Religion?. JANTZEN, Grace M.
De la teología a la mística pasando por la filosofía: Sobre el itinerario intelectual de Avicena. SARANYANA, Josep-Ignasi.
Faith and Ethical Reasoning in the Mystical Theology of St John of the Cross. SANDERLIN, David.
Mystical Experience and Non-Basically Justified Belief. LEVINE, Michael P.
Mysticism and Experience. JANTZEN, Grace M.
Paramārtha and Modern Constructivists on Mysticism: Epistemological Monomorphism verus Duomorphism. FORMAN, Robert K C.
Toward a Sound Perspective on Modern Physics: Capra's Popularization of Mysticism and Theological Approaches. CLIFTON, Robert K and REGEHR, Marilyn G.

MYTH(S)
The Conflict of Interpretations: Essays in Hermeneutics—Paul Ricoeur. IHDE, Don (ed).
Footsteps After Thought: Metaphorical Approaches from Within. VOAKE, Ronald L.
Patterns of Transcendence: Religion, Death, and Dying. CHIDESTER, David.
"Reunification and Rebuilding" in The Wisdom of Faith: Essays in Honor of Dr Sebastian Alexander Matczak, WESCOTT, Roger W.
Beyond Truth: Santayana on the Functional Relations of Art, Myth, and Religion. CONNER, Frederick W.
The Epistemological Function of Platonic Myth. STEWART, Robert Scott.
Imaginative Universals and Narrative Truth. VERENE, Donald Phillip.
Kunst und Mythos (in Greek). PANOU, S.
Mito e demittizzazione: polemica di Jaspers con Bultmann. PENZO, Giorgio.
Mito y filosofía: En torno a Mircea Eliade. AGÍS, Marcelino.
The Nazi Myth. LACOUE-LABARTHE, Philippe and NANCY, Jean-Luc.
Perceived Common Myths and Unethical Practices Among Direct Marketing Professionals. STORHOLM, Gordon.
Seven Moral Myths. ALMOND, Brenda.
Shame and Desire in the Myths of Origins. HANS, James S.
Tharp's 'Myth and Mathematics'. CHIHARA, Charles.
Vico on Mythic Figuration as Prerequisite for Philosophic Literacy. DANIEL, Stephen H.

MYTHOLOGY
Fools, Young Children and Philosophy. KENNEDY, David.
The Justification of Political Conformism: The Mythology of Soviet Intellectuals. SHLAPENTOKH, Vladimir.
Philosophy and Foolishness. HEINEGG, James.
Vico and Mythology. DALLMAYR, Fred (trans) and HORKHEIMER, Max.

NAGAO, G
What is Non-Existent and What is Remanent in Sūnyatā. DARGYAY, Lobsang.

NAGARJUNA
Comparative Philosophy and the Philosophy of Scholarship. TUCK, Andrew P.
Experience as Nothingness: A Form of Humanistic Religious Experience. RAYMOND, Menye Menye.

NAGEL, E
Ernest Nagel's Criticism of H L A Hart's Arguments for the Natural Law. HENLE, R J.
Reduction in the Social Sciences: The Future or Utopia?. SZMATKA, Jacek.

NAGEL, T
"The Objectivity of Agent Relative Values" in Inquiries into Values: The Inaugural Session of the International Society for Value Inquiry, ROBINS, Michael H.
Evolution and Skepticism. COBURN, Robert C.
Facing Diversity: The Case of Epistemic Abstinence. RAZ, Joseph.
Is Life Absurd?. WESTPHAL, Jonathan and CHERRY, Christopher.
Morality and Bad Luck. THOMSON, Judith Jarvis.
Overtones of Solipsism in Thomas Nagel's "What is it Like to Be a Bat?" and The View From Nowhere. WIDER, Kathleen.
Pain and the Quantum Leap to Agent-Neutral Value. CARLSON, George R.
El problema del realismo semántico y nuestro concepto de persona. TIRADO, Alvaro Rodriguez.

NAME(S)
Currie on Fictional Names. LAMB, Roger.
Dos teorías de la referencia en el Cratilo. VALDÉS, Margarita M.
Objects and Existence: Reflections on Free Logic. MENDELSOHN, Richard L.
Référence et identité. SEYMOUR, Michel.
Words. KAPLAN, David.

NAMING
Lingua degli angli e lingua dei bruti. DE MONTICELLI, Roberta and DI FRANCESCO, Michele.
Naming God: Moses Maimonides and Thomas Aquinas. STUBBENS, Neil A.

NANCY, J
The Retreat of the Political in the Modern Age: Jean-Luc Nancy on Totalitarianism and Community. INGRAM, David.

NARCISSISM
Plato, George Eliot, and Moral Narcissism. GOULD, Carol S.
Self-Recognition and Countermemory. STEINHART, Eric.

NARRATION
Interpretation, History and Narrative. CARROLL, Noël.
Narration and Totality. CASCARDI, Anthony J.
On the Modalities and Narrativity in Music. TARASTI, Eero.

NARRATIVE
Biblical Narrative in the Philosophy of Paul Ricoeur: A Study in Hermeneutics and Theology. VANHOOZER, Kevin J.
Narrative Experiments: The Discursive Authority of Science and Technology. ORMISTON, Gayle L.
Nietzschean Narratives. SHAPIRO, Gary.
Texts without Referents: Reconciling Science and Narrative. MARGOLIS, Joseph.
"Everything Depends on the Type of the Concepts that the Interpretation is Made to Convey". COMSTOCK, Gary L.
Feminine Perspectives and Narrative Points of View. BARWELL, Ismay.
Histories, Herstories, and Moral Traditions. MEAGHER, Sharon.
Metaphors, Narratives, and Images of AIDS. JONES, Anne Hudson.
Moral Discourse About Medicine: A Variety of Forms. GUSTAFSON, James M.
Narrative Accounts of Biblical Authority: The Need for a Doctrine of Revelation. SYKES, John.
The Narrative Reconstruction of Science. ROUSE, Joseph.
Narrative Theory: Ancient or Modern?. SAVILE, Anthony.
On Being a Meaning-Maker: Young Children's Experiences of Reading. POLAKOW, Valerie.
Politics and the Production of Narrative Identities. SILVERS, Anita.
The Primacy of Narrative in Historical Understanding. JACQUES, T Carlos.
Some Aspects of Medical Hermeneutics: The Role of Dialectic and Narrative. LOCK, James D.
Les Weltalter de Schelling: Un essai de philosophie narrative. MAESSCHALCK, M.

NATION(S)
"Mutually Acceptable Glory: Rating among Nations in Hobbes" in The Causes of Quarrel: Essays on Peace, War, and Thomas Hobbes, SACKSTEDER, William.

NATION(S)
History as Metascience: A Vichian Cue to the Understanding of the Nature and Development of Sciences. RIVERSO, Emanuele.
On Deciding Whether a Nation Deserves Our Loyalty. NATHANSON, Stephen.

NATIONAL SOCIALISM
Heidegger and Nazism. MARGOLIS, Joseph (ed).
National Socialism in the History of Being? A Discussion of Some Aspects of the Recent "L'Affaire Heidegger". SÖDER, Hans-Peter.
Philosophy and Politics: The Case of Heidegger. ZIMMERMAN, Michael E.

NATIONALISM
Hegel und Das Deutsche Erbe: Philosophie und nationale Frage zwischen Revolution und Reaktion. LOSURDO, Domenico.
"'External' Factors in the Development of Psychology in the West" in Scientific Knowledge Socialized, WILKES, Kathy.
"Rendering Unto Caesar: Religion and Nationalism" in The Wisdom of Faith: Essays in Honor of Dr Sebastian Alexander Matczak, HARRIS, Walter S.
Forgetting about Auschwitz? Remembrance as a Difficult Task of Moral Education. SCHWEITZER, Friederich.
La missione filosofica del diritto nella Napoli del giovane Mancini. OLDRINI, Guido.
Morally Privileged Relationships. DONALDSON, Thomas.
National Formation and the 'Rise of the Cultural'. JAMES, Paul.
Porous Vessels: A Critique of the Nation, Nationalism and National Character as Analytical Concepts. FARRAR JR, L L.
Sozialistische Gesellschaft und sozialistische Nation in der DDR. KOSING, Alfred.

NATIVE AMERICAN(S)
Gender Is an Organon. KEHOE, Alice B.
The Land as a Social Being: Ethical Implications From Societal Expectations. STICKEL, George W.
Ties that Bind: Native American Beliefs as a Foundation for Environmental Consciousness. BOOTH, Annie L and JACOBS, Harvey L.

NATIVISM
Connectionism and Three Levels of Nativism. RAMSEY, William and STICH, Stephen.
Language Acquisition: Growth or Learning? SAMPSON, Geoffrey.
What Is Empiricism?—I. CARRUTHERS, Peter.
What Is Empiricism?—II, Nativism, Naturalism, and Evolutionary Theory. MACDONALD, Cynthia.

NATURAL
El a priori histórico (la historia y sus hechos). SAMPEDRO, Ceferino.
Natural Signs: A Theory of Intentionality. ADDIS, Laird.
Religione e Umanità. FICHERA, Giuseppe.
Ente Natural y Artefacto en Guillermo de Ockham. LARRE, Olga L.
Intrinsic Reference and the New Theory. ADDIS, Laird.
Jan Patocka and the Idea of Natural World (in Czechoslovakian). PETRICEK JR, Miroslav.
Miracles and Natural Explanations: A Rejoinder. LARMER, Robert A.
Natural and Social Lottery, and Concepts of the Self. SADURSKI, Wojciech.
Naturnotwendigkeit und Freiheit: Zu Kants Theorie der Kausalität als Antwort auf Hume. RANG, Bernhard.
Professor Gould and the "Natural". DALCOURT, Gerard J.
A Social Constructionist Critique of The Naturalistic Theory of Emotion. RATNER, Carl.

NATURAL DEDUCTION
Fuzzy Natural Deduction. GERLA, Giangiacomo and TORTORA, Roberto.
A General Logic. SLANEY, John.
Gentzenizing Schroeder-Heister's Natural Extension of Natural Deduction. AVRON, Arnon.
Logic Based on Combinators. KOMORI, Yuichi.
Normalization and Excluded Middle, I. SELDIN, Jonathan P.

NATURAL HISTORY
The Price of Possibility. HART, W D.

NATURAL JUSTICE
Justice and Modern Moral Philosophy. REIMAN, Jeffrey.

NATURAL KINDS
The Metaphysics of Evolution. HULL, David L.
Can Abstractions Be Causes? JOHNSON, David M.
Science, Reduction and Natural Kinds. MEYER, Leroy N.
Specimens of Natural Kinds and the Apparent Inconsistency of Metaphysics Zeta. SPELLMAN, Lynne.

NATURAL LANGUAGE(S)
Meaning and Grammar: An Introduction to Semantics. CHIERCHIA, Gennaro.
Conceptual Dependency as the Language of Thought. DUNLOP, Charles E M.
Les conditions proto-logiques des langues naturelles. GRANGER, G G.
Whose Language Is It Anyway? Some Notes on Idiolects. GEORGE, Alexander.

NATURAL LAW(S)
At the Intersection of Legality and Morality: Hartian Law as Natural Law. SKUBIK, Daniel W.
Laws and Symmetry. VAN FRAASSEN, Bas C.
Natural Right and Natural Law: A Critical Introduction (Second Edition). HERVADA, Javier.
"Aquinas" in Ethics in the History of Western Philosophy, BOURKE, Vernon J.
"Two Types of Philosophical Approach to the Problem of War and Peace" in The Causes of Quarrel: Essays on Peace, War, and Thomas Hobbes, HENRICI, P.
"Is and Ought" as a Linguistic Problem. BOUKEMA, H J M.
After MacIntyre: Natural Law Theory, Virtue Ethics, and Eudaimonia. HITTINGER, Russell.
AIDS and Bowers versus Hardwick. PIERCE, Christine.
Can Legal Semiotics Contribute to Natural Law Studies?. JACKSON, Bernard S.
Derecho natural. TELLO, B D.
Ecologic-Economic Jurisprudence—The Next Step?. LEIDIG, Guido.
Ernest Nagel's Criticism of H L A Hart's Arguments for the Natural Law. HENLE, R J.
Francisco Suárez on Natural Law. CVEK, Peter P.
Hobbes alle prese con lo "stolto": La confutazione di Leviathan I. REALE, Mario.
The Humean Tradition. CARROLL, John.
Is International Law Part of Natural Law?. D'AMATO, Anthony.
Is Natural Law Ethics Obsolete?. MACHAN, Tibor R.
Kotaro Tanaka as a Natural Law Theorist. HANZAWA, Takamaro.
The Law of Nature, the Uppsala School and the Ius Docendi Affair. SUNDBERG, Jacob.
The Logic of Probabilities in Hume's Argument against Miracles. WILSON, Fred.
Love and the Natural Law. MC DERMOTT, John M.
Natural Law and the Scottish Enlightenment. HAAKONSSEN, Knud.
Natural Law Elements in Pound's Philosophy of Law?. MC LEAN, Edward B.
Natural Law in an "Auto" by Calderón. FIORE, Robert L.
Natural Law in the Huang-Lao Boshu. PEERENBOOM, R P.
Natural Law, Ownership and the World's Natural Resources. BOYLE, Joseph.
On a Similarity Between Natural Law Theories and English Legal Positivism. MC LAUGHLIN, Robert N.
On Natural Law—Aristotle. SCHALL, James V.
One More Time. MOLANDER, Bengt.
Perelman's Methodology and Natural Law Reasoning. BODENHEIMER, Edgar.
Popper and Historicist Necessities. FLEW, Antony.
A Pragmatic Version of Natural Law. WALTER, Edward.
Reducing Legal Realism to Natural Law. MILLER, Myron M.
Reflections on Natural Law: A Critical Review of the Thought of Yves R Simon. BLACK, Virginia.
De rol van het begrip intrinsieke waarde in milieu-ethische argumentaties. MERKS, K W.
Schleiermacher's "Über den Unterschied zwischen Naturgesetz und Sittengesetz". BOYD, George N.
A Skeptical Appreciation of Natural Law Theory. GINSBERG, Robert.
Something Substantial About Natural Law. FRANCIS, Richard P.
The Spanish Natural Law School. LLANO, Estela.
Stair on Natural Law and Promises. MAC CORMACK, Geoffrey.
Sulla validità della costituzione dal punto di vista del positivismo giuridico. GUASTINI, Riccardo.
To Discover Again Marriage. HERVADA, Javier.

NATURAL NUMBER(S)
Hilbert's Iterativistic Tendencies. HAND, Michael.
Monoidal Categories With Natural Numbers Object. PARÉ, Robert and ROMÁN, Leopoldo.
A Note on Natural Numbers Objects in Monoidal Categories. JAY, C Barry.
The Uniqueness of the Natural Numbers. PARSONS, Charles.

NATURALIZED EPISTEMOLOGY
RESNIK, Michael D.
Skepticism and Naturalized Epistemology. WINBLAD, Douglas G.

NATURE
Discourses on the Meaning of History. KLUBACK, William.
Divine Nature and Human Language: Essays in Philosophical Theology. ALSTON, William P.
Ein neuer Beitrag zum Verständnis Spinozas. EISENSTEIN, Israel.
Expérience et culture: Fondement d'une théorie générale de l'expérience. REALE, Miguel.
Hume and the Problem of Miracles: A Solution. LEVINE, Michael P.
Man and Nature in the Philosophical Thought of Wang-Fu-Chih. BLACK, Alison Harley.
Man and Nature: The Chinese Tradition and the Future. TANG, Yi-Jie (ed).
Nature in Asian Tradition of Thought: Essays in Environmental Philosophy. CALLICOTT, J Baird (ed).
The Nature of Man in Early Stoic Philosophy. REESOR, Margaret E.
Nature's Capacities and their Measurement. CARTWRIGHT, Nancy.
Nietzsche's Philosophy of Nature and Cosmology. MOLES, Alistair.
Ontological Investigations: Inquiry Into the Categories of Nature, Man, Society. JOHANSSON, Ingvar.
Recovery of the Measure: Interpretation and Nature. NEVILLE, Robert Cummings.
The Rehabilitation of Whitehead: An Analytic and Historical Assessment of Process Philosophy. LUCAS JR, George R.
Wesen, Freiheit und Bildung des Menschen. HAGER, Fritz-Peter.
"Creativity and the Passage of Nature" in Whitehead's Metaphysics of Creativity, EMMET, Dorothy.
"Human/Nature in Nietzsche and Taoism" in Nature in Asian Tradition of Thought: Essays in Environmental Philosophy, PARKES, Graham.
"The Japanese Experience of Nature" in Nature in Asian Tradition of Thought: Essays in Environmental Philosophy, SHANER, David Edward.
"Man and Nature in the Indian Context" in Man and Nature: The Chinese Tradition and the Future, CHATTERJEE, Margaret.
"Man versus Nature and Natural Man" in Man and Nature: The Chinese Tradition and the Future, KUIDE, Chen.
"A Metaphysical Grounding for Natural Reverence: East-West" in Nature in Asian Tradition of Thought: Essays in Environmental Philosophy, DEUTSCH, Eliot.
"On the Relationship Between Man and Nature" in Man and Nature: The Chinese Tradition and the Future, NAN-SHENG, Huang and GUANGWU, Zhao.
"Paradigms of Nature in Western Thought" in Man and Nature: The Chinese Tradition and the Future, SCHMITZ, Kenneth L.
"Quantum Nonlocality and the Description of Nature" in Philosophical Consequences of Quantum Theory: Reflections on Bell's Theorem, STAPP, Henry P.
"Science as Part of Nature" in Issues in Evolutionary Epistemology, MUNEVAR, Gonzalo.
"Slave—Master—Friend, Philosophical Reflections Upon Man and Nature" in Man and Nature: The Chinese Tradition and the Future, ZHEN, Li.
"Theories Concerning Man and Nature in Classical Chinese Philosophy" in Man and Nature: The Chinese Tradition and the Future, DAI-NIAN, Zhang.
"Toward a Middle Path of Survival" in Nature in Asian Tradition of Thought: Essays in Environmental Philosophy, KALUPAHANA, David J.
"Towards an Hermeneutics of Nature and Culture" in Man and Nature: The Chinese Tradition and the Future, FLORIVAL, Ghislaine.
"Western and Chinese Philosophy on Man and Nature" in Man and Nature: The Chinese Tradition and the Future, DE GEORGE, Richard T.
"Nature," "Substance," and "God" as Mass Terms in Spinoza's Theologico-Political Treatise. MADANES, Leiser.
"The Source" Spinoza in the Writings of Gabriel Scott. FLOISTAD, Guttorm.
Aesthetic Protectionism. GODLOVITCH, S.
Against Technocratic Hubris and Positivistic Idealism: Anti-Naturalistic and Anti-Realistic Fallacies, (Part One). LENK, Hans.
The American Founders and Classical Political Thought. ZVESPER, John.
Beauty as the Transition from Nature to Freedom in Kant's Critique of Judgement. DÜSING, Klaus.
Complementarity and the Description of Nature in Biological Science. FOLSE JR, Henry J.
The Concepts of Man and Nature in Marxism. SARKER, Sunil Kumar.
The Creator's Boundless Palace: William Bartram's Philosophy of Nature. WALTERS, Kerry S.
La culture du point de vue de l'anthropologie philosophique. COTTIER, Georges.
Culture or Nature: The Functions of the Term 'Body' in the Work in the Work

of Michel Foucault. MC WHORTER, Ladelle.
Deduction, Confirmation, and the Laws of Nature in Descartes's Principia Philosophiae. NADLER, Steven M.
The Differences Between Chinese and Western Concepts of Nature and the Trend Toward Their Convergence. ZHILIN, Li.
Emerson and the Agricultural Midworld. CORRINGTON, Robert S.
Equality of Opportunity and the Problem of Nature. BLITS, Jan H.
The Evolution of the Chinese Concept of Culture. GAWLIKOWSKI, Krzysztof.
The Familiar and the Strange: On the Limits of Praxis in the Early Heidegger. FELL, Joseph P.
La finalidad en el mundo natural según san Agustín. MAGNAVACCA, Silvia.
Fooling with Mother Nature. GAYLIN, Willard.
Gender Socialisation and the Nature/Culture Controversy: The Dualist's Dilemma. JONATHAN, Ruth.
History as Metascience: A Vichian Cue to the Understanding of the Nature and Development of Sciences. RIVERSO, Emanuele.
Humanity in Nature: Conserving Yet Creating. PETERS, Karl E.
Hume's Philosophical Schizophrenia. ERES, Gloria H.
Hypolepsis und Kompensation—Odo Marquards philosophischer Beitrag zur Diagnose und Bewältigung der Gegenwart. KERSTING, Wolfgang.
Is Nature Ever Unaesthetic?. COLEMAN, Earle J.
Kant and the Interpretation of Nature and History. MAKKREEL, Rudolf.
Man Apart and Deep Ecology: A Reply to Reed. NAESS, Arne.
Marxism, the Ecological Crisis and a Master's Attitude to Nature (in Czechoslovakian). ZNOJ, M.
Melville and Spinoza. HART, Alan.
Mens en aarde: Het ecofilosofisch dilemma in het werk van Ludwig Klages. WITZORECK, Kris.
Merleau-Ponty's nieuwe filosofie van de perceptie, de natuur en de logos. KWANT, R C.
Miracles and the Uniformity of Nature. ROOT, Michael.
Moral Autonomy in the Republic. DENT, N J H.
Moral Traditions, Ethical Language, and Reproductive Technologies. CAHILL, Lisa Sowle.
Mortal Immortals: Lucretius on Death and the Voice of Nature. NUSSBAUM, Martha C.
Natura e storia nel deismo di Diderot e Voltaire. NICOLOSI, Salvatore.
Naturaleza y causalidad en Aristóteles: Fisica II 1. BOERI, Marcelo D.
Nature and Philosophy for Children. RYAN, Mary Melville.
Nature and Revolution in Paine's Common Sense. FRUCHTMAN, Jack.
Nature and Semiosis. KRUSE, Felicia.
Nature as a Source in the History of Logic, 1870-1910. CHRISTIE, Thony.
Nature as Demonic in Thomson's Defense of Abortion. WILCOX, John T.
The Nature of Artifacts. LOSONSKY, Michael.
The Nature of Immorality. HAMPTON, Jean.
Naturhermeneutik und Ethik im Denken Heideggers. RIEDEL, Manfred.
New Connections of Man to the Nature (in Czechoslovakian). JIRIK, Vlastimil.
Nietzsche's Eternal Recurrence as Riemannian Cosmology. MOLES, Alistair.
On Schelling's Philosophy of Nature. JÄHNIG, Dieter and SOLBAKKEN, Elisabeth (trans).
On the Future of the Man-Nature Relationship (in Czechoslovakian). MUZIK, J.
Ontological Responsibility and the Poetics of Nature. LLEWELYN, John.
Philosophy and Environmental Issues. HALDANE, J J.
Reconceiving Miracles. GILMAN, James E.
Riemann's Geometry and Eternal Recurrence as Cosmological Hypothesis: A Reply. STACK, George J.
De rol van het begrip intrinsieke waarde in milieu-ethische argumentaties. MERKS, K W.
Some Reflections on Intelligence and the Nature—Nurture Issue. YAPP, Brian.
The Uniqueness and Value of Terrestrial Nature (in Czechoslovakian). SMAJS, J.
Toward a New Relation between Humanity and Nature: Reconstructing T'ien-jen-ho-i. LIU, Shu-hsien.
The Underlying Thing, the Underlying Nature and Matter: Aristotle's Analogy in Physics I 7. COOK, Kathleen C.
What is Morality All About?. HUDSON, Stephen D.
With Justice for All Beings: Educating as if Nature Matters. COHEN, Michael J.

NAZISM
Heidegger and Modernity. PHILIP, Franklin (trans).
Heidegger and Nazism. MARGOLIS, Joseph (ed).
Forgetting about Auschwitz? Remembrance as a Difficult Task of Moral

NAZISM

Education. SCHWEITZER, Friedrich.

Heidegger's Greatness and his Blindness. KEMP, T Peter.

Heideggers "Beiträge zur Philosophie" und die Politik. SCHWAN, Alexander.

The Nazi Myth. LACOUE-LABARTHE, Philippe and NANCY, Jean-Luc.

Nietzsche e il "mito" di Nietzsche: In margine a un libro su Nietzsche e il nazismo. ALFIERI, Luigi.

Nietzsche und George: Anmerkungen zu einem Buch von Heinz Raschel. WEBER, Frank.

On Heidegger's Silence. KOVACS, George.

Ontologie ohne Ethik? Zur Klärung der Heidegger-Kontroverse. RAPP, Friedrich.

Otra vez Heidegger y el nazismo. AUBENQUE, Pierre.

Philosophie et politique, un cas d'ambiguïté: "l'affaire Heidegger". SCHOUWEY, Jacques.

Savoir et croire: Sur le Pen et autres menus détails. POULIN, R.

The Use of Nazi Medical Experimentation Data: Memorial or Betrayal?. ROSENBAUM, Alan S.

NEAR-DEATH EXPERIENCE(S)

"Wisdom, Mysticism and Near-Death Experiences" in *The Wisdom of Faith: Essays in Honor of Dr Sebastian Alexander Matczak*, CLARK, Walter Houston.

NECESSARY

Necessary Moral Perfection. LEFTOW, Brian.

NECESSARY BEING

A Puzzle about Necessary Being. PEARL, Leon.

NECESSARY CONDITION(S)

Favorable Relevance and Arguments. BOWLES, George.

Metaphysics of Causation. BIGELOW, John and PARGETTER, Robert.

On Necessary Relations Between Law and Morality. ALEXY, Robert.

NECESSARY TRUTH(S)

Identity Statements and the Necessary A Posteriori. STEWARD, Helen.

NECESSITY(-TIES)

The Future: An Essay on God, Temporality, and Truth. LUCAS, J R.

God, Foreknowledge, and Freedom. FISCHER, John Martin (ed).

God, Scepticism and Modernity. NIELSEN, Kai.

Laws and Symmetry. VAN FRAASSEN, Bas C.

The Nature of Necessity. PLANTINGA, Alvin.

Necessity, Essence, and Individuation: A Defense of Conventionalism. SIDELLE, Alan.

Nietzsche's Philosophy of Nature and Cosmology. MOLES, Alistair.

"Relevant Implication and Leibnizian Necessity" in *Directions in Relevant Logic*, PARKS, Zane and BYRD, Michael.

Absolute Becoming and Absolute Necessity. SMALL, Robin.

Bernard Williams on Practical Necessity. GAY, Robert J.

The Crash of Modal Metaphysics. ROSS, James F.

Desire for All/Love of One: Tomas's Tale in *The Unbearable Lightness of Being*. DILLON, Martin C.

Early Heidegger and Wittgenstein: The Necessity of a Comprehension of Being. FAY, Thomas A.

The Essential Elements for the Possibility and Necessity of the Principle of Solidarity According to Max Scheler. IBANA, Rainer R A.

Hume on Character, Action, and Causal Necessity. JOHNSON, Clarence Sholé.

Identity as Necessity: Nozick's Objection-Kripke Replies. CHAUDHURY, Mahasweta.

Kant's Challenge: The Second Analogy as a Response to Hume. DELANEY, C.

Marx on Freedom and Necessity. BEEHLER, Rodger.

Mathematical Necessity and Reality. FRANKLIN, James.

Naturnotwendigkeit und Freiheit: Zu Kants Theorie der Kausalität als Antwort auf Hume. RANG, Bernhard.

Necessity and Contingency. CRESSWELL, M J.

On the Essential Difference between Science, Art and Philosophy, or Philosophy as the Literature of Necessity. BOULLART, Karel.

Parménide d'Élée et la fondation de la science (in Greek). KARAYANNIS, G.

Perfection and Necessity. LEFTOW, Brian.

Praxeologia della costizuione del potere. CAPOZZI, Gino.

Reply to Professor Robin Small's "Absolute Becoming and Absolute Necessity". RICHARDSON, John.

Scientific Explanation, Necessity and Contingency. WEBER, Erik.

NEED(S)

Scarcity and Modernity. XENOS, Nicholas.

Treatise on Basic Philosophy, Volume 8—Ethics: The Good and the Right. BUNGE, Mario.

"Productive Needs as Driving Forces of the Development of Science" in *Scientific Knowledge Socialized*, KRÖBER, Günther.

The Gandhian Approach to *Swadeshi* or Appropriate Technology. BAKKER, J I (Hans).

The Heart's Education: Why We Need Poetry. SWANGER, David.

NEGATION

Parmenides, Plato, and the Semantics of Not-Being. PELLETIER, Francis Jeffry.

Systems of Logic. MARTIN, Norman M.

Boolean Negation and All That. PRIEST, Graham.

Completeness and Conservative Extension Results for Some Boolean Relevant Logics. GIAMBRONE, Steve and MEYER, Robert K.

Converse Ackermann Property and Semiclassical Negation. MÉNDEZ, José M.

Essere e negazione: Per un recente volume di Gennaro Sasso. MIGNINI, Filippo.

Negación intuicionista y divergencia lógica. SCHUSTER, Federico L.

Negation and Quantification in Aristotle. WEDIN, Michael V.

Normalization and Excluded Middle, I. SELDIN, Jonathan P.

A Note on Negation. DANIELS, Charles B.

A Problem about the Meaning of Intuitionist Negation. HOSSACK, Keith G.

R-Algebras and R-Model Structures as Power Constructs. BRINK, Chris.

Resolution in Constructivism. AKAMA, Seiki.

Some Results in Some Subsystems and In an Extension of C_n. BUNDER, M W.

Subformula Semantics for Strong Negation Systems. AKAMA, Seiki.

Truth-Logics. VON WRIGHT, Georg Henrik.

Urquhart's C with Minimal Negation. MÉNDEZ, José M.

Why 'Not'?. PRICE, Huw.

NEGATIVE

L'esperienza filosofica di Enzo Paci. QUARTA, A.

Three Concepts of Tolerance. LAZARI-PAWLOWSKA, Ija.

NEGATIVITY

Negativity and Complexity: Some Logical Considerations. HIRSCH, Eli.

NEGLIGENCE

Issues Surrounding the Theories of Negligent Hiring and Failure to Fire. EXTEJT, Marian M and BOCKANIC, William N.

Reconsidering the Relationship among Voluntary Acts, Strict Liability, and Negligence in Criminal Law. ALEXANDER, Larry.

NEGOTIATION

Collaborative Collective Bargaining: Toward an Ethically Defensible Approach to Labor Negotiations. POST, Frederick R.

The Effect of Computer Intervention and Task Structure on Bargaining Outcome. JONES, Beth H and JELASSI, M Tawfik.

Group Decision and Negotiation Support in Evolving, Nonshared Information Contexts. SHAKUN, Melvin F.

The Impact of Information and Computer Based Training on Negotiators' Performance. GAUVIN, Stéphane and LILIEN, Gary L and CHATTERJEE, Kalyan.

Kampf—Verhandlung—Dialog. SCHRÖDER, Richard.

Persuasive Argumentation in Negotiation. SYCARA, Katia P.

Structuring and Simulating Negotiation: An Approach and an Example. KERSTEN, G E and BADCOCK, L and IGLEWSKI, M and MALLORY, G R.

Supporting Individuals in Group-Decision Making. KORHONEN, P and WALLENIUS, J.

NELSON, J

Comment on James Nelson's "Animals in 'Exemplary' Medical Research: Diabetes as a Case Study". FINSEN, Lawrence.

NELSON, L

'Ich habe mich wohl gehütet, alle Patronen auf einmal zu verschiessen': Ernest Zermelo in Göttingen. PECKHAUS, Volker.

NEO-CONFUCIANISM

On the Functional Unity of the "Book of Changes" (in Serbo-Croatian). SHU-HSIEN, Liu.

Response to Huang Siu-chi's Review of *Knowledge Painfully Acquired*, by Lo Ch'in-shun and Translated by Irene Bloom. BLOOM, Irene.

Tasan's "Practical Learning". SETTON, Mark.

NEO-KANTIANISM

Autobiographical Reflections—Eric Voegelin. SANDOZ, Ellis (ed).

Questions on Wittgenstein. HALLER, Rudolf.

Contemporary Trends in the Interpretation of Kant's Critical Philosophy. ZAHN, M.

Emil Lask and the Crisis of Neo-Kantianism: The Rediscovery of the Primordial World. MOTZKIN, Gabriel.

NIETZSCHE

NIEUWENTIJT, B

NIGERIAN

NIHILISM

NINETEENTH

NONSTANDARD MODELS

On Hyper-Torre Isols. DOWNEY, Rod.
On the End Extension Problem for Δ_0-PA(S). KOTLARSKI, Henryk.
Semantics for Nonstandard Languages. MURAWSKI, Roman.
Sequences in Countable Nonstandard Models of the Natural Numbers. LETH, Steven C.
Some Nonstandard Methods in Combinatorial Number Theory. LETH, Steven C.

NONVIOLENCE

On War and Morality. HOLMES, Robert L.
"The Viability of Nonviolence in Collective Life" in The Causes of Quarrel: Essays on Peace, War, and Thomas Hobbes, CHATTERJEE, Margaret.
Non-Violence, Gandhi and Our Times. SINGH, R Raj.
Non-Violence, the Core of Religious Experience in Gandhi. KUTTIANICKAL, Joseph.

NORM(S)

Limits of Philosophy: (Limits of Reality?). VERSTER, Ulrich.
The Normal and the Pathological. CANGUILHEM, Georges.
Rules, Norms, and Decisions: On the Conditions of Practical and Legal Reasoning. KRATOCHWIL, Friedrich V.
Wise Choices, Apt Feelings: A Theory of Normative Judgment. GIBBARD, Allan.
Communities of Judgment. GIBBARD, Allan.
Discourse Ethics and Civil Society. COHEN, Jean.
Efficiency, Effectiveness and Legitimation: Criteria for the Evaluation of Norms. UUSITALO, Liisa.
The Fundamental Features of Legal Rationality. GARDIES, Jean-Louis.
Impartial Application of Moral and Legal Norms: A Contribution to Discourse Ethics. GÜNTHER, Klaus.
Justification des normes: transcendantale ou pragmatique?. GRÜNEWALD, Bernward.
A Normative Conception of Coherence for a Discursive Theory of Legal Justification. GÜNTHER, Klaus.
An Objection to Kantian Ethical Rationalism. TERZIS, George N.
Ontique et deontique. KALINOWSKI, Georges.
Presumptive Norms and Norm Revision (in Hebrew). ULLMANN-MARGALIT, Edna.
Remarks on the Concept of Norm. PAULSON, Stanley L.

NORMAL

The Normal and the Pathological. CANGUILHEM, Georges.

NORMALIZATION

Normalization and Excluded Middle, I. SELDIN, Jonathan P.

NORMATIVE

Self and Others: A Study of Ethical Egoism. ÖSTERBERG, Jan.
"Comment: The Normativity of Law" in Issues in Contemporary Legal Philosophy: The Influence of H L A Hart, MAC CORMICK, Neil.
"Normative and Descriptive Issues in the Analysis of Medical Language" in Scientific Knowledge Socialized, MOULIN, Anne-Marie.
"The Normativity of Law" in Issues in Contemporary Legal Philosophy: The Influence of H L A Hart, POSTEMA, Gerald J.
Adjudication under Bentham's Pannomion. DINWIDDY, J R.
Aim-Less Epistemology?. LAUDAN, L.
Cooter and Rappoport on the Normative. DAVIS, John B.
The Function of the Press in a Free and Democratic Society. AUDI, Robert.
Justificación normativa y pertenencia. CARACCIOLO, Ricardo.
Laudan's Normative Naturalism. SIEGEL, Harvey.
Law and Morality. BICKENBACH, Jerome E.
Modern Normativity and the Politics of Deregulation. TREY, George A.
Naturalism and the Normativity of Epistemology. MAFFIE, James.
Normative Naturalism and the Role of Philosophy. ROSENBERG, Alexander.
Normative Naturalism. LAUDAN, Larry.
Objective Value and Subjective States. MENDOLA, Joseph.
The Problem of Normativity Solved or Spinoza's Stand in the Analogy/Anomaly Controversy. KLIJNSMIT, Anthony J.
The Role of Rules. WEINBERGER, Ota.
Value Judgments and Normative Claims. SINGER, Marcus G.

NORMATIVE DISCOURSE

Rules, Communities and Judgements. ZALABARDO, José L.
Tesi di Hume e sistemi di logica deontica. GALVAN, Sergio.

NORMATIVE ETHICS

Contemporary Ethics: Selected Readings. STERBA, James P.
Moral Consciousness and Communicative Action. HABERMAS, Jürgen.
Generating a Normative System. RANTALA, Veikko.
Internal Reasons and the Obscurity of Blame. WILLIAMS, Bernard.

The Limited Relevance of Analytical Ethics to the Problems of Bioethics. HOLMES, Robert L.

NORMATIVE JUDGMENT(S)

Wise Choices, Apt Feelings: A Theory of Normative Judgment. GIBBARD, Allan.
Gadamer, Objectivity, and the Ontology of Belonging. GUEN, Carroll.

NOTATION(S)

How a Note Denotes. KURKELA, Kari.

NOTHING

Meditaciones sobre la nada. COLOMBRES, Carlos A Iturralde.
Why Did Kant Bother About 'Nothing'?. VAN KIRK, Carol A.

NOTHINGNESS

Essere e negazione: Per un recente volume di Gennaro Sasso. MIGNINI, Filippo.
Experience as Nothingness: A Form of Humanistic Religious Experience. RAYMOND, Menye Menye.
Fondamento e nulla: un'alternativa?. LUGARINI, Leo.
Ser, nada y creación en el pensamiento de Nimio de Anquín. PEREZ, J R.

NOTION(S)

Notion and Object: Aspects of Late Medieval Epistemology. BROADIE, Alexander.
Notion et idée de science chez Eric Weil. BREUVART, Jean-Marie.
Unacceptable Notions of Science Held by Process-Product Researchers. CHAMBERS, John H.

NOUMENALISM

"Schopenhauer's Ethics: A View from Nowhere" in Schopenhauer: New Essays in Honor of His 200th Birthday, KOLENDA, Konstantin.

NOUN PHRASE(S)

Plural Noun Phrases and Their Readings: A Reply to Lasersohn. GILLON, Brendan S.

NOUN(S)

Nom propre et individuation chez Peirce. THIBAUD, P.

NOUS

Nous, the Concept of Ultimate Reality and Meaning in Anaxagoras. SILVESTRE, Maria Luisa.

NOVALIS

Nietzsche Contra Nietzsche: Creativity and the Anti-Romantic. DEL CARO, Adrian.

NOVEL

"The Novelist and the Camera Eye" in Cultural Hermeneutics of Modern Art: Essays in Honor of Jan Aler, PETERS, Jan.
Another Look at Novel Facts. MURPHY, Nancey.
Narration and Totality. CASCARDI, Anthony J.
Philosophy and Fiction. RICKMAN, H P.
Theory of Novel and Historical Poetics (in Czechoslovakian). SVATON, Vladimir.

NOVELTY

La pensée et la nouveauté de pensée. SCHLANGER, Judith.

NOVICK, R

L'État minimal et le droit de propriété privée selon Nozick. LAMBERT, Roger.

NOVITZ, D

Politics and the Production of Narrative Identities. SILVERS, Anita.

NOZICK, R

The Libertarian Idea. NARVESON, Jan.
Realizing Rawls. POGGE, Thomas W.
Flew on Russell on Nozick: Uncharitable Interpretations of Justice and Unjust Views of Charity. SKILLEN, Tony.
Identity as Necessity: Nozick's Objection-Kripke Replies. CHAUDHURY, Mahasweta.
The Libertarian Utopia: Robert Nozick and Aleksander Swietochowski. MIKLASZEWSKA, Justyna.
Más allá del escepticismo, a nuestro leal saber y entender. SOSA, Ernesto.
Nozick and the Sceptic: The Thumbnail Version. CRAIG, Edward.
Nozick on Self-Esteem. MASON, Andrew.

NUCLEAR DETERRENCE

Ethics and Strategic Defense: American Philosophers Debate Star Wars and Nuclear Deterrence. LACKEY, Douglas P (ed).
The Ethics of War and Peace. LACKEY, Douglas P.
Nuclear Deterrence and Moral Restraint. SHUE, Henry (ed).
Nuclear Deterrence, Morality and Realism. FINNIS, John.
On War and Morality. HOLMES, Robert L.
Posterity and Strategic Policy: A Moral Assessment of Nuclear Policy Options. BAILEY, Alison.

NUCLEAR DETERRENCE

"The Case for Deploying Strategic Defenses" in *Nuclear Deterrence and Moral Restraint*, SLOSS, Leon.

"Defending Europe: Toward a Stable Conventional Deterrent" in *Nuclear Deterrence and Moral Restraint*, UNTERSEHER, Lutz.

"Deterrence and the Moral Use of Nuclear Weapons" in *Nuclear Deterrence and Moral Restraint*, FOELBER, Robert E.

"The Dilemmas of Extended Nuclear Deterrence" in *Moral Reasoning and Statecraft: Essays Presented to Kenneth W Thompson*, MATTOX, Gale A.

"Escaping from the Bomb: Immoral Deterrence and the Problem of Extrication" in *Nuclear Deterrence and Moral Restraint*, COADY, C A J.

"Finite Counterforce" in *Nuclear Deterrence and Moral Restraint*, LEWIS, David.

"The Necessary Moral Hypocrisy of the Slide into Mutual Assured Destruction" in *Nuclear Deterrence and Moral Restraint*, QUESTER, George H.

The Immorality of Nuclear Deterrence. ARDAGH, David.

Morality and Nuclear Weapons Policy. LEE, Steven.

The Morality of Nuclear Deterrence and the Corruption of Character. LOVE JR, Charles E.

Nuclear Deterrence, Character, and Moral Education. KLEIN, J Theodore.

Nuclearism and International Law. STEGENGA, James A.

Russell's Leviathan. LIPPINCOTT, Mark S.

NUCLEAR ENERGY

Ethics and the Environmental Responsibility. DOWER, Nigel (ed).

"After Chernobyl: The Ethics of Risk-Taking" in *Ethics and the Environmental Responsibility*, SHAW, D.

NUCLEAR WAR

Arms and Judgment: Law, Morality, and the Conduct of War in the 20th Century. COHEN, Sheldon M.

The Ethics of War and Peace. LACKEY, Douglas P.

"Moral Reasoning in the Bishops' Pastoral Letter on War and Peace" in *Moral Reasoning and Statecraft: Essays Presented to Kenneth W Thompson*, KLUNK, Brian J.

"Morality, the SDI, and Limited Nuclear War" in *Nuclear Deterrence and Moral Restraint*, LEE, Steven.

NUCLEAR WEAPON(S)

Burning Conscience: The Guilt of Hiroshima. ANDERS, Gunther.

A Moral Military. AXINN, Sidney.

Posterity and Strategic Policy: A Moral Assessment of Nuclear Policy Options. BAILEY, Alison.

"Deterrence and the Moral Use of Nuclear Weapons" in *Nuclear Deterrence and Moral Restraint*, FOELBER, Robert E.

"Finite Deterrence" in *Nuclear Deterrence and Moral Restraint*, FEIVESON, Harold A.

"The Physicist and the Politicians: Niels Bohr and the International Control of Atomic Weapons" in *Moral Reasoning and Statecraft: Essays Presented to Kenneth W Thompson*, GRAIG, Ian.

Morality and Nuclear Weapons Policy. LEE, Steven.

NUMBER THEORY

Domain Extension and the Philosophy of Mathematics. MANDERS, Kenneth.

Hilbert's Iterativistic Tendencies. HAND, Michael.

Innovation and Understanding in Mathematics. KITCHER, Philip.

NUMBER(S)

see also Cardinals, Ordinals

Pythagoras Revived: Mathematics and Philosophy in Late Antiquity. O'MEARA, Dominic J.

"All is Number"? "Basic Doctrine" of Pythagoreanism Reconsidered. ZHMUD, Leonid J.

Arithmetic Based on the Church Numerals in Illative Combinatory Logic. BUNDER, M W.

Arithmetical Completeness Versus Relative Completeness. GRABOWSKI, Michal.

Completeness for Systems Including Real Numbers. BALZER, W.

Definability in Terms of the Successor Function and the Coprimeness Predicate in the Set of Arbitrary Integers. RICHARD, Denis.

Frege on the Statement of Number. SULLIVAN, David.

Minimal Representation of a Semiorder. PIRLOT, Marc.

A Number is the Exponent of an Operation. HAND, Michael.

On Plato's Philosophy of Numbers and its Mathematical and Philosophical Significance. HÖSLE, Vittorio and ADLER, Pierre (trans) and HUMPHREY, Fred (trans).

On the Complexity of Finding the Chromatic Number of a Recursive Graph I: The Bounded Case. BEIGEL, Richard and GASARCH, W I.

On the Complexity of Finding the Chromatic Number of a Recursive Graph II: The Unbounded Case. BEIGEL, R and GASARCH, W I.

On the Possibility of Mathematical Revolutions. KENNEY, Emelie.

The Roots of Mathematics Education in Russia in the Age of Peter the Great. ANELLIS, Irving H.

Sequences in Countable Nonstandard Models of the Natural Numbers. LETH, Steven C.

Some Nonstandard Methods in Combinatorial Number Theory. LETH, Steven C.

Le *Tractatus* de Wittgenstein: Considérations sur le système numérique et la forme aphoristique. HESS, Gérald.

NUREMBERG TRIALS

Obedience to Superior Orders. STUART, J M.

NURSING

The Role of Caring in a Theory of Nursing Ethics. FRY, Sara T.

NURTURE

Maternal Thinking: Toward a Politics of Peace. RUDDICK, Sara.

Some Reflections on Intelligence and the Nature—Nurture Issue. YAPP, Brian.

NUSSBAUM, M

The Subject of Love. NYE, Andrea.

NYAYA

Cut the Syllogism to its Size! Some Reflections on Indian Syllogism. AGERA, Cassian R.

The Mīmāmsā Theory of Self-Recognition. TABER, John A.

Some Features of the Technical Language of Navya-Nyāya. BHATTACHARYYA, Sibajiban.

NYE, J

The Inefficiency of Some Efficiency Comparisons: A Reply to Nye. SARAYDAR, Edward.

O'GORMAN, P

Eliminative Materialism: The Reality of the Mental, and Folk Psychology—A Reply to O'Gorman. MILLS, Stephen.

O'KEEFFE, G

Universality and Difference: O'Keeffe and McClintock. MACCOLL, San.

O'NEILL, O

Equality of Opportunity. YOUNG, Robert.

OAKESHOTT, M

Civil Association and the Idea of Contingency. MAPEL, David R.

Consciousness and History. MOULAKIS, Athanasios.

Dilemma of M Oakeshott: Oakeshott's Treatment of Equality of Opportunity in Education and His Political Philosophy. WILLIAMS, Kevin.

Michael Oakeshott as Liberal Theorist. FRANCO, Paul.

Oakeshott on the Authority of Law. FRIEDMAN, Richard B.

Spontaneous Order and the Rule of Law: Some Problems. MAC CORMICK, D Neil.

OBEDIENCE

A Moral Military. AXINN, Sidney.

Are Virtues No More Than Dispositions to Obey Moral Rules?. SCHALLER, Walter E.

Obedience to Superior Orders. STUART, J M.

Problems in the Argument of Plato's *Crito*. KAHN, Charles H.

Responsibility and Complicity. ARONSON, Ronald.

OBJECT(S)

Notion and Object: Aspects of Late Medieval Epistemology. BROADIE, Alexander.

Subject and Consciousness: A Philosophical Inquiry Into Self-Consciousness. BALABAN, Oded.

"Kant on the Modalities of Space" in *Reading Kant*, GREENWOOD, Terry.

"Realism and Realization in a Kantian Light" in *Reading Kant*, BUCHDAHL, Gerd.

A ética do poder na *História da sexualidade* de Michel Foucault. VIDEIRA, Antonio A P and PINHEIRO, Ulysses.

An Alternative to the Adverbial Theory: Dis-Phenomenalism. LAHAV, Ran.

Aristotle's Four Types of Definition. DESLAURIERS, Marguerite.

Charles S Peirce on Objects of Thought and Representation. PAPE, Helmut.

Crossroads of Skepticism: Wittgenstein, Derrida, and Ostensive Definition. MC DONALD, Henry.

A dedução dos objectos no "Tractatus". CUNHA, Rui Daniel.

Development of Collingwood's Conception of Historical Object. DAS, P S.

Existence and Reality: The Case for Pseudo-Objects. JOBE, Evan K.

A Formal Theory of Objects, Space and Time. BLIZARD, Wayne D.

Four-Dimensional Objects. VAN INWAGEN, Peter.

In the Beginning Was the Contradiction: Problems of the Philosophy of Subject and Object. BOLTUC, Piotr and KMIECIK, Witold (trans).

L'intentionalité *de dicto*, l'intentionalité *de re*, l'intentionalité *de se*. CAYLA,

OSTENSIVE INSTANCE(S)

The Acquisition of the Ostensive Lexicon: A Reply to Professor Place. STEMMER, Nathan.

OTHER MINDS

J L Austin. WARNOCK, G J.

OTHER(S)

The Question of the Other: Essays in Contemporary Continental Philosophy. DALLERY, Arleen B (ed).

"Derrida and the Ethics of the Ear" in *The Question of the Other: Essays in Contemporary Continental Philosophy,* MICHELFELDER, Diane.

"Lacan's Other and the Factions of Plato's Soul" in *The Question of the Other: Essays in Contemporary Continental Philosophy,* GRANGE, Joseph.

"The Obligation to Will the Freedom of Others, According to Jean-Paul Sartre" in *The Question of the Other: Essays in Contemporary Continental Philosophy,* ANDERSON, Thomas C.

Der Andere als Zukunft und Gegenwart. RÖMPP, Georg.

Is Ontology Fundamental?. ATTERTON, Peter (trans) and LEVINAS, Emmanuel.

Levinas's Phenomenology of the Other and Language as the Other of Phenomenology. KLEMM, David E.

Thinking About 'The Other' in Religion: It is Necessary, But is it Possible?. NEUSNER, Jacob.

To Welcome the Other: Totality and Theory in Levinas and Adorno. FLOYD, Wayne W.

Visage Versus Visages. BAUM, Mylène.

OTHERNESS

"Alma Gonzalez: Otherness as Attending to the Other" in *The Question of the Other: Essays in Contemporary Continental Philosophy,* BARBER, Michael D.

OUGHT

The Idea of a Reason for Acting: A Philosophical Argument. SCHUELER, George Frederick.

Moral Dilemmas. SINNOTT-ARMSTRONG, Walter.

"Is and Ought" as a Linguistic Problem. BOUKEMA, H J M.

Is and Ought: A Gap or a Continuity?. BLACK, Virginia.

Law as a Bridge between Is and Ought. BODENHEIMER, Edgar.

Morality: Ought or Naught?. FOLDVARY, Fred E.

Ought-Implies-Can: Erasmus Luther and R M Hare. PIGDEN, Charles R.

OWENS, D

Why Blackmail Should be Banned. EVANS, Hugh.

OWENS, J

In Defense of a Different Taxonomy: A Reply to Owens. WALKER, Valerie.

OWNERSHIP

Are Women Owner-Managers Challenging Our Definitions of Entrepreneurship? An In-Depth Survey. LEE-GOSSELIN, H and GRISÉ, J.

Natural Law, Ownership and the World's Natural Resources. BOYLE, Joseph.

Rawls and the Collective Ownership of Natural Abilities. KERNOHAN, Andrew.

Realism and Redistribution. NARDIN, Terry.

Self-Ownership, Communism and Equality—I. COHEN, G A.

Self-Ownership, Communism and Equality—II. GRAHAM, Keith.

Self-Ownership. DAY, J P.

Socio-Economic Evolution of Women Business Owners in Quebec (1987). COLLERETTE, P and AUBRY, P.

Two Theories of Ownership in German Classical Philosophy (in Czechoslovakian). SOBOTKA, Milan.

PACI, E

L'esperienza filosofica di Enzo Paci. QUARTA, A.

PACIFISM

The Ethics of War and Peace. LACKEY, Douglas P.

From Warism to Pacifism: A Moral Continuum. CADY, Duane L.

On War and Morality. HOLMES, Robert L.

Christian Pacifism and Theodicy: The Free Will Defense in the Thought of John H Yoder. PINCHES, Charles.

Pacifism and Care. DAVION, Victoria.

PAGANISM

Persuading Pagans. POTTS, S G.

PAIN(S)

Basic Moral Concepts. SPAEMANN, Robert.

Il Giogo: Alle origini della ragione: Eschilo. SEVERINO, Emanuele.

An Ethical Issue in the Psychotherapy of Pain and Other Symptoms. MERSKEY, H.

A New Approach to Regulating the Use of Animals in Science. ANDERSON, Warwick.

On Viewing Pain as a Secondary Quality. NEWTON, Natika.

Pain and the Quantum Leap to Agent-Neutral Value. CARLSON, George R.

Pain Corrigibility. BLUM, Alex.

Pleasure and Pain: Unconditional, Intrinsic Values. GOLDSTEIN, Irwin.

The Pain of Simulation on Heidegger's Philosophy of Art (in Dutch). DE SCHUTTER, Dirk.

Thinking, Poetry and Pain. CAPUTO, John D.

PAINE

The French Revolution Debate and British Political Thought. CLAEYS, Gregory.

Nature and Revolution in Paine's *Common Sense.* FRUCHTMAN, Jack.

Paine and Sieyès. DE PROSPO, R C.

PAINTING

Aesthetic Theories Concerning the Picturesque: Gilpin, Price and Knight (in Japanese). ANZAI, Shin-ichi.

Chinese Theories of Appreciation—with Particular Attention to Painting (in Japanese). KÔNO, Michifusa.

The Eclipse of Truth in the Rise of Aesthetics. KORSMEYER, Carolyn.

Jasper Johns: Strategies for Making and Effacing Art. FISHER, Philip.

Paintings and Identity. TAYLOR, Paul.

Photogenic Painting. WALKER, Pierre A (trans) and FOUCAULT, Michel.

Plato, Inquiry, and Painting. MORGAN, Michael L.

The Primacy of the Eye in Evaluating Colours and Colour Harmonies. TARANCZEWSKI, Pawel.

Thinking Eye of Karl Capek (in Czechoslovakian). HLAVACEK, Lubos.

Variations upon Variation, or Picasso Back to Bach. GOODMAN, Nelson.

Zwei Arten der Malerei: Von der Umwandelung der Interpretation der Kunst bei Hegel (in Japanese). IWAKI, Ken-ichi.

PAL, J

A Refutation of Jagat Pal's Defence of Aristotelian Square of Opposition. BASU, S and KASEM, A.

PANPSYCHISM

God and Godlings in African Ontology. DUKOR, Maduabuchi.

Santayana and Panpsychism. SPRIGGE, Timothy.

Spirit's Primary Nature is to be Secondary. KERR-LAWSON, Angus.

PANTHEISM

"Fenomenologia della metafisica: e "panteismo mistico"": Note in margine alla "Jugendgeschichte Hegels" di W Dilthey. D'ANTUONO, Emilia.

PAPIN, D

The *A Priori* Method and the *Actio* Concept Revised. RANEA, Alberto Guillermo.

PAPPAS, G

Pappas on the Role of Sensations in Reid's Theory of Perception. CUMMINS, Phillip D.

PARABLE(S)

"MacKinnon and the Parables" in *Christ, Ethics and Tragedy: Essays in Honour of Donald MacKinnon,* WHITE, Roger.

PARACONSISTENT LOGICS

The Semantic Foundations of Logic, Volume 1: Propositional Logics. EPSTEIN, Richard L.

Against Global Paraconsistency. BATENS, Diderik.

Boolean Negation and All That. PRIEST, Graham.

La distinction entre le système et l'approche du système dans la solution (in Romanian). NEGOITA, Andrei.

The Logic of Inconsistency. BUNDER, M W.

Multiply Modal Extensions of Da Costa's C_n, Logical Relativism, and the Imaginary. LOKHORST, Gert-Jan C.

New Systems of Predicate Deontic Logic. DA COSTA, Newton C A.

On a Minimal Non-Alethic Logic. GRANA, Nicola.

On the Positive Parts of the J-Systems of Arruda and Da Costa. URBAS, Igor.

An Overview of Paraconsistent Logic in the 80s. DA COSTA, Newton C A and MARCONI, Diego.

Paraconsistency and the C-Systems of DaCosta. URBAS, Igor.

Paraconsistency. URBAS, Igor.

Paraconsistent Foundations for Logic Programming. BLAIR, Howard A and SUBRAHMANIAN, V S.

A Paraconsistent Many-Valued Propositional Logic. D'OTTAVIANO, Itala M L and EPSTEIN, Richard L.

Some Results in Some Subsystems and In an Extension of C_n. BUNDER, M W.

PARADIGM(S)

"Organizational Ethics: Paradox and Paradigm" in *Papers on the Ethics of Administration,* RITCHIE, J Bonner.

PERSON(S)

"Why There is No Concept of a Person" in *The Person and the Human Mind: Issues in Ancient and Modern Philosophy*, MORTON, Adam.

Abortion Rights. EDWARDS, Rem B.

Abortion: The Right to an Argument. MEILAENDER, Gilbert.

The Central Distinction in the Theory of Corporate Moral Personhood. PFEIFFER, Raymond S.

Christianity and Humanism. LONG, Eugene T.

Comments on Mark Brown's "Why Individual Identity Matters". SWINDLER, James K.

Das Problem der Psychologischen Hinführung zur Bildung der reifen und religiösen Persönlichkeit (in Polish). BAZYLAK, Jozef and BIELECKI, Jan.

Difficoltà della filosofia pubblica (Riflessioni sul pensiero di Norberto Bobbio). POSSENTI, Vittorio.

Errant Self-Control and the Self-Controlled Person. MELE, Alfred R.

L'individuo nella città. VERNANT, Jean Pierre.

Inquiry Into Meaning and Truth. THOMAS, R S D.

Lavoro, "Lavorismo", *Otium*. POSSENTI, Vittorio.

La metafisica della Prima Persona (*Ego Sum Qui Sum*): Parte prima. ARATA, Carlo.

Metaphysical Accounts of the Zygote as a Person and the Veto Power of Facts. BOLE III, Thomas J.

Mondo, persona e storia in E De Martino: Tra Croce e Cassirer. IMBRUGLIA, Girolamo.

Parfit and the Russians. BECK, Simon.

La persona nell'esperienza morale e giuridica. BAGOLINI, Luigi.

Personhood and Moral Responsibility. LOCKE, Lawrence A.

Personhood and Personal Identity. SCHECHTMAN, Marya.

Personhood and the Land. CAMPBELL, James.

Philosophical Identification of the Dignity of Person (in Polish). GOGACZ, Mieczyslaw.

The Possibility of Computers Becoming Persons. DOLBY, R G A.

El problema del realismo semántico y nuestro concepto de persona. TIRADO, Alvaro Rodriguez.

Reply—The Possibility of Computers Becoming Persons: A Response to Dolby. CHERRY, Christopher.

Transient Natures at the Edges of Life: A Thomistic Exploration. SMITH, Philip.

The Zygote: To Be Or Not Be A Person. BEDATE, Carlos A and CEFALO, Robert C.

PERSONAL IDENTITY

see also Identity

Reincarnation: A Philosophical and Practical Analysis. PREUSS, Peter.

Thomas Reid and 'The Way of Ideas'. GALLIE, Roger D.

"Advance Directives, Self-Determination, and Personal Identity" in *Advance Directives in Medicine*, DRESSER, Rebecca S.

"Ghazali and the Avicennan Proof from Personal Identity for an Immaterial Self" in *A Straight Path: Studies in Medieval Philosophy and Culture*, MARMURA, Michael E.

Blood is Thicker Than Water: Don't Forsake the Family Jewels. BELLIOTTI, Raymond A.

Bodily Continuity, Personal Identity and Life After Death. WEI, Tan Tai.

Branching Self-Consciousness. ROVANE, Carol.

David Hume on Personal Identity and the Indirect Passions. HENDERSON, Robert S.

Egoism and Personal Identity. MAIDAN, Michael.

The Person and *The Little Prince* of St Exupéry, Part II. HETZLER, Florence M.

Personal and Impersonal Identity: A Reply to Oderberg. SPRIGGE, T L S.

Personal Expressiveness: Philosophical and Psychological Foundations. WATERMAN, Alan S.

Personal Identity and Extrinsicness. GARRETT, Brian.

Personal Identity and the Passions. MC INTYRE, Jane L.

Personal Identity, the Temporality of Agency and Moral Responsibility. LEE, Win-Chiat.

Personhood and Personal Identity. SCHECHTMAN, Marya.

Surviving Matters. SOSA, Ernest.

PERSONAL KNOWLEDGE

The Person and *The Little Prince* of St Exupéry, Part II. HETZLER, Florence M.

PERSONAL RELATIONS

"Adolescent Confidentiality and Family Privacy" in *Person to Person*, SCHOEMAN, Ferdinand.

"Commitment and the Value of Marriage" in *Person to Person*, GRAHAM, Gordon.

"The Essence of Personal Relationships and Their Value for the Individual" in *Person to Person*, WRIGHT, Paul H.

"Friends and Lovers" in *Person to Person*, THOMAS, Laurence.

"Honesty and Intimacy" in *Person to Person*, GRAHAM, George and LA FOLLETTE, Hugh.

"In Search of an Ethics of Personal Relationships" in *Person to Person*, HARDWIG, John.

"Love's Way" in *Person to Person*, GARRETT, Richard.

"Morality and Personal Relations" in *Person to Person*, DEIGH, John.

"Of Jealousy and Envy" in *Person to Person*, FARRELL, Daniel M.

"Paternalism Toward Friends" in *Person to Person*, RICHARDS, Norvin.

"Philosophers Against the Family" in *Person to Person*, SOMMERS, Christina Hoff.

"The Repair and Maintenance of Relationships" in *Person to Person*, GILMOUR, Robin and MELAMED, Tuvia.

"Trusting Ex-intimates" in *Person to Person*, BAIER, Annette.

Helping Subordinates with Their Personal Problems: A Moral Dilemma for Managers. MOBERG, Dennis J.

PERSONALISM

"The Founders of Phenomenology and Personalism" in *Reading Philosophy for the Twenty-First Century*, KOCKELMANS, Joseph J.

On Personalism and Education. HART, Richard E.

The Personalism of Austin Farrer. CONTI, Charles.

PERSONALITY

"'Sunt aliquid manes': Personalities, Personae and Ghosts in Augustan Poetry" in *Post-Structuralist Classics*, COTTERILL, Rowland.

Der Andere als Zukunft und Gegenwart. RÖMPP, Georg.

Brauchen wir eine Kategorie Persönlichkeit?. RONNEBERG, Heinz.

Can Philosophy Be Mathematized?—Probabilistic Theory of Meanings and Semantic Architectonics of Personality. NALIMOV, V V.

Ludwig Wittgenstein: Personality and Philosophy (in Czechoslovakian). STERN, Joseph P.

On Traits as Dispositions: An Alleged Truism. VAN HEERDEN, Jaap and SMOLENAARS, Anton J.

Personality and Artistic Creativity. JARRETT, James L.

PERSPECTIVE(S)

Medical Ethics: Principles, Persons, and Problems. FRAME, John M.

Aspects et perspectives du problème de la limite dans la philosophie théorique de Kant. THEIS, R.

Kant on Euclid: Geometry in Perspective. PALMQUIST, Stephen R.

PERSPECTIVISM

"A World of Hope and Optimism Despite Present Difficulties": Gadamer's Critique of Perspectivism. DAVEY, Nicholas.

Nietzsche's Synoptic and Utopian Vision. SCHROEDER, William R.

Nietzschean Perspectivism: "How Could Such a Philosophy—Dominate?". FOWLER, Mark.

Perspectivism and Postmodern Criticism. GILMOUR, John C.

Rorty and Nietzsche: Some Elective Affinities. SHAW, Daniel.

PERSUASION

Philosophical Rhetoric: The Function of Indirection in Philosophical Writing. MASON, Jeff.

Lesbian Angels and Other Matters. ZITA, Jacquelyn.

More Dyke Methods. TREBILCOT, Joyce.

A New Verdict on the 'Jury Passage': *Theaetetus* 201A-C. STRAMEL, James S.

Persuasive Argumentation in Negotiation. SYCARA, Katia P.

Philosophical Apology in the *Theaetetus*. HEMMENWAY, Scott R.

A Rhetoric of Motives: Thomas on Obligation as Rational Persuasion. HIBBS, Thomas S.

The Use and Abuse of Legal Theory: A Reply to Fish. BARASH, Carol Isaacson.

PERVERSION(S)

The Perverted Consciousness: Sexuality and Sartre. LEAK, Andrew N.

PESSIMISM

El pesimismo de Schopenhauer: sobre la differencia entre voluntad y cosa en sí. SPIERLING, Volker.

Pessimismo e umanesimo in Thomas Mann: Una riflessione etica su "Humanität" e "Humanismus". PERNECHELE, Gabriella.

El tardío pesimismo metafisico de Horkheimer. MOLINUEVO, José Luis.

PETERS, R

Philosophical Issues in Education. HAMM, Cornel M.

PETITOT, J

Il dibattito sulla razionalità oggi: un ritorno a Kant? Interviste a K O Apel & J Petitot. QUARANTA, M.

PETTIT, P

On Taking the Rabbit of Rule-Following out of the Hat of Representation: Response to 'The Reality of Rule-Following'. SUMMERFIELD, Donna M.

PHENOMENOLOGY

Whitehead and Existential Phenomenology: Is a Synthesis Possible?. RICE, Daryl H.

Who Thinks in an Abstract Manner? M Sobokta: Commentary (in Czechoslovakian). HEGEL, G W F.

Wittgenstein Never Was a Phenomenologist. REEDER, Harry P.

The Young Heidegger and Phenomenology. VAN BUREN, John.

PHILIPPINE

The Philippines: A Public Awakening. DE CASTRO, Leonardo D.

PHILOPONUS

"Philoponus on the Metaphysics of Creation" in *A Straight Path: Studies in Medieval Philosophy and Culture*, FELDMAN, Seymour.

Philoponus on the Origins of the Universe and Other Issues. OSBORNE, Catherine.

PHILOSOPHER(S)

Women Philosophers: A Bio-Critical Source Book. KERSEY, Ethel M.

"The Founders of Phenomenology and Personalism" in *Reading Philosophy for the Twenty-First Century*, KOCKELMANS, Joseph J

"The Phenomenologists" in *Reading Philosophy for the Twenty-First Century*, WOOD, Robert E.

"Philosophical Allegiance in the Greco-Roman World" in *Philosophia Togata: Essays on Philosophy and Roman Society*, SEDLEY, David.

"Philosophy, Politics, and Politicians at Rome" in *Philosophia Togata: Essays on Philosophy and Roman Society*, GRIFFIN, Miriam.

"Roman Rulers and the Philosophic Adviser" in *Philosophia Togata: Essays on Philosophy and Roman Society*, RAWSON, Elizabeth.

The Citizen Philosopher: Rousseau's Dedicatory Letter to the *Discourse on Inequality*. PALMER, Michael.

Options in African Philosophy. SOGOLO, G S.

The Philosopher as Insider and Outsider. KAMM, Frances M.

Philosophers and the Public Policy Process: Inside, Outside, or Nowhere at All?. MOMEYER, Richard W.

Philosophy and Society: On the Philosophical Heritage of Emanuel Radl (in Czechoslovakian). HEJDANEK, Ladislav.

Public Philosophy: Distinction Without Authority. MENZEL, Paul T.

Reply—Symposium on the Role of the Philosopher Among the Scientists: Nuisance or Necessity? A Reply to Baigrie. AGASSI, Joseph.

Should Lawyers Listen to Philosophers about Legal Ethics?. SMITH, M B E.

What Is and What Is Not Practical Reason?. HELLER, Agnes.

Why Philosophers Should Involve Themselves with Teaching Reasoning in the Schools. SILVERS, Anita.

PHILOSOPHICAL ANTHROPOLOGY

John of the Cross and the Cognitive Value of Mysticism. PAYNE, Steven.

Paths Toward a Clearing: Radical Empiricism and Ethnographic Inquiry. JACKSON, Michael.

"Decentering the Self: Two Perspectives from Philosophical Anthropology" in *The Question of the Other: Essays in Contemporary Continental Philosophy*, LIBERMAN, Kenneth.

The "Self" Begins to Awake: On the Philosophical Thought of Gong Zizhen. QI, Feng.

El acceso del hombre a la realidad según Xavier Zubiri. SIMONPIETRI MONEFELDT, Fannie A.

Anthropology on the Boundary and the Boundary in Anthropology. MARTIN, Dan.

Blumenberg and the Philosophical Grounds of Historiography. INGRAM, David.

Le cas Lévy-Bruhl. MERLLIÉ, Dominique.

El concepto de naturaleza. GARCIA MORIYON, Félix.

Considerações Lógicas em torno de uma Definição do Homem. CHAVES-TANNÚS, Márcio.

La culture du point de vue de l'anthropologie philosophique. COTTIER, Georges.

Dialogo sobre humanismo y existencialismo (cuarta y última parte). SILVA CAMARENA, Juan Manuel.

El enigma de la naturaleza humana. MURILLO, Ildefonso.

El enigma del animal fantastico: Bases para una antropologia y etica de la tecnica. SANCHO, Jesús Conill.

Ethnophilosophy in the Philosophical Discourse in Africa: A Critical Note. NEUGEBAUER, Christian.

Forms of Life. EMMETT, Kathleen.

Genealogies as the Language of Time: A Structural Approach—Anthropological Implications. FROUSSART, Bernard.

Grundprämisse der humanistischen Anthropologie (in Polish). OLEJNIK, Stanislaw.

Herbert Spiegelberg's Ethics: Accident and Obligation. WIGGINS, Osborne.

Hume and Davidson on Pride. ÁRDAL, Páll S.

Hume's Essays on Happiness. IMMERWAHR, John.

Intelligence artificielle et mentalité primitive. JORION, Paul.

Is Translation Possible?. HARRIS, R Thomas.

J Patocka: L'esistenza umana come "vita nella verità". DI MARCO, Chiara.

L'homme en tant qu'autocréateur; fondements anthropologiques du rejet de l'encyclique (in Polish). SZOSTEK, Andrzej.

Lavoro, "Lavorismo", *Otium*. POSSENTI, Vittorio.

Menschenbilder in pädagogiknahen Sozialwissenschaften. HUG, Theo.

The Nonduality of Life and Death: A Buddhist View of Repression. LOY, David.

Physicalism, Indeterminacy and Interpretive Science. FELEPPA, Robert.

Positivismo ed umanismo. BÜTTEMEYER, Wilhelm.

I postulati etici e metodologici fondamentali delle psichiatrie fenomenologiche. FRANCIONI, Mario.

Praxeologie als wijsgerig thema. TROOST, A.

Presence and Representation: The Other and Anthropological Writing. FABIAN, Johannes.

The Question of Relevance in Current Nigerian Philosophy. KIMMERLE, Heinz.

Reading Africa Through Foucault: V Y Mudimbe's Re-affirmation of the Subject. DIAWARA, Manthia.

Root of Man: A Note. BANDYOPADHYAY, Tirthanath.

Science—Democracy—Christianity. BRUNGS, Robert A.

Shame and Desire in the Myths of Origins. HANS, James S.

The Tao of Women and Men: Chinese Philosophy and the Women's Movement. KLEINJANS, Everett.

The Latest Philosophical Anthropology of Max Scheler (in Dutch). VEDDER, Ben.

Über Gestaltkreis und Komplementarität. BOUDIER, Henk Struyker.

Understanding Other Cultures: Studies in the Philosophical Problems of Cross-Cultural Interpretation. SANDBACKA, Carola.

William James on the Human Ways of Being. DOOLEY, Patrick.

PHILOSOPHIZING

"The 'End-of-Philosophy': An Anatomy of a Cross-Purpose Debate" in *The Institution of Philosophy: A Discipline in Crisis?*, COHEN, Avner.

"The Inevitability of Pluralism: Philosophical Practice and Philosophical Excellence" in *The Institution of Philosophy: A Discipline in Crisis?*, MANDT, A J.

"Philosophy as a Science and as a Worldview" in *The Institution of Philosophy: A Discipline in Crisis?*, CASTAÑEDA, Hector-Neri.

"Socrates and Sophia Perform the Philosophical Turn" in *The Institution of Philosophy: A Discipline in Crisis?*, RORTY, Amelie Oksenberg.

Children's Philosophy—Or: Is Motivation for Doing Philosophy a Pseudo-Problem?. MARTENS, Ekkehard.

El filosofar y el lenguaje. PIEPER, Josep.

Filosofi e filosofia nell'URSS della perestrojka. MASTROIANNI, Giovanni.

Philosophizing with Children in the Glocksee School in Hanover, Germany. HORSTER, Detlev and ALEXANDER, John V I (trans).

To Philosophize with Socrates (A Chapter from a Prepared Monography on J Patocka) (in Czechoslovakian). PALOUS, Martin.

The Value of Philosophy: A Dialogue. GINSBERG, Robert.

PHILOSOPHY

see also Metaphilosophy, Process Philosophy

The "Meditations" of Marcus Aurelius: A Study. RUTHERFORD, R B.

About Philosophy (Fourth Edition). WOLFF, Robert Paul.

Agora: Zu Ehren von Rudolph Berlinger. BERLINGER, Rudolph (and other eds).

Allāh Transcendent. NETTON, Ian Richard.

The American Evasion of Philosophy: A Genealogy of Pragmatism. WEST, Cornel.

The Changing World of Philosophy. CROWLEY, James F.

Classical American Philosophy: Essential Readings and Interpretative Essays. STUHR, John J.

Comparative Philosophy and the Philosophy of Scholarship. TUCK, Andrew P.

A Concise Dictionary of Indian Philosophy: Sanskrit Terms Defined in English. GRIMES, John A.

Connections to the World: The Basic Concepts of Philosophy. DANTO, Arthur C.

Constructions of Reason: Explorations of Kant's Practical Philosophy. O'NEILL, Onora.

The Crisis of Philosophy. MC CARTHY, Michael.

Dialectic and Contemporary Science. GRIER, Philip T (ed).

Essays in Philosophy and Education. STOTT, Laurence J.

Facts and the Function of Truth. PRICE, Huw.

First Principles, Final Ends and Contemporary Philosophical Issues. MAC INTYRE, Alasdair.

PHILOSOPHY

A Philosophic Fairytale. RICKMAN, H P.

Philosophical Books versus Philosophical Dialogue. NUSSBAUM, Martha.

A Philosophical Education. REDDIFORD, Gordon.

Philosophical Laughter: Vichian Remarks on Umberto Eco's *The Name of the Rose*. VERENE, Donald Phillip.

Philosophical Trifles (in Serbo-Croatian). LÁSZLÁO, Bulcsú.

The Philosophical Writings of Victor A Lowe (1907-1988). MC HENRY, Leemon B.

Philosophie antique et byzantine: à propos de deux nouvelles collections. O'MEARA, Dominic J.

Philosophie der Philosophiegeschichte von Hegel bis Hartmann. CEKIC, Miodrag.

Philosophie et Musique selon Schopenhauer. PICLIN, Michel.

Philosophie et politique, un cas d'ambiguïté: "l'affaire Heidegger". SCHOUWEY, Jacques.

Philosophie et religion selon Hegel. PLANTY-BONJOUR, M Guy (and others).

Philosophie und Lehre. HAGER, Nina.

Philosophie, poésie et contingent. PINSON, Jean-Claude.

Philosophische Wahrheit aus intuitivem Urdenken. MOLLOWITZ, Gerhard.

Philosophy after Wittgenstein and Heidegger. GUIGNON, Charles.

Philosophy and Literature. PALMER, Anthony.

Philosophy and Politics: The Case of Heidegger. ZIMMERMAN, Michael E.

Philosophy and Rhetoric in the *Menexenus*. COVENTRY, Lucinda.

Philosophy and Socio-Political Conversation: A Postmodern Proposal. OLIVIER, G.

Philosophy and the Cultivation of Reasoning. LIPMAN, Matthew.

Philosophy and the Devastation of the Earth (in Czechoslovakian). KOLARSKY, R and SMAJS, J.

Philosophy as (Vocational) Education. GARRISON, James W.

Philosophy as Critical Thinking. FINOCCHIARO, Maurice A.

Philosophy as Primordial Science (*Urwissenschaft*) in the Early Heidegger. KOVACS, George.

Philosophy Cannot Be Implemented in Socialism and Its Economy (in Czechoslovakian). NIKOLIC, P D.

Philosophy for Children and Aesthetic Education. HAMRICK, William S.

Philosophy for Children in its Historical Context. MULVANEY, Robert.

Philosophy for Children: An Example of the Public Dimension in Philosophy of Education. PORTELLI, John P.

Philosophy for Children: An Important Curriculum Innovation. SPLITTER, Laurance J.

Philosophy in High School: What Does It All Mean?. BENJAMIN, David.

Philosophy in South Africa: A Reply to Robert Paul Wolff. MILLER, Seumas and MAC DONALD, Ian.

Philosophy in the United States (A Dialogue of Laurent Stern and Márta Fehér) (in Hungarian). STERN, Laurent and FEHÉR, Márta.

Philosophy of Mathematics as a Theoretical and Applied Discipline. BARABASHEV, A G.

Philosophy of the Present: An Attempt at a Conceptual Specification (in Czechoslovakian). KLEIN, H D.

Philosophy Without History is Empty; History Without Philosophy is Blind. DU PLESSIS, S I M.

Philosophy, Children and Teaching Philosophy. HART, Richard E.

Philosophy: A Key to the Deaf Mind. GEISSER, Maura J.

Physiologie und Transzendentalphilosophie bei Schopenhauer. SCHMIDT, Alfred.

Pippin on Hegel. STERN, Robert.

Plato's *Lysis*: An Introduction to Philosophic Friendship. TESSITORE, Aristide.

Portia's Suitors. KUHNS, Richard and TOVEY, Barbara.

Postmodern Philosophy?. MADISON, G B.

The Practice of Philosophy for Children in Austria: How Can Children Think Philosophically?. CAMHY, Daniela G.

Pragmatic Imagination. ALEXANDER, Thomas M.

A Pragmatic Method of Reading Confused Philosophic Texts: The Case of Peirce's "Illustrations". OCHS, Peter.

Pragmatism and the Revolt Against Formalism: Revising Some Doctrines of William James. WHITE, Morton.

The Prayers of Childhood: T S Eliot's Manuscripts on Kant. HABIB, M A R.

Preface to the Publication of "P A Florenskii's Review of His Work". ABRAMOV, A I.

La pregunta por la "filosofía latinoamericana" como problema filosofico. FORNET-BETANCOURT, Raúl.

Presupposizione e verità: Il problema critico della conoscenza filosofica. MOLINARO, Aniceto.

The Principles of New Science of G B Vico and the Theory of Historical Interpretation. NOAKES, Susan (trans) and BETTI, Emilio and PINTON, Giorgio (trans).

The Problem of Consciousness and the Philosopher's Calling. MAMARDASHVILI, M K and STEWART, Philip D (trans).

The Problem of Going *from*: Science Policy and 'Human Factors' in the Experience of Developing Countries. IGNATYEV, A A.

The Problem of Going *To*: Between Epistemology and the Sociology of Knowledge. MOKRZYCKI, Edmund.

Il problema delle distinzioni nella filosofia di Spinoza. DI VONA, Piero.

Le problème du commencement dans la philosophie de Hegel. ROSEN, Menahem.

Psychological Underpinnings of Philosophy. BARTLETT, Steven J.

Pushing Thoughts With Claire. OSCANYAN, Frederick S.

The Question of Black Philosophy. JEFFERSON, Paul.

The Question of the Relation of Philosophy and Psychoanalysis: The Case of Kant and Freud. PETTIGREW, David E.

Reading Vico Three Times. SUMBERG, Theodore A.

Reasoning Skills: An Overview. CANNON, Dale and WEINSTEIN, Mark.

Recent Developments in Soviet Historiography of Philosophy. VAN DER ZWEERDE, Evert.

Recent Work in Aesthetics. JANAWAY, Christopher.

Reflective Equilibrium and the Transformation of Philosophy. NIELSEN, Kai.

The Relation of Dewey's Aesthetics to His Overall Philosophy. BURNETT, Joe R.

Remapping Modernity. COOK, Deborah.

The Role of Applied Ethics in Philosophy. MARQUIS, D.

Rorty and Nietzsche: Some Elective Affinities. SHAW, Daniel.

Santayana's Autobiography and the Development of his Philosophy. SAATKAMP JR, Herman J.

Scepticism, Certain Grounds and the Method of Reflexivity (in Dutch). VAN WOUDENBERG, R.

The Schoolman's Advocate: In Defence of the Academic Pursuit of Philosophy. THOMAS, J L H.

Schriftgemässe Philosophie als philosophische Laienmeditation?. THOMASSEN, Ber0ald.

Science, Technology, and Naturalized Philosophy. JACOBSEN, Rockney.

Self-Application in Philosophical Argumentation. JOHNSTONE JR, Henry W.

Self-Recognition and Countermemory. STEINHART, Eric.

El sentido de la indagación filosófica. DEI, H Daniel.

A Sociobiological Explanation of Strategies of Reading and Writing Philosophy. GILMAN, Roger William.

The Socratic Method and Philosophy for Children. PORTELLI, John P.

Some Prerequisites and Aspects of the Shaping of "New Thinking" Responsibility (in Czechoslovakian). JAVUREK, Z.

Some Problems About One Liberal Conception of Autonomy. SANKOWSKI, E.

Some Variations on a Metaphilosophical Theme. MARCOTTE, Edward.

The Speakerly Teacher: Socrates and Writing. KALLICK, David.

St Thomas Aquinas on the Halfway State of Sensible Being. HOFFMAN, Paul.

The State's Line: On the Change of Paradigm of Austrian Philosophy within Maria-Theresian Reform-Catholicism. GIMPL, Georg.

Step by Step in Children's Philosophy. MOSTERT, Pieter.

The Subject of Love. NYE, Andrea.

Sul concetto di filosofia nel *Fedro* platonico. ALBERT, Karl.

A Summary of Xiong Shili's Research on Philosophy Conducted in China. HAIFENG, Jing.

Teaching "Ethics in America". ROSENBAUM, Alan S.

Teaching American Philosophy. CAMPBELL, James.

Teaching as Translation: The Philosophical Dimension. JOHNSON, Tony W.

The Birth of Nietzsche's "Dionysian Philosophy" (in Serbo-Croatian). GASPAROVIC, Dubravka Kozina.

The Incongruity of Incongruity Theories of Humour (in Hebrew). KULKA, Tomas.

The Virtues of the Proprietor (Aristotle and Thomas Aquinas in Truth, Wealth and Poverty) (in Hungarian). VAN TONGEREN, Paul.

The Young Hegel—After 50 Years (in Hungarian). KONCZ, Ilona.

Thinking Skills in Science and Philosophy for Children. GAZZARD, Ann.

Thinking, Mind, the Existence of God...Transcript of a Classroom Dialogue with First-and-Second Graders in Montreal. DANIEL, Marie-France.

Three Levels of Reading Philosophy. DUHAN, Laura.

To the Lighthouse and the Feminist Path to Postmodernity. MARTIN, Bill.

Toward a History of Recent Vico Scholarship in English, Part II: 1969-1973. TAGLIACOZZO, Giorgio.

Toward a History of Recent Vico Scholarship in English, Part IV: The Vico/Venezia Conference 1978, and Its Aftermath. TAGLIACOZZO, Giorgio.

PHILOSOPHY

Toward a History of Recent Vico Scholarship in English, Part V: After Vico/Venezia (1978-1987) and Appendix. TAGLIACOZZO, Giorgio.

Toward a History of Recent Vico Scholarship in English, Part III: 1974-1977. TAGLIACOZZO, Giorgio.

The Value of Philosophy: A Dialogue. GINSBERG, Robert.

Variations on a Given Theme. KERR-LAWSON, Angus.

Vico and MacIntyre. COERS, Kathy Frashure.

Vico's Influence on Cassirer. VERENE, Donald Phillip.

Vico, Foucault, and the Strategy of Intimate Investigation. STRUEVER, Nancy S.

The Vienna Roundabout: On the Significance of Philosophical Reaction. HRACHOVEC, Herbert.

Vladimir Solov'ev on the Fate and Purpose of Philosophy. RASHKOVSKII, E B.

Was Tocqueville a Philosopher?. LAWLER, Peter A.

Weisheit—Überforderung oder Vollendung der Philosophie?. GEYER, C F.

What Is and What Is Not Practical Reason?. HELLER, Agnes.

What is Happening to the History of Ideas?. KELLEY, Donald R.

Whitehead and the New Liberals on Social Progress. MORRIS, Randall C.

Why Did Psammenitus Not Pity His Son?. BEN-ZEEV, Aaron.

Why Hegel? Heidegger and Speculative Philosophy. SCHALOW, Frank.

Why I Teach Philosophy. TORGERSON, Jon N.

Why Teachers Need Philosophy. CLARK, Charles.

Wittgenstein and Philosophy for Children. CURTIS, Barry.

Wittgenstein and the Critical Tradition. GARVER, Newton.

Wittgenstein et la philosophie. COMETTI, Jean-Pierre.

Wittgenstein on Culture and Civilization. LURIE, Yuval.

Wittgenstein's Genius. LEWIS, David.

The Words 'Same' and 'Different'. CRAWSHAY-WILLIAMS, Rupert.

Working with Philosophy for Children in Catalonia. CULLELL, Josep.

Writing and Philosophy. FISHMAN, Stephen.

El X aniversario del Primer Congreso Mundial de Filosofía Cristiana. CATURELLI, Alberto.

Young Children Generate Philosophical Ideas. MC CALL, Catherine.

Zum Philosophieverständnis bedeutender Persönlichkeiten der II, Internationale. WRONA, Vera.

PHILOSOPHY OF HISTORY

see also History

La filosofía de la historia ayer y hoy. FLÓREZ MIGUEL, Cirilo.

Filosofía y conciencia histórica. RODRÍGUEZ, Ramón.

La periodización hegeliana de la historia, vértice del conflicto interno del pensamiento hegeliano. MAYOS, Gonçal.

PHOTOGRAPHY

A Consideration of Criticism. BARRETT, Terry.

Photogenic Painting. WALKER, Pierre A (trans) and FOUCAULT, Michel.

PHYSICAL

Contemporary Models of Consciousness: Part I. BURNS, Jean E.

Intentional and Physical Relations. HOROWITZ, Amir.

On Physical Multiple Realization. ENDICOTT, Ronald P.

Wesshalb implizite Definitionen nicht genug sind. BARTELS, Andreas.

Why Supervenience?. PAPINEAU, David.

PHYSICAL SCIENCES

Texts without Referents: Reconciling Science and Narrative. MARGOLIS, Joseph.

A Critical Perspective in the Physical Sciences. ERIKSSON, Karl-Erik.

Gravity (in Dutch). KLEVER, W N A.

PHYSICAL THEORY(-RIES)

Duhem and the History and Philosophy of Mathematics. CROWE, Michael J.

Duhem and the Origins of Statics: Ramifications of the Crisis of 1903-1904. MARTIN, R N D.

The Duhemian Historiographical Project. WESTMAN, Robert S.

Essere è percepire una struttura linguistica: Il pensiero di George Berkeley quale presupposto filosofico. REBAGLIA, Alberta.

Logical Examination of Physical Theory. BARKER, Peter (trans) and ARIEW, Roger (trans) and DUHEM, Pierre.

Pierre Duhem's Conception of Natural Classification. LUGG, Andrew.

Research on the History of Physical Theories. ARIEW, Roger (trans) and BARKER, Peter (trans) and DUHEM, Pierre.

PHYSICALISM

Breaking Out of the Gricean Circle. LEVINE, Joseph.

Die kosmologischen Antinomien in der Kritik der reinen Vernunft und die moderne physikalische Kosmologie. MITTELSTAEDT, Peter and STROHMEYER, Ingeborg.

Mentalism-Cum-Physicalism vs Eliminative Materialism. O'GORMAN, P F.

More on Making Mind Matter. LE PORE, Ernest and LOEWER, Barry.

Physicalism, Indeterminacy and Interpretive Science. FELEPPA, Robert.

Physicalism, Realism and Education: A Functionalist Approach. RAINER, Valina.

Remarks on Physicalism and Reductionism. PEARCE, David.

There is No Question of Physicalism. CRANE, Tim.

Truth, Eliminativism and Disquotationalism. DAVID, Marian A.

Wittgenstein and Physicalism. HALLER, Rudolf.

PHYSICIAN(S)

"Advance Directives and the Denial of Death: Should the Conflict be Resolved?" in Advance Directives in Medicine, YOUNGNER, Stuart J.

Cost Containment Forces Physicians into Ethical and Quality of Care Compromises. JUSTIN, Renage G.

The Demand for Effectiveness, Efficiency and Equity of Health Care. MOONEY, Gavin.

The Doctor's Ethics. POWELL, D E B.

The Physician in the Technological Age. JASPERS, Karl.

Physician Investment and Self-Referral: Philosophical Analysis of a Contentious Debate. MORREIM, E Haavi.

Quality of Care and Cost Containment in the US and UK. JENNETT, Bryan.

Transparency: Informed Consent in Primary Care. BRODY, Howard.

PHYSICS

see also Quantum Mechanics

Constructivism and Science: Essays in Recent German Philosophy. BUTTS, Robert E (ed).

Dionysus Reborn: Play and the Aesthetic Dimension in Modern Philosophical and Scientific Discourse. SPARIOSU, Mihai I.

More Heat than Light: Economics as Social Physics, Physics as Nature's Economics. MIROWSKI, Philip.

The Natures of Science. MC MORRIS, Neville.

Pythagoras Revived: Mathematics and Philosophy in Late Antiquity. O'MEARA, Dominic J.

Quantum Probability—Quantum Logic. PITOWSKY, Itamar.

Reading the Mind of God: In Search of the Principle of Universality. TREFIL, James.

Thematic Origins of Scientific Thought: Kepler to Einstein—Revised Edition. HOLTON, Gerald.

"Bohr on Bell" in Philosophical Consequences of Quantum Theory: Reflections on Bell's Theorem, FOLSE JR, Henry J.

"The Concept of Structure in The Analysis of Matter" in Rereading Russell: Essays on Bertrand Russell's Metaphysics and Epistemology, DEMOPOULOS, William and FRIEDMAN, Michael.

"The Externalization of Observation: An Example from Modern Physics" in Scientific Knowledge Socialized, PINCH, Trevor J.

"From Physics to Biology: Rationality in Popper's Conception" in Issues in Evolutionary Epistemology, STOKES, Geoff.

The A Priori Method and the Actio Concept Revised. RANEA, Alberto Guillermo.

Aristotle on the Difference between Mathematics and Physics and First Philosophy. MODRAK, D K W.

Deduction, Confirmation, and the Laws of Nature in Descartes's Principia Philosophiae. NADLER, Steven M.

Die "platonische körper": Geometrische, physische, historische und epistemologische aspekte. SOFONEA, Liviu and BENKÖ, Iosif.

Duhem and Koyré on Domingo de Soto. WALLACE, William.

The Duhemian Historiographical Project. WESTMAN, Robert S.

Fisica e storia della scienza nell'opera di Pierre Duhem. RAMONI, Marco.

The Idealistic Implications of Bell's Theorem. SCHICK JR, Theodore W.

L'interprétation de la relativité. LEFETZ, L.

Logical Examination of Physical Theory. BARKER, Peter (trans) and ARIEW, Roger (trans) and DUHEM, Pierre.

Mathematics, Physics, and Corporeal Substance in Descartes. BROWN, Gregory.

Metaphysical Implications from Physics and Ecology. WITTBECKER, Alan E.

Pascal's Great Experiment. ARNOLD, Keith.

Le physicien et ses principes. RIVIER, Dominique.

Quantum Measurement and the Program for the Unity of Science. SCHARF, David C.

Relating the Physics and Religion of David Bohm. SHARPE, Kevin J.

Relativity in Mādhyamika Buddhism and Modern Physics. MANSFIELD, Victor.

PHYSIOLOGY

Physiologie und Transzendentalphilosophie bei Schopenhauer. SCHMIDT, Alfred.

PLATO

La distinción platónica entre *epistéme* y *dóxa alethés* a la luz del tratamiento del error. MARCOS DE PINOTTI, Graciela E.

Does Plato Think False Speech is Speech?. RUDEBUSCH, George.

Dooyeweerd, Bos and the *Grondmotief* of Greek Culture. RUNIA, D T.

Dos teorías de la referencia en el *Cratilo*. VALDÉS, Margarita M.

El empleo del paradigma en Platón, *Politico* 277d-283a. VIGO, Alejandro G.

The Epistemological Function of Platonic Myth. STEWART, Robert Scott.

Equality of Opportunity and the Problem of Nature. BLITS, Jan H.

Equality of Opportunity as the Noble Lie. ANDREW, Edward.

La estructura matemática de la materia en el *Timeo* de Platón. BOERI, Marcelo D.

The Ethical Dimension of Gadamer's Hermeneutical Theory. SMITH, P Christopher.

Ethos, techne y kalon en Platón. LOMBA FUENTES, Joaquín.

Filosofia dell'educazione e filosofia morale. DUCCI, Edda.

Fra Platone e Lucrezio: prime linee di una storia degli studi di filosofia antica nell'ottocento italiano. SASSI, Maria Michela.

The Hedonic Calculus in the *Protagoras* and the *Phaedo*. WEISS, Roslyn.

Heidegger spéléologue. BARNES, Jonathan.

Héraclite et l'unité des opposés. O'BRIEN, Denis.

Hobbes and Xenophon's *Tyrannicus*. BERTMAN, Martin A.

Hypothèses sur Platon et sur Nietzsche. IOANNIDI, H.

In the Beginning Was the Contradiction: Problems of the Philosophy of Subject and Object. BOLTUC, Piotr and KMIECIK, Witold (trans).

Is a Moral Organization Possible?. KLEIN, Sherwin.

Joan Kung's Reading of Plato's *Timaeus*. MUELLER, Ian.

Kantian and Platonic Conceptions of Order. STOLL, Donald.

Lectio Difficilior: le système dans la théorie platonicienne de l'âme selon interprétation de Gueroult. GAUDIN, Claude.

The Logic of the Dilemma of Participation and of the Third Man Argument. SCALTSAS, Theodore.

Logical Atomism in Plato's *Theaetetus*. RYLE, G.

Love and Beauty in Plato's *Symposium*. WHITE, F C.

Love, Beauty, and Death in Venice. WHITE, Richard.

MacIntyre's Republic. SWINDLER, J K.

Measurement, Pleasure, and Practical Science in Plato's *Protagoras*. RICHARDSON, Henry S.

Lo místico como síntesis entre bien y belleza. ELTON, María.

Moral Autonomy in the *Republic*. DENT, N J H.

More on Plato, *Meno* 82 c 2-3. SHARPLES, R W.

A New Verdict on the 'Jury Passage': *Theaetetus* 201A-C. STRAMEL, James S.

On Plato's Philosophy of Numbers and its Mathematical and Philosophical Significance. HÖSLE, Vittorio and ADLER, Pierre (trans) and HUMPHREY, Fred (trans).

On the Skeptical Influence of Gorgias's *On Non-Being*. HAYS, Steve.

The Ontological Difference and the Pre-Metaphysical Status of the Being of Beings in Plato. HUDAC, Michael C.

El origen de la energeia en Aristóteles. YEPES, Ricardo.

Over de binding van de Griekse ontologie aan het "Titanische zinperspectief'. BOS, A P.

Perceptual and Objective Properties in Plato. WHITE, Nicholas P.

Philosophy and Rhetoric in the *Menexenus*. COVENTRY, Lucinda.

Plato and Social Justice. DENT, N J H.

Plato and Totalitarianism. HALL, Robert W.

Plato on Force: Conflict Between his Psychology and Sociology and his Definition of Temperance in the *Republic*. RICE, Daryl H.

Plato's Aporetic Style. RUDEBUSCH, George.

Plato's Critique of the Poets and the Misunderstanding of his Epistemological Argumentation. WIEGMANN, Hermann.

Plato's Divided Line: A Dramatistic Interpretation. BENNE, Kenneth D.

Plato's *Euthyphro*. MORRIS, T F.

Plato's Forms: A Text That Self-Destructs to Shed Its Light. BERRY, John M.

Plato's *Ion*: The Problem of the Author. PAPPAS, Nickolas.

Plato's *Lysis*: An Introduction to Philosophic Friendship. TESSITORE, Aristide.

Plato, George Eliot, and Moral Narcissism. GOULD, Carol S.

Plato, Inquiry, and Painting. MORGAN, Michael L.

Platón filósofo-educador: valor "alusivo" de la escritura. BONAGURA, Patricia.

Platon le sceptique. ANNAS, Julia.

Platon, Arcésilas, Carnéade: Réponse à J Annas. LÉVY, Carlos.

Platonic Justice and the Republic. HALL, Robert W.

Platonic Virtue Theory and Business Ethics. KLEIN, Sherwin.

El problema del "alma mala" en la última filosofia de Platón (*Leyes* X, 896d ss). CARONE, Gabriela Roxana.

Problems in the Argument of Plato's *Crito*. KAHN, Charles H.

Reason and Passion in Plato's *Republic*. PETERS, James Robert.

A Return to Plato in the Philosophy of Substance. ZYCINSKI, Joseph.

Rhetoric as Instruction: A Response to Vickers on Rhetoric in the *Laws*. YUNIS, Harvey.

Das schöne: Gegenstand von Anschauung oder Erkenntnis?. SCHMITT, A.

Socrates' Encounter with Polus in Plato's *Gorgias*. JOHNSON, Curtis N.

Some Pleasures of Plato, *Republic* IX. STOKES, Michael.

The Subject of Love. NYE, Andrea.

Sul concetto di filosofia nel *Fedro* platonico. ALBERT, Karl.

The Newtonian Concept of Space and Time (in Polish). MAZIERSKI, Stanislaw.

The Tripartite Soul in the *Timaeus*. ROBINSON, James V.

Two Vegetarian Puns at *Republic* 372. DOMBROWSKI, Daniel A.

Virtud e interés: Fundamentos de la polis clásica y de la sociedad civil moderna. DEL BARCO, José Luis.

Virtue and Inwardness in Plato's *Republic*. KELLY, John Clardy.

Virtues and Character. WALKER, A D M.

Was Tocqueville a Philosopher?. LAWLER, Peter A

The Whole as Setting for Man: On Plato's *Timaeus*. CROPSEY, Joseph.

Der Zwang zur "geschlossenen Gesellschaft"—Ein perennes Dilemma der Utopie?. KLARER, Mario.

PLATONISM

El Concepto de Materia al Comienzo de la Escuela Franciscana de Paris. PEREZ ESTEVEZ, Antonio.

Realism, Mathematics and Modality. FIELD, Hartry.

"Schopenhauer and Platonic Ideas: A Groundwork for an Aesthetic Metaphysics" in *Schopenhauer: New Essays in Honor of His 200th Birthday*, CHANSKY, James D.

Augustine's Christian-Platonist Account of Goodness. MAC DONALD, Scott.

Fra Platone e Lucrezio: prime linee di una storia degli studi di filosofia antica nell'ottocento italiano. SASSI, Maria Michela.

Logos and Trinity: Patterns of Platonist Influence on Early Christianity. DILLON, John.

Platonische Idee und die anschauliche Welt bei Schopenhauer. KAMATA, Yasuo.

Platonism and Forms of Life. GASKIN, Richard M.

Platonismo, unicidad y metateoría. CASANAVE, Abel Lassalle.

The Roots of Contemporary Platonism. MADDY, Penelope.

Santayana's Philosophy of Love. SINGER, Irving.

PLAY

Dionysus Reborn: Play and the Aesthetic Dimension in Modern Philosophical and Scientific Discourse. SPARIOSU, Mihai I.

PLEASURE PRINCIPLE

Cremonini e le origini del libertinismo. BOSCO, Domenico.

PLEASURE(S)

Basic Moral Concepts. SPAEMANN, Robert.

Paul and the Popular Philosophers. MALHERBE, Abraham J.

"Crescas versus Maimonides on Knowledge and Pleasure" in *A Straight Path: Studies in Medieval Philosophy and Culture*, HARVEY, Warren Zev.

"The Rationality of Pleasure-Seeking Animals" in *Inquiries into Values: The Inaugural Session of the International Society for Value Inquiry*, GOLDSTEIN, Irwin.

The Argument in the *Protagoras* that No One Does What He Believes To Be Bad. MORRIS, T F.

Aristotle and Pleasure. STEWART, Robert Scott.

Epicurus on Pleasure and the Complete Life. ROSENBAUM, Stephen E.

Learning and Pleasure: Early American Perspectives. CASEMENT, William.

Measurement, Pleasure, and Practical Science in Plato's *Protagoras*. RICHARDSON, Henry S.

Pleasure and Pain: Unconditional, Intrinsic Values. GOLDSTEIN, Irwin.

Some Pleasures of Plato, *Republic* IX. STOKES, Michael.

PLENITUDE

"Problems of "Plenitude" in Maimonides and Gersonides" in *A Straight Path: Studies in Medieval Philosophy and Culture*, MANEKIN, Charles H.

PLETHON

Theosebeia in Plethon's Work: A Concept in Transition. ARGYROPOULOS, R.

PLOT(S)

The Philosophy of Horror 'or' Paradoxes of the Heart. CARROLL, Noël.

PLOTINUS

Apprehending Our Happiness: *Antilepsis* and the Middle Soul in Plotinus, *Ennead* I 4.10. SCHIBLI, H S.

L'identità del diverso. MATHIEU, Vittorio.

Origen: The Source of Augustine's Theory of Time. TZAMALIKOS, P.

POLITICAL ACTION(S)

Account" in *Inquiries into Values: The Inaugural Session of the International Society for Value Inquiry*, MARTIN, Richard.

Political Obligation and Gratitude. KLOSKO, George.

POLITICAL PHIL

see also Authority(-ties), Communism, Democracy, Ethics, Freedom, Liberalism, Libertarianism, Right(s), Social Phil, Society(-ties), State(s), Utopia

AIDS and the Good Society. ILLINGWORTH, Patricia.

Capitalism. PAUL, Ellen Frankel (ed).

Civil Disobedience. HARRIS, Paul (ed).

Civil Peace and Sacred Order: Limits and Renewals I. CLARK, Stephen R L.

Collected Works, Volume 32, Marx: 1861-1863. MARX, Karl.

Collected Works, Volume 44, Marx and Engels: 1870-1873. MARX, Karl.

The Consolations of Philosophy: Hobbes's Secret; Spinoza's Way. ROSENTHAL, Abigail L (ed).

Contre nous de la tyrannie: Des relations idéologiques entre Lumières et Révolution. BOULAD-AYOUB, Josiane.

Culture et Politique/Culture and Politics. CRANSTON, Maurice (ed).

Democracy and Dictatorship. BOBBIO, Norberto.

Democracy and Its Critics. DAHL, Robert A.

Demokrit: Texte seiner Philosophie. LOBL, Rudolf.

Eguaglianza interesse unanimità: La politica di Rousseau. BURGIO, Alberto.

Essays on Political Morality. HARE, R M.

Ethics and Strategic Defense: American Philosophers Debate Star Wars and Nuclear Deterrence. LACKEY, Douglas P (ed).

Fagothey's Right and Reason: Ethics in Theory and Practice—Ninth Edition. GONSALVES, Milton A.

Folly and Intelligence in Political Thought. KLUBACK, William.

The Good Life: Personal and Public Choices. LOUZECKY, David.

Hannah Arendt: Lectures on Kant's Political Philosophy. BEINER, Ronald (ed).

Hegel und Das Deutsche Erbe: Philosophie und nationale Frage zwischen Revolution und Reaktion. LOSURDO, Domenico.

Hegel, Heraclitus, and Marx's Dialectic. WILLIAMS, Howard.

Hobbes's System of Ideas. WATKINS, John W N.

Hobbes: War Among Nations. AIRAKSINEN, Timo (ed).

Humanisme de la liberté et philosophie de la justice, Tome II. TRIGEAUD, Jean-Marc.

The Idea of Political Theory: Reflections on the Self in Political Time and Place. STRONG, Tracy B.

Issues in Contemporary Legal Philosophy: The Influence of H L A Hart. GAVISON, Ruth (ed).

Justice and Modern Moral Philosophy. REIMAN, Jeffrey.

Justifying Legal Punishment. PRIMORATZ, Igor.

Knowledge and Politics. DASCAL, Marcelo (ed).

The Libertarian Idea. NARVESON, Jan.

Liberty and Culture: Essays on the Idea of a Free Society. MACHAN, Tibor R.

Liberty and Justice. DAY, J P.

The Logic of Political Belief: A Philosophical Analysis of Ideology. ADAMS, Ian S.

Margins of Political Discourse. DALLMAYR, Fred R.

Maternal Thinking: Toward a Politics of Peace. RUDDICK, Sara.

The Moral Foundation of Rights. SUMNER, L W.

A Moral Military. AXINN, Sidney.

Moral Reasoning and Statecraft: Essays Presented to Kenneth W Thompson. DAVIS, Reed M (ed).

The Natural Goodness of Man: On the Systems of Rousseau's Thought. MELZER, Arthur M.

Natural Right and Natural Law: A Critical Introduction (Second Edition). HERVADA, Javier.

Nuclear Deterrence and Moral Restraint. SHUE, Henry (ed).

Of the Laws of Ecclesiastical Polity (Preface, Book I, Book VIII), Richard Hooker. MC GRADE, Arthur Stephen (ed).

Political Innovation and Conceptual Change. BALL, Terence.

The Political Philosophy of the British Idealists: Selected Studies. NICHOLSON, Peter P.

The Political Theory of Liberation Theology: Toward a Reconvergence of Social Value and Science. POTTENGER, John R.

Political Writings: Thomas Paine. KUKLICK, Bruce (ed).

Politics and Process. BRENNAN, Geoffrey (ed).

Politics, Innocence, and the Limits of Goodness. JOHNSON, Peter.

Public Choice II: A Revised Edition of "Public Choice". MUELLER, Dennis C.

Realizing Rawls. POGGE, Thomas W.

Rousseau. DENT, N J H.

Rules, Norms, and Decisions: On the Conditions of Practical and Legal Reasoning. KRATOCHWIL, Friedrich V.

Selections from Political Writings, 1910-1920: Antonio Gramsci. GRAMSCI, Antonio.

Selections from Political Writings, 1921-1926: Antonio Gramsci. GRAMSCI, Antonio.

Self-Direction and Political Legitimacy: Rousseau and Herder. BARNARD, F M.

The Social and Political Thought of R G Collingwood. BOUCHER, David.

Speech, Crime, and the Uses of Language. GREENAWALT, Kent.

The Spirit of the Laws: Charles Montesquieu. COHLER, Anne M (trans).

The State and Justice: An Essay in Political Theory. FISK, Milton.

Subject and Consciousness: A Philosophical Inquiry Into Self-Consciousness. BALABAN, Oded.

The Tanner Lectures on Human Values, Volume X. PETERSON, Grethe B (ed).

Time, Freedom, and the Common Good: An Essay in Public Philosophy. SHEROVER, Charles M.

Traditions, Tyranny, and Utopias: Essays in the Politics of Awareness. NANDY, Ashis.

Typography: Mimesis, Philosophy, Politics. FYNSK, Christopher (ed).

Violence and Equality: Inquiries in Political Philosophy. HONDERICH, Ted.

Voegelin on the Idea of Race: An Analysis of Modern European Racism. HEILKE, Thomas W.

Wie kann man sagen, was nicht ist-Zur Logik des Utopischen. SCHMITZ, Heinz-Gerd.

"Evaluating the Institutions of Liberal Democracy" in *Politics and Process*, NELSON, William.

"Hobbes and the Assumption of Power" in *The Causes of Quarrel: Essays on Peace, War, and Thomas Hobbes*, CHURCHILL, R Paul.

"Introduction: Philosophy and Politics" in *The Causes of Quarrel: Essays on Peace, War, and Thomas Hobbes*, CAWS, Peter.

"The Justification of Democracy" in *Politics and Process*, PENNOCK, J Roland.

"Large Numbers, Small Costs: The Uneasy Foundations of Democratic Rule" in *Politics and Process*, BRENNAN, Geoffrey and LOMASKY, Loren E.

"Nietzsche's Musical Politics" in *Nietzsche's New Seas: Explorations in Philosophy, Aesthetics, and Politics*, GILLESPIE, Michael Allen.

"The Unity of Hobbes's Philosophy" in *Hobbes: War Among Nations*, MACHAMER, Peter and SAKELLARIADIS, Spyros.

Le "Considèrations" di Montesquieu a 250 anni dalla pubblicazione. LOCHE, Annamaria.

"The Right of a State" in Immanuel Kant's *Doctrine of Right*. LUDWIG, Bernd.

'Sustancia', 'naturaleza' y 'Dios' como términos de masa en la filosofía política de Spinoza. MADANES, Leiser.

A Continuation of Christianity (in Serbo-Croatian). KISS, Endre.

The Abortion Struggle in America. WARREN, Mary Anne.

Absolutism, Individuality and Politics: Hobbes and a Little Beyond. FLATHMAN, Richard E.

Acceleration and Restructuring: Dialectics and Problems. LAPIN, Nikolai I.

The ACLU Philosophy and the Right to Abuse the Unborn. JOHNSON, Phillip E.

Adam Schaff and the Club of Rome. KING, Alexander.

Adam Smith's Social Contract: The Proper Role of Individual Liberty and Government Intervention. COLLINS, Denis.

Adjudication under Bentham's Pannomion. DINWIDDY, J R.

Admonitions to Poland. SZCZEPANSKI, Jan and BYLINA, Maryna.

Agency, Identity, and Culture: Hannah Arendt's Conception of Citizenship. D'ENTRÈVES, Maurizio Passerin.

AIDS and *Bowers versus Hardwick*. PIERCE, Christine.

Alasdair MacIntyre: The Virtue of Tradition. ALMOND, Brenda.

Aleksei Fedorovich Losev. TAKHO-GODI, A.

Allocation and Ownership of World Resources: A Symposium Overview. KUFLIK, Arthur.

The American Founders and Classical Political Thought. ZVESPER, John.

An Analysis of Monologues and Dialogues in Political Debates. EVERTS, Diederik.

Anmerkungen zum Real Existierenden Totalitarismus und zu seinen Apologeten unter uns. MARKO, Kurt.

Are Human Rights Real?. MACHAN, Tibor R.

Arendt's Politics: The Elusive Search for Substance. SCHWARTZ, Joseph M.

Arendt, Camus, and Postmodern Politics. ISSAC, Jeffrey C.

Arendt, Republicanism and Patriarchalism. SPRINGBORG, Patricia.

An Argumentation-Analysis of a Central Part of Lenin's Political Logic. SMIT, P A.

Aristotle and the Classical Greek Concept of Despotism. RICHTER, Melvin.

Aristotle and the Value of Political Participation. MULGAN, Richard.

Aristotle's Political Naturalism. MILLER JR, Fred D.

Artificial Intelligence and Law: How To Get There From Here. MC CARTY, L Thorne.

POLITICAL PHIL

The French Revolution Debate and British Political Thought. CLAEYS, Gregory.

Friedenshandlungen und die ethischen Stellungen (in Polish). GRZEGORCZYK, Andrzej.

Friedrich Schleiermacher's Theory of the Limited Communitarian State. HOOVER, Jeffrey.

From Hemlock to Lethal Injection: The Case for Self-Execution. WALLER, Bruce N.

From Liberalism to Radicalism: Tom Paine's *Rights of Man*. KATES, Gary.

From Militancy to Ethics: On Some Forms and Problems of Militant Action in the Western World. FELDMAN, Jacqueline.

Funding the Department of Education's TRIO Programs. EKSTEROWICZ, Anthony J and GARTNER, James D.

The Future of Abortion. FLYNN, Tom.

G Shpet and His Place in the History of Russian Psychology. MITIUSHIN, A A.

The Gender Question in Criminal Law. SCHULHOFER, Stephen J.

The Generalized Others and the Concrete Other. A Response of Marie Fleming. NIELSEN, Kai.

Georg Lukács and the Ideological Fronts 1946-1949 (in Hungarian). RIPP, Zoltán.

Getting Even: The Role of the Victim. MURPHY, Jeffrie G.

The Great October, Restructuring, Politology. MSHVENIERADZE, Vladimir V.

Grounding the Rule of Law. REYNOLDS, Noel B.

Group Rights. MC DONALD, Ian.

Group Rights. SHAPARD, Leslie R.

Hacer mas legible la lectura de los acontecimientos. GRIMALDI, Rosario (trans) and HEIDEGGER, Martin.

Hannah Arendt and Leo Strauss: The Uncommenced Dialogue. BEINER, Ronald.

Hannah Arendt on Judgment, Philosophy and Praxis. KNAUER, James T.

Hart's Rule of Recognition and the United States. GREENAWALT, Kent.

Has the Revolution Been Completed?. BIALKOWSKI, Grzegorz and PETROWICZ, Lech (trans).

Hayek on Bentham. DUBE, Allison.

Hegel and the French Revolution (in Serbo-Croatian). BRUNKHORST, Hauke.

Hegel nel pensiero giuridico-politico spagnolo: Cenni storici della recezione della "Filosofia del diritto". AMENGUAL, Gabriel.

Hegel, Marx and the Cunning of Reason. PARKINSON, G H R.

Hegelianism as the Metaphysics of Revolution. ALEKSANDROWICZ, Dariusz.

Heideggers "Beiträge zur Philosophie" und die Politik. SCHWAN, Alexander.

A Historic Chance for Military-Technical Dealienation and the Building of a World Without War. BORGOSZ, Jozef and PETROWICZ, Lech (trans).

Hobbes and Xenophon's *Tyrannicus*. BERTMAN, Martin A.

Hobbes come Giano: un pensatore sulla soglia dello Stato moderno. LAMI, Gian Franco.

Hobbes e Kelsen. CATANIA, Alfonso.

Hobbes's Mortalism. JOHNSTON, David.

Hobbes's UnAristotelian Political Rhetoric. SORELL, Tom.

Hobbes: Derechos naturales, sociedad y derechos humanos. RABOSSI, Eduardo.

A Hobbesian Welfare State?. MORRIS, Christopher W.

A Hobbist Tory: Johnson on Hume. RUSSELL, Paul.

The Human Origins of *Fortuna* in Machiavelli's Thought. BALABAN, Oded.

Humanism and Political Economy. MACHAN, Tibor R.

Humanism and Socialism. SCHMITT, Richard.

The Ideal Socio-Legal Order: Its "Rule of Law" Dimension. SUMMERS, Robert S.

Immediate Legitimacy? Problems of Legitimacy in a Consensually Oriented Application of Law. MÄENPÄÄ, Olli.

In Defense of Innocents. WELLS, Donald A.

Individual Rights, Collective Interests, Public Law, and American Politics. GEORGE, Robert P.

Institutions, Arrangements and Practical Information. MAC CORMICK, Neil.

Integrity and Judicial Discretion. KASHIYAMA, Paul.

Intellectuals, Values and Society. FISK, Milton.

Intergenerational Justice and Productive Resources; A Nineteenth Century Socialist Debate. CUNLIFFE, John.

The Interpretation of Plato's *Crito*. BOSTOCK, David.

Interpreting Georges Sorel: Defender of Virtue or Apostle of Violence?. VINCENT, K Steven.

Intervencionismo y paternalismo. GARZÓN VALDÉS, Ernesto.

Ironist Theory as a Vocation: A Response to Rorty's Reply. MC CARTHY, Thomas.

Is International Law Part of Natural Law?. D'AMATO, Anthony.

Is Post-Structuralist Political Theory Anarchist?. MAY, Todd.

J S Mill and Political Violence. WILLIAMS, Geraint.

John Locke: sobre la justificación del gobierno. AMOR, Claudio O.

John Rawls et la justice. FUCHS, Erich.

John Stuart Mill on Democratic Representation and Centralization. KURER, Oskar.

John Stuart Mill on Government Intervention. KURER, O.

Journalists: A Moral Law Unto Themselves?. HARRIS, Nigel G E.

Judges Taken Too Seriously: Professor Dworkin's Views on Jurisprudence. TROPER, Michel.

The Jurisprudence of the European Court of Human Rights: Towards an Alternative Foundation of Human Rights. DURÁN Y LALAGUNA, Paloma.

Justice and the Legal Profession. GRCIC, Joseph.

Justice: Means versus Freedoms. SEN, Amartya.

La justificación de la democracia: entre la negación de la justificación y la restricción de la democracia. NINO, Carlos Santiago.

The Justification of Political Conformism: The Mythology of Soviet Intellectuals. SHLAPENTOKH, Vladimir.

Justifying Tolerance. KING, Preston.

Kant's Theory of Political Authority. CARR, Craig L.

Kant's Theory of Punishment: Deterrence in its Threat, Retribution in its Execution. BYRD, B Sharon.

L'État minimal et le droit de propriété privée selon Nozick. LAMBERT, Roger.

La correlation entre l'activité du parti et l'activité de l'Etat de la démocratie ouvrière (in Romanian). FLOREA, Ion.

Law and Morality. BICKENBACH, Jerome E.

Law and Objectivity: How People are Treated. GREENAWALT, Kent.

Law as a Bridge between Is and Ought. BODENHEIMER, Edgar.

Law as Co-ordination. FINNIS, John M.

The Law of Nature, the Uppsala School and the *Ius Docendi* Affair. SUNDBERG, Jacob.

Legal Concepts in a Natural Language Based Expert System. LEHMANN, Hubert.

Legal Reasoning as a Special Case of Moral Reasoning. PECZENIK, Aleksander.

Leninismo y Marxismo en *Historia y Conciencia de Clases*. GIGLIOLI, Giovanna.

Leo Strauss, Hobbes et la nature humaine. MALHERBE, Michel.

Leviathan and Spinoza's *Tractatus* on Revelation: Some Elements for a Comparison. PACCHI, Arrigo.

Leviathan and the Post-Modern. WILLMS, Bernard.

Lévy-Bruhl et Hegel. BOURGOIS, Bernard.

Liberal and Socialist Egalitarianism. NIELSEN, Kai.

Liberal Constitutionalism as Ideology: Marx and Habermas. WARREN, Mark.

Liberal Goods. GEISE, J P.

Liberal Neutrality: A Reply to James Fishkin. LARMORE, Charles.

Liberalism and Liberty: the Fragility of a Tradition. GRAHAM, Keith.

Liberalism and Natural End Ethics. RASMUSSEN, Douglas B.

Liberalism and Neo-Aristotelianism. PADEN, Roger.

Liberalism, Distributive Subjectivism, and Equal Opportunity for Welfare. ARNESON, Richard J.

La libertad y el concepto de lo político. DE ZAN, Julio.

The Libertarian Utopia: Robert Nozick and Aleksander Swietochowski. MIKLASZEWSKA, Justyna.

Liberty and Democracy, or Socialism?. FLEW, Antony.

Life, Liberty and Exploitation. RYAN, Cheyney.

The Limitations of Heidegger's Ontological Aestheticism. ZIMMERMAN, Michael E.

The Logic of Time in Law and Legal Expert Systems. MACKAAY, Ejan (and others).

Machiavel et la question de la Nature. EDMOND, Michel-Pierre.

Machiavel, lecteur des Anciens. ALLARD, Gérald.

Made by Contrivance and the Consent of Men. DEN HARTOGH, Govert.

Madison's Party Press Essays. SHEEHAN, Colleen A.

Making a Case for Socialism. NIELSEN, Kai.

Manichaean Responses to Zoroastrianism. SCOTT, David.

Market Equality and Social Freedom. HOLLIS, Martin.

Marxism and Psychoanalysis: An Exchange. CRAIB, Ian and KOVEL, Joel.

Marxism and Social Sciences at a New Stage. FRITZHAND, Marek and PROTALINSKI, Grzegorz (trans).

Mens Rea. HAMPTON, Jean.

Michael Oakeshott as Liberal Theorist. FRANCO, Paul.

Militancy, Violence and Democratic Rights: Indian Experience. BANERJEE, Sumanta.

POLITICAL PHIL

Mill in Parliament: The View from the Comic Papers. ROBSON, John M.

Models of Reason, Types of Principles and Reasoning: Historical Comments and Theoretical Outlines. PATTARO, Enrico.

Modern Normativity and the Politics of Deregulation. TREY, George A.

Moral and Political Implications of Pragmatism. VAN BRAKEL, J and SAUNDERS, B A C.

Moral Rights and Duties in Wicked Legal Systems. TEN, C L.

Morality and Interest. HARRISON, Bernard.

More on Self-Enslavement and Paternalism in Mill. BROWN, D G.

Murray, Niebuhr, and the Problem of the Neutral State. HUNT, Robert P.

Les mutations de l'historiographie Révolutionnaire. FURET, M François.

The Myth of Civil Disobedience. VAN DER BURG, Wibren.

National Self-determination. MARGALIT, Avishai.

Natural Law Elements in Pound's Philosophy of Law?. MC LEAN, Edward B.

Natural Law in the *Huang-Lao Boshu*. PEERENBOOM, R P.

Natural Right and Aristotle's Understanding of Justice. YACK, Bernard.

Nature and Revolution in Paine's *Common Sense*. FRUCHTMAN, Jack.

Neues zum Thema Gerechtigkeit?. STRANZINGER, Rudolf.

Neutrality and Utility. ARNESON, Richard J.

A New Approach to Regulating the Use of Animals in Science. ANDERSON, Warwick.

New Gods for Old: In Defense of Libertarianism. BRADFORD, R W.

New Social Self-Steering. GRZEGORCZYK, Andrzej and GOLEBIOWSKI, Marek (trans).

Nietzsche und George: Anmerkungen zu einem Buch von Heinz Raschel. WEBER, Frank.

Nietzsche's Politics. THIELE, Leslie Paul.

Nietzsche, Foucault and the Prospects of Postmodern Political Philosophy. BOTWINICK, Aryeh.

Nietzsche: A Radical Challenge to Political Theory?. ANSELL-PEARSON, Keith.

Nietzsche: Power as Oppression. READ, James H.

No Laughing Matter: John Stuart Mill's Establishment of Women's Suffrage as a Parliamentary Question. ROBSON, John M.

A Normative Conception of Coherence for a Discursive Theory of Legal Justification. GÜNTHER, Klaus.

Nuclearism and International Law. STEGENGA, James A.

Oakeshott on the Authority of Law. FRIEDMAN, Richard B.

Obligations of Gratitude and Political Obligation. WALKER, A D M.

On a Similarity Between Natural Law Theories and English Legal Positivism. MC LAUGHLIN, Robert N.

On Articles of the Academy of the White Deer Grotto (in Serbo-Croatian). JI-YU, Ren.

On *Begriffsgeschichte* Again. RAYNER, Jeremy.

On Deciding Whether a Nation Deserves Our Loyalty. NATHANSON, Stephen.

On Explaining Political Disagreement: The Notion of an Essentially Contested Concept. MASON, Andrew.

On Heidegger's Silence. KOVACS, George.

On Necessary Relations Between Law and Morality. ALEXY, Robert.

On the Common Saying that it is Better that Ten Guilty Persons Escape than that One Innocent Suffer: Pro and Con. REIMAN, Jeffrey and VAN DEN HAAG, Ernest.

On the Connection Between Ethology and Ecology (in Czechoslovakian). KAMARYT, J and STEINDL, R.

On the Contemporary Theory of Socialism (The October Revolution and Perestroika). SHEVCHENKO, V N.

On the Debate between China and the Soviet Union: Theoretical and Philosophical Remarks, 1963 (in Hungarian). LUKÁCS, Georg.

On the Interpretation of Laws. FRIEDMAN, Lawrence M.

On the Legitimacy of Law: A Conceptual Point of View. AARNIO, Aulis.

On the Sublime in Politics (in Serbo-Croatian). RICHIR, Marc.

Ontique et deontique. KALINOWSKI, Georges.

Origins of Natural Rights Language: Texts and Contexts, 1150-1250. TIERNEY, Brian.

Ortsbestimmungen des Politischen: Neuere Literatur zu Thomas Hobbes. ANGEHRN, Emil.

Otra vez Heidegger y el nazismo. AUBENQUE, Pierre.

Otto Neurath: Marxist Member of the Vienna Circle. JACOBS, Sturan and OTTO, Karl-Heinz.

Paine and Sieyès. DE PROSPO, R C.

La paradoja de la irrelevancia moral del gobierno y el valor epistemológico de la democracia. NINO, Carlos Santiago.

La paradoja de la libertad de expresión. MADANES, Leiser.

The Paradox of Blackmail. FEINBERG, Joel.

Le parcours Hégélien de la révolution Française. D'HONDT, M Jacques.

Parfit's Moral Arithmetic and the Obligation to Obey the Law. KLOSKO, George.

Paternalism and Democracy. SMILEY, Marion.

Perestroika as a Continuation of the October Revolution. ZAGLADIN, V V.

Philosophie et politique, un cas d'ambiguïté: "l'affaire Heidegger". SCHOUWEY, Jacques.

The Philosophy of Fate as the Basis of Education for Peace. GRZEGORCZYK, Andrzej and PETROWICZ, Lech (trans).

Philosophy of Law and the Theory of Speech Acts. AMSELEK, Paul.

Philosophy of Regional Cooperation in the Solution of Global Ecological Problems (in Czechoslovakian). MEZRICKY, V.

Plato on Force: Conflict Between his Psychology and Sociology and his Definition of Temperance in the *Republic*. RICE, Daryl H.

La Política de Aristóteles y la Democracia (II). CRUZ PRADOS, Alfredo.

La Política de Aristóteles y la Democracia. CRUZ PRADOS, Alfredo.

Political Liberalism. LARMORE, Charles.

Political Theory as an Object of Discourse. WHITE, Roger.

Political Thought and Rhetoric in Vico. JACOBITTI, Edmund E.

The Politician and the Philosopher (Some Lessons from Machiavelli). DOLGOV, Konstantin M and JARKOWSKI, Jan (trans).

Politics and Generosity. MACHAN, Tibor R.

The Politics of Justification. MACEDO, Stephen.

Porous Vessels: A Critique of the Nation, Nationalism and National Character as Analytical Concepts. FARRAR JR, L L.

Positive Retributivism. TEN, C L.

A Post-Philosophical Politics? An Interview by Danny Postel. RORTY, Richard.

Posthumous Rehabilitation and the Dust-Bin of History. LANDE, Nelson P.

Potere e ragione nella filosofia politica di Enrico Opocher. ANDREATTA, Alberto.

The Poverty of Opulence. KOLENDA, Konstantin.

The Power Principle: "Inherent Defects" Reconsidered. TOMASI, John.

Pragmatic Inquiry and Social Conflict: A Critical Reconstruction of Dewey's Model of Democracy. SMILEY, Marion.

A Pragmatic Version of Natural Law. WALTER, Edward.

Pragmatism and Precedent: A Response to Dworkin. SULLIVAN, Michael.

Pregnancy, Drugs, and the Perils of Prosecution. MARINER, Wendy K and GLANTZ, Leonard H and ANNAS, George J.

La première crise de la raison. THÉRIAULT, J Yvon.

The Problem of Bureaucracy in a Socialist State. ZAWADZKI, Sylwester and PROTALINSKI, Grzegorz (trans).

Problems in the Argument of Plato's *Crito*. KAHN, Charles H.

Protecting Fetuses from Prenatal Hazards: Whose Crimes? What Punishment?. NOLAN, Kathleen.

Punishment and Self-Defense. FLETCHER, George P.

The Radical Feminist View of Motherhood: Epistemological Issues and Political Implications. SCHEDLER, George.

Radicals, Conservatives and Moderates in Early Modern Political Thought: A Case of Sandwich Islands Syndrome?. CONDREN, C.

Raison pratique et communauté chez Fichte. MOGGACH, Douglas.

Rand Socialist?. TURNER, Dan.

Rationally Justifying Political Coercion. HARDIN, Russell.

Rawls and the Collective Ownership of Natural Abilities. KERNOHAN, Andrew.

Rawls and the Minimum Demands of Justice. MC KENNA, Edward and WADE, Maurice and ZANNONI, Diane.

Rawls on Political Community and Principles of Justice. NICKEL, James W.

Rawls, Habermas, and Real Talk: A Reply to Walzer. WARNKE, Georgia.

Rawlsian Justice and Community Planning. MARLIN, Randal.

Raz and Legal Positivism. DARE, Tim.

Reason in Law. BOBBIO, Norberto.

Reason, Revolution and Religion: Johann Benjamin Erhard's Concept of Enlightened Revolution. MARTINSON, Steven D.

Recent Work in Punishment Theory. DAVIS, Michael.

Recenti studi sullo Hegel politico. BONACINA, Giovanni.

Rechtsstaalichkeit als Moment demokratischer politischer Machtausübung. WILL, Rosemarie.

Reconsidering the Relationship among Voluntary Acts, Strict Liability, and Negligence in Criminal Law. ALEXANDER, Larry.

The Reconstruction of Political Concepts. MASON, A.

Recreational Drugs and Paternalism. HUSAK, Douglas N.

Reducing Legal Realism to Natural Law. MILLER, Myron M.

Reflections on Hobbes: Recent Work on His Moral and Political Philosophy. CURLEY, Edwin.

Reflections on Natural Law: A Critical Review of the Thought of Yves R Simon. BLACK, Virginia.

Réflexions dur le sens de l'histoire (in Greek). MICHAÉLIDÈS-NOUAROS, G.

Reification, Class and 'New Social Movements'. BROWNE, Paul.

Remarks on the Concept of Norm. PAULSON, Stanley L.

POLITICAL PHIL

Remembering and Re-Creating the Classing. CASANOVA, Pablo González.

Republic and Politics in Machiavelli and Rousseau. VIROLI, Maurizio.

Respect for Persons, Autonomy and Equality. NORMAN, Richard.

Response to Henry S Kariel's "The Feminist Subject Spinning in the Postmodern Project". NORTON, Anne.

Responsibility and Complicity. ARONSON, Ronald.

The Resurgence of the Foole. ZENZINGER, Theodore S.

The Retreat of the Political in the Modern Age: Jean-Luc Nancy on Totalitarianism and Community. INGRAM, David.

Reweaving the "One Thread" of the *Analects*. IVANHOE, Philip J.

Rhetoric and the Erasmian Defence of Religious Toleration. REMER, Gary.

Rhetoric as Instruction: A Response to Vickers on Rhetoric in the *Laws*. YUNIS, Harvey.

The Right of Self-Determination in International Law. LANGLEY, Winston.

Rights and Resources. GILBERT, Alan.

Rights to Liberty in Purely Private Matters: Part II. RILEY, Jonathan.

Robertus Britannus, 'On the Best Form of Commonwealth': A Dialogue between Pierre du Chastel and Aymar Ranconet. DYSON, R W (ed & trans) and TUDOR, H (ed & trans).

Robespierre and Revolution (in Serbo-Croatian). VEJVODA, Ivan.

The Role of Rules. WEINBERGER, Ota.

Rousseau on Reading "Jean-Jacques": *The Dialogues*. KELLY, Christopher and MASTERS, Roger D.

Rousseau, o el gobierno representativo. STRASSER, C.

The Rule of Law in the Russian Intellectual Tradition: Pre-Revolutionary Russia, the Soviet Union and Perestroika. WALICKI, Andrzej.

Russell's Leviathan. LIPPINCOTT, Mark S.

Saving Grace. BRIEN, Andrew.

Scientific and Legal Standards of Statistical Evidence in Toxic Tort and Discrimination Suits. CRANOR, Carl and NUTTING, Kurt.

Scienza politica e "nuova" scienza della politica: un conflitto "generazionale"?. LAMI, Gian Franco.

The Seventieth Anniversary of the October Revolution. SZCZEPANSKI, Jan and PETROWICZ, Lech (trans).

Should Lawyers Listen to Philosophers about Legal Ethics?. SMITH, M B E.

The Situationist International: A Case of Spectacular Neglect. PLANT, Sadie.

The Small-Republic Argument in Modern Micronesia. PETERSEN, Glenn.

Socialism is Incompatible with Humanism. SHEAFFER, Robert.

Some Aspects of the Methodology of Comparative Research in Politics. WIATR, Jerzy J.

Soviet "New Political Thinking": Reflections on the Issues of Peace and War, War and Politics. XICHENG, Yin.

Sozialistische Gesellschaft und sozialistische Nation in der DDR. KOSING, Alfred.

The Spanish Natural Law School. LLANO, Estela.

Spinoza jenseits von Hobbes und Rousseau. GEISMANN, Georg.

The State and Legitimacy. BARRY, Norman.

The State at Dusk. MAC GREGOR, David.

Statutory Interpretation and the Counterfactual Test for Legislative Intention. LEE, Win-Chiat.

The Structure of Social Revolutions (Some Remarks and Hypotheses). WITKOWSKI, Lech and PETROWICZ, Lech (trans).

Sulla validità della costituzione dal punto di vista del positivismo giuridico. GUASTINI, Riccardo.

Sur l'héritage de Hobbes. TAMINIAUX, Jacques.

Sur les Wege zur Aussprache de Heidegger. DAVID, Pascal.

A Sweet and Sour Victory in Eastern Europe. SZAKOLCZAI, Arpád and HORVÁTH, Ágnes.

The Synthesis: A Sociopolitical Critique of the Liberal Professions. ROSSIDES, Daniel.

Synthesizing Related Rules from Statutes and Cases for Legal Expert Systems. ALLEN, Layman E and PAYTON, Sallyanne and SAXON, Charles S.

T H Green's Theory of the Morally Justified Society. SIMHONY, Avital.

Taking Drugs Seriously (Liberal Paternalism and the Rationality of Preferences). CUDD, Ann E.

Terrorism, Self-Defense, and Whistleblowing. WESTRA, Laura.

The Birth of Politics (in Serbo-Croatian). HOWARD, Dick.

The Civil Revolution and Historical Materialism (in Serbo-Croatian). NOERR, Gunzelin Schmid.

The Critique and Utopia of the Subject (in Serbo-Croatian). SCHILLER, Hans-Ernst.

The Ethics Dimension of Human Attitude to the Living Environment (in Czechoslovakian). BURES, R.

The French Revolution and Thinking About the Revolution (in Serbo-Croatian). KULLASHI, Muhamedin.

The Moment of Ideology and the Human Factor in Lukác's Late Work (in Hungarian). SZABÓ, Tibor.

The Moment of the Foundation (in Serbo-Croatian). RAULET, Gérard.

The Need of Philosophy and Current Ecological Crisis (in Czechoslovakian). KOLARSKY, R.

The Problems of Czech and Slovak Culture-Political Thinking Between Both World Wars (in Czechoslovakian). BERANOVA, Vera.

The Self-Understanding of Political Modernism and the Idea of the Revolution (in Serbo-Croatian). JIMÉNEZ, Manuel.

Eine Theorie der politischen Gerechtigkeit. KERSTING, Wolfgang.

Thinking Politics without a Philosophy of History: Arendt and Merleau-Ponty. ROMAN, Joël and MICHELMAN, Stephen (trans).

Thomas Muntzer—Humanist, Reformator, Revolutionär. HERLITZIUS, Erwin and RUDOLPH, Günther.

To the Lighthouse. LEVIN, Michael.

Tocqueville and the Problem of Natural Right. EDEN, Robert.

Totalitarianism, Homogeneity of Power, Depth: Towards a Socio-Political Ontology. STEINBOCK, A J.

Totalité, temporalité et politique: Essai de typologie. LETOCHA, Danièle.

Totality, Realism, and the Type: Lukács' Later Literary Criticism as Political Theory. SHAW, Brian J.

Towards a Communication-Concept of Rational Collective Will-Formation: A Thought-Experiment. HABERMAS, Jürgen.

Towards a New Social Contract. FISHKIN, James S.

The Traditionality of Statutes. KRYGIER, Martin.

The Tragedy of National Conflicts in 'Real Socialism': The Case of the Yugoslav Autonomous Province of Kosovo. MARKOVIC, Mihailo.

Truth and Freedom: A Reply to Thomas McCarthy. RORTY, Richard.

Two Vegetarian Puns at Republic 372. DOMBROWSKI, Daniel A.

Two Visions of Liberty—Berlin and Hayek. POLANOWSKA-SYGULSKA, Beata.

Universalism as a Metaphilosophy of the New Peace Movement. KUCZYNSKI, Janusz and PETROWICZ, Lech (trans) and RODZINSKA, Aleksandra (trans).

The Use and Abuse of Legal Theory: A Reply to Fish. BARASH, Carol Isaacson.

The Use of Logical Models in Legal Problem Solving. KOWALSKI, Robert and SERGOT, Marek.

Utilitarianism and Distributive Justice: The Civil Law and the Foundations of Bentham's Economic Thought. KELLY, P J.

Utopia and Islamic Political Thought. AL-AZMEH, Aziz.

V S Solov'ev: An Attempt at a Philosophical Biography. ASMUS, V S.

The Varieties and Limitations of Legal Positivism. OTT, Walter.

Varieties of Ecological Dialectics. SIMON, Thomas W.

Violence, Law, and the Limits of Morality. CRAGG, A W.

Virtud e interés: Fundamentos de la polis clásica y de la sociedad civil moderna. DEL BARCO, José Luis.

War Against Indiscipline (WAI): Nigerian Ethical Policy. EBOH, Marie P.

War, Omnicide and Sanity: The Lesson of the Cuban Missile Crisis. SOMERVILLE, John.

Western Marxism: A Fictionalist Deconstruction. GRAY, John.

What is Conservatism?. WADLEIGH, Julian.

What Restoring Leninism Means. DAHM, Helmut and SWIDERSKI, E M (trans).

What's Left: Marx, Foucault and Contemporary Problems of Social Change. WAPNER, Paul.

When Becoming Pregnant Is a Crime. PALTROW, Lynn M.

Whither the Way?. WOHL, Andrzej and GOLEBIOWSKI, Marek (trans).

The Whole as Setting for Man: On Plato's Timaeus. CROPSEY, Joseph.

Why is There a Problem About Political Obligation?. NIELSEN, Kai.

Wittgenstein, Realism, and CLS: Undermining Rule Scepticism. LANDERS, Scott.

The World United. KOLENDA, Konstantin.

Zum Philosophieverständnis bedeutender Persönlichkeiten der II. Internationale. WRONA, Vera.

POLITICAL SCIENCE

Axioms of Cooperative Decision Making. MOULIN, Hervé.

Civil Religion in Tocqueville's Democracy in America. KORITANSKY, John C.

The Reconstruction of Political Concepts. MASON, A.

Scienza politica e "nuova" scienza della politica: un conflitto "generazionale"?. LAMI, Gian Franco.

Self-Interest in Political Life. MANSBRIDGE, Jane.

Tocqueville and the Problem of Natural Right. EDEN, Robert.

POLITICAL STRUCTURES

Equality, Political Order and Ethics: Hobbes and the Systematics of Democratic Rationality. ZIMMERMANN, Rolf.

POLITICAL THEORY

Democracy and Its Critics. DAHL, Robert A.

The Good Life: Personal and Public Choices. LOUZECKY, David.

POLITICAL THEORY

POLITICS

POLITICS

Heidegger and the Difficulties of a Postmodern Ethics and Politics. WHITE, Stephen K.

Heinrich Heine, intellectuel moderne. HÖHN, Gerhard.

Interview with Jürgen Habermas: Ethics, Politics and History. FERRY, Jean-Marc and HABERMAS, Jürgen.

J S Mill and Political Violence. WILLIAMS, Geraint.

Das Konzept einer "wahren" Politik des Friedrich Gentz. DIETRICH, Therese.

L'illuministe Simeon Marcovici—un remarquable journaliste et penseur (in Romanian). ISAR, N.

La correlation entre l'activité du parti et l'activité de l'Etat de la démocratie ouvrière (in Romanian). FLOREA, Ion.

Le développement de la science et le progrès de la société (in Romanian). MARIS, Nicolae.

Machiavel et la question de la Nature. EDMOND, Michel-Pierre.

Machiavel, lecteur des Anciens. ALLARD, Gérald.

The Make-Up of Literature. TAYLOR, Paul.

Martin Heidegger: His Philosophy and His Politics. ZUCKERT, Catherine H.

Messy Morality and the Art of the Possible—I. COADY, C A J.

The Mirror of Reproduction: Baudrillard and Reagan's America. RUBENSTEIN, Diane.

Morality, Politics and the Revolutions of 1989. O'NEILL, Onora.

Le motif de la déconstruction et ses portées politiques. LISSE, M.

Motivation et idéal dans l'action sociale (in Romanian). BARBU, Nicolae.

Noam Chomsky: An Interview. CHOMSKY, Noam and EDGLEY, Roy and OSBORNE, Peter and RÉE, Jonathan and WILSON, Deirdre.

On the Social and Political Implications of Cognitive Psychology. PRILLELTENSKY, Isaac.

On the Sublime in Politics (in Serbo-Croatian). RICHIR, Marc.

Philosophie et politique, un cas d'ambiguïté: "l'affaire Heidegger". SCHOUWEY, Jacques.

Philosophy and Politics: The Case of Heidegger. ZIMMERMAN, Michael E.

Philosophy and Society: On the Philosophical Heritage of Emanuel Radl (in Czechoslovakian). HEJDANEK, Ladislav.

Plato's Divided Line: A Dramatistic Interpretation. BENNE, Kenneth D.

Politics and the Production of Narrative Identities. SILVERS, Anita.

Politics as Soul-Making: Aristotle on Becoming Good. HOMIAK, Marcia L.

The Politics of Epistemology. WHITE, Morton.

The Politics of the Ineffable: Derrida's Deconstructionism. MC CARTHY, Thomas.

The Question of Relevance in Current Nigerian Philosophy. KIMMERLE, Heinz.

Raison pratique et communauté chez Fichte. MOGGACH, Douglas.

Rationality in Conversation and Neutrality in Politics. DEN HARTOGH, Govert.

Realism and Redistribution. NARDIN, Terry.

René Descartes n'est pas l'auteur de La naissance de la paix. WATSON, Richard A.

Scarcity and Setting the Boundaries of Political Economy. SASSOWER, Raphael.

Some Aspects of the Methodology of Comparative Research in Politics. WIATR, Jerzy J.

Soviet "New Political Thinking": Reflections on the Issues of Peace and War, War and Politics. XICHENG, Yin.

Sur l'héritage de Hobbes. TAMINIAUX, Jacques.

The Birth of Politics (in Serbo-Croatian). HOWARD, Dick.

The Theological-Political Tension in Liberalism. FULLER, Timothy.

Une conception unitaire, profondément scientifique sur la dynamique des étapes du processus (in Romanian). RUS, Vasile.

Virtud e interés: Fundamentos de la polis clásica y de la sociedad civil moderna. DEL BARCO, José Luis.

Visage Versus Visages. BAUM, Mylène.

POLITY

Of the Laws of Ecclesiastical Polity (Preface, Book I, Book VIII), Richard Hooker. MC GRADE, Arthur Stephen (ed).

Time, Freedom, and the Common Good: An Essay in Public Philosophy. SHEROVER, Charles M.

POLLOCK, J

Seeming to See Red. BAKER, Lynne Rudder.

POLLUTION

Water Quality Concerns and the Public Policy Context. MOORE, Keith M.

POLYNOMIALS

Completeness Proofs for Propositional Logic with Polynomial-Time Connectives. CROSSLEY, J N and SCOTT, P J.

On Splitting of a Recursive Set with Polynomial Time Minimal Pairs. ZHIXIANG, Chen.

Quantified Propositional Calculi and Fragments of Bounded Arithmetic. KRAJICEK, Jan and PUDLAK, Pavel.

POMPONAZZI

Pomponazzi's Critique of Aquinas' Arguments for the Immortality of the Soul. TRELOAR, John L.

POPE

The Democracy of Workers in the Light of John Paul II's Encyclical Laborem Exercens. KONDZIELA, Joachim.

John Paul II vis-à-vis Atheism and Materialism: Remarks on the Encyclical Dominum et vivificantem. TANALSKI, Dionizy and RODZINSKA, Aleksandra (trans).

La person e en tant que don dans l'enseignement de Jean-Paul II (in Polish). GALKOWSKI, Jerzy W.

A Marxist's View on the Philosophy of Peace Advanced by John Paul II. CZEMARNIK, Adam and BONIECKA, Magdalena (trans).

Towards a Theology of Peace—The Peace Doctrine of John Paul II. RAJECKI, Robert and LECKI, Maciej (trans).

POPPER

Issues in Evolutionary Epistemology. HAHLWEG, Kai (ed).

A Useful Inheritance: Evolutionary Aspects of the Theory of Knowledge. RESCHER, Nicholas.

"From Physics to Biology: Rationality in Popper's Conception" in Issues in Evolutionary Epistemology, STOKES, Geoff.

"Historicism and Rationalism" in Scientific Knowledge Socialized, KELEMEN, János.

"Popper, Natural Selection and Epiphenomenalism" in Issues in Evolutionary Epistemology, SHAW, Daniel.

Bold Hypotheses: The Bolder the Better?. CLEVELAND, Timothy and SAGAL, Paul T.

Discovery Logics. NICKLES, Thomas.

Enunciados basicos e hipótesis falsificadora en Popper. COMESAÑA, Manuel E.

Generalizaciones y explicación de la historiografía. PINCIONE, Guido M.

In Defense of Good Reasons. BERKSON, William.

La ingeniería social como método de testeo. COMESAÑA, Manuel E.

Karl Popper's Philosophy of Scientific Knowledge. NARAYAN, S Shankar.

Metafisica Todavia? (cont). SANABRIA, José Rubén.

Method and the Authority of Science. TILES, Mary E.

The Method of "Grounded Theory" in the Age-Old Debate about Induction. RODRIGUEZ, Vincent.

La metodología falsacionista y su ecología. RADNITZKY, Gerard.

Der Mythos des Rahmens am Pranger: Anderssons Antwort auf die wissenschaftsgeschichtliche Herausforderung. ALBERT, Hans.

On a Recent Objection to Popper and Miller's "Disproof" of Probabilistic Induction. HOWSON, Colin.

On the Logical Structure of Verisimilitude. GERLA, Giangiacomo and GUCCIONE, Salvatore.

Popper and Historicist Necessities. FLEW, Antony.

Positivismo ed umanismo. BÜTTEMEYER, Wilhelm.

Preference Derived from Urgency. LINDAHL, Lars.

Realismo crítico y conocimiento en Carlos Popper. DARÓS, W R.

Réflexions dur le sens de l'histoire (in Greek). MICHAÉLIDÈS-NOUAROS, G.

La revisión antihistoricista de la Revolución Francesa. SAZBÓN, José.

Riflessioni epistemologiche sull'errore. BALDINI, Massimo.

Die Situationsanalyse. WERLEN, Benno.

Some Variations on a Metaphilosophical Theme. MARCOTTE, Edward.

Teoria della argomentazione e filosofia della scienza. BARROTTA, Pierluigi.

The Logical Structure of Aesthetic Value Judgements: An Outline of a Popperian Aesthetics (in Hebrew). KULKA, Tomas.

Tolerância e interpretação. DASCAL, Marcelo.

Troubles with Popper (in Serbo-Croatian). VUJIC, Antum.

Vérisimilarité et méthodologie poppérienne. LAFLEUR, Gérald.

When Probabilistic Support is Inductive. MURA, Alberto.

POPULAR CULTURE

Postmodernist Culture: An Introduction to Theories of the Contemporary. CONNOR, Steven.

The Hypervisual Meaning of the American West. MEYER, William E H.

Towards—and Away from—an Aesthetic of Popular Culture. DOHERTY, Thomas.

POPULATION

"The Variance Allocation Hypothesis of Stasis" in Reductionism and Systems Theory in the Life Sciences: Some Problems and Perspectives, WAGNER, Günter P.

Malthus and Utilitarianism with Special Reference to the Essay on Population. HOLLANDER, Samuel.

POSTMODERISM

"Postmodern Theology as Liberation Theology: A Response to Harvey Cox" in *Varieties of Postmodern Theology*, GRIFFIN, David Ray.

"Postmortem Thought and the End of Man" in *The Question of the Other: Essays in Contemporary Continental Philosophy*, CLIFFORD, Michael.

"Reflections on the 'Crisis of Modernity'" in *The Institution of Philosophy: A Discipline in Crisis?*, DASCAL, Marcelo.

"Social Criticism Without Philosophy" in *The Institution of Philosophy: A Discipline in Crisis?*, FRASER, Nancy and NICHOLSON, Linda.

Adorno, Heidegger and Postmodernity. BRUNKHORST, H.

Arendt, Camus, and Postmodern Politics. ISSAC, Jeffrey C.

Aspectos rescatables de la cultura premoderna. MANSILLA, H C F.

Beyond Music Minus Memory?. OLIVIER, G.

Crossing the Boundaries: Educational Thought and Gender Equity. LEACH, Mary and DAVIES, Bronwyn.

The Dangers of Over-Philosophication—Reply to Arcilla and Nicholson. RORTY, Richard.

Derrida's Deconstruction of the Ideal of Legitimation. CUTROFELLO, Andrew.

Distinguishing Modern and Postmodern Theologies. MURPHY, Nancey and MC CLENDON JR, James W.

The End of Aesthetic Theory. NEGRIN, Llewellyn.

Ethics: Modern and Postmodern (in Dutch). DE WACHTER, F.

Feminism, Humanism and Postmodernism. SOPER, Kate.

Feminist Epistemology—An Impossible Project?. HALLBERG, Margareta.

Feminist Literary Criticism and the Author. WALKER, Cheryl.

The Feminist Subject Spinning in the Postmodern Project. KARIEL, Henry S.

From Rhetoric to Corporate Populism: A Romantic Critique of the Academy in an Age of High Gossip. CHRISTENSEN, Jerome.

Het gewicht van de geschiedenis: Over het waardenprobleem in de geschiedwetenschap. LORENZ, Chris.

Hacia una ecología de la razón: Consideraciones sobre la filosofía de la postmodernidad. INNERARITY, Daniel.

Heidegger and the Difficulties of a Postmodern Ethics and Politics. WHITE, Stephen K.

Kierkegaard on Doctrine: A Post-Modern Interpretation. EMMANUEL, Steven M.

Liberalism and Post-Modern Hermeneutics. NEAMAN, Elliot Yale.

Lyotard's Paralogy and Rorty's Pluralism: Their Differences and Pedagogical Implications. FRITZMAN, J M.

Menschenbilder in pädagogiknahen Sozialwissenschaften. HUG, Theo.

Modernidad y postmodernidad. INNERARITY, Daniel.

Narration and Totality. CASCARDI, Anthony J.

Nietzsche, Foucault and the Prospects of Postmodern Political Philosophy. BOTWINICK, Aryeh.

Nobodies Speaking: Subjectivity, Sex, and the Pornography Effect. FINN, Geraldine.

On Reading Postmodern Philosophy: Hiley, Redner and the End of Philosophy. COHEN, Avner.

On the Tragedy of Hermeneutical Experience. BRUNS, Gerald L.

The Origins of Post-Modernism: The Ariosto-Tasso Debate. MC KINNEY, Ronald H.

Oscar Wilde and Poststructuralism. WILLOUGHBY, Guy.

The Paranoia of Postmodernism. BYWATER, William.

Perspectivism and Postmodern Criticism. GILMOUR, John C.

Philosophy and Socio-Political Conversation: A Postmodern Proposal. OLIVIER, G.

Post-Modernism is Not a Scepticism. FUCHS, Wolfgang W.

A Post-Philosophical Politics? An Interview by Danny Postel. RORTY, Richard.

Postmodern Biblicism: The Challenge of René Girard for Contemporary Theology. WALLACE, Mark I.

Postmodern Conditions: Rethinking Public Education. KIZILTAN, Mustafa Ü and BAIN, William J and CANIZARES, Anita.

Postmodern Philosophy?. MADISON, G B.

Private Irony and Public Decency: Richard Rorty's New Pragmatism. MC CARTHY, Thomas.

The Problem of Progress. ROWE, William V.

The Recurring Postmodern: Notes on the Constitution of Musical Artworks. UUSITALO, Jyrki.

Remapping Modernity. COOK, Deborah.

Response to Henry S Kariel's "The Feminist Subject Spinning in the Postmodern Project". NORTON, Anne.

Shelf-Life Zero: A Classic Postmodernist Paper. TRAVERS, Andrew.

Thinking Politics without a Philosophy of History: Arendt and Merleau-Ponty. ROMAN, Joël and MICHELMAN, Stephen (trans).

Thinking with the Weight of the Earth: Feminist Contributions to an Epistemology of Concreteness. HOLLER, Linda.

Timely Meditations. RÉE, Jonathan.

To the Lighthouse and the Feminist Path to Postmodernity. MARTIN, Bill.

Wang Yang-ming and the Bamboos (in Serbo-Croatian). LAI, Whalen.

Weaving Chaos into Order: A Radically Pragmatic Aesthetic. SEIGFRIED, Charlene Haddock.

POSTSTRUCTURALISM

Critical Theory and Poststructuralism: In Search of a Context. POSTER, Mark.

An Introductory Guide to Post-Structuralism and Postmodernism. SARUP, Madan.

Jean Baudrillard: From Marxism to Postmodernism. KELLNER, Douglas.

Post-Structuralist Classics. BENJAMIN, Andrew (ed).

Seductive Reasoning: Pluralism as the Problematic of Contemporary Literary Theory. ROONEY, Ellen.

Stanley Cavell and Literary Skepticism. FISCHER, Michael.

The Thinking Muse: Feminism and Modern French Philosophy. ALLEN, Jeffner (ed).

"Poststructuralist Alternatives to Deconstruction" in *The Textual Sublime: Deconstruction and Its Differences*, VILLANI, Arnaud.

Doublures. SALLIS, John and BARET, Françoise (trans).

The Echo of Narcissus: Anxiety, Language and Reflexivity in "Envois". JOHNSON, Cyraina E.

Humanwissenschaft mit oder ohne Subjekt? oder Zur Kritik der Inentionalität. PRABITZ, Gerald.

Is Post-Structuralist Political Theory Anarchist?. MAY, Todd.

Le plus pur des batards (l'affirmation sans issue). KRELL, David Farrell and BARET, Françoise (trans).

Mémoires gauches. STIEGLER, Bernard.

Oscar Wilde and Poststructuralism. WILLOUGHBY, Guy.

The Situationist International: A Case of Spectacular Neglect. PLANT, Sadie.

POSTURE(S)

Human Posture: The Nature of Inquiry. SCHUMACHER, John A.

POTENCY(-CIES)

Potency, Space and Time: Three Modern Theories. CENTORE, F F.

Remarks Concerning the Doctrine of the Act and Potency. BLANDINO, Giovanni.

POTENTIALITY

Aristotle on Substance: The Paradox of Unity. GILL, Mary Louise.

POTICA, E

La conscience philosophique et la conscience morale chez Eufrosin Poteca (in Romanian). ICHIM, Viorica.

POTTS, S

Rapiers and the Religio Medici. CAREY, Jonathan Sinclair.

POUCHET, F

El Problema del Origen de la Vida. DE ASUA, Miguel J C.

POULET, G

Conscience et forme dans la pensée critique de Georges Poulet. MARTIN, Mircea.

POUND, R

Natural Law Elements in Pound's Philosophy of Law?. MC LEAN, Edward B.

POVERTY

"The Buddhist Outlook on Poverty and Human Rights" in *The Wisdom of Faith: Essays in Honor of Dr Sebastian Alexander Matczak*, PUTUWAR, Bhikkhu Sunanda.

POWER(S)

Abstract Particulars. CAMPBELL, Keith.

Democracy and Dictatorship. BOBBIO, Norberto.

Time, Freedom, and the Common Good: An Essay in Public Philosophy. SHEROVER, Charles M.

Towards a Critique of Foucault. GANE, Mike (ed).

Unruly Practices: Power, Discourse and Gender in Contemporary Social Theory. FRASER, Nancy.

"Does Deconstruction Make Any Difference?" in *The Textual Sublime: Deconstruction and Its Differences*, FISCHER, Michael.

"Hobbes and the Assumption of Power" in *The Causes of Quarrel: Essays on Peace, War, and Thomas Hobbes*, CHURCHILL, R Paul.

"The Infernal Recurrence of the Same: Nietzsche and Foucault on Knowledge and Power" in *Knowledge and Politics*, REDNER, Harry.

Le "Considèrations" di Montesquieu a 250 anni dalla pubblicazione. LOCHE, Annamaria.

'Sustancia', 'naturaleza' y 'Dios' como términos de masa en la filosofía política de Spinoza. MADANES, Leiser.

A ética do poder na *História da sexualidade* de Michel Foucault. VIDEIRA, Antonio A P and PINHEIRO, Ulysses.

POWER(S)

The Body Politic: The Embodiment of Praxis in Foucault and Habermas. LEVIN, David.

Coercion and Exploitation: Self-Transposal and the Moral Life. HAMRICK, William S.

Comments on "On the Ordering of Things: Being and Power in Heidegger and Foucault" by Hubert Dreyfus. BRUZINA, Ron.

An Empowerment Theory of Legal Norms. PAULSON, Stanley L.

Explanatory Grounds: Marx versus Foucault. GOULD, James A.

The Fifteenth Century and Divine Absolute Power. KENNEDY, L A.

Knowledge, Power, Ethics. HIRSCH, Eli.

La légitimité. GOYARD-FABRE, Simone.

Model Completeness and Direct Power. TAGHVA, Kazem.

Nietzsche: Power as Oppression. READ, James H.

On Knowlegde, Power and Michel Foucault. MEYNELL, Hugo.

On the Ordering of Things: Being and Power in Heidegger and Foucault. DREYFUS, Hubert L.

Pardes: l'écriture de la puissance. AGAMBEN, Giorgio.

The Politician and the Philosopher (Some Lessons from Machiavelli). DOLGOV, Konstantin M and JARKOWSKI, Jan (trans).

Potentia et Potestas dans les premiers écrits de B Spinoza. FERNANDEZ, Eugenio.

Potere e ragione nella filosofia politica di Enrico Opocher. ANDREATTA, Alberto.

Power and Resistance. KRIPS, Henry.

The Power Principle: "Inherent Defects" Reconsidered. TOMASI, John.

Power, Authority, and Wisdom. BAMBROUGH, Renford.

Praxeologia della costizuione del potere. CAPOZZI, Gino.

R-Algebras and *R*-Model Structures as Power Constructs. BRINK, Chris.

Rechtsstaalichkeit als Moment demokratischer politischer Machtausübung. WILL, Rosemarie.

The Semiotics of Power: Reading Michel Foucault's *Discipline and Punish*. OPHIR, Adi.

Social Power and Human Agency. KERNOHAN, Andrew.

Totalitarianism, Homogeneity of Power, Depth: Towards a Socio-Political Ontology. STEINBOCK, A J.

Uncountable Theories that are Categorical in a Higher Power. LASKOWSKI, Michael Chris.

Why is There a Problem About Political Obligation?. NIELSEN, Kai.

PRACTICAL

Fagothey's Right and Reason: Ethics in Theory and Practice—Ninth Edition. GONSALVES, Milton A.

From Salomon's House to the Land-Grant College: Practical Arts Education and the Utopian Vision of Progress. WATEROUS, Frank B.

The Meaning of BIOΣ in Aristotle's *Ethics* and *Politics*. KEYT, David.

Measurement, Pleasure, and Practical Science in Plato's *Protagoras*. RICHARDSON, Henry S.

Practical Arguments and Situational Appreciation in Teaching. PENDLEBURY, Shirley.

The Practical Element in Ancient Exact Sciences. KNORR, Wilbur R.

Practical Rationality: Some Kantian Reflections. MC CANN, Hugh J.

Praxeologie als wijsgerig thema. TROOST, A.

PRACTICAL KNOWLEDGE

"Aristotle" in *Ethics in the History of Western Philosophy*, GOMEZ-LOBO, Alfonso.

Practical Knowing: Finnis and Aquinas. SIMPSON, Peter.

PRACTICAL REASON

Constructions of Reason: Explorations of Kant's Practical Philosophy. O'NEILL, Onora.

Constructivism and Science: Essays in Recent German Philosophy. BUTTS, Robert E (ed).

Freedom and the End of Reason: On the Moral Foundation of Kant's Critical Philosophy. VELKLEY, Richard L.

Practical Reasoning. WRIGHT, Larry.

Self and Others: A Study of Ethical Egoism. ÖSTERBERG, Jan.

The Categorical Imperative and Kant's Conception of Practical Rationality. REATH, Andrews.

Courage, Relativism and Practical Reasoning. WALTON, Douglas N.

Criteria for Theories of Practical Rationality: Reflections on Brandt's Theory. POSTOW, B C.

Die Ethik—"der Schlusstein von dem ganzen Gebäude der spekulativen Vernunft". BUHR, Manfred.

A Fact About the Virtues. RAY, A Chadwick.

How to Argue about Practical Reason. WALLACE, R Jay.

Intending and Motivation. MENDOLA, Joseph.

Intending and Motivation: A Rejoinder. MELE, Alfred R.

Interpretive Bioethics: The Way of Discernment. CARSON, Ronald A.

Kant's Theory of Practical Reason. HILL JR, Thomas E.

Motivational Internalism: The Powers and Limits of Practical Reasoning. MELE, Alfred R.

Paternalism and the Rationality of the Child. EKMAN, Rosalind.

Practical Rationality: A Response. BRANDT, R B.

El principio de universalización y la razón práctica (1a parte). GUARIGLIA, Osvaldo.

El principio de universalización y la razón práctica (2a parte). GUARIGLIA, Osvaldo.

Raison pratique et communauté chez Fichte. MOGGACH, Douglas.

Sul problema della valutazione morale: A proposito della "Filosofia pratica" di Guiliano Pontara. JELLAMO, Anna.

Where the Traditional Accounts of Practical Reason Go Wrong. HURLEY, Paul.

Zur Analytizität hypothetischer Imperative. BURRI, Alex and FREUDIGER, Jürg.

PRACTICAL WISDOM

La philosophie pratique d'Aristote et sa "réhabilitation" récente. BERTI, Enrico.

PRACTICE

Conventions and Social Institutions. WEIRICH, Paul.

Praxeologia della costizuione del potere. CAPOZZI, Gino.

PRACTICE(S)

"Introduction" in *Papers on the Ethics of Administration*, WRIGHT, N Dale and MC KONKIE, Stanford S.

Grünbaum and Psychoanalysis. NASH, Margaret.

Perceptual Differences of Sales Practitioners and Students Concerning Ethical Behavior. DE CONINCK, J B and GOOD, D J.

Promises and Practices. SCANLON, Thomas.

PRADINES, M

Comparaison des doctrines de Brunschvicg et de Pradines. FOREST, Aimé.

PRAGMATIC

Interpretare l'esperienza: scienza metafisica etica nella filosofia di Ch S Peirce. CALCATERRA, Rosa.

Hermeneutical Interpretation and Pragmatic Interpretation. DASCAL, Marcelo.

The Model-Theoretic Approach in the Philosophy of Science. DA COSTA, Newton C A and FRENCH, Steven.

Op zoek naar een pragmatisch ethos. HOUTEPEN, Rob.

A Pragmatic Method of Reading Confused Philosophic Texts: The Case of Peirce's "Illustrations". OCHS, Peter.

A Pragmatic Version of Natural Law. WALTER, Edward.

PRAGMATICISM

Interpretare l'esperienza: scienza metafisica etica nella filosofia di Ch S Peirce. CALCATERRA, Rosa.

PRAGMATICS

Why You Should: The Pragmatics of Deontic Speech. FORRESTER, James W.

"The Naturalists" in *Reading Philosophy for the Twenty-First Century*, KURTZ, Paul.

The Pragmatics of What is Said. RECANATI, François.

Semantica, Pragmatica, Atti linguistici: note in margine a una polemica. SBISÀ, Marina.

Some Remarks on What Happened to John Dewey. FISHER, John.

Synonymy in Sentential Languages: A Pragmatic View. TOKARZ, Marek.

De transcendentale grondlegging van de ethiek van Karl-Otto Apel. VAN WOUDENBERG, R.

Transparency and Doubt: Understanding and Interpretation in Pragmatics and in Law. DASCAL, M and WROBLEWSKI, Jerzy.

PRAGMATISM

The American Evasion of Philosophy: A Genealogy of Pragmatism. WEST, Cornel.

Christianity and the Nature of Science: A Philosophical Investigation. MORELAND, James Porter.

William James, Public Philosopher. COTKIN, George.

"The Metaphilosophical Consequences of Pragmatism" in *The Institution of Philosophy: A Discipline in Crisis?*, OKRENT, Mark.

An Account of Peirce's Proof of Pragmatism. MC CARTHY, Jeremiah.

Changes in the Attitude of Chinese Philosophical Circles Towards Pragmatism. XUFANG, Zhan.

The Creativity of Action and the Intersubjectivity of Reason: Mead's Pragmatism and Social Theory. JOAS, Hans.

Democracy and Pragmatism in Curriculum Development. WALKER, J C.

Dialectical Materialism and Logical Pragmatism: On J E McClellan's

PRAGMATISM

"Logical Pragmatism and Dialectical Materialism". PANOVA, Elena.

The Identity of American Neo-Pragmatism; or, Why Vico Now?. MEGILL, Allan.

Justification des normes: transcendantale ou pragmatique?. GRÜNEWALD, Bernward.

Moral and Political Implications of Pragmatism. VAN BRAKEL, J and SAUNDERS, B A C.

Naturalism and Philosophy of Education. EVERS, Colin W.

Nietzsche's Synoptic and Utopian Vision. SCHROEDER, William R.

Peirce's Ultimate Logical Interpretant and Dynamical Object: A Pragmatic Perspective. ROSENTHAL, Sandra B.

A Pragmatic Analysis of Mathematical Realism and Intuitionism. BLAIS, Michel J.

Pragmatic Imagination. ALEXANDER, Thomas M.

Pragmatic Inquiry and Social Conflict: A Critical Reconstruction of Dewey's Model of Democracy. SMILEY, Marion.

Pragmatism and Precedent: A Response to Dworkin. SULLIVAN, Michael.

Pragmatism and the Revolt Against Formalism: Revising Some Doctrines of William James. WHITE, Morton.

Pragmatism and the Theory of the Reader. MC CALLUM, John.

Pragmatism, Heidegger, and the Context of Naturalism. ROSENTHAL, Sandra B.

Private Irony and Public Decency: Richard Rorty's New Pragmatism. MC CARTHY, Thomas.

Rorty and Nietzsche: Some Elective Affinities. SHAW, Daniel.

Rorty's Pragmatism and the Pursuit of Truth. BONTEKOE, Ron.

Santayana's Pragmatism and the Comic Sense of Life. LEVINSON, Henry Samuel.

Truth and Pragmatism in Higher Education. DEVINE, Phillip E.

Varieties of Pragmatism. KRAUT, Robert.

Weaving Chaos into Order: A Radically Pragmatic Aesthetic. SEIGFRIED, Charlene Haddock.

What Is the Legacy of Instrumentalism? Rorty's Interpretation of Dewey. GOUINLOCK, James.

Why Dewey Now?. SHUSTERMAN, Richard.

PRAGMATIST(S)

"The Pragmatists" in Reading Philosophy for the Twenty-First Century, MC DERMOTT, John J.

PRAUSS, G

"El aire es elástico". CAIMI, Mario P M.

PRAXIOLOGY

Logic of Action, Efficacy and Efficiency. POPA, Cornel.

Praxeologie als wijsgerig thema. TROOST, A.

PRAXIS

The Communicative Body: Studies in Communicative Philosophy, Politics, and Sociology. O'NEILL, John.

Ethics and Community. DUSSEL, Enrique D.

The Listening Self: Personal Growth, Social Change and Closure of Metaphysics. LEVIN, David Michael.

"Das Problem Theorie-Praxis in der Peripatos-Rezeption von Ciceros Staatsschrift" in Cicero's Knowledge of the Peripatos, MÜLLER, Reimar.

"Strangers in the Dark: On the Limitations of the Limits of Praxis in the Early Heidegger". SCHMIDT, Dennis J.

The Familiar and the Strange: On the Limits of Praxis in the Early Heidegger. FELL, Joseph P.

Freedom, Plurality, Solidarity: Hannah Arendt's Theory of Action. D'ENTRÈVES, Maurizio Passerin.

Hannah Arendt on Judgment, Philosophy and Praxis. KNAUER, James T.

Kant over Midden, Middel en Doel (I). VAN DER HOEVEN, J.

The Novelty of Marx's Theory of Praxis. MARGOLIS, Joseph.

Poiesis and Praxis in Fundamental Ontology. TAMINIAUX, Jacques.

Praxis and Poesis in Aristotle's Practical Philosophy. BALABAN, Oded.

Teoría y praxis: evolución de estos conceptos. PONFERRADA, Gustavo Eloy.

PREDESTINATION

"Zur Frage der Prädestination in Manichäismus und Christentum" in Agora: Zu Ehren von Rudolph Berlinger, BÖHLIG, Alexander.

Is Molinism as Bad as Calvinism?. WALLS, Jerry L.

Predestination and Freedom in Augustine's Ethics. O'DALY, Gerard.

PREDICABLE(S)

La Lógica aristotélica de los predicables. GAMBRA, Jose Miguel.

PREDICATE LOGIC

Logic for Computer Scientists. SCHÖNING, Uwe.

A Modern Formal Logic Primer, Volume I and II. TELLER, Paul.

An Algebraic Approach to Intuitionistic Modal Logics in Connection with Intermediate Predicate Logics. SUZUKI, Nobu-Yuki.

Confirmation, Paradox, and Logic. ERIKSEN, Leif.

A Content Semantics for Quantified Relevant Logics, I. BRADY, Ross T.

A Content Semantics for Quantified Relevant Logics, II. BRADY, Ross T.

First Order Logic with Empty Structures. AMER, Mohamed A.

A Formal Theory of Objects, Space and Time. BLIZARD, Wayne D.

New Systems of Predicate Deontic Logic. DA COSTA, Newton C A.

On Axiomatizability of Some Intermediate Predicate Logics (Summary). SKVORTSOV, D P.

On Finite Linear Intermediate Predicate Logics. ONO, Hiroakira.

Overlapping Types in Higher Order Predicate Calculus Based on Combinatory Logic. BUNDER, M W.

The Property (HD) in Intermediate Logics: A Partial Solution of a Problem of H Ono. MINARI, Pierluigi.

Quantified Propositional Calculi and Fragments of Bounded Arithmetic. KRAJICEK, Jan and PUDLAK, Pavel.

Relations Between Intuitionistic Modal Logics and Intermediate Predicate Logics. ONO, Hiroakira and SUZUKI, Nobu-Yuki.

PREDICATE(S)

The Nature of Man in Early Stoic Philosophy. REESOR, Margaret E.

'Saturated' and 'Unsaturated': Frege and the Nyāya. SHAW, J L.

Brouwer's Equipotence and Denumerability Predicates. FRANCHELLA, Miriam.

Conceptos y propiedades o Predicación y cópula. STRAWSON, P F.

Los modificadores de predicado y su lógica. OLLER, Carlos A.

Vagueness and Incoherence: A Reply to Burns. SCHWARTZ, Stephen P.

Vagueness Implies Cognitivism. SORENSEN, Roy A.

PREDICATION

Parmenides, Plato, and the Semantics of Not-Being. PELLETIER, Francis Jeffry.

"A Categorial Analysis of Predication: The Moral of Bradley's Regress" in Mind, Value and Culture: Essays in Honor of E M Adams, CLARK, Romane.

Aristotelian Predication, Augustine and the Trinity. RUDEBUSCH, George.

Counterparts, Logic and Metaphysics: Reply to Ramachandran. FORBES, Graeme.

Naming God: Moses Maimonides and Thomas Aquinas. STUBBENS, Neil A.

A Non-Compactness Phenomenon in Logics with Hyperintensional Predication. BONOTTO, Cinzia.

Predication in the Logic of Terms. SOMMERS, Fred.

Relevant Predication: Grammatical Characterizations. KREMER, Philip.

PREDICTION

Philosophical Consequences of Quantum Theory: Reflections on Bell's Theorem. CUSHING, James T (ed).

The Practical Element in Ancient Exact Sciences. KNORR, Wilbur R.

PREFERENCE LOGIC

Defining "Good" and "Bad" in Terms of "Better". HANSSON, Sven Ove.

PREFERENCE(S)

Rationality and Dynamic Choice: Foundational Explorations. MC CLENNEN, Edward F.

Self and Others: A Study of Ethical Egoism. ÖSTERBERG, Jan.

Adequate Representations of Condorcet Profiles. VISSER, Henk.

A Causal Theory of Intending. SHOPE, Robert K.

Democracy Without Preference. ESTLUND, David M.

A Graph-Theoretic Approach to Revealed Preference. WAKKER, Peter.

Liberalism, Distributive Subjectivism, and Equal Opportunity for Welfare. ARNESON, Richard J.

Maximization, stability of Decision, and Actions in Accordance with Reason. SOBEL, Jordan Howard.

A Methodological Assessment of Multiple Utility Frameworks. BRENNAN, Timothy J.

Minimal Representation of a Semiorder. PIRLOT, Marc.

Must Rational Preferences Be Transitive?. PHILIPS, Michael.

Neutral, Stable and Pareto-Optimal Welfare Functions. STORCKEN, A J A.

Preference Derived from Urgency. LINDAHL, Lars.

Preference-Based Deontic Logic (PDL). HANSSON, Sven Ove.

Private and Public Preferences. KURAN, Timur.

The Problems of Preference Based Morality: A Critique of "Morals by Agreement". DE MARCO, Joseph P.

The Puzzle of the Self-Torturer. QUINN, Warren S.

Queries of Psychology in Social Choice Theory. BEZEMBINDER, Th.

Utilitarianism and Preference Change. BARRY, Brian.

What is the Theory of Social Choice About?. DE SWART, H C M.

What Is Utility?. HASLETT, D W.

PROJECTION

Hermes the Interpreter. SAATKAMP JR, Herman J.

Idealization and Projection in the Empirical Sciences: Husserl versus Heidegger. KOCKELMANS, Joseph J.

Quasi-Quasi-Realism. ZANGWILL, Nick.

Reflections on Projections: Changing Conditions in Watching Film. PARKES, Graham.

PROLETARIAT

Working Class and Proletariat—On the Relation of Andries Sternheim to the Frankfurt School. MULDER, Bertus and NAUTA, Lolle.

PROMISE(S)

"Das Versprechen—problemgeschichtliche Aspekte eines rechtsphänomenologischen Paradigmas" in *Agora: Zu Ehren von Rudolph Berlinger*, WILLOWEIT, Dietmar and WILLOWEIT, Hildegard.

Callahan on Harming the Dead. SERAFINI, Anthony.

Can One Promise to Love Another?. WILSON, John.

Promises and Practices. SCANLON, Thomas.

Stair on Natural Law and Promises. MAC CORMACK, Geoffrey.

PRONOMINALIZATION

Modal Subordination and Pronominal Anaphora in Discourse. ROBERTS, Craige.

PRONOUN(S)

Descriptive Pronouns and Donkey Anaphora. NEALE, Stephen.

E-Type Pronouns and Donkey Anaphora. HEIM, Irene.

PROOF THEORY

Generalizations of the Kruskal-Friedman Theorems. GORDEEV, L.

PROOF(S)

Automated Deduction in Nonclassical Logics. WALLEN, Lincoln A.

Informal Logic: A Handbook for Critical Argumentation. WALTON, Douglas N.

Intimations of Divinity. PLATT, David.

An Account of Peirce's Proof of Pragmatism. MC CARTHY, Jeremiah.

Borges' Proof for the Existence of God. JACQUETTE, Dale.

Coherence in Cartesian Closed Categories and the Generality of Proofs. SZABO, M E.

Four Views of Arithmetical Truth. SAYWARD, Charles.

Getting Even: The Role of the Victim. MURPHY, Jeffrie G.

The Machinery of Consistency Proofs. YASUGI, Mariko.

Much Shorter Proofs: A Bimodal Investigation. CARBONE, Alessandra and MONTAGNA, Franco.

Noch einmal: Zur Rolle der Anschauung in formalen Beweisen. BENDER, Peter.

Nonstandard Methods. RICHTER, M M.

Normalization and Excluded Middle, I. SELDIN, Jonathan P.

On an Unsound Proof of the Existence of Possible Worlds. MENZEL, Christopher.

Piety and the Proofs. CLAYTON, John.

La prova a priori dell'esistenza di Dio nel Settecento inglese: da Cudworth a Hume. SCRIBANO, Emanuela.

Reflexive Consistency Proofs and Gödel's Second Theorem. SAGAL, Paul.

Resolution in Constructivism. AKAMA, Seiki.

Rigorous Proof and the History of Mathematics: Comments on Crowe. JESSEPH, Douglas.

Ross and Scotus on the Existence of God. MAYES, G Randolph.

Second Thoughts about Church's Thesis and Mathematical Proofs. MENDELSON, Elliott.

Sur l'unité de l'unique preuve de Dieu. LABBÉ, Yves.

Weak Strategy Proofness: The Case of Nonbinary Social Choice Functions. BANDYOPADHYAY, Taradas.

What Hume Actually Said About Miracles. FOGELIN, Robert J.

PROPER NAME(S)

Why Proper Names are Rigid Designators. PENDLEBURY, Michael.

PROPERTY(-TIES)

Aesthetics and the Good Life. EATON, Marcia Muelder.

A Combinatorial Theory of Possibility. ARMSTRONG, D M.

Informal Lectures on Formal Semantics. BACH, Emmon W.

Mind-Body Identity Theories. MACDONALD, Cynthia.

The Moral Case for the Free Market Economy: A Philosophical Argument. MACHAN, Tibor R.

Political Innovation and Conceptual Change. BALL, Terence.

Property, Power, and Public Choice: An Inquiry into Law and Economics—Second Ed. SCHMID, A Allan.

A Theory of Property. MUNZER, Stephen R.

"The Properties of the Intellect" in *Dialectic and Contemporary Science*, KLEVER, W N A.

"Reply to Klever's "The Properties of the Intellect"" in *Dialectic and Contemporary Science*, HARRIS, Errol E.

Are Physical Properties Dispositions?. AVERILL, Edward Wilson.

Converse Ackermann Property and Semiclassical Negation. MÉNDEZ, José M.

Gesù e la morale (rilettura di un saggio di F Costa). TARTER, Sandro.

The Hard Problem of Management is Freedom, Not the Commons. DI NORCIA, Vincent.

How We Refer to Things. CHISHOLM, Roderick M.

Hume: Justice as Property. BRETT, Nathan.

Kant on Property Rights and the Social Contract. BAYNES, Kenneth.

Monadic Π_1^1-Theories of Π_1^1-Properties. DOETS, Kees.

Negativity and Complexity: Some Logical Considerations. HIRSCH, Eli.

A Note on the Existence Property for Intuitionistic Logic with Function Symbols. DOORMAN, L M.

On Physical Multiple Realization. ENDICOTT, Ronald P.

Partition Properties and Well-Ordered Sequences. JACKSON, Steve.

Program Explanation: A General Perspective. JACKSON, Frank and PETTIT, Philip.

Recenti studi sullo I legel politico. BONACINA, Giovanni.

Resplicing Properties in the Supervenience Base. ODDIE, Graham and TICHY, Pavel.

The Simple Substitution Property of the Intermediate Propositional Logics. SASAKI, Katsumi.

Supervenience and Closure. VAN CLEVE, James.

Supervenience, Essentialism and Aesthetic Properties. CURRIE, Gregory.

PROPHECY

Maimonides on Prophecy and Human Nature: A Problem in Philosophical Interpretation. TRELOAR, John L.

PROPORTIONALITY

Ethics and Strategic Defense: American Philosophers Debate Star Wars and Nuclear Deterrence. LACKEY, Douglas P (ed).

Love, Moral Values and Proportionalism: A Response to Garth Hallett. POPE, Stephen J.

PROPOSITION(S)

see also Sentence(s), Statement(s)

Informal Logic: A Handbook for Critical Argumentation. WALTON, Douglas N.

Questions of Form: Logic and the Analytic Proposition from Kant to Carnap. PROUST, Joëlle.

Speaking from the Depths. FRANKLIN, Stephen T.

"Categorical Propositions in Relevance Logic" in *Directions in Relevant Logic*, BACON, John.

"The Différance of Translation" in *The Textual Sublime: Deconstruction and Its Differences*, ALLISON, David B.

"Propositions and Philosophical Ideas" in *Cause, Mind, and Reality: Essays Honoring C B Martin*, HINTON, J M.

"Real Implication" in *Directions in Relevant Logic*, MYHILL, John.

"Russell's Reasons for Ramification" in *Rereading Russell: Essays on Bertrand Russell's Metaphysics and Epistemology*, GOLDFARB, Warren.

"The Significance of *On Denoting*" in *Rereading Russell: Essays on Bertrand Russell's Metaphysics and Epistemology*, HYLTON, Peter.

"What One Thinks: Singular Propositions and the Content of Judgements" in *Whitehead's Metaphysics of Creativity*, KÜNNE, Wolfgang.

Acquaintance, Knowledge and Description in Russell. BAR-ELLI, Gilead.

Adams on Actualism and Presentism. KVANVIG, Jonathan L.

The Basic Notion of Justification. KVANVIG, Jonathan L and MENZEL, Christopher.

The Co-Reporting Theory of Tensed and Tenseless Sentences. SMITH, Quentin.

Declaratives Are Not Enough. BELNAP JR, Nuel D.

How to Believe the Impossible. BROWN, Curtis.

Logical Atomism in Plato's *Theaetetus*. RYLE, G.

Metaphysics in Education. ALLEN, R T.

The Propositional Objects of Mental Attitudes. DANIELS, Charles B.

Pseudo-Boolean Valued Prolog. FITTING, Melvin.

Purtill on Fatalism and Truth. CRAIG, William Lane.

Quantified Propositional Calculi and Fragments of Bounded Arithmetic. KRAJICEK, Jan and PUDLAK, Pavel.

Reply to Kvanvig: "Adams on Actualism and Presentism". ADAMS, Robert Merrihew.

Semantics of the Grammar. CROSSON, Frederick J.

Sense Experiences and their Contents: A Defence of the Propositional Account. PENDLEBURY, Michael.

The Truth about Neptune and the Seamlessness of Truth. SANFORD, David H.

Whitehead's "Theory" of Propositions. STEINBOCK, Anthony J.

PROPOSITIONAL ATTITUDES

Propositional Attitudes: An Essay on Thoughts and How We Ascribe Them. RICHARD, Mark.

Content, Thoughts and Definite Descriptions—I. MILLICAN, Peter.

Content, Thoughts and Definite Descriptions—II, The Object of Definite Descriptions. OVER, David.

Logical Competence in the Context of Propositional Attitudes. ASTROH, Michael.

PROPOSITIONAL FUNCTION(S)

Beyond the Exclusively Propositional Era. BECHTEL, William and ABRAHAMSEN, Adele A.

PROPOSITIONAL LOGIC

Logic for Computer Scientists. SCHÖNING, Uwe.

Logic: Analyzing and Appraising Arguments. GENSLER, Harry J.

The Possible Universe. TALLET, J A.

Quantum Probability—Quantum Logic. PITOWSKY, Itamar.

Schaum's Outline of Theory and Problems of Logic. NOLT, John Eric.

The Semantic Foundations of Logic, Volume 1: Propositional Logics. EPSTEIN, Richard L.

Absolutely Independent Axiomatizations for Countable Sets in Classical Logic. GRYGIEL, Joanna.

Completeness Proofs for Propositional Logic with Polynomial-Time Connectives. CROSSLEY, J N and SCOTT, P J.

Finite and Finitely Separable Intermediate Propositional Logics. BELLISSIMA, Fabio.

A Finite Model Theorem for the Propositional μ-Calculus. KOZEN, Dexter.

Interpolation in Fragments of Intuitionistic Propositional Logic. RENARDEL DE LAVALETTE, Gerald R.

Leibniz's Complete Propositional Logic. CASTAÑEDA, Hector-Neri.

Mathematics of Totalities: An Alternative to Mathematics of Sets. DISHKANT, Herman.

A Note on Stahl's Opposite System. INOUÉ, Takao.

A Paraconsistent Many-Valued Propositional Logic. D'OTTAVIANO, Itala M L and EPSTEIN, Richard L.

A Simple and General Method of Solving the Finite Axiomatizability Problems for Lambek's Syntactic Calculi. ZIELONKA, Wojciech.

The Simple Substitution Property of the Intermediate Propositional Logics. SASAKI, Katsumi.

Truth-Logics. VON WRIGHT, Georg Henrik.

PROSTITUTION

Prostitution, Exploitation and Taboo. GREEN, Karen.

PROTECTION

Maternal Thinking: Toward a Politics of Peace. RUDDICK, Sara.

The ACLU Philosophy and the Right to Abuse the Unborn. JOHNSON, Phillip E.

Illegal Products and the Question of Consumer Redress. BORNA, Shaheen.

Protecting Fetuses from Prenatal Hazards: Whose Crimes? What Punishment?. NOLAN, Kathleen.

PROTECTIONISM

Aesthetic Protectionism. GODLOVITCH, S.

PROTESTANT

Protestant Reconciliation as a Challenge for Today's Culture. HUMMEL, Gert.

PROTESTANT ETHICS

An Instrument to Measure Adherence to the Protestant Ethic and Contemporary Work Values. WAYNE, F Stanford.

PROTESTANTISM

Paul Tillich: On the Boundary between Protestantism et Marxism. STONE, Ronald H.

PROTOTYPE(S)

Empiricist Versus Prototype Theories of Language Acquisition. STEMMER, Nathan.

PROUST

"Beckett's Schopenhauerien Reading of Proust" in *Schopenhauer: New Essays in Honor of His 200th Birthday*, O'HARA, J D.

PROVABILITY

Characters and Fixed Points in Provability Logic. GLEIT, Zachary and GOLDFARB, Warren.

Much Shorter Proofs: A Bimodal Investigation. CARBONE, Alessandra and MONTAGNA, Franco.

A New Proof of the Fixed-Point Theorem of Provability Logic. REIDHAAR-OLSON, Lisa.

A Note on Stahl's Opposite System. INOUÉ, Takao.

Peano's Smart Children: A Provability Logical Study of Systems with Built-In Consistency. VISSER, Albert.

A Simplification of the Completeness Proofs for Guaspari and Solovay's R.

VOORBRAAK, Frans.

A Theory of Formal Truth Arithmetically Equivalent to ID₁. CANTINI, Andrea.

PROVIDENCE

Le origini dell'ateismo antico (terza parte). ZEPPI, Stelio.

Provvidenza: una proposta di intelligibilità del mondo. BACCARI, Luciano.

PRUDENCE

What Reason Demands. BITTNER, Rüdiger.

Models of Reason, Types of Principles and Reasoning: Historical Comments and Theoretical Outlines. PATTARO, Enrico.

PRZYWARA, E

Erich Przywara on Ultimate Reality and Meaning: *Deus Semper Major* 'God Ever Greater'. ZEITZ, James V.

PSEUDO-DIONYSIUS

"Ähnlichkeit—falscher Schein—Unähnlichkeit von Platon zu Pseudo-Dionysios Areopagitos" in *Agora: Zu Ehren von Rudolph Berlinger*, DE GANDILLAC, Maurice.

PSEUDONYM(S)

Kierkegaard, Godly Deceiver: The Nature and Meaning of His Pseudonymous Writings. HARTSHORNE, M Holmes.

PSYCHIATRY

Philosophy, Psychiatry and Neuroscience: Three Approaches to the Mind. HUNDERT, Edward M.

The Future of Psychiatry. MICHELS, Robert and MARKOWITZ, John C.

Inconscient et savoir de la folie: Freud dans le champ psychiatrique. BERCHERIE, Paul.

The Little Woman Meets Son of DSM-III. RITCHIE, Karen.

Mind-Body and the Future of Psychiatry. WALLACE IV, Edwin R.

Neuropsychology and Meaning in Psychiatry. GILLETT, Grant R.

The New Economics of Medicine: Special Challenges for Psychiatry. MORREIM, E Haavi.

I postulati etici e metodologici fondamentali delle psichiatrie fenomenologiche. FRANCIONI, Mario.

Towards a Rationalization of Biological Psychiatry: A Study in Psychobiological Epistemology. RUDNICK, Abraham.

PSYCHOANALYSIS

The Conflict of Interpretations: Essays in Hermeneutics—Paul Ricoeur. IHDE, Don (ed).

Gender Trouble: Feminism and the Subversion of Identity. BUTLER, Judith.

The Logic of Sense—Gilles Deleuze. DELEUZE, Gilles.

The Perverted Consciousness: Sexuality and Sartre. LEAK, Andrew N.

Primal Scenes: Literature, Philosophy, Psychoanalysis. LUKACHER, Ned.

Thinking Fragments: Psychoanalysis, Feminism, and Postmodernism in the Contemporary West. FLAX, Jane.

Translation and the Nature of Philosophy: A New Theory of Words. BENJAMIN, Andrew.

Le "Pari" de Pascal. BONHOEFFER, Thomas.

Le concept d'analyse généralisée ou de "non-analyse". LARUELLE, François.

Delusions, Irrationality and Cognitive Science. RUST, John.

Feminist Film Aesthetics: A Contextual Approach. SHRAGE, Laurie.

Freud, Mooij en de empiristische boeman. DERKSEN, A A.

Freud-a-til vraiment renié le pouvoir thérapeutique de la psychanalyse?. VACHON, Gérard.

Généalogie ou archéologie de la psychanalyse?. SOULEZ, Philippe.

Grünbaum and Psychoanalysis. NASH, Margaret.

Intersubjectivity and the Monadic Core of the Psyche: Habermas and Castoriadis on the Unconscious. WHITEBOOK, Joel.

Marxism and Psychoanalysis: An Exchange. CRAIB, Ian and KOVEL, Joel.

Marxismus—Subjektwissenschaft—Psychoanalyse. BRAUN, Karl-Heinz.

Materialità del testo e pratica interpretativa: la semanlisi di Julia Kristeva. BRUNO, G.

Object Relations Theory, Buddhism, and the Self: Synthesis of Eastern and Western Approaches. MUZIKA, Edward G.

Psychoanalyse: pseudo-wetenschap of geesteswetenschap?. MOOIJ, A W M.

The Question of the Relation of Philosophy and Psychoanalysis: The Case of Kant and Freud. PETTIGREW, David E.

PSYCHOBIOLOGY

Modularity, and the Psychoevolutionary Theory of Emotion. GRIFFITHS, P E.

Towards a Rationalization of Biological Psychiatry: A Study in Psychobiological Epistemology. RUDNICK, Abraham.

PSYCHOLINGUISTICS

Meaning and Mental Representation. ECO, Umberto (ed).

Reading and the Process of Reading. WINCH, Christopher.

PSYCHOLOGICAL EGOISM

The Reward Event and Motivation. MORILLO, Carolyn R.

What is Psychological Egoism?. SOBER, Elliott.

PSYCHOLOGY

see also Behaviorism, Psychiatry, Psychoanalysis

Artificial Intelligence in Psychology: Interdisciplinary Essays. BODEN, Margaret A.

Critical Theory and Society: A Reader. BRONNER, Stephen Eric (ed).

The Dual Brain, Religion, and the Unconscious. LIDDON, Sim C.

Embodiments of Mind. MC CULLOCH, Warren S.

Historical Roots of Cognitive Science. MEYERING, Theo C.

The Listening Self: Personal Growth, Social Change and Closure of Metaphysics. LEVIN, David Michael.

Mental Content. MC GINN, Colin.

The Mundane Matter of the Mental Language. MALONEY, J Christopher.

Wisdom and Humanness in Psychology: Prospects for a Christian Approach. EVANS, C Stephen.

Wittgenstein's Philosophy of Psychology. BUDD, Malcolm.

"'External' Factors in the Development of Psychology in the West" in Scientific Knowledge Socialized, WILKES, Kathy.

"On Being 'Placed' by John Milbank: A Response" in Christ, Ethics and Tragedy: Essays in Honour of Donald MacKinnon, HAUERWAS, Stanley.

Aristotle and the Functionalist Debate. GRANGER, Herbert.

Beyond Eliminativism. CLARK, Andy.

A Cast of Many: Nietzsche and Depth-Psychological Pluralism. PARKES, Graham.

Cognitiewetenschap zonder functionalisme. MEIJSING, Monica.

Complementarity and the Relation Between Psychological and Neurophysiological Phenomena. SNYDER, Douglas M.

Das Problem der Psychologischen Hinführung zur Bildung der reifen und religiösen Persönlichkeit (in Polish). BAZYLAK, Jozef and BIELECKI, Jan.

The Developmental Self-Valuing Theory: A Practical Approach for Business Ethics. JENSEN, Larry C and WYGANT, Steven A.

Die psychologischen Probleme der Frau vor dem Schwangerschaftsabbruch (in Polish). OSTROWSKA, Krystyna.

Dilthey on Psychology and Epistemology. SCANLON, John.

Disappearance and Knowledge. CLING, Andrew D.

Economics and Psychology: Estranged Bedfellows or Fellow Travellers? A Critical Synthesis. SASSOWER, Raphael.

Eliminative Materialism: The Reality of the Mental, and Folk Psychology—A Reply to O'Gorman. MILLS, Stephen.

The Ethics of Psychoactive Ads. HYMAN, Michael R and TANSEY, Richard.

Het experiment als bron van artefacten. VAN GINNEKEN, Jaap.

Free Will as Psychological Capacity and the Justification of Consequences. SCHOPP, Robert.

Freud's Phylogenetic Fantasy: An Essay Review. PARISI, Thomas.

Getting the Science Right is the Problem, Not the Solution: A Matter of Priority. MIXON, Don.

Gibson's Theory of Direct Perception and the Problem of Cultural Relativism. COSTALL, Alan and STILL, Arthur.

Gibson, Skinner and Perceptual Responses. GUERIN, Bernard.

Gödel, Escher, Bach and Dooyeweerd. VERKERK, M J.

Hay una filosofía de la ciencia en el último Wittgenstein?. MOULINES, C Ulises.

Hebrew Wisdom and Psychotheological Dialogue. GLADSON, Jerry and LUCAS, Ron.

The Impact of Feminist Research: Issues of Legitimacy. WILKINSON, Sue.

In Defence of Folk Psychology. JACKSON, Frank and PETTIT, Philip.

Individuation and Causation in Psychology. BURGE, Tyler.

Intentionality, IntenSionality and Representation. ROSENBERG, Alexander.

Interpretation Psychologized. GOLDMAN, Alvin I.

Is Socialism a Psychological Misunderstanding?. REYKOWSKI, Janusz.

It's Not that Easy Being Grue. MARTIN, Robert M.

Knowledge of the Soul. NELSON, Ralph (trans) and SIMON, Yves.

L'événement freudien: L'objet métapsychologique. ASSOUN, Paul-Laurent.

The Lack of an Overarching Conception in Psychology. SARASON, Seymour B.

Metaphysics. WEININGER, Otto and BURNS, S A M (trans).

Methodological Problems in Empirical Logic. FINOCCHIARO, Maurice A.

The Moon Is Not There When I See It: A Response to Snyder. GARRISON, Mark.

New Representationalism. WRIGHT, Edmond.

Personal Expressiveness: Philosophical and Psychological Foundations. WATERMAN, Alan S.

Personhood and Personal Identity. SCHECHTMAN, Marya.

Philosophical Functionalism. WARD, Andrew.

Plato on Force: Conflict Between his Psychology and Sociology and his Definition of Temperance in the Republic. RICE, Daryl H.

The Pluralistic Approach to the Nature of Feelings. NATSOULAS, Thomas.

Psicologia e scienze della natura in Wilhelm Wundt. CAVALLO, Giuliana.

Psychology in the First Critique. BIRD, G H.

Queries of Psychology in Social Choice Theory. BEZEMBINDER, Th.

Reflections on Hobbes: Recent Work on His Moral and Political Philosophy. CURLEY, Edwin.

Reply to Ward's "Philosophical Functionalism". DOUBLE, Richard.

A Research Strategy for Studying Telic Human Behavior. HOWARD, George S and YOUNGS, William H.

Schopenhauer y la psicología. PINILLOS, José Luis.

Sense Experiences and their Contents: A Defence of the Propositional Account. PENDLEBURY, Michael.

The Status of Content. BOGHOSSIAN, Paul A.

There is No Question of Physicalism. CRANE, Tim.

Thoughts and Their Subject: A Study of Wittgenstein's Tractatus. KANNISTO, Heikki.

The Use of Symbols in Religion from the Perspective of Analytical Psychology. MC GLASHAN, A R.

What is Psychological Egoism?. SOBER, Elliott.

What is Representation? A Reply to Smythe. LLOYD, Dan.

What's Wrong with the Syntactic Theory of Mind. EGAN, M Frances.

PSYCHOMETRY

Psychoeducational Assessment Practices for the Learning Disabled: A Philosophical Analysis. DURAN, Jane.

PSYCHOTHERAPY

An Ethical Issue in the Psychotherapy of Pain and Other Symptoms. MERSKEY, H.

Das Menschenbild in der Psychotherapie. TOMAN, Walter.

The Problem of Psychotherapeutic Effectiveness. BARTLETT, Steven J.

PUBLIC

Public Choice II: A Revised Edition of "Public Choice". MUELLER, Dennis C.

"Ethical Theory and Public Service" in Papers on the Ethics of Administration, BRADY, F Neil.

The Politics of Justification. MACEDO, Stephen.

Private and Public Preferences. KURAN, Timur.

The Public as Sculpture: From Heavenly City to Mass Ornament. NORTH, Michael.

Public Philosophy and Contemporary Pluralism. DOUGLASS, R Bruce.

Public Space in a Private Time. ACCONCI, Vito.

Three Generations of Computerized Systems for Public Administration and Implications for Legal Decision-Making. BING, Jon.

The Violence of Public Art: Do the Right Thing. MITCHELL, W J T.

Wittgenstein and Physicalism. HALLER, Rudolf.

PUBLIC GOOD

Classic Cases in Medical Ethics: Accounts of the Cases That Have Shaped Medical Ethics. PENCE, Gregory E.

Social Contract, Free Ride: A Study of the Public Goods Problem. DE JASAY, Anthony.

"Democracy: The Public Choice Approach" in Politics and Process, MUELLER, Dennis C.

Contractarianism without Foundations. SCHMIDTZ, David.

Market Equality and Social Freedom. HOLLIS, Martin.

Queries of Psychology in Social Choice Theory. BEZEMBINDER, Th.

Richard Holdsworth and the Natural Law: An Early Linguistic Turn. TRENTMAN, J A.

To the Lighthouse. LEVIN, Michael.

What is the Theory of Social Choice About?. DE SWART, H C M.

PUBLIC HEALTH

Private Hospitals in Public Health Systems. HOLM, Soren.

Who Pays for AZT: Commentary. LAMM, Richard D.

Who Pays for AZT?. PENSLAR, Robin Levin.

PUBLIC INTEREST(S)

Political Innovation and Conceptual Change. BALL, Terence.

Bentham on the Public Character of Law. POSTEMA, Gerald J.

Commentary on "The Worm and the Juggernaut". BAYLES, Michael D.

The Expert and the Public: Local Values and National Choice. GOLDSTEIN, Alfred.

The Worm and the Juggernaut: Justice and the Public Interest. LUCAS, J R.

PUBLIC OPINION

Madison's Party Press Essays. SHEEHAN, Colleen A.

Water Quality Concerns and the Public Policy Context. MOORE, Keith M.

PUBLIC POLICY(-CIES)

Democracy and Its Critics. DAHL, Robert A.

Property, Power, and Public Choice: An Inquiry into Law and Economics—Second Ed. SCHMID, A Allan.

Taking Sides: Clashing Views on Controversial Bioethical Issues (Third Edition). LEVINE, Carole (ed).

QUANTIFICATION

Logic: Analyzing and Appraising Arguments. GENSLER, Harry J.

Meaning and Grammar: An Introduction to Semantics. CHIERCHIA, Gennaro.

Systems of Logic. MARTIN, Norman M.

"Quantification, Roles and Domains" in *Meaning and Mental Representation*, FAUCONNIER, Gilles.

'Actually'. TEICHMANN, Roger.

Negation and Quantification in Aristotle. WEDIN, Michael V.

On Ockham's Supposition Theory and Karger's Rule of Inference. MARKOSIAN, Ned.

Quantified Modal Logic and the Plural *De Re*. BRICKER, Phillip.

Storia della cultura e storia sociale. VILLANI, Pasquale.

Tractatus 6.2-6.22. HUGLY, Philip and SAYWARD, Charles.

QUANTIFIER(S)

A Cut-Free Calculus for Dummett's LC Quantified. CORSI, Giovanna.

The Nonaxiomatizability of $L(Q_{\aleph_1}^2)$ By Finitely Many Schemata. SHELAH, Saharon and STEINHORN, Charles.

A Proofless Proof of the Barwise Compactness Theorem. HOWARD, Mark.

Quantifier Elimination in Separably Closed Fields of Finite Imperfectness Degree. HARAN, Dan.

Quantifiers Determined by Partial Orderings. KRYNICKI, Michal.

A Representation Theorem for Languages with Generalized Quantifiers Through Back-and-Forth Methods. PEDROSA, Renato H L and SETTE, Antonio M A.

Theory Discovery from Data with Mixed Quantifiers. KELLY, Kevin T and GLYMOUR, Clark.

Ways of Branching Quantifiers. SHER, Gila.

QUANTITATIVE

The Normal and the Pathological. CANGUILHEM, Georges.

Disciplining Qualitative Decision Exercises: Aspects of a Transempirical Protocol, I. SUTHERLAND, John W.

The Language Dependence of Accuracy. BARNES, Eric.

QUANTITY(-TIES)

The Critique of Thought: A Re-Examination of Hegel's Science of Logic. JOHNSON, Paul Owen.

QUANTUM LOGIC

Quantum Probability—Quantum Logic. PITOWSKY, Itamar.

Quantum Logics and Hilbert Spaces. GIUNTINI, Roberto.

QUANTUM MECHANICS

The Philosophy of Quantum Mechanics: An Interactive Interpretation. HEALEY, Richard.

Quantum Probability—Quantum Logic. PITOWSKY, Itamar.

"Bell's Theorem, Ideology, and Structural Explanation" in *Philosophical Consequences of Quantum Theory: Reflections on Bell's Theorem*, HUGHES, R I G.

"Bohr on Bell" in *Philosophical Consequences of Quantum Theory: Reflections on Bell's Theorem*, FOLSE JR, Henry J.

"Can You Help Your Team Tonight by Watching on TV? More Experimental Metaphysics from Einstein, Podolsky, and Rosen" in *Philosophical Consequences of Quantum Theory: Reflections on Bell's Theorem*, MERMIN, N David.

"Do Correlations Need to be Explained?" in *Philosophical Consequences of Quantum Theory: Reflections on Bell's Theorem*, FINE, Arthur.

"Holism, Separability, and the Metaphysical Implications of the Bell Experiments" in *Philosophical Consequences of Quantum Theory: Reflections on Bell's Theorem*, HOWARD, Don.

"Nonfactorizability, Stochastic Causality, and Passion-at-a-Distance" in *Philosophical Consequences of Quantum Theory: Reflections on Bell's Theorem*, REDHEAD, Michael L G.

"Relativity, Relational Holism, and the Bell Inequalities" in *Philosophical Consequences of Quantum Theory: Reflections on Bell's Theorem*, TELLER, Paul.

"Search for a Worldview Which Can Accommodate Our Knowledge of Microphysics" in *Philosophical Consequences of Quantum Theory: Reflections on Bell's Theorem*, SHIMONY, Abner.

"A Space-Time Approach to the Bell Inequality" in *Philosophical Consequences of Quantum Theory: Reflections on Bell's Theorem*, BUTTERFIELD, Jeremy.

"The Way the World Isn't: What the Bell Theorems Force Us to Give Up" in *Philosophical Consequences of Quantum Theory: Reflections on Bell's Theorem*, WESSELS, Linda.

Idealism and Quantum Mechanics. MOHANTY, J N.

The Idealistic Implications of Bell's Theorem. SCHICK JR, Theodore W.

Mādhyamika Buddhism and Quantum Mechanics: Beginning a Dialogue.

MANSFIELD, Victor.

Mediciones ideales en la mecánica cuántica. MARTÍNEZ, Sergio.

A Natural Explanation of the Existence and Laws of Our Universe. SMITH, Quentin.

Quantales and (Noncommutative) Linear Logic. YETTER, David N.

Quantum Logics and Hilbert Spaces. GIUNTINI, Roberto.

Quantum Measurement and the Program for the Unity of Science. SCHARF, David C.

Quantum Realism. FENNER, David E W.

Struggling with Causality: Schrödinger's Case. BEN-MENAHEM, Yemima.

QUANTUM PHYSICS

Beyond the Atom: The Philosophical Thought of Wolfgang Pauli. LAURIKAINEN, K V.

Nature's Capacities and their Measurement. CARTWRIGHT, Nancy.

Consciousness in Quantum Physics and The Mind-Body Problem. GOSWAMI, Amit.

Identity and Individuality in Classical and Quantum Physics. FRENCH, Steven.

QUANTUM THEORY

Mind, Brain and the Quantum: The Compound 'I'. LOCKWOOD, Michael.

Philosophical Consequences of Quantum Theory: Reflections on Bell's Theorem. CUSHING, James T (ed).

"A Background Essay" in *Philosophical Consequences of Quantum Theory: Reflections on Bell's Theorem*, CUSHING, James T.

"Bell's Theorem: A Guide to the Implications" in *Philosophical Consequences of Quantum Theory: Reflections on Bell's Theorem*, JARRETT, Jon P.

"The Explanation of Distant Action: Historical Notes" in *Philosophical Consequences of Quantum Theory: Reflections on Bell's Theorem*, MC MULLIN, Ernan.

Accardi on Quantum Theory and the "Fifth Axiom" of Probability. VAN DEN BERG, Hans and HOEKZEMA, Dick and RADDER, Hans.

Bohr, Einstein and Realism. DANIEL, Wojciech.

Compatibilidad cuántica desde una perspectiva lógica. PEREZ LARAUDOGOITIA, J.

A Modern Look at the Origin of the Universe. ODENWALD, Sten F.

The Objectivity of Quantum Probabilities. KRIPS, H.

The Pseudo-Problem of Creation in Physical Cosmology. GRÜNBAUM, Adolf.

Quantum Paradoxes and New Realism. FENNER, David E.

Toward a Sound Perspective on Modern Physics: Capra's Popularization of Mysticism and Theological Approaches. CLIFTON, Robert K and REGEHR, Marilyn G.

QUESTION(S)

Of Spirit: Heidegger and the Question. DERRIDA, Jacques.

Collingwood's Logic of Question and Answer. SOMERVILLE, James.

Domanda e definizione nella filosofia di Heidegger: Motivi E riflessioni tratti da "Was ist das-die Philosophie?". ZINGARI, Guido.

Harvey Sacks—Lectures 1964-1965. JEFFERSON, Gail (ed).

La rationalité interrogative (in Romanian). GRECU, Constantin.

Presuppositional Completeness. BUSZKOWSKI, Wojciech.

What is a Question?. COHEN, Felix S.

QUESTIONING

Heidegger als fragender Denker und als Denker der Frage. HAEFFNER, Gerd.

QUINE

Fact and Meaning. HEAL, Jane.

Necessity, Essence, and Individuation: A Defense of Conventionalism. SIDELLE, Alan.

Rationality and Relativity: The Quest for Objective Knowledge. O'GORMAN, Francis.

Thought and Language. MORAVCSIK, J M.

Truth and Objectivity. ELLIS, Brian.

Who Knows: From Quine to a Feminist Empiricism. NELSON, Lynn Hankinson.

"Epistemology Naturalized vs Epistemology Socialized" in *Scientific Knowledge Socialized*, FEHÉR, Márta.

"A Puzzle About Ontological Commitment" in *Cause, Mind, and Reality: Essays Honoring C B Martin*, JACKSON, Frank.

"Radical Philosophy and Radical History" in *The Institution of Philosophy: A Discipline in Crisis?*, MARGOLIS, Joseph.

Analyticity, Indeterminacy and Semantic Theory: Some Comments on "The Domino Theory". GREENWOOD, John D.

Counterfactuals for Free. CREATH, Richard.

The Domino Theory. KATZ, Jerrold J.

È Plausibile l'epistemologia naturalizzata di Quine?. ARTUSO, Paolo.

RATIONALISM

see also Reason

Husserl's Phenomenology and the Foundations of Natural Science. HARVEY, Charles W.

Man and Nature in the Philosophical Thought of Wang-Fu-Chih. BLACK, Alison Harley.

The Metaphysics of Epistemology: Lectures by Wilfrid Sellars. AMARAL, Pedro (ed).

Return to Reason: Critique of Enlightenment Evidentialism and a Defense of Reason and Belief in God. CLARK, Kelly James.

"Historicism and Rationalism" in *Scientific Knowledge Socialized,* KELEMEN, Jänos.

"Incommensurability, Scientific Realism and Rationalism" in *Scientific Knowledge Socialized,* PORUS, N L.

"Rationalism, Supernaturalism, and the Sociology of Knowledge" in *Scientific Knowledge Socialized,* BLOOR, David.

"Whitehead and the Dichotomy of Rationalism and Empiricism" in *Whitehead's Metaphysics of Creativity,* LECLERC, Ivor.

Bradley e Spinoza. L'iper-spinozismo di F H Bradley (seconda parte). DEREGIBUS, Arturo.

James's Religious Hypothesis Reinterpreted. JONES, Royce.

Leibniz und Ortega y Gasset. DE SALAS ORTUETA, Jaime.

Materialist Dialectic and Critique of Philosophical Irrationalism (in Czechoslovakian). JANKOV, M.

An Objection to Kantian Ethical Rationalism. TERZIS, George N.

Quelques considérations sur la signification de l'agnosticisme Kantien (in Romanian). RAMBU, Nicolae.

Racionalismo ético kantiano y amor puro. BULNES, Maria Elton.

Le rationalisme et l'analyse linguistique. AUROUX, Sylvain.

Reading Probabilismo. JEFFREY, Richard.

The Rejection of Ethical Rationalism. KAPUR, Neera Badhwar.

RATIONALITY

David Hume's Argument Against Miracles: A Critical Analysis. BECKWITH, Francis.

Dismantling Truth: Reality in the Post-Modern World. LAWSON, Hilary (ed).

Eguaglianza interesse unanimità: La politica di Rousseau. BURGIO, Alberto.

Ethics and Strategic Defense: American Philosophers Debate Star Wars and Nuclear Deterrence. LACKEY, Douglas P (ed).

God and the Burden of Proof: Plantinga, Swinburne, and the Analytic Defense of Theism. PARSONS, Keith M.

The Good Life: Personal and Public Choices. LOUZECKY, David.

Laws and Symmetry. VAN FRAASSEN, Bas C.

The Meaning of General Theoretical Sociology: Tradition and Formalization. FARARO, Thomas J.

Moral Absolutes: An Essay on the Nature and Rationale of Morality. RESCHER, Nicholas.

Paul and the Popular Philosophers. MALHERBE, Abraham J.

Philosophical Works. KALOYEROPOULOS, N A.

The Rational and the Social. BROWN, James Robert.

Rational Sex Ethics (Second Edition). ARD, Ben Neal.

Rationality and Dynamic Choice: Foundational Explorations. MC CLENNEN, Edward F.

Rationality and Relativity: The Quest for Objective Knowledge. O'GORMAN, Francis.

Self and Others: A Study of Ethical Egoism. ÖSTERBERG, Jan.

A Useful Inheritance: Evolutionary Aspects of the Theory of Knowledge. RESCHER, Nicholas.

Virtue and Self-Knowledge. JACOBS, Jonathan A.

Wise Choices, Apt Feelings: A Theory of Normative Judgment. GIBBARD, Allan.

"Aesthetic discursivity" in *Cultural Hermeneutics of Modern Art: Essays in Honor of Jan Aler,* WILLEMS, Eldert.

"Conceptions of Human Action and the Justification of Value Claims" in *Inquiries into Values: The Inaugural Session of the International Society for Value Inquiry,* BOULTING, Noel E.

"Hobbes and the Problem of Rationality" in *Hobbes: War Among Nations,* BOULTING, Noel E.

"On Seeking a Change of Environment" in *Nature in Asian Tradition of Thought: Essays in Environmental Philosophy,* HALL, David L.

"The Rationality of Pleasure-Seeking Animals" in *Inquiries into Values: The Inaugural Session of the International Society for Value Inquiry,* GOLDSTEIN, Irwin.

"Rationality, Truth and the New Fuzzies" in *Dismantling Truth: Reality in the Post-Modern World,* NEWTON-SMITH, W H.

"Relativism, Rationality, and Repression" in *Inquiries into Values: The Inaugural Session of the International Society for Value Inquiry,* JACOBS, Jonathan.

"Towards Evaluating Theories of Practical Rationality" in *Inquiries into Values: The Inaugural Session of the International Society for Value Inquiry,* POSTOW, Betsy C.

Adorno, Heidegger and Postmodernity. BRUNKHORST, H.

Alasdair MacIntyre on the Good Life and the 'Narrative Model'. BRADLEY, James.

Application on the Relevance of AI Assumptions for Social Practitioners. MURPHY, John.

Are Theories of Rationality Empirically Testable?. SMOKLER, Howard.

Aristóteles en *El Nombre de la Rosa.* GIRALT, María de los Angeles.

Bold Hypotheses: The Bolder the Better?. CLEVELAND, Timothy and SAGAL, Paul T.

Conservatism, Radicalism and Democratic Practice. SIMPSON, Evan.

Could There Be a Rationally Grounded Morality?. BOND, E J.

Criteria for Theories of Practical Rationality: Reflections on Brandt's Theory. POSTOW, B C.

Critical Rationalism: The Problem of Method in Social Sciences and Law. ALBERT, Hans.

Il dibattito sulla razionalità oggi: un ritorno a Kant? Interviste a K O Apel & J Petitot. QUARANTA, M.

The Endorsements of Interpretation. DOEPKE, Frederick.

Evolution, Rationality, and Testability. FETZER, James H.

Experience, Proper Basicality and Belief in God. PARGETTER, Robert.

Faith and Rationality. BARRETT, D C.

Figures de la rationalité dans le marxisme contemporain. MELLOS, Koula.

La filosofia del Novecento: dalla razionalità all'irrazionalità. DEL VECCHIO, Dante.

Fumerton's Puzzle. FOLEY, Richard.

Gauthier's Ethics and Extra-Rational Values: A Comment on DeMarco. CURTIS, Robert A.

How Evolutionary Biology Challenges the Classical Theory of Rational Choice. COOPER, W S.

Humanwissenschaft mit oder ohne Subjekt? oder Zur Kritik der Inentionalität. PRABITZ, Gerald.

Hume's *Tu Quoque:* Newtonianism and the Rationality of the Causal Principle. HAYNES, Michael.

The Import of the Problem of Rationality. AGASSI, Joseph.

Incommensurability, Intratextuality, and Fideism. TILLEY, Terrence W.

Just the Facts Ma'am: Informal Logic, Gender and Pedagogy. ORR, Deborah.

Justificación epistémica. LEGRIS, Javier.

Kant's Conception of Rational Action. BASU, Tora.

Kent Bach on Good Arguments. SOBEL, Jordan Howard.

Logic, Rationality and Counseling. COHEN, Elliot D.

Maximization, stability of Decision, and Actions in Accordance with Reason. SOBEL, Jordan Howard.

The Mechanics of Rationality. LEON, Mark.

Merleau-Ponty on Ultimate Problems of Rationality. VAN DER VEKEN, Jan.

Metamorphosis of the Undecidable. JANICAUD, Dominique.

A Methodological Assessment of Multiple Utility Frameworks. BRENNAN, Timothy J.

Models of Rationality. VAN STRAATEN, Zak.

Moves and Motives in the Games We Play. HOLLIS, Martin.

De nieuwe zekerheden van het hedendaags wetenschapsonderzoek. AMSTERDAMSKA, Olga and HAGENDIJK, R.

On Newton-Smith's Concept of Verisimilitude. OLCZYK, Slawoj.

On the Legitimacy of Law: A Conceptual Point of View. AARNIO, Aulis.

Philosophy of Science Naturalized? Some Problems with Giere's Naturalism. SIEGEL, Harvey.

Practical Rationality: A Response. BRANDT, R B.

Practical Rationality: Some Kantian Reflections. MC CANN, Hugh J.

El problema del "alma mala" en la última filosofia de Platón (*Leyes* X, 896d ss). CARONE, Gabriela Roxana.

Racism and Rationality: *The Need for a New Critique.* GOLDBERG, David Theo.

Rational Common Ground in the Sociology of Knowledge. KATZ, Jonathan.

The Rational Woman. SIMONS, Martin.

Rationality and Artistry in Teaching. BEYER, Landon E.

Rationality in Conversation and Neutrality in Politics. DEN HARTOGH, Govert.

The Rationality of Emotions and of Emotional Behaviour. MC CULLAGH, C Behan.

The Rationality of Rationality: Why Think Critically? Response to Siegel. ENNIS, Robert H.

Rationality, Coordination, and Convention. GILBERT, Margaret.

Rationality, Human Nature, and Lists. GERT, Bernard.

Rationality, Reasonableness and Morality. PASKE, Gerald H.

Rationality, Self-Esteem and Autonomy through Collaborative Enquiry. LANE,

REALISM

"Realism and Realization in a Kantian Light" in *Reading Kant*, BUCHDAHL, Gerd.

"Realism in the Social Sciences" in *Dismantling Truth: Reality in the Post-Modern World*, RUBEN, David.

"Why is a Philosopher?" in *The Institution of Philosophy: A Discipline in Crisis?*, PUTNAM, Hilary.

The Absolute Network Theory of Language and Traditional Epistemology. PHILIPSE, Herman.

Aesthetic Versus Moral Evaluations. GOLDMAN, Alan H.

After Experiment: Realism and Research. HEELAN, Patrick A.

Antirealism and Holes in the World. HAND, Michael.

Atomic Realism, Intuitionist Logic and Tarskian Truth. EDWARDS, Jim.

The Autonomy of Mathematics. STEINER, Mark.

Bivalenza e trascendenza. COZZO, Cesare.

Bohr, Einstein and Realism. DANIEL, Wojciech.

Causal Hermits. ROGERSON, Kenneth F.

Causation and Perception in Reid. PAPPAS, George S.

Chalmers on Unrepresentative Realism and Objectivism. SIEVERS, K H.

The Constitutional Process and the Higher Law. SHANKER, George.

Critical Realism?. FAY, Brian.

Dennett's Little Grains of Salt. MC CULLOCH, Gregory.

Desire's Desire for Moral Realism: A Phenomenological Objection to Non-Cognitivism. NELSON, James Lindemann.

A Dilemma for Internal Realism. MOSER, Paul K.

Einstein: el ideal de una ciencia sin sujeto. RIOJA, Ana.

Erkenntnistheorietischer Konstruktionismus, Minimalrealismus, empirischer Realismus. ENGELS, Eve-Marie.

Evolutionäre Erkenntnistheorie und erkenntnistheoretischer Realismus. WENDEL, Hans Jürgen.

Extragalactic Reality: The Case of Gravitational Lensing. HACKING, Ian.

From Extroverted Realism to Correspondence: A Modest Proposal. BIGELOW, John and PARGETTER, Robert.

From Kierkegaard to Cupitt: Subjectivity, the Body and Eternal Life. PATTISON, George.

Goodman's "New Riddle"—A Realist's Reprise. ELDER, Crawford L.

Heidegger and Peirce: Beyond "Realism or Idealism". BOURGEOIS, Patrick L and ROSENTHAL, Sandra B.

How to be Realistic About Inconsistency in Science. BROWN, Bryson.

Idealism and Quantum Mechanics. MOHANTY, J N.

Immanent Truth. RESNIK, Michael D.

The Inconsistency of Putnam's Internal Realism. POLAKOW, Avron.

Interpretation and Its Art Objects: Two Views. KRAUSZ, Michael.

Intuitionism as Generalization. RICHMAN, Fred.

Eine kleine Überraschung für Gehirne im Tank: Eine skeptische Notiz zu einem antiskeptischen Argument. METSCHL, Ulrich.

Maiocchi on Duhem, Howard on Duhem and Einstein: Historiographical Comments. BURIAN, Richard M.

Manifesting Realism. BLACKBURN, Simon.

Merleau-Ponty: una crítica a la teoría realista de la percepción. GARCIA, Pablo Sebastian.

Methodological Realism: An Essential Requirement of Scientific Quest. SAH, Hirendra Prasad.

Misconstruals Made Manifest: A Response to Simon Blackburn. WRIGHT, Crispin.

The Moral Atmosphere: Language and Value in Davidson. MARTIN, Bill.

New Representationalism. WRIGHT, Edmond.

NOA's Ark—Fine for Realism. MUSGRAVE, Alan.

Normative Realism, or Bernard Williams and Ethics at the Limit. MENDOLA, Joseph.

Het objectieve waarheidsbegrip in Waarder. KUIPERS, Theo A F.

Objective Value and Subjective States. MENDOLA, Joseph.

Objective Value, Realism, and the End of Metaphysics. POST, John F.

Observation, Instrumentalism, and Constructive Empiricism. GRAYBOSCH, Anthony.

Over de verhouding van conceptueel relatief en referentieel realisme. RADDER, Hans.

A Peircean Response to the Realist-Empiricist Debate. FRENCH, Steven.

Phänomenale Realität und naturalistische Philosophie. POHLENZ, Gerd.

Physicalism, Realism and Education: A Functionalist Approach. RAINER, Valina.

A Pragmatic Analysis of Mathematical Realism and Intuitionism. BLAIS, Michel J.

The Primacy of Narrative in Historical Understanding. JACQUES, T Carlos.

Prospective Realism. BROWN, Harold I.

Quantum Realism. FENNER, David E W.

Quasi-Quasi-Realism. ZANGWILL, Nick.

Reale e complesso: osservazioni sul realismo scientifico e la storia della scienza. STOMEO, A.

Realism and Reality: Some Realistic Reconsiderations. ISAAC, Jeffrey C.

Realism and Redistribution. NARDIN, Terry.

Realism and Structurism in Historical Theory: A Discussion of the Thought of Maurice Mandelbaum. LLOYD, Christopher.

Realism and the Underdetermination of Theory. CLENDINNEN, F John.

Realism in the Practice of Accounting Ethics. COTTELL JR, Philip G.

The Realism that Duhem Rejected in Copernicus. GODDU, André.

Realism versus Antirealism: The Venue of the Linguistic Consensus. POLS, Edward.

Realism, Naturalism and Culturally Generated Kinds. ELDER, Crawford L.

Realism, Reference and Theory. HARRÉ, Rom.

Realismo crítico y conocimiento en Carlos Popper. DARÓS, W R.

Realismo II: Donald Davidson. VILLANUEVA, Enrique.

Il realismo nella filosofia della scienza contemporanea. SANGUINETI, Juan José.

Realismus heute. INEICHEN, Hans.

Reducing Legal Realism to Natural Law. MILLER, Myron M.

Reference and Critical Realism. DURRANT, Michael.

Rondom realisme. RADDER, Hans.

The Status of Content. BOGHOSSIAN, Paul A.

Talking Lions and Lion Talk: Davidson on Conceptual Schemes. CRUMLEY, Jack S.

Totality, Realism, and the Type: Lukács' Later Literary Criticism as Political Theory. SHAW, Brian J.

Towards a Real Phenomenology of Logic. PERUZZI, Alberto.

Truthmongering: An Exercise. KNEZEVICH, Lily.

Truthmongering: Less is True. FINE, Arthur.

Two Concepts of the Given in C I Lewis: Realism and Foundationalism. GOWANS, Christopher W.

What is Psychological Egoism?. SOBER, Elliott.

Wittgenstein, Realism, and CLS: Undermining Rule Scepticism. LANDERS, Scott.

Zu Problemen der revolutionären Theologie Thomas Müntzers. KOLESNYK, Alexander.

REALITY

see also Being, Existence, Ontology

Basic Moral Concepts. SPAEMANN, Robert.

Beyond the Atom: The Philosophical Thought of Wolfgang Pauli. LAURIKAINEN, K V.

Cause, Mind, and Reality: Essays Honoring C B Martin. HEIL, John (ed).

Conceptual Relevance. GRÜNFELD, Joseph.

Connections to the World: The Basic Concepts of Philosophy. DANTO, Arthur C.

Conscience and the Reality of God: An Essay on the Experiential Foundations of Religious Knowledge. STATEN, John C.

Dietro il paesaggio: Saggio su Simmel. BOELLA, Laura.

Dismantling Truth: Reality in the Post-Modern World. LAWSON, Hilary (ed).

Limits of Philosophy: (Limits of Reality?). VERSTER, Ulrich.

Margins of Reality: The Role of Consciousness in the Physical World. JAHN, Robert G.

The Metaphysics of Epistemology: Lectures by Wilfrid Sellars. AMARAL, Pedro (ed).

The Nature of Existence, Volume I. MC TAGGART, John McTaggart Ellis.

Philosophical Problems (Consciousness, Reality and I). VERSTER, Ulrich.

"Clothing the Naked Truth" in *Dismantling Truth: Reality in the Post-Modern World*, LATOUR, Bruno.

"Touching Truth" in *Dismantling Truth: Reality in the Post-Modern World*, GREGORY, Richard L.

"Degrés de réalite" et "degrés de perfection" dans les *Principes de la philosophie de Descartes* de Spinoza. RAMOND, Charles.

El acceso del hombre a la realidad según Xavier Zubiri. SIMONPIETRI MONEFELDT, Fannie A.

Erich Przywara on Ultimate Reality and Meaning: *Deus Semper Major* 'God Ever Greater'. ZEITZ, James V.

Etica e realtà. SANCIPRIANO, Mario.

Existence and Reality: The Case for Pseudo-Objects. JOBE, Evan K.

Filosofia dell'educazione e filosofia morale. DUCCI, Edda.

Logical Form. MAURY, André.

Mathematical Necessity and Reality. FRANKLIN, James.

Objective Reality of Ideas in Descartes, Caterus, and Suárez. WELLS, Norman J.

On the Continuing Relevance of Whitehead. CODE, Murray.

On the Development of Knowledge. VOISVILO, E K.

Political Thought and Rhetoric in Vico. JACOBITTI, Edmund E.

Potentia et Potestas dans les premiers écrits de B Spinoza. FERNANDEZ,

REASONS

A Critique of Philosophical Conversation. WALZER, Michael.
Desires as Reasons—Discussion Notes on Fred Dretske's "Explaining Behavior: Reasons in a World of Causes". STAMPE, Dennis W.
Do Motives Matter?. GOODIN, Robert E.
In Defense of Good Reasons. BERKSON, William.
Legal Reasoning as a Special Case of Moral Reasoning. PECZENIK, Aleksander.
Methodology Is Pragmatic: A Reponse to Miller. BERKSON, William.
Moral Reasons in Confucian Ethics. SHUN, Kwong-Loi.
On Taking the Rabbit of Rule-Following out of the Hat of Representation: Response to 'The Reality of Rule-Following'. SUMMERFIELD, Donna M.
Raz and Legal Positivism. DARE, Tim.
Reasons and Reason. ROTENSTREICH, Nathan.
Reasons, Values, and Rational Action. MOSER, Paul K.
Rejoinder to Berkson's "In Defense of Good Reasons". MILLER, David.
Sources of Value. BARDEN, Garrett.
System and Training in Descartes' *Meditations*. BEYSSADE, Michelle.

RECIPROCITY

Alternative Interpretations of Aristotle on Exchange and Reciprocity. MC NEILL, Desmond.
Justice as Reciprocity versus Subject-Centered Justice. BUCHANAN, Allen.
What Children Owe Parents: Ethics in an Aging Society. POST, Stephen G.

RECOGNITION

Hart's Rule of Recognition and the United States. GREENAWALT, Kent.
Rousseau and Recognition. SHAVER, Robert.

RECONCILIATION

Hegel and the Speech of Reconcilation. STOLL, Donald.
Protestant Reconciliation as a Challenge for Today's Culture. HUMMEL, Gert.

RECONSTRUCTION

Faith on Earth: An Inquiry into the Structure of Human Faith. NIEBUHR, Richard R (ed).
Moral Consciousness and Communicative Action. HABERMAS, Jürgen.
The Evolutionary Risks of Democracy. ZOLO, Danilo.
On Historical Reconstruction of Mathematics. GABRIELIAN, O A.
Speech Act Conditions as Tools for Reconstructing Argumentative Discourse. VAN EEMEREN, Frans H and GROOTENDORST, Rob.
Suppositions in Argumentation. FISHER, Alec.

RECREATION

Sensibility and Recreational Appreciation. O'CALLAGHAN, Timothy M B.

RECURRENCE

Nietzsche's Philosophy of Nature and Cosmology. MOLES, Alistair.
Genealogies as the Language of Time: A Structural Approach—Anthropological Implications. FROUSSART, Bernard.
A Response to A A Long's "The Stoics on World-Conflagration and Everlasting Recurrence". HUDSON, Hud.
Ways Leading to Bergson's Notion of "Perpetual Present". KEBEDE, Messay.
Ways Leading to Bergson's Notion of the "Perpetual Present". KEBEDE, Messay.

RECURSION THEORY

Finite Condensations of Recursive Linear Orders. ROY, Dev K and WATNICK, Richard.
The Formal Language of Recursion. MOSCHOVAKIS, Yiannis N.
An Introduction to γ-Recursion Theory (Or What to Do in KP-Foundation). LUBARSKY, Robert S.
On the Complexity of Finding the Chromatic Number of a Recursive Graph I: The Bounded Case. BEIGEL, Richard and GASARCH, W I.
On the Complexity of Finding the Chromatic Number of a Recursive Graph II: The Unbounded Case. BEIGEL, R and GASARCH, W I.
Pairs of Recursive Structures. ASH, C J and KNIGHT, J F.
Turing *L*-Machines and Recursive Computability for *L*-Maps. GERLA, Giangiacomo.

RECURSIVE FUNCTION(S)

Arithmetic Based on the Church Numerals in Illative Combinatory Logic. BUNDER, M W.
Every Recursive Linear Ordering has a Copy in DTIME-SPACE(n,log(n)). GRIGORIEFF, Serge.
The Formal Language of Recursion. MOSCHOVAKIS, Yiannis N.
Injecting Inconsistencies Into Models of PA. SOLOVAY, Robert M.
On Infinite Series of Infinite Isols. BARBACK, Joseph.
On Splitting of a Recursive Set with Polynomial Time Minimal Pairs. ZHIXIANG, Chen.
Some Notes on Church's Thesis and the Theory of Games. ANDERLINI, Luca.

Some Restrictions on Simple Fixed Points of the Integers. MC COLM, Gregory L.

RECURSIVELY ENUMERABLE SETS

A Contiguous Nonbranching Degree. DOWNEY, Rod.
Diophantine Induction. KAYE, R.
Hyperhypersimple Sets and Δ_2 Systems. CHONG, C T.
Intervals and Sublattices of the RE Weak Truth Table Degrees, Part II: Nonbounding. DOWNEY, R G.
An Introduction to γ-Recursion Theory (Or What to Do in KP-Foundation). LUBARSKY, Robert S.
Labelling Systems and R.E. Structures. ASH, C J.
On Absoluteness. HABART, Karol.
On Hyper-Torre Isols. DOWNEY, Rod.
Pairs of Recursive Structures. ASH, C J and KNIGHT, J F.
The Recursively Enumerable Degrees have Infinitely Many One-Types. AMBOS-SPIES, Klaus and SOARE, R I.
Recursively Enumerable Sets Modulo Iterated Jumps and Extensions of Arslanov's Completeness Criterion. JOCKUSCH JR, C G (and others).

RECURSIVENESS

Recursive Solvability of Problems with Matrices. KROM, Melven and KROM, Myren.
Teoría de la recursión y lógica. DIAS, M F and PORTELA FILHO, R N A.

REDISTRIBUTION

Realism and Redistribution. NARDIN, Terry.
Taking Talents Seriously. GREEN, Simon.

REDUCTION

Addendum to "The Truth is Never Simple". BURGESS, John P.
The Formal Language of Recursion. MOSCHOVAKIS, Yiannis N.
Hilbert's Program Relativized: Proof-Theoretical and Foundational Reductions. FEFERMAN, Solomon.
Hilbert's Program Sixty Years Later. SIEG, Wilfried.
Joan Kung's Reading of Plato's *Timaeus*. MUELLER, Ian.
Physicalism, Realism and Education: A Functionalist Approach. RAINER, Valina.
Quantum Measurement and the Program for the Unity of Science. SCHARF, David C.
Reduction in the Social Sciences: The Future or Utopia?. SZMATKA, Jacek.
Relations and Reduction in Leibniz. COVER, J A.
Remarks on the Church-Rosser Property. LÓPEZ-ESCOBAR, E G K.
Science, Reduction and Natural Kinds. MEYER, Leroy N.

REDUCTION SENTENCE(S)

Discorso meta-fisico e discorso meta-forico: Derrida. PELLECCHIA, Pasquale.

REDUCTIONISM

Reductionism and Systems Theory in the Life Sciences: Some Problems and Perspectives. HOYNINGEN-HUENE, Paul (ed).
"Epistemological Reductionism in Biology" in *Reductionism and Systems Theory in the Life Sciences: Some Problems and Perspectives*, HOYNINGEN-HUENE, Paul.
"Is the Program of Molecular Biology Reductionistic?" in *Reductionism and Systems Theory in the Life Sciences: Some Problems and Perspectives*, MOHR, Hans.
"Pure, Mixed, and Spurious Probabilities and Their Significance for a Reductionist Theory of Causation" in *Scientific Explanation (Minnesota Studies in the Philosophy of Science, Volume XIII)*, PAPINEAU, David.
"Sociobiology and Reductionism" in *Reductionism and Systems Theory in the Life Sciences: Some Problems and Perspectives*, RUSE, Michael.
Aristotle on Heat, Cold, and Teleological Explanation. COHEN, Sheldon M.
Between Beanbag Genetics and Natural Selection. FALK, Raphael.
Consciousness, Brain and the Physical World. VELMANS, Max.
Does Epistemology Reduce to Cognitive Psychology?. MONTGOMERY, Richard.
Evolution in Thermodynamic Perspective: An Ecological Approach. WEBER, Bruce H (and others).
Evolutionary Anti-Reductionism: Historical Reflections. BEATTY, John.
Is Critical Thinking Guilty of Unwarranted Reductionism. HATCHER, Donald.
Methodological Individualism. TÄNNSJÖ, Torbjörn.
Philosophy and Environmental Issues. HALDANE, J J.
Quasi-Quasi-Realism. ZANGWILL, Nick.
Remarks on Physicalism and Reductionism. PEARCE, David.
Rosenberg's Rebellion. WATERS, C Kenneth.
Social Context and Historical Emergence: The Underlying Dimension of Medical Ethics. PORTO, Eugenia M.

REDUCTIVISM

Santayana's Non-Reductive Naturalism. KERR-LAWSON, Angus.

REDUNDANCY

Automated Deduction in Nonclassical Logics. WALLEN, Lincoln A.

Redundancia: Notas para su análisis. NAVARRO, Pablo E.

REED, P

Man Apart and Deep Ecology: A Reply to Reed. NAESS, Arne.

REENACTMENT

Re-enactment in Retrospect. WEINRYB, Elazar.

REFERENCE(S)

Pursuit of Truth. QUINE, W V.

What Is Said: A Theory of Indirect Speech Reports. BERTOLET, Rod.

"Reference and Its Role in Computational Models of Mental Representations" in Meaning and Mental Representation, WILKS, Yorick.

"Russelling Causal Theories of Reference" in Rereading Russell: Essays on Bertrand Russell's Metaphysics and Epistemology, FUMERTON, Richard.

"Why Perception is not Singular Reference" in Cause, Mind, and Reality: Essays Honoring C B Martin, MC LAUGHLIN, Brian P.

Aboutness and Substitutivity. MARTI, Genoveva.

Against Direct Reference. DEVITT, Michael.

Anaphoric Attitudes. CRESSWELL, M J.

Artifacts, Essence and Reference. CHAUDHURY, Mahasweta.

Belief and the Identity of Reference. DONNELLAN, Keith S.

Between Reference and Meaning. MORAVCSIK, Julius M.

Divided Reference. KVART, Igal.

E D Hirsch's Misreading of Saul Kripke. SPIKES, Michael.

How 'Russellian' Was Frege?. BELL, David.

How to Learn a Language Like a Chimpanzee. GAUKER, Christopher.

How We Refer to Things. CHISHOLM, Roderick M

Indexikalität, Wahrnehmung und Bedeutung bei Husserl. BECKER, Wolfgang.

Intrinsic Reference and the New Theory. ADDIS, Laird.

Realism, Reference and Theory. HARRÉ, Rom.

Référence et identité. SEYMOUR, Michel.

Reference in Anselm's Ontological Proof. WERTZ, S K.

Reference, Intentionality, and Nonexistent Entities. ROSENKRANTZ, Gary.

Temporal Indexicals. SMITH, Quentin.

Temptation and the Will. BIGELOW, John.

A Theory of Reference Transmission and Reference Change. BERGER, Alan.

What are Concepts?. PEACOCKE, Christopher.

What Water Is or Back to Thales. STROLL, Avrum.

REFERENTIAL OPACITY

What is Identity?. WILLIAMS, C J F.

REFERENTIALISM

Kripke e le intenzioni di riferimento. VOLTOLINI, Alberto.

REFERRING

Analytico-Referentiality and Legitimation in Modern Mathematics. ROUSSOPOULOS, George.

Kripke e le intenzioni di riferimento. VOLTOLINI, Alberto.

REFLECTION

Faith on Earth: An Inquiry into the Structure of Human Faith. NIEBUHR, Richard R (ed).

Husserl und Cohn: Widerspruch, Reflexion, und Telos in Phanomenologie und Dialektik. KLOCKENBUSCH, Reinald.

Hypothesis and the Spiral of Reflection. WEISSMAN, David.

Reflective Wisdom: Richard Taylor on Issues That Matter. DONNELLY, John (ed).

What is Identity?. WILLIAMS, C J F.

Concettualità del fondamento: Concetto e fondamento tra riflessione e speculazione. SAMONÀ, Leonardo.

Crisis Moral Communities: An Essay in Moral Philosophy. FISHER, David.

Explaining the Inexplicable: The Hypotheses of the Faculty of Reflective Judgement in Kant's Third Critique. FRICKE, Christel.

Hermeneutics and Apodicticity in Phenomenological Method. REEDER, Harry P.

Husserl's Account of Phenomenological Reflection and Four Paradoxes of Reflexivity. HOPKINS, Burt C.

Kant's Theory of the Autonomy of Reflective Judgement as an Ethics of Experiential Thinking. PILOT, Harald.

Metafora e concetto: sulla metafora dello specchio in Schelling e nel giovane Hegel. TAGLIAPIETRA, Andrea.

Of Logical Education. WILLM, J.

On the Question of the Active Role of Reflection in Marxist-Leninist Epistemology (in Czechoslovakian). HOGENOVA, A and SAFAR, Z.

Reason and Reflective Judgement: Kant on the Significance of Systematicity.

GUYER, Paul.

Reflections on Projections: Changing Conditions in Watching Film. PARKES, Graham.

Reflective Judgement and Taste. GINSBORG, Hannah.

La relation de réfléchissement pensée/langage. ROVENTA-FRUMUSANI, Daniela.

Verdad, juicio y reflexión según Tomás de Aquino. SEGURA, Carmen.

REFLECTIVE EQUILIBRIUM

Reflective Equilibrium and the Transformation of Philosophy. NIELSEN, Kai.

The Science of Man and Wide Reflective Equilibrium. BRANDT, R B.

REFLEXIVITY

The Echo of Narcissus: Anxiety, Language and Reflexivity in "Envois". JOHNSON, Cyraina E.

Husserl's Account of Phenomenological Reflection and Four Paradoxes of Reflexivity. HOPKINS, Burt C.

Les paradoxes et le langage. SEUREN, Pieter A M.

Reflexive Consistency Proofs and Gödel's Second Theorem. SAGAL, Paul.

Reflexive Ideas in Spinoza. RICE, Lee C.

The Reflexivity of Self-Consciousness: Sameness/Identity, Data for Artificial Intelligence. CASTAÑEDA, Hector-Neri.

Scepticism, Certain Grounds and the Method of Reflexivity (in Dutch). VAN WOUDENBERG, R.

Shelf-Life Zero: A Classic Postmodernist Paper. TRAVERS, Andrew.

REFORM(S)

Changes in the Social Structures of the Central- and East-European Countries. WERBLAN, Andrzej.

Educational Reform Through Philosophy for Children. SPLITTER, Laurance J.

Funding the Department of Education's TRIO Programs. EKSTEROWICZ, Anthony J and GARTNER, James D.

Looking Backward at Education Reform. HAWLEY, Willis D.

Réformisme pénal et responsabilité: une étude philosophique. BLAIS, F.

Self-Reform as Political Reform in the Writings of John Stuart Mill. EISENACH, Eldon J.

The Laborious and Painful Process of Emancipation (in Serbo-Croatian). JUNQING, Yi.

Thomas Aquinas and the Reform of Christian Education. FORTIN, Ernest L.

REFORMATION

Notion and Object: Aspects of Late Medieval Epistemology. BROADIE, Alexander.

"Wie Müntzers Religionsphilosophie an den Atheiusmus, so streifte sein politisches Programm an den Kommunismus". HÖPPNER, Joachim.

Images de la Réforme chez Pierre Bayle ou l'histoire d'une déception. WHELAN, Ruth.

Müntzer contra Luther: Der philosophische Gehalt des theologischen Konflikts. GRÜNING, Thomas.

The State's Line: On the Change of Paradigm of Austrian Philosophy within Maria-Theresian Reform-Catholicism. GIMPL, Georg.

Thomas Muntzer—Humanist, Reformator, Revolutionär. HERLITZIUS, Erwin and RUDOLPH, Günther.

Zu Problemen der revolutionären Theologie Thomas Müntzers. KOLESNYK, Alexander.

REFORMED

Evangelical Ethics and the Anabaptist-Reformed Dialogue. MOUW, Richard J and YODER, John H.

REFUSAL OF TREATMENT

"Do Living Will Statutes Embody a Claim Right or a Mere Privilege to Refuse Life-Prolonging Treatment?" in Advance Directives in Medicine, SODERBERG, William.

REFUTATION

Can the Relativist Avoid Refuting Herself?. ROOCHNIK, David L.

A New Criterion of Decidability for Intermediate Logics. SKURA, Tomasz.

A Note on Stahl's Opposite System. INOUÉ, Takao.

The Refutation of the Ontological Argument. MC GRATH, P J.

REGAN, T

Rights, Justice, and Duties to Provide Assistance: A Critique of Regan's Theory of Rights. JAMIESON, Dale.

REGRESS

Abstract Particulars. CAMPBELL, Keith.

REGULARITY(-TIES)

On Finite Models of Regular Identities. DUDEK, Józef and KISIELEWICZ, Andrzej.

On the Existence of Regular Types. SHELAH, S and BUECHLER, S.

Why Do Social Scientists Tend to See the World as Over-Ordered?. BOUDON, Raymond.

REGULATION(S)

Case Studies in Business, Society, and Ethics (Second Edition). BEAUCHAMP, Tom L.

Surrogate Motherhood: The Ethics of Using Human Beings. SHANNON, Thomas A.

Business Regulation, Business Ethics and the Professional Employee. MACKIE, Karl J.

Can There Be a Social Contract with Business?. HODAPP, Paul F.

A Legal and Economic Analysis of Insider Trading: Establishing an Appropriate Sphere of Regulation. SALBU, Steven R.

Unfree Enterprise. ESTILL, Lyle.

REGULATIVE IDEA(S)

Die Unbestimmtheit von Theorien über die menschliche Natur im chinesischen Denken. TANG, Paul C L.

REHABILITATION

Posthumous Rehabilitation and the Dust-Bin of History. LANDE, Nelson P.

REICHENBACH

The Problem of Going To: Between Epistemology and the Sociology of Knowledge. MOKRZYCKI, Edmund.

REID

Common Sense. FORGUSON, Lynd.

The Philosophy of Thomas Reid. DALGARNO, Melvin (ed).

Thomas Reid and 'The Way of Ideas'. GALLIE, Roger D.

Thomas Reid. LEHRER, Keith.

Causation and Perception in Reid. PAPPAS, George S.

Pappas on the Role of Sensations in Reid's Theory of Perception. CUMMINS, Phillip D.

Reexamining Berkeley's Notion of Suggestion. BEN-ZEEV, Aaron.

Reid and the Rights of Man. DALGARNO, Melvin.

Thomas Reid's Critique of Joseph Priestley: Context and Chronology. WOOD, Paul B.

Victor Cousin: Commonsense and the Absolute. MANNS, James W and MADDEN, Edward H.

REIFICATION

Donald Davidson's Philosophy of Language: An Introduction. RAMBERG, Bjorn T.

Reification, Class and 'New Social Movements'. BROWNE, Paul.

REIK, T

Typography: Mimesis, Philosophy, Politics. FYNSK, Christopher (ed).

REIMAN, J

The Death Penalty, Civilization, and Inhumaneness. DAVIS, Michael.

REINCARNATION

Reincarnation: A Philosophical and Practical Analysis. PREUSS, Peter.

Reincarnation and Relativized Identity. MAC INTOSH, J J.

REINER, H

El amor al prójimo en la ética fenomenológica de los valores. OLMO, Javier.

Zu Hans Reiners Wertethik. THAMM, Georg.

RELATEDNESS LOGIC

A Systematical Approach to Leibniz's Theory of Relations and Relational Sentences. MUGNAI, Massimo.

RELATION(S)

see also International Relation(s)

Hegelian/Whiteheadian Perspectives. CHRISTENSEN, Darrel E.

The Nature of Existence, Volume II. MC TAGGART, John McTaggart Ellis.

"Relativity, Relational Holism, and the Bell Inequalities" in *Philosophical Consequences of Quantum Theory: Reflections on Bell's Theorem,* TELLER, Paul.

"Rereading *Totality and Infinity*" in *The Question of the Other: Essays in Contemporary Continental Philosophy,* BERNASCONI, Robert L.

Aseity as Relational Problematic. PRATT, Douglas.

Extra-Logical Inferences. LÓPEZ-ESCOBAR, E G K.

Intentional and Physical Relations. HOROWITZ, Amir.

Interpretation of Dynamic Logic in the Relational Calculus. ORLOWSKA, Ewa.

L'indétermination, la détermination et la relation: Les trois essences de l'être. GUILLAMAUD, Patrice.

On Logical Representation and Its Consequences: The (Onto)Logical Master Premiss in Philosophy. BARTH, Else M.

Perceptual and Objective Properties in Plato. WHITE, Nicholas P.

Reachability is Harder for Directed than for Undirected Finite Graphs. AJTAI, Miklos.

The Relation of Dewey's Aesthetics to His Overall Philosophy. BURNETT, Joe R.

Relations and Reduction in Leibniz. COVER, J A.

La relazione trascendentale nella neoscolastica. VENTIMIGLIA, Giovanni.

A Systematical Approach to Leibniz's Theory of Relations and Relational Sentences. MUGNAI, Massimo.

A Theory of Command Relations. BARKER, Chris and PULLUM, Geoffrey K.

Towards a Relational Theory of Intergenerational Ethics. AGIUS, Emmanuel.

What Became of Russell's "Relation-Arithmetic"?. SOLOMON, Graham.

RELATIONISM

On Quantitative Relationist Theories. MUNDY, Brent.

RELATIONSHIP(S)

Knowledge and Politics. DASCAL, Marcelo (ed).

Person to Person. GRAHAM, George (ed).

"On the Relationship Between Man and Nature" in *Man and Nature: The Chinese Tradition and the Future,* NAN-SHENG, Huang and GUANGWU, Zhao.

Can Parents and Children Be Friends?. KUPFER, Joseph.

Couples, Canons, and the Uncouth: Spenser-and-Milton in Educational Theory. PATTERSON, Annabel.

Cross-Sex Relationships at Work and the Impact of Gender Stereotypes. DEVINE, I and MARKIEWICZ, D.

Interpersonal Knowledge According to John Macmurray. ROY, Louis.

Mentoring in Organizations: Implications for Women. BURKE, R J and MC KEEN, C A.

Morally Privileged Relationships. DONALDSON, Thomas.

The Mother-Child Relationship. HOLM, Soren.

Nietzsche: Women and Relationships of Strength. STARRETT, Shari Neller.

On the Control-Theoretic Characterization of the Self. JONES, Andrew J I.

On the Future of the Man-Nature Relationship (in Czechoslovakian). MUZIK, J.

Social Power and Human Agency. KERNOHAN, Andrew.

The Thesis. MINDER, Thomas.

Why Did Psammenitus Not Pity His Son?. BEN-ZEEV, Aaron.

Why Individual Identity Matters. BROWN, Mark T.

RELATIVE

Counterexamples to a Conjecture on Relative Categoricity. EVANS, D M.

The Doctrine of the Trinity and the Logic of Relative Identity. CAIN, James.

RELATIVISM

see also Cultural Relativism, Ethical Relativism

Ethical Theory: Classical and Contemporary Readings. POJMAN, Louis P (ed).

Feyerabend's Critique of Foundationalism. COUVALIS, George.

Moral Absolutes: An Essay on the Nature and Rationale of Morality. RESCHER, Nicholas.

Religion, Interpretation, and Diversity of Belief. GODLOVE, Terry F.

Unapologetic Theology: A Christian Voice in a Pluralistic Conversation. PLACHER, William C.

Virtue and Self-Knowledge. JACOBS, Jonathan A.

Wittgenstein and Moral Philosophy. JOHNSTON, Paul.

"Relativism, Rationality, and Repression" in *Inquiries into Values: The Inaugural Session of the International Society for Value Inquiry,* JACOBS, Jonathan.

"Why is a Philosopher?" in *The Institution of Philosophy: A Discipline in Crisis?,* PUTNAM, Hilary.

De 'natuurlijke saamhorigheid' van feiten en waarden. PELS, Dick.

Against Relativism. RADNITZKY, Gerard.

Can the Relativist Avoid Refuting Herself?. ROOCHNIK, David L.

Collingwood's Epistemological Individualism. CODE, Lorraine.

Conceptual Relativism and the Possibility of Absolute Faith. CRAIGHEAD, Houston A.

Courage, Relativism and Practical Reasoning. WALTON, Douglas N.

The Crucial Experiment of Wilhelm Johannsen. ROLL-HANSEN, Nils.

Disciplining Relativism and Truth. CLAYTON, Philip.

Epistemology as Hermeneutics: Antifoundationalist Relativism. ROCKMORE, Tom.

How Relative are Values? or Are Nazis Irrational and Why the Answer Matters. LACHS, John.

Literary Relativism. CARNEY, James D.

Moral Internalism and Moral Relativism. TILLEY, John.

Multiply Modal Extensions of Da Costa's C_n, Logical Relativism, and the Imaginary. LOKHORST, Gert-Jan C.

Notes on a Not-Relativistic Pluralism (in Hungarian). DE BOER, Theo.

Het objectieve waarheidsbegrip in Waarder. KUIPERS, Theo A F.

On a Not-Relativistic Pluralism in Philosophy (in Hungarian). PEPERZAK, Adriaan.

On Putnam's Argument for the Inconsistency of Relativism. SOLOMON, Miriam.

RELATIVISM

Over de verhouding van conceptueel relatief en referentieel realisme. RADDER, Hans.

Reasons, Rationales, and Relativisms: What's at Stake in the Conversation over Scientific. PEERENBOOM, R P.

Response to Professor Feinberg's Presidential Address: A Role for Philosophy of Education in Intercultural Research. GOLDSTONE, Peter.

A Role for Philosophy of Education in Intercultural Research: Reexamination of the Relativism-Absolutism Debate. FEINBERG, Walter.

The Sophists and Relativism. BETT, Richard.

Tolerance and the Question of Rationality. ZAPASNIK, Stanislaw and PETROWICZ, Lech (trans).

Toward the Development of a Multidimensional Scale for Improving Evaluations of Business Ethics. REIDENBACH, R E and ROBIN, D P.

Tra intenzionalismo e antirelativismo: l'interpretazione di teorie filosofiche come traduzione. VARNIER, Giuseppe.

Truth, Relativism, and Crossword Puzzles. MURPHY, Nancey.

Understanding Other Cultures: Studies in the Philosophical Problems of Cross-Cultural Interpretation. SANDBACKA, Carola.

Who Can Teach Workplace Ethics?. DAVIS, Michael.

RELATIVITY

Rationality and Relativity: The Quest for Objective Knowledge. O'GORMAN, Francis.

"Nonfactorizability, Stochastic Causality, and Passion-at-a-Distance" in *Philosophical Consequences of Quantum Theory: Reflections on Bell's Theorem*, REDHEAD, Michael L G.

"Relativity, Relational Holism, and the Bell Inequalities" in *Philosophical Consequences of Quantum Theory: Reflections on Bell's Theorem*, TELLER, Paul.

An Argument About the Relativity of Justice. DANIELS, Norman.

Does the Principle of Relativity Imply Winnie's (1970) Equal Passage Times Principle?. BROWN, Harvey R.

The End of the Absolute: A Nineteenth-Century Contribution to General Relativity. FARWELL, Ruth and KNEE, Christopher.

L'interprétation de la relativité. LEFETZ, L.

Moral Individualism: Agent-Relativity and Deontic Restraints. MACK, Eric.

Relativity in Mādhyamika Buddhism and Modern Physics. MANSFIELD, Victor.

Simultaneity and Einstein's *Gedankenexperiment*. COHEN, Michael.

The Social Relativity of Justice and Rights Thesis. HUND, John.

RELEVANCE

Four Decades of Scientific Explanation. SALMON, Wesley C.

Greek Scepticism: Anti-Realist Trends in Ancient Thought. GROARKE, Leo.

Relevant Logic: A Philosophical Examination of Inference. READ, Stephen.

"Literal Relevance" in *Directions in Relevant Logic*, PARKS-CLIFFORD, John.

"The Relevance of Relevant Logics" in *Directions in Relevant Logic*, WOODS, John.

"Relevance Principles and Formal Deducibility" in *Directions in Relevant Logic*, MAKSIMOVA, Larisa.

"Relevance, Truth and Meaning" in *Directions in Relevant Logic*, PRIEST, Graham and CROSTHWAITE, Jan.

"Relevant Implication and Leibnizian Necessity" in *Directions in Relevant Logic*, PARKS, Zane and BYRD, Michael.

"What is Relevant Implication?" in *Directions in Relevant Logic*, URQUHART, Alasdair.

Conversation, Relevance, and Argumentation. HAFT-VAN REES, M Agnes.

Explaining the Persistence of Irrelevance. MC ANINCH, Amy.

Favorable Relevance and Arguments. BOWLES, George.

More on Making Mind Matter. LE PORE, Ernest and LOEWER, Barry.

The Question of Relevance in Current Nigerian Philosophy. KIMMERLE, Heinz.

Towards a Rationalization of Biological Psychiatry: A Study in Psychobiological Epistemology. RUDNICK, Abraham.

RELEVANCE LOGIC

"'Relevance' in Logic and Grammar" in *Directions in Relevant Logic*, VAN DIJK, Teun A.

"Categorical Propositions in Relevance Logic" in *Directions in Relevant Logic*, BACON, John.

"Gentzen's Cut and Ackermann's Gamma" in *Directions in Relevant Logic*, DUNN, J Michael and MEYER, Robert K.

"Incompleteness for Quantified Relevance Logics" in *Directions in Relevant Logic*, FINE, Kit.

"Relevance Logic and Inferential Knowledge" in *Directions in Relevant Logic*, BARKER, John.

"Semantic Discovery for Relevance Logics" in *Directions in Relevant Logic*, MORGAN, Charles G.

"Semantics Unlimited I: A Relevant Synthesis of Implication with Higher Intensionality" in *Directions in Relevant Logic*, ROUTLEY, Richard.

RELEVANT LOGICS

Directions in Relevant Logic. NORMAN, Jean (ed).

Relevant Logic: A Philosophical Examination of Inference. READ, Stephen.

"The Classical Logic of Relevant Logicians" in *Directions in Relevant Logic*, KIELKOPF, Charles F.

"Conclusion: Further Directions in Relevant Logics" in *Directions in Relevant Logic*, NORMAN, Jean and SYLVAN, Richard.

"Introduction: Routes in Relevant Logic" in *Directions in Relevant Logic*, NORMAN, Jean and SYLVAN, Richard.

"Philosophical and Linguistic Inroads: Multiply Intensional Relevant Logics" in *Directions in Relevant Logic*, ROUTLEY, Richard.

"Quantification, Identity, and Opacity in Relevant Logic" in *Directions in Relevant Logic*, FREEMAN, James B.

"The Relevance of Relevant Logics" in *Directions in Relevant Logic*, WOODS, John.

"Which Entailments Entail Which Entailments?" in *Directions in Relevant Logic*, BELNAP JR, Nuel D.

Completeness and Conservative Extension Results for Some Boolean Relevant Logics. GIAMBRONE, Steve and MEYER, Robert K.

A Content Semantics for Quantified Relevant Logics, I. BRADY, Ross T.

A Content Semantics for Quantified Relevant Logics, II. BRADY, Ross T.

Converse Ackermann Property and Semiclassical Negation. MÉNDEZ, José M.

Deduction Theorems. MÉNDEZ, José M.

The Gentzenization and Decidability of RW. BRADY, Ross T.

Homophone Semantik für die relevante Aussagenlogik. READ, Stephen.

Modularity and Relevant Logic. GARSON, James.

Motivation and Demotivation of a Four-Valued Logic. FOX, John.

An Overview of Paraconsistent Logic in the 80s. DA COSTA, Newton C A and MARCONI, Diego.

Philosophical-Methodological Aspects of Relevant Logic. WOISHVILLO, E K.

Principal Type-Schemes and Condensed Detachment. HINDLEY, J Roger.

The Propositional Objects of Mental Attitudes. DANIELS, Charles B.

Prospects for Decent Relevant Factorisation Logics. URBAS, Igor and SYLVAN, Richard.

R-Algebras and R-Model Structures as Power Constructs. BRINK, Chris.

Relevant Predication: Grammatical Characterizations. KREMER, Philip.

A Routley-Meyer Affixing Style Semantics for Logics Containing Aristotle's Thesis. BRADY, Ross T.

Sequent-Systems and Groupoid Models, I. DOSEN, Kosta.

Sequent-Systems and Groupoid Models, II. DOSEN, Kosta.

Sets as Singularities in the Intensional Universe. DAYNES, Keith.

RELIABILISM

The Basic Notion of Justification. KVANVIG, Jonathan L and MENZEL, Christopher.

Two Uses of 'Know'. CLARKE JR, D S.

RELIABILITY

Justification, Reliability and Knowledge. SHOPE, Robert K.

Reliabilism and Relevant Worlds. MOSER, Paul K.

Reliability and Goldman's Theory of Justification. ALMEDER, Robert and HOFF, Franklin J.

RELIGION

see also Atheism, Buddhism, Christianity, Evil(s), Faith, God, Hinduism, Humanism, Immortality, Judaism, Metaphysics, Miracle(s), Mysticism, Theism

Allāh Transcendent. NETTON, Ian Richard.

The Anthropological Character of Theology: Conditioning Theological Understanding. PAILIN, David A.

Atheism: A Philosophical Justification. MARTIN, Michael.

Baruch or Benedict: On Some Jewish Aspects of Spinoza's Philosophy. LEVY, Ze'ev.

Beauty and Holiness: The Dialogue between Aesthetics and Religion. MARTIN JR, James Alfred.

Benevolent Living: Tracing the Roots of Motivation to God. TURNER, Dean.

Bible and Ethics in the Christian Life. BIRCH, Bruce C.

The Bitterness of Job: A Philosophical Reading. WILCOX, John T.

Body, Soul, and Life Everlasting: Biblical Anthropology and the Monism-Dualism Debate. COOPER, John W.

Christ, Ethics and Tragedy: Essays in Honour of Donald MacKinnon. SURIN, Kenneth (ed).

Civil Peace and Sacred Order: Limits and Renewals I. CLARK, Stephen R L.

The Conflict of Interpretations: Essays in Hermeneutics—Paul Ricoeur. IHDE, Don (ed).

The Confucian Creation of Heaven: Philosophy and the Defense of Ritual

RELIGION

RELIGION

Process Theology and Black Liberation: Testing the Whiteheadian Metaphysical Foundations. YOUNG, Henry James.

Process Theology: Guardian of the Oppressor or Goad to the Oppressed—An Interim Assessment. JONES, William R.

Process-Relational Christian Soteriology: A Response to Wheeler. BASINGER, David.

Properly Unargued Belief in God. LANGTRY, Bruce.

La prova a priori dell'esistenza di Dio nel Settecento inglese: da Cudworth a Hume. SCRIBANO, Emanuela.

Public Philosophy and Contemporary Pluralism. DOUGLASS, R Bruce.

Purtill on Fatalism and Truth. CRAIG, William Lane.

La question du pluralisme en théologie. MARLÉ, René.

Ragione debole e metafisica: Spunti tra vecchia e nuova apologetica. TODISCO, Orlando.

Reading Kierkegaard: Two Pitfalls and a Strategy for Avoiding Them. GOOLD, Patrick.

Reality—Realization through Self-Discipline. VEMPENY, Alice.

Reason in Mystery. KRETZMANN, Norman.

Reason, Inductive Inference, and True Religion in Hume. JANZ, Bruce.

Reasoning by Analogy in Hume's *Dialogues*. BARKER, Stephen F.

Recent Classical/Process Dialogue on God and Change. CLAYTON, Philip.

Recent Interpretations of Early Christian Asceticism. YOUNG, Robin Darling.

Recent Work in the Philosophy of Religion. ZAGZEBSKI, Linda.

Reconceiving Miracles. GILMAN, James E.

Reference and Critical Realism. DURRANT, Michael.

Reflections and Reservations Concerning Martin Buber's Dialogical Philosophy in Its Religious Dimension. THOMAS, John R.

Reformed Epistemology and Religious Fundamentalism: How Basic Are Our Basic Beliefs?. TILLEY, Terrence W.

The Refutation of the Ontological Argument. MC GRATH, P J.

Le règne de Dieu par la nature chez Thomas Hobbes. MALHERBE, Michel.

La *Regula recepta* agustiniana, germen de vida religiosa renovada. ANOZ, José.

Relating the Physics and Religion of David Bohm. SHARPE, Kevin J.

Religion a Threat to Morality: An Attempt to Throw Some New Light on Hume's Philosophy of Religion. STREMINGER, Gerhard.

Religion and Moral Meaning in Bioethics. CAMPBELL, Courtney S.

Religion and Morality: A Conceptual Understanding. BEHERA, Satrughna.

Religion and the Secularization of Bioethics. CALLAHAN, Daniel.

Religion and Truth (in Dutch). DE DIJN, H.

Religion et philosophie chez Descartes et Malebranche. GRIMALDI, Nicolas.

Religious Belief and Religious Diversity. MC KIM, Robert.

Religious Belief and Scientific Weltanschauungen. TRUNDLE, Robert.

Religious Transcendence: Scheler's Forgotten Quest. SCHALOW, Frank.

Religious Upbringing and Rational Autonomy. LAURA, Ronald S and LEAHY, Michael.

Remarques sur *Le Livre de la connaissance* de Maïmonide. STRAUSS, Leo.

A Reply to Ellin's "Streminger: 'Religion a Threat to Morality'". STREMINGER, Gerhard.

Reply to Michael Diamond's "A Modern Theistic Argument". HEBBLETHWAITE, Brian.

Response to Davis's "Doubting the Resurrection". KELLER, James A.

A Response to Sykes: Revelation and the Practices of Interpreting Scripture. JONES, L Gregory.

A Response to the Paper "Theology of Religions and Sacrifice". FRANCIS, B Joseph.

Resurrection Claims in Non-Christian Religions. HABERMAS, Gary R.

Resurrection: Critical Reflections on a Doctrine in Search of a Meaning. SCUKA, Robert F.

Revelation and Foundationalism: Towards Hermeneutical and Ontological Appropriateness. GUARINO, Thomas.

Revelation and the Bible. MAVRODES, George I.

Révélation et expérience historique des hommes. GEFFRÉ, Claude.

Review of C F Göschel's *Aphorisms: Part Three*. HEGEL, G W F and BUTLER, Clark (trans).

A Rhetoric of Motives: Thomas on Obligation as Rational Persuasion. HIBBS, Thomas S.

Ross and Scotus on the Existence of God. MAYES, G Randolph.

Sacrifice: Core of Vedic Religion and Christianity. MALIECKAL, Louis.

San Agustín y K Rahner: El amor a Dios y el amor al prójimo. GALINDO RODRIGO, José Antonio.

San Agustín y Unamuno. ZABALLOS, Juan Carlos.

Santayana's Ontology and the Nicene Creed. KERR-LAWSON, Angus.

Scepticism, Evidentialism and the Parity Argument: A Pascalian Perspective.

HOLYER, Robert.

Schriftgemässe Philosophie als philosophische Laienmeditation?. THOMASSEN, Beroald.

Science, Philosophy and Religion in the Seventeenth Century Encounter Between China and the West (in Serbo-Croatian). STANDAERT, Nicolas.

Science, Technology, and God: In Search of Believers. GOLDMAN, Steven L.

Semantics of the Grammar. CROSSON, Frederick J.

Sens et Vérité: Philosophie et théologie chez L Meyer et Spinoza. LAGREE, Jacqueline.

Sense of Humor as a Christian Virtue. ROBERTS, Robert C.

Les séquelles de la crise moderniste. MONTAGNES, Bernard.

Sibboleth ou de la Lettre. GRANEL, Gérard.

Símbolo religioso, pensamiento especulativo y libertad. SCANNONE, J C.

Six Characteristics of a Postpatriarchal Christianity. MC DANIEL, Jay.

Smarta-Varnasrama and the Law of Welfare. SWAIN, Braja Kishore.

Solamente un dios puede todavia salvarnos. SILVA CAMARENA, Juan Manuel.

Solitude in Ancient Taoism. KOCH, Philip J.

Some Emendations of Gödel's Ontological Proof. ANDERSON, C Anthony.

Soteriological Dialogue between Wesleyan Christians and Pure Land Sect Buddhism. ADAMO, David Tuesday.

Soteriology from a Christian and Hindu Perspective. JENSEN, Debra J.

Speaking for My Self. KOSINSKI, Jerzy.

St Paul and Moral Responsibility. STOHL, Johan.

The Status of the Anomaly in the Feminist God-Talk of Rosemary Reuther. JAMES, George Alfred.

Straightening the Record: Some Responses to Critics. HICK, John.

Streminger: "Religion a Threat to Morality". ELLIN, Joseph.

Struttura dell'azione e compito pubblico del cristianesimo. POSSENTI, Vittorio.

Studies in the Explanation of Issues in Biomedical Ethics: (II) On "On Play[ing] God", Etc.. ERDE, Edmund L.

Supernatural Acts and Supervenient Explanations. WHITTAKER, John H.

Sur l'unité de l'unique preuve de Dieu. LABBÉ, Yves.

Surplus Evil. SNYDER, Daniel T.

Sviluppo e senso delle annotazioni schopenhaueriane a Schelling (2 Teil). VECCHIOTTI, Icilio.

Swāmī Vivekānanda's Use of Science as an Analogy for the Attainment of *Moksa*. RAMBACHAN, Anantanand.

Talking of God—But with Whom?. VERHEY, Allen D.

Taoist Cultural Reality: The Harmony of Aesthetic Order. THOMPSON, Kirill O.

Theological Empiricism: Aspects of Johann Georg Hamann's Reception of Hume. GRAUBNER, Hans.

The Theological-Political Tension in Liberalism. FULLER, Timothy.

Theologically Unfashionable Philosophy. STUMP, Eleonore S and KRETZMANN, Norman.

Theology of Religions and Sacrifice. THACHIL, Jose.

Theosebeia in Plethon's Work: A Concept in Transition. ARGYROPOULOS, R.

Thinking About 'The Other' in Religion: It is Necessary, But is it Possible?. NEUSNER, Jacob.

Thomas Aquinas's Complete Guide to Heaven and Hell. LINDSAY, Ronald A.

Three Appeals in Peirce's Neglected Argument. ANDERSON, Douglas R.

Toward a Process-Relational Christian Soteriology. WHEELER, David L.

Towards a "Materialist" Critique of "Religious Pluralism". SURIN, Kenneth.

Translating Nishida. MARALDO, John C.

La trattazione dell'argomento ontologico nel carteggio Leibniz-Jaquelot (1702-1704). TORTOLONE, Gian Michele.

The Trinity in Universal Revelation. VILADESAU, Richard.

Truth and the Diversity of Religions. WARD, Keith.

Union with God: A Theory. OAKES, Robert.

Universalism, Hell, and the Fate of the Ignorant. DAVIS, Stephen T.

The Use of Symbols in Religion from the Perspective of Analytical Psychology. MC GLASHAN, A R.

The Value of the World as the Mystery of God in Advaita Vedanta. RAMBACHAN, Anantanand.

Verburg over Dooyeweerd. STELLINGWERFF, J.

Visits to the Sepulcher and Biblical Exegesis. STUMP, Eleonore S.

The Vulnerability of Action. ELLIS, Robert.

Die Wandlungen Gottes: Zu Rudolf Schottlaenders Beitrag *Zu Spinozas Theorie des Glaubens*. HAMMACHER, Klaus.

What Can Religion Offer Bioethics?. WIND, James P.

What Could Be the Meaning of the Idea that Morality Depends on Religion? (in Hebrew). SAGI, Avi and STATMAN, Daniel.

Why Buddhas Can't Remember Their Previous Lives. GRIFFITHS, Paul J.

REPRODUCTION(S)

Overview of the Reports of the Ethics Committee of the American Fertility Society. SPICKER, Stuart F.

Reproductive Controls and Sexual Destiny. MURPHY, Timothy F.

Sexist Dualism: Its Material Sources in the Exploitation of Reproductive Labor. LANGE, Lynda.

What Price Parenthood?. LAURITZEN, Paul.

REPUBLIC(S)

"The Son of Apollo": Themes of Plato. WOODBRIDGE, Frederick J E.

Du principe démocratique. HEINE, Heinrich and HÖHN, Gerhard (trans).

Emmanuel Kant: La liberté comme droit de l'homme et l'"Idée" de république. PONTON, Lionel.

From Liberalism to Radicalism: Tom Paine's Rights of Man. KATES, Gary.

Republic and Politics in Machiavelli and Rousseau. VIROLI, Maurizio.

REPUBLICANISM

Arendt, Republicanism and Patriarchalism. SPRINGBORG, Patricia.

Madison's Party Press Essays. SHEEHAN, Colleen A.

REPUTATION

"The Riddle of Bacon" in Early Modern Philosophy II, AGASSI, Joseph.

REQUIREMENT(S)

'Ought' Implies 'Can' and the Scope of Moral Requirements. MC CONNELL, Terrance.

Blood is Thicker Than Water: Don't Forsake the Family Jewels. BELLIOTTI, Raymond A.

A Game-Theoretical Companion to Chisholm's Ethics of Requirement. ÅQVIST, Lennart.

RESCHER, N

The Logical Limits of Science. SMITH, Joseph Wayne.

RESEARCH

Classic Cases in Medical Ethics: Accounts of the Cases That Have Shaped Medical Ethics. PENCE, Gregory E.

Academic Ethics Revisited. COTTRILL, Melville T.

Androgyny and Leadership Style. KORABIK, Karen.

Animal Models in 'Exemplary' Medical Research: Diabetes as a Case Study. NELSON, James Lindemann.

Animals, Science, and Ethics. DONNELLEY, Strachan (ed) and NOLAN, Kathleen (ed).

Are Women Different and Why are Women Thought to be Different? Theoretical and Methodological Perspectives. GREGORY, Ann.

At the Heart of Women in Management Research: Theoretical and Methodological Approaches and Their Biases. FAGENSON, Ellen A.

Attitudes of Marketing Professionals Toward Ethics in Marketing Research: A Cross-National Comparison. AKAAH, Ishmael P.

Bias, Controversy, and Abuse in the Study of the Scientific Publication System. MAHONEY, Michael J.

Can Clinical Research Be Both 'Ethical' and 'Scientific'? A Commentary Inspired by Rosser and Marquis. HOLMES, Helen Bequaert.

Career Barriers: Do We Need More Research?. CULLEN, Dallas.

Character Versus Codes: Models for Research Ethics. LOMBARDI, Louis G.

Comment on James Nelson's "Animals in 'Exemplary' Medical Research: Diabetes as a Case Study". FINSEN, Lawrence.

Confirmational Response Bias Among Social Work Journals. EPSTEIN, William M.

Critical Attitudes Inside Social Science and the Humanities—A Swedish Perspective. LIEDMAN, Sven-Eric.

Critics of Science and Research Ethics in Sweden. GUSTAFSSON, Bengt and TIBELL, Gunnar.

Cultural and Ideological Bias in Pornography Research. CHRISTENSEN, Ferrel M.

Der Kampf un den Buchstaben in der Hegel-Forschung der Gegenwart. HORSTMANN, Rolf-Peter.

Ethical Behavior Among Marketing Researchers: An Assessment of Selected Demographic Characteristics. KELLEY, S W and FERRELL, O C and SKINNER, S J.

An Ethical Problem Concerning Recent Therapeutic Research on Breast Cancer. MARQUIS, Don.

Ethics Training Programs in the Fortune 500. KOHLS, John and CHAPMAN, Christi and MATHIEU, Casey.

An Examination of Present Research on the Female Entrepreneur-Suggested Strategies for the 1990's. MOORE, Dorothy P.

Frontiers and New Vistas in Women in Management Research. SEKARAN, Uma.

Improving the Quality of Social Welfare Scholarship: Response to "Confirmational Response Bias". SCHUERMAN, John R.

Is Social Work Different? Comments on "Confirmational Response Bias".

WESTRUM, Ron.

Journals Have Obligations, Too: Commentary on "Confirmational Response Bias". HOLLANDER, Rachelle D.

Juventology: A Holistic Approach to Youth. MAHLER, Fred.

Marketing/Business Ethics: A Review of the Empirical Research. FRITSCHE, David J.

Measuring the Impact of Teaching Ethics to Future Managers: A Review, Assessment, and Recommendations. WEBER, James.

Methodology in Business Ethics Research: A Review and Critical Assessment. RANDALL, D M and GIBSON, A M.

Mind and Brain on Bergen Street. SILVER, Ruth.

The Narrative Reconstruction of Science. ROUSE, Joseph.

The New World of Research Ethics: A Preliminary Map. DAVIS, Michael.

The Offensive-Defensive Distinction in Military Biological Research. FRISINA, Michael E.

Patents and Free Scientific Information in Biotechnology: Making Monoclonal Antibodies Proprietary. MACKENZIE, Michael and KEATING, Peter.

Quality of Scholarship in Bioethics. BRODY, Baruch A.

Re-Visioning Clinical Research—Gender and the Ethics of Experimental Design. ROSSER, Sue V.

Reflections on "Confirmational Response Bias Among Social Work Journals". HOPPS, June Gary.

Research on the History of Physical Theories. ARIEW, Roger (trans) and BARKER, Peter (trans) and DUHEM, Pierre.

A Research Strategy for Studying Telic Human Behavior. HOWARD, George S and YOUNGS, William H.

Research, Myths and Expectations: New Challenges for Management Educators. GRONDIN, Deirdre.

The Responsible Use of Animals in Biomedical Research. HETTINGER, Edwin Converse.

A Role for Philosophy of Education in Intercultural Research: Reexamination of the Relativism-Absolutism Debate. FEINBERG, Walter.

Science- and Engineering-Related Ethics and Value Studies: Characteristics of an Emerging Field of Research. HOLLANDER, Rachelle D and STENECK, Nicholas H.

Scientific Problems and the Conduct of Research. HAIG, Brian.

Some Methodological Problems Associated with Researching Women Entrepreneurs. STEVENSON, Lois.

Some Remarks on Laudan's Theory of Scientific Rationality. VON ECKARDT, Barbara.

Status Arguments and Genetic Research with Human Embryos. HICKMAN, Larry.

Tra intenzionalismo e antirelativismo: l'interpretazione di teorie filosofiche come traduzione. VARNIER, Giuseppe.

Trust in Business Relations: Directions for Empirical Research. HUSTED, Bryan W.

The Women in Management Research Program at the National Centre for Management Research and Development. BURKE, R J and MIKALACHKI, D.

Women's Research and Its Inherent Critique of Society and Science. KYLE, Gunhild and JUNGEN, Britta.

RESEMBLANCE(S)

Abstract Particulars. CAMPBELL, Keith.

Metaphor. COOPER, David E.

RESENTMENT

Emotional Origins of Morality—A Sketch. THOMSON, Anne.

RESISTANCE

"Holocaust and Resistance" in Inquiries into Values: The Inaugural Session of the International Society for Value Inquiry, BAR ON, Bat-Ami.

Beyond Music Minus Memory?. OLIVIER, G.

Irresistible Desires. MELE, Alfred R.

Power and Resistance. KRIPS, Henry.

RESOLUTION

Compromise. DAY, J P.

Ethical Dilemmas and the Disputing Process: Organizations and Societies. MATHEWS, M Cash.

Resolution in Constructivism. AKAMA, Seiki.

RESOURCE(S)

Allocation and Ownership of World Resources: A Symposium Overview. KUFLIK, Arthur.

Competitive Equality of Opportunity: A Defense. GREEN, S J D.

Epistemological and Ethical Considerations in Conceptualizing and Implementing Human Resource Management. DACHLER, H Peter and ENDERLE, Georges.

High Technology Health Care. LAMM, Richard D.

RESOURCE(S)

Justice Between Age-Groups: A Comment on Norman Daniels. MC KERLIE, Dennis.

Medical Joint-Venturing: An Ethical Perspective. GREEN, Ronald M.

Resource X: Sirkin and Smith on a Neglected Economic Staple. DE VRIES, Paul H.

RESPECT

"Advance Directives: Beyond Respect for Freedom" in *Advance Directives in Medicine*, CHURCHILL, John.

The "Evils" of a Technologized Psychology in Teacher Education. ORTON, Robert E.

"Respect", "Dignity" and "Integrity": An Environmental Proposal for Ethics. WESTRA, Laura.

Equal Respect and the Enforcement of Morality. DWORKIN, Gerald.

Kant's Theory of Moral Sensibility: Respect for the Moral Law and the Influence of Inclination. REATH, A.

Paternalism and Respect for Autonomy. SCOCCIA, Danny.

The Personalization of Failure. PRATTE, Richard.

The Place of Autonomy in Bioethics. CHILDRESS, James F.

Realism and Respect. BALDNER, Kent.

Respect for Persons, Autonomy and Equality. NORMAN, Richard.

Speculations Regarding the History of *Donum Vitae*. HARVEY, John Collins.

RESPONSE(S)

Confirmational Response Bias Among Social Work Journals. EPSTEIN, William M.

Issues Management and Organizational Accounts: An Analysis of Corporate Responses to Accusation of Unethical Business. GARRETT, Dennis E and BRADFORD, Jeffrey L and MEYERS, Renee A and BECKER, Joy.

Reflections on "Confirmational Response Bias Among Social Work Journals". HOPPS, June Gary.

RESPONSIBILITY(-TIES)

Accountability in Education: A Philosophical Inquiry. WAGNER, Robert B.

Business Ethics: Where Profits Meet Value Systems. ROBIN, Donald P.

Determinism, Blameworthiness and Deprivation. KLEIN, Martha.

The Dialectic in Journalism: Toward a Responsible Use of Press Freedom. MERRILL, John Calhoun.

An Essay on Moral Responsibility. ZIMMERMAN, Michael J.

Issues in Contemporary Legal Philosophy: The Influence of H L A Hart. GAVISON, Ruth (ed).

Lawless Mind. ABELSON, Raziel.

Natural Agency: An Essay on the Casual Theory of Action. BISHOP, John.

Reflective Wisdom: Richard Taylor on Issues That Matter. DONNELLY, John (ed).

The Sanctity-of-Life Doctrine in Medicine: A Critique. KUHSE, Helga.

"Do Future Generations Matter?" in *Ethics and the Environmental Responsibility*, CAMERON, J R.

"Ethics and Responsibility" in *Papers on the Ethics of Administration*, WALTERS, Kenneth D.

Acts and Omissions. HALL, John C.

Agricultural Technology, Wealth, and Responsibility. WUNDERLICH, Gene.

Aristotle on Responsibility for Action and Character. ROBERTS, Jean.

Attitudes Towards Corporate Social Responsibility and Perceived Importance of Social Responsibility Information. TEOH, Hai Yap and SHIU, Godwin Y.

The Business and Society Course: Does It Change Student Attitudes?. WYND, William R and MAGER, John.

Business Ethics in Banking. GREEN, C F.

Business Ethics: A Literature Review with a Focus on Marketing Ethics. TSALIKIS, John and FRITZSCHE, David J.

Childhood's End: The Age of Responsibility. FRIQUEGNON, Marie-Loui.

Collective Inaction and Shared Responsibility. MAY, Larry.

Consumer Responsibility from a Social Systems Perspective. ZANARDI, William J.

The Contribution of *Nicomachean Ethics iii 5* to Aristotle's Theory of Responsibility. CURREN, Randall.

Corporate and Individual Moral Responsibility: A Reply to Jan Garrett. WERHANE, Patricia H.

Die Verantwortung des Menschen für seine natürliche Umwelt (in Polish). ROSINSKI, F M and LATAWIEC, A M.

Essential Aims and Unavoidable Responsibilities: A Response to Anscombe. COUGHLAN, Michael J.

Ethics in Education: A Comparative Study. LANE, Michael S and SCHAUPP, Dietrich.

Hospital Ethics Committees: One of the Many Centers of Responsibility. GLASER, John W.

Innere Autonomie oder Zurechnungsfähigkeit?. SCHÖNRICH, Gerhard.

Intencionalidad, responsabilidad y solidaridad: Los nuevos àmbitos del compromiso ético. SEIBOLD, J R.

Irresistible Desires. MELE, Alfred R.

Justifying Moral Initiative by Business, with Rejoinders to Bill Shaw and Richard Nunan. MULLIGAN, Thomas M.

A New Approach to Regulating the Use of Animals in Science. ANDERSON, Warwick.

Ontological Responsibility and the Poetics of Nature. LLEWELYN, John.

Personal Identity, the Temporality of Agency and Moral Responsibility. LEE, Win-Chiat.

Personhood and Moral Responsibility. LOCKE, Lawrence A.

The Price of Silence: Commentary. BERG, Kåre.

Publishing Biomedical Research: Roles and Responsibilities. RELMAN, Arnold S.

Recklessness, Omission, and Responsibility: Some Reflections on the Moral Significance of Causation. SMITH, Patricia G.

Réformisme pénal et responsabilité: une étude philosophique. BLAIS, F.

Regarding Rich's "Compatibilism Argument" and the 'Ought'-Implies-'Can' Argument. FAWKES, Don.

Responsibility and 'Free Will'. VESEY, Godfrey.

Responsibility and Complicity. ARONSON, Ronald.

The Responsibility of Socrates. STALLEY, R F.

Risiko und Entscheidung aus ethischer Sicht. RÖMER, Joachim.

Self-Deception, Human Emotion, and Moral Responsibility: Toward a Pluralistic Conceptual Scheme. WHISNER, William.

Some Prerequisites and Aspects of the Shaping of "New Thinking" Responsibility (in Czechoslovakian). JAVUREK, Z.

St Paul and Moral Responsibility. STOHL, Johan.

Talking Sense About Freedom. WARD, Andrew.

Toward a Code of Ethics for Business Ethicists. MADSEN, Peter.

Unredistributable Corporate Moral Responsibility. GARRETT, Jan Edward.

Van Inwagen on the 'Obviousness' of Libertarian Moral Responsibility. SMILANSKY, Saul.

Whistleblowing and Management Accounting: An Approach. LOEB, Stephen E and CORY, Suzanne N.

Why We Mean What We Say: The History and Use of 'Corporate Social Responsibility'. HETZNER, Candace.

REST, J

How Can Philosophers Teach Professional Ethics?. WEIL, Vivian.

RESTITUTION

Affirmative Action as a Form of Restitution. GROARKE, Leo.

Understanding and Justifying Self-Defence. SMART, B J.

RESTORATION

Michelet and Lamartine: Regicide, Passion, and Compassion. DUNN, Susan.

Preserving, Restoring, Repairing. GODLOVITCH, Stan.

RESTRAINT(S)

The Dialectic in Journalism: Toward a Responsible Use of Press Freedom. MERRILL, John Calhoun.

Moral Individualism: Agent-Relativity and Deontic Restraints. MACK, Eric.

RESURRECTION

Doubting The Resurrection: A Reply to James A Keller. DAVIS, Stephen T.

On Doubts about the Resurrection. CRAIG, William Lane.

Response to Davis's "Doubting the Resurrection". KELLER, James A.

Resurrection Claims in Non-Christian Religions. HABERMAS, Gary R.

Resurrection: Critical Reflections on a Doctrine in Search of a Meaning. SCUKA, Robert F.

Visits to the Sepulcher and Biblical Exegesis. STUMP, Eleonore S.

RETALIATION

The Morality of Nuclear Deterrence and the Corruption of Character. LOVE JR, Charles E.

RETRIBUTION

Justifying Legal Punishment. PRIMORATZ, Igor.

Fingarette and Johnson on Retributive Punishment. STEPHENSON, Wendel.

Kant's Theory of Punishment: Deterrence in its Threat, Retribution in its Execution. BYRD, B Sharon.

RETRIBUTIVE JUSTICE

Justifying Legal Punishment. PRIMORATZ, Igor.

"Comment: The Middle Way in the Philosophy of Punishment" in *Issues in Contemporary Legal Philosophy: The Influence of H L A Hart*, SCHACHAR, Yoram.

RETRIBUTIVISM

Auctions, Lotteries, and the Punishment of Attempts. DUFF, R A.

Positive Retributivism. TEN, C L.

ROUSSEAU

MELZER, Arthur M.

Nietzsche Contra Nietzsche: Creativity and the Anti-Romantic. DEL CARO, Adrian.

The Question of Jean-Jacques Rousseau—Ernest Cassirer (Second Edition). GAY, Peter (ed & trans).

Rousseau, Judge of Jean-Jacques: Dialogues—The Collected Writings of Rousseau, Volume I. MASTERS, Roger D (ed & trans).

Rousseau. DENT, N J H.

Rousseau: Selections. CRANSTON, Maurice (ed).

Scarcity and Modernity. XENOS, Nicholas.

Self-Direction and Political Legitimacy: Rousseau and Herder. BARNARD, F M.

Time, Freedom, and the Common Good: An Essay in Public Philosophy. SHEROVER, Charles M.

The Trespass of the Sign: Deconstruction, Theology and Philosophy. HART, Kevin.

Wesen, Freiheit und Bildung des Menschen. HAGER, Fritz-Peter.

"John Locke, David Fordyce, and Jean-Jacques Rousseau: On Liberty" in *Early Modern Philosophy II,* TATTON, Susan.

"Our Illusory Chains: Rousseau's Images of Bondage and Freedom" in *Culture et Politique/Culture and Politics,* WOKLER, Robert.

The Citizen Philosopher: Rousseau's Dedicatory Letter to the *Discourse on Inequality.* PALMER, Michael.

The Concept of Alienation in Janusz Korczak's Works. ROSEN, Henryk and SWIDERSKA, Ewa (trans).

Democratic Autonomy, Political Ethics, and Moral Luck. BREINER, Peter.

Das Gesetz oder das Gute? Zum Ursprung und Sinn des Formalismus in der Ethik Kants. SALA, Giovanni B.

L'idea di "Storia teoretica o congetturale" negli scritti filosofici e sul linguaggio di Adam Smith. IACONO, Alfonso M.

Immaginativa produttiva e struttura dell'immaginario nelle *Rêveries du promeneur solitaire* di Jean-Jacques Rousseau. PANELLA, Giuseppe.

The Individual and the General Will: Rousseau Reconsidered. HILEY, David R.

Naissance de l'auteur—Une Histoire de l'esthétique moderne autour de son alibi (in Japanese). SASAKI, Ken-ichi.

Republic and Politics in Machiavelli and Rousseau. VIROLI, Maurizio.

Rousseau and Recognition. SHAVER, Robert.

Rousseau on Reading "Jean-Jacques": *The Dialogues.* KELLY, Christopher and MASTERS, Roger D.

Rousseau, o el gobierno representativo. STRASSER, C.

Spinoza jenseits von Hobbes und Rousseau. GEISMANN, Georg.

The Theological-Political Tension in Liberalism. FULLER, Timothy.

Le travail de la contradiction dans le Livre I de l'*Emile.* IMBERT, Francis.

ROUTLEY, R

A Refutation of Environmental Ethics. THOMPSON, Janna.

ROUTLEY, V

A Refutation of Environmental Ethics. THOMPSON, Janna.

ROWE, W

Surplus Evil. SNYDER, Daniel T.

ROYAL SOCIETY

"Hobbes and the Royal Society" in *Perspectives on Thomas Hobbes,* MALCOLM, Noel.

ROYCE

Classical American Philosophy: Essential Readings and Interpretative Essays. STUHR, John J.

The Abbot-Royce Controversy. PEDEN, Creighton.

The Absolute, Community, and Time. WILLIAMS, Robert R.

New Documents on Josiah Royce. CLENDENNING, John and OPPENHEIM, Frank M.

When Loyalty No Harm Meant. ALLEN, R T.

RUDDICK, S

Pacifism and Care. DAVION, Victoria.

RUETHER, R

The Status of the Anomaly in the Feminist God-Talk of Rosemary Reuther. JAMES, George Alfred.

RULE OF LAW

Liberty and Justice. DAY, J P.

Comment on Robert Summers on the Rule of Law. REYNOLDS, Noel B.

Grounding the Rule of Law. REYNOLDS, Noel B.

The Ideal Socio-Legal Order: Its "Rule of Law" Dimension. SUMMERS, Robert S.

The Rule of Law in Contemporary Liberal Theory. WALDRON, Jeremy.

Spontaneous Order and the Rule of Law: Some Problems. MAC CORMICK, D Neil.

RULE UTILITARIANISM

Uncertainty in Moral Theory: An Epistemic Defense of Rule-Utilitarian Liberties. BALL, Stephen W.

RULE(S)

Dilemmas: A Christian Approach to Moral Decision Making. HIGGINSON, Richard.

Rules, Norms, and Decisions: On the Conditions of Practical and Legal Reasoning. KRATOCHWIL, Friedrich V.

"Comment: Positivism and the Foundations of Legal Authority" in *Issues in Contemporary Legal Philosophy: The Influence of H L A Hart,* BEN-MENACHEM, Hanina.

"Rule-Following in *Philosophical Investigations*" in *Wittgenstein in Focus—Im Brennpunkt: Wittgenstein,* PEARS, David.

"Wittgenstein on Breaking Rules" in *Wittgenstein in Focus—Im Brennpunkt: Wittgenstein,* FRONGIA, Guido.

Affirming the Reality of Rule-Following. PETTIT, Philip.

Are Virtues No More Than Dispositions to Obey Moral Rules?. SCHALLER, Walter E.

The Authority of Moral Rules. MOREH, J.

The Authority of the Rules of Baseball: The Commissioner as Judge. UTZ, Stephen G.

Conventions and Social Institutions. WEIRICH, Paul.

Dieu, le roi et les sujets. GUENANCIA, Pierre.

Egoism and Morality. MULHOLLAND, Leslie.

Following a Rule. WILLIAMSON, Colwyn.

Freedom and Rule-Following in Wittgenstein and Sartre. DWYER, Philip.

The Fundamental Features of Legal Rationality. GARDIES, Jean-Louis.

Malcolm on Language and Rules. BAKER, G P and HACKER, P M S.

The Naturalist Conception of Methodological Standards in Science. DOPPELT, Gerald.

Nota sobre el concepto de regla en A Tomasini Bassols. PALAVECINO, Sergio.

On Taking the Rabbit of Rule-Following out of the Hat of Representation: Response to 'The Reality of Rule-Following'. SUMMERFIELD, Donna M.

Philosophical Investigations 201: A Wittgensteinian Reply to Kripke. SUMMERFIELD, Donna M.

Règles et langage privé chez Wittgenstein: deux interprétations. SAUVÉ, Denis.

The Role of Rules. WEINBERGER, Ota.

The Rule-Following Considerations. BOGHOSSIAN, Paul A.

Rules, Communities and Judgements. ZALABARDO, José L.

Second-order Logic, Foundations, and Rules. SHAPIRO, Stewart.

Structuring and Simulating Negotiation: An Approach and an Example. KERSTEN, G E and BADCOCK, L and IGLEWSKI, M and MALLORY, G R.

Truth Rules, Hoverflies, and the Kripke-Wittgenstein Paradox. MILLIKAN, Ruth Garrett.

Virtues, Rules and the Foundations of Ethics. CLOWNEY, David.

RULER(S)

"Roman Rulers and the Philosophic Adviser" in *Philosophia Togata: Essays on Philosophy and Roman Society,* RAWSON, Elizabeth.

RUNZO, J

Conceptual Relativism and the Possibility of Absolute Faith. CRAIGHEAD, Houston A.

RUSE, M

The Structure of Biological Theories. THOMPSON, Paul.

Fundamenten, achtergronden of bondgenootschappen?. VAN DER WEELE, Cor.

Really Taking Darwin Seriously: An Alternative to Michael Ruse's Darwinian Metaethics. ROTTSCHAEFER, William A and MARTINSEN, David.

RUSSELL

A Combinatorial Theory of Possibility. ARMSTRONG, D M.

Descriptions. NEALE, Stephen.

Natural Signs: A Theory of Intentionality. ADDIS, Laird.

Rereading Russell: Essays on Bertrand Russell's Metaphysics and Epistemology. SAVAGE, C Wade (ed).

What is Identity?. WILLIAMS, C J F.

"Cause in the Later Russell" in *Rereading Russell: Essays on Bertrand Russell's Metaphysics and Epistemology,* EAMES, Elizabeth R.

"The Concept of Structure in *The Analysis of Matter*" in *Rereading Russell: Essays on Bertrand Russell's Metaphysics and Epistemology,* DEMOPOULOS, William and FRIEDMAN, Michael.

"Concepts of Projectability and the Problems of Induction" in *Rereading Russell: Essays on Bertrand Russell's Metaphysics and Epistemology,* EARMAN, John.

SALVATION

Leviathan and Spinoza's *Tractatus* on Revelation: Some Elements for a Comparison. PACCHI, Arrigo.

Solamente un dios puede todavia salvarnos. SILVA CAMARENA, Juan Manuel.

Swāmī Vivekānanda's Use of Science as an Analogy for the Attainment of *Moksa*. RAMBACHAN, Anantanand.

SAMENESS

Objetos, identidad y mismidad. CASTAÑEDA, Héctor-Neri.

SAMKHYA

A New Plausible Exposition of Sānkhya-Kārikā-9. WADHWANI-SHAH, Yashodhara.

SANCHEZ, F

Francisco Sanchez's Theory of Cognition and Vico's *verum/factum*. FAUR, José.

SANCTION(S)

"Abolishing Apartheid: The Importance of Sanctions" in *Inquiries into Values: The Inaugural Session of the International Society for Value Inquiry*, AUXTER, Thomas.

SANCTITY OF LIFE

The Sanctity-of-Life Doctrine in Medicine: A Critique. KUHSE, Helga.

"Sanctity of Life and Suicide: Tensions and Developments Within Common Morality" in *Suicide and Euthanasia*, BOYLE, Joseph.

SANDEL, M

Realizing Rawls. POGGE, Thomas W.

Sandel and the Limits of Community. ENSLIN, Penny.

SANDEL, R

Our Vantage Points: Not a View from Nowhere. LEACH, Mary.

SANITY

"Are We Losing Our Minds?" in *Mind, Value and Culture: Essays in Honor of E M Adams*, HALL, Ronald L.

War, Omnicide and Sanity: The Lesson of the Cuban Missile Crisis. SOMERVILLE, John.

SANKARA

The Place of Teaching Techniques in Samkara's Theology. SUTHREN HIRST, J G.

SANSKRIT

A Concise Dictionary of Indian Philosophy: Sanskrit Terms Defined in English. GRIMES, John A.

Sambandha and Abhisambandha. AKLUJKAR, Ashok.

SANTAYANA

Classical American Philosophy: Essential Readings and Interpretative Essays. STUHR, John J.

Beyond Truth: Santayana on the Functional Relations of Art, Myth, and Religion. CONNER, Frederick W.

The Enduring Value of Santayana's Philosophy. LACHS, John.

George Santayana and the Genteel Tradition. AARON, Daniel.

George Santayana. LACHS, John.

Hermes the Interpreter. SAATKAMP JR, Herman J.

Naturalism and Generality in Buchler and Santayana. SINGER, Beth J.

On Grue and Bleen. KERR-LAWSON, Angus.

Persons and Places. LYON, Richard C.

Santayana and Democritus—Two Mutually Interpreting Philosophical Poets. DILWORTH, David A.

Santayana and Panpsychism. SPRIGGE, Timothy.

Santayana's Autobiography and the Development of his Philosophy. SAATKAMP JR, Herman J.

Santayana's Idea of the Tragic. MC CORMICK, John E.

Santayana's Neglect of Hartshorne's Alternative. WHITTEMORE, Robert C.

Santayana's Neo-Platonism. KUNTZ, Paul G.

Santayana's Non-Reductive Naturalism. KERR-LAWSON, Angus.

Santayana's Ontology and the Nicene Creed. KERR-LAWSON, Angus.

Santayana's Philosophy of Love. SINGER, Irving.

Santayana's Pragmatism and the Comic Sense of Life. LEVINSON, Henry Samuel.

Six Aspects of Santayana's Philosophy. KERR-LAWSON, Angus.

Spirit's Primary Nature is to be Secondary. KERR-LAWSON, Angus.

Spirituality in Santayana. TEJERA, V.

Variations on a Given Theme. KERR-LAWSON, Angus.

SAPONTZIS, S

Rejoinder to Sapontzis's "Environmental Ethics and the Locus of Value". BALDNER, Kent.

SARTORIUS, R

"Comment: Positivism and the Foundations of Legal Authority" in *Issues in Contemporary Legal Philosophy: The Influence of H L A Hart*, FINNIS, John.

"Comment: Positivism and the Foundations of Legal Authority" in *Issues in Contemporary Legal Philosophy: The Influence of H L A Hart*, BEN-MENACHEM, Hanina.

SARTRE

Critical Theory and Poststructuralism: In Search of a Context. POSTER, Mark.

Existentially Speaking: Essays on the Philosophy of Literature. WILSON, Colin.

Natural Signs: A Theory of Intentionality. ADDIS, Laird.

Paths Toward a Clearing: Radical Empiricism and Ethnographic Inquiry. JACKSON, Michael.

The Perverted Consciousness: Sexuality and Sartre. LEAK, Andrew N.

The Thinking Muse: Feminism and Modern French Philosophy. ALLEN, Jeffner (ed).

"Authenticity and Historicity: On the Dialectical Ethics of Sartre" in *Inquiries into Values: The Inaugural Session of the International Society for Value Inquiry*, ZIMMERMAN, R E.

"Derrida and Sartre: Hegel's Death Knell" in *Derrida and Deconstruction*, HOWELLS, Christina M.

"Dialectical Ethics: A First Look at Sartre's Unpublished Rome Lecture Notes" in *Inquiries into Values: The Inaugural Session of the International Society for Value Inquiry*, BOWMAN, Elizabeth A and STONE, Robert V.

"From Freedom to Need: Sartre's First Two Moralities" in *Inquiries into Values: The Inaugural Session of the International Society for Value Inquiry*, ANDERSON, Thomas C.

"History as Fact and as Value: The Posthumous Sartre" in *Inquiries into Values: The Inaugural Session of the International Society for Value Inquiry*, FLYNN, Thomas.

"The Obligation to Will the Freedom of Others, According to Jean-Paul Sartre" in *The Question of the Other: Essays in Contemporary Continental Philosophy*, ANDERSON, Thomas C.

"Posthumous Anachronisms in the Work of Sartre" in *Inquiries into Values: The Inaugural Session of the International Society for Value Inquiry*, CAWS, Peter.

"Sartre's Annihilation of Morality" in *Inquiries into Values: The Inaugural Session of the International Society for Value Inquiry*, REIMAN, Jeffrey.

"Sartre" in *Ethics in the History of Western Philosophy*, BARNES, Hazel E.

"The Second Death of Jean-Paul Sartre" in *Inquiries into Values: The Inaugural Session of the International Society for Value Inquiry*, GERASSI, John.

A proposito di Jean-Paul Sartre. TOGNONATO, Claudio.

Ateismo e libertà. MONDIN, B.

Bad Faith. HYMERS, Michael.

Le cercle et le doublet: Note sur Sartre et Foucault. KNEE, Philip.

A Consideration of Sartre's View of 'Existence'. MONDAL, Sunil Baran.

The Cynicism of Sartre's "Bad Faith". SANTONI, Ronald E.

Dialogo sobre humanismo y existencialismo (cuarta y última parte). SILVA CAMARENA, Juan Manuel.

Engagement ou néantisation? (in Greek). DÉLIVOYATZIS, S.

Experience as Nothingness: A Form of Humanistic Religious Experience. RAYMOND, Menye Menye.

El Flaubert de Sartre. ZAMORA, Alvaro.

Freedom and Rule-Following in Wittgenstein and Sartre. DWYER, Philip.

Merleau-Ponty and Pseudo-Sartreanism. ZAYTZEFF, Veronique (trans).

Sartre y la ética: De la mala fe a la conversión moral. VIDIELLA, Graciela.

Sartre's Sexism Reconsidered. MUI, Constance.

Le strutture trascendentali della coscienza nel primo Sartre: ipotesi di lettura. COMOLLI, Fabrizio.

Successfully Lying to Oneself: A Sartrean Perspective. CATALANO, Joseph S.

Visage Versus Visages. BAUM, Mylène.

SASSO, G

Essere e negazione: Per un recente volume di Gennaro Sasso. MIGNINI, Filippo.

SASSOWER, R

Scarcity and the Limits of Want: Comments on Sassower and Bender. LEVINE, David.

SATISFACTION

Inductive Full Satisfaction Classes. KOTLARSKI, Henryk and RATAJCZYK, Zygmunt.

The Relationship Between Ethics and Job Satisfaction: An Empirical Investigation. VITELL, Scott J and DAVIS, D L.

Semantics for Nonstandard Languages. MURAWSKI, Roman.

Two Kinds of Satisficing. HURKA, Thomas.

SCEPTICISM

Stroud and Williams on Dreaming and Scepticism. REIN, Andrew.

Stroud's Defense of Cartesian Scepticism: A 'Linguistic' Response. GLOCK, Hans-Johann.

Universal Prescriptivism and Practical Skepticism. MC GRAY, James W.

Ward on Davidson's Refutation of Scepticism. HURTADO, Guillermo.

Wittgenstein, Realism, and CLS: Undermining Rule Scepticism. LANDERS, Scott.

Zetesis. DE OLASO, Ezequiel.

SCHAFF, A

Adam Schaff and the Club of Rome. KING, Alexander.

The Club of Rome and the Vienna Centre. FELDHEIM, Pierre.

The Dialectics of Peace Education. RAPOPORT, Anatol.

The Social Humanism of Adam Schaff. JAGUARIBE, Helio.

Sociognoseología y objectividad. MORALES, Julián.

Some Aspects of the Methodology of Comparative Research in Politics. WIATR, Jerzy J.

Whither the Way?. WOHL, Andrzej and GOLEBIOWSKI, Marek (trans).

SCHANK, R

Conceptual Dependency as the Language of Thought. DUNLOP, Charles E M.

SCHEER, R

Reply to Scheer's "What if Something Really Unheard-of Happened?". MALCOLM, Norman.

SCHEFFLER, S

Two Departures from Consequentialism. BENNETT, Jonathan.

SCHELER

The Knowledge of Values: A Methodological Introduction. LÓPEZ QUINTÁS, Alfonso (ed).

El amor al prójimo en la ética fenomenológica de los valores. OLMO, Javier.

The Essential Elements for the Possibility and Necessity of the Principle of Solidarity According to Max Scheler. IBANA, Rainer R A.

Max Scheler's Criticism of Schopenhauer's Account of Morality and Compassion. MAIDAN, Michael.

Religious Transcendence: Scheler's Forgotten Quest. SCHALOW, Frank.

The Latest Philosophical Anthropology of Max Scheler (in Dutch). VEDDER, Ben.

SCHELLING

The A Priori from Kant to Schelling. LAWRENCE, Joseph P (trans) and GRONDIN, Jean.

Dialéctica de la Revolución: Hegel, Schelling y Hölderlin ante la Revolución Francesa. INNERARITY, Daniel.

Habermas interprète de Schelling. MAESSCHALCK, Marc.

The Limits of Thought: Rosenzweig, Schelling, and Cohen. GIBBS, Robert.

Metafora e concetto: sulla metafora dello specchio in Schelling e nel giovane Hegel. TAGLIAPIETRA, Andrea.

On Schelling's Philosophy of Nature. JÄHNIG, Dieter and SOLBAKKEN, Elisabeth (trans).

The Role of the Unconscious in Schelling's System of Transcendental Idealism. SNOW, Dale.

Schelling's "On the Essence of Human Freedom": An Interpretation of the First Main Points (in Hungarian). HEIDEGGER, Martin.

Schelling's Critique of Hegel and the Beginnings of Marxian Dialectics. LAWRENCE, Joseph P (trans) and FRANK, Manfred.

Schelling: A New Beginning. LAWRENCE, Joseph P.

Sich-Wissen als Argument: Zum Problem der Theoretizität des Selbstbewusstseins. RÖMPP, Georg.

Sviluppo e senso delle annotazioni schopenhaueriane a Schelling (2 Teil). VECCHIOTTI, Icilio.

Les Weltalter de Schelling: Un essai de philosophie narrative. MAESSCHALCK, M.

SCHEMATA

An Axiom Schema of Comprehension of Zermelo-Fraenkel-Skolem Set Theory. HEIDEMA, Johannes.

G H von Wright on Explanation and Understanding: An Appraisal. MARTIN, Rex.

The Nonaxiomatizability of $L(Q^2_{\aleph_1})$ By Finitely Many Schemata. SHELAH, Saharon and STEINHORN, Charles.

SCHEMATISM

Die Anschauungsformen und das Schematismuskapitel. MUDROCH, Vilem.

SCHEMATIZATION

"The 'Universal Thinking Machine', or on the Genesis of Schematized Reasoning in the 17th Century" in Scientific Knowledge Socialized, KRÄMER-FRIEDRICH, Sybille.

SCHERVISH, M

Pareto Unanimity and Consensus. LEVI, Isaac.

SCHIFFER, S

Breaking Out of the Gricean Circle. LEVINE, Joseph.

SCHILLER

"Voyage to Syracuse: Adams—Schiller—Emerson" in Mind, Value and Culture: Essays in Honor of E M Adams, SMYTH, Richard.

The Aristotelian Character of Schiller's Ethical Ideal. CORDNER, Christopher.

Grazia e dignità dell'estetica schilleriana. DOLORES FOLLIERO, Granzia.

Libertad como gracia y elegancia. CRUZ CRUZ, Juan.

SCHIZOPHRENIA

Schizophrenia and Indeterminacy: The Problem of Validity. HUNT, Geoffrey.

SCHLEIERMACHER

Transforming the Hermeneutic Context: From Nietzsche to Nancy. ORMISTON, Gayle L (ed).

Could There Be a Mystical Core of Religion?. JANTZEN, Grace M.

Does Anxiety Explain Original Sin?. QUINN, Philip L.

The Ethical Impulse in Schleiermacher's Early Ethics. CROSSLEY JR, John P.

Friedrich Schleiermacher's Theory of the Limited Communitarian State. HOOVER, Jeffrey.

Immediacy and the Text: Friedrich Schleiermacher's Theory of Style and Interpretation. PFAU, Thomas.

New Perspectives on Schleiermacher's Ethics: An Assay. DUKE, James O.

Ritschl's Critique of Schleiermacher's Theological Ethics. BRANDT, James M.

Schleiermacher's "Über den Unterschied zwischen Naturgesetz und Sittengesetz". BOYD, George N.

Schleiermacher's Critique of Ethical Reason: Toward a Systematic Ethics. WALLHAUSSER, John.

SCHLICK

Questions on Wittgenstein. HALLER, Rudolf.

SCHMIDTZ, D

To the Lighthouse. LEVIN, Michael.

SCHMITT, C

Decisione e origine: Appunti su Schmitt e Heidegger. SCALONE, A.

El Hobbes de Schmitt. DOTTI, Jorge E.

SCHOENBERG, A

Negative Composition. HANRAHAN, Nancy Weiss.

SCHOLARSHIP

Comparative Philosophy and the Philosophy of Scholarship. TUCK, Andrew P.

Current Trends in Legal Philosophy and Jurisprudence. BRONAUGH, Richard.

Improving the Quality of Social Welfare Scholarship: Response to "Confirmational Response Bias". SCHUERMAN, John R.

Publishing Biomedical Research: Roles and Responsibilities. RELMAN, Arnold S.

Quality of Scholarship in Bioethics. BRODY, Baruch A.

SCHOLASTICISM

see also Thomism

The Possible Influence of Montaigne's "Essais" on Descartes' "Treatise on the Passions". PAULSON, Michael G.

Lorenzo Valla and Rudolph Agricola. MONFASANI, John.

Marxism and Conceptual Scholasticism. KOZYR-KOWALSKI, Stanislaw and OSZKODAR, Zbigniew (trans).

On the Scholastic or Aristotelian Roots of "Intentionality" in Brentano. RUNGGALDIER, Edmund.

The Philosophy of Language in Scholasticism (in Serbo-Croatian). GOMBOCZ, Wolfgang L.

Why St Thomas Stays Alive. MC COOL, Gerald A.

SCHOOL(S)

Essays in Philosophy and Education. STOTT, Laurence J.

Interpreting Education. EDEL, Abraham.

Reading Curriculum Theory: The Development of a New Hermeneutic. REYNOLDS, William M.

"Cicero und die 'Schule des Aristoteles'" in Cicero's Knowledge of the Peripatos, GÖRLER, Woldemar.

The False Ontology of School Climate Effects. MILLER, Steven I and FREDERICKS, Janet.

The Spanish Natural Law School. LLANO, Estela.

Towards More Effective Arts Education. GARDNER, Howard.

SCHOOLING

Literate Thinking and Schooling. LANGER, Judith.

SCIENCE

SCIENCE

SCIENCE

Francis Bacon's "Ars Inveniendi". VAN PEURSEN, C A.

Francisco Sanchez's Theory of Cognition and Vico's *verum/factum*. FAUR, José.

Freud's Phylogenetic Fantasy: An Essay Review. PARISI, Thomas.

Freud-a-til vraiment renié le pouvoir thérapeutique de la psychanalyse?. VACHON, Gérard.

Fundamenten, achtergronden of bondgenootschappen?. VAN DER WEELE, Cor.

Gedrag: wat zit er achter?. VAN DER STEEN, Wim.

Gender Is an Organon. KEHOE, Alice B.

Genetic Traits. GIFFORD, Fred.

Georg Klaus über Kybernetik und Information. STOCK, Wolfgang G.

Getting the Science Right is the Problem, Not the Solution: A Matter of Priority. MIXON, Don.

Gibbs' Paradox and Non-Uniform Convergence. DENBIGH, K G and REDHEAD, M L G.

Gibson, Skinner and Perceptual Responses. GUERIN, Bernard.

Gödel, Escher, Bach and Dooyeweerd. VERKERK, M J.

Gravity (in Dutch). KLEVER, W N A.

Harde noten om te kraken: de zachte wetenschappen. IBSCH, Elrud.

Hay una filosofía de la ciencia en el último Wittgenstein?. MOULINES, C Ulises.

Hayek and the Interpretive TUrn. MADISON, G B.

Hebrew Wisdom and Psychotheological Dialogue. GLADSON, Jerry and LUCAS, Ron.

Hegel and the Unity of Science Program. ROCKMORE, Tom.

Hegel vor dem Forum der Wissenschaftslehre Fichtes: Reinhard Lauths Untersuchungen zum Frühidealismus. ZAHN, Manfred.

Heidegger, Kant and the 'Humanism' of Science. SCHALOW, Frank.

Heideggers Kritik der neuzeitlichen Wissenschaft und Technik. PLEGER, Wolfgang H.

Henri Poincaré's Philosophy of Science. STUMP, David.

A Hermeneutic Account of Clinical Psychology: Strengths and Limits. SILVERN, Louise E.

Hermeneutics in Science and Medicine: A Thesis Understated. CHURCHILL, Larry R.

The Historical Epistemology of Gaston Bachelard and its Relevance to Science Education. SOUQUE, Jean-Pascal.

History as Metascience: A Vichian Cue to the Understanding of the Nature and Development of Sciences. RIVERSO, Emanuele.

Holism a Century Ago: The Elaboration of Duhem's Thesis. BRENNER, Anastasios A.

Homeopathie de optische metafoor van Wiersma. KIBBELAAR, Robert.

How to be Realistic About Inconsistency in Science. BROWN, Bryson.

How to Learn a Language Like a Chimpanzee. GAUKER, Christopher.

The Human Being as Subject Matter of the Philosophy of Science. BOTEZ, Angela.

The Human Brain and Human Destiny: A Pattern for Old Brain Empathy With the Emergence of Mind. ASHBROOK, James B.

Husserl's Paradox. KIDDER, Paul.

Hypothetical and Inductive Heuristics. KLEINER, Scott A.

Idealist Elements in Thomas Kuhn's Philosophy of Science. HOYNINGEN-HUENE, Paul.

The Idealistic Implications of Bell's Theorem. SCHICK JR, Theodore W.

Idealization and Projection in the Empirical Sciences: Husserl versus Heidegger. KOCKELMANS, Joseph J.

Idealized Laws, Antirealism, and Applied Science: A Case in Hydrogeology. SHRADER-FRECHETTE, K S.

Identity and Individuality in Classical and Quantum Physics. FRENCH, Steven.

The Illusory Riches of Sober's Monism. KITCHER, Philip and STERELNY, Kim and WATERS, C Kenneth.

The Import of the Problem of Rationality. AGASSI, Joseph.

Improving the Quality of Social Welfare Scholarship: Response to "Confirmational Response Bias". SCHUERMAN, John R.

In Defense of Good Reasons. BERKSON, William.

La ingeniería social como método de testeo. COMESAÑA, Manuel E.

Irony, Tragedy, and Temporality in Agricultural Systems, or, How Values and Systems are Related. BUSCH, Lawrence.

Is Kuhn's Revolution in the Philosophy of Science a Pseudo-Revolution?. RADNITZKY, G.

Is Marxism an Atheism?. FRITZHAND, Marek and RODZINSKA, Aleksandra (trans).

Is Natural Law Ethics Obsolete?. MACHAN, Tibor R.

Is Social Work Different? Comments on "Confirmational Response Bias". WESTRUM, Ron.

Is the Theory of Natural Selection Unprincipled? A Reply to Shimony. SOBER, Elliott.

János Hetényi—The Scientist, the Dilettante (in Hungarian). SZABÓ, Zoltán Z.

Jean Cavaillès' aanloop tot de wetenschapstheorie. CORTOIS, P.

Journals Have Obligations, Too: Commentary on "Confirmational Response Bias". HOLLANDER, Rachelle D.

Kant, *Naturphilosophie*, and Oersted's Discovery of Electromagnetism: A Reassessment. SHANAHAN, Timothy.

Kants Theorie der Materie und ihre Wirkung auf die zeitgenössische Chemie. CARRIER, Martin.

Karl Popper's Philosophy of Scientific Knowledge. NARAYAN, S Shankar.

L'interprétation de la relativité. LEFETZ, L.

La Cosmodicée ou Etica repetita (in Romanian). BRUCAR, Iosif.

La psychologie consonantiste et la créativité (in Romanian). STANCIULESCU, Traian Dinorel.

La rationnalité interrogative (in Romanian). GRECU, Constantin.

Lagrange's Analytical Mathematics, Its Cartesian Origins and Reception in Comte's Positive Philosophy. FRASER, Craig G.

The Language Dependence of Accuracy. BARNES, Eric.

Laudan's Normative Naturalism. SIEGEL, Harvey.

The Limits of Public Participation in Science Revealed. YOXEN, Edward.

Literatuur als bron voor historisch en sociologisch onderzoek. MASO, Benjo.

Logical Examination of Physical Theory. BARKER, Peter (trans) and ARIEW, Roger (trans) and DUHEM, Pierre.

The Logical Limits of Science. SMITH, Joseph Wayne.

Mach's "Critique of Knowledge" and the Physiology of Senses (in Czechoslovakian). JANKO, Jan.

Une Machine spéculative (informatique, intelligence artificielle et recherche cognitive). BORILLO, Mario.

Mādhyamika Buddhism and Quantum Mechanics: Beginning a Dialogue. MANSFIELD, Victor.

Maiocchi on Duhem, Howard on Duhem and Einstein: Historiographical Comments. BURIAN, Richard M.

Marxismus—Subjektwissenschaft—Psychoanalyse. BRAUN, Karl-Heinz.

La matemática y el ámbito conceptual. DE LORENZO, Javier.

Le mathématicien et ses images. DELESSERT, André.

Mathematics as Natural Science. GOODMAN, Nicolas D.

Measurement, Pleasure, and Practical Science in Plato's *Protagoras*. RICHARDSON, Henry S.

Médecine, expérience et logique. BARNES, Jonathan and BRUNSCHWIG, J (trans).

Method and the Authority of Science. TILES, Mary E.

Methodological Individualism and Explanation. TUOMELA, Raimo.

Methodological Realism: An Essential Requirement of Scientific Quest. SAH, Hirendra Prasad.

Methodology Is Pragmatic: A Reponse to Miller. BERKSON, William.

Methods of Conceptual Change in Science: Imagistic and Analogical Reasoning. NERSESSIAN, Nancy J.

La metodología falsacionista y su ecología. RADNITZKY, Gerard.

The Modal View of Economic Models. RAPPAPORT, Steven.

The Model-Theoretic Approach in the Philosophy of Science. DA COSTA, Newton C A and FRENCH, Steven.

Modeling in the Museum: On the Role of Remnant Models in the Work of Joseph Grinnell. GRIESEMER, James R.

Models of Reason, Types of Principles and Reasoning: Historical Comments and Theoretical Outlines. PATTARO, Enrico.

A Modern Look at the Origin of the Universe. ODENWALD, Sten F.

Modularity, and the Psychoevolutionary Theory of Emotion. GRIFFITHS, P E.

Moles in Motu: Principles of Spinoza's Physics. KLEVER, W N A.

The Moon Is Not There•When I See It: A Response to Snyder. GARRISON, Mark.

El movimiento accidental en Aristóteles. QUEVEDO, Amalia.

The Murky Borderland Between Scientific Intuition and Fraud. SEGERSTRALE, Ullica.

Der Mythos des Rahmens am Pranger: Anderssons Antwort auf die wissenschaftsgeschichtliche Herausforderung. ALBERT, Hans.

The Narrative Reconstruction of Science. ROUSE, Joseph.

A Natural Explanation of the Existence and Laws of Our Universe. SMITH, Quentin.

Naturaleza y función de los axiomas en la epistemología aristotélica. CASSINI, Alejandro.

The Naturalist Conception of Methodological Standards in Science. DOPPELT, Gerald.

Nature, Reality, and the Sacred: A Meditation in Science and Religion. GILKEY, Langdon.

Nel labirinto dell'informazione: i sistemi complessi. MORCHIO, Renzo.

Il neoidealismo italiano e la meccanica quantistica. MAIOCCHI, Roberto.

SCIENCE

Il neorealismo epistemologico dell' "Académie Internationale de philosophie des sciences". CASTELLANA, M.

A New Approach to Regulating the Use of Animals in Science. ANDERSON, Warwick.

A New Meaning in the History of Science: From the Logical Truth Towards the Ethical Truth. ISAC, Victor.

New Notes from Underground. ELLERMAN, Carl Paul.

The New World of Research Ethics: A Preliminary Map. DAVIS, Michael.

Newton on the Number of Colours in the Spectrum. TOPPER, David.

Niet vrouw, niet man; wat dan? De rol van biomedische kennis bij de behandeling van pseudohermafrodieten. VAN DEN WIJNGAARD, Marianne and HUYTS, Ini.

De nieuwe zekerheden van het hedendaags wetenschapsonderzoek. AMSTERDAMSKA, Olga and HAGENDIJK, R.

NOA's Ark—Fine for Realism. MUSGRAVE, Alan.

The Non-Existence of a Principle of Natural Selection. SHIMONY, Abner.

Normative Naturalism and the Role of Philosophy. ROSENBERG, Alexander.

Normative Naturalism. LAUDAN, Larry.

Notes et documents sur "Le Descartes de L Lévy-Bruhl". CAVAILLÉ, Jean-Pierre.

Notes on the Underground. CLARK, Stephen R L.

Notion et idée de science chez Eric Weil. BREUVART, Jean-Marie.

Objectividade científica: noção e questionamentos. CUPANI, Alberto.

The Objectivity of Quantum Probabilities. KRIPS, H.

Observation, Instrumentalism, and Constructive Empiricism. GRAYBOSCH, Anthony.

On Adaptation: A Reduction of the Kauffman-Levin Model to a Problem in Graph Theory and Its Consequences. SARKAR, Sahotra.

On Advancing Simple Hypotheses. OSHERSON, Daniel N and WEINSTEIN, Scott.

On Equitable Cake-Cutting, or: Caring More about Caring. HAYNES, Felicity.

On Grue and Bleen. KERR-LAWSON, Angus.

On Innertheoretical Conditions for Theoretical Terms. GÄHDE, Ulrich.

On Newton-Smith's Concept of Verisimilitude. OLCZYK, Slawoj.

On Quantitative Relationist Theories. MUNDY, Brent.

On the Essential Difference between Science, Art and Philosophy, or Philosophy as the Literature of Necessity. BOULLART, Karel.

On the Logical Structure of Verisimilitude. GERLA, Giangiacomo and GUCCIONE, Salvatore.

On the Perspectives of Research into the Philosophical and Social Aspects of Science and Technology. FROLOV, Ivan T.

One Causal Mechanism in Evolution: One Unit of Selection. KARY, Carla E.

The Only Game in Town. ACHINSTEIN, Peter.

An Operational Approach to the Dynamics of Science: Kant's Concept of Architectonic. GIUCULESCU, Alexandru.

De oppervlakkigheid van de empirisch gewende wetenschapstheorie. RIP, Arie.

Opposing Science with Art, Again? Nietzsche's Project According to Stack. SEIGFRIED, Hans.

Overview of the OTA Report Infertility: Medical and Social Choices. WHITE, Becky Cox.

Pain Corrigibility. BLUM, Alex.

Paraconsistency. URBAS, Igor.

Paradoxical Consequences of Balzer's and Gähde's Criteria of Theoreticity. SCHURZ, Gerhard.

Parménide d'Élée et la fondation de la science (in Greek). KARAYANNIS, G.

Pascal's Great Experiment. ARNOLD, Keith.

Patents and Free Scientific Information in Biotechnology: Making Monoclonal Antibodies Proprietary. MACKENZIE, Michael and KEATING, Peter.

Paul Ricoeur's Methodological Parallelism. FLEMING, Patricia Ann.

Peirce on the Progress and Authority of Science. FORSTER, Paul D.

El pensamiento económico de Hegel: Escritos recientes. CORDUA, Carla.

El pensar en la filosofía de la mente de L Wittgenstein. GIL DE PAREIJA, José L.

Phanerochemistry and Semiotic. TURSMAN, Richard.

Philoponus on the Origins of the Universe and Other Issues. OSBORNE, Catherine.

Philosophical Questions of Mathematics in Anti-Dühring. PANFILOV, V A.

Philosophy as Primordial Science (Urwissenschaft) in the Early Heidegger. KOVACS, George.

Philosophy for an 'Age of Death': The Critique of Science and Technology in Heidegger and Nishitani. HEINE, Steven.

Philosophy of Biology Under Attack: Stent Versus Rosenberg. THOMPSON, Paul.

Philosophy of Science Naturalized? Some Problems with Giere's Naturalism. SIEGEL, Harvey.

Le physicien et ses principes. RIVIER, Dominique.

Pierre Duhem's Conception of Natural Classification. LUGG, Andrew.

Pierre Duhem's The Aim and Structure of Physical Theory: A Book Against Conventionalism. MAIOCCHI, Roberto.

Place de l'homme dans l'univers. MALDAMÉ, Jean-Michel.

Positivism, Philosophy of Science, and Self-Understanding in Comte and Mill. SCHARFF, Robert C.

The Possibility of Computers Becoming Persons. DOLBY, R G A.

I postulati etici e metodologici fondamentali delle psichiatrie fenomenologiche. FRANCIONI, Mario.

The Poverty of Pluralism: A Reply to Sterelny and Kitcher. SOBER, Elliott.

The Practical Element in Ancient Exact Sciences. KNORR, Wilbur R.

The Principles of New Science of G B Vico and the Theory of Historical Interpretation. NOAKES, Susan (trans) and BETTI, Emilio and PINTON, Giorgio (trans).

Probabilism. DE FINETTI, Bruno.

The Problem of Going from: Science Policy and 'Human Factors' in the Experience of Developing Countries. IGNATYEV, A A.

The Problem of Going To: Between Epistemology and the Sociology of Knowledge. MOKRZYCKI, Edmund.

The Problem of Psychotherapeutic Effectiveness. BARTLETT, Steven J.

Programas e Promessas: Sobre o (Ab-)Uso do Jargão Computacional em Teorias Cognitivas da Mente. MENDONÇA, W P.

Prospective Realism. BROWN, Harold I.

Psicologia e scienze della natura in Wilhelm Wundt. CAVALLO, Giuliana.

Psychoanalyse: pseudo-wetenschap of geesteswetenschap?. MOOIJ, A W M.

Publishing Biomedical Research: Roles and Responsibilities. RELMAN, Arnold S.

Pythia-Sphinx Complex in Oedipus' Life: On the Reversals between the Questioning and the Answering Modes of Being. MAMALI, Catalin.

Quantum Measurement and the Program for the Unity of Science. SCHARF, David C.

Quelle est la place de l'intelligence artificielle dans l'étude de la cognition?. ANDLER, Daniel.

La radice filosofica della rivoluzione scientifica moderna. CRESCINI, Angelo.

Raising Darwin's Consciousness: Females and Evolutionary Theory. HRDY, Sarah Blaffer.

Reading Horkheimer Reading Vico: An Introduction. DALLMAYR, Fred.

The Real Objective of Mendel's Paper. MONAGHAN, Floyd V and CORCOS, Alain F.

Reale e complesso: osservazioni sul realismo scientifico e la storia della scienza. STOMEO, A.

Realism and the Underdetermination of Theory. CLENDINNEN, F John.

The Realism that Duhem Rejected in Copernicus. GODDU, André.

Realism versus Antirealism: The Venue of the Linguistic Consensus. POLS, Edward.

Il realismo nella filosofia della scienza contemporanea. SANGUINETI, Juan José.

Reason and Reflective Judgement: Kant on the Significance of Systematicity. GUYER, Paul.

A Reason for Theoretical Terms. GAIFMAN, Haim and OSHERSON, Daniel N and WEINSTEIN, Scott.

Reasons, Rationales, and Relativisms: What's at Stake in the Conversation over Scientific. PEERENBOOM, R P.

Recovering Evolution: A Reply to Eckersley and Fox. BOOKCHIN, Murray.

Reflections on "Confirmational Response Bias Among Social Work Journals". HOPPS, June Gary.

Reflexive Epistemology and Social Complexity: The Philosophical Legacy of Otto Neurath. ZOLO, Danilo.

Rejoinder to Berkson's "In Defense of Good Reasons". MILLER, David.

Relating the Physics and Religion of David Bohm. SHARPE, Kevin J.

Remarks on Physicalism and Reductionism. PEARCE, David.

Renormalizing Epistemology. LEPLIN, Jarrett.

Reply to Jahren's "Comments on Ruth Ginzberg's Paper". GINZBERG, Ruth.

Reply to Sober's "Is the Theory of Natural Selection Unprincipled? Reply to Shimony". SHIMONY, Abner.

Reply—Symposium on the Role of the Philosopher Among the Scientists: Nuisance or Necessity?. BAIGRIE, Brian.

Reply—Symposium on the Role of the Philosopher Among the Scientists: Nuisance or Necessity? A Reply to Baigrie. AGASSI, Joseph.

Reply—The Possibility of Computers Becoming Persons: A Response to Dolby. CHERRY, Christopher.

SCIENCE

Research on the History of Physical Theories. ARIEW, Roger (trans) and BARKER, Peter (trans) and DUHEM, Pierre.

Research Perspectives and the Anomalous Status of Modern Ecology. HAGEN, Joel B.

La révolution kuhnienne est-elle une fausse révolution?. RADNITZKY, Gérard.

Rhetoric and Aesthetics of History. RÜSEN, Jörn.

Robots that Learn: A Test of Intelligence. SUPPES, Patrick and CRANGLE, Colleen.

The Role of Error in Computer Science. JASON, Gary.

The Role of the Philosopher Among the Scientists: Nuisance or Necessity?. AGASSI, Joseph.

Rondom realisme. RADDER, Hans.

Rosenberg's Rebellion. WATERS, C Kenneth.

Schopenhauer y la psicología. PINILLOS, José Luis.

Science and Cultural Diversity (in Hungarian). FRESCO, Marcel F.

Science and Hermeneutics. RICKMAN, H P.

Science and Theology in Fourteenth Century: Subalternate Sciences in Oxford Commentaries on the *Sentences*. LIVESEY, Steven J.

Science Begins with Everyday Thinking. ROYER, Ron.

Science, Philosophy and Religion in the Seventeenth Century Encounter Between China and the West (in Serbo-Croatian). STANDAERT, Nicolas.

Science, Reduction and Natural Kinds. MEYER, Leroy N.

Science, Technology, and God: In Search of Believers. GOLDMAN, Steven L.

Science, Technology, and Naturalized Philosophy. JACOBSEN, Rockney.

Science, Technology, and Society: Considerations of Method. BECKWITH, Guy V.

Science- and Engineering-Related Ethics and Value Studies: Characteristics of an Emerging Field of Research. HOLLANDER, Rachelle D and STENECK, Nicholas H.

Science—Democracy—Christianity. BRUNGS, Robert A.

Scientific Explanation, Necessity and Contingency. WEBER, Erik.

Scientific Problems and the Conduct of Research. HAIG, Brian.

Scientific Rationality as Instrumental Rationality. GIERE, Ronald N.

Serendipity as a Source of Evolutionary Progress in Science. KANTOROVICH, Aharon and NE'EMAN, Yuval.

Significado, referencia e inconmensurabilidad. GAETA, Rodolfo.

La síntesis de lo uno y lo múltiple. HARRIS, Errol E.

Die Situationsanalyse. WERLEN, Benno.

Sobre la noción fregeana "extensión de un concepto". DEL PALACIO, Alfonso Avila.

Sobre la privacidad de los estados de conciencia. LARRETA, Juan Rodriguez and DORFMAN, Beatriz.

Some Recent Controversy Over the Possibility of Experimentally Determining Isotropy in the Speed of Light. CLIFTON, Robert K.

Some Remarks on Laudan's Theory of Scientific Rationality. VON ECKARDT, Barbara.

Die soziobiologische Obsoletierung des "Reichs der Zwecke". DORSCHEL, Andreas.

Species of Thought: A Comment on Evolutionary Epistemology. WILSON, David Sloan.

The Status of the Anomaly in the Feminist God-Talk of Rosemary Reuther. JAMES, George Alfred.

Strange Attraction, Curious Liaison: Clio Meets Chaos. DYKE, C.

The Structure-Nominative Reconstruction of Scientific Knowledge. BURGIN, M S.

Struggling with Causality: Schrödinger's Case. BEN-MENAHEM, Yemima.

Sulla teoria e metodica della storia. MEYER, Eduard.

T H Morgan, Neither an Epistemological Empiricist nor a "Methodological" Empiricist. VICEDO, Marga.

Tacit Metaphysical Premises of Modern Empiricism. NAHLIK, Krzysztof J.

Techne: dai Greci ai moderni e ritorno. POSSENTI, Vittorio.

Technic Aesthetics as Science (in Czechoslovakian). KLIVAR, Miroslav.

Technology in a Free Society: The New Frankenstein. BALESTRA, Dominic J.

Technology versus Science: The Cognitive Fallacy. DI NUCCI PEARCE, M Rosaria and PEARCE, David.

Teleology and Scientific Method in Kant's Critique of Judgement. BUTTS, Robert E.

Teoria della argomentazione e filosofia della scienza. BARROTTA, Pierluigi.

The Classical vs the PDP Model in Describing the Tic-Tac-Toe Game (in Hebrew). SHAGRIR, Oron.

The Logical Structure of Aesthetic Value Judgements: An Outline of a Popperian Aesthetics (in Hebrew). KULKA, Tomas.

The Newtonian Concept of Space and Time (in Polish). MAZIERSKI, Stanislaw.

Thinking with the Weight of the Earth: Feminist Contributions to an

Epistemology of Concreteness. HOLLER, Linda.

Toward a New Relation between Humanity and Nature: Reconstructing T'ien-jen-ho-i. LIU, Shu-hsien.

Toward a Sound Perspective on Modern Physics: Capra's Popularization of Mysticism and Theological Approaches. CLIFTON, Robert K and REGEHR, Marilyn G.

Towards a Typology of Experimental Errors: An Epistemological View. HON, Giora.

Truth, Relativism, and Crossword Puzzles. MURPHY, Nancey.

Two Faces of Maxwell's Demon Reveal the Nature of Irreversibility. COLLIER, John D.

Über eine unzulängliche Auffassung der methodologischen Einheit der Wissenschaft und unbefriedigende Verteidigung. JAKOWLJEWITSCH, Dragan.

Über einen neuen Versuch der Argumentation für die methodologische Einheit der Wissenschaften. JAKOWLJEWITSCH, Dragan.

Unacceptable Notions of Science Held by Process-Product Researchers. CHAMBERS, John H.

Unicidad y categoricidad de teorías. LUNGARZO, Carlos A.

Een vergelijking van inductief-statistisch redeneren en default logica. TAN, Yao-Hua.

Vérisimilarité et méthodologie poppérienne. LAFLEUR, Gérald.

Vico, Hercules, and the Lion: Figure and Ideology in the *Scienza nuova*. LUCENTE, Gregory L.

Waste and Culture. TIBERG, Nils.

Los Wertverläufe de Frege y la teoría de conjuntos. ORAYEN, Raúl.

Wesshalb implizite Definitionen nicht genug sind. BARTELS, Andreas.

What is Context?. SHANON, Benny.

When Probabilistic Support is Inductive. MURA, Alberto.

Wissenschaft, Vorurteil und Wahn. LOH, Werner.

SCIENCE FICTION

Thought Probes: Philosophy Through Science Fiction Literature (Second Edition). MILLER JR, Fred D.

Anges et hobbits: le sens des mondes possibles. LACOSTE, Jean-Yves.

SCIENTIFIC

Scientific Explanation (Minnesota Studies in the Philosophy of Science, Volume XIII). KITCHER, Philip (ed).

"'External' Factors in the Development of Psychology in the West" in *Scientific Knowledge Socialized*, WILKES, Kathy.

"The Causal Mechanical Model of Explanation" in *Scientific Explanation (Minnesota Studies in the Philosophy of Science, Volume XIII)*, WOODWARD, James.

"Extending Evolutionary Epistemology to 'Justifying' Scientific Beliefs" in *Issues in Evolutionary Epistemology*, CAMPBELL, Donald T and PALLER, Bonnie T.

"The Externalization of Observation: An Example from Modern Physics" in *Scientific Knowledge Socialized*, PINCH, Trevor J.

"The Gestalt Model of Scientific Progress" in *Scientific Knowledge Socialized*, DILWORTH, Craig.

"On the Emergence of Scientific Disciplines" in *Scientific Knowledge Socialized*, LAITKO, Hubert.

"Scientific Change and Counterfactuals" in *Scientific Knowledge Socialized*, RANTALA, Veikko.

"Scientific Explanation: The Causes, Some of the Causes, and Nothing But the Causes" in *Scientific Explanation (Minnesota Studies in the Philosophy of Science, Volume XIII)*, HUMPHREYS, Paul W.

Fools, Young Children, Animism, and the Scientific World-Picture. KENNEDY, David.

Pascal's Theory of Scientific Knowledge. ARNOLD, Keith.

Rondom realisme. RADDER, Hans.

Scientific and Legal Standards of Statistical Evidence in Toxic Tort and Discrimination Suits. CRANOR, Carl and NUTTING, Kurt.

Technology versus Science: The Cognitive Fallacy. DI NUCCI PEARCE, M Rosaria and PEARCE, David.

SCIENTIFIC LANGUAGE

Pierre Duhem's *The Aim and Structure of Physical Theory*: A Book Against Conventionalism. MAIOCCHI, Roberto.

La radice filosofica della rivoluzione scientifica moderna. CRESCINI, Angelo.

A Reason for Theoretical Terms. GAIFMAN, Haim and OSHERSON, Daniel N and WEINSTEIN, Scott.

SCIENTIFIC METHOD

Four Decades of Scientific Explanation. SALMON, Wesley C.

Klarheit und Methode: Felix Kaufmanns Wissenschaftstheorie. ZILIAN, H G.

The Nature of Social and Educational Inquiry: Empiricism versus Interpretation. SMITH, John K.

SCIENTIFIC METHOD

Philosophical Essays in Pragmatic Naturalism. KURTZ, Paul.
Scientific Explanation (Minnesota Studies in the Philosophy of Science, Volume XIII). KITCHER, Philip (ed).
"Maimonides on Aristotle and Scientific Method" in *Moses Maimonides and His Time,* KRAEMER, Joel L.
Aristotle, Demonstration, and Teaching. WIANS, William.
Differences in Style as a Way of Probing the Context of Discovery. GAVROGLU, Kostas.
Duhem in Different Contexts: Comments on Brenner and Martin. QUINN, Phillip L.
Enseignement de la théologie et méthode scientifique. DUMONT, Camille.
On Advancing Simple Hypotheses. OSHERSON, Daniel N and WEINSTEIN, Scott.
Pierre Duhem's Conception of Natural Classification. LUGG, Andrew.
La radice filosofica della rivoluzione scientifica moderna. CRESCINI, Angelo.
Reply—Symposium on the Role of the Philosopher Among the Scientists: Nuisance or Necessity?. BAIGRIE, Brian.
The Role of the Philosopher Among the Scientists: Nuisance or Necessity?. AGASSI, Joseph.
Swāmī Vivekānanda's Use of Science as an Analogy for the Attainment of *Mokṣa.* RAMBACHAN, Anantanand.
Teleology and Scientific Method in Kant's Critique of Judgement. BUTTS, Robert E.

SCIENTIFIC PHILOSOPHY

Philosophy of Science Naturalized? Some Problems with Giere's Naturalism. SIEGEL, Harvey.
Scientific Rationality as Instrumental Rationality. GIERE, Ronald N.

SCIENTIFIC REALISM

"A Background Essay" in *Philosophical Consequences of Quantum Theory: Reflections on Bell's Theorem,* CUSHING, James T.
"Incommensurability, Scientific Realism and Rationalism" in *Scientific Knowledge Socialized,* PORUS, N L.
Comment: Duhem's Middle Way. MC MULLIN, Ernan.
Peircean Scientific Realism. ALMEDER, Robert.

SCIENTIFIC REVOLUTION

"Determinants of Science Evolution in the 19th and 20th Centuries" in *Scientific Knowledge Socialized,* HÖRZ, Herbert.
"The Goals of Natural Science" in *Scientific Knowledge Socialized,* MC MULLIN, Ernan.
On the Possibility of Mathematical Revolutions. KENNEY, Emelie.
La revolución científica y las revoluciones filosóficas. ARANA, Juan.
A Scientific Dilemma: The Human Genome Project. CAVALIERI, Liebe F.

SCIENTIFIC THEORY(-RIES)

Handlexikon zur Wissenschaftstheorie. SEIFFERT, Helmut.
Klarheit und Methode: Felix Kaufmanns Wissenschaftstheorie. ZILIAN, H G.
Readings in the Philosophy of Science (Second Edition). BRODY, Baruch A.
Thematic Origins of Scientific Thought: Kepler to Einstein—Revised Edition. HOLTON, Gerald.
"Four Decades of Scientific Explanation" in *Scientific Explanation (Minnesota Studies in the Philosophy of Science, Volume XIII),* SALMON, Wesley C.
Applying Idealized Scientific Theories to Engineering. LAYMON, Ronald.
The Birth of Modern Science out of the 'European Miracle'. RADNITZKY, Gerard.
Criterios de teoricidad. LEGRIS, Javier.
Evolving Probability. KUKLA, André.
Feminist Critique of Epistemology. RUSSELL, Denise.
Jean Cavaillès' aanloop tot de wetenschapstheorie. CORTOIS, P.
On Innertheoretical Conditions for Theoretical Terms. GÄHDE, Ulrich.
On the Logical Structure of Verisimilitude. GERLA, Giangiacomo and GUCCIONE, Salvatore.
Paradoxical Consequences of Balzer's and Gähde's Criteria of Theoreticity. SCHURZ, Gerhard.
Reale e complesso: osservazioni sul realismo scientifico e la storia della scienza. STOMEO, A.
Reply—Symposium on the Role of the Philosopher Among the Scientists: Nuisance or Necessity?. BAIGRIE, Brian.
The Role of the Philosopher Among the Scientists: Nuisance or Necessity?. AGASSI, Joseph.
Rosenberg's Rebellion. WATERS, C Kenneth.
Unicidad y categoricidad de teorías. LUNGARZO, Carlos A.
Wissenschaftliche Weltauffassung zwischen Sozialrevolution und Sozialreform. NEMETH, Elisabeth.

SCIENTISM

Voegelin on the Idea of Race: An Analysis of Modern European Racism. HEILKE, Thomas W.
Wittgenstein, Mind, and Scientism. GOLDFARB, Warren.

SCIENTIST(S)

"What is the Use of a Philosophy of Science for Scientists"?. WILKES, K.
János Hetényi—The Scientist, the Dilettante (in Hungarian). SZABÓ, Zoltán Z.
Riflessioni epistemologiche sull'errore. BALDINI, Massimo.

SCOTT, G

"The Source" Spinoza in the Writings of Gabriel Scott. FLOISTAD, Guttorm.

SCOTTISH

Natural Law and the Scottish Enlightenment. HAAKONSSEN, Knud.

SCREENING

HIV and Pregnancy. ALMOND, Brenda and ULANOWSKY, Carole.
Medical Screening: AIDS, Rights, and Health Care Costs. ROTHSTEIN, Mark A.

SCRIPT(S)

The Mundane Matter of the Mental Language. MALONEY, J Christopher.

SCRIPTURE(S)

Medical Ethics: Principles, Persons, and Problems. FRAME, John M.
A Response to Sykes: Revelation and the Practices of Interpreting Scripture. JONES, L Gregory.
Schriftgemässe Philosophie als philosophische Laienmeditation?. THOMASSEN, Beroald.
Sens et Vérité: Philosophie et théologie chez L Meyer et Spinoza. LAGREE, Jacqueline.

SCRUTON, R

Philosophical Aesthetics and the Education of Teachers. REDFERN, H B.

SCULPTURE

The Public as Sculpture: From Heavenly City to Mass Ornament. NORTH, Michael.
The Violence of Public Art: *Do the Right Thing.* MITCHELL, W J T.

SEARCH(ES)

John Dewey, the "Trial" of Leon Trotsky and the Search for Historical Truth. SPITZER, Alan B.

SEARLE, J

Natural Signs: A Theory of Intentionality. ADDIS, Laird.
Can Semantics Be Syntactic?. JAHREN, Neal.
Money: A Speech Act Analysis. HADREAS, Peter.
The Role of Intention in Intentional Action. ADAMS, Frederick.
Searle ed Eco sulla metafora. BURKHARDT, Armin.
Searle on Strong AI. CAM, Philip.
Searle's Narrow Content. VAUGHAN, Rachel.
Two Consequences of Hinting. TSOHATZIDIS, Savas L.

SECHEVILLE, J

El aristotelismo de Juan de Secheville. RODRÍGUEZ, Juan Acosta.

SECONDARY QUALITY(-TIES)

Berkeley's Ideas and the Primary/Secondary Distinction. NADLER, Steven.
Of Primary and Secondary Qualities. SMITH, A D.
On Viewing Pain as a Secondary Quality. NEWTON, Natika.
Primäre und sekundäre Qualitatäten bei John Locke. KIENZLE, Bertram.

SECULAR

Building Bridges to the Right: Libertarians, Conservatives, and Humanists. HUDGINS, Edward.
Defining—and Implementing—Eupraxophy. FLYNN, T.
A Eupraxopher's Agenda: Humanism and Religion. HOFFMANN, R Joseph.
Humanism and Socialism. SCHMITT, Richard.
Libertarianism Versus Secular Humanism?. GORDON, David.
Liberty and Democracy, or Socialism?. FLEW, Antony.
Making a Case for Socialism. NIELSEN, Kai.

SECULARISM

Benevolent Living: Tracing the Roots of Motivation to God. TURNER, Dean.
Can Ethics Take Pluralism Seriously?. ENGELHARDT JR, H Tristram.
The End of the Secular Century. ROTHBARD, Murray N.
Hope in a Secular Ethic. BAKER, Robert E.
Religion and Morality: A Conceptual Understanding. BEHERA, Satrughna.
Root of Man: A Note. BANDYOPADHYAY, Tirthanath.

SECULARIZATION

Can Theology Have a Role in "Public" Bioethical Discourse?. CAHILL, Lisa Sowle.
Religion and the Secularization of Bioethics. CALLAHAN, Daniel.

SELF-INTEREST(S)

The Role of Self-Interest in Adam Smith's *Wealth of Nations*. WERHANE, Patricia H.

The Self-Interest Based Contractarian Response to the Why-Be-Moral Skeptic. SUPERSON, Anita M.

Self-Interest in Political Life. MANSBRIDGE, Jane.

The Social Conscience of Business. REILLY, Bernard J and KYJ, Myroslaw J.

Sympathy and Self-Interest: The Crisis in Mill's Mental History. GREEN, Michele.

SELF-KNOWLEDGE

Epistemic Justification: Essays in the Theory of Knowledge. ALSTON, William P.

Nietzschean Narratives. SHAPIRO, Gary.

Virtue and Self-Knowledge. JACOBS, Jonathan A.

Angelology, Metaphysics, and Intersubjectivity: A Reply to G N Casey. KAINZ, Howard P.

Anscombe on Justifying Claims to Know One's Bodily Position. LOTT, Tommy L.

Content and Self-Knowledge. BOGHOSSIAN, Paul A.

On a New Argument for the Existence of God. MARTIN, Michael.

The Role of Self-Knowledge in the *Critique of Pure Reason*. POLT, Richard F H.

Self-Knowledge and the Modern Mode of Learning. BLITS, Jan H.

Self-Knowledge of the World. ROTENSTREICH, Nathan.

To Philosophize with Socrates (A Chapter from a Prepared Monography on J Patocka) (in Czechoslovakian). PALOUS, Martin.

SELF-LOVE

L'amour-propre: Un tema secentesco tra morale e antropologia. BOSCO, Domenico.

SELF-MANAGEMENT

New Social Self-Steering. GRZEGORCZYK, Andrzej and GOLEBIOWSKI, Marek (trans).

SELF-MOTIVATION

The Developmental Self-Valuing Theory: A Practical Approach for Business Ethics. JENSEN, Larry C and WYGANT, Steven A.

SELF-PERCEPTION

The Philosophical Implications of the Use of New Information Technologies: Introductory Reflections. NIZNIK, Józef and RODZINSKA, Aleksandra (trans).

SELF-PRESERVATION

Hobbes and 'The Beautiful Axiom'. COADY, C A J.

SELF-REALIZATION

Man Apart and Deep Ecology: A Reply to Reed. NAESS, Arne.

Non-Violence, Gandhi and Our Times. SINGH, R Raj.

T H Green's Theory of the Morally Justified Society. SIMHONY, Avital.

SELF-REFERENCE

Selbstreferenz und Zeit: Die dynamische Stabilität des Bewusstseins. BERGMANN, Werner and HOFFMANN, G.

SELF-REFUTATION

Pyrrhonean Scepticism and the Self-Refutation Argument. BAILEY, Alan.

SELF-REGARDING ACTION(S)

A Reconsideration of Kant's Treatment of Duties to Oneself. PATON, Margaret.

Rights to Liberty in Purely Private Matters: Part I. RILEY, Jonathan.

SELF-VERIFICATION

The Mīmāṃsā Theory of Self-Recognition. TABER, John A.

SELFHOOD

The Person and the Human Mind: Issues in Ancient and Modern Philosophy. GILL, Christopher (ed).

"Human Persons" in *The Person and the Human Mind: Issues in Ancient and Modern Philosophy*, SMITH, Peter.

The Mīmāṃsā Theory of Self-Recognition. TABER, John A.

SELFISHNESS

Basic Moral Concepts. SPAEMANN, Robert.

SELLARS, W

The Metaphysics of Epistemology: Lectures by Wilfrid Sellars. AMARAL, Pedro (ed).

The Myth of Jones and the Mirror of Nature: Reflections on Introspection. GARFIELD, Jay L.

Phänomenale Realität und naturalistische Philosophie. POHLENZ, Gerd.

SEMANTIC MODEL(S)

A Conception of Tarskian Logic. SHER, Gila.

SEMANTICS

see also Linguistics, Meaning

The Concept of Logical Consequence. ETCHEMENDY, John.

Donald Davidson's Philosophy of Language: An Introduction. RAMBERG, Bjorn T.

Facts and the Function of Truth. PRICE, Huw.

Informal Lectures on Formal Semantics. BACH, Emmon W.

Logic and Philosophy in the Lvov-Warsaw School. WOLÉNSKI, Jan.

Meaning and Grammar: An Introduction to Semantics. CHIERCHIA, Gennaro.

Meaning and Mental Representation. ECO, Umberto (ed).

Metaphor. COOPER, David E.

Parmenides, Plato, and the Semantics of Not-Being. PELLETIER, Francis Jeffry.

Propositional Attitudes: An Essay on Thoughts and How We Ascribe Them. RICHARD, Mark.

Relevant Logic: A Philosophical Examination of Inference. READ, Stephen.

Rethinking Religion: Connecting Cognition and Culture. LAWSON, E Thomas.

The Semantic Foundations of Logic, Volume 1: Propositional Logics. EPSTEIN, Richard L.

The Structure of Biological Theories. THOMPSON, Paul.

A Theory of Content and Other Essays. FODOR, Jerry A.

"Cognitive Semantics" in *Meaning and Mental Representation*, LAKOFF, George.

"Conceptual Semantics" in *Meaning and Mental Representation*, JACKENDOFF, Ray.

"How is Meaning Mentally Represented?" in *Meaning and Mental Representation*, JOHNSON-LAIRD, Philip N.

"Identity in Intensional Logic: Subjective Semantics" in *Meaning and Mental Representation*, VAN FRAASSEN, Bas.

"Reference and Its Role in Computational Models of Mental Representations" in *Meaning and Mental Representation*, WILKS, Yorick.

"Semantic Discovery for Relevance Logics" in *Directions in Relevant Logic*, MORGAN, Charles G.

"Semantics Unlimited I: A Relevant Synthesis of Implication with Higher Intensionality" in *Directions in Relevant Logic*, ROUTLEY, Richard.

Against Global Paraconsistency. BATENS, Diderik.

Análisis semántico de los enunciados de creencia. D'ALESSIO, Juan Carlos.

The Anthropology of 'Semantic Levels' in Music. KARBUSICKY, Vladimir.

Axiomatization of the First-Order Intermediate Logics of Bounded Kripkean Heights I. YOKOTA, Shin'ichi.

Boolean Negation and All That. PRIEST, Graham.

Breaking Out of the Gricean Circle. LEVINE, Joseph.

Brentano's Criticism of the Correspondence Conception of Truth and Tarski's Semantic Theory. WOLENSKI, Jan.

Can Philosophy Be Mathematized?—Probabilistic Theory of Meanings and Semantic Architectonics of Personality. NALIMOV, V V.

Can Semantics Be Syntactic?. JAHREN, Neal.

Cause as an Implication. SYLVAN, Richard and DA COSTA, Newton.

Ceticismo semântico. DE SOUZA FILHO, Danilo Marcondes.

Cognitive Architecture and the Semantics of Belief. FORBES, Graeme.

Connectionism and the Semantic Content of Internal Representation. GOSCHKE, Thomas and KOPPELBERG, Dirk.

Conoscenza e semantica. VENTURA, Antonino.

A Content Semantics for Quantified Relevant Logics, I. BRADY, Ross T.

A Content Semantics for Quantified Relevant Logics, II. BRADY, Ross T.

Davidson's Semantic and Computational Understanding of Language (in Serbo-Croatian). BOJADZIEV, Damjan.

Did Hobbes Have a Semantic Theory of Truth?. DE JONG, Willem R.

Duality Between Modal Algebras and Neighbourhood Frames. DOSEN, Kosta.

An Elementary Proof for Some Semantic Characterizations of Nondeterministic Floyd-Hoare Logic. SAIN, Ildikó.

Extra-Logical Inferences. LÓPEZ-ESCOBAR, E G K.

Filosofar abierto. ESSLER, Wilhelm and RIVADULLA, Andrés (trans).

Form and Content in Semantics. WILKS, Yorick.

Forman and Semantic Aspects of Tibetan Buddhist Debate Logic. TILLEMANS, Tom J F.

Free from What?. BENCIVENGA, Ermanno.

Geometrical Semantics for Spatial Prepositions. SUPPES, Patrick and CRANGLE, Colleen.

Groups, I. LANDMAN, Fred.

How a Note Denotes. KURKELA, Kari.

Imagining Oneself to be Another. REYNOLDS, Steven L.

An Investigation of the Lumps of Thought. KRATZER, Angelika.

Linguists of All Countries—On Gramsci's Premise of Coherence. HELSLOOT, Niels.

SIN(S)

Andrew of Novo Castro, OFM, and the Moral Law. KENNEDY, Leonard A.

Fiat Voluntas Tua! Vício e Pecado na ética de Abelardo. ESTEVÃO, J C.

John Paul II *vis-à-vis* Atheism and Materialism: Remarks on the Encyclical *Dominum et vivificantem*. TANALSKI, Dionizy and RODZINSKA, Aleksandra (trans).

Non Posse Peccare. VAN DEN BELD, Antonie.

SINGER, P

"Constraints on *The Expanding Circle*: A Critique of Singer" in *Inquiries into Values: The Inaugural Session of the International Society for Value Inquiry*, SCHONSHECK, Jonathan.

SINGULAR TERM(S)

"The Revival of 'Fido'-Fido" in *Cause, Mind, and Reality: Essays Honoring C B Martin*, DEVITT, Michael.

Dummett's Criteria for Singular Terms. WETZEL, Linda.

SINGULARITY

The Singularity of Christian Ethics. MEILAENDER, Gilbert.

SIRKIN, G

Resource X: Sirkin and Smith on a Neglected Economic Staple. DE VRIES, Paul H.

SITUATION(S)

Art, Education, and Life-Issues. MC FEE, Graham.

An Investigation of the Lumps of Thought. KRATZER, Angelika.

Die Situationsanalyse. WERLEN, Benno.

SKILL(S)

"Freedom as a Skill" in *Culture et Politique/Culture and Politics*, MINOGUE, Kenneth.

Against Skills. HART, W.

Computer Programming As a Vehicle for Teaching Thinking Skills. NICKERSON, Raymond S.

Is Reading a "Higher Order Skill"?. MC PECK, John E.

Philosophy for Children and the Modernization of Chinese Education. MULVANEY, Robert J.

Reasoning Skills: An Overview. CANNON, Dale and WEINSTEIN, Mark.

Three Levels of Reading Philosophy. DUHAN, Laura.

Writing and Philosophy. FISHMAN, Stephen.

SKINNER, B

Accountability in Education: A Philosophical Inquiry. WAGNER, Robert B.

Gibson, Skinner and Perceptual Responses. GUERIN, Bernard.

On Mentalism, Privacy, and Behaviorism. MOORE, Jay.

Der Zwang zur "geschlossenen Gesellschaft"—Ein perennes Dilemma der Utopie?. KLARER, Mario.

SKYRMS, B

A Combinatorial Theory of Possibility. ARMSTRONG, D M.

SLAVERY

"Slave—Master—Friend, Philosophical Reflections Upon Man and Nature" in *Man and Nature: The Chinese Tradition and the Future*, ZHEN, Li.

Aristotle and the Classical Greek Concept of Despotism. RICHTER, Melvin.

Slaves Putting Themselves up for Sale. WATSON, A.

Three Approaches to Locke and the Slave Trade. GLAUSSER, Wayne.

SLEEP

The Self in Deep Sleep According to Advaita and Visistādvaita. COMANS, Michael.

SLIPKO, T

Appréciation morale des ingerences biomédiques dans le processusde de transmision (in Polish). KOWALSKI, Edmund.

Aus den Überlegungen über die Moralsprachaspekte (in Polish). RODZINSKI, A.

Die ethischen Ansichten von P Professor Tadeusz Slipko (in Polish). PODREZ, Ewa.

Matérialisme, métaphysique, éthique (in Polish). FRITZHAND, Marek.

SLIPPERY SLOPE

The Duty to Rescue and the Slippery Slope Problem. SMITH, Patricia.

Slippery Bentham: Some Neglected Cracks in the Foundation of Utilitarianism. PITKIN, Hanna Fenichel.

SLOGAN(S)

Free Will, Self-Causation, and Strange Loops. MORDEN, Michael.

SLOTE, M

Autonomy or Integrity: A Reply to Slote. WALKER, Margaret Urban.

SMELL

Odors and Private Language: Observations on the Phenomenology of Scent. ALMAGOR, Uri.

SMIT, H

Gedrag: wat zit er achter?. VAN DER STEEN, Wim.

SMITH

"Adam Smith: Skeptical Newtonianism, Disenchanted Republicanism, and the Birth of Social Science" in *Knowledge and Politics*, CREMASCHI, Sergio.

'Utility' and the 'Utility Principle': Hume, Smith, Bentham, Mill. LONG, Douglas G.

Adam Smith's "Theory" of Justice: Business Ethics Themes in *The Wealth of Nations*. DE VRIES, Paul H.

Adam Smith's Concept of the Social System. COKER, Edward W.

Adam Smith's Social Contract: The Proper Role of Individual Liberty and Government Intervention. COLLINS, Denis.

L'idea di "Storia teoretica o congetturale" negli scritti filosofici e sul linguaggio di Adam Smith. IACONO, Alfonso M.

Resource X: Sirkin and Smith on a Neglected Economic Staple. DE VRIES, Paul H.

The Role of Self-Interest in Adam Smith's *Wealth of Nations*. WERHANE, Patricia H.

SMITH, B

Can the Relativist Avoid Refuting Herself?. ROOCHNIK, David L.

SMITH, Q

The New Tenseless Theory of Time: A Reply to Smith. OAKLANDER, L Nathan.

SMOKING

The Ethics of Smoking Policies. NIXON, Judy C and WEST, Judy F.

SMOLENSKY, P

Belief, Opinion and Consciousness. CLARK, Andy.

SMULLYAN, R

A Variation on a Paradox. HAZEN, Allen.

SMYTHIES, J

Inspecting Images: A Reply to Smythies. WRIGHT, Edmond.

SNEED, J

Criterios de teoricidad. LEGRIS, Javier.

SNYDER, D

The Moon Is Not There When I See It: A Response to Snyder. GARRISON, Mark.

SOBEL, J

The Popcorn Problem: Sobel on Evidential Decision Theory and Deliberation-Probability Dynamics. EELLS, Ellery.

The Success of Hyperrational Utility Maximizers in Iterated Prisoner's Dilemma: A Response to Sobel. CURTIS, Robert A.

SOBER, E

The Illusory Riches of Sober's Monism. KITCHER, Philip and STERELNY, Kim and WATERS, C Kenneth.

Reply to Sober's "Is the Theory of Natural Selection Unprincipled? Reply to Shimony". SHIMONY, Abner.

SOCIABILITY

Sociability and Social Conflict in George Herbert Mead's Interactionism, 1900-1919. FEFFER, Andrew.

SOCIAL

El a priori histórico (la historia y sus hechos). SAMPEDRO, Ceferino.

Business Ethics: Where Profits Meet Value Systems. ROBIN, Donald P.

Disputers of the TAO: Philosophical Argument in Ancient China. GRAHAM, A C.

Man, Science, Humanism: A New Synthesis. FROLOV, Ivan T.

"Comment: Positivism and the Foundations of Legal Authority" in *Issues in Contemporary Legal Philosophy: The Influence of H L A Hart*, BEN-MENACHEM, Hanina.

"Comment: The Normativity of Law" in *Issues in Contemporary Legal Philosophy: The Influence of H L A Hart*, LYONS, David.

"The Light at the End of the Tunnel and the Light in Which We May Walk" in *The Causes of Quarrel: Essays on Peace, War, and Thomas Hobbes*, COX, Gray.

The Business and Society Course: Does It Change Student Attitudes?. WYND, William R and MAGER, John.

Corporate Social Monitoring in South Africa: A Decade of Achievement, An Uncertain Future. PAUL, Karen.

The Critique of Impure Reason: Foucault and the Frankfurt School. MC CARTHY, Thomas.

Efficiency, Effectiveness and Legitimation: Criteria for the Evaluation of Norms. UUSITALO, Liisa.

Feminist-Constructionist Theories of Sexuality and the Definition of Sex

SOCIAL

Education. DIORIO, Joseph A.

Natural and Social Lottery, and Concepts of the Self. SADURSKI, Wojciech.

Objectivity and Aesthetic Education in Its Social Context. BROWNHILL, Robert James.

On the Perspectives of Research into the Philosophical and Social Aspects of Science and Technology. FROLOV, Ivan T.

On the Social and Political Implications of Cognitive Psychology. PRILLELTENSKY, Isaac.

P F Strawson and the Social Context in Language (in Serbo-Croatian). VIDANOVIC, Dorde.

Philosophy and Socio-Political Conversation: A Postmodern Proposal. OLIVIER, G.

Promises and Practices. SCANLON, Thomas.

The Social Constitution of Action: *Objectivity and Explanation*. GREENWOOD, John D.

The Social Dynamics Between Evolution and Progress. MURESAN, Valentin.

Social Justice. WILLIAMS, Bernard.

The Structure of Social Revolutions (Some Remarks and Hypotheses). WITKOWSKI, Lech and PETROWICZ, Lech (trans).

Struttura dell'azione e compito pubblico del cristianesimo. POSSENTI, Vittorio.

The Birth of Politics (in Serbo-Croatian). HOWARD, Dick.

To the Program of Aesthetic Evolution for the Whole Society (in Czechoslovakian). CHYBA, Milos.

Vico and Bakhtin: A Prolegomenon to Any Future Comparison. JUNG, Hwa Yol.

Zur methodologischen Bedeutung des Leninschen Prinzips der "Zurückführung des Individuellen auf das Soziale". DANYEL, Jürgen.

SOCIAL CHANGE

The Listening Self: Personal Growth, Social Change and Closure of Metaphysics. LEVIN, David Michael.

The Political Theory of Liberation Theology: Toward a Reconvergence of Social Value and Science. POTTENGER, John R.

The Unknown Mechanism Moving Society. ATHAYDE, Ezequiel.

"Social Change and Epistemic Thought" in *Scientific Knowledge Socialized*, KROHN, Wolfgang.

The Impact of Feminist Research: Issues of Legitimacy. WILKINSON, Sue.

Marxist Literary Theory: A Critique. LISMAN, C David.

Reification, Class and 'New Social Movements'. BROWNE, Paul.

Utilitarianism and Reform: Social Theory and Social Change, 1750-1800. BURNS, J H.

What's Left: Marx, Foucault and Contemporary Problems of Social Change. WAPNER, Paul.

Why is the Bishops' Letter on the US Economy So Unconvincing?. REECE, William S.

SOCIAL CONDITION(S)

Weak Strategy Proofness: The Case of Nonbinary Social Choice Functions. BANDYOPADHYAY, Taradas.

SOCIAL CONSCIOUSNESS

Subject and Consciousness: A Philosophical Inquiry Into Self-Consciousness. BALABAN, Oded.

The Social Conscience of Business. REILLY, Bernard J and KYJ, Myroslaw J.

SOCIAL CONTRACT

The Consolations of Philosophy: Hobbes's Secret; Spinoza's Way. ROSENTHAL, Abigail L (ed).

Justice and Modern Moral Philosophy. REIMAN, Jeffrey.

Rousseau: Selections. CRANSTON, Maurice (ed).

Social Contract, Free Ride: A Study of the Public Goods Problem. DE JASAY, Anthony.

"Hobbes's Social Contract" in *Perspectives on Thomas Hobbes*, GAUTHIER, David.

"Toulmin to Rawls" in *Ethics in the History of Western Philosophy*, STERBA, James P.

Adam Smith's Social Contract: The Proper Role of Individual Liberty and Government Intervention. COLLINS, Denis.

Can There Be a Social Contract with Business?. HODAPP, Paul F.

Contracting for Natural Rights. FORMAN, Frank.

Democratic Sovereignty. STEWART, Don.

The Individual and the General Will: Rousseau Reconsidered. HILEY, David R.

Is Limited Government Possible?. DE JASAY, Anthony.

Kant on Property Rights and the Social Contract. BAYNES, Kenneth.

Knowing and Believing in the Original Position. CORLETT, J A.

The Myth of Civil Disobedience. VAN DER BURG, Wibren.

Obligations, Communities, and Suffering: Problems of Community Seen in

a New Light. LOEWY, Erich H.

Ortsbestimmungen des Politischen: Neuere Literatur zu Thomas Hobbes. ANGEHRN, Emil.

Reason and Agreement in Social Contract Views. FREEMAN, Samuel.

Social Contracts and Corporations: A Reply to Hodapp. DONALDSON, Thomas.

Towards a New Social Contract. FISHKIN, James S.

SOCIAL CONTROL

Freedom. BAUMAN, Zygmunt.

SOCIAL CONTROLS

Democratizing Science: A Humble Proposal. TURNER, Joseph.

SOCIAL CRITICISM

"Hermeneutics, Cultural Heritage and Social Critique" in *Reading Philosophy for the Twenty-First Century*, MC LEAN, George F.

"Social Criticism Without Philosophy" in *The Institution of Philosophy: A Discipline in Crisis?*, FRASER, Nancy and NICHOLSON, Linda.

McClellan on Quine and Social Criticism. SELMAN, Mark and ROSS, Murray.

SOCIAL DARWINISM

The Significance of Darwinian Theory for Marx and Engels. TAYLOR, Angus.

SOCIAL DETERMINISM

The Unknown Mechanism Moving Society. ATHAYDE, Ezequiel.

SOCIAL ENGINEERING

New Social Self-Steering. GRZEGORCZYK, Andrzej and GOLEBIOWSKI, Marek (trans).

SOCIAL ETHICS

Ethics and Community. DUSSEL, Enrique D.

The Political Theory of Liberation Theology: Toward a Reconvergence of Social Value and Science. POTTENGER, John R.

Atomic Energy and Moral Glue. HOLLIS, Martin.

Etica e realtà. SANCIPRIANO, Mario.

Smarta-Varnasrama and the Law of Welfare. SWAIN, Braja Kishore.

SOCIAL HISTORY

Crisi dello storicismo e "bisogno" di "Kulturgeschichte": Il caso Lamprecht. CACCIATORE, Giuseppe.

SOCIAL INSTITUTION(S)

Confucian Justice: Achieving a Humane Society. PEERENBOOM, Randall P.

SOCIAL ORDER

Jurisculture, Volume II: India. DORSEY, Gray L.

The Meaning of General Theoretical Sociology: Tradition and Formalization. FARARO, Thomas J.

L'autoreferenzialità luhmanniana: A proposito di normalizzazione dell'improbabile e improbabilità. AMATO MANGIAMELI, Agata C.

The Complexities of Spontaneous Order. DOBUZINSKIS, Laurent.

Democracy as a Spontaneous Order. DI ZIEREGA, Gus.

Friedrich Schleiermacher's Theory of the Limited Communitarian State. HOOVER, Jeffrey.

Philosophie, Ideologie et Acteurs Economique en Afrique. KIBAMBE-KIA-NKIMA, Kapongola.

SOCIAL PHIL

see also Authority(-ties), Communism, Conservatism, Equality, Ethics, Freedom, Political Phil, Progress, Punishment, Society(-ties), Utopia

Advance Directives in Medicine. HACKLER, Chris (ed).

AIDS and the Good Society. ILLINGWORTH, Patricia.

The American Evasion of Philosophy: A Genealogy of Pragmatism. WEST, Cornel.

Animal Rights and Human Obligations (Second Edition). REGAN, Tom.

Arms and Judgment: Law, Morality, and the Conduct of War in the 20th Century. COHEN, Sheldon M.

At the Intersection of Legality and Morality: Hartian Law as Natural Law. SKUBIK, Daniel W.

Autobiographical Reflections—Eric Voegelin. SANDOZ, Ellis (ed).

Burning Conscience: The Guilt of Hiroshima. ANDERS, Gunther.

Capitalism. PAUL, Ellen Frankel (ed).

The Causes of Quarrel: Essays on Peace, War, and Thomas Hobbes. CAWS, Peter (ed).

Collected Works, Volume 30, Marx: 1861-1863. MARX, Karl.

Comparative Philosophy and the Philosophy of Scholarship. TUCK, Andrew P.

The Confucian Creation of Heaven: Philosophy and the Defense of Ritual Mastery. ENO, Robert.

Critical Theory and Poststructuralism: In Search of a Context. POSTER, Mark.

Critical Theory and Society: A Reader. BRONNER, Stephen Eric (ed).

SOCIAL PHIL

Darwin in Russian Thought. VUCINICH, Alexander.

The Dialectic in Journalism: Toward a Responsible Use of Press Freedom. MERRILL, John Calhoun.

The Dialectics of Seeing: Walter Benjamin and the Arcades Project. BUCK-MORSS, Susan.

Ecological Communication. LUHMANN, Niklas.

El individuo y la feminidad. PEREZ ESTEVEZ, Antonio.

Ernst Bloch: Trame della speranza. BOELLA, Laura.

Eros, Agape and Philia: Readings in the Philosophy of Love. SOBLE, Alan (ed).

Essays in Philosophy and Education. STOTT, Laurence J.

Ethical Theory and Social Issues: Historical Texts and Contemporary Readings. GOLDBERG, David Theo.

Ethics in Government: The Moral Challenge of Public Leadership. MOORE, Mark H.

Expérience et culture: Fondement d'une théorie générale de l'expérience. REALE, Miguel.

The Fabric of This World: Inquiries into Calling, Career Choice, and the Design of Human Work. HARDY, Lee.

Fagothey's Right and Reason: Ethics in Theory and Practice—Ninth Edition. GONSALVES, Milton A.

Feminist Thought: A Comprehensive Introduction. TONG, Rosemarie.

Fourier: La Passione dell'Utopia. COLOMBO, Arrigo (ed).

Freedom. BAUMAN, Zygmunt.

French Philosophy of the Sixties: An Essay on Antihumanism. CATTANI, Mary Schnackenberg (trans).

From Warism to Pacifism: A Moral Continuum. CADY, Duane L.

Gender Trouble: Feminism and the Subversion of Identity. BUTLER, Judith.

Higher Education: An Arena of Conflicting Philosophies. SPEES, Emil Ray.

The Inner Citadel: Essays on Individual Autonomy. CHRISTMAN, John (ed).

Jürgen Habermas on Society and Politics: A Reader. SEIDMAN, Steven (ed).

Jurisculture, Volume II: India. DORSEY, Gray L.

Liberal Justice and the Marxist Critique of Education: A Study of Conflicting Research Programs. STRIKE, Kenneth A.

Liberty and Justice. DAY, J P.

The Light Shineth in Darkness. FRANK, S L.

Love and Friendship in Plato and Aristotle. PRICE, A W.

Love: Emotion, Myth, and Metaphor. SOLOMON, Robert C.

Man, Science, Humanism: A New Synthesis. FROLOV, Ivan T.

Marxism and Morality. LUKES, Steven.

The Meaning of General Theoretical Sociology: Tradition and Formalization. FARARO, Thomas J.

The Moral Case for the Free Market Economy: A Philosophical Argument. MACHAN, Tibor R.

Nature in Asian Tradition of Thought: Essays in Environmental Philosophy. CALLICOTT, J Baird (ed).

The Nature of Social and Educational Inquiry: Empiricism versus Interpretation. SMITH, John K.

Nietzsche and the Politics of Aristocratic Radicalism. DETWILER, Bruce.

The Perverted Consciousness: Sexuality and Sartre. LEAK, Andrew N.

Philosophy of Economics: On the Scope of Reason in Economic Inquiry. ROY, Subroto.

Postmodern Social Analysis and Criticism. MURPHY, John W.

Postmodernist Culture: An Introduction to Theories of the Contemporary. CONNOR, Steven.

Il Potere e l'Ipotesi: Tappe di una filosofia delle Funzioni. FRANCHINI, Raffaello.

Property, Power, and Public Choice: An Inquiry into Law and Economics—Second Ed. SCHMID, A Allan.

Public Choice II: A Revised Edition of "Public Choice". MUELLER, Dennis C.

The Question of Jean-Jacques Rousseau—Ernest Cassirer (Second Edition). GAY, Peter (ed & trans).

The Question of the Other: Essays in Contemporary Continental Philosophy. DALLERY, Arleen B (ed).

The Rational and the Social. BROWN, James Robert.

The Sanctity-of-Life Doctrine in Medicine: A Critique. KUHSE, Helga.

Scarcity and Modernity. XENOS, Nicholas.

Scientific Knowledge Socialized. HRONSZKY, Imre (ed).

The Social and Political Thought of R G Collingwood. BOUCHER, David.

The Social Context and Values: Perspectives of the Americas. MC LEAN, George F (ed).

Social Contract, Free Ride: A Study of the Public Goods Problem. DE JASAY, Anthony.

Social Philosophy and Ecological Scarcity. LEE, Keekok.

Social Theory and the Crisis of Marxism. MC CARNEY, Joseph.

Suicide and Euthanasia. BRODY, Baruch A (ed).

The Theory and Scholarship of Talcott Parsons to 1951: A Critical Commentary. WEARNE, Bruce C.

A Theory of Property. MUNZER, Stephen R.

Thinking Fragments: Psychoanalysis, Feminism, and Postmodernism in the Contemporary West. FLAX, Jane.

The Thought of Mao Tse-Tung. SCHRAM, Stuart.

Time and Change: Short But Differing Philosophies. CHACALOS, Elias Harry.

Towards a Critique of Foucault. GANE, Mike (ed).

The Unknown Mechanism Moving Society. ATHAYDE, Ezequiel.

Unruly Practices: Power, Discourse and Gender in Contemporary Social Theory. FRASER, Nancy.

Who Cares: Theory, Research and Educational Implications of the Ethic of Care. BRABECK, Mary M (ed).

Who Lives? Who Dies?: Ethical Criteria in Patient Selection. KILNER, John F.

"Abolishing Apartheid: The Importance of Sanctions" in *Inquiries into Values: The Inaugural Session of the International Society for Value Inquiry,* AUXTER, Thomas.

"Adam Smith: Skeptical Newtonianism, Disenchanted Republicanism, and the Birth of Social Science" in *Knowledge and Politics,* CREMASCHI, Sergio.

"Does Star Wars Depend on Contradiction and Deception?" in *Inquiries into Values: The Inaugural Session of the International Society for Value Inquiry,* ALLEN, Paul.

"Socializing Epistemology" in *Scientific Knowledge Socialized,* HESSE, Mary.

"'Ideology' in Marx and Engels": A Reply. MC CARNEY, J.

"System" and "Lifeworld": Habermas and the Problem of Holism. BOHMAN, James.

"The Conflation of Productivity and Efficiency in Economics and Economic History": A Comment. NYE, John Vincent.

The "Values" of Sentient Beings. FOX, Michael W.

"Wonderful Vision of a Truly Human World" (On Lukács' Conception of Communism in 1919) (in Hungarian). PERECZ, László.

'Self-Exploitation' and Workers' Co-Operatives—Or How the British Left Get Their Concepts Wrong. CARTER, Alan.

40 Jahre Philosophie in der DDR. WITTICH, Dieter.

A Bibliographical Survey on Confucian Studies in Western Languages: Retrospect and Prospect (in Serbo-Croatian). KANG, Thomas H.

A Game-Theoretical Analysis of Ecological Problems (in Hungarian). VAN ASPEREN, Gertrud M.

Abortion and Feminism. MARKOWITZ, Sally.

The Absolute, Community, and Time. WILLIAMS, Robert R.

Actions, Intentions, and Consequences: The Doctrine of Double Effect. QUINN, Warren S.

Activity-Work-Culture (in Czechoslovakian). ZLOBIN, N S.

Actualidad y fecundidad de la filosofía blondeliana. ISASI, Juan M.

Adam Smith's Concept of the Social System. COKER, Edward W.

Adequate Representations of Condorcet Profiles. VISSER, Henk.

Advertising and the Social Conditions of Autonomy. LIPPKE, Richard L.

Aesthetic Protectionism. GODLOVITCH, S.

Affirmative Action and the Doctrine of Double Effect. COONEY, William.

Affirmative Action as a Form of Restitution. GROARKE, Leo.

De afkeer van het individualisme bij Alisdair MacIntyre en de soevereiniteit van het individu. KAL, Victor.

Agricultural Technology, Wealth, and Responsibility. WUNDERLICH, Gene.

Agriculture: A War on Nature?. SURGEY, John.

AIDS, Society and Morality—A Philosophical Survey. HÄYRY, Heta and HÄYRY, Matti.

Alcoholics Anonymous Revisited. LORENZ, D C G.

Alexandru Claudian et la conscience de l'unité de l'esprit et de l'âme (in Romanian). GRIGORAS, Ioan.

Allocation of Scarce Medical Resources. BAYLES, Michael D.

Alternative Interpretations of Aristotle on Exchange and Reciprocity. MC NEILL, Desmond.

Ambition. DOMBROWSKI, Daniel A.

American Experience and the Israeli Dilemma. JACOBSOHN, Gary J.

Un ample programme d'action révolutionnaire et de perfectionnement (in Romanian). IONEL, Nicolae.

Analytical Marxism and Marx's Systematic Dialectical Theory. SMITH, Tony.

Androgyny and Leadership Style. KORABIK, Karen.

Animal Models in 'Exemplary' Medical Research: Diabetes as a Case Study. NELSON, James Lindemann.

Anmerkungen zur Autopoiesis. MOCEK, Reinhard.

Anthropology of Peace. MAZUREK, Franciszek Janusz and LECKI, Maciej (trans).

The Antithesis. BAUER, Henry.

SOCIAL PHIL

Applied Liberal Education for Engineers. LUGENBIEHL, Heinz C.

Applied Philosophy in the Post-Modern Age: An Augury. ENGELHARDT JR, H Tristram.

Architecture, Philosophy and the Public World. HALDANE, John.

Are Human Rights Real?. MACHAN, Tibor R.

Are Markets Morally Free Zones?. HAUSMAN, Daniel M.

Are There Inalienable Rights?. NELSON, John O.

Are Women Different and Why are Women Thought to be Different? Theoretical and Methodological Perspectives. GREGORY, Ann.

Are Women Owner-Managers Challenging Our Definitions of Entrepreneurship? An In-Depth Survey. LEE-GOSSELIN, H and GRISÉ, J.

Are Workers Forced to Work?. EHRING, Douglas.

The Argument in the *Protagoras* that No One Does What He Believes To Be Bad. MORRIS, T F.

An Argumentation-Analysis of a Central Part of Lenin's Political Logic. SMIT, P A.

The Artificial Inflation of Natural Rights. FLEW, Antony.

Aspectos rescatables de la cultura premoderna. MANSILLA, H C F.

Aspects socio-politiques, esthétiques et philosophiques dans l'oeuvre de Ion Heliade-Radulescu (in Romanian). DRAGOMIRESCU, Lucian.

At the Heart of Women in Management Research: Theoretical and Methodological Approaches and Their Biases. FAGENSON, Ellen A.

The Authority of the Rules of Baseball: The Commissioner as Judge. UTZ, Stephen G.

Autonomy and the Democratic Principle. BEEHLER, Rodger.

L'autoreferenzialità luhmanniana: A proposito di normalizzazione dell'improbabile e improbabilità. AMATO MANGIAMELI, Agata C.

The Availability of a Marxian Critique of Technology. KULKARNI, S G.

Bedingungen für die Aneignung und Verbreitung des Marxismus-Leninismus in afrikanischen ländern. BASTOS, Feliciano Moreira.

Begriffe im kommunikativen Handeln: Linguistische Begriffsanalyse als Rekonstruktion von Handlungsmustern. BICKES, Hans.

Belief, Doubt and Critical Thinking: Reconciling the Contraries: Response to Garrison and Phelan. BAILIN, Sharon.

Bemerkungen zu Ortega y Gassets Technikphilosophie. VAN MEEUWEN, Peter.

Bentham as Revolutionary Social Scientist. LONG, Douglas.

Bentham's Penal Theory in Action: The Case Against New South Wales. JACKSON, R V.

The Better Endowed and the Difference Principle. MC MAHON, Christopher.

Beyond Liberalism and Communitarianism: Towards a Critical Theory of Social Justice. DOPPELT, G.

Beyond Music Minus Memory?. OLIVIER, G.

Bioengineering, Scientific Activism, and Philosophical Bridges. DURBIN, Paul T.

Biological Effects of Low-Level Radiation: Values, Dose-Response Models, Risk Estimates. LONGINO, Helen E.

Biomedical Ethics: Some Lessons for Social Philosophy. BROCK, Dan W.

Biomedicine and Technocratic Power. FINKELSTEIN, Joanne L.

The Birth of the Medical Humanities and the Rebirth of the Philosophy of Medicine: The Vision of Edmund D Pellegrino. ENGELHARDT JR, H Tristram.

Bootstrapping While Barefoot (Crime Models versus Theoretical Models in the Hunt for Serial Killers). NORDBY, Jon J.

Brain Death and Brain Life: Rethinking the Connection. DOWNIE, Jocelyn.

Brain Death and the Anencephalic Newborns. TRUOG, Robert D.

Brâncusi et l'évolution de la perception (in Romanian). SMEU, Grigore.

Brauchen wir eine Kategorie Persönlichkeit?. RONNEBERG, Heinz.

La Brujería: un Invento Moderno. DÍAZ, Esther.

Buchler on Habermas on Modernity. CAHOONE, Lawrence E.

Building Bridges to the Right: Libertarians, Conservatives, and Humanists. HUDGINS, Edward.

Business Ethics, Fetal Protection Policies, and Discrimination Against Women in the Workplace. QUINN, John F.

Camus and Revolution (in Serbo-Croatian). BIEN, Joseph.

Can Legal Semiotics Contribute to Natural Law Studies?. JACKSON, Bernard S.

Can One Promise to Love Another?. WILSON, John.

Can Parents and Children Be Friends?. KUPFER, Joseph.

Can There Be a Social Contract with Business?. HODAPP, Paul F.

Capitalism, Freedom and Rhetorical Argumentation. MACHAN, Tibor R.

Career Barriers: Do We Need More Research?. CULLEN, Dallas.

Ce qui est vivant, ce qui est mort dans la philosophie d'Auguste Comte (1935). LÉVY-BRUHL, Lucien.

The Central Distinction in the Theory of Corporate Moral Personhood.

PFEIFFER, Raymond S.

The Challenge of the New Genetics. ROTHSTEIN, Mark A.

Change So As to Preserve Oneself and One's Nature: On a New Conception of Man. PECHENEV, V.

Childhood's End: The Age of Responsibility. FRIQUEGNON, Marie-Loui.

Choice, Gift, or Patriarchal Bargain? Women's Consent to *In Vitro* Fertilization in Male Infertility. LORBER, Judith.

Christianity and Humanism. LONG, Eugene T.

Christianity and Marxism: Confrontation, Dialogue, Universalism. KUCZYNSKI, Janusz.

Cinquante-six conceptions de l'androgynie. BOUCHARD, Guy.

Civil and Political Freedom in Hegel. DUQUETTE, David A.

Class—A Simple View. GRAHAM, Keith.

Classical Liberalism and its Crisis of Identity. VINCENT, Andrew.

Clinical Interpretation: The Hermeneutics of Medicine. LEDER, Drew.

The Club of Rome and the Vienna Centre. FELDHEIM, Pierre.

Coercion and Exploitation: Self-Transposal and the Moral Life. HAMRICK, William S.

Collaborative Collective Bargaining: Toward an Ethically Defensible Approach to Labor Negotiations. POST, Frederick R.

Collective Inaction and Shared Responsibility. MAY, Larry.

Comment on James Nelson's "Animals in 'Exemplary' Medical Research: Diabetes as a Case Study". FINSEN, Lawrence.

Commentary on "Hamlethics in Planning". BALKIS, Kozmas.

Commentary on "Hamlethics in Planning". HARE, R M.

Commentary on "The Expert and the Public". KRIEGER, Martin H.

Commentary on "The Worm and the Juggernaut". BAYLES, Michael D.

Commodification or Compensation: A Reply to Ketchum. MALM, H M.

The Communitarian Critique of Liberalism. WALZER, Michael.

Communities of Judgment. GIBBARD, Allan

A Comparative Study of the Representational Paradigms Between Liberalism and Socialism. KE, Gang.

The Complexities of Spontaneous Order. DOBUZINSKIS, Laurent.

Compromise. DAY, J P.

Le concept d'analyse généralisée ou de "non-analyse". LARUELLE, François.

The Concept of Alienation in Janusz Korczak's Works. ROSEN, Henryk and SWIDERSKA, Ewa (trans).

Concepts of Justice in the Scottish Enlightenment. MACKINNON, K A B.

The Concepts of Man and Nature in Marxism. SARKER, Sunil Kumar.

Confidentiality and Patient-Access to Records. SHORT, David S.

Confidentiality and Young People. GILLICK, Victoria.

Confidentiality and Young People: A G.P.'s Response. MORGAN, Huw.

Confucian Justice: Achieving a Humane Society. PEERENBOOM, Randall P.

Confucius—China's Dethroned Sage? (in Serbo-Croatian). KRAMERS, Robert P.

Connaissance, conscience et culture dans la vie spirituelle de la sociètè (in Romanian). PANA, Laura.

Consciousness, the Brain and What Matters. GILLETT, Grant R.

Consent and Fairness in Planning Land Use. SIMMONS, A John.

The Constitutional Process and the Higher Law. SHANKER, George.

The Construction, Deconstruction, and Reconstruction of Difference. ROTHENBERG, Paula.

Consumer Responsibility from a Social Systems Perspective. ZANARDI, William J.

Contexts and Essences: Indoctrination Revisited. SNOOK, Ivan.

Contracting for Natural Rights. FORMAN, Frank.

Conventions and Social Institutions. WEIRICH, Paul.

Cooter and Rappoport on the Normative. DAVIS, John B.

Cost Containment Forces Physicians into Ethical and Quality of Care Compromises. JUSTIN, Renage G.

The Creativity of Action and the Intersubjectivity of Reason: Mead's Pragmatism and Social Theory. JOAS, Hans.

The Crime of Punishment. BLUME, Robert and BLUME, Delorys.

Crisis and Programs of Identity (Notes to Debate Popular-Urban) (in Hungarian). VARDY, Péter.

Critical Attitudes Inside Social Science and the Humanities—A Swedish Perspective. LIEDMAN, Sven-Eric.

Critical Rationalism: The Problem of Method in Social Sciences and Law. ALBERT, Hans.

A Critical View of Swedish Science Policy. ELZINGA, Aant.

Critics of Science and Research Ethics in Sweden. GUSTAFSSON, Bengt and TIBELL, Gunnar.

La critique de l'utopie et de la technique chez J Ellul et H Jonas. WEYEMBERGH, Maurice.

La critique marxienne de la religion. TOSEL, André.

The Critique of Equalitarian Society in Malthus's *Essay*. GILBERT, Geoffrey.

Critique of Technological Policy in Africa. FORJE, John W.

SOCIAL PHIL

A Critique of the Deconstructionist Account of Gender Equity and Education. PIETIG, Jeanne.

Cross-Sex Relationships at Work and the Impact of Gender Stereotypes. DEVINE, I and MARKIEWICZ, D.

Cultural and Ideological Bias in Pornography Research. CHRISTENSEN, Ferrel M.

Cultural Critique and Cultural Presuppositions: The Hermeneutical Undercurrent in Critical Theory. ARNASON, Johann P.

Cultural Partnership—A Factor of Social Peace. CACKOWSKI, Zdzislaw and PACZYNSKA, Maria (trans).

Cutting Motherhood in Two: Some Suspicions Concerning Surrogacy. NELSON, Hilde and NELSON, James Lindemann.

Das Verhältnis von Verbrecherinnen zu ihren Familien (in Polish). ROSINSKI, F M.

Death and Well-Being. BIGELOW, John and CAMPBELL, John and PARGETTER, Robert.

The Death Penalty, Civilization, and Inhumaneness. DAVIS, Michael.

The Death Penalty, Deterrence, and Horribleness. Reply to Michael Davis. REIMAN, Jeffrey.

Death, Democracy and Public Ethical Choice. CUSHMAN, Reid and HOLM, Soren.

The Debate Regarding Dialectical Logic in Marx's Economic Writings. SMITH, Tony.

A Decision Support System for the Graph Model of Conflicts. KILGOUR, D Marc and FANG, Liping and HIPEL, Keith W.

Defining—and Implementing—Eupraxophy. FLYNN, T.

A Definition of Negative Liberty. PETTIT, Philip.

The Demand for Effectiveness, Efficiency and Equity of Health Care. MOONEY, Gavin.

Democracy and Technology. MARGONIS, Frank.

Democracy as a Spontaneous Order. DI ZIEREGA, Gus.

The Democracy of Workers in the Light of John Paul II's Encyclical *Laborem Exercens*. KONDZIELA, Joachim.

Democracy, Education, and Sport. ARNOLD, Peter J.

Democratic Autonomy, Political Ethics, and Moral Luck. BREINER, Peter.

The Dialectics of Peace Education. RAPOPORT, Anatol.

El dilema argumentativo de la resistencia a las perspectivas técnicas de la biología moderna. VAN DEN DAELE, Wolfgang.

Dimensioni della pace: In margine ad un recente convegno. BELLETTI, Bruno.

Discourse Ethics and Civil Society. COHEN, Jean.

The Doctoral Dissertation of Karl Marx. TEEPLE, G.

Does a Fetus Already Have a Future-like-ours?. MC INERNEY, Peter K.

Does Basing Rights on Autonomy Imply Obligations of Political Allegiance?. NICKEL, James W.

Dressing Down Dressing Up—The Philosophic Fear of Fashion. HANSON, Karen.

Le droit à la jouissance, la jouissance des droits. TZITZIS, S.

Dual-Career and Dual-Income Families: Do They Need Different Needs?. FALKENBERG, L and MONACHELLO, M.

Duquette, Hegel, and Political Freedom. BIEN, Joseph.

Eccentric Subjects: Feminist Theory and Historical Consiousness. DE LAURETIS, Teresa.

Ecologic-Economic Jurisprudence—The Next Step?. LEIDIG, Guido.

Ecologische communicatie door disciplinering van de moraal. STUY, Johan.

The Economic Efficiency and Equity of Abortion. MEEKS, Thomas J.

An Economic Newcomb Problem. BROOME, John.

Economic Participation: The Discourse of Work. CHMIELEWSKI, Philip J.

Economic Relations and their Reflection in Working People's Consciousness under Socialism (in Czechoslovakian). HELLER, J.

Economics and Hermeneutics. BERGER, Lawrence A.

Economics and Psychology: Estranged Bedfellows or Fellow Travellers? A Critical Synthesis. SASSOWER, Raphael.

Économie de la violence, violence de l'économie: Derrida et Marx. MALABOU, Catherine.

Education for Sexism: A Theoretical Analysis of the Sex/Gender Bias in Education. DAVIES, Bronwyn.

The Effect of Computer Intervention and Task Structure on Bargaining Outcome. JONES, Beth H and JELASSI, M Tawfik.

Emociones reactivas. HANSBERG, Olbeth.

The Endorsements of Interpretation. DOEPKE, Frederick.

Energy-Events and Fields. BRACKEN, Joseph A.

Engagement ou néantisation? (in Greek). DÉLIVOYATZIS, S.

The Enlightenment's Talking Cure: Habermas, *legitimation Crisis*, and the Recent Political Landscape. MARTIN, Bill.

Epicurus and Friendship. STERN-GILLET, Suzanne.

The Epistemology of Pluralism: the Basis of Liberal Philosophy. SMART, Ninian.

Equal Freedom, Rights and Utility in Spencer's Moral Philosophy. WEINSTEIN, D.

Equality of Educational Opportunity as Equality of Educational Outcomes. HOWE, Kenneth R.

Equality of Opportunity and the Problem of Nature. BLITS, Jan H.

Equality of Opportunity. YOUNG, Robert.

Equality, Political Order and Ethics: Hobbes and the Systematics of Democratic Rationality. ZIMMERMANN, Rolf.

Ergebnisse und Probleme der Entwicklung des historischen Materialismus. STIEHLER, Gottfried.

Ernest Nagel's Criticism of H L A Hart's Arguments for the Natural Law. HENLE, R J.

The Essential Elements for the Possibility and Necessity of the Principle of Solidarity According to Max Scheler. IBANA, Rainer R A.

Establishing the Moral Basis of Medicine: Edmund D Pellegrino's Philosophy of Medicine. THOMASMA, David C.

Estrategia y Táctica: La Política Como Ciencia: Marx Y Engels. SALOM, Roberto.

Ethical and Conceptual Issues in Charitable Investments, Cause Related Marketing, and Advertising. DIENHART, John W and FODERICK, Saundra I.

Ethical Principles and Medical Practices. MACKLIN, Ruth.

Ethical Problems in Competitive Bidding: The Paradyne Case. DAVIS, J Steve.

Ethics and Stochastic Processes. HARDIN, Russell.

Ethics in Bioengineering. MITCHAM, Carl.

The Ethics of Dwarf-Tossing. BABER, H E.

The Ethics of Struggle. DENYER, Tom.

A Eupraxopher's Agenda: Humanism and Religion. HOFFMANN, R Joseph.

Euthanasia, Ethics and Economics. HÄYRY, Heta and HÄYRY, Matti.

Evolución de los derechos humanos en Spinoza y en Leibniz. VERGES, S.

Evolution in Nature—Development in Society. LASZLO, Ervin.

The Evolution of the Chinese Concept of Culture. GAWLIKOWSKI, Krzysztof.

Evolutionary Biology and Naturalism. MASTERS, Roger D.

An Examination of Present Research on the Female Entrepreneur-Suggested Strategies for the 1990's. MOORE, Dorothy P.

Exile and PVS. SCHNEIDERMAN, Lawrence J.

The Expert and the Public: Local Values and National Choice. GOLDSTEIN, Alfred.

Explaining Wrongdoing. DAVIS, Michael.

F A Hayek, ce pourfendeur des droits sociaux. GIROUX, France.

Facing Diversity: The Case of Epistemic Abstinence. RAZ, Joseph.

A Family Portrait of Canada's Most Successful Female Entrepreneurs. BELCOURT, Monica.

Fear and the Limits of Human Subjectivity. CACKOWSKI, Zdzislaw and BLAIM, Artur (trans).

Feiten en waarden: de constructie van een onderscheid. PELS, Dick and DE VRIES, G.

Feminist Separatism—The Dynamics of Self-Creation. TESSIER, L J.

Feminist Social Theory and Hermeneutics: An Empowering Dialectic?. BUKER, Eloise A.

The Feminist Subject Spinning in the Postmodern Project. KARIEL, Henry S.

Fetishism, Argument, and Judgment in *Capital*. FINOCCHIARO, Maurice A.

The First Sophists and Feminism: Discourses of the "Other". JARRATT, Susan C.

Formal and Informal Management Training Programs for Women in Canada: Who Seems to Be Doing a Good Job?. LAVOIE, Dina.

Forming of an Honorable Man in Classical China: The Junzi's Education (in Serbo-Croatian). DIDIER, Michel.

A Fortnight of My Life is Missing: A Discussion of the Status of the Human 'Pre-Embryo'. HOLLAND, Allan.

Le fou stoïcien. BRAGUE, Rémi.

Foul Dealing and an Assurance Problem. PETTIT, Philip.

Four-One-Four. ANNAS, George J.

Free Will as Psychological Capacity and the Justification of Consequences. SCHOPP, Robert.

Free Will. SCHEER, Richard.

Friedrich Hayek's Moral Science. FULLER, Timothy.

From Nothing to Sociology. WOLFF, Kurt H.

Frontiers and New Vistas in Women in Management Research. SEKARAN, Uma.

The Function of the Press in a Free and Democratic Society. AUDI, Robert.

Functions of Egalitarianism in Yugoslav Society. BERNIK, Ivan.

The *Fundamental Constitutions of Carolina* as a Tool for Lockean Scholarship. MC GUINNESS, Celia.

SOCIAL PHIL

The Fundamental Features of Legal Rationality. GARDIES, Jean-Louis.

The Future of Psychiatry. MICHELS, Robert and MARKOWITZ, John C.

A Game-Theoretic Analysis of Professional Rights and Responsibilities. GAA, James C.

The Gandhian Approach to *Swadeshi* or Appropriate Technology. BAKKER, J I (Hans).

Gauthier on Cooperating in Prisoner's Dilemmas. RAINBOLT, George W.

Gender Socialisation and the Nature/Culture Controversy: The Dualist's Dilemma. JONATHAN, Ruth.

Généalogie ou archéologie de la psychanalyse?. SOULEZ, Philippe.

The Genealogy of Justice and the Justice of Genealogy. WEISS, Harold.

The Generalized Others and the Concrete Other: A Response of Marie Fleming. NIELSEN, Kai.

Gibt es einen Puls unserer Produktivkraftentwicklung?. HEDTKE, Ulrich.

God and Nation: Franz Rosenzweig's Concept of Messianism versus Polish Messianism. MARKIEWICZ, Barbara and PROTALINSKI, Grzegorz (trans).

Goffman's Revisions. MANNING, Phil.

A Graph-Theoretic Approach to Revealed Preference. WAKKER, Peter.

Group Decision and Negotiation Support in Evolving, Nonshared Information Contexts. SHAKUN, Melvin F.

The Growing Feminist Debate Over the New Reproductive Technologies. DONCHIN, Anne.

A Gynecentric Aesthetic. COX, Renée.

Habits of the Head: Tocqueville's America and Jazz. SCHNECK, Stephen Frederick.

Hamlethics in Planning: To Do or Not To Do. KAUFMAN, Jerome L.

Handlungstypen und Kriterien: Zu Habermas' "Theorie des kommunikativen Handelns". DORSCHEL, Andreas.

Health Care as a Right: Fairness and Medical Resources. HÄYRY, Matti and HÄYRY, Heta.

Hegel, die Französische Revolution und die liberale Tradition. LOSURDO, Domenico.

Heidegger and the Difficulties of a Postmodern Ethics and Politics. WHITE, Stephen K.

Heinrich Heine, intellectuel moderne. HÖHN, Gerhard.

Heterosexuality and Feminist Theory. OVERALL, Christine.

The Historical-Philosophical Change of an Involution Dialectics. IRIMIE, Ioan.

Hobbes on our Minds. ZAGORIN, Perez.

Hobbes's Persuasive Civil Science. SORELL, Tom.

Hollis on Roles and Reason. WILKERSON, T E.

Honesty in Marketing. JACKSON, Jennifer.

Hope in a Secular Ethic. BAKER, Robert E.

How Can Philosophers Teach Professional Ethics?. WEIL, Vivian.

How Evolutionary Biology Challenges the Classical Theory of Rational Choice. COOPER, W S.

How to Combine Pareto Optimality with Liberty Considerations. VALLENTYNE, Peter.

How to Define Terrorism. TEICHMAN, Jenny.

Human Ecology. JUNGEN, Britta and EGNEUS, Hans.

Human Existence and Prospective Knowledge. PANA, Laura.

The Human Factor in the Revolution and Perestroika. MINKEVICIUS, Jokubas V.

Humanism and Altruism. MADIGAN, Tim.

Humanities in Medical Education: Some Contributions. CLOUSER, K Danner.

The Hypervisual Meaning of the American West. MEYER, William E H.

Idées esthétiques et morales dans le contexte aristique et scientifique de l'oeuvre d'A Odobescu (in Romanian). DRAGOMIRESCU, Lucian.

Ideology and Epistemology: A Discussion of Mc Carney and Mills. SUSHINSKY, Mary Ann.

Imaginative Freedom and the German Enlightenment. KNELLER, Jane.

The Immorality of Nuclear Deterrence. ARDAGH, David.

The Impact of Feminist Research: Issues of Legitimacy. WILKINSON, Sue.

The Impact of Information and Computer Based Training on Negotiators' Performance. GAUVIN, Stéphane and LILIEN, Gary L and CHATTERJEE, Kalyan.

Impartial Application of Moral and Legal Norms: A Contribution to Discourse Ethics. GÜNTHER, Klaus.

The Importance of Knowledge and Trust in the Definition of Death. RIX, Bo Andreassen.

The Impossibility of a Paretian Loyalist. GÄRDENFORS, Peter and PETTIT, Philip.

In den Zeiten der Schwäche. SANDKÜHLER, Hans Jörg.

The Incarceration of Wildness: Wilderness Areas as Prisons. BIRCH, Thomas H.

Inconscient et savoir de la folie: Freud dans le champ psychiatrique. BERCHERIE, Paul.

Individual and Organizational Characteristics of Women in Managerial Leadership. ROWNEY, J I A and CAHOON, A R.

The Individual and the General Will: Rousseau Reconsidered. HILEY, David R.

Individualisierung als Emanzipationsprojekt?. TEICHMANN, Werner.

L'individuo nella città. VERNANT, Jean Pierre.

Indoctrination: A Contextualist Approach. NEIMAN, Alven M.

The Inefficiency of Some Efficiency Comparisons: A Reply to Nye. SARAYDAR, Edward.

The Inequality of Markets. ROGERSON, Kenneth F.

Initiation in Hermeneutics: An Illustration Through the Mother-and-Daughter Archetype. DARROCH-LOZOWSKI, Vivian.

Injury as Alienation in Sport. THOMAS, Carolyn E and RINTALA, Janet A.

Integralism and the Reconstruction of Society: The Idea of Ultimate Reality and Meaning in the World of P A Sorokin. JOHNSTON, Barry V.

Interpretation in Medicine: An Introduction. DANIEL, Stephen L.

Interpretive Bioethics: The Way of Discernment. CARSON, Ronald A.

Is Commercial Surrogacy Baby-Selling?. KORNEGAY, R Jo.

Is Ecology Transcending Both Marxism and Christianity?. SKOLIMOWSKI, Henryk.

Is Libertarian Free Will Worth Wanting?. SMILANSKY, Saul.

Is Limited Government Possible?. DE JASAY, Anthony.

Is Marxism an Atheism?. FRITZHAND, Marek and RODZINSKA, Aleksandra (trans).

Is Pregnancy Necessary: Feminist Concerns About Ectogenesis. MURPHY, Julien S.

Is Socialism a Psychological Misunderstanding?. REYKOWSKI, Janusz.

Is There a History of Sexuality?. HALPERIN, David M.

Is Women's Labor a Commodity?. ANDERSON, Elizabeth S.

J G Droysen: Storia universale e Kulturgeschichte. CANTILLO, Giuseppe.

Le jeu de Nietzsche dans Derrida. HAAR, Michel.

Justice as Fairness: Political or Metaphysical?. NEAL, Patrick.

Justice Between Age-Groups: A Comment on Norman Daniels. MC KERLIE, Dennis.

Justice, HMOs, and the Invisible Rationing of Health Care Resources. FLECK, Leonard M.

Justifying a Principle of Informed Consent: A Case Study in Autonomy-Based Ethics. GUNDERSON, Martin.

Justifying Punishment and the Problem of the Innocent. MARTIN, Rex.

Juventology: A Holistic Approach to Youth. MAHLER, Fred.

Kampf—Verhandlung—Dialog. SCHRÖDER, Richard.

Kant and the Interpretation of Nature and History. MAKKREEL, Rudolf.

Kant on Property Rights and the Social Contract. BAYNES, Kenneth.

Kant over midden, middel en doel II. VAN DER HOEVEN, J.

Der Kapitalismus verletzt die Menschenrechte. KÜNZLI, Arnold.

Killing, Abortion, and Contraception: A Reply to Marquis. NORCROSS, Alastair.

Knowing and Believing in the Original Position. CORLETT, J A.

Das Konzept einer "wahren" Politik des Friedrich Gentz. DIETRICH, Therese.

Kotaro Tanaka as a Natural Law Theorist. HANZAWA, Takamaro.

L'époque contemporaine et la signification axiologique de la science et de la culture (in Romanian). GHEORGHE, Elena.

L'événement freudien: L'objet métapsychologique. ASSOUN, Paul-Laurent.

L'exposé de quelques systèmes d'histoire (in Romanian). FLORU, Ion S.

L'idée d'unité et d'autonomie des formes de la culture dans la conception de Titu Maiorescu. ROSCA, I N.

L'illuministe Simeon Marcovici—un remarquable journaliste et penseur (in Romanian). ISAR, N.

L'observation: Freud et la scénographie clinique. LACOSTE, Patrick.

La conscience philosophique et la conscience morale chez Eufrosin Poteca (in Romanian). ICHIM, Viorica.

La contribution d'Anton Velini à l'enseignement philosophique du siècle passée (in Romanian). OPREA, Ioan.

La culture du travail (in Romanian). COBIANU, Maria.

La nécessité de l'affirmation d'une nouvelle pensée politique (in Romanian). FLOREA, Ion.

La polysémie des coutumes populaires (in Romanian). POPESCU, Alexandru.

La problématique du progrès dans la philosophie rationnaliste roumaine de l'entre-deux-guerres (in Romanian). TARSOLEA, Constantin.

La protoéthique ou études sur les fondements des chroniques roumaines (in Romanian). BULEANDRA, Alexandru.

La psychologie consonantiste et la créativité (in Romanian). STANCIULESCU, Traian Dinorel.

The Lacuna Between Philosophy and History. HARRIS, Leonard.

SOCIAL PHIL

The Land as a Social Being: Ethical Implications From Societal Expectations. STICKEL, George W.

Land Use Planning and Analytic Methods of Policy Analysis: Commentary on "The Expert and the Public". SHRADER-FRECHETTE, Kristin.

Lao Zi and the Xia Culture. BO, Wang.

Law as Convention. REYNOLDS, Noel B.

Le concept de crise de la culture dans la philosophie Roumaine de l'entre-deux-guerres (in Romanian). OTOVESCU, Dumitru.

Le développement de la science et le progrès de la société (in Romanian). MARIS, Nicolae.

Le plus pur des batards (l'affirmation sans issue). KRELL, David Farrell and BARET, Françoise (trans).

Le sens du nihilisme ou l'axiologie de la crise chez Nietzsche (in Romanian). GULIAN, C I.

A Legal and Economic Analysis of Insider Trading: Establishing an Appropriate Sphere of Regulation. SALBU, Steven R.

La légitimité. GOYARD-FABRE, Simone.

Leibniz's Nachklänge Im Denken und In der Dichtung von Mihai Eminescu. BOBOC, Alexandru.

Les mécanismes pentadiques de la tragédie antique (in Romanian). SURDU, Alexandru.

Les métamorphoses de l'humanisme dans le philosophie marxiste italienne (in Romanian). GHITA, Simion.

Les réalisations du socialisme dans la perspective de l'histoire (in Romanian). BAZAC, Ana.

Lesbian Angels and Other Matters. ZITA, Jacquelyn.

The Leverage of Foreigners: Multinationals in South Africa. DI NORCIA, Vincent.

Lévy-Bruhl et Durkheim: Notes biographiques en marge d'une correspondance—Lettres à L Lévy-Bruhl (1894-1915). MERLLIÉ, Dominique and DURKHEIM, Emile.

Liang Qichao and the Problematic of Social Change (in Serbo-Croatian). PFISTER, Lauren.

Liberal and Socialist Egalitarianism. NIELSEN, Kai.

Liberal Autonomy. LOMASKY, Loren E.

The Liberal Constitution: Rational Design or Evolution?. BARRY, Norman P.

Liberal Values vs Liberal Social Philosophy. CAPALDI, Nicholas.

The Liberal/Communitarian Controversy and Communicative Ethics. BAYNES, K.

Liberalism and Post-Modern Hermeneutics. NEAMAN, Elliot Yale.

Liberalism, Liberty, and Neutrality. DE MARNEFFE, Peter.

The Liberation of Caring: A Different Voice for Gilligan's "Different Voice". PUKA, Bill.

Libertarianism Versus Secular Humanism?. GORDON, David.

Lieux de l'identité freudienne: Judaïsme et Kultur. PFRIMMER, Theo.

Locke on Disagreement Over the Uses of Moral and Political Terms. MASON, Andrew.

Lukács, Adorno en de machteloze kritiek. SALMAN, Ton.

Machiavelli, Tacito, Grozio: un nesso "ideale" tra libertinismo e previchismo. SCARCELLA, Cosimo.

MacIntyre on Traditions. ANNAS, Julia.

Malthus and Utilitarianism with Special Reference to the *Essay on Population*. HOLLANDER, Samuel.

Man Cannot Change His Nature. TSIPKO, A.

Man in the System of Socioeconomic Values. DUGIN, V N.

Management Training for Women: International Experiences and Lessons for Canada. LAM, M Natalie.

Mandatory HIV Antibody Testing Policies: An Ethical Analysis. O'BRIEN, Maura.

Martin Heidegger: His Philosophy and His Politics. ZUCKERT, Catherine H.

Marx et le destin historique de la morale (in Romanian). NITA, Petre.

Marx's Use of Religious Metaphors. JEANNOT, Thomas M.

Marx, Lukes, and Human Rights. BAXTER, David.

Marxism and Conceptual Scholasticism. KOZYR-KOWALSKI, Stanislaw and OSZKODAR, Zbigniew (trans).

Marxism and Human Sociobiology: A Reply to Zhang Boshu. KEITA, Lansana.

Marxism and Surrogacy. OLIVER, Kelly.

Marxism, the Ecological Crisis and a Master's Attitude to Nature (in Czechoslovakian). ZNOJ, M.

Marxist Critical Theory, Contradictions, and Ecological Succession. CATTON, Philip.

A Marxist's View on the Philosophy of Peace Advanced by John Paul II. CZEMARNIK, Adam and BONIECKA, Magdalena (trans).

Mary of Nazareth, Feminism and the Tradition. CADEGAN, Una M and HEFT, James L.

Materialist Dialectic and Critique of Philosophical Irrationalism (in Czechoslovakian). JANKOV, M.

Matriarchale Ganzheitlichkeit gegen patriarchale Vernunft?. EIFLER, Christine.

The Meaning of Universalism: Comments on Kuczynski and McGovern. PARSONS, Howard L.

The Means of Analysis and the Future of Liberalism: A Response to Hariman. STOESZ, David.

Medical Ethics and the Death Penalty. BONNIE, Richard J.

Medical Hermeneutics: Where is the "Text" We are Interpreting. BARON, Richard J.

Medical Joint-Venturing: An Ethical Perspective. GREEN, Ronald M.

Medicine and Dialogue. ZANER, Richard M.

Mens en aarde: Het ecofilosofisch dilemma in het werk van Ludwig Klages. WITZORECK, Kris.

Mentoring in Organizations: Implications for Women. BURKE, R J and MC KEEN, C A.

Mergers, Acquisitions and the Market for Corporate Control. WERHANE, Patricia H.

Metaphors, Narratives, and Images of AIDS. JONES, Anne Hudson.

The Metaphysical Transition in Farming: From the Newtonian-Mechanical to the Eltonian Ecological. CALLICOTT, J Baird.

The Metaphysics of Communism. LURIE, Yuval.

Methodological Individualism. TÄNNSJÖ, Torbjörn.

Mill's and Other Liberalisms. GRAY, John.

Mill's Epistemology in Practice in his Liberal Feminism. TULLOCH, Gail.

Mills and Mc Carney on "Ideology" in Marx and Engels. COSTELLO, Dan.

The Mirror of Reproduction: Baudrillard and Reagan's America. RUBENSTEIN, Diane.

Misunderstanding Death on a Respirator. TOMLINSON, Tom.

Misunderstandings of Epistemic TIT for TAT: Reply to John Woods. BLAIS, Michel J.

Models of Freedom in the Modern World. WELLMER, Albrecht.

Modernizing Mortality: Medical Progress and the Good Society. CALLAHAN, Daniel.

Die Möglichkeit der Kooperation unter Egoisten: Neuere Ergebnisse spieltheoretischer Analysen. SCHÜSSLER, Rudolf.

Money: A Speech Act Analysis. HADREAS, Peter.

A Moral Case for Socialism. NIELSEN, Kai.

Moral Ideals and Social Values: The Dialectics of Legitimization. AVINERI, Shlomo.

Moral Individualism: Agent-Relativity and Deontic Restraints. MACK, Eric.

The Moral Significance of Birth. WARREN, Mary Anne.

The Moral Significance of Hard Toil: Critique of a Common Intuition. ELLIS, Ralph D.

Moral Theory: Thinking, Doing, and Living. CALLAHAN, Daniel.

Morality and Law. LETWIN, Shirley Robin.

Morality and Nuclear Weapons Policy. LEE, Steven.

The Morality of Software Piracy: A Cross-Cultural Analysis. SWINYARD, W R and RINNE, H and KENG KAU, A.

More Dyke Methods. TREBILCOT, Joyce.

More on Knowledge and the Humanities. EDEL, Abraham.

Motivation et idéal dans l'action sociale (in Romanian). BARBU, Nicolae.

Motive and Obligation in the British Moralists. DARWALL, Stephen L.

Moves and Motives in the Games We Play. HOLLIS, Martin.

Multi-Party Responses to Environmental Problems: A Case of Contaminated Dairy Cattle. MORREN JR, George E B.

Un mythe ouvert dans "Zamolxis" de Lucian Blaga (in Romanian). DADARLAT, Camil Marius.

Narrative in African Philosophy. BELL, Richard H.

National Formation and the 'Rise of the Cultural'. JAMES, Paul.

Natural and Social Lottery, and Concepts of the Self. SADURSKI, Wojciech.

Natural Law in an "Auto" by Calderón. FIORE, Robert L.

Natural Rights Liberalism. MACHAN, Tibor R.

Naturalism and Prescriptivity. RAILTON, Peter.

The Nature of Human Nature and its Bearing on Public Health Policy: An Application. KAPLAN, Mark.

Nature, Custom, and Stipulation in Law and Juriprudence. MURPHY, James Bernard.

The Nazi Myth. LACOUE-LABARTHE, Philippe and NANCY, Jean-Luc.

Neuropsychology and Meaning in Psychiatry. GILLETT, Grant R.

Neutral, Stable and Pareto-Optimal Welfare Functions. STORCKEN, A J A.

The New Consensus: The Fukuyama Thesis. FRIEDMAN, Jeffrey.

The New Economics of Medicine: Special Challenges for Psychiatry. MORREIM, E Haavi.

Nietzsche: Women and Relationships of Strength. STARRETT, Shari Neller.

Nietzschean Perspectivism: "How Could Such a Philosophy—Dominate?". FOWLER, Mark.

SOCIAL PHIL

Niklas Luhmann over ecologische communicatie. BALLIU, Julien.

No Bosses Here: Management in Worker Co-Operatives. CONN, Melanie.

Nobodies Speaking: Subjectivity, Sex, and the Pornography Effect. FINN, Geraldine.

Nonsense, Fate, and Policy Analysis: The Case of Animal Rights and Experimentation. ROE, Emery M.

Norman Bowie and Richard Rorty on Multinationals: Does Business Ethics Need 'Metaphysical Comfort?'. WICKS, Andrew C.

A Note on the Legal Liberties of Children as Distinguished from Adults. VETTERLING-BRAGGIN, Mary.

The Novelty of Marx's Theory of *Praxis*. MARGOLIS, Joseph.

Nozick on Self-Esteem. MASON, Andrew.

Obedience to Superior Orders. STUART, J M.

Obligation and Human Nature in Hume's Philosophy. COHEN, Mendel F.

Obligations of Gratitude and Political Obligation. WALKER, A D M.

The October Revolution and Spiritual Renewal of Society. NOVIKOVA, Lidia I.

Of Vision, Hope, and Courage. SKOLIMOWSKI, Henryk.

The Offensive-Defensive Distinction in Military Biological Research. FRISINA, Michael E.

Ökonomische Soziologie in Nowosibirst (Literaturbericht). SEGERT, Astrid.

On Beautiful Games. KRETCHMAR, R Scott.

On Equitable Cake-Cutting, or: Caring More about Caring. HAYNES, Felicity.

On Natural Law—Aristotle. SCHALL, James V.

On Performance-Enhancing Substances and the Unfair Advantage Argument. GARDNER, Roger.

On Realization of Human Rights. KANGER, Stig.

On the Future of the Man-Nature Relationship (in Czechoslovakian). MUZIK, J.

On the Relationship Between Law and Morality. COLEMAN, Jules.

On the Relationship of Lukács *Ontology* and the Theory of Social Formations (in Hungarian). KARIKÓ, Sándor.

Organized Religion: New Target for Professional Ethics?. BATTIN, Margaret P.

Pacifism and Care. DAVION, Victoria.

Parents Rights and Educational Policy. FORSTER, Kathie.

Paternalism and the Rationality of the Child. EKMAN, Rosalind.

Paternalism Defined. ARCHARD, David.

Per una storia della cultura. TESSITORE, Fulvio.

Perelman's Methodology and Natural Law Reasoning. BODENHEIMER, Edgar.

Performance Prestidigitation. MEIER, Klaus V.

Personhood and Moral Responsibility. LOCKE, Lawrence A.

Persuasive Argumentation in Negotiation. SYCARA, Katia P.

The Philosopher as Insider and Outsider. KAMM, Frances M.

The Philosophical Implications of the Use of New Information Technologies: Introductory Reflections. NIZNIK, Józef and RODZINSKA, Aleksandra (trans).

Philosophie und Lehre. HAGER, Nina.

Philosophie, Ideologie et Acteurs Economique en Afrique. KIBAMBE-KIA-NKIMA, Kapongola.

Philosophy and Politics: The Case of Heidegger. ZIMMERMAN, Michael E.

Philosophy and Society: On the Philosophical Heritage of Emanuel Radl (in Czechoslovakian). HEJDANEK, Ladislav.

Philosophy and the Media. HELD, Virginia.

Philosophy Cannot Be Implemented in Socialism and Its Economy (in Czechoslovakian). NIKOLIC, P D.

Philosophy for an 'Age of Death': The Critique of Science and Technology in Heidegger and Nishitani. HEINE, Steven.

Philosophy of Reservation. AGARWALA, Binod Kumar.

The Physician in the Technological Age. JASPERS, Karl.

Physician Investment and Self-Referral: Philosophical Analysis of a Contentious Debate. MORREIM, E Haavi.

Plant Closing Ethics Root in American Law. MILLSPAUGH, Peter E.

Plato and Social Justice. DENT, N J H.

Plato's *Ion*: The Problem of the Author. PAPPAS, Nickolas.

Platonic Justice and the *Republic*. HALL, Robert W.

A Plea for the Heart. EVANS, Martyn.

Pluralism and Universalist Socialism. KUCZYNSKI, Janusz and JEDYNAK, Jacek.

The Policy Implications of Differing Concepts of Risk. BRADBURY, Judith A.

Political Obligation and Gratitude. KLOSKO, George.

The Politics of the Book: The French Revolution and the Demise of Natural Rights Theory. WARNER, Stuart D.

The Politics of the Ineffable: Derrida's Deconstructionism. MC CARTHY, Thomas.

Potere e ragione nella filosofia politica di Enrico Opocher. ANDREATTA, Alberto.

Power, Authority, and Wisdom. BAMBROUGH, Renford.

Preparation for Life in Peace—Future Perspectives. SUCHODOLSKI, Bogdan.

Presumptive Norms and Norm Revision (in Hebrew). ULLMANN-MARGALIT, Edna.

Pride, Prejudice and Shyness. EWIN, R E.

Primary Goods Reconsidered. ARNESON, Richard J.

Private and Public Preferences. KURAN, Timur.

Private Hospitals in Public Health Systems. HOLM, Soren.

Private Irony and Public Decency: Richard Rorty's New Pragmatism. MC CARTHY, Thomas.

The Problem of Progress. ROWE, William V.

Probleme der Dialektik der sozialistischen Produktionsweise. HEIDLER, Angelika.

Professor Gould and the "Natural". DALCOURT, Gerard J.

Prostitution, Exploitation and Taboo. GREEN, Karen.

Protestant Reconciliation as a Challenge for Today's Culture. HUMMEL, Gert.

The Public as Sculpture: From Heavenly City to Mass Ornament. NORTH, Michael.

Public Philosophy and Contemporary Pluralism. DOUGLASS, R Bruce.

Public Space in a Private Time. ACCONCI, Vito.

Punishing Corporations: A Proposal. RISSER, David T.

Qualité et efficience—coordonate principales du développement socio-économique Roumaine (in Romanian). CORNESCU, Viorel and BUCUR, Ion.

Quality of Care and Cost Containment in the US and UK. JENNETT, Bryan.

Quel développement et pour qui?. PESTIEAU, J.

Quelques contributions de grande valeur au progrès multilatéral de la Roumanie socialiste (in Romanian). IONEL, Nicolae.

Quelques réflexions sur une thèse marxiste (in Romanian). BOTIS, Gheorghe.

Queries of Psychology in Social Choice Theory. BEZEMBINDER, Th.

The Question of Black Philosophy. JEFFERSON, Paul.

Racism and Rationality: *The Need for a New Critique*. GOLDBERG, David Theo.

Radical Relatedness and Feminist Separatism. HOWELL, Nancy R.

Il radicalismo negli Stati Uniti degli anni '80: l'anarco-ecologismo di Murray Bookchin. DONNO, A.

Rational Common Ground in the Sociology of Knowledge. KATZ, Jonathan.

Rational Reconstruction and Social Criticism: Habermas's Model of Interpretive Social Science. BAYNES, Kenneth.

The Rational Woman. SIMONS, Martin.

A Rationale for the Support of the Medium-Sized Family Farm. DANIELS, Thomas L.

Rationalising Conventions. MILLER, Seumas.

Rationality, Coordination, and Convention. GILBERT, Margaret.

Reading Horkheimer Reading Vico: An Introduction. DALLMAYR, Fred.

Reason and Agreement in Social Contract Views. FREEMAN, Samuel.

La réception du Saint-Simonisme dans l'école hégélienne: l'exemple d'Eduard Gans. WASZEK, Norbert.

Recipes, Cooking and Conflict. HELDKE, Lisa.

Recipes, Cooking, and Conflict: A Response to Heldke's Recipes for Theory. KOCH, Donald F.

Reduction in the Social Sciences: The Future or Utopia?. SZMATKA, Jacek.

Réformisme pénal et responsabilité: une étude philosophique. BLAIS, F.

Regulating AIDS Research on Infants and Children: The Moral Task of Institutional Review Boards. CARTER, Michele and WICHMAN, Alison and MC CARTHY, Charles R.

The Relevance of Deep Ecology to the Third World. JOHNS, David M.

Religious Belief and Scientific Weltanschauungen. TRUNDLE, Robert.

Remarks on the Dialogue Between Christians and Marxists. BIENIAK, Janusz and RODZINSKA, Aleksandra (trans).

Reply to Beehler's "Autonomy and the Democratic Principle". COHEN, Joshua and ROGERS, Joel.

Reproductive Controls and Sexual Destiny. MURPHY, Timothy F.

A Research Strategy for Studying Telic Human Behavior. HOWARD, George S and YOUNGS, William H.

Research, Myths and Expectations: New Challenges for Management Educators. GRONDIN, Deirdre.

Response to Janusz's "Christianity and Marxism". MC GOVERN, Arthur F and RODZINSKA, Aleksandra (trans) and PETROWICZ, Lech (trans).

The Responsible Use of Animals in Biomedical Research. HETTINGER, Edwin Converse.

Reviewing the "Subject(s)". LEACH, Mary S.

SOCIAL PHIL

La revisión antihistoricista de la Revolución Francesa. SAZBÓN, José.

Richard Holdsworth and the Natural Law: An Early Linguistic Turn. TRENTMAN, J A.

The Right to Subsistence in a "Lockean" State of Nature. SHEARMUR, Jeremy.

La risposta di Leroux a Lamennais: Il concetto di Trinità come soluzione del problema sociale. FIORENTINO, Fernando.

Robert Stevens on Offers. SWANTON, Christine.

De rol van het begrip intrinsieke waarde in milieu-ethische argumentaties. MERKS, K W.

Rousseau and Recognition. SHAVER, Robert.

The Rule of Law in Contemporary Liberal Theory. WALDRON, Jeremy.

The Sales Process and the Paradoxes of Trust. OAKES, G.

Sartre's Sexism Reconsidered. MUI, Constance.

Savoir et croire: Sur le Pen et autres menus détails. POULIN, R.

Scarcity and Setting the Boundaries of Political Economy. SASSOWER, Raphael.

Scarcity and the Limits of Want: Comments on Sassower and Bender. LEVINE, David.

Scarcity and the Turn from Economics to Ecology. BENDER, Frederic L.

Scepticism and Intellectual Freedom: The Philosophical Foundations of Kant's Politics of Publicity. LAURSEN, John C.

Schizophrenia and Indeterminacy: The Problem of Validity. HUNT, Geoffrey.

Schlüsseltechnologien—Herausforderung und Chance für moralischen Fortschritt. THIEME, Karl-Heinz.

Schumpeters Theorie der Wirtschaftsentwicklung in philosophischer Sicht. RUBEN, Peter.

Science, Technology, and God: In Search of Believers. GOLDMAN, Steven L.

A Scientific Dilemma: The Human Genome Project. CAVALIERI, Liebe F.

A Second Look at Pornography and the Subordination of Women. PARENT, W A.

Selective Termination of Pregnancy and Women's Reproductive Autonomy. OVERALL, Christine.

Self-Interest in Political Life. MANSBRIDGE, Jane.

Self-Ownership, Communism and Equality—I. COHEN, G A.

Self-Ownership, Communism and Equality—II. GRAHAM, Keith.

Self-Ownership. DAY, J P.

Self-Reform as Political Reform in the Writings of John Stuart Mill. EISENACH, Eldon J.

Selling Babies and Selling Bodies. KETCHUM, Sara Ann.

Les séquelles de la crise moderniste. MONTAGNES, Bernard.

Sexism and the Philosophical Canon: On Reading Beauvoir's *The Second Sex*. SIMONS, Margaret A.

Sexist Dualism: Its Material Sources in the Exploitation of Reproductive Labor. LANGE, Lynda.

Sexuality, Rationality, and Spirituality. TOMM, Winnifred A.

Shelf-Life Zero: A Classic Postmodernist Paper. TRAVERS, Andrew.

Should a Democrat Be in Favour of Academic Freedom?. MORROW, W E.

Should We Ration Health Care?. JECKER, Nancy S.

Simmons and the Concept of Consent: Commentary on "Consent and Fairness in Planning Land Use". FOTION, Nicholas.

A Skeptical Appreciation of Natural Law Theory. GINSBERG, Robert.

Skepticism and Happiness. KOHL, Marvin.

A Sketch for a Theory of Health. NORDENFELT, Lennart.

Slaves Putting Themselves up for Sale. WATSON, A.

Slippery Bentham: Some Neglected Cracks in the Foundation of Utilitarianism. PITKIN, Hanna Fenichel.

Sociability and Social Conflict in George Herbert Mead's Interactionism, 1900-1919. FEFFER, Andrew.

Social Choice and Social Theories. SEABRIGHT, Paul.

Social Context and Historical Emergence: The Underlying Dimension of Medical Ethics. PORTO, Eugenia M.

The Social Dynamics Between Evolution and Progress. MURESAN, Valentin.

The Social Humanism of Adam Schaff. JAGUARIBE, Helio.

Social Interpretation and Political Theory: Walzer and His Critics. WARNKE, Georgia.

Social Justice. WILLIAMS, Bernard.

Social Philosophy: The Agenda for the 'Nineties. WOLFF, Robert Paul.

Social Power and Human Agency. KERNOHAN, Andrew.

The Social Relativity of Justice and Rights Thesis. HUND, John.

Socialism and Atheism. SZCZEPANSKI, Jan and LECKI, Maciej (trans).

Socialism, Feminism and Men. MIDDLETON, Peter.

Le socialisme et le conditionnement social du bonheur. BAZAC, Ana.

La sociedad en la perspectiva informática o existe una sociología de los

computadores?. GUTIÉRREZ, Claudio.

Socio-Economic Evolution of Women Business Owners in Quebec (1987). COLLERETTE, P and AUBRY, P.

Sociognoseología y objectividad. MORALES, Julián.

Socrates' Encounter with Polus in Plato's *Gorgias*. JOHNSON, Curtis N.

Some Aspects of Medical Hermeneutics: The Role of Dialectic and Narrative. LOCK, James D.

Some Methodological Problems Associated with Researching Women Entrepreneurs. STEVENSON, Lois.

Something Akin to a Property Right: Protections for Job Security. LEE, Barbara A.

Something Substantial About Natural Law. FRANCIS, Richard P.

Soziale Sicherheit—Triebkraft ökonomischen Wachstums bei der Gestaltung der entwickelten sozialistischen Gesellschaft. HAHN, Toni and WINKLER, Gunnar.

The Specter of Communism. KRAMER, Matthew.

Spinoza et les problèmes d'une théorie de la societé commerçante. BLOM, Hans W.

Spirituality in Modern Society (in Hungarian). ZWEERMAN, Theo.

Spontaneous Order and the Rule of Law: Some Problems. MAC CORMICK, D Neil.

Sport Abjection: Steroids and the Uglification of the Athlete. FAIRCHILD, David L.

Stair on Natural Law and Promises. MAC CORMACK, Geoffrey.

A Stakeholder Apologetic for Management. SHARPLIN, Arthur and PHELPS, Lonnie D.

State, Class, and Technology in Tobacco Production. GREEN, Gary P.

Status Arguments and Genetic Research with Human Embryos. HICKMAN, Larry.

Stop or Go: Reflections of Women Managers on Factors Influencing their Career Development. ANDREW, C and CODERRE, C and DENIS, A.

Storia della cultura e storia sociale. VILLANI, Pasquale.

Strategy, Social Responsibility and Implementation. KRAFT, Kenneth L and HAGE, Jerald.

Strauss and Natural Right: A Critical Review. CVEK, Peter P.

Strauss et Nietzsche. MANENT, Pierre.

Structuring and Simulating Negotiation: An Approach and an Example. KERSTEN, G E and BADCOCK, L and IGLEWSKI, M and MALLORY, G R.

The Success of Hyperrational Utility Maximizers in Iterated Prisoner's Dilemma: A Response to Sobel. CURTIS, Robert A.

Suffrage Art and Feminism. SHEPPARD, Alice.

Supporting Individuals in Group-Decision Making. KORHONEN, P and WALLENIUS, J.

Survival Through the Generosity of Strangers. CARGAS, Harry James.

Symbolic Orders and Discursive Practices. WALKER, J C.

A Synergetic View of Institutions. WEISE, Peter and BRANDES, Wolfgang.

The Synthesis: A Sociopolitical Critique of the Liberal Professions. ROSSIDES, Daniel.

A Systematic Exploration of the Marxist Theory of Human Nature. QUANFU, Liu and ZUORONG, He.

Taking Stock: Can the Theory of Reasoned Action Explain Unethical Conduct?. RANDALL, Donna M.

Taking Talents Seriously. GREEN, Simon.

The Talloires Network—A Constructive Move in a Destructive World. RYDEN, Lars and WALLENSTEEN, Peter.

Technology in a Free Society: The New Frankenstein. BALESTRA, Dominic J.

The Concept of "Oikiá" in Classic Greek Philosophy (in Czechoslovakian). MRAZ, M.

The Conceptual Structure of Marxist Thought: Some Critical Reflections (in Serbo-Croatian). KRISHNA, Daya.

The Individuum and the Context of Individual (in Czechoslovakian). TOMEK, V.

The Subject of Historic Transformations in the Present Era (in Czechoslovakian). HAHN, E.

The Uniqueness and Value of Terrestrial Nature (in Czechoslovakian). SMAJS, J.

The Thee Generation. REGAN, Tom.

The Theme of Civilization and its Discontents in Durkheim's *Division of Labor*. MESTROVIC, Stjepan G.

The Theological-Political Tension in Liberalism. FULLER, Timothy.

Theorizing Gender: How Much of It Do We Need. HOUSTON, Barbara.

The Thesis. MINDER, Thomas.

Three Approaches to Locke and the Slave Trade. GLAUSSER, Wayne.

Three Concepts of Tolerance. LAZARI-PAWLOWSKA, Ija.

Three Generations of Computerized Systems for Public Administration and Implications for Legal Decision-Making. BING, Jon.

SOCIAL PHIL

Ties that Bind: Native American Beliefs as a Foundation for Environmental Consciousness. BOOTH, Annie L and JACOBS, Harvey L.

To Discover Again Marriage. HERVADA, Javier.

Tolerance and the Question of Rationality. ZAPASNIK, Stanislaw and PETROWICZ, Lech (trans).

Toward a Feminist Poetic of Critical Thinking. GARRISON, James W and PHELAN, Anne.

Toward a Unified Model for Social Problems Theory. JONES, Brian J and MC FALLS JR, Joseph and GALLAGHER III, Bernard J.

Towards a Creative Meaning of Marxism. RAINKO, Stanislaw and PETROWICZ, Lech (trans).

Towards a Phenomenology of Social Role. KUNINSKI, Milowit.

Towards a Relational Theory of Intergenerational Ethics. AGIUS, Emmanuel.

Towards a Theology of Peace—The Peace Doctrine of John Paul II. RAJECKI, Robert and LECKI, Maciej (trans).

Training and Women: Some Thoughts from the Grassroots. JOYCE, Glenis.

Transformations dans la manière de penser de l'homme contemporain (in Romanian). TUDOSESCU, Ion.

Le travail de la contradiction dans le Livre I de l'*Emile*. IMBERT, Francis.

Treating Animals Naturally?. ROLSTON III, Holmes.

Treating Women as Sex-Objects. SWANTON, Christine and ROBINSON, Viviane and CROSTHWAITE, Jan.

Treatment and Non-Treatment of Defective Newborns. SZAWARSKI, Zbigniew.

The Trick of the Disappearing Goal. SUITS, Bernard.

Trust and Survival: Securing a Vision of the Good Society. THOMAS, Laurence.

Trust in Business Relations: Directions for Empirical Research. HUSTED, Bryan W.

Tuning in to Whistle Blowing. GOLDBERG, David Theo.

The Two Cultures. BROUDY, Harry S.

Two Theories of Ownership in German Classical Philosophy (in Czechoslovakian). SOBOTKA, Milan.

Two-Tier Moral Codes. SMITH, Holly M.

Understanding and Justifying Self-Defence. SMART, B J.

Une conception unitaire, profondément scientifique sur la dynamique des étapes du processus (in Romanian). RUS, Vasile.

Uneven Starts and Just Deserts. WALLER, Bruce N.

Universalism: A New Way of Thinking. KUCZYNSKI, Janusz and PETROWICZ, Lech (trans) and GOLEBIOWSKI, Marek (trans).

Universalisms: Procedural, Contextualist and Prudential. FERRARA, Alessandro.

The Use of Nazi Medical Experimentation Data: Memorial or Betrayal?. ROSENBAUM, Alan S.

Uso y abuso de las nociones de "crisis" y "modelo" en Ciencias Sociales en Costa Rica. CAMACHO, Luis A.

Utilitarianism and Reform: Social Theory and Social Change, 1750-1800. BURNS, J H.

Utilitarianism and Respect for Human Life. SPRIGGE, T L S.

Utopia and Islamic Political Thought. AL-AZMEH, Aziz.

Values and Meaning: Max Weber's Approach to the Idea of Ultimate Reality and Meaning. CUNEO, Michael W.

Values of Knowledge and Values of Action in Human Conduct Structuring. PANA, Laura.

Vers une totalité-champ dans la science contemporaine (in Romanian). BIRIS, Ioan.

The Violence of Public Art: *Do the Right Thing*. MITCHELL, W J T.

Virtues and Character. WALKER, A D M.

Virtuous Lives and Just Societies. O'NEILL, Onora.

The Voices of the Medical Record. POIRIER, Suzanne and BRAUNER, Daniel J.

Was Marx an Egalitarian: Skeptical Remarks on Miller's Marx. NIELSEN, Kai.

Water Quality Concerns and the Public Policy Context. MOORE, Keith M.

Der Weg eines Mitstreiters und Kampfgefährten Lenins zum Marxismus. HEDELER, Wladislaw.

Wert und Würde der Arbeit in *Laborem Exercens* (in Polish). JUROS, Helmut.

What is Really Unethical About Insider Trading?. MOORE, Jennifer.

What is the Theory of Social Choice About?. DE SWART, H C M.

What Is Utility?. HASLETT, D W.

Who Pays for AZT: Commentary. LAMM, Richard D.

Who Pays for AZT?. PENSLAR, Robin Levin.

Why Blackmail Should be Banned. EVANS, Hugh.

Why Do Social Scientists Tend to See the World as Over-Ordered?. BOUDON, Raymond.

Why Worry about How Exploitation Is Defined? Reply to John Roemer.

REIMAN, Jeffrey.

Der Widerspruch zwischen Materiellem und Ideellem und der dialektische Materiebegriff. GEBHARDT, Birgit.

Wirtschaftslehre als Heilslehre. ALEKSANDROWICZ, Dariusz.

Wissenschaftliche Weltauffassung zwischen Sozialrevolution und Sozialreform. NEMETH, Elisabeth.

With Justice for All Beings: Educating as if Nature Matters. COHEN, Michael J.

Woman, Morality, and Fiction. ROBINSON, Jenefer and ROSS, Stephanie.

Women and AIDS: Too Little, Too Late?. BELL, Nora Kizer.

Women and Elderly Parents: Moral Controversy in an Aging Society. POST, Stephen G.

Women in Labor: Some Issues About Informed Consent. LADD, Rosalind Ekman.

The Women in Management Research Program at the National Centre for Management Research and Development. BURKE, R J and MIKALACHKI, D.

Women's Research and Its Inherent Critique of Society and Science. KYLE, Gunhild and JUNGEN, Britta.

Working Class and Proletariat—On the Relation of Andries Sternheim to the Frankfurt School. MULDER, Bertus and NAUTA, Lolle.

Worldview, Beliefs and Society: Mary Douglas' Contribution to the Study of Human Ideas on Ultimate Reality and Meaning. SPICKARD, James V.

The Worm and the Juggernaut: Justice and the Public Interest. LUCAS, J R.

Zur Diskussion um die Einheit und Vielfalt der Interessen im Sozialismus. ROTHE, Barbara and STEININGER, H.

Zur methodologischen Bedeutung des Leninschen Prinzips der "Zurückführung des Individuellen auf das Soziale". DANYEL, Jürgen.

Zur Problematik von Entwicklung und Fortschritt im soziologischen Werk Max Webers. WITTICH, Dietmar.

Der Zwang zur "geschlossenen Gesellschaft"—Ein perennes Dilemma der Utopie?. KLARER, Mario.

SOCIAL PHYSICS

More Heat than Light: Economics as Social Physics, Physics as Nature's Economics. MIROWSKI, Philip.

SOCIAL POLICY(-CIES)

Business Ethics, Corporate Good Citizenship and the Corporate Social Policy Process: A View from the US. EPSTEIN, Edwin M.

The Construction, Deconstruction, and Reconstruction of Difference. ROTHENBERG, Paula.

SOCIAL PROBLEMS

Ethical Theory and Social Issues: Historical Texts and Contemporary Readings. GOLDBERG, David Theo.

Ethics and Social Concern. SERAFINI, Anthony.

La risposta di Leroux a Lamennais: Il concetto di Trinità come soluzione del problema sociale. FIORENTINO, Fernando.

Toward a Unified Model for Social Problems Theory. JONES, Brian J and MC FALLS JR, Joseph and GALLAGHER III, Bernard J.

Uso y abuso de las nociones de "crisis" y "modelo" en Ciencias Sociales en Costa Rica. CAMACHO, Luis A.

SOCIAL PROGRESS

The Club of Rome and the Vienna Centre. FELDHEIM, Pierre.

Whitehead and the New Liberals on Social Progress. MORRIS, Randall C.

SOCIAL PSYCHOLOGY

Moral Consciousness and Communicative Action. HABERMAS, Jürgen.

SOCIAL RELATIONS

Freedom. BAUMAN, Zygmunt.

Eliminativism and Methodological Individualism. KINCAID, Harold.

Methodological Individualism and Explanation. TUOMELA, Raimo.

Plato and Social Justice. DENT, N J H.

SOCIAL RESPONSIBILITY

Paul and the Popular Philosophers. MALHERBE, Abraham J.

Corporate Responsibility: Morality Without Consciousness. SKIDD, David R A.

Ethical Problems in Competitive Bidding: The Paradyne Case. DAVIS, J Steve.

A Game-Theoretic Analysis of Professional Rights and Responsibilities. GAA, James C.

Integrating Medical Ethics with Normative Theory: Patient Advocacy and Social Responsibility. JECKER, Nancy.

Integrating Social Responsibility and Ethics into the Strategic Planning Process. ROBIN, Donald P and REIDENBACH, R Eric.

SOCIAL ROLE(S)

Higher Education: An Arena of Conflicting Philosophies. SPEES, Emil Ray.

Towards a Phenomenology of Social Role. KUNINSKI, Milowit.

SOCIAL SCIENCES

see also Economics, History, Law, Political Science

Klarheit und Methode: Felix Kaufmanns Wissenschaftstheorie. ZILIAN, H G.

"Explanation in the Social Sciences" in *Scientific Explanation (Minnesota Studies in the Philosophy of Science, Volume XIII)*, SALMON, Merrilee H.

"Realism in the Social Sciences" in *Dismantling Truth: Reality in the Post-Modern World*, RUBEN, David.

Critical Attitudes Inside Social Science and the Humanities—A Swedish Perspective. LIEDMAN, Sven-Eric.

Critical Rationalism: The Problem of Method in Social Sciences and Law. ALBERT, Hans.

Defending Laws in the Social Sciences. KINCAID, Harold.

Feitelijk expansionisme, een restrictionistische visie: praktische wetenschappen en waardevrijheid. DE VRIES, Gerard.

Harvey Sacks—Lectures 1964-1965. JEFFERSON, Gail (ed).

In Defense of Good Reasons. BERKSON, William.

La ingeniería social como método de testeo. COMESAÑA, Manuel E.

Marxism and Social Sciences at a New Stage. FRITZHAND, Marek and PROTALINSKI, Grzegorz (trans).

Menschenbilder in pädagogiknahen Sozialwissenschaften. HUG, Theo.

Methodology Is Pragmatic: A Reponse to Miller. BERKSON, William.

Rational Reconstruction and Social Criticism: Habermas's Model of Interpretive Social Science. BAYNES, Kenneth.

Realism and Reality: Some Realistic Reconsiderations. ISAAC, Jeffrey C.

Reduction in the Social Sciences: The Future or Utopia?. SZMATKA, Jacek.

Reflexive Epistemology and Social Complexity: *The Philosophical Legacy of Otto Neurath.* ZOLO, Danilo.

Rejoinder to Berkson's "In Defense of Good Reasons". MILLER, David.

Why Do Social Scientists Tend to See the World as Over-Ordered?. BOUDON, Raymond.

SOCIAL SCIENTIST(S)

Bentham as Revolutionary Social Scientist. LONG, Douglas.

Wissenschaftliche Weltauffassung zwischen Sozialrevolution und Sozialreform. NEMETH, Elisabeth.

SOCIAL SECURITY

Soziale Sicherheit—Triebkraft ökonomischen Wachstums bei der Gestaltung der entwickelten sozialistischen Gesellschaft. HAHN, Toni and WINKLER, Gunnar.

SOCIAL STRUCTURE(S)

The Confucian Creation of Heaven: Philosophy and the Defense of Ritual Mastery. ENO, Robert.

The Unknown Mechanism Moving Society. ATHAYDE, Ezequiel.

"The Phoenix" in *Scientific Knowledge Socialized*, HRONSZKY, Imre.

L'autoreferenzialità luhmanniana: A proposito di normalizzazione dell'improbabile e improbabilità. AMATO MANGIAMELI, Agata C.

Ethical Similarities in Human and Animal Social Structures. ELLOS, William J.

Sociognoseología y objectividad. MORALES, Julián.

The Unspeakable: Understanding the System of Fallacy in the Media. MC MURTRY, John.

Wissenschaftliche Weltauffassung zwischen Sozialrevolution und Sozialreform. NEMETH, Elisabeth.

SOCIAL SYSTEM(S)

Freedom. BAUMAN, Zygmunt.

Adam Smith's Concept of the Social System. COKER, Edward W.

Marx's Promethean Humanism. ABRAHAM, Kuruvilla C.

SOCIAL THEORY(-RIES)

The Unknown Mechanism Moving Society. ATHAYDE, Ezequiel.

Feminist Social Theory and Hermeneutics: An Empowering Dialectic?. BUKER, Eloise A.

L'obiettivazione della vita soggettiva nelle scienze storico-sociali e la fenomenologia trascendentale di Husserl. MASSIMILLA, Edoardo.

Rational Reconstruction and Social Criticism: Habermas's Model of Interpretive Social Science. BAYNES, Kenneth.

Social Choice and Social Theories. SEABRIGHT, Paul.

A Social Constructionist Critique of The Naturalistic Theory of Emotion. RATNER, Carl.

Towards a Creative Meaning of Marxism. RAINKO, Stanislaw and PETROWICZ, Lech (trans).

SOCIAL WELFARE

A Critical View of Swedish Science Policy. ELZINGA, Aant.

Improving the Quality of Social Welfare Scholarship: Response to "Confirmational Response Bias". SCHUERMAN, John R.

SOCIAL WORK

Confirmational Response Bias Among Social Work Journals. EPSTEIN, William M.

Is Social Work Different? Comments on "Confirmational Response Bias". WESTRUM, Ron.

Reflections on "Confirmational Response Bias Among Social Work Journals". HOPPS, June Gary.

SOCIALISM

Capitalism. PAUL, Ellen Frankel (ed).

Paul Tillich on Creativity. KEGLEY, Jacquelyn Ann K (ed).

Selections from Political Writings, 1910-1920: Antonio Gramsci. GRAMSCI, Antonio.

Selections from Political Writings, 1921-1926: Antonio Gramsci. GRAMSCI, Antonio.

Social Philosophy and Ecological Scarcity. LEE, Keekok.

Acceleration and Restructuring: Dialectics and Problems. LAPIN, Nikolai I.

Anmerkungen zum Real Existierenden Totalitarismus und zu seinen Apologeten unter uns. MARKO, Kurt.

Brauchen wir eine Kategorie Persönlichkeit?. RONNEBERG, Heinz.

Capitalism, State Bureaucratic Socialism and Freedom. NIELSEN, Kai.

Catholicism and Socialism: The Problems of Political Understanding. OPARA, Stefan and PROTALINSKI, Grzegorz (trans).

Changes in the Social Structures of the Central- and East-European Countries. WERBLAN, Andrzej.

A Comparative Study of the Representational Paradigms Between Liberalism and Socialism. KE, Gang.

Democratic Possibilities of French Revolution (in Serbo-Croatian). VUJADINOVIC, Dragica.

La deuxième crise de la raison et la critique du socialisme. MIGUELEZ, Roberto.

Economic Relations and their Reflection in Working People's Consciousness under Socialism (in Czechoslovakian). HELLER, J.

Estrategia y Táctica: La Política Como Ciencia: Marx Y Engels. SALOM, Roberto.

Functions of Egalitarianism in Yugoslav Society. BERNIK, Ivan.

Gilligan's Conception of Moral Maturity. MASON, Andrew.

The Great October, Restructuring, Politology. MSHVENIERADZE, Vladimir V.

Humanism and Socialism. SCHMITT, Richard.

Individualisierung als Emanzipationsprojekt?. TEICHMANN, Werner.

Is Socialism a Psychological Misunderstanding?. REYKOWSKI, Janusz.

L'époque contemporaine et la signification axiologique de la science et de la culture (in Romanian). GHEORGHE, Elena.

Les réalisations du socialisme dans la perspective de l'histoire (in Romanian). BAZAC, Ana.

Liberal and Socialist Egalitarianism. NIELSEN, Kai.

Liberal and Socialist Egalitarianism. NIELSEN, Kai.

Liberty and Democracy, or Socialism?. FLEW, Antony.

Making a Case for Socialism. NIELSEN, Kai.

Marx, Lukes, and Human Rights. BAXTER, David.

Materialist Dialectic and Critique of Philosophical Irrationalism (in Czechoslovakian). JANKOV, M.

A Moral Case for Socialism. NIELSEN, Kai.

On the Contemporary Theory of Socialism (The October Revolution and Perestroika). SHEVCHENKO, V N.

Philosophy Cannot Be Implemented in Socialism and Its Economy (in Czechoslovakian). NIKOLIC, P D.

Pluralism and Universalist Socialism. KUCZYNSKI, Janusz and JEDYNAK, Jacek.

The Problem of Bureaucracy in a Socialist State. ZAWADZKI, Sylwester and PROTALINSKI, Grzegorz (trans).

Probleme der Dialektik der sozialistischen Produktionsweise. HEIDLER, Angelika.

Qualité et efficience—coordonate principales du développement socio-économique Roumaine (in Romanian). CORNESCU, Viorel and BUCUR, Ion.

Quelques contributions de grande valeur au progrès multilatéral de la Roumanie socialiste (in Romanian). IONEL, Nicolae.

Quelques réflexions sur une thèse marxiste (in Romanian). BOTIS, Gheorghe.

Rand Socialist?. TURNER, Dan.

The Seventieth Anniversary of the October Revolution. SZCZEPANSKI, Jan and PETROWICZ, Lech (trans).

Socialism and Atheism. SZCZEPANSKI, Jan and LECKI, Maciej (trans).

Socialism is Incompatible with Humanism. SHEAFFER, Robert.

Socialism, Feminism and Men. MIDDLETON, Peter.

Le socialisme et le conditionnement social du bonheur. BAZAC, Ana.

Soziale Sicherheit—Triebkraft ökonomischen Wachstums bei der Gestaltung der entwickelten sozialistischen Gesellschaft. HAHN, Toni and WINKLER, Gunnar.

SOCIALISM

Sozialistische Gesellschaft und sozialistische Nation in der DDR. KOSING, Alfred.

The Tragedy of National Conflicts in 'Real Socialism': The Case of the Yugoslav Autonomous Province of Kosovo. MARKOVIC, Mihailo.

Whither the Way?. WOHL, Andrzej and GOLEBIOWSKI, Marek (trans).

Working Class and Proletariat—On the Relation of Andries Sternheim to the Frankfurt School. MULDER, Bertus and NAUTA, Lolle.

Zur Diskussion um die Einheit und Vielfalt der Interessen im Sozialismus. ROTHE, Barbara and STEININGER, H.

SOCIALIST REALISM

Socialist Realism and the Traditions of Soviet Art. ANDREEV, A L.

Socialist Realism—Yesterday, Today, and Tomorrow. IAKOVLEV, E G.

SOCIALIZATION

"What is the Use of a Philosophy of Science for Scientists"?. WILKES, K.

Gender Socialisation and the Nature/Culture Controversy: The Dualist's Dilemma. JONATHAN, Ruth.

The Liberation of Caring: A Different Voice for Gilligan's "Different Voice". PUKA, Bill.

SOCIETY(-TIES)

AIDS and the Good Society. ILLINGWORTH, Patricia.

Critical Theory and Society: A Reader. BRONNER, Stephen Eric (ed).

Eguaglianza interesse unanimità: La politica di Rousseau. BURGIO, Alberto.

Fourier: La Passione dell'Utopia. COLOMBO, Arrigo (ed).

Jürgen Habermas on Society and Politics: A Reader. SEIDMAN, Steven (ed).

Known from the Things that Are: Fundamental Theory of the Moral Life. O'KEEFE, Martin D.

Morality and Imagination: Paradoxes of Progress. TUAN, Yi-Fu.

Ontological Investigations: Inquiry Into the Categories of Nature, Man, Society. JOHANSSON, Ingvar.

Philosophia Togata: Essays on Philosophy and Roman Society. GRIFFIN, Miriam (ed).

Readings from Karl Marx. SAYER, Derek (ed).

The Social Context and Values: Perspectives of the Americas. MC LEAN, George F (ed).

Social Theory and the Crisis of Marxism. MC CARNEY, Joseph.

Unruly Practices: Power, Discourse and Gender in Contemporary Social Theory. FRASER, Nancy.

"'Character Ethics' and Organizational Life" in Papers on the Ethics of Administration, NORTON, David L.

"Liberation and Values" in The Social Context and Values: Perspectives of the Americas, DY JR, Manuel B.

Barriers Against Interdisciplinarity: Implications for Studies of Science, Technology, and Society (STS). BAUER, Henry H.

Bernard Williams and the Nature of Moral Reflection. CRAGG, A W.

Change and Crisis of Values in Modern Societies (in Hungarian). LENDVAI, Ferenc L.

Connaissance, conscience et culture dans la vie spirituelle de la sociétè (in Romanian). PANA, Laura.

Cosmology, Religion, and Society. BOWKER, John W.

A Critical View of Swedish Science Policy. ELZINGA, Aant.

Critics of Science and Research Ethics in Sweden. GUSTAFSSON, Bengt and TIBELL, Gunnar.

The Critique of Equalitarian Society in Malthus's Essay. GILBERT, Geoffrey.

Depolarizing Mathematics and Religion. VOSS, Sarah.

Energy-Events and Fields. BRACKEN, Joseph A.

Evolution in Nature—Development in Society. LASZLO, Ervin.

Functions of Egalitarianism in Yugoslav Society. BERNIK, Ivan.

Intellectuals, Values and Society. FISK, Milton.

An Introduction to Adorno's Aesthetics. EDGAR, Andrew.

Kant's Metaphysics of the Subject and Modern Society. FRIGERIO, C.

Man in the System of Socioeconomic Values. DUGIN, V N.

Philosophy and Society: On the Philosophical Heritage of Emanuel Radl (in Czechoslovakian). HEJDANEK, Ladislav.

La' risposta di Leroux a Lamennais: Il concetto di Trinità come soluzione del problema sociale. FIORENTINO, Fernando.

Science, Technology, and Society: Considerations of Method. BECKWITH, Guy V

Spirituality in Modern Society (in Hungarian). ZWEERMAN, Theo.

T H Green's Theory of the Morally Justified Society. SIMHONY, Avital.

Technology in a Free Society: The New Frankenstein. BALESTRA, Dominic J.

Trust and Survival: Securing a Vision of the Good Society. THOMAS, Laurence.

Virtuous Lives and Just Societies. O'NEILL, Onora.

What Children Owe Parents: Ethics in an Aging Society. POST, Stephen G.

Women's Research and Its Inherent Critique of Society and Science. KYLE, Gunhild and JUNGEN, Britta.

SOCIOBIOLOGY

Philosophy of Biology Today. RUSE, Michael.

Reductionism and Systems Theory in the Life Sciences: Some Problems and Perspectives. HOYNINGEN-HUENE, Paul (ed).

Who Knows: From Quine to a Feminist Empiricism. NELSON, Lynn Hankinson.

"Constraints on The Expanding Circle: A Critique of Singer" in Inquiries into Values: The Inaugural Session of the International Society for Value Inquiry, SCHONSHECK, Jonathan.

"Moral Value and the Sociobiological Reduction" in Inquiries into Values: The Inaugural Session of the International Society for Value Inquiry, JACQUETTE, Dale.

"Sociobiology and Reductionism" in Reductionism and Systems Theory in the Life Sciences: Some Problems and Perspectives, RUSE, Michael.

Darwinism as a Prohibition of Criticism: A Commentary on Friedrich August von Hayek's Theory of Moral Evolution. DORSCHEL, A.

Developmental Decomposition and the Future of Human Behavioral Ecology. KITCHER, Philip.

Does Evolutionary Biology Contribute to Ethics?. BATESON, Patrick.

Dutch Objections to Evolutionary Ethics. RICHARDS, Robert J.

Fundamenten, achtergronden of bondgenootschappen?. VAN DER WEELE, Cor.

Marxism and Human Sociobiology: A Reply to Zhang Boshu. KEITA, Lansana.

The Nature of Man—Games that Genes Play?. GÄRDENFORS, Peter.

On the Morality of Hunting. CAUSEY, Ann S.

Really Taking Darwin Seriously: An Alternative to Michael Ruse's Darwinian Metaethics. ROTTSCHAEFER, William A and MARTINSEN, David.

A Sociobiological Explanation of Strategies of Reading and Writing Philosophy. GILMAN, Roger William.

Sociobiology and Concern for the Future. JOHNSON, Andrew.

Sociobiology, Sex, and Aggression. FLAGEL, David.

Die soziobiologische Obsoletierung des "Reichs der Zwecke". DORSCHEL, Andreas.

Utilitarianism, Sociobiology, and the Limits of Benevolence. SCOCCIA, Danny.

SOCIOLOGY

Critical Theory and Society: A Reader. BRONNER, Stephen Eric (ed).

Jürgen Habermas on Society and Politics: A Reader. SEIDMAN, Steven (ed).

The Meaning of General Theoretical Sociology: Tradition and Formalization. FARARO, Thomas J.

Moral Absolutes: An Essay on the Nature and Rationale of Morality. RESCHER, Nicholas.

The Rational and the Social. BROWN, James Robert.

Science and Its Fabrication. CHALMERS, Alan.

The Theory and Scholarship of Talcott Parsons to 1951: A Critical Commentary. WEARNE, Bruce C.

"Ethics in Unethical Times—Towards a Sociology of Ethics" in The Institution of Philosophy: A Discipline in Crisis?, REDNER, Harry.

"On Recent Problems of the Sociology of Science in the Context of Karl Marx's Ideas" in Scientific Knowledge Socialized, MARKOVA, Ludmilla A.

Antwoorden op open interview-vragen als lezingen. NIJHOF, Gerhard.

Chomsky, Wittgenstein, Bloor: Zum Problem einer wissenssoziologischen Metatheorie der Linguistik. KERTÉSZ, András.

The Creativity of Action and the Intersubjectivity of Reason: Mead's Pragmatism and Social Theory. JOAS, Hans.

An Exchange on Vertical Drift and the Quest for Theoretical Integration in Sociology. BASH, Harry.

From Nothing to Sociology. WOLFF, Kurt H.

Goffman's Revisions. MANNING, Phil.

Integralism and the Reconstruction of Society: The Idea of Ultimate Reality and Meaning in the World of P A Sorokin. JOHNSTON, Barry V.

Lévy-Bruhl et Durkheim: Notes biographiques en marge d'une correspondance—Lettres à L Lévy-Bruhl (1894-1915). MERLLIÉ, Dominique and DURKHEIM, Emile.

Literatuur als bron voor historisch en sociologisch onderzoek. MASO, Benjo.

Maigret's Method. JACKSON, M W.

De nieuwe zekerheden van het hedendaags wetenschapsonderzoek. AMSTERDAMSKA, Olga and HAGENDIJK, R.

Ökonomische Soziologie in Nowosibirst (Literaturbericht). SEGERT, Astrid.

The Problem of Going from: Science Policy and 'Human Factors' in the Experience of Developing Countries. IGNATYEV, A A.

The Problem of Going To: Between Epistemology and the Sociology of Knowledge. MOKRZYCKI, Edmund.

SOCIOLOGY

Scattered Sociology: A Response to Bash. FUHRMAN, Ellsworth.

La sociedad en la perspectiva informática o existe una sociología de los computadores?. GUTIÉRREZ, Claudio.

The Uniqueness of Human Being (in Czechoslovakian). OIZERMAN, T I.

Towards a Phenomenology of Social Role. KUNINSKI, Milowit.

Zur Problematik von Entwicklung und Fortschritt im soziologischen Werk Max Webers. WITTICH, Dietmar.

SOCIOLOGY OF KNOWLEDGE

Rational Common Ground in the Sociology of Knowledge. KATZ, Jonathan.

SOCRATES

"The Son of Apollo": Themes of Plato. WOODBRIDGE, Frederick J E.

Socrates in the Apology: An Essay on Plato's Apology of Socrates. REEVE, C D C.

Socrates on Trial. BRICKHOUSE, Thomas C.

"Plato's Early Theory of Knowledge" in Epistemology (Companions to Ancient Thought: 1), WOODRUFF, Paul.

La alegoría de la caverna y su sentido. PEREZ RUIZ, F.

The Argument in the Protagoras that No One Does What He Believes To Be Bad. MORRIS, T F.

Dwellers in an Unfortified City: Death and Political Philosophy. SCHALL, James V.

The Hedonic Calculus in the Protagoras and the Phaedo: A Reply. GOSLING, J C B.

Hedonism in the Protagoras and the Sophist's Guarantee. WEISS, Roslyn.

Hypothèses sur Platon et sur Nietzsche. IOANNIDI, H.

The Interpretation of Plato's Crito. BOSTOCK, David.

Is the 'Socratic Fallacy' Socratic?. VLASTOS, Gregory.

A Matter of Life and Death in Socratic Philosophy. BRICKHOUSE, Thomas C and SMITH, Nicholas D.

A Note on Eristic and the Socratic Elenchus. BENSON, Hugh H.

Notes on a Great Erotic. MC GHEE, Michael.

On Personalism and Education. HART, Richard E.

Philosophical Apology in the Theaetetus. HEMMENWAY, Scott R.

Philosophical Books versus Philosophical Dialogue. NUSSBAUM, Martha.

Plato's Euthyphro. MORRIS, T F.

Plato's Lysis: An Introduction to Philosophic Friendship. TESSITORE, Aristide.

Platonic Education. REDFIELD, James M.

A Rejoinder to Professors Gosling and Taylor. WEISS, Roslyn.

The Responsibility of Socrates. STALLEY, R F.

The Rhetoric of Socrates. ROSSETTI, Livio.

Socrates In a New Package Helps Kids Learn to Think. BERRIAN, Annette.

Socrates' Charitable Treatment of Poetry. PAPPAS, Nickolas.

Socratic Ignorance—Socratic Wisdom. EVANS, J Claude.

The Speakerly Teacher: Socrates and Writing. KALLICK, David.

To Philosophize with Socrates (A Chapter from a Prepared Monography on J Patocka) (in Czechoslovakian). PALOUS, Martin.

Victor Cousin: frammenti socratici. RAGGHIANTI, Renzo.

What Makes Socrates a Good Man?. BRICKHOUSE, Thomas C and SMITH, Nicholas D.

SOCRATIC METHOD

"Socrates and Sophia Perform the Philosophical Turn" in The Institution of Philosophy: A Discipline in Crisis?, RORTY, Amelie Oksenberg.

Is it Possible to Teach Socratically?. SHERMAN, Rosalyn S.

A Note on Eristic and the Socratic Elenchus. BENSON, Hugh H.

Socratic Dialogue. HECKMANN, Gustav.

The Socratic Method and Philosophy for Children. PORTELLI, John P.

Socratic Teaching?. JORDAN JR, James A.

SOFTWARE

The Morality of Software Piracy: A Cross-Cultural Analysis. SWINYARD, W R and RINNE, H and KENG KAU, A.

The Role of Error in Computer Science. JASON, Gary.

SOKOLOWSKI, R

The Ego Revisited. DAUENHAUER, Bernard J.

SOLDIER(S)

A Moral Military. AXINN, Sidney.

SOLIDARITY

Can Expression Replace Reflection?. ROTENSTREICH, Nathan.

The Essential Elements for the Possibility and Necessity of the Principle of Solidarity According to Max Scheler. IBANA, Rainer R A.

Freedom, Plurality, Solidarity: Hannah Arendt's Theory of Action. D'ENTRÈVES, Maurizio Passerin.

Intencionalidad, responsabilidad y solidaridad: Los nuevos àmbitos del compromiso ético. SEIBOLD, J R.

Justice and Solidarity: On the Discussion Concerning "Stage 6". HABERMAS, Jürgen.

SOLIPSISM

Philosophy of Perception. MACLACHLAN, D L C.

On Putnam's Argument for the Inconsistency of Relativism. SOLOMON, Miriam.

Overtones of Solipsism in Thomas Nagel's "What is it Like to Be a Bat?" and The View From Nowhere. WIDER, Kathleen.

SOLITUDE

In the Onthic Human Centre: Solitariness Overcome by Solitude. AGERA, Cassian R.

Solitude in Ancient Taoism. KOCH, Philip J.

SOLOMON, R

Embarrassment and Self-Esteem. SZABADOS, Béla.

SOLOV'EV, V

V S Solov'ev: An Attempt at a Philosophical Biography. ASMUS, V S.

Vladimir Solov'ev on the Fate and Purpose of Philosophy. RASHKOVSKII, E B.

SOLUTION(S)

Adam Schaff and the Club of Rome. KING, Alexander.

Cardano: "Arithmetic Subtlety" and Impossible Solutions. KENNEY, Emelie.

A Vagueness Paradox and Its Solution. ACKERMAN, Felicia.

Waste and Culture. TIBERG, Nils.

SONG(S)

"Song and Music Drama" in What is Music?, LEVINSON, Jerrold.

SONTAG, S

Beneath Interpretation: Against Hermeneutic Holism. SHUSTERMAN, Richard.

SOPER, P

"Comment: The Obligation to Obey the Law" in Issues in Contemporary Legal Philosophy: The Influence of H L A Hart, GANS, Chaim.

SOPHISM

"Demonstrative, Dialectical and Sophistic Arguments in the Philosophy of Moses Maimonides" in Moses Maimonides and His Time, HYMAN, Arthur.

El lugar de los sofismas en la Lógica. GAMBRA, José Miguel.

SOPHISTS

"Kunst der Überlistung" oder "Reden mit Vernuft"? Zu Philosophischen Aspekten der Rhetorik. NIEHUES-PRÖBSTING, Heinrich.

Diairesis and the Tripartite Soul in the Sophist. DORTER, Kenneth.

La filosofia penale di Ippodamo e la cultura giuridica dei sofisti. ROSSETTI, Livio.

The First Sophists and Feminism: Discourses of the "Other". JARRATT, Susan C.

Hedonism in the Protagoras and the Sophist's Guarantee. WEISS, Roslyn.

The Role of the Sophists in Histories of Consciousness. JARRATT, Susan C.

Socrates' Encounter with Polus in Plato's Gorgias. JOHNSON, Curtis N.

The Sophists and Relativism. BETT, Richard.

SORA, M

Mihai Sora and the Traditions of Romanian Philosophy. NEMOIANU, Virgil.

SOREL, G

Interpreting Georges Sorel: Defender of Virtue or Apostle of Violence?. VINCENT, K Steven.

SORITES

Vagueness and Incoherence: A Reply to Burns. SCHWARTZ, Stephen P.

SOROKIN, P

Integralism and the Reconstruction of Society: The Idea of Ultimate Reality and Meaning in the World of P A Sorokin. JOHNSTON, Barry V.

SORTAL

Identity, Survival, and Sortal Concepts. BAILLIE, James.

SOSKICE, J

Reference and Critical Realism. DURRANT, Michael.

SOTERIOLOGY

Cosmology and Hindu Thought. BALSLEV, Anindita Niyobi.

Principles of Buddhism. KAWAMURA, Leslie S.

Process-Relational Christian Soteriology: A Response to Wheeler. BASINGER, David.

Soteriology from a Christian and Hindu Perspective. JENSEN, Debra J.

Toward a Process-Relational Christian Soteriology. WHEELER, David L.

SOUL(S)

see also Mind

Aristotle on Substance: The Paradox of Unity. GILL, Mary Louise.

Body, Soul, and Life Everlasting: Biblical Anthropology and the Monism-Dualism Debate. COOPER, John W.

SPEAKING

The Pragmatics of What is Said. RECANATI, François.
The Dutch Words 'besef' and 'beseffen' (in Dutch). VERHOEVEN, C.

SPECIAL EDUCATION

Psychoeducational Assessment Practices for the Learning Disabled: A Philosophical Analysis. DURAN, Jane.

SPECIES

The Death of the Animal: Ontological Vulnerability. SHAPIRO, Kenneth Joel.

SPECIFICATION

Critical Thinking as Transfer: Reconstructive Integration of Otherwise Discrete Interpretations of Experience. BRELL JR, Carl D.

SPECTRUM PROBLEM

The Boolean Spectrum of an o-Minimal Theory. STEINHORN, Charles and TOFFALORI, Carlo.
Functionalism and Inverted Spectra. COLE, David.
A Proof of Morley's Conjecture. HART, Bradd.

SPECTRUM(-TRA)

On the Generator Problem. SZWAST, Wieslaw.

SPECULATION

Metafora e concetto: sulla metafora dello specchio in Schelling e nel giovane Hegel. TAGLIAPIETRA, Andrea.
La spéculation hégélienne. BOURGEOIS, Bernard.

SPECULATIVE

"Style As the Man: From Aesthetics to Speculative Philosophy" in Analytic Aesthetics, ALTIERI, Charles.
Hume and Tetens. KUEHN, Manfred.
The Problem of Kant. HARRIS, H S.
Why Hegel? Heidegger and Speculative Philosophy. SCHALOW, Frank.

SPEECH

Limited Inc. DERRIDA, Jacques.
Saussure, Derrida, and the Metaphysics of Subjectivity. STROZIER, Robert M.
"Die abgekehrte Seite der Sprache: Zum Briefwechsel Rilke-Pasternak-Cvetaeva" in Cultural Hermeneutics of Modern Art: Essays in Honor of Jan Aler, PHILIPPOT-RENIERS, Annie.
"Unlearning to Not Speak". PAGET, M A.
Completing the Recovery of Language as an Existential Project. DAVIS, Duane H.
Does Plato Think False Speech is Speech?. RUDEBUSCH, George.
Logical Syntax as a Key to a Secret of the Guide of the Perplexed (in Hebrew). STERN, Josef.
Speech and Thought, Symbol and Likeness: Aristotle's De Interpretatione 16a3-9. POLANSKY, Ronald and KUCZEWSKI, Mark.

SPEECH ACT(S)

Conversation, Relevance, and Argumentation. HAFT-VAN REES, M Agnes.
Iterating Revolution: Speech Acts in Literary Theory. PETREY, Sandy.
Philosophy of Law and the Theory of Speech Acts. AMSELEK, Paul.
Searle's Narrow Content. VAUGHAN, Rachel.
A Speech Act Analysis of Irony. HAVERKATE, Henk.
Speech Act Conditions as Tools for Reconstructing Argumentative Discourse. VAN EEMEREN, Frans H and GROOTENDORST, Rob.
Speech Acts and Arguments. JACOBS, Scott.
Suppositions in Argumentation. FISHER, Alec.
Theory of Speech Acts (in Serbo-Croatian). IVANETIC, Nada.
What Is It To Understand a Directive Speech Act?. DORSCHEL, Andreas.

SPENCE, K

Models, Mechanisms, and Explanation in Behavior Theory: The Case of Hull Versus Spence. SMITH, Laurence D.

SPENCER

The Political Philosophy of the British Idealists: Selected Studies. NICHOLSON, Peter P.
Equal Freedom, Rights and Utility in Spencer's Moral Philosophy. WEINSTEIN, D.
Utilitarianism, Rights, and Equality. CROSSLEY, David J.

SPENGLER

Questions on Wittgenstein. HALLER, Rudolf.

SPEUSIPPUS

Ancient Non-Beings: Speusippus and Others. DANCY, R M.

SPHERE(S)

Emile Durkheim and Provinces of Ethics. CLADIS, Mark S.

SPIEGELBERG, H

The Ego Revisited. DAUENHAUER, Bernard J.
Equal Opportunity. WELLMAN, Carl.

Herbert Spiegelberg's Ethics: Accident and Obligation. WIGGINS, Osborne.
Relearning the World: On the Phenomenology of Grieving. ATTIG, Thomas.
Remarks on the Concept of Norm. PAULSON, Stanley L.

SPINOZA

Baruch or Benedict: On Some Jewish Aspects of Spinoza's Philosophy. LEVY, Ze'ev.
The Consolations of Philosophy: Hobbes's Secret; Spinoza's Way. ROSENTHAL, Abigail L (ed).
Ein neuer Beitrag zum Verständnis Spinozas. EISENSTEIN, Israel.
Elements of Modern Philosophy: Descartes through Kant. BRENNER, William H.
A Philosopher's Harvest: The Philosophical Papers of Isaac Franck. GERBER, William (ed).
Subject and Consciousness: A Philosophical Inquiry Into Self-Consciousness. BALABAN, Oded.
"The Properties of the Intellect" in Dialectic and Contemporary Science, KLEVER, W N A.
"Reply to Klever's "The Properties of the Intellect"" in Dialectic and Contemporary Science, HARRIS, Errol E.
"A Whirlwind at My Back...": Spinozistic Themes in Bernard Malamud's "The Fixer". COOK, Thomas.
"Degrés de réalite" et "degrés de perfection" dans les Principes de la philosophie de Descartes de Spinoza. RAMOND, Charles.
"Nature," "Substance," and "God" as Mass Terms in Spinoza's Theologico-Political Treatise. MADANES, Leiser.
Il "Satyricon" di Petronio e la datazione della Grammatica Ebraica Spinoziana. PROIETTI, Omero.
"The Source" Spinoza in the Writings of Gabriel Scott. FLOISTAD, Guttorm.
'Sustancia', 'naturaleza' y 'Dios' como términos de masa en la filosofía política de Spinoza. MADANES, Leiser.
Between Infinity and Community: Notes on Materialism in Spinoza and Leopardi. NEGRI, Antonio.
Bradley e Spinoza: L'iper-spinozismo di F H Bradley (I). DEREGIBUS, Arturo.
Bradley e Spinoza: L'iper-spinozismo di F H Bradley (seconda parte). DEREGIBUS, Arturo.
Des présages a l'entendement: Notes sur les présages, l'imagination et l'amour dans la lettre à P Balling. SANCHEZ-ESTOP, Juan Dominguez.
Doubt and Belief in the Tractatus De Intellectus Emendatione. BEAVERS, Anthony F and RICE, Lee C.
Einige Bemerkungen zur Bedeutung von Ewigkeit und Dauer in Spinozas Ethik. KOPPER, Joachim.
Evolución de los derechos humanos en Spinoza y en Leibniz. VERGES, S.
Leviathan and Spinoza's Tractatus on Revelation: Some Elements for a Comparison. PACCHI, Arrigo.
Un manoscritto inedito delle 'Adnotationes' al Tractatus Theologico-Politicus di Spinoza. TOTARO, Giuseppina.
Melville and Spinoza. HART, Alan.
Moles in Motu: Principles of Spinoza's Physics. KLEVER, W N A.
Natural Theology and the Concept of Perfection in Descartes, Spinoza and Leibniz. WEBB, Mark O.
On the Early Dutch Reception of the Tractatus-Theologico Politicus. VAN BUNGE, Wiep.
Per una nuova edizione del Tractatus De Intellectus Emendatione. MIGNINI, Filippo.
The Politics of Interpretation: Spinoza's Modernist Turn. LANG, Berel.
Potentia et Potestas dans les premiers écrits de B Spinoza. FERNANDEZ, Eugenio.
La priorità ontologica e gnoseologica dell'esistenza di Dio in Spinoza. NICOLOSI, Salvatore.
The Problem of Normativity Solved or Spinoza's Stand in the Analogy/Anomaly Controversy. KLIJNSMIT, Anthony J.
Il problema delle distinzioni nella filosofia di Spinoza. DI VONA, Piero.
Reflexive Ideas in Spinoza. RICE, Lee C.
Sens et Vérité: Philosophie et théologie chez L Meyer et Spinoza. LAGREE, Jacqueline.
Skeptizismus und Judentum, mit einer Einleitung und Anmerkungen von Frederick Betz und Jörg Thunecke. MAUTHNER, Fritz.
Spinoza and Finnish Literature. ELOVAARA, Raili.
Spinoza et "De Stijl". JACOBS, Cornée.
Spinoza et les problèmes d'une théorie de la societé commerçante. BLOM, Hans W.
Spinoza in Borges' Looking-Glass. ABADI, Marcelo.
Spinoza in der schönen Literatur: Bilder aus der Zeit zwischen Vormärz und Weimarer Republik. HELMES, Günther.
Spinoza in Poetry. KLEVER, Wim.
Spinoza jenseits von Hobbes und Rousseau. GEISMANN, Georg.

SPINOZA

Spinoza's Earliest Philosophical Years, 1655-61. POPKIN, Richard H.

Eine Spinoza-Reminizens in Elias Canettis autobiografischer Erzählung "Das Augenspiel". BOLLACHER, Martin.

Spinoza: de la alegría. BELTRAN, M.

A Tragic Idealist: Jacob Ostens (1630-1678). VAN BUNGE, Wiep.

Die Wandlungen Gottes: Zu Rudolf Schottlaenders Beitrag *Zu Spinozas Theorie des Glaubens.* HAMMACHER, Klaus.

Zu Spinozas Theorie des Glaubens. SCHOTTLAENDER, Rudolf.

SPIRIT(S)

see also Minds, Soul(s)

Of Spirit: Heidegger and the Question. DERRIDA, Jacques.

Absolute Spirit and Universal Self-Consciousness: Bruno Bauer's Revolutionary Subjectivism. MOGGACH, Douglas.

Berkeley's Manifest Qualities Thesis. CUMMINS, Phillip D.

The Eleventh Commandment: Sex and Spirit in Wollstonecraft and Malthus. NICHOLSON, Mervyn.

El espíritu como principio activo en Berkeley. BENÍTEZ, Laura.

Hegel on Habit. MC CUMBER, John.

Jews as a Metaphysical Species. LURIE, Yuval.

Spirit's Primary Nature is to be Secondary. KERR-LAWSON, Angus.

Spirituality in Santayana. TEJERA, V.

SPIRITUAL

Jonathan Edwards and the Sense of the Heart. WAINWRIGHT, William.

The October Revolution and Spiritual Renewal of Society. NOVIKOVA, Lidia I.

Psychomachia in Art from Prudentius to Proust. JACKSON, M J.

The Need of Philosophy and Current Ecological Crisis (in Czechoslovakian). KOLARSKY, R.

SPIRITUALISM

Spiritualismo e neoscolastica nel Novecento: L'aporia del fondamento. PENATI, Giancarlo.

SPIRITUALITY

John of the Cross and the Cognitive Value of Mysticism. PAYNE, Steven.

Of Spirit: Heidegger and the Question. DERRIDA, Jacques.

"Introduction" in *Varieties of Postmodern Theology,* GRIFFIN, David Ray.

Grazia e dignità dell'estetica schilleriana. DOLORES FOLLIERO, Granzia.

Not Bending the Knee. HOLLAND, R F.

Sexuality, Rationality, and Spirituality. TOMM, Winnifred A.

Spirituality in Modern Society (in Hungarian). ZWEERMAN, Theo.

Spirituality in Santayana. TEJERA, V.

SPLITTING

Splitting $P_\kappa\lambda$ into Stationary Subsets. MATSUBARA, Yo.

SPONTANEOUS GENERATION

Teleology and Spontaneous Generation in Aristotle: A Discussion. GOTTHELF, Allan.

SPORT(S)

Education, Movement and the Curriculum: A Philosophic Enquiry. ARNOLD, Peter J.

The Authority of the Rules of Baseball: The Commissioner as Judge. UTZ, Stephen G.

The Bioengineered Competitor?. MURRAY, Thomas H.

Democracy, Education, and Sport. ARNOLD, Peter J.

The Ethics of Dwarf-Tossing. BABER, H E.

Injury as Alienation in Sport. THOMAS, Carolyn E and RINTALA, Janet A.

On Beautiful Games. KRETCHMAR, R Scott.

Performance Prestidigitation. MEIER, Klaus V.

Sport Abjection: Steroids and the Uglification of the Athlete. FAIRCHILD, David L.

Sport, Character, and Virtue. FEEZELL, Randolph.

The Trick of the Disappearing Goal. SUITS, Bernard.

SQUARE OF OPPOSITION

Negation and Quantification in Aristotle. WEDIN, Michael V.

A Refutation of Jagat Pal's Defence of Aristotelian Square of Opposition. BASU, S and KASEM, A.

STAAL, J

Sambandha and Abhisambandha. AKLUJKAR, Ashok.

STABILITY

Almost Orthogonal Regular Types. HRUSHOVSKI, E.

A Dichotomy Theorem for Regular Types. HRUSHOVSKI, E and SHELAH, S.

Dimension of Definable Sets, Algebraic Boundedness and Henselian Fields. VAN DEN DRIES, L.

Elementary Pairs of Models. BOUSCAREN, E.

Groups With Identities. POINT, F.

Neutral, Stable and Pareto-Optimal Welfare Functions. STORCKEN, A J A.

On the Existence of Regular Types. SHELAH, S and BUECHLER, S.

Semisimple Stable and Superstable Groups. BALDWIN, J T and PILLAY, A.

Stability of Weak Second-Order Semantics. CSIRMAZ, László.

Subgroups of Stable Groups. WAGNER, Frank.

STAGE(S)

Different Conceptions of Stage in Theories of Cognitive and Moral Development. BOOM, Jan.

STAHL, G

The Conceptual Structure of the Chemical Revolution. THAGARD, Paul.

STALIN

Dialectics by Command: Revolutionism in Philosophy and the Philosophy of Revolutionism. KAPUSTIN, Mikhail.

La filosofía política marxista y la revolución. COLBERT, James.

STALINISM

Changes in the Social Structures of the Central- and East-European Countries. WERBLAN, Andrzej.

Posthumous Rehabilitation and the Dust-Bin of History. LANDE, Nelson P.

Wirtschaftslehre als Heilslehre. ALEKSANDROWICZ, Dariusz.

STALNAKER, R

Counterfactuals for Free. CREATH, Richard.

STATE OF NATURE

"Hobbes and International Relations" in *The Causes of Quarrel: Essays on Peace, War, and Thomas Hobbes,* FARRELL, Daniel M.

"Hobbes and the Concept of World Government" in *Hobbes: War Among Nations,* HUNGERLAND, Isabel C.

"Hobbes's Conception of the State of Nature from 1640 to 1651: Evolution and Ambiguities" in *Perspectives on Thomas Hobbes,* TRICAUD, François.

STATE(S)

see also Mental States

Baruch or Benedict: On Some Jewish Aspects of Spinoza's Philosophy. LEVY, Ze'ev.

Civil Peace and Sacred Order: Limits and Renewals I. CLARK, Stephen R L.

Democracy and Dictatorship. BOBBIO, Norberto.

Heidegger and Nazism. MARGOLIS, Joseph (ed).

Hobbes: War Among Nations. AIRAKSINEN, Timo (ed).

An Introductory Guide to Post-Structuralism and Postmodernism. SARUP, Madan.

The Libertarian Idea. NARVESON, Jan.

The State and Justice: An Essay in Political Theory. FISK, Milton.

"Authority and Sovereignty" in *The Causes of Quarrel: Essays on Peace, War, and Thomas Hobbes,* MARTIN, Rex.

"The Right of a State" in Immanuel Kant's *Doctrine of Right.* LUDWIG, Bernd.

Contractarianism without Foundations. SCHMIDTZ, David.

Elaborazione di temi hegeliani in Gramsci. MARINI, Giuliano.

Emile Durkheim and Provinces of Ethics. CLADIS, Mark S.

En pensamiento político en sociedades sin estado dentro del marco de un nuevo concepto de historia. MORALES, Julian.

Hobbes come Giano: un pensatore sulla soglia dello Stato moderno. LAMI, Gian Franco.

L'État minimal et le droit de propriété privée selon Nozick. LAMBERT, Roger.

Lévy-Bruhl et Hegel. BOURGOIS, Bernard.

Murray, Niebuhr, and the Problem of the Neutral State. HUNT, Robert P.

New Gods for Old: In Defense of Libertarianism. BRADFORD, R W.

On Articles of the Academy of the White Deer Grotto (in Serbo-Croatian). JI-YU, Ren.

Scienza politica e "nuova" scienza della politica: un conflitto "generazionale"?. LAMI, Gian Franco.

The State and Legitimacy. BARRY, Norman.

The State at Dusk. MAC GREGOR, David.

The State's Line: On the Change of Paradigm of Austrian Philosophy within Maria-Theresian Reform-Catholicism. GIMPL, Georg.

Eine Theorie der politischen Gerechtigkeit. KERSTING, Wolfgang.

To the Lighthouse. LEVIN, Michael.

STATEMENT(S)

Facts and the Function of Truth. PRICE, Huw.

A Doxastic Paradox. LARAUDOGOITIA, Jon Perez.

Hegel über die Rede vom Absoluten—Teil I: Urteil, Satz und Spekulativer Gehalt. GRAESER, Andreas.

STATIONARY LOGIC

Elementary Pairs of Models. BOUSCAREN, E.

STATIONARY SETS

Splitting $P_\kappa\lambda$ into Stationary Subsets. MATSUBARA, Yo.

STATISTICAL THEORY
Four Decades of Scientific Explanation. SALMON, Wesley C.

STATISTICS
Objectivism and Subjectivism in the Foundations of Statistics. COSTANTINI, Domenico.
On Newton-Smith's Concept of Verisimilitude. OLCZYK, Slawoj.

STATUS
The Rational Status of A-Moral Choices (in Hebrew). YONAH, Yossi.

STEGMUELLER, W
Criterios de teoricidad. LEGRIS, Javier.

STEIN, E
Edith Stein: Filosofia E Senso Dell'Essere. LAMACCHIA, Ada.
Edith Stein as Educator. OBEN, Freda M.
Edith Stein et la philosophie chrétienne: A propos d'Être fini et Être éternel. TILLIETTE, Xavier.
La filosofia cristiana di Edith Stein. TILLIETTE, Xavier.
Linee dell'attività filosofico-teologica della Beata Edith Stein. FABRO, Cornelio.

STEMMER, N
Comprehension and Production in Early Lexical Development: A Comment on Stemmer. HARRIS, Margaret.
Concept Acquisition and Ostensive Learning: A Response to Professor Stemmer. PLACE, Ullin T.
Empirical Versus Epistemological Considerations: A Comment on Stemmer. MORRIS, Michael.

STENIUS, E
Noch einmal: Zur Rolle der Anschauung in formalen Beweisen. BENDER, Peter.

STENT, G
Philosophy of Biology Under Attack: Stent Versus Rosenberg. THOMPSON, Paul.

STERBA, J
The Moral Significance of Hard Toil: Critique of a Common Intuition. ELLIS, Ralph D.

STERELNY, K
The Poverty of Pluralism: A Reply to Sterelny and Kitcher. SOBER, Elliott.

STERNHEIM, A
Working Class and Proletariat—On the Relation of Andries Sternheim to the Frankfurt School. MULDER, Bertus and NAUTA, Lolle.

STEVENS, R
Robert Stevens on Offers. SWANTON, Christine.

STEVENSON, C
"Moore to Stevenson" in Ethics in the History of Western Philosophy, DARWALL, Stephen.

STICH, S
Intentionality and Stich's Theory of Brain Sentence Syntax. JACQUETTE, Dale.

STIPULATION
Nature, Custom, and Stipulation in Law and Juriprudence. MURPHY, James Bernard.

STOCHASTIC
Ethics and Stochastic Processes. HARDIN, Russell.

STOICISM
The "Meditations" of Marcus Aurelius: A Study. RUTHERFORD, R B.
"Stoic Epistemology" in Epistemology (Companions to Ancient Thought: 1), ANNAS, Julia.
"Stoic Philosophy and the Concept of the Person" in The Person and the Human Mind: Issues in Ancient and Modern Philosophy, ENGBERG-PEDERSEN, Troels.
La conception stoïcienne et la conception aristotélicienne du bonheur. IRWIN, T H.
La finalidad en el mundo natural según san Agustín. MAGNAVACCA, Silvia.
Le fou stoïcien. BRAGUE, Rémi.
Il guidizio di Sant'Agostino sulla Nuova Accademia tra scetticismo ed esoterismo. FERRETTI, Silvia.
La liberté pour Aristote et les stoïciens. GAUTHIER, Pierre.
The Neo-Stoicism of Radical Environmentalism. CHENEY, Jim.

STOICS
The Nature of Man in Early Stoic Philosophy. REESOR, Margaret E.
Paul and the Popular Philosophers. MALHERBE, Abraham J.
"Cicero on Stoic Moral Philosophy and Private Property" in Philosophia

Togata: Essays on Philosophy and Roman Society, ANNAS, Julia.
The Hellenistic Version of Aristotle's Ethics. ANNAS, Julia.
A Response to A A Long's "The Stoics on World-Conflagration and Everlasting Recurrence". HUDSON, Hud.
Stoic Values. WHITE, Nicholas P.
Virtue, Praise and Success: Stoic Responses to Aristotle. IRWIN, T H.

STONE, C
The Case Against Moral Pluralism. CALLICOTT, J Baird.

STORY(-RIES)
Akrasia and Animal Rights: Philosophy in the British Primary School. COSTELLO, Patrick J M.
Experience and Nature: Teacher as Story Teller. SIMMONS JR, Michael.
Oft-Told Tales. MILLSTONE, David H.
The Propositional Objects of Mental Attitudes. DANIELS, Charles B.

STOTTLEMEIER, H
Who is Harry Stottlemeier and What Did He Discover?. JOHNSON, Tony.

STOVE, D
Stove on Inductive Scepticism. GOWER, Barry.

STRATEGY
Posterity and Strategic Policy: A Moral Assessment of Nuclear Policy Options. BAILEY, Alison.
"The Case for Deploying Strategic Defenses" in Nuclear Deterrence and Moral Restraint, SLOSS, Leon.
"Finite Deterrence" in Nuclear Deterrence and Moral Restraint, FEIVESON, Harold A.
"Morality, the SDI, and Limited Nuclear War" in Nuclear Deterrence and Moral Restraint, LEE, Steven.
Far-Sighted Equilibria in 2 x 2, Non-Cooperative, Repeated Games. AAFTINK, Jan.
Weak Strategy Proofness: The Case of Nonbinary Social Choice Functions. BANDYOPADHYAY, Taradas.
What are Goals and Joint Goals?. TUOMELA, Raimo.

STRAUSS, L
Athènes, Jérusalem, La Mecque: L'interprétation "musulmane" de la philosophie grecque chez Leo Strauss. BRAGUE, Rémi.
Deux propositions aristotéliciennes sur le droit natural chez les continentaux d'Amérique. BODÉÜS, Richard.
Hannah Arendt and Leo Strauss: The Uncommenced Dialogue. BEINER, Ronald.
Leo Strauss as Citizen and Jew. DANNHAUSER, Werner J.
Leo Strauss, Hobbes et la nature humaine. MALHERBE, Michel.
Machiavel et la question de la Nature. EDMOND, Michel-Pierre.
Strauss and Natural Right: A Critical Review. CVEK, Peter P.
Strauss et Nietzsche. MANENT, Pierre.
Tocqueville and the Problem of Natural Right. EDEN, Robert.

STRAWSON
Análisis semántico de los enunciados de creencia. D'ALESSIO, Juan Carlos.
Emociones reactivas. HANSBERG, Olbeth.
P F Strawson and the Social Context in Language (in Serbo-Croatian). VIDANOVIC, Dorde.

STREMINGER, G
Streminger: "Religion a Threat to Morality". ELLIN, Joseph.

STROUD, B
Stroud and Williams on Dreaming and Scepticism. REIN, Andrew.
Stroud's Defense of Cartesian Scepticism: A 'Linguistic' Response. GLOCK, Hans-Johann.

STRUCTURAL-COMPLETENESS
A Syntactical Characterization of Structural Completeness for Implicational Logics. WOJTYLAK, Piotr.

STRUCTURALISM
The Meaning of General Theoretical Sociology: Tradition and Formalization. FARARO, Thomas J.
Rethinking Religion: Connecting Cognition and Culture. LAWSON, E Thomas.
The Hierarchical Structure of Testing Theories. KUOKKANEN, Martti.
A Number is the Exponent of an Operation. HAND, Michael.
Realism and Structurism in Historical Theory: A Discussion of the Thought of Maurice Mandelbaum. LLOYD, Christopher.

STRUCTURE(S)
Faith on Earth: An Inquiry into the Structure of Human Faith. NIEBUHR, Richard R (ed).
The Philosophy of Horror 'or' Paradoxes of the Heart. CARROLL, Noël.
The Poetic Structure of the World: Copernicus and Kepler. HALLYN, Fernand.

SUBJECTIVITY

The Critique of Thought: A Re-Examination of Hegel's Science of Logic. JOHNSON, Paul Owen.

Inwardness and Existence: Subjectivity in/and Hegel, Heidegger, Marx, and Freud. DAVIS, Walter A.

The Past Within Us: An Empirical Approach to Philosophy of History. MARTIN, Raymond.

Saussure, Derrida, and the Metaphysics of Subjectivity. STROZIER, Robert M.

"The Development of the Principle of Subjectivity in Western Philosophy and of the Theory of Man in Chinese Philosophy" in Man and Nature: The Chinese Tradition and the Future, SHI-YING, Zhang.

"Foucault and Theory: Genealogical Critiques of the Subject" in The Question of the Other: Essays in Contemporary Continental Philosophy, GRUBER, David F.

"The Subjectivity of the Speaker" in The Question of the Other: Essays in Contemporary Continental Philosophy, KUYKENDALL, Eleanor H.

Aesthetic Consciousness and Aesthetic Non-Differentiation: Gadamer, Schiller, and Lukács. PIZER, John.

Avoiding the Subject: A Foucaultian Itinerary. SEIGEL, Jerrold.

Corps et subjectivité chez Claude Bruaire. MARQUET, Jean-François.

Fear and the Limits of Human Subjectivity. CACKOWSKI, Zdzislaw and BLAIM, Artur (trans).

From Kierkegaard to Cupitt: Subjectivity, the Body and Eternal Life. PATTISON, George.

From Nothing to Sociology. WOLFF, Kurt H.

Gadamer, Objectivity, and the Ontology of Belonging. GUEN, Carroll.

Husserl's Paradox. KIDDER, Paul.

Immaginazione produttiva e struttura dell'immaginario nelle Rêveries du promeneur solitaire di Jean-Jacques Rousseau. PANELLA, Giuseppe.

Infini et subjectivité dans la pensée classique. CHÉDIN, Jean-Louis.

Law and Objectivity: How People are Treated. GREENAWALT, Kent.

Naissance de l'auteur—Une Histoire de l'esthétique moderne autour de son alibi (in Japanese). SASAKI, Ken-ichi.

Nobodies Speaking: Subjectivity, Sex, and the Pornography Effect. FINN, Geraldine.

L'obiettivazione della vita soggettiva nelle scienze storico-sociali e la fenomenologia trascendentale di Husserl. MASSIMILLA, Edoardo.

Reviewing the "Subject(s)". LEACH, Mary S.

Subjectivity and Environmentalism. LE PORE, Ernest.

El tema principal de la fenomenología de Husserl. WALTON, Roberto J.

The Problem of "Good" in the Philosophy of Maimonides (in Hebrew). KREISEL, Howard.

Zwei Arten der Malerei: Von der Umwandelung der Interpretation der Kunst bei Hegel (in Japanese). IWAKI, Ken-ichi.

SUBJUNCTIVE(S)

Classifying Conditionals. JACKSON, Frank.

SUBLIME

The Kantian Sublime: From Morality to Art. CROWTHER, Paul.

The Textual Sublime: Deconstruction and Its Differences. SILVERMAN, Hugh J (ed).

"On Mere Sight: A Response to Paul de Man" in The Textual Sublime: Deconstruction and Its Differences, GASCHÉ, Rodolphe.

"Space, Time, and the Sublime" in The Question of the Other: Essays in Contemporary Continental Philosophy, OLKOWSKI-LAETZ, Dorothea.

On the Sublime in Politics (in Serbo-Croatian). RICHIR, Marc.

Stories of Sublimely Good Character. CALLEN, Donald.

Sublime Politics: On the Uses of an Aesthetics of Terror. CRESAP, Steven.

SUBORDINATION

A Second Look at Pornography and the Subordination of Women. PARENT, W A.

SUBSISTENCE

The Right to Subsistence in a "Lockean" State of Nature. SHEARMUR, Jeremy.

SUBSTANCE(S)

see also Attribute(s), Matter

Aristotle on Substance: The Paradox of Unity. GILL, Mary Louise.

Baruch or Benedict: On Some Jewish Aspects of Spinoza's Philosophy. LEVY, Ze'ev.

More Heat than Light: Economics as Social Physics, Physics as Nature's Economics. MIROWSKI, Philip.

The Nature of Existence, Volume I. MC TAGGART, John McTaggart Ellis.

Style, Politics and the Future of Philosophy. JANIK, Allan.

"Whitehead's Interpretation of Locke in Process and Reality" in Whitehead's Metaphysics of Creativity, SPECHT, Rainer.

"Degrés de réalité" et "degrés de perfection" dans les Principes de la philosophie de Descartes de Spinoza. RAMOND, Charles.

"Nature," "Substance," and "God" as Mass Terms in Spinoza's Theologico-Political Treatise. MADANES, Leiser.

Are There Corporeal Substances for Leibnitz? A Reaction to Stuart Brown. SILVA DE CHOUDENS, José R.

Contingencia y Analiticidad en Leibniz. ZÜRCHER, Joyce M.

La conversion à la substantialité. LE LANNOU, Jean-Michel.

The Enigma of Categories 1a20ff and Why It Matters. MATTHEWS, Gareth B.

Mathematics, Physics, and Corporeal Substance in Descartes. BROWN, Gregory.

Momenti della teoria leibniziana della sostanza nel carteggio con Arnauld. DELCÓ, Alessandro.

On the Critique of Energetism and Neoenergetism (in Czechoslovakian). ZEMAN, J.

A Return to Plato in the Philosophy of Substance. ZYCINSKI, Joseph.

SUBSTITUTION

How Epistemology Can Be a System. LEE, Donald.

The Simple Substitution Property of the Intermediate Propositional Logics. SASAKI, Katsumi.

Substitution: Marcel and Levinas. GIBBS, Robert B.

SUBSTITUTIVITY

Aboutness and Substitutivity. MARTI, Genoveva.

Paraconsistency and the C-Systems of DaCosta. URBAS, Igor.

SUBVERSION

Gender Trouble: Feminism and the Subversion of Identity. BUTLER, Judith.

SUCCESS

A Family Portrait of Canada's Most Successful Female Entrepreneurs. BELCOURT, Monica.

Success Semantics. WHYTE, J T.

Virtue, Praise and Success: Stoic Responses to Aristotle. IRWIN, T H.

SUCCESSION

Between Succession and Duration. ROTENSTREICH, Nathan.

Marxist Critical Theory, Contradictions, and Ecological Succession. CATTON, Philip.

The Rule of Succession. ZABELL, Sandy L.

SUFFERING

"Schopenhauer on Suffering, Death, Guilt, and the Consolation of Metaphysics" in Schopenhauer: New Essays in Honor of His 200th Birthday, CARTWRIGHT, David E.

Evil—A Religious Mystery: A Plea for a More Inclusive Model of Theodicy. DUPRÉ, Louis.

God and the Silencing of Job. TILLEY, Terrence W.

Obligations, Communities, and Suffering: Problems of Community Seen in a New Light. LOEWY, Erich H.

The Possibility of God. TALIAFERRO, Charles.

Schopenhauer as Moral Philosopher—Towards the Actuality of his Ethics. CARTWRIGHT, David.

Suffering, Moral Worth, and Medical Ethics: A New Beginning. LOEWY, Erich H.

SUFFICIENT CONDITION(S)

Metaphysics of Causation. BIGELOW, John and PARGETTER, Robert.

SUFFRAGE

No Laughing Matter: John Stuart Mill's Establishment of Women's Sufferage as a Parliamentary Question. ROBSON, John M.

Suffrage Art and Feminism. SHEPPARD, Alice.

SUFISM

"The Wisdom of Islam in Sufism" in The Wisdom of Faith: Essays in Honor of Dr Sebastian Alexander Matczak, OZTURK, Yasar Nuri.

SUGGESTION(S)

The Effect of Computer Intervention and Task Structure on Bargaining Outcome. JONES, Beth H and JELASSI, M Tawfik.

Reexamining Berkeley's Notion of Suggestion. BEN-ZEEV, Aaron.

Reportage as Compound Suggestion. MAY, John D.

SUICIDE

Final Choices: Autonomy in Health Care Decisions. SMITH, George P.

Suicide and Euthanasia. BRODY, Baruch A (ed).

"Death by Free Choice: Modern Variations on an Antique Theme" in Suicide and Euthanasia, ENGELHARDT JR, H Tristram.

"The Ethics of Suicide in the Renaissance and Reformation" in Suicide and Euthanasia, FERNGREN, Gary B.

"Greek Philosophers on Euthanasia and Suicide" in Suicide and Euthanasia, COOPER, John M.

"A Historical Introduction to Jewish Casuistry on Suicide and Euthanasia" in Suicide and Euthanasia, BRODY, Baruch A.

SYMPATHY

Emotional Origins of Morality—A Sketch. THOMSON, Anne.

Ethik als Grundwissenschaft: Handeln aus Klugheit, Neigung, Pflicht, Ehrfurcht, Mitleid?. FUNKEE, Gerhard.

Sympathy and Self-Interest: The Crisis in Mill's Mental History. GREEN, Michele.

SYNCHRONICITY

Initiation in Hermeneutics: An Illustration Through the Mother-and-Daughter Archetype. DARROCH-LOZOWSKI, Vivian.

SYNDICALISM

Interpreting Georges Sorel: Defender of Virtue or Apostle of Violence?. VINCENT, K Steven.

SYNERGY

Body-Vessel-Matrix: Co-creative Images of Synergetic Universe. CARTER, Nancy Corson.

A Synergetic View of Institutions. WEISE, Peter and BRANDES, Wolfgang.

SYNONYMY

On Synonymy and Ontic Modalities. ZABLUDOWSKI, Andrzej.

Synonymy in Sentential Languages: A Pragmatic View. TOKARZ, Marek.

SYNTACTIC MODEL(S)

Intentionality and Stich's Theory of Brain Sentence Syntax. JACQUETTE, Dale.

SYNTACTICS

The Structure of Biological Theories. THOMPSON, Paul.

A Comparison Between Lambek Syntactic Calculus and Intuitionistic Linear Propositional Logic. ABRUSCI, V Michele.

A Simple and General Method of Solving the Finite Axiomatizability Problems for Lambek's Syntactic Calculi. ZIELONKA, Wojciech.

What's Wrong with the Syntactic Theory of Mind. EGAN, M Frances.

SYNTAX

see also Grammar(s)

Intentionality and Extension. MATJAZ, Potrc.

The Semantic Foundations of Logic, Volume 1: Propositional Logics. EPSTEIN, Richard L.

Against Compositionality: The Case of Adjectives. LAHAV, Ran.

Bringing It About. SEGERBERG, Krister.

The Concept of Phrase Structure. MANASTER-RAMER, Alexis and KAC, Michael B.

Conceptual Dependency as the Language of Thought. DUNLOP, Charles E M.

Fuzzy Natural Deduction. GERLA, Giangiacomo and TORTORA, Roberto.

Notes on Conditional Logic. SEGERBERG, Krister.

Parmenides on What There Is. KETCHUM, Richard J.

Predication in the Logic of Terms. SOMMERS, Fred.

SYNTHESIS

The Possible Universe. TALLET, J A.

Texts without Referents: Reconciling Science and Narrative. MARGOLIS, Joseph.

The New World Synthesis. POPE, N Vivian.

La síntesis de lo uno y lo múltiple. HARRIS, Errol E.

SYNTHETIC

On the Kantian Background of Neopositivism. SAUER, Werner.

SYNTHETIC A PRIORI

"Deus ex machina" redivivus: The "Synthetic A Priori" in the Computer Age. FANG, J.

Explaining the Inexplicable: The Hypotheses of the Faculty of Reflective Judgement in Kant's Third Critique. FRICKE, Christel.

The Syntheticity of Time: Comments on Fang's Critique of Divine Computers. PALMQUIST, Stephen R.

Wittgenstein, Kant and the "Metaphysics of Experience". WILLIAMS, Meredith.

SYSTEM(S)

Probabilistic Reasoning in Intelligent Systems: Networks of Plausible Inference. PEARL, Judea.

"Neues über das Systemprogramm?" in *Agora: Zu Ehren von Rudolph Berlinger,* OESCH, Martin.

"The Way the World Isn't: What the Bell Theorems Force Us to Give Up" in *Philosophical Consequences of Quantum Theory: Reflections on Bell's Theorem,* WESSELS, Linda.

"What" and "Where" in the Human Visual System: Two Hierarchies of Visual Modules. VAINA, Lucia M.

A Conception of Tarskian Logic. SHER, Gila.

The Dynamics of Belief Systems: Foundations versus Coherence Theories. GÄRDENFORS, P.

La hiérarchie des systèmes—à la frontière de l'intuition et de la certitude. STANCIULESCU, Traian-Dinorel.

How Epistemology Can Be a System. LEE, Donald.

The Human Image System and Thinking Critically in the Strong Sense. FREEMAN, James B.

Labelling Systems and R.E. Structures. ASH, C J.

A Question of Ethics: Developing Information System Ethics. COHEN, Eli.

The Real Objective of Mendel's Paper. MONAGHAN, Floyd V and CORCOS, Alain F.

Reason and Reflective Judgement: Kant on the Significance of Systematicity. GUYER, Paul.

Some Variations on a Metaphilosophical Theme. MARCOTTE, Edward.

Tycho Brahe's Critique of Copernicus and the Copernican System. BLAIR, Ann.

SYSTEMATICS

Philosophy of Biology Today. RUSE, Michael.

"On the Unity of Systematic Philosophy and History of Philosophy" in *History and Anti-History in Philosophy,* PEPERZAK, Adriaan.

SYSTEMS ANALYSIS

El Paradigma de Sistemas: Posibilidades Para Una Práctica Social Emancipadora: Reevaluación Crítica (Primera Part). RODRÍGUEZ HÖLKEMEYER, Patricia.

SYSTEMS THEORY

Ecological Communication. LUHMANN, Niklas.

Reductionism and Systems Theory in the Life Sciences: Some Problems and Perspectives. HOYNINGEN-HUENE, Paul (ed).

"The Variance Allocation Hypothesis of Stasis" in *Reductionism and Systems Theory in the Life Sciences: Some Problems and Perspectives,* WAGNER, Günter P.

Anmerkungen zur Autopoiesis. MOCEK, Reinhard.

SZASZ, T

Lawless Mind. ABELSON, Raziel.

TABOO(S)

Prostitution, Exploitation and Taboo. GREEN, Karen.

TACITUS

Machiavelli, Tacito, Grozio: un nesso "ideale" tra libertinismo e previchismo. SCARCELLA, Cosimo.

TAKEOVER(S)

The Chainsaws of Greed: The Case of Pacific Lumber. NEWTON, Lisa H.

TALENT(S)

Taking Talents Seriously. GREEN, Simon.

Le talent. WALD, Henri.

TALKING

Analogy Sans Portrait: God-Talk as Literal But Non-Anthropomorphic. MILLER, Barry.

TANAKA, K

Kotaro Tanaka as a Natural Law Theorist. HANZAWA, Takamaro.

TAOISM

Disputers of the TAO: Philosophical Argument in Ancient China. GRAHAM, A C.

"Human/Nature in Nietzsche and Taoism" in *Nature in Asian Tradition of Thought: Essays in Environmental Philosophy,* PARKES, Graham.

"On Seeking a Change of Environment" in *Nature in Asian Tradition of Thought: Essays in Environmental Philosophy,* HALL, David L.

"Putting the Te Back into Taoism" in *Nature in Asian Tradition of Thought: Essays in Environmental Philosophy,* AMES, Roger T.

"Theft's Way": A Comparative Study of Chuang Tzu's Tao and Derridean Trace. CHIEN, Chi-Hui.

Cosmogony, the Taoist Way. PEERENBOOM, R P.

Derrida and the Decentered Universe of Ch'an Buddhism. ODIN, Steve.

Derrida and the Decentered World of K'ou-Chuan: The Deconstruction of Taoist Semiotics. SASO, Michael.

Human Nature and Its Cosmic Roots in Huang-Lao Taoism. JAN, Yun-Hua.

Lao Zi and the Xia Culture. BO, Wang.

On the Critique of Energetism and Neoenergetism (in Czechoslovakian). ZEMAN, J.

Re-Tracing the Human-Nature versus World-Nature Dichotomy: Lao Tzu's Hermeneutics for World-Building. LUSTHAUS, Dan.

Solitude in Ancient Taoism. KOCH, Philip J.

The Tao of Women and Men: Chinese Philosophy and the Women's Movement. KLEINJANS, Everett.

Taoist Cultural Reality: The Harmony of Aesthetic Order. THOMPSON, Kirill O.

A Taoist Interpretation of 'Differance' in Derrida. CHENG, Chung-Ying.

TAOISM

Virtue under Attack (in Serbo-Croatian). PAS, Julian F.

Which One Is the Real One?. GRAYBOSCH, Anthony J.

Wittgenstein and Murdock on the 'Net' in a Taoist Framework. TOMINAGA, Thomas T.

TARSKI

The Concept of Logical Consequence. ETCHEMENDY, John.

Logic and Philosophy in the Lvov-Warsaw School. WOLÉNSKI, Jan.

Truth and Objectivity. ELLIS, Brian.

Alfred Tarski i la teoria de conjunts. PLA I CARRERA, Josep.

A Conception of Tarskian Logic. SHER, Gila.

Did Hobbes Have a Semantic Theory of Truth?. DE JONG, Willem R.

Homophone Semantik für die relevante Aussagenlogik. READ, Stephen.

Sobre preórdenes y operadores de consecuencias de Tarski. CASTRO, Juan Luis and TRILLAS, Enric.

The Structure and Content of Truth. DAVIDSON, Donald.

Truth, Interpretation and Convention T. PRADHAN, R C.

Turning Tricks with Convention T: Lessons Tarski Taught Me. RICE, Martin A.

TARSKI'S THEOREM

Atomic Realism, Intuitionist Logic and Tarskian Truth. EDWARDS, Jim.

TASAN

Tasan's "Practical Learning". SETTON, Mark.

TASSO

The Origins of Post-Modernism: The Ariosto-Tasso Debate. MC KINNEY, Ronald H.

TASTE

Art of Judgement. CAYGILL, Howard.

Are Kant's "Aesthetic Judgment" and "Judgment of Tase" Synonymous?. GRACYK, Theodore A.

The Education of Taste. GOLDMAN, Alan H.

An Emendation in Kant's Theory of Taste. COHEN, Ted.

Having Bad Taste. GRACYK, Theodore A.

Kitsch and Aesthetic Education. MORREALL, John and LOY, Jessica.

The Objectivity of Taste: Hume and Kant. KULENKAMPFF, Jens.

On Taste and Excellence. HALDANE, John.

Reflective Judgement and Taste. GINSBORG, Hannah.

TAUTOLOGY(-GIES)

Reply: Flew's "Is and Ought: The 'Open-Question Argument'". BLACK, Virginia.

TAXATION

Social Contract, Free Ride: A Study of the Public Goods Problem. DE JASAY, Anthony.

TAXONOMY

An Application of Bloom's Taxonomy to the Teaching of Business Ethics. REEVES, M Francis.

A Speech Act Analysis of Irony. HAVERKATE, Henk.

TAYLOR, A

Not Bending the Knee. HOLLAND, R F.

TAYLOR, C

Does Basing Rights on Autonomy Imply Obligations of Political Allegiance?. NICKEL, James W.

Economics and Hermeneutics. BERGER, Lawrence A.

TAYLOR, P

"Respect", "Dignity" and "Integrity": An Environmental Proposal for Ethics. WESTRA, Laura.

The Life Principle: A (Metaethical) Rejection. PASKE, Gerald H.

A Refutation of Environmental Ethics. THOMPSON, Janna.

TAYLOR, R

Taylor's Defenses of Two Traditional Arguments for the Existence of God. GARAVASO, Pieranna.

TEACHER(S)

Accountability in Education: A Philosophical Inquiry. WAGNER, Robert B.

Education, Movement and the Curriculum: A Philosophic Enquiry. ARNOLD, Peter J.

Interpreting Education. EDEL, Abraham.

Reading Curriculum Theory: The Development of a New Hermeneutic. REYNOLDS, William M.

Philosophical Aesthetics and the Education of Teachers. REDFERN, H B.

TEACHING

see also Pedagogy

Philosophical Issues in Education. HAMM, Cornel M.

The Voice of Liberal Learning: Michael Oakeshott on Education. FULLER, Timothy (ed).

"Ethics in America". SCHERER, Donald.

The "Evils" of a Technologized Psychology in Teacher Education. ORTON, Robert E.

"What's Real": A Dialogue. BIELFELDT, Dennis.

Achieving the Right Distance. TAUBMAN, Peter M.

An Application of Bloom's Taxonomy to the Teaching of Business Ethics. REEVES, M Francis.

Aristotle, Demonstration, and Teaching. WIANS, William.

Can Business Ethics Be Taught? Empirical Evidence. JONES, Thomas M.

Cognitive Apprenticeship Teaching the Craft of Reading, Writing and Mathematics. COLLINS, Allan and BROWN, John Seeley and NEWMAN, Susan E.

Computer Programming As a Vehicle for Teaching Thinking Skills. NICKERSON, Raymond S.

Couples, Canons, and the Uncouth: Spenser-and-Milton in Educational Theory. PATTERSON, Annabel.

The Course in Business Ethics: Can It Work?. PAMENTAL, George L.

Critical Children: Philosophy for the Young. COLES, Martin.

Directive Teaching, Indoctrination, and the Values Education of Children. PHILLIPS, D C.

Enseignement de la théologie et méthode scientifique. DUMONT, Camille.

The Ethics of Teaching Ethics. WAITHE, Mary Ellen and OZAR, David T.

An Euler Test for Syllogisms. ARMSTRONG, Robert L and HOWE, Lawrence W.

Experience and Nature: Teacher as Story Teller. SIMMONS JR, Michael.

Explaining the Persistence of Irrelevance. MC ANINCH, Amy.

How Can Philosophers Teach Professional Ethics?. WEIL, Vivian.

The Importance of Motivation, Precision and Presence in Teaching. BRUMBAUGH, Robert S.

Logic, Language and Dewey: A Student-Teacher Dialectic. PALERMO, James and D'ERASMO, Kate.

Measuring the Impact of Teaching Ethics to Future Managers: A Review, Assessment, and Recommendations. WEBER, James.

The Moral Aspects of Reading: Response to Raitz and Edwards. NORRIS, Stephen P.

A New Verdict on the 'Jury Passage': *Theaetetus* 201A-C. STRAMEL, James S.

On Re-Visioning Philosophy. STUHR, John J.

Ontological Dependence *über Alles*. NELSON, Thomas W.

The Personalization of Failure. PRATTE, Richard.

Philosophy Outside of Schools. SHEFFER, Susannah.

Philosophy, Children and Teaching Philosophy. HART, Richard E.

Practical Arguments and Situational Appreciation in Teaching. PENDLEBURY, Shirley.

Professionalization and the Moral Jeopardy of Teaching. BOYD, Dwight.

The Single-Issue Introduction to Philosophy. WHITE, V Alan.

Socratic Dialogue. HECKMANN, Gustav.

Socratic Teaching?. JORDAN JR, James A.

The Speakerly Teacher: Socrates and Writing. KALLICK, David.

Standing Alone: Dependence, Independence and Interdependence in the Practice of Education. GRIFFITHS, Morwenna and SMITH, Richard.

The Study of Teaching and Curriculum. MALANGA, Joseph.

Teaching "Ethics in America". ROSENBAUM, Alan S.

Teaching American Philosophy. CAMPBELL, James.

Teaching and Mother Love. KLEIN, J Theodore.

Teaching and Rhetoric. MC EWAN, Hunter.

Teaching Business Ethics: Questioning the Assumptions, Seeking New Directions. FURMAN, Frida Kerner.

Teaching Business Ethics: The Use of Films and Videotapes. HOSMER, LaRue Tone and STENECK, Nicholas H.

Teaching *Elfie*. HAMRICK, William S.

Teaching Virtues and Vices. WILLIAMS, Clifford.

Teaching with a Different Ear: Teaching Ethics after Reading Carol Gilligan. SLICER, Deborah.

Teaching Workplace Ethics. DAVIS, Michael.

Teaching, Learning and Ontological Dependence. PEARSON, Allen T.

There is Relevance in the Classroom: Analysis of Present Methods of Teaching Business Ethics. STRONG, V K and HOFFMAN, A N.

Three Levels of Reading Philosophy. DUHAN, Laura.

Toward a Code of Ethics for Business Ethicists. MADSEN, Peter.

What Other Worlds Have to Say About Ontological Dependence: Is There Life in the Logical Thesis?. MC EWAN, Hunter.

Whitehead and a Committee. BRUMBAUGH, Robert S.

Who Can Teach Workplace Ethics?. DAVIS, Michael.

Why I Teach Philosophy. TORGERSON, Jon N.

Why Philosophers Should Involve Themselves with Teaching Reasoning in the Schools. SILVERS, Anita.

Why Teachers Need Philosophy. CLARK, Charles.

Writing and Philosophy. FISHMAN, Stephen.

TELEVISION
Dialogue, Distanciation, and Engagement: Toward a Logic of Televisual Communication. LANGSDORF, Lenore.

TEMPERANCE
Notes on a Great Erotic. MC GHEE, Michael.
Plato on Force: Conflict Between his Psychology and Sociology and his Definition of Temperance in the *Republic*. RICE, Daryl H.

TEMPORAL ARTS
Husserl's Concept of Inner Temporal Consciousness and Aesthetics (in Czechoslovakian). ZUSKA, Vlastimil.

TEMPORAL LOGIC
Computer Science Temporal Logics Need their Clocks. SAIN, Ildikó.
An Elementary Proof for Some Semantic Characterizations of Nondeterministic Floyd-Hoare Logic. SAIN, Ildikó.

TEMPORALITY
see also Time
The Future: An Essay on God, Temporality, and Truth. LUCAS, J R.
Nietzsche's Philosophy of Nature and Cosmology. MOLES, Alistair.
Aristotle's Theory of Time and Entropy. HUGHEN, Richard E.
Beethoven's Symphonic Style and Temporality in Music. DAHLHAUS, Carl.
God as Creator. WARD, Keith.
Incarnation and Timelessness. SENOR, Thomas D.
On Reversal of Temporality of Human Cognition and Dialectical Self. MO, Suchoon S.
Das Paradox der Zeit und die Dimensionszahl der Temporalität. FRANCK, Georg.
Personal Identity, the Temporality of Agency and Moral Responsibility. LEE, Win-Chiat.
Temporal Indexicals. SMITH, Quentin.

TENDENCY(-CIES)
A Fact About the Virtues. RAY, A Chadwick.

TENSE(S)
Being in Time: The Nature of Time in Light of McTaggart's Paradox. FARMER, David J.
"Tense and Existence" in *Cause, Mind, and Reality: Essays Honoring C B Martin*, CARGILE, James.
The Co-Reporting Theory of Tensed and Tenseless Sentences. SMITH, Quentin.
The New Tenseless Theory of Time: A Reply to Smith. OAKLANDER, L Nathan.
Tensed Facts. SWINBURNE, Richard.

TERM(S)
The Melody of Theology: A Philosophical Dictionary. PELIKAN, Jaroslav.
Albertus Magnus and the Notion of Syllogistic Middle Term. HUBBARD, J M.
A Linear Parsing Algorithm for Parenthesis Terms. FELSCHER, Walter.
Near-Equational and Equational Systems of Logic for Partial Functions, II. CRAIG, William.
On Innertheoretical Conditions for Theoretical Terms. GÄHDE, Ulrich.
Predication in the Logic of Terms. SOMMERS, Fred.
The Rank Function and Hilbert's Second E-Theorem. FERRARI, Pier Luigi.

TERMINOLOGY
Locke on Disagreement Over the Uses of Moral and Political Terms. MASON, Andrew.

TERRON, E
Hegel nel pensiero giuridico-politico spagnolo: Cenni storici della recezione della "Filosofia del diritto". AMENGUAL, Gabriel.

TERROR
Eliade's Vichianism: The Regeneration of Time and the Terror of History. VERENE, Donald Phillip.

TERRORISM
Arms and Judgment: Law, Morality, and the Conduct of War in the 20th Century. COHEN, Sheldon M.
Essays on Political Morality. HARE, R M.
Community and Civil Strife. GILBERT, Paul.
How to Define Terrorism. TEICHMAN, Jenny.
Terrorism, Self-Defense, and Whistleblowing. WESTRA, Laura.

TERTULLIAN
En torno al modalismo de Marción. ORBE, Antonio.

TEST(S)
The Effect of the *Pixie* Program on Logical and Moral Reasoning. SCHLEIFER, Michael and LEBUIS, Pierre and CARON, Anita.
Give Goodrich a Break. FIELDER, John H.

Listenaires: Thoughts on a Database. GILES, Gordon J.
Mandatory HIV Antibody Testing Policies: An Ethical Analysis. O'BRIEN, Maura.
A Simple Quantitative Test of Financial Ethics. NORTON, Edgar.

TESTABILITY
Revival of Reasoning in the Modern Age by Developing a Classroom Community of Inquiry Within College Students. SOFO, Frank.

TESTING
Drug Testing in Employment. DES JARDINS, Joseph and DUSKA, Ronald.
Old Evidence, New Theories: Two Unresolved Problems in Bayesian Confirmation Theory. EARMAN, John.
Testing as a Selection Tool: Another Old and Sticky Managerial Human Rights Issue. MUNCHUS, George.

TETENS, J
Hume and Tetens. KUEHN, Manfred.

TEXT(S)
Reading Curriculum Theory: The Development of a New Hermeneutic. REYNOLDS, William M.
Transforming the Hermeneutic Context: From Nietzsche to Nancy. ORMISTON, Gayle L (ed).
What is Music?. ALPERSON, Philip A.
"Around and About Babel" in *The Textual Sublime: Deconstruction and Its Differences*, GRAHAM, Joseph F.
"Derrida and Heidegger: The Interlacing of Texts" in *The Textual Sublime: Deconstruction and Its Differences*, CHANTER, Tina.
"Lations, Cor, Trans, Re, &c" in *The Textual Sublime: Deconstruction and Its Differences*, LEAVEY JR, John P.
Composers' Texts as Objects of Musicological Study. HEINIÖ, Mikko.
Iterating Revolution: Speech Acts in Literary Theory. PETREY, Sandy.
Knowledge and Silence: *The Golden Bowl* and Moral Philosophy. BRUDNEY, Daniel.
Origins of Natural Rights Language: Texts and Contexts, 1150-1250. TIERNEY, Brian.
Past Looking. HOLLY, Michael Ann.
Philosophy and Style: Wittgenstein and Russell. HUGHES, John.
Portia's Suitors. KUHNS, Richard and TOVEY, Barbara.
A Pragmatic Method of Reading Confused Philosophic Texts: The Case of Peirce's "Illustrations". OCHS, Peter.
Qué hacer con los textos. CASTAÑARES, Wenceslao.
Texts and Their Interpretation. GRACIA, Jorge J E.
Textuality, Totalization, and the Question of Origin in Heidegger's Elucidation of *Andenken*. FÓTI, Véronique.
Transcendental Thomism and the Thomistic Texts. KNASAS, John F X.
Victor Cousin: frammenti socratici. RAGGHIANTI, Renzo.

TEXTBOOK(S)
About Philosophy (Fourth Edition). WOLFF, Robert Paul.
A Casebook of Medical Ethics. ACKERMAN, Terrence F.
The Changing World of Philosophy. CROWLEY, James F.
Classical American Philosophy: Essential Readings and Interpretative Essays. STUHR, John J.
Contemporary Issues in Bioethics (Third Edition). BEAUCHAMP, Tom L (ed).
Critical Thinking: Consider the Verdict. WALLER, Bruce N.
Critical Thinking: Evaluating Claims and Arguments in Everyday Life—Second Edition. MOORE, Brook Noel.
Ethical Issues in Modern Medicine (Third Edition). ARRAS, John.
Ethical Theory and Social Issues: Historical Texts and Contemporary Readings. GOLDBERG, David Theo.
Ethics in America: Study Guide. NEWTON, Lisa H.
Ethics in Government: The Moral Challenge of Public Leadership. MOORE, Mark H.
Fagothey's Right and Reason: Ethics in Theory and Practice—Ninth Edition. GONSALVES, Milton A.
Feminist Thought: A Comprehensive Introduction. TONG, Rosemarie.
The Fieldston Ethics Reader. WEINSTEIN, Mark (ed).
Fundamental Concepts and Problems in Business Ethics. BUCHHOLZ, Rogene A.
Introducing Philosophy: A Text with Integrated Readings (Fourth Edition). SOLOMON, Robert C.
Introduction to Logic and Critical Thinking (Second Edition). SALMON, Merrilee H.
An Introduction to Philosophical Analysis (Third Edition). HOSPERS, John.
Landmarks in Linguistic Thought: The Western Tradition from Socrates to Saussure. HARRIS, Roy.
Logic: Analyzing and Appraising Arguments. GENSLER, Harry J.
A Logical Introduction to Philosophy. PURTILL, Richard L.
The Main Trends in Philosophy. OIZERMAN, T I.

TEXTBOOK(S)

Mathematical Methods in Linguistics. PARTEE, Barbara H.

A Modern Formal Logic Primer, Volume I and II. TELLER, Paul.

Moral Reasoning: A Philosophic Approach to Applied Ethics. FOX, Richard M.

Philosophy and the Human Condition (Second Edition). BEAUCHAMP, Tom L (ed).

Schaum's Outline of Theory and Problems of Logic. NOLT, John Eric.

Taking Sides: Clashing Views on Controversial Bioethical Issues (Third Edition). LEVINE, Carole (ed).

Understanding Symbolic Logic (Second Edition). KLENK, Virginia.

TEXTUAL CRITICISM

Against Deconstruction. ELLIS, John M.

Nietzschean Narratives. SHAPIRO, Gary.

Bruno "lulliano' nell'idealismo italiano dell'Ottocento (con un inedito di Bertrando Spaventa). SAVORELLI, Alessandro.

Metakritik und Sprache: Zu Johann Georg Hamanns Kant-Verständnis und seinen metakritischen Implikationen. MAJETSCHAK, Stefan.

New Perspectives on Schleiermacher's Ethics: An Assay. DUKE, James O.

Victor Cousin: frammenti socratici. RAGGHIANTI, Renzo.

TEXTURE(S)

Common Functional Pathways for Texture and Form Vision. VAINA, Lucia M.

THACHIL, J

A Response to the Paper "Theology of Religions and Sacrifice". FRANCIS, B Joseph.

THAI

Thailand: Refining Cultural Values. RATANAKUL, Pinit.

THALES

Aristarchus of Samos on Thales' Theory of Eclipses. LEBEDEV, Andrei V.

Johnny Head-In-The-Air and Thales. CHARPA, Ulrich.

Thales (in Greek). POTAGA, A.

Thales, Anaximander, and Infinity. DANCY, R M.

THARP, L

Introduction to 'Three Theorems of Metaphysics'. SKYRMS, Brian.

Myth and Mathematics: A Conceptualistic Philosophy of Mathematics. THARP, Leslie.

Tharp and Conceptual Logic. WANG, Hao.

Tharp's 'Myth and Mathematics'. CHIHARA, Charles.

THEATER

Theater as Art. SHPET, G.

THEISM

see also Atheism

God and the Burden of Proof: Plantinga, Swinburne, and the Analytic Defense of Theism. PARSONS, Keith M.

Return to Reason: Critique of Enlightenment Evidentialism and a Defense of Reason and Belief in God. CLARK, Kelly James.

"Confucianism and Theism" in *The Wisdom of Faith: Essays in Honor of Dr Sebastian Alexander Matczak,* HWANG, Philip H.

Atomism Between Orthodoxy and Heterodoxy. CHERCHI, Gavina.

Beyond Our Species' Potentials: Charles Hartshorne on Humanism. RUSSELL, John M.

The Doctrine of Everlasting Punishment. TALBOTT, Thomas.

Hartshorne's Neoclassical Theism and Black Theology. WALKER JR, Theodore.

Miracles as Evidence for Theism. BASINGER, David.

A Modern Theistic Argument. DIAMOND, Michael L.

The Moral Stance of Theism Without the Transcent God: Wieman and Heidegger. SHAW, Marvin C.

On Failing to Resolve Theism-Versus-Atheism Empirically. O'CONNOR, David.

Reply to Michael Diamond's "A Modern Theistic Argument". HEBBLETHWAITE, Brian.

THEME(S)

"Themes in Marxism" in *Reading Philosophy for the Twenty-First Century,* SOMERVILLE, John.

THEODICY

Atheism: A Philosophical Justification. MARTIN, Michael.

"MacKinnon and the Problem of Evil" in *Christ, Ethics and Tragedy: Essays in Honour of Donald MacKinnon,* HEBBLETHWAITE, Brian.

"Reply to Hepburn's "The Problem of Evil"" in *Dialectic and Contemporary Science,* HARRIS, Errol E.

Christian Pacificism and Theodicy: The Free Will Defense in the Thought of John H Yoder. PINCHES, Charles.

The Concept of a Strong Theodicy. SCHUURMAN, Henry.

Descartes' Doctrine of Volitional Infinity. CRESS, Donald A.

Evil—A Religious Mystery: A Plea for a More Inclusive Model of Theodicy. DUPRÉ, Louis.

God, the Demon, and the Status of Theodicies. STEIN, Edward.

Hypolepsis und Kompensation—Odo Marquards philosophischer Beitrag zur Diagnose und Bewältigung der Gegenwart. KERSTING, Wolfgang.

The Problem of Evil and the Attributes of God. KELLER, James A.

The Problem of Evil: The Unanswered Questions Argument. BEATY, Michael.

THEOLOGIAN(S)

The Darkness and the Light: A Philosopher Reflects Upon His Career—Charles Hartshorne. HARTSHORNE, Charles.

Radhakrishnan and the Ways of Oneness of East and West. ORGAN, Troy Wilson.

THEOLOGY

see also God, Miracle(s)

Allāh Transcendent. NETTON, Ian Richard.

The Anthropological Character of Theology: Conditioning Theological Understanding. PAILIN, David A.

Biblical Narrative in the Philosophy of Paul Ricoeur: A Study in Hermeneutics and Theology. VANHOOZER, Kevin J.

Christ, Ethics and Tragedy: Essays in Honour of Donald MacKinnon. SURIN, Kenneth (ed).

Conscience and the Reality of God: An Essay on the Experiential Foundations of Religious Knowledge. STATEN, John C.

Discourses on the Meaning of History. KLUBACK, William.

Divine Nature and Human Language: Essays in Philosophical Theology. ALSTON, William P.

Hermeneutics: Interpretation Theory in Schleiermacher, Dilthey, Heidegger, and Gadamer. PALMER, Richard E.

Intimations of Divinity. PLATT, David.

The Melody of Theology: A Philosophical Dictionary. PELIKAN, Jaroslav.

Our Philosophy: Allāma Muhammad Bāqir As-Sadr. INATI, Shams C (trans).

Philosophische Bemerkungen. KURTH, Rudolf.

The Political Theory of Liberation Theology: Toward a Reconvergence of Social Value and Science. POTTENGER, John R.

Primordial Truth and Postmodern Theology. GRIFFIN, David Ray.

Religious Aesthetics: A Theological Study of Making and Meaning. BURCH BROWN, Frank.

Tears. TAYLOR, Mark C.

The Trespass of the Sign: Deconstruction, Theology and Philosophy. HART, Kevin.

Unapologetic Theology: A Christian Voice in a Pluralistic Conversation. PLACHER, William C.

Varieties of Postmodern Theology. GRIFFIN, David Ray (ed).

The Wisdom of Faith: Essays in Honor of Dr Sebastian Alexander Matczak. THOMPSON, Henry O (ed).

"'Between Purgation and Illumination': A Critique of the Theology of Right" in *Christ, Ethics and Tragedy: Essays in Honour of Donald MacKinnon,* MILBANK, John.

"Aquinas's Debt to Maimonides" in *A Straight Path: Studies in Medieval Philosophy and Culture,* BURRELL, David B.

"Baubô: Theological Perversion and Fetishism" in *Nietzsche's New Seas: Explorations in Philosophy, Aesthetics, and Politics,* STRONG, Tracy B (trans) and KOFMAN, Sarah.

"Christ in the Postmodern Age: Reflections Inspired by Jean-François Lyotard" in *Varieties of Postmodern Theology,* BEARDSLEE, William A.

"The Cultural Vision of Pope John Paul II: Toward a Conservative/Liberal Postmodern Dialogue" in *Varieties of Postmodern Theology,* HOLLAND, Joe.

"Hobbes and the Problem of God" in *Perspectives on Thomas Hobbes,* PACCHI, Arrigo.

"The Postmodern Paradigm and Contemporary Catholicism" in *Varieties of Postmodern Theology,* HOLLAND, Joe.

"Postmodern Theology and A/Theology: A Response to Mark C Taylor" in *Varieties of Postmodern Theology,* GRIFFIN, David Ray.

"Postmodern Theology as Liberation Theology: A Response to Harvey Cox" in *Varieties of Postmodern Theology,* GRIFFIN, David Ray.

Il "Satyricon" di Petronio e la datazione della *Grammatica Ebraica Spinoziana.* PROIETTI, Omero.

'God-Talk' and 'Tacit' Theo-Logic. SCHWEIZER-BJELIC, Shelley and BJELIC, Dusan I.

The 'Theology' of the Hippocratic Treatise On the Sacred Disease. VAN DER EIJK, P J.

A Note on the Arabic Term 'Anniyyah/'Aniyyah/'Inniyyah (in Hebrew). HARVEY, Warren Zev and HARVEY, Steven.

Appréciation de l'oeuvre théologico-philosophique de Thomas d'Aquin au tournant des XIIIe-XIVe ss (in Polish). MORAWIEC, Edmund.

THEOLOGY

Can Theology Have a Role in "Public" Bioethical Discourse?. CAHILL, Lisa Sowle.

Christian Wolff and China: The Autonomy of Morality (in Serbo-Croatian). CHING, Julia.

Clodovis Boff on the Discipline of Theology. CUNNINGHAM, David S.

La constitucion onto-teo-logica de la metafisica. BOBURG, Felipe (trans) and HEIDEGGER, Martin.

Il credere, la rivelazione, il "nuovo pensiero" di Franz Rosenzweig. D'ANTUONO, Emilia.

Demons, Demonologists and Descartes. SCARRE, Geoffrey.

Dialogue and Theology of Religious Pluralism. VINEETH, V F.

Disciplining Relativism and Truth. CLAYTON, Philip.

Distinguishing Modern and Postmodern Theologies. MURPHY, Nancey and MC CLENDON JR, James W.

Does Philosophy 'Leave Everything as it is'? Even Theology?. BAMBROUGH, Renford.

Enseignement de la théologie et méthode scientifique. DUMONT, Camille.

From Cultural Synthesis to Communicative Action: The Kingdom of God and Ethical Theology. SCHWEIKER, William.

Groundwork for an Indian Christian Theology. MOOKENTHOTTAM, Antony.

Harde noten om te kraken: de zachte wetenschappen. IBSCH, Elrud.

Hartshorne's Neoclassical Theism and Black Theology. WALKER JR, Theodore.

Hobbes's Mortalism. JOHNSTON, David.

How Can Theology Be Moral?. O'DONOVAN, Oliver.

Incommensurability, Intratextuality, and Fideism. TILLEY, Terrence W.

Kierkegaard's Alternative Metaphysical Theology. HEYWOOD THOMAS, John.

Die Lebensgeschichte als Versöhnungsgeschichte: Eine paradigmatische Thematik spiritueller Moraltheologie. DEMMER, Klaus.

Magisterium und Moraltheologie. FUCHS, Josef.

Merleau-Ponty et la déconstruction du logocentrisme. MADISON, Gary Brent.

Method and Metaphysics: The *Via Resolutionis* in Thomas Aquinas. AERTSEN, Jan A.

Müntzer contra Luther: Der philosophische Gehalt des theologischen Konflikts. GRÜNING, Thomas.

The Notion of the Transcultural in Bernard Lonergan's Theology. LAMB, Matthew.

Petrus Damiani—ein Freund der Logik?. BUCHER, Theodor G.

Phenomenology and Theology: A Note on Bultmann and Heidegger. JONES, Gareth.

Philosophie et théologie chez Austin Farrer. HENDERSON, Edward H.

The Place of Teaching Techniques in Samkara's Theology. SUTHREN HIRST, J G.

La question du pluralisme en théologie. MARLÉ, René.

Reason in Mystery. KRETZMANN, Norman.

Recent Work in the Philosophy of Religion. ZAGZEBSKI, Linda.

Ritschl's Critique of Schleiermacher's Theological Ethics. BRANDT, James M.

Science and Theology in Fourteenth Century: Subalternate Sciences in Oxford Commentaries on the *Sentences*. LIVESEY, Steven J.

Sens et Vérité: Philosophie et théologie chez L Meyer et Spinoza. LAGREE, Jacqueline.

Six Characteristics of a Postpatriarchal Christianity. MC DANIEL, Jay.

The Status of the Anomaly in the Feminist God-Talk of Rosemary Reuther. JAMES, George Alfred.

Struttura dell'azione e compito pubblico del cristianesimo. POSSENTI, Vittorio.

Theologically Unfashionable Philosophy. STUMP, Eleonore S and KRETZMANN, Norman.

Theology of Religions and Sacrifice. THACHIL, Jose.

Theosebeia in Plethon's Work: A Concept in Transition. ARGYROPOULOS, R.

Toward a Sound Perspective on Modern Physics: Capra's Popularization of Mysticism and Theological Approaches. CLIFTON, Robert K and REGEHR, Marilyn G.

Truth, Relativism, and Crossword Puzzles. MURPHY, Nancey.

Zu Problemen der revolutionären Theologie Thomas Müntzers. KOLESNYK, Alexander.

THEOPHRASTUS

"Aristotle and Theophrastus Conjoined in the Writings of Cicero" in *Cicero's Knowledge of the Peripatos*, RUNIA, David T.

"Cicero's Knowledge of the Rhetorical Treatises of Aristotle and Theophrastus" in *Cicero's Knowledge of the Peripatos*, FORTENBAUGH, William W.

"Gibt es Spuren von Theophrasts *Phys op* bei Cicero?" in *Cicero's Knowledge of the Peripatos*, MANSFELD, Jaap.

"Theophrast in Cicero's *De finibus*" in *Cicero's Knowledge of the Peripatos*, GIGON, Olof.

El status lógico de los *topoi* aristotélicos. CHICHI, Graciela.

THEOREM(S)

Conditions on Upper and Lower Probabilities to Imply Probabilities. SUPPES, Patrick and ZANOTTI, Mario.

Introduction to 'Three Theorems of Metaphysics'. SKYRMS, Brian.

A Logic of *Good, Should*, and *Would*: Part II. GOBLE, Lou.

Three Theorems of Metaphysics. THARP, Leslie.

THEORETICAL CONCEPTS

"Foucault's Move beyond the Theoretical" in *The Question of the Other: Essays in Contemporary Continental Philosophy*, MC WHORTER, Ladelle.

The Born-Einstein Debate: Where Application and Explanation Separate. CARTWRIGHT, Nancy.

A Graph-Theoretic Approach to Revealed Preference. WAKKER, Peter.

THEORETICAL REASON

Intuición práctica y ejemplo retórico. SCHOLLMEIER, Paul and FEMENÍAS, María Luisa.

The Meaning of BIOΣ in Aristotle's *Ethics* and *Politics*. KEYT, David.

THEORETICAL TERM(S)

A Reason for Theoretical Terms. GAIFMAN, Haim and OSHERSON, Daniel N and WEINSTEIN, Scott.

THEORY(-RIES)

see also Educational Theory(-ries), Ethical Theory(-ries), Political Theory, Recursion Theory, Set Theory

Aesthetic Objects and Works of Art. TOWNSEND, Dabney.

The Growth of Knowledge: An Inquiry into the Kuhnian Theory. VERRONEN, Veli.

The Imitation of Nature. HYMAN, John.

The Normal and the Pathological. CANGUILHEM, Georges.

Reading Curriculum Theory: The Development of a New Hermeneutic. REYNOLDS, William M.

The Structure of Biological Theories. THOMPSON, Paul.

The Theory and Scholarship of Talcott Parsons to 1951: A Critical Commentary. WEARNE, Bruce C.

A Theory of Property. MUNZER, Stephen R.

"Foucault and Theory: Genealogical Critiques of the Subject" in *The Question of the Other: Essays in Contemporary Continental Philosophy*, GRUBER, David F.

"A Genotype-Phenotype Model for the Growth of Theories" in *Issues in Evolutionary Epistemology*, KANTOROVICH, Aharon.

"Legal Theory and the Problem of Sense" in *Issues in Contemporary Legal Philosophy: The Influence of H L A Hart*, DWORKIN, Ronald.

"Local Theory" in *The Question of the Other: Essays in Contemporary Continental Philosophy*, BIRMINGHAM, Peg.

"Toward an Adequate Theory of Applied Ethics". DE MARCO, Joseph P.

Analogy and Interpretation (in Polish). LUBANSKI, Mieczyslaw.

Applying Kripke's Theory of Truth. MC GEE, Vann.

The Boolean Spectrum of an o-Minimal Theory. STEINHORN, Charles and TOFFALORI, Carlo.

Bootstrapping While Barefoot (Crime Models versus Theoretical Models in the Hunt for Serial Killers). NORDBY, Jon J.

Can a Partisan be a Moralist?. GOMBERG, Paul.

Categoricity of Theories in $L_{\kappa\omega}$ with κ a Compact Cardinal. SHELAH, Saharon and MAKKAI, M.

Classical Subtheories and Intuitionism. SZYMANEK, Krzysztof.

The Classification of Small Weakly Minimal Sets, II. BUECHLER, Steven.

Conditionals and Theory Change: Revisions, Expansions, and Additions. ROTT, Hans.

The Contexts of Phenomenology as Theory. LARRABEE, Mary Jeanne.

Counterexamples to a Conjecture on Relative Categoricity. EVANS, D M.

The Crisis of Marxism and Some of Its Implications. WAMBA-DIA-WAMBA, Ernest.

Des belles paires aux beaux uples. BOUSCAREN, Elisabeth and POIZAT, Bruno.

A Dichotomy Theorem for Regular Types. HRUSHOVSKI, E and SHELAH, S.

Dirac and the Aesthetic Evaluation of Theories. MC ALLISTER, James W.

Efficiency, Effectiveness and Legitimation: Criteria for the Evaluation of Norms. UUSITALO, Liisa.

Elementary Pairs of Models. BOUSCAREN, E.

Ethische theorieën en de ontwikkeling van medische technologie. DE VRIES, Gerard.

Evolution, Phenotypic Selection, and the Units of Selection. SHANAHAN, Timothy.

THEORY(-RIES)

An Exchange on Vertical Drift and the Quest for Theoretical Integration in Sociology. BASH, Harry.
Explaining the Persistence of Irrelevance. MC ANINCH, Amy.
Finitary Algebraic Logic. MADDUX, Roger D.
Groundwork for a Subjective Theory of Ethics. SAPONTZIS, Steve F.
Grünbaum and Psychoanalysis. NASH, Margaret.
Henri Poincaré's Philosophy of Science. STUMP, David.
The Hierarchical Structure of Testing Theories. KUOKKANEN, Martti.
How to be Realistic About Inconsistency in Science. BROWN, Bryson.
Ironist Theory as a Vocation: A Response to Rorty's Reply. MC CARTHY, Thomas.
L'Évaluation des théories éthiques. BLACKBURN, Pierre.
The Language Dependence of Accuracy. BARNES, Eric.
La metodología falsacionista y su ecología. RADNITZKY, Gerard.
Michael Oakeshott as Liberal Theorist. FRANCO, Paul.
The Modal View of Economic Models. RAPPAPORT, Steven.
Model Completeness and Direct Power. TAGHVA, Kazem
Modeling in the Museum: On the Role of Remnant Models in the Work of Joseph Grinnell. GRIESEMER, James R.
Moles in Motu: Principles of Spinoza's Physics. KLEVER, W N A.
Monadic Π_1^1-Theories of Π_1^1-Properties. DOETS, Kees.
A New Model for Intuitionistic Analysis. SCOWCROFT, Philip.
The Number of Pairwise Non-Elementarily-Embeddable Models. SHELAH, Saharon.
Omega-Categoricity, Relative Categoricity and Coordinatisation. HODGES, Wilfrid and HODKINSON, I M and MACPHERSON, Dugald.
On Models of the Elementary Theory of $(Z,+,1)$. NADEL, Mark and STAVI, Jonathan.
A Proof of Morley's Conjecture. HART, Bradd.
Putnam on "Empirical Objects". STEINHOFF, Gordon.
Realism and the Underdetermination of Theory. CLENDINNEN, F John.
Realism, Reference and Theory. HARRÉ, Rom.
Recent Work in Punishment Theory. DAVIS, Michael.
Recipes, Cooking and Conflict. HELDKE, Lisa.
Scattered Sociology: A Response to Bash. FUHRMAN, Ellsworth.
Serendipity as a Source of Evolutionary Progress in Science. KANTOROVICH, Aharon and NE'EMAN, Yuval.
Sulla teoria e metodica della storia. MEYER, Eduard.
Teoría y praxis: evolución de estos conceptos. PONFERRADA, Gustavo Eloy.
A Theorem on Barr-Exact Categories, with an Infinitary Generalization. MAKKAI, Michael.
Théories complètes de paires de corps valués henseliens. LELOUP, Gérard.
Theory Discovery from Data with Mixed Quantifiers. KELLY, Kevin T and GLYMOUR, Clark.
The Theory of Ideas in Gassendi and Locke. MICHAEL, Fred S and MICHAEL, Emily.
Theory of Speech Acts (in Serbo-Croatian). IVANETIC, Nada.
To Welcome the Other: Totality and Theory in Levinas and Adorno. FLOYD, Wayne W.
Le Traité des passions de Descartes et les théories modernes de l'émotion. NEUBERG, M.
Uncountable Theories that are Categorical in a Higher Power. LASKOWSKI, Michael Chris.
Understanding Music: Remarks on the Relevance of Theory. TORMEY, Alan.
A Uniform Method for Proving Lower Bounds on the Computational Complexity of Logical Theories. COMPTON, Kevin J and HENSON, C Ward.
The Use and Abuse of Legal Theory: A Reply to Fish. BARASH, Carol Isaacson.
Virtue Ethics and Anti-Theory. LOUDEN, Robert B.
Weakly Minimal Formulas: A Global Approach. NEWELSKI, L.
Wesshalb implizite Definitionen nicht genug sind. BARTELS, Andreas.
Who Needs a Theory of Informal Logic?. DOSS, Seale.

THERAPY

see also Psychotherapy
Freud-a-til vraiment renié le pouvoir thérapeutique de la psychanalyse?. VACHON, Gérard.

THERMODYNAMICS

Evolution in Thermodynamic Perspective: An Ecological Approach. WEBER, Bruce H (and others).
Fisica e storia della scienza nell'opera di Pierre Duhem. RAMONI, Marco.
Two Faces of Maxwell's Demon Reveal the Nature of Irreversibility. COLLIER, John D.

THESIS(-SES)

Kant: An Index to Theses and Dissertations Accepted by Universities in Canada and the US, 1879-1985. GABEL, Gernot U.

THING IN ITSELF

"The Rehabilitation of Transcendental Idealism?" in Reading Kant, GUYER, Paul.
Kant's Argument for the Non-Spatiotemporality of Things in Themselves. FALKENSTEIN, Lorne.

THING(S)

The Question of Being. SOKOLOWSKI, Robert.
The Underlying Thing, the Underlying Nature and Matter: Aristotle's Analogy in Physics I 7. COOK, Kathleen C.

THINKING

see also Cognition, Critical Thinking, Reasoning
Ein neuer Beitrag zum Verständnis Spinozas. EISENSTEIN, Israel.
Maternal Thinking: Toward a Politics of Peace. RUDDICK, Sara.
Time and Change: Short But Differing Philosophies. CHACALOS, Elias Harry.
"Thinking as Writing" in Wittgenstein in Focus—Im Brennpunkt: Wittgenstein, SLUGA, Hans.
Acerca de la pregunta por la determinante de la cosa del pensar. ZUBIRÍA, Martín (trans) and HEIDEGGER, Martin.
Against Skills. HART, W.
Computer Programming As a Vehicle for Teaching Thinking Skills. NICKERSON, Raymond S.
Double Representation of the 'Paralogisms of Pure Reason' in the Two Editions of Critique of Pure Reason (in German). KOPPER, Joachim.
The Folklore of Computers and the True Art of Thinking. ROSZAK, Theodore.
Gilligan's Two Voices: An Epistemological Overview. DURAN, Jane.
Heidegger als fragender Denker und als Denker der Frage. HAEFFNER, Gerd.
Heidegger and Nietzsche on "Thinking in Values". DETMER, David.
I Think, Therefore I Can: Attribution and Philosophy for Children. ALLEN, Terry.
Integrative Thinking Is the Essential Characteristic of Creative Thinking. SONGXING, Su and GUOZHENG, Lin.
Literate Thinking and Schooling. LANGER, Judith.
Logic in the Classroom. SLADE, Christina.
Moral Theory: Thinking, Doing, and Living. CALLAHAN, Daniel.
The Novelty of Marx's Theory of Praxis. MARGOLIS, Joseph.
On the Relation Between Logic and Thinking. HENLE, Mary.
El pensar en la filosofía de la mente de L Wittgenstein. GIL DE PAREIJA, José L.
The Dutch Words 'besef' and 'beseffen' (in Dutch). VERHOEVEN, C.
Thinking Skills in Science and Philosophy for Children. GAZZARD, Ann.
Thinking, Knowing, Doing. EBLE, Kenneth.
Thinking, Poetry and Pain. CAPUTO, John D.
We Discover That Thinking Is Fun: Doing Philosophy With First Graders. BRÜNING, Barbara.

THIRD MAN ARGUMENT

The Logic of the Dilemma of Participation and of the Third Man Argument. SCALTSAS, Theodore.

THIRD WORLD

Ethnophilosophy in the Philosophical Discourse in Africa: A Critical Note. NEUGEBAUER, Christian.
The Relevance of Deep Ecology to the Third World. JOHNS, David M.

THOMAS OF YORK

El metodo filosofico segun 'Sapientiale' de Tomas de York. LÉRTORA MENDOZA, Celina A.

THOMISM

Controversies and Discussions about the Post-Council Aspect of Catholic Philosophy. BORGOSZ, Jozef and PACZYNSKA, Maria (trans).
A Conversation with Hans-Georg Gadamer. BAUR, Michael.
Die ethischen Ansichten von P Professor Tadeusz Slipko (in Polish). PODREZ, Ewa.
L'étant, l'essence et l'être. ANTONIOTTI, Louise-Marie.
Linee dell'attività filosofico-teologica della Beata Edith Stein. FABRO, Cornelio.
Thomism and Contemporary Philosophical Pluralism. CLARKE, W Norris.
Transcendental Thomism and the Thomistic Texts. KNASAS, John F X.
Why St Thomas Stays Alive. MC COOL, Gerald A.

THOMSON, J

Nature as Demonic in Thomson's Defense of Abortion. WILCOX, John T.
Thomson and the Trolley Problem. GORR, Michael.
Thomson and the Trolley Problem. POSTOW, B C.

THOREAU

Civil Disobedience. HARRIS, Paul (ed).

THOUGHT

Connections to the World: The Basic Concepts of Philosophy. DANTO, Arthur C.

El individuo y la feminidad. PEREZ ESTEVEZ, Antonio.

Folly and Intelligence in Political Thought. KLUBACK, William.

Landmarks in Linguistic Thought: The Western Tradition from Socrates to Saussure. HARRIS, Roy.

Looking Into Mind: How to Recognize Who You Are and How You Know. DAMIANI, Anthony.

Mental Content. MC GINN, Colin.

Mind, Brain and the Quantum: The Compound 'I'. LOCKWOOD, Michael.

The Natural Goodness of Man: On the Systems of Rousseau's Thought. MELZER, Arthur M.

Of Spirit: Heidegger and the Question. DERRIDA, Jacques.

Propositional Attitudes: An Essay on Thoughts and How We Ascribe Them. RICHARD, Mark.

Thought and Language. MORAVCSIK, J M.

Wittgenstein's Philosophy of Psychology. BUDD, Malcolm.

"The Identity of Thought and Being in Harris's Interpretation of Hegel's Logic" in *Dialectic and Contemporary Science*, RINALDI, Giacomo.

"Reply to Rinaldi's "The Identity of Thought and Being in Harris's Interpretation of Hegel's Logic"" in *Dialectic and Contemporary Science*, HARRIS, Errol E.

Aristotle on the Mechanics of Thought. WEDIN, M V.

Charles S Peirce on Objects of Thought and Representation. PAPE, Helmut.

Completing the Recovery of Language as an Existential Project. DAVIS, Duane H.

Conceptual Dependency as the Language of Thought. DUNLOP, Charles E M.

Conscience et forme dans la pensée critique de Georges Poulet. MARTIN, Mircea.

Dominance of the Thought on Domestication: Threat for Humanum in Our Time (in Hungarian). DUPRÉ, Wilhelm.

Explanation and the Language of Thought. BRADDON-MITCHELL, David and FITZPATRICK, John.

Franz Rosenzweig a cent'anni dalla nascita. FABRIS, Adriano.

Gebrauchssprache und Logik: Eine Philosophiehistorische Notiz zu Frege und Lotze. SCHMIT, Roger.

Hobbes's Psychology of Thought: Endeavours, Purpose and Curiosity. BARNOUW, Jeffrey.

An Investigation of the Lumps of Thought. KRATZER, Angelika.

Is This Any Way to be a Realist?. TIENSON, John L.

Language and the Problems of Knowledge (in Serbo-Croatian). CHOMSKY, Noam.

Language and Thought in Kant's Theory of Knowledge (in Hebrew). DASCAL, Marcelo and SENDEROWICZ, Yaron.

Logical Form. MAURY, André.

Mental Content and Linguistic Form. STALNAKER, Robert.

Object-Dependent Thoughts. BOËR, Steven E.

On the Typology of Modes of Thought. LI, Cheng.

La pensée et la nouveauté de pensée. SCHLANGER, Judith.

Perception: Belief and Experience. PITSON, Anthony.

La relation de réfléchissement pensée/langage. ROVENTA-FRUMUSANI, Daniela.

Simultaneity and Einstein's *Gedankenexperiment*. COHEN, Michael.

Technological Activity and Philosophical Thought. QING, Zou.

The Conceptual Structure of Marxist Thought: Some Critical Reflections (in Serbo-Croatian). KRISHNA, Daya.

Thinking Eye of Karl Capek (in Czechoslovakian). HLAVACEK, Lubos.

Thoughts and Their Subject: A Study of Wittgenstein's *Tractatus*. KANNISTO, Heikki.

The Truth about Neptune and the Seamlessness of Truth. SANFORD, David H.

Understanding the Language of Thought. POLLOCK, John L.

Utopia and Islamic Political Thought. AL-AZMEH, Aziz.

What Wittgenstein Wasn't. GILL, Jerry H.

THOUGHT EXPERIMENT(S)

The Confirmation of the Superposition Principle: The Role of a Constructive Thought Experiment in Galileo's *Discorsi*. PRUDOVSKY, Gad.

THREAT(S)

Nuclear Deterrence, Morality and Realism. FINNIS, John.

Dominance of the Thought on Domestication: Threat for Humanum in Our Time (in Hungarian). DUPRÉ, Wilhelm.

The Justification of Deterrent Violence. FARRELL, Daniel M.

Nuclearism and International Law. STEGENGA, James A.

Robert Stevens on Offers. SWANTON, Christine.

Threats and Illocutions. NICOLOFF, Franck.

Who Is the Enemy? Reflections on the Threat of Managerial Techno-Reason to the Humanities. NORDENHAUG, Theodore D.

THUCYDIDES

Le origini dell'ateismo antico (quarta parte). ZEPPI, Stelio.

TIBETAN

Patterns of Transcendence: Religion, Death, and Dying. CHIDESTER, David.

Forman and Semantic Aspects of Tibetan Buddhist Debate Logic. TILLEMANS, Tom J F.

What is Non-Existent and What is Remanent in Sūnyatā. DARGYAY, Lobsang.

TILLICH

Paul Tillich on Creativity. KEGLEY, Jacquelyn Ann K (ed).

Paul Tillich: On the Boundary between Protestantism et Marxism. STONE, Ronald H.

TIME

Being in Time: The Nature of Time in Light of McTaggart's Paradox. FARMER, David J.

Bergson. LACEY, A R.

A Commentary on Heidegger's "Being and Time". GELVEN, Michael.

Human Posture: The Nature of Inquiry. SCHUMACHER, John A.

Impermanence is Buddha-nature: Dōgen's Understanding of Temporality. STAMBAUGH, Joan.

The Infinite. MOORE, A W.

Mind, Brain and the Quantum: The Compound 'I'. LOCKWOOD, Michael.

The Nature of Existence, Volume II. MC TAGGART, John McTaggart Ellis.

Philosophical Logic and Artificial Intelligence. THOMASON, Richmond H (ed).

Realism, Mathematics and Modality. FIELD, Hartry.

Time, Freedom, and the Common Good: An Essay in Public Philosophy. SHEROVER, Charles M.

"Russell on Order in Time" in *Rereading Russell: Essays on Bertrand Russell's Metaphysics and Epistemology*, ANDERSON, C Anthony.

"Space, Time, and the Sublime" in *The Question of the Other: Essays in Contemporary Continental Philosophy*, OLKOWSKI-LAETZ, Dorothea.

"A Space-Time Approach to the Bell Inequality" in *Philosophical Consequences of Quantum Theory: Reflections on Bell's Theorem*, BUTTERFIELD, Jeremy.

"Time and Interpretation in Heraclitus" in *Post-Structuralist Classics*, BENJAMIN, Andrew.

"Deus ex machina" redivivus: The "Synthetic A Priori" in the Computer Age. FANG, J.

The Absolute, Community, and Time. WILLIAMS, Robert R.

Der Andere als Zukunft und Gegenwart. RÖMPP, Georg.

Aristotle on 'Time' and 'A Time'. WHITE, Michael J.

Bergson, Prigogine and the Rediscovery of Time. SZENDREI, Eric V.

Berkeley's Theory of Time. HESTEVOLD, H Scott.

Between Succession and Duration. ROTENSTREICH, Nathan.

Categorías puras y categorías esquematizadas. VON BILDERLING, Beatriz.

Cosmology and Hindu Thought. BALSLEV, Anindita Niyobi.

Crisis of Values and Experience of Time (in Hungarian). TARNAY, Brúnó.

Descartes on Time and Causality. SECADA, J E K.

Does the Principle of Relativity Imply Winnie's (1970) Equal Passage Times Principle?. BROWN, Harvey R.

Einige Bemerkungen zur Bedeutung von Ewigkeit und Dauer in Spinozas Ethik. KOPPER, Joachim.

An Elementary Conception of Time. AULT JR, Charles R.

Éléments de l'histoire (humains et non humains) (in Greek). DESPOTOPOULOS, K I.

Eliade's Vichianism: The Regeneration of Time and the Terror of History. VERENE, Donald Phillip.

Events Without Times An Essay On Ontology. CHISHOLM, Roderick M.

Fatalism and Time. BERNSTEIN, Mark.

A Formal Theory of Objects, Space and Time. BLIZARD, Wayne D.

Genealogies as the Language of Time: A Structural Approach—Anthropological Implications. FROUSSART, Bernard.

God and Time: Towards a New Doctrine of Divine Timeless Eternity. PADGETT, Alan G.

Hume, Strict Identity, and Time's Vacuum. COSTA, Michael J.

Is "Some-Other-Time" Sometimes Better Than "Sometime" for Proving Partial Correctness of Programs?. SAIN, Ildikó.

Kant's *Analogies* and the Structure of Objective Time. HUGHES, R I G.

Kant's Argument for the Non-Spatiotemporality of Things in Themselves. FALKENSTEIN, Lorne.

TIME

Die kosmologischen Antinomien in der Kritik der reinen Vernunft und die moderne physikalische Kosmologie. MITTELSTAEDT, Peter and STROHMEYER, Ingeborg.

L'equivoque du temps chez Aristote. BAEKERS, Stephan F.

Martin Heidegger: His Philosophy and His Politics. ZUCKERT, Catherine H.

Metaphysical Boundaries: A Question of Independence. CARTER, William R.

The New Tenseless Theory of Time: A Reply to Smith. OAKLANDER, L Nathan.

Nietzsche, Dühring, and Time. SMALL, Robin.

On Splitting of a Recursive Set with Polynomial Time Minimal Pairs. ZHIXIANG, Chen.

On the Nature of Religion. MYERS, R Thomas.

Origen: The Source of Augustine's Theory of Time. TZAMALIKOS, P.

Das Paradox der Zeit und die Dimensionszahl der Temporalität. FRANCK, Georg.

Passage and the Presence of Experience. HESTEVOLD, H Scott.

Potency, Space and Time: Three Modern Theories. CENTORE, F F.

Le problème du temps chez Paul Ricoeur. MARCONDES CESAR, C.

Ricoeur, Lonergan and the Intelligibility of Cosmic Time. PAMBRUN, James R.

Selbstreferenz und Zeit: Die dynamische Stabilität des Bewusstseins. BERGMANN, Werner and HOFFMANN, G.

El sentido de la teoría humeana del tiempo como relación filosófica. MUDROVCIC, María Inés.

The Shape of Time. CIORANESCU, Alexandre.

Stability of Weak Second-Order Semantics. CSIRMAZ, László.

Sujeto y tiempo en la "Crítica de la Razón pura". ALARCÓN, Enrique.

The Syntheticity of Time: Comments on Fang's Critique of Divine Computers. PALMQUIST, Stephen R.

Tempo e linguaggio nel pensiero di Derrida e Lyotard. MAZZARA, Giuseppe.

Tempo e spazio negli scritti inediti di Guilio Cesare Ferrari. QUARANTA, M.

Tensed Facts. SWINBURNE, Richard.

The Newtonian Concept of Space and Time (in Polish). MAZIERSKI, Stanislaw.

Tiempo e Instante. ROJAS, Jorge Ramos.

Time and Value. LIEB, Irwin C.

The Time-Like Nature of Mind: On Mind Functions as Temporal Patterns of the Neural Network. FISCHER, Roland.

Ways Leading to Bergson's Notion of "Perpetual Present". KEBEDE, Messay.

TIMELESSNESS

Boethius on Eternity. LEFTOW, Brian.

TINDAL, M

Censorship and the Displacement of Irreligion. BERMAN, David.

TOCQUEVILLE, A

"Tocqueville: La culture de la démocratie, menace pour la démocratie" in Culture et Politique/Culture and Politics, MONCONDUIT, François.

Civil Religion in Tocqueville's Democracy in America. KORITANSKY, John C.

Habits of the Head: Tocqueville's America and Jazz. SCHNECK, Stephen Frederick.

The Lack of an Overarching Conception in Psychology. SARASON, Seymour B.

Tocqueville and the Problem of Natural Right. EDEN, Robert.

Was Tocqueville a Philosopher?. LAWLER, Peter A.

TOKEN

Mustn't Whatever is Referred to Exist?. PLUMER, Gilbert.

One Self: The Logic of Experience. ZUBOFF, Arnold.

Words. KAPLAN, David.

TOLERANCE

Justifying Tolerance. KING, Preston.

Three Concepts of Tolerance. LAZARI-PAWLOWSKA, Ija.

Tolerance and the Question of Rationality. ZAPASNIK, Stanislaw and PETROWICZ, Lech (trans).

TOLERATION

"Autonomy, Toleration, and the Harm Principle" in Issues in Contemporary Legal Philosophy: The Influence of H L A Hart, RAZ, Joseph.

"Comment: Autonomy, Toleration, and the Harm Principle" in Issues in Contemporary Legal Philosophy: The Influence of H L A Hart, TEN, C L.

"Comment: Autonomy, Toleration, and the Harm Principle" in Issues in Contemporary Legal Philosophy: The Influence of H L A Hart, SHELEFF, Leon.

Difference, Diversity, and the Limits of Toleration. MC CLURE, Kirstie M.

Rhetoric and the Erasmian Defence of Religious Toleration. REMER, Gary.

Thinking About 'The Other' in Religion: It is Necessary, But is it Possible?. NEUSNER, Jacob.

Tolerância e interpretação. DASCAL, Marcelo.

TOLKIEN, J

Anges et hobbits: le sens des mondes possibles. LACOSTE, Jean-Yves.

TOLSTOY

"The Place of Schopenhauer in the Philosophical Education of Leo Tolstoi" in Schopenhauer: New Essays in Honor of His 200th Birthday, WALSH, Harry.

Artist—Work—Audience: Musings on Barthes and Tolstoy. KRUKOWSKI, Lucian.

The Life of Ivan Il'ich. PATTERSON, David.

TOMINAGA, N

Emerging from Meditation: Nakamoto Tominaga. PYE, Michael (trans).

TONALITY

Tonal Harmony as a Formal System. PYLKKÖ, Pauli.

TOOL(S)

The Fundamental Constitutions of Carolina as a Tool for Lockean Scholarship. MC GUINNESS, Celia.

TOOLEY, M

The Future of Abortion. FLYNN, Tom.

On Tooley on Salmon. DOWE, Phil.

TOPIC(S)

"Cicero's Topics and Its Peripatetic Sources" in Cicero's Knowledge of the Peripatos, HUBY, Pamela M.

TOPOI

El status lógico de los topoi aristotélicos. CHICHI, Graciela.

TOPOLOGY

Complete Local Rings as Domains. STOLTENBERG-HANSEN, V and TUCKER, J V.

The Fraenkel-Mostowski Method, Revisited. BRUNNER, Norbert.

L'axiome de normalité pour les espaces totalement ordonnés. HADDAD, Labib and MORILLON, Marianne.

Topological Models of Epistemic Set Theory. GOODMAN, Nicolas D.

Transfer Theorems for π-Monads. CUTLAND, Nigel J.

Turinici's Fixed Point Theorem and the Axiom of Choice. MANKA, Roman.

Weakly Minimal Formulas: A Global Approach. NEWELSKI, L.

TORT(S)

Scientific and Legal Standards of Statistical Evidence in Toxic Tort and Discrimination Suits. CRANOR, Carl and NUTTING, Kurt.

TORTURE

The Puzzle of the Self-Torturer. QUINN, Warren S.

TORY

A Hobbist Tory: Johnson on Hume. RUSSELL, Paul.

TOTALITARIANISM

Anmerkungen zum Real Existierenden Totalitarismus und zu seinen Apologeten unter uns. MARKO, Kurt.

Dispute over Democracy at the 17th International Philosophy Congress in Prague in 1934 (in Hungarian). ZNOJ, Milan (and others).

Plato and Totalitarianism. HALL, Robert W.

The Retreat of the Political in the Modern Age: Jean-Luc Nancy on Totalitarianism and Community. INGRAM, David.

Totalitarianism, Homogeneity of Power, Depth: Towards a Socio-Political Ontology. STEINBOCK, A J.

TOTALITY

Philosophical Works. KALOYEROPOULOS, N A.

Imagination, Totality, and Transcendence. SCHALOW, F.

Mathematics of Totalities: An Alternative to Mathematics of Sets. DISHKANT, Herman.

Narration and Totality. CASCARDI, Anthony J.

To Welcome the Other: Totality and Theory in Levinas and Adorno. FLOYD, Wayne W.

Totalité, temporalité et politique: Essai de typologie. LETOCHA, Danièle.

TOULMIN, S

"Stephen Toulmin's Theory of Conceptual Evolution" in Issues in Evolutionary Epistemology, JACOBS, Struan.

"Toulmin to Rawls" in Ethics in the History of Western Philosophy, STERBA, James P.

TOV-RUACH, L

Jealousy. WREEN, Michael.

TOWER(S)

Towers in $[\omega]^\omega$ and $^\omega\omega$. DORDAL, P L.

TOXIC SUBSTANCE(S)

Multi-Party Responses to Environmental Problems: A Case of Contaminated Dairy Cattle. MORREN JR, George E B.

TOYNBEE

Heritage and Challenge: The History and Theory of History. CONKIN, Paul K.

TRADES

Business Ethics and the International Trade in Hazardous Wastes. SINGH, Jang B and LAKHAN, V C.

TRADITION

Man and Nature: The Chinese Tradition and the Future. TANG, Yi-Jie (ed).

Philosophy—A Book. VERSTER, Ulrich.

De afkeer van het individualisme bij Alisdair MacIntyre en de soevereiniteit van het individu. KAL, Victor.

Alasdair MacIntyre: The Virtue of Tradition. ALMOND, Brenda.

Donum Vitae on Homologous Interventions: Is IVF-ET a Less Acceptable Gift than "Gift"?. CARLSON, John W.

Ethnophilosophy in the Philosophical Discourse in Africa: A Critical Note. NEUGEBAUER, Christian.

The Influence of Traditional Japanese Aesthetics on the Film Theory of Sergei Eisenstein. ODIN, Steve.

MacIntyre on Traditions. ANNAS, Julia.

The Nazi Myth. LACOUE-LABARTHE, Philippe and NANCY, Jean-Luc.

Philosophy of the Present: An Attempt at a Conceptual Specification (in Czechoslovakian). KLEIN, H D.

Het projet van de Verlichting in het licht van Hegels rechtsfilosofie. COBBEN, Paul.

Socialist Realism and the Traditions of Soviet Art. ANDREEV, A L.

Some Remarks on Laudan's Theory of Scientific Rationality. VON ECKARDT, Barbara.

The Crisis of Hermeneutical Consciousness in Modern China (in Serbo-Croatian). LUJUN, Yin.

Tradition and Reason in the History of Ethics. IRWIN, T H.

Tradition, Self-Direction, and Good Life. KOLENDA, Konstantin.

The Traditionality of Statutes. KRYGIER, Martin.

Die traditionelle chinesische Kultur und das Gegenwärtige Rechtssystem Chinas. JIAN, Mi.

TRADITIONAL LOGIC

Directions in Relevant Logic. NORMAN, Jean (ed).

"The Classical Logic of Relevant Logicians" in Directions in Relevant Logic, KIELKOPF, Charles F.

"Introduction: Routes in Relevant Logic" in Directions in Relevant Logic, NORMAN, Jean and SYLVAN, Richard.

A Refutation of Jagat Pal's Defence of Aristotelian Square of Opposition. BASU, S and KASEM, A.

TRAGEDY

Il Giogo: Alle origini della ragione: Eschilo. SEVERINO, Emanuele.

"Lessings 'tragisches Mitleid' une seine hermeneutischen Implikationen" in Cultural Hermeneutics of Modern Art: Essays in Honor of Jan Aler, HAMBURGER, Käte.

"Tragedy and Atonement" in Christ, Ethics and Tragedy: Essays in Honour of Donald MacKinnon, FORD, David F.

The Claims of Tragedy: An Essay in Moral Psychology and Aesthetics Theory. SCHIER, Flint.

Freud, Racine, and the Epistemology of Tragedy. BRODY, Jules.

Les mécanismes pentadiques de la tragédie antique (in Romanian). SURDU, Alexandru.

On the Tragedy of Hermeneutical Experience. BRUNS, Gerald L.

Santayana's Idea of the Tragic. MC CORMICK, John E.

Tragédia: uma alegoria da alienação. BOLOGNESI, Mário Fernando.

Tragedy and Nonhumans. PUTMAN, Daniel.

Tragödie des Lebens und Kunst bei Georg Simmel (in Japanese). OMORI, Atsushi.

The Woman in White: On the Reception of Hegel's Antigone. DONOUGHO, Martin.

TRAINING

Maternal Thinking: Toward a Politics of Peace. RUDDICK, Sara.

Ethics Training Programs in the Fortune 500. KOHLS, John and CHAPMAN, Christi and MATHIEU, Casey.

Formal and Informal Management Training Programs for Women in Canada: Who Seems to Be Doing a Good Job?. LAVOIE, Dina.

The Impact of Information and Computer Based Training on Negotiators' Performance. GAUVIN, Stéphane and LILIEN, Gary L and CHATTERJEE, Kalyan.

Management Training for Women: International Experiences and Lessons for Canada. LAM, M Natalie.

The Special Role of Professions in Business Ethics. DAVIS, Michael.

Students, Ethics and Surveys. HOFF, J Whitman.

Training and Women: Some Thoughts from the Grassroots. JOYCE, Glenis.

TRAITS

On Traits as Dispositions: An Alleged Truism. VAN HEERDEN, Jaap and SMOLENAARS, Anton J.

TRAJANOV, T

"Friedrich Nietzsche und Theodor Trajanov" in Agora: Zu Ehren von Rudolph Berlinger, STAMMLER, Heinrich A.

TRANQUILITY

Ataraxia: Happiness as Tranquillity. STRIKER, Gisela.

TRANSCENDENCE

In Quest of the Ordinary: Lines of Skepticism and Romanticism. CAVELL, Stanley.

An Interpretation of Religion: Human Responses to the Transcendent. HICK, John.

Patterns of Transcendence: Religion, Death, and Dying. CHIDESTER, David.

Anthropologische Prolegomena zur Metaphysik. HENRICI, Peter.

Bivalenza e trascendenza. COZZO, Cesare.

La crítica aristotélica al Bien platónico. LA CROCE, Ernesto.

Finitude et transcendance. DEPRÉ, Olivier.

Forms of Life. EMMETT, Kathleen.

Hetzelfde anders: Over de veelzinnigheid van transcendentie. PEPERZAK, Adriaan.

Imagination, Totality, and Transcendence. SCHALOW, F.

L'autre et l'immanence. GUILLAMAUD, Patrice.

Lavoro, "Lavorismo", Otium. POSSENTI, Vittorio.

Merleau-Ponty, Metaphor, and Philosophy. GILL, Jerry H.

Ontologismo e trascendenza di Dio: Note a proposito di una recente teoria. COLOMBO, Giuseppe.

Religious Transcendence: Scheler's Forgotten Quest. SCHALOW, Frank.

Semantics of Proximity: Language and the Other in the Philosophy of Emmanual Levinas. ZIAREK, Krysztof.

The Shape of Time. CIORANESCU, Alexandre.

TRANSCENDENTAL

Coleridge, Shelley, and Transcendental Inquiry: Rhetoric, Argument, Metapsychology. HODGSON, John A.

The Crisis of Philosophy. MC CARTHY, Michael.

Heidegger Interprete di Kant. COLONNELLO, Pio.

Husserl und Cohn: Widerspruch, Reflexion, und Telos in Phanomenologie und Dialektik. KLOCKENBUSCH, Reinald.

Limits of Philosophy: (Limits of Reality?). VERSTER, Ulrich.

"Creativity: A New Transcendental?" in Whitehead's Metaphysics of Creativity, FETZ, Reto Luzius.

Categorías puras y categorías esquematizadas. VON BILDERLING, Beatriz.

Concettualità del fondamento: Concetto e fondamento tra riflessione e speculazione. SAMONÀ, Leonardo.

Contemporary Trends in the Interpretation of Kant's Critical Philosophy. ZAHN, M.

Hegel and Category Theory. PIPPIN, Robert B.

How Kantian Was Hegel?. PINKARD, Terry.

Husserl, Heidegger, and Transcendental Philosophy: Another Look at the Encyclopaedia Britannica Article. CROWELL, Steven Galt.

Metaphors and the Transcendental. BENCIVENGA, Ermanno.

Physiologie und Transzendentalphilosophie bei Schopenhauer. SCHMIDT, Alfred.

Platonism and Forms of Life. GASKIN, Richard M.

Ein Protokoll aus Husserls Logikseminar vom Winter 1925. REINER, Hans and SCHUHMANN, Karl.

La relazione trascendentale nella neoscolastica. VENTIMIGLIA, Giovanni.

The Role of the Unconscious in Schelling's System of Transcendental Idealism. SNOW, Dale.

Sich-Wissen als Argument: Zum Problem der Theoretizität des Selbstbewusstseins. RÖMPP, Georg.

Transcendental Thomism and the Thomistic Texts. KNASAS, John F X.

De transcendentale grondlegging van de ethiek van Karl-Otto Apel. VAN WOUDENBERG, R.

Why Did Kant Bother About 'Nothing'?. VAN KIRK, Carol A.

Zur teleologischen Grundlage der transzendentalen Deduktion der Kategorien. ROSALES, Alberto.

TRANSCENDENTAL ARGUMENT(S)

"Atemporal Necessities of Thought: or, How Not to Bury Philosophy by History" in Reading Kant, HARRISON, Ross.

TRANSCENDENTAL ARGUMENT(S)
"How Are Transcendental Arguments Possible?" in *Reading Kant*, FÖRSTER, Eckart.
"Kant's Transcendental Arguments" in *Reading Kant*, BIRD, Graham.
"Transcendental Arguments and Scepticism" in *Reading Kant*, WALKER, Ralph C S.
Kant on Euclid: Geometry in Perspective. PALMQUIST, Stephen R.
Transcendental Arguments and Conceptual Schemes: A Reconsideration of Körner's Uniqueness Argument. MALPAS, J E.

TRANSCENDENTAL DEDUCTION
"The Identity of the Subject in the Transcendental Deduction" in *Reading Kant*, HENRICH, Dieter.
The Role of Apperception in Kant's Transcendental Deduction of the Categories. CASTAÑEDA, Héctor-Neri.

TRANSCENDENTALISM
Reading Kant. SCHAPER, Eva (ed).
"The Rehabilitation of Transcendental Idealism?" in *Reading Kant*, GUYER, Paul.
"Transcendental Idealism and the Representation of Space" in *Reading Kant*, HORSTMANN, Rolf Peter.
Prospettive teologiche nella filosofia di Husserl. MELCHIORRE, V.
Transcendentalism and Its Discontents. WHITE, Stephen L.

TRANSCENDENTALS
The Evidence of the Transcendentals and the Place of Beauty in Thomas Aquinas. JORDAN, Mark D.
Kierkegaard's View of Death. WATKIN, Julia.

TRANSFERENCE
Imagining Oneself to be Another. REYNOLDS, Steven L.

TRANSIENCY
Transient Natures at the Edges of Life: A Thomistic Exploration. SMITH, Philip.

TRANSITIVITY
Causation, Transitivity, and Causal Relata. HOLT, Dale Lynn.
Conditionals, Context, and Transitivity. LOWE, E J.
Must Rational Preferences Be Transitive?. PHILIPS, Michael.
The Puzzle of the Self-Torturer. QUINN, Warren S.
Unique Nontransitive Measurement on Finite Sets. FISHBURN, Peter C.

TRANSLATION
The Semantic Foundations of Logic, Volume 1: Propositional Logics. EPSTEIN, Richard L.
Translation and the Nature of Philosophy: A New Theory of Words. BENJAMIN, Andrew.
"Around and About Babel" in *The Textual Sublime: Deconstruction and Its Differences*, GRAHAM, Joseph F.
"*The Différance* of Translation" in *The Textual Sublime: Deconstruction and Its Differences*, ALLISON, David B.
"Entertaining Arguments: Terence *Adelphoe*" in *Post-Structuralist Classics*, HENDERSON, John.
"Lations, Cor, Trans, Re, &c" in *The Textual Sublime: Deconstruction and Its Differences*, LEAVEY JR, John P.
Āyāranga 2, 16 and Sūyagada 1, 16. BOLLÉE, W.
The Brothers James and John Bernoulli on the Parallelism between Logic and Algebra. BOSWELL, Terry.
The Dilemma of "Relevance" in the Philosophy of Education. BURBULES, Nicholas C.
From a Normative Point of View. LANCE, Mark and HAWTHORNE, John.
In Defence of Untranslatability. SANKEY, Howard.
Is Translation Relevant to Educational Relevance?. SIEGEL, Harvey.
New Light on Antiphon. BARNES, Jonathan.
Quine's Indeterminacy Thesis. LARSON, David.
The Hermeneutical Ways of the Successful Translation (in Hungarian). PAEPCKE, Fritz.
Translating Nishida. MARALDO, John C.
Translation, Art, and Culture. PERRICONE, Christopher.

TRANSLATION RULE(S)
An Empirical Basis for Charity in Interpretation. HENDERSON, David K.

TRANSMISSION
A Theory of Reference Transmission and Reference Change. BERGER, Alan.

TRANSPLANTATION
Health Care Ethics: Principles and Problems. GARRETT, Thomas M (ed).
Medical Ethics (The Encyclopedia of Health: Medical Issues). FINN, Jeffrey.
Who Lives? Who Dies?: Ethical Criteria in Patient Selection. KILNER, John F.
Designated Organ Donation: Private Choice in Social Context. KLUGE,

Eike-Henner W.
The Ethical Assessment of Innovative Therapies: Liver Transplantation Using Living Donors. SINGER, Peter (and others).
On Transplanting Human Fetal Tissue: Presumptive Duties and the Task of Casuistry. MILLER, Richard B.

TRANSUBSTANTIATION
Leibniz, Transubstantiation and the Relation between Pure and Applied Philosophy. ARMOUR, Leslie.

TRANSVALUATION
"On the Advantage and Disadvantage of Nietzsche for Women" in *The Question of the Other: Essays in Contemporary Continental Philosophy*, BERGOFFEN, Debra B.

TRAVEL
The "Notes on the Government and Population of the Kingdom of Naples" and Berkeley's Probable Route to Sicily. ALFONSO, Louis.

TREATMENT(S)
Alpha and Omega: Ethics at the Frontiers of Life and Death. YOUNG, Ernlé W D.
The Morality of Refusing to Treat HIV-Positive Patients. SILVER, Mitchell.
Treating Women as Sex-Objects. SWANTON, Christine and ROBINSON, Viviane and CROSTHWAITE, Jan.
Treatment and Non-Treatment of Defective Newborns. SZAWARSKI, Zbigniew.

TREBILCOT, J
Lesbian Angels and Other Matters. ZITA, Jacquelyn.

TREE(S)
A Diamond Example of an Ordinal Graph with no Infinite Paths. BAUMGARTNER, James E and LARSON, J A.
A Faithful Embedding of Parallel Computations in Star-Finite Models. FARKAS, E J.
Generalizations of the Kruskal-Friedman Theorems. GORDEEV, L.
The Number of Pairwise Non-Elementarily-Embeddable Models. SHELAH, Saharon.
The Primal Framework I. BALDWIN, J T and SHELAH, S.
The Recursively Enumerable Degrees have Infinitely Many One-Types. AMBOS-SPIES, Klaus and SOARE, R I.
Weak Comparability of Well Orderings and Reverse Mathematics. FRIEDMAN, Harvey M and HIRST, J L.

TREND(S)
The Main Trends in Philosophy. OIZERMAN, T I.
Backing Into Vico: Recent Trends in American Philosophy. LILLA, Mark.

TRIAL(S)
The Bitterness of Job: A Philosophical Reading. WILCOX, John T.
Socrates on Trial. BRICKHOUSE, Thomas C.

TRIANOSKY, G
Ideal Moral Codes. MAC INTOSH, Duncan.

TRINITY
"Trinity and Ontology" in *Christ, Ethics and Tragedy: Essays in Honour of Donald MacKinnon*, WILLIAMS, Rowan.
Aristotelian Predication, Augustine and the Trinity. RUDEBUSCH, George.
The Doctrine of the Trinity and the Logic of Relative Identity. CAIN, James.
Logos and Trinity: Patterns of Platonist Influence on Early Christianity. DILLON, John.
Reason in Mystery. KRETZMANN, Norman.
La risposta di Leroux a Lamennais: Il concetto di Trinità come soluzione del problema sociale. FIORENTINO, Fernando.
The Trinity in Universal Revelation. VILADESAU, Richard.

TROPE(S)
Abstract Particulars. CAMPBELL, Keith.
Is Hegel's Logic a Speculative Tropology?. SILLS, Chip.
Keith Campbell and the Trope View of Predication. MORELAND, J P.

TROTSKY, L
Marxism and Morality. LUKES, Steven.
John Dewey, the "Trial" of Leon Trotsky and the Search for Historical Truth. SPITZER, Alan B.

TRUE
Some Recent Controversy Over the Possibility of Experimentally Determining Isotropy in the Speed of Light. CLIFTON, Robert K.

TRUST
The Hiddenness of God. MC KIM, Robert.
The Impact of Trust on Business, International Security and the Quality of Life. MICHALOS, Alex C.
The Sales Process and the Paradoxes of Trust. OAKES, G.

TRUTH(S)

Kierkegaard's Use of Lessing. WHISENANT, James.

Kierkegaard, a Kind of Epistemologist. PERKINS, Robert L.

Knowledge and Truth. LEPAGE, François.

Logic and Ontology: Heidegger's "Destruction" of Logic. DASTUR, Françoise.

The Nature of Ultimate Understanding. KOVACS, George.

Nature, Reality, and the Sacred: A Meditation in Science and Religion. GILKEY, Langdon.

Neue Entwicklungen im Wahrheitsbegriff. SEUREN, Pieter A M.

A New Meaning in the History of Science: From the Logical Truth Towards the Ethical Truth. ISAC, Victor.

La nocion de verdad en el ser y el tiempo (cont). VÉLEZ, Francisco Galán.

La nocion de verdad en el ser y el tiempo (cont). VÉLEZ, Francisco Galán.

A Number is the Exponent of an Operation. HAND, Michael.

Het objectieve waarheidsbegrip in Waarder. KUIPERS, Theo A F.

Over de verhouding van conceptueel relatief en referentieel realisme. RADDER, Hans.

Parménide d'Élée et la fondation de la science (in Greek). KARAYANNIS, G.

Partial Truth, Fringes, and Motion: Three Applications of a Contradictorial Logic. PENA, Lorenzo.

Philosophical Trifles (in Serbo-Croatian). LÁSZLÁO, Bulcsú.

Philosophische Wahrheit aus intuitivem Urdenken. MOLLOWITZ, Gerhard.

Philosophy after Wittgenstein and Heidegger. GUIGNON, Charles.

Pragmatism and the Revolt Against Formalism: Revising Some Doctrines of William James. WHITE, Morton.

Presupposizione e verità: Il problema critico della conoscenza filosofica. MOLINARO, Aniceto.

The Problem with the *Fragments*: Kierkegaard on Subjectivity and Truth. PIETY, Marilyn.

Religion and Truth (in Dutch). DE DIJN, H.

Religious Upbringing and Rational Autonomy. LAURA, Ronald S and LEAHY, Michael.

Representation, Truth and the Languages of the Arts. HERMERÉN, Göran.

Rorty's Pragmatism and the Pursuit of Truth. BONTEKOE, Ron.

Skepticism and Happiness. KOHL, Marvin.

The So-Called Semantic Concept of Truth. STENIUS, Erik.

The Structure and Content of Truth. DAVIDSON, Donald.

Success Semantics. WHYTE, J T.

Sul concetto di filosofia nel *Fedro* platonico. ALBERT, Karl.

A Theory of Formal Truth Arithmetically Equivalent to ID$_1$. CANTINI, Andrea.

Three Theorems of Metaphysics. THARP, Leslie.

The Truth about Neptune and the Seamlessness of Truth. SANFORD, David H.

Truth and Convention. AZZOUNI, Jody.

Truth and Freedom: A Reply to Thomas McCarthy. RORTY, Richard.

Truth and Interpersonality: An Inquiry into the Argumentative Structure of Heidegger's *Being and Time*. RÖMPP, Georg.

Truth and Meaning in the Works of Tugendhat and Davidson (in Serbo-Croation). WYLLER, Truls.

Truth and Pragmatism in Higher Education. DEVINE, Phillip E.

Truth and the Diversity of Religions. WARD, Keith.

Truth as Disclosure: Art, Language, History. GUIGNON, Charles.

Truth in Thomas Aquinas (I). WIPPEL, John F.

Truth in Thomas Aquinas, (II). WIPPEL, John F.

Truth Rules, Hoverflies, and the Kripke-Wittgenstein Paradox. MILLIKAN, Ruth Garrett.

Truth Theoretical Semantics and Ambiguity. GILLON, Brendan S.

Truth, Definite Truth, and Paradox. YABLO, Stephen.

Truth, Eliminativism and Disquotationalism. DAVID, Marian A.

Truth, Interpretation and Convention T. PRADHAN, R C.

Truth, Relativism, and Crossword Puzzles. MURPHY, Nancey.

Truth-Logics. VON WRIGHT, Georg Henrik.

Truthmongering: An Exercise. KNEZEVICH, Lily.

Truthmongering: Less is True. FINE, Arthur.

Turning Tricks with Convention T: Lessons Tarski Taught Me. RICE, Martin A.

Varieties of Pragmatism. KRAUT, Robert.

Verdad, juicio y reflexión según Tomás de Aquino. SEGURA, Carmen.

Vérisimilarité et méthodologie poppérienne. LAFLEUR, Gérald.

La verità come inganno—L'Arte di Gorgia. VITALE, Vincenzo.

Vico on Mythic Figuration as Prerequisite for Philosophic Literacy. DANIEL, Stephen H.

Who *Needs* a Theory of Informal Logic?. DOSS, Seale.

Why Is the Ontological Proof in Descartes' Fifth Meditation?. WERTZ, S K.

Wittgenstein and Sense-Independence of Truth. PUHL, Klaus.

TRUTHFULNESS

A Note on 'Languages and Language'. HAWTHORNE, John.

TUGENDHAT, E

Innere Autonomie oder Zurechnungsfähigkeit?. SCHÖNRICH, Gerhard.

Truth and Meaning in the Works of Tugendhat and Davidson (in Serbo-Croation). WYLLER, Truls.

TUOMELA, R

Eliminativism and Methodological Individualism. KINCAID, Harold.

TURING MACHINES

Chauvinism and Science: Another Reply to Shanon. HENLEY, Tracy B.

Radical Interpretation and the Gunderson Game. WARD, Andrew.

Turing L-Machines and Recursive Computability for L-Maps. GERLA, Giangiacomo.

TVERSKY, A

Are Theories of Rationality Empirically Testable?. SMOKLER, Howard.

TWENTIETH

After the Future: Postmodern Times and Places. SHAPIRO, Gary (ed).

Against Deconstruction. ELLIS, John M.

Beauty and Holiness: The Dialogue between Aesthetics and Religion. MARTIN JR, James Alfred.

Bergson. LACEY, A R.

Beyond the Atom: The Philosophical Thought of Wolfgang Pauli. LAURIKAINEN, K V.

Biblical Narrative in the Philosophy of Paul Ricoeur: A Study in Hermeneutics and Theology. VANHOOZER, Kevin J.

The Communicative Body: Studies in Communicative Philosophy, Politics, and Sociology. O'NEILL, John.

The Darkness and the Light: A Philosopher Reflects Upon His Career—Charles Hartshorne. HARTSHORNE, Charles.

Derrida and "Différance". WOOD, David.

Derrida and Deconstruction. SILVERMAN, Hugh J (ed).

Dietro il paesaggio: Saggio su Simmel. BOELLA, Laura.

Edith Stein: Filosofia E Senso Dell'Essere. LAMACCHIA, Ada.

Existentially Speaking: Essays on the Philosophy of Literature. WILSON, Colin.

Heidegger and Modernity. PHILIP, Franklin (trans).

Heidegger and Nazism. MARGOLIS, Joseph (ed).

Husserl und Cohn: Widerspruch, Reflexion, und Telos in Phanomenologie und Dialektik. KLOCKENBUSCH, Reinald.

J L Austin. WARNOCK, G J.

Jean Baudrillard: From Marxism to Postmodernism. KELLNER, Douglas.

Nietzsche in Italy. HARRISON, Thomas (ed).

Ortega y Gasset: Aurore de la Raison Historique. LORVELLEC, Y (trans).

Philosophical Essays in Pragmatic Naturalism. KURTZ, Paul.

Questions on Wittgenstein. HALLER, Rudolf.

The Rehabilitation of Whitehead: An Analytic and Historical Assessment of Process Philosophy. LUCAS JR, George R.

Skepticism and Modern Enmity: Before and After Eliot. PERL, Jeffrey M.

Speaking from the Depths. FRANKLIN, Stephen T.

Stanley Cavell and Literary Skepticism. FISCHER, Michael.

Wittgenstein in Focus—Im Brennpunkt: Wittgenstein. MC GUINNESS, Brian (ed).

"Heideggers Kehren" in Agora: Zu Ehren von Rudolph Berlinger, BRÖCKER, Walter.

"Wittgenstein's Pre-Tractatus Manuscripts" in Wittgenstein in Focus—Im Brennpunkt: Wittgenstein, MC GUINNESS, Brian.

"Condurre tutte le metafore ad absurdum": Riflessioni filosofiche attorno alla poetica di Celan. SAMONÀ, Leonardo.

Adorno, Heidegger and Postmodernity. BRUNKHORST, H.

African Philosophy: Paulin J Hountondji—His Dilemma and Contributions. OTAKPOR, Nkeonye.

Aleksei Fedorovich Losev. TAKHO-GODI, A.

Avoiding the Subject: A Foucaultian Itinerary. SEIGEL, Jerrold.

Blondel on the Origin of Philosophy. LONG, Fiachra.

Bruce Wilshire and the Dilemma of Nontheistic Existentialism. SMITH, Quentin.

Change and Crisis of Values in Modern Societies (in Hungarian). LENDVAI, Ferenc L.

Changes in the View on Man in Our Age (in Hungarian). NYÍRI, Tamás.

A Commentary on Derrida's Reading of Hegel in Glas. CRITCHLEY, Simon.

Consciousness and History. MOULAKIS, Athanasios.

A Contribution to the Gadamer-Lonergan Discussion. BAUR, Michael.

A Conversation with Hans-Georg Gadamer. BAUR, Michael.

Las cuitas de Zarathustra: Algunas publicaciones recientes sobre Friedrich Nietzsche. KERKHOFF, Manfred.

Culture or Nature: The Functions of the Term 'Body' in the Work in the Work of Michel Foucault. MC WHORTER, Ladelle.

Desire: Direct and Imitative. COHN, Robert Greer.

TYPE(S)

Relevant Predication: Grammatical Characterizations. KREMER, Philip.
Weakly Minimal Formulas: A Global Approach. NEWELSKI, L.
Words. KAPLAN, David.

TYPOLOGY

On the Typology of Modes of Thought. LI, Cheng.

TYRANNY

Contre nous de la tyrannie: Des relations idéologiques entre Lumières et Révolution. BOULAD-AYOUB, Josiane.
Traditions, Tyranny, and Utopias: Essays in the Politics of Awareness. NANDY, Ashis.
Aristotle and the Classical Greek Concept of Despotism. RICHTER, Melvin.
Hobbes and Xenophon's Tyrannicus. BERTMAN, Martin A.

UGLINESS

Das Hässliche und die "Kritik der ästhetischen Urteilskraft". STRUB, Christian.

ULTIMATE

The Nature of Ultimate Understanding. KOVACS, George.

ULTIMATE REALITY

Baruch or Benedict: On Some Jewish Aspects of Spinoza's Philosophy. LEVY, Ze'ev.
An Interpretation of Religion: Human Responses to the Transcendent. HICK, John.
Nous, the Concept of Ultimate Reality and Meaning in Anaxagoras. SILVESTRE, Maria Luisa.
A Reflection on Lonergan's Notion of the Pure Desire to Know. MORELLI, Elizabeth A.

ULTRAFILTERS

Cofinalities of Countable Ultraproducts: The Existence Theorem. CANJAR, R Michael.
Some Principles Related to Chang's Conjecture. DONDER, Hans-Dieter and LEVINSKI, J P.

ULTRAPRODUCTS

Cofinalities of Countable Ultraproducts: The Existence Theorem. CANJAR, R Michael.
Nonstandard Methods. RICHTER, M M.

UNAMUNO

San Agustín y Unamuno. ZABALLOS, Juan Carlos.

UNANIMITY

Eguaglianza interesse unanimità: La politica di Rousseau. BURGIO, Alberto.
Pareto Unanimity and Consensus. LEVI, Isaac.

UNCERTAINTY

Action, Uncertainty, and Divine Impotence. KAPITAN, Tomis.
Decision Problems Under Uncertainty Based on Entropy Functionals. GOTTINGER, Hans W.
Uncertainty in Moral Theory: An Epistemic Defense of Rule-Utilitarian Liberties. BALL, Stephen W.
Under Stochastic Dominance Choquet-Expected Utility and Anticipated Utility Are Identical. WAKKER, Peter.

UNCONSCIOUS

The Dual Brain, Religion, and the Unconscious. LIDDON, Sim C.
Brentano on 'Unconscious Consciousness'. KRANTZ, Susan.
Contemplating Failure: The Importance of Unconscious Omission. SMITH, Patricia G.
Husserl and Freud: Time, Memory and the Unconscious. MISHARA, Aaron L.
Intersubjectivity and the Monadic Core of the Psyche: Habermas and Castoriadis on the Unconscious. WHITEBOOK, Joel.
On the Inter-relatedness of Theory and Measurement in the Study of Unconscious Processes. REINGOLD, Eyal M and MERIKLE, Philip M.
The Role of the Unconscious in Schelling's System of Transcendental Idealism. SNOW, Dale.

UNCONSCIOUSNESS

Consciousness, Unconsciousness, and Intentionality. SEARLE, John R.

UNDECIDABILITY

Decision Problem for Relatively Free Brouwerian Semilattices. IDZIAK, Pawl M.
On Halldén-Completeness of Intermediate and Modal Logics. CHAGROV, A V and ZAKHARYASHCHEV, M V.
Some Highly Undecidable Lattices. MAGIDOR, M and ROSENTHAL, J W and RUBIN, M and SROUR, G.
A Uniform Method for Proving Lower Bounds on the Computational Complexity of Logical Theories. COMPTON, Kevin J and HENSON, C Ward.

UNDERDETERMINATION

Family Resemblances and the Problem of the Under-Determination of Extension. BELLAIMEY, James E.
Realism and the Underdetermination of Theory. CLENDINNEN, F John.

UNDERGROUND

New Notes from Underground. ELLERMAN, Carl Paul.
Notes on the Underground. CLARK, Stephen R L.

UNDERSTANDING

Kants Theorie des Verstandes. SEEBOHM, Thomas M (ed).
"Musical Understanding and Musical Culture" in What is Music?, SCRUTON, Roger.
Art as Understanding. PERKINS, D N.
Beyond the Erklären-Verstehen Dichotomy. VAN NIEKERK, A A.
Dasein's Disclosedness. HAUGELAND, John.
Davidson's Semantic and Computational Understanding of Language (in Serbo-Croatian). BOJADZIEV, Damjan.
From Coffee to Carmelites. PHILLIPS, D Z.
G H von Wright on Explanation and Understanding: An Appraisal. MARTIN, Rex.
Human Understanding. ZEMACH, Eddy M.
Is Translation Possible?. HARRIS, R Thomas.
Kant's Analogies and the Structure of Objective Time. HUGHES, R I G.
Manifesting Realism. BLACKBURN, Simon.
Music and Understanding: The Concept of Understanding Applied to Listening to Music. MUNRO, Joan.
The Nature of Ultimate Understanding. KOVACS, George.
On Meaning and Understanding. PAVILIONIS, Rolandas.
The Simplicity of the Tractatus. ANSCOMBE, Elizabeth.
Verständnis für Unvernünftige. BITTNER, Rüdiger.
What Is It To Understand a Directive Speech Act?. DORSCHEL, Andreas.

UNGER, R

Beyond Capitalism and Communism: Roberto Unger's Superliberal Political Theory. BELLIOTTI, Raymond.

UNIFICATION

"Explanatory Unification and the Causal Structure of the World" in Scientific Explanation (Minnesota Studies in the Philosophy of Science, Volume XIII), KITCHER, Philip.
Dynamism of Meaningful Unification of Work and Coherence of Text (in Czechoslovakian). CERVENKA, Miroslav.
The Logic of Unification in Grammar. KASPER, Robert T and ROUNDS, William C.

UNIFORMITY

Gibbs' Paradox and Non-Uniform Convergence. DENBIGH, K G and REDHEAD, M L G.
Miracles and the Uniformity of Nature. ROOT, Michael.
Qualitative Identity and Uniformity. SCHLESINGER, George N.

UNION(S)

Union with God: A Theory. OAKES, Robert.

UNIQUENESS

Transcendental Arguments and Conceptual Schemes: A Reconsideration of Körner's Uniqueness Argument. MALPAS, J E.
Unique Nontransitive Measurement on Finite Sets. FISHBURN, Peter C.
The Uniqueness of the Natural Numbers. PARSONS, Charles.
Uniqueness, Definability and Interpolation. DOSEN, Kosta and SCHROEDER-HEISTER, Peter.
Uniqueness. KADMON, Nirit.

UNIT(S)

Are Genes Units of Inheritance?. FOGLE, Thomas.

UNITED NATIONS

Nuclearism and International Law. STEGENGA, James A.

UNITED STATES

see also American
Bribery and the United States Foreign Corrupt Practices Act. ENGLISH, Parker.
Philosophy in the United States (A Dialogue of Laurent Stern and Márta Fehér) (in Hungarian). STERN, Laurent and FEHÉR, Márta.
Préoccupations éthiques aux Etats-Unis: la "Business Ethics". GRUSON, Pascale.

UNITY

Hegel, Heraclitus, and Marx's Dialectic. WILLIAMS, Howard.
"On the Unity of Man and Heaven" in Man and Nature: The Chinese Tradition and the Future, YI-JIE, Tang.
"Die Problematik des Einen und Vielen in der geschichtlichen Entwicklung des buddhistischen Denkens" in Agora: Zu Ehren von Rudolph Berlinger

UNITY

VERDU, Alfonso.

Agustín y la unidad. CLARK, Mary T and ANOZ, José (trans).

Bemerkungen zur methodologischen Einheit der Wissenschaften. BÜHLER, Axel.

Concepts, Judgments, and Unity in Kant's Metaphysical Deduction of the Relational Categories. NUSSBAUM, Charles.

Hegel and the Unity of Science Program. ROCKMORE, Tom.

L'identità del diverso. MATHIEU, Vittorio.

Kategoriai and the Unity of Being. MALPAS, J E.

Parmenides 142b5-144e7: The "Unity is Many" Arguments. CURD, Patricia Kenig.

Reply to Kenneth K Inada. PILGRIM, Richard.

Response to Richard Pilgrim's Review of *The Logic of Unity*, by Hosaku Matsuo and Translated by Kenneth K Inada. INADA, Kenneth K.

Thomas and the Universe. JAKI, Stanley L.

Über eine unzulängliche Auffassung der methodologischen Einheit der Wissenschaft und unbefriedigende Verteidigung. JAKOWLJEWITSCH, Dragan.

Über einen neuen Versuch der Argumentation für die methodologische Einheit der Wissenschaften. JAKOWLJEWITSCH, Dragan.

Unity, Coincidence, and Conflict in the Virtues. BECKER, Lawrence C.

Validation by Touch in Kandinsky's Early Abstract Art. OLIN, Margaret.

UNIVERSAL GRAMMAR

Remarks on the Concept of "Universal Grammar". CORNILESCU, Alexandra.

UNIVERSAL(S)

Abstract Particulars. CAMPBELL, Keith.

Aristotle's Concept of the Universal. BRAKAS, George.

A Combinatorial Theory of Possibility. ARMSTRONG, D M.

Der Begriff als "nicht wirklich existierende" Einheit vieler "wirklich existerender" Individuen. KAUFMANN, Matthias.

Un desliz en la *Summa Logicae* de Guillermo de Ockham?. ROTELLA, Oscar.

Dharmakirti on Criteria of Knowledge. CHINCHORE, Mangala R.

The Formal Distinction. SWINDLER, J K.

Imaginative Universals and Historical Falsification: A Rejoinder to Professor Verene. MAC INTYRE, Alasdair.

Keith Campbell and the Trope View of Predication. MORELAND, J P.

Nom propre et individuation chez Peirce. THIBAUD, P.

The Notion of the Transcultural in Bernard Lonergan's Theology. LAMB, Matthew.

The Trinity in Universal Revelation. VILADESAU, Richard.

Wang Yang-ming and the Bamboos (in Serbo-Croatian). LAI, Whalen.

UNIVERSALISM

Christianity and Marxism: Confrontation, Dialogue, Universalism. KUCZYNSKI, Janusz.

The Meaning of Universalism: Comments on Kuczynski and McGovern. PARSONS, Howard L.

Philosophical Premises of Levinas' Conception of Judaism. LORENC, Iwona and PETROWICZ, Lech (trans).

Universalism as a Metaphilosophy of the New Peace Movement. KUCZYNSKI, Janusz and PETROWICZ, Lech (trans) and RODZINSKA, Aleksandra (trans).

Universalism Versus Love with Distinctions: An Ancient Debate Revived. WONG, David B.

Universalism, Hell, and the Fate of the Ignorant. DAVIS, Stephen T.

Universalism: A New Way of Thinking. KUCZYNSKI, Janusz and PETROWICZ, Lech (trans) and GOLEBIOWSKI, Marek (trans).

Universalisms: Procedural, Contextualist and Prudential. FERRARA, Alessandro.

UNIVERSALITY

Hetzelfde anders: Over de veelzinnigheid van transcendentie. PEPERZAK, Adriaan.

Music and Understanding: The Concept of Understanding Applied to Listening to Music. MUNRO, Joan.

Universality and Difference: O'Keeffe and McClintock. MACCOLL, San.

UNIVERSALIZABILITY

The Impracticality of Impartiality. FRIEDMAN, Marilyn.

Una nota sobre universalizabilidad. SPECTOR, Horacio.

UNIVERSALIZATION

Descriptive Pronouns and Donkey Anaphora. NEALE, Stephen.

El principio de universalización y la razón práctica (1a parte). GUARIGLIA, Osvaldo.

El principio de universalización y la razón práctica (2a parte). GUARIGLIA, Osvaldo.

Universal Prescriptivism and Practical Skepticism. MC GRAY, James W.

Zur Methodologie und Logik von "Goldene'Regel"-Argumenten: Eine Gegenposition zu Hoches Hare-Exhaustion. KESE, Ralf.

UNIVERSE

Reading the Mind of God: In Search of the Principle of Universality. TREFIL, James.

Universes. LESLIE, John.

Body-Vessel-Matrix: Co-creative Images of Synergetic Universe. CARTER, Nancy Corson.

Il luogo dell'ultima stera nei commenti tardo-antichi e medievali a "Physica" IV:5. TRIFOGLI, Cecilia.

Metaphysics. WEININGER, Otto and BURNS, S A M (trans).

A Modern Look at the Origin of the Universe. ODENWALD, Sten F.

A Natural Explanation of the Existence and Laws of Our Universe. SMITH, Quentin.

Sets as Singularities in the Intensional Universe. DAYNES, Keith.

Thomas and the Universe. JAKI, Stanley L.

UNIVERSITY(-TIES)

The Voice of Liberal Learning: Michael Oakeshott on Education. FULLER, Timothy (ed).

The Architecture of Science and the Idea of a University. FORGAN, Sophie.

Truth and Pragmatism in Higher Education. DEVINE, Phillip E.

UNIVOCITY

Univocity of the Concept of Being in the Fourteenth Century III: An Early Scotist. BROWN, Stephen F and DUMONT, Stephen D.

UNSOLVABILITY

Recursive Solvability of Problems with Matrices. KROM, Melven and KROM, Myren.

URBAN LIFE

Public Space in a Private Time. ACCONCI, Vito.

USE

Surrogate Motherhood: The Ethics of Using Human Beings. SHANNON, Thomas A.

Eguaglianza formale ed eguaglianza sostanziale dopo la rivoluzione francese. MATHIEU, Vittorio.

On the Nature of Religion. MYERS, R Thomas.

UTILITARIANISM

see also Consequentialism

Dilemmas: A Christian Approach to Moral Decision Making. HIGGINSON, Richard.

Ethical Theory: Classical and Contemporary Readings. POJMAN, Louis P (ed).

The Inner Citadel: Essays on Individual Autonomy. CHRISTMAN, John (ed).

John Stuart Mill. SKORUPSKI, John.

The Moral Foundation of Rights. SUMNER, L W.

The Political Philosophy of the British Idealists: Selected Studies. NICHOLSON, Peter P.

Self and Others: A Study of Ethical Egoism. ÖSTERBERG, Jan.

"Mill" in *Ethics in the History of Western Philosophy,* LACHS, John.

'Utilitarianism Incorporating Justice'—A Decentralised Model of Ethical Decision Making. TRAPP, Rainer W.

'Utility' and the 'Utility Principle': Hume, Smith, Bentham, Mill. LONG, Douglas G.

Actual Versus Probable Utilitarianism. STRASSER, Mark.

Étienne Dumont: Genevan Apostle of Utility. BLAMIRES, Cyprian.

A J Ayer: An Appreciation. SPRIGGE, T L S.

J S Mill y la prueba del principio de utilidad: Una defensa de *Utilitarianism* IV, (3). RABOSSI, Eduardo.

Kantian Ethics Today. FRANKENA, William K.

Malthus and Utilitarianism with Special Reference to the *Essay on Population.* HOLLANDER, Samuel.

Mill's and Other Liberalisms. GRAY, John.

Mo-Tzu: Language Utilitarianism. HANSEN, Chad.

An Ordinal Modification of Classical Utilitarianism. MENDOLA, Joseph.

Rights, Indirect Utilitarianism, and Contractarianism. HAMLIN, Alan P.

Rights, Justice, and Duties to Provide Assistance: A Critique of Regan's Theory of Rights. JAMIESON, Dale.

Slippery Bentham: Some Neglected Cracks in the Foundation of Utilitarianism. PITKIN, Hanna Fenichel.

The Social Conscience of Business. REILLY, Bernard J and KYJ, Myroslaw J.

Utilitarian Ethics and Democratic Government. RILEY, Jonathan.

Utilitarianism and Distributive Justice: The Civil Law and the Foundations of Bentham's Economic Thought. KELLY, P J.

Utilitarianism and Preference Change. BARRY, Brian.

VAN FRAASSEN, B
Observation in Constructive Empiricism: Arbitrary or Incoherent?. CORDERO, Alberto.
Realism and the Underdetermination of Theory. CLENDINNEN, F John.
Rondom realisme. RADDER, Hans.

VAN INWAGEN, P
Determinism, Blameworthiness and Deprivation. KLEIN, Martha.
How to Mind One's Ethics: A Reply to Van Inwagen. WHITE, V Alan.
Van Inwagen on the 'Obviousness' of Libertarian Moral Responsibility. SMILANSKY, Saul.

VAN SCHURMAN, A
Anna Maria van Schurman's verhouding tot de wetenschap. ROOTHAAN, Angela and VAN ECK, Caroline.

VARIABLE(S)
Quantum Probability—Quantum Logic. PITOWSKY, Itamar.
Alpha-Conversion, Conditions on Variables and Categorical Logic. CURIEN, Pierre-Louis.
Combinators and Categorial Grammar. SIMONS, Peter.
Parametrization Over Inductive Relations of a Bounded Number of Variables. MC COLM, Gregory L.

VARIETY
Relatively Point Regular Quasivarieties. CZELAKOWSKI, Janusz.
Variations upon Variation, or Picasso Back to Bach. GOODMAN, Nelson.

VASILYEV, N
The Fate of One Forgotten Idea: N A Vasiliev and His Imaginary Logic. BAZHANOV, Valentine A.
Multiply Modal Extensions of Da Costa's C_n, Logical Relativism, and the Imaginary. LOKHORST, Gert-Jan C.

VATICAN
Moral Traditions, Ethical Language, and Reproductive Technologies. CAHILL, Lisa Sowle.

VATICAN II
The Munus of Transmitting Human Life: A New Approach to Humanae Vitae. SMITH, Janet E.

VEATCH, R
Who Lives? Who Dies?: Ethical Criteria in Patient Selection. KILNER, John F.

VECTOR(S)
Margins of Reality: The Role of Consciousness in the Physical World. JAHN, Robert G.

VEDAS
Sacrifice: Core of Vedic Religion and Christianity. MALIECKAL, Louis.

VEGETARIANISM
Two Vegetarian Puns at Republic 372. DOMBROWSKI, Daniel A.

VELINI, A
La contribution d'Anton Velini à l'enseignement philosophique du siècle passée (in Romanian). OPREA, Ioan.

VELLEMAN, D
Colouring in the World. BIGELOW, John and COLLINS, John and PARGETTER, Robert.

VENEZUELAN
Corruption and Business in Present Day Venezuela. PERDOMO, Rogelio Perez.

VENINI, F
Francesco Venini: Un philosophe a Parma (1764-1772). MAMIANI, Maurizio.

VERBAL DISPUTE(S)
"Organization and Articulation of Verbal Exchanges" in From Metaphysics to Rhetoric, OLERON, Pierre.

VERBALIZATION
"Saying and Knowing" in From Metaphysics to Rhetoric, SCHLANGER, Judith.

VERBURG, M
Verburg over Dooyeweerd. STELLINGWERFF, J.

VERIFICATION
"Was heisst vollständige Verifikation?" in Wittgenstein in Focus—Im Brennpunkt: Wittgenstein, BRANDL, Johannes.
The Asymmetry of Verification and Falsification. WREEN, Michael.
G H von Wright on Explanation and Understanding: An Appraisal. MARTIN, Rex.
Is "Some-Other-Time" Sometimes Better Than "Sometime" for Proving Partial Correctness of Programs?. SAIN, Ildikó.
The Verification Principle: Another Puncture—Another Patch. WRIGHT, Crispin.

VERIFICATIONISM
The World We Found: The Limits of Ontological Talk. SACKS, Mark.
"Verificationism" in Cause, Mind, and Reality: Essays Honoring C B Martin, SMART, J J C.
Realismus heute. INEICHEN, Hans.

VERISIMILITUDE
Decision-Theoretic Epistemology. WEINTRAUB, Ruth.
On Newton-Smith's Concept of Verisimilitude. OLCZYK, Slawoj.
On the Logical Structure of Verisimilitude. GERLA, Giangiacomo and GUCCIONE, Salvatore.

VICE(S)
Paul and the Popular Philosophers. MALHERBE, Abraham J.
Fiat Voluntas Tua! Vício e Pecado na ética de Abelardo. ESTEVÁO, J C.
Ways of Wrong-Doing, the Vices, and Cruelty. MC KINNON, Christine.

VICO
The Ethics of Geometry: A Genealogy of Modernity. LACHTERMAN, David R.
Rhetorica II—Spiegelungen des Geistes: Sprachfiguren bei Vico und L Strauss. MAINBERGER, Gonsalv K.
Vico Revisited: Orthodoxy, Naturalism and Science in the Scienca Nuova. BEDANI, Gino.
"The Public Grounds of Truth": The Critical Theory of G B Vico. MALI, Joseph.
Backing Into Vico: Recent Trends in American Philosophy. LILLA, Mark.
Eliade's Vichianism: The Regeneration of Time and the Terror of History. VERENE, Donald Phillip.
Emilio Betti's Debt to Vico. NOAKES, Susan.
Francisco Sanchez's Theory of Cognition and Vico's verum/factum. FAUR, José.
From Wit to Narration: Vico's Theory of Metaphor in Its Rhetorical Context. SCHAEFFER, John D.
Hintikka and Vico: An Update on Contemporary Logic. STEINKE, Horst.
History as Metascience: A Vichian Cue to the Understanding of the Nature and Development of Sciences. RIVERSO, Emanuele.
The Identity of American Neo-Pragmatism; or, Why Vico Now?. MEGILL, Allan.
Imaginative Universals and Historical Falsification: A Rejoinder to Professor Verene. MAC INTYRE, Alasdair.
Imaginative Universals and Narrative Truth. VERENE, Donald Phillip.
J F Lyotard's The Postmodern Condition and G B Vico's De nostri temporis studiorum ratione. KIERNAN, Suzanne.
Language and the Origin of the Human Imagination: A Vichian Perspective. DANESI, Marcel.
Leading Out Into the World: Vico's New Education. ENGELL, James.
A Note on Thomas Hayne and His Relation to Leibniz and Vico. PERCIVAL, W Keith.
Political Thought and Rhetoric in Vico. JACOBITTI, Edmund E.
The Principles of New Science of G B Vico and the Theory of Historical Interpretation. NOAKES, Susan (trans) and BETTI, Emilio and PINTON, Giorgio (trans).
Reading Horkheimer Reading Vico: An Introduction. DALLMAYR, Fred.
Reading Vico Three Times. SUMBERG, Theodore A.
Rhetoric and Philosophy in Vichian Inquiry. STRUEVER, Nancy S.
Sensus Communis in Vico and Gadamer. SCHAEFFER, John D.
The Splitting of the Logos: Some Remarks on Vico and Rabbinic Tradition. FAUR, José.
Toward a History of Recent Vico Scholarship in English, Part II: 1969-1973. TAGLIACOZZO, Giorgio.
Toward a History of Recent Vico Scholarship in English, Part IV: The Vico/Venezia Conference 1978, and Its Aftermath. TAGLIACOZZO, Giorgio.
Toward a History of Recent Vico Scholarship in English, Part V: After Vico/Venezia (1978-1987) and Appendix. TAGLIACOZZO, Giorgio.
Toward a History of Recent Vico Scholarship in English, Part III: 1974-1977. TAGLIACOZZO, Giorgio.
The Vichian Elements in Susanne Langer's Thought. BLACK, David W.
A Vichian Footnote to Nietzsche's View on the Cognitive Primacy of Metaphor: An Addendum to Schrift. DANESI, Marcel.
Vico and Bakhtin: A Prolegomenon to Any Future Comparison. JUNG, Hwa Yol.
Vico and Frye: A Note. BAHTI, Timothy.
Vico and MacIntyre. COERS, Kathy Frashure.
Vico and Mythology. DALLMAYR, Fred (trans) and HORKHEIMER, Max.

VLASTOS, G
The Subject of Love. NYE, Andrea.

VLEESCHAUWER, H
"El aire es elástico". CAIMI, Mario P M.

VOCABULARY(-RIES)
La expresión de la falsedad y del error en el vocabulario agustiniano de la mentira. SÁNCHEZ MANZANO, M A.

VOCATION(S)
The Fabric of This World: Inquiries into Calling, Career Choice, and the Design of Human Work. HARDY, Lee.

VOCATIONAL EDUCATION
Philosophy as (Vocational) Education. GARRISON, James W.

VOEGELIN, E
Autobiographical Reflections—Eric Voegelin. SANDOZ, Ellis (ed).
Voegelin on the Idea of Race: An Analysis of Modern European Racism. HEILKE, Thomas W.
Consciousness and History. MOULAKIS, Athanasios.

VOID
Aristotle's Horror Vacui. THORP, John.
Wordsworth and the Zen Void. RUDY, John G.

VOLITION(S)
Descartes' Doctrine of Volitional Infinity. CRESS, Donald A.
Does Kierkegaard Think Beliefs Can Be Directly Willed?. EVANS, C Stephen.
The Trapped Infinity: Cartesian Volition as Conceptual Nightmare. REED, Edward S.

VOLTAIRE
Natura e storia nel deismo di Diderot e Voltaire. NICOLOSI, Salvatore.

VOLUNTARINESS
The Trapped Infinity: Cartesian Volition as Conceptual Nightmare. REED, Edward S.
Why is Belief Involuntary?. BENNETT, Jonathan.

VOLUNTARISM
La giustizia nella dottrina della volontà di Giovanni Duns Scoto. PIZZO, Giovanni.

VOLUNTARY ACTION(S)
On Action. GINET, Carl.
Aristotle's Compatibilism in the Nicomachean Ethics. EVERSON, Stephen.
Is Free Will Incompatible with Something or Other?. GRIFFITHS, A Phillips.
Reconsidering the Relationship among Voluntary Acts, Strict Liability, and Negligence in Criminal Law. ALEXANDER, Larry.

VON HERRMANN, F
The Co-Enactment of Heidegger's Being and Time: F W von Herrmann's Elucidation of its "Introduction". LOSCERBO, John.

VON NEUMANN, J
Correlated Equilibria and the Dynamics of Rational Deliberation. SKYRMS, Brian.
Mediciones ideales en la mecánica cuántica. MARTÍNEZ, Sergio.

VON SUTTON, T
La noción de ser en Tomás de Sutton. ECHAURI, Raúl.

VON WRIGHT, G
Expliquer et comprendre: La théorie de l'action de G H von Wright. NEUBERG, Marc.
G H von Wright on Explanation and Understanding: An Appraisal. MARTIN, Rex.
Negación intuicionista y divergencia lógica. SCHUSTER, Federico L.

VOTING
"The Democratic Order and Public Choice" in Politics and Process, ARANSON, Peter H.

VULNERABILITY
The Death of the Animal: Ontological Vulnerability. SHAPIRO, Kenneth Joel.
Foreknowledge and the Vulnerability of God. LUCAS, J R.
The Vulnerability of Action. ELLIS, Robert.

WAGNER
Nietzsche Contra Nietzsche: Creativity and the Anti-Romantic. DEL CARO, Adrian.
El arte ante las exigencias de la moral. PÖLTNER, Günther.

WAIM, G
Notion and Object: Aspects of Late Medieval Epistemology. BROADIE, Alexander.

WAISMANN, F
Metafisica Todavia? (cont). SANABRIA, José Rubén.

WAKS, L
Democracy and Technology. MARGONIS, Frank.

WALKER, A
Political Obligation and Gratitude. KLOSKO, George.

WALKER, M
Beyond Revolt: A Horizon for Feminist Ethics. LINDGREN, Ralph.

WALRAS, L
More Heat than Light: Economics as Social Physics, Physics as Nature's Economics. MIROWSKI, Philip.

WALSH, W
"Reply to Walsh's "Hegel on Morality"" in Dialectic and Contemporary Science, HARRIS, Errol E.

WALZER, M
Arms and Judgment: Law, Morality, and the Conduct of War in the 20th Century. COHEN, Sheldon M.
Communitarian Politics, the Supreme Court, and Privacy: The Continuing Need for Liberal Boundaries. LUND, William R.
Social Interpretation and Political Theory: Walzer and His Critics. WARNKE, Georgia.
Social Justice. WILLIAMS, Bernard.

WANG FU-CHIH
Man and Nature in the Philosophical Thought of Wang-Fu-Chih. BLACK, Alison Harley.

WANG FUZHI
On the Aesthetic Significance of Wang Fuzhi's Theory of the Unity of Poetry and Music, with Criticisms of Certain Biases. JIEMO, Zhang.

WANG YANG-MING
Are Knowledge and Action Really One Thing—A Study of Wang Yang-ming's Doctrine of Mind. FRISINA, Warren G.
Wang Yang-ming and the Bamboos (in Serbo-Croatian). LAI, Whalen.

WANG YUYANG
Wang Yuyang's Natural Thought on Art. TIAOGONG, Wu.

WANT(S)
Scarcity and the Limits of Want: Comments on Sassower and Bender. LEVINE, David.

WAR CRIME(S)
A Moral Military. AXINN, Sidney.
In Memoriam: Medicine's Confrontation with Evil. SEIDELMAN, William E.

WAR(S)
see also Nuclear War
Arms and Judgment: Law, Morality, and the Conduct of War in the 20th Century. COHEN, Sheldon M.
The Causes of Quarrel: Essays on Peace, War, and Thomas Hobbes. CAWS, Peter (ed)
The Ethics of War and Peace. LACKEY, Douglas P.
From Warism to Pacifism: A Moral Continuum. CADY, Duane L.
Hobbes: War Among Nations. AIRAKSINEN, Timo (ed).
Maternal Thinking: Toward a Politics of Peace. RUDDICK, Sara.
Moral Issues in Military Decision Making. HARTLE, Anthony E.
Moral Reasoning and Statecraft: Essays Presented to Kenneth W Thompson. DAVIS, Reed M (ed).
On War and Morality. HOLMES, Robert L.
"The Dilemmas of Extended Nuclear Deterrence" in Moral Reasoning and Statecraft: Essays Presented to Kenneth W Thompson, MATTOX, Gale A.
"Does Star Wars Depend on Contradiction and Deception?" in Inquiries into Values: The Inaugural Session of the International Society for Value Inquiry, ALLEN, Paul.
"Having It Both Ways: The Gradual Wrong in American Strategy" in Nuclear Deterrence and Moral Restraint, SHUE, Henry.
"On the Causes of Quarrel: Postures of War and Possibilities of Peace" in The Causes of Quarrel: Essays on Peace, War, and Thomas Hobbes, CAWS, Peter.
"Rendering Unto Caesar: Religion and Nationalism" in The Wisdom of Faith: Essays in Honor of Dr Sebastian Alexander Matczak, HARRIS, Walter S.
"War, Competition, and Religion" in The Causes of Quarrel: Essays on Peace, War, and Thomas Hobbes, GRISWOLD JR, Charles L.
"The Whiteness of the Whale" in Hobbes: War Among Nations, AIRAKSINEN, Timo.
"Winston Churchill and War in the Twentieth Century" in Moral Reasoning and Statecraft: Essays Presented to Kenneth W Thompson, STRONG,

WHITEHEAD
Susan.
On the Continuing Relevance of Whitehead. CODE, Murray.
The Philosophical Writings of Victor A Lowe (1907-1988). MC HENRY, Leemon B.
Process Theology: Guardian of the Oppressor or Goad to the Oppressed—An Interim Assessment. JONES, William R.
Some Applications of *Process and Reality I and II* to Educational Practice. BRUMBAUGH, Robert S.
Whitehead and a Committee. BRUMBAUGH, Robert S.
Whitehead and Existential Phenomenology: Is a Synthesis Possible?. RICE, Daryl H.
Whitehead and the New Liberals on Social Progress. MORRIS, Randall C.
Whitehead et Hegel: Réalisme, idéalisme et philosophie spéculative. ROCKMORE, Tom.
Whitehead's "Theory" of Propositions. STEINBOCK, Anthony J.

WHOLE(S)
Husserl's Theory of Parts and Wholes: The Dynamic of Individuating and Contextualizing Interpretation. LAMPERT, Jay.

WIEMAN, H
The Moral Stance of Theism Without the Transcent God: Wieman and Heidegger. SHAW, Marvin C.

WIERSMA, T
Homeopathie de optische metafoor van Wiersma. KIBBELAAR, Robert.

WIGGINS, D
Conceptos y propiedades o Predicación y cópula. STRAWSON, P F.
The Nature of Artifacts. LOSONSKY, Michael.
Personal Identity and Extrinsicness. GARRETT, Brian.

WIGNER, E
Mathematics as Natural Science. GOODMAN, Nicolas D.

WILDERNESS
The Incarceration of Wildness: Wilderness Areas as Prisons. BIRCH, Thomas H.

WILKERSON, T
Science, Reduction and Natural Kinds. MEYER, Leroy N.

WILL
Folly and Intelligence in Political Thought. KLUBACK, William.
Kant and the Philosophy of History. YOVEL, Yirmiyahu.
Rousseau. DENT, N J H.
Wittgenstein and Moral Philosophy. JOHNSTON, Paul.
A Cast of Many: Nietzsche and Depth-Psychological Pluralism. PARKES, Graham.
Concerning the Freedom and Limits of the Will. FRANKFURT, Harry G.
Davidson, Irrationality, and Weakness of Will. LAVELLE, Kevin C.
Descartes on Freedom of the Will. BEYSSADE, Jean-Marie.
The Emptiness of the Moral Will. WOOD, Allen W.
La giustizia nella dottrina della volontà di Giovanni Duns Scoto. PIZZO, Giovanni.
The Individual and the General Will: Rousseau Reconsidered. HILEY, David R.
Kant's Theory of Moral Sensibility: Respect for the Moral Law and the Influence of Inclination. REATH, A.
Leibniz on Locke on Weakness of Will. VAILATI, Ezio.
Lonergan's Analysis of Error: An Experiment. TEKIPPE, Terry J.
Nietzschean Perspectivism: "How Could Such a Philosophy—Dominate?". FOWLER, Mark.
On the Moral Status of Weakness of the Will. DAHL, Norman O.
On Vallicella's Critique of Heidegger. ZIMMERMAN, Michael E.
Predestination and Freedom in Augustine's Ethics. O'DALY, Gerard.
The Problem of Weakness of Will. WALKER, Arthur F.
Schopenhauer's Account of Aesthetic Experience. DIFFEY, T J.
Spirit's Primary Nature is to be Secondary. KERR-LAWSON, Angus.
Temptation and the Will. BIGELOW, John.
Towards a Communication-Concept of Rational Collective Will-Formation: A Thought-Experiment. HABERMAS, Jürgen.
La volonté en Dieu: Thomas d'Aquin et Hegel. BRITO, Emilio.

WILL TO POWER
Dionysus Reborn: Play and the Aesthetic Dimension in Modern Philosophical and Scientific Discourse. SPARIOSU, Mihai I.
Nietzsche's Philosophy of Nature and Cosmology. MOLES, Alistair.
"The Philosopher at Sea" in *Nietzsche's New Seas: Explorations in Philosophy, Aesthetics, and Politics*, HARRIES, Karsten.
Zarathustra's Dancing Dialectic. NEWELL, Waller R.

WILLIAMS, B
Autonomy or Integrity: A Reply to Slote. WALKER, Margaret Urban.

Bernard Williams and the Nature of Moral Reflection. CRAGG, A W.
Bernard Williams on Practical Necessity. GAY, Robert J.
Could There Be a Rationally Grounded Morality?. BOND, E J.
Feminist Ethics: Some Issues for the Nineties. JAGGAR, Alison M.
God, Morality, and Prudence: A Reply to Bernard Williams. TSANG, Lap-Chuen.
Kantian Ethics Today. FRANKENA, William K.
Motivational Internalism: The Powers and Limits of Practical Reasoning. MELE, Alfred R.
Rhetoric and Philosophy in Vichian Inquiry. STRUEVER, Nancy S.
Stroud and Williams on Dreaming and Scepticism. REIN, Andrew.
Through Thick and Thin: Moral Knowledge in Skeptical Times. LOUDEN, Robert B.
Why is Belief Involuntary?. BENNETT, Jonathan.

WILLING
Time and Change: Short But Differing Philosophies. CHACALOS, Elias Harry.

WILSHIRE, B
Bruce Wilshire and the Dilemma of Nontheistic Existentialism. SMITH, Quentin.

WINCH, P
Following a Rule. WILLIAMSON, Colwyn.
Witchcraft and Winchcraft. WILLIAMSON, Colwyn.

WINNER, L
"The Devaluation of Value" in *Inquiries into Values: The Inaugural Session of the International Society for Value Inquiry*, ROHATYN, Dennis.

WINNIE, J
Does the Principle of Relativity Imply Winnie's (1970) Equal Passage Times Principle?. BROWN, Harvey R.

WIREDU, K
Narrative in African Philosophy. BELL, Richard H.

WISDO, D
Kierkegaard on Faith and Freedom. POJMAN, Louis P.

WISDOM
Il Giogo: Alle origini della ragione: Eschilo. SEVERINO, Emanuele.
Reflective Wisdom: Richard Taylor on Issues That Matter. DONNELLY, John (ed).
Socrates in the Apology: An Essay on Plato's Apology of Socrates. REEVE, C D C.
The Wisdom of Faith: Essays in Honor of Dr Sebastian Alexander Matczak. THOMPSON, Henry O (ed).
"The Fear of the Lord is the Beginning of Wisdom" in *The Wisdom of Faith: Essays in Honor of Dr Sebastian Alexander Matczak*, THOMPSON, Henry O.
"Wisdom, Faith and Reason" in *The Wisdom of Faith: Essays in Honor of Dr Sebastian Alexander Matczak*, JAMES, Theodore E.
Conoscenza-sapienza-teologia oggi. SALMANN, Elmer.
Conscience, contemplation, wisdom (in Polish). GOGCZ, Mieczyslaw.
Francis Bacon's "Ars Inveniendi". VAN PEURSEN, C A.
Heidegger's Destruction of Phronesis. BERNASCONI, Robert L.
Ontologie et sagesse. TROTIGNON, P.
Philosophical Identification of the Dignity of Person (in Polish). GOGACZ, Mieczyslaw.
Power, Authority, and Wisdom. BAMBROUGH, Renford.
A Response to Robert Bernasconi's "Heidegger's Destruction of Phronesis". BROGAN, Walter.
Socratic Ignorance—Socratic Wisdom. EVANS, J Claude.
Weisheit—Überforderung oder Vollendung der Philosophie?. GEYER, C F.

WITCHCRAFT
Paths Toward a Clearing: Radical Empiricism and Ethnographic Inquiry. JACKSON, Michael.
La Brujería: un Invento Moderno. DÍAZ, Esther.
Witchcraft and Winchcraft. WILLIAMSON, Colwyn.

WITHDRAWAL
Letting and Making Death Happen—Withholding and Withdrawing Life Support: Morally Irrelevant Distinctions. GRATTON, Claude.
Letting and Making Death Happen: Is There Really No Difference? The Problem of Moral Linkage. DAGI, T F.

WITHHOLDING
Letting and Making Death Happen—Withholding and Withdrawing Life Support: Morally Irrelevant Distinctions. GRATTON, Claude.
Letting and Making Death Happen: Is There Really No Difference? The Problem of Moral Linkage. DAGI, T F.

WITKIEWICZ, S

The Primacy of the Eye in Evaluating Colours and Colour Harmonies. TARANCZEWSKI, Pawel.

WITTGENSTEIN

The Authority of Language: Heidegger, Wittgenstein, and the Threat of Philosophical Nihilism. EDWARDS, James C.

The Crisis of Philosophy. MC CARTHY, Michael.

Fact and Meaning. HEAL, Jane.

From Nietzsche to Wittgenstein: The Problem of Truth and Nihilism in the Modern World. MARTIN, Glen T.

God, Scepticism and Modernity. NIELSEN, Kai.

In Quest of the Ordinary: Lines of Skepticism and Romanticism. CAVELL, Stanley.

The Infinite. MOORE, A W.

The Language of Imagination. WHITE, Alan R.

Philosophy of Economics: On the Scope of Reason in Economic Inquiry. ROY, Subroto.

Questions on Wittgenstein. HALLER, Rudolf.

Sense and Certainty: A Dissolution of Scepticism. MC GINN, Marie.

Style, Politics and the Future of Philosophy. JANIK, Allan.

What is Identity?. WILLIAMS, C J F.

Wittgenstein and Kierkegaard: Religion, Individuality, and Philosophical Method. CREEGAN, Charles L.

Wittgenstein and Moral Philosophy. JOHNSTON, Paul.

Wittgenstein in Focus—Im Brennpunkt: Wittgenstein. MC GUINNESS, Brian (ed).

Wittgenstein's Later Philosophy. HANFLING, Oswald.

Wittgenstein's Philosophy of Psychology. BUDD, Malcolm.

"Bemerkungen zur Egologie Wittgensteins" in Wittgenstein in Focus—Im Brennpunkt: Wittgenstein, HALLER, Rudolf.

"Die Beziehung zwischen Welt und Sprache: Bemerkungen im Ausgang von Wittgensteins Tractatus" in Wittgenstein in Focus—Im Brennpunkt: Wittgenstein, ISHIGURO, Hidè.

"Die Empfindungen des Anderen: Ein Disput zwischen Cartesianer und Wittgensteinianer" in Wittgenstein in Focus—Im Brennpunkt: Wittgenstein, SPECHT, E K and ERICHSEN, N.

"Phänomenologie und Grammatik in Wittgenstein" in Wittgenstein in Focus—Im Brennpunkt: Wittgenstein, EGIDI, Rosaria.

"Russell's 1913 Theory of Knowledge Manuscript" in Rereading Russell: Essays on Bertrand Russell's Metaphysics and Epistemology, PEARS, David.

"Schopenhauer and Wittgenstein on Lonely Languages and Criterialess Claims" in Schopenhauer: New Essays in Honor of His 200th Birthday, CLEGG, Jerry S.

"Stilfragen" in Wittgenstein in Focus—Im Brennpunkt: Wittgenstein, SCHULTE, Joachim.

"Wittgenstein and Behaviourism" in Wittgenstein in Focus—Im Brennpunkt: Wittgenstein, HILMY, S Stephen.

"Wittgenstein and Phenomenology or: Two Languages for One Wittgenstein" in Wittgenstein in Focus—Im Brennpunkt: Wittgenstein, SOULEZ, Antonia.

"Wittgenstein and the Problem of Machine Consciousness" in Wittgenstein in Focus—Im Brennpunkt: Wittgenstein, NYIRI, J C.

"Wittgenstein on Breaking Rules" in Wittgenstein in Focus—Im Brennpunkt: Wittgenstein, FRONGIA, Guido.

"Wittgenstein on Ethics" in Wittgenstein in Focus—Im Brennpunkt: Wittgenstein, RADFORD, Colin.

"Wittgenstein on Meaning" in Wittgenstein in Focus—Im Brennpunkt: Wittgenstein, ZEMACH, Eddy.

"Wittgenstein's Nose" in Wittgenstein in Focus—Im Brennpunkt: Wittgenstein, STROLL, Avrum.

"Wittgenstein's Pre-Tractatus Manuscripts" in Wittgenstein in Focus—Im Brennpunkt: Wittgenstein, MC GUINNESS, Brian.

"Wittgensteins ethische Einstellung" in Wittgenstein in Focus—Im Brennpunkt: Wittgenstein, GARGANI, Aldo.

"Wittgensteins Vorwort "im Januar 1945": Quellenkritik und Interpretation" in Wittgenstein in Focus—Im Brennpunkt: Wittgenstein, STÜSSEL, Kerstin.

'God-Talk' and 'Tacit' Theo-Logic. SCHWEIZER-BJELIC, Shelley and BJELIC, Dusan I.

'If a Lion Could Talk'. CHURCHILL, John.

Aesthetics and the Insularity of Arts Educators. MC ADOO, Nick.

El análisis tractariano de los hechos relacionales: exégesis, crítica y alternativa. PEÑA, Lorenzo.

Augustine's Pretence: Another Reading of Wittgenstein's Philosophical Investigations 1. WALKER, Margaret Urban.

Avowals in the "Philosophical Investigations": Expression, Reliability, Description. VON SAVIGNY, Eike.

Black. WESTPHAL, Jonathan.

Causas y razones en la filosofía de Wittgenstein. CABANCHIK, Samuel.

Ceticismo semântico. DE SOUZA FILHO, Danilo Marcondes.

Chomsky, Wittgenstein, Bloor: Zum Problem einer wissenssoziologischen Metatheorie der Linguistik. KERTÉSZ, András.

Crossroads of Skepticism: Wittgenstein, Derrida, and Ostensive Definition. MC DONALD, Henry.

Da indiferenciação do dizer ao automaton do falar. DO CARMO SILVA, Carlos Henrique.

A dedução dos objectos no "Tractatus". CUNHA, Rui Daniel.

Dewey and Wittgenstein on the Idea of Certainty. EODICE, Alexander R.

Discourse and Metaphysics. RUTHROF, Horst.

Does Philosophy 'Leave Everything as it is'? Even Theology?. BAMBROUGH, Renford.

Duas observações sobre a gramática filosófica. MORENO, Arley R.

Early Heidegger and Wittgenstein: The Necessity of a Comprehension of Being. FAY, Thomas A.

Education and Wittgenstein's Philosophy. HAMLYN, D W.

A Farewell to Forms of Life. THOMPKINS, E F.

A Filosofia da Matemática em Wittgenstein. DE SOUSA ALVES, Vitorino.

La filosofía del cristianismo y de la religión en Wittgenstein. TORNOS, Andrés.

Freedom and Rule-Following in Wittgenstein and Sartre. DWYER, Philip.

Geometria em fragmentos: Forma e conteúdo no contexto wittgensteiniano. THEMUDO, Marina Ramos.

Gruesome Arithmetic: Kripke's Sceptic Replies. ALLEN, Barry.

Hay una filosofía de la ciencia en el último Wittgenstein?. MOULINES, C Ulises.

Jews as a Metaphysical Species. LURIE, Yuval.

L'"infaillibilité" de l'introspection: Autour de Dennett et de Wittgenstein. BOUVERESSE, Jacques.

Logical Form. MAURY, André.

Ludwig Looks at the Necker Cube: The Problem of "Seeing As" as a Clue to Wittgenstein's Philosophy. HINTIKKA, Jaakko and HINTIKKA, Merrill B.

Ludwig Wittgenstein: Personality and Philosophy (in Czechoslovakian). STERN, Joseph P.

Malcolm on Language and Rules. BAKER, G P and HACKER, P M S.

La metodología falsacionista y su ecología. RADNITZKY, Gerard.

Not Bending the Knee. HOLLAND, R F.

El pensar en la filosofía de la mente de L Wittgenstein. GIL DE PAREIJA, José L.

Philosophical Investigations 201: A Wittgensteinian Reply to Kripke. SUMMERFIELD, Donna M.

Philosophy after Wittgenstein and Heidegger. GUIGNON, Charles.

Philosophy and Style: Wittgenstein and Russell. HUGHES, John.

Pictures and Gestures. LÜDEKING, Karlheinz.

Platonism and Forms of Life. GASKIN, Richard M.

Postscript (1989): To Whom It May Concern. CAVELL, Stanley.

El problema del realismo semántico y nuestro concepto de persona. TIRADO, Alvaro Rodriguez.

Quando ser sujeito não é sujeitar-se. SUMARES, Manuel.

Règles et langage privé chez Wittgenstein: deux interprétations. SAUVÉ, Denis.

Reply to Scheer's "What if Something Really Unheard-of Happened?". MALCOLM, Norman.

The Rhetoric of Grammar: Understanding Wittgenstein's Method. BARNETT, William E.

The Rule-Following Considerations. BOGHOSSIAN, Paul A.

Rules, Communities and Judgements. ZALABARDO, José L.

Semantic Physiology: Wittgenstein on Pedagogy. MC CARTY, Luise Prior and MC CARTY, Charles.

The Simplicity of the Tractatus. ANSCOMBE, Elizabeth.

Solitary Souls and Infinite Help: Kierkegaard and Wittgenstein. HANNAY, Alastair.

Some Variations on a Metaphilosophical Theme. MARCOTTE, Edward.

Stroud's Defense of Cartesian Scepticism: A 'Linguistic' Response. GLOCK, Hans-Johann.

Syntactic Metaphor: Frege, Wittgenstein and the Limits of a Theory of Meaning. SCHNEIDER, Hans Julius.

Thoughts and Their Subject: A Study of Wittgenstein's Tractatus. KANNISTO, Heikki.

Tienen significado las contradicciones?. GÓMEZ, Astrid C and GUIBOURG, Ricardo A.

Tractatus 2:063. BLUM, Alex.

Tractatus 6.2-6.22. HUGLY, Philip and SAYWARD, Charles.

Le Tractatus de Wittgenstein: Considérations sur le système numérique et la forme aphoristique. HESS, Gérald.

Understanding Other Cultures: Studies in the Philosophical Problems of Cross-Cultural Interpretation. SANDBACKA, Carola.

WITTGENSTEIN

What Do Language Games Measure?. LORENZ, Kuno.
What if Something Really Unheard-of Happened?. SCHEER, R K.
What Wittgenstein Wasn't. GILL, Jerry H.
Wittgenstein and Kripke on the Nature of Meaning. HORWICH, Paul.
Wittgenstein and Murdock on the 'Net' in a Taoist Framework. TOMINAGA, Thomas T.
Wittgenstein and Obscurantism. CIOFFI, Frank.
Wittgenstein and Philosophy for Children. CURTIS, Barry.
Wittgenstein and Physicalism. HALLER, Rudolf.
Wittgenstein and Sense-Independence of Truth. PUHL, Klaus.
Wittgenstein and the Critical Tradition. GARVER, Newton.
Wittgenstein et la philosophie. COMETTI, Jean-Pierre.
Wittgenstein Never Was a Phenomenologist. REEDER, Harry P.
Wittgenstein on Culture and Civilization. LURIE, Yuval.
Wittgenstein on Grammar and Analytic Philosophy of Education. RIZVI, Fazal.
Wittgenstein's Genius. LEWIS, Peter.
Wittgenstein's Later Philosophy of Mind: Sensation, Privacy, and Intention. WRIGHT, Crispin.
Wittgenstein, Bodies and Meaning. NEIMAN, Alven M.
Wittgenstein, Kant and the "Metaphysics of Experience". WILLIAMS, Meredith.
Wittgenstein, Mind, and Scientism. GOLDFARB, Warren.
Wittgenstein, Realism, and CLS: Undermining Rule Scepticism. LANDERS, Scott.
Wittgenstein, Religion, Freud, and Ireland. HAYES, John.

WOLF, S

Back to Sainthood. DOMBROWSKI, Daniel A.
The Moral Importance of Free Action. BENSON, Paul.

WOLFF

Christian Wolff and China: The Autonomy of Morality (in Serbo-Croatian). CHING, Julia.
Note sur la définition wolffienne de la philosophie. ÉCOLE, Jean.

WOLFF, R

Philosophy in South Africa: A Reply to Robert Paul Wolff. MILLER, Seumas and MAC DONALD, Ian.

WOLLSTONECRAFT, M

The Eleventh Commandment: Sex and Spirit in Wollstonecraft and Malthus. NICHOLSON, Mervyn.

WOMAN

see also Feminism

Das Verhältnis von Verbrecherinnen zu ihren Familien (in Polish). ROSINSKI, F M.
Derrida, "Woman," and Politics: A Reading of Spurs. PARENS, Erik.
Eccentric Subjects: Feminist Theory and Historical Consiousness. DE LAURETIS, Teresa.

WOMEN

Feminist Thought: A Comprehensive Introduction. TONG, Rosemarie.
Who Cares: Theory, Research and Educational Implications of the Ethic of Care. BRABECK, Mary M (ed).
Women Philosophers: A Bio-Critical Source Book. KERSEY, Ethel M.
"An Ironic Mimesis" in The Question of the Other: Essays in Contemporary Continental Philosophy, MEHURON, Kate.
"On the Advantage and Disadvantage of Nietzsche for Women" in The Question of the Other: Essays in Contemporary Continental Philosophy, BERGOFFEN, Debra B.
"Unlearning to Not Speak". PAGET, M A.
Androgyny and Leadership Style. KORABIK, Karen.
Anna Maria van Schurman's verhouding tot de wetenschap. ROOTHAAN, Angela and VAN ECK, Caroline.
Are Women Different and Why are Women Thought to be Different? Theoretical and Methodological Perspectives. GREGORY, Ann.
Are Women Owner-Managers Challenging Our Definitions of Entrepreneurship? An In-Depth Survey. LEE-GOSSELIN, H and GRISÉ, J.
At the Heart of Women in Management Research: Theoretical and Methodological Approaches and Their Biases. FAGENSON, Ellen A.
La Brujería: un Invento Moderno. DÍAZ, Esther.
Business Ethics, Fetal Protection Policies, and Discrimination Against Women in the Workplace. QUINN, John F.
Comments on Ruth Ginzberg's Paper "Uncovering Gynocentric Science". JAHREN, Neal.
Die psychologischen Probleme der Frau vor dem Schwangerschaftsabbruch (in Polish). OSTROWSKA, Krystyna.
An Ethical Problem Concerning Recent Therapeutic Research on Breast Cancer. MARQUIS, Don.
An Examination of Present Research on the Female Entrepreneur-Suggested Strategies for the 1990's. MOORE, Dorothy P.
A Family Portrait of Canada's Most Successful Female Entrepreneurs. BELCOURT, Monica.
Formal and Informal Management Training Programs for Women in Canada: Who Seems to Be Doing a Good Job?. LAVOIE, Dina.
Frontiers and New Vistas in Women in Management Research. SEKARAN, Uma.
Individual and Organizational Characteristics of Women in Managerial Leadership. ROWNEY, J I A and CAHOON, A R.
Is Women's Labor a Commodity?. ANDERSON, Elizabeth S.
Lesbian Angels and Other Matters. ZITA, Jacquelyn.
Levinas and Hegel on the Woman as Home: A Comparison (in Dutch). BRÜGGEMAN-KRUIJFF, Atie T.
Management Training for Women: International Experiences and Lessons for Canada. LAM, M Natalie.
Mentoring in Organizations: Implications for Women. BURKE, R J and MC KEEN, C A.
More Dyke Methods. TREBILCOT, Joyce.
Niet vrouw, niet man; wat dan? De rol van biomedische kennis bij de behandeling van pseudohermafrodieten. VAN DEN WIJNGAARD, Marianne and HUYTS, Ini.
Nietzsche: Women and Relationships of Strength. STARRETT, Shari Neller.
No Bosses Here: Management in Worker Co-Operatives. CONN, Melanie.
No Laughing Matter: John Stuart Mill's Establishment of Women's Sufferage as a Parliamentary Question. ROBSON, John M.
Postscript (1989): To Whom It May Concern. CAVELL, Stanley.
Research, Myths and Expectations: New Challenges for Management Educators. GRONDIN, Deirdre.
A Second Look at Pornography and the Subordination of Women. PARENT, W A.
Selective Termination of Pregnancy and Women's Reproductive Autonomy. OVERALL, Christine.
Socio-Economic Evolution of Women Business Owners in Quebec (1987). COLLERETTE, P and AUBRY, P.
Some Methodological Problems Associated with Researching Women Entrepreneurs. STEVENSON, Lois.
Stop or Go: Reflections of Women Managers on Factors Influencing their Career Development. ANDREW, C and CODERRE, C and DENIS, A.
Training and Women: Some Thoughts from the Grassroots. JOYCE, Glenis.
Treating Women as Sex-Objects. SWANTON, Christine and ROBINSON, Viviane and CROSTHWAITE, Jan.
Ugly Duckling, Funny Butterfly: Bette Davis and Now, Voyager. CAVELL, Stanley.
Woman, Morality, and Fiction. ROBINSON, Jenefer and ROSS, Stephanie.
Women and Elderly Parents: Moral Controversy in an Aging Society. POST, Stephen G.
The Women in Management Research Program at the National Centre for Management Research and Development. BURKE, R J and MIKALACHKI, D.
The Women of Silence. FRANKE, Carrie.
Women's Research and Its Inherent Critique of Society and Science. KYLE, Gunhild and JUNGEN, Britta.

WOODS, J

Misunderstandings of Epistemic TIT for TAT: Reply to John Woods. BLAIS, Michel J.

WORD(S)

Landmarks in Linguistic Thought: The Western Tradition from Socrates to Saussure. HARRIS, Roy.
Translation and the Nature of Philosophy: A New Theory of Words. BENJAMIN, Andrew.
"On Truth: A Fiction" in Meaning and Mental Representation, ECO, Umberto.
"Quantification, Roles and Domains" in Meaning and Mental Representation, FAUCONNIER, Gilles.
The Acquisition of the Ostensive Lexicon: A Reply to Professor Place. STEMMER, Nathan.
How Did We Get From Simulation To Symbol?. BROOK, Donald.
El lenguaje y la palabra en Tomas de Aquino. LOBATO, Abelardo.
Words. KAPLAN, David.

WORDSWORTH

Wordsworth and the Zen Void. RUDY, John G.

WORK

The Fabric of This World: Inquiries into Calling, Career Choice, and the Design of Human Work. HARDY, Lee.

WRITING
A Pragmatic Method of Reading Confused Philosophic Texts: The Case of Peirce's "Illustrations". OCHS, Peter.
Presence and Representation: The Other and Anthropological Writing. FABIAN, Johannes.
S'entendre parler. LAPORTE, Roger.
Sens elliptique. NANCY, Jean-Luc.
Writing and Philosophy. FISHMAN, Stephen.

WRONGS
Callahan on Harming the Dead. SERAFINI, Anthony.
Explaining Wrongdoing. DAVIS, Michael.
Where Did I Go Wrong?. ZIMMERMAN, Michael J.

WUNDT, W
Psicologia e scienze della natura in Wilhelm Wundt. CAVALLO, Giuliana.

XENOPHANES
"The Beginnings of Epistemology: From Homer to Philolaus" in Epistemology (Companions to Ancient Thought: 1), HUSSEY, Edward.
Anthropomorphic Concepts of God. SCHOEN, Edward.
Xenophanes on the Moon: A Doxographicum in Aëtius. RUNIA, David T.

XIONG SHILI
A Summary of Xiong Shili's Research on Philosophy Conducted in China. HAIFENG, Jing.

YAN FU
In Search of an Image of the World: Kang Youwei and Yan Fu (in Serbo-Croatian). RADONIC, Nikola.

YEATS, W
Civil Peace and Sacred Order: Limits and Renewals I. CLARK, Stephen R L.

YIN YANG
"Toward a Middle Path of Survival" in Nature in Asian Tradition of Thought: Essays in Environmental Philosophy, KALUPAHANA, David J.

YODER, J
Christian Pacificism and Theodicy: The Free Will Defense in the Thought of John H Yoder. PINCHES, Charles.

YOGA
Reality—Realization through Self-Discipline. VEMPENY, Alice.

YOUNG, I
Feminist Ethics: Some Issues for the Nineties. JAGGAR, Alison M.

YOUNG, J
Young's Critique of Authenticity in Musical Performance. THOM, Paul.

YOUTH
Childhood's End: The Age of Responsibility. FRIQUEGNON, Marie-Loui.
Confidentiality and Young People. GILLICK, Victoria.
Confidentiality and Young People: A G.P.'s Response. MORGAN, Huw.
Juventology: A Holistic Approach to Youth. MAHLER, Fred.
Teaching Elfie. HAMRICK, William S.
Young Children Generate Philosophical Ideas. MC CALL, Catherine.

YUGOSLAVIAN
Functions of Egalitarianism in Yugoslav Society. BERNIK, Ivan.
The Tragedy of National Conflicts in 'Real Socialism': The Case of the Yugoslav Autonomous Province of Kosovo. MARKOVIC, Mihailo.

ZEN BUDDHISM
"Environmental Problematics" in Nature in Asian Tradition of Thought: Essays in Environmental Philosophy, INADA, Kenneth K.
Derrida and the Decentered Universe of Ch'an Buddhism. ODIN, Steve.
Differentialism in Chinese Ch'an and French Deconstruction: Some Test-Cases from the Wu-Men-Kuan. MAGLIOLA, Robert.
Eternal Loneliness: Art and Religion in Kierkegaard and Zen. PATTISON, George.
Wordsworth and the Zen Void. RUDY, John G.

ZERMELO
Philosophical Introduction to Set Theory. POLLARD, Stephen.
'Ich habe mich wohl gehütet, alle Patronen auf einmal zu verschiessen': Ernest Zermelo in Göttingen. PECKHAUS, Volker.

ZERMELO-FRAENKEL SET THEORY
Philosophical Introduction to Set Theory. POLLARD, Stephen.

ZEUS
Il Giogo: Alle origini della ragione: Eschilo. SEVERINO, Emanuele.

ZHU XI
On Articles of the Academy of the White Deer Grotto (in Serbo-Croatian). JI-YU, Ren.

ZIFF, P
Evaluating Art. DICKIE, George.

ZIMMERMAN, M
Reply to Zimmerman: Heidegger and the Problem of Being. VALLICELLA, William F.

ZITA, J
More Dyke Methods. TREBILCOT, Joyce.

ZOLA, E
Storied Bodies, or Nana at Last Unveil'd. BROOKS, Peter.

ZOMEREN, H
The Quarrel over Future Contingents (Louvain 1465-1475). BAUDRY, Leon.

ZOROASTRIANISM
Manichaean Responses to Zoroastrianism. SCOTT, David.

ZUBIRI, X
The Knowledge of Values: A Methodological Introduction. LÓPEZ QUINTÁS, Alfonso (ed).
El acceso del hombre a la realidad según Xavier Zubiri. SIMONPIETRI MONEFELDT, Fannie A.
El enigma del animal fantastico: Bases para una antropologia y etica de la tecnica. SANCHO, Jesús Conill.
La inersorabilità della "nuda inteligencia" in Zubiri. INCARDONA, Nunzio.

ZEA, L
Las críticas de Leopoldo Zea a Augusto Salazar Bondy. SOBREVILLA, David.

ZEMACH, E
Beardsley's Aesthetic Instrumentalism. BAILEY, George.
The Logical Limits of Science. SMITH, Joseph Wayne.

Guidance on the Use of the Author Index With Abstracts

Each entry in this section begins with the author's name and contains the complete title of the article or book, other bibliographic information, and an abstract if available. The list is arranged in alphabetical order with the author's last name first. Articles by multiple authors are listed under each author's name. Names preceded by the articles De, La, Le, etc. or the prepositions Da, De, Van, Von, etc. are usually treated as if the article or preposition were a part of the last name.

Almost all of the abstracts are provided by the authors of the articles and books; where an abstract does not appear, it was not received from the author prior to the publication of this edition. The staff of the *Index* prepares some abstracts. These abstracts are followed by "(staff)".

In order to locate all the articles and books written by a given author, various spellings of the author's name should be checked. This publication uses the form of the author's name given in the article or book. Hence, variations of an author's name may appear in this index. Particular care should be given to names that have a space, a dash, or an apostrophe in them. Because the computer sorts on each character, the names of other authors may be filed between different spellings of a given author's name.

AAFTINK, Jan. Far-Sighted Equilibria in 2 x 2, Non-Cooperative, Repeated Games. Theor Decis, 27(3), 175-192, N 89.

Consider a two-person simultaneous-move game in strategic form. Suppose this game is played over and over at discrete points in time. Suppose, furthermore, that communication is not possible, but nevertheless we observe some regularity in the sequence of outcomes. The aim of this paper is to provide an explanation for the question why such regularity might persist for many (i.e., infinite) periods. Each player, when contemplating a deviation, considers a sequential-move game, roughly speaking of the following form: if I change my strategy this period, then in the next my opponent will take his strategy 'b' and afterwards I can switch to my strategy 'a', but then I am worse off since at that outcome my opponent has no incentive to change anymore, whatever I do." Theoretically, however, there is no end to such reaction chains. In case that deviating by some player gives him less utility in the long run than before deviation, we say that the original regular sequence of outcomes is far-sighted stable for that player. It is a far-sighted equilibrium if it is far-sighted stable for both players.

AAGAARD-MOGENSEN, L. "Freedom, Religion and Socio-Logic" in The Wisdom of Faith: Essays in Honor of Dr Sebastian Alexander Matczak, THOMPSON, Henry O (ed), 1-27. Lanham, Univ Pr of America, 1989.

AARNIO, Aulis. On the Legitimacy of Law: A Conceptual Point of View. Ratio Juris, 2(2), 202-210, Jl 89.

The author outlines a conceptually oriented rational reconstruction of crisis tendencies in modern law. The connection between problems of legitimacy and the notion of rationality is emphasized and topics involving both the theory of communicative rationality and the theory of practical reasoning (especially in law) are discussed. The author concludes that a theory transcending the traditional approaches is needed. Otherwise, we shall not be able to face the questions of jurisprudence in the future, especially as regards an assessment of the relations between law and morality, between law and society and finally between law, legitimacy and democracy.

AARON, Daniel. George Santayana and the Genteel Tradition. Bull Santayana Soc, 7, 1-8, Fall 89.

ABAD, Juan Vázquez. Observaciones sobre la noción de causa en el opúsculo sobre el movimiento de Berkeley. Analisis Filosof, 6(1), 35-43, My 86.

ABADI, Marcelo. Spinoza in Borges' Looking-Glass. Stud Spinozana, 5, 29-42, 1989.

The age-long dialogue between philosophy and poetry is here illustrated by Borges' fascination for Spinoza, to whom the Argentine writer dedicated two beautiful sonnets. Borges was always drawn to Spinoza, but his evolving perception of the philosopher's message led him to deplore the geometrical armature of the Ethics. Thus in the second of these sonnets Spinoza is portrayed as a touching wizard who persists in fashioning God out of the word; philosopher and poet, both in pursuit of the absolute, are fated alike to grasp at it only by way of allusion or by the love that expects no requital.

ABBARNO, John M. "Empathy as an Objective Value" in Inquiries into Values: The Inaugural Session of the International Society for Value Inquiry, LEE, Sander H, 161-171. Lewiston, Mellen Pr, 1989.

ABBS, Peter. Aesthetic Education: A Small Manifesto. J Aes Educ, 23(4), 75-85, Wint 89.

In this essay it is argued that the aesthetic refers to a basic modality of human intelligence and that it is enhanced and developed through the symbolic forms of the arts. Furthermore it is argued that the arts, at their most profound and typical, are formally heuristic in nature and not merely hedonistic, that they apprehend meanings and values vital to our individual and communal lives. Finally, it is suggested that the arts, seen structurally, form vast symbolic orders which it is the task of arts teachers to transmit, keep alive, and relate to their students' own artistic endeavors.

ABELL, John D. A Note on the Teaching of Ethics in the MBA Macroeconomics Course. J Bus Ethics, 9(1), 21-29, Ja 90.

While there is general agreement on the need to teach ethics in the MBA classroom, there are great difficulties in completely integrating such material within the confines of an actual MBA program. This paper attempts to address these difficulties by focusing on the teaching of such issues in one particular class—MBA macroeconomics. Ethical dilemmas often arise due to failures of the market place or due to inappropriate assumptions regarding the market model. Thus, specific suggestions are offered in regard to the integration of ethical issues into the traditional macroeconomic curriculum. Suggestions are even offered as how to scale back the basic macro material so that the additional material may be accommodated. In addition to fulfilling the mandate to develop a well-educated citizenry with regard to issues of ethics and economics, the course may be structured so as to

emphasize writing skills, speaking skills, and critical analytical thinking skills.

ABELSON, Raziel. Lawless Mind. Philadelphia, Temple Univ Pr, 1988

This book offers a piecemeal, pragmatic argument for indeterministic free will as an essential feature of the mental, one which underlies and explains consciousness, intentionality and moral responsibility. Two concepts of cause are distinguished: dyadic, natural causality and triadic, psychological causality which is mediated by the agent's decision. Without this distinction, it is argued, we cannot explain transfers of responsibility, degrees of moral credit, the role of psychotherapy, degrees of excuse for misconduct, sociological understanding, and the difference between people and machines. With it, we can do this, and also solve the mind-body problem.

ABRAHAM, Kuruvilla C. Marx's Promethean Humanism. J Dharma, 14(2), 139-157, Ap-Je 89.

ABRAHAMSEN, Adele A and BECHTEL, William. Beyond the Exclusively Propositional Era. Synthese, 82(2), 223-253, F 90.

Contemporary epistemology has assumed that knowledge is represented in sentences or propositions. However, a variety of extensions and alternatives to this view have been proposed in other areas of investigation. We review some of these proposals, focusing on (1) Ryle's notion of knowing how and Hanson's and Kuhn's account of theory-laden perception in science; (2) extensions of simple propositional representations in cognitive models and artificial intelligence; (3) the debate concerning imagistic versus propositional representations in cognitive psychology; (4) recent treatments of concepts and categorization which reject the notion of necessary and sufficient conditions; and (5) parallel distributed processing (connectionist) models of cognition. This last development is especially promising in providing a flexible, powerful means of representing information nonpropositionally, and carrying out at least simple forms of inference without rules. Central to several of the proposals is the notion that much of human cognition might consist in pattern recognition rather than manipulation of rules and propositions.

ABRAMOV, A I. Preface to the Publication of "P A Florenskii's Review of His Work". Soviet Stud Phil, 28(3), 31-39, Wint 89-90.

ABRUSCI, V Michele. A Comparison Between Lambek Syntactic Calculus and Intuitionistic Linear Propositional Logic. Z Math Log, 36(1), 11-15, 1990.

Lambek syntactic calculus, created by Lambek in 1958 and used in linguistics, is a fragment of noncommutative intuitionistic linear logic. The paper is an investigation of the syntax and semantics of both Lambek syntactic calculus and noncommutative intuitionistic linear logic.

ABRUSCI, V Michele and GIRARD, Jean-Yves and VAN DE WIELE, Jacques. Some Uses of Dilators in Combinatorial Problems, II. J Sym Log, 55(1), 32-40, Mr 90.

We introduce sequences of ordinal numbers, called "increasing F-sequences" (where F is a dilator). By induction on dilators, we prove that every increasing F-sequence terminates. "Inverse Goodstein sequences" are particular increasing F-Sequences: we show that the theorem "every inverse Goodstein sequence terminates" is not provable in the theory ID_1.

ACCONCI, Vito. Public Space in a Private Time. Crit Inquiry, 16(4), 900-918, Sum 90.

ACHINSTEIN, Peter. The Only Game in Town. Phil Stud, 58(3), 179-201, Mr 90.

ACHTENBERG, Deborah. The Role of the Ergon Argument in Aristotle's Nicomachean Ethics. Ancient Phil, 9 (1), 37-47, Spr 89.

In this essay it is argued that the ergon argument is central to Aristotle's Nicomachean Ethics since virtue, for Aristotle, is the first completion relative to ergon and completions of things different in kind are themselves different. The human ergon is rational action. By itself it is incomplete: we aim at what we think is a good, but our aim may be bad or may fail to inform the particulars with which action has to do. Virtue brings our ergon to completion: it makes right both the aim and the means.

ACKERMAN, Felicia. A Vagueness Paradox and Its Solution. Midwest Stud Phil, 14, 395-398, 1989.

ACKERMAN, Terrence F and STRONG, Carson. A Casebook of Medical Ethics. New York, Oxford Univ Pr, 1989

ADAMO, David Tuesday. Soteriological Dialogue between Wesleyan Christians and Pure Land Sect Buddhism. J Dharma, 14(4), 366-375, O-D 89.

The aim of this essay is to encourage dialogue among people of different religious tradition. A concrete example is given as to how a dialogue could take place between Christians and Pure Land Sect Buddhism according to Shinran. The conclusion is that it is better to dialogue in order to understand one another than to strife.

ADAMS, E Maynard. "Where I Stand: Response to the Essays" in *Mind, Value and Culture: Essays in Honor of E M Adams*, WEISSBORD, David (ed), 357-394. Atascadero, Ridgeview, 1989.

This is my response to the sixteen essays by others in the book. The main purpose of the essay is to clarify the positions I have advocated in my earlier writings. The major topics discussed are (1) the derangement of the modern Western mind; (2) categories and categorical analysis; (3) value realism; (4) meaning and the mental; (5) perception and the language of appearing; (6) ethics and the humanities; and (7) religion, God, and humanism. I argue for a realistic theory of the categories in general, especially the humanistic categories of value, meaning, subjectivity, and personhood.

ADAMS, Frederick. The Role of Intention in Intentional Action. Can J Phil, 19(4), 511-531, D 89.

What is the causal (functional) role of an intention in an (intended) intentional action? We sketch and defend a control model of the role of intention in intentional action. Intentions set the goal of the action, and are involved in the guidance and control of the bodily movements that yield the action. We contrast our control model of intention with Searle's attempt to carve a distinction between kinds and functional roles of intentions. We demonstrate the advantages of our control model at providing a unified account of the role intention in intentional action and at solving puzzles of causal deviance.

ADAMS, Frederick. Tertiary Waywardness Tamed. Critica, 21(61), 117-125, Ap 89.

Myles Brand has catalogued two kinds of deviant causal chains that threaten to undermine causal theories of intentional action—"antecedential" and "consequential" causal waywardness. Alfred Mele claims to have found a third kind of deviant chain that previously has gone unnoticed—"tertiary" waywardness. Furthermore, Mele claims that solutions to antecedential and consequential waywardness will not work for tertiary waywardness. I show that a theory based on a cybernetic model of feedback-controlled behavior will handle all three types of causal deviance and preserve a causal theory of intentional action.

ADAMS, Ian S. *The Logic of Political Belief: A Philosophical Analysis of Ideology*. New York, Barnes & Noble, 1989

This book analyses the nature and scope of ideology, arguing that these are purely philosophical questions which cannot be settled by social science or traditional political theory. Ideology is shown to be a particular form of ethical understanding having a distinctive logic and structure, similar in many ways to religion. At its centre is a moralised conception of human nature, implying the kind of life human beings ought to live. Ideology is concerned with justifying action in terms of moral identity. It has no necessary relation to social class or fanaticism or even politics. Non-political ideologies are possible.

ADAMS, Robert Merrihew. Reply to Kvanvig: "Adams on Actualism and Presentism". Phil Phenomenol Res, 50(2), 299-301, D 89.

ADDANTE, Pietro. La "fucina del mondo". Filosofia, 40(2), 209-215, My-Ag 89.

ADDIS, Laird. Intrinsic Reference and the New Theory. Midwest Stud Phil, 14, 241-257, 1989.

The theory of natural signs, according to which reference to something requires a property of a person's mind that intrinsically points to that something, is defended against the "new theory of reference," according to which at least some of the conditions of reference are external to a person's mind. It is argued that the new theory of reference is neither a theory insofar as it merely describes the external conditions for *saying* that someone has referred or else prescribes how to use 'refer', nor is it about reference insofar as it ignores the crucial constituent of reference—the intentional connection.

ADDIS, Laird. *Natural Signs: A Theory of Intentionality*. Philadelphia, Temple Univ Pr, 1989

It is argued that every intentional state contains a *natural sign*, an entity that represents by its very nature, as against the theory that to be aware of something is merely to be in some relation to it and the theory that whatever is in the mind only conventionally rather than naturally represents. The simplicity of natural signs is defended, and a new account of what it is to think of something nonexistent is developed. It is further argued that natural sign theory, while endorsing the ontological uniqueness and irreducibility of intentionality, is fully consistent with the scientific worldview.

ADKINS, Arthur. "Plato" in *Ethics in the History of Western Philosophy*, CAVALIER, Robert J (ed), 1-31. New York, St Martin's Pr, 1988.

This essay is part of a volume devoted to the study of moral philosophers in their context and tradition. For Socrates/Plato there was no already-existing tradition of moral philosophy. This essay (a) studies Platonic ethics in the

context of Greek pre-philosophical values, and the problems to which they led, in extant Greek sources from Homer to the fourth century BC, and (b) traces links between those values and the serious ethical and political problems that accompanied them and the problems which Plato treats as most important and tries to solve in his works.

ADLER, Jonathan E. Epistemics and the Total Evidence Requirement. Philosophia (Israel), 19(2-3), 227-243, O 89.

In *Epistemology and Cognition* (Harvard, 1986), Alvin I Goldman argues against the total evidence requirement as making demands that are not feasible for finite, epistemic agents. The argument depends upon two alleged counterexamples. The examples are challenged, as part of a broader challenge to the claims of naturalistic epistemology to be in competition with, and an improvement upon, traditional epistemological views.

ADLER, Jonathan E. Particularity, Gilligan, and the Two-Levels View: A Reply. Ethics, 100(1), 149-156, O 89.

Hare's two-level distinction is that between principles functional under the constraints of everyday thinking, and the fundamental principles we appeal to when no constraints infringe upon thinking. The two-level view provides a defense against a range of objections to impartialist moral theories. Specifically, an example of Larry Blum's meant to show that there are moral reasons which are not impartialist, but particularistic, fails on a two-levels impartialism. Further, while Carol Gilligan's work does not, as has been alleged, challenge impartialist moral theory, some of her most interesting claims gain plausibility under a two-levels view.

ADLER, Pierre (trans) and HÖSLE, Vittorio and HUMPHREY, Fred (trans). On Plato's Philosophy of Numbers and its Mathematical and Philosophical Significance. Grad Fac Phil J, 13(1), 21-63, 1988.

AERTSEN, Jan A. Method and Metaphysics: The *Via Resolutionis* in Thomas Aquinas. New Scholas, 63(4), 405-418, Autumn 89.

AGAMBEN, Giorgio. *Pardes*: l'écriture de la puissance. Rev Phil Fr, 180(2), 131-145, Ap-Je 90.

AGARWALA, Binod Kumar. Philosophy of Reservation. Indian Phil Quart, 17(2), 125-146, Ap 90.

Equality of opportunity and compensation for past injustice as legitimate state purposes behind the policy of reservation fail to justify caste as criterion of reservation require introduction of means test, and lead to high percentage of reservation and other difficulties. Group equality also leads to undesirable consequences as legitimate state purpose behind policy of reservation. So it is argued that reduction of caste prejudice and caste consciousness against certain castes is the only legitimate state purpose which justifies caste as criterion of reservation, which does not require means test and which leads only to very low percentage of reservation.

AGASSI, Joseph. The Import of the Problem of Rationality. Method Sci, 23(2), 61-74, 1990.

AGASSI, Joseph. Reply—Symposium on the Role of the Philosopher Among the Scientists: Nuisance or Necessity? A Reply to Baigrie. Soc Epistem, 3(4), 319, O-D 89.

AGASSI, Joseph. "The Riddle of Bacon" in *Early Modern Philosophy II*, TWEYMAN, Stanley (ed), 103-136. Delmar, Caravan Books, 1988.

Robert Leslie Ellis, editor of Sir Francis Bacon's *Works* and best interpreter of Bacon to date, asked, why is Bacon admired? As all previous answers to this question are defective, here is mine. Bacon's great idea is his doctrine of prejudice. It is scientific radicalism: we must begin by cleaning our slates. This led to modern science as we know it and to political radicalism. Shallow and unscholarly as he was, Bacon is the greatest modern philosopher.

AGASSI, Joseph. The Role of the Philosopher Among the Scientists: Nuisance or Necessity? Soc Epistem, 3(4), 297-309, O-D 89.

Scientists consider philosophers nuisances because they, the scientists, violate their own inductivist philosophy of science and make bold conjectures and best them. Thus, scientists who allow bold conjectures are not hostile to philosophers. Philosophers are often servile to scientists. Had they studied the empirical methods empirically, they would render some of their work scientific and cooperate with some scientists.

AGAZZI, Evandro. Can Knowledge Be Acquired Through Contradiction? Stud Soviet Tho, 39(3-4), 205-208, Ap-My 90.

AGERA, Cassian R. Cut the Syllogism to its Size! Some Reflections on Indian Syllogism. Indian Phil Quart, 16(4), 465-477, O 89.

AGERA, Cassian R. In the Onthic Human Centre: Solitariness Overcome by Solitude. J Dharma, 14(2), 121-138, Ap-Je 89.

AGÍS, Marcelino. Mito y filosofía: En torno a Mircea Eliade.

Pensamiento, 46(183), 337-344, Jl-S 90.

It is not up to philosophy to discover philosophical topics. Mircea Eliade defends a mythical-religious-based starting point for reflection. An awakening to philosophical problems occurs in the context of the ancient societies thanks to messages revealed through the sacred: the true source of meaning and of orientation in a world with numerous gaps in knowledge. And although primitive man did not possess an abstract or theoretical language, his symbols had the function of overcoming this deficiency, facilitating his understanding of realities outside the utilitarian daily sphere. In this way, the ancient world has left behind an important legacy, which can be detected in the first philosophers, and of which we are also heirs.

AGIUS, Emmanuel. Towards a Relational Theory of Intergenerational Ethics. Bijdragen, 3, 293-313, 1989.

The growing moral concern for unborn generations points to the need of an adequate ethical theory. The aim of our study is to lay down the groundwork for an ethical theory suited to express adequately today's concern for posterity. We feel that the ethical theories adopted so far are not fully equipped to tackle this social issue. Convinced that an adequate approach to the problem under study needs a solid metaphysical basis, we are therefore attempting to construct an intergenerational ethical theory based on the philosophical insights of process thought which sees reality as interrelated and interdependent. Since humanity, nature and God are all involved in the future generations issue, we redefine these notions from a relational standpoint. (edited)

AGUADO, Javier Fernández. Deus, causa sui en Descartes. Sapientia, 44(173), 211-220, Jl-S 89.

AHRENS, John (ed) and PAUL, Ellen Frankel (ed) and MILLER JR, Fred D (ed) and PAUL, Jeffrey (ed). Capitalism. Cambridge, Blackwell, 1989

The essays in this volume address some of the central moral and conceptual questions arising out of the nature of capitalism. Some address the connection between capitalism and such moral notions as freedom, self-ownership and community. Others consider the role that efficiency plays in the justification of capitalism. And others are concerned with the methodological difficulties involved in comparing existing capitalist and socialist systems. Together, these essays delineate some of the concepts which are central to the ongoing debate between capitalism and socialism.

AIRAKSINEN, Timo (ed) and BERTMAN, Martin A (ed). Hobbes: War Among Nations. Brookfield, Gower, 1989

AIRAKSINEN, Timo. "The Whiteness of the Whale" in Hobbes: War Among Nations, AIRAKSINEN, Timo (ed), 51-69. Brookfield, Gower, 1989.

This paper deals with a paradox of war and fear. The point is that Hobbes's social philosophy concentrates on civil war but international war is also a severe threat to one's safety. Several interpretations of this thesis are introduced and evaluated.

AJTAI, M. First-Order Definability on Finite Structures. Annals Pure Applied Log, 45(3), 211-225, D 89.

If k is a fixed positive integer, G is a graph with n vertices, v_1, $v_2 \epsilon G$ then the property $dG(v_1, v_2)$ less than or equal to k can be easily defined by a first-order formula with at most $2+2 \log_2 k$ quantifiers. Let M be a finite structure with n elements. We may consider G as a binary relation on the universe M. Using the relations of M may help to define the given property of G. (E.g., the number k may be coded by one of the relations.) However, we prove that if n is sufficiently large compared to k, then the given property cannot be defined by a first-order formula whose length does not depend on k even if we are allowed to use in this formula the arbitrary relations given on M. This result implies that the existential first-order formulas form a nontrivial hierarchy on finite structures in a strong sense.

AJTAI, Miklos. Reachability is Harder for Directed than for Undirected Finite Graphs. J Sym Log, 55(1), 113-150, Mr 90.

Although it is known that reachability in undirected finite graphs can be expressed by an existential monadic second-order sentence, our main result is that this is not the case for directed finite graphs (even in the presence of certain "built-in" relations, such as the successor relation). The proof makes use of Ehrenfeucht-Fraïssé games, along with probabilistic arguments. However, we show that for directed finite graphs with degree at most k, reachability is expressible by an existential monadic second-order sentence.

AKAAH, Ishmael P. Attitudes of Marketing Professionals Toward Ethics in Marketing Research: A Cross-National Comparison. J Bus Ethics, 9(1), 45-53, Ja 90.

The study reported here examines, in the context of Crawford's (1970) items, differences in research ethics attitudes among marketing professionals in Australia, Canada, Great Britain, and the United States. The study results indicate the lack of significant differences in research ethics attitudes among marketing professionals in the four countries. This finding is interpretable as implying the generalizability of the results of previous research ethics studies involving "domestic" (United States) marketing professionals as respondents.

AKAMA, Seiki. Resolution in Constructivism. Log Anal, 30(120), 385-399, D 87.

The aim of this paper is to formalize the resolution principle proposed by J A Robinson in the framework of constructive logic. As is well known, this method is based on indirect proof. Such a proof, in general, is not permitted in constructive logic because of its lack of the excluded middle. Thus, it becomes important to discuss whether the classical interpretation remains valid for resolution from the viewpoint of constructivism. Fortunately, one of the constructive logics, called strong negation system, enables us to give a positive answer to the question under some restrictions.

AKAMA, Seiki. Subformula Semantics for Strong Negation Systems. J Phil Log, 19(2), 217-226, My 90.

AKLUJKAR, Ashok. Sambandha and Abhisambandha. J Indian Phil, 17(3), 299-307, S 89.

In Word Order in Sanskrit and Universal Grammar, J F Staal understands sambandha and abhisambandha respectively as 'relation of one word to another within a sentence' and 'order or arrangement of words (= anupurvya or anupurvi)' and proposes that the distinction between the two served to delimit the scope of grammar (vyakarana). This paper points out that no distinction of the kind Staal makes exists, that the distinction had no role in delimiting the scope of grammar, and that it is wrong to set up abhisambandha as a synomyn of anupurvi and anupurvya.

AL-AZMEH, Aziz. Utopia and Islamic Political Thought. Hist Polit Thought, 11(1), 9-19, Spr 90.

Muslim political theory, construed from works of belles lettres and of jurisprudence, treats of the phenomenon of absolute power, and of the legal attributes of rule. At the moment when general religious-moral injunctions are separated from statecraft and from technical jurisprudence, they tend to regard early Muslim paradigms as a utopian order to be recreated by political action. This is a very recent phenomenon, and is currently known under the name of fundamentalism. It is at variance with the realism and legalism of Islamic practice.

ALANEN, Lilli. Descartes's Dualism and the Philosophy of Mind. Rev Metaph Morale, 94(3), 391-413, Jl-S 89.

This paper examines Descartes's view of man and the understanding involved in the notion of the mind-body union. The aim is to spell out the implications of Descartes's distinction between different and incomparable primary notion and related kinds of knowledge, which due to the misleading but influential Rylean version of Descartes's mind-body dualism have remained largely unnoticed in the contemporary Anglo-American debate.

ALARCÓN, Enrique. Sujeto y tiempo en la "Crítica de la Razón pura". Anu Filosof, 20(1), 199-206, 1987.

ALBERT, Hans. Critical Rationalism: The Problem of Method in Social Sciences and Law. Ratio Juris, 1(1), 1-19, Mr 88.

The author characterizes the model of rationality devised by critical rationalism in opposition to the classic model of rationality and as an alternative to this. He illustrates and criticizes the trichotomous theory of knowledge which, going back to Max Scheler, is received in a secularized version by Habermas and Apel, also under the influence of the hermeneutic tradition of Heidegger and Gadamer and of the so-called "critical theory" of Max Horkheimer and Theodor Adorno. The author criticizes historicism as it expects to be an alternative to naturalism and not to make use of the method based on scientific laws. The author proposes as an example of technological social science the model developed in economics starting from Adam Smith. With regard to legal theories, natural law is rejected because of its sociomorphic cosmology. It is proposed that legal science as social technology has two parts. One part aims at efficient interpretations of valid law (for the space-time region concerned) and a second part aims at the construction of efficient norms for the modification of valid law by legislation.

ALBERT, Hans. Der Mythos des Rahmens am Pranger: Anderssons Antwort auf die wissenschaftsgeschichtliche Herausforderung. Z Phil Forsch, 44(1), 85-97, 1990.

It is shown how Andersson repudiates ideas and arguments of Kuhn, Lakatos and Feyerabend and gives a critical reconstruction of Popper's falsificationism with the conclusion that in principle the Popperian views on this topic are acceptable.

ALBERT, Karl. Sul concetto di filosofia nel Fedro platonico. Riv Filosof Neo-Scolas, 81(2), 219-223, Ap-Je 89.

The article is a part of my book *Über Platons Begriff der Philosophie* (Academia Verlag Richarz, St. Augustin 1989), and tries to show that the usual meaning about Plato's concept of philosophy as a permanent and endless search is caused by modern and not by Platonic thinking. An exact interpretation of the Phaedrus and other dialogues proves that Plato describes philosophy as the way to the last and final aim which the philosopher can really attain: the immediate knowledge of the 'good' or the 'one'.

ALBERTS, Kelly T. The Self and First Person Metaphysics. Int Stud Phil, 22(1), 3-20, 1990.

ALBIZU, Edgardo. Pensar despues de Heidegger. Rev Filosof (Mexico), 22(66), 375-387, S-D 89.

ALDRICH, Virgil. "Philosophical 'Ins' and 'Outs'" in *Mind, Value and Culture: Essays in Honor of E M Adams*, WEISSBORD, David (ed), 183-190. Atascadero, Ridgeview, 1989.

The essay's aim is to show senses of prepositions such as 'in' and 'out' that are not metaphorical and yet are irreducible to literal uses, such as 'in the drawer'. Examples: 'in the picture', 'in the person'. But pictures and persons have bodies that 'show' what is in the person or the picture, thus presenting or representing items in the world. Bodies, functioning thus, are not just 'physical objects'. Adams's theory on such counts is too mentalistic.

ALEKSANDROWICZ, Dariusz. Hegelianism as the Metaphysics of Revolution. Dialec Hum, 15(3-4), 129-138, Sum-Autumn 88.

The author interprets the Hegelian philosophy as the main intellectual source of the revolutionary myth, which constitutes the metaphysical background of the theory and practice of the Marxist-Leninist political project. Seen in the light of this view, Lenin's theory of the Party turns out to be an answer to both a political and a philosophical problem, which acquires its legitimacy within the framework of the Hegelian tradition.

ALEKSANDROWICZ, Dariusz. Wirtschaftslehre als Heilslehre. Conceptus, 23(60), 51-64, 1989.

The discussion of the concept of cognition represented by the so-called 'dialectical philosophy' leads beyond the limits of an epistemological argumentation. This follows from the fundamental principle of this philosophy, according to which only such thinking which is related to the 'true being' can claim to be true. In Marxism-Leninism-Stalinism as well as in the Marcuse-Horkheimer School this being is conceived of as a form of society where the regulation of the socio-economic process based on the market economy has been eliminated and replaced by the 'plan of production' which at the same is an aspect of the general 'plan of salvation'. It is the liberation of *production* from *economy* what is considered here to be the main condition of the salvation. This philosophy has found its materialization in the really existing socialist system of the Soviet type.

ALES BELLO, Angela. Tradizione medievale e innovazione umanistica. Aquinas, 32(3), 545-550, S-D 89.

ALESSI, Adriano. La struttura metafisica dell'esistente. Aquinas, 32(2), 353-380, My-Ag 89.

ALEXANDER, Donald. Bioregionalism: Science or Sensibility? Environ Ethics, 12(2), 161-173, Sum 90.

The current interest in bioregionalism, stimulated in part by Kirkpatrick Sale's *Dwellers in the Land*, shows that people are looking for a form of political praxis which addresses the importance of region. In this paper, I argue that much of the bioregional literature written to date mystifies the concept of region, discounting the role of subjectivity and culture in shaping regional boundaries and veers toward a simplistic view of "nature knows best." Bioregionalism can be rehabilitated, provided we treat it not as a "revealed wisdom" for the reconstruction of human society, but as a sensibility and environmental ethic that can infuse our work even as we make use of the functional regionalisms that increasingly shape people's consciousness. I conclude by citing Lewis Mumford's concept of a region as capturing the dialectical interplay of natural and cultural elements.

ALEXANDER, John V I (trans) and HORSTER, Detlev. Philosophizing with Children in the Glocksee School in Hanover, Germany. Thinking, 8(3), 23-24, 1989.

ALEXANDER, Larry. Reconsidering the Relationship among Voluntary Acts, Strict Liability, and Negligence in Criminal Law. Soc Phil Pol, 7(2), 84-104, Spr 90.

In this article I analyze the relationship among three principles of Anglo-American criminal law: the voluntary act principle (no criminal liability in the absence of a voluntary act); the strict liability principle (criminal liability can be predicated solely on a voluntary act); and the negligence principle (as an alternative to strict liability, criminal liability can be predicated on a voluntary act plus negligence). I conclude that the first two

principles are in tension with one another and that the second and third principle collapse into one another. I then state what I see as the implications of these conclusions.

ALEXANDER, Thomas M. Pragmatic Imagination. Trans Peirce Soc, 26(3), 325-348, Sum 90.

ALEXY, Robert. On Necessary Relations Between Law and Morality. Ratio Juris, 2(2), 167-183, Jl 89.

The author's thesis is that there is a conceptually necessary connection between law and morality which means legal positivism must fail as a comprehensive theory. The substantiation of this thesis takes place within a conceptual framework which shows that there are at least 64 theses to be distinguished, concerning the relationship of law and morality. The basis for the author's argument in favour of a necessary connection is formed by the thesis that individual legal norms and decisions as well as whole legal systems necessarily make a claim to correctness. The explication of this claim within the frame of discourse theory shows that the law has a conceptually necessary, ideal dimension, which connects law with a procedural, universalistic morality.

ALFIERI, Luigi. Nietzsche e il "mito" di Nietzsche: In margine a un libro su Nietzsche e il nazismo. Riv Int Filosof Diritto, 66(3), 497-514, Jl-S 89.

ALFONSO, Louis. The "Notes on the Government and Population of the Kingdom of Naples" and Berkeley's Probable Route to Sicily. Berkeley News, 11, 20-27, 1989-90.

ALLARD, Gérald. Machiavel, lecteur des Anciens. Laval Theol Phil, 46(1), 43-63, F 90.

Machiavel, homme d'action et d'expérience, auteur du trop fameux *Prince*, était un lecteur des historiens, penseurs et philosophes de l'Antiquité. Une lecture attentive du *Prince* fournit quelques faits qui illustrent cette thèse. À cette fin, les oeuvres d'Hérodien, de Plutarque et de Cicéron sont examinées et comparées aux mots et prises de position du *Prince*.

ALLEN, Barry. Gruesome Arithmetic: Kripke's Sceptic Replies. Dialogue (Canada), 28(2), 257-264, 1989.

Kripke's *Wittgenstein on Rules and Private Language* has enlivened recent discussion of Wittgenstein's later philosophy. Yet it is possible to disengage his interpretive thesis from its supporting argumentation. This leaves an intriguing skeptical argument which Kripke first powerfully advances, then tries to halt. But contrary to the impression his argument may leave, Kripke's solution and the position it concedes to the Skeptic are deeply allied. I demonstrate their common assumption, and show that Kripke's solution begs the Skeptic's question. Furthermore, we can live with the Skeptic, whose argument usefully contributes to a kind of nominalism in the philosophy of truth.

ALLEN, Jeffner (ed) and YOUNG, Iris Marion (ed). *The Thinking Muse: Feminism and Modern French Philosophy*. Bloomington, Indiana Univ Pr, 1989

Marking a radical shift in the traditional philosophical separation between muse (female) and thinker (male), this book revises the scope and methods of philosophical reflection. These engaging essays by American feminists bring together feminist philosophy, existential phenomenology, and recent currents in French poststructuralist thought. The authors consider a broad range of modern French philosophers, including Camus, Cixous, Derrida, Foucault, Irigaray, Kristeva, Merleau-Ponty, Sartre, and Wittig. While finding gaps, biases, and silences in their writings, the authors show that the thinkers discussed provide fruitful modes of discourse, both for critique and for positive reflection. At the same time the essays illustrate the creation of feminist philosophical styles that give rise to positive accounts of women's experience. The editors provide an excellent introductory overview, making this an ideal book for courses in feminist theory and philosophy and modern French thought.

ALLEN, Layman E and PAYTON, Sallyanne and SAXON, Charles S. Synthesizing Related Rules from Statutes and Cases for Legal Expert Systems. Ratio Juris, 3(2), 272-318, Jl 90.

Different legal expert systems may be incompatible with each other: a user in characterizing the same situation by answering the questions presented in a consultation can be led to contradictory inferences. Such systems can be "synthesized" to help users avoid such contradictions by alerting them that other relevant systems are available to be consulted as they are responding to questions. An example of potentially incompatible, related legal expert systems is presented here—ones for the New Jersey murder statute and the celebrated Quinlan case, along with one way of synthesizing them to avoid such incompatibility.

ALLEN, Paul. "Does Star Wars Depend on Contradiction and Deception?" in *Inquiries into Values: The Inaugural Session of the International Society for*

Value Inquiry, LEE, Sander H , 429-440. Lewiston, Mellen Pr, 1989.

To what extent is the US government using deception and various forms of distorted thinking to sell SDI to the American people? We analyze seven lines of reasoning which the administration seems to be resorting to in order to justify its promotion of SDI. We conclude that all seven are products of confusion, contradiction, or deception. Finally we suggest a theory to explain how the key proponent of SDI, Reagan, could have justified in his own mind his enthusiasm for SDI.

ALLEN, R T. The Arousal and Expression of Emotion by Music. Brit J Aes, 30(1), 57-61, Ja 90.

The idea of 'arousal' is ambiguous and can refer to (1) 'evoking' an emotion which is the counterpart to that in the music (e.g., fear to malice or anger); (2) 'communicating' or arousing the *same* emotion in the listener as in the music; (3) 'provoking' an emotion towards itself and to the emotion or lack of emotion in it (e.g., scorn towards its sentimentality). 'Arousal' therefore presupposes, and so cannot be identified with, an emotion already 'in' the music. We do not attribute emotions to music by way of analogy with people, but as a continuation of our original perception of the world as 'affective' or 'physiognomical' (cf. Katz and Wertheimer). We then depersonalise the world but can still respond to things as having emotions and attitudes within them.

ALLEN, R T. Metaphysics in Education. J Phil Educ, 23(2), 159-169, Wint 89.

Recent philosophy of education has ignored metaphysics. P H Hirst's arguments against its relevance are refuted and his own theory of education presupposes a specific metaphysics. Metaphysical beliefs necessarily help to determine the selection of the curriculum, especially by permitting or debarring given items. Examples of metaphysics in the curriculum: the metaphysical presuppositions of natural science; the world-views embodied in literature, even naturalistic fiction; the question of escapism raised by all fiction, and thus the question of what is the real world; and the particular ontology embodied in each language or in every language.

ALLEN, R T. When Loyalty No Harm Meant. Rev Metaph, 43(2), 281-294, D 89.

Loyalty has been little discussed in modern philosophy (Bryant, Royce, Ladd) and has not been distinguished sufficiently from fidelity or faithfulness to one's word, promise or pledge. But loyalty can be owed apart from any promise or pledge. Its object is either a concrete and personal being or a pledge to something not concrete nor personal. In both, it is loyalty to something already existing. The modern view of man as self-defining subject who creates all his obligations is incompatible with any loyalty (and piety) owed apart from one's pledging it, and explains the reduction of loyalty to fidelity.

ALLEN, Terry. Doing Philosophy with Children. Thinking, 7(3), 23-28, 1988.

ALLEN, Terry. I Think, Therefore I Can: Attribution and Philosophy for Children. Thinking, 8(1), 14-18, 1989.

ALLISON, David B. "The *Différance* of Translation" in *The Textual Sublime: Deconstruction and Its Differences*, SILVERMAN, Hugh J (ed), 177-190. Albany, SUNY Pr, 1990.

ALMAGOR, Uri. Odors and Private Language: Observations on the Phenomenology of Scent. Human Stud, 13(3), 253-274, Jl 90.

This article discusses three dimensions of odor perception: "Primordial," social and individual, concentrating on the latter. It takes the arguments against private language put forward by Wittgenstein and his interpreters in support of an argument for the existence of a phenomenological basis of odor sensation, whose meaning is not always that of the "olfactory given" in the public realm or that of typically known odors in society. Such an approach enables us not only to argue that some aspects of odor sensation resemble the notion of a "private language" but also to better understand the individual's scent perception and experiences.

ALMEDER, Robert. Peircean Scientific Realism. Hist Phil Quart, 6(4), 357-364, O 89.

In this paper I examine Peirce's view that scientific inquiry will come to some final theory better than all available others. After showing that the latter was in fact Peirce's view, I examine the reasons one might offer in defense of the view and conclude that we certainly do have persuasive reasons for thinking Peirce's position is correct. In all of this the most important question is whether the number of nontrivial empirically answerable questions is finitely many. I argue for the affirmative. Given that, plus indefinite progress by way of answering more and more questions in the course of time without end, a final set of nontrivial answers will emerge.

ALMEDER, Robert and HOFF, Franklin J. Reliability and Goldman's

Theory of Justification. Philosophia (Israel), 19(2-3), 165-187, O 89.

In this essay we argue that Goldman's theory of justification is defective because it is neither a necessary nor a sufficient condition for a person being justified in what she believes that her belief be reliably produced or caused in any humanly specifiable way. We examine various replies and defenses of reliabilism and argue that they are defective. What renders a belief justified has nothing to do with the way in which the belief is caused to come about.

ALMEIDA, Michael J. Deontic Logic and the Possibility of Moral Conflict. Erkenntnis, 33(1), 57-71, Jl 90.

Standard dyadic deontic logic (as well as standard deontic logic) has recently come under attack by moral philosophers who maintain that the axioms of standard dyadic deontic logic are biased against moral theories which generate moral conflicts. Since moral theories which generate conflicts are at least logically tenable, it is argued, standard dyadic deontic logic should be modified so that the set of logically possible moral theories includes those which generate such conflicts. I argue that (1) there are only certain types of moral conflicts which are interesting, and which have worried moral theorists, (2) the modification of standard dyadic deontic logic along the lines suggested by those who defend the possibility of moral conflicts makes possible only uninteresting types of moral conflicts, and (3) the general strategy of piecemeal modification standard dyadic deontic logic is misguided: the possibility of interesting moral conflicts cannot be achieved in that way.

ALMOND, Brenda. Alasdair MacIntyre: The Virtue of Tradition. J Applied Phil, 7(1), 99-103, Mr 90.

Liberal individualism is attacked by Alasdair MacIntyre on the grounds that it is based on a rejection of tradition in favour of individual preferences. He argues that the pursuit of a universal culture and a universal morality promote a rootless cosmopolitanism, that individuals cannot be conceived of in abstraction from particularities of character, history and circumstance, and that liberal education is a process of deprivation rather than enrichment. However, while this analysis succeeds in identifying important defects of modern liberal societies, it is based on a false conception of liberalism, which is in fact based on strong and distinctive values.

ALMOND, Brenda and ULANOWSKY, Carole. HIV and Pregnancy. Hastings Center Rep, 20(2), 16-21, Mr-Ap 90.

Testing women of childbearing age for HIV infection and disclosure of HIV status should be examined from three interlocking perspectives—women's personal concerns, the interests of caregivers, and those of the community. In the absence of specific objections, testing for HIV infection should be considered a routine procedure in prenatal care.

ALMOND, Brenda. Seven Moral Myths. Philosophy, 65(252), 129-136, Ap 90.

Ethics addresses the question of how to live, individually and socially. Educators should be concerned with this question, but too often offer those they teach a smorgasbord of moral fare, rather than simple fundamental values based on a common human nature. This is the result of the prevalence of certain myths or errors of moral reasoning, centrally connected with relativism, and involving the notions of toleration and neutrality, liberalism and permissiveness.

ALONI, Nimrod. The Three Pedagogical Dimensions of Nietzsche's Philosophy. Educ Theor, 39(4), 301-306, Fall 89.

In this article I present Nietzsche as a counternihilistic philosopher-educator and argue that the guiding principle of his philosophy is the exploration of cultural conditions and ways of life that could lift man to higher modes of existence. I have organized the pedagogical elements of his works in terms of aim, groundwork, and example: *aiming* to liberate humanity from the state of nihilism toward healthier and nobler modes of existence, *groundwork* that is manifested in his pedagogical anthropology, and the *example* that he sets for "doing" the type of education necessary for the elevation and enhancement of man.

ALPERSON, Philip A. *What is Music?*. New York, Haven, 1987

A comprehensive discussion of problems in the philosophy of music. The book contains an essay by the editor on the history of philosophical reflections on music and a long essay by Francis Sparshott on the limits and grounds of the aesthetics of music. There are also articles by other contemporary philosophers on aspects of musical meaning (formal, emotional, representational and semiotic), music composition and performance, song and music drama, the evaluation of music, music and history, musical understanding and the challenge of contemporary music. The emphasis throughout is on musical practice broadly conceived. All the essays are written for this volume.

ALPERSON, Philip. "Introduction: The Philosophy of Music" in *What is*

Music?, ALPERSON, Philip A , 1-30. New York, Haven, 1987.

An overview of problems in the philosophy of music. The essay contains a historical account of philosophical reflections on music and an examination of the views of leading contemporary philosophers on topics including musical meaning, musical composition and performance, song and music drama, the evaluation of music, music and history, musical understanding and the challenge of contemporary music. The author argues for a movement from a normative *aesthetics of music* which takes as its focus music in the fine art tradition to a *philosophy of music* which takes as its object the entire range and significance of music as a human practice.

ALPERSON, Philip. "Music as Philosophy" in *What is Music?*, ALPERSON, Philip A , 193-210. New York, Haven, 1987.

A discussion of the possibility that instrumental music be considered philosophical. It is observed that generations of philosophers have construed the meaning of instrumental music in metaphysical terms, appealing to many different aspects of musical theory and practice. The author argues that instrumental music cannot directly assert philosophical truths because it is not adequately propositional in nature. However, he defends the view that music may be considered philosophical in a more limited but nontrivial sense, offering a typology of ways ("genetic," "illustrative," "component," "emblematic," and "paradigmatic") in which music can play a role in the activity of philosophical inquiry.

ALSTON, Kal. Bipolar Disorders: The Unifying Possibilities of Friendship and Feminist Theory. Proc Phil Educ, 45, 76-80, 1989.

ALSTON, William P. *Divine Nature and Human Language: Essays in Philosophical Theology*. Ithaca, Cornell Univ Pr, 1990

These essays deal with basic issues concerning epistemic concepts, positions, and orientations, as well with the more specific topic of one's knowledge of one's own conscious states. Part I deals with foundationalism, defending a form of the view. Part II examines concepts of justification and considers the relation of justification and knowledge. Part III looks at internalist and externalist approaches to epistemology. Part IV is concerned with the epistemology of self-knowledge.

ALSTON, William P. *Epistemic Justification: Essays in the Theory of Knowledge*. Ithaca, Cornell Univ Pr, 1990

The book is divided into three parts. The first group of essays is devoted to the kind of meaning terms carry in application to God and to what is involved in referring to God. The second deals with issues concerning divine knowledge, divine eternity, and other aspects of the divine nature. The third part is concerned with divine activity in the world and with God as the foundation of ethics.

ALSTON, William P. Goldman on Epistemic Justification. Philosophia (Israel), 19(2-3), 115-131, O 89.

Despite basic agreement I find the following difficulties: (1) making justification hang on conformity with permission rules gets into difficulties over voluntary control of belief. (2) Belief forming processes are better thought of in terms of input-output "mechanisms" each of which embodies a certain function. (3) If any reliable belief forming process confers justification, then beliefs could be justified even if they are not based on anything of which the subject is or could be aware.

ALTIERI, Charles. Life After Difference: The Positions of the Interpreter and the Positionings of the Interpreted. Monist, 73(2), 269-295, Ap 90.

Most theory of interpretation concentrates on aspects of validity. This essay asks how interpretive activity makes visible needs and powers that have considerable ethical significance. Interpreters adopt each of the singular pronoun positions in English, revealing needs and powers characteristic of each, and demonstrating specific dispositional capacities fundamental for ethical action. Thereby we understand better the role of the first person in making ethical commitments and the very different processes characterizing third person concerns for accommodating criteria and second person concerns for reverence and adjustment over time. These last two stances mark one another's necessity and one another's limits.

ALTIERI, Charles. "Style *As* the Man: From Aesthetics to Speculative Philosophy" in *Analytic Aesthetics*, SHUSTERMAN, Richard (ed), 59-84. Cambridge, Blackwell, 1989.

Attempting to illustrate limitations in analytic aesthetics, this essay takes a Wittgensteinian approach to clarifying what seems provocative in the concept of style. Style cannot be equated with signature but must be understood as an aspect of performative agency that shows why we cannot account for such agency by traditional psychoanalytic or idealist models of subjectivity. Wittgenstein provides a much better alternative by focussing on the grammatical capacity of the "as" to define personal investments without inviting claims about deep inwardness. Style is revealed by the modal adjustments characterizing *how* agency is woven into processes of thinking

and doing.

ALTIZER, Thomas J J. *The Self-Embodiment of God*. Lanham, Univ Pr of America, 1987

God is the sole subject of this meditation, and insofar as the meditation is realized the sole speaker as well. Yet it is God as speaker who is the subject of this meditation. Only when God disappears as object, or as 'God', does God fully speak. In that, God's speech is fully speech and silence ends. The ending of silence is identical with the beginning of total speech whose actualization is apocalypse.

ALTMAN, Andrew. "Glory, Respect, and Violent Conflict" in *The Causes of Quarrel: Essays on Peace, War, and Thomas Hobbes*, CAWS, Peter (ed), 114-127. Boston, Beacon Pr, 1989.

ALVARÉ, Helen M and CHOPKO, Mark E and HARRIS, Phillip. The Price of Abortion Sixteen Years Later. Nat Forum, 69(4), 18-22, Fall 89.

AMARAL, Pedro (ed). *The Metaphysics of Epistemology: Lectures by Wilfrid Sellars*. Cambridge, Abacus Pr, 1989

AMATO MANGIAMELI, Agata C. L'autoreferenzialità luhmanniana: A proposito di normalizzazione dell'improbabile e improbabilità. Riv Int Filosof Diritto, 66(3), 482-493, Jl-S 89.

AMBOS-SPIES, Klaus and SOARE, R I. The Recursively Enumerable Degrees have Infinitely Many One-Types. Annals Pure Applied Log, 44(1-2), 1-23, O 89.

AMENGUAL, Gabriel. Hegel nel pensiero giuridico-politico spagnolo: Cenni storici della recezione della "Filosofia del diritto". Arch Stor Cult, 3, 375-408, 1990.

AMER, Mohamed A. First Order Logic with Empty Structures. Stud Log, 48(2), 169-177, Je 89.

For first order languages with no individual constants, empty structures and truth values (for sentences) in them are defined. The first order theories of the empty structures and of all structures (the empty ones included) are axiomatized with modus ponens as the only rule of inference. Compactness is proved and decidability is discussed. Furthermore, some well-known theorems of model theory are reconsidered under this new situation. Finally, a word is said on other approaches to the whole problem.

AMES, Roger T (ed) and CALLICOTT, J Baird (ed). *Nature in Asian Tradition of Thought: Essays in Environmental Philosophy*. Albany, SUNY Pr, 1989

William Irwin Thompson, Harold Morowitz, and Baird Callicott argue that ecology represents nature to be internally related, systemically integrated, and unified. Resonant concepts of nature may repose in Asian traditions of thought. Tu Wei-Ming, Graham Parkes, David Hall, Roger Ames, and Robert Neville explore the complementary environmental attitudes and values in the Chinese world view; Hubertus Tellenbach and Bin Kimura, David Shaner, and William LaFleur, the Japanese world view; Francis Cook, David Inada, and David Kalupahana, the Buddhist world view; Eliot Deutsch and Gerald Larson, the Indian world view. These traditions provide a rich conceptual resource for contemporary environmental philosophy.

AMES, Roger T and CALLICOTT, J Baird. "The Asian Traditions as a Conceptual Resource for Environmental Philosophy" in *Nature in Asian Tradition of Thought: Essays in Environmental Philosophy*, CALLICOTT, J Baird (ed), 1-21. Albany, SUNY Pr, 1989.

Environmental problems allegedly are rooted in Western traditions of thought. Accordingly, environmental philosophers have suggested that Eastern traditions of thought provide more ecologically resonant and environmentally benign world views. Comparative environmental philosophy is risky, but at the very least Asian traditions of thought may provide (1) a perspective from which to criticize otherwise unconscious assumptions at the foundations of the Western tradition; (2) a rich vocabulary to articulate the conceptually resonant revolutionary new paradigm in Western science; and (3) a conceptual resource for the development of indigenous Asian environmental ethics.

AMES, Roger T and CALLICOTT, J Baird. "Epilogue: On the Relation of Idea and Action" in *Nature in Asian Tradition of Thought: Essays in Environmental Philosophy*, CALLICOTT, J Baird (ed), 279-289. Albany, SUNY Pr, 1989.

Asian traditions of thought cognitively resonate with contemporary ecological ideas and environmental ideals, yet Asia is as environmentally degraded as the West. This paradox may be explained in part by the intellectual colonization of the East by the West. More deeply, ideas and ideals are only indirectly and imperfectly linked to behavior. Nevertheless, they are not utterly inefficacious. *Homo sapiens* is a precocious, weedy species. A systemic concept of nature sets limits for successful human exploitation of nature, a relational concept of human nature connects human welfare with the nature's welfare, and environmental values may moderate man's adverse environmental impact.

AMES, Roger T. "Putting the *Te* Back into Taoism" in *Nature in Asian Tradition of Thought: Essays in Environmental Philosophy*, CALLICOTT, J Baird (ed), 113-143. Albany, SUNY Pr, 1989.

AMOR, Claudio O. John Locke: sobre la justificación del gobierno. Rev Filosof (Argentina), 2(2), 157-177, N 87.

This paper deals with the justification of the existence of authorities in Locke's *Second Treatise*. The starting point is the interpretation of the law of nature as a quasi-juridical system: the epistemic-motivational requirements involved in its administration, and its satisfactibility in the given social conditions are examined. This analysis connects Locke with the vindication of a majority rule restricted in its scope.

AMOR, José Alfredo. La Hipótesis Generalizada del Continuo (HGC) y su relación con el Axioma de Elección (AE). Critica, 21(62), 55-66, Ag 89.

The so-called generalized continuum hypothesis is the sentence: Any subset of the power set of an infinite set is or of cardinality less or equal than the cardinality of the set, or of the cardinality of all the power set; the purpose of the article is to give, in Zermelo Fraenkel set theory, a proof that it implies the axiom of choice in the form: the power set of any well orderable set is well orderable, by giving an adequate definition of cardinal number of a set that doesn't depend of axiom of choice but depending from foundation axiom.

AMSELEK, Paul. Philosophy of Law and the Theory of Speech Acts. Ratio Juris, 1(3), 187-223, D 88.

The object of this paper is to throw light on the reciprocal exchanges between legal philosophy and the theory of speech acts (as developed by Austin and Searle). The first part concerns the contributions to legal philosophy made by the theory of speech acts with a view to developing new perspectives. The second part deals with the contributions of legal philosophy to speech act theory.

AMSTERDAMSKA, Olga and HAGENDIJK, R. De nieuwe zekerheden van het hedendaags wetenschapsonderzoek. Kennis Methode, 14(1), 60-83, 1990.

By rejecting old certainties about scientific rationalism and replacing them with the idea that scientific knowledge is a contingent outcome of social interaction, the constructivist theories of science have demolished the traditional fact/value distinction that underpinned most studies of the social and political controversies involving science and technology. In their analyses of such controversies, these new approaches raise new questions about issues which have not been debated earlier and introduce new sociological certainties to replace the old epistemological ones. The paper argues that because the various versions of constructivism—the strong programme, the micro-constructivism of Karin Knorr-Cetina, and the translation approach of Bruno Latour—are based on substantially different sociological assumptions, their ability to contribute to public discussions about science differs profoundly. (edited)

AMUNDSEN, Darrel W. "Suicide and Early Christian Values" in *Suicide and Euthanasia*, BRODY, Baruch A (ed), 77-153. Norwell, Kluwer, 1989.

AMUNDSON, Ron. "The Trials and Tribulations of Selectionist Explanations" in *Issues in Evolutionary Epistemology*, HAHLWEG, Kai (ed), 413-432. Albany, SUNY Pr, 1989.

Evolutionary epistemologists stress similarities among natural selection, trial and error learning, and other selective mechanisms of change. It is infrequently recognized that selectionist scientific theories have typical kinds of competitors, which competitors show similarities of their own. The challenges are often well founded and have led to modification or rejection of selectionist theories. This paper cites historical cases showing persistent patterns in selectionist/nonselectionist debates. The patterns expose a set of "Central Conditions" for the force of selectionist explanations, whatever their domain. Implications are drawn for the limits of selectionist explanation, and for the project of evolutionary epistemology itself.

ANDEREGGEN, Ignacio E M. Diferencias en la comprensión medioeval del *De divinis nominibus* de Dionisio Areopagita. Sapientia, 44(173), 197-210, Jl-S 89.

ANDERLINI, Luca. Some Notes on Church's Thesis and the Theory of Games. Theor Decis, 29(1), 19-52, Jl 90.

This paper considers games in normal form played by Turing machines. The machines are fed as input all the relevant information and then are required to play the game. Some 'impossibility' results are derived for this set-up. In particular, it is shown that no Turing machine exists which will always play the correct strategy given its opponent's choice. Such a result also generalizes to the case in which attention is restricted to economically optimizing machines only. The paper also develops a model of knowledge.

This allows the main results of the paper to be interpreted as stemming out of the impossibility of always deciding whether a player is rational or not in some appropriate sense.

ANDERS, Gunther and EATHERLY, Claude. *Burning Conscience: The Guilt of Hiroshima*. New York, Paragon House, 1989

ANDERSON, C Anthony (ed) and SAVAGE, C Wade (ed). *Rereading Russell: Essays on Bertrand Russell's Metaphysics and Epistemology*. Minneapolis, Univ of Minn Pr, 1989

ANDERSON, C Anthony. "Russell on Order in Time" in *Rereading Russell: Essays on Bertrand Russell's Metaphysics and Epistemology*, SAVAGE, C Wade (ed), 249-263. Minneapolis, Univ of Minn Pr, 1989.

A critical analysis of Bertrand Russell's construction of instants of time out of events (in "On Order in Time") is given. The author proposes a set of axioms about events as the best for the purpose and disputes Russell's claim that the existence of instants, thus constructed, cannot be proved. The analysis is defended against various objections due to Russell himself and arising from the theory of relativity. There is a discussion concerning the acceptability of constructions generally, and It is urged that the adoption of Russell's analysis of events is superior to taking instants as primitives.

ANDERSON, C Anthony. Some Emendations of Gödel's Ontological Proof. Faith Phil, 7(3), 291-303, Jl 90.

Kurt Gödel's version of the ontological argument was shown by J Howard Sobel to be defective, but some plausible modifications in the argument result in a version which is immune to Sobel's objection. A definition is suggested which permits the proof of some of Gödel's axioms.

ANDERSON, Douglas R. Three Appeals in Peirce's Neglected Argument. Trans Peirce Soc, 26(3), 349-362, Sum 90.

In this paper I examine Peirce's "Neglected Argument" by assessing the relationship of the three arguments in the "nest": the humble argument, the neglected argument proper, and the argument from scientific inquiry. In looking at these through the lens of Peirce's categoriology of persons, I see the "Neglected Argument" making belief in the reality of God hinge on three appeals: an appeal to feeling, an appeal to willing, and an appeal to thinking.

ANDERSON, Elizabeth S. Is Women's Labor a Commodity? Phil Pub Affairs, 19(1), 71-92, Wint 90.

The author criticizes the practice of commercial surrogate motherhood in the light of a theory of commodity values. The theory proposes some conditions under which it is appropriate to treat a good as a commodity or to sell it on the market. It is argued that commercial surrogate motherhood improperly treats women's reproductive powers, and children, as commodities, and that in doing so it fails to give women and children proper respect and consideration.

ANDERSON, Kevin. The Marcuse-Dunayevskaya Dialogue, 1954-1979. Stud Soviet Tho, 39(2), 89-109, Mr 90.

The extensive correspondence between Herbert Marcuse (1898-1979) and Raya Dunayevskaya (1910-1987) covers the years 1954 to 1979. During this period they debated several issues: (1) The bulk of the correspondence covers their dialogue over the relation of Hegel to Marx. (2) They also discussed the effects of automation and other technological changes on the working class, and its relation to other oppositional social groups such as Blacks, youth and women. (3) Finally, they argued over what type of critique to make of established communist societies. Their dialogue sheds new light on some of their major published writings.

ANDERSON, Lyle V. "What is it to be Moral?" in *Inquiries into Values: The Inaugural Session of the International Society for Value Inquiry*, LEE, Sander H , 15-26. Lewiston, Mellen Pr, 1989.

There are two well-known but purportedly disparate paradoxes of action. The epistemic paradox (EP) is that a person who is self-deceived must be said to believe p as a necessary condition for his or her coming to believe (simultaneously) that ~p. The metaphysical paradox (MP) is neither a deterministic nor indeterministic process of "character transformation" beginning with a being that was *not* responsible for any of its "decisions" and yielding a being who was responsible both for its decisions and for having the sort of character that would make those decisions. My goal is to show how (1) Aristotle's theory of deliberation provides EP and MP resolutions that share crucial features, and (2) this may force us to rethink the epistemic links between metaphysics and ethics.

ANDERSON, Susan Leigh. Evil. J Value Inq, 24(1), 43-53, Ja 90.

In this paper I attempt to define an "evil action." I argue that an evil action must be done consciously, voluntarily and willfully, and the agent must cause a minimum of harm, or allow a minimum of harm to be done, to at least one other person. Typically, the agent feels himself to be more powerful than, or superior to, the victim(s). It also appears to be the case that what the agent's motive is in acting may be relevant to our deciding to call an action evil, or at least in determining the degree of evilness.

ANDERSON, Thomas C. "From Freedom to Need: Sartre's First Two Moralities" in *Inquiries into Values: The Inaugural Session of the International Society for Value Inquiry*, LEE, Sander H , 315-334. Lewiston, Mellen Pr, 1989.

ANDERSON, Thomas C. "The Obligation to Will the Freedom of Others, According to Jean-Paul Sartre" in *The Question of the Other: Essays in Contemporary Continental Philosophy*, DALLERY, Arleen B (ed), 63-74. Albany, SUNY Pr, 1989.

His posthumous notebooks on ethics show that Sartre never held that human beings are inevitably in conflict. Rather he advanced arguments to prove that every human being should will the freedom of others. I present Sartre's argument from universal responsibility and his arguments from interdependency (political and psychological). I conclude that one version of the argument from psychological dependency does demonstrate that I should not interfere with, but strive to increase, the freedom of others. A question remains about the extension of this notion of the other.

ANDERSON, Tyson. Kalupahana on *Nirvāna*. Phil East West, 40(2), 221-234, Ap 90.

ANDERSON, W French. Genetics and Human Malleability. Hastings Center Rep, 20(1), 21-24, Ja-F 90.

ANDERSON, W French. Human Gene Therapy: Why Draw a Line? J Med Phil, 14(6), 681-693, D 89.

Despite widespread agreement that it would be ethical to use somatic cell gene therapy to correct serious diseases, there is still uneasiness on the part of the public about this procedure. The basis for this concern lies less with the procedure's clinical risks than with fear that genetic engineering could lead to changes in human nature. Legitimate concerns about the potential for misuse of gene transfer technology justify drawing a moral line that includes corrective germline therapy but excludes enhancement interventions in both somatic and germline contexts.

ANDERSON, Warwick. A New Approach to Regulating the Use of Animals in Science. Bioethics, 4(1), 45-54, Ja 90.

ANDIAPPAN, P and REAVLEY, M. Discrimination Against Pregnant Employees: An Analysis of Arbitration and Human Rights Tribunal Decisions in Canada. J Bus Ethics, 9(2), 143-149, F 90.

Recent arbitration and human rights boards of inquiry cases involving discrimination against pregnant employees are reviewed. A comparison is made between remedies available under each procedure. It is suggested that the human resource managers review their policies and procedures relevant to this issue to ensure that they do not have the effect or intent of discriminating against pregnant employees.

ANDLER, Daniel. Quelle est la place de l'intelligence artificielle dans l'étude de la cognition? Rev Int Phil, 44(172), 62-86, 1990.

ANDRADE, Ciro Schmidt. Heraclito de efeso entre la experiencia y la razon. Rev Filosof (Mexico), 22(65), 207-220, My-Ag 89.

ANDREATTA, Alberto. Potere e ragione nella filosofia politica di Enrico Opocher. Riv Int Filosof Diritto, 66(2), 215-239, Ap-Je 89.

ANDREEV, A L. Socialist Realism and the Traditions of Soviet Art. Soviet Stud Phil, 28(4), 71-78, Spr 90.

ANDREW, C and CODERRE, C and DENIS, A. Stop or Go: Reflections of Women Managers on Factors Influencing their Career Development. J Bus Ethics, 9(4-5), 361-367, Ap-My 90.

The purpose of this paper is to discuss how women managers themselves interpret the factors that constrain and those that facilitate management careers for women. We will do this by first reviewing some of the interpretations that have been put forward in the academic literature to explain the relatively small number of women managers and particularly the small number of very senior women managers. In the light of these interpretations, we will examine the opinions of a sample of intermediate and senior women managers in the public and private sectors in Ontario and Quebec. More specifically we will look at their answers to questions about what blocks and what facilitates management careers for women generally and what obstacles they themselves have met. We will then compare their interpretations of their own career development with the interpretations that exist in the literature.

ANDREW, Edward. Equality of Opportunity as the Noble Lie. Hist Polit Thought, 10(4), 577-595, Wint 89.

ANDREWS, Kenneth R (ed) and DAVID, Donald K (ed). *Ethics in Practice: Managing the Moral Corporation*. Boston, Harvard Bus Schl Pr, 1989

This anthology presents ethical and legal perspectives on artificial insemination, fertility drugs, embryo transfer, gestational surrogacy, surrogate motherhood, fetal monitoring, nonreproductive uses of fetuses, and other issues. In addition to discussions explaining the technology and underlying biology, the work includes case studies of concrete moral dilemmas that provoke reflection. Contributors include Lori Andrews, George Annas, Michael Bayles, Arthur Caplan, Gena Corea, Mary Mahowald, Thomas Murray, Lawrence Nelson, John Robertson, Carol Smart, Hans Tiefel, LeRoy Walters, Hon. Robert Wilentz, Richard Zaner, as well as the Ethics Committee of the American Fertility Society and the Congregation for the Doctrine of the Faith.

ANDREWS, Lori B. Control and Compensation: Laws Governing Extracorporeal Generative Materials. J Med Phil, 14(5), 541-560, O 89.

The Vatican *Instruction* advocates laws banning *in vitro* fertilization, gamete donation, embryo donation, and surrogate motherhood. The OTA Report *Infertility* provides a range of policy choices for handling these reproductive procedures. The choice among these alternative regulations needs to be developed within the framework of the right to privacy of the US Constitution, which provides support for an approach that allows the progenitors to control the uses made of their generative materials and to receive compensation for them, subject to laws which facilitate informed consent and attempt to assure quality.

ANEESH. The Birth of God. Indian Phil Quart, SUPP 17(2), 11-19, Ap 90.

ANELLIS, Irving H. Distortions and Discontinuities of Mathematical Progress: A Matter of Luck, A Matter of Time, ... A Matter of Fact. Philosophica, 43(1), 163-196, 1989.

Mathematical progress is not always linear, but frequently depends upon the vagaries of style, of luck, of timing, and of the presentation and interpretation of fact. This is illustrated through the detailed presentation of four not very well known examples from the history of mathematics.

ANELLIS, Irving H. The Roots of Mathematics Education in Russia in the Age of Peter the Great. Phil Math, 5(1-2), 23-55, 1990.

ANGEHRN, Emil. Ortsbestimmungen des Politischen: Neuere Literatur zu Thomas Hobbes. Phil Rundsch, 37(1-2), 1-26, 1990.

ANGELL, R B. "Deducibility, Entailment and Analytic Containment" in *Directions in Relevant Logic*, NORMAN, Jean (ed), 119-143. Norwell, Kluwer, 1989.

ANNAS, George J. Four-One-Four. Hastings Center Rep, 19(5), 27-29, S-O 89.

ANNAS, George J and MARINER, Wendy K and GLANTZ, Leonard H. Pregnancy, Drugs, and the Perils of Prosecution. Crim Just Ethics, 9(1), 30-41, Wint-Spr 90.

ANNAS, Julia. "Cicero on Stoic Moral Philosophy and Private Property" in *Philosophia Togata: Essays on Philosophy and Roman Society*, GRIFFIN, Miriam (ed), 151-173. New York, Clarendon/Oxford Pr, 1989.

The paper discusses a passage in De Officiis III where Cicero compares the positions of the Stoics Diogenes and Antipater in cases where rights (e.g., property rights) are involved. The paper argues that Cicero mistakes the point of the debate, and discusses, with reference to other texts, the early and middle Stoic position on the relevance of property and other institutional rights to difficult cases for moral judgment.

ANNAS, Julia. The Hellenistic Version of Aristotle's Ethics. Monist, 73(1), 80-96, Ja 90.

The article discusses some aspects of a Hellenistic account of Aristotle's ethics in Arius Didymus. It is argued that the account is an intelligent restatement of Aristotelian ethics in answer to Stoic ethics.

ANNAS, Julia. MacIntyre on Traditions. Phil Pub Affairs, 18(4), 388-404, Fall 89.

The article is a discussion review of Alasdair MacIntyre's book *Whose Justice? Which Rationality?* The review focuses on MacIntyre's notion of a tradition and his claim that there is no neutral tradition-independent notion of rationality which can adjudicate between different traditions. The review attempts to distinguish between a stronger and a weaker form of MacIntyre's claims.

ANNAS, Julia. Platon le sceptique. Rev Metaph Morale, 95(2), 267-291, Ap-Je 90.

The article discusses the sceptical New Academy's interpretation of Plato as a sceptic. The first part discusses Arcesilaus's reintroduction of Socratic method, and the reading of the Socratic dialogues and the *Theaetetus* implied by this. The second part discusses arguments probably used by the later, more moderate Academy for a reading of Plato's more dogmatic dialogues in a way consistent with scepticism.

dialogues in a way consistent with scepticism.

ANNAS, Julia. "Stoic Epistemology" in *Epistemology (Companions to Ancient Thought: 1)*, EVERSON, Stephen (ed), 184-203. New York, Cambridge Univ Pr, 1989.

The article gives an account of the development of Stoic epistemology, in particular the continuing debate with the Sceptics. It is argued that this debate exposes the issue between (in modern terms) internalist and externalist accounts of knowledge.

ANOZ, José (trans) and CLARK, Mary T. Agustín y la unidad. Augustinus, 34(135-136), 293-304, Jl-D 89.

ANOZ, José. La *Regula recepta* agustiniana, germen de vida religiosa renovada. Augustinus, 34(133-134), 155-172, Ja-Je 89.

ANSCOMBE, Elizabeth. The Simplicity of the *Tractatus*. Critica, 21(63), 3-16, D 89.

ANSCOMBE, G E M. A Comment on Coughlan's "Using People". Bioethics, 4(1), 62, Ja 90.

ANSCOMBE, G E M. Elementos y esencias. Anu Filosof, 22(2), 9-16, 1989.

ANSCOMBRE, Jean-Claude and DUCROT, Oswald. "Argumentativity and Informativity" in *From Metaphysics to Rhetoric*, MEYER, Michel (ed), 71-87. Norwell, Kluwer, 1989.

ANSELL-PEARSON, Keith. Nietzsche: A Radical Challenge to Political Theory? Rad Phil, 54, 10-18, Spr 90.

This essay critically examines recent work on Nietzsche in political theory, focussing attention on the claim that his philosophy of power contains the basis for articulating a postmodern conception of human agency. It argues that a synthesis of Kant's ethics and Nietzsche's philosophy of power cannot provide a solution to the antinomies of modern political life since for Nietzsche the relationship between autonomy and morality is one of mutual exclusivity. This argument is situated in the context of a reading of Nietzsche's relationship to the tradition of modern political thought deriving from Rousseau.

ANTISERI, Dario. Falibilismo razionale e fede cristiana. Sapienza, 42(3), 295-308, Jl-S 89.

ANTONIOTTI, Louise-Marie. L'étant, l'essence et l'être. Rev Thomiste, 90(2), 289-306, Ap-Je 90.

ANZAI, Shin-ichi. Aesthetic Theories Concerning the Picturesque: Gilpin, Price and Knight (in Japanese). Bigaku, 40(2), 36-49, Autumn 89.

According to the fundamental assumption of the picturesque aesthetics, the "painter's eye" or "picturesque eye," the eye conversant with painting, is privileged to discover "the picturesque" hidden from the common eyes. This is done (often with the assistance of imagination) by abstracting the purely visual qualities of objects and disregarding their utilitarian, moral or emotional contents. Because of circularity and conventionality, the picturesque aesthetics have been criticised since Romanticism. Nevertheless, these aestheticians themselves found the tradition of painting not so much an unassailable authority as an endless succession of experiments towards better ways of seeing nature. (edited)

AOYAMA, Hiroshi. Barwise and Etchemendy's Theory of Truth. Auslegung, 16(1), 59-72, Wint 90.

Barwise and Etchemendy have recently presented a novel solution to the Liar paradox in their very attractive book *The Liar: An Essay in Truth and Circularity*. Their solution is given in the theory of truth which they have developed using Austin's account of truth. Their theory of truth is well developed both philosophically and technically. In this paper, we will first look at the philosophical aspect of their theory of truth and then give some criticisms of it.

APOSTLE, Hippocrates G (trans) and DOBBS, Elizabeth A (trans) and PARSLOW, Morris A (trans) and ARISTOTLE,. *Aristotle's Poetics*. Grinnell, Peripatetic Pr, 1990

APPELBAUM, David. *Making the Body Heard: The Body's Way Toward Existence*. New York, Lang, 1989

A study of body-consciousness through the phenomenon of cognitive arrest. Cognitive arrest occurs when the automatic processes of mental activity are brought to a stop by an aesthetic, emotional, or intellectual object. An attempt is made to contrast the body's form of perception with the intellect's, and to clarify the former's relation to existence. The line of analysis takes up various suggestions on the approach to self-consciousness as idea and practice.

AQUILA, Richard E. Consciousness as Higher-Order Thought: Two Objections. Amer Phil Quart, 27(1), 81-88, Ja 90.

The view that consciousness is the appropriate targeting of mental states as objects of higher-order states implies that one might notice a sound yet fail to notice one's consciousness of it. Short of further objectionable alternatives, the view is also unable to account for the fact that certain perceptual states are not of the sort to occur unconsciously at all. A Husserlian alternative is briefly sketched: conscious mental states are instances of mental directedness *through* states that might or might not themselves be mental. They are states of affairs or events with the irreducible *form* of directedness through the latter as their material.

ÅQVIST, Lennart. A Game-Theoretical Companion to Chisholm's Ethics of Requirement. Acta Phil Fennica, 38, 327-347, 1985.

ARANA, Camilo Reynaud. La filosofia dialogica de Martin Buber misterio y magia del "encuentro". Rev Filosof (Mexico), 22(65), 228-234, My-Ag 89.

ARANA, Juan. La doble significación científica y filosófica de la evolución del concepto de fuerza de Descartes a Euler. Anu Filosof, 20(1), 9-42, 1987.

ARANA, Juan. La revolución científica y las revoluciones filosóficas. Anu Filosof, 22(2), 17-35, 1989.

ARANSON, Peter H. "The Democratic Order and Public Choice" in *Politics and Process*, BRENNAN, Geoffrey (ed), 97-148. New York, Cambridge Univ Pr, 1989.

Four problems afflict the ability of decision processes in representative democracies to render social choices that reflect citizen's preferences: rational abstention, rational ignorance, disequilibrium, and rent-seeking. Each problem results in the degradation of citizens' welfare. This essay reviews the sources and characteristics of each of these problems. It argues that these problems emerge endogenously to politics in representative democracies. It then shows that attempts to correct any one of these problems will exacerbate at least one of the others.

ARATA, Carlo. La metafisica della Prima Persona *(Ego Sum Qui Sum)*: Parte prima. Riv Filosof Neo-Scolas, 81(2), 181-200, Ap-Je 89.

ARBIB, Michael A. A Piagetian Perspective on Mathematical Construction. Synthese, 84(1), 43-58, Jl 90.

In this paper, we offer a Piagetian perspective on the construction of the logico-mathematical schemas which embody our knowledge of logic and mathematics. Logico-mathematical entities are tied to the subject's activities, yet are so constructed by reflective abstraction that they result from sensorimotor experience only via the construction of intermediate schemas of increasing abstraction. The 'axiom set' does not exhaust the cognitive structure (schema network) which the mathematician thus acquires. We thus view 'truth' not as something to be defined within the closed 'world' of a formal system but rather in terms of the schema network within which the formal system is embedded. We differ from Piaget in that we see mathematical knowledge as based on social processes of mutual verification which provide an external drive to any 'necessary dynamic' of reflective abstraction within the individual. From this perspective, we argue that axiom schemas tied to a preferred interpretation may provide a necessary intermediate stage of reflective abstraction en route to acquisition of the ability to use formal systems in abstracto.

ARCHARD, David. Paternalism Defined. Analysis, 50(1), 36-42, Ja 90.

In this article I provide a definition of paternalism which I believe improves on others that have been offered. Someone behaves paternalistically towards another if they deny or diminish the other's choice in respect of some state of affairs concerning the other's good, doing so in the main because of a belief that this promotes the other's good and discounting the other's belief that this behaviour does not promote their own good. I introduce a number of examples to illustrate and defend this definition which is a morally neutral one.

ARCILLA, René V. Edification, Conversation, and Narrative: Rortyan Motifs for Philosophy of Education. Educ Theor, 40(1), 35-39, Wint 90.

ARCILLA, René V. The Greatest Metaphysics Ever Told? Proc Phil Educ, 45, 41-44, 1989.

ARD, Ben Neal. *Rational Sex Ethics (Second Edition)*. New York, Lang, 1989

This book is a critique of conventional sex morality and a humanistic offering of more rational alternatives in a more scientific sex ethics. The author discusses adolescents and sex, premarital and extramarital sex, birth control, abortion, sex and guilt, problematic sex behavior, safer sex (in an era of herpes, AIDS, etc.), and in a philosophical and psychological manner, discusses science and ethics. The point of view set forth in this book is perhaps best called scientific humanism. Essentially this book is an extension of the democratic ideal into the sexual sphere. Instead of conventional sex morality the author offers a more rational sex ethics.

ARDAGH, David. The Immorality of Nuclear Deterrence. Int Phil Quart, 30(3), 343-358, S 90.

This paper argues that nuclear deterrence strategy (NDS) is immoral. Section I outlines some moral intuitions regarding limits on deterrent threat-making disclosed in ordinary domestic and legal contexts and suggests that NDS flouts these intuitions. Section II further specifies these moral intuitions as they are articulated in the "natural law/just war" tradition; applies them to NDS; and confirms that NDS is substantially at odds with this moral tradition. Section III outlines and rejects two arguments for NDS which appear to be left standing by Section II's analysis: first, that NDS can meet the excepting conditions to the principle that it is wrong to threaten what it would be wrong to do; second, that NDS is not fundamentally intended, but only quasi-intended by its proponents. Section IV offers some speculation on why we do not abandon NDS even though it is on reflection immoral.

ÁRDAL, Páll S. Hume and Davidson on Pride. Hume Stud, 15(2), 387-394, N 89.

ARENELLA, Peter. Character, Choice, and Moral Agency: The Relevance of Character to our Moral Culpability Judgments. Soc Phil Pol, 7(2), 59-83, Spr 90.

This essay considers the attributes a person must possess to justify treating him as someone worthy of moral address and evaluation by examining a "rational choice" and character-based conception of moral agency. The author claims that the rational choice model offers an inadequate account of a moral agent's necessary attributes because it treats the actor's capacity to reason instrumentally as his only salient moral characteristic and permits the imposition of moral blame of actors who lack the capacity to comply with governing moral norms for moral reasons. He argues that the capacity for moral motivation is a necessary attribute of moral agency and suggests that only a character-based model can explain how this capacity develops and functions.

ARGYROPOULOS, R. Theosebeia in Plethon's Work: A Concept in Transition. Philosophia (Athens), 17-18, 391-395, 1987-88.

ARIEW, Roger (trans) and BARKER, Peter (trans) and DUHEM, Pierre. Logical Examination of Physical Theory. Synthese, 83(2), 183-188, My 90.

Duhem summarizes his philosophy of science, beginning from the "truism" that individual elements in a scientific system are inseparable for purposes of application or appraisal, and deriving both the thesis most commonly associated with his name, that elements of a scientific system are not separately falsifiable, and the thesis that observations are theory laden. Newtonian inductivists are criticized for ignoring the latter; Cartesian hypothetico-deductivists for destroying science's ability to achieve consensus by privileging a particular metaphysics. Duhem rejects atomism (Lorentz's electron theory) on the same grounds as Cartesianism, and contrasts his own view with pragmatic instrumentalism. Metaphysics is not the starting point of theory but the endpoint of science's historical development. Duhem may therefore, in a qualified sense, count as a convergent realist.

ARIEW, Roger. Christopher Clavius and the Classification of the Sciences. Synthese, 83(2), 293-300, My 90.

I discuss two questions: (1) would Duhem have accepted the thesis of the continuity of scientific methodology? and (2) to what extent is the Oxford tradition of classification/subalternation of sciences continuous with early modern science? I argue that Duhem would have been surprised by the claim that scientific methodology is continuous; he expected at best only a continuity of physical theories, which he was trying to isolate from the perpetual fluctuations of methods and metaphysics. I also argue that the evidence does not support the conclusion that early modern doctrines about mathematics and physics are continuous with the subalternation of sciences from Grosseteste, Bacon, and the theologians of fourteenth-century Oxford. The official and dominant context for early modern scientific methodology seems to have been progressive Thomism, and early modern thinkers seem to have pitted themselves against it.

ARIEW, Roger (trans) and BARKER, Peter (trans) and DUHEM, Pierre. Research on the History of Physical Theories. Synthese, 83(2), 189-200, My 90.

Reviewing his research in the history of statics and dynamics, Duhem argues that Energetics is the modern heir to the principle of "saving the phenomena" that originated in Greek astronomy. Jordanus de Nemore's school surpassed ancient statics by introducing the principle of virtual work, while Parisian nominalists prepared the way for modern dynamics. After the condemnation of 1277 loosened the hold of Aristotelian theory, Ockham rehabilitated Philoponus's account of projectiles. Buridan, followed by Oresme, Albert of Saxony, and Leonardo, adopted impetus as the foundation of dynamics and introduced a law of inertia. Similar antecedents for the law of fall culminated

in Domingo de Soto. The reception of these principles by Galileo and his contemporaries led to the modern science of mechanics. But the metaphysics of imperceptible bodies and hidden motions played no role in these advances, confirming Duhem's logical analysis of scientific method, and the primacy of Energetics as their descendant.

ARISAKA, Yoko and FEENBERG, Andrew. Experiential Ontology: The Origins of the Nishida Philosophy in the Doctrine of Experience. Int Phil Quart, 30(2), 173-205, Je 90.

The thesis of this article is that Kitaro Nishida (1870-1945), Japan's leading philosopher in this century, should be interpreted primarily against the background of the Continental tradition. The article discusses his relation to the many Western thinkers who influenced him. Nishida's first book developed a version of William James's theory of "radical empiricism," but later, under the influence of Fichte, Husserl, and Hegel, Nishida elaborated a dialectical phenomenology. The article argues that, like many of his European contemporaries, Nishida attempted to conceive immediate experience as an ontological absolute.

ARISTOTLE and APOSTLE, Hippocrates G (trans) and DOBBS, Elizabeth A (trans) and PARSLOW, Morris A (trans). *Aristotle's Poetics*. Grinnell, Peripatetic Pr, 1990

ARMOUR, Leslie. Leibniz, Transubstantiation and the Relation between Pure and Applied Philosophy. Phil Context, 19, 33-46, 1989.

Leibniz wrestled for many years with the problem of transubstantiation. It was a key issue in the resolution of the confrontations between Catholic orthodoxy and the "new" (post-Cartesian) philosophy as well as of the tensions between Catholics and protestants in Europe. I argue that a connection between Leibniz's metaphysics and his political and moral theory was necessitated by his belief that a just order in human affairs must reflect the harmony of the universe. This belief dictated the course of his investigations, and, in following them, we learn something about the relations between theoretical and applied philosophy.

ARMSTRONG, A H. On Not Knowing too Much About God. Philosophy, 25, 129-145, 89 Supp.

ARMSTRONG, D M. "C B Martin, Counterfactuals, Causality, and Conditionals" in *Cause, Mind, and Reality: Essays Honoring C B Martin*, HEIL, John (ed), 7-15. Norwell, Kluwer, 1989.

The paper begins with some personal reminiscences of C B Martin. It goes on to argue for the importance of his truth-maker doctrine, and its application to counterfactuals. His singularist theory of causation is then discussed, and the question of truth-makers for dispositions.

ARMSTRONG, D M. *A Combinatorial Theory of Possibility*. New York, Cambridge Univ Pr, 1989

ARMSTRONG, D M and MC CALL, Storrs. God's Lottery. Analysis, 49(4), 223-224, O 89.

When Cantor's definition of equinumerousness as one-one correspondence is pitted against the intuition that no set can be the same size as one of its own proper subsets, which side wins? An answer is given by God's lottery, in which God offers choices between different sets of lottery tickets.

ARMSTRONG, Robert L and HOWE, Lawrence W. An Euler Test for Syllogisms. Teach Phil, 13(1), 39-46, Mr 90.

Citing both pedagogical and theoretical difficulties with the Venn diagram method of testing syllogisms, we propose an alternative method based on Euler Circles. Our method works for all categorical syllogisms and is based on the indirect or counterexample method of formal proof. It rejects the restrictive Boolean interpretation of existence in favor of the intuitive, traditional Aristotelian assumption that everything exists in some sense or other. Critical questions about the existential content of terms are deferred to postlogical analysis in the same manner that questions about the soundness of arguments are discussed after the evaluation of validity.

ARMSTRONG, T J (trans) and SPAEMANN, Robert. *Basic Moral Concepts*. New York, Routledge, 1989

The book is an introduction into ethical thinking dealing with the problems of the relativity of good and evil, justice and self-interest, responsibility, utilitarianism, and the role of the individual in society. It points out and discusses the philosophical importance of upbringing and education. Ethical relativism is criticized on the basis of the concept of the unconditional reflecting the tradition of ethical thinking from Plato and Aristotle to Kant and modern theories of value. The concluding chapter characterizes equanimity as the attitude to what we cannot change.

ARMSTRONG-BUCK, Susan. Nonhuman Experience: A Whiteheadian Analysis. Process Stud, 18(1), 1-18, Spr 89.

The article is an application of Whitehead's system to recent findings concerning nonhuman experience, particularly primate experience. I discuss research concerning nonhuman aesthetic and moral experience, nonverbal thinking, language, consciousness and self-consciousness, and deception. I also provide a Whiteheadian account of self-consciousness and a fourfold typology of self-consciousness as agent, public, introspective and pure. The article demonstrates that in some respects animal consciousness is closer to human consciousness than Whitehead believed.

ARNASON, Johann P. Cultural Critique and Cultural Presuppositions: The Hermeneutical Undercurrent in Critical Theory. Phil Soc Crit, 15(2), 125-149, 1989.

ARNAULT, Lynne. Talking 'Bout a Revolution: Feminism, Historicism, and Liberal Moral Theory. Logos (USA), 10, 39-55, 1989.

In my paper I attempt to support feminist efforts to effect a radical transformation of liberal moral epistemology by taking a representative liberal theory—R M Hare's universal prescriptivism—and critically analyzing one of its central notions, the notion of "taking the standpoint of the other." Hare's characterization of "taking the standpoint of the other" as a monological process commits him to denying the epistemic significance of social factors and social politics in the construction of the knowing subject. I argue that when it is conceived as a monological process of deliberation, "taking the standpoint of the other" is methodologically hubristic, epistemologically problematic, and grounded in an inadequate understanding of what constitutes the "standpoints" or situations of others. Only by moving toward a *dialogical* model of moral deliberation and a critical *social* understanding of the conditions governing dialogical interchange, can liberal moral theory's ideal of impartiality be rehabilitated.

ARNESON, Richard J. Liberal Egalitarianism and World Resource Distribution: Two Views. J Value Inq, 23(3), 171-190, S 89.

Two varieties of liberal egalitarianism are distinguished: a Lockean and a welfare egalitarian position. The implications of each doctrine with respect to world resource distribution are explored. The varieties of egalitarianism converge on the judgment that large resource transfers from rich to poor countries are required by distributive justice. A final section of the paper briefly considers how best to enforce worldwide distributive justice obligations.

ARNESON, Richard J. Liberalism, Distributive Subjectivism, and Equal Opportunity for Welfare. Phil Pub Affairs, 19(2), 158-194, Spr 90.

"Distributive subjectivism" is the claim that for purposes of determining what should count as fair shares from the standpoint of distributive justice, the appropriate measure of a person's resources is the welfare or rational preference satisfaction level that those resources enable her to reach. I defend distributive subjectivism along with the partial explication of "fair shares" as provision of equal opportunity for welfare. I rebut criticisms of distributive subjectivism developed by Richard Brandt, Amartya Sen, John Rawls, and Ronald Dworkin.

ARNESON, Richard J. Neutrality and Utility. Can J Phil, 20(2), 215-240, Je 90.

ARNESON, Richard J. Paternalism, Utility and Fairness. Rev Int Phil, 43(170), 409-437, 1989.

The principle of antipaternalism holds that restriction of a person's liberty to carry out a voluntarily chosen course of conduct should never be imposed for the purpose of benefitting either that person herself or others who voluntarily consent to be affected by that conduct. John Stuart Mill offers utilitarian arguments for this principle in On Liberty. Recently Joel Feinberg has appealed to an ideal of personal sovereignty to support a version of antipaternalism. Against Mill and Feinberg I argue that antipaternalism is unfair insofar as it conflicts with a reasonable concern for the welfare of worse-off members of society.

ARNESON, Richard J. Primary Goods Reconsidered. Nous, 24(3), 429-454, Je 90.

This essay challenges John Rawls's claim that the measure of interpersonal comparisons of advantage and disadvantage for purposes of a theory of justice should be primary social goods. Instead a welfare or rational preference satisfaction standard is defended. Neither the Kantian turn in Rawls's recent writings nor his appeal to the fact of pluralism provides a sound defense of the primary good notion. Nor does Rawls's invocation of the voluntary character of preferences discredit a welfare standard.

ARNHART, Larry. On Jaffa's Reading of Aristotle's *Nichomachean Ethics*. Polis, 6(2), 127-138, 1986.

Of the many teachings in Aristotle's *Nicomachean Ethics* that are difficult to interpret, none is more critical for one's understanding of the book than the relationship between moral and intellectual virtue. A survey of the major studies of the *Ethics* written over the last few decades will reveal a variety of theories to explain the connection between Aristotle's account of the life of moral virtue, in the early parts of the book, and his account of the

philosophic life, near the end of the book. Although little scholarly attention has been given to Harry Jaffa's work on the *Ethics*, I believe Jaffa offers the most cogent solution to the problem. But since I also believe there are some difficulties in his interpretation, I will suggest a revised version of his argument that avoids the difficulties.

ARNOLD, Keith. Pascal's Great Experiment. Dialogue (Canada), 28(3), 401-415, 1989.

Pascal invented the methodology of experimentation. The Great Experiment exemplified his scientific theories about design, analysis and truth-seeking in scientific research. Pascal's experiment was deceptively simple; in structure, it was the most important experiment in the history of science and in scientific epistemology. It is historically significant because it was the very first controlled experiment in science. It is philosophically important because it embodied modern views on the formulation and testing of hypotheses, and because it established standards for the analysis of experiments, and for tracking empirical truths.

ARNOLD, Keith. Pascal's Theory of Scientific Knowledge. J Hist Phil, 27(4), 531-544, O 89.

Pascal believed a theory of knowledge requires two complementary parts. One is the faculty of mind he called *le coeur*, which we would call intuition or insight. The complement to this is the faculty of mind Pascal named *l'esprit*, which is the ability to reason, to solve problems, to evaluate evidence, and to construct proofs. Pascal's theory of reasoning, measurement and experimentation, within a theory of knowledge, originates and illustrates a form of intuitionism. His theory of scientific knowledge develops from an instrumentalist theory of mind and cognition, and into a theory of experimental methods and scientific decision making.

ARNOLD, Peter J. Democracy, Education, and Sport. J Phil Sport, 16, 100-110, 1989.

ARNOLD, Peter J. *Education, Movement and the Curriculum: A Philosophic Enquiry*. Philadelphia, Falmer Pr, 1989

Two questions underly the contemporary educational debate. The first is: 'On what grounds should a subject be taught in schools?' The second is: 'How can it be satisfactorily evaluated?' The purpose of this work is to provide answers to both these questions in relation to what is customarily called 'physical education', by exploring the relationship between the concept of education and the concept of movement and to see what implications this has for the teacher and for curriculum planning. The aim is that the book will not only provide a sound introduction to discussion about the educational basis of physical activities in the context of school life, but be of practical use when it comes to making decisions about why a particular programme should be adopted and how it can be reasonably appraised. (edited)

ARONSON, Ronald. Responsibility and Complicity. Phil Papers, 19(1), 53-73, Ap 90.

What does reflection on the Holocaust have to teach us about apartheid? Beginning with Sartre's notion of responsibility, we can begin to construct a spiral of complicity and responsibility to explain different kinds and degrees of participation in evil. This model can be used to assess responsibility for apartheid. This is an expansion and revision of a lecture originally given in South Africa.

ARRAS, John and RHODEN, Nancy. *Ethical Issues in Modern Medicine (Third Edition)*. Mountain View, Mayfield, 1989

ARREGUI, Jorge Vicente. Metafísica del yo y hermenéutica diltheyana de la vida. Anu Filosof, 21(1), 97-121, 1988.

ARRELL, Douglas. Exemplification Reconsidered. Brit J Aes, 30(3), 233-243, Jl 90.

According to Nelson Goodman, exemplification is reference from an object to certain of its predicates. In my non-nominalist version, exemplification involves an unspoken agreement between a communicator and a recipient to apply certain perceptual and/or conceptual categories to an object. This view of exemplification avoids many of the problems critics have noted in Goodman's treatment of it. I use the term *exemplificatory system* to refer to a system of perceptual and/or conceptual categories that is used exclusively for exemplificatory communication. Certain art forms, such as classical music and classical ballet, make use of such a system.

ARTUSO, Paolo. È Plausibile l'epistemologia naturalizzata di Quine? Filosofia, 40(3), 255-282, S-D 89.

ASH, C J. Labelling Systems and R.E. Structures. Annals Pure Applied Log, 47(2), 99-119, My 90.

This paper provides a generalisation and simplification of the metatheorem obtained in the author's "Recursive labelling systems and stability of recursive structures in hyperarithmetical degrees." The proof is basically the same as in this previous paper, and the author does not repeat this, describing instead how it should be modified. In the improved metatheorem, metric spaces are abandoned and the desideratum assumes the form that $\overset{U}{N} E(I_n)$ is r.e. As an example, it is shown how the main result of "Pairs of recursive structures" by Ash and Knight may be proved as easily for r.e. structures as for recursive ones.

ASH, C J and KNIGHT, J F. Pairs of Recursive Structures. Annals Pure Applied Log, 46(3), 211-234, Ap 90.

Many constructions concerning recursive functions involve constructing a uniformly recursive sequence, A_n, of structures such that, for each n, A_n is isomorphic to the given structure B_n or C_n according to where n is or is not in a given (non-recursive) set S. This paper considers an obviously necessary condition, involving recursive infinitary sentences of the ordinal complexity corresponding to the position of the set S in Kleene's hyperarithmetical hierarchy, and proves that this condition is also sufficient, subject to various further reasonable recursive assumptions. These converses require technically advanced methods of recursion theory previously developed by the authors.

ASHBROOK, James B. The Human Brain and Human Destiny: A Pattern for Old Brain Empathy With the Emergence of Mind. Zygon, 24(3), 335-356, S 89.

The human brain combines empathy and imagination via the old brain which sets our destiny in the evolutionary scheme of things. This new understanding of cognition is an emergent phenomenon—basically an expressive ordering of reality as part of "a single natural system." The holographic and subsymbolic paradigms suggest that we live in a contextual universe, one which we create and yet one in which we are required to adapt. The inadequacy of the new brain—especially the left hemisphere's rational view of destiny—is replaced by a view of a new relatedness in reality in which human destiny comes from and depends upon the mutual interchange between the new brain (cultural knowledge) and the old brain (genetic wisdom) for the survival of what is significant to the whole systemic context in which we live.

ASHER, Nicholas. Belief, Acceptance and Belief Reports. Can J Phil, 19(3), 327-361, S 89.

ASMUS, V S. V S Solov'ev: An Attempt at a Philosophical Biography. Soviet Stud Phil, 28(2), 66-95, Fall 89.

ASSOUN, Paul-Laurent. L'événement freudien: L'objet métapsychologique. Rev Int Phil, 43(171), 461-479, 1989.

ASTROH, Michael. Logical Competence in the Context of Propositional Attitudes. Commun Cog, 23(1), 3-44, 1990.

The present paper introduces a constructive semantics for logical constants and propositional attitudes in general. Terms of the first kind are explicated as normative specifications of an assertoric structure. Terms of the second kind specify the actual performance of assertions and of other kinds of representations. This systematic differentiation provides a semantical account of logical and other constants in the context of a propositional attitude. They indicate a logical and semantical commitment of a person having this attitude with respect to a proposition determined by the meaning of these constants. Finally, this general understanding of propositional attitudes and of logical constants occurring in their scope is translated into a set of schematic rules. Similar to game-theoretical conceptions of validity a formal argumentation procedure ARFLC provides a constructivist concept of logical implication. It pertains to propositional attitudes without the paradoxical presupposition of logical omniscience. On the contrary, the rules of this normative semantics offer sufficient means in order to justify a restricted analogue of Aristotle's rule of necessitation for the case of propositional attitudes.

ATHAYDE, Ezequiel. *The Unknown Mechanism Moving Society*. Salvador, CEPA, 1989

ATLAS, Jay David. *Philosophy without Ambiguity: A Logico-Linguistic Essay*. New York, Clarendon/Oxford Pr, 1989

This book expounds and defends a new conception of the relation between truth and meaning. The thesis is that the sense of a sense-general sentence radically underdetermines (independently of indexicality) its truth-conditional content. This linguistic analysis sheds new light on problems of meaning, truth, falsity, negation, existence, presupposition, and implicature. The book demonstrates how the concept of ambiguity has been misused and confused with other concepts of meaning, and how the interface between semantics and pragmatics has been misunderstood. The problems discussed will interest those working in philosophy, linguistics, cognitive psychology, and artificial intelligence.

ATTERTON, Peter (trans) and LEVINAS, Emmanuel. Is Ontology Fundamental? Phil Today, 33(2), 121-129, Sum 89.

In this 1951 essay Levinas calls into question the traditional primacy accorded to comprehension and knowledge within human experience. The contestation, which makes no exception of Heideggerian ontology, its main focus, is waged in the name of the ethical relation as a relation of discourse. The Other, through the expression of her or his face, is said to elude thematization and comprehension, and thus resist appropriation and exploitation. The essay ends with a derivation of a list of themes which determine the trajectory Levinas's thought will later follow.

ATTIG, Thomas. Relearning the World: On the Phenomenology of Grieving. J Brit Soc Phenomenol, 21(1), 53-66, Ja 90.

It is crucial to understand the impacts of bereavement and the growing process phenomenologically, i.e., as experienced by the bereaved. Husserlian and Heideggerian analyses of processes of reconstituting the life world following bereavement are offered as a means of demonstrating the capacity of phenomenological analysis to illuminate such centrally important experiences.

ATWELL, John E. "Doers and their Deeds: Schopenhauer on Human Agency" in *Schopenhauer: New Essays in Honor of His 200th Birthday*, VON DER LUFT, Eric (ed), 21-23. Lewiston, Mellen Pr, 1989.

This essay examines Schopenhauer's account of the relation between doers and their deeds. It is determined that Schopenhauer puts forth both a version of agent-causation (the agent as will is the "ground" of his actions) and a version of agent-reductionism (the agent is the moral character of his actions). Though these theories need not be incompatible, a third theory—the imputability thesis (one is not responsible for actions done out of character) proves anomalous, and in fact incompatible with Schopenhauer's will-body identity thesis; and that is disastrous.

AUBENQUE, Pierre. Otra vez Heidegger y el nazismo. Rev Filosof (Spain), 1, 157-169, 1987-88.

AUBRY, P and COLLERETTE, P. Socio-Economic Evolution of Women Business Owners in Quebec (1987). J Bus Ethics, 9(4-5), 417-422, Ap-My 90.

Two years after a five-year longitudinal study was undertaken in 1986, distinct characteristics of the female entrepreneur in Quebec are starting to emerge. This paper draws a general portrait of the female entrepreneur and examines certain features that have not been extensively studied in the past: age, family status, size and type of business, partnerships, motivation, obstacles, financing, and income evolution.

AUDI, Robert. Causalist Internalism. Amer Phil Quart, 26(4), 309-320, O 89.

Internalist theories of justification take it to be based on grounds that are in some sense accessible to the subject. Causalist theories of justification hold that a ground justifies a belief only if the belief is causally sustained or produced by it. Many philosophers have thought that since we do not have internal access to causal connections, a causalist theory of justification cannot be internalist. This paper sets out an internalist account of justification, sharpens the problem of reconciling it with a causal condition on justification, and argues that given a proper understanding of internalism and a balanced appraisal of skepticism, the prospects for reconciliation are good.

AUDI, Robert. The Function of the Press in a Free and Democratic Society. Pub Affairs Quart, 4(3), 203-215, Jl 90.

AUDI, Robert. Internalism and Externalism in Moral Epistemology. Logos (USA), 10, 13-37, 1989.

This paper sets forth the distinction between internalist and externalist theories in epistemology and extends it to ethics. It is applied to consequentialist, Kantian, and virtue theories; and its implications for a number of major issues in metaethics, for instance subjectivism, non-cognitivism, and reductive naturalism, are developed. On the basis of this general account of internalist and externalist ethical theories, the paper partially assesses the resources of two representative specimens, a Kantian internalism and a utilitarian consequentialism. A major task here is to confront each with the question of how the moral assessment of action is related to the moral appraisal of character. It is argued that while both positions encounter difficulties in adequately answering this question, consequentialist externalist theories, but not Kantian internalist theories, are subject to a *normative cleavage*, a disparity between the assessment of action and the appraisal of character. The former, but not the latter theories, cannot adequately explain the relation between these two kinds of appraisal.

AULT JR, Charles R. An Elementary Conception of Time. Thinking, 6(4), 2-7, 1986.

AUMANN, Robert J. *Lectures on Game Theory*. Boulder, Westview Pr,

1989

AUNE, Bruce. "Epistemically Justified Opinion" in *The Current State of the Coherence Theory*, BENDER, John W (ed), 215-230. Norwell, Kluwer, 1989.

The theories of epistemic justification offered in recent years are generally developed as contributions to a theory of knowledge. It is argued here that such theories exaggerate the importance of knowledge for a sound epistemology and also, perhaps as a consequence, take an ill-advised foundational or coherentist form. A new concept of epistemic justification is, accordingly, introduced. Since the new concept has interesting affinities with the coherentist conception of epistemic justification recently proposed by Laurence BonJour, the latter is critically discussed. Critical remarks are also directed to a Bayesian theory that provides another, increasingly popular alternative.

AUROUX, Sylvain. Le rationalisme et l'analyse linguistique. Dialogue (Canada), 28(2), 203-233, 1989.

AUXIER, Randall E. Dewey on Religion and History. SW Phil Rev, 6(1), 45-58, Ju 90.

This paper examines Dewey's wider views of traditions and institutions by closely examining the more particular things he says about history (from the 1938 *Logic*) and organized religion (from *A Common Faith*). It is argued that a refusal to think critically about the history of the institution through which one engages in a given social practice (i.e., worship) leads inevitably to an insidious institutional orthodoxy which usually fails to engender those experiences for which the institution was created. Rorty's account of Dewey on traditions is found inadequate in its failure to fully consider the positive role of traditions and institutions.

AUXTER, Thomas. "Abolishing Apartheid: The Importance of Sanctions" in *Inquiries into Values: The Inaugural Session of the International Society for Value Inquiry*, LEE, Sander H , 441-457. Lewiston, Mellen Pr, 1989.

This paper is an examination of the nature of apartheid from a moral point of view. It also examines and rejects the arguments of those who wish us to take a very gradual approach to dismantling the system. The conclusion is that everyone should share the sense of urgency expressed by the African majority, through religious groups and unions, as well as through the African National Congress, that a comprehensive set of sanctions should be imposed in order to "quarantine apartheid." The paper ends with reflections on the nature of the decision to abolish apartheid.

AVERILL, Edward Wilson. Are Physical Properties Dispositions? Phil Sci, 57(1), 118-132, Mr 90.

Several prominent philosophers have held that physical properties are dispositions. The aim of this paper is to establish the following conjunction: if the thesis that physical properties are dispositions is unsupplemented by controversial assumptions about dispositions, it entails a contradiction; and if it is so supplemented the resulting theory has the consequence that either many worlds which seem to be possible worlds are not possible worlds or some properties which seem to be identical are not identical. In this way it is shown that a dispositional account of physical properties is implausible.

AVINERI, Shlomo. Moral Ideals and Social Values: The Dialectics of Legitimization. Dialec Hum, 16(1), 209-213, Wint 89.

AVIRAM, Roni. An Appeal for Total Intellectual Openness. Thinking, 5(2), 26-27, 1984.

AVIRAM, Ronni. Is the Ideal of the Overman Possible? (in Hebrew). Iyyun, 38(3-4), 228-264, Jl-O 89.

The aim of this paper is to present the Nietzschean ideal of the Overman as a concrete and coherent ideal in spite of prima facie contradictions characterizing it. In the first part of the paper four groups of prima facie contradictions on four successive levels (the epistemological, ontological, psychological and developmental) are presented and analysed. In the second part, each of the prima facie contradictions pertaining to these four groups is separately discussed. It is shown that (a) it is possible to form interpretative hypotheses that eliminate each of these contradictions; (b) all these hypotheses are compatible and many of them complement each other. From the discussion as a whole there gradually emerges one inclusive interpretation of the ideal of the Overman depicting it as referring—coherently—to a hierarchy of concrete psychological types.

AVRON, Arnon. Gentzenizing Schroeder-Heister's Natural Extension of Natural Deduction. Notre Dame J Form Log, 31(1), 127-135, Wint 90.

Our purpose here is to provide an example of how the use of the Gentzen-type sequential calculus considerably simplifies a complex Natural Deduction formalism. The formalism is that of Schroeder-Heister's system of higher-order rules. We show that the notions of Schroeder-Heister's that are the most difficult to handle (discharge functions and subrules) become

redundant in the Gentzen-type version. The complex normalization proof given by Schroeder-Heister can be replaced therefore by a standard cut-elimination proof. It turns out also that the unusual form of some of the elimination rules of Schroeder-Heister corresponds to the natural, standard form of antecedent rules in sequential calculi.

AVSHALOM, Asnat and BALABAN, Oded. The Ontological Argument Reconsidered. J Phil Res, 15, 279-310, 1990.

The ontological argument—first proposed by St. Anselm and subsequently developed by Descartes, Leibniz, Kant, Hegel and Marx—furnishes a key to understanding the relationship between thought and reality. In this article we shall focus on Hegel's attitude towards the ontological argument as set out in his *Science of Logic*, where it appears as a paradigm of the relationship between thought and reality. It should be remarked, moreover, that our choice of the subject was not random and that it was selected for the reason that belief in God is a preeminent social reality, inasmuch as faith in God creates His existence. Therefore, an investigation of the concept of God is an inquiry into the most profound recesses of human consciousness. The great opponents of the ontological argument, from Hume down to our day—and even Kant—have based their arguments upon the fundamental empiricist assertion that existential judgments are not analytical. In this paper we attempt to defend the ontological argument against its opponents.

AXINN, Sidney. *A Moral Military*. Philadelphia, Temple Univ Pr, 1989

This studies "laws of warfare" from a philosophical standpoint. Taking a natural-law view of the Geneva and Hague Conventions, and a Kantian position on ethical theory, this book argues for the seriousness of the concepts of war crime and of military honor, but limits honorable military activity by a strict interpretation of the notion of a war crime. Chapters deal with morality, prisoners of war, spying, war crimes, the dirty-hands theory of command, nuclear weapons, terrorism and covert operations.

AXINN, Sidney. Moral Style. J Value Inq, 24(2), 123-133, Ap 90.

To be moral is to choose a moral style. "Style" is defined as preference for a certain balance of type I and type II risk of error. Moral patterns are classified by a square of opposition applied to beneficiaries of a moral sacrifice. It is assumed that Kant's categorical imperative gives the parameters of style that can be called moral. Therefore, within Kant's parameters, Kantians can choose more than one moral style, more than one way of treating people as ends. Moral styles require temperamental and aesthetic dispositions.

AYLESWORTH, Gary E (ed) and SILVERMAN, Hugh J (ed). *The Textual Sublime: Deconstruction and Its Differences*. Albany, SUNY Pr, 1990

This book addresses the question of deconstruction by asking what it is and by asking about its alternatives. To what extent does deconstruction derive from a philosophical stance, and to what extent does it depend upon a set of strategies, moves, and rhetorical practices that result in criticism? Special attention is given to the formulations offered by Jacques Derrida (in relation to Heidegger's philosophy) and by Paul de Man (in relation to Kant's theory of the sublime and its implications for criticism). And what, in deconstructive terms, does it mean to translate from one textual corpus into another? Is it a matter of different theories of translation or of different practices? And what of difference itself? Does not difference already invoke the possibility of deconstruction's "others"? Althusser, Adorno, and Deleuze are offered as exemplary cases. Includes extensive editors' introductory materials and a substantial bibliography.

AZZOUNI, Jody. Truth and Convention. Pac Phil Quart, 71(2), 81-102, Je 90.

"Truth by convention" as positivists meant it, and as Quine criticizes it, is an amalgam of *two* notions. I separate them, grant Quine's claim that mathematical *truth* depends on the empirical sciences, but show that conventionality (understood algorithmically) still has epistemic content. The resulting view provides a sharp epistemic distinction between mathematics and the empirical sciences.

BABER, H E. The Ethics of Dwarf-Tossing. Int J Applied Phil, 4(4), 1-5, Fall 89.

Most people consider dwarf-tossing, a sport in which participants compete to see how far they can throw a dwarf across a large air mattress, at the very least offensive. Indeed, The Little People of America, an organization of dwarfs and midgets, have proposed that the practice be prohibited by law. Afficionados of the sport, however, including the dwarf (who is a willing and well-paid participant) argue that any such interference would constitute unwarranted paternalism. I argue that dwarf-tossing is indeed wrong and ought to be discouraged because it harms unwilling nonparticipants, specifically other little people.

BACCARI, Luciano. Provvidenza: una proposta di intelligibilità del mondo. Aquinas, 32(3), 411-433, S-D 89.

BACH, Emmon W. *Informal Lectures on Formal Semantics*. Albany, SUNY Pr, 1988

BACHARACH, Michael. Commodities, Language, and Desire. J Phil, 87(7), 346-368, Jl 90.

This paper examines the role of language in trade and explicates the notion of commodity. The dominant form of trade is without inspection, through verbal descriptions contained in 'notional' offers. A 'commodity' is a type so traded. The commonsense beliefs which language mastery requires are modelled by a shared Bayesian prior, which in turn yields a notion of the informativeness of a predicate 'F'. If and only if 'F' is informative enough, commodity trade in Fs Pareto-improves on trade by inspection in them. These considerations provide a capital-theoretic component in the explanation of a community's conceptual repertoire.

BACON, John. "Categorical Propositions in Relevance Logic" in *Directions in Relevant Logic*, NORMAN, Jean (ed), 197-203. Norwell, Kluwer, 1989.

While 'Men are a subset of mortals' goes over into classical formal implication in relevance logic, 'All men are mortal' poses a problem. It is neither a generalized relevant conditional nor a generalized intuitionistic conditional. Restricted quantification doesn't really help either. Categoricals must rather be construed as generalized conditional assertions in the sense of Nuel D Belnap Jr. and Ruth Manor. The task indicated is thus to extend relevance logic to include conditional assertion.

BACON, John. Van Cleve versus Closure. Phil Stud, 58(3), 239-242, Mr 90.

In "Supervenience, Necessary Coextension, and Reducibility" (*Philosophical Studies* 49, 1986, 163-176), among other results, I showed that weak or ordinary supervenience is equivalent to Jaegwon Kim's strong supervenience, given certain assumptions: S4 modality, the usual modal conception of properties as class-concepts, and diagonal closure or resplicing of the set of base properties. This last means that any mapping of possible worlds into extensions of base properties counts itself as a base property. James Van Cleve attacks the modal conception of property and diagonal closure. To me it seems desperate to reject diagonal closure merely in order to save supervenience-materialism. But I concede that it may be unacceptable in the context of a sparser theory of properties.

BADCOCK, L and KERSTEN, G E and IGLEWSKI, M and MALLORY, G R. Structuring and Simulating Negotiation: An Approach and an Example. Theor Decis, 28(3), 243-273, My 90.

Negotiation is a complex and dynamic decision process during which parties' perceptions, preferences, and roles may change. Modeling such a process requires flexible and powerful tools. The use of rule-based formalism is therefore expanded from its traditional expert system type technique, to structuring and restructuring nontrivial processes like negotiation. Using rules, we build a model of a negotiation problem. Some rules are used to infer positions and reactions of the parties, other rules are used to modify problem representation when such a modification is necessary. We illustrate the approach with a contract negotiation case between two large companies. We also show how this approach could help one party to realize that negotiations are being carried on against their assumptions and expectations.

BADÍA CABRERA, Miguel A. Hume y la incurable ineficacia de la filosofía contra la superstición. Rev Latin De Filosof, 15(3), 293-305, N 89.

It has been suggested that Hume did not share the Enlightenment's optimism because for him philosophy cannot overthrow superstition since most men are by a fateful temperament beyond the reach of her call. This paper rejects that interpretation as being at odds with important doctrines which Hume held in different works and with Hume's conception about the nature and ultimate ends of his philosophical investigation. It also defends an alternative interpretation: an attenuated yet still enlightened optimism, which shows that philosophy has an extensive beneficial influence on society, and is a perpetual check to the errors and evils of superstition.

BAECHLER, Jean. "Les cultures et la culture politiques de l'Europe" in *Culture et Politique/Culture and Politics*, CRANSTON, Maurice (ed), 16-28. Hawthorne, de Gruyter, 1988.

BAEKERS, Stephan F. L'equivoque du temps chez Aristote. Arch Phil, 53(3), 461-477, Jl-S 90.

In addition to the definition of time as 'number of movement', Aristotle in *Physics* IV, 10-14 incidentally refers to a second sense of time, that as an encompassing condition (ο ποτε ον) precedes defined time. For the purpose of philosophical elucidation (that, as also has been argued by E Martineau, forms the necessary supplement to philological analysis) an interpretation of this second sense of time is given in connection with the Aristotelian notion of Eternity (αιων) and with Heidegger's conception of 'Worldtime' (*Weitzeit*).

BAER, Joachim T (trans) and EICHENWALD, I I and KATZ, Nina J (trans). "A Note on Schopenhauer (1910) (also in German)" in *Schopenhauer: New Essays in Honor of His 200th Birthday*, VON DER LUFT, Eric (ed), 139-158. Lewiston, Mellen Pr, 1989.

BAER, Joachim T. "Die Ästhetik des russischen Symbolismus und ihre Beziehung zu Schopenhauer" in *Schopenhauer: New Essays in Honor of His 200th Birthday*, VON DER LUFT, Eric (ed), 24-39. Lewiston, Mellen Pr, 1989.

BAGOLINI, Luigi. La persona nell'esperienza morale e giuridica. Riv Int Filosof Diritto, 66(2), 240-249, Ap-Je 89.

BAHM, Archie J. "Comparative Axiology: Western, Indian and Chinese Theory Compared" in *Inquiries into Values: The Inaugural Session of the International Society for Value Inquiry*, LEE, Sander H , 255-262. Lewiston, Mellen Pr, 1989.

Values are somewhat alike in all cultures, but two kinds of differing emphases can be observed in Western, Indian and Chinese civilizations: I. Intrinsic goodness is often identified with feelings of enjoyment: (1) of satisfactions, (2) of freedom from both desires and satisfactions, and (3) of willing acceptance of both desires, satisfactions and frustrations, respectively. II. Intrinsic goodness is often identified with forms or formlessness: (1) with real (especially eternal) forms, (2) with pure formlessness (Nirguna Brahman), and (3) with harmonious successions of opposing forms, respectively.

BAHTI, Timothy. Vico and Frye: A Note. New Vico Studies, 3, 119-129, 1985.

BAIER, Annette. "Trusting Ex-intimates" in *Person to Person*, GRAHAM, George (ed), 269-281. Philadelphia, Temple Univ Pr, 1989.

Three fictional cases of typical let-down by ex-intimates are discussed. Ex-intimates are vulnerable to such let-downs as breach of confidence, and neglect of what was left in their care (pets, art works). The intimacy itself confers especial value on some things (symbolic gifts) and these are especially vulnerable to the neglect which estrangement can bring. General morals are drawn concerning what we risk, as well as what we gain, from intimate relationships that we outlive.

BAIGRIE, Brian. Reply—Symposium on the Role of the Philosopher Among the Scientists: Nuisance or Necessity? Soc Epistem, 3(4), 311-318, O-D 89.

BAILEY, Alan. Pyrrhonean Scepticism and the Self-Refutation Argument. Phil Quart, 40(158), 27-44, Ja 90.

This article argues that the Pyrrhonist's use of Agrippa's five tropes does commit the Pyrrhonist to a form of global scepticism about rational justification. However, it is then shown that the objection that such scepticism is dialectically self-defeating can be disarmed by distinguishing between the mature Pyrrhonist's assessment of his negative epistemological arguments and the assessment forced upon his philosophic opponents by their own rationalistic code.

BAILEY, Alison. *Posterity and Strategic Policy: A Moral Assessment of Nuclear Policy Options*. Winchester, Unwin Hyman, 1989

The unthinkable nature of nuclear war has caused policy makers to speak and strategize about nuclear war in an unacceptable value-free manner which ignores humanistic concerns. Philosophical skills and philosophers' familiarity with moral issues can be used to introduce value issues into the nuclear debate revealing the absurdity of present US policy. The author surveys three current policy options in detail and reveals the moral flaws of each, arguing that 'security' policy must account for our obligations to future persons. If defense policy is to have any meaning, it must consider humanity in the context of a human narrative. The concluding chapter provides a guideline and step-by-step procedure for arsenal reduction to a temporary minimal deterrent.

BAILEY, George. Beardsley's Aesthetic Instrumentalism. Int Stud Phil, 21(3), 63-70, 1989.

I argue that although Eddy Zemach is unsuccessful in his attempt to show that Monroe Beardsley's concept of aesthetic experience is flawed, nonetheless Zemach reveals serious problems for aesthetic theories that combine an instrumental notion of aesthetic value with a noninstrumental notion of aesthetic objects. Developing Zemach's basic insights, I show that in Beardsley's aesthetic theory an object's instrumentally acquired worth lacks a necessary connection either with an object's aesthetic properties or with an experience's aesthetic value, making it incorrect for Beardsley to classify judgments of an object's instrumental value as *aesthetic* judgments.

BAILEY, Leonard L. Organ Transplantation: A Paradigm of Medical Progress. Hastings Center Rep, 20(1), 24-28, Ja-F 90.

Transplantation clearly exemplifies progress in medical science and technology. The transplantation process is traced from its relevant clinical origins in the 1950s, speculating on the directions this "new therapy" might have taken under the glow of contemporary ethical "light." Comparison is made with the development of open heart surgery and circulatory assist devices. Rather than supporting containment of medical progress on moral-ethical grounds, a plea is made for enhanced moral wisdom and patience with an eye to "predictive bioethics." Inevitably, *progress happens.* This fact alone suggests the need for pause and reflection as antecedents of bioethical commentary.

BAILIN, Sharon. Belief, Doubt and Critical Thinking: Reconciling the Contraries: Response to Garrison and Phelan. Proc Phil Educ, 45, 315-319, 1989.

This paper, a response to "Toward a Feminist Poetic of Critical Thinking" by Garrison and Phelan, argues that the authors unfairly criticize contemporary theories of critical thinking for advocating doubt, fault finding, and certainty. Rather, these theories advocate apportioning belief and doubt to the evidence, are based on a fallibilist epistemology, and are compatible with the acknowledgement that knowledge is constructed. The paper further argues that the poetic dialectic advocated by Garrison and Phelan in which contraries are tolerated is untenable and that acceptance of contradiction would mean the end of inquiry.

BAILLIE, Harold W (ed) and GARRETT, Thomas M (ed) and GARRETT, Rosellen M (ed). *Health Care Ethics: Principles and Problems.* Englewood Cliffs, Prentice-Hall, 1989

BAILLIE, James. Identity, Survival, and Sortal Concepts. Phil Quart, 40(159), 183-194, Ap 90.

I contest the following assumptions regarding the conditions of diachronic identity for natural kind members: (1) That there is a principle whereby *a* and *b* can be located on a single continuous spatio-temporal path, and thereby be identified as stages of the same continuant particular; (2) That the identification of *a* and *b* must be sortal-governed; (3) That a particular cannot change kind-membership without contravening its identity-conditions. I argue that these issues are best treated in terms of Derek Parfit's 'Relation R' rather than in terms of the identity relation.

BAIN, William J and KIZILTAN, Mustafa Ü and CAÑIZARES, Anita. Postmodern Conditions: Rethinking Public Education. Educ Theor, 40(3), 351-369, Sum 90.

In the first section, within a framework modeled after Foucault's theory of discourse and Lyotard's analysis of the postmodern condition, we reconceptualize "public education" and outline the structure of a postmodern problematic. From this standpoint, the challenge of postmodernity lies in its destabilization of the metanarratives of modernity which have long sustained public education, the imminent postmodern fallout being the fracture and the dislocation of public education as a discursive formation. In the second section, we reconsider the idea of enlightenment and reconstitute it through the principle of "limit-attitude." We propose a transgressive mode of thought as the basis for public education.

BAIRD, Robert M (ed) and ROSENBAUM, Stuart E (ed). *Euthanasia: The Moral Issues.* Buffalo, Prometheus, 1989

This work poses the moral dilemmas of euthanasia or mercy killing and provides a collection of essays that clarify the issues and present alternative views. Included is material by prominent thinkers such as Koop, Rachels, Sullivan, Fletcher, and Engelhardt. Also included are provocative essays by physicians recently appearing in the *Journal of the American Medical Association* and the *New England Journal of Medicine.* By analyzing the arguments of these essays, readers will be able to reach tentative conclusions, and become better equipped to make difficult decisions of their own concerning these matters.

BAJER, Jiri. New Hypothesis on the Theme of Janacek's "Russian" Opera (in Czechoslovakian). Estetika, 27(1), 28-34, 1990.

BAK, Nelleke. Can a Political Theory of Education Be Objective? S Afr J Phil, 9(2), 95-100, My 90.

Two questions are addressed. Firstly, to the question of whether a theory of education is necessarily political, the author answers 'yes', since to theorize is to articulate socially and historically situated practices which are directly influenced by political considerations. To the second question of whether such a theory of education can be objective, the author again answers in the affirmative, rearticulating the notion of 'objective' as meaning intersubjective standards of rationality, as expressed through rational discourse which, in turn, constitutes a rational and thus accessible social reality. Although this does not mean that rationality is an absolute, what it does mean is that at this stage, it is the only viable common court of appeal.

BAKER, G P and HACKER, P M S. The Last Ditch. Phil Quart, 39(157), 471-477, O 89.

BAKER, G P and HACKER, P M S. Malcolm on Language and Rules. Philosophy, 65(252), 167-179, Ap 90.

BAKER, Judith. The Metaphysical Construction of Value. J Phil, 86(10), 505-513, O 89.

BAKER, Lynne Rudder. Seeming to See Red. Phil Stud, 58(1-2), 121-128, Ja-F 90.

In "Understanding the Language of Thought," John Pollock offers a semantics for Mentalese. Along the way, he raises many deep issues concerning, among other things, the indexicality of thought, the relations between thought and communication, the function of 'that'-clauses and the nature of introspection. Regrettably, I must pass over these issues here. Instead, I shall focus on Pollock's views on the nature of appearance and its role in interpreting the language of thought. I shall examine two aspects of Pollock's views: (i) the distinction between comparative and noncomparative senses of 'red', and (ii) the construal of narrow content in terms of input states and rational architecture. Consideration of the former will call into question the coherence of the distinction; consideration of the latter will suggest that comparative appearance states cannot play the theoretical role that Pollock assigns to them.

BAKER, Robert E. Hope in a Secular Ethic. Bridges, 1(3-4), 93-101, Fall-Wint 89.

Since the rate of advance in science and technology outstrips our ability to assess their implications for society and the individual, it is argued that a new educational imperative has emerged: literacy in science, technology and ethics. Further, since many people do not embrace a traditional religion, ethical literacy means that a secular approach to ethical thought needs to be considered. Our hope for a sustainable and worthwhile future depends on citizens literate in science, technology and ethics so that they might effectively participate in the scientific and technological decisions that will affect them.

BAKKER, J I (Hans). The Gandhian Approach to *Swadeshi* or Appropriate Technology. J Agr Ethics, 3(1), 50-88, 1990.

This is an examination of the significance of Gandhi's social philosophy for development. It is argued that, when seen in light of Gandhi's social philosophy, the concepts of appropriate technology and basic needs take on new meaning. The Gandhian approach can be identified with the *original* "basic needs" strategy for international development. Gandhi's approach helps to provide greater equity, or "distributive justice," by promoting technology that is appropriate to "basic needs." Gandhi's social philosophy has been neglected by most development specialists, with only a few exceptions. This analysis attempts to draw out some aspects of M K Gandhi's background and his thinking about *swadeshi* and *swaraj.* (edited)

BALABAN, Oded. The Hermeneutics of the Young Marx: According to Marx's Approach to the Philosophy of Democritus and Epicurus. Diogenes, 148, 28-41, Wint 89.

This paper is an attempt to reconstruct Marx's own philosophical presuppositions in his efforts to interpret ancient atomistic philosophy and attempts to throw light on the beginning of his critical method. In the history of philosophy, the atomistic physics of Epicurus and of Democritus have been considered as very similar. Marx considers this similarity as only apparent. He also indicates that there is even an *inner contradiction* in each of those theories. Marx also intended to explain the reasons for this contradiction.

BALABAN, Oded. The Human Origins of *Fortuna* in Machiavelli's Thought. Hist Polit Thought, 11(1), 21-36, Spr 90.

Scholars have tended to discuss whether Machiavelli regarded *fortuna* to be amenable to human governance. *Fortuna* commonly appears in human consciousness as a force which is extrinsic to men's deeds, since the results of their actions are not the results that were consciously intended. However, Machiavelli's use of the term can be elucidated as referring to the consequences of the activity of men rather than to a natural phenomenon. Accordingly, *Fortuna* is different from providence, accident or chance, and different also from conscious human achievement. The governability of fortune can only be understood within the framework of this approach. It is proposed a model of human activity as a key to understanding Machiavelli's use of the term.

BALABAN, Oded. On Justice and Legitimation: A Critique of Jürgen Habermas' Concept of "Historical Reconstructivism". Z Phil Forsch, 44(2), 273-277, 1990.

It is shown that the Thrasymachus-Socrates controversy in Plato's *Republic* can be interpreted as a controversy between two necessarily different kinds of political consciousness. This is explained by criticizing the three modern interpretations of Plato's concept of justice: normativism, empiricism and Habermas's historical reconstructivism.

BALABAN, Oded and AVSHALOM, Asnat. The Ontological Argument Reconsidered. J Phil Res, 15, 279-310, 1990.

The ontological argument—first proposed by St. Anselm and subsequently developed by Descartes, Leibniz, Kant, Hegel and Marx—furnishes a key to understanding the relationship between thought and reality. In this article we shall focus on Hegel's attitude towards the ontological argument as set out in his *Science of Logic*, where it appears as a paradigm of the relationship between thought and reality. It should be remarked, moreover, that our choice of the subject was not random and that it was selected for the reason that belief in God is a preeminent social reality, inasmuch as faith in God creates His existence. Therefore, an investigation of the concept of God is an inquiry into the most profound recesses of human consciousness. The great opponents of the ontological argument, from Hume down to our day—and even Kant—have based their arguments upon the fundamental empiricist assertion that existential judgments are not analytical. In this paper we attempt to defend the ontological argument against its opponents.

BALABAN, Oded. *Praxis* and *Poesis* in Aristotle's Practical Philosophy. J Value Inq, 24(3), 185-198, Jl 90.

The purpose of the paper is to bridge the gap between the Aristotelian concept of *praxis* and the 20th century values of modern commentators. It is argued that their adherence to these values prevents them from understanding Aristotle. In Aristotle's philosophy there are two kinds of human activity: *Praxis* and *Poesis*. In *Praxis* the activity is an end in itself; in *poesis* it is a means to an end. In order to understand them, a distinction is made between two Aristotelian concepts of *telos*: *Telos* as the goal of the activity, and *telos* as the activity itself.

BALABAN, Oded. *Subject and Consciousness: A Philosophical Inquiry Into Self-Consciousness*. Totowa, Rowman & Littlefield, 1990

A new approach to understanding human consciousness based on a distinction between content and form—allowing a further distinction between consciousness and different kinds of self-consciousness. Accordingly, there are proposed alternative interpretations of Plato, Protagoras, Spinoza, Freud, Machiavelli, Hegel, Marx, Stirner, Sartre, Marcuse, Habermas, etc. To clarify the constitutive function of self-consciousness the principal versions of the ontological argument, from Anselm to Marx, are critically analyzed. Finally, the distinction between content and form is applied to that between politics and ideology, criticizing normativism, empiricism, and Habermas's historical reconstructivism.

BALDINI, Massimo. Riflessioni epistemologiche sull'errore. Sapienza, 43(1), 57-65, Ja-Mr 90.

BALDNER, Kent. Realism and Respect. Between Species, 6(1), 1-8, Wint 90.

In this article I endorse the view that humans have obligations with respect to living and nonliving parts of the natural environment. I do this by examining and rejecting an argument by Steven Sapontzis that concludes that we have a moral obligation to prevent some natural predation. I argue that such a position would commit us to claiming that there is something morally wrong with the very fabric of the natural world, a view I find to be paternalistic. I then argue that it is the ecosystem taken as a whole that is the proper bearer of moral value.

BALDNER, Kent. Rejoinder to Sapontzis's "Environmental Ethics and the Locus of Value". Between Species, 6(1), 10-11, Wint 90.

BALDUS, Bernd. "Somatic Evolution and Cultural Form" in *Issues in Evolutionary Epistemology*, HAHLWEG, Kai (ed), 258-277. Albany, SUNY Pr, 1989.

The use of evolutionary theory for the analysis of sociocultural processes has been hindered by the difficulty of finding suitable social equivalents of units of selection, fitness maximization, and form-generating processes in biological evolution. This gap can be bridged by returning to Darwin's original understanding of evolution as working on the somatic properties of actively adapting individuals. Evolution can then be seen as an internally guided structure-producing process which relies on blind genetic as well as environmental resources. Such a view is much more compatible with data typically found in the social sciences.

BALDWIN, J T and SHELAH, S. The Primal Framework I. Annals Pure Applied Log, 46(3), 235-264, Ap 90.

This paper begins a series developing a setting for abstract classification theory. The aim is to provide a common framework for first order stability theory and generalizations to, e.g., infinitary logic.

BALDWIN, J T and PILLAY, A. Semisimple Stable and Superstable Groups. Annals Pure Applied Log, 45(2), 105-127, D 89.

This paper explores the relation between various notions of simplicity (no normal subgroups) and definable simplicity (no definable normal subgroups)

in stable groups. The importance of definability concepts in the study of algebraic groups is an underlying theme. It concludes with a technical analysis of superstable groups with monomial U-rank.

BALESTRA, Dominic J. Technology in a Free Society: The New Frankenstein. Thought, 65(257), 155-168, Je 90.

BALKIS, Kozmas. Commentary on "Hamlethics in Planning". Bus Prof Ethics J, 6(2), 79-82, Sum 87.

BALL, Stephen W. Uncertainty in Moral Theory: An Epistemic Defense of Rule-Utilitarian Liberties. Theor Decis, 29(2), 133-160, S 90.

The purpose of this essay is to defend utilitarianism from the popular objection that it makes moral theory depend improperly upon *uncertain* factual information and calculations which may produce violations of individual rights or liberties. This objection is a more subtle variant of the general Kantian complaint that utilitarianism makes morality improperly *contingent* upon empirical facts about historical, socioeconomic circumstances, the consequences of actions, institutions, etc., thereby allowing individual liberties to be sacrificed in order to maximize the collective welfare. Three main arguments connected with the uncertainty-objection are delineated in Rawls's work and are seen to be fallacious. It is concluded that a suitably sophisticated form of rule-utilitarianism need not base liberty on any impermissible kind of uncertainty in moral theory. This analysis is contrary not only to what Rawlsians and other Kantians nowadays typically argue or assume in criticizing utilitarianism, but also to what some of the leading critics of Rawls have said about his anti-utilitarian stance.

BALL, Terence and FARR, James (ed) and HANSON, Russell L (ed). *Political Innovation and Conceptual Change*. New York, Cambridge Univ Pr, 1989.

BALLARD, B W. Marxist Challenges to Heidegger on Alienation and Authenticity. Man World, 23(2), 121-141, Ap 90.

BALLIU, Julien. Niklas Luhmann over ecologische communicatie. Tijdschr Stud Verlich Denken, 17(1-2), 137-152, 1989.

A summary of Luhmann's main ideas on the relationship between societal differentiation and the difficulties of a global ecological strategy.

BALOGH, Imre. Response to Dietrich's "Computationalism". Soc Epistem, 4(2), 155-157, Ap-Je 90.

The target paper argues for the acceptance of the notion of computationalism based on the Church-Turing thesis as the foundation of the study of intelligence. In this commentary it is suggested that the failings of current computational models of intelligence are mistakenly taken as indicating that Turing computability is inadequate for computing intelligence. It is argued that these failings do not indicate that our current notions of "computable" are inadequate, only that the current computational formalism is not suitable for modeling intelligence. To capture this distinction between suitability and adequacy the notion of computational fitness is introduced.

BALSLEV, Anindita Niyobi. Cosmology and Hindu Thought. Zygon, 25(1), 47-58, Mr 90.

This paper outlines some major ideas concerning cosmogony and cosmology that pervade the Hindu conceptual world. The basic source for this discussion is the philosophical literature of some of the principal schools of Hindu thought, such as Vaisesika, Sānkhya, and Advaita Vedānta, focusing on the themes of cosmology, time, and soteriology. The core of Hindu philosophical thinking regarding these issues is traced back to the Rk Vedic cosmogonical speculations, analyzed, and contrasted with the "views of the opponent." The relevance of the Hindu worldview for overcoming the conflict between science and religion is pointed out.

BALZER, W. Completeness for Systems Including Real Numbers. Stud Log, 48(1), 67-75, Mr 89.

The usual completeness theorem for first-order logic is extended in order to allow for a natural incorporation of real analysis. Essentially, this is achieved by building in the set of real numbers into the structures for the language, and by adjusting other semantical notions accordingly. We use many-sorted languages so that the resulting formal systems are general enough for axiomatic treatments of empirical theories without recourse to elements of set theory which are difficult to interpret empirically. Thus we provide a way of applying model theory to empirical theories without "tricky" detours. Our frame is applied to axiomatizations of three empirical theories: classical mechanics, phenomenological thermodynamics, and exchange economics.

BAMBROUGH, Renford. Does Philosophy 'Leave Everything as it is'? Even Theology? Philosophy, 25, 225-236, 89 Supp.

BAMBROUGH, Renford. Power, Authority, and Wisdom. SW Phil Rev, 4(1), 19-31, Ja 88.

BAMFORD, Greg. Watkins and the Pragmatic Problem of Induction. Analysis, 49(4), 203-205, O 89.

Watkins proposes a neo-Popperian solution to the pragmatic problem of induction. He asserts that evidence can be used noninductively to prefer the principle that corroboration is more successful over all human history than that, say, counter-corroboration is more successful either over this same period or in the future. Watkins's argument for rejecting the first counter-corroborationist alternative is beside the point, however, as whatever is the best strategy over all human history is irrelevant to the pragmatic problem of induction since we are not required to act in the past, and his argument for rejecting the second presupposed induction.

BANDMAN, Bertram. The Adolescent's Rights to Freedom, Care and Enlightenment. Thinking, 4(1), 21-27, 1982.

BANDYOPADHYAY, Taradas. Weak Strategy Proofness: The Case of Nonbinary Social Choice Functions. Theor Decis, 27(3), 193-205, N 89.

It is now well known that under some eminently acceptable behavioral rule in comparing various power sets every nonimposed, binary, multivalued social choice mechanism is strategy-proof or oligarchic. Various attempts have been made to resolve the paradox either by relaxing binariness or by weakening the notion of strategy-proofness. By relaxing both binariness and the notion of strategy-proofness this paper shows that the trade-off between weak strategy-proofness and various unacceptable power structures, such as oligarchy or dictatorship, would remain intact.

BANDYOPADHYAY, Tirthanath. Root of Man: A Note. Indian Phil Quart, 17(2), 251-259, Ap 90.

BANERJEE, Sumanta. Militancy, Violence and Democratic Rights: Indian Experience. Phil Soc Act, 16(2), 51-56, Ap-Je 90.

BANU, Beatrice (ed) and WEINSTEIN, Mark (ed). *The Fieldston Ethics Reader*. Lanham, Univ Pr of America, 1988

The Fieldston Reader introduces students to significant moral problems using critical thinking skills. Short pieces of classic and contemporary literature serve as vehicles for exploring ethical issues. All selections have been chosen for their appropriateness for secondary and junior college students as well as literary quality and relevance to issues confronting thoughtful adolescents.

BAO, Zhiming. Language and World View in Ancient China. Phil East West, 40(2), 195-219, Ap 90.

The paper investigates the philosophical issues concerning language discussed in ancient China, and shows that there is a common linguistic presupposition underlying the discussions across the various schools of thought. The conception of language, which is an integral part of their conception of the world and its relation to man, provides the perspective with which to look at the formulations and solutions of the linguistic issues that characterize the writings of Confucians, the Logicians, among others.

BĀQIR AS-SADR, Allāma Muhammad and INATI, Shams C (trans). *Our Philosophy: Allāma Muhammad Bāqir As-Sadr*. London, Muhammadi Trust, 1987

The main purpose of the work is to point out the benefits of Islam over capitalism and communism. A discussion of the disagreements among certain philosophical notions and the dialectical method upon which modern materialism rests follows. The causal laws governing the universe and the conflict between materialism and theology are considered, and a notion of the world in light of philosophical laws is formed. It is claimed that thoughts are not mechanically conditioned by the requirements of the community, but are rather the result of free motives that induce one to create a system in harmony with one's community.

BAR ON, Bat-Ami. "Holocaust and Resistance" in *Inquiries into Values: The Inaugural Session of the International Society for Value Inquiry*, LEE, Sander H , 495-508. Lewiston, Mellen Pr, 1989.

In this paper I examine the moral importance attached to resistance to the holocaust. I argue that by assigning resistance a moral priority over and above other morally worthy actions one empties much of life during the holocaust of moral meaning. I also argue that in the case of the Jews, or any other victim proper, the moral prioritization of resistance to the holocaust brings with it an unnecessary moral burden.

BAR-ELLI, Gilead. Acquaintance, Knowledge and Description in Russell. Russell, 9(2), 133-156, Wint 89-90.

There is a puzzling ambivalence in Russell's treatment of "knowledge by description," which seems to render it incoherent: it is presented as a kind of knowledge of objects, while under analysis it vanishes into what remains propositional knowledge, and acquaintance. I try to explain the deep motivation for this by the idea that knowledge by description is the Russellian ancestor of knowledge about objects, and by the claim that the notion of a proposition being about an object is essential for the conceptual resources needed for explaining the epistemic character of acquaintance, and thus for the very idea of objective knowledge.

BARABASHEV, A G. Philosophy of Mathematics as a Theoretical and Applied Discipline. Phil Math, 4(2), 121-128, 1989.

The theme of the article is to show an examination of the two directions in the contemporary philosophy of mathematics—fundamental and nonfundamental. It involves the description of the nonfundamental philosophy of mathematics.

BARAD, Judith. Hartshorne and the Metaphysics of Animal Rights. Between Species, 5(3), 160-164, Sum 89.

BARASH, Carol Isaacson. The Use and Abuse of Legal Theory: A Reply to Fish. Phil Soc Crit, 15(2), 183-197, 1989.

BARBA, Juan L. A Modal Version of Free Logic. Topoi, 8(2), 131-135, S 89.

Kripke's relational models have proved to be suitable for several nonclassical logical systems, such as intuitionistic, many-valued or relevance logics. The aim of this paper is to present a Kripkean semantics for the supervaluational free logic developed by E Bencivenga (1980) and prove equivalence with Bencivenga's semantics. A certain quantificational modal logic will be proposed and it will be shown how to translate supervaluational free sentences into the modal language.

BARBACK, Joseph. On Infinite Series of Infinite Isols. J Sym Log, 53(2), 443-462, Je 88.

BARBER, Michael D. "Alma Gonzalez: Otherness as Attending to the Other" in *The Question of the Other: Essays in Contemporary Continental Philosophy*, DALLERY, Arleen B (ed), 119-126. Albany, SUNY Pr, 1989.

This article begins by describing a young Mexican girl's attentiveness to an elderly man in congested traffic. The author explores the "because motives" (in Alfred Schutz's sense) shaping her attentiveness, including her mythic background. Her attitude contrasts with a more restrictive technological attitude which tends to ignore or truncate Others' attitudes toward the world. Finally, the mythic worldview can be seen to be further along the route to Jürgen Habermas's communicative rationality than a technological worldview.

BARBIERI, Marcello. La creazione dell'informazione. Epistemologia, 11(2), 283-292, Jl-D 88.

According to a widespread belief, the only thing which is able to generate true novelties in the world is a chance event, an accident or an error. Today, this conclusion seems to be accepted in virtually all scientific fields, from mathematics to biology, to the point that many authors have expressed it as a universal principle: the principle that "no system...can produce anything new unless the system contains some source of the random" (G Bateson). Here, however, it is proposed that a more general version of epigenesis can be held, because of a new principle which states that it is mathematically possible to obtain not only a convergent generation of form, but also a convergent generation of information. (edited)

BARBU, Nicolae. Motivation et idéal dans l'action sociale (in Romanian). Rev Filosof (Romania), 35(6), 539-542, N-D 88.

BARDEN, Garrett. Sources of Value. Method, 7(2), 132-140, O 89.

Sources of value are distinguished into material and formal sources. The formal source and first principle of value is the responsible subject. The material sources are the actual situation, preferences, desires, orientations, etc. The subject expresses responsibility by giving intelligible reasons for action and by accepting those reasons as sufficient. One's tradition provides reasons that eventually each actor must, more or less clearly, take the tradition or its rejection upon him or her self and there are no unquestionable reasons beyond the actor's responsibility, and no unquestionable axioms, natural or cultural, from which values may be deduced.

BARET, Françoise (trans) and SALLIS, John. Doublures. Rev Phil Fr, 180(2), 349-360, Ap-Je 90.

A reading of several texts by Jacques Derrida on Husserl and on Saussure. The reading is oriented to the figure of doubling.

BARET, Françoise (trans) and KRELL, David Farrell. Le plus pur des batards (l'affirmation sans issue). Rev Phil Fr, 180(2), 229-238, Ap-Je 90.

BARKER, Chris and PULLUM, Geoffrey K. A Theory of Command Relations. Ling Phil, 13(1), 1-34, F 90.

BARKER, Evelyn M. Beardsley's Theory of Analogy. Inform Log, 11(3), 185-194, Fall 89.

The paper defends analogical arguments against Monroe C Beardsley's claim that they are "inherently fallacious," pointing out diverse forms, and irreplaceable utility in practical and philosophical reasoning.

BARKER, John. "Relevance Logic and Inferential Knowledge" in *Directions in Relevant Logic*, NORMAN, Jean (ed), 317-326. Norwell, Kluwer, 1989.

BARKER, Peter (trans) and ARIEW, Roger (trans) and DUHEM, Pierre. Research on the History of Physical Theories. Synthese, 83(2), 189-200, My 90.

Reviewing his research in the history of statics and dynamics, Duhem argues that Energetics is the modern heir to the principle of "saving the phenomena" that originated in Greek astronomy. Jordanus de Nemore's school surpassed ancient statics by introducing the principle of virtual work, while Parisian nominalists prepared the way for modern dynamics. After the condemnation of 1277 loosened the hold of Aristotelian theory, Ockham rehabilitated Philoponus's account of projectiles. Buridan, followed by Oresme, Albert of Saxony, and Leonardo, adopted impetus as the foundation of dynamics and introduced a law of inertia. Similar antecedents for the law of fall culminated in Domingo de Soto. The reception of these principles by Galileo and his contemporaries led to the modern science of mechanics. But the metaphysics of imperceptible bodies and hidden motions played no role in these advances, confirming Duhem's logical analysis of scientific method, and the primacy of Energetics as their descendant.

BARKER, Peter. Copernicus, the Orbs, and the Equant. Synthese, 83(2), 317-323, My 90.

I argue that Copernicus accepted the reality of celestial spheres on the grounds that the equant problem is unintelligible except as a problem about real spheres. The same considerations point to a number of generally unnoticed liabilities of Copernican astronomy, especially gaps between the spheres, and the failure of some spheres to obey the principle that their natural motion is to rotate. These difficulties may be additional reasons for Copernicus's reluctance to publish, and also stand in the way of strict realism as applied to *De Revolutionibus*, although a realistic astronomy may be envisioned as a goal for Copernicus's research program.

BARKER, Peter (trans) and ARIEW, Roger (trans) and DUHEM, Pierre. Logical Examination of Physical Theory. Synthese, 83(2), 183-188, My 90.

Duhem summarizes his philosophy of science, beginning from the "truism" that individual elements in a scientific system are inseparable for purposes of application or appraisal, and deriving both the thesis most commonly associated with his name, that elements of a scientific system are not separately falsifiable, and the thesis that observations are theory laden. Newtonian inductivists are criticized for ignoring the latter; Cartesian hypothetico-deductivists for destroying science's ability to achieve consensus by privileging a particular metaphysics. Duhem rejects atomism (Lorentz's electron theory) on the same grounds as Cartesianism, and contrasts his own view with pragmatic instrumentalism. Metaphysics is not the starting point of theory but the endpoint of science's historical development. Duhem may therefore, in a qualified sense, count as a convergent realist.

BARKER, Stephen F. Reasoning by Analogy in Hume's *Dialogues*. Inform Log, 11(3), 173-184, Fall 89.

BARNARD, F M. *Self-Direction and Political Legitimacy: Rousseau and Herder*. New York, Clarendon/Oxford Pr, 1988

What social life ought to be like to make self-direction and legitimacy *possible* was, as Herder put it, the "great theme" that linked him with Rousseau. The book variously probes this common theme by exploring the relation between nature and culture, freedom and autonomy, selfhood and mutuality, and touches on such problematic notions as will, accountability, teleology, rationality, and historical-political consciousness. It attempts to show that Herder, like Rousseau, profoundly affected the transformation of states into nation-states, and of subjects into citizens, and thereby highlighted important features of a world-view which persists into the present day.

BARNES, Annette. When Do We Deceive Others? Analysis, 50(3), 197-202, Je 90.

I argue that interpersonal deception always requires something more than some form of epistemic irresponsibility; the deceiver must also get the deceived to believe something the deceiver knows or truly believes to be false. Examples in the current literature which may at first sight seem to pose difficulties for this view do not on closer inspection pose these difficulties. If, therefore, philosophers want to model self-deception on interpersonal deception, they must come to terms with the difficulty of explaining how people can get themselves to believe propositions which they know or truly believe to be false.

BARNES, Eric. The Language Dependence of Accuracy. Synthese, 84(1), 59-95, Jl 90.

David Miller has demonstrated to the satisfaction of a variety of philosophers that the accuracy of false quantitative theories is language dependent (cf. Miller 1975). This demonstration renders the accuracy-based mode of comparison for such theories obsolete. The purpose of this essay is to supply an alternate basis for theory comparison which in this paper is deemed the 'knowledge-based' mode of quantitative theory comparison. It is argued that the status of a quantitative theory as knowledge depends primarily on the 'soundness' of the measurement procedure which produced the theory; such soundness is invariant, on my view, under Milleresque translations. This point is the basis for the linguistic invariance of 'knowledgelikeness'. When the aim of science is not construed simply in terms of the 'truthlikeness' or accuracy of theories, but in terms of the knowledge such theories embody, Miller's language dependence problem is overcome. One result of this analysis is that the possibility of objective scientific progress is restored, a possibility that Miller's analysis has *prima facie* defeated.

BARNES, Hazel E. "Sartre" in *Ethics in the History of Western Philosophy*, CAVALIER, Robert J (ed), 335-365. New York, St Martin's Pr, 1988.

Sartre's phenomenological ontology brought him finally, via his own interpretation of Marxism, to an ethics of communal responsibility. Starting with the notion of a radically free consciousness striving to make a self authentically in a world of solitary individuals whose original relation is conflict, Sartre later postulated a revolutionary group whose members are "healed of alienation" by virtue of the group itself acting as a mediating Third. In consciousness' relation to its ego, in dyadic human interaction, and even in a truly free society, choice and action can be realized only through an objectification which tends to become reification.

BARNES, Jonathan (ed) and GRIFFIN, Miriam (ed). *Philosophia Togata: Essays on Philosophy and Roman Society*. New York, Clarendon/Oxford Pr, 1989

This volume assembles a selection of papers originally delivered at the seminar on Philosophy and Roman Society in the University of Oxford. The papers, contributed by ancient philosophers, Roman historians and classical scholars, concentrate on the first century BC, a well-documented period in which the interaction of philosophy and Roman life can be examined. There are chapters on such key figures as Posidonius, Antiochus of Ascalon, Philodemus, Lucretius, Cicero, and Plutarch, as well as general essays on philosophy and politics and philosophy and religion. There is also an analytical bibliography.

BARNES, Jonathan. "Antiochus of Ascalon" in *Philosophia Togata: Essays on Philosophy and Roman Society*, GRIFFIN, Miriam (ed), 51-96. New York, Clarendon/Oxford Pr, 1989.

BARNES, Jonathan. Heidegger spéléologue. Rev Metaph Morale, 95(2), 173-195, Ap-Je 90.

An examination of Heidegger's account of Plato's Cave, the article comes to the depressing conclusion that Heidegger is not worth reading.

BARNES, Jonathan and BRUNSCHWIG, J (trans). Médecine, expérience et logique. Rev Metaph Morale, 94(4), 437-481, O-D 89.

BARNES, Jonathan. New Light on Antiphon. Polis, 7(1), 2-5, 1987.

BARNES, Jonathan. "Some Ways of Scepticism" in *Epistemology (Companions to Ancient Thought: 1)*, EVERSON, Stephen (ed), 204-224. New York, Cambridge Univ Pr, 1989.

In the works of Sextus Empiricus, scepticism is presented in its most elaborate and challenging form. This book investigates—both from an exegetical and from a philosophical point of view—the chief argumentative forms which ancient scepticism developed. Thus the focus is on the Agrippan aspect of Sextus's Pyrrhonism. The author gives a lucid explanation and analysis of these arguments, both individually and as constituent parts of a sceptical system. For, taken together, they amount to a formidable and systematic challenge to any claim to knowledge or rational belief. The challenge has in fact had a great influence on the history of philosophy. But it has never been met.

BARNETT, John H and KARSON, Marvin J. Managers, Values, and Executive Decisions. J Bus Ethics, 8(10), 747-771, O 89.

A study of 513 executives researched decisions involving ethics, relationships and results. Analyzing personal values, organization role and level, career stage, gender and sex role with decisions in ten scenarios produced conclusions about both the role of gender, subjective values, and the other study variables and about situational relativity, gender stereotypes, career stages, and future research opportunities.

BARNETT, William E. The Rhetoric of Grammar: Understanding Wittgenstein's Method. Metaphilosophy, 21(1-2), 43-66, Ja-Ap 90.

I approach the method of Wittgenstein's later philosophy by investigating the *rhetoric* of the texts. Wittgenstein's two main objectives are to provide a method for describing grammar and to show how grammatical descriptions shed light on philosophical problems. A rhetorical study examines how Wittgenstein's writings and lectures are designed to realize these objectives.

I conclude that Wittgenstein's method is a function of this rhetoric. Two consequences of this are that 'language-games' are purely heuristic devices free of theoretical or ontological commitments and that Wittgenstein's remarks are meant to expose *pre*-theoretical conceptions which affect philosophical thinking.

BARNOUW, Jeffrey. Hobbes's Psychology of Thought: Endeavours, Purpose and Curiosity. Hist Euro Ideas, 10(5), 519-545, 1989.

Hobbes is wrongly thought to have mechanized the mind in such a way as to exclude purpose and spontaneity from human thinking. His adaptation from mechanics of a conative model for motions of the mind made for a clearer understanding of how intended goals have effect in the determination of human action, and like Aristotle he made orientation to an end central to ordered thought. But since ends are not different from means intrinsically and are relative to human desires, Hobbes converts the Aristotelian theme of the natural desire of knowledge (of or by way of causes) into a novel idea of curiosity which provides a new principle for the coherence of thought: curiosity as the desire to know the undiscovered effects of causes in our power, which may become new ends.

BARON, Marcia. "Patriotism and Liberal Morality" in *Mind, Value and Culture: Essays in Honor of E M Adams*, WEISSBORD, David (ed), 269-300. Atascadero, Ridgeview, 1989.

This paper examines the tension between an approach which sees impartiality and the impersonal point of view to be central to morality and an approach which emphasizes special ties (of family, community, etc.). It does so by challenging MacIntyre's claim that a proponent of "impersonal morality" (or "liberal morality") cannot consistently regard patriotism as a virtue. I develop a conception of patriotism which, while replete with particularity, is consistent with impersonal morality and is arguably a virtue.

BARON, Richard J. Medical Hermeneutics: Where is the "Text" We are Interpreting. Theor Med, 11(1), 25-28, Mr 90.

The present paper is a commentary on an article by Drew Leder. Leder identifies a series of 'texts' in the clinical encounter, emphasizes the central role of interpretation in making sense of each of these texts, and articulates ordering principles to guide the interpretive work. The metaphor of clinical work as textual explication, however, creates the expectation that there is a text somewhere to be found. Such an expectation invites doctors and patients to search for the text and runs the risk of conceptualizing patients as more static than they are. If one is to use the textual metaphor, one must appreciate the radical extent to which the clinical encounter is a mutually produced and shifting entity. The qualities of mutuality and indeterminacy are not those one usually associates with texts. One might ultimately be better served by a different metaphor based more directly on uncertainty.

BARR, James. Literality. Faith Phil, 6(4), 412-428, O 89.

Although the concept of the literal is very widely used in the discussion of biblical interpretation, it has seldom been deeply analysed. "Conservative" understandings of the Bible are often thought of as literal, but it is equally true that "critical" views are built upon literality. In some relations, literality seems to imply physicality, in others to mean exactitude in the rendering of "spiritual" realities. In Christianity the relation of Christians to the laws of the Old Testament is a prime area of application of these categories. Are the silences of the Bible to be taken as "literally" as its words? And does literality give us access to *intentions*?

BARR, Robert R (trans) and DUSSEL, Enrique D. *Ethics and Community*. Maryknoll, Orbis Books, 1988

This book examines the insights provided by liberation theology concerning morality and differing ethical systems. It examines what two ethical systems, community ethics and social morality, have to say about ten questions basic to ethics (good and evil, personal vs. social sin, relative morals vs. absolute ethics, etc.). The author then examines ways in which the two systems address ten contemporary issues. (staff)

BARRALL, Mary Rose. "Values and Family Relations" in *Inquiries into Values: The Inaugural Session of the International Society for Value Inquiry*, LEE, Sander H , 459-475. Lewiston, Mellen Pr, 1989.

The aim is to uncover the status of values in the modern family. After a study of "value" from a philosophical viewpoint, the ontologico-social foundation of the family is investigated. The interpersonal relations among the members, parenthood, the needs of the family, love, friendship and sexuality are discussed. Personal freedom, as fundamental value for domestic love relations, is presented vis-a-vis both traditional family virtues and contemporary reevaluation of the same. They demand a radically new approach to interpersonal relations.

BARRET-KRIEGEL, Blandine. "Dimension européenne de la culture politique de l'Etat moderne" in *Culture et Politique/Culture and Politics*, CRANSTON, Maurice (ed), 51-54. Hawthorne, de Gruyter, 1988.

BARRET-KRIEGEL, Blandine. Politique-(s) de Descartes? Arch Phil, 53(3), 371-388, Jl-S 90.

"Cartesian policy" may be understood according to three meanings: (1) Political theory is excluded together with history. (2) Moral policy is reduced to freedom as "générosité." (3) In political action there seems to be a kind of Cartesian "Christian policy."

BARRETT, D C. Faith and Rationality. Philosophy, 24, 135-143, 88 Supp.

BARRETT, Terry. A Consideration of Criticism. J Aes Educ, 23(4), 23-35, Wint 89.

This article presents differing attitudes, beliefs, and practices of several contemporary art critics, many of whom criticize photographs. It considers critics' perceived roles with the publications and audiences for whom they write, their formative backgrounds, stances toward criticism, relationships toward artists, with implications for teaching about criticism within aesthetic education. Criticism is presented as a positive endeavor engaged in by people who are learned and enthusiastic about art, work within artworld contexts, and write to persuade audiences about their views of artworks.

BARROTTA, Pierluigi. Teoria della argomentazione e filosofia della scienza. Epistemologia, 11(2), 255-276, Jl-D 88.

The aim of this paper is to show how the theory of argumentation put forward by C Perelman could clarify some of the traditional problems of the philosophy of science—especially in the light of discussions on the incommensurability of scientific theories. (edited)

BARRY, Brian. Utilitarianism and Preference Change. Utilitas, 1(2), 278-282, N 89.

It has been claimed (e.g., by Rawls) that if we ascribe value to want-satisfaction this entails that people should modify their preferences constantly so as to have easily satisfied wants. This claim is without merit. In the statement 'It is good that I get what I want', the relevant wants are those I actually have. It is not a derivation from some notion of the value of want-satisfaction in the abstract.

BARRY, Norman P. The Liberal Constitution: Rational Design or Evolution? Crit Rev, 3(2), 267-282, Spr 89.

This article analyses the contributions of F A von Hayek to constitutional theory and puts them in a context of liberal individualist jurisprudence. It describes the antirationalist basis of Hayek's thought and the claim that spontaneous legal systems, such as the common law, contain more knowledge than could be captured in a legal code. It argues that an extreme antirationalistic jurisprudence is inadequate to sustain a liberal individualist social philosophy. It critically analyses Hayek's reform proposals, based on a new separation of powers between command-issuing and rule-making legislative bodies, and compares this to liberal contractarianism.

BARRY, Norman. The State and Legitimacy. Philosophy, 24, 191-206, 88 Supp.

Liberal political economists have tried to construct a normative theory of the state: a theory that justifies its activities on the ground that it is a conduit for the expression of people's subjective wants for collective goods and services. It is shown that this cannot satisfactorily explain the existence of law and government. Conservatives argue that the legitimacy of the state can only be explained in terms of tradition. But this can provide no legitimating criteria for the range of its activity. It is maintained that legitimacy is a function of subjective choice expressed through received constitutional rules.

BARRY, Robert L. *Medical Ethics: Essays on Abortion and Euthanasia*. New York, Lang, 1989

This book examines the moral aspects of taking life at the beginning and end of the life spectrum. It discusses the morality of abortion, the nature of the human person, procedures for ending neonatal life, removal of nutrition and fluids, the problems and paradoxes of mercy killing and the jurisprudence of life-ending decisions. The book approaches these topics from a counter-establishment standpoint and raises hard questions for those who would justify terminating the lives of the unborn, newly born and elderly.

BARTELS, Andreas. Wesshalb implizite Definitionen nicht genug sind. Erkenntnis, 32(2), 269-281, Mr 90.

At least some physical concepts get their meaning neither by "operational definition" nor by their mathematical role ("implicit definition"). A detailed discussion of the example of Schwarzschild mass in general relativity theory yields that generalizations of central empirical relations play an important role in extending the meaning of "old" Newtonian mass to the "new" Schwarzschild mass term. The latter is identified as successor of the former one, because in the "weak field limit" the term becomes empirically indistinguishable from the Newtonian mass term. Limit relations therefore not only bring about empirical comparability of theories, but also semantical comparability ("commensurability") of their concepts.

BARTH, Else M. On Logical Representation and Its Consequences: The (Onto)Logical Master Premiss in Philosophy. Commun Cog, 22(3-4), 337-356, 1989.

BARTLETT, Steven J. The Problem of Psychotherapeutic Effectiveness. Method Sci, 23(2), 75-86, 1990.

Hundreds of evaluative studies of psychotherapy still leave the issue unsettled. This paper argues that such studies have ignored the major determinant of therapeutic effectiveness, the role of a patient's belief in a successful outcome in therapy. It makes little sense to claim that a certain therapy is effective or ineffective in itself; rather, there is a relation of mutual interaction among three terms: a patient's ability to learn in a psychological context, a therapist's ability to teach, and the capacity of an approach to therapy to engender in the patient the necessary belief in its effectiveness.

BARTLETT, Steven J. Psychological Underpinnings of Philosophy. Metaphilosophy, 20(3-4), 295-305, Jl-O 89.

In an earlier paper in this journal (Vol. 17, No. 1, 1986, pp. 1-13), the author looked at ways in which philosophical positions become self-encapsulating ideologies, and tried to examine why it is that communication between philosophical standpoints is so difficult. In this paper, the author looks at the same phenomenon, but from the point of view of the personality structure of philosophers themselves. A psychological description is given of the philosophical personality.

BARUSS, Imants. Categorial Modelling of Husserl's Intentionality. Husserl Stud, 6(1), 25-41, 1989.

Category-theoretic constructions involved in the definition of Grothendieck topoi are used to model conscious mental acts. Correspondences are made between acts and objects, time and arrows, directedness and sheaves, and the objects of consciousness and germs. The power of this categorial modelling becomes evident when it is seen that the impact of future events on the present is captured by the presence of a pretopology and made possible by the compatibility condition. Set-theoretic possible worlds accounts of Husserl's intentionality can be recovered from this more comprehensive modelling by considering the partial sections over a site generated by germs.

BARWELL, Ismay. Feminine Perspectives and Narrative Points of View. Hypatia, 5(2), 63-75, Sum 90.

The search for a unified and coherent feminine aesthetic theory could not be successful because it relies upon "universals" which do not exist and assumes simple parallels among psychological, social and aesthetic structures. However, with an apparatus of narrative points of view, one can demonstrate that individual narrative texts are organized from a feminine point of view. To this extent, the intuition that there is a feminine aesthetic can be vindicated.

BARWISE, Jon. "On the Circumstantial Relation between Meaning and Content" in *Meaning and Mental Representation*, ECO, Umberto (ed), 23-39. Bloomington, Indiana Univ Pr, 1988.

This article is an attempt to show that the relational theory of meaning can provide a bridge between two views about language, one that accounts for the ability of speakers to convey information, and so impart knowledge, the other which recognizes the importance of the speaker's intentions. The article also explores consequences of this view for the theory of literary interpretation.

BASH, Harry. An Exchange on Vertical Drift and the Quest for Theoretical Integration in Sociology. Soc Epistem, 3(3), 229-246, Jl-S 89.

If substantive concerns of sociology are arrayed along a vertical axis of relative phenomenal and conceptual complexity, the discipline is seen to embrace several distinct analytic levels. Their respective boundaries function as base-lines from which emergent properties arise, and as dead-ends for reductionist chains. Not merely aggregative, these complexities reflect qualitative discontinuities which are rooted in relatively discrete constructions of reality. Parallelisms in other disciplines are cited. To integrate various extant theories *in* sociology, the possibility for a unified theory *of* sociology is probed.

BASINGER, David. Miracles as Evidence for Theism. Sophia (Australia), 29(1), 56-59, Ap 90.

In an ongoing dialogue, Robert Larmer and I have been discussing whether the undisputed occurrence of certain conceivable events would require all honest, thoughtful individuals to acknowledge that God has intervened in earthly affairs. I argue that there is no reason to believe that a nontheist who acknowledged certain healings to be strong evidence for theism but did not see such evidence as outweighing what she viewed as the stronger counterevidence, and thus remained a nontheist, could justifiably be accused of adopting a dogmatic, uncritical question-begging stance.

BASINGER, David. Process-Relational Christian Soteriology: A Response to Wheeler. Process Stud, 18(2), 114-117, Sum 89.

This article is a response to David Wheeler's discussion of the relationship between the soteriological positions of evangelical and process thinkers. I conclude that while there are points at which the two schools of thought are similar, the differences between process thought (of the Whiteheadian variety) and evangelical thought are far more basic and profound than the differing terminology they employ might indicate.

BASTOS, Feliciano Moreira. Bedingungen für die Aneignung und Verbreitung des Marxismus-Leninismus in afrikanischen ländern. Deut Z Phil, 37(9), 867-869, 1989.

BASU, S and KASEM, A. A Refutation of Jagat Pal's Defence of Aristotelian Square of Opposition. Indian Phil Quart, 17(2), 261-270, Ap 90.

The aim of this article is to argue against the contention that the traditional doctrine of the square of opposition can be refuted by modern logic (which uses the language of first order predicate logic) only if it admits an empty domain of discourse at the cost of involving inconsistency in other parts of the system. By emphasising the distinction between "empty predicate" and "empty domain of discourse" this article establishes that modern logic consistently admits the former in refuting the doctrine of traditional square, and also claims that this admission is consistent with semantic and logical intuitions.

BASU, Tora. Kant's Conception of Rational Action. Indian Phil Quart, 16(4), 393-408, O 89.

The article seeks to find out a definition of rational action in Kant's ethical system. Kant's idea of rational action is differentiated from that of his predecessors. The resulting definition is, "A rational act is that which is done in accordance with the idea of a practical principle." Questions like whether the division of these practical principles into moral (morally good) and nonmoral (morally not good) ones is exhaustive do arise: could there be principles of rational action that were nonuniversal but without content and principles of action that were universal without having a moral import? The finding of this paper is that according to Kant, no practical principle can be either the one or the other.

BATENS, Diderik. Against Global Paraconsistency. Stud Soviet Tho, 39(3-4), 209-229, Ap-My 90.

BATESON, Patrick. Does Evolutionary Biology Contribute to Ethics? Biol Phil, 4(3), 287-301, Jl 89.

Human propensities that are the products of Darwinian evolution may combine to generate a form of social behavior that is not itself a direct result of such pressure. This possibility may provide a satisfying explanation for the origin of socially transmitted rules such as the incest taboo. Similarly, the regulatory processes of development that generated adaptations to the environment in the circumstances in which they evolved can produce surprising and sometimes maladaptive consequences for the individual in modern conditions. These combinatorial aspects of social and developmental dynamics leave a subtle but not wholly uninteresting role for evolutionary biology in explaining the origins of human morality.

BATTA, Nirmala Devi. Descartes in the Hegelian Perspective. Indian Phil Quart, SUPP 16(4), 21-28, O 89.

BATTERSBY, Mark E. Critical Thinking as Applied Epistemology: Relocating Critical Thinking in the Philosophical Landscape. Inform Log, 11(2), 91-100, Spr 89.

This paper argues that epistemology, like ethics, can be divided into meta, normative, and applied, and that the content of most informal logic courses (as critical thinking courses are usually described by philosophy faculty) is actually "applied epistemology": instruction in the practical application of the norms that establish "justified belief." It is also argued that "applied epistemology" will generate as interesting and significant problems for epistemology (e.g., the proper role of appeal to authority) as applied ethics has for ethical theory.

BATTIN, M Pabst. The Least Worst Death. Nat Forum, 69(4), 36-38, Fall 89.

BATTIN, Margaret P. Organized Religion: New Target for Professional Ethics? J Soc Phil, 20(1-2), 125-130, Spr-Fall 89.

Is it possible to use the conceptual apparatus of (secular) applied ethics—already employed in such fields as medical ethics, law ethics, business ethics, and other professional-ethics fields—to critique a new target: organized religion? This paper sketches the advantages and limitations of such an approach.

BAUDRY, Leon and GUERLAC, Rita (trans). *The Quarrel over Future Contingents (Louvain 1465-1475)*. Norwell, Kluwer, 1989

BAUER, Henry H. Barriers Against Interdisciplinarity: Implications for

Studies of Science, Technology, and Society (STS). Sci Tech Human Values, 15(1), 105-119, Wint 90.

Interdisciplinary work is intractable because the search for knowledge in different fields entails different interests, and thereby different values too; and the different possibilities of knowledge about different subjects also lead to different epistemologies. Thus differences among practitioners of the various disciplines are pervasive and aptly described as cultural ones, and interdisciplinary work requires transcending unconscious habits of thought. Two sorts of interdisciplinary effort seem to have been successful: specific, delimited problems have been solved by teams in what is actually multidisciplinary rather than interdisciplinary work and new disciplines have sprung up at the intersections of existing ones. STS fits neither of those patterns.

BAUER, Henry. The Antithesis. Soc Epistem, 4(2), 215-227, Ap-Je 90.

Many examples are given to illustrate the contention that differences among disciplines are cultural rather than just concern with different fields of knowledge. Practitioners of the various disciplines vary in religious affiliation, political persuasion, and the like as well as in epistemic beliefs. Chemists and historians, for example, differ from one another not as do collectors of stamps and collectors of coins, say, but rather as do Frenchmen and Germans. There are obvious implications for academic life and interdisciplinary activities.

BAUGH, Bruce. Left-Wing Elitism: Adorno on Popular Culture. Phil Lit, 14(1), 65-78, Ap 90.

The aim of this article is to show that T W Adorno's and Herbert Marcuse's critique of popular culture rests on a misunderstanding of popular art. Marcuse and Adorno see popular art as providing pleasure, whereas emancipatory art arouses anxiety in virtue of its "difficulty." Yet popular art, properly understood, can be emancipatory in just the way Adorno and Marcuse require.

BAUM, Mylène. Visage Versus Visages. Phil Theol, 4(2), 187-205, Wint 89.

I aim here to confront texts of Levinas and Sartre in an attempt to rethink the relation of the political to the ethical in the early eighties in France. The method is essentially to try to think a passage from one domain into the other without privileging politics over ethics or vice versa while uncovering their organic and dialectical interaction, a subject that can only be touched upon via the bridging metaphor of a Visage that can liberate oneself from the totalization of egoity. My purpose, thus, is not to confront Levinas and Sartre but to allow them to embark on a dialogue constructed around the paradigm of the question of the Other.

BAUMAN, Zygmunt. *Freedom*. Minneapolis, Univ of Minn Pr, 1988

Freedom is considered as a social relation. In the contemporary stage of modern society seduction replaces repression as method of social control. Consumer freedom moves into the place occupied by work—as the link between life-world, social integration and sytemic reproduction. Individual freedom becomes, first and foremost, freedom of the consumer.

BAUMGARTNER, James E and LARSON, J A. A Diamond Example of an Ordinal Graph with no Infinite Paths. Annals Pure Applied Log, 47(1), 1-10, Ap 90.

BAUR, Michael. A Contribution to the Gadamer-Lonergan Discussion. Method, 8(1), 14-23, Mr 90.

Much literature on Gadamer and Lonergan has focussed on the purported similarities between the two; this essay is meant as a "corrective" to that literature. A significant difference between the two thinkers has to do with their diverging views concerning the explanatory ideal of science. Lonergan argues that it is possible to develop a single explanatory viewpoint which can comprehend and integrate the diverse forms of human inquiry from physics to theology; Gadamer denies this possibility. It is argued, in conclusion, that an adequate understanding of both Gadamer and Lonergan must take such differences into account.

BAUR, Michael. A Conversation with Hans-Georg Gadamer. Method, 8(1), 1-13, Mr 90.

In this interview, Gadamer responds to questions on a number of related issues, including the failure of metaphysics, the neo-Thomism of Bernard Lonergan, the Western philosophical and theological traditions, the situation of the modern age, modern science, and Heidegger's thought. Throughout the interview, Gadamer expresses his conviction that we moderns must learn to live in "two worlds"—one which is accessible to the canons of theoretical explanation, and the other which is accessible only through the regulative ideas of practical reason; in other words, not all truth can be mediated intellectually.

BAXTER, David. Marx, Lukes, and Human Rights. Soc Theor Pract, 15(3),

355-373, Fall 89.

BAXTER, Donald L M. Hume on Virtue, Beauty, Composites, and Secondary Qualities. Pac Phil Quart, 71(2), 103-118, Je 90.

Hume's account of virtue (and beauty) entails that distinct things—a quality in the contemplated and a perception in the contemplator—are the same thing—a given virtue. I show this inconsistency is consistent with his intent. A virtue is a composite of quality and perception, and for Hume a composite is distinct things—the parts—falsely supposed to be a single thing. False or unsubstantiated supposition is for Hume the basis of most of our beliefs. I end with an argument that for Hume secondary qualities are composites, not powers.

BAYEROVA, Marie. Husserl—Bolzano I (in Czechoslovakian). Estetika, 27(2), 105-127, 1990.

BAYLES, Michael D. Allocation of Scarce Medical Resources. Pub Affairs Quart, 4(1), 1-16, Ja 90.

This paper argues for allocating scarce medical resources primarily on the basis of proportional individual benefit. Principles of social worth, responsibility, and randomization are criticized but retained as secondary principles. Individual benefit is analyzed as proportional increase in opportunity for a life found valuable. The view is illustrated generally and in allocating in vitro fertilization to patients.

BAYLES, Michael D. Commentary on "The Worm and the Juggernaut". Bus Prof Ethics J, 6(2), 61-65, Sum 87.

This is a brief commentary on a companion article by J R Lucas on the British Inquiry procedure for planning highways. Four sets of questions based on different principles of justice should be answered to justify projects. Professional planning involves a mixture of adversarial adjudication and professional service decision-making models. Citizens or their elected representatives should be involved early in the planning and have the final say.

BAYLES, Michael D. Prenatal Harm and Privacy Rights. Nat Forum, 69(4), 28-30, Fall 89.

This article considers what types of laws might be justified to restrict the conduct of pregnant women risking the health of fetuses. Laws are justified if acceptable reasons for them outweigh reasons against them and the net advantage is greater than for any alternative (including no law). While the prevention of harm supports such laws, women's rights to liberty and bodily integrity oppose them. The prevention of harm might outweigh women's rights and justify criminal, tort, or compulsory treatment laws. However, I conclude that the net advantage favors laws conferring benefits—free and available education, prenatal care, nutrition, and abortion.

BAYLES, Michael D. *Professional Ethics (Second Edition)*. Belmont, Wadsworth, 1989

BAYNE, Steven R. On the Appearance of Contingency: A Rejoinder to Blum. Philosophia (Israel), 19(4), 457-460, D 89.

BAYNES, K. The Liberal/Communitarian Controversy and Communicative Ethics. Phil Soc Crit, 14(3-4), 293-313, 1988.

The author examines three issues in the dispute between liberals and their communitarian critics—the concept of the self, the distinction between the right and the good, and the justification of political principles. The author then argues that Habermas's model of communicative ethics improves on weaknesses in each position while also drawing on the particular strengths of liberalism.

BAYNES, Kenneth. Dialectic and Deliberation in Aristotle's Practical Philosophy. SW Phil Rev, 6(2), 19-42, Jl 90.

Although recent interpretations generally agree that Aristotle's model of practical reasoning is not simply instrumental or calculative, the connections between an alternative reading and other features of his practical philosophy (such as his discussion of friendship) have not been drawn out. Drawing upon Gadamer's interpretation, it is argued that "phronesis" is a form of dialectic practiced among friends in an attempt to determine the right thing to do. Some consequences for Aristotle's interpretation of the practical syllogism are also indicated.

BAYNES, Kenneth. Kant on Property Rights and the Social Contract. Monist, 72(3), 433-453, Jl 89.

The essay argues that, having earlier defended a labor theory similar to Locke's, Kant subsequently develops a unique theory of property rights in connection with his own conception of practical reason (or moral autonomy). Central to this later theory is the notion that these rights depend not on a relation between persons and things, but on a (counterfactual) agreement between free and equal persons. A reconstruction of the "deduction" of the right to "intelligible possession" contained in the *Rechtslehre* emphasizes its introduction as a "permissive law" and considers the originality of Kant's position within the natural law tradition. The essay ends with a discussion of the distinctive features and problems connected with Kant's theory of the social contract as a basis of political legitimacy.

BAYNES, Kenneth. Rational Reconstruction and Social Criticism: Habermas's Model of Interpretive Social Science. Phil Forum, 21(1-2), 122-145, Fall-Wint 89-90.

BAZAC, Ana. Les réalisations du socialisme dans la perspective de l'histoire (in Romanian). Rev Filosof (Romania), 36(3), 216-219, My-Je 89.

BAZAC, Ana. Le socialisme et le conditionnement social du bonheur. Phil Log, 32(3-4), 179-183, Jl-D 88.

BAZHANOV, Valentine A. The Fate of One Forgotten Idea: N A Vasiliev and His Imaginary Logic. Stud Soviet Tho, 39(3-4), 333-341, Ap-My 90.

The article traces the life and logical inheritance of Kazan University Professor N A Vasiliev—the forerunner of nonclassical logic, foremost paraconsistent and multi-valued. In his imaginary, non-Aristotelian logic free of the laws of contradiction and excluded middle and constructed, according to Vasiliev by Lobachevsky method, new classes of judgments were introduced, ideas of the plurality of logics and metalogic have been realized. The status of Gödel theorems and the principle of external premises are discussed.

BAZYLAK, Jozef and BIELECKI, Jan. Das Problem der Psychologischen Hinführung zur Bildung der reifen und religiösen Persönlichkeit (in Polish). Stud Phil Christ, 25(1), 221-236, 1989.

In der Arbeit wurde die Bildung der reifen Persönlichkeit besprochen mit der Berücksichtung aller Elemente, die sie bilden. Es wurden auch experimentale Forschungen besprochen, die das religiöse Leben betreffen d.h. religiöse Haltungen mit der Persönlichkeit und ihre Aufgabe in der Bildung der Persönlichkeit. Der Autor unterstrich die Notwendigkeit der Bildung der eigentlichen religiösen Haltungen. Er sprach sich Für die Stärkung der Überzeugungskraft sowie des Erkenntnisund des Willensbereiches der religiösen Haltungen aus.

BEABOUT, Greg. Morphine Use for Terminal Cancer Patients. Phil Context, 19, 49-57, 1989.

BEAKLEY, Brian. Response to Dietrich's "Computationalism". Soc Epistem, 4(2), 157-162, Ap-Je 90.

My response challenges three central tenets of Dietrich's position on computational explanation, favoring instead a more liberal and general account. Against his claim that "causal" and "computational" explanations are mutually exclusive, I argue that—at least on van Fraassen's view—the opposition is illusory. Second, I suggest that, contrary to Dietrich's conclusion, functional analyses at the program level do provide acceptable explanations. Finally, I conclude likewise that what Dietrich terms "nonproductive functions" (where competence, and not just performance, is intrinsically limited) can legitimately figure in computational explanations.

BEARDS, Andrew. Creator and Causality: A Critique of Pre-Critical Objections. Thomist, 53(4), 573-586, O 89.

The article is a brief outline of central elements in Bernard Lonergan's argument for the existence of God. This argument is situated within the context of traditional and contemporary debates on epistemology and metaphysics, and Lonergan's basic strategy is described as an explication of conditions implicit in the activity of criticism.

BEARDSLEE, William A (ed) and GRIFFIN, David Ray (ed) and HOLLAND, Joe (ed). *Varieties of Postmodern Theology*. Albany, SUNY Pr, 1989

BEARDSLEE, William A. "Christ in the Postmodern Age: Reflections Inspired by Jean-François Lyotard" in *Varieties of Postmodern Theology*, GRIFFIN, David Ray (ed), 63-80. Albany, SUNY Pr, 1989.

Two senses of "postmodern" are distinguished: a broader postmodernism (which the article espouses) which moves beyond the determinism of classic modern scientific thought, and a "severe" postmodernism, close to nihilism, which is seen in literature and philosophy. As a representative of the latter, a work of J-F Lyotard is examined and questioned. A "distributive" Christology appropriate to the postmodern world is sketched.

BEARDSLEE, William A. "Cornel West's Postmodern Theology" in *Varieties of Postmodern Theology*, GRIFFIN, David Ray (ed), 149-155. Albany, SUNY Pr, 1989.

Cornel West's theology, with its roots in the Afro-American Christian tradition and in American neo-pragmatism, is appreciated for its perception of the role that traditional metaphysics played in establishing the status quo. It is suggested that West's theological affirmations could be more strongly based in a postmodern metaphysics such as that of process thought.

BEATTY, John. Evolutionary Anti-Reductionism: Historical Reflections. Biol Phil, 5(2), 197-210, Ap 90.

BEATY, Michael and TALIAFERRO, Charles. God and Concept Empiricism. SW Phil Rev, 6(2), 97-105, Jl 90.

David Blumenfeld employs a version of concept empiricism to argue that there cannot be an omnipotent, omniscient being. We argue that Blumenfeld's defense of concept empiricism is inadequate and his argument fails.

BEATY, Michael. The Problem of Evil: The Unanswered Questions Argument. SW Phil Rev, 4(1), 57-64, Ja 88.

A theist does not need a theodicy, if her belief in God is to be rational. The assertion that one does need a theodicy is to suggest a formulation of the problem of evil I call "the unanswered questions" argument, an argument suggested by both Philo of Hume's *Dialogues Concerning Natural Religion* and Ivan of Dostoevsky's *The Brothers Karamazov*. I argue that it does not follow from the inability of the theist to answer questions like "Why does God permit these kinds of evils?" that belief in God is irrational.

BEAUCHAMP, Tom L. *Case Studies in Business, Society, and Ethics (Second Edition)*. Englewood Cliffs, Prentice-Hall, 1989

BEAUCHAMP, Tom L (ed) and WALTERS, Leroy (ed). *Contemporary Issues in Bioethics (Third Edition)*. Belmont, Wadsworth, 1989

BEAUCHAMP, Tom L (ed) and FEINBERG, Joel (ed) and SMITH, James M. (ed). *Philosophy and the Human Condition (Second Edition)*. Englewood Cliffs, Prentice-Hall, 1989

BEAUCHAMP, Tom L. "Suicide in the Age of Reason" in *Suicide and Euthanasia*, BRODY, Baruch A (ed), 183-219. Norwell, Kluwer, 1989.

BEAUDE, Joseph. Bérulle, Malebranche et l'amour de Dieu. Rev Phil Fr, 179(2), 163-176, Ap-Je 89.

BEAUJOUR, Michel. "Rhetoric and Literature" in *From Metaphysics to Rhetoric*, MEYER, Michel (ed), 151-168. Norwell, Kluwer, 1989.

BEAVERS, Anthony F. Desire and Love in Descartes' Late Philosophy. Hist Phil Quart, 6(3), 279-294, Jl 89.

BEAVERS, Anthony F and RICE, Lee C. Doubt and Belief in the *Tractatus De Intellectus Emendatione*. Stud Spinozana, 4, 93-119, 1988.

We argue that Spinoza has a consistent account of the nature of doubt and belief in the *TIE*, and that this account, while not expounded explicitly in the *Ethics*, remains the consistent background for much of the development there. Finally, Spinoza's account of belief is defended against the cognitivist theory of propositional attitudes which is offered by thinkers such as Bennett and Braithwaite.

BECHTEL, William and ABRAHAMSEN, Adele A. Beyond the Exclusively Propositional Era. Synthese, 82(2), 223-253, F 90.

Contemporary epistemology has assumed that knowledge is represented in sentences or propositions. However, a variety of extensions and alternatives to this view have been proposed in other areas of investigation. We review some of these proposals, focusing on (1) Ryle's notion of *knowing how* and Hanson's and Kuhn's account of theory-laden perception in science; (2) extensions of simple propositional representations in cognitive models and artificial intelligence; (3) the debate concerning imagistic versus propositional representations in cognitive psychology; (4) recent treatments of concepts and categorization which reject the notion of necessary and sufficient conditions; and (5) parallel distributed processing (connectionist) models of cognition. This last development is especially promising in providing a flexible, powerful means of representing information nonpropositionally, and carrying out at least simple forms of inference without rules. Central to several of the proposals is the notion that much of human cognition might consist in *pattern recognition* rather than manipulation of rules and propositions.

BECHTEL, William. "An Evolutionary Perspective on the Re-Emergence of Cell Biology" in *Issues in Evolutionary Epistemology*, HAHLWEG, Kai (ed), 433-457. Albany, SUNY Pr, 1989.

BECK, Clive. Is There Really Development? An Alternative Interpretation. J Moral Educ, 18(3), 174-185, O 89.

It is usually assumed by developmentalists that the changes in morality which typically take place from childhood through adolescence to adulthood represent *improvement*, at least in moral judgment and also, on the whole, in general moral functioning. In this paper, I maintain that there is, on average, no moral improvement from middle childhood to adulthood: the morality of children and adolescents is no less (and no more) appropriate than that of adults, given their respective socio-political situations. In order to support this claim, I offer a number of arguments and an alternative interpretation of the phenomena which have been taken to support developmentalism. I conclude with a reaffirmation of the importance of moral education, but suggest that it must proceed not in a top-down manner but rather with children, adolescents and adults working together to improve the morality of our society and the global community.

BECK, Lewis White (ed). *Kant: Selections.* New York, Macmillan, 1988

This textbook-anthology contains all of the Prize Essay, *Prolegomena, Foundations of Metaphysics of Morals, Idea for a Universal History, Perpetual Peace,* and *What Is Enlightenment?*; and major parts of the Inaugural Dissertation, the letter to Herz, and the three *Critiques*. All are revisions of earlier translations, mostly those by Beck. It contains an extensive biographical and philosophical introduction suitable for students and a "bibliographical essay" and advice for teachers. Each selection is accompanied by an introduction and notes. The material on the *Critique of Judgment* is unique in its exposition of the organization and significance of this work.

BECK, Simon. Parfit and the Russians. Analysis, 49(4), 205-209, O 89.

Derek Parfit provides, in *Reasons and Persons,* an account of how some of our moral concepts will be affected on accepting his reductionist view of personal identity. He uses as a central illustration of the way commitment is affected his example of the nineteenth-century Russian. This paper argues that Parfit's description of the example is seriously misleading, and that commitment is a much more complex matter in Parfit's world than he acknowledges.

BECKER, Joy and GARRETT, Dennis E and BRADFORD, Jeffrey L and MEYERS, Renee A. Issues Management and Organizational Accounts: An Analysis of Corporate Responses to Accusation of Unethical Business. J Bus Ethics, 8(7), 507-520, Jl 89.

When external groups accuse a business organization of unethical practices, managers of the accused organization usually offer a communicative response to attempt to protect their organization's public image. Even though many researchers readily concur that analysis of these communicative responses is important to our understanding of business and society conflict, few investigations have focused on developing a *theoretical framework* for analyzing these communicative strategies used by managers. In additon, research in this area has suffered from a *lack of empirical investigation.* In this paper we address both of these weaknesses in the existing literature. (edited)

BECKER, Lawrence C. Unity, Coincidence, and Conflict in the Virtues. Philosophia (Israel), 20(1-2), 127-143, Jl 90.

This paper argues for an ordinal account of the unity of the virtues (1) by showing the importance of a neglected class of questions about the coherence of lists of virtues (coincidence problems); (2) by organizing conventional accounts of the unity of the virtues in a perspicuous way, and showing that they fail to solve coincidence problems; and (3) by describing the sorts of ordinal accounts that are available, sketching the outlines of one organized around a vaguely Aristotelian notion of practical wisdom, and indicating how it would handle coherence questions of all sorts, including those of coincidence.

BECKER, Neal C and CUDD, Ann E. Indefinitely Repeated Games: A Response to Carroll. Theor Decis, 28(2), 189-195, Mr 90.

In a recent volume of this journal John Carroll argued that there exist only uncooperative equilibria in indefinitely repeated prisoner's dilemma games. We show that this claim depends on modeling such games as finitely but indefinitely repeated games, which reduce simply to finitely repeated games. We propose an alternative general model of probabilistically indefinitely repeated games, and discuss the appropriateness of each of these models of indefinitely repeated games.

BECKER, Werner. "Schopenhauers Kritik des kategorischen Imperativs" in *Schopenhauer: New Essays in Honor of His 200th Birthday,* VON DER LUFT, Eric (ed), 40-50. Lewiston, Mellen Pr, 1989.

The Kantian ethic is interpreted by Schopenhauer as a secularization of Christian morals: the Kantian "ought to" supposedly is the internalization of the commanding role of the Christian God. According to Schopenhauer this internalization acts as a cause for the logically questionable structure of the "moral subject": for Kant the "moral subject" simultaneously is the lawgiver and the follower of ethical norms. Schopenhauer, however, goes only half the way with his criticism, because his own moral philosophy sanctions the Christian-Kantian opposition of egoism and altruism in an even stronger form.

BECKER, Wolfgang. Indexikalität, Wahrnehmung und Bedeutung bei Husserl. Conceptus, 24(61), 51-71, 1990.

According to Husserl the reference of the demonstrative pronoun 'this' is always determined by a perception belonging to the context of the utterance 'this'. I elucidate how to understand demonstrative reference on the basis of Husserl's general concept of meaning, his analysis of occasional expressions and his conception of perception. In his analysis of indexical expressions and in linking demonstrative reference and perception, Husserl attempts to account for the egocentric determination of the reference of 'this' and at the same time the intersubjective intelligibility of this expression in perception statements.

BECKWITH, Francis. *David Hume's Argument Against Miracles: A Critical Analysis.* Lanham, Univ Pr of America, 1989

This book is a presentation and critical analysis of Hume's argument against miracles. In addition, this work contains a critique of contemporary rehabilitations of Hume's argument by Flew, Nowell-Smith, and McKinnon, and a defense of the kalam cosmological argument for God's existence. The author concludes that the concept of miracle is perfectly coherent and that it is possible that one can enough evidence to be epistemically justified in believing that one has occurred. This book also includes a discussion on the nature of evidential standards and how they are similar to scientific law in their grounding.

BECKWITH, Guy V. Science, Technology, and Society: Considerations of Method. Sci Tech Human Values, 14(4), 323-339, Autumn 8.

The article attributes the many conflicting theories about the nature and direction of contemporary technological society to the revolutionary and paradoxical character of technology itself. Commentators come to very different conclusions about the same basic phenomena; but their differences, while reflecting divergent assumptions and intellectual styles, also reveal contradictions within the subject matter. Dialectical and historical methods are introduced as ways to redefine the basic terms involved, augment traditional studies, and indicate directions for authentic interdisciplinary research. A non-Hegelian approach can help resolve problems of method and interpretation in the field of science, technology, and society, and reveal new possibilities for rational action and effective social control.

BECLEANU-IANCU, Adela. Iosif Brucar—penseur rationaliste et historien de la philosophie roumaine (in Romanian). Rev Filosof (Romania), 35(5), 479-488, S-O 88.

BEDANI, Gino. *Vico Revisited: Orthodoxy, Naturalism and Science in the Scienca Nuova.* New York, St Martin's Pr, 1989

This study relocates Vico's major work within the naturalistic system of thought from which it emerged. The *Scienza Nuova* is thus shown to have a more coherent set of reference points than has often been supposed. This leads to a number of far-reaching reinterpretations of major aspects of Vico's philosophy. Naturalistic currents of thought, moreover, were highly suspect within the church in Naples. This book examines in a systematic manner the consequences of Vico's difficulties. Historical and textual evidence is used to highlight an undercurrent of discourse which also has important implications for our understanding of the *Scienza Nuova.*

BEDATE, Carlos A and CEFALO, Robert C. The Zygote: To Be Or Not Be A Person. J Med Phil, 14(6), 641-645, D 89.

It is no longer possible to claim that the biological characteristics of the future adult are already determined at conception. After all, a zygote may develop into a hydatidiform mole rather than into a human being. The development of an individual human person is determined by genetically and nongenetically coded molecules within the embryo, together with the influence of the maternal environment. Consequently, it is an error to regard the zygote's chromosomal (and other) DNA as sufficient to determine the uniqueness of the future individual.

BEDAU, Mark. Against Mentalism in Teleology. Amer Phil Quart, 27(1), 61-70, Ja 90.

BEDNARSKI, F W. Le principe constitutif des valeurs morales dans l'éthique de S Thomas d'Aquin (in Polish). Stud Phil Christ, 25(1), 59-78, 1989.

L'auteur s'efforce de prouver que saint Thomas d'Aquin a bien exposé la question du principe constitutif de la valeur morale, c'est-à-dire, de la bonte reelle du comportement humain; tandis que le mal est plutôt une privation de la valeur, laquelle n'est pas un idéal hors d'atteindre mais une realite accessible. La nature humaine, integrale et ordoneé, est le fondement de la valeur morale et non son principe constitutif. Par contre la conformité du comportement humain à la nature de l'homme en accord avec les exigences de la raison bien orientée a la vraie fin dernière de la vie humaine—voila vraiment le principe constitutif de bonté morale, parce que la rationalité est la distinction spécifique de la nature humaine, mais la conduite humaine n'est raisonnable que dans la concordance avec la finalité de la vie humaine, et en conséquence quand les moyens sont ordonnés à la fin et les fins secondaires subordonnées à la vraie fin dernière de l'homme. (edited)

BEDNARZ JR, John (trans) and LUHMANN, Niklas. *Ecological Communication.* Chicago, Univ of Chicago Pr, 1989

BEEHLER, Rodger. Autonomy and the Democratic Principle. Can J Phil, 19(4), 575-581, D 89.

Joshua Cohen and Joel Rogers have recently argued (in their important book *On Democracy*, 1983) that the claim of persons to autonomy proceeds from their status as free and equal members of a democratic association exercising sovereignty. I argue, first, that Cohen and Rogers neglect a defining feature of autonomy, and, secondly, that they mistake the relation of autonomy to democracy. The democratic association, by securing freedom, secures a necessary (but not sufficient) condition of autonomy. However, the democratic association does not *license* the claim to autonomy, which is prior to (and survives) the free association.

BEEHLER, Rodger. Freedom and Authenticity. J Applied Phil, 7(1), 39-44, Mr 90.

The essay enquires whether action that authentically expresses the self who acts constitutes freedom. Features of authentic action that tempt toward this assimilation are identified, and a recent theory of freedom that propounds the assimilation is examined. An illustrative example of authentic action in conditions of unfreedom is discussed. Reasons are proposed for judging the equation of freedom with authenticity a mistake. Noted in particular is the error of confusing the subjective condition of authentic choice with the objective circumstance of unconstrained interpersonal relations.

BEEHLER, Rodger. Marx on Freedom and Necessity. Dialogue (Canada), 28(4), 545-552, 1989.

In the third volume of *Capital* Karl Marx distinguishes between a realm of freedom and a realm of necessity. G A Cohen and others have argued that the passage reveals Marx viewing labour in post-capitalist society as bound always to be unsatisfying, a marked shift from his 1840s expectation that such labour would be unalienating. The essay establishes that when the passage is carefully elucidated Cohen's charge is seen to be unwarranted. A further allegation that the passage is incompatible with late remarks by Marx on the Gotha programme is also considered, and a reading that reconciles the two passages proposed.

BEETS, S Douglas and KILLOUGH, Larry N. The Effectiveness of a Complaint-Based Ethics Enforcement System: Evidence from the Accounting Profession. J Bus Ethics, 9(2), 115-126, F 90.

Many professions, in order to enforce their ethics codes, rely on a complaint-based system, whereby persons who observe or discover ethics violations may file a complaint with an authoritative body. The authors assume that this type of system may encourage ethical behavior when practitioners believe that a punishment is likely to result from a failure to adhere to the rules. This perceived likelihood of punishment has three components: detection risk, reporting risk, and sanction risk. A survey of potential violation witnesses related to the accounting profession revealed that the profession's complaint-based enforcement system may not provide practitioners with the necessary disincentive to refrain from code violations.

BEGGS, Joyce M and LANE, Michael S. Corporate Goal Structures and Business Students: A Comparative Study of Values. J Bus Ethics, 8(6), 471-478, Je 89.

Are the values of business students of today synchronized with the reality of the present business environment? 222 business students rated the importance of 20 corporate goals. Moreover, the students rated the same goals as they perceived chief executive officers (CEOs) would have rated them. Significant differences were found between the two ratings, with students ranking social and employee-oriented goals as more important than they perceived CEOs would have.

BEHERA, Satrughna. Religion and Morality: A Conceptual Understanding. Indian Phil Quart, SUPP 17(2), 21-34, Ap 90.

The relationship between morality and religion as most often is considered non-distinguishable or the former takes to be dependent on the latter. In this paper I shall not attempt a comprehensive explanation of all possible relationships in which morality can be dependent on religion. Rather I have attempted to show the conceptual distinction between religion and morality and pointed out that moral principles cannot be justified by being derived logically from religious beliefs or doctrines. I come to the conclusion that religion and morality are conceptually different and each has a conceptual framework of its own.

BEIGEL, R and GASARCH, W I. On the Complexity of Finding the Chromatic Number of a Recursive Graph II: The Unbounded Case. Annals Pure Applied Log, 45(3), 227-246, D 89.

A recursive graph is a graph whose edge set and vertex set are both recursive. We determine the difficulty of determining the chromatic number of a graph. The two parameters of difficulty are the Turing degree of the oracle required, and the number of queries to that query that are required. We also investigate recursive chromatic numbers (which require queries to a

set much harder than the halting set), the effect of allowing queries to a weaker set, and the effect of being able to ask p queries at a time.

BEIGEL, Richard and GASARCH, W I. On the Complexity of Finding the Chromatic Number of a Recursive Graph I: The Bounded Case. Annals Pure Applied Log, 45(1), 1-38, N 89.

We study the difficulty of computing the chromatic number (respectively, the recursive chromatic number) of a recursive graph, given a bound on that number. We show that a logarithmic number of queries to an oracle for the halting problem (respectively, the third level of the arithmetic hierarchy) are necessary and sufficient. These results are tight with respect to both parameters: number of queries and power of oracle.

BEINER, Ronald. Hannah Arendt and Leo Strauss: The Uncommenced Dialogue. Polit Theory, 18(2), 238-254, My 90.

Hannah Arendt and Leo Strauss are two of the most influential figures in twentieth-century political philosophy. They knew each other, were in fact colleagues at the height of their respective careers, and yet neither acknowledges or addresses the work of the other in their published writings. Were a dialogue between them to materialize, what would it look like? What would be the main points of theoretical contention? The question of nature and history, of naturalism and historicism, turns out to be a less important source of disagreement than at first appears. A more promising locus of debate is the relation between philosophy and politics, and the implications of this relation for the issue of human equality.

BEINER, Ronald (ed). *Hannah Arendt: Lectures on Kant's Political Philosophy*. Chicago, Univ of Chicago Pr, 1989

BELCOURT, Monica. A Family Portrait of Canada's Most Successful Female Entrepreneurs. J Bus Ethics, 9(4-5), 435-438, Ap-My 90.

In an attempt to study the factors contributing to the decision to become an entrepreneur, an intensive interview survey of 36 successful women entrepreneurs was conducted. The importance of paternal occupation and psychodynamic interactions with both the mother and father was highlighted. The study revealed mirror images of the patterns found to be correlated with male entrepreneurship.

BELL, David. How 'Russellian' Was Frege? Mind, 99(394), 267-277, Ap 90.

In the wake of Gareth Evans's account of Frege's thought, in *The Varieties of Reference*, a number of commentators have assimilated Frege's views on singular terms and the sense of denotationless proper names to those of Russell. I argue that this assimilation is wrong. In particular, I argue that the attribution of a number of specific theses by Evans to Frege cannot be sustained. I further suggest that these specific claims can be plausibly attributed to Frege only against the background of a certain general interpretation of Frege's overall goals, concepts, and methods. This general interpretation too, it is argued, is indefensible. An alternative is outlined.

BELL, Nora Kizer. Women and AIDS: Too Little, Too Late? Hypatia, 4(3), 3-22, Fall 89.

Many authors examine the governmental, the scientific, and the sexual politics of AIDS. Many of these same authors tell the AIDS story within the context of decrying homophobia. The implications of that story, however, have a troubling significance for women. This essay proposes to move the discussion of the sexual politics of AIDS beyond the confines of homophobia and to highlight issues not widely discussed outside of AIDS activist circles—issues which are having, and will continue to have, profound effects on women.

BELL, Richard H. Narrative in African Philosophy. Philosophy, 64(249), 363-379, Jl 89.

Current African philosophers characterize their philosophy as moving toward a more "critical" and "scientific" consensus, thus conforming more with contemporary European and Anglo-American developments. It is also understood to have its own cultural focus related to postcolonial realities and the pluralism within African culture. Within this current discussion, however, elements of traditional culture and its oral tradition are largely rejected. This essay argues that aspects of the oral tradition practiced within communities and that African literature and its iconic traditions—what are called the *narrative* aspects of philosophy—be given more serious consideration as primary data for an African philosophy. The argument is supported through a review of some current thinkers such as Paulin Hountondju and Wole Soyinka and a discussion of the importance of the African *palaver* and the arts of Africa as viable means of critical self-expression.

BELL, Richard H. On Trusting One's Own Heart: Scepticism in Jonathan Edwards and Soren Kierkegaard. Hist Euro Ideas, 12(1), 105-116, 1990.

The article discusses the positive role of scepticism in understanding religious experience. Special attention is paid to two texts: Jonathan Edwards's

Religious Affections and Soren Kierkegaard's *On Authority and Revelation*. I conclude that religious experience can be understood in the context of a qualified subjective testimony, checked by sacred texts within a religious tradition and by the grammar of one's life.

BELLA, David and KING, Jonathan. Common Knowledge of the Second Kind. J Bus Ethics, 8(6), 415-430, Je 89.

Although most of us "know" that human beings cannot and should not be replaced by computers, we have great difficulties saying why this is so. This paradox is largely the result of institutionalizing several fundamental misconceptions as to the nature of both trustworthy "objective" and "moral" knowledge. Unless we transcend this paradox, we run the increasing risks of becoming very good at counting without being able to say what is worth counting and why. The degree to which this is occurring is the degree to which the computer revolution is already over—and the degree to which we human beings have lost.

BELLAIMEY, James E. Family Resemblances and the Problem of the Under-Determination of Extension. Phil Invest, 13(1), 31-43, Ja 90.

Various commentators have said that Wittgensteinian family resemblances cannot determine the extension of a concept. I examine three proposed solutions to this problem, and evaluate them in relation to Wittgenstein's texts. None of them is truly Wittgensteinian.

BELLETTI, Bruno. Dimensioni della pace: In margine ad un recente convegno. Sapienza, 42(2), 207-209, Ap-Je 89.

BELLIOTTI, Raymond A. Blood is Thicker Than Water: Don't Forsake the Family Jewels. Phil Papers, 18(3), 265-280, N 89.

I address the problem of nonvoluntary moral requirements—certain demands of morality which do not arise from explicit and discrete volitional acts. My thesis is that humans have a general moral requirement to preserve and maintain value; constituents of personal identity such as our inherited legacy (genetic make-up, family, nation, culture, and traditions) and noninherited attachments, commitments, and properties possess objective value regardless of whether particular individuals acknowledge explicitly that value; moral requirements are generated in part by the fact that as the repository of such value I am better placed than others to understand and preserve it simply by being who I am; and as the repository of that value I therefore bear a special responsibility to a particular segment of the shared human heritage. Thus, my objective metaphysical constitution—who I am—has moral implications for what I must do.

BELLIOTTI, Raymond. Beyond Capitalism and Communism: Roberto Unger's Superliberal Political Theory. Praxis Int, 9(3), 321-334, O 89.

I will here explore the "superliberal" political theory and program advanced recently by Roberto Unger. First, I will outline his theory of persons, which forms the background argument for his programmatic vision. Second, I will adumbrate the structure of his general prescriptions for legal and institutional transformation. Third, I will explain several criticisms that have been or could be levied against Unger's thesis, and, where possible, anticipate Unger's response to those critical attacks. In so doing, I will underscore several of Unger's methodological presuppositions and aspirations.

BELLISSIMA, Fabio. Finite and Finitely Separable Intermediate Propositional Logics. J Sym Log, 53(2), 403-420, Je 88.

The author introduces the concept of "finitely separable (FS) class of Kripke frames." An intermediate propositional logic L is said to be an FS-logic if the class of L-frames is FS (all the most-studied intermediate logics are FS). An effective and semantic procedure to axiomatize FS-logics is given, and it is shown that each FS-logic has the finite model property.

BELLISSIMA, Fabio. A General Treatment of Equivalent Modalities. J Sym Log, 54(4), 1460-1471, D 89.

A classical problem of modal logic consists in determining the number of non-equivalent modalities available in a certain system. The paper deals with this problem, without referring to particular logics but considering the whole class of normal modal logics. One result: there is a continuum of P(L)'s, where P(L) reflects the set of the classes of L-equivalent modalities, for a given L.

BELLISSIMA, Fabio. Infinite Sets of Nonequivalent Modalities. Notre Dame J Form Log, 30(4), 574-582, Fall 89.

The set of irreducible nonequivalent modalities for a class of normal modal logics is determined. All the logics considered (KT, KD, K4, KB, among others) have this set infinite.

BELLISSIMA, Fabio. Post Complete and 0-Axiomatizable Modal Logics. Annals Pure Applied Log, 47(2), 121-144, My 90.

BELLU, Niculae. La place de Fichte dans l'ouverture de la perspective ontologique sur l'éthique (in Romanian). Rev Filosof (Romania), 35(6), 553-561, N-D 88.

BELNAP JR, Nuel D. "Conjunctive Containment" in *Directions in Relevant Logic*, NORMAN, Jean (ed), 145-156. Norwell, Kluwer, 1989.

BELNAP JR, Nuel D. Declaratives Are Not Enough. Phil Stud, 59(1), 1-30, My 90.

BELNAP JR, Nuel D. Linear Logic Display. Notre Dame J Form Log, 31(1), 14-25, Wint 90.

BELNAP JR, Nuel D. "Which Entailments Entail Which Entailments?" in *Directions in Relevant Logic*, NORMAN, Jean (ed), 185-196. Norwell, Kluwer, 1989.

BELSHAW, Christopher. Scepticism and Madness. Austl J Phil, 67(4), 447-451, D 89.

BELTRAN, M. Spinoza: de la alegría. Pensamiento, 46(183), 333-336, Jl-S 90.

The aim of the paper is to describe the ways in which morally correct actions, in Spinoza's *Ethics*, depend on the affection of joy (*laetitia*), understood as the transition of a man from a less to a greater perfection. And, more importantly, that really good joys—as mirth (*hilaritas*) and self-approval (*acquiescentia in se ipso*)—rely on the intuitive knowledge of God. This knowledge involves the will's propensity to desires that do not undermine happiness (*beatitudo*), and the impossibility of a real evil for the good man.

BEN-MENACHEM, Hanina. "Comment: Positivism and the Foundations of Legal Authority" in *Issues in Contemporary Legal Philosophy: The Influence of H L A Hart*, GAVISON, Ruth (ed), 76-82. New York, Clarendon/Oxford Pr, 1987.

BEN-MENAHEM, Yemima. Struggling with Causality: Schrödinger's Case. Stud Hist Phil Sci, 20(3), 307-334, S 89.

When one considers the schematic division between 'orthodox' and 'deviant' quantum theoreticians, one usually takes Schrödinger to belong to the latter camp. It is held that he, just like Einstein, could not come to terms with the inherently acausal nature of quantum mechanics. Since it is known that in the early twenties Schrödinger was rather sceptical about causality, it is suggested by several historians that Schrödinger changed his position, converting to the causal view in the mid-twenties. In this paper the author argues that Schrödinger did not change his views in any substantial way with regard to causality. (edited)

BEN-SHAMMAI, Haggai. "Saadya's Goal in his *Commentary on Sefer Yezira*" in *A Straight Path: Studies in Medieval Philosophy and Culture*, LINK-SALINGER, Ruth (ed), 1-9. Washington, Cath Univ Amer Pr, 1988.

BEN-ZEEV, Aaron. Reexamining Berkeley's Notion of Suggestion. Conceptus, 23(59), 21-30, 1989.

Berkeley's criticism on Descartes's intellectualist approach on perception seems to be adequate, but the empiricist element in his own alternative rules out innate perceptual capacities which are required to make sense both of the richness of perceptual experience and of recent findings concerning neonate perceptions. This problem in Berkeley's account can be overcome by adopting and developing some of the views of Thomas Reid. One important consequence of this is that sensation and perception can no longer be regarded as two separate stages, but must rather be seen as two inseparable aspects of perceptual experience: feeling and information.

BEN-ZEEV, Aaron. Why Did Psammenitus Not Pity His Son? Analysis, 50(2), 118-126, Mr 90.

This paper discusses the nature of pity and self-pity and their connection to the subject-object distance. I argue that in very close relations (such as those between father and son) pity is unlikely to emerge.

BENCIVENGA, Ermanno. Free from What? Erkenntnis, 33(1), 9-21, Jl 90.

It is argued that the contrast between classical and free quantification theories is best understood within the context of Kant's Copernican revolution: classical quantification theory is the most natural logic for the transcendental realist, and free quantification theory the most natural for the transcendental idealist. The discussion is then extended to semantics for free and modal logics.

BENCIVENGA, Ermanno. *Looser Ends: The Practice of Philosophy*. Winchester, Unwin Hyman, 1989

This is a collection of eleven papers, nine of which are published elsewhere, with an introduction. Topics range from logic to ethics, from aesthetics to the philosophy of language. The common theme is a conception of philosophy as a gamelike, liberating activity that breaks the barriers of convention.

BENCIVENGA, Ermanno. Metaphors and the Transcendental. Metaphilosophy, 21(3), 189-203, Jl 90.

A view of conceptual analysis is presented, which makes it consist of the straining of words and phrases outside their ordinary contexts. The straining occurs through seeing those words and phrases as examples relevant to other contexts, which is a first step toward a mixing of the contexts and ultimately the creation of new linguistic practices.

BENCIVENGA, Ermanno. Why Three Dimensions? Phil Stud, 59(1), 113-114, My 90.

An argument is proposed to the effect that space as experienced must have at least three dimensions. The moral of the argument is that we need a third dimension to account for the possibility of our being wrong.

BENDER, Frederic L. Scarcity and the Turn from Economics to Ecology. Soc Epistem, 4(1), 93-113, Ja-Mr 90.

This is a critical examination of neoclassical economics' postulate of inherent scarcity linked to its assumption of desire without limit. It is argued that this assumption is philosophically naive and that the scarcity postulate based on it is ideological and, even if considered merely as an empirical claim, quite likely untrue. Critiques of the neoclassical paradigm from both Marxist and deep-ecological perspectives are found to reflect the real situation of advanced capitalism much more accurately than does neoclassicism.

BENDER, John W. "Coherence, Justification, and Knowledge: The Current Debate" in *The Current State of the Coherence Theory*, BENDER, John W (ed), 1-14. Norwell, Kluwer, 1989.

This essay compares the coherence theories of Keith Lehrer and Laurence BonJour on nine major points, and critically evaluates the positions taken. Also, the relational and systemic senses of coherence are distinguished.

BENDER, John W (ed). *The Current State of the Coherence Theory*. Norwell, Kluwer, 1989

Twenty-six new essays by recognized epistemologists on the subject of the coherence theory of knowledge. Most are focused critically upon either Keith Lehrer's or Laurence BonJour's theory. An introductory essay compares the theories on nine basic points. Detailed replies by Lehrer and BonJour are included.

BENDER, John W and DAVIS, Wayne A. "Fundamental Troubles with the Coherence Theory" in *The Current State of the Coherence Theory*, BENDER, John W (ed), 52-68. Norwell, Kluwer, 1989.

Coherence of a belief to the body of other beliefs a person holds is neither a necessary nor sufficient condition for the empirical justification of that belief, we argue. We make the non-necessity claim in discussing the question of basic beliefs. The more interesting debate, however, concerns whether coherence is ever sufficient for epistemic justification. The paper offers two arguments for the insufficiency thesis. The first argues that a coherence measure fails to capture the inferential structure of a set of beliefs and that that structure is important to justification. The second argument claims that coherence will not yield justification even if the background system is entirely true—because the system might be a set of lucky guesses. (This should not be confused with the "isolation argument" which objects that purely fictitious systems can be coherent.) These arguments are directed primarily toward Keith Lehrer's version of the coherence theory; however, certain suggestions of Laurence BonJour also are considered.

BENDER, Peter. Noch einmal: Zur Rolle der Anschauung in formalen Beweisen. Stud Leibniz, 21(1), 98-100, 1989.

A mathematical proof is more than a sequence of logical propositions. It includes also epistemological, cognitive, social, and didactical aspects. The article is a response to a paper by Struve (*Studia Leibnitiana* 1986:89ff) which was a response to an article by Stenius (*Studia Leibnitiana* 1981:133ff).

BENHABIB, Seyla. In the Shadow of Aristotle and Hegel: Communicative Ethics and Current Controversies in Practical Philosophy. Phil Forum, 21(1-2), 1-31, Fall-Wint 89-90.

The article discusses recent objections raised against the project of a "communicative ethics" from a neo-Aristotelian and neo-Hegelian perspective. These objections are summarized as skepticism about universalizability procedures in ethics; the relation between the right and the good; the relation between morality and politics; concepts of the self; and problems of moral judgment. I conclude that these objections, although requiring considerable modification of communicative ethics, as formulated initially by Karl-Otto Apel and Jürgen Habermas, cannot lead to its rejection. This ethical theory remains a viable and compelling reformulation of a universalist ethics.

BENIS-SINACEUR, Hourya. *Ars inveniendi* et théorie des modèles. Dialogue (Canada), 27(4), 591-613, Wint 88.

The aim of this paper is to reassess some cardinal ideas of Leibniz in the light of the methods and goals of model theory. It is a leitmotiv in Abraham Robinson's work that, as well as Leibniz wanted logic to be an *ars inveniendi*

for mathematics, model theory has to "produce useful tools for the development of actual mathematics." This paper tries to clarify the meaning and the far-reaching consequences of such a statement by comparing the method of logical analysis of the mathematical language to Leibniz's concepts of 'analysis' and 'characteristica'. Some results of Alfred Tarski and Abraham Robinson are briefly sketched in order to give evidence of the contemporary achievement of what Leibniz wished logic to be.

BENÍTEZ, Laura. El espíritu como principio activo en Berkeley. Analisis Filosof, 6(1), 23-34, My 86.

The problem considered in this paper is the activity of the subject or spirit as it appears in the *PHK* and in the *Philosophical Commentaries*. Berkeley's proposal centres on the idea of the soul as activity, showing a positive desire to retain the idea while remaining within the traditional conception of the spirit as a substance. This is an open problem in the theory. Hence it is necessary to give an account of its different versions to establish its significance with modern philosophical discussions of Berkeley's views on this matter as well as discussions of the limits of his conception.

BENJAMIN, Andrew (ed). *Post-Structuralist Classics*. New York, Routledge, 1988

BENJAMIN, Andrew. "Time and Interpretation in Heraclitus" in *Post-Structuralist Classics*, BENJAMIN, Andrew (ed), 106-131. New York, Routledge, 1988.

BENJAMIN, Andrew. *Translation and the Nature of Philosophy: A New Theory of Words*. New York, Routledge, 1989

BENJAMIN, David. Philosophy in High School: What Does It All Mean? Thinking, 8(4), 43-44, 1990.

BENJAMIN, Martin. Philosophical Integrity and Policy Development in Bioethics. J Med Phil, 15(4), 375-389, Ag 90.

Critically examining what most people take for granted is central to philosophical inquiry. Philosophers who accept positions on policy making commissions, task forces, or committees cannot, however, play the same uncompromisingly critical role in this capacity as they do in the classroom or in their personal research or writing. Still, philosophers have much to contribute to such bodies, and they can do so without compromising their integrity or betraying themselves as philosophers.

BENJAMIN, Martin. *Splitting the Difference: Compromise and Integrity in Ethics and Politics*. Lanham, Univ Pr of America, 1990

Can we ever compromise on matters of ethical principle without compromising our integrity? If so, when—and how? In addressing these and related questions the book examines the meanings of compromise, the nature of integrity, the relationships between practical and theoretical ethics, the importance of judgment, and the connection between personal ethics and political compromise, especially as it applies to abortion. Philosophical reason, though limited in its capacity to settle complex ethical controversies, is of undeniable importance in helping, through compromise, to contain them.

BENKÖ, Iosif and SOFONEA, Liviu. Die "platonische körper": Geometrische, physische, historische und epistemologische aspekte. Phil Log, 32(1-2), 63-73, Ja-Je 88.

BENNE, Kenneth D. Plato's Divided Line: A Dramatistic Interpretation. Proc Phil Educ, 45, 363-373, 1989.

BENNETT, Jonathan. Two Departures from Consequentialism. Ethics, 100(1), 54-66, O 89.

Samuel Scheffler's *The Rejection of Consequentialism* discusses two possible departures from consequentialism: one permits an agent sometimes to give special weight to his own premoral desires, the other requires the agent sometimes to obey deontological rules. Scheffler characterizes the former as involving an agent-centred prerogative, and the latter as involving agent-centred restrictions; and his book is built on the assumption that a single concept of agent-centredness is at work in both. In this article it is argued that that assumption is false: the two have in common only that they depart from consequentialism, and the apparent unity of this work of Scheffler's is illusory.

BENNETT, Jonathan. Why is Belief Involuntary? Analysis, 50(2), 87-107, Mr 90.

This paper seeks to explain why it is absolutely, conceptually impossible to immediately start believing something just because one wants to, as distinct from voluntarily starting a causal chain that will lead to one's acquiring a belief. Previous attempts to explain this—notably by Bernard Williams—are criticised. A new explanation is proposed, and also subjected to fatal criticisms. No successful explanation is offered: the paper presents a negative result.

BENSON, Hugh H. A Note on Eristic and the Socratic Elenchus. J Hist Phil, 27(4), 591-599, O 89.

In this essay I attempt to respond to the objection that on the nonconstructivist account of the Socratic elenchus the distinction between the elenchus and eristic collapses. (According to the nonconstructivist account the elenchus can establish no more than the consistency or inconsistency of the interlocutors' beliefs.) The relevant difference between the elenchus and eristic, I argue, is that while they both establish an inconsistency in what the interlocutor says, only the former establishes an inconsistency in what the interlocutor believes. As a result only the former can generate genuine perplexity.

BENSON, Paul. The Moral Importance of Free Action. S J Phil, 28(1), 1-18, Spr 90.

This paper discusses a traditional view of the moral importance of free agency. According to this view, what it is rational to believe about free agency matters morally because it bears on the rational defensibility of practices of responsibility-attribution. P F Strawson has criticized this view, and Susan Wolf and Jonathan Bennett have offered related objections. This paper presents a defense of the traditional view, arguing that the very distinction between reactive and objective attitudes upon which these objections rely is best understood through one version of the traditional view.

BERANOVA, Vera. The Problems of Czech and Slovak Culture-Political Thinking Between Both World Wars (in Czechoslovakian). Estetika, 26(4), 208-217, 1989.

BERCEANU, Barbu B. Sur la signification logique et linguistique de la négation (in Romanian). Rev Filosof (Romania), 36(2), 174-180, Mr-Ap 89.

BERCHERIE, Paul. Inconscient et savoir de la folie: Freud dans le champ psychiatrique. Rev Int Phil, 43(171), 525-539, 1989.

BERCIANO VILLALIBRE, Modesto. Arte y Ontología en Martin Heidegger (2a parte). Logos (Mexico), 17(51), 29-54, S-D 89.

Heidegger critica otras reflexiones filosóficas sobre el ente. Lo que es realmente un ente lo revela la obra de arte. Esta muestra al ente en el contexto del ser, de la verdad y de la historia. Nietzsche no entendió así el arte y dio de él una interpretación defectuosa. La poesia hace ver al ente en el evento del mundo, compuesto de cielo, tierra, dioses y mortales. Por todas estas razones el arte podria ser el punto de partida para una nueva reflexión sobre el ente y para una nueva ontología.

BEREZDIVIN, Ruben. "Drawing: (An) Affecting Nietzsche: With Derrida" in Derrida and Deconstruction, SILVERMAN, Hugh J (ed), 92-107. New York, Routledge, 1989.

BERG, Kåre. The Price of Silence: Commentary. Hastings Center Rep, 20(3), 34-35, My-Je 90.

BERGER, Alan. A Theory of Reference Transmission and Reference Change. Midwest Stud Phil, 14, 180-198, 1989.

BERGER, Henrik H. Life-World and System at Habermas (in Hungarian). Magyar Filozof Szemle, 2-3, 352-363, 1989.

BERGER, Lawrence A. Economics and Hermeneutics. Econ Phil, 5(2), 209-233, O 89.

BERGMANN, Werner and HOFFMANN, G. Selbstreferenz und Zeit: Die dynamische Stabilität des Bewusstseins. Husserl Stud, 6(2), 155-175, 1989.

BERGOFFEN, Debra B. "On the Advantage and Disadvantage of Nietzsche for Women" in The Question of the Other: Essays in Contemporary Continental Philosophy, DALLERY, Arleen B (ed), 77-88. Albany, SUNY Pr, 1989.

Placing Nietzsche's reputation as a misogynist in question, I argue that his critique of western culture indirectly but necessarily undermines patriarchy. For Nietzsche, historical consciousness is nihilistic and must be transvaluated. For feminists the bipolarization of time according to gender (where the male is situated in the valued temporality of history and creativity, and the female is enclosed in the devaluated other time of re-creative cosmic rhythms) must be overcome. Nietzsche's eternal recurrence offers feminists a disruption of patriarchal temporality and an androgynous-heterosexual vision of time where the otherness of the feminine is affirmed as sexism is undone.

BERGSON, Henri and SOULEZ, Philippe. La correspondance Bergson/Lévy-Bruhl—Lettres à L Lévy-Bruhl (1889-1932). Rev Phil Fr, 179(4), 481-492, O-D 89.

BERGSTRÖM, Matti. Music and the Living Brain. Acta Phil Fennica, 43, 135-153, 1988.

An analysis of the sources of music and art is made on the basis of brain research. The brain consists of a dipole with a primitive chaos-generator and

a developed order-generator. In between is the "Self," situated between an inner, chaotic, and an outer, ordered environment. To cope with the fear for the corresponding "Unknowns" ("demons") the Self has to produce "antibodies" which bind these demons: information for the outer and art for the inner environment (describing thus a "symmetry of fear"). The music of each historical epoch thus mirrors the fears of its time and helps mankind to survive.

BERKOWITZ, Sheldon T and NEWMAN, Louis E. Commentary: C-Section for Organ Donation. Hastings Center Rep, 20(2), 22-23, Mr-Ap 90.

The authors consider whether a C-section should be performed on a pregnant woman at 38 weeks to save her congenitally malformed fetus with anencephaly for the purpose of making its organs available for donation. They argue that such surgery is not medically indicated or morally justified in that the risks to the mother outweigh any possible psychological or medical benefits (except to a potential organ recipient) that could result from successful transplantation of this infant's organs. The mother's right to decide the course of her own pregnancy (autonomy) should not override medical judgments about what treatment is indicated.

BERKSON, William. In Defense of Good Reasons. Phil Soc Sci, 20(1), 84-91, Mr 90.

Sir Karl Popper's well-known theory of scientific method has sometimes been dismissed on the grounds that it implies absurdities such as "We have no knowledge" and "We can never learn from observation." Popper's theory, in this view, does not rise above a sterile skepticism. This view of Popper's work had always struck me as a simple failure to understand Popper. However, David Miller's recent article, "A Critique of Good Reasons," has convinced me that I was mistaken; for Miller, an excellent and orthodox defender of Popper, portrays Popper's ideas in a manner startlingly close to the hostile caricature. Popper's work, I believe, contains two significant errors which lend plausibility to the caricature. These are (a) the assumption that positive reasons are useless and irrelevant to the rational assessment of alternatives, and (b) the claim that belief is irrelevant to rationality. Here, I want to dispose of the first error and show that Popper's core ideas survive without it. By making an explicit case for the first assumption, Miller has, contrary to his intention, constructed a reductio ad absurdum of it.

BERKSON, William. Methodology Is Pragmatic: A Reponse to Miller. Phil Soc Sci, 20(1), 95-98, Mr 90.

BERLEANT, Arnold. "The Eighteenth Century Assumptions of Analytic Aesthetics" in History and Anti-History in Philosophy, LAVINE, T Z (ed), 256-274. Norwell, Kluwer, 1989.

The literature of analytic aesthetics draws support from three principles formulated during the eighteenth century: that art be construed as separate objects, that they possess a special status, and that they be regarded with a unique, disinterested attitude. These principles are anachronistic in the face of the demand of the contemporary arts for direct engagement and active participation in its workings and for the continuity of art with other objects and experiences.

BERLEANT, Arnold. "Musical De-Composition" in What is Music?, ALPERSON, Philip A, 239-254. New York, Haven, 1987.

Musical creation is usually thought of as composition, ordering musical materials by rules, patterns, and forms. This essay argues that creation in music is rather a process of generation, carrying out the dynamic forces inherent in the tonal materials. This process applies to tones, motives, repetition, cadences, modulation, and classical forms, and it is exemplified by musical memory, by performance, including improvisation, and by apppreciation. The immediacy of musical experience reflects the sensory directness of sound, and both creation and appreciation consist in elaborating the potentialities of particular tonal materials.

BERLINGER, Rudolph (and other eds). Agora: Zu Ehren von Rudolph Berlinger. Amsterdam, Rodopi, 1988

BERMAN, David. Censorship and the Displacement of Irreligion. J Hist Phil, 27(4), 601-604, O 89.

BERMAN, Lawrence V. "The Ideal State of the Philosophers and Prophetic Laws" in A Straight Path: Studies in Medieval Philosophy and Culture, LINK-SALINGER, Ruth (ed), 10-22. Washington, Cath Univ Amer Pr, 1988.

BERMAN, Ronald. Cultural History and Cultural Materialism. J Aes Educ, 24(1), 111-121, Spr 90.

BERNASCONI, Robert L. "The Double Concept of Philosophy" and the Place of Ethics in Being and Time. Res Phenomenol, 18, 41-57, 1988.

The paper presents Heidegger's introduction of fundamental ontology as an attempt to avoid the problems encountered by the philosophy of worldviews.

By drawing on the analysis of metontology from *The Metaphysical Foundations of Logic*, it is argued that the alleged opposition between the ontological and the ontic proves more complex than is usually recognized. Heidegger did not attempt to establish a science purged of all worldviews, as should already be clear from the fact that a specific factical ideal of existence, the philosophical "worldview," has a dominant place in *Being and Time*.

BERNASCONI, Robert L. Descartes in the History of Being: Another Bad Novel? Res Phenomenol, 17, 75-102, 1987.

By contrasting Heidegger's interpretation of Descartes in the 1920s with the reading he gave in the late 1930s, this essay attempts to clarify the impact Heidegger's conception of the history of Being had on his understanding of Descartes. Particular attention is paid to the contrast between (1) Heidegger's initially highly critical account in which Descartes's claims to novelty are challenged, and (2) his subsequent attempt to give Descartes his traditional place as the founder of modern philosophy on a nontraditional (nonepistemological) basis.

BERNASCONI, Robert L. Heidegger's Destruction of Phronesis. S J Phil, SUPP(28), 127-147, 1989.

The paper issues a challenge to the dominant ways of reading Heidegger's *Being and Time* by taking the published portion of the book as already a repetition and destruction of the history of ontology and not as, for example, a phenomenological description in the familiar sense. The particular example considered is that of the discussion of worldhood in sections 15 to 18 which is read with reference to Aristotle's account of practical reason in the *Ethics*. The reading is supported by reference to Heidegger's lectures and manuscripts from the 1920s.

BERNASCONI, Robert L. "Rereading *Totality and Infinity*" in *The Question of the Other: Essays in Contemporary Continental Philosophy*, DALLERY, Arleen B (ed), 23-34. Albany, SUNY Pr, 1989.

Levinas's commentators understand the face to face relation either empirically as a concrete experience or transcendentally as the condition for the possibility of ethics. Levinas appears to authorize both interpretations in a way that cannot easily be reconciled. I suggest that a reading of the second part of *Totality and Infinity*, "Interiority and Economy," shows that Levinas employs the languages of transcendental philosophy and empiricism, not to unite them into a transcendental empiricism, but to set them in opposition. Levinas courts contradiction in order to introduce his readers to the face to face as a rupture of ordinary experience and conceptuality.

BERNET, Rudolf. Derrida et la voix de son maitre. Rev Phil Fr, 180(2), 147-166, Ap-Je 90.

BERNET, Rudolf. Husserl and Heidegger on Intentionality and Being. J Brit Soc Phenomenol, 21(2), 136-152, My 90.

BERNET, Rudolf. "On Derrida's 'Introduction' to Husserl's *Origin of Geometry*" in *Derrida and Deconstruction*, SILVERMAN, Hugh J (ed), 139-153. New York, Routledge, 1989.

BERNIK, Ivan. Functions of Egalitarianism in Yugoslav Society. Praxis Int, 9(4), 425-432, Ja 90.

BERNSTEIN, Mark. Fatalism and Time. Dialogue (Canada), 28(3), 461-471, 1989.

BERNSTEIN, Mark. Fatalism Revisited. Metaphilosophy, 21(3), 270-281, Jl 90.

Fatalism tells us that whatever happens had to happen. This thesis has, in contemporary times, been treated derisively. My aim is to show that this attitude is not completely warranted. I do this by making clear the question-begging nature of a debate on fatalism conducted by Richard Taylor and Peter van Inwagen.

BERNSTEIN, Richard L. "Hermeneutics and Its Anxieties" in *Reading Philosophy for the Twenty-First Century*, MC LEAN, George F (ed), 3-17. Lanham, Univ Pr of America, 1989.

BERRIAN, Annette. Socrates In a New Package Helps Kids Learn to Think. Thinking, 5(3), 43-44, 1984.

BERRY, John M. Plato's Forms: A Text That Self-Destructs to Shed Its Light. SW Phil Rev, 4(1), 111-119, Ja 88.

BERTAGNA, Mario. Buridano e le consequenze. Teoria, 9(2), 27-43, 1989.

BERTELLONI, Francisco. De la política como ontoteología a la política como teología. Rev Filosof (Argentina), 2(2), 119-134, N 87.

This paper deals with the antecedents of the Medieval political thought on the basis of the M S Ripoll 109. The evolution of this thought from Aquinas to Ockham is also briefly analyzed.

BERTHOLD-BOND, Daniel. Freud's Critique of Philosophy. Metaphilosophy, 20(3-4), 274-294, Jl-O 89.

The article explores Freud's critique of philosophy, emphasizing his attempt to expose the limitations of the philosophic tendency to construct metaphysical *Weltanschauungen*. I show how there is a curious ambiguity entailed by this critique: on the one hand, Freud is out to show how the need for philosophy is at a close; but on the other hand, he is ambivalent about this closure of philosophy, and seeks to re-open a path to it through a reconstruction of its form. I conclude that the Freudian reconstruction tentatively puts forward an invitation to dialogue between philosophy and psychoanalysis.

BERTI, Enrico. La philosophie pratique d'Aristote et sa "réhabilitation" récente. Rev Metaph Morale, 95(2), 249-266, Ap-Je 90.

Contrast between the Aristotelizing practical philosophy of today, represented in Germany especially by H G Gadamer, J Ritter and their followers, and Aristotle's theories on *phronesis* and *ethos*, in order to show that these theories, in the Stagirite's thought, don't play, against the opinion of those interpreters, the rôle of the whole practical philosophy.

BERTMAN, Martin A (ed) and AIRAKSINEN, Timo (ed). *Hobbes: War Among Nations*. Brookfield, Gower, 1989

BERTMAN, Martin A. Hobbes and Xenophon's *Tyrannicus*. Hist Euro Ideas, 10(5), 507-517, 1989.

Hobbes separates himself from the classical tradition in not having a doctrine of tyranny. The Socratic tradition, Xenophon, Plato, and Aristotle base politics on psychology; so does Hobbes. Therefore, the contention between the Socratic tradition and Hobbes is how psychology should be seen and taken account for expressing a political theory. Strauss is discussed in his dispute with Kojève on the Xenophon dialogue.

BERTMAN, Martin A. Kierkegaard and/or Philosophy. Hist Euro Ideas, 12(1), 117-126, 1990.

BERTMAN, Martin A. "What is Alive in Hobbes" in *Hobbes: War Among Nations*, AIRAKSINEN, Timo (ed), 1-14. Brookfield, Gower, 1989.

To highlight the anti-Platonic view of Hobbes on the concept of action, his view is compared to Plotinus. Hobbes's politics, with its view of action, is fundamentally linked to a crucial metaphysical decision about action.

BERTOLET, Rod. *What Is Said: A Theory of Indirect Speech Reports*. Norwell, Kluwer, 1990

While the practice of changing a speaker's words in reporting what he or she has said is virtually universal, the principles governing the acceptability of such substitutions are poorly understood. This book develops a theory of such indirect speech reports, or what is said. It is argued that what is said is generally a function of what the speaker refers to, and what the speaker predicates of the thing referred to. Each of these notions is analyzed in terms of the speaker's intentions. The proper theory of indirect speech reports is a pragmatic rather than a semantic theory.

BETT, Richard. Carneades' Distinction Between Assent and Approval. Monist, 73(1), 3-20, Ja 90.

Carneades, like other ancient sceptics, faced the Stoics' objection that the universal withholding of assent would render action impossible. In response, Carneades is said to have drawn a distinction between assent and "approval"; the selective "approval" of impressions makes choice and action possible, yet approval falls short of full-scale assent. The article examines whether this intermediate notion of approval is intelligible; the conclusion is that it is intelligible, but only if the concept of assent, as originated by the Stoics, undergoes some alteration. The outcome of the dispute is therefore an inevitable stalemate.

BETT, Richard. The Sophists and Relativism. Phronesis, 34(2), 139-169, 1989.

It is frequently alleged that the Sophists were relativists. I argue that there is little if any reason to accept this claim. The argument begins with an analysis of the term "relativism" itself, as standardly understood. There follows an examination of numerous ideas and activities attributed to the Sophists, with a view to determining whether they exemplify relativism, as earlier defined. The conclusion is that, with the possible exception of Protagoras's "Man the Measure" doctrine, they do not.

BETTI, Emilio and NOAKES, Susan (trans) and PINTON, Giorgio (trans). The Principles of New Science of G B Vico and the Theory of Historical Interpretation. New Vico Studies, 6, 31-50, 1988.

BEUCHOT, Mauricio. Escepticismo en la Edad Media: el caso do Nicolás de Autrecourt. Rev Latin De Filosof, 15(3), 307-319, N 89.

BEUCHOT, Mauricio. La esencia y la existencia en Tomas de Aquino. Rev Filosof (Mexico), 22(65), 149-165, My-Ag 89.

BEYER, Landon E. Rationality and Artistry in Teaching. Proc Phil Educ, 45, 212-216, 1989.

BEYSSADE, Jean-Marie. Descartes on Freedom of the Will. Grad Fac Phil J, 13(1), 81-96, 1988.

The Cartesian notion of human freedom is discussed according to *Principles* Part I article 39: there are some significant differences between *Meditations* and *Principles* on that topic, and even between the original Latin text of *Principia* and the French authorized translation of 1647. The freedom experience of which is collected in article 39 is neither the enlightened freedom of Meditation IV nor the rejection of evidence. Knowledge of first principles is strictly distinguished from science of proven conclusions, in order to compare the certainty of our freedom with the *cogito*, and solve the inconsistency of a comprehensible infinity.

BEYSSADE, Michelle. System and Training in Descartes' *Meditations*. Grad Fac Phil J, 13(1), 97-114, 1988.

The relationships between two aspects of Descartes's *Meditations*, order of reasons, demonstration or system, on one side, and experience, exercise or training, on the other side, are explained with an example (Med III AT, VII, 36-IX, 28). This passage, which cannot be understood except as training—a new exercise of doubt after the *cogito*—brings some doctrinal teaching and throws some light on the system: it shows what exactly doubt strikes, and allows us to defend Descartes against the charge of circularity.

BEZEMBINDER, Th. Queries of Psychology in Social Choice Theory. Method Sci, 22(1), 11-22, 1989.

This essay discusses the confinements of social choice theory and argues that these confinements keep the theory away from dealing with the decision procedures often followed in complex decision issues. The essay considers the problems of psychology that need be resolved for crossing these confinements. The confinements considered arise from problems concerning (i) fixed pre-given alternatives, (ii) using non-utility information, (iii) fairness in amalgamations and decision procedures, (iv) time invariance.

BHASKAR, Roy. *Reclaiming Reality: A Critical Introduction to Contemporary Philosophy*. New York, Routledge, 1989

BHATTACHARYYA, Sibajiban. Some Features of the Technical Language of Navya-Nyāya. Phil East West, 40(2), 129-149, Ap 90.

The technical language of Navya-Nyaya uses concepts like *limitor, determiner*, etc., to deal with sentences expressing cognition like perception, inference, memory, belief, doubt, supposition. As such sentences are not extensional, Navya-Nyaya distinguishes between what is cognised and the mode under which what is cognised is cognised. Limitor, in the technical language, determines the mode of cognition and is also used to express quantity of cognition, universality, particularity, etc. The concept of determiner is used to show what predicate is asserted of what subject in the same cognition.

BIAGIOLI, Mario. The Anthropology of Incommensurability. Stud Hist Phil Sci, 21(2), 183-209, Je 90.

This essay proposes a new interpretation of linguistic incommensurability among competing scientific paradigms. Here incommensurability is no longer presented only as a phenomenon originating from the different linguistic structures of competing theories but it is also connected to the strategies of noncommunication developed by groups of scientists operating in specific disciplinary hierarchies and power structures. My conclusion is not that what had previously been discussed as linguistic incommensurability is just the result of strategic unwillingness to communicate, but that the integration of the linguistic and the socio-anthropological approaches to incommensurability offer a more complex view of scientific change.

BIALKOWSKI, Grzegorz and PETROWICZ, Lech (trans). Has the Revolution Been Completed? Dialec Hum, 15(3-4), 107-115, Sum-Autumn 88.

BICCHIERI, Christina. Counterfactuals and Backward Induction. Philosophica, 44(2), 101-118, 1989.

In certain types of games, common knowledge of rationality leads to inconsistencies. I show that a theory of the game that includes a model of belief revision can contain both the assumption that players are rational and that rationality is common knowledge among them without generating inconsistencies.

BICKENBACH, Jerome E. Law and Morality. Law Phil, 8(3), 291-300, D 89.

BICKES, Hans. Begriffe im kommunikativen Handeln: Linguistische Begriffsanalyse als Rekonstruktion von Handlungsmustern. Conceptus, 23(60), 81-97, 1989.

Communicative (linguistic) acts follow rule-governed action-patterns. The unit used for reconstructing such action-patterns is the (linguistic) sign.

"Concepts" can be understood as strategies for the solving or problems or as action plans. Concepts are interpreted as signifies of signs, with the latter regarded as minimal cognitive units. In this paper a structuralist view of concepts will be proposed (analogous to the Sneed-Stegmüller view of scientific theories), according to which signifies are reconstructed as set-theoretical structures. The knowledge of the meaning of a sign is equivalent to the ability to use the sign (intentionally) within the framework of a communicative act. Thus the knowledge of meanings (resp. of "concepts") is equal to the knowledge of (successful) communicative acts, i.e., it is to be seen within a social dimension.

BIELECKI, Jan and BAZYLAK, Jozef. Das Problem der Psychologischen Hinführung zur Bildung der reifen und religiösen Persönlichkeit (in Polish). Stud Phil Christ, 25(1), 221-236, 1989.

In der Arbeit wurde die Bildung der reifen Persönlichkeit besprochen mit der Berücksichtung aller Elemente, die sie bilden. Es wurden auch experimentale Forschungen besprochen, die das religiöse Leben betreffen d.h. religiöse Haltungen mit der Persönlichkeit und ihre Aufgabe in der Bildung der Persönlichkeit. Der Autor unterstrich die Notwendigkeit der Bildung der eigentlichen religiösen Haltungen. Er sprach sich Für die Stärkung der Überzeugungskraft sowie des Erkenntnisund des Willensbereiches der religiösen Haltungen aus.

BIELFELDT, Dennis. "What's Real": A Dialogue. Teach Phil, 12(3), 235-241, S 89.

In this article I present an original dialogue written to challenge first-year philosophy students to consider alternatives to the myth of the given. I describe how the dialogue is used in getting students interested in the question of the role of language in issues of ontology and epistemology.

BIELFELDT, Dennis. Luther, Metaphor, and Theological Language. Mod Theol, 6(2), 121-135, Ja 90.

I believe there is an implicit theological semantics at work in the texts of Martin Luther, a semantics which (1) squares both with the propositional content and existential address of his theological language, (2) is consistent with the paradoxical nature of theological language as "human words about God's Word," and (3) allows for the "identity in difference" between the incommensurable languages of philosophy and theology. I argue that his theological language can be modeled as an extended interaction metaphor over and against the language of philosophy. Through a collision of "earthly" meanings a "heavenly" sense is established allowing reference to the theological realm.

BIEN, Joseph. Camus and Revolution (in Serbo-Croatian). Filozof Istraz, 30(3), 911-923, 1989.

The author is examining the positions of Albert Camus as regards social change, namely his concepts of rebellion and revolution. Particularly, he analyses Camus's negative remarks on theoretical and practical activities of Rousseau, St. Just, Marx and Marxists (mostly laid out in The Rebel). The author considers Camus's accusations for confused at least at three points: concerning divine right monarchs and monarchies, general will and the will of all and the dialectic of history (revolution). Camus is not able to step outside the immediate in order to recognize that the alternatives for human history are not the static absolute of God or communism, or in terms of practical activities those of the rebels' radical isolation and of revolutionary terror. As a conclusion the author examines Camus's behavior facing the complex social crisis, and ends with the statement that Camus's claims on behalf of suffering humanity although honest were not sufficient and practically turned out to be the lack of action that is also a sort of action that covers all violence in the name of justice.

BIEN, Joseph. Duquette, Hegel, and Political Freedom. SW Phil Rev, 6(2), 111-113, Jl 90.

BIENENSTOCK, Myriam. "The Logic of Political Life: Hegel's Conception of Political Philosophy" in *Knowledge and Politics*, DASCAL, Marcelo (ed), 145-170. Boulder, Westview Pr, 1988.

To clarify the relationship between Hegel's conception of philosophy and his political thought, the author first contends that the attempt to characterize Hegel's so-called "dialectical" approach by opposing it to "positivism" rests upon an unsatisfactory account of the meaning of Hegel's philosophical enterprise as a whole. She then examines one central feature of Hegel's enterprise: the transformation of "representations" into "thoughts," of "thoughts" into a "concept"; and she claims that Hegel's political philosophy itself shares this overall purpose of his system: it consists in a kind of conceptual clarification.

BIENIAK, Janusz and RODZINSKA, Aleksandra (trans). Remarks on the Dialogue Between Christians and Marxists. Dialec Hum, 15(3-4), 187-193, Sum-Autumn 88.

The paper was read at the Polish-Soviet philosophical conference (Warsaw,

October 1987). It was made in connection with the author's activity in (existing 1986-1989) the Consultative Board attached to the Chairman of the Council of State. It should give arguments for introducing into the state an effective world outlook equality and tolerance. In detail, it was a polemic with an article of a Marxist philosopher Zdzislaw Cackowski, "Cultural Partnership—A Factor of Social Peace." In spite of that author an obstacle for cultural partnership is not religion but only all totalism and all inequality.

BIER, Jean Paul. "Die Polyglottie als Stilfigur: *Der Fall Doderer*" in *Cultural Hermeneutics of Modern Art: Essays in Honor of Jan Aler*, DETHIER, Hubert (ed), 205-221. Amsterdam, Rodopi, 1989.

A descriptive attempt to define and locate the main constructive functions of polyglottic elements in the novels of Heimito von Doderer. Based on an original typology (the differences of style production and reception), the hermeneutic approach makes a new codification of the phenomenon possible in the German written literature from the nineteenth century on.

BIERI, Peter. "Scepticism and Intentionality" in *Reading Kant*, SCHAPER, Eva (ed), 77-113. Cambridge, Blackwell, 1989.

BIGELOW, John and COLLINS, John and PARGETTER, Robert. Colouring in the World. Mind, 99(394), 279-288, Ap 90.

BIGELOW, John and CAMPBELL, John and PARGETTER, Robert. Death and Well-Being. Pac Phil Quart, 71(2), 119-140, Je 90.

BIGELOW, John and PARGETTER, Robert. From Extroverted Realism to Correspondence: A Modest Proposal. Phil Phenomenol Res, 50(3), 435-460, Mr 90.

BIGELOW, John and PARGETTER, Robert. Metaphysics of Causation. Erkenntnis, 33(1), 89-119, Jl 90.

BIGELOW, John. Temptation and the Will. Amer Phil Quart, 27(1), 39-49, Ja 90.

BILLMAN, Dorrit and PETERSON, Justin. Critique of Structural Analysis in Modeling Cognition: A Case Study of Jackendoff's Theory. Phil Psych, 2(3), 283-296, 1989.

Modeling cognition by structural analysis of representation leads to systematic difficulties which are not resolvable. We analyse the merits and limits of a representation-based methodology to modeling cognition by treating Jackendoff's *Consciousness and the Computational Mind* as a good case study. We note the effects this choice of methodology has on the view of consciousness he proposes, as well as a more detailed consideration of the computational mind. The fundamental difficulty we identify is the conflict between the desire for modular processors which map directly onto representations and the need for dynamically interacting control. Our analysis of this approach to modeling cognition is primarily directed at separating merits from problems and inconsistencies by a critique internal to this approach; we also step outside the framework to note the issues it ignores.

BILOW, Scott H. Future Persons and the Justification of Education. Proc Phil Educ, 45, 320-330, 1989.

The paper argues that children have the right to education in virtue of their status as "future persons" and discusses the content of this right.

BIMEL, Walter. En torno a Heidegger. Rev Filosof (Mexico), 22(66), 332-348, S-D 89.

BINEHAM, Jeffery L. The Cartesian Anxiety in Epistemic Rhetoric: An Assessment of the Literature. Phil Rhet, 23(1), 43-62, 1990.

BING, Jon. Three Generations of Computerized Systems for Public Administration and Implications for Legal Decision-Making. Ratio Juris, 3(2), 219-236, Jl 90.

The paper is concerned with the introduction of computerized systems into public administration. As a basis for the assessment of current systems, a brief history of such systems is offered. Not only are "legal information systems" discussed, but the access to factual information is also dealt with. Three generations of systems in public administration are indicated: the first generation emphasized use of data bases and computers for calculation, as well as "computer-oriented legislation." The second generation lifted the forms, which structure the case work, onto the computer screens. And the third generation is being born from the current efforts to design integrated work stations, using knowledge based methods. On this background, a discussion of impact on legal decision making is offered, emphasizing the replacement of vague by strict criteria, and the re-use of pre-collected factual information. A final note addresses the problem of reviewing or supervising such systems.

BIRCH, Bruce C and RASMUSSEN, Larry L. *Bible and Ethics in the Christian Life*. Minneapolis, Augsburg, 1989

BIRCH, Thomas H. The Incarceration of Wildness: Wilderness Areas as Prisons. Environ Ethics, 12(1), 3-26, Spr 90.

Even with the very best intentions, Western culture's approach to wilderness and wildness, the otherness of nature, tends to be one of imperialistic domination and appropriation. Nevertheless, in spite of Western culture's attempt to gain total control over nature by imprisoning wildness in wilderness areas, which are meant to be merely controlled "simulations" of wildness, a real wildness, a real otherness, can still be found in wilderness reserves. This wildness can serve as the literal ground for the subversion of the imperium, and consequently as the basis for the practical establishment of and residence in what Wendell Berry has called the "landscape of harmony." Here all land becomes wild sacred space that humans consciously come to reinhabit. In this subversive potential lies the most fundamental justification for the legal establishment of wilderness reserves.

BIRD, Frederick and WATERS, James A. Attending to Ethics in Management. J Bus Ethics, 8(6), 493-497, Je 89.

Based on analysis of interviews with managers about the ethical questions they face in their work, a typology of morally questionable managerial acts is developed. The typology distinguishes acts committed against-the-firm (non-role and role-failure acts) from those committed on-behalf-of-the-firm (role-distortion and role-assertion acts) and draws attention to the different nature of the four types of acts. The argument is made that senior management attention is typically focused on the types of acts which are least problematical for most managers, and that the most troublesome types are relatively ignored.

BIRD, G H. Psychology in the First *Critique*. S Afr J Phil, 8(3-4), 166-175, N 88.

In this article it is argued that the objection to Kant's position in the *Critique*—that it includes psychological claims, which are themselves untenable—is itself ill-founded, insofar as these commentators do not spend much time in explaining the mistake. To them it is transparently obvious. The purpose of this article is to examine some of the background to Kant's account of psychology in the *Critique* and elsewhere with the aim of showing that there is good reason not to ascribe these supposed mistakes to Kant. Though some of the central points in favour of the view that Kant's *Critique* rests on certain mistakes will be rehearsed, it is shown that the argument cannot be decisive. For one motive for identifying these claimed errors is very deeply embedded in the history of Kant interpretation.

BIRD, Graham. "Kant's Transcendental Arguments" in *Reading Kant*, SCHAPER, Eva (ed), 21-39. Cambridge, Blackwell, 1989.

The paper surveys what I take to be the central features of Kant's so-called transcendental arguments. It concentrates specifically on the Refutation of Idealism and the Second Analogy. The claim is that philosophers, such as Stroud, have misunderstood the nature of these arguments, and that specifically they do not function in the context of traditional scepticism as has been often supposed. There is some concluding criticism of the obscurities of Stroud's views on scepticism.

BIRIS, Ioan. Vers une totalité-champ dans la science contemporaine (in Romanian). Rev Filosof (Romania), 36(2), 160-166, Mr-Ap 89.

BIRMINGHAM, Peg. "Local Theory" in *The Question of the Other: Essays in Contemporary Continental Philosophy*, DALLERY, Arleen B (ed), 205-212. Albany, SUNY Pr, 1989.

BIRMINGHAM, Robert L. On Legal Proof. Austl J Phil, 67(4), 479-486, D 89.

In criminal and civil lawsuits, the prosecutor or plaintiff must establish the defendant's guilt or liability. Recently, Davidson and Pargetter explained that proof beyond a reasonable doubt requires more than high probability. Likewise, proof by a preponderance of the evidence requires more than probability exceeding .5. We comment upon their explanation that the probability must also be robust, resilient, or stable, an idea first held by Peirce. Using a Scandinavian theory of evidence stated by Sahlin and Gärdenfors, we sketch a competing explanation: the prosecutor or plaintiff must establish a causal connection between the evidence and the event to be proved.

BIRÓ, Balázs. Isomorphic But Not Lower Base-Isomorphic Cylindric Algebras of Finite Dimension. Notre Dame J Form Log, 30(2), 262-267, Spr 89.

This article deals with Serény's theorem giving sufficient conditions for two cylindric set algebras (Cs's) to be lower base-isomorphic, a cylindric algebra version of Vaught's theorem on the existence of prime models of atomic theories in countable languages. It is proved that Serény's theorem requires all the conditions given in its statement. Here the necessity of the condition of the infinite-dimensionality of the given Cs's is proved via constructing isomorphic but not lower base-isomorphic Cs's of any finite dimension greater than one. A model-theoretical corollary of the above dependence is stated also.

BISHOP, John. *Natural Agency: An Essay on the Casual Theory of Action.* New York, Cambridge Univ Pr, 1989

The author argues that it is possible to reconcile our "ethical perspective" (according to which we are capable of responsible action) with a naturalistic view of human behavior. He offers a critical treatment of arguments which seem to support skepticism about the possibility of "natural agency," and argues that this form of skepticism can be defeated provided a causal theory of action is defensible. The prospects for a successful defence of such a theory are investigated in detail with special emphasis placed on methods of overcoming the problem of causal deviance.

BITTNER, Rüdiger. Verständnis für Unvernünftige. Z Phil Forsch, 43(4), 577-592, O-D 89.

BITTNER, Rüdiger and TALBOT, Theodore (trans). *What Reason Demands.* New York, Cambridge Univ Pr, 1980

This work is concerned with morality. Beginning with the question "Why should I be moral?" it moves on, in light of objections, to a fundamental query, "*Should* I be moral?" Resolving that we should not, on a vernacular conception, the author moves on to consideration of guides to action based upon morality-less rationality, arguing prudence and autonomy as proper guides. (staff)

BITZER, Lloyd F (ed) and CAMPBELL, George. *The Philosophy of Rhetoric (Revised Edition).* Carbondale, So Illinois Univ Pr, 1988

BJELIC, Dusan I and SCHWEIZER-BJELIC, Shelley. 'God-Talk' and 'Tacit' Theo-Logic. Mod Theol, 6(4), 341-366, Jl 90.

BLACK, Alison Harley. *Man and Nature in the Philosophical Thought of Wang-Fu-Chih.* Seattle, Univ Washington Pr, 1987

BLACK, Carolyn. "Foundations" in *The Current State of the Coherence Theory*, BENDER, John W (ed), 200-204. Norwell, Kluwer, 1989.

The thesis is that some recent coherentist criticism of the purportedly basic elements of foundationalism, notably that of Laurence BonJour in *The Structure of Empirical Knowledge*, fails to apply to a certain type of foundation. After describing some of the criticism I examine an account of grounds in the later philosophy of Wittgenstein which I then modify so as to suggest what we take to be the case as basic. One of BonJour's central claims against foundationalism is that the only justification for empirical belief is other empirical belief. I contend that this is false and that we can initiate a sound foundationalism with bases which are neither true nor false nor simply empirical.

BLACK, David W. The Vichian Elements in Susanne Langer's Thought. New Vico Studies, 3, 113-118, 1985.

Although Susanne Langer never committed herself to a serious study of Vico, this essay argues that there are significant elements of Vichian theory that may have been refracted to Langer during her studies of Ernst Cassirer. Langer appears to be struggling with a theory of the imagination which not only parallels Vico's own theory but which retraces in a highly conceptual manner the perception of imaginative universals that Vico presents in a more narrative fashion.

BLACK, Deborah L. The 'Imaginative Syllogism' in Arabic Philosophy: A Medieval Contribution to the Philosophical Study of Metaphor. Med Stud, 51, 242-267, 1989.

BLACK, Virginia. Is and Ought: A Gap or a Continuity? Vera Lex, 9(1), 13-16, 1989.

The naturalistic fallacy is inappropriate at the level of moral foundations. Moral norms are not questionable when they inhere in basic conditions. Certainly there are contexts in which it is necessary sharply to contrast what exists with what ought to exist or ought to be done. Prominent among these are morally unacceptable situations. And there are others. But the alleged "is-ought gap" has been carried too far. Positing unquestionable, invariant aspects of human nature is necessary to avoid a counterproductive utopianism in morals. And certain social constants make it otiose to allege that some other condition ought to prevail. A discontinuous "ought" out of some philosopher's head and not grounded in social realities provides a formula for "anything goes."

BLACK, Virginia. Reflections on Natural Law: A Critical Review of the Thought of Yves R Simon. Vera Lex, 9(2), 10-13, 1989.

The Tradition of Natural Law by the late Yves R Simon is remarkable for its fresh insights into, and defense of, the Aristotelian-Thomistic natural-ends tradition, to which, in my view, Aristotle's "what is due" augments natural ends with an account of necessary adjustment and finesse in matters of justice. Simon's language is startlingly original in its deep sensitivity both to the ramifications of this line of thought and to their lasting (and hence current) applicability. I take up a number of Thomistic declarations that I think require

expulsion, e.g., Thomas's error in believing exchange values must be equal or his error in believing interest is morally inadmissible. But these are not natural law derivatives and are easily expelled. The book is worthy to be taken as a guide to classic, mainstream natural law thought.

BLACK, Virginia. Reply: Flew's "Is and Ought: The 'Open-Question Argument'". Vera Lex, 9(2), 14, 1989.

Some ethical naturalists claim a logical connection between certain factual and valuational statements since these thinkers belong broadly to the camp that associates morality with human nature. Various arguments try to establish this connection. Flew asserts that to do this we need to "insist upon the wrongness of some sort of behaviour which can be described in non-moral terms." This must not be a tautology but "a substantial moral claim." And by way of illustration he offers: "Is it morally licit for me to cause someone else to suffer...because his...sufferings provide me with sadistic satisfaction?" I reply that the foregoing is still a kind of tautology since "sadistic," as well as being descriptive, *entails* moral disapprovability. Nevertheless some tautologies can serve a remindful function and are necessary in ethical theory.

BLACKBURN, Pierre. L'Évaluation des théories éthiques. Rev Int Phil, 43(170), 379-389, 1989.

When evaluating ethical theories, we typically must use crucial but unwarranted (or poorly warranted) background theories, principles or data. However, these elements are particularly problematic when used to refute or immunize a given ethical theory confronted with moral intuitions. Illustrative examples of this: (1) the use of the principle of diminishing marginal utility of wealth by classical welfare economists; (2) the use of the maximin rule of choice by Rawls; (3) the use, by Harsanyi, of the "principle" according to which utility is maximized by the non-imposition of overburdening moral obligations.

BLACKBURN, Simon. Filling in Space. Analysis, 50(2), 62-65, Mr 90.

BLACKBURN, Simon. Manifesting Realism. Midwest Stud Phil, 14, 29-47, 1989.

In this paper I describe various positions against which the 'antirealist' polemic of Dummett and Wright might appear to be directed. I argue that either they are fit only for straw men, or they are immune to the arguments. I urge instead a more traditional approach to the issue of realism.

BLACKWELL, Kenneth. "Portrait of a Philosopher of Science" in *Rereading Russell: Essays on Bertrand Russell's Metaphysics and Epistemology*, SAVAGE, C Wade (ed), 281-293. Minneapolis, Univ of Minn Pr, 1989.

Russell held that the pursuit and attainment of scientific truth was an "impersonal" activity, and so enlarged the self. This essay pursues details of this evaluation of science, i.e., its ethical content for those engaged in it.

BLAIM, Artur (trans) and CACKOWSKI, Zdzislaw. Fear and the Limits of Human Subjectivity. Dialec Hum, 15(3-4), 223-231, Sum-Autumn 88.

Fear is a signal of danger and subjective premise of counteractivity. It gives rise to prospective vigilance, from which consciousness originates as its most developed form. Two factors enhancing fear: a cognitive *impossibility of recognizing and localizing of a danger* and a practical one, *powerlessness in front of a danger*. In their extreme positions both of them transform fear into FEAR. The final term of FEAR may be a total demission including resignation, giving up even a symbolic counteractivity in front of a danger *DANGER*.

BLAIR, Ann. Tycho Brahe's Critique of Copernicus and the Copernican System. J Hist Ideas, 51(3), 355-377, Jl-S 90.

BLAIR, Howard A and SUBRAHMANIAN, V S. Paraconsistent Foundations for Logic Programming. J Non-Classical Log, 5(2), 45-73, N 88.

Paraconsistent logics are useful for reasoning about very large knowledge bases, which may contain inconsistencies. We present a notion of knowledge base defined by a set of formulae of a many-valued logic whose truth values form a complete lattice which may be inconsistent in the two-valued sense with inconsistency represented by the top of the truth-value lattice. We give a model theory for these knowledge bases and characterize models by an operator on structures. As a step toward computational efficiency a proof procedure based on AND/OR tree searching is given along with soundness and completeness results.

BLAIS, F. Réformisme pénal et responsabilité: une étude philosophique. Philosophiques, 16(2), 293-325, Autumn 89.

The main objective of this paper is to criticize some propositions of the social doctrine of penal reformism (the social doctrine which favors a therapeutic attitude toward a criminal rather than a punitive one). The perspective adopted is that of the responsibility in the different theoretical constructions of the penal reformism doctrine (medico-legal, determinist and the strict-liability). I will explicate some thesis on the subject and I will do, in my conclusion, some critical commentaries on the difficulties that these three versions of penal reformism face when they have to give a coherent and morally acceptable point of view of the problem of responsibility.

BLAIS, Michel J. Misunderstandings of Epistemic TIT for TAT: Reply to John Woods. J Phil, 87(7), 369-374, Jl 90.

An earlier paper ("Epistemic TIT FOR TAT," *Journal of Philosophy*, LXXXIV, 8 [August 1987]: 363-375) analogically modeled epistemic collectivism upon A Rappaport's TIT FOR TAT Prisoner's Dilemma strategy: a *nice*, *provocable*, *forgiving*, *clear*, *robust* strategy suffices to illuminate cooperative behavior in the "knowledge game," without invoking moral trust. This paper answers John Woods's criticism ("The Maladroitness of Epistemic TIT FOR TAT," *Journal of Philosophy*, LXXXVI, 6 [June 1989]: 324-331). Purported counterexamples are defused by showing that 'cooperation' and 'defection' within the knowledge game have been misconstrued, and the demand that the analogical model be formalized is shown to be unreasonable.

BLAIS, Michel J. A Pragmatic Analysis of Mathematical Realism and Intuitionism. Phil Math, 4(1), 61-85, 1989.

Classical logic is usually portrayed as having an ontologically realist "Platonist" basis; mathematical objects and truths exist independently of the knower. Intuitionist logic has a more resolutely constructive basis; no mathematical object or truth can exist unless the knowing subject has the appropriate intuition. A pragmatic analysis based on the abolition of the boundary between the formal and the empirical, on fallibilism and on internalism shows that it is not necessary to choose between the two, because both have pragmatically unsound assumptions. A priori elements need not entail Platonism; constructivity need not constrain within intuitionist bounds.

BLAMIRES, Cyprian. Étienne Dumont: Genevan Apostle of Utility. Utilitas, 2(1), 55-70, My 90.

BLANCHOT, Maurice. Grâce (soit rendue) à Jacques Derrida. Rev Phil Fr, 180(2), 167-173, Ap-Je 90.

BLANDINO, Giovanni. G Blandino's Further Reply to A Alessi. Aquinas, 32(3), 551-552, S-D 89.

BLANDINO, Giovanni. Remarks Concerning the Doctrine of the Act and Potency. Aquinas, 32(2), 337-352, My-Ag 89.

The author denies the validity of the doctrine of act and potency. In this article he discusses with A Alessi, professor of metaphysics in the Pontificia Università Salesiana.

BLANDINO, Giovanni. Remarks on General Neo-Thomistic Metaphysics: The Contribution of Christian Revelation to Philosophy. Aquinas, 32(1), 57-71, Ja-Ap 89.

The author accepts all the theses of Neo-Thomistic metaphysics, except the thesis of the act and potency. He underlines that the principal ideas of Thomistic metaphysics are due not to Aristotle, but to the indication of Judeo-Christian revelation.

BLANSHARD, Brand. "Harris on Internal Relations" in *Dialectic and Contemporary Science*, GRIER, Philip T (ed), 3-20. Lanham, Univ Pr of America, 1989.

BLASS, Andreas and SHELAH, Saharon. Near Coherence of Filters III: A Simplified Consistency Proof. Notre Dame J Form Log, 30(4), 530-538, Fall 89.

In the model obtained from a model of the continuum hypothesis by iterating rational perfect set forcing $\aleph_2$ times with countable supports, every two nonprincipal ultrafilters on ω have a common image under a finite-to-one function.

BLITS, Jan H. Equality of Opportunity and the Problem of Nature. Educ Theor, 40(3), 309-319, Sum 90.

Equality of opportunity, once honored as the guiding principle of liberalism, has recently fallen into disrepute. Some critics accept the principle that nature is a proper standard for justice but deny that opportunity is ever really equal; others deny that natural differences are morally respectable on the grounds that they are no less arbitrary than artificial ones. At the same time, the problem of nature—i.e., nature as a *problem*—has been missing from the debate. This paper, stepping back from the current debate, shows the crucial significance of that missing problem.

BLITS, Jan H. Hobbesian Dualism: Hobbes's Theory of Motion. S J Phil, 28(2), 135-147, Sum 90.

Although scholars have long emphasized the central importance of motion in Hobbes's philosophy, they seem to take for granted that what Hobbes means by motion when he defines it as a continual change of place is the

same as what he means by it when he calls motion the cause of all that exists. This paper, challenging the traditional understanding, shows that motion has two radically different meanings, or levels of meaning, for Hobbes. Locomotion becomes purely imaginary motion, while real motion becomes power *per se*.

BLITS, Jan H. Self-Knowledge and the Modern Mode of Learning. Educ Theor, 39(4), 293-299, Fall 89.

This paper explores the tension inherent within the modern mode of study, epitomized by the scientific method, between thinking for oneself and self-knowledge.

BLIZARD, Wayne D. A Formal Theory of Objects, Space and Time. J Sym Log, 55(1), 74-89, Mr 90.

The two statements "Two different objects cannot occupy the same place at the same time" and "An object cannot be in two different places at the same time" are axioms of our everyday understanding of objects, space and time. We develop a first-order theory OST (Objects, Space and Time) in which formal equivalents of these two statements are taken as axioms. Using the theory OST, we uncover other fundamental principles of objects, space and time. We attempt to understand the logical nature of these principles, to investigate their formal consequences, and to identify logical alternatives to them.

BLOM, Hans W. Spinoza et les problèmes d'une théorie de la societé commerçante. Stud Spinozana, 4, 281-301, 1988.

Spinoza's youthful experience as a tradesman is related to his mature views on the role of economic behavior and economic institutions as a factor in societal development. Insights from economic history, history of economic thought and political philosophy are brought to bear on the issue. It is shown that some of the central Spinozan tenets capture problems he confronted while in business himself. Next, it is concluded that precisely these tenets make Spinoza's economic and political theory remarkably ahead of his time.

BLOM, Tannelie and NIJHUIS, Ton. Contingency, Meaning and History. Philosophica, 44(2), 33-59, 1989.

BLOM, Tannelie and NIJHUIS, Ton. Geschiedenis en contingentie: Een nieuw perspectief op historisch verklaren. Kennis Methode, 13(4), 362-381, 1989.

BLONDEL, Eric. "Ist das Lachen philosophisch? Bruchstücke einer Metaphysik des Lachens" in *Agora: Zu Ehren von Rudolph Berlinger*, BERLINGER, Rudolph (and other eds), 1-10. Amsterdam, Rodopi, 1988.

BLOOM, Alfred H. The Privileging of Experience in Chinese Practical Reasoning. J Chin Phil, 16(3-4), 297-307, D 89.

The paper presents a series of experiments, undertaken with Taiwanese, Hong Kong and American subjects, which suggests that while Americans tend to feel relatively comfortable in accepting purely hypothetical premises for the sole purpose of inferring what would follow if the premises were true, Chinese tend to resist such purely speculative theoretical activity, asking that the premises make sense within their own experience before feeling comfortable in extrapolating from them. The paper then explores the possible role of this observed difference in conceptual inclination in explaining broader cross-cultural differences in the areas of education, contractual relations and moral thinking.

BLOOM, Irene. Response to Huang Siu-chi's Review of *Knowledge Painfully Acquired*, by Lo Ch'in-shun and Translated by Irene Bloom. Phil East West, 39(4), 459-463, O 89.

BLOOR, David. "Rationalism, Supernaturalism, and the Sociology of Knowledge" in *Scientific Knowledge Socialized*, HRONSZKY, Imre (ed), 59-74. Norwell, Kluwer, 1989.

BLUM, Alex. Bayne on Kripke. Philosophia (Israel), 19(4), 455-456, D 89.

This article responds to a criticism of Kripke on the identity theory and criticizes Kripke in turn. [There is a serious printing omission of three lines.]

BLUM, Alex. Pain Corrigibility. Manuscrito, 11(2), 127-128, O 88.

We try to show how it is that being in pain is not equivalent to knowing that one is in pain.

BLUM, Alex. *Tractatus* 2:063. Phil Invest, 12(4), 325-326, O 89.

An explanation is offered which obviates some apparent difficulties.

BLUM, Peter. Heidegger and Rorty on "The End of Philosophy". Metaphilosophy, 21(3), 223-238, Jl 90.

Both Martin Heidegger and Richard Rorty herald "the end of philosophy," i.e., the end of a tradition running from Plato through Descartes and Kant. Rorty ostensibly relies in part on Heidegger's critique of Western metaphysics, but rejects the latter's talk of "Being" as lapsing back into metaphysics. This amounts to separating a negative (critical) strand from a positive (substantive) strand in Heidegger's thought. I advance the claim that Rorty's reading of Heidegger is highly problematic in this regard, and that Rorty himself lapses more clearly than Heidegger.

BLUME, Delorys and BLUME, Robert. The Crime of Punishment. Humanist, 49(6), 12-15,44, N-D 89.

BLUME, Robert and BLUME, Delorys. The Crime of Punishment. Humanist, 49(6), 12-15,44, N-D 89.

BLUMENFELD, Karen. Dilemmas of Disclosure: Ethical Issues in Environmental Auditing. Bus Prof Ethics J, 8(3), 5-27, Fall 89.

BO, Wang. Lao Zi and the Xia Culture. Chin Stud Phil, 21(4), 34-69, Sum 90.

BOBBIO, Norberto and KENNEALY, Peter (trans). *Democracy and Dictatorship*. Minneapolis, Univ of Minn Pr, 1989

BOBBIO, Norberto. Reason in Law. Ratio Juris, 1(2), 97-108, Jl 88.

The problem of the relationship between "reason" and "law" has two different meanings depending on whether the first or the second of the two terms is considered to be the most important one. These two different meanings are revealed in the expressions "law of reason" and "legal reason," respectively. In the first expression, "reason" is meant in its strong sense, that is, the faculty of grasping the essence of things, while in the second, "reason" is meant in a weak sense, the ability to reason (calculate, infer, discuss). "Law of reason" and "legal reason" correspond to two different moments of the legal universe, the creation and, respectively, the application of law. Strong reason is that which discovers the rules to be obeyed, while weak reason is that which applies rules to an actual case. The first is legislating reason, while the second is judging reason. (edited)

BOBOC, Alexandru. Leibniz's Nachklänge im Denken und in der Dichtung von Mihai Eminescu. Phil Log, 32(3-4), 203-209, Jl-D 88.

BOBOC, Alexandru. Technics and the Ontology of the Human Being Nowadays. Phil Log, 32(1-2), 33-39, Ja-Je 88.

BOBURG, F. Hegel y la revolucion Francesa. Rev Filosof (Mexico), 22(65), 235-242, My-Ag 89.

BOBURG, Felipe (trans) and HEIDEGGER, Martin. La constitucion onto-teo-logica de la metafisica. Rev Filosof (Mexico), 22(66), 300-319, S-D 89.

BOCHENSKI, Joseph M. Die fünf Wege. Frei Z Phil Theol, 36(3), 235-265, 1989.

Mathematical-logical commentary to the proofs of existence of God in Aquinas's *Summa Theologiae*. Only the second proof is acceptable.

BOCKANIC, William N and EXTEJT, Marian M. Issues Surrounding the Theories of Negligent Hiring and Failure to Fire. Bus Prof Ethics J, 8(4), 21-34, Wint 89.

BODEN, Margaret A. *Artificial Intelligence in Psychology: Interdisciplinary Essays*. Cambridge, MIT Pr, 1989

This collection of the author's recent essays discusses how AI and computational ideas are being used in psychology. Most essays are accessible to a wide audience, and the author's introduction gives an overview. Searle's attack on AI, for example, is challenged. Issues in animal, developmental, visual, and educational psychology are addressed.

BODENHEIMER, Edgar. Law as a Bridge between Is and Ought. Ratio Juris, 1(2), 137-153, Jl 88.

Law has variously been described as part of empirical social reality or as a set of normative prescriptions defining desirable conduct. The author takes the view that a legal system normally represents an amalgam of "is" and "ought" elements. It is operative in part as a living law of actual human conduct, in another part as an instrumentality for transforming unfulfilled social ideals or goals into reality. A different blending of "is" and "ought" factors often occurs in the judicial process, when an application of given legal norms is combined with some injection of law deemed desirable by the judges.

BODENHEIMER, Edgar. Perelman's Methodology and Natural Law Reasoning. Vera Lex, 7(1), 2,8, 1987.

BODÉÜS, Richard. Deux propositions aristotéliciennes sur le droit natural chez les continentaux d'Amérique. Rev Metaph Morale, 94(3), 369-389, Jl-S 89.

BOËR, Steven E. Object-Dependent Thoughts. Phil Stud, 58(1-2), 51-85, Ja-F 90.

BOERI, Marcelo D. La estructura matemática de la materia en el *Timeo* de Platón. Rev Filosof (Argentina), 3(2), 107-125, N 88.

Very often historians and philosophers of science have regarded Plato as a thinker who was devoted to hinder the development of science. The author of this article maintains that this is not due to chance but it is the effect of uncritical acceptance of some scholars. This paper deals with the main problems of the Platonic theory of elements; some difficulties concerning stereometric construction are analyzed as well as some arguments explaining the philosophical issues of Plato's doctrine of matter. Finally, it is suggested what the Platonic theory of elements might stand for in the history of scientific ideas.

BOERI, Marcelo D. Naturaleza y causalidad en Aristóteles: *Fisica* II 1. Rev Filosof (Argentina), 1(1-2), 41-58, N 86.

This paper is dedicated to study the Aristotelian notion of nature. Basic text is *Physics* II 1, although some passages of *Metaphysics* V 4 are included too. The main purpose of this article is to point out in what sense the nature is a form of causality. The work is divided in three *items*: (1) the general definition of nature ("the nature is a principle, it means, cause of motion in that to which it inheres primarily of itself") and the objects that are produced by nature; (2) the treatment of nature from a point of view of the matter; and (3) the nature from the point of view of the form.

BOGDAN, Deanne. From Stubborn Structure to Double Mirror: The Evolution of Northrop Frye's Theory of Poetic Creation and Response. J Aes Educ, 23(2), 33-43, Sum 89.

This paper poses two questions: what can The Great Code tell us about Northrop Frye's theory of poetic response; the second, what can the answer to the first question disclose about Frye's theory of literature. Frye's earlier work enunciates a framework for response to literature that devolves upon his acceptance of T S Eliot's dissociation of sensibility as psychological reality. In The Great Code, however, we perceive a shift in his angle of vision, with respect both to response and to poetic creation. This shift turns on the engagement/detachment paradigm fusing into the act of reading as a single but "complex dialectical process."

BOGDAN, Deanne. Joyce, Dorothy, and Willie: Literary Literacy as Engaged Reflection. Proc Phil Educ, 45, 168-182, 1989.

This paper describes and analyzes the reader response journals of students in their initial assignment within a study unit on the relationship between William and Dorothy Wordsworth. In doing so, the paper explores a conception of literary literacy as "engaged reflection," and suggests the ways in which the students' response journals, in their first foray into the feminist critique of Romanticism, demonstrate pertinent interrelationships between English Studies and Women's Studies with respect to both substantive theoretical issues and pedagogical practice.

BOGEN, James. "Coherentist Theories of Knowledge Don't Apply to Enough Outside of Science" in The Current State of the Coherence Theory, BENDER, John W (ed), 142-159. Norwell, Kluwer, 1989.

Coherentist theories of the kind advocated by BonJour fail to give an adequate account of epistemic responsibility in two kinds of cases for which an epistemological theory should provide an account. The first includes a wide variety of ordinary, nonscientific beliefs (e.g., my belief that my name is 'Bogen', and that Thelonius Monk composed 'I Mean You' after 1935, and a cook's belief that his sauce needs more cheese). Here coherentist tests for epistemic responsibility require access to a belief system whose specification makes the requirement psychologically realistic. The second class includes scientific beliefs (e.g., Newton's belief that gravitation is a universal force which acts uniformly). Here there are accessible systems which approximate to those coherentism requires. But the application of coherentist tests leads typically to the conclusion that scientists are epistemically irresponsible—an unacceptable result. The paper concludes with some methodological remarks about how to pursue a more plausible sort of coherentism.

BOGHOSSIAN, Paul A. Content and Self-Knowledge. Phil Topics, 17(1), 5-26, Spr 89.

This paper argues that, given a certain apparently inevitable thesis about content, we could not know our own thoughts. The thesis is that the content of a thought is determined by its relational properties. This skeptical conclusion is reached by showing that our thoughts are not known to us by inference, and, indeed, could not be so known if a plausible internalism about justification is true. It is further argued that our thoughts could not be known on the basis of 'inner observation' or, finally, on the basis of nothing (as in Tyler Burge's recent view). The overall aim of the paper is not to promote skepticism but understanding: by highlighting the conditions under which self-knowledge is not possible, we shall better understand the condition under which it is.

BOGHOSSIAN, Paul A. The Rule-Following Considerations. Mind, 98(392), 507-549, O 89.

The paper consists of an extended critique of Kripke's discussion of 'rule-following' and of the extensive secondary literature to which it has given rise. Among the issues discussed are the reality of meaning, the privacy of meaning, the reducibility of meaning, the relation between meaning and rule-following and the relation between meaning and community. The paper argues for a robust realism about meaning: a realist, nonreductionist and judgment-independent conception, one which sustains no obvious animus against private language.

BOGHOSSIAN, Paul A. The Status of Content. Phil Rev, 99(2), 157-184, Ap 90.

It is argued that standard formulations of irrealist construals of content discourse—error theories and nonfactualist conceptions—are unstable and self-undermining. A new formulation—in the form of a deflationist conception of truth and reference—is attempted and also found wanting.

BÖHLIG, Alexander. "Zur Frage der Prädestination in Manichäismus und Christentum" in *Agora: Zu Ehren von Rudolph Berlinger*, BERLINGER, Rudolf (and other eds), 11-29. Amsterdam, Rodopi, 1988.

BOHM, David. Insight and Reason: The Role of Ratio in Education. Thinking, 5(1), 24-26, 1983.

BÖHM, Peter. "Ob das ächte Schöne erkannt werden könne?" in *Agora: Zu Ehren von Rudolph Berlinger*, BERLINGER, Rudolph (and other eds), 31-49. Amsterdam, Rodopi, 1988.

For the first time due recognition is given to two of Karl Philipp Moritz's essays. These writings of 1789 focus on the factuality of existing works of art. After the attempts to gain a clear and well-founded concept of beauty had fallen short, as neither the correlation of an autonomous subject and an equally autonomous work of art (1785) proved successful in establishing an understanding of the idea of beauty nor the irrational knowledge thereof (1788), Moritz now (1789) tests if the idea of beauty can be traced from all works of art by way of finding their common quality.

BOHMAN, James F. "Participating in Enlightenment" in *Knowledge and Politics*, DASCAL, Marcelo (ed), 264-289. Boulder, Westview Pr, 1988.

Despite his emphasis on the public sphere as a political institution, Jürgen Habermas has never developed a normative democratic theory. However, his remarks on the legitimacy of modern states indicate that such a theory would be highly cognitive and based on a description of the ideal conditions regulating participation in a process of communication issuing in a general will: a free, uncoerced consensus formed in public discourse. Such a cognitive notion of democracy as participation in public discourse also requires the critique of ideology, understood as corrective reflection on undetected restrictions on communication that permit cognitively and morally inadequate decisions.

BOHMAN, James. "System" and "Lifeworld": Habermas and the Problem of Holism. Phil Soc Crit, 15(4), 381-401, 1989.

BOHMAN, James. Critical Theory as Metaphilosophy. Metaphilosophy, 21(3), 239-252, Jl 90.

One of the basic problems of modern philosophy is to define its relation to the results of the sciences. Many argue that various sciences can replace philosophical disciplines; others claim that they only transform them. The critical theory of the Frankfurt School represents a sustained attempt to elaborate this latter, cooperative relationship between philosophy and the social sciences and is arguably the most fruitful metaphilosophical position among contemporary, competing alternatives.

BOJADZIEV, Damjan. Davidson's Semantic and Computational Understanding of Language (in Serbo-Croatian). Filozof Istraz, 30(3), 951-954, 1989.

The main concern of the paper is to evaluate the applicability of Davidson's semantics to a computational understanding of language. First, the role of a theory of truth in characterizing sentence meaning and logical form is briefly discussed; closer attention is then paid to the connection between meaning and belief in (radical) interpretation. As might have been predicted, the suggested conclusion is that the value of Davidson's semantics for computational semantics lies not so much in its concrete proposals as in its general orientation and results—its "desubstantialization of meaning." The popular objection to the effect that a computer cannot really understand, grasp the meaning, since it merely manipulates formal symbols, is thus undermined "from within," by exposing the formal core of its notions of meaning and understanding.

BOLE III, Thomas J. Metaphysical Accounts of the Zygote as a Person and the Veto Power of Facts. J Med Phil, 14(6), 647-653, D 89.

That the soul of a human person is infused at conception is a metaphysical claim. But given its traditional articulation, it has the empirical consequence that the zygote must have a substantial continuity with the adult person, a

continuity which is already determined at conception. This empirical consequence is contradicted by the fact that the zygote may become a hydatidiform mole, or several persons. The metaphysical claim is falsified by the facts.

BOLLACHER, Martin. Eine Spinoza-Reminizens in Elias Canettis autobiografischer Erzählung "Das Augenspiel". Stud Spinozana, 5, 103-118, 1989.

In volume three of his autobiography, published in 1987 under the title *Das Augenspiel*, Elias Canetti depicts the Jewish scholar Dr. Abraham Sonne (Avraham Ben Yitzhak) as a distinctive personality with a singularly impressive aura, who—in the Vienna of the mid-thirties—became his esteemed teacher and represented for him an absolute intellectual and moral authority. In this work—and this is an aspect which critics have failed to notice up to now—the historical figure of Dr. Sonne conceals behind his contours the image of the philosopher Spinoza as it was developed during the Spinoza-Renaissance in the age of Goethe: Spinoza (Sonne) appears as the type of Jewish thinker functioning in a context of unprotected freedom who knows how to keep his integrity amidst the structures of power and control and who—a true Salomonic sage—lives, thinks, and acts in the spirit of selflessness and common sense—a totally exceptional figure and yet an exemplar humanae vitae.

BOLLÉE, W. Āyāranga 2, 16 and Sūyagada 1, 16. J Indian Phil, 18(1), 29-52, Mr 90.

The paper edits, translates and discusses two chapters of the old Jain texts Āyāranga 2,16 and Sūyagada 1,16 whose titles do not fit their form and may have been exchanged. Both chapters depict an eminent monk's qualities that lead him up to final emancipation. Yet the former, metrical chapter is called "Liberation," whereas the second, prose chapter is named "The Song." The paper's author adopts Schubring's exchange theory and proposes to translate Gāha by 'eulogy' instead of 'song' in the latter chapter's title.

BOLOGNESI, Mário Fernando. Tragédia: uma alegoria da alienação. Trans/Form/Acao, 12, 23-35, 1989.

Vladímir Maiakóvski's first theater play, called *Vladímir Maiakóvsky: A Tragedy*, written in 1913, was elaborated by using an abstract symbolism. The metaphor of the characters, the metonymy in the poetry and the displacement of the main focus of the play from the subject's action towards the object contributed to the production of scenic images of alienation. The main procedure used by the author is allegory.

BOLOTIN, David. The Concerns of Odysseus: An Introduction to the *Odyssey*. Interpretation, 17(1), 41-57, Fall 89.

BOLTUC, Piotr and KMIECIK, Witold (trans). In the Beginning Was the Contradiction: Problems of the Philosophy of Subject and Object. Dialec Hum, 15(3-4), 177-185, Sum-Autumn 88.

Knowledge in the modern period is based on two perspectives. The first is the perspective of the subject; it leads to the philosophy of the cogito, the bundle theory, the sense-data theory, etc. The second is the perspective of the object; it leads to uncritical materialism and takes the primitiveness of the world of objects for granted. For it, subjectivity is not reducible to objecthood. I argue that these two perspectives are not contradictory but complementary to each other and represent two sides of the knowledge we have. But I do not reject the monism if developed in a non-(post)modern epistemological perspective.

BON JOUR, Laurence. "Replies and Clarifications" in *The Current State of the Coherence Theory*, BENDER, John W (ed), 276-292. Norwell, Kluwer, 1989.

BONACINA, Giovanni. Recenti studi sullo Hegel politico. Filosofia, 41(1), 103-116, Ja-Ap 90.

BONAGURA, Patricia. Platón filósofo-educador: valor "alusivo" de la escritura. Anu Filosof, 22(2), 37-55, 1989.

BOND, E J. Could There Be a Rationally Grounded Morality? J Phil Res, 15, 15-45, 1990.

Williams claims that the only *particular* moral truths, and perhaps the only moral truths of any kind, are nonobjective, i.e., culture-bound. For Lovibond we have moral truths when an assertion-condition is satisfied, and that is determined by the voice of the relevant moral authority as embodied in the institutions of the *sittlich* morality. According to MacIntyre one must speak from within a living tradition for which there can be no external rational grounding. However, if my criticisms of traditional philosophical ethics are sound, such relativist and historicist views are unjustified, and the project of seeking a rationally grounded morality is perfectly in order.

BONEVAC, Daniel. Paradoxes of Fulfillment. J Phil Log, 19(3), 229-252, Ag 90.

BONHOEFFER, Thomas. Le "Pari" de Pascal. Rev Theol Phil, 122(2), 189-202, 1990.

The famous text by Pascal, replaced in its biographical context and reconsidered in the light of mathematics, of psychoanalysis and of Lutheran, hermeneutical theology.

BONIECKA, Magdalena (trans) and CZEMARNIK, Adam. A Marxist's View on the Philosophy of Peace Advanced by John Paul II. Dialec Hum, 14(1), 209-217, Wint 87.

BONJOUR, Laurence. Reply to Solomon's "Apriority and Metajustification in BonJour's 'Structure of Empirical Knowledge'". Phil Phenomenol Res, 50(4), 779-782, Je 90.

BONNIE, Richard J. Medical Ethics and the Death Penalty. Hastings Center Rep, 20(3), 12-18, My-Je 90.

This article critiques ethical arguments against conducting forensic evaluations of capital defendants or condemned prisoners and against treating prisoners found incompetent for execution, and considers the impact of widespread professional abstention on the legal system. It concludes that arguments for abstention by forensic evaluators are grounded mainly in personal moral scruples against capital punishment, rather than in tenets of professional ethics, but that abstention would be ethically required if the evaluator's scruples preclude objectivity. It also concludes that treatment of incompetent prisoners known to want treatment is ethically permissible but that treatment for the sole purpose of readying the prisoner for execution is not.

BONOTTO, Cinzia. A Non-Compactness Phenomenon in Logics with Hyperintensional Predication. J Phil Log, 18(4), 383-398, N 89.

Hyperintensional predicates are those which can assume different truth values on terms having equal intensions but different senses (e.g., "to believe that..."). In the paper, Bressan's semantics for a logic with these predicates is considered and it is proved that compactness fails: a set X of formulas is characterized such that every finite subset of it is satisfiable, but X itself is not. The details of the proof focus the conditions under which an arbitrary semantics presents the same phenomena. A consequence of the result is that the relative notion of "logical consequence" is not axiomatizable.

BONSOR, Jack A. An Orthodox Historicism? Phil Theol, 4(4), 335-350, Sum 90.

This essay suggests the possible form of an orthodox historicism. The essay begins by examining the historicism of Heidegger and Gadamer. It then proposes how a theology might appear which places the faith in conversation with this historicism.

BONTEKOE, Ron. Rorty's Pragmatism and the Pursuit of Truth. Int Phil Quart, 30(2), 221-244, Je 90.

It is argued first, that the "conversational turn" which Rorty, as an advocate of tolerance, wants philosophy to take would, ironically, be disastrous for tolerance, and second, that Rorty's rejection of the pursuit of truth is unwarranted given our ability to improve the effectiveness of our languages.

BOOKCHIN, Murray. Recovering Evolution: A Reply to Eckersley and Fox. Environ Ethics, 12(3), 253-274, Fall 90.

Robyn Eckersley claims erroneously that I believe humanity is currently equipped to take over the "helm" of natural evolution. In addition, she provides a misleading treatment of my discussion of the relationship of first nature (biological evolution) and second nature (social evolution). I argue that here positivistic methodology is inappropriate in dealing with my processual approach and that her Manichaean contrast between biocentrism and anthropocentrism virtually excludes any human intervention in the natural world. I argue that Warwick Fox deals with my views on society's relationship to nature in a simplistic, narrowly deterministic, and ahistorical manner. I fault both of my deep ecology critics for little or no knowledge of my writings. I conclude with an outline of a dialectical naturalism that treats nature as an evolutionary process-not simply as a scenic view—and places human and social evolution in a graded relationship with natural evolution. I emphasize that society and humanity can no longer be separated from natural evolution and that the kind of society we achieve will either foster the development of first nature or damage the planet beyond repair. (edited)

BOOLOS, George S and JEFFREY, Richard C. *Computability and Logic (Third Edition)*. New York, Cambridge Univ Pr, 1989

BOOM, Jan. Different Conceptions of Stage in Theories of Cognitive and Moral Development. J Moral Educ, 18(3), 208-217, O 89.

The concept 'development stage' seems to be going through a revival (cf. Commons and Richards, 1984; Levin, 1986). Three positions regarding the conceptualization of development stages can be distinguished. Piaget's original formulations are presented as a starting point (Piaget, 1960).

Trends in the subdiscipline of developmental psychology concerned with the study of cognitive development are then shortly reviewed and contrasted with trends in the subdiscipline concerned with the study of moral development. In the field of moral development research, Kohlberg has proposed a hard-structural stage model which subscribes to Piaget's criteria while in the field of cognitive development most of the stage criteria specified by Piaget are regarded as untenable and the weaker notion of 'sequence' has become popular. By relating this divergence in interpretation and appreciation to trends in the methodology and theory of research concerning moral development, reasons for maintaining a hard-structural stage model are made intelligible. Characteristic of the Kohlbergian stage concept is an interest in meaning structures, structured wholeness and hierarchical integration.

BOOTH, Annie L and JACOBS, Harvey L. Ties that Bind: Native American Beliefs as a Foundation for Environmental Consciousness. Environ Ethics, 12(1), 27-43, Spr 90.

In this article we examine the specific contributions Native American thought can make to the ongoing search for a Western ecological consciousness. We begin with a review of the influence of Native American beliefs on the different branches of the modern environmental movement and some initial comparisons of Western and Native American ways of seeing. We then review Native American thought on the natural world, highlighting beliefs in the need for reciprocity and balance, the world as a living being, and relationships with animals. We conclude that Native American ideas are important, can prove inspirational in the search for a modern environmental consciousness, and affirm the arguments of both deep ecologists and ecofeminists.

BOPP, JR, James. Choosing Death for Nancy Cruzan. Hastings Center Rep, 20(1), 42-44, Ja-F 90.

BORALEVI, Lea Campos (ed) and CRANSTON, Maurice (ed). *Culture et Politique/Culture and Politics*. Hawthorne, de Gruyter, 1988

BORGES, Bento Itamar. Os Sentidos da "Crítica". Educ Filosof, 2(3), 61-79, Jl-D 87.

BORGOSZ, Jozef and PACZYNSKA, Maria (trans). Controversies and Discussions about the Post-Council Aspect of Catholic Philosophy. Dialec Hum, 14(1), 233-248, Wint 87.

BORGOSZ, Jozef and PETROWICZ, Lech (trans). A Historic Chance for Military-Technical Dealienation and the Building of a World Without War. Dialec Hum, 15(3-4), 241-250, Sum-Autumn 88.

BORICIC, Branislav R. A Note on Sequent Calculi Intermediate Between LJ and LK. Stud Log, 47(2), 151-157, Je 88.

We prove that every finitely axiomatizable extension of Heyting's intuitionistic logic has a corresponding cut-free Gentzen-type formulation. It is shown how one can use this result to find the corresponding normalizable natural deduction system and to give a criterion for separability of considered logic. Obviously, the question how to obtain an effective definition of a sequent calculus which corresponds to a concrete logic remains a separate problem for every logic.

BORILLO, Mario. Une Machine spéculative (informatique, intelligence artificielle et recherche cognitive). Rev Int Phil, 44(172), 47-61, 1990.

The central issue in cognitive research is the interaction between material and symbolic structures of cognitive processes. On the other hand, the essential of computer science—the point that differentiates it from physics and from mathematics (or logic)—is the same type of dynamic imbrication: as an empirical discipline, it describes and realizes, at instant t, the materialization of some previously known logical structures and processes; as a formal discipline, it is a theory of the computational behaviour of the material realization of these structures. The consequences of this deep homology for the knowledge of human mind are discussed.

BORNA, Shaheen. Illegal Products and the Question of Consumer Redress. J Bus Ethics, 8(6), 499-505, Je 89.

Despite the enormous size of the illicit market in the United States, there is a paucity of research concerning the rights of consumers of illegal products. In this article it is argued that the illicit nature of a transaction should not deny consumers the right to safety and redress. Recognition of these rights is not only in line with the public policy goal, i.e., protecting public interests, but it can also serve as a deterrent factor for the sales of illegal products.

BOROBIO, Luis. Forma y contenido del arte. Anu Filosof, 22(1), 113-124, 1989.

BOROBIO, Luis. La moral en las artes figurativas. Anu Filosof, 20(2), 115-119, 1987.

BORUAH, Bijoy H. Fictional Emotion, Quasi-Desire and Background Relief. Indian Phil Quart, 16(4), 409-417, O 89.

In *Art and Imagination* Roger Scruton offers an analysis of aesthetic emotions as an 'imagined counterpart' of real-life emotions. The key to this analysis is his theory of imagination, according to which imagination is a species of 'unasserted' thought essentially contrasted with belief. While belief is at the heart of real-life emotions, aesthetic emotions are founded on imagination. Despite this difference in the structure of these two emotions, our response to works of art is said to be similar to our response to real life. As Scruton writes: 'to find a work of art sad is to respond to it in the way I respond to a man when I am "touched" by his sadness'. In this paper my aim is to critically discuss Scruton's account of aesthetic emotion *vis-a-vis*, on the one hand, the contrast between imagination and belief and, on the other hand, the analysis of real-life emotions in terms of belief and desire. I shall try to show how his treatment of the problem is inadequate, and what can be done to make up for this deficiency. I shall end with a general note on the possibility of our response to fiction.

BOS, A P. Over de binding van de Griekse ontologie aan het "Titanische zinperspectief'. Phil Reform, 55(1), 34-47, 1990.

BOSCO, Domenico. L'*amour-propre*: Un tema secentesco tra morale e antropologia. Riv Filosof Neo-Scolas, 81(1), 27-67, Ja-Mr 89.

BOSCO, Domenico. Cremonini e le origini del libertinismo. Riv Filosof Neo-Scolas, 81(2), 255-293, Ap-Je 89.

BOSLEY, Richard. Virtues and Vices: East and West. J Chin Phil, 16(3-4), 387-409, D 89.

BOSTOCK, David. The Interpretation of Plato's *Crito*. Phronesis, 35(1), 1-20, 1990.

The arguments of Plato's *Crito* appear at first sight to require obedience to any and every law. The article discusses three interpretations which attempt to avoid this result, and argues that none of them can be accepted. Finally it offers some grounds for saying that Plato did genuinely intend to claim that absolutely all laws should be obeyed.

BOSWELL, Terry. The Brothers James and John Bernoulli on the Parallelism between Logic and Algebra. Hist Phil Log, 11(2), 173-184, 1990.

A short seventeenth-century text, sometimes cited as one of the first essays in mathematical logic, is introduced, translated and evaluated. Although by no means sharing the depth and magnitude of the investigations by Leibniz being undertaken at the same time, and although in particular not yet applying algebraic symbolism to logical structures, the treatise is of historical interest as an early published attempt to trace out analogies between logical and mathematical form, and may be viewed as a preliminary step toward the formalization of logic.

BOTEZ, Angela. The Human Being as Subject Matter of the Philosophy of Science. Phil Log, 32(1-2), 41-46, Ja-Je 88.

BOTIS, Gheorghe. Quelques réflexions sur une thèse marxiste (in Romanian). Rev Filosof (Romania), 35(6), 577-584, N-D 88.

BOTTANI, Livio. Metafisica e metaforica. Sapienza, 42(4), 415-434, O-D 89.

The purpose of the work is to point out the mistake of Heidegger's and Derrida's statement that between metaphysics and metaphorics exists a negative connection for which the metaphor subsists only within the sphere of metaphysics. The conclusion is that, in accordance with Ricoeur and Jüngel, metaphorics can prelude metaphysics but not necessarily, and moreover that meta-physics as theoretical ambit of word's enigma can positively connected with meta-phorics as the dimension of language's productivity.

BOTTANI, Livio. Mondo sociale, mimesi e violenza in R Girard. Sapienza, 43(2), 197-206, Ap-Je 90.

The purpose of this work is to try to specify a few of the peculiarities of Girard's thought. Between the social world and mimesis of human nature as naturally violent there is an essential connection. To break this connection is the goal which Girard ascribes to the Gospel and the Old Testament. Their teaching was to hold out the natural man's violence. (edited)

BOTTERILL, George. "Human Nature and Folk Psychology" in *The Person and the Human Mind: Issues in Ancient and Modern Philosophy*, GILL, Christopher (ed), 165-185. New York, Clarendon/Oxford Pr, 1989.

The paper explores the idea that a shared conception of human nature informs folk-psychology. It is pointed out that there is a genuine *non-sceptical* problem of other minds, and that the existence of this problem of interpretation is consistent with standard accounts of the structure of folk-psychology. After considering various ways in which the problem of interpretation might be resolved in practice, the paper concludes that it is the possession of folk-psychology itself, particularly as a means of self-presentation, that constitutes human nature.

BOTWINICK, Aryeh. Nietzsche, Foucault and the Prospects of Postmodern Political Philosophy. Manuscrito, 12(2), 117-154, O 89.

I proceed by first marshalling some pronouncedly skeptical and relativist passages in some of Nietzsche's key works and indicating the problematic to which they give rise. Next, I argue against Deleuze's postmodernist construal of the dominant tensions in Nietzsche's work. I then go on to try and show how recurring patterns of argument in Nietzsche's work—as well as some of his most famous metaphors—can be mobilized to restore consistency on the issues of skepticism and relativism. After that, and much more tentatively, I propose a conservative reading of Nietzsche's moral theory in keeping with my conservative reading of his epistemology. Next, I try to illustrate some major tensions in Foucault's thought, which undermine the viability of his postmodernism. Finally, I summarize my case against postmodernism.

BOUCHARD, Guy. Cinquante-six conceptions de l'androgynie. Dialogue (Canada), 28(4), 609-636, 1989.

Beyond the masculine and feminine stereotypes, the concept of androgyny tries to sketch a new kind of person, even a new kind of society. The objections raised against it are less based on a real disagreement than on an incomplete consideration of the relevant problems: this is what the paper shows by an analysis of 16 definitions of androgyny. This analysis yields a set of basic elements whose combination generates the 56 notions of androgyny, and allows a discussion of the main issues they raise in the context of an emerging new society without discrimination between the sexes.

BOUCHER, David. The Social and Political Thought of R G Collingwood. New York, Cambridge Univ Pr, 1989

BOUDIER, Henk Struyker. Über Gestaltkreis und Komplementarität. Man World, 23(2), 143-155, Ap 90.

Historische Untersuchungen zeigen, dass zwischen dem holländischen Arzt und Anthropologen F J J Buytendijk (1887-1974) und dem Vater der anthropologischen Medizin, Viktor von Weizsäcker (1886-1957) enge Beziehungen bestanden haben. Besonders gross war Buytendijks Bedeutung für den zentralen Begriff der anthropologischen Medizin, den Begriff "Gestaltkreis". Wie sich aus der Korrespondenz, die hier besprochen werden soll, ergibt, hat Buytendijk wesentlich zu der Ausarbeitung dieses Begriffes beigetragen. Der dem Begriff "Gestaltkreis" verwandte Begriff "Komplementarität" wurde durch Viktor von Weizsäckers Neffe, Carl Friedrich von Weizsäcker (1912 geboren) entwickelt.

BOUDON, Raymond. Why Do Social Scientists Tend to See the World as Over-Ordered? Philosophica, 44(2), 15-31, 1989.

BOUKEMA, H J M. "Is and Ought" as a Linguistic Problem. Vera Lex, 9(1), 16,28, 1989.

BOULAD-AYOUB, Josiane. Contre nous de la tyrannie: Des relations idéologiques entre Lumières et Révolution. Lasalle, Hurtubise, 1989

The political concepts and values as worked out by eighteenth-century French philosophers are studied in their pragmatical relationships with the discourse and the institutions of the French Revolution to bring out their ideological determinations and regulative action in the political struggles and the polemical debates of the time. The corpus analyzed is composed mostly of the works of the Encyclopedists, Rousseau, Saint-Just and Robespierre. Following the Kantian interpretation of the French Revolution, my conclusions assess the cultural and symbolical nature of the changes then taking place as also their signification and their range.

BOULLART, Karel. On the Essential Difference between Science, Art and Philosophy, or Philosophy as the Literature of Necessity. Commun Cog, 22(3-4), 285-301, 1989.

BOULTING, Noel E. "Conceptions of Human Action and the Justification of Value Claims" in *Inquiries into Values: The Inaugural Session of the International Society for Value Inquiry*, LEE, Sander H , 173-193. Lewiston, Mellen Pr, 1989.

BOULTING, Noel E. "Hobbes and the Problem of Rationality" in *Hobbes: War Among Nations*, AIRAKSINEN, Timo (ed), 179-189. Brookfield, Gower, 1989.

BOUNDAS, Constantin V (ed) and DELEUZE, Gilles and LESTER, Mark (trans). *The Logic of Sense—Gilles Deleuze*. New York, Columbia Univ Pr, 1990

BOURDIEU, Pierre. "The Historical Genesis of a Pure Aesthetic" in *Analytic Aesthetics*, SHUSTERMAN, Richard (ed), 147-160. Cambridge, Blackwell, 1989.

This article intends to question the ambition of capturing a transhistoric or an ahistoric essence of the work of art: the eye of the art lover is a product of history. The experience of the work of art as being immediately endowed with meaning and value is the result of the accord between the cultured habitus and the artistic field. The categories which are used in order to perceive and appreciate the work of art (like the adjectives used to express the main binary oppositions of the aesthetic judgment) are doubly bound to the historical context: linked to a situated and dated social universe, they become subject of usages which are themselves socially marked by the social position of the users.

BOURGEOIS, Bernard. La filosofía revolucionaria de la Revolución. Anu Filosof, 22(1), 9-26, 1989.

BOURGEOIS, Bernard. La spéculation hégélienne. Rev Theol Phil, 121(3), 273-289, 1989.

BOURGEOIS, Patrick L and ROSENTHAL, Sandra B. Heidegger and Peirce: Beyond "Realism or Idealism". SW Phil Rev, 4(1), 103-110, Ja 88.

In both the phenomenological ontology of Martin Heidegger and the pragmatism of Charles Peirce, the rejection of the Kantian phenomenal/noumenal distinction leads to a rejection of the alternatives of realism or idealism as well. In their respective denials of such an existential or ontological gap between appearance or phenomena and the ontologically real, they each establish a fundamental intentional unity between man and world which cannot be understood within the framework of realism or of idealism and which reveals deeply rooted affinities between the two positions.

BOURGEOIS, Patrick L and ROSENTHAL, Sandra B. The Philosophy of the Act and the Phenomenology of Perception: Mead and Merleau-Ponty. S J Phil, 28(1), 77-90, Spr 90.

Mead and Merleau-Ponty each portray the perceptual field as a field of spatially and temporally located, ontologically "thick" or resisting objects which are essentially related to the horizon of world, which allow for the very structure of the sensing which gives access to them, and whose manner of emergence undercuts the problematics of the subject-object split. This essay surveys this perceptual field as a focus for eliciting their more fundamental shared understanding of the dimensions of human activity which underlie its emergence.

BOURGEOIS, Patrick L and ROSENTHAL, Sandra B. Sensation, Perception and Immediacy: Mead and Merleau-Ponty. SW Phil Rev, 6(1), 105-111, Ja 90.

A focus on the relation between sensation and the perceptual object in the philosophies of G H Mead and Maurice Merleau-Ponty points toward their shared views of perception as non-reductionistic and holistic, as inextricably tied to the active role of the sensible body, and as involving a new understanding of the nature of immediacy within experience. This essay explores these shared views.

BOURGOIS, Bernard. Lévy-Bruhl et Hegel. Rev Phil Fr, 179(4), 449-451, O-D 89.

BOURKE, Vernon J. "Aquinas" in *Ethics in the History of Western Philosophy*, CAVALIER, Robert J (ed), 98-124. New York, St Martin's Pr, 1988.

Thomas Aquinas changed western ethics from Christian Platonism to a more naturalistic moral theory in which Aristotle's ethics played a role. Besides the *Summa of Theology* and Book III, *Summa contra Gentiles*, seven other writings indicate how Aquinas used analyses of human virtue, natural law precepts, and right reason to develop this new ethics. His handling of some special problems (homicide in self-defence, usury, gambling, just war) illustrates how Thomistic ethics works. It influenced later ethics: the Spanish Commentators, Cambridge Platonists and Caroline Casuists, and recent moralities of human virtue.

BOUSCAREN, E. Elementary Pairs of Models. Annals Pure Applied Log, 45(2), 129-137, D 89.

We give a survey of some recent results and some remaining questions concerning the model theory of elementary pairs of models of a complete first-order theory, in the language with a new predicate for the small model of the pair.

BOUSCAREN, Elisabeth and POIZAT, Bruno. Des belles paires aux beaux uples. J Sym Log, 53(2), 434-442, Je 88.

BOUVERESSE, Jacques. L'"infaillibilité" de l'introspection: Autour de Dennett et de Wittgenstein. Rev Theol Phil, 122(2), 217-233, 1990.

BOWIE, Norman E. "The Paradox of Profit" in *Papers on the Ethics of Administration*, WRIGHT, N Dale (ed), 97-120. Albany, SUNY Pr, 1988.

BOWKER, John W. Cosmology, Religion, and Society. Zygon, 25(1), 7-23, Mr 90.

It is a mistake to assume that science and religion are competing accounts of the same subject matter, so that either science supersedes religion or religion

anticipates science. Using the question of cosmic origins as an example, I argue that the basic task of religion is not the scientific one of establishing the most accurate account of the origin of the universe. Rather, as illustrated from Jewish, Hindu, Chinese, and Buddhist thought, religion uses a variety of cosmologies to help specify the necessary terms and conditions on which human social life is possible in particular ecological niches.

BOWLES, George. Favorable Relevance and Arguments. Inform Log, 11(1), 11-17, Wint 89.

The actual or attributed favorable relevance of one proposition to another is a necessary condition of the former's being a premise and the latter the conclusion of an argument, because a group of propositions constitutes an argument only if some of them are, or at least are said to be, (good) reasons for another; and something is a (good) reason for something else only if it is favorably relevant to it. Moreover, attributed, rather than actual, favorable relevance is a necessary condition for an argument. For only thus can we avoid a prohibition against calling some arguments 'arguments'.

BOWLES, George. Professor Kasachkoff on Explaining and Justifying. Inform Log, 11(2), 107-110, Spr 89.

The purpose of this paper is critically to examine the five arguments that Tziporah Kasachkoff offers in "Explaining and Justifying" (*Informal Logic*, Vol. X, No. 1 (Winter 1988), pp. 21-30) for her claim that the evaluation of a discourse is affected by whether the discourse is an explanation or a justificatory argument. I conclude that none succeeds.

BOWMAN, Elizabeth A and STONE, Robert V. "Dialectical Ethics: A First Look at Sartre's Unpublished Rome Lecture Notes" in *Inquiries into Values: The Inaugural Session of the International Society for Value Inquiry*, LEE, Sander H, 335-361. Lewiston, Mellen Pr, 1989.

BOYD, Dwight. Professionalization and the Moral Jeopardy of Teaching. Proc Phil Educ, 45, 102-118, 1989.

This paper addresses the question, "What is being professionalized in the professionalization of teaching?" It first analyzes the moral stance of the teacher in ways designed both to reveal its complexity and to explicate its necessity. Questions are then raised about whether two structural requirements of professionalization can accommodate this essential dimension of teaching.

BOYD, George N. Schleiermacher's "Über den Unterschied zwischen Naturgesetz und Sittengesetz". J Relig Ethics, 17(2), 41-49, Fall 89.

Schleiermacher's Berlin Academy lecture took issue with the Kantian-Fichtean view of the radical difference between natural law and moral law, arguing that moral law, like natural law, is fundamentally descriptive of being, not prescriptive and independent of any embodiment in moral action. This essay seeks to generalize Schleiermacher's argument that a teleological premise underlies and provides whatever force is possessed by Kant's abstract imperative into an argument for the presence of a teleological premise in any normative ethic. Finally it summarizes and comments on Schleiermacher's remarkable outline of biological evolution.

BOYLE, Joseph M and FINNIS, John and GRISEZ, Germain. *Nuclear Deterrence, Morality and Realism*. New York, Oxford Univ Pr, 1988

Nuclear deterrence expresses a conditional choice to kill noncombatants, a choice irreconcilable with traditional morality. Having fully surveyed official threats and systems, we examine the crucial conceptual and strategic questions: Why are conditional choices morally decisive? Why can't deterrence be a bluff? Or purely counterforce? We then argue that neither deterrence nor unilateral disarmament can be justified by the other's bad consequences, and that all consequentialist justifications are inevitably incoherent. Exploring the foundations of ethics, we conclude to an ethics of killing similar to common morality's, and try to identify the specific duties of policy makers, military personnel and citizens.

BOYLE, Joseph. Natural Law, Ownership and the World's Natural Resources. J Value Inq, 23(3), 191-207, S 89.

BOYLE, Joseph. "Sanctity of Life and Suicide: Tensions and Developments Within Common Morality" in *Suicide and Euthanasia*, BRODY, Baruch A (ed), 221-250. Norwell, Kluwer, 1989.

BOZICEVIC, Vanda. Verbal and Pictorial Signification (in Serbo-Croatian). Filozof Istraz, 30(3), 989-1001, 1989.

The aim of this article is to propose semantic criteria for the differentiation between verbal and pictorial modes of signifying. Starting with Peirce's differentiation between symbols and icons, as well as de Saussure's definition of language as an arbitrary and linear sign system, leaning on Goodman's theory of notation, as well as on his critical abandoning of the notion of similarity as the traditional explanation of pictorial representation. The possible criteria, such as natural vs. conventional, arbitrary vs. nonarbitrary, atomistic vs. holistic, syntactically and semantically differentiated vs. syntactically and semantically dense, are thoroughly examined and discussed. Finally, the discussion reaches the conclusion that none of the proposed pairs of notions offer a strict criterion for the differentiation between verbal and pictorial. The criterion that the author suggests redefines Peirce's differentiation between symbols and icons, replacing the notion of similarity by the notion of referential use of perceptual codes.

BRABECK, Mary M (ed). *Who Cares: Theory, Research and Educational Implications of the Ethic of Care.* Westport, Greenwood Pr, 1989

This book presents the work of scholars from philosophy, theology, psychology, and education who critically examine the ethic of care. The book begins with a historical discussion of caring as described by women philosophers of the past two millenia. Further chapters discuss the ethic of care; the gender relatedness of care; the political and psychological price of attributing care to women; the socialization experiences that shape and develop the caring response and the caring self; the relationship between care and rationality and between care and justice; the distinction between a theory of care based on the norms of society and moral philosophy; ethical framework of Black, Third World, and "pink collar" women.

BRACKEN, Joseph A. Energy-Events and Fields. Process Stud, 18(3), 153-165, Fall 89.

The author argues that Whiteheadian "societies" should be understood as environments or fields for the psychic energy-events ("actual occasions") taking place within them. Furthermore, these fields possess an objective unity and exercise a collective agency derivative from the agency of their interrelated constituent occasions. Unlike actual occasions, however, societies are not themselves subjects of experience which make "decisions" with respect to their self-constitution. Where a society thus appears to act as a unified subject of experience (as in the case of a human being), it does so through the actual occasions constitutive of its principal subsociety, namely, the "soul."

BRACKIN, Stephen H. Partitions with no Coarsenings of Higher Degree. Z Math Log, 35(4), 363-366, 1989.

There exist partitions of the natural numbers into an infinite number of classes such that these partitions have no coarsenings of higher Turing degree. The proof is similar to the proof of an analogous result for sets, but uses the Simpson-Carlson Dual Ellentuck theorem in place of the Galvin-Prikry theorem.

BRADBURY, Judith A. The Policy Implications of Differing Concepts of Risk. Sci Tech Human Values, 14(4), 380-399, Autumn 8.

The author draws on the policy analysis literature to delineate the linkage between conceptualization of risk and the formulation and proposed solution of risk-related policy problems. Two concepts of risk are identified: (1) a concept of risk as a physically given attribute of hazardous technologies, and (2) a concept of risk as a socially constructed attribute. The argument is advanced that the social construction of risk provides a firm, theoretical basis for the design of policy. The discussion links the perception, management, and communication of risk to the more fundamental issue of the nature and role of science and technology.

BRADDON-MITCHELL, David and FITZPATRICK, John. Explanation and the Language of Thought. Synthese, 83(1), 3-29, Ap 90.

In this paper we argue that the insistence by Fodor et al. that the language of thought hypothesis must be true rests on mistakes about the kinds of explanations that must be provided of cognitive phenomena. After examining the canonical arguments for the LOT, we identify a weak version of the LOT hypothesis which we think accounts for some of the intuitions that there must be a LOT. We then consider what kinds of explanation cognitive phenomena require, and conclude that three main confusions lead to the invalid inference of the truth of a stronger LOT hypothesis from the weak and trivial version. These confusions concern the relationship between syntax and semantics, the nature of higher-level causation in cognitive science, and differing roles of explanations invoking intrinsic structures of minds on the one hand, and aetiological or evolutionary accounts of their properties on the other.

BRADFORD, Jeffrey L and GARRETT, Dennis E and MEYERS, Renee A and BECKER, Joy. Issues Management and Organizational Accounts: An Analysis of Corporate Responses to Accusation of Unethical Business. J Bus Ethics, 8(7), 507-520, Jl 89.

When external groups accuse a business organization of unethical practices, managers of the accused organization usually offer a communicative response to attempt to protect their organization's public image. Even though many researchers readily concur that analysis of these communicative responses is important to our understanding of business and society conflict, few investigations have focused on developing a *theoretical*

framework for analyzing these communicative strategies used by managers. In additon, research in this area has suffered from a *lack of empirical investigation*. In this paper we address both of these weaknesses in the existing literature. (edited)

BRADFORD, R W. New Gods for Old: In Defense of Libertarianism. Free Inq, 9(4), 5-7, Fall 89.

BRADIE, Michael. "Evolutionary Epistemology as Naturalized Epistemology" in *Issues in Evolutionary Epistemology*, HAHLWEG, Kai (ed), 393-412. Albany, SUNY Pr, 1989.

The theory of biological evolution suggests that the human capacity for knowledge and belief is shaped by evolutionary forces and should be treated and analyzed by the methods of science. Evolutionary epistemologies are attempts to carry out this agenda. This paper explores the relationship between two programs in current evolutionary epistemology: (1) the evolution of cognitive mechanisms and (2) the evolution of knowledge, and the wider domain of naturalistic epistemologies in general. The relevance of the theory of evolution for progarm 1 is clear but problematic for program 2.

BRADLEY, James. Alasdair MacIntyre on the Good Life and the 'Narrative Model'. Heythrop J, 31(3), 324-326, Jl 90.

BRADY, F Neil. "Ethical Theory and Public Service" in *Papers on the Ethics of Administration*, WRIGHT, N Dale (ed), 225-241. Albany, SUNY Pr, 1988.

The primary purpose of this paper is to illustrate the practical application of ethical theory to the reasoning underlying landmark Supreme Court cases. It shows how the form of ethical reasoning used is determined by the issue: the issue of equality is basically formalistic; the issue of freedom is primarily utilitarian; and the issue of property, originally utilitarian, has required a formalistic approach in recent decades. The paper then briefly examines the status of ethical theory for the public administrator's use of discretionary power.

BRADY, Ross T. A Content Semantics for Quantified Relevant Logics, I. Stud Log, 47(2), 111-127, Je 88.

We present an algebraic-style of semantics, which we call a "content semantics," for quantified relevant logics based on the weak system BBQ. We show soundness and completeness for all quantificational logics extending BBQ and also treat reduced modelling for all systems containing BB^dQ. The key idea of content semantics is that true entailments $A \rightarrow B$ are represented under interpretation I as content containments, i.e. $I(A)$ less than or equal to $I(B)$ (or, the content of A contains that of B). This is opposed to the truth-functional way which represents true entailments as truth-preservations over all set-ups (or worlds), i.e. $(\forall a \epsilon K)$ (if $I(A, a) = T$ then $I(B, a) = T$).

BRADY, Ross T. A Content Semantics for Quantified Relevant Logics, II. Stud Log, 48(2), 243-257, Je 89.

In Part I, we presented an algebraic-style of semantics, which we called "content semantics," for quantified relevant logics based on the weak system BBQ. We showed soundness and completeness with respect to the *unreduced* semantics of BBQ. In part II, we proceed to show soundness and completeness for extensions of BBQ with respect to this type of semantics. We introduce *reduced* semantics which requires additional postulates for primeness and saturation. We then conclude by showing soundness and completeness for BB^dQ and its extensions with respect to this reduced semantics.

BRADY, Ross T. The Gentzenization and Decidability of RW. J Phil Log, 19(1), 35-73, F 90.

BRADY, Ross T. A Routley-Meyer Affixing Style Semantics for Logics Containing Aristotle's Thesis. Stud Log, 48(2), 235-241, Je 89.

We provide a semantics for relevant logics with addition of Aristotle's Thesis, $\sim(A \rightarrow \sim A)$ and also Boethius, $(A \rightarrow B) \rightarrow \sim(A \rightarrow \sim B)$. We adopt the Routley-Meyer affixing style of semantics but include in the model structures a regulatory structure for all interpretations of formulae, with a view to obtaining a less ad hoc semantics than those previously given for such logics. Soundness and completeness are proved, and in the completeness proof, a new corollary to the Priming Lemma is introduced (c.f. *Relevant Logics and their Rivals I*, Ridgeview, 1982).

BRAGUE, Rémi. Athènes, Jérusalem, La Mecque: L'interprétation "musulmane" de la philosophie grecque chez Leo Strauss. Rev Metaph Morale, 94(3), 309-336, Jl-S 89.

BRAGUE, Rémi. Le fou stoïcien. Rev Phil Fr, 180(2), 175-184, Ap-Je 90.

BRAKAS, George. *Aristotle's Concept of the Universal.* Hildesheim, Olms, 1988

This work argues that Aristotle's concept of the universal went through three phases. According to his early view, a universal is an existent asserted of several other existents (a particular being asserted of none). It tries to clarify this concept by explicating the two major terms of its definition, 'an existent' (on) and 'is asserted of'. It explains 'an existent' on the basis of his doctrine of the categories and 'is asserted of' (or 'is said of') on the basis of his early theory of the simple statement. According to his middle view, a universal is still an existent, but it is now distinguished from particulars by being in several other existents. According to his late view, a universal is no longer an actually existing thing at all, but a mere potency.

BRANDES, Wolfgang and WEISE, Peter. A Synergetic View of Institutions. Theor Decis, 28(2), 173-187, Mr 90.

In this paper we attempt to demonstrate how, in the course of human cooperation, compulsions and forces come into existence which compel individuals into regularities of behavior. These behavioral regularities are labelled institutions; the approach selected is called synergetic, since it considers institutions to be the result of combined human actions. The compulsions and forces which emerge from human cooperation are generated by the individuals' dependencies, struggles for independence, and preferences. Whereas individuals act freely as subjects, they become objects under the compulsions and forces of compressed social interdependence.

BRANDL, Johannes. "Was heisst vollständige Verifikation?" in Wittgenstein in Focus—Im Brennpunkt: Wittgenstein, MC GUINNESS, Brian (ed), 227-247. Amsterdam, Rodopi, 1989.

Wittgenstein meint, nur ein endliches Verifikationsverfahren könne einem Satz Sinn verleihen. Darin unterscheidet er sich sowohl vom alten Verifikationismus des Wiener Kreises als auch von neueren Bedeutungstheorien, die den Satzsinn durch die Bedingungen des berechtigten Behauptens erklären wollen. Es wird gezeigt, dass beide Positionen in einen Regress münden, sobald sie Wittgensteins Forderung nach vollständiger Verifizierbarkeit ernst nehmen. Weder der epistemische Begriff des "endgültigen" Verifizierens noch der semantische Begriff der "ausgezeichneten" Verifikation kommen ohne einen externen Bezugspunkt wie Wahrheit oder Rationalität aus. Da Wittgenstein jedes Verbindungsglied ablehnt, das noch zwischen den Satz und seine Verifikation treten kann, bleibt für ihn als Ideal der Vollständigkeit nur der Punkt, an dem sich die Erklärungskraft einer zue Demonstration vorgeführten Verifikation erschöpft. Zue Erläuterung dieser Position wird auf die Tractatus-These der internen Relationen und auf das Argument des Regelfolgens zurückgegriffen.

BRANDON, E P. On What Isn't Learned in School. Thinking, 5(4), 22-28, 1985.

BRANDS, Maarten. "Political Culture: Pendulum Swing of a Paradigm?" in Culture et Politique/Culture and Politics, CRANSTON, Maurice (ed), 130-137. Hawthorne, de Gruyter, 1988.

BRANDT, James M. Ritschl's Critique of Schleiermacher's Theological Ethics. J Relig Ethics, 17(2), 51-72, Fall 89.

The interpreter of Friedrich Schleiermacher's theological ethics faces a historical paradox: on the one hand, Schleiermacher's theological ethics have been judged by many to be inadequate, and on the other hand, careful analysis of his major work in theological ethics (Die christliche Sitte or Sittenlehre) is lacking. This essay considers Albrecht Ritschl's complaint about the status of the ethical in Schleiermacher's theological system and responds with an analysis of the latter's view of theology and of Christian piety. It concludes that Schleiermacher accords ethics a definite and significant place in his theological system.

BRANDT, R B. Practical Rationality: A Response. Phil Phenomenol Res, 50(1), 125-130, S 89.

BRANDT, R B. The Science of Man and Wide Reflective Equilibrium. Ethics, 100(2), 259-278, Ja 90.

The aim is to identify some problems and puzzles in Rawls's conception of reflective equilibrium, to consider what he thinks reflective equilibrium shows, and to compare his result with asking the question what sort of moral system we should want for our society if we were fully rational and expected to live a lifetime in it.

BRANDT, Reinhard. "Analytic/Dialectic" in Reading Kant, SCHAPER, Eva (ed), 179-195. Cambridge, Blackwell, 1989.

The work first analyses the genesis and structure of the concept of analysis and dialectic as a "logic of truth" and a "logic of appearance" in the Kritik der reinen Vernunft. This is followed by an investigation into the changes the system underwent in the 80s. Both in the Kritik der praktischen Vernunft and the "Kritik der ästhetischen Urteilskraft," dialectic is entrusted with the deduction of ideas (the highest Good, the transcendental) which are

essential to the possibility of morality and aesthetic judgment.

BRANDT, Reinhard. Feder und Kant. Kantstudien, 80(3), 249-264, 1989.

This paper outlines the philosophical writings of J G H Feder as a whole and then the point of dissension with respect to Kant and his transcendental idealism. After a brief discussion of the various general forms of idealism, the conclusion is reached that Feder's commonsense realism fails to overcome the way-of-ideas and is subject to Kant's critique, on the other hand, however, that Kant does not consider idealism refuted even after 1781, thus implicitly acknowledging the correctness of Feder's objection.

BRANDT, Richard B. Comment on Chad Hansen's "Language Utilitarianism". J Chin Phil, 16(3-4), 381-385, D 89.

BRANN, Eva. Excellence and the Pursuit of Ideas. Thinking, 5(3), 2-7, 1984.

BRANQUINHO, João. Are Salmon's 'Guises' Disguised Fregean Senses? Analysis, 50(1), 19-24, Ja 90.

My paper contains an argument for a negative answer to the question which constitutes its title. In particular, I examine a claim which has been recently advanced by Graeme Forbes to the effect that Salmon's Millian analysis of belief ascriptions might be regarded as a mere notational variant of a certain version of a neo-Fregean theory, in which case the notion of a guise as employed in the former sort of account would turn out to be indistinguishable from the notion of a Fregean sense as employed in the later sort of account. Forbes's claim is deemed unsound on the basis that his neo-Fregean analysis does not yield the same consequences, concerning the truth-values of certain belief reports, as Salmon's account.

BRANTE, Thomas. Empirical and Epistemological Issues in Scientists' Explanations of Scientific Stances: A Critical Synthesis. Soc Epistem, 3(4), 281-295, O-D 89.

BRATMAN, Michael E. Dretske's Desires. Phil Phenomenol Res, 50(4), 795-800, Je 90.

BRAUN, Karl-Heinz. Marxismus—Subjektwissenschaft—Psychoanalyse. Deut Z Phil, 37(9), 834-842, 1989.

BRAUNER, Daniel J and POIRIER, Suzanne. The Voices of the Medical Record. Theor Med, 11(1), 29-39, Mr 90.

The medical record, as a managerial, historic, and legal document, serves many purposes. Although its form may be well established and many of the cases documented in it 'routine' in medical experience, what is written in the medical record nevertheless records decisions and actions of individuals. Viewed as an interpretive 'text', it can itself become the object of interpretation. This essay applies literary theory and methodology to the structure, content, and writing style(s) of an actual medical record for the purpose of exploring the relationship between the forms and language of medical discourse and the daily decisions surrounding medical treatment. The medical record is shown to document not only the absence of a consistent treatment plan for the patient studied but also a breakdown in communication between different health professionals caring for that patient. The paper raises questions about the kind of education being given to house staff in this instance. The essay concludes with a consideration of how such situations might be more generally avoided.

BREAZEALE, Daniel. Lange, Nietzsche, and Stack: The Question of "Influence". Int Stud Phil, 21(2), 91-103, 1989.

BREINER, Peter. Democratic Autonomy, Political Ethics, and Moral Luck. Polit Theory, 17(4), 550-574, N 89.

BRELL JR, Carl D. Critical Thinking as Transfer: Reconstructive Integration of Otherwise Discrete Interpretations of Experience. Educ Theor, 40(1), 53-68, Wint 90.

BRENNAN, Geoffrey and LOMASKY, Loren E. "Large Numbers, Small Costs: The Uneasy Foundations of Democratic Rule" in Politics and Process, BRENNAN, Geoffrey (ed), 42-59. New York, Cambridge Univ Pr, 1989.

Economists typically attempt to explain voting as wealth-maximizing behavior. A major source of embarrassment for this view is that, under reasonable assumptions of cost and expected return, individuals in large-number electorates will not vote. Nonetheless, millions do. We propose a revised model in which voting is understood primarily as maximizing expressive returns. Some consequences are (i) individuals will rationally vote otherwise than they would choose were they decisive; (ii) policies may emerge that are suboptimal for everyone; (iii) electoral outcomes, relative to private activity, will manifest extremes of both altruism and malice. We conclude by developing normative implications of the model.

BRENNAN, Geoffrey (ed) and LOMASKY, Loren E (ed). Politics and

Process. New York, Cambridge Univ Pr, 1989

The ten contributions to this volume from philosophers, economists, and political scientists evaluate democratic principles and processes as mechanisms through which individual preferences are translated into public policies. Although the essays represent a diverse range of interests and methodologies, each addresses the problem of imperfections that attend the translation process. The authors appraise the status of democratic institutions and foundational democratic theory in light of these imperfections.

BRENNAN, Timothy J. A Methodological Assessment of Multiple Utility Frameworks. Econ Phil, 5(2), 189-208, O 89.

Economics has been criticized because it models preferences as if all choices are comparable. Proposed "multiple utility" alternatives distinguish either among hierarchies or preference or between community and private values. Economic models, however, can readily be adapted to deal with the logical or empirical problems motivating these proposals. Attempts to capture the moral standing of choices through their distinctions among preferences or values exemplify the "naturalistic fallacy." Successful and desirable reform of economics requires direct analyses of the morality of preferences and concept of agency; formalist "multiple utility" frameworks are of little help.

BRENNER, Anastasios A. Holism a Century Ago: The Elaboration of Duhem's Thesis. Synthese, 83(3), 325-335, Je 90.

Duhem first expounds the holistic thesis, according to which an experimental test always involves several hypotheses, in articles dating from the 1890s. Poincaré's analysis of a recent experiment in optics provides the incentive, but Duhem generalizes this analysis and develops a highly original methodological position. He is led to reject inductivism. I will endeavor to show the crucial role history of science comes to play in the development of Duhem's holism.

BRENNER, William H. *Elements of Modern Philosophy: Descartes through Kant.* Englewood Cliffs, Prentice-Hall, 1989

This is an elegant, perspicuous presentation of key ideas and arguments of classical modern philosophers, along with samples of their writings: *Monadology*; excerpts from Spinoza's *Ethics*, Locke's *Essay*, Berkeley's *Principles*, Kant's first *Critique*. It is meant to be supplemented with complete texts from Descartes and Hume.

BRENNER-GOLOMB, N and VAN BRAKEL, J. Putnam on Davidson on Conceptual Schemes. Dialectica, 43(3), 263-269, 1989.

In *Dialectica* 41, 1987, Putnam claims to refute Davidson's objection to conceptual relativity by showing that knowledge of a *chosen* conceptual scheme (CS) is necessary for answering questions of existence, and thus, is a constraint on interpretation. Using his examples we defend Davidson's claim that their interpretation is a condition for attributing a CS to the speaker. We show that Putnam's discussion of the debate between Kant and Leibniz, or Carnap and the Polish Logician, displays all the characteristics of ascribing beliefs and a *language scheme* simultaneously, rather than choosing a CS and then considering which sentences are true.

BRENTANO, Franz and LAUNAY, Marc B (trans). L'origine de la connaissance morale, traduit par M B de Launay. Rev Metaph Morale, 95(1), 3-32, Ja-Mr 90.

BRETT, Nathan. Hume: Justice as Property. Man Nature, 6, 55-72, 1987.

Hume claims to show that justice is an artificial virtue. But he in fact argues that *property* rules have a basis in convention. With Locke, he claims that "to convince us that where there is no property there can be no injustice, is only necessary to define the terms...." The paper explores the skeptical possibility that Hume never managed to say a word about justice because this supposed logical connection does not exist. In partial defense of Hume, however, it is argued that the conventions which he sees as constitutive of property have impartiality and reciprocity built into them.

BREUVART, Jean-Marie. Notion et idée de science chez Eric Weil. Arch Phil, 52(4), 589-609, O-D 89.

The author tries to revisit Weil's communication entitled *La Science et la Civilisation Moderne ou le Sens de l'Insensé*, in the light of Kantian terms of notion and idea. The notion of a science, as devoid of any human interest, contrasts with the ideal of science, which has become more and more insistent in the quest of life's sense, and yet more and more senseless. On the other hand, the coherently discoursing philosopher tries to maintain as accepted two levels of coherent discourse, namely that discourse of science which is not attached to human interest, and that which characterizes the reasonable and sensible life. Pic de la Mirandole and Pomponazzi, inasmuch as they have been studied by Weil, both appear to prepare such a conception of relationships and differences between scientific research and reasonable life. Thus, they are contributing to define the very touchstone of a sane modernity, without appealing to a transcendent principle of unity,

nor confusing the two mentioned levels of coherence.

BRIANCESCO, Eduardo. Lenguaje y misterio en Anselmo de Canterbury. Pat Med, 10, 57-63, 1989.

BRICKER, Phillip. Quantified Modal Logic and the Plural *De Re*. Midwest Stud Phil, 14, 372-394, 1989.

Modal sentences of the form "Every F might be G" and "Some F must be G" have a threefold ambiguity. In addition to the familiar readings *de dicto* and *de re*, there is a third reading on which they are examples of the *plural de re*: they attribute a modal property to the F's plurally in a way that cannot in general be reduced to an attribution of modal properties to the individual F's. The plural *de re* readings of modal sentences cannot be captured within standard quantified modal logic. I consider various strategies for extending standard quantified modal logic so as to provide analyses of the readings in question. I argue that the ambiguity in question is associated with the scope of the general term 'F'; and that plural quantifiers can be introduced for purposes of representing the scope of a general term. Moreover, plural quantifiers provide the only fully adequate solution that keeps within the framework of quantified modal logic.

BRICKHOUSE, Thomas C and SMITH, Nicholas D. A Matter of Life and Death in Socratic Philosophy. Ancient Phil, 9 (2), 155-165, Fall 89.

In this paper we argue that Socrates believes that everyone is better off dead. This belief, we argue, does not contradict either his famous profession of ignorance of what happens at death nor his conviction that certain lives are, and certain lives are not, worth living. Finally, we show why Socrates thinks that all human beings have reason to make themselves as good as possible while they are alive in spite of the fact that a better condition awaits them at death.

BRICKHOUSE, Thomas C and SMITH, Nicholas D. *Socrates on Trial.* Princeton, Princeton Univ Pr, 1989

This book attempts to provide an exhaustive historical and philosophical commentary on Plato's *Apology of Socrates*. Contrary to the received interpretation of the *Apology*, the authors argue that Plato's Socrates makes a sincere attempt to persuade the jury of his innocence.

BRICKHOUSE, Thomas C and SMITH, Nicholas D. What Makes Socrates a Good Man? J Hist Phil, 28(2), 169-179, Ap 90.

This paper attempts to explain why Socrates is convinced that he is a good person even through he lacks the moral virtue he says he has spent his life seeking.

BRIDGES, Douglas S. A General Constructive Intermediate Value Theorem. Z Math Log, 35(5), 433-435, 1989.

BRIEN, Andrew. Can God Forgive Us Our Trespasses? Sophia (Australia), 28(2), 35-42, Jl 89.

In his paper "Can God Forgive Us Our Trespasses?" (*Sophia*, Vol. 25, July 1986, pp. 4-10), David Londey argues that it is logically impossible for an ideal moral agent (IMA) to forgive and act rightly. In my paper I argue that his argument fails for at least two reasons. First, it is invalid due to equivocation between types of 'ought' in his argument. Second, even if the argument were valid, it cannot guarantee the truth of the conclusion because it rests upon Londey's account of forgiveness, which is, itself, false. The paper has three sections. In the first section I set out the distinction between 'oughts'. In the second section I consider the validity of the argument in the light of this. In the third section I consider Londey's account of forgiveness.

BRIEN, Andrew. Saving Grace. Crim Just Ethics, 9(1), 52-59, Wint-Spr 90.

Jeffrie Murphy has argued that "mercy," as it is usually understood, is incompatible with the duties that a judge is thought to have in a criminal trial. Murphy, however, recently presented a strategem to save grace and show that it is, in principle, possible for a judge in a criminal case to be merciful. In this paper I argue that not only is Murphy's strategem unsuccessful but, more importantly, it is unnecessary. In the first part I set out the arguments—or as I shall refer to them, conundrums—Murphy uses to show that the relationship of mercy to legal justice is problematic. In the second part I set out Murphy's strategem to cope with these conundrums. In the third part I present my arguments against Murphy's strategem.

BRIGHOUSE, M H. Blackburn's Projectivism—An Objection. Phil Stud, 59(2), 225-233, Je 90.

This article explores Simon Blackburn's neo-emotivist alternative to J L Mackie's 'error' theory of ethics. It argues that proper justification of his subjectivist position on the phenomenology of value judgments requires at least a system of rules of translation from English to his artificial 'expressivist' language. Not only does Blackburn not provide this, but there are intuitively meaningful sentences in the moral fragment of English for which there are not even ad hoc equivalents in the expressivist language. Hence, he fails to justify his thoroughgoing subjectivism.

BRINGSJORD, Selmer. Grim on Logic and Omniscience. Analysis, 49(4), 186-189, O 89.

In this paper an argument, due to Patrick Grim, that there can be no omniscient being because of work done by Cantor is attacked—partly by appeal to axiomatic set theories other than ZF, partly by appeal to things not even God can know.

BRINK, Chris. R-Algebras and R-Model Structures as Power Constructs. Stud Log, 48(1), 85-109, Mr 89.

In relevance logic it has become commonplace to associate with each logic both an algebraic counterpart and a relational counterpart. The former comes from the Lindenbaum construction; the latter, called a model structure, is designed for semantical purposes. Knowing that they are related through the logic, we may enquire after the algebraic relationship between the algebra and the model structure. This paper offers a complete solution for the relevance logic obtained from the standard relevance logic R of Anderson and Belnap by adding to it a Boolean negation operator over and above its own De Morgan negation operator. Namely, the algebras and model structures for this logic can be obtained from each other, and represented in terms of each other, by application of power constructions. (edited)

BRINTON, Alan. Agnosticism and Atheism. Sophia (Australia), 28(3), 2-6, O 89.

BRION-GUERRY, Liliane. "Signification des modifications morphologiques de la coupole: LE TEMPS et le temps" in Cultural Hermeneutics of Modern Art: Essays in Honor of Jan Aler, DETHIER, Hubert (ed), 105-118. Amsterdam, Rodopi, 1989.

BRITO, Emilio. Infinité et omniprésence divines: Thomas d'Aquin et Hegel. G Metaf, 11(2), 163-190, My-Ag 89.

BRITO, Emilio. La volonté en Dieu: Thomas d'Aquin et Hegel. Rev Phil Louvain, 87(76), 391-426, Ag 89.

The present study compares the Thomist doctrine of the will in God with the Hegelian theory of the will of the Idea and of the freedom of the Spirit. Hegel's Idea, which, unlike Thomas's God, lacks any truly ecstatic volitional tendency, articulates only the assimilating moment of the self-knowledge of the absolute Spirit. But Thomas does not sufficiently show the link between divine freedom, which Hegel is wrong to deny, and the necessary rationality of divine freedom, which Hegel perceived in depth. Hence an attempt has been made, finally, to decipher the absoluteness of freedom in conciliating the Thomist projection of possibles with the Hegelian introjection of necessity.

BROAD, C D (ed) and MC TAGGART, John McTaggart Ellis. The Nature of Existence, Volume I. New York, Cambridge Univ Pr, 1988

This volume is a reprint of McTaggart's now-classic defense of idealism which was originally published in 1927. The entire work (2 volumes) represents the author's theory of the nature of the universe. Volume 1 sets out "to determine as far as possible the characteristics which belong to all that exists, or which belong to existence as a whole." (staff)

BROAD, C D (ed) and MC TAGGART, John McTaggart Ellis. The Nature of Existence, Volume II. New York, Cambridge Univ Pr, 1988

This volume is a reprint of McTaggart's now-classic defense of idealism which was originally published in 1927. The entire work (2 volumes) represents the author's theory of the nature of the universe. Volume 2 is an "empirical inquiry into the consequences of theoretical or practical interest that can be drawn from the general nature of the universe." (staff)

BROADIE, Alexander. Notion and Object: Aspects of Late Medieval Epistemology. New York, Oxford Univ Pr, 1989

BROCK, Dan W. Biomedical Ethics: Some Lessons for Social Philosophy. J Soc Phil, 20(1-2), 108-115, Spr-Fall 89.

BRÖCKER, Walter. "Heideggers Kehren" in Agora: Zu Ehren von Rudolph Berlinger, BERLINGER, Rudolph (and other eds), 51-56. Amsterdam, Rodopi, 1988.

BRODY, Baruch A. "A Historical Introduction to Jewish Casuistry on Suicide and Euthanasia" in Suicide and Euthanasia, BRODY, Baruch A (ed), 39-75. Norwell, Kluwer, 1989.

It is often claimed that traditional Jewish casuistry is committed to a belief in the sanctity of human life. This essay reviews the many conditions under which this casuistry allowed for suicide, passive euthanasia, and (perhaps) active euthanasia. It concludes that traditional Jewish casuistry was trying to balance several different values such as the great value of human life, a strong prohibition against taking innocent life, integrity in one's commitment to God, and the legitimacy of avoiding cruel and painful deaths.

BRODY, Baruch A. Quality of Scholarship in Bioethics. J Med Phil, 15(2),

161-178, Ap 90.

This paper identifies four major forms of scholarship in bioethics: empirical research, the articulation of mid-level principles of bioethics, the relating of these principles to fundamental moral theories, and discussions of the bioethical implications of legal principles and health delivery policies. It develops a reflective equilibrium approach to the relation between these four forms of scholarship. It then presents, in light of this approach, criteria for quality research in each of these forms of scholarship in bioethics.

BRODY, Baruch A and GRANDY, Richard E. Readings in the Philosophy of Science (Second Edition). Englewood Cliffs, Prentice-Hall, 1989

This second edition updates the first edition by including two new sections (one on space and time and the other on biology) and emphasizing many recent authors (Achinstein, Cartwright, Hacking, Laudan, Salmon, and van Fraassen). It retains from the first edition the basic structure of three major sections, one on theories, one on explanation and causality, and one on the confirmation of scientific hypotheses.

BRODY, Baruch A (ed). Suicide and Euthanasia. Norwell, Kluwer, 1989

This volume analyses the history of philosophical thought on suicide and euthanasia and discusses the implication of that history for the contemporary debate. The historical section contains an essay by John Cooper on Greek views, Baruch Brody on Jewish casuistry, Darrel Amundsen on Christian values, Gary Ferngren on Renaissance and Reformation views, and Tom Beauchamp on views during the Enlightenment. Joseph Boyle and Tris Engelhardt debate the implications of the historical views for the contemporary discussion.

BRODY, Howard. Transparency: Informed Consent in Primary Care. Hastings Center Rep, 19(5), 5-9, S-O 89.

Current legal standards of informed consent send the wrong message to physicians about moral and legal expectations, by focusing too much on information disclosure. A "transparency" model that sees consent as a conversation process can better enhance good medical practice and patient autonomy without foreclosing appropriate judicial review. Transparency calls for the physician to "think out loud" in making the medical recommendation, thereby inviting optimal patient participation.

BRODY, Jules. Freud, Racine, and the Epistemology of Tragedy. Phil Lit, 14(1), 1-23, Ap 90.

Freud invented a new ontology in which Eros replaces the Logos of the Greeks as linchpin of human behavior. Racine revolutionized tragedy, traditionally concerned with religious and social conflicts, by making instinctual satisfaction the motor principle in human conduct. In both the Freudian and Racinian anthropologies crisis arises from the encounter between the individual's claim to happiness and the repressions of society. The tragic hero resolves his crisis through a gradual advance in moral insight, reminiscent of the progress in self-knowledge achieved by neurotics in classical psychoanalytic therapy.

BROGAN, Walter. "Plato's Pharmakon: Between Two Repetitions" in Derrida and Deconstruction, SILVERMAN, Hugh J (ed), 7-23. New York, Routledge, 1989.

This article is about reading Derrida reading Plato. It develops three major themes: (1) Plato's suppression of writing; the effects of this decision that produces a system of metaphysical oppositions and effaces an 'originary' or arche-writing in Plato's texts. (2) Derrida's deconstructive strategy in pursuing the force of the Greek word pharmakon in Plato's text. (3) The deployment in Plato's writing of deconstructive strategies which demand a "double reading" and disrupt the univocity of Platonism.

BROGAN, Walter. A Response to Robert Bernasconi's "Heidegger's Destruction of Phronesis". S J Phil, SUPP(28), 149-153, 1989.

BRONAUGH, Richard. Current Trends in Legal Philosophy and Jurisprudence. Eidos, 8(1), 67-77, Je 89.

BRONIAK, Christopher. "Duty or Virtue?" as a Metaethical Question. Dialogos, 25(55), 139-150, Ja 90.

BRONNER, Stephen Eric (ed) and KELLNER, Douglas MacKay (ed). Critical Theory and Society: A Reader. New York, Routledge, 1989

This book is an anthology of writings by the most influential members of the "Frankfurt School." The book includes essays by Theodor Adorno, Walter Benjamin, Jürgen Habermas, Max Horkheimer, Herbert Marcuse, and others. Divided into sections dealing with psychology, sociology, cultural criticism, and other areas, this is an interdisciplinary collection which also contains a historical introduction.

BROOK, Donald. How Did We Get From Simulation To Symbol? Austl J Phil, 67(4), 452-468, D 89.

Representation is conceived in terms of the substitutability of one thing for another in relation to some causally determined outcome. Representational devices are classified as simulation, matching and symbolization. Simulation is basic and is explained in terms of perceptual failure. A possibility for the emergence of symbolism within the natural biological evolutionary process is adduced. The apparently unnatural transition from insensate discriminating mechanisms to perceiving and symbolizing (language-using) organisms is seen to be naturally attainable.

BROOKS, Daniel R (and others). Entropy and Information in Evolving Biological Systems. Biol Phil, 4(4), 407-432, O 89.

Integrating concepts of maintenance and of origins is essential to explaining biological diversity. The unified theory of evolution attempts to find a common theme linking production rules inherent in biological systems, explaining the origin of biological order as a manifestation of the flow of energy and the flow of information on various spatial and temporal scales, with the recognition that natural selection is an evolutionarily relevant process. Biological systems persist in space and time by transforming energy from one state to another in a manner that generates structures which allow the system to continue to persist. Macroevolutionary processes are neither reducible to, nor autonomous from, microevolutionary processes. (edited)

BROOKS, Peter. Storied Bodies, or Nana at Last Unveil'd. Crit Inquiry, 16(1), 1-32, Autumn 89.

BROOME, John. An Economic Newcomb Problem. Analysis, 49(4), 220-222, O 89.

The theory of 'rational expectations' provides a perfect example of a practical Newcomb problem.

BROSIO, Richard A. Teaching and Learning for Democratic Empowerment: A Critical Evaluation. Educ Theor, 40(1), 69-81, Wint 90.

The purpose of this work Is to analyze critically the work of motivational theorists in education who have made unrealistic claims for democratic empowerment, without taking into consideration adequately the awesome power of capitalist hegemony. An exaggerated view of human agency has resulted from a necessary attack upon reductionist and deterministic aspects of Marxist theory. The dangerous and laborious work needed to make the school and society more democratic will require a sober and realistic grasp of what is possible. Like Dewey, the motivational theorists can formulate an idea of a democratic society and communicate it to their students.

BROUDY, Harry S. The Two Cultures. J Aes Educ, 21(4), 87-94, Wint 87.

The article tries to clarify C P Snow's distinction between the two cultures and their import for education in the sciences and the humanities, which are usually taught by separate faculties in the university. Students expect different outcomes from them and rightly so. The subject matter of the sciences originates in the desire to understand physical phenomena; of the humanities to understand the images of justice, liberty, honesty, courage, beauty. Their reality lies in the power of imagination to create belief and a willingness to warrant that belief by faith. The arts express in images for feeling what other disciplines have tried to establish as fact.

BROWN, Bryson. How to be Realistic About Inconsistency in Science. Stud Hist Phil Sci, 21(2), 281-294, Je 90.

It might be supposed that realist forms of cognitive commitment can be made only to consistent theories. This paper argues the contrary. Using paraconsistent logic, it develops a form of cognitive commitment that tolerates inconsistency, and allows room for characteristically realist positions about reference and the properties of entities referred to.

BROWN, Charles S. Husserl, Intentionality, and Cognitive Architecture. SW Phil Rev, 6(1), 65-72, Ja 90.

In this paper it is argued that the Dreyfus and McIntyre comparisons of Husserl and Fodor are flawed because of their uncritical acceptance of what has become known as the Fregean interpretation of Husserl's theory of intentionality. The interpretation is faulty insofar as it takes Husserl's notion of perceptual content to be a Fregean sense, i.e., an abstract, conceptual, intensional entity which picks out the object of the perceptual act. I shall also show that as we leave the Fregean reading of Husserl behind we move farther away from the language of thought model advocated by Fodor and closer to a so-called connectionist model.

BROWN, Curtis. How to Believe the Impossible. Phil Stud, 58(3), 271-285, Mr 90.

One sometimes believes a singular proposition in virtue of believing a general proposition, and sometimes, in virtue of believing a sentence one understands to be true, believes the proposition expressed by the sentence; in either case one can, in virtue of believing a contingent proposition, believe an impossibility. Richard Foley has argued that contradictory *de re* beliefs are "reducible to" noncontradictory *de dicto* beliefs, and that, if one

believes contradictory sentences to be true, one must fail to understand one of them. Depending on their interpretation, Foley's claims either are false or do not rule out belief in the impossible.

BROWN, D G. More on Self-Enslavement and Paternalism in Mill. Utilitas, 1(1), 144-150, My 89.

Mill's rejection of contracts of self-enslavement is not a lapse into strong paternalism. It declines to create a power without denying any right or restricting any freedom. In general freedom of association is paradoxical in needing implementation by enforceable undertakings, hence by unfreedom. Such provision for enforcement may be too high a cost in liberty in the cases of marriage, personal services, engagements not for money or money's worth, or (the extreme case) self-enslavement.

BROWN, Graham. God's Unchanging Knowledge of the World. Sophia (Australia), 28(2), 2-12, Jl 89.

After giving reasons for thinking that Boethius's conception of an eternal being is coherent, it is argued that such a being could, logically speaking, be omniscient. The key to defending such a position is avoidance of certain erroneous conceptions of what it is to know something. These misconceptions derive from confusing the object of knowledge with true propositions that are known about the object. The several effects of this confusion are traced by examining a common account of omniscience and some arguments that omniscience requires change in the knower.

BROWN, Gregory. Mathematics, Physics, and Corporeal Substance in Descartes. Pac Phil Quart, 70(4), 281-302, D 89.

I undertake to examine how Descartes understood the relationship between physics and mathematics. My thesis is that what distinguishes the objects of mathematics from those of physics on Descartes's view is that the former are considered in abstraction from a material substratum while the latter are considered as involving a material substratum. Since it has often been maintained that Descartes identified matter with extension, and hence rejected the notion of a material substratum, I attempt in the first part of my paper to establish the textual basis for ascribing a substratum view to Descartes. In the second part of the paper, I present the case for my thesis concerning Descartes's account of the difference between the objects of mathematics and those of physics.

BROWN, Harold I. Prospective Realism. Stud Hist Phil Sci, 21(2), 211-242, Je 90.

Prospective realism holds that the attempt to learn the nature of the world is a reasonable aim for science to pursue and that our ability to pursue this aim has been increasing through the development of instruments that extend our observational range. In Part I the realist aim is defended as *prima facie* legitimate and I argue that extant antirealist arguments do not show that this aim cannot be successfully pursued. In Part II, I argue that indirect realist account of perception allows us to understand the use of instrumentation as an extension of our normal perceptual abilities.

BROWN, Harvey R. Does the Principle of Relativity Imply Winnie's (1970) Equal Passage Times Principle? Phil Sci, 57(2), 313-324, Je 90.

The kinematical principle of Equal Passage Times (EPT) was introduced by Winnie in his 1970 derivation of the relativistic coordinate transformations compatible with arbitrary synchrony conventions in one-dimensional space. In this paper, the claim by Winnie and later Giannoni that EPT is a direct consequence of the relativity principle is questioned. It is shown that EPT, given Einstein's 1905 postulates, is equivalent to the relativistic (synchrony independent) clock retardation principle, and that for standard synchrony it reduces to an isotropy condition for contraction (and dilation) effects.

BROWN, James Robert (ed) and BUTTS, Robert E (ed). *Constructivism and Science: Essays in Recent German Philosophy*. Norwell, Kluwer, 1989

BROWN, James Robert. *The Rational and the Social*. New York, Routledge, 1989

BROWN, John Seeley and COLLINS, Allan and NEWMAN, Susan E. Cognitive Apprenticeship Teaching the Craft of Reading, Writing and Mathematics. Thinking, 8(1), 2-10, 1989.

BROWN, Lee. Resurrecting Hegel to Bury Art. Brit J Aes, 29(4), 303-315, Autumn 89.

I argue that (1) Danto's derivation of his "death of art" from Hegel's is implausible, that (2) Danto's thesis is dubious in itself, that (3) Danto should not want to agree with Hegel anyway, that (4) the evidence Danto's brings to bear really shows, not that art is dead, but that the developmental concept of it is bankrupt. The paper notes further that (5) if Danto had capitalized upon his own observations on the market forces that drive the "breakthrough" ideology of art, he might have recast his thesis in less sensational but more plausible terms. (edited)

BROWN, Mark A. Action and Ability. J Phil Log, 19(1), 95-114, F 90.

This paper explores two ways of connecting a logic of action with a logic of ability: (1) by treating actions as exercised abilities, and (2) by treating abilities as possibilities of action. In (1), a completely axiomatized logic of action appears as a specialization of a logic of ability. In (2), the system of (1) is augmented with a normal possibilitation operator. A logic of ability equivalent to that from which (1) started reappears as a subsystem of this augmented logic. Throughout, stress is put on the importance of reliability of outcomes in both action and ability.

BROWN, Mark T. Why Individual Identity Matters. SW Phil Rev, 6(1), 99-104, Ja 90.

BROWN, Stephen F. "Richard Fishacre on the Need for "Philosophy"" in *A Straight Path: Studies in Medieval Philosophy and Culture*, LINK-SALINGER, Ruth (ed), 23-36. Washington, Cath Univ Amer Pr, 1988.

BROWN, Stephen F and DUMONT, Stephen D. Univocity of the Concept of Being in the Fourteenth Century III: An Early Scotist. Med Stud, 51, 1-129, 1989.

This is the edition of a text that is one of the most detailed expositions of John Duns Scotus's doctrine on the univocity of the concept of being (39-129), with an introduction that shows that these questions are important for the historical light they shed on Scotus's contemporaries Richard of Conington, Robert Cowton, and William of Alnwich, as well as the clarifications they offer for Scotus's own teaching on univocity (1-38).

BROWN, Stuart. Christian Averroism, Fideism and the 'Two-fold Truth'. Philosophy, 25, 207-223, 89 Supp.

BROWN, William R. Two Traditions of Analogy. Inform Log, 11(3), 161-172, Fall 89.

The study seeks to demonstrate that predictive and proportional analogy are distinct first in their logical structure and then in their pragmatics and their place in the history of ideas. Predictive analogy is treated as a complete argument form and proportional analogy as a relation that enters into various argument forms. The distinction is traced historically with key emphasis on Mill, whose overwhelming emphasis on predictive analogy has been perpetuated through generations of textbooks. Theory of legal reasoning is cited as a specialized area where the application of Mill's conception may be misleading.

BROWNE, Paul. Philosophy as Exile from Life: Lukacs' 'Soul and Form'. Rad Phil, 53, 20-30, Autumn 89.

BROWNE, Paul. Reification, Class and 'New Social Movements'. Rad Phil, 55, 18-24, Sum 90.

BROWNHILL, Robert James. Objectivity and Aesthetic Education in Its Social Context. J Aes Educ, 21(3), 29-44, Fall 87.

BRUCAR, Iosif. La Cosmodicée ou Etica repetita (in Romanian). Rev Filosof (Romania), 35(5), 479-488, S-O 88.

BRUDNEY, Daniel. Knowledge and Silence: *The Golden Bowl* and Moral Philosophy. Crit Inquiry, 16(2), 397-437, Wint 89.

BRUECKNER, Anthony. Scepticism about Knowledge of Content. Mind, 99(395), 447-451, Jl 90.

BRÜGGEMAN-KRUIJFF, Atie T. Levinas and Hegel on the Woman as Home: A Comparison (in Dutch). Tijdschr Filosof, 51(3), 444-485, S 89.

This essay contains an investigation of the meaning of the feminine and the position of women in Levinas, in *Totalité et Infini*, as well as in Hegel's *Phenomenology of Spirit*. The article has two parts. In the first part, an attempt is made to trace the meaning of the feminine in Levinas's defence of subjectivity. The second part of the study is directed to Hegel's *Phenomenology of Spirit*, especially the section which deals with the spirit, part A, "The true spirit, morality" and of that, paragraph a, the moral world, the human and divine law, male and female; and paragraph b, the moral act, human and divine knowledge, guilt and fate. (edited)

BRULAND, Esther Byle. Evangelical and Feminist Ethics: Complex Solidarities. J Relig Ethics, 17(2), 139-160, Fall 89.

Evangelicalism was a major source of feminism in the nineteenth century, but it also gave women mixed messages about the use of their newfound agency. The uneasy relations of evangelicalism and feminism have continued in the twentieth century, but there are new signs of a growing rapprochement. Evangelical feminists read and draw upon the work of other Christian feminists, and are making attempts to integrate feminist concerns and perspectives into a more inclusive theology and ethics. Similarities of method and focus between the two groups facilitate this process, though substantial areas of challenge and difference remain.

BRUMBAUGH, Robert S. The Importance of Motivation, Precision and Presence in Teaching. Thinking, 6(2), 15-19, 1985.

BRUMBAUGH, Robert S. Some Applications of *Process and Reality* I

and II to Educational Practice. Educ Theor, 39(4), 385-390, Fall 89.

Whitehead's *Process and Reality* analyzes the evolution of intelligence, with its precise discriminations, from an earlier evolutionary stage of concrete feeling. The selective attention of vision and abstraction is achieved at the prices of overlooking concrete things and presences which give learning its motivation. Thus the more efficiently one "covers the material" of abstract discipline the less interesting it is and the less difference it makes to captive students. There is in fact one optimum pattern of teaching and learning that follows from Whitehead's technical analysis of process and reality; the article explains what this is.

BRUMBAUGH, Robert S. Whitehead and a Committee. Process Stud, 18(3), 166-172, Fall 89.

Whitehead was a leading member of the committee that wrote a new degree syllabus for an M.A. in history and philosophy of science for University College, London. The syllabus, here reproduced, fills in some background of *Science and the Modern World*, and directs attention to problems that continued to occupy Whitehead in *Process and Reality* and *Modes of Thought*. It is a typical example of his way of applying his philosophical theories to educational applications. (edited)

BRUMBAUGH, Robert. Coins and Classical Philosophy. Teach Phil, 12(3), 243-255, S 89.

This article is based on an exhibit, "Coins and Classical Philosophy," that we have had annually at Yale. Coins and captions illuminate the classical conception of the fit of ideal and actual; direct attention to the solidity that gives new meaning for the modern reader to Plato's metaphor of physical reality as "minted space"; show alternative definitions of women, with no single common stand on "feminism." We see in coin portraiture the descent from idealized to (sometimes downright ugly) portraiture of individual rulers as philosophy moves from the Hellenic to the Hellenistic Age. There are other associations and items as well.

BRUNGS, Robert A. Science—Democracy—Christianity. Thought, 64(255), 377-398, D 89.

The growth in the biological sciences in itself poses opportunities as well as concomitant problems. It is taking place in the increasingly privatized culture of the United States. It will have significant effects on that culture. High technology in and by itself will not destroy democratic society. It will, however, broaden and deepen existing social, political and religious crises. Science/technology and democracy must reverse the secularizing tendencies which dominate them and return to their Christian roots if they are to maintain their success. Both are in grave danger.

BRÜNING, Barbara. We Discover That Thinking Is Fun: Doing Philosophy With First Graders. Thinking, 5(3), 19-24, 1984.

BRÜNING, Barbara. What Kind of Girl is Pippi Longstocking, Anyway? Thinking, 5(3), 35-36, 1984.

BRUNKHORST, H. Adorno, Heidegger and Postmodernity. Phil Soc Crit, 14(3-4), 411-424, 1988.

Brunkhorst uses the Heidegger debate to juxtapose Adorno's modernism to the 'postmodernism' of Heidegger and others, including Rorty and Lyotard. In contrast to Heidegger, Brunkhorst finds Adorno's modernity to be more informed by Enlightenment categories. Starting with Adorno's suggestion that "ratio" must "transcend" the self-preservation of instrumental thought, Brunkhorst interprets Adorno as moving in a somewhat universalist direction. According to this interpretation, although Adorno would agree with Heidegger's critique of "identifying thought," he would find the category of "rational identity" something much more positive than did Heidegger. In contrast to Heidegger, Adorno's critique of instrumentality has a strong ethical component.

BRUNKHORST, Hauke. Hegel and the French Revolution (in Serbo-Croatian). Filozof Istraz, 30(3), 741-751, 1989.

Die Grundidee von Hegels politischer Philosophie betrachtet der Verfasser als *doppelte Realisierung des modernen Prinzips der Einzelnheit*. Während sich dieses Prinzip der Subjektivität in der Bürgerlichen Gesellschaft als Atomismus des Privateigentums realisiert, realisiert es sich im modernen Staat als "allgemeines Leben" in einer "Vereinigung als solcher". Es ist die mit der Französischen Revolution durchgesetzte Einsicht, dass der moderne Staat das allgemeine Leben durch eine radikale *Aufhebung des Privateigentums am Staat* verwirklichen muss. Auch dieses Motiv zieht sich wie ein roter Faden durch Hegels ganzes Werk.

BRUNNER, Norbert. The Fraenkel-Mostowski Method, Revisited. Notre Dame J Form Log, 31(1), 64-75, Wint 90.

Permutation models generated by isomorphic topological groups satisfy the same choice principles (Boolean combinations of injectively bounded statements). As an application the group Jp of p-adic integers is characterized: A monothetic linear group G generates a model that satisfies the same choice principles that hold in the model corresponding to Jp iff the G-model satisfies the well-orderable selection principle, and ACq holds, q prime, iff $q \neq p$. The main result is a strengthening of a previous theorem of Pincus: All Fraenkel-Mostowski-Specker independence proofs concerning choice principles can be proved in finite support models.

BRUNNER, Norbert. Set Mappings on Dedekind Sets. Notre Dame J Form Log, 30(2), 268-270, Spr 89.

Hajnal's free set principle is equivalent to the axiom of choice, and some of its variants for Dedekind-finite sets are equivalent to countable forms of the axiom of choice.

BRUNO, G. Materialità del testo e pratica interpretativa: la semanlisi di Julia Kristeva. Il Protag, 6(9-10), 33-48, Je-D 86.

BRUNS, Gerald L. On the Tragedy of Hermeneutical Experience. Res Phenomenol, 18, 191-204, 1988.

BRUNSCHWIG, J (trans) and BARNES, Jonathan. Médecine, expérience et logique. Rev Metaph Morale, 94(4), 437-481, O-D 89.

BRUNSCHWIG, J (trans) and FREDE, Michael (trans). Les origines de la notion de cause. Rev Metaph Morale, 94(4), 483-511, O-D 89.

BRUNT, P A. "Philosophy and Religion in the Late Republic" in *Philosophia Togata: Essays on Philosophy and Roman Society*, GRIFFIN, Miriam (ed), 174-198. New York, Clarendon/Oxford Pr, 1989.

BRUZINA, Ron. Comments on "On the Ordering of Things: Being and Power in Heidegger and Foucault" by Hubert Dreyfus. S J Phil, SUPP(28), 97-104, 1989.

BRUZINA, Ronald. Die Notizen Eugen Finks zur Umarbeitung von Edmund Husserls "Cartesianischen Meditationen". Husserl Stud, 6(2), 97-128, 1989.

This article is an edition of notes written by Eugen Fink relating to the revision proposals he prepared for Edmund Husserl for a second stage of revision of the latter's *Cartesian Meditations* of 1929. Dating from 1929 to 1933, Fink's notes provide supplementary materials for understanding the texts now published in Eugen Fink, *VI. Cartesianische Meditation*, Bd 1-2, Husserliana Dokumente II/1-2, Dordrecht: Kluwer, 1988. The editor of these notes has provided an explanatory introduction and footnotes to the texts.

BUCHANAN, Allen. Justice as Reciprocity versus Subject-Centered Justice. Phil Pub Affairs, 19(3), 227-252, Sum 90.

BUCHANAN, James M. "Contractarian Presuppositions and Democratic Governance" in *Politics and Process*, BRENNAN, Geoffrey (ed), 174-182. New York, Cambridge Univ Pr, 1989.

This paper clarifies the relationship between contractarianism and majoritarian democracy. Contractarianism presupposes political equality, but political equality does not imply majoritarian decision making either in enforcing law or in changing law. Majority rule is only one of several means of making collective choices within the allowed limits of the constitution.

BUCHDAHL, Gerd. "Realism and Realization in a Kantian Light" in *Reading Kant*, SCHAPER, Eva (ed), 217-249. Cambridge, Blackwell, 1989.

The chapter seeks to give a precise distinction between two different types of realism in Kant, leading also to a fresh interpretation of the vexed Kantian problem of the 'affection of sensibility by objects'. A complex graphical representation is given of the relationships that exist between different Kantian uses of the notion of 'thing', in terms of various 'stations' in Kant's account of the 'realization' of the 'thing', or, in the opposite direction, of its 'reduction', leading to a clarification of the Kantian 'thing in itself', the 'transcendental object', etc., with 'reduction-realization' defining the transcendental process.

BUCHER, Theodor G. Petrus Damiani—ein Freund der Logik? Frei Z Phil Theol, 36(3), 267-310, 1989.

Among historians there is a tendency to minimize Damiani's quarrel with logic, a position which has been suggested by several philosophers during the last few decades. An analysis, however, of four selected passages from *De divina omnipotentia* gives evidence of a confusion on different levels: Damiani imputes the mistakes from his private theory of knowledge to logic, a curious result for a formal logic which is reduced to the modus ponens rule. Trapped by his own metaphors he denies the principle of noncontradiction.

BUCHHOLZ, Rogene A. *Fundamental Concepts and Problems in Business Ethics*. Englewood Cliffs, Prentice-Hall, 1989

This book delves into basic questions of business ethics in laymen's terms dealing with them so that their significance in the real world is readily apparent. Each chapter asks a different question such as why be moral, what decisions have ethical dimensions, how can moral judgments be

justified, can a corporation be made moral, and so forth. The answers to these questions are fundamental to an understanding of the moral significance of business behavior. Cases help reinforce the practical applications that these ethical issues have in common business practices.

BUCK-MORSS, Susan. *The Dialectics of Seeing: Walter Benjamin and the Arcades Project*. Cambridge, MIT Pr, 1990

BUCUR, Ion and CORNESCU, Viorel. Qualité et efficience—coordonate principales du développement socio-économique Roumaine (in Romanian). Rev Filosof (Romania), 36(2), 134-141, Mr-Ap 89.

BUDD, Malcolm. Music and the Expression of Emotion. J Aes Educ, 23(3), 19-29, Fall 89.

BUDD, Malcolm. *Wittgenstein's Philosophy of Psychology*. New York, Routledge, 1989

BUECHLER, S and SHELAH, S. On the Existence of Regular Types. Annals Pure Applied Log, 45(3), 277-308, D 89.

BUECHLER, Steven. The Classification of Small Weakly Minimal Sets, II. J Sym Log, 53(2), 625-635, Je 88.

BÜHLER, Axel. Bemerkungen zur methodologischen Einheit der Wissenschaften. Conceptus, 23(59), 99-102, 1989.

BUHR, Manfred. Die Ethik—"der Schlussstein von dem ganzen Gebäude der spekulativen Vernunft". Stud Soviet Tho, 38(3), 193-202, O 89.

BUIJS, Joseph A. Attributes of Action in Maimonides. Vivarium, 27(2), 85-102, N 89.

Maimonides maintains that attributes of action provide an alternative to negative attributes when talking about God. Yet how is it that such attribution avoids the difficulties that, according to Maimonides, necessitate a negative language? An answer lies in his theory of predication and in his theory of action. In both he deviates from Aristotle. In his theory of predication, he offers a distinct kind of predication in addition to the essential and accidental predication of Aristotle. In his theory of action, he distinguishes both human and divine agency from natural causation.

BUKER, Eloise A. Feminist Social Theory and Hermeneutics: An Empowering Dialectic? Soc Epistem, 4(1), 23-39, Ja-Mr 90.

This essay focuses on the question "Can hermeneutics contribute to the development of an epistemological strategy for feminist social theory?" It proceeds by examining five epistemological issues that confront feminist social analysts and by showing how hermeneutics, especially as developed by Hans-Georg Gadamer and Paul Ricoeur, can help develop approaches to these issues: (1) objectivity; (2) the problem of language and cultural contexts in social analysis; (3) praxis and the integration of theory and political action; (4) the problem of tradition in social critique; (5) the problem of reflection and social critique.

BUKOVSKY, Lev and COPLÁKOVÁ-HARTOVÁ, E. Minimal Collapsing Extensions of Models of ZFC. Annals Pure Applied Log, 46(3), 265-298, Ap 90.

BULEANDRA, Alexandru. La protoéthique ou études sur les fondements des chroniques roumaines (in Romanian). Rev Filosof (Romania), 35(5), 451-460, S-O 88.

BULNES, Maria Elton. Racionalismo ético kantiano y amor puro. Anu Filosof, 22(2), 133-146, 1989.

BUNDER, M W. Arithmetic Based on the Church Numerals in Illative Combinatory Logic. Stud Log, 47(2), 129-143, Je 88.

In the early thirties, Church developed predicate calculus within a system based on lambda calculus. Rosser and Kleene developed Arithmetic within this system, but using a Godelization technique showed the system to be inconsistent. Alternative systems to that of Church have been developed, but so far more complex definitions of the natural numbers have had to be used. The present paper based on a system of illative combinatory logic developed previously by the author, does allow the use of the Church numerals. Given a new definition of equality all the Peano-type axioms of Mendelson except one can be derived. A rather weak extra axiom allows the proof of the remaining Peano axiom. *Note*. The illative combinatory logic used in this paper is similar to the logic employed in computer languages such as ML.

BUNDER, M W. The Logic of Inconsistency. J Non-Classical Log, 6(1), 57-62, My 89.

BUNDER, M W. Overlapping Types in Higher Order Predicate Calculus Based on Combinatory Logic. J Non-Classical Log, 6(1), 33-44, My 89.

BUNDER, M W. Some Results in Some Subsystems and In an Extension of C_n. J Non-Classical Log, 6(1), 45-56, My 89.

BUNGAY, Stephen. *Beauty and Truth: A Study of Hegel's Aesthetics*.

New York, Clarendon/Oxford Pr, 1987

This book, the first in English to attempt a full theoretical analysis of Hegel's philosophy of art, examines Hegel's central thesis, that both Beauty and Truth can be understood in terms of systematic coherence, and that art, as a purveyor of Truth, embodies and reflects the beliefs of societies from which it comes.

BUNGE, Mario. *Treatise on Basic Philosophy, Volume 8—Ethics: The Good and the Right*. Norwell, Kluwer, 1989

A monograph on value theory and ethics based on the hypothesis that values and moral norms have biological, psychological and social roots and functions, whence they can be investigated scientifically. Rights-only doctrines, as well as duties-only ones, are criticized, and so are individualist and collectivist theories. The ethical theory proposed in this book, called "agathonism," is realistic but not absolutistic, systemist but not holistic, and consequentialist but not utilitarian. It proposes substantive value judgments and moral principles in addition to analyses of axiological and ethical concepts and principles.

BURBIDGE, John. The First Chapter of Hegel's Larger *Logic*. Owl Minerva, 21(2), 177-183, Spr 90.

Commentators criticize the first chapter of Hegel's larger *Logic* because it appears to lack logical necessity. Hegel himself argues that the logic is a plastic discourse. This suggests that one has to take seriously the *process* of implication—of moving from one term to another—and not simply the structure. At the same time Hegel stresses understanding as the culminating stage of logical development, following from dialectical and speculative reason. By recognizing the role of fixed distinctions, we can identify the transitional stages that move by way of "Becoming" to "*Dasein*," so that their necessity becomes evident.

BURBULES, Nicholas C. The Dilemma of "Relevance" in the Philosophy of Education. Proc Phil Educ, 45, 187-196, 1989.

This essay offers a definition of "relevance" appropriate to philosophy of education. In so doing, it seeks to avoid two dichotomous positions, namely, that either philosophy must be relevant to be worthwhile, or that it has no responsibilities for relevance whatsoever. Instead, I recommend that "relevance" be seen as a process of translation, in which points of relevance can be established in particular cases; this process is an educative process that stands to benefit both the philosopher and the practitioner.

BURBULES, Nicholas C. Equal Opportunity or Equal Education? Educ Theor, 40(2), 221-226, Spr 90.

This essay is a critical response to an earlier article by Kenneth Howe, "In Defense of Outcomes-Based Conceptions of Equal Educational Opportunity." My essay focuses on the question of what constitutes an "opportunity" where children are concerned.

BURCH BROWN, Frank. *Religious Aesthetics: A Theological Study of Making and Meaning*. Princeton, Princeton Univ Pr, 1990

This book breaks with formalist and purist aesthetics in order to show that aesthetics has a major though largely neglected role to play in the study of religion and in the practice of theology. Proposing a "neo-aesthetic" approach supported by a critical reconsideration of aspects of Kant's *Critique of Judgment*, the author analyzes ways in which religious artifacts, rituals, and modes of thought employ aesthetic forms and styles, thus appealing partly to imagination and taste (broadly defined).

BURDICK, Howard. On Davidson and Interpretation. Synthese, 80(3), 321-345, S 89.

Davidson's theory of interpretation, I argue, is vulnerable to a number of significant difficulties, difficulties which can be avoided or resolved by the more Quinean approach which I develop. (edited)

BURES, R. The Ethics Dimension of Human Attitude to the Living Environment (in Czechoslovakian). Filozof Cas, 37(5), 691-703, 1989.

The deteriorating ecological situation in the world has necessitated change in the human approach to nature. The question arises whether and how this relationship can come to be a subject of moral regulation and how it affects or alters the nature and concept of ethics. The author believes that the foundation of the moral dimension of the attitude to nature lies in the fact that the ecological situation is, in actual fact, a limiting factor of mankind's sound development and vent its very survival. He argues in favour of an anthropocentric approach to the problem in hand, especially as a methodological vantage point for practical behaviour. The author goes on to stress that an anthropocentric attitude is not identical with man's predatory approach to nature. On the contrary, care for nature and efforts to preserve it intact rank high among the most important human interests. (edited)

BURGE, Tyler. Individuation and Causation in Psychology. Pac Phil Quart, 70(4), 303-322, D 89.

BURGER, Ronna. Nemesis. Grad Fac Phil J, 13(1), 65-79, 1988.

Nemesis or righteous indignation concludes the list of the virtues in Book II of Aristotle's *Nicomachean Ethics*; it alone fails to appear in the subsequent analysis. This essay askes what that disappearance, if intended, might mean. Righteous indignation is an experience of pain at a perceived discrepancy between external reward and desert; it rests on the expectation of a precise but natural correlation between character and fortune. In this *nemesis* is found to be the psychological counterpart to the theoretical demand for precision in ethical inquiry, which Aristotle rejects as a standard both inappropriate and inevitably disappointing.

BURGESS, Craig. Kant's Key to the Critique of Taste. Phil Quart, 39(157), 484-492, O 89.

BURGESS, J A. Vague Objects and Indefinite Identity. Phil Stud, 59(3), 263-287, Jl 90.

BURGESS, John P. Addendum to "The Truth is Never Simple". J Sym Log, 53(2), 390-392, Je 88.

BURGIN, M S. The Structure-Nominative Reconstruction of Scientific Knowledge. Epistemologia, 11(2), 235-254, Jl-D 88.

In this paper we propose an informal exposition of the structure approach in the philosophy of science. Scientific knowledge is here considered as a collection of scientific theories. Each scientific theory has logico-linguistic, model-representing, pragmatic-procedural, and problem-heuristical subsystems and a subsystem of ties. The pivotal methodological concept for the exact description of these subsystems is the named set. We also outline the possibility of applying the structure-nominative approach to certain problems in the philosophy of science.

BURGIO, Alberto. *Eguaglianza interesse unanimità: La politica di Rousseau*. Napoli, Bibliopolis, 1989

Alla vigilia della rivoluzione, la Francia é il luogo d'osservazione dal quale Rousseau immagina le possibili soluzioni di dilemmi politici ancor oggi cruciali. Che cosa intendiamo quando, parlando di una società, diciamo che esse é libera? In che rapporto sta la libertà dei suoi membri con la loro eguaglianza? Che relazione collega la giustizia alla possibilità di perseguire il proprio interesse individuale? Cos'ha a che fare tutto questo con la ragione? La definizione del confine tra pubblico e privato e tra dirriti individuali e collettivi; dell'identità personale dei singoli in rapporto alla loro dimensione sociale; delle idee di egoismo e razionalità, di interesse particolare e bene pubblico, di autonomia e obbligo, di merito e bisogno, sono i nodi della rete con la quale la teoria politica rousseauiana cerca, a più riprese, di rispondere a questi interrogativi e di comprendere la realtà del proprio tempo per governarne in forme razionali il movimento.

BURIAN, Richard M. Maiocchi on Duhem, Howard on Duhem and Einstein: Historiographical Comments. Synthese, 83(3), 401-408, Je 90.

These comments center on the methodological stance that Howard and Maiocchi recommend to us when we are doing history of philosophy. If Howard and Maiocchi are right, both Duhem and Einstein developed closely related versions of conventionalism and realism, and in both of their philosophies the conventionalist and realist moments were mutually compatible. Duhem's holism and, arguably, Einstein's as well, denies the need for across-the-board literalism, and both of them had important reasons for denying that convergence was required or even desirable for realism. Thus, for those who are caught up in the current disputes, serious consideration of the discrepancies between the standard current versions of realism and conventionalism and the positions that contextualist analyses reveal to have been advocated by Duhem and Einstein may uncover some of the tacit assumptions that impede the resolution or advancement of our disputes.

BURKE, R J and MC KEEN, C A. Mentoring in Organizations: Implications for Women. J Bus Ethics, 9(4-5), 317-332, Ap-My 90.

This paper reviews the literature on the mentoring process in organizations and why mentoring can be critical to the career success of women managers and professionals. It examines some of the reasons why it is more difficult for women to find mentors than it is for men. Particular attention is paid to potential problems in cross-gender mentoring. A feminist perspective is then applied to the general notion of mentorships for women. The paper concludes with an examination of what organizations can do to further mentor relationships and an agenda for further research in this area.

BURKE, R J and MIKALACHKI, D. The Women in Management Research Program at the National Centre for Management Research and Development. J Bus Ethics, 9(4-5), 447-453, Ap-My 90.

NCMRD initiated the Women in Management Research Program in January 1988. One of the objectives of the program is to help managers and policy makers deal with issues arising from women's increased participation in managerial and professional jobs backing research to help arrive at solutions to the problems being encountered both by institutions and by women themselves. Significant research funds have been raised from the private sector and ten projects have been funded to date. This article describes the early development of the program and its research mandate.

BURKEY, John. Descartes, Skepticism, and Husserl's Hermeneutic Practice. Husserl Stud, 7(1), 1-27, 1990.

Husserl's commentary on the content of Descartes's *Meditations* is pieced together according to the order of argument of the *Meditations*. This reconstruction aims to show precisely what Husserl found valuable, what he rejected, and why. Husserl's double-edged hermeneutic, as well as his truncated reading of the *Meditations*, are found to have their primary source in Descartes's (mis)handling of skepticism.

BURKHARDT, Armin. Searle ed Eco sulla metafora. Teoria, 9(1), 139-157, 1989.

BURKHARDT, Hans and DEGEN, Wolfgang. Mereology in Leibniz's Logic and Philosophy. Topoi, 9(1), 3-13, Mr 90.

BURLINGAME, Charles E. "A Reflection on Naturalistic Accounts of Language" in *Inquiries into Values: The Inaugural Session of the International Society for Value Inquiry*, LEE, Sander H , 27-35. Lewiston, Mellen Pr, 1989.

Imagine a poor soul who had come to feel the folly of attempting to find peace or happiness by forcing others to acquiesce to himself since the very act of presuming another passes a judgment upon both which no amount of coming together will erase. Imagine further that such a fool is struck by this thought, not merely on the psychological level, not merely on the sociopolitical level, but also on the level of his thinking about language, a thinking which is guided by naturalistic accounts of language, and which led this solitary individual to an even deeper awareness of his alienation.

BURMS, A. Fiction, Self-Deception, Contemplation (in Dutch). Tijdschr Filosof, 52(1), 3-16, Mr 90.

How can it be explained that we are able to be captivated by fictions and to sympathize with characters about whom we know that they are merely the figments of someone's imagination? In the current debate about this question it is often taken for granted that the interest in fiction is a peculiar deviation from something which is to be considered as perfectly rational and normal, viz. our interest in what really happened. In this article, however, I try to describe a perspective from which our interest in what really happened turns out to be as paradoxical and peculiar as our interest in fiction. In the final part of the article I try to explain how the interest in artistic fictions can be related to the traditional ideal of contemplation. (edited)

BURNETT, Joe R. The Relation of Dewey's Aesthetics to His Overall Philosophy. J Aes Educ, 23(3), 51-54, Fall 89.

BURNS, J H. Bentham and Blackstone: A Lifetime's Dialectic. Utilitas, 1(1), 22-40, My 89.

BURNS, J H. Utilitarianism and Reform: Social Theory and Social Change, 1750-1800. Utilitas, 1(2), 211-225, N 89.

BURNS, Jean E. Contemporary Models of Consciousness: Part I. J Mind Behav, 11(2), 153-171, Spr 90.

BURNS, Robert M. The Divine Simplicity in St Thomas. Relig Stud, 25(3), 271-293, S 89.

Aquinas's arguments for divine simplicity are essentially attempts to specify the nature of the source of cosmic intelligibility. They fail because no account is taken of the possibility of complexity as opposed to compositeness in the first principle, even though Aquinas eventually resorts to it in his defence of the doctrine of the Trinity. Moreover he fails to reconcile divine simplicity with omniscience and free will. His preoccupation with divine simplicity is traced to the influence of Arabic Neoplatonized Aristotelianism mediated especially through Avicenna and Maimonides. More satisfactory approaches are found in Plotinus, Marius Victorinus, Al-Ghazali, and Schelling.

BURNS, S A M (trans) and WEININGER, Otto. Metaphysics. J Phil Res, 15, 311-327, 1990.

This is a translation of a posthumous essay by the Viennese philosopher-psychologist, Otto Weininger (1880-1903). His main book, *Sex and Character*, was published in 1903 (English version, 1906). Many distinguished Viennese were deeply influenced by Weininger; among them was Ludwig Wittgenstein, who paid tribute to him even late in his life. In particular, he is known to have admired the present essay and its foray into "animal psychology." The investigation of the significance for human psychology of dogs and other animals is part of a larger scheme which Weininger sketches, to investigate the symbolism of all kinds of things. His ultimate goal is to reveal the relationship between the microcosm of the human consciousness and the macrocosm of the external universe. Hence

the title, "Metaphysics."

BURRELL, David B. "Aquinas's Debt to Maimonides" in *A Straight Path: Studies in Medieval Philosophy and Culture*, LINK-SALINGER, Ruth (ed), 37-48. Washington, Cath Univ Amer Pr, 1988.

Aquinas lived in an interfaith, intercultural intellectual situation, and the greatest proof was his debt to Moses Maimonides: for the strategy of argumentation regarding the "eternity" of the world, for the pattern of reasoning regarding God's existence, and even for the question of "divine names," although Aquinas's more sophisticated semantics led him to a more nuanced solution. All this argues for a re-visioning of the medieval philosophical world, as one in which Jewish, Christian, and Islamic philosophers were treating common subjects in a shared idiom.

BURRI, Alex and FREUDIGER, Jürg. Zur Analytizität hypothetischer Imperative. Z Phil Forsch, 44(1), 98-105, 1990.

In *Foundations of the Metaphysics of Morals* Kant makes a distinction between categorical and hypothetical imperatives and claims that the latter are analytic. By analyzing their logical structure we show that his claim is false.

BUSCH, Lawrence. Irony, Tragedy, and Temporality in Agricultural Systems, or, How Values and Systems are Related. Agr Human Values, 6(4), 4-11, Fall 89.

In the last decade the systems approach to agricultural research has begun to subsume the older reductionist approaches. However, proponents of the systems approach often accept without critical examination a number of features that were inherited from previously accepted approaches. In particular, supporters of the systems approach frequently ignore the ironies and tragedies that are a part of all human endeavors. They may also fail to consider that all actual systems are temporally and spatially bounded. By incorporating such features into a systems perspective, it becomes possible to consider them as involving the manipulation of things, the reconstruction of institutions, and the reformulation of policies in accordance with democratic goals and objectives as part of a single web of interrelationships.

BUSH, Judith R (trans) and MASTERS, Roger D (ed & trans) and KELLY, Christopher (ed & trans). *Rousseau, Judge of Jean-Jacques: Dialogues—The Collected Writings of Rousseau, Volume I*. Hanover, Univ Pr New England, 1990

BUSZKOWSKI, Wojciech. Presuppositional Completeness. Stud Log, 48(1), 23-34, Mr 89.

Some notions of the logic of questions (presupposition of a question, validation, entailment) are used for defining certain kinds of completeness of elementary theories. Presuppositional completeness, closely related to ω-completeness, is shown to be fulfilled by strong elementary theories like Peano arithmetic. (edited)

BUTCHVAROV, Panayot. The Demand for Justification in Ethics. J Phil Res, 15, 1-14, 1990.

The common belief that the epistemic credentials of ethics are quite questionable, and therefore in need of special justification, is an illusion made possible by the logical gap between reason and belief. This gap manifests itself sometimes even outside ethics. In ethics its manifestations are common, because of the practical nature of ethics. The attempt to cover it up takes the form of exorbitant demands for justification and often leads to espousing noncognitivism.

BUTLER, Clark (trans) and HEGEL, G W F. Review of C F Göschel's *Aphorisms: Part Three*. Clio, 18(4), 379-385, Sum 89.

BUTLER, Judith. Foucault and the Paradox of Bodily Inscriptions. J Phil, 86(11), 601-607, N 89.

Foucault argues in *Discipline and Punish* and in *The History of Sexuality*, Vol. I, that there is no body prior to the workings of culture, discourse, and power. His view of the body as culturally constructed appears, then, to be a very strong view in which the very materiality of the body is itself structured and presented through cultural means. In his reflections on his own genealogical method, however, Foucault appears to contradict his refutation of the possibility of a prediscursive body and argues implicitly that the body is a dynamic point of resistance to "history," externally related to cultural meanings, and further, that all histories, quite apart from their specific formulations, create historical meanings through the subjection of the body. I argue that Foucault's view of history as an act of inscription on the body paradoxically undermines his claim that the body is culturally constructed in the strong sense.

BUTLER, Judith. *Gender Trouble: Feminism and the Subversion of Identity*. New York, Routledge, 1989

This is a feminist philosophical inquiry into the category of "women," the sex/gender distinction, and the political consequences of the fundamental categories by which sexed persons are described. The book reviews and criticizes psychoanalytic theory, Foucault, French feminism, anthropology and performance theory.

BÜTTEMEYER, Wilhelm. Positivismo ed umanismo. G Crit Filosof Ital, 68(2), 225-234, My-Ag 89.

BUTTERFIELD, Jeremy. "A Space-Time Approach to the Bell Inequality" in *Philosophical Consequences of Quantum Theory: Reflections on Bell's Theorem*, CUSHING, James T (ed), 114-144. Notre Dame, Univ Notre Dame Pr, 1989.

The Bell theorem for stochastic hidden variables makes two contentious assumptions, completeness and locality. I analyse these, by taking the hidden variable and apparatus settings as total physical states of appropriate spacetime regions. I show that the assumptions are very weak; and *pace* Jarrett et al., that they are not implied by relativity's prohibition on superluminal causation.

BUTTS, Robert E (ed) and BROWN, James Robert (ed). *Constructivism and Science: Essays in Recent German Philosophy*. Norwell, Kluwer, 1989.

BUTTS, Robert E. Teleology and Scientific Method in Kant's Critique of Judgement. Nous, 24(1), 1-16, Mr 90.

Kant endeavors to harmonize the maxims of mechanism and teleology as research strategies. (1) He proposes two kinds of causal orders. (2) Reflection on ends of nature discovers organisms, which cannot be understood solely by reference to efficient causes. (3) Application of this biological model of purposiveness to the nexus of empirical laws constituting known nature shows that nature can only be understood as designed. (4) Therefore, a teleological principle is an a priori presupposition of any scientific inquiry. Because we must necessarily think of nature as designed we are justified in applying the principle of mechanism.

BUTTS, Robert E (ed) and WHEWELL, William. *Theory of Scientific Method—William Whewell*. Indianapolis, Hackett, 1989.

The selections in this volume include William Whewell's seminal 19th-century studies of the logic of induction (with his critique of Mill's theory), arguments for his realist view that science discovers necessary truths about nature, and exercises in the epistemology and ontology of science. The book's arrangement sets forth a coherent statement of the historically important philosophy of science whose influence has never been greater: every one of Whewell's fundamental ideas about the philosophy of science is presented here. The introductory essay provides an overview of the main features of Whewell's theory of scientific method.

BYK, Christian. *Donum Vitae*: Civil Law and Moral Values. J Med Phil, 14(5), 561-573, O 89.

The *Instruction* reminds us that reproductive medicine has become part of our social reality and as such justifies the intervention of public authorities. The *Instruction* suggests relevant principles which should guide appropriate legislation. This essay analyzes how far the French government has taken these fundamental principles into account.

BYLINA, Maryna and SZCZEPANSKI, Jan. Admonitions to Poland. Dialec Hum, 16(2), 87-91, Spr 89.

BYRD, B Sharon. Kant's Theory of Punishment: Deterrence in its Threat, Retribution in its Execution. Law Phil, 8(2), 151-200, Ag 89.

Kant's theory of punishment is commonly regarded as purely retributive in nature, and indeed much of his discourse seems to support that interpretation. Still, it leaves one with certain misgivings regarding the internal consistency of his position. Perhaps the problem lies not in Kant's inconsistency nor in the senility sometimes claimed to be apparent in the *Metaphysic of Morals*, but rather in a superimposed, modern yet monistic view of punishment. Historical considerations tend to show that Kant was discussing not one, but rather two facets of punishment, each independent but nevertheless mutually restrictive. (edited)

BYRD, Michael and PARKS, Zane. "Relevant Implication and Leibnizian Necessity" in *Directions in Relevant Logic*, NORMAN, Jean (ed), 179-184. Norwell, Kluwer, 1989.

BYWATER, William. The Paranoia of Postmodernism. Phil Lit, 14(1), 79-84, Ap 90.

The image of the postmodern critic which Stanley Fish creates in the closing essays of *Is There a Text in This Class?* resembles the image of the paranoid personality which David Shapiro describes in *Neurotic Styles*. A comparison between these two works yields insights into how the paranoia of postmodernism perpetuates itself thus placing limits on the horizon of thought.

CABANCHIK, Samuel M. Certeza, duda escéptica y saber. Critica, 21(62), 67-92, Ag 89.

Traditionally, the skeptic has been considered as a threat to our claims to true and justified knowledge. Also, certainty appears to be as the highest possible degree of knowledge. Knowledge and certainty are thus opposed to skepticism. This paper wants to show that 'certainty' and knowledge are, probably, incompatible notions, and that the possibility of a doubt about the assumed certainty is a necessary condition to distinguish between belief and knowledge, and to construe any kind of knowledge. (edited)

CABANCHIK, Samuel. Causas y razones en la filosofía de Wittgenstein. Analisis Filosof, 7(1), 29-45, My 87.

The aim of the paper is to refine the conceptual distinction between causes and reasons, following Wittgenstein's views. It is argued that, as a philosophical instrument, the distinction is essential to discussions about the explanation of actions and the nature of mind. It is also claimed that the distinction is important to cognitivism and, in general, to computational models of mind.

CABRERA, Julio. Significado literal: entre la profunda necesidad de una construcción y la mera nostalgia. Critica, 21(61), 103-116, Ap 89.

CACCIATORE, Giuseppe. Crisi dello storicismo e "bisogno" di "Kulturgeschichte": Il caso Lamprecht. Arch Stor Cult, 1, 257-281, 1988.

CACINOVIC-PHUOVSKI, Nadezda. Classicism and Revolution (in Serbo-Croatian). Filozof Istraz, 30(3), 821-827, 1989.

Das Thema dieses Aufsatzes ist ein Aspekt der oft beschriebenen "erborgten Sprache" der Französischen Revolution von 1789, des Anlehnen an den römischen Republikanismus mit Elementen der Graecomanie. In der Gestalt und Werk Davids ist ein Klassizismus am Werke, dem man zugestanden hat, eine Ausnahme in der sonst durchgehenden Verbrüderung zwischen der neoantiken Form und dem konservativen Lager zu sein. Er wird auch hier als Wendepunkt und "Drehscheibe" verstanden, der einer Reihe von neuen Elementen in der Institutionalisierung der autonomen Kunst als der Bestätigung der bürgerlichen Subjektivität zum Durchbruch verhalf. Dabei wurde der Klassizismus als Modestil zum Vehikel, den gesellschaftlichen Druck nicht in die Richtung der pragmatischen Unterwerfung der Kunst sondern in der Richtung einer institutionellen Garantie für ihren Eigenbereich zu wenden; der restliche Druck wurde in frühe Formen der Ästhetisierung der Politik (die grossen öffentlichen Feier) abgezweigt.

CACKOWSKI, Zdzislaw and PACZYNSKA, Maria (trans). Cultural Partnership—A Factor of Social Peace. Dialec Hum, 14(1), 35-41, Wint 87.

CACKOWSKI, Zdzislaw and BLAIM, Artur (trans). Fear and the Limits of Human Subjectivity. Dialec Hum, 15(3-4), 223-231, Sum-Autumn 88.

Fear is a signal of danger and subjective premise of counteractivity. It gives rise to prospective vigilance, from which consciousness originates as its most developed form. Two factors enhancing fear: a cognitive *impossibility of recognizing and localizing of a danger* and a practical one, *powerlessness in front of a danger*. In their extreme positions both of them transform fear into FEAR. The final term of FEAR may be a total demission including resignation, giving up even a symbolic counteractivity in front of a danger DANGER.

CADBURY, William and POAGUE, Leland. The Possibility of Film Criticism. J Aes Educ, 23(4), 5-22, Wint 89.

This essay considers the relevance of Monroe Beardsley's aesthetics to film criticism. Against the view that "aesthetic" criticism prizes the "organic" over the historical it is observed that Beardsley rejects "organic" as a value-term and that Beardsley's view of interpretation is exactly a matter of connecting work to world and in accord with knowledges which are deeply connected to (changing) social reality. Against the view that aesthetic criticism is ideologically blind to its complicity with the status quo it is observed that Beardsley provides extended and subtle examples (prefiguring much latter-day film criticism) or moral analyses of art works.

CADEGAN, Una M and HEFT, James L. Mary of Nazareth, Feminism and the Tradition. Thought, 65(257), 169-189, Je 90.

CADY, Duane L. *From Warism to Pacifism: A Moral Continuum*. Philadelphia, Temple Univ Pr, 1989

This book proposes a framework for understanding the spectrum of positions on morality and war. At one extreme is war realism, the view that morality is irrelevant to war. The moral restraint of the just war tradition is seen in increasing degrees ultimately relating to a range of pacifist views from pragmatic through nuclear, technological and epistemological to absolute pacifism. Our cultural predisposition to "warism" misguides values and institutions as do sexism and racism. Common objections to pacifism, a range of positive peace conceptions, and a brief history of the idea of pacifism are all considered.

CAHILL, Lisa Sowle. Can Theology Have a Role in "Public" Bioethical Discourse? Hastings Center Rep, 20(4), Supp 10-14, Jl-Ag 90.

This essay examines the grounds on which church-based groups may legitimately influence public policy debates, even granting that policy may not impose religious convictions or practices on dissenters. Policy discourse is actually a meeting ground of various religious, moral, and philosophical traditions. No moral or political debates are completely tradition-free. Rather, traditions and their representatives enter into dialogue about common practical concerns with a shared commitment to self-criticism and openness. Specifically religious traditions can challenge dominant values and institutions, while joining in efforts to achieve consensus on concrete issues.

CAHILL, Lisa Sowle. Moral Traditions, Ethical Language, and Reproductive Technologies. J Med Phil, 14(5), 497-522, O 89.

The Vatican Instruction on reproductive technologies and the OTA report, Infertility, both use "rights" language to advance quite different views of the same subject matter. The former focuses on the rights and welfare of the embryo and the protection of the family, while the latter stresses the freedom and rights of couples. This essay uses the work of Alasdair MacIntyre and Jeffrey Stout to consider the different traditions grounding these definitions of rights. It is proposed that a potentially effective mediating language could be that of "human nature," and argued that donor methods raise more serious moral objections that homologous ones.

CAHOON, A R and ROWNEY, J I A. Individual and Organizational Characteristics of Women in Managerial Leadership. J Bus Ethics, 9(4-5), 293-316, Ap-My 90.

Women are making a substantial impact on the employment market, both in terms of overall numbers as well as by appointment to male-dominated organizational roles. Research on women in leadership positions within organizations has concentrated on two main foci: firstly, the identification of relevant individual and organizational characteristics and secondly, on the impact of these variables on the women in management roles. This paper presents the findings from a series of studies in relation to these broad dimensions.

CAHOONE, Lawrence E. Buchler on Habermas on Modernity. S J Phil, 27(4), 461-477, Wint 89.

The work of Justus Buchler is used to critique and to suggest a reformulation of certain ideas in Jurgen Habermas's Theory of Communicative Action, most especially his analysis of modernity in terms of the conflict between "lifeworld" and "system." The difficulties of this dualistic analysis are examined. A Buchlerian "pluralistic" alternative is suggested, for which the pathologies of modernity are attributed, not to the dominance of the system, but to the condition of dominance per se, that is, the reduction of effective plurality.

CAIANIELLO, Silvia. Finitezza ed eticità nel pensiero storico di J G Droysen. Arch Stor Cult, 2, 305-323, 1989.

CAIMI, Mario P M. "El aire es elástico". Rev Filosof (Spain), 2, 109-126, 1989.

CAIN, James. The Doctrine of the Trinity and the Logic of Relative Identity. Relig Stud, 25(2), 141-152, Je 89.

I explore one way in which the theory of relative identity (developed along lines suggested by Geach's writings) can be used to understand the way language functions in Trinitarian doctrine. This includes a discussion of reduplicative propositions.

CALANDRA, A. Seeking Out Alternatives. Thinking, 7(3), 41, 1988.

CALCATERRA, Rosa. Interpretare l'esperienza: scienza metafisica etica nella filosofia di Ch S Peirce. Rome, Ianua, 1989

CALDERA, Rafael Tomas. Primo cadit ens. Anu Filosof, 22(2), 57-94, 1989.

CALEO, Marcello. Cosa è pensare: Saggio sulle "Categorie" di Aristotele. Sapienza, 42(4), 435-452, O-D 89.

CALLAHAN, Daniel. Modernizing Mortality: Medical Progress and the Good Society. Hastings Center Rep, 20(1), 28-37, Ja-F 90.

The control of health care costs will not be achieved unless there is a change in some underlying values of the health care system. The most central value is the belief in unlimited medical progress. This article contends that such a view of progress is no longer financially feasible or socially sensible. In its place should be put a greater effort to improve on human care of the sick, not medically based care.

CALLAHAN, Daniel. Moral Theory: Thinking, Doing, and Living. J Soc Phil, 20(1-2), 18-24, Spr-Fall 89.

How should the moral philosopher think about his or her own moral life while working on technical issues? It is argued that the moral philosopher has to understand not only formal moral theory, but have a drive for self-knowledge

and knowledge of the culture of which he or she is a part. Moral theory divorced from such understanding is likely to be thin.

CALLAHAN, Daniel. Religion and the Secularization of Bioethics. Hastings Center Rep, 20(4), Supp 2-4, Jl-Ag 90.

CALLAHAN, Joan C and KNIGHT, James W. Preventing Birth: Contemporary Methods and Related Moral Controversies. Salt Lake City, Univ of Utah Pr, 1989

Written to contribute to the public understanding of contemporary birth control methods and the moral issues surrounding these methods, this work includes detailed descriptions of reproductive anatomy and physiology, methods ranging from sophisticated "rhythm" techniques to induced abortion, and detailed discussions of moral issues such as elective abortion, holding women legally liable for fetal harm, rerodutive harm in the workplace, national funding for birth control research, and international family planning policies.

CALLAN, Eamonn. Godless Moral Education and Liberal Tolerance. J Phil Educ, 23(2), 267-281, Wint 89.

CALLEN, Donald. Stories of Sublimely Good Character. Phil Lit, 14(1), 40-52, Ap 90.

CALLENDER, Craig Adam. Function, Contemplation, and Eudaimonia. Dialogue (PST), 32(2-3), 33-38, Ap 90.

In the continuing debate concerning whether Aristotle has an "intellectualist" or "comprehensive" conception of the good in the Nicomachean Ethics, I argue for the supremacy of the "intellectualist" position. I claim "eudaimonia" to consist in one dominant good, contemplation, rather than a plurality of more or less equal goods. I also contend that man's distinctive function should be understood as the "top" of a being's hierarchical structure of supportive functions, and that contemplation is this "top."

CALLICOTT, J Baird and AMES, Roger T. "The Asian Traditions as a Conceptual Resource for Environmental Philosophy" in Nature in Asian Tradition of Thought: Essays in Environmental Philosophy, CALLICOTT, J Baird (ed), 1-21. Albany, SUNY Pr, 1989.

Environmental problems allegedly are rooted in Western traditions of thought. Accordingly, environmental philosophers have suggested that Eastern traditions of thought provide more ecologically resonant and environmentally benign world views. Comparative environmental philosophy is risky, but at the very least Asian traditions of thought may provide (1) a perspective from which to criticize otherwise unconscious assumptions at the foundations of the Western tradition; (2) a rich vocabulary to articulate the conceptually resonant revolutionary new paradigm in Western science; and (3) a conceptual resource for the development of indigenous Asian environmental ethics.

CALLICOTT, J Baird. The Case Against Moral Pluralism. Environ Ethics, 12(2), 99-124, Sum 90.

Despite Christopher Stone's recent argument on behalf of moral pluralism, the principal architects of environmental ethics remain committed to moral monism. Moral pluralism fails to specify what to do when two or more of its theories indicate inconsistent practical imperatives. More deeply, ethical theories are embedded in moral philosophies and moral pluralism requires us to shift between mutually inconsistent metaphysics of morals, most of which are no longer tenable in light of postmodern science. A univocal moral philosophy—traceable to David Hume's and Adam Smith's theory of moral sentiments, grounded in evolutionary biology by Charles Darwin, and latterly extended to the environment by Aldo Leopold—provides a unified, scientifically supported world view and portrait of human nature in which multiple, lexically ordered ethics are generated by multiple human, "mixed," and "biotic" community memberships.

CALLICOTT, J Baird and AMES, Roger T. "Epilogue: On the Relation of Idea and Action" in Nature in Asian Tradition of Thought: Essays in Environmental Philosophy, CALLICOTT, J Baird (ed), 279-289. Albany, SUNY Pr, 1989.

Asian traditions of thought cognitively resonate with contemporary ecological ideas and environmental ideals, yet Asia is as environmentally degraded as the West. This paradox may be explained in part by the intellectual colonization of the East by the West. More deeply, ideas and ideals are only indirectly and imperfectly linked to behavior. Nevertheless, they are not utterly inefficacious. Homo sapiens is a precocious, weedy species. A systemic concept of nature sets limits for successful human exploitation of nature, a relational concept of human nature connects human welfare with the nature's welfare, and environmental values may moderate man's adverse environmental impact.

CALLICOTT, J Baird. "The Metaphysical Implications of Ecology" in Nature in Asian Tradition of Thought: Essays in Environmental Philosophy,

CALLICOTT, J Baird (ed), 51-64. Albany, SUNY Pr, 1989.

The classical Western paradigm of nature is material, reductive, particulate, aggregative, quantitative, and mechanical. The natural paradigm emerging from the new physics and ecology is energetic, insubstantial, systemic, holistic, integrative, internally related, and organic. The distinction between self and nature blurs. If the intrinsic value of self may be taken as a given, and no crisp distinction between self and world is possible, then the intrinsic value of nature is reached.

CALLICOTT, J Baird. The Metaphysical Transition in Farming: From the Newtonian-Mechanical to the Eltonian Ecological. J Agr Ethics, 3(1), 36-49, 1990.

Modern agriculture is subject to a metaphysical as well as an ethical critique. As a casual review of the beliefs associated with food production in the past suggests, modern agriculture is embedded in and informed by the prevailing modern world view, Newtonian mechanics, which is bankrupt as a scientific paradigm and unsustainable as an agricultural motif. A new holistic, organic world view is emerging from ecology and the new physics marked by four general conceptual features: each level of organization from atoms to ecosystems (1) exhibits emergent properties, (2) exerts downward causation from whole to part, (3) is a systemically integrated whole, (4) the parts of which are internally related. Organic agriculture has been favourably compared with industrial agriculture by the United States National Academy of Science's Board on Agriculture. Aldo Leopold was among the first to criticize industrial agriculture and to envision a new motif for agriculture informed by ecology. A future postmodern ecological agriculture will help to solve the ethical problems engendered by modern mechanical agriculture.

CALLICOTT, J Baird (ed) and AMES, Roger T (ed). *Nature in Asian Tradition of Thought: Essays in Environmental Philosophy*. Albany, SUNY Pr, 1989

William Irwin Thompson, Harold Morowitz, and Baird Callicott argue that ecology represents nature to be internally related, systemically integrated, and unified. Resonant concepts of nature may repose in Asian traditions of thought. Tu Wei-Ming, Graham Parkes, David Hall, Roger Ames, and Robert Neville explore the complementary environmental attitudes and values in the Chinese world view; Hubertus Tellenbach and Bin Kimura, David Shaner, and William LaFleur, the Japanese world view; Francis Cook, David Inada, and David Kalupahana, the Buddhist world view; Eliot Deutsch and Gerald Larson, the Indian world view. These traditions provide a rich conceptual resource for contemporary environmental philosophy.

CAM, Philip. Searle on Strong AI. Austl J Phil, 68(1), 103-108, Mr 90.

CAMACHO, Luis A. Uso y abuso de las nociones de "crisis" y "modelo" en Ciencias Sociales en Costa Rica. Rev Filosof (Costa Rica), 26, 9-17, D 88.

The term "crisis" is so often used in recent books and articles by social scientists in Costa Rica that the conclusion could be drawn that we are always in crisis and that, therefore, nothing new is said when a particular epoch is characterized as critical. As to the term "model," two very different meanings are usually confused in the pre-analytical way it is used: as a socio-economic structure to be explained, and as a graphic representation useful in explanation. The oft-quoted expression "crisis of the model" merely compounds the confusion.

CAMACHO, Luis. "On Technology and Values" in *The Social Context and Values: Perspectives of the Americas*, MC LEAN, George F (ed), 125-139. Lanham, Univ Pr of America, 1989.

The first aim of the paper is to offer a description of how technological changes influence values. Several stages in the impact of technology in daily lives are distinguished, and different types of conflict are analyzed and assessed. The main purpose of the discussion is to establish some criteria for making moral judgments about changes in values. An analysis of the shift from change in values to change as the most important value is provided.

CAMARENA, Juan M S. Dialogo sobre humanismo y existencialismo (tercera parte). Rev Filosof (Mexico), 22(65), 123-131, My-Ag 89.

CAMERON, J R. "Do Future Generations Matter?" in *Ethics and the Environmental Responsibility*, DOWER, Nigel (ed), 57-78. Aldershot, Avebury, 1989.

This chapter explores the basis of the obligation we feel to respect the interests of future generations. Views which ground it in affection for our descendants (Passmore), or a morality based on self interest, social contract or rights are found wanting. Utilitarianism lacks the concept of fairness, which seems central here. Rawls's account of justice as fairness cannot apply, since we cannot form a society with those to whom the obligation is owed. The (admittedly vague) respect-for-persons account seems most nearly to capture the basis of the obligation. A trans-generational version of the

veil-of-ignorance is offered; the apparently limitless extent of our obligation to the totality of our successors is considered.

CAMHY, Daniela G and SOMMERMEIER, Rolf (trans). How Does the Child Benefit from "Philosophy for Children"? Thinking, 6(3), 32, 1986.

CAMHY, Daniela G. The Practice of Philosophy for Children in Austria: How Can Children Think Philosophically? Thinking, 5(4), 54-57, 1985.

CAMPBELL, Courtney S. Religion and Moral Meaning in Bioethics. Hastings Center Rep, 20(4), Supp 4-10, Jl-Ag 90.

The place of religious scholarship in bioethics hinges on (1) a reiteration of bioethics as a genuinely interdisciplinary endeavor; (2) a recognition of the vitality of prophetic voices in bioethics to complement applied decision making about moral quandaries; (3) an acknowledgement that insistence upon a common moral language risks impoverishing general moral discourse; and (4) sensitivity to how bioethics issues are most frequently embedded in the lives of persons and communities whose stories and traditions can enhance moral perception and imagination.

CAMPBELL, Donald T and PALLER, Bonnie T. "Extending Evolutionary Epistemology to 'Justifying' Scientific Beliefs" in *Issues in Evolutionary Epistemology*, HAHLWEG, Kai (ed), 231-257. Albany, SUNY Pr, 1989.

CAMPBELL, George and BITZER, Lloyd F (ed). *The Philosophy of Rhetoric (Revised Edition)*. Carbondale, So Illinois Univ Pr, 1988

CAMPBELL, James. Personhood and the Land. Agr Human Values, 7(1), 39-43, Wint 90.

This paper discusses the sense of human fulfillment elaborated in the writings of Wendell Berry. The initial section considers the relationship between freedom and social and geographical rootedness; and the second section considers in greater detail how agriculture and personal fulfillment are intertwined in Berry's work. In the concluding section, consideration is given to the degree to which agriculture may be said to be the proper form of human life.

CAMPBELL, James. Teaching American Philosophy. Teach Phil, 12(4), 375-398, D 89.

This paper is an attempt to survey the field of American philosophy for teachers who would like to teach a course in American philosophy. I consider a number of different kinds of possible courses and suggest what I think would be the best starting point. I also offer a survey of the primary and secondary literature in American philosophy with the intention of assisting the introductory teacher.

CAMPBELL, John and BIGELOW, John and PARGETTER, Robert. Death and Well-Being. Pac Phil Quart, 71(2), 119-140, Je 90.

CAMPBELL, Keith. Abstract Particulars. Cambridge, Blackwell, 1990

This book takes up, defends, and elaborates D C Williams's thesis that the fundamental ontological category is that of abstract particulars, that is, particular cases of qualities and relations. It provides a new resemblance treatment of the problem of universals, and argues that relations can be regarded, in most if not quite all cases, as supervenient on their terms. Considerations from first philosophy are presented as supporting a field theory of the natural world, and the benefits of abstract particularism for the human sciences briefly indicated.

CANARY, Catherine and ODEGARD, Douglas. Deductive Justification. Dialogue (Canada), 28(2), 305-320, 1989.

CAÑAS, José Luis. Tres niveles de conocimiento en la filosofía de Gabriel Marcel. Pensamiento, 46(181), 49-74, Ja-Mr 90.

En el seno de la dispersa y asistemática obra filosófica de G Marcel podemos distinguir claramente tres niveles de conocimiento, que corresponden a otras tres vertientes de la realidad cada vez más profundas: 1. nivel de la *encarnación*, donde el hombre aparece como espíritu encarnado ("mi cuerpo"); 2. nivel de la *comunión*, de la intersubjetividad, de la unión con los demás a través del diálogo, el amor, la fidelidad, la esperanza..., y, finalmente, 3. nivel de la *trascendencia*, de la participación en el ser, de la "exigencia ontológica...".

CANDIESCU, Calin. The Principle of Contextual *Bedeutung* and Triadic Semantics with Frege. Phil Log, 32(1-2), 113-127, Ja-Je 88.

CANGUILHEM, Georges and FAWCETT, Carolyn R and COHEN, Robert S (trans). *The Normal and the Pathological*. Cambridge, Zone Books, 1989

The normal and the pathological are terms used for structures, activities, individual or collective situations proper to living beings and especially to man. The relation of a fact and a norm is its positive or negative value. Can the assessment of behaviors (in medicine, psychology, law and jurisprudence) be reduced to noting a necessity? Is a living being's disease a fact similar to universal attraction? The author maintains that diseases are not merely predetermined effects, but are revealing of a normative regulation proper to living beings and man.

CAÑIZARES, Anita and KIZILTAN, Mustafa Ü and BAIN, William J. Postmodern Conditions: Rethinking Public Education. Educ Theor, 40(3), 351-369, Sum 90.

In the first section, within a framework modeled after Foucault's theory of discourse and Lyotard's analysis of the postmodern condition, we reconceptualize "public education" and outline the structure of a postmodern problematic. From this standpoint, the challenge of postmodernity lies in its destabilization of the metanarratives of modernity which have long sustained public education, the imminent postmodern fallout being the fracture and the dislocation of public education as a discursive formation. In the second section, we reconsider the idea of enlightenment and reconstitute it through the principle of "limit-attitude." We propose a transgressive mode of thought as the basis for public education.

CANJAR, R Michael. Cofinalities of Countable Ultraproducts: The Existence Theorem. Notre Dame J Form Log, 30(4), 539-542, Fall 89.

CANNON, Dale and WEINSTEIN, Mark. Reasoning Skills: An Overview. Thinking, 6(1), 29-33, 1985.

The article attempts to develop a comprehensive conception of reasoning skills that explains the place of philosophical inquiry among the various kinds of reasoning and in the development of skill or competence in their practice. It defines philosophical reasoning as a matter of clarifying and improving the conceptual tools with which one thinks and reasons about other things. A novel taxonomy is developed which recognizes four dimensions of reasoning: formal, informal, interpersonal, and philosophical, and discusses representative examples of each dimension. The article goes on to explain the relation of this conception of philosophical reasoning to the traditional discipline of philosophy and to develop a case for recognizing an essentially moral component to human reasoning in terms of its interpersonal dimension.

CAÑÓN, Camino. John Stuart Mill: su concepción de la Lógica. Pensamiento, 46(183), 257-284, Jl-S 90.

En esta presentación de la concepción milliana de la Lógica deductiva, ponemos de manifiesto su relevancia respecto de los puntos siguientes: 1.—Referente obligado para la adscripción o confrontación con posiciones psicologistas contemporáneas. 2.—Los intentos de absorción del viejo *Organon* por el nuevo baconiano sólo pueden hacerse a costa de ignorar la autonomía de la Lógica como Lógica formal. 3.—Ejemplar metodológico para el establecimiento de las relaciones entre compromiso ontológico y posición epistemológica. 4.—Tratamiento diferenciado y complementario de la Lógica como ciencia y como arte, según una epistemología empirista y unos criterios prácticos utilitaristas.—Criticamos las posiciones de Mill desde una concepción de la Lógica deductiva como Lógica formal, no psicologista.

CANTILLO, Giuseppe. J G Droysen: Storia universale e Kulturgeschichte. Arch Stor Cult, 1, 81-136, 1988.

CANTINI, Andrea. A Theory of Formal Truth Arithmetically Equivalent to ID$_1$. J Sym Log, 55(1), 244-259, Mr 90.

We present a theory VF of partial truth over Peano arithmetic and we prove that VF and ID$_1$ have the same arithmetical content. The semantics of VF is inspired by van Fraassen's notion of supervaluation.

CANTRELL, Carol H. Analogy as Destiny: Cartesian Man and the Woman Reader. Hypatia, 5(2), 7-19, Sum 90.

Feminist studies in the history and philosophy of science have suggested that supposedly neutral and objective discourses are shaped by pairs of dualisms, which though value-laden are assumed to inhere in the order of nature. These hierarchical pairs devalue women, particularly their bodies and their labor, as they sanction the domination of nature. Readers of literature can draw on these studies to address texts and genres which do not thematize gender but rather purport to portray "the human condition." Samuel Beckett's *Molloy*, with its clear structure of Cartesian divisions, provides a dramatic example of how an examination of dualisms reveals the presence of a language of gender informing a minimalist literary text.

CAPALDI, Nicholas. Liberal Values vs Liberal Social Philosophy. Phil Theol, 4(3), 283-296, Spr 90.

This paper is a contribution toward the clarification of the meaning and evolution of liberalism. Liberal values are distinguished from liberal social philosophy. Liberal values, specifically individuality, government by consent of the governed, and private property in a capitalist economy are modern despite their clear classical and medieval origins. Liberal social philosophy consists of ontological realism, epistemological invididualism, and axiological teleology. Liberal social philosophy is classical, and it reflects an attempt to rationalize modern values with a classical philosophy. I argue that liberal social philosophy is seriously flawed, and when it is modified for modern contexts it is inimical to liberal values. Liberal values are better understood and more defensible, as well as more compatible with nonliberal values, when divorced from liberal social philosophy.

CAPOZZI, Gino. Praxeologia della costizuione del potere. Riv Int Filosof Diritto, 66(2), 250-289, Ap-Je 89.

CAPPELLETTI, Angel J. Vida y evolución en la filosofía griega. Pensamiento, 46(182), 225-240, Ap-Je 90.

Partiendo del concepto griego de "physis" se exponen las teorías de los primeros filósofos jónicos sobre la vida integrada en la primera materia viva y divina (hilozoísmo); Anaxágoras y Empédocles marcan una diferenciación de factores que siguen la línea ascendente de la vida hasta las concepciones superiores de Platón y Aristóteles. La segunda parte atiende al tema de la evolución; señala aproximaciones a ella ya en los jónicos, más en Empédocles y Parménides, y relaciona la misma concepción fijista de Aristóteles, gracias a su labor clasificadora, con las modernas teorías evolucionistas.

CAPRON, Alexander Morgan. The Burden of Decision. Hastings Center Rep, 20(3), 36-41, My-Je 90.

Despite good reasons for judicial intervention in some bioethics, judges ought to be reluctant routinely to accept a decision-making role—in place of patients, families, physicians and others directly involved—in most medical treatment cases; principles and arguments are presented against judicially "immunizing" decision making at the bedside.

CAPUTO, C. Parlando di segni, di Hjelmslev e di filosofia del linguaggio. Il Protag, 6(9-10), 127-137, Je-D 86.

CAPUTO, John D Beyond Aestheticism: Derrida's Responsible Anarchy. Res Phenomenol, 18, 59-73, 1988.

CAPUTO, John D. Derrida, a Kind of Philosophy: A Discussion of Recent Literature. Res Phenomenol, 17, 245-259, 1987.

CAPUTO, John D. "Disseminating Originary Ethics and the Ethics of Dissemination" in *The Question of the Other: Essays in Contemporary Continental Philosophy*, DALLERY, Arleen B (ed), 55-62. Albany, SUNY Pr, 1989.

CAPUTO, John D. "Mysticism and Transgression: Derrida and Meister Eckhart" in *Derrida and Deconstruction*, SILVERMAN, Hugh J (ed), 24-39. New York, Routledge, 1989.

CAPUTO, John D. Thinking, Poetry and Pain. S J Phil, SUPP(28), 155-181, 1989.

CARACCIOLO, Alberto. Leopardi e il nichilismo. G Metaf, 11(1), 41-49, Ja-Ap 89.

CARACCIOLO, Ricardo. Justificación normativa y pertenencia. Analisis Filosof, 8(1), 37-67, My 88.

An analysis of the question of the normative justification of decisions, especially the judicial decisions, is presented in this paper. To this end, two different uses of the term "decision" are distinguished and two correlative notions of justification of norms and of acts are suggested. This analysis aims especially at a discussion of the conditions of justification of norms based on deductive relations. Grounded on the strong conceptual connection between the justification of an act and that of its result, the argument tries to show that alternative responses are conditioned by the way in which membership of individual norms to a normative system is defined. To that purpose, four possible models of membership are discussed from the point of view of their respective suitability to the standard conception about judicially produced norms. It is held that the problems of adjustment of the justification deductive model, represented by the common notion of "judicial syllogism," result from disregarding the fact that the identification of a system also depends on decisions about the meaning of the language in which the norms are expressed.

CARAHER, Brian G. "Recovering the Figure of J L Austin in Paul de Man's *Allegories of Reading*" in *The Textual Sublime: Deconstruction and Its Differences*, SILVERMAN, Hugh J (ed), 139-146. Albany, SUNY Pr, 1990.

This essay examines traces of Paul de Man's effort to grapple with the speech-act theory and terminology of J L Austin. De Man reinstates a contrast between "constative" and "performative" conceptions of language in *Allegories of Reading*. The "deconstruction" of this problematic contrast has already been performed by Austin's *How to Do Things with Words*, yet de Man posits it once again to help generate his deconstructive practice. De Man's key philosophical and rhetorical strategy is to presuppose a positivist paradigm that disables a performative conception of rhetorical utterance and linguistically-mediated knowledge.

CARAMELEA, Vasile V (and others). The National Axiological Anthropological Atlas: A "Chart" of the Premiss Values of the Romanian People's Culture (I). Phil Log, 32(1-2), 47-58, Ja-Je 88.

CARBONE, Alessandra and MONTAGNA, Franco. Much Shorter Proofs: A Bimodal Investigation. Z Math Log, 36(1), 47-66, 1990.

CARBONE, Alessandra and MONTAGNA, F. Rosser Orderings in Bimodal Logics. Z Math Log, 35(4), 343-358, 1989.

CAREY, Jonathan Sinclair. Rapiers and the Religio Medici. Ethics Med, 6(2), 28-29, Sum 90.

CARGAS, Harry James. Survival Through the Generosity of Strangers. Bridges, 1(3-4), 119-133, Fall-Wint 89.

CARGILE, James. "Tense and Existence" in *Cause, Mind, and Reality: Essays Honoring C B Martin*, HEIL, John (ed), 161-172. Norwell, Kluwer, 1989.

It is argued that contrary to the "B theory" there is such a property as being present, and that, contrary to the "A theory" propositions do not change truth values. Further, that it is not possible to refer to what does not exist *simpliciter* (*pace* Meinong) but perfectly possible to refer to what does not exist *yet* (*pace* the "Generality of Predictions Thesis"). Further, that even if a meaning is given the idea of a "tenseless" translation of a statement, it is not true that any principles of logic require such formulations.

CARLSON, George R. Pain and the Quantum Leap to Agent-Neutral Value. Ethics, 100(2), 363-367, Ja 90.

T Nagel holds that the "awfulness" of anyone's pain provides *anyone else* with reason for wanting it to stop and is consequently bad for all, *period* (*Tanner Lectures*, p. 108). I believe that the hard facts about pain cannot sustain any such quantum leap to agent-neutral value. Accordingly, I argue that the allegation that pain is agent-neutrally bad is not supported by Nagel's claim about the equal awfulness of anyone's pains, unless there are reasons (such as Nagel fails to provide) for concluding that this awfulness, itself, is agent-neutral.

CARLSON, Jeffrey. Ogden's 'Appropriateness' and Religious Plurality. Mod Theol, 6(1), 15-28, O 89.

CARLSON, John W. *Donum Vitae* on Homologous Interventions: Is IVF-ET a Less Acceptable Gift than "Gift"? J Med Phil, 14(5), 523-540, O 89.

Donum Vitae argues that, by failing to respect the connection between the conjugal act and procreation, in vitro fertilization—even in the homologous or "simple case," where both gametes come from a married couple and the resulting embryo is transferred to the wife—shows itself to be morally unacceptable. On the other hand, the document refers approvingly to other technological interventions which "facilitate" or "assist" the conjugal act in achieving its objective. Although none of the latter interventions are mentioned by name, the recently developed gamete intrafallopian transfer (GIFT) and certain associated techniques have found favor with many orthodox Roman Catholic thinkers, as well as with some church authorities. The present article explores this situation in the Catholic moral tradition, and offers reasons for believing that, given relevantly similar conditions, if GIFT if morally acceptable so also is homologous IVF-ET.

CARNEY, James D. Literary Relativism. J Aes Educ, 21(3), 5-16, Fall 87.

CARON, Anita and SCHLEIFER, Michael and LEBUIS, Pierre. The Effect of the *Pixie* Program on Logical and Moral Reasoning. Thinking, 7(2), 12-16, 1987.

CARONE, Gabriela Roxana. El problema del "alma mala" en la última filosofia de Platón (*Leyes* X, 896d ss). Rev Filosof (Argentina), 3(2), 143-163, N 88.

This paper deals with some difficulties arisen in *Laws* X, where at least two souls are said to be concerned in the governance of the universe: beneficent soul and soul capable of working the opposite. After examining the argument that leads to that postulation, we weigh different possible interpretations of the maleficent soul. We conclude that, though the dialogue finally discards the hypothesis of an evil soul ruling the whole cosmos by asserting God's care of the world, an irrational faculty of the World-Soul, inferior to the governing rational part, may be assumed as a potential source of physical disorders here on earth.

CARPENTER, Bob and MORRILL, Glyn. Compositionality, Implicational Logics, and Theories of Grammar. Ling Phil, 13(4), 383-392, Ag 90.

According to (Frege's) principle of compositionality, the meaning of a linguistic expression is to be analysed as a function of the meaning of its components, and their mode of combination. The paper shows how a construal of this principle for natural language, together with an assumption that meanings fit a simply typed function space, derives effects achieved by the Theta-Criterion in Government-Binding Theory, and Completeness and Coherence Conditions in Lexical-Functional Grammar. The demonstration exploits the relationship between functional types and implicational logics, and is interpreted as providing semantic rationalisation for apparently arbitrary syntactic principles.

CARR, Craig L. Kant's Theory of Political Authority. Hist Polit Thought, 10(4), 719-731, Wint 89.

This discussion addresses the legitimacy of Kant's notion of political authority. It is argued that Kant's appeal to political authority is not inconsistent with his moral philosophy, as is frequently supposed. The article concludes that Kant's notion of coercion provides the bridge that reconciles his use of political authority with his notion of moral autonomy.

CARR, Indira Mahalingam. Communication, Grice, and Languageless Creatures. Indian Phil Quart, 17(2), 223-250, Ap 90.

This paper shows that the possibility of languageless creatures communicating in the full sense (i.e., in the human sense) under relevant circumstances does exist. And to this end an account of the meaning of an utterance is explicated in terms of the utterer's intention to produce an effect of a broadly cognitive or epistemic kind in an audience—a position that draws heavily on Grice's paper "Meaning." Further, the relevant circumstances under which the languageless creatures could be said to communicate are given.

CARRIER, Martin. Kants Theorie der Materie und ihre Wirkung auf die zeitgenössische Chemie. Kantstudien, 81(2), 170-210, 1990.

Kant's theory of matter is reconstructed and his views about and impact on chemistry are studied. His early "monadological" conception is analyzed and compared to other dynamical approaches of the period. His later attempt to regard matter as a continuum and to derive some of its properties from the interaction of forces is reconstructed. His conception of chemistry is examined and compared to the notion of some chemists who were inspired by Kant's work.

CARRION, Rejane. Depois do ceticismo. Manuscrito, 11(2), 113-123, O 88.

Scepticism casts doubt—in a very rigorous and consequential way—about our ability to reach true justifiable beliefs. In order to preserve the possibility of communication and action (which depends upon shared beliefs), the sceptic appeals either to a language devoid of assertive illocutionary force or else to a natural or practical domain. The latter provides certainties which are neither *grounded* nor *subject to doubt*. In this paper an attempt is made to show that both ways are blocked for a contemporary sceptic. This fact forces him, at the very least, to become much more radical.

CARROLL, John. The Humean Tradition. Phil Rev, 99(2), 185-219, Ap 90.

Within the Humean tradition, no adequate account of laws of nature is possible. There are two reasons for this conclusion. The first is that the initially most plausible attempts to give such an account fail. This, in part, is argued through criticisms of David Lewis's account and an account discernible in Brian Skyrms's *Causal Necessity*. The second reason for the anti-Humean conclusion is of a more general nature. An argument is advanced showing that Humeans have mistakenly presupposed that lawhood *supervenes* on non-nomic, nominalistic considerations.

CARROLL, Noël. Interpretation, History and Narrative. Monist, 73(2), 134-166, Ap 90.

CARROLL, Noël. *The Philosophy of Horror 'or' Paradoxes of the Heart*. New York, Routledge, 1990

CARROLL, William and FURLONG, John. Teaching Reasoning With Computers. Thinking, 5(4), 29-32, 1985.

CARRUTHERS, Peter. What Is Empiricism?—I. Aris Soc, SUPP 64, 63-79, 1990.

The paper asks whether empiricism can be construed so as to allow for the possibility of innate knowledge and concepts, arguing that it can. The core of empiricism consists in the demand that claims to knowledge should be constrained by our best theory of the mind's powers and natural modes of access to reality. Classic empiricists rejected innateness because the only explanation of it available at the time, concerned intervention in the human mind by God. But given a theory of evolution, their opposition should evaporate. The paper also argues that the constraint in question is a reasonable one.

CARSON, Ronald A. Interpretive Bioethics: The Way of Discernment. Theor Med, 11(1), 51-59, Mr 90.

This paper critically appraises the applied action-guide approach to bioethics and finds it wanting in two ways: it is tethered to a social contract view of the doctor-patient relationship that is largely incompatible with experiences of illness and care; and, as a formalist doctrine, it lacks critical edge and tends toward accommodationism. An alternative approach is recommended that involves interpreting moral experience by means once associated with the rhetorical arts—practical reasoning, hermeneutics, casuistry, and thick description.

CARSON, Thomas L. Could Ideal Observers Disagree?: A Reply to Taliaferro. Phil Phenomenol Res, 50(1), 115-124, S 89.

In *The Status of Morality* I argue that Firth's version of the ideal observer theory commits him to an extreme version of moral relativism. Firthian ideal observers could disagree in their attitudes about all possible moral questions. I also propose an alternative version of the ideal observer theory which I believe commits us to a moderate version of moral relativism. In "Relativizing the Ideal Observer Theory" Charles Taliaferro defends Firth's formulation of the ideal observer theory. He also rejects my claim that Firth is committed to relativism. In this paper I defend my views against Taliaferro's criticisms.

CARTER, Alan. 'Self-Exploitation' and Workers' Co-Operatives—Or How the British Left Get Their Concepts Wrong. J Applied Phil, 6(2), 195-199, O 89.

In this article I examine the concept 'self-exploitation' and its use in criticizing workers' co-operatives. I argue that the concept is incoherent and that the kind of exploitation which members of workers' co-ops actually face is 'market-exploitation'. Moreover, some of the criticisms of workers' co-ops which are made by those who employ the confused concept 'self-exploitation' are shown to be inapposite when 'market-exploitation' is recognised to be the real problem. I conclude with a discussion of the reasons for the acceptance of the misguided concept 'self-exploitation' by a number on the Left in Britain today.

CARTER, Alan. On Individualism, Collectivism and Interrelationism. Heythrop J, 31(1), 23-38, Ja 90.

CARTER, Michele and WICHMAN, Alison and MC CARTHY, Charles R. Regulating AIDS Research on Infants and Children: The Moral Task of Institutional Review Boards. Bridges, 2(1-2), 63-73, Spr-Sum 90.

Acquired Immunodeficiency Syndrome (AIDS) has created ethical dilemmas for research investigators as well as other healthcare professionals. One difficult problem facing research investigators and Institutional Review Boards (IRBs) (committees required to review and approve proposed research involving human subjects before the projects can be initiated) is to determine if, when, and under what circumstances it is permissible to conduct research involving children and infants infected with the AIDS virus as research subjects. The authors review existing Health and Human Services (HHS) regulations for the Protection of Human Subjects, present a prototypical case involving an infant infected with the AIDS virus, and conclude that the regulations provide a suitable framework for IRBs to consider the ethical problems facing pediatric AIDS research.

CARTER, Nancy Corson. Body-Vessel-Matrix: Co-creative Images of Synergetic Universe. Zygon, 25(2), 151-165, Je 90.

In his essay "Goddesses of the Twenty-first Century," R Buckminster Fuller's use of woman and goddess as metaphor suggests a fruitful source of images illuminating synergetic principles. Using five images, clustered as body-vessel-matrix, the article suggests an epistemology and a heuristic for connecting the personal-physical and the universal-metaphysical. These images are (1) the Egyptian goddess Nut, (2) the Greek earth goddesses, (3) Neolithic Maltese goddess temples, (4) the double spiral, and (5) the Apollo Mission's Earth photographs. These images are intended as transformational synergetic/ecofeminist figures to replace images of deprivation, alienation, and destruction with images of abundance, intimacy, and co-creation.

CARTER, William R. Metaphysical Boundaries: A Question of Independence. Austl J Phil, 67(3), 263-276, S 89.

CARTER, William. Changing the Minimal Subject. Phil Stud, 57(2), 217-226, O 89.

CARTWRIGHT, David E. "Schopenhauer on Suffering, Death, Guilt, and the Consolation of Metaphysics" in *Schopenhauer: New Essays in Honor of His 200th Birthday*, VON DER LUFT, Eric (ed), 51-66. Lewiston, Mellen Pr, 1989.

I herein elucidate a number of Schopenhauer's most provocative claims concerning the guilt of being within the context of his analysis of the human need for metaphysics. I argue that Schopenhauer's metaphysics involves two conflicting requirements: namely, that it provides a correct and comprehensive description of human experience and that it consoles the metaphysician concerning the all-pervasive nature of suffering and death. I conclude that Schopenhauer's remarks concerning existential guilt, suffering, death, and eternal justice reveal more about Schopenhauer's personality than they do about the universal structure of being.

CARTWRIGHT, David. Schopenhauer as Moral Philosopher—Towards the Actuality of his Ethics. Schopenhauer Jahr, 70, 54-65, 1989.

CARTWRIGHT, Nancy. The Born-Einstein Debate: Where Application and Explanation Separate. Synthese, 81(3), 271-282, D 89.

Application in science has its own structure, distinct from the structure of theoretical science, and therefore needs its own philosophy. The covering power of a formal scientific theory is no guide to its explanatory power. Explanation is too much to ask of a fundamental scientific theory. This is seen by considering two strands of the Born-Einstein debate: first the explanatory power of quantum mechanics and second, the reality of unobserved properties. The function of theoretical physics is to describe rather than to explain. Some techniques are a standard part of theory; while some are *ad hoc* to the problems at hand. Very few of the derivations in mathematical physics are explanatory. This shows distinctly separate structures for theory and for application.

CARTWRIGHT, Nancy. "Capacities and Abstractions" in *Scientific Explanation (Minnesota Studies in the Philosophy of Science, Volume XIII)*, KITCHER, Philip (ed), 349-356. Minneapolis, Univ of Minn Pr, 1989.

CARTWRIGHT, Nancy. *Nature's Capacities and their Measurement*. New York, Clarendon/Oxford Pr, 1989

CASANAVE, Abel Lassalle. Platonismo, unicidad y metateoría. Rev Filosof (Argentina), 2(1), 3-20, My 87.

This paper is devoted to analyze the possibility of supporting the tenet we call "moderate Platonism." We conclude that arguments based upon results that stem in first order logic do not offer enough evidence for this standpoint. After rejecting this approach, we resort to stronger systems, specifically infinitary languages, and regard them as a promissory way for foundations.

CASANOVA, Pablo González. Remembering and Re-Creating the Classing. Dialec Hum, 16(2), 165-170, Spr 89.

CASCARDI, Anthony J. Narration and Totality. Phil Forum, 21(3), 277-294, Spr 90.

CASEMENT, William. Learning and Pleasure: Early American Perspectives. Educ Theor, 40(3), 343-349, Sum 90.

Early American thinkers conceived of learning largely in terms of its application to practical ends: religious, political, economic, social, moral. A summary is given of this utilitarian perspective, followed by exposition of a subordinate perspective that is seldom mentioned in current accounts of early American thought: the connections of learning with pleasure. The connections sometimes linked pleasure with utility, but there is also evidence of an appreciation for the activity of learning as pleasurable inherently. References are made to such notable early Americans as Benjamin Rush, Simeon Doggett, Noah Webster, Benjamin Franklin, Samuel Knox, Samuel Smith, Thomas Jefferson, John Adams.

CASEY, Gerard N. Angelic Interiority. Irish Phil J, 6(1), 82-118, 1989.

In this article I examine St. Thomas's application of some basic metaphysical and epistemological principles to purely intellectual beings (angels). I consider an apparent inconsistency in St. Thomas's angelology having to do with an angel's transparency to self but not to other angels and I attempt to show both *that* is not an inconsistency and *why* it is not an inconsistency. The dissolution of the inconsistency depends crucially upon the distinction of *esse naturale*, *esse intentionale* and *esse intelligibile* from one another; and upon a clear grasp of the role of the will as a principle of interiority in all created intellectual beings.

CASPARY, William R. Judgments of Value in John Dewey's Theory of Ethics. Educ Theor, 40(2), 155-169, Spr 90.

CASSINI, Alejandro. Naturaleza y función de los axiomas en la epistemología aristotélica. Rev Filosof (Argentina), 1(1-2), 75-97, N 86.

This paper deals with the Aristotelian concept of axioms, and analyzes its function in the model of demonstrative science explained in the *Posterior Analytics*. It argues that the axioms are not premises of scientific deduction, nor rules of inference which manage the axiomatic construction of any science. Nevertheless, they are a certain kind of rule, but not logical rules. They are metascientific rules that set up necessary conditions for the statements of all sciences, including their proper principles.

CASSINI, Alejandro. Poder causal, experiencia y conceptos *a priori*. Rev Filosof (Argentina), 3(1), 3-15, My 88.

The paper considers the justification of the objectivity of causal relations. First, it criticizes some aspects of Hume's approach to the topic. Then it sketches an analysis of causation in terms of causal powers and production of events. Finally, it postulates the general concept of causal power as *a priori*, i.e., as a necessary condition for the experience of objects. Nevertheless, this *a priori* concept is conceived as acquired from a kind of preobjective experience.

CASSIRER, Ernst and GAY, Peter (ed & trans). *The Question of Jean-Jacques Rousseau—Ernest Cassirer (Second Edition)*. New Haven, Yale Univ Pr, 1989

CASTAÑARES, Wenceslao. Qué hacer con los textos. Dialogo Filosof, 6(2), 241-246, My-Ag 90.

El comentario de texto, como método específico en la enseñanza de la filosofía, encuentra dificultades prácticas que bloquean su eficacia y desaniman a profesores y alumnos. En este breve trabajo se analizan las causas de esas dificultades y se aportan las líneas de su posible solución, en lo que se refiere a los presupuestos teóricos y prácticos que deben ponerse en juego a la hora de abordar esta necesaria tarea didáctica.

CASTAÑEDA, Hector-Neri. Leibniz's Complete Propositional Logic. Topoi, 9(1), 15-27, Mr 90.

CASTAÑEDA, Hector-Neri. Moral Obligation, Circumstances, and Deontic Foci (A Rejoinder to Fred Feldman). Phil Stud, 57(2), 157-174, O 89.

Feldman has replied to my proof that his dyadic calculus is not adequate as a formalization of the logic of moral reparation. In spite of some polemical smoke, the reply is clear and candid. It shows how the paradoxes are so close to the surface of his solution. Then he brings in additional data to show how his solution may appear to be in error. These data corroborate the deontic focus/circumstance distinction and establish that the appearance of error is not just an appearance.

CASTAÑEDA, Hector-Neri. "The Multiple Faces of Knowing: The Hierarchies of Epistemic Species" in *The Current State of the Coherence Theory*, BENDER, John W (ed), 231-241. Norwell, Kluwer, 1989.

Knowledge is coherence, of course. It is hierarchical and it must have a base. This need not be an absolute foundation. In any case each particular state of knowing or of justified belief must have a base consisting of a relevant hierarchy of background assumptions and, especially, takens-for-granted. These are non-justified justifiers. No local epistemic base need be an absolute foundation. The next major claims are these: Each epistemic base determines a species of justified believing or knowing, and perhaps species fall under different types; perhaps the species are determinates and they and their determinables are captured only schematically in definition schemata. In support of this multiple-species view of knowledge a family of diverse humdrum-type cases of knowing is marshaled. The hypothesis that debates in epistemology involve arguments from different species of knowledge is corroborated by a well-known dispute between Keith Lehrer and Alvin Goldman. (edited)

CASTAÑEDA, Héctor-Neri. Objetos, identidad y mismidad. Analisis Filosof, 9(1), 1-39, My 89.

The concepts of identity and sameness are necessary for thinking: through them our finite minds break reality into units of experience and, in general, into thinkable referential units. In this work the author analyses the nature of the identity and sameness of the objects of the world, as structures that make possible human experience. (edited)

CASTAÑEDA, Hector-Neri. Paradoxes of Moral Reparation: Deontic Foci versus Circumstances. Phil Stud, 57(1), 1-21, S 89.

Several families of deontic paradoxes are discussed to show that deontic logic is two-sorted, built on the focus/circumstance distinction. Ponder: (A) "Dan is obligated to do the following: go to help Jones, to notify Jones that he is coming if he goes, and notify him that he is not coming if he does not go." This implies that Dan is obligated to go to help Jones; but it does not imply what notification Dan should send. This depends on the actual *circumstance* of whether he goes to help or not. Any formal calculus that lets (A) imply that Dan is obligated to notify Jones that he is coming to help is inadequate for deontic logic. For example, Fred Feldman's dyadic deontic calculus fails this test.

CASTAÑEDA, Hector-Neri. "Philosophy as a Science and as a Worldview" in *The Institution of Philosophy: A Discipline in Crisis?*, COHEN, Avner (ed), 13-33. La Salle, Open Court, 1989.

CASTAÑEDA, Hector-Neri. The Reflexivity of Self-Consciousness: Sameness/Identity, Data for Artificial Intelligence. Phil Topics, 17(1), 27-58, Spr 89.

The hierarchical structure of self-consciousness is analyzed. It involves (a) a hierarchy of reflexivities having as its base the mere external reflexivity of any reflexive relation, (b) a hierarchy of states of consciousness, and (c) a hierarchy of *I*-representations: the *I*-strands. The investigation shows also a manifold of sameness relations. An *I* is merely an ephemeral subjective hypostasis which is posited as the same as its external thinker. The unity of consciousness cannot proceed from an *I*, but is built upwards from the different contents and their monitorial processes.

CASTAÑEDA, Héctor-Neri. The Role of Apperception in Kant's Transcendental Deduction of the Categories. Nous, 24(1), 147-157, Mr 90.

CASTAÑEDA, Hector-Neri. Semantic Holism Without Semantic Socialism: Twin Earths, Thinking, Language, Bodies, and the World. Midwest Stud Phil, 14, 101-126, 1989.

This is a first round in defense of both a methodological epistemic physicalism and a semantic holism, which grounds doxastic cooperation, without endorsing the semantic socialism, which is said to ensue from Hilary Putnam's celebrated Twin-Earth and Twin-Pomeranian arguments, and Tyler Burge's challenging Twin-Arthritis thought experiments.

CASTELLANA, M. Il neorealismo epistemologico dell' "Académie Internationale de philosophie des sciences". Il Protag, 6(9-10), 5-31, Je-D 86.

This essay for the first time wants to point out the important and original contributions given to the philosophy of science by the "Académie Internationale de Philosophie des Sciences" (AIPS), for its 40 years of activity (1947-1987). The AIPS, which was founded by S Dockx, has developed a unitary epistemological project which has involved scientists and philosophers, epistemologists and historians of science of various countries. Above all the philosophy of physics has been deeply studied and particularly the known contrasts between the two "great systems" of the twentieth century (relativity and quantum mechanics). (edited)

CASTRO, Barry. Business Ethics and Business Education: A Report from a Regional State University. J Bus Ethics, 8(6), 479-486, Je 89.

My central point is that the recent wave of interest in business ethics is an opportunity to review the whole enterprise of undergraduate business education. Business ethics, taught as if the students, faculty, curriculum and organization of the business school were important parts of the subject matter, is a way both to affirm the seriousness of ethical inquiry and to build an increased sense of collegial responsibility for the overall curriculum students are asked to undertake.

CASTRO, Edgardo. Antropología y evolucionismo. Sapientia, 44(173), 233-235, Jl-S 89.

CASTRO, Edgardo. Orden-desorden, a propósito de *Il nome della rosa*. Sapientia, 44(174), 295-304, O-D 89.

CASTRO, J. Nondeterministic ω-Computations and the Analytical Hierarchy. Z Math Log, 35(4), 333-342, 1989.

Classically, Turing machines define languages by accepting or not finite strings over some finite (usually binary) alphabet. Many problems related to these notions (e.g., determining whether a given machine accepts any word, or whether two machines define the same language) are known to be complete in certain degrees of Keene's arithmetical hierarchy. In this note, Turing machines that accept infinite words—a more recent concept—are considered, and problems like those quoted above are shown to be complete in certain degrees of the analytical hierarchy. Moreover, these results give instances of natural complete problems for the analytical hierarchy.

CASTRO, Juan Luis and TRILLAS, Enric. Sobre preórdenes y operadores de consecuencias de Tarski. Theoria (Spain), 4(11), 419-425, F-My 89.

CASULLO, Albert. Perceptual Space Is Monadic. Phil Phenomenol Res, 50(1), 131-134, S 89.

In a recent paper, I defended the *monadic theory* of perceptual space: (MT) Objects in the visual field have their location by virtue of monadic positional properties. The defense involved (a) responding to some objections; and (b) offering an independent argument in support of the theory. Lorne Falkenstein offers two objections to my defense of (MT). He maintains that a purely relational account of locations in visual space is possible and that my account involves a tacit reliance on spatial relations. In this paper I argue that these objections are not convincing.

CATALANO, George D. Animals in the Research Laboratory: Science or Pseudoscience? Between Species, 6(1), 17-21, Wint 90.

A consideration of the ethics of using animals in research laboratories is undertaken using Popper's falsifiability criterion. Popper's criterion maintains that a theory is scientific if and only if a crucial experiment which can falsify it is specified in advance. An analysis of the data from the experiments/observations dealing with tuberculosis, flu, and other vaccines demonstrates that the use of animals leads only to trivial verification rather than to predictions and thus represents the pseudoscience of a degenerating research programme.

CATALANO, Joseph S. Successfully Lying to Oneself: A Sartrean Perspective. Phil Phenomenol Res, 50(4), 673-693, Je 90.

The crux of the argument is a distinction between a thetic and nonthetic consciousness. The point is that, for Sartre, translucency does not imply a thetic, or delineated, conceptual awareness. It is thus possible to be nonthetically aware of one's behavior, and still misrepresent this awareness conceptually to oneself. Beyond this, it is also possible to frame one's conceptual misrepresentations so that one eventually believes in them. Tension, of course, exists, but it is conceived by the individual to be the "normal" tension experienced by everyone.

CATANIA, Alfonso. Hobbes e Kelsen. Riv Int Filosof Diritto, 66(3), 407-423, Jl-S 89.

CATTANI, Mary Schnackenberg (trans) and FERRY, Luc and RENAUT, Alain. French Philosophy of the Sixties: An Essay on Antihumanism. Amherst, Univ of Mass Pr, 1990

The focus of this text is the philosophic interpretation of the French revolt in 1968. The interpretations of the French postmodernists of the revolt, and their attempt to find a nonmetaphysical form of humanism to explain the revolt are explicated. (staff)

CATTON, Philip. Marxist Critical Theory, Contradictions, and Ecological Succession. Dialogue (Canada), 28(4), 637-653, 1989.

CATURELLI, Alberto. El X aniversario del Primer Congreso Mundial de Filosofía Cristiana. Sapientia, 44(174), 310-313, O-D 89.

CAUCHY, Venant and CHRÉTIEN, Émile. Intervention: Entretien avec Monsieur Venant Cauchy. Philosophiques, 17(1), 127-141, 1990.

CAUSEY, Ann S. On the Morality of Hunting. Environ Ethics, 11(4), 327-343, Wint 89.

The controversy between hunting apologists and their anti-hunting antagonists continues to escalate. Numerous attempts to settle the issue have failed in part because the participants have often not distinguished and treated separately the various activities labeled "hunting." Those who participate in hunting fall into one of two categories: shooters or sport hunters. Shooters are those whose ultimate goals do not depend on hunting but can be met in other ways; sport hunters are those who take immense pleasure in the hunt itself and who kill in order to have had an authentic hunting experience. Discussion of the morality of hunting (as opposed to its prudence) is properly restricted to the moral evaluation of the desire of sport hunters to kill for pleasure. This desire can be explained by biological/evolutionary concepts and defended as morally neutral. Neither the animal protectionists nor the utilitarian apologists recognize that violent death is part of nature and that man's desire to participate in it can be both natural and culturally valuable. Though well-intentioned, utilitarianism is an impotent ethical defense of hunting because it can judge only the prudence, not the morality, of hunting.

CAVADI, Augusto. Pensiero sobrio e fede cristiana. Sapienza, 42(3), 319-335, Jl-S 89.

CAVAILLÉ, Jean-Pierre. Notes et documents sur "Le Descartes de L Lévy-Bruhl". Rev Phil Fr, 179(4), 453-463, O-D 89.

CAVALIER, Robert J (ed) and GOUINLOCK, James (ed) and STERBA, James P (ed). Ethics in the History of Western Philosophy. New York, St Martin's Pr, 1988

This book presents the central ideas in the moral theory of major thinkers from Plato to Rawls. An acknowledged expert on the ethical theory of each philosopher characterises these ideas as they developed out of the historical context in which they were actually formulated. The cultural and intellectual conditions that generated each philosophy are set forth, and when pertinent, the personal experience of the philosopher as well. Accordingly the interested reader as well as the professional scholar will find in this book the actual intent and meaning of the greatest moral theories in the Western tradition.

CAVALIERI, Liebe F. A Scientific Dilemma: The Human Genome Project. Bridges, 2(1-2), 17-25, Spr-Sum 90.

When a discovery is so fundamental that it can be applied to manipulate or rearrange basic components of natural systems—as nuclear fission can, for example—it behooves us to be extraordinarily prudent about its use. The discovery that DNA is the genetic substance started a scientific revolution that has culminated in the Human Genome Project, a gigantic undertaking aimed at locating all the genes and identifying all of the genetic components of human DNA. This knowledge will make possible improved methods for diagnosis of genetic diseases. From this we can expect to arise not only benefits but also severe social stresses: problems of priorities, confusion between medical and cosmetic considerations, the development of procedures that involve the manipulation of future generations, and a variety of psychological stresses and social negatives. (edited)

CAVALLO, Giuliana. Psicologia e scienze della natura in Wilhelm Wundt. Filosofia, 40(3), 357-415, S-D 89.

CAVELL, Stanley. In Quest of the Ordinary: Lines of Skepticism and Romanticism. Chicago, Univ of Chicago Pr, 1988

CAVELL, Stanley. Postscript (1989): To Whom It May Concern. Crit Inquiry, 16(2), 248-289, Wint 89.

CAVELL, Stanley. Ugly Duckling, Funny Butterfly: Bette Davis and Now, Voyager. Crit Inquiry, 16(2), 213-247, Wint 89.

CAWS, Peter (ed). The Causes of Quarrel: Essays on Peace, War, and Thomas Hobbes. Boston, Beacon Pr, 1989

The main focus of this book (the proceedings of a conference under the same title held at The George Washington University in 1987, to commemorate the 400th anniversary of Hobbes's birth and the 200th of the American Constitution), is on the application of Hobbes's theories of human nature and conflict to the international scene. Among the less predictable topics covered, given this setting, are conflicts among cultures, the role of glory in international affairs, nonviolence, and anarchy. The last part of the book is devoted to the possibility of a positive concept of peace and the prospects for its realization.

CAWS, Peter. "Introduction: Philosophy and Politics" in The Causes of Quarrel: Essays on Peace, War, and Thomas Hobbes, CAWS, Peter (ed), 1-12. Boston, Beacon Pr, 1989.

This essay describes the genesis of an interest in the philosophy of peace in reflections provoked by the Cold War and the Mafia, establishes the connection with Hobbes through the concept of diffidence, discusses Hobbes's realism in connection with the eccentricities of the peace movement, and suggests a sense in which the existence of nuclear weapons is functionally equivalent to some aspects of Hobbesian sovereignty. It also gives a preview of other contributions to the book to which it serves as an introduction.

CAWS, Peter. "On the Causes of Quarrel: Postures of War and Possibilities of Peace" in The Causes of Quarrel: Essays on Peace, War, and Thomas Hobbes, CAWS, Peter (ed), 170-182. Boston, Beacon Pr, 1989.

War, like peace, has two sets of connotations, corresponding respectively to general conditions and formal structure. War involves a willingness to use death as an instrument of policy, but many interests sustain it, including that of some of those who risk their own death, whether for the sake of the risk itself or of its attendant benefits. This essay looks at the structure of command and countermand, at the relevance of human nature (and second nature), at the history of American warlikeness (or lack of it), and at the prospects for a positive peace.

CAWS, Peter. "Posthumous Anachronisms in the Work of Sartre" in Inquiries into Values: The Inaugural Session of the International Society for Value Inquiry, LEE, Sander H , 363-373. Lewiston, Mellen Pr, 1989.

Readings of Sartre's posthumous works, e.g., volume II of the Critique, forget why they were not published by him. In spite of his sympathy for Marx, Sartre ceased to believe in the Marxist account of the intelligibility of history; this explains why he abandoned the project of the Critique. Failure to take account of volume IIi of L'Idiot distorts Sartre's mature position, which should be taken to rest on a view of the later published works as pieces that fit into a coherent picture, and is quite revolutionary enough without trying to make it into orthodox Marxism.

CAYGILL, Howard. Art of Judgement. Cambridge, Blackwell, 1989

This book discusses the history of the problem of judgement from Hobbes to Kant. It argues that judgement is aporetic, and that the aporia of judgement informs logical, aesthetic and political judgement.

CAYLA, Fabien. L'intentionalité de dicto, l'intentionalité de re, l'intentionalité de se. Arch Phil, 53(3), 431-459, Jl-S 90.

Intentionality as a mark of the mental is widely recognized. But some philosophers think that this peculiar relation holds primarily between a thinker and his objects of thought, and is secondarily but not necessarily focused onto the world, while others think that intentionality is essentially a matter of thought about objects, that is about particular res. What matters here is the kind of intentional object involved in the individuation of mental states as content of propositional attitudes.

CEBIK, L B. Knowledge or Control as the End of Art. Brit J Aes, 30(3), 244-255, Jl 90.

Danto's Hegelian prediction for art's death, as it approaches self-knowledge and a combination of post-mortem freedom and subservience, rests upon his limited notion of artworld. Expanding that notion into art realm—the entire social substructure of art—reveals that art's approach to self-knowledge is an approach to self-control, free of external influence. Philosophy does not disenfranchise art; rather art disenfranchises philosophy.

CEFALO, Robert C and BEDATE, Carlos A. The Zygote: To Be Or Not To Be A Person. J Med Phil, 14(6), 641-645, D 89.

It is no longer possible to claim that the biological characteristics of the future adult are already determined at conception. After all, a zygote may develop into a hydatidiform mole rather than into a human being. The development of an individual human person is determined by genetically and nongenetically coded molecules within the embryo, together with the influence of the maternal environment. Consequently, it is an error to regard the zygote's chromosomal (and other) DNA as sufficient to determine the uniqueness of the future individual.

CEKIC, Miodrag. Philosophie der Philosophiegeschichte von Hegel bis Hartmann. Man World, 23(1), 1-22, Ja 90.

In this paper the author discusses the conceptions of the subject and the method of the history of philosophy by Hegel, Windelband, Dilthey, Hartmann, and other philosophers of the history of philosophy. The conceptions of history of philosophy by all those philosophers are functionally dependent on their conceptions of philosophy. In addition to discussing the conceptions of the history of philosophy, of those four philosophers, the author presents his own critical comments. (edited)

CENTORE, F F. Potency, Space and Time: Three Modern Theories. New Scholas, 63(4), 435-462, Autumn 89.

Philosophical thought today is dominated by one of two views of reality. One places the emphasis on quantity and spatial arrangements of parts outside of parts; the other emphasizes the becoming-temporality aspect of the world. There is, though, a third, much more ancient, position which combines the pertinent aspects of both of the other two views, and which is today becoming better and better supported by the latest scientific evidence, especially from microscopy.

CERNOHORSKY, I. Some Notes on the Existentialist Concept of Human Freedom (in Czechoslovakian). Filozof Cas, 37(6), 840-847, 1989.

Linking up to a revival of interest in the issue of the freedom of man and society in the contemporary world, this article singles out some solutions of this question in the existential philosophy of Martin Heidegger, Karl Jaspers and Jean-Paul Sartre within the context of their philosophical reflections. The author focuses his attention primarily on J-P Sartre, possibly the best known of the philosophers in Czechoslovakia, and his conception of freedom. In this context, the author analyzes the impact of existentialism and its concept of freedom on arts and literature.

CERRATO, C and FATTOROSI-BARNABA, M. Graded Modalities, III. Stud Log, 47(2), 99-109, Je 88.

We go on along the trend of two previous papers (Fattorosi-Barnaba and De Caro, "Graded modalities, I" (1985) and De Caro, "Graded modalities, II" (1988)), giving an axiomatization of $S4^0$ and proving its completeness and compactness with respect to the usual reflexive and transitive Kripke models. To reach this result, we use techniques from De Caro (1988), with suitable adaptations to our specific case. (edited)

CERVENKA, Miroslav. Dynamism of Meaningful Unification of Work and Coherence of Text (in Czechoslovakian). Estetika, 27(1), 54-60, 1990.

CHACALOS, Elias Harry. *Time and Change: Short But Differing Philosophies*. Rockville, Potomac Pr, 1989

This book explores differing perspectives of some realities important to life and existence. The editor takes the view that although experts do a great deal of good, their narrow-mindedness also does harm. This book allows new ideas into public consideration. (staff)

CHADWICK, Ruth F. The Market for Bodily Parts: Kant and Duties to Oneself. J Applied Phil, 6(2), 129-139, O 89.

The demand for bodily parts such as organs is increasing, and individuals in certain circumstances are responding by offering parts of their bodies for sale. Is there anything wrong in this? Kant had arguments to suggest that there is, namely that we have duties towards our own bodies, among which is the duty not to sell parts of them. Kant's reasons for holding this view are examined, and found to depend on a notion of what is intrinsically degrading. Rom Harré's recent revision of Kant's argument, in terms of an obligation to preserve the body's organic integrity, is considered. Harré's view does not rule out all acts of selling, but he too ultimately depends on a test of what is intrinsically degrading. Both his view and Kant's are rejected in favour of a view which argues that it does make sense to speak of duties towards our own bodies, grounded in the duty to promote the flourishing of human beings, including ourselves. This provides a reason for opposing the sale of bodily parts, and the current trend towards the market ethic in health care provision.

CHAFFIN, Deborah. "Hegel, Derrida, and the Sign" in *Derrida and Deconstruction*, SILVERMAN, Hugh J (ed), 77-91. New York, Routledge, 1989.

In his focus on the problematic of the sign—on writing and language generally—Derrida develops an alternative to the traditional systematic relegation of the sign to the status of transition. On the basis of his critique of the history of the concept of the sign in Hegel, Derrida seeks to effect a *displacing* and *transgressive* 'appropriation' of Hegelian logic. I show, first, that such a project is bound intimately to Derrida's understanding of Hegelian *Aufhebung*. This context elicits the sense in which Derrida's reading of Hegel is *transformational*. I consider, second, the import of this transformation by focusing on Derrida's interpretation of Hegelian *Aufhebung*. Finally, I argue that important aspects of the Hegelian arguments concerning the role and function of contradiction are still valid and should be considered outside their Derridian affiliation.

CHAGROV, A V and ZAKHARYASHCHEV, M V. On Halldén-Completeness of Intermediate and Modal Logics. Bull Sect Log, 19(1), 21-24, Mr 90.

CHAKRABARTY, Alpana. The Theory of Complimentarity and Mind-Body Dualism: A Critique. Indian Phil Quart, 17(2), 193-207, Ap 90.

CHALIER, Agnes. Are There Categories in Chinese Philosophy? (in Serbo-Croatian). Filozof Istraz, 29(2), 467-471, 1989.

Chinese thought differs from Western thought. Western thought is based on the concept of ontology (in the sense of the Aristotelian *Metaphysics*) and Aristotle's categories. My question was how the specific Chinese domain of thought has been constituted. Chinese tradition directs our attention to the facts concerning the relation of man to the universe. There are two words to express 'category': fanshou and lei. They indicate different figures: the first one expresses the idea of field division, the second one refers to the gesture of putting something together. Zoù Yan, with his theory of wuxing, five elements was first to use a concept of categories. Dong Zhong Zhu, one of the most famous Confucianist scholars, brings a new idea concerning nature, developing a new relation between nature, human nature and social nature. The concept of *Sprachlichkeit* helps us to understand how the categories of nature became philosophical discourse. The nature is an immanent principle with a circular movement like the play between yin and yang. The Chinese categories seem to express a world like a natura rerum, with some hidden correspondences.

CHALMERS, Alan. *Science and Its Fabrication*. Minneapolis, Univ of Minn Pr, 1990

The failure of traditional, positivist inspired, attempts to defend the distinctive epistemological status of science has led to a situation where skeptical attacks on science are common. This book is an attempt to rectify this situation. Aided by historical examples that are not too technically demanding, the author shows how a qualified defence of science is possible that occupies middle ground between ideological glorifications and radical denials of it. The way is thus prepared for an appreciation of science for what it is worth as well as a clarification of its limitations.

CHALMETA, Gabriel. Intuición estética e intuición ética en Jacques Maritain. Anu Filosof, 20(2), 139-147, 1987.

CHAMBERS, John H. The Aesthetic-Artistic Domain, Criticism, and Teaching. J Aes Educ, 23(3), 5-18, Fall 89.

Notions of the artistic-aesthetic are basic to all aesthetic encounters. Works of art being forms of practice *within* the world, and recent writing having strongly modified the meanings of the aesthetic subject, object and relationship, how adults and children grasp the artistic-aesthetic will depend both upon their experience of the artistic-aesthetic and upon the art criticism they have encountered. School teachers have normally understood neither this unique epistemological status of the artistic-aesthetic, nor the importance of experience and criticism, construing the artistic-aesthetic mainly as a vehicle for other subjects.

CHAMBERS, John H. Unacceptable Notions of Science Held by Process-Product Researchers. Proc Phil Educ, 45, 81-95, 1989.

CHAMBLISS, J J. Educational Theories: Ideas of Things to Do. Proc Phil Educ, 45, 262-270, 1989.

CHAN, Wing-Tsit. *Chu Hsi: New Studies*. Honolulu, Univ of Hawaii Pr, 1989

Chu Hsi (1130-1200) was indisputably the most influential Chinese thinker after Confucius and Mencius. Because his philosophy of Neo-Confucianism dominated East Asian thought and institutions for centuries, scholars in Asia and the West have concentrated on his philosophical doctrines and political career, leaving much of his personal life and character unaccounted for. In this volume, the world's leading authority of Chu Hsi present aspects of his life and thought that have hitherto been overlooked.

CHANSKY, James D. "Schopenhauer and Platonic Ideas: A Groundwork for an Aesthetic Metaphysics" in *Schopenhauer: New Essays in Honor of*

His 200th Birthday, VON DER LUFT, Eric (ed), 67-81. Lewiston, Mellen Pr, 1989.

This article clarifies the meaning Schopenhauer gives to the Platonic Ideas and establishes their centrality within his metaphysics as the proper objects of metaphysical knowledge. This answers the question of the possibility of metaphysics given Schopenhauer's rejection of any metaphysics of Pure Reason. As aesthetic objects, the Platonic Ideas reveal to perception the inner essence of things by being the clearest phenomenal expressions of that essence, that is, of the will. In this way we come to know *what* the world is beyond being merely objects for a subject. It is argued that Schopenhauer's metaphysics is, therefore, an aesthetic one.

CHANTER, Tina. "Derrida and Heidegger: The Interlacing of Texts" in *The Textual Sublime: Deconstruction and Its Differences*, SILVERMAN, Hugh J (ed), 61-68. Albany, SUNY Pr, 1990.

CHANTEUR, Janine. "L'individualisme dans ses rapports avec la culture et la politique" in *Culture et Politique/Culture and Politics*, CRANSTON, Maurice (ed), 86-94. Hawthorne, de Gruyter, 1988.

CHAPELLE, A. L'itinéraire philosophique de Claude Bruaire: de Hegel à la métaphysique. Rev Phil Fr, 180(1), 5-12, Ja-Mr 90.

CHAPELLE, A. Présence de Hegel en France: G Fessard et Claude Bruaire. Rev Phil Fr, 180(1), 13-26, Ja-Mr 90.

CHAPMAN, Christi and KOHLS, John and MATHIEU, Casey. Ethics Training Programs in the Fortune 500. Bus Prof Ethics J, 8(2), 55-72, Sum 89.

CHARLES, Daniel. Heidegger on Hermeneutics and Music Today. Acta Phil Fennica, 43, 154-166, 1988.

CHARLES, David. "Intention" in *Cause, Mind, and Reality: Essays Honoring C B Martin*, HEIL, John (ed), 33-52. Norwell, Kluwer, 1989.

CHARPA, Ulrich. Johnny Head-In-The-Air and Thales. Thinking, 5(3), 32-34, 1984.

CHATTERJEE, Kalyan and GAUVIN, Stéphane and LILIEN, Gary L. The Impact of Information and Computer Based Training on Negotiators' Performance. Theor Decis, 28(3), 331-354, My 90.

This paper presents the results of an experiment on negotiation, designed to measure the impact of (1) computerized training and (2) information on negotiators' performance. The paper is structured as follows. First, we review the literature on negotiation training. Second, we develop a conceptual framework to link various forms of negotiation support systems to joint and individual negotiation performance. Third, we present the negotiation paradigm—a bilateral monopoly—and the computerized training system we used. Regarding training, our results show an asymmetric impact on individual performance levels and, unexpectedly, a negative impact on negotiators' joint performance. In contrast, more information improves both individual and joint performance. Finally, we discuss these results, and outline further research questions.

CHATTERJEE, Margaret. "Man and Nature in the Indian Context" in *Man and Nature: The Chinese Tradition and the Future*, TANG, Yi-Jie (ed), 85-99. Lanham, Univ Pr of America, 1989.

CHATTERJEE, Margaret. "The Viability of Nonviolence in Collective Life" in *The Causes of Quarrel: Essays on Peace, War, and Thomas Hobbes*, CAWS, Peter (ed), 128-138. Boston, Beacon Pr, 1989.

CHAUDHURY, Mahasweta. Artifacts, Essence and Reference. Indian Phil Quart, 17(1), 63-73, Ja 90.

CHAUDHURY, Mahasweta. Identity as Necessity: Nozick's Objection-Kripke Replies. Indian Phil Quart, 16(3), 283-289, Jl 89.

CHAVES-TANNÚS, Márcio. Considerações Lógicas em torno de uma Definição do Homem. Educ Filosof, 2(3), 5-8, Jl-D 87.

Thesis: Man is in essence a being in movement and subject to change, neither more nor less than a being in movement and subject to change. Thus everything human is in a state of uninterrupted movement and is ceaselessly changing. This thesis entails moral consequences that are worth exploring in detail; however, the purpose of this essay is merely to test its logical foundations. The object and outcome of the paper is to show the self-destructive nature of this thesis from the standpoint of logic.

CHÉDIN, Jean-Louis. Infini et subjectivité dans la pensée classique. Rev Metaph Morale, 94(2), 229-250, Ap-Je 89.

La métaphysique classique (ou post-classique) n'a pas son point de départ dans la subjectivité, comme le soutient une interprétation devenue quasi-dominante, mais plutôt dans l'"être-à-l'infini" de la substance (finie), qui représente la condition originaire de la subjectivité. Ainsi en particulier, chez Descartes et Leibniz. Le kantisme toutefois répond, partiellement, aux critères de la métaphysique de la subjectivité.

CHENEY, Jim. The Neo-Stoicism of Radical Environmentalism. Environ Ethics, 11(4), 293-325, Wint 89.

Feminist analysis has convinced me that certain tendencies within that form of radical environmentalism known as deep ecology—with its supposed rejection of the Western ethical tradition and its adoption of what looks to be a feminist attitude toward the environment and our relationship to nature—constitute one more chapter in the story of Western alienation from nature. In this paper I deepen my critique of these tendencies toward alienation within deep ecology by historicizing my critique in the light of a development in the ancient world that is disquietingly similar to the rise of deep ecology in recent times—namely, the rise of Stoicism in the wake of the breakup of the ancient polis.

CHENG, Anne. What is Chinese Philosophy? (in Serbo-Croatian). Filozof Istraz, 29(2), 383-389, 1989.

Etant donné qu'il est impossible de fournir une réponse, sinon exhaustive, du moins satisfaisante à une question aussi vaste, cet article se propose de la saisir d'un point de vue particulier, mais néanmoins significatif. Il s'agit de tenter de spécifier le caractère de la "philosophie chinoise" comme une forme cosmologique de pensée, par contraste avec les constructions intellectuelles abstraites qui constituent la tradition philosophique occidentale. Cela n'exclue pas, néanmoins, une certaine rationalité; mais cette rationalité est de type analogique et corrélatif plutôt que logique et déductif. (edited)

CHENG, Chung-Ying. A Taoist Interpretation of 'Differance' in Derrida. J Chin Phil, 17(1), 19-30, Mr 90.

CHERCHI, Gavina. Atomism Between Orthodoxy and Heterodoxy. Teoria, 9(1), 187-213, 1989.

CHERRY, Christopher and WESTPHAL, Jonathan. Is Life Absurd? Philosophy, 65(252), 199-203, Ap 90.

Nagel claims that we are like ants and that life, seen from an 'external' perspective, is absurd. We argue that the 'external' perspective is just another optional *internal* perspective, that life is not absurd, as demonstrated by art and faith, and that the metaphor of the ant is false, both to human beings and to ants. The lives of ants are filled with significance, for ants.

CHERRY, Christopher. Reply—The Possibility of Computers Becoming Persons: A Response to Dolby. Soc Epistem, 3(4), 337-348, O-D 89.

R G A Dolby has argued on several counts that it is intelligible—and useful—to treat machines of certain kinds as persons. Against this it is argued that such an extensional change involves a radical and unprecedented shift in the *meaning* of 'person'. Human beings are paradigm persons; and a necessary (though not a sufficient) condition of personhood is sentience. That Artefacts cannot conceivably be sentient may be shown by a variety of reductive considerations, and in particular by exposing as exclusively psychological and aesthetic pressures to attribute mental states to machines.

CHICHI, Graciela. El status lógico de los *topoi* aristotélicos. Rev Latin De Filosof, 15(2), 131-145, Jl 89.

In this paper I try to expose and examine two contemporary interpretations with regard to the logical status of the Aristotelian *tópoi* starting from a Theophrastus's passage conserved by Alexander Aphrodisias. I try to show the resemblance of Aristotle's *tópoi* with Theophrastus's *paraggelmatikoi tópoi* and, finally, its function as inference in nonformal argumentative schemes.

CHIDESTER, David. *Patterns of Transcendence: Religion, Death, and Dying*. Belmont, Wadsworth, 1990

This fascinating study explores the ways that people of many different cultures approach death and dying; how they act in the face of death and how they discover meaning through religion, myth and cultural values. The book samples cultures as diverse as the Australian Aborigines, Hindus, Buddhists, and Christians. The author brings the reader to the present with a chapter on death and dying in contemporary America. (edited)

CHIEN, Chi-Hui. "Theft's Way": A Comparative Study of Chuang Tzu's Tao and Derridean Trace. J Chin Phil, 17(1), 31-49, Mr 90.

CHIERCHIA, Gennaro and MC CONNELL-GINET, Sally. *Meaning and Grammar: An Introduction to Semantics*. Cambridge, MIT Pr, 1990

This book is a self-contained introduction to natural language semantics that addresses the major theoretical questions in the field and shows how the machinery of logical semantics can be used in the empirical study of natural language. The work deals with the following issues: quantification and logical form, the syntax/semantics interface, context and presuppositions, speech acts, the philosophical foundations of semantics, modalities, generalized quantifiers.

CHIEREGHIN, Franco. "Vivere" e "vivere bene": Note sul concetto aristotelico di πρᾶξις. Rev Metaph Morale, 95(1), 57-74, Ja-Mr 90.

CHIHARA, Charles. Tharp's 'Myth and Mathematics'. Synthese, 81(2), 153-165, N 89.

CHILDRESS, James F. The Place of Autonomy in Bioethics. Hastings Center Rep, 20(1), 12-17, Ja-F 90.

CHINCHORE, M. Post-Udayana Nyaya Reactions to Dharmakirti's Vadanyaya: An Evaluation. Indian Phil Quart, 17(1), 1-31, Ja 90.

In the post-Udayana-Nyāya tradition attempts were made to rebut Dharmakīrti's views concerning *Nigrahasṭānas* as expressed in his *Vādanyāya*. Principally there are two such attempts, viz., the *Anvīkṣānayatattvabodha* of Vardhamāna and the *Nyāya-Sūtra-Vrtti* of Visvanātha, representative of two trends reacting to Dharmakīrti. This paper aims at understanding their arguments and evaluating their significance.

CHINCHORE, Mangala R. Dharmakirti on Criteria of Knowledge. Indian Phil Quart, 16(3), 319-344, Jl 89.

In this paper I intend to consider Dharmakīrti's two important criteria of knowledge, viz. *Avisamvadana* or *Avisamvadakatva* and *A(vi)jñatarthaprakasakatva*, explain their rationale and bring out the role they play in our epistemic enterprise. The paper has three sections. The first investigates into the need and necessity of the criteria under consideration. The second seeks to highlight their nature and role, while the last intends to study significant implications of them.

CHING, Julia. Christian Wolff and China: The Autonomy of Morality (in Serbo-Croatian). Filozof Istraz, 29(2), 441-448, 1989.

The contemporary philosophical world neglects the eighteenth century German thinker Christian Wolff as a figure who has been superseded by Immanuel Kant. It is generally ignorant of his historical contributions, especially his struggles for the independence of moral philosophy vis-à-vis pietist theology. This is especially highlighted by Wolff's lecture or discourse on "The Practical Philosophy of the Chinese" (1721), a performance which led to his expulsion from Prussia and a Europe-wide controversy over such issues as the permissibility of comparing Confucius with Jesus Christ, and of affirming the positive value of the philosophy of the pagan Chinese to a Christian Europe, but even more, over the question of academic freedom in eighteenth century Europe. The quality of Wolff's understanding of China is an interesting question in itself, but this article concentrates more on the use Wolff made of China and Chinese philosophy in his efforts to liberate philosophy from dominance of theology.

CHISHOLM, Roderick M. Events Without Times An Essay On Ontology. Nous, 24(3), 413-427, Je 90.

Making use of tense and of four undefined philosophical concepts (exemplification, necessity, state and part), this paper sets forth a theory of events that is simpler than its alternatives. Unlike most of these alternatives, it presupposes that questions about what would be an adequate *language* for describing events cannot be answered without first constructing a general ontology and theory of categories. It exhibits events as contingent states of contingent substances and attempts to show that what is known about temporality can be expressed without presupposing that "times" are substantival entities. And it proposes solutions to familiar philosophical puzzles about time and events.

CHISHOLM, Roderick M. How We Refer to Things. Phil Stud, 58(1-2), 155-164, Ja-F 90.

CHISHOLM, Roderick M. Monads, Nonexistent Individuals and Possible Worlds: Reply to Rosenkrantz. Phil Stud, 58(1-2), 173-175, Ja-F 90.

CHISHOLM, Roderick M. The Status of Epistemic Principles. Nous, 24(2), 209-215, Ap 90.

The paper describes that sense of "theory of knowledge" that requires the formulation of normative supervenience principles. In the simplest cases such principles are conditionals in which the non-normative antecedents describe certain states of consciousness and the antecedents describe the epistemic justification that supervenes upon these states. Such principles provide the foundation for further principles in which the antecedents describe a combination of normative and non-normative conditions. More complex principles may then be formulated in which the antecedents are purely normative.

CHISHOLM, Roderick M. *Theory of Knowledge (Third Edition)*. Englewood Cliffs, Prentice-Hall, 1989

CHMIELEWSKI, Philip J. Economic Participation: The Discourse of Work. Int Phil Quart, 30(3), 331-342, S 90.

CHOMSKY, Noam. Language and the Problems of Knowledge (in Serbo-Croatian). Filozof Istraz, 30(3), 925-950, 1989.

There is an innate structure that determines the framework within which thought and language develop, down to quite precise and intricate details. Language and thought are awakened in the mind, and follow a largely predetermined course, much like other biological properties. They develop in a way that provides a rich structure of truths of meaning. Our knowledge in these areas, and I believe elsewhere—even in science and mathematics—is not derived by induction, by applying reliable procedures, and so on; it is not grounded or based on "good reasons" in any useful sense of these notions. Rather, it grows in the mind, on the basis of our biological nature, triggered by appropriate experience, and in a limited way shaped by experience that settles options left open by the innate structure of mind. The result is an elaborate structure of cognitive systems, systems of knowledge and belief, that reflects the very nature of the human mind, a biological organ like others, with its scope and limits.

CHOMSKY, Noam and EDGLEY, Roy and OSBORNE, Peter and RÉE, Jonathan and WILSON, Deirdre. Noam Chomsky: An Interview. Rad Phil, 53, 31-40, Autumn 89.

CHONG, C T. Hyperhypersimple Sets and Δ_2 Systems. Annals Pure Applied Log, 44(1-2), 25-38, O 89.

CHOPKO, Mark E and HARRIS, Phillip and ALVARÉ, Helen M. The Price of Abortion Sixteen Years Later. Nat Forum, 69(4), 18-22, Fall 89.

CHRÉTIEN, Émile and CAUCHY, Venant. Intervention: Entretien avec Monsieur Venant Cauchy. Philosophiques, 17(1), 127-141, 1990.

CHRISTENSEN, Darrel E. *Hegelian/Whiteheadian Perspectives*. Lanham, Univ Pr of America, 1989

This is a collection of essays on phenomenology, that examines the perspectives of Hegel and Whitehead on realities, more explicitly, temporal reality from the retrospective, present, and prospective origins. (staff)

CHRISTENSEN, Ferrel M. Cultural and Ideological Bias in Pornography Research. Phil Soc Sci, 20(3), 351-375, S 90.

This paper argues that our culture's traditional antisexual attitudes have seriously compromised much scientific research on the "effects" of pornography. It does so by examining a number of examples of explanation of data, perception of data and perception of values by the researchers, revealing a pattern of bias in all three.

CHRISTENSEN, Jerome. From Rhetoric to Corporate Populism: A Romantic Critique of the Academy in an Age of High Gossip. Crit Inquiry, 16(2), 438-465, Wint 89.

CHRISTIE, Thony. *Nature* as a Source in the History of Logic, 1870-1910. Hist Phil Log, 11(1), 1-3, 1990.

By using examples drawn from the periodical *Nature*, I show that research into the history of logic in the nineteenth century involves journals and periodicals which are normally not considered as standard sources for logic or its history.

CHRISTMAN, John (ed). *The Inner Citadel: Essays on Individual Autonomy*. New York, Oxford Univ Pr, 1989

This collection, which combines previously published pieces with original work, focusses on the concept of individual autonomy and its relation to human freedom. In the editor's introduction and in an essay by Joel Feinberg, the various construals of 'autonomy', and debates surrounding that idea, are surveyed. Attention in various pieces is given to the "hierarchical-self" model of autonomy, and criticisms of this view are represented. Discussions are conducted concerning the relation between autonomy and other values, such as utility. A bibliography is included. Contributors: Gerald Dworkin, Jon Elster, Feinberg, Harry Frankfurt, Russell Hardin, Lawrence Haworth, Thomas Hill, Jr., James Rachels, David A J Richards, William Ruddick, Irving Thalberg, Gary Watson, Susan Wolf, and Robert Young.

CHUNG, Albert C. Lectures on the I Ching (in Serbo-Croatian). Filozof Istraz, 29(2), 547-557, 1989.

The variations in the I Ching hexagram manifest by both the contrastabilities and invertabilities which are different fundamentally from the traditional Aristotelian logic of the categorical propositions in the concepts of contraries and contradictories. According to the latter, two propositions are said to be contradictories, if one is the denial of the other, i.e., if they cannot be either both true or both false. But that is not the case with either the contrastabilities or invertabilities of the I Ching. As a matter of fact, all of the 64 hexagrams are true in their own respective merits, simply because all of them are based upon the principles of empiricism, and also comply with the principle of I Ching dialectic logic which rests upon the principle of ever change. The essay also points out that the dialectic logic of the I Ching differs from that of the Hegelian; the latter failed to stick to the principle of change, while the dialectics of I Ching never deviate from it.

CHURCH, Jennifer. Judgment, Self-Consciousness, and Object Independence. Amer Phil Quart, 27(1), 51-60, Ja 90.

There are good reasons, mostly deriving from Kant, for supposing that the ability to make judgments presupposes some recogniton of an objective world. Just what the relevant sense of objectivity is, and whether the recognition of such objectivity in turn presupposes some sort of self-consciousness, is less clear. This paper is an attempt to articulate and assess the relevant arguments and to distinguish between the sort of judgments that do presuppose self-consciousness and those that do not. Requirements on perceptual judgment, practical judgment, and theoretical judgment are considered. It is argued that judgments involving negation or conditionals do presuppose self-consciousness.

CHURCHILL, John. 'If a Lion Could Talk'. Phil Invest, 12(4), 308-324, O 89.

Wittgenstein's remark "If a lion could talk we could not understand him" suggests radical incommensurability between humans and animals. But in fact Wittgenstein's view of language, with its emphasis on "the natural history" of humanity, his discussios of the bodily, behavioral, and social nature of language, and his remarks on animals suggest strongly that commensuration and, hence, communication between humans and animals are matters of degree, varying according to degrees of resemblance in physiology and behavior. This conclusion coheres with Wittgenstein's attacks on Cartesian concepts of mind and the place of human beings in the world.

CHURCHILL, John. "Advance Directives: Beyond Respect for Freedom" in *Advance Directives in Medicine*, HACKLER, Chris (ed), 171-179. New York, Praeger, 1989.

Discussion of advance directives for medical treatment has centered on the problems of competence and autonomy. Emphasis on freedom and the procedures of moral choice has obscured issues about the quality of such choices. Freedom itself implies concepts of selfhood, community, and narrativity that supply substantive criteria for the evaluation of choices expressed in advance directives. In particular, the shape given to a life by a narrative sense of self should provide a basis for the evaluation of advance directives concerning the pursuit or withholding of medical treatments at the end of life.

CHURCHILL, Larry R. Hermeneutics in Science and Medicine: A Thesis Understated. Theor Med, 11(2), 141-144, Je 90.

Drew Leder's "Clinical Interpretation: The Hermeneutics of Medicine" is an essay which understates its case and thereby opens itself to misinterpretation. This response to Leder argues for a more thorough-going hermeneutic for both medicine and science. At the conceptual as well as the practical level, modern medicine and its scientific foundations are hermeneutic enterprises. The purpose of this essay is to argue that we should not back away from this more radical thesis. Embracing it will result in less alienation of physicians from patients, and of physicians from the tasks of medicine.

CHURCHILL, R Paul. "Hobbes and the Assumption of Power" in *The Causes of Quarrel: Essays on Peace, War, and Thomas Hobbes*, CAWS, Peter (ed), 13-22. Boston, Beacon Pr, 1989.

CHURCHLAND, Paul. Response to Dietrich's "Computationalism". Soc Epistem, 4(2), 162-165, Ap-Je 90.

CHYBA, Milos. To the Program of Aesthetic Evolution for the Whole Society (in Czechoslovakian). Estetika, 26(3), 129-138, 1989.

CILLIERS, F P. The Brain, the Mental Apparatus and the Text: A Post-Structural Neuropsychology. S Afr J Phil, 9(1), 1-8, F 90.

Although neuropsychological descriptions of the brain are becoming much more detailed, explanations of the brain's higher functions—perception, memory and consciousness—remain unsatisfactory. By developing descriptions of the brain in poststructural terms, these issues can be constituted in a different discourse. A poststructural model of the brain is developed by relating neurological information with poststructural description of language. This process is facilitated by Derrida's reading of Saussure on the one hand, and of Freud's neuropsychology on the other. Such a model of the brain is then related to a recent technological development known as neural networks or connectionism. This technology is already finding practical applications in the computational environment.

CIOFFI, Frank. Wittgenstein and Obscurantism. Aris Soc, SUPP 64, 1-23, 1990.

CIORANESCU, Alexandre. The Shape of Time. Diogenes, 149, 1-21, Spr 90.

Le temps étant un concept aveugle, l'imagination se le représente suivant deux modules traditionnels, le cercle et la ligne droite. Ces deux images conditionnent toute la métaphysique et la littérature. Le cercle implique l'assurance de l'éternel retour des choses et des âmes. La ligne droite suppose une ascension vers l'éternité ou, pour l'homme moderne, vers le progrès et subsidiairement vers l'angoisse existentielle et vers l'évasion de la terreur de l'histoire.

CLADIS, Mark S. Emile Durkheim and Provinces of Ethics. Interpretation, 17(2), 255-273, Wint 89-90.

Durkheim describes four spheres of social life—the domestic, the civil, the professional, and the universal or general. Each sphere has its own specific moral reasoning and vocabulary. What some social philosophers, such as MacIntyre, would deplore and label moral fragmentation, Durkheim calls "provinces of ethics"—historically fashioned spheres of morality. I highlight how Durkheim articulates a plurality of morals in the idiom of social traditions and commitment to common goods. He fashions a mixed vocabulary (an assortment of liberal and communitarian values). This vocabulary, I argue, enables us to maintain commitment to noble features of both liberal and communitarian ways of thinking.

CLAEYS, Gregory. The French Revolution Debate and British Political Thought. Hist Polit Thought, 11(1), 59-80, Spr 90.

An examination of several hundred pamphlets on both sides of the 'Burke-Paine debate' demonstrates that the intellectual centre of gravity in much of the *popular* debate was not the nature of the Lockean contract nor the limits of republican virtue, but instead, through the critique of 'levelling', the relationship between economic inequality and social progress, manners, and commerce, or broadly, 'civilisation'. The central argument levelled against the Painites was not that their language of rights was too extreme, but that their implicit economic programme threatened the general progress of commerce and culture. Paine himself was a 'modern' republican sympathetic to commerce, but his followers were lambasted with an argument against republican primitivism generally.

CLARK, Andy. Belief, Opinion and Consciousness. Phil Psych, 3(1), 139-154, 1990.

The paper considers two recent accounts of the difference between human and animal thought. One deflationary account, due to Daniel Dennett, insists that the only real difference lies in our ability to use words and sentences to give artificial precision and determinacy to our mental contents. The other, due to Paul Smolensky, conjectures that we at times deploy a special purpose device (the conscious rule interpreter) whose task is to deal with public, symbolically coded data and commands. Both these accounts make a crucial error. They offer what is in effect an extra top-level processor to soothe our realist/classical prejudices. But in each case the extra ingredient turns out to be explanatorily hollow. Appealing to language use and language processing alone mistakes a cognitive effect for a cognitive cause. I argue instead that we need to seek a more profound architectural condition which may ground our conscious linguistic abilities but *also* explains a variety of deeper facts. I sketch a picture which seems to meet those needs and draw out its implications for the debates about belief and about classical artificial intelligence.

CLARK, Andy. Beyond Eliminativism. Mind Lang, 4(4), 251-279, Wint 89.

CLARK, Charles. Why Teachers Need Philosophy. J Phil Educ, 23(2), 241-252, Wint 89.

CLARK, H Westley and NELSON, Lawrence J and GOLDMAN, Robert L and SCHORE, Jean E. Taking the Train to a World of Strangers: Health Care Marketing and Ethics. Hastings Center Rep, 19(5), 36-43, S-O 89.

CLARK, Kelly James. *Return to Reason: Critique of Enlightenment Evidentialism and a Defense of Reason and Belief in God*. Grand Rapids, Eerdmans, 1990

The evidentialist objector's assessment of the rationality of religious belief is doubly defective. In unfairly condemning theistic proofs, they unjustifiably rely on evidence acceptable to theist and atheist alike. With a person-relative notion of proof, the theist may have adequate evidence of God's existence. Evidentialism is also belief in God because it mistakenly treats belief in God like belief in a scientific hypothesis; it is also an irrational principle of rationality which maintains an impossibly high and self-refuting standard. A Reidian, fallibilist approach to rationality is defended.

CLARK, Kelly James. Spanish Common Sense Philosophy. Hist Phil Quart, 7(2), 207-226, Ap 90.

Spanish philosophy in the early 19th century, marked by a commitment to common sense, was influenced by Thomas Reid and the French Jesuit, Buffier. Chief among the Spanish thinkers is Father Jaime Balmes (1810-1848). This essay examines (1) Balmes's critique of Descartes's assumption of universal doubt; (2) his rejection of the arbitrary preference of consciousness and reasoning; (3) the repudiation of Cartesian foundationalism—that knowledge all noninferential knowledge is either self-evident, evident to the senses or incorrigible; (4) his understanding of common sense and regress argument; (5) his understanding of philosophical method; and (6) his arguments against Cartesian skepticism.

CLARK, Mary T and ANOZ, José (trans). Agustín y la unidad. Augustinus, 34(135-136), 293-304, Jl-D 89.

CLARK, Mary T. "Willing Freely According to Thomas Aquinas" in *A Straight Path: Studies in Medieval Philosophy and Culture*, LINK-SALINGER, Ruth (ed), 49-56. Washington, Cath Univ Amer Pr, 1988.

CLARK, Romane. "A Categorial Analysis of Predication: The Moral of Bradley's Regress" in *Mind, Value and Culture: Essays in Honor of E M Adams*, WEISSBORD, David (ed), 117-130. Atascadero, Ridgeview, 1989.

According to Adams, the grammar of an expression indicates the categorical nature of what is semantically associated with it. For instance, "that something is semantically located by a predicate indicates that it has the categorical status of a property." Using this as a test case of his notion of "Categorical Analysis," we consider the complexity of English predicates to evaluate the claim that they "semantically locate" properties. Doing this leads as well to a version of Bradley's Regress which is a valid *reductio ad absurdum* of certain "connectionist" views of predication, but of certain Fregean ones too.

CLARK, Stephen R L. *Civil Peace and Sacred Order: Limits and Renewals I*. New York, Clarendon/Oxford Pr, 1989

A restatement of traditional, pluralist and 'anarcho-conservative' political philosophy. The State has authority over our natural allegiances only insofar as it stands for a higher law. That law demands attention to the interests of the global and historical community. This is the first volume of a neo-Platonizing trilogy.

CLARK, Stephen R L. How to Reason About Value Judgments. Philosophy, 24, 173-190, 88 Supp.

People in general and examination candidates in particular are expected to have opinions about important civil questions, but do not like to defend them. Opinion mongering is often exempted from rational criticism, as being a form of self-expression. Examination questions, accordingly, must often be occasions for the art of rhetoric rather than philosophy: even as such, they can be more or less well crafted. True philosophy, of a Socratic kind, does not forget the requirements of truth and rationality, and for that reason is unlikely to lead to straightforward answers of the kind sought by pollsters, and too many examination papers.

CLARK, Stephen R L. Notes on the Underground. Inquiry, 33(1), 27-37, Mr 90.

The victory of Ellerman's technetronic civilization is indeed a fearful prospect, but one that is much less plausible than he allows. His imagined makers, as was pointed out forty-odd years ago by C S Lewis, could themselves have no criterion of right action or right belief, nor could they sensibly expect—either on secular or on theistic suppositions—to be able to control the world forever.

CLARK, Stephen R L. "Reason as *Daimōn*" in *The Person and the Human Mind: Issues in Ancient and Modern Philosophy*, GILL, Christopher (ed), 187-206. New York, Clarendon/Oxford Pr, 1989.

A consciously unconventional, and anti-conventionalist, discussion of ancient claims that there is something in each of us (Nous, or the Real Self) that matters more than anything else, and is in some way identically the same in all its manifestations.

CLARK, Stephen R L. World Religions and World Orders. Relig Stud, 26(1), 43-57, Mr 90.

Religions can be considered, by analogy with the modern conception of species, as historically defined traditions lacking any identifiable essence. What traditions have the potential for being world religions, ideologies capable of providing the sort of community feeling necessary for world order in the absence of a world-state ruling by military force? Different sorts of religion are considered, including syncretic spiritualism and naturism, and characterized under different polarities. None are entirely satisfactory, or likely, and it may be that the most successful would, to traditionally pious souls, be the most diabolical.

CLARK, Walter Houston. "Wisdom, Mysticism and Near-Death Experiences" in *The Wisdom of Faith: Essays in Honor of Dr Sebastian Alexander Matczak*, THOMPSON, Henry O (ed), 29-34. Lanham, Univ Pr of America, 1989.

CLARKE JR, D S. Two Uses of 'Know'. Analysis, 50(3), 188-190, Je 90.

This is a criticism of Goldman's reliabilist condition for knowledge, the condition that an agent must be able to discriminate relevant alternatives in order to have propositional knowledge. It is argued that this is a condition for nonpropositional source knowledge, but not for propositional redundancy avoidance knowledge.

CLARKE, W Norris. Thomism and Contemporary Philosophical Pluralism.

Mod Sch, 67(2), 123-139, Ja 90.

The article notes the recent historical change in the status of Thomism within the Catholic intellectual community from being the sole dominant system of philosophy to a context of pluralism as one among several other irreducible modes of doing philosophy. The hermeneutical necessity of such a shift in our day is noted. The relations between Thomism and the principal other modes of contemporary Western philosophy are then worked out on the analogy of relations between nations: active collaboration, peaceful coexistence, border disputes, and open warfare, with respect to phenomenology, analytic philosophy, Kantianism, empiricism, hermeneutics, postmodernism.

CLASSEN, C Joachim. "Die Peripatetiker in Cicero's *Tuskulanen*" in *Cicero's Knowledge of the Peripatos*, FORTENBAUGH, William W (ed), 186-200. New Brunswick, Transaction Books, 1989.

The paper first states basic principles one should bear in mind when studying Cicero's philosophical writings, before dealing with the influence on the Tusculans, of Aristotle, the Peripatetics and particular Peripatetic philosophers. The relevant passages are discussed, and it is shown that Cicero is not interested in tenets of individuals, but has used Peripatetic methods and absorbed much of their teaching, rejecting only their view that emotions or passions may be 'mean states' and trying to reconcile their threefold division of *virtus/bona corporis* and *fortunae* with the Stoic distinction of *bona* and *commoda*.

CLAYTON, Jay. Narrative and Theories of Desire. Crit Inquiry, 16(1), 33-53, Autumn 89.

This article identifies two paradigms of desire that have become influential in recent literary theory: the essentialist, which views desire as a primal force, aligned with Eros, and the structuralist, which, following Lacan, views desire as the displacement of energy, an insatiable search for an absent object. Through analyses of the theories of narrative found in Peter Brooks, Leo Bersani, and Teresa de Lauretis, the article demonstrates that both paradigms produce ahistorical accounts of literature. The implications of a historical theory of desire for literary studies are outlined in conclusion.

CLAYTON, John. Piety and the Proofs. Relig Stud, 26(1), 19-42, Mr 90.

CLAYTON, Philip. Disciplining Relativism and Truth. Zygon, 24(3), 315-334, S 89.

Imre Lakatos's philosophy of science can provide helpful leads for theological methodology, but only when mediated by the disciplines that lie between the natural sciences and theology. The questions of relativism and truth are used as indices for comparing disciplines, and Lakatos's theory of natural science is taken as the starting point. Major modifications of Lakatos's work are demanded as one moves from the natural sciences, through economics, the interpretive social sciences, literary theory, and into theology. Although theology may consist of Lakatosian research programs, it also includes programs of interpretation and programs for living. This conclusion must influence our definition of theological truth and our assessment of theological relativism.

CLAYTON, Philip. Recent Classical/Process Dialogue on God and Change. Process Stud, 18(3), 194-203, Fall 89.

The article isolates and discusses four central questions in the debate between classical and process theories of God and change. Recent critiques of the theology of Wolfhart Pannenberg by three Whiteheadians (John Cobb, Jr., David Polk, Lewis Ford), and Pannenberg's response, set the stage for an evaluation of the long-term prospects for process/classical agreement. Particular attention is paid to the themes of being and becoming, personal identity, the part/whole relationship, and the Trinity. The primacy of the future in Ford and Pannenberg offers important common ground for a meeting of the two traditions.

CLEARY, Denis (trans) and ROSMINI, Antonio and WATSON, Terence (trans). *Conscience*. Durham, Rosmini, 1989

CLEGG, Jerry S. "Schopenhauer and Wittgenstein on Lonely Languages and Criterialess Claims" in *Schopenhauer: New Essays in Honor of His 200th Birthday*, VON DER LUFT, Eric (ed), 82-100. Lewiston, Mellen Pr, 1989.

The article explores the two questions of what Wittgenstein meant by "ordinary language" and why he insisted on its being the sole provenance of philosophy. The answers to both questions lie in his repudiation of a theory once held by him, and derived from Schopenhauer, that saw the numenal side of man as capable of speaking a language only it could understand. Wittgenstein's use of "criterion" and "criterion of identity"—both borrowed from Schopenhauer—show that his defense of ordinary language is, indeed, a repudiation of his early Schopenhauerian habits of thought.

CLEMENT, Grace. Is the Moral Point of View Monological or Dialogical? The Kantian Background of Habermas' Discourse Ethics. Phil Today, 33(2),

159-173, Sum 89.

In this essay, I examine Habermas's discourse ethics against its Kantian backdrop. First, I show how Habermas's dialogical model improves upon Kant's monological model. Then I defend a Kantian rejoinder to discourse ethics, namely that an ethics with personal as well as social applications will require monological as well as dialogical deliberations. The discourse model must have a derivative personal application.

CLENDENNING, John and OPPENHEIM, Frank M. New Documents on Josiah Royce. Trans Peirce Soc, 26(1), 131-145, Wint 90.

This article discusses and describes the contents of a large newly acquired addition to the Papers of Josiah Royce, Harvard University Archives. The material includes Royce unpublished manuscripts (1 box), incoming correspondence (4 boxes), logicalia (1 box), correspondence of Royce and Head families (5 boxes), family photographs (1 box), manuscripts of Katherine Royce (1 box), notebooks, diaries, etc. (1 box), Royce's published work (2 boxes), miscellanea (4 boxes). Appendix A lists Royce's correspondents alphabetically. Appendix B prints letters by Royce and Peirce.

CLENDINNEN, F John. "Evolutionary Explanation and the Justification of Belief" in *Issues in Evolutionary Epistemology*, HAHLWEG, Kai (ed), 458-474. Albany, SUNY Pr, 1989.

If there is any point to thinking, naturalism cannot dispense with the need to evaluate the norms used in appraising our conclusions. Scientific theories, like evolution, cannot provide the sole rational grounds of the reasoning used to judge them. However, given the basic rationality of methods, theory may substantially increase our rational confidence in the conclusions method reaches. The initial justification may rest on the reflexive use of thought in exploring its possibilities and limitations, and the acceptance of the possibility of so doing is no challenge to the naturalistic perspective on humans.

CLENDINNEN, F John. Realism and the Underdetermination of Theory. Synthese, 81(1), 63-90, O 89.

The main theme is that theorizing serves empirical prediction. This is used as the core of a counter to contemporary antirealist arguments. Different versions of the thesis that data underdetermines theory are identified and it is shown that none which are acceptable differentiate between theory selection and prediction. Criteria sufficient for the former are included amongst those necessary for the latter, and obviously go beyond mere compatibility with data. Special attention is given to causal process theories. It is argued that the only empirically equivalent alternatives which can be constructed to any theory of this kind must be parasitic on that theory; so a choice for the original theory cannot be avoided. Once this is established, a positive case for taking a realist position can be developed.

CLEVELAND, Timothy and SAGAL, Paul T. Bold Hypotheses: The Bolder the Better? Ratio, 2(2), 109-121, D 89.

When scientists want an explanation of some puzzling or problematic event or phenomenon should they propose the boldest conceivable hypothesis? According to Popper's influential conjecture and refutation methodology they should, since such hypotheses are susceptible to more severe tests. This answer depends, however, on a certain notion of "boldness" or "measure of boldness" which leads to a dilemma. The solution is that there are two senses of "boldness," a *logical*, and a *psychological* sense, which go unrecognized and are confused or conflated in the Popperian account. What scientists want are hypotheses bold in the logical, but not in the psychological sense—hypotheses which, on the proposed account, will have both the virtues of boldness and conservatism. With this account, which will be elucidated in terms of subjective probability, one will see more clearly the kinds of reasoning which are involved when a hypothesis is proposed for testing. In fact, one will see that the reasoning involved in the context of discovery is not independent of reasoning in the context of justification.

CLIFFORD, Michael. "Postmortem Thought and the End of Man" in *The Question of the Other: Essays in Contemporary Continental Philosophy*, DALLERY, Arleen B (ed), 213-221. Albany, SUNY Pr, 1989.

CLIFTON, Robert K. Some Recent Controversy Over the Possibility of Experimentally Determining Isotropy in the Speed of Light. Phil Sci, 56(4), 688-696, D 89.

The most recent attempt at factually establishing a "true" value for the one-way velocity of light is shown to be faulty. The proposal consists of two round-trip photons travelling first in vacuo and then through a medium of refractive index n before returning to their common point of origin. It is shown that this proposal, as well as a similar one considered by Salmon (1977), presupposes that the one-way velocities of light are equal to the round-trip value. Furthermore, experiments of this type, involving regions of space with varying refractive indices, cannot "single out" any factual value for the Reichenbach-Grünbaum ε factor thus posing no threat to the conventionalist thesis.

CLIFTON, Robert K and REGEHR, Marilyn G. Toward a Sound Perspective on Modern Physics: Capra's Popularization of Mysticism and Theological Approaches. Zygon, 25(1), 73-104, Mr 90.

Fritjof Capra's *The Tao of Physics*, one of several popularizations paralleling Eastern mysticism and modern physics, is critiqued, demonstrating that Capra gives little attention to the differing philosophies of physics he employs, utilizing whatever interpretation suits his purposes, without prior justification. The same critique is applied and similar conclusions drawn, about some recent attempts at relating theology and physics. In contrast, we propose the possibility of maintaining a cogent relationship between these disciplines by employing theological hypotheses to account for aspects of physics that are free from interpretive difficulties, such as the ability to create mathematical structures with extraordinary predictive success.

CLING, Andrew D. Disappearance and Knowledge. Phil Sci, 57(2), 226-247, Je 90.

Paul Churchland argues that the continuity of human intellectual development provides evidence against folk psychology and traditional epistemology, since these latter find purchase only at the later stages of intellectual development. He supports this contention with an analogy from the history of thermodynamics. Careful attention to the thermodynamics analogy shows that the argument from continuity does not provide independent support for eliminative materialism. The argument also rests upon claims about continuity which do not support the claim that the continuity of intellectual development is evidence for the elimination of folk psychology. Traditional epistemology and folk psychology should not yet be abandoned.

CLINTON, W David. "Ethics and Diplomacy" in *Moral Reasoning and Statecraft: Essays Presented to Kenneth W Thompson*, DAVIS, Reed M (ed), 37-51. Lanham, Univ Pr of America, 1988.

CLOUSER, K Danner and GERT, Bernard. A Critique of Principlism. J Med Phil, 15(2), 219-236, Ap 90.

The authors use the term "principlism" to refer to the practice of using "principles" to replace both moral theory and particular moral rules and ideals in dealing with the moral problems that arise in medical practice. The authors argue that these "principles" do not function as claimed, and that their use is misleading both practically and theoretically. The "principles" are in fact not guides to action, but rather they are merely names for a collection of sometimes superficially related matters for consideration when dealing with a moral problem. The "principles" lack any systematic relationship to each other, and they often conflict with each other. These conflicts are unresolvable, since there is no unified moral theory from which they are all derived. For comparison the authors sketch the advantages of using a unified moral theory.

CLOUSER, K Danner. Humanities in Medical Education: Some Contributions. J Med Phil, 15(3), 289-301, Je 90.

The author discusses the contribution of humanities teaching in medical education. Five "qualities of mind" specifically engendered by the humanistic disciplines are isolated, delineated, and illustrated: critical abilities, flexibility of perspective, nondogmatism, discernment of values, and empathy and self-knowledge.

CLOUTIER, Yvan. La Prétention amoraliste. Rev Int Phil, 43(170), 342-351, 1989.

Many moral philosophers use the "amoralist fiction" in order to answer the question "Why should I be moral?" The paper examines three figures of the amoralist: (a) the psychopath, (b) the one who refuses moral judgment, (c) the one who refuses to act accordingly. The normal individual has a minimum moral affectivity, a minimum moral judgment and the capacity to act accordingly. So it is like asking "Why should I imagine considering the fact that I am a being who has imagination as an indispensable feature?" The issue becomes the relation to one's "moral constitution." One can be moral or immoral, never amoral.

CLOWNEY, David. Virtues, Rules and the Foundations of Ethics. Philosophia (Israel), 20(1-2), 49-68, Jl 90.

The author argues that a theory of the virtues is an irreducibly important part of moral theory, but that it cannot be the only part. The first section discusses the work of Philippa Foot on the foundations and limits of virtues ethics, concluding that Foot's account of the virtues depends on deontological and axiological notions. The second section is a more general comparison of deontological and aretaic theories of ethics, indicating their relative strengths and weaknesses and their mutual interdependence.

CLULEE, Nicholas H. *John Dee's Natural Philosophy: Between Science and Religion*. New York, Routledge, 1988

This study delineates the character of John Dee's natural philosophy and defines its place in both Dee's career and sixteenth-century attempts to understand the natural world. An intensive examination of the major expressions of his natural philosophy suggests that his thinking was individual and developed considerably as he attempted to find in nature expression for increasing religious impulses and sought to define an intellectual role for himself within sixteenth-century court culture. His ideas were strongly influenced by Roger Bacon and other medieval sources, on which he gradually grafted an idiosyncratic blend of renaissance magical and occult ideas.

COADY, C A J. "Escaping from the Bomb: Immoral Deterrence and the Problem of Extrication" in *Nuclear Deterrence and Moral Restraint*, SHUE, Henry (ed), 163-225. New York, Cambridge Univ Pr, 1989.

COADY, C A J. Hobbes and 'The Beautiful Axiom'. Philosophy, 65(251), 4-17, Ja 90.

Self-preservation plays a central but elusive role in Hobbes's moral theory. The best construal of Hobbes should not ground his emphasis upon self-preservation in any form of egoism, but rather in an ethical tradition stretching back at least to the Stoics. This has the advantage that the general rationality of self-preservation is more secure than the supposed rationality of any version of egoism. Moreover, the notion of self-interest is dangerously unclear. Nonetheless, Hobbes's monism about self-preservation leads to a serious problem concerning noncooperation in the moral enterprise.

COADY, C A J. Messy Morality and the Art of the Possible—I. Aris Soc, SUPP 64, 259-279, 1990.

COBBEN, Paul. 'Communicatief handelen' als theoretisch grondbegrip. Alg Ned Tijdschr Wijs, 81(4), 241-263, O 89.

"Communicative action" is the central concept of Jürgen Habermas's most recent work. In this article the concept has been subjected to a critical survey. The conclusions could be summarized as follows: (1) As a transformation of Kantian transcendental philosophy the theory of communicative action does not overcome the old paradigma. Hegel's critics on Kant also concern Habermas. (2) Habermas has good reasons for the transformation just mentioned. Traditional philosophy failed to understand human autonomy in terms that are appropriate to finite beings. To save the project of Enlightenment means to solve this problem. Habermas pretends that the theory of communicative action is able to fulfill this task. Analysis of the merits and limitations of the pretension however tempers this optimistic view.

COBBEN, Paul. Het projet van de Verlichting in het licht van Hegels rechtsfilosofie. Alg Ned Tijdschr Wijs, 82(3), 212-231, Jl 90.

At the present day the thesis is defended that the concept of the autonomous subject is not compatible to tradition. For that reason the Enlightenment project had to fail. This thesis gives occasion to a review of Hegel's *Grundlinien der Philosophie des Rechts*. The book contains a philosophical reflection on the concept of the autonomous subject. It is argued that in Hegel's vision the concept is not incompatible with tradition. The *Philosophy of Right* on the contrary leads to a determination of the transcendental conditions to which tradition has to conform in order to be valid as a manifestation of the autonomous subject. At the end of the article some suggestions are made for a better realization of this program.

COBIANU, Elena. La morale dans le contexte des sciences de l'homme chez Constantin Leonardescu (in Romanian). Rev Filosof (Romania), 36(1), 66-72, Ja-F 89.

COBIANU, Maria. La culture du travail (in Romanian). Rev Filosof (Romania), 36(1), 37-40, Ja-F 89.

COBURN, Robert C. Evolution and Skepticism. Pac Phil Quart, 71(1), 1-13, Mr 90.

COCCHIARELLA, Nino B. "Russell's Theory of Logical Types and the Atomistic Hierarchy of Sentences" in *Rereading Russell: Essays on Bertrand Russell's Metaphysics and Epistemology*, SAVAGE, C Wade (ed), 41-62. Minneapolis, Univ of Minn Pr, 1989.

It is shown in this paper that the theory of logical types Russell was committed to after 1913 (as described in his lectures on logical atomism and in his introduction to the 1925 second edition of *Principia Mathematica, PM*) amounts to no more than ramified second-order logic, a fragment of the full theory of types described in the 1910-13 *PM*, and, in particular, a fragment in which Russell's construction of mathematics is no longer possible. Russell's 1908 theory of logical types is also described and distinguished from his 1910-13 theory. How Russell came to be committed to three different theories of types over these different periods is explained in terms of Russell's changing views on the notion of a logical subject.

CODE, Lorraine. Collingwood's Epistemological Individualism. Monist,

72(4), 542-567, O 89.

Although Collingwood's relativism, historicism, antirealism, and idealism appear to cast him as a 'free-spirited' philosopher (in Ernest Sosa's taxonomy), I argue that his *individualism* makes the aptness of that characterisation less clear. In working out his famous reenactment thesis, Collingwood seems to exempt the historian—hence, too, the epistemologist—from the strictures of 'locatedness' that constrain all of the knowledge-seeking enterprises that he (i.e., the historian) studies. The implications of this exemption, which I elaborate, reveal that an adequate characterization of 'free-spiritedness' in philosophy requires a theory of specifically situated subjectivity and human agency.

CODE, Murray. On the Continuing Relevance of Whitehead. Int Stud Phil, 21(3), 85-93, 1989.

The question of the relevance and importance of Whitehead's approach to philosophy is discussed in the context of a note on the recent book *Alfred North Whitehead*, by Paul G Kuntz. This book is a timely reminder that Whitehead raises and provides a solution to a fundamental question of philosophy: how best can one become clear and rational in the attempt to wed the systematic to the speculative in our expressions of the orderly aspects of nature?

CODERRE, C and ANDREW, C and DENIS, A. Stop or Go: Reflections of Women Managers on Factors Influencing their Career Development. J Bus Ethics, 9(4-5), 361-367, Ap-My 90.

The purpose of this paper is to discuss how women managers themselves interpret the factors that constrain and those that facilitate management careers for women. We will do this by first reviewing some of the interpretations that have been put forward in the academic literature to explain the relatively small number of women managers and particularly the small number of very senior women managers. In the light of these interpretations, we will examine the opinions of a sample of intermediate and senior women managers in the public and private sectors in Ontario and Quebec. More specifically we will look at their answers to questions about what blocks and what facilitates management careers for women generally and what obstacles they themselves have met. We will then compare their interpretations of their own career development with the interpretations that exist in the literature.

COERS, Kathy Frashure. Vico and MacIntyre. New Vico Studies, 4, 131-133, 1986.

This essay indicates the relevance of the thought of Giambattista Vico to Alasdair MacIntyre's *After Virtue: A Study in Moral Theory*. It argues that the heart of MacIntyre's Vichianism is to be found in his interpretation of the historical context of the Aristotelian tradition and in the contrast between this tradition and the mentality of twentieth-century man. If ethics is grounded in politics, then such ethical concepts as the virtues have a functional relationship to living well in a given society. These concepts are developments of poetic memory in that such memory informs them.

COHEN, Avner. "The 'End-of-Philosophy': An Anatomy of a Cross-Purpose Debate" in *The Institution of Philosophy: A Discipline in Crisis?*, COHEN, Avner (ed), 105-110. La Salle, Open Court, 1989.

COHEN, Avner (ed) and DASCAL, Marcelo (ed). *The Institution of Philosophy: A Discipline in Crisis?*. La Salle, Open Court, 1989

COHEN, Avner. On Reading Postmodern Philosophy: Hiley, Redner and the End of Philosophy. Praxis Int, 9(4), 381-399, Ja 90.

COHEN, Avner. Scepticism and *Angst*: The Case of David Hume. Manuscrito, 11(2), 49-66, O 88.

This paper is an attempt to examine the intimate psychological and phenomenological environment which gives rise to philosophical scepticism as exemplified in the case of David Hume. The paper consists of two different and distinct inquiries. The first is an "internal" one, a quasi-phenomenological inquiry into the intimate nature of scepticism as special philosophical experience. My source for this inquiry is the philosophical text alone. My primary contention here is that there is a close kinship, both phenomenological and conceptual, between the experience of total scepticism and the existentialist notion of *Angst*. The notion of *Angst*, I argue, is the phenomenological side of the radical thesis of scepticism. The second inquiry attempts to extend this phenomenological point by linking it into an "external" psycho-historical evidence from Hume's biography. Here I attempt to place the origins of *Angst* in a broader historical-biographical context. As such the paper is an attempt to utilize a psycho-historical investigation as a way to make a philosophical (or metaphilosophical) point.

COHEN, Carl. Militant Morality: Civil Disobedience and Bioethics. Hastings Center Rep, 19(6), 23-25, N-D 89.

COHEN, Cynthia B (ed) & others. Ethics Committees. Hastings Center

Rep, 19(5), 21-26, S-O 89.

COHEN, Cynthia B (ed). Ethics Committees. Hastings Center Rep, 20(2), 29-34, Mr-Ap 90.

COHEN, Eli. A Question of Ethics: Developing Information System Ethics. J Bus Ethics, 8(6), 431-437, Je 89.

This study develops a pedagogy for the teaching of ethical principles in information systems (IS) classes, and reports on an empirical study that supports the efficacy of the approach. The proposed pedagogy involves having management information systems professors lead questioning and discussion on a list of ethical issues as part of their existing IS courses. The rationale for this pedagogy involves (1) the maturational aspects of ethics, and (2) the importance of repetition, challenge, and practice in developing a personal set of ethics. A study of IS ethics using a pre-post test design found that classes receiving such treatment significantly improved their performance on an IS ethics questionnaire.

COHEN, Elliot D. Logic, Rationality and Counseling. Int J Applied Phil, 5(1), 43-49, Spr 90.

In the theory of counseling it is commonplace to distinguish between counseling approaches that are "directive" and those that are not. Whereas the former are didactic and evaluative, the latter are non-didactic and non-judgmental. Nonetheless, both sorts of approaches admit the value of client *autonomy*. This paper sketches a model of counseling that clarifies the extent of legitimate therapeutic directiveness, while also making sense of the notion of client autonomy. The proposed model is interdisciplinary, a fusion between cognitive-behavioral therapy on the one hand, and applied logic and philosophy on the other.

COHEN, Felix S. What is a Question? Thinking, 4(3-4), 57-60, 1982.

COHEN, G A. Self-Ownership, Communism and Equality—I. Aris Soc, SUPP 64, 25-44, 1990.

Marxism has failed to distinguish itself sufficiently thoroughly from left-wing libertarianism, which affirms the principle of self-ownership and is egalitarian with respect to non-human resources (only). This failure disfigures both the Marxian account of capitalist exploitation and the Marxian account of how communism, that is, a society of uncoerced equality, is possible.

COHEN, Hermann. Commentaire de la Critique de la Raison pure de Kant (1907). Rev Metaph Morale, 94(2), 165-170, Ap-Je 89.

COHEN, Jean. Discourse Ethics and Civil Society. Phil Soc Crit, 14(3-4), 315-337, 1988.

COHEN, Joshua and ROGERS, Joel. Reply to Beehler's "Autonomy and the Democratic Principle". Can J Phil, 19(4), 583-587, D 89.

COHEN, Mark R. "Maimonides' Egypt" in *Moses Maimonides and His Time*, ORMSBY, Eric L (ed), 21-34. Washington, Cath Univ Amer Pr, 1989.

COHEN, Mendel F. Obligation and Human Nature in Hume's Philosophy. Phil Quart, 40(160), 316-341, Jl 90.

It is shown that in spite of appearances to the contrary Hume holds that moral judgments are fully universalizable and that his account of moral obligation is a response to attacks on his sentimentalism. It is argued that this defense of his account of the "foundation of morals" together with his conception of both the nature of obligation and the "practicality of morals" leads him to insist that the moral sentiments of human beings across space and time are far more uniform than he knew them to be.

COHEN, Michael J. With Justice for All Beings: Educating as if Nature Matters. Between Species, 5(4), 220-223, Fall 89.

COHEN, Michael. Simultaneity and Einstein's *Gedankenexperiment*. Philosophy, 64(249), 391-396, Jl 89.

COHEN, Richard A. "Absolute Positivity and Ultrapositivity: Husserl and Levinas" in *The Question of the Other: Essays in Contemporary Continental Philosophy*, DALLERY, Arleen B (ed), 35-43. Albany, SUNY Pr, 1989.

COHEN, Richard. Non-in-difference in the Thought of Emmanuel Levinas and Franz Rosenzweig. Grad Fac Phil J, 13(1), 141-153, 1988.

A close examination and explanation of the terms and relations meant by Rosenzweig and Levinas in their characterization of the I-Other relation as the "non-in-difference" of the self to the other. Non-in-difference of the I to the other is revealed to be the central positive "inspiration" shared by both thinkers. This formula not only recalls Hegelian philosophy, it is specifically designed to mark Rosenzweig's and Levinas's overcoming of the absoluteness, the rational comprehensiveness of the idealist synthesis of identity and difference.

COHEN, Robert S (trans) and CANGUILHEM, Georges and FAWCETT, Carolyn R. *The Normal and the Pathological*. Cambridge, Zone Books, 1989.

The normal and the pathological are terms used for structures, activities, individual or collective situations proper to living beings and especially to man. The relation of a fact and a norm is its positive or negative value. Can the assessment of behaviors (in medicine, psychology, law and jurisprudence) be reduced to noting a necessity? Is a living being's disease a fact similar to universal attraction? The author maintains that diseases are not merely predetermined effects, but are revealing of a normative regulation proper to living beings and man.

COHEN, Sheldon M. Aristotle on Heat, Cold, and Teleological Explanation. Ancient Phil, 9 (2), 255-270, Fall 89.

I argue that Aristotle believes that nonteleological processes can account for some aspects of the development of the embryo, but not for others.

COHEN, Sheldon M. *Arms and Judgment: Law, Morality, and the Conduct of War in the 20th Century*. Boulder, Westview Pr, 1989.

COHEN, Ted. An Emendation in Kant's Theory of Taste. Nous, 24(1), 137-145, Mr 90.

A suggestion of a way to license the use of concepts in adjudicating conflicts in taste.

COHEN, Ted. Reflections on One Idea of Collingwood's Aesthetics. Monist, 72(4), 581-585, O 89.

An argument for the salience of the idea that the only serious distinction is the one between art and non-art.

COHLER, Anne M (trans) and MILLER, Basia C (trans) and STONE, Harold (trans) and MONTESQUIEU, Charles. *The Spirit of the Laws: Charles Montesquieu*. New York, Cambridge Univ Pr, 1989.

COHN, Robert Greer. Desire: Direct and Imitative. Phil Today, 33(4), 318-329, Wint 89.

René Girard's concept of desire which heavily features imitation is excessively unidimensional. There is also a deep ("metaphoric": high and low) *direct* desire which is in constant dialectical play with "mimetic desire." In his *Theory of the Emotions* Adam Smith alluded to this full dialectic of spontaneous or original desire versus "custom." Originality in this sense is important in Proust whom Girard misuses: the love for Gilberte or Odette is clearly stated by Proust to be as pure and spontaneous as simple "animal" desire, e.g., for mother milk (there are *also* mimetic phases of this love).

COKER, Edward W. Adam Smith's Concept of the Social System. J Bus Ethics, 9(2), 139-142, F 90.

This essay will postulate that Adam Smith's view of society was formulated out of historical influences far broader than generally conceded by many commentators in economic thought. Smith's basic behavioral concepts of sympathy and self-interest are significant contributions to economic thought as are his philosophy of human nature being based on liberty and freedom and not simply the creation of wealth. The vectors of influence that converged on Adam Smith were of varied and even contradictory natures. Yet the result of this collision of philosophical forces was clearly an event of significance in the history of philosophical and economic thought.

COLBERT, James. La filosofía política marxista y la revolución. Anu Filosof, 22(2), 95-112, 1989.

COLE, David. Functionalism and Inverted Spectra. Synthese, 82(2), 207-222, F 90.

Functionalism predicts that where systematic transformations of sensory input occur and are followed by behavioral accommodation in which normal function of the organism is restored such that the causes and effects of the subject's psychological states return to those of the period prior to the transformation, there will be a return of qualia or subjective experiences to those present prior to the transform. A transformation of this type that has long been of philosophical interest is the possibility of an inverted spectrum. Hilary Putnam argues that the physical possibility of *acquired* spectrum inversion refutes functionalism. The author argues, however, that in the absence of empirical results no *a priori* arguments against functionalism, such as Putnam's, can be cogent. (edited)

COLEMAN, Dorothy P. Interpreting Hume's *Dialogues*. Relig Stud, 25(2), 179-190, Je 89.

The author defends the traditional identification of Philo with Hume by showing that the passages in the *Dialogues* considered most problematic for this view are in fact *required* by Hume's assessment of the nature and limitations of religious belief. A systematic approach for interpreting these passages is adapted from Hume's criticism of fallacious concepts of external existence in the *Treatise of Human Nature*.

COLEMAN, Earle J. Is Nature Ever Unaesthetic? Between Species, 5(3), 138-146, Sum 89.

This essay explores negative replies to the question: Is nature ever ugly? First, illustrations that appear to tell in favor of an affirmative reply are rebutted by a turn to contextualism, according to which there is no ugliness if one has adopted the proper perspective. I then argue that although certain purported cases of the unaesthetic do vanish in the face of a contextual perspective, another account is needed in order to explain the simple, nonrelational beauty of a single tone or color patch. Next, a Taoist model of aesthetic appreciation is used to explain simple beauty as well as the omnipresence of aesthetic value.

COLEMAN, Jules. On the Relationship Between Law and Morality. Ratio Juris, 2(1), 66-78, Mr 89.

Instead of being embarrassed and uneasy about the implications of the separation thesis, positivists should welcome the fact that they cannot account for the obligatoriness of law. The rule of recognition is only a social rule and introduces no grounds for obligation.

COLEMAN, Jules. "Rationality and the Justification of Democracy" in *Politics and Process*, BRENNAN, Geoffrey (ed), 194-220. New York, Cambridge Univ Pr, 1989.

COLES, Martin. Critical Children: Philosophy for the Young. Thinking, 7(2), 26-28, 1987.

COLES, Romand. Shapiro, Genealogy, and Ethics. Polit Theory, 17(4), 575-579, N 89.

COLL, Alberto R. "Christianity and Statecraft in International Relations" in *Moral Reasoning and Statecraft: Essays Presented to Kenneth W Thompson*, DAVIS, Reed M (ed), 3-22. Lanham, Univ Pr of America, 1988.

COLLERETTE, P and AUBRY, P. Socio-Economic Evolution of Women Business Owners in Quebec (1987). J Bus Ethics, 9(4-5), 417-422, Ap-My 90.

Two years after a five-year longitudinal study was undertaken in 1986, distinct characteristics of the female entrepreneur in Quebec are starting to emerge. This paper draws a general portrait of the female entrepreneur and examines certain features that have not been extensively studied in the past: age, family status, size and type of business, partnerships, motivation, obstacles, financing, and income evolution.

COLLETT, Alan. Literature, Criticism, and Factual Reporting. Phil Lit, 13(2), 282-296, O 89.

Truman Capote's *In Cold Blood*, it is argued, is the successful result of an intention to create a literary work whose literariness is inseparable from the truth or falsity of its reporting sentences. The book is, therefore, an effective counterexample to the claim that all literature, including novels dealing with real historical events, is properly regarded as fictional.

COLLETT, Alan. Literature, Fiction and Autobiography. Brit J Aes, 29(4), 341-352, Autumn 89.

COLLIER, John D. Two Faces of Maxwell's Demon Reveal the Nature of Irreversibility. Stud Hist Phil Sci, 21(2), 257-268, Je 90.

COLLINS, Allan and BROWN, John Seeley and NEWMAN, Susan E. Cognitive Apprenticeship Teaching the Craft of Reading, Writing and Mathematics. Thinking, 8(1), 2-10, 1989.

COLLINS, Denis. Adam Smith's Social Contract: The Proper Role of Individual Liberty and Government Intervention. Bus Prof Ethics J, 7(3-4), 119-146, Fall-Wint 88.

COLLINS, H M. "The Meaning of Experiment: Replication and Reasonableness" in *Dismantling Truth: Reality in the Post-Modern World*, LAWSON, Hilary (ed), 82-92. New York, St Martin's Pr, 1989.

Replicability is an essential idea in empirical sciences. The question remains: does this have any methodological payoff? The answer is no because in ill-understood areas, what counts as a replication is not clear. Replicability is necessary but the notion can only be applied after the existence of the phenomenon in question has been established.

COLLINS, John and BIGELOW, John and PARGETTER, Robert. Colouring in the World. Mind, 99(394), 279-288, Ap 90.

COLLOPY, Bart and DUBLER, Nancy and ZUCKERMAN, Connie. The Ethics of Home Care: Autonomy and Accommodation. Hastings Center Rep, 20(2), Supp 1-16, Mr-Ap 90.

COLOMBO, Arrigo (ed) and TUNDO, Laura (ed). *Fourier: La Passione dell'Utopia*. Milan, Angeli, 1988

COLOMBO, Giuseppe. Ontologismo e trascendenza di Dio: Note a proposito di una recente teoria. Riv Filosof Neo-Scolas, 81(3), 478-491, JI-S 89.

COLOMBRES, Carlos A Iturralde. Meditaciones sobre la nada. Sapientia, 44(174), 249-272, O-D 89.

COLOMER, Eusebi. Heidegger, pensador del tiempo indigente.

Pensamiento, 46(181), 3-21, Ja-Mr 90.

Partiendo de un aforismo de *De la experiencia del pensar* y en torno a la tríada: ser, hombre, lenguaje, el ensayo esboza, en clave dialéctica, una visión sintética del pensamiento de Martin Heidegger, y por cierto sobre el sombrío telón de fondo de nuestro tiempo indigente, ateológico y postmetafísico, del que este pensamiento es trágico testimonio.

COLONNELLO, Pio. *Croce e i Vociani*. Geneva, Stud Ed Di Cultura, 1984

COLONNELLO, Pio. *Heidegger Interprete di Kant*. Geneva, Stud Ed Di Cultura, 1981

COLTESCU, Viorel. Sur le status théorique de la philosophie moderne du langage (in Romanian). Rev Filosof (Romania), 36(1), 40-49, Ja-F 89.

COLWELL, Gary. God, the Bible and Circularity. Inform Log, 11(2), 61-73, Spr 89.

A standard religious example of circular reasoning has repeatedly appeared in numerous textbooks on informal logic. With variations it reads essentially like this: "God exists because the Bible says so, and we know that what the Bible says is true because it is The Revealed Word of God." It is argued here that this example is either not an argument, or, if it is an argument, it is not a circular argument, or if it is a circular argument, it is not a viciously circular argument. In any case there is no cause for worry among believers.

COMANS, Michael. The Self in Deep Sleep According to Advaita and Visistādvaita. J Indian Phil, 18(1), 1-28, Mr 90.

COMESAÑA, Manuel E. Enunciados basicos e hipótesis falsificadora en Popper. Analisis Filosof, 7(1), 19-27, My 87.

According to Popper, a theory is falsified by accepting basic statements which contradict it, but only if such basic statements describe "reproducible effects," or, in other words, only if they corroborate "falsifying hypotheses." This view wrongly presents as a general requirement what only holds for experimental testing in theoretical science. If the basic statement describes a nonreproducible fact whose observation is not problematic (as it happens with "There is a family of white ravens in the New York zoo"), then it refutes a universal statement ("All ravens are black") without corroborating any falsifying hypothesis.

COMESAÑA, Manuel E. La ingeniería social como método de testeo. Rev Filosof (Argentina), 4(1), 21-40, My 89.

According to Popper, scientific knowledge of society can grow only if it tries to give response to practical problems of social life. The aim of this paper is to show that such "technological approach of social science" finds epistemological justification on Popper's plausible ideas about empirical testing of theories.

COMETTI, Jean-Pierre. Wittgenstein et la philosophie. Etudes, 371(3), 195-207, S 89.

La pensée de Wittgenstein privilégie la conscience du pluriel et du possible par rapport à celle de l'unique, de l'identique et de l'inexorable. Le souci éthique n'est pas étranger à son effort pour débusquer les sophismes de toutes sortes auxquels, selon lui, les super-ordres et les super-concepts de la philosophie servent souvent d'abri.

COMNINOU, Maria. To Rectify an Amoral Design. Between Species, 5(3), 165-167, Sum 89.

It is argued that life on planet earth has evolved as if by an engineering design based on efficiency, self-sufficiency, renewability and productivity. This design has led to acceptance of killing as a necessity in nature. The human race has historically tried to draw a circular boundary to protect certain beings from killing, but without much success. The animal rights movement, still fraught with controversy in its embryonic stage, has as a goal to extend the boundary as far as it can practically go.

COMOLLI, Fabrizio. Le strutture trascendentali della coscienza nel primo Sartre: ipotesi di lettura. Riv Filosof Neo-Scolas, 81(1), 107-137, Ja-Mr 89.

COMPTON, Kevin J and HENSON, C Ward. A Uniform Method for Proving Lower Bounds on the Computational Complexity of Logical Theories. Annals Pure Applied Log, 48(1), 1-79, JI 90.

A new method for obtaining lower bounds on the computational complexity of logical theories is presented. It extends widely used techniques for proving the undecidability of theories by interpreting models of a theory already known to be undecidable. New inseparability results related to the well-known inseparability result of Trakhtenbrot and Vaught are the foundation of the method. Their use yields hereditary lower bounds (i.e., bounds which apply uniformly to all subtheories of a theory). By means of interpretations lower bounds can be transferred from one theory to another. Complicated machine codings are replaced by much simpler definability considerations, viz., the kinds of binary relations definable with short formulas on large finite sets. Numerous examples are given, including new proofs of essentially all previously known lower bounds for theories, and lower bounds for various theories of finite trees, which turn out to be particularly useful.

COMSTOCK, Gary L. "Everything Depends on the *Type* of the Concepts that the Interpretation is Made to Convey". Mod Theol, 5(3), 215-237, Ap 89.

Contemporary Christian theologians are concerned with the ethical significance of the Bible's narratives. Major proposals for how one ought to construe the moral relevance of Scripture have come from "pure narrativists" like Hans Frei and "impure narrativists" like David Tracy. I argue that both approaches have difficulties, and turn to the Jewish thinker, Max Kadushin, for a new approach. The answer centers on what Kadushin calls "value-concepts."

CONDREN, C. Radicals, Conservatives and Moderates in Early Modern Political Thought: A Case of Sandwich Islands Syndrome? Hist Polit Thought, 10(3), 525-542, Autumn 89.

The set of terms radical, moderate and conservative is used almost universally to describe political texts/authors of the late medieval/early modern period. Varieties of careless use are widely illustrated. It is then argued that even when carefully used the terms are misleading and anachronistic. Definitional strategies are discussed. The origins of the terms and the distance between metaphor and formal conceptualisation help explain the misleading conspectus the use of the terms has created.

CONE, Edward T. "Music and Form" in *What is Music?*, ALPERSON, Philip A , 131-146. New York, Haven, 1987.

Musical form involves succession, agglutination, and accretion. That is, a composition can be fruitfully studied from the points of view of its details, its articulative factors, and its unifying principles. Roughly, these aspects correspond to the rhythmic, melodic, and harmonic components of a composition. But rhythm, the most basic of the elements, informs all three aspects. Even the generic patterns—"musical forms"—are explicable in terms of rhythm; they must be experienced as processes rather than as abstract designs. So considered, musical form is itself expressive, both in its adherence to and in its contravention of norms. Its control of rhythm makes musical expression possible; its constraints make it tolerable.

CONKIN, Paul K and STROMBERG, Roland N. *Heritage and Challenge: The History and Theory of History*. Arlington Heights, Forum Pr, 1989

This book includes a history of historical writing by Roland Stormberg, and a series of essays on the critical philosophy of history by Paul Conkin. These essays (on definitions of history, the relation of history to the generalizing sciences, causation, objectivity, and the use of history) reflect a loosely pragmatic orientation. Conkin distinguishes historical inquiry from the social and physical sciences by differences in subject, form, and use, but not method. He defends a circumspect form of objectivity, one tied to rules or conventions, which he justifies largely by the human purposes they serve.

CONN, Melanie. No Bosses Here: Management in Worker Co-Operatives. J Bus Ethics, 9(4-5), 373-376, Ap-My 90.

This article examines the worker co-op structure as a workplace option for women. The appeal of the model for women is described in terms of the opportunity for skill development and control over workplace conditions. The structure also presents some unique challenges for training since all members participate in management functions. The author describes a six-month course, "Co-operative Employment for Women" which trained women in co-operative business development.

CONNER, Frederick W. Beyond Truth: Santayana on the Functional Relations of Art, Myth, and Religion. Bull Santayana Soc, 5, 17-26, Fall 87.

Truth, as Santayana used the term, is correspondence, but in dealing with the possibilities of acceptable affirmation he goes considerably beyond this limited conception, first to "knowledge," which he conceives in the pragmatic sense of imagination disciplined by punishment, and, second, to expression by symbolic means of things held dear. Ultimate in this development is the expression of a detached contemplation in which one goes beyond the biological necessities of picking and choosing and comes to love and understand all things for the good to which they imperfectly aspire. Here rests the author's legendary devotion to art, myth, and religion despite their indifference to literal truth.

CONNOR, Steven. *Postmodernist Culture: An Introduction to Theories of the Contemporary*. Cambridge, Blackwell, 1989

This book explores and contrasts the definitions of postmodernity in a number of different disciplines and cultural areas, including philosophy, political theory, architecture, art, photography, literature, drama, film, TV and video, popular culture and contemporary cultural politics. Examining the

institutional frames of postmodern theory, it develops the view that postmodern theory simultaneously promotes openness and contains it; the custodial force of postmodern theory therefore being part of the condition of postmodernity. The book concludes with an investigation of the languages of postmodern theory and a consideration of the possibility of a cultural-political ethics after postmodernism.

CONROY, Fran. Learning to be Human: Confucian Resources for Person-Centered Education. Personalist Forum, 6(1), 27-49, Spr 90.

CONSIGNY, Scott. Dialectical, Rhetorical, and Aristotelian Rhetoric. Phil Rhet, 22(4), 281-287, 1989.

CONSTANTE, Alberto. La alegria del arte: Hegel y Heidegger. Rev Filosof (Mexico), 22(66), 349-353, S-D 89.

CONTI, Charles. The Personalism of Austin Farrer. Personalist Forum, 5(2), 83-118, Fall 89.

CONWAY, Daniel W. Literature as Life: Nietzsche's Positive Morality. Int Stud Phil, 21(2), 41-53, 1989.

CONWAY, Daniel W. Overcoming the *Übermensch*: Nietzsche's Revaluation of Values. J Brit Soc Phenomenol, 20(3), 211-224, O 89.

Nietzsche is best known as a relentless critic whose constructive agenda betrays a horrifying naivete. Perhaps the most notorious of his constructive prescriptions is his call for a "revaluation of values" that would catalyze our transcendence of nihilism. Nietzsche's allusions to the agent ostensibly responsible for executing his agenda, the world-historical *Übermensch*, suggest that this revaluation of values would involve a radical break from the bankrupt values of modernity. But Nietzsche neither anticipates nor prophesies a redemption of modernity. Because he identifies our perceived need for redemption as symptomatic of nihilism, he intends the proposed revaluation of values to eliminate the basis of this felt need.

CONWAY, Stephen. Bentham on Peace and War. Utilitas, 1(1), 82-101, My 89.

COOK, Deborah. Madness and the Cogito: Derrida's Critique of *Folie et déraison*. J Brit Soc Phenomenol, 21(2), 164-174, My 90.

In "Cogito et Histoire de la Folie," Derrida challenges Foucault's reading of Descartes's natural and hyperbolic exclusions of madness from the truth of the *cogito*. Derrida's criticisms of Foucault are often flawed because the former's interpretation of Descartes is highly problematic. The author questions Derrida's reading of Descartes and argues for Foucault's. At the end of the paper, however, aspects of Foucault's reading of the hyperbolic hypothesis are also disputed as is the form of exclusion Foucault claimed was practised in the classical age.

COOK, Deborah. Remapping Modernity. Brit J Aes, 30(1), 35-45, Ja 90.

This paper is primarily a critique of the position Habermas takes with respect to the work of Derrida and Foucault in his "Modernity—An Incomplete Project." The essay also takes into account discussions of modernity and postmodernity in the writings of Andreas Huyssen and Frederick Jameson. The author concludes that the work of Derrida and Foucault is not postmodern because it does not adopt the philosophical positions these writers claim it adopts and because their work should be interpreted as a response to problems raised by the Enlightenment.

COOK, Kathleen C. The Underlying Thing, the Underlying Nature and Matter: Aristotle's Analogy in Physics *I 7*. Apeiron, 22(4), 105-119, D 89.

COOK, Thomas. "A Whirlwind at My Back...": Spinozistic Themes in Bernard Malamud's "The Fixer". Stud Spinozana, 5, 15-28, 1989.

The article deals with Spinozistic themes in *The Fixer*, a prize-winning novel by Bernard Malamud. The novel is a fictionalized account of a criminal case in Czarist Russia. In the novel, as in the actual historical case, an innocent Jew is accused by the anti-Semitic authorities of "ritual murder" and is imprisoned for two years without trial. Before his arrest, the accused read some works by Spinoza and found them inspiring, though he understood little. In the course of his imprisonment, he realizes the truth of Spinoza's doctrines regarding the interconnectedness of all things and the intelligible order underlying apparent chaos. His increasing understanding of these Spinozistic principles helps to transform him from a confused and passive victim to an active and effective opponent of tyranny.

COONEY, William. Affirmative Action and the Doctrine of Double Effect. J Applied Phil, 6(2), 201-204, O 89.

This article attempts to show that affirmative action can be supported by the doctrine of double effect which recognises distinctions between desired and unintended effects such that the responsibility for acts falls on the side of the former rather than the latter. With this doctrine it may also be seen why affirmative action programmes cannot be simply equated with numerical quota systems, nor can they be called discriminatory, at least not under the definition of discrimination utilised.

COOPER, David E. Irony and 'The Essence of Writing'. Phil Papers, 18(1), 53-73, My 89.

Literary critics from Schlegel to Barthes have claimed that irony is an essential dimension of literature. Such claims need, first, to be disambiguated. They are then found to suffer from implausible extrapolations from some genuine features of the trope of irony, wrongly held to characterize all literary writing, and from mistaken analyses of ironic meaning.

COOPER, David E. *Metaphor*. Cambridge, Blackwell, 1986

The book falls into four chapters. In the first, the question of why metaphor has become such a popular topic of discussion is addressed. In Chapter 2, issues of metaphorical meaning are examined, with the author developing and defending the claim that (fresh) metaphors have no meaning. In the next chapter, a theory is advanced, in terms of speakers' need for 'intimacy', of why metaphor is such a pervasive feature of discourse. Finally, the question of metaphorical truth is explored.

COOPER, John M. "Greek Philosophers on Euthanasia and Suicide" in *Suicide and Euthanasia*, BRODY, Baruch A (ed), 9-38. Norwell, Kluwer, 1989.

COOPER, John W. *Body, Soul, and Life Everlasting: Biblical Anthropology and the Monism-Dualism Debate*. Grand Rapids, Eerdmans, 1989

COOPER, Neil. Aristotle's Crowning Virtue. Apeiron, 22(3), 191-205, S 89.

This paper contends that Aristotle in his account of the *megalopsychos* in his ethical works, is likely to have been following the methodology of the *Posterior Analytics* (97b 7-25), that this methodology seduced him into trying to produce an impossible unitary account, that in fact he provided merely a compromise between the Achillean and Socratic types distinguished in *PoA* and that he had in the *endoxa* the materials for a more admirable crowning virtue, less repellent to "modern sympathies" and more easily integrated with his other ethical doctrines.

COOPER, W E and KING-FARLOW, John. A Case for Capital Punishment. J Soc Phil, 20(3), 64-76, Wint 89.

Independent from the standard deterrence and retributivist considerations, capital punishment might be justified by linking it to the saving of innocent lives.

COOPER, W S. How Evolutionary Biology Challenges the Classical Theory of Rational Choice. Biol Phil, 4(4), 457-481, O 89.

A fundamental philosophical question that arises in connection with evolutionary theory is whether the fittest patterns of behavior are always the most rational. Are fitness and rationality fully compatible? When behavioral rationality is characterized formally as in classical decision theory, the question becomes mathematically meaningful and can be explored systematically by investigating whether the optimally fit behavior predicted by evolutionary process models is decision-theoretically coherent. Upon investigation, it appears that in nontrivial evolutionary models the expected behavior is *not* always in accord with the norms of the standard theory of decision as ordinarily applied. (edited)

COOPER, Wesley E. The Metaphysics of Leisure. Phil Context, 19, 59-73, 1989.

In the light of a review of recent literature about leisure, I connect leisure to self-expression under conditions of full information and vivid awareness.

COPLÁKOVÁ-HARTOVÁ, E and BUKOVSKY, Lev. Minimal Collapsing Extensions of Models of ZFC. Annals Pure Applied Log, 46(3), 265-298, Ap 90.

COPP, David. Explanation and Justification in Ethics. Ethics, 100(2), 237-258, Ja 90.

Confirmation theory is a new approach to naturalistic moral realism. Its fundamental thesis is that a normative moral theory is justified just in case it is empirically confirmed according to the canons of scientific methodology. It rests on claims about the existence of genuine moral explanations. I argue that an important skeptical position remains open even if these claims are granted, for moral explanations are "incidental" explanations. They are genuine explanations that invoke moral concepts but no moral standard can be justified on the basis of its role in successful explanations. Hence, a skeptic can accept moral explanations while holding that no moral standard is credible. I explore various objections to my claim and conclude by attempting to explain why moral explanations are incidental.

CORCOS, Alain F and MONAGHAN, Floyd V. The Real Objective of Mendel's Paper. Biol Phil, 5(3), 267-292, Jl 90.

According to the traditional account Mendel's paper on pea hybrids reported a study of inheritance and its laws. Hence, Mendel came to be known as "The Father of Genetics." This paper demonstrates that, in fact, Mendel's objective in his research was finding the empirical laws which describe the formation of hybrids and the development of their offspring over several generations. (edited)

CORDERO, Alberto. Observation in Constructive Empiricism: Arbitrary or Incoherent? Critica, 21(61), 75-102, Ap 89.

This paper argues against the plausibility of constructive empiricism as a philosophy of science. The standard general arguments for the doctrine are found to be invalid. The specific rationale for constructive empiricism advanced by Van Fraassen in *The Scientific Image* is then examined and found to be based exclusively on abstract decision theory and selected facts about the human species. It is shown that a philosophy so motivated is unable to prevent its own collapse under the weight of numerous other "facts" about the human species.

CORDNER, Christopher. The Aristotelian Character of Schiller's Ethical Ideal. Int Stud Phil, 22(1), 21-36, 1990.

Schiller's ethical and aesthetic views have long been regarded as essentially Kantian, or at least as a ready extension of Kant's views. I argue that there are deep differences between Kant and Schiller, and that these are best understood if Schiller is thought of in relation to an Aristotelian tradition of ethical thought. (I urge a close resemblance between Schiller and Aristotle, rather than an influence on Schiller by Aristotle.) I argue that Schillerian grace, and also Schiller's idea of the aesthetic state, is close in significance to Aristotle's idea, in the *Nicomachean Ethics*, of the noble.

CORDUA, Carla. El pensamiento económico de Hegel: Escritos recientes. Dialogos, 25(55), 159-167, Ja 90.

A critical study of recent writings on the origins and content of Hegel's economic ideas. In particular, writings in English and German of the last ten years are considered. W Ver Eecke's "Relation between Economics and Politics in Hegel," N Rotenstreich's "Needs and Interdependence: On Hegel's Conception and its Aftermath" and N Waszek's "Hegels schottische Bettler" are discussed in some detail. Various interpretations of Hegel's acceptance of the existence of poverty in the modern state are considered.

CORLETT, J A. Knowing and Believing in the Original Position. Theor Decis, 27(3), 241-256, N 89.

I describe John Rawls's concept of the original position, a concept which plays a crucial role in his theory of justice. Then I provide an internal critique of this concept, arguing that there is some incoherence concerning the following Rawlsian claims: (1) that the parties in the original position are free and equal rational persons; (2) that the goal and outcome of the original position is a social contract; (3) that Rawls's principles of justice would be chosen in the original position; (4) that the persons behind the veil of ignorance in the original position know their own or another's social position; and (5) that persons in the actual world can at any time participate in the original position. My argument is not that such incoherence proves the end of Rawls's theory of justice, but that his concept of the manner by which principles of justice are selected and agreed on by rational agents needs rethinking.

CORLETT, J Angelo. The "Modified Vendetta Sanction" as a Method of Corporate-Collective Punishment. J Bus Ethics, 8(12), 937-942, D 89.

Shannon Shipp argues for the "Modified Vendetta Sanction" as a method of corporate-collective punishment. He claims that this sanction evades the difficulties of Peter French's "Hester Prynne Sanction." In this paper I argue that, though the Modified Vendetta Sanction evades the problems that Shipp poses for it, it fails to evade some of the difficulties that I pose for French's method. Moreover, there are some difficulties that plague the Modified Vendetta Sanction which do not count against the Hester Prynne Sanction. Therefore, if my analysis holds, then Shipp's method neither improves significantly on the "Hester Prynne Sanction" nor is unproblematic in its own right. The significance of this paper is that it foils yet another attempt by some corporate punishment theorists to establish the plausibility of a method of corporate-collective punishment.

CORNBLIT, Oscar. Acontecimientos y leyes en la explicación histórica. Analisis Filosof, 8(2), 141-159, N 88.

According to one of the prevailing views concerning historic explanation, historic narrative is in itself an adequate type of explanation to which there is no need to add any additional scheme in order to complete it. Opposed to this view is the Hempelian deductive-nomological explanation (DN) which considers narration as an explanatory sketch to be reformulated by expliciting the laws which supposedly sustain the narrative argument. By examining this debate one sees that narration fulfills the conditions of objectivity and independent testability which are often required as adequacy conditions for all kinds of explanation. Furthermore, narration doesn't contain an implicit appeal to generalization, even though it nearly always employs a casual language. These conclusions support the autonomous character of narration as an explanatory style. (edited)

CORNESCU, Viorel and BUCUR, Ion. Qualité et efficience—coordonate principales du développement socio-économique Roumaine (in Romanian). Rev Filosof (Romania), 36(2), 134-141, Mr-Ap 89.

CORNILESCU, Alexandra. Remarks on the Concept of "Universal Grammar". Phil Log, 32(1-2), 129-146, Ja-Je 88.

CORRINGTON, Robert S. Conversation between Justus Buchler and Robert S Corrington. J Speculative Phil, 3(4), 261-274, 1989.

This conversation took place on August 18th, 1982 in the home of Professor Buchler. In it, Buchler, author of five systematic works of philosophy including his seminal *Metaphysics of Natural Complexes* (1966, 2nd expanded edition 1989), discusses his conception of naturalism, the nature of metaphysics, the possibility of a conception of God, his own concept of "judgment," and the nature and limits of sign theory. He also sheds light on his reading of Locke, Dewey, and Husserl as they relate to what has been termed "ordinal naturalism." Also, clarifications are made of his key concept of "natural complex."

CORRINGTON, Robert S. Emerson and the Agricultural Midworld. Agr Human Values, 7(1), 20-26, Wint 90.

The metaphor of the "midworld" refers to Emerson's conception of the realm between the human process and nature. In his earlier writings, poetry served as a linguistic midworld that made it possible for the self to relate to the innumerable orders of nature. By the 1840s Emerson's thought had taken a much more skeptical turn and had moved decisively away from his earlier linguistic idealism. As a consequence, his conception of the nature of the midworld changed. The more humble work of the farmer came to represent more clearly the actual development of the midworld. In agricultural production, the basic features of nature became more directly available to the self. By the 1870s Emerson recognized that the farmer and the poet were both representatives of the midworld that made nature actual to the human process.

CORSI, Giovanna. A Cut-Free Calculus for Dummett's LC Quantified. Z Math Log, 35(4), 289-301, 1989.

CORSI, Giovanna. A Logic Characterized by the Class of Connected Models with Nested Domain. Stud Log, 48(1), 15-22, Mr 89.

The main aim of this paper is to introduce the logic QE-LC whose language contains the 'existence' predicate E and which is characterized by the class of connected (Kripke) E-models with nested domains.

CORTI, E C. Libertad y necesidad en el "cur Deus homo" de San Anselmo de Canterbury. Stromata, 45(3-4), 339-368, Jl-D 89.

CORTINA, Juan Luis. La reflexión gnoseológica de Francisco Canals Vidal. Pensamiento, 46(181), 103-114, Ja-Mr 90.

The purpose of the work is to show the importance of research which has been carried out during the last forty years on the essence of knowledge. Especially relevant are what Canals calls "praecognita" or "pre-existent knowledge" which is prior to any reflexive structure but is in no way innate, being rather "connatural" either sensorial or intellectual. This work also vindicates the reality of the individual concrete human being as a thinking person and defends Aquinas's doctrine of "the word of the mind" (verbum mentis), related to Aristotle's thought. It strongly rejects any unidimensional and univocal interpretation or knowledge and emphasises the exclusive connection between language and thought.

CORTOIS, P. Jean Cavaillès' aanloop tot de wetenschapstheorie. Tijdschr Filosof, 52(1), 100-120, Mr 90.

The article proposes a key to Cavaillès' posthumous treatise *Sur la logique et la théorie de la science*. The author's premature death (1944) explains the difficulty of the too-condensed text. Through a number of critical analyses of two interwoven logical traditions—transcendental logic (Kant, Husserl) and the logicist canon of science (from Leibniz to Carnap)—Cavaillès reaches his own point of departure for a doctrine of science. Neither a transcendental *cogito* nor the mirage of ultimate form can account for the internal necessity underlying the unpredictable progression of mathematized theories: the essence of science consists in autonomous conceptual dynamics.

CORY, Suzanne N and LOEB, Stephen E. Whistleblowing and Management Accounting: An Approach. J Bus Ethics, 8(12), 903-916, D 89.

In this paper, we consider the licensing of and codes of ethics that affect the accountant not in public accounting, the potential for an accountant not in public accounting encountering an ethical conflict situation, and the moral responsibility of such accountant when faced with an ethical dilemma. We review an approach suggested by the National Association of Accountants

for dealing with an ethical conflict situation including that association's position on whistleblowing. We propose another approach based on the work of De George (1981), in which both internal and external whistleblowing are possible alternatives, for use by management accountants in an ethical conflict situation. Finally, we consider the implications of our analysis for management accounting. While most of the analysis centers on management accountants, we note the likely applicability of the analysis to accountants in the public sector.

COSTA, Filippo. La logica di Hegel come testo filosofico (I). Teoria, 9(1), 17-40, 1989.

COSTA, Margarita. La deliberación en Hobbes. Cuad Filosof, 20(32), 47-55, My 89.

Aristotle's theory of deliberation is briefly dealt with at the beginning of the paper, to emphasize that in this, as in other respects, Hobbes departs from tradition. An analysis of Hobbes's definition of deliberation, as stated in *The Elements of Law* and in *Leviathan*, shows that in both renderings stress is laid on the nonrational aspects of the process. The obvious relation between the terms "deliberation" and "liberty" is subsequently analysed, as is also the reference to possibility and the will. The paper closes with a comparison between Aristotle's and Hobbes's views on deliberation, pointing first to some similarities between them and then to their differences, which spring from divergent conceptions of man's nature.

COSTA, Michael J. Hume, Strict Identity, and Time's Vacuum. Hume Stud, 16(1), 1-16, Ap 90.

How can Hume accommodate the existence of ideas such as strict identity or a vacuum, since he believes that no possible impression could provide an instance of them? The solution is found in Hume's account of general ideas as dispositions to connect appropriate instances. The dispositions representing strict identity and a vacuum connect incompatible (but psychologically associated) instances. For strict identity, it is instances of unity and number. For a vacuum, it is instances of extension and empty distance. The similarity between the cases makes it helpful to think of strict identity as time's vacuum.

COSTALL, Alan and STILL, Arthur. Gibson's Theory of Direct Perception and the Problem of Cultural Relativism. J Theor Soc Behav, 19(4), 433-441, D 89.

James Gibson's perceptual theory was directed against the dualisms of traditional psychology. His own work, however, seems to invoke a dichotomy between individual and socialized perception. It is argued that this unresolved dualism arose from his early concern with the problem of cultural relativism and the social stereotyping of perception. In his early work, he proposed a separate realm of 'literal perception', i.e., awareness that is essentially individual and pre-social. Despite radical developments in his later theory, he continued to return to this early solution of the problem of relativism when considering the influence of language on perception.

COSTANTINI, Domenico. Objectivism and Subjectivism in the Foundations of Statistics. Erkenntnis, 31(2-3), 387-396, S 89.

The difference between Carnap's and de Finetti's conceptions of probability does not consist of a couple of requirements, as Carnap asserted in a letter to de Finetti. The paper is intended to give a theoretical justification for this denial. In order to do this, the author stresses the difference between (tolerant) objectivism and (radical) subjectivism. The difference is discussed in statistical terms. The discussion is faced with respect to predictive inferences, a type of statistical inference that both Carnap and de Finetti advocate in many occasions.

COSTELLO, Dan. Mills and Mc Carney on "Ideology" in Marx and Engels. Phil Forum, 21(4), 463-470, Sum 90.

A defense of the interpretation of Marx and Engels's concept of ideology proposed by Joe McCarney in his book *The Real World of Ideology* (Humanities Press, 1980) from the specific criticisms levelled against it by Charles Mills in his article "'Ideology' in Marx and Engels" (*The Philosophical Forum* 16(4), Summer 1985), with some thoughts on the relevance of their differences for the theory and practice of contemporary Marxism.

COSTELLO, Patrick J M. *Akrasia* and Animal Rights: Philosophy in the British Primary School. Thinking, 8(1), 19-27, 1989.

The purpose of this article is to show that children are capable of engaging, in a competent and often skilful manner, in philosophical debate. A substantial dialogue, in which children discuss problems relating to weakness of will and animal rights, is offered. I conclude that the teaching of philosophy to children can do much to counteract the prejudices and uncritical thinking which are a fact of everyday adult life.

COTKIN, George. *William James, Public Philosopher*. Baltimore, Johns Hopkins U Pr, 1990

By placing William James's life and thought within the context of intellectual and cultural history, *William James, Public Philosopher* contends that James's philosophy was deeply engaged with the problems of his historical era: the crisis of individualism, the implications of Darwinism, the *tedium vitae* of modernity, and the challenge of imperialism. In turn, James's professional philosophy became a public intervention influenced by these issues. *Pragmatism*, for example, is to be understood as a philosophical attempt to reconcile a discourse of heroism with the dangerous implications of freedom within the context of the Spanish-American War.

COTTELL JR, Philip G. Realism in the Practice of Accounting Ethics. Bus Prof Ethics J, 7(2), 27-50, Sum 88.

Most of the literature about professional ethics concentrates upon either utilitarian or deontologism or some combination thereof for theoretical support. This paper examines professional ethics from the viewpoint of ethical realism, a system which has been suggested by several twentieth century philosophers. An understanding and acceptance of ethical realism can enable future accounting researchers to study and explain the fluid aspects of accounting ethics as well as the interacting, or lack thereof, between the ethics of the profession and the ethics expected in a public policy context.

COTTERILL, Rowland. "'*Sunt aliquid manes*': Personalities, Personae and Ghosts in Augustan Poetry" in *Post-Structuralist Classics*, BENJAMIN, Andrew (ed), 227-244. New York, Routledge, 1988.

COTTIER, Georges. La culture du point de vue de l'anthropologie philosophique. Rev Thomiste, 89(3), 405-425, Jl-S 89.

COTTOM, Daniel. Purity. Crit Inquiry, 16(1), 173-198, Autumn 89.

COTTRILL, Melville T. Academic Ethics Revisited. Bus Prof Ethics J, 8(1), 57-64, Spr 89.

COUGHLAN, Michael J. Essential Aims and Unavoidable Responsibilities: A Response to Anscombe. Bioethics, 4(1), 63-65, Ja 90.

G E M Anscombe charged that in 'Using People' (*Bioethics* 4, 55-61) Coughlan made the erroneous assumption that the principle of double effect is meant to exonerate a causer of any evils so long as they are not intended as means or end. Coughlan defends himself against the charge and counters that Anscombe and other supporters of the principle of double effect habitually and erroneously assume that one is not responsible for the evil consequences of one's good actions.

COUGHLAN, Michael J. Using People. Bioethics, 4(1), 55-61, Ja 90.

The principle that (full) human beings may not be used as means to an end that is good for other humans and the broader 'Pauline' principle, that one may not do evil in order to procure good, constrain consequentialism. But, if taken as exceptionless principles, then, particularly in areas of public-policy decision making, they lead to morally unacceptable conclusions in the form of policies which would cause far more deaths than would be necessary to achieve our ends for no reason other than to avoid any of those deaths being necessary to achieve those ends.

COULOUBARITSIS, Lambros. "Dialectic, Rhetoric and Critique in Aristotle" in *From Metaphysics to Rhetoric*, MEYER, Michel (ed), 95-110. Norwell, Kluwer, 1989.

COUVALIS, George. *Feyerabend's Critique of Foundationalism*. Brookfield, Gower, 1989

This book concentrates on Feyerabend's arguments in the works which preceded *Against Method*. It focuses on three central claims: that foundationalist empiricism is both epistemologically and ethically flawed; that the growth of science is not cumulative; and that some theories are incommensurable. It argues that Feyerabend's arguments for these claims are basically correct, but that the claims are consistent with realism rather than with an incoherent relativism. The book also contains a detailed discussion of some central criticisms of the early Feyerabend. It argues that incommensurability is not a serious problem, and that Feyerabend's theory of meaning is superior to the causal theory.

COVENTRY, Lucinda. Philosophy and Rhetoric in the *Menexenus*. J Hellen Stud, 109, 1-15, 1989.

The article considers the seriousness and purpose of Plato's *Menexenus*. It concludes that Plato is using the traditional form of the general speech to explore the corruption of contemporary Athenian rhetoric and politics and contrasting these with Socratic philosophy as the only guide to well-being in a state.

COVEOS, Costis M. Autonomy and the Death of the Arts. Phil Invest, 13(1), 1-17, Ja 90.

"Art is dead" has no factual content. It is a *form of representation*; it points to a way of viewing art: namely not as a continuum but as a group of autonomous (quasi-biological) entities, that eventually decay and die. This

way of representing art expands the notion of autonomy—a core element of the notion of a work of art—to the particular arts and art styles as well as to art in general. It thus explains why certain forms of expression fit no longer into the mould of our civilization. This age does not express itself in the arts.

COVER, J A. Relations and Reduction in Leibniz. Pac Phil Quart, 70(3), 185-211, S 89.

Did Leibniz endorse a reducibility thesis about inter-monadic relations? Nowadays we are invited to answer "no," and to see moreover that no such thesis is workable. Following a brief account of reduction generally and its asymmetric features in particular, I argue that current treatments of Leibnizian reducibility fail, and argue further that the Leibnizian metaphysic underwrites a plausible supervenience account of the reducibility of relations. The paper concludes with a reply to two important objections.

COWARD, Harold. Derrida and Bhartrhari's Vākyapadīya on the Origin of Language. Phil East West, 40(1), 3-16, Ja 90.

This article compares the views of a traditional Indian (Hindu) philosopher of language, Bhartrhari, with the modern Western deconstructionist view of language of Derrida. Both see time, as the sequencing of language, to be its basic character and language's constituting source. Both seek to show how the unitary Word manifests itself in experience as the diversity of speech and writing—without recourse to an external other (God or Logos). For both language is neither logocentric nor empty of reality (the Buddhist view) but is a dynamic becoming that is itself the very stuff of our experience of reality.

COX, Gray. "The Light at the End of the Tunnel and the Light in Which We May Walk" in *The Causes of Quarrel: Essays on Peace, War, and Thomas Hobbes*, CAWS, Peter (ed), 162-169. Boston, Beacon Pr, 1989.

COX, Renée. A Gynecentric Aesthetic. Hypatia, 5(2), 43-62, Sum 90.

In the proposed gynecentric aesthetic, which follows the work of Heide Göttner-Abendroth and Alan Lomax, aesthetic activity would function to integrate the individual and society. Intellect, emotion and action would combine to achieve a synthesis of body and spirit. Song and dance would involve the equal expressions of all participants, and aesthetic structures would reflect this egalitarianism. The erotic would be expressed as a vital, positive force, divorced from repression and pornography. The emphasis would be off aesthetic objects to be coveted, hoarded and contemplated, and on dynamic process, fully engaging and socially significant.

COY, Janet. "From Patient to Agent: On the Implication of the Values Shift in Informed Consent" in *Inquiries into Values: The Inaugural Session of the International Society for Value Inquiry*, LEE, Sander H , 647-675. Lewiston, Mellen Pr, 1989.

This paper examines the apparent shift in values in the doctrine of informed consent, i.e., from the duty to protect a patient from harm—even if the harm is the result of the patient's own choice—to the duty of respecting a patient's autonomy. These conflicting duties have resulted in two different perspectives for approaching the issue of informed consent: the "harm-avoidance model" and the "autonomy-enhancing model." Implications of the two models are compared and the author concludes that if informed consent is to be genuinely based on the value of respecting patient autonomy, then important implications have not yet been appreciated.

COZZO, Cesare. Bivalenza e trascendenza. Teoria, 9(2), 63-86, 1989.

CRAGG, A W. Bernard Williams and the Nature of Moral Reflection. Dialogue (Canada), 28(3), 355-363, 1989.

In *Ethics and the Limits of Philosophy*, Bernard Williams implies that Socrates' view that an unexamined life is not worth living, and that to live a moral life requires that one engage in moral reflection is either misleading or mistaken. Williams argues that not only is reflection not helpful, it can result in the destruction of moral knowledge. The purpose of my article is to examine these claims. I argue that while Williams gives us good reasons for reexamining the role of modern moral theory, his attack on the role of reflection in shaping a good life is not convincing.

CRAGG, A W. Violence, Law, and the Limits of Morality. Law Phil, 8(3), 301-318, D 89.

This paper argues that the moral foundations of law lie in the need to avoid violence. Violence has both an immoral and an antimoral character. However, morality itself contains within it the seeds of violence. The function of legal systems I argue is to overcome this defect through binding law governed adjudication whose central function is nonviolent dispute resolution. This both explains why coercion is justified in the enforcement of law, identifies the limits to its use and provides criteria for the moral evaluation of legal systems.

CRAGG, C Brian. "Evolution of the Steam Engine" in *Issues in Evolutionary Epistemology*, HAHLWEG, Kai (ed), 313-356. Albany, SUNY Pr, 1989.

CRAIB, Ian and KOVEL, Joel. Marxism and Psychoanalysis: An Exchange. Rad Phil, 55, 25-30, Sum 90.

CRAIG, Edward (trans) and SPITZLEY, Thomas. Davidson and Hare on Evaluations. Ratio, 3(1), 48-63, Je 90.

This paper has two parts. In the first I discuss Davidson's view of evaluations: what is the meaning and function of *prima facie*, 'all-things-considered' and 'sans phrase' judgments, and what is the role of his principle of continence? In the (shorter) second part I try to exploit Davidson's insights to elucidate the position of Hare: what is it to treat moral judgment as a *prima facie*, or as a critical moral judgment, and when *is* a moral judgment a critical moral judgment?

CRAIG, Edward. Nozick and the Sceptic: The Thumbnail Version. Analysis, 49(4), 161-162, O 89.

In approximately 500 words it is argued that the 'tracking' analysis of knowledge can only be used against epistemic scepticism if a certain proposition, itself equivalent to the defeat of scepticism, has already been established. As a weapon against scepticism the 'tracking' analysis is therefore either impotent or redundant.

CRAIG, William L. 'Nice Soft Facts': Fischer on Foreknowledge. Relig Stud, 25(2), 235-246, Je 89.

CRAIG, William Lane. Aquinas on God's Knowledge of Future Contingents. Thomist, 54(1), 33-79, Ja 90.

A thorough examination of the primary texts, dealing with God's timeless *scientia visionis* and analyzing the implications for Thomas's theory of time, the doctrine of God's knowing all things through His essence, and the doctrine of God's knowledge as the cause of things.

CRAIG, William Lane. On Doubts about the Resurrection. Mod Theol, 6(1), 53-75, O 89.

In a recent article, James Keller has expressed what he calls "Christian doubts" about Jesus' resurrection. He presses two objections against the rationality of belief in that event as traditionally construed: (I) we cannot today reconstruct what the resurrection involved because there is no clear, historically reliable account of what the resurrection was thought to be by those who directly experienced the Easter event, and (II) we do not have sufficient evidence to make it rational to believe that the resurrection is part of a pattern of nonnatural events in which God has acted for similar ends, yet such a belief is essential to the rationality of belief in Jesus' resurrection. In this piece, I wish to take issue with both of Keller's objections.

CRAIG, William Lane. Purtill on Fatalism and Truth. Faith Phil, 7(2), 229-234, Ap 90.

Richard Purtill's discussion of theological fatalism, while having the merit of discerning the reduction of theological to logical fatalism, nevertheless fails both the refute either an Ockhamist or a Molinist solution to the problem and to offer adequate justification for the denial of bivalence for future contingent propositions.

CRAIG, William. Near-Equational and Equational Systems of Logic for Partial Functions, II. J Sym Log, 54(4), 1181-1215, D 89.

CRAIGHEAD, Houston A. Conceptual Relativism and the Possibility of Absolute Faith. Sophia (Australia), 29(2), 2-16, Jl 90.

This paper investigates whether, given a relativistic theory of truth, religious beliefs can be held as objectively true. The first section examines the view of Joseph Runzo in this regard. The second section evaluates Runzo's "cognitive relativism" and his way of making religious faith compatible with it. The last section suggests two other ways of claiming objective truth in a relativistic system. The principle argument here is based on Schubert Ogden's view that affirming the worthwhileness of anything at all entails a deeper affirmation of an ultimate ground of all affirmation—that belief in God (at least in this sense) is a necessary belief.

CRANE, Tim. There is No Question of Physicalism. Mind, 99(394), 185-206, Ap 90.

We examine the various definitions and defences of physicalism that have been offered in recent philosophy, and argue that no nontrivial version of physicalism is true. Physicalists need to define the physical in a way that (a) exludes the mental; and (b) shows why physics has the ontological authority that other sciences lack. Physicalists have used the following notions in attempting thus to define and defend physicalism: reducibility to physics, causation, laws and supervenience. We show why all these attempts fail.

CRANGLE, Colleen and SUPPES, Patrick. Geometrical Semantics for Spatial Prepositions. Midwest Stud Phil, 14, 399-422, 1989.

The main aim of this article is to propose a classification of the kinds of geometry that underlie the basic meaning of various spatial prepositions. For example, the preposition *on* assumes an orientation of verticality that is missing from standard Euclidean geometry. On the other hand, the geometry underlying many uses of the preposition *in* is much weaker than Euclidean geometry, being mainly topological in character. We also consider prepositions that require assigning orientation to figures and shapes. Finally, some attention is given to space-time geometry as required for prepositions used in action sentences.

CRANGLE, Colleen and SUPPES, Patrick. Robots that Learn: A Test of Intelligence. Rev Int Phil, 44(172), 5-23, 1990.

Inattention to learning is characteristic of foundational discussions of artificial intelligence and of cognitive science in philosophy. The focus on intentionality has dominated much of the debate between philosophers and computer scientists about the nature of artificial intelligence. Detailed theories of learning provide a framework for a more adequate philosophical analysis of artificial intelligence or of intelligence in general. We attempt to provide one such analysis specifically aimed at tasks that robots need to master in order to claim any genuine learning ability. Finally, we present a detailed example of how we might expect a robot to learn through instruction by the use of ordinary language.

CRANOR, Carl and NUTTING, Kurt. Scientific and Legal Standards of Statistical Evidence in Toxic Tort and Discrimination Suits. Law Phil, 9(2), 115-156, My 90.

Many legal disputes turn on scientific, especially statistical, evidence. Traditionally scientists have accepted only that statistical evidence which satisfies a 95 percent rule—that is, only evidence which has less than 5 percent probability of resulting from chance. The rationale for this rule is the reluctance of scientists to accept anything less than the best-supported new knowledge. The rule reflects the internal needs of scientific practice. However, when uncritically adopted as a rule for admitting legal evidence, the seemingly innocuous 95 percent rule distorts the balance of interests historically protected by the legal system. In particular, plaintiffs in toxic tort and employment discrimination suits are effectively held to a heavier burden of proof in showing that their injuries were more probably than not caused by the defendant's actions. The result is that too many victims of toxic torts or employment discrimination cannot win legal redress for their injuries. (edited)

CRANSTON, Maurice (ed) and BORALEVI, Lea Campos (ed). *Culture et Politique/Culture and Politics*. Hawthorne, de Gruyter, 1988

CRANSTON, Maurice (ed). *Rousseau: Selections*. New York, Macmillan, 1988

This book argues that Rousseau's lesser-known writings are as important to an understanding of his philosophy as are his best-known works. Besides an introductory essay it includes translations from neglected passages of *Emile*, the *Essay on the Origin of Languages*, as well as the *Confessions*, the *Letter to M. d'Alembert*, and the two *Discourses*.

CRAWFORD, Donald W. Aesthetics in Discipline-Based Art Education. J Aes Educ, 21(2), 227-239, Sum 87.

CRAWSHAY-WILLIAMS, Rupert. The Words 'Same' and 'Different'. Thinking, 6(3), 38-39, 1986.

CREATH, Richard. Counterfactuals for Free. Phil Stud, 57(1), 95-101, S 89.

CREEGAN, Charles L. *Wittgenstein and Kierkegaard: Religion, Individuality, and Philosophical Method*. Cambridge, Abacus Pr, 1989

CREERY, Walter E (ed) and TWEYMAN, Stanley (ed). *Early Modern Philosophy II*. Delmar, Caravan Books, 1988

CREMASCHI, Sergio. "Adam Smith: Skeptical Newtonianism, Disenchanted Republicanism, and the Birth of Social Science" in *Knowledge and Politics*, DASCAL, Marcelo (ed), 83-110. Boulder, Westview Pr, 1988.

Both Smith's epistemology and his politics lead to a stalemate. The former is under the opposing pulls of an essentialist idea of knowledge and of a pragmatist approach to the history of science. The latter still tries to provide a foundation for a natural law, while conceiving it as nonabsolute and changeable. The consequences are (i) inability to complete both the political and the epistemological works projected by Smith; (ii) decentralization of the social order, giving rise to several partial orders, such as that of the market.

CRESAP, Steven. Sublime Politics: On the Uses of an Aesthetics of Terror. Clio, 19(2), 111-125, Wint 90.

Burke's theory of the sublime helps us understand how we use aesthetic values to deal with our political regimes. Insofar as political regimes use power, they can be experienced as sublime. The sublime experience is a power exchange, from object to subject. But it might also be a power drain, which would leave us helpless toward our regimes. Includes analyses of the uses of beauty and sado-masochism.

CRESCINI, Angelo. La radice filosofica della rivoluzione scientifica moderna. G Metaf, 10(3), 393-420, S-D 88.

CRESS, Donald A. Descartes' Doctrine of Volitional Infinity. S J Phil, 28(2), 149-164, Sum 90.

CRESSWELL, M J. Anaphoric Attitudes. Phil Papers, 19(1), 1-18, Ap 90.

The paper explores the semantic treatment of anaphoric pronouns in attitude contexts. It tries to solve certain puzzles which arise when anaphora is treated by variable binding. One solution involves analysing some desires as within the scope of a belief operator. Another solution offers a treatment of a desire as conditional on a belief.

CRESSWELL, M J. Necessity and Contingency. Stud Log, 47(2), 145-149, Je 88.

The paper considers the question of when the operator *L* of necessity in modal logic can be expressed in terms of the operator Δ meaning 'it is non-contingent that'.

CRIMMINS, Mark. Having Ideas and Having the Concept. Mind Lang, 4(4), 280-294, Wint 89.

What is the relation between having the concept of a given property and being able to form beliefs that things have the property? I claim that what is required for the latter is having an idea (a particular representation) with the property as its content. What is required for the former is having a normal such idea. I claim that, although blind persons cannot have the concept of redness, they can have beliefs about it. I sketch the connection of these points to an account of belief reporting.

CRIMMINS, Mark and PERRY, John. The Prince and the Phone Booth: Reporting Puzzling Beliefs. J Phil, 86(12), 685-711, D 89.

Beliefs are concrete particulars containing ideas of properties and notions of things, which also are concrete. The claim made in a belief report is that the agent has a belief (i) whose content is a specific singular proposition, and (ii) which involves certain of the agent's notions and ideas in a certain way. No words in the report stand for the notions and ideas, so they are unarticulated constituents of the report's content (like the relevant place in "it's raining"). The belief puzzles (Hesperus, Cicero, Pierre) involve reports about two different notions. So the analysis gets the puzzling truth values right.

CRITCHLEY, Simon. A Commentary on Derrida's Reading of Hegel in *Glas*. Bull Hegel Soc Gt Brit, 18, 6-32, Autumn-Wint 88.

This article attempts to give a detailed commentary on Derrida's most extended, important and hitherto largely undiscussed reading of Hegel in *Glas*. Particular attention is paid to Derrida's discussion of Hegel's interpretation of *Antigone* and the discussion of religion in the *Phenomenology of Spirit*. Broadly, I argue that Derrida's deconstructive reading of Hegel attempts to locate the nonmetaphysical (metaphysics understood in Heidegger's sense) moment in dialectical thinking.

CROCKER, David A. La naturaleza y la práctica de una ética del desarrollo. Rev Filosof (Costa Rica), 26, 49-56, D 88.

This is the last of two articles concerned with the need for and nature of an ethics of "Third World development." The present essay locates such an ethics in the context of "development theory-practice." The elements of a development theory-practice are (1) scientific understanding, (2) scientific and metaphysical assumptions, (3) critique, (4) forecast, (5) selection and justification of the best future and ethical principles, (6) strategic recommendations, and (7) development practice. The essay identifies some ethical issues with respect to Costa Rican development and concludes by briefly considering how a development ethics should be practiced and what role philosophers should play therein.

CROPSEY, Joseph. The Whole as Setting for Man: On Plato's *Timaeus*. Interpretation, 17(2), 165-191, Wint 89-90.

CROSBY, John F and DE LEANIZ CAPRILE, Ignacio García (trans). Son Ser y Bien realmente convertibles? Una Investigación Fenomenológica. Dialogo Filosof, 6(2), 170-194, My-Ag 90.

Se establecen en este trabajo las diferencias entre la concepción tomista del "esse" y la concepción fenomenológica, especialmente apoyada en la filosofía de Von Hildebrand, de valor. El valor aparece con un carácter absoluto, mientras que el "bonum"—idéntico con el "esse"—tiene un cierto carácter relativo—aunque no relativista—, por ser el mismo ser en cuanto apetecido. Se muestra con profusión de argumentos que el valor no es reducible al ser, concebido por la filosofía tomista, pero que tampoco se debe entender la relación entre ser y valor en un sentido dualista radical. El valor no es una característica constitutiva del ser sustancial, pero sí una característica "consecuencial" del mismo, por lo que no puede concebirse al margen del ser mismo.

CROSSLEY JR, John P. The Ethical Impulse in Schleiermacher's Early Ethics. J Relig Ethics, 17(2), 5-24, Fall 89.

Freedom is Schleiermacher's key ethical concept. Human life in general, however, is causally determined. Freedom is actualized only in the inner life, in feeling and imagination. Inner life, however, is the domain of religion, of consciousness of the infinite, and the source of free human fellowship. Thus freedom is tied to religion. This paper analyzes Schleiermacher's concept of religion and relates it to freedom in its connection with determinism. It attempts to demonstrate that religion is the foundation of the moral life in a way that does not compromise the relative autonomy of morality, but rather makes moral life possible.

CROSSLEY, David J. Utilitarianism, Rights, and Equality. Utilitas, 2(1), 40-54, My 90.

This paper discusses Bentham's dictum, "everybody to count for one and nobody for more than one." Section I considers, and rejects, both Spencer's claim that the dictum announces rights presupposed by the utility principle and interpretations of the dictum as a formal impartiality constraint. Section II argues that the dictum proclaims a moral right, namely an immunity-right. This immunity is a second-order relation, grounded on first order normative relations which are discovered, upon analysis of the utilitarian conception of the good and of the maximization goal, to be entailed by the utility principle.

CROSSLEY, David. Self-Conscious Agency and the Eternal Consciousness: Ultimate Reality in Thomas Hill Green. Ultim Real Mean, 13(1), 3-20, Mr 90.

This paper examines the main themes of the first two books of T H Green's *Prolegomena to Ethics*: that an analysis of experience reveals a spiritual principle whose activities are responsible for the unified system of relations that constitutes reality, and that finite human agents participate in the historical development of this ultimate spiritual principle. This generates two problems. First, is the doctrine of reproduction—that the Eternal Consciousness reproduces itself in human knowledge and actions—coherent? Secondly, what is "given" in human experience? Green's employment of the notion of feeling is considered in the context of the latter question.

CROSSLEY, J N and SCOTT, P J. Completeness Proofs for Propositional Logic with Polynomial-Time Connectives. Annals Pure Applied Log, 44(1-2), 39-52, O 89.

We introduce a conservative extension of propositional calculus which allows conjunctions and disjunctions of variable length. Consistency, completeness and decidability for both classical and intuitionistic systems are given provided some simple conditions on the formation of propositional letters are satisfied. We describe an application to PROLOG programming in the context of databases.

CROSSON, Frederick J. Semantics of the Grammar. Faith Phil, 7(2), 218-228, Ap 90.

Newman's intent to analyze the nature of religious language in the *Grammar of Assent* leads him to focus on two issues, the distinction between notional and real apprehension/assent, and the role of images in religious as opposed to theological affirmations. Both issues have been diversely interpreted, in part because Newman's empiricist language sometimes constrains what he wants to say. Taking as point of departure his central insight that religious assent rests on the apprehension of God as present, I analyze the role of assent and of images accordingly.

CROSTHWAITE, Jan and PRIEST, Graham. "Relevance, Truth and Meaning" in *Directions in Relevant Logic*, NORMAN, Jean (ed), 377-397. Norwell, Kluwer, 1989.

The paper argues that a number of the problems that beset Davidson's account of meaning arise solely in virtue of interpreting the English conditional (and in particular, its occurrence in the T-scheme) as a material conditional, and that these problems are avoided if the conditional is interpreted as a relevant one. It also shows that this is technically possible by constructing a Tarski-type theory of truth for a language containing a relevant conditional in a relevant metalanguage.

CROSTHWAITE, Jan and SWANTON, Christine and ROBINSON, Viviane. Treating Women as Sex-Objects. J Soc Phil, 20(3), 5-20, Wint 89.

CROWE, Michael J. Duhem and the History and Philosophy of Mathematics. Synthese, 83(3), 431-447, Je 90.

The first part of this paper consists of an exposition of the views expressed by Pierre Duhem in his *Aim and Structure of Physical Theory* concerning the philosophy and historiography of mathematics. The second part provides a critique of these views, pointing to the conclusion that they are in need of reformulation. In the concluding third part, it is suggested that a number of the most important claims made by Duhem concerning physical theory, e.g., those relating to the 'Newtonian method', the limited falsifiability of theories, and the restricted role of logic, can be meaningfully applied to mathematics.

CROWELL, Steven Galt. Husserl, Heidegger, and Transcendental Philosophy: Another Look at the Encyclopaedia Britannica Article. Phil Phenomenol Res, 50(3), 501-518, Mr 90.

This essay interprets Husserl's first draft of his *Encyclopaedia Britannica* article and Heidegger's suggestions for revision, outlining a new way of reading the Husserl/Heidegger relationship. It is argued that these sources do not show Heidegger rejecting Husserl's transcendental phenomenology but rather, in specific disagreement over the phenomenological status of the "ego" and the "world," reinterpreting transcendental phenomenology as an ontological achievement, in a sense of "ontology" which itself derives in important ways from Husserl's transcendental reflection on the constitution of meaning. The essay argues that there is a significant sense in which Heidegger accepts the transcendental-phenomenological reduction.

CROWLEY, James F. *The Changing World of Philosophy*. Belmont, Wadsworth, 1989

CROWTHER, Paul. *The Kantian Sublime: From Morality to Art*. New York, Clarendon/Oxford Pr, 1989

CRUMLEY, Jack S. Talking Lions and Lion Talk: Davidson on Conceptual Schemes. Synthese, 80(3), 347-371, S 89.

This essay is a reconstruction and defense of Davidson's argument against the intelligibility of the notion of conceptual scheme. After presenting a brief clarification of Davidson's argument in 'On the Very Idea of a Conceptual Scheme', I turn to reconstructing Davidson's argument. Unlike many commentators, and occasionally Davidson, who hold that the motive force of the argument is the Principle of Charity (or the denial of the Third Dogma), I argue that there is a further principle which underlies the argument. This principle I call the Strong Discrimination Principle. Strong Discrimination Principle meets certain objections to Davidson's argument, but I show how the principle clarifies the realist position. In particular, I show how a line of argument advanced by Rorty and Putnam against (metaphysical) realism can be rejected.

CRUZ CRUZ, Juan. Libertad como gracia y elegancia. Anu Filosof, 20(2), 121-138, 1987.

CRUZ PRADOS, Alfredo. La Política de Aristóteles y la Democracia (II). Anu Filosof, 21(2), 9-32, 1988.

The author of this work attempts to clarify the true meaning of Aristotle's *Politics*, and in this context, to discover the value of democracy for this philosopher. Contrary to more common interpretations, the author states that *Politics* is a book with an intrinsic structural and doctrinal unity. Aristotle is neither a utopic idealist nor a pragmatic conservative: he takes into account all the circumstances without ignoring the tendency towards an ideal regime. Democracy—which has to be distinguished from the Republic—is always an imperfect form of government for Aristotle, who propounds measures so that power remains in the hands of the "selected few."

CRUZ PRADOS, Alfredo. La Política de Aristóteles y la Democracia. Anu Filosof, 21(1), 9-34, 1988.

CSIRMAZ, László. Stability of Weak Second-Order Semantics. Stud Log, 47(3), 193-202, S 88.

By extending the underlying data structure by new elements, we also extend the input/output relation generated by a program, i.e., no existing run is killed, and no new one lying entirely in the old structure is created. We investigate this stability property for the weak second order semantics derived from nonstandard time models. It turns out that the light face, i.e., parameterless collection principle always induces stable semantics, but the bold face one may be unstable. We give an example where an elementary extension kills a 'bold face run', showing also that the light face semantics is strictly weaker than the bold face one.

CUA, A S. The Status of Principles in Confucian Ethics. J Chin Phil, 16(3-4), 273-296, D 89.

This paper explores the question on the possibility of accommodating ethical principles in Confucian ethics construed as an ethics of virtue. Four theses are considered: (1) subordination, (2) double language, (3) coordination, and (4) complementarity. The last thesis, from the point of view of the Confucian concern with arbitration rather than adjudication of conflict, is proposed for further inquiry, along with an initial statement of some principles as preconditions for intercultural discourse.

CUDD, Ann E and BECKER, Neal C. Indefinitely Repeated Games: A Response to Carroll. Theor Decis, 28(2), 189-195, Mr 90.

In a recent volume of this journal John Carroll argued that there exist only uncooperative equilibria in indefinitely repeated prisoner's dilemma games. We show that this claim depends on modeling such games as finitely but indefinitely repeated games, which reduce simply to finitely repeated

games. We propose an alternative general model of probabilistically indefinitely repeated games, and discuss the appropriateness of each of these models of indefinitely repeated games.

CUDD, Ann E. Sensationalized Philosophy: A Reply to Marquis's "Why Abortion is Immoral". J Phil, 87(5), 262-264, My 90.

This paper responds to a paper by Don Marquis, "Why Abortion is Immoral," *Journal of Philosophy*, 86, 4 (April 1989): 183-202. Marquis argues that abortion is immoral because fetuses have what he calles a "future-like-ours." I point out that even if fetuses have futures-like-ours, this gives them only a *prima facie* right to life, which may well be overridden by their mothers' rights. I also point out ways in which Marquis overstates the claims of the authorities he cites.

CUDD, Ann E. Taking Drugs Seriously (Liberal Paternalism and the Rationality of Preferences). Pub Affairs Quart, 4(1), 17-31, Ja 90.

In this paper I address the question of whether a liberal society may, on grounds of paternalism, outlaw the use of (recreational) drugs. I argue that any such liberal paternalism must be based on the claim that it is irrational to take drugs. I then examine various arguments for this claim and conclude that although preferences to take drugs are sometimes irrational, they may also be rational. I argue that since the government is not in a position to discriminate the rational from the irrational cases, there is no liberal paternalist rationale for making drugs illegal.

CUGNO, Alain. Le désir de Dieu dans L'affirmation de Dieu de Claude Bruaire. Rev Phil Fr, 180(1), 27-33, Ja-Mr 90.

CULLELL, Josep. Working with Philosophy for Children in Catalonia. Thinking, 8(3), 18-22, 1989.

CULLEN, Dallas. Career Barriers: Do We Need More Research? J Bus Ethics, 9(4-5), 353-360, Ap-My 90.

Research on career barriers has stressed the commonalities among women, and the ways in which women can develop the personal and professional skills they need to demonstrate their commitment to the organization. However, this individualistic focus is not appropriate for dealing with the problem of combining career and family responsibilities. Our research focus must now turn to the commonalities among organizations, and the ways in which different organizational structures and cultures are more or less responsive to women. A study of Canadian National Sport Organizations illustrates some of the issues in this approach.

CUMMINS, Phillip D. Berkeley's Manifest Qualities Thesis. J Hist Phil, 28(3), 385-401, Jl 90.

I formulate Berkeley's Manifest Qualities Thesis (MQT) as a sensible thing has only those qualities it is perceived to have. After showing its centrality to Berkeley's philosophy, by linking it to his denials of material substances and material causes, I investigate what can be said in support of it on four different construals of "sensible thing." Of these construals, two are neutral between realist and idealist interpretations of Berkeley, the other two are clearly idealistic. I argue that MQT can be secured only under one of the idealistic construals.

CUMMINS, Phillip D. Berkeley's Unstable Ontology. Mod Sch, 67(1), 15-32, N 89.

Berkeley's dualistic account of the main categories of entities is characterized with reference to four complementary classes, non-sensible perceivers (spirits), non-perceiving sensibles (ideas), sensible perceivers, and non-sensible non-perceivers, the first two of which have members and the second two of which are devoid of members. Berkeley's arguments for (a) there are no sensible perceivers, (b) there are no non-sensible non-perceivers, and (c) only spirits are causes, are held to rest upon principles which can be maintained only by construing sensible qualities as sensations. Since sensations are states of spirits, the surface dualism is founded upon spiritualistic monism.

CUMMINS, Phillip D. Pappas on the Role of Sensations in Reid's Theory of Perception. Phil Phenomenol Res, 50(4), 755-762, Je 90.

I challenge George Pappas's contention that there are both philosophical and textual grounds for holding that for Reid sensations are constituents of rather than merely concomitants of perceptions. The philosophical ground is that the latter option generates an inconsistency for Reid in cases in which sensations are perceived. I question the inconsistency by arguing that generating it requires a very implausible thesis about joint effects of a single cause. I also question Pappas's textual evidence that for Reid sensations are sometimes perceived.

CUMMISKEY, David. Consequentialism, Egoism, and the Moral Law. Phil Stud, 57(2), 111-134, O 89.

Kant did not adequately consider consequentialist *normative* theories. Kant's arguments focus on questions of moral motivation and the *justification* of normative principles and he argues that the *determining ground* of the will must be a formal principle of duty. Nonetheless, even if the arguments for this conclusion succeed, they do not show that the *material* or content of the basic normative principle does not involve promoting the good. Kant's arguments may show that a moral agent does not promote the good because of inclination, but they do not rule out a duty-based consequentialism: that is, a duty-based justification of a principle of right which is consequentialist in structure.

CUNEO, Michael W. Values and Meaning: Max Weber's Approach to the Idea of Ultimate Reality and Meaning. Ultim Real Mean, 13(2), 84-95, Je 90.

CUNHA, Rui Daniel. A dedução dos objectos no "Tractatus". Rev Port Filosof, 45(2), 225-246, Ap-Je 89.

This article seeks first to elucidate and then refute the argument appearing in the ontological context of the *Tractatus* in favor of the existence of absolutely simple objects. It begins by presenting Frege's semantical thesis, which lends itself to be applied to the argument found in 2.0211-2.0212 of this work: it is this application which is at the root of this argument's untenable interpretation. The introduction of the idea, "analysis of an expression," is crucial: it can be contrasted to Russell's analysis as it is practiced in his theory of descriptions. A correct understanding of what analysing a proposition means in the *Tractatus* allows us to explain the argument. The argument's refutation on the thesis that the ontological force of the argument depends on an ensemble of semantical theses, found in the *Tractatus*, but which are subsequently rejected by Wittgenstein in the *Philosophische Untersuchungen*. The groundlessness of those theses implies the failure of the argument.

CUNLIFFE, John. Intergenerational Justice and Productive Resources; A Nineteenth Century Socialist Debate. Hist Euro Ideas, 12(2), 227-238, 1990.

This paper examines a debate on intergenerational justice and property regimes, in which the key participants were Marx, Bakunin, and De Paepe. There was agreement only that each generation was the custodian rather than the owner of the planet, which should be passed on in an undiminished form. There was disagreement over the property regime most conducive to any such ethic, ranging from communal ownership of all productive resources to full private property in all resources. Each of the proposed regimes involved three contested distinctions: between natural and produced resources; between productive and nonproductive resources; and between private or common ownership.

CUNNINGHAM, David S. Clodovis Boff on the Discipline of Theology. Mod Theol, 6(2), 137-158, Ja 90.

Clodovis Boff's important work *Theology and Praxis* attempts to define the boundaries of theology as a discipline. Boff describes the epistemological and ontological status of various "degrees" of theology, and evaluates the place of each. He argues for a critical and dialectical relationship between theory and praxis. This article offers a sustained analysis of Boff's account; it examines the warrants for his position, and brings his work into conversation with recent works in critical theory, philosophical hermeneutics, and theological method. Although the paper criticizes some of Boff's positions, it commends his analysis of the "boundaries of theology."

CUPANI, Alberto. Objectividade científica: noção e quiestionamentos. Manuscrito, 13(1), 25-54, Ap 90.

Discussion of scientific objectivity is one of the most frequent subjects in contemporary epistemology and philosophy of science. This paper presents the traditional view on objectivity, analyzes its different aspects and presuppositions, identifies some objections to that view and comments on their value.

CURD, Patricia Kenig. *Parmenides* 142b5-144e7: The "Unity is Many" Arguments. S J Phil, 28(1), 19-35, Spr 90.

In the opening passages of the second hypothesis of the *Parmenides* Plato constructs two sets of arguments to show that the One is many. This paper explores the question of why two different arguments for the same conclusion are given, and suggests that consideration of these arguments can help us to understand some of Plato's purposes in the second part of the *Parmenides*. I proceed by looking at the two arguments in some detail and drawing some conclusions from them; I then conclude with some brief comments on Plato's use of the part-whole relation.

CURIEN, Pierre-Louis. Alpha-Conversion, Conditions on Variables and Categorical Logic. Stud Log, 48(3), 319-360, S 89.

CURLEY, Edwin. Reflections on Hobbes: Recent Work on His Moral and Political Philosophy. J Phil Res, 15, 169-250, 1990.

In this article I attempt to survey work on Hobbes within the period from 1975 to 1989. The text is restricted almost exclusively to work in English on

topics in moral and political philosophy. The bibliography is more comprehensive, including work on other aspects of Hobbes's philosophy and work written in a variety of other languages. (edited)

CURLEY, Thomas V. The Right to Education: An Inquiry Into Its Foundations. Thinking, 5(3), 8-14, 1984.

In this article, the author reflects upon that section of the United Nations Universal Declaration of Rights dealing with the right to education in order to determine whether there is such a universal right. After exploring the meaning of the term, 'right', the author contends that there are sufficient grounds for claiming such a right provided it is set within its historical and social context.

CURREN, Randall. The Contribution of *Nicomachean Ethics* iii 5 to Aristotle's Theory of Responsibility. Hist Phil Quart, 6(3), 261-277, Jl 89.

Aristotle's remarks on the voluntariness of states of character in EN iii 5 are prompted by an objection to his claim that carelessness is sufficient for responsibility. This seems to limit the scope of the discussion to people who, like those who are voluntarily drunk, have experienced at their own hands a loss of ability to exercise care. The aim of this paper is to take this limitation of scope seriously. The resulting reinterpretation of iii 5 overturns many of the assumptions underlying previous interpretations, and it eliminates a number of apparent problems in Aristotle's account.

CURRIE, Gregory. Supervenience, Essentialism and Aesthetic Properties. Phil Stud, 58(3), 243-257, Mr 90.

Two kinds of supervenience—weak and strong—are considered as candidates for expressing the supervenience of aesthetic properties. It has been argued that weak and strong supervenience are equivalent. I deny this, and say the result depends on a controversial assumption about property closure. I claim that weak supervenience, when applied to the aesthetic, reduces to a triviality. I consider what might be an appropriate *supervenience base* for the strong supervenience of aesthetic properties. Finally, I apply these results to argue that aesthetic properties are not *essential* properties of works.

CURTIS, Barry. Wittgenstein and Philosophy for Children. Thinking, 5(4), 10-19, 1985.

Wittgenstein said that philosophical questions are like an illness, and that the task of the philosopher is to cure himself and others through a variety of therapies. Is the Philosophy for Children Program doing a disservice by infecting young children with this disease? No, for philosophical illness, according to Wittgenstein, arises out of a misunderstanding of the grammar of our language. So children already have this illness at a very early age. Far from causing the disease, the Philosophy for Children Program can be seen as a kind of "preventative medicine," insofar as it brings the philosophical questions of children out in the open and provides kids with techniques for "dissolving" them before they grow too large.

CURTIS, Robert A. Gauthier's Ethics and Extra-Rational Values: A Comment on DeMarco. J Soc Phil, 20(3), 92-98, Wint 89.

CURTIS, Robert A. The Success of Hyperrational Utility Maximizers in Iterated Prisoner's Dilemma: A Response to Sobel. Dialogue (Canada), 28(2), 265-274, 1989.

CUSHING, James T. "A Background Essay" in *Philosophical Consequences of Quantum Theory: Reflections on Bell's Theorem*, CUSHING, James T (ed), 1-24. Notre Dame, Univ Notre Dame Pr, 1989.

CUSHING, James T (ed). *Philosophical Consequences of Quantum Theory: Reflections on Bell's Theorem*. Notre Dame, Univ Notre Dame Pr, 1989.

CUSHMAN, Reid and HOLM, Soren. Death, Democracy and Public Ethical Choice. Bioethics, 4(3), 237-252, Jl 90.

CUTLAND, Nigel J. Transfer Theorems for π-Monads. Annals Pure Applied Log, 44(1-2), 53-62, O 89.

Benninghofen and Richter (*Fundamenta Mathematicae* 128) developed a theory of *pi-monads* (or *superfinitesimals*), designed to give a natural and applicable extension of Robinson's idea of monads in nonstandard analysis. Pi-monads play the role of monads of nonstandard points; they are not genuine monads, and are not internal objects. Thus a new and complicated transfer principle (*topological transfer*), found by Benninghofen and Richter, was needed to describe some of the properties of pi-monads. The paper under review gives an accessible exposition of the Benninghofen-Richter theory, and isolates certain transfer principles for pi-monads that are both applicable and comprehensible by comparison with topological transfer, and some applications are given.

CUTROFELLO, Andrew. Derrida's Deconstruction of the Ideal of Legitimation. Man World, 23(2), 157-173, Ap 90.

In an early work, Derrida calls attention to Husserl's distinction between two regulative ideals of interpretation: textual univocity and textual equivocity. After explicating this distinction and relating it to Derrida's later practice of deconstructive criticism, I give an analysis of "différance"—the conceptual crucible whose peculiar logic organizes Derrida's deconstructive work. This analysis outlines Derrida's critique of Hegelian dialectic, and concludes with an account of Derridian deconstruction as both playful and deciphering, disseminative and dialectical. Finally, a deconstructive argument against one-sided programs of legitimation theory—such as that of Habermas—is broached.

CVEK, Peter P. Francisco Suárez on Natural Law. Vera Lex, 9(2), 3-4,7, 1989.

This paper is a brief exposition of Francisco Suarez's theory of law, with special attention paid to his concept of the natural (moral) law. In contrast with the standard voluntarist interpretation, the author maintains that Suarez attempted to develop a composite theory of law, as a middle ground between the extremes of voluntarism and intellectualism. In so doing, Suarez brought the medieval debate concerning the essence of law into modern model discourse and, in effect, became the starting point for the development of the modern understanding of natural law.

CVEK, Peter P. Strauss and Natural Right: A Critical Review. Vera Lex, 8(2), 2-3, 1988.

This article is a critical review of Leo Strauss's *Natural Right and History*, originally published in 1953. The review evaluates the now common distinction between the modern natural rights theories of Hobbes, Locke, Rousseau and the classical natural right teachings of Plato and Aristotle, with special reference to the doctrine of natural law. I suggest that reliance on this conceptual scheme often conceals more than it reveals about the history of the natural law tradition.

CYZYK, Mark. Conscience, Sympathy, and Love: Ethical Strategies toward Confirmation of Metaphysical Assertions in Schopenhauer. Dialogue (PST), 32(1), 24-31, O 89.

In this article the author emphasizes the radical interrelatedness of Schopenhauer's metaphysics and ethics (a feature common to any monistic idealism) and attempts to show how the discussions in Book Four of *The World As Will and Representation* of emotional and moral notions—specifically conscience, sympathy, love, and to a certain extent, dread—can be read as further evidence, or at least in an illustrative, heuristic way, for the metaphysical assertion in Book Two that the world is will.

CZEIZEL, Andrew. The Price of Silence: Commentary. Hastings Center Rep, 20(3), 33, My-Je 90.

CZELAKOWSKI, Janusz. Relatively Point Regular Quasivarieties. Bull Sect Log, 18(4), 138-145, D 89.

CZEMARNIK, Adam and BONIECKA, Magdalena (trans). A Marxist's View on the Philosophy of Peace Advanced by John Paul II. Dialec Hum, 14(1), 209-217, Wint 87.

D'ALESSIO, Juan Carlos. Análisis semántico de los enunciados de creencia. Rev Filosof (Argentina), 3(1), 17-25, My 88.

This paper describes the semantical analysis of belief sentences in Carnap and Strawson. It makes some critics to certain common features of both philosophers, and concludes that their account is unsatisfactory, specially with respect to the pragmatic dimension of language.

D'AMATO, Anthony. Is International Law Part of Natural Law? Vera Lex, 9(1), 8, 1989.

D'AMBROSIO, Ubiratan. On Ethnomathematics. Phil Math, 4(1), 3-14, 1989.

Ethnomathematics is a research program in the history of ideas, with clear pedagogical implications. Based on a new interpretation of the history and philosophy motivated by the etymology of mathematics as the *tics* (techne) of the *mathema* (explanation, understanding), the program looks into the sociocultural roots of the generation, of transmission and of diffusion of knowledge. It bears close relation with cultural aspects of cognition and goes deeper into the relations between arts, the sciences and religion.

D'ANTUONO, Emilia. "Fenomenologia della metafisica: e "panteismo mistico": Note in margine alla "Jugendgeschichte Hegels" di W Dilthey. Arch Stor Cult, 2, 199-211, 1989.

D'ANTUONO, Emilia. Il credere, la rivelazione, il "nuovo pensiero" di Franz Rosenzweig. Arch Stor Cult, 1, 291-301, 1988.

D'ENTRÈVES, Maurizio Passerin. Agency, Identity, and Culture: Hannah Arendt's Conception of Citizenship. Praxis Int, 9(1-2), 1-24, Ap-Jl 89.

D'ENTRÈVES, Maurizio Passerin. Freedom, Plurality, Solidarity:

Hannah Arendt's Theory of Action. Phil Soc Crit, 15(4), 317-350, 1989.

D'ERASMO, Kate and PALERMO, James. Logic, Language and Dewey: A Student-Teacher Dialectic. Thinking, 8(1), 11-13, 1989.

D'HONDT, Jacques. "Hegel et Hölderlin: *Le sens d'une rencontre*" in *Cultural Hermeneutics of Modern Art: Essays in Honor of Jan Aler*, DETHIER, Hubert (ed), 223-231. Amsterdam, Rodopi, 1989.

Le destin de l'amitié qui lia Hölderlin et Hegel est significatif. Communiant d'abord dans l'admiration de la jeunesse, de la Révolution française, de l'action, tous deux durent se contenter de l'inaction et, à certains égards du silence mais en se séparant pour aller, l'un à la poésie et à la folie, l'autre à la contemplation théorique. Ils illustraient ainsi, à leur manière, l'inertie de l'Allemagne de l'époque, face à l'impétuosité française.

D'HONDT, M Jacques. Le parcours Hégélien de la révolution Française. Bull Soc Fr Phil, 83(4), 115-158, O-D 89.

Hegel defines the French Revolution as a historic process which covers the period 1789 to 1830. Consequently he puts together all diverse and sometimes violently opposing political ideas which quickly succeeded one another during this period. He does not agree with them all morally or even politically but he does not want just to judge them. He mainly intends to understand what happened and describe it in a rational way. Therefore one can consider him as the true philosopher of the French Revolution even though he is not himself a revolutionary.

D'ORS, Angel. Sobre las "Obligationes" de Juan de Holanda. Anu Filosof, 21(2), 33-70, 1988.

In this paper, we analyze in detail the 'Obligationes' of John of Holland, in contrast with the 'De Arte Obligatoria' of the MS.306 of Merton College, in the light of the contemporary discussions on the meaning of the differences between the doctrines of Burley and Swyneshed. Special attention is paid to the criteria of pertinence, and to the way in which the problems raised by the reflexivity and composition in the context of the doctrine of obligations are faced. John of Holland seems to hold a middle position between Burley and Swyneshed, so that his work is particularly enlightening.

D'OTTAVIANO, Itala M L and EPSTEIN, Richard L. A Paraconsistent Many-Valued Propositional Logic. Rep Math Log, 22, 89-103, 1988.

In a previous paper D'Ottaviano and da Costa introduced a propositional system called J_3, which is a three-valued system with two distinguished truth-values, which is paraconsistent and also reflects aspects of modal logics. D'Ottaviano also extended the system to first-order J_3-theories. In this paper the authors give a technical development of J_3 and discuss the intuitions behind the logic. The system is presented in two different ways, depending on the choice of primitive connectives. The interdefinability of the connectives, the relation between J_3 and the classical propositional logic and the notions of consistency and completeness are discussed. A set-assignment semantics for J_3 using falsity as a default truth-value is also presented.

DA COSTA, Newton C A and FRENCH, Steven. Belief and Contradiction. Critica, 20(60), 3-11, D 88.

DA COSTA, Newton C A and FRENCH, Steven. The Model-Theoretic Approach in the Philosophy of Science. Phil Sci, 57(2), 248-265, Je 90.

An introduction to the model-theoretic approach in the philosophy of science is given and it is argued that this program is further enhanced by the introduction of *partial* structures. It is then shown that this leads to a natural and intuitive account of both "iconic" and mathematical models and of the role of the former in science itself.

DA COSTA, Newton C A. New Systems of Predicate Deontic Logic. J Non-Classical Log, 5(2), 75-80, N 88.

We present a strong system L of first-order predicate logic, which includes a powerful logic of action in the sense of von Wright, as well as the deontic operators. L can be extended to a higher-order logic and can also be modified in several ways, giving rise, for instance, to paraconsistent and paracomplete logical formalisms.

DA COSTA, Newton C A and MARCONI, Diego. An Overview of Paraconsistent Logic in the 80s. J Non-Classical Log, 6(1), 5-32, My 89.

In this paper we aim at giving a sketch of some aspects of the state of development of paraconsistent logic in the 80s. Our exposition will not aim at completeness. Given the development of the literature in the field, completeness is out of the question in a paper like ours. However, we delineate not only the theoretical accomplishments, but also the more important applications of paraconsistent logic in philosophy, mathematics, the sciences, and technology.

DA COSTA, Newton and SYLVAN, Richard. Cause as an Implication. Stud Log, 47(4), 413-427, D 88.

An appropriately unprejudiced logical investigation of causation as a type of implication relation is undertaken. The implication delineated is bounded syntactically. The developing argument then leads to a very natural process analysis, which demonstrably captures the established syntactical features. Next relevantly-based semantics for the resulting logical theory are adduced, and requisite adequacy results delivered. At the end of the tour, further improvements are pointed out, and the attractive terrain beyond present developments is glimpsed.

DACHLER, H Peter and ENDERLE, Georges. Epistemological and Ethical Considerations in Conceptualizing and Implementing Human Resource Management. J Bus Ethics, 8(8), 597-606, Ag 89.

As an example of applied social science, the field of human resource management is used to show that ethical problems are not only those of carrying out research, of professional conduct, and of the "distribution fairness" of social science knowledge. A largely overlooked ethical issue is also the implicit choices that are made as an integral part of research and implementation. First, an analysis is undertaken of the implicit assumptions, values and goals that derive from the conception of human problems in work organizations as "managing human resources." Secondly, it is argued that such a conception is in fact a socially constructed reality with "real" consequences and not a reflection of "objective" states of human and social nature with which we have to live. Thirdly, to the extent that our implicit assumptions are in part based upon conceptual choices that are made by individuals or as a collective act of a discipline or work organization, the development of an ethical framework that could guide such choices becomes a crucial challenge for business ethics.

DADARLAT, Camil Marius. Un mythe ouvert dans "Zamolxis" de Lucian Blaga (in Romanian). Rev Filosof (Romania), 36(3), 249-255, My-Je 89.

DAGI, T F. Letting and Making Death Happen: Is There Really No Difference? The Problem of Moral Linkage. J Med Human, 11(2), 81-90, Sum 90.

DAHL, Norman O. On the Moral Status of Weakness of the Will. Logos (USA), 10, 133-156, 1989.

This paper investigates whether weakness of the will is something we should always try to eliminate in ourselves, taking up three arguments that deny that it is. The first points to cases like Huckleberry Finn. The second appeals to consequentialist considerations. The third rests on the denial of one form of the unity of virtues. The first two arguments fail. The third turns out to be inconclusive. Tentative conclusions drawn are that we should try to eliminate weakness of the will; and that where we should, it is because it robs people of autonomy and integrity.

DAHL, Robert A. Democracy and Its Critics. New Haven, Yale Univ Pr, 1989

DAHL, Robert A. "The Pseudodemocratization of the American Presidency" in The Tanner Lectures on Human Values, Volume X, PETERSON, Grethe B (ed), 33-72. Salt Lake City, Univ of Utah Pr, 1989.

DAHL, Tor. The Corporation and Its Employees: A Case Story. J Bus Ethics, 8(8), 641-645, Ag 89.

One of the main objectives in the information society is to improve the quality of life. Paying attention to the needs of people seems to be a key element in good ethical behaviour, says the author, managing director of Manpower Scandinavia. In defining these needs, Manpower used Abraham Maslow's famous pyramid, his hierarchy of needs, as a model for trying to satisfy in practice the needs on each level. However, they went a step further, asking: what comes after Maslow? To mean something for others; togetherness and that people can be trusted and that they seek a purpose with their work, came out as answers. In his paper the author tells us how Manpower Scandinavia has developed a written set of values, which function as a basis for action and guidelines for behaviour, and where the key idea behind it all is to let people be self-managed. Furthermore, he shows us how Manpower has organised the company according to this conviction. If you really have faith in people and show them trust, they will show you trust in return. Then you have a good basis for ethical behavior, the author concludes his paper.

DAHLHAUS, Carl. Beethoven's Symphonic Style and Temporality in Music. Acta Phil Fennica, 43, 281-292, 1988.

DAHM, Helmut and SWIDERSKI, E M (trans). What Restoring Leninism Means. Stud Soviet Tho, 39(1), 55-76, F 90.

DAI-NIAN, Zhang. "Theories Concerning Man and Nature in Classical Chinese Philosophy" in Man and Nature: The Chinese Tradition and the Future, TANG, Yi-Jie (ed), 3-12. Lanham, Univ Pr of America, 1989.

DAJKA, Balazs (ed) and HRONSZKY, Imre (ed) and FEHER, Marta (ed). Scientific Knowledge Socialized. Norwell, Kluwer, 1989

DAJKA, Balázs. "Two Uses of Functional Explanation" in Scientific Knowledge Socialized, HRONSZKY, Imre (ed), 365-374. Norwell, Kluwer, 1989.

DALCOURT, Gerard J. Professor Gould and the "Natural". Int J Applied Phil, 5(1), 75-77, Spr 90.

In a recent article J A Gould claimed that homosexuality "cannot be rejected by any definition of the unnatural." He then presented seven definitions of "natural" and gave his reasons why none of them excludes homosexuality. I argue that when we examine each of his main points, none of them stand up very well and that therefore he has not established his conclusion in any firm sense.

DALE, A J. Why are Italians More Reasonable than Australians? Analysis, 49(4), 189-194, O 89.

DALGARNO, Melvin (ed) and MATTHEWS, Eric (ed). The Philosophy of Thomas Reid. Norwell, Kluwer, 1989

DALGARNO, Melvin. Reid and the Rights of Man. Man Nature, 4, 81-94, 1985.

The attachment of Thomas Reid, the Scottish philosopher, to the Rights of Man ideology is argued to be no aberration. While it may be at variance with the reception of his philosophy in postrevolutionary France, and a philosophical reputation in opposition to Hume, as an essentially conservative, counterrevolutionary thinker, it is integral to the core of his philosophy. It stems from the same commitment to principles of common sense authority. In expounding a philosophical foundation for theses expressed in the language of rights, Reid has generally unrecognised claims to be regarded as a significant theorist of rights.

DALLERY, Arleen B (ed) and SCOTT, Charles E (ed). The Question of the Other: Essays in Contemporary Continental Philosophy. Albany, SUNY Pr, 1989

DALLMAYR, Fred R. Margins of Political Discourse. Albany, SUNY Pr, 1989

DALLMAYR, Fred. Reading Horkheimer Reading Vico: An Introduction. New Vico Studies, 5, 57-62, 1987.

DALLMAYR, Fred (trans) and HORKHEIMER, Max. Vico and Mythology. New Vico Studies, 5, 63-77, 1987.

DALMIYA, Vrinda. Coherence, Truth and the 'Omniscient Interpreter'. Phil Quart, 40(158), 86-94, Ja 90.

DALTON, Dan R and RECHNER, Paula L. On the Antecedents of Corporate Severance Agreements: An Empirical Assessment. J Bus Ethics, 8(6), 455-462, Je 89.

This study of major corporations (n = 481) provides an empirical assessment of the effects of several corporate governance variables (CEO duality, boards of director composition, officers and directors common stock holdings, institutional common stock holdings, number of majority owners) on the adoption of so-called severance agreements. A discriminant analysis indicates a significant multivariate function. Wilks lambda univariate analyses suggest that the percentage of common stock held by owners and directors and number of majority stock holders are the more robust discriminators.

DAMIANI, Anthony. Looking Into Mind: How to Recognize Who You Are and How You Know. Burdett, Larson, 1990

This book is a guide to discovering the spiritual significance of everyday living. It is a treatment of the two most fundamental issues in conscious self-development: (1) how to meditate, and (2) the relation between the inner and outer dimensions of one's life. Living sincerely, being totally self-honest, and being responsive to the meanings embedded in one's everyday experience are discussed as the most direct of all valid spiritual paths. Meditation and study of spiritual teachings enter as valuable elements of, but not substitutes for, such a lifestyle. (edited)

DAMNJANOVIC, Milan. "L'esthétique de demain" in Cultural Hermeneutics of Modern Art: Essays in Honor of Jan Aler, DETHIER, Hubert (ed), 3-11. Amsterdam, Rodopi, 1989.

I have presented the situation of aesthetics today considering (1) aesthetics as a modern science, an autonomous science with its specific method, and (2) aesthetics as philosophy of art, as a philosophical discipline in the traditional meaning of metaphysics. With the radical historicity was lost the confidence to the science: against method like against science. In the postmetaphysical epoch was lost the traditional system of philosophy. The new point of departure will be the aesthetic or artistic experience, and the new aesthetics the generative aesthetics: philosophical-scientific elaborated art-view and world-view of artist.

DANCY, R M. Ancient Non-Beings: Speusippus and Others. Ancient Phil,

9 (2), 207-243, Fall 89.

The idea that some things are not beings was ascribed by Aristotle to the atomists. This helps to substantiate a controversial claim: that, according to Aristotle, Speusippus thought the One was not a being. Speusippus can be provided with an argument for that view based on his rejection of the Theory of Forms and of the associated thesis, adopted by Aristotle, that what causes things to be F is itself F; Speusippus claims, instead, that what causes everything to be F cannot be F; hence the One, which causes whatever there is to be, is not itself a being.

DANCY, R M. Thales, Anaximander, and Infinity. Apeiron, 22(3), 149-190, S 89.

This paper reconstructs the initial stages of Milesian thought as follows: Thales supposed the *arche*, the 'principle' of 'beginning', was water, but also supposed that there was only just so much of it. Anaximander thought this indefensible, and argued that the *arche*, whatever it was, had to be unlimited in size. This is all he meant by calling it '*apeiron*', 'unlimited'. But from this conclusion he argued to the further conclusion that it had to be qualitatively indeterminate, intermediate between any two contrary qualities.

DANDEKAR, Natalie. Contrasting Consequences: Bringing Charges of Sexual Harrassment Compared with Other Cases of Whistleblowing. J Bus Ethics, 9(2), 151-158, F 90.

The phenomenon of whistleblowing seems puzzling in that whistleblowing presumably brings a wrongful practice to the attention of those with power to correct the situation. In this respect, whistleblowers act to serve the public interest in defeating harmful, illegal and unjust practices. Yet these persons suffer vilification and worse, not only from their fellow employees, but from members of the general public as well. Cases in which members of a discriminated minority report instances of job discrimination, and especially instances of sexual harassment resemble other cases in which an employee reports corporate or bureaucratic misdeeds. Examining the differences, and what seem to be underlying causes of these differences, provides some insight into the factors that set limits to the practice of whistleblowing in a democratic society. (edited)

DANESI, Marcel. Language and the Origin of the Human Imagination: A Vichian Perspective. New Vico Studies, 4, 45-56, 1986.

In all discussions on the origins of language, one particular viewpoint (gesture theory, osmosis, etc.) generally dominates the hypotheses put forward and/or the conclusions reached. In Giambattista Vico's *New Science*, on the other hand, a kind of integrated view of language phylogenesis is elaborated which cogently synthesizes the various viewpoints into a coherent description. At the core of Vico's theory is the role played by figurative language in the primordial acts of symbolic consciousness. Vico's theory is here assessed in the light of current work in archeology, linguistics, and psychology.

DANESI, Marcel. A Vichian Footnote to Nietzsche's View on the Cognitive Primacy of Metaphor: An Addendum to Schrift. New Vico Studies, 5, 157-164, 1987.

In his course on rhetoric, Nietzsche emphasizes the crucial role that metaphor plays in philosophical discourse and, ultimately, in cognition. His conclusion is that reality outside of the figuration universe created by language is an illusion. Giambattista Vico also gives metaphor a primary role in cognition, but he sees it as a creative force, not an obstacle to the understanding of the external world. It allows humans to carry images in their mind of what is "perceived" as experientially meaningful. The two viewpoints are compared and assessed in the light of current theories on metaphor.

DANIEL, Marie-France. Thinking, Mind, the Existence of God...Transcript of a Classroom Dialogue with First-and-Second Graders in Montreal. Thinking, 7(3), 21-22, 1988.

DANIEL, Stephen H. Vico on Mythic Figuration as Prerequisite for Philosophic Literacy. New Vico Studies, 3, 61-72, 1985.

Vico's discovery of mythic forms of thought historically at the base of rational inquiry opens the possibility that such sense-based metaphorical forms still infect the character of thought itself. This suggests that philological and etymological analyses reveal the close ties between the language of myth and that of supposedly purified philosophic discourse. In Vico's account, the language of philosophy itself emerges as meaningful only in terms of its genetic association with the image-based metaphors of prerational thought. Within the discourse of myth one finds the figural characters central in grounding Vico's doctrine of certainty and his account of ingenuity.

DANIEL, Stephen L. Interpretation in Medicine: An Introduction. Theor Med, 11(1), 5-8, Mr 90.

This is the editor's introduction to an issue of the journal devoted to the development of an interpretive perspective in the philosophy of medicine. This development is seen to be an adaptation of hermeneutical theory as practiced in the humanities, with textual interpretation serving as a model for the doctor-patient relationship. Summaries are given of the issue's subsequent essays treating the theory and practice of interpretation as applied to clinical diagnosis and treatment, the medical record, and bioethics. Suggestions are given for projects which might further advance the hermeneutical turn in medicine.

DANIEL, Wojciech. Bohr, Einstein and Realism. Dialectica, 43(3), 249-261, 1989.

The Bohr-Einstein debate on the interpretation of quantum mechanics may be viewed as a discussion on the epistemological status of knowledge gained by physics. It is shown that in fact the advent of quantum theory has led, in a new context, to an old philosophical controversy between epistemological realism (held by Einstein) and phenomenalism (held by Bohr). An inquiry into this controversy, taking into account the contemporary understanding of quantum mechanics based on the axiomatic study of its foundations, leads to the conclusion that contrary to widespread opinion, it is perfectly possible to formulate quantum mechanics in an entirely realistic manner according to the postulate of Einstein. We demonstrate that Bohr's epistemology, in which the role of experimental arrangements in the physical description is taken as a starting point, does not necessarily imply phenomenalism, but may be justifiably considered as a complementary standpoint to the realistic epistemology of Einstein, which is based on the notion of a mental construction which pictures reality.

DANIELS, Charles B. Note on Colourization. Brit J Aes, 30(1), 68-70, Ja 90.

This paper responds to James Young's "In Defence of Colourization" (*British Journal of Aesthetics* 28, 368-72). It argues that Young is correct in concluding that colorization is not wrong because it interferes with artists' freedom of expression. Despite disagreement with presuppositions Young makes, it argues further that he is correct in his conclusion that colorizing films is not immoral.

DANIELS, Charles B. A Note on Negation. Erkenntnis, 32(3), 423-429, My 90.

Informally, classical negation can be taken to mean 'it is not true that', and intuitionist negation to mean 'it's demonstrable that it isn't demonstrable that'. In this paper a third notion, *story negation*, is put forward where negation means 'it is false that'. Reasons connected with truth and falsehood in stories are offered for rejecting contraposition and even modus tolens for this negation. A complete first-degree axiomatization is provided.

DANIELS, Charles B. The Propositional Objects of Mental Attitudes. J Phil Log, 19(3), 317-342, Ag 90.

It is argued that mental attitudes like *believing that* have two objects, (a) propositions which are true or false and (b) mental contents which contain all their indexical features. Both are required to account for our judgments concerning when people do and do not believe the same things. Often people are judged to believe the same thing because their beliefs are about the same things, they believe the same propositions. A theory is put forward in which propositions are taken to be sets of stories, not sets of possible worlds. A sound and complete axiomatization is provided.

DANIELS, Norman. An Argument About the Relativity of Justice. Rev Int Phil, 43(170), 361-378, 1989.

DANIELS, Norman. The Biomedical Model and Just Health Care: Reply to Jecker. J Med Phil, 14(6), 677-680, D 89.

DANIELS, Thomas L. A Rationale for the Support of the Medium-Sized Family Farm. Agr Human Values, 6(4), 47-53, Fall 89.

The current financial stress in the countryside and the future of the family farm are likely to be major issues in the formulation of the 1990 Farm Bill. Medium-sized commercial family farms may be especially targeted for support. These farms are the basis of rural economies and settlement patterns in many parts of nonmetropolitan America. Two possible changes in farm policy are debt restructuring and the decoupling of farm payments from commodity production. Many medium-sized family farms continue to face substantial debt problems, but most of these farms could be viable with some debt restructuring. Commodity programs have become extremely expensive and encourage overproduction and the consolidation of farming resources into ever larger units. Federal farm programs may become based on need, with a sensitivity to differences in regional farming systems. Such a policy could support medium-sized family farms, slow the growth in superfarms, reduce surpluses, and reduce the overall cost of farm programs.

DANNHAUSER, Werner J. Leo Strauss as Citizen and Jew. Interpretation, 17(3), 433-447, Spr 90.

I discuss the controversies surrounding the allegiance of Leo Strauss to his country and his faith, seeking to understand both of them as aspects of the primary allegiance of Leo Strauss to philosophy. As a citizen of the United States, Strauss tended toward conservatism without ever becoming a Conservative. He was a critical but committed adherent of liberal democracy. As a Jew he was a proud scholar who felt deeply about the Jewish people but held fast to his intellectual integrity, exploring the tensions between Athens and Jerusalem while seeking to do justice to them both.

DANTO, Arthur C. *Connections to the World: The Basic Concepts of Philosophy*. San Francisco, Harper & Row, 1989

DANYEL, Jürgen. Zur methodologischen Bedeutung des Leninschen Prinzips der "Zurückführung des Individuellen auf das Soziale". Deut Z Phil, 37(10-11), 979-989, 1989.

DARE, Tim. Raz and Legal Positivism. Eidos, 8(1), 11-33, Je 89.

Joseph Raz has defended an especially pure version of legal positivism. Since law is intended precisely to settle controversial moral and political questions, it would defeat its own purpose if it allowed appeal to moral considerations in identifying the existence or content of law. Law avoids this result by providing its subjects with 'exclusionary' reasons for action, which not only militate directly for or against particular actions, but also prohibit recourse to ordinary reasons which do militate directly. The idea that we can distinguish between exclusionary and ordinary reasons is central to Raz's theory. This paper critically examines this idea. If it cannot be sustained, the purity of Raz's positivism must be compromised, and we will have less reason to distinguish Raz from less pure positivists such as Austin and Hart.

DARGYAY, Lobsang. What is Non-Existent and What is Remanent in Sūnyatā. J Indian Phil, 18(1), 81-91, Mr 90.

The question of what remains after Sūnyatā is fully realized was addressed by G M Nagao, D S Ruegg, and S Yamaguchi. In light of their achievements this contribution will be minimal. I wish merely to continue the studies initiated by Nagao is his article on 'What Remains in Sūnyatā' and to extend those studies into the field of Tibetan philosophy. In order to provide the appropriate contextual background I shall first summarize the *Smaller Discourse on Emptiness* (*Cūlasuññata-sutta*), and secondly, I shall provide an expository account of Nagao's thought. Following that, I shall investigate the various Tibetan interpretations of the crucial sentence "What is remanent in Sūnyatā." The passage dealing with the Tibetan interpretations will focus on two issues: (1) Dol-po-pa's interpretation of "what is remanent in Sūnyatā," in particular in the light of the *Abhidharmasamuccaya*; and (2) Tibetan comments on *Ratnagotravibhāga*, I v. 154-155 and its commentary, traditionally attributed to Asanga.

DARÓS, W R. Realismo crítico y conocimiento en Carlos Popper. Pensamiento, 46(182), 179-200, Ap-Je 90.

El realismo, como el idealismo, son sistemas de pensamientos y, en cuanto tales, creaciones de los hombres. El idealismo, en última instancia es monista. El realismo es radicalmente pluralista. Para K Popper tanto el realismo como el idealismo son afirmaciones, en principio, indemostrables e irrefutables. Acepta el *realismo crítico* como la conjetura más sensata, aunque siempre criticable. Sin la aceptación del realismo crítico, la verdad, la discusión, la libertad, la investigación carecen de sentido. Popper acepta estos valores, pero los somete constantemente a la crítica intersubjetiva.

DARROCH-LOZOWSKI, Vivian. Initiation in Hermeneutics: An Illustration Through the Mother-and-Daughter Archetype. Human Stud, 13(3), 237-251, Jl 90.

DARWALL, Stephen L. Autonomist Internalism and the Justification of Morals. Nous, 24(2), 257-267, Ap 90.

A precis of a longer APA address. A distinction is made between two different philosophical motivations for the internalist construal of justificational weight in terms of motivational force. One is the naturalistic impulse to reduce the normative to features of nature. The second is the desire to connect practical reasons to an understanding of autonomous agency, as what is realized in the practical thinking of a free rational agent. An approach of the second sort is sketched as a way of answering the question, "why be moral?"

DARWALL, Stephen L. Motive and Obligation in the British Moralists. Soc Phil Pol, 7(1), 133-150, Autumn 89.

This paper undertakes two main tasks. First, I investigate the way the concept of obligation came to function as a term of fundamental justification, first in the 17th century natural law tradition, and then in the writings of the 18th century British moralists, and how it became related in this literature to motivation. Second, I illustrate, using Shaftesbury as an example, how one source of this link was an emerging view about the relation between obligation and autonomy that was in some respects similar to Kant's.

DARWALL, Stephen. "Moore to Stevenson" in *Ethics in the History of*

Western Philosophy, CAVALIER, Robert J (ed), 366-398. New York, St Martin's Pr, 1988.

As a contribution to a collection of essays aiming to provide a broad overview of the history of ethics, this essay discusses major themes in English-speaking ethical philosophy of the first half of the twentieth century, focussing particularly on G E Moore, W D Ross, and Charles Stevenson. Some attention is also given to locating their views in a broader social and intellectual context.

DAS, P S. Development of Collingwood's Conception of Historical Object. Indian Phil Quart, 17(2), 209-222, Ap 90.

Collingwood's theory of history is a story of continual change—both ontological and epistemological. Earlier he was a realist but later became an objective idealist. In his earlier life, he maintained that history is a study of given fact and is a perception. Later he came to view history as the reenactment of past thought and is an inference. For on realistic assumption the historian and the object remain in two unbridged poles and that idea led to the 'breakdown of history'. However, historical thought is a universal thought that can be shared by all.

DASCAL, M and WROBLEWSKI, Jerzy. Transparency and Doubt: Understanding and Interpretation in Pragmatics and in Law. Theoria (Spain), 4(11), 427-450, F-My 89.

DASCAL, Marcelo (ed) and COHEN, Avner (ed). *The Institution of Philosophy: A Discipline in Crisis?*. La Salle, Open Court, 1989

DASCAL, Marcelo. Hermeneutical Interpretation and Pragmatic Interpretation. Phil Rhet, 22(4), 239-259, 1989.

DASCAL, Marcelo (ed) and GRUENGARD, Ora (ed). *Knowledge and Politics*. Boulder, Westview Pr, 1988

The links between the political and epistemological theories of thirteen philosophers, ranging from Aristotle and Hobbes to Habermas and Feyerabend, are examined in self-contained essays specially written for this book. The aim was to elucidate the nature of the connections—if any—between the doctrines held by the same thinker in two traditionally different philosophical disciplines. The main general finding was that such connections are neither strictly logical nor merely circumstantial. They rather have a variety of 'strategical' rationales. The introductory essay classifies, analyzes, and exemplifies the kinds of 'strategies of connection' discernible in the essays.

DASCAL, Marcelo and SENDEROWICZ, Yaron. Language and Thought in Kant's Theory of Knowledge (in Hebrew). Iyyun, 39(2), 151-175, Ap 90.

Why is there no theory of language in Kant's writings? We purport to show that a theory of language is a necessity for Kant's theory of knowledge. This is apparent, among other things, if one reflects on how 'empirical concepts' are possible on the basis of Kant's theory of judgment. The conclusion is that, while badly needed for Kant, a theory of language cannot be trivially supplied on the basis of his epistemology, for the very same arguments that show its need also show its impossibility within the Kantian framework.

DASCAL, Marcelo. "Reflections on the 'Crisis of Modernity'" in *The Institution of Philosophy: A Discipline in Crisis?*, COHEN, Avner (ed), 217-240. La Salle, Open Court, 1989.

The radicality of recent critiques of philosophy displays some recurrent features: (a) a deliberate search for paradox; (b) an ostensive disdain for *tu quoque* counterarguments; (c) a 'discourse egalitarianism': all discourse levels and types are on a par; (d) a rejection of the categories, distinctions, methods and strategies of (classical) Reason; (e) a notion of criticism that goes deeper than refutation or denial. A cyclic model of the dynamics of confrontations is proposed, in order to account for the radicality of the current episode of the centuries-old opposition between philosophical 'constructionists' and 'deconstructionists'.

DASCAL, Marcelo. Tolerância e interpretação. Critica, 21(62), 3-28, Ag 89.

An argument in favor of tolerance is developed here, based on a critique of the 'naive semantic' model of language understanding. This model, as illustrated both by Popper and Mao Tse-Tung, presumes the objectivity and context-independence of the understanding of discourse (texts included). On this view, criticism of 'wrong' views is a purely logical matter, having to do with the detection of inconsistencies, lack of evidence, or other logical insufficiencies of the criticized views. Against this, it is argued that the semantic rules of language are always insufficient to determine the "meaning" of a text or other piece of discourse. (edited)

DASTUR, Françoise. Logic and Ontology: Heidegger's "Destruction" of Logic. Res Phenomenol, 17, 55-74, 1987.

DAUENHAUER, Bernard J. The Ego Revisited. J Brit Soc Phenomenol, 21(1), 48-52, Ja 90.

I argue that the views of the "I" presented in Robert Sokolowski's *Moral Action* and Herbert Spiegelberg's *Steppingstones Toward an Ethics for Fellow Existers* provide a way of construing what it is to be a human being which can successfully resist many recent attacks upon notions of the self, ego, person, or subject.

DAUENHAUER, Bernard. History's Sources: Reflections on Heidegger and Ricoeur. J Brit Soc Phenomenol, 20(3), 236-247, O 89.

Martin Heidegger and Paul Ricoeur have each contributed substantial clarifications to the question of the sources whence the study of history springs. Though Ricoeur is critical of parts of Heidegger's treatment of this topic, I show that their respective contributions can readily be synthesized. Then, in a final section, I sketch one way in which their contributions, when synthesized, shed light upon the conditions for responsible political practice.

DAUER, Francis. Art and Art Criticism: A Definition of Art. Metaphilosophy, 21(1-2), 111-132, Ja-Ap 90.

DAVENPORT, Manuel. False Reports: Misperceptions, Self Deceptions or Lies? SW Phil Rev, 6(1), 113-121, Ja 90.

Why are estimates of enemy losses in time of war so inaccurate that it is often difficult for commanders to determine whether they are winning or losing? Perceptions do vary in terms of individual capacity to withstand stress. Should we, then, by means of training or selection identify and utilize those whose personal perceptual and valuational systems are affected least by stress? As an analysis of the Yamamoto shootdown reveals, those most resistant to stress are most highly predisposed to self-deception, which enhances combat readiness but leads to unreliable reports, and those least predisposed to self-deception are most indecisive, which leads to careful reporting but impairs combat readiness.

DAVEY, Earl. The Cognitive in Aesthetic Activity. J Aes Educ, 23(2), 107-112, Sum 89.

Art, as an object of scrutiny and meditation, provides a way of seeing and comprehending, a way of experiencing an imaginative vision of reality. This process is not intellectually passive, but properly characterized by a high order of thinking and feeling. In this brief essay the author treats of the cognitive in aesthetic activity and provides two examples in support of the argument; the first is taken from T S Eliot's *Four Quartets* and the second from Handel's *Giulio Cesare*.

DAVEY, Nicholas. "A World of Hope and Optimism Despite Present Difficulties": Gadamer's Critique of Perspectivism. Man World, 23(3), 273-294, Jl 90.

A critical examination of the different bases of Gadamer's and Nietzsche's approach to meaning: an attempt to view Gadamer's 'foundationlessism' as a possible riposte to Nietzschean nihilism: an argument to suggest that Gadamer is right to criticise Nietzsche's nihilistic-perspectival stance but incorrect in the formulation of his alternative.

DAVID, Donald K (ed) and ANDREWS, Kenneth R (ed). *Ethics in Practice: Managing the Moral Corporation*. Boston, Harvard Bus Schl Pr, 1989

This anthology presents ethical and legal perspectives on artificial insemination, fertility drugs, embryo transfer, gestational surrogacy, surrogate motherhood, fetal monitoring, nonreproductive uses of fetuses, and other issues. In addition to discussions explaining the technology and underlying biology, the work includes case studies of concrete moral dilemmas that provoke reflection. Contributors include Lori Andrews, George Annas, Michael Bayles, Arthur Caplan, Gena Corea, Mary Mahowald, Thomas Murray, Lawrence Nelson, John Robertson, Carol Smart, Hans Tiefel, LeRoy Walters, Hon. Robert Wilentz, Richard Zaner, as well as the Ethics Committee of the American Fertility Society and the Congregation for the Doctrine of the Faith.

DAVID, Marian A. Truth, Eliminativism and Disquotationalism. Nous, 23(5), 599-614, D 89.

The semantic concept of truth is naturally analyzed in terms of some notion of meaning. It is proposed that the so-called disquotational theory of truth is best understood as a consequence of a physicalist and eliminativist attitude toward this notion: a physicalist who is an eliminativist with respect to the relevant notion of meaning is likely to adopt disquotationalism. It is argued that disquotationalism is not a sensible theory of truth. It has too many unacceptable consequences. The result has at least an indirect bearing on eliminativism: if disquotationalism fails, eliminativism with respect to the relevant notion of meaning becomes unattractive.

DAVID, Pascal. *Sur les Wege zur Aussprache de Heidegger*. Heidegger Stud, 5, 173-179, 1989.

This article by Heidegger, published in 1937, is an attempt to elucidate how a real understanding between German and French peoples is to be

understood, and by which means it may be reached. What is a people? In complete and radical opposition to Nazi biological and racial ideology, Heidegger determines the essence of a people as a spiritual one, requesting its receptivity to the other ways of life, including the life of the mind and creation of other peoples. This condition may enable a dialogue between peoples to be fruitful.

DAVIDSON, Arnold (trans) and HADOT, Pierre and WISSING, Paula (trans). Forms of Life and Forms of Discourse in Ancient Philosophy. Crit Inquiry, 16(3), 483-505, Spr 90.

Dans cette leçon inaugurale de la chaire d'Histoire de la pensée hellénistique et romaine, au Collège de France (Paris), l'auteur se propose de décrire la philosophie antique, non pas du point de vue de l'histoire des doctrines, mais comme un phénomène social et spirituel, comme une quête de la sagesse qui provoque une rupture entre le philosophe et le "quotidien". Cette approche concrète du phénomène philosophique permet aussi d'aborder les oeuvres philosophiques de l'Antiquité avec une méthodologie nouvelle, notamment en considérant que leur structure et leur contenu sont étroitement liés à des conduites orales.

DAVIDSON, Donald. The Structure and Content of Truth. J Phil, 87(6), 279-328, Je 90.

Various deflationary views of truth are rejected on the ground that they cannot capture what is common to the concept of truth as applied to specific languages. It is argued that correspondence theories are empty or unintelligible. Views that reduce truth to what is in some sense epistemically accessible are either false or trivial. An alternative account is offered which makes truth an irreducible concept essential to the description and explanation of thought and action. The account combines a theory of meaning with a version of Bayesian decision theory.

DAVIDSON, Herbert A. "*Averrois Tractatus de Animae Beatitudine*" in *A Straight Path: Studies in Medieval Philosophy and Culture*, LINK-SALINGER, Ruth (ed), 57-73. Washington, Cath Univ Amer Pr, 1988.

DAVIES, Brian. Does God Create Existence? Int Phil Quart, 30(2), 151-157, Je 90.

DAVIES, Bronwyn and LEACH, Mary. Crossing the Boundaries: Educational Thought and Gender Equity. Educ Theor, 40(3), 321-332, Sum 90.

DAVIES, Bronwyn. Education for Sexism: A Theoretical Analysis of the Sex/Gender Bias in Education. Educ Phil Theor, 21(1), 1-19, 1989.

An analysis of the literature in relation to sexism and educational processes is undertaken. It is argued that while access and positive affirmation of femaleness are necessary as long as access is denied and femaleness marginalized that genuine equity will not be achieved until the male/female dualism is recognized as a social/linguistic construction that needs to be undone.

DAVIES, Paul. Difficult Friendship. Res Phenomenol, 18, 149-173, 1988.

DAVIES, Stephen. "The Evaluation of Music" in *What is Music?*, ALPERSON, Philip A , 303-325. New York, Haven, 1987.

Primarily, individual musical works are valued for giving pleasure when considered for "their own sakes." Such evaluations presuppose familiarity with the type of music being considered and are subject to justification. An interest in listening to many musical works has further, but incidental, benefits. A parallel is drawn: just as kind acts are their own reward, so too is the pleasure taken in individual musical works; but just as kindness would not be valued in general were it not for its wider social consequences, so a concern with music would not be valued were it not for benefits which go beyond the pleasure afforded to the listener.

DAVION, Victoria. Pacifism and Care. Hypatia, 5(1), 90-100, Spr 90.

I argue there is no pacifist commitment implied by the practice of mothering, contrary to what Ruddick suggests. Using violence in certain situations is consistent with the goals of this practice. Furthermore, I use Ruddick's valuable analysis of the care for particular individuals involved in this practice to show why pacifism may be incompatible with caring passionately for individuals. If giving up passionate attachments to individuals is necessary for pacifist commitment as Ghandi claims, then the price is too high.

DAVIS, Caroline Franks. *The Evidential Force of Religious Experience*. New York, Oxford Univ Pr, 1989

DAVIS, Charles. Our Modern Identity: The Formation of Self. Mod Theol, 6(2), 159-171, Ja 90.

DAVIS, D L and VITELL, Scott J. The Relationship Between Ethics and Job Satisfaction: An Empirical Investigation. J Bus Ethics, 9(6), 489-494, Je 90.

The relationship between ethics and job satisfaction for MIS professionals is examined empirically. Five dimensions of job satisfaction are examined: (1) satisfaction with pay, (2) satisfaction with promotions, (3) satisfaction with co-workers, (4) satisfaction with supervisors, and (5) satisfaction with the work itself. These dimensions of satisfaction are compared to top management's ethical stance, one's overall sense of social responsibility and an ethical optimism scale (i.e., the degree of optimism that one has concerning the positive relationship between ethics and success in his/her company). Results indicate that MIS professionals are more satisfied with the various dimensions of their jobs when top management stresses ethical behavior and when they are optimistic about the relationship between ethics and success within their firms. The one exception to this is pay satisfaction which is unrelated to these constructs. One's sense of social responsibility is also relatively unrelated to job satisfaction.

DAVIS, Donald L and VITELL, Scott J. Ethical Beliefs of MIS Professionals: The Frequency and Opportunity for Unethical Behavior. J Bus Ethics, 9(1), 63-70, Ja 90.

The frequency and opportunity for unethical behavior by MIS professionals is examined empirically. In addition, the importance of top management's ethical stance, one's sense of social responsibility and the existence of codes of ethics in determining perceptions of the frequency and opportunity for unethical behavior are tested. Results indicate that MIS professionals are perceived as having the opportunity to engage in unethical practices, but that they seldom do so. Additionally, successful MIS professionals are perceived as ethical. Finally, while company codes of ethics were uncommon, top management was seen as supporting high ethical standards.

DAVIS, Duane H. Completing the Recovery of Language as an Existential Project. J Brit Soc Phenomenol, 21(2), 175-184, My 90.

Since the time of Aristotle, most of the results of Western philosophical inquiries into language have been flawed due to the presupposed ontological hierarchy of thought, speech, and written discourse (écriture). Speech is presumed to be derivative of thought, and écriture to be derivative of speech. I appropriate two contemporary critiques of this hierarchy: Calvin O Schrag is shown to recover speech as an existential project, while Gerhard Ebeling's notion of the word-event effects the same style of recovery of écriture. Finally, the ethical nature of language is revealed by the completion of this recovery.

DAVIS, J Steve. Ethical Problems in Competitive Bidding: The Paradyne Case. Bus Prof Ethics J, 7(2), 3-25, Sum 88.

The purpose of this paper is to outline the important problems which may occur in competitive bidding situations, and to illustrate some of these issues with a case study. Most problems are associated with deception or lack of social responsibility by the vendor, or with the buyer's unfairness in selecting a vendor. Many important issues are illustrated by the Paradyne case, in which the Social Security Administration awarded the largest contract in their history for small computer systems to equip their field offices.

DAVIS, John B. Cooter and Rappoport on the Normative. Econ Phil, 6(1), 139-146, Ap 90.

DAVIS, Lawrence H. The Importance of Reverence. Faith Phil, 7(2), 135-148, Ap 90.

Is it more important to love God, or to revere Him? On the account of reverence I give, it differs both from literal "fear" of God and from love—but the latter only if certain Humean views are incorrect. Assuming my account, it follows that reverence is virtually a prerequisite for love. Also, there are reasons to think God is more concerned with asking reverence from humanity than with asking for their love. In these respects, at least, reverence is more important.

DAVIS, Lawrence H. Self-Consciousness in Chimps and Pigeons. Phil Psych, 2(3), 249-260, 1989.

Chimpanzee behaviour with mirrors makes it plausible that they can recognise themselves as themselves in mirrors, and so have a 'self-concept'. I defend this claim, and argue that roughly similar behavior in pigeons, as reported, does not in fact make it equally plausible that they also have this mental capacity. But for all that it is genuine, chimpanzee self-consciousness may differ significantly from ours. I describe one possibility I believe consistent with the data, even if not very plausible: that the chimpanzee is aware of itself only as a material being, and not as a subject of any psychological states. As I try to make clear, this possibility exists even if the chimpanzee has psychological states, and is aware of some of them.

DAVIS, Michael. Avoiding the Tragedy of Whistleblowing. Bus Prof Ethics J, 8(4), 3-19, Wint 89.

Whistleblowing is a normal response to an organization's failure to use bad news. An organization can reduce the need for whistleblowing by improving the flow of information within it, especially the flow of "bad news." A

combination of procedural, educational, and structural changes are suggested. Individuals can reduce the likelihood of having to become whistleblowers not only by looking for an organization in which bad news flows easily but also by developing the political skills that help get bad news through ordinary channels.

DAVIS, Michael. The Death Penalty, Civilization, and Inhumaneness. Soc Theor Pract, 16(2), 245-259, Sum 90.

Should the death penalty be abolished even if criminals deserve death for what they did? Reiman and Bedau have each recently published a substantial article answering, Yes. The argument each makes—"the argument from inhumaneness"—is attractive because it addresses nonconsequentialists in their own terms (without entanglement in issues of desert). But the attraction is deceptive. The argument can be made only on an analysis of inhumaneness narrow enough to permit the strong moral criticism we save for inhumane penalties. Neither Reiman nor Bedau seems to have presented such an analysis.

DAVIS, Michael and KADISH, Mortimer R. Defending the Hearsay Rule. Law Phil, 8(3), 333-352, D 89.

DAVIS, Michael. Explaining Wrongdoing. J Soc Phil, 20(1-2), 74-90, Spr-Fall 89.

This paper has three objectives: (1) to provide some evidence that evil will, weakness of will, self-deception, and moral immaturity, even together, will not explain much wrongdoing of concern to students of professional or business ethics; (2) to add one interesting alternative to the explanations now available ("microscopic vision"); and (3) to suggest the practical importance of that alternative (by, for example, an examination of the *Challenger* disaster).

DAVIS, Michael. The New World of Research Ethics: A Preliminary Map. Int J Applied Phil, 5(1), 1-10, Spr 90.

This paper (a) briefly describes the history of research ethics as a field and the topics it today includes; (b) summarizes what little we know about the apparent crisis in *scientific* research; and (c) outlines the practical responses to that crisis. We seem to have entered a period where at least some of the sciences will become more like the traditional professions (law, medicine, engineering, and so on).

DAVIS, Michael. Recent Work in Punishment Theory. Pub Affairs Quart, 4(3), 217-232, Jl 90.

This is a brief history of punishment theory over the last 25 years, identifying both large trends and important individual works. Punishment theory is taken to include (a) the justification of punishment as an institution, (b) the justification of a particular social arrangement for punishing, (c) the setting of statutory penalties, (d) justification of individual sentences, and (e) pardoning and other forms of clemency. Special attention is given to the startling resurgence of retributivism during the last 15 years.

DAVIS, Michael. The Special Role of Professions in Business Ethics. Bus Prof Ethics J, 7(2), 51-62, Sum 88.

Professionals have a special role to play in business ethics. They are qualified for that role by both training and motivation in a way business people generally are not. The argument for this unorthodox thesis includes an analysis of professions making ethics (rather than knowledge) central. Any (morally decent) person who joins a profession will be motivated accordingly.

DAVIS, Michael. Teaching Workplace Ethics. Thinking, 8(4), 33-42, 1990.

Though the focus of this paper is teaching *workplace* ethics, much of the analysis should apply to teaching ethics of any sort. The paper has four parts. Part One briefly introduces the subject by explaining how the paper came to be. Part Two analyzes five misconceptions that can get in the way of teaching workplace ethics. Part Three applies the insights gained in Part Two to a specific classroom situation. Part Four consists of four sample problems suitable for classroom use.

DAVIS, Michael. Who Can Teach Workplace Ethics? Teach Phil, 13(1), 21-38, Mr 90.

Philosophers are being flooded by requests to teach professional students the ethics of their own profession because faculty of professional schools tend to feel inadequate in teaching ethics. This paper considers seven "fears" that can inspire such discomfort, explaining what makes each *seem* reasonable and suggesting arguments to show professional faculty why in fact it is not. The arguments stress the difference between teaching ethics and teaching virtue.

DAVIS, Reed M (ed). *Moral Reasoning and Statecraft: Essays Presented to Kenneth W Thompson*. Lanham, Univ Pr of America, 1988

DAVIS, Stephen T. Doubting The Resurrection: A Reply to James A Keller.

Faith Phil, 7(1), 99-111, Ja 90.

In this paper, I reply to James A Keller's criticisms of my "Is It Possible to Know That Jesus Was Raised from the Dead?" I first discuss three of Keller's arguments about the New Testament evidence for the resurrection of Jesus. I then respond to two philosophical criticisms Keller makes of my original article. Finally, I argue that Keller has paid insufficient attention to several powerful arguments that support the thesis that Jesus was genuinely raised from the dead.

DAVIS, Stephen T. Universalism, Hell, and the Fate of the Ignorant. Mod Theol, 6(2), 173-186, Ja 90.

DAVIS, Susan E. Pro-Choice: A New Militancy. Hastings Center Rep, 19(6), 32-33, N-D 89.

DAVIS, Walter A. *Inwardness and Existence: Subjectivity in/and Hegel, Heidegger, Marx, and Freud.* Madison, Univ Wisconsin Pr, 1989

The fundamental conflict in criticism today is between deconstruction and humanism, between the poststructuralist proclaimers of "the death of the subject" and those who would reaffirm traditional humanistic concepts and values. Rather than taking sides in the debate, the author sets out to transcend it, to show that genuine subjectivity—and an adequate theory of subject—begins only when one steps beyond the conceptual limitations of both humanism and deconstruction. In taking that "step beyond," he invites the reader to join him in the effort to recapture the complexity of personal existence by confronting the question: what is the human subject's relationship to himself or herself? The author argues that the answer to that question requires the achievement of a principled dialectical integration of four contexts of thought that are frequently opposed: Hegelian phenomenology, existentialism, Marxism, and psychoanalysis. (edited)

DAVIS, Wayne A and BENDER, John W. "Fundamental Troubles with the Coherence Theory" in *The Current State of the Coherence Theory*, BENDER, John W (ed), 52-68. Norwell, Kluwer, 1989.

Coherence of a belief to the body of other beliefs a person holds is neither a necessary nor sufficient condition for the empirical justification of that belief, we argue. We make the non-necessity claim in discussing the question of basic beliefs. The more interesting debate, however, concerns whether coherence is ever sufficient for epistemic justification. The paper offers two arguments for the insufficiency thesis. The first argues that a coherence measure fails to capture the inferential structure of a set of beliefs and that that structure is important to justification. The second argument claims that coherence will not yield justification even if the background system is entirely true—because the system might be a set of lucky guesses. (This should not be confused with the "isolation argument" which objects that purely fictitious systems can be coherent.) These arguments are directed primarily toward Keith Lehrer's version of the coherence theory; however, certain suggestions of Laurence BonJour also are considered.

DAVLANTES, Nancy. The Eminently Practical Mr Hume or Still Relevant After All These Years. Hume Stud, 16(1), 45-56, Ap 90.

DAVSON-GALLE, Peter. Interpreting Arguments and Judging Issues. Inform Log, 11(1), 41-45, Wint 89.

The paper argues that arguments by Jonathan Berg and Trudy Govier (in earlier issues of *Informal Logic*) to the effect that the point of argument analysis is the understanding of what the author meant are unpersuasive; and that the appropriate attitude to take to reading the arguments of others is to view them as mere stimuli to one's own thought, a role that does not have "high fidelity" interpretation as a precondition.

DAWSON, Karen and GAZE, Beth. Distinguishing Medical Practice and Research: The Special Case of IVF. Bioethics, 3(4), 301-319, O 89.

The distinctions between medical practice and research, and research which is therapeutic and nontherapeutic, are used to analyse the position of embryo research. Where it is designed to improve in vitro fertilization treatment, embryo research affects not only the embryo, but also the woman to whom the embryo may later be transferred. Although such research may be difficult to classify, it is argued that the effect of the research (or of not doing it) on a woman's treatment cannot be overlooked in the debate over embryo experimentation.

DAY, J P. Compromise. Philosophy, 64(250), 471-485, O 89.

This essay examines one familiar and important way of resolving conflicts of claims, which philosophers have neglected. Confusions are removed, and our ambivalent attitude to compromise is explained by drawing the necessary distinctions. In *Ethics* it is morally wrong for A *to compromise* (tr) B, but often morally right for A *to compromise* (intr) with B. It is morally wrong for A *to compromise* (tr) moral principles X and Y, but often morally right for A *to compromise* (intr) between X and Y. The application of these findings to *Politics* is illustrated by a consideration of the American compromise of 1850 on slavery.

DAY, J P. *Liberty and Justice.* Wolfeboro, Croom Helm, 1987

The book elucidates liberty and justice, which are the central concepts of social and political thought. But since they are significantly linked to most of the other key notions in this domain, the book accordingly provides a unified treatment of social and political philosophy as a whole. It consists of thirteen interconnected essays in which are discussed, e.g., Do offers, like threats, curtail liberty? Are retributive punishment and compensatory discrimination justifiable? What does 'the Rule of Law' mean, and how is the rule of law related to civil liberty? Is justice indefeasible, and why is it believed to be so? How does collective liberty differ from individual liberty? Does Locke solve the problem of religious liberty? Is economic liberty the means to economic justice?

DAY, J P. Self-Ownership. Locke News, 20, 77-85, 1989.

This essay has two purposes: (I) to interpret Locke's thesis on the self-ownership of man (Locke's SOT); (II) to suggest Locke's reasons for maintaining his SOT. On (I), it is contended that Locke's SOT is that every freeman is the 'joint property' of himself and of God. This interpretation resolves the apparent inconsistency between 'Every freeman is owned by himself' (which is the first premiss of Locke's deontological argument to prove 'Every freeman owns what he has made'), and 'Every freeman is owned by God' (which is the reason for Locke's objections to suicide and self-enslavement). On (II), it is suggested that Locke's reasons are (1) Everything except God has been made by God or by man; (2) God made man in some respects like himself; and (3) All makers own what they have made.

DAY, Susan G and TROTTER, R Clayton and LOVE, Amy E. Bhopal, India and Union Carbide: The Second Tragedy. J Bus Ethics, 8(6), 439-454, Je 89.

The paper examines the legal, ethical, and public policy issues involved in the Union Carbide gas leak in India which caused the deaths of over 3000 people and injury to thousands of people. The paper begins with a historical perspective on the operating environment in Bhopal, the events surrounding the accident, then discusses an international situation audit examining internal strengths and weaknesses, and external opportunities and threats faced by Union Carbide at the time of the accident. There is a discussion of management of the various interests involved in international public relations and ethical issues. A review of the financial ratio analysis of the company prior and subsequent to the accident follows, then an examination of the second tragedy of Bhopal—the tragic failure of the international legal system to adequately and timely compensate victims of the accident. The paper concludes with recommendations towards public policy, as well as a call for congressional action regarding international safety of US-based multinational operations.

DAY, Timothy Joseph. "Circularity, Non-Linear Justification and Holistic Coherentism" in *The Current State of the Coherence Theory*, BENDER, John W (ed), 134-141. Norwell, Kluwer, 1989.

The coherence theory is sometimes accused of circularity in its response to the regress problem. To answer this charge coherentists have appealed to a nonlinear theory of inferential justification. This is in contrast to a linear theory that treats inferential justification as imposing an ordering relation on a set of beliefs. In this paper, I consider the response to the charge of circularity that Laurence BonJour gives in his book *The Structure of Empirical Knowledge*. I argue that the coherentist response to regressive circularity does not depend on any nonlinear theory of inferential justification. Instead the coherence theory uses inference in a way that the issue of circularity does not arise. BonJour himself actually develops such a theory. The coherence theory can make use of the same sorts of inferences as any theory of justification. Hence, there is no reason for BonJour to introduce a nonlinear theory of inferential justification. The real issue is whether there is inferential justification (linear or not) in the sense required to generate the regress.

DAYNES, Keith. Sets as Singularities in the Intensional Universe. Stud Log, 48(1), 111-128, Mr 89.

This paper is motivated by the search for a natural and deductively powerful extension of classical set theory. A theory of properties U is developed, based on a system of relevant logic related to RQ. In U the set $\{a,b,c,...\}$ is identified with the property $[x: x=a \lor x=b \lor x=c...]$. The universe of all sets V, is identified with the property of being a hereditary set. The main result is that relevant implication $\rightarrow$ collapses to material implication $\supset$ for sentences with quantifiers restricted to V. This demonstrates the naturalness of the system. However, an apparent lack of deductive power leads to the conclusion that the best extension of classical set theory is to be found in intensional theories with the unrestricted comprehension schema based on weak relevant logics. The author has obtained similar collapses of $\rightarrow$ to $\supset$ for these systems.

DE ASUA, M J C. Alberto Magno y los últimos unicornios. Stromata, 45(3-4), 407-422, Jl-D 89.

Albert's treatment of the unicorn, in his *De animalibus*, is considered in detail. This case study shows the character of much of Albert's biological works: its empirical character and its relationship to the Aristotelian theoretical framework. Albert's consideration of the fabulous beasts marks a departure from the symbolic and allegorical approach of the previous medieval traditions of natural history. (edited)

DE ASUA, Miguel J C. El Problema del Origen de la Vida. Manuscrito, 12(1), 71-89, Ap 89.

This paper proposes a rational reconstruction, according to a modified version of the methodology of research programs of I. Lakatos, of the polemic about the origin of life, from the 17th century onwards, with special emphasis on the Pasteur-Pouchet controversy. Two research programs are considered (the biogenist and the abiogenist). Their hard cores, as well as their positive and negative heuristic are detailed. The biogenist 'program' comprises the hypothesis and experiments by Needham, Appert, Pouchet, Bastian and Bernard; the abiogenist, those of Spallanzani, Schwann, Ure, von Helmholtz, Schulze, von Dusch, Schröder, Pasteur and Tyndall. The reconstruction of the controversy is divided into three periods: (1) antecedents, (2) the polemic Pasteur-Pouchet, (3) subsequent developments. Within each of these periods the progressive or regressive character of the 'programs' under consideration is established.

DE BARY, William Theodore. "The Trouble with Confucianism" in *The Tanner Lectures on Human Values, Volume X*, PETERSON, Grethe B (ed), 131-183. Salt Lake City, Univ of Utah Pr, 1989.

These lectures deal with the relationship between the Chinese state and the involvement with it of Confucians both as officials and as scholars, the latter often speaking, as did Confucius and Mencius, with a prophetic voice, invoking transcendent values to criticize the established order. Contrary to Max Weber, the Confucians did not lack such a prophetic role in respect to rulers; where they differed from the Hebrew prophets was rather in their relationship to the people, and in the role the people were expected to play.

DE BOER, Theo. Notes on a Not-Relativistic Pluralism (in Hungarian). Magyar Filozof Szemle, 2-3, 331-339, 1989.

DE CASTRO, Leonardo D. The Philippines: A Public Awakening. Hastings Center Rep, 20(2), 27-28, Mr-Ap 90.

DE CONINCK, J B and GOOD, D J. Perceptual Differences of Sales Practitioners and Students Concerning Ethical Behavior. J Bus Ethics, 8(9), 667-676, S 89.

This study investigates specific behavioral perceptual differences of ethics between practitioners and students enrolled in sales classes. Respondents were asked to indicate their beliefs to issues related to ethics in sales. A highly significant difference was found between mean responses of students and sales personnel. Managers indicated a greater concern for ethical behavior and less attention to sales than did the students. Students indicated a strong desire for success regardless of ethical constraints violated.

DE DIJN, H. Religion and Truth (in Dutch). Tijdschr Filosof, 51(3), 407-426, S 89.

Religion and science are altogether too different to be rationally incompatible (or compatible). If—as is done here—one defends such a thesis, one seems to sever the link between religion and truth. This link seems to many to be really essential: is not the highest requirement of a person, especially a religious person, "to live in the truth"? And is it not necessary for rational beings to try and give a rational justification for one's religious beliefs? But perhaps "the truth" which is of such importance to the religious person is not a theoretical truth; perhaps "to live in the truth" is not a matter of trying not to be fooled or of being prepared to change one's views according to new and better information. Furthermore, the desire for independent justification seems either incompatible with religious belief or rather pointless. The link between religion and truth can only be seriously discussed if one understands the relationship between religious beliefs and attitudes like truthfulness, trust, obedience to authority, etc. (edited)

DE FINETTI, Bruno. Probabilism. Erkenntnis, 31(2-3), 169-223, S 89.

DE GANDILLAC, Maurice. "Ähnlichkeit—falscher Schein—Unähnlichkeit von Platon zu Pseudo-Dionysios Areopagitos" in *Agora: Zu Ehren von Rudolph Berlinger*, BERLINGER, Rudolph (and other eds), 93-107. Amsterdam, Rodopi, 1988.

After having examined, from Plato to Plotinus, the devaluation of the image, appearance and wrong-resemblance connecting in the categories of reflection and illusion, the author shows in Aristotle's *Poetics* a relative apologizing of the deformation (cathartic overstatement in the tragedy, caricatural shrinking in the comedie) and finally draws out the Pseudo-Areopagyte the notion of knowledge by dissimilarity suitable in theology to the ineffable Transcendant, and of which he proposes here an aesthetic transposition in the field of recent painting.

DE GARIS, Hugo. Moral Dilemmas Concerning the Ultra Intelligent Machine. Rev Int Phil, 44(172), 131-138, 1990.

Within one to two human generations, it is likely that computer technology will be capable of building brain-like computers containing millions if not billions of artificial neurons. This development will allow neuroengineers and neurophysiologists to combine forces to discover the principles of the functioning of the human brain. These principles will then be translated into more sophisticated computer architectures, until a point is reached in the 21st century when the primary global political issue will become, "Who or what is to be dominant species on this planet—human beings, or artilects (artificial intellects)?" A new branch of applied moral philosophy is needed to study the profound implications of the prospect of life in a world in which it is generally recognised to be only a question of time before our computers become smarter than we are. Since human beings could never be sure of the attitudes of advanced artilects towards us, due to their unfathomable complexity and possible "Darwinian" self-modification, the prospect of possible hostilities between human beings and artilects cannot be excluded.

DE GEORGE, Richard T. "The Marxists" in *Reading Philosophy for the Twenty-First Century*, MC LEAN, George F (ed), 289-313. Lanham, Univ Pr of America, 1989.

After describing Marx's method, the article distinguishes and characterizes four groups of contemporary Marxists: critical, humanistic, scientific, and analytic. Each emphasizes one aspect of original Marxism and together help a reader evaluate that doctrine.

DE GEORGE, Richard T. "Western and Chinese Philosophy on Man and Nature" in *Man and Nature: The Chinese Tradition and the Future*, TANG, Yi-Jie (ed), 143-148. Lanham, Univ Pr of America, 1989.

Western philosophy can be characterized as dualistic, containing both a dichotomy of subject and object and a notion of transcendence, and hence as opposed to Chinese thought, which is monistic and emphasizes immanence. The paper examines whether these differences can be traced to environmental differences, whether the philosophical differences are sufficient to account for the Western approach to and development of science, and whether Western and Chinese philosophy can be made compatible.

DE GRIJS, Ferdinand. About the Question on God's Government of the World (in Dutch). Bijdragen, 4, 358-372, 1989.

How do theologians treat words and notions from the past? This problem is concretized by the question whether God reigns over the world, and includes the traditional notion 'gubernatio mundi'. This evokes a problem as regards content: how is divine government of the world consonant with daily experience of all sorts of evil? A problem of methodology is being raised as well: in what manner can this notion of 'gubernatio mundi' be used in present-day theology? This methodological question forms the actual issue of this paper. Because of the alleged contradiction to daily experience, in contemporary theology the notion of 'gubernatio mundi' is frequently replaced with another, preferably with 'regnum dei', and that often without any serious theological verification. It is tentatively concluded that 'Kingdom of God' has to be defined as a concept for God's plan, put into action with free human beings in this history, that becomes realized now and again, here and there. 'Divine government' has to be circumscribed as a concept for the faith in God, through which we are certain—without knowing how—that God directs everything for the better. (edited)

DE JASAY, Anthony. Is Limited Government Possible? Crit Rev, 3(2), 283-309, Spr 89.

DE JASAY, Anthony. *Social Contract, Free Ride: A Study of the Public Goods Problem*. New York, Oxford Univ Pr, 1989

DE JONG, Willem R. Did Hobbes Have a Semantic Theory of Truth? J Hist Phil, 28(1), 63-88, Ja 90.

DE LAURETIS, Teresa. Eccentric Subjects: Feminist Theory and Historical Consiousness. Fem Stud, 16(1), 115-150, Spr 90.

DE LEANIZ CAPRILE, Ignacio García (trans) and CROSBY, John F. Son Ser y Bien realmente convertibles? Una Investigación Fenomenológica. Dialogo Filosof, 6(2), 170-194, My-Ag 90.

Se establecen en este trabajo las diferencias entre la concepción tomista del "esse" y la concepción fenomenológica, especialmente apoyada en la filosofía de Von Hildebrand, de valor. El valor aparece con un carácter absoluto, mientras que el "bonum"—idéntico con el "esse"—tiene un cierto carácter relativo—aunque no relativista—, por ser el mismo ser en cuanto apetecido. Se muestra con profusión de argumentos que el valor no es reducible al ser, concebido por la filosofía tomista, pero que tampoco se debe entender la relación entre ser y valor en un sentido dualista radical. El valor no es una característica constitutiva del ser sustancial, pero sí una característica "consecuencial" del mismo, por lo que no puede concebirse al margen del ser mismo.

DE LORENZO, Javier. La matemática y el ámbito conceptual. Rev Filosof (Spain), 1, 43-53, 1987-88.

DE MAN, Paul. "Phenomenality and Materiality in Kant" in *The Textual Sublime: Deconstruction and Its Differences*, SILVERMAN, Hugh J (ed), 87-108. Albany, SUNY Pr, 1990.

DE MARCO, Joseph P. "Toward an Adequate Theory of Applied Ethics". Int J Applied Phil, 4(4), 45-51, Fall 89.

We examine R B Brandt's recent attempt to show how a utilitarian position can meet the pragmatic demands of application. His proposal begins with a provisional acceptance of current practices, which are to be subsequently modified by using the principle of utility. We claim his proposal is inconsistent, because utility is not subject to pragmatic testing, and is unduly authoritarian, because it accepts rules which are not subject to principled review. Although we believe Brandt is moving in the right direction, his solution to the problem of application is inadequate.

DE MARCO, Joseph P and FOX, Richard M. *Moral Reasoning: A Philosophic Approach to Applied Ethics*. Orlando, Holt Rinehart Winst, 1989

Attempting to bridge the gap between theory and practice, the book analyzes principles and techniques required for moral decision making and develops a theory of applied ethics. It begins with issues about the nature of morality and the logic of moral reasoning. Then Kantianism, utilitarianism, natural law, contractarianism, pragmatism, and existentialism are explained and criticized. Insights from this analysis are used to form a system of principle and rules, and the system is applied in reasoning about social issues and individual acts. The last chapters focus on case studies in bioethics, business ethics, and personal life.

DE MARCO, Joseph P. The Problems of Preference Based Morality: A Critique of "Morals by Agreement". J Soc Phil, 20(3), 77-91, Wint 89.

In this paper I examine the role of preference in Gauthier's *Morals by Agreement*. I argue that Gauthier incorporates a number of values into his analysis, such as freedom and harm avoidance, that go beyond individual preferences. This violates his explicit attempt to base morality on individual rationality. I pay special attention to the second part of Gauthier's book, where he presents an analysis of acceptable preferences. I believe that this part of his work fails. The failure is instructive; I argue that an adequate moral theory cannot be founded on the rational pursuit of individual preference.

DE MARNEFFE, Peter. Liberalism, Liberty, and Neutrality. Phil Pub Affairs, 19(3), 253-274, Sum 90.

Liberalism has recently been associated with the doctrine that the state should remain neutral between conceptions of the good. This article distinguishes two different principles of neutrality and argues that the principle of neutrality—neutrality of grounds—that is fundamental to theoretical liberalism does not entail the principle of neutrality—concrete neutrality—that is typically appealed to in order to ground rights to individual liberty. The article focuses on the work of John Rawls and Ronald Dworkin, and includes concluding reflections on the implications of the argument for the separation of church and state.

DE MARTELAERE, Patricia. A Taste for Hume. Ratio, 2(2), 122-137, D 89.

The purpose of this article is threefold. First, I would like to offer a brief but systematic survey of Hume's main ideas in 'The Standard of Taste'. Next, I wish to explore more thoroughly two most important topics, viz. the idea of Beauty and the idea of a causal link between the work of art and the observer, supplemented by material from Hume's other writings and mainly from the *Treatise of Human Nature*. Finally, I will venture to suggest as a hypothesis a comprehensively 'aesthetic' interpretation of Hume's entire philosophy, with the inclusion of his seemingly independent epistemology. In particular the famous mechanism of *belief*, with its irritatingly obscure element of 'feeling' could, in my opinion, gain a more positive content if turned into a kind of 'cognitive taste'.

DE MONTICELLI, Roberta and DI FRANCESCO, Michele. Lingua degli angli e lingua dei bruti. Teoria, 9(1), 69-137, 1989.

DE MOSS, David J. Acquiring Ethical Ends. Ancient Phil, 10(1), 63-79, Spr 90.

According to Aristotle, the practically wise person decides through the rational process of deliberation what means are appropriate for pursuing ethical ends. The question examined in this essay is: How does the practically wise person rationally acquire these ends? Two answers to this question are rejected: (1) One deliberates about ends, and (2) Ends are not rationally acquired. The answer defended is that just as scientific first principles are, according to Aristotle, acquired by induction, so are ethical

ends. The essay explores in detail the structure of this special inductive process.

DE MUL, Jos. The Development of Aesthetic Judgment: Analysis of a Genetic-Structuralist Approach. J Aes Educ, 22(2), 55-71, Sum 88.

This article offers a philosophical analysis of M Parsons's genetic-structuralist theory of the development of aesthetic judgment (cp. M Parsons, *How We Understand Art*, Cambridge 1987). The author argues that, although Parsons's theory avoids several problems that are connected with traditional theories about aesthetic development, important questions remain. Among the problems discussed are the relations between descriptive and evaluative claims to aesthetic development, between the logic and dynamics of aesthetic development, and between horizontal and vertical (re)construction of the aesthetic domain. Attention is also paid to the relation between intellectual, moral and aesthetic development.

DE OLASO, Ezequiel. Zetesis. Manuscrito, 11(2), 7-32, O 88.

We do not have a satisfactory analysis of what Hellenistic skepticism understood by *zetesis*. However, it is the term used by Sextus Empiricus to characterize skepticism at the very beginning of *Outlines of Pyrrhonism*. This paper purports to show that *zetesis* refers to one of the most important activities, if not the main one, of pyrrhonian skepticism. Likewise, it is shown that the presupposition that *zetesis* always refers to an open investigation, utterly free from suppositions, is the cause of the problems of understanding the meaning of this term in pyrrhonian skepticism. The paper suggests that the nature of skeptical *zetesis* is mainly refutatory, and following this hypothesis a reconstruction of the skeptical attitude in general is offered.

DE PIERRIS, Graciela. Subjective Justification. Can J Phil, 19(3), 363-382, S 89.

I draw the distinction between "objective" and "subjective" justification and discuss problems of underdetermination in the attribution of subjective justification. I use the Achilles and the Tortoise regress as an illustration of this underdetermination and also to make the more radical claim that there are difficulties in principle in the attribution of subjective justification. The moral is that naturalistic approaches to epistemology that attempt to retain normative concepts face serious problems. Thus the choices left open are either Quinean descriptive naturalism or attributions of subjective justification drawing from resources provided by rational reconstructions of knowledge in terms of objective justification.

DE PROSPO, R C. Paine and Sieyès. Thought, 65(257), 190-202, Je 90.

DE REUCK, Anthony. "Culture in Conflict" in *The Causes of Quarrel: Essays on Peace, War, and Thomas Hobbes*, CAWS, Peter (ed), 50-63. Boston, Beacon Pr, 1989.

DE SALAS ORTUETA, Jaime. Leibniz und Ortega y Gasset. Stud Leibniz, 21(1), 87-97, 1989.

DE SCHUTTER, Dirk. The Pain of Simulation on Heidegger's Philosophy of Art (in Dutch). Bijdragen, 1, 38-67, 1990.

In his meditation on art Heidegger tries to show how art is given the ability to overcome the twentieth-century metaphysical constellation that is characterized by nihilism and technological rationalism. Whereas technology wills the complete control over the totality of beings, art respects the identity of beings: art breathes the assumption that this identity cannot be appropriated, not because it belongs to the beings as an unalienable property, but rather because it affects them with the gift of otherness that forever imprints upon them the mark of a lack. In the same way nihilism has forgotten the finitude of beings: art frees the space and time to experience this finitude. This is an experience of tearing grief: it does not conquer the negativity of death, but abides with it in a mixture of release and dissimulation. (edited)

DE SOUSA ALVES, Vitorino. A Filosofia da Matemática em Wittgenstein. Rev Port Filosof, 45(2), 161-188, Ap-Je 89.

The author examines Wittgenstein's criticism of the foundations of mathematics in the two phases of his logical and philosophical thought. He begins by situating it in relation to the three schools which discussed the logical foundations of mathematics: logicism, intuitionism, and formalism. In the first phase of the *Tractatus*, we can see Wittgenstein as a logicist. His originality resides in his not deriving arithmetic from the calculus of classes, as did Russell, but from propositional calculus that he generalizes. Wittgenstein considers mathematics as a simple "logical method." In the second phase of *Remarks*, manuscripts and copies, dating between 1927 and 1944, Wittgenstein changed his thinking. Now he believes that mathematics founds itself independently of pure logic. He discovers beyond "symbols" there are relations for "meanings" and "uses." (edited)

DE SOUZA FILHO, Danilo Marcondes. Ceticismo semântico. Manuscrito, 11(2), 95-112, O 88.

The discussion begins with Wittgenstein's *skeptical paradox* regarding the notion of following a rule, as interpreted by Kripke. On this interpretation, there is ultimately no justification for rule-governed linguistic behavior, since it is always possible to subsume a deviant use under a nonstandard application of the rule. The objections raised by Baker and Hacker to Kripke's interpretation are examined. According to these authors, one should reject the skeptical paradox itself: the relation between rule and use should be construed as an *internal*, grammatical relation, which does not require, consequently, a justification in the traditional sense.

DE SWART, H C M. What is the Theory of Social Choice About? Method Sci, 22(1), 1-10, 1989.

The purpose of an election is to determine a social choice, given the individual preferences of society members. Using mathematical-logical models several election systems are considered: the voting procedure, the Borda rule and the majority rule. All these systems turn out to have very unpleasant properties. Next we discuss Arrow's impossibility theorem, which roughly says that no "election system" (more precisely, no social welfare function) can exist which satisfies a number of particular conditions.

DE TIENNE, André. Peirce's Early Method of Finding the Categories. Trans Peirce Soc, 25(4), 385-406, Fall 89.

DE VRIES, G and PELS, Dick. Feiten en waarden: de constructie van een onderscheid. Kennis Methode, 14(1), 7-13, 1990.

DE VRIES, Gerard. Ethische theorieën en de ontwikkeling van medische technologie. Kennis Methode, 13(3), 278-294, 1989.

DE VRIES, Gerard. Feitelijk expansionisme, een restrictionistische visie: praktische wetenschappen en waardevrijheid. Kennis Methode, 14(1), 44-59, 1990.

DE VRIES, Paul H. Adam Smith's "Theory" of Justice: Business Ethics Themes in *The Wealth of Nations*. Bus Prof Ethics J, 8(1), 37-55, Spr 89.

DE VRIES, Paul H. Resource X: Sirkin and Smith on a Neglected Economic Staple. Bus Prof Ethics J, 6(4), 47-64, Wint 87.

Economist Gerald Sirkin believes that there is one essential but depletable resource that is generally overlooked in our economic analyses and policies. This "Resource X" is a cluster of ethical values that historically engender business vitality and economic growth. I defend Sirkin's extraordinary perspective as both true and justifiable. Moreover, I argue that philosopher/economist Adam Smith's published writings on ethics provide a richly endowed reserve of this precious economic staple, "Resource X." Smith's ethics provides an integrated philosophical perspective that complements Sirkin. Smith also avoids some of the false dichotomies and hazardous detachments that disable numerous other modern ethicists.

DE WACHTER, F. Ethics: Modern and Postmodern (in Dutch). Tijdschr Filosof, 52(2), 207-229, Je 90.

In celebration of the centennial of the Institute of Philosophy of the Catholic University of Leuven, a series of lectures was organized to outline the evolution of various philosophical disciplines in the timespan 1889-1989. The lecture on ethics was an attempt to depict the transition from foundational and universalist ethics into a hermeneutical type of ethics that is antifoundational and particularistic. Such can be interpreted as a transition from modernity into postmodernity, or from ethics into postethics; it is the abandonment of the belief that ethics might offer a rational legitimation of ethical principles, or that such principles might be shown to be universal dictates of reason. (edited)

DE ZAN, Julio. La libertad y el concepto de lo político. Cuad Filosof, 20(33), 31-39, O 89.

Starting from the positive and the negative senses of political liberty as set against each other by I Berlin and N Bobbio, the concept of politics assumed by each author is made explicit. It is shown that those concepts had already been formally discussed by Hegel, whose criticism had brought to light their contradictions and the unfeasibility of either of those forms of liberty if taken in isolation. Precisely, on that double criticism rests the Hegelian working up of those two concepts and his attempt to think them both together. The discussion of Hegel's answer to that claim, through his exposition of the dialectic constitution of free will and his own conception of politics, remains open.

DECORTE, Jos. Saint Anselm of Canterbury on Ultimate Reality and Meaning. Ultim Real Mean, 12(3), 177-191, S 89.

The article aims at introducing people to the religious context of the ontological argument, i.e., the religious meaning and purpose of the *Proslogion* itself. In fact, the proof of God's existence stands at the beginning of a pious and zealous quest for God. Prescinding from the discussion about the validity of the proof the author focuses on the structure of the *Proslogion* (and of that search), on the meaning of the two formulae (IQM—quidquam

maius quam cogitari nequit), their connection and relationship with hope (cf. A Stolz, H de Lubac).

DECREUS, F. Entre positivisme et anarchie? Trois voies de recherche dans la construction des theories en science litteraire. Commun Cog, 22(3-4), 249-261, 1989.

DEELY, John. *Basics of Semiotics*. Bloomington, Indiana Univ Pr, 1990

DEGEN, Wolfgang and BURKHARDT, Hans. Mereology in Leibniz's Logic and Philosophy. Topoi, 9(1), 3-13, Mr 90.

DEI, H Daniel. El sentido de la indagación filosófica. Rev Filosof (Costa Rica), 26, 71-76, D 88.

Philosophy is essentially an act of freedom. As the same existence of the man, its interrogations take place in the tension of the ambiguity of the open and final questions about life meaning. In this occupation of fidelity to the truth and freedom it expresses a testimony of critical implacable conscience before a contractured world for the oppression of the securities and the most different sedative forms of ideological legitimations.

DEIGH, John. "Morality and Personal Relations" in *Person to Person*, GRAHAM, George (ed), 106-123. Philadelphia, Temple Univ Pr, 1989.

The essay offers an account of morality's prohibitions and requirements that emphasizes their place in the regulation of social relations. The account follows from consideration of personal relations, relations between friends and among the members of a family, and how moral prohibitions and requirements work to keep such relations stable and amicable and to restore them to good order when they become ruptured. The essay concludes with criticism of rationalist accounts of morality that treat it as an abstract system of rules and ignore or deemphasize the place of its prohibitions and requirements in the regulation of social relations.

DEJNOZKA, Jan. The Ontological Foundation of Russell's Theory of Modality. Erkenntnis, 32(3), 383-418, My 90.

Prominent thinkers such as Kripke and Rescher hold that Russell has no modal logic, even that Russell was indisposed toward modal logic. In Part I, I show that Russell had a modal logic which he repeatedly described and that Russell repeatedly endorsed Leibniz's multiplicity of possible worlds. In Part II, I describe Russell's theory as having three ontological levels. In Part III, I describe six Parmenidean theories of being Russell held, including: literal in 1903, universal in 1912, timeless in 1914, transcendental in 1918-1948. The transcendental theory underlies the primary level of Russell's modal logic. In Part IV, I examine Rescher's view that Russell and modal logic did not mix.

DEL BARCO, Jose Luis. La utopía de lo supremo y el conocimiento metafísico de Dios. Anu Filosof, 21(2), 119-134, 1988.

DEL BARCO, José Luis. Virtud e interés: Fundamentos de la polis clásica y de la sociedad civil moderna. Pensamiento, 46(181), 75-102, Ja-Mr 90.

Frente a la desconexión que mantienen en el pensamiento moderno, en la filosofía clásica ética y política se hallan íntimamente unidas. Por eso, para Aristóteles el final de la ética constituye el comienzo de la política. El voluntarismo moderno convierte a la razón en *ancilla voluntatis*, rompiendo la armonía entre ética y política. El hombre pone la razón al servicio de la pasión (Hobbes). De ese modo, los medios se justifican *a posteriori*: son morales si sirven para conservar el poder (Maquiavelo). Mas la consideración del desnudo interés como *ultima ratio* anula la posibilidad de la razón política. De ahí, la necesidad de recuperar la noción de verdad práctica.

DEL CARO, Adrian. Dionysian Classicism, or Nietzsche's Appropriation of an Aesthetic Norm. J Hist Ideas, 50(4), 589-605, O-D 89.

To redirect the focus of philosophy from metaphysics to life-consummation, Nietzsche borrowed freely from Goethe's philosophy of life and his classicism. The new classicism envisioned by Nietzsche is antiromantic, anti-idealistic, and for most of his productive years he appropriated and elaborated Goethe's and Germany's classical tradition. Ultimately Nietzsche had to reject even Goethe's views on the classical, in favor of his own hybrid "Dionysian classicism." This essay accomplishes a historical overview of the Dionysian from an aesthetic to a philosophical concept, and offers a concrete example of how Nietzsche worked with major sources and borrowed from tradition in order to emerge as a leading cultural critic.

DEL CARO, Adrian. *Nietzsche Contra Nietzsche: Creativity and the Anti-Romantic*. Baton Rouge, Louisiana St Univ Pr, 1989

DEL PALACIO, Alfonso Avila. Sobre la noción fregeana "extensión de un concepto". Analisis Filosof, 8(1), 19-35, My 88.

This paper tries to clarify the Fregean notions of *function, concept, course of values*, and *extension*. According to Frege, a function is the reference of an expression with gaps; the function itself also has gaps and yields an object when those gaps are filled. Each function has a course of values and different functions can yield the same course of values. Concepts are functions having one argument which yield the truth for those objects which fall under the concept and which otherwise yield the false. The extension of a concept is its course of values. According to my interpretation, a Fregean function behaves like a skeleton that connects the objects that fill the gaps with the objects that arise when the gaps are filled. Therefore, one can say that a function is a mode of connecting objects, and the course of values is the connection itself, taken as a Fregean object. On these terms, a concept is a mode of connecting objects with truth-values, and its extension is the connection itself; in other words, a concept is a way of grouping objects (those that fall under the concept) and the extension is the grouping or "set" that is defined by that way of grouping objects.

DEL VECCHIO, Dante. La filosofia del Novecento: dalla razionalità all'irrazionalità. Sapienza, 42(2), 203-206, Ap-Je 89.

DELANEY, C. Kant's Challenge: The Second Analogy as a Response to Hume. Dialogue (PST), 32(2-3), 51-56, Ap 90.

In the essay I consider the manner and extent to which Kant's second Analogy demonstrates the objective necessity of the causal principle. I argue that the adequacy of the Analogy as a response to "Hume's Challenge" ultimately depends upon what in general we wish to regard as a "response" to a skeptical challenge. If a response must proceed from basic epistemological principles that the skeptic would himself accept, then the Analogy is a failure. If, on the other hand, one takes a skeptical challenge to be neutralized if the premises upon which it relies cannot account for an undeniable feature of our experience, then Kant's argument is not so clearly ineffective.

DELCÓ, Alessandro. Momenti della teoria leibniziana della sostanza nel carteggio con Arnauld. Filosofia, 41(1), 63-88, Ja-Ap 90.

DELESSERT, André. Le mathématicien et ses images. Rev Theol Phil, 121(3), 241-257, 1989.

Mathematical texts give all upon mathematics except what makes them interesting. One can seek, beyond their logical aspects, something which is of archetypical nature. One notion which appears in this direction is that of "image": a constellation of thought objects, which is at once recognizable and can give rise to reflexion. Some examples are given: the functional relation, the pairs finite-infinite, discrete-continuous, the identification process. Comments with references to facts like the axiom of choice are made. Some analogies are suggested with known myths such as the "Eternal Return."

DELEUZE, Gilles and DELEUZE, Gilles and MASSUMI, Brian (trans). A Thousand Plateaus: Capitalism and Schizophrenia. Minneapolis, Univ of Minn Pr, 1987

DELEUZE, Gilles and LESTER, Mark (trans) and BOUNDAS, Constantin V (ed). The Logic of Sense—Gilles Deleuze. New York, Columbia Univ Pr, 1990

DELEUZE, Gilles and MASSUMI, Brian (trans) and DELEUZE, Gilles. A Thousand Plateaus: Capitalism and Schizophrenia. Minneapolis, Univ of Minn Pr, 1987

DÉLIVOYATZIS, S. Engagement ou néantisation? (in Greek). Philosophia (Athens), 17-18, 168-181, 1987-88.

Nous essayons ici d'étudier les possibilités de rencontre entre une philosophie phénoménologique d'inspiration cartésienne, comme celle de Sartre, et la pratique marxiste à travers la lecture que Merleau-Ponty entreprend de la pensée politique sartrienne avant, bien Sûr, la Critique de la raison dialectique. Le point central différenciant Sartre, qui conçoit le sujet comme "néantisation", de Merleau-Ponty, qui voit dans l'homme un "engagement" de principe, reste le problème de la communication intérieur (conscience)-extérieur (être). (edited)

DELON, Françoise. Extensions Séparées et immédiates des corps valués. J Sym Log, 53(2), 421-428, Je 88.

The notion of separated extension of valued fields was introduced by Baur. He showed that extensions of maximal fields are separated. We prove that, when (K,v) is Henselian with residual characteristic 0, then $(K,v) \subset (L,w)$ is separated iff L is linearly disjoint over K from each immediate extension of K.

DEMMER, Klaus. Die Lebensgeschichte als Versöhnungsgeschichte: Eine paradigmatische Thematik spiritueller Moraltheologie. Frei Z Phil Theol, 36(3), 375-393, 1989.

It is the intention of the article to shed light on the proper interrelation between moral theology and spiritual theology. The integral well-being of the moral subject demands a permanent attempt to reconcile oneself with all implications of one's life project, therefore a high degree of truthfulness is asked for. One has to discover all those elements which are incoherent with one's life choice to come to full integration and maturity. Moral theology has

to sharpen its own intellectual tools.

DEMOPOULOS, William and FRIEDMAN, Michael. "The Concept of Structure in The Analysis of Matter" in Rereading Russell: Essays on Bertrand Russell's Metaphysics and Epistemology, SAVAGE, C Wade (ed), 183-199. Minneapolis, Univ of Minn Pr, 1989.

DEN HARTOGH, Govert. Made by Contrivance and the Consent of Men. Interpretation, 17(2), 193-221, Wint 89-90.

The Second Treatise tells a tale about people leaving the state of nature because of its "inconveniences," and entering political society by unanimous agreement. Recent interpretation tends to accept this story, not as a description of presumed historical fact, but as a theoretical justification of limited government on the basis of abstract principles within the framework of a hypothetical contract. I argue that (1) the principal historical element in Locke's account is social convention, not individual consent; (2) this element is of fundamental importance to Locke's concerns; (3) it makes his theory philosophically superior to any exclusively hypothetical contract theory of political obligation.

DEN HARTOGH, Govert. Rationality in Conversation and Neutrality in Politics. Analysis, 50(3), 202-205, Je 90.

DENBIGH, K G and REDHEAD, M L G. Gibbs' Paradox and Non-Uniform Convergence. Synthese, 81(3), 283-312, D 89.

It is only when mixing two or more pure substances along a reversible path that the entropy of the mixing can be made physically manifest. It is not, in this case, a mere mathematical artifact. This mixing requires a process of successive stages. In any finite number of stages, the external manifestation of the entropy change, as a definite and measurable quantity of heat, is a fully continuous function of the relevant variables. It is only at an infinite and unattainable limit that a non-uniform convergence occurs. And this occurs when considered in terms of the number of stages together with a 'distinguishability parameter' appropriate to the particular device which is used to achieve reversibility. These considerations, which are of technological interest to chemical engineers, resolve a paradox derived in chemical theory called Gibbs' Paradox.

DENECKE, Klaus. Hyperidentities of Dyadic Algebras. Z Math Log, 35(4), 303-310, 1989.

DENIS, A and ANDREW, C and CODERRE, C. Stop or Go: Reflections of Women Managers on Factors Influencing their Career Development. J Bus Ethics, 9(4-5), 361-367, Ap-My 90.

The purpose of this paper is to discuss how women managers themselves interpret the factors that constrain and those that facilitate management careers for women. We will do this by first reviewing some of the interpretations that have been put forward in the academic literature to explain the relatively small number of women managers and particularly the small number of very senior women managers. In the light of these interpretations, we will examine the opinions of a sample of intermediate and senior women managers in the public and private sectors in Ontario and Quebec. More specifically we will look at their answers to questions about what blocks and what facilitates management careers for women generally and what obstacles they themselves have met. We will then compare their interpretations of their own career development with the interpretations that exist in the literature.

DENT, N J H. Moral Autonomy in the Republic. Polis, 9(1), 52-77, 1990.

Liberal critics of Plato's Republic criticise him for ignoring the moral autonomy of persons, their right to form and to express their own moral ideas. It is argued that this criticism is superficial. Neither Plato, nor his liberal critics, wish all moral views to be held and acted on; they both wish to set limits to what is acceptable. The true source of disagreement is over the scope of reason in human affairs; Plato understands that narrowly; his liberal critics in a broad, permissive, way.

DENT, N J H. Plato and Social Justice. Polis, 6(2), 78-115, 1986.

Plato has been said to argue, in the Republic, that each person owes, in justice, all their life to discharging their function in the state. It is argued that this is to misunderstand Plato. He argues that we have a supreme duty to discharge our function in the state, but this is not an all-consuming duty. Space is left for people to pursue personal ends. Plato did not hold that our social rôle exhausted our individual good in society.

DENT, N J H. Rousseau. Cambridge, Blackwell, 1988

DENYER, Tom. The Ethics of Struggle. Polit Theory, 17(4), 535-549, N 89.

DEPRÉ, Olivier. Finitude et transcendance. Rev Phil Louvain, 87(76), 516-530, Ag 89.

This paper is a critical presentation of the third volume of the "Etudes d'anthropologie philosophique": Figures de la finitude (Gh. Florival, ed.),

Paris, Louvain-la-Neuve; Vrin, Peeters, 1988. It is shown that the anthropological contributions of this book are mainly concerned with the connection between finitude and transcendence. A first group of contributions deals with the problems of "anguish and affectivity" by M Heidegger and E Levinas. A second one points out the problems of relationships between ethics and politics. Other contributions on Buddhism and Islam form the third section about the intercultural dialogue. Each of these themes points to the internal tension between the condition of the man and the openness to his own truth.

DEREGIBUS, Arturo. Bradley e Spinoza: L'iper-spinozismo di F H Bradley (seconda parte). G Metaf, 11(1), 3-39, Ja-Ap 89.

DEREGIBUS, Arturo. Bradley e Spinoza: L'iper-spinozismo di F H Bradley (I). G Metaf, 10(3), 339-392, S-D 88.

DEREGIBUS, Arturo. Pascal: scienza, filosofia, religione. Filosofia, 40(3), 295-356, S-D 89.

DERISI, Octavio N. Naturaleza del conocimiento humano: El significado de la abstracción en Santo Tomás (III). Sapientia, 44(173), 163-170, Jl-S 89.

Compuesto de cuerpo y alma espiritual, el hombre se vale de dos conocimientos, intimamente unidos: el sensitivo, que es una intuición o aprehensión inmediata de la realidad, sin intermediarios. Este conocimiento no aprehende el ser o la realidad y el yo como tal. El entendimiento inteligible, a través de la abstracción del conocimiento sensitivo, aprehende el ser o esencia de las cosas y sabe que las cosas son y que él es. El trabajo denuncia los errores tanto del sensismo antiguo y moderno, como del espiritualismo exagerado racionalismo, que escinde estos dos conocimientos y por caminos diversos conducen al inmanentismo. Sólo por la abstracción es posible la unión de estos dos conocimientos, que permiten la aprehensión de la realidad como tal.

DERKSEN, A A. Freud, Mooij en de empiristische boeman. Alg Ned Tijdschr Wijs, 82(3), 232-236, Jl 90.

This is a reply to Mooij's article "Psycho-analysis: Pseudo-science or Geisteswissenschaft" (ANTW 82 (1990), 45-53). I argue that Mooij is engaged in fighting an empiricist of his own making. This leads him to misrepresent both my position and that of Freud. I further argue that in his defense of Freud Mooij neglects the burden of proof which rests with Freud—as Freud himself realized. Mooij's hermeneutic turn does not help Freud with his truth claims either. Recasting psychoanalysis as a Geisteswissenschaft leaves unimpeded the obligation to give support for one's claims. As Mooij does not provide this support, I see no reason to change my previous conclusion, to wit, that Freud's theory suffers from the First Sin of Pseudo-science, the Great Lack of Decent Evidence.

DERRIDA, Jacques and LYOTARD, Jean-François. Épreuves d'écriture—Notes du traducteur. Rev Phil Fr, 180(2), 269-292, Ap-Je 90.

DERRIDA, Jacques. Limited Inc. Evanston, Northwestern Univ Pr, 1988

DERRIDA, Jacques. Of Spirit: Heidegger and the Question. Chicago, Univ of Chicago Pr, 1989

DERRIDA, Jacques. On Reading Heidegger. Res Phenomenol, 17, 171-185, 1987.

DERRY, Robbin. An Empirical Study of Moral Reasoning Among Managers. J Bus Ethics, 8(11), 855-862, N 89.

Current research in moral development suggests that there are two distinct modes of moral reasoning, one based on a morality of justice, the other based on a morality of care. The research presented here examines the kinds of moral reasoning used by managers in work-related conflicts. Twenty men and twenty women were randomly selected from the population of first-level managers in a Fortune 100 industrial corporation. In open-ended interviews each participant was asked to describe a situation of moral conflict in her or his work life. The results indicated a clearly preferred mode of moral reasoning among the participants who described moral conflicts. Nearly all of these predominated with a justice orientation. These findings suggest that a correlation between gender and preferred mode may be context specific.

DERRY, Robbin and GREEN, Ronald M. Ethical Theory in Business Ethics: A Critical Assessment. J Bus Ethics, 8(7), 521-533, Jl 89.

How is ethical theory used in contemporary teaching in business ethics? To answer this question, we undertook a survey of 25 of the leading business ethics texts. Our purpose was to examine the ways in which normative moral theory is introduced and applied to cases and issues. We focused especially on the authors' views of the conflicts and tensions posed by basic theoretical debates. How can these theories be made useful if fundamental tensions are acknowledged? Our analysis resulted in a typology, presented here, of the ways in which normative theory, and the difficulties within it, are handled in business ethics texts. We conclude that there is a serious lack of

clarity about how to apply the theories to cases and a persistent unwillingness to grapple with tensions between theories of ethical reasoning. These deficiencies hamper teaching and ethical decision making.

DES JARDINS, Joseph and DUSKA, Ronald. Drug Testing in Employment. Bus Prof Ethics J, 6(3), 3-21, Fall 87.

Contrary to what seems to be a growing trend in favor of drug testing in the workplace, we argue that it is seldom legitimate to override an employee's privacy by using such tests. In arguing against the two major justifications of drug testing, we outline those few cases when testing can be appropriate. We conclude by considering certain limitations which must be placed upon those specific cases.

DESCARTES, Rene and VOSS, Stephen H (trans). *The Passions of the Soul—Rene Descartes*. Indianapolis, Hackett, 1989

DESLAURIERS, Marguerite. Aristotle's Four Types of Definition. Apeiron, 23(1), 1-26, Mr 90.

This paper is a discussion of the four types of definition enumerated in the *Posterior Analytics* 2.10. I argue that Aristotle considers these to be four discrete types, distinguished according to their objects and functions. To do this, I first show that according to Aristotle, there are two kinds of object for definition: self-explanatory and non-self-explanatory items. I then show that in each case it is possible to start from a prescientific definition—a definition that does not state the cause—and proceed to a definition that does state the cause.

DESMOND, William. "Schopenhauer, Art, and the Dark Origin" in *Schopenhauer: New Essays in Honor of His 200th Birthday*, VON DER LUFT, Eric (ed), 101-122. Lewiston, Mellen Pr, 1989.

An exploration of the metaphysical underpinnings of Schopenhauer's view of art, this paper examines the following topics: the Kantian heritage in Schopenhauer in relation to genius; the idea of the universal in Schopenhauer's and Hegel's aesthetics in relation to Plato; the claim that the grounding origin is dark, that is, on the other side of the principle of sufficient reason as this applies to phenomena; the legacy of the dark origin in Nietzsche. (edited)

DESPOTOPOULOS, K I. Éléments de l'histoire (humains et non humains) (in Greek). Philosophia (Athens), 17-18, 97-119, 1987-88.

I. L'histoire. L'histoire est un ensemble phantasmagorique d'actions, d'épreuves et de créations de l'humanité, encadrées dans le temps abstrait de l'Univers, tout en constituant un temps concret. 2. Les éléments non-humains de l'histoire. 3. La terre, fondement de l'histoire. 4-5. Les incidences d'évènements géodynamiques et de changements géophysiques sur l'histoire. 6. Les éléments extra-spatiaux et extra-temporels, et leur rayonnement sur l'histoire. 7. L'espace historique. 8. Le temps historique. 9. L'homme face aux éléments non-humains de l'histoire. (edited)

DESTRÉE, Pierre. Une mise à l'épreuve d'Aristote à partir de Heidegger. Rev Phil Louvain, 87(76), 629-639, N 89.

This paper is a critical review of Rémi Brague's important book, *Aristote et la question du monde* (Paris, PUF, 1988). Brague successfully shows that the core-concept of *Being and Time*, the being-in-the-world, can be found in all the work of Aristotle. So, if it's true that he was the thinker who deepest influenced Heidegger, we have consequently the task to read Aristotle as the first phenomenologist.

DETHIER, Hubert (ed) and WILLEMS, Eldert (ed). *Cultural Hermeneutics of Modern Art: Essays in Honor of Jan Aler*. Amsterdam, Rodopi, 1989

DETHIER, Hubert. "The Modern Religion of Art" in *Cultural Hermeneutics of Modern Art: Essays in Honor of Jan Aler*, DETHIER, Hubert (ed), 119-134. Amsterdam, Rodopi, 1989.

DETMER, David. Heidegger and Nietzsche on "Thinking in Values". J Value Inq, 23(4), 275-283, D 89.

DETWILER, Bruce. *Nietzsche and the Politics of Aristocratic Radicalism*. Chicago, Univ of Chicago Pr, 1990

This book argues that there is a significant political dimension in Nietzsche's writings, although politics were by no means his central concern. Nietzsche deliberately undermines the fundamental assumptions of the West's most prominent political traditions while developing his own disturbing but original political vision arising from his commitment to "the enhancement of man." Detwiler argues that Nietzsche's strategies for undermining existing hierarchies (a major source of his appeal for the left) culminate in an artistic alternative to western morality that allies him with the radical right and that has paradoxical affinities with fascism.

DEUTSCH, Eliot. "A Metaphysical Grounding for Natural Reverence: East-West" in *Nature in Asian Tradition of Thought: Essays in Environmental Philosophy*, CALLICOTT, J Baird (ed), 259-265. Albany, SUNY Pr, 1989.

I argue for the possibility of a creative relationship, which I call "natural reverence," obtaining between persons and nature which may inform the basic decision makings involved in the issues of environmental ethics today. Contrasting Kant's treatment of the sublime with certain ideas to be found in Indian philosophy, namely the idea of karma as involving modes of human *making*, I try to show the manner in which nature can become value-laden and how we can work with nature in a manner analogous to that of an artist working with his/her medium in a kind of creative play.

DEUTSCHER, Max. "Remembering 'Remembering'" in *Cause, Mind, and Reality: Essays Honoring C B Martin*, HEIL, John (ed), 53-72. Norwell, Kluwer, 1989.

The article reassesses, after 25 years, the influential paper "Remembering" (*Philosophical Review* 1965) by C B Martin and Max Deutscher. It places "remembering" within a larger cluster of ideas involving repetition and retention. While it gives further support, and defence against main criticisms, of the 'causal' criterion for remembering, it makes a radical new distinction concerning the notion of re-presentation.

DEVINE, I and MARKIEWICZ, D. Cross-Sex Relationships at Work and the Impact of Gender Stereotypes. J Bus Ethics, 9(4-5), 333-338, Ap-My 90.

Organizations pride themselves on their creation of rational structures based primarily on a male perspective of interaction. Workers are expected to set aside interpersonal behaviours that do not directly contribute to task performance. As more women enter management, norms concerning appropriate interpersonal relationships at work are undergoing strain. In addition, the phenomenon of mutual sexual attractions between co-workers is demanding attention. This study systematically describes attitudes, attributions and anticipated consequences of mutual sexual attractions at work. Findings suggest that gender stereotypes are significant factors in people's judgments of persons involved in sexual attractions at work.

DEVINE, Phillip E. Truth and Pragmatism in Higher Education. Int J Applied Phil, 5(1), 67-74, Spr 90.

I here argue that the contemporary crisis in American higher education arises from the influence of the pragmatist tradition, which subordinates the life of the mind to the agenda either of the political and economic elite, or of some other group to which a given professor may give his allegiance. The article includes an extended critique of Richard Rorty's *Irony, Contingency, Solidarity*.

DEVITT, Michael. Against Direct Reference. Midwest Stud Phil, 14, 206-240, 1989.

The paper distinguishes several theories of names associated with "direct reference," including the "causal" theory and the "'Fido'-Fido" theory. It traces the origins of those theories in the works of Donnellan, Kaplan, and Kripke. It argues that the causal theory does not support the 'Fido'-Fido theory, contrary to received opinion, and that the strategies of Salmon and others for avoiding traditional Fregean objections to the 'Fido'-Fido theory fail. In this argument the importance of the question, "What is the semantic task?", is emphasized. The paper offers an alternative view of the meaning of a name based on the causal theory.

DEVITT, Michael. "The Revival of 'Fido'-Fido" in *Cause, Mind, and Reality: Essays Honoring C B Martin*, HEIL, John (ed), 73-94. Norwell, Kluwer, 1989.

The revival of the 'Fido'-Fido theory of names has come mainly from philosophers influenced by the works of Donnellan, Kaplan, and Kripke. The paper distinguishes the theory from several others, particularly the "causal" theory. It argues that the causal theory does not support the 'Fido'-Fido theory, contrary to received opinion, and that the strategies of Salmon and others for avoiding traditional Fregean objections to the 'Fido'-Fido theory fail. In this argument the importance of the question, "What is the semantic task?," is emphasized. The paper offers an alternative view of the meaning of a name based on the causal theory.

DEWASHI, Mahadev. Is Causal Relation Asymmetrical. Indian Phil Quart, SUPP 16(4), 1-8, O 89.

DEWASHI, Mahadev. Temporal Versus Manipulability Theory of Causal Asymmetry. Indian Phil Quart, SUPP 17(1), 15-23, Ja 90.

DI COSTANZO, Giuseppe. Meinecke e Dilthey. Arch Stor Cult, 1, 283-289, 1988.

DI FRANCESCO, Michele and DE MONTICELLI, Roberta. Lingua degli angli e lingua dei bruti. Teoria, 9(1), 69-137, 1989.

DI MARCO, Chiara. J Patocka: L'esistenza umana come "vita nella verità". Aquinas, 32(3), 553-561, S-D 89.

DI NORCIA, Vincent. An Enterprise/Organization Ethic. Bus Prof Ethics J, 7(3-4), 61-79, Fall-Wint 88.

Since we have no valid ethical theory one must derive ethics from the

institutions involved. In this essay I focus on two central aspects of business: as enterprise and organization. The idea of ethical excellence helps reinterpret the product-market functions of an enterprise, showing how it transcends purely technical and financial norms. It also requires one to think of the firm as a social institution crosscut by mutual exchanges and obligations.

DI NORCIA, Vincent. The Hard Problem of Management is Freedom, Not the Commons. Bus Prof Ethics J, 6(3), 57-71, Fall 87.

DI NORCIA, Vincent. The Leverage of Foreigners: Multinationals in South Africa. J Bus Ethics, 8(11), 864-872, N 89.

This article argues that foreign multinational corporations (MNCs) in South Africa cannot evade an ethical choice, how best to exercise their leverage against apartheid? Disinvestment is only one, ambiguous option. MNCs need clear ethical goals and an effective strategy. Both arise from the political economy of the MNC. It involves three relationships, between the MNC parent and its subsidiary; the MNC home society and host society; and the MNC home state and host state. That political economy explains the MNC's dependency and modernization effects. Those effects give foreigners some leverage against apartheid; but an effective and ethical MNC strategy is needed. It involves four goals: dismantling apartheid, a mixed economy, full democracy, and a negotiated peace. It suggests a sequence of MNC/home state options from Do Nothing or Divest to More Corporate Activism, Home State Support, and International Sanctions. But victory is not around the corner; rather, we are all condemned to freedom.

DI NUCCI PEARCE, M Rosaria and PEARCE, David. Technology versus Science: The Cognitive Fallacy. Synthese, 81(3), 405-419, D 89.

There are fundamental differences between the explanation of scientific change and the explanation of technological change. The differences arise from fundamental differences between scientific and technological knowledge and basic disanalogies between technological advance and scientific progress. Given the influence of economic markets and industrial and institutional structures on the development of technology, it is more plausible to regard technological change as a continuous and incremental process, rather than as a process of Kuhnian crises and revolutions.

DI VONA, Piero. Il problema delle distinzioni nella filosofia di Spinoza. Stud Spinozana, 4, 147-164, 1988.

The question of distinctions is fundamental for an understanding of Spinoza's philosophy. It arises at the very beginning of the *Ethics* (E1Ax1), and governs the principal articulations of the Dutch philosopher's doctrine—substance and mode, substance and attribute, attribute and mode—as well as the inner relations which flow from the distinctions Spinoza draws between individuals and modes, and between modes of diverse attributes and a mediating atttribute. Among other things, the problem of distinctions bears upon such issues as the relation of essence and existence within God's modes, attributes and properties in God, and the nature and limitations of the modal distinction in Spinoza. While it does not aim at a complete resolution of the problem of distinctions, the article does strive to explicate the difficulties, and to underline the main implications which follow from Spinoza's thought.

DI ZIEREGA, Gus. Democracy as a Spontaneous Order. Crit Rev, 3(2), 206-240, Spr 89.

DIACONESCU, Carmen. Le concept de style culturel et le monde des valeurs (in Romanian). Rev Filosof (Romania), 35(6), 570-577, N-D 88.

DIAMOND, Michael L. A Modern Theistic Argument. Mod Theol, 6(3), 287-293, Ap 90.

A theistic argument is put forward by Brian Hebblethwaite (in *The Ocean of Truth: A Defence of Objective Theism*, Cambridge University Press, 1988): an argument to God from the nature of *truth*. In this article Hebblethwaite's argument is stated, its nature examined, its logical status and its credibility are assessed. Also discussed is its place within a cumulative case for theistic belief. The argument is found to be *a posteriori* in character, broadly conforming to recognised canons of rationality and, being grounded in the nature of reality, of considerable potential to convince the unbeliever. That is, even apart from its companion arguments of the cumulative defence.

DIAS, M F and PORTELA FILHO, R N A. Teoría de la recursión y lógica. Rev Filosof (Argentina), 2(2), 107-117, N 87.

This expositive paper is devoted to show some relations between logic and recursivity, particularly recursivity as applied to completeness-proof in first order logic.

DIAWARA, Manthia. Reading Africa Through Foucault: V Y Mudimbe's Re-affirmation of the Subject. Quest, 4(1), 74-93, Je 90.

DÍAZ, Esther. La Brujería: un Invento Moderno. Manuscrito, 12(2), 65-82, O 89.

This paper follows Foucault's thought and deals with one of the constituents of non-reason: witchcraft. The difference between sorcery and witchcraft is examined as well as the social and legal framework which made possible witch-hunting in the 16th and 17th centuries. The analysis further tries to show the modes of discourse which set up the notion of the diabolical. The figure of the woman as a privileged object of persecution is underlined. A Western feminine image from the 11th to the 17th century is disclosed. In both "courteous love" and witchcraft the woman is conceived in contradistinction to the figure of the Virgin Mary. An interpretation of the meaning of these three figures is suggested, and a relationship between the confinement of witches in the 18th century and hysteria in 19th century positivism is advanced.

DIAZ, Ruben. "The Person: Experience of Transcendence Through Immanence" in *The Social Context and Values: Perspectives of the Americas*, MC LEAN, George F (ed), 161-191. Lanham, Univ Pr of America, 1989.

The human person is not an abstraction but a historical process to be experienced by man. He lives his experience in a concrete social and natural context, becoming aware of his personal existence while he is acting. His action follows to his being. From his immanent existence he is aware of his own transcendence and, through his personal transcendence he can discover gradually the transcendent being. The purpose of my work was to show history as a pathway to transcendence and even to the encounter with the transcendent person, God.

DICKIE, George. *Evaluating Art*. Philadelphia, Temple Univ Pr, 1988

In this book I advance an instrumentalist theory of art evaluation. I discuss the views of Ziff, Beardsley, Sibley, Goodman, Wolterstorff, Hume, Vermazen, and Urmson, and I criticize their views, organize their insights, fill in gaps, and work out a theory of art evaluation. The instrumentalist view I develop admits the artistic value or disvalue of the aesthetic qualities, the representational and other cognitive characteristics, and the moral characteristics of art. Following Hume, the view developed is a relativistic one. The view, following Vermazen, allows for a limited comparison of the values of works of art. An attempt is made to work out a basis for specific evaluations, that is, for evaluation such as "This work is good," "This work is excellent," etc.

DICKINSON, Anthony and HEYES, Cecilia. The Intentionality of Animal Action. Mind Lang, 5(1), 87-104, Spr 90.

DIDIER, Michel. Forming of an Honorable Man in Classical China: The Junzi's Education (in Serbo-Croatian). Filozof Istraz, 29(2), 489-498, 1989.

Two notions, denoting the same concept in both Western and Chinese philosophy, are explained in this paper. Each individual has to develop the notions in order to maintain peace, welfare and social harmony. The Western tradition describes the concept as "the honorable man," the Chinese as "junzi." The author explores the two basic meanings of the latter: "prince, king, emperor" is the first meaning, "wise duke, sage a friend of sagehood" the second one.

DIENHART, John W and FODERICK, Saundra I. Ethical and Conceptual Issues in Charitable Investments, Cause Related Marketing, and Advertising. Bus Prof Ethics J, 7(3-4), 47-59, Fall-Wint 88.

DIETRICH, Eric. Computationalism. Soc Epistem, 4(2), 135-154, Ap-Je 90.

Computationalism is the hypothesis that cognizing is computing partial recursive functions. The task of the computational cognitive scientist is discovering the functions and explaining them as the execution of algorithms. This paper is intended to be the computationalist's manifesto; it spells out what the computationalist is and is not committed to. For example, computationalists are not committed to any claims about which functions are computed by a cognizer, nor how they are computed; they are committed to the claim that both humans and computers have intentionality; and they deny that, when making decisions, humans willfully select among alternatives.

DIETRICH, Therese. Das Konzept einer "wahren" Politik des Friedrich Gentz. Deut Z Phil, 38(4), 346-353, 1990.

The article reconstructs a discussion about the relation between theory/philosophy and practice from 1793. It shows that the major political writer Friedrich Gentz (1764-1832), the translator of Edmund Burke's (1729-1797) *Reflections on the Revolution in France* (1790), called for a "pragmatic theory of wisdom" as a substitute for the "German theory of the French Revolution." The article seeks a line in Kant's work *Über den Gemeinspruch* as a polemic with Gentz. It may be all right in theory, but is no use in practice—Gentz, the man of honour, feels entitled to disdain theory.

DIEZ, Amparo. Enunciados de identidad. Anu Filosof, 21(2), 135-143, 1988.

DIFFEY, T J. "The Evaluation of Works of Art" in *Cultural Hermeneutics of Modern Art: Essays in Honor of Jan Aler*, DETHIER, Hubert (ed), 135-150. Amsterdam, Rodopi, 1989.

Contemporary art provides little room for the spectator; it offers little worth seeing. Many works are resistant to the kinds of comparative evaluative judgments encouraged by traditional works and analysed by Hume. Much contemporary art is beyond evaluation. We can specify what aesthetic standards were used traditionally but cannot say what ours are. "Experimental" is often treated as an intrinsic value of contemporary art; this is irrational since "experimental" can only be instrumental. Interpretation has displaced evaluation. We ask of an art work what it means, where the eighteenth century asked: is it good?

DIFFEY, T J. Schopenhauer's Account of Aesthetic Experience. Brit J Aes, 30(2), 132-142, Ap 90.

First a brief exposition is given of Schopenhauer's aesthetics of representational art, but not music, reconstructed from his *World as Will and Idea*. The influence of this aesthetics upon Anglo-American aesthetics since World War Two is then examined. The paper concludes with an account of the problems Schopenhauer's aesthetics poses for us now.

DILLEY, Frank B. The Free-Will Defence and Worlds Without Moral Evil. Int J Phil Relig, 27(1-2), 1-15, Ap 90.

Steven E Boër's claim that the free-will defence fails because God could (a) have created people who are allowed to attempt to do evil and also, (b) have prevented them from actually accomplishing that evil by an appropriate "coincidence" miracle, has previously been refuted by the present author. This paper replies to an effort by Robert McKim to overcome the alleged defects in Boër's argument by offering a modification. My claim is that far from improving on Boër's original argument, the McKim modification undermines what little was persuasive about Boër's case without offering any compensating advantages which would make Boër's case more plausible.

DILLON, John. Logos and Trinity: Patterns of Platonist Influence on Early Christianity. Philosophy, 25, 1-13, 89 Supp.

DILLON, John. Salomon Ibn Gabirol's Doctrine of Intelligible Matter. Irish Phil J, 6(1), 59-81, 1989.

An attempt to relate Ibn Gabirol's doctrine of intelligible matter to earlier Neoplatonic doctrine, particularly that of Plotinus in *Ennead* II4. Possible intermediaries are discussed, particularly Isaac Israeli, and pseudo-Empedocles, in the *Book of the Five Substances*.

DILLON, Martin C. Desire for All/Love of One: Tomas's Tale in *The Unbearable Lightness of Being*. Phil Today, 33(4), 347-357, Wint 89.

This is an attempt to test deconstructive techniques of interpretation in the context of Kundera's novel, *The Unbearable Lightness of Being*. The novel describes the lovesex relation between its two major characters and tacitly questions whether the destiny of the relation is essential or accidental. I try to show (1) that the binary opposition in whose terms the question is posed is misconceived, but (2) that an appeal to *differance* does not improve our understanding of the issues. I then (3) provide a nondeconstructive reading of the novel that offers a competitive model of the role of metaphor in interpreting narrative.

DILWORTH, Craig. "The Gestalt Model of Scientific Progress" in *Scientific Knowledge Socialized*, HRONSZKY, Imre (ed), 299-311. Norwell, Kluwer, 1989.

DILWORTH, David A. The Critique of Logocentrism, or (Else) Derrida's Dead Line. J Chin Phil, 17(1), 5-18, Mr 90.

DILWORTH, David A. Santayana and Democritus—Two Mutually Interpreting Philosophical Poets. Bull Santayana Soc, 7, 9-19, Fall 89.

DIMA, Teodor. De la "révélation" et de l' "irrationnel" dans la "Connaissance luciférienne" (in Romanian). Rev Filosof (Romania), 36(2), 149-154, Mr-Ap 89.

DINGBO, Wu. 1987 Controversy Over the Evaluations of Confucius. J Chin Phil, 16(3-4), 419-436, D 89.

DINWIDDY, J R. Adjudication under Bentham's Pannomion. Utilitas, 1(2), 283-289, N 89.

DIORIO, Joseph A. Feminist-Constructionist Theories of Sexuality and the Definition of Sex Education. Educ Phil Theor, 21(2), 23-31, 1989.

Work and sex pervade contemporary life. Both are central to personal identity, and to where individuals position themselves or to where they are placed within society. Despite parallels in the influence they have on human lives, work and sex have been dealt with very differently within educational theory. Work has long been recognized as theoretically central to education, and much literature has examined the definition and origins of work and its connection with education from a range of competing perspectives. Sex has rarely been seen as theoretically problematical by educators. The recent development of constructionist theories of sexuality, while as yet having little impact on discussion of sex education, nonetheless pose important questions for the ways in which such education can be conceptualized, and how its purposes and subject matter should be defined. (edited)

DISHKANT, Herman. Mathematics of Totalities: An Alternative to Mathematics of Sets. Stud Log, 47(4), 319-326, D 88.

I dare say, a set is contranatural if some pair of its elements has a nonempty intersection. So, we consider only collections of disjoint nonempty elements and call them totalities. We propose the propositional logic *TT*, where a proposition letters some totality. The proposition is true if it letters the greatest totality. There are five connectives in *TT*, and the last is called plexus. The truth of σ * π means that any element of the totality σ has a nonempty intersection with any element of the totality π. An imbedding *G* of the classical predicate logic *CPL* in *TT* is defined. A formula *f* of *CPL* is a classical tautology if and only if *G(f)* is always true in *TT*. So, mathematics may be expounded in *TT*, without quantifiers. (edited)

DO CARMO SILVA, Carlos Henrique. Da indiferenciação do dizer ao *autómaton* do falar. Rev Port Filosof, 45(2), 247-285, Ap-Je 89.

The present study is a critical essay on the question of language's limits in Wittgenstein's thought. The view of this study observes how Wittgensteinian method proceeds. This investigation adopts a pluralistic model of speech, from several points of view, which not only allow to deconstruct the pseudo-unity of reason, but also make possible to investigate about the inner limits of Wittgenstein's analysis. As a conclusion, the author points out, not only the outlines of the so-called "rethoric moral" of language in Wittgenstein philosophy, but also to original views. (edited)

DOBBS, Elizabeth A (trans) and APOSTLE, Hippocrates G (trans) and PARSLOW, Morris A (trans) and ARISTOTLE,. *Aristotle's Poetics*. Grinnell, Peripatetic Pr, 1990

DOBBS-WEINSTEIN, Idit. "Medieval Biblical Commentary and Philosophical Inquiry" in *Moses Maimonides and His Time*, ORMSBY, Eric L (ed), 101-120. Washington, Cath Univ Amer Pr, 1989.

The paper examines Maimonides' and Aquinas's biblical exegetical practice as an instance of philosophical prudence through an inquiry into their respective approaches to interpretation in general, to that of the Book of Job in particular. In contrast to the predominant scholarship on the questions of providence and theodicy which address the tension between divine knowledge, human freedom and evil, this study focuses upon the possibility, nature and scope of human knowledge of providence. The conclusion reached is that for both thinkers Job's transgression consists of an intellectual hubris of a kind that precludes a true understanding of providence and of evil.

DOBSON, John. The Role of Ethics in Global Corporate Culture. J Bus Ethics, 9(6), 481-488, Je 90.

Whatever ethnic, religious, or other cultural boundaries may have evolved through history, a global corporate culture is increasingly subsuming these traditional divisions. Multinational corporations, internationally linked securities markets, and omnipresent communication networks characterize this global corporate culture. The dynamics of corporate culture centres on the intricate web of contractual relations between stakeholders. This study addresses the question of how these stakeholder contracts can be most efficiently enforced. Three alternative contractual enforcement mechanisms are identified: the legal system, a generally accepted moral code, and stakeholders' desire to build and maintain reputations. Each alternative is critically evaluated and conclusions are drawn as to the relative feasibility and desirability of each enforcement mechanism.

DOBUZINSKIS, Laurent. The Complexities of Spontaneous Order. Crit Rev, 3(2), 241-266, Spr 89.

An evolutionary vision of natural and societal self-organizing processes is well on the way to replacing the conventional "scientific method." F A Hayek's analysis of the notion of "spontaneous order" is a significant contribution to this new paradigm. The libertarian implications Hayek derives from it, however, are open to question. An exploration of the ecology of spontaneous social orders is proposed as an alternative context of interpretation.

DOEPKE, Frederick. The Endorsements of Interpretation. Phil Soc Sci, 20(3), 277-294, S 90.

Support is given to Habermas's argument that we interpret thoughts only by seeing persons as actually justified in their circumstances. Habermas holds further that his argument extends to moral thinking, in that we understand it only by actually taking the moral point of view, and he thinks this is illustrated

by Kohlberg's theory of moral development. While this illustration is denied here on the ground that Kohlberg's theory accepts Rawls's theory of justice, it is argued that the extension to morality can be made with a theory like Gewirth's, in which morality appears as a form of rationality.

DOERINGER, Franklin M. Unto the Mountain: Toward a Paradigm for Early Chinese Thought. J Chin Phil, 17(2), 135-156, Je 90.

This piece seeks to reappraise the "paradigm" within which we discuss early Chinese thought to avoid what Edward Said in *Orientalism* calls Western scholarship's "formidable structure of cultural domination." Using Foucault's notion of an "archaeology of knowledge" which looks below the symbolic level of thought, it suggests we bypass that domination by deriving our discourse about early Chinese thought from the study of concrete "exemplars" in the sinitic tradition instead of the Western philosophic legacy. As an illustration, it analyses some Han Chinese artifacts associated with cosmology to discuss three paradigmatic aspects of early Chinese thought: centricity, circularity, and circumfluency.

DOETS, Kees. Monadic Π_1^1-Theories of Π_1^1-Properties. Notre Dame J Form Log, 30(2), 224-240, Spr 89.

Axiomatizations are provided for the monadic universal second-order theories of scattered orderings, well-orderings, complete orderings, the ordering of the natural numbers, of the reals, and of well-founded trees. Proofs employ the Ehrenfeucht-Fraïssé-game.

DOHERTY, Thomas. Towards—and Away from—an Aesthetic of Popular Culture. J Aes Educ, 22(4), 31-43, Wint 88.

In departments of history, literature, communication, and combinations thereof, the traditional doctrine of a qualitative cultural hierarchy, of the unquestioned superiority of one kind of art over another, is not so much under assault as in full retreat. Political criteria have replaced aesthetic judgments in the bulk of popular culture criticism.

DOLBY, R G A. The Possibility of Computers Becoming Persons. Soc Epistem, 3(4), 321-336, O-D 89.

DOLGOV, Konstantin M and JARKOWSKI, Jan (trans). The Politician and the Philosopher (Some Lessons from Machiavelli). Dialec Hum, 15(3-4), 59-66, Sum-Autumn 88.

DOLORES FOLLIERO, Granzia. Grazia e dignità dell'estetica schilleriana. Aquinas, 32(1), 107-130, Ja-Ap 89.

DOMBROWSKI, Daniel A. Ambition. J Soc Phil, 20(3), 130-137, Wint 89.

The purpose of this article is to show that a consideration of Plato's and Aristotle's thought on ambition (*philotimia*) can contribute both to contemporary efforts to understand ambition and to the effort to develop a "virtue-based" ethics.

DOMBROWSKI, Daniel A. Back to Sainthood. Phil Today, 33(1), 56-62, Spr 89.

J O Urmson's theory of supererogation is defended against the criticisms of Elizabeth Pybus and Susan Wolf.

DOMBROWSKI, Daniel A. Two Vegetarian Puns at *Republic* 372. Ancient Phil, 9 (2), 167-171, Fall 89.

The purpose of this article is to point out two puns which help in determining the relationship between the first city in the *Republic* and Plato's own views regarding vegetarianism.

DONALDSON, Thomas. Morally Privileged Relationships. J Value Inq, 24(1), 1-15, Ja 90.

Should we favor fellow citizens, friends, family members and neighbors over non-family members, foreigners, and other global inhabitants? This article isolates a set of principles for determining the justified range of partiality. Utilizing thought experiments that consider hypothetical worlds devoid of favoritism, it concludes that one is frequently justified in exhibiting partiality to persons even in instances where traditional moral theory espouses impartiality. But it also argues that in some instances we are much less justified in exhibiting partiality than many suppose, in particular, to fellow citizens in contrast to foreigners—at least where "partiality" is defined to exclude hidden considerations of impartial morality. It follows that there is greater justification for partiality towards friends and family members than towards fellow citizens.

DONALDSON, Thomas. Social Contracts and Corporations: A Reply to Hodapp. J Bus Ethics, 9(2), 133-137, F 90.

In this reply to Professor Hodapp's criticism of my social contract theory, I focus on the misinterpretations I believe Professor Hodapp makes of the social contract tradition as well as my version of the contract. By misinterpreting the underlying purpose of social contract theory, he neglects the contract's heuristic or "functional" dimension, something that leads him to downplay the importance of the contract as a conceptual catalyst. And by adopting an overly narrow notion of rationality, he imagines circularity where none exists. Later, Professor Hodapp questions the effect of the contract upon individual liberties, and in doing so broaches a critical issue. But I attempt to show that his concerns are eliminated by close attention to the theory itself.

DONATO, Eugenio. "Ending/Closure: On Derrida's Margining of Heidegger" in *The Textual Sublime: Deconstruction and Its Differences*, SILVERMAN, Hugh J (ed), 37-51. Albany, SUNY Pr, 1990.

DONCHIN, Anne. The Growing Feminist Debate Over the New Reproductive Technologies. Hypatia, 4(3), 136-149, Fall 89.

A critical review of four recent works that reflect current conflicts and tensions among feminists regarding new reproductive technologies: *In Search of Parenthood* by Judith Lasker and Susan Borg; *Ethics and Human Reproduction* by Christine Overall; *Made to Order*, Patricia Spallone and Deborah Steinberg, eds.; and *Reproductive Technologies: Gender, Motherhood and Medicine*, Michelle Stanworth, ed. Their positions are evaluated against the background of growing feminist dialogue about the future of reproduction and the bearing of reproductive innovations on such related issues as racism, sexuality, motherhood and abortion.

DONDER, Hans-Dieter and LEVINSKI, J P. Some Principles Related to Chang's Conjecture. Annals Pure Applied Log, 45(1), 39-101, N 89.

We determine the consistency strength of the negation of the transversal hypothesis. We also study other variants of Chang's conjecture.

DONNELLAN, Keith S. Belief and the Identity of Reference. Midwest Stud Phil, 14, 275-288, 1989.

It has been argued that the theory of "direct reference" involves an unacceptable paradox about belief. Saul Kripke's paper "A Puzzle about Belief" generates the paradox from certain plausible principles about belief ascription, principles, he holds, that the opponents of the direct reference view must accept. The present paper accepts Kripke's general strategy for defending the direct reference theory, but argues that the paradox involves our concept of belief itself, not merely principles of disquotation and translation. It suggests an analogy with the kind of situation involved in the paradox of the ship of Theseus.

DONNELLEY, Strachan (ed) and NOLAN, Kathleen (ed). Animals, Science, and Ethics. Hastings Center Rep, 20(3), Supp 1-32, My-Je 90.

This special supplement is the result of a Hastings Center Project, "The Ethics of Animal Experimentation and Research." The project involved a multidisciplinary group of animal researchers and welfarists, veterinarians, physicians, and bioethicists. The group tried systematically to develop a position that was at once pro animal welfare and pro legitimate science—a "troubled middle" position between more extreme animal rightists and human welfarists. There are sections on the moral status of animals, the ethical justification of animal experiments, animal suffering and cultural anthropomorphism, TACUCs, and the adequacy of present federal regulations of animal use in science.

DONNELLY, John (ed). Reflective Wisdom: Richard Taylor on Issues That Matter. Buffalo, Prometheus, 1989

A collection of 29 of Richard Taylor's essays (some previously unpublished) on a wide range of issues: the search for wisdom, the meaning of life, the mysterious relationship between self and world, liberty and the nature of government, the evidence for various religious claims, hedonism, the concepts of rights and justice, the nature of ethics, virtue, and the search for personal happiness, love and friendship, marriage, materialism, and fatalism. The editor provides a general introduction, along with introductory remarks that precede each of the book's five parts. Taylor offers herein a vision of philosophy as wonder and insight, along with conceptual analysis.

DONNELLY, William J and MILLER, Gary A. The Treadway Commission Recommendations for Education: Professor's Opinions. Bus Prof Ethics J, 8(4), 83-92, Wint 89.

Our study was developed to obtain information about the beliefs and perceptions of accounting professors regarding the four specific recommendations made by the Treadway Commission for educators. A questionnaire was developed and sent to 500 members of the American Accounting Association. The professors we surveyed strongly agreed with the four Treadway recommendations for educators. Fraudulent financial reporting and ethics issues need to be integrated into accounting curriculum. All accounting courses, not just auditing, need to be included. Increased coverage of ethics issues is strongly supported.

DONNO, A. Il radicalismo negli Stati Uniti degli anni '80: l'anarco-ecologismo di Murray Bookchin. Il Protag, 6(9-10), 49-64, Je-D 86.

DONOUGHO, Martin. The Language of Architecture. J Aes Educ, 21(3), 53-67, Fall 87.

This article enquires into the analogy that has commonly been drawn between architecture and language. It asks first what "language" might mean: a logical model, speech act model, involving double articulation or a generative grammar, or *langue* vs *parole*, as behaviorist, or Goodmanian. It then examines which architectural features might correspond to these definitions, coming to a sceptical conclusion. Finally, a notion of style as code or convention is defended.

DONOUGHO, Martin. "Music and History" in *What is Music?*, ALPERSON, Philip A , 327-348. New York, Haven, 1987.

This article looks briefly at the historicality of music. It begins by observing that music has only recently acquired a history, and examines modes of writing it. It proceeds to music in history, where the latter is more than artistic or high culture, and then to the history of aesthetic theories that sponsor music as practice.

DONOUGHO, Martin. The Woman in White: On the Reception of Hegel's *Antigone*. Owl Minerva, 21(1), 65-89, Fall 89.

This article examines Hegel's ethico-political approach to the play, and outlines the controversies surrounding it in the 150 years following. It goes on to answer some criticisms by clearing up misconceptions; in particular, it focusses on Hegel's distinction between ancient and modern psychology. Finally it sketches Hegel's theory of tragedy as both mode of presentation and mimesis of ethical content.

DONOVAN, Peter. Neutrality in Religious Studies. Relig Stud, 26(1), 103-115, Mr 90.

What counts as 'neutrality' in the academic study of religion? The answer will be found in actual cases rather than in theory and generalization. 'Observer-neutrality' and 'participant-neutrality' are found to be largely unattainable, and 'role-neutrality' is offered as the notion most likely to find an application in practice. Whether the study of religion can be role-neutral about its own methodology, and whether it should attempt to be, are further questions considered.

DOOLEY, Patrick. William James on the Human Ways of Being. Personalist Forum, 6(1), 75-85, Spr 90.

My paper argues that James's concept of man centers upon our ability to select a variety of ways of being from reality's rich reservoir. I begin with his effort to capture the raw, undifferentiated, primordial stuff available to experience, "a blooming, buzzing confusion." Next I examine his contrast of normal, adult human consciousness with that of dogs and other animals on one hand, infants and the insane, on the other. Third I discuss James's celebration of humans' practical, survival-oriented goals as well as our "useless," nonutilitarian interests. My reading of James, then, stresses his catholic tolerance of variety and plurality in the human ways of being.

DOORMAN, L M. A Note on the Existence Property for Intuitionistic Logic with Function Symbols. Z Math Log, 36(1), 17-21, 1990.

The existence property for intuitionistic first order logic is reconsidered. This property is proved by Prawitz for an arbitrary language without function symbols. A generalization is outlined in the paper. For the generalization we use the unification theorem, known from the resolution method in automated theorem proving. With this theorem the complexity of the terms in a derivation is minimized.

DOPPELT, G. Beyond Liberalism and Communitarianism: Towards a Critical Theory of Social Justice. Phil Soc Crit, 14(3-4), 271-292, 1988.

DOPPELT, Gerald. The Naturalist Conception of Methodological Standards in Science. Phil Sci, 57(1), 1-19, Mr 90.

In this essay, the author criticizes Laudan's view that methodological rules in science are best understood as hypothetical imperatives, for example, to realize cognitive aim A, follow method . The author criticizes his idea that such rules are best evaluated by a naturalized philosophy of science which collects the empirical evidence bearing on the soundness of these rules. The author's claim is that this view yields a poor explanation of (1) the role of methodological rules in establishing the rationality of scientific practices, (2) the debates scientists have over rival methodological rules, and (3) the reasons on the basis of which scientists actually embrace, challenge, or transform methodological rules. (edited)

DORDAL, P L. Towers in $[\omega]^\omega$ and $^\omega\omega$. Annals Pure Applied Log, 45(3), 247-276, D 89.

DORE, Clement. More on the Possibility of God. Faith Phil, 7(3), 340-343, Jl 90.

In this paper, I draw a distinction between two kinds of impossibility and maintain that one is entitled to suppose that they do not obtain, in the absence of a reason to think that they do. I claim that there is no reason to think that the first kind obtains with respect to God and that, though there are non-negligible arguments that the second kind does, my argument for the possibility of God, which appeared in an earlier volume of this journal, adequately rebuts those arguments.

DORFMAN, Beatriz and LARRETA, Juan Rodriguez. Sobre la privacidad de los estados de conciencia. Analisis Filosof, 7(2), 77-95, N 87.

DÖRING, Klaus. Gab es eine Dialektische Schule? Phronesis, 34(3), 293-310, 1989.

Until recently, students of ancient philosophy have generally believed that Diodorus Cronus was a member of the Megarian school founded by Socrates' pupil Euclides of Megara. In 1977, however, David Sedley claimed that Diodorus should be associated with the so-called Dialectical school. The article argues against this view. The main results are (1) There are no testimonies which suggest that we should distinguish between Megarians and Dialecticians. (2) The so-called Dialectical school never existed; it is a construct of ancient historians of philosophy.

DORITY, Barbara. Feminist Moralism, "Pornography," and Censorship. Humanist, 49(6), 8-9,46, N-D 89.

The issue of "pornography" has engendered intense debate within the feminist movement. Most feminists exhibit a classic moralistic, pro-censorship mindset. Many feminist leaders promote Minneapolis-style anti-pornography ordinances. The author, executive director of the Washington Coalition Against Censorship and founder of the Northwest Feminist Anti-Censorship Taskforce (NW-FACT), argues that this viewpoint diverts attention from the real issues, is anti-sex, demeans women who have made a decision to work in the sex industry, and jeopardizes civil liberties. A rational analysis is necessary to overcome longstanding feminist dogma and demagoguery and restore integrity to the movement.

DORSCHEL, A. Darwinism as a Prohibition of Criticism: A Commentary on Friedrich August von Hayek's Theory of Moral Evolution. Int J Moral Soc Stud, 5(1), 55-66, Spr 90.

Friedrich August von Hayek, Economic Science Nobel prizewinner, has proposed an applied Darwinian theory of moral evolution of which the sole explanans is supposed to be the physical survival of social structures. Insofar as a group ethos is seen to be the result of natural selection, not the conscious choice of the agents of reason and the will who comprise the group, it is exempt from being criticised by them. This type of reasoning contains a genetic fallacy, and has the form of a manifest contradiction in arguing against all argumentation, or of precluding thought from thinking. Certain significant aspects of the object to be explained, i.e., morality, remain unexplained in the proposed theory.

DORSCHEL, Andreas. Handlungstypen und Kriterien: Zu Habermas' "Theorie des kommunikativen Handelns". Z Phil Forsch, 44(2), 220-252, 1990.

In seiner "Theorie des kommunikativen Handelns" hat Jürgen Habermas vorgeschlagen, drei Typen rationalen Handelns zu unterscheiden: instrumentelles Handeln, strategisches Handeln, kommunikatives Handeln. Diese Unterscheidung kann Habermas zufolge entlang dreier Kriterien gezogen werden: die Handlungstypen praesupponierten jeweils verschiedene "ontologische Voraussetzungen", d.i. die Bezugnahme auf verschiedene "Welten" ("subjective Welt" vs. "objektive Welt" vs. "soziale Welt"), seien auf verschiedene Typen von Motivation bezogen ("empirische Motivation" vs. "rationale Motivation"), und implizierten unterschiedliche "Einstellungen" der Aktoren ("Erfolgsorientierung" vs. "Verstaendigungsorientierung"). Demgegenüber wird die These vertreten, dass die ersten beiden Kriterien unbrauchbar sind, und das dritte mit Schwierigkeiten behaftet ist.

DORSCHEL, Andreas. Die soziobiologische Obsoletierung des "Reichs der Zwecke". Gregorianum, 71(1), 5-22, 1990.

In view of the theory of the genetic foundations of social behaviour of organisms (man included) which is called sociobiology, the author analyzes the endeavour which tries to legitimate by the science of nature a cynic anthropology. This endeavour presupposes that man is a machine, rejects the determination at which the great practical philosophy arrives about man as a being which has its end in itself, declares illusive the unity of subjectivity, and negates man's morality and free choice. A sketch of a critique of this doctrine is presented, in a rough outline, and then in relation to one of the theorems, namely that of genetic determinism.

DORSCHEL, Andreas. What Is It To Understand a Directive Speech Act? Austl J Phil, 67(3), 319-340, S 89.

The concept of "conditions of fulfillment" or "compliance" or "satisfaction" has been introduced by some authors in order to provide analyses of meaning which are just as adequate to directive speech acts as truth-conditional semantics are (claimed to be) adequate to assertive speech

acts. It is argued that this aim is missed. Most analyses (except those of some primitive cases) will remain throughout incomplete as long as they are not supplemented by a specification of conditions of normative validity. In the case of several illocutionary verbs they can be substituted by conditions under which the speaker could make use of sanctions against the hearer.

DORSEY, Gray L. *Jurisculture, Volume II: India*. New Brunswick, Transaction Books, 1990

Jurisculture studies historical attempts to form and govern authentic, effective, and just societies by adapting prevailing beliefs about reality, knowing, and desiring to serve the ends of survival, well-being, and higher aspirations. Volume II looks at prevailing beliefs of traditional India in the Vedas, Jainism, Buddhism, carvakian materialism, the great epic poems (*Ramayana* and *Mahabharata*), and the six orthodox systems of Hindu philosophy, and traces the influences of these beliefs in society and family life from 1500 BC to AD 1500.

DORTER, Kenneth. Diairesis and the Tripartite Soul in the *Sophist*. Ancient Phil, 10(1), 41-61, Spr 90.

The *Republic* and its predecessors interpret sophistry as the employment of reason in the service of the appetites (or spiritedness). But although the *Sophist* defines sophistry in several ways, none of which is entirely satisfactory, it never discusses this earlier approach. It proceeds entirely in terms of material products rather than value-laden goals. The tripartite soul is not mentioned, and attentiveness to difference of value is actively discouraged. At the same time, however, the dialogue abounds with allusions to the tripartite soul and value. My essay explores this tension and suggests a resolution that also explains the six preliminary definitions and the purpose of the trilogy as a whole.

DOSEN, Kosta. Duality Between Modal Algebras and Neighbourhood Frames. Stud Log, 48(2), 219-234, Je 89.

This paper presents duality results between categories of neighbourhood frames for modal logic and categories of modal algebras (i.e., Boolean algebras with an additional unary operation). These results extend results of Goldblatt and Thomason about categories of relational frames for modal logic.

DOSEN, Kosta. Sequent-Systems and Groupoid Models, I. Stud Log, 47(4), 353-385, D 88.

The purpose of this paper is to connect the proof theory and the model theory of a family of propositional logics weaker than Heyting's. This family includes systems analogous to the Lambek calculus of syntactic categories, systems of relevant logic, systems related to BCK algebras, and, finally, Johansson's and Heyting's logic. This paper lays the ground for a kind of correspondence theory for axioms of logics with implication weaker than Heyting's, a correspondence theory analogous to the correspondence theory for modal axioms of normal modal logics. The first part of the paper contains the first two sections, which deal with sequent-systems and Hilbert-formulations. The second part, which will appear in the next issue of this journal, deals with groupoid models. (edited)

DOSEN, Kosta. Sequent-Systems and Groupoid Models, II. Stud Log, 48(1), 41-65, Mr 89.

The purpose of this paper is to connect the proof theory and the model theory of a family of propositional logics weaker than Heyting's. This family includes systems analogous to the Lambek calculus of syntactic categories, systems of relevant logic, systems related to BCK algebras, and, finally, Johansson's and Heyting's logic. This paper lays the ground for a kind of correspondence theory for axioms of logics with implication weaker than Heyting's, a correspondence theory analogous to the correspondence theory for modal axioms of normal modal logics. This is the sequel to the first part of the paper, which appeared in a previous issue of this journal. The first part contained sections on sequent-systems and Hilbert-formulations, and here is the third section on groupoid models. This second part is meant to be read in conjunction with the first part. (edited)

DOSEN, Kosta and SCHROEDER-HEISTER, Peter. Uniqueness, Definability and Interpolation. J Sym Log, 53(2), 554-570, Je 88.

Starting from a notion of a consequence relation which captures only the structural aspects of logic, we prove generalizations of Craig's interpolation lemma and Beth's definability theorem which are not restricted to the syntactic categories of nonlogical constants.

DOSS, Seale. Who *Needs* a Theory of Informal Logic? Inform Log, 11(2), 111-118, Spr 89.

DOTTI, Jorge E. El Hobbes de Schmitt. Cuad Filosof, 20(32), 57-69, My 89.

The aim of this paper is to expose the main features of Carl Schmitt's interpretation of Thomas Hobbes. The author distinguishes three moments in

Schmitt's thought, but deals mainly with the second (namely with *Der Leviathan in der Staatslehre des Thomas Hobbes*, from 1938) and the third, which comprises the "Hinweise" to the 1963 edition of *Der Begriff des Politischen* and the article *Die Vollendung der Reformation* (1965). According to Schmitt, the leading idea of Hobbes: political philosophy is the attempt to restore the broken natural unity between the temporal and the spiritual powers. The Leviathan protects the individual liberty of conscience, and therefore rejects the illegitimate claims of the *potestates indirectae*, first of all the Catholic Church. After analysing Schmitt's version of the problem of transcendence in the Hobbesian system, the author proposes his own interpretation of the concept of "atheist" and of the idea of "God" in the work of 1651.

DOTTI, Jorge E. La razón en su uso regulativo y el a priori del "sistema" en la primera Crítica. Rev Filosof (Spain), 1, 83-103, 1987-88.

The appendix to the Transcendental Dialectic in the first *Critique* opens the Kantian *transcendental epistemology*. The categorial synthesis cannot work as condition of "systems," because it would cancel the contingency of such concepts dealing with species/genera features of Nature. Kant coordinates regulative reason with a more formal use of judgment and develops the interesting notion of "ideal objects." But the *transcendental* dimension of the third faculty is lacking: the unsolved problem is the specifically transcendental a priori of "not given" universals.

DOUBLE, Richard. Reply to Ward's "Philosophical Functionalism". Behaviorism, 17(2), 159-160, Fall 89.

In "Philosophical Functionalism" (*Behaviorism*, 1989), Andrew Ward claims that my "The Computational Model of the Mind and Philosophical Functionalism" (*Behaviorism*, 1987) begs the question against philosophical functionalism by assuming that sensations possess nonrelational characteristics that cannot be explained in funtional terms. In this reply I point out that my argument does not claim this, but only the much weaker premise that sensations appear to have such characteristics. I then show how the latter is strong enough to discredit philosophical functionalism.

DOUBLE, Richard. Sayre-McCord on Evaluative Facts. S J Phil, 28(2), 165-169, Sum 90.

In "Moral Theory and Explanatory Impotence" (*Essays on Moral Realism*, Cornell, 1988), Geoffrey Sayre-McCord argues that the preferability of some explanations over others demonstrates the existence of evaluative facts, thereby showing the existence of one type of value. In this paper, I argue that the preferability of explanations must be understood in such a way as to make clear the uselessness of such evaluative facts to the moral realist's case for the objectivity of values. Although there are many evaluative facts, they provide no reason to suppose that there are values in addition to the valuings done by persons.

DOUGLASS, R Bruce. Public Philosophy and Contemporary Pluralism. Thought, 64(255), 343-361, D 89.

DOW, Tsung-I. Das philosophische Menschenbild: Eine konfuzianische Sicht. Conceptus, 24(61), 35-42, 1990.

The fundamental concern of the Confucian philosophical undertaking was to understand man through the following questions: What is a man? How does one become a man? And why should one strive for the highest good to fulfill the meaning of man? The characteristics of the Confucians' answer were based on their assertion of the unity of what is, with what should be, the innate goodness in human nature, the dignity of man, and the primacy of harmonious balance in a twofold nature of world development. This view is unique because they see cognition as a process of harmonization of subject and object through the creativity of man, the unifier. Confucians focus on filial piety as the vehicle for actualizing *Ren*-reciprocal altruism which derives from the ontological assumption of a dialectical monist world outlook crystalized in Yin-Yang symbolic relationship.

DOWDALL, Terence and STEERE, Jane. On Being Ethical in Unethical Places: The Dilemmas of South African Clinical Psychologists. Hastings Center Rep, 20(2), 11-15, Mr-Ap 90.

Practicing under the social and economic conditions created by apartheid, South African clinical psychologists face the task of questioning both the traditional values and the traditional social role of their profession. Dilemmas of trust, confidentiality, and professional competence highlight the limits of professional ethical codes.

DOWE, Phil. On Tooley on Salmon. Austl J Phil, 67(4), 469-471, D 89.

DOWER, Nigel (ed). *Ethics and the Environmental Responsibility*. Aldershot, Avebury, 1989

Six professional philosophers cover various ethical issues raised by environmental problems. The book covers an introduction to environmental ethics, an examination of the metaphysics of environmentalism, the relevance of future generations, the treatment of animals, the constraints and opportunities for environmental protection raised by democracy, and the ethics of risk-taking in the nuclear industry. The issues are for the most part discussed from a human-centred perspective rather than that of deep ecology.

DOWER, Nigel. "What is Environmental Ethics?" in *Ethics and the Environmental Responsibility*, DOWER, Nigel (ed), 11-37. Aldershot, Avebury, 1989.

In this chapter, which introduces the book, I identify three dimensions of moral responsibility which are highlighted by environmental issues: local/global; human/nonhuman; present/future. Responsibility for the unintended and cumulative consequences of our actions is seen as the hallmark of environmental ethics. The need for a reevaluation of the nature of "the good life"/quality of life is stressed in the light of questioning the economic growth paradigm.

DOWNEY, R G. Intervals and Sublattices of the RE Weak Truth Table Degrees, Part II: Nonbounding. Annals Pure Applied Log, 44(3), 153-172, O 89.

It is shown that there exists an r.e. weak truth table degree $a \neq 0$ such that for all c less than or equal to a if the weak truth table degrees between 0 and c (inclusive) form a lattice, then c = 0.

DOWNEY, Rod. A Contiguous Nonbranching Degree. Z Math Log, 35(4), 375-383, 1989.

The author constructs the degree of the title answering a technical question of Stob. The techniques introduced have found other applications.

DOWNEY, Rod. On Hyper-Torre Isols. J Sym Log, 54(4), 1160-1166, D 89.

According to a theorem of Barback, a regressive isol is hereditarily odd/even (i.e., each predecessor has parity). Using this result the author constructs a co-simple hyper-torre isol.

DOWNIE, Jocelyn. Brain Death and Brain Life: Rethinking the Connection. Bioethics, 4(3), 216-226, Jl 90.

DRABMAN, Randy. A Philosopher's Stone in the Hands of Children: Using Classical Philosophy to Teach Children Mathematical Concepts. Thinking, 6(4), 19-27, 1986.

DRAGOMIRESCU, Lucian. Aspects socio-politiques, esthétiques et philosophiques dans l'oeuvre de Ion Heliade-Radulescu (in Romanian). Rev Filosof (Romania), 36(3), 240-245, My-Je 89.

DRAGOMIRESCU, Lucian. Idées esthétiques et morales dans le contexte aristique et scientifique de l'oeuvre d'A Odobescu (in Romanian). Rev Filosof (Romania), 36(1), 58-66, Ja-F 89.

DRAGONETTI, Carmen and TOLA, Fernando. La estructura de la mente según la escuela idealista budista (Yogachara). Pensamiento, 46(182), 129-147, Ap-Je 90.

Después de una somera información sobre las principales tendencias de la filosofía de la India, la escuela idealista budista y la teoría de las Tres Naturalezas, el artículo trata de la estructura de la mente en dicha escuela. La mente está formada por la conciencia-receptáculo, constituida por las impresiones subliminales dejadas por experiencias anteriores, y por la conciencia-función (conocimiento sensorial, mental y conciencia de "yo"), constituida a su vez por las impresiones subliminales hechas conscientes. Esta teoría explica la posición idealista extrema de la escuela. El artículo termina ocupándose de la teoría de la Mente Pura, que corona la concepción de la estructura de la mente propia de la filosofía budista idealista.

DRAGONETTI, Carmen and TOLA, Fernando. Some Remarks on Bhartrhari's Concept of Pratibhā. J Indian Phil, 18(2), 95-112, Je 90.

The word *pratibhā* is a very important one. It expresses some fundamental concepts. We start mentioning three of them, which have been analyzed in some valuable works. Other meanings, equally fundamental, will come to light when we study what Bhartrhari teaches about *pratibhā*. (edited)

DRANGE, Theodore M. Liar Syllogisms. Analysis, 50(1), 1-7, Ja 90.

Liar syllogisms are syllogisms yielding paradoxes similar to the Paradox of the Liar. Here is a self-referential example: (A) (1): (A) is not valid or else (A)'s premises are not both true. (2): But (A) *is* valid. (3): Hence, (A)'s premises are not both true. Since (2) is true, whether the second disjunct of (1) is classified as "true" or "false," a contradiction is derivable. To solve the problem, the "Dismissal Approach" dismisses liar syllogisms as "defective arguments with all their self-referential components truthvalueless." I reject this solution because it is counterintuitive and because some liar syllogisms are *not* self-referential.

DRESSER, Rebecca S. "Advance Directives, Self-Determination, and Personal Identity" in *Advance Directives in Medicine*, HACKLER, Chris (ed),

155-170. New York, Praeger, 1989.

In this chapter, I examine certain assumptions underlying the view that the advance directive is an appropriate mechanism to guide medical decision making on behalf of incompetent patients. I discuss the concept of changing selves over time and argue that the ability of a competent person to control future treatment should be limited when the former choices fail to protect the interests of the subsequent incompetent patient.

DRETSKE, Fred. Reply to Reviewers of "Explaining Behavior: Reasons in a World of Causes". Phil Phenomenol Res, 50(4), 819-839, Je 90.

Professors Stich and Millikan question my use of indication (or information) as a basis on which to build a semantics of thought. They also ask about my use of teleological concepts (indicator *functions*) in my analysis of mental representation. Professor Stampe argues that I fail to capture the rationalizing aspect of desire and Bratman that I have *two* theories about the intentional content of desire. Tuomela challenges my idea that explanations in terms of reasons always provide *structuring* causes of action. While conceding some points and clarifying others, the general theory about the way reasons explain behavior is amplified and defended.

DREYER, P S. Purpose as Historical Category (in Dutch). S Afr J Phil, 8(3-4), 182-186, N 88.

This article is an investigation into the concept of purpose or end as a fundamental category in the understanding of the past. Firstly a contrast is made between the concepts of purpose and *telos*, of which the latter is considered to be a concept in the metaphysics of history. Then the concept of purpose is analysed as a fundamental concept functioning in the practical existence of man. Thirdly a contrast is made between purpose and cause as categories of historical understanding.

DREYFUS, Hubert L. On the Ordering of Things: Being and Power in Heidegger and Foucault. S J Phil, SUPP(28), 83-96, 1989.

DROIT, Roger-Pol. "Schopenhauer et le Bouddhisme: Une 'Admirable Concordance'" in *Schopenhauer: New Essays in Honor of His 200th Birthday*, VON DER LUFT, Eric (ed), 123-138. Lewiston, Mellen Pr, 1989.

DROST, Mark P. The Primacy of Perception in Husserl's Theory of Imagining. Phil Phenomenol Res, 50(3), 569-582, Mr 90.

In the *Logical Investigations* Husserl outlines two distinct situations in which one speaks of an image: (a) there is the imaginal act in which one perceived physical object is an image of another perceivable object, and (b) there is the imaginal act in which a mental content is an intermediate in the intention of an object. In each case Husserl shows that the interpretation of anything as an image presupposes an object intentionally given to consciousness. Of the two imaginal acts, I argue that the first is logically dependent on a perceptual intention, and that the second is explicable in terms of a perceptual intention rather than in terms of pictorial representation. I conclude that nonmental images cannot be a paradigm for understanding the situation in which an image is a mental event, that images cannot be the basis for perceptual acts, and that Husserl is not committed to a picture theory of mental images.

DRUON, Michèle. "Deconstructing the Subject: An Ethical Paradox in the French Post-Structuralist Discourse" in *Inquiries into Values: The Inaugural Session of the International Society for Value Inquiry*, LEE, Sander H, 263-272. Lewiston, Mellen Pr, 1989.

The deconstruction of the classical conception of the subject through three main models of overdetermination—language, ideology, the unconscious—is generally perceived as the neutral product of an epistemological theory in the French deconstructionist discourse. But the opposite values given two of these models—ideology, the unconscious—simultaneously reveal the ethical dimension of deconstruction and its paradox, since both of these models imply a self-alienation. After analysis, this contradiction appears to originate in an impossible desire to differentiate oneself from the alienating scene of power, which paradoxically leads to a desire for self-alienation through the "other scene" of the unconscious. This wish for self-alienation, or self-deconstruction ultimately reveals a desire to exorcize the subject in oneself as a figure of power. Thus the deconstructed subject becomes a symptom of a hidden guilt, or the last figure of an impossible innocence.

DRYZEK, John S. Green Reason: Communicative Ethics for the Biosphere. Environ Ethics, 12(3), 195-210, Fall 90.

Exclusively instrumental notions of rationality not only reinforce attitudes conducive to the destruction of the natural world, but also undermine attempts to construct environmental ethics that involve more harmonious relationships between humans and nature. Deep ecologists and other ecological critics of instrumental rationality generally prefer some kind of spiritual orientation to nature. In this paper I argue against both instrumental rationalists and ecological spiritualists in favor of a communicative

rationality which encompasses the natural world. I draw upon both critical theory and recent scientific intimations of agency in nature.

DU PLESSIS, S I M. Philosophy Without History is Empty; History Without Philosophy is Blind. S Afr J Phil, 8(3-4), 187-189, N 88.

This article is a concise appreciation of H J de Vleeschauwer's life and scholarship, written from personal experience. The author places in perspective de Vleeschauwer's life and work, from which the latter's greatness emerges as both man and scholar.

DUBE, Allison. Hayek on Bentham. Utilitas, 2(1), 71-87, My 90.

DUBLER, Nancy and COLLOPY, Bart and ZUCKERMAN, Connie. The Ethics of Home Care: Autonomy and Accommodation. Hastings Center Rep, 20(2), Supp 1-16, Mr-Ap 90.

DUBROVSKY, David and STANKEVICH, Vladimir (trans). *The Problem of the Ideal*. Chicago, Progress, 1988

DUCCI, Edda. Filosofia dell'educazione e filosofia morale. Aquinas, 32(2), 183-192, My-Ag 89.

DUCROT, Oswald and ANSCOMBRE, Jean-Claude. "Argumentativity and Informativity" in *From Metaphysics to Rhetoric*, MEYER, Michel (ed), 71-87. Norwell, Kluwer, 1989.

DUDEK, Józef and KISIELEWICZ, Andrzej. On Finite Models of Regular Identities. Notre Dame J Form Log, 30(4), 624-628, Fall 89.

It is a known result of Austin that there exist nonregular identities with all nontrivial models being infinite. In this note a certain analogue of this result for regular identities is presented and some remarks in this connection are given.

DUDMAN, V H. Vive la Révolution. Mind, 98(392), 591-603, O 89.

Responding to generous critical attention in Jonathan Bennett's 'Phlogiston' article (*Mind* 1988), this note defends the grammatical approach to conditionals, urging the primacy of the grammatical distinction between having 'if' externally prefixed to a sentence ('If she fell she was probably killed') and having it first word of a subordinate clause ('If she falls/fell/had fallen she will be/would be/would have been killed'). In neither case is the received ternary analysis into antecedent, consequent and binary operator grammatically tenable, it is argued, but especially not in the second one. The title gratefully acknowledges an encomium of Bennett's.

DUFF, R A. Auctions, Lotteries, and the Punishment of Attempts. Law Phil, 9(1), 1-37, F 90.

The article criticises two recent attempts to show that it may be just to punish attempts less severely than completed crimes: Michael Davis's version of the "unfair advantage" theory of sentencing, which relies on an imagined auction of licences to commit crimes ('Why Attempts Deserve Less Punishment than Complete Crimes' (1986) 5 *Law and Philosophy* 1); and David Lewis's argument that we should explain, and perhaps justify, this practice as a "penal lottery" ('The Punishment that Leaves Something to Chance' (1989) 18 *Philosophy and Public Affairs* 53). I show why both these arguments fail, and sketch an alternative argument of my own.

DUGIN, V N. Man in the System of Socioeconomic Values. Soviet Stud Phil, 28(4), 16-24, Spr 90.

DUHAN, Laura. Three Levels of Reading Philosophy. Teach Phil, 12(4), 355-360, D 89.

Three levels of reading a philosophical text are identified: reading to understand (1) the English sentences, (2) the philosopher's pattern of reasoning, and (3) the philosopher's core concepts and the relationships between them. Analogies are drawn to three levels in learning to play a piece of music and learning to play basketball. Techniques for encouraging students to attend to all three levels are illustrated using a passage from Aristotle's *Nicomachean Ethics*.

DUHEM, Pierre and BARKER, Peter (trans) and ARIEW, Roger (trans). Logical Examination of Physical Theory. Synthese, 83(2), 183-188, My 90.

Duhem summarizes his philosophy of science, beginning from the "truism" that individual elements in a scientific system are inseparable for purposes of application or appraisal, and deriving both the thesis most commonly associated with his name, that elements of a scientific system are not separately falsifiable, and the thesis that observations are theory laden. Newtonian inductivists are criticized for ignoring the latter; Cartesian hypothetico-deductivists for destroying science's ability to achieve consensus by privileging a particular metaphysics. Duhem rejects atomism (Lorentz's electron theory) on the same grounds as Cartesianism, and contrasts his own view with pragmatic instrumentalism. Metaphysics is not the starting point of theory but the endpoint of science's historical development. Duhem may therefore, in a qualified sense, count as a convergent realist.

DUHEM, Pierre and ARIEW, Roger (trans) and BARKER, Peter (trans).

Research on the History of Physical Theories. Synthese, 83(2), 189-200, My 90.

Reviewing his research in the history of statics and dynamics, Duhem argues that Energetics is the modern heir to the principle of "saving the phenomena" that originated in Greek astronomy. Jordanus de Nemore's school surpassed ancient statics by introducing the principle of virtual work, while Parisian nominalists prepared the way for modern dynamics. After the condemnation of 1277 loosened the hold of Aristotelian theory, Ockham rehabilitated Philoponus's account of projectiles. Buridan, followed by Oresme, Albert of Saxony, and Leonardo, adopted impetus as the foundation of dynamics and introduced a law of inertia. Similar antecedents for the law of fall culminated in Domingo de Soto. The reception of these principles by Galileo and his contemporaries led to the modern science of mechanics. But the metaphysics of imperceptible bodies and hidden motions played no role in these advances, confirming Duhem's logical analysis of scientific method, and the primacy of Energetics as their descendant.

DUKE, James O. New Perspectives on Schleiermacher's Ethics: An Assay. J Relig Ethics, 17(2), 73-76, Fall 89.

DUKOR, Maduabu. African Cosmology and Ontology. Indian Phil Quart, 16(4), 367-391, O 89.

I shall attempt in this paper to expose and analyse the ancient African ontology and cosmology. It is not a critique as such but an exposition. I intend to analyse African myths about God as well as the concepts of myth. Finally I shall examine the relationship between African cosmology and the unified field theory.

DUKOR, Maduabuchi. God and Godlings in African Ontology. Indian Phil Quart, 17(1), 75-89, Ja 90.

Africans believed in the existence of a Supreme being as well as other lesser beings like divinities, gods, ancestors and so on. The Supreme being manifest himself through these lesser gods and objects of nature. This belief has a pantheistic undertone, but it is precisely panpsychic. The fact that they believed in one Supreme creator means that they were not atheistic or purely polytheistic. I therefore would refer to African metaphysical world view as Theistic Panpsychism. Theistic Panpsychism reconciles the transcendental and the immanence conceptions of God in African culture.

DUMITRU, Mircea. Essentialisme et logique modale (in Romanian). Rev Filosof (Romania), 36(1), 87-91, Ja-F 89.

DUMONT, Camille. Enseignement de la théologie et méthode scientifique. Gregorianum, 71(3), 441-463, 1990.

"Teaching" and "science" are notions that cannot be applied univocally to theology. Teaching implies that the mind masters its object scientifically through human methods; but who can master the knowledge which God alone possesses? There is need for God's Word himself to become Teacher (John 1,18). Thus, in the schools the sacra pagina will open itself up to become sacra doctrina. The method of theology is therefore always subordinate to a transcendent knowledge which finally remains inaccessible to any merely human science. Is science thereby degraded or on the contrary enhanced? Thomas Aquinas developed the idea of "subalternation." Blondel spoke of a science based on Christ "verified and realised in us." Today hermeneutics discovers that only the Glory of ultimate reality is capable of giving meaning to all the figures that announce it in human history and knowledge. On the other hand, the avatars of nominalism show that reducing theology and science to univocity results in perverting science as such.

DUMONT, Stephen D and BROWN, Stephen F. Univocity of the Concept of Being in the Fourteenth Century III: An Early Scotist. Med Stud, 51, 1-129, 1989.

This is the edition of a text that is one of the most detailed expositions of John Duns Scotus's doctrine on the univocity of the concept of being (39-129), with an introduction that shows that these questions are important for the historical light they shed on Scotus's contemporaries Richard of Conington, Robert Cowton, and William of Alnwich, as well as the clarifications they offer for Scotus's own teaching on univocity (1-38).

DUNCAN, Elmer. "Do We Need a General Theory of Value?" in Inquiries into Values: The Inaugural Session of the International Society for Value Inquiry, LEE, Sander H , 37-46. Lewiston, Mellen Pr, 1989.

What is the purpose of a general theory of value? It has sometimes been argued, e.g., by Ralph Barton Perry, that the purpose is to resolve all cases of value—in ethics, aesthetics, religion (?), economics, etc.—into one account, to show that they all share a common property. The purpose of the present paper is to show that this is not possible, because there is no such "common something," in any important sense. If this is their goal, all such general theories must be either false or trivial.

DUNLOP, Charles E M. Conceptual Dependency as the Language of

Thought. Synthese, 82(2), 275-296, F 90.

Roger Schank's research in AI takes seriously the ideas that understanding natural language involves mapping its expressions into an internal representation scheme and that these internal representations have a syntax appropriate from computational operations. It therefore falls within the computational approach to the study of mind. This paper discusses certain aspects of Schank's approach in order to assess its potential adequacy as a (partial) model of cognition. This version of the Language of Thought hypothesis encounters some of the same difficulties that arise for Fodor's account.

DUNN, J Michael and MEYER, Robert K. "Gentzen's Cut and Ackermann's Gamma" in Directions in Relevant Logic, NORMAN, Jean (ed), 229-240. Norwell, Kluwer, 1989.

DUNN, Susan. Michelet and Lamartine: Regicide, Passion, and Compassion. Hist Theor, 28(3), 275-295, O 89.

In their histories of the French Revolution, Michelet and Lamartine traced the moral failure of the Jacobin Revolution to the pitiless regicide. Politically, Jacobin mercilessness served the royalist cause; morally it discredited republican ideology for decades to come. Pity was central to Michelet's and Lamartine's concepts of political morality but it also extended to their attitudes toward historiography. They envisioned pity as the basis for historiography and as the fundamental moral mission for the historian. The question of pity for Louis XVI was a vehicle for exploring the relationship between ethics and politics and for examining the role of pity in the writing of history.

DUNNE, Brenda J and JAHN, Robert G. Margins of Reality: The Role of Consciousness in the Physical World. San Diego, Harcourt Brace Jov, 1987

This book reexamines the role of consciousness in the light of a new body of experimental data on the interaction of human operators with various technical devices and information-processing systems. Many philosophical fibers are required to sift these results into a coherent model; but once the essential concepts are in place, human consciousness indeed emerges endowed with an active component. By virtue of the manner in which it exchanges information with its environment, orders that information, and interprets it, consciousness has the ability to bias probabilistic processes, and thereby to avail itself of certain margins of reality.

DUNPHY, William. "Maimonides' Not-So-Secret Position on Creation" in Moses Maimonides and His Time, ORMSBY, Eric L (ed), 151-172. Washington, Cath Univ Amer Pr, 1989.

DUPRÉ, Louis. Evil—A Religious Mystery: A Plea for a More Inclusive Model of Theodicy. Faith Phil, 7(3), 261-280, Jl 90.

Major problems in modern theodicy derive from a rationalist conception of God—alien to living faith—and from an abstract, theologically neutral definition of good and evil. The alternative model here proposed rests on a more intimate union of finite with infinite Being which, on the one hand, allows the creature a greater autonomy and responsibility, and, on the other hand, enables the Creator to share in the suffering of his creatures and thereby to redeem them.

DUPRÉ, Wilhelm. Dominance of the Thought on Domestication: Threat for Humanum in Our Time (in Hungarian). Magyar Filozof Szemle, 2-3, 287-302, 1989.

DUQUETTE, David A. Civil and Political Freedom in Hegel. SW Phil Rev, 6(1), 37-44, Ja 90.

A new tendency in Hegel scholarship is to portray Hegel's political theory as essentially democratic, and even socialistic in its implications. In order to challenge this view I examine Hegel's conception of institutionalized freedom in order to show that, even on more modest claims of Hegel's "pluralism," there are some difficulties for democrats in his view of the state, particularly with his ideas of political freedom and participation.

DURÁN Y LALAGUNA, Paloma. The Jurisprudence of the European Court of Human Rights: Towards an Alternative Foundation of Human Rights. Vera Lex, 8(2), 17-18, 1988.

DURAN, Jane. Gilligan's Two Voices: An Epistemological Overview. Phil Context, 19, 75-80, 1989.

DURAN, Jane. Psychoeducational Assessment Practices for the Learning Disabled: A Philosophical Analysis. Phil Soc Sci, 20(2), 183-194, Je 90.

Four lines of argument are adduced to support the contention that current disease-modeled approaches to learning disability (LD) are inadequate and that a more environmentally-centered approach should be utilized. The first argument employs philosophy of science to criticize the blatant operationalism of the extant theorizing, while noting that the theories frequently try to employ a realist slant. The second line of argument attacks the disease model itself, employing the work of other philosophers who have noted the extent to which "disease" is a value-laden construct. Still another line notes that, at first glance, current work on paternalism might seem to provide some kind of rationale for LD placement, but that this is probably not the case. The fourth line of argument adverts to the possibility that sociopolitical motivations underlie some of the labeling efforts. It is concluded that current efforts are fruitless and that a new definitional effort is needed, one which specifically cites the locus of disability as the classroom environment.

DURBIN, Paul T. Bioengineering, Scientific Activism, and Philosophical Bridges. Bridges, 2(1-2), 27-41, Spr-Sum 90.

It is possible to focus the controversy over biotechnology or bioengineering on specific concerns or problems rather than on "grand" fears of escaping cell cultures or a bioengineered "brave new world." If we do this, a problem arises about how best to deal with these more limited problems. This article, building on the tradition of George Herbert Mead and John Dewey, proposes that scientists, academic engineers, philosophers, and others interested in these problems work in activist fashion—alongside the actual decision makers in these areas—to bring about the most reasonable and most practical solutions to these problems. For philosophers, this means a special kind of bridge-building via applied ethics. The paper concludes with an appeal to applied ethicists to undertake this approach.

DURKHEIM, Emile and MERLLIÉ, Dominique. Lévy-Bruhl et Durkheim: Notes biographiques en marge d'une correspondance—Lettres à L Lévy-Bruhl (1894-1915). Rev Phil Fr, 179(4), 493-514, O-D 89.

DURRANT, Michael. Reference and Critical Realism. Mod Theol, 5(2), 133-143, Ja 89.

In her book *Metaphor and Religious Language* Dr. Janet Martin Soskice attempts to explain how it is possible to refer to God, or, more generally how it is possible for theological terms to be 'reality depicting'. This paper presents a challenge to her account. Whilst not unsympathetic to her 'realist' approach, I argue that (i) her account of reference in general and hence of theological reference is unsatisfactory and rejectable; (ii) her critical realist position entails certain unacceptable consequences for Christian theology; (iii) her own 'critical realist' position turns out to be not consistently statable.

DÜSING, Klaus. Beauty as the Transition from Nature to Freedom in Kant's Critique of Judgement. Nous, 24(1), 79-92, Mr 90.

The transition from nature to freedom, made possible by the beautiful, has first an empirical-anthropological meaning. The consideration of the beautiful liberates from the coercion of the senses and makes disposed for an habitual moral attitude. That transition has second a fundamental transcendental sense. The free and harmonious play of imagination and understanding, which is brought about in the consideration of the beautiful, opens us prospects of the intellectual substrate of humanity, which is no more to be thought as something indeterminable, but as a spontaneity, which means under moral laws: freedom.

DUSKA, Ronald and DES JARDINS, Joseph. Drug Testing in Employment. Bus Prof Ethics J, 6(3), 3-21, Fall 87.

Contrary to what seems to be a growing trend in favor of drug testing in the workplace, we argue that it is seldom legitimate to override an employee's privacy by using such tests. In arguing against the two major justifications of drug testing, we outline those few cases when testing can be appropriate. We conclude by considering certain limitations which must be placed upon those specific cases.

DUSSEL, Enrique D and BARR, Robert R (trans). *Ethics and Community*. Maryknoll, Orbis Books, 1988

This book examines the insights provided by liberation theology concerning morality and differing ethical systems. It examines what two ethical systems, community ethics and social morality, have to say about ten questions basic to ethics (good and evil, personal vs. social sin, relative morals vs. absolute ethics, etc.). The author then examines ways in which the two systems address ten contemporary issues. (staff)

DUTTON, Michael. From Facts to Theory: The Emergence of the Feudal Relics Debate within Chinese Marxism (in Serbo-Croatian). Filozof Istraz, 29(2), 415-433, 1989.

This paper deals with the theoretical effects of the redeployment of the slogan 'seeking truth from facts' in current post-Gang of Four theoretical work. It argues that an epistemologically based reading of the 'facts' slogan which would condemn it as empiricist is inadequate and fails to note conjunctural considerations. In place of this reading, the paper asserts that it was under the banner of 'seeking truth from facts' that more sophisticated theoretical work was possible. This was nowhere more clearly demonstrated than in the recent and highly controversial debate around the issue of 'feudal relics'. The theoretical ramifications of works which assert the centrality of 'feudal relics' is then explored and a critique of the underlying humanism of

this response offered.

DWORETZ, Steven M. *The Unvarnished Doctrine: Locke, Liberalism, and the American Revolution*. Durham, Duke Univ Pr, 1990

Historians have reinterpreted the political thought of the American Revolution in terms of a "republican" tradition, in relation to which John Locke's liberalism, once deemed the substance of Revolutionary ideology, appears irrelevant or hostile. This book challenges this deliberalization of Revolutionary thought. It shows how the Revolutionists argued in the language and theory of Locke's *Two Treatises*. It also explores the influential New England clergy's affinity for Locke. The ministers admired Locke's writings on politics, epistemology, and religion; and they cited "Locke on Government" not merely for expediency, but also because they sympathized with the underlying theistic liberalism which emerges from those texts.

DWORKIN, Gerald. Equal Respect and the Enforcement of Morality. Soc Phil Pol, 7(2), 180-193, Spr 90.

DWORKIN, Ronald. "Legal Theory and the Problem of Sense" in *Issues in Contemporary Legal Philosophy: The Influence of H L A Hart*, GAVISON, Ruth (ed), 9-20. New York, Clarendon/Oxford Pr, 1987.

DWYER, Philip. Freedom and Rule-Following in Wittgenstein and Sartre. Phil Phenomenol Res, 50(1), 49-68, S 89.

What Sartre means by 'existence precedes essence' is sketched, and how this notion captures the gist of Wittgenstein's later critique of his early conception of language is shown. A detailed comparison of Sartre and Wittgenstein revolves around Wittgenstein's account of rule-following. His arguments against meaning as something which transcends and determines the *use* of words duplicates Sartre's arguments against any notion of a human essence determining human action in general. In debunking the illusion of a metaphysical essence of either language or human existence, both analyses put freedom at the centre of the language-game and of human life generally.

DY JR, Manuel B. "Liberation and Values" in *The Social Context and Values: Perspectives of the Americas*, MC LEAN, George F (ed), 193-210. Lanham, Univ Pr of America, 1989.

The purpose of the article is to trace the movement of liberation of the person, in particular, the social person, and the values incarnated in this movement. Freedom is not irreconcilable with determination but manifests itself in the act of commitment. The movement of liberation is the dialectic of freedom and nature in the different but interrelated dimensions of man (work, language and power). In this movement, freedom becomes a response to the values of justice, truth and love, values grounded on the dignity of the person.

DYCK, Stephen. Some Applications of Positive Formulas in Descriptive Set Theory and Logic. Annals Pure Applied Log, 46(2), 95-146, F 90.

DYKE, C. Strange Attraction, Curious Liaison: Clio Meets Chaos. Phil Forum, 21(4), 369-392, Sum 90.

DYLLICK, Thomas. Ecological Marketing Strategy for Toni Yogurts in Switzerland. J Bus Ethics, 8(8), 657-662, Ag 89.

Whoever enters a food store in Switzerland, nowadays, most probably passes by a conspicuous crate for depositing empty glass containers for Toni yogurts. But who actually would know that the story behind the recyclable glass containers is one of the most interesting and informative cases, where one company successfully integrated ecological considerations of society-at-large into their company's marketing strategy, making it eventually a great business success. It is an encouraging story for those who are trying to find ways to include a sense of social responsibility into company policies without calling for more state intervention to bring it about. It is a sobering story at the same time, leaving little doubt that there are no easy and undisputed solutions for complex and ambiguous problems.

DYSON, R W (ed & trans) and TUDOR, H (ed & trans). Robertus Britannus, 'On the Best Form of Commonwealth': A Dialogue between Pierre du Chastel and Aymar Ranconet. Hist Polit Thought, 11(1), 37-58, Spr 90.

EAMES, Elizabeth R. "Cause in the Later Russell" in *Rereading Russell: Essays on Bertrand Russell's Metaphysics and Epistemology*, SAVAGE, C Wade (ed), 264-280. Minneapolis, Univ of Minn Pr, 1989.

The concept of cause is of central importance in the post-1920 work of Bertrand Russell. In the construction of matter it binds events into the "lines" and "centers" necessary for physics. In the construction of mind, it links and discriminates objects perceived, remembered, imagined, or inferred and the particulars of experience. Questions are raised concerning a circularity in Russell's concept of cause as both itself constructed and as a postulate of that construction, and concerning the viability, in the later Russell, of a physical realism that had abandoned the principle of acquaintance.

EARLE, William. "The Evanescent Authority of Philosophy" in *Dialectic and*

Contemporary Science, GRIER, Philip T (ed), 203-212. Lanham, Univ Pr of America, 1989.

EARMAN, John. "Concepts of Projectability and the Problems of Induction" in *Rereading Russell: Essays on Bertrand Russell's Metaphysics and Epistemology*, SAVAGE, C Wade (ed), 220-233. Minneapolis, Univ of Minn Pr, 1989.

EARMAN, John. Old Evidence, New Theories: Two Unresolved Problems in Bayesian Confirmation Theory. Pac Phil Quart, 70(4), 323-340, D 89.

EASTHOPE, Antony. "Derrida's Epistemology" in *The Textual Sublime: Deconstruction and Its Differences*, SILVERMAN, Hugh J (ed), 207-212. Albany, SUNY Pr, 1990.

While sharing with much Anglo-American philosophy a rejection of empiricist epistemology, Derrida in "Structure Sign and Play" risks re-generating a binary between empiricism and the "play" of discourse. This essay calls on a Marxist tradition in epistemology especially as developed by Althusser to breach any opposition between a supposedly unmediated access to truth and the construction of knowledge as an effect of discourse.

EATHERLY, Claude and ANDERS, Gunther. *Burning Conscience: The Guilt of Hiroshima*. New York, Paragon House, 1989

EATON, Marcia Muelder. *Aesthetics and the Good Life*. Madison, F Dickinson Univ Pr, 1989

The author argues that the *aesthetic* is characterized by delight taken in intrinsic features of objects traditionally considered worthy of sustained attention. Applied aesthetic problems, such as assessment of environmental resources, would benefit from taking such traditions seriously. Measuring what matters aesthetically, and determining what constitutes a rational life, requires humanistic investigations that provide contexts that reflect value systems. The history of art and aesthetics cannot be separated from the history of society.

EATON, Marcia. Laughing at the Death of Little Nell: Sentimental Art and Sentimental People. Amer Phil Quart, 26(4), 269-282, O 89.

A survey of the uses and analyses of 'sentimental' reveals that understanding sentimentality (and why, when, and how it creates bad art and bad people) requires recognizing that the aesthetic and the ethical are not as distinct as it has often been claimed. Indeed, 'sentimental' is used in both ethical and aesthetic assessment, and its use in the one always involves considerations from the other realm.

EBERT, Theodor. Wo beginnt der Weg der Doxa? Phronesis, 34(2), 121-138, 1989.

Taking up a proposal made by G Calogero in 1936, the paper argues for a transposition of Parmenides fr. 8, 34-41 behind 8, 52. It is claimed that this alteration yields a better test on philological as well as on philosophical grounds. The proposed new arrangement would make fr. 8, 34-41 the starting point of the Doxa-part in Parmenides' poem.

EBLE, Kenneth. Thinking, Knowing, Doing. Thinking, 6(2), 20-24, 1985.

EBOH, Marie P. War Against Indiscipline (WAI): Nigerian Ethical Policy. Phil Soc Act, 16(2), 23-30, Ap-Je 90.

War Against Indiscipline (WAI) like Moral Rearmament, is a militant action aimed at revolutionising a society. Because it is edictally enforced, its morality is obfuscated by militancy and the use of decrees. The objective of this article is to highlight the importance, timeliness and positive impact of WAI and also to argue for its ethicality. Our submission is that a genuine ethical programme should be trusted and accepted even when it is launched by a questionable military government.

ECCLES, John C. *Evolution of the Brain: Creation of the Self*. New York, Routledge, 1990

The story of hominid evolution to Homo Sapiens Sapiens is the most wonderful story that can be told. It was the only chance of our existence as human beings. This book conforms with the Darwinist hypothesis of biological evolution. But it goes beyond the materialist concepts of Darwinism in the last three chapters where there is consideration of the most extraordinary evolutionary happenings: firstly the emergence of consciousness in the higher animals; secondly the even more remarkable transcendence when Hominids experienced self-consciousness. It is argued that there can be no physicalist explanation of this mysterious emergence of consciousness and self-consciousness in a hitherto *mindless world*. Philosophical consideration of the coming-to-be of each unique self leads on to the religious concept of the creation of each soul.

ECHAURI, Raúl. La noción de ser en Tomás de Sutton. Pat Med, 10, 49-55, 1989.

Au fur et à mesure que se multiplient les études autour de la pensée et les écrits de ce dominicain anglais qui vécut vers la fin du XIIIe. siècle,

s'approfondit la conviction—soutenue déjà par Ét. Gilson dans son livre *L'être et l'essence*—qui signale en T. de S. l'un des rares disciples du maître d'Aquin (peut-être le premier) qui aurait su voir ce que l'A nomme "le visage authentique de la métaphysique thomiste", c'est-à-dire cette interprétation de celle-ci qui, au lieu de privilégier l'*essentia* dans l'analyse de la structure du réel, comme le feront du plupart des expositeurs dans une attitude que l'A attribue à l'influence des *Theoremata de esse et essentia* de Gilles de Rome, met l'accent sur l'*esse*, de telle sorte qu'on pourrait parler d'une métaphysique *existentielle* chez Thomas d'Aquin. (edited)

ECO, Umberto (ed) and SANTAMBROGIO, Marco (ed) and VIOLI, Patrizia (ed). *Meaning and Mental Representation*. Bloomington, Indiana Univ Pr, 1988

ECO, Umberto. La natura sprecona, i codici e lo struscio. Epistemologia, 11(2), 333-340, Jl-D 88.

Information is a slippery word. There is a hidden ambiguity in it, and perhaps a game like "Scrabble" may help us to grasp it. When the various letters of the game are mixed at random on the board, the information of the set, according to Shannon's formula, is maximum. When the game is over, on the other hand, the letters displayed on the pieces are arranged in words which make sense, and we have a maximum of what is more properly referred to as meaning, rather than information. There are, of course, linguistic hindrances, limiting the number of possible combinations of letters. Such hindrances could be considered as codes, determining the final meaning. (edited)

ECO, Umberto. "On Truth: A Fiction" in *Meaning and Mental Representation*, ECO, Umberto (ed), 41-59. Bloomington, Indiana Univ Pr, 1988.

ÉCOLE, Jean. Note sur la définition wolffienne de la philosophie. Stud Leibniz, 21(2), 205-208, 1989.

Für sich genommen, könnte die von Wolff vorgeschlagene Definition der Philosophie als Wissenschaft von allen Möglichkeiten zur Vermutung Anlass geben, dass Wolff vom Gegenstand jener Disziplin jeden Bezug auf das Verwirklichte ausschlösse. Wenn man diese Definition jedoch sorgfältig im Lichte der sie begleitenden Erläuterungen, die auf seine Konzeption des Möglichen Bezug nehmen, interpretiert, wird im Gegenteil deutlich, dass sie der Philosophie zur Aufgabe stellt zu erklären, weshalb bestimmte Möglichkeiten eher verwirklicht sind als andere, oder—wenn man lieber möchte—den Übergang der Essenz zur Existenz aufzuhellen. Denn im strengen Sinne, den er diesem Begriff beilegt, ist das Mögliche das, was existieren könnte, weil es nicht widerspruchsvoll ist. Da er ferner das Sein im allgemeinen durch diese innere Möglichkeit des Existierens definiert, reduziert er es auf die Essenz, welche er auf diese Weise streng von der Existenz trennt. Daraus ergibt sich das Problem zu bestimmen, auf welche Weise und aus welchem Grunde die Existenz zur Essenz hinzutreten kann.

EDEL, Abraham. *Interpreting Education*. Buffalo, Prometheus, 1989

The book considers what role philosophy can play as a resource for education in a changing world. Topics dealt with include variant (and competing) bases for normative educational judgments, a moral agenda for contemporary education, central curricular issues (from the science-humanities dichotomy to the liberal-vocational confrontation), critical concepts of rationality, impartiality, autonomy, relativity. Among illustrative specific problems dealt with are grading, the role of sports, teacher-student relations. Emphasis falls throughout on the cooperative handling of issues by philosophy and education, as against philosophical mandates for educational application.

EDEL, Abraham. More on Knowledge and the Humanities. J Aes Educ, 21(4), 95-101, Wint 87.

Current distinction between science as cumulative and humanities as noncumulative is found a dubious move to keep science and humanities apart. This discontinuity, entrenched in education, has been maintained by successive metaphysical and epistemological gambits using such dichotomies as nature-spirit, quantity-quality, objective-subjective, nomothetic-ideographic, fact-value. These are now crumbling, and perspectives of continuity, with discipline boundary-making a historical-functional enterprise open to reconstruction in the light of advancing knowledge and philosophical refinement, deserves present consideration. It entails also unfreezing present educational structures.

EDELSON, Thomas. Does Artificial Intelligence Require Artificial Ego? A Critique of Haugeland. J Phil Res, 15, 251-262, 1990.

John Haugeland, in *Artificial Intelligence: The Very Idea*, predicts that it will not be possible to create systems which understand discourse about people unless those systems share certain characteristics of people, specifically what he calls "ego involvement." I argue that he has failed to establish this. In fact, I claim that his argument fails at two points. First, he has not established that it is impossible to understand ego involvement without simulating the processes which underlie it. Second, even if the first point be granted, the conclusion does not follow, for it is possible to *simulate* ego involvement without *having* it.

EDEN, Robert. Tocqueville and the Problem of Natural Right. Interpretation, 17(3), 379-387, Spr 90.

EDGAR, Andrew. An Introduction to Adorno's Aesthetics. Brit J Aes, 30(1), 46-56, Ja 90.

The paper explicates T W Adorno's work on art, situating Adorno within the tradition of 19th century German philosophy (specifically of Kant, Hegel and Marx). Secondly the relationship between the sociology of art and aesthetics in this tradition is explored. For Adorno formalist aesthetics responds to a logic within art. However, art is also a product of society, and art works are produced from materials and concepts that are social in origin. Adorno argues that art works can be judged aesthetically only if their aesthetic structures are seen as critical responses to the social content crystalised within them.

EDGLEY, Roy and CHOMSKY, Noam and OSBORNE, Peter and RÉE, Jonathan and WILSON, Deirdre. Noam Chomsky: An Interview. Rad Phil, 53, 31-40, Autumn 89.

EDIE, James M. Husserl Versus Derrida. Human Stud, 13(2), 103-118, Ap 90.

EDMAN, Irwin. Intimations of Philosophy in Early Childhood. Thinking, 7(1), 13-18, 1987.

EDMOND, Michel-Pierre. Machiavel et la question de la Nature. Rev Metaph Morale, 94(3), 347-352, Jl-S 89.

EDWARDS, Jack and RAITZ, Keith L. Teaching Reading and Educating Persons. Proc Phil Educ, 45, 334-343, 1989.

EDWARDS, James C. *The Authority of Language: Heidegger, Wittgenstein, and the Threat of Philosophical Nihilism*. Gainesville, Univ S Florida Pr, 1990

The book offers a reading of Heidegger and Wittgenstein in relation to the threat of a wholesale collapse in epistemic and ethical authority, which some philosophers call the threat of *nihilism*. It is argued that such a threat depends upon a particular conception of language, and thus of the self, a conception challenged (in very different ways) by Heidegger and by Wittgenstein. The book then evaluates the respective merits of the two challenges, arguing that Wittgenstein's response is superior.

EDWARDS, Jim. Atomic Realism, Intuitionist Logic and Tarskian Truth. Phil Quart, 40(158), 13-26, Ja 90.

The author considers the generalization of the intuitionist account of the meanings of mathematical statements to empirical discourse. He argues that one plausible antirealist argument for rejecting classical logic is consistent with the supposition that atomic sentences are bivalent even if undecidable. The resulting conception of truth makes atomic sentences bivalent, all sentences Tarskian, but nonatomic sentences are not known to be bivalent. The author contrasts this conception of truth with Crispin Wright's generalization of intuitionistic truth as superassertibility, and offers a brief defense of the manifestability in usage of the author's conception of truth.

EDWARDS, Paul. Heidegger's Quest for Being. Philosophy, 64(250), 437-470, O 89.

According to Heidegger, man has "forgotten" Being and it was his task to bring human beings back to a "commitment" to and "remembrance" of Being. By "Being" Heidegger means what we normally mean by existence. Things like pieces of chalk or houses exist, but when we look for existence in them we cannot find it. Heidegger concludes that Being is ineffable. The main aim of the present article is to show that Heidegger's search for Being is a pseudo-inquiry. It is based on the mistaken assumption that existence is the most basic characteristic of existing things. "Exists" is not the name of a characteristic, but a logical constant. It follows that expressions like "forgottenness of Being" and "commitment to Being" are nonsensical.

EDWARDS, Rem B. Abortion Rights. Nat Forum, 69(4), 19-24, Fall 89.

The conservative position on abortion gives neoconceptuses full and equal moral standing from conception and holds that genetic completeness is sufficient for personhood. This makes almost every human cell a person and every finger prick murder. Neoconceptuses lack all the traits of paradigm personhood; minorities exemplify them; thus minorities and majorities have nothing to fear from abortion but should be intimidated if their value is equal to, thus no greater than a single cell neoconceptus. The conservative "benefit of the doubt" argument confuses "is x a person?" with "is a person x?" Conservatives illicitly assume that potentialities equal actualities. Other points are developed.

EELLS, Ellery. The Popcorn Problem: Sobel on Evidential Decision Theory and Deliberation-Probability Dynamics. Synthese, 81(1), 9-20, O 89.

I defend evidential decision theory and the theory of deliberation-probability dynamics from a recent criticism advanced by Jordan Howard Sobel. I argue that his alleged counterexample to the theories, called the 'Popcorn Problem' is not a genuine counterexample.

EGAN, M Frances. What's Wrong with the Syntactic Theory of Mind. Phil Sci, 56(4), 664-674, D 89.

Stephen Stich has argued that psychological theories that instantiate his syntactic theory of mind are to be preferred to content-based or representationalist theories, because the former can capture and explain a wider range of generalizations about cognitive processes than the latter. Stich's claims about the relative merits of the syntactic theory of mind are unfounded. Not only is it false that syntactic theories can capture psychological generalizations that content-based theories cannot, but a large class of behavioral regularities, readily explained by content-based theories, appears to be beyond their explanatory reach.

EGGERMAN, Richard W. Kantian Strict Duties of Benevolence. SW Phil Rev, 6(1), 81-88, Ja 90.

Kant claims an alignment between strict duties and those discoverable by the text for contradiction in conception. Similarly, he claims an alignment between broad duties and those discoverable by contradiction in the will. I challenge these claimed alignments. Once they are surrendered, I argue there are Kantian grounds for some strict duties of beneficence, even in fairly minor cases of assisting others.

EGGERMAN, Richard W. Why Should We Care About the General Happiness? SW Phil Rev, 4(1), 79-85, Ja 88.

We can give reasons why agents should sometimes sacrifice for the welfare of other agents seen as individuals. However, the utilitarian view can commit an agent to severe sacrifice for the trivial interests of other agents, just in case the number of other agents who will be benefitted is sufficiently large. This indefensible outcome is a natural outcome of the utilitarian pooling of individual interests. The pooling move is both artificial and potentially dangerous.

EGIDI, Rosaria. "Phänomenologie und Grammatik in Wittgenstein" in *Wittgenstein in Focus—Im Brennpunkt: Wittgenstein*, MC GUINNESS, Brian (ed), 185-205. Amsterdam, Rodopi, 1989.

Die Aufgabe, die diese Arbeit sich stellt, ist, zwei entscheidende Momente in der Entwicklung der philosophischen Psychologie Wittgensteins zu verdeutlichen. Darüber hinaus wird versucht, einige Hinweise auf Material zu geben, das bei einer weitergreifenden und gründlicheren Rekonstruktion dieser Momente zu berücksichtigen wäre: (A) das Moment der phänomenologischen "Versuchung" im Kontext der ersten und mittleren Phase des Wittgensteinschen Denkens und (B) das Moment der grammatischen Wende, die seine spätere Deutung der visuellen Phänomene einleitet und die sich als die Ausarbeitung seiner antipsychologischen Erkenntnistheorie erweist.

EGNEUS, Hans and JUNGEN, Britta. Human Ecology. Phil Soc Act, 15(3-4), 47-57, Jl-D 89.

EHRING, Douglas. The 'Only t_1 Through t_2' Principle. Analysis, 49(4), 176-177, O 89.

I argue that Humean and Neo-Humean theories of causation are incompatible with a causal theory of identity. Whether two object stages are stages of the same object does not depend upon any event which occurs after the time of the occurrence of those two stages. But on a Humean or Neo-Humean theory of causation, whether two stages are causally connected will depend upon how the world unfolds *after* those stages occur.

EHRING, Douglas. Are Workers Forced to Work? Can J Phil, 19(4), 589-602, D 89.

G A Cohen, in his "The Structure of Proletarian Unfreedom," addresses the classical Marxist claim that workers are forced to sell their labour power under capitalism. On Cohen's analysis this claim is ambiguous, i.e., the term "proletariat" has two importantly different senses. In the collective sense, Cohen argues, workers are subject to coercion, but in the distributive sense, they are not coerced. In this paper, I argue that Cohen has not established that the proletariat, in the distributive sense, are not forced to sell their labour power.

EICHENWALD, I I and KATZ, Nina J (trans) and BAER, Joachim T (trans). "A Note on Schopenhauer (1910) (also in German)" in *Schopenhauer: New Essays in Honor of His 200th Birthday*, VON DER LUFT, Eric (ed), 139-158. Lewiston, Mellen Pr, 1989.

EIFLER, Christine. Matriarchale Ganzheitlichkeit gegen patriarchale Vernunft? Deut Z Phil, 37(9), 843-582, 1989.

EISENACH, Eldon J. Self-Reform as Political Reform in the Writings of John Stuart Mill. Utilitas, 1(2), 242-258, N 89.

This essay explores the ways in which Mill's stress on self or inward culture might be reconciled to his more systematic social and political theory. Beginning with Mill's recognition of how and why these enterprises are now divided, the path to reconciliation requires us to relate self or inward culture to self-reform and then to connect self-reform to actors in the reform of the larger society. Mill's theory of self-development, or "laws of the mind" is then related to his larger theory of social change.

EISENBERG, Paul. Was Hegel a Panlogicist? Nous, 24(1), 159-167, Mr 90.

It is argued that panlogicism, understood as the doctrine that all that exists is, or else is merely the expression of, a fundamentally mental or spiritual entity, God or *Geist*, is a traditional but mistaken interpretation of Hegel. Granted, his concern to preserve certain standard terms and views within philosophy invites to such a confusion; but one must remember that this Hegelian preservation is also a cancellation (*Aufhebung*). Particular attention is paid to a passage from the *Phenomenology* which Glockner for one took to be, in effect, the proof text for establishing Hegel's commitment to panlogism; a quite different interpretation of that passage is suggested.

EISENSTEIN, Israel. *Ein neuer Beitrag zum Verständnis Spinozas*. Konigstein, Athenaum, 1989

EKMAN, Rosalind. Paternalism and the Rationality of the Child. Thinking, 6(1), 15-19, 1985.

EKSTEROWICZ, Anthony J and GARTNER, James D. Funding the Department of Education's TRIO Programs. Pub Affairs Quart, 4(3), 233-247, Jl 90.

During the Reagan administration, the Education Department's TRIO program operated within a political environment that exhibited ideological conflicts between administration and congressional goals concerning education policy. In essence, the Reagan administration desired to cut funding for educational programs like TRIO while the Congress resisted such cuts and even, upon occasion, restored program funding. The administration responded by slashing support and evaluation funds, leaving program specialists in the difficult position of monitoring programs with less resources. The authors propose the institution of Congressional/Administration Support and Evaluation (CASE) task forces as a means for both establishing a closer connection between program and support funding and bridging interbranch ideological and political conflicts concerning educational policy.

ELDER, Crawford L. Goodman's "New Riddle"—A Realist's Reprise. Phil Stud, 59(2), 115-135, Je 90.

Goodman argues that "blue" and "green" differ from "grue" and "bleen" only in respect of entrenchment, hence that entrenchment determines projectibility. This paper argues that "blue" and "green" differ also in being tied, in certain sorts of objects, to certain causal powers, while "grue" and "bleen" are disengaged from the way the world works. For while one can try to concoct "grue"-like predicates for "causal powers" too, one either winds up with powers magically affected by observedness-before-T—something not even Goodman can allow—or with "powers" that do not amount to producing any effect.

ELDER, Crawford L. Realism, Naturalism and Culturally Generated Kinds. Phil Quart, 39(157), 425-444, O 89.

Realism asserts mind-independence: no components of the world are such that, if beliefs get formed about them, those beliefs are bound to be true, just because of being about those components and being held by their holders. But what about culturally generated kinds—jokes and insults, pencils, marriages? These seem created and shaped by a culture's beliefs; so have they the mind-independence which realism requires? *Naturalist* realists must answer: "in some cases, yet." Consequently, they must deny that terms designating such kinds conform to the "description theory" of reference. This paper shows that sometimes, such terms refer "indexically."

ELDERS, Lédon. St Thomas et la métaphysique du "liber de causis". Rev Thomiste, 89(3), 427-442, Jl-S 89.

ELGIN, Catherine Z and GOODMAN, Nelson. "Changing the Subjects" in *Analytic Aesthetics*, SHUSTERMAN, Richard (ed), 190-196. Cambridge, Blackwell, 1989.

ELÍCEGUI, Juan M O. La unidad perdida del proyecto arquitectónico. Anu Filosof, 20(1), 221-228, 1987.

ELLERMAN, Carl Paul. New Notes from Underground. Inquiry, 33(1), 3-26, Mr 90.

An American underground man examines arguments to evidence his thesis that Huxley's 'really revolutionary revolution in the souls and flesh of human beings' is being fomented by respected scientific rationalists. Believing that *Homo sapiens* is an evolutionary error, these benevolent intellectuals wish to alter the human gene pool in order to circumvent genosuicide. Seeking to awaken the educated public to ominous events of evolutionary enormity, the underground man prods humanist philosophers by impiously debunking the Socratic dream of reason, the Enlightenment mystique, and the millennial myth of freedom, provocatively supporting the revolution of the scientific rationalists, as if they had perceived aright. (edited)

ELLIN, Joseph. Streminger: "Religion a Threat to Morality". Hume Stud, 15(2), 295-300, N 89.

ELLIOT, Robert. The Rights of Future People. J Applied Phil, 6(2), 159-169, O 89.

It has been argued by some that the present nonexistence of future persons entails that whatever obligations we have towards them are not based on rights which they have or might come to have. This view is refuted. It is argued that the present nonexistence of future persons is no impediment to the attribution of rights to them. It is also argued that, even if the present nonexistence of future persons *were* an impediment to the attribution of rights to them, the rights they will have when they come into existence constitute a constraint on present actions. Both arguments build on a suggestion of Joel Feinberg's. Also, three arguments are considered which, while they do not highlight the nonexistence issue, are related to it. (edited)

ELLIS, Brian. *Truth and Objectivity*. Cambridge, Blackwell, 1990

This book explores the implications of scientific realism for ontology, theories of truth, and epistemology. It is argued that scientific realism implies an ontology of natural kinds, natural properties and natural processes—all with their own distinct essences; a naturalistic theory of truth, according to which truth is what it is right epistemically to believe; and a naturalistic values-based epistemology. Given this epistemology, it is argued that objective knowledge is possible only if there are natural kinds, natural properties and natural processes, and that such knowledge is limited to such kinds, properties and processes.

ELLIS, John M. *Against Deconstruction*. Princeton, Princeton Univ Pr, 1989

This is a sustained analysis of the theoretical position known as deconstruction. It analyzes the major deconstructive themes and the modes of thought, ideas and arguments through which deconstructionists claim to enlarge our view of meaning in language. Particular attention is given to Derrida's reading of Saussure, which emerges as muddled and uncomprehending. Deconstruction's major themes are not original and useful but instead reformulations of the most persistent and regressive underlying attitudes of traditional criticism. In spite of its claims to theoretical sophistication, deconstruction is an inherently antitheoretical position, one which diminishes the role of theoretical reflection in language, literature and philosophy.

ELLIS, Ralph D. Afferent-Efferent Connections and Neutrality-Modifications in Perceptual and Imaginative Consciousness. Man World, 23(1), 23-33, Ja 90.

This paper attempts to correlate introspective examination of conscious events with corresponding neurological processes in order to answer a question posed by Dennett and others: If there is a similarity between what is happening in my consciousness (and in my brain) when I *see* an object and what is happening when I merely imagine or remember the same object, how do we account for this similarity? The solution proposed is that the imaginative consciousness of 'looking for' something occurs in the efferent part of the brain, whereas the consciousness of 'looking at' that same object combines a similar efferent function with corresponding inputs from the afferent system.

ELLIS, Ralph D. The Moral Significance of Hard Toil: Critique of a Common Intuition. Phil Forum, 21(3), 343-358, Spr 90.

The notion that people should be rewarded proportionately to how hard they work is a common one, and has recently been supported, e.g., by James Sterba on Rawlsian grounds. Such arguments involve the difficulty that inequality of outcome is to be justified by a supposed equality of opportunity, yet it is obvious that, if the gap between winners and losers in a game becomes too wide, then the person in a Rawlsian original position (or any other objective observer) would not consider equality of opportunity sufficient to justify the change of losing so severely; moreover, he might prefer not to play that particular game for such high stakes.

ELLIS, Robert. The Vulnerability of Action. Relig Stud, 25(2), 225-233, Je 89.

ELLMAN, Ira Mark. Can Others Exercise an Incapacitated Patient's Right to Die? Hastings Center Rep, 20(1), 47-50, Ja-F 90.

The author distinguishes between the ethical issues present in the case of Cruzan v. Harmon and the legal issues as the case is framed before the United States Supreme Court. In *Cruzan*, the Missouri Supreme Court decided that the physicians attending a comatose patient could not disconnect her from equipment supplying life sustaining nutrients on the request of her family, where the patient herself left no instructions indicating her own preferences. While agreeing with most commentators that this decision is wrong, both ethically and legally, the essay concludes that nonetheless it would be an even greater error for the Supreme Court to establish the new constitutional rule that would be required for it to reverse the Missouri court.

ELLOS, William J. Ethical Similarities in Human and Animal Social Structures. Between Species, 5(4), 211-218, Fall 89.

ELOVAARA, Raili. Spinoza and Finnish Literature. Stud Spinozana, 5, 59-80, 1989.

The article deals with the relationship between Spinoza and five Finnish authors, with special attention given to Eeva-Liisa Manner. All five authors are familiar with Spinoza's thought, in particular with his concept of God, pantheism, determinism and freedom. Manner and V A Koskenniemi each wrote a poem actually called "Spinoza." Koskenniemi's sonnet gives Spinoza and his pantheism a romantic colouring. Manner's apparently simple poem is in fact highly complex, showing the philosopher as a failed rationalist and an incipient intuitionist. This poem deserves the status of "a creative comment" on Spinoza.

ELSTER, Jon. "Marxism and Individualism" in *Knowledge and Politics*, DASCAL, Marcelo (ed), 189-206. Boulder, Westview Pr, 1988.

ELTON, Maria. La autofundamentación de la conciencia y la liberación del espíritu. Anu Filosof, 21(2), 71-88, 1988.

Fénelon, como Descartes, demuestra la existencia de Dios a partir de la duda. Pero si para Descartes la duda es una mera operación crítica del pensamiento que antecede a la evidencia, para Fénelon la duda es una crisis de fe, un estado psicológico mas profundo. Al describir filosóficamente ese estado, Fénelon explica que la fe es un movimiento de la voluntad del hombre que se encuentra con la voluntad de Dios, en el vacío de todo discurso racional que tenga su origen en el amore propio. Ese encuentro implica un conocimiento humano que es unión con Dios, y no mera representación intelectual.

ELTON, María. Lo místico como síntesis entre bien y belleza. Anu Filosof, 20(2), 149-158, 1987.

El propósito de este artículo es averiguar si existe una relación entre el bien y la belleza, a partir de la interpretación de algunos textos de Platón y de Fénelon. En esos textos se dice, en síntesis, que la contemplación de la belleza en sí es amor, preferencia por otro, salida de sí, ausencia de goce en el sentido de autoafirmación personal y, por tanto, la mejor actitud moral. Esa interpretación implica la afirmación de que se puede amar desinteresadamente, y se aparta de la interpretación intelectualista del arte propia del Renacimiento.

ELZINGA, Aant. A Critical View of Swedish Science Policy. Phil Soc Act, 15(3-4), 7-21, Jl-D 89.

EMAD, Parvis and MALY, Kenneth. Poetic Saying as Beckoning: The Opening of Hölderlin's *Germanien*. Res Phenomenol, 19, 121-138, 1989.

EMMANUEL, Steven M. Kierkegaard on Doctrine: A Post-Modern Interpretation. Relig Stud, 25(3), 363-378, S 89.

In this essay it is argued that Kierkegaard presupposes an essentially postmodern view of religious doctrine. The essay is divided into three parts. In the first, I present a brief exposition of the regulative theory of doctrine as that is developed by George Lindbeck. In the second, it is shown how the salient features of the regulative proposal can be traced in the development of the Kierkegaardian theory of subjectivity. And in the final part, I address some of the conceptual difficulties with the regulative view, in particular the relation it posits between rules and truth.

EMMET, Dorothy. "Creativity and the Passage of Nature" in *Whitehead's Metaphysics of Creativity*, RAPP, Friedrich (ed), 59-69. Albany, SUNY Pr, 1990.

EMMETT, Kathleen. Forms of Life. Phil Invest, 13(3), 213-231, Jl 90.

Wittgenstein's remarks about "forms of life" have been interpreted in two startlingly different ways. Bernard Williams, Lynne Rudder-Baker and Jonathan Lear take our forms of life to be transcendental limits on anything human. The anthropological interpretation takes forms of life to be variable practices and expectations which differ from one culture or historical period to another. I argue that the transcendental reading misunderstands the connection between grammar and necessity. Lear et al. wrongly suppose that the necessity we attach to certain practices within our forms of life can be transferred to the forms of life themselves. Such necessity is purely an artifact of grammar, not a transcendental limit on humanness.

EMMETT, Kathleen. Must Intentional States Be IntenSional? Behaviorism,

17(2), 129-136, Fall 89.

I argue that intenSionality (opacity) is a feature of the intentional states (states with content) of language users. An animal's beliefs, if true, are true under any description of their content. This point is directed against Alexander Rosenberg who thinks that attempts to naturalize intentional explanation have failed because they have rendered intentional states nonintenSional. (See Rosenberg, "Intentional Psychology and Evolutionary Biology," *Behaviorism* 14, nos 1 and 2.) I argue that naturalization proceeds if we restrict intenSionality to the psychological states of language users, and I offer independent evidence for the plausibility of this restriction.

ENDERLE, Georges and DACHLER, H Peter. Epistemological and Ethical Considerations in Conceptualizing and Implementing Human Resource Management. J Bus Ethics, 8(8), 597-606, Ag 89.

As an example of applied social science, the field of human resource management is used to show that ethical problems are not only those of carrying out research, of professional conduct, and of the "distribution fairness" of social science knowledge. A largely overlooked ethical issue is also the implicit choices that are made as an integral part of research and implementation. First, an analysis is undertaken of the implicit assumptions, values and goals that derive from the conception of human problems in work organizations as "managing human resources." Secondly, it is argued that such a conception is in fact a socially constructed reality with "real" consequences and not a reflection of "objective" states of human and social nature with which we have to live. Thirdly, to the extent that our implicit assumptions are in part based upon conceptual choices that are made by individuals or as a collective act of a discipline or work organization, the development of an ethical framework that could guide such choices becomes a crucial challenge for business ethics.

ENDICOTT, Ronald P. On Physical Multiple Realization. Pac Phil Quart, 70(3), 212-224, S 89.

I respond to those who claim that the "multiple realizability" argument has been vitiated by the fact that physical properties are also multiply realized. First, mental properties have distinct realization bases, and only they can be realized with respect to the entire range of physical properties. Second, the appeal to multiply realized physical properties wrongly presupposes that multiple realization provides a *criterion* for being mental or nonphysical. But other criteria are used to make an initial classification into psychological vs. physical types; and then multiple realization enters to answer the question naturally raised about intertheoretic identity.

ENGBERG-PEDERSEN, Troels. "Stoic Philosophy and the Concept of the Person" in *The Person and the Human Mind: Issues in Ancient and Modern Philosophy*, GILL, Christopher (ed), 109-135. New York, Clarendon/Oxford Pr, 1989.

The article attempts to bring out the central content of a notion of personhood or human individuality, which it claims to be the official one in European philosophy up to the early modern period, by showing its roots in an understanding of practical rationality as elaborated by the Stoics. It then compares and contrasts the Stoic understanding of the individual with the one that underlies two modern accounts, in Bernard Williams's discussion of the distinction between practical and factual deliberation in *Ethics and the Limits of Philosophy* and Thomas Nagel's discussion of freedom in *The View from Nowhere*.

ENGEL, Pascal. Interprétation et mentalité prélogique. Rev Phil Fr, 179(4), 543-558, O-D 89.

ENGEL, S Morris. The Many Faces of Amphiboly. Metaphilosophy, 20(3-4), 347-355, Jl-O 89.

ENGEL-TIERCELIN, Claudine. C S Peirce et le projet d'une "logique du vague". Arch Phil, 52(4), 553-579, O-D 89.

Peirce's logic of vagueness covers what is usually meant today by works in semantics concerning the vagueness of ordinary language or by researches in the field of nonstandard logic (e.g., Peirce's triadic logic). But it is mainly a project grounded in a certain semiotical and ontological conception of formal logic. In that sense, Peirce's logic of vagueness is everywhere: it is part and parcel of his semiotical realism. It is a general theory of the vagueness surrounding signs (their meanings as well as their references). Despite its specificity, Peirce's project gives precious indications for contemporary researches on vagueness and on the well- or ill-founded reasons one may have to abandon classical logic.

ENGELHARDT JR, H Tristram. "Advance Directives and the Right to Be Left Alone" in *Advance Directives in Medicine*, HACKLER, Chris (ed), 141-154. New York, Praeger, 1989.

ENGELHARDT JR, H Tristram. Applied Philosophy in the Post-Modern Age: An Augury. J Soc Phil, 20(1-2), 42-48, Spr-Fall 89.

Given the substantial arguments in the 20th century against the possibility of rationally establishing any particular moral philosophy as intellectually canonical, the broad cultural success of applied philosophy and the interest in theories of justice are incongruous at best. Despite skeptical arguments which may undermine applied, cultural needs which promote interest in applied philosophy are likely to become more intense. Applied philosophy will be challenged to develop strategies for living with content-full moralities and the pluralism of moral visions.

ENGELHARDT JR, H Tristram. The Birth of the Medical Humanities and the Rebirth of the Philosophy of Medicine: The Vision of Edmund D Pellegrino. J Med Phil, 15(3), 237-241, Je 90.

ENGELHARDT JR, H Tristram. Can Ethics Take Pluralism Seriously? Hastings Center Rep, 19(5), 33-34, S-O 89.

ENGELHARDT JR, H Tristram. "Death by Free Choice: Modern Variations on an Antique Theme" in *Suicide and Euthanasia*, BRODY, Baruch A (ed), 251-280. Norwell, Kluwer, 1989.

ENGELL, James. Leading Out Into the World: Vico's New Education. New Vico Studies, 3, 33-47, 1985.

Vico's thoughts on education stress exercise of the imagination rather than emphasis on technique and method, especially when the student is young. Early specialization must be avoided. Poetry and rhetoric help to humanize knowledge and, along with philosophy, stress education as a general end rather than a series of often disconnected means. Imaginative facility with language can transform inert knowledge into the realm of social and moral use. Affinities with Bacon and Schelling are noted. Vico's ideas remain relevant in an era characterized by specialization. His views are in *The New Science*, *De nostri temporis studiorum ratione*, and *De mente heroica*.

ENGELS, Eve-Marie. Erkenntnistheorietischer Konstruktionismus, Minimalrealismus, empirischer Realismus. Z Phil Forsch, 44(1), 28-54, 1990.

In recent discussions about evolutionary epistemology, realism and constructionism usually are held to be two incompatible positions. Advocates of evolutionary epistemology maintain that their theory is necessarily combined with realism, whereas their opponents reject this kind of realism as being a metaphysical position, and sometimes they plead for constructionism as an alternative to realism. The author shows that (empirical) realism and (epistemological) constructionism are compatible and even indispensable for an evolutionary epistemology, and that constructionism does not imply arbitrariness but has its foundations in a "minimal realism."

ENGELS, Frederick and MARX, Karl. *Collected Works, Volume 30, Marx: 1861-1863*. New York, Intl Publ, 1989

ENGELS, Frederick and MARX, Karl. *Collected Works, Volume 31, Marx: 1861-1863*. New York, Intl Publ, 1989

ENGELS, Frederick and MARX, Karl. *Collected Works, Volume 44, Marx and Engels: 1870-1873*. New York, Intl Publ, 1990

ENGLER, Gideon. Aesthetics in Science and in Art. Brit J Aes, 30(1), 24-34, Ja 90.

The importance in science of the aesthetic criteria of symmetry, simplicity, order, coherence, unity, elegance and harmony, is examined. A comparison with art supports the view that aesthetic appreciation in science and in art possess close affinity.

ENGLISH, Parker. Bribery and the United States Foreign Corrupt Practices Act. Int J Applied Phil, 4(4), 13-23, Fall 89.

ENNIS, Robert H. The Rationality of Rationality: Why Think Critically? Response to Siegel. Proc Phil Educ, 45, 402-405, 1989.

Harvey Siegel has attempted to provide a universally applicable rational defense of rationality (and, he claims, of critical thinking). Ennis responds by showing crucial weaknesses in Siegel's defense and by proposing a defense strategy that should fit most situations. Siegel defended rationality by showing that a person who seeks a justification of rationality is presupposing the appropriateness of giving reasons. Ennis responds by noting that such a defense, if it worked, would be binding only on someone seeking a justification of rationality, and thus would not be a defense of rationality. But, he argues, the defense does not even work for people seeking a justification of rationality. Being committed to the appropriateness of reasons does not commit one to rationality, because one might be only committed to the appropriateness of giving reasons that actually are irrational—hardly a commitment to rationality.

ENO, Robert. *The Confucian Creation of Heaven: Philosophy and the Defense of Ritual Mastery*. Albany, SUNY Pr, 1990

This book explores the earliest Confucian texts to find coherent structural principles linking the various facets of Confucian doctrine. Its central theme

is that the coherence of early Confucianism emerges only when doctrine is viewed as a function of the unique ritual practice of the early Confucian community. Exploring the systematic relation between practice and theory through analysis of metaphysical doctrines and their background, it is suggested that Confucianism represents a species of "synthetic" philosophy, distinct from the analytical traditions of the West.

ENSLIN, Penny. Sandel and the Limits of Community. Proc Phil Educ, 45, 249-257, 1989.

Communitarian critiques of liberalism challenge liberal conceptions of the self in society, and hence liberal conceptions of education. Michael J Sandel's *Liberalism and the Limits of Justice* is a notable example of a communitarian critique of liberalism. This paper argues against Sandel's constitutive conception of community as an alternative to Rawls's sentimental conception of community. Assuming that *apartheid* is a social doctrine to which the reader will be opposed, the paper argues that Sandel's constitutive notion of community is problematic, by showing how the *apartheid* doctrine of education reflects just such a constitutive conception of community.

EODICE, Alexander R. Dewey and Wittgenstein on the Idea of Certainty. Phil Today, 34(1), 30-38, Spr 90.

This paper compares Dewey's view of certainty with that of Wittgenstein in an attempt to derive a concept of the kind of certainty required for inquiry. I suggest that this kind of certainty is not epistemic but pragmatic. 'Certainty' is not defined in terms of a special kind of knowledge of a privileged class of propositions; instead it refers to a set of background assumptions which are, strictly speaking, neither known nor unknown but acknowledged.

EPSTEIN, Edwin M. Business Ethics, Corporate Good Citizenship and the Corporate Social Policy Process: A View from the US. J Bus Ethics, 8(8), 583-595, Ag 89.

Within the American context, the term corporate good citizenship, a rather vague and somewhat dated notion, bears little relationship to the concept of business ethics. Whereas the latter refers to systematic reflection on the moral significance of the institutions, policies and behavior of business actors in the normal course of their business operations, the former is a subset of the broader notion of corporate social responsibility and denotes, generally, discretionary, possibly altruistic, "nonbusiness" relationships between business organizations and diverse community stakeholders. A newer concept, the corporate social policy process, provides analytical linkages between business ethics and corporate good citizenship which can be useful to business scholars and operating managers alike. (edited)

EPSTEIN, Richard L and D'OTTAVIANO, Itala M L. A Paraconsistent Many-Valued Propositional Logic. Rep Math Log, 22, 89-103, 1988.

In a previous paper D'Ottaviano and da Costa introduced a propositional system called J_3, which is a three-valued system with two distinguished truth-values, which is paraconsistent and also reflects aspects of modal logics. D'Ottaviano also extended the system to first-order J_3-theories. In this paper the authors give a technical development of J_3 and discuss the intuitions behind the logic. The system is presented in two different ways, depending on the choice of primitive connectives. The interdefinability of the connectives, the relation between J_3 and the classical propositional logic and the notions of consistency and completeness are discussed. A set-assignment semantics for J_3 using falsity as a default truth-value is also presented.

EPSTEIN, Richard L. *The Semantic Foundations of Logic, Volume 1: Propositional Logics*. Norwell, Kluwer, 1990

This is the first book to present the history, philosophy, and mathematics of the major systems of modern propositional logic. Classical logic, modal logics, many-valued logics, intuitionism, paraconsistent logics, and analytic implication are each examined in separate chapters. Each begins with a motivation in the originators' own terms, followed by the standard formal semantics and syntax and completeness theorem. One chapter summarizes translation between the logics with a general theory of translation. (edited)

EPSTEIN, William M. Confirmational Response Bias Among Social Work Journals. Sci Tech Human Values, 15(1), 9-38, Wint 90.

This article reports the results of a study of confirmational response bias among social work journals. A contrived research paper with positive findings and its negative mirror image were submitted to two different groups of social work journals and to two comparison groups of journals outside social work. The quantitative results, suggesting bias, are tentative; but the qualitative findings based upon an analysis of the referee comments are clear and consistent. Few referees from prestigious or nonprestigious social work journals prepared reviews that were knowledgeable, scientifically astute, or objective. The best reviews came from journals outside of social work or from journals that are accepted as social work journals but originate with other disciplines.

ERDE, Edmund L. Studies in the Explanation of Issues in Biomedical Ethics: (II) On "On Play[ing] God", Etc.. J Med Phil, 14(6), 593-615, D 89.

A previous essay (Erde, 1988) tracked the influence of the major Western historical paradigm of the great chain of being through various positions taken about abortion. This essay shows the paradigm's influence on our language—especially in animating the use of "god" and phrases like "playing god." This is important given the prevalence of religious values in bioethics debates and the pervasiveness of the language. I hunt unsuccessfully for a meaning that could serve as a moral principle, and I show how these phrases are rooted in the paradigm. I conclude that all that such language can do is offer the pretense that there is a specific absolute ground for forbidding something which could otherwise be morally acceptable. But such language is nearly senseless, and worse still, it is immoral in that it cuts off reflection and debate.

ERES, Gloria H. Hume's Philosophical Schizophrenia. Pac Phil Quart, 71(1), 14-22, Mr 90.

ERICHSEN, N and SPECHT, E K. "Die Empfindungen des Anderen: Ein Disput zwischen Cartesianer und Wittgensteinianer" in *Wittgenstein in Focus—Im Brennpunkt: Wittgenstein*, MC GUINNESS, Brian (ed), 305-334. Amsterdam, Rodopi, 1989.

Cartesianer und Wittgensteinianer diskutieren über die logischen Grundlagen der Empfindungssprache. Mit einem Gedankenexperiment suggeriert der Cartesianer die Notwendigkeit, "private Objekte" anzunehmen. Der Wittgensteinianer deckt die "grammatische Täuschung" auf, der der Cartesianer dabei unterliegt. Nun sucht dieser, seinen Ansatz zu retten, indem er die Empfindungen des anderen als "theoretische Entitäten" (etwa im Rahmen der Hirnphysiologie) konstruiert: Neucartesianismus. Bestimmte empirische Befunde könnten ihn dabei aber in das Dilemma bringen, entweder seine Theorie oder seine "natürliche Einstellung" zum anderen Menschen aufzugeben. Allerdings bleibt auch dem Wittgensteinianer ein ähnliches Dilemma letztlich nicht erspart.

ERIKSEN, Leif. Confirmation, Paradox, and Logic. Phil Sci, 56(4), 681-687, D 89.

Paul Horwich has formulated a paradox which he believes to be even more virulent than the related Hempel paradox. I show that Horwich's paradox, as originally formulated, has a purely logical solution, hence that it has no bearing on the theory of confirmation. On the other hand, it illuminates some undesirable traits of classical predicate logic. A revised formulation of the paradox is then dealt with in a way that implies a modest revision of Nicod's criterion.

ERIKSSON, Karl-Erik. A Critical Perspective in the Physical Sciences. Phil Soc Act, 15(3-4), 23-27, Jl-D 89.

ESSLER, Wilhelm K. Selbst das Selbst ist nicht Selbst. Erkenntnis, 32(3), 295-340, My 90.

The Buddhist triad of body, speech and mind and the concept of self as their function are analysed from an analytic philosopher's point of view. Buddhism is seen as an empirical religion with intersubjective operationalisations of its concepts. The mind is not observable but can be found by empirical methods in the traces of its actions, which can be found in the utterances of speech. Semantical and other paradoxes do not permit the location of mind within the hierarchy of languages. Mind has an active aspect by choosing a suitable frame of reference for every activity of the aspect of speech and is thus irreducible to that aspect. Mind is the space, the essence, indescribable by language, of possible frames of reference for perception and cognition. This absolute aspect of the mind corresponds to an absolute aspect of the self, unique by *identitas indiscernibilium*, which cannot be perceived, but can be found by the exercise of awareness; while the relative self corresponds to the individual form of cognition and does not therefore presuppose a semantical regress of ever richer metalanguages.

ESSLER, Wilhelm and RIVADULLA, Andrés (trans). Filosofar abierto. Rev Filosof (Spain), 2, 155-168, 1989.

ESTEVÁO, J C. *Fiat Voluntas Tua!* Vício e Pecado na ética de Abelardo. Trans/Form/Acao, 12, 85-96, 1989.

Abelardo, na sua ética, desqualifica a noção de "vício" em favor da noção de "pecado". Esta passagem não é apenas um pressuposto do autor, mas decorre necessariamente tanto de sua posição enquanto lógico quanto de sua crítica dos filósofos estóicos que pôde conhecer.

ESTILL, Lyle. Unfree Enterprise. J Bus Ethics, 9(1), 39-43, Ja 90.

In the completely unregulated microcomputer industry, ethical restrictions to business are often self-imposed or put in place by the suppliers of product. This article addresses the problems which can arise from the implementation of "authorization" programs. It is the history of one product's success in the

Canadian marketplace, from the US vendor, to the Canadian distributor, to computer dealers, to the end-user. The focus is on an authorization program, applied after the fact, to a local market which was unwilling to abide by the program's good intent.

ESTLUND, David M. Democracy Without Preference. Phil Rev, 99(3), 397-423, Jl 90.

A normative democratic theory must specify what proper democratic voting is. A common account of democratic votes sees them as expressions of individual preferences over social alternatives, where this usually means desires, interests, dispositions to choose, or reports of one of these three. *No preference interpretation of voting can jointly meet three reasonable conditions on the interpretation of democratic votes: activity—votes must be acts; advocacy—votes must have some practical valence; aggregability—votes must be on some common topic. There is an interpretation that succeeds where preference interpretations fail, namely that votes are opinions on the common interest.*

ESTLUND, David M. Mutual Benevolence and the Theory of Happiness. J Phil, 87(4), 187-204, Ap 90.

Imagine just two people, each of whom has no desire other than for the satisfaction of the other's desire. The structure of this case is important for moral theory, by way of the havoc it wreaks on the notions of benevolence and happiness. As an example, this loop will be shown to occur under certain assumptions of Butler's moral psychology. The loop problem puts a certain pressure on a satisfaction conception of happiness. Butler himself may have held an interesting alternative conception of happiness which is not subject to the loop and its associated problems.

ESTRELLA, Jorge. Die Philosophie und ihre Missbildungen. Conceptus, 24(61), 3-16, 1990.

In the same way as medicine is distinct from quackery, there also is a difference between philosophy proper and some adulterated forms of discourse, that should thus not be called *philosophical*. The author names and analyses four of these malformations that are prevailing in our societies: pedagogicality, confusionism, quotationism, and ideologism. In sum, this essay is intended to supply a mere theory of knowledge with an ethics of knowing.

ETCHEMENDY, John. *The Concept of Logical Consequence*. Cambridge, Harvard Univ Pr, 1990

In this book, I argue that the standard, model-theoretic account of logical consequence is mistaken, and that its acceptance has resulted in a variety of confusions in logic and the philosophy of logic.

ÉTIENNE, Jacques. Bergson et l'idée de causalité. Rev Phil Louvain, 87(76), 589-611, N 89.

From his *Time and Free Will* to *The Two Sources of Morality and Religion* via *Matter and Memory* and *Creative Evolution*, the idea of causality reveals some of Bergson's great preoccupations: the irreducibility of psychic to physical phenomena, of duration to homogeneous space, of freedom to its prerequisites, of an event to that which precedes it, finally, of personal creativity open to that which is universally human to passivity in which impersonal and particular social pressure triumphs.

EVANS, C S. Is Kierkegaard an Irrationalist: Reason, Paradox, and Faith. Relig Stud, 25(3), 347-362, S 89.

Kierkegaard is often denigrated as an irrationalist on the grounds that he advocated belief in the Incarnation, understood as a formal contradiction. I give both textual and philosophical arguments that when Kierkegaard called the Incarnation the absolute paradox he meant that it was an apparent contradiction, but not that it involved a formal contradiction. The tension between faith and reason is not necessary but arises when reason makes imperialistic claims to have no limits. Faith is not based on evidence but is grounded in an encounter which transforms the individual, including the attitudes and values which permeate the thinking of the individual.

EVANS, C Stephen. Does Kierkegaard Think Beliefs Can Be Directly Willed? Int J Phil Relig, 26(3), 173-184, D 89.

This article discusses the question as to whether Kierkegaard thought beliefs were under the direct control of the will. Contrary to many interpretations which see Kierkegaard as holding the untenable position that beliefs can be directly created by volitions, I argue that Kierkegaard's claim is only the noncontroversial one that beliefs can be brought about by the will through indirect means. The role of will is illuminated by a discussion of Kierkegaard's quasi-Humean, nonfoundationalist epistemology. With respect to religious beliefs, willing is necessary, not to make myself believe what I know is untrue, but to create moral qualities essential to grasping religious truth.

EVANS, D M. Counterexamples to a Conjecture on Relative Categoricity.

Annals Pure Applied Log, 46(2), 201-209, F 90.

EVANS, Hugh. Why Blackmail Should be Banned. Philosophy, 65(251), 89-94, Ja 90.

David Owens contended in "Should Blackmail Be Banned?" (*Philosophy*, Vol. LXV, No. 246, 1988) that blackmail should be banned because it is irrational to enter such a contract. It is argued that this is wrong, because it is likely that entering the contract increases the chances of the desired result, particularly if the payment will be refunded should the desired result not be achieved. Harming people is generally impermissible; publishing information is an exception to this because of the importance of free speech. Blackmailing someone to pay money rather than have information published cannot fall under such an exception and is therefore wrong.

EVANS, J Claude. Deconstructing the Declaration: A Case Study in Pragrammatology. Man World, 23(2), 175-189, Ap 90.

In "Declarations of Independence" (*New Political Science* 5, 1986, 7-15), Jacques Derrida claims that it is systematically undecidable whether the force of the Declaration is constative or performative, and that this confusion is essential for the desired effect of the Declaration. I argue that much of Derrida's analysis is based on a systematic neglect of historical context: undecidability and "*différance*" are read into, not out of the text and context of the Declaration.

EVANS, J Claude. Phenomenological Deconstruction: Husserl's Method of *Abbau*. J Brit Soc Phenomenol, 21(1), 14-25, Ja 90.

This essay traces the genesis of the term "deconstruction" from Derrida through Heidegger to Husserl's use of the term "*Abbau.*" It criticizes Gasche's interpretation of the Husserlian method of *ABBAU* as well as David Carr's interpretation. Finally, it offers an interpretation of the method of *Abbau* as Husserl presents it in texts ranging from 1921 to *Experience and Judgment.*

EVANS, J Claude. Socratic Ignorance—Socratic Wisdom. Mod Sch, 67(2), 91-109, Ja 90.

This essay undertakes a dialogical reading of some of Plato's early "Socratic" dialogues, arguing that the famous "what is it?" question turns out to be something of a red herring when approached from this perspective rather than from the perspective of the so-called Theory of Ideas. Socratic virtue is not rooted in a substantive knowledge of the *eidos* of piety, virtue or justice, but in a kind of action: inquiry undertaken in the awareness of one's ignorance. This activity is itself capable of making us better human beings and of giving shape to human life.

EVANS, Martyn. A Plea for the Heart. Bioethics, 4(3), 227-231, Jl 90.

Brain-centred conceptions of death (upon which vital-organ transplantation depends) are shown to rely on metaphysical views of the uniqueness of the brain in relation to what is characteristic of human life. Rival versions of brain-centred conceptions of death are shown to conflict in expressly metaphysical and moral terms. Thus such conceptions represent moral claims (rather than scientific descriptions) and may be challenged as such. A challenge is offered, affirming the primacy of generally held attitudes on moral understanding, and, thence, the vital significance of the spontaneously beating heart.

EVERS, Colin W. Naturalism and Philosophy of Education. Educ Phil Theor, 19(2), 11-21, 1987.

EVERSON, Stephen. Aristotle's Compatibilism in the *Nicomachean Ethics.* Ancient Phil, 10(1), 81-103, Spr 90.

Aristotle's discussion of voluntary action in the *EN* is best understood within a determinist account of action. His claim that an action is compelled if its cause lies outside the agent seems at first sight a desperate attempt to distinguish a class of actions for which the agent is not responsible: desperate because on this criterion, a compelled action would not seem to be an *action* at all. We can make sense of this, and explain how the emotions are also voluntary, if we take his claim to be that voluntary actions can be causally explained by reference to the agent's character rather than to his human nature.

EVERSON, Stephen. "Epicurus on the Truth of the Senses" in *Epistemology (Companions to Ancient Thought: 1),* EVERSON, Stephen (ed), 161-183. New York, Cambridge Univ Pr, 1989.

Epicurus's claim that 'all perceptions are true' has traditionally been taken to be a rather naive attempt to rebut scepticism. This assumes falsely, however, that the objects of perception, with which perceptions must accord to be true, are what the perceptions represent to the subject. When it is seen that the latter are solid objects, whilst the former are the atoms which impact on the sense-organs, Epicurus turns out to provide a quite sophisticated and naturalistic perceptual epistemology.

EVERSON, Stephen (ed). *Epistemology (Companions to Ancient*

Thought: 1). New York, Cambridge Univ Pr, 1989

The collection seeks critically to present central arguments in ancient epistemology in such a way as to reveal their depth and sophistication. It contains papers by Edward Hussey, Paul Woodruff, Gail Fine, Christopher Taylor, Stephen Everson, Julia Annas, Jonathan Barnes, Michael Frede and Myles Burnyeat and covers the period from Homer to Sextus Empiricus and the medical empiricists.

EVERTS, Diederik. An Analysis of Monologues and Dialogues in Political Debates. Commun Cog, 22(3-4), 375-381, 1989.

EWBANK, Michael B. Diverse Orderings of Dionysius's *Triplex via* by Saint Thomas Aquinas. Med Stud, 52, 82-109, 1990.

EWELL JR, John W. Dai Zhen: The Unity of the Moral Nature (in Serbo-Croatian). Filozof Istraz, 29(2), 527-531, 1989.

Chu Hsi, faced with the views of Mencius and Ch'eng I on the source of morality, made a masterful synthesis: he posited a place in the human mind that the pattern of heaven-and-earth might inhabit, while admitting that one's everyday mind, however it tended toward the pattern, still encountered tremendous obstacles in attaining to it. Yet this solution created a divided mind as well as a certain ambivalence toward the feelings and attachments of everyday life. Dai Zhen rescued human feelings and tastes for the moral life. Specifically, he argues that just as all men like certain things, the tastes of all men—including their moral tastes—can be educated and perfected. The sage, then, does not overcome his common human feelings, he simply develops and refines them.

EWIN, R E. Pride, Prejudice and Shyness. Philosophy, 65(252), 137-154, Ap 90.

EXTEJT, Marian M and BOCKANIC, William N. Issues Surrounding the Theories of Negligent Hiring and Failure to Fire. Bus Prof Ethics J, 8(4), 21-34, Wint 89.

FABIAN, Johannes. Presence and Representation: The Other and Anthropological Writing. Crit Inquiry, 16(4), 753-772, Sum 90.

Must representing the Other in anthropology go together with denying the Other's presence in the world of the representer? Alternatives are explored by approaching representation as praxis and reviewing some practices of writing as representation, including the option of not-writing. The aim is recognition of the Other that is not limited to, dictated by, representations of the Other.

FABRIS, Adriano. Franz Rosenzweig a cent'anni dalla nascita. Teoria, 9(1), 231-240, 1989.

FABRO, Cornelio. Linee dell'attività filosofico-teologica della Beata Edith Stein. Aquinas, 32(2), 193-256, My-Ag 89.

FACIO, Tatiana. Hegel y Marcuse: El Ideal o la Forma Estética. Rev Filosof (Costa Rica), 26, 125-132, D 88.

The concept of "aesthetic form" in H Marcuse finds in Hegel's aesthetics the way to oppose to sociologism in art and to make of aesthetics the form of expression that can have a subversive potential in a world limited by solidified oppositions.

FAGENSON, Ellen A. At the Heart of Women in Management Research: Theoretical and Methodological Approaches and Their Biases. J Bus Ethics, 9(4-5), 267-274, Ap-My 90.

This paper examines the dominant theoretical approaches in the field of women in management (WIM) that have been applied to explain women's limited ability to assume organizational positions of significant power. The propositions of traditional (gender-centered and organization structure perspectives) and a newer theoretical perspective (gender-organization-system approach) are discussed. It is proposed that the theories embraced by WIM researchers bias the factors they examine, the methodologies they employ, the statistical techniques they apply, the results they obtain and the conclusions they reach. This is shown to be a particular problem with the gender-centered and organization structure perspectives and not the gender-organization-system approach.

FAIRCHILD, David L. Sport Abjection: Steroids and the Uglification of the Athlete. J Phil Sport, 16, 74-88, 1989.

FALK, Raphael. Between Beanbag Genetics and Natural Selection. Biol Phil, 5(3), 313-325, Jl 90.

The encounter between the Darwinian theory of evolution and Mendelism could be resolved only when reductionist tools could be applied to the analysis of complex systems. The instrumental reductionist interpretation of the hereditary basis of continuously varying traits provided mathematical tools which eventually allowed the construction of the "Modern Synthesis" of the theory of evolution. When genotypic as well as environmental variance allow the isolation of parts of the system, it is possible to apply Mendelian reductionism, that is, to treat the phenotypic trait as if it is causally determined by discrete "genes for" the trait. However, such a "beanbag genetics" approach obscures the system's eye-view. (edited)

FALK, W D. Humanism. Personalist Forum, 5(2), 69-81, Fall 89.

FALKENBERG, L and MONACHELLO, M. Dual-Career and Dual-Income Families: Do They Have Different Needs? J Bus Ethics, 9(4-5), 339-351, Ap-My 90.

Dual-earner families have been treated as if they are a homogenous group of individuals having to cope with similar demands. Yet these families vary in their rationale for both spouses working outside the home (from financial necessity to personal growth) and the responsibilities each spouse assumes in the home. Given the variations in work and home responsibilities it is proposed that members of dual-earner families should be studied on the basis of (1) the rationale each spouse has for working, (b) the responsibility each spouse assumes in the home, and (c) the gender of the spouse. A model delineating the different problems experienced by individuals within these subgroups is developed based on an extensive review of the literature.

FALKENSTEIN, Lorne. Kant's Account of Sensation. Can J Phil, 20(1), 63-88, Mr 90.

Various remarks Kant makes about intuition, space, and sensation commit him to the view that sensations are physical states of the body of the perceiving subject. This paper examines the reasons for this conclusion, some of the major difficulties associated with it, and its implications for Kant's empirical realism.

FALKENSTEIN, Lorne. Kant's Argument for the Non-Spatiotemporality of Things in Themselves. Kantstudien, 80(3), 265-283, 1989.

Kant's problematic conclusion, that we can know that things in themselves are not in space or time, is shown to follow directly from his claim that space and time are manners of disposition or forms of arrangement in which various items are presented to us in intuition. This argument is not strong enough to rule out certain well-defined senses in which things in themselves could possibly be spatiotemporal, but it does show that any sense in which things in themselves could be in space or time would bear no relation to the spatiotemporal features of appearances.

FANG, J. "Deus ex machina" redivivus: The "Synthetic A Priori" in the Computer Age. Phil Math, 4(2), 217-232, 1989.

Emphasis is on the "pragmatic" if not simply "operational" virtue of maintaining the Kantian bifurcation of synthetic vs. analytic a priori, especially in the light of manifest limits relative to the temporal aspect of computation in the current age of computers, and this, against the fashion since Ayer's flagrant abuse of Deus ex machina in his linguistic turn for the monolithic monopoly of the analytic a priori. To be reconsidered here is the oft-neglected nature of mathematics in the manner practiced by "working" mathematicians: *one at a time* for specific problems—never *once for all* [problems].

FANG, J. Is Philosophy, As Is, "Bunk"? Phil Math, 5(1-2), 142-150, 1990.

Philosophical emphasis here is on "assembling" than "dissembling" which has already gone far enough (via very "professional" specialization or more recently via deconstructionism—as is flagrantly the case of the late de Man who would defend his Nazi past via his dogma). The surrealistic loss in touch with reality is exemplified here through the insight of William L Shirer, the *practicing* historian (in his latest book, 1989) vs. *academic* historians. Meden again (nothing in excess)!—so warned Aristotle long ago, but philosophy in academic excesses has turned "bunk"!

FANG, Liping and KILGOUR, D Marc and HIPEL, Keith W. A Decision Support System for the Graph Model of Conflicts. Theor Decis, 28(3), 289-311, My 90.

A comprehensive decision support system called GMCA (graph model for conflict analysis) implementing the multi-player graph model for analyzing conflicts is developed. GMCA contains algorithms for the rapid computation of a wide range of solution concepts, thereby enabling decision makers to take account of the diversity of human behavior. Using an engineering case study, the key features of GMCA are illustrated.

FARARO, Thomas J. *The Meaning of General Theoretical Sociology: Tradition and Formalization*. New York, Cambridge Univ Pr, 1989

The main objectives of the book are to set out a conception of a research tradition focussed on general theoretical knowledge in sociology and to show how its key problems are defined and studied in formal terms. Topics treated in sequential terms are the philosophy and methodology of general theoretical sociology; a dynamical systems formulation of its key problems; formal studies in action theory and social order; and synthesizing theory construction centered on social structural analysis.

FARÍAS, Victor and MARGOLIS, Joseph (ed) and ROCKMORE, Tom (ed).

Heidegger and Nazism. Philadelphia, Temple Univ Pr, 1989

This is the English translation of Victor Farias's *Heidegger et le Nazisme*. It is enlarged and extensively altered by the addition of new and replacement materials from the German edition. Also, substantive errors and errors in the Notes have been corrected. The editors provide a new introductory statement.

FARKAS, E J. A Faithful Embedding of Parallel Computations in Star-Finite Models. Stud Log, 47(3), 203-212, S 88.

The purpose of this paper is to show that there exist star-finite tree-structured sets in which the computations of parallel programs can be faithfully embedded, and that the theory of star-finite sets and relations therefore provides a new tool for the analysis of non-deterministic computations.

FARMER, David J. *Being in Time: The Nature of Time in Light of McTaggart's Paradox*. Lanham, Univ Pr of America, 1990

FARR, James (ed) and BALL, Terence and HANSON, Russell L (ed). *Political Innovation and Conceptual Change*. New York, Cambridge Univ Pr, 1989

FARRAR JR, L L. Porous Vessels: A Critique of the Nation, Nationalism and National Character as Analytical Concepts. Hist Euro Ideas, 10(6), 705-720, 1989.

A critique of the nation, nationalism and national character must confront the paradox that these concepts are widely regarded as distinctive features of the modern world yet difficult to define. Precisely this significance, however, demands a definition which is suggested here as a composite of the three concepts. This definition is criticised and then defended by drawing on the extensive debate over the concepts. In the process they are found not only to be determined by but also to determine a host of concepts constituting the basic framework of social analysis. Far from being an empty semantic exercise, the debate proves to have fundamental implications for our understanding of history. Finally it is argued that the criticism of the national concepts can be applied to all concepts and thus implicates the entire intellectual enterprise.

FARRELL, Daniel M. "Hobbes and International Relations" in *The Causes of Quarrel: Essays on Peace, War, and Thomas Hobbes*, CAWS, Peter (ed), 64-77. Boston, Beacon Pr, 1989.

I summarize Hobbes's famous argument for the rationality of submitting, as individuals, to a certain form of political sovereignty, and I then explore the implications of that argument for the question of whether some equally strong form of inter-state or international political association would be just as rational for nations. I argue that it would be rational, from the standpoint of strict national self-interest, for any but the strongest states, but that it appears not to be rational, from that standpoint, for the very strongest.

FARRELL, Daniel M. Intention, Reason, and Action. Amer Phil Quart, 26(4), 283-295, O 89.

FARRELL, Daniel M. The Justification of Deterrent Violence. Ethics, 100(2), 301-317, Ja 90.

Deterrent violence is violence aimed at inducing others not to do something we want them not to do. I investigate the relevance of antecedent warnings and *threats* to the justifiability of such violence and show that a comprehensive theory of deterrent violence can be grounded entirely on plausible principles of justifiable self-defense.

FARRELL, Daniel M. "Of Jealousy and Envy" in *Person to Person*, GRAHAM, George (ed), 245-268. Philadelphia, Temple Univ Pr, 1989.

This is an attempt to say exactly what it is to be jealous, what it is to be envious, and how the two differ. In addition I discuss some of the various claims that are sometimes made about what each of these emotions "shows" about the jealous or envious individual. Some of the material on jealousy is reprinted from an earlier paper; the work on envy is new.

FARRELL, Martin D. En busca de la voluntad de Dios. Analisis Filosof, 6(2), 97-102, N 86.

FARWELL, Ruth and KNEE, Christopher. The End of the Absolute: A Nineteenth-Century Contribution to General Relativity. Stud Hist Phil Sci, 21(1), 91-121, Mr 90.

This paper considers the geometric ideas of Riemann and Clifford in the latter half of the nineteenth century and their philosophical implications. Both are credited with the anticipation of certain aspects of general relativity: Riemann's work centred on the *nature* of physical space, whereas Clifford suggested *using* the geometry of physical space to describe a theory of all physical quantities. The latter thus proposed the geometrisation of physics, a new philosophy which was to lie at the heart of general relativity in 1916 and underlie subsequent developments in theoretical physics.

FASOLO, Aldo. Ontogenesi della forma e informazione. Epistemologia,

11(2), 325-331, Jl-D 88.

An important achievement of the nowadays developmental biology is the awareness that simplistic mechanical or genetic models of the ontogeny are not tenable. In order to understand the regulatory architecture of the embryo (i.e., how differential patterns of gene activity are instituted) it is necessary to explain not only the mechanisms of cell differentiation but also the inheritance of the form. This conceptual shift means that if the developmental processes are ultimately controlled by, and require, the activity of the genome, nonetheless development can be regarded as a historical cascade of complex stochastic interactions among the different cells. Accordingly, development is considered as an evolutionary process, where selection seemingly occurs also at cellular level and it involves cell groups more than individual cells.

FATTOROSI-BARNABA, M and CERRATO, C. Graded Modalities, III. Stud Log, 47(2), 99-109, Je 88.

We go on along the trend of two previous papers (Fattorosi-Barnaba and De Caro, "Graded modalities, I" (1985) and De Caro, "Graded modalities, II" (1988)), giving an axiomatization of $S4^0$ and proving its completeness and compactness with respect to the usual reflexive and transitive Kripke models. To reach this result, we use techniques from De Caro (1988), with suitable adaptations to our specific case. (edited)

FAUCONNIER, Gilles. "Quantification, Roles and Domains" in *Meaning and Mental Representation*, ECO, Umberto (ed), 61-80. Bloomington, Indiana Univ Pr, 1988.

FAUR, José. Francisco Sanchez's Theory of Cognition and Vico's *verum/factum*. New Vico Studies, 5, 131-146, 1987.

FAUR, José. The Splitting of the *Logos*: Some Remarks on Vico and Rabbinic Tradition. New Vico Studies, 3, 85-103, 1985.

FAWCETT, Carolyn R and CANGUILHEM, Georges and COHEN, Robert S (trans). *The Normal and the Pathological*. Cambridge, Zone Books, 1989

The normal and the pathological are terms used for structures, activities, individual or collective situations proper to living beings and especially to man. The relation of a fact and a norm is its positive or negative value. Can the assessment of behaviors (in medicine, psychology, law and jurisprudence) be reduced to noting a necessity? Is a living being's disease a fact similar to universal attraction? The author maintains that diseases are not merely predetermined effects, but are revealing of a normative regulation proper to living beings and man.

FAWKES, Don. Regarding Rich's "Compatibilism Argument" and the 'Ought'-Implies-'Can' Argument. SW Phil Rev, 6(2), 123-124, Jl 90.

FAY, Brian. *Critical* Realism? J Theor Soc Behav, 20(1), 33-41, Mr 90.

FAY, Thomas A. Early Heidegger and Wittgenstein: The Necessity of a Comprehension of Being. J Brit Soc Phenomenol, 20(3), 248-256, O 89.

When one thinks of early Wittgenstein, that is the Wittgenstein of the *Tractatus*, who clearly and unequivocally denounces all metaphysical statements as nonsense, and of the Heidegger of *Sein und Zeit* who undertook that monumental work for the purpose of "founding" ontology anew, it would seem that what we have are two unalterably and irreconcilably opposed foes. I should like to argue here however that their thought may be brought into a dialogue which will prove profitable and illuminating, particularly on their notion of the necessity of a comprehension of Being.

FEENBERG, Andrew and ARISAKA, Yoko. Experiential Ontology: The Origins of the Nishida Philosophy in the Doctrine of Experience. Int Phil Quart, 30(2), 173-205, Je 90.

The thesis of this article is that Kitaro Nishida (1870-1945), Japan's leading philosopher in this century, should be interpreted primarily against the background of the Continental tradition. The article discusses his relation to the many Western thinkers who influenced him. Nishida's first book developed a version of William James's theory of "radical empiricism," but later, under the influence of Fichte, Husserl, and Hegel, Nishida elaborated a dialectical phenomenology. The article argues that, like many of his European contemporaries, Nishida attempted to conceive immediate experience as an ontological absolute.

FEEZELL, Randolph. Sport, Character, and Virtue. Phil Today, 33(3), 204-220, Fall 89.

FEFERMAN, Solomon. Hilbert's Program Relativized: Proof-Theoretical and Foundational Reductions. J Sym Log, 53(2), 364-384, Je 88.

FEFFER, Andrew. Sociability and Social Conflict in George Herbert Mead's Interactionism, 1900-1919. J Hist Ideas, 51(2), 233-254, Ap-Je 90.

George H Mead, following the lead of John Dewey at the University of Chicago, developed his innovative interactive theories of the social self in response to the problems of contemporary industrial life in Chicago and other industrial cities at the turn of the century. This essay explores the contentious political environment in which Mead wrote his theories, and the divided political discourse from which he drew and for which he developed his arguments. The essay concludes that Mead's theory followed the ambiguous contours of actual social change and political dispute in Chicago between 1894 and 1919.

FEHÉR, István M. "Fundamental Ontology and Political Interlude: Heidegger as Rector of the University of Freiburg" in *Knowledge and Politics*, DASCAL, Marcelo (ed), 316-351. Boulder, Westview Pr, 1988.

Heidegger's political involvement is often seen either as a regrettable mistake, independent of his philosophy, or as having links to it—but then all the worse for his philosophy! This paper offers a hermeneutic reevaluation of this alternative. Part One gives an outline of Heidegger's philosophy up to *Being and Time*. Part Two offers a reconstruction of Heidegger's conduct as rector. The assumption is that the meaning of his involvement should be unfolded against the background of his philosophy and of historical cieumstances rather than stripped out of (both philosophical and historical) context.

FEHÉR, István. Eigentlichkeit, Gewissen und Schuld in Heideggers "Sein und Zeit". Man World, 23(1), 35-62, Ja 90.

Theme of the paper is the central role which conscience and guilt have in Heidegger's conception of authenticity in *Being and Time*. In a first step, a closer analysis is offered of the chapter about conscience, focusing on the concepts of guilt, conscience, and ground. It is then shown, in a second step, how far what these concepts imply bear upon the whole systematic project of the work, and are responsible for its fragmentary character. The results of the analysis are finally connected, in a third step, to Heidegger's later development included his "Kehre" and his much debated political involvement.

FEHER, Marta (ed) and HRONSZKY, Imre (ed) and DAJKA, Balazs (ed). *Scientific Knowledge Socialized*. Norwell, Kluwer, 1989

FEHÉR, Márta. "Epistemology Naturalized vs Epistemology Socialized" in *Scientific Knowledge Socialized*, HRONSZKY, Imre (ed), 75-96. Norwell, Kluwer, 1989.

What the paper argues for is to historicize and to sociologize the goals and, by that, the methodologies of science. The author suggests the separating of the problem of rationality from that of progress. Thus, she argues, we should not try to derive either scientific rationality from the progress of science (as Laudan did) or progress from rationality (as Lakatos and others did). Scientific progress ought rather be linked to that of society.

FEHÉR, Marta. The Essential Tension. Stud Soviet Tho, 39(3-4), 231-239, Ap-My 90.

Borrowing the title of my paper from Kuhn's famous (1977) paper, I intend to refer by it to that age-old tension which subsists between actual and ideal science. That is to say, my topic is that well-known fact that what scientists actually do differs essentially from what they should do according to the norms and requirements of scientific methodology prescribed by philosophers of science. The paper tries to show how important role inconsistencies play in actual science.

FEHÉR, Márta and STERN, Laurent. Philosophy in the United States (A Dialogue of Laurent Stern and Márta Fehér) (in Hungarian). Magyar Filozof Szemle, 4, 508-530, 1989.

FEILING, Carlos. Argumentos no son razones. Rev Latin De Filosof, 15(2), 147-157, Jl 89.

Since the pioneering work by Stephen Toulmin, many articles and books have been published in the area of "Informal Logic." However, some important advances, e.g., on the "*ad*" fallacies, have been hindered by the fact that answers to the crucial question, *What is an argument?* tend to conflate the logical and extralogical aspects of argumentative *discourse*. In this article I make a methodological proposal for informal logic or, as I prefer to call it, the "Theory of Argumentative Discourse." It consists of introducing two distinct notions, "argument" and "argumentation," which roughly correspond to the logical and extralogical aspects of argumentative discourse and can be jointly used to evaluate it.

FEINBERG, Joel (ed) and BEAUCHAMP, Tom L (ed) and SMITH, James M. (ed). *Philosophy and the Human Condition (Second Edition)*. Englewood Cliffs, Prentice-Hall, 1989

FEINBERG, Joel. The Paradox of Blackmail. Ratio Juris, 1(1), 83-95, Mr 88.

The author questions himself about what is known as "the paradox of blackmail," that is, the fact that blackmail is the result of the combination of two ways of behaving which are often both lawful if taken individually, but unlawful once they are connected. The author also examines whether the harm principle typical of liberal orders provides the justification (the rationale) for the assumption of blackmail as a crime, or whether it is instead necessary to turn to another justificatory basis: the exploitation principle. However, as this principle leads to legal moralism, it opposes a liberal ethics. Thus, one is faced with the dilemma of either accepting the harm principle thus decriminalizing blackmail, or accepting the exploitation principle and going against principles of liberalism. To escape this dilemma the author distinguishes between various types (five categories) of blackmail, concluding that only non-paradoxical types fit the commonsense expectation of criminalization.

FEINBERG, Walter. Response to Francis Schrag's "Response to Feinberg's 'Foundationalism and Recent Critiques of Education'". Educ Theor, 40(2), 219, Spr 90.

FEINBERG, Walter. A Role for Philosophy of Education in Intercultural Research: Reexamination of the Relativism-Absolutism Debate. Proc Phil Educ, 45, 2-19, 1989.

I explore the argument between relativists and absolutists in light of the imperative for action required by educational situations and argue for a conception of respect that takes into account both positions without fully accepting either.

FEIVESON, Harold A. "Finite Deterrence" in *Nuclear Deterrence and Moral Restraint*, SHUE, Henry (ed), 271-291. New York, Cambridge Univ Pr, 1989.

The strategic arsenals of the US and the Soviet Union each contain over 10,000 nuclear warheads with a total destructive power equivalent to over 70,000 Hiroshima bombs. This is a hundred or more times larger than what could destroy either country as a modern state. The principal rationale for the huge size of the arsenals is that thousands of warheads are required for counterforce attacks on the other side's nuclear forces. But such attacks are not credible; they would be virtually indistinguishable from attacks directly on populations. There is now every reason and opportunity to reduce each side's strategic arsenal to a highly survivable "finite deterrence" force of about 2000 warheads with much of the counterforce potential stripped out of the force.

FELDHEIM, Pierre. The Club of Rome and the Vienna Centre. Dialec Hum, 16(2), 11-20, Spr 89.

FELDMAN, David Henry. The Child as Craftsman. Thinking, 6(1), 20-24, 1985.

FELDMAN, Fred. Concerning the Paradox of Moral Reparation and Other Matters. Phil Stud, 57(1), 23-39, S 89.

FELDMAN, Fred. F M Kamm and the Mirror of Time. Pac Phil Quart, 71(1), 23-27, Mr 90.

According to the "Deprivation Approach" early death is bad for us because it deprives us of the goods we would have enjoyed if we had lived longer. Lucretius raised a puzzle for this view: if early death is bad for us for the cited reason, then why isn't "late birth" bad for us for a corresponding reason? F M Kamm attempts to answer Lucretius. She appeals to "The Terror Factor" and "The Insult Factor." I claim that her attempt fails. For each of these factors, there is a temporal mirror image—if early death is bad because of these factors, then late birth would be equally bad because of their mirror images.

FELDMAN, Fred. On Dying as a Process. Phil Phenomenol Res, 50(2), 375-390, D 89.

To say that a thing is dying, in the process sense, is to say (roughly) that it is in a "terminal decline," that it is "heading toward death." After examining and rejecting several proposed analyses of the concept of dying as a process, I present my own. When an organism is dying, it is engaged in a process consisting of the sequential decrease of the thing's vital properties; a process which, if allowed to reach its conclusion without interference, will terminate with the death of the organism. I discuss the virtues of this analysis, and its weaknesses.

FELDMAN, Jacqueline. From Militancy to Ethics: On Some Forms and Problems of Militant Action in the Western World. Phil Soc Act, 16(2), 31-43, Ap-Je 90.

The drastic changes that militant action have undergone in France in the last decades are discussed. After a historical sketch, the student movement of May 68, a turning point, is shown to have opened new forms of militancy. Ethics, once the preserve of philosophers, has become implanted through the whole society. Phases in individual itineraries are considered: the moral revolt of youth, the learning of the complexity of reality, maturity which tries

to keep the subtle balance between ethics and efficiency. Crucial ethical moments of militant action are pointed out: consciousness-raising, possible slippages, inevitable contradictions.

FELDMAN, Jan. New Thinking about the "New Man": Developments in Soviet Moral Theory. Stud Soviet Tho, 38(2), 147-163, Ag 89.

Recent developments in Soviet thinking about morality appear to contrast with the tradition of moral instrumentalism and consequentialism. A narrowing of the concept of acceptable behavior on the part of the state is occurring, accompanied by an emerging recognition of the sanctity of the individual. By contrast, the definition of moral behavior on the part of the individual is being expanded to include a variety of activities hitherto condemned as inimical to the moral code of the New Soviet Man. But while moving in a promising direction, Soviet moral theory has yet to create a firm foundation for individual moral autonomy. For moral autonomy to overcome its traditional subordination to politics, Soviets must go the final yard and enunciate and codify a "socialist" doctrine of natural rights.

FELDMAN, Richard. Goldman on Epistemology and Cognitive Science. Philosophia (Israel), 19(2-3), 197-207, O 89.

In *Epistemology and Cognition* Alvin Goldman says that his goal "is to redirect and restructure the field of epistemology" because epistemology "needs help from the cognitive sciences." In this paper I argue that Goldman's proposed restructuring of epistemology is less radical than it may initially appear. Those who maintain the autonomy of epistemology need not oppose his view, since his new epistemology includes an autonomous part coextensive with traditional epistemology. Goldman counts as part of epistemology an empirical inquiry into the nature of the processes that lead to the formation of beliefs. This is a separate enterprise which may require help from the cognitive sciences.

FELDMAN, Richard. "Lehrer's Coherence Theory of Knowledge" in *The Current State of the Coherence Theory*, BENDER, John W (ed), 69-76. Norwell, Kluwer, 1989.

In two recent papers Keith Lehrer has developed the coherence theory of knowledge and justification that he originally proposed in *Knowledge*. The current theory is that a person knows a proposition if and only if the proposition is justified relative to the person's actual acceptance system and relative to every acceptance system that can be constructed out of the actual system by eliminating falsehoods and replacing them by their true denials. Justification relative to a system is spelled out in terms of coherence with that system, and a proposition coheres with a system provided it is more reasonable to believe that proposition than its competitors on the basis of that system. Although it is difficult to assess the merits of his theory, it appears that the theory avoids skeptical implications only by making it too easy to have knowledge and justification, and it also appears that the theory does not avoid some variations on standard Gettier-style counterexamples. (edited)

FELDMAN, Seymour. "Philoponus on the Metaphysics of Creation" in *A Straight Path: Studies in Medieval Philosophy and Culture*, LINK-SALINGER, Ruth (ed), 74-85. Washington, Cath Univ Amer Pr, 1988.

FELEPPA, Robert. Physicalism, Indeterminacy and Interpretive Science. Metaphilosophy, 21(1-2), 89-110, Ja-Ap 90.

Quine's indeterminacy of translation thesis can be seen as a skeptical commentary on problems of interpretive objectivity in cultural anthropology, particularly those that concern tensions between objectivity and interpreter bias. I examine the import of the general thesis and of remarks of Quine's directed specifically to anthropology for interpretation-based ethnography. I argue that although the ontological status Quine grants physical theory might be seen as exhibiting an unjustified discriminatory attitude toward the social sciences, adoption of Quine's ontological position does not necessarily threaten interpretive anthropology's scientific status.

FELL, Joseph P. The Familiar and the Strange: On the Limits of *Praxis* in the Early Heidegger. S J Phil, SUPP(28), 23-41, 1989.

Citing evidence of Martin Heidegger's dissatisfaction with certain interpretations of the "primacy" of "readiness to hand" in *Being and Time*, this paper seeks to reassess his interrelating of readiness and presentness by correlating relevant passages in *Being and Time*, *The Basic Problems of Phenomenology*, *What Is Metaphysics?*, and *The Essence of Ground*. It is shown that adequate interpretation of the interrelation of readiness and presentness requires consideration of (1) the relative priorities of inauthentic and authentic temporality, (2) the several senses of presentness, and (3) the extent to which praxis is limited by the disclosure of nature.

FELPERIN, Howard. "The Anxity of American Deconstruction" in *The Textual Sublime: Deconstruction and Its Differences*, SILVERMAN, Hugh J (ed), 147-161. Albany, SUNY Pr, 1990.

FELSCHER, Walter. A Linear Parsing Algorithm for Parenthesis Terms. Z

Math Log, 35(4), 359-362, 1989.

FEMENÍAS, María Luisa and SCHOLLMEIER, Paul. Intuición práctica y ejemplo retórico. Cuad Filosof, 20(33), 41-48, O 89.

Assume that we have a faculty of theoretical intuition, through which we intuit theoretical principles, and a faculty of practical intuition, through which we intuit practical principles. Could we justify or verify our theoretical and practical intuitions in the same way? Despite recent attempts to do so, one would think not. For we assume that we have two different faculties grasping principles of different kinds. We would thus ask what method or technique we could use to justify or to verify our practical principles. Aristotle suggests that an art of discourse and an inductive technique might serve to justify practical intuitions about our ends. The art is rhetoric and the technique argument by example. After all, rhetoric is an art concerned with discourse of a practical kind, and example is an argument of an inductive sort.

FENNER, David E W. Quantum Realism. J Speculative Phil, 4(2), 161-167, 1990.

In "Representation and Reality in Quantum Mechanics" (J Spec Phil, 3(2), 1989) Barbara J Bennett argues that to preserve, in the face of quantum mechanics, a tenable commitment to realism (whose keystone tenet, for her, is observer-independence) we must opt for a "mathematical realism." I argue (i) that "realism" need not be observer-independent, (ii) that "mathematical realism" is not the same as "empirical" realism, and (iii) that realism may be retained in spite of the quantum paradoxes, if observer-independence is redefined or sacrificed.

FENNER, David E. Quantum Paradoxes and New Realism. Dialogue (PST), 32(1), 15-23, O 89.

Neither traditionally formulated realism nor instrumentalism is adequate as a conceptual model for dealing with the paradoxes which arise out of quantum theory. I propose that we remedy this by adding to our definition of realism a narrowly defined tenet which calls for the addition of the subject in those microphysical interactions which, on the face of the overwhelming empirical evidence, call for it.

FERNANDEZ, Eugenio. Potentia et Potestas dans les premiers écrits de B Spinoza. Stud Spinozana, 4, 195-223, 1988.

This study seeks to establish that *potentia* and *potestas* are not only decisive categories in the mature writings of Spinoza, but also that they are already present in his early writings as embryonic forces which provide an interpretive path and also configure the ontological and political space which is occupied by the notion of freedom. This approach provides an interesting explanation of the means by which, beginning with the analysis of the imaginary and the use that power makes of it in order to consolidate servitude, one may construct a philosophy of *potentia* which is, indivisibly, ontological, epistemological, ethical and political.

FERNGREN, Gary B. "The Ethics of Suicide in the Renaissance and Reformation" in *Suicide and Euthanasia*, BRODY, Baruch A (ed), 155-181. Norwell, Kluwer, 1989.

The sixteenth and seventeenth centuries form an important transitional period in the development of the ethics of suicide. Montaigne and Charron marked the first departure from the Augustinian view that suicide was a sin precluding repentance. While Protestants condemned suicide, they were more hopeful than Catholics regarding the possibility of God's forgiveness. Perhaps because of her religious development England was in the forefront of the discussion of suicide. During the seventeenth century a non-Christian position was formulated that divorced the morality of suicide from theological considerations. Long a minority view, it gained many supporters during the Enlightenment.

FERNHOUT, Harry. Moral Education as Grounded in Faith. J Moral Educ, 18(3), 186-198, O 89.

Inquiry into the grounding of moral education inevitably raises questions of the relation of morality and religion. To break through this perplexing issue, it is helpful to shift conceptual ground and focus on moral education as grounded in faith. Consistent with Cantwell Smith and Tillich, faith can be understood as that which is of ultimate concern, that which is the focus of trust and commitment. Kohlberg's theory is examined in this essay as a test case for the claim that moral education is grounded in faith. If it makes sense to regard moral education as grounded in faith, then the issue of the grounding of moral education in a pluralistic society becomes acute. The concept of pluralism is examined, and a strategy of fostering the public educational expression of varying convictional orientations is proposed. (edited)

FERRAND DE PIAZZA, Hortensia. "Values in an Historical, Socio-Cultural Context" in *The Social Context and Values: Perspectives of the Americas*, MC LEAN, George F (ed), 41-74. Lanham, Univ Pr of America, 1989.

FERRARA, Alessandro. Universalisms: Procedural, Contextualist and Prudential. Phil Soc Crit, 14(3-4), 243-269, 1988.

Two promising attempts to reconcile ethical universalism with a genuine acceptance of the pluralism of life-forms are examined. Habermas's "procedural" universalism, reconstructed from his writings on the "discourse-ethic" and on communicative action, is contrasted with the "contextualist" approach developed by two representatives of communitarianism, Walzer and MacIntyre. While Habermas's distinction between form and content of ethical judgment is shown to be problematical and inadequate for dealing with the issue of competing conceptual schemes, the communitarian approach, preferable in that respect, seems unable to block norms sanctioned by a wicked society. Finally, some considerations are offered concerning a *prudential* universalism, capable of overcoming these difficulties.

FERRARI, Giovanni. "Hesiod's Mimetic Muses and the Strategies of Deconstruction" in *Post-Structuralist Classics*, BENJAMIN, Andrew (ed), 45-78. New York, Routledge, 1988.

A discussion of the current use to which Jacques Derrida's work is put in classical studies. The particular focus of the discussion is an interpretation by Derridean classicists of the couplet spoken by the Muses in the prologue to Hesiod's *Theogony*. It is argued that theirs is a misinterpretation, due to their imposing on the text anachronistically 'metaphysical realist' assumptions (in Hilary Putnam's sense). An examination of 'Limited Inc. a b c...' traces these assumptions back to Derrida, and contends that he is saddling himself with unnecessary metaphysical baggage. An approach to Archaic Greek texts is proposed which avoids the Derridean distortion.

FERRARI, Pier Luigi. The Rank Function and Hilbert's Second E-Theorem. Z Math Log, 35(4), 367-373, 1989.

A proof of Hilbert's second epsilon theorem is provided which corrects Flannagan's proof by modifying the definition of rank. The new definition of rank allows to prove that a word is proper if and only if its rank is 1, and to simplify various steps of the proof. This provides a unified version of the proof of Hilbert's second epsilon theorem, which was not available before.

FERRELL, O C and FRAEDRICH, John. An Empirical Examination of Three Machiavellian Concepts: Advertisers Versus the General Public. J Bus Ethics, 8(9), 687-694, S 89.

This paper examines the perceived ethics of advertisers and the general public relative to three ethical concepts. Based on the survey findings, it can be concluded that with regard to the ethically laden concepts of manipulation, exploitation, and deviousness, advertisers are perceptually as ethical as the general public. The research also clarifies some of the differences between ethics and Machiavellianism.

FERRELL, O C and KELLEY, S W and SKINNER, S J. Ethical Behavior Among Marketing Researchers: An Assessment of Selected Demographic Characteristics. J Bus Ethics, 9(8), 681-688, Ag 90.

This study considers the relationship between perceptions of ethical behavior and the demographic characteristics of sex, age, education level, job title, and job tenure among a sample of marketing researchers. The findings of this study indicate that female marketing researchers, older marketing researchers, and marketing researchers holding their present job for ten years or more generally rate their behavior as more ethical.

FERRER, Urbano. Fin y valor de la acción: recorrido histórico-sistemático. Anu Filosof, 22(1), 125-134, 1989.

The notion of end in Kant appears as a negative limit for the action, whereas in Scheler, the end is based on the valuable, objective content, given tendentially. Both authors incur for a priori/effective experience dualism. The hermeneutics of Ricoeur, on the other hand, connect the effective experience with values and ends through the reciprocal mediation between subject and motives. As a systematic conclusion we contrast, within the action, the *relational* character of the end which orientates it with the *absolute* nature of the value which qualifies it, without any prejudice to the real identity of either.

FERRETTI, Silvia. Il guidizio di Sant'Agostino sulla Nuova Accademia tra scetticismo ed esoterismo. Filosofia, 41(2), 155-183, My-Ag 90.

FERRY, Jean-Marc and HABERMAS, Jürgen. Interview with Jürgen Habermas: Ethics, Politics and History. Phil Soc Crit, 14(3-4), 433-439, 1988.

FERRY, Luc and CATTANI, Mary Schnackenberg (trans) and RENAUT, Alain. *French Philosophy of the Sixties: An Essay on Antihumanism*. Amherst, Univ of Mass Pr, 1990

The focus of this text is the philosophical interpretation of the French revolt in 1968. The interpretations of the French postmodernists of the revolt, and their attempt to find a nonmetaphysical form of humanism to explain the revolt are explicated. (staff)

FERRY, Luc and PHILIP, Franklin (trans) and RENAUT, Alain. *Heidegger and Modernity*. Chicago, Univ of Chicago Pr, 1990

The authors investigate the debate within French intellectualism regarding the relationship of Heidegger and Nazism. They consider the relations between Heidegger's phenomenology and his politics, and conclude that Heidegger's critique against modernity is flawed by ambiguities. (staff)

FETZ, Reto Luzius. "Creativity: A New Transcendental?" in *Whitehead's Metaphysics of Creativity*, RAPP, Friedrich (ed), 189-208. Albany, SUNY Pr, 1990.

FETZER, James H. Evolution, Rationality, and Testability. Synthese, 82(3), 423-439, Mr 90.

Cosmides, Wason, and Johnson-Laird, among others, have suggested evidence that reasoning abilities tend to be domain specific, insofar as humans do not appear to acquire capacities for logical reasoning that are applicable across different contexts. Unfortunately, the significance of these findings depends upon the specific variety of 'logical reasoning' under consideration. Indeed, there seem to be at least three grounds for doubting such conclusions, since (1) tests of reasoning involving the use of *material conditionals* may not be appropriate for representing ordinary thinking, especially when it concerns causal processes involving the use of *causal conditionals* instead; (2) tests of domain specificity may fail to acknowledge the crucial role fulfilled by rules of inference, such as *modus ponens* and *modus tollens*, which appear to be completely general across different contexts; and (3) tests that focus exclusively upon *deductive reasoning* may misinterpret findings involving the use of *inductive reasoning*, which is of primary importance for human evolution.

FICHERA, Giuseppe. *Religione e Umanità*. Catania, CUECM, 1987

L'A. illustra il cammino compiuto dall'umanità per giungere a Dio. Dalla preistoria ad oggi, l'uomo ha seguito tre vie: quelle della *natura*, della *ragione* e della *fede*. Nella sua indagine storico-culturale, dalla religiosità preistorica alla recente "teologia della morte di Dio", l'A. fa rilevare il fallimento di tutti e tre i tipi di approccio alla divinità e, pertanto, la crisi della religione tradizionale nel mondo occidentale e cristiano. L'A. propende per una prospettiva agnostica sul piano teoretico e releva che il recupero dei valori religiosi oggi si può avere soltanto sul piano etico-sociale, e più precisamente in una religiosità ispirata ai valori fondamentali dell'etica cristiana.

FIELD, Hartry. *Realism, Mathematics and Modality*. Cambridge, Blackwell, 1989

FIELDER, John H. Give Goodrich a Break. Bus Prof Ethics J, 7(1), 3-25, Spr 88.

FIESER, James. Is Hume a Moral Skeptic? Phil Phenomenol Res, 50(1), 89-105, S 89.

Using J L Mackie's analysis of moral skepticism as a point of reference, I argue that, as a normative theory, Hume's account of morality is not skeptical since he is offering a relatively optimistic consequentialist theory of right and wrong action. As a metaethical theory, however, I argue that Hume is a weak metaethical skeptic insofar as he denies that morality is independent of the existence and character of human beings. He should not be considered a thorough or strong metaethical skeptic, though, since he advances a moral theory which is firmly grounded in human instinct.

FILIPPI, Silvana. Heidegger y la noción tomista de verdad. Anu Filosof, 22(1), 135-158, 1989.

This work tries to show notable concidences that—without forgetting the differences—can be observed between the conception of truth by Heidegger and Thomas Aquinas. Supporting that thesis three aspects from both philosophers are comparatively examined: the notion, the originary place and the scope of truth. This analysis considers then the Heideggerian conception of truth presented by him in *Sein und Zeit*, and at the same time it tries to determine the accurate sense of the Thomist doctrine of truth as *adaequatio intellectus et rei*, frequently misinterpreted because of the transformation that it suffered during modern age.

FINE, Arthur. "Do Correlations Need to be Explained?" in *Philosophical Consequences of Quantum Theory: Reflections on Bell's Theorem*, CUSHING, James T (ed), 175-194. Notre Dame, Univ Notre Dame Pr, 1989.

This paper takes up the question of whether stable correlations between sequences of randomly occurring events inherently call for explanation. The context of the discussion is the Bell theorem, for which we give a new derivation. We also take up the issue of locality, and show that some form of determinism is required by attempts to derive a breakdown in locality from the failure of the Bell inequalities. We conclude by suggesting an

indeterminist view that sees correlations *between* outcomes sequences as part of the same natural order as probabilistic patterns *internal* to the sequences themselves.

FINE, Arthur. Truthmongering: Less is True. Can J Phil, 19(4), 611-616, D 89.

This is a response to Lily Knezevich's critique (*Canadian J Phil* 19 (1989) 603-10) of a general line of argument against acceptance or consensus theories of truth (ideal or not), proposed by the author in chapter 8 of *The Shaky Game* (Chicago, 1986). In response the argument is clarified, expanded and defended.

FINE, Gail. "Knowledge and Belief in *Republic* V-VII" in *Epistemology* (Companions to Ancient Thought: 1), EVERSON, Stephen (ed), 85-115. New York, Cambridge Univ Pr, 1990.

FINE, Kit. "Incompleteness for Quantified Relevance Logics" in *Directions in Relevant Logic*, NORMAN, Jean (ed), 205-225. Norwell, Kluwer, 1989.

Propositional relevance logic is complete for a certain relational semantics. It is shown that the natural extension of the logic to quantifiers is not complete for the natural extension of the semantics.

FINK, Eugen and GILLESPIE, Michael Allen (trans). "Nietzsche's New Experience of World" in *Nietzsche's New Seas: Explorations in Philosophy, Aesthetics, and Politics*, GILLESPIE, Michael Allen (ed), 203-219. Chicago, Univ of Chicago Pr, 1989.

FINKELSTEIN, Joanne L. Biomedicine and Technocratic Power. Hastings Center Rep, 20(4), 13-16, Jl-Ag 90.

Our willing employment of sophisticated medicine to control and change the way we look and act rests on a deeper conviction that technological developments and scientific discoveries are proper and useful measures of human progress. The implication of this is that any interest in shaping the future capacities of humans through biomedical techniques can transform medicine into a latent agent of social engineering. Foucault's analysis of medicine's professionalism in the nineteenth century is a useful chart of modern medicine's current trajectory.

FINN, Geraldine. Nobodies Speaking: Subjectivity, Sex, and the Pornography Effect. Phil Today, 33(2), 174-182, Sum 89.

FINN, Jeffrey and MARSHALL, Eliot L. *Medical Ethics (The Encyclopedia of Health: Medical Issues)*. New York, Chelsea House, 1990

Should a hospital spend millions of dollars saving the life of 1 critically ill child, or should it use this same money to provide prenatal care to 20 pregnant women? Should a lengthy test period be required for drugs that may successfully treat AIDS? What rights do women who want to begin or end a pregnancy have? Articles concerning such complex medical questions appear in newspapers virtually every day. This book describes the nature of these issues—including abortion, euthanasia, drug testing on terminally ill patients, and funding for organ transplants and other expensive procedures. It also examines health-insurance policies, discussing the financial assistance that the poor and elderly receive when they get sick and contrasting American practices with those of other countries. The book stresses the complex—and often conflicting—moral principles upon which health-related laws are based and uses vivid case studies to reveal the human dilemmas that result when principles meet reality in life-and-death situations.

FINNIS, John M. Law as Co-ordination. Ratio Juris, 2(1), 97-104, Mr 89.

The concept of co-ordination problems helps solve the problem of authority and obligation in legal theory, but only if the concept is carefully distinguished from the game-theoretical concept of co-ordination problems and their solutions. After explaining the game-theoretical concept, the author defends its application to legal theory by reviewing the exchange he has had with Joseph Raz about the authority of law. Extending that debate, he argues that criticisms from Raz and others miss the point of the co-ordination thesis; its primary benefit is that it illuminates the source of law's moral authority in the way law enables individuals to co-ordinate their actions for the common good without imposing a national common enterprise upon them.

FINNIS, John. "Comment: Positivism and the Foundations of Legal Authority" in *Issues in Contemporary Legal Philosophy: The Influence of H L A Hart*, GAVISON, Ruth (ed), 62-75. New York, Clarendon/Oxford Pr, 1987.

FINNIS, John and BOYLE, Joseph M and GRISEZ, Germain. *Nuclear Deterrence, Morality and Realism*. New York, Oxford Univ Pr, 1988

Nuclear deterrence expresses a conditional choice to kill noncombatants, a choice irreconcilable with traditional morality. Having fully surveyed official threats and systems, we examine the crucial conceptual and strategic questions: Why are conditional choices morally decisive? Why can't deterrence be a bluff? Or purely counterforce? We then argue that neither deterrence nor unilateral disarmament can be justified by the other's bad consequences, and that all consequentialist justifications are inevitably incoherent. Exploring the foundations of ethics, we conclude to an ethics of killing similar to common morality's, and try to identify the specific duties of policy makers, military personnel and citizens.

FINOCCHIARO, Maurice A. Fetishism, Argument, and Judgment in *Capital*. Stud Soviet Tho, 38(3), 237-244, O 89.

FINOCCHIARO, Maurice A. Methodological Problems in Empirical Logic. Commun Cog, 22(3-4), 313-335, 1989.

Empirical logic is defined as the empirical (but normative) study of reasoning, involving the formulation, testing, clarification, and systematization of concepts and principles for the interpretation, the evaluation, and the sound practice of reasoning. This enterprise is distinguished from the experimental psychology of reasoning, and it is defended from number of methodological objections.

FINOCCHIARO, Maurice A. Philosophy as Critical Thinking. Thinking, 8(2), 2-3, 1989.

FINOCCHIARO, Maurice A. Siegel on Critical Thinking. Phil Soc Sci, 19(4), 483-492, D 89.

FINSEN, Lawrence. Comment on James Nelson's "Animals in 'Exemplary' Medical Research: Diabetes as a Case Study". Between Species, 5(4), 205-210, Fall 89.

FIORE, Robert L. Natural Law in an "Auto" by Calderón. Vera Lex, 9(2), 1-2, 1989.

FIORENTINO, Fernando. La risposta di Leroux a Lamennais: Il concetto di Trinità come soluzione del problema sociale. Sapienza, 43(1), 41-56, Ja-Mr 90.

FISCHER, John Martin (ed). *God, Foreknowledge, and Freedom*. Stanford, Stanford Univ Pr, 1989

This is an anthology composed of contemporary articles on the relationship between God's foreknowledge and human freedom. There is a substantial introduction which locates the articles within a larger historical and analytical grid.

FISCHER, Michael. "Does Deconstruction Make Any Difference?" in *The Textual Sublime: Deconstruction and Its Differences*, SILVERMAN, Hugh J (ed), 23-30. Albany, SUNY Pr, 1990.

This paper examines some of the claims made on behalf of deconstruction by its opponents and advocates. I specifically discuss the accusation that it is dangerous or nihilistic and the hope that it is liberating or subversive. Drawing on work by Christopher Norris and J Hillis Miller, I conclude that deconstruction does make a difference, although not the revolutionary difference its proponents have longed for and its critics have feared. Deconstruction reinforces established political and educational arrangements rather than damaging or overturning them.

FISCHER, Michael. *Stanley Cavell and Literary Skepticism*. Chicago, Univ of Chicago Pr, 1989

This book applies Stanley Cavell's analysis of skepticism to the controversies surrounding poststructuralist literary theory, particularly works by Jacques Derrida, J Hillis Miller, Paul de Man, and Stanley Fish. The book argues that there are significant affinities between deconstruction and the skeptical questioning discussed by Cavell. Cavell's work on external-world and other-minds skepticism permits a fresh view of deconstruction and shows why some attacks against deconstruction (most notably those by M H Abrams and Charles Altieri) have failed.

FISCHER, Norman. "Marxism and Ecology" in *Inquiries into Values: The Inaugural Session of the International Society for Value Inquiry*, LEE, Sander H , 299-305. Lewiston, Mellen Pr, 1989.

FISCHER, Roland. The Time-Like Nature of Mind: On Mind Functions as Temporal Patterns of the Neural Network. Diogenes, 147, 52-76, Fall 89.

Evolution-learning-perception-cognition and dreaming-hallucinations, i.e., the process of *mind*, unfolds while displaying more and more time-like (information) and less and less space-like (energy) features. The unitary nature of this process is the result of a temporal selection process, with the selected time patterns re-expressed in spatially localized movements. Brain matter and its mind are complementary domains of a hermeneutic circle: they legitimate reality, i.e., the interpretation of their interactions, while they themselves are legitimated by the interpretation. The contemporary key concepts that contribute to the understanding of mind as self-experience in time are rhythmicity, excitability, re-entrant propagation and spontaneous organization.

FISHBURN, Peter C. Unique Nontransitive Measurement on Finite Sets. Theor Decis, 28(1), 21-46, Ja 90.

Two themes in the theory of measurement that have been studied extensively in the past few years are numerical representations of nontransitive binary comparison structures and uniqueness in finite measurement systems. This paper brings the two together by exploring the solutions to a nontransitive, additive model that are unique up to multiplication by a positive constant. The model relates to various contexts including decision under risk, evaluation of objectives, comparative probability, and voting theory. The family of unique solutions for the model is shown to be extremely rich and varied.

FISHER, Alec. Suppositions in Argumentation. Argumentation, 3(4), 401-413, N 89.

The atheist who begins to argue his case by saying, 'Suppose there is an omniscient Being of the sort in which Christians believe...' is employing a very familiar move in argumentation. However, most books on argumentation theory ignore 'suppositions' completely. Searle omits suppositions entirely from his taxonomy of speech acts and this appears to lead to a similar omission in *Speech Acts in Argumentative Discussions* by van Eemeren and Grootendorst. This paper argues that 'suppositional argument' is elegant, powerful and extremely common, that the correct way to understand it is based on Gottlob Frege's distinction between 'asserted' and 'unasserted' propositions and hence that suppositions are neither assertions nor (and this is more important) assertives. The paper discusses the connections between suppositions and conditionals; it argues that argumentation theory which ignores suppositions is systematically misleading; and it concludes by indicating some possible developments in argumentation theory.

FISHER, David. Crisis Moral Communities: An Essay in Moral Philosophy. J Value Inq, 24(1), 17-30, Ja 90.

FISHER, John. Some Remarks on What Happened to John Dewey. J Aes Educ, 23(3), 54-60, Fall 89.

FISHER, Philip. Jasper Johns: Strategies for Making and Effacing Art. Crit Inquiry, 16(2), 313-354, Wint 89.

FISHKIN, James S. "In Quest of the Social Contract" in *Politics and Process*, BRENNAN, Geoffrey (ed), 183-193. New York, Cambridge Univ Pr, 1989.

FISHKIN, James S. Towards a New Social Contract. Nous, 24(2), 217-226, Ap 90.

FISHMAN, Stephen. Writing and Philosophy. Teach Phil, 12(4), 361-374, D 89.

An examination of philosophy classes which emphasize pre-writing in contrast with those focussing on finished texts. Pre-writing is favored as a way of developing (1) student paradigms of "good writing," (2) "personal contexts" for student papers, and (3) new questions about topics students prematurely believe they have exhausted. Various explanations of the success of pre-writing are explored, and detailed assignments are presented to illustrate the author's pre-writing strategies.

FISK, Milton. Intellectuals, Values and Society. Phil Soc Crit, 15(2), 151-165, 1989.

The characteristically liberal position that freedom is violated by imposing conceptions of the good is discussed. It is argued that the liberal defense of freedom is nonetheless a defense of a conception of the good, one that varies with context. The alternative is proposed that intellectuals rooted in given social groups can advocate conceptions of the good without threatening freedom.

FISK, Milton. *The State and Justice: An Essay in Political Theory*. New York, Cambridge Univ Pr, 1989

FITTING, Melvin. Pseudo-Boolean Valued Prolog. Stud Log, 47(2), 85-91, Je 88.

A generalization of conventional Horn clause logic programming is proposed in which the space of truth values is a pseudo-Boolean or Heyting algebra, whose members may be thought of as evidences for propositions. A minimal model and an operational semantics is presented, and their equivalence is proved, thus generalizing the classic work of Van Emden and Kowalski.

FITZPATRICK, John and BRADDON-MITCHELL, David. Explanation and the Language of Thought. Synthese, 83(1), 3-29, Ap 90.

In this paper we argue that the insistence by Fodor et al. that the language of thought hypothesis must be true rests on mistakes about the kinds of explanations that must be provided of cognitive phenomena. After examining the canonical arguments for the LOT, we identify a weak version of the LOT hypothesis which we think accounts for some of the intuitions that there must be a LOT. We then consider what kinds of explanation cognitive phenomena require, and conclude that three main confusions lead to the invalid inference of the truth of a stronger LOT hypothesis from the weak and trivial version. These confusions concern the relationship between syntax and semantics, the nature of higher-level causation in cognitive science, and differing roles of explanations invoking intrinsic structures of minds on the one hand, and aetiological or evolutionary accounts of their properties on the other.

FLAGEL, David. Sociobiology, Sex, and Aggression. Eidos, 7(2), 137-153, D 88.

In both *Sociobiology: The New Synthesis* and *On Human Nature*, Edward O Wilson suggests that human males are genetically predisposed to be more aggressive than human females. I argue that Wilson ignores much available evidence which suggests that females (both human and nonhuman) can be as aggressive as males. I conclude by suggesting that female aggression is much more pronounced than Wilson supposes and that his mistaken conclusion is the result of his not recognizing that female aggression is often expressed in more subtle and less overt ways than is male aggression.

FLAM, Leopold. "L'esthétique et le sacré" in *Cultural Hermeneutics of Modern Art: Essays in Honor of Jan Aler*, DETHIER, Hubert (ed), 151-158. Amsterdam, Rodopi, 1989.

FLANAGAN, Owen. Virtue and Ignorance. J Phil, 87(8), 420-428, Ag 90.

In "The Virtues of Ignorance," Julia Driver (*J Phil* 86(7), July 1989, 373-384) discusses the question of whether there exists some class of virtues that require as a necessary ingredient that she who possesses or displays any one of them lacks knowledge. Many recent writers have pointed to an ineliminable tension between our ethical and personal ideals. If successful, Driver's argument would establish the existence of a different, but equally ineliminable tension: between our ethical and epistemic ideals. I argue that there are no virtues of ignorance.

FLANNERY, Richard and LOUZECKY, David. *The Good Life: Personal and Public Choices*. Atascadero, Ridgeview, 1989

We defend that favorite American position, individualism, as the only social philosophy with broad enough support to be used, and we argue that without the conception of a good life individualism is senseless. The good life is composed of intimate companionships and quality work in a free society; the personal and the public cannot be separated. We also discuss self-development, privacy, rationality, equality, justice, and democratic politics.

FLATHMAN, Richard E. Absolutism, Individuality and Politics: Hobbes and a Little Beyond. Hist Euro Ideas, 10(5), 547-568, 1989.

FLAUMENHAFT, Mera J. Seeing Justice Done: Aeschylus' *Oresteia*. Interpretation, 17(1), 69-109, Fall 89.

Agamemnon explores justice in communities where outsiders have no view into the affairs of private families. Clytemnestra stages a symbolic drama, exhibiting the violator before punishing him. *Libation Bearers* opens a passageway between the restricted views and cyclic revenge of *Agamemnon* and the full view and justice in *Eumenides*, where publicly-staged trials resemble theatrical dramas. Orestes is acquitted and the deities of revenge are assimilated into an enlightened civic order. There is a price to pay. We must continue to learn from Argos, as well as Athens, while constituting our own judicial and penal institutions.

FLAX, Jane. *Thinking Fragments: Psychoanalysis, Feminism, and Postmodernism in the Contemporary West*. Berkeley, Univ of Calif Pr, 1989

With the demise of objectivist notions of truth, knowledge, self, and power, intellectuals have devised new modes of thinking, as exemplified by the development of psychoanalysis, feminism and postmodernism. Each addresses at least one aspect of what has become most problematic to modern individuals: how to come to terms with self, gender, knowledge and power without resorting to concepts that stress objectivity, universal knowledge and a unitary self. None of the theories sufficiently addresses these questions. Despite their failures, these modes of theorizing are our best tools thus far, compelling us to use them even while we grapple with their problems.

FLECK, Leonard M. Just Health Care (II): Is Equality Too Much? Theor Med, 10(4), 301-310, D 89.

In a previous essay I criticized Engelhardt's libertarian conception of justice, which grounds the view that society's obligation to assure access to adequate health care for all is a matter of beneficence. Beneficence fails to capture the moral stringency associated with many claims for access to health care. In the present paper I argue that these claims are really matters of justice proper, where justice is conceived along moderate egalitarian lines, such as those suggested by Rawls and Daniels, rather than strong egalitarian lines. Further, given the empirical complexity associated with the

distribution of contemporary health care, I argue that what we really need to address the relevant policy issues adequately is a theory of *health care justice*, as opposed to an all-purpose conception of justice. Daniels has made an important start toward that goal, though there are some large policy areas which I discuss that his account of health care justice does not really speak to. Finally, practical matters of health care justice really need to be addressed in a 'non-ideal' mode, a framework in which philosophers have done little.

FLECK, Leonard M. Justice, HMOs, and the Invisible Rationing of Health Care Resources. Bioethics, 4(2), 97-120, Ap 90.

FLEMING, John E. Business Ethics: Diversity and Integration. Bus Prof Ethics J, 6(4), 81-88, Wint 87.

FLEMING, Patricia Ann. Paul Ricoeur's Methodological Parallelism. Human Stud, 13(3), 221-236, Jl 90.

FLETCHER, George P. Defensive Force as an Act of Rescue. Soc Phil Pol, 7(2), 170-179, Spr 90.

This article explores the relationship of the Western conception of self-defense as permissive intervention to the Judaic notion that the roots of self-defense are a duty rather than a right to act. What is lacking in the latter is the recognition that the taking of any human life, regardless of the circumstances, must to some degree be wrong.

FLETCHER, George P. Punishment and Self-Defense. Law Phil, 8(2), 201-215, Ag 89.

A legal system that seeks to be self-administering would enthrone self-defense as the primary mode of suppressing aggressive intrusions, state punishment being a continuation of the same repressive measures. But each of these institutions has come to stand for a particular conception of merit in using force against criminal acts. Self-defense defends and reinforces the rightful and lawful order of cooperation among autonomous individuals. Punishment goes beyond the maintenance of the lawful order by realizing an imperative to avoid the injustice of suffering unsanctioned crime.

FLETCHER, Joseph. Genetic Control. Nat Forum, 69(4), 43-45, Fall 89.

Some diseases are transmitted by contagion, others by reproduction. Carriers of genetic disorders are exactly like Typhoid Mary. Should we not have control by law of at least some genetic disorders, in the interest of innocent offspring and the social good, just as we have of syphilis and diphtheria? Arguments for and against genetic control are canvassed and the case for control is offered.

FLEW, Antony. The Artificial Inflation of Natural Rights. Vera Lex, 8(2), 4,6, 1988.

The fundamental distinction is between option rights—rights to be left alone—and welfare rights—rights to be supplied with some good. In eighteenth century declarations, only rights of the former kind were claimed as natural and universal, but in the twentieth century the latter proliferate and tend to predominate. It is argued that it is impossible to produce an adequate justificatory rationale for any determinate set or system of natural and universal welfare rights.

FLEW, Antony. Is and Ought: The "Open Question Argument". Vera Lex, 9(2), 14, 1989.

FLEW, Antony. Liberty and Democracy, or Socialism? Free Inq, 9(4), 14-15, Fall 89.

Insisting that the criterion of democratic legitimacy must be, not whether a regime was voted in, but whether it can in due course be voted out, this paper argues that there is abundant experiential reason for believing it practically impossible to combine a fully socialist command economy with a pluralist, democratic political system. Certainly the Institute of Marxist-Leninism in Moscow has always recognized that "under socialism, once the working class has implemented the liquidation of the private ownership of the means of production, then there remains no ground for any opposition parties counter-balancing the Communist Party."

FLEW, Antony. Popper and Historicist Necessities. Philosophy, 65(251), 53-64, Ja 90.

Popper contends that, though there are sociological laws of nature, there neither are nor could be natural laws of historical development. But since laws of nature assert physical (as opposed to logical) necessities and physical (as opposed to logical) impossibilities, and since agents necessarily cannot be necessitated to do whatever it is which they choose to do, there neither are nor could be any such natural laws necessitatingly determining the senses of human actions. Therefore, a fortiori, there neither are nor could be any historicist natural laws of historical development. A less sympathetic critique of Carr's *What Is History?* follows.

FLICHMAN, Eduardo H. The Causalist Program: Rational or Irrational Persistence? Critica, 21(62), 29-53, Ag 89.

El análisis de las conexiones nomológicas se confunde a menudo con el de la causación. Mi propuesta, que se basa en las ideas de Bertrand Russell, plantea tratar el primer problema (programa acausalista) en contextos científicos, y rechazar el viejo programa causalista, viciado de imprecisión y antropomorfismo. Intento explicar por qué aun los análisis más sofisticados de la causación recaen en las dificultades que pretenden eludir (por ejemplo, en el problema de la asimetría). Mi intención principal es tratar de explicar por qué creo que el causalista es un típico programa degenerativo, en el sentido de Lakatos. También intento contestar ciertas preguntas acerca de la racionalidad, la objetividad y el progreso, en relación con los programas causalista y acausalista. (edited)

FLOISTAD, Guttorm. "The Source" Spinoza in the Writings of Gabriel Scott. Stud Spinozana, 5, 185-201, 1989.

The article purports to show the influence of Spinoza's philosophy of nature in the writings of the Norwegian author Gabriel Scott. An English translation of the Ethics and several books on Spinoza's philosophy with Scott's notes were found in his library. Scott also wrote a poem celebrating Spinoza as "a redeemer to himself and others." Spinoza's influence is clearly present in the interpretation of the Christian God in terms of nature. Whenever Marcus, the fisherman, attends the local church service and tries to understand God, his eyes are captured by the nature and the natural forces outside.

FLOREA, Ion. La correlation entre l'activité du parti et l'activité de l'Etat de la démocratie ouvrière (in Romanian). Rev Filosof (Romania), 35(5), 439-445, S-O 88.

FLOREA, Ion. La nécessité de l'affirmation d'une nouvelle pensée politique (in Romanian). Rev Filosof (Romania), 36(3), 220-226, My-Je 89.

FLORENSKII, P V and POLOVINKIN, S M. P A Florenskii's Review of His Work. Soviet Stud Phil, 28(3), 40-51, Wint 89-90.

FLÓREZ MIGUEL, Cirilo. La filosofía de la historia ayer y hoy. Dialogo Filosof, 6(1), 52-81, Ja-Ap 90.

FLORIVAL, Ghislaine. "Towards an Hermeneutics of Nature and Culture" in Man and Nature: The Chinese Tradition and the Future, TANG, Yi-Jie (ed), 71-83. Lanham, Univ Pr of America, 1989.

FLORU, Ion S. L'exposé de quelques systèmes d'histoire (in Romanian). Rev Filosof (Romania), 36(3), 256-270, My-Je 89.

FLOYD, Wayne W. To Welcome the Other: Totality and Theory in Levinas and Adorno. Phil Theol, 4(2), 145-170, Wint 89.

Emmanuel Levinas argued for the priority of the ethical—over the theoretic-other, vis-à-vis the prevailing modern, idealistic philosophies of totality. This essay argues that too facile a turn from epistemology to ethics, however, risks eviscerating the very role that theory—as "critical"—plays in the sustenance of the valuation of the Other. An alternative understanding of theory, the essay proposes, hinges on the negative dialectics of Adorno.

FLYNN, Bernard. "Derrida and Foucault: Madness and Writing" in Derrida and Deconstruction, SILVERMAN, Hugh J (ed), 201-218. New York, Routledge, 1989.

This article analyzes the debate between Derrida and Foucault that was begun with Derrida's critical reading of Foucault's Madness and Civilization (Histoire de la folie a l'age classique). Foucault responded in his article, "Cogito Incogito: Foucault's 'My Body, This Paper, This Fire'." Derrida never answered this response. I "took the liberty" of constructing a response for him, based on his writings. Derrida's critical remarks address Foucault's project of writing an archeology of the silence which is imposed on madness in the classical age by the voice of reason, and his consideration of Descartes's treatment of madness in the Meditations where it is both evoked and dismissed. My constructed response is based on Derrida's reading of Austin, particularly the opposition between event and the recontextualizing possibilities generated by writing. (edited)

FLYNN, T. Defining—and Implementing—Eupraxophy. Free Inq, 10(3), 16-18, Sum 90.

Secular humanism as lifestance encompasses atheism, materialism, rationalism, agnosticism, pragmatism, etc. These terms neglect the emotional, communitarian aspects of humanist living. The author endorses Paul Kurtz's coinage "eupraxophy," which defines the humanist stance but avoids religious terminology. Humanist groups should likewise avoid temptations to emulate each function of outmoded church congregations. Being secular, humanists may seek rites of passage outside their community of belief. Eupraxophic communities should concentrate on moral education of children and on creating a sense of community for members.

FLYNN, Thomas. "History as Fact and as Value: The Posthumous Sartre" in Inquiries into Values: The Inaugural Session of the International Society for Value Inquiry, LEE, Sander H , 375-390. Lewiston, Mellen Pr, 1989.

Relying especially on posthumously published material, I show that Sartre's

interest in the philosophy of history dates from the late 1930s and that his resultant concept of the historical process evolved from a descriptive, through an interpretative to an evaluative one: in effect, that soon after the War, without discounting the concept of historical fact so central to his early reflections, he adopted a concept of "History" as value to be fostered in our social life.

FLYNN, Tom. The Future of Abortion. Free Inq, 9(4), 44-46, Fall 89.

FODERICK, Saundra I and DIENHART, John W. Ethical and Conceptual Issues in Charitable Investments, Cause Related Marketing, and Advertising. Bus Prof Ethics J, 7(3-4), 47-59, Fall-Wint 88.

FODOR, Jerry A. Making Mind Matter More. Phil Topics, 17(1), 59-79, Spr 89.

FODOR, Jerry A. A Theory of Content and Other Essays. Cambridge, MIT Pr, 1990

FODOR, Jerry. Remnants of Meaning by Stephen Schiffer. Phil Phenomenol Res, 50(2), 409-423, D 89.

FOELBER, Robert E. "Deterrence and the Moral Use of Nuclear Weapons" in Nuclear Deterrence and Moral Restraint, SHUE, Henry (ed), 115-162. New York, Cambridge Univ Pr, 1989.

FOGELIN, Robert J. What Hume Actually Said About Miracles. Hume Stud, 16(1), 81-86, Ap 90.

Contrary to the standard interpretations, this essay shows that Hume, in Section X of the Enquiry Concerning Human Understanding, explicitly put forward an a priori argument intended to show that, by the nature of the case, there must always be adequate empirical evidence establishing that a reported miracle could not have taken place.

FOGELIN, Robert and SINNOTT-ARMSTRONG, Walter and MOOR, James. A Defence of Modus Tollens. Analysis, 50(1), 9-16, Ja 90.

Ernest Adams recently discussed an apparent counterexample to modus tollens: A asserts (1) If it rained, it didn't rain hard; B asserts (2) it rained hard; but it is paradoxical to conclude (3) it didn't rain. Adams avoids this paradox by claiming that (1) cannot be a material conditional, because A would not accept its contrapositive. We argue that (1) can be a material conditional; modus tollens is valid; Adams's contrapositive explanation fails; and no paradox arises, because it is illegitimate to draw conclusions from assertions when they can't both be true, and (1)-(2) can't both be true, given 'If it rained hard, it rained'.

FOGLE, Thomas. Are Genes Units of Inheritance? Biol Phil, 5(3), 349-371, Jl 90.

Definitions of the term 'gene' typically superimpose molecular genetics onto Mendelism. What emerges are persistent attempts to regard the gene as a 'unit' of structure and/or function, language that creates multiple meanings for the term and fails to acknowledge the diversity of gene architecture. I argue that coherence at the molecular level requires abandonment of the classical unit concept and recognition that a gene is constructed from an assemblage of domains. Hence, a domain set (1) conforms more closely to empirical evidence for genetic organization of DNA regions capable of transcription and (2) has ontological properties lacking in the traditional unit definition.

FOLDVARY, Fred E. Morality: Ought or Naught? Vera Lex, 9(1), 16, 1989.

FOLEY, Richard. Fumerton's Puzzle. J Phil Res, 15, 109-113, 1990.

There is a puzzle that is faced by every philosophical account of rational belief, rational strategy, rational planning or whatever. I describe this puzzle, examine Richard Fumerton's proposed solution to it and then go on to sketch my own preferred solution.

FOLMAN, Shoshana and SARIG, Gissi. Intercultural Rhetorical Differences in Meaning Construction. Commun Cog, 23(1), 45-92, 1990.

Recent research seems to challenge Robert Kaplan's contrastive rhetoric hypothesis, a phenomenon which might have an effect on EFL written communication instruction. Three studies were set out to further test this hypothesis. We wanted to find out if and to what extent rhetorical structures preferred by native Hebrew speakers differ from those preferred by native English speakers when constructing meaning in reading and in writing in their native languages. Findings are presented and discussed in light of an oral to written diagnostic model developed for this study. On the basis of this analysis, the possible relationship between writing instructional norms or practices and intercultural rhetorical preferences are suggested. Implications for future research are drawn. (edited)

FOLSE JR, Henry J. "Bohr on Bell" in Philosophical Consequences of Quantum Theory: Reflections on Bell's Theorem, CUSHING, James T (ed), 254-271. Notre Dame, Univ Notre Dame Pr, 1989.

Bohr's unique idiom in characterizing his framework of complementarity bears the stamp of his personal and professional history. From the sometimes strange things Bohr said in reply to EPR, this paper constructs what he would have said about Bell phenomena and "translates" it into the language of contemporary discussions of "separability." The result enlightens our understanding of Bohr's disagreement with Einstein as well as revealing complementarity as a realist interpretation of physics. Though Bohr qua physicist sees no need to develop a quantum era philosophy of nature, complementarity provides a possible framework for such an ontological undertaking.

FOLSE JR, Henry J. Complementarity and the Description of Nature in Biological Science. Biol Phil, 5(2), 211-224, Ap 90.

Niels Bohr developed the framework of complementarity for resolving paradoxes in atomic physics, but he claimed his viewpoint also could resolve disputes over teleological explanations in biology. His position is related to three stages in this controversy: the mechanist/vitalist debate, which shaped Bohr's outlook and led him to reject the ontological defense of teleological explanations, the positivist declaration that the debate was a pseudo-problem, which Bohr also repudiated, and the current "autonomist"/"provincialist" debate to which Bohr's viewpoint contributes by presenting an interactionist ontology defending the irreducibility of teleological explanations.

FORBES, Graeme. Cognitive Architecture and the Semantics of Belief. Midwest Stud Phil, 14, 84-100, 1989.

In this paper I apply the semantics I develop in "The Indispensability of Sinn" (*Philosophical Review*, 1990) to be Mates problem. I criticize the views of Salmon and Burge about substitution of synonyms in belief attributions.

FORBES, Graeme. Counterparts, Logic and Metaphysics: Reply to Ramachandran. Analysis, 50(3), 167-173, Je 90.

In this paper I discuss some criticisms by Murali Ramachandran of my reformation of Lewis's counterpart theory to accommodate contingent existence. I object to Ramachandran's own formulation on the grounds that it midhandles predication and contingent identity.

FORD, David F. "Tragedy and Atonement" in *Christ, Ethics and Tragedy: Essays in Honour of Donald MacKinnon*, SURIN, Kenneth (ed), 117-130. New York, Cambridge Univ Pr, 1989.

FOREST, Aimé. Comparaison des doctrines de Brunschvicg et de Pradines. G Metaf, 11(2), 191-215, My-Ag 89.

FORGAN, Sophie. The Architecture of Science and the Idea of a University. Stud Hist Phil Sci, 20(4), 405-434, D 89.

An analysis of the architectural and scientific context of university buildings in 19th Century Britain. The background to building, the plan, and layout of lecture halls and laboratories are examined in relation to educational theory, the meaning of different architectural styles, the imposition of discipline and systematic instruction. It is argued that spatially and intellectually science became integrated into the idea of a liberal education, but tensions remained, especially with regard to workshop and industrial facilities.

FORGUSON, Lynd. Common Sense. New York, Routledge, 1989

This book investigates the network of shared beliefs which guides our everyday behaviour. From an interdisciplinary perspective drawing on both philosophical analysis and recent research in cognitive development, *Common Sense* outlines the nature and scope of the common sense view of the world and traces its development in children. The author critically surveys the sceptical attacks on common sense realism by philosopher-psychologists of the seventeenth and eighteenth centuries. He examines the attempts by Reid and Moore to defend common sense against these attacks, and presents a new defence of common sense based on recent discoveries in the field of cognitive development.

FORJE, John W. Critique of Technological Policy in Africa. Phil Soc Act, 15(3-4), 102-112, Jl-D 89.

FORMAN, Frank. Contracting for Natural Rights. Vera Lex, 8(2), 13-14,20, 1988.

FORMAN, Robert K C. Paramārtha and Modern Constructivists on Mysticism: Epistemological Monomorphism verus Duomorphism. Phil East West, 39(4), 393-418, O 89.

Modern "constructivist" accounts of mysticism (Steven Katz, Robert Gimello, Wayne Proudfoot, etc.), which maintain that mystical experiences result from the constructive, world-building mental activities, are compared with (9th century yogacara Buddhist) Paramartha's constructivism. Both argue that generally experiences result from the shaping influences of background set, beliefs, etc. Modern constructivists hold that such construction apply as described to mysticism. Paramartha however holds that constructive activities are the initiating problematic of the Buddhist path: in mystical states they cease utterly. Article argues for Paramartha, suggesting that there are two epistemological structures: ordinary (conditioned) and mystical (unconditioned).

FORMENT, Eudaldo. El problema del *cogito* en san Agustin. Augustinus, 34(133-134), 7-30, Ja-Je 89.

FORNET-BETANCOURT, Raúl. La cuestion de dios en el pensar de Heidegger. Rev Filosof (Mexico), 22(66), 400-411, S-D 89.

FORNET-BETANCOURT, Raúl. En torno a Heidegger: Entrevista de Raúl Fornet-Betancourt y Klaus Hedwig con Walter Biemel. Logos (Mexico), 17(51), 13-28, S-D 89.

FORNET-BETANCOURT, Raúl. La pregunta por la "filosofia Latinoamericana" como problema filosofico. Rev Filosof (Mexico), 22(65), 166-188, My-Ag 89.

FORREST, Peter. New Problems with Repeatable Properties and with Change. Nous, 24(4), 543-556, S 90.

Suppose an object goes round a closed circuit arriving back where it started. Suppose, in addition, that it has a certain property specified by a vector. If space is curved, then, apparently, the object need never change with respect to this property, yet it comes back with a different property. The author's resolution of this paradox implies that repeatable properties do not play as fundamental a role as he, and many others, would like to think. It also implies that material objects are best thought of as continuants rather than as the sums of time-slices.

FORRESTER, James W. Why You Should: The Pragmatics of Deontic Speech. Hanover, Univ Pr New England, 1989

FORRESTER, John. "Lying on the Couch" in *Dismantling Truth: Reality in the Post-Modern World*, LAWSON, Hilary (ed), 145-165. New York, St Martin's Pr, 1989.

The contestatory character of truth-claims leads to the genealogy of the importance of claims concerning truth, in Augustine's attack on lying, in Nietzsche's and Jankelevitch's expressivist conceptions of truth-telling, in the Cartesian project of securing truth by confronting 'being deceived'. The unstable social foundations of truth-telling are revealed by Koyré on the lie and the secret and Sacks on the limits of serious talk. Psychoanalysis discards the distinction between truth and fiction, thus shifting the notion of what its reality is, but also creating a description of medical and social relations which are based on implicit, 'performative' relations of authority.

FÖRSTER, Eckart. "How Are Transcendental Arguments Possible?" in *Reading Kant*, SCHAPER, Eva (ed), 3-20. Cambridge, Blackwell, 1989.

FORSTER, Kathie. Parents Rights and Educational Policy. Educ Phil Theor, 21(1), 47-52, 1989.

This article addresses the issue of whether parents have a right to make educational decisions on their child's behalf; now far this right would extend; and what obligations this right would impose on other parties in the educational process such as teachers and administrators. I argue that parents' right does not merely rest upon the duties of parents to safeguard the interests of their children but also on the fact that parents' own interests are vitally bound up with their children's well-being. While there are limits to the rights of parents to make educational decisions for their children (not the least of these being the emerging rights of the children themselves), I conclude that on these grounds parents do have a right to participate in educational decision making and, consequently, schools and systems have an obligation to provide for this participation.

FORSTER, Paul D. Peirce on the Progress and Authority of Science. Trans Peirce Soc, 25(4), 421-452, Fall 89.

This paper argues that Peirce has a well-developed and systematic defence of the view that science is self-corrective. Peirce's concept of inferential validity is described and the validity of each form of inference is demonstrated. The precise sense in which science can be said to be self-corrective is outlined in detail. Finally, it is argued that the self-corrective thesis is insufficient to establish science as the ultimate cognitive authority. Rather, to make that case appeal must be made to Peirce's categories. Thus Peirce's vindication of science is shown to be inseparable from the broader foundations of his philosophical system.

FORSTER, Thomas. A Consistent Higher-Order Theory Without a (Higher-Order) Model. Z Math Log, 35(5), 385-386, 1989.

The theory of negative types (Wang, *Mind* 1952) is a higher order theory which is consistent (compactness) but can be shown (without use in the metatheory of the axioms of choice or foundation—or even replacement) to have no standard higher-order models.

FORTENBAUGH, William W (ed). *Cicero's Knowledge of the Peripatos*. New Brunswick, Transaction Books, 1989

This book investigates the extent to which Cicero knew Peripatetic authors and used their material in composing his dialogues. The areas covered include logic and rhetoric, physics and doxography, psychology, theology and politics. The primary emphasis is on Cicero's knowledge of Aristotle, but Theophrastus and other members of the school also receive serious attention.

FORTENBAUGH, William W. "Cicero's Knowledge of the Rhetorical Treatises of Aristotle and Theophrastus" in *Cicero's Knowledge of the Peripatos*, FORTENBAUGH, William W (ed), 39-60. New Brunswick, Transaction Books, 1989.

FORTI, M and HINNION, R. The Consistency Problem for Positive Comprehension Principles. J Sym Log, 54(4), 1401-1418, D 89.

FORTIN, Ernest L. Thomas Aquinas and the Reform of Christian Education. Interpretation, 17(1), 3-17, Fall 89.

FOSTER, Stephen Paul. Different Religions and the Difference They Make: Hume on the Political Effects of Religious Ideology. Mod Sch, 66(4), 253-274, My 89.

This paper deals with Hume's view of church-state relations and of the effects of religious ideology on political behavior, views developed primarily in his *History of England*, essays, and the *Natural History of Religion*. Hume argues that polytheistic religions, while theologically unsophisticated, are mythopoetic, do not advance truth claims, and hence are tolerant. Monotheism's rise, its co-option of philosophy, Hume sees as setting the stage for early modern religious conflagration. Hume examines two "perversions" of "true religion," *superstition* and *enthusiasm*, forms he links with political extremism.

FÓTI, Véronique. Textuality, Totalization, and the Question of Origin in Heidegger's Elucidation of *Andenken*. Res Phenomenol, 19, 43-58, 1989.

FOTION, Nicholas. Simmons and the Concept of Consent: Commentary on "Consent and Fairness in Planning Land Use". Bus Prof Ethics J, 6(2), 21-24, Sum 87.

The concept of consent has its home in one-to-one settings such as those found in medicine. Land-use planning is not such a setting. It makes sense, therefore, to ask whether that concept has any explanatory power when we are concerned with such planning. Does "We have community consent" explain better what has been gained than does "The community has agreed—in accord with its democratic procedures—to this project." Community consent is not an easy concept to understand. Unfortunately, in his article on land-use planning, Simmons does little to explain to us what the nature and force of that concept is.

FOUCAULT, Michel and WALKER, Pierre A (trans). Photogenic Painting. Crit Texts, 6(3), 1-12, 1989.

FOWLER, Corbin. "In Defense of Ethical Absolutism" in *Inquiries into Values: The Inaugural Session of the International Society for Value Inquiry*, LEE, Sander H , 47-56. Lewiston, Mellen Pr, 1989.

In this essay I shall outline an ideal utilitarian theory of ethics, construing intrinsic moral good and evil as absolutes, and I shall defend ethical absolutism against several objections posed by ethical subjectivism and ethical relativism. I will argue that these venerable objections are inconclusive (and in some cases self-defeating)—hence pose no serious challenge to ethical absolutism.

FOWLER, D P. "Lucretius and Politics" in *Philosophia Togata: Essays on Philosophy and Roman Society*, GRIFFIN, Miriam (ed), 120-150. New York, Clarendon/Oxford Pr, 1989.

FOWLER, Mark. Nietzschean Perspectivism: "How Could Such a Philosophy—Dominate?". Soc Theor Pract, 16(2), 119-162, Sum 90.

FOX, Ivan. On the Nature and Cognitive Function of Phenomenal Content—Part I. Phil Topics, 17(1), 81-117, Spr 89.

FOX, John. Motivation and Demotivation of a Four-Valued Logic. Notre Dame J Form Log, 31(1), 76-80, Wint 90.

Belnap offers two arguments for the usefulness of four-valued logic. I argue that one of them, which rests on interpreting valuations as states of our information, when taken seriously collapses into an argument for two-valued logic in which relevance is lost, and that the other, resting on Scott's thesis, is not an argument for its usefulness.

FOX, Michael Allen. "Schopenhauer on the Need for Metaphysics" in *Schopenhauer: New Essays in Honor of His 200th Birthday*, VON DER LUFT, Eric (ed), 159-164. Lewiston, Mellen Pr, 1989.

An attempt is made in this essay to indicate that Schopenhauer may be classed with those thinkers who regard metaphysics as a "natural disposition" (Aristotle, Bradley, Heidegger), the source of which is deep-seated human needs and yearnings. Through an analysis of Schopenhauer's principal essay on this subject, his thoughts on death, evil and the truth-claims of metaphysics are examined. Born in self-awareness and in revolt against the facticity, finiteness and vanity of existence, Schopenhauer's metaphysics is seen to be strikingly existential and to unite Eastern and Western traditions.

FOX, Michael W. The "Values" of Sentient Beings. Between Species, 5(3), 158-159, Sum 89.

FOX, Richard M and DE MARCO, Joseph P. *Moral Reasoning: A Philosophic Approach to Applied Ethics*. Orlando, Holt Rinehart Winst, 1989

Attempting to bridge the gap between theory and practice, the book analyzes principles and techniques required for moral decision making and develops a theory of applied ethics. It begins with issues about the nature of morality and the logic of moral reasoning. Then Kantianism, utilitarianism, natural law, contractarianism, pragmatism, and existentialism are explained and criticized. Insights from this analysis are used to form a system of principle and rules, and the system is applied in reasoning about social issues and individual acts. The last chapters focus on case studies in bioethics, business ethics, and personal life.

FRAEDRICH, John and FERRELL, O C. An Empirical Examination of Three Machiavellian Concepts: Advertisers Versus the General Public. J Bus Ethics, 8(9), 687-694, S 89.

This paper examines the perceived ethics of advertisers and the general public relative to three ethical concepts. Based on the survey findings, it can be concluded that with regard to the ethically laden concepts of manipulation, exploitation, and deviousness, advertisers are perceptually as ethical as the general public. The research also clarifies some of the differences between ethics and Machiavellianism.

FRAME, John M. *Medical Ethics: Principles, Persons, and Problems*. Phillipsburg, Presbyterian & Ref, 1988

The book asks whether the traditional evangelical Christian commitment to biblical authority is concretely helpful in dealing with the more difficult ethical cases—cases not specifically mentioned in scripture. By methodological analysis and case studies it argues an affirmative answer.

FRANCHELLA, Miriam. Brouwer's Equipotence and Denumerability Predicates. Teoria, 9(2), 45-55, 1989.

The aim is to understand why Brouwer has split the classical equipotence and denumerability predicates and has given just those new ones. I point out that the splitting is due to the fact that the intuitionistic "bijective correspondence"—present in both definitions—requires to find *effectively* the image. The various equipotence predicates are then obtained by the distinction between identity and congruence and by the composition of the predicates "larger or equal" and "smaller or equal" in all their expressions. The denumerability predicates come from the nuances of the concept of "at most denumerable."

FRANCHI, Alfredo. "Sub ratione ardui": Paura e speranza nella filosofia. Sapienza, 42(2), 149-165, Ap-Je 89.

FRANCHINI, Raffaello. *Il Potere e l'Ipotesi: Tappe di una filosofia delle Funzioni*. Bologna, Morano, 1989

FRANCIONI, Mario. I postulati etici e metodologici fondamentali delle psichiatrie fenomenologiche. Filosofia, 40(3), 283-293, S-D 89.

FRANCIS, B Joseph. A Response to the Paper "Theology of Religions and Sacrifice". J Dharma, 14(4), 340-342, O-D 89.

Sacrifice, in the Indian context, should include the aspect of moving from the unconscious to the conscious. The unconscious is the vibrant relationship one enjoys with all of reality and the conscious is the awareness of such a relationship. The point of contact with the Judeo-Christian view is the celebration of relationship which varies in its concrete manifestation or expression.

FRANCIS, Richard P. Something Substantial About Natural Law. Vera Lex, 8(2), 10-11, 1988.

FRANCIS, Richard. "The Holocaust's Ideological Perversion of Value" in *Inquiries into Values: The Inaugural Session of the International Society for Value Inquiry*, LEE, Sander H , 509-517. Lewiston, Mellen Pr, 1989.

The abuse of power, tolerated to maintain social order, can lead to the ideological perversion of our civilizing values. By making innocent victims to be criminals, terror is directed against them. The Nazi regime, in its anti-Semitic hysteria, blamed the Jews for its conflicts and sought their eradication. The Jews, in their two-thousand-year diaspora, while integrated as citizens of many countris, were regularly perceived as despicable foreigners, without effective protection. Thus, the expert, relentless ideological propaganda of totalitarian states accused powerless Jews of a conspiracy to rule the world, frustrating imperialist ambitions of anti-Semitic governments. Stripped of all rights, all of the Jews and other undesirables, wherever they lived, were subject to be murdered in gas chambers and crematoria of the Holocaust, our century's efficient way to slaughter millions of innocents. This dramatic collapse of all ethical standards still endangers us, by dishonoring human life and betraying our traditional values.

FRANCK, Georg. Das Paradox der Zeit und die Dimensionszahl der Temporalität. Z Phil Forsch, 43(3), 449-471, Jl-S 89.

The incompatibility of physical and historical time is reconstructed within the Kantian concept of time as 'form of vision'. Within this framework temporal experience reveals itself as a process including the representation of temporally different processes. The traditional paradoxes of tense—and particularly McTaggart's paradox—appear as problems of this nested kind of processuality. The analysis of remembering and anticipating as actual processes representing temporally different processes strongly suggests that the process of temporal awareness has more than one dimension of time.

FRANCK, Isaac and GERBER, William (ed). *A Philosopher's Harvest: The Philosophical Papers of Isaac Franck*. Washington, Georgetown Univ Pr, 1988

This is a collection of essays by the Jewish scholar Isaac Franck. Subjects covered by the essays include man's knowledge of God, freedom and determinism, and psychological concerns. Works by Maimonides, Aquinas and Spinoza are considered. (staff)

FRANCO, Paul. Michael Oakeshott as Liberal Theorist. Polit Theory, 18(3), 411-436, Ag 90.

Contrary to the predominant view of Oakeshott as a conservative thinker, this article contends that Oakeshott's political philosophy—especially his theory of civil association in *On Human Conduct*—is best understood as a restatement or reformulation of liberalism. Not uncritical of traditional liberal doctrine, this restatement seeks to purge liberalism of some of its more questionable ethical and metaphysical assumptions, i.e., its atomism and its materialism or economism. In this connection, Oakeshott's affinity with the Hegelian or idealist tradition of political philosophy is brought out. The article concludes with a consideration of Oakeshott's restatement in the context of the contemporary debate over liberalism, showing that it in many ways transcends the limitations of both the "deontological" and "communitarian" alternatives.

FRANK, Daniel H. "Humility as a Virtue: A Maimonidean Critique of Aristotle's Ethics" in *Moses Maimonides and His Time*, ORMSBY, Eric L (ed), 89-99. Washington, Cath Univ Amer Pr, 1989.

FRANK, Manfred and LAWRENCE, Joseph P (trans). Schelling's Critique of Hegel and the Beginnings of Marxian Dialectics. Ideal Stud, 19(3), 251-268, S 89.

The author shows how consistently Schelling maintained the transreflexive nature of being. He asserted this in opposition to Hegel, whose "proof" that being is reflexive in nature presupposes what it wants to demonstrate by defining being at the outset as pure self-relation. Schelling, in contrast, did not begin on the level of metaphysical assertion, but with a clear insight into the dependency of self-consciousness upon a prior, and absolutely unmediated, identity. According to Frank's understanding, the positioning of being beyond relation results from an experience of the conditionality of both reason and selfhood. In terms of such conditionality, Schelling emerges as a kind of dialectical materialist, the precursor of Feuerbach and Marx.

FRANK, S L and JAKIM, Boris (trans). *The Light Shineth in Darkness*. Athens, Ohio Univ Pr, 1989

In this work the author attempts to combine "the neglected truth of the mysterious power of sin in the world" with "faith in the positive value of the world as a creation of God and as an expression, in its primordial foundation, of the holy essence of God." This combination leads to a clear discrimination between Christ's absolute truth and its always imperfect embodiment in the world—between the essential salvation of the world and its protection from evil. On the other hand it leads to a perception of the nature of moral creativity as a dramatic Divine-human process of the healing of the world through the imbedding in it of its Divine primordial ground and the battle against dark human willfullness. (edited)

FRANKE, Carrie. The Women of Silence. Proc Phil Educ, 45, 150-153, 1989.

FRANKENA, William K. Kantian Ethics Today. J Phil Res, 15, 47-55, 1990.

Kantian ethics is both very much alive and very much under attack in recent moral philosophy, and so I propose to review some of the discussion, though I must say in advance that my review will have to be incomplete and oversimplified in various ways.

FRANKFURT, Harry G. Concerning the Freedom and Limits of the Will. Phil Topics, 17(1), 119-130, Spr 89.

FRANKLIN, James. Mathematical Necessity and Reality. Austl J Phil, 67(3), 286-294, S 89.

Einstein and most philosophers have thought there cannot be mathematical truths which are at once necessary and about reality. The article argues against this. *Prima facie* examples such as "It is impossible to tile my bathroom floor with (equally-sized) regular pentagonal tiles" are given, and defended against objections such as those based on the supposed purely logical or hypothetical nature of mathematics.

FRANKLIN, Stephen T. *Speaking from the Depths*. Grand Rapids, Eerdmans, 1989

This work breaks new ground in exploring some of the hermeneutical implications of Whitehead's philosophy. The book arises out of the author's quest to find a way of explaining how human language can speak of God. Whitehead's profound metaphysical vision—developed in his central work, *Process and Reality*, and in other writings—engages the author's quest. This book presupposes previous study in philosophy and theology as well as some knowledge of Whitehead's metaphysical system. (edited)

FRASER, Craig G. Lagrange's Analytical Mathematics, Its Cartesian Origins and Reception in Comte's Positive Philosophy. Stud Hist Phil Sci, 21(2), 243-256, Je 90.

An examination of the origins and reception of Lagrange's mathematical philosophy is used in order to illuminate his conception of analysis. His analytical approach is situated within a methodological tradition dominated by Malebranche and d'Alembert. The specific interpretation that Comte conferred upon Lagrange's doctrines is documented and contrasted with Cauchy's understanding of analysis. A prominent theme of the paper concerns the changing relationship within algebraic analysis of pure and applied mathematics.

FRASER, Nancy and NICHOLSON, Linda. "Social Criticism Without Philosophy" in *The Institution of Philosophy: A Discipline in Crisis?*, COHEN, Avner (ed), 283-301. La Salle, Open Court, 1989.

We argue that, in their respective attempts to develop paradigms of "social criticism without philosophy," postmodernism and feminism have been prey to complementary shortcomings. The anti-essentialism and anti-foundationalism of postmodernism have been purchased at the cost of the robustness of social criticism, while the robustness of some feminist social criticism has been achieved at the cost of a continued appeal to essential natures. We propose a postmodern feminism that avoids both these problems. The result is social criticism without philosophy, but not without political bite.

FRASER, Nancy. Unruly Practices: Power, Discourse and Gender in Contemporary Social Theory. Minneapolis, Univ of Minn Pr, 1989

This book brings together a series of widely discussed essays in feminism and social theory. Read together, they constitute a sustained critical encounter with leading European and American approaches to social theory. In addition, I develop a new and original socialist-feminist critical theory that overcomes many of the limitations of current alternatives. First, in a series of critical essays, I sort the wheat from the chaff in the work of Michel Foucault, the French deconstructionists, Richard Rorty, and Jürgen Habermas. Then, in a group of constructive essays, I incorporate their respective strengths in a new critical theory of late-capitalist political culture.

FRAZEE, Jerome. A New Symbolic Representation for the Algebra of Sets. Hist Phil Log, 11(1), 67-75, 1990.

The algebra of sets has, basically, two different types of symbols. One type of symbol defines another set from two other sets. A second type of symbol makes a proposition about two sets. When the construction of these two types of symbols is based on the same four-dot matrix as the logic symbols described in a previous paper, the three symbol types then dovetail together into a harmonious whole that greatly simplifies derivation in the algebra of sets. (edited)

FREDE, Dorothea. "Constitution and Citizenship: Peripatetic Influence on Cicero's Political Conception in the *De re publica*" in *Cicero's Knowledge of the Peripatos*, FORTENBAUGH, William W (ed), 77-100. New Brunswick, Transaction Books, 1989.

Cicero's depiction of an ideal state in *De re publica*, though tailored to fit the Roman political situation, shows Peripatetic influence in its theoretical framework (book 1): the state as a community based on justice, utility and gregariousness; the separation of power as executive (magistrate) legislative-deliberative (council), and judicative (Law courts). A Greek source is evident also in the evaluation of different kinds of constitutions and in the explanation of their origin: Aristotle's theory of degenerate forms (*parabaseis*) of constitutions. Although these conceptions are derived from Aristotle's *Politics*, it cannot be the direct source, because the metaphysical underpinnings are not developed, such as the conception of a 'natural citizenship' with teleological justification for the right to participate in politics. A more popular work of the Aristotelian school must be Cicero's source, most likely the work by Theophrastus referred to also in the De Finibus V.11.

FREDE, Michael. "An Empiricist View of Knowledge: Memorism" in *Epistemology (Companions to Ancient Thought: 1)*, EVERSON, Stephen (ed), 225-250. New York, Cambridge Univ Pr, 1989.

FREDE, Michael (trans) and BRUNSCHWIG, J (trans). Les origines de la notion de cause. Rev Metaph Morale, 94(4), 483-511, O-D 89.

FREDERICK, Robert E and HOFFMAN, W Michael. The Individual Investor in Securities Markets: An Ethical Analysis. J Bus Ethics, 9(7), 579-589, Jl 90.

In this paper we consider whether one type of individual investor, which we call "at risk" investors, should be denied access to securities markets to prevent them from suffering serious financial harm. We consider one kind of paternalistic justification for prohibiting at risk investors from participating in securities markets, and argue that it is not successful. We then argue that restricting access to markets is justified in some circumstances to protect the rights of at risk investors. We conclude with some suggestions about how this might be done.

FREDERICKS, Janet and MILLER, Steven I. The False Ontology of School Climate Effects. Educ Theor, 40(3), 333-342, Sum 90.

Theories concerning so-called "climate effects" have become an important empirical claim in the formulation of educational policies related to establishing "effective" schools. The authors argue that climate effects are based on suspect ontological claims which conflate a variety of separate empirical findings into a composite measure of dubious theoretical status. It is suggested that school effectiveness policies are better served by incorporating naturalistic forms of inquiry.

FREEMAN, James B. The Human Image System and Thinking Critically in the Strong Sense. Inform Log, 11(1), 19-40, Wint 89.

Strong sense critical thinking involves overcoming egocentric and sociocentric tendencies by entertaining the world views of others. The concept of the image system sheds light on what egocentricity, sociocentricity, world view mean. Our image system gives us a picture of our world and our place in it. Its developmental sources lie both in our experience and in our needs for meaning and ego-defense. It filters information, predisposing us to make prejudiced, uncritical judgments. By gaining insight into its growth and dynamics, one may transcend its effects. Hence, study of the image system should contribute to strong sense critical thinking.

FREEMAN, James B. "Quantification, Identity, and Opacity in Relevant Logic" in *Directions in Relevant Logic*, NORMAN, Jean (ed), 305-316. Norwell, Kluwer, 1989.

The paradoxes Quine and others have discussed in connection with substitution of identicals within and quantification into the scope of modal operators or verbs of propositional attitude also arise in relevant contexts. However, keeping to an objectual interpretation of the quantifiers avoids maintaining that quantification into relevant contexts is meaningless, or that occurrences of singular terms within such contexts are "not purely referential." The substitution interpretation or construing the quantifier as ranging over intensional entities also has plausibility. Ultimately, a theory with two styles of quantifiers may be more satisfying in explicating quantification and identity in relevant contexts.

FREEMAN, Samuel. Reason and Agreement in Social Contract Views. Phil Pub Affairs, 19(2), 122-157, Spr 90.

This work discusses the structure of Rawls's and Gauthier's contractarian arguments, focusing on the role of social agreement in their views, and how it is connected with different conceptions of practical reason. Against the contention that a social agreement plays no significant role in Rawls's account, it is argued that Rawls's version of the social contract is closely tied to his conception of practical reason, public justification, and the social bases of autonomy.

FRENCH, Marilyn. Is There a Feminist Aesthetic? Hypatia, 5(2), 33-42, Sum 90.

FRENCH, Peter A. Moral Education, Liberal Education, and Model Building. Thinking, 4(1), 10-18, 1982.

FRENCH, Peter. "What Can You Do with Art?" in *Inquiries into Values: The Inaugural Session of the International Society for Value Inquiry*, LEE, Sander H , 557-568. Lewiston, Mellen Pr, 1989.

What sort of protection ought to be afforded to works of art? Does it make sense to protect artworks from alteration and destruction regardless of the wishes of their creators? This paper discusses these questions and relates them to the concept of artwork integrity and its moral implications. It also examines the problem of defining what makes something a work of art.

FRENCH, Steven and DA COSTA, Newton C A. Belief and Contradiction. Critica, 20(60), 3-11, D 88.

FRENCH, Steven. Identity and Individuality in Classical and Quantum Physics. Austl J Phil, 67(4), 432-446, D 89.

The individuality of elementary particles is discussed in the context of both classical and quantum physics. It is argued that two broad views—referred to as 'Lockean' and 'Space-Time' individuality, respectively—can be consistently maintained in both domains. This is taken to support the claim that more than one metaphysical package may be consistent with a given physical theory.

FRENCH, Steven and DA COSTA, Newton C A. The Model-Theoretic Approach in the Philosophy of Science. Phil Sci, 57(2), 248-265, Je 90.

An introduction to the model-theoretic approach in the philosophy of science is given and it is argued that this program is further enhanced by the introduction of *partial* structures. It is then shown that this leads to a natural and intuitive account of both "iconic" and mathematical models and of the role of the former in science itself.

FRENCH, Steven. A Peircean Response to the Realist-Empiricist Debate. Trans Peirce Soc, 25(3), 292-307, Sum 89.

The purpose of this paper is to point out the similarities which exist between the realism-scepticism debate in general philosophy and the realist-empiricist debate in philosophy of science and to suggest that Peirce's response to the former might profitably be applied to the latter. The paper concludes by making some connections between fallibilist realism and recent formal work on 'pragmatic' or 'partial' truth.

FRESCO, Marcel F. Science and Cultural Diversity (in Hungarian). Magyar Filozof Szemle, 2-3, 315-322, 1989.

FREUDENTHAL, Gideon. "Otto Neurath: From Authoritarian Liberalism to Empiricism" in *Knowledge and Politics*, DASCAL, Marcelo (ed), 207-240. Boulder, Westview Pr, 1988.

Logical positivism was said by Otto Neurath to be the "philosophy of the socialist proletariat" and thus dependent on political views. The paper argues that Neurath's epistemology was indeed dependent on his political views (by constraints of consistency) but that these coincided with Eduard Bernstein's liberal interpretation of Marxism in political economy, sociology and politics. The paper argues further that it is the concept of man that ties together sociology, politics and epistemology and that the liberal concentration on the sphere of distribution, neglecting production, could not be the basis of a historical materialist epistemology but only of empiricism.

FREUDENTHAL, Gideon. "Towards a Social History of Newtonian Mechanics: Boris Hessen and Henryk Grossmann Revisited" in *Scientific Knowledge Socialized*, HRONSZKY, Imre (ed), 193-212. Norwell, Kluwer, 1989.

Hessen's and Grossmann's essays are reinterpreted and integrated into a comprehensive historical and philosophical theory of science. In this interpretation, previous technology determined the material and cognitive means of Newtonian science. Drawing on the author's *Atom and Individual in the Age of Newton* (1986), it is further argued that Newton's interpretation of the analytic-synthetic method was dependent on a general metaphysics of essential properties of individuals both physical and moral that determined the structure of explanation in physics as well as in social philosophy, and that this metaphysics was in turn dependent on socio-economic views typical to the rising bourgeoisie of the time.

FREUDIGER, Jürg and BURRI, Alex. Zur Analytizität hypothetischer Imperative. Z Phil Forsch, 44(1), 98-105, 1990.

In *Foundations of the Metaphysics of Morals* Kant makes a distinction between categorical and hypothetical imperatives and claims that the latter are analytic. By analyzing their logical structure we show that his claim is false.

FREUNDLIEB, Dieter. Deconstructionist Metaphysics and the Interpretation of Saussure. J Speculative Phil, 4(2), 105-131, 1990.

Apart from a short discussion of the specific problems that arise if one tries to criticize a philosophical position which is as radical as that of Derridean deconstruction, this paper pursues two aims: it argues that Derrida's principle of 'difference' is more metaphysical in a negative sense than anything to be found in the tradition Derrida attacks, and it attempts to demonstrate that Derrida's interpretation of Saussure's work as an example of the traditional hostility towards writing is untenable.

FRICKE, Christel. Explaining the Inexplicable: The Hypotheses of the Faculty of Reflective Judgement in Kant's Third Critique. Nous, 24(1), 45-62, Mr 90.

FRIEDMAN, Harvey M and HIRST, J L. Weak Comparability of Well Orderings and Reverse Mathematics. Annals Pure Applied Log, 47(1), 11-29, Ap 90.

FRIEDMAN, Harvey. The Equivalence of the Disjunction and Existence Properties for Modal Arithmetic. J Sym Log, 54(4), 1456-1459, D 89.

FRIEDMAN, Jeffrey. The New Consensus: The Fukuyama Thesis. Crit Rev, 3(3-4), 373-410, Sum-Fall 89.

Fukuyama's argument that we have recently reached "The End of History" is defended against writers who fail to appreciate the Hegelian meaning of Fukuyama's "Endism," but is criticized for using simplistic dichotomies that evade the economic and ideological convergence of East and West. Against Fukuyama, the economic critique of socialism, revisionist scholarship on early Soviet economic history, and the history of the libertarian ideas of Rousseau, Kant, Hegel and Marx are deployed to show that history "ended" years ago: the creeds of the First and Second Worlds sprang from common assumptions; and even before Eastern European reform movements, both sides of the Iron Curtain had moved to economies that are neither capitalist nor socialist.

FRIEDMAN, Lawrence M. On the Interpretation of Laws. Ratio Juris, 1(3), 252-262, D 88.

The essay is an attempt to examine aspects of legal interpretation from an external, sociological point of view. "Interpretation," in its normal juristic sense, is primarily a process in which decision makers with secondary legitimacy link their decisions to authority of primary legitimacy. The type of legitimacy which is dominant within the legal system greatly influences the style of interpretation—in "closed" systems, where the stock of premises is fixed, "legalism" will abound. Legal interpretation is not concerned with what a text really means, in any literal sense; and standards for judging legal interpretation are different from the standards of judging other forms of communication, for example, literature. Indeed, a judge can be considered great precisely because of his creative acts of misinterpretation.

FRIEDMAN, Marilyn. The Impracticality of Impartiality. J Phil, 86(11), 645-656, N 89.

Impartiality, I argue, is an impracticable abstract ideal. It is not confirmably attainable in a direct way in practice, either through the method of universalization or the requirements of the contractual model, nor by means of the contemporary analysis of impartial reasons in terms of universality and neutrality. In place of these approaches, I recommend the alternative practice of aiming to eliminate particular named partialities one by one as their substantive manifestations are recognized. Intersubjective dialogue, I suggest, plays a practically necessary role in this recognition of specific partialities.

FRIEDMAN, Michael and DEMOPOULOS, William. "The Concept of Structure in *The Analysis of Matter*" in *Rereading Russell: Essays on Bertrand Russell's Metaphysics and Epistemology*, SAVAGE, C Wade (ed), 183-199. Minneapolis, Univ of Minn Pr, 1989.

FRIEDMAN, Richard B. Oakeshott on the Authority of Law. Ratio Juris, 2(1), 27-40, Mr 89.

The author explains Michael Oakeshott's distinctive theory of law through an explanation of its notion of authority. He explains the view that modern states are ambiguous, consisting partly of *civil associations* and partly of *enterprise associations*. Authority is not a function of people's attitudes to those in power, but exists when a government's action is itself accepted as sufficient reason for unconditional obedience. Authority in this sense cannot exist in enterprise association, commitment to which must be contingent on the fulfillment of purposes common to all participants. But modern states are compulsory associations, different from each. Furthermore, authority could never be justified on a rational choice model, which must always be teleological in character. Because this means there can be no solution to the problem of political obligation, all philosophy can do is describe abstractly the Rule of Law state which does reconcile authority and liberty.

FRIEDMAN, Sy D. Coding Over a Measurable Cardinal. J Sym Log, 54(4), 1145-1159, D 89.

FRIGERIO, C. Kant's Metaphysics of the Subject and Modern Society. S Afr J Phil, 8(3-4), 176-181, N 88.

Modern man lives a life of paradoxes and contradictions in a society the order of which, in many instances, contradicts the very value system on which it claims to be founded. In this article it is argued that the contradictions we experience at praxis level are not instances of unfulfilled prescriptions or incorrect applications of the system, but rather a reflection of contradictions existing at theoretical level. At this level the conception of man we have inherited from Descartes and Kant is the main premiss to the value system which both prescribes and justifies the social order of today. In this article attempts are made to expose the contradictions existing in Descartes's

and Kant's metaphysics of subjectivity which, it is argued, are the real root of the paradoxes existing at praxis level in contemporary society. From this the author is led to concur with Foucault's claim that 'it is no longer possible to think in our day other than in the void left by man's disappearance'.

FRIQUEGNON, Marie-Loui. Childhood's End: The Age of Responsibility. Thinking, 4(3-4), 20-24, 1982.

FRISCH, Morton J. Edmund Burke and the American Constitution. Interpretation, 17(1), 59-67, Fall 89.

FRISINA, Michael E. The Offensive-Defensive Distinction in Military Biological Research. Hastings Center Rep, 20(3), 19-22, My-Je 90.

This article defends the moral justification of US military medical personnel conducting biological research. Opponents of this research contend that any medical research conducted by the military necessarily will lead to a biological weapons race. The author argues that vaccine and therapeutic drug therapy medical research constitutes defensive research against biological weapons of potential adversaries of the US. As such, this research upholds the principle of beneficence, a historic component of the health care professions, and consequently is morally justifiable.

FRISINA, Warren G. Are Knowledge and Action Really One Thing—A Study of Wang Yang-ming's Doctrine of Mind. Phil East West, 39(4), 419-447, O 89.

I examine what Wang meant by *chih hsing ho-i* (the unity of knowledge and action), setting this slogan into the context of his own thought and that of his Neo-Confucian predecessors. My aim is to demonstrate that Wang intended his phrase literally. Knowledge and action are, *in all their forms, really one thing*. I show this by arguing that Wang developed *chih hsing ho-i* to render the epistemological practices of his day consistent with the central metaphysical claims of the Confucian tradition as he understood them. In short, I claim that to understand *chih hsing ho-i* we must begin with the metaphysical presuppositions upon which it was founded.

FRISINA, Warren G. Knowledge as Active, Aesthetic, and Hypothetical. Phil Today, 33(3), 245-263, Fall 89.

This article examines the relation between Dewey's metaphysics and epistemology, arguing that knowledge is best understood as active aesthetic and hypothetical. For Dewey, knowledge is active because it is a species of the dynamic activity constituting experience and existence. The aesthetic dimension of knowledge is rooted in the link Dewey draws between knowledge, biology, and art. Finally, the hypothetical character of knowledge is drawn from Dewey's description of symbol systems and their development.

FRITSCHE, David J. Marketing/Business Ethics: A Review of the Empirical Research. Bus Prof Ethics J, 6(4), 65-79, Win 87.

The empirical literature on marketing/business ethics published during the past 25 years is reviewed. The literature focusses on personal values, types of ethical issues faced and the impact of organizations, their goals and culture. The paper ends with a summary of empirical findings to date. It is encouraging to find similar findings from research using different samples, and different methodologies.

FRITZHAND, Marek and RODZINSKA, Aleksandra (trans). Is Marxism an Atheism? Dialec Hum, 16(2), 109-120, Spr 89.

FRITZHAND, Marek and PROTALINSKI, Grzegorz (trans). Marxism and Social Sciences at a New Stage. Dialec Hum, 15(3-4), 53-58, Sum-Autumn 88.

FRITZHAND, Marek. Matérialisme, métaphysique, éthique (in Polish). Stud Phil Christ, 25(1), 47-58, 1989.

L'auteur du présent article attire l'attention sur la grande importance dans l'oeuvre philosophique du père professeur Slipko de son ouvrage en trois tomes consacré à l'éthique générale et particulière. Cet ouvrage est lié à la tradition des oeuvres monumentales d'éthique chrétienne, mais c'est toutefois un ouvrage moderne, traitant les problèmes actuels et demeurant en liaison vivante avec la pratiques des temps présents. La façon éclairée et humaniste du professeur Slipko de comprendre le dialogue entre la chrétienté et le marxisme permet à l'auteur de cet article d'entreprendre une discussion objective concernant ce qui différencie et ce qui est commun aux partenaires du dialogue. L'auteur de l'article essaie de démontrer que les divergences sont en ce cas remarquablement plus restreintes que l'on ne le suppose généralement; il démontre plus particulièrement que le marxisme n'est pas porcément lié à l'atheisme.

FRITZMAN, J M. Lyotard's Paralogy and Rorty's Pluralism: Their Differences and Pedagogical Implications. Educ Theor, 40(3), 371-380, Sum 90.

The postmodern philosophies of Jean-François Lyotard and Richard Rorty seem similar. Nevertheless, there are significant differences between

Lyotard's paralogy and Rorty's pluralism. The pedagogical implications of paralogy and pluralism are quite distinct. Lyotardian paralogy may be read as overcoming the deficiencies of Rortyan pluralism. However, there cannot be criteria which would decide between them.

FRITZSCHE, David J and TSALIKIS, John. Business Ethics: A Literature Review with a Focus on Marketing Ethics. J Bus Ethics, 8(9), 695-743, S 89.

In recent years, the business ethics literature has exploded in both volume and importance. Because of the sheer volume and diversity of this literature, a review article was deemed necessary to provide focus and clarity to the area. The present paper reviews the literature on business ethics with a special focus in marketing ethics. The literature is divided into normative and empirical sections, with more emphasis given to the latter. Even though the majority of the articles deal with the American reality, most of the knowledge gained in easily transferable to other nations.

FRIZEN, Werner. "Der alte Schopenhauer schlohweiss—ich und geschichte in Günter Grass' Romanen"" in *Schopenhauer: New Essays in Honor of His 200th Birthday*, VON DER LUFT, Eric (ed), 165-187. Lewiston, Mellen Pr, 1989.

FROLOV, Ivan T. *Man, Science, Humanism: A New Synthesis*. Buffalo, Prometheus, 1990

FROLOV, Ivan T. On the Perspectives of Research into the Philosophical and Social Aspects of Science and Technology. Dialec Hum, 15(3-4), 7-18, Sum-Autumn 88.

FRONGIA, Guido. "Wittgenstein on Breaking Rules" in *Wittgenstein in Focus—Im Brennpunkt: Wittgenstein*, MC GUINNESS, Brian (ed), 263-284. Amsterdam, Rodopi, 1989.

Among the rules which govern the "language-games" discussed by Wittgenstein there are some which seem to have particular functions which can be more effectively brought to light by considering the logical and pragmatic effects of their breakage. Indeed, if we extend progressively the analysis of possible breakages of such rules from particular language-games to broader and broader areas of language, we arrive at a point where (as happened in the *Tractatus*) it seems possible to draw a limit between what, in general terms, is endowed with sense, and what is devoid of it. This possibility, offered by a "rule-breaking" approach, also opens a promising perspective from which to look afresh at some classical problems connected with skepticism.

FROST, Thomas B. In Defense of the Causal Representative Theory of Perception. Dialogue (PST), 32(2-3), 43-50, Ap 90.

In my essay I detail and defend what I believe to be the most acceptable theory of perception: the causal representative theory, or CRT. The paper is divided into three sections: in the first section I show how the CRT is superior to its main competitor, direct realism; in the second I explain how we can claim knowledge of an independent reality that we don't directly experience; finally I defend the CRT from the criticisms made by William Cooney in *Dialogue*, October 1985.

FROUSSART, Bernard. Genealogies as the Language of Time: A Structural Approach—Anthropological Implications. Diogenes, 149, 41-64, Spr 90.

The article aims at showing that the age reached by individuals when various genealogical events occur (marriages, births, deaths), similar to words, endowed with form and meaning, obeys a grammatical type organisation. Thanks to an adequate transformation system and descriptive brochure the exploitation of genealogies is deeply improved. The application of this analysis to one case of heart attack shows that the age of the deceased undoubtedly obeys an emplacement syntax as if the defunct had chosen that particular moment to die. The concealed order brought to light by observations is interpreted within the frame of "menetic theory."

FRUCHTMAN, Jack. Nature and Revolution in Paine's *Common Sense*. Hist Polit Thought, 10(3), 421-438, Autumn 89.

Thomas Paine, one of the most influential writers of the late eighteenth century, provided a rationale for political revolution grounded in his theory of nature. For Paine, God made human beings with the natural ability to reflect his own inventive creativity. Although they could never mirror God's perfection, people could improve life by producing democratic constitutions and sound economies. One important invention, when necessary, was political revolution. In arguing that revolution was well within the people's natural capabilities, Paine advanced a powerful justification for the elimination of corrupt kings and aristocrats who threatened the people's very humanity.

FRY, Sara T. The Role of Caring in a Theory of Nursing Ethics. Hypatia, 4(2), 88-103, Sum 89.

The development of nursing ethics as a field of inquiry has largely relied on theories of medical ethics that use autonomy, beneficence, and/or justice as foundational ethical principles. Such theories espouse a masculine approach to moral decision making and ethical analysis. This paper challenges the presumption of medical ethics and its associated system of moral justification as an appropriate model for nursing ethics. It argues that the value foundations of nursing ethics are located within the existential phenomenon of human caring within the nurse/patient relationship instead of in models of patient good or rights-based notions of autonomy as articulated in prominent theories of medical ethics. Models of caring are analyzed and a moral-point-of-view (MPV) theory with caring as a fundamental value is proposed for the development of a theory of nursing ethics. This type of theory is supportive to feminist medical ethics because it focuses on the subscription to, and not merely the acceptance of, a particular view of morality.

FUCHS, Erich. John Rawls et la justice. Rev Theol Phil, 122(2), 253-260, 1990.

FUCHS, Josef. Magisterium und Moraltheologie. Frei Z Phil Theol, 36(3), 395-407, 1989.

FUCHS, Wolfgang W. Post-Modernism is Not a Scepticism. Man World, 22(4), 393-402, D 89.

The purpose of the article is to examine the popular claim that postmodern philosophical thought is a form of scepticism. Analyzing scepticism in both its classical and modern versions, the author shows their basic incompatibilities with the thought of Nietzsche and Derrida, two exemplars of postmodernism. He concludes that postmodernism is not a scepticism. He then speculates about the grounds its critics might have for trying to identify postmodernism with scepticism.

FUHRMAN, Ellsworth. Scattered Sociology: A Response to Bash. Soc Epistem, 3(3), 247-249, Jl-S 89.

FUHRMANN, André. Reflective Modalities and Theory Change. Synthese, 81(1), 115-134, O 89.

A reflective modality is a unary sentence-forming operator N associated with the closure condition: if a sentence A is (not) in a set T, then NA (not-NA) is in T. A reflectively closed theory is a deductively closed set of sentence satisfying the above closure condition. The paper explores the prospects for defining adequate contraction and revision operations (in the sense of Alchourron, Gärdenfors and Makinson) on reflectively closed theories.

FULLER, Timothy. Friedrich Hayek's Moral Science. Ratio Juris, 2(1), 17-26, Mr 89.

F A Hayek's defense and analysis of the liberal state built on rule of law is both a moral and a scientific enterprise. The author shows that Hayek favors rule of law because it seeks to protect moral agency. It is procedurally rather than morally restrictive because men cannot easily know moral truth. Markets are included in Hayek's analysis not because they produce wealth but because they promote moral agency.

FULLER, Timothy. The Theological-Political Tension in Liberalism. Phil Theol, 4(3), 267-281, Spr 90.

The tension in liberal political theory between religious commitment and political citizenship is examined first within the framework of Rousseau's political theory, and secondly within the context of Hegel's account of the state. I conclude with some reflections upon the tension as it occurs among contemporary political theorists.

FULLER, Timothy (ed) and OAKESHOTT, Michael. *The Voice of Liberal Learning: Michael Oakeshott on Education*. New Haven, Yale Univ Pr, 1989

Oakeshott's education essays, collected, edited and introduced by Timothy Fuller, show universities as special places of learning where scholars congregate to keep learning and to teach. Universities have no definable, external purpose. Humanity would achieve little if limited merely to utilitarian pursuits. The university's differentiating idea is to pursue learning for its own sake wherein the how and what of learning are inseparable and equally eligible for philosophic reflection, only incidentally bearing practical fruit, an unrehearsed intellectual adventure in becoming human, preferring conversation to victory, and where political demands are extrinsic to teaching and learning.

FULLINWIDER, Robert K. Against Theory, or: Applied Philosophy—A Cautionary Tale. Metaphilosophy, 20(3-4), 222-234, Jl-O 89.

FULLINWIDER, Robert K. Moral Conventions and Moral Lessons. Soc Theor Pract, 15(3), 321-338, Fall 89.

FULLINWIDER, S P. Hermann von Helmholtz: The Problem of Kantian Influence. Stud Hist Phil Sci, 21(1), 41-55, Mr 90.

Description of how Helmholtz built Kantian epistemology into his sensory physiology and in the process conflated transcendental lawlikeness with "theoretical lawlikeness" (that presupposed in nature by the possibility of discovering empirical laws).

FUMERTON, Richard. "Russelling Causal Theories of Reference" in *Rereading Russell: Essays on Bertrand Russell's Metaphysics and Epistemology*, SAVAGE, C Wade (ed), 108-118. Minneapolis, Univ of Minn Pr, 1989.

I argue that a Russellian analysis of names can incorporate whatever is plausible in a causal theory in such a way as to make it immune to the causal theorist's objections while acknowledging one interesting insight about referential opacity.

FUNKE, Gerhard. "Homo conscius sui" in *Agora: Zu Ehren von Rudolph Berlinger*, BERLINGER, Rudolph (and other eds), 57-91. Amsterdam, Rodopi, 1988.

The article stresses the aspect of last foundation as heart of the philosophical anthropology. This discipline is understood as one "radical" approach to the final aim of all philosophical investigation: last foundation. From Husserl to Kant, man is described as person, capable of responsibility for his acts. Thus, anthropology has to determine man as self-conscious: "Homo conscius sui."

FUNKEE, Gerhard. Ethik als Grundwissenschaft: Handeln aus Klugheit, Neigung, Pflicht, Ehrfurcht, Mitleid? Schopenhauer Jahr, 70, 19-42, 1989.

"Ethik als Grundwissenschaft" Fragt nach der Letztbegrundung des Verhaltens, das allgemein sittlich genannt werden kann. Solche Begründung ist nicht gegeben durch ethische Positionen, die an die Gesichtspunkte eines Handelns aus Klugheit geheftet sind, wie etwa in den verschiedenen Spielarten einer Günterethik bei Leibniz und Herder, ebenso nicht durch die Pflichtenethik Kants, nicht durch Goethes Seinsethik als Ehrfurchtsethik und schließlich auch nicht durch Schopenhauers Mitleidsethik. Demgegenüber kann die "Ethik als Grundwissenschaft" mit dem Prinzip der Selbstlosigkeit ein Lefztbegründendes in Hinsicht auf das 'Wie' des sittlichen Verhaltens angeben.

FURASH, Gary. Frank Jackson's Knowledge Argument Against Materialism. Dialogue (PST), 32(1), 1-6, O 89.

This essay examines an argument against physicalism made by Frank Jackson, the "Knowledge argument," which concerns the discovery of new knowledge in a situation which, according to physicalism, there is nothing new to be learned. Several recent criticisms of this argument by physicalists are considered. The author concludes that the argument points out a basic flaw in physicalism.

FURET, M François. Les mutations de l'historiographie Révolutionnaire. Bull Soc Fr Phil, 83(3), 77-110, Jl-S 89.

The actual historiography of the French Revolution seems to me to be dominated by a return to political analysis and reflection which has been from the restriction of its definition through social and economic factors. The opposition between political and social rights which has obsessed so many generations of scholars leaves room to the rediscovery of the birth of the world of the autonomous individual, so difficult to link into a political body. (edited)

FURLEY, David J. "Aristotelian Material in Cicero's De natura deorum" in *Cicero's Knowledge of the Peripatos*, FORTENBAUGH, William W (ed), 201-219. New Brunswick, Transaction Books, 1989.

FURLONG, John and CARROLL, William. Teaching Reasoning With Computers. Thinking, 5(4), 29-32, 1985.

FURMAN, Frida Kerner. Teaching Business Ethics: Questioning the Assumptions, Seeking New Directions. J Bus Ethics, 9(1), 31-38, Ja 90.

An examination of leading textbooks suggests the predominance of a principle-based model in the teaching of business ethics. The model assumes that by teaching students the rudiments of ethical reasoning and ethical theory, we can hope to create rational, independent, autonomous managers who will apply such theory to the many quandary situations of the corporate world. This paper challenges these assumptions by asking the following questions: (1) Is the acquisition of principle-based ethical theory unproblematic? (2) What is the transferability of classroom learning to the business context? (3) Is it appropriate to consider complementary models in the teaching of business ethics? The last question is approached from the perspective of virtues-based ethics, from the insights of feminist ethics, and from a culturally grounded orientation to moral values and norms.

FYNSK, Christopher. "The Choice of Deconstruction" in *The Textual Sublime: Deconstruction and Its Differences*, SILVERMAN, Hugh J (ed), 5-12. Albany, SUNY Pr, 1990.

FYNSK, Christopher. Noise at the Threshold. Res Phenomenol, 19, 101-120, 1989.

FYNSK, Christopher (ed) and LACOUE-LABARTHE, Philippe. *Typography: Mimesis, Philosophy, Politics*. Cambridge, Harvard Univ Pr, 1989

GAA, James C. A Game-Theoretic Analysis of Professional Rights and Responsibilities. J Bus Ethics, 9(3), 159-169, Mr 90.

Professions are granted autonomy by society, to regulate their own affairs. In return for the economic benefits autonomy grants to professions, society expects professions to act in a socially responsible manner. This paper presents a game-theoretic analysis of the relationship between society and professions, which shows that the relationship is unstable in the face of opportunities for professions to renege on the "social contract." It also shows how periodic controversies regarding the degree to which professionals act in the "public interest" are expected to occur periodically, and how they are resolved.

GABEL, Gernot U. *Index to Theses on German Philosophy Accepted by Universities of Great Britain & Ireland, 1900-1985*. Koln, Gemini, 1990

The bibliography lists the titles of master's theses and doctoral dissertations on topics relevant to German philosophers or philosophical schools which were accepted by universities in Great Britain and Ireland in the period 1900 to 1985. The 665 entries, an increase of 35 percent over the first edition, are listed alphabetically by name of the author. The bibliography concludes with a detailed subject index.

GABEL, Gernot U. *Kant: An Index to Theses and Dissertations Accepted by Universities in Canada and the US, 1879-1985*. Koln, Gemini, 1989

The bibliography lists the titles of dissertations and theses on Kant which were accepted for PhD or Masters degrees by universities in Canada and the United States. Inclusion was limited to items which either mention the philosopher or one of his works in the title. The 502 entries are arranged in chronological order. The work concludes with an author and a subject index.

GABRIELIAN, O A. On Historical Reconstruction of Mathematics. Phil Math, 4(2), 112-120, 1989.

The treatment of the history of mathematics of New Ages has been carried out through the method of historical reconstruction which allows the recreation of the image of mathematics that corresponds to the epoch. The concrete idea of mathematics (that of motion) which had proved to be significant in the development of mathematics has been analyzed. This idea comes out also as a specific feature of dominant views of the corresponding period of history and culture.

GADAMER, Hans-Georg and HEILKE, Thomas W (trans). "The Drama of Zarathustra" in *Nietzsche's New Seas: Explorations in Philosophy, Aesthetics, and Politics*, GILLESPIE, Michael Allen (ed), 220-231. Chicago, Univ of Chicago Pr, 1989.

GADAMER, Hans-Georg. "Im Schatten des Nihilismus" in *Cultural Hermeneutics of Modern Art: Essays in Honor of Jan Aler*, DETHIER, Hubert (ed), 233-244. Amsterdam, Rodopi, 1989.

GAETA, Rodolfo. Significado, referencia e inconmensurabilidad. Rev Latin De Filosof, 16(1), 80-86, Mr 90.

GAETA, Rodolfo. Sobre una presunta inconsecuencia acerca de la noción de función en la doctrina de Frege. Analisis Filosof, 7(1), 13-17, My 87.

GÄHDE, Ulrich. On Innertheoretical Conditions for Theoretical Terms. Erkenntnis, 32(2), 215-233, Mr 90.

Two innertheoretical conditions for theoretical terms are described: (1) theoretical terms (with respect to some empirical theory T) are underdetermined by T's axioms (if only the nontheoretical terms are given); (2) they can, however, be determined with the help of axioms plus suitable special laws. It is shown that these two characteristics of theoretical terms are responsible both for the remarkable ability of empirical theories to adapt to new or modified sets of data as well as for the occurrence of holistic phenomena. Finally, it is demonstrated how these conditions can be used as a tool for the identification of theoretical terms.

GAIFMAN, Haim and OSHERSON, Daniel N and WEINSTEIN, Scott. A Reason for Theoretical Terms. Erkenntnis, 32(2), 149-159, Mr 90.

The presence of nonobservational vocabulary is shown to be necessary for wide application of a conservative principle of theory revision.

GAINES, Jeffrey J. Maine de Biran and the Body-Subject. Phil Today, 34(1), 67-79, Spr 90.

The idea of a union between mind and body, and of a productive tension between them, found one of its paradigmatic expressions in the thought of Maine de Biran (1766-1824). He developed a notion not only of what was later called the "subjective body" (as in M Henry), but of something closer to

Merleau-Ponty's "flesh," as a tension between the two "layers" of a body that is *at once* subjective and objective, seeing and seen, touching and touched, etc. This essay is an attempt to introduce his work on the body to an American audience.

GALAVOTTI, Maria Carla. Anti-Realism in the Philosophy of Probability: Bruno de Finetti's Subjectivism. Erkenntnis, 31(2-3), 239-261, S 89.

Known as an upholder of subjectivism, Bruno de Finetti (1906-1985) put forward a totally original philosophy of probability. This can be qualified as a combination of empiricism and pragmatism within an entirely coherent antirealistic perspective. The paper aims at clarifying the central features of such a philosophical position, which is not only incompatible with any perspective based on an objective notion, but cannot be assimilated to other subjective views of probability either.

GALE, Richard M. Lewis' Indexical Argument for World-Relative Actuality. Dialogue (Canada), 28(2), 289-304, 1989.

David Lewis has appealed to the alleged indexicality of "actual" to show that no world is actual simpliciter. It is argued (1) "actual" is not an indexical term; and (2) even if it were, it would not follow that actuality is world-relative.

GALINDO RODRIGO, José Antonio. San Agustín y K Rahner: El amor a Dios y el amor al prójimo. Augustinus, 34(135-136), 305-330, Jl-D 89.

GALISON, Peter. Aufbau/Bauhaus: Logical Positivism and Architectural Modernism. Crit Inquiry, 16(4), 709-752, Sum 90.

GALKOWSKI, Jerzy W. La person e en tant que don dans l'enseignement de Jean-Paul II (in Polish). Stud Phil Christ, 25(2), 29-41, 1989.

GALLAGHER III, Bernard J and JONES, Brian J and MC FALLS JR, Joseph. Toward a Unified Model for Social Problems Theory. J Theor Soc Behav, 19(3), 337-356, S 89.

The article argues for the importance of conceptualizing social problems through a two-dimensional theory. Specifically, our position would extend current constructionist accounts by formally considering the objective dimension (evidence of the social harm associated with a problem) in relation to the subjective dimension (public opinion about the seriousness of a problem). Unemployment and sex roles are developed as case studies of the theoretical model.

GALLIE, Roger D. Of Particles. Locke News, 16, 23-33, 1985.

In III vii of his essay Locke maintains that *is* and *is not* are the general marks of the mind affirming or denying. In the Port Royal grammar est is said to be used to signify affirmation but it emerges more clearly that the manner of signification is different from the case of 'affirmation' and nouns in general. Both views neglect the fact that sentences involving 'is' can occur as constituents of compound sentences whose affirmation need not involve affirmation of constituent sentences.

GALLIE, Roger D. *Thomas Reid and 'The Way of Ideas'*. Norwell, Kluwer, 1989

This book introduces the reader to central areas of Reid's philosophical concern, the areas of perception, conception, signification of words, causality, active power, personhood and first principles being the main ones covered. Where possible, important positions of contemporaries, e.g., Hume, or near contemporaries, e.g., Locke and Arnauld, are presented and Reid's views in response to these positions is given through careful exposition and adequate quotation. They are then assessed in an analytic but sympathetic spirit.

GALLOIS, André. Occasional Identity. Phil Stud, 58(3), 203-224, Mr 90.

In my paper I defend the view that it is possible for things that are distinct at one time to be identical at another. The main argument I consider against that view is the argument that it contravenes Leibniz's Law. I attempt to show that the objection from Leibniz's Law is question-begging.

GALVAN, Sergio. Tesi di Hume e sistemi di logica deontica. Epistemologia, 11(2), 183-210, Jl-D 88.

Hume's thesis includes two problems: the problem of the reducibility of normative language to descriptive language and the problem of the derivability of normative formulae from descriptive ones. This paper intends to deal only with the latter of these two problems (even though the results achieved are of some benefit to the former, too) and, moreover, from a strictly logical point of view. This essay includes an elaboration of the method adopted by Kutschera in order to apply it to alethic systems of deontic logic and consequently to extend the underivability results of normative propositions from descriptive ones. Besides, the essay deals with the question of the underivability of normative propositions even from those descriptive propositions which have a modal structure, and it briefly outlines the underivability results which can be achieved also in this field. (edited)

GAMBRA, Jose Miguel. La Lógica aristotélica de los predicables. Anu Filosof, 21(2), 89-118, 1988.

This paper tries to systematize what can be called the first Aristotle's formal logic. This logic, previous to the *Prior Analytics*, uses functions like "A is said of B as a genus" (or as an accident, etc.). At first, a complete list of this type of function is offered; then the laws of the logic of predicables, drawn principally from texts of the *Categories* and the *Topica*, are displayed. The conclusion shows that this logic is necessary to an adequate interpretation of some Aristotelian fallacies as the sophism of accident and the sophism *secunum quid et simpliciter*.

GAMBRA, José Miguel. El lugar de los sofismas en la Lógica. Rev Filosof (Spain), 1, 7-26, 1987-88.

This paper tries to elucidate in what sense fallacies are a logical theme. In the first part some actual theories, like the ones of G Massey and R George, are discussed. The second part offers a definition of formal sophism based on the medieval distinction between *causa apparentiae* and *causa defectus* of a sophism. It concludes that fallacies are not a subject matter of formal logic as a theoretical discipline, but of logic as a practical science and also to dialectic or argumentation theory.

GANE, Mike (ed). *Towards a Critique of Foucault*. New York, Routledge, 1986

This collection of essays considers the work of Michel Foucault. It presents and begins a critique of the fundamental assumptions of Foucault's analysis of history and language. It leads to an analysis of Foucault's political position and discusses the uses to which his theories can be put and how they have been used. The book is designed to clarify the issues at stake in Foucault's work as they are seen to feed into the modern debate over the nature and effect of structures of power and knowledge.

GANS, Chaim. "Comment: The Obligation to Obey the Law" in *Issues in Contemporary Legal Philosophy: The Influence of H L A Hart*, GAVISON, Ruth (ed), 180-190. New York, Clarendon/Oxford Pr, 1987.

GARAVASO, Pieranna. Taylor's Defenses of Two Traditional Arguments for the Existence of God. Sophia (Australia), 29(1), 31-41, Ap 90.

In 1963, in the first edition of his book *Metaphysics*, Richard Taylor presented two interesting defenses of the cosmological and design arguments for the existence of God. Surprisingly, even after the third edition has appeared, his defense of the cosmological argument has passed relatively unnoticed, and while his novel account of the argument from design has provoked a fair amount of critical discussion, little attention is given to Taylor's reply contained in the same text. In this paper, we attempt to show that Taylor's defenses contain some new and interesting moves. However, we conclude that they ultimately fail to provide rational grounds for belief in the existence of God.

GARAY SUÁREZ-LLANOS, Jesús. La libertad en S Anselmo. Anu Filosof, 20(1), 43-72, 1987.

GARCÍA MARQUÉS, Alfonso. La polémica sobre el ser en el Avicena y Averroes latinos. Anu Filosof, 20(1), 73-103, 1987.

GARCIA MATEO, R. La relación Krause/krausismo como problema hermenéutico. Pensamiento, 45(180), 425-445, O-D 89.

Determinar la originalidad del krausismo español, sobre todo en lo que concierne a Julián Sanz del Río, es una de las cuestiones más debatidas. Tanto los que la afirman como los que la discuten pasan por alto el problema hermenéutico que ella conlleva. A este tema, unido al de la relación de Krause con el idealismo alemán, pretende introducir el presente artículo. Al mismo tiempo se pone de manifiesto el amplio y transcendental contexto filosófico que el krausismo implica cuando se lo contempla desde sus fuentes alemanas.

GARCIA MORIYON, Felix. El concepto de naturaleza. Dialogo Filosof, 5(3), 392-407, S-D 89.

GARCIA, J L A. Deserved Punishment. Law Phil, 8(2), 263-277, Ag 89.

The essay contrasts the thesis that deserved punishment is punishment which, as deserved, is *obligatory* with the weaker thesis that it is punishment which, as deserved, is *permissible*. The author first outlines an account of the meaning of desert-claims which entails only the weaker thesis and then defends this account against criticisms levied in a recent article that it is ambiguous, cannot explain the moral significance of desert, justifies letting people profit from their crimes, and permits unequal treatment. The essay proceeds to a critique of George Sher's view of deserved punishment, faulting Sher for (1) his reliance on an implausible understanding of benefits, (2) his inability to justify the punishment of crime-victims for their own crimes, and (3) the inadequacy of his defense of mercy. Finally, the author sketches a role-centered conception of morality within which it becomes clearer how deserved punishment can be justified as the victim's ties to the criminal, and the role-responsibilities derivative therefrom, are vitiated by the latter's misdeeds.

GARCIA, Jorge. "Do the Numbers Count: A Value-Theoretic Response" in *Inquiries into Values: The Inaugural Session of the International Society for Value Inquiry*, LEE, Sander H , 57-66. Lewiston, Mellen Pr, 1989.

This essay considers questions raised by a controversial essay of John Taurek's: Is the death of two persons a worse thing than is the death of one? And, if so, what, if any, difference does it make in proper moral reasoning? Briefly put, the author's answers, respectively, are 'Yes' and 'Not much'. (edited)

GARCIA, Jorge. The Primacy of the Virtuous. Philosophia (Israel), 20(1-2), 69-91, Jl 90.

This essay argues that treating certain virtue-concepts as morally basic helps us comprehend and defend two controversial features of ordinary morality. First, I sketch a virtue-based defense of "agent-centered" restrictions against Scheffler's challenge, contrasting my defense with one appealing to Sen's suggestion objective values are of position-relative. Second, I sketch a virtue-based defense of the ordinary view that agents should give preference to the interests of kinfolk against Parfit's charge that this is unacceptably "self-defeating." Finally, I argue that concepts of virtuous attitudes and action are prior to concepts of virtuous character and of right action.

GARCIA, Pablo S. F H Bradley y E E Harris: acerca de la relación mente-cuerpo. Rev Filosof (Argentina), 1(1-2), 31-40, N 86.

The purpose of this article is to introduce a line of argumentation which takes account of the mind-body problem, as it is present in the neo-Hegelian British thought, specially considering the influence of scientific knowledge.

GARCIA, Pablo Sebastian. Merleau-Ponty: una crítica a la teoría realista de la percepción. Rev Filosof (Argentina), 3(1), 43-51, My 88.

This paper describes Merleau-Ponty's critic of realistic theory of perception and points out some difficulties. It also suggests that there is an implicit argument in Merleau-Ponty's reasoning.

GARCÍA-BARÓ, Miguel. Recusación del atomismo ontológico. Rev Filosof (Spain), 1, 55-81, 1987-88.

GÄRDENFORS, P. The Dynamics of Belief Systems: Foundations versus Coherence Theories. Rev Int Phil, 44(172), 24-46, 1990.

This paper contrasts two types of theories for belief revision systems: *foundational theories* which hold that one needs to keep track of the *justifications* for one's beliefs; and *coherence theories* which emphasize the importance of *minimal changes* maintaining the *consistency* of beliefs. These two types of theories are illustrated by Doyle's TMS system and the AGM theory for belief revision respectively. I argue, with the aid of some examples, that justifications of beliefs can be handled within a coherence theory of the AGM by exploiting the information contained in the *epistemic entrenchment* of the beliefs.

GÄRDENFORS, Peter and PETTIT, Philip. The Impossibility of a Paretian Loyalist. Theor Decis, 27(3), 207-216, N 89.

Amartya Sen has argued the impossibility of the Paretian liberal. While his abstract argument is compelling, the concrete significance of the conclusion is in some doubt. This is because it is not clear how important liberalism in his sense is; in particular it is not clear that the sort of liberalism required for the impossibility result is a compelling variety. We show that even if the argument cannot be used to establish the inconsistency of Paretianism and common-or-garden liberalism, it can be adapted to prove a parallel impossibility. This is the impossibility of combining the Pareto criterion with a loyalty constraint involving certain claim-rights rather than liberty-rights. The impossibility of the Paretian loyalist is of interest in itself but it is also interesting for the light it throws on the source of Sen-style impossibilities.

GÄRDENFORS, Peter. Induction, Conceptual Spaces, and AI. Phil Sci, 57(1), 78-95, Mr 90.

A computational theory of induction must be able to identify the projectible predicates, that is to distinguish between which predicates can be used in inductive inferences and which cannot. The problems of projectibility are introduced by reviewing some of the stumbling blocks for the theory of induction that was developed by the logical empiricists. The author's diagnosis of these problems is that the traditional theory of induction, which started from a given (observational) language in relation to which all inductive rules are formulated, does not go deep enough in representing the kind of information used in inductive inferences. (edited)

GÄRDENFORS, Peter. The Nature of Man—Games that Genes Play? Acta Phil Fennica, 38, 9-24, 1985.

This paper discusses some of the philosophically fundamental assumptions of *sociobiology*. First, it is argued that it is misleading to treat the genes as separate 'individuals', let alone individuals with intentions. Second, it is

shown that the *reduction claims* made by Wilson and others, maintaining that the social sciences can be reduced to sociobiology, are far too strong. The concluding part of the paper suggests that sociobiology may provide us with new perspectives on the nature of man. Using aggression as an example, it is argued that sociobiology allows us to see human emotions as *dispositions* rather than as *drives*.

GÄRDENFORS, Peter. Semantics, Conceptual Spaces and the Dimensions of Music. Acta Phil Fennica, 43, 9-27, 1988.

In contrast to semantic theories where language is mapped onto possible worlds, a theory which treats semantics as a relation between language and a conceptual structure is outlined. This structure is called a *conceptual space* and it is construed from a number of 'quality dimensions'. As an application a brief analysis of *metaphors* is given. The second part of the paper discusses the relevance of conceptual spaces for understanding the 'dimensions' of *music*.

GARDIES, Jean-Louis. The Fundamental Features of Legal Rationality. Ratio Juris, 1(3), 241-251, D 88.

The aim of this paper is to clarify the logical structure of a code connecting together some distinctions already introduced by different authors: a distinction between primary norms and secondary norms, the latter being implied by the provisions describing institutions in the indicative: a distinction between norms the content of which concerns a state and those the content of which concerns a behaviour which is itself function of several states; a distinction, among the primary norms, of the norms of competence by which a normative power can be delegated to an individual; lastly a distinction between regulative rules and constitutive rules.

GARDNER, Howard. Towards More Effective Arts Education. J Aes Educ, 22(1), 157-167, Spr 88.

If arts education is to be maximally effective, it must take into account these four factors: (1) the philosophical underpinnings and rationale for such education; (2) psychological accounts of learning in the arts; (3) a full account of past and current artistic practices; (4) the ecology of the educational system within which education will occur. Following a description of Project Zero, a long-term research endeavor in arts education, the author describes two on-going projects: (1) Project Spectrum, an effort to assess artistic and other intelligences in preschool children; (2) Arts PROPEL, an effort to improve artistic curricula and assessment at the middle and high school levels.

GARDNER, Roger. On Performance-Enhancing Substances and the Unfair Advantage Argument. J Phil Sport, 16, 59-73, 1989.

The purpose of this essay was to determine if current policies restricting the use of performance enhancing substances in sport could be ethically validated on grounds of unfair advantage. Logical argumentation revealed, to the contrary, that appeals to the moral issue of fairness cannot provide a compelling justificatory defense for proscription.

GAREWICZ, Jan. Erkennen und Erleben: Ein Beitrag zu Schopenhauers Erlösungslehre. Schopenhauer Jahr, 70, 75-83, 1989.

GARFIELD, Jay L. Epoche and Sūnyatā: Skepticism East and West. Phil East West, 40(3), 285-307, Jl 90.

GARFIELD, Jay L. The Myth of Jones and the Mirror of Nature: Reflections on Introspection. Phil Phenomenol Res, 50(1), 1-26, S 89.

The attack on givenness in Sellars's "Empiricism and the Philosophy of Mind" has been incorrectly taken to entail eliminative materialism. I articulate Sellars's attack on givenness and characterize the eliminativist arguments of Churchland, Rorty, and Feyerabend. I argue that their use of the myth of Jones is unsuccessful, and that it in fact requires not eliminativism but realism about mental states. Eliminativists, I argue, covertly adopt a pernicious form of givenness and a Lockean model of introspection incompatible with the central morals of the myth of Jones. Finally, I defend a realistic Sellarsian model of introspection and of belief-ascription.

GARGANI, Aldo. "Wittgensteins ethische Einstellung" in *Wittgenstein in Focus—Im Brennpunkt: Wittgenstein*, MC GUINNESS, Brian (ed), 67-84. Amsterdam, Rodopi, 1989.

Es gibt eine enge Vergindung zwischen Wittgensteins ethischer Einstellung und seiner Ablehnung des philosophischen Theoretisierens. Wittgenstein betrachtet es als Aufgabe des Menschen, in sich selbst mit Mut hinunterzusteigen, um durch eine sprachliche Analyse seine innere Natur zu enthüllen. Wittgenstein arbeitet den Unterschied zwischen oberflächlichen und tiefergehenden ethischen Einstellungen als sprachphilosophischen Unterschied zwischen *Oberflächengrammatik* und *Tiefengrammatik* heraus. Die von Wittgenstein so beziechnete Oberflächengrammatik ruft die grammatischen Täuschungen hervor, die für die Sublimierung und Idealisierung der philosophischen Theorien verantwortlich sind.

GARRETT, Brian. Personal Identity and Extrinsicness. Phil Stud, 59(2), 177-194, Je 90.

GARRETT, Dennis E and BRADFORD, Jeffrey L and MEYERS, Renee A and BECKER, Joy. Issues Management and Organizational Accounts: An Analysis of Corporate Responses to Accusation of Unethical Business. J Bus Ethics, 8(7), 507-520, Jl 89.

When external groups accuse a business organization of unethical practices, managers of the accused organization usually offer a communicative response to attempt to protect their organization's public image. Even though many researchers readily concur that analysis of these communicative responses is important to our understanding of business and society conflict, few investigations have focused on developing a *theoretical framework* for analyzing these communicative strategies used by managers. In additon, research in this area has suffered from a *lack of empirical investigation*. In this paper we address both of these weaknesses in the existing literature. (edited)

GARRETT, Jan Edward. Unredistributable Corporate Moral Responsibility. J Bus Ethics, 8(7), 535-545, Jl 89.

Certain cases of corporate action seem especially resistant to a shared moral evaluation. The theory that sometimes a corporation's moral responsibility cannot be redistributed, even in principle, to the individuals involved, seems quite attractive. This doctrine of unredistributable corporate moral responsibility (UCMR) is, however, ultimately indefensible. This paper reexamines cases cited in defense of UCMR and takes up the attempt to defend it by identifying corporate moral agency with corporate practices. A further section explores the claim that UCMR is a convention distinct from, yet compatible with, traditional "natural" notions of responsibility. The final section develops a notion of combined akratic agency to provide an alternate explanation, compatible with rejection of UCMR, of the phenomena which make the doctrine attractive. (edited)

GARRETT, Richard. "Love's Way" in *Person to Person*, GRAHAM, George (ed), 124-145. Philadelphia, Temple Univ Pr, 1989.

GARRETT, Rosellen M (ed) and GARRETT, Thomas M (ed) and BAILLIE, Harold W (ed). *Health Care Ethics: Principles and Problems*. Englewood Cliffs, Prentice-Hall, 1989

GARRETT, Thomas M (ed) and BAILLIE, Harold W (ed) and GARRETT, Rosellen M (ed). *Health Care Ethics: Principles and Problems*. Englewood Cliffs, Prentice-Hall, 1989

GARRISON, James W. Greene's Dialectics of Freedom and Dewey's Naturalistic Existential Metaphysics. Educ Theor, 40(2), 193-209, Spr 90.

GARRISON, James W. Philosophy as (Vocational) Education. Educ Theor, 40(3), 391-406, Sum 90.

GARRISON, James W and PHELAN, Anne. Toward a Feminist Poetic of Critical Thinking. Proc Phil Educ, 45, 304-314, 1989.

GARRISON, Mark. The Moon Is Not There When I See It: A Response to Snyder. J Mind Behav, 11(2), 225-232, Spr 90.

GARSON, James. Modularity and Relevant Logic. Notre Dame J Form Log, 30(2), 207-223, Spr 89.

A practical system of reasoning must be both correct and efficient. An efficient system which contains a large body of information can not search for the proof of a conclusion from all information available. Efficiency requires that deduction of the conclusion be carried out in a modular way using only a relatively small and quickly identified subset of the total information. One might assume that data modularity is incompatible with correctness, where a system is correct for a logic *L* iff it proves exactly what is valid in *L*. We point out that modularity and correctness are indeed incompatible if the logic in question is classical. On the other hand, the two desiderata are compatible for relevance logic. Furthermore, Horn clause resolution theorem proving is modular (this helps explain its relative efficiency) and the logic for which it is correct is relevance logic not classical logic.

GARTNER, James D and EKSTEROWICZ, Anthony J. Funding the Department of Education's TRIO Programs. Pub Affairs Quart, 4(3), 233-247, Jl 90.

During the Reagan administration, the Education Department's TRIO program operated within a political environment that exhibited ideological conflicts between administration and congressional goals concerning education policy. In essence, the Reagan administration desired to cut funding for educational programs like TRIO while the Congress resisted such cuts and even, upon occasion, restored program funding. The administration responded by slashing support and evaluation funds, leaving program specialists in the difficult position of monitoring programs with less resources. The authors propose the institution of Congressional/Administration Support and Evaluation (CASE) task forces as a means for both establishing a closer connection between program and support funding and bridging interbranch ideological and political conflicts concerning educational policy.

GARVER, Eugene. The Moral Virtues and the Two Sides of *Energeia*. Ancient Phil, 9 (2), 293-312, Fall 89.

Morally virtuous actions are the subject of praise in the judgments of communities. Aristotle's moral virtues are *energeiai* or actualities in two distinct senses: they actualize the soul and so fulfill the human potential, and in addition they are activities as opposed to *kineseis*, motions, and so are ends in themselves and not merely instrumental activity. The connections among these three properties of the moral virtues is not evident, or necessary. It is only under certain political conditions that they are even extensionally equivalent. Aristotle's achievement is to show the interconnections of the two sides of *energeia*, activity as opposed to potency and activity as opposed to motion, and to use their correlation to show why the actions conventionally praised are praiseworthy.

GARVER, Newton. Wittgenstein and the Critical Tradition. Hist Phil Quart, 7(2), 227-240, Ap 90,

Critical philosophy, founded by Kant, must be conceived independently of his work. The key is that critical criteria must be neither dogmatic nor subject to an endless regress, and therefore must be self-referential. Thus Kant holds that the very criteria required to make sense of science not only impugn speculative metaphysics but also make critical philosophy legitimate. Wittgenstein's *Tractatus* was a magnificent critical failure, honoring the tradition in the way it condemned itself. The concept of grammar, as both a familiar language-game and the source of critical criteria, makes his later work a conspicuously successful version of critical philosophy.

GARZÓN VALDÉS, Ernesto. Intervencionismo y paternalismo. Rev Latin De Filosof, 16(1), 3-24, Mr 90.

After rejecting the analogy between personal autonomy and state sovereignty and questioning the strong relationship usually believed to exist between the right to self-determination of a people and the prohibition of any type of intervention, criteria are proposed which permit to identify some cases where intervention in the internal affairs of other countries is ethically permitted. An ethically justifiable intervention must—just like cases of legal paternalism within a state—satisfy two necessary and jointly sufficient conditions: (1) the intervened country must be unable to overcome on its own some real ill, due to a basic incompetence in the area where the intervention takes place, and (2) the intervention may not be aimed at manipulating the intervened country for the benefit of the intervening power. Both conditions are not easily satisfied. This explains the difficulty of justifying interventions, but it does not permit to conclude that they are *always* unjustifiable.

GASARCH, W I and BEIGEL, Richard. On the Complexity of Finding the Chromatic Number of a Recursive Graph I: The Bounded Case. Annals Pure Applied Log, 45(1), 1-38, N 89.

We study the difficulty of computing the chromatic number (respectively, the recursive chromatic number) of a recursive graph, given a bound on that number. We show that a logarithmic number of queries to an oracle for the halting problem (respectively, the third level of the arithmetic hierarchy) are necessary and sufficient. These results are tight with respect to both parameters: number of queries and power of oracle.

GASARCH, W I and BEIGEL, R. On the Complexity of Finding the Chromatic Number of a Recursive Graph II: The Unbounded Case. Annals Pure Applied Log, 45(3), 227-246, D 89.

A recursive graph is a graph whose edge set and vertex set are both recursive. We determine the difficulty of determining the chromatic number of a graph. The two parameters of difficulty are the Turing degree of the oracle required, and the number of queries to that query that are required. We also investigate recursive chromatic numbers (which require queries to a set much harder than the halting set), the effect of allowing queries to a weaker set, and the effect of being able to ask *p* queries at a time.

GASCHÉ, Rodolphe. "On Mere Sight: A Response to Paul de Man" in *The Textual Sublime: Deconstruction and Its Differences*, SILVERMAN, Hugh J (ed), 109-115. Albany, SUNY Pr, 1990.

GASKIN, Richard M. Can Aesthetic Value Be Explained? Brit J Aes, 29(4), 329-340, Autumn 89.

There is a difference in point of explicability between ethical and aesthetic evaluations: there is a sense in which the aesthetic is inexplicable. This had to do with the ontological status of aesthetic objects as concrete universals.

GASKIN, Richard M. Platonism and Forms of Life. Auslegung, 16(1), 1-16, Wint 90.

GASPAROVIC, Dubravka Kozina. The Birth of Nietzsche's "Dionysian Philosophy" (in Serbo-Croatian). Filozof Istraz, 29(2), 639-658,

1989.

Nietzsches posthum veröffentlichtes Werk *Ecce homo*, seine Selbstdarstellung wird als Leitfaden in dieser Arbeit über die Geburt des Dionysischen und Nietzscheschen dionysischen Philosophie genommen. Das Dionysische ist auf Grund seiner eigenen Aussagen, wie auch der interpretation einer der erfolgreichsten Nietzsche-Interpreten—K.-H. Volkmann-Schluck, als Kern seines Philosophierens betrachtet worden, als sein "einziger Gedanke" im Heideggerschen Sinne dieses Wortes. Diesem Gedanken hat Nietzsche nicht nur seinen Erstling—*Die Geburt der Tragödie*, sondern sein ganzes Leben geopfert. Unmittelbar vor seiner Umnachtung korrigierte er das Druckmanuskript der *Dionysos-Dithyramben*. Diese Arbeit ist als ein Abriss des Gebärens dieses Gedankens und nicht als dessen Explikation gedacht worden.

GATES, Eugene. The Female Voice: Sexual Aesthetics Revisited. J Aes Educ, 22(4), 59-68, Wint 88.

GAUDIN, Claude. Lectio Difficilior: le système dans la théorie platonicienne de l'âme selon interprétation de Gueroult. Phronesis, 35(1), 47-82, 1990.

Could Plato's thought be seen as a system? That is what is examined here, starting with the two papers by Gueroult, one on Phaedo, the other on Laws X. Their assumption is that these dialogues are built according to a similar conception of physics and mathematics. The former is concerned with a dialectical and argumentative process, the latter, dialectical, as well, builds on the constructive meaning of the word. Several arguments are developed against that interpretation: How the two meanings of dialectics can be connected together? Why the dialectical process must be mixed with dogmatic and heterogeneous themes?

GAUKER, Christopher. How to Learn a Language Like a Chimpanzee. Phil Psych, 3(1), 31-53, 1990.

This paper develops the hypothesis that languages may be learned by means of a kind of cause-effect analysis. This hypothesis is developed through an examination of E Sue Savage-Rumbaugh's research on the abilities of chimpanzees to learn to use symbols. Savage-Rumbaugh herself tends to conceive of her work as aiming to demonstrate that chimpanzees are able to learn the 'referential function' of symbols. Thus the paper begins with a critique of this way of viewing the chimpanzee's achievements. The hypothesis that Savage-Rumbaugh's chimpanzees learn to use symbols by means of cause-effect analysis is then supported through a detailed examination of the tasks they have learned to perform. Next, it is explained how language learning in humans might be conceptualized along similar lines. The final section attempts to explain how the pertinent cause-effect analysis ought to be conceived.

GAUKROGER, Stephen. *Cartesian Logic: An Essay on Descartes's Conception of Inference*. New York, Oxford Univ Pr, 1989

The book provides an account of Descartes's conception of deductive inference as an instantaneous grasp guided only by the natural light of reason. It is argued that this conception is principally a reaction to late scholastic and humanist conceptions of reason, rather than to Aristotelian syllogistic, and that it plays a pivotal role in the development of an understanding of the nature of inference. The consequences of Descartes's conception for his work in mathematics and natural philosophy are explored, and it is compared with those of Aristotle and Leibniz.

GAUTHIER, David. "Hobbes's Social Contract" in *Perspectives on Thomas Hobbes*, ROGERS, G A J (ed), 125-152. New York, Clarendon/Oxford Pr, 1988.

GAUTHIER, Pierre. La liberté pour Aristote et les stoïciens. Rev Thomiste, 89(4), 609-621, O-D 89.

GAUTHIER, Yvon. Finite Arithmetic with Infinite Descent. Dialectica, 43(4), 329-337, 1989.

Finite, or Fermat arithmetic, as we call it, differs from Peano arithmetic in that it does not involve the existence of an infinite set (of natural numbers) or Peano's induction postulate. Fermat's method of infinite descent takes the place of bound induction, and we show that a constructivist interpretation of logical connectives and quantifiers can account for the predicative finitary nature of Fermat's arithmetic. A non-set-theoretic arithmetical logic thus seems best suited to a constructivist-inspired number theory.

GAUVIN, Stéphane and LILIEN, Gary L and CHATTERJEE, Kalyan. The Impact of Information and Computer Based Training on Negotiators' Performance. Theor Decis, 28(3), 331-354, My 90.

This paper presents the results of an experiment on negotiation, designed to measure the impact of (1) computerized training and (2) information on negotiators' performance. The paper is structured as follows. First, we review the literature on negotiation training. Second, we develop a conceptual framework to link various forms of negotiation support systems to joint and individual negotiation performance. Third, we present the negotiation paradigm—a bilateral monopoly—and the computerized training system we used. Regarding training, our results show an asymmetric impact on individual performance levels and, unexpectedly, a negative impact on negotiators' joint performance. In contrast, more information improves both individual and joint performance. Finally, we discuss these results, and outline further research questions.

GAVIN, William J. William James, Dieu et la possibilité actuelle. Arch Phil, 52(4), 529-538, O-D 89.

Critics often attack James's philosophy for being overly nominalistic or subjectivistic, or more specifically for not asserting the real status of generals, of "actual possibility." In this paper I offer one defense against such criticisms. Specifically, a careful analysis of James's statements of God (as found in *Pragmatism*) is extremely revealing. In these statements, James works towards a position of actual possibility, as might be verbalized in terms of the "contrary-to-fact" conditional. Such a position forces James, acting as an empiricist, to conclude that the "really real" is broader than the logical, and essentially so.

GAVISON, Ruth. "Comment: Legal Theory and the Problem of Sense" in *Issues in Contemporary Legal Philosophy: The Influence of H L A Hart*, GAVISON, Ruth (ed), 21-34. New York, Clarendon/Oxford Pr, 1987.

A comment on a condensed version of Dworkin's *Law's Empire*, presented in a conference in honour of H L A Hart, Jerusalem 1984. Argues that Dworkin's criticism of all existing legal theories as misguided is misplaced, that his own interpretivist approach is illuminating on some issues and misleading on others, and that the 'classical' distinctions between law and legal theory and between law and adjudication, challenged by Dworkin, are indispensable to an adequate understanding of law. A defence of general jurisprudence.

GAVISON, Ruth (ed). *Issues in Contemporary Legal Philosophy: The Influence of H L A Hart*. New York, Clarendon/Oxford Pr, 1987

This collection of essays and comments on subjects on the forefront of contemporary legal philosophy is unified around central themes in H L A Hart's work. It was originally presented in an international conference in honour of H L A Hart, Jerusalem 1984. Three subjects are covered. On legal theory and the obligation to obey the law articles include contributions by Dworkin, Sartorius, Postema, Greenawalt, with comments by Hart himself, Finnis, MacCormick, and Lyons. On criminal responsibility and punishment contributors include Kadish, Morawetz, Primoraz and Moore. On the enforcement of morality a paper by Raz is commented upon by C L Ten.

GAVROGLU, Kostas. Differences in Style as a Way of Probing the Context of Discovery. Philosophica, 45(1), 53-75, 1990.

The purpose of the paper is to examine the possibilities offered by Hacking's arguments about national styles of scientific discourse in the study of low temperature work in England and the Netherlands. The notion of affinity with respect to a specific style of reasoning is introduced. The work of J Dewar, who liquefied hydrogen, is compared to that of H Kamerlingh Onnes, who liquefied helium. It becomes possible to discern distinct differences in style between the two, and some of these differences are analytically discussed.

GAWLIKOWSKI, Krzysztof. The Evolution of the Chinese Concept of Culture. Dialec Hum, 16(2), 195-208, Spr 89.

GAY, Peter (ed & trans) and CASSIRER, Ernst. *The Question of Jean-Jacques Rousseau—Ernest Cassirer (Second Edition)*. New Haven, Yale Univ Pr, 1989

GAY, Robert J. Bernard Williams on Practical Necessity. Mind, 98(392), 551-569, O 89.

Williams has pointed to a recognizable type of experience, which can single out one consideration in a situation as the one on which I *must* act. He rightly says that it is independent of systems of ethical thinking and ideas of (Mackie-style) objective values. But he considers that it can be explained away. I reconstruct three lines of explanation from Williams's writings ("Practical Necessity," "The Makropulos Case," "Ethics and the Fabric of the World") and criticize these. And I explain how the experience might be something irreducible which could properly be a basis for a moral outlook.

GAYLIN, Willard. Fooling with Mother Nature. Hastings Center Rep, 20(1), 17-21, Ja-F 90.

GAZE, Beth and DAWSON, Karen. Distinguishing Medical Practice and Research: The Special Case of IVF. Bioethics, 3(4), 301-319, O 89.

The distinctions between medical practice and research, and research which is therapeutic and nontherapeutic, are used to analyse the position of embryo research. Where it is designed to improve in vitro fertilization fertilization treatment, embryo research affects not only the embryo, but also the woman to whom the embryo may later be transferred. Although such research may be difficult to classify, it is argued that the effect of the research (or of not doing it) on a woman's treatment cannot be overlooked in the debate over embryo experimentation.

GAZZARD, Ann. Philosophy for Children and the Piagetian Framework. Thinking, 5(1), 10-13, 1983.

GAZZARD, Ann. Thinking Skills in Science and Philosophy for Children. Thinking, 7(3), 32-40, 1988.

GEACH, Peter. Amor y eternidad: La filosofía idealista de McTaggart. Anu Filosof, 22(1), 27-34, 1989.

GEBHARDT, Birgit. Der Widerspruch zwischen Materiellem und Ideellem und der dialektische Materiebegriff. Deut Z Phil, 37(12), 1101-1110, 1989.

Ausgehend von einem Fazit der theoretischen Diskussion zur Kategorie Materie nach 40 Jahren DDR-Philosophie werden Defizite und Probleme aufgezeigt, die letztendlich aus der Dogmatisierung der Materieauffassung auf wenige Kernaussagen, insbesondere auf das Primär-Sekundär-Schema resultierten. Die Autorin versucht, einen eigenen Ansatz für die Bestimmung der dialektischen Kategorie Materie zu begrunden, wobei vor allem die Widersprüchlichkeit zwischen Materiellem und Ideellem als konstituives Moment für den Materiebegriff dargestellt wird. Zentrum der Argumentation bildet die Funktion des Materiebegriffs in der Geschichte des philosophischen Denkens im allgemeinen und in den Frühschriften von Marx und Engels im besonderen.

GEFFRÉ, Claude. Révélation et expérience historique des hommes. Laval Theol Phil, 46(1), 3-16, F 90.

Comme l'atteste la crise moderniste, il est difficile d'articuler ensemble révélation divine et expérience humaine. Une réflexion de type herméneutique cherche à montrer que non seulement révélation et expérience ne s'opposent pas mais que l'expérience est un moment intrinsèque de la révélation. Au point de départ de la révélation chrétienne, c'est l'expérience de l'événement Jésus-Christ qui a suscité une pluralité de témoignages interprétatifs. Et tout au long des siècles, il n['y aura pas de tradition vivante et donc d'actualisation de la révélation sans une réinterprétation créatrice. L'actualité permanente du message chrétien dans l'Église repose sur une corrélation mutuelle et critique entre l'expérience chrétienne fondamentale et notre expérience historique. D'où l'importance de faire un bon diagnostic du contenu de notre expérience historique.

GEIMAN, Kevin Paul. Habermas' Early Lifeworld Appropriation: A Critical Assessment. Man World, 23(1), 63-83, Ja 90.

GEISE, J P. Liberal Goods. Int J Moral Soc Stud, 5(2), 95-115, Sum 90.

Under pressure from their communitarian critics, many exponents of political liberalism have felt compelled to abandon their traditional hope of speaking for all humans in all circumstances. Only by doing so have they thought they could situate their liberalism. Other liberal theorists, anxious to preserve liberalism's universalist aspirations, have continued to construct political visions that remain susceptible to the charge that they are remote from the actual affairs of human beings. The present essay contends that there is a way to bridge the gap between a liberalism that is practical yet parochial and one that is universalistic yet unsituated. The way to achieve this is through an examination of the concrete desires of liberal citizens. This examination reveals that these desires both accord with universal, liberal principles and sustain a practical model of decision making.

GEISMANN, Georg. Spinoza jenseits von Hobbes und Rousseau. Z Phil Forsch, 43(3), 405-431, Jl-S 89.

In literature, Spinoza as a "political philosopher" is again and again placed in an ideational line with Hobbes and Rousseau. It is argued in this article that Spinoza is not at all a philosopher of right and law and that there is no attempt in his work to legitimize the domination of the state or of certain rules of domination. The political thought of Spinoza fits rather into the line of empirical analysts and theorists of politics.

GEISSER, Maura J. Philosophy: A Key to the Deaf Mind. Thinking, 6(2), 33-40, 1985.

GELLATLY, Angus R H. "Influences on the Conception of Logic and Mind" in Scientific Knowledge Socialized, HRONSZKY, Imre (ed), 245-263. Norwell, Kluwer, 1989.

This paper brings together recent work in the psychology of reasoning and the sociology of knowledge. The author argues against both a mental logic account of reasoning and a 'discovery' view of logic itself. It is suggested that the mental model approach to reasoning and a relativist epistemology are well suited to one another.

GELLMAN, Jerome I. "Freedom and Determinism in Maimonides' Philosophy" in Moses Maimonides and His Time, ORMSBY, Eric L (ed), 139-150. Washington, Cath Univ Amer Pr, 1989.

The purpose of this study is to determine Maimonides' view on free will and determinism in the Guide of the Perplexed. I argue, against Pines and Altman, that Maimonides favored free will. This is supported by a close exegesis of Guide 2:48.

GELLMAN, Jerome I. Kierkegaard's Fear and Trembling. Man World, 23(3), 295-304, Jl 90.

A new interpretation of Fear and Trembling is offered wherein for Kierkegaard the story of the sacrifice of Isaac is an allegory—about self-definition and possibility vs. Hegelian public morality, rather than about a particular act, that transgresses morality.

GELVEN, Michael. A Commentary on Heidegger's "Being and Time". DeKalb, No Illinois Univ Pr, 1989

This is a revised edition of the original commentary published in 1970. An entirely new 20-page introduction, plus major revisions on the chapters on authenticity, truth, and history are included. A new postscript discusses the development in the later Heidegger. This is a section-by-section commentary on Being and Time which has been well received for twenty years because it is clearly written.

GÉLY, Raphaël. Bibliographie de Claude Bruaire. Rev Phil Fr, 180(1), 89-93, Ja-Mr 90.

GENSLER, Harry J. Logic: Analyzing and Appraising Arguments. Englewood Cliffs, Prentice-Hall, 1989

This is an introductory logic textbook, covering formal logic (syllogisms, propositional logic, quantificational logic, and modal logic) and informal logic (inductive reasoning, meaning and definitions, fallacies, etc.). It uses innovative methods for testing arguments and real-life examples, and is accompanied by the LogiCola instructional software program which runs on IBM compatibles.

GENTILE, Francesco. "Culture et politique européenne chez Montesquieu" in Culture et Politique/Culture and Politics, CRANSTON, Maurice (ed), 29-40. Hawthorne, de Gruyter, 1988.

GEORGE, Alexander. Whose Language Is It Anyway? Some Notes on Idiolects. Phil Quart, 40(160), 275-298, Jl 90.

This article examines and ultimately rejects two theses about idiolects, or the languages of individuals. The first (recently espoused by Donald Davidson) is that reflection about communication involving 'deviant' speech (e.g., malaprops) shows that idiolects so vary with the moment that linguists and philosophers are wrong to assume there is a shared and stable body of information that is, or would be, sufficient for communication. The second (advanced by Michael Dummett) is that the notion of an idiolect cannot be made sense of without appeal to a prior communal language. Against the first, it is argued that most students of language do not make this assumption, which is, at any rate, not clearly cast into doubt by the communicational phenomena in question. Against the second, it is shown how one can analyze a speaker's being in linguistic error without countenancing anything more than linguistic beliefs of individual speakers at particular times, i.e., without postulating a communal language.

GEORGE, Robert P. Individual Rights, Collective Interests, Public Law, and American Politics. Law Phil, 8(2), 245-261, Ag 89.

This article criticizes an influential liberal conception of individual rights and collective interests and proposes, as an alternative, a conception drawn from the tradition of natural law theory. It also criticizes Ronald Dworkin's attempt to derive a right to pornography from a general right to be treated by one's government with equal concern and respect.

GERASSI, John. "The Second Death of Jean-Paul Sartre" in Inquiries into Values: The Inaugural Session of the International Society for Value Inquiry, LEE, Sander H , 391-399. Lewiston, Mellen Pr, 1989.

GERBER, Rona M. Gratitude and the Duties of Grown Children Towards Their Aging Parents. Int J Applied Phil, 5(1), 29-34, Spr 90.

GERBER, William (ed) and FRANCK, Isaac. A Philosopher's Harvest: The Philosophical Papers of Isaac Franck. Washington, Georgetown Univ Pr, 1988

This is a collection of essays by the Jewish scholar Isaac Franck. Subjects covered by the essays include man's knowledge of God, freedom and determinism, and psychological concerns. Works by Maimonides, Aquinas and Spinoza are considered. (staff)

GERGYE, László. Formation of Philosophical Views of the Young Bessenyei in the Mirror of His Poem "On Spirit" (in Hungarian). Magyar Filozof Szemle, 2-3, 165-182, 1989.

L'étude s'occupe de l'analyse d'un long "discours en vers" de György Bessenyei intitulé De l'âme. Elle essaie de reconstruire ses sources philosophiques à l'aide du texte. En interprétant, en systématisant les vues de la philosophie de Bessenyei, on peut relever le fait que l'auteur donne dans le poème institulé *De l'âme* l'analyse de trois ensembles des problèmes. Dans le premier, Bessenyei traite du rapport entre l'âme et Dieu du point de vue épistémologique-ontologique. Dans le deuxième, il développe sa pensée de la sensibilité corporelle selon laquelle l'âme est soumise au corps. Enfin, dans le troisième, Bessenyei cherche à concilier la volonté libre de l'âme avec la volonté divine. (edited)

GERHARDT, V. What is a Rational Being? (in German). S Afr J Phil, 8(3-4), 155-165, N 88.

Against the background of contemporary attacks on rationality and the subject, the author addresses the question: What is a rational being? His starting point is the so-called change in Kant's position: while man and reason are two sides of the same coin in the *Critique of Pure Reason*, Kant replaces man by 'rational beings' in the development of his moral philosophy. The author develops a theory of rationality on Kantian lines which also bridges this gap. He argues that reason cannot function on its own; it is necessarily linked to will which in its turn presupposes aims (of general nature: for all rational beings and for all similar situations), action and spontaneity. Each of these in its turn has yet further conditions of possibility, *inter alia* choice (freedom), sensation and knowledge (including self-knowledge), the abilities to find relations and to deduce, and the possibility of failure. The end result is that only man complies with all the conditions for rationality. (edited)

GERHART, Mary and RUSSELL, Allan Melvin. The Cognitive Effect of Metaphor. Listening, 25(2), 114-126, Spr 90.

GERLA, Giangiacomo and TORTORA, Roberto. Fuzzy Natural Deduction. Z Math Log, 36(1), 67-77, 1990.

Many systems of fuzzy logic have since been proposed as formal counterparts of approximate reasoning, obtained via suitable fuzzyfications of the ordinary Hilbert-type logical systems. Here we explore the possibility of introducing very general fuzzy analogues of the classical systems of natural deduction; in particular a consequence operator is defined and examined which associates to every fuzzy subset of assumptions the related fuzzy subset of consequences. This approach turns out to be an extension both of ordinary natural deduction and of the fuzzy logic as proposed by J Pavelka. Also, compactness and completeness are examined.

GERLA, Giangiacomo and GUCCIONE, Salvatore. On the Logical Structure of Verisimilitude. Epistemologia, 12(1), 161-165, Ja-Je 89.

As is well known, Popper's comparative theory of verisimilitude meets with several obstacles. This paper is an attempt to bypass such obstacles by a suitable modification of Popper's definition of falsity contents and truth contents.

GERLA, Giangiacomo. Pointless Metric Spaces. J Sym Log, 55(1), 207-219, Mr 90.

We propose and examine a system of axioms for the pointless space theory in which "regions," "inclusion," "distance" and "diameter" are assumed as primitives and the concept of point is derived. It is shown that a point-free approach to Euclidean geometry is possible as devised by Lobachevski, Whitehead, Tarski and other authors.

GERLA, Giangiacomo. Turing *L*-Machines and Recursive Computability for *L*-Maps. Stud Log, 48(2), 179-192, Je 89.

We propose the notion of partial recursiveness and strong partial recursiveness for fuzzy maps. We prove that a fuzzy map *f* is partial recursive if and only if it is computable by a Turing fuzzy machine and that *f* is strongly partial recursive and deterministic if and only if it is computable via a deterministic Turing fuzzy machine. This gives a simple and manageable tool to investigate about the properties of the fuzzy machines.

GERLACH, Hans-Martin. Heidegger und das Problem der Metaphysik. Deut Z Phil, 37(9), 824-833, 1989.

In der Philosophiegeschichte führte Metaphysikzerstörung ständig zu ihrer Neugeburt, deutlich wird dies besonders bei Kant. Nach Hegel sind es besonders Marx und Heidegger, die neue Wege in der Metaphysikkritik gehen. Während Marx spekulative Vernunftsmetaphysik historisch konkret auf dem Boden sinnlich-praktischer Aneignung der Wirklichkeit durch den menschen auflöst, geht Heidegger in "Sein und Zeit" mit der zeitlich endlichen menschlichen Existenz gegen bisherige Metaphysik vor. In seiner Spätphase orientiert er sich wesentlich auf Kritik europäischer Rationalitätsentwicklung, die zur Verfalls- und Verbergungsgeschichte des Seins wurde und aus der nur ein "neues Denken" erlösen kann.

GERT, Bernard and CLOUSER, K Danner. A Critique of Principlism. J Med Phil, 15(2), 219-236, Ap 90.

The authors use the term "principlism" to refer to the practice of using "principles" to replace both moral theory and particular moral rules and ideals in dealing with the moral problems that arise in medical practice. The authors argue that these "principles" do not function as claimed, and that their use is misleading both practically and theoretically. The "principles" are in fact not guides to action, but rather they are merely names for a collection of sometimes superficially related matters for consideration when dealing with a moral problem. The "principles" lack any systematic relationship to each other, and they often conflict with each other. These conflicts are unresolvable, since there is no unified moral theory from which they are all derived. For comparison the authors sketch the advantages of using a unified moral theory.

GERT, Bernard. Rationality, Human Nature, and Lists. Ethics, 100(2), 279-300, Ja 90.

In this paper I show that all of the standard attempts to define rationality by means of a procedure or a formula fail. I defend the account of rationality that I presented in *Morality: A New Justification of the Moral Rules* (Oxford, 1988) showing that it is the only account that allows rationality to serve as the fundamental normative concept. The two most striking features of my account of rationality are (1) irrationality is taken as more basic than rationality, and (2) irrationality is defined by means of a list rather than by a procedure or a formula.

GETHMANN-SIEFERT, Annemarie. Heidegger and Hölderlin: The Over-Usage of "Poets in an Impoverished Time". Res Phenomenol, 19, 59-88, 1989.

GETZ, Kathleen A. International Codes of Conduct: An Analysis of Ethical Reasoning. J Bus Ethics, 9(7), 567-577, Jl 90.

Four international codes of conduct (those of the International Chamber of Commerce, the Organization for Economic Cooperation and Development, the International Labor Organization, and the United Nations Commission on Transnational Corporations) are analyzed to determine the ethical bases of the behaviors they prescribe for multinational enterprises (MNEs). Although the four codes emphasize different aspects of business behavior, there is substantial agreement regarding many of the moral duties of MNEs. It is suggested that MNEs are morally bound to recognize the codes and to take them into account when engaging in international business.

GEWIRTH, Alan. "Are There Any Natural Rights?" in *Mind, Value and Culture: Essays in Honor of E M Adams*, WEISSBORD, David (ed), 249-268. Atascadero, Ridgeview, 1989.

After critically examining H L A Hart's 1955 article having the same title, I present six conditions of a successful argument for natural rights. I then show that natural rights are based on the needs of human agency, and I set forth a dialectical argument for natural rights that satisfies the six conditions. I conclude by indicating three ways in which my theory of the contents of natural rights differs from Hart's theory.

GEYER, C F. Weisheit—Überforderung oder Vollendung der Philosophie? Tijdschr Filosof, 51(3), 427-443, S 89.

"Von den sogenannten "östlichen Weisheiten" geht gegenwärtig eine unübersehbare Faszination aus. Dagegen weckt der Titel "Weisheit" bei der Frage nach einem Äquivalent im eigenen kulturellen Zusammenhang allenfalls Assoziationen an eher im Umkreis der Religion angesiedelte Heilslehren, an allgemeine Regeln der "Lebensklugheit" oder aber an eine philosophische Esoterik, die mit dem Selbstverständnis der Philosophie als akademischer Disziplin wenn überhaupt dann nur am Rande zu tun hat."

GHEORGHE, Elena. L'époque contemporaine et la signification axiologique de la science et de la culture (in Romanian). Rev Filosof (Romania), 36(2), 121-127, Mr-Ap 89.

GHITA, Simion. Les métamorphoses de l'humanisme dans le philosophie marxiste italienne (in Romanian). Rev Filosof (Romania), 35(5), 494-501, S-O 88.

GHOSH-DASTIDAR, Koyeli. The Morality of Animals. Indian Phil Quart, 16(4), 419-432, O 89.

GIACALONE, Robert A and KNOUSE, Stephen B. Justifying Wrongful Employee Behavior: The Role of Personality in Organizational Sabotage. J Bus Ethics, 9(1), 59-61, Ja 90.

The role that personality plays in the justification of organizational sabotage behavior was examined. In a two-phase study, 120 business students were first surveyed to create a list of 51 methods of sabotage. In the second phase, 274 other business students rated justifiability of the 51 methods and completed Machiavellian and hostility scales. A factor analysis of the justification ratings yielded four factors: (1) methods of sabotaging company profits and production, (2) informational sabotage, (3) violent and illegal methods, and (4) traditional labor methods of sabotage. A 2 (high versus low Machiavellianism) x 2 (high versus low hostility) ANOVA upon factor scores for justifiability revealed significant main effects for hostility and significant interactive effects on Factors 1 and 2. Results were discussed in terms of differences in management and blue collar methods of sabotage and in terms of a self-presentational approach to justification of sabotage.

GIACOIA JUNIOR, Oswaldo. O grande experimento: sobre a oposição entre eticidade (*Sittlichkeit*) e autonomia em Nietzsche. Trans/Form/Acao, 12, 97-132, 1989.

Elegendo motivo principal da exposição a noção nietzscheana de eticidade do costume (*Sittlichkeit der Sitte*), este trabalho procura ressaltar a posição estratégica ocupada pela reflexão sobre a procedência dos valores morais na crítica da metafísica tradicional empreendida por Nietzsche, bem como a especificidade da contribuição deste filósofo para o tratamento do tema em questão.

GIAMBRONE, Steve and MEYER, Robert K. Completeness and Conservative Extension Results for Some Boolean Relevant Logics. Stud Log, 48(1), 1-14, Mr 89.

This paper present completeness and conservative extension results for the Boolean extensions of the relevant logic *T* of Ticket Entailment, and for the contractionless relevant logics *TW* and *RW*. Some surprising results are shown for adding the sentential constant *t* to these Boolean relevant logics; specifically, the Boolean extensions with *t* are conservative of the Boolean extensions without *t*, but not of the original logics with *t*. The special treatment required for the semantic normality of *T* is also shown along the way.

GIAMMUSSO, Salvatore. Individuo, tradizioni e pluralismo dei valori. Arch Stor Cult, 2, 251-302, 1989.

GIBBARD, Allan. Communities of Judgment. Soc Phil Pol, 7(1), 175-189, Autumn 89.

GIBBARD, Allan. *Wise Choices, Apt Feelings: A Theory of Normative Judgment.* Cambridge, Harvard Univ Pr, 1990

GIBBS, Robert B. Substitution: Marcel and Levinas. Phil Theol, 4(2), 171-185, Wint 89.

The subject is under siege. In many disciplines the self that modern thought established and fortified has fallen to critique. But while many explore the implications for epistemology, for literary theory, for psychology, or for history and social thought, few writers have pondered the question in terms of ethics. After all, ethics must rest on a subject, a person who makes choices and decides for various reasons to commit acts in one's own name. I suggest that ethics can survive the fracturing, decentering, deconstructing of the self. A selection of passages from Marcel and Levinas is offered, with commentary.

GIBBS, Robert. The Limits of Thought: Rosenzweig, Schelling, and Cohen. Z Phil Forsch, 43(4), 618-640, O-D 89.

I display how the construction in Part I of Rosenzweig's *Star of Redemption* is a pure construction of a set of inverted elements (God, World, Man), allowing Rosenzweig to discover the logical conditions for knowing that we do not know something. Schelling provides Rosenzweig with insight into the contraction of the self which precedes freedom; while Cohen's purity appears as a translation of *creatio ex nihilo*. Rosenzweig transforms both in laying a logical foundation for his empirical theological system.

GIBSON, A M and RANDALL, D M. Methodology in Business Ethics Research: A Review and Critical Assessment. J Bus Ethics, 9(6), 457-471, Je 90.

Using 94 published empirical articles in academic journals as a data base, this paper provides a critical review of the methodology employed in the study of ethical beliefs and behavior of organizational members. The review revealed that full methodological detail was provided in less than one half of the articles. Further, the majority of empirical research articles expressed no concern for the reliability or validity of measures, were characterized by low response rates, used convenience samples, and did not offer a theoretic framework, hypotheses, or a definition of ethics. Several recommendations, including a reviewer rating form addressing methodological decisions and inclusion of methodologists on the review panel, are offered to improve methodological rigor in published ethics research.

GIBSON, Kevin. Ranken on Disharmony and Business Ethics. J Applied Phil, 6(2), 209-213, O 89.

This article is a response to Nani Ranken's paper "Morality in Business: Disharmony and Its Consequences" (*Journal of Applied Philosophy*, Vol. 4, p. 41). There she attacked the analogy sometimes made between businesses and persons, and concluded that businesses cannot be regarded as moral agents. Her thesis relies centrally on a very strict notion of a person's 'true good'. By exploring and expanding the concepts of 'true good' and 'moral agency' we are able to recover a sense in which businesses are indeed members of the moral community. Moreover,

admitting businesses to the moral community also provides a working framework to examine the claim that what is good for business is in harmony with the dictates of morality.

GIERE, Ronald N. Scientific Rationality as Instrumental Rationality. Stud Hist Phil Sci, 20(3), 377-384, S 89.

This paper replies to Harvey Siegel's critique of my program for naturalizing the philosophy of science as developed in *Explaining Science: A Cognitive Approach*. Siegel believes it is possible to discover epistemological principles that are *autonomous* from science, principles that provide criteria for *categorical* rationality among scientists. The naturalist believes that there is no autonomous realm of epistemological principles. This is not to deny that there are better and worse ways of attempting to do science, but the corresponding principles of rationality are only *instrumental*, or conditional. They establish empirical connections between research strategies and the goals of research.

GIFFORD, Fred. Genetic Traits. Biol Phil, 5(3), 327-347, Jl 90.

Recognizing that all traits are the result of an interaction between genes and environment, I offer a set of criteria for nevertheless making sense of our practice of singling out certain traits as genetic ones, in effect making a distinction between "causes" and "mere conditions." The central criterion is that a trait is genetic if it is genetic differences that make the differences in that trait variable in a given population. A second criterion requires that genetic traits be individuated in a way that matches what some genetic factors cause specifically. Clarifying our causal and classificatory language here can help us to avoid confusions of both theoretical and practical significance.

GIGLIOLI, Giovanna. Leninismo y Marxismo en *Historia y Conciencia de Clases*. Rev Filosof (Costa Rica), 26, 113-124, D 88.

This is the third and last of a series of articles dedicated to the role of Leninism in *History and Class Consciousness*. It shows how Lukacs's original conception of dialectics eternizes, through its Hegelian categories, the Leninist thesis of world revolutionary years.

GIGON, Olof. "Theophrast in Cicero's De finibus" in *Cicero's Knowledge of the Peripatos*, FORTENBAUGH, William W (ed), 159-185. New Brunswick, Transaction Books, 1989.

GIL DE PAREIJA, José L. El pensar en la filosofía de la mente de L Wittgenstein. Anu Filosof, 21(1), 123-131, 1988.

GILBERT, Alan. Rights and Resources. J Value Inq, 23(3), 227-247, S 89.

GILBERT, Geoffrey. The Critique of Equalitarian Society in Malthus's *Essay*. Phil Soc Sci, 20(1), 35-55, Mr 90.

The attack on perfectibilism in T R Malthus's *Essay on Population* (1798) is methodologically hollow. Malthus presents himself as a Newtonian empiricist, yet his analysis of equalitarian society is entirely abstract. Godwinian equality is debunked by means of a thought experiment. Malthus fails to take note of a variety of historical instances of equalitarian social practice (Sparta, the Moravians, and so on), thus undermining his empiricist posture. This deficiency in the critique of equality is remedied, to some degree, in the fifth edition of the *Essay* (1817), where Malthus finally cites some of the historical evidence relevant to an assessment of equalitarianism.

GILBERT, Margaret. Rationality and Salience. Phil Stud, 57(1), 61-77, S 89.

A number of authors, including Thomas Schelling and David Lewis, have envisaged a model of the generation of action in coordination problems in which salience plays a crucial role. Empirical studies suggest that human subjects are likely to try for the salient combination of actions, a tendency leading to fortunate results. Does *rationality* dictate that one aim at the salient combination? Some have thought so, thus proclaiming that salience is all that is needed to resolve coordination problems for agents who are rational in the sense of game theory. I argue against this position; rational agents will not necessarily aim for the salient. It remains to explain how the salient comes to be chosen by human beings. Various possibilities are noted. One involves a mechanism invoked by Hume and Wittgenstein in other contexts: we may project an unreasoned compulsion onto reason, falsely believing that rationality dictates our choice of the salient.

GILBERT, Margaret. Rationality, Coordination, and Convention. Synthese, 84(1), 1-21, Jl 90.

Philosophers using game-theoretical models of human interactions have, I argue, often overestimated what sheer rationality can achieve. (References are made to David Gauthier, David Lewis, and others.) In particular I argue that in coordination problems rational agents will not necessarily reach a unique outcome that is most preferred by all, nor a unique 'coordination equilibrium' (Lewis), nor a unique Nash equilibrium. Nor are things helped by the addition of a successful precedent, or by common knowledge of generally accepted personal principles. Commitments like those generated by agreements may be necessary for rational expectations to arise. Social conventions, construed as group principles (following the analysis in my book *On Social Facts*), would suffice for this task.

GILBERT, Paul. El acto de ser: Un don. Rev Filosof (Mexico), 23(67), 28-52, Ja-Ap 90.

GILBERT, Paul. Community and Civil Strife. J Applied Phil, 7(1), 3-14, Mr 90.

What kind of threat does terrorism pose to a community? Two models of terrorism are introduced. The Unjust War model views terrorism as an attack on the innocent, but thereby misidentifies its criminal character. The Political Crime model regards it as violence for political ends, by-passing democratic channels. This misconstrues the terrorist's aim of waging war against a state whose legitimacy he contests. Associated with the models of terrorism are two conceptions of community, the Communitarian and the Hobbesian, respectively. While the Communitarian conception sees the community as independent of the state, the Hobbesian identifies them, thus assimilating an attack on the state to a threat to the community. The Hobbesian conception, however, even when amplified by democratic theory, provides inadequate resources to rebut a challenge to the state's legitimacy, in particular one concerning territorial boundaries. Arguments for permitting secession are discussed. The communitarian conception may be able to ground legitimacy claims, but it may also justify some terrorist campaigns as needed to preserve communities.

GILES, Gordon J. Listenaires: Thoughts on a Database. Brit J Aes, 30(2), 166-174, Ap 90.

350 people in England and Italy were asked to characterise pieces from the 'serious' musical repertoire in terms of emotions, colours and images. There was a large degree of agreement among responses. The data is shown to support such claims as Frank Sibley makes for an objectivity of aesthetic judgements—at least in respect of descriptions which are couched in terms of emotions.

GILKEY, Langdon. Nature, Reality, and the Sacred: A Meditation in Science and Religion. Zygon, 24(3), 283-298, S 89.

Many scientists now recognize the participation of the knower in the known. Not many admit, however, that scientists rely upon intuitions about reality commonly attributed to philosophy and religion: that sensory experience relates us to an order in nature congruent with our minds and of value congruent with our fulfilled being. Nature has disclosed itself to scientists—albeit fragmentarily—as power, life, order, and unity or meaning. In science these remain limit questions, raised but unanswered. In the unity of these qualities, assumed by science, the sacred begins to appear. Addressing the limit questions, not only of scientific but of human experience, is the province of philosophy and religion.

GILL, Christopher. "The Human Being as an Ethical Norm" in *The Person and the Human Mind: Issues in Ancient and Modern Philosophy*, GILL, Christopher (ed), 137-163. New York, Clarendon/Oxford Pr, 1989.

How does the idea of human nature function as a reason in ancient ethical theory? This essay raises this question in relation to Aristotle and the Stoics. The main thesis is that the idea functions in these contexts as an ethical norm, presupposing ethical commitment, and not as a way of grounding ethical life from outside as Bernard Williams suggests in connection with Aristotle. In this respect, the idea functions in a way that is comparable to that of 'person', as deployed by David Wiggins.

GILL, Christopher (ed). *The Person and the Human Mind: Issues in Ancient and Modern Philosophy*. New York, Clarendon/Oxford Pr, 1989

This collection of unpublished essays explores analogous issues in ancient Greek and modern philosophy relating to the concepts of person and human being. The essays on ancient philosophy reappraise the concept of person and ask whether this notion can be distinguished from our conception of work essential to our existence as human beings. The essays on Greek philosophy take up the related questions of what being human entails in ancient ethics and psychology, and whether we should regard ourselves essentially as human or natural beings.

GILL, Jerry H. Merleau-Ponty, Metaphor, and Philosophy. Phil Today, 34(1), 48-66, Spr 90.

The aim of this essay is to ascertain Merleau-Ponty's view of the nature of philosophical activity by focusing on his theory of metaphor and especially on his prolific *use* of metaphor in his own philosophical writing. The conclusion is that Merleau-Ponty thought of metaphorical thought and speech as crucial to philosophical activity.

GILL, Jerry H. What Wittgenstein Wasn't. Int Phil Quart, 30(2), 207-220, Je 90.

GILL, Mary Louise. *Aristotle on Substance: The Paradox of Unity*. Princeton, Princeton Univ Pr, 1989

This book explores a fundamental tension in Aristotle's metaphysics: how can an entity such as a living organism—a composite generated through the imposition of form on a preexisting matter—have the conceptual unity that Aristotle demands of primary substances? The author bases her treatment of the problem of unity, and of Aristotle's solution, on a reassessment of matter and its relation to form. She argues that material substances are subverted by matter and maintained by form, which controls the matter to serve a positive end. The unity of substances thus involves a dynamic relation between resistant materials and directive form.

GILLESPIE, Michael Allen. "Nietzsche's Musical Politics" in *Nietzsche's New Seas: Explorations in Philosophy, Aesthetics, and Politics*, GILLESPIE, Michael Allen (ed), 117-149. Chicago, Univ of Chicago Pr, 1989.

GILLESPIE, Michael Allen (trans) and FINK, Eugen. "Nietzsche's New Experience of World" in *Nietzsche's New Seas: Explorations in Philosophy, Aesthetics, and Politics*, GILLESPIE, Michael Allen (ed), 203-219. Chicago, Univ of Chicago Pr, 1989.

GILLESPIE, Michael Allen (ed) and STRONG, Tracy B (ed). *Nietzsche's New Seas: Explorations in Philosophy, Aesthetics, and Politics*. Chicago, Univ of Chicago Pr, 1989

GILLETT, Grant R. Consciousness, the Brain and What Matters. Bioethics, 4(3), 181-198, Jl 90.

Consciousness is one basis on which we make medical decisions about quality of life. An account of consciousness should explain what it is, its relation to brain function and its ethical relevance. Consciousness is analysed as a holistic complex of related abilities and is linked to the functions of the cerebral cortex. The reason we take special account of the experiences of conscious individuals is that they themselves can form attitudes and make choices about such experiences.

GILLETT, Grant R. Neuropsychology and Meaning in Psychiatry. J Med Phil, 15(1), 21-39, F 90.

The relationship between "causal" and "meaningful" (Jaspers) influences on behavior is explored. The nature of meaning essentially involves rules and the human practices in which they are imparted to a person and have a formative influence on that person's thinking. The meanings that come to be discerned in life experience are then important in influencing the shape of that person's conduct. The reasoning and motivational structures that develop on this basis are realized by the shape of the neural processing networks that constitute the mature human brain. This implies that meaning is not only realized by brain microstructure but, in part, explains its workings. This in turn entails that in psychiatry we must continue to avail ourselves both of neuropsychology/neurobiology and of dynamic/meaningful explanation.

GILLICK, Victoria. Confidentiality and Young People. Ethics Med, 4(2), 21-23, 1988.

Since 1974 the British government has attempted to curb the rise in schoolgirl pregnancies by means of free and secret contraception and abortion. Within a decade, this policy, combined with intense ideological and commercial propaganda, had encouraged a teenage 'copulation explosion', accompanied by record levels of disease, pregnancies and abortions. In 1984 a historic High Court ruling upheld parental authority, by reestablishing the medical age of consent at 16 years, thereby outlawing the government's policy of secrecy. Despite vigorous opposition by the media and the birth control lobby, this ruling succeeded in achieving a substantial reduction in the incidence of under-age sex and its consequences.

GILLON, Brendan S. Plural Noun Phrases and Their Readings: A Reply to Lasersohn. Ling Phil, 13(4), 477-485, Ag 90.

The author had concluded in earlier work (Ling Phil 10(2)) that, among other things, the full range of readings to which plural English demonstrative noun phrases are liable are in one-to-one correspondence with the number of minimal covers of the noun phrase's denotation. This conclusion has been challenged by Peter Lasersohn on both theoretical and empirical grounds. The author points out, first, that Lasersohn's theoretical objection is based on a single premiss, asserted without any supporting argumentation, evidence, or citation of supporting literature; and second, that the empirical objection, while having some initial plausibility, cannot be sustained under critical scrutiny.

GILLON, Brendan S. Truth Theoretical Semantics and Ambiguity. Analysis, 50(3), 178-182, Je 90.

Davidson has proposed that a semantic theory for a natural language should emulate truth conditional semantic theories for artificial languages, first developed by Tarski. Kathryn Parsons and L Jonathan Cohen think that his proposal founders on the phenomenon of lexical ambiguity. The author shows that, in fact, there is a straightforward treatment of lexical ambiguity which follows, virtually directly, from Davidson's own explicitly stated assumptions.

GILMAN, James E. Reconceiving Miracles. Relig Stud, 25(4), 477-487, D 89.

I reject the Humean approach to the possibility of miracles and offer a tradition-constituted approach which argues for the possibility of miracles. The Humean tradition, I argue, is based on three false assumptions: one, that the laws of nature are prescriptive and hence inevitable; two, that consequently miracles must be conceived as violations of laws of nature and hence impossible; and three, that miracles so conceived must therefore be ascertainable by nontheists and theists alike. In contrast, I argue, one, that laws of nature explain "dispositional properties" of natural processes and allow for novelty and creativity; two, that miracles properly conceived are occurrences whose proximate, sufficient, and necessary cause is God; and three, that miracles are therefore possible and ascertainable only to those whose presuppositions include belief in God.

GILMAN, Roger William. A Sociobiological Explanation of Strategies of Reading and Writing Philosophy. Phil Forum, 21(3), 295-323, Spr 90.

The "plain style" rhetoric of analytic philosophy is given a sociobiological explanation, using the concept of "territoriality" to interpret the social work of the analytic style of philosophizing. The argument claims the following: (1) all styles of reading and writing (even those—like the analytic, plain style—which deny it) imply a point of view toward a subject, audience, and author; (2) a style of reading and writing may be consistent or inconsistent with the beliefs, values, and attitudes asserted, or with the strategy of arriving at these; (3) taking a point of view is a self-interested (adaptive) behavior because it is an element of persuasion—a way of defending intellectual property; (4) helping behavior can be regarded as self-interested behavior; (5) analytic, plain style rhetoric (which regards itself as disinterested, helping behavior) can be regarded as self-interested (or "territorial") behavior; (6) all self-interested behavior can and should be judged for its moral and political consequences.

GILMOUR, John C. Perspectivism and Postmodern Criticism. Monist, 73(2), 233-246, Ap 90.

Nietzsche's account of interpretation has a strong impact on postmodern cultural criticism. This paper employs Anselm Kiefer's painting, *Sulamith*, to demonstrate the advantages of Nietzsche's perspectivism and genealogical analysis over Greenberg's modernist criticism. It argues that Nietzschean thought clarifies questions raised by Kiefer's work: questions about intertextuality, cultural memory, and the role of myths in history. In contrast, modernism's assumptions about objectives interpretation, continuity in history, and purely aesthetic art fail when confronted by the conflicting signs *Sulamith* contains. Finally, the paper considers how Deleuze and Foucault expand Nietzsche's interpretation theory and discusses the way his understanding of tragedy fits with postmodern interpretive practices.

GILMOUR, Robin and MELAMED, Tuvia. "The Repair and Maintenance of Relationships" in *Person to Person*, GRAHAM, George (ed), 155-166. Philadelphia, Temple Univ Pr, 1989.

GILROY JR, John D. Hartshorne on the Ultimate Issue in Metaphysics. Process Stud, 18(1), 38-56, Spr 89.

This article addresses a crucial issue for process philosophy: how, if at all, can eternal metaphysical categories be explained? I argue that an explanation can be found in the metaphysics of Charles Hartshorne, though he has yet to endorse my main thesis that contingent divine states can indirectly necessitate the existence of the categories they contain. I defend his position, as here interpreted, from attacks by Robert Neville, David Pailin and Houston Craighead.

GIMPL, Georg. The State's Line: On the Change of Paradigm of Austrian Philosophy within Maria-Theresian Reform-Catholicism. Topoi, 8(2), 75-96, S 89.

The idea of an *Austrian philosophy* here in focus is not considered only as a reaction against *German Idealism* which would have been born at the end of the 19th century. It is much more the schisma of the *Reformation*, and thereafter the *confessionalistic* prototypes of a *true philosophy*, which are responsible for this polarisation: the philosophical movements became distinct nationally as part of their general process of secularization. One milestone in this differentiation process must be seen in the reforms of philosophy within Maria-Theresian Reform-Catholicism. The highly *pragmatic* values in the further development of *Josefinism* preclude Austria from the "*philosophical revolution*" in Germany, and thus pave the way quite early for a *scientific* outlook on the world. *Don't think, but look!* (L Wittgenstein).

GINET, Carl. Justification: It Need not Cause but it Must be Accessible. J Phil Res, 15, 93-107, 1990.

This paper argues that a fact which constitutes part of a subject's being justified in adopting an action or a belief at a particular time need not be part of what induced the subject to adopt that action or belief but it must be something to which the subject had immediate access. It argues that similar points hold for justification of the involuntary acquisition of a belief and for the justification of continuing a belief (actively or dispositionally).

GINET, Carl. *On Action*. New York, Cambridge Univ Pr, 1990

The book's questions: What distinguishes actions from other sorts of events? How are actions individuated? What makes an action intentional? What is required to have alternative actions open to one? What makes true an explanation of one's action in terms of one's reasons for it? Some major claims: all voluntary bodily exertion begins with mental willing of the exertion; all actions are marked by their beginning with mental events having a special "actish" quality; determinism is incompatible with an agent's having alternative actions open; an action not determined by its antecedents may nevertheless be one the agent did for reasons.

GINSBERG, Robert. A Skeptical Appreciation of Natural Law Theory. Vera Lex, 7(2), 1-2,5, 1987.

GINSBERG, Robert. "The Teaching of Values in Higher Education" in *Inquiries into Values: The Inaugural Session of the International Society for Value Inquiry*, LEE, Sander H , 593-602. Lewiston, Mellen Pr, 1989.

Three popular arguments current in American educational circles are countered: that values cannot be taught, that if they could be taught they should not, and that if they could be taught then a traditional doctrine should be taught. The positive argument is made that values are inescapably taught, by the very way in which we teach people, and that the identity of those values should include intellectual courage, honesty, respect, and cooperation.

GINSBERG, Robert. The Value of Philosophy: A Dialogue. J Value Inq, 24(1), 31-42, Ja 90.

The question of the value of philosophy is an unavoidable one for philosophy, especially for the philosophy of value. Philosophy is valuable as having second thoughts. This reflective curiosity about everything, including itself, gives us a second chance in life. While philosophy may not be decisive in its inquiry into subject matters, it does decidedly reveal ourselves as the subject who pursues inquiry. But the pursuit of inquiry presupposes the continued existence of the world. Philosophy must now save that world.

GINSBORG, Hannah. Reflective Judgement and Taste. Nous, 24(1), 63-78, Mr 90.

In the *Critique of Judgment*, Kant claims that taste consists in the exercise of reflective judgment. This claim has seemed puzzling to many commentators, given that reflective judgment appears to consist in the capacity for engaging in systematic natural science. I try to defend the claim by suggesting a new interpretation of reflective judgment as the capacity to take one's perceptual states to be intersubjectively valid with respect to particular objects. I argue that this interpretation accounts both for the role assigned to reflective judgment in the context of scientific enquiry, and for its role in judgments of taste.

GINZBERG, Ruth. Reply to Jahren's "Comments on Ruth Ginzberg's Paper". Hypatia, 5(1), 178-180, Spr 90.

This is a reply to Neal Jahren's "Comments" on my paper, "Uncovering Gynocentric Science," which appeared in a 1987 issue of *Hypatia* 2 (3).

GIORGINI, Giovanni. Crick, Hampshire and MacIntyre or Does an English-Speaking Neo-Aristotelianism Exist? Praxis Int, 9(3), 249-272, O 89.

GIRALT, Maria de los Angeles. Aristóteles en *El Nombre de la Rosa*. Rev Filosof (Costa Rica), 26, 109-112, D 88.

Brother William of Baskerville is the responsible person to look into the deep mysteries of the cruel assassination of some friars. Brother William moves about between an irrational world and the Aristotelian universe of reason. Roger Bacon and William of Ockham are his allies in his search for truth. So we enter into the Library labyrinth in search of irreverent books. It is there where the greatest scandal is hidden in Aristotele's *Poetics*. *The Name of the Rose* is the unveiling of the mystery: the fight between the forces of Hell and the forces of goodness.

GIRARD, Jean-Yves and ABRUSCI, V Michele and VAN DE WIELE, Jacques. Some Uses of Dilators in Combinatorial Problems, II. J Sym Log, 55(1), 32-40, Mr 90.

We introduce sequences of ordinal numbers, called "increasing F-sequences" (where F is a dilator). By induction on dilators, we prove that every increasing F-sequence terminates. "Inverse Goodstein sequences" are particular increasing F-Sequences: we show that the theorem "every inverse

Goodstein sequence terminates" is not provable in the theory ID₁.

GIRARD, René. Love Delights in Praises: A Reading of *The Two Gentlemen of Verona*. Phil Lit, 13(2), 231-247, O 89.

The Two Gentlemen of Verona very directly reflects Shakespeare's discovery of memetic desire. The Valentine-Proteus relationship of childhood friendship is one of "good" imitation suddenly transformed into mimetic rivalry. Valentine does all he can to incite a desire for his woman friend in Proteus, whose name signifies the constant metamorphosis of mimetic desire.

GIRARDET, Klaus M. "'Naturrecht' bei Aristoteles und bei Cicero (*De legibus*): Ein Vergleich" in *Cicero's Knowledge of the Peripatos*, FORTENBAUGH, William W (ed), 114-132. New Brunswick, Transaction Books, 1989.

In dem Aufsatz werden Aussagen des Aristeteles (rhet.I 13; NE V 1o; (MM) I 33) und Ciceros (de legibus) über das "von Natur Rechte" miteinander verglichen. Es treten fundamentale Unterschiede zutage. Cicero verdankte dem Peripatos, ebenso wie Platon und der Stoa, sicher manche Anregung. Aber das eine vollkommene konzeptionelle Einheit bildende, auf reformpolitische Realisierung abzielende Gedankengebäuge der Rechtstheorie von de legibus ist genuin ciceronianisch.

GIROUX, France. F A Hayek, ce pourfendeur des droits sociaux. Laval Theol Phil, 45(3), 351-359, O 89.

L'auteur s'est fixé ici comme objectif d'évaluer la faisabilité et la cohérence du projet de société hayékien favorable à la dissolution des droits sociaux. À la suite de l'analyse de ce projet néo-libéral, l'auteur conclut que sa réalisation susciterait une série de dissensus susceptibles de provoquer une crise sociale. De plus, la théorie juridique et politique de Hayek accuse certaines incohérences qui, au lieu d'éclairer le débat à propos du bien et du mal-fondé des droits sociaux, ne peuvent conduire qu'à une impasse. En fait, l'examen de l'évolution de la société industrielle nous permet d'envisager, de manière légitime, la prise en compte de nouveaux droits sociaux.

GIUCULESCU, Alexandru. An Operational Approach to the Dynamics of Science: Kant's Concept of Architectonic. Phil Log, 32(1-2), 153-161, Ja-Je 88.

Both theory of science and history of science are merging in the concept of dynamics of science, since all forms of scientific knowledge are to be dealt with from a synchronic as well as from a diachronic point of view. The genesis of scientific theories is to be explained not only as determined by the development of inner factors but also as a sui generis answer to outer forces. Generally speaking, the development of any science is a process more or less continuous with periods of stability followed either by oscillations or by sudden interruptions. For the study of the dynamics of science several conceptual ways have been advanced, some of them as alternative solutions. This paper is aiming to present a Kantian approach to the dynamics of science, as it may be construed from the *Critique of Pure Reason*.

GIUNTINI, Roberto. Quantum Logics and Hilbert Spaces. Teoria, 9(2), 3-26, 1989.

In this paper we will be concerned with some logico-algebraic structures arising from the *standard* approach to quantum mechanics and from the *operational* formulation of quantum mechanics. In particular, we will show that most of these logics cannot be characterized by their corresponding Hilbert-space realizations. As it is well known, Hilbert-space theory plays an essential role in the axiomatization of quantum mechanics both in the standard (von Neumann) and in the operational formulation. Why Hilbert spaces play such a role is not clearly understood yet. In this paper, we will not take into account this question, and we will give the Hilbert-space axiomatization of quantum mechanics for granted.

GJELSVIK, Olav. On the Location of Actions and Tryings: Criticism of an Internalist View. Erkenntnis, 33(1), 39-56, Jl 90.

J Hornsby has argued that the view that actions are internal events is a consequence of a Davidsonian approach to actions. The aim of this paper is to show that actions are not internal events, and that this is compatible with a causal theory of actions. I locate three important problems the internalist fails to handle properly, problems which arise because the relationship between actions and bodily movements is thought of as that of cause and effect. We can reject this latter thesis, and reject internalism, without rejecting the essentials of the causal view.

GLADSON, Jerry and LUCAS, Ron. Hebrew Wisdom and Psychotheological Dialogue. Zygon, 24(3), 357-376, S 89.

When understood as a potential resolution for the epistemological impasse between psychology and religion, Hebrew wisdom presents a model for dialogue. Noting that wisdom exhibits a special interest in human dispositions and behavior, the authors compare Viktor Frankl's logotherapy and Adlerian psychology with Proverbs and uncover a biblical, empirical approach to psychology which indirectly incorporates the religious dimension.

GLANTZ, Leonard H and MARINER, Wendy K and ANNAS, George J. Pregnancy, Drugs, and the Perils of Prosecution. Crim Just Ethics, 9(1), 30-41, Wint-Spr 90.

GLASER, John W. Hospital Ethics Committees: One of the Many Centers of Responsibility. Theor Med, 10(4), 275-288, D 89.

Ethical reality is coextensive with human dignity. Therefore, one essential way to understand ethics is as the systematic effort to discern the imperatives of human dignity. Seeing ethics in this way highlights the fact that health care institutions have many centers of ethical responsibility (CERs)—the Chief Executive Officer, Board of Trustees, senior management team, etc. The Ethics Committee is only one such CER and not the most important one. These other CERs will benefit from identifying (1) the fact that they are consistently dealing with ethical reality and making ethical decisions; (2) some critical elements of good ethical decision making: (i) having the appropriate community; (ii) making the guiding value priorities explicit and specific; (iii) gaining skill in using the needed intellectual tools; and (iv) fashioning appropriate process and structure for discernment.

GLAUSSER, Wayne. Three Approaches to Locke and the Slave Trade. J Hist Ideas, 51(2), 199-216, Ap-Je 90.

Locke is an anti-slavery theorist who participated in the slave trade. There are three ways to account for this discrepancy. One, Locke's conduct simply deviates from his theory; two, Locke does manage to accommodate theory to practice, but only by a conspicuously tortured logic; and three, Locke's involvement with slavery is part of the fabric of his philosophy (which lays a foundation for capitalist development; for racism; or for forfeiture of natural rights). Any effective approach will recognize within Locke's work a destabilizing competition of values.

GLEIT, Zachary and GOLDFARB, Warren. Characters and Fixed Points in Provability Logic. Notre Dame J Form Log, 31(1), 26-36, Wint 90.

Some basic theorems about provability logic—the system of modal logic that reflects the behavior of formalized probability predicates in theories such as arithmetic—are given simplified, model-theoretic proofs. The theorems include the Fixed Point Theorem of de Jongh and Sambin, the Craig Interpolation Theorem, and the Beth Definability Theorem. Attention is also paid to the complexity of models for formulas in this logic.

GLENN JR, James R. Business Curriculum and Ethics: Student Attitudes and Behavior. Bus Prof Ethics J, 7(3-4), 167-185, Fall-Wint 88.

This paper reports results from a national survey of graduate (M.B.A.) and undergraduate business students' ethical attitudes and practices. The findings reviewed are (1) students' assessment of whether ethics was adequately stressed in their business education and whether a separate ethics course should be included in their degree program; (2) their perceptions of the pressure in their future work environment to compromise their personal values and their ability to resist that pressure; and (3) their actual behavior—whether they had resisted the pressure in their present academic environment to cheat. Implications for education—admissions, curriculum, pedagogy, faculty development, and future research—are offered.

GLOBUS, Gordon G. Heidegger and Cognitive Science. Phil Today, 34(1), 20-29, Spr 90.

Dreyfus has argued in a Heideggerian vein that digital computers can't do what Dasein can. The recent development of "connectionism" reopens the question. These new machines are spontaneous, self-organizing rather than other-organized, holistic, and situated, and so might conceivably do what Dasein does. Heidegger's thought is considered both pre- and post-*Kehre* from this connectionist perspective. There is a coherence between the lighting process of the *Spiegel-Spiele* and the self-organizing process of neural nets. Despite the great difference between Heidegger and a cognitive science that is technological exemplar of the *Gestell*, an openness to their interface is called for.

GLOCK, Hans-Johann. Stroud's Defense of Cartesian Scepticism: A 'Linguistic' Response. Phil Invest, 13(1), 44-64, Ja 90.

The core of Stroud's rehabilitation of Cartesian scepticism is his attack on anti-sceptical arguments provided by linguistic philosophy. I argue against Stroud that 'linguistic anti-scepticism' can reveal the nonsensicality of scepticism, by criticizing his use, against Austin, of verification-transcendent possibilities and of unforeseen events. Finally, I reject Stroud's second line of defense, his contrast between the use of epistemic concepts and their 'real meaning' by developing Wittgenstein's suggestion that there are linguistic limits to meaningful doubt and that language is not responsible to reality in the way envisaged by sceptics.

GLOUBERMAN, M. Error Theory: Logic, Rhetoric, and Philosophy. J Speculative Phil, 4(1), 37-65, 1990.

Philosophers sometimes use a rhetorical technique—'modelling'—in dealing with opposed theories. Aristotle's representation of the Milesians as overplaying the *Aristotelian* material cause is a good example. Relative to a generalised definition of rhetoric, I argue that this kind of treatment is essential in philosophy. Specifically, the metaphysician must deal with the possibility of error about reality, and that makes essential a consideration of theorists—error-makers—as distinct from matters of pure theory. Some farther-reaching metaphilosophical implications of the unavoidability of the rhetorical infusion are sketched.

GLOUBERMAN, M. The Sense/Intellect Continuum in Early Modern Philosophy: A Critique of Analytic Interpretation. Mod Sch, 67(1), 49-70, N 89.

Kant's 'critical' view, that sensibility and understanding are entirely distinct cognitive stems, and the pre-Kantian view, that sense-based representation is a 'confused' version of reason-based representation, relate as two *bona fide* theoretical contenders, not, as per modern 'analytic' interpretation, as a legitimate candidate for acceptance to a muddle. The contrast, as attention to context reveals, is rooted in a specific thesis about the *relationality* of sense-based cognition. Kant and his predecessors take different lines not on the *relationality*, but on whether it is ultimate.

GLYMOUR, Clark and KELLY, Kevin T. Theory Discovery from Data with Mixed Quantifiers. J Phil Log, 19(1), 1-33, F 90.

Convergent realists desire scientific methods that converge reliably to informative, true theories over a wide range of theoretical possibilities. Much attention has been paid to the problem of induction from quantifier-free data. In this paper, we employ the techniques of formal learning theory and model theory to explore the reliable inference of theories from data containing alternating quantifiers. We obtain a hierarchy of inductive problems depending on the quantifier prefix complexity of the formulas that constitute the data, and we provide bounds relating the quantifier prefix complexity of the data to the quantifer prefix complexity of the theories that can be reliably inferred from such data without background knowledge. We also examine the question whether there are theories with mixed quantifiers that can be reliably inferred with closed, universal formulas in the data, but not without.

GOBLE, Lou. A Logic of *Good, Should,* and *Would*: Part I. J Phil Log, 19(2), 169-199, My 90.

Truth-conditions are defined for statements of the form 'it is good that p', 'it is bad that p', and 'it ought to be that p' in a way that locates these operators firmly in a framework of subjunctives 'it would be the case that p'. It is neglect of the subjunctive character of deontic functions that gives rise to the familiar paradoxes of deontic logic.

GOBLE, Lou. A Logic of *Good, Should,* and *Would*: Part II. J Phil Log, 19(3), 253-276, Ag 90.

The first part of this paper introduced a system of deontic logic in which deontic concepts of 'good' and 'should' contain a subjunctive component, 'would'. In this part that system is presented in full formal detail, both axiomatically and semantically. The axiomatic system is proved to be consistent and complete with respect to its semantical interpretation.

GODDU, André. The Realism that Duhem Rejected in Copernicus. Synthese, 83(2), 301-315, My 90.

Pierre Duhem rejected unambiguously the strong version of realism that he believed was held by Copernicus. In fact, Copernicus seems to have recognized that this theory was at best only approximately true. Duhem regarded even the belief in probably true explanations as misguided. Nevertheless, Duhem recognized that, even if metaphysical intuition does not enter into the content of physical theories, the rejection of hypotheses could be explained only by appeal to common sense. Hence, Duhem held a qualified instrumentalism according to which physical theories are not realist, but the terms of ordinary experience and empirical laws are realist. Accordingly, Duhem rejected the complete subordination of science to philosophy as well as the complete separation of science from philosophy. (edited)

GODFREY, Raymond. Democritus and the Impossibility of Collision. Philosophy, 65(252), 212-217, Ap 90.

GODFREY-SMITH, Peter. Misinformation. Can J Phil, 19(4), 533-550, D 89.

"Misinformation" is a critical survey of recent attempts within informational (or "indicator") semantics to deal with the problem of misrepresentation. It discusses the theories of Fodor, Dretske, Stalnaker and others, and argues that none of these proposals can solve the problem. I also suggest that there are reasons why no information theory is likely to work.

GODLOVE, Terry F. *Religion, Interpretation, and Diversity of Belief.* New York, Cambridge Univ Pr, 1989

GODLOVITCH, S. Aesthetic Protectionism. J Applied Phil, 6(2), 171-180, O 89.

Aesthetic protectionists think nature worth preserving and protecting from harm on aesthetic rather than moral grounds. Their outlook can be compared with the drive to shelter and sustain artworks. As such, protectionists seem rather like curators. However, this kind of attention to natural objects leads to a minimisation of the significance of the naturalness of those objects. This raises questions about the protectionist's real regard for nature. By examining what in nature is aesthetically worthy of protection, and then asking how far one is entitled to go in one's protective mission, it transpires that protectionists have no special stake in sustaining the independence of nature. Indeed, its independence often conspires against their aims. Since that very independence is essential to the natural, protectionism is exposed as having no intrinsic regard for nature.

GODLOVITCH, Stan. Preserving, Restoring, Repairing. J Aes Educ, 23(3), 39-47, Fall 89.

GOGACZ, Mieczyslaw. Philosophical Identification of the Dignity of Person (in Polish). Stud Phil Christ, 25(1), 181-207, 1989.

The literature of the subject shows that dignity is identified with the person, or with one of its properties, or with relation, which is bandaged by person with surrounded beings. Therefore dignity appears like a freely pointed element, which distinguishes person. It is not a separate being structure. That state of the problem induces to undertake strictly philosophical researches, which lie in establishing internal and examined object. (edited)

GOGCZ, Mieczyslaw. Conscience, contempolation, wisdom (in Polish). Stud Phil Christ, 25(2), 65-71, 1989.

Conscience is man's interior tendency to make good and avoid evil. Conscience is, because of intellectual reception of principles of being, a tendency of will to being as shown by intellect to will as good. Contemplation is giving evidence with the help of intellect and will that personal relations are persisting. Wisdom is an intellectual capacity of connecting the effects with the causes. By the same it is the grasp of the dependence between good and truth. It is recognition whether the being is giving us the good while being opened. When the being is causing good, out intellect advises will to tie the relations upon this being. This relation shelters us, because good shelters us always.

GOLASZEWSKA, Maria. Between the Philosophy of Art and Microaesthetics. Rep Phil, 13, 3-14, 1989.

GOLDBERG, David Theo. *Ethical Theory and Social Issues: Historical Texts and Contemporary Readings.* Orlando, Holt Rinehart Winst, 1989

The book presents the history of ethical theory with a firm theoretical foundation for exploring contemporary moral and legal issues. It includes selections on theory from Plato to MacIntyre, as well as eight topics of current relevance, from sexual morality and AIDS to political violence.

GOLDBERG, David Theo. Racism and Rationality: *The Need for a New Critique.* Phil Soc Sci, 20(3), 317-350, S 90.

Two classes of argument, logical and moral, are usually offered for the general assumption that racism is inherently irrational. The logical arguments involve accusations concerning stereotyping (category mistakes and empirical errors resulting from overgeneralization) as well as inconsistencies between attitudes and behavior and inconsistencies in beliefs. Moral arguments claim that racism fails as means to well-defined ends, or that racist acts achieve ends other than moral ones. Based on a rationality-neutral definition of racism, it is argued in this article that none of these arguments establish exhaustively that racism is inherently irrational. Ways are suggested to proceed in condemning racism(s) as morally and socially unacceptable, independent of the irrationality claim.

GOLDBERG, David Theo. Tuning in to Whistle Blowing. Bus Prof Ethics J, 7(2), 85-94, Sum 88.

GOLDBLATT, Robert. Varieties of Complex Algebras. Annals Pure Applied Log, 44(3), 173-242, O 89.

This paper presents results about varieties of Boolean algebras with operators, many of which were inspired by results in the model theory of modal logics. It includes, for example, an algebraic version of the proof that an elementary class of Kripke frames determines a canonical logic. The general objective is to show that the "modal case" is an instance of a more general theory about multi-argument operators that forms a chapter of universal algebra.

GOLDFARB, Warren and GLEIT, Zachary. Characters and Fixed Points in Provability Logic. Notre Dame J Form Log, 31(1), 26-36, Wint 90.

Some basic theorems about provability logic—the system of modal logic that reflects the behavior of formalized probability predicates in theories such as arithmetic—are given simplified, model-theoretic proofs. The theorems include the Fixed Point Theorem of de Jongh and Sambin, the Craig Interpolation Theorem, and the Beth Definability Theorem. Attention is also paid to the complexity of models for formulas in this logic.

GOLDFARB, Warren. Herbrand's Theorem and the Incompleteness of Arithmetic. Iyyun, 39(1), 45-64, Ja 90.

A proof of the incompleteness of arithmetic is presented that does not require any self-referential sentence. Instead, Herbrand's theorem is exploited to show directly that the formalization of a sort of consistency assertion is underivable. This assertion is, roughly, that in any given formal derivation the quantifiers can be given appropriate numerical evaluations; thus it expresses a minimal precondition of Hilbert's program.

GOLDFARB, Warren. "Russell's Reasons for Ramification" in *Rereading Russell: Essays on Bertrand Russell's Metaphysics and Epistemology*, SAVAGE, C Wade (ed), 24-40. Minneapolis, Univ of Minn Pr, 1989.

GOLDFARB, Warren. Wittgenstein, Mind, and Scientism. J Phil, 86(11), 635-642, N 89.

GOLDHILL, Simon. "Desire and the Figure of Fun: Glossing Theocritus 11" in *Post-Structuralist Classics*, BENJAMIN, Andrew (ed), 79-105. New York, Routledge, 1988.

This article explores the problem of framing with specific regard to Theocritus's eleventh *Idyll*. It discusses the problems that arise for the security of meaning from the relationship of difference between frame and content. In the case of Theocritus's poetry, it is found that the figure of fun in the satire on desire shifts to implicate the control of the sophisticated reader faced by the naive pastoral.

GOLDING, Martin P. "Agreements with Hostage-Takers" in *Hobbes: War Among Nations*, AIRAKSINEN, Timo (ed), 154-167. Brookfield, Gower, 1989.

GOLDMAN, Alan H. Aesthetic Qualities and Aesthetic Value. J Phil, 87(1), 23-37, Ja 90.

Broadly evaluative aesthetic properties, such as beauty or artistic merit, supervene on more narrowly evaluative aesthetic properties, such as grace or power. The latter supervene on nonevaluative or basic aesthetic properties. These are phenomenal properties and relations among them. The relevant relations are formal, expressive and representational, and historical (relations to properties of other artworks in a tradition). There are no interesting aesthetic principles linking nonevaluative properties to evaluations (such that these properties always contribute positive value). There can be none because of the uniqueness of artworks and because of irresolvable differences in taste. Nevertheless, it can be explained why the sorts of relations mentioned above tend to contribute aesthetic value, and this paper suggests such explanations.

GOLDMAN, Alan H. Aesthetic Versus Moral Evaluations. Phil Phenomenol Res, 50(4), 715-730, Je 90.

GOLDMAN, Alan H. "BonJour's Coherentism" in *The Current State of the Coherence Theory*, BENDER, John W (ed), 125-133. Norwell, Kluwer, 1989.

This paper argues that BonJour's requirement of internal coherence of belief systems is both not necessary for knowledge and insufficient when added to true belief. It is not sufficient because the problem of incompatible but fully coherent belief systems still looms despite the addition of a requirement for continuous observational input. An example that illustrates the problem is provided. The same example shows that BonJour's criterion of justification does not indicate probable truth. In order to demonstrate truth and knowledge, epistemologists begin with foundational beliefs (shown to be possible despite BonJour's argument to the contrary). They then infer to an external relation (in addition to truth) as the source of knowledge. To validate this source, they must adopt an interpersonal viewpoint missing from BonJour's internalist picture.

GOLDMAN, Alan H. The Education of Taste. Brit J Aes, 30(2), 105-116, Ap 90.

GOLDMAN, Alvin I. "BonJour's *The Structure of Empirical Knowledge*" in *The Current State of the Coherence Theory*, BENDER, John W (ed), 105-114. Norwell, Kluwer, 1989.

Despite the sophistication of BonJour's defense of coherentism, the book faces a number of serious problems. First, it is difficult to see how his notion of a "standard" of justification is compatible with his metajustification requirement. Second, the metajustification requirement creates an objectionable circularity in the theory. Third, BonJour's arguments for the metajustification requirement seem to rest, ultimately, on level-confusions. The metajustification requirement is central to BonJour's conception of

internalism. But, as Brueckner has shown, BonJour's attempt to defend coherentist internalism has insuperable problems. Although BonJour denies the existence of basic empirical beliefs, his doxastic presumption in effect creates a class of beliefs that qualify as basic. There are also some technical problems in BonJour's formulation of coherentism. More serious yet is the fact that BonJour has no *unified* theory of justification. Since *a priori* justification requires neither coherence nor metajustification, the account is badly bifurcated.

GOLDMAN, Alvin I. Interpretation Psychologized. Mind Lang, 4(3), 161-185, Autumn 89.

No account of interpretation can be philosophically helpful unless it jibes with a psychologically correct account of how people interpret others. The two most popular approaches to interpretation, viz., the charity (or rationality) approach and the folk-theory approach, are both psychologically implausible. The simulation, or empathy, theory is more defensible. On this account, the interpreter "projects" himself into the agent's shoes and infers further states of the agent by applying his own cognitive processes to the simulated state. Evidence to support the simulation approach is adduced, and some philosophical morals are drawn.

GOLDMAN, Alvin I. Metaphysics, Mind, and Mental Science. Phil Topics, 17(1), 131-145, Spr 89.

Two kinds of metaphysics are distinguished: descriptive and prescriptive. Descriptive metaphysics tries to describe and explain our folk ontology, i.e., the entities and properties posited in naive, prereflective thought. Prescriptive metaphysics proposes a "correct" ontology, which might differ dramatically from folk ontology. The paper argues that cognitive science can contribute to both types of metaphysics. It can help explain the nature and sources of our folk ontology, and it can provide evidence to support revisions in our ontological posits. Identity and color are among the specific topics used to illustrate these theses.

GOLDMAN, Alvin I. Replies to the Commentators. Philosophia (Israel), 19(2-3), 301-324, O 89.

GOLDMAN, Louis. Homer, Literacy, and Education. Educ Theor, 39(4), 391-400, Fall 89.

Homer, who links preliterate and literate culture, is the first written record in Western civilization, and as such formulated the value system of his time and helped mold the value system to come. There is a conservative aspect to Homer insofar as his formulations are accepted by succeeding generations. But in his central focus on the *hero*, Homer also sets in motion ideas of individualism, competition and progress which lead to the transformation of culture rather than its mere perpetuation.

GOLDMAN, Robert L and NELSON, Lawrence J and CLARK, H Westley and SCHORE, Jean E. Taking the Train to a World of Strangers: Health Care Marketing and Ethics. Hastings Center Rep, 19(5), 36-43, S-O 89.

GOLDMAN, Steven L. Science, Technology, and God: In Search of Believers. Bridges, 2(1-2), 43-56, Spr-Sum 90.

While science and technology are more powerful than religion as forces for change at work in modern societies, they are not substitutes for religion. The current perception of science and technology as increasingly problematic for society is thus not usefully interpretable as an illustration of false gods or gods that have failed. The social impact of science and technology since the Renaissance can only be understood in terms of the deliberate social actions that enabled them as agents of secular social change while concurrently disabling religion. The distinctive power of science and technology derives from the social context of their practice and selective exploitation, not from their intrinsic natures.

GOLDSTEIN, Alfred. The Expert and the Public: Local Values and National Choice. Bus Prof Ethics J, 6(2), 25-41, Sum 87.

GOLDSTEIN, Irwin. Pleasure and Pain: Unconditional, Intrinsic Values. Phil Phenomenol Res, 50(2), 255-276, D 89.

That *all* pleasure is good and *all* pain bad in itself is an eternally valid ethical principle. The common claim that some pleasure is not good, or some pain not bad, is mistaken. Strict *particularism* (ethical decisions must be made case by case; there are no sound universal normative principles) and *relativism* (all good and bad are relative to society) are among the ethical theories we may refute through an appeal to pleasure and pain. Daniel Dennett, Philippa Foot, R M Hare, Gilbert Harman, Immanuel Kant, J L Mackie, and Jean-Paul Sartre are among the many philosophers discussed.

GOLDSTEIN, Irwin. "The Rationality of Pleasure-Seeking Animals" in *Inquiries into Values: The Inaugural Session of the International Society for Value Inquiry*, LEE, Sander H , 131-136. Lewiston, Mellen Pr, 1989.

Pleasure-seeking animals, including the most primitive, are to some extent rational. Intrinsically, pleasure is better than pain; there is reason to desire pleasure and prefer it to pain. In desiring pleasure and avoiding pain, an animal's dispositions towards these experiences are appropriate and guided by reason.

GOLDSTEIN, Laurence. *The Philosopher's Habitat: Introduction to Investigations in, and Applications of, Modern Philosophy*. New York, Routledge, 1990

This book introduces the reader to all the main areas of philosophy by selecting a large number of problems which are currently engaging philosophers and which can be made intelligible to the absolute beginner. The stress is on those problems which illustrate modern philosophy's engagement with other disciplines. The procedure of traditional texts is inverted. Instead of starting out with the contributions of the major historical figures, we deal with current debates at the interfaces between philosophy, science, culture and practical life and, in so doing, come to appreciate how the stage was set by the great writers of the past.

GOLDSTICK, D. One Commends Something By Attributing the Property of Goodness To It (Penultimate Word). Int Stud Phil, 22(1), 73-75, 1990.

COLDSTICK, Danny and MILLS, Charles W. A New Old Meaning of "Ideology". Dialogue (Canada), 28(3), 417-432, 1989.

For decades, "ideology" has been one of the most influential concepts in Marxist theory. But the corresponding claims attributed to Marx about the sociology of belief and the cognitive deficiencies of political thought have always been deeply problematic. In this paper we advance the radically novel interpretation that "ideology" does not refer generally to ideas, or class ideas, or bourgeois ideas, or socially determined ideas (the standard candidates), but rather specifically to the "superstructure" and "superstructuralism." This implies that a significant proportion of exegesis and commentary on Marx's views on the social determination of belief actually rests on mistaken premises.

GOLDSTONE, Peter. Response to Professor Feinberg's Presidential Address: A Role for Philosophy of Education in Intercultural Research. Proc Phil Educ, 45, 20-26, 1989.

GOLEBIOWSKI, Marek (trans) and GRZEGORCZYK, Andrzej. New Social Self-Steering. Dialec Hum, 15(3-4), 251-254, Sum-Autumn 88.

Society may be defined as a kind of potentially self-steering social group. In the mechanism of this self-steering the role of public opinion constantly increases in our century. A constant development of the awareness of universal values impacts the decision makers by means of different forms of social debate.

GOLEBIOWSKI, Marek (trans) and KUCZYNSKI, Janusz and PETROWICZ, Lech (trans). Universalism: A New Way of Thinking. Dialec Hum, 15(3-4), 27-51, Sum-Autumn 88.

GOLEBIOWSKI, Marek (trans) and WOHL, Andrzej. Whither the Way? Dialec Hum, 16(2), 139-147, Spr 89.

GOLOMB, Jacob. Kierkegaard's Ironic Ladder to Authentic Faith. Iyyun, 39(2), 177-210, Ap 90.

This essay deals with some aspects of Kierkegaard's thought that have a direct bearing on the issue of authenticity: the existential dialectics of authenticity, the motif of enticement, the revolt against a given ethos, irony and literature, the return to origins, extreme existential experiences, the emphasis upon passion and commitment—in Kierkegaard's case the passion of religious faith. Kierkegaard's views of authenticity are critically examined and defended against some criticisms. (edited)

GOMBERG, Paul. Can a Partisan be a Moralist? Amer Phil Quart, 27(1), 71-79, Ja 90.

Moral universalism implies that we are all bound by a common morality. Situations where we must take sides in a life and death struggle—such as rebellions at Nazi death camps—put universalist conceptions under stress. For we do not believe that we share a moral community with SS men. Moral universalism can be defended, but this defense depends on doubtful assumptions about the course of human history. On Marx's conception of history, where class violence is inevitable, universalist moral conceptions are less tenable. Thus Marx's amoralism is a consequence of his conception of history.

GOMBERG, Paul. Consequentialism and History. Can J Phil, 19(3), 383-403, S 89.

Consequentialism has been criticized on the grounds that a consequentialist morality is too demanding and that such a morality distorts and constricts our personalities. These criticisms are rejected here. Given optimistic conceptions of our possible future and our ability to contribute to it, we can motivate a very demanding consequentialist life. Defenders of consequentialism such as Parfit and Railton share the pessimism of consequentialism's critics and very questionable views about the relationship between our interests and the interests of others.

GOMBOCZ, Wolfgang L. The Philosophy of Language in Scholasticism (in Serbo-Croatian). Filozof Istraz, 30(3), 1011-1029, 1989.

Der Autor versucht in diesem Text die philosophische Auseinandersetzung mit der Sprache in der Scholastik darzustellen. Diese philosophische Auseinandersetzung mit Sprachlichem in sehr verschiedenen Hinsichten wurde im europäischen Mittelalter von Anfang an auf's Engste mit der Logik (im weiten Sinne des Triviums von Grammatik, Rhetorik und Logik) ver—knüpft. Die "Sprachphilosophie" erscheint auf der Bühne des abendländisch-mittelalterlichen Denkens hauptsächlich und zunächst in Verbindung mit der Logik; sie wird als philosophische Semantik und Grammatik, als Bedeutungslehre also, sowie als Erörterung damit zusammenhängender mentaler Phänomene betrieben. Diese philosophische Sprachtheorie der Mettelzeit hat ihren Ausgangspunkt in der Interpretation der aristotelischperipatetischen Texte der sog. Logica vetus. Die Entfaltung der sich daraus ergebenden Reflexionen auf das implizite semantische Fundament ist dadurch gekennzeichnet, dass sich ein von konkreten, individuellen Gegenständen ausgehender Aristotelismus gegenüber den platonisierenden Deutungen der Logica vetus mehr und mehr durchsetzt.

GÓMEZ, Astrid C and GUIBOURG, Ricardo A. Tienen significado las contradicciones? Analisis Filosof, 9(1), 77-91, My 89.

Should we interpret meaning as a certain real entity expressed by words? Or rather as a property of words, which may or may not consist in a relationship between them and entities that are alien to them? In the first case we are led to conclude that contradictions are meaningless. But if this is so, the same must apply to tautologies, which implies a negation of the logical structure of language. In the second case we become aware of a disturbing similarity between the meaningfulness of contradictions and the meaninglessness of the expressions Russell calls syntactically impossible. The danger implied is, then, similar to that of the previous alternative. A pragmatic solution consists in introducing an idea resembling the mathematical notion of *limit*: the contradiction is the limit of the proposition when its designation approaches infinity; the tautology represents the opposite limit, when its designation approaches zero. (edited)

GÓMEZ, Carlos. Kolakowski y la religión: reflexiones sobre un texto de Dostoievski. Pensamiento, 46(182), 201-224, Ap-Je 90.

En su reciente obra sobre la religion, Kolakowski ha llevado a cabo un impresionante alegato en favor de la filosofía de la religión, al tratar de mostrar la vigencia, en varios sentidos, de la famosa sentencia de Dostoievski "Si Dios no existe, todo está permitido". Señalaré, en un primer momento, sus planteamientos centrales, para realizar a continuación una serie de comentarios críticos, referidos sobre todo al ámbito moral.

GOMEZ-LOBO, Alfonso. "Aristotle" in *Ethics in the History of Western Philosophy*, CAVALIER, Robert J (ed), 32-59. New York, St Martin's Pr, 1988.

The aim of this chapter is to provide a unified account of the moral philosophy found in the *Nicomachean Ethics*. After a sketch of Aristotle's life with some references to his adherence to Athenian values, three central topics are discussed: Aristotle's doctrine of practical knowledge (a strong version of cognitivism), his conception of the good (happiness is inclusive of all virtues), and his conception of the right (relativity of the mean does not imply moral relativism).

GOMEZ-LOBO, Alfonso. The Ergon Inference. Phronesis, 34(2), 170-184, 1989.

Aristotle's inference of the definition of *eudaimonia* in the *Nicomachean Ethics* has been commonly understood in a way which commits him to some form of fallacious naturalism or inference from fact to value. This view of the *ergon* inference is prompted to some extent by the fact that commentators rarely make an effort to identify the premises of the argument and also by the fact that, as I shall try to show, some key terms employed therein have been misunderstood. The purpose of the present paper is to show by means of a detailed analysis of Aritotle's text that the most commonly held view of the argument cannot be right and that he does not infer the notion of the human good from facts about human nature.

GONSALVES, Milton A. *Fagothey's Right and Reason: Ethics in Theory and Practice—Ninth Edition*. Columbus, Merrill, 1989

GONZALEZ, Orestes J. Tomás de Aquino: la aprehensión del "acto de ser". Anu Filosof, 22(2), 147-159, 1989.

GONZI, Andrea. Circolarità di condizione in L'homme et le langage di Jean Brun. Filosofia, 40(2), 203-207, My-Ag 89.

GOOD, D J and DE CONINCK, J B. Perceptual Differences of Sales Practitioners and Students Concerning Ethical Behavior. J Bus Ethics, 8(9), 667-676, S 89.

This study investigates specific behavioral perceptual differences of ethics between practitioners and students enrolled in sales classes. Respondents were asked to indicate their beliefs to issues related to ethics in sales. A highly significant difference was found between mean responses of students and sales personnel. Managers indicated a greater concern for ethical behavior and less attention to sales than did the students. Students indicated a strong desire for success regardless of ethical constraints violated.

GOODIN, Robert E. Do Motives Matter? Can J Phil, 19(3), 405-419, S 89.

GOODMAN, Dena. The Martin Guerre Story: A Non-Persian Source for Persian Letter CXLI. J Hist Ideas, 51(2), 311-316, Ap-Je 90.

GOODMAN, L E. "Matter and Form as Attributes of God in Maimonides' Philosophy" in *A Straight Path: Studies in Medieval Philosophy and Culture*, LINK-SALINGER, Ruth (ed), 86-97. Washington, Cath Univ Amer Pr, 1988.

Combatting Cartesian dualism, Spinoza adapts Maimonides' solution to the problem of God's absolute simplicity, treating thought and extension as distinct ways in which God is manifest to us. In Maimonides' *Guide to the Perplexed* matter is linked with what we find arbitrary in nature, thus with God's will; form or mind, with what seems rational, thus with divine wisdom. But in reality God has no attributes distinct from His Identity. Spinoza departs from Maimonides in treating the "attributes" as actually constitutive of God (since intellect apprehends things as they are) but retains the idea that their plurality is only notional.

GOODMAN, Nelson and ELGIN, Catherine Z. "Changing the Subjects" in *Analytic Aesthetics*, SHUSTERMAN, Richard (ed), 190-196. Cambridge, Blackwell, 1989.

GOODMAN, Nelson. Variations upon Variation, or Picasso Back to Bach. Acta Phil Fennica, 43, 167-178, 1988.

GOODMAN, Nicolas D. Mathematics as Natural Science. J Sym Log, 55(1), 182-193, Mr 90.

GOODMAN, Nicolas D. Topological Models of Epistemic Set Theory. Annals Pure Applied Log, 46(2), 147-167, F 90.

GOOLD, Patrick. Reading Kierkegaard: Two Pitfalls and a Strategy for Avoiding Them. Faith Phil, 7(3), 304-315, Jl 90.

Soren Kierkegaard is an important thinker, especially important for those who wish to understand Christian faith. His elusive style, however, and certain distancing techniques make him particularly difficult to understand. The recent history of writings on Kierkegaard reveals a strong tendency to fall into one of two erroneous modes of interpretation. This essay is an attempt to rescue Kierkegaard both from muggings by 'rigorous' philosophers and from the morganatic embraces of postmodernists. It reviews the classical sources of each of these sorts of reading of Kierkegaard, exposes their mistakes, and suggests several appropriate principles of interpretation.

GOOSSENS, Charles. "Ethical Relativity and Empirical Evaluation of Normative Propositions" in *Inquiries into Values: The Inaugural Session of the International Society for Value Inquiry*, LEE, Sander H , 195-217. Lewiston, Mellen Pr, 1989.

Ethical relativity in this study is not primarily conceived of as relativity of different moralities to different cultures but as relativity of moral propositions to specific social phenomena such as commitments of people in a community. Truth of normative, including moral, propositions is truth in the perspective of relevant dynamic social phenomena. The paper provides an analysis of 'the internal perspective' of normative truth. Truth of normative propositions can be empirically assessed because of the characteristic relationship between truth of such propositions and dynamic social phenomena. The study is presented as exploring new areas of research.

GOPNIK, Alison. Developing the Idea of Intentionality: Children's Theories of Mind. Can J Phil, 20(1), 89-113, Mr 90.

Recently a large amount of empirical research in developmental psychology has investigated children's understanding of the mind, their "folk psychology." This research is reviewed here. There appears to be an important change in children's understanding of belief at about age three. At this point, though not before, children begin to think of beliefs as intentional, that is they conceive of beliefs as mental entities that represent a physical world. This research supports the "theory theory" of the development of "folk psychological" concepts.

GORANKO, Valentin. Modal Definability in Enriched Languages. Notre Dame J Form Log, 31(1), 81-105, Wint 90.

The paper deals with polymodal languages combined with standard semantics defined by means of some conditions on the frames. So a notion of "polymodal base" arises which provides various enrichments of the classical modal language. One of these enrichments, viz., the base $L(R,-R$, with modalities over a relation and over its complement, is the paper's main paradigm. The modal definability (in the spirit of van Benthem's correspondence theory) of arbitrary and Δ-elementary classes of frames in this base and in some of its extensions, e.g., $L(R,-R,R^{-1},-R^{-1})$, $L(R,-R,\neq)$ etc., is described, and numerous examples of conditions definable there, as well as undefinable ones, are adduced.

GORDEEV, L. Generalizations of the Kruskal-Friedman Theorems. J Sym Log, 55(1), 157-181, Mr 90.

Kruskal proved that finite trees are well-quasi-ordered by hom(e)omorphic embeddability. Friedman observed that this statement is not provable in predicative analysis. Friedman also proposed some stronger variants of the Kruskal theorem dealing with finite labeled trees under hom(e)omorphic embeddability with a certain gap-condition, where labels are arbitrary finite ordinals from a fixed initial segment of ω. Schütte and Simpson proved that the one-dimensional case of Friedman's limit statement dealing with finite labeled intervals is not provable in Peano arithmetic. However, Friedman's gap-condition fails for finite trees labeled with transfinite ordinals. In a previous paper, I proposed another gap-condition and proved the resulting one-dimensional modified statements for all (countable) transfinite ordinal-labels. (edited)

GORDON, Colin (trans) and LE DOEUFF, Michèle. *The Philosophical Imaginary*. Stanford, Stanford Univ Pr, 1990

GORDON, David. Libertarianism Versus Secular Humanism? Free Inq, 9(4), 22-23, Fall 89.

GORDVITZ, Samuel. Moral Conflict in Public Policy. Nat Forum, 69(4), 31-32, Fall 89.

GÖRES, Jörn. "Die hermeneutische Funktion des Literaturmuseums" in *Cultural Hermeneutics of Modern Art: Essays in Honor of Jan Aler*, DETHIER, Hubert (ed), 159-166. Amsterdam, Rodopi, 1989.

GÖRLER, Woldemar. "Cicero und die 'Schule des Aristoteles'" in *Cicero's Knowledge of the Peripatos*, FORTENBAUGH, William W (ed), 246-263. New Brunswick, Transaction Books, 1989.

Cicero is well acquainted with Peripatetic philosophers from Theophrastus up to his own time. But he does not approve of their philosophical tenets and quotes them but rarely. Some general conclusions may be drawn as to Cicero's reliability as a "source author": Wherever Cicero cites his authority he may be trusted. More often, however, his statements about Greek philosophers (given in vague and general terms) are thoroughly tinged with his own philosophical convictions. Verbatim quotations of Greek 'sources' are to be found only where Cicero says so, explicitly. All other passages are of his own wording and should not be regarded as 'fragments'.

GORMAN, Michael. Response to Dietrich's "Computationalism". Soc Epistem, 4(2), 165-167, Ap-Je 90.

This response argues that computationalism comes perilously close to behaviorism. Both 'black-box' the mind, the latter by ignoring it and the former by substituting programs for mental processes. The computer is a potentially fruitful metaphor that often becomes a Procrustean bed.

GÓRNIAK-KOCIKOWSKA, Krystyna. Martin Buber—A Jew from Galicia. Dialec Hum, 16(1), 171-181, Wint 89.

Martin Buber's philosophy has diverse roots. He spent his childhood and teenage in the multinational and multicultural city of Lvov, a major city of Galicia, which was at that time part of the Austrian-Hungarian monarchy, but had its own very specific cultural and "existential" atmosphere. The article asks whether it was any influence of these years on Buber's future work. The answer is yes. Not only Hasidism, but also some other phenomena of the Galician culture stimulated Buber. The article presents some of them. Buber is regarded as a symbol of synthesis of differences; the environment of his early years was a very good place to work out this ability.

GORR, Michael. Thomson and the Trolley Problem. Phil Stud, 59(1), 91-100, My 90.

I argue that Judith Thomson's solution to the trolley problem appears to account for our intuitions but is theoretically unsatisfactory because it attaches moral significance to factors that are devoid of it. I also criticize James Montmarquet's proposed solution.

GOSCHKE, Thomas and KOPPELBERG, Dirk. Connectionism and the Semantic Content of Internal Representation. Rev Int Phil, 44(172), 87-103, 1990.

GOSLING, J C B. The Hedonic Calculus in the *Protagoras* and the *Phaedo*: A Reply. J Hist Phil, 28(1), 115-116, Ja 90.

GOSWAMI, Amit. Consciousness in Quantum Physics and The Mind-Body Problem. J Mind Behav, 11(1), 75-96, Wint 90.

Following the lead of von Neumann and Wigner, Goswami (1989) has developed a paradox-free interpretation of quantum mechanics based on the idealistic notion that consciousness collapses the quantum wave function. This solution of quantum measurement theory sheds a considerable amount of light on the nature of consciousness. Quantum theory is applied to the mind-brain problem and a solution (quantum functionalism) is proposed for the paradox of the causal potency of the conscious mind and of self-reference. Cognitive and neurophysiological data in support of the present theory are also reviewed.

GOSWAMI, Roshmi. On the "Incompleteness" of a Musical Work. Indian Phil Quart, 16(3), 345-355, Jl 89.

It has been said that a musical composition is essentially incomplete, and that it needs completion through performance. I wish, in this paper, to discuss this contention and some issues connected with it. But before doing that, it is essential first of all to determine what precisely is the identity of a piece of music as a work of art. For this would, I believe, bring out some powerful peculiarities of music as a work of art.

GOTT, V S. The Dialectics of the Unity of Linearity and Non-linearity of Physical Processes (in Czechoslovakian). Filozof Cas, 37(6), 773-782, 1989.

During the study of real physical phenomena, the dialectics of concepts reflects the objective dialectics of these phenomena. This also holds true of the examination of the relationship between linearity and nonlinearity. While linearity tends to mirror a disposition towards stability, equilibrium, towards the preservation of the determinateness of structure, nonlinearity expresses a tendency towards upsetting the equilibrium and structure, towards upsetting existing stability. A link-up between linearity and nonlinearity is capable of more adequately reflecting real processes, spelling out, as it does, a unity involving stability and variability which creates the most profound substance of each movement, and hence also of moving matter. Seen in this light, the philosophical significance of the unity of linearity and nonlinearity inheres in the fact such a unity may be used to specify the content of the categories of motion and development. The terms linearity and nonlinearity simultaneously discharge a major epistemological function, connected with the mathematization and formulization of scientific knowledge. (edited)

GOTTHELF, Allan. Teleology and Spontaneous Generation in Aristotle: A Discussion. Apeiron, 22(4), 181-193, D 89.

Aristotle's mature theory of spontaneous generation and his evident denial that spontaneous generations have a teleological character pose an intriguing dilemma to interpretations of his natural teleology that test it on an irreducibility thesis. In this brief discussion I try to spell out the GA III.11 account of spontaneous generation more precisely than has been done in previous discussions of this problem, and offer a resolution of that dilemma consistent with my own interpretation of the teleology.

GOTTINGER, Hans W. Decision Problems Under Uncertainty Based on Entropy Functionals. Theor Decis, 28(2), 143-172, Mr 90.

This essay intends to define the role of entropy, in particular, the role of the maximum entropy criterion with respect to decision analysis and information economics. By considering the average opportunity loss interpretation, the basic hypothesis for Shannon's derivation can be derived from properties of decision problems. Using the representation Bayes Boundary it is possible to show that selecting a single probability from a set by the maximum entropy criterion corresponds to a minimax criterion for decision making. Since problems of randomly accessing and storing information as well as communicating information can often be stated in terms of coding problems, this result might be used to develop strategies for minimizing retrieval time or communications costs.

GOUDSMIT, Arno L. Kleine epistemologie van de kikvors-retina. Kennis Methode, 14(2), 237-241, 1990.

GOUINLOCK, James (ed) and CAVALIER, Robert J (ed) and STERBA, James P (ed). *Ethics in the History of Western Philosophy*. New York, St Martin's Pr, 1988

This book presents the central ideas in the moral theory of major thinkers from Plato to Rawls. An acknowledged expert on the ethical theory of each philosopher characterises these ideas as they developed out of the historical context in which they were actually formulated. The cultural and intellectual conditions that generated each philosophy are set forth, and when pertinent, the personal experience of the philosopher as well. Accordingly the interested reader as well as the professional scholar will find in this book the actual intent and meaning of the greatest moral theories in the Western tradition.

GOUINLOCK, James. "Dewey" in *Ethics in the History of Western Philosophy*, CAVALIER, Robert J (ed), 306-334. New York, St Martin's Pr, 1988.

GOUINLOCK, James. What Is the Legacy of Instrumentalism? Rorty's Interpretation of Dewey. J Hist Phil, 28(2), 251-269, Ap 90.

GOULD, Carol S. Plato, George Eliot, and Moral Narcissism. Phil Lit, 14(1), 24-39, Ap 90.

GOULD, James A. Explanatory Grounds: Marx versus Foucault. Dialogos, 25(55), 133-138, Ja 90.

GOVIER, Trudy. Analogies and Missing Premises. Inform Log, 11(3), 141-152, Fall 89.

This paper explores the issue of whether analogies are a type of argument logically distinct from deductive arguments and arguments depending on inductive generalization. Using the 'missing premise' device, so-called a priori analogies can be turned into deductively valid arguments. I consider this strategy and argue, for a variety of reasons, that it should not be adopted.

GOVIER, Trudy. *God, the Devil and the Perfect Pizza: Ten Philosophical Questions*. Peterborough, Broadview Pr, 1989

The author uses dialogue form to wrestle with questions about the existence of God and the external world, free will, artificial intelligence and other philosophical problems. (staff)

GOWANS, Christopher W. Two Concepts of the Given in C I Lewis: Realism and Foundationalism. J Hist Phil, 27(4), 573-590, O 89.

It is usually assumed that what Lewis says about the given in *Mind and the World-Order* (MWO) and *An Analysis of Knowledge and Valuation* (AKV) is essentially the same, and that both works are defenses of foundationalism. However, this assumption faces two problems: first, it is difficult to bring Lewis's diverse remarks on the given into coherence, especially when those in MWO are compared with those in AKV; and second, though AKV is a defense of foundationalism, there is much in MWO that can be read as a critique of foundationalism. In this paper a different reading of Lewis is proposed, one that avoids these problems. This is developed by going farther back in Lewis, to his Harvard Ph.D. dissertation, *The Place of Intuition in Knowledge* (PIK). By tracing Lewis's discussion of the given from PIK through MWO up to AKV, it is shown that the phrase 'the given' is used to refer to two different doctrines, and that Lewis's position on foundationalism undergoes a fundamental change, roughly, from indifference to rejection to acceptance.

GOWER, Barry. David Hume and the Probability of Miracles. Hume Stud, 16(1), 17-31, Ap 90.

GOWER, Barry. Mellor on Inductive Scepticism. Phil Quart, 40(159), 233-240, Ap 90.

GOWER, Barry. Stove on Inductive Scepticism. Austl J Phil, 68(1), 109-112, Mr 90.

GOYARD-FABRE, Simone. La légitimité. Rev Theol Phil, 122(2), 235-252, 1990.

Though it may be admitted that legitimacy confers to power its plenitude and strength, the concept of legitimacy responds nonetheless to founding principles which affiliate it to a variety of doctrinal models. As shown in the cohesion between the concepts of legitimacy and legality, the complex and indecisive nature of the criteria of legitimacy points to its fundamentally problematic status, which, just as politics itself, cannot remain axiologically neutral.

GRABOWSKI, Michal. Arithmetical Completeness Versus Relative Completeness. Stud Log, 47(3), 213-220, S 88.

In this paper we study the status of the arithmetical completeness of dynamic logic. We prove that for finitistic proof systems for dynamic logic results beyond arithmetical completeness are very unlikely. The role of the set of natural numbers is carefully analyzed.

GRACELY, Edward J. Comment on Shrader-Frechette's "Parfit and Mistakes in Moral Mathematics". Ethics, 100(1), 157-159, O 89.

Real but imperceptible benefits and harms have been proposed by Parfit as a solution to certain ethical paradoxes. I defend an alternative approach. A minuscule stimulus, such as an extra drop of water to a thirsty person, has its physiological effect on top of the random "noise" already present in the perceptual system. On occasion, the noise will be close enough to a perceptual threshold that the extra stimulus causes the latter to be crossed. Although the stimulus is only "perceived" in a limited sense, its real effect on the perceptual process helps explain its moral relevance.

GRACIA, Jorge J E. Texts and Their Interpretation. Rev Metaph, 43(3), 495-542, Mr 90.

The aim of this paper is to provide an understanding of the nature of interpretations of texts, their object and function, and of the difficulties that historians of philosophy encounter when they try to produce them. The paper is divided into four parts, dealing respectively with texts, authors, audiences, and interpretations. The main theses of the paper are two: first, interpretations are texts added to other texts; second, their function is to create the conditions that will help reproduce in the contemporary audience mental phenomena similar to those that would have been produced in the audience contemporary with the original text.

GRACYK, Theodore A. Are Kant's "Aesthetic Judgment" and "Judgment of Tase" Synonymous? Int Phil Quart, 30(2), 159-172, Je 90.

Kant asserts both that feeling is the basis of aesthetic judgment and that judgment is the basis of feeling. Some commentators resolve this by distinguishing the "judging of the object" from the "judgment of taste"; this interpretation is revised in light of Kant's emphasis on the nonconceptual status of aesthetic judgments and the empirical component of judgments of taste. Judgments of taste involve a sequence of judgments, in which feeling provides the nonconceptual aesthetic judgment concerning the representation of the object, followed by a conceptually determinate judgment concerning the empirical object.

GRACYK, Theodore A. Having Bad Taste. Brit J Aes, 30(2), 117-131, Ap 90.

People frequently judge that others have bad taste, but such judgments are seldom justified. The author argues that taste involves both hedonic and judgmental elements, and that no person has universally good taste. Departure from good taste is often confused with having bad taste, but the former does not demonstrate the latter. Based on these conclusions, he suggests a set of necessary and sufficient conditions for having bad taste.

GRACYK, Theodore A. Pornography as Representation: Aesthetic Considerations. J Aes Educ, 21(4), 103-121, Wint 87.

The article challenges recent attempts to define pornography as necessarily defaming and degrading women. Specifically, it considers the criteria for pornography offered by A Dworkin and C MacKinnon and rejects the criteria as too broad to exclude many nondefamatory films, books, etc. It is argued that any precise criteria will be similarly inadequate, because they cannot capture the sensitivity to context required to identify both subject matter and a work's expressed attitude to that subject matter.

GRADINAROV, Plamen. Laugāksi Bhāskara on Inference: Problems of Generalizing Ideation in Comparative Light. J Indian Phil, 17(3), 225-264, S 89.

GRAESER, Andreas. Hegel über die Rede vom Absoluten—Teil I: Urteil, Satz und Spekulativer Gehalt. Z Phil Forsch, 44(2), 175-193, 1990.

GRAHAM, A C. Conceptual Schemes and Linguistic Relativism in Relation to Chinese (in Serbo-Croatian). Filozof Istraz, 29(2), 587-605, 1989.

Philosophers tend to think of conceptual schemes as systems of propositions presupposed as true, explorers of other cultures rather as classificatory and syntactic structures. On the latter approach one can accept the relativity of propositions to incommensurable schemes without the undermining of truth which seems to follow from the former. 'The cat sat on the mat' and Chinese Mao wo tsai hsi-tzu-shang are not intertranslatable; the latter unlike the former could be true even if the cat has only just begun to sit, false if the mat was not made of straw. But a bilingual speaker who saw the cat will accept both as confirmed by observation. (edited)

GRAHAM, A C. Disputers of the TAO: Philosophical Argument in Ancient China. La Salle, Open Court, 1989

GRAHAM, George and LA FOLLETTE, Hugh. "Honesty and Intimacy" in Person to Person, GRAHAM, George (ed), 167-181. Philadelphia, Temple Univ Pr, 1989.

Examination of the role of honesty in intimate relationships, which includes a defense of the thesis that dishonesty is never justified in an intimate relationship. Two types of honesty are distinguished and the role of sensitivity in intimacy is counterpointed with the role of honesty.

GRAHAM, George. Melancholic Epistemology. Synthese, 82(3), 399-422, Mr 90.

Too little attention has been paid by philosophers to the cognitive and epistemic dimensions of emotional disturbances such as depression, grief, and anxiety and to the possibility of justification or warrant for such conditions. The chief aim of the present paper is to help to remedy that deficiency with respect to depression. Taxonomy of depression reveals two distinct forms: depression (1) with intentionality and (2) without intentionality. Depression with intentionality can be justified or unjustified, warranted or unwarranted. I argue that the effort of Aaron Beck to show that depressive reasoning is necessarily illogical and distorted is flawed. I identify an essential characteristic of that depression which is a mental illness. Finally, I describe the potential of depression to provide credal contact with important truths.

GRAHAM, George (ed) and LA FOLLETTE, Hugh (ed). Person to Person. Philadelphia, Temple Univ Pr, 1989

A collection of mostly original essays by philosophers and psychologists on the ethics of personal relationships, including such topics as parental obligations to children, trust and intimacy among friends, and family privacy.

GRAHAM, Gordon. "Commitment and the Value of Marriage" in Person to Person, GRAHAM, George (ed), 199-212. Philadelphia, Temple Univ Pr, 1989.

This paper explores traditional Christian conceptions of marriage and asks whether a secularized notion of 'commitment' can secure the same sort of value for a relationship between two people. The conclusion is that it cannot, and that secular conceptions of marriage rest upon social contingencies which need not prevail.

GRAHAM, Joseph F. "Around and About Babel" in The Textual Sublime: Deconstruction and Its Differences, SILVERMAN, Hugh J (ed), 167-176. Albany, SUNY Pr, 1990.

GRAHAM, Keith. Class—A Simple View. Inquiry, 32(4), 419-436, D 89.

The aim is to defend the starting point of Marx's theory of class, which is located in a definition of the working class in the Communist Manifesto. It is a definition solely in terms of separation from productive resources and a need to sell one's labour power, and it is closely connected with Marx's thesis that the population in capitalism has a tendency to polarize. That thesis conflicts with the widely held belief in the growth of a large middle class, unaccounted for by Marx. Moreover, recent critics have argued that this definition fails even in its own terms. The definition is refurbished so as to withstand these objections. But is there any point in using it? Does it serve to pick out the exploited producers as Marx intended? It does, once due attention is given to the idea of the collective worker, which is central in the volume of Capital which Marx himself published. That idea makes plain that it is an irreducibly corporate entity which is productive and subject to exploitation. The structural conditions for membership of that entity remove Marx's view from any simple identification of working-class membership with manual or lowly labour. (edited)

GRAHAM, Keith. Liberalism and Liberty: the Fragility of a Tradition. Philosophy, 24, 207-223, 88 Supp.

My discussion in this lecture is structured as follows. In section 1 I consider the nature of philosophical enquiry and its affinity to liberalism. In section 2 I lay out some of the basic components of liberal theory and explore their interrelations. In section 3 I discuss two challenges to liberalism: one concerning the conception of liberty which it involves and one concerning the way in which it introduces the idea of legitimate political authority. In section 4 I suggest that these problems, to do with the values of liberalism, arise on the basis of a prior conception of individuals which is in need of modification. In a brief concluding section 5 I indicate the need for a postliberal political theory.

GRAHAM, Keith. Self-Ownership, Communism and Equality—II. Aris Soc, SUPP 64, 45-61, 1990.

A response to G A Cohen's claim that Marxism fails to dissociate itself from the self-ownership principle, with harmful results. Stress is laid on collective aspects of Marx's claims about the capitalist dynamic, the nature of the future society and the route for reaching it. In capitalism, the surplus product is held to be collectively produced and outside the scope of the principle. Correspondingly, productive resources in the future society will be collectively owned and thus not under individual control. The route to that society requires motivation via collective identification, of a form to which the self-ownership principle is irrelevant.

GRAIG, Ian. "The Physicist and the Politicians: Niels Bohr and the International Control of Atomic Weapons" in Moral Reasoning and Statecraft: Essays Presented to Kenneth W Thompson, DAVIS, Reed M (ed), 105-131. Lanham, Univ Pr of America, 1988.

GRAMSCI, Antonio and HOARE, Quintin (ed) and MATHEWS, John (trans). Selections from Political Writings, 1910-1920: Antonio Gramsci. Minneapolis, Univ of Minn Pr, 1990

Antonio Gramsci is considered one of the most influential thinkers of the twentieth century. The selections in this volume, the first of two, span the period from his initial involvement in Italian politics to the "Red Years" of 1919-1920, and feature texts by Bordiga and Tasca from their debates with Gramsci. They trace Gramsci's development as a revolutionary socialist during the First World War, the impact of his thoughts concerning the Russian Revolution and his involvement in the general strike and factory occupations of 1920. Also included are his reactions to the emerging fascist movement and his contributions to the early stages of the debate about the establishment of the Communist Party of Italy.

GRAMSCI, Antonio and HOARE, Quintin (ed & trans). Selections from Political Writings, 1921-1926: Antonio Gramsci. Minneapolis, Univ of

Minn Pr, 1990

This is a second volume of Gramsci's political writings. It details events during the rise of the Italian Communist party. The concerns of the writing focus on contemporary Marxist issues such as the functioning of working class power and the implications of proletarian internationalism. (staff)

GRANA, Nicola. On a Minimal Non-Alethic Logic. Bull Sect Log, 19(1), 25-29, Mr 90.

A minimal non-alethic logic A can be employed as a basis for a deontic logic that does not exclude ab inintio moral dilemmas as real deadlocks, and considers them only as prima facie difficulties. The deontic logic founded on A is also compatible with the existence of deontic gaps, i.e., deontic situations whose proper deontic status cannot be directly settled. Consequently, A may be the starting point of systems of deontic logic apt to cope with ethical and juridical issues of fundamental nature.

GRANDY, Richard E. "A Modern Inquiry Into the Physical Property of Colors" in Mind, Value and Culture: Essays in Honor of E M Adams, WEISSBORD, David (ed), 229-245. Atascadero, Ridgeview, 1989.

I attempt to show that most arguments against the reality of colors are either question begging or depend on an incorrect identification of the physical structure in question. I distinguish the question whether determinate colors exist from whether determinable colors exist. I argue for a positive answer to the first and give a sketch of the physical structure involved; I argue for a much more equivocal answer to the second.

GRANDY, Richard E. On Grice and Language. J Phil, 86(10), 514-525, O 89.

GRANDY, Richard E and BRODY, Baruch A. Readings in the Philosophy of Science (Second Edition). Englewood Cliffs, Prentice-Hall, 1989

This second edition updates the first edition by including two new sections (one on space and time and the other on biology) and emphasizing many recent authors (Achinstein, Cartwright, Hacking, Laudan, Salmon, and van Fraassen). It retains from the first edition the basic structure of three major sections, one on theories, one on explanation and causality, and one on the confirmation of scientific hypotheses.

GRANEL, Gérard. Sibboleth ou de la Lettre. Rev Phil Fr, 180(2), 185-206, Ap-Je 90.

GRANGE, Joseph. "Lacan's Other and the Factions of Plato's Soul" in The Question of the Other: Essays in Contemporary Continental Philosophy, DALLERY, Arleen B (ed), 157-174. Albany, SUNY Pr, 1989.

This is a comparison of Lacan's psychoanalytic theory with Plato's tripartite concept of the soul. Language is seen as determinative of human personality. From this perspective culture and the unconscious are viewed as the great formative influences on human growth and development. Poetry and philosophy are considered as the regions within which being and being human flourish.

GRANGER, G G. Les conditions proto-logiques des langues naturelles. Philosophiques, 16(2), 245-256, Autumn 89.

Is it possible to state nonempirical requisites for an object, fact or artefact, to obtain symbolical functioning? If so, their status could be named proto-logical, insofar as they bear upon forms, like logic, but ought to be more primitive than logical determinations. The purpose of this paper is to discuss five notions which may be considered candidates for the functional role of proto-logical universals of natural languages: plurality of the levels of "articulations," the concept of full-fledged sentence, "anchorage" of enunciated sentences to enunciation, proper names, the correlation rheme-theme. Such universals are not meant to correspond to classes of symbols, but to typical functions, diversely embodied in grammatical structures. To trace them—or others—should be one of the tasks of philosophy of language, in its relationship with linguistic investigations.

GRANGER, Herbert. Aristotle and the Functionalist Debate. Apeiron, 23(1), 27-49, Mr 90.

The paper considers both the functionalist and anti-functionalist interpretations of Aristotle's psychology. They are both incorrect for the same reason because they both take the soul to be a set of 'powers' construed as 'dispositional properties'. Instead, Aristotle's soul resists classification as a 'property', or even as a 'thing'. It is what might be called a 'power-thing', and its true nature, although unclear, is clear enough to reveal its incompatibility with functionalism.

GRANOFF, Phyllis. The Biographies of Siddhasena: A Study in the Texture of Allusion and the Weaving of a Group-Image (Part I). J Indian Phil, 17(4), 329-384, D 89.

GRANT, Hardy. Geometry and Medicine: Mathematics in the Thought of Galen of Pergamum. Phil Math, 4(1), 29-34, 1989.

This paper describes Galen's confidence in the sureness of mathematical reasoning and conclusions, and his attempts to use mathematical methods in physiology and medicine. The balance in his work between quasi-Euclidean deduction from first principles on the one hand, and empirical methods on the other, is also discussed.

GRATTAN-GUINNESS, H (ed) and POST, E L. The Modern Paradoxes. Hist Phil Log, 11(1), 85-91, 1990.

The text is transcribed from a paper of 1935 in which E L Post (1897-1954) creates a temporal set theory in which objects of thought are pukka, and so may belong to (i.e., join) already existent sets. Possibilities of paradox are in the offing, which he considers. I survey the Nachlass from which the manuscript is drawn and also the mentalistic philosophy evident in this and other writings.

GRATTAN-GUINNESS, I. The Manuscripts of Emil L Post. Hist Phil Log, 11(1), 77-83, 1990.

Post's Nachlass has recently been made available to the public in an archive in the USA. After a short summary of his life and career, this article indicates the character and content of the manuscripts, and their significance is assessed. Two short passages are transcribed; and, as a separate item, a paper of the 1930s on the paradoxes is reproduced.

GRATTON, Claude. Letting and Making Death Happen—Withholding and Withdrawing Life Support: Morally Irrelevant Distinctions. J Med Human, 11(2), 75-80, Sum 90.

This article examines the proposition that there are no inherent moral distinctions between withholding and withdrawing care. The two decisions have traditionally been perceived in different lights; the courts treat them differently; and they appear different to many clinicians. The difference can be explained by the idea of moral linkage: there exist moral considerations which, though theoretically separable from acts and decisions examined out of context, are not always separable in any practical way. In that sense, withholding and withdrawing care are not the same. The conditions under which one decision is justifiable may differ substantially from the conditions which license the other. Moral linkage explains why withholding care may be allowable under circumstances in which withdrawing care is not even though there is not necessarily any moral difference between these two acts.

GRAUBNER, Hans. Theological Empiricism: Aspects of Johann Georg Hamann's Reception of Hume. Hume Stud, 15(2), 377-385, N 89.

GRAY, John. Mill's and Other Liberalisms. Crit Rev, 2(2-3), 12-35, Spr-Sum 88.

GRAY, John. Western Marxism: A Fictionalist Deconstruction. Philosophy, 64(249), 403-408, Jl 89.

GRAYBOSCH, Anthony J. Which One Is the Real One? Phil Theol, 4(4), 365-384, Sum 90.

This paper examines the phenomena of falling in love and of love using Baudelaire's poem, "Which Is the Real One?" as impetus. The author asks why love is often focused toward an individual and why an individual often makes such a monumental difference when love should be a more universal experience. The focus of the Romantic poets on the individual is criticized, and Taoist and anti-romantic conceptions of love are considered.

GRAYBOSCH, Anthony. Observation, Instrumentalism, and Constructive Empiricism. SW Phil Rev, 6(2), 1-17, Jl 90.

GRCIC, Joseph. Justice and the Legal Profession. Int J Applied Phil, 5(1), 51-56, Spr 90.

GRECU, Constantin. La rationnalité interrogative (in Romanian). Rev Filosof (Romania), 35(6), 543-547, N-D 88.

GREEN, C F. Business Ethics in Banking. J Bus Ethics, 8(8), 631-634, Ag 89.

Companies do have ethical responsibility and are not protected by limited liability from the consequences of their actions. A company's record and the preception of its ethics affect its reputation and ensure long-term success or failure. The financial community has a history of placing moral considerations above legal or opportunistic expedients. But we are often exposed to moral dangers and the dangers of contamination are increasing. Deregulation and the technological revolution are sharpening ethical conflicts. Bankers' role is one of stewardship based on trust. We are trusted by those who ask us to look after their money and we have a duty to lend that money responsibly. (edited)

GREEN, Gary P. State, Class, and Technology in Tobacco Production. Agr Human Values, 6(4), 54-61, Fall 89.

Recent debates over the persistence of family farms have focused on the importance of "naturalistic" obstacles to the capitalist development of agriculture. According to these arguments, the existence of these barriers in some realms of agricultural production precludes the development of wage labor. I argue, however, that in many instances these obstacles are based primarily on political factors. To demonstrate this thesis I illustrate how the tobacco program until recently has proved to be an obstacle to consolidation and structural change in tobacco production. (edited)

GREEN, Karen. Prostitution, Exploitation and Taboo. Philosophy, 64(250), 525-534, O 89.

A rational ground for judging prostitution immoral is defended by taking into account features of human moral psychology which enable a stable and well-ordered society to reproduce itself. These include the preconditions for the acquisition, by children, of a sense of justice and other moral sentiments.

GREEN, Michele. Sympathy and Self-Interest: The Crisis in Mill's Mental History. Utilitas, 1(2), 259-277, N 89.

GREEN, Ronald M and DERRY, Robbin. Ethical Theory in Business Ethics: A Critical Assessment. J Bus Ethics, 8(7), 521-533, Jl 89.

How is ethical theory used in contemporary teaching in business ethics? To answer this question, we undertook a survey of 25 of the leading business ethics texts. Our purpose was to examine the ways in which normative moral theory is introduced and applied to cases and issues. We focused especially on the authors' views of the conflicts and tensions posed by basic theoretical debates. How can these theories be made useful if fundamental tensions are acknowledged? Our analysis resulted in a typology, presented here, of the ways in which normative theory, and the difficulties within it, are handled in business ethics texts. We conclude that there is a serious lack of clarity about how to apply the theories to cases and a persistent unwillingness to grapple with tensions between theories of ethical reasoning. These deficiencies hamper teaching and ethical decision making.

GREEN, Ronald M. Medical Joint-Venturing: An Ethical Perspective. Hastings Center Rep, 20(4), 22-26, Jl-Ag 90.

An examination of some of the leading ethical issues raised by medical joint-venturing, the practice of physicians investing in facilities to which they refer patients. After reviewing the most important ethical arguments for and against these practices, the discusssion calls for an outright ban on such referral practices.

GREEN, Ronald M. Method in Bioethics: A Troubled Assessment. J Med Phil, 15(2), 179-197, Ap 90.

This discussion is a critical assessment of the methods employed by some leading writers in the field of bioethics. The author agrees with those in the field who regard its primary or essential method as moral philosophy, but he nevertheless finds a prevalent tendency among bioethical writers merely to apply received moral principles to issues and to avoid penetrating theoretical analysis, even when such analysis is unavoidably required. He explains these deficiencies in terms of the exigencies of interdisciplinary work and the affinity of much early bioethics with policy- or legislatively-oriented "public ethics." The discussion ends with a call for increased theoretical sophistication in this field.

GREEN, S J D. Competitive Equality of Opportunity: A Defense. Ethics, 100(1), 5-32, O 89.

This article mounts a philosophical defence of a version of equality of opportunity, commonly known as "competitive equality of opportunity," against radical egalitarian, conservative, pluralist, libertarian and formalist criticisms. It argues that competitive equality of opportunity is a theory of social justice most appropriately applied to those social goods generally called "social offices." It concludes that a just form of allocation for these goods should be maintained in society, at once motivated by the ideal of the human good of self-realization, and regulated by the principle of proportionality, through a system of competitive initial compensation.

GREEN, Simon. Taking Talents Seriously. Crit Rev, 2(2-3), 202-219, Spr-Sum 88.

This article directs critical attention to the radical egalitarian theory of equality of resources, defined as equality of talents, or nontransferable resources. It argues that this theory is flawed conceptually by its inability to distinguish, *ex ante*, between individual resources and personal choices and empirically by its incapacity to confront the revelation problem well known in economic theory. It is contended, finally, that these problems are compounded by the fact that most human talents are identified, as well as utilised, only under social conditions of individual uncertainty and competitive risk taking.

GREENAWALT, Kent. "Comment: The Obligation to Obey the Law" in *Issues in Contemporary Legal Philosophy: The Influence of H L A Hart*, GAVISON, Ruth (ed), 156-179. New York, Clarendon/Oxford Pr, 1987.

This comment in a volume honoring H L A Hart compares Philip Soper's claim that respect for those in authority underlies a broad obligation to obey the

law with Hart's own suggestion that the duty of fair play is most important. The comment concludes that respect for those in authority is a duty that has relatively little strength and a breadth less encompassing than Soper supposes. The duty of fair play has greater significance. Its force is not, as John Rawls has assumed, limited to fair political regimes. Within such regimes, it establishes a prima facie obligation to obey many, but not all, laws.

GREENAWALT, Kent. Hart's Rule of Recognition and the United States. Ratio Juris, 1(1), 40-57, Mr 88.

This essay explores the implication of H L A Hart's rule of recognition for identifying ultimate standards of law in the United States. The effort reveals that these standards are much more complex than is commonly supposed. Not all of the federal constitution is part of the "ultimate" rule of recognition, and much else must be included in that rule. The analysis uncovers many possibilities for how ultimate standards relate to derivative standards that are omitted or barely hinted at in Hart's account. Some of these possibilities pose genuine difficulty for Hart's basic theory and help illuminate the relation of conventional and normative elements in an adequate account of law, a subject addressed in the final section of the essay.

GREENAWALT, Kent. Law and Objectivity: How People are Treated. Crim Just Ethics, 8(2), 31-45, Sum-Fall 89.

This essay has two main subjects. It first considers legal issues, mainly in criminal law, as to which more or less objective or subjective approaches might be used. It addresses factual perceptions, quality of judgment, linguistic understandings, immediate aims, ultimate motivations, and control. The broad theme is that deciding how objective or subjective standards of liability should be is highly complex. The essay's second main subject is classifications that differentially affect groups, either because membership in the group is directly taken into account or because crucial characteristics correlate with membership. It discusses possible justifications and application of terms like "bias."

GREENAWALT, Kent. *Speech, Crime, and the Uses of Language*. New York, Oxford Univ Pr, 1989

The book explores the three-way relationship between the idea of freedom of speech, the law of crimes, and the many uses of language. It considers free speech as a political principle, first analyzing justifications commonly advanced for free speech and the kinds of communications to which a principle of free speech applies. Focusing on threats and solicitations to crime, it then examines what kinds of criminal liability raise free speech problems. The second half of the book considers what should count as "speech" within the First Amendment and what standards courts should use to decide if criminal statutes are unconstitutional.

GREENE, Maxine. Creating, Experiencing, Sense-Making: Art Worlds in Schools. J Aes Educ, 21(4), 11-23, Wint 87.

GREENWOOD, John D. Analyticity, Indeterminacy and Semantic Theory: Some Comments on "The Domino Theory". Phil Stud, 58(1-2), 41-49, Ja-F 90.

This paper presents some critical comments on J J Katz's paper on "The Domino Theory," focusing on some problems with respect to Katz's objections to Quine's rejection of the analytic-synthetic distinction. It is suggested that Katz's abandonment of the Fregean link between sense and reference in order to preserve intensionalism against recent critiques by Putnam and Kripke exposes his account of linguistic meaning to the full force of Quinian scepticism.

GREENWOOD, John D. Kant's Third Antinomy: Agency and Causal Explanation. Int Phil Quart, 30(1), 43-57, Mr 90.

It is argued that Kant failed to resolve an ontological problem generated by the Third Antinomy, and that the conflict between explanations in terms of human agency and causal explanations in terms of ontologically sufficient conditions is an empirical question. Kant's transcendental argument for the universality of the causal principle does not preclude agency explanations. This is because it is not a necessary condition for epistemic experience that events are represented as having ontologically sufficient conditions; it is sufficient that they are represented as having necessary enabling conditions only.

GREENWOOD, John D. The Social Constitution of Action: *Objectivity and Explanation*. Phil Soc Sci, 20(2), 195-207, Je 90.

It is argued in this article that human actions may be said to be socially constituted: as being behavior that is constituted as human action by social relations and by participant agent and collective representations of behavior. In contrast to recent social constructionist accounts, it is argued that the social constitution of action does not pose any threat to the objectivity of classification or explanation in social psychological science. It does mark some significant ontological differences between natural and social psychological phenomena that have implications for the university and generality, but not the adequacy, of explanations of socially constituted human actions.

GREENWOOD, Terry. "Kant on the Modalities of Space" in *Reading Kant*, SCHAPER, Eva (ed), 117-139. Cambridge, Blackwell, 1989.

GREGORY, Ann. Are Women Different and Why are Women Thought to be Different? Theoretical and Methodological Perspectives. J Bus Ethics, 9(4-5), 257-266, Ap-My 90.

The existing literature on gender differences and stereotyping is reviewed in this article. Three theoretical perspectives are discussed: person-centred, organization-centred, and gender context, followed by a review concerning both the findings of the research, a critique of the research methodologies used, and suggestions for future research. The article concludes by suggesting other areas in the field of women in management to which little if any attention has been drawn and recommending some research methodologies which would be applied.

GREGORY, Richard L. "Touching Truth" in *Dismantling Truth: Reality in the PostModern World*, LAWSON, Hilary (ed), 93-100. New York, St Martin's Pr, 1989.

GREISCH, Jean. Du dialogue référentiel au dialogisme transcendantal: L'itinéraire philosophique de Francis Jacques. Rev Metaph Morale, 95(1), 75-93, Ja-Mr 90.

GRIEDER, Alfons. Husserl and the Origin of Geometry. J Brit Soc Phenomenol, 20(3), 277-289, O 89.

GRIER, Philip T (ed). *Dialectic and Contemporary Science*. Lanham, Univ Pr of America, 1989

A critical anthology of articles on the work of Errol E Harris. The articles address his neo-Hegelian philosophy of nature and contemporary science, his commentary on Hegel's logic, his theistic account of the problem of evil, his choice between Hegelian and Kantian ethical theory, a problem of Spinoza interpretation connected with his work, his argument concerning the inevitable failure of representational theories of knowledge, and the ideal of reason in philosophical reflection.

GRIER, Philip T. The End of History, and the Return of History. Owl Minerva, 21(2), 131-144, Spr 90.

GRIESEMER, James R. Modeling in the Museum: On the Role of Remnant Models in the Work of Joseph Grinnell. Biol Phil, 5(1), 3-36, Ja 90.

Accounts of the relation between theories and models in biology concentrate on mathematical models. In this paper I consider the dual role of models as representations of natural systems and as a material basis for theorizing. In order to explicate the dual role, I develop the concept of a remnant model, a material entity made from parts of the natural system(s) under study. I present a case study of an important but neglected naturalist, Joseph Grinnell, to illustrate the extent to which mundane practices in a museum setting constitute theorizing. I speculate that historical and sociological analyses of institutions can play a specific role in the philosophical analysis of model-building strategies.

GRIFFIN, David Ray. "Introduction" in *Varieties of Postmodern Theology*, GRIFFIN, David Ray (ed), 1-7. Albany, SUNY Pr, 1989.

GRIFFIN, David Ray. "Liberation Theology and Postmodern Philosophy: A Response to Cornel West" in *Varieties of Postmodern Theology*, GRIFFIN, David Ray (ed), 129-148. Albany, SUNY Pr, 1989.

GRIFFIN, David Ray. "Postmodern Theology and A/Theology: A Response to Mark C Taylor" in *Varieties of Postmodern Theology*, GRIFFIN, David Ray (ed), 29-61. Albany, SUNY Pr, 1989.

GRIFFIN, David Ray. "Postmodern Theology as Liberation Theology: A Response to Harvey Cox" in *Varieties of Postmodern Theology*, GRIFFIN, David Ray (ed), 81-94. Albany, SUNY Pr, 1989.

GRIFFIN, David Ray and SMITH, Huston. *Primordial Truth and Postmodern Theology*. Albany, SUNY Pr, 1989

GRIFFIN, David Ray (ed) and BEARDSLEE, William A (ed) and HOLLAND, Joe (ed). *Varieties of Postmodern Theology*. Albany, SUNY Pr, 1989

GRIFFIN, Miriam (ed) and BARNES, Jonathan (ed). *Philosophia Togata: Essays on Philosophy and Roman Society*. New York, Clarendon/Oxford Pr, 1989

This volume assembles a selection of papers originally delivered at the seminar on Philosophy and Roman Society in the University of Oxford. The papers, contributed by ancient philosophers, Roman historians and classical scholars, concentrate on the first century BC, a well-documented period in which the interaction of philosophy and Roman life can be examined. There are chapters on such key figures as Posidonius, Antiochus of Ascalon,

Philodemus, Lucretius, Cicero, and Plutarch, as well as general essays on philosophy and politics and philosophy and religion. There is also an analytical bibliography.

GRIFFIN, Miriam. "Philosophy, Politics, and Politicians at Rome" in *Philosophia Togata: Essays on Philosophy and Roman Society*, GRIFFIN, Miriam (ed), 1-37. New York, Clarendon/Oxford Pr, 1989.

GRIFFIN, Robert S and NASH, Robert J. Individualism, Community, and Education: An Exchange of Views. Educ Theor, 40(1), 1-18, Wint 90.

GRIFFITHS, A Phillips. Is Free Will Incompatible with Something or Other? Philosophy, 24, 101-119, 88 Supp.

GRIFFITHS, Morwenna and SMITH, Richard. Standing Alone: Dependence, Independence and Interdependence in the Practice of Education. J Phil Educ, 23(2), 283-293, Wint 89.

Independence—or autonomy—is usually seen as a desirable state of human beings, and, therefore, as a central aim of education. This paper explores the idea that the largely unreflective approval given to independence not only conceals a number of mutually incoherent concepts of independence, but also prevents us from understanding the nature of dependence. We argue that there is a need to reconceptualise both independence (and autonomy) and dependence and that this is an essential part of the educational project of enabling human beings to flourish.

GRIFFITHS, P E. The Degeneration of the Cognitive Theory of Emotions. Phil Psych, 2(3), 297-313, 1989.

The type of cognitive theory of emotion traditionally espoused by philosophers of mind makes two central claims. First, that the occurrence of propositional attitudes is essential to the occurrence of emotions. Second, that the identity of a particular emotional state depends upon the propositional attitudes that it involves. In this paper I try to show that there is little hope of developing a theory of emotion which makes these claims true. I examine the underlying defects of the programme, and show that several recent variants fail to repair these defects. Furthermore, even if such a theory could be developed, it would not achieve many of the things that we look to a theory of emotion for. I argue that philosophers should turn their attention to new and more promising approaches. These have been developed by various of the special sciences, while philosophy has remained enthralled by traditional, propositional attitude psychology.

GRIFFITHS, P E. Modularity, and the Psychoevolutionary Theory of Emotion. Biol Phil, 5(2), 175-196, Ap 90.

It is unreasonable to assume that our prescientific emotion vocabulary embodies all and only those distinctions required for a scientific psychology of emotion. The psychoevolutionary approach to emotion yields an alternative classification of certain emotion phenomena. The new categories are based on a set of evolved adaptive responses, or affect-programs, which are found in all cultures. The triggering of these responses involves a modular system of stimulus appraisal, whose evaluations may conflict with those of higher-level cognitive processes. Whilst the structure of the adaptive responses is innate, the contents of the system which triggers them are largely learnt. The circuits subserving the adaptive responses are probably located in the limbic system. This theory of emotion is directly applicable only to a small sub-domain of the traditional realm of emotion. It can be used, however, to explain the grouping of various other phenomena under the heading of emotion, and to explain various characteristic failings of the prescientific conception of emotion.

GRIFFITHS, Paul J. Why Buddhas Can't Remember Their Previous Lives. Phil East West, 39(4), 449-451, O 89.

This piece argues that, given standard Buddhist definitions of memory (smrti), a fully awakened Buddha cannot have it. Therefore, a fortiori, a Buddha cannot remember its previous lives.

GRIGORAS, Ioan. Alexandru Claudian et la conscience de l'unité de l'esprit et de l'âme (in Romanian). Rev Filosof (Romania), 36(3), 236-239, My-Je 89.

GRIGORIEFF, Serge. Every Recursive Linear Ordering has a Copy in DTIME-SPACE(n,log(n)). J Sym Log, 55(1), 260-276, Mr 90.

GRIMALDI, Nicolás. El arte y el mal. Anu Filosof, 20(2), 9-22, 1987.

GRIMALDI, Nicolas. Religion et philosophie chez Descartes et Malebranche. Arch Phil, 53(2), 229-244, Ap-Je 90.

Although Descartes had discovered all the truths which can be deduced by reason alone, how could we account with the fact that Malebranche had nevertheless to develop a new philosophy? Is it not due to the fact that without faith reason appears unable to solve the problems that it poses? But it is not then in the field of the relationship between religion and philosophy that Malebranche should be distinguished from Descartes, and is it not precisely there that one should look for the origin of his own philosophy?

GRIMALDI, Rosario (trans) and HEIDEGGER, Martin. Hacer mas legible la lectura de los acontecimientos. Rev Filosof (Mexico), 22(66), 297-299, S-D 89.

GRIMES, John A. A Concise Dictionary of Indian Philosophy: Sanskrit Terms Defined in English. Albany, SUNY Pr, 1989

This volume provides a comprehensive dictionary of Indian philosophical terms, providing the terms in both devanagari script and roman transliteration with the translation. If offers special meanings of words used as technical terms within particular philosophical systems. Cross-referencing has been provided and various charts are included that provide information regarding relationships, categories, and source books relevant to individual schools.

GRISÉ, J and LEE-GOSSELIN, H. Are Women Owner-Managers Challenging Our Definitions of Entrepreneurship? An In-Depth Survey. J Bus Ethics, 9(4-5), 423-433, Ap-My 90.

In the Quebec city area, 400 women owner-managers of business in the three industrial sectors answered a detailed questionnaire, and 75 of these subsequently underwent in-depth interviews. The main dimensions explored were the characteristics of the entrepreneurs and their firms, the experience of starting a business, the success criteria used, and their vision for the future of their firms. The results suggest the importance, to these women, of a model of "small and stable business." This is not a transitory phase for their firm: most choose and value such a scale of business, and they seek recognition for what they do. This model seems to represent an innovative adaptation to their professional, social, family and personal demands and challenges our definitions of entrepreneurship and of "serious business."

GRISEZ, Germain and FINNIS, John and BOYLE, Joseph M. Nuclear Deterrence, Morality and Realism. New York, Oxford Univ Pr, 1988

Nuclear deterrence expresses a conditional choice to kill noncombatants, a choice irreconcilable with traditional morality. Having fully surveyed official threats and systems, we examine the crucial conceptual and strategic questions: Why are conditional choices morally decisive? Why can't deterrence be a bluff? Or purely counterforce? We then argue that neither deterrence nor unilateral disarmament can be justified by the other's bad consequences, and that all consequentialist justifications are inevitably incoherent. Exploring the foundations of ethics, we conclude to an ethics of killing similar to common morality's, and try to identify the specific duties of policy makers, military personnel and citizens.

GRISWOLD JR, Charles L. "War, Competition, and Religion" in The Causes of Quarrel: Essays on Peace, War, and Thomas Hobbes, CAWS, Peter (ed), 23-35. Boston, Beacon Pr, 1989.

The problem of the political role of religion is one of the controlling themes of the Enlightenment. A major aspect of the problem concerns religious civil war: how is that type of strife to be minimized? In this paper I look at the 'classical', Platonic solution proposed in Laws X, show its differences with Hobbes's solution in the Leviathan, and then examine the American Enlightenment, where a synthesis of Platonic and Hobbesian elements is proposed (I consider some of the background for that solution as presented by Adam Smith), as well as the philosophical assumptions the American solution commits to.

GRIZE, Jean-Blaise. "To Reason While Speaking" in From Metaphysics to Rhetoric, MEYER, Michel (ed), 37-48. Norwell, Kluwer, 1989.

GROARKE, Leo. Affirmative Action as a Form of Restitution. J Bus Ethics, 9(3), 207-213, Mr 90.

Though the common sense defense of affirmative action (or "employment equity") appeals to principles of restitution, philosophers have tried to defend it in other ways. In contrast, I defend it by appealing to the notion of restitution, arguing (1) that alternative attempts to justify affirmative action fail; and (2) that ordinary affirmative action programs need to be supplemented and amended in keeping with the principles this suggests.

GROARKE, Leo. Greek Scepticism: Anti-Realist Trends in Ancient Thought. Toronto, McGill-Queens U Pr, 1990

The most common interpretation of ancient scepticism maintains that it rejects all belief and is therefore self-defeating and incompatible with life. Some commentators have taken issue with such views, though they have not found a convincing way to reconcile belief with universal epoche. The present book attempts to resolve the difficulty by arguing that the sceptics reject a specifically realist account of truth (aletheia), adopting antirealist notions of belief. Recent scholarship on the sceptics is discussed.

GRONDIN, Deirdre. Research, Myths and Expectations: New Challenges for Management Educators. J Bus Ethics, 9(4-5), 369-372, Ap-My 90.

During the late seventies and early eighties unprecedented numbers of women attempted to "reach the top" of the corporate hierarchies. This paper examines three factors which have handicapped management educators in preparing these women to meet this objective. It also discusses the impact of these factors on research in management education.

GRONDIN, Jean and LAWRENCE, Joseph P (trans). The A Priori from Kant to Schelling. Ideal Stud, 19(3), 202-221, S 89.

The author traces the history of the concept of the A Priori through German Idealism. He contends that the concept was crucial for Kant and Schelling and of minor importance for Hegel. He links it to the Platonic doctrine of recollection, whereby giving Kant's metaphysical concerns their due. His primary contention is that Schelling deepens the notion of the a priori until he discovers that at its heart lies not that which can be rationally constructed, but that which is given prior to any construction, the a priori Unbegreifliche. This is the incomprehensible facticity of Being itself, which cannot be deduced since it is presupposed by any deduction.

GRONDIN, Jean. La conclusion de la Critique de la raison pure. Kantstudien, 81(2), 129-144, 1990.

The purpose of this article is to enquire whether there is a conclusion to Kant's Critique of Pure Reason, that is a concluding answer to the overriding question of the book on the possibility of metaphysics. The article argues there is such a (positive) outcome and that it is to be found in the canon of pure reason.

GRONDIN, Jean. Habermas und das Problem der Individualität. Phil Rundsch, 36(3), 187-205, 1989.

This critical presentation of Habermas's later work (Nachmetaphysisches Denken, 1988) argues that the theory of communicative action rests upon political presuppositions that aren't always spelled out with full clarity. Also questioned is Habermas's notion of necessary idealisations at the root of language. In their most acceptable version they amount to a reactivation of hermeneutics' claim to universality. In all consequence the idea that the theory of communicative action wants to allow and not suppress the free development of individuality should lead to a political theory close to liberalism.

GRONDIN, Jean. L'herméneutique comme science rigoureuse selon Emilio Betti (1890-1968). Arch Phil, 53(2), 177-198, Ap-Je 90.

Pre-Heideggerian hermeneutics has often been seen as an attempt to develop a methodology of the human sciences. If this project goes back to the later 19th century, this hermeneutic methodology of the human sciences was carried through for the first time after Heidegger, and against his ontological conception of interpretation, in the work of the Italian jurist Emilio Betti (1890-1968). This paper will present, on the occasion of his centenary, the main tenets as well as the limits of his hermeneutic theory. The symmetry of Betti's and Gadamer's hermeneutics will be stressed: whereas the jurist Betti finds his paradigm of understanding in the contemplative activity of the philologist, Gadamer, whose formation was mainly philological, takes his inspiration from the juridical model in order to put forward his universal hermeneutics of application.

GROOTENDORST, Rob and VAN EEMEREN, Frans H. Speech Act Conditions as Tools for Reconstructing Argumentative Discourse. Argumentation, 3(4), 367-383, N 89.

According to the pragma-dialectical approach to argumentation, for analysing argumentative discourse, a normative reconstruction is required which encompasses four kinds of transformations. It is explained in this paper how speech act conditions can play a part in carrying out such a reconstruction. It is argued that integrating Searlean insights concerning speech acts with Gricean insights concerning conversational maxims can provide us with the necessary tools. For this, the standard theory of speech acts has to be amended in several respects and the conversational maxims have to be translated into speech act conditions. Making use of the rules for communication thus arrived at, and starting from the distribution of speech acts in a critical discussion as specified in the pragma-dialectical model, it is then demonstrated how indirect speech acts are to be transformed when reconstructing argumentative discourse.

GROSMAN, Brian A. Corporate Loyalty, Does It Have a Future? J Bus Ethics, 8(7), 565-568, Jl 89.

A promotion of concepts of corporate family and employee participation as well as euphemisms which stress employee-employer long-term continuity makes the loss of loyalty flowing from downsizings and mass firings as well as corporate restructurings more difficult both for the employer and employee. The promotion of reciprocal obligations between employer and employee misleads both into a belief system which is to their mutual disadvantage. Corporate semantics that soften employment realities and the implications of dislocation with positive rhetoric increases the sense of failure and guilt on the part of both employer and employee. Unrealistic expectations create hostility. If employment dislocation is seen as part of a continual economic evolution, not shrouded in semantic double-speak, loss of employment no longer becomes an outrageous affront to the dignity of those involved but rather a normal process of economic change and renewal.

GROSSBERG, R. The Classification of Excellent Classes. J Sym Log, 54(4), 1359-1381, D 89.

GROSSMAN, Morris. "Performance and Obligation" in *What is Music?*, ALPERSON, Philip A, 255-281. New York, Haven, 1987.

GROSSMAN, Reinhardt. *The Fourth Way: A Theory of Knowledge.* Bloomington, Indiana Univ Pr, 1990

The author argues that a realistic ontology in regard to perceptual, physical, and mathematical objects can be combined with an empiricistic theory of knowledge. In the first part of the book he shows that the traditional distinction between primary and secondary qualities inevitably leads to idealism. In the second part, he argues against the common view that knowledge of mental states is infallible. In the third part, the author concludes that logic, arithmetic, and set theory concern matters of fact and that we discover these facts empirically.

GROVER, Robinson A. "Hobbes and the Concept of International Law" in *Hobbes: War Among Nations*, AIRAKSINEN, Timo (ed), 79-90. Brookfield, Gower, 1989.

There is a disparity in Hobbes's treatment of individuals and nations in the state of nature. Hobbes asserts that nations are currently in a state of war with each other, as are individuals in the state of nature. A careful analysis of his writings reveals few differences in his treatment of individuals and nations. In theory, Hobbes should judge both conditions equally harshly, but he does not recommend an absolute sovereign be placed over nations as he does for individuals. The reason for this difference seems to lie in Hobbes's historical antecedents, not in his philosophical arguments.

GRUBER, David F. "Foucault and Theory: Genealogical Critiques of the Subject" in *The Question of the Other: Essays in Contemporary Continental Philosophy*, DALLERY, Arleen B (ed), 189-196. Albany, SUNY Pr, 1989.

Attempts to utilize Foucault's genealogical investigations of the modern forms of subjectivity as a revitalization of theory too easily overlook the linkages between the theoretical mentality and the very assumptions of subjectivity that Foucault's efforts put into question. This paper briefly traces the ways in which theory constitutes its objects and subjects rather than simply observing that which it discovers already existing or merely aiding in their historical emergence. Genealogical emphases on these processes of production and on the interrogation of concrete subjectivities should be sustained against our inclinations to return to theory that presents itself as safely, passively reflective.

GRUBER, David F. Foucault's Critique of the Liberal Individual. J Phil, 86(11), 615-621, N 89.

Foucault's genealogies of the practices of constituting recent concrete individualities challenge liberalism's arrogance that its individuality is necessary for social criticism. In the wake of liberalism we find not autonomous individuals but the fractured, useful but docile individuals of the disciplines and the human sciences. Liberalism is not irrelevant but is fully implicated; its rhetoric of political and judicial rights of individuals is compliantly deferential to the disciplinary apparatus. Critical thinking which wishes only to revitalize liberalism's individuality is dismally futile, repeating its complicity. Critical thinking should not seek to emancipate our individuality, but to liberate us from our individuality.

GRUENGARD, Ora (ed) and DASCAL, Marcelo (ed). *Knowledge and Politics.* Boulder, Westview Pr, 1988

The links between the political and epistemological theories of thirteen philosophers, ranging from Aristotle and Hobbes to Habermas and Feyerabend, are examined in self-contained essays specially written for this book. The aim was to elucidate the nature of the connections—if any—between the doctrines held by the same thinker in two traditionally different philosophical disciplines. The main general finding was that such connections are neither strictly logical nor merely circumstantial. They rather have a variety of 'strategical' rationales. The introductory essay classifies, analyzes, and exemplifies the kinds of 'strategies of connection' discernible in the essays.

GRUGAN, Arthur A. Heidegger: Preparing to Read Hölderlin's *Germanien*. Res Phenomenol, 19, 139-167, 1989.

GRÜNBAUM, Adolf. The Pseudo-Problem of Creation in Physical Cosmology. Epistemologia, 12(1), 3-31, Ja-Je 89.

According to some cosmologists, the big bang cosmogony and even the (now largely defunct) steady-state theory pose a *scientifically insoluble*

problem of matter-energy creation. But I argue that the genuine problem of the origin of matter-energy or of the universe has been fallaciously transmuted into the pseudo-problem of creation by an external cause. A fortiori, it emerges that the initial "true" and "false" so-called "vacuum" states of quantum cosmology do *not* vindicate biblical divine creation ex nihilo at all.

GRÜNBERG, Ludwig. "Are Values Objective?" in *Inquiries into Values: The Inaugural Session of the International Society for Value Inquiry*, LEE, Sander H, 219-227. Lewiston, Mellen Pr, 1989.

GRUND, Cynthia. Metaphors, Counterfactuals and Music. Acta Phil Fennica, 43, 28-53, 1988.

The aim of this article is to provide some perspectives on metaphor by treating it in a manner reminiscent of and inspired by David Lewis's treatment of fiction in his article "Truth in Fiction." Important groundwork for the program is provided by Alan Tormey in his paper "Metaphors and Counterfactuals." In conclusion, it is suggested that the resultant approach captures some of the distinctions needed in addressing the truth or falsity of certain statements about music.

GRÜNEWALD, Bernward. Justification des normes: transcendantale ou pragmatique? Rev Theol Phil, 122(1), 1-14, 1990.

La première partie de cet article analyse les propositions centrales de la pragmatique transcendantale pour la justification des normes; ces propositions reposent sur l'affirmation de l'"incontournabilité" de la situation d'argumentation. On y discute cette "incontournabilité". La deuxième partie cherche à corriger la position du problème tout en conservant les avantages de la conception pragmatique transcendantale. On y remplace la situation d'argumentation par un acte vraiment "incontournable", à savoir notre conscience pratique (ou notre vouloir en général), qui révèle la volonté générale comme condition de possibilité de cette conscience pratique.

GRÜNFELD, Joseph. *Conceptual Relevance.* Atlantic Highlands, Gruner, 1989

This work, a phenomenological look at the nature of reality, particularly as gleaned from scientific investigation, examines several possible relations of our (inherently linguistic) concepts of the world with the world as independently existing. The criteria of consistency and utility define the value of our science, and the question of objectivity, applied both to science and the world, is seen as a chief assessing factor. (staff)

GRÜNING, Thomas. Müntzer contra Luther: Der philosophische Gehalt des theologischen Konflikts. Deut Z Phil, 37(12), 1093-1100, 1989.

Der philosophische Gehalt des theologischen Konflikts zwischen Luther und Müntzer besteht in der kontroversen Diskussion der Frage: Wie ist menschliche Wesensverwirklichung möglich? Präziser: In welchem Verhältnis stehen weltliche Taten (Werke) und christlicher Glauben? Das europäische Bürgertum fand in Luthers Theologie einen Weg, christliches Armutsgebot und Nächstenliebe mit bürgerlichem Gewinnstreben und Konkurrenzkampf zu harmonisieren. Müntzers Theologie schliesst dies radikal aus.

GRUSON, Pascale. Préoccupations éthiques aux Etats-Unis: la "Business Ethics". Etudes, 371(4), 327-337, O 89.

Since economic growth is nowadays the main challenge liberal societies have to face, corporations' responsibilities and powers have been increasing. This is the starting point for research in business ethics. To be efficient, corporations have to be free from heavy taxes. The counterpart of the so-called "deregulation policy" in the US has been drastic cuts in welfare state programs. This may seem rather paradoxical in a society so proud of democratic achievements. But corporations may help to overcome such a paradox. As concerns applied ethics, the scope of business ethics is clear. Economic growth is the key point for further improvement in social justice. (edited)

GRYGIEL, Joanna. Absolutely Independent Axiomatizations for Countable Sets in Classical Logic. Stud Log, 48(1), 77-84, Mr 89.

The notion of absolute independence, considered in this paper, has a clear algebraic meaning and is a strengthening of the usual notion of logical independence. We prove that any consistent and countable set in classical propositional logic has an absolutely independent axiomatization.

GRZEGORCZYK, Andrzej. Friedenshandlungen und die ethischen Stellungen (in Polish). Stud Phil Christ, 25(1), 141-159, 1989.

Man kann das Kriegsübel als eine Lebensvernichtung und eine Zerstörung der anderen Humanwerte bestimmen. Das Friedensgut bestimmen wir als eine gegenseitige Hilfe unter den Menschen beim Kommen zu den Werten. Die Friedenshandlungen betreffen das Kriegsübelsvermeiden und das Friedensgutverstärken. Diese Handlungen können mit der utilitaristischen, solidaristischen oder absolutistischen Ethik begründet werden. Viele von der positiven Handlungen können mit jeder von den oben erwähnten Versionen des ethischen Angagierens begründet werden. Die absolutische Begründung scheint es aber als die, die dem Christentumsgeite am meisten entspricht.

GRZEGORCZYK, Andrzej and GOLEBIOWSKI, Marek (trans). New Social Self-Steering. Dialec Hum, 15(3-4), 251-254, Sum-Autumn 88.

Society may be defined as a kind of potentially self-steering social group. In the mechanism of this self-steering the role of public opinion constantly increases in our century. A constant development of the awareness of universal values impacts the decision makers by means of different forms of social debate.

GRZEGORCZYK, Andrzej and PETROWICZ, Lech (trans). The Philosophy of Fate as the Basis of Education for Peace. Dialec Hum, 14(1), 167-172, Wint 87.

A vision of mankind grappling with conditions that have been imposed upon it, gives one a sense of community of human fate. This vision enables us for the reconciliation with those who gravely ruined our life (like Nazis or communists in recent times). The experience of the 20th century was an experience of some extremeness. It reflects the dialectic of the extremeness of our thinking. But it culminates in very fruitful self-criticisms of the end of our century.

GUANGWU, Zhao and NAN-SHENG, Huang. "On the Relationship Between Man and Nature" in *Man and Nature: The Chinese Tradition and the Future*, TANG, Yi-Jie (ed), 103-112. Lanham, Univ Pr of America, 1989.

GUARDA, Victor and SOMMERMEIER, Rolf (trans). How Does the Child Benefit from "Philosophy for Children"? Thinking, 6(3), 30-31, 1986.

GUARIGLIA, Osvaldo. El principio de universalización y la razón práctica (1a parte). Critica, 20(60), 31-54, D 88.

Regarding the universalization principle and its applications to specific cases, there has been a tendency to intermingle the principle with universalizability criteria. In this paper, I show a *scheme* of the universalization principle in order to clarify its logical structure and the concepts that must be specified in each case so that the principle can be applied significantly. The analysis of the elements involved in moral discourse will show to what extent the significative application of the universalization scheme presupposes a dense weave of semantic, pragmatic and logico-practico rules that constitute the first level from which moral judgments arise.

GUARIGLIA, Osvaldo. El principio de universalización y la razón práctica (2a parte). Critica, 21(61), 3-41, Ap 89.

In this paper, I will examine the function of the universalizability principle in the field of moral argumentation and its main role as *ultimate rule of practical reason*, to which it grants its particular form of objectivity. As an alternative to the contemporary crisis of the concept of "practical reason," I shall try to offer an examination of the irreplaceable contribution of the universalization principal to a reconstructive notion of practical reason as ultimate ground for valid moral judgments.

GUARINO, Thomas. Revelation and Foundationalism: Towards Hermeneutical and Ontological Appropriateness. Mod Theol, 6(3), 221-235, Ap 90.

Postmodern philosophy, characterized by words such as fissure, incommensurability and difference, reflects decentered and nonfoundationalist thinking. To what extent does postmodernism affect the concept of Revelation which stresses the integrity, identity and continuity of faith and doctrine? This article examines traditional ontological and hermeneutical strategies, delineates the challenges posed by Heidegger and Gadamer, and concludes with a brief analysis of the 'phenomenological' hermeneutics of David Tracy and the "radical" hermeneutics of John Caputo. The author suggests that the interplay of presence and absence, called for in varying degrees by postmodern thinkers, should be more fully incorporated into contemporary theories of revelation.

GUASTINI, Riccardo. Sulla validità della costituzione dal punto di vista del positivismo giuridico. Riv Int Filosof Diritto, 66(3), 424-436, Jl-S 89.

Is constitution valid from the viewpoint of legal positivism? It depends on the concepts of 'validity'. Three versions of positivism are distinguished, each one involving a different concept. (1) In normative theory 'validity' means identifiability according to meta-rules of recognition; hence constitution is neither valid nor invalid, lacking any meta-rule governing its production and/or contents. (2) In realistic jurisprudence 'validity' means effectiveness; hence the validity of constitution is a matter of empirical social science. (3) In legalistic (quasi-positivistic) meta-ethics 'validity' means binding force; hence the validity of constitution amounts to the evaluative problem of

political obligation.

GUCCIONE, Salvatore and GERLA, Giangiacomo. On the Logical Structure of Verisimilitude. Epistemologia, 12(1), 161-165, Ja-Je 89.

As is well known, Popper's comparative theory of verisimilitude meets with several obstacles. This paper is an attempt to bypass such obstacles by a suitable modification of Popper's definition of falsity contents and truth contents.

GUEN, Carroll. Gadamer, Objectivity, and the Ontology of Belonging. Dialogue (Canada), 28(4), 589-608, 1989.

GUENANCIA, Pierre. Dieu, le roi et les sujets. Arch Phil, 53(3), 403-420, Jl-S 90.

In two letters (April 15th 1630 and January 1646) Descartes compares God to a king who institutes laws in his kingdom or gives an order to his subjects. If it's possible to compare the way God establishes freely the truths and the king his laws, does it enable us to say that men are to God what his subjects are to their king? The Cartesian doctrine of freedom and of the similarity between God and man is opposed to the fact that these two relations—essentially different—should constitute an analogy. But, more generally, to what extent do the forms of imagination allow us to represent the notions of understanding?

GUERIN, Bernard. Gibson, Skinner and Perceptual Responses. Behavior Phil, 18(1), 43-54, Spr-Sum 90.

The theoretical proposals of the present paper derive from the assumptions of both Gibson (1966, 1979) and Skinner (1953, 1974). Both these authors have proposed new ways to think and talk about psychology which have not yet become dominant. To talk about psychology in their way requires changing some of our most basic assumptions. The first aim of this paper is to highlight some of their common assumptions. It will be shown that there are remarkable similarities between some of the views of Gibson and Skinner (cf. Costall, 1984). Even when one author has not fully discussed a topic, the other's position is often implied nonetheless. The second aim of the paper is to draw out further implications from their work. The result is a coherent view of perception which includes new ways of thinking about stimuli and memory. It is not a view, however, that Gibson or Skinner might fully agree with since it attempts to go beyond their views. The paper will first deal with perception and the concept of "stimuli," and then show the implications of this for memory and cognition.

GUERIN, Ignasi Miralbell. La revolución semántica de Guillermo de Ockham. Anu Filosof, 21(1), 35-50, 1988.

GUERLAC, Rita (trans) and BAUDRY, Leon. *The Quarrel over Future Contingents (Louvain 1465-1475)*. Norwell, Kluwer, 1989

GUEST, Gérard. Anabase—Acheminement vers l'amont de la "présupposition"—Le chemin de *Sein und Zeit*. Heidegger Stud, 5, 79-133, 1989.

GUIBOURG, Ricardo A and GÓMEZ, Astrid C. Tienen significado las contradicciones? Analisis Filosof, 9(1), 77-91, My 89.

Should we interpret meaning as a certain real entity expressed by words? Or rather as a property of words, which may or may not consist in a relationship between them and entities that are alien to them? In the first case we are led to conclude that contradictions are meaningless. But if this is so, the same must apply to tautologies, which implies a negation of the logical structure of language. In the second case we become aware of a disturbing similarity between the meaningfulness of contradictions and the meaninglessness of the expressions Russell calls syntactically impossible. The danger implied is, then, similar to that of the previous alternative. A pragmatic solution consists in introducing an idea resembling the mathematical notion of *limit*: the contradiction is the limit of the proposition when its designation approaches infinity; the tautology represents the opposite limit, when its designation approaches zero. (edited)

GUIGNON, Charles. Philosophy after Wittgenstein and Heidegger. Phil Phenomenol Res, 50(4), 649-672, Je 90.

The question is: how does the thought of Heidegger and the later Wittgenstein lead to such different postfoundationalist views as those of Charles Taylor and Richard Rorty? I consider how the "phenomenology of everyday life" in Heidegger and Wittgenstein shows (1) that understanding is dependent on a social background of meanings, and (2) that the sense of reality embodied in our actions is prestructured by language. This picture of everydayness is holistic, antidualistic and nonfoundationalist. I conclude by focusing the debate between Taylor and Rorty, suggesting that Taylor's reading of our current philosophical situation is more viable.

GUIGNON, Charles. Truth as Disclosure: Art, Language, History. S J Phil, SUPP(28), 105-120, 1989.

Throughout his life, Heidegger tried to formulate a conception of truth as the play of disclosure and concealment, and an "expressivist" ontology which treats Being as an event of coming-into-presence. I trace Heidegger's accounts of how truth emerges in what I call "exemplary beings"—Dasein in the early writings; the artwork or "the thing" in the later works. Unifying strands in these accounts are (1) a constitutive view of language as preshaping what shows up, and (2) a vision of history as a future-directed happening realized through the actions of future generations.

GUILLAMAUD, Patrice. L'autre et l'immanence. Rev Metaph Morale, 94(2), 251-272, Ap-Je 89.

Although there seems to be a contradiction between Michel Henry's philosophy considered as an ontology of sheer immanence and Emmanuel Lévinas's viewed as a metaphysics of absolute transcendence or radical otherness, we are attempting to bring out the similarity of philosophical thought processes at hand in both outlooks. We intend to show that, in taking up the same set of themes, they represent a similar effort to get away from the western monism of ontological manifestation thought of as both representation and intention, and to achieve a synthesis between metaphysics and phenomenology.

GUILLAMAUD, Patrice. L'indétermination, la détermination et la relation: Les trois essences de l'être. Rev Phil Louvain, 87(76), 427-469, Ag 89.

Whereas monist ontologies subsume indeterminacy, determination and relation under one single fundamental essence, we have put forward the speculative hypothesis, that indeed indeterminacy, determination and relation are in themselves three different essences or absolute spheres of Being. On the ground of this hypothesis, and in the course of studying some of today's ontologies, we have established these three essences to be ontologically, coexistentially and as opposed to immanence, the three phenomenological essences of transcendence, absolutely separate from one another. This can be expressed in concrete terms as consciousness as otherness, thing, relation from the consciousness to nature.

GUIN, Philip. A Bold Adventure. Thinking, 8(2), 7-8, 1989.

GUITIÉRREZ, Pedro Stepanenko. La concepción berkelayana del yo. Analisis Filosof, 6(1), 45-54, My 86.

GULIAN, C I. Le sens du nihilisme ou l'axiologie de la crise chez Nietzsche (in Romanian). Rev Filosof (Romania), 36(3), 279-285, My-Je 89.

GUNDERSON, Martin. Justifying a Principle of Informed Consent: A Case Study in Autonomy-Based Ethics. Pub Affairs Quart, 4(3), 249-265, Jl 90.

GÜNTHER, Klaus. Impartial Application of Moral and Legal Norms: A Contribution to Discourse Ethics. Phil Soc Crit, 14(3-4), 425-432, 1988.

GÜNTHER, Klaus. A Normative Conception of Coherence for a Discursive Theory of Legal Justification. Ratio Juris, 2(2), 155-166, Jl 89.

The author introduces a normative conception of coherence, derived from a pragmatic interpretation of the application of norms to concrete cases. A distinction is made between the justification of a norm and its application. In the case of moral norms, justification and application can be analysed as two different discursive procedures which give rise to different aspects of the principle of impartiality. Impartial justification requires a procedure by which all interests concerned are taken into account whereas impartial application requires a procedure where all features of a situation are considered. The complete description of a concrete case makes necessary a coherent interpretation of all the valid norms which are prima facie applicable. This requirement of an ideal coherent system of norms is restricted to interpretive "paradigms" in the case of legal norms, because it is necessary to produce singular judgments under the restrictive conditions of scarce time and incomplete knowledge.

GUOZHENG, Lin and SONGXING, Su. Integrative Thinking Is the Essential Characteristic of Creative Thinking. Chin Stud Phil, 21(2), 74-93, Wint 89-90.

At home and abroad, in recent theoretical studies concerning the nature of creative thought, the theory of divergent thinking has played an extremely important role. This essay proposes some disagreements with this traditional opinion; for we believe that it is integrative thinking that is the essence of creative thought. Our reason is this: Creative thought is realized through cognitive activity, and cognitive activity is always, continuously, in a process of combination. (edited)

GUR-ARYE, Miriam. "Comment: A Theory of Complicity" in *Issues in Contemporary Legal Philosophy: The Influence of H L A Hart*, GAVISON, Ruth (ed), 304-310. New York, Clarendon/Oxford Pr, 1987.

This comment demonstrates that the two main assumptions on which Kadish's article "A Theory of Complicity" are based ought not necessarily to be considered part of the law of complicity. First, we may need the doctrine of complicity, and not that of causation, even where the actions of the principal

offender are not fully volitional; that is, even where the principal is not criminally liable. Second, to hold one person liable, under the doctrine of complicity, for the volitional actions of another who is criminally liable, does not require that "his liability must rest on the liability of the other," as Kadish believes.

GURTLER, Gary M. Plotinus and Byzantine Aesthetics. Mod Sch, 66(4), 275-284, My 89.

A stronger case can be made for Plotinus's influence on Byzantine art than did A Grabar in the 1940s. It is based on the continuity of Plotinus with his Greek predecessors, especially his perceptual realism and theory of the image. Plotinus is not the source of inverse perspective, as Grabar claimed, but of the world view behind it. Thus different artistic expressions, classical Greek and Byzantine, share the same intellectual grounding, through Plotinus's mediation.

GURWITSCH, Aron and SEEBOHM, Thomas M (ed). *Kants Theorie des Verstandes*. Norwell, Kluwer, 1990

The volume presents: (1) "Kant's Transcendental Deduction in Leibnizian Perspective"—draft of a German book; (2) "The Concept of Consciousness in Kant and Husserl"—German essay published first Kant-Studien 1964; (3) "A Study of Kant's Conception of the Human Mind"—unpublished English outline of a research project; (4) "The Leibniz in Kant"—lecture, edited by L Embree. The unpublished material is taken from the Archives of the Center for Advanced Research in Phenomenology. Preface and an appendix deal with the general development of Gurwitsch's thoughts on Kant and his philosophy.

GUSTAFSON, James M. Moral Discourse About Medicine: A Variety of Forms. J Med Phil, 15(2), 125-142, Ap 90.

Moral evaluations of medical research and care focus on different issues, e.g., clinical choices, public policy and cultural values. Technical ethical concepts and arguments do not suffice for all issues. Analysis of the literature suggests that, in addition to ethical discourse, prophetic, narrative, and policy discourse function morally. The article characterizes each of these forms, and suggests the insufficiency of each if it is taken to be the only mode of analysis.

GUSTAFSSON, Bengt and TIBELL, Gunnar. Critics of Science and Research Ethics in Sweden. Phil Soc Act, 15(3-4), 59-74, Jl-D 89.

GUTIÉRREZ, Claudio. La sociedad en la perspectiva informática o existe una sociología de los computadores? Rev Filosof (Costa Rica), 26, 33-40, D 88.

The advent of AI has made epistemology an empirical science. The advent of distributed computing is making computer science one of the "soft" sciences. The era of the unerring computer is over: communication problems in distributed computing have created the fallible computer, which errs exactly for the same causes as the human brain: "Errare complexum est." Computer science is using social science models to solve networking problems. A "boomerang effect" may benefit the social sciences.

GUTIÉRREZ, Gilberto. La decisión moral: principios universales, reglas generales y casos particulares. Rev Filosof (Spain), 1, 127-155, 1987-88.

The whole point of moral reasoning is to reach a personal decision in the particular case. But this process must not be conceived of as one of applying the rules of a code by way of deduction. Particular cases cannot be subsumed under rules in the way conclusions are driven under premisses. As opposed to acting on principles, talk of abiding by rules overlooks the role of risk-taking and creativity in moral decisions. The 'codicial' model of practical reasoning misrepresents the true nature of rationality, autonomy and freedom in moral agency.

GUTTING, Gary. *Michel Foucault's Archaeology of Scientific Reason*. New York, Cambridge Univ Pr, 1989

GUYER, Paul. Kant's Conception of Empirical Law—I. Aris Soc, SUPP 64, 221-242, 1990.

GUYER, Paul. Reason and Reflective Judgement: Kant on the Significance of Systematicity. Nous, 24(1), 17-43, Mr 90.

GUYER, Paul. "The Rehabilitation of Transcendental Idealism?" in *Reading Kant*, SCHAPER, Eva (ed), 140-167. Cambridge, Blackwell, 1989.

HAAKONSSEN, Knud. Natural Law and the Scottish Enlightenment. Man Nature, 4, 47-80, 1985.

The paper provides a comprehensive survey of the spread through Europe of Protestant natural law doctrine from Grotius and Pufendorf to the middle of the eighteenth century and outlines the complexity of this doctrine. Special attention is paid to such concepts as 'natural law', 'obligation', 'natural rights', 'perfect/imperfect rights', and 'justice'. It is argued that differences over these issues among the natural lawyers were continued into the moral philosophy of the Scottish Enlightenment.

HAAPARANTA, Leila. Frege's Doctrine of Being. Acta Phil Fennica, 39, 1-182, 1985.

This work seeks to find out why Frege distinguished between identity, predication, two concepts of existence, and class-inclusion in his *Begriffsschrift*. An adequate answer calls for a philosophical reconstruction of his notation. The interpretational framework is based on the observation that Frege's logic was meant to be a Leibnizian universal language, and the hypothesis that Frege relied on Kant's epistemological doctrines. The conclusion is that Frege's Kantianism led him to distinguish objects in themselves from objects as we know them and that this very aim also gave rise to the different formalizations for the different meanings of 'is' in *Begriffsschrift*.

HAAR, Michel. Heidegger and the God of Hölderlin. Res Phenomenol, 19, 89-100, 1989.

HAAR, Michel. Le jeu de Nietzsche dans Derrida. Rev Phil Fr, 180(2), 207-227, Ap-Je 90.

HAAR, Michel. The Question of Human Freedom in the Later Heidegger. S J Phil, SUPP(28), 1-16, 1989.

HABART, Karol. On Absoluteness. Z Math Log, 35(5), 469-480, 1989.

Absoluteness of formulas will be tried to be studied as a condition on constants of set theory as for some sense of real existence, i.e., as a distinction between "obscure" and "less obscure" ones. In the case of theories this distinction corresponds with the possibility to have a Platonistic approach to this theory in contrast to the common formalistic one. In this sense first- and second-order arithmetic will be compared.

HABERMAS, Gary R. Resurrection Claims in Non-Christian Religions. Relig Stud, 25(2), 167-177, Je 89.

The chief purpose of this article is to investigate several non-Christian religious claims that certain historical rabbis, prophets, gurus or 'messiahs' rose from the dead. Can it be ascertained if any of these teachings has a historical basis? It is concluded that none of these specific claims can be established by historical or other critical methodology. For example, there is a plethora of naturalistic alternative theories which could possibly apply to these cases. Thus, there is a distinct difference between a claim to be resurrected and the establishing of such on critical grounds.

HABERMAS, Jürgen and FERRY, Jean-Marc. Interview with Jürgen Habermas: Ethics, Politics and History. Phil Soc Crit, 14(3-4), 433-439, 1988.

HABERMAS, Jürgen and SEIDMAN, Steven (ed). *Jürgen Habermas on Society and Politics: A Reader*. Boston, Beacon Pr, 1989

For more than three decades Habermas has attempted to supply foundations for a reconstructed critical social theory that provides a critical analysis of modernity. This anthology brings together in one volume his most important writings on society, the state and social theory.

HABERMAS, Jürgen. Justice and Solidarity: On the Discussion Concerning "Stage 6". Phil Forum, 21(1-2), 32-52, Fall-Wint 89-90.

HABERMAS, Jürgen and LENHARDT, Christian (trans) and WEBER NICHOLSEN, Shierry (trans). *Moral Consciousness and Communicative Action*. Cambridge, MIT Pr, 1990

HABERMAS, Jürgen. Towards a Communication-Concept of Rational Collective Will-Formation: A Thought-Experiment. Ratio Juris, 2(2), 144-154, Jl 89.

Contractarian theories are meant to settle the issue of when political authority meets the conditions of rational legitimacy. The author addresses the same issue, but using different premises and a different conceptual frame. He takes as his point of departure the two basic problems which rational collective will-formation refers to—conflict-resolution and goal attainment. He then introduces the codes of law and power, with which such will-formation can be institutionalized. The legitimation gap that then still remains open can be filled by a practical reason which is not limited simply to morality but also permeates the procedures of law application, policy-formation and legislation. These preliminary considerations remain within the limits of a thought-experiment.

HABIB, M A R. The Prayers of Childhood: T S Eliot's Manuscripts on Kant. J Hist Ideas, 51(1), 93-113, Ja-Mr 90.

This paper analyses three hitherto undiscovered manuscripts on Kant, written by T S Eliot while a graduate student at Harvard. The paper examines Eliot's comparison of the categories of Plato, Aristotle and Kant; his attack on Herbert Spencer's positivism and agnosticism, and his rejection of Kant's ethics. The paper yields these conclusions: Eliot's view of Kant informed his ideas on Bradley. It is in the treatment of Kant, rather than Bradley, that Eliot's arguments extend to subjects which retained his lifelong interest (ethics, religion, humanism). Finally, the Kant manuscripts clarify two

contradicting attitudes, classical and romantic, in Eliot's work.

HABSCHEID, Walter J. "Zur Philosophie des Zivilprozessrechts, insbesondere zum Prinzip der Fairness" in *Agora: Zu Ehren von Rudolph Berlinger*, BERLINGER, Rudolph (and other eds), 293-306. Amsterdam, Rodopi, 1988.

The paper argues that civil procedural law is more than a collection of technical legal rules, that it aims at the realisation of substantive justice, a philosophy which is inherent in its institutions. One of the principles governing civil procedure is the rule of fairness, "the primary virtue of all social institutions" (Rawls).

HACKER, P M S and BAKER, G P. The Last Ditch. Phil Quart, 39(157), 471-477, O 89.

HACKER, P M S and BAKER, G P. Malcolm on Language and Rules. Philosophy, 65(252), 167-179, Ap 90.

HACKETT, Jeremiah. "Averroes and Roger Bacon on the Harmony of Religion and Philosophy" in *A Straight Path: Studies in Medieval Philosophy and Culture*, LINK-SALINGER, Ruth (ed), 98-112. Washington, Cath Univ Amer Pr, 1988.

The paper argues that Roger Bacon's *Opus maius* fulfills the same purpose in the West as Averroes' *The Decisive Treatise* did in the World of Islam. Both works defend the uses of demonstrative argument in religious discourse. An account is given of the manner in which both Averroes and Bacon present the role of dialectical, demonstrative and rhetorical argument. First, there is an outline of Averroes' teaching in *The Decisive Treatise*. This is followed by an account of scientific knowledge in Bacon's *Opus maius*. It ends with an account of Averroes as a source for Bacon's moral philosophy.

HACKING, Ian. Extragalactic Reality: The Case of Gravitational Lensing. Phil Sci, 56(4), 555-581, D 89.

My *Representing and Intervening* (1983) concludes with what it calls an experimental argument for scientific realism about entities. The argument is evidently inapplicable to extragalactic astrophysics, but leaves open the possibility that there might be other grounds for scientific realism in that domain. Here I argue for antirealism in astrophysics, although not for any particular kind of antirealism. The argument is conducted by a detailed examination of some current research. It parallels the last chapter of (1983). Both represent the methodological opinion that abstract or semantic realism/antirealism debates are empty, and typically lead to confused or wrong conclusions because they pay so little attention to the details of a science.

HACKLER, Chris (ed) and MOSELEY, Ray (ed) and VAWTER, Dorothy E (ed). *Advance Directives in Medicine*. New York, Praeger, 1989

HADDAD, Labib and MORILLON, Marianne. L'axiome de normalité pour les espaces totalement ordonnés. J Sym Log, 55(1), 277-283, Mr 90.

We show that the following property (LN) holds in the basic Cohen model as sketched by Jech: The order topology of any linearly ordered set is normal. This proves the independence of the axiom of choice from LN in ZF, and thus settles a question raised by G Birkhoff (1940) which was partly answered by van Douwen (1985).

HADEN, N Karl. Of Paradigms, Saints and Individuals: The Question of Authenticity. Dialogue (PST), 32(1), 7-14, O 89.

Amidst the incommensurability of modern moral theories, the prospects of founding an ethical theory on the basis of a paradigmatic individual is one of the most promising features of virtue ethics. But what kind of person qualifies as a moral paradigm? In this essay special attention is given to the concept of sainthood in relation to a dilemma posed in recent literature: will one be moral or authentic? *Contra* the position that authenticity entails psychological egoism, the author maintains that authenticity is a necessary condition of sainthood.

HADOT, Pierre and DAVIDSON, Arnold (trans) and WISSING, Paula (trans). Forms of Life and Forms of Discourse in Ancient Philosophy. Crit Inquiry, 16(3), 483-505, Spr 90.

Dans cette leçon inaugurale de la chaire d'Histoire de la pensée hellénistique et romaine, au Collège de France (Paris), l'auteur se propose de décrire la philosophie antique, non pas du point de vue de l'histoire des doctrines, mais comme un phénomène social et spirituel, comme une quête de la sagesse qui provoque une rupture entre le philosophe et le "quotidien". Cette approche concrète du phénomène philosophique permet aussi d'aborder les oeuvres philosophiques de l'Antiquité avec une méthodologie nouvelle, notamment en considérant que leur structure et leur contenu sont étroitement liés à des conduites orales.

HADREAS, Peter. Money: A Speech Act Analysis. J Soc Phil, 20(3), 115-129, Wint 89.

The thesis of this paper is that the use of money depends upon a set of linguistic commitments. The linguistic commitments implied in the use of money are uncovered through speech-act theory. Speech-act theory shows that the use of money demands the maintenance of a patchwork of promissory relations which, in turn, are grounded upon varieties of trust. This analysis of money illuminates the inter-subjective bonds which successful fiscal practices depend upon and suggests what is elemental to their repair.

HAEFFNER, Gerd. Heidegger als fragender Denker und als Denker der Frage. Bijdragen, 2, 157-171, 1990.

HAFT-VAN REES, M Agnes. Conversation, Relevance, and Argumentation. Argumentation, 3(4), 385-393, N 89.

This paper deals with the explanation the maxim of relevance provides for the way utterances in argumentative discourse follow each other in an orderly and coherent fashion. Several senses are distinguished in which utterances can be considered relevant. It is argued that an utterance can be considered relevant as an interactional act, as an illocutionary act, as a propositional act, and as an elocutionary act. These four kinds of relevance manifest the rational organization of discourse, which is aimed at bringing about mutual alignment between the participants, enabling them jointing to work out certain interactional outcomes that are acceptable to both of them.

HAGBERG, Garry. Artistic Intention and Mental Image. J Aes Educ, 22(3), 63-75, Fall 88.

HAGE, Jerald and KRAFT, Kenneth L. Strategy, Social Responsibility and Implementation. J Bus Ethics, 9(1), 11-19, Ja 90.

This paper correlates community service goals from 82 business firms with various organizational characteristics, including goals, niches, structure, context, and performance. The results demonstrate that community-service goals are positively correlated with prestige goals, assets goals, superior-design niche, net assets size, and performance on income to net assets. Community-service goals, however, were not significantly correlated with profit goals, low-price niche, multiplicity of outputs, workflow continuity, qualifications, or centralization, as expected.

HAGEN, Joel B. Research Perspectives and the Anomalous Status of Modern Ecology. Biol Phil, 4(4), 433-455, O 89.

Ecology has often been characterized as an "immature" scientific discipline. This paper explores some of the sources of this alleged immaturity. I argue that the perception of immaturity results primarily from the fact that historically ecologists have based their work upon two very different approaches to research.

HAGENDIJK, R and AMSTERDAMSKA, Olga. De nieuwe zekerheden van het hedendaags wetenschapsonderzoek. Kennis Methode, 14(1), 60-83, 1990.

By rejecting old certainties about scientific rationalism and replacing them with the idea that scientific knowledge is a contingent outcome of social interaction, the constructivist theories of science have demolished the traditional fact/value distinction that underpinned most studies of the social and political controversies involving science and technology. In their analyses of such controversies, these new approaches raise new questions about issues which have not been debated earlier and introduce new sociological certainties to replace the old epistemological ones. The paper argues that because the various versions of constructivism—the strong programme, the micro-constructivism of Karin Knorr-Cetina, and the translation approach of Bruno Latour—are based on substantially different sociological assumptions, their ability to contribute to public discussions about science differs profoundly. (edited)

HAGER, Fritz-Peter. Wesen, Freiheit und Bildung des Menschen. Berne, Haupt, 1989

Das Buch stellt anhand von herausragenden Beispielen aus der Geschichte des europäischen Erziehungs- und Bildungsdenkens dar, wie die zentrale Frage nach dem Sinn der Bildung und dem Ziel der Erziehung auf der Grundlage eines philosophischen Menschenbildes, welches das Wesen und die Freiheit des Menschen aufzeigt, beantwortet worden ist und beantwortet werden kann. Schwerpunkte der Untersuchung sind Platons Philosophie der Paideia und ihre Nachwirkung in der Geschichte der Pädogogik, die Aufklärungsphilosophie des 17. und 18. Jahrhunderts und die Existenzphilosophie des 20. Jahrhunderts mit ihren respektiven pädagogischen Konsequenzen sowie die geisteswissenschaftliche Pädagogik des 19. und des 20. Jahrhunderts.

HAGER, Nina. Philosophie und Lehre. Deut Z Phil, 37(10-11), 936-944, 1989.

There is no obligatory scheme for teaching dialectical materialism for all university teachers. We attach great importance to creative thinking which naturally depends on individual possibilities. Researches in other fields of philosophy must be taken into consideration more vigorously. Teaching must be based on the development of modern natural and other sciences; students should also understand more about logic and methods of leading sciences.

HAHLWEG, Kai and HOOKER, C A. "Evolutionary Epistemology and Philosophy of Science" in Issues in Evolutionary Epistemology, HAHLWEG, Kai (ed), 21-150. Albany, SUNY Pr, 1989.

In this paper the authors collaborate in the exposition of a naturalistic approach to problems in the philosophy of science. An evolutionary model which is phrased in terms of the evolution of complex regulatory structures is put forward by Hahlweg. He argues that science can be understood as such a system, and that scientific method evolves and improves in the course of scientific evolution. Hooker integrates this model into his evolutionary naturalist realism and makes a case for the identity of biological and scientific evolution by arguing that information as a functional term can be reduced to underlying causal structure.

HAHLWEG, Kai (ed) and HOOKER, C A (ed). Issues in Evolutionary Epistemology. Albany, SUNY Pr, 1989

This book provides a thorough philosophical examination of theories of evolutionary epistemology. It is divided into four parts: Part I introduces several new approaches to evolutionary epistemology, Part II attempts to widen the scope of evolutionary epistemology, either by tackling more traditional epistemological issues, or by applying evolutionary models to new areas of inquiry such as the evolution of culture or of intentionality; Part III critically discusses specific problems in evolutionary epistemology; and Part IV deals with the relationship of evolutionary epistemology to the philosophy of mind.

HAHN, E. The Subject of Historic Transformations in the Present Era (in Czechoslovakian). Filozof Cas, 37(4), 519-526, 1989.

Erich Hahn's study represents a stimulating entry in the ongoing debate pertaining to the interdependence of class and panhuman interests. It is an attempt at characterizing the social subject in the novel conditions of the present-day world, particularly as regards the depiction of continuity and discontinuity in relation to the classical concept of such categories as mankind, class, or individual. The focal point of this analysis lies in the relationship between class and panhuman interests. The author proceeds in particular from the joint SED-SPD document dedicated to ideological controversies concerning common security. While searching for a common denominator of interests, the author inevitably places considerable accent on joint practical actions.

HAHN, Toni and WINKLER, Gunnar. Soziale Sicherheit—Triebkraft ökonomischen Wachstums bei der Gestaltung der entwickelten sozialistischen Gesellschaft. Deut Z Phil, 38(1), 64-68, 1990.

Social security is an achievement of socialism. It depends on concrete individual experiences if it will become to a drive of economic growth. Especially young people are meaning, that there are restrictions of social security. In fact, this only exists if it is more than a system of social maintenance and rights. It has to include possibilities for responsible self-determination the quality of life. "From each according to his abilities" in work is required and also "to each according to his performance." It has to be guaranteed the "right of social inequality" following unequal achievement just as have to be excluded leveling equality and misuse of social rights.

HAIFENG, Jing. A Summary of Xiong Shili's Research on Philosophy Conducted in China. Chin Stud Phil, 21(1), 3-19, Fall 89.

HAIG, Brian. Scientific Problems and the Conduct of Research. Educ Phil Theor, 19(2), 22-32, 1987.

HÁJEK, Alan. Probabilities of Conditionals—Revisited. J Phil Log, 18(4), 423-428, N 89.

I present a result that counts against the hypothesis that the probability of a conditional equals the corresponding conditional probability: $P(\text{if } A \text{ then } C) = P(C/A)$ ($P(a) > 0$). Admittedly, this hypothesis has already been challenged in the literature, most notably by Lewis's triviality results. However, I drop certain contested assumptions of these earlier works. I show: for any finite model with more than two worlds, there is no binary operation $\rightarrow$ such that $P(A \rightarrow C) = P(C/A)$. The result against the hypothesis, with $\rightarrow$ interpreted as a conditional, is an immediate corollary.

HALDANE, J J. Philosophy and Environmental Issues. Int J Moral Soc Stud, 5(1), 79-91, Spr 90.

Examination of the central notions employed in contemporary discussions of large-scale environmental issues and policies shows them to have philosophical character. This is most obviously so where the ideas involved are normative—concerning the good, or what ought to be done—but it is also so in the case of such (proto-)metaphysical ideas as those of Nature and the Environment. The present essay considers something of this philosophical character as well as reflecting on the prospects of a normative philosophy of the environment. In discussing the latter, it examines changing conceptions of how theory and conduct might be related and draws upon traditions of speculative and practical thought to be found in classical antiquity and in the mediaeval period.

HALDANE, John. Architecture, Philosophy and the Public World. Brit J Aes, 30(3), 203-217, Jl 90.

Contemporary philosophers invited to consider relevant difficulties raised by modern urban redevelopment might think to approach these issues from the direction of either social philosophy or aesthetics. Among other aims this paper is concerned to show that no accurate identification of the problems, and hence no adequate prescription for their solution, is possible unless *both* perspectives are adopted—or merged. Architecture being the paradigm of a public art, its philosophical examination is an exercise in social aesthetics. The discussion proceeds by examining the debate about city architecture initiated by the Prince of Wales.

HALDANE, John. Chesterton's Philosophy of Education. Philosophy, 65(251), 65-80, Ja 90.

This is a study of the educational philosophy of Chesterton. It considers his credentials as a philosopher, noting that several distinguished thinkers, including Aurel Kolnai, Ernst Bloch, Etienne Gilson and John Anderson, cite his work with respect, and it explores something of the character of his views about the role of philosophy and the nature of education, showing them to be closely related to the epistemology, metaphysics and value theory of Aquinas.

HALDANE, John. Metaphysics in the Philosophy of Education. J Phil Educ, 23(2), 171-183, Wint 89.

The essay considers current preoccupations about the condition and future course of philosophy of education and it proposes a reexamination of the project of devising an educational philosophy in answer to the question: what is education for? It rejects arguments to the effect that the metaphysical and axiological presuppositions of any nonrelativist answer to this question must be incoherent and it outlines the structure of a teleological account of the aim of education.

HALDANE, John. On Taste and Excellence. J Aes Educ, 23(2), 17-20, Sum 89.

Taste is a set of capacities associated with refined sensibilities and such refinement is usually the product of education. It involves the discernment and pursuit of value and hence is a virtue worth cultivating. Yet, for various (bad) reasons little attention has been given to the place of taste in education. This short essay examines that neglect.

HALL, David L. "On Seeking a Change of Environment" in *Nature in Asian Tradition of Thought: Essays in Environmental Philosophy*, CALLICOTT, J Baird (ed), 99-111. Albany, SUNY Pr, 1989.

HALL, John C. Acts and Omissions. Phil Quart, 39(157), 399-408, O 89.

HALL, R. "Adams on the Mind: Mind as Meaning and as Agent" in *Mind, Value and Culture: Essays in Honor of E M Adams*, WEISSBORD, David (ed), 173-182. Atascadero, Ridgeview, 1989.

HALL, Robert W. Plato and Totalitarianism. Polis, 7(2), 105-114, 1988.

HALL, Robert W. Platonic Justice and the *Republic*. Polis, 6(2), 116-126, 1986.

HALL, Roland. Some Uses of *Imagination* in the British Empiricists: A Preliminary Investigation of Locke, as Contrasted with Hume. Locke News, 20, 47-62, 1989.

HALL, Ronald L. "Are We Losing Our Minds?" in *Mind, Value and Culture: Essays in Honor of E M Adams*, WEISSBORD, David (ed), 191-206. Atascadero, Ridgeview, 1989.

HALLBERG, Margareta. Feminist Epistemology—An Impossible Project? Rad Phil, 53, 3-7, Autumn 89.

This article outlines some of the main problems raised by the recent epistemological turn in feminist theory. It is argued that there is a tension in feminist philosophy of science between objectivism and relativism which cannot be overcome. It is also argued that the concept of "experience" when used as a basis for knowledge is extremely complicated to cope with. Finally, the idea that science and its philosophy are completely genderized is rejected.

HALLER, Rudolf (ed) and MC GUINNESS, Brian (ed). *Wittgenstein in Focus—Im Brennpunkt: Wittgenstein*. Amsterdam, Rodopi, 1989

HALLER, Rudolf. "Bemerkungen zur Egologie Wittgensteins" in *Wittgenstein in Focus—Im Brennpunkt: Wittgenstein*, MC GUINNESS, Brian (ed), 353-373. Amsterdam, Rodopi, 1989.

In Wittgensteins früher Ich-Lehre wird die Existenz eines metaphysischen Subjekts, eines von Gott und Welt unabhängigen Ich augenommen, das nicht nur als eine Grenze ontologisch bestimmt wird. Wittgensteins spätere Frage nach dem "diametralen Gegenteil des Solipsismus" gibt einige Rätsel auf: Es kann kein Realismus sein. Was ist es sonst? Wittgensteins Betrachtungen der Jahre nach 1929 ändern die Gesichtspunkte der Interpretation. Unmittelbare Erfahrungen sind so wenig personbezogen wie der Hinweis auf ein Subjekt notwendig ist für die Beschreibung einer Erfahrung. Wittgensteins anti-cartesischer Standpunkt wird dadurch deutlich gemacht, dass er zwei Wege probiert, die Unwichtigkeit des Ausdrucks "ich" aufzuzeigen: erstens, den Weg der Elimination des Ich, zweitens, den Aufweis der Bedeutungslosigkeit der egozentrischen Perspektive, die keinen ausgezeichneten Platz in der Weltbeschreibung einnimmt.

HALLER, Rudolf. *Questions on Wittgenstein*. Lincoln, Univ of Nebraska Pr, 1988

The book deals mainly with questions which normally are not to be investigated in the vast literature on Wittgenstein: the background in Austrian philosophy with questions like: was Wittgenstein a Neo-Kantian, a neo-positivist, a Sceptic? Or on Wittgenstein's relations to Weininger and Spengler, and finally on the role of a common way of human acting and forms of life in Wittgenstein's philosophy. Contrary to most interpreters, Wittgenstein's ultimate point of view is described as praxiological foundationalism.

HALLER, Rudolf. Wittgenstein and Physicalism. Critica, 21(63), 17-32, D 89.

The main question of the paper concerns the question if Wittgenstein himself was a physicalist. In order to answer the question we have to look at Neurath and Carnap on the one hand and Wittgenstein's claim to be the "main source" of Carnap's physicalism. The solution is given in the fact that already the language we learn is the so-called physical language.

HALLIBURTON, David. "Concealing Revealing: A Perspective on Greek Tragedy" in *Post-Structuralist Classics*, BENJAMIN, Andrew (ed), 245-267. New York, Routledge, 1988.

HALLYN, Fernand and LESLIE, Donald M (trans). *The Poetic Structure of the World: Copernicus and Kepler*. Cambridge, Zone Books, 1990

Confronted with a scientific text, the historian of science tries to define its signification, the epistemologist its theoretical status. "Poetics" of science proposes another approach. It studies the work of a scientist as an event embedded in a wider field of images, symbols, texts and practices. Scientific imagination is *not* fundamentally different from a mythic or poetic imagination. The sun-centered universe of Copernicus and Kepler is inseparable from the aesthetic, theological and rhetorical imperatives of both Neoplatonism and Mannerism in the sixteenth century. Closely related notions of harmony, symmetry and proportion inform cosmology as well as music and painting. This book offers the first comprehensive, full-scale study of these relations in these particularly important cases.

HALPERIN, David M. Is There a History of Sexuality? Hist Theor, 28(3), 257-274, O 89.

HALPIN, John F. Counterfactual Analysis: Can the Metalinguistic Theory Be Revitalized? Synthese, 81(1), 47-62, O 89.

This paper evaluates the recent trend to renounce the similarity approach to counterfactuals in favor of the older metalinguistic theory. I try to show, first, that the metalinguistic theory cannot work in anything like its present form (the form described by many in the last decade who claim to be able to solve Goodman's old problem of cotenability). This is so, I argue, because the metalinguistic theory requires laws of nature of a sort that we (apparently) do not have: current physical theory cannot underwrite the metalinguistic theory. Second, I draw from the first point a motivation for the similarity approach, a motivation based on theoretical considerations apart from the standard ones of pretheoretical intuition.

HAMBURGER, Käte. "Lessings 'tragisches Mitleid' une seine hermeneutischen Implikationen" in *Cultural Hermeneutics of Modern Art: Essays in Honor of Jan Aler*, DETHIER, Hubert (ed), 245-259. Amsterdam, Rodopi, 1989.

HAMLIN, Alan P. Rights, Indirect Utilitarianism, and Contractarianism. Econ Phil, 5(2), 167-187, O 89.

There have been a number of attempts to argue that indirect or two-level utilitarianism of one type or another can succeed in grounding substantive individual rights. This paper confronts these various arguments and claims that they all fail—indirectly consequentialist and welfarist arguments cannot support substantive rights. However, the argument points to the possibility of a more contractarian basis for rights. A discussion of the role and status of rights in social evaluation and decision making provides the starting point for the discussion of the indirect utilitarian arguments advanced by Gray, Pettit, Sumner and others.

HAMLYN, D W. Education and Wittgenstein's Philosophy. J Phil Educ, 23(2), 213-222, Wint 89.

The paper, which is a version of a lecture given to commemorate the centenary of Wittgenstein's birth, seeks to show that although Wittgenstein wrote nothing on philosophy of education, despite incidental remarks on teaching and learning, his thought has definite implications for the subject. Wittgenstein's emphasis on forms of life and on practice provides a context without which the growth of understanding cannot itself be properly understood. Such understanding must not be construed as something purely formal; its background of forms of behaviour affects what is educationally possible.

HAMLYN, D W. *In and Out of the Black Box: On the Philosophy of Cognition*. Cambridge, Blackwell, 1990

The book presents the argument that contemporary cognitive science suffers from an acceptance of the legacy of behaviourism while reacting against it, through an inadequate attention to the nature of the input and output to the human system. Recourse is had to the idea of inner representations, without a satisfactory examination of the nature of perception (input) and behaviour or action (output). Cognition in general presupposes knowledge, agency, and aspects of affective and social life, and the intervening cognitive processes must equally be construed in those terms.

HAMLYN, D W. The Problem of the External World. Philosophy, 24, 1-13, 88 Supp.

The paper investigates the senses in which the world may be thought external, and argues that none of them supports doubt about the possibility of knowledge of the world. Scepticism sometimes depends on certain erroneous conceptions of perception, especially those which lead to belief in 'inner, representational states'. How we perceive things depends on the satisfaction of certain general conditions—on what concepts we have, on the kind of senses we have, and so on a kind of anthropocentricity; but this does not prevent objectivity, even in the case of secondary qualities.

HAMM, Cornel M. *Philosophical Issues in Education*. Philadelphia, Falmer Pr, 1989

Many of the ideas presented in this introductory book in philosophy of education have been expressed elsewhere in a manner beginning students find difficult to grasp. Here these ideas together with new ones are expressed simply and clearly without sacrificing the rigour necessary for understanding complex philosophical matters. This is achieved by eliminating unnecessary philosophical jargon, by use of tables and diagrams where appropriate, and by coherent organization of ideas. The main distinctive features of the book are its clarity, currency, and completeness.

HAMMACHER, Klaus. Die Wandlungen Gottes: Zu Rudolf Schottlaenders Beitrag *Zu Spinozas Theorie des Glaubens*. Stud Spinozana, 4, 247-262, 1988.

According to Schottlaender—as well as to Hans Jonas in his renowned lecture *Der Gottesbegriff nach Auschwitz*—there only remains a universally gracious, but not omnipotent God to be conceivable. Schottlaender's and Jonas's ideas of a God acting at the same time world-immanently are opposed to a transcendence, which, however, does not mean a transeunt acting according to Schottlaender's distinctions. This transcendence does not pass on from the cause to the effect, but becomes true as a beneficial efficacy in a change of the attitude towards being and fellow being. This implies a change of our inner strengths, which we mean along with the concept of God. I try to associate Schottlaender's appeal to the reality of beneficial efficacy in belief with a new doctrine of emotions which takes up Spinoza's theory of affections. (edited)

HAMMOND, David M. The Influence of Newman's Doctrine of Assent on the Thought of Bernard Lonergan. Method, 7(2), 95-115, O 89.

The article traces the development of what became a key influence in Bernard Lonergan's thought: Newman's doctrine of assent. The research is based on extensive use of Lonergan's unpublished manuscripts, letters and other materials.

HAMPSHIRE, Stuart. *Innocence and Experience*. Cambridge, Harvard Univ Pr, 1989

HAMPTON, Jean. "Hobbes's Science of Moral Philosophy" in *Knowledge and Politics*, DASCAL, Marcelo (ed), 48-67. Boulder, Westview Pr, 1988.

Hobbes's various remarks on morality are reviewed with the aim of explaining why he called his moral theory a "science." The theory is presented as an anti-Aristotelian, proto-Humean approach to morality, which not only fits well with Hobbes's psychological pronouncements but also provides a plausible foundation for his political conclusions.

HAMPTON, Jean. "Hobbesian Reflections on Glory as a Cause of Conflict" in *The Causes of Quarrel: Essays on Peace, War, and Thomas Hobbes*, CAWS, Peter (ed), 78-96. Boston, Beacon Pr, 1989.

This article explores how someone such as Hobbes could argue that a desire for "glory" precipitates conflict. Glory is linked to the notion of self-worth, and an argument is given to the effect that if one has a certain conception of what it is to have worth, emotional reactions such as hate, envy and revenge are inevitable in situations where one believes one's worth is threatened. These reactions often result in violence, and perhaps (in social contexts) civil war.

HAMPTON, Jean. *Mens Rea*. Soc Phil Pol, 7(2), 1-28, Spr 90.

Despite its importance to the criminal law, philosophers and legal theorists have found it difficult to say what legal *mens rea* is. This article develops a positive theory of *mens rea*, understood as legal culpability, and connects it to conceptions of moral and rational culpability. On this account, all three kinds of culpability arise from what is called a "defiant" state of mind.

HAMPTON, Jean. The Nature of Immorality. Soc Phil Pol, 7(1), 22-44, Autumn 89.

This article explores the question of why people behave immorally, what it is for someone to be culpable for a wrongdoing, and what it means to say of someone that she has a 'bad' or 'immoral' or 'evil' character. Different meta-ethical theories purporting to explain the authority of moral action implicitly assume different and often mutually inconsistent accounts of why and when we fail to be moral, and analysis shows that all of these accounts of moral failure are problematic.

HAMRICK, William S. Coercion and Exploitation: Self-Transposal and the Moral Life. J Brit Soc Phenomenol, 21(1), 67-79, Ja 90.

HAMRICK, William S. Philosophy for Children and Aesthetic Education. J Aes Educ, 23(2), 55-67, Sum 89.

HAMRICK, William S. A Real-Life Brain. Thinking, 6(4), 18, 1986.

HAMRICK, William S. Some Concrete Approaches to Nature in *Kio and Gus*. Thinking, 7(2), 40-45, 1987.

HAMRICK, William S. Teaching *Elfie*. Thinking, 8(2), 9-11, 1989.

HAND, Michael. Antirealism and Holes in the World. Philosophy, 65(252), 218-224, Ap 90.

J J C Smart has claimed that semantical (Dummettian) antirealism must posit "holes in the world," corresponding to meaningful sentences that lack truth-value. James O Young charges that Smart is mistaken. I examine Young's defense of antirealism and find it unsuccessful. Young identifies truth with warranted assertibility, but keeps a realistic conception of reality, thus avoiding holes. I also clarify and defend Smart's claim.

HAND, Michael. Hilbert's Iterativistic Tendencies. Hist Phil Log, 11(2), 185-192, 1990.

Serious difficulties attend the reading of David Hilbert's 1925 classic paper 'On the Infinite'. I claim that the peculiarities of presentation plaguing certain parts of that paper, as well as of the earlier 'On the Foundations of Logic and Arithmetic' (1904), are due to a tension between two incompatible semantical approaches to numerical statements of elementary arithmetic, and accordingly two incompatible metaphysical conceptions of the natural numbers. One of these approaches is the referential, or model-theoretical one; the other is the iterativist's approach. I draw out the two tendencies in these works, with more attention paid to Hilbert's iterativistic tendency because of the unfamiliarity of iterativism generally. I begin with an exposition of this view.

HAND, Michael. A Number is the Exponent of an Operation. Synthese, 81(2), 243-265, N 89.

The natural numbers are not objects, i.e., a referential account of the truth of numerical statements is inappropriate. Instead, natural numbers are *controls on iterations*. The semantics and ontology of this view (iterativism) are presented in detail, and its attendant epistemology is contrasted with that of Platonistic structuralism.

HANFLING, Oswald. *Wittgenstein's Later Philosophy*. Albany, SUNY Pr, 1989

The opening chapter is on Wittgenstein's *Tractatus* and the following chapter, on meaning and use, attempts to locate the essential difference between his earlier and later positions. Subsequent chapters deal with privacy, objectivity versus "conventionalism," and *On Certainty*. A major theme throughout is Wittgenstein's insistence that in philosophy "we must do away with all *explanation*, and description alone must take its place." It is shown that this principle has often been ignored or misunderstood by both sympathetic and hostile readers of Wittgenstein, resulting in various misunderstandings of his position.

HANNAY, Alastair. "Politics and Feyerabend's Anarchist" in *Knowledge* *and Politics*, DASCAL, Marcelo (ed), 241-263. Boulder, Westview Pr, 1988.

The message of Feyerabend's epistemological anarchism is: restore to both creative scientists and the general public freedom of decision in matters of knowledge. In an epistemological context it is natural to regard the freedom here as designed to improve science, but both *Against Method* and *Science in a Free Society* argue as if the democratization of science served humanitarian ends outside the scope of knowledge. In order to accommodate these ends a version of epistemological anarchism would have to be formulated in which the individual's right to form its own scientific choices was made basic. But there is no guarantee that protecting such a right will promote rather than prevent discovery.

HANNAY, Alastair. Solitary Souls and Infinite Help: Kierkegaard and Wittgenstein. Hist Euro Ideas, 12(1), 41-52, 1990.

A prima facie similarity between remarks by Wittgenstein and views expressed by Kierkegaard's pseudonym Anti-Climacus in *The Sickness Unto Death* dissolves under closer inspection, but both can be incorporated in a greater unity if the remarks are understood, on the one hand, as stemming from one who grasps the problem to which Christianity is a solution, and the views, on the other, as stemming from one who has adopted the solution.

HANRAHAN, Nancy Weiss. Negative Composition. Phil Soc Crit, 15(3), 273-291, 1989.

HANS, James S. Shame and Desire in the Myths of Origins. Phil Today, 33(4), 330-346, Wint 89.

HANSBERG, Olbeth. Emociones reactivas. Critica, 20(59), 5-21, Ag 88.

HANSBERG, Olbeth. Emociones y creencias. Rev Latin De Filosof, 15(2), 201-213, Jl 89.

The author's concern in this paper is to examine certain theses proposed by cognitivist theories about the relationship between emotion and belief. Due to the great variety of states we call emotions and to the fact that they do not constitute a unitary class, it is important to examine particular emotions and special cases to avoid undue simplification. When we go into particular cases we observe that with certain emotions a perception of 'seeing something as' is more relevant to the emotion than a specific belief. Although in general we believe things are as we see them, there are cases when our rational beliefs conflict with our perceptions. On the other hand, there are emotions like love and hate, which hardly ever taken sentential complements and of which we cannot say that they are determined or generated by specific beliefs. (edited)

HANSEN, Chad. Mo-Tzu: Language Utilitarianism. J Chin Phil, 16(3-4), 355-380, D 89.

Mo-tzu assumes that language programs motivations and guides behavior. A shared language grounds social cooperation. His analysis of prescriptive discourse focuses on the word, not the sentence. My explanatory model is computer machine language. The instruction set consists of a stack of words. Each step in the execution of the set requires that we test for the condition indicated by the current word. We apply language in guiding action by the ability to make distinctions. The discourse content and the dispositions to discriminate should lead to universal benefit—hence language utilitarianism.

HANSER, Matthew. Harming Future People. Phil Pub Affairs, 19(1), 47-70, Wint 90.

Derek Parfit argues that an action cannot, in the morally relevant sense, harm someone who (a) has a life worth living and (b) would not have existed had the action not been performed. Parfit uses this conclusion to support an "impersonal" form of consequentialism. I argue that many actions satisfying Parfit's conditions *do* harm people in the morally relevant sense, and that those which don't provide no support for a general consequentialism.

HANSON, Barbara Gail. Parallogic: As Mind Meets Context. Diogenes, 147, 77-91, Fall 89.

Parallogic models the relationship between mind and context by suggesting that systems of logic are context specific and therefore parallel. Thus, perceived departures in mental process, reasoning, may be more apparent than real. Parallogic suggests a way of separating breakdowns in mental process from shifts in systems of logic. The model emerges from a linkage between general systems theory and constructivist thought. It suggests a two-stage diagnosis process which first rules out aberrations of observation point before focusing on individual pathology.

HANSON, Karen. Dressing Down Dressing Up—The Philosophic Fear of Fashion. Hypatia, 5(2), 107-121, Sum 90.

This paper examines a philosophical hostility to fashionable dress, locating its sources in philosophy's suspicion of change; anxiety about surfaces and the inessential; failures in the face of death; and disdain for, denial of, the

human body and human passivity. Feminist concerns about fashion should be radically different from those of traditional philosophy. Whatever our ineluctable worries about desire and death, appropriate anger and impatience with the merely superficial, and genuine need to mark off the serious from the trivial, feminism may still be a corrective therapy for philosophy's bad humor and self-deception on the subject of beautiful clothes.

HANSON, Russell L (ed) and BALL, Terence and FARR, James (ed). *Political Innovation and Conceptual Change*. New York, Cambridge Univ Pr, 1989

HANSSON, Sven Ove. Defining "Good" and "Bad" in Terms of "Better". Notre Dame J Form Log, 31(1), 136-149, Wint 90.

Monadic predicates for "good" and "bad" are inserted into structures already containing the dyadic predicate "better." A set of logical properties for "good" and "bad" is proposed, and a complete characterization is given of the pairs of monadic predicates that have these properties. It is argued that "good" and "bad" can indeed be defined in terms of "better," and a definition is given that is more generally applicable than those previously proposed.

HANSSON, Sven Ove. A Note on the Deontic System DL of Jones and Pörn. Synthese, 80(3), 427-428, S 89.

Andrew Jones and Ingmar Pörn have constructed a system of deontic logic in which many of the paradoxical results of standard deontic logic seem to disappear (*Synthese* 65:275-290, 1985). It is shown that some of the paradoxes, including Ross's paradox, reappear in their system in a somewhat different form.

HANSSON, Sven Ove. Preference-Based Deontic Logic (PDL). J Phil Log, 19(1), 75-93, F 90.

A new possible world semantics for deontic logic is proposed. Its intuitive basis is that prohibitive predicates (such as "wrong" and "prohibited") have the property of negativity, i.e., that what is worse than something wrong is itself wrong. The logic of prohibitive predicates is built on this property and on preference logic. Prescriptive predicates are defined in terms of prohibitive predicates, according to the well-known formula "ought" = "wrong that not." In this preference-based deontic logic (PDL), those theorems that give rise to the paradoxes of standard deontic logic (SDL) are not obtained. (E.g., $O(p \& q) \rightarrow Op \& Oq$ and $Op \rightarrow O(p \vee q)$) are theorems of SDL but not of PDL.) The more plausible theorems of SDL, however, can be derived in PDL.

HANZAWA, Takamaro. Kotaro Tanaka as a Natural Law Theorist. Vera Lex, 7(1), 5,10,24-25, 1987.

Kotaro Tanaka (1890-1974), a professor, the Chief Justice of the Supreme Court and the Judge of the International Court of Justice, was a prominent natural law theorist in modern Japan. Although brought up in the scholarly world where Neo-Kantian epistemology prevailed, Tanaka, a converted Catholic from a Protestant fundamentalist sect, achieved a remarkable breakthrough in constructing his theory of world law and universal commercial law on the basis of Thomistic natural law theory with which he carried on his strenuous fight against the ultra-nationalism of pre-war Japan.

HARAN, Dan. Quantifier Elimination in Separably Closed Fields of Finite Imperfectness Degree. J Sym Log, 53(2), 463-469, Je 88.

An explicit primitive recursive procedure of quantifier elimination is given for the elementary theory of separably closed fields of a fixed characteristic and a fixed finite imperfectness degree.

HARDIN, Russell. Ethics and Stochastic Processes. Soc Phil Pol, 7(1), 69-80, Autumn 89.

Traditional moral theories often do not readily fit major policy issues. Theories that focus on the rightness of particular act-kinds have special difficulties with large-scale stochastic problems. Policies to deal with such problems are inherently directed at consequences and imply tradeoffs between individuals, at least ex ante. Consider smallpox vaccination: some died because they were vaccinated but far fewer died from the vaccination than would have died without general vaccination. One cannot have a sensible principle on vaccination per se in the way one might have a general principle on lying as right or wrong independently of its likely consequences.

HARDIN, Russell. Rationally Justifying Political Coercion. J Phil Res, 15, 79-91, 1990.

The central problem of political philosophy is how to justify coercion by government. For political theories that are based in a rational accounting of the interests of the polity, citizens must have consented at least indirectly to coercion. Such indirect consent to coercion is plausible for ordinary contexts such as, for example, submitting to legally enforceable contracts. Unfortunately, however, Hobbesian mutual advantage, contemporary contractarian, and Lockean natural rights theories, all of which ground the state in rational interests at least in large part, can justify government coercion only in principle. They cannot justify coercion by actual states. In practice, these theories are morally indeterminate.

HARDWIG, John. "In Search of an Ethics of Personal Relationships" in *Person to Person*, GRAHAM, George (ed), 63-81. Philadelphia, Temple Univ Pr, 1989.

Philosophers thinking about ethics have tacitly presupposed a context in which we mean little or nothing to each other. Consequently, what we now think of as ethics is almost entirely the ethics of impersonal relationships. These theories of ethics ignore important considerations in personal relationships; even worse, they often urge us to act in ways that would clearly be inappropriate in, even destructive to personal relationships. I offer some considerations for developing an ethics of personal relationships. However, this is just a beginning. Until we have more fully explored the ethics of personal relationships, pronouncements about "the moral point of view" are premature.

HARDWIG, John. What About the Family? Hastings Center Rep, 20(2), 5-10, Mr-Ap 90.

Medical ethics has ignored the interests of the patient's family in medical treatment decisions. But these interests are often affected by treatment decisions and sometimes should even override the interests of the patient. Recognizing the legitimacy of family members' interests forces basic changes in medical ethics. Fidelity to the patient must be rejected in favor of an ethics of fairness to all members of the family. We must also abandon our focus on patient autonomy or acknowledge Kant's insight that patient autonomy and dignity sometimes require patients to choose treatments that are not the treatments they want.

HARDY, Lee. *The Fabric of This World: Inquiries into Calling, Career Choice, and the Design of Human Work*. Grand Rapids, Eerdmans, 1990

In this work, the author seeks to explain and apply the Christian concept of work as vocation. It is composed of four chapters. The first chapter reviews the history of the philosophy of labor. The second chapter explicates the concept of vocation as inaugurated by the Protestant tradition. The third chapter applies the practical implications of the concept of vocation to the issue of career choice. The fourth chapter works out the implications of the concept of vocation for job design.

HARE, R M. Commentary on "Hamlethics in Planning". Bus Prof Ethics J, 6(2), 83-87, Sum 87.

Kaufman, apart from his misuse of 'relativist' to mean 'consequentialist', gives a perfect illustration of the use in applied ethics of the distinction between levels of moral thinking (see my *Moral Thinking* (1981)). Disregarding his 'ethically unaware', his 'ethically hyperactives' operate only at the intuitive level, his consequentialists only at the critical level, and his 'ethical hybrids' at both levels (as they should); but his actual subjects were perhaps not clear enough to do this effectively).

HARE, R M. *Essays on Political Morality*. New York, Clarendon/Oxford Pr, 1989

This book reprints 'Political Obligation' (T Honderich (ed.), *Social Ends and Political Means*, 1976), 'On Terrorism' (*JVI* 13 (1979)), 'Rules of War' (*Ph Pub Aff* 1 (1972)), 'Philosophy and Practice: Some Issues about War and Peace' (A P Griffiths (ed.), *Philosophy and Practice*, 1985), 'Rights, Utility and Universalization' (R G Frey (ed.), *Utility and Rights* (1984)), 'Utility and Rights' (*Nomos* 24 (1984)), 'Arguing about Rights' (*Emory Law Journal* 33 (1984)), 'Liberty and Equality' (*Social Philosophy and Policy* 2 (1984)), 'What is Wrong with Slavery' (*Ph Pub Aff* 8 (1979)), 'Liberty, Equality and Fraternity in S Africa' (*Ph Forum* 18 (1986)), 'Justice and Equality' (J Arthur et al. (eds.), *Justice and Economic Distribution*, 1978), 'Punishment and Retributive Justice' (*Philosophical Topics* 14 (1986)), 'Contrasting Methods of Environmental Planning' (R S Peters (ed.), *Nature and Conduct*, 1975), and 'Moral Reasoning about the Environment' (*J App Ph* 4 (1987)). It also contains 'The Role of Philosophers in the Legislative Process', 'Rebellion' and 'The Rights of Employees'.

HARGROVE, Eugene C. *Foundations of Environmental Ethics*. Englewood Cliffs, Prentice-Hall, 1989

This book examines the foundations of environmental ethics in terms of a reconstruction of the history of ideas behind environmental thought, focusing on the negative effects of philosophical and land use attitudes and the positive contribution of scientific and aesthetic attitudes in the modern period. Approaching environmental ethics from the perspectives of weak anthropocentrism and moral pluralism, Hargrove argues that its foundations are fundamentally aesthetic. The book culminates with an ontological argument for nature preservation in terms of natural beauty.

HARKER, W John. Literary Communication: The Author, the Reader, the

Text. J Aes Educ, 22(2), 5-14, Sum 88.

The paper argues that it is the interplay through the text between the author's intentional artifice and the reader's attentional construction and reconstruction of meaning that describes the arena of interpretive activity in literature and the communicative framework within which this activity takes place.

HARMAN, Gilbert. The Simplest Hypothesis. Critica, 20(59), 23-42, Ag 88.

People sometimes are more inclined to believe one hypothesis rather than another because of the simplicity of the first hypothesis. The simplicity of a theory in this sense cannot be merely the simplicity of the way in which the theory is represented, because any hypothesis can be given an extremely simple representation. But the simplicity of the theory may involve the simplicity of the explanations that the theory provides: i.e., the simplicity of the representations of the connections that the theory allows between the theory and the data to be explained.

HARNAD, Stevan. Response to Dietrich's "Computationalism". Soc Epistem, 4(2), 167-172, Ap-Je 90.

According to "computationalism," to be thinking is to be computing certain propositional functions. Searle has tried to show that this is just mindless symbol manipulation; whatever "meaning" it has is parasitic on the mind of the interpreter. Dietrich argues that symbols *are* meaningful to the symbol manipulator itself because their meanings are used in operations such as look-up. I show that if you refrain from interpreting the symbols it is clear that no meaning whatsoever is involved or "used." Hence computationalism is just a form of hermeneutics.

HARRÉ, Rom. Realism, Reference and Theory. Philosophy, 24, 53-68, 88 Supp.

The argument is based on four distinctions: bivalence and referential realism: theories as logical structures and theories as descriptions of models; linguistic and materialist accounts of reference; empiricist and dispositionalist defences of realism. It is argued that a philosophy of science based on a conjunction of the first member of each pair of contrasts is incoherent, and that only by developing an account of science based on a conjunction of the second of the contrasting pairs can a defensible realism be thought out.

HARRIES, Karsten. Heidegger and the Problem of Style in Interpretation. Irish Phil J, 6(2), 250-274, 1989.

HARRIES, Karsten. "The Philosopher at Sea" in *Nietzsche's New Seas: Explorations in Philosophy, Aesthetics, and Politics*, GILLESPIE, Michael Allen (ed), 21-44. Chicago, Univ of Chicago Pr, 1989.

HARRIS, Errol E. "Reply to Blanshard's "Harris on Internal Relations"" in *Dialectic and Contemporary Science*, GRIER, Philip T (ed), 21-27. Lanham, Univ Pr of America, 1989.

HARRIS, Errol E. "Reply to Earle's "The Evanescent Authority of Philosophy"" in *Dialectic and Contemporary Science*, GRIER, Philip T (ed), 213-217. Lanham, Univ Pr of America, 1989.

HARRIS, Errol E. "Reply to Hepburn's "The Problem of Evil"" in *Dialectic and Contemporary Science*, GRIER, Philip T (ed), 125-135. Lanham, Univ Pr of America, 1989.

HARRIS, Errol E. "Reply to Klever's "The Properties of the Intellect"" in *Dialectic and Contemporary Science*, GRIER, Philip T (ed), 179-182. Lanham, Univ Pr of America, 1989.

HARRIS, Errol E. "Reply to Lucas's "Science and Teleological Explanations"" in *Dialectic and Contemporary Science*, GRIER, Philip T (ed), 51-54. Lanham, Univ Pr of America, 1989.

HARRIS, Errol E. "Reply to Muller's "The *Pons Asinorum* in Philosophy" in *Dialectic and Contemporary Science*, GRIER, Philip T (ed), 199-202. Lanham, Univ Pr of America, 1989.

HARRIS, Errol E. "Reply to Rinaldi's "The Identity of Thought and Being in Harris's Interpretation of Hegel's Logic"" in *Dialectic and Contemporary Science*, GRIER, Philip T (ed), 89-90. Lanham, Univ Pr of America, 1989.

HARRIS, Errol E. "Reply to Rockmore's "System and History: Harris on Hegel's Logic"" in *Dialectic and Contemporary Science*, GRIER, Philip T (ed), 105-107. Lanham, Univ Pr of America, 1989.

HARRIS, Errol E. "Reply to Smith's "Harris's Commentary on Hegel's Logic"" in *Dialectic and Contemporary Science*, GRIER, Philip T (ed), 65-68. Lanham, Univ Pr of America, 1989.

HARRIS, Errol E. "Reply to Walsh's "Hegel on Morality"" in *Dialectic and Contemporary Science*, GRIER, Philip T (ed), 153-160. Lanham, Univ Pr of America, 1989.

HARRIS, Errol E. La síntesis de lo uno y lo múltiple. Rev Filosof (Argentina), 3(2), 87-106, N 88.

This paper is concerned with the old philosophical issue of the One and the Many. The author analyzes this problem in different philosophers and he shows the fact that the modern empirical sciences prove that the world is a single system; but this unity involves the many. Finally, there are pointed out the problems that the dualism between matter and mind implies as well as the solipsism and the idealism. It is also suggested the necessity of a new starting point according to the empirical discoveries in sciences.

HARRIS, H S. The Problem of Kant. Bull Hegel Soc Gt Brit, 19, 18-27, Spr-Sum 89.

This is an essay on the relation between the Critical Philosophy and Hegel's *Phenomenology of Spirit*. It is also a critical study and appreciation of Robert Pippin's book *Hegel's Idealism*. The thesis maintained is that "Hegel was the greatest disciple that Kant ever had." But he was great because he was committed to the resolution of the problems raised by Kant's system as a *whole*. Kant boasted that he had criticized Reason in order to make room for faith. Hegel responded by developing a "critical method" to show that "faith" in anything beyond the pale of actual experience is quite unnecessary.

HARRIS, James R. A Comparison of the Ethical Values of Business Faculty and Students: How Different Are They? Bus Prof Ethics J, 7(1), 27-49, Spr 88.

Ethical values of graduating business seniors in an AACSB accredited institution were compared with those of their faculty. Ethical values were measured across five constructs: (1) fraud, (2) coercive power, (3) influence dealing, (4) self-interest, and (5) deceit. Statistically significant differences were observed only within the domain of fraud, the graduating business seniors expressing greater tolerance for these types of behaviors than their faculty. No differences were observed in the ethical value measures within the student group by major area of study. Within the faculty, however, economists were found to profess significantly different ethical values than their peers in other departments.

HARRIS, Leonard. The Lacuna Between Philosophy and History. J Soc Phil, 20(3), 110-114, Wint 89.

HARRIS, Margaret. Comprehension and Production in Early Lexical Development: A Comment on Stemmer. Mind Lang, 4(3), 229-234, Autumn 89.

HARRIS, Nigel G E. Journalists: A Moral Law Unto Themselves? J Applied Phil, 7(1), 75-85, Mr 90.

Journalists often take themselves as having a moral duty to protect their sources. If the sources in question leak information from government departments, government ministers will consider themselves as having the moral right to demand that the journalists disclose the identity of those sources. This creates conflicts of value between what journalists and ministers consider to be right. It is argued not only that traditional moral theories cannot resolve such moral conflicts, but that they are in a sense a good thing. A world in which the conflicts occur may be considered to be better than one in which they are prevented from occurring, for one can expect to have both effective journalism and effective government only in the former. The most important consequence of this view is that it makes the professional ethics of journalism (and, by implication, those of other professions) into something more than the mere application of universal moral rules to the various situations in which those who work in the profession are liable to find themselves.

HARRIS, Paul (ed). *Civil Disobedience*. Lanham, Univ Pr of America, 1989

Recent theoretical literature on civil disobedience has been dominated by two themes: What is civil disobedience? How can civil disobedience be morally justified, particularly in a democracy? Consideration of these questions inevitably leads to other major problems in political and moral theory. The articles and extracts in this collection cover the main points of contest in the modern literature on civil disobedience. The contributors are Hugo Adam Bedau, Ronald Dworkin, Joel Feinberg, Abe Fortas, Clyde Frazier, Alan Gewirth, Paul Harris, Martin Luther King, Jr., Wilson Carey McWilliams, Paul F Power, Harry Prosch, John Rawls, Bruce Sievers, and Herbert J Storing.

HARRIS, Phillip and CHOPKO, Mark E and ALVARÉ, Helen M. The Price of Abortion Sixteen Years Later. Nat Forum, 69(4), 18-22, Fall 89.

HARRIS, R Thomas. Is Translation Possible? Diogenes, 149, 105-121, Spr 90.

The paper develops in a discursive fashion Heidegger's thought on translation. Examples are used from the Japanese as well as the author's experience to bring to light a rather tenuous and as yet to be clearly

articulated ground between Eastern and Western traditions that shape and guide what we call our thinking. The paper shows that this ground only emerges with an awareness of the difference between these traditions. An attempt is made to articulate those differences and in so doing, the reader is invited to glimpse such a ground.

HARRIS, Roy and TAYLOR, Talbot J. *Landmarks in Linguistic Thought: The Western Tradition from Socrates to Saussure*. New York, Routledge, 1989

HARRIS, Walter S. "Rendering Unto Caesar: Religion and Nationalism" in *The Wisdom of Faith: Essays in Honor of Dr Sebastian Alexander Matczak*, THOMPSON, Henry O (ed), 35-50. Lanham, Univ Pr of America, 1989.

HARRISON, Bernard. Morality and Interest. Philosophy, 64(249), 303-322, Jl 89.

HARRISON, Ross. "Atemporal Necessities of Thought: or, How Not to Bury Philosophy by History" in *Reading Kant*, SCHAPER, Eva (ed), 43-54. Cambridge, Blackwell, 1989.

Defends the possibility of transcendental arguments. Shows that it is possible to establish the steps required by such arguments as necessary steps; hence that such arguments are not temporally or contextually relative.

HARRISON, Thomas (ed). *Nietzsche in Italy*. Saratoga, Anma Libri, 1988

This a collection of papers explores the influence Italy had on Nietzsche at the end of his life as well as the influence Nietzsche has had on Italian philosophy. Many of the essays were first read at the "Nietzsche in Italy" conference hosted by the Department of French and Italian at Stanford University in 1986. (staff)

HART, Alan. Melville and Spinoza. Stud Spinozana, 5, 43-58, 1989.

Herman Melville purchased an edition of Bayle's *Dictionary* in 1849. It contains Bayle's version of Spinoza's philosophy. Melville refers to Spinoza in *Moby Dick* and echoes of Bayle's interpretation can be found there and in *Billy Budd*.

HART, Bradd. A Proof of Morley's Conjecture. J Sym Log, 54(4), 1346-1358, D 89.

HART, David K. "The Sympathetic Organization" in *Papers on the Ethics of Administration*, WRIGHT, N Dale (ed), 67-95. Albany, SUNY Pr, 1988.

HART, H L A. "Comment: Legal Theory and the Problem of Sense" in *Issues in Contemporary Legal Philosophy: The Influence of H L A Hart*, GAVISON, Ruth (ed), 35-42. New York, Clarendon/Oxford Pr, 1987.

HART, James G. Constitution and Reference in Husserl's Phenomenology of Phenomenology. Husserl Stud, 6(1), 43-72, 1989.

HART, Kevin. *The Trespass of the Sign: Deconstruction, Theology and Philosophy*. New York, Cambridge Univ Pr, 1989

This study poses two questions, seeks to demonstrate that they are intimately related, then examines several aspects of this relationship. One question—What is deconstruction?—is very new, while the other—What is the relationship between metaphysics and theology?—is very old indeed. Upon Hart's reading, however, some of the earliest answers to the second question also partially answer the first. If this is so, metaphysics, theology and deconstruction have always existed in a covert economy; and in realising this, we can come to a better understanding of all three.

HART, Richard E. On Personalism and Education. Personalist Forum, 6(1), 51-74, Spr 90.

This paper elaborates on such philosophic notions as dialogue, life experience, instrumentalism, and motivation as they relate to a theory of education. It utilizes leading concepts from Socrates, John Dewey, Martin Buber and the tradition of American personalism in arguing for a return to a genuine person-centered approach to teaching and learning. The final section discusses efforts currently underway at one school, Bloomfield College in New Jersey, to realize and manifest the person-centered approach, thus enabling students to reach their peak potentials in a highly diverse and competitive world.

HART, Richard E. Philosophy, Children and Teaching Philosophy. Thinking, 8(3), 25-26, 1989.

A brief report on a paper delivered by Gareth Matthews at the Eastern Division APA meeting in 1988. The special session was sponsored by the American Association of Philosophy Teachers and Matthews's paper was entitled "Teaching Philosophy as Reconstructing Childhood." A stimulating commentary was offered by Karen J Warren. Reflecting on his in-class work with children, Matthews described a child's natural condition of puzzlement and how puzzlement incites philosophy. Philosophy thus becomes, for Matthews, a systematic and disciplined way of dealing with questions that can and do occur to young children. As teachers of philosophy we would do well to seek to recover in our classrooms this childlike fascination with the very questions that may have prompted our own initial interest in the field. The report concludes with comments on the growth, in numbers and professional importance, of the American Association of Philosophy Teachers.

HART, W D. The Cake Problem. Acta Phil Fennica, 38, 25-35, 1985.

When two people have a cake to divide between themselves, it seems fair that one cut and the other choose first. It is not difficult to generalize this rule from two to many people. If it also be required that the amount of cake available for division should vary with the rule chosen for dividing it, then a miniature of Rawls's conception of justice as fairness emerges from the solution to the problem.

HART, W D. The Price of Possibility. Pac Phil Quart, 70(3), 225-239, S 89.

Why is modality of philosophical interest? Objective modal truths should answer to possibilities independent of our conceptions of them. But then it is obscure how we might have epistemic access to such possibilities, especially given the natural analogy that sensuous imagination is to knowledge of mere possibility as perception is to knowledge of actuality. For actuality acts on us causally through perception, while it seems axiomatic that mere possibility be utterly inert to us. Yet the cost, both to philosophy itself and to our conception of deliberation among alternative courses of action, of ceasing to take possibility seriously seems very high.

HART, W. Against Skills. Thinking, 5(1), 35-44, 1983.

HARTLE, Anthony E. *Moral Issues in Military Decision Making*. Lanham, Univ Pr of America, 1989

This study identifies the moral framework within which American military professionals function and argues that three primary factors shape professional military ethics: the exigencies of combat, the laws of war, and the core values of the society served. The latter two result in a distinctive American professional military ethic. Numerous case studies clarify the nature of the ethic and its application. The discussion also concludes that American military professionals can be described as filling a partially differentiated role, which is to say that the moral guidance that applies may call for actions that are different from those appropriate for a general member of society.

HARTSHORNE, Charles. *The Darkness and the Light: A Philosopher Reflects Upon His Career—Charles Hartshorne*. Albany, SUNY Pr, 1990

HARTSHORNE, M Holmes. *Kierkegaard, Godly Deceiver: The Nature and Meaning of His Pseudonymous Writings*. New York, Columbia Univ Pr, 1990

This work is a biographical sketch as well as an analysis of Kierkegaard's pseudonymous writings. The thesis of the book is that Kierkegaard's statement that "in the pseudonymous works there is not a single word that is mine" must not be taken as poetic denial, but rather must be taken as truth. Kierkegaard was employing "Socratic irony" to bring light to false viewpoints and to ultimately "impart honesty to Christendom." (staff)

HARTZ, Glenn A. Desire and Emotion in the Virtue Tradition. Philosophia (Israel), 20(1-2), 145-165, Jl 90.

Tom Beauchamp has recently asked "What's So Special About the Virtues?" I argue that the virtue tradition's distinctiveness lies in its ability to explain the moral dimension of states of mind like desires and emotions. By contrast, modern theories tend to concentrate exclusively on action, and are unable to give a rich account of such states of mind. I explore logical and causal connections between desires and emotions, and use one of Aquinas's insights to provide fresh motivation for Aristotle's emphasis on emotions as reliable indicators of one's ethical character.

HARVEY, Charles W. Epistemology, Ergo Politics: Critique of a Correlation. Soc Theor Pract, 16(1), 43-59, Spr 90.

This essay argues that two common correlations made between epistemic stances and socio-political stances are unjustified. It shows how those who argue that truth is "made" (e.g., Adorno) are accused of sliding into authoritarian forms of social control by those who argue that truth is "found" (e.g., Russell), whereas those who argue that truth is found are accused of sliding into authoritarian forms of social control by those who argue that truth is made. It is then argued that these claims cannot be supported at either a common sense or a social-scientific level. Counterexamples are then given to each set of claims. The essay concludes by arguing that the epistemic distinction that motivates the debate is itself spurious.

HARVEY, Charles W. *Husserl's Phenomenology and the Foundations of Natural Science*. Athens, Ohio Univ Pr, 1989

The key operative concepts of Husserl's phenomenology, "epoche," "reduction," and "constitution," are interpreted in terms of the problems that arose from the metaphysical foundations supplied to modern physical

science. The book shows how the attempt to provide these foundations to modern physical science spawned the problems to which Husserl's phenomenology was meant to supply an answer. At the center of these problems are the appearance-reality, and the mind-body dichotomy. The reading of Husserl offered here locates his thought squarely in the "revolt against dualism," it functions as propaedeutic to an understanding of Husserl's philosophy of natural science, and it offers the apparatus for, and the beginnings of, a Husserlian response to his contemporary critics.

HARVEY, Charles W. Husserl's Phenomenology as Critique of Epistemic Ideology. Int Phil Quart, 30(1), 33-42, Mr 90.

The essay describes some of the commonly expressed correlations between epistemic and socio-political stances. It shows how foundationalist philosophies have been correlated with fascistic and totalitarian forms of political control, and how Husserl's philosophy has been classed in this group. The essay then shows that Husserl's philosophy is not one that demands absolute foundations for knowledge, and thereby not one that implies totalitarian forms of political rule. It is argued, finally, that the opposite is true: Husserl's philosophy is inherently a critical philosophy.

HARVEY, Charles W. Reflections on Charles S Brown's "Husserl, Intentionality, and Cognitive Architecture". SW Phil Rev, 6(2), 119-122, Jl 90.

These comments attempt to show that a classic philosophical problem lies just below the surface of the debate between Jerry Fodor's "language model of thought" and Adrian Cussins's prelinguistic "connectionist" approach to problems in AI. The classical philosophical problem is the problem of the prelinguistically given and its relation to the conceptually articulate. I claim that while the AI debate might result in some *mechanical* advances in imitating human thought, it cannot advance *phenomenological* understanding of the relation between the prelinguistic and the conceptual.

HARVEY, Irene E. "Derrida, Kant, and the Performance of Paregonality" in *Derrida and Deconstruction*, SILVERMAN, Hugh J (ed), 59-76. New York, Routledge, 1989.

HARVEY, Irene E. "The *Différance* Between Derrida and de Man" in *The Textual Sublime: Deconstruction and Its Differences*, SILVERMAN, Hugh J (ed), 73-86. Albany, SUNY Pr, 1990.

HARVEY, John Collins. Speculations Regarding the History of *Donum Vitae*. J Med Phil, 14(5), 481-491, O 89.

HARVEY, Steven and HARVEY, Warren Zev. A Note on the Arabic Term 'Anniyyah/'Aniyyah/'Inniyyah (in Hebrew). Iyyun, 38(2), 167-172, Ap 89.

Despite his *via negativa*, Maimonides states in *Guide*, I:58, that we can apprehend God's 'nyh; see J Stern's essay in this issued. S Pines has argued that this unusual Arabic term originated as a transliteration of the Greek *einai* or *on*. God's 'aniyyah would thus be His *being*. Others derive the term from the Arabic 'an or 'anna. God's 'anniyyah would thus be His *quoditas*: we cannot know what He is, only *that* He is. Still others derive the term from the Arabic 'ana. God's 'aniyyah would thus be His Egoism: God is the Ego of the cosmos. Yet others derive the term from the Arabic 'inna. We cannot describe God, but can emphatically affirm Him. All four explications are theologically suggestive, and each might be claimed to fit Maimonides' views. However, the fourth is found in Alfarabi's *Kitab al-Alfaz* and *Kitab al-Haruf*. Given Maimonides' high regard for Alfarabi's logical works, he too probably understood the term as derived from "indeed," and vocalized it 'inniyyah. The explication is also apt in light of Stern's remarks on the "syntactical problem of attributes." (edited)

HARVEY, Warren Zev and HARVEY, Steven. A Note on the Arabic Term 'Anniyyah/'Aniyyah/'Inniyyah (in Hebrew). Iyyun, 38(2), 167-172, Ap 89.

Despite his *via negativa*, Maimonides states in *Guide*, I:58, that we can apprehend God's 'nyh; see J Stern's essay in this issued. S Pines has argued that this unusual Arabic term originated as a transliteration of the Greek *einai* or *on*. God's 'aniyyah would thus be His *being*. Others derive the term from the Arabic 'an or 'anna. God's 'anniyyah would thus be His *quoditas*: we cannot know what He is, only *that* He is. Still others derive the term from the Arabic 'ana. God's 'aniyyah would thus be His Egoism: God is the Ego of the cosmos. Yet others derive the term from the Arabic 'inna. We cannot describe God, but can emphatically affirm Him. All four explications are theologically suggestive, and each might be claimed to fit Maimonides' views. However, the fourth is found in Alfarabi's *Kitab al-Alfaz* and *Kitab al-Haruf*. Given Maimonides' high regard for Alfarabi's logical works, he too probably understood the term as derived from "indeed," and vocalized it 'inniyyah. The explication is also apt in light of Stern's remarks on the "syntactical problem of attributes." (edited)

HARVEY, Warren Zev. "Crescas versus Maimonides on Knowledge and

Pleasure" in *A Straight Path: Studies in Medieval Philosophy and Culture*, LINK-SALINGER, Ruth (ed), 113-123. Washington, Cath Univ Amer Pr, 1988.

HASLETT, D W. What Is Utility? Econ Phil, 6(1), 65-94, Ap 90.

This article examines the concepts of "utility" and of "personal welfare" and the relationship between them. The objections to the two main competing models of utility—the preference (or desire) model and the experience model—are discussed, and a "compromise" model that avoids the objections to each main model is set out and defended.

HATCHER, Donald. A Critique of Critical Thinking. Thinking, 6(4), 14-16, 1986.

This paper presents a series of arguments for including instruction in formal logic in any critical thinking course and criticizes the tendency of most critical thinking texts for emphasizing only informal approaches to reasoning.

HATCHER, Donald. Is Critical Thinking Guilty of Unwarranted Reductionism. J Thought, 24(1-2), 94-111, Spr-Sum 89.

Critical thinking texts and courses have been accused of being overly analytic and employing methods that are reductionistic. I argue that the analytic methods of critical thinking instruction can be employed to evaluate claims made in any discipline, and that those who claim that there are alternative methods of evaluation imply an unacceptable form of epistemological relativism.

HATTIANGADI, J N. "The Physical Manifestation of Empirical Knowledge" in *Issues in Evolutionary Epistemology*, HAHLWEG, Kai (ed), 545-558. Albany, SUNY Pr, 1989.

HAUERWAS, Stanley. "On Being 'Placed' by John Milbank: A Response" in *Christ, Ethics and Tragedy: Essays in Honour of Donald MacKinnon*, SURIN, Kenneth (ed), 197-201. New York, Cambridge Univ Pr, 1989.

HAUGELAND, John. Dasein's Disclosedness. S J Phil, SUPP(28), 51-73, 1989.

HAUSMAN, Carl R. In and Out of Peirce's Percepts. Trans Peirce Soc, 26(3), 271-308, Sum 90.

Analyzes the relation between percepts and perceptual judgments. Begins with Bernstein's "Peirce's Theory of Perception" shows how the mediating function of the percipuum is complicated by a distinction—which Peirce seems to assume—between two senses of "percept": (1) the initial, pre-interpreted constraint on perception, and (2) the provisionally completed object of the interpetive judgment. Perception moves from "the medad" of percept (1) through abductive inference in judgment to the formed judgment with its object, percept (2) the dynamical object constrains percept (1) and percept (2); percept (2) is also interpretatively constrained and thus is an immediate object.

HAUSMAN, Daniel M. Are Markets Morally Free Zones? Phil Pub Affairs, 18(4), 317-333, Fall 89.

This essay examines David Gauthier's claim in *Morals by Agreement* that perfectly competitive markets are "morally free zones" in which there are no moral constraints on individual conduct. This claim is both indefensible and false. In all complicated social interactions, including those mediated by perfectly competitive markets, individual conduct affects the interests of others and is subject to moral appraisal.

HAUTAMAKI, Antti. Points of View and their Logical Analysis. Acta Phil Fennica, 41, 1-156, 1986.

The purpose of the work is to explicate the concept of point of view and to develop a logical calculus for points of view. The basic concept is that of determinable (or attribute). A determinable is a functional term, such as 'age' or 'colour' together with a set of mutually exclusive determinate values, like red and blue. A point of view is a finite set of determinables (attributes). In the given logic points of view are expressed in syntax by attaching finite lists of determinable indices to terms. A complete axiomatization of the logic is presented. Some philosophical applications are given (modal and free logics, relative identity, structure of theories, dialectics).

HAVAS, Katalin G. Dialectic and Inconsistency in Knowledge Acquisition. Stud Soviet Tho, 39(3-4), 189-198, Ap-My 90.

Separations and the naming of that which was separated is a necessary activity on the basis of which natural languages came into being and use. The dialectical approach does not mean trying to deliver cognition from this activity, but to take it into account. The paper deals with some kind of inconsistencies which follow from separations introduced into reality by our reflective mind. In some cases inconsistency can be eliminated through the extension of the universe of discourse and in some other cases the problem can be solved by changing the subdivision of the universe.

HAVERKATE, Henk. A Speech Act Analysis of Irony. J Prag, 14(1), 77-109, F 90.

The aim of this paper is to show that the category of verbal irony can be properly described within the framework of the theory of speech acts. It is argued that speakers make use of irony in order to produce certain perlocutionary effects on their hearers, the principal ones being to break their patterns of expectation, and involve them in a type of verbal interaction that is characterized by interpersonal distance. The paper starts with a critical evaluation of traditional definitions, which, for the greater part, qualify irony as a rhetoric or stylistic figure of speech. Conceptually, these definitions are centered around two criteria: (1) saying the opposite of what you mean, and (2) saying something different from what you mean. It is the thesis of this paper that both these criteria can be integrated into a homogeneous pragmalinguistic frame of reference. That is to say, taking into account the componential structure of the speech act, the above criteria are found to play an essential part in the analysis of the propositional and the illocutionary component of the speech act, respectively.

HAWLEY, Willis D. Looking Backward at Education Reform. Thinking, 8(4), 10-11, 1990.

HAWTHORNE, James. "Giving up Judgment Empiricism: The Bayesian Epistemology of Bertrand Russell and Grover Maxwell" in *Rereading Russell: Essays on Bertrand Russell's Metaphysics and Epistemology*, SAVAGE, C Wade (ed), 234-248. Minneapolis, Univ of Minn Pr, 1989.

HAWTHORNE, John and LANCE, Mark. From a Normative Point of View. Pac Phil Quart, 71(1), 28-46, Mr 90.

Translation is indexical in the sense that the correctness of a translation depends not just on features of the linguistic community being translated, but also on that of the translator. This indexicality is preserved even if the language community being translated has the ability to formulate claims about what its words mean. The best explanation of this phenomenon involves changing our conception of the activity of translation. In translating, one devises a set of rules which are to govern communication between the members of two communities and lead to the formation of a single large linguistic community.

HAWTHORNE, John. A Note on 'Languages and Language'. Austl J Phil, 68(1), 116-118, Mr 90.

In 'Languages and Language', David Lewis claims that a community uses some particular language L by virtue of conventions of truthfulness and trust in L prevailing in that community. Unfortunately, Lewis's proposal has as a consequence the exclusion of long sentences from our language. This difficulty besets not only Lewis's account but, moreover, any convention-based account of language use. Hence no purely convention-based account of language use is possible.

HAYES, John. Wittgenstein, Religion, Freud, and Ireland. Irish Phil J, 6(2), 191-249, 1989.

This article is, firstly, an attempt to give a comprehensive account of Ludwig Wittgenstein's visits to and stays in Ireland; secondly, an examination of Wittgenstein's primary relationship there, viz., to the psychiatrist, Maurice O'Connor Drury; and thirdly, an investigation of the record of that relationship with an eye to seeing what it reveals of Wittgenstein's view on psychiatry (mainly Freud's) and religion. Ray Monk, Wittgenstein's most recent biographer, has said that Drury's record provides perhaps more information than any other secondary source on the 'spiritual and moral attitudes that informed Wittgenstein's life and work'.

HAYNES, Felicity. On Equitable Cake-Cutting, or: Caring More about Caring. Educ Phil Theor, 21(2), 12-22, 1989.

It is fallacious to presume simply because there are fewer women in mathematics and science, that they are being discriminated against. Apple's distinction between property rights and person rights is used to indicate that Federal government policy to increase participation of women in these areas is based on a definition of equity which has an economic base, rather than a democratic one. If Gilligan's gender distinctions are accurate, the current equity policy in the white paper may well be inequitable in important respects for women, and equity only possible after a radical deconstruction of epistemological assumptions of success and national wealth.

HAYNES, Michael. Hume's *Tu Quoque*: Newtonianism and the Rationality of the Causal Principle. Man Nature, 7, 131-139, 1988.

Hume regarded himself as the Newton of the moral sciences. Yet in devastating the rationality of any belief in necessary connection, he would seem to have made mincemeat of a dynamics, like Newton's, that is based upon (causal) force. Therein lies a problem. We can, however, make sense of Hume's move if we view it as a *tu quoque* directed against Leibniz, whose (Cartesian) action by contact is thereby rendered ostensibly as "occult" as Newton's (alleged) action at a distance, thereby defusing the celebrated criticism of Newtonian gravitational attraction.

HÄYRY, Heta and HÄYRY, Matti. AIDS, Society and Morality—A Philosophical Survey. Philosophia (Israel), 19(4), 331-361, D 89.

The article surveys some of the most important philosophical literature on acquired immune deficiency syndrome (AIDS), published during 1985-88. The topics prevalent in the literature include the tension between the individual and society; the legitimacy of quarantines, quarantine-like measures and legal restrictions on high-risk behaviour; the optimal nature of health education; questions in testing for the AIDS virus; and the duties of the medical personnel as regards confidentiality and equal treatment. A liberal response to these issues is developed throughout the article.

HÄYRY, Heta and HÄYRY, Matti. Euthanasia, Ethics and Economics. Bioethics, 4(2), 154-161, Ap 90.

Those who hold traditionalist views on medical ethics have often argued that euthanasia ought to remain illegal, since its legalisation would have a 'frightening symbolic value' for the disabled and the elderly. More recently, however, some of these theorists have also suggested that publicly funded medical services should not be extended to older people. Yet it seems that the 'symbolic value' of not treating people on the grounds of old age is considerably more frightening than the 'symbolic value' of legalising voluntary euthanasia. In the article it is argued that the official acceptance of voluntary euthanasia ought to be preferred to any traditionalist solutions in dealing with the economic problems facing health care systems today.

HÄYRY, Heta and HÄYRY, Matti. Health Care as a Right: Fairness and Medical Resources. Bioethics, 4(1), 1-21, Ja 90.

There is a growing feeling in many Western countries that every human being has an equal right to health, or an equal right to health care. If this popular feeling is to be taken seriously, the allocation of medical resources ought to be arranged in a fair and equitable manner. It is argued in this article, however, that there are no universally acceptable criteria for preferring some kinds of medical need over others. The only remaining possibility seems to be that medical resources must be radically increased at the expense of less important nonmedical budgetary allocations.

HÄYRY, Matti and HÄYRY, Heta. AIDS, Society and Morality—A Philosophical Survey. Philosophia (Israel), 19(4), 331-361, D 89.

The article surveys some of the most important philosophical literature on acquired immune deficiency syndrome (AIDS), published during 1985-88. The topics prevalent in the literature include the tension between the individual and society; the legitimacy of quarantines, quarantine-like measures and legal restrictions on high-risk behaviour; the optimal nature of health education; questions in testing for the AIDS virus; and the duties of the medical personnel as regards confidentiality and equal treatment. A liberal response to these issues is developed throughout the article.

HÄYRY, Matti and HÄYRY, Heta. Euthanasia, Ethics and Economics. Bioethics, 4(2), 154-161, Ap 90.

Those who hold traditionalist views on medical ethics have often argued that euthanasia ought to remain illegal, since its legalisation would have a 'frightening symbolic value' for the disabled and the elderly. More recently, however, some of these theorists have also suggested that publicly funded medical services should not be extended to older people. Yet it seems that the 'symbolic value' of not treating people on the grounds of old age is considerably more frightening than the 'symbolic value' of legalising voluntary euthanasia. In the article it is argued that the official acceptance of voluntary euthanasia ought to be preferred to any traditionalist solutions in dealing with the economic problems facing health care systems today.

HÄYRY, Matti and HÄYRY, Heta. Health Care as a Right: Fairness and Medical Resources. Bioethics, 4(1), 1-21, Ja 90.

There is a growing feeling in many Western countries that every human being has an equal right to health, or an equal right to health care. If this popular feeling is to be taken seriously, the allocation of medical resources ought to be arranged in a fair and equitable manner. It is argued in this article, however, that there are no universally acceptable criteria for preferring some kinds of medical need over others. The only remaining possibility seems to be that medical resources must be radically increased at the expense of less important nonmedical budgetary allocations.

HAYS, Robert G and REISNER, Anne E. Media Ethics and Agriculture: Advertiser Demands Challenge Farm Press's Ethical Practices. Agr Human Values, 6(4), 40-46, Fall 89.

The agricultural communicator is a key link in transmitting information to farmers. If agricultural communicators' ethics are compromised, the resulting biases in news production could have serious detrimental effects on the quality of information conveyed to farmers. But, to date, agricultural communicators' perceptions of ethical problems they encounter at work has not been examined. This study looks at the dimensions of ethical concerns for

topic area (agricultural) journalists as defined by practitioners. To determine these dimensions, we sent open-ended questionnairs to members of two professional agricultural journalist associations. Agricultural communicators overwhelmingly focus on one specific threat to objectivity—advertising pressure. Respondents indicated that agricultural journalists' responses to advertising pressure adversely affected the entire profession. The editors' and reporters' perceptions of advertising pressure clearly indicate that advertising abuses are a clear and present danger and one worthy of far more attention than it has previously received. (edited)

HAYS, Steve. On the Skeptical Influence of Gorgias's On Non-Being. J Hist Phil, 28(3), 327-337, Jl 90.

HAZELETT, Richard and TURNER, Dean. Benevolent Living: Tracing the Roots of Motivation to God. Pasadena, Hope, 1990

This book attempts to define happiness, to distinguish between wise and unwise ways of pursuing it, and to determine what the conditions are that make it possible and enduring. Both empirically and creatively, the book examines every major aspect of the problem of happiness—the economics, politics, sociology, psychology, aesthetics and ethics of the sense of well-being and joy in being alive. The book not only talks of achieving a comprehensive philosophy of happiness but actually develops one that can be represented as solid and of distinct value in the face of sophisticated criticism.

HAZEN, A P. The Mathematical Philosophy of Contact. Philosophy, 65(252), 205-211, Ap 90.

A sophism purports to draw physical conclusions from topological premisses: bodies occupy sets of points, neither open nor closed sets can adjoin, ergo, bodies cannot touch. This paradox commits the fallacy of misplaced concreteness. It is dissolved when the conception of spatial points as real existents is replaced by one that sees them as constructed by Whitehead's method of extensive abstraction.

HAZEN, Allen. A Variation on a Paradox. Analysis, 50(1), 7-8, Ja 90.

If I am telling the truth, we are in deep trouble. Think about it.

HAZLITT, Henry. The Foundations of Morality. Lanham, Univ Pr of America, 1988

HEACOCK, Marian V and MC GEE, Gail W. Whistleblowing: An Ethical Issue in Organizational and Human Behavior. Bus Prof Ethics J, 6(4), 35-46, Wint 87.

Whistleblowing is an extremely crucial issue for organizations, employees, and the public at large. Therefore, it is important that we develop greater understanding of the whistleblowing process, including its predictors and effects. This paper provides a brief overview of the whistleblowing literature, including descriptive, theoretical, and empirical. Based on this review, we offer some suggestions regarding specific delineations of whistleblowing for use by organizations, and make recommendations for future whistleblowing research.

HEAL, Jane. Fact and Meaning. Cambridge, Blackwell, 1989

Some have thought that Quine and Wittgenstein hold similar sceptical views about meaning on similar 'holistic' grounds. The book argues that this is not so. Both do indeed emphasise the dissimilarity between the concepts of natural science and those of semantics and psychology. But Quine's empiricism leads him to an ultimately incoherent meaning scepticism, whereas Wittgenstein's view of the interdependence of concepts and interests leads to a nonsceptical outcome and a different view about what 'realism' should amount to.

HEALEY, Richard. The Philosophy of Quantum Mechanics: An Interactive Interpretation. New York, Cambridge Univ Pr, 1989

This book presents a new interpretation of quantum mechanics. In this interpretation, a quantum measurement is a physical interaction within a compound system, correlating the dynamical states of measured system and (quantum mechanical) apparatus; whereas the quantum state provides (via the Born rules) a summary of numerical information concerning probabilistic dispositions realized in such interactions. The distinction between dynamical and quantum states is the key to the dissolution of the measurement problem. The further idea that the dynamical state of a compound quantum system is not always determined by those of its components permits a novel understanding of EPR-type correlations.

HEBBLETHWAITE, Brian. "MacKinnon and the Problem of Evil" in Christ, Ethics and Tragedy: Essays in Honour of Donald MacKinnon, SURIN, Kenneth (ed), 131-145. New York, Cambridge Univ Pr, 1989.

In this paper I argue, against Donald MacKinnon, that, properly understood, the 'privatio boni' analysis of the ontological status of evil is a *necessary* element in Christian metaphysics, that the problem of evil *must* in the end find a theoretical solution, and that tragedy *cannot* be an ultimate category to a

Christian view of the world. To refuse to press these theoretical questions is to rest content with an incoherent faith. Practical commitment is no substitute for theodicy.

HEBBLETHWAITE, Brian. Reply to Michael Diamond's "A Modern Theistic Argument". Mod Theol, 6(3), 295-296, Ap 90.

HECKMANN, Gustav. Socratic Dialogue. Thinking, 8(1), 34-37, 1989.

HEDELER, Wladislaw. Der Weg eines Mitstreiters und Kampfgefährten Lenins zum Marxismus. Deut Z Phil, 37(12), 1111-1120, 1989.

HEDTKE, Ulrich. Gibt es einen Puls unserer Produktivkraftentwicklung? Deut Z Phil, 38(4), 328-337, 1990.

HEELAN, Patrick A. After Experiment: Realism and Research. Amer Phil Quart, 26(4), 297-308, O 89.

Theory making and experimentation are two differently constituted research roles. This essay takes a new look at the complex relationships between them. The philosophical perspective is taken from hermeneutical phenomenology. Husserl's "geometrizing" of the phenomenon as a perceptual invariance under transformations of its profiles is applied to experimental phenomena prepared by standardized laboratory performance. Performance, however, after Heidegger, is a mode of ontological interpretation or hermeneutics. Consequently, the function of theory is to model the transformational structure of the scientific phenomenon as an ontological structure and to name its profiles. This analysis justifies the general thesis that scientific phenomena are new "naturalized" perceptual objects. This account also gives legitimacy to the claim that moral, social, historical, religious, artistic, technological, and prudential factors operate side by side with theory and data at the core of scientific research.

HEFT, James L and CADEGAN, Una M. Mary of Nazareth, Feminism and the Tradition. Thought, 65(257), 169-189, Je 90.

HEGEL, G W F and BUTLER, Clark (trans). Review of C F Göschel's *Aphorisms: Part Three*. Clio, 18(4), 379-385, Sum 89.

HEGEL, G W F. Who Thinks in an Abstract Manner? M Sobokta: Commentary (in Czechoslovakian). Filozof Cas, 38(1-2), 177-187, 1990.

Hegel's article entitled "Wer denk abstrakt?" has not yet been translated into Czech even though several comments on it have appeared in Hegel-Studien, the latest of which was Gencho Donchev's study "Wer denkt abstrakt? und die Phänomenologie des Geistes" (Hegel-Studien, vol. 12, 1977, pp. 190-200). In a broader analysis of Hegel's method leading from the abstract to the concrete the author points to the parallel existing between article 32 and 256 in Philosophie des Rechts and Marx's characterization of this particular method in Grundrissse der Kritik der politischen ökonomie. (edited)

HEGENBARTH, Siegfried. "Krise des Fortschritts—Umkehr zur Zukunft": Zu einigen Aspekten religiöser Welt-und Fortschrittssicht. Deut Z Phil, 37(10-11), 956-966, 1989.

The article, basing on a theoretical study published in 1989, examines the developments of meaning about "Epoch" and "Progress" in the Roman Catholic Church and the discussions of the World Council of Churches since the sixties. From a Marxist point of view the authors accentuate the differential ideological and religious particularly of Christian thinking in our time. Referring to the concept of "Change to the World" and to the ethical axiom of the "Unity of Peace and Justice"—the biblical tradition of "Shalom"—they vote for a cooperation between Christians and Marxists in common responsibility for the future of mankind.

HEIDEGGER, Martin and ZUBIRÍA, Martín (trans). Acerca de la pregunta por la determinante de la cosa del pensar. Rev Filosof (Mexico), 22(66), 320-331, S-D 89.

HEIDEGGER, Martin and BOBURG, Felipe (trans). La constitucion onto-teo-logica de la metafisica. Rev Filosof (Mexico), 22(66), 300-319, S-D 89.

HEIDEGGER, Martin and GRIMALDI, Rosario (trans). Hacer mas legible la lectura de los acontecimientos. Rev Filosof (Mexico), 22(66), 297-299, S-D 89.

HEIDEGGER, Martin. *Hegel's Concept of Experience*. San Francisco, Harper & Row, 1989

HEIDEGGER, Martin. Schelling's "On the Essence of Human Freedom": An Interpretation of the First Main Points (in Hungarian). Magyar Filozof Szemle, 4, 434-507, 1989.

HEIDEGGER, Martin. Vom Ursprung des Kunstwerks: Erste Ausarbeitung. Heidegger Stud, 5, 5-22, 1989.

HEIDEMA, Johannes. An Axiom Schema of Comprehension of Zermelo-Fraenkel-Skolem Set Theory. Hist Phil Log, 11(1), 59-65, 1990.

Unrestricted use of the axiom schema of comprehension, 'to every mathematically (or set-theoretically) describable property there corresponds the set of all mathematical (or set-theoretical) objects having that property', leads to contradiction. In set theories of the Zermelo-Fraenkel-Skolem (ZFS) style suitable instances of the comprehension schema are chosen ad hoc as axioms, e.g., axioms which guarantee the existence of unions, intersection, pairs, subsets, empty set, power sets and replacement sets. It is demonstrated that a uniform syntactic description may be given of *acceptable* instances of the comprehension schema, which include all of the axioms mentioned, and which in their turn are theorems of the usual versions of ZFS set theory.

HEIDLER, Angelika. Probleme der Dialektik der sozialistischen Produktionsweise. Deut Z Phil, 37(10-11), 1035-1040, 1989.

HEIL, John (ed). *Cause, Mind, and Reality: Essays Honoring C B Martin*. Norwell, Kluwer, 1989

The essays in this volume are intended to be free-standing philosophical contributions honoring a widely influential but under-appreciated philosopher. Contributions (all but one of which were written expressly for the volume) focus on metaphysical and historical topics (Locke, causality, reference, materialism, verificationism, and the like) associated with Martin's published and unpublished work. Contributors include D M Armstrong, James Cargile, David Charles, Max Deutscher, Michael Devitt, Ian Hinckfuss, J M Hinton, Frank Jackson, Brian P McLaughlin, Brian Medlin, Graham Nerlich, Kai Nielsen, U T Place, Daniel Shaw, J J C Smart, and Paul Snowdon.

HEIL, John. Minds Divided. Mind, 98(392), 571-583, O 89.

In an effort to cope with puzzles associated with the ascription of certain sorts of irrational thoughts and deeds, some theorists—most notably Donald Davidson and David Pears—have suggested that we regard the mind as *divided* or *partitioned*. I examine a line of reasoning that might be taken to motivate such a conception, and argue that, on the whole, we have available simpler, more plausible and attractive explanations of the species of irrationality for which the model of the divided mind seems most apt.

HEILKE, Thomas W (trans) and GADAMER, Hans-Georg. "The Drama of Zarathustra" in *Nietzsche's New Seas: Explorations in Philosophy, Aesthetics, and Politics*, GILLESPIE, Michael Allen (ed), 220-231. Chicago, Univ of Chicago Pr, 1989.

HEILKE, Thomas W (trans) and JANZ, Curt Paul. "The Form-Content Problem in Nietzsche's Conception of Music" in *Nietzsche's New Seas: Explorations in Philosophy, Aesthetics, and Politics*, GILLESPIE, Michael Allen (ed), 97-116. Chicago, Univ of Chicago Pr, 1989.

HEILKE, Thomas W. *Voegelin on the Idea of Race: An Analysis of Modern European Racism*. Baton Rouge, Louisiana St Univ Pr, 1990

HEIM, Irene. E-Type Pronouns and Donkey Anaphora. Ling Phil, 13(2), 137-177, Ap 90.

HEIM, Michael. Grassi's Experiment: The Renaissance through Phenomenology. Res Phenomenol, 18, 233-263, 1988.

HEINAMAN, Robert. Aristotle and the Mind-Body Problem. Phronesis, 35(1), 83-102, 1990.

HEINE, Heinrich and HÖHN, Gerhard (trans). Du principe démocratique. Rev Metaph Morale, 94(2), 147-151, Ap-Je 89.

HEINE, Steven. Philosophy for an 'Age of Death': The Critique of Science and Technology in Heidegger and Nishitani. Phil East West, 40(2), 175-193, Ap 90.

An analysis of the critique of science and technology in the thought of Heidegger and Nishitani in light of the "convergence thesis," which argues for the parallel between philosophy of religion and science, with emphasis on the ethical as well as the metaphysical implications in the criticism. The article begins to develop an "ethics of uncertainty" by viewing the Heidegger-Nishitani position in relation to the principles of uncertainty and complementarity.

HEINEGG, James. Philosophy and Foolishness. Thinking, 8(4), 7-9, 1990.

HEINIÖ, Mikko. Composers' Texts as Objects of Musicological Study. Acta Phil Fennica, 43, 293-299, 1988.

HEJDANEK, Ladislav. Philosophy and Society: On the Philosophical Heritage of Emanuel Radl (in Czechoslovakian). Filozof Cas, 38(1-2), 59-86, 1990.

This study, written in 1983 on the occasion of the anniversary of the death of Emanuel Rádl, an outstanding Czech thinker, sets out to expound his concept of philosophy and specify his place in society and political life in comparison with some other philosophers and some contemporary topical problems facing Czech philosophers. Tying on to Komensky, Rádl views philosophy as a programme of worldwide correction of things in the service of truth. His concept of truth is distinctly polemically non-Greek, and links up to the tradition viewing truth as more powerful than everything real and above everything real, prevailing and overcoming all things. Of particular importance for the present and the future are Rádl's thought on the democracy of philosophy and philosophers, i.e., on a certain type of leadership to which philosophers are predestined and also on the necessity of philosophy becoming comprehensible to the broadest strata without whose sympathies and support it can never hope to exist. (edited)

HELD, Virginia. Philosophy and the Media. J Soc Phil, 20(1-2), 116-124, Spr-Fall 89.

HELDKE, Lisa. Recipes, Cooking and Conflict. Hypatia, 5(1), 165-170, Spr 90.

This paper addresses Koch's concern about whether a coresponsible theorist can engage in inquiry with a theorist who is "beyond the pale." On what grounds, he asks, can a coresponsible inquirer argue against one who uses a racist, sexist, or classist model for inquiry? I argue that, in such situations, the coresponsible inquirer brings to inquiry both a theoretical framework, or "attitude," and a set of practical concerns which manifest that attitude.

HELLER, Agnes. The Contingent Person and the Existential Choice. Phil Forum, 21(1-2), 53-69, Fall-Wint 89-90.

HELLER, Agnes. Unknown Masterpiece. Phil Soc Crit, 15(3), 205-239, 1989.

HELLER, Agnes. What Is and What Is Not Practical Reason? Phil Soc Crit, 14(3-4), 391-410, 1988.

HELLER, J. Economic Relations and their Reflection in Working People's Consciousness under Socialism (in Czechoslovakian). Filozof Cas, 37(6), 795-811, 1989.

The author approaches the problem of studying social consciousness on the basis of analyzing economic relations and class-oriented social structures of socialism. He comes out against a very frequent view which proceeds from the methodological basis comprising an insufficient distinction between actual socio-economic differences between classes and groups and differences of a professional nature. The author goes on to stress the need of respecting the relative independence of the reflection of socio-economic, professional-employment ones on the other. He presents a brief outline of the concept of class-social structure of socialist society, based on the distinction between the position of the working class and the socio-economically dual position of other groups of working people. (edited)

HELMES, Günther. Spinoza in der schönen Literatur: Bilder aus der Zeit zwischen Vormärz und Weimarer Republik. Stud Spinozana, 5, 119-149, 1989.

This paper takes a critical look at pictures of Spinoza in German literature in the 19th and early 20th centuries. In that period, authors turn their attention to Spinoza especially in the decades before and after the Revolution of March 1848, in the decade before World War I, and at the end of the Weimar Republic. This leads to the assumption that not only historico-cultural correlations and the world of ideas had a determining influence on the picture of Spinoza as it was formed in these periods, but contemporary history as well. As a whole, the pictures of Spinoza mirror the ambivalent history of bourgeois ideology in the 19th and 20th century. (edited)

HELSLOOT, Niels. Linguists of All Countries—On Gramsci's Premise of Coherence. J Prag, 13(4), 547-566, Ag 89.

The Italian Marxist politician Antonio Gramsci deserves to be seen as a linguist and a philosopher of language. His casual remarks on language contain a compelling methodology, implying a view of society that permits a fruitful criticism of theories of knowledge by its inclusion of knowledge in the pursuit of social unity. This, in its turn, leads to a dissolution of the problematical distinction between objective and subjective meaning, similar to those concepts of language developed by Saussure and Wittgenstein, but more explicitly politicized. What is historically accepted as 'linguistic unity', 'agreement', or 'understanding', changes within social struggle. Therefore, Gramsci starts from difference, in order to strive towards unity. Up to this point, his linguistics is extremely useful. The impact of his work, however, is that to strive for unity is something one should always do (his 'principle of coherence'). This claim (complemented by the linguistics of the Marxist Volosinov (Bakhtin)) leads to an elaboration on Gramsci that also allows for nonconformist political strategies (a 'principle of translatability').

HEMMENWAY, Scott R. Philosophical Apology in the Theaetetus. Interpretation, 17(3), 323-346, Spr 90.

Two speeches in Plato's Theaetetus, Socrates' well-known description of himself as a midwife and the "digression" in the middle of the dialogue,

wherein Socrates contrasts the philosopher and the public orator, have apologetic dimensions; they are, in part, attempts by Socrates to account for, and hence correct, his and the philosopher's undeserved public reputation. A careful reading of these passages in their dramatic contexts as philosophical apologies reveals interesting parallels to the Apology, insights into some of the major themes of the Theaetetus, and a fuller appreciation of Socratic philosophy as portrayed in Plato's dialogues.

HENDERSON, David K. An Empirical Basis for Charity in Interpretation. Erkenntnis, 32(1), 83-103, Ja 90.

In codifying the methods of translation, several writers have formulated maxims that would constrain interpreters to construe their subjects as (more or less) rational speakers of the truth. Such maxims have come to be known as versions of the principle of charity. W V O Quine suggests an empirical, not purely methodological, basis for his version of that principle. Recently, Stephen Stich has criticized Quine's attempt to found the principle of charity in translation on information about the probabilities of various sorts of mistakes. Here I defend Quine's approach. These issues have important implications for the supposed a priori status of human rationality.

HENDERSON, Edward H. Philosophie et théologie chez Austin Farrer. Arch Phil, 53(1), 49-74, Ja-Mr 90.

This is an introduction to Austin Farrer's philosophical and theological thought. Austin Farrer has been called the Anglican communion's one genius of the century, yet his work has been neglected. I try to show how he harmonized profound philosophy, traditional belief, and practical faith by focusing upon action: in philosophy upon the analysis of personal and interpersonal agency as the clue both to being and knowing; and in theology upon the 'lived' or practiced meaning of Christian belief. I explain how Farrer used the action clue in philosophical theology, considering the logic of faith, the idea of God, God's action in the world, and the problem of evil. Then I show how the action clue proves fruitful also in Farrer's practical and ascetical works as he disucsses Christology, the Trinity, prayer, and the sacraments. So we come to see his great achievement: the union of profound and original philosophy with traditional Christian belief and practical faith.

HENDERSON, John. "Entertaining Arguments: Terence Adelphoe" in Post-Structuralist Classics, BENJAMIN, Andrew (ed), 192-226. New York, Routledge, 1988.

HENDERSON, Robert S. David Hume on Personal Identity and the Indirect Passions. Hume Stud, 16(1), 33-44, Ap 90.

To answer the question of why we have "so great a propension to ascribe an identity to these successive impressions" which make up experience, Hume says we must distinguish "betwixt personal identity, as it regards our thought or imagination, and as it regards our passions or the concern we take in ourselves." This paper concentrates on the second part of the distinction and especially on the discussion of the indirect passions in book II of the Treatise. It shows that pride, humility, love and hatred are an important part of Hume's answer to the above question.

HENLE, Mary. On the Relation Between Logic and Thinking. Thinking, 5(1), 27-34, 1983.

HENLE, R J. Ernest Nagel's Criticism of H L A Hart's Arguments for the Natural Law. Vera Lex, 7(2), 18-20, 1987.

I examine Ernest Nagel's three criticisms of H L A Hart's, "The Minimum Good Sense of Natural Law." I reject the first criticism, that Hart's principle provides no guide for the detail of positive law. I agree with the second and third criticisms that (ii) Hart provides no standard for replacing unjust laws and that (iii) Hart's "survival" principle contradicts human history. Finally, I deny that Hart's position is, in any sense, a defense of natural law.

HENLEY, Tracy B. Chauvinism and Science: Another Reply to Shanon. J Theor Soc Behav, 20(1), 93-95, Mr 90.

Several recent theorists, including Shanon, have concerned themselves with reasons why machines cannot think. While thought in the areas has become more developed, and numerous stumbling blocks to AI have been identified, most objections still contain a certain element of humanistic chauvinism. This paper attempts to illustrate this, and to underscore the continued viability of the Turing test as an empirical way to say "if machines can think."

HENRICH, Dieter. "The Identity of the Subject in the Transcendental Deduction" in Reading Kant, SCHAPER, Eva (ed), 250-280. Cambridge, Blackwell, 1989.

HENRICI, P. "Two Types of Philosophical Approach to the Problem of War and Peace" in The Causes of Quarrel: Essays on Peace, War, and Thomas Hobbes, CAWS, Peter (ed), 149-161. Boston, Beacon Pr, 1989.

HENRICI, Peter. Anthropologische Prolegomena zur Metaphysik. Bijdragen, 3, 254-262, 1989.

A la suite de Kant, l'A. s'interroge sur les fondements anthropologiques de la métaphysique: pourquoi l'homme, de tous temps, a-t-il développé une forme de métaphysique? Elle résulte de la constatation des limites existentielles de l'homme. La constatation d'une limite implique celle d'une possibilité qui diffère de la réalité et cette dernière constatation implique celle d'un être-autre, transcendant par rapport au simple donné.

HENRY, Anne. "La réception de Schopenhauer en France" in *Schopenhauer: New Essays in Honor of His 200th Birthday*, VON DER LUFT, Eric (ed), 188-215. Lewiston, Mellen Pr, 1989.

HENRY, Barbara. Epistemologia e neocriticismo in un dibattito degli anni 1912-1914 fra Cassirer e Heidegger. Arch Stor Cult, 3, 445-458, 1990.

HENRY, Michel. "Schopenhauer: une philosophie première" in *Schopenhauer: New Essays in Honor of His 200th Birthday*, VON DER LUFT, Eric (ed), 216-231. Lewiston, Mellen Pr, 1989.

HENSON, C Ward and COMPTON, Kevin J. A Uniform Method for Proving Lower Bounds on the Computational Complexity of Logical Theories. Annals Pure Applied Log, 48(1), 1-79, JI 90.

A new method for obtaining lower bounds on the computational complexity of logical theories is presented. It extends widely used techniques for proving the undecidability of theories by interpreting models of a theory already known to be undecidable. New inseparability results related to the well-known inseparability result of Trakhtenbrot and Vaught are the foundation of the method. Their use yields hereditary lower bounds (i.e., bounds which apply uniformly to all subtheories of a theory). By means of interpretations lower bounds can be transferred from one theory to another. Complicated machine codings are replaced by much simpler definability considerations, viz., the kinds of binary relations definable with short formulas on large finite sets. Numerous examples are given, including new proofs of essentially all previously known lower bounds for theories, and lower bounds for various theories of finite trees, which turn out to be particularly useful.

HEPBURN, Ronald. "The Problem of Evil" in *Dialectic and Contemporary Science*, GRIER, Philip T (ed), 111-124. Lanham, Univ Pr of America, 1989.

To Errol Harris the world is a developing scale of forms, progressively more complex and integrated, and involving gradation in degree of finitude, lack and defect. Evil is 'incident upon finiteness'—and no argument for atheism. The essay attempts a critical appraisal of Harris's theodicy: the question of God's decision to create rather than not create, knowing the cost in suffering for finite sentient beings. Harris sees the cosmic totality as capable of a consummation in which its evil is overcome and annulled. This possibility is critically discussed.

HERLITZIUS, Erwin and RUDOLPH, Günther. Thomas Muntzer— Humanist, Reformator, Revolutionär. Deut Z Phil, 37(12), 1057-1070, 1989.

A rough understanding of the German Peasant War even in terms of the earliest burgher reform (1517-1525) mainly preferred Thomas Müntzer's political doctrine. But his religious achievements are of initial account. God's speech is supposed to be the everlasting essence in the laymen's strive for social justice and equality. Faith has come alive as reason. Müntzer is one of those who fostered the Protestant movement self-reliantly; he abolished the Latin ritual even before Luther. Inquiries about the European Renaissance should take due notice of the different streams of early Bible humanism with its integrable publication and communication, affiliated to the rediscovery of ancient literature and art.

HERMAN, Barbara. Murder and Mayhem: Violence and Kantian Casuistry. Monist, 72(3), 411-431, JI 89.

This essay examines what can be said about acts of violence in Kantian ethics using what has come to be called "the Categorical Imperative procedure." It is argued that (1) acts of noncoercive violence are rejected *not* by the arguments associated with perfect duties but by those associated with imperfect duties; (2) the resulting prohibition establishes a deliberative presumption (only) against violence as a means; (3) the casuistry of violence requires a conception of *value* elicited from the argument establishing the prohibition. (Violence in self-defense is the illustrative example.)

HERMERÉN, Göran. Representation, Truth and the Languages of the Arts. Acta Phil Fennica, 43, 179-209, 1988.

HERNDON, James F. Ethics Instruction and the Constitution. Thinking, 7(1), 6-11, 1987.

HERRERA UBICO, Silvia. El bien del arte en Etienne Gilson. Anu Filosof, 20(2), 165-172, 1987.

HERVADA, Javier. *Natural Right and Natural Law: A Critical Introduction (Second Edition)*. Pamplona, Univ Navarra, 1990

The aim of this book is to introduce a synthetical exposition of the notions of

justice and rights, according to the classical juridical realism. Specially exposes the concepts of natural law and natural right. The analyzed topics are justice, right and natural right, human person, law and natural law. Edited in Spanish (Spain and Mexico), English and Italian.

HERVADA, Javier. To Discover Again Marriage. Vera Lex, 8(2), 12, 1988.

After looking upon the actual panorama of so many proposals about marriage, the first and most urgent task of today's thought is to discover what marriage really is. Before all, marriage is not only a fact, not even a fact legally regulated. Marriage is a juridical tie, born of the consent of the two parts, a tie having mutual rights and duties. Secondly, marriage is a tie of natural law which arises from the reciprocal agreement.

HERZOG, Don. "David Hume: Crusading Empiricist, Skeptical Liberal" in *Knowledge and Politics*, DASCAL, Marcelo (ed), 69-82. Boulder, Westview Pr, 1988.

HESLEP, Robert D. A Questionable Resurrection. Proc Phil Educ, 45, 300-303, 1989.

HESS, Gérald. Le *Tractatus* de Wittgenstein: Considérations sur le système numérique et la forme aphoristique. Rev Theol Phil, 121(4), 389-406, 1989.

The article attempts to show that the philosophy of the *Tractatus* is inseparably connected with the form of the work. The contents allow two formal aspects to be exhibited: the aphoristic style and the numeric system. The author analyses these in relationship to the ideas presented by Wittgenstein. The study points out finally the role of the reader in any reflexion upon the limits of language. It also brings out a kind of rationality which could be interpreted as intuition.

HESSE, Mary. "Socializing Epistemology" in *Scientific Knowledge Socialized*, HRONSZKY, Imre (ed), 3-26. Norwell, Kluwer, 1989.

Normative philosophies of science have been criticised by sociologists who claim to find no norms in scientific practice. The paper attempts to define the concept of "conceptual system," and argues that any socially recognized cognitive system, such as "western" science, must incorporate internal social norms, and these can be analysed by methods which include those of traditional epistemology. Nontraditional cognitive models from general sociology and the anthropology of nonwestern cultures can also be exploited in both macro- and micro-social studies of science.

HESTEVOLD, H Scott. Berkeley's Theory of Time. Hist Phil Quart, 7(2), 179-192, Ap 90.

The standard interpretation of Berkeley's theory of time is formulated; this interpretation has been defended by I C Tipton, George Pitcher, and A C Grayling. Following several objections to interpreting Berkeley in the standard way, an alternative interpretation is developed and defended. The alternative both resolves a paradox of resurrection to which Berkeley alludes and preserves his account of creation.

HESTEVOLD, H Scott. Passage and the Presence of Experience. Phil Phenomenol Res, 50(3), 537-552, Mr 90.

After objecting to a defense of "transitory time" (TT)—the view that events undergo "passage"—offered by M M Schuster, TT *is* defended by appealing to (a) the doctrine that experiences, necessarily, may be known to be present and (b) A N Prior's argument involving the appropriateness of certain attitudes toward future and past events. It is argued that D H Mellor's tenseless analysis of the presence of experience offers no reason to abandon either defense of TT.

HETÉNYI, János. Detailed Analysis of the *Philosophia Harmonistica* (Introduced and Notes by Zoltán Z Szabó) (in Hungarian). Magyar Filozof Szemle, 2-3, 205-261, 1989.

HETTINGER, Edwin C. What is Wrong With Reverse Discrimination? Bus Prof Ethics J, 6(3), 39-55, Fall 87.

This discussion evaluates the alleged injustice of reverse discrimination. The charges that reverse discrimination is inefficient, involves unjustified stereotyping, creates a new form of racism and sexism, and violates the most qualified person's rights, deserts, or entitlements are all shown to be deficient. The reasons which do explain reverse discrimination's injustice—namely, it judges people on the basis of involuntary characteristics and places a larger than fair share of the burden of achieving an egalitarian society on the shoulders of white males, without compensating them for this sacrifice—only show that it is unjust in a relatively weak sense.

HETTINGER, Edwin Converse. The Responsible Use of Animals in Biomedical Research. Between Species, 5(3), 123-131, Sum 89.

This article is a critique of Carl Cohen's *New England Journal of Medicine* defense of animal experimentation. It argues that (1) Cohen relies on an attenuated notion of capacity and an unjustifiable form of speciesism when he rejects biomedical research using severely retarded humans while advocating the use of equally psychologically sophisticated animals; (2) Cohen ignores the frequent misuse of animals in biomedical research and overlooks the abundant alternatives; (3) critics of the biomedical use of animals need not be opposed to all uses of animals—they can accept limited uses of animals based on their degree of psychological sophistication.

HETZLER, Florence M. The Person and *The Little Prince* of St Exupéry, Part I. Thinking, 7(3), 2-7, 1988.

HETZLER, Florence M. The Person and *The Little Prince* of St Exupéry, Part II. Thinking, 8(1), 44-45, 1989.

HETZLER, Florence. "Interdisciplinarity as Value" in *Inquiries into Values: The Inaugural Session of the International Society for Value Inquiry*, LEE, Sander H , 603-614. Lewiston, Mellen Pr, 1989.

HETZNER, Candace. Why We Mean What We Say: The History and Use of 'Corporate Social Responsibility'. Bus Prof Ethics J, 6(3), 23-37, Fall 87.

HEYD, David. "Comment: Intentions and *Mens Rea*" in *Issues in Contemporary Legal Philosophy: The Influence of H L A Hart*, GAVISON, Ruth (ed), 271-276. New York, Clarendon/Oxford Pr, 1987.

Intentions cannot be individuated like objects or events, that is, independently of other entities. They must be individuated through their objects. There are two possible candidates for such objects: actions and propositions. But actions can function as individuating criteria only under descriptions which turn out to be themselves intentional in nature. And intentions, which look promising (being objectively identifiable) are also of little use because in the context of intention they are identified relative to the agent's subjective beliefs and intentions. This circularity casts doubts over Michael Moore's project of intention-individuation.

HEYD, Thomas. Locke's Simple Ideas, the Blooming, Buzzing Confusion, and Quasi-Photographic Perception. Locke News, 20, 17-33, 1989.

HEYD, Thomas. Reply to Roth: Locke Is Not a Cartesian with Respect to Knowledge of our Own Existence. Int Phil Quart, 29(4), 463-467, D 89.

This paper *rejects* the suggestion that for Locke there may be instances of knowledge that are *not* mediated by ideas. The intuition of our own existence is a case of 'direct and immediate' knowledge, according to R J Roth. I point out that, despite some appearances, the *Essay does not* warrant Roth's reading; intuition of the self, according to Locke's *Essay*, is not a matter of direct acquaintance with a real thing in the Cartesian manner.

HEYES, Cecilia and DICKINSON, Anthony. The Intentionality of Animal Action. Mind Lang, 5(1), 87-104, Spr 90.

HEYWOOD THOMAS, John. Kierkegaard's Alternative Metaphysical Theology. Hist Euro Ideas, 12(1), 53-63, 1990.

Kierkegaard was inspired by a passion for metaphysics and sought a new metaphysical theology. Set against the background of Danish philosophy and theology of the early 19th century, his rejection of the fashionable metaphysical theology was itself the development of an alternative and his avowedly religious authorship was a metaphysical clarification of Christian discipleship. The alternative metaphysical theology is characterised in the six theses: (i) truth is subjectivity; (ii) harmonising Christianity and philosophy misinterprets Christianity; (iii) proof of God is impossible; (iv) logic and existence are separate; (v) the Incarnation is an event not an idea; (vi) sin shows the mystery of time.

HIBBS, Thomas S. A Rhetoric of Motives: Thomas on Obligation as Rational Persuasion. Thomist, 54(2), 293-309, Ap 90.

HICK, John. An Interpretation of Religion: Human Responses to the Transcendent. New Haven, Yale Univ Pr, 1989

HICK, John. The Logic of God Incarnate. Relig Stud, 25(4), 409-423, D 89.

This is a critique of Thomas Morris's proposal in *The Logic of God Incarnate* (1986) that the idea of divine incarnation can be understood on the model of two minds, a human mind enclosed within a divine mind, with the latter having full cognitive access to the former but the former only occasional access to the latter. The critique, which suggests the failure of Morris's attempt to render a Chalcedonian-type dogma intelligible, claims that cognitive access is not sufficient to constitute incarnation, and that Morris is unable to explain how, since two wills are also required, Jesus was genuinely free to sin and yet necessarily sinless.

HICK, John. Straightening the Record: Some Responses to Critics. Mod Theol, 6(2), 187-195, Ja 90.

A response to the recent criticisms of John Hick's pluralistic interpretation of

religion by Gavin D'Costa (*Theology and Religious Pluralism* and *John Hick's Theology of Religions*) and Chester Gillis (*A Question of Final Belief: John Hick's Pluralistic Theory of Salvation*). Issues include whether Hick's interpretation covertly presupposes the Christian concept of God; whether it takes account of nontheistic as well as theistic forms of religion; whether its eschatology is compatible with the rest of the hypothesis; and the way in which the notion of myth is used. The writer concludes that D'Costa's and Gillis's criticisms can be rejected.

HICKMAN, Larry. Status Arguments and Genetic Research with Human Embryos. SW Phil Rev, 4(1), 45-55, Ja 88.

After reviewing numerous contributions to the literature, I argue that status as an individual of the human species cannot be attributed to an embryo of human provenance prior to the 14th day after fertilization. The strongest status claim that can be supported is that such embryos are "dividuals" and human species tissue. It follows from this that those who seek to prohibit experimentation with embryos of human provenance cannot rely on status arguments to support their claims, but must turn to some other type of argument.

HICKS, Michael. *Energeia* and "The Work Itself". J Aes Educ, 21(3), 69-75, Fall 87.

The well-established categories of music as (a) a set of objects ("pieces") and (b) an act of "performance" are subverted by the notational and structural complexities of twentieth-century music. A notation in a sketch by Stravinsky provides a frame for a discussion of that subversion, particularly with respect to how fully formed a "piece" must be in the mind or on paper. Increasingly indeterminate scores—akin to unfinished sketches—necessitate new categories, such as "conjectural objects" and "proformance." Moreover, the modern dissemination of music through electronically reproductive media at once erodes and reinforces the historical idea of "works."

HIDALGO, Cecilia. Inconmensurabilidad y criterios de identidad de esquemas conceptuales. Analisis Filosof, 8(1), 69-78, My 88.

Different interpretations and references of the incommensurability thesis are presented for a new assessment of the theoretical import of relativistic and antirelativistic claims. The discussion is set in the framework of the thesis relevant for the relativism and universalism. The paper focuses on the criteria stated for the existence of divergent conceptual schemes. Two main types of criteria are outlined: criteria of translatability and criteria of correlation between linguistic and extralinguistic (cognitive or perceptual) behavior.

HIDALGO-SERNA, Emilio and PINTON, Giorgio (trans). Metaphorical Language, Rhetoric, and *Comprehensio*: J L Vives and M Nizolio. Phil Rhet, 23(1), 1-11, 1990.

HIGGINSON, Richard. Dilemmas: A Christian Approach to Moral Decision Making. Louisville, Westminster Pr, 1988

HILEY, David R. The Individual and the General Will: Rousseau Reconsidered. Hist Phil Quart, 7(2), 159-178, Ap 90.

I offer an interpretation of Rousseau, within the context of the recent debate between liberalism and communitarianism, that offers a basis for individual diversity that liberalism and critics of mass society defend within the context of irreducibly common social values that the communitarian critics of liberalism require.

HILL JR, Thomas E. Kant's Theory of Practical Reason. Monist, 72(3), 363-383, Jl 89.

This paper presents, in summary without detailed textual exegesis, a reconstruction of Kant's theory of practical reason and some comparison with contemporary theories. Among the conclusions: (1) Nonmoral practical reasoning is governed by the hypothetical imperative, a nonsubstantive, nonmaximizing principle, fully compatible with moral imperatives, and supposedly analytic of ideal rationality but often violated. (2) Kant's claims that rational wills have negative freedom and autonomy are not merely, or primarily, metaphysical theses, but characterizations of the rational deliberative point of view and what constitutes good reasons for action. (3) Though Kant denies that familiar substantive principles are necessary principles of rationality, he argues for a nonhypothetical rational standard that implies that there are agent-neutral reasons to value the rational agency of each person. The theory, however, does not demand unrestricted impartiality.

HILLESHEIM, James W. Nietzschean Images of Self-Overcoming: Response to Rosenow. Educ Theor, 40(2), 211-215, Spr 90.

HILMY, S Stephen. "Wittgenstein and Behaviourism" in *Wittgenstein in Focus—Im Brennpunkt: Wittgenstein*, MC GUINNESS, Brian (ed), 335-352. Amsterdam, Rodopi, 1989.

Many have interpreted Wittgenstein as advocating a form of behaviourism. Through an examination of Wittgenstein's own remarks about behaviourism, and further textual evidence from his notebooks, it is shown that categorizing Wittgenstein as a 'behaviourist', of whatever ilk, serves not merely to obstruct an appreciation of his thinking, but perversely to distort Wittgenstein's views by flying in the face of the central critical thrusts of his later philosophy.

HINCHLIFF, Mark. Plantinga's Defence of Serious Actualism. Analysis, 49(4), 182-185, O 89.

HINCKFUSS, Ian. "Locke's Ideas, Abstraction, and Substance" in *Cause, Mind, and Reality: Essays Honoring C B Martin*, HEIL, John (ed), 95-109. Norwell, Kluwer, 1989.

It is argued that Locke's idea of '*Idea*' was univocal, was not a mental image idea of 'idea', and was probably indistinguishable from the idea of 'idea' that is prevalent today. It is shown that Locke's idea of '*Idea*' is no more equivocal or inconsistent than the idea of 'computer routine'. Locke's recursive characterisation of ideas included abstraction as a formation mechanism of new ideas from old. There was nothing inconsistent about Locke's theory of abstraction. The idea of a 'substance' can be generated as what Locke would have called an abstract or general idea.

HINDLEY, J Roger. Principal Type-Schemes and Condensed Detachment. J Sym Log, 55(1), 90-105, Mr 90.

The condensed detachment rule, or Rule D, was first proposed for the propositional logic of implication by Carew Meredith. It is a combination of modus ponens with a minimal amount of substitution. This paper defines Rule D carefully and shows that it is equivalent to the algorithm for computing principal types in combinatory logic and lambda calculus. (A short introduction to principal types is included.) From this equivalence the completeness of Rule D is derived for classical and for intuitionistic implicational logic. In contrast, Rule D is shown to be incomplete for two weaker systems, BCK-logic and BCI-logic.

HINNION, R and FORTI, M. The Consistency Problem for Positive Comprehension Principles. J Sym Log, 54(4), 1401-1418, D 89.

HINTIKKA, Jaakko. The Cartesian *Cogito*, Epistemic Logic, and Neuroscience: Some Surprising Interrelations. Synthese, 83(1), 133-157, Ap 90.

HINTIKKA, Jaakko and HINTIKKA, Merrill B. Ludwig Looks at the Necker Cube: The Problem of "Seeing As" as a Clue to Wittgenstein's Philosophy. Acta Phil Fennica, 38, 36-48, 1985.

Wittgenstein's different comments on ambiguous figures help to confirm the interpretation offered in *Investigating Wittgenstein*. In the *Tractatus* seeing the same configuration of physical objects in two different ways was supposed to show that the objects we have to assume are phenomenological, not physical. Conversely, "seeing as" became a problem for Wittgenstein when he gave up phenomenological languages. He had to explain, not only the possibility of seeing a figure in different ways, but also the spontaneity (noninterpretational character) of "seeing as." That Wittgenstein's comments conform to our interpretation is seen also from his use of the term "aspect."

HINTIKKA, Merrill B and HINTIKKA, Jaakko. Ludwig Looks at the Necker Cube: The Problem of "Seeing As" as a Clue to Wittgenstein's Philosophy. Acta Phil Fennica, 38, 36-48, 1985.

Wittgenstein's different comments on ambiguous figures help to confirm the interpretation offered in *Investigating Wittgenstein*. In the *Tractatus* seeing the same configuration of physical objects in two different ways was supposed to show that the objects we have to assume are phenomenological, not physical. Conversely, "seeing as" became a problem for Wittgenstein when he gave up phenomenological languages. He had to explain, not only the possibility of seeing a figure in different ways, but also the spontaneity (noninterpretational character) of "seeing as." That Wittgenstein's comments conform to our interpretation is seen also from his use of the term "aspect."

HINTON, J M. "Propositions and Philosophical Ideas" in *Cause, Mind, and Reality: Essays Honoring C B Martin*, HEIL, John (ed), 173-190. Norwell, Kluwer, 1989.

The article asks when, if ever, we are entitled to assume that some given philosophical idea, view or thesis is a classical proposition—a truth or falsehood—without taking a view as to its truth. An extremely restrictive answer is provisionally favoured. The question, and answer, are extended to nonphilosophical items. Although a response to Michael Dummett's initiatives, the article neither accepts Dummett's view that such assumptions are 'Realist', nor sees the question as belonging to the theory of meaning.

HIPEL, Keith W and KILGOUR, D Marc and FANG, Liping. A Decision Support System for the Graph Model of Conflicts. Theor Decis, 28(3), 289-311, My 90.

A comprehensive decision support system called GMCA (graph model for conflict analysis) implementing the multi-player graph model for analyzing conflicts is developed. GMCA contains algorithms for the rapid computation of a wide range of solution concepts, thereby enabling decision makers to take account of the diversity of human behavior. Using an engineering case study, the key features of GMCA are illustrated.

HIRSCH, Eli. Knowledge, Power, Ethics. Manuscrito, 12(2), 49-63, O 89.

In the introduction to "L'usage des ploisirs" Foucault describes a complicated and multifaceted philosophical shift which took place in his mind and led him to redefine the nature of his genealogical project. The philosophical break embodied in this shift cannot be ignored: Foucault's philosophy seems to collapse into the philosophical tradition, and to forego almost all of its earlier revolutionary elements. The aim of this paper is to point out the crucial importance of this shift for the understanding of Foucault's philosophical activity as a whole, and thus to show that what appears to be a collapse into the tradition is rather a step forward: that it does not negate Foucault's radicalism but rather clarifies its content and establishes its validity. (edited)

HIRSCH, Eli. Negativity and Complexity: Some Logical Considerations. Synthese, 81(2), 217-241, N 89.

The author attempts to develop certain distinctions between positive and negative terms, and between simple and complex terms, by appealing exclusively to the logical properties of terms. It is shown that these attempts must fail, for the most part, but that some interesting results can be salvaged from them.

HIRSCHMAN, Albert O. "Two Hundred Years of Reactionary Rhetoric: The Case of the Perverse Effect" in *The Tanner Lectures on Human Values, Volume X*, PETERSON, Grethe B (ed), 1-31. Salt Lake City, Univ of Utah Pr, 1989.

HIRSHFELD, Joram. Nonstandard Combinatorics. Stud Log, 47(3), 221-232, S 88.

Ramsey type theorems are theorems of the form: "if certain sets are partitioned at least one of the parts has some particular property." In its finite form, Ramsey's theory will ask how big the partitioned set should be to assure this fact. Proofs of such theorems usually require a process of multiple choice, so that this apparently "pure combinatoric" field is rich in proofs that use ideal guides in making the choices. Typically they may be ultrafilters or points in the compactification of the given set. It is, therefore, not surprising that nonstandard elements are much more natural guides in some of the proofs and in the general abstract treatment. (edited)

HIRST, J L and FRIEDMAN, Harvey M. Weak Comparability of Well Orderings and Reverse Mathematics. Annals Pure Applied Log, 47(1), 11-29, Ap 90.

HITTINGER, Russell. After MacIntyre: Natural Law Theory, Virtue Ethics, and Eudaimonia. Int Phil Quart, 29(4), 449-461, D 89.

The essay contends that the project of recovering natural law theory requires something more than retrieving discourse about either the virtues or basic goods. While these may be constituent parts of human well-being, one does not need natural law theory for the purpose of such lists of natural goods or virtues. Rather, if natural law theory has any constructive role to play, it must be enquiry into a teleological principle for how the goods are to be ordered.

HLAVACEK, Lubos. Aesthetic Thinking of Karel Capek (in Czechoslovakian). Estetika, 26(4), 218-232, 1989.

HLAVACEK, Lubos. Thinking Eye of Karl Capek (in Czechoslovakian). Estetika, 27(1), 1-27, 1990.

HOARE, Quintin (ed & trans) and GRAMSCI, Antonio. *Selections from Political Writings, 1921-1926: Antonio Gramsci*. Minneapolis, Univ of Minn Pr, 1990.

This is a second volume of Gramsci's political writings. It details events during the rise of the Italian Communist party. The concerns of the writing focus on contemporary Marxist issues such as the functioning of working class power and the implications of proletarian internationalism. (staff)

HOARE, Quintin (ed) and GRAMSCI, Antonio and MATHEWS, John (trans). *Selections from Political Writings, 1910-1920: Antonio Gramsci*. Minneapolis, Univ of Minn Pr, 1990

Antonio Gramsci is considered one of the most influential thinkers of the twentieth century. The selections in this volume, the first of two, span the period from his initial involvement in Italian politics to the "Red Years" of 1919-1920, and feature texts by Bordiga and Tasca from their debates with Gramsci. They trace Gramsci's development as a revolutionary socialist during the First World War, the impact of his thoughts concerning the Russian Revolution and his involvement in the general strike and factory occupations of 1920. Also included are his reactions to the emerging fascist movement and his contributions to the early stages of the debate about the establishment of the Communist Party of Italy.

HOCHBERG, Herbert. "Russell's Paradox, Russellian Relations, and the Problems of Predication and Impredicativity" in *Rereading Russell: Essays on Bertrand Russell's Metaphysics and Epistemology*, SAVAGE, C Wade (ed), 63-87. Minneapolis, Univ of Minn Pr, 1989.

HODAPP, Paul F. Can There Be a Social Contract with Business? J Bus Ethics, 9(2), 127-131, F 90.

Professor Donaldson in his book *Corporations and Morality* has attempted to use a social contract theory to develop moral principles for regulating corporate conduct. I argue in this paper that his attempt fails in large measure because what he refers to as a social contract theory is, in fact, a weak functionalist theory which provides no independent basis for evaluating business corporations. I further argue that given the nature of a morality based on contract and the nature of the modern corporation, it is highly unlikely that any plausible contract theory of business ethics can be developed.

HODGES, Wilfrid and HODKINSON, I M and MACPHERSON, Dugald. Omega-Categoricity, Relative Categoricity and Coordinatisation. Annals Pure Applied Log, 46(2), 169-199, F 90.

Let L,L' be countable first order languages with L' $\subseteq$ L, such that there is a unary relation symbol P in L\L'. Let T be a complete L-theory with infinite models. If M $\models$ T let P(B) be the substructure induced on {x: M $\models$ Px}. Then T is *relatively categorical* if, whenever M,M' are models of T with P(M) = P(M') there is an isomorphism M → M' which is the identity on P(M). Various conditions are examined which, together with relative categoricity, guarantee that M is algebraic over P(M), or is coordinatisable over P(M).

HODGSON, John A. *Coleridge, Shelley, and Transcendental Inquiry: Rhetoric, Argument, Metapsychology*. Lincoln, Univ of Nebraska Pr, 1989

HODKINSON, I M and HODGES, Wilfrid and MACPHERSON, Dugald. Omega-Categoricity, Relative Categoricity and Coordinatisation. Annals Pure Applied Log, 46(2), 169-199, F 90.

Let L,L' be countable first order languages with L' $\subseteq$ L, such that there is a unary relation symbol P in L\L'. Let T be a complete L-theory with infinite models. If M $\models$ T let P(B) be the substructure induced on {x: M $\models$ Px}. Then T is *relatively categorical* if, whenever M,M' are models of T with P(M) = P(M') there is an isomorphism M → M' which is the identity on P(M). Various conditions are examined which, together with relative categoricity, guarantee that M is algebraic over P(M), or is coordinatisable over P(M).

HOEKZEMA, Dick and VAN DEN BERG, Hans and RADDER, Hans. Accardi on Quantum Theory and the "Fifth Axiom" of Probability. Phil Sci, 57(1), 149-157, Mr 90.

In this paper we investigate Accardi's claim that the "quantum paradoxes" have their roots in probability theory and that, in particular, they can be evaded by giving up Bayes's rule, concerning the relation between composite and conditional probabilities. We reach the conclusion that, although it may be possible to give up Bayes's rule and define conditional probabilities differently, this contributes nothing to solving the philosophical problems which surround quantum mechanics.

HOFF, Franklin J and ALMEDER, Robert. Reliability and Goldman's Theory of Justification. Philosophia (Israel), 19(2-3), 165-187, O 89.

In this essay we argue that Goldman's theory of justification is defective because it is neither a necessary nor a sufficient condition for a person being justified in what she believes that her belief be reliably produced or caused in any humanly specifiable way. We examine various replies and defenses of reliabilism and argue that they are defective. What renders a belief justified has nothing to do with the way in which the belief is caused to come about.

HOFF, J Whitman. Students, Ethics and Surveys. J Bus Ethics, 8(10), 823-825, O 89.

In a recent article in this journal Grant and Broom reported on a survey which they conducted concerning student attitudes toward ethics. They suggest that while their findings are only preliminary, such surveys can help instructors and schools to determine what type of ethical training a person from a particular demographic background might need. Likewise they may very well help a student's future employer determine the ethics he or she has based on the type of institution he or she attended. However, it is my contention that there are a number of problems inherent in the process and the interpretation which Grant and Broom suggest. I discuss these problems herein.

HOFFMAN, A N and STRONG, V K. There is Relevance in the Classroom: Analysis of Present Methods of Teaching Business Ethics. J Bus Ethics, 9(7), 603-607, Jl 90.

In 1988 the *Journal of Business Ethics* published a paper by David Mathison entitled "Business Ethics Cases and Decision Models: A Call for Relevancy in the Classroom." Mathison argued that the present methods of teaching business ethics may be inappropriate for MBA students. He believes that faculty are teaching at one decision-making level and that students are and will be functioning on another (lower) level. The purpose of this paper is to respond to Mathison's arguments and offer support for the present methods and materials used to teach Master level ethics classes. The support includes suggested class discussion ideas and assignments.

HOFFMAN, Frank J. More on Blasphemy. Sophia (Australia), 28(2), 26-34, Jl 89.

HOFFMAN, Paul. St Thomas Aquinas on the Halfway State of Sensible Being. Phil Rev, 99(1), 73-92, Ja 90.

HOFFMAN, W Michael and FREDERICK, Robert E. The Individual Investor in Securities Markets: An Ethical Analysis. J Bus Ethics, 9(7), 579-589, Jl 90.

In this paper we consider whether one type of individual investor, which we call "at risk" investors, should be denied access to securities markets to prevent them from suffering serious financial harm. We consider one kind of paternalistic justification for prohibiting at risk investors from participating in securities markets, and argue that it is not successful. We then argue that restricting access to markets is justified in some circumstances to protect the rights of at risk investors. We conclude with some suggestions about how this might be done.

HOFFMANN, G and BERGMANN, Werner. Selbstreferenz und Zeit: Die dynamische Stabilität des Bewusstseins. Husserl Stud, 6(2), 155-175, 1989.

HOFFMANN, R Joseph. A Eupraxopher's Agenda: Humanism and Religion. Free Inq, 10(3), 19-21, Sum 90.

This article responds to the humanist agenda outlined in Paul Kurtz's 1988 book, *Eupraxophy*. The secular humanist critique of religion is often delimited by an emphasis on the positivist indictment of theistic language. Eupraxophy moves beyond that limitation to the articulation of a humanistic ethic which does not look to religious paradigms for legitimation. Eupraxophy as a "philosophy of the good" challenges contemporary religion to examine the source of its own normative ethic and provides that the bulk of the social-moral agenda of Christian churches is derived from the theories of 19th century free thought and libertarian groups. The article attempts to suggest the importance of humanists' reasserting their claim to a liberal agenda and of opposing the efforts of some religious groups to identify constructive ethical/moral discourse as "essentially" religious or "Christian" in nature.

HOGAN, David. Moral Authority and the Antinomies of Moral Theory: Francis Wayland and Nineteenth-Century Moral Education. Educ Theor, 40(1), 95-119, Wint 90.

HOGENOVA, A and SAFAR, Z. On the Question of the Active Role of Reflection in Marxist-Leninist Epistemology (in Czechoslovakian). Filozof Cas, 37(6), 783-794, 1989.

This theoretical study sets itself the task of highlighting the intricate problems connected with the active role of reflection in the realm of human consciousness. The authors make use of several inspiring stimuli, drawn from their studies of phenomenological texts, which tend to develop and sometimes incorrectly overestimate the subjective aspect of the cognitive process. They single out several major aspects of the process of the reflection of objective and subjective reality, aspects that were critically analyzed for example by Kant. The authors also refer to the specific features of the processuality of reflections constituting themselves in various modes of psychological activities such as memories, phantasy or symbols. The article is primarily designed to serve in teaching the theory of reflection in Marxism-Leninism courses at universities. (edited)

HÖHN, Gerhard (trans) and HEINE, Heinrich. Du principe démocratique. Rev Metaph Morale, 94(2), 147-151, Ap-Je 89.

HÖHN, Gerhard. Heinrich Heine, intellectuel moderne. Rev Metaph Morale, 94(2), 151-164, Ap-Je 89.

HOLCOMB III, Harmon R. Cognitive Dissonance and Scepticism. J Theor Soc Behav, 19(4), 411-432, D 89.

Cognitive dissonance theory employs 'independence principles' to reveal self-deceptive logic. When applied to reasoning about true beliefs, they reveal a fallacy in thinking that we turn our true beliefs into knowledge through acts of justification. The fallacy lies in tacitly both affirming and denying that valuations of ends (valued objects, including true beliefs) are performed independently of valuations of means (methods for obtaining valued objects, including evidence-gathering). Instances of the fallacy in the literature on scepticism are exposed.

HOLLAND, Allan. A Fortnight of My Life is Missing: A Discussion of the Status of the Human 'Pre-Embryo'. J Applied Phil, 7(1), 25-37, Mr 90.

Summed up in the coinage of the term 'pre-embryo' is the denial that human beings, as such, begin to exist from the moment of conception. This denial, which may be thought to have significant moral implications, rests on two kinds of reason. The first is that the pre-embryo lacks the characteristics of a human being. The second is that the pre-embryo lacks what it takes to be an individual human being. The first reason, I argue, embodies an untenable view of what it is to be human. The second reason exploits certain logical difficulties which arise over the possibility of twinning. I question the relevance of the appeal to such difficulties and conclude that there is no good reason for denying that a human being begins to exist from the moment of conception.

HOLLAND, Joe (ed) and GRIFFIN, David Ray (ed) and BEARDSLEE, William A (ed). *Varieties of Postmodern Theology*. Albany, SUNY Pr, 1989

HOLLAND, Joe. "The Cultural Vision of Pope John Paul II: Toward a Conservative/Liberal Postmodern Dialogue" in *Varieties of Postmodern Theology*, GRIFFIN, David Ray (ed), 95-127. Albany, SUNY Pr, 1989.

HOLLAND, Joe. "The Postmodern Paradigm and Contemporary Catholicism" in *Varieties of Postmodern Theology*, GRIFFIN, David Ray (ed), 9-27. Albany, SUNY Pr, 1989.

HOLLAND, R F. Not Bending the Knee. Phil Invest, 13(1), 18-30, Ja 90.

This work is directed mainly towards the question: Why might the philosophy of religion present itself to a sympathetic enquirer as particularly difficult territory? The enquiry takes shape initially around two remarks of Wittgenstein taken from 'Culture and Value', and subsequently around material taken from Vol. II of A E Taylor's 'The Faith of a Moralist'. The discussion ends with a quotation from Conor Cruise O'Brien.

HOLLANDER, Rachelle D. Journals Have Obligations, Too: Commentary on "Confirmational Response Bias". Sci Tech Human Values, 15(1), 46-49, Wint 90.

Journals have a responsibility to foster responsible editorial and peer review practices, in addition to responsible authorship practices. This commentary considers ways to do this. It considers the controversial study of peer review practice in social work, reported on in this same issue of *STHV*, in this light, suggesting that a general grant of consent by journals to deceptive submissions that satisfy standards for good research may be justified, as a way to assure responsible editorial practice. Finally, it notes that the central application of a principle of informed consent is as a protection for the weak; when the powerful call on it, it appears uncomfortably self-serving.

HOLLANDER, Rachelle D and STENECK, Nicholas H. Science- and Engineering-Related Ethics and Value Studies: Characteristics of an Emerging Field of Research. Sci Tech Human Values, 15(1), 84-104, Wint 90.

The National Science Foundation began a program to support research and related educational projects about the ethical and value aspects of scientific and technological research, development and its applications in the mid-1970s. This article studies and characterizes 172 projects that have been supported. It reflects on the relationship between this area of study and the larger area of studies in science, technology and society. Arguing that the intellectual and institutional dimensions of this area of study are still unclear, the article ends with some recommendations for strengthening the progress that has been made.

HOLLANDER, Samuel. Malthus and Utilitarianism with Special Reference to the *Essay on Population*. Utilitas, 1(2), 170-210, N 89.

HOLLER, Linda. Thinking with the Weight of the Earth: Feminist Contributions to an Epistemology of Concreteness. Hypatia, 5(1), 1-23, Spr 90.

This essay proposes a possible direction for feminist epistemology—an embodied rationality that defines the process of knowing as a dialogue with particulars or the "things themselves." On the grounds that modern reality is marked by abstract projects of *homo mensura*, I argue that the task of postmodernism is to ground cognition in the world by breaking the habit of looking *at* the world, as if from a distance, and by ceasing to think about the world as if it were composed of a collection of objects-in-general.

HÖLLHUBER, Ivo. Antonio Rosmini, Michele Federico Sciacca e Hans-Eduard Hengstenberg: un paragone. Filosofia, 40(2), 139-150, My-Ag 89.

HOLLINGER, Dennis. Can Bioethics Be Evangelical? J Relig Ethics, 17(2), 161-179, Fall 89.

A lack of theological reflection in bioethics raises the question, "Can bioethics be theological?" as necessarily prior to the narrower question, "Can bioethics by Evangelical?" Bioethics abounds with descriptive analysis, but normative analysis—especially such analysis based in theological concerns—is much less frequent and is not at the center of focus. Given this tangential relationship of theological inquiry to bioethics, how can a highly confessional movement like evangelicalism contribute to it? In this essay I contend that evangelical theological reflection *can* contribute to debate concerning bioethics, but only by modifying some of its past styles of ethical discourse among both the intellectual and the popular evangelical community.

HOLLINGSHEAD, Greg. Sources for the *Ladies' Library*. Berkeley News, 11, 1-9, 1989-90.

My purpose is to specify first, four previously unidentified sources used by Berkeley to create the *Ladies' Library*; second, 35 brief linking passages almost certainly by Berkeley himself (of these, 15 are provided in full); third, 11 passages (totalling approximately 27,000 words) that remain to be identified. The new sources are from John Kettlewell, Mary Astell, the Messieurs du Port Royal, and John Tillotson.

HOLLIS, Martin. Atomic Energy and Moral Glue. J Phil Educ, 23(2), 185-193, Wint 89.

An enterprise culture rewards the energies of social atoms but erodes public spirit and its own moral glue. This sets a dilemma for moral education, which neither the Prime Minister's version of Christianity nor the Home Secretary's invocation of Edmund Burke can resolve. We need to teach a positive kind of individualism where duties are prior to rights and citizenship embodies a principle of public affections.

HOLLIS, Martin. Market Equality and Social Freedom. J Applied Phil, 7(1), 15-23, Mr 90.

Conflicts between the good of each and the good of all are often presented in terms of freedom versus equality, with liberals pulled one way by libertarians and the other by social democrats. When we distinguish between negative and positive notions not only of freedom but also of equality, the liberal freedom 'to pursue our own good in our own way' is a positive freedom involving a negative idea of equality (or 'equity'). Yet 'equity' is not strong enough to deal with the problem of public goods. Trust is a public good, essential if markets are to work and dependable only where there is a moral commitment to a positive basic equality among citizens.

HOLLIS, Martin. Moves and Motives in the Games We Play. Analysis, 50(2), 49-62, Mr 90.

Game theory abstracts to an ideal-type world where agents are hyperrational. Paradoxes result. The paper traces them to the Humean moral psychology behind the standard notion of instrumentally rational action. Kantian and Wittgensteinian alternatives are to be considered. Rational agents need psychological 'grit' to give content to their preferences, epistemic 'dust' to make them opaque to one another and moral 'glue' to fix their relationships.

HOLLY, Michael Ann. Past Looking. Crit Inquiry, 16(2), 371-396, Wint 89.

The essay speculates on the rhetorical ways in which works of art can be read as prefiguring their own historiographic response. By reference to Burckhardt, Wittgenstein, Nietzsche, and Lacan, the argument is made that paintings, especially from the Renaissance, mandate the kind of roles later historians play out before them.

HOLM, Soren and CUSHMAN, Reid. Death, Democracy and Public Ethical Choice. Bioethics, 4(3), 237-252, Jl 90.

HOLM, Soren. The Mother-Child Relationship. Ethics Med, 6(2), 32-34, Sum 90.

The moral relevance of special relations (e.g., family ties) have been repeatedly questioned, but common sense indicates that such relations do matter morally, but how much do they matter? This question can only be answered if we can identify the important attributes of these relationships. Through an analysis of H C Andersen's story "The Story of a Mother" the paper proceeds to show that love, sacrifice, and concern for the good of the child are integral attributes of the mother-child relationship, and that any moral analysis of this relationship must recognize these attributes.

HOLM, Soren. Private Hospitals in Public Health Systems. Hastings Center Rep, 19(5), 16-20, S-O 89.

Several European countries have in recent years experienced a growth in private medicine, in what was previously predominantly public health care systems. This development gives rise to new inequalities in health care, and the article explores the moral status of these inequalities. It is argued that they can be divided into inequalities of access, inequalities of quality, and inequality of amenities. It is shown that any substantial inequalities of access or quality would undermine the justness of health care provision, and would furthermore be likely to lead to a loss of utility.

HOLMES, Arthur F. Ethical Monotheism and the Whitehead Ethic. Faith Phil, 7(3), 281-290, Jl 90.

Whitehead's rejection of a coercive divine lawgiver is well known, but the underlying ethic which led him in that direction needs to be examined. Arguing that he is an ethical naturalist with an aesthetic theory of value, and an act utilitarian, I find that this gives priority to eros over agape, limits moral responsibility, and obscures the depth of moral evil.

HOLMES, Helen Bequaert. A Call to Heal Medicine. Hypatia, 4(2), 1-8, Sum 89.

Authors in the special issue of *Hypatia*, "Feminist Ethics and Medicine," seem called to heal ethics, medicine, and the new field—medical ethics. After explaining why feminists should feel this calling, I group authors' contributions as responses to questions: (1) Why hasn't medical ethics already healed medicine? (2) What role should 'caring' play in ethics? (3) Must we first heal science? (4) Are we setting up health and the perfectly functioning body as virtues? (5) Why hasn't the plethora of medical ethics books helped? (6) How do our sisters in sociology help us heal medicine?

HOLMES, Helen Bequaert. Can Clinical Research Be Both 'Ethical' and 'Scientific'? A Commentary Inspired by Rosser and Marquis. Hypatia, 4(2), 156-168, Sum 89.

Problems with clinical research that create conflicts between doctors' therapeutic and research obligations may be fueled by a rigid view of science as determiner of truth, a heavy reliance on statistics, and certain features of randomized clinical trials. I suggest some creative, feminist approaches to such research and explore ways to provide choice for patients and to use values in directing both therapy and science—to enhance the effectiveness of each.

HOLMES, Robert L. The Limited Relevance of Analytical Ethics to the Problems of Bioethics. J Med Phil, 15(2), 143-159, Ap 90.

Philosophical ethics comprises metaethics, normative ethics and applied ethics. These have characteristically received analytic treatment by twentieth-century Anglo-American philosophy. But there has been disagreement over their interrelationship to one another and the relationship of analytical ethics to substantive morality—the making of moral judgments. I contend that the expertise philosophers have in either theoretical or applied ethics does not equip them to make sounder moral judgments on the problems of bioethics than nonphilosophers. One cannot "apply" theories like Kantianism or consequentialism to get solutions to practical moral problems unless one knows which theory is correct, and that is a metaethical question over which there is no consensus. On the other hand, to presume to be able to reach solutions through neutral analysis of problems is unavoidably to beg controversial theoretical issues in the process. Thus, while analytical ethics can play an important clarificatory role in bioethics, it can neither provide, nor substitute for, moral wisdom.

HOLMES, Robert L. On War and Morality. Princeton, Princeton Univ Pr, 1989

This book argues that, contrary to political realists, morality applies fully to international relations, and to warfare in particular. The just war tradition does not, however, succeed in justifying war. Because war inevitably involves killing innocent people, I argue that war cannot be morally justified. As an alternative to war, I propose a system of nonviolent civilian defense.

HOLMES, Stephen. "John Stuart Mill: Fallibilism, Expertise, and the Politics-Science Analogy" in *Knowledge and Politics*, DASCAL, Marcelo (ed), 125-143. Boulder, Westview Pr, 1988.

HOLMSTRÖM, Ghita. Wills, Purposes and Actions. Acta Phil Fennica, 38, 49-62, 1985.

HOLT, Dale Lynn. Causation, Transitivity, and Causal Relata. J Phil Res, 15, 263-277, 1990.

I consider an alleged example of a nontransitive causal chain, on the basis of which J Lee has argued that causation is nontransitive. I show that his analysis of the example rests on too coarse-grained an approach to causal relata. I develop a fine-grained analysis of events which owes much to Dretske's notion of an allomorphic event, and I use this analysis to show that in the example all the genuine causal chains are indeed transitive. It emerges that when fine-grained analyses of events are possible, causal contexts are allomorphically sensitive.

HOLTON, Gerald. Thematic Origins of Scientific Thought: Kepler to Einstein—Revised Edition. Cambridge, Harvard Univ Pr, 1988

HOLYER, Robert. Scepticism, Evidentialism and the Parity Argument: A Pascalian Perspective. Relig Stud, 25(2), 191-208, Je 89.

It is commonly argued that sceptical arguments used in defense of religious belief establish no more than a state of parity between the believer and his challenger and therefore do not provide any positive epistemic support for religious belief. Drawing on Pascal, I sketch a naturalist position in which sceptical arguments are used to revise and contextualize epistemic standards and thereby are part of a larger strategy to provide positive epistemic support. I then argue that this option has been insufficiently considered in some recent discussions of sceptical arguments, specifically those of Anthony O'Hear, M Jamie Ferreira and Terence Penelhum.

HOMIAK, Marcia L. Politics as Soul-Making: Aristotle on Becoming Good. Philosophia (Israel), 20(1-2), 167-193, Jl 90.

Aristotle claims that human beings are naturally political animals, i.e., they fully express their characteristic human powers only in a political community. Such persons are also morally virtuous and are marked by a psychological unity. In their souls there is no conflict between the rational and nonrational desires. I take up the relationship between these claims and show how political activity can transform and educate both the rational and nonrational parts of the soul. I argue that we become good by practicing the most generalizable human activity, which is essentially political activity.

HON, Giora. Towards a Typology of Experimental Errors: An Epistemological View. Stud Hist Phil Sci, 20(4), 469-504, D 89.

This paper is concerned with the problem of experimental error. The prevalent view that experimental errors can be dismissed as a tiresome but trivial blemish on the method of experimentation is criticized. It is stressed that the occurrence of errors in experiments constitutes a permanent feature of the attempt to test theories in the physical world, and this feature deserves proper attention. It is suggested that a classification of types of experimental error may be useful as a heuristic device in studying the nature of these errors. However, the standard classification of systematic and random errors is mathematically based and as such does not focus on the causes of the errors, their origins, or the contexts in which they arise. A new typology of experimental errors is therefore proposed whose criterion is epistemological. This typology reflects the various stages that can be discerned in the execution of an experiment, each stage constituting a category of a certain type of experimental error. The proposed classification consists of four categories which are illustrated by historical cases.

HONDERICH, Ted. Violence and Equality: Inquiries in Political Philosophy. New York, Routledge, 1989

The book inquires into the moral justification, if any, of political violence of the left. There are chapters on feelings about violence and inequality, the principle of equality, acts and omissions, political obligation, democracy and democratic violence, and four conclusions about violence of the left.

HONNETH, Axel. Atomism and Ethical Life: On Hegel's Critique of the French Revolution. Phil Soc Crit, 14(3-4), 359-368, 1988.

HOOKER, C A (ed) and HAHLWEG, Kai (ed). Issues in Evolutionary Epistemology. Albany, SUNY Pr, 1989

This book provides a thorough philosophical examination of theories of evolutionary epistemology. It is divided into four parts: Part I introduces several new approaches to evolutionary epistemology; Part II attempts to widen the scope of evolutionary epistemology, either by tackling more traditional epistemological issues, or by applying evolutionary models to new areas of inquiry such as the evolution of culture or of intentionality; Part III critically discusses specific problems in evolutionary epistemology; and Part IV deals with the relationship of evolutionary epistemology to the philosophy of mind.

HOOKER, C A and HAHLWEG, Kai. "Evolutionary Epistemology and Philosophy of Science" in *Issues in Evolutionary Epistemology*, HAHLWEG, Kai (ed), 21-150. Albany, SUNY Pr, 1989.

In this paper the authors collaborate in the exposition of a naturalistic approach to problems in the philosophy of science. An evolutionary model which is phrased in terms of the evolution of complex regulatory structures is put forward by Hahlweg. He argues that science can be understood as such a system, and that scientific method evolves and improves in the course of scientific evolution. Hooker integrates this model into his evolutionary naturalist realism and makes a case for the identity of biological and scientific evolution by arguing that information as a functional term can be reduced to underlying causal structure.

HOOKER, Michael. "Vaticinal Visions and Pedagogical Prescriptions" in *Mind, Value and Culture: Essays in Honor of E M Adams*, WEISSBORD, David (ed), 326-345. Atascadero, Ridgeview, 1989.

This article forecasts some changes that will occur in society as the result of a world-wide shift from an energy-based economy to one based on information. The author recommends some changes that should be made in education to accommodate changes elsewhere in society.

HOOKER, Richard and MC GRADE, Arthur Stephen (ed). Of the Laws of Ecclesiastical Polity (Preface, Book I, Book VIII), Richard Hooker. New York,

Cambridge Univ Pr, 1989

HOOKWAY, Christopher. Critical Common-Sensism and Rational Self-Control. Nous, 24(3), 397-411, Je 90.

HOOVER, Jeffrey. Friedrich Schleiermacher's Theory of the Limited Communitarian State. Can J Phil, 20(2), 241-260, Je 90.

In his theory of the state Schleiermacher outlines three primary spheres of social interaction which are more or less free of state intervention, namely, the church, academia, and the domain of "free sociality." The latter of these provides for the unfettered pursuit of *private* or *common* goods within noninstitutional and voluntary associations. This article shows how Schleiermacher attempts to combine the pluralism and individualism of "free sociality" with a conception of the state that is communitarian, i.e., one which takes as its primary aim the promotion of *communal* goods.

HOPFMANN, Arndt. Zum Verhältnis von Entwicklung und Unterentwicklung. Deut Z Phil, 37(10-11), 1022-1028, 1989.

This discussion paper is a contribution to a debate—launched by G Söder—on the dialectics of development and underdevelopment from a philosophical point of view. The authors support the following positions: (1) underdevelopment is neither stagnation nor a natural social stage before development; (2) it is historically a specific result of capitalist production and reproduction on global scale; (3) this world economic system works nowadays in two directions, that is reproduction *and* reduction of underdevelopment in the Third World; (4) the latter process can be measured adequately only by complex socioeconomic criteria.

HOPKINS, Burt C. Husserl's Account of Phenomenological Reflection and Four Paradoxes of Reflexivity. Res Phenomenol, 19, 180-194, 1989.

The paper defends Husserl's phenomenological account of reflection. The paradox of accessing preobjective experience in the objectivating regard of reflection is shown to appeal to an "essence" of reflexivity and make an unwarranted ontological distinction between the reflective and unreflective. The problem of infinite regression is denied, showing instead phenomenology's infinite task of unfolding the horizontal fringe co-intended in the reflective gaze. The hermeneutical critique of reflexivity is shown to appeal to a traditional understanding of inner perception as well as originate in distinctions won through transcendental reflection. Derrida's critique is also refuted and found to presuppose eidetic distinctions.

HÖPPNER, Joachim. "Wie Müntzers Religionsphilosophie an den Atheiusmus, so streifte sein politisches Programm an den Kommunismus". Deut Z Phil, 37(12), 1082-1092, 1989.

Muntzer's theology is pointed out as a chief character of a typical people's pantheism, in which basic principles are integrated with those of a solidary egalitarianism, and in such a way as a beginning of a diverse tradition of both ideological and socio-political emancipation apart from bourgois reformation and enlightenment (Anabaptists, Paracelsus, Franck, Andreae, Arnold, Dippel).

HOPPS, June Gary. Reflections on "Confirmational Response Bias Among Social Work Journals". Sci Tech Human Values, 15(1), 39-45, Wint 90.

HORGAN, Terence and TIENSON, John. Representations without Rules. Phil Topics, 17(1), 147-174, Spr 89.

We argue (1) that in order for a cognitive system to deal successfully with its environment (as organisms do), it needs syntactically structured mental representations that interact with each other in ways that depend upon their structure and content; and (2) that the relevant kind of processing is not describable by exceptionless rules statable over the representations themselves. Connectionism, we argue, appears to have the potential for showing how there can be cognitive processing that is structure sensitive and content sensitive without being rule governed.

HORKHEIMER, Max and DALLMAYR, Fred (trans). Vico and Mythology. New Vico Studies, 5, 63-77, 1987.

HOROWITZ, Amir. Intentional and Physical Relations. Manuscrito, 13(1), 55-67, Ap 90.

According to Brentano, all and only mental phenomena are characterized by their *intentionality*. The author tries to show in part A of this paper that intentional relations are 'essential' in a way physical relations are not, since the former are necessary while the latter are contingent. In part B, he argues that physical 'relations' are not real relations, and that they can be fully described in a nonrelational language. Mental relations, on the other hand, cannot be fully described in a nonrelational language. If so, no psychophysical reduction is possible. In part C it is shown that mental 'relations' too are not *real* relations, but that nevertheless their intentionality distinguishes mental acts sharply from physical acts and excludes the possibility of psychophysical reduction. (edited)

HORSTER, Detlev and ALEXANDER, John V I (trans). Philosophizing with Children in the Glocksee School in Hanover, Germany. Thinking, 8(3), 23-24, 1989.

HORSTMAN, Klasien. Biologische constructies en sociale feiten: Obstakels in het onderzoek naar gezondheidsproblemen van vrouwen. Kennis Methode, 14(1), 84-103, 1990.

In this article some problems in women's studies are described which stem from a so-called 'constructivist' approach of health problems of women. Many 'constructivist' analyses reject the 'hard facts' of medicine and biology and turn the attention to the meanings each woman gives to menopause, menstruation, etc., by herself. The author demonstrates that this 'constructivism' is a kind of upside-down realism, which is not an adequate strategy to understand the power of medicine. Argued is that constructivism a kind of pragmatism will be a better instrument to understand in which way medicine influences women's lives, and how easy or how hard it is to transform these practices.

HORSTMANN, Rolf Peter. "Transcendental Idealism and the Representation of Space" in *Reading Kant*, SCHAPER, Eva (ed), 168-176. Cambridge, Blackwell, 1989.

HORSTMANN, Rolf-Peter. Der Kampf un den Buchstaben in der Hegel-Forschung der Gegenwart. Phil Rundsch, 37(1-2), 60-79, 1990.

HORVÁTH, Ágnes and SZAKOLCZAI, Arpád. A Sweet and Sour Victory in Eastern Europe. Rad Phil, 55, 40-42, Sum 90.

HORWICH, Paul. Wittgenstein and Kripke on the Nature of Meaning. Mind Lang, 5(2), 105-121, Sum 90.

Kripke has argued that there is no fact of the matter concerning what we mean by our words, and he attributes this sceptical thesis to Wittgenstein. It is shown here, first, that the facts of meaning are naturalistic facts about the use of words; second, and contrary to Kripke's arguments, that the infinite, normative implications of meaning can thereby be accommodated; and third, that this was Wittgenstein's own view of the matter.

HÖRZ, Herbert. "Determinants of Science Evolution in the 19th and 20th Centuries" in *Scientific Knowledge Socialized*, HRONSZKY, Imre (ed), 139-155. Norwell, Kluwer, 1989.

Determinanten sind Gesetze und Bedingungen. Zu den Gesetzen gehören u.a. die Dialektisierung der Wissenschaften als Einheit von Mathematisierung und Humanisierung und die wachsende Komplexität von Aufgaben und Entscheidungssituationen. Bedingungen sind u.a. die Verwissenschaftlichung der Gesellschaft, die Politisierung der Wissenschaften und der steigende administrative Aufwand für die Organisation der Wissenschaften.

HÖRZ, Herbert. Enzyklopädie als Aktionswissen? Deut Z Phil, 37(9), 813-823, 1989.

Das Werk der französischen Enzyklopädisten diente durch Aufklärung der Vorbereitung der Revolution. Gegenwärtig dominieren Spezialwissen einerseits und Wissenschaftskritik andererseits. Gefordert wird die Synthese des Wissens als Orientierung des Handelns. Deshalb wird die Forderung begründet, Enzyklopädie als Aktionswissen zu verstehen.

HÖSLE, Vittorio and ADLER, Pierre (trans) and HUMPHREY, Fred (trans). On Plato's Philosophy of Numbers and its Mathematical and Philosophical Significance. Grad Fac Phil J, 13(1), 21-63, 1988.

HOSMER, LaRue Tone and STENECK, Nicholas H. Teaching Business Ethics: The Use of Films and Videotapes. J Bus Ethics, 8(12), 929-936, D 89.

Audio-visual material is extremely useful in the teaching of business ethics, yet no bibliography of the commercially available films and videotapes seems to be available. We have prepared a formal listing, complete with titles, descriptions, sources, prices and a brief evaluation, and have explained our selection and use of this material.

HOSPERS, John. *An Introduction to Philosophical Analysis (Third Edition)*. Englewood Cliffs, Prentice-Hall, 1988

HOSSACK, Keith G. A Problem about the Meaning of Intuitionist Negation. Mind, 99(394), 207-219, Ap 90.

HOUSTON, Barbara. Theorizing Gender: How Much of It Do We Need. Educ Phil Theor, 21(1), 20,24-30, 1989.

In this paper I consider Bronwyn Davies' theoretical analysis of the sex/gender bias in education. In particular, I argue that Davies' preferred theory of gender, a postmodern one, affords us descriptions of options which obscure the alternatives available, mask the political dangers associated with some of them, and, in general, is a theory of gender which cannot support the changes we desire. Thus, I conclude that, contrary to stated claims, it is a theory of gender which fails to offer the greatest potential for establishing equitable practice.

HOUTEPEN, Rob. Op zoek naar een pragmatisch ethos. Kennis Methode, 14(2), 222-229, 1990.

HÖVELMANN, Gerd H. Técnica o imagen del mundo? Dialogo Filosof, 5(3), 364-379, S-D 89.

HOVIS, R Corby. What Can the History of Mathematics Learn from Philosophy? Phil Math, 4(1), 35-57, 1989.

One influential interpretation of Newton's formulation of his calculus has regarded his work as an organized, cohesive presentation, shaped primarily by technical issues and implicitly motivated by a knowledge of the form which a "finished" calculus should take. Offered as an alternative to this view is a less systematic and more realistic picture, in which both philosophical and technical considerations played a part in influencing the structure and interpretation of the calculus throughout Newton's mathematical career. This analysis sees the development of Newton's calculus not principally as a calculated movement toward "rigorous" justification (in the sense of Cauchy, Weierstrass, and their nineteenth-century contemporaries) and refinement of techniques, but as an evolution in the light of his involvement in debates over philosophical and scientific issues central to the rise of modern philosophy and science in the seventeeth and early eighteenth centuries.

HOWARD, Dick. The Birth of Politics (in Serbo-Croatian). Filozof Istraz, 30(3), 791-797, 1989.

Il s'agit d'une conférence qui se propose d'esquisser un projet de recherches qui s'avance petit-à-petit. L'auteur se propose trois buts. Tout d'abord, il cherche à démontrer la priorité de la démocratie sur toute autre forme de politique moderne. Il s'y emploie par des voies aussi bien philosophiques qu'historiques. De point de vue théroqie, il développe les implications des arguments élaborés dans son livre, *From Marx to Kant*. Ceci se présente concrètement sous la forme d'une analyse comparée des révolutions américaines, françaises et 'prussiennes.' L'auteur s'explique d'ailleurs sur l'inclusion de cette dernière expérience et l'exclusion de la Révolution anglaise. Ces trois figures représentent les trois formes possibles d'une entrée sociale en modernité. L'auteur y applique les catégories de genèse, normativité et d'origine—expliquées dans son livre mentionné ci-dessus—afin d'expliquer la priorité d'une politique démocratique dans nos sociétés contemporaines.

HOWARD, Don. Einstein and Duhem. Synthese, 83(3), 363-384, Je 90.

Pierre Duhem's often unrecognized influence on twentieth-century philosophy of science is illustrated by an analysis of his significant if also largely unrecognized influence on Albert Einstein. Einstein's first acquaintance with Duhem's *La Théorie physique, son objet et sa structure* around 1909 is strongly suggested by his close personal and professional relationship with Duhem's German translator, Friedrich Adler. The central role of a Duhemian holistic, underdeterminationist variety of conventionalism in Einstein's thought is examined at length, with special emphasis on Einstein's deployment of Duhemian arguments in his debates with neo-Kantian interpreters of relativity and in his critique of the empiricist doctrines of theory testing advanced by Schlick, Reichenbach, and Carnap. Most striking is Einstein's 1949 criticism of the verificationist conception of meaning from a holistic point of view, anticipating by two years the rather similar, but more famous criticism advanced independently by Quine in "Two Dogmas of Empiricism."

HOWARD, Don. "Holism, Separability, and the Metaphysical Implications of the Bell Experiments" in *Philosophical Consequences of Quantum Theory: Reflections on Bell's Theorem*, CUSHING, James T (ed), 224-253. Notre Dame, Univ Notre Dame Pr, 1989.

HOWARD, George S and YOUNGS, William H. A Research Strategy for Studying Telic Human Behavior. J Mind Behav, 10(4), 393-411, Autumn 89.

Numerous writers have recently called for reform in psychological theorizing and research methodology designed to appreciate the teleological, active agent capacities of humans. This paper presents three studies that probe individual's abilities to volitionally control their eating behavior. These investigations suggest one way that researchers might consider the operation of telic powers in human action. Rather than seeing teleological explanations as rivals to the more traditional causal explanations favored in psychological research, this paper elaborates a position that sees human volition as a causal force embedded in (and influenced by) the traditional causal influences studied in psychological research. Finally, the theoretical and methodological refinements suggested here and elsewhere are seen against the backdrop of a philosophy of science that sees change as a more gradual, evolutionary process, rather than the Kuhnian, revolutionary process.

HOWARD, Mark. A Proofless Proof of the Barwise Compactness Theorem.

J Sym Log, 53(2), 597-602, Je 88.

We prove a theorem (1.7) about partial orders which can be viewed as a version of the Barwise compactness theorem which does not mention logic. The Barwise compactness theorem is easily equivalent to 1.7 + "Every Henkin set has a model." We then make the observation that 1.7 gives us the definability of forcing for quantifier-free sentences in the forcing language and use this to give a direct proof of the truth and definability lemmas of forcing.

HOWARD, V A. Expression as Hands-on Construction. J Aes Educ, 22(1), 133-141, Spr 88.

Expression is sometimes passive, sometimes subjective, sometimes uncontrolled, sometimes surprising. The negative aim of this paper is to head off those who would substitute the word 'always' for the word 'sometimes' in the preceding sentence. The positive aim is to sketch a portrait of the quest for expression showing it to be as discerning as it is feeling—a matter of making and, therefore, for the most part a "hands on" constructive affair.

HOWE, Kenneth R. Equal Opportunity *Is* Equal Education (within Limits). Educ Theor, 40(2), 227-230, Spr 90.

HOWE, Kenneth R. Equality of Educational Opportunity as Equality of Educational Outcomes. Proc Phil Educ, 45, 292-299, 1989.

HOWE, Kenneth R. In Defense of Outcomes-Based Conceptions of Equal Educational Opportunity. Educ Theor, 39(4), 317-336, Fall 89.

HOWE, Lawrence W and ARMSTRONG, Robert L. An Euler Test for Syllogisms. Teach Phil, 13(1), 39-46, Mr 90.

Citing both pedagogical and theoretical difficulties with the Venn diagram method of testing syllogisms, we propose an alternative method based on Euler Circles. Our method works for all categorical syllogisms and is based on the indirect or counterexample method of formal proof. It rejects the restrictive Boolean interpretation of existence in favor of the intuitive, traditional Aristotelian assumption that everything exists in some sense or other. Critical questions about the existential content of terms are deferred to postlogical analysis in the same manner that questions about the soundness of arguments are discussed after the evaluation of validity.

HOWELL, Nancy R. Radical Relatedness and Feminist Separatism. Process Stud, 18(2), 118-126, Sum 89.

This article is an interpretation of feminist separatism. A definition of separatism is developed using the works of Mary Daly and Janice Raymond. Following an analysis of the concept of separatism, it is suggested that the Whiteheadian understanding of judgment, propositions, and internal relations contributes to the construction of a more radical separatism as a challenge to the patriarchal worldview.

HOWELLS, Christina M. "Derrida and Sartre: Hegel's Death Knell" in *Derrida and Deconstruction*, SILVERMAN, Hugh J (ed), 169-181. New York, Routledge, 1989.

The article compares Derrida's treatment of Hegel and Genet in *Glas* with Sartre's account of Genet and use of Hegel in *Saint Genet, Comédien et martyr*, with particular reference to the philosophers' aim of escaping totalization within the mechanisms of the Hegelian dialectic. It shows Derrida's work as in part a response to Sartre's earlier study, and focuses on the paradoxes and problems entailed in both critics' attempts to avoid recuperation, and in their desire to read Genet's work in terms of its philosophical and ethical effects.

HOWSON, Colin. On a Recent Objection to Popper and Miller's "Disproof" of Probabilistic Induction. Phil Sci, 56(4), 675-680, D 89.

Dunn and Hellman's objection to Popper and Miller's alleged disproof of inductive probability is considered and rejected. Dunn and Hellman base their objection on a decomposition of the incremental support $P(h/e)-P(h)$ of h by e dual to that of Popper and Miller, and argue, dually to Popper and Miller, to a conclusion contrary to the latter's that all support is deductive in character. I contend that Dunn and Hellman's dualizing argument fails because the elements of their decomposition are not supports of *parts* of h. I conclude by reinforcing a different line of criticism of Popper and Miller due to Redhead.

HOWSON, Colin. Subjective Probabilities and Betting Quotients. Synthese, 81(1), 1-8, O 89.

This paper addresses the problem of why the conditions under which standard proofs of the Dutch Book argument proceed should ever be met. In particular, the condition that there should be odds at which you would be willing to bet indifferently for or against are hardly plausible in practice, and relaxing it and applying Dutch book considerations gives only the theory of upper and lower probabilities. It is argued that there are nevertheless admittedly rather idealised circumstances in which the classic form of the Dutch book argument is valid.

HOYNINGEN-HUENE, Paul. "Epistemological Reductionism in Biology" in *Reductionism and Systems Theory in the Life Sciences: Some Problems and Perspectives*, HOYNINGEN-HUENE, Paul (ed), 29-44. Norwell, Kluwer, 1989.

HOYNINGEN-HUENE, Paul. Idealist Elements in Thomas Kuhn's Philosophy of Science. Hist Phil Quart, 6(4), 393-401, O 89.

HOYNINGEN-HUENE, Paul (ed) and WUKETITS, Franz M (ed). *Reductionism and Systems Theory in the Life Sciences: Some Problems and Perspectives*. Norwell, Kluwer, 1989

HRACHOVEC, Herbert. The Vienna Roundabout: On the Significance of Philosophical Reaction. Topoi, 8(2), 121-129, S 89.

This paper investigates philosophical work done in Vienna after the Second World War. It is argued that it is based on reaction against the revolutionary advances of the Viennese Circle, grounded in a dubious concept of *philosophia perennis*. This has not turned out to be a productive enterprise. Nevertheless it is a state of affairs that has to be acknowledged as historically unavoidable for any new development to originate from this particular place.

HRDY, Sarah Blaffer. Raising Darwin's Consciousness: Females and Evolutionary Theory. Zygon, 25(2), 129-137, Je 90.

Early studies of primate social behavior were distorted by observational, methodological, and ideological biases that caused researchers to overlook active roles played by females in the social lives of monkeys. Primatology provides a particularly well-documented case illustrating why research programs in the social and natural sciences need multiple studies that enlist researchers from diverse backgrounds.

HROCH, Jaroslav. Vantage Points of H G Gadamer's Philosophical Thinking (Plato, Herder, Goethe, Hegel) (in Czechoslovakian). Filozof Cas, 38(1-2), 132-146, 1990.

The author of this article focuses his attention on the first period of the development of H-G Gadamer's philosophical thinking in the years 1920 to 1947. In this context he demonstrates that Gadamer's concept of understanding stems from an existentially ethicizing interpretation of the Socratic-Platonian dialogue as educationally operating communicative action, based on the idea of the dialogic nature of truth. The author goes on to subject to a critical analysis Gadamer's studies and essays in Hegel, Herder and Goethe, in which the philosopher displayed endeavours for an original synthesis of the humanistic legacy of German classical philosophy and the traditions of conservative liberalism and Christianity. The final part of the article is devoted to a critical analysis of Gadamer's effort to find a way out of the crisis of bourgeois consciousness in a novel, ethically oriented concept of rationality which would be capable of contributing towards the revitalization of the original humanistic content and meaning of European science.

HRONSZKY, Imre. "The Phoenix" in *Scientific Knowledge Socialized*, HRONSZKY, Imre (ed), 97-121. Norwell, Kluwer, 1989.

HRONSZKY, Imre (ed) and FEHER, Marta (ed) and DAJKA, Balazs (ed). *Scientific Knowledge Socialized*. Norwell, Kluwer, 1989

HRUSHOVSKI, E. Almost Orthogonal Regular Types. Annals Pure Applied Log, 45(2), 139-155, D 89.

Let p,q be non-orthogonal regular types over B, in a stable theory. We show that at most three parameters from p are needed to witness the non-orthogonality with $q^{(\omega)}$, and classify completely the situations in which two or three are in fact necessary; they are all classical. Partial results are obtained in the case when ω is replaced by a finite $n < \omega$.

HRUSHOVSKI, E and SHELAH, S. A Dichotomy Theorem for Regular Types. Annals Pure Applied Log, 45(2), 157-169, D 89.

HUBBARD, J M. Albertus Magnus and the Notion of Syllogistic Middle Term. Thomist, 54(1), 115-122, Ja 90.

HUBIK, S. Concerning the Issue of Points of Departure of Environmental Ethics (in Czechoslovakian). Filozof Cas, 37(5), 677-690, 1989.

The author traces in his article selected attempts made by Western philosophers and theoreticians at constituting foundations of an environmental ethics. He goes on to analyze the implications of the major programme postulate, which was spelt out by J B Callicott, T Regan and others and which claimed that the key prerequisite for the constitution of an environmental ethics was the formation of a nonanthropocentric theory of values. (edited)

HÜBSCHER, Arthur (ed) and SCHOPENHAUER, Arthur and PAYNE, E F J (trans). *Manuscript Remains, Volume IV: The Manuscript Books of 1830-1852 and Last Manuscripts*. New York, St Martin's Pr, 1990

HUBY, Pamela M. "Cicero's *Topics* and Its Peripatetic Sources" in *Cicero's Knowledge of the Peripatos*, FORTENBAUGH, William W (ed), 61-76. New Brunswick, Transaction Books, 1989.

What is the origin of the list of Topics in Cicero's *Topics* and other works? Aristotle's primarily dialectical topics were transferred to rhetoric and law, and Cicero's inept treatment suggests a Greek original designed for different purposes. The fifth-century Martianus Capella has a similar list and, separately, some propositional logic identical with that embedded in Cicero's list. Both may have a post-Chrysippean Stoic original. Boetius claims to give a list of topics from Themistius, but that is confused. Cicero's account of what a topic is may come from Theophrastus, but his sources are many.

HUDAC, Michael C. The Ontological Difference and the Pre-Metaphysical Status of the Being of Beings in Plato. Man World, 23(2), 191-203, Ap 90.

The article begins by outlining key aspects of Heidegger's thinking on the ontological difference and metaphysics. The discussion then moves to consider Heidegger's reading of Plato, finding it most often highly thoughtful and informative, if not always consistent. The question is posed concerning whether in certain of Plato's texts Being is thought in a way that Heidegger would regard as pre-metaphysical. In the concluding section, some suggestions for such a reading are given.

HUDAK, Brent and WOODS, John. By Parity of Reasoning. Inform Log, 11(3), 125-139, Fall 89.

We argue that arguments from analogy are a particular type of meta-argument, viz., arguments by parity of reasoning. Given this, we show that two arguments are analogous when they share a deep structure (which in the case of arguments from analogy amounts to logical form). Hence we show that such arguments stand or fall together.

HUDGINS, Edward. Building Bridges to the Right: Libertarians, Conservatives, and Humanists. Free Inq, 9(4), 9-12, Fall 89.

HUDSON, Hud. A Response to A A Long's "The Stoics on World-Conflagration and Everlasting Recurrence". S J Phil, 28(1), 149-158, Spr 90.

I examine a recent attempt by A A Long to give a reading of the Stoic doctrine of everlasting recurrence which utilizes a circular theory of time. Although Long can thus avoid traditional objections to the claim that the members in a world-order are numerically identical with and indiscernible from their counterparts in other world-orders, I argue that on this reading the supposed infinite series of world-orders collapses into a single world-order which, in addition to other difficulties, yields an impoverished and ultimately unacceptable sense of "recurrence." Finally, I defend a different reading of this doctrine.

HUDSON, Stephen D. What is Morality All About? Philosophia (Israel), 20(1-2), 3-13, Jl 90.

HUG, Theo. Menschenbilder in pädagogiknahen Sozialwissenschaften. Conceptus, 23(60), 3-22, 1989.

In former pedagogical anthropologies there was always a tendency to develop standardised and idealistic conceptions of human being. By looking at a selection of examples one can prove that anthropological conceptions of human beings are also contained in theories of modern social sciences, on which the pedagogical thinking continuously refers to. Given the variety of heterogeneous scientific paradigms and the development of specialised disciplines in pedagogy the question arises of how to integrate this cosmos of conceptions. This question will be critically discussed within the framework of the ongoing discourse about postmodernism.

HUGHEN, Richard E. Aristotle's Theory of Time and Entropy. SW Phil Rev, 6(1), 19-27, Ja 90.

Aristotle denied that time was an entity or thing that could exist independently of objects or things—in this respect, his theory is quite modern. He recognized the relationship of time and motion and consequently defines time as the measure or number of a continuous motion taken without qualification. In this paper I reconstruct Aristotle's theory of time using entropy as the 'continuous motion taken without qualification' and note that this helps to explain several passages in the *Physics* that seem quite obscure otherwise, but in the final analysis an entropic interpretation cannot rescue his theory from certain shortcomings.

HUGHES, John. Philosophy and Style: Wittgenstein and Russell. Phil Lit, 13(2), 332-339, O 89.

A study and comparison of the characteristic forms of writing employed by Wittgenstein and Russell, indicating something of the complex and various ways in which personality constitutes a source and context for philosophical thought, and is evident within it.

HUGHES, Paul. Disparate Conceptions of Moral Theory. Phil Context, 19, 9-20, 1989.

This article describes the ultimate differences between "action" oriented and "agent" centered moral theories in an attempt to clarify recent criticisms of modern moral philosophy. These criticisms claim that modern moral philosophy violates moral agency by reducing the moral life to nothing more than consistent adherence to decision procedures. But, as Aristotle and other virtue theorists have made clear, there is far more to the moral life than mere conformity to rules or the performance of "right" actions. I urge in particular that what gets "lost" in act morality is the individual's "particularity," which is a function, in part, of her embeddedness in a social context.

HUGHES, R I G. "Bell's Theorem, Ideology, and Structural Explanation" in *Philosophical Consequences of Quantum Theory: Reflections on Bell's Theorem*, CUSHING, James T (ed), 195-207. Notre Dame, Univ Notre Dame Pr, 1989.

HUGHES, R I G. Kant's *Analogies* and the Structure of Objective Time. Pac Phil Quart, 71(2), 141-163, Je 90.

HUGLY, Philip and SAYWARD, Charles. Can There Be a Proof That Some Unprovable Arithmetic Sentence Is True? Dialectica, 43(3), 289-292, 1989.

A common theme of logic texts is that the Gödel incompleteness result shows that some unprovable statement of arithmetic is true, or, at least, that determining whether arithmetic truth is axiomatizable is a logical or mathematical issue. Against this common theme we argue that the issue is a philosophical issue that has not been settled.

HUGLY, Philip and SAYWARD, Charles. Tractatus 6.2-6.22. Phil Invest, 13(2), 126-136, Ap 90.

Implicit in Tractatus 6.2-6.22 are the ideas that the content of mathematical propositions consists in their use outside of mathematics, and that outside of mathematics these propositions function as rules, primarily rules of inference. These ideas are elaborated and defended.

HUH, Woo-Sung. The Philosophy of History in the "Later" Nishida: A Philosophic Turn. Phil East West, 40(3), 343-374, Jl 90.

This essay argues that Nishida pursued two main lines of thought. These lines are the development of a philosophy of self-consciousness in his pre-1931 corpus and the philosophy of history-politics in his later writings. Nishida's later philosophy may be seen as his effort to overcome his earlier sharp distinction between homo interior and homo exterior. The familiar characterization of pure experience as the motif of Nishida's entire philosophy must be amended. Since acts of self-consciousness and historical entities are not similar enough to be treated by forms of self-consciousness, Nishida's turn to the philosophy of history is a wrong turn.

HULL, David L. *The Metaphysics of Evolution*. Albany, SUNY Pr, 1989

Fourteen papers deal with such topics as the variability of the human species, Charles Darwin and evolution, issues in contemporary evolutionary biology, the principles of biological classification, the role of history in science, and sociobiology.

HULL, Richard T (ed). *Ethical Issues in the New Reproductive Technologies*. Belmont, Wadsworth, 1990

HUMMEL, Gert. Protestant Reconciliation as a Challenge for Today's Culture. Dialec Hum, 14(1), 121-126, Wint 87.

HUMPHREY, Fred (trans) and HÖSLE, Vittorio and ADLER, Pierre (trans). On Plato's Philosophy of Numbers and its Mathematical and Philosophical Significance. Grad Fac Phil J, 13(1), 21-63, 1988.

HUMPHREYS, Paul W. "Scientific Explanation: The Causes, Some of the Causes, and Nothing But the Causes" in *Scientific Explanation (Minnesota Studies in the Philosophy of Science, Volume XIII)*, KITCHER, Philip (ed), 283-306. Minneapolis, Univ of Minn Pr, 1989.

A detailed theory of causal explanations is based on the use of contributing and counteracting causes that operate invariantly across contexts. The theory is able to provide true explanations when our knowledge is incomplete, and it provides a unified approach to both deterministic and probabilistic explanations. It rejects the view that specification of probability values is essential for an adequate explanation and concludes with arguments against the need for an erotetic account of explanation.

HUND, John. The Social Relativity of Justice and Rights Thesis. Vera Lex, 8(2), 1,18-19, 1988.

HUNDERT, Edward M. *Philosophy, Psychiatry and Neuroscience: Three Approaches to the Mind*. New York, Clarendon/Oxford Pr, 1989

HUNGERLAND, Isabel C. "Hobbes and the Concept of World Government" in *Hobbes: War Among Nations*, AIRAKSINEN, Timo (ed), 35-50. Brookfield, Gower, 1989.

HUNT, David Paul. Middle Knowledge: The "Foreknowledge Defense". Int J Phil Relig, 28(1), 1-24, Ag 90.

In response to the objection (from Robert Adams and others) that counterfactuals of freedom are not sufficiently "grounded" to serve as objects of divine knowledge, some defenders of middle knowledge have argued that it is at least no *worse* off than foreknowledge in this respect; so if foreknowledge is deemed coherent, despite the threat of "ungroundedness," middle knowledge should be likewise. I focus on the employment of this strategy in a recent article by Richard Otte, and show that it is undermined by significant differences between foreknowledge and middle knowledge as well as a failure to appreciate the force of the "grounding" objection.

HUNT, Geoffrey. Schizophrenia and Indeterminacy: The Problem of Validity. Theor Med, 11(1), 61-78, Mr 90.

The paper attempts to account for the confusion over the validity of the concept of 'schizophrenia' in terms of two closely related aspects of conceptual indeterminacy. Firstly, it is identified on the basis of a breakdown in intelligibility, but what constitutes such a breakdown is indeterminate. Secondly, the concept sits between the categories of natural disease or illness on the one hand, and character trait or moral failing or gift on the other. This entails an indeterminacy in attempting to define the role that physiological explanation could have. Light may be thrown on the concept by exploring a distinction between a life story in which the schizophrenic condition emerges as the conclusion of the story and a causal process in which the condition is the end result or final consequence.

HUNT, Robert P. Murray, Niebuhr, and the Problem of the Neutral State. Thought, 64(255), 362-376, D 89.

HUNTER, Graeme. The Fate of Thomas Hobbes. Stud Leibniz, 21(1), 5-20, 1989.

This is an analysis of Thomas Hobbes's lengthy controversy with Bishop Bramhall concerning the question of freedom. I argue that because the presuppositions concerning the new science, which underly Hobbes's fatalism, are not even understood, much less shared, by Bramhall, their discussion fails to be decisive. Its historical importance lies in partly anticipating the solutions later proposed by Spinoza and Leibniz.

HURKA, Thomas. Two Kinds of Satisficing. Phil Stud, 59(1), 107-111, My 90.

Michael Slote has defended a moral view that he calls "satisficing consequentialism." Less demanding than maximizing consequentialism, it requires only that agents bring about consequences that are "good enough." I argue that Slote's characterization of satisficing is ambiguous. His idea of consequences' being "good enough" admits of two interpretations, with different implications in (some) particular cases. One interpretation I call "absolute-level" satisficing, the other "comparative" satisficing. Once distinguished, these versions of satisficing appear in a very different light. Absolute-level satisficing is indeed plausible and attractive, at least for subjective-good versions of consequentialism; comparative satisficing is not.

HURLEY, Paul. Where the Traditional Accounts of Practical Reason Go Wrong. Logos (USA), 10, 157-166, 1989.

The many disagreements between Humeans and Kantians regarding practical reason and moral judgment have served to obscure their fundamental shared assumption: the assumption that there are given desires. Granted this assumption, the Humean and Kantian accounts *do* seem to provide exhaustive alternatives—either practical reason, hence moral judgment, is grounded in such given desires; or practical reason, hence moral judgment, is independent of, and capable of standing in opposition to, the ends dictated by the agent's given desires. The assumption, however, should *not* be granted. It is merely a special case of the appeal to a foundational "given," and the powerful arguments against any such appeal to a given theoretical foundation can readily be extended to the practical domain. With the assumption eliminated, the Humean and Kantian accounts no longer present themselves as exhaustive alternatives. Indeed, a third alternative suggests itself, one capable of incorporating the strong points of each of the other accounts, while avoiding their shortcomings.

HURTADO, Guillermo. Ward on Davidson's Refutation of Scepticism. Critica, 21(63), 75-81, D 89.

This paper shows that (1) there is no guarantee of symmetry in the radical interpretation process. Even if we grant that an omniscient being is intelligible and that he can interpret us, it does not follow—as recently claimed—that we can interpret him. (2) From the intelligibility of a speaker who has no false beliefs it does not follow that (2.1) we can interpret him, or he us, for our beliefs can have radically different subject matters; (2.2) we are not grossly mistaken about the world, for such a speaker may have a very small set of beliefs about the world.

HUSAK, Douglas N. Recreational Drugs and Paternalism. Law Phil, 8(3),

353-381, D 89.

I argue that criminal laws against the use of recreational drugs are especially unlikely to be justified instances of paternalistic interference. The paternalistic case for anti-drug legislation rests on dubious empirical assumptions and unwarranted generalizations from worst-case scenarios.

HUSSEY, Edward. "The Beginnings of Epistemology: From Homer to Philolaus" in *Epistemology (Companions to Ancient Thought: 1)*, EVERSON, Stephen (ed), 11-38. New York, Cambridge Univ Pr, 1989.

HUSTED, Bryan W. Trust in Business Relations: Directions for Empirical Research. Bus Prof Ethics J, 8(2), 23-40, Sum 89.

HUTTON, Patrick H. Vico's Significance for the New Cultural History. New Vico Studies, 3, 73-84, 1985.

This essay considers the way in which Giambattista Vico's *New Science* (1744) provides a theoretical framework for recent studies in the history of collective mentalities. It explains how historiographical issues raised by Vico are addressed in the historical writings of pioneers in this field, such as Johan Huizinga, Lucien Febvre, Robert Mandrou, Norbert Elias, Michel Foucault, and Carlo Ginzburg.

HUYTS, Ini and VAN DEN WIJNGAARD, Marianne. Niet vrouw, niet man; wat dan? De rol van biomedische kennis bij de behandeling van pseudohermafrodieten. Kennis Methode, 13(4), 382-395, 1989.

Based on what knowledge and according to what images of masculinity and feminity treated physicians people born as intersex? Physicians used more traditional images of feminity and masculinity in the practice of construction of 'normal' women and men than fundamental researchers. Whilst the latter could afford to produce carefully balanced knowledge, in treatment, unambiguous criteria on which to base decisions remained highly desirable. Since there was (and is) a high degree of task-uncertainty in the field of medical practice, mechanisms to reduce the insecurity could be found. The simplification of results of fundamental research is an example of this.

HWANG, Philip H. "Confucianism and Theism" in *The Wisdom of Faith: Essays in Honor of Dr Sebastian Alexander Matczak*, THOMPSON, Henry O (ed), 51-62. Lanham, Univ Pr of America, 1989.

HYLTON, Peter. "The Significance of *On Denoting*" in *Rereading Russell: Essays on Bertrand Russell's Metaphysics and Epistemology*, SAVAGE, C Wade (ed), 88-107. Minneapolis, Univ of Minn Pr, 1989.

HYMAN, Arthur. "Demonstrative, Dialectical and Sophistic Arguments in the Philosophy of Moses Maimonides" in *Moses Maimonides and His Time*, ORMSBY, Eric L (ed), 35-51. Washington, Cath Univ Amer Pr, 1989.

HYMAN, John. *The Imitation of Nature*. Cambridge, Blackwell, 1989

HYMAN, Michael R and TANSEY, Richard. The Ethics of Psychoactive Ads. J Bus Ethics, 9(2), 105-114, F 90.

Many of today's ads work by arousing the viewer's emotions. Although emotion-arousing ads are widely used and are commonly thought to be effective, their careless use produces a side-effect: the *psychoactive ad*. A psychoactive ad is any emotion-arousing ad that can cause a meaningful, well-defined group of viewers to feel extremely anxious, to feel hostile toward others, or to feel a loss of self-esteem. We argue that, because some ill-conceived psychoactive ads can cause harm, ethical issues must arise during their production. Current pretesting methods cannot identify the potentially psychoactive ads; therefore, we offer some tentative guidelines for reducing the number of viewers harmed by psychoactive ads.

HYMERS, Michael. Bad Faith. Philosophy, 64(249), 397-402, Jl 89.

Responding to Leslie Stevenson's analysis of bad faith (*Philosophy* 58) and Jeffrey Gordon's criticism of Sartre—which assumes this analysis (*Philosophy* 60)—I argue for an understanding of Sartre's position as one which treats bad faith as the reflective affirmation of an ambiguous claim about some state of affairs, one "private" interpretation of which is compatible with that state of affairs, and another "public" interpretation of which is not. I anticipate and rebut a reformulation of Gordon's criticism.

IACONO, Alfonso M. L'idea di "Storia teoretica o congetturale" negli scritti filosofici e sul linguaggio di Adam Smith. Teoria, 9(2), 113-133, 1989.

IAKOVLEV, E G. Socialist Realism—Yesterday, Today, and Tomorrow. Soviet Stud Phil, 28(4), 79-87, Spr 90.

IBANA, Rainer R A. The Essential Elements for the Possibility and Necessity of the Principle of Solidarity According to Max Scheler. Phil Today, 33(1), 42-55, Spr 89.

The possibility and the necessity of the principle of solidarity in Max Scheler's philosophy depend on the acting person's level of personhood and level of social unity. Solidarity aims to promote both the values of the individual person and the values of social units. The fulfillment of both the individual person and the social unit are achieved within the context of the objective order of values.

IBAÑEZ, Alejandro Herrera. La noción de existencia en la ontología de Berkeley. Analisis Filosof, 6(1), 13-22, My 86.

I examine Section 33 of the *Principles of Human Knowledge* in order to reconstruct Berkeley's ontology. After examining this and other passages from the *Philosophical Commentaries* I conclude that existence does not fit in Berkeley's picture of the world as an idea, much less as an abstract idea. After showing several tensions in his ontology I conclude that existence must be a primitive notion of a relational property. *Esse est percipi*, therefore, is a description, not a definition.

IBSCH, Elrud. Harde noten om te kraken: de zachte wetenschappen. Alg Ned Tijdschr Wijs, 82(1), 54-62, Ja 90.

The publication of the series 'Philosophy of Science' by Martinus Nijhoff (The Hague) deserves both our attention and a critical discussion. The author has chosen the books on 'Theology' and 'Literary Studies', both belonging to the humanities. This means that they have been conceived of as belonging to the hermeneutic tradition. Developments in the philosophy of sciences and in the natural sciences have led to the principle of the 'unity of method' and happened to be a challenge for the rather 'weak' methodological claims of the humanities. Literary scholarship and theology, however, cannot simply be transformed into a science, because there are—at the very core of both disciplines—domains which resist intersubjective testing. (edited)

ICHIM, Viorica. La conscience philosophique et la conscience morale chez Eufrosin Poteca (in Romanian). Rev Filosof (Romania), 36(3), 245-249, My-Je 89.

IDALOVICHI, Israel. Grundprinzipien einer kritischen Dialektik zwischen Kant und Hegel. Kantstudien, 80(3), 324-344, 1989.

IDEL, Moshe. "Some Conceptions of the Land of Israel in Medieval Jewish Thought" in *A Straight Path: Studies in Medieval Philosophy and Culture*, LINK-SALINGER, Ruth (ed), 124-141. Washington, Cath Univ Amer Pr, 1988.

IDZIAK, Pawl M. Decision Problem for Relatively Free Brouwerian Semilattices. Rep Math Log, 22, 39-50, 1988.

The paper shows that finitely generated free algebras from any variety of Brouwerian semilattices (as well as Heyting algebras) containing a non-linear subdirectly irreducible member form a class with a hereditarily undecidable first order theory. Another problem solved is decidability of any single free Heyting algebra. In the paper it is shown that the 1-generated algebra is decidable, while the question for another one is answered—in negative—in a subsequent paper.

IGLEWSKI, M and KERSTEN, G E and BADCOCK, L and MALLORY, G R. Structuring and Simulating Negotiation: An Approach and an Example. Theor Decis, 28(3), 243-273, My 90.

Negotiation is a complex and dynamic decision process during which parties' perceptions, preferences, and roles may change. Modeling such a process requires flexible and powerful tools. The use of rule-based formalism is therefore expanded from its traditional expert system type technique, to structuring and restructuring nontrivial processes like negotiation. Using rules, we build a model of a negotiation problem. Some rules are used to infer positions and reactions of the parties, other rules are used to modify problem representation when such a modification is necessary. We illustrate the approach with a contract negotiation case between two large companies. We also show how this approach could help one party to realize that negotiations are being carried on against their assumptions and expectations.

IGNATOW, Assen. The Dialectic of Freedom in Nikolai Berdjaev. Stud Soviet Tho, 38(4), 273-289, N 89.

This paper is devoted to Berdjaev's doctrine of freedom. This great Russian Christian thinker draws a distinction between the uncreated "meonic" irrational freedom and the created human freedom which passes two stages: "freedom from..." and "freedom to...." Berdjaev shows the antinomies of the first kind of freedom which can lead to self-destruction. The paradoxical antinomies of the first freedom are resolved in the final, creative freedom. Berdjaev's philosophy of freedom is deeper than French existentialism and, of course, than scientist determinism. It is one of the most important attempts to clarify this metaphysical mystery.

IGNATYEV, A A. The Problem of Going *from*: Science Policy and 'Human Factors' in the Experience of Developing Countries. Soc Epistem, 3(3), 217-227, Jl-S 89.

IHDE, Don (ed) and RICOEUR, Paul. *The Conflict of Interpretations: Essays in Hermeneutics—Paul Ricoeur*. Evanston, Northwestern Univ Pr, 1988

IHODA, Jaime I. Σ1/2 Sets of Reals. J Sym Log, 53(2), 636-642, Je 88.

In this work we study the relationships between different regularity properties for Sigma (1,2) sets of reals. We show that the only implications for Sigma (1,2) sets are: Measurability implies category, category implies K-sigma regularity, and the Ramsey property implies K-sigma regularity. Also parameter forms of these results are true. (edited)

IHODA, Jaime I. Strong Measure Zero Sets and Rapid Filters. J Sym Log, 53(2), 393-402, Je 88.

We prove that cons(ZF) inplies cons(ZF + Borel conjecture + there exists a Ramsey ultrafilter). We also prove some results on strong measure zero sets from the existence of generalized Luzin sets. We study the relationships between strong measure zero sets and rapid filters on ω.

ILLINGWORTH, Patricia. AIDS and the Good Society. New York, Routledge, 1990.

The question of whether or not coercive policies designed to slow the spread of HIV/AIDS can be morally justified is considered from within a liberal framework. It is argued that (1) the behavior which transmits HIV is self-regarding and therefore that coercive measures cannot be justified according to the strong harm principle, and (2) social conditions which are themselves unjustifiable have fostered the high-risk behavior of gay men and IV drug users such that this behavior may not be autonomous. On the basis of the weak harm principle the conditions which have interfered with autonomy need to be changed. Not only are coercive policies unjustifiable by both the weak and strong harm principles, but gay men and IV drug users with HIV/AIDS ought to be compensated.

IMBERT, Francis. Le travail de la contradiction dans le Livre I de l'Emile. Rev Metaph Morale, 94(2), 205-228, Ap-Je 89.

A comparative reading of Emile's first and definitive versions' introductory pages permits to estimate the theoretical and practical importance of contradiction for J J Rousseau. The aim of the educative praxis is "the union into one" of a "double subject": the education of the natural man and that of the citizen. The work of unifying the contraries implicates both not to reduce contradictions to ordinary "differences" and to get out of an antagonistic union of the contraries.

IMBRUGLIA, Girolamo. Mondo, persona e storia in E De Martino: Tra Croce e Cassirer. Arch Stor Cult, 3, 339-361, 1990.

IMMERWAHR, John. Hume's Essays on Happiness. Hume Stud, 15(2), 307-324, N 89.

IMURA, Akira. Autonomie der Kunst in der Ästhetischen Theorie Adornos (in Japanese). Bigaku, 40(2), 13-24, Autumn 89.

Adornos Ästhetische Theorie ist als ambivalente Theorie über die Autonomie der Kunst charakterisiert. Er verteidigt die Autonomie der Kunst als Abgehobenheit von der Gesellschaft, obwohl er den avantgardischen Versuch der Aufhebung der autonomen Kunst als notwendigen Anspruch vesteht. Seine Forderung ist nicht die Verweigerung, sondern die Rettung des ästhetischen Scheins, in dem das autonome Kunstwerk das utopische Moment als augenblicklichen Glück verspricht. Aber Adorno sagt nicht nur die Massen- und engagierte Kunst, sonder auch die rezeptive Seite der Kunst überhaupt ab, weil auch das autonome Kunstwerk den Gefahr nicht vermeiden kann, in Heteronomie zur Warenwelt zurückzufallen, sobald der Schein in Beziehung zur Wirklichkeit kommt. (edited)

INADA, Kenneth K. "Environmental Problematics" in Nature in Asian Tradition of Thought: Essays in Environmental Philosophy, CALLICOTT, J Baird (ed), 231-245. Albany, SUNY Pr, 1989.

Environmental problems stem from the dichotomous nature of man. The Buddhist views this nature as expressions of ordinary experience, but there is another dimension to experience which, though functioning in the ordinary experiential realm, is non-attached to any empirical elements and therefore depicts a detached form of existence. The tension between the attached and detached forms of existence is resolved by the capture of emptiness in experience which, in turn, brings forth the realization of a holistic and balanced nature of existence.

INADA, Kenneth K. Response to Richard Pilgrim's Review of The Logic of Unity, by Hosaku Matsuo and Translated by Kenneth K Inada. Phil East West, 39(4), 453-456, O 89.

The response was prompted by a totally erroneous interpretation of Matsuo's novel epistemological framework. The reviewer attempted to understand Buddhist doctrines by way of Western categories which on surface seems plausible but, in essence, is impossible. For the epistemic notions expounded in Buddhism are based on the unique nature of emptiness, not in the literal sense but in its full (plenum) existential sense. This is the source of the nature of the Buddhist middle way which is not sought between being and nonbeing at all.

INATI, Shams C (trans) and BĀQIR AS-SADR, Allāma Muhammad. Our Philosophy: Allāma Muhammad Bāqir As-Sadr. London, Muhammadi Trust, 1987.

The main purpose of the work is to point out the benefits of Islam over capitalism and communism. A discussion of the disagreements among certain philosophical notions and the dialectical method upon which modern materialism rests follows. The causal laws governing the universe and the conflict between materialism and theology are considered, and a notion of the world in light of philosophical laws is formed. It is claimed that thoughts are not mechanically conditioned by the requirements of the community, but are rather the result of free motives that induce one to create a system in harmony with one's community.

INCARDONA, Nunzio. La inersorabilità della "nuda inteligencia" in Zubiri. G Metaf, 11(1), 127-142, Ja-Ap 89.

INEICHEN, Hans. Realismus heute. Z Phil Forsch, 43(3), 534-537, Jl-S 89.

INGENKAMP, Heinz Gerd. Dreimal keine höflichkeit. Schopenhauer Jahr, 70, 151-160, 1989.

INGRAM, David. Blumenberg and the Philosophical Grounds of Historiography. Hist Theor, 29(1), 1-15, F 90.

In The Legitimacy of the Modern Age (2nd revised edition, 1976) and Work on Myth (1979) Hans Blumenberg argues that we can no more write the history of ideas without notions of progress and novelty than we can without notions of continuity. Yet he argues that discontinuity, or epochal change, is also a necessary condition for experiencing historical progress. This issue is closely connected to the legitimacy of the modern age as at once comparably progressive and uniquely original—in short, as uniquely rational—with respect to the epochs that preceded it. Analyzing difficulties in the concept of rational autonomy and justification that appear in the above texts, I contend that neither work establishes a transcendental warrant for the historiographic deployment of categories of progress and novelty.

INGRAM, David. The Retreat of the Political in the Modern Age: Jean-Luc Nancy on Totalitarianism and Community. Res Phenomenol, 18, 93-124, 1988.

INNERARITY, Daniel. Dialéctica de la Revolución: Hegel, Schelling y Hölderlin ante la Revolución Francesa. Anu Filosof, 22(1), 35-54, 1989.

This paper analyzes the meaning that the French Revolution had in forming German idealism. The three-sided meaning of the term "revolution" is studied as a transition from nature to liberty, as a political revindication, and as a realization of God's Kingdom from the idealist conception of liberty. I criticize those theories which—starting from Lukács—do not notice the continuity existing between the youthful desires of liberation which lie in the origin of German idealism, and its later speculative development.

INNERARITY, Daniel. Hacia una ecología de la razón: Consideraciones sobre la filosofía de la postmodernidad. Anu Filosof, 21(1), 133-142, 1988.

INNERARITY, Daniel. Modernidad y postmodernidad. Anu Filosof, 20(1), 105-129, 1987.

INOUÉ, Takao. A Note on Stahl's Opposite System. Z Math Log, 35(5), 387-390, 1989.

Stahl's opposite system SP is a Hilbert-style sentential calculus deriving all well-formed formulas whose negation are provable in classical propositional logic. It is a remarkable fact that SP does not use usual provability relation. In this paper a Hilbert-style axiomatization of predicate opposite system SC is given on the basis of Stahl's idea. Moreover the author proposes Gentzen-style sequent calculi OP and OC corresponding to the Hilbert-style systems SP and SC, respectively. This result is one of the very answers to Stahl's suggestion in his paper.

IOANNIDI, H. Hypothèses sur Platon et sur Nietzsche. Philosophia (Athens), 17-18, 310-324, 1987-88.

IONEL, Nicolae. Un ample programme d'action révolutionnaire et de perfectionnement (in Romanian). Rev Filosof (Romania), 35(6), 533-537, N-D 88.

IONEL, Nicolae. Quelques contributions de grande valeur au progrès multilatéral de la Roumanie socialiste (in Romanian). Rev Filosof (Romania), 36(1), 19-23, Ja-F 89.

IRIMIE, Ioan. The Historical-Philosophical Change of an Involution Dialectics. Phil Log, 32(3-4), 219-224, Jl-D 88.

IRVINE, William B. Insider Trading: An Ethical Appraisal. Bus Prof Ethics J, 6(4), 3-33, Wint 87.

In my paper, I discuss the ethical ramifications of insider trading, i.e., the buying or selling of securities on the basis of privileged information. I argue *against* the standard view that anyone who engages in insider trading wrongs the shareholders of a company and is therefore engaged in moral misconduct. Instead, I suggest that the real moral culprits in typical cases of insider trading are the corporate directors who needless harm the shareholders by withholding from them information that they have a right to possess—viz., information concerning a takeover offer.

IRWIN, T H. Le caractère aporétique de la *Métaphysique* d'Aristote. Rev Metaph Morale, 95(2), 221-248, Ap-Je 90.

IRWIN, T H. La conception stoïcienne et la conception aristotélicienne du bonheur. Rev Metaph Morale, 94(4), 535-576, O-D 89.

IRWIN, T H. Tradition and Reason in the History of Ethics. Soc Phil Pol, 7(1), 45-68, Autumn 89.

IRWIN, T H. Virtue, Praise and Success: Stoic Responses to Aristotle. Monist, 73(1), 59-79, Ja 90.

ISAAC, Jeffrey C. Realism and Reality: Some Realistic Reconsiderations. J Theor Soc Behav, 20(1), 1-31, Mr 90.

ISAC, Ionut. Quelques repères de l'épistémologie contemporaine (in Romanian). Rev Filosof (Romania), 36(3), 293-299, My-Je 89.

ISAC, Victor. A New Meaning in the History of Science: From the Logical Truth Towards the Ethical Truth. Phil Log, 32(1-2), 147-152, Ja-Je 88.

ISAR, N. L'illuministe Simeon Marcovici—un remarquable journaliste et pensuer (in Romanian). Rev Filosof (Romania), 35(5), 464-471, S-O 88.

ISASI, Juan M. Actualidad y fecundidad de la filosofía blondeliana. Pensamiento, 46(183), 285-303, Jl-S 90.

El trabajo, a la vez que señala el cultivo selectivo que hoy se sigue haciendo de la filosofía blondeliana en ámbitos amplios de la cultura, subraya sobre todo la fecunda actualidad de su pensamiento. En su dialéctica se hallan intuiciones muy valiosas para encarar, con éxito, inquietudes y problemas de la más acuciante actualidad como las antinomias libertad-necesidad, autonomía-heteronomia, hombre-Dios.

ISERSON, Kenneth V. Commentary: Prehospital DNR Orders. Hastings Center Rep, 19(6), 17-19, N-D 89.

Prehospital care (i.e., ambulance services) is designed to allow physician-extenders to save lives. Yet the emergency medical systems operate under rigid guidelines that generally require full resuscitation to be performed on all patients they are called for who are in cardio-pulmonary arrest. This action uses scarce resources and demoralizes both families and providers. Problems arise when CPR and adjunctive measures are used on terminally ill patients who explicitly do not want this care. There is a need for prehospital protocols to address DNR that can be easily executed by patients, understood and recognized by prehospital care providers, and permitted by regulatory agencies.

ISHIGURO, Hidè. "Die Beziehung zwischen Welt und Sprache: Bemerkungen im Ausgang von Wittgensteins *Tractatus*" in *Wittgenstein in Focus—Im Brennpunkt: Wittgenstein*, MC GUINNESS, Brian (ed), 49-66. Amsterdam, Rodopi, 1989.

Theories of understanding and of language use cannot be detached from theories of truth and reference as many have recently attempted to say. Wittgenstein's early picture theory and his theory of reference (*Bedeutung*) is part and parcel of his view on understanding meaningful sentences (*Sätze*), and the use of expressions. His later theory of meaning as use of expressions is inseparable from his view on what kind of objects these expressions refer to. As logical analysis is a quest for definiteness of sense and is not reductionism, not all objects of the *Tractatus* are of one kind. Singular propositions have no privileged role in linking language to the world. Understanding propositions with proper names or with demonstratives imply understanding of general propositions. This does not entail a definite description view of the sense of proper names. It does suggest that demonstrative pronouns are often not used anaphorically and never purely ostensively.

ISKANDER, Awad A. An Isomorphism Between Rings and Groups. Notre Dame J Form Log, 30(4), 513-529, Fall 89.

Bijective functors S and T are constructed, by a uniform algorithm, between a category R of commutative nonassociative rings and a category G of nilpotent groups such that for any ring A in R and any group B in G, TSA is isomorphic to A and STB is isomorphic to B. If L is a subclass of R, then L has a decidable elementary theory iff. SL has a decidable elementary theory. The free nilpotent class 3 group on 2 generators is assigned to the ring of integers and the class of nilpotent class 2 groups in G is assigned to the class of nonassociative Boolean rings.

ISSAC, Jeffrey C. Arendt, Camus, and Postmodern Politics. Praxis Int, 9(1-2), 48-71, Ap-Jl 89.

IVANETIC, Nada. Theory of Speech Acts (in Serbo-Croatian). Filozof Istraz, 30(3), 1031-1042, 1989.

Es wird ein Überblick über interaktionalistische (pragmatische) Disziplinen in der Linguistik gegeben. Zugleich geht man auf ihre Terminologie, Ziele und Methoden ein. Besondere Aufmerksamkeit wird der Sprechakttheorie und der Frage der Sprechaktkonstitution gewidmet.

IVANHOE, Philip J. Reweaving the "One Thread" of the *Analects*. Phil East West, 40(1), 17-33, Ja 90.

A study of Confucius's version of the golden Rule, including a critical review of past scholarship on the issue and an analysis of the rule's ethical implications. The author argues that Confucius's version of the Golden Rule has two fundamental aspects: one, which commands fidelity to a traditionalist ethic and another, which regulates this adherence to rules by appealing to individual intuitions revealed by the imaginative act of placing oneself in another's place.

IVRY, Alfred L. "Averroes and the West: The First Encounter/Nonencounter" in *A Straight Path: Studies in Medieval Philosophy and Culture*, LINK-SALINGER, Ruth (ed), 142-158. Washington, Cath Univ Amer Pr, 1988.

The view of Averroes held by Scholastic philosophers was based entirely on the 13th century translations of his Aristotelian commentaries. He was regarded as a secular Aristotelian, his attempts to synthesize religion and reason unknown. This paper documents those attempts, arguing that Western familiarity with them might have altered the conflict between the arts and theology faculties in 13th century Paris. This theme is illustrated by an analysis of Averroes' *Prooemium* to *Metaphysics Lambda* in his *Long Commentary on the Metaphysics*, in which all distinctive and problematic issues are ignored.

IWAKI, Ken-ichi. Zwei Arten der Malerei: Von der Umwandelung der Interpretation der Kunst bei Hegel (in Japanese). Bigaku, 40(3), 12-23, Wint 89.

Die Malerei ist diejenige Kunst, die die Realen durch die Farben als die Besonderung des Lichts auf deren ideellen Beziehungen reduziert. Dieses Prinzip der Malerei als Subjektivisierung der Welt entspricht der Weltanschauung des Christentums, dessen Prinzip auch die Subjektivität, m.a.W. die Innigkeit des Gemüts ist. Deshalb ist die Malerei nach Hegel erst in der Welt des Christentums vollendet und seitdem das Paradigma der bildenden Künste geworden (edited)

JACKENDOFF, Ray. "Conceptual Semantics" in *Meaning and Mental Representation*, ECO, Umberto (ed), 81-97. Bloomington, Indiana Univ Pr, 1988.

JACKSON, Bernard S. Can Legal Semiotics Contribute to Natural Law Studies? Vera Lex, 7(1), 9,14,18, 1987.

This article briefly surveys the history of legal semiotics, and outlines the principal claims of different approaches. The school of Greimas looks for legal manifestations of generally applicable "elementary structures of signification," on both syntagmatic and paradigmatic axes. But it makes no claim to the innateness of such structures. This view is compared with a version of the "deep structure" of law based on Chomsky. In contrast to these and other formalist approaches, there are also historical accounts of legal discourse, emphasising pragmatic dimensions. It is suggested that these approaches are not incompatible. All share in common a denial of the normativity of the legal system, in any sense other than a set of claims constructed in particular discourses.

JACKSON, Christine M. The Fiery Fight for Animal Rights. Hastings Center Rep, 19(6), 37-39, N-D 89.

JACKSON, Frank. Classifying Conditionals. Analysis, 50(2), 134-147, Mr 90.

Consider (1) If Booth had not killed Lincoln, someone else would have; (2) if Booth does not kill Lincoln, someone else will; and (3) if Booth did not kill Lincoln, someone else did. Many writers agree that (1) is importantly different from (3). The issue this paper is concerned with is where then to place (2). A number of recent writers have argued that (2) should go with (1). I argue that (2) should go with (3).

JACKSON, Frank and PETTIT, Philip. In Defence of Folk Psychology. Phil Stud, 59(1), 31-54, My 90.

Eliminativists have raised the question of whether beliefs and desires exist. Their view is that beliefs and desires are the posits of a theory, dubbed folk psychology, and so that, like the posits of any theory, they are open to challenge. We agree that beliefs and desires are indeed to be thought of as the posits of a theory but that despite this, it is virtually certain that they exist. We describe the kind of theory we take folk psychology to be, namely, a species of commonsense functionalism, and explain how, given this account, it is virtually certain that beliefs and desires exist.

JACKSON, Frank and PETTIT, Philip. Program Explanation: A General Perspective. Analysis, 50(2), 107-117, Mr 90.

Some properties are causally relevant for a certain effect, others are not. In this paper we describe a problem for our understanding of this notion and then offer a solution in terms of the notion of a program explanation.

JACKSON, Frank. "A Puzzle About Ontological Commitment" in *Cause, Mind, and Reality: Essays Honoring C B Martin*, HEIL, John (ed), 191-199. Norwell, Kluwer, 1989.

Plausibly, a theory is ontologically committed to Ks if it entails that Ks exist. But a necessary truth is entailed by any theory. Hence, if Ks exist iff Ks exist necessarily, it cannot be that one theory is committed to Ks and another theory is not. This appears to threaten the Quinean tradition of assessing theories in part in terms of their ontological commitments, at least in the case of entities that exist iff they exist necessarily. I argue that we can avoid this untoward result without abandoning the classical position that a necessary truth is entailed by anything.

JACKSON, Jennifer. Honesty in Marketing. J Applied Phil, 7(1), 51-60, Mr 90.

To what extent is honesty or truthfulness morally obligatory in trade and advertising practices? It is argued here that while we have a general right, in business as elsewhere, not to be lied to, we have no general right, either in our business or other pursuits, not to be deliberately deceived. Certain restrictions on deceptive practices in trade and advertising, even unintentionally deceptive practices, are, even so, morally defensible: viz., where the practice would mislead reasonable people to a material degree or where it would mislead especially vulnerable people who are predictably unreasonable. It is suggested that a code of practice for trade and advertising which exaggerates the degree of truthfulness which is morally obligatory may actually be corrupting in effect.

JACKSON, M J. Psychomachia in Art from Prudentius to Proust. Brit J Aes, 30(2), 159-165, Ap 90.

The purpose of the article is to trace the concept of spiritual warfare, psychomachia, in examples of literature and art from Prudentius to Proust. The external warfare found in Prudentius's poem, *Psychomachia*, and in the sculpture of Romanesque churches and Gothic cathedrals becomes an internal warfare in Giotto's Arena Chapel at Padua and in Proust's *A la recherche du temps perdu*. In exploring the spiritual warfare of the novel attention is drawn to Proust's use of Giotto, Mâle and Ruskin.

JACKSON, M W. Maigret's Method. J Value Inq, 24(3), 169-183, Jl 90.

In this paper I argue that Georges Simenon's fictional detective M Jules Maigret employs a method of inquiry, though M Maigret often explicitly denies being methodical. The method he does in fact use is ethno-methodology.

JACKSON, Michael. *Paths Toward a Clearing: Radical Empiricism and Ethnographic Inquiry*. Bloomington, Indiana Univ Pr, 1989

JACKSON, R V. Bentham's Penal Theory in Action: The Case Against New South Wales. Utilitas, 1(2), 226-241, N 89.

JACKSON, Steve. Partition Properties and Well-Ordered Sequences. Annals Pure Applied Log, 48(1), 81-101, Jl 90.

This paper is concerned with well-ordered sequences, both of sets of ordinals and of sets of reals. The axiom of determinacy is assumed throughout. For each Suslin cardinal κ we consider the pointclass of sets A such that there is no κ^+ increasing sequence of sets reducible to A. We show that for successor or regular κ that this contains the κ-Suslin sets and is closed under countable unions, intersections, and complements. Some results concerning longer unions and intersection are given, as well as results concerning non-increasing sequences. Finally, for κ having the strong partition property, best possible bounds are given for the lengths of well-ordered sequences of subsets of the finite successors of κ. These results bear on the question of the GCH in the HOD of L(R), where R is the reals.

JACOBITTI, Edmund E. Political Thought and Rhetoric in Vico. New Vico Studies, 4, 73-88, 1986.

JACOBS, Bart. The Inconsistency of Higher Order Extensions of Martin-Löf's Type Theory. J Phil Log, 18(4), 399-422, N 89.

Martin-Löf's constructive type theory forms the basis of this paper. His central notions of category and set, and their relations with Russell's type theories, are discussed. It is shown that addition of an axiom—treating the category of propositions as a set and thereby enabling higher order quantification—leads to inconsistency. This theorem is a variant of Girard's paradox—which is a translation into type theory of Mirimanoff's paradox (concerning the set of all well-founded sets). The occurrence of the contradiction is explained in set theoretical terms. Crucial here is the way a

proof-object of an existential proposition is understood. It is shown that also Russell's paradox can be translated into type theory. The type theory extended with the axiom mentioned above contains constructive higher order logic, but even if one only adds constructive second order logic to type theory the contradictions arise.

JACOBS, Cornée. Spinoza et "De Stijl". Stud Spinozana, 5, 177-183, 1989.

The contributors to the periodical *De Stijl* (1917-1931) weren't only interested in visual arts and architecture, but also in philosophy. The influence of theosophy on the creation of images and formulation of theories by the contributors to *De Stijl* has been pointed out in various art-historical studies. Less well known is the influence of Spinoza. Both Vilmos Hustà and Georges Vantongerloo have been profoundly influenced by *Ethica*, and Theo van Doesburg, Piet Mondrian and Gino Severini make explicit reference to Spinoza. *Ethica* is also included in the recommended reading in *De Stijl*. Following a sketch of the development of Mondrian's painting, which is illustrative for *De Stijl*, a number of themes and examples are elaborated in the article.

JACOBS, Harvey L and BOOTH, Annie L. Ties that Bind: Native American Beliefs as a Foundation for Environmental Consciousness. Environ Ethics, 12(1), 27-43, Spr 90.

In this article we examine the specific contributions Native American thought can make to the ongoing search for a Western ecological consciousness. We begin with a review of the influence of Native American beliefs on the different branches of the modern environmental movement and some initial comparisons of Western and Native American ways of seeing. We then review Native American thought on the natural world, highlighting beliefs in the need for reciprocity and balance, the world as a living being, and relationships with animals. We conclude that Native American ideas are important, can prove inspirational in the search for a modern environmental consciousness, and affirm the arguments of both deep ecologists and ecofeminists.

JACOBS, Jonathan A. *Virtue and Self-Knowledge*. Englewood Cliffs, Prentice-Hall, 1988

The book develops an account of the relations between self-determination, moral character, and self-knowledge. The main claims are that virtue is the maximal exercise of rational agency and that the more fully one exercises rational agency in leading their life, the more fully they are able to unify and understand their life-history. Moreover, this understanding promotes further effective exercises of self-determination and is partially constitutive of happiness. The claims, with their sources chiefly in Aristotle and Kant, are defended against some important modern critiques of the ideal of rational self-mastery.

JACOBS, Jonathan. "Relativism, Rationality, and Repression" in *Inquiries into Values: The Inaugural Session of the International Society for Value Inquiry*, LEE, Sander H, 137-147. Lewiston, Mellen Pr, 1989.

JACOBS, Scott. Speech Acts and Arguments. Argumentation, 3(4), 345-365, N 89.

Speech act theory seems to provide a promising avenue for the analysis of the functional organization of argument. The theory, however, might be taken to suggest that arguments are a homogeneous class of speech act with a specifiable illocutionary force and a single set of felicity conditions. This suggestion confuses the analysis of the meaning of speech act verbs with the analysis of the pragmatic structure of actual language use. Suggesting that arguments are conveyed through a homogeneous class of linguistic action overlooks the way in which the context of activity and the form of expression organize the argumentative functions performed in using language. An alternative speech act analysis would treat folk terminology as a heuristic entry point into the development of a technical analysis of the myriad argumentative functions and structures to be found in natural language use. This would lead to a thorough-going pragmatic analysis of the rational and functional design of speech acts in argumentation.

JACOBS, Struan. "Stephen Toulmin's Theory of Conceptual Evolution" in *Issues in Evolutionary Epistemology*, HAHLWEG, Kai (ed), 510-523. Albany, SUNY Pr, 1989.

Salient features of the (supposedly) evolutionary metascience in Toulmin's *Human Understanding* are described, assessed and rejected. By its own standards the theory is untenable. Designed to supersede the generic relativist interpretation (exemplified by Kuhn and Collingwood) of conceptual change as marked by revolutionary mutations or breaks, that is the sort of historiography Toulmin unwittingly offers.

JACOBS, Sturan and OTTO, Karl-Heinz. Otto Neurath: Marxist Member of the Vienna Circle. Auslegung, 16(2), 175-189, Sum 90.

An exposition of Neurath's thought, designed to show its systematic character. Elements dealt with include his theory of history, Marxism and physicalism, metascience, and sociology as part of unified science.

JACOBS, Wilhelm G. *Zwischen Revolution und Orthodoxie?*. Stuttgart, Frommann-Holzboog, 1989

JACOBSEN, Rockney. Science, Technology, and Naturalized Philosophy. Eidos, 7(2), 155-174, D 88.

Redrawing the borders between philosophy and science disturbs our view of science as much as our view of philosophy. Quine's call for a replacement of philosophy by science rests on a Kantian misconception of the history of philosophy, and Rorty's reaction to naturalized philosophy (his edifying hermeneutics) rests on an overly Baconian conception of science. The naturalization of philosophy is better seen as a reconciliation of philosophy with its pre-Kantian past, together with a view of science as enjoying a principled autonomy *vis-à-vis* technology.

JACOBSOHN, Gary J. American Experience and the Israeli Dilemma. Vera Lex, 7(2), 16-17,20, 1987.

JACOBSON, Anne Jaap. Inductive Scepticism and Experimental Reasoning in Moral Subjects in Hume's Philosophy. Hume Stud, 15(2), 325-338, N 89.

JACOBSON, Pauline. Raising as Function Composition. Ling Phil, 13(4), 423-475, Ag 90.

JACOBY, Henry. Empirical Functionalism and Conceivability Arguments. Phil Psych, 2(3), 271-282, 1989.

Functionalism, the philosophical theory that defines mental states in terms of their causal relations to stimuli, overt behaviour, and other inner mental states, has often been accused of being unable to account for the qualitative character of our experiential states. Many times such objections to functionalism take the form of conceivability arguments. The author argues that if the conceivability arguments were successful against functionalism, then they would be successful against their alternative materialist views as well. So the conceivability arguments alone do not provide a good reason for materialists to abandon functionalism. It is further argued that functionalism is best understood to be an empirical theory, and if it is so understood then the conceivability arguments have no force against it at all. A further consequence that emerges is that on an empirical functionalist view, qualia, if real, are properties in the domain of psychology. (edited)

JACQUES, T Carlos. The Primacy of Narrative in Historical Understanding. Clio, 19(3), 197-214, Spr 90.

The essay presents an argument against Louis O Mink's claim that narrative, as the central cognitive instrument for historical knowledge, is not something objective that is discovered in reality, but is rather something that the historian invents or projects onto historical facts. Against this antirealist thesis, it is argued that historical reality is itself ordered by a narrative structure.

JACQUETTE, Dale. Borges' Proof for the Existence of God. J Speculative Phil, 4(1), 83-88, 1990.

In *Dreamtigers*, Jorge Luis Borges presents a partially whimsical '*Argumentum Ornithologicum*' proof for the existence of God, based on the problem of the speckled hen, according to which God must exist to guarantee the determinate number of birds seen but unknown and uncounted by the subject in a passing moment of imagination. The argument is criticized as invalid under Fred I Dretske's distinction between epistemic and nonepistemic seeing, but a disanalogy between imagination and ordinary vision is suggested, which may recommend Borges' argument for further serious philosophical discussion.

JACQUETTE, Dale. Intentionality and Stich's Theory of Brain Sentence Syntax. Phil Quart, 40(159), 169-182, Ap 90.

Stephen P Stich maintains that causal interactions of brain sentence tokens with neural mechanisms are sufficient to explain intelligent behavioral phenomena in a purely syntactical theory of mind without resort to the intentional concepts or representational content of traditional folk psychology. It is shown that the analysis is inadequate to provide identity criteria for brain sentence tokens in the absence of semantic correlations, especially for ideologically distant subjects. The concept of pure syntax on which Stich's projected mature cognitive science rests is exposed as a myth of artificial intelligence and mechanist philosophy of mind.

JACQUETTE, Dale. "Moral Value and the Sociobiological Reduction" in *Inquiries into Values: The Inaugural Session of the International Society for Value Inquiry*, LEE, Sander H , 685-694. Lewiston, Mellen Pr, 1989.

The synthesis of sociology and biology in the new science of sociobiology provides decision-theoretical explanations of social phenomena in terms of the reproductive self-interest of the individual members of a society. Sociobiology further projects the reduction of normative value, ethical choice, and moral belief as aspects of learned cultural practices under sociobiological principles. There is however an asymmetry in the kind of explanations that can be given in sociobiology, though this problem has been overlooked by even its most severe critics. It is argued that the theory cannot support satisfactory teleological or teleological-reductive explanations of reproductively unsuccessful social behavior, and that this limitation in particular undermines the effort to advance a sociobiological interpretation of ethics. The difficulties encountered by sociobiological reductions of moral value are explored in connection with practical reasoning about the genetically self-defeating social mechanisms of mass celibacy, abortion, suicide and global nuclear war.

JACQUETTE, Dale. Presupposition and Foundational Asymmetry in Metaphysics and Logic. Phil Math, 4(1), 15-22, 1989.

Alternative simplified models of presuppositional relations between logic and metaphysics are sketched, including a traditional unidirectional schema with logic as ultimate foundation, an exact equivalence taxonomy, and two different forms of presuppositional interdependence. Bidirectional presupposition does not imply equivalence, since logic is intuitively characterized as more foundational than metaphysics in the sense that metaphysics presupposes the whole rather than a mere proper part of logic, while logic presupposes a mere proper part rather than the whole of metaphysics.

JAGGAR, Alison M. Feminist Ethics: Some Issues for the Nineties. J Soc Phil, 20(1-2), 91-107, Spr-Fall 89.

This paper sketches recent feminist contributions to five main areas of debate in contemporary ethics. These areas are equality and difference, impartiality, moral subjectivity, autonomy and moral epistemology and anti-epistemology. I emphasise how feminist thinking on these topics is continuous with, rather than radically discontinuous from, much work by philosophers who are not explicitly feminist.

JAGUARIBE, Helio. The Social Humanism of Adam Schaff. Dialec Hum, 16(2), 21-35, Spr 89.

JAHN, Robert G and DUNNE, Brenda J. *Margins of Reality: The Role of Consciousness in the Physical World*. San Diego, Harcourt Brace Jov, 1987

This book reexamines the role of consciousness in the light of a new body of experimental data on the interaction of human operators with various technical devices and information-processing systems. Many philosophical fibers are required to sift these results into a coherent model; but once the essential concepts are in place, human consciousness indeed emerges endowed with an active component. By virtue of the manner in which it exchanges information with its environment, orders that information, and interprets it, consciousness has the ability to bias probabilistic processes, and thereby to avail itself of certain margins of reality.

JÄHNIG, Dieter and SOLBAKKEN, Elisabeth (trans). On Schelling's Philosophy of Nature. Ideal Stud, 19(3), 222-230, S 89.

The author argues that Schelling's philosophy is best understood as a transformation within idealism. By turning his attention to nature, Schelling discovered a realm that is rationally ordered—but inexplicably so. Nature displays an after-the-fact reality. Comprehended as self-production, nature is the proper home of free beings and not, as for Fichte, a barrier for them to overcome. Schelling's recognition of the autonomous structure of nature leads to the ethical imperative that is prominent in his middle period, that is, the imperative to sacrifice the narrow standpoint of the self in order to acknowledge and affirm otherness.

JAHREN, Neal. Can Semantics Be Syntactic? Synthese, 82(3), 309-328, Mr 90.

The author defends John R Searle's Chinese Room argument against a particular objection made by William J Rapaport called the 'Korean Room'. Foundational issues such as the relationship of 'strong AI' to human mentality and the adequacy of the Turing Test are discussed. Through undertaking a *Gedankenexperiment* similar to Searle's but which meets new specifications given by Rapaport for an AI system, the author argues that Rapaport's objection to Searle does not stand and that Rapaport's arguments seem convincing only because they assume the foundations of strong AI at the outset.

JAHREN, Neal. Comments on Ruth Ginzberg's Paper "Uncovering Gynocentric Science". Hypatia, 5(1), 171-177, Spr 90.

Ruth Ginzberg has proposed a model for a gynocentric science that might constitute a paradigm as described by Kuhn. The author argues that Ginzberg's model lacks certain essential features of paradigms as described by Kuhn. The differences may stem from more fundamental disagreements between them, including the possibility that some essential features of Ginzberg's gynocentric science place it outside the intended scope of Kuhn's analysis.

JAKI, Stanley L. Thomas and the Universe. Thomist, 53(4), 545-572, O 89.

JAKIM, Boris (trans) and FRANK, S L. *The Light Shineth in Darkness*. Athens, Ohio Univ Pr, 1989

In this work the author attempts to combine "the neglected truth of the mysterious power of sin in the world" with "faith in the positive value of the world as a creation of God and as an expression, in its primordial foundation, of the holy essence of God." This combination leads to a clear discrimination between Christ's absolute truth and its always imperfect embodiment in the world—between the essential salvation of the world and its protection from evil. On the other hand it leads to a perception of the nature of moral creativity as a dramatic Divine-human process of the healing of the world through the imbedding in it of its Divine primordial ground and the battle against dark human willfullness. (edited)

JAKOWLJEWITSCH, Dragan. Über eine unzulängliche Auffassung der methodologischen Einheit der Wissenschaft und unbefriedigende Verteidigung. Conceptus, 24(61), 91-103, 1990.

JAKOWLJEWITSCH, Dragan. Über einen neuen Versuch der Argumentation für die methodologische Einheit der Wissenschaften. Conceptus, 23(59), 91-98, 1989.

JAMBOR, Mishka. A Dialogue with God. Indian Phil Quart, SUPP 16(3), 5-26, Jl 89.

The 'Dialogue' explores a number of issues within the broad category of 'the relationship of the human being with the Divine'. The spokesperson is a woman who may or may not exhibit a feminist attitude to religion and who may not represent the typical male style of philosophising about God. Some of the issues discussed are the following: (1) elaboration of human refusal of God—another perspective on atheism; (2) God/the Absolute as the only substance and the only consciousness in the universe; stunning practical implications of this alleged fact; (3) examination of surrender; does it matter to whom one surrenders?; (4) human divinity and the emptiness of the self—an attempt to bridge the two conceptions.

JAMES, David N. On Colorizing Films: A Venture into Applied Aesthetics. Metaphilosophy, 20(3-4), 332-340, Jl-O 89.

The paper takes a critical look at the three most philosophically interesting objections to colorization. The creative intention argument mistakenly assumes that creative intentions should delimit allowable modifications of art in the public domain. The integrity of the artwork argument conflates autographic and allographic works, and thereby fails to recognize the difference this makes to claims about respecting unique works. The best experience argument rests on the dubious claim that low-grade aesthetic experiences are worse than no aesthetic experiences. I conclude that the case against colorization has not been proven.

JAMES, George Alfred. The Status of the Anomaly in the Feminist God-Talk of Rosemary Reuther. Zygon, 25(2), 167-185, Je 90.

Scripture, the creeds, and tradition have provided the raw material that theology has attempted to refine. The contribution of much recent theology comes from new insight into these materials by women, blacks, and the Third World, often as examined by analytic tools derived from post-Christian ideologies. The theology of Rosemary Ruether stands out because of her choice of sources, among which she includes documents excoriated as heretical by what she calls the patriarchal orthodoxy of the early Christian church. Because of this it is useful to examine this type of theology in relation to other theological inquiries of recent years. The thesis of this paper is that, in her ability to incorporate source material hitherto regarded as heretical, Ruether has demonstrated the scientific character of this kind of theology.

JAMES, Paul. National Formation and the 'Rise of the Cultural'. Phil Soc Sci, 19(3), 273-290, S 89.

Social theorists from various perspectives have suggested that the sphere of the 'cultural' has with the coming of modernity and postmodernity emerged into dominance. One version of this, developed by the philosopher Ernest Gellner, argues for the predominance of culture over structure. This article uses Gellner's and others' work on the nation-state to critically examine the status of that argument. It concludes that Gellner's theory of the nation rests upon a deeply flawed theory of social formations, one which fails to escape the iron cage of Weberian orthodoxy.

JAMES, Theodore E. "Wisdom, Faith and Reason" in *The Wisdom of Faith: Essays in Honor of Dr Sebastian Alexander Matczak*, THOMPSON, Henry O (ed), 63-78. Lanham, Univ Pr of America, 1989.

JAMIESON, Dale. Rights, Justice, and Duties to Provide Assistance: A Critique of Regan's Theory of Rights. Ethics, 100(2), 349-362, Ja 90.

This essay begins with an overview of the powerful and sophisticated theory of rights put forward by Tom Regan in his recent book, *The Case for Animal Rights*. I argue that the theory founders on its account of duties of assistance, and on its prescription for how to resolve conflicts of rights. I claim that plausible responses to these difficulties would begin to close the gap between Regan's theory and utilitarian alternatives.

JAN, Yun-Hua. Human Nature and Its Cosmic Roots in Huang-Lao Taoism. J Chin Phil, 17(2), 215-233, Je 90.

JANAWAY, Christopher. Recent Work in Aesthetics. Phil Books, 30(4), 193-201, O 89.

The following books (published 1984-88) are briefly reviewed: Mary Mothersill, *Beauty Restored*; Salim Kemal, *Kant on Fine Art*; Anthony Savile, *Aesthetic Reconstructions*; Mary McCloskey, *Kant's Aesthetic*; Stephen Halliwell, *Aristotle's Poetics*; Stephen Bungay, *Beauty and Truth: A Study of Hegel's Aesthetics*; Anthony O'Hear, *The Element of Fire*; George Dickie, *The Art Circle: A Theory of Art*; B R Tilghman, *But Is it Art?*; Arthur Danto, *The Philosophical Disenfranchisement of Art*; Malcolm Budd, *Music and the Emotions: The Philosophical Theories*; Flint Schier, *Deeper into Pictures*; Richard Wollheim, *Painting as an Art*; Anne Sheppard, *Aesthetics: An Introduction to the Philosophy of Art*

JANICAUD, Dominique. Metamorphosis of the Undecidable. Grad Fac Phil J, 13(1), 125-140, 1988.

JANICH, Peter. "Truth as Success of Action: The Constructive Approach in the Philosophy of Science" in *Scientific Knowledge Socialized*, HRONSZKY, Imre (ed), 313-326. Norwell, Kluwer, 1989.

JANIK, Allan. *Style, Politics and the Future of Philosophy*. Norwell, Kluwer, 1989

Fifteen essays explore the relation between style and substance in the work of Heidegger, Wittgenstein and Lichtenberg, the implications of the later Wittgenstein for politics and social science, the role of politics in the life of an animal that talks and the vistas that the later Wittgenstein opens up for the future of philosophy. These studies provide an alternative scenario to that of Richard Rorty with respect to philosophy's future in a middle ground between Habermas and the postmodernists.

JANKO, Jan. Mach's "Critique of Knowledge" and the Physiology of Senses (in Czechoslovakian). Filozof Cas, 38(1-2), 118-131, 1990.

This article analyzes the origin and maturation of Mach's "critique of knowledge," depending on the logic of Mach's research in the field of physiology of senses. The prevailing specific conditions in the research into the physiology of senses eventually resulted in growing scepticism towards the existing philosophical and methodological foundations. Even though the philosophical implications of Mach's "critique of knowledge" did mark a step back, a return to the already overcome positions of Berkeley and Hume, the accent laid on the active role of the subject in scientific learning constitutes a valuable rational core of this approach. Moreover, one should not ignore the fact that Mach criticized scientific learning from the "inside," as a theorizing natural scientist and not as an external philosophical commentator of the cognitive process in natural sciences. (edited)

JANKOV, M. Materialist Dialectic and Critique of Philosophical Irrationalism (in Czechoslovakian). Filozof Cas, 37(4), 487-500, 1989.

This article examines the problems of materialist dialectic and critique of philosophical irrationalism, aiming at an analysis of some issues connected with this subject. First and foremost, the author studies the philosophical nature and functions of contemporary irrationalism, its position and role in the present-day ideological struggle. Another group of problems is formed by the relationship between rationalism and irrationalism in contemporary bourgeois philosophy. A third group of problems centres around the relationship between present-day irrationalism and materialist dialectic. A fourth group of problems pertains to continued explication of the dialectical type of rationality, to a more adequate construction of the dialectical model. A fifth group of problems revolves around the relationship between the rational in social reality, especially under the conditions of socialism. (edited)

JANKOVIC, Milan. Aesthetic Function and Dynamics of Meaningful Unification (in Czechoslovakian). Estetika, 26(3), 158-163, 1989.

JANSANA, Ramón. On the Mathematical Content of the Theory of Classes KM. Z Math Log, 35(5), 399-412, 1989.

In the paper "On the necessary use of Abstract Set Theory" H Friedman gives a proposition independent of ZFC but decided in the theory of classes Kelley-Morse. This proposition is proved independent of ZFC by arguments different from the standard forcing ones. In the present paper we show that for every sentence prove independent of ZFC by forcing using a set of forcing conditions, the corresponding sentence can be proved independent from KM + Choice. In order to do it we develop the method of Boolean-valued models for the theory KM + Global Choice.

JANSSENS, C J A M and VAN BRAKEL, J. Davidson's Omniscient Interpreter. Commun Cog, 23(1), 93-100, 1990.

In response to the skeptic's argument that a speaker and interpreter might understand one another on the basis of shared but erroneous beliefs, Davidson has provided an argument in which he asks us to imagine an interpreter who is omniscient. Davidson's omniscient interpreter also plays a role in his argument that the possibility of communication implies a form of realism. (edited)

JANTZEN, Grace M. Could There Be a Mystical Core of Religion? Relig Stud, 26(1), 59-71, Mr 90.

JANTZEN, Grace M. Mysticism and Experience. Relig Stud, 25(3), 295-315, S 89.

In this article I first explore William James's understanding of mysticism and religious experience, and then measure that understanding against the accounts of two actual mystics, Bernard of Clairvaux and Julian of Norwich, who, for all their differences, may be taken as paradigms of the Christian mystical tradition. I argue that judging from these two cases, James's position is misguided and inadequate. Since James's account has been of enormous influence in subsequent thinking about mysticism, it follows that if his understanding of mysticism is inadequate, so is much of the work that rests upon it.

JANTZEN, Grace. 'Where Two Are to Become One': Mysticism and Monism. Philosophy, 25, 147-166, 89 Supp.

JANZ, Bruce. Reason, Inductive Inference, and True Religion in Hume. Dialogue (Canada), 27(4), 721-726, Wint 88.

For Hume, an inference can be called reasonable despite the fact that it cannot attain deductive certainty. This means that, in any particular case, Hume would be able to accept more than one inference as reasonable. A case in point involves Hume's comments on religion. Some argue that Hume's position against superstition and enthusiasm holds for religion in general. I argue that Hume wished to separate superstition and enthusiasm from true religion. I also argue that Hume would be able to consistently allow someone else to hold to true religion and be called reasonable, while he himself probably did not.

JANZ, Curt Paul and HEILKE, Thomas W (trans). "The Form-Content Problem in Nietzsche's Conception of Music" in *Nietzsche's New Seas: Explorations in Philosophy, Aesthetics, and Politics*, GILLESPIE, Michael Allen (ed), 97-116. Chicago, Univ of Chicago Pr, 1989.

JARDINE, David W. On the Humility of Mathematical Language. Educ Theor, 40(2), 181-191, Spr 90.

JARKOWSKI, Jan (trans) and DOLGOV, Konstantin M. The Politician and the Philosopher (Some Lessons from Machiavelli). Dialec Hum, 15(3-4), 59-66, Sum-Autumn 88.

JARRATT, Susan C. The First Sophists and Feminism: Discourses of the "Other". Hypatia, 5(1), 27-41, Spr 90.

In this essay, I explore the parallel between the historical exclusions of rhetoric from philosophy and of women from fields of rational discourse. After considering the usefulness and limitations of deconstruction for exposing marginalization by hierarchical systems, I explore links between texts of the sophists and feminist proposals for rewriting/rereading history by Cixous, Spivak, and others. I conclude that sophistic rhetoric offers a flexible alternative to philosophy as an intellectual framework for mediating theoretical oppositions among contemporary feminisms.

JARRATT, Susan C. The Role of the Sophists in Histories of Consciousness. Phil Rhet, 23(2), 85-95, 1990.

JARRETT, James L. Personality and Artistic Creativity. J Aes Educ, 22(4), 21-29, Wint 88.

JARRETT, Jon P. "Bell's Theorem: A Guide to the Implications" in *Philosophical Consequences of Quantum Theory: Reflections on Bell's Theorem*, CUSHING, James T (ed), 60-79. Notre Dame, Univ Notre Dame Pr, 1989.

The experimentally observed predictions of quantum mechanics violate the Bell-type inequalities, casting doubt on local realism. This paper surveys the implications of Bell-type arguments through a discussion of some of the premises in these arguments and an examination of several results linking various of these premises to each other and (via Bell's theorem) to Bell-type inequalities. While relativity and the quantum "connectedness" associated with Bell-type experiments appear not to be in outright conflict, neither is there a thoroughgoing harmony between them.

JASON, Gary. Fallacies are Common. Inform Log, 11(2), 101-106, Spr 89.

This article is a rejoinder to a reply to the author's earlier paper, "Are Fallacies Common?" The thesis that fallacies as standardly defined in logic texts are common in political discourse is defended, and several points about the principle of charity are made.

JASON, Gary. Hedging as a Fallacy of Language. Inform Log, 10(3), 169-175, Fall 88.

In this article a neglected fallacy of language (hedging) is discussed, and fitted into the fallacies of language most commonly discussed in textbooks. Moreover, a perspective is sketched which expands the traditional scope of fallacies of language (which tends to equate them with just the fallacies of ambiguity).

JASON, Gary. The Role of Error in Computer Science. Philosophia (Israel), 19(4), 403-416, D 89.

The aim of this paper is to explore the concept of error as it applies to software science. The term "error" is defined for software. Four levels of software are distinguished, and error at each level discussed, along with the methods developed to counter that error.

JASPERS, Karl. The Physician in the Technological Age. Theor Med, 10(3), 251-267, S 89.

Jaspers argues that modern advances in the natural sciences and in technology have exerted transforming influence on the art of clinical medicine and on its ancient Hippocratic ideal, even though Plato's classical argument about slave physicians and free physicians retains essential relevance for the physician of today. Medicine should be rooted not only in science and technology, but in the humanity of the physician as well. This essay, written in 1959, reflects Jaspers's lifelong preoccupation with the philosophical *meaning* of medicine (he received his MD degree in 1909) and the totality of the human person. It should significantly enhance our own comprehension of medical power, dangers, reasoning, and accomplishments. (edited)

JAUREGUI, Claudia and VIGO, Alejandro G. Algunas consideraciones sobre la Refutación del Idealismo. Rev Filosof (Argentina), 2(1), 29-41, My 87.

This paper deals with some assumptions of the *Refutation of Idealism*. First, it analyzes the function of inner sense in the consciousness of the own existence. Secondly, it points out that the permanent element required by the formal structure of inner sense may not be provided either by the 'I' nor by the pure forms of intuition, but only by the outer objects. Lastly, it emphasizes some aspects of the time-space relation presupposed in the proof.

JAVUREK, Z. Some Prerequisites and Aspects of the Shaping of "New Thinking" Responsibility (in Czechoslovakian). Filozof Cas, 37(6), 868-876, 1989.

JAY, C Barry. A Note on Natural Numbers Objects in Monoidal Categories. Stud Log, 48(3), 389-393, S 89.

JAY, Gregory S. "Paul de Man and the Subject of Literary History" in *The Textual Sublime: Deconstruction and Its Differences*, SILVERMAN, Hugh J (ed), 123-137. Albany, SUNY Pr, 1990.

JAYANT, Asha. Cultural Basis for Political Thought: A Lesson from Kautilya and Hobbes. Indian Phil Quart, SUPP 16(3), 27-32, Jl 89.

JEANNOT, Thomas M. Marx's Use of Religious Metaphors. Int Phil Quart, 30(2), 135-150, Je 90.

The "embryology" of Marxist criticism is situated within the womb of Young Hegelian theological criticism. Marx's break with the Young Hegelians was a break with their theological mode of theorizing. Thereafter, Marx was concerned with religion and theology only as metaphors. The metaphorical function of religion and theology in Marx's mature criticism is to signal the presence of a mystification. Theoretical mystification consists in presenting some subject-matter in an abstract, "otherworldly" fashion, in isolation from "this-worldly" practices. Bourgeois political economy reflects the concrete, material mystification of economic relationships in the capitalist mode of production.

JECKER, Nancy S. Moral Epistemology: Historical Lessons and Contemporary Concerns. Med Human Rev, 4(2), 9-22, Jl 90.

Recent feminist scholarship claims to locate an unbridgeable gulf between women's moral thinking and sensibilities on the one hand, and currently favored moral theories on the other. A growing number of feminists have come to doubt the metaethical assumptions that drive contemporary theories and the epistemological framework to which these theories are wedded. This essay identifies common themes in contemporary feminist critiques, places these themes in historical perspective, and shows how the recent history of ethics bears on present debates and should give feminists pause.

JECKER, Nancy S. Should We Ration Health Care? J Med Human, 10(2), 77-90, Fall-Wint 89.

The paper begins by drawing a distinction between "allocation"—the distribution of resources between different categories, and "rationing"—the distribution of scarce resources within a single category. I argue that the current allocation of funds to health care makes some form of rationing unavoidable. The paper next considers proposals by Daniel Callahan and Norman Daniels supporting age rationing publicly-financed life-extending medical care. I provide reasons for doubting that either argument succeeds. The final section of the paper sets forth an alternative approach which holds that if people have any rights to health care, then they have a right to a decent minimum.

JECKER, Nancy S. Towards a Theory of Age-Group Justice. J Med Phil, 14(6), 655-676, D 89.

Norman Daniels's and Daniel Callahan's recent work attempts to develop and deepen theories of justice in order to accommodate intergenerational moral issues. Elsewhere, I have argued that Callahan's arguments furnish inadequate support for the age rationing policy he accepts. This essay therefore examines Daniels's account of age rationing, together with the complex theory of age-group justice that buttresses it. Sections one and two trace the main features of Daniels' prudential lifespan approach. Section three calls into question the theory's conformity to liberal tenets. The next section attempts to show that the outcome of the prudential approach fails to match our considered judgments. The brief final section offers a broader perspective on the task of articulating a liberal theory of age-group justice.

JECKER, Nancy. Integrating Medical Ethics with Normative Theory: Patient Advocacy and Social Responsibility. Theor Med, 11(2), 125-139, Je 90.

It is often assumed that the chief responsibility medical professionals bear is patient care and advocacy. The meeting of other duties, such as ensuring a more just distribution of medical resources and promoting the public good, is not considered a legitimate basis for curtailing or slackening beneficial patient services. It is argued that this assumption is often made without sufficient attention to foundational principles of professional ethics; that once core principles are laid bare this assumption is revealed as largely unwarranted; and, finally, that these observations at the level of moral theory should be reflected, in various ways, in medical practice. Specifically, this essay clarifies a tension that exists between different kinds of moral principles and explores the possibility of dissipating that tension by shoring up foundational principles. The paper begins by setting out three alternative models of how best to balance patient advocacy responsibilities with broader social responsibilities. It then turns to critically assess these models and argue that one has several advantages over the others.

JEDYNAK, Jacek and KUCZYNSKI, Janusz. Pluralism and Universalist Socialism. Dialec Hum, 16(1), 215-222, Wint 89.

JEFFERSON, Gail (ed). Harvey Sacks—Lectures 1964-1965. Human Stud, 12(3-4), 1-408, D 89.

JEFFERSON, Paul. The Question of Black Philosophy. J Soc Phil, 20(3), 99-109, Wint 89.

JEFFREY, Richard C and BOOLOS, George S. *Computability and Logic (Third Edition)*. New York, Cambridge Univ Pr, 1989

JEFFREY, Richard. Reading *Probabilismo*. Erkenntnis, 31(2-3), 225-237, S 89.

JELASSI, M Tawfik and JONES, Beth H. The Effect of Computer Intervention and Task Structure on Bargaining Outcome. Theor Decis, 28(3), 355-377, My 90.

This paper reports on a study that examined the impact of computer presentation of suggested solutions during negotiation, in bargaining situations that can be characterized as integrative or distributive. It was found that in the integrative task, the bargainers achieved higher joint outcomes when presented with suggestions. They had a more negative perception of the negotiation atmosphere, however. In the distributive task, the suggestions did not help achieve joint gains, but it lessened negative attitudes of the bargainers. Bargainers who received suggestions felt both they and their partner had been somewhat more flexible, cooperative, considerate, and less suspicious. Thus, regardless of negotiation situation, the suggestions resulted in some benefit to the negotiators.

JELLAMO, Anna. Sul problema della valutazione morale: A proposito della "Filosofia pratica" di Guiliano Pontara. Riv Int Filosof Diritto, 66(3), 468-481, Jl-S 89.

JENNETT, Bryan. Quality of Care and Cost Containment in the US and UK. Theor Med, 10(3), 207-215, S 89.

Many activities of doctors in the acute hospital sector do not improve patient outcome because they are inappropriate. Curtailing interventions that are unnecessary (because the patient is not bad enough) or are unsuccessful (because the condition is too advanced) could both save resources and improve care. Rational rationing depends on knowledge about the expected benefits of various technologies when used in different clinical circumstances.

JENNINGS, Bruce. Bioethics as Civic Discourse. Hastings Center Rep, 19(5), 34-35, S-O 89.

Can a pluralistic society engage in a serious discourse about the good without threatening civil liberties and toleration? This article briefly reviews the debate between liberals and communitarians on this issue, and relates it to bioethics. It argues that public ethics need not—and should not—be limited to conceptions of justice or right alone. A sense of shared purpose and respect must rely on an underlying vision of the common good and the good for individuals. Bioethics shoud help to refine that vision.

JENSEN, Debra J. Soteriology from a Christian and Hindu Perspective. J Dharma, 14(4), 353-365, O-D 89.

This paper examined Simone Weil's reading of the Bhagavad-Gita and selected Upanishads. Weil's *Notebooks* were used as the main source for this examination although other works were drawn upon when they were helpful. The paper attempted to identify the specific passages from these Hindu texts which appeared to have most importance for Weil in the development of her soteriological thought. In so doing it sought to establish where Weil's views differed from these texts and where they differed. The Gita's concept of 'actionless action' emerged as most significant for Weil. An important difference was found to lie in Weil's Christology.

JENSEN, Henning. Kant and Moral Integrity. Phil Stud, 57(2), 193-205, O 89.

A main objection to Kant's theory of moral worth is that whereas he claims that only actions performed from the motive of duty have moral worth, most people are convinced that right actions performed out of motives such as love or compassion are normally judged preferable to the same actions done from the sense of duty. I argue that a conclusive answer to this objection is contained within Kant's theory. Criticizing recent discussions of this issue, I contend that a correct approach consists of applying some neglected aspects of Kant's position concerning integrity, autonomy, and our perfect duties to ourselves and others.

JENSEN, Larry C and WYGANT, Steven A. The Developmental Self-Valuing Theory: A Practical Approach for Business Ethics. J Bus Ethics, 9(3), 215-225, Mr 90.

Ethics in business has been an increasingly controversial and important topic of discussion over the last decade. Debate continues about whether ethics should be a part of business, but also includes how business can implement ethical theory in day-to-day operations. Most discussions focus on either traditional moral philosophy, which offers little of practical value for the business community, or psychological theories of moral reasoning, which have been shown to be flawed and incomplete. The theory presented here is called the Developmental Self-Valuing Theory, and adapts the general psychological theory of Albert Bandura for ethics in business. (edited)

JESSEPH, Douglas. Rigorous Proof and the History of Mathematics: Comments on Crowe. Synthese, 83(3), 449-453, Je 90.

Duhem's portrayal of the history of mathematics as manifesting calm and regular development is traced to his conception of mathematical rigor as an essentially static concept. This account is undermined by citing controversies over rigorous demonstration from the eighteenth and twentieth centuries.

JI-YU, Ren. On Articles of the Academy of the White Deer Grotto (in Serbo-Croatian). Filozof Istraz, 29(2), 499-504, 1989.

The author analyzes the articles of the Academy of the White Deer Grotto, which was one of Zhu Xi's educational institutions where he chose to devote his whole life to train a qualified elite for feudal society. He shows that in these articles we can find an underlying social significance, and he takes them as Zhu's political policy rather than as his educational policy, his religious ideas rather than philosophical ideas. In Zhu Xi's doctrine of unity of state and religion the author finds the common phenomenon in the medieval feudal society.

JIAN, Mi. Die traditionelle chinesische Kultur und das Gegenwärtige Rechtssystem Chinas. Stud Soviet Tho, 38(1), 55-76, Jl 89.

JIDA, Yan. David Hume's Doctrine of Moral Judgment. Chin Stud Phil, 21(2), 49-58, Wint 89-90.

Within his intellectual system as a whole, David Hume's thoughts in the area of ethics, or moral philosophy, are very rich and abundant, and occupy an important place in the history of the development of modern European ethics. This essay shall focus on discussing and introducing, within Hume's ethics, his doctrine and teachings in the area of moral judgment, or moral evaluation.

JIEMO, Zhang. On the Aesthetic Significance of Wang Fuzhi's Theory of the Unity of Poetry and Music, with Criticisms of Certain Biases. Chin Stud Phil, 21(3), 26-53, Spr 90.

JIMENEZ MORENO, Luis. Filosofía-Formación. Dialogo Filosof, 5(3), 408-415, S-D 89.

JIMÉNEZ, Manuel. The Self-Understanding of Political Modernism and the Idea of the Revolution (in Serbo-Croatian). Filozof Istraz, 30(3), 899-910, 1989.

Der Autor betrachtet zwei Denktraditionen die die Selbstaufassung der politischen Moderne geprägt haben: einerseits die liberale Tradition von Locke bis Hayek, andererseits die demokratische Tradition im Zeichen Rousseaus. Damit wird die Geschichte der Grundrechte und die Kompromisse die die politische Prinzipien, von den die Grundrechte inspiriert worden waren eingegangen sind, verglichen. Endlich versucht der Autor Habermasche Diskursethik und "the original position" von John Rawls als zwei zeitgenössischen Antworten auf Grundfragen der politischen Moderne kritisch nachzuprüfen.

JINSHAN, Liu. On Ji Kang's "Aestheticist" Aesthetic Thought. Chin Stud Phil, 21(4), 70-93, Sum 90.

JIRACEK, Pavel. Semantisation of Sounds and Its Meaning by Contents Interpretation of a Lyrical Poem (in Czechoslovakian). Estetika, 26(3), 152-157, 1989.

JIRIK, Vlastimil. New Connections of Man to the Nature (in Czechoslovakian). Estetika, 26(4), 233-247, 1989.

JOAS, Hans. The Creativity of Action and the Intersubjectivity of Reason: Mead's Pragmatism and Social Theory. Trans Peirce Soc, 26(2), 165-194, Spr 90.

This text was originally written as a preface to the German pocketbook edition of Joas's book on G H Mead. It contains a retrospect—after ten years—of research on Mead; a comparison of the pragmatist model of action to action theory in sociology; a discussion of the relationship between pragmatist and discourse ethics; and an evaluation of Rorty's neo-pragmatism.

JOBE, Evan K. Existence and Reality: The Case for Pseudo-Objects. S J Phil, 28(2), 171-191, Sum 90.

This is an attempt to furnish a plausible account of our discourse about things having no location in the spacetime world—things such as possibilities, classes, properties, number, sense-data, fictional characters, etc. It is argued that the meaning relations of our language generate a category of objects ("pseudo-objects") that, although forming no part of the real world, can nevertheless correctly be said to exist. The position defended represents something of a middle ground between various pairs of traditionally opposed views such as those of the realists versus the nominalists, the sense-datum theorists versus their critics, etc.

JOCKUSCH JR, C G (and others). Recursively Enumerable Sets Modulo Iterated Jumps and Extensions of Arslanov's Completeness Criterion. J Sym Log, 54(4), 1288-1323, D 89.

JOHANSSON, Ingvar. *Ontological Investigations: Inquiry Into the Categories of Nature, Man, Society*. New York, Routledge, 1989

The book is a theory of categories in the realist and Aristotelian sense of the word. It contains many discussions around topics within so-called metaphysics, e.g., the mind-body problem, immanent realism and tendencies. But it aims at synthetic metaphysics. Present-day ontological systems, it is argued, suffer from a failure to grasp relations of existential dependence. The theory tries to reconcile a conception of nature as something purely physical with the categories of action and intentionality. Social states of affairs have, it is claimed, their essence in nested intentionality.

JOHNS, David M. The Relevance of Deep Ecology to the Third World. Environ Ethics, 12(3), 233-252, Fall 90.

Although Ramachandra Guha has demonstrated the importance of cross-cultural dialogue on environmental issues and has much to tell us about the problems of wilderness preservation in the Third World, I argue that Guha is partly wrong in claiming that deep ecology equates environmental protection with wilderness protection and simply wrong in calling wilderness protection untenable or incorrect as a global strategy for environmental protection. Moreover, I argue that the deep ecology distinction between anthropocentrism and biocentrism is useful in dealing with the two major problems which Guha identifies as undermining the health of the planet—overconsumption and militarism. Although it is true that preservation of wilderness will not be successful unless human social dynamics are taken into consideration, nevertheless, a biocentrism which integrates critical social theory can provide the basis for an ethic that undercuts the environmental degradation from overconsumption and militarism more effectively than a human-centered system.

JOHNSON, Andrew. Sociobiology and Concern for the Future. J Applied Phil, 6(2), 141-148, O 89.

Despite its excesses, sociobiology can make a useful contribution to ethics, if it is recognised that it need not impinge on free will, and if the 'naturalistic fallacy' can be avoided. This contribution is the central concept of evolutionary stability, and the implication which can be drawn from it, that concern for the future is a basic part of human nature. In stable societies, such concern is manifested as fear of change, or strict adherence to tradition, but modern ideas of progress have engendered a cavalier attitude to the more distant future, and current ethical systems cannot get to grips with duties towards future generations. It is suggested that the popularity of sociobiology and the present-day interest in conservation both reflect an aspect of human nature which has too long been neglected by moralists.

JOHNSON, Clarence Sholé. Hume on Character, Action, and Causal Necessity. Auslegung, 16(2), 149-164, Sum 90.

In the *Treatise*, Hume argues against the Lockean and Cartesian theses that causal necessity is a feature of objects by virtue of which objects behave as they do. Hume's own view is that causal necessity is nothing but a human propensity to infer the existence of a member in a regularly conjunctive pair from the existence of the other member. The present study shows that the causal necessity that emerges in Hume's discussion of the relation between character and action flatly contradicts his positive account; indeed, that Hume tacitly advances a version of the theory he rejects.

JOHNSON, Curtis N. Socrates' Encounter with Polus in Plato's *Gorgias*. Phoenix, 43(3), 196-216, Autumn 89.

In his cross-examination by Socrates, Polus begins by asserting that it is better to do wrong than to be wronged, but, stumbling into self-contradiction, is forced to reverse his position. I show in this essay that the cause of Polus's undoing was his willingness to agree to certain Socratic assertions in the course of the elenchus that he could easily have challenged. The result of his failure to challenge them was an easy victory for Socrates, but one that was earned at the expense of an apparent manipulation of Polus by Plato.

JOHNSON, Cyraina E. The Echo of Narcissus: Anxiety, Language and Reflexivity in "Envois". Int Stud Phil, 22(1), 37-50, 1990.

The relationship of "Envois" to philosophy, literature and 18th century English novels is analyzed through a discussion of subjective anxiety as an aspect of poststructuralism's concern with the role of language in the construction of identity and in the communicative act. Through a comparison with the concept of subjectivity in Richardson's *Pamela*, "Envois" is described as "originary" (as the 18th century English novels are often called) in itself, both in its constitution as a philosophical/literary treatise (introducing a new way of writing and reading philosophy) and as a method of portraying the complexity of subjective existence in 20th century reality.

JOHNSON, David M. Can Abstractions Be Causes? Biol Phil, 5(1), 63-77, Ja 90.

The Empiricist or Lockean view says natural kinds do not exist objectively in nature but are practical categories reflecting use of words. The Modern, Ostensive view says they do exist, and one can refer to such a kind by ostention and recursion, assuming his designation of it is related causally to the kind itself. However, this leads to a problem: kinds are abstract repeatables, and it seems impossible that abstractions could have causal force. In defence of the Modern view, I suggest we can think of kinds as—or as like—ecological niches existing in nature, which are causally effective by virtue of the fact that they predictively determine (some) properties of the things that happen to occupy them.

JOHNSON, Fred. Analogical Arguings and Explainings. Inform Log, 11(3), 153-160, Fall 89.

Johnson takes arguings and explainings to be more fundamental than arguments and explanations. The former require agents for their explication. Johnson contends that the texts fail to recognize that many ordinary analogical arguments and explanations have a deductive structure. According to Johnson, analogies are often used to state general principles, which are a part of the structure of analogical arguments and explanations. Johnson compares his analysis of analogies with Levi's analysis of legal reasoning and with Aristotle's analysis of "reasoning by example."

JOHNSON, Fred. Models for Modal Syllogisms. Notre Dame J Form Log, 30(2), 271-284, Spr 89.

A semantics is presented for Storrs McCall's separate axiomatizations of Aristotle's accepted and rejected polysyllogisms. The polysyllogisms under discussion are made up of either assertoric or apodeictic propositions. The semantics is given by associating a property with a pair of sets: one set consists of things having the property essentially and the other of things having it accidentally. A completeness proof and a semantic decision procedure are given.

JOHNSON, Galen A. Merleau-Ponty's Early Aesthetics of Historical Being: The Case of Cézanne. Res Phenomenol, 17, 211-225, 1987.

JOHNSON, Paul J. "Death, Identity and the Possibility of a Hobbesian Justification for World Government" in *Hobbes: War Among Nations*, AIRAKSINEN, Timo (ed), 70-78. Brookfield, Gower, 1989.

JOHNSON, Paul Owen. *The Critique of Thought: A Re-Examination of Hegel's Science of Logic*. Brookfield, Gower, 1988

This is the first full-scale commentary on Hegel's *Science of Logic* since McTaggart's work in 1910. It is a complete reappraisal of that work that was made necessary by the radical transformation of our conception of Hegel's philosophy. It concludes that logic is no mere *a priori* system, but implicitly a thorough-going critique of contemporary thought, and that the true merit of Hegel's work lies not in the creation of a new metaphysical method but in his concentration on the concepts themselves in his efforts to resolve metaphysical conflicts. (edited)

JOHNSON, Peter. *Politics, Innocence, and the Limits of Goodness*. New York, Routledge, 1988

JOHNSON, Phillip E. The ACLU Philosophy and the Right to Abuse the Unborn. Crim Just Ethics, 9(1), 48-51, Wint-Spr 90.

The ACLU philosophy opposes in all cases the prosecution of pregnant women for abuse of the unborn child by drug use or other harmful behavior. Some proponents deny that the expectant mother even has a moral obligation to refrain from conduct causing permanent damage to the child. This paper concurs that prosecution of expectant mothers is often counterproductive, but argues for a standard of family morality which includes an obligation to refrain from conduct likely to cause a child to be born with substantial health defects.

JOHNSON, Ralph H. Massey on Fallacy and Informal Logic: A Reply. Synthese, 80(3), 407-426, S 89.

In "The Fallacy Behind Fallacies," Massey criticizes the notion of fallacy and in particular informal logic texts. In this article, I examine Massey's criticisms. It turns out that they hinge upon the way he conceptualizes the idea of fallacy. I have some criticisms and suggestions to make about how it might be done better. I also suggest a way of understanding the respective precincts of formal and informal logic and conclude that there need be no tension between them.

JOHNSON, Tony W. Teaching as Translation: The Philosophical Dimension. Thinking, 8(3), 34-38, 1989.

JOHNSON, Tony. Who is Harry Stottlemeier and What Did He Discover? Thinking, 7(4), Supp 6-9, 1988.

JOHNSON-LAIRD, Philip N. "How is Meaning Mentally Represented?" in *Meaning and Mental Representation*, ECO, Umberto (ed), 99-118. Bloomington, Indiana Univ Pr, 1988.

JOHNSTON, Barry V. Integralism and the Reconstruction of Society: The Idea of Ultimate Reality and Meaning in the World of P A Sorokin. Ultim Real Mean, 13(2), 96-108, Je 90.

Sorokin's Integral philosophy was the product of a complex lifelong struggle with ultimate questions of society, humanity and the transcendent. A sociology of knowledge approach is used to discuss its development and to demonstrate the intertwining of biography and ideas. The first, formal, Integral statement came from Sorokin's 2,500 year study of social order and change: *Social and Cultural Dynamics*. It was further developed in his analysis of the contemporary crisis of civilization and advanced from epistemology to a theory of social action and reform in his later study of altruism. What began as sociological theory culminated in a philosophy of action whose goal was the reconstruction of society.

JOHNSTON, David. Hobbes's Mortalism. Hist Polit Thought, 10(4), 647-663, Wint 89.

JOHNSTON, Paul. *Wittgenstein and Moral Philosophy*. New York, Routledge, 1989

JOHNSTONE JR, Henry W. Self-Application in Philosophical Argumentation. Metaphilosophy, 20(3-4), 247-261, Jl-O 89.

I aim to clarify the scope of philosophical arguments exploiting self-application. (I deliberately use this term rather than the more common but less accurate "self-reference.") I argue that many valid philosophical arguments fall beyond this scope. They are ad hominem but not self-applicational. Yet the point of any philosophical argument is to invite the person under attack to apply an epithet to himself/herself. In this sense of self-application, valid philosophical arguments are all self-applicational.

JONATHAN, Ruth. Gender Socialisation and the Nature/Culture

Controversy: The Dualist's Dilemma. Educ Phil Theor, 21(2), 40-48, 1989.

This article reexamines the controversy over the roles of nature and nurture in gender formation. It argues that both the popular "traditional" and popular "radical" views of the origins of gender are a priori, assuming the truth respectively of metaphysical and normative dualism. If dualist commitments are suspended, the nature/culture controversy becomes an illusory dilemma. A dialectical model of natural/cultural interaction is therefore proposed, which reveals the cultural parameters of natural evolution as well as the natural parameters of cultural evolution. The implication of a dialectical model of gender formation for schooling practices and the minimising of stereotyping are discussed, and the gender debate resituated in the context of social discussion.

JONES JR, William A. Student Views on "Ethical" Issues: A Situational Analysis. J Bus Ethics, 9(3), 201-205, Mr 90.

This paper reports on selected attitudes of a sample of third-year undergraduate business students in a major urban university. The focus of the research is on respondent perceptions of certain aspects of the employee-employer relationship. Such issues as use of the company car for a personal trip, use of the company copy machine for personal copies, calling in sick when some personal time is needed, eating at the very best restaurant on a business trip and others are explored. Half of the students surveyed were asked to respond as though they were employees of the company. The other half were asked to respond as though they were the president of the company. Both groups seemed to reflect a certain amount of "flexibility" in their responses to the issues presented. The assumed position of the respondent, the "situation," did influence the responses given.

JONES, Andrew J I. Deontic Logic and Legal Knowledge Representation. Ratio Juris, 3(2), 237-244, Jl 90.

The current literature in the artificial intelligence and law field reveals uncertainty concerning the potential role of deontic logic in legal knowledge representation. For instance, the Logic Programming Group at Imperial College has shown that a good deal can be achieved in this area in the absence of explicit representation of the deontic notions. This paper argues that some rather ordinary parts of the law contain structures which, if they are to be represented in logic, will call for use of a reasonably sophisticated deontic logic.

JONES, Andrew J I. On the Control-Theoretic Characterization of the Self. Acta Phil Fennica, 38, 63-70, 1985.

The paper offers an outline and criticism of the characterization of the concept of the self in I Pörn, "Kierkegaard and the Study of the Self," *Inquiry* 27, 1984. The task is not to assess Pörn's interpretation of Kierkegaard. Rather, the paper sees the basic framework Pörn uses—a hierarchically organized structure of interconnected information-feedback control loops—as a potentially valuable tool in the analysis of the self concept, but raises some doubts about the way Pörn actually defines the principles governing the construction of that hierarchy. In particular, it is not clear that these principles, as Pörn defines them, permit an adequate representation of the self's awareness of rifts or incongruencies in the self.

JONES, Andrew J I and PÖRN, Ingmar. A Rejoinder to Hansson. Synthese, 80(3), 429-432, S 89.

JONES, Anne Hudson. Metaphors, Narratives, and Images of AIDS. Med Human Rev, 4(1), 7-16, Ja 90.

JONES, Beth H and JELASSI, M Tawfik. The Effect of Computer Intervention and Task Structure on Bargaining Outcome. Theor Decis, 28(3), 355-377, My 90.

This paper reports on a study that examined the impact of computer presentation of suggested solutions during negotiation, in bargaining situations that can be characterized as integrative or distributive. It was found that in the integrative task, the bargainers achieved higher joint outcomes when presented with suggestions. They had a more negative perception of the negotiation atmosphere, however. In the distributive task, the suggestions did not help achieve joint gains, but it lessened negative attitudes of the bargainers. Bargainers who received suggestions felt both they and their partner had been somewhat more flexible, cooperative, considerate, and less suspicious. Thus, regardless of negotiation situation, the suggestions resulted in some benefit to the negotiators.

JONES, Brian J and MC FALLS JR, Joseph and GALLAGHER III, Bernard J. Toward a Unified Model for Social Problems Theory. J Theor Soc Behav, 19(3), 337-356, S 89.

The article argues for the importance of conceptualizing social problems through a two-dimensional theory. Specifically, our position would extend current constructionist accounts by formally considering the objective dimension (evidence of the social harm associated with a problem) in relation to the subjective dimension (public opinion about the seriousness of a problem). Unemployment and sex roles are developed as case studies of the theoretical model.

JONES, Gareth. Phenomenology and Theology: A Note on Bultmann and Heidegger. Mod Theol, 5(2), 161-179, Ja 89.

JONES, L Gregory. A Response to Sykes: Revelation and the Practices of Interpreting Scripture. Mod Theol, 5(4), 343-348, Jl 89.

John Sykes criticizes Hans Frei and Stanley Hauerwas for having inadequate doctrines of revelation. Sykes proposes that Ronald Thiemann's account provides the outlines of a coherent understanding of revelation. But Sykes's use of Thiemann is unsatisfactory. Indeed Thiemann's account raises more problems that it solves. The response outlines those problems and suggests an alternative account of revelation that encompasses both God's advent to humanity in Jesus Christ and the continuing rediscovery and re-presentation of Jesus Christ by contemporary Christian communities.

JONES, Robert F. Montaigne, Encoder and Decoder, in Propria Persona. Commun Cog, 22(3-4), 263-276, 1989.

JONES, Royce. James's Religious Hypothesis Reinterpreted. SW Phil Rev, 6(2), 79-96, Jl 90.

The continuity of "The Will to Believe" with "The Sentiment of Rationality" is demonstrated through an exposition of the two articles which omits as superfluous any account of genuine options and emphasizes the generality of the Religious Hypothesis. It is argued that the Religious Hypothesis satisfies the conditions of rationality set forth in "The Sentiment of Rationality" and that James does not provide a license for wishful thinking. A brief history of the criticism of "The Will to Believe" is provided.

JONES, Thomas M. Can Business Ethics Be Taught? Empirical Evidence. Bus Prof Ethics J, 8(2), 73-94, Sum 89.

Debate on the effectiveness of ethics education for business students continues to rage. This paper reviews the existing evidence and tests the effect of two types of ethics "interventions." A brief ethics module, suitable for teaching large numbers of students, was found to be marginally effective in promoting moral development. An ethics elective course showed considerable promise in promoting moral development. Evidence also indicated a possible negative effect of business education on moral development.

JONES, William R. Process Theology: Guardian of the Oppressor or Goad to the Oppressed—An Interim Assessment. Process Stud, 18(4), 268-281, Wint 89.

JONSEN, Albert R. Bentham in a Box. Nat Forum, 69(4), 33-35, Fall 89.

JORDAN JR, James A. Socratic Teaching? Thinking, 4(3-4), 25-29, 1982.

JORDAN, Mark D. The Evidence of the Transcendentals and the Place of Beauty in Thomas Aquinas. Int Phil Quart, 29(4), 393-407, D 89.

JORION, Paul. Intelligence artificielle et mentalité primitive. Rev Phil Fr, 179(4), 541, O-D 89.

JOYCE, Glenis. Training and Women: Some Thoughts from the Grassroots. J Bus Ethics, 9(4-5), 407-415, Ap-My 90.

Current assumptions and values with respect to management training for women are examined. A number of suggestions for change are made. The thrust of the changes will move us toward ensuring that education for women does not remain "education for frustration," that is, education which gives women the desire for change in a world that remains the same.

JUDOVITZ, Dalia. "Derrida and Descartes: Economizing Thought" in *Derrida and Deconstruction*, SILVERMAN, Hugh J (ed), 40-58. New York, Routledge, 1989.

JUENGST, Eric T and WEIL, Carol J. "Interpreting Proxy Directives" in *Advance Directives in Medicine*, HACKLER, Chris (ed), 21-37. New York, Praeger, 1989.

We criticize current standards for proxy decision making found in legal instructions to holders of durable powers of attorney for health care. We argue that the "explicit instructions" interpretation of the substituted judgment standard and the "medical indications" interpretation of the best interest standard should be supplemented with at least four other interpretations, which we call the "analogy test," the "worldwide test," the "special personal interests test" and the "reasonable person test."

JUFFRAS, A. "Cassirer's Theory of History" in *History and Anti-History in Philosophy*, LAVINE, T Z (ed), 188-214. Norwell, Kluwer, 1989.

One asks two things. What is Cassirer's theory of history? How does he actually write history? Cassirer claims to be recreating the spirit of an age in each of his histories. If this is what he is doing, then he is engaged in archeo-cultural anthropology, not history. However, his individual "histories" are chapters in the progress toward freedom. The "spirit" of the various ages

which he describes are the Aristotelian material factors that enter into a longer history. This history, as he has written it over the course of several volumes (each a "spirit" of an age), despite his "theory," is a standard history; that is, an explanation of how the ideal of freedom has grown. His methodology for discovering the "spirit of the age" is excessively subjective.

JUNG, Hwa Yol. Mikhail Bakhtin's Body Politic: A Phenomenological Dialogics. Man World, 23(1), 85-99, Ja 90.

JUNG, Hwa Yol. Vico and Bakhtin: A Prolegomenon to Any Future Comparison. New Vico Studies, 3, 157-165, 1985.

JUNGEN, Britta and EGNEUS, Hans. Human Ecology. Phil Soc Act, 15(3-4), 47-57, Jl-D 89.

JUNGEN, Britta and KYLE, Gunhild. Women's Research and Its Inherent Critique of Society and Science. Phil Soc Act, 15(3-4), 41-45, Jl-D 89.

JUNQING, Yi. The Laborious and Painful Process of Emancipation (in Serbo-Croatian). Filozof Istraz, 29(2), 435-440, 1989.

In the article the author analyzes the situation in contemporary Chinese philosophy, which is, as he states, in the process of emancipation and reform. The essence and the direction of the emancipation, according to the author, have three basic aspects: the problem of humanism and alienation, the fate of traditional Chinese culture, and the problem of the transformation of dialectical and historical materialism. The author concludes by giving the process of emancipation a good chance of success.

JUROS, Helmut. Wert und Würde der Arbeit in *Laborem Exercens* (in Polish). Stud Phil Christ, 25(2), 7-28, 1989.

JUSTIN, Renage G. Cost Containment Forces Physicians into Ethical and Quality of Care Compromises. Theor Med, 10(3), 231-238, S 89.

Contemporary cost containment measures ignore patients' need for privacy, destroy long-term doctor-patient relationships, and demand ethical and standard of care compromises. Economic considerations have distracted the physician, and he/she no longer focuses primarily on the patient's welfare. The superficiality of the doctor-patient relationship and the cost-cutting efforts have jointly contributed to the deterioration of the quality of medical care. The purpose of this paper is to illustrate that the care physicians dispense in the office is adversely affected by cost containment regulations.

KAC, Michael B and MANASTER-RAMER, Alexis. The Concept of Phrase Structure. Ling Phil, 13(3), 325-362, Je 90.

KADISH, Mortimer R and DAVIS, Michael. Defending the Hearsay Rule. Law Phil, 8(3), 333-352, D 89.

KADMON, Nirit. Uniqueness. Ling Phil, 13(3), 273-324, Je 90.

KAGAN, Shelly. *The Limits of Morality*. New York, Clarendon/Oxford Pr, 1989

Most of us believe that there are limits to the sacrifices that morality can demand of us; we do not think that we are morally required to make our greatest possible contribution to the overall good. It is also widely believed that certain types of acts are simply forbidden, even when necessary for promoting the overall good. Despite the intuitive appeal of these views, I argue that neither cannot be adequately defended. My book thus offers a sustained attack on two of the most fundamental features of commonsense morality.

KAHN, Charles H. Problems in the Argument of Plato's *Crito*. Apeiron, 22(4), 29-43, D 89.

The *Crito* takes no stand on the question of whether violating the law is ever morally justified, despite modern attempts to derive a civil disobedience doctrine from it. The argument is largely ad hoc and ad hominem and resistant to generalization as political theory. The central claim is that Socrates' escape would be unjust because escape would be an act whose maxim is incompatible with the principle of effective legality. A new construal of the *Crito*'s argument is offered and several problems with the argument are discussed.

KAHN, Tamar Joy (ed) and WALTERS, LeRoy (ed). *Bibliography of Bioethics, Volume 15*. Washington, Kennedy Inst Ethics, 1989

KAIN, Philip J. Kant and the Possibility of Uncategorized Experience. Ideal Stud, 19(2), 154-173, My 89.

If it were possible to have organized experience without bringing the categories of the understanding into play, the Transcendental Deduction of the *Critique of Pure Reason* would be doomed to failure. In several places, however, Kant seems to admit that organized experience is, in fact, possible without the categories. The most important of these cases is that of aesthetic judgments—judgments of the beautiful and of the sublime—which clearly involve ordered experience and seem to occur without employing the categories. I argue that this contraction is merely apparent and I try to resolve it.

KAIN, Philip J. Kant's Political Theory and Philosophy of History. Clio, 18(4), 325-345, Sum 89.

The importance of Kant's political thought can best be understood if we do two things: if we compare it to political theory as it existed before Kant and if we see how it fundamentally depends upon his philosophy of history. It is Kant's philosophy of history that allows him to take a major step beyond previous political thinkers. Kant brings together for the first time two projects which had traditionally remained separate. He develops a theory of the ideal state and also a philosophy of history, i.e., a theory of how to actually realize the ideal state in history.

KAINZ, Howard P. Angelology, Metaphysics, and Intersubjectivity: A Reply to G N Casey. Irish Phil J, 6(1), 119-132, 1989.

This is a reply to Casey's challenge to my suggestion in *"Active and Passive Potency" in Thomistic Angelology* that there is an inconsistency in Aquinas's contention that an angel would be endowed with completely transparent self-knowledge and yet be subject to opacities in knowledge of other angels. The root of the disagreement is the Thomistic doctrine that there can be a completely spiritual potency. I argue that a potency which is responsible for opacity is at least analogous to what we designate as corporeality; and that, in any case, there is an important commensurability between self-knowledge and knowledge of the other.

KAL, Victor. De afkeer van het individualisme bij Alisdair MacIntyre en de soevereiniteit van het individu. Alg Ned Tijdschr Wijs, 81(4), 285-303, O 89.

After introducing into the main argument of MacIntyre's work, which says that morality and its justification are possible only when the individual is conceived as embedded in a tradition and a community, the article criticizes this anti-individualism where it leaves no place to any individually inspired and motivated, sovereign attitude and responsibility. The article argues that MacIntyre's firm rejection of all kinds of moral intuition, and his preoccupation with justification, brings him, in *After Virtue* and in *Whose Justice? Which Rationality?* equally, near to some sort of traditionalism.

KALANSURIA, A D P. The Dhamma and the Notion of 'Perception': A Conceptual Technique Made Explicit. Indian Phil Quart, 16(3), 291-302, Jl 89.

The aim of this paper is to elicit the nature of the notion of 'perception' in the Buddha's Dhamma. Philosophically speaking, in a discussion of this kind, one cannot ignore the same notion current in Western epistemologies, with special reference to those in recent philosophies in the English-speaking world. It shall be shown, at the end, that the Buddhist notion of 'perception' is not epistemological, and therefore Buddhist philosophers who concentrated heavily on 'epistemology', err.

KALINOWSKI, Georges. Ontique et deontique. Riv Int Filosof Diritto, 66(3), 437-449, Jl-S 89.

KALLICK, David. The Speakerly Teacher: Socrates and Writing. Metaphilosophy, 20(3-4), 341-346, Jl-O 89.

KALOYEROPOULOS, N A. *Philosophical Works*. Geneva, Ion, 1988

KALUPAHANA, David J. "Toward a Middle Path of Survival" in *Nature in Asian Tradition of Thought: Essays in Environmental Philosophy*, CALLICOTT, J Baird (ed), 247-256. Albany, SUNY Pr, 1989.

KAMARYT, J and STEINDL, R. On the Connection Between Ethology and Ecology (in Czechoslovakian). Filozof Cas, 37(5), 704-715, 1989.

Ethology closely connected with ecology and genetics, is currently one of the fastest growing biological disciplines. In terms of their theoretical content and their practical implications for industry, agriculture and medicine, these sciences influence the totality of contemporary cultural and civilization transformations. The close interconnection between ecology and ethology, which in the 19th century was perceived in biological classifications in more methodological terms, has nowadays come to the fore quite forcefully, also due to its contents and due to the urgent need of finding a practical solution to burning global problems, ecological crises and the necessity of grappling with a number of adverse civilization factors. (edited)

KAMATA, Yasuo. Platonische Idee und die anschauliche Welt bei Schopenhauer. Schopenhauer Jahr, 70, 84-93, 1989.

KAMIKURA, Tsuneyuki. L'esthétique de l'intuition chez Jacques Maritain (in Japanese). Bigaku, 40(2), 1-12, Autumn 89.

Jacques Maritain définit l'essence de l'art comme l'intuition poétique. Réduire l'art en acte de l'esprit rend difficile le traitement théorique des éléments matériels dans l'oeuvre d'art. Cependant il a tenu à cette position, parce que la subjectivité qui est capable d'entrer en communion avec l'homme comme personne ne s'est jamais établi dans son système philosophique. Dans le domaine de l'art l'artiste, l'homme comme personne, joue le rôle principale pour faire les choses qui existent seulement pour être belles. La philosophie de l'art chez Maritain est indispensable pour sa philosophie totale. Cela s'éclaircira par cet article.

KAMM, F M. Harming Some to Save Others. Phil Stud, 57(3), 227-260, N 89.

KAMM, Frances M. The Philosopher as Insider and Outsider. J Med Phil, 15(4), 347-374, Ag 90.

Philosophers may play the role of insider, e.g., serving as advisor to government commissions, or of outsider, commenting on the work of such commissions. Each role may raise dilemmas. It is argued that as insider the philosopher's primary duties should be to clarify and inform, as well as philosophize with the commissioners, and help them stay on a course in which moral considerations are given their proper weight in the preparation of commission reports. The outsider philosopher can comment both on how close a report comes to being perfect of its type, and how far short of an ideal philosophical analysis even a perfect government report is. (edited)

KAMPE, Cornelius. "Can There Be Equal Opportunity Without a Merit Principle" in *Inquiries into Values: The Inaugural Session of the International Society for Value Inquiry*, LEE, Sander H, 615-631. Lewiston, Mellen Pr, 1989.

The paper presents some arguments to show that egalitarian thought in the form that it takes in John Rawls's *A Theory of Justice*, and as later interpreted and defended by Kai Nielsen, does not accommodate competitive equality of opportunity. The problem with pure egalitarian principles is that they emphasize the end point in distributions to the exclusion of a competitive component, and thereby disallow a justifying role for equal opportunity in distribution of benefits. In the hypothetical case where conditions of fair equality of opportunity are ideally fulfilled, "competition" is reduced to a form of lottery. We are left with an equal chance to receive benefits. Since no personal attributes in the form of talents or motivations are, for Rawls, ever deserved, the moral point of making competitive equality of opportunity fair, is lost.

KANE, Robert. Two Kinds of Incompatibilism. Phil Phenomenol Res, 50(2), 219-254, D 89.

Two kinds of incompatibilist theories of freedom (theories denying that freedom is compatible with determinism) are distinguished, agent cause (AC) theories and teleological intelligibility (TI) theories. The former postulate some kind of nonevent (or nonoccurrent) cuasation to account for free agency, the latter do not. AC theories are the most common ones in traditional and contemporary discussion of free will, but they are flawed. By contrast, traditional writing gives only the barest hints about what TI theories might look like. After discussing the difficulties of AC theories, the paper develops and defends a TI theory in some detail.

KANELLOPOULOS, P. La philosophie de Hegel (in Greek). Philosophia (Athens), 17-18, 13-40, 1987-88.

Ce sont des pages du 246ème chapitre de l'"Histoire de l'Esprit Européen" de Panayotis Canellopoulos. Ce chapitre a été écrit par l'auteur à son âge de quatre vingt quatre ans, quelques semaines avant sa mort. Après la mention de la division tripartite de l'Esprit en "subjectif", "objectif" et "absolu", est présentée, commentée et critiquée la philosophie de l'Histoire notamment, telle qu'elle se dégage des ouvrages de Hegel, publiés par lui-même, ou de ses cours, publiés après sa mort. L'auteur en fait le commentaire et la critique en fonction de sa connaissance profonde de l'Historie de la philosophie. (edited)

KANG, Thomas H. A Bibliographical Survey on Confucian Studies in Western Languages: Retrospect and Prospect (in Serbo-Croatian). Filozof Istraz, 29(2), 575-586, 1989.

Based on a collection of over 5,000 items of bibliographical data, which will be published as the first bibliography on Confucian studies in Western languages, this intensive survey highlights the following points: (a) the historical roles of the Western studies in the development of philosophical and religious concepts of Confucianism and in the dissemination of Confucianism throughout the world by translating, studying, and publishing of Confucian classics in Western languages; (b) the Confucian influence in Europe; (c) the strength and weakness of Western studies; (d) status quo of Confucian studies in the West in contrast with other major religions. Suggestions are also made in this survey: (a) to modernize Confucianism by reinterpreting it to cope with the changing world, and by making an independent study separate from Chinese philosophical and religious studies; (b) to reexport some of the outstanding Western studies of Confucianism to the East; and (c) to amalgamate the Confucian and Western heritages as a new heritage of all mankind to serve a new age.

KANGER, Stig. On Realization of Human Rights. Acta Phil Fennica, 38, 71-78, 1985.

KANNISTO, Heikki. Thoughts and Their Subject: A Study of

Wittgenstein's *Tractatus*. Acta Phil Fennica, 40, 1-184, 1986.

KANTOROVICH, Aharon. "A Genotype-Phenotype Model for the Growth of Theories" in *Issues in Evolutionary Epistemology*, HAHLWEG, Kai (ed), 171-184. Albany, SUNY Pr, 1989.

Evolutionary epistemology neglects ontogeny, which according to evolutionary biology constitutes an indispensable part of the selection cycle in nature. In this paper it is suggested that the development of a dynamic theory within the framework of a research program be taken as the counterpart of ontogeny. According to this model the body of unfalsifiable hard-core ideas is the analogue of the genotype, whereas the theory, which is adjusted to observational data, is the analogue of the phenotype. It is shown how the "ontogenetic" process of theory development is intertwined within a cybernetic model of selection in science.

KANTOROVICH, Aharon and NE'EMAN, Yuval. Serendipity as a Source of Evolutionary Progress in Science. Stud Hist Phil Sci, 20(4), 505-529, D 89.

KANY-TURPIN, José and PELLEGRIN, Pierre. "Cicero and the Aristotelian Theory of Divination by Dreams" in *Cicero's Knowledge of the Peripatos*, FORTENBAUGH, William W (ed), 220-245. New Brunswick, Transaction Books, 1989.

KAPITAN, Tomis. Action, Uncertainty, and Divine Impotence. Analysis, 50(2), 127-133, Mr 90.

Agency is exercised only through intentional action, hence, via intending courses of action. To intend is to prepare oneself for the exertion of effort, and no one would do this without assuming that (i) there is a need for effort in order to bring about a desired result, (ii) there is a chance of success, and (iii) the future is yet open as regards the action in question. But for rational agents, these assumptions must antedate intending, in which case intentional action implies an antecedent uncertainty about what will be. Therefore, no omniscient being can act intentionally.

KAPLAN, Caren (trans) and KOFMAN, Sarah. "'Ça cloche'" in *Derrida and Deconstruction*, SILVERMAN, Hugh J (ed), 108-138. New York, Routledge, 1989.

KAPLAN, David. Words. Aris Soc, SUPP 64, 93-119, 1990.

KAPLAN, Francis. Le dieu de Claude Bruaire. Rev Phil Fr, 180(1), 35-45, Ja-Mr 90.

KAPLAN, Mark. The Nature of Human Nature and its Bearing on Public Health Policy: An Application. Soc Epistem, 3(3), 251-259, Jl-S 89.

KAPUR, Neera Badhwar. The Rejection of Ethical Rationalism. Logos (USA), 10, 99-131, 1989.

Ethical rationalism, as I define it, is the view found in Kant, Gauthier, and, perhaps, others, that our moral agency—our ability to articulate, justify, and act on, moral principles—must be defined in terms of our rational nature, understood as being logically independent of our emotional nature. I argue that rationalism is contradicted by the moral data, and that there are no good data-independent reasons for accepting it. An analysis of our patterns of moral perception, evaluation, and response reveals that these essentially involve our emotional nature. I use friendship as a central test of adequacy of rationalist moral conceptions.

KAPUSTIN, Mikhail. Dialectics by Command: Revolutionism in Philosophy and the Philosophy of Revolutionism. Soviet Stud Phil, 28(2), 6-29, Fall 89.

KAR, Gitangshu. Is a Work of Art Symbol of Feeling or an Image of Experience? Indian Phil Quart, SUPP 16(4), 9-13, O 89.

In this paper I have tried to make out a case for saying that a work of art is an image of experience, rather than a symbol. Symbol is an arbitrarily accepted sign to stand for something mostly beyond itself. Whereas an image ensues but out of a resemblance for certain thing. "Every knowledge begins with Experience." Artwork too imparts knowledge—of images of experiences—experiences of perceptual objects, ideas and feeling fused together in the minds of the artists and embodied by them in the work of art. Art therefore is the creation of images of feeling out of experience.

KARAYANNIS, G. Parménide d'Élée et la fondation de la science (in Greek). Philosophia (Athens), 17-18, 258-271, 1987-88.

Dans l'article présent on decrit les points de la philosophie de Parménide dont la valeur, la signification et le contenu—avant tout—consistent à la constatation qu'ils conduisent à la fondation et à l'édification de la science, telle quelle on conçoit aujourd'hui sous l'aspect du savoir profond et exhaustif et sous l'aspect de l'effort systématique pour la conquête de la connaissance. (edited)

KARBUSICKY, Vladimir. The Anthropology of 'Semantic Levels' in Music. Acta Phil Fennica, 43, 54-69, 1988.

KARIEL, Henry S. The Feminist Subject Spinning in the Postmodern Project. Polit Theory, 18(2), 255-272, My 90.

KARIKÓ, Sándor. On the Relationship of Lukács *Ontology* and the Theory of Social Formations (in Hungarian). Magyar Filozof Szemle, 5, 604-617, 1989.

Die wagehalsigen Zielsetzungen der *Ontologie* von Lukács, die Originalität seines Ausgangspunktes, die moderne Aufarbeitung mancher Teilfragen und ihre imponierenden Interpretationen lassen ahnen, dass der Verfasser mit seiner Philosophie eine dauernde Wirkung in unserer Philosophie und in unserem fachwissenschaftlichen Denken hinterliesse. Bei der Aufarbeitung dieses grossartigen Werkes ist es eine wichtige Aufgabe die Frage zu beantworten, ob Lukács mit seiner Ontologie in der Lage ist, Zusammenhänge in der Geschichtsphilosophie oder in der Theorie der Gesellschaftsformationen aufzustellen. (edited)

KARNS, J E and SCHADLER, F P. The Unethical Exploitation of Shareholders in Management Buyout Transactions. J Bus Ethics, 9(7), 595-602, Jl 90.

The accurate pricing of securities in the capital markets depends upon the markets being both efficient and fair. In management buyout transactions (MBOs), the price bid by inside managers enhances the efficient pricing of securities but raises a reasonable doubt about the fairness to existing shareholders. This study addresses this fairness question in MBOs and offers short-term and long-term legal alternatives which allow both the efficiency and fairness criteria to be met. In the short-term the case law established in the *Basic v. Levinson* decision for merger negotiation disclosures should be applied to MBO transactions. Over the longer horizon, legislative changes should be made to existing securities laws. Applying the investor protection principles of the 1933 and 1934 securities acts to MBO transactions will suppress the temptation of managers to extract shareholder wealth for their personal gain.

KARSON, Marvin J and BARNETT, John H. Managers, Values, and Executive Decisions. J Bus Ethics, 8(10), 747-771, O 89.

A study of 513 executives researched decisions involving ethics, relationships and results. Analyzing personal values, organization role and level, career stage, gender and sex role with decisions in ten scenarios produced conclusions about both the role of gender, subjective values, and the other study variables and about situational relativity, gender stereotypes, career stages, and future research opportunities.

KARY, Carla E. One Causal Mechanism in Evolution: One Unit of Selection. Phil Sci, 57(2), 290-296, Je 90.

The theory of evolution is supported by the theory of genetics, which provides a single causal mechanism to explain the activities of replicators and interactors. A common misrepresentation of the theory of evolution, however, is that interaction (involving interactors) and transmission (involving replicators) are distinct causal processes. Sandra Mitchell (1987) is misled by this. I discuss why only a single causal mechanism is working in evolution and why it is sufficient. Further, I argue that Mitchell's mistaken view of the causal mechanism in evolution prevents her from resolving the conflict between Dawkins and Brandon. I conclude that the unit-of-selection question remains very much alive.

KASANEN, Eero and MAULA, Erkka. Chez Fermat A.D. 1637. Philosophica, 43(1), 127-162, 1989.

This paper discusses Fermat's "Last Theorem" from philosophical, historical, heuristic and number theoretical angles. A novel heuristic scenario is suggested. It enables a proof of FLT for even exponents without restrictions, and a proof reconstruction according to which it is impossible to solve the Diophantine equation $x^{2k+1} + y^{2k+1} = z^{2k+1}$, as the proof leads to a variant of the Liar Paradox. All methods used are known from Fermat's own works.

KASEM, A and BASU, S. A Refutation of Jagat Pal's Defence of Aristotelian Square of Opposition. Indian Phil Quart, 17(2), 261-270, Ap 90.

The aim of this article is to argue against the contention that the traditional doctrine of the square of opposition can be refuted by modern logic (which uses the language of first order predicate logic) only if it admits an empty domain of discourse at the cost of involving inconsistency in other parts of the system. By emphasising the distinction between "empty predicate" and "empty domain of discourse" this article establishes that modern logic consistently admits the former in refuting the doctrine of traditional square, and also claims that this admission is consistent with semantic and logical intuitions.

KASHIYAMA, Paul. Integrity and Judicial Discretion. Eidos, 8(1), 35-46, Je 89.

One of the controversial claims made by Ronald Dworkin's theories of law and legal reasoning is that "law as integrity" succeeds in eliminating the necessity of judicial discretion. In this brief paper, I argue that we have reasons to doubt the truth of this claim since Dworkin's arguments are incomplete. One major difficulty is the question concerning how the "best" interpretations of different judges should concur with an interpretation of what the law ought to be, i.e., the "right" answer. Dworkin's notions of "inclusive" and "pure" integrity, though suggestive, are as yet underdeveloped to make the "necessary" connection between law and political morality. This leaves intact the plausibility of the claim defending the need and hence the acceptability of internally consistent, but discretionary, judicial decisions.

KASPER, Robert T and ROUNDS, William C. The Logic of Unification in Grammar. Ling Phil, 13(1), 35-58, F 90.

KASPRISIN, Lorraine. Literature as a Way of Knowing: An Epistemological Justification for Literary Studies. J Aes Educ, 21(3), 17-27, Fall 87.

KASS, Alex and SCHANK, Roger. "Knowledge Representation in People and Machines" in *Meaning and Mental Representation*, ECO, Umberto (ed), 181-200. Bloomington, Indiana Univ Pr, 1988.

KASS, Leon R. Practicing Ethics: Where's the Action? Hastings Center Rep, 20(1), 5-12, Ja-F 90.

KATES, Gary. From Liberalism to Radicalism: Tom Paine's *Rights of Man*. J Hist Ideas, 50(4), 569-587, O-D 89.

The first and second parts of *Rights of Man* contain contradictory ideologies. Part One (1791) served as an apology for the Marquis de LaFayette and ignored the burgeoning democratic movement in Paris. Part Two (1792) rejected LaFayette's political principles in favor of a more radical conception of democracy. Thus Paine's ideas fundamentally changed during the French Revolution.

KATZ, Jerrold J. The Domino Theory. Phil Stud, 58(1-2), 3-39, Ja-F 90.

This paper argues that the principal criticisms of intensionalism over the last several decades of Anglo-American philosophy all depend on Quine's argument in "Two Dogmas of Empiricism," in particular, Quine's argument for the indeterminacy of translation, Davidson's argument for replacing the intensionalist paradigm with the Tarskian paradigm, the argument for an extensionalist possible worlds semantics, Putnam's criticisms of intensionalism, and Burge's arguments against semantic individualism. The paper explains how these arguments depend on Quine and why they fail.

KATZ, Jonathan. Rational Common Ground in the Sociology of Knowledge. Phil Soc Sci, 19(3), 257-271, S 89.

The critique of positivism which has led to the relativization of rationality is sketched. Despite the collapse, within this critique, of the analytic/synthetic distinction, and the resulting semantic holism, despite the incommensurability between languages, and thus beliefs, of cultures distant from our own, it is argued that there are nonetheless global and invariant conditions on rationality.

KATZ, Leo. The Assumption of Risk Argument. Soc Phil Pol, 7(2), 138-169, Spr 90.

Assumption of risk arguments are made all the time. Sometimes they persuade; sometimes they sound preposterous. What is odd is that when they sound preposterous, it is often very hard to say why they sound preposterous. This essay tried to outline some of the chief reasons beyond the two or three most familiar ones: the indeterminancy of the argument in some circumstances, the special problems posed by collective assumption of risk, the phenomenon of victimless injuries, the incommensurability of choices under extreme uncertainty, the built-in qualifications of conditional promises, the immorality of avoiding certain gambles, and the inappropriateness of the argument in the criminal law.

KATZ, Nina J (trans) and EICHENWALD, I I and BAER, Joachim T (trans). "A Note on Schopenhauer (1910) (also in German)" in *Schopenhauer: New Essays in Honor of His 200th Birthday*, VON DER LUFT, Eric (ed), 139-158. Lewiston, Mellen Pr, 1989.

KAUFMAN, Jerome L. Hamlethics in Planning: To Do or Not To Do. Bus Prof Ethics J, 6(2), 67-77, Sum 87.

KAUFMANN, Matthias. Der Begriff als "nicht wirklich existierende" Einheit vieler "wirklich existierender" Individuen. Z Phil Forsch, 43(3), 509-518, Jl-S 89.

The problem of individuation is complementary to the better-known problem of universals. It turns out to be unsolvable for different variants of medieval conceptual realism. However, the medieval nominalist solution—to take mainly physical objects as individuals existing *extra animam* and as immediately given while concepts are only beings *in anima*—seems to be untenable facing the unperceptible objects of modern science. Nevertheless, to accept the difference between existence in the sense of modern logic and existence as the subsistence of physical things is to give

the possibility of maintaining a nominalist position without being committed to conceptual reductionism.

KAWAMURA, Leslie S. Principles of Buddhism. Zygon, 25(1), 59-72, Mr 90.

This paper presents Buddhism as a path theory in which the adherent practices mindfulness in order to see the world as-it-is. The world as presented in a human situation is an interdependently originating process to which one can bring meaning but in which meaning is not inherent. The conceptualizing process by which one concretizes reality is the foundation on which human frustrations and dis-ease arise. However, it is by this conceptualizing process that one establishes a cosmological view of the universe. The soteriological consideration in Buddhism is to realize that reality created by the mind is like an illusion, a concretization of an interdependently originating process into a substantive reality. Through this realization one can remove the delusion created by mind and see reality as-it-is.

KAYE, R. Diophantine Induction. Annals Pure Applied Log, 46(1), 1-40, Ja 90.

It is shown that Matijasevic's theorem on the diophantine representation of R.E. predicates is provable in the subsystem of first-order Peano arithmetic formed by restricting the induction scheme to diophantine formulas with no parameters. The associated subsystem of bounded diophantine induction (where induction is only available for diophantine formulas in which the roots are bounded by a polynomial in the induction variable) is also considered. A rather general conservation result relating parameter-free induction to parameter-induction is given, and all these results are applied to give some new structure-theorems for nonstandard models of bounded diophantine induction.

KAYE, Richard. Parameter-Free Universal Induction. Z Math Log, 35(5), 443-456, 1989.

Theories axiomatized by the axioms for nonnegative parts of discretely ordered rings together with the parameter-free scheme of induction for purely universal formulas (both with and without a polynomial bound on the quantified variables) in the usual first-order language of arithmetic with symbols for addition, multiplication and the order relation are investigated. The consistency strengths of these theories are determined relative to other theories, via several conservation results. Structural properties of nonstandard models of these theories are studied and related to questions of proving the MRDP theorem in weak fragments of arithmetic.

KE, Gang. A Comparative Study of the Representational Paradigms Between Liberalism and Socialism. Phil Soc Sci, 20(1), 5-34, Mr 90.

Traditionally, debates over the issue of representation in liberalism and in socialism focused on such questions as who or whose interests should be represented in order to attest to the legitimacy of representation. In this article, a different and more fundamental approach is achieved by asking how the representation is accomplished. At this methodological point, liberalism and socialism diverge in their understanding of representative government: each follows its own philosophical paradigm(s) that underly and justify its position. Differences between liberal and socialist understandings of representation are analytically compared in three pairs of categories: (a) micro versus macro, (b) individual versus class, and (c) the formalistic versus the substantive. The most crucial differences between the social systems are found in the last pair of categories—the formalistic versus the substantive approach to representation—because different understandings of central concepts such as democracy, freedom, and equality stem from these two frameworks.

KEARNS, John T. Lesniewski's Strategy and Modal Logic. Notre Dame J Form Log, 30(2), 291-307, Spr 89.

Lesniewski used formal systems and artificial languages to capture and explore concepts expressed in ordinary language. This strategy, which is the appropriate strategy for the philosophical logician, is illustrated by developing a system of modal logic to investigate the concept of analyticity. The ordinary concept of analyticity applies only to sentences; it is *de dicto*. This is a shortcoming of the ordinary concept, which is overcome by extending the concept to constitute the corresponding *de re* concept. A semantic account and a deductive system are developed for a first-order language with identity to capture this concept. The system is shown to be sound and complete with respect to the semantic account.

KEATING, Peter and MACKENZIE, Michael. Patents and Free Scientific Information in Biotechnology: Making Monoclonal Antibodies Proprietary. Sci Tech Human Values, 15(1), 65-83, Wint 90.

In this paper we examine the evolution of the biomedical field of Hybridoma/Monoclonal Antibodies with detailed examples of the three types of patent claims—basic, application techniques and specific antibodies—that have emerged there. We then analyse the impact of these claims and their legal histories on (a) the free flow of scientific information, and (b) the activity of scientific researchers. We conclude that such patent claims present severe restrictions for both, not only in the Monoclonal area but in general, amounting to a subtle but significant shift in the political economy of science and technology.

KEBEDE, Messay. Ways Leading to Bergson's Notion of "Perpetual Present". Diogenes, 149, 22-40, Spr 90.

KEBEDE, Messay. Ways Leading to Bergson's Notion of the "Perpetual Present". Phil Today, 33(3), 275-287, Fall 89.

Why and how does something start to exist? Hegel conceived time as unfolding: particularities originate from and return to the universal. This logic fails to grasp time as creation. For Nietzsche, mobility has no given goal; this finite and yet changing world can only be will to power. Its secret is to change its own recurrence into novelty. This finite and yet insatiable power, Bergson conceives it as perpetual present or duration. Time is not unrolling as an after and a before; it returns upon itself to accomplish its alteration (self-creation). Being is time, not in time.

KEGLEY, Jacquelyn Ann K. "History and Philosophy of Science: Necessary Partners or Merely Roommates?" in *History and Anti-History in Philosophy*, LAVINE, T Z (ed), 237-255. Norwell, Kluwer, 1989.

This article addresses the relationships between science, philosophy of science and history of science and concludes that all three are interpretaive projects while the philosophy of science and the history of science are complementary endeavors. The scientist and philosopher who do not understand the history of their disciplines suffer a distortion of memory and thus of self-understanding. Historians and philosophers who do not study science with care cannot interpret with wisdom that which they seek to interpret.

KEGLEY, Jacquelyn Ann K (ed). *Paul Tillich on Creativity*. Lanham, Univ Pr of America, 1989

For Paul Tillich creativity was a fundamental axiom of his philosophical theology. Human creativity involves participation in the Ground of Being which puts one in touch with both the positive aspects of being and the Demonic. The volume begins with an essay on "Creativity in Tillich" by Manfred O Meitzen followed by the reactions of ten respondents. The volume also includes Tillich's newly translated essay on "The Demonic" and "Class Struggle and Religious Socialism," never published in English. Recent essays by Lewis Ford ("Tillich, Whitehead and Creativity") and Ann Bedford Ulanov (Tillich and the feminine) complete the volume.

KEHOE, Alice B. Gender Is an Organon. Zygon, 25(2), 139-150, Je 90.

Gender is a social construct. Technically, it is a grammatical structuring category that may refer to sex, as is typical of Indo-European languages, or to another set of features such as animate versus inanimate, as is typical of Algonkian languages. Religion and science—organons for rendering existential experience intelligible—have always been used by the dominant class as instruments of power, and therefore in Western cultures have been entangled with legitimization of a congeries of concepts collocated with male gender. This paper illustrates the social construction of this congeries by contrasting it with non-Western usages and valuations. (edited)

KEISLER, H Jerome (and others). Descriptive Set Theory Over Hyperfinite Sets. J Sym Log, 54(4), 1167-1180, D 89.

The separation, uniformization, and other properties of the Borel and projective hierarchies over hyperfinite sets are investigated and compared to the corresponding properties in classical descriptive set theory. The techniques used in this investigation also provide some results about countably determined sets and functions, as well as an improvement of an earlier theorem of Kunen and Miller.

KEITA, Lansana. Marxism and Human Sociobiology: A Reply to Zhang Boshu. Biol Phil, 5(1), 79-83, Ja 90.

KELEMEN, Jänos. "Historicism and Rationalism" in *Scientific Knowledge Socialized*, HRONSZKY, Imre (ed), 347-364. Norwell, Kluwer, 1989.

KELESSIDOU, A. Entretiens avec Panayotis Kanellopoulos de *L'Archive de Philosophie et de Théorie des Sciences* (in Greek). Philosophia (Athens), 17-18, 456-466, 1987-88.

L'Archive de Philosophie et de Théorie des Sciences, la Revue fondée en Grèce en 1929 par J Théodoracopoulos, K Tsatsos, I Tsamados et P Kanellopoulos, comprend 11 études de P Kannelopouos, 4 articles concernant des personnalités éminentes de l'époque et deux traductions ("La Philosophie existentielle" de Jaspers et "Le mythe et la vie" de W Schütz). Les traits caractéristiques des études sont: le refus du fanatisme—qui fait que l'auteur repousse également l'idéalisme inauthentique et le matérialisme intransigeant—le souffle créateur et la méthode critique et militante. Les

études appartiennent: à la Philosophie de l'Historie, la Philosophie Politique, la Sociologie et la Philosophie Contemporaine. (edited)

KELLER, James A. Accepting the Authority of the Bible: Is It Rationally Justified? Faith Phil, 6(4), 378-397, O 89.

This paper provides an answer to this question: is the Christian of today rationally justified in using the views expressed in the Bible as a (or the) standard for what she should accept for her own beliefs and practices. I argue against trying to answer this question on the basis of some alleged character of the biblical writings (e.g., their inerrancy or inspiredness). Such a thesis would itself have to be rationally justified, as would the interpretations and applications of biblical writings made by a Christian of today who held the thesis. Instead she should seek to understand how the writers' faith was expressed in their views and use that understanding to guide her as she constructs (or adopts) a set of beliefs by which to express her faith today. I argue that using the Bible in this way and the conclusions reached in doing so are rationally justified.

KELLER, James A. The Problem of Evil and the Attributes of God. Int J Phil Relig, 26(3), 155-171, D 89.

In discussions of the probabilistic argument from evil, some defenders of theism have recently argued that evil has no evidential force against theism. They base their argument on the claim that there is no reason to think that we should be able to discern morally sufficient reasons which God presumably has for permitting the evil which occurs. In this paper I try to counter this argument by discussing factors which suggest that we should generally be able to discern why God permits evil events. I close by suggesting that the theist use the evidential force which evil does have as a reason to question her understanding of the divine attributes.

KELLER, James A. Response to Davis's "Doubting the Resurrection". Faith Phil, 7(1), 112-116, Ja 90.

This article is a response to Stephen T Davis's reply to my article on reasons why Christian theists may doubt that Jesus was raised in the sense that his body was restored to life, somewhat transformed, and emerged from the tomb to be seen (in the ordinary sense of that term) by certain eyewitnesses. In addition to responding to some points Davis raised, I defend my earlier claim that because we lack contemporary descriptions, by the eyewitnesses, of what was later referred to as "seeing Jesus," we have no way to be sure what was involved in the experience to which this phrase refers.

KELLEY, Donald R. What is Happening to the History of Ideas? J Hist Ideas, 51(1), 3-25, Ja-Mr 90.

"What is happening to the history of ideas?" suggests three sub-questions: (1) What has the history of ideas been? This involves a survey of the practice of intellectual history and especially the problem of "the philosophy of the history of philosophy" from the "eclecticism" of the Enlightenment down to that of Arthur O Lovejoy. (2) How has it been written? This question leads to a review of changes in the "history of ideas" in the fifty years since Lovejoy proposed his agenda. (3) What should it be? This question has no answer but opens a discussion of recent attitudes, assumptions, and methods surrounding modern (and "postmodern") issues in philosophy, literary theory, and intellectual, "disciplinary," and cultural history.

KELLEY, S W and FERRELL, O C and SKINNER, S J. Ethical Behavior Among Marketing Researchers: An Assessment of Selected Demographic Characteristics. J Bus Ethics, 9(8), 681-688, Ag 90.

This study considers the relationship between perceptions of ethical behavior and the demographic characteristics of sex, age, education level, job title, and job tenure among a sample of marketing researchers. The findings of this study indicate that female marketing researchers, older marketing researchers, and marketing researchers holding their present job for ten years or more generally rate their behavior as more ethical.

KELLNER, Douglas MacKay (ed) and BRONNER, Stephen Eric (ed). *Critical Theory and Society: A Reader*. New York, Routledge, 1989

This book is an anthology of writings by the most influential members of the "Frankfurt School." The book includes essays by Theodor Adorno, Walter Benjamin, Jürgen Habermas, Max Horkheimer, Herbert Marcuse, and others. Divided into sections dealing with psychology, sociology, cultural criticism, and other areas, this is an interdisciplinary collection which also contains a historical introduction.

KELLNER, Douglas. *Jean Baudrillard: From Marxism to Postmodernism*. Stanford, Stanford Univ Pr, 1989

This book provides the first critical analysis of a theorist who has been identified in recent years with postmodern theory. The text critically dissects the three stages of Baudrillard's development thus far: (1) his early attempt to develop a synthesis of Marxism and semiology in producing a "political economy of the sign" and critical theory of the consumer society; (2) his theory of postmodern society; and (3) the metaphysical turn of the 1980s.

The influence of Marx, Freud, semiology, Bataille, Derrida, McLuhan, and Foucault on Baudrillard's work is noted, as well as his attempts to break with these "references" and to produce his own unique theory. The final chapter presents a critical analysis of the later Baudrillard which is used as a case study of the problems of metaphysics.

KELLY, Christopher (ed & trans) and MASTERS, Roger D (ed & trans) and BUSH, Judith R (trans). *Rousseau, Judge of Jean-Jacques: Dialogues—The Collected Writings of Rousseau, Volume I.* Hanover, Univ Pr New England, 1990

KELLY, Christopher and MASTERS, Roger D. Rousseau on Reading "Jean-Jacques": *The Dialogues.* Interpretation, 17(2), 239-253, Wint 89-90.

KELLY, John Clardy. Virtue and Inwardness in Plato's *Republic.* Ancient Phil, 9 (2), 189-205, Fall 89.

KELLY, Kevin T and GLYMOUR, Clark. Theory Discovery from Data with Mixed Quantifiers. J Phil Log, 19(1), 1-33, F 90.

Convergent realists desire scientific methods that converge reliably to informative, true theories over a wide range of theoretical possibilities. Much attention has been paid to the problem of induction from quantifier-free data. In this paper, we employ the techniques of formal learning theory and model theory to explore the reliable inference of theories from data containing alternating quantifiers. We obtain a hierarchy of inductive problems depending on the quantifier prefix complexity of the formulas that constitute the data, and we provide bounds relating the quantifier prefix complexity of the data to the quantifer prefix complexity of the theories that can be reliably inferred from such data without background knowledge. We also examine the question whether there are theories with mixed quantifiers that can be reliably inferred with closed, universal formulas in the data, but not without.

KELLY, Mary Ann. "Schopenhauer's Influence on Hardy's *Jude the Obscure*" in *Schopenhauer: New Essays in Honor of His 200th Birthday,* VON DER LUFT, Eric (ed), 232-246. Lewiston, Mellen Pr, 1989.

Hardy's reading in Schopenhauer in the years following 1883 appears to have influenced his composition of *Tess of the D'Urbervilles* and *Jude the Obscure.* Close textual analysis reveals that idealistic illusions, irrational compulsions, and an appreciation of Schopenhauerian ethics are woven into both novels, but Hardy's emphasis on Schopenhauer's underlying assumption that "all love...is sympathy" seems demonstrated with particular insistence in *Jude the Obscure.* Injustice to one's fellows apparently became more worthy of condemnation in Hardy's eyes as he assimilated Schopenhauer's ideas.

KELLY, Michael J. Should Competence Be Coerced?: Commentary. Hastings Center Rep, 20(4), 31-32, Jl-Ag 90.

KELLY, Michael. The Gadamer-Habermas Debate Revisited: The Question of Ethics. Phil Soc Crit, 14(3-4), 369-389, 1988.

I investigate the implications of the Gadamer/Habermas debate for philosophical ethics by asking: How is critical ethical reflection possible? I discuss the differences between a conception of ethical reflection partially derived from Gadamer's philosophical hermeneutics and Habermas's recent "discourse ethics" based on the theory of communicative action. In the final section, I explore the possibility of a mediation of these two conceptions of philosophical ethics.

KELLY, Michael. MacIntyre, Habermas, and Philosophical Ethics. Phil Forum, 21(1-2), 70-93, Fall-Wint 89-90.

I first analyze Alasdair MacIntyre's notion of tradition-bound moral-practical rationality. I then contrast MacIntyre's ethics with Jürgen Habermas's "universal proceduralism," arguing that, although MacIntyre's theory seems incompatible with Habermas's, they can in fact be rendered compatible, at least on a methodological level. Finally, I analyze MacIntyre's account of how a tradition develops its rationality by resolving its moral crises, and then discuss the consequences of this account for philosophical ethics.

KELLY, Michaeleen. Commentary on "An Empirical Study of Moral Reasoning Among Managers". J Bus Ethics, 8(11), 863-864, N 89.

Managerial reasoning is characteristic of a care-relationship ethics (1) if a corporation provides certain community values to corporate members not reducible to their self-interested economic or professional objectives; (2) if such values are generated by a division of labor based on interdependence, reciprocity and concern for another's self-realization; (3) if it's based on promoting an ethical corporate self independent of its economic value. Such an ethic is appropriate, given employees' tremendous personal contributions, the unique position of private industry to provide distinctive resources without committing extensive social resources, and due to its potential for reducing managerial moral fragmentation and hypocrisy.

KELLY, P J. Utilitarianism and Distributive Justice: The Civil Law and the

Foundations of Bentham's Economic Thought. Utilitas, 1(1), 62-81, My 89.

KEMP, T Peter. Heidegger's Greatness and his Blindness. Phil Soc Crit, 15(2), 107-124, 1989.

A contribution to the debate about *Heidegger and Nazism.* The author argues, that what is ill-fated about Heidegger's philosophy is not simply that it lacks an ethics, but that it at the same time concerns the whole and lacks an ethics. It was therefore not incompatible with a "hating of strangers" and with an enormous German intellectual arrogance. Heidegger certainly felt himself to be above those who expressed this hate and this arrogance in a more vulgar form, but he could not dissociate himself radically from their way of thinking. (edited)

KENG KAU, A and SWINYARD, W R and RINNE, H. The Morality of Software Piracy: A Cross-Cultural Analysis. J Bus Ethics, 9(8), 655-664, Ag 90.

Software piracy is a damaging and important moral issue, which is widely believed to be unchecked in particular areas of the globe. This cross-cultural study examines differences in morality and behavior toward software piracy in Singapore versus the United States, and reviews the cultural histories of Asia versus the United States to explore why these differences occur. The paper is based upon pilot data collected in the US and Singapore, using a tradeoff analysis methodology and analysis. The data reveal some fascinating interactions between the level of ethical transgression and the rewards of consequences which they produce.

KENNEALY, Peter (trans) and BOBBIO, Norberto. *Democracy and Dictatorship.* Minneapolis, Univ of Minn Pr, 1989

KENNEDY, David. Fools, Young Children and Philosophy. Thinking, 8(4), 2-6, 1990.

Both fool and young child speak the secret language—paradoxical, transcendent babble—of the prelapsarian world. Both fool and child are voices within us, marginalized by adulthood, both bestial and heavenly. The child figure in Western myth, literature and religion is emblematic of the unity of knowledge and being, or aesthetic non-differentiation of subject and object. The child figure's nonsense, like the fool's, stops the world, and throws accepted meanings into question. Insofar as philosophy is an activity which throws all of existence into question while evoking its most fundamental meaning, it is paradigmatic of fools and young children.

KENNEDY, David. Fools, Young Children, Animism, and the Scientific World-Picture. Phil Today, 33(4), 374-381, Wint 89.

Both the historical fool (e.g., Lear's) and the young child are marginal to the adult world-picture. When with the rise of modernism the West switched from the oral/aural, panvital cosmos of the ancient and medieval world to the silent, visual cosmos of literacy, the young child was left behind, in that all the young child's ontological and epistemological convictions—animism, finalism, artificialism—are on the side of the ancients. In the panmechanistic cosmos of the moderns, the young child has become a fool, but also prophet of a world-view that is moving dialectically beyond monistic materialism.

KENNEDY, L A. The Fifteenth Century and Divine Absolute Power. Vivarium, 27(2), 125-152, N 89.

This article proves that a preoccupation with divine absolute power, which began about 1300 and dominated the fourteenth century, was still strong on the eve of the Reformation among Ockhamists and Scotists. The Ockhamists studied are Gabriel Biel, John Major, and James Almain; the Scotists, Nicholas de Orbellis, Paul Scriptoris, and Nicholas Denyse. Their teaching concerning divine absolute power is studied in the physical, intellectual, moral, and supernatural orders. The article also shows that Thomists were almost unaffected by this doctrine and frequently opposed it. The Thomists examined are John Capreolus, Denys the Carthusian, and Cardinal Cajetan.

KENNEDY, Leonard A. Andrew of Novo Castro, OFM, and the Moral Law. Fran Stud, 48(26), 28-39, 1988.

This work illustrates the moral theory of a philosopher who has adopted an extreme doctrine of divine absolute power, a doctrine extremely common in the fourteenth and fifteenth centuries. Andrew teaches that charity is not required for eternal life, that God can deceive us, and that all moral laws (except the necessity of obeying God) are changeable by divine absolute power. His *Commentary on the Sentences* contains the most sustained treatise on the arbitrariness of the moral law which the author has encountered.

KENNEY, Emelie. Cardano: "Arithmetic Subtlety" and Impossible Solutions. Phil Math, 4(2), 195-216, 1989.

Cardano's work on complex numbers created little excitement in his lifetime, yet these objects caused a stir in later generations. This paper examines Cardano's reputation and work in an attempt to clarify why this was the case. A presentation of and commentary on pertinent sections of Cardano's seminal work, the *Ars Magna*, is offered. Cardano is placed in a historic tradition, and the difficulties he experienced with respect to negative numbers are noted. Cardano's explicit expectation that calculations must be useful is emphasized.

KENNEY, Emelie. On the Possibility of Mathematical Revolutions. Phil Math, 5(1-2), 114-123, 1990.

We argue that in mathematics there are no scientific revolutions, in Kuhn's sense. Some ideas do meet with resistance. Indeed, infinitesimals, divergent series, and square roots of negatives were not immediately accepted as legitimate mathematical objects. Their appearance, however, did not throw the mathematical community into an uproar, although square roots of negatives did generate much hostility, particularly in nineteenth century England. Yet the ultimate acceptance of these objects did not cause a replacement of one paradigm by another; rather, mathematics was enriched via new problems and research areas, and the concept of number was enlarged to admit complex numbers.

KERKHOFF, Manfred. Las cuitas de Zarathustra: Algunas publicaciones recientes sobre Friedrich Nietzsche. Dialogos, 25(55), 169-197, Ja 90.

In this review-article I discuss the problems Nietzsche faced with the project of letting Zarathustra die; therefore, I evaluate several theories on the composition of *Thus Spoke Zarathustra*. (Books reviewed, among others: D F Krell, *Postponements*; W B Warner, *Chance and the Text of Experience*; J L Farrell (ed), C G Jung, *Nietzsche's Zarathustra*; L Lampert, *Nietzsche's Teaching*; K G Higgins, *N's Zarathustra*; G Shapiro, *Nietzschean Narratives*.)

KERNOHAN, Andrew. Rawls and the Collective Ownership of Natural Abilities. Can J Phil, 20(1), 19-28, Mr 90.

This article attempts to clarify the meaning of Rawls's claim that, as a consequence of the difference principle, the natural talents of persons are common property. The difference principle assigns different incomes to talents than would be assigned by the market. But there is much more to self-ownership than just a right to charge what the market will bear for the exercise of a talent. Consequently, liberal egalitarian constraints on rewards to talents do not deny self-ownership in a significant way.

KERNOHAN, Andrew. Social Power and Human Agency. J Phil, 86(12), 712-726, D 89.

Definitions of A's power over B frequently appeal to features of A and B as human agents. Steven Lukes defines power in terms of A's affect on B's real interests. Alvin Goldman employs the notion of A's getting what A wants. William Connolly stresses A's responsibility for actions which affect B. The article criticizes these three definitions for being unable to comprehend forms of social power which interfere with autonomous human agency, forms such as nonrational persuasion, cultural normalization and gender formation.

KERR, Fergus. "Idealism and Realism: An Old Controversy Dissolved" in *Christ, Ethics and Tragedy: Essays in Honour of Donald MacKinnon*, SURIN, Kenneth (ed), 15-33. New York, Cambridge Univ Pr, 1989.

KERR-LAWSON, Angus. On Grue and Bleen. Bull Santayana Soc, 1, 12-16, Fall 83.

KERR-LAWSON, Angus. Santayana's Non-Reductive Naturalism. Trans Peirce Soc, 25(3), 229-250, Sum 89.

Santayana was a naturalist, but his materialism was entirely nonreductive; it is strikingly similar to the antireductionist naturalism recently discussed by Strawson. However, Santayana's theory is formulated in ontological terms, rather than in terms of linguistic reductions. It is argued that Santayana's writings are in the same antireductionist spirit as those of Strawson, but are led by the ontological approach to a more radical split from reductive materialism.

KERR-LAWSON, Angus. Santayana's Ontology and the Nicene Creed. Bull Santayana Soc, 7, 26-32, Fall 89.

KERR-LAWSON, Angus. Six Aspects of Santayana's Philosophy. Bull Santayana Soc, 4, 28-33, Fall 86.

KERR-LAWSON, Angus. Spirit's Primary Nature is to be Secondary. Bull Santayana Soc, 2, 9-14, Fall 84.

KERR-LAWSON, Angus. Variations on a Given Theme. Bull Santayana Soc, 5, 34-40, Fall 87.

KERSEY, Ethel M. *Women Philosophers: A Bio-Critical Source Book*. Westport, Greenwood Pr, 1989

This work developed from the discovery that there existed no biographical dictionaries of women philosophers, and few references to women in textbooks on the history of philosophy. Intended to fill that void, the book covers more than 170 women born before 1920 who wrote about or

pondered questions of Western intellectual life. The volume includes extensive bibliographies of both primary and secondary works about each philosopher. An in-depth introduction establishes the context for the reference, and an appendix provides charts showing women philosophers by century, nationality and discipline. An index of names completes the source book.

KERSTEN, G E and BADCOCK, L and IGLEWSKI, M and MALLORY, G R. Structuring and Simulating Negotiation: An Approach and an Example. Theor Decis, 28(3), 243-273, My 90.

Negotiation is a complex and dynamic decision process during which parties' perceptions, preferences, and roles may change. Modeling such a process requires flexible and powerful tools. The use of rule-based formalism is therefore expanded from its traditional expert system type technique, to structuring and restructuring nontrivial processes like negotiation. Using rules, we build a model of a negotiation problem. Some rules are used to infer positions and reactions of the parties, other rules are used to modify problem representation when such a modification is necessary. We illustrate the approach with a contract negotiation case between two large companies. We also show how this approach could help one party to realize that negotiations are being carried on against their assumptions and expectations.

KERSTING, Wolfgang. Hypolepsis und Kompensation—Odo Marquards philosophischer Beitrag zur Diagnose und Bewältigung der Gegenwart. Phil Rundsch, 36(3), 161-186, 1989.

KERSTING, Wolfgang. Eine Theorie der politischen Gerechtigkeit. Z Phil Forsch, 43(3), 472-488, Jl-S 89.

KERTÉSZ, András. Chomsky, Wittgenstein, Bloor: Zum Problem einer wissenssoziologischen Metatheorie der Linguistik. Z Phil Forsch, 44(1), 68-84, 1990.

Starting from what Kripke calls "Wittgenstein's sceptical paradox," the paper raises the question of whether Chomsky's views on language and Wittgenstein's ideas of rule-following are really incompatible. As a result, it is shown that on the background of a sociological interpretation of Wittgenstein's work as put forward by Bloor both the paradox and the alleged contrast between Chomsky and Wittgenstein can be resolved.

KERVEGAN, Jean-Francois. Le problème de la fondation de l'éthique: Kant, Hegel. Rev Metaph Morale, 95(1), 33-55, Ja-Mr 90.

La critique virulente menée par Hegel du formalisme, de l'ineffectivité et du dualisme de la "vision morale du monde", les implications anti-kantiennes de la distinction qu'il fait entre *Moralität* et *Sittlichkeit* ne doivent pas masquer son adhésion fondamentale au principe kantien de l'autonomie de la volonté rationnelle. Un examen de la conception hegelienne de la moralité révèle cette proximité. La philosophie pratique de Hegel apparaît, notamment par l'analyse qu'elle propose de la structure logique de l'action, non pas comme le rejet, mais comme l'expression vraie de la fondation rationnelle de l'éthique entreprise par Kant.

KESE, Ralf. Zur Methodologie und Logik von "Goldene 'Regel"-Argumenten: Eine Gegenposition zu Hoches Hare-Exhaustion. Kantstudien, 81(1), 89-98, 1990.

KESSIDIS, T. Die ethischen Schriften des Aristoteles (in Greek). Philosophia (Athens), 17-18, 325-355, 1987-88.

Im Rahmen einer kurzen Einleitung in die Nikomachische Ethik versucht der verfasser dieses Aufsatzes eine Bewertung der aristotelischen Schrift und ihre Einordnung innerhalb des ganzen Werkes des Aristoteles. Der Aufsatz von Kessidis bezieht sich noch auf die Aristoteles' Kritik an Platons ethischen Idealismus, wobei Aristoteles die objektive Existenz der platonischen Idee des Guten als unnützlich für praktische Gut ablehnt. Der V. findet diese Kritik zum Teil ungerecht und versucht in diesem Punkt Aristoteles und Platon in Einklang zu bringen. (edited)

KETCHUM, Richard J. Parmenides on What There Is. Can J Phil, 20(2), 167-190, Je 90.

Part I provides an original interpretation of the fragments dealing with the way of truth. I interpret "It is," as "What can be thought of is something or other," and "It is not," as "What can be thought of is nothing at all." Thus, the equivalence of "nothing" with "what is not" is sustained and all of fragments 2-7 are either true or highly plausible. Parmenides' mistake occurs in fragment 8 where he confuses "x is not something (or other)," with "x is not anything," in the arguments for changelessness and continuity. In Part II, I compare my interpretation with those of others.

KETCHUM, Sara Ann. Selling Babies and Selling Bodies. Hypatia, 4(3), 116-127, Fall 89.

I will argue the free market in babies or in women's bodies created by an institution of paid surrogate motherhood is contrary to Kantian principles of personhood and to the feminist principle that men do not have—and cannot gain through contract, marriage, or payment of money—a right to the sexual or reproductive use of women's bodies.

KETTNER, Matthias. Hegels "Sinnliche Gewissheit": Diskursanalytischer Kommentar. Frankfurt, Campus, 1990

This study provides a complete sequential analysis and reconstruction of one of Hegel's most important arguments against ontological atomism and for Hegel's "idealistic" views concerning the nonrepresentation base of our epistemic relation to the world. Hegel's opening arguments of the *Phenomenology of Spirit* are critically evaluated against the background of recent discussions about singular demonstrative reference, essential indexical expressions and their referential role, and the impossibility of reference to conceptually bare particulars. The author discerns in Hegel's text on *Sense-Certainty* two lines of arguments, one "dialectical" line concerning the nature of appearance, and another line of arguments which concern language. The author shows that Hegel's "dialectical" analysis of sense-certainty suffers from a theory of language which capitalizes on descriptive word-meaning. Hegel's views on sense-certainty draw on pragmatic features of singular demonstrative reference but fail to theoretically account for these features.

KEYT, David. The Meaning of ΒΙΟΣ in Aristotle's *Ethics* and *Politics*. Ancient Phil, 9 (1), 15-21, Spr 89.

KHAN, Rahat Nabi. Outline of a Doctrine of Aesthetic Education. Diogenes, 147, 111-124, Fall 89.

KHLENTZOS, Drew. Anti-Realism Under Mind? Dialectica, 43(4), 315-328, 1989.

Antirealism claims that the classical or realist conception of truth as verification-transcendent is incoherent. Our grasp of the meanings of statements from any given class is to be assimilated to a grasp of their assertibility or deniability conditions. In this paper I present an apparent counterexample to the antirealist's positive claim which derives from the traditional problem of other minds.

KIAMIE, Kimberly A. Neurophilosophy and the Logic-Causation Argument. Dialogue (PST), 32(2-3), 39-42, Ap 90.

This article covers Patricia Churchland's position on eliminative materialism and her conclusions that all mental states are reducible to brain states. By comparing the points made in the Lewis-Anscombe debate concerning the nature of mental events to Churchland's conclusions, the author finds her position to be generally well founded. However, Churchland's position on reductionism is not as solid as she upholds it to be.

KIBAMBE-KIA-NKIMA, Kapongola. Philosophie, Ideologie et Acteurs Economique en Afrique. Quest, 4(1), 18-41, Je 90.

This article discusses the present social order in Africa. In the opinion of the author, current political, ideological and philosophical issues are intimately related with social and economical realities, determined by the 'dominated capitalist mode of production'. At the level of ideology this is expressed for instance in mystifying political discourse that refuses to use the terms 'exploitation' and 'dependence'. The African continent harbours authentic ideologies which could stimulate economic actors. Practical life shows the significance of these ideologies.

KIBBELAAR, Robert. Homeopathie de optische metafoor van Wiersma. Kennis Methode, 13(3), 333-337, 1989.

KIDD, I G. "Posidonius as Philosopher-Historian" in *Philosophia Togata: Essays on Philosophy and Roman Society*, GRIFFIN, Miriam (ed), 38-50. New York, Clarendon/Oxford Pr, 1989.

KIDDER, Paul. Husserl's Paradox. Res Phenomenol, 17, 227-242, 1987.

As Husserl allows in *The Crisis of the European Sciences and Transcendental Phenomenology*, phenomenology's procedure of rendering everything objective something subjective seems paradoxical: a part of the world seems to be constituting the very whole of which it is part. Husserl attempts to resolve this paradox by distinguishing two kinds of subjectivity: an extramundane, constituting ego; and an intramundane, constituted human being. Gadamer, among others, has criticized this resolution and raises the interesting alternative suggestion that the paradox might not be the sort of thing we should expect or desire to overcome.

KIDDER, Paul. Lonergan's Negative Dialectic. Int Phil Quart, 30(3), 299-309, S 90.

The transcendental pivot of Lonergan's philosophy is to be found in intellectual operations rather than in mental contents or products. To defend such a transcendentalism, one must refute those who would deny the existence, availability, or relevance of the cognitional operations in question. This paper follows the course of Lonergan's refutation, which employs primarily the notion of performative self-contradiction. Lines of

objection to Lonergan's defense are then considered, including a kind of objection that regards Lonergan's elenctic strategy as empty eristic, and a kind that views contradiction as an inevitable phenomenon rather than a corrigible defect.

KIELKOPF, Charles F. "The Classical Logic of Relevant Logicians" in *Directions in Relevant Logic*, NORMAN, Jean (ed), 87-93. Norwell, Kluwer, 1989.

This paper was prepared for a 1974 conference on entailment and relevance preserving implications. It is shown that for every classically valid argument: A therefore B, which is unacceptable in entailment system E, there is an argument: A,T therefore B, with T a classical tautology, which is acceptable in the entailment systems. Since classical logicians regard: A therefore B and A,T therefore B as equivalent, entailment systems do not tell classical logicians that certain arguments, such as disjunctive syllogism, are unacceptable.

KIENZLE, Bertram. Primäre und sekundäre Qualitatäten bei John Locke. Stud Leibniz, 21(1), 21-41, 1989.

KIERNAN, Suzanne. J F Lyotard's The Postmodern Condition and G B Vico's *De nostri temporis studiorum ratione*. New Vico Studies, 4, 101-112, 1986.

The essay explores parallels between two pamphlets written nearly 300 years apart—1708 and 1979—in response to similar exigencies. Both are critiques of a crisis perceived in the institution that in each case gives rise to them—the university. Addressing an audience beyond the institution's confines, both writers see that crisis as symptomatic of a wider crisis in contemporary knowledge. As a corrective to (over-)specialisation, Vico proposes the exercise of fantasy and imagination, and the cultivation of rhetoric ("wisdom dressed in its best finery"). Lyotard valorises "paralogical" thinking and "narrative knowledge." Both authors inquire into the source, transmission, accumulation and "legitimation" of knowledge, and confront the "sublime" as the mind's response to objects of knowledge that it is unable to comprehend.

KILGOUR, D Marc and FANG, Liping and HIPEL, Keith W. A Decision Support System for the Graph Model of Conflicts. Theor Decis, 28(3), 289-311, My 90.

A comprehensive decision support system called GMCA (graph model for conflict analysis) implementing the multi-player graph model for analyzing conflicts is developed. GMCA contains algorithms for the rapid computation of a wide range of solution concepts, thereby enabling decision makers to take account of the diversity of human behavior. Using an engineering case study, the key features of GMCA are illustrated.

KILLINGLEY, D H. Yoga-Sūtra IV, 2-3 and Vivekānanda's Interpretation of Evolution. J Indian Phil, 18(2), 151-179, Je 90.

Swami Vivekananda (1862-1902) held that ancient India had anticipated Darwinian evolution. In this connection he frequently quoted a passage from Patanjali's *Yoga-Sutra*, identifying Patanjali's concept of collective progress. His interpretation, formed in New York in 1895-96, transforms both evolution and yoga; it supports and is motivated by his contrast of spiritual Hinduism with material Western thought. His view of Darwin is coloured by popularizers such as Haeckel.

KILLOUGH, Larry N and BEETS, S Douglas. The Effectiveness of a Complaint-Based Ethics Enforcement System: Evidence from the Accounting Profession. J Bus Ethics, 9(2), 115-126, F 90.

Many professions, in order to enforce their ethics codes, rely on a complaint-based system, whereby persons who observe or discover ethics violations may file a complaint with an authoritative body. The authors assume that this type of system may encourage ethical behavior when practitioners believe that a punishment is likely to result from a failure to adhere to the rules. This perceived likelihood of punishment has three components: detection risk, reporting risk, and sanction risk. A survey of potential violation witnesses related to the accounting profession revealed that the profession's complaint-based enforcement system may not provide practitioners with the necessary disincentive to refrain from code violations.

KILNER, John F. Who Lives? Who Dies?: Ethical Criteria in Patient Selection. New Haven, Yale Univ Pr, 1990

Who should receive lifesaving health care resources as it becomes increasingly clear that all in need cannot? Drawing upon an original study of US medical directors, cross-cultural research in Kenya, and numerous case studies, the author probes the justifications and weaknesses of sixteen criteria such as the patient's value to society, age, ability to pay, and quality of life. Other criteria examined include types of medical, social, and personal criteria. The book concludes with a chapter proposing a particular set of criteria, followed by extensive notes and references to most of the literature in the field.

KILVINGTON, Richard and KRETZMANN, Norman and KRETZMANN, Barbara Ensign. *The Sophismata of Richard Kilvington.* New York, Cambridge Univ Pr, 1990

Richard Kilvington was a 14th-century English philosopher, one of the "Oxford Calculators." His *Sophismata* is a subtly ordered series of 48 philosophical puzzles designed to raise and settle issues in natural philosophy (having to do with change, motive power, velocity, or strength) and in epistemology. This volume contains a historical introduction, an English translation, and a philosophical commentary. A companion volume (published by Oxford for the British Academy) contains the edition of the Latin text, based on 20 manuscripts.

KIM, Jaegwon. Supervenience as a Philosophical Concept. Metaphilosophy, 21(1-2), 1-27, Ja-Ap 90.

The first part of the paper traces the evolution of the supervenience concept (including a discussion of its relation to the concept of "emergence"), and reviews the recent literature concerning this concept. In the second part, the following three aspects of supervenience are distinguished and discussed: supervenience as a relation of property covariance, supervenience as a dependency relation, and supervenience as a nonreductive relation. The problem of "explaining" specific supervenience claims is also discussed.

KIMMERLE, Heinz. The Question of Relevance in Current Nigerian Philosophy. Quest, 4(1), 66-73, Je 90.

The question of relevance of philosophical work is asked everywhere at any time. In current Nigerian philosophy it is connected with the problem whether African traditional thought forms an important or even necessary contribution to the philosophical work in Africa today. Sogolo sees a dilemma between "Africanists" and "Western orientated philosophers," because the first group claims relevance, but remains "descriptive." Bodunrin argues that relevance and a high standard of philosophy also in Africa can be combined.

KINCAID, Harold. Defending Laws in the Social Sciences. Phil Soc Sci, 20(1), 56-83, Mr 90.

This article defends laws in the social sciences. Arguments against social laws are considered and rejected based on the "open" nature of social theory, the multiple realizability of social predicates, the macro and/or teleological nature of social laws, and the inadequacies of belief-desire psychology. The more serious problem that social laws are usually qualified ceteris paribus is then considered. How the natural sciences handle ceteris paribus laws is discussed and it is argued that such procedures are possible in the social sciences. The article ends by arguing that at least some social research is roughly as well as confirmed as good work in evolutionary biology and ecology.

KINCAID, Harold. Eliminativism and Methodological Individualism. Phil Sci, 57(1), 141-148, Mr 90.

Tuomela (this issue, pp. 96-103) raises several objections to the analysis and critique of methodological individualism in my paper, "Reduction, Explanation and Individualism" (*Phil Sci* 53, 1986). In what follows I reply to those criticisms, arguing, among other things, that (1) the alleged reductions provided by Tuomela and others fail, because they either presuppose rather than eliminate social predicates or do not avoid the problem of multiple realizations; (2) supervenience does not guarantee that the social sciences are reducible, because merely describing supervenience bases leaves numerous questions unanswered, and (3) the eliminativism that Tuomela favors verges on being self-refuting and is highly implausible short of a detailed empirical critique of the social sciences, something Tuomela does not provide and something there is little reason to think can be provided. (edited)

KINCZEWSKI, Kathryn. "Is Deconstruction an Alternative?" in *The Textual Sublime: Deconstruction and Its Differences*, SILVERMAN, Hugh J (ed), 13-22. Albany, SUNY Pr, 1990.

In this paper I address the implicit notion of choice between one school of literary criticism over another. In the imaginary encounter staged between two leading theoreticians of the day, Paul de Man appears more than somewhat relieved to finally be able to identify Michael Riffaterre's blind spot. In the shift from a stylistics to a semiotics to a hermeneutics of reading, Riffaterre has never in fact left behind his own critique of semiotics. Nor can Paul de Man. Originally written in 1982, this essay traces the path that de Man's posthumous writings on the aesthetic ideology were to follow.

KING, Alexander. Adam Schaff and the Club of Rome. Dialec Hum, 16(2), 5-10, Spr 89.

KING, Jonathan and BELLA, David. Common Knowledge of the Second Kind. J Bus Ethics, 8(6), 415-430, Je 89.

Although most of us "know" that human beings cannot and should not be replaced by computers, we have great difficulties saying why this is so. This paradox is largely the result of institutionalizing several fundamental misconceptions as to the nature of both trustworthy "objective" and "moral" knowledge. Unless we transcend this paradox, we run the increasing risks of becoming very good at counting without being able to say what is worth counting and why. The degree to which this is occurring is the degree to which the computer revolution is already over—and the degree to which we human beings have lost.

KING, Preston. Justifying Tolerance. Hist Polit Thought, 10(4), 733-743, Wint 89.

KING, Richard. *Sūnyatā and Ajāti*: Absolutism and the Philosophies of Nāgārjuna and Gaudapāda. J Indian Phil, 17(4), 385-405, D 89.

Gaudapāda aligns himself with the Vedāntic tradition in that he attributes a permanent self (*ātman*) or essence (*svabhāva*) to reality, but has clearly been influenced by Mādhyamika arguments. In chapter 24 of the *Mūla-Madhyamaka-kārikā* Nāgārjuna outlines the absolutistic consequences of essentialism (*svabhāva-vāda*). The contrasting perspectives of Nājārjuna and Gaudapāda can be seen in their attempts to reconcile the incompatibility of the notion that one can have an entity which has an essence yet is still capable of change. Nāgārjuna rejects the "essentialist" view as absolutistic (i.e., denying change), while Gaudapāda rejects the idea of change, opting for an absolutistic "essentialism."

KING-FARLOW, John and COOPER, W E. A Case for Capital Punishment. J Soc Phil, 20(3), 64-76, Wint 89.

Independent from the standard deterrence and retributivist considerations, capital punishment might be justified by linking it to the saving of innocent lives.

KISIEL, Chester (trans) and PLUZANSKI, Tadeusz and KISIEL, Krystyna (trans). The Dialogue of Grand Theories for Peace. Dialec Hum, 14(1), 173-184, Wint 87.

KISIEL, Krystyna (trans) and PLUZANSKI, Tadeusz and KISIEL, Chester (trans). The Dialogue of Grand Theories for Peace. Dialec Hum, 14(1), 173-184, Wint 87.

KISIELEWICZ, Andrzej and DUDEK, Józef. On Finite Models of Regular Identities. Notre Dame J Form Log, 30(4), 624-628, Fall 89.

It is a known result of Austin that there exist nonregular identities with all nontrivial models being infinite. In this note a certain analogue of this result for regular identities is presented and some remarks in this connection are given.

KISS, Endre. A Continuation of Christianity (in Serbo-Croatian). Filozof Istraz, 30(3), 843-849, 1989.

Durch die Erörterung der Nietzscheschen zweideutigen Beurteilung der Französischen Revolution kommt der Verfasser zum wohl offen paradoxen Schluss, dass die Französische Revolution Nietzsche überhaupt nicht um ihrer selbst willen interessierte, sondern als eine Station in der Entwicklung einer Einstellung, die er—als logische Konsequenz seiner ganzen Philosophie—als seine grösste Feindin ansah. So erwies sich dieses grösste Ereignis seines jahrhunderts für den Denker des nächsten Dezenniums bloss als Epiphänomen: *Fortsetzung des Christentums durch die Französische Revolution.* Der Verführer ist *Rousseau*.

KITCHER, Philip. Developmental Decomposition and the Future of Human Behavioral Ecology. Phil Sci, 57(1), 96-117, Mr 90.

I attempt to complement my earlier critiques of human sociobiology, by offering an account of how evolutionary ideas might legitimately be employed in the study of human social behavior. The main emphasis of the paper is the need to integrate studies of proximate mechanisms and their ontogenesis with functional/evolutionary research. Human psychological complexity makes it impossible to focus simply on specific types of human behavior and ask for their functional significance. For any of the kinds of behavior patterns that have occupied human sociobiologists, the underlying proximate mechanisms are very likely to be linked to a broad spectrum of types of behavior, and we cannot expect that natural selection will have acted directly on any individual element from this spectrum. I illustrate this general point with a specific example, considering the traditional sociobiological account of human incest-avoidance and outlining an alternative approach to the phenomena. The example is intended to show the possibility of a more rigorous and sophisticated successor to human sociobiology, which I call "human behavioral ecology."

KITCHER, Philip. The Division of Cognitive Labor. J Phil, 87(1), 5-22, Ja 90.

KITCHER, Philip. "Explanatory Unification and the Causal Structure of the World" in *Scientific Explanation (Minnesota Studies in the Philosophy of Science, Volume XIII)*, KITCHER, Philip (ed), 410-505. Minneapolis, Univ of Minn Pr, 1989.

KITCHER, Philip and STERELNY, Kim and WATERS, C Kenneth. The Illusory Riches of Sober's Monism. J Phil, 87(3), 158-161, Mr 90.

KITCHER, Philip. Innovation and Understanding in Mathematics. J Phil, 86(10), 563-564, O 89.

KITCHER, Philip (ed) and SALMON, Wesley C (ed). *Scientific Explanation (Minnesota Studies in the Philosophy of Science, Volume XIII)*. Minneapolis, Univ of Minn Pr, 1989

KIVINEN, S Albert. Apocalyptic Anticipations. Acta Phil Fennica, 38, 79-90, 1985.

KIVY, Peter. "How Music Moves" in *What is Music?*, ALPERSON, Philip A , 147-163. New York, Haven, 1987.

Those who think listening to music is a moving experience think that it moves in virtue of arousing in listeners the emotions that it is expressive of: anger, fear, joy, melancholy and the like—what I call the garden-variety emotions. Others deny that music can arouse the garden-variety emotions, and hence tend to be seen as denying that listening to music can be a moving experience. I argue in the present paper that music cannot arouse the garden-variety emotions, except in aesthetically irrelevant ways, but that, nevertheless, listening to music is a moving experience.

KIVY, Peter. A New Music Criticism? Monist, 73(2), 247-268, Ap 90.

I try to show in this paper that expressive properties, like other musical properties, can and often do function as part of the syntactical structure of music. I argue that it makes a big syntactical difference whether, for example, a musical resolution goes from the dark side of the musical spectrum to the light side or from light to light.

KIZILTAN, Mustafa Ü and BAIN, William J and CAÑIZARES, Anita. Postmodern Conditions: Rethinking Public Education. Educ Theor, 40(3), 351-369, Sum 90.

In the first section, within a framework modeled after Foucault's theory of discourse and Lyotard's analysis of the postmodern condition, we reconceptualize "public education" and outline the structure of a postmodern problematic. From this standpoint, the challenge of postmodernity lies in its destabilization of the metanarratives of modernity which have long sustained public education, the imminent postmodern fallout being the fracture and the dislocation of public education as a discursive formation. In the second section, we reconsider the idea of enlightenment and reconstitute it through the principle of "limit-attitude." We propose a transgressive mode of thought as the basis for public education.

KLARER, Mario. Der Zwang zur "geschlossenen Gesellschaft"—Ein perennes Dilemma der Utopie? Conceptus, 23(60), 37-49, 1989.

In their utopian works *Politeia* and *Walden Two*, Plato and Skinner advocate a "closed society," which they try to reach and maintain through analogous strategies. The most dominant feature of the two utopias certainly is education, which directly or indirectly all other themes depend on: for example, steps that precede education per se (including eugenics, birth and marriage control, and the loosening or abolition of family ties), as well as proposals for social stratification together with thoughts on how to maintain stable classes, and finally the discussion of freedom and laws. This article juxtaposes these thematic areas of both works in a formal analysis and tries to point out crucial analogies in their deep structures.

KLEIN, H D. Philosophy of the Present: An Attempt at a Conceptual Specification (in Czechoslovakian). Filozof Cas, 37(6), 877-886, 1989.

KLEIN, Horst. Bemerkungen zum Begriff "Austromarxismus". Deut Z Phil, 37(9), 853-859, 1989.

Mit dem Begriff "Austromarxismus" verbinden sich unterschiedliche Vorstellungen vom Marxismusverständnis. Vor dem ersten Weltkrieg galt er als Synonym für "marxistisches Denken in Österreich" bzw. "österreichische Marxisten", bezogen auf O Bauer, M Adler, R Hilferding u.a., die einen wertvollen Beitrag für die Entwicklung der marxistischen Theorie leisteten. Es kann jedoch nicht vom Begriff auf das Denken bezeichneter Theoretiker geschlossen werden, da dieses sehr unterschiedlich war. Seit den 2oer Jahren wurde der Begriff von der stalinistischen Dogmatik mit Revisionismus und Opportunismus gleichgesetzt. Desungeachtet gehört der "Austromarxismus" zum Kulturgut der internationalen Arbeiterbewegung.

KLEIN, J Theodore. Nuclear Deterrence, Character, and Moral Education. Proc Phil Educ, 45, 388-391, 1989.

This response to Love's paper on morality and nuclear deterrence interprets Love as heavily weighing corruption of character among the moral costs of involvement in nuclear deterrence. Love recommends temporarily continuing nuclear deterrence while seeking extrication from it. While being in agreement with much in Love's paper, this response questions whether the proposed alternative is a better option than unilateral disarmament in all situations. The response also suggests somewhat different views of morality and character from those developed in Love's paper.

KLEIN, J Theodore. Teaching and Mother Love. Educ Theor, 39(4), 373-383, Fall 89.

The paper claims that the practice of mother love well provides an ideal for teaching. Mother love is distinguished from gender associations and from other kinds of love, and an analogy between teaching and mothering is explored. Emphasized in the account of mother love are the balancing of preservation and growth interests, and the virtue of attentiveness. Mother love, when practiced well, is seen as taking into account students' vulnerability, distancing from self, and responding inclusively. Support is given to the view that it is good for teachers to practice mother love well.

KLEIN, Martha. *Determinism, Blameworthiness and Deprivation*. New York, Clarendon/Oxford Pr, 1990

This book is designed to cast new light on the debate, between compatibilists and incompatibilists, about moral responsibility and determinism. The author explores the relationship between deprivation and desert, argues that the traditional view of the debate—as one which centres on the could-have-acted-otherwise condition—should be abandoned, and suggests acceptance of a *new* compatibilist approach which will meet the needs of justice more fully than the usual proposals from either side.

KLEIN, Martha. Morality and Justice in Kant. Ratio, 3(1), 1-20, Je 90.

Kant's puzzling claims about duty, inclination and moral motivation have been said to spring from a commitment to justice. But his *explicit* arguments contain no references to justice. In this paper, it is argued that Kant provides three *implicit* arguments, involving problems of justice, to which his claims can be seen as attempted solutions. It is also argued that we can solve these problems without resorting, as Kant does, to the belief that duty-inspired motivation has its source in a noumenal world. The solution proposed involves using one aspect of Kant's conception of duty in a radically non-Kantian way.

KLEIN, Sherwin. Is a Moral Organization Possible? Bus Prof Ethics J, 7(1), 51-73, Spr 88.

KLEIN, Sherwin. Platonic Virtue Theory and Business Ethics. Bus Prof Ethics J, 8(4), 59-82, Wint 89.

Difficulties in the standard use of ethical theory (teleological and deontological) in business ethics are examined. This position is, then, contrasted with a Platonic (virtue-based) approach. The value of the Platonic view in ethically evaluating corporate cultures, analyzing business virtue, and in addressing what is probably our deepest problem in business ethics is emphasized.

KLEINER, Scott A. Hypothetical and Inductive Heuristics. Philosophica, 45(1), 77-113, 1990.

As a method for conceptual innovation, abduction is found wanting because explanatory power is no indicator of truth unless the explanation is in already credible terms. Inductive extension of concepts between domains of established similarity, as found in Newton's *vera causa* method, was successfully applied by Darwin in inventing natural selection and is flexible and efficacious as a heuristic for conceptualization.

KLEINJANS, Everett. The Tao of Women and Men: Chinese Philosophy and the Women's Movement. J Chin Phil, 17(1), 99-127, Mr 90.

KLEMM, David E. Levinas's Phenomenology of the Other and Language as the Other of Phenomenology. Man World, 22(4), 403-426, D 89.

KLENK, Virginia. *Understanding Symbolic Logic (Second Edition)*. Englewood Cliffs, Prentice-Hall, 1989

KLEVER, W N A. Gravity (in Dutch). Tijdschr Filosof, 52(2), 280-314, Je 90.

Gravity was a major theme in the seventeenth century scientific discussion. Trendsetters in the renewal of natural science were Galilei and Descartes. The first required a unified theory of all phenomena of gravity; the second provided one with his vortex-hypothesis, which explained gravity by the mechanical push of subtile bodies of the vortex. This conception was tested and generally followed by Christiaan Huygens, whereas Newton presented the laws of the so-called 'attraction' by which he did not at all indicate the causes of those laws of motion. Spinoza comes on the scene of polemics as a critical Cartesian. Motion was explained by Descartes, but not so the rest of bodies or the equilibrium in the power relation between opposite forces, neither the reason why in some cases the particles form a hard body. Full-fledged mechanism and consistent determinism led Spinoza to account for rest and solidity in the same way, namely by means of the pressure of small mostly invisible bodies in the whirling environment. (edited)

KLEVER, W N A. Moles in Motu: Principles of Spinoza's Physics. Stud Spinozana, 4, 165-194, 1988.

Spinoza is known as a philosopher. But close reading of all his texts shows that physics is more than marginal in his work. Cartesian physics is taken over, but also criticised for its irrational and metaphysical components. Major differences are that according to Spinoza motion is constitutive for matter, that bodies represent a quantity of motion, that the unity of bodies is the effect of pressure, that besides motion also rest is paid for; further one finds elements of a theory of equilibrium and of general relativity. This physics provides a format for modern developments.

KLEVER, W N A. "The Properties of the Intellect" in *Dialectic and Contemporary Science*, GRIER, Philip T (ed), 161-177. Lanham, Univ Pr of America, 1989.

The last paragraph (198) of Spinoza's unfinished *Treatise on the Emendation of the Intellect* enumerates its properties, instead of giving a definition. Analysis of this collection of properties and their comparison with other texts shows the crucial value of this much neglected passage and offers a key for the interpretation of the whole treatise, including the problem of why it remained unfinished.

KLEVER, Wim. Spinoza in Poetry. Stud Spinozana, 5, 81-102, 1989.

The analysis of Spinoza-poems written by his friends (Balling, Bouwmeester and Bronckhorst), by later authors (Saint-Evremond, Herder, Schiller, Voltaire, Von Stein, Nietzsche) and by twentieth century poets (Babits, Borges, Verwey, Sachs, Artaud, Zweig, Celan, Achterberg and others) shows the details (essentials in the perception, imagery in expression) of Spinoza's presence in world literature.

KLIJNSMIT, Anthony J. The Problem of Normativity Solved or Spinoza's Stand in the Analogy/Anomaly Controversy. Stud Spinozana, 4, 305-314, 1988.

KLIVAR, Miroslav. Technic Aesthetics as Science (in Czechoslovakian). Estetika, 27(1), 35-42, 1990.

KLOCKENBUSCH, Reinald. *Husserl und Cohn: Widerspruch, Reflexion, und Telos in Phanomenologie und Dialektik*. Norwell, Kluwer, 1989

Das Buch ist eine kritisch-systematische Untersuchung der Phänomenologie Edmund Husserls und der Dialektik Jonas Cohns. Unter Hinzuziehung der "Theorie der Dialektik" Cohns arbeitet der Verfasser bezüglich der "Formalen und transzendentalen Logik" Husserls heraus, dass teleologische Strukturen dem Programm einer "Kritik der logischen Vernunft" immanent sind, wie dies in ähnlicher Weise für die Dialektik des Freiburger Neukantianers Cohn gilt. Bei der Frage, ob trotz der Konvergenz beider philosophischen Konzepte die jeweiligen Logikverständnisse und Methoden inkompatibel sind, wird ausführlich auf die Bedeutung von "widersprüchen" für die Dialektik bei Cohn, andererseits auf die "Kritik des Satzes vom Widerspruch" durch Husserl und das Problem möglicher Paradoxien in der Phänomenologie eingegangen. Der Verfasser kommt zu einem neuartigen ("entscheidungstheoretischen") Lösungsansatz bezüglich des "Problems des transzendentalen Psychologismus" und des damit zusammenhängenden "Paradoxons der Subjektivität". (edited)

KLOESEL, Christian J W (ed) and PEIRCE, Charles S. *Writings of Charles S Peirce: A Chronological Edition, Volume 4, 1879-1884*. Bloomington, Indiana Univ Pr, 1989

KLOSKO, George. Parfit's Moral Arithmetic and the Obligation to Obey the Law. Can J Phil, 20(2), 191-213, Je 90.

Though consequentialist theories of political obligation have been widely criticized, a series of arguments presented by Derek Parfit are now believed to have given this position new life. Parfit's presentation, which is intended to correct "five mistakes in moral mathematics," can be extended to account for the most central of our political obligations, the obligation to obey the law. This paper takes a closer look at Parfit's moral arithmetic and attempts to demonstrate the continuing difficulties with consequentialist theories of political obligation.

KLOSKO, George. Political Obligation and Gratitude. Phil Pub Affairs, 18(4), 352-358, Fall 89.

A D M Walker's recent attempt to ground political obligations upon a principle of gratitude ("Political Obligation and the Argument from Gratitude," *Philosophy and Public Affairs*, 17, 1988) is subject to criticism. Most important, Walker's position appears to be unable to meet an important criterion that theories of political obligation should satisfy that political obligations be sufficiently strong to require compliance with the onerous burdens of citizenship.

KLUBACK, William. *Discourses on the Meaning of History*. New York, Lang, 1988

KLUBACK, William. *Folly and Intelligence in Political Thought*. New York, Lang, 1990

KLUGE, Eike-Henner W. Designated Organ Donation: Private Choice in Social Context. Hastings Center Rep, 19(5), 10-16, S-O 89.

KLUNK, Brian E. "Moral Reasoning in the Bishops' Pastoral Letter on War and Peace" in *Moral Reasoning and Statecraft: Essays Presented to Kenneth W Thompson*, DAVIS, Reed M (ed), 151-164. Lanham, Univ Pr of America, 1988.

KMIECIK, Witold (trans) and BOLTUC, Piotr. In the Beginning Was the Contradiction: Problems of the Philosophy of Subject and Object. Dialec Hum, 15(3-4), 177-185, Sum-Autumn 88.

Knowledge in the modern period is based on two perspectives. The first is the perspective of the subject; it leads to the philosophy of the cogito, the bundle theory, the sense-data theory, etc. The second is the perspective of the object; it leads to uncritical materialism and takes the primitiveness of the world of objects for granted. For it, subjectivity is not reducible to objecthood. I argue that these two perspectives are not contradictory but complementary to each other and represent two sides of the knowledge we have. But I do not reject the monism if developed in a non-(post)modern epistemological perspective.

KNAPPE, Ulrich. Theoretische und methodologische Probleme der Erforschung und Propagierung der Geschichte. Deut Z Phil, 37(10-11), 1040-1043, 1989.

Am 27.April 1989 fand in Berlin(Ost) ein Kolloquium aus Anlass des 100.Jahrestages der Gründung der II.Internationale statt. *Referat*: Die Geschichte der marxistischen Philosophie ist widersprüchlich und von Bedeutung für das Erkennen gesellschaftstheoretischer Probleme der Gegenwart. Philosophische Auffassungen von R Luxemburg, K Liebknecht, O Bauer, G Lukacs, K Kautsky und N Bucharin wurden vorgestellt (siehe: Philosophie für eine neue Welt. Berlin 1989). *Diskussion*: steilnehmer aus der Sowjetunion, der BRD, der DDR, der Ungarischen Vr. *Probleme*: Verknüpfung marxistischen und nichtmarxistischen Denkens; Klassen-und allgemeinmenschliche Interessen; Leninismus; Weiterentwicklung und Abkehr vom Marxismus in der II. und III. Internationale; Auseinandersetzung mit dem "strukturalistischen Marxismus".

KNASAS, John F X. Transcendental Thomism and the Thomistic Texts. Thomist, 54(1), 81-95, Ja 90.

Some time ago Fr. Joseph Donceel published an unchallenged article alleging that American Thomism was too *a posteriori* in its appreciation of Aquinas's metaphysical stance. Donceel counters by spotlighting various Thomistic texts that speak of an *a priori* contribution of the intellect to human knowledge. The texts cited by Donceel are all found in Maréchal's *Cahier V*. There Maréchal mentions many others besides. By employing the Maréchalian collection, I seek to determine if Aquinas is an *a priorist*. The texts include De Ver. I, 4, ad 5m; De Ver. XXII, 2 ad 1m; S.T. I, 84, 5; S.T. I, 88, 3c; De Ver. X, 6c; In IV Meta. lect. 6; S.T. I, 84, 6c; C.G. I, 43.

KNAUER, James T. Hannah Arendt on Judgment, Philosophy and Praxis. Int Stud Phil, 21(3), 71-83, 1989.

Arendt's theory of judgment illuminates the problematic relationship between mind and action in her thought. In particular, it reveals that The Life of the Mind was not a turning from the *vita activa* to the *vita contemplativa*. Instead, in her last work Arendt continued to argue that our humanity arises out of a world-building activity in which appearance is primary and the disinterestedness of the theorist is grounded in that of the political actor. *The Life of the Mind* shows more clearly than before that acting and judging are two moments in the praxis of human community.

KNEE, Christopher and FARWELL, Ruth. The End of the Absolute: A Nineteenth-Century Contribution to General Relativity. Stud Hist Phil Sci, 21(1), 91-121, Mr 90.

This paper considers the geometric ideas of Riemann and Clifford in the latter half of the nineteenth century and their philosophical implications. Both are credited with the anticipation of certain aspects of general relativity: Riemann's work centred on the *nature* of physical space, whereas Clifford suggested *using* the geometry of physical space to describe a theory of all physical quantities. The latter thus proposed the geometrisation of physics, a new philosophy which was to lie at the heart of general relativity in 1916 and underlie subsequent developments in theoretical physics.

KNEE, Philip. Le cercle et le doublet: Note sur Sartre et Foucault. Philosophiques, 17(1), 113-126, 1990.

This paper suggests two possible directions for a dialogue between Sartre and Foucault: a reading of the Sartrean ambivalences on the subject, morality and politics in the light of the characterization of the modern épistémè in *The Order of Things*; and, inversely, a critical approach of the Foucaldian conception of power and knowledge through the anthropology of the *Critique of Dialectical Reason*.

KNELLER, Jane. Imaginative Freedom and the German Enlightenment. J Hist Ideas, 51(2), 217-232, Ap-Je 90.

This paper argues that Kant's account of imaginative freedom suggests the possibility that political and moral progress may be intimately connected with our ability to make universally valid aesthetic judgments. For his own moral theory, it suggests a solution to the difficult problem of how reason can command us to strive to bring about the highest good—a moral world—on earth. Given the possibilities that Kant's aesthetic theory hold out to morality, the former may be seen as a missing link between earlier Enlightenment views on the didactic nature of art and later views such as Schiller's on aesthetic education.

KNEZEVICH, Lily. Truthmongering: An Exercise. Can J Phil, 19(4), 603-609, D 89.

Arthur Fine has motivated his natural ontological attitude by developing several arguments against both realist and antirealist conceptions of truth. This "curse on both your houses" approach vilifies antirealist attempts to analyze truth as "truthmongering." In this paper I distinguish three arguments in Fine's work against a Putnam-style analysis of truth in terms of ideal rational acceptability. I then proceed to offer refutations of these arguments, my contention being that in each of his arguments, Fine is either committing an epistemic fallacy, or relying on a very awkward and unacceptable doctrine of the significance of theorizing about truth. Finally, I suggest a more liberalized notion of what analysis itself is about utilizing the Carnapian notion of explication.

KNIGHT, J F and ASH, C J. Pairs of Recursive Structures. Annals Pure Applied Log, 46(3), 211-234, Ap 90.

Many constructions concerning recursive functions involve constructing a uniformly recursive sequence, A_n, of structures such that, for each n, A_n is isomorphic to the given structure B_n or C_n according to where n is or is not in a given (non-recursive) set S. This paper considers an obviously necessary condition, involving recursive infinitary sentences of the ordinal complexity corresponding to the position of the set S in Kleene's hyperarithmetical hierarchy, and proves that this condition is also sufficient, subject to various further reasonable recursive assumptions. These converses require technically advanced methods of recursion theory previously developed by the authors.

KNIGHT, James W and CALLAHAN, Joan C. Preventing Birth: Contemporary Methods and Related Moral Controversies. Salt Lake City, Univ of Utah Pr, 1989

Written to contribute to the public understanding of contemporary birth control methods and the moral issues surrounding these methods, this work includes detailed descriptions of reproductive anatomy and physiology, methods ranging from sophisticated "rhythm" techniques to induced abortion, and detailed discussions of moral issues such as elective abortion, holding women legally liable for fetal harm, reroductive harm in the workplace, national funding for birth control research, and international family planning policies.

KNOBLOCK, John (trans) and XUNZI,. Xunzi: A Translation and Study of the Complete Works, Volume II—Books 7-16. Stanford, Stanford Univ Pr, 1990

KNORR, Wilbur R. The Practical Element in Ancient Exact Sciences. Synthese, 81(3), 313-328, D 89.

When ancient mathematical treatises lack expositions of numerical techniques, what purposes could ancient mathematical theories be expected to serve? Ancient writers only rarely address questions of this sort directly. Possible answers are suggested by surveying geometry, mechanics, optics, and spherics to discover how the mathematical treatments imply positions on this issue. This survey shows the ways in which these ancient theoretical inquiries reflect practical activity in their fields. This account, in turn, suggests that the authors may have intended their theorems not to predict, but to explain phenomena. We may then consider what kind of explanations they were seeking.

KNOUSE, Stephen B and GIACALONE, Robert A. Justifying Wrongful Employee Behavior: The Role of Personality in Organizational Sabotage. J Bus Ethics, 9(1), 59-61, Ja 90.

The role that personality plays in the justification of organizational sabotage behavior was examined. In a two-phase study, 120 business students were first surveyed to create a list of 51 methods of sabotage. In the second phase, 274 other business students rated justifiability of the 51 methods and completed Machiavellian and hostility scales. A factor analysis of the justification ratings yielded four factors: (1) methods of sabotaging company profits and production, (2) informational sabotage, (3) violent and illegal methods, and (4) traditional labor methods of sabotage. A 2 (high versus low Machiavellianism) x 2 (high versus low hostility) ANOVA upon factor scores for justifiability revealed significant main effects for hostility and significant interactive effects on Factors 1 and 2. Results were discussed in terms of differences in management and blue collar methods of sabotage and in terms of a self-presentational approach to justification of sabotage.

KOCH, Donald F. Recipes, Cooking, and Conflict: A Response to Heldke's Recipes for Theory. Hypatia, 5(1), 156-164, Spr 90.

This paper contends that Heldke's recipe analogy can be reworked to help us deal with those who hold beliefs and practice activities that are contrary to our own. It draws upon the work of William James and John Dewey to develop a practical approach to such conflict situations.

KOCH, Philip J. Solitude in Ancient Taoism. Diogenes, 148, 78-91, Wint 89.

KOCKELMANS, Joseph J. "The Founders of Phenomenology and Personalism" in Reading Philosophy for the Twenty-First Century, MC LEAN, George F (ed), 161-212. Lanham, Univ Pr of America, 1989.

KOCKELMANS, Joseph J. "Hermeneutics and Modern Art" in Cultural Hermeneutics of Modern Art: Essays in Honor of Jan Aler, DETHIER, Hubert (ed), 39-58. Amsterdam, Rodopi, 1989.

In this essay the criticism which hermeneuticists of the classical tradition have levelled against hermeneutic phenomenology is discussed critically insofar as such a discussion is directly relevant to modern art. It is argued that hermeneutic phenomenology rejects the metaphysical assumptions on which both the classical hermeneutic theory and the classical treatises on aesthetics rest. This criticism implies that in some instances the meaning of the hermeneutic canons is to be reinterpreted accordingly.

KOCKELMANS, Joseph J. Idealization and Projection in the Empirical Sciences: Husserl versus Heidegger. Hist Phil Quart, 6(4), 365-380, O 89.

The article describes what according to Husserl on the one hand and Heidegger on the other is constitutive for the scientificity of the empirical sciences. The essay focuses mainly on the natural sciences and shows in particular how both authors try to avoid the problem of indiction.

KOFMAN, Sarah and KAPLAN, Caren (trans). "'Ça cloche'" in Derrida and Deconstruction, SILVERMAN, Hugh J (ed), 108-138. New York, Routledge, 1989.

KOFMAN, Sarah and STRONG, Tracy B (trans). "Baubô: Theological Perversion and Fetishism" in Nietzsche's New Seas: Explorations in Philosophy, Aesthetics, and Politics, GILLESPIE, Michael Allen (ed), 175-202. Chicago, Univ of Chicago Pr, 1989.

Nietzsche is not only not a misogynist but in fact presents us with a profound new understanding of woman. Whereas perversion and degeneracy may seem attached to the feminine in Nietzsche's thought, Nietzsche also recognizes that seduction is the art of Dionysos. The affirmative woman, like Nietzsche's art itself, is profound in her superficiality and is a reflection of ascending life.

KOFMAN, Sarah. "Beyond Aporia" in Post-Structuralist Classics, BENJAMIN, Andrew (ed), 7-44. New York, Routledge, 1988.

KOGAN, Barry S. "'What Can We Know and When Can We Know It': On the Active Intelligence and Human Cognition" in Moses Maimonides and His Time, ORMSBY, Eric L (ed), 121-137. Washington, Cath Univ Amer Pr, 1989.

KOGAN, Barry S. "The Problem of Creation in Late Medieval Jewish Philosophy" in A Straight Path: Studies in Medieval Philosophy and Culture, LINK-SALINGER, Ruth (ed), 159-173. Washington, Cath Univ Amer Pr, 1988.

KOHL, Marvin. Skepticism and Happiness. Free Inq, 10(3), 40-47, Sum 90.

Truthfulness may demand that we be agnostic skeptics, but it does not follow that happiness demands the same thing. Not only does affective happiness often demand little by way of truth but even reflective happiness often requires that we do not believe it is wrong to believe anything upon insufficient evidence. For there is a substantial amount of evidence indicating that some illusions (and I suspect some false beliefs) promote mental health, including the ability to be happy.

KOHLI, Wendy. Engaging the New Literacy: A "Way In" to Philosophy of Education. Proc Phil Educ, 45, 183-186, 1989.

KOHLS, John and CHAPMAN, Christi and MATHIEU, Casey. Ethics Training Programs in the Fortune 500. Bus Prof Ethics J, 8(2), 55-72, Sum 89.

KOLARSKY, R and SMAJS, J. Philosophy and the Devastation of the Earth (in Czechoslovakian). Filozof Cas, 37(5), 617-623, 1989.

The article sets out to show in what sense the current ecological crisis grows up to be a truly philosophical problem. Basing their observations on contemporary data, the authors point to changes occurring in the relationship between culture and nature. They assert that the present-day ecological crisis does indeed constitute a philosophical problem in its own right, representing an impetus for reflecting on fundamental philosophical concepts, the subject of philosophy and its history. This reflection may, as it were, be of significance for efforts to tackle the current ecological crisis insofar as the philosophical concepts themselves tend to change into instruments for the formulation of objectives and insofar as they serve as a communication basis.

KOLARSKY, R. The Need of Philosophy and Current Ecological Crisis (in Czechoslovakian). Filozof Cas, 37(5), 624-631, 1989.

The present-day ecological crisis amounts to a separation of the life of contemporary humankind, constituting a crisis of the human home; at the same time it is a philosophical crisis, a crisis of philosophy. The question arises in this connection what is the need of philosophy, called forth by the contemporary ecological crisis. The concept of philosophy as a spiritual home (Hegel, Husserl) is stimulating for the philosophical reflection of the present-day ecological crisis because the devastation of society's spiritual life constitutes one of the causes of the current ecological crisis. The contemporary devastation of the Earth attests not only the untenable nature of material life but also the limited character of spiritual life, it testifies to the fact spiritual life is, in actual fact, saddled with a certain spiritlessness in the sense of a blindness towards its ecological ramifications. (edited)

KOLENDA, Konstantin. The Poverty of Opulence. Humanist, 50(5), 31-32, S-O 90.

The heedless pursuit of personal wealth facilitates a slide into unethical and even criminal behavior: condoning shady, questionable deals and colluding with individuals who operate on the edges or outside the law, those who cook the books and launder drug money. Even when no law is explicitly broken, it is morally inexcusable to take irresponsible risks with unsuspecting depositor's savings.

KOLENDA, Konstantin. "Schopenhauer's Ethics: A View from Nowhere" in Schopenhauer: New Essays in Honor of His 200th Birthday, VON DER LUFT, Eric (ed), 247-256. Lewiston, Mellen Pr, 1989.

Schopenhauer moves beyond Kant and proclaims that the thing-in-itself can be not only thought but also known. The noumenon acquires a voice, and the voice is Schopenhauer's. It is in his character as a Platonic Idea that the Will reveals its true nature. Schopenhauer thought that he was speaking in moral language, but his utterances do not meet the conditions of moral discourse. His extreme noumenalism prevents him from having credible ethics.

KOLENDA, Konstantin. Tradition, Self-Direction, and Good Life. J Speculative Phil, 4(2), 132-145, 1990.

John Kekes's attempt to reconcile the claims of tradition, community, and convention with the desire for freedom, individuality, and self-direction is only partly successful. Good life can be better described in a vocabulary that does not invoke the notion of balance but instead takes into account the demands of moral pluralism. For that purpose, the notion of "fashioned life" may prove to be useful.

KOLENDA, Konstantin. The World United. Humanist, 49(6), 49-50, N-D 89.

It is encouraging that the world's nations have begun to cooperate on more and more projects, including the establishment of regulations for the use of oceans and the sharing of meterorological information. Extending their areas of cooperation, the nations of the world are also more likely to embark successfully on such all-encompassing projects as space exploration. United, we not only stand but move forward as well.

KOLESNYK, Alexander. Zu Problemen der revolutionären Theologie Thomas Müntzers. Deut Z Phil, 37(12), 1071-1081, 1989.

KOMORI, Yuichi. Logic Based on Combinators. Bull Sect Log, 18(3), 100-104, O 89.

The system BCKT (Y Komori, "Illative combinatory logic based on BCK-logic," Mathematica Japonica 34 (1989), 585-596) is illative combinatory logic based on BCK-logic. For lack of contraction, the system BCKT is so weak that we cannot develop mathematics in it. So, in order to treat mathematics in it, we introduce the system BCK+CP in this paper. CP is the contraction rule for proposition. It is shown that BCKT+CP is not weaker than the intuitionistic simple type theory.

KONCZ, Ilona. The Young Hegel—After 50 Years (in Hungarian). Magyar Filozof Szemle, 5, 550-563, 1989.

Der Aufsatz vertritt die These, dass das Buch von Georg Lukács, vor allem dessen "Jenaer Kapitel", heute, nach 50 Jahren, unter mindestens zwei Aspekten überholt ist. Erstens ist die Chronologie, auf deren Grund Lukács versucht hat, Hegels Jenaer Philosophie darzustellen, veraltet—seitdem Heinz Kimmerle die Ergebnisse seiner philologischer Arbeit in der

Hegel-Studien (1967) veröffentlicht hat. Vor allem war es unmöglich, aufgrund dieser alten Chronologie, die wahre Bedeutung der sog. Zweitens versucht der Autor nachzuweisen: die Weise, nach dem Lukács bei der Untersuchung der Texte des jungen Hegels immer von den Feststellungen von Marx, Engels und Lenin ausgeht, ist der Schuld daran, dass die Urteile von Lukács sich oft als unrichtig erweisen. (edited)

KONDO, Michiro. Simple Completeness Proof of Lemmon's SO:5. Rep Math Log, 22, 3-8, 1988.

KONDZIELA, Joachim. The Democracy of Workers in the Light of John Paul II's Encyclical Laborem Exercens. Dialec Hum, 14(1), 49-55, Wint 87.

KÖNIGSHAUSEN, Johann-Heinrich. "Grundsätzliches der platonischen σκεψις von guter Rede und guter Schrift im Phaidros" in Agora: Zu Ehren von Rudolph Berlinger, BERLINGER, Rudolph (and other eds), 109-127. Amsterdam, Rodopi, 1988.

According to the author, Plato's criticism of written language is based in his Logos-theory. The arguments leading to Plato's criticism of written language are the same as those leading to his criticism of good and bad speech. The article refers to Plato's dialogue "Phaidros" as well as to the literature by Hans Krämer, Ernst Heitsch, and Thomas A Szlezák.

KÖNIGSHAUSEN, Johann-Heinrich. Ursprung und Thema von Ersten Wissenschaft. Amsterdam, Rodopi, 1989

The book provides a complete discussion of the central theme of Aristotle's Metaphysics. The author makes a point of tracing back the old dispute about the character of metaphysics as "theology" or "ontology" to a more basic question. The theme of metaphysics is to be seen out of the original meaning of any search for knowledge. The author shows the strong connection between Met. I (especially chapters 1 and 2), Met. III, and Met. IV. In the second part of the book a commentary to the fourth book of Metaphysics is given. The special literature is widely discussed.

KÔNO, Michifusa. Chinese Theories of Appreciation—with Particular Attention to Painting (in Japanese). Bigaku, 40(4), 36-46, Spr 90.

Something of Chinese theories of art appreciation can be comprehended from the literature concerning painting. There are the mentions of seals and signatures, types of paper and silk for paintings, and viewpoints for judging paintings, calligraphies and other art objects. Essentially the areas of aesthetic appreciation and concern can be classified into five groups. These are (1) the knowledge of materials, (2) the connoisseurship of materials, (3) the critical evaluation of artists, (4) the aesthetic appraisal for artistic change over time, and (5) the commentary on the essential quality of painting. As these points are often subtle and complicated, it is not easy to comprehend the depth of their meaning. However, by taking up one point at a time, it is possible to discover interesting transitions in attitudes toward art. (edited)

KOONS, Robert C. A Representational Account of Mutual Belief. Synthese, 81(1), 21-45, O 89.

Although the notion of common or mutual belief plays a crucial role in game theory, economics and social philosophy, no thoroughly representational account of it has yet been developed. In this paper, I propose two desiderata for such an account, namely, that it take into account the possibility of inconsistent data without portraying the human mind as logically and mathematically omniscient. I then propose a definition of mutual belief which meets these criteria. This account takes seriously the existence of computational limitations. Finally, I point out that the epistemic 'logic' (or theory) needed to make the definition work is subject to the Kaplan/Montague Paradox of the Knower. I argue that this is not a defect of the account, and I discuss briefly the bearing of recent work on the paradox of the Liar upon this problem.

KOPELMAN, Loretta M. What Is Applied About "Applied" Philosophy? J Med Phil, 15(2), 199-218, Ap 90.

"Applied" is a technical term describing a variety of new philosophical enterprises. The author examines and rejects the view that these fields are derivative. Whatever principles, judgments, or background theories that are employed to solve problems in these areas are either changed by how they are used, or at least the possibility exists of their being changed. Hence we ought to stop calling these endeavors "applied," or agree that the meaning of "apply" will have to include the possibility that what is applied may be changed. The so-called applied fields of philosophy, therefore, are not derivative. The strongest cases to the contrary are the foundationalist views that what we apply is epistemically privileged. Different foundationalist views take different principles, judgments, or background theories to be epistemically privileged. Strong and weak versions of each of these foundationalist views are considered but none establish these fields as derivative.

KOPPELBERG, Dirk and GOSCHKE, Thomas. Connectionism and the Semantic Content of Internal Representation. Rev Int Phil, 44(172), 87-103,

1990.

KOPPER, Joachim. Double Representation of the 'Paralogisms of Pure Reason' in the Two Editions of *Critique of Pure Reason* (in German). S Afr J Phil, 8(3-4), 148-154, N 88.

On the basis of the antinomy of reason Kant attempts in the transcendental aesthetic and the transcendental analytic to express the metaphysical tendency of reason in critical thinking. He finds, however, that this investigation does not get him to the true nature of knowing—something is left out. He finds the missing link to be the judgment, 'I think'. In this article the author traces the development of Kant's thinking about the subject and how he fits it into his transcendental system.

KOPPER, Joachim. Einige Bemerkungen zur Bedeutung von Ewigkeit und Dauer in Spinozas Ethik. Z Phil Forsch, 43(3), 432-448, Jl-S 89.

Eternity and duration are two concepts of human thinking through which man tries to comprehend the existence of the world and of his own in its truth. The whole of our thinking is composed of an active comprehension in which the world has a mere temporal existence and of a 'passive' knowledge in which the world is known as eternal and whom time and space are nothing but the manifestation of the eternal. But these two moments of thinking remain separated from each other in Spinoza's *Ethica*.

KORAB-KARPOWICZ, W J. A Point of Reconciliation Between Schopenhauer and Hegel. Owl Minerva, 21(2), 167-175, Spr 90.

Schopenhauer's world as Will and Idea is very different from Hegel's world as Spirit. Nevertheless, by taking into account their views of aesthetics, I have attempted to provide a limited reconciliation between Schopenhauer and Hegel, and to show that their presentations of art, and particularly of architecture, are only apparently contradictory. In fact, they express two different, yet compatible and complementary pictures of reality, as it can be seen from different angles.

KORABIK, Karen. Androgyny and Leadership Style. J Bus Ethics, 9(4-5), 283-292, Ap-My 90.

Research on leadership has either ignored women or focused on sex differences. This paper illustrates how both of these strategies have been detrimental to women. An alternative conception based on sex-role orientation is presented and the research relating androgyny to leadership style and managerial effectiveness is reviewed. It is proposed that adopting an androgynous management style may help women to overcome the negative effects of sex-stereotyping in the workplace.

KORHONEN, P and WALLENIUS, J. Supporting Individuals in Group-Decision Making. Theor Decis, 28(3), 313-329, My 90.

Pooling of different resources is typical among the member countries of the Council of Mutual Economic Assistance participating in joint large-scale construction projects. The problem faced by the members of the Council is to decide, how much of various resources each country should contribute to a construction project. In this paper we present a general approach to supporting individuals involved in such negotiations. We formulate the problem as a multiple criteria/multiple decision-maker model and use our approach to finding a compromise solution for the resource pooling problem within the Council of Mutual Economic Assistance. The approach is implemented on a computer, tested and illustrated using a prototypical example.

KORITANSKY, John C. Civil Religion in Tocqueville's *Democracy in America*. Interpretation, 17(3), 389-400, Spr 90.

KORNBLITH, Hilary. Introspection and Misdirection. Austl J Phil, 67(4), 410-422, D 89.

Some epistemologists offer epistemic advice to truth seeking agents, advice which is designed to improve their epistemic performance. Historically, the faculty of introspection has played a significant role in such advice. It is argued in this paper that introspection is ill-suited to play such a role. Indeed, the value of introspection in the project of epistemic self-improvement is inversely proportional to the need for such improvement. Those who are most in need of epistemic improvement will be harmed most by seeking aid from introspection. Introspection is unlikely to improve an agent's epistemic position, but it is likely to make a bad situation worse. These claims are illustrated by an examination of the views of Chisholm and BonJour; it is argued, however, that they apply to all internalist epistemologies.

KORNBLITH, Hilary. "The Unattainability of Coherence" in *The Current State of the Coherence Theory*, BENDER, John W (ed), 207-214. Norwell, Kluwer, 1989.

I argue in this paper that the ideal of belief acquisition which coherence theorists propose is unattainable. In section I, I discuss Laurence BonJour's internalist coherence theory and argue that it fails on its own terms: the ideal which BonJour proposes cannot be met. In section II, I discuss Gilbert Harman's externalist coherence theory and argue that it proposes an ideal which is beyond the powers of any human being to realize; indeed, it proposes an ideal which cannot be realized by any information processing device whatsoever. I conclude that human beings do not and cannot arrive at their beliefs by determining whether they cohere with beliefs already held. In section III, I discuss an argument due to Jerry Fodor which suggests that the only alternative to a holistic account of the fixation of belief is skepticism. I propose a way to elude the horns of this dilemma.

KORNEGAY, R Jo. Is Commercial Surrogacy Baby-Selling? J Applied Phil, 7(1), 45-50, Mr 90.

This essay considers a common objection to commercial surrogacy on the grounds that the child is treated as a commodity for sale by the surrogate and the commissioning couple. I analyse one prevalent argument for the view that commercial surrogacy is a kind of baby-selling, not service-selling. I conclude that this argument rests on an implausible interpretation of what the reproductive services are. I defend an alternative interpretation of typical surrogacy agreements. Furthermore, I argue that this interpretation fails to support the conclusion that the surrogate is primarily or exclusively selling a baby, rather than her reproductive services. My primary concern is to diagnose a conceptual error in an argument against surrogacy. However, the interpretation of surrogacy arrangements that is defended helps to shift the focus from the issue of whether or not the child is degraded to the issue of whether or not the surrogate degrades herself or is degraded by the commissioning couple.

KORSGAARD, Christine M. Kant's Analysis of Obligation: The Argument of *Foundationsl*. Monist, 72(3), 311-340, Jl 89.

Most of the moves in the current debate about whether moral motivation is internal or external to moral judgment were anticipated in the eighteenth century British debate between the Rationalists and the Sentimenalists about obligation. The problem in both cases is how the thought of duty can at once motivate and bind every rational agent. By reconstructing Kant's argument in the first section of the *Foundations*, this paper shows how Kant solves this problem. Only a law willed autonomously can motivate through the thought of its bindingness, and so only an action dictated by such a law can be obligatory.

KORSGAARD, Christine. "Kant" in *Ethics in the History of Western Philosophy*, CAVALIER, Robert J (ed), 201-243. New York, St Martin's Pr, 1988.

My aim is to provide a sympathetic account of Kant's ethics in its historical setting. For Kant, the death of speculative metaphysics and the birth of the Rights of Man are not independent events: together they constitute the resolution of the Enlightenment debate about the power of reason. Theoretical reason is unable to answer the questions of metaphysics, about God, freedom, and immortality. But this conclusion prepares the way for an extension in the power of practical reason. Practical reason directs that every human being be regarded as unconditionally valuable. This provides a rational foundation for morality and a moral foundation for liberal politics and religion.

KORSMEYER, Carolyn. The Eclipse of Truth in the Rise of Aesthetics. Brit J Aes, 29(4), 293-302, Autumn 89.

Although philosophers usually place the advent of modern aesthetics in the eighteenth century, there is considerable earlier discussion of the nature of art and perception. An emphasis on cognition and on truth as a value of art characterizes the earlier periods, in contrast with empiricist interest in beauty and what later will be termed aesthetic pleasure. This essay discusses some of the early literature, focussing on visual art, and questions whether the accepted periodization of aesthetics is still satisfactory, given recent shifts of interest in philosophy of art.

KORTHALS, Michiel. Art and Morality: Critical Theory About the Conflict and Harmony between Art and Morality. Phil Soc Crit, 15(3), 241-251, 1989.

During the Enlightenment it was obvious that the cultural spheres science, art, and morality and law composed a unity. Nowadays, because of the conflicts between these three spheres, this unity is not taken for granted. The Frankfurt School (critical theory) responded differently to the question of the relationship between the two cultural spheres morality and art. Horkheimer argued that morality is more important than art, Marcuse argued the opposite and Adorno joined him, although on totally different grounds. Habermas tries to solve the unity on a procedural level. The author argues that in the case of conflict, art should give way to morality.

KOSING, Alfred. Sozialistische Gesellschaft und sozialistische Nation in der DDR. Deut Z Phil, 37(10-11), 913-924, 1989.

KOSINSKI, Jerzy. Speaking for My Self. Dialec Hum, 14(1), 117-120, Wint 87.

KOSKENNIEMI, Martti. "The Hobbesian Structure of International Legal Discourse" in *Hobbes: War Among Nations*, AIRAKSINEN, Timo (ed), 168-178. Brookfield, Gower, 1989.

KOSTELANETZ, Richard (ed). *Esthetics Contemporary—Revised Edition*. Buffalo, Prometheus, 1989

This is the ten-year anniversary revised edition, which includes over a dozen new essays. It expands upon its predecessor with more than 50 contributions by today's experts in esthetics. (staff)

KOTLARSKI, Henryk and RATAJCZYK, Zygmunt. Inductive Full Satisfaction Classes. Annals Pure Applied Log, 47(3), 199-223, Je 90.

KOTLARSKI, Henryk. On the End Extension Problem for Δ_o-PA(S). Z Math Log, 35(5), 391-397, 1989.

KOVACS, George. The Nature of Ultimate Understanding. Ultim Real Mean, 13(1), 61-68, Mr 90.

These considerations (1) unearth the main questions and the basic issues regarding the human capacity to discern ultimate meaning and reality, describe (2) the nature and (3) the qualities of ultimate understanding, and (4) indicate some conclusions for the methodology of ultimate understanding. This analysis represents a prolegomenon to the question about the possibility and the nature of ultimate understanding, of the dynamics of wonder about ultimate meaning and being.

KOVACS, George. On Heidegger's Silence. Heidegger Stud, 5, 135-151, 1989.

These reflections examine the nature and the motivations of Heidegger's involvement in National Socialism in Germany. They (1) expand the range of questions that ought to be asked regarding his attitudes and actions, (2) assess his understanding of, response to, or silence about the historical phenomena and events of that time in the light of his philosophy, and (3) indicate some concluding questions and insights about the extent of his failure and the final significance of his thought as a whole.

KOVACS, George. Philosophy as Primordial Science (*Urwissenschaft*) in the Early Heidegger. J Brit Soc Phenomenol, 21(2), 121-135, My 90.

This study examines the essence of philosophy according to Heidegger's earliest lecture courses at the University of Freiburg given in 1919. They include (1) a reflection on the way the question about the essence of philosophy originates in the early Heidegger; (2) the analysis of his idea of philosophy as primordial science, as his search for the method (and "matter") of thinking and knowing; and (3) an assessment of the significance, nature, and of the final horizon of his insights.

KOVEL, Joel and CRAIB, Ian. Marxism and Psychoanalysis: An Exchange. Rad Phil, 55, 25-30, Sum 90.

KOWALSKI, Edmund. Appréciation morale des ingerences biomédiques dans le processusde de transmision (in Polish). Stud Phil Christ, 25(1), 79-92, 1989.

Le Père Slipko, à la base de la vision spirituelle de l'homme et en adoptant le monde des valeurs, inchangeable et objectif fondé sur la nature humaine (intégrale et ordonné vers un but) et en admettant lecaractère stable et absolue des normes morales, indique les normes qui défendent l'homme (apartir de sa conception jusqu'au moment de la nature humaine (intégrale et ordonnée vers un but) et en admettant le caractère stable et absolue des normes morales, indique les normes qui déferdent l'homme (apartir de sa conception jusqu'áu moment de la tout utilitarisme, naturalisme, ou traitement instrumentuel. La dignité de la personne humaine détermine les limites axiologiques de l'admissibilité de l'ingérence biomedique dans la structure somatique et psychologique de l'homme. (edited)

KOWALSKI, Gary. The Ethics Crunch: Can Medical Science Advance Without the Use of Animals? Between Species, 6(1), 22-24, Wint 90.

KOWALSKI, Robert and SERGOT, Marek. The Use of Logical Models in Legal Problem Solving. Ratio Juris, 3(2), 201-218, Jl 90.

The authors describe a logic programming approach to the representation of legislative texts. They consider the potential uses of simple systems which incorporate a single, fixed interpretation of a text. These include assisting in the routine administration of complex areas of the law. The authors also consider the possibility of constructing more complex systems which incorporate several, possibly conflicting interpretations. Such systems are needed for dealing with ambiguity and vagueness in the law. Moreover, they are more suitable than single interpretation systems for helping to test proposed legislation and for helping to give citizens advice.

KOZEN, Dexter. A Finite Model Theorem for the Propositional μ-Calculus. Stud Log, 47(3), 233-241, S 88.

We prove a finite model theorem and infinitary completeness result for the propositional μ-calculus. The construction establishes a link between finite model theorems for propositional program logics and the theory of well-quasi-orders.

KOZYR-KOWALSKI, Stanislaw and OSZKODAR, Zbigniew (trans). Marxism and Conceptual Scholasticism. Dialec Hum, 15(3-4), 151-167, Sum-Autumn 88.

KRAEMER, E R. Is the Best Really Necessary? Analysis, 50(1), 42-43, Ja 90.

In response to Stephen Grover's recent attempt (*Analysis* 48:4) to argue that in order for God's goodness to remain inviolate this must be the best of all possible worlds, I explain how God's goodness could be preserved *without* this world's having to be the best possible.

KRAEMER, Joel L. "Maimonides on Aristotle and Scientific Method" in *Moses Maimonides and His Time*, ORMSBY, Eric L (ed), 53-88. Washington, Cath Univ Amer Pr, 1989.

KRAFT, Kenneth L and HAGE, Jerald. Strategy, Social Responsibility and Implementation. J Bus Ethics, 9(1), 11-19, Ja 90.

This paper correlates community service goals from 82 business firms with various organizational characteristics, including goals, niches, structure, context, and performance. The results demonstrate that community-service goals are positively correlated with prestige goals, assets goals, superior-design niche, net assets size, and performance on income to net assets. Community-service goals, however, were not significantly correlated with profit goals, low-price niche, multiplicity of outputs, workflow continuity, qualifications, or centralization, as expected.

KRAJICEK, Jan and PUDLAK, Pavel. Quantified Propositional Calculi and Fragments of Bounded Arithmetic. Z Math Log, 36(1), 29-46, 1990.

We investigate a relation between bounded arithmetic and propositional calculus. The main tool is a translation of bounded arithmetical formulas into quantified Boolean formulas and a transformation of arithmetical proofs into proofs in propositional calculus. This brings information both about fragments of bounded arithmetic and propositional calculus.

KRÄMER, Hans. "Thomas Alexander Szlezák, Platon und die Schriftlichkeit der Philosophie" in *Agora: Zu Ehren von Rudolph Berlinger*, BERLINGER, Rudolph (and other eds), 417-439. Amsterdam, Rodopi, 1988.

Szlezák's book is a refutation of Schleiermacher and his modern followers by Schleiermacher's own method, i.e., a careful analysis of the scenic and dramatic structure of the dialogues and their hints to the unwritten doctrines in the central part of each work. So the new paradigm of Platonic scholarship, which combines the two branches of tradition (the dialogues and the relations of Plato's teaching in the Academy), is supported against the previous Romantic one. The second part of the review defends Szlezák's results against misunderstandings and errors of recent critics in a detailed argumentation.

KRAMER, Matthew. The Specter of Communism. Polit Theory, 17(4), 607-637, N 89.

Over the past decade, G A Cohen's reinterpretation of Marxism has achieved preeminence in the English-speaking world. Cohen's work is here subjected to a three-pronged critique—from an analytic perspective, which reveals flaws in some of Cohen's key arguments; from a rhetorical perspective, which shows that Cohen's language puts into question some of his substantive insights; and from a deconstructionist perspective, which demonstrates that Cohen's Marxist priorities (wherein materiality is privileged over sociality) have overturned themselves.

KRÄMER-FRIEDRICH, Sybille. "The 'Universal Thinking Machine', or on the Genesis of Schematized Reasoning in the 17th Century" in *Scientific Knowledge Socialized*, HRONSZKY, Imre (ed), 179-191. Norwell, Kluwer, 1989.

The 17th-century paradigm of technical action gains meaning not only in the case of the so-called factual truths (*Tatsachenwahrheiten*) of natural sciences, but also in the case of the truths of reason (*Vernunftwahrheiten*) for mathematics and logic and for the rationalistic concept of reason in general. To support this, the genesis of a regulative idea is analysed, metaphorical expressed as "the idea of the universal thinking machine." It is the assumption that reasoning can in principle be mechanized.

KRAMERS, Robert P. Confucius—China's Dethroned Sage? (in Serbo-Croatian). Filozof Istraz, 29(2), 569-573, 1989.

Confucius, China's greatest sage, has been much criticised in modern China, beginning with the May Fourth movement in 1919 when the slogan "Down with the Confucian shop" epitomised the revolt of young intellectuals against the remnants of a too-rigid social morality. Western philosophy and science, and later especially Marxist-Leninist thought, provided the catalyzers for a critical reevaluation of the Chinese identity. The article traces the ups and downs of this modern reevaluation through the contributions of one of China's foremost philosophers, Professor Feng Youlan, who after a long Marxist peregrination seems to have come back to his positive evaluation of Neo-Confucian idealism. This may point the way towards a renewed attempt at philosophical and cultural synthesis between China and the modern West.

KRANTZ, Susan. Brentano on 'Unconscious Consciousness'. Phil Phenomenol Res, 50(4), 745-753, Je 90.

In *Psychology from an Empirical Standpoint*, Brentano argues that an 'unconscious consciousness' is not possible. I focus on his use in this argument of the principle of the infallibility of inner perception. By contrast with the view he argues against, it becomes plain that Brentano discusses sense perception in an idealistic or subjectivist mode. Yet Brentano insists that he is a realist, and not guilty of 'psychologism', precisely because he adheres to the infallibility of inner perception and denies unconscious consciousness. Thus we encounter in Brentano a version of what may be called phenomenological realism.

KRAPIEC, Mieczyslaw A and RODZINSKA, Aleksandra (trans). The Human Dimension of Christian Culture—The Common Heritage of the Nations of Europe. Dialec Hum, 14(1), 5-23, Wint 87.

KRATOCHWIL, Friedrich V. *Rules, Norms, and Decisions: On the Conditions of Practical and Legal Reasoning*. New York, Cambridge Univ Pr, 1989

KRATZER, Angelika. An Investigation of the Lumps of Thought. Ling Phil, 12(5), 607-653, O 89.

KRAUSZ, Michael. Interpretation and Its Art Objects: Two Views. Monist, 73(2), 222-232, Ap 90.

The author idealizes two contrasting views of interpretation in art: constructionist and realist. He argues that, as regards limiting admissible interpretations in art, they need not be opposed. He indicates what considerations may constrain the range of ideally admissible interpretations for the constructionist, and why realism as such will not restrict the range of ideally admissible interpretations. He offers criticisms of each of these positions, and indicates some points at which there might be some promise for reconciliation between them. He concludes by making some strategic suggestions to advance the discussion.

KRAUT, Robert. Varieties of Pragmatism. Mind, 99(394), 157-183, Ap 90.

"Pragmatism" includes positions concerning a variety of issues: the relation between truth and warranted assertibility, the status of bivalence and referential semantics, the explanatory role (if any) of semantical notions, the bifurcation of language into expressive and descriptive components, the scope of justificatory holism, the status of epistemically privileged representations, and the "primacy of social practice." But it is not clear how the positions often designated as "pragmatist" relate to one another. My goal is to explore Richard Rorty's characterizations of pragmatism—especially the position he calls "epistemological behaviorism"—and note some of the interconnections among them.

KRAYE, Jill. Aristotle's God and the Authenticity of *De mundo*: An Early Modern Controversy. J Hist Phil, 28(3), 339-358, Jl 90.

This article shows how a number of thinkers from the fifteenth to the eighteenth century were influenced to either reject or accept the Aristotelian authenticity of the Greek treatise *De mundo* on the basis of its presentation of a providential God.

KREISEL, Howard. The Problem of "Good" in the Philosophy of Maimonides (in Hebrew). Iyyun, 38(3-4), 183-208, Jl-O 89.

This paper argues that Maimonides never uses "good" as a purely subjective notion. The main part of the paper focuses on two areas where Maimonides appears to use "good" as a subjective notion. It further explores the question whether Maimonides recognizes a system of morality belonging to the theoretical intellect and having the epistemological status of "truth" or of the "intelligibles." The paper concludes with a discussion of the question why Maimonides employs the expression, "the Torah speaks in the language of the sons of man," in regard to the verse, "And God saw that it was good." (edited)

KRELL, David Farrell. "'Knowledge is Remembrance': Diotima's Instruction at *Symposium* 207c 8 - 208b 6" in *Post-Structuralist Classics*, BENJAMIN, Andrew (ed), 160-172. New York, Routledge, 1988.

KRELL, David Farrell. Daimon Life, Nearness and Abyss: An Introduction to Za-ology. Res Phenomenol, 17, 23-53, 1987.

Heidegger's relation to life-philosophy is examined critically, with attention both to *Being and Time* and the later work; special care is taken with the 1929-1930 lectures on theoretical biology. "Life" proves to be central to Heidegger's thought on *to daimonion*, the overpowering and the holy.

KRELL, David Farrell and BARET, Françoise (trans). Le plus pur des batards (l'affirmation sans issue). Rev Phil Fr, 180(2), 229-238, Ap-Je 90.

KREMER, Klaus. Zur ontologischen Differenz: Plotin und Heidegger. Z Phil Forsch, 43(4), 673-694, O-D 89.

The article elucidates that Plotinus's conception of being and Heidegger's are two incommensurable concepts. Yet Plotinus also distinguishes between "being" (Sein) and "existing" (Seiendes). Plotinus, however, does not consider this difference to be the crucial ontological difference, but rather the difference of the Ohne (= Hen) to everything, which is either "being" or "existing." This One, the God of Plotinus, is neither a "something" nor "the highest form of existing," as Heidegger imputes to occidental metaphysics. In order that all things existing may be derived from the One, the One may be neither "being" nor "existing." This difference is more radical than Heidegger's "ontological difference."

KREMER, Philip. Relevant Predication: Grammatical Characterizations. J Phil Log, 18(4), 349-382, N 89.

This paper reformulates and decides a certain conjecture in Dunn's 'Relevant Predication 1: The Formal Theory' (*Journal of Philosophical Logic* 16, 347-381, 1987). This conjecture of Dunn's relates his object-language characterisation of a property's being *relevant in a variable x* to certain grammatical characterisations of relevance, analogous to some given by Helman, in 'Relevant Implication and Relevant Functions' (to appear in *Entailment: The Logic of Relevance and Necessity*, vol. 2, by Alan Ross Anderson, Nuel Belnap, and J Michael Dunn et el.). In the course of the investigation this paper also investigates Kit Fine's semantics for quantified relevance logics, which appears in his appropriately titled 'Semantics for Quantified Relevance Logics' (*Journal of Philosophical Logic* 17, 27-59, 1988).

KREMNITZER, Mordechai. "Comment: Intentions and *Mens Rea*" in *Issues in Contemporary Legal Philosophy: The Influence of H L A Hart*, GAVISON, Ruth (ed), 277-286. New York, Clarendon/Oxford Pr, 1987.

KRETCHMAR, R Scott. On Beautiful Games. J Phil Sport, 16, 34-43, 1989.

KRETZMANN, Barbara Ensign and KRETZMANN, Norman and KILVINGTON, Richard. *The Sophismata of Richard Kilvington*. New York, Cambridge Univ Pr, 1990

Richard Kilvington was a 14th-century English philosopher, one of the "Oxford Calculators." His *Sophismata* is a subtly ordered series of 48 philosophical puzzles designed to raise and settle issues in natural philosophy (having to do with change, motive power, velocity, or strength) and in epistemology. This volume contains a historical introduction, an English translation, and a philosophical commentary. A companion volume (published by Oxford for the British Academy) contains the edition of the Latin text, based on 20 manuscripts.

KRETZMANN, Norman. Reason in Mystery. Philosophy, 25, 15-39, 89 Supp.

With the aim of defending and furthering philosophical theology, I distinguish it from natural theology, set out two connected goals of it, address the concerns of the Reformed epistemologists, and then turn to a consideration of the most formidable objections against philosophical theology as carried out in the Middle Ages, and some of the ways those objections were dealt with, focusing on Aquinas and Bonaventure on the mystery of the Trinity.

KRETZMANN, Norman and KRETZMANN, Barbara Ensign and KILVINGTON, Richard. *The Sophismata of Richard Kilvington*. New York, Cambridge Univ Pr, 1990

Richard Kilvington was a 14th-century English philosopher, one of the "Oxford Calculators." His *Sophismata* is a subtly ordered series of 48 philosophical puzzles designed to raise and settle issues in natural philosophy (having to do with change, motive power, velocity, or strength) and in epistemology. This volume contains a historical introduction, an English translation, and a philosophical commentary. A companion volume (published by Oxford for the British Academy) contains the edition of the Latin text, based on 20 manuscripts.

KRETZMANN, Norman and STUMP, Eleonore S. Theologically Unfashionable Philosophy. Faith Phil, 7(3), 329-340, Jl 90.

KRIEGER, Martin H. Commentary on "The Expert and the Public". Bus Prof Ethics J, 6(2), 47-50, Sum 87.

KRIPS, H. The Objectivity of Quantum Probabilities. Austl J Phil, 67(4), 423-431, D 89.

KRIPS, Henry. Power and Resistance. Phil Soc Sci, 20(2), 170-182, Je 90.

The exercises of modern power which Foucault discusses constitute counterexamples to traditional views of the nature of power. Foucault's views are extended to provide an account of the nature of resistance.

KRISHNA, Daya. The Conceptual Structure of Marxist Thought: Some Critical Reflections (in Serbo-Croatian). Filozof Istraz, 29(2), 631-638, 1989.

The article seeks to apply the methodology developed in connection with the study of some classical Indian texts to Marx's thought. The methodology consists in articulating the concepts used in any text and the different possible interrelationships between them in the light of the multifarious questions that may be asked with respect to them in order to see how the thought can be developed further. The philosophical issues behind the approach may be seen in the author's paper, "Thinking vs. Thought" published in the *Journal of the Indian Council of Philosophical Research* (Vol. V, No. 2, Jan.-April, 1988) and illustrated in the book, *India's Intellectual Traditions: Attempts at Conceptual Reconstructions* (Delhi, Motilal Banarsidas, 1987).

KRÖBER, Günther. "Productive Needs as Driving Forces of the Development of Science" in *Scientific Knowledge Socialized*, HRONSZKY, Imre (ed), 157-164. Norwell, Kluwer, 1989.

In order to become productive as a real driving force for the development of science a social need has to fulfill some conditions: it has to refer to the given standard of science and technology; it has to be able to effectively regulate the conditions of scientific work; it has to prove that it can be formulated as a concrete technical or scientific problem, that the prevailing standard of science allows to work on it and that the prevailing standard of production allows to make practical use of the results.

KROH, M. Concerning the Problems Surrounding "Theoretical Consciousness" (in Czechoslovakian). Filozof Cas, 37(6), 827-839, 1989.

The first part of the article deals with problems connected with concepts "current" and "theoretical consciousness." The author criticizes their widespread interpretation as different layers or levels of the social consciousness together with outcoming logical contradictions. In contradiction to the criticized conception the author proposes an investigation of the problem from the point of view of the dialectics of subjective and objective moments in the social consciousness. In connection with the preceding the author speaks about two basic types of production and reproduction of the social theories: authoritarian and democratic. He proves that only the last one corresponds with the essence of socialism. (edited)

KROHN, Franklin B and MILNER, Laura M. The AIDS Crisis: Unethical Marketing Leads to Negligent Homicide. J Bus Ethics, 8(10), 773-780, O 89.

The purpose of this paper is to demonstrate how condom manufacturers and their marketers have failed to adequately promote their product to the male homosexual population (gays). Inasmuch as the AIDS syndrome constitutes a major life-threatening danger and that gays appear to be particularly vulnerable, failure to aggressively promote a known preventive such as condoms to gays constitutes negligent homicide. The method used here defines what is traditionally viewed as a viable "target market," analyzes the major elements of marketing with regard to gays, and examines the neglect of condom promotion by their manufacturers. It is concluded that condom marketers have failed to promote a known protection against AIDS to a highly susceptible group. That group would normally be seen as a highly attractive market for condoms and were it not for homophobia, marketers would zealously pursue more aggressive promotion of condoms to gays.

KROHN, Wolfgang and KÜPPERS, Günter. "Self-Organization: A New Approach to Evolutionary Epistemology" in *Issues in Evolutionary Epistemology*, HAHLWEG, Kai (ed), 151-170. Albany, SUNY Pr, 1989.

The essay specifies several shortcomings characteristic of the attempts to combine evolutionary with epistemological aspects of knowledge. Most important is that the self-referentiality of scientific knowledge and the self-organization of social systems don't allow for an independent definition of variation and selection. On the basis of the theory of self-organizing systems the essay attempts to develop new ideas as to how social interaction and formation of knowledge operate on each other and exemplifies these in the case of production of scientific knowledge.

KROHN, Wolfgang. "Social Change and Epistemic Thought" in *Scientific Knowledge Socialized*, HRONSZKY, Imre (ed), 165-178. Norwell, Kluwer, 1989.

The essay attempts to outline a conceptual model for analyzing the emergence of new 'validity claims of knowledge'. In trying to avoid the shortcomings of the genetic fallacy it draws upon ideas from the genetic epistemology of Jean Piaget. In its historical part the essay focusses on the Baconian dictum "knowledge is power" as an example of a new validity

claim, reconstructs its social origins, epistemic meaning and justification.

KROM, Melven and KROM, Myren. Recursive Solvability of Problems with Matrices. Z Math Log, 35(5), 437-442, 1989.

The *Mortality Problem* for a finite set of n x n matrices is to determine whether there is a product of matrices from the set that is equal to the zero matrix. An *Equality of Entry Problem* for a finite set of n x n matrices is to determine whether there is a product of matrices from the set that is equal to a matrix in which the entries in certain specified entry positions are equal. This paper concerns the recursive solvability of mortality problems and equality of entry problems.

KROM, Myren and KROM, Melven. Recursive Solvability of Problems with Matrices. Z Math Log, 35(5), 437-442, 1989.

The *Mortality Problem* for a finite set of n x n matrices is to determine whether there is a product of matrices from the set that is equal to the zero matrix. An *Equality of Entry Problem* for a finite set of n x n matrices is to determine whether there is a product of matrices from the set that is equal to a matrix in which the entries in certain specified entry positions are equal. This paper concerns the recursive solvability of mortality problems and equality of entry problems.

KRUKOWSKI, Lucian. Artist—Work—Audience: Musings on Barthes and Tolstoy. Brit J Aes, 30(2), 143-148, Ap 90.

Within the triadic schema, "artist-work-audience," I situate the aesthetic theories of Tolstoi and Barthes as asserting the dominance of "audience" over the other parts—but for different reasons. Tolstoi's "audience" is both the source and beneficiary of the utopian values that justify art. For Barthes, the above triad is renamed as "scriptor-text-reader," and "reader" functions as the field within which all the parts are emancipated from the decadent implications of the replaced terms.

KRUKOWSKI, Lucian. Contextualism and Autonomy in Aesthetics. J Aes Educ, 24(1), 123-134, Spr 90.

KRUMHOLZ, Linda and LAUTER, Estella. Annotated Bibliography on Feminist Aesthetics in the Visual Arts. Hypatia, 5(2), 158-172, Sum 90.

KRUSE, Felicia. Nature and Semiosis. Trans Peirce Soc, 26(2), 211-224, Spr 90.

Charles Peirce developed an extremely broad concept of sign interpretation, according to which everything in the universe can function as a sign and signification is in a certain sense characteristic of the universe as a whole. One problem that emerges from this concept is whether it is possible for Peirce to account for anything's not being a sign. This essay argues that Peirce's distinction of immediate, dynamic, and final interpretants articulates the conditions for Peircean semiosis and thereby provides the constraints that make it impossible for everything in the Peircean universe to be unqualifiedly a sign.

KRYGIER, Martin. The Traditionality of Statutes. Ratio Juris, 1(1), 20-39, Mr 88.

The author begins by sketching the characteristics or elements of every tradition. Some reasons are then suggested for the propensity of so many authors to contrast statutes with other, allegedly more traditional kinds of law. However, it is argued that statutes are deeply embedded, along with customary and judge-made law, in the highly traditional practices of law and that this matters much more than is commonly suspected. The thesis being defended here is not merely that law includes traditions along with rules, principles, maxims, and so on, but rather that legal systems should be understood as traditions, albeit highly complex ones. Not only are ancient legal systems (the Talmudic, for example) held to be traditional; modern legal positive orders are viewed as being traditional too. Finally, the concept of "communities of interpretation" is applied to the contemporary posited statutes which are believed by many to be a distinguishing feature of modern legal systems.

KRYNICKI, Michal. The Non-Definability Notion and First Order Logic. Stud Log, 47(4), 429-437, D 88.

The theorem to the effect that the language L_Δ introduced in "On a formalization of the non-definedness notion" (A Hoogewijs, *Z Math Log* 25, 1979) is mutually interpretable with the first order language is proved. This yields several model-theoretical results concerning L_Δ.

KRYNICKI, Michal. Quantifiers Determined by Partial Orderings. Z Math Log, 36(1), 79-86, 1990.

KUÇURADI, Ioanna. Different Concepts of Dialectics: Methods and Views. Stud Soviet Tho, 39(3-4), 257-264, Ap-My 90.

The purpose of the paper is to show, by tracing selectively—from Plato to Sartre—the main changes in the meaning of the term 'dialectics'; (a) how these changes have led to the ambiguity of the term 'method' prevailing today; (b) that this ambiguity is due to the double function or role that Hegel ascribes to dialectics, who uses it as a *principle of deduction*, as well as an *approach to reality*; as a consequence of which (c) 'method' now denotes not only the steps formally followed in doing something, i.e., a special way followed in carrying out *different activities*, but also a general view (ontological, epistemological, etc.), in its role of approach, i.e., a special assumption or theory applied to explain given facts. This distinction between the two meanings of 'method' leads us to a conclusion concerning the evaluation of Marxist dialectics, as well as of every 'method' in the sense of 'approach'.

KUCZEWSKI, Mark and POLANSKY, Ronald. Speech and Thought, Symbol and Likeness: Aristotle's *De Interpretatione* 16a3-9. Apeiron, 23(1), 51-63, Mr 90.

It is crucial for understanding the opening passage of Aristotle's *De Interpretatione* to comprehend several key terms within it: "symbol," "sign," "likeness," and "affections of the soul." These have recently been taken in diverse, and often unlikely, ways. We connect "likeness" and "affections of the soul" to the doctrine of cognition in the *De Anima*, which is alluded to in the passage, and we offer a view of "symbol" and "sign" which fits the evidence. These accounts of the details of the passage reveal its general meaning, which is basically that attributed to it by traditional commentators.

KUCZYNSKI, Janusz. Christianity and Marxism: Confrontation, Dialogue, Universalism. Dialec Hum, 14(1), 67-87, Wint 87.

I would like to limit my paper to three parts and in the first part to present the most recent important attempt made by Christians at interpreting the relation between religion and Marxism; I have in mind a far-reaching discussion entitled "Is Atheism Essential to Marxism?" published in the *Journal of Ecumenical Studies* (No. 3: 1985), edited by P Mojzes. The second part of the paper contains my positive counterproposal to this discussion, together with certain concretizations and applications of my conception of universalism. The third part, which actually constitutes a logical consequence of my views, envisages a type of Marxism which could develop within the general perspective of universalism, also in confrontation with Christianity.

KUCZYNSKI, Janusz and JEDYNAK, Jacek. Pluralism and Universalist Socialism. Dialec Hum, 16(1), 215-222, Wint 89.

KUCZYNSKI, Janusz and PETROWICZ, Lech (trans) and RODZINSKA, Aleksandra (trans). Universalism as a Metaphilosophy of the New Peace Movement. Dialec Hum, 16(2), 61-78, Spr 89.

KUCZYNSKI, Janusz and PETROWICZ, Lech (trans) and GOLEBIOWSKI, Marek (trans). Universalism: A New Way of Thinking. Dialec Hum, 15(3-4), 27-51, Sum-Autumn 88.

KUEHN, Manfred. Hume and Tetens. Hume Stud, 15(2), 365-375, N 89.

KUFLIK, Arthur. Allocation and Ownership of World Resources: A Symposium Overview. J Value Inq, 23(3), 249-258, S 89.

KUHNS, Richard and TOVEY, Barbara. Portia's Suitors. Phil Lit, 13(2), 325-331, O 89.

Suitors described in Act I, Scene ii of *The Merchant of Venice* are identified, and reasons given for the identifications. They are five of Shakespeare's important teachers and predecessors. Philosophical implications for the drama are stated.

KUHSE, Helga. *The Sanctity-of-Life Doctrine in Medicine: A Critique*. New York, Clarendon/Oxford Pr, 1987

It is widely believed that all human lives, regardless of their quality or kind, are equally valuable and inviolable. It is also widely believed that it is possible to combine this view with a limited duty of life-preservation: whilst it is always wrong to kill a patient, it is not always wrong to withhold life-sustaining treatment, foreseeing that the patient will die as a consequence. This book challenges the consistency of this view by examining the difference between killing and allowing to die in terms of causation, intention and the traditional distinction between ordinary and extraordinary means of treatment.

KUIDE, Chen. "Man versus Nature and Natural Man" in *Man and Nature: The Chinese Tradition and the Future*, TANG, Yi-Jie (ed), 131-141. Lanham, Univ Pr of America, 1989.

KUIPER, M. Dialects of Aestheticism (in Dutch). Tijdschr Filosof, 52(1), 41-61, Mr 90.

Attempts to solve philosophical problems from the point of view of language-use have been very fruitful, but if language becomes the sole principle by which knowledge is accounted for, serious strains emerge. This article ventures to criticize the conception of historical knowledge as being—for any part of it that is more than the statement of simple fact—essentially the product of the creative powers of language. This argument is developed by analysing the work of two philosophers, Michel

Foucault and Hayden White, who both hold that our image of the past is the result of the aesthetic and creative power of language: although they share a common starting point in *aestheticism*, Foucault and White are at odds over central issues in their theories. As a consequence we can read the philosophy of the one as a criticism of the philosophy of the other. Such a reading unveils the paradoxical structure inherent in aestheticism. (edited)

KUIPERS, Theo A F. Het objectieve waarheidsbegrip in Waarder. Kennis Methode, 14(2), 198-211, 1990.

In the past twenty years many philosophers have developed an allergy with respect to speaking freely about statements being objectively true or false. This applies even to so-called referential realists such as Hacking and Radder. It is argued that they do better to leave the allergy to the diehard empiricists who prefer refraining from any ontological hypothesis to explaining the success of natural science and common sense. (edited)

KUKLA, André. Evolving Probability. Phil Stud, 59(2), 213-224, Je 90.

Garber contrasts two models for dealing with logical learning within a Bayesian framework. The *evolving probability model* (EPM) stipulates only that we should eliminate incoherencies when we are apprised of them. According to the *conditionalization model* (CM), logical truths may be assigned nontrivial probabilities; upon discovering a proof of a logical truth, we are to raise its probability to 1 and conditionalize our other beliefs accordingly. I argue that EPM is not a modification of classical Bayesianism, but a description of how the classical theory is to be used. The adoption of CM would not obviate the need for EPM.

KUKLA, André and KUKLA, Rebecca. Meaning Holism and Intentional Psychology. Analysis, 49(4), 173-175, O 89.

The doctrine of meaning holism is seen by Fodor as incompatible with intentional psychology on the grounds that it precludes the formulation of a certain type of psychological generalization. However, most of the laws constituting intentional psychology are of a different, more general type, to which meaning holism poses no threat. Hence the apparent conflict is illusory.

KUKLA, Rebecca and KUKLA, André. Meaning Holism and Intentional Psychology. Analysis, 49(4), 173-175, O 89.

The doctrine of meaning holism is seen by Fodor as incompatible with intentional psychology on the grounds that it precludes the formulation of a certain type of psychological generalization. However, most of the laws constituting intentional psychology are of a different, more general type, to which meaning holism poses no threat. Hence the apparent conflict is illusory.

KUKLICK, Bruce (ed) and PAINE, Thomas. *Political Writings: Thomas Paine*. New York, Cambridge Univ Pr, 1989

KUKSEWICZ, Zdzislaw. Gilles d'Orléans était-il averroïste? Rev Phil Louvain, 88(77), 5-24, F 90.

Giles of Orleans is generally considered to be an Averroist. However, an examination of his *Quaestiones super De generatione* undermines this view: the author analyses the solutions proposed by Giles to the problems of the eternity of the world in the past (and of creation), and the problems of the intellect and of determinism. Giles does not defend Averroist theses in any of these matters. In conclusion none of the three characteristics of an Averroist text is to be found in these *Quaestiones*: Averroes does not appear as a major source; the typical Averroist theses are rejected; the solutions proposed always respect Christian orthodoxy. In other words, Giles is not an Averroist in this text.

KULENKAMPFF, Jens. The Objectivity of Taste: Hume and Kant. Nous, 24(1), 93-110, Mr 90.

In two points at least, Kant's *Critique of Aesthetic Judgment* can be read as an answer to Hume's essay *Of the Standard of Taste*. First, can there be a standard of taste—as Hume affirms and Kant denies? Second, do judgments of taste ascribe to their object objective value, as Kant contends, or subjective value, as Hume seems to hold? I shall deal with these questions in turn. And I shall finish with a third part that tries to sketch Kant's theory of objective aesthetic value.

KULKA, Jiri. Segmentation, Stratification and Semiotic Transformation in Art Communication (in Czechoslovakian). Estetika, 26(3), 139-151, 1989.

KULKA, Tomas. The Incongruity of Incongruity Theories of Humour (in Hebrew). Iyyun, 39(2), 223-235, Ap 90.

In the literature on humour and laughter it is customary to distinguish between three traditional theories: the superiority theory, the relief from restraint theory, and the incongruity theory. The incongruity theory is today the most popular mainly because its rivals are considered discredited. It is considered to be particularly well suited to account for humorous laughter and amusement occasioned by jokes. This article is not concerned with the question whether the concept of incongruity adequately covers all cases of laughter. For it is argued that the incongruity theory is inadequate even for those cases for which it is thought to be especially well suited. It is shown that the incongruity theory does not (and indeed cannot) account either for the pleasurable effect of jokes, or for aesthetic pleasure. (edited)

KULKA, Tomas. The Logical Structure of Aesthetic Value Judgements: An Outline of a Popperian Aesthetics (in Hebrew). Iyyun, 38(2), 87-102, Ap 89.

The purpose of this essay is to suggest an outline of Popperian aesthetics. I try to show that the main ideas of Popper's philosophy of science can be adapted to the philosophy of art. I suggest that the principle of falsifiability, which plays a central role in Popper's philosophy of science, can be applied to aesthetics. (edited)

KULKARNI, S G. The Availability of a Marxian Critique of Technology. Indian Phil Quart, 17(1), 33-47, Ja 90.

KULLASHI, Muhamedin. The French Revolution and Thinking About the Revolution (in Serbo-Croatian). Filozof Istraz, 30(3), 889-898, 1989.

Gegenstand dieser Studie ist die Bedeutung, die die Französische Revolution für die relevanteste Strömung innerhalb der jugoslawischen Philosophie—das Denken der Revolution—anzunehmen im Begriff ist. Sich auf das umfangreiche Werk Kangrgas stützend versucht der Verfasser dieser Studie, die Leitgedanken ausfindig zu machen, anhand derer die Besonderheit von Kangrgas Interpretation dieser von der Französischen Revolution sowie vom Klassischen deutschen Idealismus ausgelösten zweifachen Wende klar wird. (edited)

KUNEN, Kenneth. Where MA First Fails. J Sym Log, 53(2), 429-433, Je 88.

If 0 is any singular cardinal of cofinality w_1, we produce a forcing extension in which MA holds below 0 but fails at 0. The failure is due to a partial order which splits a gap of size 0 in $P(w)$.

KUNINSKI, Milowit. Towards a Phenomenology of Social Role. Rep Phil, 13, 37-49, 1989.

KÜNNE, Wolfgang. "What One Thinks: Singular Propositions and the Content of Judgements" in Whitehead's Metaphysics of Creativity, RAPP, Friedrich (ed), 117-126. Albany, SUNY Pr, 1990.

KUNTZ, Paul G. Santayana's Neo-Platonism. Bull Santayana Soc, 3, 9-21, Fall 85.

KÜNZLI, Arnold. Der Kapitalismus verletzt die Menschenrechte. Dialec Hum, 16(2), 171-185, Spr 89.

KUOKKANEN, Martti. The Hierarchical Structure of Testing Theories. Erkenntnis, 32(2), 235-267, Mr 90.

The first part of the paper sketches the hierarchical structure of testing empirical theories. The structuralist theory-concept is essentially revised especially more adequate for the reconstruction of mathematical social theorizing. The second part of the paper evaluates critically the structuralist notion of theoreticity. The analysis of four examples of typical mathematical social theorizing, i.e., "linear mathematical modelling," proposes that there really are hierarchical structures of different "theoretical levels" in mathematical social theorizing and that the adequate notion of theoreticity should take into account these structures in an appropriate way. The paper contains no technical innovations in the area of mathematical modelling, but the nature of the paper is methodological and philosophical.

KUPFER, Joseph. Can Parents and Children Be Friends? Amer Phil Quart, 27(1), 15-26, Ja 90.

Fundamental features of the ideal parent-adult child relationship keep it from being true or complete friendship. Adult children can't be as autonomous as their parents in the relationship because parents are more responsible for the children's identity. Parents exercise greater autonomy when the child is young, resulting in their opinions and values carrying over into the adult child's life. Secondly, parents and adult children lack the true separateness needed for the union which defines friendship. These basic features, however, enable the ideal parent-child relationship to have uniquely valuable qualities which are missing from even the best of friendships: mutual identification, stability, aesthetic closure, parent-child love.

KUPFER, Joseph. Suicide: Its Nature and Moral Evaluation. J Value Inq, 24(1), 67-81, Ja 90.

This paper clarifies what suicide is and provides a schema for its moral evaluation. When an individual takes his own life it is suicide unless one of two conditions obtains: he did not truly "choose" his death, or there is an alternate description/intention of the act. The moral evaluation of suicides groups them into three classes: the laudable, "acceptable," and immoral. The laudable are other-regarding. Acceptable suicides involve the agent in disvaluing her own life. And immoral suicides either use the death as a

means to evil ends or spring from weak character.

KÜPPERS, Günter and KROHN, Wolfgang. "Self-Organization: A New Approach to Evolutionary Epistemology" in Issues in Evolutionary Epistemology, HAHLWEG, Kai (ed), 151-170. Albany, SUNY Pr, 1989.

The essay specifies several shortcomings characteristic of the attempts to combine evolutionary with epistemological aspects of knowledge. Most important is that the self-referentiality of scientific knowledge and the self-organization of social systems don't allow for an independent definition of variation and selection. On the basis of the theory of self-organizing systems the essay attempts to develop new ideas as to how social interaction and formation of knowledge operate on each other and exemplifies these in the case of production of scientific knowledge.

KURAN, Timur. Private and Public Preferences. Econ Phil, 6(1), 1-26, Ap 90.

KURATA, Reijiro and SHIMODA, M. Some Combinatorial Principles Equivalent to Restrictions of Transfinite Induction Up to Γ_0. Annals Pure Applied Log, 44(1-2), 63-69, O 89.

KURER, O. John Stuart Mill on Government Intervention. Hist Polit Thought, 10(3), 457-480, Autumn 89.

KURER, Oskar. John Stuart Mill on Democratic Representation and Centralization. Utilitas, 1(2), 290-299, N 89.

The article examines Mill's argument on centralization and democratic representation. It questions the commonly held view that Mill was favourably inclined towards decentralization, and shows that his centralist tenets are the result of his fear of the consequences of mass participation in politics. Centralization is used as a means to reduce the dangers emanating from participation, and Mill emerges less of an advocate of participatory democracy than it is commonly thought.

KURKELA, Kari. How a Note Denotes. Acta Phil Fennica, 43, 70-96, 1988.

The paper analyses conventional music notation as a means of communication and as a language applying methods used in possible world semantics and model-theoretical semantics. It carries on with some questions dealt with in the book Note and Tone by the same author. A detailed analysis of a fragment of notation is presented, some essential terms, such as sound structure and musical work, are explicated, and relationships between notation, performance and musical work are clarified.

KURODA, S Y. An Explanatory Theory of Communicative Intentions. Ling Phil, 12(6), 655-681, D 89.

The formal theory of communicative intentions presented in Kuroda (1986) ("A Formal Theory of Speech Acts," Linguistics and Philosophy 9) is shown to provide deductive proofs of three different interpretations for Grice's formula for nonnatural meaning (Paul Grice, "Meaning," Philosophical Review 66).

KURTH, Rudolf. Philosophische Bemerkungen. New York, Lang, 1989

Das Buch bringt eine systematisch geordnete Sammlung von "Bemerkungen"—d.h. von Aphorismen, Ketten von zusammenhängenden Aphorismen und kurzen Aufsätzen; u.a. zur Ersten Philosophie, Religion, Ethik, Ästhetik und Erziehung. Die Bemerkungen, methodisch bewusst vollzogen, richten sich zum grossen Teil auf konkrete Dinge. Sie sind durchdrungen von einem Grundbewusstsein, das sich etwa mit den folgenden Stichworten umschreiben lässt: das Wirkliche als Erscheinung; Transzendenz; Freiheit als Verantwortung; Handeln als Einheit von Denken und Wollen; Geist als Einheit von Fühlen und Denken; Vernunft als Wille und Liebe zur Wahrheit.—Maximen der Form: "Einfach, knapp, klar, genau."

KURTZ, Paul. Militant Atheism Versus Freedom of Conscience. Free Inq, 9(4), 24-32, Fall 89.

KURTZ, Paul. "The Naturalists" in Reading Philosophy for the Twenty-First Century, MC LEAN, George F (ed), 215-244. Lanham, Univ Pr of America, 1989.

KURTZ, Paul. Philosophical Essays in Pragmatic Naturalism. Buffalo, Prometheus, 1990

KUTTIANICKAL, Joseph. Non-Violence, the Core of Religious Experience in Gandhi. J Dharma, 14(3), 227-246, Jl-S 89.

KUYKENDALL, Eleanor H. "The Subjectivity of the Speaker" in The Question of the Other: Essays in Contemporary Continental Philosophy, DALLERY, Arleen B (ed), 145-155. Albany, SUNY Pr, 1989.

KUYS, Thieu. Knowledge, Criticism, and Coherence. Phil Stud, 57(1), 41-60, S 89.

This paper introduces a novel perspective on the theory of knowledge that relates the standards of knowing to the standards of criticism. It is argued that this perspective leads to a new method for constructing and evaluating theories of knowledge. In applying this method it is found that one can give independent arguments in support of a coherence condition of knowing as has been defended by Keith Lehrer and Laurence BonJour. However, the method also explains why Lehrer's fourth condition is defective, and shows how it can be improved.

KVANVIG, Jonathan L. Adams on Actualism and Presentism. Phil Phenomenol Res, 50(2), 289-298, D 89.

Adams has recently argued for the temporal dependency thesis (TDT). The TDT claims that no singular propositions about an individual and no "thisnesses" of individuals exist prior to the existence of the individual in question. Adams claims the TDT follows from an acceptable version of actualism. This paper argues that the argument for this thesis is flawed. More importantly, it is argued that if the argument is accepted, there is an analogue of actualism, presentism, which is as adequate as Adams's version of actualism, and which implies that there are no singular propositions of "thisnesses" about objects which no longer exist. Since Adams agrees that the truth of this position constitutes a problem for his view, his view ought to be rejected.

KVANVIG, Jonathan L and MENZEL, Christopher. The Basic Notion of Justification. Phil Stud, 59(3), 235-261, Jl 90.

There are three important kinds of justification: personal (as in "S is justified in believing p"); propositional (as in "p is justified for S"); and doxastic (as in "S justifiably believes p"). The question we address is whether any one of these three is basic, and argue that propositional justification has this status. This conclusion is important in that most versions of reliabilism require that doxastic justification is the basic kind. Hence our conclusion implies that the most common reliabilist theories of justification are false.

KVANVIG, Jonathan L. The Haecceity Theory and Perspectival Limitation. Austl J Phil, 67(3), 295-305, S 89.

The haecceity theory claims that all awareness is best analyzed in terms of a two-place relation between a person and a proposition, and that self-awareness can be explained as a special case of propositional awareness. Self-awareness is differentiated from ordinary awareness in that it involves awareness of one's own haecceity, a property one has essentially which no one else has and which can only be grasped by oneself. This paper argues that the haecceity theory is the last best hope for a dyadic theory of the intentional attitudes, but that it is plagued by self-referential inconsistency. Thus, it concludes that no dyadic theory of the intentional attitudes can be correct.

KVART, Igal. Divided Reference. Midwest Stud Phil, 14, 140-179, 1989.

KWANT, R C. Merleau-Ponty's nieuwe filosofie van de perceptie, de natuur en de logos. Tijdschr Filosof, 51(4), 669-695, D 89.

KYJ, Myroslaw J and REILLY, Bernard J. The Social Conscience of Business. Bus Prof Ethics J, 7(3-4), 81-101, Fall-Wint 88.

The issue of social ethics and its meaning become critical when space, time, and distances are narrowed by the expansion of technology, the potentials of indestructible chemicals and biologicals, the internationalization of product and financial markets, the multinational drug firm, and the marketing, communications, and information changes which deny the limitations of traditional markets. Therefore, ethical theory and practice begin with agreements on the categories of what is good and what is valuable, both for the individual and the society. This involves the development of categories of ethical values as they define relationships between corporations and their environments.

KYLE, Gunhild and JUNGEN, Britta. Women's Research and Its Inherent Critique of Society and Science. Phil Soc Act, 15(3-4), 41-45, Jl-D 89.

KYLE, Judy A. Managing Philosophical Discussions. Thinking, 5(2), 19-22, 1984.

LA CROCE, Ernesto. La crítica aristotélica al Bien platónico. Rev Filosof (Argentina), 4(2), 79-96, N 89.

This paper considers the Aristotelian criticisms to the Platonic concept of the Good. They are divided into two groups: (a) against the Good as "Idea" or "Form"; (b) against the Good as "principle." The paper analyses the differences between the criticisms in Nicomachean Ethics and in Eudemian Ethics. Then, it discusses six Aristotelian arguments against the Good as Idea or Form, as well as some modern interpretations of them. Lastly, a long argument against the Good as principle is considered, following some remarks stated by J Brunschwig. It concludes that both groups of criticisms try to establish the same point: each thing tends to its own good, and this is a particular good, neither an absolute nor a unique Good.

LA FOLLETTE, Hugh (ed) and GRAHAM, George (ed). Person to Person. Philadelphia, Temple Univ Pr, 1989

A collection of mostly original essays by philosophers and psychologists on the ethics of personal relationships, including such topics as parental

obligations to children, trust and intimacy among friends, and family privacy.

LA FOLLETTE, Hugh. "Animal Rights and Human Wrongs" in Ethics and the Environmental Responsibility, DOWER, Nigel (ed), 79-90. Aldershot, Avebury, 1989.

This essay, written for a nonphilosophical audience, argues that there are substantial moral limits on how we should treat nonhuman animals. We have conflicting attitudes toward animals: while virtually everyone recognizes we cannot treat animals just anyway we please, we uncritically accept the use of animals for food and in medical research. We should eliminate these conflicts by formally recognizing the moral status of animals.

LA FOLLETTE, Hugh and GRAHAM, George. "Honesty and Intimacy" in Person to Person, GRAHAM, George (ed), 167-181. Philadelphia, Temple Univ Pr, 1989.

Examination of the role of honesty in intimate relationships, which includes a defense of the thesis that dishonesty is never justified in an intimate relationship. Two types of honesty are distinguished and the role of sensitivity in intimacy is counterpointed with the role of honesty.

LABARRIÈRE, Jean-Louis. "The Political Animal's Knowledge According to Aristotle" in Knowledge and Politics, DASCAL, Marcelo (ed), 33-47. Boulder, Westview Pr, 1988.

This paper examines a double question: that of the knowledge required in order to be a political animal and that of the status of such a knowledge which can't be a science according to the Aristotelian criteria. It shows that man is not the only political animal, but that his logos establishes his political superiority because he can deliberate on what is good for the city. The status of this deliberation justifies that politics can't be a science because we deliberate only on the things which can be otherwise while the object of science is what can't be otherwise.

LABBÉ, Yves. Sur l'unité de l'unique preuve de Dieu. Rev Thomiste, 90(2), 194-229, Ap-Je 90.

LABRADA, Maria Antonia. La imagen del hombre en la teoría kantiana del genio. Anu Filosof, 21(2), 145-154, 1988.

The purpose of the work is to study the faculties which constitute genius. The conclusion is that the infinite of objectivity is not expressed in creativity. This fact limits the Kantian theory of genius to the familiar bounds of critical philosophy. Thus, it is possible to assert that Kantian philosophy, including that which refers to the theory of genius and artistic creation, is a philosophy of nature and a philosophy of the finite spirit.

LACEY, A R. Bergson. New York, Routledge, 1989

The book aims to give a critical survey of Bergson's thought from the broadly 'analytical' standpoint prevalent in current English-speaking philosophy. This is not Bergson's own standpoint, but the book tries to steer between unsympathetic rejection and uncritical overestimation; it does not go into the history of ideas, or trace influences on or of Bergson. The topics cover space and time (including durée, and a brief note on Bergson's debate with Einstein), free will, change and substance, perception and memory, instinct and intelligence and intuition, biology (including the élan vital), the cosmic, and morality and religion.

LACHS, John. The Enduring Value of Santayana's Philosophy. Bull Santayana Soc, 6, 1-13, Fall 88.

LACHS, John. George Santayana. Bull Santayana Soc, 2, 15-22, Fall 84.

LACHS, John. How Relative are Values? or Are Nazis Irrational and Why the Answer Matters. S J Phil, 28(3), 319-328, Fall 90.

LACHS, John. Human Natures. Proc Amer Phil Ass, 63(7), 29-39, Je 90.

LACHS, John. "Mill" in Ethics in the History of Western Philosophy, CAVALIER, Robert J (ed), 244-270. New York, St Martin's Pr, 1988.

LACHTERMAN, David R. The Ethics of Geometry: A Genealogy of Modernity. New York, Routledge, 1989

Are ancient and modern thought essentially discontinuous and substantively opposed? By exploring the roles of construction in Euclidean and Cartesian mathematics, the author tries to establish an affirmative answer. The mark of modernity, in mathematics as well as in philosophy, is construction. The ethos of the moderns is poïetic; Euclid's geometry, once the now-orthodox Kantian, i.e., constructivistic, interpretation has been undermined, discloses itself as the exemplar of theoretical phronesis. In this light so-called postmodernism is a coda to radical modernity.

LACKEY, Douglas P (ed). Ethics and Strategic Defense: American Philosophers Debate Star Wars and Nuclear Deterrence. Belmont, Wadsworth, 1989

LACKEY, Douglas P. The Ethics of War and Peace. Englewood Cliffs, Prentice-Hall, 1989

LACKEY, Douglas P. *God, Immortality, Ethics: A Concise Introduction to Philosophy*. Belmont, Wadsworth, 1989

LACOSTE, Jean-Yves. Anges et hobbits: le sens des mondes possibles. Frei Z Phil Theol, 36(3), 341-373, 1989.

LACOSTE, Patrick. L'observation: Freud et la scénographie clinique. Rev Int Phil, 43(171), 480-505, 1989.

LACOUE-LABARTHE, Philippe and NANCY, Jean-Luc. The Nazi Myth. Crit Inquiry, 16(2), 291-312, Wint 89.

Nazi ideology did work through a very specific relationship to the category and to the intellectual-emotional tool of *myth*. First, because nazism takes, in a totalitarian and racist way, the heritage of a fundamental problem of Germany: this one of *identification*. Myth is precisely conceived in our tradition as an "identificatory mechanism." People and State as *total work of art* is mean and goal of such a process. This implies also (which may be shown with Rosenberg's *Myth of the XXth Century*) that the Aryan/Nazi myth is not a myth among others, but the proper figure, and essence, of myth itself. It presents the power of forming or "typing" oneself. The self-formation of the self (subjectivity in philosophical meaning) and the "collective egoism" of this formation as a nation (racism) are strongly bounded here.

LACOUE-LABARTHE, Philippe and FYNSK, Christopher (ed). *Typography: Mimesis, Philosophy, Politics*. Cambridge, Harvard Univ Pr, 1989

LADD, Rosalind Ekman. Women in Labor: Some Issues About Informed Consent. Hypatia, 4(3), 37-45, Fall 89.

Women wishing hospital admission for childbirth are asked to sign very general pre-admission consent forms. The use of such forms suggests that women in labor are considered incompetent to give informed consent. This paper explores some of the problems with advance directives and general consent, and argues that since women in labor are not generally incompetent, it is not appropriate to require this kind of consent of them.

LADRIERE, Jean. "Logic and Argumentation" in *From Metaphysics to Rhetoric*, MEYER, Michel (ed), 15-35. Norwell, Kluwer, 1989.

LAFLEUR, Gérald. Vérisimilarité et méthodologie poppérienne. Dialogue (Canada), 28(3), 365-390, 1989.

This article shows that (1) Karl Popper's qualitative theory of verisimilitude is consistent with his method of conjectures, corroborations and refutations; (2) nevertheless this theory, when considered from an intuitive point of view, is too strong; (3) the Popperian system can overcome the formal proof proposed by Pavel Tichy in 1974 against Popper's theory. Finally, the paper provides a new definition of verisimilitude which seems logically sound, intuitively satisfactory and more intimately linked to the Popperian methodology than Popper's original definition.

LAFON, Guy. L'homme du désir. Etudes, 371(3), 257-266, S 89.

LAFRANCE, Guy. Égalité et justice: une idée de l'homme. Rev Int Phil, 43(170), 352-360, 1989.

LAGERSPETZ, Eerik. A Conventionalist Theory of Institutions. Acta Phil Fennica, 44, 1-166, 1989.

This work deals with the question of how social rules and practices exist. The author defends the thesis that they are self-grounding—their existence is based on general beliefs that they exist, and on the role those beliefs play in the practical reasoning of relevant individuals. This practical role is due to the coordinative function of rules and practices. The analysis is applied to two major social institutions—the monetary system and the law. Included are discussions on various philosophical, social and legal theories, including the theories of Thomas Hobbes, H L A Hart, David Lewis, James Buchanan and John Searle.

LAGERSPETZ, Eerik. "Hobbes's Logic of Law" in *Hobbes: War Among Nations*, AIRAKSINEN, Timo (ed), 142-153. Brookfield, Gower, 1989.

The basic properties of a Hobbesian sovereign are illimitability, indivisibility and continuity. These properties follow logically from Hobbes's idea that laws are commands, and from the pragmatics of commanding acts. According to Hobbes, commanding-obedience relationships are transitive and asymmetric. By using an argument based on infinite regress, Hobbes proves that a supreme commanding authority has to exist. This argument runs through the history of modern legal theory, and it appears, e.g., in Austin, Kant and Kelsen.

LAGO BORNSTEIN, Juan Carlos. La educación ética: una asignatura pendiente. Dialogo Filosof, 6(1), 82-88, Ja-Ap 90.

LAGREE, Jacqueline. Sens et Vérité: Philosophie et théologie chez L Meyer et Spinoza. Stud Spinozana, 4, 75-91, 1988.

Although both Lodewijk Meyer and Spinoza had access to Clauberg's *Logica* in which an elaborated theory of interpretation is developed,

including the distinction of immediate meaning, true meaning and truth, their respective use of these distinctions in the hermeneutics of scripture differs considerably. Meyer denies the validity of the distinction of true meaning and truth in the very case of scripture, because God who is omniscient and omniprovident has foreseen the progress of human understanding, and that is why every interpretation of scriptural texts that conforms with truth can be judged to meet the true meaning of those texts. Spinoza always takes care to stick to the principle of a strictly historical, i.e., a contextual analysis, even if there is a meaning of the text that conforms to reason. Otherwise people would become dependent on the philosophers' authority in understanding scripture, and thus all freedom of religious thought would be abolished. (edited)

LAHAV, Ran. Against Compositionality: The Case of Adjectives. Phil Stud, 57(3), 261-279, N 89.

I argue against the prevalent view that natural language is compositional, in the sense that the meanings of compound expressions are functions of the meanings of their constituents. My strategy is to examine the actual behavior of natural language expressions, in particular of adjectives. I argue that the applicability conditions of an adjective depend on the noun to which it is applied. Consequently, there is an element in the meaning of an adjective which is not constant across linguistic contexts; which means that adjectives do not behave compositionally.

LAHAV, Ran. An Alternative to the Adverbial Theory: Dis-Phenomenalism. Phil Phenomenol Res, 50(3), 553-568, Mr 90.

I offer an alternative to the prevalent adverbial account of what is traditionally described (misleadingly, as I argue) as objects of experience. I start by rejecting the adverbial theory on the ground that despite its ontological elegance, it violates the phenomenological facts. I then present a picture which is no less ontologically elegant, but at the same time is faithful to phenomenological considerations. The theory consists of two parts: a phenomenological thesis about the inner structure of "objects of experience," and an ontological thesis which identifies "objects of experience" with physical events undergone by cognizers.

LAHAV, Ran. Bergson and the Hegemony of Language. S J Phil, 28(3), 329-342, Fall 90.

I argue that Henri Bergson's views on the nature of experience constitute a fundamental metaphilosophical criticism of traditional mainstream philosophical methodologies. According to Bergson, our experience consiitutes a flux of qualities that escapes analysis and description. I argue that this is at bottom a methodological claim about the attitude from which the world is to be investigated philosophically. Bergson can be seen as exposing and questioning the traditional presupposition that the proper philosophical attitude which grants us an epistemic access to reality is analytic and descriptive.

LAI, Whalen. Wang Yang-ming and the Bamboos (in Serbo-Croatian). Filozof Istraz, 29(2), 505-516, 1989.

LAITKO, Hubert. "On the Emergence of Scientific Disciplines" in *Scientific Knowledge Socialized*, HRONSZKY, Imre (ed), 213-223. Norwell, Kluwer, 1989.

LAKHAN, V C and SINGH, Jang B. Business Ethics and the International Trade in Hazardous Wastes. J Bus Ethics, 8(11), 889-899, N 89.

The annual production of hazardous wastes, which was less than 10 million metric tonnes in the 1940s, is now in excess of 320 million metric tonnes. These wastes are, in the main, by-products of industrial processes that have contributed significantly to the economic development of many countries which, in turn, has led to lifestyles that also generate hazardous wastes. The phenomenal increase in the generation of hazardous wastes coupled with various barriers to local disposal has led to the thriving international trade in these environmentally hazardous substances. This paper examines the nature of the international trade in hazardous wastes and the ethical issues associated with such business activity.

LAKOFF, George. "Cognitive Semantics" in *Meaning and Mental Representation*, ECO, Umberto (ed), 119-154. Bloomington, Indiana Univ Pr, 1988.

LAKOMSKI, Gabriele. Against Feminist Science: Harding and the Science Question in Feminism. Educ Phil Theor, 21(2), 1-11, 1989.

The relationship between gender and science, and specifically the question of whether there is, or can be, a feminist science, has, for good reason, become central in feminist theorizing. For if science is masculine, and characterized by an empiricist epistemology as claimed by major feminist writers, then science systematically misrepresents the world by misrepresenting the experience of women. The consequence feminists have drawn from their analysis issued in a number of alternative feminist epistemologies which in various ways attempt to redress the problem. This article examines one prominent exploration of the thesis that science is androcentric. Sandra Harding not only examines the epistemological proposals of other feminists, she also offers an outline for a new feminist theory of science which is to replace the "unity of science" thesis of the Vienna Circle. It is argued here that Harding's proposal is incoherent. (edited)

LAM, M Natalie. Management Training for Women: International Experiences and Lessons for Canada. J Bus Ethics, 9(4-5), 385-406, Ap-My 90.

In Canada, there is growing recognition that women play an increasingly important role in the working world. Management training programs for women have been considered as a route to prepare women to be more effective managers. This paper highlights some of the major issues and concerns being discussed outside Canada by those engaged in management education and training for women—objectives and content of programs, nature of participants, training methods, choice of trainers, organization and evaluation of programs. References are made to a few international programs to illustrate how some of these concerns have been addressed. Implications for training programs in Canada, from both practical as well as research points of view, are discussed.

LAMACCHIA, Ada. Edith Stein: Filosofia E Senso Dell'Essere. Cambridge, Abacus Pr, 1989

LAMB, Matthew. The Notion of the Transcultural in Bernard Lonergan's Theology. Method, 8(1), 48-73, Mr 90.

This essay shows how Lonergan's notion of the concrete universal and the transcultural breaks through the antinomies set up by both empiricism and idealism. Philosophical and theological consequences of this breakthrough are also discussed.

LAMB, Roger. Currie on Fictional Names. Austl J Phil, 68(1), 113-115, Mr 90.

This is a brief discussion of Gregory Currie's semantics for the fictive uses of fictional names as it appears in his 'Fictional Names' (AJP Dec 88). His problem is how to represent the content of stories so that 'unique identification' of characters is achieved. His solution is to introduce into the content of the story a narrator who produces a text. I suggest the unhappy result of this maneuver is an infinite regress of 'embedded cloned stories' nested within the story.

LAMBEK, J. On Some Connections Between Logic and Category Theory. Stud Log, 48(3), 269-278, S 89.

LAMBERT, Roger. L'État minimal et le droit de propriété privée selon Nozick. Rev Metaph Morale, 95(1), 95-113, Ja-Mr 90.

LAMI, Gian Franco. Hobbes come Giano: un pensatore sulla soglia dello Stato moderno. Riv Int Filosof Diritto, 66(3), 515-519, Jl-S 89.

LAMI, Gian Franco. Scienza politica e "nuova" scienza della politica: un conflitto "generazionale"? Riv Int Filosof Diritto, 66(2), 374-381, Ap-Je 89.

LAMM, Richard D. High Technology Health Care. Nat Forum, 69(4), 14-17, Fall 89.

LAMM, Richard D. Who Pays for AZT: Commentary. Hastings Center Rep, 19(5), 32, S-O 89.

LAMMENRANTA, Markus. Nelson Goodman on Emotions in Music. Acta Phil Fennica, 43, 210-216, 1988.

According to Nelson Goodman's theory of symbols, a piece of music expresses the properties that it possesses metaphorically and that it refers to. Because of his nominalism, Goodman, however, insists that all talk about properties must be analyzable into talk about predicates and other labels. So it is labels that are actually expressed. What are the required emotion labels? Three views are considered: the emotion labels can be understood as (1) linguistic terms, (2) self-referring musical events, or (3) mental images. It is argued that Goodman's theory must allow the reference to mental images to be plausible at all.

LAMPERT, Jay. Husserl's Theory of Parts and Wholes: The Dynamic of Individuating and Contextualizing Interpretation. Res Phenomenol, 19, 195-212, 1989.

LANCE, Mark and HAWTHORNE, John. From a Normative Point of View. Pac Phil Quart, 71(1), 28-46, Mr 90.

Translation is indexical in the sense that the correctness of a translation depends not just on features of the linguistic community being translated, but also on that of the translator. This indexicality is preserved even if the language community being translated has the ability to formulate claims about what its words mean. The best explanation of this phenomenon involves changing our conception of the activity of translation. In translating, one devises a set of rules which are to govern communication between the

members of two communities and lead to the formation of a single large linguistic community.

LANDE, Nelson P. Posthumous Rehabilitation and the Dust-Bin of History. Pub Affairs Quart, 4(3), 267-286, Jl 90.

I advance three arguments to the effect that justice calls for the posthumous rehabilitation of the Bolshevik Oppositionists. First I examine the nature of rehabilitation, and in particular the notion of the restoration of one's good name. My first argument is that one has a right to his good name and to its restoration, even if it is violated posthumously. I examine the notion of the posthumous violation of one's rights, and criticize the views of Joel Feinberg and George Pitcher in this regard. My next two arguments entail that there is a duty to preserve the memories of the Oppositionists, and thus to seek their rehabilitation. First I argue that the duty to show respect for the ideals of the October Revolution, insofar as they are worthy, entails the duty to honor those Oppositionists who exemplified them. Second I argue that there is a duty based on gratitude to remember those who contributed a measure of good to the world by helping to secure the preservation of a variety of ideals, amongst them those of the October Revolution.

LANDERS, Scott. Wittgenstein, Realism, and CLS: Undermining Rule Scepticism. Law Phil, 9(2), 177-203, My 90.

LANDESMAN, Charles. Color and Consciousness: An Essay in Metaphysics. Cambridge, Abacus Pr, 1989

This work reviews various dispositional, microstate, and subjectivist accounts of secondary qualities and finds that their views about color cannot be defended. In their place, the book defends color skepticism according to which nothing has any color even though many things appear to have color. Color skepticism which is based upon scientific realism must be distinguished from the more radical Cartesian skepticism which attempts to cast doubt upon science altogether.

LANDESMAN, Charles. "Reflections on Hobbes: Anarchy and Human Nature" in The Causes of Quarrel: Essays on Peace, War, and Thomas Hobbes, CAWS, Peter (ed), 139-148. Boston, Beacon Pr, 1989.

LANDMAN, Fred. Groups, I. Ling Phil, 12(5), 559-605, O 89.

LANDMAN, Fred. Groups, II. Ling Phil, 12(6), 723-744, D 89.

LANE, Michael S and BEGGS, Joyce M. Corporate Goal Structures and Business Students: A Comparative Study of Values. J Bus Ethics, 8(6), 471-478, Je 89.

Are the values of business students of today synchronized with the reality of the present business environment? 222 business students rated the importance of 20 corporate goals. Moreover, the students rated the same goals as they perceived chief executive officers (CEOs) would have rated them. Significant differences were found between the two ratings, with students ranking social and employee-oriented goals as more important than they perceived CEOs would have.

LANE, Michael S and SCHAUPP, Dietrich. Ethics in Education: A Comparative Study. J Bus Ethics, 8(12), 943-949, D 89.

This study reports the results of a survey designed to assess the impact of education on the perceptions of ethical beliefs of students. The study examines the beliefs of students from selected colleges in an eastern university. The results indicate that beliefs which students perceive are required to succeed in the university differ among colleges. Business and economics students consistently perceive a greater need for unethical beliefs than students from other colleges.

LANE, Neil R. Rationality, Self-Esteem and Autonomy through Collaborative Enquiry. Thinking, 8(3), 41-49, 1989.

LANG, Berel. The Politics of Interpretation: Spinoza's Modernist Turn. Rev Metaph, 43(2), 327-356, D 89.

Beyond its specific reading of the Bible, Spinoza's Tractatus provides a general theory of interpretation which includes the claim for an intrinsic relation between interpretation and politics. In "secularizing" the biblical text, Spinoza anticipates (and criticizes in anticipation) interpretative theories based on the 'Hermeneutic Circle'; his own theory includes a conception of textual meaning as fixed and historically (although not necessarily personally) intentional.

LANG, Daniel G. "Human Rights and the Founding Fathers" in Moral Reasoning and Statecraft: Essays Presented to Kenneth W Thompson, DAVIS, Reed M (ed), 53-66. Lanham, Univ Pr of America, 1988.

The American Constitution's framers' view of human rights pulled them in two directions when applied to foreign policy. The assertion of the universality of human rights gave Americans cause to try to export republicanism. On the other hand, the relative lack of American power, the logic of nonintervention, and the realization that the American model would not fit all situations gave Americans pause. For many of the framers, this tension was resolved through a policy which promoted human rights indirectly: support for the balance of power system, neutral rights, and free trade.

LANG, Dieter. "Über philosophische Ethik: Probleme angelsächsischer und skandinavischer Positionen" in *Agora: Zu Ehren von Rudolph Berlinger*, BERLINGER, Rudolph (and other eds), 129-140. Amsterdam, Rodopi, 1988.

LANGE, Lynda. Sexist Dualism: Its Material Sources in the Exploitation of Reproductive Labor. Praxis Int, 9(4), 400-407, Ja 90.

LANGENFUS, William L. Consequentialism in Search of a Conscience. Amer Phil Quart, 27(2), 131-141, Ap 90.

Consequentialism, some have held, can be regarded as specifying an ultimate criterion of rightness without at the same time requiring the general inculcation of a direct motivation to act in accordance with it. The purpose of this paper is to show that this "criterion/motivation separation" leaves an important motivational gap in the theory. It cannot account for the general development of a robust moral conscience which, it is argued, has significant consequentialist relevance. It is argued that neither of the two strategies most commonly used to fill this gap is successful.

LANGENFUS, William L. Implications of a Self-Effacing Consequentialism. S J Phil, 27(4), 479-493, Wint 89.

A "self-effacing" consequentialism (the term coined by Derek) is one that morally requires the exclusive, general inculcation of a nonconsequentialist conception of morality. It is argued that a self-effacing consequentialism has a social role in reforming certain aspects of "common-sense morality"; however, this is inherently limited by the need to couch any revisionary arguments to that end in "common-sense" (and not consequentialist) terms.

LANGER, Judith. Literate Thinking and Schooling. Thinking, 8(3), 29-30, 1989.

LANGER, Susanne Katherina. *Mind: An Essay on Human Feeling*. Baltimore, Johns Hopkins U Pr, 1988

LANGLEY, Winston. The Right of Self-Determination in International Law. Quest, 4(1), 4-17, Je 90.

The objective of the article is to look at the relationship between the norm of self-determination and the developmental aspirations of Third World peoples, in particular, and the world in general. It pursues that objective by defining the *self* in which the right inheres, examining the scope and reach of the right possessed by that self, and looking at the links of that right to certain preferred international arrangements.

LANGSDORF, Lenore. Dialogue, Distanciation, and Engagement: Toward a Logic of Televisual Communication. Inform Log, 10(3), 151-168, Fall 88.

The discussion relies on the work of Ricoeur, Perelman, Havelock, Innis, and Ong in identifying similarities and differences in kinesthetic, oral, written, and televisual reasoning, in order to consider the extent to which practices of interpreting, evaluating, and constructing argumentation in those media are transferable.

LANGTRY, Bruce. Hume, Probability, Lotteries and Miracles. Hume Stud, 16(1), 67-74, Ap 90.

Hume's main argument against rational belief in miracles might seem to rule out rational belief in other antecedently improbable occurrences as well—for example, a certain person's having won the lottery. Dorothy Coleman has recently defended Hume against the lottery counterexample, invoking Hume's distinction between probability of chances and probability of causes. I argue that Coleman's defence fails.

LANGTRY, Bruce. Properly Unargued Belief in God. Int J Phil Relig, 26(3), 129-154, D 89.

This paper defends the following thesis: there are professional philosophers in our culture today who do not have and have never had a good argument for the existence of God, and who are nevertheless epistemically justified in believing that God exists.

LAPIN, Nikolai I. Acceleration and Restructuring: Dialectics and Problems. Dialec Hum, 15(3-4), 67-83, Sum-Autumn 88.

LAPORTE, Roger. S'entendre parler. Rev Phil Fr, 180(2), 239-246, Ap-Je 90.

LARA, Tiago Adão. Filosofia e Filosofia da Educação. Educ Filosof, 2(3), 15-24, Jl-D 87.

Based on the differences between the concepts of metaphysics and the dialectics of philosophy, it is important to emphasise the necessity of reflecting the philosophy of education as a commitment to the many ideas of education which have been developed historically so as to indicate its social origins, its humanistic perspectives and limitations. At the same time, it is necessary to go beyond the stage of criticism which is currently in vogue to

the development of alternative projects that reflect a renewed mental process. This project should also reflect a new way of thinking no longer based on the metaphysical concept of absolutes and abstract ideas.

LARAUDOGOITIA, Jon Perez. A Doxastic Paradox. Analysis, 50(1), 47-48, Ja 90.

We can accept as true, propositions which are false or even self-contradictory. But can mere belief in the truth of certain propositions lead us into contradiction? It is shown in this article that such situations can arise, by analysing the structure of a test which anybody can, in principle, be submitted to. The problem is related with the preface paradox and with a classical argument by Prior.

LARGEAULT, J. Cinq questions à propos de l'épistémologie. Rev Phil Fr, 179(3), 297-310, Jl-S 89.

LARKIN, Edward T. "Goethe's Moral Thinking" in *Inquiries into Values: The Inaugural Session of the International Society for Value Inquiry*, LEE, Sander H , 273-278. Lewiston, Mellen Pr, 1989.

Through an analysis of Goethe's comments, conversations and literary texts this paper exemplifies the legitimacy of an approach to literature which seeks to establish an author's ethical stance. Goethe understands morality to be divine, i.e., transcendent, yet accessible to man as he expands his self-consciousness and finds accommodation with societal norms. Morality, while inherently individualistic, supercedes subjectivity and finds a correlate in the laws of nature. It presupposes freedom of choice, but is bound by the individual's demon, the transgression of which defines immorality. Art may only indirectly and never intentionally be moralistic for it then ceases to be art.

LARMER, Robert A. Miracles and Natural Explanations: A Rejoinder. Sophia (Australia), 28(3), 7-12, O 89.

In his article "Miracles and Natural Explanation" David Basinger takes issue with the claim I advanced in my earlier article "Miracles and Criteria" that only a dogmatic and uncritical assumption that nature is in fact an isolated system can explain the insistence of some philosophers that, no matter what the event and no matter what the context in which it occurs, it is always more rational to live in the faith that such an event has a natural explanation rather than believe it a miracle. Basinger urges that my argument contains two basic confusions. In reply, I argue that both his objections are mistaken.

LARMORE, Charles. Liberal Neutrality: A Reply to James Fishkin. Polit Theory, 17(4), 580-581, N 89.

LARMORE, Charles. Political Liberalism. Polit Theory, 18(3), 339-360, Ag 90.

Liberalism should be understood as a minimal moral conception. It then depends on moral commitments which are neutral with respect to the general ideals of individualism and tradition. In this form it becomes an appropriate response to the problem of reasonable disagreement about the good life. It can be called "political liberalism" since the individualist treatment of persons it requires is a strictly political norm, applicable to persons in their role as citizens. It does not express a broader individualism about the sources of value.

LARMORE, Charles. The Right and the Good. Philosophia (Israel), 20(1-2), 15-32, Jl 90.

The nature of moral value assumes two fundamentally different forms, depending on whether the notion of good, as in Greek ethics, or the notion of right, as in modern ethics, is thought to be more basic. This essay explores the reasons why the modern priority of the right should still be affirmed, and also some of the difficulties confronting this position.

LARRABEE, Mary Jeanne. The Contexts of Phenomenology as Theory. Human Stud, 13(3), 195-208, Jl 90.

Edmund Husserl requires transcendental phenomenology to be self-critical. This essay initiates this critique by describing phenomenology as a theory that is a noema correlated with a phenomenologist's theorizing and by indicating the temporal-historical dimensions that such an assessment must investigate. These dimensions include both the essential history of phenomenology within the broader contexts of Western intellectual endeavors and the genetic elements functioning within a phenomenologist's activities, where 'phenomenologist' may indicate either the originary thinker of the theory—here, Husserl—or the reactivating thinker who is currently practicing phenomenology.

LARRE, Olga L. Ente Natural y Artefacto en Guillermo de Ockham. Manuscrito, 13(1), 87-96, Ap 90.

The distinction between *ens naturalis* and *artefactum* is usually taken to be satisfactorily established in Aristotelism by the well-known text of the *Physics*. A significant revision of this distinction was proposed by William of Ockham. Against the background of a poor scientific and technological development, Ockham offers a theory of *ens naturalis* and *artefactum* that could be adequate to later technological conditions. This article studies Ockham's theory as developed in the *Summula Philosophiae Naturalis* (Pars I, cap. 25-6).

LARRETA, Juan Rodríguez. Democracia y moral: Respuesta a Nino. Analisis Filosof, 6(2), 83-95, N 86.

LARRETA, Juan Rodríguez and DORFMAN, Beatriz. Sobre la privacidad de los estados de conciencia. Analisis Filosof, 7(2), 77-95, N 87.

LARSON, David. Quine's Indeterminacy Thesis. SW Phil Rev, 4(1), 65-70, Ja 88.

As is well known, Quine distinguishes between the underdetermination which all empirical theories suffer and the special indeterminacy suffered by theories of translation. I argue that the underdetermination of the theory being translated is responsible for the indeterminacy of its translation. I show how the notions of indeterminacy and underdetermination may nevertheless be distinguished either with or without the scientific realism which Quine may or may not hold.

LARSON, Gerald James. "'Conceptual Resources' in South Asia for 'Environmental Ethics'" in *Nature in Asian Tradition of Thought: Essays in Environmental Philosophy*, CALLICOTT, J Baird (ed), 267-277. Albany, SUNY Pr, 1989.

LARSON, J A and BAUMGARTNER, James E. A Diamond Example of an Ordinal Graph with no Infinite Paths. Annals Pure Applied Log, 47(1), 1-10, Ap 90.

LARSON, Jean A. Martin's Axiom and Ordinal Graphs: Large Independent Sets or Infinite Paths. Annals Pure Applied Log, 47(1), 31-39, Ap 90.

LARUELLE, François. Le concept d'analyse généralisée ou de "non-analyse". Rev Int Phil, 43(171), 506-524, 1989.

LASKOWSKI, Michael Chris. Uncountable Theories that are Categorical in a Higher Power. J Sym Log, 53(2), 512-530, Je 88.

In this paper we prove three theorems about first-order theories that are categorical in a higher power. The first theorem asserts that such a theory either is totally categorical or these exist prime and minimal models over arbitrary base sets. The second theorem shows that such theories have a natural notion of dimension that determines the models of the theory up to isomorphism. From this we conclude that $I(T, \aleph_\alpha) = \aleph_0 + |\alpha|$ where $\aleph_\alpha =$ the number of formulas modulo *T*-equivalence provided that *T* is not totally categorical. The third theorem gives a new characterization of these theories.

LÁSZLÁO, Bulcsú. Philosophical Trifles (in Serbo-Croatian). Filozof Istraz, 30(3), 973-978, 1989.

Der Autor antwortet auf die Frage: nach dem Verhältnis von nichts zu etwas; nach der Unmöglichkeit des Denkens ausserhalb sprachlicher Kategorien; nach dem Subjekt und dem Objekt; nach dem Gleichen und Verschiedenen; nach der Wahrheit, nach der Kongruenz von Sprache, Zeit und Raum; nach dem Übersetzen des Textes und des Kontextes; nach der gleichen Struktur verschiedener Sprachen; nach der Richtung des Schreibverlaufs von unten nach oben; nach dem Nicht-Bestehen einer besonderen Befehlsform für die erste Person Singular und der Form des Reflexivpronomens *sebe* ('sich') im Nominativ. Der Autor schreibt über die Wahrheit: "Die Wahrheit liegt nicht in der Sprache, sondern ausserhalb, kann aber ohne diese nicht bestehen. Die Wahrheit ist die gewortete überprüfte Tatsache der Wirklichkeit. Sie wird durch die Sprache ausgedrückt, aber, ob das, was behauptet wird, in der Tat wahrhaftig ist, wird von dem Orakel, also ein Subjekt ausserhalb des Systems, festgestellt. In diesem Sinn ist die *Wahrheit in der Sprache* das Verhältnis dessen, was ausgesprochen wurde zu dem, was dargelegt, oder worauf verwiesen wurde."

LASZLO, Ervin. Evolution in Nature—Development in Society. Dialec Hum, 16(2), 159-164, Spr 89.

LATAWIEC, A M and ROSINSKI, F M. Die Verantwortung des Menschen für seine natürliche Umwelt (in Polish). Stud Phil Christ, 25(2), 121-137, 1989.

Im vorliegenden Artikel wurden 2 prinzipielle Verhaltenweisen: die sakrale und profane gegenüber der Umwelt hervorgehoben; beide haben eine sehr lange Tradition und ihre Befürworter berufen sich auf theologische und philosophische Argumente. Die Bedrohung der Umwelt bedeutet eine ernste Gefährdung der physischen und psychischen Integrität des Menschen; er muss sich dessen bewusst werden, dass er nicht nur Rechte gegenüber der Natur hat, aber auch moralische Pflichten, deren Begründung in vorliegender Arbeit erörtert wurde.

LATAWIEC, Anna. Transplantation du cerveau—une chance pour

l'humanité ou bien une menace? (in Polish). Stud Phil Christ, 25(1), 93-109, 1989.

Après une présentation de la structure, de l'évolution et du functionnement du cerveau humain, ainsi que de l'histoire des recherches et des expériences biologiques et médicales, on été présentés les principaux problèmes éthiques liés à la transplantation. Cette présentation a tenu compte de deux aspects différents: du point de vue du donneur et du point vue du receveur de l'organe transplanté. Le présent article est une tentative de justification de la thèse que la transplantation du cerveau est une opération acceptable à condition qu'elle n'est pas une atteinte à la dignité de la personne humaine à son droit de vivre. Deux genres de transplantation du cerveau sont donc acceptables: lorsque le donneur est en même temps receveur et lorsque est implanté un produit artificiel (ce qui n'est pas encore pratiqué). les autres genres de transplantation de cerveau entrainent la mise à mort du donneur et sont pour celà moralement inadmissibles.

LATOUR, Bruno. "Clothing the Naked Truth" in *Dismantling Truth: Reality in the Post-Modern World*, LAWSON, Hilary (ed), 101-126. New York, St Martin's Pr, 1989.

LAUDAN, L. Aim-Less Epistemology? Stud Hist Phil Sci, 21(2), 315-322, Je 90.

This paper responds to Harvey Siegel's thesis that epistemic rationality is fundamentally different from instrumental rationality. It shows that the former is a proper species of the latter.

LAUDAN, Larry. Normative Naturalism. Phil Sci, 57(1), 44-59, Mr 90.

Normative naturalism is a view about the status of epistemology and philosophy of science; it is a meta-epistemology. It maintains that epistemology can both discharge its traditional normative role *and* nonetheless claim a sensitivity to empirical evidence. The first sections of this essay set out the central tenets of normative naturalism, both in its epistemic and its axiological dimensions; later sections respond to criticisms of that species of naturalism from Gerald Doppelt, Jarrett Leplin and Alex Rosenberg.

LAUDER, Robert E. The Accuracy of Atheism and the Truth of Theism. Sophia (Australia), 28(3), 40-48, O 89.

Atheists have claimed that God is nothing but a human projection, that God-talk is only talk about man. The partial insight into the connection between God-talk and human experience had by many atheists can be used and deepened by theists. God-talk is *also* talk about human experience. By exploring human experiences such as future, freedom and truth we can reflect on and speak about God as the source and deepest dimension of these experiences. God is the absolute future and radical beauty and ultimate truth that underlies all our experiences of future, beauty and truth.

LAUFER, Romain. "Rhetoric and Politics" in *From Metaphysics to Rhetoric*, MEYER, Michel (ed), 183-197. Norwell, Kluwer, 1989.

LAUNAY, Marc B (trans) and BRENTANO, Franz. L'origine de la connaissance morale, traduit par M B de Launay. Rev Metaph Morale, 95(1), 3-32, Ja-Mr 90.

LAURA, Ronald S and LEAHY, Michael. Religious Upbringing and Rational Autonomy. J Phil Educ, 23(2), 253-265, Wint 89.

In this article, we consider two recent objections to the religious upbringing of children: (1) that by implanting beliefs which characteristically resist falsification, such an upbringing violates the liberal idea of rational autonomy; and (2) that a religious upbringing closes children's minds to alternatives to which rational autonomy requires their minds to remain open. We refute (1) by showing that *all* belief systems are underpinned by a class of beliefs we call *epistemically primitive*, a fundamental characteristic of which is resistance to falsification. We overcome (2) by showing that religious beliefs can be fervently, but *corrigibly* held.

LAURIKAINEN, K V. *Beyond the Atom: The Philosophical Thought of Wolfgang Pauli*. New York, Springer, 1988

LAURITZEN, Paul. A Feminist Ethic and the New Romanticism—Mothering as a Model of Moral Relations. Hypatia, 4(2), 29-44, Sum 89.

This paper claims that recent attempts to draw on the maternal experiences of women in order to articulate an ethic of care and compassion is a new romanticism. Like earlier romantic views, it is both attractive and potentially dangerous. The paper examines the basic claims of this new romanticism in order to identify both its strengths and weaknesses. I conclude that there are at least two versions of this new romanticism, one that relies primarily on the experiences of child-*bearing* in grounding an ethic of care and compassion, and a second that relies primarily on child-*rearing*. I suggest that the former version of the new romanticism is deeply flawed because such a view ought to be unacceptable to women and will be inaccessible to men.

LAURITZEN, Paul. What Price Parenthood? Hastings Center Rep, 20(2), 38-46, Mr-Ap 90.

This paper explores various feminist objections to reproductive technology in the light of the author's experience of treating for infertility. In particular the paper focuses on claims that reproductive technology is coercive, devalues motherhood, reduces procreation to the production of a commodity and will inevitably lead to genetic engineering. The author concludes that there are indeed reasons to be concerned about each of these, and that we should approach further developments in reproductive technology cautiously.

LAURSEN, John C. Scepticism and Intellectual Freedom: The Philosophical Foundations of Kant's Politics of Publicity. Hist Polit Thought, 10(3), 439-455, Autumn 89.

LAUTER, Estella and KRUMHOLZ, Linda. Annotated Bibliography on Feminist Aesthetics in the Visual Arts. Hypatia, 5(2), 158-172, Sum 90.

LAUTER, Estella. Re-enfranchising Art: Feminist Interventions in the Theory of Art. Hypatia, 5(2), 91-106, Sum 90.

Feminist analyses of the roles gender has played in art lead to an alternative theory that emphasizes art's complex interactions with culture(s) rather than the autonomy within culture claimed for it by formalism. Focusing on the visual arts, I extrapolate the new theory from feminist research and compare it with formalist precepts. Sharing Arthur Danto's concern that art has been disenfranchised in the twentieth century by its preoccupation with theory, I claim that feminist thought re-enfranchises art by revisioning its relationship to its contexts.

LAVELLE, Kevin C. Davidson, Irrationality, and Weakness of Will. Logos (USA), 10, 89-98, 1989.

In "How Is Weakness of Will Possible?" Donald Davidson argues that *akrasia* is best explained as irrationality on the part of a choosing agent. I believe he is mistaken in reducing incontinence to irrationality, and I argue that the legitimacy of his claim rests on a failure to distinguish between judgments which issue from 'mere preferences', and judgments which arise from more deeply seated value beliefs or principles. While both types of judgments issue from value beliefs (or 'pro-attitudes' as Davidson terms them) and are related in that way, it is not obvious that judgments arising from 'mere preference' provide sufficient rational ground for thinking that transgressing them is 'irrational' in any useful sense of the term irrational.

LAVINE, T Z (ed) and TEJERA, V (ed). *History and Anti-History in Philosophy*. Norwell, Kluwer, 1989

LAVINE, T Z. "The Interpretive Turn from Kant to Derrida: A Critique" in *History and Anti-History in Philosophy*, LAVINE, T Z (ed), 32-121. Norwell, Kluwer, 1989.

LAVOIE, Dina. Formal and Informal Management Training Programs for Women in Canada: Who Seems to Be Doing a Good Job? J Bus Ethics, 9(4-5), 377-383, Ap-My 90.

The increasing complexity of Canadian businesses in a changing marketplace indicates that women as well as men managers will have to be well trained to be able to position themselves in this new environment with a certain degree of success and personal happiness. As management educators, we have to accept an important share in this responsibility. This paper examines some of the factors that should be considered by those who want to develop management training programs for the future women managers or entrepreneurs.

LAWLER, Peter A. Was Tocqueville a Philosopher? Interpretation, 17(3), 401-414, Spr 90.

Tocqueville did not call himself a philosopher. In fact, he clearly distinguished himself from the philosophers. His work contains a criticism of their self-destructive misanthropy. Nevertheless, he did not reject the truth of the fundamental uncertain or contingency of human existence revealed by philosophic inquiry. His task was to surpass the philosophers from a human perspective by teaching human beings how to live well as human beings with that truth. He believed himself to be a "new kind" of "liberal," because he was a partisan of distinctively human liberty.

LAWRENCE, Joseph P (trans) and GRONDIN, Jean. The A Priori from Kant to Schelling. Ideal Stud, 19(3), 202-221, S 89.

The author traces the history of the concept of the A Priori through German Idealism. He contends that the concept was crucial for Kant and Schelling and of minor importance for Hegel. He links it to the Platonic doctrine of recollection, whereby giving Kant's metaphysical concerns their due. His primary contention is that Schelling deepens the notion of the a priori until he discovers that at its heart lies not that which can be rationally constructed, but that which is given prior to any construction, the a priori Unbegreifliche. This is the incomprehensible facticity of Being itself, which cannot be deduced since it is presupposed by any deduction.

LAWRENCE, Joseph P (trans) and FRANK, Manfred. Schelling's Critique of Hegel and the Beginnings of Marxian Dialectics. Ideal Stud, 19(3), 251-268, S 89.

The author shows how consistently Schelling maintained the transreflexive nature of being. He asserted this in opposition to Hegel, whose "proof" that being is reflexive in nature presupposes what it wants to demonstrate by defining being at the outset as pure self-relation. Schelling, in contrast, did not begin on the level of metaphysical assertion, but with a clear insight into the dependency of self-consciousness upon a prior, and absolutely unmediated, identity. According to Frank's understanding, the positioning of being beyond relation results from an experience of the conditionality of both reason and selfhood. In terms of such conditionality, Schelling emerges as a kind of dialectical materialist, the precursor of Feuerbach and Marx.

LAWRENCE, Joseph P. Schelling: A New Beginning. Ideal Stud, 19(3), 189-201, S 89.

Schelling's philosophy is introduced under the title of a "new beginning" not only because his work has been unduly neglected in the Anglo-American tradition, but because his conception of "positive philosophy" provides the most promising avenue for a new beginning of philosophy itself, which in our own era has been declared dead by a variety of schools. What Heidegger poetically and prophetically evokes as the coming *Ereignis* of a new but indescribable way of thinking, Schelling concretely elaborates as a philosophy capable of penetrating even those sources, such as myth and art, which are themselves not articulated in the sphere of the concept. This is decisive, for philosophy's highest concern is with Being itself, which is given prior to any conceptual derivation.

LAWSON, E Thomas and MC CAULEY, Robert N. *Rethinking Religion: Connecting Cognition and Culture*. New York, Cambridge Univ Pr, 1990

A critique of interpretive approaches to the study of religion, and a proposal, instead, of a cognitive explanatory theory which acknowledges the contributions of intellectualist, symbolist and structuralist theories but goes beyond them. The book presents a formal system for representing ritual actions that can be paired with a religious conceptual scheme to yield both descriptions of ritual acts and universal principles for all religious ritual systems. The theory makes use of strategies available from the cognitive sciences.

LAWSON, Hilary (ed). *Dismantling Truth: Reality in the Post-Modern World*. New York, St Martin's Pr, 1989

In this collection of essays, the editors have brought together leading philosophers, scientists and social scientists—among them Richard Rorty, Bruno Latour, Richard Gregory, John Forrester and W N Newton-Smith—to question the rhetoric of scientific truth. The essays apply philosophical accounts of truth to the specific practices of science, and show how science has implications for the nature of truth in general. They look at the debate between those who advocate a realist truth and those who wish to dismantle such a truth, and they ask the question our culture is beginning to face: how the postmodern world can be represented when truth in the conventional sense no longer exists. (edited)

LAYMON, Ronald. Applying Idealized Scientific Theories to Engineering. Synthese, 81(3), 353-371, D 89.

The problem for the scientist created by using idealizations is to determine whether failures to achieve experimental fit are attributable to experimental error, falsity of theory, or of idealization. Even in the rare case when experimental fit within experimental error is achieved, the scientist must determine whether this is so because of a true theory and fortuitously cancelling idealizations, or due to a fortuitous combination of false theory and false idealizations. For the engineer, the problem seems rather different. Experiment for the engineer reveals the closeness of predictive fit that can be achieved by theory and idealization for a particular case. If the closeness of fit is good enough for some practical purpose, the job is done. If not, or there are reasons to consider variation, then the engineer needs to know how well the experimentally determined closeness of fit will extrapolate to new cases. This paper focuses on engineering measures of closeness of fit and the projectibility of those measures to new cases.

LAZARI-PAWLOWSKA, Ija. Three Concepts of Tolerance. Dialec Hum, 14(1), 133-146, Wint 87.

The word "tolerance" is being defined in many different ways. The two concepts that are most often found in the contemporary literature are the concept of negative and the concept of positive tolerance. According to the negative concept tolerance consists in nonopposition to beliefs and actions considered as wrong. According to the positive concept—in a favourable approval or even support of somebody's otherness. Tolerance in the third sense expects an active intervention but combined with desisting from the use of compulsion and any violent means against those whose convictions or practices we do not accept.

LE DOEUFF, Michèle and GORDON, Colin (trans). *The Philosophical Imaginary.* Stanford, Stanford Univ Pr, 1990

LE LANNOU, Jean-Michel. La conversion à la substantialité. Rev Phil Fr, 180(1), 61-69, Ja-Mr 90.

LE PORE, Ernest and LOEWER, Barry. Absolute Truth Theories for Modal Languages as Theories of Interpretation. Critica, 21(61), 43-73, Ap 89.

Donald Davidson, Gilbert Harman, and in particular John Wallace have identified some difficulties in constructing absolute truth theories for languages containing intensional operators. Wallace argues that the standard recursion clause for negation has no analogue for "necessity" and a range of other intensional operators. Anil Gupta and Christopher Peacocke respond to Wallace by devising truth theories which, though containing a straightforward recursion clause for "necessity," are not false. In this paper, we argue that though Gupta and Peacocke circumvent Wallace's objection, there is a cost: the truth theories they propose cannot function as theories of interpretation for any language. Since we have argued that the firmest grip we have on theories of interpretation is supplied by truth theories, this cost is too high. We then consider possible world semantics for modal languages and argue that such theories cannot be converted into truth theories suitable for interpretation. Lastly, we sketch an adequate semantic account for modal languages, qua theories of interpretation, by viewing modalities as predicates, much as Davidson proposes we view propositional attitude ascriptions.

LE PORE, Ernest and LOEWER, Barry. More on Making Mind Matter. Phil Topics, 17(1), 175-191, Spr 89.

In this paper we discuss the question whether there is any causal role for content properties to play. First we discuss considerations which may lead one to worry that content properties are causally impotent. These worries arise from combining certain physicalistic commitments with the view that content properties are not reducible to physical properties. So we formulate a nonreductive physicalism and then canvass some reasons for thinking that content properties are not reducible to physical basic properties. We then consider three responses which attempt to characterize a causal role and show that content properties play this role.

LE PORE, Ernest. Subjectivity and Environmentalism. Inquiry, 33(2), 197-214, Je 90.

The main thesis of this paper is that the most cogent demands of subjectivity, at least with respect to questions concerning the contents of our thoughts, can be accommodated within an objectivist framework. I begin with two theses: (1) *Subjectivity*: I can know (the contents of) my own thoughts without appeal to any knowledge of features external to my mind; (2) *Environmentalism*: (The contents of) my thoughts are determined by features external to my mind, at least in this sense: without causal and/or social interaction between my internal states and various external features, these internal states would not have the particular contents they have and therefore would not be the mental states they are. (edited)

LE PORE, Ernest and LOEWER, Barry. You Can Say *That* Again. Midwest Stud Phil, 14, 338-356, 1989.

In "Truth and Meaning" (1967) Donald Davidson proposed that a Tarskian truth theory for a language L can be (the heart of) a theory of meaning for L. In "On Saying That" (1968) he proposed a radically novel approach, the paratactic account, to the logical form of indirect discourse. The two proposals are related in a number of ways. The paratactic account claims to show how to construct a truth theory for languages containing indirect discourse. The truth theoretic account of meaning provides motivation and support for the paratactic account. Our primary aim is to motivate the paratactic account and defend it from certain widely known criticisms.

LEACH, Mary S. Reviewing the "Subject(s)". Educ Phil Theor, 21(1), 21,30-33, 1989.

LEACH, Mary and DAVIES, Bronwyn. Crossing the Boundaries: Educational Thought and Gender Equity. Educ Theor, 40(3), 321-332, Sum 90.

LEACH, Mary. Our Vantage Points: Not a View from Nowhere. Proc Phil Educ, 45, 258-261, 1989.

LEAHY, Michael and LAURA, Ronald S. Religious Upbringing and Rational Autonomy. J Phil Educ, 23(2), 253-265, Wint 89.

In this article, we consider two recent objections to the religious upbringing of children: (1) that by implanting beliefs which characteristically resist falsification, such an upbringing violates the liberal idea of rational autonomy; and (2) that a religious upbringing closes children's minds to alternatives to which rational autonomy requires their minds to remain open. We refute (1) by showing that *all* belief systems are underpinned by a class of beliefs we call *epistemically primitive*, a fundamental characteristic of which is resistance to falsification. We overcome (2) by showing that religious beliefs can be fervently, but *corrigibly* held.

LEAK, Andrew N. *The Perverted Consciousness: Sexuality and Sartre.* New York, St Martin's Pr, 1989

A fresh look at the Sartrean corpus, using a nonreductive psychoanalytic approach. Sartre's ambivalent attitude towards Freudian psychoanalysis is traced through his representational strategies and the development of his own theory of sexuality. Sartre's texts are seen as the product of a tension between a powerful will to express and the insistence of a core of unconscious 'scenarios'. This struggle within the texts (both fiction and theory) is seen as ultimately positive: the Sartrean 'text' is the productive interweaving of the strands of conscious and unconscious determinants into a whole which remains open to the reader.

LEAVEY JR, John P. "Lations, Cor, Trans, Re, &c" in *The Textual Sublime: Deconstruction and Its Differences*, SILVERMAN, Hugh J (ed), 191-202. Albany, SUNY Pr, 1990.

LEBEDEV, A. The Imagery of Lampadedromia in Heraclitus. Philosophia (Athens), 17-18, 233-257, 1987-88.

LEBEDEV, Andrei V. Aristarchus of Samos on Thales' Theory of Eclipses. Apeiron, 23(2), 77-85, Je 90.

LEBER, Gary. We Must Rescue Them. Hastings Center Rep, 19(6), 26-27, N-D 89.

LEBLANC, Hugues and ROEPER, Peter. On Relativizing Kolmogorov's Absolute Probability Functions. Notre Dame J Form Log, 30(4), 485-512, Fall 89.

LEBRUN, Gérard. Berkeley ou le sceptique malgré lui. Manuscrito, 11(2), 33-48, O 88.

This paper presents an aspect of what might be called the difference in spirit between Hume and Berkeley exactly where the analysis of Hume seems to be strictly connected with that of Berkeley. Why does Hume, in the *First Enquiry*, presume to rank Berkeley among the masters of Scepticism, when immaterialism's purpose was precisely to eradicate Scepticism? Obviously there must be an ambiguity associated with the word "Scepticism" here. According to Berkeley, it means a distrust of the resources of our knowledge, whereas in Hume's opinion Berkeley's unavoidable "Scepticism" means a discrepancy with common belief. In order to localize this dissent, I compare a text from the *Principles* with a chapter of the *Treatise*. (edited)

LEBUIS, Pierre and SCHLEIFER, Michael and CARON, Anita. The Effect of the *Pixie* Program on Logical and Moral Reasoning. Thinking, 7(2), 12-16, 1987.

LEBUS, Bruce. Moral Dilemmas: Why They Are Hard To Solve. Phil Invest, 13(2), 110-125, Ap 90.

I argue that there are genuine moral dilemmas. The position that all moral dilemmas can be ethically resolved is rejected. Terrence McConnell's arguments against the existence of dilemmas are examined. I agree with him that one cannot show that there are moral dilemmas by merely pointing to difficult cases of conflict. It is necessary to explain what prevents opposing obligations from being resolved. I analyze two dilemmas (Sartre's case of the young French man and Sophie's dilemma from *Sophie's Choice*) to show how irresolvable moral conflict can arise. Finally, I contend that moral dilemmas challenge the principles of deontic logic.

LECKI, Maciej (trans) and MAZUREK, Franciszek Janusz. Anthropology of Peace. Dialec Hum, 14(1), 185-200, Wint 87.

Man (people) who lives in various communities is the only creator and bearer of peace. Anthropology of peace must have a realistic conception of the human person and his dignity. Anthropology of peace perceives the value of peace already in the very structure of man's needs. Man needs peace just like he needs joy and happiness. Anthropology of peace should make use of the concept of the human family (familia humana) instead of international community. This approach will also bring to the foreground the idea of man as the bearer and "creator" of peace. Peace is not only a value which preconditions the actualization of all other values but it constitutes a value in itself—a personal value—the moral competence of peace. The moral competence of peace would be conceived as a synthesis of all the other moral competences. Considering that peace constitutes a personalist and humanistic value everything ought to be done to secure and maintain it by humanistic means: education, dialogue, international cooperation, development and implementation of human rights.

LECKI, Maciej (trans) and SZCZEPANSKI, Jan. Socialism and Atheism. Dialec Hum, 14(1), 43-47, Wint 87.

LECKI, Maciej (trans) and RAJECKI, Robert. Towards a Theology of Peace—The Peace Doctrine of John Paul II. Dialec Hum, 14(1), 201-208, Wint 87.

LECLERC, Ivor. "Whitehead and the Dichotomy of Rationalism and Empiricism" in *Whitehead's Metaphysics of Creativity*, RAPP, Friedrich (ed), 1-20. Albany, SUNY Pr, 1990.

LECLERC, Marc. Being and the Sciences: The Philosophy of Gaston Isaye. Int Phil Quart, 30(3), 311-329, S 90.

LEDDY, Thomas. Practical George and Aesthete Jerome Meet the Aesthetic Object. S J Phil, 28(1), 37-53, Spr 90.

George Dickie's "The Myth of the Aesthetic Attitude" argues that there is no such thing as the aesthetic attitude. I criticize Dickie's position from a romantic/phenomenological standpoint. Contra Dickie, consideration of aesthetic issues *beyond* art is inseparable from consideration of the aesthetic *within* art. Dickie neglected the fundamental role of inspiration in the aesthetic experiences of artists. I distinguish between "strong" and "weak" aesthetic attitudes and explore this distinction in terms of a confrontation between two characters who originally appeared in Dickie's *The Art Circle*, practical George and aesthete Jerome. The paper concludes with some comments on kitsch.

LEDER, Drew. Clinical Interpretation: The Hermeneutics of Medicine. Theor Med, 11(1), 9-24, Mr 90.

I argue that clinical medicine can best be understood not as a purified science but as a hermeneutical enterprise: that is, as involved with the interpretation of texts. The literary critic reading a novel, the judge asked to apply a law, must arrive at a coherent reading of their respective texts. Similarly, the physician interprets the 'text' of the ill person: clinical signs and symptoms are read to ferret out their meaning, the underlying disease. However, I suggest that the hermeneutics of medicine is rendered uniquely complex by its wide variety of textual forms. I discuss four in turn: the "experiential text" of illness as lived out by the patient; the "narrative text" constituted during history-taking; the "physical text" of the patient's body as objectively examined; and the "instrumental text" constructed by diagnostic technologies. I further suggest that certain flaws in modern medicine arise from its refusal of a hermeneutic self-understanding. In seeking to escape all interpretive subjectivity, medicine has threatened to expunge its primary subject—the living, experiencing patient.

LEDER, Drew. Flesh and Blood: A Proposed Supplement to Merleau-Ponty. Human Stud, 13(3), 209-219, Jl 90.

This article seeks to critique and supplement Merleau-Ponty's phenomenology of the lived body. Merleau-Ponty focuses upon the body's sensorimotor capacities; even his ontological notion of the "flesh" is built upon the body as perceiver and perceived. I argue that Merleau-Ponty neglects the "visceral" dimension of embodiment. Beneath our surface organs there lies a domain of anonymous functions: digestion, circulation, and the like. We emerge from such "viscerality" when we are born, and nightly descend into it in sleep. I argue that this visceral dimension has profound philosophical significance, despite its neglect by professional philosophers.

LEDUC-FAYETTE, Denise. Du retour à l'origine. Rev Phil Fr, 180(1), 47-57, Ja-Mr 90.

LEE, Barbara A. Something Akin to a Property Right: Protections for Job Security. Bus Prof Ethics J, 8(3), 63-81, Fall 89.

Although for most workers their job is their only source of income, most workers in the private sector have no property right in their job. The article examines the common law of wrongful discharge and concludes that this doctrine is inferior to statutory protection. Montana's wrongful discharge statute is examined briefly. The article concludes that a uniform approach to protecting employee job rights is necessary but unlikely to occur in the present political and judicial climate.

LEE, Donald. How Epistemology Can Be a System. SW Phil Rev, 4(1), 1-18, Ja 88.

LEE, Keekok. *Social Philosophy and Ecological Scarcity*. New York, Routledge, 1989

Modern civilisation assumes there is no ecological (absolute) scarcity. Economics, political and social philosophy also assume it. Belated recognition of this error requires reconceptualisation which this book does for social philosophy. "What is the good person/life/society?" cannot be answered without considering the entropic impact of actions on the natural world. This involves rejecting external (material) goods via economic (exponential) growth using ecologically insensitive technology to promote the good life as understood by bourgeois and state capitalism. It leads to a social vision akin to Fourier's and Morris's based on acquiring internal goods via the artistic mode of production.

LEE, Sander H. "The Essence of Human Experience in David Lynch's *Blue Velvet*" in *Inquiries into Values: The Inaugural Session of the International*

Society for Value Inquiry, LEE, Sander H , 569-583. Lewiston, Mellen Pr, 1989.

In *Blue Velvet*, a film David Lynch wrote as well as directed, themes worthy of a Freud, Nietzsche, or Schopenhauer are conveyed. Lynch demonstrates that our feeble human attempts to pretend that rationality can be successfully imposed both on nature and ourselves is doomed to failure. The best of us are irresistably drawn to the degrading, the brutal, and the violent, yet those who are most successful are those who can control their drives, hiding them when it's to their advantage and yet satisfying them when they can get away with it. Thus, the important role of "seeing" in the film is also explored.

LEE, Sander H. *Inquiries into Values: The Inaugural Session of the International Society for Value Inquiry*. Lewiston, Mellen Pr, 1989

This volume is an anthology of selected papers presented at the inaugural meetings of *The International Society for Value Inquiry*, held in Arundel, England in August of 1988. The book contains 54 essays. Section one contains 19 essays on issues relating to general value theory and the relation of rationality to values. Section two has 14 essays examining moral questions in the context of a variety of historical perspectives including contemporary developments in Marxian and Sartrean theory. Section three contains 22 essays on applied contemporary issues including the Holocaust, apartheid, education, medicine, and aesthetic issues in areas such as contemporary film criticism.

LEE, Steven. Morality and Nuclear Weapons Policy. Phil Pub Affairs, 19(1), 93-106, Wint 90.

This is a review essay of John Finnis, Joseph M Boyle, Jr., and Germain Grisez, *Nuclear Deterrence, Morality and Realism* (Oxford: Clarendon Press, 1987). The authors, rejecting a consequentialist approach, argue that nuclear deterrence is morally prohibited because it involves an intention to kill innocents. But their anti-consequentialist arguments are inadequate. Their realism is in their argument that the required abandoning of nuclear deterrence is likely to lead to Soviet domination of the West. But this argument makes selective use of the kinds of consequentialist considerations earlier rejected, and leads them to offer moral advice in a way inconsistent with their own moral theory.

LEE, Steven. "Morality, the SDI, and Limited Nuclear War" in *Nuclear Deterrence and Moral Restraint*, SHUE, Henry (ed), 381-416. New York, Cambridge Univ Pr, 1989.

Based on its potential war-limiting capability, the SDI is claimed to be morally advantageous. The chief advantage claimed is that SDI defenses would completely eliminate damage in a nuclear war, allowing the US to abandon nuclear deterrence. A secondary advantage claimed is that, even if SDI defenses would only partially limit damage, this would enhance deterrence and lessen the risk of war. SDI defenses would have neither of these moral advantages, but would have serious moral disadvantages.

LEE, Steven. "A Positive Concept of Peace" in *The Causes of Quarrel: Essays on Peace, War, and Thomas Hobbes*, CAWS, Peter (ed), 183-192. Boston, Beacon Pr, 1989.

This essay explores the claim that a proper concept of peace regards peace as a positive state involving the presence of cooperation or justice, not merely the absence of violence. First, a positive concept of peace is elaborated, partly in reaction to proposals by Gray Cox and Peter Caws elsewhere in the volume. Second, I consider whether one should adopt a positive rather than a negative concept of peace. Finally, the relevance of this to our state of mutual assured destruction is examined. The danger is that nuclear weapons seem to make positive peace impossible while falsely appearing to obviate the need for it.

LEE, Win-Chiat. Personal Identity, the Temporality of Agency and Moral Responsibility. Auslegung, 16(1), 17-29, Wint 90.

In this article, I argue against Derek Parfit's thesis that the Reductionist View of personal identity renders the Extreme Claim more defensible. The Extreme Claim supposedly rejects the idea of personal moral responsibility for one's past acts. I argue that in using the Reductionist View to defend the Extreme Claim, we need to construct out of some psychological connections a temporally extended agent who lasts long enough to commit an act, but not long enough to be responsible for the act after it has been completed. The arbitrariness of this kind of construct is explained.

LEE, Win-Chiat. Statutory Interpretation and the Counterfactual Test for Legislative Intention. Law Phil, 8(3), 383-404, D 89.

In this paper I examine the counterfactual test for legislative intention as used in *Riggs v. Palmer*. The distinction between the speaker's meaning approach and the constructive interpretation approach to statutory interpretation, as made by Dworkin in *Law's Empire*, is explained. I argue that Dworkin underestimates the potential of the counterfactual test in making the speaker's meaning approach more plausible. I also argue that Dworkin's reasons for rejecting the counterfactual test, as proposed in *Law's Empire*, are either too weak or unsound. A deeper reason for rejecting the counterfactual test as a method for the speaker's meaning approach is proposed in this paper. The difference between the counterfactual test and other tests for legislative intention which seem also to make use of counterfactual conditions is explained.

LEE-GOSSELIN, H and GRISÉ, J. Are Women Owner-Managers Challenging Our Definitions of Entrepreneurship? An In-Depth Survey. J Bus Ethics, 9(4-5), 423-433, Ap-My 90.

In the Quebec city area, 400 women owner-managers of business in the three industrial sectors answered a detailed questionnaire, and 75 of these subsequently underwent in-depth interviews. The main dimensions explored were the characteristics of the entrepreneurs and their firms, the experience of starting a business, the success criteria used, and their vision for the future of their firms. The results suggest the importance, to these women, of a model of "small and stable business." This is not a transitory phase for their firm: most choose and value such a scale of business, and they seek recognition for what they do. This model seems to represent an innovative adaptation to their professional, social, family and personal demands and challenges our definitions of entrepreneurship and of "serious business."

LEEDS, Stephen. Levi's Decision Theory. Phil Sci, 57(1), 158-168, Mr 90.

Suppose my utilities are representable by a set of utility assignments, each defined for atomic sentences; suppose my beliefs are representable by a set of probability assignments. Then each of my utility assignments together with each of my probability assignments will determine a utility assignment to non-atomic sentences, in a familiar way. This paper is concerned with the question, whether I am committed to all the utility assignments so constructible. Richard Jeffrey (1984) says (in effect) "no," Isaac Levi (1974) says "yes." I argue for "no," and raise in passing a problem for Levi.

LEFEBVRE, Jean Pierre. The Undiscoverable Fraternity (in Serbo-Croatian). Filozof Istraz, 30(3), 763-771, 1989.

L'auteur traite la réception de la Révolution française chez les intellectuels contemporains, c'est-à-dire les répercussions des événements de 1789, 1792, 1804 dans les oeuvres des deux plus grands poètes allemands, Heinrich Heine et Friedrich Hölderlin, qui gardaient une sympathie immense pour la cause révolutionnaire, surtout pour le concept d'égalité.

LEFETZ, L. L'interprétation de la relativité. Rev Phil Fr, 179(3), 311-341, Jl-S 89.

LEFORT, Claude. How Did You Become a Philosopher? Thinking, 6(2), 7-12, 1985.

LEFTOW, Brian. Boethius on Eternity. Hist Phil Quart, 7(2), 123-142, Ap 90.

In their "Eternity," Eleonore Stump and Norman Kretzmann claim that such authors as Boethius conceive of God's eternity as an "atemporal duration." Stump and Kretzmann have recently tried to defend the concept of atemporal duration against an attack by Paul Fitzgerald. I argue that their defense fails, then offer a different defense and a somewhat different concept of atemporal duration.

LEFTOW, Brian. God and Abstract Entities. Faith Phil, 7(2), 193-217, Ap 90.

Alvin Plantinga's *Does God Have a Nature?* has ignited debate over God's relations to abstract entities. Recently Thomas Morris and Christopher Menzel have suggested a way to maintain that God creates all abstract entities, including those attributes which He instances essentially. After defending the Morris-Menzel position against some initial objections, I argue that it generates the unacceptable consequence that God creates Himself and fails to secure the claim that God creates His nature. In closing I suggest that Aquinas's claim that God is "purely actual" may avoid the problems of Morris and Menzel's view and secure the relation of God to abstract entities which they favor.

LEFTOW, Brian. Individual and Attribute in the Ontological Argument. Faith Phil, 7(2), 235-242, Ap 90.

William Rowe has recently charged that Anselm's *Proslogion* 2 argument for God's existence contains a question-begging premise. I offer a reading of the argument on which that premise begs no questions. The reading is based on the suggestion that Anselm's vacillation between talking of that-than-which-no-greater-can-be-conceived as an individual and as an attribute is not sloppiness, but instead reflects a feature of his concept of that-than-which-no-greater-can-be-conceived.

LEFTOW, Brian. Is God an Abstract Object? Nous, 24(4), 581-598, S 90.

Before Duns Scotus, most philosophers agreed that God is identical with His necessary intrinsic attributes—omniscience, omnipotence, etc. This identity

thesis was a component of widely held doctrines of divine simplicity, which stated that God exemplifies no metaphysical distinctions, including that between subject and attribute. The identity thesis seems to render God an attribute, an abstract object. This paper argues that the identity thesis follows from a basic theistic belief and does not render God abstract. It also discusses how one might move from the identity thesis to the full doctrine of divine simplicity and shows that the identity thesis generates a new ontological argument for God's existence.

LEFTOW, Brian. A Leibnizian Cosmological Argument. Phil Stud, 57(2), 135-155, O 89.

I explicate and defend Leibniz's argument from "eternal truths" to the existence of God. I argue that necessary beings can be caused to exist, showing how one can apply a counterfactual analysis to such causation, then argue that if such beings can be caused to exist, they are.

LEFTOW, Brian. Necessary Moral Perfection. Pac Phil Quart, 70(3), 240-260, S 89.

Traditional theists sometimes claim that God is *de re* necessarily morally perfect, i.e., that the individual who is God lacks the very ability to do wrong. Several recent writers have argued that *de re* necessary moral perfection is impossible. I argue that they are wrong and attempt to make sense of necessary moral perfection.

LEFTOW, Brian. Perfection and Necessity. Sophia (Australia), 28(3), 13-20, O 89.

Steven Makin has recently offered a defense of *Proslogion* 3's ontological argument. I argue that this defense does not succeed. En route I argue against the claims that (a) any necessary being is greater than any contingent being; (b) there is a firm logical link between conceivable greatness and possible greatness.

LEGAULT, Georges A. La parole du philosophe éthicien est-elle crédible? Philosophiques, 17(1), 21-43, 1990.

This article aims to trace the basic agreements necessary to the articulation of ethics today. The author proposes that research be oriented on the dialogical aspect of speech, proposing to insist thus upon reasons to believe and upon the sharing of meaning sharing rather than upon the foundational aspect of ethical language. The orientation supposes that the role of philosophy be redefined, that ethics be centered on human deliberation and that corroborations be searched with other human sciences, namely moral development psychology and psychoanalysis.

LEGRIS, Javier. Criterios de teoricidad. Rev Filosof (Argentina), 1(1-2), 5-16, N 86.

The aim of this paper is to make a characterization of the theoreticity criterion risen within the structural view of scientific theories developed by J S Sneed in his *The Logical Structure of Mathematical Physics* and W Stegmüller in the second part of his *Theorie und Erfahrung*. First we begin by exposing the critics to the traditional criterion based on the distinction between theoretical and observational concepts and to the relativization to theories proposed by C G Hempel (section 1). Section 2 is dedicated to Sneed's criterion. Related to it some general references about the structural view are given. As example of the criterion it is analysed the theoretical character of mass and force in classical particle mechanics (section 3). Finally the last section is devoted to some philosophical consequences of the criterion.

LEGRIS, Javier. Justificación epistémica. Rev Filosof (Argentina), 4(1), 3-19, My 89.

The definition of knowledge as "justified true belief" leads to paradoxical and problematic situations as many authors have pointed out. Those problems and paradoxes arise because justification is understood as a type of foundation. In this paper I present a new conception of epistemic justification. Here justification is defined in terms of *intersubjective standards*: The belief of a person a is justified if and only if a has obtained it according to intersubjective standards of rationality. These intersubjective standards are patterns or criteria which are regarded by the persons within an "epistemic community" as valid and reliable for characterising a belief as justified. I also present some principles for justified belief according to this characterization.

LEHE, Robert T. Coherence and the Problem of Criterion. Ideal Stud, 19(2), 112-120, My 89.

It is generally thought to be impossible to give a non-question-begging justification of any candidate for the fundamental criterion of truth, because any attempted justification of the criterion would have to appeal to that criterion itself, the justification of which is at issue. I argue that coherence is one candidate for the criterion of truth which can be given a justification which, while admittedly circular, is not question-begging. I attempt to provide the justification, and to respond to objections to coherence as the criterion of truth.

LEHMANN, Hubert. Legal Concepts in a Natural Language Based Expert System. Ratio Juris, 3(2), 245-253, Jl 90.

A new approach to the formalization of concepts used in legal reasoning such as *obligation* and *cause* is presented. The formalization is based on the linguistic use of the concepts both in legal language and in ordinary language, and has been motivated by work on a legal expert system with a natural language interface. Particularly for the concept of obligation this yields quite different results from those obtained by the usual approach of deontic logic: so-called paradoxes are avoided, quantification over obligations becomes possible, no restriction to a "single-agent system" is required, and collisions of obligations can be formulated.

LEHNERT, Wendy G. "The Analysis of Nominal Compounds" in *Meaning and Mental Representation*, ECO, Umberto (ed), 155-179. Bloomington, Indiana Univ Pr, 1988.

LEHRER, Keith. "Coherence and the Truth Connection: A Reply to My Critics" in *The Current State of the Coherence Theory*, BENDER, John W (ed), 253-275. Norwell, Kluwer, 1989.

LEHRER, Keith. *Theory of Knowledge*. Boulder, Westview Pr, 1990

The book is a textbook in the theory of knowledge, but it contains a constructive defense of the coherence theory of knowledge. The chapter titles of the book provide an outline of the contents. They are as follows: (1) The Analysis of Knowledge; (2) Truth and Acceptance; (3) The Foundation Theory: Infallible Foundationalism; (4) Fallible Foundations; (5) The Explanatory Coherence Theory; (6) Internal Coherence and Personal Justification; (7) Coherence, Truth, and Undefeated Justification; (8) Externalism and Epistemology Naturalized; (9) Skepticism.

LEHRER, Keith. *Thomas Reid*. New York, Routledge, 1989

This book on Thomas Reid is a complete account of his philosophical system based on his published books. It is an account of his theory of conception, perception, reasoning, evidence, morality, and agency among other topics. Reid's epistemology combines a nativist account of faculties of conception and belief with a naturalized theory of evidence containing elements of foundationalism, coherentism and reliablism. Reid's moral theory combines a nativist account of a moral faculty with a libertarian view of agency. What results is a unified theory of innate faculties of the mind producing the justified beliefs of common sense. The ultimate defense of common sense, according to Reid, is the trustworthiness of our innate faculties.

LEIDIG, Guido. Ecologic-Economic Jurisprudence—The Next Step? Vera Lex, 8(2), 15-16,26, 1988.

LELAS, Srdjan. "A Plea for an Interactionist Epistemology" in *Scientific Knowledge Socialized*, HRONSZKY, Imre (ed), 327-345. Norwell, Kluwer, 1989.

After we have been aware for quite some time that the traditional epistemology had been "a spectator theory of knowledge" (Dewey) based on "ocular metaphor" and "mirror imagery" (Rorty), we are in search for an interactionist epistemology. In order to characterize epistemologically relevant interaction living beings are open, i.e., interacting, systems are carefully examined. Humans, however, add to the basic interaction a mediation of their artefacts. Production and existence of artefacts involve and give rise to peculiar cognitive dynamics which shed a new light on human cognition, its historical development, and the situation in modern physics.

LELOUP, Gérard. Théories complètes de paires de corps valués henseliens. J Sym Log, 55(1), 323-339, Mr 90.

We try to generalize Ax-Kochen-Ershov's theorem to pairs of Hensel fields (K⊂L,v) with residue fields of characteristic 0, showing that the pair's theory is given by the theories of the pair of residue fields and of the pair of value groups. It is possible to generalize in the case of separated pairs (i.e., L is linearly disjoint from any extension field of K) or dense pairs (for the valuation's topology). Adding new predicates to the theory of the pair of residue fields, and using the two previous cases, we can study more pairs.

LEMOS, Noah M. "Epistemic Priority and Coherence" in *The Current State of the Coherence Theory*, BENDER, John W (ed), 178-187. Norwell, Kluwer, 1989.

There are two related topics considered in this paper. The first concerns the status of basic beliefs and the thesis of epistemic priority, and the second concerns the justification of observational and introspective beliefs within a coherentist approach to justification. These issues are related since the proponents of coherence theories typically deny the thesis of epistemic priority and the existence of basic beliefs, and since those sympathetic to the thesis typically maintain that our introspective beliefs are among the clearest examples of basic beliefs. In the first section I consider an argument by

Laurence BonJour against the existence of basic beliefs and the thesis of epistemic priority. This argument presupposes a certain view of what is required for justification. In the second section I argue that this view of justification presents problems for BonJour's positive account of the warrant of observational and introspective beliefs. In the third section I consider a brief proposal by Roderick Firth in response to the objection that coherence theories cut off justification from the world.

LEMOS, Noah M. Warrant, Emotion, and Value. Phil Stud, 57(2), 175-192, O 89.

In this paper I consider two sorts of grounds for judgments of intrinsic value. These two grounds are what Brentano calls the experience of "correct" or "fitting" emotion and the experience of blind emotion, i.e., emotion not experienced as correct. I consider briefly how the epistemic role of such experiences is related to the views of contemporary writers such as John McDowell and to the thesis of epistemic priority. I defend the epistemic role of such experiences against various objections.

LENDVAI, Ferenc L. Change and Crisis of Values in Modern Societies (in Hungarian). Magyar Filozof Szemle, 2-3, 340-345, 1989.

LENHARDT, Christian (trans) and HABERMAS, Jürgen and WEBER NICHOLSEN, Shierry (trans). *Moral Consciousness and Communicative Action*. Cambridge, MIT Pr, 1990

LENK, Hans. Against Technocratic Hubris and Positivistic Idealism: Anti-Naturalistic and Anti-Realistic Fallacies, (Part One). SW Phil Rev, 4(1), 87-94, Ja 88.

LENKA, Laxminarayan. Meaning N and Meaning NN—An Exposition of the Unformed Gricean Intention. Indian Phil Quart, SUPP 17(2), 1-9, Ap 90.

The main purpose is to point 'intention' out of the five ways H P Grice distinguishes nonnatural meaning from natural meaning in his paper "Meaning." Intending Grice's threefold utterer's intention to be the formed, polished or refined kind, the pointed 'intention' is concluded to be the *unformed Gricean intention*. (Formulation of the said threefold intention is discussed by Lenka in the same journal's vol. XVII, No. 4, October 1990.)

LENZEN, Wolfgang. On Leibniz's Essay *Mathesis rationis*. Topoi, 9(1), 29-59, Mr 90.

LEON, Mark. The Mechanics of Rationality. S J Phil, 28(3), 343-366, Fall 90.

The paper examines the relation between rationality and mechanism. What is contested is the thesis that, if at base our functioning were mechanical, we could not be genuinely rational, we could not believe or act for a reason. It is argued that on the contrary, not only can the rational and mechanical coincide, more strongly the operation of reason requires a mechanism of a certain sort; for the mechanical system enables the operation of reason.

LEONARD, George J. Emerson, Whitman, and Conceptual Art. Phil Lit, 13(2), 297-306, O 89.

Those who share in the "intellectual tendency" M H Abrams called "Natual Supernaturalism" believe that paradise can be found in the common day, in mere real things. They must at best, like Emerson and Whitman, tolerate art's objects—"hypocritical rubbish," "toys"—as temporary training aids, as children's "gymnastics of the eye." Emerson quite logically yearns for the day when the arts can "die" (his word). The 1960s conceptualist attacks on the art object were wrongly thought radically, frighteningly, new; even, by Arthur Danto, the "end of art." They were Natural Supernaturalism's logical climax.

LEPAGE, François. Knowledge and Truth. Dialectica, 43(3), 215-229, 1989.

In this paper I will strive towards three main objectives. First of all, I will try to show that a very commonplace property of knowledge, that of yielding truth, can be used to characterize an ideal and radical notion of knowledge. It will be argued that this property generates a basic and autonomous concept of knowledge, i.e., a purely logical concept of knowledge that can be clearly separated from the psychological, intentional or epistemological aspects of knowledge. What results can thus be regarded as a kind of reduction of the concept of knowledge to that of truth. This reduction will be expressed by means of a criterion which a relation between an agent and a sentence must satisfy in order to be interpreted as exemplifying the relation of knowing. Secondly, I will offer an analysis of presuppositional knowledge which shows how the very strong and ideal notion of knowledge previously developed can be useful in interpreting the ordinary use of "knowing." My third and last objective will be to use this criterion to characterize formally the semantic interpretation associated to a rational and competent agent, i.e., the space of his knowledge.

LEPLIN, Jarrett. Renormalizing Epistemology. Phil Sci, 57(1), 20-33, Mr

90.

The fact that the goals and methods of science, as well as its empirical conclusions, are subject to change, is shown to allow at once for (a) the objectivity of warrant for knowledge claims; (b) the absence of a priori standards from epistemology; (c) the normative character of epistemology; and (d) the rationality of axiological innovation. In particular, Laudan's attempt to make axiological constraints undercut epistemic realism is confuted.

LÉRTORA MENDOZA, Celina A. El metodo filosofico segun 'Sapientiale' de Tomas de York. Rev Filosof (Mexico), 23(67), 53-62, Ja-Ap 90.

LESJAK, Gregor. Hegel and Daodejing (in Serbo-Croatian). Filozof Istraz, 29(2), 607-615, 1989.

The author deals with two basic problems in this paper. Hegel's interpretation of Chinese philosophy is discussed first, and Hegel's relation towards the oriental religion in general is explored in greater detail. Hegel's understanding of the relation is then connected with the Daodejing's philosophy.

LESLIE, Donald M (trans) and HALLYN, Fernand. *The Poetic Structure of the World: Copernicus and Kepler*. Cambridge, Zone Books, 1990

Confronted with a scientific text, the historian of science tries to define its signification, the epistemologist its theoretical status. "Poetics" of science proposes another approach. It studies the work of a scientist as an event embedded in a wider field of images, symbols, texts and practices. Scientific imagination is *not* fundamentally different from a mythic or poetic imagination. The sun-centered universe of Copernicus and Kepler is inseparable from the aesthetic, theological and rhetorical imperatives of both Neoplatonism and Mannerism in the sixteenth century. Closely related notions of harmony, symmetry and proportion inform cosmology as well as music and painting. This book offers the first comprehensive, full-scale study of these relations in these particularly important cases.

LESLIE, John. Demons, Vats and the Cosmos. Phil Papers, 18(2), 169-188, S 89.

Could not a vat-brain learn English so well that it noticed no difference when transferred into a real head which genuinely talked it? Could it not have learned how to refer to real rocks? Reality extends far beyond the verifiable; which is fortunate, because modern cosmological speculations extend likewise. But there is no uniquely correct answer to what a vat-brain's words mean, or what ours mean. Interacting with a computer-based pattern, a vat-brain might be interacting with something worth calling a real person, genuinely worth loving. Berkeley's or Spinoza's world might contain real rocks and people.

LESLIE, John. Is the End of the World Nigh? Phil Quart, 40(158), 65-72, Ja 90.

Carter's anthropic principle says observers must find themselves in a life-permitting universe, and are specially likely to inhabit a spatiotemporal region where life is specially likely. A variant, also originated by Carter, says you are unlikely to find yourself at a date such that almost all humans live later. (Compare, perhaps, how the ball marked with your name is unlikely to be drawn quickly from an urn containing thousands.) This gives you additional grounds for thinking that mankind will not survive long. Maybe high-energy physics will produce a phase transition which kills us all.

LESLIE, John. *Universes*. New York, Routledge, 1989

Force strengths, particle masses, the cosmic expansion rate, and many other cosmologically important numbers, seem fine tuned for producing life. Did God select them? Alternatively, do there exist many "universes," huge cosmic domains with perhaps very varied properties, living beings then observing only the perhaps very rare life-permitting ones? Though sometimes called "anthropic" this last idea concerns all intelligent beings, not just human observers. This book discusses alleged evidence of fine tuning, mechanisms for generating very varied universes, types of anthropic principle, and whether God (particularly if pictured Neoplatonically) would be more plausible than universes in vast numbers.

LESTER, Mark (trans) and DELEUZE, Gilles and BOUNDAS, Constantin V (ed). *The Logic of Sense—Gilles Deleuze*. New York, Columbia Univ Pr, 1990

LETH, Steven C. Sequences in Countable Nonstandard Models of the Natural Numbers. Stud Log, 47(3), 243-264, S 88.

Two different equivalence relations on countable nonstandard models of the natural numbers are considered. Properties of a standard sequence A are correlated with topological properties the equivalence classes of the transfer of A. This provides a method for translating results from analysis into theorems about sequences of natural numbers.

LETH, Steven C. Some Nonstandard Methods in Combinatorial Number Theory. Stud Log, 47(3), 265-278, S 88.

A combinatorial result about internal subsets of *N is proved using the Lebesgue Density Theorem. This result is then used to prove a standard theorem about difference sets of natural numbers which provides a partial answer to a question posed by Erdös and Graham.

LETOCHA, Danièle. Totalité, temporalité et politique: Essai de typologie. Rev Univ Ottawa, 57(4), 9-31, O-D 87.

The text deals with the relations between *cultural structures* and *logics* of *political action* in the Western world. It proposes a speculative typology. Four successive, nonlinear types are presented with the status of totalities analogous to Foucault's "*episteme*": the archaic, the Greek, the modern and the contemporary. They are compared with each other from the standpoints of *extrinsic foundational principle*, the role of the *sacred*, the production of *meaning*, the definition of political *order/disorder* and the *aim* of action. The differences between these four totalities is accounted for through their respective conceptions of *time*.

LETTENBAUER, Wilhelm. "Literatur und Religion zu Dostjevskijs Erzählkunst" in *Agora: Zu Ehren von Rudolph Berlinger*, BERLINGER, Rudolph (and other eds), 331-354. Amsterdam, Rodopi, 1988.

LETWIN, Shirley Robin. "Culture, Individuality, and Deference" in *Culture et Politique/Culture and Politics*, CRANSTON, Maurice (ed), 73-85. Hawthorne, de Gruyter, 1988.

LETWIN, Shirley Robin. Morality and Law. Ratio Juris, 2(1), 55-65, Mr 89.

The controversy over law and morality between positivists and normativists is largely a result of failure on both sides to understand the idea of authority. The author argues that Plato, Aristotle, Aquinas and Hobbes held a common notion of legal authority that was distinctively moral. They all saw the virtue of law (and the source of legal obligation) in the equal protection it provides for all against the disorder to which passion makes men vulnerable, and not in the justice of its provisions. Michael Oakeshott, among contemporary theorists, best illustrates this approach to a resolution of the differences between positivists and normativists.

LETWIN, Shirley Robin. "The Morality of Democracy and the Rule of Law" in *Politics and Process*, BRENNAN, Geoffrey (ed), 221-234. New York, Cambridge Univ Pr, 1989.

The morality of democracy gives the rule of law priority over the democratic way of constituting a government. Law that does not dictate outcomes but sets conditions to be observed when individuals pursue the projects they choose is the only way of resolving disagreements peacefully in a domain where indisputable knowledge is necessarily absent. Though democracy is inseparable from the rule of law, the converse is not true; for it is conceivable that the rule of law may flourish, perhaps even more effectively, under other forms of government. Where the greatest danger lies has to be decided for every set of circumstances. It is a prudential judgment that cannot be determined in advance for all times and places. It follows that a commitment to the morality of democracy obliges us to decide whether democracy should be preferred here and now not on grounds of lofty moral principle but on hard considerations of expediency.

LEVI, Albert William. Literature, Philosophy, and the Imagination. J Aes Educ, 22(4), 9-20, Wint 88.

LEVI, Isaac. Pareto Unanimity and Consensus. J Phil, 87(9), 481-492, S 90.

Seidenfeld, Kadane, and Schervish [J Phil 86 (1989), 225-244] offer an argument showing that two Bayesian decision makers engaged in joint decision making who differ in their probability and utility judgments can reach a Bayesian evaluation of the available options which obeys Pareto unanimity except by letting the views of one of the decision makers be legislated. This paper argues that Pareto unanimity should be modified as a condition on consensus so as to allow "compromises" between the decision makers. In this way, the convexity conditions on indeterminate probabilities and utilities may be satisfied.

LEVI, Isaac. Possibility and Probability. Erkenntnis, 31(2-3), 365-386, S 89.

LEVIN, David Michael. Existentialism at the End of Modernity: Questioning the I's Eyes. Phil Today, 34(1), 80-95, Spr 90.

This essay reflects on the role of existentialism in a critique of modern philosophy and culture which has carried us forward to the end of modernity. The essay then examines the resources of existentialism to see whether this movement can contribute to the new set of challenges and adventures, opportunities and prospects engaging us at the beginning of a postmodern epoch. The analysis is formulated in terms of the human capacity for vision, since it is argued that modernity was shaped and closed by the hegemony of the visual paradigm.

LEVIN, David Michael. *The Listening Self: Personal Growth, Social Change and Closure of Metaphysics.* New York, Routledge, 1989

This book attempts to go beyond the ego of bourgeois history affirmed by Freudian psychology, proposing an account of personal growth and progressive social change based on the development of our capacity for listening in a "practice of the self." These issues are situated within an examination of how the subordination of listening in a vision-dominated epistemology and culture is related to the closure of metaphysics and oppressive closures in everyday life. Arguing that ethical and political life requires the realization of our communicative potentials, this book demonstrates how listening contributes to the ideal speech situation and rational consensus-formation that Habermas describes in his theory of communicative action.

LEVIN, David. The Body Politic: The Embodiment of Praxis in Foucault and Habermas. Praxis Int, 9(1-2), 112-132, Ap-Jl 89.

This paper is a critical examination of Foucault and Habermas, focused on their theoretical conceptualizations of the human body and on how they understand the body to figure in praxis. Merleau-Ponty's phenomenology is used to argue that Foucault's "body" cannot embody a praxis of resistance, and to show how Habermas's "communicative rationality" and "discourse ethics" are already prefigured by, and may be experientially grounded in, the nature of the body of lived experience.

LEVIN, Michael. To the Lighthouse. Philosophia (Israel), 19(4), 471-474, D 89.

This article replies to a criticism of my defense of a Hobbesian minimal state. It is argued that Hobbesian bargainers can distinguish between security and positive public goods, so need not endorse a Hobbesian welfare state.

LEVIN-WALDMAN, Oren M. Dilemmas of Plant Closing Policy in Liberal Society: Equality, Rights, Justice. Pub Affairs Quart, 4(1), 33-53, Ja 90.

LEVINAS, Emmanuel and ATTERTON, Peter (trans). Is Ontology Fundamental? Phil Today, 33(2), 121-129, Sum 89.

In this 1951 essay Levinas calls into question the traditional primacy accorded to comprehension and knowledge within human experience. The contestation, which makes no exception of Heideggerian ontology, its main focus, is waged in the name of the ethical relation as a relation of discourse. The Other, through the expression of her or his face, is said to elude thematization and comprehension, and thus resist appropriation and exploitation. The essay ends with a derivation of a list of themes which determine the trajectory Levinas's thought will later follow.

LEVINE, Carole (ed). *Taking Sides: Clashing Views on Controversial Bioethical Issues (Third Edition).* Guilford, Dushkin, 1989

LEVINE, David. Scarcity and the Limits of Want: Comments on Sassower and Bender. Soc Epistem, 4(1), 115-119, Ja-Mr 90.

This comment responds to two papers dealing with economic theory and its postulate of the scarcity of means relative to wants. A critique of the scarcity postulate is presented in brief followed by an outline of an alternative approach to thinking about the origin and limits of want. This alternative focuses on the qualitative rather than quantitative dimension of want. Emphasizing the qualitative dimension suggests limits of want and has relevance for the ecological perspective of one of the authors addressed.

LEVINE, Joseph. Breaking Out of the Gricean Circle. Phil Stud, 57(2), 207-216, O 89.

LEVINE, Michael P. Alvin I Goldman's Epistemology and Cognition: An Introduction. Philosophia (Israel), 19(2-3), 209-225, O 89.

LEVINE, Michael P. *Hume and the Problem of Miracles: A Solution.* Norwell, Kluwer, 1989

Hume's argument against justified belief in miracles cannot be properly understood apart from his analysis of causation. It is argued that Hume's position has never been correctly interpreted because its connection with his more general metaphysics has never been adequately examined. To understand Hume's view of miracles the following question must be answered: Why did Hume think that one could justifiably believe that an *extraordinary* event had occurred, but that one could *never* justifiably believe a *miracle* had occurred? This book offers a sustained treatment of that question. It is also argued that it makes no significant difference whether Hume's central argument is interpreted as an *a priori* or an *a posteriori* argument; and that his argument is applicable both to belief based on testimony and direct experience of a miracle. In Part II the central question addressed is whether or not anyone can justifiably believe a miracle to have occurred given a contemporary epistemological perspective. The relevance of Hume's essay for the issue of the possibility of justified belief in miracles

from this perspective is examined.

LEVINE, Michael P. Mystical Experience and Non-Basically Justified Belief. Relig Stud, 25(3), 335-345, S 89.

LEVINE, Shellie-helene. The Child-As-Philosopher: A Critique of the Presuppositions of Piagetian Theory. Thinking, 5(1), 1-9, 1983.

LEVINSKI, J P and DONDER, Hans-Dieter. Some Principles Related to Chang's Conjecture. Annals Pure Applied Log, 45(1), 39-101, N 89.

We determine the consistency strength of the negation of the transversal hypothesis. We also study other variants of Chang's conjecture.

LEVINSON, Henry Samuel. Santayana's Pragmatism and the Comic Sense of Life. Bull Santayana Soc, 6, 14-24, Fall 88.

Santayana's *Realms of Being* is pragmatic because it abandons foundational metaphysics and epistemology for reflection on human finitude; accepts the Romantics' claim that the varieties of human discourse help manage life's difficulties but rejects their view that poetry provides a key to metaphysical disclosure; asserts that existence is utterly contingent; and characterizes knowledge as sound opinion. It is comic because it takes joy as seriously as meanness and explores ways to celebrate earthbound, mortal delight (as do Peirce, James, and Dewey). This suggests that Sidney Hook's construal of pragmatism as tragic is polemical, not definitive.

LEVINSON, Jerrold. Colourization Ill-Defended. Brit J Aes, 30(1), 62-67, Ja 90.

LEVINSON, Jerrold. "Song and Music Drama" in *What is Music?*, ALPERSON, Philip A, 283-301. New York, Haven, 1987.

In this essay I consider what distinguishes song from music in general, investigate the interactions of the components of a paradigm western art song, consider how song is to be evaluated as compared with purely instrumental music, and finally, discuss some problems of song used for dramatic purposes (music drama, or opera).

LÉVY, Carlos. Platon, Arcésilas, Carnéade: Réponse à J Annas. Rev Metaph Morale, 95(2), 293-306, Ap-Je 90.

The purpose of this article is to give an interpretation of the New Academy's philosophy quite different from the one defended by J Annas. In our opinion, the reading of the whole testimonies relating to this school suggests a greater complexity than what is embraced by the concept of skepticism, at least in its neo-Pyrrhonian version. We believe that Arcesilas and Carneades, instead of confining Plato within the limits of skepticism, have accepted—in their own way—the whole Platonician legacy. Thus the burden of tradition seems more important in the history of the Academy than it is generally admitted.

LEVY, David. "Smith and Kant Respond to Mandeville" in *Early Modern Philosophy II*, TWEYMAN, Stanley (ed), 25-39. Delmar, Caravan Books, 1988.

A comparison of moral motivation in the writings of Smith and Kant by reference to the challenge posed by Mandeville's motivational skepticism.

LEVY, Ze'ev. *Baruch or Benedict: On Some Jewish Aspects of Spinoza's Philosophy.* New York, Lang, 1989

This book investigates various aspects of the controversial relations between Spinoza's philosophy and his Jewish background. It examines some important trends of medieval Jewish philosophy on the shaping of Spinoza's thought—particularly the impact of Maimonides. The book elucidates the differences between Spinoza and his predecessors in regard to Bible criticism, and dwells extensively on the concepts of substance and pantheism. It also discusses Spinoza's views of Judaism and the Jewish people, the relationship between state and religion, and some problems of Spinoza's "Hebrew Grammar."

LÉVY-BRUHL, Lucien. Ce qui est vivant, ce qui est mort dans la philosophie d'Auguste Comte (1935). Rev Phil Fr, 179(4), 479-480, O-D 89.

LÉVY-BRUHL, Lucien. Descartes et l'esprit cartésien (1922). Rev Phil Fr, 179(4), 464-469, O-D 89.

LÉVY-BRUHL, Lucien. L'esprit cartésien et l'histoire (1936). Rev Phil Fr, 179(4), 470-474, O-D 89.

LEWIN, Renato A. Involutions Defined By Monadic Terms. Stud Log, 47(4), 387-389, D 88.

We prove that there are two involutions defined by monadic terms that characterize Monadic Algebras. We further prove that the variety of Monadic Algebras is the smallest variety of Interior Algebras where these involutions give rise to an interpretation from the variety of Bounded Distributive Lattices into it.

LEWIS, David. "Finite Counterforce" in *Nuclear Deterrence and Moral*

Restraint, SHUE, Henry (ed), 51-114. New York, Cambridge Univ Pr, 1989.

The article advocates a form of nuclear deterrence in which the response even to a major nuclear attack would be limited to second-strike counterforce warfare, with efforts to avoid collateral death and destruction. It argues (1) that no worse threat is needed to achieve adequate deterrence; (2) that the nuclear use envisaged would be morally acceptable; (3) that second-strike counterforce attacks, though mediocre as a means of preventing harm, would probably be beneficial on balance; and (4) that weapons suited for modest, second-strike counterforce would not create much pressure to preempt.

LEWIS, Peter. Collingwood on Art and Fantasy. Philosophy, 64(250), 547-556, O 89.

The aim of this paper is to show how Collingwood attempts to incorporate the idea that art involves the renunciation of fantasy into the theory of art he constructs in *The Principles of Art*. Collingwood's distinction between make-believe and imagination forms the basis of his rejection of psychoanalytic theories of art. Collingwood accounts for bad art in terms of his notion of 'corruption of consciousness', which subsumes the concept of fantasy. George Eliot's *Middlemarch* is employed to illustrate Collingwood's thesis.

LEWIS, Peter. Wittgenstein's Genius. Phil Invest, 13(3), 246-257, Jl 90.

A consideration of Wittgenstein's reflections on the nature of genius in *Culture and Value*. Wittgenstein accepts the traditional dichotomy between talent, or skilfulness, and genius, or originality of the soil and originality of the seed. The latter distinction is illustrated in the relationship of Breuer and Freud, though it is Freud's genius which enables us to identify Breuer's contribution as the seed of the psychoanalytic method. Wittgenstein's remark that 'the measure of genius is character' is discussed in relation to Freud's career and Beethoven's symphonies.

LEYDESDORFF, Loet and VAN DER MEULEN, Barend. Effecten en gevolgen van wetenschapsbeleid voor de filosofiebeoefening aan de Nederlandse universiteiten. Alg Ned Tijdschr Wijs, 82(3), 173-193, Jl 90.

During the last five years, the Dutch Faculties of Philosophy went through a period of transition. First, in 1982, the national government introduced a new system of financing research at the universities. In 1983, a drastic reduction in the budget for philosophy was proposed. In 1987 a Visiting Committee reported on the weak and strong areas of Dutch philosophy and made proposals about a policy to strengthen Dutch philosophy. This study explores the possibilities of indicating the effects of the institutional reorganizations on the study of philosophy at the Faculties, using scientometric methods. Moreover at the end some remarks are made on possibilities for a functional policy.

LEYVRAZ, Jean-Pierre. Variations sur Schopenhauer et la musique. Rev Theol Phil, 121(4), 377-388, 1989.

This article emphasises the important part played by music in Schopenhauer's "World as will and representation." The four books of this work are considered and the role of music is linked to the "repetition" of the first two books in the last ones. The world of sensation and causation, of conflict, reflects itself in music, where pain and conflict reveal their pacified essence.

LI, Cheng. On the Typology of Modes of Thought. Chin Stud Phil, 21(3), 3-25, Spr 90.

LI-TIAN, Fang. "Liu Zongyuan's and Liu Yuxi's Theories of Heaven and Man" in *Man and Nature: The Chinese Tradition and the Future*, TANG, Yi-Jie (ed), 25-32. Lanham, Univ Pr of America, 1989.

LIBERMAN, Kenneth. "Decentering the Self: Two Perspectives from Philosophical Anthropology" in *The Question of the Other: Essays in Contemporary Continental Philosophy*, DALLERY, Arleen B (ed), 127-142. Albany, SUNY Pr, 1989.

LIDDON, Sim C. *The Dual Brain, Religion, and the Unconscious*. Buffalo, Prometheus, 1989.

This work explores the religious, mystical aspects of the human unconscious. It is the author's opinion that traditional psychology has failed to adequately explain such phenomena. He draws on the findings of psychology, psychotherapy, religion, anthropology, philosophy and neurology to gain a better understanding of this type of subjective human experience. (staff)

LIEB, Irwin C. Time and Value. Rev Metaph, 43(3), 475-494, Mr 90.

LIEDMAN, Sven-Eric. Critical Attitudes Inside Social Science and the Humanities—A Swedish Perspective. Phil Soc Act, 15(3-4), 35-40, Jl-D 89.

LIEDTKA, Jeanne M. Value Congruence: The Interplay of Individual and Organizational Value Systems. J Bus Ethics, 8(10), 805-815, O 89.

This paper focuses on the individual manager making difficult decisions within the context of the organization in which he or she is a member. It proposes a method for examining the interplay of individual and corporate value systems, offering a value congruence model. Hypotheses are generated concerning the varying nature of the value conflicts faced by managers. These are then evaluated based upon interview data from a cross-section of managers in two organizations. The impact of differing organizational value systems is discussed, as well as the implications of the study for research in this area.

LIKIERMAN, Andrew. Ethical Dilemmas for Accountants: A United Kingdom Perspective. J Bus Ethics, 8(8), 617-629, Ag 89.

The paper provides an introduction to some of the professional ethical dilemmas facing an accountant in the United Kingdom. The first part deals with those dilemmas which accountants would normally accept are covered by the term "ethics." These include the problems associated with adequately fulfilling a duty to shareholders and conflicts of interest (including whistleblowing) by the accountant acting as independent auditor or as an employee. The second part deals with wider aspects of ethical dilemmas stemming from reconciling the implicit understanding that the accountant is being objective with the fact that accounting rules make it very difficult to sustain that objectivity.

LILIEN, Gary L and GAUVIN, Stéphane and CHATTERJEE, Kalyan. The Impact of Information and Computer Based Training on Negotiators' Performance. Theor Decis, 28(3), 331-354, My 90.

This paper presents the results of an experiment on negotiation, designed to measure the impact of (1) computerized training and (2) information on negotiators' performance. The paper is structured as follows. First, we review the literature on negotiation training. Second, we develop a conceptual framework to link various forms of negotiation support systems to joint and individual negotiation performance. Third, we present the negotiation paradigm—a bilateral monopoly—and the computerized training system we used. Regarding training, our results show an asymmetric impact on individual performance levels and, unexpectedly, a negative impact on negotiators' joint performance. In contrast, more information improves both individual and joint performance. Finally, we discuss these results, and outline further research questions.

LILLA, Mark. Backing Into Vico: Recent Trends in American Philosophy. New Vico Studies, 4, 89-100, 1986.

LINDAHL, Lars. Preference Derived from Urgency. Acta Phil Fennica, 38, 91-109, 1985.

The concepts 'more urgent' and 'preferable', though different, are interrelated. In the essay, preferability is conceived of as a relation between alternatives, urgency as a relation between properties of alternatives. It is shown that a preferability ordering of alternatives can be derived from an urgency ordering of properties of the alternatives. Postulates and proofs are formulated. Applicatory examples from politics are suggested; references are made to the theory of value of Carl Menger and the doctrines of piecemeal engineering and moral urgency of Karl Popper. (A misprint occurs on p. 99, line 3 from the bottom: read 'Qb' instead of 'Qa'.)

LINDGREN, Ralph. Beyond Revolt: A Horizon for Feminist Ethics. Hypatia, 5(1), 145-150, Spr 90.

The suggestion here is that casting the project of feminist ethics in confrontational language, rooted in a rebellion picture of moral epistemology, impedes the further development of that very project. Four commonplace examples are offered to make this suggestion plausible. I urge instead a pluralistic approach to styles of moral thinking and propose that the project of feminist ethics would be better served by casting it in the language of reconciliation.

LINDOP, Clive. Harry 17: Judgment, Perspective and Philosophy. Thinking, 8(3), 39-40, 1989.

Examines Justus Buchler's notions of judgment and perspective, the role of philosophy in the articulation of each, and the application of these ideas in the Philosophy for Children programs. Traditional philosophic expositions give a distorted picture of the individual, one's representation of the world and communication with others. Philosophy for Children, heeding Buchler, remedies this by featuring, as central characters in the novels, children who exemplify the different modes of experience and judgment, thus engaging pupils in articulation of perspective in ways other than their habitual personal one.

LINDSAY, Ronald A. Thomas Aquinas's Complete Guide to Heaven and Hell. Free Inq, 10(3), 38-39, Sum 90.

This article summarizes, in a humorous fashion, the orthodox Christian philosopher's conception of the afterlife. All quotes are from the Supplement to Part Three of the Summa Theologica. Problems with this conception are discussed; in particular, the Christian philosopher's understanding of the afterlife diverges sharply from the understanding of the ordinary layperson. The article suggests that the ordinary layperson may not find the prospect of immortality attractive as it is described by the philosopher.

LINGIS, Alphonso. The Elemental Imperative. Res Phenomenol, 18, 3-21, 1988.

LINK-SALINGER, Ruth (ed). A Straight Path: Studies in Medieval Philosophy and Culture. Washington, Cath Univ Amer Pr, 1988

LINTS, Richard. Irresistibility, Epistemic Warrant and Religious Belief. Relig Stud, 25(4), 425-433, D 89.

LINVILLE, Mark D. On Goodness: Human and Divine. Amer Phil Quart, 27(2), 143-152, Ap 90.

This article begins by reconstructing a Kantian argument to show that essential divine goodness is both a necessary condition of the truth of divine command morality and a sufficient condition for its falseness. Further, it is argued that if Kantian libertarianism is true, then the very notion of an essentially morally perfect being is contradictory. The article then attempts to construct a coherent version of divine command morality in full recognition of the constraints set by these important Kantian criticisms.

LIPKIN, Robert. Intimacy and Confidentiality in Psychotherapeutic Relationships. Theor Med, 10(4), 311-330, D 89.

This article explores the relations among and between intimacy, psychotherapeutic relationships and moral advice. The article concludes that a psychotherapeutic relationship is not usefully explained in terms of intimacy. Instead, a psychiatric relationship is a form of moral advice, and it is this dimension of a psychotherapeutic relationship as a form of moral advice that poses a natural limit to the confidentiality necessary for engaging in psychotherapy.

LIPMAN, Matthew. Philosophy and the Cultivation of Reasoning. Thinking, 5(4), 33-41, 1985.

A look at what philosophy has to offer the elementary school student in terms of the improvement of reasoning. Consideration is given to the contributions of the philosophical subdivisions of ethics, epistemology, etc., and to the analysis by students of their own mental acts (believing, knowing, wishing, hoping, etc.). Also, a summary of some results of educational testing of philosophy in the classroom.

LIPMAN, Matthew. Philosophy for Children and Critical Thinking. Thinking, 7(4), Supp 10-12, 1988.

This brief article considers the distinguishing characteristics of *critical thinking* (that it is aimed at the making of *judgments*; that it is guided or controlled by *criteria*; that it is *sensitive to context*; and that it is *self-correcting*), and attempts to show that these traits are outstandingly achieved by the Philosophy for Children curriculum.

LIPMAN, Matthew and SHARP, Ann Margaret. Philosophy for Children: A Traditional Subject in a Novel Format. Thinking, 7(4), Supp 2-5, 1988.

An examination of alternative curricula for the teaching of thinking, and a closer look at Philosophy for Children. The article concludes with a set of claims regarding those achievements which are peculiar to Philosophy for Children.

LIPPINCOTT, Mark S. Russell's Leviathan. Russell, 10(1), 6-29, Sum 90.

This article documents and examines the residual influence of Thomas Hobbes's political metaphor of absolute power, the leviathan, in Bertrand Russell's numerous works on the prospects for international peace. This Hobbesian influence was most dramatically revealed in Russell's brief and highly controversial advocacy of an American preemptive nuclear strike against the Soviet Union following the Second World War. While other commentators have seen this episode as an aberration in Russell's political thought, Russell viewed the temporary American nuclear monopoly as a unique Hobbesian opportunity to end the international 'state of nature' and set the preconditions for world government.

LIPPKE, Richard L. Advertising and the Social Conditions of Autonomy. Bus Prof Ethics J, 8(4), 35-58, Wint 89.

John Galbraith charges that advertising is an aspect of the capacity of corporations to impose their interests on others. I concur with this judgment and seek to more systematically develop and support it. I develop an account of autonomy and argue that advertising suppresses it by inducing in persons the uncritical acceptance of the consumer lifestyle. I emphasize that the impact of advertising is a function not only of its methods and content but also of the availability of other social conditions of autonomy.

LIPPOLIS, Laura. Costituzione e realità attuale: A proposito di un convegno tenuto a Lecce. Riv Int Filosof Diritto, 66(3), 494-496, Jl-S 89.

LISMAN, C David. Marxist Literary Theory: A Critique. J Aes Educ, 22(2),

73-85, Sum 88.

LISSE, M. Le motif de la déconstruction et ses portées politiques. Tijdschr Filosof, 52(2), 230-250, Je 90.

LISTON, Daniel P. Capitalist Schools: Explanation and Ethics in Radical Studies of Schooling. New York, Routledge, 1988

LISZKA, James Jakob. Peirce's Interpretant. Trans Peirce Soc, 26(1), 17-62, Wint 90.

I attempt to justify a broader and more comprehensive interpretation of Peirce's interpretant than is typically made. The interpretant cannot be reduced to either sense or reference, but is a third aspect of meaning which incorporates both of these aspects in a process of sign translation. Translation is not understood as synonymy but as growth. In turn, sign translation gets its determination and direction from the community of sign users engaged in the right sort of inquiry. Under this account of the interpretant, value, purpose and meaning are incorporated in a more coherent way.

LIU, Shu-hsien. Toward a New Relation between Humanity and Nature: Reconstructing T'ien-jen-ho-i. Zygon, 24(4), 457-468, D 89.

The traditional Chinese idea of t'ien-jen-ho-i (Heaven and humanity in union) implies that humanity has to live in harmony with nature. As science and technology progress, however, the idea appears increasingly outmoded, and it becomes fashionable to talk about overcoming nature. Ironically, though, the further science reaches the more clearly are its limitations exposed. The exploitation of nature not only endangers many life forms on earth but threatens the very existence of the human species. I propose that a reconstruction of the traditional Chinese idea of T'ien-jen-ho-i will help us envisage a new and salutary relation between humanity and nature.

LIVESEY, Steven J. Science and Theology in Fourteenth Century: Subalternate Sciences in Oxford Commentaries on the *Sentences*. Synthese, 83(2), 273-292, My 90.

Both Pierre Duhem and his successors emphasized that medieval scholastics created a science of mechanics by bringing both observation and mathematical techniques to bear on natural effects. Recent research into medieval and early modern science has suggested that Aristotle's subalternate sciences also were used in this program, although the degree to which the theory of subalternation had been modified is still not entirely clear. This paper focuses on the English tradition of subalternation between 1310 and 1350, and concludes with a discussion of the theory advanced by Thomas Claxton early in the fifteenth century.

LIVINGSTON, Kenneth R. Concepts, Categories, and Epistemology. Philosophia (Israel), 19(2-3), 265-300, O 89.

Empirical studies by psychologists are reviewed with special attention to the theoretical conclusions drawn from the data by psychologists (and some philosophers). It is argued that psychological theories of concepts and categories are founded on a number of implicit epistemological assumptions of generally antirealist character. This epistemological antirealism is in conflict with the realism that seems to characterize the current paradigm of research in cognitive psychology. It is suggested that a more thorough-going realism is possible which is nevertheless consistent with the empirical findings currently available and the shape of this realism is sketched in very broad strokes. As proposed, however, this realism would require abandonment of the concept of representation in favor of a more directly causal theory of brain-world interaction.

LLANO, Estela. The Spanish Natural Law School. Vera Lex, 9(2), 5, 1989.

The article proposes to give a vision very brief of the so-called Spanish Natural Law School, established by a series of theologians and jurists of the XVI and XVII centuries. This group of authors constitutes one of the most famous schools of natural law. The article gives the names of the authors best known, with a concise reference to the fundamental line of his thoughts. At the footnote, it is given a bibliographical and select reference, so that the interested reader may widen the knowledge of the school.

LLEWELYN, J. Glasnostalgia. Bull Hegel Soc Gt Brit, 18, 33-42, Autumn-Wint 88.

LLEWELYN, John. Belongings. Res Phenomenol, 17, 117-136, 1987.

LLEWELYN, John. "On the Saying that Philosophy Begins in *Thaumazein*" in *Post-Structuralist Classics*, BENJAMIN, Andrew (ed), 173-191. New York, Routledge, 1988.

This paper comments on the relationship between stupidity and the stupefaction of the wonder with which philosophers since Socrates have said philosophy begins. These comments are then related to the analysis of forms of wonder conducted by Heidegger in the *Grundfragen der Philosophie*.

LLEWELYN, John. Ontological Responsibility and the Poetics of Nature. Res Phenomenol, 19, 3-26, 1989.

LLOYD, Christopher. Realism and Structurism in Historical Theory: A Discussion of the Thought of Maurice Mandelbaum. Hist Theor, 28(3), 296-325, O 89.

LLOYD, Dan. What is Representation? A Reply to Smythe. Behaviorism, 17(2), 151-154, Fall 89.

This is a reply to William Smythe's "The Case for Cognitive Conservatism: A Critique of Dan Lloyd's Approach to Mental Representation" (*Behaviorism* 17, 63-75, Spring 1989). Smythe charged that representations à la Lloyd are too simple, vague in content, and missing the necessary condition of interpretation. This brief reply to those challenges touches on themes more fully developed in *Simple Minds* (MIT Press/Bradford Books, 1989).

LO BUE, Salvatore. La teoria dello spazio immaginario in Leopardi. G Metaf, 11(1), 51-64, Ja-Ap 89.

LOBATO, Abelardo. El lenguaje y la palabra en Tomas de Aquino. Rev Filosof (Mexico), 22(65), 132-148, My-Ag 89.

LOBL, Rudolf. *Demokrit: Texte seiner Philosophie*. Amsterdam, Rodopi, 1988

LOCHE, Annamaria. Le "Considèrations" di Montesquieu a 250 anni dalla pubblicazione. G Crit Filosof Ital, 68(1), 100-104, Ja-Ap 89.

LOCK, James D. Some Aspects of Medical Hermeneutics: The Role of Dialectic and Narrative. Theor Med, 11(1), 41-49, Mr 90.

This essay constructs an argument for a dialectic between the scientific and clinical aspects of medicine using the hermeneutical approach of Paul Ricoeur as a theoretical and philosophical guide. Additionally, the relationship between this dialectic and narrative case histories is examined as a way of expressing this abstract and theoretical concept in more concrete terms.

LOCKE, Lawrence A. Personhood and Moral Responsibility. Law Phil, 9(1), 39-66, F 90.

LOCKWOOD, Michael. *Mind, Brain and the Quantum: The Compound 'I'*. Cambridge, Blackwell, 1989

The book presents a new approach to the mind-body problem, drawing together considerations from the philosophy of mind, cognitive science, neurophysiology and fundamental physics. Connections are drawn between the traditional mind-body problem and the measurement problem in quantum mechanics. It is argued (following Russell) that awareness reveals the intrinsic character of that part or aspect of our own brains whose activities are constitutive of conscious mentality—but that such direct acquaintance with our own brains must be governed by some preferred set of brain *observables*, in the quantum-mechanical sense. A time observable plays a crucial role here.

LOEB, Louis E. The Priority of Reason in Descartes. Phil Rev, 99(1), 3-43, Ja 90.

Descartes is committed to *the priority of reason*: the proper use of sense-perception requires submitting the beliefs it generates to tests for correction by reason, but not *vice versa*. I show that this commitment cannot be explained by the greater truth-conduciveness of reason; the priority of reason rests on the greater psychological irresistibility of reason, together with the adoption of permanence in belief as a doxastic objective. I consider the bearing of my interpretation on the problem of the Cartesian circle. I also argue that Descartes's epistemological position has affinities with that of Hume.

LOEB, Stephen E and CORY, Suzanne N. Whistleblowing and Management Accounting: An Approach. J Bus Ethics, 8(12), 903-916, D 89.

In this paper, we consider the licensing of and codes of ethics that affect the accountant not in public accounting, the potential for an accountant not in public accounting encountering an ethical conflict situation, and the moral responsibility of such accountant when faced with an ethical dilemma. We review an approach suggested by the National Association of Accountants for dealing with an ethical conflict situation including that association's position on whistleblowing. We propose another approach based on the work of De George (1981), in which both internal and external whistleblowing are possible alternatives, for use by management accountants in an ethical conflict situation. Finally, we consider the implications of our analysis for management accounting. While most of the analysis centers on management accountants, we note the likely applicability of the analysis to accountants in the public sector.

LOECK, Gisela. Descartes' Logic of Magnitudes. Dialectica, 43(4), 339-372, 1989.

The paper presents a paradigmatic part of the logic of magnitudes, an invention of Descartes, different from alethic formal logic, but a proper formal logic *sui generis*. Descartes's logic consists of corporeal—geometrical and physical—devices that behave like deductive calculi, generating inferences of magnitudes from magnitudes. Its syntactic elements are magnitudes as corporeal entities, whose connections can be characterized by various magnitudinal connectives, distinguished from those of alethic logic. The paper presents two kinds of orthogonal and the congruence connectives applying them (1) to line segments and (2) to physical magnitudes. It describes the value semantics and the interpretative semantics of these connections, the inference rules they take part in, states the conditions for validity and theoremhood, and compares it to model theory. It shows that one of the orthogonal connections displays the ontic and logical properties of Descartes's *ideae innatae*, whereas the other displays those of Descartes's *ideae factae*, and shows that the physical law $m \cdot v = p$ regarded as an orthogonal connection is an *idea innata*.

LOECK, Gisela. Remarks On Teaching "Barefoot" Philosophy. Thinking, 5(3), 25-31, 1984.

LOEWER, Barry and LE PORE, Ernest. Absolute Truth Theories for Modal Languages as Theories of Interpretation. Critica, 21(61), 43-73, Ap 89.

Donald Davidson, Gilbert Harman, and in particular John Wallace have identified some difficulties in constructing absolute truth theories for languages containing intensional operators. Wallace argues that the standard recursion clause for negation has no analogue for "necessity" and a range of other intensional operators. Anil Gupta and Christopher Peacocke respond to Wallace by devising truth theories which, though containing a straightforward recursion clause for "necessity," are not false. In this paper, we argue that though Gupta and Peacocke circumvent Wallace's objection, there is a cost: the truth theories they propose cannot function as theories of interpretation for any language. Since we have argued that the firmest grip we have on theories of interpretation is supplied by truth theories, this cost is too high. We then consider possible world semantics for modal languages and argue that such theories cannot be converted into truth theories suitable for interpretation. Lastly, we sketch an adequate semantic account for modal languages, qua theories of interpretation, by viewing modalities as predicates, much as Davidson proposes we view propositional attitude ascriptions.

LOEWER, Barry and LE PORE, Ernest. More on Making Mind Matter. Phil Topics, 17(1), 175-191, Spr 89.

In this paper we discuss the question whether there is any causal role for content properties to play. First we discuss considerations which may lead one to worry that content properties are causally impotent. These worries arise from combining certain physicalistic commitments with the view that content properties are not reducible to physical properties. So we formulate a nonreductive physicalism and then canvass some reasons for thinking that content properties are not reducible to physical basic properties. We then consider three responses which attempt to characterize a causal role and show that content properties play this role.

LOEWER, Barry and LE PORE, Ernest. You Can Say *That* Again. Midwest Stud Phil, 14, 338-356, 1989.

In "Truth and Meaning" (1967) Donald Davidson proposed that a Tarskian truth theory for a language L can be (the heart of) a theory of meaning for L. In "On Saying That" (1968) he proposed a radically novel approach, the paratactic account, to the logical form of indirect discourse. The two proposals are related in a number of ways. The paratactic account claims to show how to construct a truth theory for languages containing indirect discourse. The truth theoretic account of meaning provides motivation and support for the paratactic account. Our primary aim is to motivate the paratactic account and defend it from certain widely known criticisms.

LOEWY, Erich H. Obligations, Communities, and Suffering: Problems of Community Seen in a New Light. Bridges, 2(1-2), 1-16, Spr-Sum 90.

A sense of obligation, irrespective of how it might be variously constituted, is essential to ethical function. In this paper, the various notions of obligation are examined briefly and the notions of social contract and community are then related to the way in which obligation is perceived. It is suggested that the capacity to suffer is the principal condition that endows entities with moral worth. An ethic predicated on the capacity to suffer can, therefore, underwrite a more realistic and workable notion of a beneficent community. The paper concludes that such an ethic not only necessitates the responsible use of biotechnology and entails a decent respect for future generations, but demands an active concern with social justice.

LOEWY, Erich H. Suffering, Moral Worth, and Medical Ethics: A New Beginning. Bridges, 1(3-4), 103-117, Fall-Wint 89.

LOGLI, Paul A. Drugs in the Womb: The Newest Battlefield in the War on

Drugs. Crim Just Ethics, 9(1), 23-29, Wint-Spr 90.

The reported incidence of drug-related births has risen dramatically over the last several years. The legal system and, in particular, local prosecutors have attempted to properly respond to the suffering, death, and economic costs which result from a pregnant woman's use of drugs. The ensuing debate has raised serious constitutional and practical issues which are far from resolution. Prosecutors have achieved mixed results in using current criminal and juvenile statutes as a basis for legal action intended to prosecute mothers and protect children. As a result, state and federal legislators have begun the difficult task of drafting appropriate laws to deal with the problem, while at the same time acknowledging the concerns of medical authorities, child protection groups, and advocates for individual rights.

LOH, Werner. Wissenschaft, Vorurteil und Wahn. Conceptus, 23(59), 31-48, 1989.

Delusion, prejudice and science overlap and are interlaced. Nevertheless there are no systematic researches about these connections. In demarcation from religion an integrating concept will be proposed, that defines "science," "prejudice" and "delusion" from autogenious proofs. "Delusion" will be specified as prejudice, which is regulated in reflection by other prejudices. The proof of a prejudice will be adapted to the maintenance of a concept. The development of modern knowledge may be considered also as a competition of prejudices.

LOIACONO, James. "Liberation as Autonomy and Responsibility" in *The Social Context and Values: Perspectives of the Americas*, MC LEAN, George F (ed), 75-121. Lanham, Univ Pr of America, 1989.

LOKHORST, Gert-Jan C. Multiply Modal Extensions of Da Costa's C_n, Logical Relativism, and the Imaginary. J Non-Classical Log, 5(2), 7-22, N 88.

How should *our* logic express what *other* logics deem necessary? How should we give a rational account of forms of rationality which are different from ours? The present paper answers these questions. It shows how to enrich logical systems with operators which describe what is necessary, rational and imaginary according to other systems. Although only Da Costa's paraconsistent calculi are treated in detail, the construction is generally applicable. As a result the thesis of logical relativism—people from different cultures may live in different cognizable worlds—may henceforth be discussed in terms of modal logic and possible world semantics.

LOMASKY, Loren E (ed) and BRENNAN, Geoffrey (ed). *Politics and Process*. New York, Cambridge Univ Pr, 1989

The ten contributions to this volume from philosophers, economists, and political scientists evaluate democratic principles and processes as mechanisms through which individual preferences are translated into public policies. Although the essays represent a diverse range of interests and methodologies, each addresses the problem of imperfections that attend the translation process. The authors appraise the status of democratic institutions and foundational democratic theory in light of these imperfections.

LOMASKY, Loren E and BRENNAN, Geoffrey. "Large Numbers, Small Costs: The Uneasy Foundations of Democratic Rule" in *Politics and Process*, BRENNAN, Geoffrey (ed), 42-59. New York, Cambridge Univ Pr, 1989.

Economists typically attempt to explain voting as wealth-maximizing behavior. A major source of embarrassment for this view is that, under reasonable assumptions of cost and expected return, individuals in large-number electorates will not vote. Nonetheless, millions do. We propose a revised model in which voting is understood primarily as maximizing expressive returns. Some consequences are (i) individuals will rationally vote otherwise than they would choose were they decisive; (ii) policies may emerge that are suboptimal for everyone; (iii) electoral outcomes, relative to private activity, will manifest extremes of both altruism and malice. We conclude by developing normative implications of the model.

LOMASKY, Loren E. Liberal Autonomy. Phil Theol, 4(3), 297-309, Spr 90.

Theorists increasingly turn to autonomy (rather than liberty per se) as a grounding value for liberalism. This is, I argue, an ill-advised strategy. If autonomy is understood to differ from (negative) liberty insofar as it demands from agents significantly greater feats of self-determination, then it is not clear that autonomy is worth having. And, irrespective of whether autonomy is judged to be valuable, autonomy-based liberalisms either prescribe essentially the same constraints as classical liberalism—and thus are politically innocuous—or else require that the state act non-neutrally with respect to its citizens—and thus are illiberal.

LOMBA FUENTES, Joaquín. Ethos, techne y kalon en Platón. Anu Filosof, 20(2), 23-70, 1987.

LOMBARD, Lawrence Brian. Causes, Enablers, and the Counterfactual

Analysis. Phil Stud, 59(2), 195-211, Je 90.

In this paper, I consider an objection to the counterfactual analysis of event causation based on a case devised by Jonathan Bennett. The case, in conjunction with the counterfactual analysis, implies falsely that heavy rainstorms are causes of fires. I suggest that, while the case does pose a problem for the counterfactual analysis, that analysis might overcome the objection, if it is so revised as to take account of the distinction between a genuine cause of an event and a cause of a condition the obtaining of which merely makes it possible for one event to be a cause of another.

LOMBARDI, Louis G. Character Versus Codes: Models for Research Ethics. Int J Applied Phil, 5(1), 21-28, Spr 90.

The article examines two models for research ethics: an emphasis on rules or codes, which is related to Kantian ethics, and reliance on the development of character, on the model of Aristotle's ethics. The two models are evaluated, based in part on their applicability to the current environment in academia. The article closes with an attempt to delineate appropriate roles for each model.

LOMBARDINI, Siro. Fede e filosofia. Sapienza, 42(3), 337-348, Jl-S 89.

LONG, Douglas G. 'Utility' and the 'Utility Principle': Hume, Smith, Bentham, Mill. Utilitas, 2(1), 12-39, My 90.

LONG, Douglas. Bentham as Revolutionary Social Scientist. Man Nature, 6, 115-145, 1987.

LONG, Eugene T. Christianity and Humanism. Personalist Forum, 5(2), 119-136, Fall 89.

LONG, Eugene T. The Gifford Lectures and the Glasgow Hegelians. Rev Metaph, 43(2), 357-384, D 89.

LONG, Fiachra. Blondel on the Origin of Philosophy. Phil Today, 33(1), 21-27, Spr 89.

This paper examines Blondel's views on the nature and scope of philosophy particularly as outlined in two articles written for the *Annales de philosophie chrétienne* in 1906. These articles ask how important it is for philosophy to retain its formal expression. If philosophy flows naturally from a person's life, how important are big words and learned treatises? On the other hand, some people view philosophy as a scholarly form of learning requiring mastery over technical terms just like any other science. So what is the origin of philosophy? Blondel suggests an interesting compromise.

LONG, R James. "Richard Fishacre's Way to God" in *A Straight Path: Studies in Medieval Philosophy and Culture*, LINK-SALINGER, Ruth (ed), 174-182. Washington, Cath Univ Amer Pr, 1988.

Was Richard Fishacre (d. 1248) among those mentioned by Aquinas who assert that the existence of God is self-evident? Although Fishacre constructs ten arguments for the existence of God, more than any other scholastic thitherto, they lack the intellectual rigor of the Thomistic proofs. Indeed the proposition "God exists" is virtually self-evident for Fishacre (and other Augustinians) on the grounds that without God's illuminating presence the human mind would know nothing; therefore, who sees something in the presence of light, sees the light more than the object.

LONGINO, Helen E. Biological Effects of Low-Level Radiation: Values, Dose-Response Models, Risk Estimates. Synthese, 81(3), 391-404, D 89.

Predictions about the health risks of low-level radiation combine two sorts of measures. One estimates the amount and kinds of radiation released into the environment, and the other estimates the adverse health effects. A new field called health physics integrates and applies nuclear physics to cytology to supply both these estimates. It does so by first determining the kinds of effects different types of radiation produce in biological organisms, and second, by monitoring the extent of these effects produced by given levels of exposure. This essay examines the interplay between evidential constraints and external, contextual interests and values in studying the biological hazards of radiation. By analyzing the debate over linear vs. quadratic dose response models, the essay focuses on problems of developing quantitative, rather than qualitative, estimates of the risks of increased cancer incidence in an exposed population.

LONGUENESSE, Béatrice and WAXMAN, Wayne (trans). Actuality in Hegel's Logic. Grad Fac Phil J, 13(1), 115-124, 1988.

LOOMIS, David E. EUCLID: Rhetoric in Mathematics. Phil Math, 5(1-2), 56-72, 1990.

Sustaining wonder is the task of philosophical rhetoric. This essay traces Euclid's rhetoric from the pretextual, "visual" wonder at the existence of any regular solid, to wonder about the conditions of such an existence; to a choice about which "natural" landmarks to choose as the means of articulating spatial intuitions and wonder at the refusal of the straight and the curved to measure one another; from the invention of instruments to measure space to wonder at the "natural" correctness these instruments exhibit; to the incommensurability of some spatial magnitudes, their refusal to behave like rational numbers; all of which lead to the complete articulation of the regular solids, but also back to deeper wonder about where they began; is there anything at all "given" in that synthetic a priori called spatial intuition?

LOPARIC, Zeljko. Kant e o ceticismo. Manuscrito, 11(2), 67-83, O 88.

It is commonly held that the triumph over Hume aimed at by Kant was a new foundation of traditional metaphysics understood as science of the supra-sensible. The present article shows that this view must be rejected. It establishes, in the first place, that far from trying to diminish the impact of Hume's critique of metaphysics Kant actually generalized and thus radicalized his criticism. If Kant can still be called a foundationalist in the domain of theoretical philosophy, it is because he has laid foundations of empirical and not of metaphysical knowledge. A second tenet of the article is that Kant cannot be viewed as a traditional foundationalist on grounds of his attempt to establish metaphysical foundations of free action either. For these foundations are based on a new concept of meaning of practical ideas which is entirely different from that of reference to a given object. Kant's practical metaphysics is therefore a theory completely at variance with traditional metaphysics requiring the rethinking of all traditional first principles.

LOPARIC, Zeljko. A propos du Cartésianisme Gris de Marion. Manuscrito, 11(2), 129-133, O 88.

LÓPEZ DOMÍNGUEZ, Virginia E. Sobre Dios como orden moral del universo: Fichte y el golpe de gracia a la teología dogmática. Rev Latin De Filosof, 15(3), 321-334, N 89.

This article tries to establish the place that the religious doctrine, enunciated in the Fichte's *Atheismus-Schriften*, occupies in the philosophical system of this author, especially its relation with subjectivity's philosophy, and secondary with regard to the philosophy of religion from Berlin, examining the concept of God as moral order in opposition to the substance-God postulated by dogmatic philosophies.

LÓPEZ QUINTÁS, Alfonso. La enseñanza de la ética a través de la literatura. Anu Filosof, 20(2), 71-84, 1987.

Las obras literarias de calidad describen experiencias humanas básicas y ponen al descubierto los procesos que articulan entre sí tales experiencias, de modo singular los procesos de vértigo o fascinación y los proyectos de éxtasis o creatividad. Mediante su teoria del "juego creador" y de los "ámbitos de realidad" (field of reality), el autor explica cómo puede el lector rehacer las experiencias y procesos nucleares de la vida humana y disc ernir cuáles son constructivos y cuáles destructivos. Es una via fecunda para la formación de los jóvenes en la ética y para el logro de una ética que puedan compartir creyentes y no creyentes.

LÓPEZ QUINTÁS, Alfonso (ed). *The Knowledge of Values: A Methodological Introduction*. Lanham, Univ Pr of America, 1989

Any solidly developed theory of values must include the dynamic nature of reality, the existence of "objects" and "ambits," the concept of play as the foundation of ambits or fields of possibilities of action under certain norms, the relation between creative play and the birth of meaning, the mutual empowerment of the relations of immediacy and distance in the phenomnon of *presence*, the harmonization of objectivist and the ludic attitudes in the face of the real, a clear idea of the polar opposition between the experience of vertigo and ecstasy, the connection between opening to the real and participation.

LOPEZ, Raul. "Aesthetics in the Context of Historicity, Moral Education and Character Development" in *The Social Context and Values: Perspectives of the Americas*, MC LEAN, George F (ed), 141-159. Lanham, Univ Pr of America, 1989.

LÓPEZ-ESCOBAR, E G K. Extra-Logical Inferences. J Non-Classical Log, 5(2), 23-43, N 88.

LÓPEZ-ESCOBAR, E G K. Remarks on the Church-Rosser Property. J Sym Log, 55(1), 106-112, Mr 90.

A reduction algebra is defined as a set with a collection of partial unary functions (called reduction operators). Motivated by the lambda calculus, the Church-Rosser property is defined for a reduction algebra and a characterization is given for those reduction algebras satisfying CRP and having a measure respecting the reductions. The characterization is used to give (with 20/20 hindsight) a more direct proof of the strong normalization theorem for the impredicative second order intuitionistic propositional calculus.

LOPTSON, Peter. Phenomenological Skepticism in Hume. S J Phil, 28(3), 367-388, Fall 90.

This paper explores skepticism in Hume not as a justificatory challenge for

beliefs about the world but as the condition Hume thinks human nature places us in. Hume is argued to hold that our environment-responsive perceptual/cognitive equipment predisposes us to external enduring object constitution, independently of cues provided us by that environment. This is intended (by Hume) as an empirical thesis in scientific psychology. In this light Hume is seen as a sort of empirical proto-Kantian. Hume then faces the challenge of how or whether human beings can rationally engage in science, Hume assuming without argument that we can.

LORAUX, Nicole. La métaphore sans métaphore: A propos de l' "Orestie". Rev Phil Fr, 180(2), 247-268, Ap-Je 90.

LORBER, Judith. Choice, Gift, or Patriarchal Bargain? Women's Consent to In Vitro Fertilization in Male Infertility. Hypatia, 4(3), 23-36, Fall 89.

This paper explores the reasons why women who are themselves fertile might consent to undergo in vitro fertilization (IVF) with an infertile male partner. The reasons often given are desire to have that particular man's child, or altruism, giving a gift to the partner. Although ethically, the decision should be completely woman's prerogative, because IVF programs usually treat the couple as a unit, she may be offered few other options by the medical staff. In social terms, whether the woman is or is not infertile may be immaterial because in either situation, if she wants to try to have a biological child and maintain the relationship, she may have to make a patriarchal bargain and undergo in vitro fertilization.

LORENC, Iwona and PETROWICZ, Lech (trans). Philosophical Premises of Levinas' Conception of Judaism. Dialec Hum, 16(1), 157-170, Wint 89.

What purposes does Levinas's vision of Judaism serve in his philosophy? This question has inspired me to offer these remarks. A reference to Judaism as a source is such a vision of culture which, being alternative to the generally accepted paradigm of West European culture, would offer a chance for endowing the ideas of humanism and universalism with new contents. He wants to indicate the area which makes it possible to leave the structures of pure thinking, to go beyond totalizing thinking. Using philosophical means, Levinas proclaims the necessity of going beyond philosophy.

LORENZ, Chris. Het gewicht van de geschiedenis: Over het waardenprobleem in de geschiedwetenschap. Kennis Methode, 14(1), 129-162, 1990.

The purpose of this article is to analyze the problem of values in history. This problem is investigated via three authors—P Blaas, F R Ankersmit and J Rüsen—who are more or less representative for historism, postmodernism and the critical conception of history. The analysis shows that both historism and postmodernism produce inconsistencies dealing with the problem of values and that these can be avoided through the pragmatical approach advocated by J Rüsen.

LORENZ, D C G. Alcoholics Anonymous Revisited. Int J Applied Phil, 4(4), 69-75, Fall 89.

The philosophical basis of the Twelve Steps of Alcoholics Anonymous is examined in the light of Western tradition. In contrast to phallocentric linear concepts of personality and character, AA is based on a concept of personality as process. The program of recovery integrates subjective and objective factors, hence its ideological compatibility with feminist, dialectic materialist, and contemporary counterculture views of reality and freedom.

LORENZ, Kuno. What Do Language Games Measure? Critica, 21(63), 59-73, D 89.

Both in the *Tractatus* (T) and in the *Philosophical Investigations* (PU) Wittgenstein (W) uses 'Bild' (picture) to convey metaphorically the function of a ('Satz') resp. a sentence-radical. The change of meaning for both terms between T and PU which is implied by the change from a level of explanation (>meta-competence<, T) to a level of description (>object-competence<, PU) can be expressed in a Peircean terminology: pictures function as *symbolic* representations in T, as a means of *iconic* representations in PU. Hence, language-games being rational reconstructions (W: measuring rods) in PU in order to *show* what *shows itself* in T are W's version of iconic representations and thus the paradigm case of perceptual knowledge. Finally, using a dialogue-model for acquiring the competence to perform and to recognize an action, a generalization of language-games is set up to account for pragmatic *and* semiotic competence even in case of mere nonverbal activity.

LORMAND, Eric. Framing the Frame Problem. Synthese, 82(3), 353-374, Mr 90.

The frame problem is widely reputed among philosophers to be one of the deepest and most difficult problems of cognitive science. This paper discusses three recent attempts to display this problem: Dennett's problem of ignoring obviously irrelevant knowledge, Haugeland's problem of efficiently keeping track of salient side effects, and Fodor's problem of avoiding the use of 'kooky' concepts. In a negative vein, it is argued that these problems bear nothing but a superficial similarity to the frame problem of AI, so that they do not provide reasons to disparage standard attempts to solve it. More positively, it is argued that these problems are easily solved by slight variations on familiar AI themes. Finally, some discussion is devoted to more difficult problems confronting AI.

LORVELLEC, Y (trans) and PIERRE, C. *Ortega y Gasset: Aurore de la Raison Historique*. France, Klincksieck, 1986

LOSCERBO, John. The Co-Enactment of Heidegger's *Being and Time*: F W von Herrmann's Elucidation of its "Introduction". Heidegger Stud, 5, 183-200, 1989.

LOSONCY, Thomas. "St Augustine" in *Ethics in the History of Western Philosophy*, CAVALIER, Robert J (ed), 60-97. New York, St Martin's Pr, 1988.

LOSONSKY, Michael. Locke on the Making of Complex Ideas. Locke News, 20, 35-46, 1989.

LOSONSKY, Michael. The Nature of Artifacts. Philosophy, 65(251), 81-88, Ja 90.

The author argues against the Aristotelian view of artifacts, namely that artifacts do not have natures, essences or special nomological properties. This view can be found in Aristotle, Leibniz, David Wiggins, and Stephen Schwartz. The opposing view maintains that artifacts have natures, and it can be found in Marx and Hilary Putnam. After defending the Aristotelian view from a criticism due to Hilary Kornblith, the author argues that an artifact's internal structure, purpose, and manner of use constitutes its nature. The author supports his argument with examples, especially from traffic science and horology (the science of clocks).

LOSURDO, Domenico. *Hegel und Das Deutsche Erbe: Philosophie und nationale Frage zwischen Revolution und Reaktion*. Cologne, Pahl-Rugenstein, 1989

The author studies Hegel's evolution with particular attention to the German national question, the history of the Hegelian school and that of Hegel's fortune until the Second World War. He underlines the meaning of a cultural policy which tended to a philosophical elaboration of the results of the French Revolution, and which will be definitively defeated in 1848. This defeat will tragically count on German history. How Carl Schmitt observed, with Hitler's coming to power, "Hegel is, so to speak, dead": the tragedy of the extermination camps should be incomprehensible without the destruction of that universal concept of man to which Hegel had given a form philosophically perfect.

LOSURDO, Domenico. Hegel, die Französische Revolution und die liberale Tradition. Deut Z Phil, 38(4), 338-345, 1990.

Hegel, accused by Haym of being the theoretician of the Restoration, goes in fact even further than any liberal tradition in justifying revolutions that have signalled the birth of the modern world. The attitude he adopts towards the French Revolution is one of particular significance: where liberal tradition condemns the event the moment it pursues the material claims of the plebians, Hegel explains it and justifies it as the social upheaval that develops from the rebellion against "der fürchterliche harte Druck, der auf dem Volke lastete" and puts an end to the shame of "dem Schweisse des Volkes abgepressten Summen" that sustained the luxury of the parasitic nobility.

LOTT, Tommy L. Anscombe on Justifying Claims to Know One's Bodily Position. Phil Invest, 12(4), 293-307, O 89.

In her widely read work *Intention*, Anscombe introduced the case of a man knowing the position of his limbs as a paradigm of what she called "knowledge without observation." She wanted to account for the fact that normally a person with eyes closed can tell the position of an extended limb, but cannot usually report *how* she knows its position, by denying that sense experience provides the evidential ground for that person's claims to know her bodily position. In support of Anscombe, I argue that questions which demand evidence for my claims to know my bodily position are generally misguided, for there is an important asymmetry between what warrants my claims regarding my bodily position and what warrants the claims of others regarding my bodily position.

LOTT, Tommy L. "Hobbes on International Relations" in *Hobbes: War Among Nations*, AIRAKSINEN, Timo (ed), 91-98. Brookfield, Gower, 1989.

Hobbes's interpreters have sometimes been led by their own emphasis on his pre-social paradigm of the state of nature to overlook his frequent references to certain facts about the world. I aim to make clear how he intended his remarks regarding the state of nature to apply to international relations. My account reconciles certain implications of his political theory with his reluctance to state the case for an international sovereign.

LOUDEN, Robert B. Through Thick and Thin: Moral Knowledge in Skeptical Times. Logos (USA), 10, 57-72, 1989.

In this essay I examine the currently popular distinction between specific or "thick" and general or "thin" moral concepts, with special reference to the way in which the terms are used by Bernard Williams in his book *Ethics and the Limits of Philosophy* (Cambridge: Harvard University Press, 1985). In Section I, I argue, *contra* Williams, that this distinction cannot be made satisfactorily by invoking the properties of world-guidedness, rule-governedness, and action-guidingness. In Section II, I challenge his claim that traditional societies rely primarily on thick concepts and modern ones rely primarily on thin concepts. Finally, in Section III, I argue for the necessity of a type of moral knowledge which employs both thick as well as thin concepts.

LOUDEN, Robert B. Virtue Ethics and Anti-Theory. Philosophia (Israel), 20(1-2), 93-114, Jl 90.

In this essay I address the issue of whether virtue ethics is best interpreted as an anti-theory. After first analyzing the concepts of "ethical theory" and "anti-theory," I go on to argue that virtue ethics, contrary to initial appearances, does not constitute a philosophical brief against the enterprise of ethical theory *per se*. Rather, it is a protest against certain modern assumptions concerning what ethical theory should look like as well as an attempt to return us to more realistic avenues of moral reflection.

LOUZECKY, David and FLANNERY, Richard. *The Good Life: Personal and Public Choices*. Atascadero, Ridgeview, 1989

We defend that favorite American position, individualism, as the only social philosophy with broad enough support to be used, and we argue that without the conception of a good life individualism is senseless. The good life is composed of intimate companionships and quality work in a free society; the personal and the public cannot be separated. We also discuss self-development, privacy, rationality, equality, justice, and democratic politics.

LOVE JR, Charles E. The Morality of Nuclear Deterrence and the Corruption of Character. Proc Phil Educ, 45, 378-387, 1989.

LOVE, Amy E and TROTTER, R Clayton and DAY, Susan G. Bhopal, India and Union Carbide: The Second Tragedy. J Bus Ethics, 8(6), 439-454, Je 89.

The paper examines the legal, ethical, and public policy issues involved in the Union Carbide gas leak in India which caused the deaths of over 3000 people and injury to thousands of people. The paper begins with a historical perspective on the operating environment in Bhopal, the events surrounding the accident, then discusses an international situation audit examining internal strengths and weaknesses, and external opportunities and threats faced by Union Carbide at the time of the accident. There is a discussion of management of the various interests involved in international public relations and ethical issues. A review of the financial ratio analysis of the company prior and subsequent to the accident follows, then an examination of the second tragedy of Bhopal—the tragic failure of the international legal system to adequately and timely compensate victims of the accident. The paper concludes with recommendations towards public policy, as well as a call for congressional action regarding international safety of US-based multinational operations.

LOWE, E J. Conditionals, Context, and Transitivity. Analysis, 50(2), 80-87, Mr 90.

It is argued that the standard examples purportedly demonstrating the nontransitivity of subjunctive conditionals are in fact much more plausibly interpreted as showing that such conditionals are highly context-dependent, with transitivity being preserved within context. An alternative to the Stalnaker-Lewis style of semantics for such conditionals is proposed which licenses transitivity but not certain other patterns of inference standardly regarded as fallacious where subjunctive conditionals are concerned, such as contraposition and strengthening the antecedent.

LOWE, E J. Impredicative Identity Criteria and Davidson's Criterion of Event Identity. Analysis, 49(4), 178-181, O 89.

W V Quine has recently charged Donald Davidson's well-known criterion of event identity with vicious circularity because it quantifies over events themselves in attempting to individuate events, i.e., it is 'impredicative'. I argue that although Davidson's criterion is indeed defective, impredicativity is not as such a fatal defect in an identity criterion.

LÖWENHARD, Percy. "The Mind-Body Problem: Some Neurobiological Reflections" in *Reductionism and Systems Theory in the Life Sciences: Some Problems and Perspectives*, HOYNINGEN-HUENE, Paul (ed), 85-135. Norwell, Kluwer, 1989.

LOY, David. The Nonduality of Life and Death: A Buddhist View of Repression. Phil East West, 40(2), 151-174, Ap 90.

Existential psychoanalysis argues that our primal repression is not sex but death; the repressed returns symbolically as all the compulsive ways we try to make ourselves immortal. The Buddhist claim of "no-self" carries this a step further: even death-fear projects the problem into the future; my deepest dread is the quite valid suspicion that "I" don't really exist. The consequence is that our sense-of-self is always shadowed by a sense-of-*lack*, which it always tries to escape. Dogen implies that life-confronting-death is an unconscious game each of us is playing with him/herself. This conclusion is used to criticize Heidegger's *Being and Time*.

LOY, Jessica and MORREALL, John. Kitsch and Aesthetic Education. J Aes Educ, 23(4), 63-73, Wint 89.

We trace the origins of Kitsch to the Industrial Revolution and the ensuing loss of two traditional sources of aesthetic sensibility: familiarity with nature and craft skills. Then we discuss the increasing aesthetic deprivation of our postindustrial age, especially our hunger for instant, passive aesthetic experiences. We close by presenting several cultural and aesthetic lessons to be learned from Kitsch, and then suggesting specific ways to use Kitsch in the arts curriculum.

LUBANSKI, Mieczyslaw. Analogy and Interpretation (in Polish). Stud Phil Christ, 25(1), 209-219, 1989.

Analogy is a kind of similarity of objects and interpretation is coordination of objects of one kind with conditions (axioms) formulated in an abstract manner. The paper puts forward a thesis in which analogy and interpretation (more precisely: the activity of searching for analogy between objects and interpreting given conditions) are scientifically originative activities aiming, so to speak, in opposite directions. If given objects are analogical, general conditions which characterize them can be quoted; similarly, when interpreting a set of conditions we find objects which fulfill them, i.e., are analogical objects. Using the terms theory and model we can say that analogy and interpretation are scientifically originative activites leading respectively from models to theories and from theories to models. Thus the activities are related.

LUBARSKY, Robert S. An Introduction to γ-Recursion Theory (Or What to Do in KP-Foundation). J Sym Log, 55(1), 194-206, Mr 90.

Reverse mathematics is the program of finding just which fundamental principles are needed to prove standard mathematical theorems. In classical recursion theory, this project takes the form of finding out just how much induction on the natural numbers it is necessary to assume in order to obtain some particular recursion-theoretic fact. This paper extends this program to higher recursion theory, more precisely to alpha-recursion theory. It shows that KP (admissible set theory) with the foundation scheme restricted to Σ_1 formulas does not prove theorems of Sacks and Shore, by constructing a model of such a theory with a minimum non-recursive r.e. degree.

LÜBCKE, Poul. Kierkegaard and Indirect Communication. Hist Euro Ideas, 12(1), 31-40, 1990.

The article offers an interpretation of the distinction between "direct" and "indirect communication" in *Concluding Unscientific Postscript*, Kierkegaard's *Journal* and *Training into Christianity*. It criticises the traditional interpretation of Kierkegaard's notion of indirect communication as embodying a *semantic* theory about how to use language to express what is really ineffable. Instead of attributing such a mysterious theory to Kierkegaard, it is argued that the term "indirect communication" does not belong to *semantics* but applies to certain *speech acts*, more specifically to certain *perlocutionary acts* intended to produce a specific *perlocutionary effect*, namely the effect of prompting listeners to make a decision.

LUCAS JR, George R. *The Rehabilitation of Whitehead: An Analytic and Historical Assessment of Process Philosophy*. Albany, SUNY Pr, 1989

The book argues in favor of a critical reassessment of the purely *philosophical* significance of Whitehead's thought within the framework of major themes in current analytic philosophy, viewed against the backdrop of major historical trends in European and American thought since the Enlightenment. It discusses the relationship of Whitehead's thought to current epistemology of science, to the antifoundationalism debate, as well as to modal logic, action theory, and philosophy of mind, concluding with Bell's theorem and recent discussion of relativity physics and quantum mechanics.

LUCAS JR, George R. "Science and Teleological Explanations: A Comment on Errol Harris's Project" in *Dialectic and Contemporary Science*, GRIER, Philip T (ed), 29-50. Lanham, Univ Pr of America, 1989.

Lucas describes an older tradition of metaphysics of science, represented by neo-Hegelian idealist like R G Collingwood and festschrift-honoree, Errol E Harris. This is compared with the recent re-emergence of a *non*-metaphysical or "pragmatic teleology" in the life and cognitive sciences: "functionalism" (Jerry Fodor), or the "intentional stance" (Daniel Dennett). These new and old models of teleological explanation in science differ with regard to theism,

which Lucas holds to be an unwarranted inference even in the older, idealistic mode.

LUCAS, J R. Foreknowledge and the Vulnerability of God. Philosophy, 25, 119-128, 89 Supp.

LUCAS, J R. *The Future: An Essay on God, Temporality, and Truth*. Cambridge, Blackwell, 1989

This book is about the logic of future-tensed statements, the ontological status of the future, and their theological significance. It argues that tense logic is a special sort of modal logic, and develops a version of dated tense-logic with a special "tree-semantics" that assigns truth-values to· statements about the present and past, but not to contingent statements about the future. This accords with our intuitive belief that the present and past are real, but the future does not yet exist. The worries of Aristotle and others about fatalism and theological determinism are resolved, and an altered theology sketched.

LUCAS, J R. The Worm and the Juggernaut: Justice and the Public Interest. Bus Prof Ethics J, 6(2), 51-59, Sum 87.

LUCAS, Ron and GLADSON, Jerry. Hebrew Wisdom and Psychotheological Dialogue. Zygon, 24(3), 357-376, S 89.

When understood as a potential resolution for the epistemological impasse between psychology and religion, Hebrew wisdom presents a model for dialogue. Noting that wisdom exhibits a special interest in human dispositions and behavior, the authors compare Viktor Frankl's logotherapy and Adlerian psychology with Proverbs and uncover a biblical, empirical approach to psychology which indirectly incorporates the religious dimension.

LUCENTE, Gregory L. Vico, Hercules, and the Lion: Figure and Ideology in the *Scienza nuova*. New Vico Studies, 6, 85-94, 1988.

This essay treats the intertwining effects of figure, etymology, and ideology in Vico's *Scienza nuova*. The first step is analysis of these notions in Vico's work; the second is an understanding of the way Vico's own text both forms and is formed by questions of figuration and questions of ideology, or worldview.

LUCIER, Ruth. "Policies for Hunger Relief: Moral Considerations" in *Inquiries into Values: The Inaugural Session of the International Society for Value Inquiry*, LEE, Sander H , 477-493. Lewiston, Mellen Pr, 1989.

In this essay it is suggested that food aid has moral ramifications stemming from present limitations on the aid available for distribution. In light of such limitations, it is argued, a partialist ethic is a morally sound (and preferable) option. Justifications are suggested for several criteria that legitimize preferential treatment for (1) persons whose means of livelihood have been adversely affected by the potential donors, (2) children in food-short countries, and (3) women farmers in third world countries whose work contributes directly to domestic food supplies—particularly where such supplies are made available to the least advantages persons in the social order.

LÜDEKING, Karlheinz. Pictures and Gestures. Brit J Aes, 30(3), 218-232, Jl 90.

According to his own testimony, Ludwig Wittgenstein was forced to abandon his picture-theory of language (advocated in the *Tractatus*) because it couldn't explain the meaning of a gesture. Having learnt his lesson from this failure, Wittgenstein later was very conscious of the significance of gestures. Most remarkable in this respect is his tendency to refer to gestures in order to elucidate the meaning of works of art. The article explores the consequences of this way of understanding art (in terms of the language of the body) and indicates certain similarities with the views of Nietzsche, Merleau-Ponty and Aby Warburg.

LUDWIG, Bernd. "The Right of a State" in Immanuel Kant's *Doctrine of Right*. J Hist Phil, 28(3), 403-415, Jl 90.

It is a widely accepted opinion that the *Doctrine of Right* is an imperfect product of Kant's later life, affected by the author's senility. This article shows (by focusing on the 'Right of a State') there is strong evidence that the printed version of 1797 delivers not the text Kant intended to publish, but an incorrect composition out of his manuscript, being assembled by third hand. In the paper the originally intended text is reconstructed by following the internal cross-references given by the author.

LUDWIG, Walter D. Aristotle's Conception of the Science of Being. New Scholas, 63(4), 379-404, Autumn 89.

This paper argues for the harmony of ontology and theology in Aristotle's *Metaphysics*. The science whose object is *all* beings in respect to their *being* must focus upon the primary instance of being—namely, divine substance. The latter's final causality establishes and defines the relation between the primary and secondary senses of being. By ascertaining the nature of the being of divine substance, it becomes possible to determine the nature of the being of all other things. This knowledge provides the basis of discerning the attributes, principles, and causes of all beings in respect to their being.

LUDWIG, Walter D. Hegel's Conception of Absolute Knowing. Owl Minerva, 21(1), 5-19, Fall 89.

Absolute knowing in Hegel's *Phenomenology of Spirit* consists of a unique view of the relation between such moments of spirit as subject and object, freedom and necessity, individual and society. By drawing not merely from the final chapter of the book, but from passages found throughout the work, this paper concludes that this relation is one of "unity in difference." In this relation, the opposed moments are different in the sense of *incommensurable*, yet they form a unity in that each such opposite must contain the meaning of the other. This is a unity that preserves the radical opposition.

LUFT, Eric V D. The Cartesian Circle: Hegelian Logic to the Rescue. Heythrop J, 30(4), 403-418, O 89.

This is neither a Descartes paper nor a Hegel paper, but one which tries to determine a general philosophical truth about the human relation to God. Accordingly, we examine the problem of the Cartesian circle not historically, in terms of Descartes's formulation of it, but speculatively, in terms of the problem itself. We find that Kenley Dove's interpretation of Hegel's logic of contrast, determination, and individuality is useful toward showing the atomic character of the whole insight, as opposed to Descartes's own belief that he reasoned linearly in the second and third Meditations.

LUFT, Eric V D. Hegel and Judaism: A Reassessment. Clio, 18(4), 361-378, Sum 89.

LUGARINI, Leo. Fondamento e nulla: un'alternativa? G Metaf, 11(1), 99-114, Ja-Ap 89.

LUGENBIEHL, Heinz C. Applied Liberal Education for Engineers. Int J Applied Phil, 4(4), 7-11, Fall 89.

The discussion demonstrates the value of, and need for, a focus on applied liberal education in the context of professional education. It develops, from among several models, an appropriate conception of liberal education, shows how traditional forms of liberal education can be deficient in the context of professional education, and proposes how these deficiencies can be overcome. Emphasized are ways of integrating traditional approaches of the humanities with contemporary professional contexts.

LUGG, Andrew. Pierre Duhem's Conception of Natural Classification. Synthese, 83(3), 409-420, Je 90.

Duhem's discussion of physical theories as natural classifications is neither antithetical nor incidental to the main thrust of his philosophy of science. Contrary to what is often supposed, Duhem does not argue that theories are better thought of as economically organizing empirical laws than as providing information concerning the nature of the world. What he is primarily concerned with is the character and justification of the scientific method, not the logical status of theoretical entities. The crucial point to notice is that he took the principle of the autonomy of physics to be of paramount importance and he developed the conception of natural classification in opposition to accounts of physical theories that contravened it.

LUHMANN, Niklas and BEDNARZ JR, John (trans). *Ecological Communication*. Chicago, Univ of Chicago Pr, 1989

LUJUN, Yin. The Crisis of Hermeneutical Consciousness in Modern China (in Serbo-Croatian). Filozof Istraz, 29(2), 365-381, 1989.

This article reflects critically on three contemporary influential approaches—the Neo-traditionalist, the dogmatic Marxist, and the pro-modernist versions of tradition—towards the reconstructions of Chinese philosophy. It reveals that the three approaches, though radically different, mistreat tradition as a thing of the past and fail to see the hermeneutical disclosure of human language through which tradition transfers itself meaningfully into the present. Meanwhile, this article proposes a new hermeneutical approach that redefines the relation of tradition to the present. The new approach aims to shift the focus of interpretation from on the discovery of the "original spirit," "historical laws," or "usefulness" of tradition to on the hermeneutical relevances of tradition to modern China, and thereby restoring a "meaningful" rather than merely "historical" continuity between traditional and modern Chinese philosophy.

LUKACHER, Ned. *Primal Scenes: Literature, Philosophy, Psychoanalysis*. Ithaca, Cornell Univ Pr, 1986

This book presents a critical articulation of the radical hermeneutic procedures of Sigmund Freud and Martin Heidegger in an effort to pose the question of the relation between Heidegger's deconstructive "history of Being" and Freud's psychoanalytic determination of the "primal scene." The

implications of this articulation are pursued in genealogical terms in order to determine both the progenitors and the heirs of this radicalization of hermeneutic method. To this end there are extensive readings of Shakespeare, Hegel, Marx, Balzac, Henry James, Dickens, Lacan, and Derrida.

LUKÁCS, Georg. On the Debate between China and the Soviet Union: Theoretical and Philosophical Remarks, 1963 (in Hungarian). Magyar Filozof Szemle, 5, 631-654, 1989.

LUKES, Steven. *Marxism and Morality*. New York, Oxford Univ Pr, 1987

LUND, William R. Communitarian Politics, the Supreme Court, and Privacy: The Continuing Need for Liberal Boundaries. Soc Theor Pract, 16(2), 191-215, Sum 90.

This paper evaluates the charge that communitarian political theory might allow prejudicial or other irrational treatment of minorities. An analysis of the theory's preferred approach to constitutional interpretation, which denies a strong right of privacy, concludes that this concern is fully warranted. Absent this right, deprivations of liberty will occur without a serious evaluation of the impartiality of the reasons used to justify such coercion, and we ought instead to defend the right of privacy as a procedural mechanism guaranteeing the relative neutrality of democratic outcomes.

LUNDBERG, Randolph. Mill on Moral Wrong. Nous, 24(4), 557-580, S 90.

A key element in John Stuart Mill's view of moral wrong is the natural desire to retaliate. In Mill's view, a rule of moral obligation must not only be socially beneficial, but must guard against a kind of consequence that arouses a desire to retaliate in a universally sympathetic spectator. The paper presents evidence for these claims, and shows how they explain some distinctive properties of Mill's moral view, including his special attitude toward consequences for the agent, the limit he places on obligations of beneficence, and his policy on exceptions to rules of moral obligation. Also considered are the related work of David Lyons, and an important question of classification: is Mill's moral view utilitarian?

LUNGARZO, Carlos A. Unicidad y categoricidad de teorías. Rev Filosof (Argentina), 1(1-2), 17-30, N 86.

The underlying concept of this paper is that problems of existence in formal sciences obtain greater ontological support when the objects to which a theory "refers" can be characterized without ambiguity. If certain axioms "define" the objects which satisfy them all its models must be isomorphies. The cardinality theorem strongly limits this possibility, specially for theories which admit infinite models. It is said that Morley theorem as well as some highly technical results on stable theories have relevant philosophical implications, showing that the underlying "ontology" of the model theory seems to have a more "concrete" reality than it is currently thought. The paper points out the factibility of platonism, which seems to be the most adequate conception with mathematical common sense.

LUNTLEY, Michael. On the Critique of Values. Inquiry, 32(4), 399-417, D 89.

On a familiar conception of the business of ethics, we are set to produce theories which codify our intuitive conception of values. And on this conception, the notion of a theory is that of an account which, in providing the epistemological backing to our intuitive valuations, *overrules* our intuitive grasp of our moral lives. An intuitionist faces a dilemma: Without an epistemological backing intuitions of value seem unsuited to deliver moral truth, and yet if a theoretical backing is provided this then threatens the autonomy of the intuitions which become little more than rules of thumb. In this paper, an alternative notion of theorizing in morals is outlined which, although providing the resources to criticize our intuitive grasp of values, does not provide an overruling theory. A critical theory of values is outlined which acts as a filter on those of our moral intuitions which produce conflict. The account is a dynamic notion of critique although, unlike, say, Habermas's, it does not depend on a conception of an end-state to which the dynamic aims.

LURIE, Yuval. Jews as a Metaphysical Species. Philosophy, 64(249), 323-347, Jl 89.

There are certain remarks in *Culture and Value* in which Wittgenstein writes about Jews and about what he describes as their "Jewish Mind." He draws there a distinction between two spiritual forces which operate in western culture. One force is powerful and original, the other is sophisticated and imitative. Jews, according to Wittgenstein, embody the latter force. This distinction between the spiritual nature of Jews and non-Jews is just one aspect of an overall metaphysical distinction he draws between culture and civilization. He also believes that culture is now being replaced by civilization. It is this view also which clearly aligns Wittgenstein's thinking with the Romantic tradition in philosophy. Due to the political events in the thirties, and the changes which occurred in his philosophical views, Wittgenstein abandoned his prior references to the "Jew." However, he never abandoned the metaphysical view which was its basis.

LURIE, Yuval. The Metaphysics of Communism. Ratio, 3(1), 21-39, Je 90.

Communism has many faces, and yet it also reduces to a single matter: the abolition of private property. For many, this alone is reason enough to oppose the establishment of a communist society. Do communists have any justification for their attempt to establish a society in which private property is to be abolished? I intend to discuss this question in only one limited context: in regard to the justification, if there is any, which serves Karl Marx in his work for the establishment of a communist society.

LURIE, Yuval. Wittgenstein on Culture and Civilization. Inquiry, 32(4), 375-397, D 89.

Wittgenstein's remarks on the nature of culture presuppose a view according to which there is an important difference between culture and civilization. This view aligns his thinking to that of the Romantic tradition in philosophy. It also leads him to perceive 'the disappearance of a culture' in our time. In many of his remarks on art and certain artists he expresses this view by attempting to clarify the different ways in which the spirit of man is manifested in modern times (in arts, science, and industry) as opposed to how it is manifested in an age of culture. This article undertakes to describe and explain the remarks which lead him to this view. It then considers whether Wittgenstein was, in fact, correct in his evaluation regarding the disappearance of a culture.

LUSTHAUS, Dan. Re-Tracing the Human-Nature versus World-Nature Dichotemy: Lao Tzu's Hermeneutics for World-Building. J Chin Phil, 17(2), 187-214, Je 90.

LYCAN, William G. "Ideas of Representation" in *Mind, Value and Culture: Essays in Honor of E M Adams*, WEISSBORD, David (ed), 207-228. Atascadero, Ridgeview, 1989.

This paper surveys some naturalistic theories of intentionality, and defends the Sellarsian position that propositional attitudes are physically realized mental representations in our brains. The view is defended particularly against a powerful objection urged by R M Chisholm and by E M Adams: that the representational character of the brain states in question depends covertly on a prior notion of intentional content for propositional attitudes. A "psychosemantics" is briefly sketched.

LYCAN, William G. Mental Content in Linguistic Form. Phil Stud, 58(1-2), 147-154, Ja-F 90.

Robert Stalnaker has argued against the "linguistic" paradigm for the understanding of belief and thought, and against the apparent hyperintensionality of belief contexts. The present paper rebuts Stalnaker's arguments and defends a representational account of belief that withstands them.

LYNCH, Abbyann. The Price of Silence: Commentary. Hastings Center Rep, 20(3), 31-32, My-Je 90.

LYON, Richard C. Persons and Places. Bull Santayana Soc, 3, 1-8, Fall 85.

LYONS, David. "Comment: The Normativity of Law" in *Issues in Contemporary Legal Philosophy: The Influence of H L A Hart*, GAVISON, Ruth (ed), 114-126. New York, Clarendon/Oxford Pr, 1987.

This is a comment on Gerald Postema's paper on the normativity of law. "Normativity" can mean that one always has (or there always is) some good moral reason to comply with legal requirements; or it can mean that law tells people how to behave (which does not imply that one ever had or that there ever is good reason to comply). The crucial consideration is what is done to people in the name of the law, which typically requires justification; not the beliefs or intentions of officials, which do not necessarily justify what they do.

LYOTARD, Jean-François and DERRIDA, Jacques. Épreuves d'écriture—Notes du traducteur. Rev Phil Fr, 180(2), 269-292, Ap-Je 90.

MAC CAULL, W A. Positive Definite Functions Over Regular f-Rings and Representations as Sums of Squares. Annals Pure Applied Log, 44(3), 243-257, O 89.

MAC CORMACK, Geoffrey. Stair on Natural Law and Promises. Vera Lex, 7(1), 13,16, 1987.

This note distinguishes the different senses in which Stair uses the term 'natural law' and argues that he employs reason to deduce God's will as to the circumstances in which a human by an 'act of will' may surrender (even by a unilateral promise) part of his freedom to another.

MAC CORMICK, D Neil. Spontaneous Order and the Rule of Law: Some Problems. Ratio Juris, 2(1), 41-54, Mr 89.

Two conservative theorists, F A Hayek and Michael Oakeshott, have advanced theories of law with important and plausible central theses focusing on the rule of law. The author argues, however, that in each case the theorist—or at least some of his followers on the contemporary British and American political scene—have wrongly inferred strong conclusions from these theories which are inimical to the welfare state. In conclusion, the author points to possible ways of reconciling rule of law to social justice.

MAC CORMICK, Neil. "Comment: The Normativity of Law" in *Issues in Contemporary Legal Philosophy: The Influence of H L A Hart*, GAVISON, Ruth (ed), 105-113. New York, Clarendon/Oxford Pr, 1987.

This paper makes three points: first, that legal rights and obligations are 'jurisdictionally relative', by contrast with moral rights and obligations, which are universalistic (but this does not mean that the concept 'obligation' or 'right' has a different meaning); second, that the concept of 'detachment' is different as between detached legal statements and detached moral statements; third, that the justifying reasons for judicial commitment to legal systems must be moral, but this does not entail a natural law conclusion.

MAC CORMICK, Neil. The Ethics of Legalism. Ratio Juris, 2(2), 184-193, Jl 89.

"Legalism" is defined as requiring that all matters of legal regulation and controversy ought so far as possible to be conducted in accordance with predetermined rules of considerable generality and clarity. Thus there may be moral limits on governments which ban them from acting on the substantive moral merits of situations with which they have to deal. This is most important in public law, but also applies in private law, e.g., in cases involving property. Hume, Kant, and Hayek are examined in respect of their case for legalism; Alexy and Finnis also reviewed. Autonomy is the foundation for legalism, and justifies "ethical positivism," in T Campbell's phrase. Critical legal studies (Unger, Kelman, Kennedy et al.), however, challenge legalism's premises. But the "critical" arguments against reification merely raise, they do not settle, the issue about the politics of legalism and the desirability of legal dogmatics. With all faults, legalism is a prerequisite of free government.

MAC CORMICK, Neil. Institutions, Arrangements and Practical Information. Ratio Juris, 1(1), 73-82, Mr 88.

A restatement of an institutionalist theory of law is attempted with particular reference to legal reasoning and legal rights. Use is made of Ota Weinberger's concept of "practical information," focusing on both its momentary and diachronic aspects. Momentary practical information corresponds to the need to know which conduct is required of us at a given moment. The diachronic practical information becomes relevant whenever we wish to stabilize the practical information and to reduce the likelihood of change regarding our ways of acting. Furthermore, the momentary information is given sense only against the background of the diachronic one. Among the different types of diachronic practical information particular importance is ascribed to legal "institutions" such as contracts and rights. Legal "institutions" are conceived as founded on various sets of rules. Rules may then increase the number of facts in the world: those special kinds of facts which are represented by social phenomena.

MAC DONALD, Graham. Biology and Representation. Mind Lang, 4(3), 186-200, Autumn 89.

Some philosophers have turned to biology in their attempt to naturalise intentionality. The article looks at two attempts which use biological functionality to underpin 'representation'. The first, Fred Dretske's, is found to be inadequate partly as a consequence of a deficient view of what functionality consists in. After defending a selectionist account of functions, I look at Papineau's recent attempt to 'functionalise' representation. This is also found deficient. The problem in general: it will invalidate all biological-reductionist accounts of intentionality.

MAC DONALD, Ian and MILLER, Seumas. Philosophy in South Africa: A Reply to Robert Paul Wolff. Phil Forum, 21(4), 442-450, Sum 90.

In the first part of this paper we argue that R P Wolff's account in this journal of philosophy in South Africa seriously distorts the situation here. Analytic philosophers have had, and continue to have, a far greater concern with practical ethical political issues than Wolff admits. In the second part of this paper we address the question, "What ought the role of philosophy in South Africa be?"

MAC DONALD, Scott. Augustine's Christian-Platonist Account of Goodness. New Scholas, 63(4), 485-509, Autumn 89.

I examine Augustine's development and defense of his universality thesis, the thesis that everything that exists is good. The thesis is strategically important to him because it is inconsistent with Manichaean dualism and is entailed by the doctrine that there is a highest good, a doctrine to which the Manichaeans themselves are committed. I argue that Augustine's strategy of refuting Manichaeanism by arguing for the universality thesis turns on an equivocation in his use of the notion of corruption. Moreover, I claim that his discussion of the universality thesis does not involve a particular view about the nature of goodness, though a late text from *De civitate Dei* XII suggests one.

MAC GREGOR, David. The State at Dusk. Owl Minerva, 21(1), 51-64, Fall 89.

This paper offers a reinterpretation of Hegel's theory of the state, and critically examines neo-Marxist political theory from an Hegelian perspective. Neo-Marxism's resistance to Hegel's notion of the autonomy of the state from civil society has crippled its account of modern politics. Similarly, neo-Marxism's lack of a coherent theory of the family has weakened its understanding of the role of women and men in government. The paper argues for the contemporary relevance of Hegel's concepts of private property, the universal class and the corporation. These Hegelian formulations are at the root of Marx's political theory, but they also go beyond Marx.

MAC INTOSH, Duncan. Ideal Moral Codes. S J Phil, 28(3), 389-408, Fall 90.

Ideal rule utilitarianism says: a moral code C is correct if its acceptance maximizes utility; (a) Right action is compliance with C. But what if we cannot accept C? Rawls and L Whitt suggest: C is correct if accepting it maximizes among codes we *can* accept; (a). But what if merely *reinforcing* a code we *can't* accept would maximize? G Trianosky suggest: C is correct if reinforcing it maximizes; (b) Right action is reinforcing C. I object to this and argue: C is correct if both accepting and reinforcing C would maximize and if C is reinforcible; (c) Right action is coming as close as possible to perfect acceptance of and compliance with C.

MAC INTOSH, Duncan. Modality, Mechanism and Translational Indeterminacy. Dialogue (Canada), 28(3), 391-399, 1989.

Ken Warmbröd thinks Quine agrees that: translation is determinate (D) if it is D what speakers would say in all possible circumstances (PCs); what things would do in merely PCs is determined (Dd) by what their subvisible mechanisms would dispose them to do on the evidence of: (e) what like actual mechanisms make like actual things do actually; what speakers say is Dd by their neural mechanisms (NMs). Warmbröd infers that NMs make translation D. I argue that (e) underdetermines what our NMs would make us say in merely PCs. So translation is indeterminate, but so are the dispositions of physical mechanisms.

MAC INTOSH, J J. Reincarnation and Relativized Identity. Relig Stud, 25(2), 153-165, Je 89.

In this paper I spell out the arguments which show that, contrary to the claims of Hick and others (including, in the past, the present writer), reincarnation in a different body is logically impossible in the absence of a continuing soul. I then investigate the possibility that relativizing identity (which seems to invalidate one of the arguments used to show the logical impossibility of reincarnation) might allow reincarnation in again, and show that reincarnation can be shown to be logically impossible in this context as well.

MAC INTYRE, Alasdair. *First Principles, Final Ends and Contemporary Philosophical Issues*. Milwaukee, Marquette Univ Pr, 1990

This is an investigation into the place of first principles within that conception of a perfected science, the achievement of which, so it is argued, is the final end of rational enquiry, as understood by Aristotle and by Aquinas. Their account of first principles is contrasted with that advanced by Cartesians and others for whom appeal to first principles has an epistemological function. The project of a genealogy of contemporary anti-Thomistic standpoints is proposed.

MAC INTYRE, Alasdair. Imaginative Universals and Historical Falsification: A Rejoinder to Professor Verene. New Vico Studies, 6, 21-30, 1988.

This criticism of Vico focusses upon the relationship of the imaginative to the conceptual universal, as expounded by Donald Verene. It is argued against Verene that Vico's view is defective. Vico's relationship to Plato is examined and his philosophy of history is also criticized.

MACCOLL, San. Universality and Difference: O'Keeffe and McClintock. Hypatia, 5(2), 149-157, Sum 90.

This is a critique of the idea of universality in art and science that considers the examples of Georgia O'Keeffe's work as an artist and Barbara McClintock's work as a scientist. A consideration of their lives and work brings out their differences in the inherently male fields of art and science. Their underlying commonality is found in a shared view of nature involving fluidity, concern for detail, and caring and feeling, traits often characterized as "female." This enables each of them to assert her own identity in her work and contributes to its remarkable success.

MACDONALD, Cynthia. *Mind-Body Identity Theories*. New York, Routledge, 1989

The purpose of the book is twofold: first, to provide a survey of the recent history of mind-body identity theories; and second, to provide a detailed defense of one such theory. Part One concentrates on the type-type identity theories of Smart and Place, the causal role identity theories of Lewis and Armstrong, and the token identity theories of Kim and Davidson. Part Two constructs an original defense of nonreductive monism in the light of a view of events known as the property exemplification account.

MACDONALD, Cynthia. Weak Externalism and Mind-Body Identity. Mind, 99(395), 387-404, Jl 90.

Mind-body identity theories have been repeatedly subjected to the charge that since intentional mental properties supervene on objects external to persons' bodies, no intentional state (type or token) can be identical with any internal physical phenomenon of a person's body. The author argues that the claim that objects external to persons' bodies are partly constitutive of their intentional states, while being incompatible with type-type identity theories, in no way prejudices the truth of token identity theories. The position advanced, weak externalism, is externalist with respect to intentional mental types but not with respect to tokens of those types.

MACDONALD, Cynthia. What Is Empiricism?—II, Nativism, Naturalism, and Evolutionary Theory. Aris Soc, SUPP 64, 81-92, 1990.

The paper addresses the issue of whether empiricism is compatible with nativism. The argument it discusses is that the core of empiricism lies in its commitment to naturalism, and there are naturalistic (evolutionary-biological) accounts of nativism, so empiricists can be nativists. The author argues, first, that evolutionary-biological accounts of nativism require assuming that content itself can be biologized, and this assumption is highly dubious; and second, that there are problems (concerning truth and justification) with extending a biological account of how a belief might come to be innate to cover innate knowledge consistently with empiricism.

MACEDO, Leosino Bizinoto. A Segurança em Descartes. Educ Filosof, 2(3), 41-60, Jl-D 87.

MACEDO, Stephen. The Politics of Justification. Polit Theory, 18(2), 280-304, My 90.

In the quest for reasonable agreement amidst diversity, liberals have a tendency to minimize the deep implications of liberal politics (see esp. John Rawls and Charles Larmore). Liberal politics shapes our lives deeply, pervasively, and relentlessly. Liberalism and its commitment to public reasonableness is at odds with many religious beliefs and other deep personal commitments. Since these conflicts can be evaded only by embracing a noble fib, they should be openly confronted even if that means admitting religious controversies into politics. Better to moderate our expectations about agreement than to inhibit critical reason.

MACHAMER, Peter and SAKELLARIADIS, Spyros. "The Unity of Hobbes's Philosophy" in *Hobbes: War Among Nations*, AIRAKSINEN, Timo (ed), 15-34. Brookfield, Gower, 1989.

Critics have tended to view Hobbes in either of two ways: first, that Hobbes is simply wrong to think that natural philosophy is in the least way relevant to politics, or, second, that Hobbes, in principle, thinks he can, and, in fact, attempts to, reduce politics to physics. In this paper we show what truth there is to both these claims. We shall argue that neither is completely correct. Attempting to reconcile the insights behind these two positions will involve laying out the architectonic of Hobbes's philosophy and examining the interconnection of its various levels. In particular, we will show how Hobbes's version of a nominalistic theory of language acts to unify the various parts of his philosophy.

MACHAN, Tibor R. Are Human Rights Real? Humanist, 49(6), 28-29,36, N-D 89.

This article responds to Delos McKown's criticism of natural rights in which the author argues that no such rights are possible and what rights exist amount to no more than positive or legislated permissions by the government (of whatever kind). I argue that positive rights are recorded acknowledgments of principles by which human beings in communities must relate to each other *qua* human beings (as distinct from members of the same family, friends, colleagues), in virtue of the kind of entities they are—i.e., in virtue of their nature. Since human beings are moral agents, responsible to conduct themselves properly *and* the authors of their own conduct, they require "moral space," defined by natural rights.

MACHAN, Tibor R. Capitalism, Freedom and Rhetorical Argumentation. J Applied Phil, 6(2), 215-218, O 89.

In this reply to a criticism of my "The Virtue of Freedom in Capitalism" by Alan Haworth (J Applied Phil, 6, 97-107, 1989), I answer various charges made by Haworth, notably that I have not managed to link the principle of private property rights with the idea of morally responsible conduct. I reiterate the point that to act morally responsibly it is necessary (but not sufficient) to have a sphere of personal jurisdiction (or what Nozick calls "moral space").

MACHAN, Tibor R. Humanism and Political Economy. Free Inq, 9(4), 21-22, Fall 89.

Humanists, following mainly Marx, are often fond of collectivist political-economic organizations. Yet this does not follow from humanism per se. Whether humanism favors capitalism or socialism, for example, has much to do with how central individuality is to human nature. If human beings are essentially collective entities (Marx: "The human essence is the true collectivity of man"), then socialism would be more suited to them as their economic arrangement in society. But if individuality is central, as I hold and briefly argue in this note, then capitalism is a more suitable arrangement since this system is more able to address diverse wants and needs of individuals in societies.

MACHAN, Tibor R. Is Natural Law Ethics Obsolete? Vera Lex, 9(1), 1-2,10,23, 1989.

Some, e.g., John Gray (in his *Liberalism*), argue that because of modern science and empiricism, natural law ethics, including natural rights liberalism, cannot succeed as a theory. They believe that the teleological underpinnings of the conception of human nature needed for such a normative stance has been ruled out. But there is no reason to hold this. First, it is scientism, not science per se, that is antiteleological; second, empiricism as the candidate for the right epistemology is by no means a shoe-in; third, there is scientific evidence for teleology—e.g., in Roger W Sperry's conception of consciousness.

MACHAN, Tibor R. *Liberty and Culture: Essays on the Idea of a Free Society.* Buffalo, Prometheus, 1989

This is a collection of previously published newspaper and magazine essays expressing arguments, analyses, and opinions that reflect a libertarian viewpoint from an ethical egoist/objectivist frame of reference. The essays appeared in publications ranging from the *New York Times* and the *Chicago Tribune* to the *Orange Country Register* and the *Humanist*.

MACHAN, Tibor R. *The Moral Case for the Free Market Economy: A Philosophical Argument.* Lewiston, Mellen Pr, 1988

This work, growing out of five lectures given in Stockholm, Sweden, outlines what the author regards as the moral case for the free market capitalist political economic system. First the compatibility of science and free will is established. Then a teleological ethical egoism or individualism is defended. From this the socioeconomic principles of natural individual human rights are derived. In particular, property rights are defended on the grounds that (a) individuals often deserve holdings and (b) ought to enjoy a sphere of exclusive jurisdiction where their moral life is in their own control. Finally, objections to capitalism are considered and answered.

MACHAN, Tibor R. Natural Rights Liberalism. Phil Theol, 4(3), 253-265, Spr 90.

Some critics of natural rights liberalism—*a la* Locke and his contemporary champions—dismiss the stance on grounds that scientific empiricism and the demise of teleology clearly spell doom for it. In this essay I argue that the health of empiricism is itself in far greater question than some alternative epistemologies, which then opens certain metaphysical paths that may lead to the revival of a form of teleological explanation. Although admittedly natural rights liberalism presupposes that human beings have fundamental free choices they can make and that these may be evaluated as regards the ends they further, this approach does not fly in the face of some scientific orthodoxy and, thus, may succeed.

MACHAN, Tibor R. Politics and Generosity. J Applied Phil, 7(1), 61-73, Mr 90.

This paper argues that generosity as a moral virtue is only consistently and fully possible to practise in the kind of polity that upholds natural individual human rights, including the basic negative right to private property. The paper sketches a characterisation of generosity and explains the sense in which it can be a moral virtue. Some of the assumptions underlying the concept of moral virtue are considered and it is argued that contrary to some recent claims, it is possible to conceptualise as well as to practise moral virtues in our age. Yet it is also shown that certain political prerequisites are necessary for practising generosity. Furthermore, it is shown that there cannot be any generosity involved in a polity in which one is forced to share one's wealth with those who might be the beneficiaries of generous conduct. Finally, it is argued that even in a polity with a very limited government some acts of official generosity are possible.

MACK, Eric. Moral Individualism: Agent-Relativity and Deontic Restraints. Soc Phil Pol, 7(1), 81-111, Autumn 89.

This essay characterizes and seeks to render plausible a doctrine of deontic restraints and the moral rights correlative to those restraints as one of the two complementary facts of moral individualism. The core of the individualist theory of the good, the agent-relativity of values, is defended against standard objections and alternatives. The core of its theory of the right is deontic constraints on the means by which agent-relative values may be pursued. These constraints comprise the form that each individual's practical recognition of others as beings with separate and equally ultimate ends of their own must take.

MACKAAY, Ejan (and others). The Logic of Time in Law and Legal Expert Systems. Ratio Juris, 3(2), 254-271, Jl 90.

Research on an expert system regarding unemployment insurance law has pointed to the difficulties of explicitly representing temporal relations. The question has been addressed in the artificial intelligence literature with respect to planning systems and linguistic analysis. The approaches adopted do not appear to be directly transposable to legal discourse. The problem seems so far to have escaped notice amongst researchers attempting to develop legal expert systems. The paper explores in a preliminary way how lawyers use temporal concepts. It is submitted that "legal time" only partly overlaps with real time. A sketch of a formalization of temporal relations in law, following J F Allen's approach, is presented.

MACKENZIE, Michael and KEATING, Peter. Patents and Free Scientific Information in Biotechnology: Making Monoclonal Antibodies Proprietary. Sci Tech Human Values, 15(1), 65-83, Wint 90.

In this paper we examine the evolution of the biomedical field of Hybridoma/Monoclonal Antibodies with detailed examples of the three types of patent claims—basic, application techniques and specific antibodies—that have emerged there. We then analyse the impact of these claims and their legal histories on (a) the free flow of scientific information, and (b) the activity of scientific researchers. We conclude that such patent claims present severe restrictions for both, not only in the Monoclonal area but in general, amounting to a subtle but significant shift in the political economy of science and technology.

MACKIE, Karl J. Business Regulation, Business Ethics and the Professional Employee. J Bus Ethics, 8(8), 607-616, Ag 89.

The differences in business reactions to legal regulation, and the nature of business moralities, are examined through the eyes of an 'expert' group—in-house lawyers. The research indicates that lawyers inevitably provide a degree of control through their technical expertise, but that they also identify strongly with their companies and emphasise shared ethics rather than ethical differences between lawyers and their employers. This can partly be explained by their integration with the company but also rests on the problematic nature of law and regulatory controls in relation to organisations within the community. In-house lawyers therefore reject a 'policing' role in favour of a 'counselling' role. Since they perceive themselves as part of a shared culture of ethics, they also avoid a leadership role. However, the article suggests that the nature of legal judgment should assist lawyers towards such a role, while recognising that organisational 'statesmanship' must be constrained by organisational culture and the wider community culture of ethical standards.

MACKINNON, K A B. Concepts of Justice in the Scottish Enlightenment. Vera Lex, 7(2), 14-15, 1987.

The concepts of justice of five writers in eighteenth century Scotland are outlined and contrasted. While James Balfour criticised the narrow utilitarianism of David Hume's account of justice as the mere respecting of conventional property rights, two of his more famous critics, Adam Smith and Thomas Reid, also disagreed between themselves about whether justice could demand positive actions as well as prohibiting injury to the natural rights of others. Without going as far as Reid's welfarism, Lord Kames set out an evolutionary view which held that duties of benevolence could develop into duties of justice.

MACKLIN, Ruth. Ethical Principles and Medical Practices. Nat Forum, 69(4), 25-27, Fall 89.

MACLACHLAN, D L C. *Philosophy of Perception.* Englewood Cliffs, Prentice-Hall, 1989

The central purpose of this book is to introduce the problem of perception through the deployment of the traditional causal representative theory. Answers are offered to some standard objections, such as the idea that the theory can be reduced to solipsism, and the argument for an alternative account in terms of how things appear to the subject. Although it is conceded in the final chapters that there are emerging problems not handled by the traditional theory, the thesis is that this theory contains an important element of truth, which must be preserved in the dialectical development of a more adequate account.

MACMILLAN, C J B. The Search for Theory in Process-Product Research: Response to Chambers. Proc Phil Educ, 45, 96-100, 1989.

MACPHERSON, Dugald and HODGES, Wilfrid and HODKINSON, I M. Omega-Categoricity, Relative Categoricity and Coordinatisation. Annals Pure Applied Log, 46(2), 169-199, F 90.

Let L,L´ be countable first order languages with L´ ⊆ L, such that there is a unary relation symbol P in L\L´. Let T be a complete L-theory with infinite models. If M ⊨ T let P(B) be the substructure induced on {x: M⊨ Px}. Then T is *relatively categorical* if, whenever M,M´ are models of T with P(M) = P(M´) there is an isomorphism M → M´ which is the identity on P(M). Various conditions are examined which, together with relative categoricity, guarantee that M is algebraic over P(M), or is coordinatisable over P(M).

MADANES, Leiser. "Nature," "Substance," and "God" as Mass Terms in Spinoza's *Theologico-Political Treatise*. Hist Phil Quart, 6(3), 295-302, Jl 89.

MADANES, Leiser. 'Sustancia', 'naturaleza' y 'Dios' como términos de masa en la filosofía política de Spinoza. Rev Latin De Filosof, 15(2), 183-199, Jl 89.

A division fallacy is detected in one of Spinoza's main political arguments by which he concludes that right is determined by power (*TTP*, chap. 16). It is argued that if 'God', 'nature' and 'substance' can be considered as mass-terms denoting stuffs, the division fallacy can be avoided and the cogency of Spinoza's argument is thus assured.

MADANES, Leiser. La paradoja de la libertad de expresión. Cuad Filosof, 20(32), 25-35, My 89.

It is well known that Spinoza was strongly influenced by Hobbes's political thought. It is well known, too, that Spinoza was one of the staunchest advocates of freedom of thought and conscience during the XVII century. Yet, seldom has Hobbes been interpreted as favouring these basic individual freedoms. Hobbes thought that as sovereignty became more absolute and stable, more individual freedoms, including freedom of speech and expression, could be granted. Some relevant paragraphs of *Leviathan*, chapter 18, are examined in detail in order to show this rather unnoticed side of Hobbes's political philosophy.

MADDEN, Edward H and MANNS, James W. Victor Cousin: Commonsense and the Absolute. Rev Metaph, 43(3), 569-589, Mr 90.

This paper aims to clarify the extent to which Cousin's philosophy (which he termed "eclecticism") was dependent, respectively, on the philosophy of Thomas Reid and on the absolute idealists, particularly Schelling. We find that Cousin's epistemology leans heavily on Reid, and that Reid's commonsense approach supplies the very criteria in terms of which philosophical views are to be evaluated and either included in or excluded from Cousin's eclecticism. We find also that the alleged absolute idealist influence on his work has been considerably exaggerated (at times by Cousin himself), and that in fact the German "idealist" who most influenced Cousin was Leibniz.

MADDUX, Roger D. Finitary Algebraic Logic. Z Math Log, 35(4), 321-332, 1989.

If transitive closure is added to the finitary algebraic logic presented in *A Formalization of Set Theory without Variables*, by A Tarski and S Givant, American Mathematical Society, Colloquium Publications 41, 1987, the resulting extension is not finitely axiomatizable. On the other hand, three finitely axiomatizable extensions are constructed by adding nonlogical operations. Finally, there is a natural correspondence between first order structures and relation algebras with quasi-projections, so that a first order sentence is logically valid if and only if its translation into an equation is true in all relation algebras.

MADDY, Penelope. Believing the Axioms, I. J Sym Log, 53(2), 481-511, Je 88.

Philosophers often claim that mathematical axioms are obvious or self-evidently true, but this does not match the practice of modern set theory. In fact, set theorists offer a wide range of arguments for and against axiom candidates, and the description and evaluation of these arguments presents an important challenge to the philosopher. The paper and its sequel ('Believing the axioms', II, *JSL* 53 (1988), pp. 736-64) take a first step in the direction of such an account.

MADDY, Penelope. The Roots of Contemporary Platonism. J Sym Log, 54(4), 1121-1144, D 89.

Despite its pretheoretic appeal, Platonism in the philosophy of mathematics has suffered a checkered career. In recent years, however, it has enjoyed something of a comeback. This paper traces the roots of this resurgence to the shortcomings of the three great schools proposed in the early decades of this century. The various Platonistic programs now under development are

briefly described.

MADIGAN, Tim. Humanism and Altruism. Free Inq, 9(4), 46-47, Fall 89.

MADIGAN, Tim. Moral Education and a Critical Thinking: The Humanist Perspective. Free Inq, 10(1), 4, Wint 89-90.

A brief examination of the misconception that moral education courses can be taught apart from other courses in the curriculum.

MADISON, G B. Hayek and the Interpretive Turn. Crit Rev, 3(2), 169-185, Spr 89.

MADISON, G B. Postmodern Philosophy? Crit Rev, 2(2-3), 166-182, Spr-Sum 88.

MADISON, Gary Brent. Merleau-Ponty et la déconstruction du logocentrisme. Laval Theol Phil, 46(1), 65-79, F 90.

L'auteur montre que la philosophie de Merleau-Ponty, comme philosophie de l'ambiguïté, constitue une tentative réussie de déconstruire le logocentrisme ou l'inversionisme philosophique traditionnel, et de miner, par conséquent, ses applications contemporaines: la simulation cognitive et l'intelligence artificielle aussi bien que la logique informelle ou la "critique des raisonnements".

MADSEN, Peter. Toward a Code of Ethics for Business Ethicists. Bus Prof Ethics J, 7(3-4), 147-166, Fall-Wint 88.

The reasons for the adoption of a code of ethics for business ethicists are discussed and critically examined. It is concluded that there is a need for such a code given the various activities of business ethicists that present ethical problems and dilemmas for them.

MÄENPÄÄ, Olli. Immediate Legitimacy? Problems of Legitimacy in a Consensually Oriented Application of Law. Law Phil, 8(3), 319-331, D 89.

The legitimatory basis of law should be analyzed as an evolving process. Conventionally emphasis is laid on the enactment stage as the predominant legitimatory basis for law. It is argued that a wider and more procedurally oriented view is both necessary and possible. The legitimatory procedures and bases may alter on a continuum. The subsequent legitimatory processes can be presented as overlapping and intermingling. Legitimacy can, to a considerable extent, even be provided immediately in the application process of law. Certain qualitative requirements and restrictions are necessary, however, insofar as the degree of immediacy increases.

MAESSCHALCK, M. Les *Weltalter* de Schelling: Un essai de philosophie narrative. Laval Theol Phil, 46(2), 131-148, Je 90.

Le renouveau des recherches schellingiennes depuis les années 50 a montré la fécondité de la période des *Weltalter*. Cependant, si l'on a puisé à cette source intuitive, on n'a pas montré comment Schelling y maintient une liberté proprement spéculative par rapport à ses sources mystiques. Il nous semble que les récentes analyses de Ricoeur dans *Temps et récit* permettent de mieux saisir la liberté du philosophe, à l'oeuvre dans un essai de structuration narrative de la relation de création. Dans ce récit des origines se découvre un sens des rapports de la liberté et de l'histoire dans son imprévisible nouveauté, qui démarque radicalement Schelling de Hegel, son vieux rival.

MAESSCHALCK, Marc. La fondation de l'autonomie chez Descartes: Lecture entre Brunschvicg et Derrida. Rev Phil Louvain, 88(77), 25-47, F 90.

To read Descartes through the eyes of Brunschvicg and Derrida is to lend an ear to French rationalism, which implants itself with Descartes in the tradition of European thought. But it is also to recognize the premisses of a thought of finiteness and of existential difference, which weakens the pretentions of rationalism and finally makes it possible to understand the as yet unthought truth in it. Autonomy is perhaps less a title to glory for reason than the sign of its finitude divided between the denial of a will to know and the humiliation of its realisation. In this cleft between creative madness and the patience of time enters the courageous responsibility of man, consisting in being accountable for time, basing himself on his finite ego.

MAESSCHALCK, Marc. Habermas interprète de Schelling. Arch Phil, 52(4), 639-658, O-D 89.

The interpretation of Schelling by Habermas is also a critique of Hegel, Marx and the Marxist tradition, Bloch, Löwith and Marcuse. In the first Weltalter he finds the true meaning of present in history. The value of the Kairos is manifest in the last philosophy, but the religious should not be disqualified.

MAESSCHALCK, Marc. Questions sur le langage poétique à partir de Roman Jakobson. Rev Phil Louvain, 87(76), 470-503, Ag 89.

The investigation of poetic language presupposes the epistemological clarification of the intellectual operation of reading. This requirement leads us to dismiss Jakobson momentarily in order to explore in turn the thought of Todorov, then that of Merleau-Ponty, who justifies more fully his reference to the pathology of language in order to indicate that language belongs to the structures that constitute existence, finally, even more radically, the thought of Heidegger, Gadamer and Ricoeur, in order to pause in the distance that separates the original and the derived, the appeal of the work of art and its translation. (edited)

MAFFIE, James. Naturalism and the Normativity of Epistemology. Phil Stud, 59(3), 333-349, Jl 90.

Epistemology plays an indisputably normative role in our affairs; it is this which is commonly argued to prevent epistemology's being naturalized. I propose a descriptivist account of epistemology. Epistemic judgments, concepts, and properties are essentially descriptive and only hypothetically and contingently normative. Epistemology enjoys an intimate relationship with human conduct and motivation—and is therefore normative—in virtue of its centrality and widespread utility as a means to our variable ends. Epistemology becomes normative only within the framework of instrumental reason and its normativity is parasitic upon that of the latter.

MAGEL, Charles R. Keyguide to Information Sources in Animal Rights. Jefferson, McFarland, 1989

MAGER, John and WYND, William R. The Business and Society Course: Does It Change Student Attitudes? J Bus Ethics, 8(6), 487-491, Je 89.

The purpose of this research was to determine if there is a significant difference in the attitudes of students toward situations involving ethical decisions before and after taking a course in Business and Society. A simulated before and after design was used with Clark's personal business ethics and social responsibility scale serving as the measurement instrument. The result of the study indicated that the Business and Society class had no statistically significant impact on student attitudes.

MAGIDOR, M and ROSENTHAL, J W and RUBIN, M and SROUR, G. Some Highly Undecidable Lattices. Annals Pure Applied Log, 46(1), 41-63, Ja 90.

MAGLIOLA, Robert. Differentialism in Chinese Ch'an and French Deconstruction: Some Test-Cases from the Wu-Men-Kuan. J Chin Phil, 17(1), 87-97, Mr 90.

I argue there is a deconstructive para-tradition in Ch'an surpassing French deconstruction: "differential" Ch'an takes logic-as-deconstructed to be liberating bliss (Nagarjuna's second truth) and affirms logic as conventionally valid (Nagarjuna's first truth). Wu-men's Case 43, treated in the original Chinese, enacts reinscription by way of the Chinese words ts'u and pei, which carry opposite meanings on the first semantic level but equivalent meanings on the second. This maneuver is shown to function by way of logic-as-deconstructed, and not by way of mystical paradox ("centric" Ch'an). Case 38 is treated in terms of postmodern "lack," carnavalesque, and alterity.

MAGNAVACCA, Silvia. La finalidad en el mundo natural según san Agustín. Rev Filosof (Argentina), 3(1), 27-42, My 88.

This paper is devoted to show that Saint Augustine's notion about finality in Nature is based on his metaphysical concept of pondus. It also deals with Aristotelian and Stoic antecedents of this Augustinian theory. Last, it indicates briefly that his point of view is still standing in Middle Ages.

MAGNELL, Thomas. "Moore's Attack on Naturalism" in Inquiries into Values: The Inaugural Session of the International Society for Value Inquiry, LEE, Sander H , 67-87. Lewiston, Mellen Pr, 1989.

With his answer to "What is meant by 'good'?" G E Moore attacked naturalism and fashioned subsequent discussions of the meaning of 'good'. The four parts of his answer, that 'good' signifies a property, that the property is non-natural, that the property is simple and that 'good' is indefinable, are each examined. Particular attention is given to his tacit realism, his reliance on the complementarity of his classificatory terms and his use of the open question argument. As Moore's arguments are found to be too weak to support the last three parts of his answer, his attack on naturalism is deemed to be unsuccessful.

MAGNUS, Bernd. Self-Consuming Concepts. Int Stud Phil, 21(2), 63-71, 1989.

MAHLER, Fred. Juventology: A Holistic Approach to Youth. Phil Log, 32(1-2), 19-31, Ja-Je 88.

MAHONEY, Jack. An International Look at Business Ethics: Britain. J Bus Ethics, 9(7), 545-550, Jl 90.

Interest in business ethics is not new in Britain and has been increasing recently. Business companies have responded over the years with various organisational initiatives, including the British Institute of Management and the Christian Association of Business Executives; and interest in corporate mission statements and codes of conduct is growing. As a formal subject for study and teaching, however, business ethics is still in a rudimentary form,

dependent on work in the United States. However, official reports, conferences, and new Centres are indicators of growing interest. As teaching begins to develop British business ethics has to identify its own agenda, and especially in the light of 1992 and the implementation of the Single European Act.

MAHONEY, Michael J. Bias, Controversy, and Abuse in the Study of the Scientific Publication System. Sci Tech Human Values, 15(1), 50-55, Wint 90.

MAIDAN, Michael. Egoism and Personal Identity. G Metaf, 11(2), 293-302, My-Ag 89.

A number of contemporary philosophers have tried to show that egoism hangs on a 'substantialist' view of personal identity. Following Hume, they dismiss such notion together with the moral standpoint which they associate with it. In fact, any theory of morality requires a 'substantialist' view of personal identity. The paper suggests that an egoist feels justified in behaving as if the interests of other people were less demanding than his own because he feels that the former are known to him in a direct and immediate way whereas he knows about the latter in a derivative way only.

MAIDAN, Michael. Max Scheler's Criticism of Schopenhauer's Account of Morality and Compassion. J Brit Soc Phenomenol, 20(3), 225-235, O 89.

Though Scheler broadly agrees with Schopenhauer's rejection of the traditional accounts of pity, he criticizes Schopenhauer's reduction of pity to a metaphysical category and the attempt to make pity the central fact in moral life. Instead, Scheler advocates love as the fundamental fact of morality. After reviewing Scheler's arguments, the paper shows that, though Scheler's criticism is pertinent, his own account of morality in terms of love is not immune to the same arguments.

MAINBERGER, Gonsalv K. Rhetorica I—Reden mit Vernunft: Aristoteles, Cicero, Augustinus. Stuttgart, Frommann-Holzboog, 1988

This is Part One of a two-volume series which is intended as a contribution to the history of rhetoric and knowledge. In light of the Aristotelian theory of knowledge, rhetoric is the theory of conjectural reasoning of which the author explores the inner state and potentiality. Also examined are the contributions of Cicero and Augustine. (edited)

MAINBERGER, Gonsalv K. Rhetorica II—Spiegelungen des Geistes: Sprachfiguren bei Vico und L Strauss. Stuttgart, Frommann-Holzboog, 1988

A barely discovered yet productive ferment of postmodernism is the rhetorical use of reason. This thesis is one of the motives of research for this, the second volume of a two-part series on the history of rhetoric and knowledge. Two rhetorically conceived models of the conjectural use of reason are brought to light: Vico's Metaphysics and Levi-Strauss's Mythologica. This work invites philosophers to take a new look at rhetoric and outlines a philosophy of finiteness. (edited)

MAIOCCHI, Roberto. Il neoidelismo italiano e la meccanica quantistica. G Crit Filosof Ital, 68(1), 78-99, Ja-Ap 89.

MAIOCCHI, Roberto. Pierre Duhem's The Aim and Structure of Physical Theory: A Book Against Conventionalism. Synthese, 83(3), 385-400, Je 90.

I reject the widely held view that Duhem's 1906 book La Théorie physique is a statement of instrumentalistic conventionalism, motivated by the scientific crisis at the end of the nineteenth century. By considering Duhem's historical context I show that his epistemological views were already formed before the crisis occurred; that he consistently supported general thermodynamics against the new atomism; and that he rejected the epistemological views of the latter's philosophical supporters. In particular I show that Duhem rejected Poincaré's account of scientific language, Le Roy's view that laws are definitions, and the conventionalist's use of simplicity as the criterion of theory choice. Duhem regarded most theory choices as decidable on empirical grounds, but made historical context the main determining factor in scientific change.

MAITLAND, Ian. Rights in the Workplace: A Nozickian Argument. J Bus Ethics, 8(12), 951-954, D 89.

There is a growing literature that attempts to define the substantive rights of employees in the workplace, a.k.a. the duties of employers toward their employees. Following Nozick, this article argues that—so long as there is a competitive labor market—to set up a class of moral rights in the workplace invades workers' rights to freely choose the terms and conditions of employment they judge best.

MAJETSCHAK, Stefan. Metakritik und Sprache: Zu Johann Georg Hamanns Kant-Verständnis und seinen metakritischen Implikationen. Kantstudien, 80(4), 447-471, 1989.

MAJOR, René. A coup de dé(s). Rev Phil Fr, 180(2), 293-302, Ap-Je 90.

MAKKAI, M and SHELAH, Saharon. Categoricity of Theories in $L_{\kappa\omega}$ with κ a Compact Cardinal. Annals Pure Applied Log, 47(1), 41-97, Ap 90.

MAKKAI, Michael. A Theorem on Barr-Exact Categories, with an Infinitary Generalization. Annals Pure Applied Log, 47(3), 225-268, Je 90.

Let C be a small Barr-exact category, reg(C,Set) the category of all regular functors from C to the category of small sets. A form of M Barr's full embedding theorem states that the evaluation functor $e: C \rightarrow [Reg(C, Set), Set]$ is full and faithful. We prove that the essential image of e consists of the functors that preserve all small products and filtered colimits. The concept of κ-Barr-exact category is introduced, for κ any infinite regular cardinal, and the natural generalization to κ-Barr-exact categories of the above result is proved. The treatment combines methods of model theory and category theory. Some applications to module categories are given.

MAKKREEL, Rudolf. The Genesis of Heidegger's Phenomenological Hermeneutics and the Rediscovered "Aristotle Introduction" of 1922. Man World, 23(3), 305-320, Jl 90.

In the first part of this paper I use Heidegger's early unpublished lectures to consider his efforts to apply phenomenological theories of intuition and meaning clarification to what he saw as the Diltheyan project of interpreting life and history. I show a progression from a concern with understanding through the *having* of intuitive evidence to an interest in fulfilling our interpretation of life in terms of the meaning of *being*. After pointing to a tension between these themes of having and being in Heidegger's early lectures, I then make use of the rediscovered "Aristoteles-Einleitung" of 1922 to resolve this tension.

MAKKREEL, Rudolf. Kant and the Interpretation of Nature and History. Phil Forum, 21(1-2), 169-181, Fall-Wint 89-90.

My purpose is to examine Kant's views on interpreting nature and history and to attempt to see them as coherent by relating them to his theory of reflective judgment. With this reconstruction of a Kantian conception of interpretation it is possible to shed new light on Kant's approach to political history. I propose that reflective judgments as defined in the *Critique of Judgment* be conceived primarily as interpretive and only derivatively as either aesthetic or teleological. This approach to reflective judgments creates a spectrum of them ranging from the noncognitive to the cognitive and from the aesthetic to the practical.

MAKSIMOVA, Larisa. "Relevance Principles and Formal Deducibility" in *Directions in Relevant Logic*, NORMAN, Jean (ed), 95-97. Norwell, Kluwer, 1989.

MALABOU, Catherine. Économie de la violence, violence de l'économie: Derrida et Marx. Rev Phil Fr, 180(2), 303-324, Ap-Je 90.

MALANGA, Joseph. The Study of Teaching and Curriculum. Thinking, 8(1), 38-43, 1989.

MALBREIL, G. Malebranche et le libertin. Rev Phil Fr, 179(2), 177-191, Ap-Je 89.

MALCOLM, Noel. "Hobbes and the Royal Society" in *Perspectives on Thomas Hobbes*, ROGERS, G A J (ed), 43-66. New York, Clarendon/Oxford Pr, 1988.

MALCOLM, Norman. Reply to Scheer's "What if Something Really Unheard-of Happened?". Phil Invest, 13(2), 165-168, Ap 90.

MALDAMÉ, Jean-Michel. Place de l'homme dans l'univers. Rev Thomiste, 90(1), 109-131, Ja-Mr 90.

MALHERBE, Abraham J. *Paul and the Popular Philosophers*. Philadelphia, Fortress Pr, 1989

The book consists of eleven previously published articles which demonstrate Paul's familiarity with popular philosophy, particularly Stoicism and Cynicism. Paul is seen to have adopted, and then adapted literary and rhetorical conventions, self-descriptions, and techniques aimed at bringing about moral transformation in others from his philosophical contemporaries. Four of the studies show that interpreters of Paul, within and outside of the New Testament, presented him in philosophic terms. One of the studies sketches in detail some of the differences among Cynics.

MALHERBE, Michel. Leo Strauss, Hobbes et la nature humaine. Rev Metaph Morale, 94(3), 353-367, Jl-S 89.

MALHERBE, Michel. Le règne de Dieu par la nature chez Thomas Hobbes. Arch Phil, 53(2), 245-259, Ap-Je 90.

In the kingdom of God by nature (*De Cive XV, Leviathan XXXI*), religion is founded on the act of faith by which, submitting to the omnipotence of God, believers acknowledge God's sovereignty. Although its causes can be traced back, this act is, as such, original, because its essence is political and not moral, even if it leads to the service of God, rendered in morality, when believers suppose that the laws of nature are moral laws. Such a faith is

irrational by its principle; but, when one tries to justify it, it shows a regressive rationality: God sovereignty is justified by His natural right and moral obligation proceeds from the natural obligation of fear.

MALI, Joseph. "The Public Grounds of Truth": The Critical Theory of G B Vico. New Vico Studies, 6, 59-83, 1988.

MALIECKAL, Louis. Sacrifice: Core of Vedic Religion and Christianity. J Dharma, 14(4), 313-328, O-D 89.

MALLORY, G R and KERSTEN, G E and BADCOCK, L and IGLEWSKI, M. Structuring and Simulating Negotiation: An Approach and an Example. Theor Decis, 28(3), 243-273, My 90.

Negotiation is a complex and dynamic decision process during which parties' perceptions, preferences, and roles may change. Modeling such a process requires flexible and powerful tools. The use of rule-based formalism is therefore expanded from its traditional expert system type technique, to structuring and restructuring nontrivial processes like negotiation. Using rules, we build a model of a negotiation problem. Some rules are used to infer positions and reactions of the parties, other rules are used to modify problem representation when such a modification is necessary. We illustrate the approach with a contract negotiation case between two large companies. We also show how this approach could help one party to realize that negotiations are being carried on against their assumptions and expectations.

MALM, H M. Commodification or Compensation: A Reply to Ketchum. Hypatia, 4(3), 128-135, Fall 89.

I defend the permissibility of paid surrogacy arrangements against the arguments Sara Ketchum advances in "Selling Babies and Selling Bodies." I argue that the arrangements cannot be prohibited out of hand on the grounds that they treat persons as objects of sale, because it is possible to view the payments made in these arrangements as compensation for the woman's services. I also argue that the arguments based on exploitation and parental custodial rights fail to provide adequate grounds for prohibiting the arrangements.

MALONEY, J Christopher. It's Hard to Believe. Mind Lang, 5(2), 122-148, Sum 90.

Belief attribution exploits different and occasionally conflicting criteria. This suggests that there may be different kinds of psychological states captured by these criteria. Thus it is argued that the folk psychological notion of belief may mask a heterogeneity of psychological states.

MALONEY, J Christopher. *The Mundane Matter of the Mental Language*. New York, Cambridge Univ Pr, 1989

This book advances the thesis that cognition involves the deployment of a mental language, a system of mental representation that is essentially a linguistic system. While this thesis is in league with classical artificial intelligence, it is complemented with the idea that genuine mental representation must be implemented in matter of a certain sort. A causal theory of the contents of mental representations is advanced, and an attempt is made to show how a theory of mental representation that posits a mental language can accommodate qualia and consciousness.

MALPAS, J E. *Kategoriai* and the Unity of Being. J Speculative Phil, 4(1), 13-36, 1990.

This paper begins by considering the classificatory role of the Aristotelian *Kategoriai*. This classificatory role is presented as primarily ontological rather than logical. But it is only by virtue of their having a central ontological role that the *Kategoriai* can operate as classifications at all. The development of this ontological role is parallel to the development of Aristotle's metaphysical concerns towards an account in the *Metaphysics* which integrates the *Kategoriai* with the *archai* themselves. Thus the paper concludes that the *Kategoriai* should ultimately be seen as representing an articulation of the proper 'unity' of being.

MALPAS, J E. Transcendental Arguments and Conceptual Schemes: A Reconsideration of Körner's Uniqueness Argument. Kantstudien, 81(2), 232-251, 1990.

Stephan Körner has claimed that transcendental deductions in general, and Kant's deduction in particular, are impossible. Körner's position is reconsidered in the light of Eva Schaper's reply to Körner. One of Schaper's arguments against Körner, an argument which makes use of the notion of translatability, is shown to closely resemble Donald Davidson's argument against the very idea of a conceptual scheme. This leads to a brief comparison between Davidson's antisceptical, antirelativistic position and that of Kant. Davidson's position shows there is a basic incoherence in the idea of transcendental deduction and in the arguments of both Körner and Schaper. The conclusion is that transcendental deduction is impossible, but also unnecessary.

MALTER, Rudolf. "Abstraktion, Begriffsanalyse, und Urteilskraft in Schopenhauers Erkenntnislehre" in *Schopenhauer: New Essays in Honor of His 200th Birthday*, VON DER LUFT, Eric (ed), 257-272. Lewiston, Mellen Pr, 1989.

MALY, Kenneth and EMAD, Parvis. Poetic Saying as Beckoning: The Opening of Hölderlin's *Germanien*. Res Phenomenol, 19, 121-138, 1989.

MAMALI, Catalin. Pythia-Sphinx·Complex in Oedipus' Life: On the Reversals between the Questioning and the Answering Modes of Being. Phil Log, 32(3-4), 257-270, Jl-D 88.

MAMARDASHVILI, M K and STEWART, Philip D (trans). The Problem of Consciousness and the Philosopher's Calling. Soviet Stud Phil, 29(1), 6-26, Sum 90.

MAMIANI, Maurizio. Francesco Venini: Un philosophe a Parma (1764-1772). G Crit Filosof Ital, 68(2), 213-224, My-Ag 89.

MANAKOS, Jannis. On a Subtheory of the Bernays-Gödel Set Theory. Z Math Log, 35(5), 413-414, 1989.

A (proper) subtheory T of the impredicative Bernays-Gödel set theory is presented containing, nevertheless, a model of this theory. In T, the objects of the universe are called neutrally objects, sets are defined as the elements of one-elemented objects, and classes as the objects containing only sets. Non-classes are not forbidden. The conclusion is reached that the concept of non-elements is not necessary in set theory with classes.

MANASTER-RAMER, Alexis and KAC, Michael B. The Concept of Phrase Structure. Ling Phil, 13(3), 325-362, Je 90.

MANDERS, Kenneth. Domain Extension and the Philosophy of Mathematics. J Phil, 86(10), 553-562, O 89.

Starting from a logical analysis of domain extension constructions, we analyse how such constructions can enhance understandability of a prior subject matter, and compare the analysis with historical developments in mathematics. This provides a theoretical, epistemological basis for the utility of complex numbers, geometrical points at infinity, and similar mathematical objects; it opens up perspectives for nonformalist philosophical views of mathematics, which account for the significance of specific mathematical structures.

MANDT, A J. "The Inevitability of Pluralism: Philosophical Practice and Philosophical Excellence" in *The Institution of Philosophy: A Discipline in Crisis?*, COHEN, Avner (ed), 77-101. La Salle, Open Court, 1989.

MANEKIN, Charles H. "Problems of "Plenitude" in Maimonides and Gersonides" in *A Straight Path: Studies in Medieval Philosophy and Culture*, LINK-SALINGER, Ruth (ed), 183-194. Washington, Cath Univ Amer Pr, 1988.

According to Hintikka, Aristotle's modal theory implies acceptance of the classical "principle of plenitude" ("No genuine possibility can remain forever unrealized"); this "statistical" interpretation of modality in Aristotle has been extended by Knuuttila to the medieval Arab and scholastic philosophers. In this paper I examine some applications of the principle of plenitude in the writings of the Jewish philosophers Moses Maimonides and Levi Gersonides. I argue that although both essentially accept the principle, Maimonides restricts its application in order to avoid philosophical and theological difficulties. I also show how Gersonides uses the principle against Averroes' harmonizing interpretation of Aristotle's modal logic.

MANENT, Pierre. Strauss et Nietzsche. Rev Metaph Morale, 94(3), 337-345, Jl-S 89.

MANKA, Roman. Turinici's Fixed Point Theorem and the Axiom of Choice. Rep Math Log, 22, 15-19, 1988.

Turinici's generalization of the Caristi fixed point theorem is equivalent to the axiom of choice. Its specialization to Hausdorff spaces can be proved without choice.

MANNING, Phil. Goffman's Revisions. Phil Soc Sci, 19(3), 341-343, S 89.

Erving Goffman's reputation as a cynic stems from his text, *The Presentation of Self in Everyday Life*, which portrays the self as a manipulative confidence trickster. However, matters are more complicated than they first appear. There are two versions of the text, one published in 1956, the other in 1959, and Goffman's revisions to the latter quietly challenge the cynicism of the former. Focussing on these revisions makes the text look rather different. Goffman has two voices in *The Presentation of Self* and the aim of this paper is to allow each to be heard.

MANNO, Ambrogio Giacomo. *Lo storicismo di W Dilthey (Il problema di dio nei grandi pensatori, Volume Quinto)*. Napoli, Loffredo, 1990

MANNS, James W and MADDEN, Edward H. Victor Cousin: Commonsense and the Absolute. Rev Metaph, 43(3), 569-589, Mr 90.

This paper aims to clarify the extent to which Cousin's philosophy (which he termed "eclecticism") was dependent, respectively, on the philosophy of Thomas Reid and on the absolute idealists, particularly Schelling. We find that Cousin's epistemology leans heavily on Reid, and that Reid's commonsense approach supplies the very criteria in terms of which philosophical views are to be evaluated and either included in or excluded from Cousin's eclecticism. We find also that the alleged absolute idealist influence on his work has been considerably exaggerated (at times by Cousin himself), and that in fact the German "idealist" who most influenced Cousin was Leibniz.

MANSBRIDGE, Jane. Self-Interest in Political Life. Polit Theory, 18(1), 132-153, F 90.

From the ancient Greeks to before World War II, even thinkers who made self-interest the basis of political life usually incorporated some role for non-self-interested behavior, both benevolent and malevolent. Both civic republicans and the framers of modern liberalism, including Adam Smith and James Madison, promoted public spirit. After the war, many social sciences, including "rational choice" in political science, tried to construct models of human behavior, e.g., democracy, on self-interest alone. By 1980, however, this assumption had begun to fade in every discipline, including economics. Few now defend self-interest as the dominant source of behavior in all political contexts.

MANSFELD, Jaap. Chrysippus and the *Placita*. Phronesis, 34(3), 311-342, 1989.

MANSFELD, Jaap. "Gibt es Spuren von Theophrasts *Phys op* bei Cicero?" in *Cicero's Knowledge of the Peripatos*, FORTENBAUGH, William W (ed), 133-158. New Brunswick, Transaction Books, 1989.

MANSFIELD, Victor. Mādhyamika Buddhism and Quantum Mechanics: Beginning a Dialogue. Int Phil Quart, 29(4), 371-391, D 89.

A philosophic analysis of the Middle Way Buddhist conception of emptiness is first presented. Then the philosophic foundations of quantum mechanics are explored through a nontechnical derivation of Bell's Inequality and a discussion of its experimental refutation. The paper shows the intimate relationship between the Middle Way Buddhist conception of emptiness, the experimental refutation of Bell's Inequality, and the fundamental principles of quantum mechanics. It is hoped that these comparisons, contrasts, and applications spark a dialogue between those concerned with the philosophic ramifications of quantum mechanics and those interested in an ancient path to liberation.

MANSFIELD, Victor. Relativity in Mādhyamika Buddhism and Modern Physics. Phil East West, 40(1), 59-72, Ja 90.

Many Middle Way Buddhist scholars and translators equate the pivotal principle of dependent arising with relativity from physics. I discuss the philosophic structure of Middle Way Buddhism and then nontechnically present relativity in modern physics. There are some significant parallels between these two very different disciplines. But because physical relativity formulates the laws of physics in a reference frame independent, or absolute, way and stresses other frame independent quantities, we may not equate physical relativity with dependent arising. Such an identification generates misunderstanding, since dependent arising leads to a fully nonaffirming negation.

MANSILLA, H C F. Aspectos rescatables de la cultura premoderna. Rev Filosof (Costa Rica), 26, 41-48, D 88.

The goal of this essay is to place emphasis on some aspects of premodern, i.e., pre-industrial culture in Latin America, and more especially in the Andean area. These aspects contain some preservable and valuable elements for human conviviality. The essay is a part of the present debate of postmodernism. The base of the analysis is the thesis that the present development of Latin American countries exhibits many negative factors, which are not due to backwardness, but to a second-class modernization: too many too big towns, ecological disarrays, isolation of the individual, demographic explosion, mass phenomena of alienation, etc. Among the preservable aspects of the traditional order one can find the extended family as a shelter of practical solidarity, genuine religiosity as counterbalance to anthropocentrical ideologies, and aristocratic conception of art as a public aesthetics of high value and firmness.

MAPEL, David R. Civil Association and the Idea of Contingency. Polit Theory, 18(3), 392-410, Ag 90.

This essay argues that the idea of contingency is the key to understanding Michael Oakeshott's *On Human Conduct*. The idea of contingency explains why Oakeshott mistakenly thinks that civil association is the only form of political association compatible with freedom. It also makes sense of Oakeshott's antifoundational conception of authority. By focusing on the idea of contingency, this essay defends Oakeshott against those critics who argue that civil association is an impossible abstraction and against those who argue that it presupposes a self-defeating historicism.

MARALDO, John C. Translating Nishida. Phil East West, 39(4), 465-496, O 89.

MARCEL, Gabriel. Mi relación con Heidegger. Dialogo Filosof, 5(3), 348-363, S-D 89.

MARCHAL, Bruno. Des fondements théoriques pour l'intelligence artificielle et la philosophie de l'esprit. Rev Int Phil, 44(172), 104-117, 1990.

MARCHETTI, Cesare. Del valore: Chi crea l'informazione? Epistemologia, 11(2), 317-324, Jl-D 88.

Biological systems are the most prolific creators of information in terms of matching structures. Matching is the key word because the structures have to satisfy the very demanding condition of long-term species survival. The basic mechanism, to be broadly interpreted, is to make a variant (mutation) of a preexisting structure and to test the viability of the new object within the context (selection). *Selection then is the value assigning machine*. Our thesis is that syntactic language is the next step in information processing and storing, above DNA, and operates on the same principles as DNA. Certainly, cultural innovations diffuse inside social systems exactly as mutant species with equivalent hierarchical structures. (edited)

MARCIL-LACOSTE, Louise. L'égalité au dix'huitième siècle: l'importance de l'*aequanimitas*. Man Nature, 7, 117-129, 1988.

L'analyse du corpus du Trésor de la Langue Française concernant le XVIIIe siècle à partir de la notion d'égalité permet de mettre en cause plusieurs généralisations courantes concernant la manière dont l'égalité fut esquissée au cours des Lumières. En particulier, la notion d'équanimité a joué un rôle majeur dans l'articulation entre une éthique individuelle et une éthique politique, articulation dont on trouve le point culminant chez Diderot.

MARCILLA CATALÁN, Javier. El hombre como imagent de Dios en la especulación agustiniana. Augustinus, 34(133-134), 119-154, Ja-Je 89.

MARCONDES CESAR, C. Le problème du temps chez Paul Ricoeur. Il Protag, 6(9-10), 65-72, Je-D 86.

MARCONI, Diego and DA COSTA, Newton C A. An Overview of Paraconsistent Logic in the 80s. J Non-Classical Log, 6(1), 5-32, My 89.

In this paper we aim at giving a sketch of some aspects of the state of development of paraconsistent logic in the 80s. Our exposition will not aim at completeness. Given the development of the literature in the field, completeness is out of the question in a paper like ours. However, we delineate not only the theoretical accomplishments, but also the more important applications of paraconsistent logic in philosophy, mathematics, the sciences, and technology.

MARCOS DE PINOTTI, Graciela E. La distinción platónica entre *epistéme* y *dóxa alethés* a la luz del tratamiento del error. Rev Filosof (Argentina), 2(2), 135-155, N 87.

The unsuccessful discussion of *Theatetus*'s false judgment is usually considered a digression with no connection at all with Plato's attack to the second definition of knowledge. This paper argues that it is rather a *reductio* of it. 188a-c shows that the *epistéme—dóxa alethés* identification is self-contradictory as it requires a previous distinction between what truth and falsity are. Nevertheless, falsehood cannot be explained. The argument brings out interesting consequences concerning Platonic conception of error.

MARCOTTE, Edward. Some Variations on a Metaphilosophical Theme. Int Stud Phil, 21(3), 49-61, 1989.

MARCUS, Ruth Barcan. Possibilia and Possible Worlds. Grazer Phil Stud, 25-26, 107-134, 1985-86.

Four questions are raised about the semantics of quantified modal logic (QML). Does QML admit possible objects, i.e., possibilia? Is it plausible to admit them? Can sense be made of such objects? Is QML committed to the existence of possibilia? The conclusions are that QML, generalized as in Kripke, would seem to accommodate possibilia, but they are rejected on philosophical and semantical grounds. Things must be encounterable, directly nameable and a part of the actual order before they may plausibly enter into the identity relation. QML is not committed to possibilia in that the range of variables may be restricted to actual objects. Support of the conclusions requires some discussion of substitution puzzles; also, the semantical distinction between proper names which are directly referring, and descriptions even where the latter are "rigid designators." Views of W V Quine, B Russell, A Donnellan, D Kaplan as well as S Kripke are invoked or evaluated in conjunction with these issues.

MARCZUK, Stanislaw. "Problems of Value in Marxist Philosophy" in *Inquiries into Values: The Inaugural Session of the International Society for*

Value Inquiry, LEE, Sander H , 307-314. Lewiston, Mellen Pr, 1989.

MARGA, Andrei. La méthodologie et l'éthique herméneutiques (in Romanian). Rev Filosof (Romania), 35(5), 501-510, S-O 88.

MARGALIT, Avishai. Bar-Hillel: The Man and his Philosophy of Mathematics. Iyyun, 39(1), 7-12, Ja 90.

MARGALIT, Avishai. National Self-determination. J Phil, 87(9), 439-461, S 90.

MARGOLIS, Joseph. "The Eclipse and Recovery of Analytic Aesthetics" in *Analytic Aesthetics*, SHUSTERMAN, Richard (ed), 161-189. Cambridge, Blackwell, 1989.

The reasons for the noticeable decline in analytic aesthetics are analyzed both in terms of general tendencies in analytic philosophy (notably through W V Quine and Richard Rorty) and specifically in terms of the systematic views of Monroe Beardsley, Nelson Goodman, Arthur Danto, and Joseph Margolis. A number of suggestions are aired regarding the prospects for the recovery of analytic aesthetics informed by certain salient themes drawn from European currents.

MARGOLIS, Joseph (ed) and ROCKMORE, Tom (ed) and FARÍAS, Victor. *Heidegger and Nazism*. Philadelphia, Temple Univ Pr, 1989

This is the English translation of Victor Farias's *Heidegger et le Nazisme*. It is enlarged and extensively altered by the addition of new and replacement materials from the German edition. Also, substantive errors and errors in the Notes have been corrected. The editors provide a new introductory statement.

MARGOLIS, Joseph. Interpretation at Risk. Monist, 73(2), 312-330, Ap 90.

Stanley Rosen has charged that interpretation is impossible if human nature is not constant through history. The argument is shown to be inadequate, and its conclusion, false. The counterthesis explores the views of Aristotle and Protagoras and the pertinent views of Gadamer, Derrida, and Foucault. The essential issue concerns the conditions of reference and reidentification and the viability of description and interpretation where reidentification can be secured though the "nature" of what is referred to may change. An illustration is drawn from the critical practice of Harold Bloom.

MARGOLIS, Joseph. The Novelty of Marx's Theory of *Praxis*. J Theor Soc Behav, 19(4), 367-388, D 89.

Marx's theory of *praxis* is construed essentially as a theory of thinking, and is taken to mark what is most original in his work as a philosopher. Effectively, this is to emphasize that thinking has a history and is in a sense "produced" under praxical conditions. The issue is explored in textual terms, in terms of canonical views of thinking and in terms of deviant thinkers like Roberto Unger and Michel Foucault.

MARGOLIS, Joseph. "On the Semiotics of Music" in *What is Music?*, ALPERSON, Philip A , 211-236. New York, Haven, 1987.

The general features of a Saussurean (structuralist) semiotics are specified and shown to be ill-fitted to both natural language and natural communicative processes (music, in particular). Other semiotic approaches are examined, including the views of Arthur Danto, Nelson Goodman, Abraham Moles (an information-theoretic approach), Susanne Langer, Jean Jacques Nattiez, Leonard Meyer, and others more briefly. Difficulties are collected; and the general prospects of a rigorous semiotics are taken to be dim, although there is no denying that human culture in general, and music in particular, exhibit semiotic features.

MARGOLIS, Joseph. "Radical Philosophy and Radical History" in *The Institution of Philosophy: A Discipline in Crisis?*, COHEN, Avner (ed), 243-247. La Salle, Open Court, 1989.

The problem of recovering metaphysical and epistemological questions under the condition of radical history is explored through a review of a variety of influential thinkers. It is shown that some leading thinkers are attracted to a notion of radical history or radical contingency (Quine, for instance) and yet posit invariances that they could not then defend; and that some philosophers, embracing the implications of radical history and radical contingency (Rorty) are prepared to abandon philosophy altogether. The present effort steers a middle course between these two alternatives.

MARGOLIS, Joseph. *Texts without Referents: Reconciling Science and Narrative*. Cambridge, Blackwell, 1989

This book presents among other things an ontology of cultural entities and phenomena, a theory of history, and a theory of reference. These issues are integrated in the service of a systematic philosophy (continuing the trilogy of which it is a part) committed to construing the natural sciences as human sciences, rejecting all forms of cognitive privilege, and recovering the principal questions of philosophy under the condition of radical history.

MARGONIS, Frank. Democracy and Technology. Proc Phil Educ, 45, 276-279, 1989.

MARIAN, Marin. Quelques repésentants de l'Esthétique musicale Roumaine (in Romanian). Rev Filosof (Romania), 36(2), 142-149, Mr-Ap 89.

MARINER, Wendy K and GLANTZ, Leonard H and ANNAS, George J. Pregnancy, Drugs, and the Perils of Prosecution. Crim Just Ethics, 9(1), 30-41, Wint-Spr 90.

MARINI, Gaetano. Della scommessa legislativa sulla discrezionalità dei giudici. Riv Int Filosof Diritto, 66(2), 290-314, Ap-Je 89.

MARINI, Giuliano. Elaborazione di temi hegeliani in Gramsci. Arch Stor Cult, 3, 315-338, 1990.

MARIS, Nicolae. Le développement de la science et le progrès de la société (in Romanian). Rev Filosof (Romania), 36(1), 23-27, Ja-F 89.

MARITAIN, J. Extrait d'une lettre à L Lévy-Bruhl (1904). Rev Phil Fr, 179(4), 475-477, O-D 89.

MARKAKIS, M. The Notion of Chance and the Metaphysics of P Kanellopoulos (in Greek). Philosophia (Athens), 17-18, 467-475, 1987-88.

An attempt is being made in this paper to examine the notion of chance, using the framework of Panayotis Kanellopoulos's metaphysics as our main point of departure. Major points of determinism analysis are being examined to indicate its inadequacy *per se* when it deals with processes of nature as well as with processes of mind, to conclude that its antithesis to indeterminism is being overcome on the basis of probability theory. While the probability theory founds the probable and not the chance event, the existence of change is being assumed especially by several statistical notions such as "degrees of freedom" taken into account to isolate probability systems from external influences and to solve simultaneous equations related to these systems. Mathematical foundation of change is being also supported by modern experimental psychology on the processes of mind which, although does not prove directly the existence of freedom in the realm of human understanding, at least it does not renounce it. The thesis is being finally formulated that the notion of chance is an expression of nature as well as in the sphere of human consciousness.

MARKER, Rita L. Euthanasia, the Ultimate Abandonment. Ethics Med, 6(2), 21-25, Sum 90.

MARKIEWICZ, Barbara and PROTALINSKI, Grzegorz (trans). God and Nation: Franz Rosenzweig's Concept of Messianism versus Polish Messianism. Dialec Hum, 16(1), 149-156, Wint 89.

The purpose of this paper is to analyse the concept of the Jewish nation and national existence of Franz Rosenzweig. This notion plays a very important role in Rosenzweig's thought—it is a basis of his idea of Messianism as a new version of the philosophy of history. In comparing Rosenzweig's philosophy with the Polish Messianism of the 19th century I make an effort to formulate the main features of an idea that I call "national existentialism." (edited)

MARKIEWICZ, D and DEVINE, I. Cross-Sex Relationships at Work and the Impact of Gender Stereotypes. J Bus Ethics, 9(4-5), 333-338, Ap-My 90.

Organizations pride themselves on their creation of rational structures based primarily on a male perspective of interaction. Workers are expected to set aside interpersonal behaviours that do not directly contribute to task performance. As more women enter management, norms concerning appropriate interpersonal relationships at work are undergoing strain. In addition, the phenomenon of mutual sexual attractions between co-workers is demanding attention. This study systematically describes attitudes, attributions and anticipated consequences of mutual sexual attractions at work. Findings suggest that gender stereotypes are significant factors in people's judgments of persons involved in sexual attractions at work.

MARKO, Kurt. Anmerkungen zum Real Existierenden Totalitarismus und zu seinen Apologeten unter uns. Stud Soviet Tho, 38(2), 165-181, Ag 89.

Es wird vor dem "neuen Denken", das Gorbatschow zugeschrieben wird, gewarnt. Es ist bloss new speak, das der Bevölkerung der Länder in kommunistischer Hand und den Westen für die Erhaltung des Machtapparats Sowjetunion gewinnen soll. Denn das Ziel der Systemrenovierung ist dessen Fortbestand, also des Sowjetimperiums und seines Hegemonialverbandes unter sich wandelnden Verhältnissen. Westlichen Illusionen werden die Erfahrungen von Sowjetbürgern—Mstislav Rostropowitsch, Galina Wischnewskaja und Alexander Sinowjew—privilegiert und exiliert—entgegengehalten. Durch Gorbatschows Renovierungsversuch sind die bleibenden Erkenntnisse der Totalitarismus-Theorien nicht überholt, nur werden sie, weil im Westen die Wunschwelt störend, negiert, so der Selbsttäuschung der freien Welt Vorschub leistend.

MARKOSIAN, Ned. On Ockham's Supposition Theory and Karger's Rule of Inference. Fran Stud, 48(26), 40-52, 1988.

Elizabeth Karger has suggested an interpretation of Ockham's theory of the modes of common personal supposition ("TM") according to which the purpose of TM is to provide certain distinctions that Ockham will use in formulating a unified theory of immediate inference among certain kinds of sentences. Karger presents a single, powerful rule of inference that incorporates TM distinctions and that is meant to codify Ockham's theory of immediate inference. I raise an objection to Karger's rule, thereby calling into doubt the interpretation of Ockham that is based on attributing that rule to him.

MARKOVA, Ludmilla A. "On Recent Problems of the Sociology of Science in the Context of Karl Marx's Ideas" in *Scientific Knowledge Socialized*, HRONSZKY, Imre (ed), 123-137. Norwell, Kluwer, 1989.

Sociality of science is considered as a problem; it can be understood in different ways. Science exists in society as if in two forms: science as a totality of final results, functioning in society, and science as a production of new knowledge in the process of creativity. In the first case the external causality dominates, in the second, science is considered as self-determined, self-organized, as composed of unique events. In other words, we deal here with universal labour and cooperative labour in Karl Marx's terminology.

MARKOVIC, Mihailo. The Tragedy of National Conflicts in 'Real Socialism': The Case of the Yugoslav Autonomous Province of Kosovo. Praxis Int, 9(4), 408-424, Ja 90.

MARKOWITZ, John C and MICHELS, Robert. The Future of Psychiatry. J Med Phil, 15(1), 5-19, F 90.

Psychiatry is rapidly changing. The authors review the history of psychiatry in the United States, its gradual integration into medicine and society, and the dialectic between its "biologic" and "mentalist" outlooks. After describing the current state of the profession and its knowledge base, they discuss the likely future of the field: psychiatry's projected mode of practice and economics; its future as a science for understanding human behavior; its expected boundaries with other treatment disciplines; its anticipated relationship with academia and with the community at large; and internal issues for the profession. Unprecedented internal and external pressures on the field are likely to require important reconceptualizations of psychiatry both by its members and by the rest of the American public.

MARKOWITZ, Sally. Abortion and Feminism. Soc Theor Pract, 16(1), 1-17, Spr 90.

Feminist defenses of abortion often invoke a woman's right to control her own body. However, many feminists are ambivalent about the general right to autonomy upon which this defense rests. Instead, a more explicitly feminist defense will follow from the claim that women are oppressed in our society and the commitment to end this oppression. As an oppressed group, then, women cannot be required to make sacrifices which will systematically worsen their position. This approach leaves open the possibility that such a right might not be necessary in societies which are truly sexually egalitarian.

MARKS, Joel. Integrating Oriental Philosophy into the Introductory Curriculum. Teach Phil, 12(3), 221-233, S 89.

The typical "Introduction to Philosophy" in the United States and elsewhere limits consideration to the "Western" tradition that began in ancient Greece. But there are other great traditions of philosophy, which such a course does not properly neglect. This article considers in particular the "Eastern" traditions that began in ancient China and India. Various issues—pedagogic, philosophic, metaphilosophic—are discussed, and suggestions made to enable East and West to meet in the introductory philosophy course.

MARKWORTH, Tino. *Johann Gottfried Herder: A Bibliographical Survey, 1977-1987*. Hurth-Efferen, Gabel, 1990

This work gives a bibliographical listing of literature on Johann Gottfried Herder published from 1977 to 1987, a period not covered by the first comprehensive Herder bibliography (Berlin/Weimar, Aufbau Verlag, 1978). The survey lists English and German publications whose titles are explicitly related to Herder or his works. The 481 references are presented in chronological order. Moreover, four different indices (author index, name index, subject index, index of Herder's works) are given to facilitate locating desired literature.

MARLÉ, René. La question du pluralisme en théologie. Gregorianum, 71(3), 465-486, 1990.

Theological pluralism is not new. In the Middle Ages several theological "schools" coexisted. A narrowing down of theological thought happened with the confessional controversies of the 16th century, and later in opposition to the rationalism of the Enlightenment. Theology must therefore build itself up in dialogue: dialogue between faith and the cultural contexts in which faith seeks to express itself; dialogue also between persons with diverse functions within the Church and who hold different responsibilities for her mission. (edited)

MARLIN, Randal. Rawlsian Justice and Community Planning. Int J Applied Phil, 4(4), 36-43, Fall 89.

Rawls's theory of justice can have practical application, it is argued, because it did in fact have application in the case of some complex community planning concerning traffic controls—a case in which the author was centrally involved. Application specifically of the difference principle was not without problems, described in the text; but as interpreted by the author it had significant impact on the outcome.

MARMURA, Michael E. "Ghazali and the Avicennan Proof from Personal Identity for an Immaterial Self" in *A Straight Path: Studies in Medieval Philosophy and Culture*, LINK-SALINGER, Ruth (ed), 195-205. Washington, Cath Univ Amer Pr, 1988.

MARQUET, Jean-François. Corps et subjectivité chez Claude Bruaire. Rev Phil Fr, 180(1), 71-78, Ja-Mr 90.

MARQUIS, D. The Role of Applied Ethics in Philosophy. SW Phil Rev, 6(1), 1-18, Ja 90.

This was the 1989 Presidential Address of the Southwestern Philosophical Society. Some reasons for scepticism concerning the role of applied ethics in philosophy seem compelling. Nevertheless, philosophers bring skills to applied ethics that members of other disciplines often do not bring. Also, the resolution of some issues in applied ethics requires the philosophical treatment of fundamental areas of disagreement. This can be shown through an analysis of the nature of some of those issues.

MARQUIS, Don. An Ethical Problem Concerning Recent Therapeutic Research on Breast Cancer. Hypatia, 4(2), 140-155, Sum 89.

The surgical treatment of breast cancer has changed in recent years. Analysis of the research that led to these changes yields apparently good arguments for all of the following: (1) The research yielded very great benefits for women. (2) There was no other way of obtaining these benefits. (3) This research violated the fundamental rights of the women who were research subjects. This sets a problem for ethics at many levels.

MARRONE, Pierpaolo. Prima e terza persona: Un recente contributo alla "Philosophy of Mind". Aquinas, 32(1), 141-151, Ja-Ap 89.

MARSH, James L. The Play of Difference/Différance in Hegel and Derrida. Owl Minerva, 21(2), 145-153, Spr 90.

MARSH, Robert Charles (ed) and RUSSELL, Bertrand. *Logic and Knowledge: Bertrand Russell, Essays 1901-1950*. Winchester, Unwin Hyman, 1988

First published in 1956, *Logic and Knowledge* was an anticipation of the 28 volumes of the collected papers of Bertrand Russell now being prepared. It contains the text of 10 essays written by Russell between 1901-50, each of them a milestone in Russell's philosophical work. It has the advantage that the editor was in close communication with the author through the preparation of the text and that when required he provided correct readings of corrupt or ambiguous passages. The editor, then in residence in Cambridge, is now a retired member of the faculty of the University of Chicago.

MARSHALL, Eliot L and FINN, Jeffrey. *Medical Ethics (The Encyclopedia of Health: Medical Issues)*. New York, Chelsea House, 1990

Should a hospital spend millions of dollars saving the life of 1 critically ill child, or should it use this same money to provide prenatal care to 20 pregnant women? Should a lengthy test period be required for drugs that may successfully treat AIDS? What rights do women who want to begin or end a pregnancy have? Articles concerning such complex medical questions appear in newspapers virtually every day. This book describes the nature of these issues—including abortion, euthanasia, drug testing on terminally ill patients, and funding for organ transplants and other expensive procedures. It also examines health-insurance policies, discussing the financial assistance that the poor and elderly receive when they get sick and contrasting American practices with those of other countries. The book stresses the complex—and often conflicting—moral principles upon which health-related laws are based and uses vivid case studies to reveal the human dilemmas that result when principles meet reality in life-and-death situations.

MARSHALL, Ernest C. Artistic Convention and the Issue of Truth in Art. J Aes Educ, 23(3), 69-76, Fall 89.

The paper addresses the question, whether and in what sense, works of art can be said to express something either true or false, by criticizing premise

(3) in the following argument against the view that there is truth in art: (1) For something to be either true or false it must have meaning; (2) meaning is not possible without the presence of certain sorts of conventions; (3) such conventions are absent in art; therefore, works of art cannot be true (or false). I conclude that such conventions are present and that the above argument thus fails.

MARSOOBIAN, Armen. Does Metaphysics Rest on an Agrarian Foundation? A Deweyan Answer and Critique. Agr Human Values, 7(1), 27-32, Wint 90.

This paper provides an analysis of John Dewey's appreciation of the effects of the emergence of agriculture on the patterns of Western thought. It shows the role played by this agrarian theme in Dewey's own critique of the dominant values inherent in Western metaphysics.

MARTENS, Ekkehard. Children's Philosophy—Or: Is Motivation for Doing Philosophy a Pseudo-Problem? Thinking, 4(1), 33-36, 1982.

MARTI, Genoveva. Aboutness and Substitutivity. Midwest Stud Phil, 14, 127-139, 1989.

The paper examines critically the traditional, extensionalist, doctrine of substitutivity according to which codesignative singular terms should be intersubstitutable *salva veritate*. The claim is that some of the intuitive assumptions proponents of the doctrine appeal to in order to support the extensionalist principle of substitutivity, when properly analyzed, turn out to provide strong reasons to reject the extensionalist approach to substitutivity.

MARTIN JR, James Alfred. *Beauty and Holiness: The Dialogue between Aesthetics and Religion*. Princeton, Princeton Univ Pr, 1990

MARTIN, Bill. The Enlightenment's Talking Cure: Habermas, *Legitimation Crisis*, and the Recent Political Landscape. SW Phil Rev, 4(1), 33-43, Ja 88.

MARTIN, Bill. How Marxism Became Analytic. J Phil, 86(11), 659-666, N 89.

Marx was rarely clear about what explanatory models he employed in his theoretical works. This failure is the main philosophical reason for welcoming the development of analytical Marxism. The work of G A Cohen and Jon Elster is examined here, with the following aims in mind: (1) to question whether Marxism should be fully naturalized; (2) to raise the question of the cost of naturalizing, and thereby de-Hegelianizing Marxism; (3) to question the place of the concept of rationality in Cohen and Elster, and the relation of that concept to language and social practice; (4) to clarify the debate between methodological individualism and methodological collectivism. In conclusion, I maintain that a type of nonfunctionalist methodological collectivism is possible.

MARTIN, Bill. The Moral Atmosphere: Language and Value in Davidson. SW Phil Rev, 6(1), 89-97, Ja 90.

MARTIN, Bill. *To the Lighthouse* and the Feminist Path to Postmodernity. Phil Lit, 13(2), 307-315, O 89.

This essay uses Virginia Woolf's *To the Lighthouse* to articulate two points of convergence between feminism and postmodernism: (1) the subversion of philosophy by literature; (2) the deconstruction and recreation of the self. The characters in the novel are shown to have affinities with G E Moore, Bertrand Russell, and Ludwig Wittgenstein. The critical framework employed is based in the philosophies of Luce Irigaray and Jacques Derrida.

MARTIN, Dan. Anthropology on the Boundary and the Boundary in Anthropology. Human Stud, 13(2), 119-145, Ap 90.

This work engages in boundary testing on several fronts, but most notably the disciplinary. It follows a kind of structuralist program, but with biography, not myth, as the basis. Then, finding its way through poststructuralist (Bourdieu, Douglas) understandings of 'embodiment', it reaches synthesis in a particular aspect of Indo-Tibetan mandala symbolism. It turns the tables on the sociocultural constructionist theories of emotion, suggesting that emotions possess formative power over both the social and the intellectual structures.

MARTIN, Glen T. *From Nietzsche to Wittgenstein: The Problem of Truth and Nihilism in the Modern World*. New York, Lang, 1989

Part One offers a complete interpretation of Nietzsche's philosophy as an expression of the problems of truth, value, and relativism in the modern world and examines his vision of existence beyond "nihilism." Part Two examines Wittgenstein's lifetime philosophical project as addressing, in a radically new way, the overcoming of nihilism through realizing "the groundlessness of the human situation," thereby restoring "truth" to its legitimate place within the conventions of language. Part Three juxtaposes Nietzsche's "metaphysical scepticism" with Wittgenstein's "new way of seeing" (linked to "Buddhist" philosophy) and explores the spiritual implications for modern man of seeing clearly "the limits" of language.

MARTIN, James E. "Value, Cognition, and Cognitive Sciences: Three Questions about Psychological Accounts" in *Inquiries into Values: The*

Inaugural Session of the International Society for Value Inquiry, LEE, Sander H , 709-719. Lewiston, Mellen Pr, 1989.

This paper proposes an interpretation of psychological phenomena in terms of value. An account of those phenomena requires that we see them as realizing values which are taken to be as objective as the phenomena themselves. In this context, we criticize the vision of science presupposed by most cognitive scientists as incompatible with coherent description, explanation and argument concerning those data which are the focus of much cognitive scientific investigation. The outlines of an alternative perspective are sketched.

MARTÍN, José Pablo. El Pseudo-Justino en la historia del aristotelismo. Pat Med, 10, 3-19, 1989.

Parmi les quatre traités appartenant à l'école syro-chrétienne du Ve siècle et faussement attribués à l'apologiste Justin, occupe une place privilégiée la *Confutatio dogmatum quorundam Aristotelis*. Ce traité admet l'hylémorphisme aristotélicien, et c'est à partir de celui-ci qu'il rejette d'autres thèses cosmologiques de l'Estagirite, telles que la primauté du mouvement local, l'éternité du ciel, l'impossibilité de changement chez les astres. De cette sorte, et même avant Jean Philopon, il a dévancé les critiques au système aristotélicien que dix siècles plus tard fera Galilée.

MARTIN, Michael. *Atheism: A Philosophical Justification*. Philadelphia, Temple Univ Pr, 1990

The aim of this book is to provide good reasons for being an atheist. I present a comprehensive critique of the arguments for the existence of a theistic God and a defense of arguments against the existence of God. Part I is a defense of negative atheism, the position of not believing that a God exists. In part II a justification is provided for positive atheism, the position of disbelieving that God exists. In the book's conclusion I consider what would and would not follow if my main arguments were widely accepted.

MARTIN, Michael. On a New Argument for the Existence of God. Int J Phil Relig, 28(1), 25-34, Ag 90.

In a recent article in *Modern Theology* Augustine Shutte presents what he believes is a new argument for the existence of the Christian God. Although I do not consider if Shutte's argument is really new, I show that his argument is not sound and thus that he is unsuccessful in demonstrating that the Christian God exists.

MARTIN, Mircea. *Conscience* et *forme* dans la pensée critique de Georges Poulet. Phil Log, 32(1-2), 99-111, Ja-Je 88.

MARTIN, Norman M. *Systems of Logic*. New York, Cambridge Univ Pr, 1989

The book is a study of logical systems, developed from an abstract viewpoint. Basic notions of logical structure are developed from the concept of finite sequence and logical systems are developed and compared, with major emphasis on the notion of logical operation, developed as a kind of syntactic function subject to some normality conditions. Greatest detail in application is on the level of propositional logic, but there is also treatment of strict implications as well as extension of the basic methodology to quantification.

MARTIN, R N D. Duhem and the Origins of Statics: Ramifications of the Crisis of 1903-1904. Synthese, 83(3), 337-355, Je 90.

Much speculation of the sources of Duhem's historical interests fails to account for the major shifts in these interests: neither his belief in the continuous development of physics nor his Catholicism, when his Church was encouraging the study of generally Aristotelian scholastic thought, led to any interest in mediaeval science before 1904. Equally, his own claim that he was merely testing his views on the nature of physical theory is easily squared only with earlier work with no trace of mediaeval science. Behind this discontinuity lies a major crisis. Though not a positivist, Duhem had based all his work on assumptions acceptable to positivist. One of these, the sterility of the Middle Ages, was refuted by his chance discovery of evidence of genuine mediaeval science in the autumn of 1903, but that left the doctrine of scholastic sterility intact.

MARTIN, Raymond. *The Past Within Us: An Empirical Approach to Philosophy of History*. Princeton, Princeton Univ Pr, 1989

What are historical interpretations? Why do we interpret the past as we do, rather than in some other way or not at all? Are there realistic alternatives? If not, why not? If there are, what are they and why don't we adopt them? The author begins by diagnosing a basic flaw in the dominant analytic approach to these and related questions: namely, the focus on conceptual analysis and what is possible in principle, rather than on actual historical controversies and what is possible in fact. He then proposes an alternative empirical approach that uses case studies to help determine what makes one historical interpretation better than its competitors.

MARTIN, Rex. "Authority and Sovereignty" in *The Causes of Quarrel: Essays on Peace, War, and Thomas Hobbes*, CAWS, Peter (ed), 36-49. Boston, Beacon Pr, 1989.

The paper has three parts. In the first I sketch out the notion of political authority and identify one pattern—which I call the externalist pattern—for justifying such authority. I then provide an argument against this pattern and suggest an alternative to it. In the second part I turn to the issue of sovereignty. I treat sovereignty as a special case of authority. Specifically, it is that case in which (a) there is (and can be) one and only one body said to have rule-issuing authority. (b) The rules issued by this body oblige absolutely or at least strictly. And (c) the sovereign body is all-powerful; it can do anything. Arguments that there must be one such obligation-creating, all-powerful, rule-issuing body in a system of political authority constitute arguments for sovereignty. I examine and attempt to discredit one such sample argument, that of Hobbes. In the third part, I address an important implication of the failure of the Hobbesian argument.

MARTIN, Rex. Collingwood's Claim that Metaphysics is a Historical Discipline. Monist, 72(4), 489-525, O 89.

This paper provides an account of metaphysics as the study of "absolute presuppositions" (Collingwood's term) and interprets his claim about metaphysics as a denial that metaphysical statements are like Kantian synthetic a priori propositions. The author addresses a possible further elaboration of Collingwood's claim: that the dominant goal of metaphysics is the same as that of standard historical inquiry. Another possible elaboration is that metaphysics, like history, is concerned with a process of development. And this claim is plausible and is the very point Collingwood had in mind. The author tries to make clearer the particular notion of development intended here by treating it as temporal development and as progressive development. One interesting and novel result of the interpretation advanced in this paper is that it brings together and unifies Collingwood's earlier account of scale of forms analysis with his later doctrine that metaphysics is a form of historical study. (edited)

MARTIN, Rex. G H von Wright on Explanation and Understanding: An Appraisal. Hist Theor, 29(2), 205-233, My 90.

Section one is concerned with von Wright's main model for explanations of the sort he called "intentionalist," where an action (of an agent) is accounted for by reference to certain beliefs or thoughts that the agent had. Section two addresses von Wright's view as to the ground of connection (the "tie") between such efficacious reasons and the actions performed. The paper turns next to a critique of von Wright's account of intentionalist explanation on two points: (a) the role of understanding or intelligibility, often called *Verstehen* (section three), and (b) von Wright's claim that actions, in being explained intentionalistically, are not thereby *causally* explained (section four). The paper concludes with a brief fifth section.

MARTIN, Rex. Justifying Punishment and the Problem of the Innocent. J Soc Phil, 20(1-2), 49-67, Spr-Fall 89.

The paper begins with a brief characterization of punishment. The central claim is then made that punishment would be justified in a system of civil rights if (1) it prevents or at least substantially deters violations of rights while at the same time being necessary to this particular task (either in that no alternative can do the job at all or that none can do it as well). Of course, we realize that punitive sanctions often infringe rights of the violator; accordingly, we must also require (drawing here on the notion of the competitive weight of rights) that (2) the right protected is not outweighed by the right infringed by sanction and that it cannot be substantially better protected by a sanction that infringes a right of roughly the same weight (or, of course, one of even lesser weight). Thus, one important ground for punitive sanctions in a system of rights is overall necessity (as in 1 above). On this same ground, a policy of punishing only adjudged violators would be incorporated in the background institution—the trial system—that served to admit people, upon determination of their guilt, into the practice of punishment.

MARTIN, Richard. "Some Records of Political Obligation during the Third Reich: An Empirical Account" in *Inquiries into Values: The Inaugural Session of the International Society for Value Inquiry*, LEE, Sander H , 519-537. Lewiston, Mellen Pr, 1989.

Political participation understood apart from extreme circumstances, as if it were limited to voting or interest group activities undermines the importance of conscience for those who choose to participate in public life by resisting the orders of the state. This study examines case studies of resistance by bureaucrats to the Third Reich's extermination of the Jews. Those who chose resistance to the death bureaucracy were found to exist even in the context of great personal danger. The common aspect of each case was their unwillingness to heed the counsels of despair pointing to the uselessness of resistance.

MARTIN, Robert M. It's Not that Easy Being Grue. Phil Quart, 40(160), 299-315, Jl 90.

If t is future, we cannot tell now whether someone means *green* or Goodman's *grue* by 'green'. Had some of us meant grue* (whose t is past) by 'green', systematic disagreement about colour-attribution would have arisen at t. That this has not happened shows that we had a predisposition against grue*. This must be innate; for we could not have learned before t not to use grue*, and there is no bar (such as logical peculiarity) about thinking that way. This has no evolutionary explanation because before t, grue*-thought conferred the same fitness as green-thought.

MARTINEZ, Juana M. Experiencia y comprensión: Estudio a través del arte como lenguaje. Anu Filosof, 21(1), 143-150, 1988.

MARTÍNEZ, Luis. El no al 2x2=4 de León Chestov. Pensamiento, 46(182), 241-249, Ap-Je 90.

MARTINEZ, Roy. Socrates and Judge Wilhelm: A Case of Kierkegaardian Ethics. Phil Today, 34(1), 39-47, Spr 90.

In Kierkegaard's authorship Socrates is the paradigm of the human way of living. In the schema of the stages as delineated in the pseudonymous works, however, Judge Wilhelm features as the premier spokesman of ethical existence. By establishing a structural correlation between Plato's *Apology* and Kierkegaard's *Either/Or*, I attempt to show that Wilhelm is a caricature of Socrates.

MARTÍNEZ, Sergio. Mediciones ideales en la mecánica cuántica. Critica, 20(60), 13-30, D 88.

As a series of investigations have shown, the interpretation of the change upon measurement in quantum mechanics described by the "projection postulate," as a purely statistical formula, is clear. This formula, here denoted by VNL, is a version of the conditional expectation in Hilbert spaces, and this mathematical result can be given a solid physical interpretation in terms of quantum statistics. In this paper, the author proposes that the change of state on measurement described by the formula VNL can be understood as a change on individual states along the line of Von Neumann's initial proposal for interpreting nonmaximal measurements. The author discusses the objections raised by Lüders and others to Von Neumann's idea and show that they do not apply to the interpretation proposed here. (edited)

MARTINOT, Steve. The Abyss and the Circle: A Cyclo-Analysis of *Being and Time*. Auslegung, 16(1), 73-96, Wint 90.

MARTINSEN, David and ROTTSCHAEFER, William A. Really Taking Darwin Seriously: An Alternative to Michael Ruse's Darwinian Metaethics. Biol Phil, 5(2), 149-173, Ap 90.

Michael Ruse has proposed in his recent book *Taking Darwin Seriously* and elsewhere a new Darwinian ethics distinct from traditional evolutionary ethics, one that avoids the latter's inadequate accounts of the nature of morality and its failed attempts to provide a naturalistic justification of morality. Ruse argues for a sociobiologically based account of moral sentiments, and an evolutionarily based causal explanation of their function, rejecting the possibility of ultimate ethical justification. We find that Ruse's proposal distorts, overextends and weakens both Darwinism and naturalism. So we propose an alternative Darwinian metaethics that both remedies the problems in Ruse's proposal and shows how a Darwinian naturalistic account of the moral good in terms of human fitness avoids the naturalistic fallacy and can provide genuine, even if limited, justifications for substantive ethical claims. Thus, we propose to really take Darwin seriously.

MARTINSON, Steven D. Reason, Revolution and Religion: Johann Benjamin Erhard's Concept of Enlightened Revolution. Hist Euro Ideas, 12(2), 221-226, 1990.

MARTIRANO, Maurizio. Scienze della cultura e storiografia filosofica in Ernst Cassirer. Arch Stor Cult, 3, 409-444, 1990.

MARVAN, George J. Language of Cognition—Cognition of Language (in Serbo-Croatian). Filozof Istraz, 30(3), 979-988, 1989.

The main purpose of this brief outline is to examine the definition stating that "Language is the means of communication and thinking." This definition, though overwhelmingly relevant for the vast majority of linguists and linguistic disciplines, is just the first and hence the most superficial approximation we use to understand language. There are some levels of language which are purely linguistic, hence unexplainable by the definition. Serbo-Croatian is used to demonstrate that the native speaker does not only operate within the synchronic structure (as the tradition sees it), but also within the spatial and retrospective (diachronic) dimensions which by no means are identical by their linguistic constructs. The extra-communicative function (function of the communicative function) possesses an underestimated and underutilized potential able to create from the areas of tension the zones of peace. This potential is available to us not because of the communicative facilities of language *addressing our minds but because of its extra-communicative values able to talk to our hearts and souls.*

MARX, Karl and ENGELS, Frederick. *Collected Works, Volume 30, Marx: 1861-1863*. New York, Intl Publ, 1989

MARX, Karl and ENGELS, Frederick. *Collected Works, Volume 31, Marx: 1861-1863*. New York, Intl Publ, 1989

MARX, Karl. *Collected Works, Volume 32, Marx: 1861-1863*. New York, Intl Publ, 1990

MARX, Karl and ENGELS, Frederick. *Collected Works, Volume 44, Marx and Engels: 1870-1873*. New York, Intl Publ, 1990

MASO, Benjo. Literatuur als bron voor historisch en sociologisch onderzoek. Kennis Methode, 13(3), 315-332, 1989.

MASON, A. The Reconstruction of Political Concepts. Int J Moral Soc Stud, 4(3), 245-258, Autumn 89.

This paper considers Felix Oppenheim's attempt to produce value-free reconstructions of political concepts that are moral notions in ordinary discourse so that political scientists will be able to reach agreement on their empirical application. If political concepts are moral notions in ordinary discourse (as Oppenheim concedes), then they describe from the moral point of view. Oppenheim's program requires that they be redesigned to describe from a nonmoral point of view. But if this were achieved, we would have created new concepts, not merely refined existing ones. Furthermore, the definitions that Oppenheim gives of political concepts can be interpreted differently: the application of these definitions will be in doubt, sometimes in cases that have been regarded as important by political theorists. We have reason to think that when these cases arise, political scientists will interpret the definitions differently, so will continue to disagree.

MASON, Andrew. Gilligan's Conception of Moral Maturity. J Theor Soc Behav, 20(2), 167-179, Je 90.

Gilligan should continue to regard moral maturity as at least partly the result of the integration of an ethics of care with an ethics of rights, rather than in the way she has recently proposed, as a gestalt switch between them. Focusing on the way in which an appreciation of each ethic might transform the other, shows that there is a question insufficiently addressed by Gilligan, viz., how this process might transform a person's understanding of the relation between justice and the provision of care for the needy.

MASON, Andrew. Locke on Disagreement Over the Uses of Moral and Political Terms. Locke News, 20, 63-75, 1989.

In Book III of the *Essay*, Locke argues that disagreements over the proper use of moral and political terms such as 'freedom', 'equality' and 'democracy', which stand for ideas of mixed modes, occur (in general) because people use these terms to signify different ideas. The view that there is a failure of communication between those who apply terms such as these differently, and that disputes occur and persist because of a lack of precision in our use of language, is tacitly accepted by many. However, the theoretical underpinnings of such a view are rarely made explicit; I propose to examine Locke's account, which I think is deserving of serious consideration, in order to see whether it can provide the necessary foundations.

MASON, Andrew. Nozick on Self-Esteem. J Applied Phil, 7(1), 91-98, Mr 90.

This paper considers Robert Nozick's account of self-esteem, as presented in *Anarchy, State, and Utopia*. I criticise three aspects of it. First, the claim that people gain self-esteem only when they believe that they possess greater quantities than others of some valued talent or attribute. Secondly, the view that there will always be a conflict of interests between people over the acquisition of self-esteem. Thirdly, the proposal that the most promising way to improve levels of self-esteem across a society is to educate people so that they value a number of different activities and attributes. I argue against Nozick that there are noncomparative standards of doing something well or successfully that provide a person with a means of self-assessment; there is no necessary conflict of interests over the acquisition of self-esteem; reforming basic social and economic institutions is a promising way for a society to increase levels of self-esteem.

MASON, Andrew. On Explaining Political Disagreement: The Notion of an Essentially Contested Concept. Inquiry, 33(1), 81-98, Mr 90.

Although the notion of an essentially contested concept may shed light on the logic of disputes over the proper application of some key political terms, it nevertheless plays no genuine role in *explaining* the intractability of these disputes. The notion of an essentially contested concept is defended against some influential criticisms, showing how it is possible for one conception of an essentially contested concept to be justifiably regarded as superior to other competing conceptions. Two possible answers are distinguished to the question of why disputes over essentially contested concepts should be regarded as inevitable, but neither provides us with a plausible explanation for why they are so intractable. Disagreements over the proper use of key political concepts are better explained by features of moral and political discourse, such as the short reach of 'intellectual authority' and the fact that consensus is not one of its primary aims, in conjunction with empirical hypotheses from the social sciences, rather than by essential contestedness theses.

MASON, Jeff. *Philosophical Rhetoric: The Function of Indirection in Philosophical Writing.* New York, Routledge, 1989

The purpose of *Philosophical Rhetoric* is to reveal the rhetorical strategies which are at work in all philosophical writings, including those which expressly deny them. Rhetoric in philosophy is defined as the use of arguments and actions to persuade an audience of a truth which transcends the arguments presented. Rhetoric in philosophy is also defined by reference to techniques of indirect communication, understood as a kind of perlocutionary action. It concludes with a discussion of the importance of metaphor and other linguistic devices in the writing and reception of philosophy.

MASSIMILLA, Edoardo. L'obiettivazione della vita soggettiva nelle scienze storico-sociali e la fenomenologia trascendentale di Husserl. Arch Stor Cult, 2, 213-237, 1989.

MASSUMI, Brian (trans) and DELEUZE, Gilles and DELEUZE, Gilles. *A Thousand Plateaus: Capitalism and Schizophrenia.* Minneapolis, Univ of Minn Pr, 1987

MASTERS, Roger D. Evolutionary Biology and Naturalism. Interpretation, 17(1), 111-126, Fall 89.

Contemporary research in the life sciences challenges the common understanding of human nature and history. Findings in the study of hominid evolution, ethology, neurophysiology, sociobiology, and linguistics can no longer be ignored by anyone seriously interested in human political and social behavior. A "naturalistic" approach to human behavior has three principal consequences. First, it can provide a new foundation for the social sciences. Second, it can offer an objective basis for moral judgment. Finally, it can give us a deeper understanding of our species' place in the world.

MASTERS, Roger D and KELLY, Christopher. Rousseau on Reading "Jean-Jacques": The Dialogues. Interpretation, 17(2), 239-253, Wint 89-90.

MASTERS, Roger D (ed & trans) and KELLY, Christopher (ed & trans) and BUSH, Judith R (trans). *Rousseau, Judge of Jean-Jacques: Dialogues—The Collected Writings of Rousseau, Volume I.* Hanover, Univ Pr New England, 1990

MASTROIANNI, Giovanni. Filosofi e filosofia nell'URSS della perestrojka. G Crit Filosof Ital, 68(1), 105-113, Ja-Ap 89.

MATERNA, Pavel. Do We Need a Restriction of the Law of Contradiction? Bull Sect Log, 18(3), 121-125, O 89.

The paper applies Tichy's criticism of the formalist approach to the laws of logic (see Sidorenko's article in *Bull Sect Log* 17:3/4, 1988). It is shown that the laws of logic cannot be "restricted" or modified due to a choice of formal axioms, where the meanings of constants are not given in advance. These laws hold unrestrictedly because they are defined for logical functions given independently of any formalisation. Besides, Tichy's (and Frege's) two-dimensional concept of proof is mentioned.

MATET, Pierre. Some Filters of Partitions. J Sym Log, 53(2), 540-553, Je 88.

After considering two different representations of a given Ramsey ultrafilter as a filter of partitions, the paper proceeds to study those filters that can be associated with Hindman's theorem (in the same way Ramsey ultrafilters are associated with Ramsey's theorem) and with the extension thereof due to Milliken and Taylor.

MATHAUSER, Zdenek. Edmund Husserl and Russian Philosophy (in Czechoslovakian). Filozof Cas, 38(1-2), 107-117, 1990.

The attitude of contemporary Soviet philosophy to Husserl's phenomenology is motivated not only by today's enhanced independence of philosophical thought in the USSR but also historically. In addition to the spiritual world of Russian symbolism, mention should also be made of Russian "mystic rationalism," a movement emerging at the turn of the century and tying on to Leibniz's concrete idealism and the domestic tradition of universal empiricism. After providing some bibliographic data pertaining to the impact of phenomenology in the first and second decades of the 20th century, the author proceeds to discuss the effect phenomenology had on some Russian philosophers who live outside their home country since the early 1920s as well as the two most distinguished Husserlians living in the Soviet Union. The author then goes on to distinguish the attitude of

present-day Soviet philosophers dealing with phenomenology into a confrontational and consequential one. (edited)

MATHEWS, John (trans) and GRAMSCI, Antonio and HOARE, Quintin (ed). *Selections from Political Writings, 1910-1920: Antonio Gramsci.* Minneapolis, Univ of Minn Pr, 1990

Antonio Gramsci is considered one of the most influential thinkers of the twentieth century. The selections in this volume, the first of two, span the period from his initial involvement in Italian politics to the "Red Years" of 1919-1920, and feature texts by Bordiga and Tasca from their debates with Gramsci. They trace Gramsci's development as a revolutionary socialist during the First World War, the impact of his thoughts concerning the Russian Revolution and his involvement in the general strike and factory occupations of 1920. Also included are his reactions to the emerging fascist movement and his contributions to the early stages of the debate about the establishment of the Communist Party of Italy.

MATHEWS, M Cash. Ethical Dilemmas and the Disputing Process: Organizations and Societies. Bus Prof Ethics J, 8(1), 25-35, Spr 89.

The traditional anthropological research on dispute resolution has focused on disputes between and among individuals and small groups in non-industrialized societies. In this article, the analysis is based on an anthropological perspective in comparing the resolving of disputes in non-industrialized societies to similar processes within modern organizations. The modes of dispute processing examined are (1) "lumping it," (2) avoidance, (3) negotiation, (4) mediation, (5) adjudication, and (6) self-help. Modern organizations are viewed as types of societies, in which these modes are used to resolve disputes over illegal or unethical activity.

MATHIEU, Casey and KOHLS, John and CHAPMAN, Christi. Ethics Training Programs in the Fortune 500. Bus Prof Ethics J, 8(2), 55-72, Sum 89.

MATHIEU, Deborah R. Commentary: C-Section for Organ Donation. Hastings Center Rep, 20(2), 23-24, Mr-Ap 90.

MATHIEU, Vittorio. Eguaglianza formale ed eguaglianza sostanziale dopo la rivoluzione francese. Filosofia, 40(3), 243-254, S-D 89.

MATHIEU, Vittorio. L'identità del diverso. G Metaf, 10(3), 441-451, S-D 88.

MATJAZ, Potrc. Intentionality and Extension. Ljubljana, Univ Ljubljana, 1989

MATSUBARA, Yo. Splitting $P_\kappa\lambda$ into Stationary Subsets. J Sym Log, 53(2), 385-389, Je 88.

We show that if κ is an inaccessible cardinal then $P_\kappa\lambda$ splits into $\lambda^{<\kappa}$ many disjoint stationary subsets. We also show that if $P_\kappa\lambda$ carries a strongly saturated ideal then the nonstationary ideal cannot be λ^+-saturated.

MATTEY, G J. "Personal Coherence, Objectivity, and Reliability" in *The Current State of the Coherence Theory*, BENDER, John W (ed), 38-51. Norwell, Kluwer, 1989.

The isolation argument purports to show that the existence of a relation of coherence among what one accepts need not reflect the structure of the world, and hence is inadequate as a criterion of justification. Lehrer defends his coherence theory by claiming that complete justification involves the reliability of the acceptance system and the acceptance of that reliability. This is supposed to establish the connection between justification and truth. I argue that Lehrer's defense is only partially successful, applying to reflective acceptance alone. His coherence theory is too permissive to establish the truth connection for unreflective belief.

MATTHEN, Mohan. The Four Causes in Aristotle's Embryology. Apeiron, 22(4), 159-179, D 89.

MATTHEN, Mohan. Intensionality and Perception: A Reply to Rosenberg. J Phil, 86(12), 727-733, D 89.

MATTHEN, Mohan. "Intentional Parallelism and the Two-Level Structure of Evolutionary Theory" in *Issues in Evolutionary Epistemology*, HAHLWEG, Kai (ed), 559-569. Albany, SUNY Pr, 1989.

All materialists, whether reductionists or not, believe that mental states are characterizable neurologically. They also believe, unless of an eliminativist bent, that these same states are intentionally characterizable. The existence of law-like generalizations at both levels constitutes the "intentional parallelism" of the title. It is argued that only through an evolutionary characterization of intentional content can a satisfactory naturalistic account of this parallelism be given.

MATTHEWS, Eric (ed) and DALGARNO, Melvin (ed). *The Philosophy of Thomas Reid.* Norwell, Kluwer, 1989

MATTHEWS, Eric. "The Metaphysics of Environmentalism" in *Ethics and the Environmental Responsibility*, DOWER, Nigel (ed), 38-56. Aldershot,

Avebury, 1989.

This paper defends a version of anthropocentric ethics in relation to environmental issues. Values are necessarily related to purposes and interests, so nature cannot have intrinsic value. Arguments based on the 'new physics', on the ecological interdependence of humanity with the rest of nature and on the rejection of Cartesian dualism are insufficient to establish the contrary. However, radical environmentalist concerns can largely be accommodated within a human-centred ethic, provided that the notion of 'human interest' is taken to include more than selfish or short-term human concerns.

MATTHEWS, Gareth B. Egocentric Phenomenalism and Conservation in Piaget. Behaviorism, 17(2), 119-128, Fall 89.

Piaget claims that as young children we are all egocentric phenomalists and that, in growing up, we become, by stages, both less egocentric and less phenomenalistic. Piaget's attempts to support these claims, however, are plagued by a basic incoherence. Moreover, the claims themselves obscure some of the most striking results from Piaget's famous experiments on the conservation of substance, weight and volume.

MATTHEWS, Gareth B. The Enigma of *Categories* 1a20ff and Why It Matters. Apeiron, 22(4), 91-104, D 89.

I discuss three interpretations of Aristotle's definition of 'in a subject' at *Categories* 1a24-5—one associated with Michael Frede, one with G E L Owen and one with John Ackrill. I consider whether Ammonius's commentary on the *Categories*—particularly his treatment of the fragrance in the apple that leaves the apple and comes to us—should lead us to settle on one of the three interpretations. Finally, I sketch the "metaphysics of containers" presented in the *Categories* and try to explain why the definitional question is important for assessing that metaphysical doctrine.

MATTOX, Gale A. "The Dilemmas of Extended Nuclear Deterrence" in *Moral Reasoning and Statecraft: Essays Presented to Kenneth W Thompson*, DAVIS, Reed M (ed), 133-150. Lanham, Univ Pr of America, 1988.

MAULA, Erkka and KASANEN, Eero. Chez Fermat A.D. 1637. Philosophica, 43(1), 127-162, 1989.

This paper discusses Fermat's "Last Theorem" from philosophical, historical, heuristic and number theoretical angles. A novel heuristic scenario is suggested. It enables a proof of FLT for even exponents without restrictions, and a proof reconstruction according to which it is impossible to solve the Diophantine equation $x^{2k+1} + y^{2k+1} = z^{2k+1}$, as the proof leads to a variant of the Liar Paradox. All methods used are known from Fermat's own works.

MAURER, Armand A. "Maimonides and Aquinas on the Study of Metaphysics" in *A Straight Path: Studies in Medieval Philosophy and Culture*, LINK-SALINGER, Ruth (ed), 206-215. Washington, Cath Univ Amer Pr, 1988.

The essay compares the views of Maimonides and Aquinas on the place of metaphysics in education. They agree that a long preparation in the liberal arts and sciences is needed before undertaking metaphysics. It should not be taught to the young. They also agree that there are divine gifts superior to all rational speculation, such as prophecy and mysticism. But their conceptions of these gifts and their relation to the natural sciences and metaphysics were widely different. They did not see eye to eye on the nature of metaphysics itself or its relation to scriptural theology or prophecy.

MAURY, André. Logical Form. Acta Phil Fennica, 38, 110-132, 1985.

In Wittgenstein's *Tractatus* logical form or "the form of reality" is a condition of factual truth. Yet the question whether a proposition fulfills this condition of truth is undecidable. So factual truth is, in the end, undecidable. This problem is discussed with reference to Wittgenstein's view of meaning as use, and to realism and antirealism as regards linguistic rules. It turns out that none of the options discussed give a satisfactory solution of the problem. It is also shown that a semantics in terms of "truth-conditions" collapses into a semantics in terms of rules.

MAUTHNER, Fritz. Skeptizismus und Judentum, mit einer Einleitung und Anmerkungen von Frederick Betz und Jörg Thunecke. Stud Spinozana, 5, 275-307, 1989.

The text published here for the first time, with introduction and annotations, represents the original German manuscript (ca. 1921) of Fritz Mauthner's (1849-1923) essay on "Scepticism and the Jews," which appeared in The *Menorah Journal* (New York) in 1924. In the introduction the editors consider the genesis of manuscript and translation, compare both versions, outline the history and aims of *The Menorah Journal*, then turn to Mauthner's life and career, with focus on the development of his radical skepticism and critique of language. (edited)

MAVRODES, George I. Revelation and the Bible. Faith Phil, 6(4), 398-411, O 89.

Jesus said to Peter, "Flesh and blood has not revealed this to you, but my Father who is in heaven." This looks like a noetic miracle which happened in (or to) Peter. Must all Christians have a comparable miracle in themselves, or does the Bible enable us to apprehend, in some "natural" way, the revelations made to prophets and apostles long ago? I suggest that we need not have a single answer to this question, and that the "mix" of revelation and reason, natural and supernatural noetic elements, may be different in various believers.

MAY, John D. Reportage as Compound Suggestion. Inform Log, 10(3), 113-131, Fall 88.

Journalistic narrative prose is rich in suggestion. By voicing a single narrative ("X happened") statement in a supposedly nonfiction context, sender invites receiver to impute intelligibility, ascertainability, feasibility, topicality and speaker sincerity, as well as veracity, to the terms of an account. Conversely, when a narrative statement passes through a 'news-giving' medium, receivers are deterred from appraising those invited inferences. Similar inducements come from pseudo-narrative statements. Meanwhile, some narratives convey other suggestions. Without being explicit they invite extra-logical inferences about event locations, agent numbers, chronologies, relative importance, and determinants, as well as current practicabilities. Awareness of such suggestions is the first step toward distinguishing between prudent and foolhardy inferences.

MAY, Larry. Collective Inaction and Shared Responsibility. Nous, 24(2), 269-277, Ap 90.

Inaction leads to serious harm in the world, just as certainly as intentional, active wrongdoing. Yet, inaction, especially collective inaction, presents difficult problems for theories of responsibility. These difficulties may be formulated in terms of the following questions: why, among the countless things members of a group fail to do, should certain failures be singled out as constituting "collective inactions"? And how should blame for the harmful consequences of these inactions be apportioned within the group? I address this first, conceptual question in Section I, and I address the second, normative question in Section II.

MAY, Larry. "Hobbes" in *Ethics in the History of Western Philosophy*, CAVALIER, Robert J (ed), 125-154. New York, St Martin's Pr, 1988.

This is meant to be a general overview of Hobbes's moral philosophy. Of special importance are Hobbes's concepts of self-interest, contract and law. A theme which runs throughout the essay is the connection between being morally obligated and avoiding self-contradiction. This connection is shown to be essential for understanding how the laws of nature, which for Hobbes are the basic moral rules, are binding. The essay concludes by arguing that Hobbes's moral philosophy is consistent with traditional natural law doctrine in several important respects.

MAY, Todd. Is Post-Structuralist Political Theory Anarchist? Phil Soc Crit, 15(2), 167-182, 1989.

Post-structuralism, in its rejection of the Marxist tradition, has embraced and deepened a tradition long neglected in political philosophy: anarchism. It is argued that thinkers like Deleuze, Foucault, and Lyotard have offered a new anarchism, shorn of the traditional and unnecessary commitment to humanism. By jettisoning humanism, post-structuralists are able to articulate a truly anarchist political philosophy that concentrates upon the multiple and irreducible network of oppressions and struggles that constitute the political field.

MAYES, G Randolph. Ross and Scotus on the Existence of God. Thomist, 54(1), 97-114, Ja 90.

In his *Philosophical Theology* James Ross claims to have uncovered an assumption essential to the proof of God's existence advanced by Duns Scotus: the equivalence of logical and real possibility. Ross argues that the omission is reparable, and that Scotus's proof is ultimately satisfactory. In this paper I examine his claim and determine that while Scotus may have believed there to be a significant connection between these two concepts, his proof of God does not depend on it. Ross's attempt to rework the Scotist demonstration merits consideration on its own terms, however. In calling attention to the relation between real and metaphysical possibility, Ross has hit on a way of circumventing one of the major impediments to the acceptability of Scotus's original proof: the infinite regress of causes. Since Scotus argues against the possibility of the infinite regress in copious detail, we must wonder whether he could have countenanced the alternate route suggested by Ross. While I shall argue that indeed Ross's gambit is flawed in a way that Scotus may have foreseen, his proof nevertheless deserves recognition as an original and noteworthy contribution to the literature.

MAYOS, Gonçal. La periodización hegeliana de la historia, vértice del conflicto interno del pensamiento hegeliano. Pensamiento, 46(183), 305-332, Jl-S 90.

Hegel pasa de periodizar su filosofía de la historia en cuatro etapas a hacerlo en tres (en *Die Vernunft in der Geschichte*). Este hecho en principio menor parece responder a una profunda evolución en su pensamiento. Inciden en este cambio: tanto el esfuerzo por dar una interpretación plenamente especulativa—y acorde con su sistema—de la historia, como la relativización del ideal griego juvenil y la progresiva mayor identificación con el cristianismo; así como el paso—correlativo—de ver la realización del principio de la reconciliación ya no en la Revolución francesa, sino en la Reforma protestante.

MAYS, Wolfe and SHARP, Ann Margaret. Thinking Skill Programs: An Analysis. Thinking, 7(4), 2-11, 1988.

This paper deals with the attempt to develop thinking skills programmes to improve intellectual performance. It aims to give an account and an analysis of the principles on which they are based. Starting with Binet's mental orthopaedics it then considers the CORT system of de Bono, Feuerstein's Mediated Learning and Lipman's Philosophy for children. It compares these programmes and examines some of the criticisms levelled against them. It concludes that there seems some evidence that an adequate system of cognitive education will in some measure improve pupils' powers of judgment and also their motivation.

MAZIERSKI, Stanislaw. The Newtonian Concept of Space and Time (in Polish). Stud Phil Christ, 25(2), 139-153, 1989.

Ancient Greeks did not create a clear theory of space and did not distinguish the concept of place from the concept of space. They had different notions of time. In the trend of realistic philosophy (Aristotle) time was closely connected with motion, in the idealistic trend (Plato) it was considered to be the image of eternity. Newton fluctuated between empiricism and metaphysics. As a physicist he tried to infer his statements from phenomena, but in practice he went beyond the limits of experience. He accepted the concept of absolute time and absolute space. To prove the existence of absolute space he performed the experiment with a rotating bucket filled with water. Einstein rejected the concept of absolute space and absolute time as he considered it to be inconsistent with the Newtonian system of physics.

MAZUREK, Franciszek Janusz and LECKI, Maciej (trans). Anthropology of Peace. Dialec Hum, 14(1), 185-200, Wint 87.

Man (people) who lives in various communities is the only creator and bearer of peace. Anthropology of peace must have a realistic conception of the human person and his dignity. Anthropology of peace perceives the value of peace already in the very structure of man's needs. Man needs peace just like he needs joy and happiness. Anthropology of peace should make use of the concept of the human family (familia humana) instead of international community. This approach will also bring to the foreground the idea of man as the bearer and "creator" of peace. Peace is not only a value which preconditions the actualization of all other values but it constitutes a value in itself—a personal value—the moral competence of peace. The moral competence of peace would be conceived as a synthesis of all the other moral competences. Considering that peace constitutes a personalist and humanistic value everything ought to be done to secure and maintain it by humanistic means: education, dialogue, international cooperation, development and implementation of human rights.

MAZZARA, Giuseppe. Tempo e linguaggio nel pensiero di Derrida e Lyotard. G Metaf, 11(2), 307-311, My-Ag 89.

MC ADOO, Nick. Aesthetics and the Insularity of Arts Educators. Brit J Aes, 30(1), 14-23, Ja 90.

My main purpose is to contrast the aesthetician's synoptic view of the arts with the tendency of arts educators to see their own subject in isolation from the concerns of other art forms. Current trends towards a narrow formalism and contempt for nonaesthetic significance in the teaching of music and painting, together with the mirror opposite trend in the teaching of literature, have fragmented arts faculties. I argue that such divisions are incoherent and that arts education would be far more effective if students were introduced to common aspects of a variety of art forms.

MC ALLISTER, James W. Dirac and the Aesthetic Evaluation of Theories. Method Sci, 23(2), 87-102, 1990.

The paper investigates the role which P A M Dirac attributed to aesthetic judgements in the endorsement and rejection of scientific theories.

MC ANINCH, Amy. Explaining the Persistence of Irrelevance. Proc Phil Educ, 45, 136-139, 1989.

MC ANINCH, Stuart A. The Educational Theory of Mary Sheldon Barnes: Inquiry Learning as Indoctrination in History Education. Educ Theor, 40(1), 45-52, Wint 90.

MC CALL, Catherine. Young Children Generate Philosophical Ideas.

Thinking, 8(2), 22-41, 1989.

MC CALL, Storrs and ARMSTRONG, D M. God's Lottery. Analysis, 49(4), 223-224, O 89.

When Cantor's definition of equinumerousness as one-one correspondence is pitted against the intuition that no set can be the same size as one of its own proper subsets, which side wins? An answer is given by God's lottery, in which God offers choices between different sets of lottery tickets.

MC CALLUM, John. Pragmatism and the Theory of the Reader. S Afr J Phil, 9(2), 68-88, My 90.

Under the broad rubric of reader-oriented literary studies, it is possible to distinguish three different kinds of projects: *formalist* projects which identify rhetorical modes of address and their effectiveness; *empirical* projects which involve the positive identification of readers and their social environment; and *foundationalist* projects in terms of which particular interpretive strategies are justified by an appeal to an account of interpretation in general. Arguing that both formalist and empirical projects rely on foundationalist projects in order to *justify* their approaches, the article sets out a critique of foundationalism as it manifests itself in the Theory of the Reader. This critique is divided roughly into two sections. The first deals with the identification of the foundationalist strategies which provide the underpinnings of phenomenological, psychological, historical and sociological reader studies, while the second deals with the critique proper, where a number of arguments are mustered from the ranks of pragmatists such as Richard Rorty and Stanley Fish who suggest that *any* foundationalist project is doomed to failure.

MC CANN, Hugh J. Practical Rationality: Some Kantian Reflections. J Phil Res, 15, 57-77, 1990.

Recent views on practical rationality harmonize well with a fundamentally Kantian conception of the foundations of morality. Rationality in practical thinking is not a matter of valid reasoning, or of following maximization principles. From an agent-centered perspective, it consists in observing certain standards of consistency. In themselves, these standards lack the force of duties, hence there can be no irresolvable conflict between rationality and morality. Furthermore, the Kantian test of universalization for maxims of actions may be seen as adapting agent-centered standards of consistency to the task of specifying moral duties, so that objective rationality and morality are one and the same.

MC CARNEY, J. "'Ideology' in Marx and Engels": A Reply. Phil Forum, 21(4), 451-462, Sum 90.

MC CARNEY, Joseph. Social Theory and the Crisis of Marxism. New York, Verso, 1990

MC CARTHY, Barry. "Adult Friendships" in Person to Person, GRAHAM, George (ed), 32-45. Philadelphia, Temple Univ Pr, 1989.

MC CARTHY, Charles R and CARTER, Michele and WICHMAN, Alison. Regulating AIDS Research on Infants and Children: The Moral Task of Institutional Review Boards. Bridges, 2(1-2), 63-73, Spr-Sum 90.

Acquired Immunodeficiency Syndrome (AIDS) has created ethical dilemmas for research investigators as well as other healthcare professionals. One difficult problem facing research investigators and Institutional Review Boards (IRBs) (committees required to review and approve proposed research involving human subjects before the projects can be initiated) is to determine if, when, and under what circumstances it is permissible to conduct research involving children and infants infected with the AIDS virus as research subjects. The authors review existing Health and Human Services (HHS) regulations for the Protection of Human Subjects, present a prototypical case involving an infant infected with the AIDS virus, and conclude that the regulations provide a suitable framework for IRBs to consider the ethical problems facing pediatric AIDS research.

MC CARTHY, Jeremiah. An Account of Peirce's Proof of Pragmatism. Trans Peirce Soc, 26(1), 63-113, Wint 90.

MC CARTHY, Michael. The Crisis of Philosophy. Albany, SUNY Pr, 1989

This book explores the reconception of philosophy brought about by momentous theoretical and cultural changes of the last two centuries. The metaphilosophical programs of Frege, Husserl, Wittgenstein, Carnap, Sellars, Dewey, Quine and Rorty are carefully presented and an assessment is made of their merits and limitations. The dialectical assessment climaxes in a defense of Bernard Lonergan's integrative strategy rooted in cognitional theory. Lonergan's philosophical project is structurally developed and shown to be continuous with philosophy's historic purposes and equal to the exigencies of the present.

MC CARTHY, Thomas. The Critique of Impure Reason: Foucault and the Frankfurt School. Polit Theory, 18(3), 437-469, Ag 90.

MC CARTHY, Thomas. Ironist Theory as a Vocation: A Response to

Rorty's Reply. Crit Inquiry, 16(3), 644-655, Spr 90.

MC CARTHY, Thomas. The Politics of the Ineffable: Derrida's Deconstructionism. Phil Forum, 21(1-2), 146-168, Fall-Wint 89-90.

MC CARTHY, Thomas. Private Irony and Public Decency: Richard Rorty's New Pragmatism. Crit Inquiry, 16(2), 355-370, Wint 89.

MC CARTY, Charles and MC CARTY, Luise Prior. Semantic Physiology: Wittgenstein on Pedagogy. Proc Phil Educ, 45, 231-243, 1989.

MC CARTY, L Thorne. Artificial Intelligence and Law: How To Get There From Here. Ratio Juris, 3(2), 189-200, Jl 90.

This paper offers a survey of the current state of artificial intelligence and law, and makes recommendations for future research. Two main areas of investigation are discussed: the practical work on intelligent legal information systems, and the theoretical work on computational models of legal reasoning. In both areas, the knowledge representation problem is identified as the most important issue facing this field.

MC CARTY, Luise Prior and MC CARTY, Charles. Semantic Physiology: Wittgenstein on Pedagogy. Proc Phil Educ, 45, 231-243, 1989.

MC CARTY, Richard. Business and Benevolence. Bus Prof Ethics J, 7(2), 63-83, Sum 88.

While business activity and the profit motive seem incompatible with morally worthy benevolence, benevolent business activities such as "cause-related marketing" are becoming increasingly more common. The profit motive does not preclude truly benevolent business activities if virtuous business people are sometimes willing to forego maximum profit for the good of others.

MC CAULEY, Robert N and LAWSON, E Thomas. *Rethinking Religion: Connecting Cognition and Culture*. New York, Cambridge Univ Pr, 1990

A critique of interpretive approaches to the study of religion, and a proposal, instead of a cognitive explanatory theory which acknowledges the contributions of intellectualist, symbolist and structuralist theories but goes beyond them. The book presents a formal system for representing ritual actions that can be paired with a religious conceptual scheme to yield both descriptions of ritual acts and universal principles for all religious ritual systems. The theory makes use of strategies available from the cognitive sciences.

MC CLELLAN, James E. Call to Coalition: A Response to Selman and Ross. Proc Phil Educ, 45, 55-60, 1989.

Selman and Ross's objections to "Canpro" are answered in detail. Insistence on Q(uine)-consistent use of epistemic predicates does not negate "empathy" with victims of injustice. A Q-consistent interpretation of 'believes that Y' shown to have exactly the explanatory power such predication has in ordinary usage, does not require quantifying into opaque contexts. Q-consistent theory held necessary for effective action to stop worldwide war against children. Soft-headed liberals invited to join with radicals in calling a worldwide teachers conference on education for peace.

MC CLENDON JR, James W and MURPHY, Nancey. Distinguishing Modern and Postmodern Theologies. Mod Theol, 5(3), 191-214, Ap 89.

MC CLENNEN, Edward F. *Rationality and Dynamic Choice: Foundational Explorations*. New York, Cambridge Univ Pr, 1990

The best argument for the ordering and independence axioms of the standard theory of expected-utility and subjective probability is that non-conformity makes one liable to a pragmatically costly form of dynamic inconsistency. The argument, however, invokes an overly restrictive conception of rational dynamic choice. What emerges is a much more liberal theory of individual choice, within which both the expected-utility hypothesis, and determinate subjective probabilities, are seen to be problematic. The analysis also yields a surprising bonus: rational interdependent choice (the object of game theory) needs to be reconceptualized along much more "cooperative" lines.

MC CLURE, Kirstie M. Difference, Diversity, and the Limits of Toleration. Polit Theory, 18(3), 361-391, Ag 90.

MC COLM, Gregory L. Parametrization Over Inductive Relations of a Bounded Number of Variables. Annals Pure Applied Log, 48(2), 103-134, Jl 90.

We present a Parameterization Theorem for (positive elementary) inductions that use a bounded number of variables. We investigate associated halting problem(s) on classes of finite structures and on solitary 'unreasonable' structures. These results involve the complexity of the inductive relations—and the complexity of the structure or class of structures on which these relations live. We also apply this Parameterization Theorem to Moschovakis closure ordinals, to determine when the closure ordinal is greater than w, and to investigate the closure ordinals of unreasonable structures.

MC COLM, Gregory L. Some Restrictions on Simple Fixed Points of the Integers. J Sym Log, 54(4), 1324-1345, D 89.

A function is *recursive* (in given operations) if its values are computed explicitly and uniformly in terms of other "previously computed" values of itself and (perhaps) other "simultaneously computed" recursive functions. Here, "explicitly" includes definition by cases. We investigate those recursive functions on the structure $N = \langle \omega, 0, succ, pred \rangle$ that are computed in terms of themselves only, without other simultaneously computed recursive functions.

MC CONNELL, Terrance. 'Ought' Implies 'Can' and the Scope of Moral Requirements. Philosophia (Israel), 19(4), 437-454, D 89.

This paper examines two contexts in ethical theory that some have thought support the claim that attempts, rather than actions, are what are morally required of agents. In each context there is an appeal to the principle that 'ought' implies 'can'. I begin by explaining how I think appeals to this principle typically work. I conclude that not only do the contexts in question not demonstrate that moral requirements range over attempts, but also that any argument in support of that conclusion has serious obstacles to overcome.

MC CONNELL-GINET, Sally and CHIERCHIA, Gennaro. *Meaning and Grammar: An Introduction to Semantics*. Cambridge, MIT Pr, 1990

This book is a self-contained introduction to natural language semantics that addresses the major theoretical questions in the field and shows how the machinery of logical semantics can be used in the empirical study of natural language. The work deals with the following issues: quantification and logical form, the syntax/semantics interface, context and presuppositions, speech acts, the philosophical foundations of semantics, modalities, generalized quantifiers.

MC COOL, Gerald A. Why St Thomas Stays Alive. Int Phil Quart, 30(3), 275-287, S 90.

MC CORMICK, John E. Santayana's Idea of the Tragic. Bull Santayana Soc, 1, 1-11, Fall 83.

MC CORMICK, Peter. Interpretation in Aesthetics: Theories and Practices. Monist, 73(2), 167-180, Ap 90.

MC CULLAGH, C Behan. The Rationality of Emotions and of Emotional Behaviour. Austl J Phil, 68(1), 44-58, Mr 90.

Amelie O Rorty has distinguished two senses of rationality, a narrow sense of being logically derived from accepted premises, and a broad sense of being 'appropriately formed to serve our thriving'. This paper argues that emotions are generally not rational in the narrow sense; and that while generic emotions may be rational in the broad sense, particular emotions may not. The views of Solomon, Warnock and de Sousa on this subject are shown to be inadequate. The paper goes on to characterize emotional behaviour as behaviour constrained by emotion, and argues that kinds of emotional behaviour can be rational in the broad sense, but that particular instances are rational in neither sense, unless they express rationally cultivated emotions.

MC CULLOCH, Gregory. Dennett's Little Grains of Salt. Phil Quart, 40(158), 1-12, Ja 90.

MC CULLOCH, Gregory. Honderich on the Indispensability of the Mental. Analysis, 50(1), 24-29, Ja 90.

MC CULLOCH, Warren S. *Embodiments of Mind*. Cambridge, MIT Pr, 1988

In this collection of 21 essays and lectures the author pursues a physiological theory of knowldge that touches on philosophy, neurology, and psychology. (edited)

MC CUMBER, John. Hegel on Habit. Owl Minerva, 21(2), 155-164, Spr 90.

Though given only the briefest of discussions in his System, Hegel's concept of habit plays important roles in some of the major transitions of that System. Attention to it can also, I argue, reconcile the three disparate ways Hegel refers to his own historical period: as one of decline, of disruption, and of the "emergence of Spirit" into the sunlight.

MC CUMBER, John. Is a Post-Hegelian Ethics Possible? Res Phenomenol, 18, 125-147, 1988.

MC DANIEL, Jay. Six Characteristics of a Postpatriarchal Christianity. Zygon, 25(2), 187-217, Je 90.

Christianity is best understood not as a set of timeless doctrines, but as a historical movement capable of change and growth. In this respect, Christianity is like a science. Heretofore, most instances of Christianity have exhibited certain ways of thinking that, taken as a whole, have led to the subordination of women (and the Earth and animals as well) to men in power. This article describes these ways of thinking, then contrasts six ways of thinking and acting that can inform postpatriarchal Christianity and science.

MC DERMOTT, John J. "The Pragmatists" in *Reading Philosophy for the Twenty-First Century*, MC LEAN, George F (ed), 245-263. Lanham, Univ Pr of America, 1989.

MC DERMOTT, John M. Love and the Natural Law. Vera Lex, 9(1), 11-12, 1989.

Natural law theories vary according to their understanding of nature and its necessities: are its laws objectively universal or subjectively particular? Love is also interpreted as eros or agape, physical or ecstatic. The underlying problem involves the relation of absolute to relative, infinite to finite. Love exhibits the same paradoxical structure as thought—only if thought is seen to reflect love's mystery can it avoid being destroyed by its own conundrums. So necessity and ecstatic freedom are united, and an absolute norm for scientific probabilities as asymptotic approximations is established. Theorists should confirm natural signs of love in family, etc.

MC DONALD, Henry. Crossroads of Skepticism: Wittgenstein, Derrida, and Ostensive Definition. Phil Forum, 21(3), 261-276, Spr 90.

MC DONALD, Ian. Group Rights. Phil Papers, 18(2), 117-136, S 89.

MC DONALD, Ross A and VICTOR, Bart. Towards the Integration of Individual and Moral Agencies. Bus Prof Ethics J, 7(3-4), 103-118, Fall-Wint 88.

MC DOWELL, John. "One Strand in the Private Language Argument" in *Wittgenstein in Focus—Im Brennpunkt: Wittgenstein*, MC GUINNESS, Brian (ed), 285-303. Amsterdam, Rodopi, 1989.

In reflecting about experience, philosophers are prone to fall into a dualism of conceptual scheme and preconceptual given, according to which the most basic judgments of experience are grounded in nonconceptual impingements on subjects of experience. This idea is dubiously coherent: relations of grounding or justification should hold between conceptually structured items. This thought has been widely applied to 'outer' experience; at least some of the Private Language Argument can be read as applying it to 'inner' experience. In this light, Wittgenstein's suggestion that a sensation is 'not a something' seems infelicitous. The main point of this reading of Wittgenstein is in Richard Rorty's *Philosophy and the Mirror of Nature*; but Rorty locates the point in the context of a subtle materialism, and a 'communitarian' substitute for first-person authority, which seem non-Wittgensteinian.

MC DOWELL, John. Peacocke and Evans on Demonstrative Content. Mind, 99(394), 255-266, Ap 90.

MC EVOY, James. Philosophie fondamentale. Rev Phil Louvain, 87(76), 626-628, N 89.

MC EVOY, John G. Lavoisier, Priestley, and the *Philosophes*: Epistemic and Linguistic Dimensions to the Chemical Revolution. Man Nature, 8, 91-98, 1989.

The chemical revolution was an integral part of the Enlightenment. The Enlightenment notion of the self-defining subject established a unitary framework of regulative principles, dealing with the relation between science and metaphysics, the method of analysis, and the relation between thought and language, which were variously interpreted in the opposing views that Lavoisier and Priestley developed about the ontology of chemistry, the nature of experimentation, the reform of the chemical nomenclature, and the institutional organization of science. This study concentrates on some of the epistemic and linguistic issues raised by this scientific dialectic in a way that delimits Foucault's notion of the classical *episteme*.

MC EWAN, Hunter. Teaching and Rhetoric. Proc Phil Educ, 45, 203-211, 1989.

MC EWAN, Hunter. What Other Worlds Have to Say About Ontological Dependence: Is There Life in the Logical Thesis? Educ Theor, 40(3), 381-390, Sum 90.

The article demonstrates the paradoxes that arise from the traditional debate over the relationship between teaching and learning. A new approach is proposed that focuses attention on the logical relationship between content taught and content learned. A number of alternatives are considered, depending on the nature of the logical connection. An argument is made for a more pluralistic conception of how teaching something can be connected to learning it—one that corresponds to the relationship between a text and a reader.

MC FALLS JR, Joseph and JONES, Brian J and GALLAGHER III, Bernard J. Toward a Unified Model for Social Problems Theory. J Theor Soc Behav, 19(3), 337-356, S 89.

The article argues for the importance of conceptualizing social problems

through a two-dimensional theory. Specifically, our position would extend current constructionist accounts by formally considering the objective dimension (evidence of the social harm associated with a problem) in relation to the subjective dimension (public opinion about the seriousness of a problem). Unemployment and sex roles are developed as case studies of the theoretical model.

MC FEE, Graham. Art, Education, and Life-Issues. J Aes Educ, 22(3), 37-48, Fall 88.

MC GARY, Howard. Forgiveness. Amer Phil Quart, 26(4), 343-351, O 89.

A primary purpose of this paper is to argue that forgiveness is a virtue, but that this virtue does not require a duty to forgive if a duty to forgive is correlated with a right to be forgiven. It is argued that good reasons for forgiving or failing to forgive can be self-pertaining and that genuine cases of forgiveness involve the overcoming of potentially harmful feelings like resentment. This account of forgiveness explains why a correct account of forgiveness is not as voluntaristic as it is often made out to be.

MC GEE, Gail W and HEACOCK, Marian V. Whistleblowing: An Ethical Issue in Organizational and Human Behavior. Bus Prof Ethics J, 6(4), 35-46, Wint 87.

Whistleblowing is an extremely crucial issue for organizations, employees, and the public at large. Therefore, it is important that we develop greater understanding of the whistleblowing process, including its predictors and effects. This paper provides a brief overview of the whistleblowing literature, including descriptive, theoretical, and empirical. Based on this review, we offer some suggestions regarding specific delineations of whistleblowing for use by organizations, and make recommendations for future whistleblowing research.

MC GEE, Vann. Applying Kripke's Theory of Truth. J Phil, 86(10), 530-539, O 89.

The methods Kripke develops in his "Outline of a Theory of Truth" are utilized to give a theory of truth for a language within the language itself, without recourse to a richer metalanguage. The plan is to treat 'true' as a vague predicate, and to develop an account according to which '"p" is true' is definitely true, definitely untrue, or unsettled according as 'p' is definitely true, definitely untrue, or unsettled. 'Definitely true' is likewise treated as a vague predicate, and Kripke's techniques are employed to develop, with the object language, a consistent theory of both truth and definite truth.

MC GEE, Vann. Conditional Probabilities and Compounds of Conditionals. Phil Rev, 98(4), 485-541, O 89.

A probabilistic theory of conditionals is developed, based upon the idea that the subjective probability of an indicative conditional "If p then q" is the probability q would acquire if we learned p with certainty, and we learned nothing else. The central thesis governing the probability calculus is that, if p and r are incompatible, conditional-free statements, then r and "If p then q" are probabilistically independent. Arguments supporting the thesis are based upon Dutch book theory and upon Jeffrey probability kinematics. Using the thesis, one derives the law that, for simple conditionals, the probability of a conditional is the conditional probability of the consequent given the antecedent, yet one does not run afoul of the Lewis triviality theorem. A probabilistic account of validity is given, with a complete and decidable deductive calculus, and probabilistic validity is shown to coincide with validity in a modified version of Stalnaker's possible-world semantics.

MC GHEE, Michael. Notes on a Great Erotic. Phil Invest, 13(3), 258-272, Jl 90.

The Great Erotic is Socrates. Doubts are raised about the condemnation offered by Nietzsche and an attempt made to show that Plato's Socrates is closer than Nietzsche realises to the latter's views about the possibility of transforming the passions. This discussion provides the context for an attempt to show how Plato wavers between an account of 'harmony' that depends upon 'continence' (the *Republic*) and one that depends upon 'temperance' (the *Symposium*). This is related to an expressivist view of values that sees them as reflecting the systematic changes of orientation or real preference described by Diotima.

MC GINN, Colin. *Mental Content*. Cambridge, Blackwell, 1989

MC GINN, Marie. *Sense and Certainty: A Dissolution of Scepticism*. Cambridge, Blackwell, 1988

This book is concerned with the question whether there is a satisfactory rebuttal of external world scepticism. It argues that the justifications the sceptic requires cannot be given, but that his conclusion is both beyond belief and in conflict with common sense; this makes both scepticism and the dogmatic assumption of common sense unsatisfactory. It attempts to construct a nondogmatic defence of common sense, by giving an account of the nature of the judgments that form the framework of our practice, which shows why the absence of justification is not a lack. Philosophers discussed include Wittgenstein, Moore, Austin, Cavell, Stroud.

MC GLASHAN, A R. The Use of Symbols in Religion from the Perspective of Analytical Psychology. Relig Stud, 25(4), 501-520, D 89.

MC GOVERN, Arthur F and RODZINSKA, Aleksandra (trans) and PETROWICZ, Lech (trans). Response to Janusz's "Christianity and Marxism". Dialec Hum, 14(1), 89-92, Wint 87.

McGovern wrote "Is Atheism Essential to Marxism?" for the *Journal of Ecumenical Studies* (Summer, 1985). He argued that Marxist socialism need not be atheistic. Kuczynski responded in *Dialectics and Humanism*, arguing that McGovern effectively calls for Marxists to give up their atheism. McGovern rejects that interpretation, and agrees that neither Christianity nor Marxism should seek dominance. He argues also that a humanistic materialism which stresses human initiative in transforming society, a humanism Kuczynski views as essential to Marxism, does not conflict with contemporary Christian views about change.

MC GOVERN, Edythe M. Opening the Door to Moral Education. Free Inq, 10(1), 14-20, Wint 89-90.

MC GOWAN, William H. Berkeley Kicking His Own Stones. Indian Phil Quart, 16(4), 433-446, O 89.

When Samuel Johnson kicked the stone in his celebrated refutation of Berkeley's immaterialism he was, in effect, repeating what Berkeley unwittingly had already done in his own life efforts. The use of Berkeley's biography to criticize his own theory—in this case, to show its insufficient recognition of material recalcitrance—defies current academic propriety, which seeks to avoid the genetic fallacy. Yet both Berkeley's pragmatism and his precociousness invite a testificatory reading of his biography.

MC GRADE, Arthur Stephen (ed) and HOOKER, Richard. *Of the Laws of Ecclesiastical Polity (Preface, Book I, Book VIII), Richard Hooker*. New York, Cambridge Univ Pr, 1989

MC GRATH, P J. The Refutation of the Ontological Argument. Phil Quart, 40(159), 195-212, Ap 90.

MC GRAY, James W. Universal Prescriptivism and Practical Skepticism. Phil Papers, 19(1), 37-51, Ap 90.

The aim of this paper is to evaluate Hare's moral theory. Its weakness is a practical one. It is anything but easy to apply, and one is almost never sure one has applied it properly. Most of Hare's own work in applied ethics amounts to guesswork or rules so general that they are almost useless in practice. The 'moral' is that applied ethics is extremely difficult, and its claims are almost always tentative.

MC GUINNESS, Brian (ed) and HALLER, Rudolf (ed). *Wittgenstein in Focus—Im Brennpunkt: Wittgenstein*. Amsterdam, Rodopi, 1989

MC GUINNESS, Brian. "Wittgenstein's Pre-*Tractatus* Manuscripts" in *Wittgenstein in Focus—Im Brennpunkt: Wittgenstein*, MC GUINNESS, Brian (ed), 35-47. Amsterdam, Rodopi, 1989.

There has recently come to light a list of manuscripts and typescripts with instructions for their disposal, which suggest a number of hypotheses concerning the composition of Wittgenstein's only printed work, the *Tractatus*. In this article an attempt is made at identifying these documents with the help of biographical facts of the period 1914-1918. As a result it becomes highly improbable that many of the notebooks from which the *Tractatus* was composed have been lost. Rather it is suggested that the various stages of the "Prototractatus" can finally be traced on the basis of the now-available evidence.

MC GUINNESS, Celia. The *Fundamental Constitutions of Carolina* as a Tool for Lockean Scholarship. Interpretation, 17(1), 127-143, Fall 89.

MC HENRY, Leemon B. The Philosophical Writings of Victor A Lowe (1907-1988). Trans Peirce Soc, 25(3), 333-339, Sum 89.

This brief article is an appreciative survey of Victor Lowe's philosophical writings, and focuses attention on his contributions to American philosophy, and especially that of A N Whitehead.

MC INERNEY, Peter K. Does a Fetus Already Have a Future-like-ours? J Phil, 87(5), 264-268, My 90.

The article argues that a fetus is not related to a personal future in the same way that a normal adult human is related to his or her personal future. In opposition to Marquis, the article argues that at its time a fetus does not already have a personal future of which it can be deprived. For this reason, killing a fetus is morally very different from killing a normal adult human.

MC INERNY, Ralph. La importancia de la Poética para entender la Etica aristotélica. Anu Filosof, 20(2), 85-93, 1987.

MC INERNY, Ralph. La materia prima es conocida por analogía. Rev Filosof (Argentina), 2(2), 99-105, N 87.

There are many of Aristotle's concepts that were interpreted again by Aquinas in his work. This paper is concerned with the Aristotelian concept of matter and it points out the peculiar interpretation made by Thomas. Firstly, the author explains the way in which Aquinas understands the expression κατ αναλογιαν when is said that the prime matter is known by analogy. Secondly, it when is said that the prime matter is known by analogy. Secondly, it is indicated the Thomistic sense of analogy; lastly, it is suggested how Thomas extends analogically the term "matter" and its importance in order to understand the thesis according to the intellectual knowledge is immaterial.

MC INTYRE, Jane L. Character: A Humean Account. Hist Phil Quart, 7(2), 193-206, Ap 90.

MC INTYRE, Jane L. Personal Identity and the Passions. J Hist Phil, 27(4), 545-557, O 89.

In two places in the *Treatise* Hume distinguishes "personal identity as it regards our thought or imagination" from personal identity "as it regards the passions." Book I discusses only the former, but Book II, "Of the Passions," contains no explicit examination of personal identity. The article argues that Hume recognized issues about personal identity, particularly *concern* with the past and the future, that could not be addressed within the confines of the theory of the imagination in Book I. It is argued, however, that the theory of the passions in Book II of the *Treatise* can explain self-concern, and thereby provides the resources for completing Hume's account of personal identity.

MC KEEN, C A and BURKE, R J. Mentoring in Organizations: Implications for Women. J Bus Ethics, 9(4-5), 317-332, Ap-My 90.

This paper reviews the literature on the mentoring process in organizations and why mentoring can be critical to the career success of women managers and professionals. It examines some of the reasons why it is more difficult for women to find mentors than it is for men. Particular attention is paid to potential problems in cross-gender mentoring. A feminist perspective is then applied to the general notion of mentorships for women. The paper concludes with an examination of what organizations can do to further mentor relationships and an agenda for further research in this area.

MC KENNA, Edward and WADE, Maurice and ZANNONI, Diane. Rawls and the Minimum Demands of Justice. J Value Inq, 24(2), 85-108, Ap 90.

We demonstrate that by focusing on Rawls's view of the nature of the person and on his use of the Aristotelian Principle it is possible to counter many of the criticisms made against Rawls. In particular, we show why Rawls is correct in asserting that individuals in the original position will not use the principle of insufficient reason to assign probabilities to unknown states of nature, nor will they accept the principle of utility for the purposes of distributing primary goods. We then show, however, that the use of the Aristotelian Principle is more likely to lead to a distribution principle which guarantees minimum basic necessities than it is to lead to the difference principle.

MC KERLIE, Dennis. Justice Between Age-Groups: A Comment on Norman Daniels. J Applied Phil, 6(2), 227-234, O 89.

Norman Daniels suggests that the just distribution of resources between different age-groups is determined by the choice a prudential agent would make in budgeting resources over the different temporal stages of a single life. He calls this view the "prudential lifespan account" of justice between age-groups. Daniels thinks that the view recommends a rough kind of equality in resources between age-groups. I argue that in the case of a single life prudence would choose an unequal distribution of resources. Consequently, using prudence to model distribution between age-groups might severely restrict the share of resources assigned to the elderly. If we think that extreme inequality between age-groups would be unjust, we should continue to think of justice between age-groups as a problem concerned with the relationship between different lives. But we should apply the requirement of equality to the temporal parts of lives, not just to complete lives.

MC KIM, Robert. The Hiddenness of God. Relig Stud, 26(1), 141-161, Mr 90.

The plausibility of various attempts to account for the fact that, if God exists, the existence and nature of God are unclear and puzzling to human beings is discussed. These attempts to account for God's hiddenness include appeals to God's infinity, to human finitude, to human sin, and to the desirability of our being in a position to choose our religious beliefs. I argue that the fact that God is hidden suggests both that our beliefs about God should be held tentatively and that it probably is not important which such beliefs are held.

MC KIM, Robert. Religious Belief and Religious Diversity. Irish Phil J, 6(2), 275-302, 1989.

There is deep and widespread disagreement among the main religious traditions on numerous issues which are central to those traditions. This suggests that the religions are dealing with areas of some mystery and perplexity, and that if one is going to hold religious beliefs, one should hold them tentatively.

MC KINNEY, Ronald H. The Origins of Post-Modernism: The Ariosto-Tasso Debate. Phil Today, 33(3), 232-244, Fall 89.

In this essay I examine the sixteenth century quarrel in the Italian literary Renaissance between Ariosto and Tasso. I attempt to show the similarities and differences between this battle between the "ancients" and "moderns" and that between "Modernists" and "Postmodernists" today. Both are shown to revolve around the perennial problem of the One and the Many. However, any historiographic simplicity is avoided by revealing the inevitable paradoxes that arise in drawing parallels between these two debates.

MC KINNON, Christine. Ways of Wrong-Doing, the Vices, and Cruelty. J Value Inq, 23(4), 319-335, D 89.

MC KONKIE, Stanford S and WRIGHT, N Dale. "Introduction" in *Papers on the Ethics of Administration*, WRIGHT, N Dale (ed), 1-20. Albany, SUNY Pr, 1988.

MC LAUGHLIN, Brian P. Incontinent Belief. J Phil Res, 15, 115-126, 1990.

Alfred Mele has recently attempted to direct attention to a neglected species of irrational belief which he calls 'incontinent belief'. He has devoted a paper and an entire chapter (chapter eight) of his book, *Irrationality* (Oxford University Press, 1987) to explaining its logical possibility. In what follows, I will appeal to familiar facts about the difference between belief and action to make a case that it is *entirely unproblematic* that incontinent belief is logically possible. In the process, I will call into question the philosophical interest of incontinent belief. If what I say is correct, incontinent belief does not warrant the attention of philosophers of mind.

MC LAUGHLIN, Brian P. "Why Perception is not Singular Reference" in *Cause, Mind, and Reality: Essays Honoring C B Martin*, HEIL, John (ed), 111-120. Norwell, Kluwer, 1989.

MC LAUGHLIN, Robert N. On a Similarity Between Natural Law Theories and English Legal Positivism. Phil Quart, 39(157), 445-462, O 89.

MC LEAN, Edward B. Natural Law Elements in Pound's Philosophy of Law? Vera Lex, 7(2), 11-13, 1987.

MC LEAN, George F (ed) and TANG, Yi-Jie (ed) and ZHEN, Li (ed). *Man and Nature: The Chinese Tradition and the Future*. Lanham, Univ Pr of America, 1989

MC LEAN, George F. "The Evolution of Approaches to Philosophy" in *Reading Philosophy for the Twenty-First Century*, MC LEAN, George F (ed), 59-76. Lanham, Univ Pr of America, 1989.

MC LEAN, George F. "Hermeneutics and Heritage" in *Man and Nature: The Chinese Tradition and the Future*, TANG, Yi-Jie (ed), 57-70. Lanham, Univ Pr of America, 1989.

The paper treats the relation of hermeneutics to the development, reception and application of values. It identifies the mode and role of social critique in relation to tradition as bearer of values. The mutual complementarity of the two is noted, which points to the foundational importance of tradition and cultural heritage considered as the work of freedom unveiling transcendent values.

MC LEAN, George F. "Hermeneutics, Cultural Heritage and Social Critique" in *Reading Philosophy for the Twenty-First Century*, MC LEAN, George F (ed), 19-56. Lanham, Univ Pr of America, 1989.

MC LEAN, George F. "Hermeneutics, Historicity and Values" in *The Social Context and Values: Perspectives of the Americas*, MC LEAN, George F (ed), 15-39. Lanham, Univ Pr of America, 1989.

The article treats the significance of cultural heritage for the contemporary change. Using the hermeneutics of H G Gadamer, it studies first the constitution of tradition, with special attention to the roles of community, time and authority. Second, the application of a cultural heritage to the present is studied in terms of a dialogue of horizons by a method of question and answer. Finally, this is related to critical hermeneutics.

MC LEAN, George F (ed). *Reading Philosophy for the Twenty-First Century*. Lanham, Univ Pr of America, 1989

MC LEAN, George F (ed) and PEGORARO, Olinto (ed). *The Social Context and Values: Perspectives of the Americas*. Lanham, Univ Pr of America, 1989

The first part of this work, largely by Latin American philosophers, treats

hermeneutics and the socio-historical context of values. Its chapters concern historicity, hermeneutics and the sociological and psychoanalytic critique of values. The second part treats the relation of value horizons to liberation from four points of view: the phenomenological and existential philosophy of the person, technological development, aesthetics and religion.

MC MAHON, Christopher. The Better Endowed and the Difference Principle. Analysis, 49(4), 213-216, O 89.

This article argues that if Rawls's difference principle must look plausible to people outside the original position, who know their attributes, Nozick is right in thinking that it leaves something to be desired. For on one natural way of measuring the effects of the transition from a regime of strict equality to a regime of the difference principle, the transition would not, as it seems, benefit those better endowed with natural and social advantages in a way that those worse endowed could not object to. Rather it would benefit those worse endowed in a way that the better endowed could object to.

MC MAHON, Christopher. Managerial Authority. Ethics, 100(1), 33-53, O 89.

This paper considers whether morality requires that managerial decisions be made democratically by employees. Three conceptions of the legitimacy of managerial authority are examined. It is argued that contractual obligations undertaken in a labor market cannot ground managerial authority. Then the possibility of applying to managerial contexts two conceptions usually reserved for governments is considered. It is argued that nondemocratic managerial structures, such as those typical of capitalism, can satisfy one of these conceptions but not the other. The paper concludes by considering the implications of this result for the moral acceptability of the typical capitalist arrangement.

MC MAHON, Christopher. Openness. Can J Phil, 20(1), 29-46, Mr 90.

The paper provides an account of morally valuable openness. Openness is presented as involving not merely refraining from deception but also eliminating ignorance and disabusing people of false beliefs. A principle of openness is formulated and defended as a moral requirement. Openness is mapped onto Chisholm and Feehan's taxonomy of deception, and the greater wrongness of lying as opposed to other forms of deception is discussed.

MC MORRIS, Neville. *The Natures of Science*. Madison, F Dickinson Univ Pr, 1989

This book makes attempts to examine some of the intellectual roots of what we now know as science, and to fashion a historical sketch of its development. It also challenges the monolithic view of science, and amasses evidence to persuade us that science is a much more multifaceted structure than is often assumed. One result arising from these attempts is that science's roots in the *episteme* of Aristotle have never dried up, and indeed science is seen to have long flourished as the best example of epistemology.

MC MULLIN, Ernan. Comment: Duhem's Middle Way. Synthese, 83(3), 421-430, Je 90.

Duhem attempted to find a middle way between two positions he regarded as extremes, the conventionalism of Poincaré and the scientific realism of the majority of his scientific colleagues. He argued that conventionalism exaggerated the arbitrariness of scientific formulations, but that belief in atoms and electrons erred in the opposite direction by attributing too much logical force to explanatory theories. The instrumentalist sympathies so apparent in Duhem's writings on the history of astronomy are only partially counterbalanced by his view that science is progressing toward a 'natural classification' of the world.

MC MULLIN, Ernan. "The Explanation of Distant Action: Historical Notes" in *Philosophical Consequences of Quantum Theory: Reflections on Bell's Theorem*, CUSHING, James T (ed), 272-302. Notre Dame, Univ Notre Dame Pr, 1989.

Traces the principle of contact action in Aristotle and Descartes, and then goes on to discuss the way in which Kepler and Newton transformed the issue of explaining apparent action at a distance. The dual status of gravity as cause and as effect faced Newton with a dilemma he was never able to overcome successfully.

MC MULLIN, Ernan. "The Goals of Natural Science" in *Scientific Knowledge Socialized*, HRONSZKY, Imre (ed), 27-58. Norwell, Kluwer, 1989.

Prediction and explanation of natural phenomena are concerns that go a long way back in the human story. This essay (1) traces the gradual formation of a precise and successful predictive practice in ancient Babylonia and of an explanatory practice in ancient Greece; (2) shows that the two kinds of practices coexisted uneasily for many centuries until they were blended more or less successfully in the natural science of the late seventeenth century, and (3) derives some morals for contemporary philosophy of science from this historical narrative.

MC MURTRY, John. The Unspeakable: Understanding the System of Fallacy in the Media. Inform Log, 10(3), 133-150, Fall 88.

This article argues that there is a deep structure of unreason which operates beneath the reach of current tools of logical detection: (i) because its fallacy lies not in what is asserted in making a case, but in what is ruled out *from* being asserted in making a case; and (ii) because the bearer of its fallacy is not the premiss or inference of any route of assertion, but an overall *field* of assertion and silence. The article focuses its analysis on the contemporary print media, but the structure of falsehood it discloses can be detected across cultures and sign systems. Its operations are shown to conform to four principles of selection and exclusion which determine what is and what is not communicated in any given social regime.

MC NEILL, Desmond. Alternative Interpretations of Aristotle on Exchange and Reciprocity. Pub Affairs Quart, 4(1), 55-68, Ja 90.

MC PECK, John E. Is Reading a "Higher Order Skill"? Proc Phil Educ, 45, 154-162, 1989.

MC TAGGART, John McTaggart Ellis and BROAD, C D (ed). *The Nature of Existence, Volume I*. New York, Cambridge Univ Pr, 1988

This volume is a reprint of McTaggart's now-classic defense of idealism which was originally published in 1927. The entire work (2 volumes) represents the author's theory of the nature of the universe. Volume 1 sets out "to determine as far as possible the characteristics which belong to all that exists, or which belong to existence as a whole." (staff)

MC TAGGART, John McTaggart Ellis and BROAD, C D (ed). *The Nature of Existence, Volume II*. New York, Cambridge Univ Pr, 1988

This volume is a reprint of McTaggart's now-classic defense of idealism which was originally published in 1927. The entire work (2 volumes) represents the author's theory of the nature of the universe. Volume 2 is an "empirical inquiry into the consequences of theoretical or practical interest that can be drawn from the general nature of the universe." (staff)

MC WHORTER, Ladelle. Culture or Nature: The Functions of the Term 'Body' in the Work in the Work of Michel Foucault. J Phil, 86(11), 608-614, N 89.

In some passages of Foucault's work, *body* appears to mean "that which is to be liberated" or "that which pre-exists disciplinary regimes." If so, Foucualt would stand with some feminists and environmental philosophers who attempt to revalue nature as opposed to culture. This article asserts, however, that *body* in Foucault's discourse names not an unchanging given behind changing cultural forms; on the contrary, it names change itself, or movements of differing, to use a less reifiable term. In conclusion, this article situates Foucault in opposition to the entire nature/culture debate.

MC WHORTER, Ladelle. "Foucault's Move beyond the Theoretical" in *The Question of the Other: Essays in Contemporary Continental Philosophy*, DALLERY, Arleen B (ed), 197-203. Albany, SUNY Pr, 1989.

Despite some commentators' suggestions, Foucault is not a theorist; on the contrary, in Foucault's discourse theoretical thinking is itself in question, for two reasons. First, theory traditionally bears a conception of truth as constant and of knowledge as adequate reflection of that constant reality. Second, even when theory posits truth as historical, it still holds truth to be a unitary totality during a given epoch. Foucault's genealogical analysis stands opposed to theory since it seeks to historicize and de-totalize knowledge and truth.

MEAGHER, Sharon. Histories, Herstories, and Moral Traditions. Soc Theor Pract, 16(1), 61-84, Spr 90.

Much recent commentary on Carol Gilligan's research on moral development and gender notes a similarity between the "different voice" articulated by Gilligan and the virtue theory presented by Alasdair MacIntyre. This article explores this comparison, asking what the stories of MacIntyre and Gilligan can say to one another, and what this means more generally for moral theory. The comparison between MacIntyre and Gilligan is especially noteworthy in regard to the role that narrative plays in their work.

MEDLIN, Brian. "Objectivity and Ideology in the Physical and Social Sciences" in *Cause, Mind, and Reality: Essays Honoring C B Martin*, HEIL, John (ed), 201-220. Norwell, Kluwer, 1989.

The intellectual objective is to discredit some fashionable relativisms, the practical one to discredit the educational philistinism of Australian governments. These objectives are approached from a plausible account of the social generation of the ideal of objectivity in modern societies. It is alleged that the relativist positions in question are both incoherent and pernicious. In the context of the global ecological crisis, rigorous objectivity

is a necessary condition for human survival. Such objectivity is not known to be unattainable and yet certain kinds of relativism militate against its attainment. They are therefore a threat to human survival.

MEEHAN, Kenneth A. Evaluation of a Philosophy for Children Project in Hawaii. Thinking, 8(4), 20-23, 1990.

MEEKS, Thomas J. The Economic Efficiency and Equity of Abortion. Econ Phil, 6(1), 95-138, Ap 90.

Judith Thomson's assertion of the right to abort human beings is evaluated against standard economic criteria. Equity is discussed in terms of utilitarianism, Nozick's minimal state, and Rawls's social contract. Plausible applications of the criteria are generally consistent with the inequity and inefficiency of aborting human beings. Would-be abortees as a class could in effect bribe their way to birth. The hard cases yield appropriately weaker conclusions. Thomson's own assumptions, when appropriately extended, support a strong argument *against* aborting human beings. Efficiency is not found to be ethically neutral, and the neat distinction between the normative and positive here dissolves.

MEGILL, Allan. The Identity of American Neo-Pragmatism; or, Why Vico Now? New Vico Studies, 5, 99-116, 1987.

MEHURON, Kate. "An Ironic Mimesis" in *The Question of the Other: Essays in Contemporary Continental Philosophy*, DALLERY, Arleen B (ed), 89-101. Albany, SUNY Pr, 1989.

MEIER, Klaus V. Performance Prestidigitation. J Phil Sport, 16, 13-33, 1989.

This paper addresses and attempts to resolve some current definitional issues concerning the nature of sport, games, and play. A definition of 'game' is presented; the nature of 'sport' is delineated; a claim is forwarded that all sports are games, but not all games are sport; and 'play' is discussed in connection with both sport and games. The major protion of the paper concerns itself with the presentation and defense of a model (in the form of a Venn diagram) depicting the essential characteristics of, and interrelationships among, sport, games, and play.

MEIJSING, Monica. Cognitiewetenschap zonder functionalisme. Alg Ned Tijdschr Wijs, 81(4), 304-321, O 89.

Cognitive science's reliance upon representational entities raises the question which position in the philosophy of mind forms (part of) the foundation for this new science. Generally, functionalism is thought to be the philosophy of cognitive science. This article tries to show, however, that functionalism, both in its realist reading (Fodor) and in its instrumentalist reading (Dennett), cannot give a consistent account of cognitive science's (real or putative) representational entities and of the intentionality involved. Even Dennett's recent elaboration of his brand of functionalism cannot solve these problems. It is argued that the double-aspect theory offers a way out of these problems, and is, moreover, much more compatible with the actual nature of psychological explanations in cognitive science.

MEILAENDER, Gilbert. Abortion: The Right to an Argument. Hastings Center Rep, 19(6), 13-16, N-D 89.

MEILAENDER, Gilbert. The Singularity of Christian Ethics. J Relig Ethics, 17(2), 95-120, Fall 89.

The shape of the moral life is determined for Christians at least in part by beliefs peculiar to Christians, and a perennial problem for Christian ethics is relating that peculiar understanding to more general claims about moral knowledge. Since the problem is perennial, I propose not to solve it but to think about it. I do so by considering first the sense in which Christian ethics may be a kind of "insider's" ethic—the shared language of believers. Despite the strengths of such a view, it may too greatly restrict both human and divine freedom. Having considered its difficulties from both those angles, I return to the sense of Christian life as a tradition of conduct in order to illustrate the importance of such a vision in our cultural setting.

MELAMED, Tuvia and GILMOUR, Robin. "The Repair and Maintenance of Relationships" in *Person to Person*, GRAHAM, George (ed), 155-166. Philadelphia, Temple Univ Pr, 1989.

MELCHIORRE, V. Prospettive teologiche nella filosofia di Husserl. Riv Filosof Neo-Scolas, 81(2), 201-218, Ap-Je 89.

In a fragment of his maturity (1931-1932), Husserl speaks of the idea of God as a constitutive principle of every movement of conscience. On this basis the author follows the development of Husserl's analysis of conscience and finds out the transcendental conditions of possibility, which are ultimately metaphysical and theological as Husserl himself acknowledges in his maturity. Thus reference to an unfounded foundation generates interesting parallelisms with Heidegger's thought. Another interesting comparison is suggested with regard to hermeneutic philosophy: the foundation of being, either regarded as immanence in the flux of life, or as transcendence remains in itself unspeakable or speakable only through images, through its giving itself in the finiteness of time and space.

MELCIC, Dunja. "Interpretation and Solidarity"—An Interview with Richard Bernstein. Praxis Int, 9(3), 201-219, O 89.

MELE, Alfred R. Akratic Feelings. Phil Phenomenol Res, 50(2), 277-288, D 89.

This paper characterizes a feeling-analogue of full-blown akratic action, establishes its possibility, and sketches an explanation of its occurrence. The etiology of many feelings is complex, involving desires, habits of interpretation, learned patterns of emotional response, physiological considerations, etc. The evaluations grounding an individual's better judgments about matters of feeling need neither fully fix nor exactly gauge the causal power of feeling-influencing items. If there is a mismatch between the determinants of a feeling and the agent's better judgment, and if, despite this disparity, what the agent feels or continues to feel is subject to his control, akratic feelings are possible.

MELE, Alfred R. Errant Self-Control and the Self-Controlled Person. Pac Phil Quart, 71(1), 47-59, Mr 90.

This paper defends a traditional, quasi-Aristotelian conception of the self-controlled person while accommodating two points that the background of this conception speaks against: (1) the self of self-control is not properly identified with "reason"; (2) some exercises of self-control are *errant*, serving behavior that conflicts with the agent's consciously held better judgment. Despite the truth of (2), there is a tight fit between the better judgments of self-controlled individuals and their behavior. The chief burden of the paper is to establish this conjunctive thesis. Its aim is to foster a deeper appreciation of the nature of self-control.

MELE, Alfred R. Exciting Intentions. Phil Stud, 59(3), 289-312, Jl 90.

The paper addresses a conditional question: If there is a specific motivational role that intention plays in all cases of overt intentional action, in virtue of what features of intention does it play that role? A popular answer is rejected: It is argued that intentions to A do not essentially incorporate preponderant motivation (wanting most) to A and that the motivational role of intention in intentional action does not rest upon that alleged feature of intention. An alternative answer is developed, one emphasizing the "settledness" encompassed in intending or the executive nature of intention—something irreducible to preponderant wanting.

MELE, Alfred R. Intending and Motivation: A Rejoinder. Analysis, 50(3), 194-197, Je 90.

This paper rebuts J Mendola's criticism ("Intending and Motivation," *Analysis* 50 [1990]) of arguments that the author has presented elsewhere against the thesis that an agent intends to A only if she is preponderantly motivated to A. The structure of the author's strategy in previous work on the topic ("Intending and the Balance of Motivation," *Pacific Philosophical Quarterly* 65 [1984]; *Irrationality*, Oxford University Press, 1987; "Exciting Intentions," *Philosophical Studies* 59 [1990]) is set out; and it is argued, against this background, that Mendola's objections miss their mark.

MELE, Alfred R. Irresistible Desires. Nous, 24(3), 455-472, Je 90.

This paper advances a new analysis of irresistible desire. The analysis features a distinction between unconquerable and uncircumventable desires as well as accounts of three species of inability with respect to intentional action: epistemic (in a broad sense), motivational, and executive. A traditional analysis of irresistible desire is attacked—one framed in terms of what an agent would have done if she had taken there to be good and sufficient reason for not acting on a given desire.

MELE, Alfred R. Motivational Internalism: The Powers and Limits of Practical Reasoning. Philosophia (Israel), 19(4), 417-436, D 89.

Motivational internalism about practical reasoning is, very roughly, the thesis that all reasoning-produced motivation is partly derivative from motivation already present in the reasoner. The paper develops a particular version of this thesis, argues that it has decisive advantages over externalist competitors, and shows that it does not entail the normative internalist thesis that reasons for action and practical rationality are dependent upon antecedent motivation. Work on the topic by Aristotle, Cohon, Darwall, Frankena, Hume, Korsgaard, Reid, and B Williams is discussed.

MELÉE, Domènec. Organization of Work in the Company and Family Rights of the Employees. J Bus Ethics, 8(8), 647-655, Ag 89.

The duty to respect, protect and help the family rights is related very closely with the organization of work in the firm. This paper summarizes and illustrates, using mini-case studies, the relationship between the organization of work in companies and the family rights and duties of employees.

MELENDO, Tomás. "Αρχή y ἐναντίωσιζ: su nexo en el pensamiento preparmenideo". Anu Filosof, 20(1), 131-165, 1987.

MELLING, David J. *Understanding Plato*. New York, Oxford Univ Pr, 1987

MELLOS, Koula. Figures de la rationalité dans le marxisme contemporain. Rev Univ Ottawa, 57(4), 79-97, O-D 87.

MELZER, Arthur M. *The Natural Goodness of Man: On the Systems of Rousseau's Thought*. Chicago, Univ of Chicago Pr, 1990

"The natural goodness of man," Rousseau proclaims, is the hidden key to the perplexities of the human condition—and also to those of his seemingly contradictory writings, which are actually disassembled fragments of a rigorous system rooted in that principle. The present work attempts to reassemble this system. The first two parts restore the original significance of Rousseau's principle and examine the arguments offered to prove it. Part three unfolds the *Social Contract* as a precise consequence of this principle. The result is not only a comprehensive new presentation of Rousseau but a far-ranging meditation on human nature and politics, and on the vexed history of western thinking on these subjects.

MENDELSOHN, Richard L. Objects and Existence: Reflections on Free Logic. Notre Dame J Form Log, 30(4), 604-623, Fall 89.

It is usual in free logic to regard free variables and constants as alike, and to distinguish them semantically from bound variables. In the present treatment, by contrast, variables are handled uniformly, while individual constants are regarded as surface artifacts to be fleshed out for deep-structure predicate constructions. Philosophical reasons are presented to support this interpretation, and the logical construction is described informally. The main idea involves a threefold refinement of Quine's Russellian treatment of proper names. First, the existence clause is eliminated. Second, uniqueness is made a formal aspect of the symbolization of singular predicates. Third, no scope distinction is marked in the surface structure, as with Russell's iota-notation, so that, although a sentence involving a singular term might be read in different ways, corresponding to a difference in the way scope is reckoned, the sentence is treated in the logic as if that scope is unknown.

MENDELSON, Elliott. Second Thoughts about Church's Thesis and Mathematical Proofs. J Phil, 87(5), 225-233, My 90.

It is widely held that Church's Thesis (CT) cannot be proved because it equates a precise concept with an intuitive notion. Challenging this view, the article points out that half of CT has a proof that is as convincing and rigorous as any known mathematical proof. Thus, there is no inherent reason why intuitive concepts cannot be proved equivalent to (allegedly) precise concepts. Four examples of other well-accepted "theses" in logic and mathematics provide historical support to this contention. It is also noted that precise concepts are ultimately based on intuitive notions.

MÉNDEZ, José M. Converse Ackermann Property and Semiclassical Negation. Stud Log, 47(2), 159-167, Je 88.

A propositional logic S has the "Converse Ackermann Property" (CAP) if $(A\rightarrow)\rightarrow C$ is unprovable in S when C does not contain $\rightarrow$. In "A Routley-Meyer semantics for Converse Ackermann Property" (*Journal of Philosophical Logic*, 16 (1987), pp. 65-76) I showed how to derive positive logical systems with the CAP. There I conjectured that each of these positive systems were compatible with a so-called "semiclassical" negation. In the present paper I prove that this conjecture was right. Relational Routley-Meyer type semantics are provided for each one of the resulting systems (the positive systems plus the semiclassical negation).

MÉNDEZ, José M. Deduction Theorems. Rep Math Log, 22, 9-13, 1988.

A logic L is *implicative* if the sole connective of L is the conditional; a logic has the "Converse Ackermann Property" (CAP) if non-necessitive propositions are not derivable from necessitive ones. In this paper we prove deduction theorems for the implicative fragments with the CAP of the following propositional logics: *Ticket Entailment, Entailment, Relevance Logic, Modal Logic* S4 and *Intuitionistic Logic*. Next, and using the deduction theorems, we define a natural deduction system for each one of these implicative fragments with the CAP.

MÉNDEZ, José M. Urquhart's C with Minimal Negation. Bull Sect Log, 19(1), 15-20, Mr 90.

MENDOLA, Joseph. Intending and Motivation. Analysis, 50(3), 190-193, Je 90.

Many writers on intention claim that someone x intends to A only if x is preponderantly motivated to A, more motivated to A than to do something incompatible. In his book *Irrationality* and in "Intending and the Balance of Motivation," Alfred Mele contends that this popular thesis is false. I argue that his case does not establish his contention.

MENDOLA, Joseph. Normative Realism, or Bernard Williams and Ethics at the Limit. Austl J Phil, 67(3), 306-318, S 89.

Recent arguments for normative realism have centered on attempts to meet a demand on normative facts articulated by Harman, that they be required for explanations of uncontroversial phenomena. This paper argues that another argument for normative realism should take precedence, an argument suggested by Williams's skeptical discussion of moral objectivity in *Ethics and the Limits of Philosophy*.

MENDOLA, Joseph. Objective Value and Subjective States. Phil Phenomenol Res, 50(4), 695-713, Je 90.

There has been a revival of interest in moral realism, but many recent discussions have not focused on specifying plausible examples of normative facts, and this may have left the abstract discussion of their possibility unsatisfying. I argue that there are plausible examples of normative facts. In particular, I argue that there are phenomenal states which are an essential part of some pleasure and pain and which have, as a matter of objective fact, the normative properties of intrinsic objective value or disvalue.

MENDOLA, Joseph. An Ordinal Modification of Classical Utilitarianism. Erkenntnis, 33(1), 73-88, Jl 90.

Classical utilitarianism is notoriously insensitive to the *distribution* of pleasure and pain, and hence seems to offend our moral intuition that distribution matters. This insensitivity is underwritten by a second counterintuitive feature of the view—its *arithmetization* of pleasure and pain. Many suspect that it does not make sense to speak of an exact sum of pleasures in the way which classical utilitarianism requires and which supports distribution insensitivity. This paper proposes a modification of classical utilitarianism which fares better in these two ways, which does not require an arithmetization of pleasure and which is sensitive to distribution.

MENDONÇA, W P. Intelligence artificielle et signification: À propos des limites et des possibilités des sciences cognitives. Philosophiques, 17(1), 3-19, 1990.

In the literature on artificial intelligence, the author distinguishes two approaches: the technological approach and the cognitivist approach. He shows that the parallels made between human intelligence and artificial intelligence within the cognitivist approach do not go without saying, and that the theses on artificial intelligence are largely dependent upon certain rationalist and empiricist speculations of classical philosophy. He exposes the principal problem that then encounters an understanding of human intelligence in the light of the cognitivist approach, namely the necessity to obliterate the semantic dimension and to profess a radical solipsism, and he pleads for an understanding of human intelligence commensurable with what it is in culture rather than in machines.

MENDONÇA, W P. Programas e Promessas: Sobre o (Ab-)Uso do Jargão Computacional em Teorias Cognitivas da Mente. Manuscrito, 12(1), 91-108, Ap 89.

According to a widespread view, computational theories of the mind of the type commonly proposed in cognitive psychology and artificial intelligence differ from earlier conceptions in the accuracy of the conceptual instruments which they use: the introduction of the vocabulary of computational sciences in psychology would make possible the elaboration of precise hypotheses about the so-called cognitive processes, being, thus, equivalent to a methodical discipline of our thinking on man as a being capable of thinking and speaking. I argue in this paper that this view is untenable. (edited)

MENN, Stephen. Descartes and Some Predecessors on the Divine Conservation of Motion. Synthese, 83(2), 215-238, My 90.

Here I reexamine Duhem's question of the continuity between medieval dynamics and early modern conservation theories. I concentrate on the heavens. For Aristotle, the motions of the heavens are eternally constant (and thus mathematizable) because an eternally constant divine Reason is their mover. Duhem thought that impetus and conservation theories, by extending sublunar mechanics to the heavens, made a divine renewer of motion redundant. By contrast, I show how Descartes derives his law of conservation by extending Aristotelian celestial dynamics to the earth. Descartes argues that motion is intrinsically linear, not circular. But he agrees that motion is mathematically intelligible only where divine Reason moves bodies in a constant and eternal motion. Descartes strips bodies of active powers, leaving God as the only natural mover; thus *both* celestial *and* sublunar motions are constant, and uniformly mathematizable. The law of conservation of the *total quantity* of motion is an attempt to harmonize the constancy derived *a priori* with the phenomenal inconstancy of sublunar motions.

MENZEL, Christopher and KVANVIG, Jonathan L. The Basic Notion of Justification. Phil Stud, 59(3), 235-261, Jl 90.

There are three important kinds of justification: personal (as in "S is justified in believing p"); propositional (as in "p is justified for S"); and doxastic (as in "S justifiably believes p"). The question we address is whether any one of these three is basic, and argue that propositional justification has this status. This conclusion is important in that most versions of reliabilism require that doxastic justification is the basic kind. Hence our conclusion implies that the most common reliabilist theories of justification are false.

MENZEL, Christopher. On an Unsound Proof of the Existence of Possible Worlds. Notre Dame J Form Log, 30(4), 598-603, Fall 89.

In this paper, an argument of Alvin Plantinga's for the existence of abstract possible worlds is shown to be unsound. The argument is based on a principle Plantinga calls "Quasicompactness," due to its structural similarity to the notion of compactness in first-order logic. The principle is shown to be false.

MENZEL, Paul T. Public Philosophy: Distinction Without Authority. J Med Phil, 15(4), 411-424, Ag 90.

An assumed core of normative ethical principles may constitute a philosophically proper framework within which public policy should be formulated, but it seldom provides any substantive solutions. To generate public policy on bioethical issues, participants still need to confront underlying philosophical controversies. Professional philosophers' proper role in that process is to clarify major philosophical options, to press wider-ranging consistency questions, and to bring more parties into the philosophical debate itself by arguing for particular substantive claims. Though questions of fact that mediate final policy conclusions frequently fall outside philosophical competence, one sort of fact, lack of political support, should seldom cause philosophers to stand aside; philosophers still have an important role as critics of culture, politics, and profession. They have no authority, however, on even the philosophical presuppositions of public policy.

MENZIES, Peter and NEANDER, Karen. David Owens on Levels of Explanation. Mind, 99(395), 459-466, Jl 90.

This paper is concerned with the thesis that the supervenience of the nonphysical on the physical entails that explanations in the special sciences are always underwritten by physical explanations. The paper examines objections to this thesis made by David Owens in 'Levels of Explanation' (*Mind* 98, 1989). The paper concludes that the thesis properly formulated escapes Owens's objections.

MENZIES, Peter. Probabilistic Causation and Causal Processes: A Critique of Lewis. Phil Sci, 56(4), 642-663, D 89.

This paper examines a promising probabilistic theory of singular causation developed by David Lewis. I argue that Lewis's theory must be made more sophisticated to deal with certain counterexamples involving preemption. These counterexamples appear to show that in the usual case singular causation requires an unbroken causal process to link cause with effect. I propose a new probabilistic account of singular causation, within the framework developed by Lewis, which captures this intuition.

MERCHANT, Carolyn. Environmental Ethics and Political Conflict: A View from California. Environ Ethics, 12(1), 45-68, Spr 90.

I examine three approaches to environmental ethics and illustrate them with examples from California. An egocentric ethic is grounded in the self and based on the assumption that what is good for the individual is good for society. A homocentric ethic is grounded in society and is based on the assumption that policies should reflect the greatest good for the greatest number of people and that, as stewards of the natural world, humans should conserve and protect nature for human benefit. An ecocentric ethic is grounded in the cosmos, or whole environment, and is based on the assignment of intrinsic value to nonhuman nature. This threefold taxonomy may be useful in identifying underlying ethical assumptions in cases where ethical dilemmas and conflicts of interest develop among entrepreneurs, government agencies, and environmentalists. (edited)

MERCIER, A. Le temps de la préhistoire et la venue de l'homme et des cultures sur la terre. Philosophia (Athens), 17-18, 153-167, 1987-88.

Animals understand the meaning of some signs, but never invent them. Human beings have been able to give a meaning to their knowledge, creeds, habits and techniques, grounding thus Culture which consists in the transmission of these four modes of being. An oldest social division probably existed between chiefs, shamans and other people with their various occupations. Most probably shamans were the oldest people to reflect upon the "Problem of Time": possibly this is the origin of Myth. The (hypothetical) Great Myth concerns Time and seems to imply sexuality, because the latter amounts to a form of knowledge and to a mastery of temporality. Yet Time remains—since the beginning of man's prehistoric existence—the source of paradoxes and hence the reason for philosophizing.

MERIKLE, Philip M and REINGOLD, Eyal M. On the Inter-relatedness of Theory and Measurement in the Study of Unconscious Processes. Mind Lang, 5(1), 9-28, Spr 90.

In the present paper we identify the a priori assumptions underlying the dissociation paradigm employed by researchers on the unconscious. We argue that definitional chaos, and implicit assumptions that are rarely acknowledged, fuel the often futile controversy between 'believers' and 'nonbelievers' in the unconscious. We analyze the logical status of inferences based on the dissociation paradigm, and critique two major approaches to the measurement of consciousness. We then describe two alternative approaches which avoid the conceptual and methodological pitfalls of previous approaches, and thus have the potential to provide more conclusive evidence regarding the nature of conscious versus unconscious processes.

MERKS, K W. De rol van het begrip intrinsieke waarde in milieu-ethische argumentaties. Bijdragen, 2, 139-156, 1990.

MERLLIÉ, Dominique. Le cas Lévy-Bruhl. Rev Phil Fr, 179(4), 419-448, O-D 89.

MERLLIÉ, Dominique and DURKHEIM, Emile. Lévy-Bruhl et Durkheim: Notes biographiques en marge d'une correspondance—Lettres à L Lévy-Bruhl (1894-1915). Rev Phil Fr, 179(4), 493-514, O-D 89.

MERMIN, N David. "Can You Help Your Team Tonight by Watching on TV? More Experimental Metaphysics from Einstein, Podolsky, and Rosen" in Philosophical Consequences of Quantum Theory: Reflections on Bell's Theorem, CUSHING, James T (ed), 38-59. Notre Dame, Univ Notre Dame Pr, 1989.

MERRILL, John Calhoun. The Dialectic in Journalism: Toward a Responsible Use of Press Freedom. Baton Rouge, Louisiana St Univ Pr, 1989

MERRILL, John W L. UFA Fails in the Bell-Kunen Model. J Sym Log, 55(1), 284-296, Mr 90.

MERSKEY, H. An Ethical Issue in the Psychotherapy of Pain and Other Symptoms. Bioethics, 4(1), 22-32, Ja 90.

Patients may consult physicians about pain or other somatic symptoms and find themselves involved in psychological treatment. This provides a potential discrepancy between the aims of physicians and patients, and disruptions of the patient's life, which he might not anticipate, follow from the psychological treatment of what was supposed to be a physical disorder. Because the physician has more knowledge of the potential hazards than the patient, who is not warned of them, a weak form of paternalism develops, albeit in a fiduciary relationship. The ethical solution is that the patient provides "ignorant consent."

MERTZ, David. Response to Dietrich's "Computationalism". Soc Epistem, 4(2), 172-176, Ap-Je 90.

MESKIN, Jacob. From Phenomenology to Liberation: The Displacement of History and Theology in Levinas's Totality and Infinity. Phil Theol, 4(2), 119-144, Wint 89.

The paper seeks to establish a kinship between the philosophy of Levinas and the theology of liberation. In their separate domains, these two enterprises reveal to us a portrait of late, twentieth-century intellectual work which refuses to abandon eschatological urgency. Philosophy and theology may meet, outside of both of their own homes, on a journey toward the other, in ethics.

MESTROVIC, Stjepan G. The Theme of Civilization and its Discontents in Durkheim's Division of Labor. J Theor Soc Behav, 19(4), 443-456, D 89.

METSCHL, Ulrich. Eine kleine Überraschung für Gehirne im Tank: Eine skeptische Notiz zu einem antiskeptischen Argument. Z Phil Forsch, 43(3), 519-527, Jl-S 89.

This paper is concerned with Professor Putnam's recent argument that 'we' cannot be brains in a vat. It is argued that brains in a vat are in situation parallel to that of the prisoner of the hangman paradox. In addition some remarks are made concerning metaphysical realism and the idea of consistency.

METZINGER, Thomas. Kriterien für eine Theorie zur Lösung des Leib-Seele-Problems. Erkenntnis, 32(1), 127-145, Ja 90.

The article presents a critical survey of the philosophical discussion of the mind-body problem since the collapse of Rylean behaviourism. The major theories (identity theories, supervenience, emergentist materialism, dualist interactionism and functionalism) are sketched and briefly evaluated with regard to their advantages and disadvantages. The conclusion is that no satisfactory theory about the relation between mental and neurophysiological states exists today, but considerable progress has been made regarding the contours of this cluster of problems. A catalogue of criteria which every future theory concerning the mind-body problem must fulfill is given at the end.

MEYER, Eduard. Sulla teoria e metodica della storia. Arch Stor Cult, 2,

359-411, 1989.

MEYER, Leroy N. Science, Reduction and Natural Kinds. Philosophy, 64(250), 535-546, O 89.

MEYER, Michel. "Foreword—The Modernity of Rhetoric" in From Metaphysics to Rhetoric, MEYER, Michel (ed), 1-7. Norwell, Kluwer, 1989.

MEYER, Michel (ed). From Metaphysics to Rhetoric. Norwell, Kluwer, 1989

MEYER, Michel. "Toward an Anthropology of Rhetoric" in From Metaphysics to Rhetoric, MEYER, Michel (ed), 111-136. Norwell, Kluwer, 1989.

MEYER, Robert K and GIAMBRONE, Steve. Completeness and Conservative Extension Results for Some Boolean Relevant Logics. Stud Log, 48(1), 1-14, Mr 89.

This paper present completeness and conservative extension results for the Boolean extensions of the relevant logic T of Ticket Entailment, and for the contractionless relevant logics TW and RW. Some surprising results are shown for adding the sentential constant t to those Boolean relevant logics; specifically, the Boolean extensions with t are conservative of the Boolean extensions without t, but not of the original logics with t. The special treatment required for the semantic normality of T is also shown along the way.

MEYER, Robert K and DUNN, J Michael. "Gentzen's Cut and Ackermann's Gamma" in Directions in Relevant Logic, NORMAN, Jean (ed), 229-240. Norwell, Kluwer, 1989.

MEYER, William E H. The Hypervisual Meaning of the American West. Phil Today, 33(1), 28-41, Spr 89.

In order to understand all aspects of American culture—art, literature, philosophy, religion, and even science—you must first acknowledge the hypervisual essence of that culture. Emerson's dictum—"that which others hear, I see"—becomes the purpose and conclusion of this investigation into the paradigmatic "hypervisual meaning of the American West." There can be no European method or terminology which is applicable to this radical look at American forms.

MEYERING, Theo C. Historical Roots of Cognitive Science. Norwell, Kluwer, 1989

MEYERS, Renee A and GARRETT, Dennis E and BRADFORD, Jeffrey L and BECKER, Joy. Issues Management and Organizational Accounts: An Analysis of Corporate Responses to Accusation of Unethical Business. J Bus Ethics, 8(7), 507-520, Jl 89.

When external groups accuse a business organization of unethical practices, managers of the accused organization usually offer a communicative response to attempt to protect their organization's public image. Even though many researchers readily concur that analysis of these communicative responses is important to our understanding of business and society conflict, few investigations have focused on developing a theoretical framework for analyzing these communicative strategies used by managers. In additon, research in this area has suffered from a lack of empirical investigation. In this paper we address both of these weaknesses in the existing literature. (edited)

MEYNELL, Hugo A. Fish Fingered: Anatomy of a Deconstructionist. J Aes Educ, 23(2), 5-15, Sum 89.

The works of Wordsworth and Jane Austen are priceless cultural treasures, and any account of literature and literary value which implies, as does the work of Fish, that we might as well in the last analysis set ourselves to value any trivial corpus of words as the works of these two writers of genius, is accordingly dangerous. The remedy is a general account of how we come to know what is true and good; against this background an account can be given of what is meant by works of literature, and why some are of greater value than others.

MEYNELL, Hugo. On Knowlegde, Power and Michel Foucault. Heythrop J, 30(4), 419-432, O 89.

There are certain defects in Foucault's writings which make them less effective and beneficial a force in morals, politics and the critique of institutions than they would otherwise be. Chief among these defects is lack of a coherent idea of the good, and of the human mental capacities which favour attainment of truth and avoidance of error. It is suggested how these defects might be remedied.

MEZEI, György Iván. Vagueness and Meaning in Lukács' Ontology. Stud Soviet Tho, 39(3-4), 265-272, Ap-My 90.

Although the paper recapitulates the basic characteristics of G Lukács's project in social philosophy, it is intended as a rough case-study in the methodology of the humanities and social studies. The established logic of the twentieth century is founded on the study of mathematics and the sciences which are pursued in the spirit of the Cartesian principle *clare et distincte*. In order to be able to handle vagueness, which is always to some extent uneliminable from the humanities and the social studies one needs, as opposed to the established logical paradigm, as well as to amplifying vagueness, say, in paraconsistent logic, a new paradigm of methodology, including patterns of deconstructing vague phenomena and restructuring the furnished meaning.

MEZRICKY, V. Philosophy of Regional Cooperation in the Solution of Global Ecological Problems (in Czechoslovakian). Filozof Cas, 37(5), 666-676, 1989.

Global problems are known to exist in virtually all walks of human societies, affecting relations both between individuals and between various communities. In many cases, this impact is positive, as corroborated by the example of the European continent. As far as Europe is concerned, ecological problems have resulted in the adoption of a number of legal and especially political documents which contain explicitly worded basic principles of a philosophy of regional cooperation among states with different socio-political systems. This has paved the way for fostering exemplary regional collaboration. Of key importance is the recognition of the priority of panhuman values in interstate relations. These values include the value of natural balance. The already defined praxiological postulates which are expected to safeguard the protection of this particular value, however, call for a legal definition so the protection of this value could be enforceable and could be permanently ensured.

MICHAEL, Emily and MICHAEL, Fred S. The Theory of Ideas in Gassendi and Locke. J Hist Ideas, 51(3), 379-399, Jl-S 90.

MICHAEL, Fred S and MICHAEL, Emily. The Theory of Ideas in Gassendi and Locke. J Hist Ideas, 51(3), 379-399, Jl-S 90.

MICHAELIDES, K. Die Hermeneutik der schriftlichen, mündlichen und innerlichen Rede bei Platon (in Greek). Philosophia (Athens), 17-18, 297-309, 1987-88.

Im platonischen *Phaidros* behandelt Sokrates das grosse Thema der Kunst der Reden und insbesondere die Rede in ihrer schriftlichen Form. Die schriftliche Rede ist, nach Sokrates: (a) eine entfremdete, in Zeichen gebundene Rede, ein Abbild der lebendigen Rede, (b) sie bietet keinen Zugang zur Wahrheit sondern bleibt im Schein verfangen, (c) sie ist monologisch und unpersönlich und (d) sie ist starr und der Missdeutung ausgeliefert. (edited)

MICHAÉLIDÈS-NOUAROS, G. Réflexions dur le sens de l'histoire (in Greek). Philosophia (Athens), 17-18, 41-96, 1987-88.

Le présent essai est divisé en trois parties: Dans la première partie on examine d'abord des questions philosophiques ayant trait au problème fondamental du sens de l'histoire et par la suite une série de problèmes méthodologiques concernant la méthode d'étude et d'interprétation des événements historiques. L'investigation du sens de l'histoire comprend l'examen des questions suivantes: (a) La marche de l'histoire est-elle un produit de la volonté de l'homme ou bien l'effet des forces surnaturelles de la Providence Divine ou du Destin? (b) La nature humaine est-elle identique à tous les hommes et à toutes les époques historiques? (c) est-il possible de connaître l'histoire *réelle* de l'humanité ou cela est impossible, comme il est affirmé par certains auteurs, notamment Popper? (edited)

MICHALOS, Alex C. The Impact of Trust on Business, International Security and the Quality of Life. J Bus Ethics, 9(8), 619-638, Ag 90.

The theses supported in this essay are that the world is to some extent constructed by each of us, that it can and ought to be constructed in a more benign way, that such construction will require more trust than most people are currently willing to grant, and that most of us will be better off if most of us can manage to be more trusting in spite of our doubts.

MICHALSON JR, Gordon E. Kierkegaard's Debt to Lessing: Response to Whisenant. Mod Theol, 6(4), 379-384, Jl 90.

MICHALSON JR, Gordon E. Moral Regeneration and Divine Aid in Kant. Relig Stud, 25(3), 259-270, S 89.

MICHAM, Carl. La ética ingenieril norteamericana: problems y promesas. Rev Filosof (Costa Rica), 26, 57-63, D 88.

This essay traces the traditional engineering ethics of obedience to its military origins and the ideology of technological progress. It then considers the rise of an alternative professional ethics of responsibility for the public welfare, and describes one of the key events in North American engineering experience (the Bay Area Rapid Transit case) that has led engineers to seek new ways to protect whistle blowers. There is also an annotated bibliography of recent literature on the new field of engineering ethics.

MICHELFELDER, Diane. "Derrida and the Ethics of the Ear" in *The Question of the Other: Essays in Contemporary Continental Philosophy*, DALLERY, Arleen B (ed), 47-54. Albany, SUNY Pr, 1989.

This paper discusses the question of where to situate Derrida's thinking with regards to ethics—inside or outside its borders. I argue that, although it is not an ethics in the conventional sense of being a search for a fundamental principle or value on which to base decision making, it can be seen as having an ethical dimension. This dimension is connected to the role that memory plays in a structure that on Derrida's view implicates the ear: the structure of textuality.

MICHELMAN, Stephen (trans) and ROMAN, Joël. Thinking Politics without a Philosophy of History: Arendt and Merleau-Ponty. Phil Soc Crit, 15(4), 403-422, 1989.

MICHELS, Robert and MARKOWITZ, John C. The Future of Psychiatry. J Med Phil, 15(1), 5-19, F 90.

Psychiatry is rapidly changing. The authors review the history of psychiatry in the United States, its gradual integration into medicine and society, and the dialectic between its "biologic" and "mentalist" outlooks. After describing the current state of the profession and its knowledge base, they discuss the likely future of the field: psychiatry's projected mode of practice and economics; its future as a science for understanding human behavior; its expected boundaries with other treatment disciplines; its anticipated relationship with academia and with the community at large; and internal issues for the profession. Unprecedented internal and external pressures on the field are likely to require important reconceptualizations of psychiatry both by its members and by the rest of the American public.

MICHIELSEN, Peter. Philosophy and Literature: Their Relationship in the Works of Paul de Man. Commun Cog, 22(3-4), 277-284, 1989.

MIDDLETON, Peter. Socialism, Feminism and Men. Rad Phil, 53, 8-19, Autumn 89.

Discusses two areas of conceptual difficulty for men trying to develop a progressive politics of masculinity: oppression and sexual difference. Oppression operates only in terms of collectivities, and does not, as is often tacitly assumed, describe experience or intention. Sexual difference theory has defined men in terms of an absolute relation to language, and therefore, like the global use of the term oppression to define men, made it difficult for men to develop a theoretical understanding of ways to take an active role in changing oppressive masculinities.

MIDGLEY, Mary. Practical Solutions. Hastings Center Rep, 19(6), 44-45, N-D 89.

MIGLIOLI, Pierangelo (and others). Some Results on Intermediate Constructive Logics. Notre Dame J Form Log, 30(4), 543-562, Fall 89.

Some techniques for the study of intermediate constructive logics are illustrated. In particular a general characterization is given of maximal constructive logics from which a new proof of the maximality of MV (Medvedev's logic of finite problems) can be obtained. Some semantical notions are also introduced, allowing a new characterization of MV, from which a new proof of a conjecture of Friedman's and a new family of principles valid in MV can be extracted.

MIGNINI, Filippo. Essere e negazione: Per un recente volume di Gennaro Sasso. G Crit Filosof Ital, 68(2), 248-257, My-Ag 89.

MIGNINI, Filippo. Per una nuova edizione del *Tractatus De Intellectus Emendatione*. Stud Spinozana, 4, 15-35, 1988.

The article suggests a list of corrections to the Gebhardt edition of the *TIE*, prepared following a methodical examination of the OP and NS. Such an examination is the only criterion which we can adopt in order to trace back to the original wording of a text which, probably, ended up in the hands of the author's friends and publishers only after his death. In all likelihood, the style of the Latin manuscript was corrected with the translation in mind, and perhaps even after the latter had been made. Nor can we exclude the possibility that the authors may have made some changes to Glazemaker's Dutch translation. With reference to the page and line of the Gebhardt edition, the reading to be corrected is indicated and the suggested amendment can be read after the colon. The aim of this article is to constitute an initial contribution towards a new edition of the *TIE*.

MIGUELEZ, Roberto. La deuxième crise de la raison et la critique du socialisme. Rev Univ Ottawa, 57(4), 63-78, O-D 87.

MIHAI, Gheorghe. Sur la structure particulière du dialogue argumentatif. Phil Log, 32(3-4), 225-234, Jl-D 88.

MIKALACHKI, D and BURKE, R J. The Women in Management Research Program at the National Centre for Management Research and Development. J Bus Ethics, 9(4-5), 447-453, Ap-My 90.

NCMRD initiated the Women in Management Research Program in January 1988. One of the objectives of the program is to help managers and policy makers deal with issues arising from women's increased participation in managerial and professional jobs backing research to help arrive at solutions to the problems being encountered both by institutions and by women themselves. Significant research funds have been raised from the private sector and ten projects have been funded to date. This article describes the early development of the program and its research mandate.

MIKLASZEWSKA, Justyna. The Libertarian Utopia: Robert Nozick and Aleksander Swietochowski. Rep Phil, 13, 51-60, 1989.

MILANO, Andrea. Cristianesimo e metafisica: Tra "ragione debole" e "fede ignava". Sapienza, 42(3), 245-293, Jl-S 89.

MILBANK, John. "'Between Purgation and Illumination': A Critique of the Theology of Right" in *Christ, Ethics and Tragedy: Essays in Honour of Donald MacKinnon*, SURIN, Kenneth (ed), 161-196. New York, Cambridge Univ Pr, 1989.

The essay reexamines the Kantian assumptions of modern theology, arguing that they permeate 'liberal' and 'neo-orthodox' theologies alike. It is contended that transcendentalist presuppositions are always in league with political liberalism, and tend to make problematic any notions of analogy or participation. The work of Donald MacKinnon is examined in support of these contentions. On the positive side, it is argued that a 'metacritical' linguistic turn overcomes transcendentalism and helps us to recover, in a 'postmodern' guise, ideas of participation which ground a nonliberal 'common good'.

MILES, Murray. Heidegger and the Question of Humanism. Man World, 22(4), 427-451, D 89.

Through detailed exegesis of the text of the "Letter on Humanism" it is argued that Heidegger's rejection of all past 'humanisms' (Roman, Christian, Marxian, and Sartrean) cannot be interpreted as itself another humanism, nor as a nonhumanistic alternative to past humanisms. Heidegger's position is profoundly *anti*-humanistic, though the deliberate esotericism of the "Letter on Humanism" is apt to disguise this fact.

MILL, John Stuart and ROBSON, John M (ed). *Miscellaneous Writings (Collected Works of John Stuart Mill, Volume 31)*. Buffalo, Univ of Toronto Pr, 1989.

MILL, John Stuart. The Role of Logic in Education. Thinking, 5(4), 20-21, 1985.

MILL, John Stuart and ROBSON, John M (ed) and MOIR, Martin (ed) and MOIR, Zawahir (ed). *Writings on India (Collected Works of John Stuart Mill, Volume 30)*. Buffalo, Univ of Toronto Pr, 1990

MILLAR, Alan. Experience and the Justification of Belief. Ratio, 2(2), 138-152, D 89.

It is widely accepted that a person's beliefs can derive justification from other beliefs which the person has, but there is a serious question whether, and if so how, a person's beliefs can derive justification from that person's current sensory experiences. As Davidson sees it the problem is that states which are not themselves 'beliefs or other propositional attitudes' cannot be 'logically related' to beliefs and thus cannot justify beliefs. It is argued that while sensory experiences should be distinguished from propositional attitudes they may, nevertheless, contribute to the justification of beliefs. The argument is set within the framework of a general approach to derived justification.

MILLER JR, Fred D (ed) and PAUL, Ellen Frankel (ed) and PAUL, Jeffrey (ed) and AHRENS, John (ed). *Capitalism*. Cambridge, Blackwell, 1989

The essays in this volume address some of the central moral and conceptual questions arising out of the nature of capitalism. Some address the connection between capitalism and such moral notions as freedom, self-ownership and community. Others consider the role that efficiency plays in the justification of capitalism. And others are concerned with the methodological difficulties involved in comparing existing capitalist and socialist systems. Together, these essays delineate some of the concepts which are central to the ongoing debate between capitalism and socialism.

MILLER JR, Fred D. Aristotle's Political Naturalism. Apeiron, 22(4), 195-218, D 89.

MILLER JR, Fred D and PAUL, Jeffrey. Communitarian and Liberal Theories of the Good. Rev Metaph, 43(4), 803-830, Je 90.

MILLER JR, Fred D and SMITH, Nicholas D. *Thought Probes: Philosophy Through Science Fiction Literature (Second Edition)*. Englewood Cliffs, Prentice-Hall, 1989

MILLER, Alexander. An Objection to Wright's Treatment of Intention. Analysis, 49(4), 169-173, O 89.

Crispin Wright has recently suggested that 'intentional and sensational states...are, in effect, "secondary": that subjects' best judgements fix the

extension of the truth predicate among ascriptions of belief, desire, and feeling to them'. In this paper I argue that on Wright's own conditions for a class of concepts being 'secondary', it cannot be correct to construe the concept of intention as secondary in that sense.

MILLER, Barry. Analogy Sans Portrait: God-Talk as Literal But Non-Anthropomorphic. Faith Phil, 7(1), 63-84, Ja 90.

The impression is sometimes given that the analogical character of God-talk could be established only by providing an account of the particular form that the analogy would take. In this paper I argue that it can be established without having to endorse any particular form of analogy at all: the former question is quite independent of the latter. As I present it, the argument for the analogical character of God-talk is based on two doctrines. One is the classical theistic doctrine of the divine simplicity; the other is the doctrine that some propositions are logically simple in the sense of having no *sub*-propositional logical parts.

MILLER, Basia C (trans) and COHLER, Anne M (trans) and STONE, Harold (trans) and MONTESQUIEU, Charles. *The Spirit of the Laws: Charles Montesquieu*. New York, Cambridge Univ Pr, 1989

MILLER, David. Rejoinder to Berkson's "In Defense of Good Reasons". Phil Soc Sci, 20(1), 92-94, Mr 90.

Berkson fails to recognise that in addition to the epistemological infinite regress exposed by traditional scepticism, which discredits all arguments, justificatory or critical, that aspire to yield conclusiveness or certainty, there is a methodological infinite regress embodied in the fallacy of begging the question, which discredits all arguments, conclusive or inconclusive, that aspire to furnish justification or support. 'A Critique of Good Reasons' was concerned only with the methodological issue.

MILLER, Gary A and DONNELLY, William J. The Treadway Commission Recommendations for Education: Professor's Opinions. Bus Prof Ethics J, 8(4), 83-92, Wint 89.

Our study was developed to obtain information about the beliefs and perceptions of accounting professors regarding the four specific recommendations made by the Treadway Commission for educators. A questionnaire was developed and sent to 500 members of the American Accounting Association. The professors we surveyed strongly agreed with the four Treadway recommendations for educators. Fraudulent financial reporting and ethics issues need to be integrated into accounting curriculum. All accounting courses, not just auditing, need to be included. Increased coverage of ethics issues is strongly supported.

MILLER, James. Carnivals of Atrocity: Foucault, Nietzsche, Cruelty. Polit Theory, 18(3), 470-491, Ag 90.

MILLER, Myron M. Reducing Legal Realism to Natural Law. Vera Lex, 7(2), 3-5, 1987.

Legal realisms like those of Hans Kelson and Alex Hagerstrom are shown to accept a set of descriptive assumptions to perform the task of justifying positive law. This is compared with the task of formulating any scientific theory, arguing that, as in any effective scientific explanation, the intelligibility of regularities assumes that the world is of such-and-such a structure. Similarly, the theoretic assumptions for legal realism posit that the structure of legal decisions is such-and-such. But then it is argued that so long as this is intelligible, this rests on the acceptance of natural law.

MILLER, Peter. Descartes' Legacy and Deep Ecology. Dialogue (Canada), 28(2), 183-202, 1989.

The Cartesian legacy in axiology is that values are conceived to be dependent upon (human) subjects. Deep ecology finds natural objects and systems to be valuable in their own right, and thus their value would seem to be independent of human valuing. Of three responses to this tension, informed and enriched anthropocentrism, projectionism, and extended naturalism, the author finds the last to be most harmonious with deep ecology and sketches several lines of explanation and defense.

MILLER, Richard B. Dog Bites Man: A Defence of Modal Realism. Austl J Phil, 67(4), 476-478, D 89.

The recent attempt by William Lycan to find fault with what he calls "Mad Dog Modal Realism" is compared to other recent criticism and examined in its own right. Lycan objects that Lewis cannot explicate the crucial notion of a world without implicitly invoking the notion of possibility, which it is meant to explain. It is admitted that this would be a grave, even fatal, flaw in any philosophical account of modality. But examination of Lewis's work shows that he can define "world" without modal notions while, ironically, Lycan is forced to admit that he cannot do so himself.

MILLER, Richard B. Neoteny and the Virtues of Childhood. Metaphilosophy, 20(3-4), 319-331, Jl-O 89.

The way philosophers conceive human development has important ramifications not only for the applied ethical issue of children's rights but also for philosophical theories of language, epistemology and education. Gareth Matthew's discussion of (1) the Preform Model, (2) the Logical Model, and (3) the Recap Model is reexamined. These are found to be inadequate but not mutually exclusive and in need of supplementation from the (4) Neoteny Model. Neoteny, the retention of youthful traits into adulthood, is found especially helpful in explaining human intelligence.

MILLER, Richard B. On Transplanting Human Fetal Tissue: Presumptive Duties and the Task of Casuistry. J Med Phil, 14(6), 617-640, D 89.

The procurement of fetal tissue for transplantation may promise great benefit to those suffering from various pathologies, e.g., neural disorders, diabetes, renal problems, and radiation sickness. However, debates about the use of fetal tissue have proceeded without much attention to ethical theory and application. Two broad moral questions are addressed here, the first formal, the second substantive: Is there a framework from other moral paradigms to assist in ethical debates about the transplantation of fetal tissue? Does the use of fetal tissue entail cooperation in abortion? To answer these questions the author develops a theoretical framework by combining the paradigm of just-war reasoning with canons governing the use of cadaverous tissue. (edited)

MILLER, Richard B. There Is Nothing Magical about Possible Worlds. Mind, 99(395), 453-457, Jl 90.

Alex Rosenberg has argued that David Lewis's genuine modal realism conflicts with the time-honored belief in the singularity of time. The multiplicity of distinct spaces and times is indeed required by genuine modal realism. However the arguments for the necessary singularity of space or time support only the singularity of actual space and time and assume that time is essentially McTaggert's A-series. On the contrary genuine modal realism does not conflict with the singularity of actual time and it assumes the objective reality of the B-series.

MILLER, Seumas. Derrida and the Indeterminacy of Meaning. S Afr J Phil, 9(1), 24-27, F 90.

A key doctrine in the account of language, propounded by Jacques Derrida, is that meaning is radically indeterminate. Derrida's argument for this indeterminacy appears to rest on his rejection of 'presence' and his commitment to meaning being wholly relational and essentially contextual. This argument fails in virtue of the falsity of its premises.

MILLER, Seumas and MAC DONALD, Ian. Philosophy in South Africa: A Reply to Robert Paul Wolff. Phil Forum, 21(4), 442-450, Sum 90.

In the first part of this paper we argue that R P Wolff's account in this journal of philosophy in South Africa seriously distorts the situation here. Analytic philosophers have had, and continue to have, a far greater concern with practical ethical political issues than Wolff admits. In the second part of this paper we address the question, "What ought the role of philosophy in South Africa be?"

MILLER, Seumas. Rationalising Conventions. Synthese, 84(1), 23-41, Jl 90.

Conformity by an agent to a convention to which the agent is a party is rational only if the agent prefers to conform given the other parties conform and believes the others will conform. But this justification is inadequate; what, for example, is the justification for this belief? The required rational justification requires recourse to (a) preferences for general conformity (as opposed to merely conditional preferences for one's own conformity) and (b) procedures. An agent adopts a procedure when he chooses to perform a whole set of future actions, as opposed to a single action.

MILLER, Steven I and FREDERICKS, Janet. The False Ontology of School Climate Effects. Educ Theor, 40(3), 333-342, Sum 90.

Theories concerning so-called "climate effects" have become an important empirical claim in the formulation of educational policies related to establishing "effective" schools. The authors argue that climate effects are based on suspect ontological claims which conflate a variety of separate empirical findings into a composite measure of dubious theoretical status. It is suggested that school effectiveness policies are better served by incorporating naturalistic forms of inquiry.

MILLICAN, Peter. Content, Thoughts and Definite Descriptions—I. Aris Soc, SUPP 64, 167-203, 1990.

MILLIKAN, Ruth Garrett. Seismograph Readings for "Explaining Behavior". Phil Phenomenol Res, 50(4), 807-812, Je 90.

Dretske's views in *Explaining Behavior* are vacillating both concerning what functions are and concerning what indication is. Indication cannot play the role he assigns to it in the learning history of an organism.

MILLIKAN, Ruth Garrett. Truth Rules, Hoverflies, and the Kripke-Wittgenstein Paradox. Phil Rev, 99(3), 323-353, Jl 90.

A naturalist solution to the Kripke-Wittgenstein paradox is offered. The solution is based on a biological theory of the nature of an ability or competence. A result is that it is just as easy to explain how a speaker might exhibit through his practice a grasp of correspondence truth rules as to explain how he might grasp unification ones. This blocks one route of Putnam's and Dummett's retreat from realism.

MILLS, Charles W. Determination and Consciousness in Marx. Can J Phil, 19(3), 421-445, S 89.

One of Marx's most famous and controversial claims is that socio-economic causality has an important influence on the genesis and development of ideas. But although this thesis is so central to historical materialism, it is nowhere given a detailed explication, and many commentators have seen it as self-undermining or completely implausible. This paper attempts to unpack the notion of socio-economic determination, arguing that the traditional monocausal interpretation is misleading, and that if it is replaced by a multicausal one, many of the standard objections to Marx's thesis may be overcome.

MILLS, Charles W and GOLDSTICK, Danny. A New Old Meaning of "Ideology". Dialogue (Canada), 28(3), 417-432, 1989.

For decades, "ideology" has been one of the most influential concepts in Marxist theory. But the corresponding claims attributed to Marx about the sociology of belief and the cognitive deficiencies of political thought have always been deeply problematic. In this paper we advance the radically novel interpretation that "ideology" does not refer generally to ideas, or class ideas, or bourgeois ideas, or socially determined ideas (the standard candidates), but rather specifically to the "superstructure" and "superstructuralism." This implies that a significant proportion of exegesis and commentary on Marx's views on the social determination of belief actually rests on mistaken premises.

MILLS, Stephen. Eliminative Materialism: The Reality of the Mental, and Folk Psychology—A Reply to O'Gorman. Irish Phil J, 6(1), 148-163, 1989.

MILLSPAUGH, Peter E. Plant Closing Ethics Root in American Law. J Bus Ethics, 9(8), 665-670, Ag 90.

The harsh consequences of the American plant closing epidemic in recent years on workers, their families, and their communities, have raised widespread ethical and moral concerns. In the early 1970s, a diverse group of academics, social activists, public policy analysts, and special interest organizations developed a number of legislative proposals designed to restrict closings by law. The proposals encountered many formidable obstacles in an increasingly hostile free-market environment. The business community was itself moved to assume some of the burdens precipated by closures either unilaterally or through collective bargaining. At the same time, powerful business interests tenaciously fought the enactment of mandatory closing restrictions into law. Nevertheless, through a prolonged and tortuous odyssey, the requirements of advanced notice and worker severance pay have now begun to root in law. Their success stands as evidence of a continuing American public policy receptivity to ethics-driven concerns.

MILLSTONE, David H. Oft-Told Tales. Thinking, 8(3), 31-33, 1989.

MILNE, Peter. Scotching the Dutch Book Argument. Erkenntnis, 32(1), 105-126, Ja 90.

Consistent application of coherence arguments shows that fair betting quotients are subject to constraints that are too stringent to allow their identification with either degrees of belief or probabilities. The pivotal role of fair betting quotients in the Dutch Book Argument, which is said to demonstrate that a rational agent's degrees of belief are probabilities, is thus undermined from both sides.

MILNER, Laura M and KROHN, Franklin B. The AIDS Crisis: Unethical Marketing Leads to Negligent Homicide. J Bus Ethics, 8(10), 773-780, O 89.

The purpose of this paper is to demonstrate how condom manufacturers and their marketers have failed to adequately promote their product to the male homosexual population (gays). Inasmuch as the AIDS syndrome constitutes a major life-threatening danger and that gays appear to be particularly vulnerable, failure to aggressively promote a known preventive such as condoms to gays constitutes negligent homicide. The method used here defines what is traditionally viewed as a viable "target market," analyzes the major elements of marketing with regard to gays, and examines the neglect of condom promotion by their manufacturers. It is concluded that condom marketers have failed to promote a known protection against AIDS to a highly susceptible group. That group would normally be seen as a highly attractive market for condoms and were it not for homophobia, marketers would zealously pursue more aggressive promotion of condoms to gays.

MINARI, Pierluigi. The Property (HD) in Intermediate Logics: A Partial

Solution of a Problem of H Ono. Rep Math Log, 22, 21-25, 1988.

MINDER, Thomas. The Thesis. Soc Epistem, 4(2), 201-213, Ap-Je 90.

MINKEVICIUS, Jokubas V. The Human Factor in the Revolution and Perestroika. Dialec Hum, 15(3-4), 85-92, Sum-Autumn 88.

MINOGUE, Kenneth. "Freedom as a Skill" in *Culture et Politique/Culture and Politics*, CRANSTON, Maurice (ed), 95-109. Hawthorne, de Gruyter, 1988.

MIROIU, Adrian. Le rôle des théorèmes du type Löwenheim-Skolem dans la logique des prédicats du premier ordre (in Romanian). Rev Filosof (Romania), 36(1), 97-107, Ja-F 89.

MIROWSKI, Philip. *More Heat than Light: Economics as Social Physics, Physics as Nature's Economics*. New York, Cambridge Univ Pr, 1989

Starting with the work of Emile Meyerson, this book shows how anthropomorphic metaphors of body, motion and value are central to the mathematicization of the disciplines of physics and economics. The first third describes the impact of cultural/economic ideas upon physics, particularly in the instance of the doctrine of the conservation of energy, whereas the remainder shows how neoclassical economics developed as an appropriation of the energy metaphor in both mathematics and rhetoric. The history is used to shed light on the vexed question of whether or not economics is a science.

MISHARA, Aaron L. Husserl and Freud: Time, Memory and the Unconscious. Husserl Stud, 7(1), 29-58, 1990.

MITCHAM, Carl. Ethics in Bioengineering. J Bus Ethics, 9(3), 227-231, Mr 90.

Bioengineering, as the decisive extension of engineering action to human life itself, constitutes a fundamental enlargment of the technical realm, and calls for a commensurate expansion of ethical reflection. In fact, the engineering profession has been actively pursuing the development of new ethical codes, and the promotion of ethics by bioengineers both in the United States and on the international level deserves philosophical recognition and support.

MITCHELL, Jeff. Danto, Dewey and the Historical End of Art. Trans Peirce Soc, 25(4), 469-501, Fall 89.

My paper examines Arthur Danto's contention that art has reached the end of its historical development from a Deweyan perspective. I argue that Danto's analysis of the metaphorlike nature of the work of art is insightful, but that the conclusions about the history of art which he then draws are mistaken. Dewey's notion of the esthetic experience is introduced as a way of appreciating the value of Danto's analysis of the work of art without commitment to the thesis about the historical end of art.

MITCHELL, W J T. The Violence of Public Art: *Do the Right Thing*. Crit Inquiry, 16(4), 880-889, Sum 90.

MITIUSHIN, A A. G Shpet and His Place in the History of Russian Psychology. Soviet Stud Phil, 28(2), 45-58, Fall 89.

MITTELSTAEDT, Peter and STROHMEYER, Ingeborg. Die kosmologischen Antinomien in der Kritik der reinen Vernunft und die moderne physikalische Kosmologie. Kantstudien, 81(2), 145-169, 1990.

MIXON, Don. Getting the Science Right is the Problem, Not the Solution: A Matter of Priority. J Theor Soc Behav, 20(2), 97-110, Je 90.

Psychology's practice of emulating the natural sciences has meant that unsatisfactory accomplishments are blamed on getting the science wrong and reforms are centered on getting the science right. The paper argues that putting method before problem is so entrenched in institutionalized practice that psychology will not create a set of distinctive problems until it can give problem priority over method. The chief work of the essay is to clarify issues and to weaken two of the chief supports—justification by science and fear of appearing unscientific—of psychology's 110-year project of science-by-emulation.

MO, Suchoon S. On Reversal of Temporality of Human Cognition and Dialectical Self. J Mind Behav, 11(1), 37-46, Wint 90.

In terms of temporality of logic, the relation between "before" and "after" is an inverse relation, as is the relation between intension and extension. Reversal of temporality of human cognition is accompanied by corresponding reversal between intension and extension. Such reversal is based on lateral reversal of brain hemisphere locus of time information. A similar inverse relation exists between self as subject and self as object. Extreme objectification of self is associated with brain hemisphere lateral reversal of time information, indicating that subject-object reversal is similar in nature to reversal of temporality of cognition. Dialectical nature of self is based on contradiction between self as subject and self as object. Synthesis arising from such contradiction may be regarded as reality of self.

MOBERG, Dennis J. Helping Subordinates with Their Personal Problems: A Moral Dilemma for Managers. J Bus Ethics, 9(6), 519-531, Je 90.

When subordinates ask managers for help with their personal problems, it creates moral dilemmas for their managers. Managers are contractually obliged to maintain equivalent relations between their subordinates and that is compromised when one subordinate makes this kind of request. By applying deontological principles to this dilemma, additional options are revealed, and the moral duties managers owe their subordinates in these situations are clarified.

MOCEK, Reinhard. Anmerkungen zur Autopoiesis. Deut Z Phil, 38(4), 354-362, 1990.

MODRAK, D K W. Aristotle on the Difference between Mathematics and Physics and First Philosophy. Apeiron, 22(4), 121-139, D 89.

In *Nicomachean Ethics* VI 8, Aristotle contrasts mathematics with physics and philosophy. The paper addresses the puzzle this raises: in what respect does first philosophy, which is the study of an immaterial first principle, resemble physics? The answer that is developed and defended here is, in brief, that the principles of first philosophy like those of physics and unlike mathematical axioms are ultimately justified through an appeal to observation and sense experience.

MODRAK, D K W. Aristotle The First Cognitivist? Apeiron, 23(1), 65-75, Mr 90.

In *Mind and Imagination in Aristotle*, Michael Wedin gives a comprehensive account of Aristotle's philosophy of mind that assimilates Aristotle's positions to those of modern cognitivism. The paper is a critical discussion of the successes and failures of this interpretative strategy. While acknowledging the importance of insights gained through examining Aristotle's positions within the context of modern philosophy of mind, the author argues for a more moderate position than Wedin's, one which grants similarities but also recognizes the significant differences between Aristotle's objectives and modern ones.

MOGGACH, Douglas. Absolute Spirit and Universal Self-Consciousness: Bruno Bauer's Revolutionary Subjectivism. Dialogue (Canada), 28(2), 235-256, 1989.

Bruno Bauer formulates an ontology of freedom through a critique of the Hegelian notion of substantiality and a consequent reassessment of the doctrines of absolute and objective spirit. He invests the individual self-consciousness with an infinite creative power, and attempts to develop an immanent concept of universality to distinguish this transformative energy from immediate, particularistic consciousness, the domain of egoistic material interest shaped heteronomously by the existing order. For Bauer, the pure productive self-activity behind all limited, concrete forms of embodiment is the true element of freedom and the essence of history.

MOGGACH, Douglas. Raison pratique et communauté chez Fichte. Rev Univ Ottawa, 57(4), 33-48, O-D 87.

Fichte's practical philosophy addresses the problem of mutual recognition, seeking to legitimate individuality and to reintegrate it into a rational whole. He distinguishes two structures of recognition, analytical and synthetic. The analytical model (right), based on private appropriation, delimits spheres of particularity and subsumes them under general laws in a formal-legal community. The synthetic model (morality) postulates self-legislation where individuals reach beyond their particularistic limits in willing the universal moral law. Fichte's attempt to define the sphere of morality retains in its end-means problematic the individualistic premises and the formal subsumption model of the sphere of right.

MOHANTA, Dilipkumar. Is Jayarasi a Materialist? Indian Phil Quart, SUPP 16(3), 1-4, Jl 89.

MOHANTY, J N. Idealism and Quantum Mechanics. Hist Phil Quart, 6(4), 381-391, O 89.

MOHR, Hans. "Is the Program of Molecular Biology Reductionistic?" in *Reductionism and Systems Theory in the Life Sciences: Some Problems and Perspectives*, HOYNINGEN-HUENE, Paul (ed), 137-159. Norwell, Kluwer, 1989.

MOIR, Martin (ed) and ROBSON, John M (ed) and MILL, John Stuart and MOIR, Zawahir (ed). *Writings on India (Collected Works of John Stuart Mill, Volume 30)*. Buffalo, Univ of Toronto Pr, 1990

MOIR, Zawahir (ed) and ROBSON, John M (ed) and MILL, John Stuart and MOIR, Martin (ed). *Writings on India (Collected Works of John Stuart Mill, Volume 30)*. Buffalo, Univ of Toronto Pr, 1990

MOKRZYCKI, Edmund. The Problem of Going *To*: Between Epistemology and the Sociology of Knowledge. Soc Epistem, 3(3), 205-216, Jl-S 89.

An attempt is made to define the theoretical situation in which the philosophy of science has found itself as a result of the crisis of the seventies. It is argued that the crisis has not resulted in new paradigms. The turn toward history has been neutralized, and the turn toward sociology miscarried. Though logically the philosophy of science is faced with a choice between the return to epistemology and evolution in the direction of a social science of science, realistically it is fated to blocking its developmental possibilities in both directions.

MOLANDER, Bengt. One More Time. Acta Phil Fennica, 38, 133-148, 1985.

MOLES, Alistair. Nietzsche's Eternal Recurrence as Riemannian Cosmology. Int Stud Phil, 21(2), 21-35, 1989.

The paper argues that Nietzsche's doctrine of eternal recurrence, considered as cosmological hypothesis, is made more plausible if the influence of Friedrich Zoellner is recognized. Zoellner was among the first to apply Bernhard Riemann's geometry of positively curved space to constructing a model of the universe which reconciles the law of conservation of energy with the second law of thermodynamics by making it impossible for energy to dissipate to infinity. Nietzsche read Zoellner's book; however, his version of the model entails that the universe is bounded in time as well as space: the same events recur.

MOLES, Alistair. *Nietzsche's Philosophy of Nature and Cosmology*. New York, Lang, 1989

This work argues for the plausibility of construing Nietzsche as a philosopher of nature, and demonstrates that his doctrine of eternal recurrence, as a hypothesis concerning the universe, is loosely entailed by his conceptions of inorganic nature, the necessity of events, temporality and space. The key to understanding this entailment is that Nietzsche's conception of space must be understood as Riemannian (finite yet unbounded, and with positive curvature). Nietzsche's access to this conception of space is almost certainly through his reading an important book by the Leipzig astrophysicist, Friedrich Zöllner.

MOLINA, Jorge. Definiciones impredicativas. Rev Filosof (Argentina), 2(1), 43-66, My 87.

This paper attempts first to examine the issue of whether circular definitions must be avoided in mathematics. Second, granted that the answer is affirmative, the question arises whether they can really be avoided.

MOLINARO, Aniceto. Presupposizione e verità: Il problema critico della conoscenza filosofica. Aquinas, 32(3), 435-444, S-D 89.

MOLINUEVO, José Luis. El tardío pesimismo metafísico de Horkheimer. Rev Filosof (Spain), 1, 115-126, 1987-88.

MOLLOWITZ, Gerhard. Bewährung-aus-sich-selbst als Kriterium der philosophischen Wahrheit. Schopenhauer Jahr, 70, 205-225, 1989.

MOLLOWITZ, Gerhard. Philosophische Wahrheit aus intuitivem Urdenken. Schopenhauer Jahr, 70, 189-205, 1989.

MOMEYER, Richard W. Philosophers and the Public Policy Process: Inside, Outside, or Nowhere at All? J Med Phil, 15(4), 391-409, Ag 90.

Three standard tasks undertaken by applied ethicists engaged in the public policy process are identifying value issues, clarifying concepts and meanings, and analyzing arguments. I urge that these should be expanded to include making specific moral judgments and advocating positions and policies. Three objections to philosophers/ethicists' engagement in the formation of public policy are advanced and evaluated: philosophers necessarily do public policy badly, doing it at all compromises one's integrity as a seeker after truth, and frequently participation is in the service of a repressive status quo that is structured simultaneously to preclude radical change and to co-opt ethicists. Finally, however, I argue that those who would be 'applied ethicists' cannot avoid all participation in some form of a public policy process; that engagement holds the hope as well for improved ethical theory; that the preferred form of participation is frequently from outside of establishment bodies; and that wherever philosophers do involve themselves in policy formulation, this is best done in the expanded sense urged at the outset.

MONACHELLO, M and FALKENBERG, L. Dual-Career and Dual-Income Families: Do They Have Different Needs? J Bus Ethics, 9(4-5), 339-351, Ap-My 90.

Dual-earner families have been treated as if they are a homogenous group of individuals having to cope with similar demands. Yet these families vary in their rationale for both spouses working outside the home (from financial necessity to personal growth) and the responsibilities each spouse assumes in the home. Given the variations in work and home responsibilities it is proposed that members of dual-earner families should be studied on the basis of (1) the rationale each spouse has for working, (b) the responsibility each spouse assumes in the home, and (c) the gender of the spouse. A

model delineating the different problems experienced by individuals within these subgroups is developed based on an extensive review of the literature.

MONAGHAN, Floyd V and CORCOS, Alain F. The Real Objective of Mendel's Paper. Biol Phil, 5(3), 267-292, Jl 90.

According to the traditional account Mendel's paper on pea hybrids reported a study of inheritance and its laws. Hence, Mendel came to be known as "The Father of Genetics." This paper demonstrates that, in fact, Mendel's objective in his research was finding the empirical laws which describe the formation of hybrids and the development of their offspring over several generations. (edited)

MONCONDUIT, François. "Tocqueville: La culture de la démocratie, menace pour la démocratie" in *Culture et Politique/Culture and Politics*, CRANSTON, Maurice (ed), 67-72. Hawthorne, de Gruyter, 1988.

MONDAL, Sunil Baran. A Consideration of Sartre's View of 'Existence'. Indian Phil Quart, SUPP 17(1), 5-13, Ja 90.

MONDIN, B. Ateismo e libertà. Sapienza, 43(1), 3-20, Ja-Mr 90.

MONDIN, Battista. Un tratado de teología natural de Octavio N Derisi. Sapientia, 44(174), 308-310, O-D 89.

MONFASANI, John. Lorenzo Valla and Rudolph Agricola. J Hist Phil, 28(2), 181-200, Ap 90.

The article argues that Valla and Agricola differed significantly in their approach to philosophy, logic, and rhetoric. Indeed, Agricola's *De inventione dialectica* may be seen as an antidote to Valla's teaching. Furthermore, contrary to the opinion of Lisa Jardine, Valla was not an Academic sceptic. He was, in fact, hostile to scepticism. Finally, it is probably wrong to read scepticism into Agricola's *De inventione dialectica*.

MONTAGNA, F and CARBONE, Alessandra. Rosser Orderings in Bimodal Logics. Z Math Log, 35(4), 343-358, 1989.

MONTAGNA, Franco and CARBONE, Alessandra. Much Shorter Proofs: A Bimodal Investigation. Z Math Log, 36(1), 47-66, 1990.

MONTAGNES, Bernard. Les séquelles de la crise moderniste. Rev Thomiste, 90(2), 245-270, Ap-Je 90.

MONTERO, Fernando. En defensa de la objectividad. Rev Filosof (Spain), 2, 65-86, 1989.

The aim of this paper is to defend the intentional objectivity studied by Husserl, against the interpretation of the object made by authors of the analytical tradition such as Frege, Russell, and Searle. To that end, the paper examines the problem of objective identity and the processes of semantical identification, both those that express the identity of one and the same object by means of different denominations, and those that verify the identity of the named object by means of an empirical fulfillment. In both cases, it is concluded that the meaning and its fulfillment can only be analyzed appealing to the object spoken of or perceived.

MONTES, Raúl Iturrino. Husserlian Ontology of Cultural Objects. Dialogos, 25(55), 125-132, Ja 90.

In this paper, after making a rather schematic and partial presentation of Husserl's idea of regional ontologies, we expound some regional categories commanding the sphere of cultural objects, of which ideality is more closely examined. Finally, a critical remark is made concerning Karl Popper's theory of ideality and understanding in the human sciences. It is acknowledged that we here only *announce* aspects of the phenomenological analysis of cultural objects which deserve separate and detailed treatment.

MONTESANO, Aldo. On the Definition of Risk Aversion. Theor Decis, 29(1), 53-68, Jl 90.

Two definitions of risk aversion have recently been proposed for nonexpected utility theories of choice under uncertainty: the former refers the measure of risk aversion directly to the risk premium; the latter defines risk aversion as a decreasing preference for an increasing risk. When the von Neumann-Morgenstern utility function exists both these definitions indicate an agent as a risk averter if his or her utility function is concave. Consequently, the two definitions are equivalent. However, they are no longer equivalent when the von Neumann-Morgenstern utility function does not exist and a nonexpected utility theory is assumed. (edited)

MONTESQUIEU, Charles and COHLER, Anne M (trans) and MILLER, Basia C (trans) and STONE, Harold (trans). *The Spirit of the Laws: Charles Montesquieu*. New York, Cambridge Univ Pr, 1989

MONTGOMERY, Richard. Does Epistemology Reduce to Cognitive Psychology? Philosophia (Israel), 19(2-3), 245-263, O 89.

Alvin Goldman's reliabilist epistemology, as elaborated in *Epistemology and Cognition*, paves the way for an intertheoretic reduction of what he calls *primary individual epistemology* to cognitive psychology. The main dimensions of epistemic evaluation that Goldman identifies, *reliability, power*, and *speed*, already play a role in cognitive explanations. Moreover, the *normative* status of epistemology is not, as Goldman claims, a roadblock to successful reduction. The only difference between primary individual epistemology and cognitive psychology is a *pragmatic* one: their objectives differ.

MONTOYA, Rocío Basurto. El concepto de libertad en Humano, demasiado humano de Nietzsche. Logos (Mexico), 17(51), 71-79, S-D 89.

MOOIJ, A W M. Psychoanalyse: pseudo-wetenschap of geesteswetenschap? Alg Ned Tijdschr Wijs, 82(1), 44-53, Ja 90.

In this article an aspect of Grünbaum's critique of Freud is discussed, originally formulated in 'The Foundations of Psychoanalysis: A Philosophical Critique' (1984), along the modifications as were put forward by A A Derksen. At the core of this critique is a criticism of the so-called Tally Argument, the thesis ascribed to Freud that only true interpretations could be effective in psychoanalytic treatment. The argument which is brought in against this thesis is that in this matter Freud did not specifically have an externally measurable effectiveness in view. Instead he defined the way of finding truth in the psychoanalytic context: essential is to gain insight in an intrapsychic reality, which insight may bring about, in an internal way, changes in the psychic reality.

MOOKENTHOTTAM, Antony. Groundwork for an Indian Christian Theology. J Dharma, 14(4), 343-352, O-D 89.

MOONEY, Gavin. The Demand for Effectiveness, Efficiency and Equity of Health Care. Theor Med, 10(3), 195-205, S 89.

Effectiveness, efficiency and equity in health care are discussed in this article against the background of concerns that 'cost containment' may lead to reductions in quality of care. It is suggested that effectiveness is best seen from the patient's point of view and that it relates to more than simply improved health status. Efficiency and equity are better viewed from a societal stance. The paper discusses the role of the medical profession in effectiveness, efficiency and equity and argues that the role of medical doctors needs to be constrained.

MOOR, James and SINNOTT-ARMSTRONG, Walter and FOGELIN, Robert. A Defence of Modus Tollens. Analysis, 50(1), 9-16, Ja 90.

Ernest Adams recently discussed an apparent counterexample to modus tollens: A asserts (1) If it rained, it didn't rain hard; B asserts (2) it rained hard; but it is paradoxical to conclude (3) it didn't rain. Adams avoids this paradox by claiming that (1) cannot be a material conditional, because A would not accept its contrapositive. We argue that (1) can be a material conditional; modus tollens is valid; Adams's contrapositive explanation fails; and no paradox arises, because it is illegitimate to draw conclusions from assertions when they can't both be true, and (1)-(2) can't both be true, given 'If it rained hard, it rained'.

MOORE, A W. The Infinite. New York, Routledge, 1990

This book, which covers all aspects of the infinite from the mathematical to the mystical, is in two parts. In the first part the author traces the history of the topic. In the second part he draws on various technical results, and on the early work of Wittgenstein, to develop his own account of the infinite, arguing that there are fundamental links between the infinite and the ineffable. In a final chapter on human finitude, these and other links are traced out, and the book culminates in a discussion of death.

MOORE, Brook Noel and PARKER, Richard. *Critical Thinking: Evaluating Claims and Arguments in Everyday Life—Second Edition*. Mountain View, Mayfield, 1989

MOORE, Dorothy P. An Examination of Present Research on the Female Entrepreneur-Suggested Strategies for the 1990's. J Bus Ethics, 9(4-5), 275-281, Ap-My 90.

Intensive investigations into female entrepreneurships are a relatively recent research phenomenon. Advances in the past five years, while dramatic, find the field in an initial stage of paradigm development. Individual studies appear fragmented, unrelated, and seem to describe only small segments of the female entrepreneurial population and more frequently than not apply theoretical tools developed in other areas which are neither reliable or valid. This article examines a number of current research and methodological issues, presents a descriptive analysis of the traditional and modern female entrepreneur, suggests focal areas for research oriented toward the establishment of typologies, models and theory development.

MOORE, F C T. A Problem about Higher Order Desires. Acta Phil Fennica, 38, 149-155, 1985.

Coordination problems can arise in any social context where independent action is possible for participants. Certain results, such as the Prisoner's Dilemma, suggest that these problems are insoluble in principle. For, contrary to a common view, Prisoner's Dilemma arises as well for altruistic as

for self-seeking agents. The paper explores a line of solution through higher-order desires or preferences, such that the parties prefer their own first order preferences to accord with those of the other party. But the paper ends in paradox: the solution will only work if it does not work.

MOORE, Jay. On Mentalism, Privacy, and Behaviorism. J Mind Behav, 11(1), 19-36, Wint 90.

The present paper examines three issues from the perspective of Skinner's radical behaviorism: (a) the nature of mentalism, (b) the relation between behaviorism and mentalism, and (c) the nature of behavioristic objections to mentalism. Mentalism is characterized as a particular orientation to the explanation of behavior that entails an appeal to inner causes. Methodological and radical behaviorism are examined with respect to this definition, and methodological behaviorism is held to be mentalistic by virtue of its implicit appeal to mental phenomena in the account of how knowledge is gained from scientific endeavors. Finally, it is noted that the behavioristic objection to mentalism is pragmatic: mentalism interferes with the effective explanation of behavioral events.

MOORE, Jennifer. What is Really Unethical About Insider Trading? J Bus Ethics, 9(3), 171-182, Mr 90.

Insider trading is illegal, and is widely believed to be unethical. It has received widespread attention in the media and has become, for some, the very symbol of ethical decay in business. For a practice that has come to epitomize unethical business behavior, however, insider trading has received surprisingly little ethical analysis. This article critically examines the principal ethical arguments against insider trading: the claim that the practice is unfair, the claim that it involves a "misappropriation" of information and the claim that it harms ordinary investors and the market as a whole. The author concludes that each of these arguments has some serious deficiencies; no one of them by itself provides a sufficient reason for outlawing insider trading. This does not mean, however, that there are no reasons for prohibiting the practice. The author argues that the real reason for outlawing insider trading is that it undermines the fiduciary relationship that lies at the heart of American business.

MOORE, Keith M. Water Quality Concerns and the Public Policy Context. Agr Human Values, 6(4), 12-20, Fall 89.

National water quality concerns are creating momentum for legislation that takes a proactive stance toward agricultural practices involving agrichemicals. In response, the Environmental Protection Agency has asked the states to design appropriate non-point source pollution policies. This article examines the issues involved in two ways. First, it reviews the literature on previous conservation policies and discusses the implications for stricter regulation. Second, in order to determine the public opinion context for non-point source pollution policies, it examines the responses of a sample of Oklahoma rural leaders to a set of environmental, water quality, political, economic, and family farm orientation items developed in previous surveys. The analysis considers areas of agreement and disagreement related to socio-economic status, education, and extent of involvement in farming. It concludes that although Oklahoma's rural leaders are concerned about water quality problems, an environmentally sound formulation of rural values has yet to develop. The most serious obstacle appears to be the perceived threat of environmental regulations to the variability of production agriculture.

MOORE, Mark H. *Ethics in Government: The Moral Challenge of Public Leadership*. Englewood Cliffs, Prentice-Hall, 1990

Designed both for practitioners in, and students of, government, this book explores the nature of the particular moral obligations and ethical dilemmas which face public officials within a democracy. It uses real life case studies, with commentaries, to uncover issues of leadership, official discretion, stewardship of public resources; and obligations to colleagues, subordinates, and to the democratic process.

MOORE, Michael. Choice, Character, and Excuse. Soc Phil Pol, 7(2), 29-58, Spr 90.

MOORE, Michael. "Intentions and *Mens Rea*" in Issues in Contemporary Legal Philosophy: The Influence of H L A Hart, GAVISON, Ruth (ed), 245-270. New York, Clarendon/Oxford Pr, 1987.

MOORS, Kent F. The Argument Against a Dramatic Date for Plato's *Republic*. Polis, 7(1), 6-31, 1987.

MOORS, Kent F. Chthonic Themes in Plato's *Republic*. Dialogos, 25(55), 29-37, Ja 90.

MORALES, Julian. En pensamiento político en sociedades sin estado dentro del marco de un nuevo concepto de historia. Anu Filosof, 22(1), 159-170, 1989.

Concepts as history, thought and organization are consubstantial to mankind, for this reason it is complicated to assume a univocal conception of history, and we are inclined towards a history of political thought as progress. Clans are primitive societies, as social wholes determined by consanguinity lines. Organization is realized through distribution of functions. When cooperation is developed, it passes from the clan to the local group. When clans agglutinate as tribes, ideological and suprastructural levels appear. People talk political organization when tribal unity is produced, but political activity begins when the approach between myth and political thought is realized (theocratic conception of city-state). It can be said that political organization exists as such, and so states formed by the birth of empires, because of its territorial dimensions, its organized sedentary life, its military groups and its stabilized economy.

MORALES, Julián. Sociognoseología y objectividad. Anu Filosof, 20(1), 207-219, 1987.

MORAN, Richard. Seeing and Believing: Metaphor, Image, and Force. Crit Inquiry, 16(1), 87-112, Autumn 89.

Metaphor is called a *figurative* use of language, and discussions of it frequently allude to images or something picture-like to describe its functioning. And part of this functioning is described in terms of a certain rhetorical or persuasive *force* that is thought to be peculiar to metaphorical language. This paper tries to account for the association of the idioms of 'imagery' and 'force' in discussions of literary metaphor, and criticizes various other ways in which the association has been construed. Various parallels are drawn between metaphors and images in their problematic relations to assertion and belief, and in the course of this I discuss at length Donald Davidson's denial that a metaphorical utterance means or says anything distinct from its literal meaning. Davidson's view is ultimately rejected, although it forces the defender of metaphoric-meaning to distinguish the assertoric from the non-assertoric dimensions of metaphor. Understanding the type of thinking involved in the composition and comprehension of literary metaphor requires attention to both aspects.

MORAVCSIK, J M. *Thought and Language*. New York, Routledge, 1990

This book defends a realist ontology in philosophy of language, criticizes causalism and behaviorism, and sketches an "objectual" account of cognition. It also presents a new theory of lexical meaning according to which meanings of words are explanatory schemes, to be filled in in predictable but context-dependent ways. Underlying this theory is a conception of humans not as labelling and information gathering creatures, but as primarily explanation seeking creatures.

MORAVCSIK, Julius M. Between Reference and Meaning. Midwest Stud Phil, 14, 68-83, 1989.

As the meaning of a word like 'emergency' shows, meaning does not determine reference. Two people can agree on the meaning of this word, but disagree on what counts in a particular context as emergency. The paper develops a 3-level analysis—apart from indexicality—that generates meaning, then contexts for reference, and criteria for reference. This analysis is shown to affect most lexical items in a language like English, and thus needs to be incorporated as a key element in an adequate semantics for natural languages.

MORAVCSIK, Julius M. The Role of Virtues in Alternatives to Kantian and Utilitarian Ethics. Philosophia (Israel), 20(1-2), 33-48, Jl 90.

This paper articulates a conceptually distinct alternative to both utilitarianism and deontic ethics. It shows also that accounts of virtues can be made parts of either deontic ethics, or utilitarian moral theories. The distinctive approach makes the specification of aim for life and character fundamental, denies the distinction between moral and nonmoral virtues, and derives appropriate ways of dealing with each other from the right aim and character.

MORAWETZ, Thomas. "Comment: The Middle Way in the Philosophy of Punishment" in *Issues in Contemporary Legal Philosophy: The Influence of H L A Hart*, GAVISON, Ruth (ed), 221-237. New York, Clarendon/Oxford Pr, 1987.

MORAWIEC, Edmund. Appréciation de l'oeuvre théologico-philosophique de Thomas d'Aquin au tournant des XIIIe-XIVe ss (in Polish). Stud Phil Christ, 25(2), 73-87, 1989.

Des le début, l'oeuvre théologico-philosophique de Thomas d'Aquin a recontre une appréciation qui s'est manifestée par la critique et par l'acceptation. Ce qui est devenu l'objet de l'appréciation c'est, contenue dans l'oeuvre la doctrine chrétienne vue du point de vue de sa position face à la philosophie d'Aristote. L'article se propose de reproduire les positions directes prises face à la doctrine de Thomas d'Aquin par les théologiens et les philosophes chrétiens et non chrétiens qui lui sont les plus proches quant au temps. Les plus proches, car le sujet de l'article embrase la période de la seconde moitié du XIIIe s. et la première du XIVe s. (edited)

MORAWSKI, Stefan. "Revolution und Avantgarde: *Vor und nach 1917*"

in *Cultural Hermeneutics of Modern Art: Essays in Honor of Jan Aler*, DETHIER, Hubert (ed), 167-182. Amsterdam, Rodopi, 1989.

The article is a part of a quite large study on the topic. It deals with the intricate interrelations between the artistic circles considering the avant garde ideology as the very embodiment of the revolutionary movement which should bring justice and freedom to the world out of joint. This happened all over Europe. However, when the October revolution won its crusade of setting the world right, it occurred the constantly growing hiatus between the artistic visions and the ruling establishment. The artists were indeed revolutionary anarchist-minded visionaries, the party officials could not stomach the avant garde because it was (a) too difficult for masses as well as for them, and (b) imprinted with the spirit of dissent menacing the new social order.

MORCHIO, Renzo. Nel labirinto dell'informazione: i sistemi complessi. Epistemologia, 11(2), 305-316, Jl-D 88.

Terms like form, structure, information and the like have invaded practically all fields of scientific research, and although this is, in itself, a healthy sign of expansion, it must be said that we need to use them with a great deal of caution if we are to avoid ominous misunderstandings. A scientific definition of the terms, in fact, requires that they are stripped of a great many number of meanings that they normally have in everyday language, and this is a mixed blessing, because what is gained in rigour is often lost in range and suppleness. (edited)

MORDEN, Michael J. The Salesperson: Clerk, Con Man or Professional? Bus Prof Ethics J, 8(1), 3-23, Spr 89.

MORDEN, Michael. Free Will, Self-Causation, and Strange Loops. Austl J Phil, 68(1), 59-73, Mr 90.

Compatibilism is a doctrine concerning how free we have to be in order to be free *enough* (viz., free enough to be morally responsible). We reach this level when our self-awareness allows us to become one of the causes of our own behavior. Clearly this view requires that we make sense of the concept of self-causation. Douglas Hofstadter's discussion of "strange loops" is crucial for defending this position and helpful for interpreting other variants on compatibilism from the recent literature.

MOREH, J. The Authority of Moral Rules. Theor Decis, 27(3), 257-273, N 89.

The wide gap between the prescriptions of moral rules and actual human behaviour is attributed to two factors which undermine the authority of moral rules, the one mainly affecting people's behaviour as individuals, and the other their behaviour as members of collectives. (a) Morality suffers from an inner tension: if it allows exemptions, e.g., that lying may be used as a retaliatory or protective measure, then its domain is eroded; if it allows no exceptions, it is too stringent and it is flouted. Hence the moral agent who is the upholder of morality is also the transgressor of its rules. (b) Groups have evolved hostile and oppressive institutions for dealing with each other. In the setting up of these institutions and in the practising of them, individual moral responsibility is attenuated to vanishing point, so that moral rules are ineffectual in a large area of human interaction.

MOREHOUSE, Richard. A Model for the Evaluation of Moral Education. Thinking, 4(1), 2-9, 1982.

Philip Phenix's *Realms of Meaning* is used as a conceptual framework for placing moral education within a larger framework and for assessing the strengths and weaknesses of four different approaches to moral education: value classification, moral reasoning, value analysis, and philosophy for children. After examining the place of moral education within the general curriculum, the four major approaches to moral education are evaluated in terms of materials available to teachers and students, the training needed to effectively conduct the program and the comprehensiveness of the theoretical background.

MORELAND, J P. Keith Campbell and the Trope View of Predication. Austl J Phil, 67(4), 379-393, D 89.

After comparing extreme nominalism (qualities do not exist), nominalism (qualities are abstract particulars called tropes), and realism (qualities are universals), I focus on the nominalist views of Keith Campbell. His understanding of a nominalist assay of qualities and quality-instances is stated and subjected to criticism. The criticisms center on Campbell's use of the distinction of reason to analyze a trope. I conclude that Campbell's views are incoherent.

MORELLI, Elizabeth A. A Reflection on Lonergan's Notion of the Pure Desire to Know. Ultim Real Mean, 13(1), 50-60, Mr 90.

This paper critically examines Lonergan's notion of the pure desire to know, outlining its place in his works, and analyzing the nature of this desire. Modern objections to the existence of such a desire, from Nietzsche, Foucault, and Rorty, are presented. They are answered in terms of

Lonergan's own arguments for its existence. Finally, the question of the relationship of the pure desire to know and the will to power is discussed. The conclusion is reached that the two are equiprimordial, neither is reducible to the other; but that they are dialectically linked.

MORENO, Antonio. Finality and Intelligibility in Biological Evolution. Thomist, 54(1), 1-31, Ja 90.

MORENO, Arley R. Duas observações sobre a gramática filosófica. Manuscrito, 12(2), 83-115, O 89.

The present work compares the Wittgensteinian project of 'philosophy-as-therapy', in the form of a grammatical description of the rules of the use of language, with two other philosophical projects, apparently quite distinct: the archaeology/genealogy of Foucault and the stylistic approach of Granger. The comparison aims at stressing the differences and similarities between these approaches. The paper tries to show that the grammatical, on the one hand, is not an exploration of the vague, nor, in renouncing the transcendental, is it a plunge into the empirical—as in Foucault. On the other hand, regarded as the philosophy of concept, and not of the conscience, the grammatical is not necessarily built up upon a priori transcendental foundations as in Granger. The aim of these considerations is to prepare the field for a more detailed analysis with respect to the theoretical status of therapeutic discourse as proposed by Wittgenstein—suggesting that the notion of a language game plays a determining role in this context.

MORETTI, Alberto. Sobre la objeción de Orayen a la semántica de Meinong. Cuad Filosof, 20(33), 49-54, O 89.

It is pointed out that there is an implicit premiss in the argument by means of which Orayen concludes that Meinong's ontology is inconsistent. It is shown that this is an objectionable premiss but nevertheless the essentials of the argument are apt to prove the nonplausibility of Meinong's theory.

MORGAN, Charles G. "Semantic Discovery for Relevance Logics" in *Directions in Relevant Logic*, NORMAN, Jean (ed), 241-267. Norwell, Kluwer, 1989.

MORGAN, Huw. Confidentiality and Young People: A G.P.'s Response. Ethics Med, 4(2), 24-25, 1988.

As a Christian GP it seems clear to me that what is threatened by any ruling that doctors have a duty of confidentiality towards minors is no less than the integrity of the family, and particularly the duty, responsibility and right of parents to care for and guide their children. In this paper I propose to do four things. Firstly (and briefly), to consider the purpose of confidentiality from a medical viewpoint; secondly, to outline the particular problems that confidentiality towards young people poses; thirdly, to illustrate these problems with two case histories; and finally to consider the lessons we must learn from these.

MORGAN, Michael L. Plato, Inquiry, and Painting. Apeiron, 23(2), 121-145, Je 90.

MORILLO, Carolyn R. The Reward Event and Motivation. J Phil, 87(4), 169-186, Ap 90.

The paper sketches a theory of motivation based on empirical studies of the rewarding nature of electrical stimulation of the brain, and of many drugs. The theory speculates that (1) all positive motivation is anchored in *internal* reward events, (2) there is only one *ultimate* object of (positive) motivation, and (3) we intrinsically desire these reward events *because* they are intrinsically satisfying, they are not intrinsically satisfying *because* we desire them. The theory challenges philosophical theories of motivation often appealed to in criticisms of psychological egoism, and also challenges the adequacy of belief-desire models for explaining action.

MORILLON, Marianne and HADDAD, Labib. L'axiome de normalité pour les espaces totalement ordonnés. J Sym Log, 55(1), 277-283, Mr 90.

We show that the following property (LN) holds in the basic Cohen model as sketched by Jech: The order topology of any linearly ordered set is normal. This proves the independence of the axiom of choice from LN in ZF, and thus settles a question raised by G Birkhoff (1940) which was partly answered by van Douwen (1985).

MOROWITZ, Harold J. "Biology as a Cosmological Science" in *Nature in Asian Tradition of Thought: Essays in Environmental Philosophy*, CALLICOTT, J Baird (ed), 37-49. Albany, SUNY Pr, 1989.

MORPURGO-TAGLIABUE, Guido. Non replica, chiarimento. Teoria, 9(2), 173-175, 1989.

MORREALL, John and LOY, Jessica. Kitsch and Aesthetic Education. J Aes Educ, 23(4), 63-73, Wint 89.

We trace the origins of Kitsch to the Industrial Revolution and the ensuing loss of two traditional sources of aesthetic sensibility: familiarity with nature and craft skills. Then we discuss the increasing aesthetic deprivation of our

postindustrial age, especially our hunger for instant, passive aesthetic experiences. We close by presenting several cultural and aesthetic lessons to be learned from Kitsch, and then suggesting specific ways to use Kitsch in the arts curriculum.

MORREIM, E Haavi. The New Economics of Medicine: Special Challenges for Psychiatry. J Med Phil, 15(1), 97-119, F 90.

The ongoing economic overhaul of medicine creates two basic imperatives—boosting profits and containing costs—that pose special ethical and philosophical challenges for psychiatry. Because insurance coverage still favors inpatient care, pressures to raise revenues translate into a corresponding pressure on psychiatry as a whole to expand its diagnostic categories, and on individual psychiatrists to ascribe these diagnoses liberally and to hospitalize as many patients as possible. Reciprocally, cost containment requires all physicians to justify their care as clearly as possible and to eliminate those interventions that are not of demonstrable value. An economics-driven reorganization of psychiatry therefore poses serious philosophical challenges, not only for the profession and its future, but for the clinical care of patients. (edited)

MORREIM, E Haavi. Physician Investment and Self-Referral: Philosophical Analysis of a Contentious Debate. J Med Phil, 15(4), 425-448, Ag 90.

A new economic phenomenon, in which physicians refer their patients to ancillary facilities of which they themselves are owners or substantial investors, present a 'laboratory' for assessing philosophers' potential contributions to public policy issues. In this particular controversy, 'prohibitionists' who wish to ban all such self-referral focus on the dangers that patients and payers may receive or be billed for unnecessary or poor-quality care. 'Laissez-fairists', in contrast, argue that self-referral should be freely permitted, with a reliance on personal ethics and internal professional monitoring to guard against abuse. Undue government regulation, they argue, infringes providers' and patients' economic freedom, and stifles the competition that can yield better quality care at lower prices. (edited)

MORREN JR, George E B. Multi-Party Responses to Environmental Problems: A Case of Contaminated Dairy Cattle. Agr Human Values, 6(4), 30-39, Fall 89.

This paper presents a framework for exploring the temporal and behavioral aspects of the responses of various involved parties that may lead to governmental intervention in situations involving exposure of the public to hazardous substances. The activities of key individuals are closely scrutinized. Relevance of the framework to agricultural and food concerns is also indicated. The exemplary case is the contamination of livestock in Michigan that began in 1973, but other cases are discussed that conform closely to the pattern described by the framework.

MORRILL, Glyn and CARPENTER, Bob. Compositionality, Implicational Logics, and Theories of Grammar. Ling Phil, 13(4), 383-392, Ag 90.

According to (Frege's) principle of compositionality, the meaning of a linguistic expression is to be analysed as a function of the meaning of its components, and their mode of combination. The paper shows how a construal of this principle for natural language, together with an assumption that meanings fit a simply typed function space, derives effects achieved by the Theta-Criterion in Government-Binding Theory, and Completeness and Coherence Conditions in Lexical-Functional Grammar. The demonstration exploits the relationship between functional types and implicational logics, and is interpreted as providing semantic rationalisation for apparently arbitrary syntactic principles.

MORRIS, Christopher W. A Hobbesian Welfare State? Dialogue (Canada), 27(4), 653-673, Wint 88.

MORRIS, Michael. Empirical Versus Epistemological Considerations: A Comment on Stemmer. Mind Lang, 4(3), 222-228, Autumn 89.

MORRIS, Randall C. Whitehead and the New Liberals on Social Progress. J Hist Ideas, 51(1), 75-92, Ja-Mr 90.

This article aims to contribute to the task of reconstructing Whitehead's political beliefs through a detailed comparison of his theory of social progress with those advanced by L T Hobhouse and J S Mill. It begins by outlining certain key ideas concerning progress contained in Whitehead's metaphysics. It then examines the concepts of uniformity and force which Whitehead identifies as the main threats to social progress. These dangers are shown to be related not only to the principles of order and novelty in his metaphysics, but also correspond closely to the concerns of the new liberals with individuality and sociability.

MORRIS, T F. The Argument in the *Protagoras* that No One Does What He Believes To Be Bad. Interpretation, 17(2), 291-304, Wint 89-90.

MORRIS, T F. Plato's *Euthyphro*. Heythrop J, 31(3), 309-323, Jl 90.

Time after time Euthyphro is stymied because he cannot say what the gods like. If we knew what the gods like we could be pious, for we could try to give them what they like. But the dialogue takes as unproblematic that the gods care about people—to whom they give all good things—and especially that they care that people act justly. Thus piety would entail preventing people from acting unjustly (Socrates). Euthyphro exemplifies impiety because he does not care if he is doing wrong in the sight of the gods.

MORRIS, T. Kierkegaard on Despair and the Eternal. Sophia (Australia), 28(3), 21-30, O 89.

An exegetical study of *Works of Love*. I explain how preference makes erotic love and friendship really be self-love. They are in despair because they involve treating the other as if she/he were eternal, i.e., as an idol. I explain how not having the eternal is being in despair. The only way to escape our desperate search for that which will secure us in happiness is to relate to that which is about us through a sense of duty. Otherwise, we select something and treat it as an idol.

MORRIS, William Edward. Knowledge and the Regularity Theory of Information. Synthese, 82(3), 375-398, Mr 90.

Fred Dretske's *Knowledge and the Flow of Information* is an extended attempt to develop a philosophically useful theory of information. Dretske adapts central ideas from Shannon and Weaver's mathematical theory of communication, and applies them to some traditional problems in epistemology. In doing so, he succeeds in building for philosophers a much-needed bridge to important work in cognitive science. The payoff for epistemologists is that Dretske promises a way out of a long-standing impasse—the Gettier problem. He offers an alternative model of knowledge as *information-based belief*, which purports to avoid the problems justificatory accounts face. This essay looks closely at Dretske's theory. I argue that while the information-theoretic framework is attractive, it does not provide an adequate account of knowledge. And there seems to be no way of tightening the theory without introducing some version of a theory of justification—the very notion Dretske's theory was designed to avoid.

MORRISON, Donald. The Ancient Sceptic's Way of Life. Metaphilosophy, 21(3), 204-222, Jl 90.

MORROW, W E. Should a Democrat Be in Favour of Academic Freedom? S Afr J Phil, 9(2), 89-94, My 90.

Section I of the article shows why a democrat should, rationally, be ambivalent about academic freedom. Section II discusses the O'Brien affair at the University of Cape Town and tries to bring on to the agenda some aspects of the opposition to O'Brien's visit. Section III claims that academic freedom is not a right but a privilege. It defends the view that truth is constructed in and by the practices of critical enquiry, and, in terms of a distinction between two conceptions of ideology, shows in what way there is a conceptual link between the search for truth and the striving for justice. It is argued that although academic work is highly vulnerable to itself being ideological, it can be anti-ideological. It is claimed that academic work has a special contribution to make to the maintenance of a just and democratic society but that there is no way to sustain or regulate the practices of critical enquiry except by acknowledging the collective authority of academics. (edited)

MORSE, M Steven. Liabilities and Realities Faced in Biomedical Engineering. Nat Forum, 69(4), 46-47, Fall 89.

Biomedical engineering is a science that is just now coming of age. It encompasses a broad multitude of technical domains and may be defined as the application or modification of engineering science to interface man's technology with the human machine. Because of the proximity to the human machine, biomedical engineers must go beyond the merely technical and carefully consider the moral, ethical, and societal ramifications of their work. Good ideas are often lost or altered to allow the engineer to conform to the realities posed by liabilities.

MORTON, Adam. Double Conditionals. Analysis, 50(2), 75-79, Mr 90.

Examples are given of an irreducibly three-place conditional. An analysis of its content is given, which distinguishes it from reducible three-place conditionals such as 'if p then if q then r' and 'if p and q then r'. (The relation to 'if p then (if p and q then r)' is misstated in the article. A correction will appear.) At the end of the paper, connections are made with the idea of a law of nature.

MORTON, Adam. "Why There is No Concept of a Person" in *The Person and the Human Mind: Issues in Ancient and Modern Philosophy*, GILL, Christopher (ed), 39-59. New York, Clarendon/Oxford Pr, 1989.

Definitions of personhood in terms of second order beliefs and desires, such as Frankfurt's, run into difficulties about the indexical aspect of self-knowledge. I describe cases in which there seems to be no objective

matter of fact whether a creature is a full or a marginal person, or whether a creature at one time is the same person as a creature at another time. Some of these cases can actually occur. Moral implications are suggested.

MOSCHOVAKIS, Yiannis N. The Formal Language of Recursion. J Sym Log, 54(4), 1216-1252, D 89.

MOSELEY, Ray (ed) and HACKLER, Chris (ed) and VAWTER, Dorothy E (ed). *Advance Directives in Medicine*. New York, Praeger, 1989

MOSER, Paul K. A Dilemma for Internal Realism. Phil Stud, 59(1), 101-106, My 90.

This paper shows that Hilary Putnam's internal realism faces a fatal dilemma. The dilemma arises from Putnam's claim that the notion of "how things are" makes no sense. This paper shows that Putnam's claim either presupposes the notion of how things are or generates an unacceptable endless regress.

MOSER, Paul K. *Knowledge and Evidence*. New York, Cambridge Univ Pr, 1988

This book develops a foundationalist account of empirical knowledge according to which nonconceptual awareness and inference to best explanation play a central role. The book also deals with the conditions for belief and truth, the nature of rational belief, the Gettier problem, the internalism-externalism debate, and the problem of the criterion.

MOSER, Paul K. "Lehrer's Coherentism and the Isolation Objection" in *The Current State of the Coherence Theory*, BENDER, John W (ed), 29-37. Norwell, Kluwer, 1989.

Among coherence theories of epistemic justification, Keith Lehrer's version is second to none in its originality, detail, and precision. It is, without a doubt, the most refined coherence theory in circulation. In this paper I ask whether Lehrer's coherentism withstands the familiar isolation objection to epistemic coherentism. Part 1 outlines Lehrer's coherentism in its most recent garb. Part 2 states the isolation objection to coherentism without relying on the troublesome metaphor of "cutting off" empirical justification from the world. And Part 3 argues that Lehrer's coherentism falls prey to the isolation objection because of a deficiency shared by all versions of epistemic coherentism.

MOSER, Paul K. Reasons, Values, and Rational Action. J Phil Res, 15, 127-151, 1990.

This paper outlines an account of rational action. It distinguishes three species of reasons: motivating reasons, evidential reasons, and normative reasons. It also contends that there is a univocal notion of reason common to the notions of motivating reasons, evidential reasons, and normative reasons. Given this thesis, the paper explains how we can have a unified theory of reasons for action. It also explains the role of values in rational action. It sketches an affective approach to value that contrasts with prominent desire-satisfaction approaches.

MOSER, Paul K. Reliabilism and Relevant Worlds. Philosophia (Israel), 19(2-3), 155-164, O 89.

MOSER-VERREY, Monique. L'Emergence de la notion d'intérêt dans l'esthétique des Lumières. Man Nature, 6, 193-207, 1987.

MOSES, M. Decidable Discrete Linear Orders. J Sym Log, 53(2), 531-539, Je 88.

Three classes of decidable discrete linear orders with varying degrees of effectiveness are investigated. We consider how a classical order type may lie in relation to these three classes, and we characterize by their order types elements of these classes that have effective nontrivial self-embeddings.

MOSKOP, John C. "Choosing Among the Alternatives" in *Advance Directives in Medicine*, HACKLER, Chris (ed), 9-19. New York, Praeger, 1989.

After a brief statement of the benefits of advance directives regarding life-prolonging medical care, this essay examines two questions: (1) How should advance directives by formally recognized in the law? (2) Which kind of advance directive is most likely to achieve the goals of its author? The essay argues that many current natural death statutes unduly restrict patients' options to forego life-prolonging treatment. Among the different kinds of advance directives available to individuals, the essay argues that proxy directives have several distinct advantages over more traditional living wills.

MOSTERT, Pieter. Step by Step in Children's Philosophy. Thinking, 5(4), 58-60, 1985.

MOTT, Peter D. The Elderly and High Technology Medicine: A Case for Individualized, Autonomous Allocation. Theor Med, 11(2), 95-102, Je 90.

The issues involved in decision making about the aggressiveness of future medical care for older persons are explored. They are related to population trends, the heterogeneity of older persons and a variety of factors involved in individual preferences. Case studies are presented to illustrate these points, as well as a review of pertinent literature. The argument is offered that, considering these many factors, a system of flexible, individualized care by informed patient preference, is more rational than the rationing of technological services by age.

MOTZKIN, Gabriel. Emil Lask and the Crisis of Neo-Kantianism: The Rediscovery of the Primordial World. Rev Metaph Morale, 94(2), 171-190, Ap-Je 89.

MOULAKIS, Athanasios. Consciousness and History. Riv Int Filosof Diritto, 66(3), 450-467, Jl-S 89.

The article juxtaposes two philosophical views of history as a field of experience and as a mode of understanding. It compares Michael Oakeshott's view of history with that of Eric Voegelin. The comparison helps bring out the distinctive character of each thinker's philosophical framework.

MOULIN, Anne-Marie. "Normative and Descriptive Issues in the Analysis of Medical Language" in Scientific Knowledge Socialized, HRONSZKY, Imre (ed), 287-296. Norwell, Kluwer, 1989.

MOULIN, Hervé. Axioms of Cooperative Decision Making. New York, Cambridge Univ Pr, 1988.

The modern theory of normative economics relies heavily on the axiomatic approach. Similar axioms often apply to very different problems. This point of view yields a unified treatment of utilitarianism (including inequality indexes), cooperative games (including the Shapley value and nucleolus), public decision mechanisms (including the pivotal mechanism), voting and social choice.

MOULIN, Léo. "Quelques réflexions sur le thème "culture et politique"" in Culture et Politique/Culture and Politics, CRANSTON, Maurice (ed), 3-15. Hawthorne, de Gruyter, 1988.

La première réflexion qui m'est venue à l'esprit devant le thème proposé est qu'il est bien difficile, sinon impossible, de le traiter. Des centaines de spécialistes ont parlé de l'Europe. D'autres centaines, sinon des milliers, ont traité des rapports de la culture avec la politique. Et enfin un nombre tout aussi impressionnant de professeurs ont tenté de démêler l'écheveau, quaisiment inextricable, qu'a produit la conjonction des recherches et des réflexions des "européeanistes" et des politistes. La deuxième réflexion est venue peu après: comme ces vins de classe dans lesquels les tasteurs détectent, au départ du bouquet, un premier, puis un second, puis un troisième rang de saveurs de plur en plus profondes et de plus en plus subtiles. Elle m'a amené à croire que, ayant déjà moi'même beaucoup écrit sur le thème proposé, il était sans doute possible d'avoir quelque chose à dire qui serait, sinon la synthèse de mes réflexions sur le thème proposé, du moins l'état actuel de mes réflexions. Et cela en suivant pas à pas le Mémoire qui nous a été proposé.

MOULINES, C Ulises. Hay una filosofía de la ciencia en el último Wittgenstein? Theoria (Spain), 4(11), 327-342, F-My 89.

MOURÉLOS, Georges. "La polyphonie des herméneutiques dans l'art contemporain" in Cultural Hermeneutics of Modern Art: Essays in Honor of Jan Aler, DETHIER, Hubert (ed), 59-75. Amsterdam, Rodopi, 1989.

L'auteur s'applique à établir la diversité des systèmes de référence dans le domaine de l'art contemporain, à la base desquels on peut procéder à l'interprétation d'une oeuvre. Il choisit comme principal domaine de recherches la littérature, tout en faisant allusion aux autres formes de l'art. Il prend comme centres de gravité l'auteur et l'oeuvre, considérés de plusieurs points de vue. Il arrive ainsi à dégager les principales caractéristiques et les limites de chacun de ces modes d'explication, qui s'échelonnent sur plusieurs niveaux, tout en montrant que c'est dans le domaine de l'art que le terme "herméneutique" trouve une de ses plus fructueuses applications.

MOUTSOPOULOS, E. Art as an Axiology of Man. Philosophia (Athens), 17-18, 120-152, 1987-88.

The article is a general introduction to artistic reality as a means of axiological evaluation of human existence. It focuses on the problems of art in human life, on aesthetics as opposed to philosophy of art, to the history of the whole problematic, to the system of aesthetic categories, to the passage from creativity to creation, to the dialectics of artistic creation, to artistic techniques and styles, to the mythical dimensions of art, to personal, social and transcendent references in art, to falsifications of artistic creation and to art as a value in itself. Art can give to all human beings a more meaningful life. As Plato has put it, "man's whole life needs good rhythm and harmony," and "a life without art is not worth being lived."

MOUW, Richard J and YODER, John H. Evangelical Ethics and the Anabaptist-Reformed Dialogue. J Relig Ethics, 17(2), 121-137, Fall 89.

The recent resurgence of evangelical social action has been accompanied by some serious attention to issues in ethical thought. Evangelical scholars have been engaged in a search for ethical "roots," for traditions of

theological-ethical discourse that can give shape to twentieth century ethical explorations. Of special interest to many in this regard are the longstanding tensions between Anabaptist and Reformed thought. In this essay we argue against the "received wisdom" that there is a strict polarity between these two perspectives. The ethical differences between the Reformed and Anabaptist communities are in fact "intra-family" ones that emerge out of some important commonalities. The exploration of these commonalities, we suggest, is crucial for the development of a healthier evangelical ethical perspective.

MOYAL, Georges J D. "...Quod circulum non commiserim..." Quartae Responsiones. Dialogue (Canada), 28(4), 569-588, 1989.

The text of the Meditations alone suffices to show Descartes innocent of any circularity in his proofs of the existence of God, for the 'proofs' of the Third Meditation are actually heuristic devices leading to an intuition of God's existence intricately woven into the cogito, while the ontological proof in the Fifth Meditation is provisionally detached from the order of discoveries, and thus does not depend on the clear and distinct. However, if the Second and Fourth replies are taken into account, they reveal an implicit critical philosophy at work in the Meditations, which renders the charge of circularity all the more implausible.

MRAZ, M. The Concept of "Oikiá" in Classic Greek Philosophy (in Czechoslovakian). Filozof Cas, 37(5), 716-733, 1989.

The author of this article sets himself the task of contributing to the clarification of the concept of "oikiá" in Greek philosophy from its early days up to Aristotle. With a view to the present-day ecological problems this concept is analyzed as an expression of the ancient view of man's relationship to his immediate environs, to the people who are close to him and to those parts of nature with which he comes into daily contact. (edited)

MSHVENIERADZE, Vladimir V. The Great October, Restructuring, Politology. Dialec Hum, 15(3-4), 99-105, Sum-Autumn 88.

MUDROCH, Vilem. Die Anschauungsformen und das Schematismuskapitel. Kantstudien, 80(4), 405-415, 1989.

The second edition of Kant's Critique of Pure Reason places far greater emphasis on space than the first edition. Excluded from the revisions is the chapter on schematism; as the article argues it was left unchanged largely for architectonic reasons. Space was included in the second edition wherever the transition from general epistemological considerations to statements dealing with matter and motion occurs, i.e., where reference to the First Metaphysical Foundations of Science is made. Schematism, however, concerns general epistemological arguments and thus requires time, which is the more abstract form of intuition than space.

MUDROVCIC, María Inés. El sentido de la teoría humeana del tiempo como relación filosófica. Rev Filosof (Argentina), 4(1), 41-48, My 89.

Time is not a problem frequently associated to Hume's philosophy. Nevertheless, there is a special temporal character in Hume's epistemology. This paper deals with this topic and the difficulties that it involves.

MUELLER, Dennis C. "Democracy: The Public Choice Approach" in Politics and Process, BRENNAN, Geoffrey (ed), 78-96. New York, Cambridge Univ Pr, 1989.

This paper discusses the main contributions of public choice theory to our knowledge of democratic processes. Three main questions are discussed: (1) Why does government exist? (2) Why do rational individuals vote? (3) What are the normative properties of the outcomes from this voting process? It is argued that public choice provides good answers to the first and third questions, but is unable to answer the second question adequately with the rational egoist models it usually employs.

MUELLER, Dennis C. Public Choice II: A Revised Edition of "Public Choice". New York, Cambridge Univ Pr, 1989.

This book represents a substantial revision, expansion and updating of its predecessor. All major issues of collective decision making are discussed using the methodology of public choice. These include why government exists, the properties of majority rule and other voting rules, voting with the feet, two-party and multiparty representation systems, rent seeking, bureaucracy, political business cycles, the growth of government, why people vote, social welfare functions, Arrowian welfare functions, social contracts and constitutions, and redistribution.

MUELLER, Ian. Joan Kung's Reading of Plato's Timaeus. Apeiron, 22(4), 1-27, D 89.

The core of this paper is a presentation of Joan Kung's interpretation of the Timaeus based on her published writings and unpublished materials left at her untimely death in 1987. An attempt is made to relate Kung's ideas to developments in contemporary philosophy. There is an excursus on stylometry in which G E L Owen's stylometric arguments for assigning the

Timaeus a date earlier than the generally accepted one are shown to fail.

MUGNAI, Massimo. A Systematical Approach to Leibniz's Theory of Relations and Relational Sentences. Topoi, 9(1), 61-81, Mr 90.

MUGUERZA, Javier. "The Alternative of Dissent" in *The Tanner Lectures on Human Values, Volume X*, PETERSON, Grethe B (ed), 73-129. Salt Lake City, Univ of Utah Pr, 1989.

Human rights are moral demands rather than "moral rights" (Dworkin). Anyway, they are prior to its legal recognition. Its foundation through a "factual consensus" (Bobbio), like the one embodied in the Universal Declaration of Human Rights, is obviously insufficient since factuality is not in itself a warrant to the rationality of such an agreement. On the other hand, its foundation through an "ideal" on "counterfactual consensus" (Apel, Habermas) seems to pose more problems than it could ever solve. As a result, it is suggested here the possible suitability of exploring into an attempt of a "negative foundation" of human rights on the basis of "dissensus."

MUGUERZA, Javier. José Ferrater Mora: De la materia a la razón pasando por la ética. Rev Latin De Filosof, 15(2), 219-238, Jl 89.

MUI, Constance. Sartre's Sexism Reconsidered. Auslegung, 16(1), 31-41, Wint 90.

Margery Collins's and Christine Pierce's first documentation of Sartre's sexism (1973) has had the profound effect in feminist scholarship of discrediting a vast tradition of feminist writings, beginning with those of Simone de Beauvoir, which have adopted Sartre's ontology of freedom as a philosophical reference point. This paper argues that Sartre, in spite of himself, has set up a system which ironically committed him to giving woman at least an equal, if not more primordial, ontological status as man. This argument seeks to qualify Collins's and Pierce's original thesis by situating it within the broader context of Sartrean ontology. One cannot infer from the sexist analogies of slime and holes the claim that woman occupies an inferior ontological status. To do so would be to overlook the delightful irony in his ontology: in spite of his ill feelings toward woman, woman nevertheless prevails as a full-fledged consciousness in that ontology. Such clarification of the status of woman in Sartre's system would rescue Beauvoir's writings from the specific charges of sexism regarding her philosophical reference point.

MUKENGEBANTU, Paul. L'unité de l'oeuvre philosophique de Paul Ricoeur. Laval Theol Phil, 46(2), 209-222, Je 90.

La Poétique, dernière partie de la *Philosophie de la volonté*, qui devait traiter de la libération de la volonté, n'a pas encore paru. On serait tenté de penser que les multiples préoccupations philosophiques de Paul Ricoeur l'ont détourné de ce projet initial ou l'ont amené à en différer la réalisation. L'auteur du présent article est d'un autre avis. Pour lui, les longs détours qui caractérisent la démarche de Ricoeur ne sont ni des déviations, ni d'encombrantes parenthèses. Par ailleurs, *La Poétique* n'est pas seulement anticipée figurativement par l'oeuvre déjà réalisée; elle reste le terme vers lequel tend l'oeuvre entière depuis son commencement.

MUKHOPADHYAY, Debabrata. On Gettier's Notion of Knowledge and Justification. Indian Phil Quart, 16(4), 447-464, O 89.

Gettier's claim that a justified true belief may not be knowledge (Edmund L Gettier, "Is Justified True Belief Knowledge?", *Analysis*, Vol. 23, Blackwell, 1963) seems to presuppose some more criteria (other than being justified true belief) to be fulfilled by a proposition for its being someone's knowledge. The paper attempts to show (i) that Gettier's claim is based on his two notions, e.g., notion of knowing a disjunctive proposition and notion of justification, and (ii) that none of these two notions is acceptable implying thereby that none of the two Gettier cases establishes his claim.

MULDER, Bertus and NAUTA, Lolle. Working Class and Proletariat—On the Relation of Andries Sternheim to the Frankfurt School. Praxis Int, 9(4), 433-445, Ja 90.

MULGAN, Richard. Aristotle and the Value of Political Participation. Polit Theory, 18(2), 195-215, My 90.

In Aristotle's political theory, is political participation essential for the good life? His theory of ethical virtue and external goods in the *Ethics* requires the social life of friends and family but not specifically political activity. The virtuous will accept office if it is offered but will not suffer deprivation if it is not. In the *Politics*, the 'political animal' argument implies living under law but not active participation. Citizenship is defined in terms of political participation but such participation is not essential for the good life. However, the emphasis on leisure in Books VII and VIII does not imply moral rejection of political life.

MULHOLLAND, Leslie A. "Autonomy, Extended Sympathy, and the Golden Rule" in *Inquiries into Values: The Inaugural Session of the International Society for Value Inquiry*, LEE, Sander H , 89-98. Lewiston,

Mellen Pr, 1989.

I examine the question, implicit in the rule, 'do unto others as you would have them do unto you', of how we are to determine who the others are. I argue that in part the answer is provided by Kant's contention that others are those who are like oneself, rational beings. But against Kant, I maintain that others can include any being whose place one could imagine oneself occupying as a result of the ordinary course of nature. One has a duty to others, including animals, to the extent of the reversibility.

MULHOLLAND, Leslie. Egoism and Morality. J Phil, 86(10), 542-550, O 89.

I distinguish between 'act egoism', the egoism of a person who aims to maximize utilities wihtout limit, and 'rule egoism', the egoism of a person who aims to maximize utilities through constrained cooperation with others. An act egoist cannot demonstrate how the act egoist can adopt the limits of moral rules. Thus rule egoism is impossible. To adopt the limits of a moral rule, a person must be able to override egoistic aims and goals by a motive supplied by the rule itself. Morality is possible only if egoistic considerations do not determine rational behaviour.

MÜLLER, Paola. Nominare l'essenza divina: La distinzione XXII dell'*Ordinatio* di Ockham. Riv Filosof Neo-Scolas, 81(2), 224-254, Ap-Je 89.

MULLER, Philippe. "The *Pons Asinorum* in Philosophy" in *Dialectic and Contemporary Science*, GRIER, Philip T (ed), 185-198. Lanham, Univ Pr of America, 1989.

This article was written in honor of E E Harris, and tries to discern the key argument in his thought. It is shown that Harris gives us the means of classifying the writings posing as philosophy between what is valid and what is not. Only the valid works refute or disregard entirely the representative doctrine of knowledge, that is one where all knowledge is supposed to originate in sense impressions caused by external stimuli. That has the consequence to drop out all positivism, semanticism, Wittgensteinism and empiro-criticism, and to allow only for Hegelian types of thought.

MÜLLER, Reimar. "Das Problem Theorie-Praxis in der Peripatos-Rezeption von Ciceros Staatsschrift" in *Cicero's Knowledge of the Peripatos*, FORTENBAUGH, William W (ed), 101-113. New Brunswick, Transaction Books, 1989.

MULLIGAN, Thomas M. Justifying Moral Initiative by Business, with Rejoinders to Bill Shaw and Richard Nunan. J Bus Ethics, 9(2), 93-103, F 90.

In this paper I respond to separate criticisms by Bill Shaw (*JBE*, July 1988) and Richard Nunan (*JBE*, December 1988) of my paper "A Critique of Milton Friedman's Essay 'The Social Responsibility of Business Is to Increase its Profits'" (*JBE*, August 1986). Professors Shaw and Nunan identify several points where my argument could benefit from clarification and improvement. They also make valuable contributions to the discussion of the broad issue area of whether and to what extent business should exercise moral initiative. My objectives are (1) to show, with the aid of examples (inspired by Shaw) and the addition of one point of correction (inspired by Nunan), that my disapproving critique of Friedman's famous argument remains sound, (2) to show that Professor Shaw's argument contains serious problems, and (3) to build on the base laid by my critics by developing important reasons why business should exercise moral initiative.

MULVANEY, Robert J. Philosophy for Children and the Modernization of Chinese Education. Thinking, 7(2), 7-11, 1987.

MULVANEY, Robert. Philosophy and the Education of the Community. Thinking, 6(2), 2-6, 1985.

MULVANEY, Robert. Philosophy for Children in its Historical Context. Thinking, 6(3), 2-8, 1986.

MÜNCH, Dieter. The Early Work of Husserl and Artificial Intelligence. J Brit Soc Phenomenol, 21(2), 107-120, My 90.

MUNCHUS, George. Testing as a Selection Tool: Another Old and Sticky Managerial Human Rights Issue. J Bus Ethics, 8(10), 817-820, O 89.

The intent of this paper is to state testing's definition and purpose within the selection process. A brief review of the current trend toward the increased use of testing in the selection process. An actual example of the increased use of testing in both the public and private sector is illustrated. Some discussion regarding future trends of testing—genetic screening, personality test, honsety test, etc., are also presented as issues of concern.

MUNDY, Brent. On Quantitative Relationist Theories. Phil Sci, 56(4), 582-600, D 89.

Mundy (1983) presented the formal apparatus of certain relationist theories of space and space-time taking quantitative relations as primitive. The present paper discusses the philosophical and physical interpretation of such theories, and replies to some objections to such theories and to relationism is general raised in Field (1985). Under an appropriate second-order naturalistic Platonist interpretation of the formalism, quantitative relationist theories are seen to be entirely comparable to spatialist ones in respect of the issues raised by Field. Moreover, it appears that even if accepted as sound, Field's general line of criticism would not diminish the significance of relationism for philosophy of science, since this derives primarily from its connection to physical rather than to mathematical or philosophical ontology.

MUNÉVAR, Gonzalo. Naturalismo prescriptivo: epistemología. Rev Filosof (Spain), 2, 31-42, 1989.

MUNEVAR, Gonzalo. "Science as Part of Nature" in *Issues in Evolutionary Epistemology*, HAHLWEG, Kai (ed), 475-487. Albany, SUNY Pr, 1989.

MUNRO, Joan. Music and Understanding: The Concept of Understanding Applied to Listening to Music. Proc Phil Educ, 45, 140-149, 1989.

MUNZ, Peter. "Taking Darwin Even More Seriously" in *Issues in Evolutionary Epistemology*, HAHLWEG, Kai (ed), 278-293. Albany, SUNY Pr, 1989.

In current theories of cultural evolution, selection is taken to be natural in that the most adapted is the most favoured. But in cultural association, in contrast to biological speciation, solidarity and the exclusion of aliens have to be maintained artificially. Therefore, the features most favoured by selection tend to be false beliefs and nonadaptive practices because they are more exclusive and more distinctive and hence more solidarity promoting than adaptive ones. Most current theories are therefore mistaken and we must look for a criterion of selection other than the natural selection of the most adapted.

MUNZER, Stephen R. *A Theory of Property*. New York, Cambridge Univ Pr, 1990

This book argues for the justification of some rights of private property while showing why many unequal distributions of private property are indefensible. It offers a new "pluralist" theory of justification that rests on three main principles: utility and efficiency, justice and equality, and desert based on labor. This interdisciplinary book moves with assurance among philosophy, law, and economics. Its argument integrates analyses of the great classical theorists with discussion of contemporary philosophers.

MURA, Alberto. When Probabilistic Support is Inductive. Phil Sci, 57(2), 278-289, Je 90.

This note makes a contribution to the issue raised in a paper by Popper and Miller (1983) in which it was claimed that probabilistic support is purely deductive. Developing R C Jeffrey's remarks, a new general approach to the crucial concept of "going beyond" is here proposed. By means of it a quantitative measure of the *inductive component* of a probabilistic inference is reached. This proposal leads to vindicating the view that typical *predictive* probabilistic inferences by enumeration and analogy are *purely inductive*.

MURAWSKI, Roman. Semantics for Nonstandard Languages. Rep Math Log, 22, 105-114, 1988.

The aim of this paper is to give account of the concept of satisfaction and truth for nonstandard formulas. We shall present the notion of a nonstandard satisfaction class which extends Tarski's notion of satisfaction, show some of its properties and discuss their philosophical and methodological consequences. We shall indicate also some applications of satisfaction classes.

MURAY, Leslie A. Confessional Postmodernism and the Process-Relational Vision. Process Stud, 18(2), 83-94, Sum 89.

The article is an appreciative critique of the confessional postmodernism of Stanley Hauerwas from a process perspective. It critiques Hauerwas's development of an ethics of character and virtue by claiming that this development (1) rests in what lends itself to a substantialist view of the self, (2) is reinforced by an "essentialist" understanding of Christianity, and (3) that such an understanding culminates in a separatist notion of the church-world relation. A more adequate view of these three interrelated issues is presented based on the conceptuality of process thought.

MURESAN, Valentin. The Social Dynamics Between Evolution and Progress. Phil Log, 32(1-2), 3-10, Ja-Je 88.

MURILLO, Ildefonso. El enigma de la naturaleza humana. Dialogo Filosof, 5(3), 380-391, S-D 89.

MURNION, William E. The Ideology of Social Justice in Economic Justice For All. J Bus Ethics, 8(11), 847-854, N 89.

Although both the American Catholic bishops and their commentators seem to agree that the economics pastoral is capitalist, if anything, in its ideology,

a careful reading of the pastoral shows that the principle of social justice implicit in it is actually socialist, indeed communist, in nature. The bishops arrived at such a principle because of their interpretation of the biblical sense of justice as entailing a "preferential option for the poor." To justify this option on a rational basis, they developed a theory of social justice that may be summarized in the principle, familiar from Marx's writings, "From each according to one's ability, to each according to one's needs." Whether or not the bishops intended such a convergence in principle, this development sets them at odds with the capitalist ideology of the United States.

MURPHY, James Bernard. Nature, Custom, and Stipulation in Law and Juriprudence. Rev Metaph, 43(4), 751-790, Je 90.

MURPHY, Jeffrie G. Getting Even: The Role of the Victim. Soc Phil Pol, 7(2), 209-225, Spr 90.

This essay gives some limited support to the victims' rights movement by arguing that fulfilling crime victims' desires for revenge may be one legitimate purpose of criminal punishment.

MURPHY, John W. *Postmodern Social Analysis and Criticism*. Westport, Greenwood Pr, 1989

This book examines the historical development of postmodern thought and its effect on contemporary social and political institutions. It draws on the works of Lyotard, Foucault, Derrida, Heidegger and other postmodern thinkers. (staff)

MURPHY, John. Application on the Relevance of AI Assumptions for Social Practitioners. Soc Epistem, 3(4), 349-354, O-D 89.

Rather than simply crunching numbers, computers are illustrated to manipulate symbols. Computers, in other words, are based on a world-view, and thus are not value-free devices. Furthermore, the philosophical assumptions that underpin computerization may influence negatively the therapeutic encounter. The consequences of this world-view (or Micro-world) are examined in this paper.

MURPHY, Julien S. Is Pregnancy Necessary: Feminist Concerns About Ectogenesis. Hypatia, 4(3), 66-84, Fall 89.

To what extent are women obliged to be child-bearers? If reproductive technology could offer some form of ectogenesis, would feminists regard it as a liberating reproductive option? Three lines of reproductive rights arguments currently used by feminists are applied to ectogenesis. Each fails to provide strong grounds for prohibiting it. Yet, there are several ways in which ectogenesis could contribute to women's oppression, in particular, if it were used to undermine abortion rights, reinforce traditional views of fertility, increase fetal rights in pregnancy, and perpetuate the unequal distribution of scarce medical resources. A rethinking of women's relationship to pregnancy is needed in order to challenge ectogenetic research.

MURPHY, Nancey. Another Look at Novel Facts. Stud Hist Phil Sci, 20(3), 385-388, S 89.

MURPHY, Nancey and MC CLENDON JR, James W. Distinguishing Modern and Postmodern Theologies. Mod Theol, 5(3), 191-214, Ap 89.

MURPHY, Nancey. Truth, Relativism, and Crossword Puzzles. Zygon, 24(3), 299-314, S 89.

Neither the correspondence nor the coherence theory of truth does justice to the truth claims made in science and theology. I propose a new definition that relates truth to solving puzzles. I claim that this definition is more adequate than either of the traditional theories and that it offers two additional benefits: first, it provides grounds for a theory regarding the relations between theology and science that may stand up better to philosophical scrutiny than does critical realism; and second, it blocks the move to relativism based on recognition of the plurality of perspectives and the historical and social conditioning of knowledge.

MURPHY, Timothy F. Reproductive Controls and Sexual Destiny. Bioethics, 4(2), 121-142, Ap 90.

Given reported hypotheses that homosexual orientation in adult males might be eliminated by prenatal hormone treatments during prenatal development, various arguments considering the morality of controlling the adult sexual orientation of children are considered. It is held that only an argument that such interventions are heterosexist succeeds as a moral objection to possible interventions. Heterosexism is defined as the doctrine that heterosexual orientation is by nature and consequence superior to forms of homerotic sexuality. On the other hand, because it is important to preserve respect for individual reproductive decisions it is argued that such interventions are not the kinds of immoralities that should be forbidden and sanctioned by law.

MURRAY, Michael. Ingarden and the End of Phenomenological Aesthetics. Res Phenomenol, 19, 171-179, 1989.

MURRAY, Thomas H. The Bioengineered Competitor? Nat Forum,

69(4), 41-42, Fall 89.

The use of anabolic steroids by athletes seeking a competitive advantage tests the limits of the morally acceptable exercise of individual liberty. In addition to the physical side-effects of the drug, other harms include rewarding those who cheat and disadvantaging honest athletes, as well as the deformation of one's character that comes with cheating and deception. Using human Growth Hormone (hGH) to make normal children taller, in order to gain for them the advantages that height brings in this culture, creates similar moral problems. Biotechnology will require vexed judgments about the proper balance between liberty and other values crucial to sustaining a decent community.

MUSGRAVE, Alan. NOA's Ark—Fine for Realism. Phil Quart, 39(157), 383-398, O 89.

Arthur Fine says that scientific realism is dead, drowned by floods of criticism. In its place he puts the *natural ontological attitude*, NOA, pronounced 'Noah' (or 'Knower'). Fine thinks NOA is a minimalist view which is neither realist nor antirealist. This paper argues that NOA is either so minimalist as to be empty, or a thoroughly realist view so that in NOA's Ark the realist can sail happily above the floods of criticism.

MUZIK, J. On the Future of the Man-Nature Relationship (in Czechoslovakian). Filozof Cas, 37(5), 632-643, 1989.

This article is based on the well-known facts concerning the ongoing deterioration of the natural environment at the hands of contemporary society, an aggravation which has gradually reached the stage wherein it jeopardizes the very biological foundations of mankind. This, indeed, is a problem which necessitates an effective solution that, in turn, presupposes thorough knowledge of its general causes, which have to be sought in the historical development of social—and especially production—practice. Nonetheless, world views of ordinary people, including a world-view settlement of their relationship with nature, are known to co-shape the concrete objectives of such a practice. The author studies the individual phases of this relationship at the level of the image of the world, of value orientations and of life programmes. (edited)

MUZIKA, Edward G. Object Relations Theory, Buddhism, and the Self: Synthesis of Eastern and Western Approaches. Int Phil Quart, 30(1), 59-74, Mr 90.

MYDLARSKI, H. Du moraliste classique au moraliste des Lumières où la naissance des sciences humaines. Man Nature, 5, 131-139, 1986.

MYDLARSKI, Henri. Les fondements du savoir dans la pensée moraliste des Lumières. Man Nature, 7, 141-148, 1988.

Les moralistes des Lumières inscrivent l'irrationalité du coeur au centre des exigences physico-mathématiques que commande la science, aucun discours ne se tenant sur le mode exogène. Simultanément, ils font remonter la faculté cognitive aux temps où se seraient constitués monde, hommes et hérédités. D'où une conception moniste de l'ambivalence par laquelle le "moi" et la raison réfléchissent les expressions d'un Logos irisées en unité. En d'autres termes, ils posent la réalité/vérité comme consubstantielle à l'être et son intelligence comme l'effet d'un clonage cosmique à l'échelle humaine.

MYERS, R Thomas. On the Nature of Religion. Relig Hum, 24(3), 132-138, Sum 90.

Religion is the sum total of our knowledge and theory of the past and present, and the spirit with which we extrapolate into the future, or into the unknown. Religion is what the individual or the group does with its concept of time, as a guide to behavior.

MYERS, Richard. Christianity and Politics in Montesquieu's *Greatness and Decline of the Romans*. Interpretation, 17(2), 223-238, Wint 89-90.

MYHILL, John. "Real Implication" in *Directions in Relevant Logic*, NORMAN, Jean (ed), 157-165. Norwell, Kluwer, 1989.

NADEL, Mark and STAVI, Jonathan. On Models of the Elementary Theory of (Z,+,1). J Sym Log, 55(1), 1-20, Mr 90.

NADLER, Steven M. *Arnauld and the Cartesian Philosophy of Ideas*. Princeton, Princeton Univ Pr, 1989

After examining Arnauld's commitment to the fundamental principles of Descartes's philosophy, the author analyses the Arnauld-Malebranche debate over ideas. Arnauld, he argues, was a direct-realist in regard to perception. Moreover, Arnauld's "content" theory of representative ideas provides a sophisticated analysis of the intentionality of mental acts. This philosophical side of Arnauld's theory is looked at in both its historico-philosophical and theological context.

NADLER, Steven M. Deduction, Confirmation, and the Laws of Nature in Descartes's *Principia Philosophiae*. J Hist Phil, 28(3), 359-383, Jl 90.

Descartes's method in establishing the laws of nature in the *Principia* is rather obscured by the mixture of *a priori* argumentation from metaphysical premises and empirical corroboration. This paper argues that, contrary to the traditional interpretation, according to which the confirmation of the laws is completely a priori, Descartes's method in establishing them is more hypothetico-deductive, and relies on experimental confirmation.

NADLER, Steven M. "Ideas and Perception in Malebranche" in *Early Modern Philosophy II*, TWEYMAN, Stanley (ed), 41-60. Delmar, Caravan Books, 1988.

This paper argues that in spite of the traditional, representationalist interpretation of Malebranche's theory of ideas, the role ideas play in perception is not that of immaterial objects directly perceived instead of bodies. Rather, the intellectual apprehension of ideas informs our perceptual acquaintance with the world, and contributes the cognitive or conceptual element necessary to perception.

NADLER, Steven. Berkeley's Ideas and the Primary/Secondary Distinction. Can J Phil, 20(1), 47-61, Mr 90.

It is argued that while Berkeley's attack on Locke's epistemological distinction between primary quality ideas and secondary quality ideas is essential to his antimaterialist project, he himself is ultimately committed to an epistemological distinction between those ideas which succeed in making known their archetypal models in God, and those that do not. For Berkeley, this distinction is primarily suggested by his solution to the problem of God's pain.

NAESS, Arne. *Man Apart* and Deep Ecology: A Reply to Reed. Environ Ethics, 12(2), 185-192, Sum 90.

Peter Reed has defended the basis for an environmental ethic based upon feelings of awe for nature together with an existentialist absolute gulf between humans and nature. In so doing, he has claimed that there are serious difficulties with Ecosophy T and the terms, *Self-realization* and *identification with nature*. I distinguish between discussions of ultimate norms and the penultimate deep ecology platform. I also clarify and defend a technical use of *identification* and attempt to show that awe and identification may be compatible concepts.

NAHLIK, Krzysztof J. Tacit Metaphysical Premises of Modern Empiricism. Rep Phil, 13, 83-92, 1989.

NAISHTAT, Francisco. Teoría lógica y argumentación. Rev Latin De Filosof, 15(2), 159-182, Jl 89.

The article aims at analyzing some neuralgic topics lying at the core of formal logic and argumentation, such as *formal validity*, *logical form* and *apriority*. The two main questions considered successively by the author are: (I) Is there any *extrasystematic* criterion to characterize the idea of deductiveness, i.e., one that does not depend on the preliminary given of some formal language? (II) Can nondeductive argumentation be formalized? While (I) belongs to the foundations of formal logic and is very connected to the current diversification of logical theory, (II) involves the very problematic relationship between *probability* and *formal necessity*.

NALEZINSKI, Alix. "Questions Philosophers Ask": Response to Michael Baur. Eidos, 8(1), 91-98, Je 89.

Michael Baur argues that ancient and medieval philosophers were predominantly interested in metaphysics, ethics, and aesthetics and not "the issues of knowing and objectivity" (epistemology) as prior concerns to be worked out in order to serve as a basis for the discussion of what can be known about metaphysics, ethics, and aesthetics. Philosophers beginning with Descartes reversed this order. I argue, in response, that ancient and medieval thinkers did discuss the issue of knowing as a prior concern to the discussion of other topics.

NALIMOV, V V. Can Philosophy Be Mathematized?—Probabilistic Theory of Meanings and Semantic Architectonics of Personality. Phil Math, 4(2), 129-146, 1989.

In the present paper we wish to demonstrate the way the language of mathematical notions can be applied to reveal the philosophical ideas. Earlier I was engaged in the application of probabilistically oriented mathematics in science and technology. In the recent fifteen years I have been trying to do the same in philosophy by developing the probabilistic model of consciousness. Strange as it may seem, my initial premises are very close to Plato's metaphysics, and that enables us to show that absolute idealism can contribute not only to contemporary philosophy, but also to science. Here we somewhat anticipate the future and answer the question to be included into the program of the next, 9th Congress in Brighton.

NAN-SHENG, Huang and GUANGWU, Zhao. "On the Relationship Between Man and Nature" in *Man and Nature: The Chinese Tradition and the Future*, TANG, Yi-Jie (ed), 103-112. Lanham, Univ Pr of America, 1989.

NANCY, Jean-Luc. Elliptical Sense. Res Phenomenol, 18, 175-190, 1988.

To think of "sense" as a permanent alteration of sense (meaning). How the passion of writing is related to this. This article is an hommage to Jacques Derrida's work.

NANCY, Jean-Luc and LACOUE-LABARTHE, Philippe. The Nazi Myth. Crit Inquiry, 16(2), 291-312, Wint 89.

Nazi ideology did work through a very specific relationship to the category and to the intellectual-emotional tool of *myth*. First, because nazism takes, in a totalitarian and racist way, the heritage of a fundamental problem of Germany: this one of *identification*. Myth is precisely conceived in our tradition as an "identificatory mechanism." People and State as *total work of art* is mean and goal of such a process. This implies also (which may be shown with Rosenberg's *Myth of the XXth Century*) that the Aryan/Nazi myth is not a myth among others, but the proper figure, and essence, of myth itself. It presents the power of forming or "typing" oneself. The self-formation of the self (subjectivity in philosophical meaning) and the "collective egoism" of this formation as a nation (racism) are strongly bounded here.

NANCY, Jean-Luc. Sens elliptique. Rev Phil Fr, 180(2), 325-347, Ap-Je 90.

Analysis of Derrida's main theme, as this one of a *sense* which doesn't have (or make) an achievement: not a *meaning*. (Second, extended version of "Elliptical Sense," published in *Research in Phenomenology*, vol. XVIII, 1988.)

NANDY, Ashis. *Traditions, Tyranny, and Utopias: Essays in the Politics of Awareness*. New York, Oxford Univ Pr, 1987

This book takes a cross-cultural view of the concepts of compassion, freedom, dissent and oppression. It examines the process by which Western views of normality, masculinity and technological rationality have, through colonialist oppression, replaced the views of the oppressed. The author believes that institutional oppression has repressed a more egalitarian, democratic world vision for the individual and the community. (staff)

NARAGON, Steve. Kant on Descartes and the Brutes. Kantstudien, 81(1), 1-23, 1990.

Despite Kant's belief in a universal causal determinism among phenomena and his rejection of any noumenal agency in brutes, he nevertheless rejected Descartes's hypothesis that brutes are machines. Explaining Kant's response to Descartes forms the basis for this discussion of the nature of consciousness and matter in Kant's system. Kant's numerous remarks on animal psychology—as found in his lecture notes and reflections on metaphysics and anthropology—suggest a theory of consciousness and self-consciousness at odds with that traditionally ascribed to him.

NARAYAN, S Shankar. Karl Popper's Philosophy of Scientific Knowledge. Indian Phil Quart, SUPP 17(1), 1-4, Ja 90.

Science being perhaps the most successful of human intellectual endeavours, has attracted studies of its epistemology. Popper's important contribution to this field is his demarcation criteria for science from metaphysics; that a scientific theory is falsifiable and its validity is its ability to withstand the test of falsification. According to Popper, scientific theory is not the result of induction based on empirical data but a conjecture which is either validated or invalidated by empirical data. It is a process of conjecture, refutation and a new conjecture to overcome the refutation and so on. Every refutation by a new observation results in a more universal theory resulting in the genuine growth of scientific knowledge. Does scientific knowledge reveal the true laws operating in the material world or is it only a mental construct to relate the phenomenological events in a rational and economic manner without any necessary correlation to the material world as it really is? Popper as a critical realist believes in a material world and its natural laws independent of the observer and that scientific knowledge leads to them asymptotically.

NARDIN, Terry. Realism and Redistribution. J Value Inq, 23(3), 209-225, S 89.

Political realism distinguishes ordinary and emergency situations. Morality does not apply in the latter, which are governed by "necessity"—that is, by prudence in the pursuit of communal interests. Some realists find a moral rationale for prudential action, others do not. Because different policies further communal interests, depending on circumstances, realism lacks a consistent position on resource distribution. Realists disagree about which distributive criteria are best and the scope of the community within which distribution should occur. Forms of realism that do not distinguish morality and prudence confuse the pursuit of national or global interests with justice.

NARVESON, Jan. *The Libertarian Idea*. Philadelphia, Temple Univ Pr, 1988

This book provides a generally sympathetic exposition and defense of libertarianism, the thesis that the basic rights are (negative) liberty rights. It defends this not on intuitionist but on contractarian grounds. Various applicational contexts are considered, with some surprises, e.g., that the

traditional 'minimal state' is not necessarily what issues from this view. A substantial section on moral theory occupies a central position. Considerable space is devoted to rebutting critiques of private property rights.

NASH, Margaret. Grünbaum and Psychoanalysis. Phil Psych, 2(3), 325-343, 1989.

This paper argues that Adolf Grünbaum's evaluation of the scientific status of psychoanalysis is marred by its failure to locate Freud's notion of natural science. Contrary to his claims, Grünbaum does not assess Freud's theory on Freud's own terms. The presuppositions that Grünbaum brings to the question of the scientific status of psychoanalysis are problematic and his criticisms and methodological restrictions may not be defensible when psychoanalysis is taken to develop methodologically out of medical science rather than out of physics. I question the adequacy of the epistemological and methodological norms that Grünbaum brings to his analysis and I examine his arguments against the scientific credibility of Freud's theoretical claims. I argue that Grünbaum fails to consider the tension between clinical practice and psychoanalytic theory, ignores the evolution of Freud's thought and distorts and simplifies the complexity of the domain under investigation. Therefore his conclusions regarding the scientific credibility and evaluation of psychoanalysis are questionable.

NASH, Robert J and GRIFFIN, Robert S. Individualism, Community, and Education: An Exchange of Views. Educ Theor, 40(1), 1-18, Wint 90.

NASR, Seyyed Hossein. Existence (*wujūd*) and Quiddity (*māhiyyah*) in Islamic Philosophy. Int Phil Quart, 29(4), 409-428, D 89.

This paper deals with the meaning of *wujud* and *mahiyyah* in various schools of Islamic thought. It begins by turning attention to the significance of this subject for Islamic philosophy as well as theology and even certain schools of Sufism. It traces the history of the subject from al-Farabi and Ibn Sina to Suhrawardi, Fakhr al-Din al-Razi and later Islamic philosophers such as Mir Damad and Mulla Sadra. The essay then deals with the basic distinction made by Ibn Sina between necessity, contingency and impossibility which forms the basis of the ontology of Islamic philosophers. (edited)

NATHANSON, Bernard. Operation Rescue: Domestic Terrorism or Legitimate Civil Rights Protest? Hastings Center Rep, 19(6), 28-32, N-D 89.

NATHANSON, Stephen. On Deciding Whether a Nation Deserves Our Loyalty. Pub Affairs Quart, 4(3), 287-298, Jl 90.

NATSOULAS, Thomas. The Pluralistic Approach to the Nature of Feelings. J Mind Behav, 11(2), 173-217, Spr 90.

NAUTA, Lolle and MULDER, Bertus. Working Class and Proletariat—On the Relation of Andries Sternheim to the Frankfurt School. Praxis Int, 9(4), 433-445, Ja 90.

NAVARRO, Pablo E. Redundancia: Notas para su análisis. Analisis Filosof, 7(2), 135-140, N 87.

This paper exposes different problems arising from redundant normative systems. First, I analyze the probable existence of redundant norms, when "norms" is taken, as in the hylectic conception, to be the meaning of certain linguistic expressions. My aim is to show, in a simple way, the probable use of redundant norms in resolving normative inconsistencies. I also consider the substitution of a normative system by a similar one without explicit derogation and analyze the derogation of norms by mere redundance.

NAVIA, Luis E. *Pythagoras: An Annotated Bibliography*. New York, Garland, 1990

This descriptive bibliography on Pythagoras provides information on more than 1100 books, articles, dissertations, poetical and artistic works, and other kinds of works on Pythagoras and Pythagoreanism. It includes annotated entries on works in a variety of languages (English, French, German, Spanish, Russian, Latin, Greek, etc.), published since 1600. It divides the materials into eleven sections: bibliographical works, source collections, studies on the sources, general works, philosophical studies, Socrates and Plato, the testimony of Aristotle, mathematics and science, music and art, literature, and miscellanea. It furnishes comprehensive indexes.

NE'EMAN, Yuval and KANTOROVICH, Aharon. Serendipity as a Source of Evolutionary Progress in Science. Stud Hist Phil Sci, 20(4), 505-529, D 89.

NEAL, Patrick. Justice as Fairness: Political or Metaphysical? Polit Theory, 18(1), 24-50, F 90.

The author's purpose is to test Rawls's claim that his theory of justice as fairness can be coherently understood as deriving from a political, rather than a metaphysical, foundation. The author argues that Rawls fails to establish this claim, and that success in this endeavor would require that

Rawls abandon the Kantian interpretation of his theory for something resembling more an "Hegelian interpretation."

NEALE, Stephen. *Descriptions*. Cambridge, MIT Pr, 1990

NEALE, Stephen. Descriptive Pronouns and Donkey Anaphora. J Phil, 87(3), 113-150, Mr 90.

NEAMAN, Elliot Yale. Liberalism and Post-Modern Hermeneutics. Crit Rev, 2(2-3), 149-165, Spr-Sum 88.

NEANDER, Karen and MENZIES, Peter. David Owens on Levels of Explanation. Mind, 99(395), 459-466, Jl 90.

This paper is concerned with the thesis that the supervenience of the nonphysical on the physical entails that explanations in the special sciences are always underwritten by physical explanations. The paper examines objections to this thesis made by David Owens in 'Levels of Explanation' (*Mind* 98, 1989). The paper concludes that the thesis properly formulated escapes Owens's objections.

NEDERMAN, Cary J. Conciliarism and Constitutionalism: Jean Gerson and Medieval Political Thought. Hist Euro Ideas, 12(2), 189-209, 1990.

This essay argues that it is a mistake to look to medieval doctrines of conciliarism for the foundations of modern constitutional thought. By examination of the conciliar theory of Jean Gerson, the paper demonstrates that conciliarism is essentially consistent with the main stream of medieval political philosophy, which stressed personalized conceptions of rulership and corporatist ideas of community. By contrast, modern constitutionalism assumes individualized rights and personal consent, as well as impersonal notions of office and the limitation of power. At best, Gerson's conciliarism is "constitutionalist" in a different, medieval sense.

NEDERMAN, Cary J. Knowledge, Virtue and the Path to Wisdom: The Unexamined Aristotelianism of John of Salisbury's *Metalogicon*. Med Stud, 51, 268-286, 1989.

I argue that John of Salisbury's *Metalogicon* (1159) draws more heavily on Aristotelian doctrines than has previously been suspected. Specifically, the *Metalogicon* embraces two important Aristotelian claims: first, knowledge is only possessed once the knower has formed a stable disposition, which is acquired through regular and rigorous practice; and second, no lesson is rightly learned which is not in accordance with the mean between excess and deficiency. From this Aristotelian foundation is constructed John's account of how education leads to the attainment of wisdom.

NEEDHAM, Paul. 'Would Cause'. Acta Phil Fennica, 38, 156-182, 1985.

A definition is proposed of the subjunctive connective 'would cause' in terms of a modal conditional for which a semantics is sketched in possible world terms. Denying what corresponds to Lewis's 'centering' condition makes it possible to include a nontrivial sufficiency clause in the definition, which also includes a sine qua non condition and what is called a causal priority condition. Some consequences are discussed—in particular, restrictions on transitivity.

NEGOITA, Andrei. La distinction entre le système et l'approche du système dans la solution (in Romanian). Rev Filosof (Romania), 36(1), 91-96, Ja-F 89.

NEGRI, Antonio. Between Infinity and Community: Notes on Materialism in Spinoza and Leopardi. Stud Spinozana, 5, 151-176, 1989.

NEGRIN, Llewellyn. The End of Aesthetic Theory. Phil Soc Crit, 15(3), 253-271, 1989.

Throughout its history, the viability of aesthetics has been questioned. This essay focuses on two attempts to deconstruct aesthetics—those of Weitz and Bennett—both of which are derived from very different philosophical traditions. It is argued that these challenges to aesthetic theory result from the fact that the conditions which gave rise to aesthetics at the same time have paradoxically undermined the possibility of aesthetics. Furthermore, it is argued that while the discipline of aesthetics is in one sense impossible, nevertheless, it is in another inescapable. Consequently, while there have been concerted efforts to transcend aesthetics, none have succeeded.

NEHAMAS, Alexander. Different Readings: A Reply to Magnus, Solomon, and Conway. Int Stud Phil, 21(2), 73-80, 1989.

NEIMAN, Alven M. Indoctrination: A Contextualist Approach. Educ Phil Theor, 21(1), 53-61, 1989.

My paper is meant to critically examine the presuppositions operating within the debate among analytic philosophers over the idea of indoctrination. I argue (from a perspective sympathetic both to Rorty's pragmatism and MacIntyre's historicism) that the search for necessary and sufficient conditions here, as in other fields of philosophy, is futile. Finally, I suggest ways of interpreting the results of that search in a constructive way and propose, in the spirit of Wittgenstein, a way in which philosophers of

education might carry on discussions of indoctrination that would have real implications for practice.

NEIMAN, Alven M. Wittgenstein, Bodies and Meaning. Proc Phil Educ, 45, 244-248, 1989.

In this paper I respond to David and Louise McCarty's claim (in their paper also in the *Proceedings* concerning Wittgenstein's views on teaching. I discuss and contest their notion of Wittgensteinian semantics as "semantic physiology." In conclusion I suggest how for Wittgenstein meaning is constituted, and how education is to be understood in the light of these remarks.

NEL, Deon and PITT, Leyland. Business Ethics: Defining the Twilight Zone. J Bus Ethics, 8(10), 781-791, O 89.

This paper examines the issue of ethics policy in organizations. While the actions of top management may be the single most important factor in fostering corporate behaviour of a high ethical standard, there should be policy where policy is needed. The perceptions of three managerial groups—top- marketing- and purchasing managers—are compared regarding firstly, whether they see a need for policy on a range of ethically contentious issues, and secondly whether they believe there is policy covering these issues in their own organizations. No significant differences between the three groups of managers were found, either with regard to their perceptions of needs for policy, or as far as the existence thereof is concerned. However, an overall comparison of need for policy and the existence of policy showed a significant difference on the scenarios presented to respondents. Furthermore, the study identifies grey areas of ethics in business where managers believe policy is needed, but is not perceived to exist. The use of an ethics policy matrix in organizations is suggested as a practical tool for the examination of ethically contentious issues.

NELKIN, Dorothy. Dangerous Diagnostics. Nat Forum, 69(4), 2-6, Fall 89.

NELKIN, Norton. Categorising the Senses. Mind Lang, 5(2), 149-165, Sum 90.

The thesis of "Categorising the Senses" is that two questions about the senses need to be separated out: How did we ever come to the idea of five separate senses? And what is the best way for a psychological science to categorize the senses? It is argued that, however the first question is decided (and suggestions are given), the second question should be answered in terms of the kinds of cognitive results (in terms of the kind of information the entity comes to have) and not in terms of the phenomenology of the entity's states.

NELSON, Hilde and NELSON, James Lindemann. Cutting Motherhood in Two: Some Suspicions Concerning Surrogacy. Hypatia, 4(3), 85-94, Fall 89.

Surrogate motherhood—at least if carefully structured to protect the interests of the women involved—seems defensible along standard liberal lines which place great stress on free agreements as moral bedrocks But feminist theories have tended to be suspicious about the importance assigned to this notion by mainstream ethics, and in this paper, we develop implications of those suspicions for surrogacy. We argue that the practice is inconsistent with duties parents owe to children and that it compromises the freedom of surrogates to perform their share of those duties. Standard liberal perspectives tend to be insensitive to such considerations; we propose a view which takes more seriously the moral importance of the causal relationship between parents and children, and which therefore illuminates rather than obscures the stake that women and children have in surrogacy.

NELSON, James Lindemann. Animal Models in 'Exemplary' Medical Research: Diabetes as a Case Study. Between Species, 5(4), 195-204, Fall 89.

Animal research is often attacked on prudential, as well as moral grounds. I suggest that diabetes research generally counts as an instance of 'exemplary medical research', i.e., animal research for which there is a plausible utilitarian defense. However, surprisingly strong moral criticisms can be leveled against even such exemplary research. Responding to them requires restructuring not just our laboratories but the role of animals in the moral community altogether.

NELSON, James Lindemann and NELSON, Hilde. Cutting Motherhood in Two: Some Suspicions Concerning Surrogacy. Hypatia, 4(3), 85-94, Fall 89.

Surrogate motherhood—at least if carefully structured to protect the interests of the women involved—seems defensible along standard liberal lines which place great stress on free agreements as moral bedrocks. But feminist theories have tended to be suspicious about the importance assigned to this notion by mainstream ethics, and in this paper, we develop implications of those suspicions for surrogacy. We argue that the practice is inconsistent with duties parents owe to children and that it compromises the freedom of surrogates to perform their share of those duties. Standard liberal perspectives tend to be insensitive to such considerations; we propose a view which takes more seriously the moral importance of the causal relationship between parents and children, and which therefore illuminates rather than obscures the stake that women and children have in surrogacy.

NELSON, James Lindemann. Desire's Desire for Moral Realism: A Phenomenological Objection to Non-Cognitivism. Dialogue (Canada), 28(3), 449-460, 1989.

David Wiggins, Mark Platts, and Sabina Lovibond have all offered versions of a "phenomenological argument" in defense of moral realism. The argument appeals to our inability to act on our values if we don't regard them as, in some sense, holding independently of our beliefs and desires. Lovibond has developed this argument most thoroughly, connecting it to a Wittgensteinian notion of language. This article offers an assessment of her project.

NELSON, John O. Are There Inalienable Rights? Philosophy, 64(250), 519-524, O 89.

This paper aims to show that, even using Nichol's minimal definition, "inalienable" = "not waivable and not forfeitable except in overriding circumstances," no rights are inalienable. If rights are construed as existing independently of duties, then as unconditioned goods of our own they may always be waived. If their unalienableness rests on a connection to some duty, the duty must be one that necessarily exists and the connection in question a necessary one. But even if the first condition can be fulfilled the second cannot be.

NELSON, John O. Hume's Missing Shade of Blue Re-viewed. Hume Stud, 15(2), 353-363, N 89.

NELSON, John O. Was Aristotle a Functionalist? Rev Metaph, 43(4), 791-802, Je 90.

NELSON, Lawrence J and CLARK, H Westley and GOLDMAN, Robert L and SCHORE, Jean E. Taking the Train to a World of Strangers: Health Care Marketing and Ethics. Hastings Center Rep, 19(5), 36-43, S-O 89.

NELSON, Lynn Hankinson. *Who Knows: From Quine to a Feminist Empiricism*. Philadelphia, Temple Univ Pr, 1990

Building on Quine's work, I establish a framework for a much-needed dialogue between feminist science critics and other scientists and scholars about the nature of science. Specifically, I make a case for a feminist empiricism, a view of science that can account for its obvious success in explaining and predicting experience, and can encompass feminist insights into relationships between gender, politics, and science. I conclude that empiricism can survive the demise of individualism and that the evolving network of our theories does and should incorporate political views, including those shaped by, and shaping in turn, our experiences of gender.

NELSON, Mark T. Intuitionism and Conservatism. Metaphilosophy, 21(3), 282-293, Jl 90.

Some critics of moral intuitionism claim that intuitionism is inherently noetically conservative because it enshrines whatever intuitions a subject begins with, making those intuitions immune from criticism. Some critics argue further that moral intuitionism is also politically conservative as well, because any theory which protects that noetic *status quo* will also protect the sociopolitical *status quo*. I defend a version of moral intuitionism from both charges.

NELSON, R J. *The Logic of Mind (Second Edition)*. Norwell, Kluwer, 1989

The book presents a mechanist theory of mind and argues that intentional attitudes, including perception, can be explained in terms of systems of recursive rules (nondeterministic automata). The theory does not assume contentful states of belief and desire but reduces them to functional rules which are embodied in extensional statements that reflect the logical characteristics of the intensional: failure of substitutivity; non-truth functionality; and resistance to quantification from the outside, in short, reflects opacity without itself having opaque contexts. The first half of the book explains the basis of computability theory and draws comparisons with other functionalist theories such as those of Fodor.

NELSON, Ralph (trans) and SIMON, Yves. Knowledge of the Soul. Thomist, 54(2), 269-291, Ap 90.

The general disorder in the field of psychology prompted this study of the epistemological nature of psychology. It is important to make distinctions between different kinds of psychology, and to recognize their complementarity. Moral psychology is to be distinguished from applied psychology, a kind of technology. Theoretical psychology is divided into positive and philosophical. Though the author indicates the dangers implicit

in applied psychology, he remains positive about it. He notes the unfortunate confusion between philosophical and positive psychology and argues for boundary maintenance. He ends with cautionary advice about the use and misuse of terminology in the field of psychology.

NELSON, Thomas W. Ontological Dependence *über Alles*. Proc Phil Educ, 45, 288-291, 1989.

Pearson has raised putative counterexamples to Fenstermacher's notion of "ontological dependence." I show that these counterexamples do not work and that Fenstermacher's notion is sound, given the audience of social scientists at which it is aimed. Fenstermacher's paper remains a strong argument for a noncausal, antipositivist relation between the concepts "teaching" and "learning."

NELSON, William. "Evaluating the Institutions of Liberal Democracy" in *Politics and Process*, BRENNAN, Geoffrey (ed), 60-77. New York, Cambridge Univ Pr, 1989.

Justifying democracy is justifying a specific set of *institutions*—a structure of rights and authority. This problem is no harder, and no easier, than justifying an economic system, including rights of private property. In both cases, some moral conception must be assumed. I assume a contractualist conception. By this standard, *no* system of institutions, *in either area*, will be perfect. The dream of "perfect procedural justice" is a dream that won't come true. Consequently, we cannot avoid, in either area, relying on the good character of those who will exercise authority.

NEMETH, Elisabeth. Wissenschaftliche Weltauffassung zwischen Sozialrevolution und Sozialreform. Conceptus, 24(61), 73-90, 1990.

In his social-technological utopias Otto Neurath after World War I intended to supersede the monetarian and economic system in a rigid way by a centralized system of Naturalwirtschaft. This seems to be anachronistic, even scandalous, these days. However, there can clearly be seen a growing interest concerning the positions in philosophy and theory of science formulated by Otto Neurath within the Vienna Circle during the twenties and the thirties. In this paper I want to show that both of these aspects in the work of Otto Neurath are related to each other, which also could be seen as two periods. Neurath's intention during and after World War I, to find theoretical and practical means to make transparent and calculable social structures, is related to the goal he aimed to as a member of the Vienna Circle, to make intelligible and controllable the scientific knowledge by showing its historicity and its depending on social factors.

NEMETZ, Anthony. "The Classical Philosophers" in *Reading Philosophy for the Twenty-First Century*, MC LEAN, George F (ed), 77-107. Lanham, Univ Pr of America, 1989.

NEMOIANU, Virgil. Mihai Sora and the Traditions of Romanian Philosophy. Rev Metaph, 43(3), 591-605, Mr 90.

The article provides basic information on Romanian philosophy and on the ways it relates to Western thinking. The evolution of Romanian philosophy is not coherent or integrated. It has nevertheless a unifying concern. This is the effort to preserve the gains of the Western rationalist-empirical mainstream while placing them inside a broad variety of other modes of approaching reality that are mostly nonrationalist. Thus empiricism and rationalism are relativized (Blaga, Noica, Florian, Eliade) in ways that anticipate Derrida, Rorty, and Feyerabend. Mihai Sora managed, in the last ten years, to enrich this Romanian philosophical tradition with ethical and sociopolitical dimensions that freed it of any anti-Western and antimodernist suggestions and yet kept its focus on imperfection, heteronomy and nuance as epistemological units.

NENON, Thomas J. Which Beings are Exemplary? Comments on Charles Guignon's "Truth as Disclosure: Art, Language, History". S J Phil, SUPP(28), 121-126, 1989.

NERLICH, Graham. "Motion and Change of Distance" in *Cause, Mind, and Reality: Essays Honoring C B Martin*, HEIL, John (ed), 221-234. Norwell, Kluwer, 1989.

Relativity changed the concept of motion, in ways examined and itemised. A classical view is that position consists of relations of distance and angle among observable bodies; motion is change of these relations. Thus motion in the context just of kinematics is wholly symmetrical; dynamics defines the privileged frames of classical mechanics. In special relativity motion referred to non-inertial frames is not possible even in kinematics due to the strong symmetries of Minkowski space-time. In general relativity the expansion of space cuts the link between motion and distance change. The classical view fails.

NERODE, A and REMMEL, J B. Complexity-Theoretic Algebra II: Boolean Algebras. Annals Pure Applied Log, 44(1-2), 71-99, O 89.

NERSESSIAN, Nancy J. Methods of Conceptual Change in Science:

Imagistic and Analogical Reasoning. Philosophica, 45(1), 33-52, 1990.

Conceptual change is a significant component of all major changes of theory in science. Fine-structure analyses of the transition periods between theories show, contrary to the most influential characterizations, conceptual change is continuous, but not simply cumulative. Accounting for the historical data requires a new method for investigating the dynamics of how conceptual structures change: a "cognitive-historical" method. This method is illustrated by an account of how imagistic and analogical reasoning function in the construction of scientific representations.

NETTON, Ian Richard. *Allāh Transcendent*. New York, Routledge, 1989

This work examines the role of God in medieval Islamic philosophy and theology, using modern literary modes of criticism derived from structuralism, poststructuralism and semiotics. The author focuses on major Islamic and Arab thinkers of the Middle Ages from Al-Kindi to Ibn al-Arabi, to study the nature, function, role and development of their God, and relates the views of each to the textual and intellectual history of which he is a product. In the process, the author traces the development of the Neoplatonic God out of the Qur'anic God.

NEUBERG, M. Le *Traité des passions* de Descartes et les théories modernes de l'émotion. Arch Phil, 53(3), 479-508, Jl-S 90.

In his analysis of Descartes's treatise of *The Passions of the Soul*, the author shows its methodological relevance to contemporary studies of emotion. Descartes has established the conceptual patterns which are being used by the two competing modern approaches to emotion: the physiological and the cognitive theory of emotion. Moreover, the Cartesian text is a remarkable illustration of the difficulties inherent to these approaches to emotion.

NEUBERG, Marc. Expliquer et comprendre: La théorie de l'action de G H von Wright. Rev Phil Louvain, 88(77), 48-78, F 90.

In his writings on the problem of explaining and describing action, G H von Wright has elaborated a most subtle argumentation in support of a noncausal approach to this problem. The author of this essay shows that, though the criticisms produced by von Wright against the causal theory of action are sound, his own conception implies several paradoxical consequences whose justification appears to be doubtful. According to the author, the reason why neither the causalists nor von Wright have succeeded in producing a satisfactory solution of the problem of action, resides in a joint presupposition of theirs, namely their conviction that the corporal movements which form an action are natural events. The author points out that this presupposition is far from evident and he shows that its rejection makes it possible to restate the problem of action in a more promising way.

NEUGEBAUER, Christian. Ethnophilosophy in the Philosophical Discourse in Africa: A Critical Note. Quest, 4(1), 42-64, Je 90.

NEUSNER, Jacob. Thinking About 'The Other' in Religion: It is Necessary, But is it Possible? Mod Theol, 6(3), 273-285, Ap 90.

NEVILLE, Robert C. "Units of Change—Units of Value" in *Nature in Asian Tradition of Thought: Essays in Environmental Philosophy*, CALLICOTT, J Baird (ed), 145-149. Albany, SUNY Pr, 1989.

The essay proposes that the analysis of complex ethical issues would be greatly aided by a social and natural science that traces how the worths of things are changed by transitions through change-points in systems. A Taoist theory of change is advocated, in conjunction with a theory of systems and objective value.

NEVILLE, Robert Cummings. *Recovery of the Measure: Interpretation and Nature*. Albany, SUNY Pr, 1989

This work is the second installment in the author's planned three-volume *Axiology of Thinking*. The focus of the present volume is to address the issue of interpretation from a hermeneutical theory which is situated within the context of the philosophy of nature. The argument given is intended to provide a nonmodernist and nonpostmodernist theory of interpretation. (staff)

NEWELL, Waller R. Zarathustra's Dancing Dialectic. Interpretation, 17(3), 415-432, Spr 90.

NEWELSKI, L. Weakly Minimal Formulas: A Global Approach. Annals Pure Applied Log, 46(1), 65-94, Ja 90.

Let T be a countable weakly minimal unidimensional theory and A a set of parameters. We determine the number of models of $T(A)$ in power $|A| + c$, depending on topological properties of the set of types realized in A.

NEWMAN, Amy. Aestheticism, Feminism, and the Dynamics of Reversal. Hypatia, 5(2), 20-32, Sum 90.

Postmodern aestheticism is defined as a way of thinking that privileges the art of continual reversal. The dynamics of reversal operate according to a

theoretical model that, historically speaking, has been the vehicle for blatantly masculinist ideologies. This creates problems for feminist thinking that would appropriate the postmodern conception of the subjectivity of the artist or the aestheticist dissolution of the distinction between life and art.

NEWMAN, Louis E and BERKOWITZ, Sheldon T. Commentary: C-Section for Organ Donation. Hastings Center Rep, 20(2), 22-23, Mr-Ap 90.

The authors consider whether a C-section should be performed on a pregnant woman at 38 weeks to save her congenitally malformed fetus with anencephaly for the purpose of making its organs available for donation. They argue that such surgery is not medically indicated or morally justified in that the risks to the mother outweigh any possible psychological or medical benefits (except to a potential organ recipient) that could result from successful transplantation of this infant's organs. The mother's right to decide the course of her own pregnancy (autonomy) should not override medical judgments about what treatment is indicated.

NEWMAN, Susan E and COLLINS, Allan and BROWN, John Seely. Cognitive Apprenticeship Teaching the Craft of Reading, Writing and Mathematics. Thinking, 8(1), 2-10, 1989.

NEWTON, Lisa H. The Chainsaws of Greed: The Case of Pacific Lumber. Bus Prof Ethics J, 8(3), 29-61, Fall 89.

The article explores the ethical implications of hostile takeovers, especially where such takeovers have a detrimental impact on the natural environment. The story of Maxxam's takeover of Pacific Lumber is told, and the effects of that takeover on financial institutions, communities, labor (loggers), the political process and the forests themselves are evaluated. An effort is made to adumbrate an ethic for environmental industries generally and for special cases like the Sequoia forests in particular.

NEWTON, Lisa H. *Ethics in America: Study Guide*. Englewood Cliffs, Prentice-Hall, 1989

The *Study Guide* was designed as a companion volume for the Ethics in America television series. After two introductory chapters on the terms and traditions of moral reasoning, it tracks the series through ten topics in ethics (autonomy, distributive justice, privacy, etc.). Each of the ten chapters contains a short introductory essay on the focal term, a summary of the video presentation, a synthesis of historical materials, and various aids to instruction. A summary chapter concludes the work.

NEWTON, Natika. Error in Action and Belief. Philosophia (Israel), 19(4), 363-401, D 89.

NEWTON, Natika. On Viewing Pain as a Secondary Quality. Nous, 23(5), 569-598, D 89.

Wittgenstein was mistaken in thinking that we might refer to 'pain-patches' in external objects; pain is always in the body. But he was right that pain is not an essentially private (subjective) event. I analyze pain as a secondary quality in Locke's sense, located in a part of the body and having the power to cause sensations in a subject. Feeling a pain is, like seeing red, having a perceptual experience. I argue that this analysis corresponds exactly to the scientific account, and answer objections to this view of pain. More specifically, I argue that pain is an *intrinsic* rather than a *relative* property, as these categories are understood by McGinn and Shoemaker. Finally I argue that my analysis satisfies Peacocke's requirements that perceptual experiences have both sensational and representational properties, and I briefly discuss the related issue of sensation qualia.

NEWTON-SMITH, W H. "Rationality, Truth and the New Fuzzies" in *Dismantling Truth: Reality in the Post-Modern World*, LAWSON, Hilary (ed), 23-42. New York, St Martin's Pr, 1989.

NG, Yew-Kwang. What Should We Do About Future Generations? Impossibility of Parfit's Theory X. Econ Phil, 5(2), 235-253, O 89.

Parfit's requirements for an ideal Theory X cannot be fully met since the Mere Addition Principle and Non-Antiegalitarianism imply the Repugnant Conclusion: Theory X does not exist. However, since the Repugnant Conclusion is really compelling, the Impersonal Total Principle should be adopted for impartial comparisons concerning future generations. Nevertheless, where our own interests are affected, we may yet choose to be partial, trading off our concern for future (or others') goodness with our self-interests. Theory X' (maximization of number-dampened total utility) meets all Parfit's requirements except the Mere Addition Principle in less compelling cases.

NICHOLS, Terence L. Miracles, the Supernatural, and the Problem of Extrinsicism. Gregorianum, 71(1), 23-41, 1990.

Miracles involve a supernatural causality which in some cases suspends physical laws. But in such cases God acts through created forms, intrinsically and incarnationally, not extrinsically or magically. Thus a miraculous healing is not truly instantaneous: it is an acceleration and empowering of natural healing processes. The parallel is with grace, which heals and elevates nature without suppressing or violating it. But God's supernatural causality is not limited to extraordinary events like miracles: it is widespread and may be present even in ordinary events. Nonetheless miracles remain important visible signs of this wider presence and activity of God in history.

NICHOLSON, Linda and FRASER, Nancy. "Social Criticism Without Philosophy" in *The Institution of Philosophy: A Discipline in Crisis?*, COHEN, Avner (ed), 283-301. La Salle, Open Court, 1989.

We argue that, in their respective attempts to develop paradigms of "social criticism without philosophy," postmodernism and feminism have been prey to complementary shortcomings. The anti-essentialism and anti-foundationalism of postmodernism have been purchased at the cost of the robustness of social criticism, while the robustness of some feminist social criticism has been achieved at the cost of a continued appeal to essential natures. We propose a postmodern feminism that avoids both these problems. The result is social criticism without philosophy, but not without political bite.

NICHOLSON, Mervyn. The Eleventh Commandment: Sex and Spirit in Wollstonecraft and Malthus. J Hist Ideas, 51(3), 401-421, Jl-S 90.

NICHOLSON, Peter P. *The Political Philosophy of the British Idealists: Selected Studies*. New York, Cambridge Univ Pr, 1990

A reassessment of some of the central ideas of the political philosophy of the nineteenth century Hegelians, particularly F H Bradley, T H Green and Bernard Bosanquet, once extremely influential. The principal topics covered are Bradley on social morality and self-realisation; Green on the common good, rights and the right to private property, freedom, and state action (compared with Spencer and Mill); and Bosanquet on the general will, democracy, and international politics. These ideas are defended, and the common criticisms of them rejected as unsympathetic and misconceived. There are extensive bibliographies of these and other British Idealists, and of the secondary literature.

NICKEL, James W. Does Basing Rights on Autonomy Imply Obligations of Political Allegiance? Dialogue (Canada), 28(4), 531-544, 1989.

This paper criticizes Charles Taylor's essay, "Atomism." The first section reconstructs Taylor's argument that grounding rights on autonomy commits one to belong to, support, and give obedience to those institutions which create the environment in which autonomy can be developed. Subsequent sections evaluate the argument's premises. It is concluded that the most one can hope to get from Taylor's argument is that one who grounds rights in autonomy has good moral reasons to sustain an autonomy-supporting environment. The alleged path from autonomy-based rights to a full-fledged theory of political obligation does not go through.

NICKEL, James W. Rawls on Political Community and Principles of Justice. Law Phil, 9(2), 205-216, My 90.

This essay examines Rawls's attempt to develop a notion of political community compatible with his style of liberalism. Community, or "social unity," exists according to Rawls when there is an overlapping consensus on a political conception of justice. This essay (1) argues that Rawls's account of community exaggerates the role of political philosophy in shaping a consensus; (2) criticizes Rawls's argument that stronger forms of community cannot be achieved in modern democracies without oppression; and (3) argues that having an overlapping consensus on a political conception of justice is not itself sufficient for having political community.

NICKERSON, Raymond S. Computer Programming As a Vehicle for Teaching Thinking Skills. Thinking, 4(3-4), 42-48, 1982.

NICKLES, Thomas. Discovery Logics. Philosophica, 45(1), 7-32, 1990.

The paper addresses the questions whether there a logic of discovery that has in fact guided scientific research and whether in principle there could be such a logic. The paper concludes that there is no usable, fully general or content-neutral logic of discovery, but that there are many empirically justified logics of discovery in the sense of routine problem-solving methods. These assist in the solution of novel problems also, but such "logics" typically postdate rather than explain the major breakthroughs. Scientific methods are laden with substantive content, not a priori.

NICKLES, Thomas. Heuristic Appraisal: A Proposal. Soc Epistem, 3(3), 175-188, Jl-S 89.

Heuristic appraisal (HA) is the evaluation of the promise and expected fertility of a problem, theory, research program, proposal, instrument, or technique, its ability to handle difficulties blocking progress and to generate new lines of research. HA is fundamental to economy of research and should be a central topic of methodology of science and technology. Yet philosophers of science have largely ignored the topic. How are heuristic assessments made? How does HA relate to epistemic appraisal? I briefly critique some standard answers and formulate a proposal for addressing such questions.

NICOLET, Daniel. Langage et raison: Philosophie, linguistique et ce qui leur ressemble. Rev Theol Phil, 121(4), 353-375, 1989.

From a Wittgensteinian point of view, this article emphasizes the incommensurability between philosophical (pseudo-)theories and scientific (Galilean-style) theories about language. For instance, recent developments in Saussurian linguistics demonstrate that classical notions like "constative/performative" or "illocutory force/propositional content," etc., are not necessary for semantical description of natural languages. They belong rather to a philosophical (indeed linguistical) mythology. The proposed solution of the difficulty consists in a combination of Wittgenstein's dichotomy natural science/philosophy with his sense/truth distinction. Furthermore, this combination suggests a new interpretation for Wittgenstein's definition of the task of philosophy.

NICOLOFF, Franck. Threats and Illocutions. J Prag, 13(4), 501-522, Ag 89.

This paper tries to demonstrate that threats cannot be assimilated to illocutionary acts. Menacing is shown to be a very special type of perlocution, which cannot be held to be a counterexample to the "conventionalist" theory of speech acts, for which all illocutions are convention-constituted actions. The analysis proposed tends to confirm that theory, and discredit the rival "intentionalist" thesis of illocutions.

NICOLOSI, Salvatore. Natura e storia nel deismo di Diderot e Voltaire. Sapienza, 42(2), 121-148, Ap-Je 89.

NICOLOSI, Salvatore. La priorità ontologica e gnoseologica dell'esistenza di Dio in Spinoza. Sapienza, 43(2), 121-143, Ap-Je 90.

NIEBUHR, H Richard and NIEBUHR, Richard R (ed). *Faith on Earth: An Inquiry into the Structure of Human Faith*. New Haven, Yale Univ Pr, 1989

NIEBUHR, Richard R (ed) and NIEBUHR, H Richard. *Faith on Earth: An Inquiry into the Structure of Human Faith*. New Haven, Yale Univ Pr, 1989

NIEHUES-PRÖBSTING, Heinrich. "Kunst der Überlistung" oder "Reden mit Vernuft"? Zu Philosophischen Aspekten der Rhetorik. Phil Rundsch, 37(1-2), 123-152, 1990.

NIELSEN, Kai. Capitalism, State Bureaucratic Socialism and Freedom. Stud Soviet Tho, 38(4), 291-297, N 89.

NIELSEN, Kai. The Generalized Others and the Concrete Other: A Response of Marie Fleming. Indian Phil Quart, 17(2), 163-171, Ap 90.

NIELSEN, Kai. *God, Scepticism and Modernity*. Ottawa, Univ of Ottawa Pr, 1989

It is argued that the idea of an anthropomorphic God of any sort is untenable. It is false that such a God exists. It is further argued that nonanthropormorphic conceptions of God are so problematic as to be incoherent. There is an extensive discussion of familiar criticisms of this last point and attempts are made to answer them.

NIELSEN, Kai. Liberal and Socialist Egalitarianism. J Soc Phil, 20(1-2), 137-154, Spr-Fall 89.

NIELSEN, Kai. Liberal and Socialist Egalitarianism. Laval Theol Phil, 46(1), 81-96, F 90.

Responding to some criticisms of my *Equality and Liberty*, I elucidate and defend a conception of socialist egalitarianism. I contrast this with Rawlsian egalitarianism, specify the scope of its application and articulate a conception of equality of condition rooted in a principle which prescribes a commitment (under conditions of material abundance) to providing conditions which secure, as far as that is feasible, the equal satisfaction of needs.

NIELSEN, Kai. Making a Case for Socialism. Free Inq, 9(4), 12-14, Fall 89.

NIELSEN, Kai. A Moral Case for Socialism. Crit Rev, 3(3-4), 542-553, Sum-Fall 89.

A moral case for socialism is made, eschewing efficiency arguments—as crucial as they are in other contexts. The best feasible models of socialism and capitalism are compared with respect to such fundamental values as well-being, rights, autonomy, equality and justice. It is argued that a feasible democratic socialism is superior in all these dimensions to even the best feasible forms of capitalism.

NIELSEN, Kai. "On Being Ontologically Unserious" in *Cause, Mind, and Reality: Essays Honoring C B Martin*, HEIL, John (ed), 235-259. Norwell, Kluwer, 1989.

NIELSEN, Kai. Reflective Equilibrium and the Transformation of Philosophy. Metaphilosophy, 20(3-4), 235-246, Jl-O 89.

NIELSEN, Kai. Was Marx an Egalitarian: Skeptical Remarks on Miller's Marx. Rev Int Phil, 43(170), 438-450, 1989.

NIELSEN, Kai. Why is There a Problem About Political Obligation? J Value Inq, 24(3), 235-240, Jl 90.

NIEZNANSKI, Edward. Gödels Beweis für die Existens des *Summum Bonum* (in Polish). Stud Phil Christ, 25(2), 89-102, 1989.

In diesem Aufsatz wird am Anfang die Gödels Originalversion (Handschrift) des ontologischen Gottesbeweises dargestellt. Danach treten die Interpretationen dieses Beweises von Dana Scott, Johannes Czermak, Wilhelm Essler, Geo Siegwart und Otto Muck hervor. Alle Überlegungen führen zum Schluss, dass jede Semantik vom Kripke's Typ für das Gödelschen System als die möglichen Welten nur die Booleschen Algebren w_i enthält, die bei dem Individuenbereich U_i mit der Pontezmenge 2^{U_i} gleich sind. Nur in diesem Fall kann die "Göttlichkeit" als Durchschnitt aller positiven Eigenschaften, d.h. der Durchschnitt aller Elemente des Ultrafilters in der Algebra w_i, die einelementige Menge sein.

NIINILUOTO, Ilkka. Remarks on the Logic of Imagination. Acta Phil Fennica, 38, 183-202, 1985.

This paper employs possible worlds semantics to develop a systematic framework for studying the syntax and the semantics of imagination sentences. Following Hintikka's treatment of propositional attitudes like knowledge and perception, the propositional construction "a imagines that p" is taken as the basic form to which other sentences (such as "a imagines b," "a imagines an F") are reduced through quantifiers ranging over 'world lines', i.e., functions picking out individuals from the relevant possible worlds or scenes. This intensional analysis is compared and contrasted with Barwise and Perry's situation semantics. It is also suggested that the logic of imagination helps us to understand some peculiarities of fictional discourse.

NIJHOF, Gerhard. Antwoorden op open interview-vragen als lezingen. Kennis Methode, 14(2), 183-197, 1990.

The status of responses to open questions in qualitative sociological research is discussed. In such research reports the responses are often presented both as homogeneous representations of the opinion of the respondent and as sources for the interpretation of the researcher. Both of these research practices are being criticized. After an exploration of these critiques, two solutions are presented: (1) the approach of the text of a response as heterogeneous rather than homogeneous, more specific as a representation of a process of 'internal reading' in the text; (2) the description of this reading-process instead of the interpretation of it by the researcher.

NIJHUIS, Ton and BLOM, Tannelie. Contingency, Meaning and History. Philosophica, 44(2), 33-59, 1989.

NIJHUIS, Ton and BLOM, Tannelie. Geschiedenis en contingentie: Een nieuw perspectief op historisch verklaren. Kennis Methode, 13(4), 362-381, 1989.

NIKKELS, Eveline. *"O Mensch—Gib Acht": Friedrich Nietzsches Bedeutung Für Gustav Mahler*. Amsterdam, Rodopi, 1989

NIKOLIC, P D. Philosophy Cannot Be Implemented in Socialism and Its Economy (in Czechoslovakian). Filozof Cas, 37(4), 526-536, 1989.

This article proceeds from V I Lenin's philosophical heritage and especially from his tenet, saying that he who undertakes an analysis of partial issues without a previous solution of general questions is bound to "bump" at every step into those general questions. Regrettably, social scientists in general and economists in particular are nowadays known to be ignoring Lenin's philosophical legacy in this respect. (edited)

NINO, Carlos Santiago. La justificación de la democracia: entre la negación de la justificación y la restricción de la democracia. Analisis Filosof, 6(2), 103-114, N 86.

NINO, Carlos Santiago. La paradoja de la irrelevancia moral del gobierno y el valor epistemológico de la democracia. Analisis Filosof, 6(2), 65-82, N 86.

The article deals with this apparent paradox about the irrelevance of law and government to practical reasoning: laws do not provide by themselves operative reasons for justifying decisions without resort to autonomous moral principles; but the latter could justify by themselves the decisions without need of the laws, thus making them superfluous. The solution adopted depends on questioning the assumption of the paradox that we can know moral reasons by individual reflection alone and defending the epistemic value, on matters of public morality, of collective discussion and of a democratic system of government, which essentially involves that discussion.

NITA, Petre. Marx et le destin historique de la morale (in Romanian). Rev Filosof (Romania), 35(5), 489-494, S-O 88.

NIXON, Judy C and WEST, Judy F. The Ethics of Smoking Policies. J Bus Ethics, 8(6), 409-414, Je 89.

Smoking has long been declared a health hazard. In 1964, the US Surgeon General revealed that smoking was related to lung cancer. Subsequent reports linked smoking to numerous other health problems. Recent statements by the Surgeon General indicated smokers do have the right to decide to continue or quit; however, their choice to continue cannot interfere with the nonsmoker's right to breathe smoke-free air. The full impact of adverse health consequences of involuntary smoking may not be recognized yet. Smoke is now known to affect everyone who breathes it. Even when one doesn't smoke, the nonsmoker is susceptible to the ill effects because of inhaling smoke. Are smoking policies justified? Companies are disovering that smoking has a negative economic and ethical impact on business. Smoking has been linked to increased health care costs, reduced productivity, increased absenteeism, and lowered morale. (edited)

NIZNIK, Józef and RODZINSKA, Aleksandra (trans). The Philosophical Implications of the Use of New Information Technologies: Introductory Reflections. Dialec Hum, 16(2), 187-193, Spr 89.

In very preliminary remarks, the author outlines some of the cognitive and epistemological effects of computerization and artificial intelligence projects. He argues that the new information technology leads to the redefinition of information and knowledge. It creates "epistemological compulsion" affecting human consciousness, the intellectual processes of man and the self-perception of man. This self-perception also has an impact on man's perception of nature. The paper has been designed as an introduction to a more comprehensive study.

NOAKES, Susan. Emilio Betti's Debt to Vico. New Vico Studies, 6, 51-57, 1988.

Betti's *General Theory of Interpretation* builds upon a principle of Vico's *New Science* to develop a hermeneutics focussed on the relation between interpretation and action. Vico's idea that the principle underlying anything humans produce is to be found in the "modifications" of the human mind allows Betti to treat such topics as the relation between literature and economics and the "style" of various economic systems. Betti's premises for the analysis of mass culture, as well, are based on the Vichian model of historical recurrence. (A translation of a lecture on Vico which Betti gave in Perugia in 1957 precedes this article.)

NOAKES, Susan (trans) and BETTI, Emilio and PINTON, Giorgio (trans). The Principles of New Science of G B Vico and the Theory of Historical Interpretation. New Vico Studies, 6, 31-50, 1988.

NOERR, Gunzelin Schmid. The Civil Revolution and Historical Materialism (in Serbo-Croatian). Filozof Istraz, 30(3), 865-878, 1989.

Die Marxschen und marxistischen Beschreibungen und Deutungen der Französischen Revolution haben das Verdienst, nachdrücklich auf die Bedeutung politisch-ökonomischer Strukturen und sozialer Klassen-gegensätze und Interessenwidersprüuche hingewiesen zu haben, sodass diese Dimension auch in grundsätzlich anderen Interpretationsansätzen nicht mehr ausser Acht gelassen werden konnte. Der Vergleich zwischen der historisch-materialistischen Interpretation der Französischen Revolution und den mit Allgemeinheitsanspruch formulierten Theoremen gesellschaftlicher Entwicklung deigt, dass die letzteren selbst im Fall der Analyze der bürgerlichen Gesellschaft, auf die hin sie primär konzipiert scheinen, nicht hinreichen.

NOLAN, Kathleen (ed) and DONNELLEY, Strachan (ed). Animals, Science, and Ethics. Hastings Center Rep, 20(3), Supp 1-32, My-Je 90.

This special supplement is the result of a Hastings Center Project, "The Ethics of Animal Experimentation and Research." The project involved a multidisciplinary group of animal researchers and welfarists, veterinarians, physicians, and bioethicists. The group tried systematically to develop a position that was at once pro animal welfare and pro legitimate science—a "troubled middle" position between more extreme animal rightists and human welfarists. There are sections on the moral status of animals, the ethical justification of animal experiments, animal suffering and cultural anthropomorphism, TACUCs, and the adequacy of present federal regulations of animal use in science.

NOLAN, Kathleen. Protecting Fetuses from Prenatal Hazards: Whose Crimes? What Punishment? Crim Just Ethics, 9(1), 13-23, Wint-Spr 90.

Potential threats to fetal well-being are myriad, ranging from genetic abnormalities and environmental pollution to infectious diseases and use of nicotine, alcohol, cocaine, and other drugs by pregnant women. While a focus on the children who are expected to manifest the consequences of prenatal exposures can ground a general moral obligation to promote fetal well-being, defining the boundaries of this obligation is complicated. The intentions of pregnant women and the inherent morality of their prenatal activities carry moral weight, perhaps more than the risk of harmful consequences to their children. Autonomy and justice concerns combine with pragmatic concerns about the efficacy of imposing criminal liability, however, to dictate against legal efforts to coerce or punish women who engage in potentially harmful behaviors.

NOLT, John Eric and ROHATYN, Dennis. *Schaum's Outline of Theory and Problems of Logic*. New York, McGraw-Hill, 1988

Intended to function either as a stand-alone textbook or supplement, this volume includes chapters on argument structure, argument evaluation, the propositional calculus, truth tables and refutation trees, categorical syllogisms, the predicate calculus, fallacies, induction, the probability calculus, and extensions of formal logic. Both formal and informal points of view are covered. It contains 524 solved problems.

NOONAN, Harold W. Vague Identity Yet Again. Analysis, 50(3), 157-162, Je 90.

The paper defends Gareth Evans's argument against vague identity. It appeals to a principle I name the principle of the diversity of the definitely dissimilar to defend the thesis that vague identity statements owe their indeterminacy to vagueness in language.

NORCROSS, Alastair. Killing, Abortion, and Contraception: A Reply to Marquis. J Phil, 87(5), 268-277, My 90.

This is a reply to Marquis's paper, "Why Abortion Is Immoral." Marquis argues that almost all abortions are seriously immoral, because they share the central wrong-making feature of standard killings. I argue that Marquis fails to distinguish morally between contraception and abortion. I also argue that an attempt to distinguish contraception from abortion by appeal to a parsimonious ontology does not provide a morally relevant distinction. I conclude that Marquis is unable to distinguish morally between contraception and abortion without appealing to morally relevant features other than what he calls the "wrong-making feature of one's being killed."

NORD, Warren. "The Humanities and the Modern Mind" in *Mind, Value and Culture: Essays in Honor of E M Adams*, WEISSBORD, David (ed), 13-54. Atascadero, Ridgeview, 1989.

NORDBY, Jon J. Bootstrapping While Barefoot (Crime Models versus Theoretical Models in the Hunt for Serial Killers). Synthese, 81(3), 373-389, D 89.

Investigating random homicides involves constructing models of an odd sort. While the differences between these models and scientific models are radical, calling them models is justified both by functional and structural similarities. Serial homicide investigations illustrate the marked difference between theoretical models in science and the models applied in these criminal investigations. This is further illustrated by considering Glymourian bootstrapping in attempts to solve such homicides. The solutions that result differ radically from explanations in science that are confirmed or disconfirmed by occurrences. Unlike the scientist, the flatfoot gumshoe is also barefoot: he is bereft of a general, determinative theoretical frame. This result shows that criminal investigations do not apply 'science' in the Galilean sense.

NORDENFELT, Lennart. A Sketch for a Theory of Health. Acta Phil Fennica, 38, 203-217, 1985.

In this article a holistic theory of health is presented. Health is defined as a person's ability to reach his vital goals. Diseases are characterized as such bodily and mental processess which tend to compromise health. The major analyses of the paper concern the concepts of "ability" and "vital goal." The relation between ability and context is emphasized. Different approaches to the definition of "vital goal" are scrutinized. The author proposes the idea that the realization of a vital goal is a necessary condition for the subject's longterm minimal happiness.

NORDENHAUG, Theodore D. Who Is the Enemy? Reflections on the Threat of Managerial Techno-Reason to the Humanities. Personalist Forum, 6(1), 5-25, Spr 90.

NORHOLM, Ingrid. Kio and Gus Teach Henrik to Read. Thinking, 6(2), 31-32, 1985.

NORMAN, Jean and SYLVAN, Richard. "Conclusion: Further Directions in Relevant Logics" in *Directions in Relevant Logic*, NORMAN, Jean (ed), 399-437. Norwell, Kluwer, 1989.

NORMAN, Jean (ed) and SYLVAN, Richard (ed). *Directions in Relevant Logic*. Norwell, Kluwer, 1989

NORMAN, Jean and SYLVAN, Richard. "Introduction: Routes in Relevant Logic" in *Directions in Relevant Logic*, NORMAN, Jean (ed), 1-24. Norwell, Kluwer, 1989.

NORMAN, Richard. Respect for Persons, Autonomy and Equality. Rev Int Phil, 43(170), 323-341, 1989.

Though the concept of "respect for persons" has its original home in Kant's moral philosophy, it also has a wider intuitive appeal which survives its detachment from that original context. In this paper I shall try to locate that appeal. I shall sketch what I take to be a tenable version of the concept and the role which it can play in ethical thinking, and I shall then spell out some of its implications for political thought, especially through its connections with the concepts of "autonomy" and "equality."

NORRIS, Christopher. "Reading Donald Davidson: Truth, Meaning and Right Interpretation" in *Analytic Aesthetics*, SHUSTERMAN, Richard (ed), 97-122. Cambridge, Blackwell, 1989.

NORRIS, Stephen P. The Moral Aspects of Reading: Response to Raitz and Edwards. Proc Phil Educ, 45, 344-348, 1989.

Borrowing a distinction offered by Passmore, Raitz and Edwards argue that reading should not be taught as a closed capacity but, rather, as an open one. However, use of Passmore's distinction risks focusing educational debate upon what is and what is not totally masterable, instead of upon central philosophical questions concerning what is more important to teach. Thus, educational philosophers should turn their attention to such questions as why children ought to learn to read well, and what ethical and moral issues arise when interpreting texts.

NORTH, Michael. The Public as Sculpture: From Heavenly City to Mass Ornament. Crit Inquiry, 16(4), 860-879, Sum 90.

This article investigates a common metaphor in contemporary art, that of the public as sculpture. Behind the metaphor lies that assumption that modern art becomes public by including the public itself, by engaging the collective experience of space. The history of the metaphor of the public as sculpture shows, however, that it has contradictory implications: it begins as a model of participatory democracy but is always converted to authoritarian uses. The article concludes that contemporary public projects that begin with revolutionary or avant-garde sentiments also often end with authoritarian results. Projects that avoid this outcome do so by using space to reanimate the public's power to debate controversial political questions.

NORTMANN, Ulrich. Über die Stärke der Aristotelischen Modallogik. Erkenntnis, 32(1), 61-82, Ja 90.

The author aims at comparing as to logical strength the Aristotelian system of modal syllogisms with familiar modern systems of modal predicate logic such as PL+T, PL+S4, etc. An essential prerequisite consists in seeking formulas of modal predicate logic apt to depict the logical forms of, say, Aristotelian apodeictic propositions. Conclusions are: there is a way of symbolizing Aristotelian modal propositions to the effect that most Aristotelian theorems (including such controversial ones as the validity of Barbara with assertoric major and contingent minor) are true at least in relation to PL+S5. Aristotle's technique of converting universally negative apodeictic propositions is shown to be in a sense equivalent to PL+S5.

NORTON, Anne. Response to Henry S Kariel's "The Feminist Subject Spinning in the Postmodern Project". Polit Theory, 18(2), 273-279, My 90.

NORTON, David Fate. "Hume" in *Ethics in the History of Western Philosophy*, CAVALIER, Robert J (ed), 155-200. New York, St Martin's Pr, 1988.

NORTON, David L. "'Character Ethics' and Organizational Life" in *Papers on the Ethics of Administration*, WRIGHT, N Dale (ed), 47-66. Albany, SUNY Pr, 1988.

NORTON, Edgar. A Simple Quantitative Test of Financial Ethics. J Bus Ethics, 8(7), 561-564, Jl 89.

This paper reports on a survey sent to financial executives at 405 small corporations. A cover letter assured recipients all survey responses would be anonymous and that the enclosed $5 check was to be considered payment for completing and returning the survey. The letter requested the check be returned or destroyed if the survey was not going to be completed and returned. In a quantitative test of financial ethics, the proportion of cancelled checks and checks returned with a completed survey is compared to the proportion of completed and returned surveys. Based on the Z test statistic, the null hypothesis of equal proportions was accepted, implying ethical behavior by the group of executives in this test. Suggestions are given for future research.

NOSKE, Frits. "Visible and Audible 'Art Nouveau': The Limits of Comparison" in *Cultural Hermeneutics of Modern Art: Essays in Honor of Jan Aler*, DETHIER, Hubert (ed), 183-193. Amsterdam, Rodopi, 1989.

NOTTURNO, M A. Critical Generosity or Cognitive Growth? The Case for Epistemological Buddhism. Metaphilosophy, 20(3-4), 306-318, Jl-O 89.

This article introduces and defends epistemological Buddhism—a pluralist epistemology which rejects commitment to belief as an inappropriate response to the twentieth century's loss of certainty. It regards interpretation as fundamental to knowledge and criticism as fundamental to interpretation. But it argues that criticism should aim at understanding, as opposed to discrediting, conflicting interpretations. In distinguishing pluralism regarding truth from pluralism regarding knowledge, it defends the latter against charges of incoherency, arguing that it is possible to view the world from opposing perspectives and that understanding the world from such perspectives is what constitutes cognitive growth in a pluralistic universe.

NOVAK, David. Bioethics and the Contemporary Jewish Community. Hastings Center Rep, 20(4), Supp 14-17, Jl-Ag 90.

This article deals with the growing response by Jewish ethicists to the revolution in biomedical technology. It delineates three different approaches: (1) a presentation of what Jewish tradition has held to be normative for gentiles as well as Jews; (2) a presentation of what Jewish tradition should hold to be normative for gentiles as well as Jews based on natural rights type reasoning; (3) a presentation of what can be presented from Jewish tradition as normative for gentiles as well as Jews based on commonalities between Judaism and Christianity. The last approach is advocated by the author.

NOVICK, Alvin. Civil Disobedience in Times of AIDS. Hastings Center Rep, 19(6), 35-36, N-D 89.

NOVIKOVA, Lidia I. The October Revolution and Spiritual Renewal of Society. Dialec Hum, 15(3-4), 195-204, Sum-Autumn 88.

NOXON, James. "Alternative Readings: Hume and His Commentators" in *Early Modern Philosophy II*, TWEYMAN, Stanley (ed), 7-24. Delmar, Caravan Books, 1988.

NÚÑEZ LADEVÉZE, Luis. La definición como significado textual. Anu Filosof, 20(1), 167-195, 1987.

NUSSBAUM, Charles. Concepts, Judgments, and Unity in Kant's Metaphysical Deduction of the Relational Categories. J Hist Phil, 28(1), 89-103, Ja 90.

In the Metaphysical Deduction Kant claims that judgmental unity and the synthetic unity of the manifold rest on "the same function." If this is the case, how, then, do we distinguish between analytical and synthetic operations? But if the functions are not the same, how can the forms of judgment serve as a "clue" for the discovery of the categories? The difficulty can be resolved if Kant's "same function" is understood as syntactical formation, rather than as the production of unity in the extension of a concept. This, in turn, suggests a connection between synthesis, pure intuition, and the logic of relations.

NUSSBAUM, Martha C. Mortal Immortals: Lucretius on Death and the Voice of Nature. Phil Phenomenol Res, 50(2), 303-351, D 89.

NUSSBAUM, Martha. Philosophical Books versus Philosophical Dialogue. Thinking, 6(2), 13-14, 1985.

NUTTING, Kurt and CRANOR, Carl. Scientific and Legal Standards of Statistical Evidence in Toxic Tort and Discrimination Suits. Law Phil, 9(2), 115-156, My 90.

Many legal disputes turn on scientific, especially statistical, evidence. Traditionally scientists have accepted only that statistical evidence which satisfies a 95 percent rule—that is, only evidence which has less than 5 percent probability of resulting from chance. The rationale for this rule is the reluctance of scientists to accept anything less than the best-supported new knowledge. The rule reflects the internal needs of scientific practice. However, when uncritically adopted as a rule for admitting legal evidence, the seemingly innocuous 95 percent rule distorts the balance of interests historically protected by the legal system. In particular, plaintiffs in toxic tort and employment discrimination suits are effectively held to a heavier burden of proof in showing that their injuries were more probably than not caused by the defendant's actions. The result is that too many victims of toxic torts or employment discrimination cannot win legal redress for their injuries. (edited)

NUYEN, A T. Art and the Rhetoric of Allusion. S J Phil, 27(4), 495-510, Wint 89.

According to Danto, art works represent metaphorically and thus invite interpretation. Danto's view of art is very close to Gadamer's. For Gadamer, art is a game of interpretation and understanding the elements of which are "play, symbol and festival." The paper compares and contrasts the two views, and develops an account of art as "allusion." It is argued that the notion of "allusion" neatly captures and unifies the features of art identified by Danto and Gadamer.

NUYEN, A T. Sense, Reason and Causality in Hume and Kant. Kantstudien, 81(1), 57-68, 1990.

It is argued that Hume has two notions of causation, one psychological and the other philosophical. Kant's criticism of Hume overlooks the fact that Hume's scepticism is directed only at the latter. At the psychological level, Hume could have accepted Kant's argument without abandoning his own account of causation. The real difference between Hume and Kant is that Hume is not and Kant is concerned with the conditions for the possibility of sense experience. Hume is concerned only with the philosophical inferences

we can draw, having experienced the world in a certain way.

NUYEN, A T. Some Heideggerian Reflections on Euthanasia. Metaphilosophy, 21(1-2), 133-140, Ja-Ap 90.

The opposition to euthanasia seems to stem from an attitude toward death that Heidegger would call inauthentic. Since death is an existential condition of Dasein insofar as Dasein is being-toward-death, authenticity requires that we wrench ourselves from the influence of the society (the "they-self") and face death with anxiety, not fear. Dasein is also being-in-the-world and among-others, and as such it is better to involve others in one's death than to face it in isolation.

NYE, Andrea. The Subject of Love. J Value Inq, 24(2), 135-153, Ap 90.

Plato's theory of love has been criticized by Gregory Vlastos, Martha Nussbaum, and others for bypassing the unique individual subject of love for an abstract ideal. I argue in this paper that Diotima's teaching on love in the *Symposium* is different from Plato's as expressed in the *Phaedrus*. Nussbaum and Vlastos assume an autonomous subject who is incapable of love; because of this, they have not understood Diotima who understands the subject of love as relational.

NYE, John Vincent. "The Conflation of Productivity and Efficiency in Economics and Economic History": A Comment. Econ Phil, 6(1), 147-152, Ap 90.

NYENHUIS, Gerald. Dos caras de la hermeneutica. Rev Filosof (Mexico), 22(65), 221-227, My-Ag 89.

This article, written in Spanish, comments on the ways that the present emphasis on hermeneutics makes itself known. The article affirms that hermeneutics presents itself in two basic forms: it can be seen as a logic of validation or as a phenomenology of understanding. The article further affirms that if we choose the logic of validation as the only legitimate form of hermeneutics, then an understanding of it as the phenomenology of understanding is ruled out. But, on the other hand, if we choose to approach hermeneutics as a phenomenology of understanding, the logic of validation can find a place in it too. The article, then, is an apology for the latter point of view.

NYIRI, J C. "Wittgenstein and the Problem of Machine Consciousness" in *Wittgenstein in Focus—Im Brennpunkt: Wittgenstein*, MC GUINNESS, Brian (ed), 375-394. Amsterdam, Rodopi, 1989.

For any given society, its particular technology of communication has far-reaching consequences, not merely as regards social organization, but on the epistemic level as well. Plato's name-theory of meaning represents the transition from the age of primary orality to that of literacy; Wittgenstein's use-theory of meaning stands for the transition from the age of literacy to that of a second orality (audio-visual communication, electronic information processing). On the basis of a use-theory of meaning the problem of machine consciousness, to which the later Wittgenstein again and again returned, is capable of a nonessentialist solution: appropriate changes in our form of life might well entail a radically different psychological language-game.

NYÍRI, Tamás. Changes in the View on Man in Our Age (in Hungarian). Magyar Filozof Szemle, 2-3, 303-314, 1989.

O'BRIEN, Denis. Héraclite et l'unité des opposés. Rev Metaph Morale, 95(2), 147-171, Ap-Je 90.

Plato and Aristotle presumably read the same text of Heraclitus, and yet they come up with entirely opposite accounts of its meaning. Plato thinks that Heraclitus and Empedocles disagree; Aristotle, that they agree. Scholars have failed to solve this conundrum, because they have failed to recognise in the fragments of Heraclitus the obscure alternative forms of the law of the unity of opposites. Aristotle (wrongly) took one formulation of the law of the unity of opposites to imply an endless succession of the one and the many, and therefore the agreement of Heraclitus with Empedocles.

O'BRIEN, Maura. Mandatory HIV Antibody Testing Policies: An Ethical Analysis. Bioethics, 3(4), 273-300, O 89.

O'CALLAGHAN, Paul. La metafísica de la esperanza y del deseo en Gabriel Marcel. Anu Filosof, 22(1), 55-92, 1989.

"The first half of this study examines Marcel's doctrine on hope as a feature of man's being, developed from within the very process in which hope arises: the inadequacy of desire; despair; intersubjectivity; grace. The second half looks into a series of gray areas in his thought: hope's illusory character, theological basis; relationship to freedom, and especially its opposition to desire. Historically, the latter is the result of his rejection of Spinozean naturalism, and speculatively because his reflection is slightly tinged by an anticosmic spiritualism."

O'CALLAGHAN, Timothy M B. Sensibility and Recreational Appreciation. J Aes Educ, 22(3), 25-35, Fall 88.

O'CONNELL, Patrick F. Aelred of Rievaulx and the "Lignum Vitae" of Bonaventure: A Reappraisal. Fran Stud, 48(26), 53-79, 1988.

O'CONNOR, David K. Two Ideals of Friendship. Hist Phil Quart, 7(2), 109-122, Ap 90.

We tend to classify our relationships according to degree of intimacy: acquaintances, friends, close friends, best friends. Aristotle instead classifies friendships on the basis of what common goal the friends pursue in partnership: pleasure-friends, utility-friends, goodness-friends. The paper outlines these contrasting ideals of friendship as intimacy and as partnership and considers the different accounts they lead to of (i) what limits how many good friends people can have and (ii) what is required to love a friend for himself. I conclude with a discussion of the place of altruism and intimacy in the Aristotelian ideal.

O'CONNOR, David. Levine on Hare on Camus' Assumption. Sophia (Australia), 28(3), 31-39, O 89.

The philosophical credentials of the debate between optimists and pessimists over the meaning of life have been challenged by, among others, Baier, Edwards, Nielson, and Hare. Against that background, Michael P Levine recently argued in support of a key assumption in the debate. My argument is that Levine fails to sustain the assumption in question.

O'CONNOR, David. On Failing to Resolve Theism-Versus-Atheism Empirically. Relig Stud, 26(1), 91-103, Mr 90.

Both the argument from evil and the theistic responses to it are predicated on the assumption that, in thought-experiments, the condition of the world can be compared both with how the world would be if God existed and with how it would be if God did not exist. From those comparisons conclusions are drawn about God's existence being confirmed or disconfirmed by the state of the world. But if those comparisons could never be legitimately made, those conclusions could not be drawn. I show that those comparisons cannot, in principle, be made.

O'CONNOR, David. On the Problem of Evil's Still Not Being What It Seems. Phil Quart, 40(158), 72-78, Ja 90.

The points I shall make in reply to P J McGrath's criticisms of my 'On the Problem of Evil's Not Being What It Seems' fall into three groups. First I will show that he seriously misrepresents my position and that, accordingly, his attacks upon it fail. Second, I will point out significant defects in the solution that he goes on to propose to the problem of evil. And third, I will sketch out an argument for my conclusion about God and all evil that was not in my original paper.

O'DALY, Gerard. Predestination and Freedom in Augustine's Ethics. Philosophy, 25, 85-97, 89 Supp.

O'DONOVAN, Oliver. How Can Theology Be Moral? J Relig Ethics, 17(2), 81-94, Fall 89.

A tension exists between the disciplines of theology, which seeks to discern the rational order of what is believed and to impose intellectual discipline on its presentation, and moral thought, which is practical in nature, thought-towards-action. More fully expressed, this tension is found in three antinomies: that theology is declarative, while moral thought is deliberative; that theology is evangelical, while moral thought is problematic; and that while theology is Christocentric, moral thought must be generic. This essay argues that despite the tension inherent in its dual focus, moral theology can be an authentic enterprise, proceeding via a dialectic within these three antinomies.

O'GORMAN, Francis. Rationality and Relativity: The Quest for Objective Knowledge. Brookfield, Gower, 1989.

The central theme of this work is that mainstream philosophy is operating with inadequate theories of knowledge. As an alternative, the author develops 'the learning feedback model'. This model, located in a historical context from Aristotle to Wittgenstein, develops a dynamic conception of human knowledge. The work ranges from the naturalization of epistemology to the realism-constructive empiricism debate, and develops an intriguing conception of the objectivity of morality.

O'GORMAN, P F. Mentalism-Cum-Physicalism vs Eliminative Materialism. Irish Phil J, 6(1), 133-147, 1989.

The central thesis is that Churchland's eliminative materialism, though a logical possibility, fails to stand up to the current evidence available. Given the viewpoint of physicalism, the superimposition of our folk psychological model of the mind, modified to eliminate any strands of Cartesian dualism, on to a biological-neurophysiological model of a human being is a better research programme than eliminative materialism.

O'HAGAN, Timothy. Searching for Ancestors. Rad Phil, 54, 19-22, Spr 90.

The author engages in a light-hearted biographical sketch of Alasdair

MacIntyre's trajectory since the 1960s and in some slightly more serious reflections on the author's latest work *Whose Justice? Which Rationality?* In it he disengages a rational kernel (the irreducible presence of context and hermeneutics) and a mystical shell (a millenarian pessimism about the disintegration wrought by Enlightenment "liberalism"). For MacIntyre, "things fall apart, the centre cannot hold, mere anarchy is loosed upon the world." The solution lies in recuperating a shared, "healthy" tradition, allegedly located in "Augustinian Christianity." The author questions both the critique of liberalism and the proposed countermodel.

O'HARA, J D. "Beckett's Schopenhauerien Reading of Proust" in *Schopenhauer: New Essays in Honor of His 200th Birthday*, VON DER LUFT, Eric (ed), 273-292. Lewiston, Mellen Pr, 1989.

O'KEEFE, Martin D. *Known from the Things that Are: Fundamental Theory of the Moral Life*. Houston, Ctr Thomistic Stud, 1987

This book sets out to answer a primary question of ethics: What can the individual, relying on his powers of observation and reasoning alone, know about the moral life, especially in light of contemporary society's materialism, hedonism, and subjectivity concerning right and wrong? The volume begins with a brief introduction to philosophy and ethics. Part II examines the theory of ethics: What is human conduct? What are "good" and "evil" acts? Part III discusses the practical nature of ethics: our relationships to ourselves, to others, and to God. (edited)

O'LOUGHLIN, Thomas. Knowing God and Knowing the Cosmos: Augustine's Legacy of Tension. Irish Phil J, 6(1), 27-58, 1989.

Part of Augustine's influence is a tension regarding the study of the cosmos. As God's handiwork it deserves study, but compared with the Creator (and Man's transcendent destiny) it hardly merits attention. Indeed such attention might distract the investigator from his true goal. Augustine believes there must be new criteria and a new basis for such study. Genesis 1 (the Hexaemeron) and a number of other scriptural texts are crucial in providing the framework for this new cosmology. The article examines this underlying tension, these texts, and the basic structure Augustine envisages for cosmology in the *Confessiones*, the *De doctrina christiana* and the *De Genesi ad litteram*.

O'MEARA, Dominic J. Philosophie antique et byzantine: à propos de deux nouvelles collections. Frei Z Phil Theol, 36(3), 471-478, 1989.

O'MEARA, Dominic J. Le problème du discours sur l'indicible chez Plotin. Rev Theol Phil, 122(2), 145-156, 1990.

This article examines the reasons Plotinus has for asserting the ineffability of the ultimate source of reality, the One. It is argued that Plotinus explains the possibility of speaking about the One in such a way as to preserve its ineffability: such speaking is in fact about our nature and that of the world, whose lack of self-sufficiency points beyond itself. Some final remarks concern the place and function of language in the context of soul's return to the One.

O'MEARA, Dominic J. *Pythagoras Revived: Mathematics and Philosophy in Late Antiquity*. New York, Clarendon/Oxford Pr, 1989

O'NEILL, John. *The Communicative Body: Studies in Communicative Philosophy, Politics, and Sociology*. Evanston, Northwestern Univ Pr, 1989

This book is a series of articles by one author on the work of Merleau-Ponty. The discussion centers on Merleau-Ponty's phenomenological analysis of the human body, and also on his work in politics, history, and language. (staff)

O'NEILL, Onora. *Constructions of Reason: Explorations of Kant's Practical Philosophy*. New York, Cambridge Univ Pr, 1989

This approach to Kant's account of practical reason undertakes three main tasks. The first is to offer an account of Kant's constructivist vindication of reason and to analyse its implications for the relation of theory and practice, and in particular for his accounts of autonomy and morality. The second is to offer a reading of Kant's ethics which is neither formalistic nor rigoristic, and which takes virtues as well as justice seriously. The third is to explore the distance between Kant's ethics and recent depictions of 'Kantian ethics' offered both by its advocates and by its opponents.

O'NEILL, Onora. Morality, Politics and the Revolutions of 1989. Aris Soc, SUPP 64, 281-294, 1990.

An attempt to rechart the connections between morality and politics in the wake of the revolutions of 1989. For a long time this terrain has been divided between discussions of acts of state, discussions of the fate of the powerless and discussions of less well defined moral dilemmas of "normal" politics. The writings of Vaclav Havel suggest another view, in which the powerlessness of individuals may form the matrix for a certain sort of civic courage and ultimately political transformation. Havel's critique of western liberalism is briefly discussed.

O'NEILL, Onora. Universal Laws and Ends-In-Themselves. Monist, 72(3),

341-361, Jl 89.

Kant perplexingly claims that the various Formulations of the Categorical Imperative are equivalent, and yet that the Formula of Universal Law and the Formula of the End in Itself provide respectively the form and the matter of morality. However, a reading of these formulae and the Formula of the Kingdom of Ends can be provided which sustains both the equivalence claims and the insistence that the formulae determine distinct aspects of morality. This reading relies mainly upon an extensive analysis of Kant's notion of a maxim, careful consideration of the different positions that the formulae have in the text of Kant's *Groundwork*, and insistence that all formulations must be interpreted as providing a dual criterion respectively for perfect and imperfect duties.

O'NEILL, Onora. Virtuous Lives and Just Societies. J Soc Phil, 20(1-2), 25-30, Spr-Fall 89.

Neither the contemporary advocates of justice nor the contemporary friends of the virtues have vindicated the division of intellectual labour on which both insist. The arguments suggest rather that traditional connections between investigations of justice and of the virtues should and can be resumed.

OAKES, G. The Sales Process and the Paradoxes of Trust. J Bus Ethics, 9(8), 671-679, Ag 90.

This essay explores a major ethical variable in personal sales: trust. By analyzing data drawn from life insurance sales, the essay supports the thesis that the role of the agent and the exigencies of personal sales create certain antinomies of trust that compromise the sales process. As a result, trust occupies a problematic and apparently paradoxical position in the sales process. On the one hand, success in personal sales is held to depend upon trust. On the other hand, because the techniques required to form trust in personal sales nullify the conditions under which trust is possible, these instruments of trust formation are self-defeating.

OAKES, Robert. Union with God: A Theory. Faith Phil, 7(2), 165-176, Ap 90.

The experience of "union with God," i.e., experience the phenomenological core of which can be expressed as *dissolution-of-self-in-God*, arguably constitutes the most spiritually significant sort of religious experience. However, it is well known that canonical theistic metaphysics—by virtue of its (anti-pantheistic) insistence upon an unbridgeable bifurcation between Creator and creature—rules out the literal veridicality of such experience. Alternatively, whatever the *phenomenological* significance of "unitive" religious experience, traditional theism must deny that there can occur literal or *ontological mergings* of finite selves with God. Our purpose is to construct the rudiments of a theory designed to establish that classical theism is perfectly compatible with the view that "unitive" religious experience has serious ontological import; moreover, our proposal has the "practical" advantage of accounting well for the profound *conviction* among the phenomenological subjects of such experience of having "become one" with God.

OAKES, Robert. The Wrath of God. Int J Phil Relig, 27(3), 129-140, Je 90.

OAKESHOTT, Michael and FULLER, Timothy (ed). *The Voice of Liberal Learning: Michael Oakeshott on Education*. New Haven, Yale Univ Pr, 1989

Oakeshott's education essays, collected, edited and introduced by Timothy Fuller, show universities as special places of learning where scholars congregate to keep learning and to teach. Universities have no definable, external purpose. Humanity would achieve little if limited merely to utilitarian pursuits. The university's differentiating idea is to pursue learning for its own sake wherein the how and what of learning are inseparable and equally eligible for philosophic reflection, only incidentally bearing practical fruit, an unrehearsed intellectual adventure in becoming human, preferring conversation to victory, and where political demands are extrinsic to teaching and learning.

OAKLANDER, L Nathan. The New Tenseless Theory of Time: A Reply to Smith. Phil Stud, 58(3), 287-292, Mr 90.

Quentin Smith has argued (*Philosophical Studies*, 1987, pp. 371-392) that the token-reflexive and the date versions of the new tenseless theory of time are open to insurmountable difficulties. I argue that Smith's central arguments are irrelevant since they rest upon methodological assumptions accepted by the old tenseless theory, but rejected by the new tenseless theory.

OBEN, Freda M. Edith Stein as Educator. Thought, 65(257), 113-126, Je 90.

OBERHOLZER, C K. Man's Yearnings (in Dutch). S Afr J Phil, 8(3-4), 190-197, N 88.

By looking at man's yearnings the author attempts to answer Kant's question: what must man be to be truly human? He attacks the biological homeostatic view of human needs and the accompanying view that man has a dual nature. According to the author these views rest on a confusion—taking structural continuity for continuity in essence. The author shows that the humanness of man is constituted by man's open-endedness which involves freedom and responsibility, values and norms, a history and consiousness of the future. All these in their turn imply intersubjectivity. In this context talk of human needs is out of place whereas yearnings are expressive of the humanness of man and thus provide a basis for an account of the essentially human.

OBRADORS, Pedro J M. Etienne Gilson ante las falsas interpretaciones del pensamiento de Santo Tomás de Aquino. Sapientia, 44(173), 185-196, Jl-S 89.

OBTULOWICZ, A. Categorical and Algebraic Aspects of Martin-Löf Type Theory. Stud Log, 48(3), 299-317, S 89.

OCHS, Peter. A Pragmatic Method of Reading Confused Philosophic Texts: The Case of Peirce's "Illustrations". Trans Peirce Soc, 25(3), 251-291, Sum 89.

Charles Peirce's method for "How to Make Our Ideas Clear" also suggests a method for how to make confused writing clear. I derive this "Pragmatic Method of Reading" from Peirce's 1877-78 "Illustrations of the Logic of Science" and then apply it as a method of clarifying confusions in those same Illustrations. On a preliminary reading, the Illustrations appear to offer self-contradictory claims. According to a pragmatic reading, these claims exhibit the competing influences in Peirce's early thought of two sets of incompatible leading tendencies: one a "pragmatic realism," the other a "pragmatic conceptualism."

ODDIE, Graham and TICHY, Pavel. Resplicing Properties in the Supervenience Base. Phil Stud, 58(3), 259-269, Mr 90.

John Bacon has recently argued that weak and strong supervenience are equivalent. He employs a novel closure principle: related classes of properties must be closed under 'resplicing'. This requirement is shown to render supervenience both too narrow and too wide. It rules out perfectly good supervenience bases, and permits counterintuitive relations of supervenience. If the approach is amended to rectify the former shortcoming the latter persists. This is because Bacon's strong and weak supervenience are both equivalent to old-style weak supervenience. This furnishes further arguments that weak supervenience is too weak to do the work required of it.

ODEGARD, Douglas and CANARY, Catherine. Deductive Justification. Dialogue (Canada), 28(2), 305-320, 1989.

ODENWALD, Sten F. A Modern Look at the Origin of the Universe. Zygon, 25(1), 25-45, Mr 90.

I review the modern theory of the origin of the universe as astronomers and physicists are coming to understand it during the last decades of the twentieth century. An unexpected discovery of this study is that the story of "cosmogenesis" cannot be completely told unless we understand the fundamental nature of matter, space, and time. In the context of modern cosmology space has become not only the bedrock (so to speak) of our physical existence, it may yield a fuller understanding of the universe itself.

ODIN, Steve. Derrida and the Decentered Universe of Ch'an Buddhism. J Chin Phil, 17(1), 61-86, Mr 90.

ODIN, Steve. The Influence of Traditional Japanese Aesthetics on the Film Theory of Sergei Eisenstein. J Aes Educ, 23(2), 69-81, Sum 89.

OESCH, Martin. "Neues über das Systemprogramm?" in *Agora: Zu Ehren von Rudolph Berlinger*, BERLINGER, Rudolph (and other eds), 141-164. Amsterdam, Rodopi, 1988.

The research of the so-called idealistic "Systemprogramm" from the end of the 18th century has resulted in traces of a paper agitating the society. The essay appropriates this thesis and it is discussed if a leading member of the "Society of free men" in Jena, von Berger, was the author of basic ideas of this fragment. By comparing sentences and terms of his early work one can imagine this thesis. We know about the relation between the free men and F Schlegel. Oesch assumes that he was involved in final editorial work of the programme. Many concepts in "Athenaeums Fragmenten" show this.

OESTERREICH, Peter L. Die Idee einer existentialontologischen Wendung der Rhetorik in M Heideggers "Sein und Zeit". Z Phil Forsch, 43(4), 656-672, O-D 89.

Der Aufsatz stellt Heideggers methodische Idee einer existentialontologischen Wendung der klassischen Rhetorik heraus. Rhetorikaffine Passagen in *Sein und Zeit* sind dabei einerseits die explizite Aneignung der aristotelischen *Rhetorik* in den Analysen von *Befindlichkeit* und *Stimmungen* und andererseits die verborgene Rezeption der *quinque artes* in der *Verstehen-Auslegung-Rede*-Struktur. Dem stehen rhetorikrepugnante Tendenzen wie Heideggers unreflektierte *Pathosrhetorik der Eigentlichkeit* und die negative Perspektivierung der öffentlichen Rede als *Gerede* entgegen, die die Aussicht auf eine fundamentalrhetorische Erneuerung der Philosophie wieder verschliessen.

ÖFFENBERGER, Niels. La logica polivalente *in Statu Nascendi*. Teoria, 9(2), 57-62, 1989.

OIKKONEN, Juha. On Ehrenfeucht-Fraïssé Equivalence of Linear Orderings. J Sym Log, 55(1), 65-73, Mr 90.

OIZERMAN, T I. *The Main Trends in Philosophy*. Chicago, Progress, 1988

The author considers history of philosophy as a specific form of development through differentiation, divergences, polarisations and integrations of doctrines especially of materialist and idealist ones which make the main trends in philosophy. The author concludes that the quests for a correct outlook on the world and the tragic delusions and misconceptions, the battle of the trends, which is sometimes perceived as a permanent philosophical scandal are not the searches, torments and delusions of individual philosophers but are the spiritual drama of all humanity.

OIZERMAN, T I. The Uniqueness of Human Being (in Czechoslovakian). Filozof Cas, 37(4), 537-552, 1989.

This article is devoted to the relationship between the social and biological components of human being, aspects which are known to form a unity of contradictions. In the process of manufacturing humans alter the physical environment, while changing their own nature as well. Unlike animals, man is the product of an interaction among human beings, that make up society. In this way, man is being shaped as a social being in the course of his individual development (its biological development included); in this sense, man is a creation of society, its history and culture. In fact, social being gives rise to man as a social individual. (edited)

OKRENT, Mark. Heidegger and Davidson (on Haugeland). S J Phil, SUPP(28), 75-81, 1989.

OKRENT, Mark. Individuation and Intentional Ascriptions. Phil Phenomenol Res, 50(3), 461-480, Mr 90.

OKRENT, Mark. "The Metaphilosophical Consequences of Pragmatism" in *The Institution of Philosophy: A Discipline in Crisis?*, COHEN, Avner (ed), 177-198. La Salle, Open Court, 1989.

OLCZYK, Slawoj. On Newton-Smith's Concept of Verisimilitude. Conceptus, 23(59), 67-76, 1989.

This paper contains a discussion of the new definition of verisimilitude presented by Newton-Smith in his book *The Rationality of Science*. Detailed examination of the concept seems to be instructive despite the fact that the author acknowledges it as being flawed. As a result of the analysis presented in this paper the conclusion can be drawn that it is not possible to explicate verisimilitude with the help of statistics.

OLDRINI, Guido. La missione filosofica del diritto nella Napoli del giovane Mancini. G Crit Filosof Ital, 68(1), 1-17, Ja-Ap 89.

OLEJNIK, Stanislaw. Grundprämisse der humanistischen Anthropologie (in Polish). Stud Phil Christ, 25(1), 161-180, 1989.

Den Menschen kann man nicht zum Niveau einer von der Tierspezies zurückführen. Obwohl er mit der Tierwelt in einem strengen Zusammenhang steht, bildet er eine eigenartige, selbständige Welt. Die Antworten auf die Frage: "Was (wer) der Mensch ist", sind sehr verschieden. Man unternimmt immer wieder neue Versuche um die Eigenschaften der Menschen verschiedener Rassen, Nationen, Kulturen und Geschichtsepochen festzustellen, also die, die die Hauptmerkmale des Menschen bilden. Der Verfasser dieses Aufsatzes ist überzeugt, dass man alle Menscheneigenschaften zu vier Eigenschaften zurückführen kann und diese vier Eigenschaften machen den Gegenstand seiner Erörterung aus. Er untersucht also den Menschen der Reihe nach als ein Leib-seelischwesen, ein sich entwickelndes Wesen, ein transzendentales und soziales Wesen. Diese vier richtig verstandenen Dimensionen des Menschentums bilden di Grundprämisse der humanistischen Anthropologie.

OLERON, Pierre. "Organization and Articulation of Verbal Exchanges" in *From Metaphysics to Rhetoric*, MEYER, Michel (ed), 49-69. Norwell, Kluwer, 1989.

OLIN, Margaret. Validation by Touch in Kandinsky's Early Abstract Art. Crit Inquiry, 16(1), 144-172, Autumn 89.

OLIVER, Kelly. Marxism and Surrogacy. Hypatia, 4(3), 95-115, Fall 89.

In this article, I argue that the liberal framework—its autonomous individuals with equal rights—allows judges to justify enforcing surrogacy contracts. More importantly, even where judges do not enforce surrogacy contracts, the liberal framework conceals gender and class issues which insure that the surrogate will lose custody of her child. I suggest that Marx's analysis of estranged labor can reveal the class and gender issues which the liberal framework conceals.

OLIVER, Kelly. Revolutionary Horror: Nietzsche and Kristeva on the Politics of Poetry. Soc Theor Pract, 15(3), 305-320, Fall 89.

By juxtaposing Nietzsche's analysis of poetry to Kristeva's, I bring Nietzsche into the foreground of Kristeva's most well known contribution to semiology, the semiotic/symbolic distinction, as well as Kristeva's suggestion that poetry is revolutionary language. Kristeva's semiotic/symbolic distinction is prefigured by Nietzsche's tone/gesture distinction. Kristeva's suggestion that semiosis seeps into poetic language is prefigured by Nietzsche's suggestion that a bodily Dionysian force motivates poetry. Even Kristeva's "powers of horror" and its association with the maternal are prefigured by Nietzsche's horrifying "womb of being." Both describe horror as an aesthetic phenomenon, and I analyze the political implications of this move.

OLIVERAS, Elena. Espacialidad de la metáfora. Rev Filosof (Argentina), 4(2), 97-106, N 89.

The paper deals with the nature of metaphor. It considers both the fields of language and visual arts. First, it states that metaphor in general implies the transference of terms based on resemblance or likeness. Then, it compares the fundamental features of metaphor with those of the other tropes (metonymy and synecdoche) and points out its differences. Finally, it concludes that metaphor has a specific spatiality that is present not only in iconic metaphors but also in linguistic ones.

OLIVIER, G. Beyond Music Minus Memory? S Afr J Phil, 9(1), 9-17, F 90.

In this article the prospects of music in contemporary society are explored in the light of Kundera's remark that pop music represents 'music minus memory'. The social relevance of pop music, combined with its critical impotence as an agent for social change is noted, together with the social irrelevance of traditional art music. The views of Stahl on the possibility of moving beyond the stage of forgetting in music's history are pursued at length. Stahl sees avant-garde electronic music as capable of introducing a new era of a nonmanipulative relationship between man and sound. The therapeutic value of electronic music is linked with Schopenhauer's aesthetics before concluding with thoughts on a postmodern music of resistance. (edited)

OLIVIER, G. Philosophy and Socio-Political Conversation: A Postmodern Proposal. S Afr J Phil, 9(2), 101-109, My 90.

In this article the possibility is examined of applying neopragmatist Richard Rorty's concept of philosophy as conversation to the kind of socio-political situation where opponents face the difficult task of negotiating under conditions where misunderstanding, clashing interests and discursive dominance seem to preclude agreement from the outset. It is argued that, although Rorty uses the notion of conversation primarily in the context of his painstaking dismantling of mainstream modern western philosophy (conceived of as primarily epistemological), it may justifiably be applied to the kind of socio-political situation described above, and instantiated in current conditions in South Africa. (edited)

OLKOWSKI-LAETZ, Dorothea. "Space, Time, and the Sublime" in *The Question of the Other: Essays in Contemporary Continental Philosophy*, DALLERY, Arleen B (ed), 175-185. Albany, SUNY Pr, 1989.

OLLER, Carlos A. Los modificadores de predicado y su lógica. Analisis Filosof, 7(1), 47-53, My 87.

This paper introduces two sets of axioms which are adequate to give an account of the inferential behavior of two different kinds of predicate modifiers—those called "standard" and "negators" by R Clark. These axiomatic systems also prove useful to explain the behavior of certain modifiers of predicate modifiers, which are treated as (complex) predicate modifiers.

OLMO, Javier. El amor al prójimo en la ética fenomenológica de los valores. Dialogo Filosof, 6(2), 195-212, My-Ag 90.

Tras referirse a unos pasajes del Antiguo Testamento en los que aparecen las primeras formulaciones del mandato del amor al prójimo y destacar el carácter nuevo y la importancia esencial que ese mandato adquiere en el Nuevo Testamento, el artículo se centra en la exposición, muy apoyada en citas textuales, de las interpretaciones que han hecho del mandamiento evangélico los principales representantes de la llamada Etica Fenomenológica de los Valores: Max Scheler, Nicolai Hartmann, Hans Reiner y Dietrich von Hildebrand. A fin de situar adecuadamente esas interpretaciones en la obra de los pensadores citados, se las presenta en el marco de un apretado resumen de la Filosofía Moral de cada uno de ellos.

ŌMORI, Atsushi. Tragödie des Lebens und Kunst bei Georg Simmel (in Japanese). Bigaku, 41(1), 1-11, Sum 90.

Was Georg Simmel im Vergleich zu den anderen gleichzeitigen

Lebensphilosophen, z.B. Wilhelm Dilthey, auszeichnet, besteht darin, dass er die dialektische Bewegung des Lebens selbst durchschaut hat. Das Leben ist, als immer sich selbst überschreitende Macht, als absatzloses Fliessen, (Mehr-Leben), aber zugleich ist es, in dem Sinne, dass das jeweils vom Leben Geschaffene immer schon als das absolute Andere jenseits des Lebens selbst steht, (Mehr-als-Leben). Das Leben kann immer nur in den jeweils von sich selbst geschaffenen Formen aussprechen, aber doch gehen sie sogleich in die ganz andere Ordnung ein, als sie geschaffen werden. Die beiden Seiten des Lebens sollen durch die geschichtliche Entwicklung nicht versöhnt werden. Simmel sieht in den gleichzeitigen kulturellen Richtungen, z.B. Expressionismus in der Kunst und Mystizismus in der Religion, die äussersten Ergebnisse der Widerlegung des Lebens. (edited)

ONO, Hiroakira. On Finite Linear Intermediate Predicate Logics. Stud Log, 47(4), 391-399, D 88.

An intermediate predicate logic S_n^+ ($n > 0$) is introduced and investigated. First, a sequent calculus GS_n is introduced, which is shown to be equivalent to S_n^+ and for which the cut elimination theorem holds. In section 2, it will be shown that S_n^+ is characterized by the class of all linear Kripke frames of the height n.

ONO, Hiroakira and SUZUKI, Nobu-Yuki. Relations Between Intuitionistic Modal Logics and Intermediate Predicate Logics. Rep Math Log, 22, 65-87, 1988.

Resemblance between modal operators and quantifiers has been often discussed. For example, modal operators of modal logic S5 behave just like quantifiers of the classical logic. So, it will be expected that the similar relation will hold between many pairs of an intuitionistic modal logic and an intermediate predicate logic. This paper treats the problem and proves some fundamental results on it. Among other things, countably many examples of pairs of logics are explicitly given, for which the above relation holds, by making use of the translation theorem proved early in the paper.

ONWURAH, Emeka. Investigating the Case of Religion and Humanism. J Dharma, 14(2), 158-164, Ap-Je 89.

The burden of the paper is whether or not man needs God today since the theme of humanism, freedom, stresses man's capacity for self-realization through reason alone. However, considering his unlimited potentials, man assumes the title "Lord of all." But does this imply unaided control of the universe? Unfortunately, man is by nature paradoxical and the misuse of his freedom culminates in self-destruction. So the key to understanding man lies beyond himself, and his values are lost outside his relationship with God. Consequently, man is not self-sufficient. Therefore the humanist, though on the right track, cannot live fully without God.

OPARA, Stefan and PROTALINSKI, Grzegorz (trans). Catholicism and Socialism: The Problems of Political Understanding. Dialec Hum, 14(1), 57-65, Wint 87.

OPHIR, Adi. Beyond Good-Evil: A Plea for a Hermeneutic Ethics. Phil Forum, 21(1-2), 94-121, Fall-Wint 89-90.

Some, if not most evils are socially produced and distributed, a fact ignored by theories of distributive justice. On the basis of a social ontology that considers evils as social objects, the social contract is reformulated as an agreement regarding the present sharing of suffering, its voluntary conversion, and future elimination. Both reconstructivist and communitarian conceptions of justice are thus revised and limited in scope. The social distribution of evils is always at stake in cultural-political conflicts of interpretations, hence the crucial role of hermeneutic ethics in moral argumentation.

OPHIR, Adi. The Semiotics of Power: Reading Michel Foucault's *Discipline and Punish*. Manuscrito, 12(2), 9-34, O 89.

This paper is an attempt to relate Foucault's interpretative strategy to his concept of power on the one hand, and to his analysis of power, especially the semiotics of power as exemplified in *Discipline and Punish*, on the other hand. (edited)

OPPENHEIM, Frank M and CLENDENNING, John. New Documents on Josiah Royce. Trans Peirce Soc, 26(1), 131-145, Wint 90.

This article discusses and describes the contents of a large newly acquired addition to the Papers of Josiah Royce, Harvard University Archives. The material includes Royce unpublished manuscripts (1 box), incoming correspondence (4 boxes), logicalia (1 box), correspondence of Royce and Head families (5 boxes), family photographs (1 box), manuscripts of Katherine Royce (1 box), notebooks, diaries, etc. (1 box), Royce's published work (2 boxes), miscellanea (4 boxes). Appendix A lists Royce's correspondents alphabetically. Appendix B prints letters by Royce and Peirce.

OPREA, Ioan. La contribution d'Anton Velini à l'enseignement philosophique

du siècle passée (in Romanian). Rev Filosof (Romania), 35(5), 460-464, S-O 88.

ORAMO, Ilkka. Artistic and Aesthetic Value. Acta Phil Fennica, 43, 217-227, 1988.

ORAYEN, Raúl. Sobre objetos posibles y Meinong: una respuesta a Moretti. Cuad Filosof, 20(33), 55-56, O 89.

ORAYEN, Raúl. Los Wertverläufe de Frege y la teoría de conjuntos. Analisis Filosof, 8(1), 1-18, My 88.

This paper tries to make clear and precise the relationship between Frege's theory of extensions and set theory. First, it is shown that, even though Frege's notion of the extension of a concept is ontologically different from the notion of set, Frege's extensions can "represent" sets for two reasons: (i) they are similar to characteristic functions of sets, and (ii) there are enough Fregean extensions to build a one-to-one correspondence between intuitive sets and those extensions (which is what makes it possible to represent each set by just one extension). Secondly, it is shown that Frege's extensions constitute a model of the inconsistent set theory called "The ideal calculus."

ORBE, Antonio. En torno al modalismo de Marción. Gregorianum, 71(1), 43-65, 1990.

ORGAN, Troy Wilson. *Radhakrishnan and the Ways of Oneness of East and West*. Athens, Ohio Univ Pr, 1989

Part One is a critical evaluation of the work of Radhakrishnan. Part Two examines eight ways of oneness of East and West—annihilation, assimilation, domination, accommodation, integration, synthesis, polarization, and omegalization—and concludes that polarization is the best way of oneness. Much of the illustrative material of Part Two comes from the writings of Radhakrishnan.

ORLICKI, Andrzej. On Lifting of ω-Operations From the Category of Sets to the Category of Enumerated Sets. Z Math Log, 35(5), 457-468, 1989.

What does it mean that any ω-operation has a lift to the category of enumerated sets? This question is not trivial, because this category is not complete. In the paper two possible ways to answer this question are given. The paper is devoted to the study of the existence of such lifts. Covariant hom-functors (which have been studied by the author in a previous paper) are used.

ORLOWSKA, Ewa. Interpretation of Dynamic Logic in the Relational Calculus. Bull Sect Log, 18(4), 132-137, D 89.

ORMISTON, Gayle L and SASSOWER, Raphael. *Narrative Experiments: The Discursive Authority of Science and Technology*. Minneapolis, Univ of Minn Pr, 1989

An examination of experimentation with certain prominent themes recurrent in the current literature of science and technology studies. Particular attention is given the "performative" function of language and the kinds of authority assigned and attributed to scientific and technological discourses. Using the notion that "use creates," the authority of selected "radical" philosophical perspectives—Feyerabend, Kuhn, Rorty—is questioned in terms of the "metaphysics" each utilizes and for what purposes. The final sections of the book are devoted to an analysis of the differences between discursive replacement and discursive displacement as each is used in certain scientific and philosophic contexts.

ORMISTON, Gayle L (ed). *Transforming the Hermeneutic Context: From Nietzsche to Nancy*. Albany, SUNY Pr, 1990

This book presents contemporary analyses of interpretation by some of the most prominent figures in contemporary philosophy and literary criticism. These essays question and transform traditional statements on the aims, methods, and techniques of interpretation (many of which are presented in the companion volume, *The Hermeneutic Tradition: From Ast to Ricoeur*, SUNY, 1990). The essays included in this volume demonstrate how contemporary discussions of interpretation are necessarily sent back to reread the hermeneutic tradition. This volume traces the differences in interpretive perspectives generated in the writings of Nietzsche, Foucault, Blondel, Kristeva, Derrida, Frank, Hamacher, and Nancy.

ORMSBY, Eric L (ed). *Moses Maimonides and His Time*. Washington, Cath Univ Amer Pr, 1989

The work is a volume of nine essays on various aspects of the life and works of Maimonides by Christian and Jewish scholars. Two essays on Maimonides in Spain and in Egypt (by N Roth and M Cohen) are followed by examinations of his contributions to logic (A Hyman), method (J Kraemer), ethics (D Frank), exegesis (I Dobbs-Weinstein), epistemology (B Kogan), and metaphysics (J Gellman and W Dunphy).

ORR, Deborah. Just the Facts Ma'am: Informal Logic, Gender and Pedagogy. Inform Log, 11(1), 1-10, Wint 89.

ORTIZ IBARZ, José M. La justificación del mal y el nacimiento de la Estética: Leibniz y Baumgarten. Anu Filosof, 21(1), 151-157, 1988.

ORTIZ-BUONAFINA, M and TSALIKIS, John. Ethical Beliefs' Differences of Males and Females. J Bus Ethics, 9(6), 509-517, Je 90.

This study investigates the differences in ethical beliefs between males and females. 175 business students were presented with four scenarios and given the Reidenbach-Robin instrument measuring their ethical reactions to these scenarios. Contrary to previous research, the results indicate that the two groups have similar ethical beliefs, and they process ethical information similarly.

ORTON, Robert E. The "Evils" of a Technologized Psychology in Teacher Education. Proc Phil Educ, 45, 360-362, 1989.

ORTON, Robert E. Two "Representative" Approaches to the Learning Problem. Educ Phil Theor, 21(1), 66-71, 1989.

If the learner constructs her own knowledge, where does the "plan" for her construction originate? Present-day researchers often seek this plan in a knowledge representation. Some cognitive psychologists represent (or picture) a learner's knowledge using a propositional network. Piaget hypothesized that the learner represents (or constructs) her knowledge by reflecting on her action. Propositional representations are functional in the sense that they are easy to implement on machines, whereas structures built from reflective abstraction are functional in the sense that they help the learner cope with her environment. Possible curricular implications of these different approaches to representation are mentioned.

OSBORNE, Catherine. Philoponus on the Origins of the Universe and Other Issues. Stud Hist Phil Sci, 20(3), 389-395, S 89.

A review article assessing (a) Richard Sorabji, editor, *Philoponus and the Rejection of Aristotelian Science* (London 1987) and (b) Philoponus, *Against Aristotle on the Eternity of the World*, translated by Christian Wildberg (London 1987). It discusses the impact of Philoponus on the history of science, and the contribution of the articles in Sorabji's volume to illuminating his influence. It also examines Wildberg's approach to assembling fragments of a lost work, affirming that it is methodologically sound.

OSBORNE, Peter and CHOMSKY, Noam and EDGLEY, Roy and RÉE, Jonathan and WILSON, Deirdre. Noam Chomsky: An Interview. Rad Phil, 53, 31-40, Autumn 89.

OSCANYAN, Frederick S. Pushing Thoughts With Claire. Thinking, 8(4), 46-47, 1990.

OSERS, Ewald (trans) and SAFRANSKI, Rüdiger. *Schopenhauer and the Wild Years of Philosophy*. Cambridge, Harvard Univ Pr, 1990

The author provides a detailed biography of Schopenhauer, examining his philosophy in relation to his predecessors and contemporaries. (staff)

OSHERSON, Daniel N and WEINSTEIN, Scott. On Advancing Simple Hypotheses. Phil Sci, 57(2), 266-277, Je 90.

We consider drawbacks to scientific methods that prefer simple hypotheses to complex ones that cover the same data. The discussion proceeds in the context of a precise model of scientific inquiry.

OSHERSON, Daniel N and GAIFMAN, Haim and WEINSTEIN, Scott. A Reason for Theoretical Terms. Erkenntnis, 32(2), 149-159, Mr 90.

The presence of nonobservational vocabulary is shown to be necessary for wide application of a conservative principle of theory revision.

ÖSTERBERG, Jan. *Self and Others: A Study of Ethical Egoism*. Norwell, Kluwer, 1988

The main aim of this study is to single out the most plausible versions of *Ethical Egoism* (EE), roughly the thesis that one ought to act so as to achieve what is in one's best interest, and assess their validity. The hitherto unwritten history of EE is sketched, and it is argued that no valid argument either for or against EE has been given. It is shown, however, that, for conceptual or metaphysical reasons, no version of EE is tenable. A consequence of this is that the modern view of practical rationality, conceptually connected with EE, is not tenable either.

OSTERFELD, David. "Radical Federalism: Responsiveness, Conflict, and Efficiency" in *Politics and Process*, BRENNAN, Geoffrey (ed), 149-173. New York, Cambridge Univ Pr, 1989.

A decentralized, federal structure of government is a necessary condition for fulfillment of the democratic ideal of government by the people. The single most effective check on the predations of the ruler, whether democratic or autocratic, is the ability of citizens to vote with their feet. The less expensive "exit" becomes, the more effective the constraint on the rulers. Thus, the concept of consent applies to local but not to national levels of government. Similarly, it is argued that a plethora of small communities reduces conflict since dissatisfied citizens can join communities more to their liking. And government efficiency is enhanced by competition between communities for citizen-clients.

OSTROWSKA, Krystyna. Die psychologischen Probleme der Frau vor dem Schwangerschaftsabbruch (in Polish). Stud Phil Christ, 25(2), 103-119, 1989.

In der Arbeit wurde der Versuch unternommen die Entschlüsse der Frau zum Schwangerschaftsabbruch als einen schwerwiegenden Aufgabenbereich darzustellen. Die Erlebnisse der betroffenen Frauen. sowie die daraus folgenden theoretischen Überlegungen stützen sich auf 3,5 Jahre dauernde Praxis psychologischer Beratungen von Frauen, die sich bei einer Warschauer Klinik zum Schwangerschaftsabbruch gemeldet hatten. (edited)

OSZKODAR, Zbigniew (trans) and KOZYR-KOWALSKI, Stanislaw. Marxism and Conceptual Scholasticism. Dialec Hum, 15(3-4), 151-167, Sum-Autumn 88.

OTAKPOR, Nkeonye. African Philosophy: Paulin J Hountondji—His Dilemma and Contributions. Indian Phil Quart, 17(2), 173-191, Ap 90.

OTOVESCU, Dumitru. Lo concept do crise do la culture dans la philosophie Roumaine de l'entre-deux-guerres (in Romanian). Rev Filosof (Romania), 36(3), 227-235, My-Je 89.

OTT, Walter. The Varieties and Limitations of Legal Positivism. Vera Lex, 7(1), 17,25, 1987.

The reason why the positivists developed so many different theories (analytical jurisprudence, German legal positivism, Kelsen's "Pure Theory," psychological realism, sociological realism, institutional positivism) is the following: all these theories base on stipulations stating a certain meaning of the word "law," but not on a lexical definition which can be proved to be true. The author proposes that in order to cope with the problems of Nazi law a certain minimum content should already be guaranteed in the term "law." But for research in areas of legal history or legal sociology a positivistic concept of law is appropriate.

OTTE, Michael. Der Charakter der Mathematik zwischen Philosophie und Wissenschaft. Philosophica, 43(1), 79-126, 1989.

OTTO, Karl-Heinz and JACOBS, Sturan. Otto Neurath: Marxist Member of the Vienna Circle. Auslegung, 16(2), 175-189, Sum 90.

An exposition of Neurath's thought, designed to show its systematic character. Elements dealt with include his theory of history, Marxism and physicalism, metascience, and sociology as part of unified science.

OVER, David. Content, Thoughts and Definite Descriptions—II, The Object of Definite Descriptions. Aris Soc, SUPP 64, 205-220, 1990.

This paper gives an interpretation of the referential/attributive distinction for uses of definite descriptions. The referential use occurs when the speaker uses the description with effective reference, i.e., when the speaker knows which object the description refers to. Such a use is related to the constructive justification of assertions. Similarly, the attributive use of descriptions is related to noneffective reference and the nonconstructive justification of assertions.

OVERALL, Christine. Heterosexuality and Feminist Theory. Can J Phil, 20(1), 1-17, Mr 90.

The paper examines the significance and the effects, for women, of the heterosexual institution, which is the systematized set of social standards, customs, and expected practices that both regulate and restrict romantic and sexual relationships between persons of different sexes in late twentieth-century western culture. Rejecting an essentialist interpretation of sexual orientations, the paper discusses the politics of heterosexuality, the object of the heterosexual institution, and its harms and benefits. Raising questions about the possibility of a feminist heterosexuality, it concludes by exploring the concepts of women's choice of and responsibility for being heterosexual.

OVERALL, Christine. Selective Termination of Pregnancy and Women's Reproductive Autonomy. Hastings Center Rep, 20(3), 6-11, My-Je 90.

Selective termination is used to eliminate a fetus at risk of a disability, or to reduce the number of fetuses in the uterus. This paper argues that the "demand" for selective termination must be understood as a socially constructed response to prior medical interventions in women's reproductive processes; that selective termination is a "grim option" chosen because the alternatives—abortion of all the fetuses, or maintaining the multiple pregnancy to term—are unacceptable; and that selective termination does not violate any alleged "rights" of the fetuses. The paper concludes by proposing measures to change the conditions that produce multiple pregnancies.

OWEN, David. Benne's Plato and the Theater of Ideas: Response to Benne. Proc Phil Educ, 45, 374-377, 1989.

OWENS, David. Disjunctive Laws. Analysis, 49(4), 197-202, O 89.

If we disjoin two arbitrary lawlike generalisations, we obtain a new disjunctive generalisation. I argue that these disjunctive generalisations are not, in general, lawlike generalisations, despite the fact that they support predictions and counterfactual suppositions. This is for two reasons: (a) they are not confirmed by their instances in the way that laws are confirmed by their instances, and (b) they do not explain their instances in the way that laws explain their instances.

OWENS, Joseph I. Contradictory Belief and Cognitive Access. Midwest Stud Phil, 14, 289-316, 1989.

OWENS, Wayne D. Radical Concrete Particularity: Heidegger, Lao Tzu and Chuang Tzu. J Chin Phil, 17(2), 235-255, Je 90.

This paper is an exploration of how the thought of Martin Heidegger and the arch-Taoists, Lao Tzu and Chuang Tzu, converge on what I call the radical concrete particularity of things. I argue that this convergence is a consequence of the correspondence of *Ereignis* to Tao and *gelassenheit* to *wu-wei*.

OZAR, David T and WAITHE, Mary Ellen. The Ethics of Teaching Ethics. Hastings Center Rep, 20(4), 17-21, Jl-Ag 90.

OZTURK, Yasar Nuri. "The Wisdom of Islam in Sufism" in *The Wisdom of Faith: Essays in Honor of Dr Sebastian Alexander Matczak*, THOMPSON, Henry O (ed), 79-90. Lanham, Univ Pr of America, 1989.

Sufism is the Islamic answer to the longing of the human spirit towards the essence of the universe, Allah, God. It is an Islamic institution rooted in revelation, the Koran and the tradition of the Prophet. The dominant character is action. This is the fundamental difference between the Moksha of Indian mysticism and the concept of Nirvana of Buddhism. The education of the sufi takes place along the thorny highways and byways of life. This is the only way of service to man. Escape from the world cannot be a measure of sufi perfection. Sufi thought accords minimal value to a God-man union achieved at the cost of abandoning the world and man. So, sufism is a religious-Islamic mysticism. The sufi is a disciple of the Koran and Sunna (the tradition of the Prophet) before being philosopher or poet.

PACCHI, Arrigo. "Hobbes and the Problem of God" in *Perspectives on Thomas Hobbes*, ROGERS, G A J (ed), 171-187. New York, Clarendon/Oxford Pr, 1988.

The guiding thread of the discussion the author develops, perusing all Hobbes's works, is provided by the supposed tension between Hobbes's assertions of absolute unknowableness of God's attributes and his claims of the demonstrability of God's existence. The author's analysis plays down both this tension (by pointing out Hobbes's conception of *hypothesis*) and the *theological* meaning and status of God's existence, which thus reveals a striking and paradoxical function of foundation and warrant of the materialistic and deterministic order of reality.

PACCHI, Arrigo. Leviathan and Spinoza's *Tractatus* on Revelation: Some Elements for a Comparison. Hist Euro Ideas, 10(5), 577-593, 1989.

PACHO GARCÍA, Julián. La "parte pura" de las ciencias de la naturaleza: Observaciones sobre el fundamentalismo kantiano. Theoria (Spain), 4(11), 471-490, F-My 89.

Kant claims that natural sciences require a "pure part" (*reiner Teil*), which has to be formulated a priori by philosophy. This pure part is enunciated by Kant in his *Metaphysische Anfangsgründen der Naturwissenschaften* in relation to Newton's *Principia*, whose steps it closely follows. This Kantian work also represents an instance of classical "foundation" by philosophy in the particular sciences. In this paper the particularities of Kant's foundation in Newton's physics come under close scrutiny, and his huge speculative effort on this issue is shown to be equivocant in content, inconsistent in form and probably useless.

PACZYNSKA, Maria (trans) and BORGOSZ, Jozef. Controversies and Discussions about the Post-Council Aspect of Catholic Philosophy. Dialec Hum, 14(1), 233-248, Wint 87.

PACZYNSKA, Maria (trans) and CACKOWSKI, Zdzislaw. Cultural Partnership—A Factor of Social Peace. Dialec Hum, 14(1), 35-41, Wint 87.

PADEN, Roger. Liberalism and Neo-Aristotelianism. Int Stud Phil, 22(1), 51-58, 1990.

This essay examines Charles Larmore's attempt to defend the concept of liberal neutrality against the attacks advanced by several post-structuralist philosophers on the liberal conception of the self. It is argued that Larmore's attempt fails, although, it is suggested, a more self-consciously Aristotelian defence may be possible.

PADGETT, Alan G. God and Time: Towards a New Doctrine of Divine Timeless Eternity. Relig Stud, 25(2), 209-215, Je 89.

Rejecting the traditional view of divine eternity associated with Boethius and Aquinas, proposes a new doctrine of God's timelessness. God is "relatively" timeless, in that (i) he is not in any Measured Time, (ii) his life is not limited to the time of our space-time universe, (iii) he is not subject to the negative aspects of the passage of time, such as death or inability to complete a task in a specific amount of time. God is still temporal in some sense, yet he also transcends our created temporal process.

PAEPCKE, Fritz. The Hermeneutical Ways of the Successful Translation (in Hungarian). Magyar Filozof Szemle, 4, 413-433, 1989.

PAGET, M A. "Unlearning to Not Speak". Human Stud, 13(2), 147-161, Ap 90.

PAILIN, David A. *The Anthropological Character of Theology: Conditioning Theological Understanding*. New York, Cambridge Univ Pr, 1990

After clarifying what is meant by faith, belief, theology and reason, and how they are related to each other, this critique of theological judgements examines how theistic understanding is conditioned by the nature of human rationality. In order to fulfill its role in such understanding, the concept of God combines a cosmic projection of human self-awareness with the regulative ideas of rational reflection; it is influenced by the ways in which religious experience and supposed revelation are apprehended; and it is modified by what is considered to meet fundamental human needs and to provide a satisfying understanding of reality as a whole.

PAINE, Thomas and KUKLICK, Bruce (ed). *Political Writings: Thomas Paine*. New York, Cambridge Univ Pr, 1989

PAL, Jagat. Modern Analysis of Syllogistic Logic: A Critical Reflection. Indian Phil Quart, 16(3), 303-317, Jl 89.

The purpose of this paper is to examine modern analysis of syllogistic logic. It is concerned with one of the fundamental doctrines of syllogistic logic, namely, the doctrine of square of opposition. I have tried to show that modern analysis fails in refuting the Aristotelian doctrine. Instead of refuting the doctrine it rather supports the doctrine.

PALAU, Gladys. Lógicas divergentes y principios lógicos: Un análisis crítico de algunas tesis de Susan Haack. Rev Latin De Filosof, 16(1), 47-66, Mr 90.

This article analyses some of the theses sustained by Susan Haack in her book *Deviant Logic*. It has two principal goals: first, to demonstrate that Haack's arguments are not sufficiently conclusive to defend a global change in classical logic, in the case where the rival system is a divergent one; on the second, that there exist good reasons to defend local reforms of classical logic for this same situation.

PALAVECINO, Sergio. Nota sobre el concepto de regla en A Tomasini Bassols. Rev Latin De Filosof, 15(2), 215-217, Jl 89.

PALERMO, James and D'ERASMO, Kate. Logic, Language and Dewey: A Student-Teacher Dialectic. Thinking, 8(1), 11-13, 1989.

PALERMO, James. Rereading Aristotle and Dewey on Educational Theory: A Deconstruction. Proc Phil Educ, 45, 271-274, 1989.

PALLER, Bonnie T and CAMPBELL, Donald T. "Extending Evolutionary Epistemology to 'Justifying' Scientific Beliefs" in *Issues in Evolutionary Epistemology*, HAHLWEG, Kai (ed), 231-257. Albany, SUNY Pr, 1989.

PALMER, Anthony. Philosophy and Literature. Philosophy, 65(252), 155-166, Ap 90.

PALMER, Michael. The Citizen Philosopher: Rousseau's Dedicatory Letter to the *Discourse on Inequality*. Interpretation, 17(1), 19-39, Fall 89.

I enter the controversy over Rousseau's dedicatory letter to the *Discourse on the Origin and Foundations of Inequality Among Men*, dedicated to the city of his birth, the republic of Geneva. Is Rousseau sincere or saucy in his praise of republican Geneva? I suggest that he is both and more; that the letter, addressed explicitly to Rousseau's erstwhile fellow-citizens of Geneva, is addressed implicitly to the *philosophes* of Enlightenment Europe with the intention of enlightening them, by the exemplary method, concerning how cosmopolitan philosophers should speak to patriotic citizens.

PALMER, Richard E. *Hermeneutics: Interpretation Theory in Schleiermacher, Dilthey, Heidegger, and Gadamer*. Evanston, Northwestern Univ Pr, 1988

PALMGREN, Erik and STOLTENBERG-HANSEN, Viggo. Domain Interpretations of Martin-Löf's Partial Type Theory. Annals Pure Applied Log, 48(2), 135-196, Jl 90.

Partial type theory without universes is modelled in the category of effective Scott-Ershov domains, in order to give meaning to the iteration type (which makes the fixed point operator definable). We interpret families of types as continuously varying domains and elements of types as continuous functions.

The intensional identity type is given a natural interpretation in terms of maximal common informational content. Finally an adequacy theorem is proved, stating that a term of partial type theory terminates (under lazy evaluation) if, and only if, its interpretation is not the least element of the domain.

PALMQUIST, Stephen R. Kant on Euclid: Geometry in Perspective. Phil Math, 5(1-2), 88-113, 1990.

Kant's theoretical philosophy does not depend, as is often assumed, on the absolute validity of outmoded scientific viewpoints, such as Euclidean geometry. A perspectival interpretation of Kant's first *Critique* reveals that, far from asserting the absolute validity of the classical theories of Euclidean geometry, Aristotelian logic, and Newtonian physics, Kant ties their views in each case to a particular, well-defined perspective, which actually *limits* their validity, and in so doing, prepares the way for the modern developments in geometry, logic, and physics. The distinction between the transcendental and empirical perspectives on geometry is examined in detail as an example.

PALMQUIST, Stephen R. The Syntheticity of Time: Comments on Fang's Critique of Divine Computers. Phil Math, 4(2), 233-235, 1989.

J Fang attempts to avoid mixing theology with philosophy of mathematics by arguing that mathematical calculations cannot be analytic a priori because they take time. This article responds with three objections: (1) propositions are analytic or synthetic, not calculations; (2) the temporality of calculations is irrelevant to the debate over the status of mathematics; (3) Kant's notion of synthetic a priori can be used to prove computers are human, not divine, machines. If a mathematical proposition is synthetic a priori, it ought to be a necessary condition for the possibility of mathematics in general.

PALOS, Ana Maria and WELCH, John R. Apuntes sobre el pensamiento matemático de Ramón Llull. Theoria (Spain), 4(11), 451-459, F-My 89.

PALOUS, Martin. To Philosophize with Socrates (A Chapter from a Prepared Monography on J Patocka) (in Czechoslovakian). Filozof Cas, 38(1-2), 45-58, 1990.

The author presents a dual interpretation of Socrates in the work of Jan Patocka: viewed in ethical and metaphysical terms, Patocka's reflections on the philosophical heritage of Socrates then give rise to the concept of philosophy in the Socratic spirit which—in Patocka's view—means a radical transformation of one's life orientation and self-understanding by man and also thanks to Socrates' knowing ignorance—represents human understanding relating to the whole, always as insufficient and unrooted in any thesis, always ever actively reverting to reality in an experience of transcendency—overcoming oneself and in participation in the process of imparting sense to it.

PALTROW, Lynn M. When Becoming Pregnant Is a Crime. Crim Just Ethics, 9(1), 41-47, Wint-Spr 90.

PAMBRUN, James R. Ricoeur, Lonergan and the Intelligibility of Cosmic Time. Thomist, 54(3), 471-498, Jl 90.

This article aims to examine the foundations of our affirmation of the objectivity and intelligibility of cosmic time. It pursues this investigation within the study of time presented in volume 3 of Ricoeur's *Time and Narrative*. Ricoeur has shown the importance of maintaining a reference to cosmic experience within his interpretation of human action and history. Our article suggests that an interpretation of cosmic time guided by an understanding of the structures of reasoning and cognitional operations, exemplified especially in Chapter 5 of Lonergan's *Insight*, complements and informs the cosmological moment appropriated within Ricoeur's hermeneutics of human action and history.

PAMENTAL, George L. The Course in Business Ethics: Can It Work? J Bus Ethics, 8(7), 547-551, Jl 89.

An examination of 99 syllabi for undergraduate courses in business ethics, collected by the Center for Business Ethics at Bentley College, reveals that half the courses are offered to freshmen and sophomores. Because of the fact that these students will have minimal knowledge of the functional areas of business firms, and because these courses rely heavily on case analysis, it is likely that the students in these courses are not able to deal effectively with the material in the course. Therefore, any expectation that the business ethics course will raise the students' ethical sensitivity when considering business problems or decisions is unrealistic.

PANA, Laura. Connaissance, conscience et culture dans la vie spirituelle de la société (in Romanian). Rev Filosof (Romania), 36(2), 127-134, Mr-Ap 89.

PANA, Laura. Human Existence and Prospective Knowledge. Phil Log, 32(3-4), 185-196, Jl-D 88.

PANA, Laura. Values of Knowledge and Values of Action in Human

Conduct Structuring. Phil Log, 32(1-2), 11-18, Ja-Je 88.

PANELLA, Giuseppe. Immaginazione produttiva e struttura dell'immaginario nelle *Rêveries du promeneur solitaire* di Jean-Jacques Rousseau. Arch Stor Cult, 3, 365-373, 1990.

PANFILOV, V A. Philosophical Questions of Mathematics in *Anti-Dühring*. Phil Math, 4(2), 147-153, 1989.

The article deals with Engels, philosophy of mathematics statements on objective and dialectical character of mathematical truths, on practically-objective status and actively-material origin of mathematics abstractions and axioms, on the object and method of mathematical knowledge. It is pointed out that principles of practice, development and contradictoriness of cognition are basic ones for a philosophical analysis of mathematics. The principal character and up-to-dateness of Engels's direction for the necessity of dialectical cognition of mathematics to develop both philosophy and mathematics is stressed.

PANOU, S. Kunst und Mythos (in Greek). Philosophia (Athens), 17-18, 182-190, 1987-88.

Der Mythos ist von Anfang an Sprache der Transzendenz in seiner bescheidensten Form Sprache der Transzendenz des Menschen in seinem Verhältnis zur Natur. Jedes grosse Kunstwerk ist ein Mythos. Was man "Verfremdung" des Wirklichen nennt, ist in Wirklichkeit ein mythisches Bild des Wirklichen. Die Kunst ist durch die Konstruktion von Mythen eine exemplarische Form des schöpferischen Aktes des Menschen, der die Zukunft des Menschen errichtet. (edited)

PANOVA, Elena. Dialectical Materialism and Logical Pragmatism: On J E McClellan's "Logical Pragmatism and Dialectical Materialism". Stud Soviet Tho, 38(4), 261-271, N 89.

PAPADIS, D. Das Eudaimonie-Problem und seine aristotelische Lösung (in Greek). Philosophia (Athens), 17-18, 356-390, 1987-88.

Die Eudaimonie-Lehre des Aristoteles ist das Thema dieses Aufsatzes. Vor der eigentlichen Behandlung des Themas wird kurz Bezug genommen auf die Kritik Kants und des Marxismus an der altgriechischen Ethik. Von Kant wird ihr nämlich vorgeworfen, dass sie eudaimonistisch bzw. heteronom sei, und seitens des Marxismus, dass sie unter anderem eudaimonistische und individualistisch sei und ausserdem dass sie keine Rücksicht auf die sozialpolitischen Umstände nehme. Zu allen diesen Vorwürfen wird hier kritisch Stellung genommen, wobei sie als unberechtigt erwiesen werden. (edited)

PAPAGEORGIOU, C I. Four or Five Types of Democracy in Aristotle? Hist Polit Thought, 11(1), 1-8, Spr 90.

The paper attempts to provide arguments in defence of Schlosser's emendation of the first classification of types of democracy in Aristotle (*Politics*, 1291b30-92a39) in order to account for four variants of democracy, in compliance with the other two classifications of types of democracy in Aristotle (1292b22-93a11 and 1318a7-19b33).

PAPE, Helmut. Charles S Peirce on Objects of Thought and Representation. Nous, 24(3), 375-395, Je 90.

PAPINEAU, David. "Pure, Mixed, and Spurious Probabilities and Their Significance for a Reductionist Theory of Causation" in *Scientific Explanation (Minnesota Studies in the Philosophy of Science, Volume XIII)*, KITCHER, Philip (ed), 307-348. Minneapolis, Univ of Minn Pr, 1989.

This first half of this paper argues that there are only terminological differences between the traditional view, that causes determine their effects, and the "statistical-relevance" view, that causes increase the probability of their effects. The second half of the paper then uses distinctions made in the first half, in particular the distinctions between "pure," "mixed," and "spurious" probabilities, to show how facts of causation can be reduced to facts of correlational dependence.

PAPINEAU, David. Why Supervenience? Analysis, 50(2), 66-71, Mr 90.

Take any category of "special" events which have some physical effects, such as mental events. Papineau argues that the *completeness of physics* implies that any such special category must supervene on physics. He proceeds via a lemma of "no independent causal powers," which claims that all effects of such special events must be fixed by physical features of those events, and appeals to the thought that a difference which cannot show up in differential effects is no difference at all. He concludes with some observations on how "physics" should be understood for supervenience to be both plausible and contentful.

PAPPAS, George S. Abstract General Ideas in Hume. Hume Stud, 15(2), 339-352, N 89.

PAPPAS, George S. Causation and Perception in Reid. Phil Phenomenol Res, 50(4), 763-766, Je 90.

PAPPAS, Nickolas. Plato's *Ion*: The Problem of the Author. Philosophy, 64(249), 381-389, Jl 89.

The *Ion*'s main charge against poetry is not, as commonly thought, that poets and their readers are ignorant. That is rather a secondary or supporting claim. According to the dialogue's principal argument, poetry is worse than mere ignorance because it seduces its audience away from the search for truth. Poetry binds its audience to the person of its author, and thus leads the audience to prefer a single point of view—Homer on charioteering—over a general account of charioteering. This same diagnosis of poetry as perspectival, and therefore more perverse than simple ignorance, may also be seen to underlie the antipoetic arguments of *Republic* 10.

PAPPAS, Nickolas. Socrates' Charitable Treatment of Poetry. Phil Lit, 13(2), 248-261, O 89.

In Plato's *Protagoras* (338e-348a), Socrates interprets a poem of Simonides' and finds Simonides to be restating his own beliefs. Rather than see this passage (as others have) as simply a parody of interpretation, I read it as an exemplification of the interpretive principle of charity. Socrates' use of the principle of charity is part of his hostility toward poetry: it is his strategy for weaning the reader from the person of the author.

PARÉ, Robert and ROMÁN, Leopoldo. Monoidal Categories With Natural Numbers Object. Stud Log, 48(3), 361-376, S 89.

PARENS, Erik. Derrida, "Woman," and Politics: A Reading of *Spurs*. Phil Today, 33(4), 291-301, Wint 89.

The first aim of this piece is to present the argument of *Spurs*. The second aim is to begin to ask what the political ramifications of that argument are. I urge the reader to appreciate the brilliance of Derrida's undermining of Nietzsche's antifeminism, as well as to remember that the same strategy of reading works equally well at undermining feminism.

PARENT, W A. A Second Look at Pornography and the Subordination of Women. J Phil, 87(4), 205-211, Ap 90.

PAREYSON, Luigi. Le "Letture dai Vangeli" di Antonio Maddalena. Filosofia, 40(2), 127-137, My-Ag 89.

PARGETTER, Robert and BIGELOW, John and COLLINS, John. Colouring in the World. Mind, 99(394), 279-288, Ap 90.

PARGETTER, Robert and BIGELOW, John and CAMPBELL, John. Death and Well-Being. Pac Phil Quart, 71(2), 119-140, Je 90.

PARGETTER, Robert. Experience, Proper Basicality and Belief in God. Int J Phil Relig, 27(3), 141-163, Je 90.

PARGETTER, Robert and BIGELOW, John. From Extroverted Realism to Correspondence: A Modest Proposal. Phil Phenomenol Res, 50(3), 435-460, Mr 90.

PARGETTER, Robert and BIGELOW, John. Metaphysics of Causation. Erkenntnis, 33(1), 89-119, Jl 90.

PARISI, Giorgio. Aristotele, Platone e l'IBM. Epistemologia, 11(2), 293-298, Jl-D 88.

The origin of human knowledge has been the object of one of the most ancient disputes in philosophy. According to Aristotle, man knows nothing when he is born, and has to learn everything on the basis of the data that come from the outside world. According to Plato, on the other hand, man already has innate ideas at birth, even if he is not aware of them, and any act of learning is, in reality, an act of remembering. Today, the research into artificial intelligence seems to be able to contribute some genuinely new ideas to this very old and venerable controversy. One can ask, in fact, whether it is possible to build machines which behave in a "creative" way, for example a machine which can learn from experience. (edited)

PARISI, Thomas. Freud's Phylogenetic Fantasy: An Essay Review. Biol Phil, 4(4), 483-494, O 89.

This essay examines the recently discovered draft of Freud's last metapsychology paper. The author makes use of Holton's concept of "thematic commitments" to argue that Freud's work, like that of other revolutionaries, such as Darwin and Newton, reveals background commitments which are extrinsic to the intellectual or scientific work itself, but which are nonetheless crucial to a complete understanding of that work. In Freud's case, however, these thematic commitments overlap and replace elements of the empirical domain, forcing a reexamination of Freud's often stated claim that he was taking a strictly inductive approach to his work.

PARK, Woosuk. The Problem of Individuation for Scotus: A Principle of Indivisibility or a Principle of Distinction. Fran Stud, 48(26), 105-123, 1988.

The aim of this article is to answer the question what the problem of individuation for Duns Scotus was. It turns out that for Scotus the problem of individuation was primarily the problem of identifying the principle of indivisibility of an individual into subjectlike parts. But Scotus thought that he

had solved the problem of numerical difference as well, since numerical difference is derived from a formally distinct entity which is the principle of indivisibility. Also, Suarez's interpretation of Scotus's problem as that of the ontological status of individuality rather than that of individuation will be critically examined.

PARKER, Kelly. C S Peirce and the Philosophy of Religion. S J Phil, 28(2), 193-212, Sum 90.

The essay challenges the view that Peirce's writings on religion are superfluous and late developments, incompatible with the rest of his philosophy. Only his writings prior to "A Neglected Argument for the Reality of God" are considered. Religion is identified as the instinctual apprehension of purposiveness in nature, and is seen to complement rational, scientific apprehension. In Peirce's view, religious practice in the church community should serve to nurture elements of harmony, goodness, and unity in experience. Religion and science both contribute to the evolution of "concrete reasonableness," in distinct but equally important ways.

PARKER, Richard and MOORE, Brook Noel. *Critical Thinking: Evaluating Claims and Arguments in Everyday Life—Second Edition*. Mountain View, Mayfield, 1989

PARKES, Graham. A Cast of Many: Nietzsche and Depth-Psychological Pluralism. Man World, 22(4), 453-470, D 89.

While the Western philosophical tradition has generally conceived of the self as something unitary, an idea of the multiple self began to emerge toward the end of the last century. A major proponent of this idea was Friedrich Nietzsche, and this essay traces its development in his writings against the background of similar ideas in the work of William James, Sigmund Freud, C G Jung, and the contemporary American psychologist James Hillman. The metaphor of the self as a kind of theater company is suggested as helpful for realizing the advantages of psychical multiplicity while minimizing the risk of disintegration.

PARKES, Graham. "Human/Nature in Nietzsche and Taoism" in *Nature in Asian Tradition of Thought: Essays in Environmental Philosophy*, CALLICOTT, J Baird (ed), 79-97. Albany, SUNY Pr, 1989.

PARKES, Graham. Reflections on Projections: Changing Conditions in Watching Film. J Aes Educ, 21(3), 77-82, Fall 87.

This essay argues that the conditions under which films are viewed, more various now than they ever have been, affect the aesthetic experience far more than is generally recognized. Of special significance are the changes brought about by the rise of videotape as a medium through which films are viewed, and the consequent shift from context of public ritual to a domestic situation of privacy and relative intimacy. The advantages of control and replay-ability offered by the videotape recorder are balanced against the powerful somatic effects of viewing a film on a larger-than-life screen as a member of a greater community.

PARKINSON, G H R. Hegel, Marx and the Cunning of Reason. Philosophy, 64(249), 287-302, Jl 89.

Hegel argues that history manifests the 'cunning of reason', i.e., that people who act in their own particular and selfish interests are at the same time governed by the universal laws of the dialectic. This paper argues that a similar concept is implicit in Marx's philosophy of history. The thesis may seem implausible, in that Marx's philosophy of history is thought to be very different from Hegel's: 'materialist' rather than 'idealist'. Yet Marx, like Hegel, sees history as a progress towards a more rational order of things. This rational order is brought about by the revolutionary proletariat, and the parallel to the 'cunning of reason' is the proletariat's anger at its lot, which is an important historical factor.

PARKS, Zane and BYRD, Michael. "Relevant Implication and Leibnizian Necessity" in *Directions in Relevant Logic*, NORMAN, Jean (ed), 179-184. Norwell, Kluwer, 1989.

PARKS-CLIFFORD, John. "Literal Relevance" in *Directions in Relevant Logic*, NORMAN, Jean (ed), 59-75. Norwell, Kluwer, 1989.

This article traces an attempt to meet felt objections to validating ampliating arguments (e.g., Addition) by producing a satisfying proof system, incorporating some further desiderata. The final system is system is equivalent to Perry's Analytic Implication as demodalized by Dunn. Appendices give the proof of equivalence, extension to the modal version, and discuss possible quantified versions.

PARRY, William T. "Analytic Implication: Its History, Justification and Varieties" in *Directions in Relevant Logic*, NORMAN, Jean (ed), 101-118. Norwell, Kluwer, 1989.

PARSLOW, Morris A (trans) and APOSTLE, Hippocrates G (trans) and DOBBS, Elizabeth A (trans) and ARISTOTLE,. *Aristotle's Poetics*. Grinnell,

Peripatetic Pr, 1990

PARSONS, Charles. The Uniqueness of the Natural Numbers. Iyyun, 39(1), 13-44, Ja 90.

PARSONS, Howard L. The Meaning of Universalism: Comments on Kuczynski and McGovern. Dialec Hum, 14(1), 93-97, Wint 87.

Kuczynski and McGovern agree most Marxists are atheistic; McGovern thinks they need not be. McGovern finds Kuczynski's universalism "attractive"—the common human values of biological life, family, education, production, communities, equality, partnership, and movement toward a united human community. The author takes the most inclusive concrete universal to be the creative advance of the ecological system. To facilitate it we must overcome the ruinous tendencies of starvation, joblessness, indebtedness, militarism, imperialism, war, racism, and pollution and move toward equality, peace, justice, and development. Marxists, Christians, and others should unite in this mission.

PARSONS, Keith M. *God and the Burden of Proof: Plantinga, Swinburne, and the Analytic Defense of Theism*. Buffalo, Prometheus, 1989

The evidentialist challenge holds that theists must bear the burden of proof in their debates with nontheists. Alvin Plantinga argues that theism should not be considered irrational, even if it cannot meet the evidentialist challenge. I claim that Plantinga's arguments succeed, but that they have consequences that other theists are likely to reject. I also argue that Richard Swinburne's cosmological argument fails as an effort to meet the burden of proof. Finally, I contend that the problem of evil allows atheists to meet the burden of proof in arguing against God's existence.

PARTEE, Barbara H. *Mathematical Methods in Linguistics*. Norwell, Kluwer, 1990

PAS, Julian F. Virtue under Attack (in Serbo-Croatian). Filozof Istraz, 29(2), 559-568, 1989.

Both the *Tao Te Ching* and the *Chuang-tzu* criticize the Confucian ethical value system. Their fiercest attacks against Confucian "Virtue" are found in the so-called "primitivist" chapters 8-11: Confucian sages were the real cause of the collapse of true "virtue" of the *Chuang-tzu*, and of the darkening of Tao: they have introduced external standards and thus created confusion and ultimately disorder. This accusation is questionable, since K'ung-tzu also wanted to bring the country back to a morally coherent society. Trying to discover Confucius's own ultimate standard of ethics, it appears to be his belief in T'ien or Heaven, a metaphysical concept transcending the human nature of individuals, yet ultimately grounded in that nature. In that sense, Confucianism and Taoism are closer in their views than one would expect. Other systems rely on different foundations: in Christianity, for example, ethics are based on divine revelation, but implicitly also on 'natural' law. What is the foundation of Marxist ethics? Further study is needed here, also to find out whether it is possible to discover a basis for morality which is universal, transcending time, space and all kinds of particularities.

PASKE, Gerald H. The Life Principle: A (Metaethical) Rejection. J Applied Phil, 6(2), 219-225, O 89.

In *Respect for Nature* Paul W Taylor argues that there is a moral obligation to respect all living things. I argue that there is no such obligation. Taylor presents three basic premises for his position. The first two are shown to be mistaken but not necessary for Taylor's argument. The third, that being a nonsentient *teleological* centre of life confers moral significance, while necessary, fails to be rationally compelling. I argue that (1) the relevant concept of teleology as readily applies to inanimate objects as it does to nonsentient life forms. (2) The inanimate-nonsentient distinction (at the relevant molecular level) is founded upon a continuum which offers no basis sufficient to justify The Life Principle. (3) The concept of teleology, as used by Taylor, is too unclear and ill-founded to serve as the basis for a rationally compelling argument.

PASKE, Gerald H. Rationality, Reasonableness and Morality. Logos (USA), 10, 73-88, 1989.

Several philosophers have attempted to provide a rational basis for morality, including R M Hare, Alan Gewirth, and David Gauthier. Each of these three offers distinct concepts of rationality such that rationality can allow no internal logical conflicts. I distinguish rationality from reasonableness by arguing that a person can get caught by logical conflicts and yet remain reasonable. I further argue that reason rather than rationality underlies morality. I next argue that all three attempts to rationally justify morality fail. Finally, I argue that though an amoralist need not be irrational, it is unreasonable to choose to be an amoralist.

PASKINS, Barrie. "Pride and International Relations" in *Christ, Ethics and Tragedy: Essays in Honour of Donald MacKinnon*, SURIN, Kenneth (ed), 146-160. New York, Cambridge Univ Pr, 1989.

PATOCKA, Jan. Can Philosophy Perish? (in Czechoslovakian). Filozof Cas, 38(1-2), 3-21, 1990.

Dabei entsteht die Metaphysik selbst aus vorsokratischen Erwägungen über ein latentes, vergorgenes Prinzip und ihre wichtigste Spannung besteht darin, dass sie ohne Nichtgegenständliches nicht möglich, ist, dass sie aber nur gegenständlich denkt. Diese Zwiespältigkeit hat dann zur Folge, dass die Metaphysiken eher eine in der gegenständlichen Welt wissenschaftlich anwendbare Ordnung als akzeptable Wahrheiten über das übersinnliche Seiende zum Resultat haben; hier erblickt der Autor das Kernstück der Idee vom notwendigen Übergang von der Metaphysik zur Wissenschaft. (edited)

PATOCKA, Jan. "Europa und sein Erbe: Skizze zu einer Geschichtsphilosophie" in *Agora: Zu Ehren von Rudolph Berlinger*, BERLINGER, Rudolph (and other eds), 165-184. Amsterdam, Rodopi, 1988.

PATON, Margaret. A Reconsideration of Kant's Treatment of Duties to Oneself. Phil Quart, 40(159), 222-232, Ap 90.

PATTARO, Enrico. Models of Reason, Types of Principles and Reasoning: Historical Comments and Theoretical Outlines. Ratio Juris, 1(2), 109-122, Jl 88.

The author distinguishes between scientific and prudential reason (practical wisdom) in Aristotle with reference to the nature of the principles assumed as premises, and to the method of inference. In the history of thought these two models of reason are believed not only to be proper to science and, respectively, ethics, but also, at times, to be the scientific model proper to ethics (for example, in natural law doctrines) and the prudential model proper to science. Mixed models are also given in the history of thought: scientific-prudential (for example, in Thomas Aquinas) and prudential-scientific. Furthermore, some aspects of the relationship between authority and reason are examined.

PATTEE, H H. Response to Dietrich's "Computationalism". Soc Epistem, 4(2), 176-181, Ap-Je 90.

Dietrich defines computationalism as the hypothesis that cognition is the computation of functions. The essence of a function is its unambiguous determinism that is only ideally realized by formal, discrete symbols manipulated by syntactical procedures or programs. This methodology can *describe* cognitive activities; but the central issue in cognitive theory is whether the brain is better *explained* as a programmable computer of functions, or as a nonprogrammable dynamical network. The fact that dynamical networks can be *described* by a programmable computation is not the issue, since all dynamics can be so described. In physical theory, symbols are grounded only by nonformalizable measurements that are established by observables of the theory. Without measurements computation is meaningless syntax. We have yet to find how the brain establishes observables, or at what level it begins to manipulate discrete symbols. Computationalism is only a formal methodology that is intrinsically incapable of explaining the existence and meaning of symbols. (edited)

PATTERSON, Annabel. Couples, Canons, and the Uncouth: Spenser-and-Milton in Educational Theory. Crit Inquiry, 16(4), 773-793, Sum 90.

PATTERSON, David. The Life of Ivan Il'ich. Thought, 65(257), 143-154, Je 90.

PATTERSON, Richard. Conversion Principles and the Basis of Aristotle's Modal Logic. Hist Phil Log, 11(2), 151-172, 1990.

Aristotle founds his modal syllogistic, like his plain syllogistic, on a small set of 'perfect' or obviously valid syllogisms. The rest he reduces to those, usually by means of modal conversion principles. These principles are open to more than one reading, however, and they are in fact invalid on one traditional reading (de re), valid on the other (de dicto). It is argued here that this way of framing the contrast is not Aristotelian, and that an interpretation involving modal *copulae* allows us to see how these principles, and the modal system as a whole, are to be understood in light of close and precise connections to Aristotle's essentialist metaphysics.

PATTERSON, Sarah. The Explanatory Role of Belief Ascriptions. Phil Stud, 59(3), 313-332, Jl 90.

PATTISON, George. A Drama of Love and Death: Michael Pedersen Kierkegaard and Regine Olsen Revisited. Hist Euro Ideas, 12(1), 79-91, 1990.

The article discusses the presence in Kierkegaard's authorship of his father, Michael Peter Kierkegaard, and the fiancee whose love he renounced, Regine Olsen. These figures are not seen biographically, however, but as ideal types, representing, in a highly dramatic manner, an essential conflict in which Kierkegaard sees all human life as entangled. This illustrates how, in Kierkegaard's view, the self cannot be defined in terms of a static, monadic nucleus, but exists as a process in which the contradictions represented by these figures play a key role.

PATTISON, George. Eternal Loneliness: Art and Religion in Kierkegaard and Zen. Relig Stud, 25(3), 379-392, S 89.

PATTISON, George. From Kierkegaard to Cupitt: Subjectivity, the Body and Eternal Life. Heythrop J, 31(3), 295-308, Jl 90.

Taking note of Don Cupitt's claim that Kierkegaard stands close to the position he develops in *Taking Leave of God*, the article examines Kierkegaard's views on the relation of subjectivity (a) to psychosomatic life and (b) to eternal life, compares and contrasts them with Cupitt's and concludes that the two thinkers are operating with profoundly different religious values.

PAUL, Ellen Frankel (ed) and MILLER JR, Fred D (ed) and PAUL, Jeffrey (ed) and AHRENS, John (ed). *Capitalism*. Cambridge, Blackwell, 1989

The essays in this volume address some of the central moral and conceptual questions arising out of the nature of capitalism. Some address the connection between capitalism and such moral notions as freedom, self-ownership and community. Others consider the role that efficiency plays in the justification of capitalism. And others are concerned with the methodological difficulties involved in comparing existing capitalist and socialist systems. Together, these essays delineate some of the concepts which are central to the ongoing debate between capitalism and socialism.

PAUL, Jeffrey (ed) and PAUL, Ellen Frankel (ed) and MILLER JR, Fred D (ed) and AHRENS, John (ed). *Capitalism*. Cambridge, Blackwell, 1989

The essays in this volume address some of the central moral and conceptual questions arising out of the nature of capitalism. Some address the connection between capitalism and such moral notions as freedom, self-ownership and community. Others consider the role that efficiency plays in the justification of capitalism. And others are concerned with the methodological difficulties involved in comparing existing capitalist and socialist systems. Together, these essays delineate some of the concepts which are central to the ongoing debate between capitalism and socialism.

PAUL, Jeffrey and MILLER JR, Fred D. Communitarian and Liberal Theories of the Good. Rev Metaph, 43(4), 803-830, Je 90.

PAUL, Karen. Corporate Social Monitoring in South Africa: A Decade of Achievement, An Uncertain Future. J Bus Ethics, 8(6), 463-469, Je 89.

Corporate social monitoring has reached its most systematic form and has had the most practical impact with regard to companies doing business in South Africa. This paper discusses the economic clinate for US business in South Africa both historically and currently, the conflicting pressures experienced by US companies remaining there, and the effectiveness of strategies aimed to create pressure for companies to withdraw, including divestment resolutions, purchasing restrictions, and sanctions. (edited)

PAULSON, Michael G. *The Possible Influence of Montaigne's "Essais" on Descartes' "Treatise on the Passions"*. Lanham, Univ Pr of America, 1988

Montaigne's *Essais*, although unsystematic, seem to have provided a basis for Descartes's *Treatise* in the former's definition and examples of the primitive and composite passions or emotions. The present study shows similarities in structures and form between the two great writers and tentatively concludes that Descartes consciously borrows from Montaigne in the *Treatise* as well as in other works.

PAULSON, Stanley L. An Empowerment Theory of Legal Norms. Ratio Juris, 1(1), 58-72, Mr 88.

Traditionally legal theorists, whenever engaged in controversy, have agreed on one point: legal norms are par excellence rules which impose obligations. The author examines this assumption, which from another perspective (that of constitutional law, for instance) appears less obvious. In fact, constitutional rules are commonly empowering norms, norms which do not create duties but powers. To this objection many theorists would reply that empowering rules are incomplete and that they are to be understood as parts of duty-creating rules. A different position from this traditional stance is that defended in Kelsen's later writings, according to which the fundamental type of norm is the empowering norm. The author discusses Kelsen's three theories on the "ideal form" or structure of the legal norm, with special attention to the third of these, the empowerment theory.

PAULSON, Stanley L. Remarks on the Concept of Norm. J Brit Soc Phenomenol, 21(1), 3-13, Ja 90.

PAVILIONIS, Rolandas. On Meaning and Understanding. Acta Phil Fennica, 38, 218-246, 1985.

An approach is suggested according to which (a) meaning is part of individual conceptual systems and only in abstraction from them is it part of the so-called 'semantics of natural language'; (b) natural language acquisition is based upon the existence of sufficiently cognitively rich

conceptual structures; (c) understanding is interpretation in a conceptual system made up of interrelated concepts, forming cognitively basic subsystems of belief and knowledge.

PAVKOVIC, Aleksandar. "Skepticism and the Senses in Hume's 'Treatise'" in *Early Modern Philosophy II*, TWEYMAN, Stanley (ed), 61-74. Delmar, Caravan Books, 1988.

In the section "Of scepticism with regard to the senses" of the *Treatise*, Hume argues that the senses are not the cause of our belief in external objects. Although his arguments do not follow the standard skeptical patterns, they concern the way perceived items phenomenally appear to their perceiver and thus, like the standard skeptical arguments, they concern the evidence of sense. Hume in effect argues that since perceived items do not and cannot phenomenally appear as external to the perceiver, the senses do not cause this belief of ours. For this purpose he does not need to assume that perceived items are contingently or necessarily mind-dependent.

PAWLOWSKI, Tadeusz. Ästhetischer Subjektivismus. Conceptus, 23(59), 3-19, 1989.

According to aesthetic objectivism, aesthetic values exist independently of perceiving subjects, and are eternal, immutable, and the same for all. In view of the obvious variety and variability of aesthetic judgments, subjectivists take this position to be false and suggest instead that aesthetic values are connected with the emotions and experiences of the person pronouncing a judgment. This position in turn raises some problems which I investigate in this paper. Firstly I distinguish five fundamental variants of subjectivism, some of which differ considerably from others. I then attempt to show that the main arguments adduced by subjectivists can neither refute objectivism nor provide an adequate justification for subjectivism. Finally I discuss a number of facts which cannot satisfactorily be accounted for by subjectivism.

PAYNE, E F J (trans) and SCHOPENHAUER, Arthur and HÜBSCHER, Arthur (ed). *Manuscript Remains, Volume IV: The Manuscript Books of 1830-1852 and Last Manuscripts*. New York, St Martin's Pr, 1990

PAYNE, Steven. *John of the Cross and the Cognitive Value of Mysticism*. Norwell, Kluwer, 1990

This new study of mysticism's cognitive value develops an alternative approach based on detailed analysis of one major mystic, John of the Cross (1542-1591), using the results in an "explanatory inference" that it is reasonable to regard contemplative consciousness as a cognitive mode of experience. Initial chapters explore John's epistemology, philosophical anthropology, and account of spiritual development, showing how these challenge popular theories of mysticism (e.g., of James and Stace). Later chapters defend the hypothesis that mysticism is a cognitive mode of experience, by answering classical objections, and arguing that this hypothesis provides as good an explanation of the data as any reasonable alternative.

PAYTON, Sallyanne and ALLEN, Layman E and SAXON, Charles S. Synthesizing Related Rules from Statutes and Cases for Legal Expert Systems. Ratio Juris, 3(2), 272-318, Jl 90.

Different legal expert systems may be incompatible with each other: a user in characterizing the same situation by answering the questions presented in a consultation can be led to contradictory inferences. Such systems can be "synthesized" to help users avoid such contradictions by alerting them that other relevant systems are available to be consulted as they are responding to questions. An example of potentially incompatible, related legal expert systems is presented here—ones for the New Jersey murder statute and the celebrated Quinlan case, along with one way of synthesizing them to avoid such incompatibility.

PEACOCKE, Christopher. What are Concepts? Midwest Stud Phil, 14, 1-28, 1989.

Concepts are individuated by their possession conditions. A possession condition for a concept is a true, noncircular statement of the form: the concept F is that concept C to possess which a thinker must meet the condition A(C). Plausible examples of this form are given, and its connection with the level of semantic value is investigated. The 'systematicity' of thought built up from concepts is derived from *a priori* constraints on possession conditions. The theory is also used to steer a middle course between the more extreme views of Dummett and McDowell on concept mastery, and to treat some of the tensions in Wittgenstein's *Tractatus*.

PEARCE, David. Musical Expression: Some Remarks on Goodman's Theory. Acta Phil Fennica, 43, 228-243, 1988.

PEARCE, David. "The Problem of Incommensurability: A Critique of Two Instrumentalist Approaches" in *Scientific Knowledge Socialized*, HRONSZKY, Imre (ed), 385-398. Norwell, Kluwer, 1989.

PEARCE, David. Remarks on Physicalism and Reductionism. Acta Phil Fennica, 38, 247-271, 1985.

PEARCE, David and DI NUCCI PEARCE, M Rosaria. Technology versus Science: The Cognitive Fallacy. Synthese, 81(3), 405-419, D 89.

There are fundamental differences between the explanation of scientific change and the explanation of technological change. The differences arise from fundamental differences between scientific and technological knowledge and basic disanalogies between technological advance and scientific progress. Given the influence of economic markets and industrial and institutional structures on the development of technology, it is more plausible to regard technological change as a continuous and incremental process, rather than as a process of Kuhnian crises and revolutions.

PEARL, Judea. *Probabilistic Reasoning in Intelligent Systems: Networks of Plausible Inference*. San Mateo, Morgan Kaufmann, 1988

This book explores the applicability of probabilistic methods to tasks requiring automated reasoning under uncertainty. It provides a computation-minded interpretation of probability theory, an interpretation that exposes the qualitative nature of this centuries-old formalism. Its epistemological foundations, its compatibility with human intuition, and most importantly, its amenability to network representations and to parallel and distributed computation. From this vantage point the book gives a coherent account of probability as a language for reasoning with partial beliefs and binds it, in a unifying perspective, with other artificial intelligence (AI) approaches to uncertainty, such as the Dempster-Shafer formalism, truth maintenance systems, and nonmonotonic logic.

PEARL, Leon. A Puzzle about Necessary Being. Philosophy, 65(252), 229-231, Ap 90.

I argue contrary to Stephen Makin's "The Ontological Argument" (*Philosophy* 63, No. 243) that one can't show that necessary being is a meaningful concept by the use of modal notions involving the exemplification of concepts. For conceptual coherence provides, at best, a necessary condition for necessary exemplification, not a sufficient one. What then could there possibly be about a concept beyond its coherence that would necessitate its exemplification. I suspect there is none.

PEARS, David. "Rule-Following in *Philosophical Investigations*" in *Wittgenstein in Focus—Im Brennpunkt: Wittgenstein*, MC GUINNESS, Brian (ed), 249-261. Amsterdam, Rodopi, 1989.

The negative part of Wittgenstein's treatment of rule-following in the *Philosophical Investigations* is a critique of Platonic theories of meaning. The main argument, summarized in sections 201-202 is a reductio: if Platonism were true, the difference between obeying and disobeying a linguistic rule would vanish. For Platonism requires the rule-follower to have in his mind something which will completely determine in advance all the correct applications of a descriptive word, but this is a requirement that could not be conceivably satisfied. The analogy which Wittgenstein finds for the Platonist's "super-idealization" of the rule-follower's mental equipment—the analogy of the "machine-as-symbol" (sections 193-194) indicates the connection between his treatment of this topic and his philosophy of mathematics.

PEARS, David. "Russell's 1913 *Theory of Knowledge* Manuscript" in *Rereading Russell: Essays on Bertrand Russell's Metaphysics and Epistemology*, SAVAGE, C Wade (ed), 169-182. Minneapolis, Univ of Minn Pr, 1989.

PEARSON, Allen T. Teaching, Learning and Ontological Dependence. Proc Phil Educ, 45, 280-287, 1989.

PECHENEV, V. Change So As to Preserve Oneself and One's Nature: On a New Conception of Man. Soviet Stud Phil, 29(1), 55-69, Sum 90.

PECHEY, Graham. Boundaries Versus Binaries: Bakhtin In/Against the History of Ideas. Rad Phil, 54, 23-31, Spr 90.

The article attempts to identify what sort of philosophy (if any) Bakhtin practises, in texts that are not always directly 'philosophical'. Focusing in particular on *Problems of Dostoevsky's Poetics*, a text that might be called personalist or existentialist in cast, it shows how his critique of the classical speculative dialectic in favour of 'dialogue' (in his special, extended sense) rests on a parody of the latter. It also argues the political bearings of that text of 1929 by suggesting that there is a homology between Bakhtin's idea of novelistic 'polyphony' and Gramsci's idea of civil society as a space of the dialogical negotiation of power. Finally, it attempts to dissociate Bakhtin from the politically compromised project of the US liberal academy and links him instead with those 'hero-ideologues' of the narrative of decolonization (like Fanon and Freire) who speak critically and dialogically from the margins of Western rationality and imperialist hegemony.

PECKHAUS, Volker. 'Ich habe mich wohl gehütet, alle Patronen auf einmal zu verschiessen': Ernest Zermelo in Göttingen. Hist Phil Log, 11(1), 19-58, 1990.

Zermelo's Göttingen period (1897-1910) can be regarded as the most fruitful period in his scientific career. Nevertheless, up till now there have been no investigations which enable us to embed his work in its biographical and social contexts. This study tries to partially fill the gap, concentrating on two major themes: (1) the historical context of the development of Zermelo's early work on the foundations of set theory; (2) the prehistory and particulars of his lectureship for mathematical logic and related topics, this lectureship, which he was awarded in 1907, being the first step taken in Germany towards the establishment of this subject as a separate mathematical discipline. Both will be seen in close connection with the first phase of Hilbert's programme of founding mathematics. (edited)

PECZENIK, Aleksander. Legal Reasoning as a Special Case of Moral Reasoning. Ratio Juris, 1(2), 123-136, Jl 88.

Moral statements are related to some ought- and good-making facts. If at least one of these facts exists then it is reasonable that an action in question is *prima facie* good and obligatory. If all of these facts take place, then it is reasonable that the action is definitively good and obligatory. Yet, moral reasoning is relatively uncertain. The law is more "fixed." Legal interpretatory statements ought to express a compromise between the literal sense of the law and moral considerations. They can be to a high degree both coherent and accepted. One may emotionally reject them but most people have a disposition to endorse a coherent and commonly accepted value system.

PEDEN, Creighton. The Abbot-Royce Controversy. Relig Hum, 24(1), 17-23, Wint 90.

PEDROSA, Renato H L and SETTE, Antonio M A. A Representation Theorem for Languages with Generalized Quantifiers Through Back-and-Forth Methods. Stud Log, 47(4), 401-411, D 88.

We obtain in this paper a representation of the formulae of extensions of $L_{\omega\omega}$ by generalized quantifiers through functors between categories of first-order structures and partial isomorphisms. The main tool in the proofs is the back-and-forth technique. As a corollary we obtain the Caicedo's version of Fraïssé's theorem characterizing elementary equivalence for such languages. We also discuss informally some geometrical interpretations of our results.

PEERENBOOM, R P. Buddhist Process Ethics: Dissolving the Dilemmas of Substantialist Metaphysics. Indian Phil Quart, 16(3), 247-268, Jl 89.

Buddhist process ontology, together with the corrollary notions of non-egoity, momentariness and conditioned origination, challenge fundamental ethical assumptions in regard to the nature of the self as an ethical agent, to moral autonomy and, consequently, to the possibility and justifiability of assigning moral responsibility. Understanding the ethical agent not as an atomistic individual but as a person-in-a-social-and-natural-context who both conditions and is conditioned by his or her constituting relationships militates against a dualistic, either-or reading of freedom and determinism, and diffuses ethical responsibility over the whole community.

PEERENBOOM, R P. Cosmogony, the Taoist Way. J Chin Phil, 17(2), 157-174, Je 90.

PEERENBOOM, R P. Natural Law in the *Huang-Lao Boshu*. Phil East West, 40(3), 309-329, Jl 90.

The recent discovery of long lost manuscripts known as the *Huang-Lao Boshu* has made possible reassessment of classical Chinese philosophies of law. In contrast to the sage-dependent "rule of man" of Confucianism, Huang-Lao, like legalism, espouses a rule of law. However, unlike legalism's positive law, Huang-Lao advances natural law where the laws of the human social order are predicated on and implicate the Way/dao, construed as a predetermined cosmic order encompassing both the human and nonhuman realms.

PEERENBOOM, R P. Reasons, Rationales, and Relativisms: What's at Stake in the Conversation over Scientific. Phil Today, 34(1), 3-19, Spr 90.

Philosophers of science have saddled Quine, Kuhn, Feyerabend and Rorty with the *prima facie* absurd positions of "anything-goes relativism," "cognitive egalitarianism," total incommunicability across paradigms and even "irrationalism." Such criticisms miss the thrust of the latter group's arguments as an attack on the Enlightenment-Kantian quest for an account of rational theory choice which grounds the decision process in the "discovered" foundations of a permanent, neutral algorithm allowing for "rational closure" in adjudicating conflicting claims. Yet that there are no foundational or theory-neutral epistemic standards does not entail that there are no standards whatsoever for theory choice given one's past experiences, goals, beliefs and so forth.

PEERENBOOM, Randall P. Confucian Justice: Achieving a Humane Society. Int Phil Quart, 30(1), 17-32, Mr 90.

Classical and contemporary contractarian theories of justice begin with a zero sum assumption of atomistic individuals in competition over scarce goods. They aim to ensure the ability of society to function and the means to resolve potential conflicts by providing a minimum level of security to the individual, often in the guise of protecting individual ("inalienable" or "natural") rights and liberties. Confucianism, by contrast, aims at a more robust justice. The goal is to foster a human state in which social beings rather than atomistic individuals realize their maximum potential in and through the achievement of a harmonious social order. One seeks positive sum solutions to interpersonal conflicts by beginning not with abstract, ahistorical, universal ethical or rational principles but with the context-specific goals, values, interests of the particular parties concerned.

PEERENBOOM, Randall P. A Coup d'État in Law's Empire: Dworkin's Hercules Meets Atlas. Law Phil, 9(1), 95-113, F 90.

In Law's Empire, Ronald Dworkin advances two incompatible versions of law as integrity. On the strong thesis, political integrity understood as coherence in fundamental moral principles constitutes an overriding constraint on justice, fairness and due process. On the weak thesis, political integrity, while a value, is not to be privileged over justice, fairness, and due process, but to be weighed along with them. I argue that the weak thesis is superior on both of Dworkin's criteria: fit and justifiability. However, the weak thesis must be amended to allow for coherence in policies as well as in principles: the social consequences of legal decisions must be taken into account.

PEGORARO, Olinto (ed) and MC LEAN, George F (ed). The Social Context and Values: Perspectives of the Americas. Lanham, Univ Pr of America, 1989

The first part of this work, largely by Latin American philosophers, treats hermeneutics and the socio-historical context of values. Its chapters concern historicity, hermeneutics and the sociological and psychoanalytic critique of values. The second part treats the relation of value horizons to liberation from four points of view: the phenomenological and existential philosophy of the person, technological development, aesthetics and religion.

PEGORARO, Olinto. "Ethics and Historicity" in The Social Context and Values: Perspectives of the Americas, MC LEAN, George F (ed), 3-13. Lanham, Univ Pr of America, 1989.

PEIRCE, Charles S and KLOESEL, Christian J W (ed). Writings of Charles S Peirce: A Chronological Edition, Volume 4, 1879-1884. Bloomington, Indiana Univ Pr, 1989

PEIRCE, Michael. Domination, Legitimation and Law: Introducing Critical Legal Studies. Eidos, 8(1), 47-66, Je 89.

PEITCHINIS, Stephen G. Government Spending and the Budget Deficit. J Bus Ethics, 9(7), 591-594, Jl 90.

The business community of Canada manifests questionable moral and ethical standards in its criticism of government spending, since it itself bears considerable responsibility for the increase in government spending and budget deficits. The contradiction arises from the failure of the business community to recognize the liberalization of society at large and the associated social responsibility for the well-being of its citizens; a well-being manifested in income maintenance programmes, in access to education and training, in health care, and others. The failure to recognize such expectations is manifested in its failure to provide adequately for the retirement of its employees, for the health care of its employees, for laid-off and separated employees, thereby shifting the burden to government. (edited)

PEKARSKY, Daniel. Dewey's Conception of Growth Reconsidered. Educ Theor, 40(3), 283-294, Sum 90.

With attention to some competing accounts of Dewey's views, this paper offers a sympathetic, but not uncritical, interpretation of Dewey's conception of growth. This interpretation highlights the ways in which Dewey's view resembles and differs from that of some other significant "growth-theorists." It is argued that although the ideal of growth as Dewey understands it cannot carry all the moral weight that he sometimes places on its shoulders, it can be very helpful in guiding the attention of educational theorists and educators to some critically important questions concerning the process and aims of education.

PELIKAN, Jaroslav. The Melody of Theology: A Philosophical Dictionary. Cambridge, Harvard Univ Pr, 1988

PELLECCHIA, Pasquale. Discorso meta-fisico e discorso meta-forico: Derrida. Aquinas, 32(1), 17-55, Ja-Ap 89.

PELLECCHIA, Pasquale. Discorso meta-forico e discorso meta-fisico: Heidegger. Aquinas, 32(3), 445-486, S-D 89.

PELLECCHIA, Pasquale. Discorso meta-forico e discorso meta-fisico: Ricoeur. Aquinas, 32(2), 257-300, My-Ag 89.

PELLEGRIN, Pierre and KANY-TURPIN, José. "Cicero and the Aristotelian Theory of Divination by Dreams" in Cicero's Knowledge of the Peripatos, FORTENBAUGH, William W (ed), 220-245. New Brunswick, Transaction Books, 1989.

PELLEGRIN, Pierre. De l'explication causale dans la biologie d'Aristote. Rev Metaph Morale, 95(2), 197-219, Ap-Je 90.

PELLEREY, Roberto. Idéologie e conoscenza scientifica: La fondazione delle scienze umane nella gnoseologia sensita idéologique. Epistemologia, 12(1), 65-89, Ja-Je 89.

The Idéologie of Destutt de Tracy, Cabanis, Dégérando, Volney and Thurot is the threshold between the 18th and the 19th century which carries out the transition of philosophy from speculative investigation to a critical apparatus organizing the specific contents of the new sciences. The Idéologie is almost a general anthropology which founds the different fields of knowledge: the new biology of the Institut National Idéologique, the psychology of Maine de Biran, anthropology as a science of ethnographical data, sociology as an inquiry on human society, economy, history, physiology and finally the Idéologie "proprement dite" as an analysis of the physiological processes which generate mental events. It is the task of the Idéologie to connect the different fields of knowledge and to try to synthesize the data coming from them with general laws. (edited)

PELLETIER, Francis Jeffry. Parmenides, Plato, and the Semantics of Not-Being. Chicago, Univ of Chicago Pr, 1990

In the Sophist, Plato gives an account of predication which is designed to overturn an argument of Parmenides' that would have discourse be impossible. This book examines the interpretations that have been given for the Sophist and concludes that both a "correspondence account" (which associates a specific portion of reality with each sentence, including negative sentences) and a "backdrop account" (which gives certain relationships amongst the forms as necessary preconditions for language) are required to make sense of Plato's position. Novel in the interpretation is the emphasis placed on different sorts of "generic/kind statements" within the backdrop theory, and the identification of a syntactic correlate for this in the text of the Sophist.

PELLING, Christopher. "Plutarch: Roman Heroes and Greek Culture" in Philosophia Togata: Essays on Philosophy and Roman Society, GRIFFIN, Miriam (ed), 199-232. New York, Clarendon/Oxford Pr, 1989.

PELS, Dick. De 'natuurlijke saamhorigheid' van feiten en waarden. Kennis Methode, 14(1), 14-43, 1990.

PELS, Dick and DE VRIES, G. Feiten en waarden: de constructie van een onderscheid. Kennis Methode, 14(1), 7-13, 1990.

PEÑA, L. Flew on Entitlements and Justice. Int J Moral Soc Stud, 4(3), 259-263, Autumn 89.

A Flew has argued that redistributionism in any form is in fact incompatible with justice, which hinges on what entitlements people have to hold their own. This paper shows that the only entitlements that can rightly be called upon within a justice theory are those which have not been secured by use of force or deception or any other guilty means. Now, the hugely widespread resort to such means entails that no holding is to be deemed legitimate unless and until it is proved to have been acquired in a blameless way through transactions with people having gained their goods and money in a likewise irreproachable way and so on and so forth. Hence, the fresh start Flew brands seems to be wholly justified.

PEÑA, Lorenzo. El análisis tractariano de los hechos relacionales: exégesis, crítica y alternativa. Analisis Filosof, 9(1), 41-76, My 89.

Wittgenstein's Tractarian ontology has been interpreted in several ways. A construal is put forward to the effect that things are taken to include relations, while a state of affairs is a combination of things through a linkage or combination way. Combination ways are the structures of respective states of affairs, one for each situation. This ontology is flawed by its failing to give a real account of what constitutes a relational fact. An alternative to Wittgenstein's approach is then sketched: a relational fact is not a static combination of things, but a (nontemporal) transition consisting in a relation's passing from the subject to the term. Such a passage is elucidated along the lines of a similar approach to motion already set forth elsewhere: through a combinatory paraconsistent logic, which allows us to look upon transitions or process as conjunctions of being and not-being. (edited)

PEÑA, Lorenzo. Partial Truth, Fringes, and Motion: Three Applications of a Contradictorial Logic. Stud Soviet Tho, 39(3-4), 283-312, Ap-My 90.

The paper argues that we can make good sense of the idea of contradictory truths—as implemented in a paraconsistent infinite-valued system of logic, which is here put forward—in three fields—which have claimed to be amenable to contradictorial treatments by the dialectical tradition—namely those of partial truth, fringes of application of sundry predicates, and motion. The first is that, when a predicate correctly or truthfully applies to a part of some object but not to other parts thereof, it can only be said with partial truth that the object satisfies that predicate or has the property it denotes. The second problem arises because many predicates can be neither completely assigned to some things nor completely withheld from them. The third problem is nothing else but Zeno's paradox of the arrow. The paper's gist is that in all cases true contradictions stem from graduality in things.

PENATI, Giancarlo. Spiritualismo e neoscolastica nel Novecento: L'aporia del fondamento. G Metaf, 11(2), 303-306, My-Ag 89.

PENCE, Gregory E. *Classic Cases in Medical Ethics: Accounts of the Cases That Have Shaped Medical Ethics*. New York, McGraw-Hill, 1990

This book examines 16 famous cases in depth: Karen Quinlan, Elizabeth Bouvia, Dutch mercy-killing, Baby Louise Brown's in vitro fertilization, Baby M's Surrogate Gestation, Kenneth Edelin's abortion trial, Baby Jane Doe, Philadelphia Head-Injury Experiment on Primates, Tuskegee Syphilis Study, Christiaan Barnard's heart transplant, Barney Clark's artificial heart, Baby Fae, involuntary psychiatric commitment (Joyce Brown vs. Ed Koch), decreasing teenage pregnancy, genetic markers, and mandatory AIDS testing. Each chapter contains a historical review, legal synopsis, update, and extended discussion of ethical/philosophical issues. Annotated Contents and Name/Subject Indexes are included.

PENDLEBURY, Michael. Sense Experiences and their Contents: A Defence of the Propositional Account. Inquiry, 33(2), 215-230, Je 90.

A number of philosophers are committed to the view that sense experiences, insofar as they have contents, have propositional contents, but this is more often tacitly accepted than argued for in the literature. This paper explains the propositional account and presents a basic case in support of it in a simple and straightforward way which does not involve commitment to any specific philosophical theory of perception.

PENDLEBURY, Michael. Why Proper Names are Rigid Designators. Phil Phenomenol Res, 50(3), 519-536, Mr 90.

PENDLEBURY, Shirley. Practical Arguments and Situational Appreciation in Teaching. Educ Theor, 40(2), 171-179, Spr 90.

Gary Fenstermacher claims that the practical argument may serve as a device for understanding and evaluating how teachers deliberate. Opponents reject this as a barren route. Much of the discussion, on both sides, is muddled. One of the purposes of the article is to sort out the middle; the other is to argue that deliberation in teaching, if it is any good, relies crucially on situational appreciation. The argument is advanced as part of an Aristotelian account of practical reasoning in teaching.

PENNOCK, J Roland. "The Justification of Democracy" in *Politics and Process*, BRENNAN, Geoffrey (ed), 11-41. New York, Cambridge Univ Pr, 1989.

This essay deals broadly with modes of justifying both the ideal and the practical forms of democracy. The ideal, I argue, does not depend upon any one ethical theory. Certain facts of human rationality, autonomy, and sociality are fundamental. From them follows a powerful case for maximizing liberty and equality. I then provide arguments and evidence in support of the proposition that political institutions, varying in form from country to country but all conforming to the concept of liberal democracy, are more likely than any rivals to approximate the ideal, all the while recognizing that certain minimal conditions are essential.

PENSKY, Max. On the Use and Abuse of Memory: Habermas, "Anamnestic Solidarity," and the *Historikerstreit*. Phil Soc Crit, 15(4), 351-380, 1989.

In his arguments against "neoconservative" historians in the German *Historikerstreit*, Jürgen Habermas presents the view that collective memory establishes a solidarity with the oppressed past, and that this "anamnestic solidarity" carries ethical as well as political consequences. Habermas draws chiefly on the late work of Walter Benjamin for this conception. I reconstruct Habermas's reading of Benjamin, showing the special problems involved in transforming Benjamin's essentially theological understanding of remembrance into a critique of contemporary neoconservatism. I argue that, while this conception does constitute a powerful critique, it also reveals the aporetic dimension of the discourse ethic of Habermas's *Theory of Communicative Action*.

PENSLAR, Robin Levin. Who Pays for AZT? Hastings Center Rep, 19(5), 30-31, S-O 89.

PENZO, Giorgio. Mito e demittizzazione: polemica di Jaspers con Bultmann. Aquinas, 32(3), 487-512, S-D 89.

PEPERZAK, Adriaan. "From Intentionality to Responsibility: On Levinas's Philosophy of Language" in *The Question of the Other: Essays in*

Contemporary Continental Philosophy, DALLERY, Arleen B (ed), 3-21. Albany, SUNY Pr, 1989.

Starting from the central concept of Husserlian phenomenology, intentionality, this article shows how Levinas retrieved it and reduced it to the more radical, "pre-original" and "an-archic" "principle" of a responsibility that precedes all freedom of choice.

PEPERZAK, Adriaan. Hetzelfde anders: Over de veelzinnigheid van transcendentie. Alg Ned Tijdschr Wijs, 82(1), 15-25, Ja 90.

Discussion with O Duintjer and Martin Heidegger on the last metaphilosophical horizon of all attempts at writing a metaphysics or an ontology.

PEPERZAK, Adriaan. On a Not-Relativistic Pluralism in Philosophy (in Hungarian). Magyar Filozof Szemle, 2-3, 323-330, 1989.

What are the conditions of a philosophical pluralism that does not fall into the contradictions of a nonrelative relativism?

PEPERZAK, Adriaan. "On the Unity of Systematic Philosophy and History of Philosophy" in *History and Anti-History in Philosophy*, LAVINE, T Z (ed), 19-31. Norwell, Kluwer, 1989.

In this simplified presentation of the conclusions of his book *System and History*, the author argues for the thesis that a clear distinction between research in the history of philosophy and engagement in thematic philosophy is impossible. The concepts of kinship and conversation permit to think their unbreakable unity.

PEPPERELL, Keith C. Democracy and Schooling: An Essentially Contested Relationship. Proc Phil Educ, 45, 226-230, 1989.

PERCIVAL, Philip. Fitch and Intuitionistic Knowability. Analysis, 50(3), 182-187, Je 90.

Classically, $p \rightarrow \Diamond Kp \mid - p \rightarrow Kp$. Against the suggestion that an anti-realist will insist on reasoning intuitionistically, this paper defends the view that this entailment is a reductio of the anti-realist thesis that all truths are knowable. Intuitionistically, $p \rightarrow \Diamond Kp$ entails both that no proposition is forever undecided and the equivalence of not Kp and not p. It is argued that no extant constructivist semantics warrants these consequences—indeed, that no acceptable semantics could do so.

PERCIVAL, W Keith. A Note on Thomas Hayne and His Relation to Leibniz and Vico. New Vico Studies, 6, 97-101, 1988.

PERDOMO, Rogelio Perez. Corruption and Business in Present Day Venezuela. J Bus Ethics, 9(7), 555-566, Jl 90.

Venezuelan media present corruption as a major problem of the country, and a research conducted by the author shows managers perceive it as business ethics' main issue. The corruption type addressed to in this article is the collusion between public officials and private managers for illegal or undue profits. Corruption in this form is related to the longstanding policy of state intervention and overregulation of the economy in order to industrialize the country. The issue analyzed is the perception of corruption as a major political and social problem. Corruption is pervasive in many societies but it is not perceived as a central problem. The explanation for this perception in Venezuela is the increased impoverishment of people as a consequence of present economic crisis (the corrupt person is perceived as taking from my pocket) and the openness and pluralistic character of the political system. Moral indignation and scandal is the result of this new feature of Venezuelan society. Changes in the economic policies and the awareness of corruption seem to establish the basis to overcome the perception of corruption as the paramount problem it is now.

PERECZ, László. "Wonderful Vision of a Truly Human World" (On Lukács' Conception of Communism in 1919) (in Hungarian). Magyar Filozof Szemle, 5, 535-549, 1989.

Der Aufsatz rekonstruiert die Kommunismusauffassung der Schriften von Georg Lukács zur Zeit der Ungarischen Räterepublik. Er beweist, dass die grundlegenden Zeichen dieser Kommunismusauffassung der Messianismus, die Institutionsfeindlichkeit und die Bestrebung auf die Ergreifung der Organisationsprinzipien der neuen Gesellschaft sind. Er analysiert ausführlich die—von Lukács abgefassten—zwei grundlegenden Organisationsprinzipien: die Sitte und die Kultur. Die folgerungen des Aufsatzes sind (den Ergebnissen der früheren Forschungen von der Seite des Kommunismusbildes beitragend): im Jahr 1919 ist Lukács ein radikaler Utopist, seine Auffassung ist noch kaum marxistisch und in seiner Tätigkeit kommen der Philosoph und der Politiker in Widerspruch.

PERELMAN, Chaïm. "Formal Logic and Informal Logic" in *From Metaphysics to Rhetoric*, MEYER, Michel (ed), 9-14. Norwell, Kluwer, 1989.

PERELMAN, Chaïm. Rhetoriques. Brussels, Univ Bruxelles, 1989

PEREZ ESTEVEZ, Antonio. *El Concepto de Materia al Comienzo de la*

Escuela Franciscana de Paris. Zulia, Univ Zulia, 1976

This book presents a study on the concept of matter in an important period of medieval ages (Franciscan School in Paris). The author finds out that, side by side of the formalistic current led by Thomas Aquinas in which matter is despised, there exists another current, represented by the Franciscan School, in which matter performs a fundamental role. Bonaventure's matter is a mysterious entity with an essential relation to form. Matter gives existence to the individuum, that is, makes it to endure in being or to be located in place and time. The matter of Richard of Middletown has a stronger and more complicated entity; as fundamentum and subject of change is an entity compound of actuality and potentiality. Matter keeps being important in Franciscan School and overcomes the difficult formalistic period of these ages to spring up again strong and powerful in Giordano Bruno.

PEREZ ESTEVEZ, Antonio. *El individuo y la feminidad*. Zulia, Univ Zulia, 1989

This book gathers four studies or dialogues with important thinkers of the past, to develop the main ideas on the individual and on femininity: "Language in Merleau-Ponty," "Marcuse and Negative Thought," "Life's Notion in Nietzsche," "Femininity and Reason in Western Thought." Philosophy and politics have in history refused to accept as positive and human the values linked to the individual and to femininity. This book implies an effort to discover and to incorporate such values in the course of the western culture to make it more human.

PEREZ LARAUDOGOITIA, J. Compatibilidad cuántica desde una perspectiva lógica. Pensamiento, 45(180), 489-497, O-D 89.

PEREZ RUIZ, F. La alegoría de la caverna y su sentido. Pensamiento, 45(180), 385-424, O-D 89.

En la alegoría de la caverna hay aspectos importantes que se ven fcilmente olvidados o mal comprendidos: en primer lugar, sobre el contexto próximo y remoto de la alegoría, cuyo fin no es corregir, sino completar la exposición anterior; en segundo, sobre el mismo contenido de la imagen, que comprende diversos planos cada uno con su peculiaridad propia y en continuidad y discontinuidad entre sí, y en tercero, sobre el sentido de algunos de sus elementos (situación original del hombre, doble conversión, fuego en el mundo inferior, sombras en el superior, doble movimiento descendente teórica y prácticamente).

PEREZ, J R. Ser, nada y creación en el pensamiento de Nimio de Anquín. Stromata, 45(3-4), 369-406, Jl-D 89.

PERKINS, D N. Art as Understanding. J Aes Educ, 22(1), 111-131, Spr 88.

PERKINS, Robert L. Kierkegaard, a Kind of Epistemologist. Hist Euro Ideas, 12(1), 7-18, 1990.

Kierkegaard was deeply concerned with the problem of truth. His thought is not so much antirational as it is an effort to reform and broaden the sense of rationality by bringing epistemology back to the situation of the subject in the ordinary lived world. He rejects the Cartesian and Hegelian constructions in favor of the effort the subject makes to found itself. This effort considerably shifts the sense of the empirical from "data" and "facts" to edification as the basis of epistemology. His concept of "subjective truth" avoids subjectivism, arbitrariness and self-deception by the uncompromising demand that subjective truth be morally and religiously upbuilding.

PERL, Jeffrey M. *Skepticism and Modern Enmity: Before and After Eliot*. Baltimore, Johns Hopkins U Pr, 1989

PERNECHELE, Gabriella. Pessimismo e umanesimo in Thomas Mann: Una riflessione etica su "Humanität" e "Humanismus". Filosofia, 41(2), 185-212, My-Ag 90.

PEROLI, Enrico. Cornelia de Vogel fra vecchio e nuovo paradigma ermeneutico nell'interpretazione di Platone. Riv Filosof Neo-Scolas, 81(3), 347-392, Jl-S 89.

PEROV, I V. The Problem of the Historicity of Values. Soviet Stud Phil, 28(4), 6-15, Spr 90.

PERRICONE, Christopher. Artist and Audience. J Value Inq, 24(3), 199-212, Jl 90.

In this essay I argue, assuming the work of art to be fully realized upon its reception by an audience, that it is important to understand that philosophies of art have quasi-political agendas. I examine what I call the collaborationist view (R G Collingwood being its representative), the contentionist view (the "philosopher" and pianist Glenn Gould being its representative), and art as context (F Nietzsche being its representative). I find the last view most sound—a mean between the extremes of the first two views.

PERRICONE, Christopher. St Augustine's Idea of Aesthetic Interpretation. Ancient Phil, 9 (1), 95-107, Spr 89.

Through a close reading mainly of *Confessions* 12, 16, I show how

Augustine argues that *Holy Scripture* (and by implication non-holy scriptures, i.e., literary artworks) generates a plurality of interpretations. Augustine says explicitly, there is no one right interpretation of Moses' words: "In the beginning...." On this ground, I develop the ideas of fecundity and charity as necessary conditions of full interpretation of literary artworks.

PERRICONE, Christopher. Translation, Art, and Culture. Clio, 19(1), 1-16, Fall 89.

First, I discuss the nature and problems of translation from the point of view of working translators. Second, I argue that no translation (qua translation) of a literary work is a work of art. Finally, I place translated works in the class of cultural objects and draw out some implications (mostly negative) of what cultural objects mean.

PERRY, John and CRIMMINS, Mark. The Prince and the Phone Booth: Reporting Puzzling Beliefs. J Phil, 86(12), 685-711, D 89.

Beliefs are concrete particulars containing ideas of properties and notions of things, which also are concrete. The claim made in a belief report is that the agent has a belief (i) whose content is a specific singular proposition, and (ii) which involves certain of the agent's notions and ideas in a certain way. No words in the report stand for the notions and ideas, so they are unarticulated constituents of the report's content (like the relevant place in "it's raining"). The belief puzzles (Hesperus, Cicero, Pierre) involve reports about two different notions. So the analysis gets the puzzling truth values right.

PERRY, Leslie R. Creativity and Routine. J Aes Educ, 22(4), 45-57, Wint 88.

PERSZYK, Kenneth J. What's Wrong with Impossible Objects? Phil Papers, 18(3), 241-251, N 89.

Meinongians claim that in addition to objects which exist (at some time), there are possible and impossible objects. With the developments of various versions of possible-worlds semantics and modal logics, one might say that hostility to possible objects has abated somewhat, though Meinongian claims that they do not exist or have being in any sense and that some of them are concrete individuals or particulars are highly contentious. Hostility to impossible objects, on the other hand, remains undiminished, if it has not intensified. (edited)

PERUZZI, Alberto. Towards a Real Phenomenology of Logic. Husserl Stud, 6(1), 1-24, 1989.

The paper deals with the phenomenological roots of logic, and suggests a strict link of such roots with concepts of category theory. The project stems from a new consideration of the philosophy of logic developed by Husserl. Differences between this approach and intuitionism are examined. The objectivity of logical constructions is seen from the viewpoint of natural epistemology. An essential complementary of descriptive and constructive components is reached and related to formal developments in category theory.

PESSINA, Adriano. Oltre l'imperativo categorico—Bergson e la fondazione dell'esperienza morale: L'etica della pressione. Riv Filosof Neo-Scolas, 81(1), 68-106, Ja-Mr 89.

Questo saggio costituisce la prima parte di un'indagine dedicata all'etica di Bergson. L'oggetto affrontato è la morale della pressione. Contestualizzata la riflessione di Bergson nel dibattito riguardante la possibilità di dare dignità scientifica all'etica, si sono evidenziate le modalità con cui viene corretta l'impostazione positivistica. Il suo tentativo di fondare metafisicamente l' etica della pressione e di procedere verso una progressiva abolizione del valore dell'obbligazione morale a favore di un'etica di stampo vitalistico pone molteplici interrogativi.

PESTIEAU, J. Quel développement et pour qui? Philosophiques, 16(2), 327-346, Autumn 89.

This paper is divided into two parts. In the first one, the author tries to categorize the different strands in the criticism of development. In the second part, the author discusses the values which could give a sound direction to development. (edited)

PETERS, James Robert. Reason and Passion in Plato's *Republic*. Ancient Phil, 9 (2), 173-187, Fall 89.

I argue that, for Plato, reason is itself a passionate drive in the *psyche* that seeks to create order and harmony according to the pattern of the Good. Reason's distinctive passion for creating a complete, ordered self motivates the philosopher-king to rule and not merely seek the harmony of the philosopher's private, individual *psyche*. Plato's theory of passionate rationality also explains Plato's insistence in the *Republic* that only a *psyche* trained to love beauty and order can succeed in the dialectical quest for ultimate knowledge.

PETERS, Jan. "The Novelist and the Camera Eye" in *Cultural Hermeneutics*

of Modern Art: Essays in Honor of Jan Aler, DETHIER, Hubert (ed), 195-203. Amsterdam, Rodopi, 1989.

Novelists have been influenced by films and in recent years several authors have tried to define the content of the expression 'cinematographic quality' of a novel, mainly in order to discover in what ways the art of writing over the years has been changed by the techniques of filmic narration. Three books dealing with this question are discussed here.

PETERS, Karl E. Humanity in Nature: Conserving Yet Creating. Zygon, 24(4), 469-485, D 89.

Developing a scientifically grounded philosophy of cosmic evolution, and using the moral norm of completeness as dynamic harmony, this paper argues that humans are a part of nature in both its conserving and emergent aspects. Humans are both material and cultural, instinctual-emotional and rational, creatures and creators, and carriers of stability and change. To ignore any of the multifaceted aspects of humanity in relation to the rest of nature is to commit one of a number of fallacies that are grounded in a dualistic-conquest mentality. Examples of some new developments in philosophy and ethology, metaphorical images, and ritual show how to overcome dualism in favor of a dynamic harmony of humanity within nature.

PETERSEN, Glenn. The Small-Republic Argument in Modern Micronesia. Phil Forum, 21(4), 393-411, Sum 90.

Current political and constitutional questions in the Federated States of Micronesia are placed within a larger context of political theory. The republic as a small, face-to-face community was a Greek ideal; its practicality was praised by Montesquieu and Rousseau; its relevance for the newly independent United States was promoted by the Anti-Federalists. Today, the people of Pohnpei island retain traditional polities, still functioning well, that are much like the Greek republics. The Pohnpeians argue that their political system is still relevant and should serve as a model for their modern nation-state. The continued relevance of the small republic argument is demonstrated.

PETERSON, Grethe B (ed). *The Tanner Lectures on Human Values, Volume X*. Salt Lake City, Univ of Utah Pr, 1989

PETERSON, Justin and BILLMAN, Dorrit. Critique of Structural Analysis in Modeling Cognition: A Case Study of Jackendoff's Theory. Phil Psych, 2(3), 283-296, 1989.

Modeling cognition by structural analysis of representation leads to systematic difficulties which are not resolvable. We analyse the merits and limits of a representation-based methodology to modeling cognition by treating Jackendoff's *Consciousness and the Computational Mind* as a good case study. We note the effects this choice of methodology has on the view of consciousness he proposes, as well as a more detailed consideration of the computational mind. The fundamental difficulty we identify is the conflict between the desire for modular processors which map directly onto representations and the need for dynamically interacting control. Our analysis of this approach to modeling cognition is primarily directed at separating merits from problems and inconsistencies by a critique internal to this approach; we also step outside the framework to note the issues it ignores.

PETERSON, Philip. "How Reasonable is Lehrer's Coherence Theory? Beats Me" in *The Current State of the Coherence Theory*, BENDER, John W (ed), 77-93. Norwell, Kluwer, 1989.

Keith Lehrer offers a probabilistic approach to a coherence theory of *justification*. Very recently, Lehrer has slightly modified this conception of knowledge possession by substituting so-called ultra-system justification for personal and verific justification and undefeatedness. A requirement that any theory of knowledge should satisfy is *non-iteration*. The mere possibility of knowing that one know that p, however, does not violate *non-iteration*. On Lehrer's account, *a priori* knowledge—i.e., an empiristic account of and/or substitute for it—is explained through the notion of rational consent. One's acceptance of something is "intuitive" only if the appropriate form of rational consent holds. But any case of rational consent is *not* easy to observe or determine, so that conscious knowledge that an acceptance *is* intuitive is difficult. As a result, knowing that one knows that p wherein acceptance of p is an intuition is practically impossible. (edited)

PETITDEMANGE, Guy. Jacques Derrida. Etudes, 371(4), 355-369, O 89.

PETREY, Sandy. Iterating Revolution: Speech Acts in Literary Theory. Phil Soc Crit, 15(3), 291-306, 1989.

PETRICEK JR, Miroslav. Jan Patocka and the Idea of Natural World (in Czechoslovakian). Filozof Cas, 38(1-2), 22-44, 1990.

This article attempts to place Patocka's concept of the natural world of our life (*Lebenswelt*) into broader contexts and traces its development from its first treatment in Patocka's book *Natural World as a Philosophical Problem* to his

texts from the last period. A comparison between Patocka's concept and the parallel development of structuralism betrays some identical points: just like in French structuralism, coming to the forefront in Patocka's phenomenology is more or less a dynamic approach to the problems under scrutiny (concept of life movements). In conclusion the author ponders the role of language in Husserl's phenomenology, the critique of this conception in J Derrida and J Lacan and considers the implications of such a discussion in the light of Patocka's transition from phenomenology to phenomenological philosophy and to "Post-European" problems.

PETRO, Nicolai N. "Detente, Human Rights and Soviet Behavior" in *Moral Reasoning and Statecraft: Essays Presented to Kenneth W Thompson*, DAVIS, Reed M (ed), 67-83. Lanham, Univ Pr of America, 1988.

Human rights and detente are widely assumed to reinforce one another. The argument of this paper is that while reinforcement occurs in some instances, this does not diminish the underlying conflict between pursuing these two objectives simultaneously. A detailed examination of emigration and trade patterns between the USSR and the US shows that correlations are not translated into improvements for all human rights. Indeed, improved emigration was gained partly by ignoring domestic human rights violations in the USSR.

PETROWICZ, Lech (trans) and BIALKOWSKI, Grzegorz. Has the Revolution Been Completed? Dialec Hum, 15(3-4), 107-115, Sum-Autumn 88.

PETROWICZ, Lech (trans) and BORGOSZ, Jozef. A Historic Chance for Military-Technical Dealienation and the Building of a World Without War. Dialec Hum, 15(3-4), 241-250, Sum-Autumn 88.

PETROWICZ, Lech (trans) and LORENC, Iwona. Philosophical Premises of Levinas' Conception of Judaism. Dialec Hum, 16(1), 157-170, Wint 89.

What purposes does Levinas's vision of Judaism serve in his philosophy? This question has inspired me to offer these remarks. A reference to Judaism as a source is such a vision of culture which, being alternative to the generally accepted paradigm of West European culture, would offer a chance for endowing the ideas of humanism and universalism with new contents. He wants to indicate the area which makes it possible to leave the structures of pure thinking, to go beyond totalizing thinking. Using philosophical means, Levinas proclaims the necessity of going beyond philosophy.

PETROWICZ, Lech (trans) and GRZEGORCZYK, Andrzej. The Philosophy of Fate as the Basis of Education for Peace. Dialec Hum, 14(1), 167-172, Wint 87.

A vision of mankind grappling with conditions that have been imposed upon it, gives one a sense of community of human fate. This vision enables us for the reconciliation with those who gravely ruined our life (like Nazis or communists in recent times). The experience of the 20th century was an experience of some extremeness. It reflects the dialectic of the extremeness of our thinking. But it culminates in very fruitful self-criticisms of the end of our century.

PETROWICZ, Lech (trans) and MC GOVERN, Arthur F and RODZINSKA, Aleksandra (trans). Response to Janusz's "Christianity and Marxism". Dialec Hum, 14(1), 89-92, Wint 87.

McGovern wrote "Is Atheism Essential to Marxism?" for the *Journal of Ecumenical Studies* (Summer, 1985). He argued that Marxist socialism need not be atheistic. Kuczynski responded in *Dialectics and Humanism*, arguing that McGovern effectively calls for Marxists to give up their atheism. McGovern rejects that interpretation, and agrees that neither Christianity nor Marxism should seek dominance. He argues also that a humanistic materialism which stresses human initiative in transforming society, a humanism Kuczynski views as essential to Marxism, does not conflict with contemporary Christian views about change.

PETROWICZ, Lech (trans) and SZCZEPANSKI, Jan. The Seventieth Anniversary of the October Revolution. Dialec Hum, 15(3-4), 93-98, Sum-Autumn 88.

PETROWICZ, Lech (trans) and WITKOWSKI, Lech. The Structure of Social Revolutions (Some Remarks and Hypotheses). Dialec Hum, 15(3-4), 117-127, Sum-Autumn 88.

PETROWICZ, Lech (trans) and ZAPASNIK, Stanislaw. Tolerance and the Question of Rationality. Dialec Hum, 14(1), 147-158, Wint 87.

Analysing the situation that has arisen in the humanities at the close of the 20th century, the philosopher cannot avoid the question of whether it is possible to create a philosophy that would be universal knowledge expressing the experience of people living in various areas of civilization. The continuing cultural differences and ideological contradictions make the answer to this question one of the most important moral imperatives. However, the philosopher cannot ignore the fact that the contemporary sciences dealing with culture have considerably undermined the trust in the form of reason that was shaped in Western culture over the past two hundred years. Today one finds it more difficult than ever before to free oneself from historical relativism. Nonetheless, the overcoming of historism is a necessity, since historism gives rise to skepticism, and the latter could only mean the destruction of Western culture. This fundamental question is at the root of the present essay. The aims of the essay are limited. It raises the question of whether the idea of tolerance could contribute to the creation of a new, constructive philosophical universalism.

PETROWICZ, Lech (trans) and RAINKO, Stanislaw. Towards a Creative Meaning of Marxism. Dialec Hum, 15(3-4), 139-150, Sum-Autumn 88.

PETROWICZ, Lech (trans) and KUCZYNSKI, Janusz and RODZINSKA, Aleksandra (trans). Universalism as a Metaphilosophy of the New Peace Movement. Dialec Hum, 16(2), 61-78, Spr 89.

PETROWICZ, Lech (trans) and KUCZYNSKI, Janusz and GOLEBIOWSKI, Marek (trans). Universalism: A New Way of Thinking. Dialec Hum, 15(3-4), 27-51, Sum-Autumn 88.

PETTIGREW, David E. The Question of the Relation of Philosophy and Psychoanalysis: The Case of Kant and Freud. Metaphilosophy, 21(1-2), 67-88, Ja-Ap 90.

PETTIT, Philip. Affirming the Reality of Rule-Following. Mind, 99(395), 433-439, Jl 90.

This discusses an objection by Donna Summerfield to my paper, "The Reality of Rule-Following." It describes the objection to my account of rules and rule following and shows that it is off target. It also argues that the sort of theory I defend is going to be an elusive target for any such line of attack.

PETTIT, Philip and PRICE, Huw. Bare Functional Desire. Analysis, 49(4), 162-169, O 89.

It seems that no set of beliefs could guarantee any action. Is this an argument for the necessity of desire? No. It is only an argument for a *ceteris paribus* qualification. And if it were an argument for the necessity of desire at the origin of action, it would also establish, absurdly, the necessity of desire at the origin of reference.

PETTIT, Philip. A Definition of Negative Liberty. Ratio, 2(2), 153-158, D 89.

Negative liberty is subject to almost as many indeterminacies as positive liberty. This paper identifies the main indeterminacies and argues a line on how they ought to be resolved. On the account offered, a person is free to perform a certain sort of activity if and only if no one interferes or would interfere with him in doing so and no one credibly threatens such interference. As it is understood here, interference must be intentional or at least negligent and it may take the form either of preventing the agent from performing the action or frustrating him in doing so, by imposing suitable costs.

PETTIT, Philip. Foul Dealing and an Assurance Problem. Austl J Phil, 67(3), 341-344, S 89.

Many-party prisoner's dilemmas come in two sorts, sorts that are associated respectively with free rider and foul dealer problems. David Schmidtz argues that foul dealer problems raise a distinctive assurance problem, and that this undermines some claims in an earlier paper of mine, but he is mistaken, although the observation he makes is of interest. The assurance problem in question arises under certain contingencies but it arises for both sorts of prisoner's dilemmas.

PETTIT, Philip and GÄRDENFORS, Peter. The Impossibility of a Paretian Loyalist. Theor Decis, 27(3), 207-216, N 89.

Amartya Sen has argued the impossibility of the Paretian liberal. While his abstract argument is compelling, the concrete significance of the conclusion is in some doubt. This is because it is not clear how important liberalism is in his sense is; in particular it is not clear that the sort of liberalism required for the impossibility result is a compelling variety. We show that even if the argument cannot be used to establish the inconsistency of Paretianism and common-or-garden liberalism, it can be adapted to prove a parallel impossibility. This is the impossibility of combining the Pareto criterion with a loyalty constraint involving certain claim-rights rather than liberty-rights. The impossibility of the Paretian loyalist is of interest in itself but it is also interesting for the light it throws on the source of Sen-style impossibilities.

PETTIT, Philip and JACKSON, Frank. In Defence of Folk Psychology. Phil Stud, 59(1), 31-54, My 90.

Eliminativists have raised the question of whether beliefs and desires exist. Their view is that beliefs and desires are the posits of a theory, dubbed folk psychology, and so that, like the posits of any theory, they are open to challenge. We agree that beliefs and desires are indeed to be thought of as the posits of a theory but that despite this, it is virtually certain that they exist.

We describe the kind of theory we take folk psychology to be, namely, a species of commonsense functionalism, and explain how, given this account, it is virtually certain that beliefs and desires exist.

PETTIT, Philip and JACKSON, Frank. Program Explanation: A General Perspective. Analysis, 50(2), 107-117, Mr 90.

Some properties are causally relevant for a certain effect, others are not. In this paper we describe a problem for our understanding of this notion and then offer a solution in terms of the notion of a program explanation.

PFAU, Thomas. Immediacy and the Text: Friedrich Schleiermacher's Theory of Style and Interpretation. J Hist Ideas, 51(1), 51-73, Ja-Mr 90.

PFEIFER, Karl. *Actions and Other Events: The Unifier-Multiplier Controversy.* New York, Lang, 1989

This book is a general defence of Donald Davidson's and G E M Anscombe's 'unifying' approach to the individuation of actions and other events against objections raised by Alvin I Goldman and others. It is argued that, ironically, Goldman's rival 'multiplying' account is itself vulnerable to these objections, whereas Davidson's account survives them. Although claims that the unifier-multiplier dispute is not really substantive are shown to be unfounded, some room for limited agreement over the ontological status of events is indicated. Davidson's causal criterion of event identity is then defended against charges of triviality or inadequacy. It is concluded that Davidson's criterion is not primarily a criterion for arriving at particular judgments of individuation, but a metaphysical standard for the correctness of such judgments, however arrived at.

PFEIFFER, Raymond S. The Central Distinction in the Theory of Corporate Moral Personhood. J Bus Ethics, 9(6), 473-480, Je 90.

Peter French has argued that conglomerate collectivities such as business corporations are moral persons and that aggregate collectivities such as lynch mobs are not. Two arguments are advanced to show that French's claim is flawed. First, the distinction between aggregates and conglomerates is, at best, a distinction of degree, not kind. Moreover, some aggregates show evidence of moral personhood. Second, French's criterion for distinguishing aggregates and conglomerates is based on inadequate grounds. Application of the criterion to specific cases requires an additional judgment of a pragmatic nature which undermines any attempt to demonstrate French's thesis that actual conglomerates are moral persons and aggregates are not. Thus, French's theory is seriously lacking both empirical basis and empirical relevance.

PFISTER, Lauren. Liang Qichao and the Problematic of Social Change (in Serbo-Croatian). Filozof Istraz, 29(2), 391-413, 1989.

After providing a brief historical background to his work, this essay develops the problem of social change as found in Liang Qichao's early writings (1902-1903) from Japan. In particular, it focuses on certain sections of his highly influential series of articles entitled "The Theory of the New Citizen." Utilizing Paul Ricoeur's fourfold hermeneutic analysis of text and his threefold conception of ideology, the arguments of Liang regarding the need for China to transcend its traditional moorings in Confucian moral philosophy are revealed. In this process, Liang's complex personality, his ideological critiques, and his propagandistic tendencies are all sifted out, so that the major philosophical aporia regarding social change in Liang's philosophy is identified. A brief reflection on the interest of contemporary Chinese scholars in Liang provides some sense of the current status of Liang's philosophical impact as well as points out its analogue in contemporary China's philosophical concerns.

PFRIMMER, Theo. Lieux de l'identité freudienne: Judaïsme et Kultur. Rev Int Phil, 43(171), 540-570, 1989.

PHAN, Peter C. Gender Roles in the History of Salvation: Man and Woman in the Thought of Paul Evdokimov. Heythrop J, 31(1), 53-66, Ja 90.

PHELAN, Anne and GARRISON, James W. Toward a Feminist Poetic of Critical Thinking. Proc Phil Educ, 45, 304-314, 1989.

PHELPS, Lonnie D and SHARPLIN, Arthur. A Stakeholder Apologetic for Management. Bus Prof Ethics J, 8(2), 41-53, Sum 89.

Whom does management serve? The classical theory of the firm assumes that management acts to maximize shareholder wealth. From an agency theory perspective management is viewed as servant (agent) of a variety of constituents (principals). The shareholder may not be preeminent. Each group—communities, creditors, customers, employees, and shareholders—claims throughputs of value commensurate with its power to engage management as agent in its transactions with other stakeholders.

PHILIP, Franklin (trans) and FERRY, Luc and RENAUT, Alain. *Heidegger and Modernity*. Chicago, Univ of Chicago Pr, 1990

The authors investigate the debate within French intellectualism regarding the relationship of Heidegger and Nazism. They consider the relations between Heidegger's phenomenology and his politics, and conclude that Heidegger's critique against modernity is flawed by ambiguities. (staff)

PHILIPPOT-RENIERS, Annie. "Die abgekehrte Seite der Sprache: Zum Briefwechsel Rilke-Pasternak-Cvetaeva" in *Cultural Hermeneutics of Modern Art: Essays in Honor of Jan Aler*, DETHIER, Hubert (ed), 261-271. Amsterdam, Rodopi, 1989.

PHILIPS, Michael. Must Rational Preferences Be Transitive? Phil Quart, 39(157), 477-483, O 89.

Preferences for states of affairs based on more than one criteria can be both rational and intransitive. One class of intransitivities occurs when a criterion that is subordinate with respect to certain pairwise choices becomes dominant with respect to others. This change in ranking can occur when the difference between objects with respect to the criterion passes a threshold. (When the difference is below the threshold, criterion *a* dominates criterion *b*; when it passes the threshold criterion *b* dominates criterion *a*.)

PHILIPSE, Herman. The Absolute Network Theory of Language and Traditional Epistemology. Inquiry, 33(2), 127-178, Je 90.

Paul Churchland provides us with the intellectual tools for constructing a unified scientific *Weltanschauung*. His network theory of language implies a provocative view of the relation between science and common sense. This paper contains a critical examination of Churchland's network theory of language, which is the foundation of his philosophy. It is argued that the network theory should be seen as deriving its point from traditional empiricism. The network theory enables the empiricist to resist the phenomenalistic temptations inherent in his position, and to build a realist philosophy on the basis of the representative theory of perception. This interpretation is confirmed by the fact that the representative theory is presupposed by Churchland's main argument in favour of the network view. (edited)

PHILLIPS, D C. Directive Teaching, Indoctrination, and the Values Education of Children. Soc Theor Pract, 15(3), 339-353, Fall 89.

After revisiting arguments for rejecting indoctrinatory methods in education, the paper focuses upon the defence of directive moral education by George Sher and William Bennett in the *Journal of Philosophy* (1982). They argue that directive methods are acceptable for use with young children prior to the age of reason. In reply, it is argued that this is self-defeating: if children cannot use reason then they will not be able to apply the principles that have been directively inculcated, and so these children will not be able to act morally or use principles to deal with novel situations.

PHILLIPS, D Z. From Coffee to Carmelites. Philosophy, 65(251), 19-38, Ja 90.

PHILLIPS, Linda M. Specific Content Knowledge is Not Necessary for Good Reading. Proc Phil Educ, 45, 163-167, 1989.

The claim that increased knowledge and information (i.e., content) about a subject is the major determinant of improved reading is challenged. It misrepresents the relation between decoding and comprehension, and the role of background knowledge in comprehension. I argue that decoding and comprehension go hand-in-hand. Evidence from my research is used to show that differences in comprehension occurred *not* on the basis of having knowledge specific to the reading context, but rather on the basis of students' ability to think critically with the information available to them, that is information from their general background knowledge and the text.

PHILLIPSON, N T. *Hume.* New York, St Martin's Pr, 1989

PIATEK, Zdzislawa. Anti-Anthropocentrism as a Value in Science. Rep Phil, 13, 73-81, 1989.

PICLIN, Michel. Philosophie et Musique selon Schopenhauer. Schopenhauer Jahr, 70, 94-106, 1989.

PIEPER, Josep. El filosofar y el lenguaje. Anu Filosof, 21(1), 73-83, 1988.

PIERCE, Christine. AIDS and *Bowers versus Hardwick*. J Soc Phil, 20(3), 21-32, Wint 89.

PIERRE, C and LORVELLEC, Y (trans). *Ortega y Gasset: Aurore de la Raison Historique*. France, Klincksieck, 1986

PIETERSMA, H. Knowledge and Being in Merleau-Ponty. Man World, 23(2), 205-223, Ap 90.

This is an examination of Merleau-Ponty's metaphysical doctrine as found in Part Two, Chapter 3, of the *Phenomenology of Perception*. I attempt to set out the argument, which begins with a certain analysis of the distinctively cognitive nature of sensuous-bodily awareness and ends with the metaphysical thesis that time is the measure of being. Interpreting the horizonality of perception as a basic metaphysical fact, he suggests that for both percipient and object *to be* is to occupy a place in a field which in the last analysis is temporal, a thesis which makes the cognitive status of

perception itself problematic.

PIETERSMA, Henry. The Problem of Knowledge and Phenomenology. Phil Phenomenol Res, 50(1), 27-47, S 89.

PIETIG, Jeanne. A Critique of the Deconstructionist Account of Gender Equity and Education. Educ Phil Theor, 21(1), 20,22-24, 1989.

PIÉTRI, Gaston. L'indifférence religieuse: un aboutissement. Etudes, 371(4), 371-383, O 89.

PIETY, Marilyn. The Problem with the *Fragments*: Kierkegaard on Subjectivity and Truth. Auslegung, 16(1), 43-57, Wint 90.

Kierkegaard's stated objective in the *Fragments* is to compare the "Socratic" interpretation of the relation of the individual to the truth with a possible alternative. The thesis of this article is that the "Interlude" section of the *Fragments* represents a deliberate subversion of the pretended objectivity of the work. The article concludes that Kierkegaard's aim, in the *Fragments*, is to reveal indirectly that an objective resolution to the question of the manner in which one is related to the truth is impossible and that hence, such a resolution must come by way of an appeal to one's subjective experience.

PIEVATOLO, M Chiara. Ermeneutica e storia nel pensiero di Karl Löwith. Arch Stor Cult, 2, 63-83, 1989.

PIGDEN, Charles R. Geach on 'Good'. Phil Quart, 40(159), 129-154, Ap 90.

According to Geach (1956) 'good' is attributive. This disposes of a non-natural property of goodness answering to the predicative 'good' and opens the way for a naturalistic and Aristotelian ethic. I argue that 'good' has predicative and attributive uses. Moorean goodness may be metaphysically suspect, but it is grammatically in order. In everyday contexts 'good' can be both action-guiding and descriptive. 'Good' must be understood in terms of contextually specified requirements, and can only be used to found a naturalistic ethic if the requirements themselves are 'naturalistic'. But you cannot extract credible naturalistic requirements from the human biological function.

PIGDEN, Charles R. Ought-Implies-Can: Erasmus Luther and R M Hare. Sophia (Australia), 29(1), 2-30, Ap 90.

There is an antinomy in Hare's thought between Ought-Implies-Can and No-Indicatives-from-Imperatives. Luther resolved this antinomy in the 16th century. He thought the necessity of Divine foreknowledge made it impossible for sinners to do otherwise than sin. Erasmus objected that this violates Ought-Implies-Can. Luther showed that Ought-Implies-Can is not a logical truth. Ought conversationally implies Can, only because Ought-Implies-Can is a background *moral* belief. If Ought-Implies-Can is treated as a *moral* principle, Erasmus's argument for free will can be revived. But it does not 'prove' Pelagianism as Luther supposed.

PIKE, Nelson. Alston on Plantinga and Soft Theological Determinism. Int J Phil Relig, 27(1-2), 17-39, Ap 90.

PILGRIM, Richard. Reply to Kenneth K Inada. Phil East West, 39(4), 457, O 89.

PILLAY, A and BALDWIN, J T. Semisimple Stable and Superstable Groups. Annals Pure Applied Log, 45(2), 105-127, D 89.

This paper explores the relation between various notions of simplicity (no normal subgroups) and definable simplicity (no definable normal subgroups) in stable groups. The importance of definability concepts in the study of algebraic groups is an underlying theme. It concludes with a technical analysis of superstable groups with monomial U-rank.

PILOT, Harald. Kant's Theory of the Autonomy of Reflective Judgement as an Ethics of Experiential Thinking. Nous, 24(1), 111-135, Mr 90.

PINCH, Trevor J. "The Externalization of Observation: An Example from Modern Physics" in *Scientific Knowledge Socialized*, HRONSZKY, Imre (ed), 225-244. Norwell, Kluwer, 1989.

PINCHES, Charles. Christian Pacifism and Theodicy: The Free Will Defense in the Thought of John H Yoder. Mod Theol, 5(3), 239-255, Ap 89.

In this paper I draw on the Christian theological pacifism of John H Yoder to construct a "theodicy" not susceptible to the charges of ahistorical abstraction leveled recently by Ken Surin against the theodicies of contemporary philosophers such as Plantinga and Swinburne. While Yoder's alternative is more promising than its more philosophical cousins it is open to further criticism as well, which criticism I offer in the paper's final section.

PINCHES, Charles. Hauerwas Represented: A Response to Muray. Process Stud, 18(2), 95-101, Sum 89.

The express purpose of this article is to defend the thought of Stanley Hauerwas against criticisms leveled from the process-relational perspective of Leslie Muray. In addition, theological challenges are made of process theology and affinities between the Christian virtue thinking of Hauerwas and process thought as articulated by Muray are cautiously noted.

PINCIONE, Guido M. Generalizaciones y explicación de la historiografía. Analisis Filosof, 6(2), 125-137, N 86.

PINEAU, Lois. Date-Rape: A Feminist Analysis. Law Phil, 8(2), 217-243, Ag 89.

This paper shows how the mythology surrounding rape enters into a criterion of 'reasonableness' which operates through the legal system to make women vulnerable to unscrupulous victimization. It explores the possibility for changes in legal procedures and presumptions that would better serve women's interests and leave them less vulnerable to sexual violence. This requires that we reformulate the criterion of consent in terms of what is reasonable from a woman's point of view.

PINHEIRO, Ulysses and VIDEIRA, Antonio A P. A ética do poder na *História da sexualidade* de Michel Foucault. Manuscrito, 12(2), 35-48, O 89.

This article examines some concepts and hypotheses presented by Foucault in the first volume of his *Histoire de la sexualité—La volonté de savoir*—from the vantage point of the reformulation made in the second volume—*L'usage des plaisirs*. The study of this change is important to understand Foucault's work, since it reveals the transformation of one of his fundamental concepts: that of power. In *L'usage des plaisirs* Foucault separates the ethical sphere from that of power. The main question that guides our investigation is: what is the role of ethics in the context described in *La volonté de savoir*, in which power has a central place? Or: how does ethics (subjectivation) act in the dichotomy subject *x* object in the human sciences (which have the subject as its object)? Is it separated from power? With these questions we intend to emphasize the differences between the two first volumes of Foucault's *Histoire de la sexualité*.

PINILLOS, José Luis. Schopenhauer y la psicología. Rev Filosof (Spain), 2, 43-52, 1989.

PINKARD, Terry. The Categorial Satisfaction of Self-Reflexive Reason. Bull Hegel Soc Gt Brit, 19, 5-17, Spr-Sum 89.

PINKARD, Terry. How Kantian Was Hegel? Rev Metaph, 43(4), 831-838, Je 90.

PINKAVA, J. A Philosophical (Hermeneutical) Survey of Modern Abstract Art (in Czechoslovakian). Filozof Cas, 37(4), 553-574, 1989.

This article analyzes some interpretations of modern (primarily abstract) art in the period, beginning with the 20th Congress of the Communist Party of the Soviet Union and during the 1960s, predominantly from a Marxist point of view. Doubts were at that time cast on the very sense of such an art, and its importance was acknowledged only in the case of the application of design to certain categories of fine arts. The study goes on to discuss the views, propounded by the two distinguished aestheticians, Lifshic and Reingardt, describing their ideological conclusions as non-Marxist, as being under the sway of obsolete norms. Assuming the standpoints of dialectical Marxism, the author of this article goes out of his way to rehabilitate abstractionism as well as later trends in arts, restoring them to their previous positions from which they had been dislodged by ideologically deformed interpretations. (edited)

PINSON, Jean-Claude. Philosophie, poésie et contingent. Arch Phil, 53(2), 213-228, Ap-Je 90.

Even when it proposes, as in the works of Hegel, to "save" the phenomena in full, the philosophical discourse does not really succeed in seizing (and at once disdains) the *this* in its most contingent individuality. The poetic speech is more capable of catching it, as this article will attempt to show it from an *incipit* of a novel by Claude Simon. The poetic speech makes thus the truth of an unknown dimension of the being which Heidegger calls Earth emerge. Alone an ontology of the difference is liable to provide this poetic valorisation of the infra-conceptual with an adequate "home." As far as literary hermeneutics are concerned, it results in the necessity of a method which must be particularly heedful of the most factual details through which this veiled dimension of the being forms itself.

PINTON, Giorgio (trans) and HIDALGO-SERNA, Emilio. Metaphorical Language, Rhetoric, and *Comprehensio*: J L Vives and M Nizolio. Phil Rhet, 23(1), 1-11, 1990.

PINTON, Giorgio (trans) and NOAKES, Susan (trans) and BETTI, Emilio. The Principles of New Science of G B Vico and the Theory of Historical Interpretation. New Vico Studies, 6, 31-50, 1988.

PIPPIN, Robert B. Hegel and Category Theory. Rev Metaph, 43(4), 839-848, Je 90.

PIPPIN, Robert. Hegel's Idealism: Prospects. Bull Hegel Soc Gt Brit, 19, 28-41, Spr-Sum 89.

PIPPIN, Robert. "Irony and Affirmation in Nietzsche's *Thus Spoke Zarathustra*" in *Nietzsche's New Seas: Explorations in Philosophy, Aesthetics, and Politics*, GILLESPIE, Michael Allen (ed), 45-71. Chicago, Univ of Chicago Pr, 1989.

PIRLOT, Marc. Minimal Representation of a Semiorder. Theor Decis, 28(2), 109-141, Mr 90.

In a multicriteria decision problem it may happen that the preference of the decision maker on some criterion is modeled by means of a semiorder structure. If the available information is qualitative, one often needs a numerical representation of the semiorder. We investigate the set of representations of a semiorder and show that, once a unit has been fixed, there exists a minimal representation. This representation can be calculated by linear programming and exhibits some interesting properties: all values are integer multiples of the unit and are as scattered as possible in the sense that, in the set of all representations contained in the same bounded interval, the minimal representation is a representation for which the minimal distance between two values is maximal. The minimal representation can also be interpreted as a generalisation of the rank function associated to linear orders.

PITKIN, Hanna Fenichel. Slippery Bentham: Some Neglected Cracks in the Foundation of Utilitarianism. Polit Theory, 18(1), 104-131, F 90.

Bentham's theorizing displays recurrent patterns of unacknowledged ambiguity confounding conventional criticism. The "Greatest Happiness Principle" can have no unique solutions. Central terms expand and contract in meaning unpredictably, creating and dissolving tautologies. The full utilitarian system involves so many interrelated variables, each unstable in meaning (psychology vs. ethics vs. prudence vs. legislation; private vs. public; apparent vs. real interest; natural harmony vs. legislation vs. education for prudence vs. education for benevolence), that proving it *cannot* be made coherent is difficult. Nevertheless, it probably cannot.

PITOWSKY, Itamar. The Physical Church Thesis and Physical Computational Complexity. Iyyun, 39(1), 81-99, Ja 90.

PITOWSKY, Itamar. *Quantum Probability—Quantum Logic*. New York, Springer, 1989

PITSON, Anthony. Perception: Belief and Experience. S J Phil, 28(1), 55-76, Spr 90.

The central theme of this paper is the relation in perception between belief and experience. I argue that while nonepistemic theorists of perception are right that perception generally involves the occurrence of experience which is not itself reducible to belief and its acquisition, this leaves the essential claim of the epistemic theory intact. For while perception typically involves, in addition to belief, experience with a character which reflects both the modality in which it occurs and the nature of what is perceived, the occurrence of experience with this dual character is dependent upon the epistemic component of perception.

PITT, Leyland and NEL, Deon. Business Ethics: Defining the Twilight Zone. J Bus Ethics, 8(10), 781-791, O 89.

This paper examines the issue of ethics policy in organizations. While the actions of top management may be the single most important factor in fostering corporate behaviour of a high ethical standard, there should be policy where policy is needed. The perceptions of three managerial groups—top- marketing- and purchasing managers—are compared regarding firstly, whether they see a need for policy on a range of ethically contentious issues, and secondly whether they believe there is policy covering these issues in their own organizations. No significant differences between the three groups of managers were found, either with regard to their perceptions of needs for policy, or as far as the existence thereof is concerned. However, an overall comparison of need for policy and the existence of policy showed a significant difference on the scenarios presented to respondents. Furthermore, the study identifies grey areas of ethics in business where managers believe policy is needed, but is not perceived to exist. The use of an ethics policy matrix in organizations is suggested as a practical tool for the examination of ethically contentious issues.

PITTS, Andrew M and TAYLOR, Paul. A Note on Russell's Paradox in Locally Cartesian Closed Categories. Stud Log, 48(3), 377-387, S 89.

PIZER, John. Aesthetic Consciousness and Aesthetic Non-Differentiation: Gadamer, Schiller, and Lukács. Phil Today, 33(1), 63-72, Spr 89.

In *Truth and Method*, Gadamer condemns the tendency to make the realm of art an autonomous sphere purged of quotidian reality. This tendency stems from the "abstraction" of "aesthetic consciousness," and leads either to the elimination of the real world (Schiller) or the dissolution of the artwork (Lukács). Gadamer's own doctrine of "aesthetic non-differentiation" attempts to overcome such abstracting by denying a distinction between the artwork's aesthetic component and its character as an experienced phenomenon. This essay would demonstrate that Schiller and Lukács are more in concordance with Gadamer in this aspect of aesthetics than Gadamer realizes.

PIZZO, Giovanni. "Malita" e "odium Dei" nella dottrina della volontà di Giovanni Duns Scoto. Riv Filosof Neo-Scolas, 81(3), 393-415, Jl-S 89.

PIZZO, Giovanni. La giustizia nella dottrina della volontà di Giovanni Duns Scoto. Riv Filosof Neo-Scolas, 81(1), 3-26, Ja-Mr 89.

PLA I CARRERA, Josep. Alfred Tarski i la teoria de conjunts. Theoria (Spain), 4(11), 343-417, F-My 89.

The work on set theory made by A Tarski in the years 1924-1950 is very interesting, but little known. We develop partial questions in set theory in the moment that A Tarski intervenes and his contributions and also influences. The principal aims in this development are (1) the axiom of choice (AC) and its equivalents; (2) the general continuum hypothesis (GCH) and the AC; (3) the dual trichotomy principle; (4) the inaccessible cardinals and its relation with the AC and the GCH; (5) the notion of finite set and its relation with the AC and the GCH; (6) the almost disjoint set and its relation with the GCH; and finally, (7) the results in Berkeley.

PLACE, Ullin T. Concept Acquisition and Ostensive Learning: A Response to Professor Stemmer. Behaviorism, 17(2), 141-145, Fall 89.

The alternative offered by Professor Stemmer to cognitivist theories of the process whereby general terms acquire their meaning is criticised in its turn on the grounds that it presents an oversimplified view of the complex processes involved in the acquisition of word meanings.

PLACE, Ullin T. "Low Claim Assertions" in Cause, Mind, and Reality: Essays Honoring C B Martin, HEIL, John (ed), 121-135. Norwell, Kluwer, 1989.

'Low claim assertions' is the title of an unpublished paper, now lost, written by C B Martin in 1954. Martin argued that the effect of prefacing an assertion with a phrase such as 'It seems', 'looks', 'sounds' or 'feels to me as if' is to withdraw that claim that things actually are as they seem to be, thereby converting an assertion about the public world into a description of a private experience. This paper is cited as the source both of the writer's discussion of the 'phenomenological fallacy' in 'Is consciousness a brain process?' and of J J C Smart's concept of 'topic neutrality'.

PLACHER, William C. Unapologetic Theology: A Christian Voice in a Pluralistic Conversation. Louisville, Westminster Pr, 1989

Recent trends in philosophy provide an interesting context for doing Christian theology. The Enlightenment project of finding some universally secure foundation for rational inquiry seems to have failed (even in sophisticated recent versions like those of Habermas and Rawls). But that need not drive us to the kind of radical relativism represented by Rorty, Foucault, and some followers of Wittgenstein. A middle path traced out by Gadamer, Walzer, and MacIntyre, among others, offers a model for thinking about controversies between theology and science, dialogues among different religions, and the debate between revisionist and postliberal theology.

PLANT, Sadie. The Situationist International: A Case of Spectacular Neglect. Rad Phil, 55, 3-10, Sum 90.

PLANTINGA, Alvin. The Nature of Necessity. New York, Clarendon/Oxford Pr, 1989

This book, one of the first full-length studies of the modalities to emerge from the debate to which Saul Kripke, David Lewis, Ruth Marcus and others have contributed, is an exploration and defence of the notion of modality de re, the idea that objects have both essential and accidental properties. The argument is developed by means of the notion of possible worlds and ranges over key problems including the nature of essence, trans-world identity, negative existential propositions, and the existence of unactual objects in other possible worlds. In the final chapter the author applies his logical theories to the elucidation of two problems in the philosophy of religion: the problem of evil and the ontological argument. The first of these, the problem of reconciling the moral perfection and omnipotence of God with the existence of evil, can, he concludes, be resolved, and the second given a sound formulation. The book ends with an appendix on Quine's objection to quantified modal logic. This paperback edition is a reprint of the original work, which was first published in 1974. (edited)

PLANTY-BONJOUR, M Guy (and others). Philosophie et religion selon Hegel. Bull Soc Fr Phil, 84(1), 1-32, Ja-Mr 90.

PLATT, David. Intimations of Divinity. New York, Lang, 1989

The book explores the perplexing issue of our knowledge of God. Must we line up with those who believe that any knowledge of God is impossible, or should we agree with those who feel that knowledge of God is strongly established? Relying on neither formal proof nor appeal to revelation, the book argues for a creative middle ground where divinity manifests itself through intimations in experience. The work argues that divinity manifests

itself at the phenomenological level, while explicit ontological commitment is made when one embraces a theistic God. Experience of divinity is contrasted with experience of things and persons.

PLATTS, Mark. What Should a Theory of Meaning Do? Critica, 20(59), 43-67, Ag 88.

PLEGER, Wolfgang H. Heideggers Kritik der neuzeitlichen Wissenschaft und Technik. Z Phil Forsch, 43(4), 641-655, O-D 89.

PLOMER, Aurora. Merleau-Ponty on Sensations. J Brit Soc Phenomenol, 21(2), 153-163, My 90.

Merleau-Ponty's Phenomenology of Perception starts with an attack on the concept of 'sensation'. I argue that Merleau-Ponty's objections are inspired by the Gestaltists but that Merleau-Ponty departs from the Gestaltists in the general doubts which he raises about the capacity of science to explain perceptual phenomena.

PLUMER, Gilbert. Mustn't Whatever is Referred to Exist? S J Phil, 27(4), 511-528, Wint 89.

Some hold that proper names and indexicals are "Kaplan rigid": they designate their designata even in worlds where the designata don't exist. An argument they give for this is based on the analogy between time and modality. It is shown how this argument gains forcefulness at the expense of carefulness. Then the argument is criticized as forming a part of an inconsistent philosophical framework, the one with which David Kaplan and others operate. An alternative account of a certain class of negative existentials is developed, one which eliminates both the inconsistency and the need for Kaplan rigidity.

PLUZANSKI, Tadeusz and KISIEL, Krystyna (trans) and KISIEL, Chester (trans). The Dialogue of Grand Theories for Peace. Dialec Hum, 14(1), 173-184, Wint 87.

POAGUE, Leland and CADBURY, William. The Possibility of Film Criticism. J Aes Educ, 23(4), 5-22, Wint 89.

This essay considers the relevance of Monroe Beardsley's aesthetics to film criticism. Against the view that "aesthetic" criticism prizes the "organic" over the historical it is observed that Beardsley rejects "organic" as a value-term and that Beardsley's view of interpretation is exactly a matter of connecting work to world and in accord with knowledges which are deeply connected to (changing) social reality. Against the view that aesthetic criticism is ideologically blind to its complicity with the status quo it is observed that Beardsley provides extended and subtle examples (prefiguring much latter-day film criticism) or moral analyses of art works.

PODREZ, Ewa. Die ethischen Ansichten von P Professor Tadeusz Slipko (in Polish). Stud Phil Christ, 25(1), 9-46, 1989.

Der Aufsatz ist ein Versuch, die Hauptideen der ethischen Ansichten des Professors Tadeusz Slipko SJ zu charakterisieren. Das wissenschaftliche Werk dieses Verfassers auf dem Gebiet der Ethik konzentriert sich hauptsächlich um zwei Faden herum: einerseits um die Vertiefung und Befestigung depositi doctrinalis der christlichen Moralphilosophie in der Thomistischen Richtung, und anderseits um die inhaltliche und formale Bereicherung dieser Philosophie mit neuen Problemen, Untersuchungen und Entscheidungen. Die beiden erwähnten Faden oder Ideen haben sowohl das Slipkos Programm der Ethik in Einzelheiten als auch Seine Forschungslinien bestimmt.

POGGE, Thomas W. Realizing Rawls. Ithaca, Cornell Univ Pr, 1989

Part One defends Rawls's focus on basic social institutions, and his maximin idea, against the criticisms of Nozick and Sandel. Part Two critically develops Rawls's criterion of justice—accommodating basic social and economic needs under the first principle; education, employment, and health care under the opportunity principle; and leisure under the difference principle. Part Three shows, on internal and external grounds, that Rawls's conception must today apply to the world at large. Properly specified, Rawls's criterion yields plausible priorities for global institutional reform and can help move international relations from modus vivendi toward overlapping consensus on values.

POHLENZ, Gerd. Phänomenale Realität und naturalistische Philosophie. Z Phil Forsch, 44(1), 106-142, 1990.

POINT, F. Groups With Identities. Annals Pure Applied Log, 45(2), 171-188, D 89.

We characterize the soluble groups which admit a disjunction of monoidal identities. This notion has been introduced by M Boffa and is equivalent to admitting the elimination of inverses. We use the result of Rosenblatt that a finitely generated soluble group which does not contain the free monoid on two generators is quasi-nilpotent. We also obtain partial results for the class of elementary amenable groups and its subclass of locally finite groups.

POIRIER, Suzanne and BRAUNER, Daniel J. The Voices of the Medical

Record. Theor Med, 11(1), 29-39, Mr 90.

The medical record, as a managerial, historic, and legal document, serves many purposes. Although its form may be well established and many of the cases documented in it 'routine' in medical experience, what is written in the medical record nevertheless records decisions and actions of individuals. Viewed as an interpretive 'text', it can itself become the object of interpretation. This essay applies literary theory and methodology to the structure, content, and writing style(s) of an actual medical record for the purpose of exploring the relationship between the forms and language of medical discourse and the daily decisions surrounding medical treatment. The medical record is shown to document not only the absence of a consistent treatment plan for the patient studied but also a breakdown in communication between different health professionals caring for that patient. The paper raises questions about the kind of education being given to house staff in this instance. The essay concludes with a consideration of how such situations might be more generally avoided.

POIZAT, Bruno and BOUSCAREN, Elisabeth. Des belles paires aux beaux uples. J Sym Log, 53(2), 434-442, Je 88.

POJMAN, Louis P (ed). *Ethical Theory: Classical and Contemporary Readings*. Belmont, Wadsworth, 1989

POJMAN, Louis P. Kierkegaard on Faith and Freedom. Int J Phil Relig, 27(1-2), 41-61, Ap 90.

This article is a defense of my position on Kierkegaard's views on faith and freedom against the charge of David Wisdo that I have misconstrued those views. I argue that (1) Kierkegaard is a volitionist, believing that we can obtain beliefs by willing to have them; (2) faith, for Kierkegaard, involves the will; and (3) Kierkegaard is engaged in giving a philosophical explanation of faith.

POLAKOW, Avron. The Inconsistency of Putnam's Internal Realism. Manuscrito, 12(1), 39-53, Ap 89.

Putnam's new theory of internal realism has replaced his previous theory of metaphysical realism. It is not always clear why Putnam now calls himself a "realist." In this paper it is claimed that Putnam still relies on rigid designation as a ground for realism, even if rigid designation has been stripped of its metaphysically realist interpretation. This papers seeks to trace the reasons for this, beginning with how he interprets "realism" (part I), his treatment of Tarski's criterion T of correspondence (part II), his own principle of indeterminacy of reference (part III), and its comparison to the principle of rigid designation (part IV). In the final section, it is shown that the watered down principle of rigid designation is too weak for any realist position, internal or otherwise (part V).

POLAKOW, Valerie. On Being a Meaning-Maker: Young Children's Experiences of Reading. Thinking, 6(1), 9-14, 1985.

The author uses a social phenomenological approach to explore the meaning of literacy for a young child. The experiences and perceptions of four young kindergarten children are chronicled, as they reflect on what it means to read. The author concludes that reading has been "de-meaned" by an atomized storyless curriculum, severing the engagement with text, and argues that experiencing the storied lived-world is critical for young children on the brink of emergent literacy. Promoting the transformative possibilities of meaning-making gives a word-world experience to young children and makes a lived encounter with literacy possible.

POLANOWSKA-SYGULSKA, Beata. Two Visions of Liberty—Berlin and Hayek. Rep Phil, 13, 61-72, 1989.

POLANSKY, Ronald and KUCZEWSKI, Mark. Speech and Thought, Symbol and Likeness: Aristotle's *De Interpretatione* 16a3-9. Apeiron, 23(1), 51-63, Mr 90.

It is crucial for understanding the opening passage of Aristotle's *De Interpretatione* to comprehend several key terms within it: "symbol," "sign," "likeness," and "affections of the soul." These have recently been taken in diverse, and often unlikely, ways. We connect "likeness" and "affections of the soul" to the doctrine of cognition in the *De Anima*, which is alluded to in the passage, and we offer a view of "symbol" and "sign" which fits the evidence. These accounts of the details of the passage reveal its general meaning, which is basically that attributed to it by traditional commentators.

POLIN, Raymond. "La fonction politique des intellectuels" in *Culture et Politique/Culture and Politics*, CRANSTON, Maurice (ed), 55-66. Hawthorne, de Gruyter, 1988.

La fonction politique des intellectuels pose un problème si intensément vécu à l'époque actuelle qu'on ne peut y voir clair et le considérer sans passion qu'à condition de prendre assez de hauteur et de le poser tout d'abord dans les termes philosophiques les plus généraux. On s'aperçoit alors qu'il s'agit d'un problème très classique: le problème du rapport de la théorie et de la pratique, ou en tout cas, celui du théoricien et de l'homme d'action.

POLKA, Brayton. Interpretation and the Bible: The Dialectic of Concept and Content in Interpretive Reading. J Speculative Phil, 4(1), 66-82, 1990.

POLLARD, D E B. Authors Without Paradox. Brit J Aes, 29(4), 363-366, Autumn 89.

Walter Glannon has recently argued that no communicable meaning can be imputed to fictional texts. The irreferential nature of such texts is taken to deprive them of anything other than subjective content. In reply, it is argued that Glannon's case is based on faulty assumptions and the misapplication of some recent work in the field of propositional attitudes, more specifically his use of the distinction between 'wide' and 'narrow' content. He thus fails to substantiate his claim that literary authorship is inherently paradoxical.

POLLARD, Denis E B. Troubles with Fiction. Philosophy, 65(251), 95-98, Ja 90.

POLLARD, Stephen. *Philosophical Introduction to Set Theory*. Notre Dame, Univ Notre Dame Pr, 1990

This book uses philosophical reflection on the foundations of mathematics as motivation for a technical survey of the rudiments of Cantorian set theory. Its aim is to make transfinite set theory intelligible to the educated nonspecialist while clarifying some aspects of the philosophical debate swirling around the foundations of the formal sciences.

POLLOCK, John L. Understanding the Language of Thought. Phil Stud, 58(1-2), 95-120, Ja-F 90.

This paper develops a theory of content for the language of thought. Different kinds of content are distinguished. (1) It is argued that introspection apprises us only of syntactical features, not semantical features. (2) A functional account of narrow content is proposed. (3) Propositional content is defined in terms of narrow content together with indexical parameters. (4) Content-ascriptions using "that"-clauses are analyzed in terms of the author's general theory of language (in *Language and Thought*). "That"-clauses describe contents, but do not uniquely identify either propositional content or narrow content. (Note that this is an early version of material updated in *How to Build a Person*.)

POLOVINKIN, S M and FLORENSKII, P V. P A Florenskii's Review of His Work. Soviet Stud Phil, 28(3), 40-51, Wint 89-90.

POLS, Edward. Realism versus Antirealism: The Venue of the Linguistic Consensus. Rev Metaph, 43(4), 717-749, Je 90.

POLT, Richard F H. The Role of Self-Knowledge in the *Critique of Pure Reason*. Auslegung, 16(2), 165-173, Sum 90.

PÖLTNER, Günther. El arte ante las exigencias de la moral. Anu Filosof, 20(2), 95-109, 1987.

POMA, Andrea. La metafora dei "due labirinti" e le sue implicazioni nel pensiero di Leibniz. Filosofia, 41(1), 13-62, Ja-Ap 90.

PONFERRADA, Gustavo Eloy. Teoría y praxis: evolución de estos conceptos. Sapientia, 44(174), 273-294, O-D 89.

PONSSARD, Jean-Pierre. Self Enforceable Paths in Extensive Form Games. Theor Decis, 29(1), 69-83, Jl 90.

This paper explores the idea of forward induction for extensive games. It interprets this idea as a general behavioral principle the technical details of which have to be worked out in each specific case. Because of its cooperative ingredient, this approach should be contrasted with the usual approaches of noncooperative game theory which are rooted in individual rationality.

PONTON, Lionel. Emmanuel Kant: La liberté comme droit de l'homme et l'"Idée" de république. Laval Theol Phil, 45(3), 361-378, O 89.

Tributaire de l'Aufklärung et contemporain de la Révolution française, Kant est le premier grand défenseur de la liberté qui consiste "à faire un *usage public* de sa raison dans tous les domaines" et le premier à formuler, à l'adresse des rois, ce qu'il considère comme "le devoir moral" de tendre vers la constitution *républicaine*, la seule qui soit parfaitement conforme aux droits de l'homme. S'il qualifie ceux-ci "d'attributs indissociables de l'essence des citoyens", il ne les associe pas toujours aux droits strictement politiques. Même dans la constitution républicaine *selon la lettre*, seuls les citoyens dits actifs ont droit de vote et peuvent accéder aux responsabilités publiques. Quand les rois autocrates gouvernent "selon la méthode républicaine", ce que Kant juge acceptable faute de mieux, le peuple n'a pas à donner son consentement à la législation et il n'a pas droit de vote. (edited)

POOLE, Ross. Nietzsche: The Subject of Morality. Rad Phil, 54, 2-9, Spr 90.

Nietzsche's genealogy of morals is also a genealogy of a certain conception of moral agency, involving a distinction between the subject and its actions, freedom of will, and guilt. Nietzsche argued that this conception is a fiction created and sustained by the reactive hatred of those who are afraid to act. The project of 'becoming what one is' aimed at reconstructing a self which is beyond morality. Nietzsche's 'positive nihilism', the doctrine of eternal recurrence, and the concept of the *übermensch*, are all aspects of the project of self-making and the overcoming both of morality and the moral subject.

POPA, Cornel. Logic of Action, Efficacy and Efficiency. Phil Log, 32(3-4), 235-248, Jl-D 88.

The aim of this paper is first to pay homage to the Polish school of praxiology and especially to one of its leaders and outstanding scientists, Professor Tadeusz Pszczolowski. Second, I intend to reveal the intrinsic connection between a more comprehensive understanding of the logic of action and descriptive and appreciative praxiology. Third, I wish to outline the praxiological relevance of the concept of method and the possibility to analyse it in the frame of modal logic and logical theory of human actions. Fourth, I would like to define two main praxiological concepts, efficacy and efficiency, by using teleological, performative and axiological functors. Further down, some short remarks are made on the relation between actional initial states, goal states and sequences of operations or programs as instrumentalization of the goals. We shall conclude our discussion with some remarks on human action rationality from the point of view of the logical theory of action.

POPA, Cornel. Préliminaires à une théorie logique des méthodes pratiques (in Romanian). Rev Filosof (Romania), 36(2), 181-184, Mr-Ap 89.

POPARDA, Oana. Trois lectures cartésiennes de la théorie du gouvernement-liage de N Chomsky. Phil Log, 32(1-2), 81-87, Ja-Je 88.

POPE, N Vivian. The New World Synthesis. Phil Math, 4(1), 23-28, 1989.

On the levels of science which deal with quanta, nature appears more 'cinematographic' than mechanical, its dimensions being observational (i.e., relativistic) video-projections out of pure quantum-information rather than features of any classical, continuous 'void'. This article shows, by means of a computer analogy, how a systematic resynthesis of science might be achieved along these new conceptual lines.

POPE, Stephen J. Love, Moral Values and Proportionalism: A Response to Garth Hallett. Heythrop J, 31(2), 199-205, Ap 90.

POPESCU, Alexandru. La polysémie des coutumes populaires (in Romanian). Rev Filosof (Romania), 35(6), 547-553, N-D 88.

POPKIN, Richard H. "Condorcet's Epistemology and His Politics" in *Knowledge and Politics*, DASCAL, Marcelo (ed), 111-124. Boulder, Westview Pr, 1988.

POPKIN, Richard H. "Newton and Maimonides" in *A Straight Path: Studies in Medieval Philosophy and Culture*, LINK-SALINGER, Ruth (ed), 216-229. Washington, Cath Univ Amer Pr, 1988.

POPKIN, Richard H. Spinoza's Earliest Philosophical Years, 1655-61. Stud Spinozana, 4, 37-55, 1988.

POR, Peter and WALKER, R Scott (trans). Fin de Siècle, End of the "Globe Style"? The Concept of Object in Contemporary Art. Diogenes, 147, 92-110, Fall 89.

The historical style—as it stood when at its peak between the "Lumières" and the turn towards modernism—is the form of creation and existence through which art undertakes the mission of ancient transcendent systems and transforms it into its own categories. The great filiation of the theories of historical style (Wölfflin, Riegl, Walzel) aims at conceptualizing the same ideal: an artistic synthesis—absolute, in terms of construction, relative, in terms of historical phenomenon—between *poiésis* and *techné*, idea and matter. The last blossoming of this artistical ideal was the *"fin de siècle"* period. The turn towards modern in art as well as in criticism happened through a radical break-away from this period and this ideal in general. It is precisely the eternal schism which was to be the creative principle behind, on the one side, the works of the *poiésis*, *eidos* (Eliot, Schönberg, Klee, etc.), and, on the other side, the works of the matter, and *techné* (lettrisme, repetitive music, Max Bill). Modern art and modern criticism are no longer conceived as creating a style.

POREBSKI, Czeslaw. Das Problem der "Zusammensetzung" der Werte. Rep Phil, 13, 15-25, 1989.

PORÉE, Jérôme. L'innocence de l'être-pour la mort. Arch Phil, 52(4), 611-637, O-D 89.

The problem of the beginning of philosophy in a phenomenological reduction instead of the Heideggerian idea of human reality manifested by death is set the apriority of evil with consequences in epistemology, anthropology and ontology.

PÖRN, Ingmar and JONES, Andrew J I. A Rejoinder to Hansson. Synthese, 80(3), 429-432, S 89.

PORTELA FILHO, R N A and DIAS, M F. Teoría de la recursión y lógica. Rev Filosof (Argentina), 2(2), 107-117, N 87.

This expositive paper is devoted to show some relations between logic and recursivity, particularly recursivity as applied to completeness-proof in first order logic.

PORTELLI, John P. Philosophy for Children: An Example of the Public Dimension in Philosophy of Education. Eidos, 7(2), 183-194, D 88.

This paper presents and briefly comments on the development, aims and assumptions of the idea and practice of doing philosophy for children which, it is suggested, fulfills the "public dimension" of philosophy of education. It also outlines possible objections to this endeavour and replies to such objections.

PORTELLI, John P. The Socratic Method and Philosophy for Children. Metaphilosophy, 21(1-2), 141-161, Ja-Ap 90.

The purpose of this article is twofold: (i) to examine the nature of the Socratic method by focusing on the role of the teacher and the nature of questioning; (ii) to explore some of the implications of following the Socratic method in doing philosophy with children by focusing on "facts and discussions," "the Socratic Fallacy," "answers and discussions" and "neutrality and interests." This article offers and defends an interpretation of the Socratic method and its application for developing philosophical discussions with children.

PORTO, Eugenia M. Social Context and Historical Emergence: The Underlying Dimension of Medical Ethics. Theor Med, 11(2), 145-165, Je 90.

I argue that work in medical ethics which attempts to humanize medicine without examining hidden assumptions (about medicine's ontology, explanations, goals, relationships) has the *dehumanizing* effect of legitimating practices which treat persons as abstractions. After illustrating the need to reexamine the field of medical ethics and the doctor-patient relationship in particular, I use Foucault's work to provide a social, historical framework for discussion. This background begins to demonstrate that doctor-patient relationships cannot be made satisfactory by new hospital policies or interpersonal skills, but have deep-rooted problems due to medicine's place in social history. Real progress requires social or structural change.

PORUS, N L. "Incommensurability, Scientific Realism and Rationalism" in *Scientific Knowledge Socialized*, HRONSZKY, Imre (ed), 375-383. Norwell, Kluwer, 1989.

An important and real problem of scientific rationality is hidden under the vaguely formulated problem of incommensurability. The notion of incommensurability has not only methodological but psychological function; it inspires the philosophy of science to search for the "realistic" conception of scientific rationality. "Scientific realists" as well as neo-instrumentalists, adherents and opponents of the incommensurability-thesis, in spite of principal epistemological controversies between them, agree that the nontraditional theory of scientific rationality should be based on historical, contextual, pragmatic analysis of the growth of scientific knowledge. It opens the perspectives for the fruitful discussion between them.

POSER, Hans. "Whitehead's Cosmology as Revisable Metaphysics" in *Whitehead's Metaphysics of Creativity*, RAPP, Friedrich (ed), 94-114. Albany, SUNY Pr, 1990.

POSSENTI, Vittorio. Difficoltà della filosofia pubblica (Riflessioni sul pensiero di Norberto Bobbio). Filosofia, 40(2), 151-174, My-Ag 89.

POSSENTI, Vittorio. Lavoro, "Lavorismo", *Otium*. Filosofia, 41(2), 135-154, My-Ag 90.

POSSENTI, Vittorio. Struttura dell'azione e compito pubblico del cristianesimo. Sapienza, 43(1), 21-39, Ja-Mr 90.

POSSENTI, Vittorio. Techne: dai Greci ai moderni e ritorno. Riv Filosof Neo-Scolas, 81(2), 294-307, Ap-Je 89.

POST, E L and GRATTAN-GUINNESS, H (ed). The Modern Paradoxes. Hist Phil Log, 11(1), 85-91, 1990.

The text is transcribed from a paper of 1935 in which E L Post (1897-1954) creates a temporal set theory in which objects of thought are pukka, and so may belong to (i.e., join) already existent sets. Possibilities of paradox are in the offing, which he considers. I survey the *Nachlass* from which the manuscript is drawn and also the mentalistic philosophy evident in this and other writings.

POST, Frederick R. Collaborative Collective Bargaining: Toward an Ethically Defensible Approach to Labor Negotiations. J Bus Ethics, 9(6), 495-508, Je 90.

In this paper I explain the present adversarial collective bargaining process

(ACB) and then critique it on legal and ethical grounds. A new methodology, that I describe as the collaborative collective bargaining process (CCB), will then be explained and similarly critiqued. I argue that replacing the present ACB model with the CCB model will result in better long-term results for all parties concerned. This is because the ACB model is comparable, in many respects, to the adversarial process used in court litigation. It is a combat model based on power. I argue that, in sharp contrast, CCB can foster an environment which encourages candor and truthfulness. (edited)

POST, John F. Objective Value, Realism, and the End of Metaphysics. J Speculative Phil, 4(2), 147-160, 1990.

POST, Stephen G. Interacting with Other Worlds: A Review of Books from the Park Ridge Center. Med Human Rev, 4(2), 45-54, Jl 90.

This is a review of books published on religious traditions and medicine, published by the Park Ridge Center.

POST, Stephen G. What Children Owe Parents: Ethics in an Aging Society. Thought, 64(255), 315-325, D 89.

POST, Stephen G. Women and Elderly Parents: Moral Controversy in an Aging Society. Hypatia, 5(1), 83-89, Spr 90.

The human life span has been extended considerably, and among the very old, women outnumber men by a large margin. Thus, the aging society cannot be adequately addressed without taking into account the experience of women in specific. This article focuses on women as caregivers for aging parents. It critically assesses what some women philosophers are saying about the basis and limits of these caregiving duties.

POSTEMA, Gerald J. Bentham on the Public Character of Law. Utilitas, 1(1), 41-61, My 89.

POSTEMA, Gerald J. "The Normativity of Law" in *Issues in Contemporary Legal Philosophy: The Influence of H L A Hart*, GAVISON, Ruth (ed), 81-104. New York, Clarendon/Oxford Pr, 1987.

POSTER, Mark. *Critical Theory and Poststructuralism: In Search of a Context*. Ithaca, Cornell Univ Pr, 1989

This book seeks to test a synthesis of the discourses of critical social theory and poststructuralism in relation to the emergent context of the mode of information (electronically mediated communication). The book concludes with a study of the family in Orange County, California as illuminated by these theoretical trends.

POSTOW, B C. Criteria for Theories of Practical Rationality: Reflections on Brandt's Theory. Phil Phenomenol Res, 50(1), 69-87, S 89.

My goal is to identify and articulate possible criteria for the evaluation of normative theories of practical rationality. In addition to noting the criteria used by Richard Brandt, I identify the criteria implicit in various evaluations of his theory. An example of such a criterion is the requirement that the theory explain how rational desires are *appropriate* to an understanding of certain facts rather than merely *caused* by an understanding of them.

POSTOW, B C. Thomson and the Trolley Problem. S J Phil, 27(4), 529-537, Wint 89.

Judith Jarvis Thomson supports a moral principle that I call the permissible diversion hypothesis by arguing that this principle succeeds where others fail in accommodating our moral intuitions about various imaginary cases. I try to show that her principle does not accommodate her intuitions about the various cases best, and I also raise some doubts about Thomson's general manner of argumentation.

POSTOW, Betsy C. "Towards Evaluating Theories of Practical Rationality" in *Inquiries into Values: The Inaugural Session of the International Society for Value Inquiry*, LEE, Sander H, 149-160. Lewiston, Mellen Pr, 1989.

My aim is to shed light on the factors that should be considered in accepting or rejecting a theory of rationality conditions for ultimate preferences or goals. I use the wide reflective equilibrium (WRE) model as an example of a possible criterion for evaluating normative ethical theories. After suggesting a few refinements in WRE to meet certain objections, I sketch the WREPR model, an analogue of WRE which expresses a possible criterion for the evaluation of normative theories of practical rationality, including rationality conditions on ultimate preferences and goals. Finally, I suggest that in order to make an informed decision whether to accept a theory such as WREPR, we must identify, classify, and compare various possible criteria for the evaluation of theories of practical rationality.

POTAGA, A. Thales (in Greek). Philosophia (Athens), 17-18, 220-232, 1987-88.

Leader of the ancient Greek mathematicians and founder of theoretic geometry, the porisms of which he applies to near and remote reality (as engineer and astronomer respectively), with his innovating method to combine mathematics with physics for the explanation of phenomena, Thales of Miletus is the first, according to tradition, who enters the field of "Physiologia," becoming thus not only the first natural philosopher, as usually considered, but also the example for both the Platonic dialectician and the Aristotelian sage, who possesses the "Καθ ολου επιστημην" and seeks the First Principles and Causes. The vital property of his first principle, the water—which is also the first ontological principle in the history of philosophy—to create life and animate everything, is the main reason for characterising the philosophy of which Thales is the leader as hylozoistic philosophy.

POTEAT, William H. "For Whom is the Real Existence of Values a Problem: Or, An Attempt to Show that the Obvious is Plausible" in *Mind, Value and Culture: Essays in Honor of E M Adams*, WEISSBORD, David (ed), 147-169. Atascadero, Ridgeview, 1989.

POTTENGER, John R. *The Political Theory of Liberation Theology: Toward a Reconvergence of Social Value and Science*. Albany, SUNY Pr, 1989

In its attempt to deal with contemporary social problems of political oppression and poverty, liberation theology incorporates Marxist social analysis in Christian process theology to restore a normative dimension to modern social science. In this study, I assess liberation theology's methodology for social theorizing, especially as it applies to political hermeneutics and praxis, problems associated with the incorporation of Marxist social analysis, and the moral justifications for legal, extralegal, and revolutionary political behavior, including the use of violence. I argue that for theoretical success, liberation theology should consider more carefully the arguments from the Frankfurt School of critical theory on religion and politics.

POTTS, S G. Persuading Pagans. Ethics Med, 4(2), 28-29,32, 1988.

In medical ethics the Christian perspective is prominent but only one among many others. In a democracy the Christian must persuade and not impose upon the non-Christian (or "pagan"). Successful persuasion avoids all reference to specifically Christian premises such as faith in the truth of the Bible, and relies solely on reasoned argument. Aquinas held that reason alone was sufficient for the non-Christian to arrive at the truths of Natural Law, though Christians through their faith, have access to an extra dimension (analogous to the contours on a moral map) from which to view those truths more clearly.

POULIN, R. Savoir et croire: Sur le Pen et autres menus détails. Philosophiques, 16(2), 359-371, Autumn 89.

POWELL, D E B. The Doctor's Ethics. Ethics Med, 6(2), 26-27, Sum 90.

Ethical issues in medicine have largely concerned contentious subjects such as abortion and euthanasia, or the allocation of resources coupled with an emphasis on patient rights and autonomy. The doctor's own moral stance is neglected. Thus the doctor's autonomy may conflict with an employer's or with the patient's. The state's role may contradict the doctor's own moral stance. Hitherto this has often had a religious or humanitarian basis. In the absence of such motivation or philosophy the doctor with a religious reference system could be placed under increasing pressure to conform.

PRABITZ, Gerald. Humanwissenschaft mit oder ohne Subjekt? oder Zur Kritik der Inentionalität. Conceptus, 23(60), 65-80, 1989.

The debate between methodological individualism (Jon Elster) and so-called poststructuralism (Pierre Bourdieu) is to be discussed regarding the different textual strategies. Elster takes off with subjective intentional action and by developing an enlarged concept of rationality tries to lance an efficient attack on functionalism. Bourdieu on the other hand conceives of subjective action as being determined by and dependent on a world of symbolic forms. The concrete reasoning of the two concepts is shown, their underlying logic is made visible and the point is made, that notwithstanding the seemingly similar vocabulary there is a maximum of difference of meaning resulting from the altogether different contexts.

PRADHAN, R C. Truth, Interpretation and Convention T. Indian Phil Quart, 17(2), 147-162, Ap 90.

PRADO, José Julián. Thomas Hobbes: La razón-cálculo. Cuad Filosof, 20(32), 9-23, My 89.

This article analyses the meaning of a modern idea of rationality established by Thomas Hobbes: rationality as a human practice of a linguistic and combinatory character. This idea implies a problematic relation—of a semantic kind—between reason and sensory thought. The new rational pattern introduces epistemological structures, which potentiate the technologic dimension of science and, at the same time, restrict its cognitive possibilities. Finally, the actual validity of the Hobbesian idea of calculating reason is brought to light in the attempts to apply the computational model to the mind and in the problems arising from the constraint of practical reason within the limits of a purely technological rationality.

PRAKASH, Madhu Suri. On Being a Dewey Teacher Today. Proc Phil Educ, 45, 125-135, 1989.

PRASAD, Rajendra. Discussion: Professor Devaraja on the Emergence of Facts. Indian Phil Quart, 16(4), 479-491, O 89.

PRATT, Douglas. Aseity as Relational Problematic. Sophia (Australia), 28(2), 13-25, Jl 89.

Aseity is a key concept undergirding the traditional Judeo-Christian doctrine of God. Theologically it affirms the conception of God as having no beginning and owing existence to none. Philosophically, aseity functions as the technical term for the judgment that God's existence is necessary. A kind of "conceptual fulcrum," aseity summarizes and undergirds the notion that God is *both* uncaused *and* unrelated to any other. God is thus conceived as having no "need," in any sense, to relate to that which is not Gods-self. But does the self-existence of aseity necessarily imply ontological self-sufficiency of Deity?

PRATTE, Richard. The Personalization of Failure. Proc Phil Educ, 45, 349-359, 1989.

PREGEANT, Russell. Christological Grounds for Liberation Praxis. Mod Theol, 5(2), 113-132, Ja 89.

This article examines the christologies of three contemporary theologians—Jon Sobrino, Schubert Ogden, and Rosemary Ruether—in search of an adequate christological grounding for liberation theology. The discussion focuses on three areas of concern: (1) the theological norm that establishes adequacy to Christian tradition, (2) the mode by which this norm authorizes liberation praxis, and (3) the specific content that the term "liberation" receives through the norm and mode of authorization. The final section offers a constructive proposal that, although indebted to Ogden and to process thought for its basic structure, draws upon the insights of Sobrino, Ruether, and others.

PRESKILL, Stephen. Educating for Democracy: Charles W Eliot and the Differentiated Curriculum. Educ Theor, 39(4), 351-358, Fall 89.

The author contends that as an increasingly diverse group of students sought a high school education at the beginning of the 20th century, Charles W Eliot, the president of Harvard University and outspoken educational reformer, withdrew his support for a rigorous liberal education for all students and publicly advocated vocational education for immigrants and working class students. The author furthermore maintains that Eliot's endorsement of curriculum differentiation helped to make tracking a fixture in almost every American high school.

PRESKILL, Stephen. Strong Democracy, The Ethic of Caring and Civil Education. Proc Phil Educ, 45, 217-225, 1989.

PREUSS, Peter. *Reincarnation: A Philosophical and Practical Analysis.* Lewiston, Mellen Pr, 1989

The book is a response to the question: does reincarnation occur and what difference would it make if it did? The two parts of this question divide the book into two parts. In the first part a number of peripheral issues are dealt with, and then the apparent evidence for reincarnation is presented and its presuppositions about memory and personal identity are discussed. The conclusion is that reincarnation occurs. In the second part the significance of this conclusion is discussed.

PREVE, Costanzo. Kritische Ontologie als Philosophie der Freiheit (in Serbo-Croatian). Filozof Istraz, 29(2), 659-669, 1989.

Der Verfasser kritisiert als "metaphysische" verschiedene Lösungen dieses Problems, die die gegenwärtige philosophische Diskussion bezeichnen (von Stalinismus zu gegenwärtigen neubürgerlichen Synthesen, von Habermas zu abendländischem Marxismus, und endlich bis zu einigen der bekanntesten Denker aus dem italienischen philosophischen Panorama). Der Autor meint, einige Lösungen des späten Lukács seien im wesentlichen richtig, aber sie benötigten eine weitere aktuelle Bearbeitung, indem Lukács trotz allem einem anderen historischen Zeitalter, das heute als vollendet erscheint, gehörte. (edited)

PRICE, A W. *Love and Friendship in Plato and Aristotle.* New York, Clarendon/Oxford Pr, 1989

Though persons are separate, their lives need not be: one person's life may overflow into another's, so that helping the other is a way of serving oneself. This idea, which is common to Plato and Aristotle and unifies their treatments of love and friendship, is fully explored for the first time here. They apply their views not only to lovers and friends (especially of the same sex), but also to members of a household, and even of a city-state, in a way that promises to resolve the old dichotomy between egoism and altruism.

PRICE, A W. "Plato and Freud" in *The Person and the Human Mind: Issues in Ancient and Modern Philosophy*, GILL, Christopher (ed), 247-270. New York, Clarendon/Oxford Pr, 1989.

PRICE, Huw and PETTIT, Philip. Bare Functional Desire. Analysis, 49(4), 162-169, O 89.

It seems that no set of beliefs could guarantee any action. Is this an argument for the necessity of desire? No. It is only an argument for a *ceteris paribus* qualification. And if it were an argument for the necessity of desire at the origin of action, it would also establish, absurdly, the necessity of desire at the origin of reference.

PRICE, Huw. *Facts and the Function of Truth.* Cambridge, Blackwell, 1989

Many areas of philosophy employ a distinction between factual and nonfactual uses of language. This book examines the various ways in which this distinction is normally elucidated, and argues that all are unsatisfactory. The argument suggests that the search for a sharp distinction is misconceived. The book develops an alternative approach, based on a novel theory of the function and origins of truth. The central hypothesis is that the main role of the normative notion of truth is to encourage speakers to argue, with long-run behavioural advantages. This theory offers a fresh perspective on the disagreement between 'realists' and their critics in contemporary philosophy.

PRICE, Huw. Why 'Not'? Mind, 99(394), 221-238, Ap 90.

The paper discusses the function and possible aetiology of negation in natural language, and applies the discussion to Dummett's argument for antirealism. I argue that the most plausible aetiology favours the development of classical rather than intuitionist negation. I conclude by considering the objection that classical rule of double negation elimination might nevertheless be unjustifiable, in an important sense. I suggest in reply that there is no need for the classicist to concede that this rule is a logical principle at all: rather it may be regarded simply a transformation licensed by grammar.

PRICE, Richard M. The Distinctiveness of Early Christian Sexual Ethics. Heythrop J, 31(3), 257-276, Jl 90.

The author argues that the sexual ethics of the pagan world of the first two centuries (including Stoic and Platonic teaching) exerted little influence on the sexual ethics of the early Christian church, which were significantly different in content and utterly different in motivation, arising as they did not from philosophical principles but from the special themes of the Gospel and the distinctive self-identity of the early church.

PRIEST, Graham. Boolean Negation and All That. J Phil Log, 19(2), 201-215, My 90.

A standard objection to orthodox solutions to the semantic paradoxes is that they maintain consistency only by requiring the language in question to be expressively incomplete. It might be suggested that paraconsistent solutions maintain nontriviality only by a similar device; in particular, the language cannot contain "Boolean Negation." The paper defends paraconsistent solutions against this charge. It argues that Boolean Negation, characterised semantically, makes perfectly good sense, but does not lead to triviality. Characterised proof-theoretically, it does lead to triviality, but then it fails quite standard tests for having any sense.

PRIEST, Graham and CROSTHWAITE, Jan. "Relevance, Truth and Meaning" in *Directions in Relevant Logic*, NORMAN, Jean (ed), 377-397. Norwell, Kluwer, 1989.

The paper argues that a number of the problems that beset Davidson's account of meaning arise solely in virtue of interpreting the English conditional (and in particular, its occurrence in the T-scheme) as a material conditional, and that these problems are avoided if the conditional is interpreted as a relevant one. It also shows that this is technically possible by constructing a Tarski-type theory of truth for a language containing a relevant conditional in a relevant metalanguage.

PRILLELTENSKY, Isaac. On the Social and Political Implications of Cognitive Psychology. J Mind Behav, 11(2), 127-136, Spr 90.

PRIMORATZ, Igor. *Justifying Legal Punishment.* Atlantic Highlands, Humanities Pr, 1989

The book is a treatise on the moral justification of legal punishment. While the philosophy of punishment is largely dominated by utilitarian and "mixed" theories, this book argues for a purely retributive view: all the main questions facing a theory of punishment are answered in terms of just retribution, without any concessions to social expediency. In addition to the basic tenets any consistently retributive theory would include, the book also advances the controversial thesis that punishment is a right of the offender. A separate chapter deals with the issue of capital punishment, offering a qualified defense of such punishment for the crime of murder.

PRIMORATZ, Igor. "The Middle Way in the Philosophy of Punishment" in *Issues in Contemporary Legal Philosophy: The Influence of H L A Hart*, GAVISON, Ruth (ed), 193-220. New York, Clarendon/Oxford Pr, 1987.

I discuss four attempts at a compromise between the utilitarian and retributive theories of punishment: Ewing's "educative theory," Quinton's reduction of retributivism to a logical point, rule-utilitarianism, and Hart's theory of punishment as a practice justified by its "general justifying aim," to be pursued within certain constraints of justice. All except the last are exposed to the standard objections to the utilitarian theory. Hart's account is immune to most such objections; but it incorporates only "negative retributivism," and thus could justify nonpunishment of the guilty and their disproportionately lenient punishment. I also argue for "positive retributivism," which precludes such practices.

PRING, Richard. Subject-Centred Versus Child-Centred Education—A False Dualism. J Applied Phil, 6(2), 181-194, O 89.

Changing fashions in how the school curriculum is organised are sometimes seen as a regular shift from child-centred to subject-centred education, and back again. At the present moment, the British Government is enforcing 'subject-centredness', partly as a reaction to criticism of declining standards attributed to less rigorous child-centred approaches. On the other hand, other Government initiatives hark back to child-centred principles. This apparent paradox is partly resolved through a closer analysis of one particular tradition of 'child-centred' education, and of what is represented by 'subjects'. Such analyses take us necessarily into ethics and epistemology.

PROIETTI, Omero. Il "Satyricon" di Petronio e la datazione della *Grammatica Ebraica* Spinoziana. Stud Spinozana, 5, 253-272, 1989.

Spinoza owns a famous edition of Petronius, namely Valesius's 1669 edition, founded on the Traurino codex, discovered a few years before. Spinoza's utilizations of the *Satyricon* enables us to establish the "terminus post quem" for the composition of the *Compendium Grammatices Linguae Hebraeae*. In agreement with the research on the "grammatica universalis" of the group *Nil volentibus arduum* this work continues a line of high, theological-political intervention, which occupies the years from 1670 onwards and which perhaps also encompassed the project of a Dutch translation of the *Pentateuch*. (edited)

PROTALINSKI, Grzegorz (trans) and OPARA, Stefan. Catholicism and Socialism: The Problems of Political Understanding. Dialec Hum, 14(1), 57-65, Wint 87.

PROTALINSKI, Grzegorz (trans) and MARKIEWICZ, Barbara. God and Nation: Franz Rosenzweig's Concept of Messianism versus Polish Messianism. Dialec Hum, 16(1), 149-156, Wint 89.

The purpose of this paper is to analyse the concept of the Jewish nation and national existence of Franz Rosenzweig. This notion plays a very important role in Rosenzweig's thought—it is a basis of his idea of Messianism as a new version of the philosophy of history. In comparing Rosenzweig's philosophy with the Polish Messianism of the 19th century I make an effort to formulate the main features of an idea that I call "national existentialism." (edited)

PROTALINSKI, Grzegorz (trans) and FRITZHAND, Marek. Marxism and Social Sciences at a New Stage. Dialec Hum, 15(3-4), 53-58, Sum-Autumn 88.

PROTALINSKI, Grzegorz (trans) and ZAWADZKI, Sylwester. The Problem of Bureaucracy in a Socialist State. Dialec Hum, 16(2), 93-108, Spr 89.

PROTO, M. Gramsci, Mariàtegui e la teologia della liberazione. Il Protag, 6(9-10), 73-85, Je-D 86.

PROUST, Joëlle. *Questions of Form: Logic and the Analytic Proposition from Kant to Carnap*. Minneapolis, Univ of Minn Pr, 1989

PROUVOST, Géry. Approche herméneutique d'une méthodologie propre à la métaphysique chrétienne. Rev Thomiste, 89(4), 622-629, O-D 89.

PROUVOST, Géry. La constitution ontothéologique de la métaphysique chrétienne. Rev Thomiste, 90(2), 230-244, Ap-Je 90.

Le présent essai se propose d'assumer le concept de "constitution ontothéologique" comme une caractéristique positive de la métaphysique. Engageant un dialogue critique avec le procès contemporain de l'ontothélogie, il aboutit à la conclusion suivante: si Dieu n'est pas, l'être non plus n'est pas. Ou si l'on veut: c'est ou prix de l'affirmation de Dieu comme Être que l'être est. Une telle affirmation, philosophiquement e'tablie, permet alors de vérifier la fe condité speculative de la Révélation judeo-chretienne dans la figure de'oute par Etienne Gilson sous le nom de "metaphysique de l'Exode."

PRUDOVSKY, Gad. The Confirmation of the Superposition Principle: The Role of a Constructive Thought Experiment in Galileo's *Discorsi*. Stud Hist Phil Sci, 20(4), 453-468, D 89.

My aim in this paper is to analyse a Galilean thought experiment which, I

believe, serves as the first and the most important justification in the *Discorsi* for the superposition principle. To substantiate this claim I first introduce the context in which the superposition experiment is found in Galileo's text, then describe the experiment itself and analyse its contribution to the whole book. In this analysis a new interpretation of the Galilean argumentation is suggested. This is shown by establishing a connection between the above-mentioned thought experiment, on the one hand, and the superposition principle and trajectory motion, on the other. I then proceed to compare my analysis to that of Kuhn of yet another Galilean thought experiment. I shall end the paper with a short remark on the way my conclusion can be applied to the historiographical debate on whether Galileo was an 'empiricist' or a 'rationalist'.

PRZELECKI, Marian. Morality without Moral Judgment. Dialec Hum, 14(1), 127-131, Wint 87.

PUCCI, Pietro. "Banter and Banquets for Heroic Death" in *Post-Structuralist Classics*, BENJAMIN, Andrew (ed), 132-159. New York, Routledge, 1988.

PUDLAK, Pavel and KRAJICEK, Jan. Quantified Propositional Calculi and Fragments of Bounded Arithmetic. Z Math Log, 36(1), 29-46, 1990.

We investigate a relation between bounded arithmetic and propositional calculus. The main tool is a translation of bounded arithmetical formulas into quantified Boolean formulas and a transformation of arithmetical proofs into proofs in propositional calculus. This brings information both about fragments of bounded arithmetic and propositional calculus.

PUHL, Klaus. Wittgenstein and Sense-Independence of Truth. Phil Invest, 13(3), 232-245, Jl 90.

The claim of this paper is that a version of a principle actually informs Wittgenstein's later philosophy of language which in the *Tractatus* guaranteed the possibility of the factual truth of a sentence. The principle claims that the sense of a sentence cannot be dependent on the truth of another sentence. Section 1 begins with a brief outline of the role of this principle in the *Tractatus*. Sections 2 and 3 then discuss Wittgenstein's critique of Russell's causal analysis of sense. Russell fails because he violates the sense-independence of truth.

PUKA, Bill. The Liberation of Caring: A Different Voice for Gilligan's "Different Voice". Hypatia, 5(1), 58-82, Spr 90.

Recent literature portrays caring as a psychological, social, and ethical orientation associated with female gender identity. This essay focuses on Gilligan's influential view that "care" is a broad theme of moral development which is underrepresented in dominant theories of human development such as Kohlberg's theory. An alternative hypothesis is proposed portraying care development as a set of circumscribed coping strategies tailored to dealing with sexism. While these strategies are practically effective and partially "liberated," from the moral point of view, they also reflect the debilitating influences of sexist socialization even at the highest level. Gilligan and her colleagues seem to misidentify these inadequacies of mature care. This alternative hypothesis is briefly related to the critical and feminist tradition. Then it is supported with Gilligan's own research and interpretive text.

PUKA, William. "Ethical Caring: Pros, Cons, and Possibilities" in *Inquiries into Values: The Inaugural Session of the International Society for Value Inquiry*, LEE, Sander H , 99-113. Lewiston, Mellen Pr, 1989.

This essay considers the ethic of caring in moral development and its relevance for the benevolence tradition in philosophy. It also takes up the critique of justice and patriarchy in Kohlberg's theory offered by Gilligan in the ethical lines of critical theory and feminism. The presumed relationship between Gilligan's position and Kohlberg's is challenged, along with claims regarding the moral adequacy of care. Finally, various interpretive hypotheses and counterhypotheses are posed for developing care's case psychologically and philosophically.

PULLUM, Geoffrey K and BARKER, Chris. A Theory of Command Relations. Ling Phil, 13(1), 1-34, F 90.

PURDY, Laura M. Feminists Healing Ethics. Hypatia, 4(2), 9-14, Sum 89.

The field of ethics is enjoying a much-needed renaissance. Traditional theories and approaches are appropriately coming under fire, although not every new idea will stand time's test. Feminist thinking suggests that we at least emphasize the importance of women and their interests, focus on issues specially affecting women, rethink fundamental assumptions, incorporate feminist insights and conclusions from other areas, and be consistent with respect to our concerns about equality by paying attention to race and class.

PURI, Vinod K and WEBER, Leonard J. Limiting the Role of the Family in Discontinuation of Life Sustaining Treatment. J Med Human, 11(2), 91-98, Sum 90.

In matters of discontinuation of life-sustaining treatment, traditional role of the family to speak on behalf of the incompetent patient is questionable. We explore the reasons why physicians perceive patient autonomy to be transferrable to family members. Principle of patient autonomy may not suffice when futile treatment is demanded and may serve to erode the ethical integrity of medical profession. An enhanced role for bioethics committees is proposed when physicians propose to discontinue life-sustaining treatment against the wishes of the patient or their families.

PURTILL, Richard L. *A Logical Introduction to Philosophy*. Englewood Cliffs, Prentice-Hall, 1989

This volume combines an introduction to logic with an introduction to philosophy. The text moves from the beginnings of philosophy in ancient Greece through contemporary philosophy, and from the simplest systems of logic through the elements of probability theory and the logic of modality. Thus, philosophy and logic are learned together and cast mutual light upon each other. Including numerous examples from the great philosophers, the text presents patterns for analyzing and constructing complex philosophical arguments. In addition, the book features a new, simplified method of checking arguments for validity and practice doing proofs.

PUTMAN, Daniel. Some Distinctions on the Role of Metaphor in Music. J Aes Educ, 23(2), 103-106, Sum 89.

Discussions about the role of metaphor in human knowledge have important implications for understanding music. I utilize some recent work in linguistics to clarify what is meant by "metaphor" in music and argue that music always utilizes what some linguists have called orientational metaphors. Such metaphors put the epistemic status of music in a new light and support the claim that it is possible to learn through musical experience.

PUTMAN, Daniel. Tragedy and Nonhumans. Environ Ethics, 11(4), 345-353, Wint 89.

The concept of tragedy has been central to much of human history; yet, twentieth-century philosophers have done little to analyze what tragedy means outside of the theater. Utilizing a framework from MacIntyre's *After Virtue*, I first discuss what tragedy is for human beings and some of its ethical implications. Then I analyze how we use the concept with regard to nonhumans. Although the typical application of the concept to animals is thoroughly anthropocentric, I argue first that the concept of tragedy can be applied directly to nonhumans (a) because the loss of potential for some nonhumans may be as great or greater than loss of potential for some humans to whom the concept applies and (b) because tragedy depends on what is valued and, for those creatures that do not conceptualize death, the destruction of the present moment through pain and suffering is the ultimate loss, and second that self-awareness in the human sense is not necessary for tragedy.

PUTNAM, Hilary. "Why is a Philosopher?" in *The Institution of Philosophy: A Discipline in Crisis?*, COHEN, Avner (ed), 61-75. La Salle, Open Court, 1989.

PUTUWAR, Bhikkhu Sunanda. "The Buddhist Outlook on Poverty and Human Rights" in *The Wisdom of Faith: Essays in Honor of Dr Sebastian Alexander Matczak*, THOMPSON, Henry O (ed), 91-99. Lanham, Univ Pr of America, 1989.

PYE, Michael (trans) and TOMINAGA, Nakamoto. *Emerging from Meditation: Nakamoto Tominaga*. Honolulu, Univ of Hawaii Pr, 1990

PYLKKÖ, Pauli. Tonal Harmony as a Formal System. Acta Phil Fennica, 43, 300-322, 1988.

QI, Feng. The "Self" Begins to Awake: On the Philosophical Thought of Gong Zizhen. Chin Stud Phil, 21(1), 50-84, Fall 89.

QING, Zou. Technological Activity and Philosophical Thought. Chin Stud Phil, 21(2), 32-48, Wint 89-90.

QUANFU, Liu and ZUORONG, He. A Systematic Exploration of the Marxist Theory of Human Nature. Chin Stud Phil, 21(2), 59-73, Wint 89-90.

QUARANTA, M. Il dibattito sulla razionalità oggi: un ritorno a Kant? Interviste a K O Apel & J Petitot. Il Protag, 6(9-10), 121-125, Je-D 86.

QUARANTA, M. Tempo e spazio negli scritti inediti di Guilio Cesare Ferrari. Il Protag, 6(9-10), 179-187, Je-D 86.

QUARTA, A. L'esperienza filosofica di Enzo Paci. Il Protag, 6(9-10), 145-152, Je-D 86.

QUESTER, George H. "The Necessary Moral Hypocrisy of the Slide into Mutual Assured Destruction" in *Nuclear Deterrence and Moral Restraint*, SHUE, Henry (ed), 227-270. New York, Cambridge Univ Pr, 1989.

The entire history of aerial bombing campaigns, and of mutual nuclear deterrence, has necessarily been shrouded in euphemisms and obfuscations, as military targets where the pretended object of attack, but collateral damage to civilians was the actual goal. But such hypocrisy has indeed been more useful than an honest appraisal would have been, probably

reducing the likelihood of war in the nuclear age.

QUEVEDO, Amalia. El concepto aristotélico de violencia. Anu Filosof, 21(2), 155-170, 1988.

Violence represents, in Aristotle, one of the senses of real necessity: exactly the one that is contrary to hypothetical necessity which is characteristic of the natural phenomena and of the artificial productions (*Physics* II, 7-9); whatever, supposing the end, thwarts it, is violent. The Aristotelic expression *para physin* admits two senses: a broad one according to which it designates what is marginated from nature (*praeter naturam*) and a strict one according to which it designates what is directly contrary to nature (*contra natura*). In an ample sense, the unforeseen, which is a cause by accident is *para physin*; in a strict sense is *para physin* the violence, which as the unforeseen refers to the efficient cause, but it is not *kata symbebekos*, but *kath' hauto*.

QUEVEDO, Amalia. El movimiento accidental en Aristóteles. Anu Filosof, 22(2), 161-172, 1989.

Aristotle differentiates in the movement per se and per accidens. The movement per se is divided into natural and violent. Also the movement per accidens is divided into accidental movement—the one of the beings that do not move by themselves, but exist in something that moves—and the movement of parts that only move with the movement of the whole. Of the ones that move per accidens, some have a movement of their own while others do not accept other movement than the accidental one: such is the case of the soul that only admits the accidental movement.

QUILICI, Leana. Metafisica e teoria dei saperi da Mabillon a Dom Deschamps. Arch Stor Cult, 1, 151-217, 1988.

QUINE, W V. *Pursuit of Truth*. Cambridge, Harvard Univ Pr, 1990

QUINN, John F. Business Ethics, Fetal Protection Policies, and Discrimination Against Women in the Workplace. Bus Prof Ethics J, 7(3-4), 3-27, Fall-Wint 88.

QUINN, John F. Moral Theory and Defective Tobacco Advertising and Warnings (The Business Ethics of *Cipollone versus Liggett Group*). J Bus Ethics, 8(11), 831-840, N 89.

Traditional moral theories help corporate decision makers understand what position consumers, like Rose Cipollone, in *Cipollone vs Liggett Group*, will take against cigarette manufacturers who fail to warn of the dangers of smoking, conceal data about addiction and other dangers from the public, as well as continue to neutralize the warnings on cigarettes by deceptive advertisements.

QUINN, Philip L. Does Anxiety Explain Original Sin? Nous, 24(2), 227-244, Ap 90.

This paper is devoted to a critical examination of the account of hereditary sin set forth in Kierkegaard's *The Concept of Anxiety*. It begins with summaries of Kant's theory of radical evil and Schleiermacher's theory of original sin and argues that both these theories confront serious philosophical problems. It then proceeds to make a case that Kierkegaard's account solves those problems and so represents a genuine advance in the search for a defensible version of the traditional doctrine of original sin.

QUINN, Phillip L. Duhem in Different Contexts: Comments on Brenner and Martin. Synthese, 83(3), 357-362, Je 90.

These comments consist of reflections on the papers Anastasios Brenner and R N D Martin presented at the Conference on Pierre Duhem: Historian and Philosopher of Science. I argue they present nicely complementary accounts of Duhem's turn to history of science: Brenner emphasizes reasons internal to Duhem's philosophical concern with scientific methodology while Martin highlights reasons derived from the broader context of Duhem's engagement with religious controversies of his culture. I go on to suggest that seeing Duhem in this broader perspective can help us cope with the conflicts between science and religion in our own culture.

QUINN, Warren S. Actions, Intentions, and Consequences: The Doctrine of Double Effect. Phil Pub Affairs, 18(4), 334-351, Fall 89.

A version of the doctrine of double effect is defined and defended. As defined in light of objections by Hart and Bennett, it rules not merely against choices in which harm or something close to harm is directly intended, but against any choice involving a direct intention to affect someone where that will, intentionally or unintentionally, bring harm. The doctrine is defended along vaguely Kantian lines: choices that the doctrine rules against are harder to justify because they involve not only harm but a distinctive, if difficult to characterize, morally offensive presumption that the victim is available for one's purposes.

QUINN, Warren S. The Puzzle of the Self-Torturer. Phil Stud, 59(1), 79-90, My 90.

A problem-case is presented (involving choices of imperceptible increases of physical stimuli tied to tangible economic rewards) in which natural preferences lead, under standard principles of rational choice, to unwise overall choices. A solution to the problem is offered which involves challenging a central principle of received theories of rational choice.

QUINTON, Anthony. "The Varieties of Value" in *The Tanner Lectures on Human Values, Volume X*, PETERSON, Grethe B (ed), 185-210. Salt Lake City, Univ of Utah Pr, 1989.

QUIRK, Michael J. Jesus and Interpretation: Sheehan's Hermeneutic Radicalism. Mod Theol, 6(2), 197-209, Ja 90.

Thomas Sheehan's *The First Coming* contends that the Gospels, when "deconstructed" in the light of modern historical criticism, are documents of Jesus' "absolute absence" and herald the "end of religion." I argue that Sheehan's unusual conclusion is a result of his flawed conception of interpretation as *hairesis* or radical choice, which underestimates the historically situated position of all interpreters and the inescapable authority of theological traditions.

RABINOWICZ, Woldzimierz. Stable and Retrievable Options. Phil Sci, 56(4), 624-641, D 89.

An option available to an agent is stable if it maximizes expected utility on the hypothetical assumption that the agent is going to choose it. As is well known, some decision problems lack a stable solution. Paul Weirich has recently proposed a decision principle which prescribes that the option chosen should be at least weakly stable—or "weakly ratifiable," to use his terminology. According to him, full stability is an excessively strong demand. I shall argue that Weirich's proposal conflicts with the familiar condition of dominance. But I shall also prove that this difficulty can be avoided if we replace weak stability by "moderate" stability—where the latter property is somewhat stronger than the former. The paper ends with a discussion of the relevance of retrievability to theories of choiceworthiness and practical reason. (edited)

RABOSSI, Eduardo. Hobbes: Derechos naturales, sociedad y derechos humanos. Cuad Filosof, 20(32), 37-46, My 89.

RABOSSI, Eduardo. J S Mill y la prueba del principio de utilidad: Una defensa de *Utilitarianism IV*, (3). Analisis Filosof, 7(1), 1-12, My 87.

After reviewing standard criticisms to Mill's thesis about desirable/desired, it is argued that Mill is involved in a metatheoretical task: making explicit adequacy conditions of proofs about moral ends. This task differs from that of proving, as a matter of fact, that human beings desire happiness as an end. Mill follows a similar strategy concerning the sequence individual/general happiness. The paper pursues the line of argument started by E Hall, M Warnock and J Klenig.

RACHELS, James. "Morality, Parents, and Children" in *Person to Person*, GRAHAM, George (ed), 46-62. Philadelphia, Temple Univ Pr, 1989.

RACHELS, James. "Why Darwin is Important for Ethics" in *Mind, Value and Culture: Essays in Honor of E M Adams*, WEISSBORD, David (ed), 301-325. Atascadero, Ridgeview, 1989.

RACIONERO, Quitín. Ciencia e historia en Leibniz. Rev Filosof (Spain), 2, 127-154, 1989.

RADDER, Hans and VAN DEN BERG, Hans and HOEKZEMA, Dick. Accardi on Quantum Theory and the "Fifth Axiom" of Probability. Phil Sci, 57(1), 149-157, Mr 90.

In this paper we investigate Accardi's claim that the "quantum paradoxes" have their roots in probability theory and that, in particular, they can be evaded by giving up Bayes's rule, concerning the relation between composite and conditional probabilities. We reach the conclusion that, although it may be possible to give up Bayes's rule and define conditional probabilities differently, this contributes nothing to solving the philosophical problems which surround quantum mechanics.

RADDER, Hans. Over de verhouding van conceptueel relatief en referentieel realisme. Kennis Methode, 14(2), 212-215, 1990.

RADDER, Hans. Rondom realisme. Kennis Methode, 13(3), 295-314, 1989.

RADFORD, C. Driving to California. Phil Invest, 12(4), 281-292, O 89.

RADFORD, Colin. "Wittgenstein on Ethics" in *Wittgenstein in Focus—Im Brennpunkt: Wittgenstein*, MC GUINNESS, Brian (ed), 85-114. Amsterdam, Rodopi, 1989.

According to Wittgenstein's mature philosophy, no 'language game' or 'form of life' is inherently philosophically problematic. However real, practical moral problems undermine the objectivity of morality, which as moral beings we cannot abandon. This problem is both philosophical and 'real'. Morality therefore undermines the later Wittgenstein's whole account of philosophy, i.e., its nature, how such problems are resolved, and its

relation with the rest of our lives. Perhaps that is why he virtually never mentions ethics in his writings after 1932-3.

RADLOFF, Bernhard. *Das Gestell* and *L'écriture*: The Discourse of Expropriation in Heidegger and Derrida. Heidegger Stud, 5, 23-46, 1989.

This article shows how Derrida's refusal of the question of being implicates an understanding of being which sets the limits of his interpretation of technology. Because the question of being is not asked, the question of the essence of technology cannot be raised. Heidegger defines the essence of technology (*das Gestell*) as the consummate form of representational thinking. The philosophy of *l'écriture*, which attempts a metatechnical "grounding" of technological thinking, belongs to the essence of technology; yet it cannot articulate this belonging-to and remains within the purview of representational thinking.

RADNITZKY, G. Is Kuhn's Revolution in the Philosophy of Science a Pseudo-Revolution? Int Stud Phil, 22(1), 77-78, 1990.

In his latest book *Kritik und Wissenschaftsgeschichte* (*Criticism and the History of Science*, 1988), Gunnar Andersson clarifies the logical aspects of falsification and metalogical relationships between falsification, prediction and explanation. By analyzing the case studies on which Kuhn and Feyerabend have based their arguments for the incommensurability thesis, he shows that thesis to be untenable. A decisive criticism of the "new philosophy of science" is given. In the process Popper's methodology is developed further. It is shown that the "Kuhn Revolution" is indeed a pseudo-revolution.

RADNITZKY, Gerard. Against Relativism. Conceptus, 23(60), 99-110, 1989.

Relativism in its various forms has become the mainstream tendency in philosophy, from epistemology to the philosophy of science, and its influence on ethics and political philosophy has been considerable. What are its main tenets? How can its popularity be explained, and, most importantly, how do the key contentions of relativism withstand a critical examination? (1) Criticism of the Criticism of Tradition often Leads to Relativism. (2) The Objectivist and the Relativist Approach Lead to Different Positions with Respect to Explanation, Probability, the Role of Logic, and Rational Theory Preference. (3) The Relevance of the Objectivism-Relativism Debate for Political Philosophy and for Politics.

RADNITZKY, Gerard. The Birth of Modern Science out of the 'European Miracle'. S Afr J Phil, 9(2), 59-67, My 90.

(1) The development of science forms part of the rise of Western civilization, which is a special case of cultural evolution. (2) Our intellectual make-up is the result of biological and cultural evolution combined. (3) A distinction is introduced between 'primary theories' and 'secondary theories'. The former are closely linked to our cognitive sensory apparatus; the latter are the result of attempts to meet the demand for an explanation of phenomena that cannot be explained in terms of 'primary theories'. (4) Two subsets of 'secondary theories' are compared: spiritualistic and scientific theories. (5) The rise of scientific thinking, of intertheoretical competition, is one of the earmarks of the 'European Miracle'. How (and when and why) did the West grow rich? (6) The explanation given focuses on institutional arrangements, in particular on limited government. It leads to the question of why did those institutions arise in Europe. Finally, the consequences of institutional arrangements for scientific progress and innovation are examined.

RADNITZKY, Gerard. La metodología falsacionista y su ecología. Rev Filosof (Spain), 1, 27-41, 1987-88.

RADNITZKY, Gérard. La révolution kuhnienne est-elle une fausse révolution? Arch Phil, 53(2), 199-212, Ap-Je 90.

Falsificationist methodology has been challenged by means of case studies culled from the history of science. That criticism hinges on two methodological problems: the problem of how empirically to test theoretical systems, and the problem of how to criticize, how to "test" basic statements. A close scrutiny of some of the classical case studies shows that they do not prove what they claim to prove. Some ideas, which Popper has only sketched, are elaborated, e.g., how unproblematic test statements can be deduced from problematic ones with the help of auxiliary hypotheses. Hence, the so-called incommensurability thesis dissolves. In the event, the challenge to falsificationism from the history of science has led to a processing, to an upgrading of falsificationist methodology. (edited)

RADONIC, Nikola. In Search of an Image of the World: Kang Youwei and Yan Fu (in Serbo-Croatian). Filozof Istraz, 29(2), 617-629, 1989.

Starting from an interest for problems of China entering into the modern era, this text deals with basic ideas of Kang Youwei and Yan Fu, the first significant representatives of the process of intellectual change and cultural transformation in China at the end of the 19th century. In relation to trends of traditional thought, moral utopia of Kang Youwei and Social Darwinism of

Yan Fu are seen as a continuity in discontinuity. A reconstruction of picture of the world as a whole is found to be a basic characteristic of their intellectual preoccupation, but particular significance they have lies in the fact that, besides continuing the tradition, they introduced new ideas which marked the intellectual scene of the 20th century China.

RAFALKO, Robert J. Corporate Punishment: A Proposal. J Bus Ethics, 8(12), 917-928, D 89.

This is an exercise in logic and creative thinking. I shall argue that no good reasons exist for the supposition that corporations have rights independent of the rights and interests of the persons they serve and that the error of treating corporations as though they do have autonomous rights derives from a sloppy argument from analogy. I shall further argue that the analogy of corporations to citizens, though pushed too far by some courts and lawmakers, remains a useful analogy if its logical relations can be cleaned up and clarified. Finally, I shall conclude this essay by employing the refurbished analogy in such a way that it yields a proposal for more effective criminal punishment for corporate wrongdoing.

RAGEP, F Jamil. Duhem, the Arabs, and the History of Cosmology. Synthese, 83(2), 201-214, My 90.

Duhem has generally been understood to have maintained that the major Greek astronomers were instrumentalists. This view has emerged mainly from a reading of his 1908 publication To Save the Phenomena. In it he sharply contrasted a sophisticated Greek interpretation of astronomical models (for Duhem this was that they were mathematical contrivances) with a naive insistence of the Arabs on their concrete reality. But in Le Système du monde, which began to appear in 1913, Duhem modified his views on Greek astronomy considerably; his more subtle understanding included the recognition that many Greeks subordinated mathematical astronomy to physical theory. But he could not completely repudiate his earlier views about Greek astronomy in part because his extreme nineteenth century prejudices led him to continue to insist on a clear-cut demarcation between Greek and Arabic astronomy. The inevitable result is a certain unevenness in the Système and some glaring inconsistencies.

RAGGHIANTI, Renzo. Victor Cousin: frammenti socratici. G Crit Filosof Ital, 68(1), 18-44, Ja-Ap 89.

RAGUSSIS, Michael. Representation, Conversion, and Literary Form: Harrington and the Novel of Jewish Identity. Crit Inquiry, 16(1), 113-143, Autumn 89.

RAILTON, Peter. "Explanation and Metaphysical Controversy" in Scientific Explanation (Minnesota Studies in the Philosophy of Science, Volume XIII), KITCHER, Philip (ed), 220-252. Minneapolis, Univ of Minn Pr, 1989.

RAILTON, Peter. Naturalism and Prescriptivity. Soc Phil Pol, 7(1), 151-174, Autumn 89.

Naturalistic theories of intrinsic value—theories that explicate the notion of intrinsic value in terms that might pass muster in empirical science—have typically had difficulty in explaining the relation of the explicans to the explicandum and in capturing the normativity of explicandum. A five-element strategy for accomplishing these tasks is outlined, and applied to the case of hedonism. This strategy involves an a posteriori identification of explicans with explicandum; an explanatory role for the explicans, including explanation of intuitive judgments employing the explicandum; and a defense of this identificatory reduction as tolerably revisionist and non-undermining under critical reflection.

RAINBOLT, George W. Gauthier on Cooperating in Prisoner's Dilemmas. Analysis, 49(4), 216-220, O 89.

In Morals by Agreement David Gauthier attempts to show that it is rational to cooperate in prisoners' dilemmas. According to Gauthier, the utility cooperators gain when they correctly identify other cooperators and receive the cooperation payoff will outweigh the utility lost when they mistake non-cooperators for cooperators and receive the sucker payoff. It is argued that this argument depends on an implicit and false assumption—that people have equal abilities to conceal their dispositions and detect the dispositions of others.

RAINBOLT, George W. Mercy: An Independent, Imperfect Virtue. Amer Phil Quart, 27(2), 169-173, Ap 90.

Mercy raises two puzzles. How can mercy be a virtue when it requires tampering with justice? How is it that no one has a right to mercy given that if one shows mercy to one person, one must show mercy to every relevantly similar person? The first puzzle is resolved once one sees that mercy is an independent virtue—that it can conflict with justice without being any less a virtue. The second puzzle is resolved once one sees that mercy is an imperfect virtue—that one has considerable discretion in manifesting it.

RAINER, Valina. Physicalism, Realism and Education: A Functionalist

Approach. Educ Phil Theor, 19(2), 47-56, 1987.

RAINKO, Stanislaw and PETROWICZ, Lech (trans). Towards a Creative Meaning of Marxism. Dialec Hum, 15(3-4), 139-150, Sum-Autumn 88.

RAITZ, Keith L and EDWARDS, Jack. Teaching Reading and Educating Persons. Proc Phil Educ, 45, 334-343, 1989.

RAJAEE, Farhang. "Ethics and Politics in a Religious Political Tradition" in Moral Reasoning and Statecraft: Essays Presented to Kenneth W Thompson, DAVIS, Reed M (ed), 23-35. Lanham, Univ Pr of America, 1988.

RAJECKI, Robert and LECKI, Maciej (trans). Towards a Theology of Peace—The Peace Doctrine of John Paul II. Dialec Hum, 14(1), 201-208, Wint 87.

RAKOVER, Sam S. Incommensurability: The Scaling of Mind-Body Theories as a Counter Example. Behaviorism, 17(2), 103-118, Fall 89.

An opponent thesis to that of incommensurability—the commensurability approach—is proposed. The new thesis is based on the delineation of an empirical comparative metatheory for comparing theories of different paradigms. The method of multidimensional scaling (MDS) together with the proximity-predictability hypothesis (PP hypothesis) instantiate and substantiate this metatheory. The scaling of mind body theories, and the confirmation of certain predictions derived from MDS and the PP hypothesis concerning the relations that exist among these theories, are brought as actual examples supporting the present paper's approach.

RAMACHANDRAN, Murali. Contingent Identity in Counterpart Theory. Analysis, 50(3), 163-166, Je 90.

A slight modification to the translation scheme for David Lewis's counterpart theory I put forward in 'An Alternative Translation Scheme for Counterpart Theory' (Analysis 49.3 (1989)) is proposed. The motivation for this change is that it makes for a more plausible account of contingent identity. In particular, contingent identity is accommodated without admitting the contingency of self-identity.

RAMACHANDRAN, Murali. Sense and Schmidentity. Phil Quart, 39(157), 463-471, O 89.

RAMACHANDRAN, Murali. Unsuccessful Revisions of CCT. Analysis, 50(3), 173-177, Je 90.

In this note, I respond to objections advanced by Graeme Forbes in 'Counterparts, Logic and Metaphysics: Reply to Ramachandran' (Analysis 50.3 (1990)) against my proposed translation scheme for David Lewis's counterpart theory ('An Alternative Translation Scheme for Counterpart Theory', Analysis 49.3 (1989)). I also show that his attempts to avoid certain problems I pointed out for his canonical counterpart theory do not in fact work.

RAMBACHAN, Anantanand. Swāmī Vivekānanda's Use of Science as an Analogy for the Attainment of Moksa. Phil East West, 40(3), 331-342, Jl 90.

Vivekananda came under the influence of various strands of Western thought and was concerned to harmonize the findings of religion and science. This study aims (a) to clarify the scientific model which he used for validating his religious views and (b) to analyze the parallels which he traced between this model and the claims of rajayoga. Finally, (c) I attempt a critical assessment of his achievement in equating the processes and findings of science with those of rajayoga. His parallels are possible only through a radical simplification of the scientific method.

RAMBACHAN, Anantanand. The Value of the World as the Mystery of God in Advaita Vedanta. J Dharma, 14(3), 287-297, Jl-S 89.

In an attempt to affirm God as an absolute and limitless reality, some interpreters of the Advaita tradition deny the reality of the world. It is possible, however, to formulate an understanding of the world and its relationship to God which affirms its value and the value of life in it. The world can be seen as the expression of God's plenitude, not to be completely equated with God, or to be seen as utterly distinct from God. It is admittedly mysterious and indefinable in its relationship to God, but not unreal or nonexistent. In affirming God, the world does not have to be denied.

RAMBERG, Bjorn T. Charity and Ideology: The Field Linguist as Social Critic. Dialogue (Canada), 27(4), 637-651, Wint 88.

RAMBERG, Bjorn T. Donald Davidson's Philosophy of Language: An Introduction. Cambridge, Blackwell, 1989

RAMBU, Nicolae. The Abyssal Categories of Blaga's Apriorism. Phil Log, 32(1-2), 95-98, Ja-Je 88.

RAMBU, Nicolae. Quelques considérations sur la signification de l'agnosticism Kantien (in Romanian). Rev Filosof (Romania), 36(2), 166-173, Mr-Ap 89.

RAMOND, Charles. "Degrés de réalite" et "degrés de perfection" dans les *Principes de la philosophie de Descartes* de Spinoza. Stud Spinozana, 4, 121-146, 1988.

Such notions as "the degrees of reality" and "the degrees of perfection" play a major part in the A posteriori proofs of God's existence in the demonstrations of both Descartes and Spinoza. The present study, whilst offering a comparison between Descartes's geometric abstract of the *Answers to the Second Set of Objections* and Spinoza's *Principles of Descartes' Philosophy*, shows that all the notable differences between the two texts hinge upon the notion of "degrees of reality" and "degrees of perfection." Light is thrown on the philosophical issue raised by this comparison. The question is: as far as reality as such is concerned, can one choose between a quantitative conception—i.e., by degrees—and a qualitative one—i.e., without degrees?

RAMONI, Marco. Fisica e storia della scienza nell'opera di Pierre Duhem. Epistemologia, 12(1), 33-63, Ja-Je 89.

During the last decades, philosophical researchers have changed their opinion about Pierre Duhem's epistemological position. Under a conventionalistic theory of scientific method, they discovered a realistic interpretation of theories in his picture of the history of science. According to this view, Duhem's thought must be taken into account at two different levels: a conventionalistic analysis of scientific method, and a general image of science in which history is used for carrying on a realistic attempt aimed at establishing a "natural classification." In my opinion, this ambiguity in Duhem's philosophy may be removed considering his scientific work. (edited)

RAMSEY, W. Response to Dietrich's "Computationalism". Soc Epistem, 4(2), 181-183, Ap-Je 90.

RAMSEY, William and STICH, Stephen. Connectionism and Three Levels of Nativism. Synthese, 82(2), 177-205, F 90.

Along with the increasing popularity of connectionist language models has come a number of provocative suggestions about the challenge these models present to Chomsky's arguments for nativism. The aim of this paper is to assess these claims. We begin by reconstructing Chomsky's "argument from the poverty of the stimulus" and arguing that it is best understood as three related arguments, with increasingly strong conclusions. Next, we provide a brief introduction to connectionism and give a quick survey of recent efforts to develop networks that model various aspects of human linguistic behavior. Finally, we explore the implications of this research for Chomsky's arguments. Our claim is that the relation between connectionism and Chomsky's views on innate knowledge is more complicated than many have assumed, and that even if these models enjoy considerable success the threat they pose for linguistic nativism is small.

RANDALL, D M and GIBSON, A M. Methodology in Business Ethics Research: A Review and Critical Assessment. J Bus Ethics, 9(6), 457-471, Je 90.

Using 94 published empirical articles in academic journals as a data base, this paper provides a critical review of the methodology employed in the study of ethical beliefs and behavior of organizational members. The review revealed that full methodological detail was provided in less than one half of the articles. Further, the majority of empirical research articles expressed no concern for the reliability or validity of measures, were characterized by low response rates, used convenience samples, and did not offer a theoretic framework, hypotheses, or a definition of ethics. Several recommendations, including a reviewer rating form addressing methodological decisions and inclusion of methodologists on the review panel, are offered to improve methodological rigor in published ethics research.

RANDALL, Donna M. Taking Stock: Can the Theory of Reasoned Action Explain Unethical Conduct? J Bus Ethics, 8(11), 873-882, N 89.

Extensive interest in business ethics has developed accompanied by an increase in empirical research on the determinants of unethical conduct. In setting forth the theory of reasoned action, Fishbein and Ajzen (1975) maintained that research attention on such variables as personality traits and demographic characteristics is misplaced and, instead, researchers should focus on behavioral intentions and the beliefs that shape those intentions. This study summarizes business ethics research which tests the theory of reasoned action and suggests directions for further research.

RANEA, Alberto Guillermo. The *A Priori* Method and the *Actio* Concept Revised. Stud Leibniz, 21(1), 42-68, 1989.

RANG, Bernhard. Naturnotwendigkeit und Freiheit: Zu Kants Theorie der Kausalität als Antwort auf Hume. Kantstudien, 81(1), 24-56, 1990.

RANTALA, Veikko. Generating a Normative System. Acta Phil Fennica, 38, 272-281, 1985.

RANTALA, Veikko. Musical Work and Possible Events. Acta Phil Fennica, 43, 97-109, 1988.

RANTALA, Veikko. "Scientific Change and Counterfactuals" in *Scientific Knowledge Socialized*, HRONSZKY, Imre (ed), 399-408. Norwell, Kluwer, 1989.

RAPHAEL, D D and SAKAMOTO, Tatsuya. Anonymous Writings of David Hume. J Hist Phil, 28(2), 271-281, Ap 90.

This article publishes and discusses the text of a manuscript memorandum written by George Chalmers in 1788 which supports a recent conjecture by David Raynor that Hume was the author of an anonymous review of Adam Smith's *Theory of Moral Sentiments* in 1759. The memorandum also reports that Hume published and then retracted a pamphlet against Archibald Stewart, Lord Provost of Edinburgh when the Jacobites occupied the city in 1745. The authors show that the source of Chalmers's information was David Callander, a talented pupil of Adam Smith and a nephew of Hume's friend Michael Ramsay. (edited)

RAPHAEL, D D. "Hobbes on Justice" in *Perspectives on Thomas Hobbes*, ROGERS, G A J (ed), 125-152. New York, Clarendon/Oxford Pr, 1988.

Hobbes has a distinctive view of justice, defining it (in *Leviathan*) as the performance of covenants. The main purpose of this unusual definition is to support the absolute authority of the sovereign, who does not surrender any rights under the social contract of an instituted commonwealth or the implicit covenant of an acquired commonwealth. It follows that acts of the sovereign cannot be called injustice or injury, though they can be contrary to equity. Hobbes's account of equity shows that he supports the egalitarian against the meritarian concept of distributive justice, though he does not classify it as justice.

RAPOPORT, Amnon and WEG, Eythan. Effects of Fixed Costs in Two-Person Sequential Bargaining. Theor Decis, 28(1), 47-71, Ja 90.

Rubinstein (1982) considered the problem of dividing a given surplus between two players sequentially, and then proposed a model in which the two players alternately make and respond to each other's offers through time. He further characterized the perfect equilibrium outcomes, which depend on the players' time preferences and order of moves. Using both equal and unequal bargaining cost conditions and an unlimited number of rounds, two experiments were designed to compare the perfect equilibrium model to alternative models based on norms of fairness. We report analyses of final agreements, first offers, and number of bargaining rounds, which provide limited support to the perfect equilibrium model, and then conclude by recommending a shift in focus from model testing to specification of the conditions favoring one model over another.

RAPOPORT, Anatol. The Dialectics of Peace Education. Dialec Hum, 16(2), 47-59, Spr 89.

The two features of dialectics, inquiry into meanings of concepts pervading conventional wisdom and emphasis on continual change of meanings and their referents, are perceived as highly relevant to peace education. It is suggested that special emphasis be placed on the radical changes in the perception of war and the "adaptations" of the institution of war to changing social environments. In particular, the demarcation lines between the traditional parties to social struggles (ethnic, national, class) are now beginning to be redrawn between the Warriors, serving the war machine, and the Victims, comprising the entire human race.

RAPP, Friedrich. Ontologie ohne Ethik? Zur Klärung der Heidegger-Kontroverse. Z Phil Forsch, 43(4), 695-701, O-D 89.

With reference to the omnibus volume: *Heidegger und die praktische Philosophie*, Frankfurt 1988, it is pointed out that a prima facie distinction must be made between Heidegger's involvement in Nazi politics and his philosophical teaching. The decisive question is whether his type of philosophy (and not just the person Heidegger) has an affinity to the voluntarism and irrationalism of the Third Reich. It turns out that by exclusively concentrating on the Being-question Heidegger leaves a void for ethical and political theory that can be filled in different ways.

RAPP, Friedrich. "Whitehead's Concept of Creativity and Modern Science" in *Whitehead's Metaphysics of Creativity*, RAPP, Friedrich (ed), 70-93. Albany, SUNY Pr, 1990.

Whitehead sets out to do justice to the phenomena of creative novelty by means of a universal category of creativity. By contrast, science offers analytic dissection, mechanistic models and the experimental method in order to arrive at well-defined mathematical dependency relations. Thus the full concreteness of novelty is reduced toward the combination of already existing elements and the natural laws governing their behaviour, i.e., toward the already known. In terms of conceptual precision and empirical verifiability, Whitehead's speculative cosmology cannot compare with modern science. But the sciences pay the price of accounting for nature in terms of lifeless uniformity.

RAPP, Friedrich (ed) and WIEHL, Reiner (ed). *Whitehead's Metaphysics of Creativity*. Albany, SUNY Pr, 1990

The book contains twelve articles which were first presented at the International Whitehead Symposium held in Bad Homburg, West Germany, in October, 1983. The papers centre around the concept of creativity basic to Whitehead's novel system of categories which accords becoming priority over being. The book's four chapters treat Whitehead's place in the history of philosophy, the mutual dependence between the results obtained in empirical research and their metaphysical interpretation, the cosmological and the anthropological dimensions in Whitehead's philosophy and finally the relationship between the philosophical and the theological interpretations of creativity.

RAPPAPORT, Steve. Bonjour's Objection to Traditional Foundationalism. Dialogue (Canada), 28(3), 433-448, 1989.

In *The Structure of Empirical Knowledge* Bonjour criticizes traditional foundationalism, which holds that basic empirical beliefs are justified by states of direct awareness. He says the direct awarenesses which allegedly warrant basic beliefs are either cognitive, or they are noncognitive. If cognitive, direct awarenesses require justification and so cannot stop the regress of justification. But if noncognitive, direct awarenesses cannot justify anything. In either case traditional foundationalism fails. Grasping the second horn of Bonjour's dilemma, I argue that noncognitive direct awarenesses can warrant basic beliefs. The case relies on Davidson's notion of a state of affairs making true a proposition, and Swain's distinction between evidential and causal reasons.

RAPPAPORT, Steven. The Modal View of Economic Models. Philosophica, 44(2), 61-80, 1989.

The modal view holds that theoretical models in economics consist of truths about hypothetical objects, while applied models are true or false statements about the real world. The alternatives are the lawlike generalization and structuralist accounts of economic models. The former claims models are collections of generalizations about the real world, and the latter is an application to economic models of the structuralist view of scientific theories held by Suppes, Van Fraassen, et al. I argue that the modal view is preferable to the lawlike generalization view because it is more consistent with the use of nondescriptive models in economics. And I argue the modal view is better than the structuralist account because it is a more accurate description of the way economists actually handle their models.

RASHKOVSKII, E B. Vladimir Solov'ev on the Fate and Purpose of Philosophy. Soviet Stud Phil, 28(3), 5-16, Wint 89-90.

The main problem of the article is the structural correlation between the foundations of V Solov'ev's metaphysics and other parts of his great philosophical synthesis (epistemology, anthropology, ethics, philosophy of history, etc.). Successes and shortcomings of this correlation are analysed.

RASMUSSEN, Douglas B. Liberalism and Natural End Ethics. Amer Phil Quart, 27(2), 153-161, Ap 90.

Could liberalism find support from a natural end ethics? Rawlsian/Dworkinian liberalism is described, and the compatibility of this version of liberalism with a natural end ethics is considered. The following questions are addressed: (a) What does it mean to say there is an unequivocal interpretation of the human *telos*?; (b) How is the principle of universalizability to be interpreted by a natural end ethics?; (c) What are the proper concerns of social justice for a natural end ethics?; and (d) Can a natural end ethics ever provide a basis for legal tolerance of activities which are not in accord with the human *telos*? Rawlsian/Dworkinian liberalism is shown to be incompatible with a natural end ethics, but it is noted that there is another version of liberalism which suggests itself as a possibility.

RASMUSSEN, Larry L and BIRCH, Bruce C. *Bible and Ethics in the Christian Life*. Minneapolis, Augsburg, 1989

RASMUSSEN, Stig Alstrup. Supervaluational Anti-Realism and Logic. Synthese, 84(1), 97-138, Jl 90.

It is argued that nonrevisionary Dummettian antirealism does not exist. In particular, the hope of retaining classical logic in an antirealistically acceptable manner, either by appeal to semantical holism or supervaluational semantics, is doomed. The paper is best seen in the context of S A Rasmussen and J Ravnkilde, "Realism and Logic," Synthese 52, 1982, and C Wright, "Realism, Bivalence and Classical Logic," in C Wright, Realism, Meaning and Truth, Oxford 1987.

RATAJCZYK, Zygmunt and KOTLARSKI, Henryk. Inductive Full Satisfaction Classes. Annals Pure Applied Log, 47(3), 199-223, Je 90.

RATANAKUL, Pinit. Thailand: Refining Cultural Values. Hastings Center Rep, 20(2), 25-27, Mr-Ap 90.

RATNER, Carl. A Social Constructionist Critique of The Naturalistic Theory of Emotion. J Mind Behav, 10(3), 211-230, Sum 89.

The doctrine that emotions are products of natural mechanisms is critiqued from a social constructionist perspective. Evidence marshalled in support of the naturalistic theory is also subjected to critical analysis and found wanting. The social constructionist theory of emotion is proposed as more adequate than the naturalistic theory. Since emotion exemplifies psychological phenomena in general, the social constructionist theory that explains it is considered worthy of explaining the entire range of psychological phenomena.

RATZAN, Richard M and SPICKER, Stuart F. *Ars Medicina et Conditio Humana* Edmund D Pellegrino, MD, on His 70th Birthday. J Med Phil, 15(3), 327-341, Je 90.

In his writings, Edmund Pellegrino analyzes four deficiencies in the humanity of those who fall ill: the loss of (1) freedom of action, (2) freedom to make rational choices, (3) freedom from the power of others, and (4) a sense of the integrity of the self. Since Pellegrino's analysis and commitment to virtue-based ethics preceded much of the attention later given by philosophers to the importance of the moral principle of *autonomy* (in contrast to *beneficence*) in patient care, it is helpful to trace the source of his commitment to virtue-based ethics and his account of freedom to Aristotle's analysis of the human soul, as an entelechy of an intact and healthy living organism that, unimpeded by illness, moves itself to act, to actualize its intellectual potential in the form of making rational choices, and to free itself from the power of others by remaining independent and without need of continuous assistance, while at the same time retaining the integrity of a unified self that can act, think, and choose for itself autonomously.

RAULET, Gérard. The Moment of the Foundation (in Serbo-Croatian). Filozof Istraz, 30(3), 799-819, 1989.

Toute révolution, et ce fut le cas de la Révolution française, entraine à la fois la formation d'une pratique nouvelle et la constitution d'un discours politique nouveau. Partant de la notion du paradoxe des "identités de remplacement", l'auteur a choisi pour projet de rechercher à travers la modernité les traces d'une prise de conscience du moment révolutionnaire, une réflexion archéologique qui prend ici la forme d'un triptyque: Hölderlin et l'impossible identification du "Prince de la Fête"; Kleist et la rédemption, ou recréation de l'Etat; Büchner enfin et son impitoyable critique de la représentation. Is s'agit donc d'interroger le "moment révolutionnaire" comme césure dans la continuité historique.

RAV, Yehuda. Philosophical Problems of Mathematics in the Light of Evolutionary Epistemology. Philosophica, 43(1), 49-78, 1989.

A new foundational philosophy of mathematics is developed in the spirit of evolutionary epistemology. Mathematics is seen as a two-tiered web: (1) a *logico-operational level* based on cognitive mechanisms which have become fixed in the course of evolution in adaptation to the real world; (2) a *thematic level* determined by culture and social needs and hence in a continuous process of growth. The interplay between these levels is analyzed in detail and an account is proposed for the applicability of mathematics, a subject normally neglected by the traditional schools in the philosophy of mathematics. The essay first introduces the reader to evolutionary epistemology and an extensive bibliography is provided.

RAWSON, Elizabeth. "Roman Rulers and the Philosophic Adviser" in *Philosophia Togata: Essays on Philosophy and Roman Society*, GRIFFIN, Miriam (ed), 233-257. New York, Clarendon/Oxford Pr, 1989.

RAY, A Chadwick. A Fact About the Virtues. Thomist, 54(3), 429-451, Jl 90.

The thesis that virtues cannot be displayed in bad actions or in excess seems defeasible today only through a stipulative definition. I argue that the thesis can be taken as factual if actions are understood teleologically. Bad actions apparently exhibiting a virtue aim at goods in ways manifesting loves not conducive to happiness, and so do not exhibit the virtue in question. I also uphold the role of loves in the virtues.

RAY, Christopher. Paradoxical Tasks. Analysis, 50(2), 71-74, Mr 90.

This paper presents a development of an argument due to James Thomson: that an infinite super-task involves a paradox—the so-called 'lamp paradox'. Here we consider what happens when two lamps are operated in parallel. Although no logical paradox is involved, there seems to be a rational paradox associated with such super-tasks.

RAYMOND, Menye Menye. Experience as Nothingness: A Form of Humanistic Religious Experience. J Dharma, 14(2), 173-189, Ap-Je 89.

RAYNER, Jeremy. On Begriffsgeschichte Again. Polit Theory, 18(2), 305-307, My 90.

RAZ, Joseph. "Autonomy, Toleration, and the Harm Principle" in *Issues in*

Contemporary Legal Philosophy: The Influence of H L A Hart, GAVISON, Ruth (ed), 313-333. New York, Clarendon/Oxford Pr, 1987.

The article, since superceded by the author's *The Morality of Freedom*, explores some moral consequences of the ideal of personal autonomy. It argues that autonomy presupposes value pluralism, including the conflict-ridden type of competitive pluralism. But autonomy itself encourages a certain measure of toleration. While not requiring neutrality, it puts a limit to the ability of governments to pursue moral, and other ideals, especially by coercive means.

RAZ, Joseph. Facing Diversity: The Case of Epistemic Abstinence. Phil Pub Affairs, 19(1), 3-46, Wint 90.

Rawls's recent writings on the foundations of his theory are based on three precepts: The theory of justice has limited applicability, shallow foundations, autonomy and it is based on epistemic abstinence. The different strands are traced, and the tensions between them explored. The case for accommodating diversity through embracing epistemic abstinence is criticised. Nagel has recently argued more powerfully that liberalism rests on the acceptance of a special epistemic stance for political decisions. This argument is also discussed and criticised.

READ, James H. Nietzsche: Power as Oppression. Praxis Int, 9(1-2), 72-87, Ap-Jl 89.

The purpose of this essay is to discuss critically Nietzsche's view of power. I show why Nietzsche believes that in practice power is always *oppressive*—why the power of one always diminishes the power of another. But at the same time, while accepting some of Nietzsche's crucial premises, I criticize the conclusions he draws. I maintain that even if one accepts Nietzsche's premise that a "will to power" underlies all human motives, one need not conclude that the power of one necessarily comes at the expense of the power of another.

READ, Stephen. Homophone Semantik für die relevante Aussagenlogik. Conceptus, 23(59), 77-89, 1989.

The calculus *R* of relevant logic was developed to show that a formal account of logic could be given in which relevance was respected. Later, it was given a possible-worlds semantics, in which the consequence relation was classical. It was criticised for giving a non-homophonic truth-condition to 'not' and 'if', one in which similarly sounding signs in object and metalanguage were understood differently. To give a homophonic semantics, one must replace the classical consequence relation by a relevant one. Using this, a homophonic semantics adequate in Tarski's sense is developed, and soundness and completeness of *R* are proven.

READ, Stephen. *Relevant Logic: A Philosophical Examination of Inference*. Cambridge, Blackwell, 1989

The logician's central concern is with the validity of argument. A logical theory ought, therefore, to provide a general criterion of validity. Giving such a criterion requires describing the philosophical basis and the formal theory of a logic in which the premises of a valid argument are relevant to its conclusion. I provide an elegant natural deduction proof theory embracing classical, relevant and modal logics, and prove the theories sound and complete with respect to the appropriate semantics. These technical results are then reviewed and underpinned by a proof-conditional analysis of the meaning of the logical connectives.

REALE, Mario. Hobbes alle prese con lo "stolto": La confutazione di *Leviathan* I. Teoria, 9(1), 41-67, 1989.

REALE, Miguel. *Expérience et culture: Fondement d'une théorie générale de l'expérience*. Bordeaux, Biere, 1990

One of the fundamental problems of our time consists in elaborating a theory of knowledge and at the same time, a theory of experience, in an attempt to reconstruct a correlation between nature and culture, in particular, between natural science and human science. This book attempts to reconstruct a correlation between nature and culture, a general theory of experience. (staff)

REAMER, Frederic G. Should Competence Be Coerced?: Commentary. Hastings Center Rep, 20(4), 30-31, Jl-Ag 90.

This commentary discusses a case involving a forensic patient whose attorney suggests that he refuse psychotropic medication to avoid trial in criminal court. Refusal of medication may mean a return of the patient's psychotic symptoms. The commentary critically examines the forensic patient's right to refuse medication and the ethics of the attorney involved in the case.

REATH, A. Kant's Theory of Moral Sensibility: Respect for the Moral Law and the Influence of Inclination. Kantstudien, 80(3), 284-302, 1989.

This paper explains how respect for the moral law functions in moral motivation, and outlines Kant's general theory of motivation. Respect has an intellectual aspect (recognition of the moral law as an overriding reason) and an affective aspect. Since the former is primary, respect is not a motive that exerts a force on the will. Thus, for it to limit inclinations, inclinations must motivate by being viewed as justifying reasons. A balance of forces model of the will must be rejected for a model in which all action is motivated by reasons taken by the agent to have justifying force.

REATH, Andrews. The Categorical Imperative and Kant's Conception of Practical Rationality. Monist, 72(3), 384-410, Jl 89.

This paper examines Kant's derivation of a substantive moral conception from the nature of practical reason (a part of Kant's derivation of the moral law from practical reason), by reconstructing the introduction of the Formula of Universal Law (FUL) in the first two sections of the *Groundwork*. First, it explains how, according to *Groundwork*, I, the concept of morality implicit in ordinary thought leads to the FUL; that is, how the formal features of moral reasons lead to a principle for determining what moral reasons there are in a given situation. The paper then examines Kant's conception of practical reason, and explains a second derivation of the FUL given in *Groundwork*, II, which traces it to the nature of practical reason. The argument of the paper is that, in Kant's view, moral choice is the most complete realization of an ideal of rationality found in all forms of choice—that moral reasoning extends a concern for justification and evaluation found in all forms of choice.

REAVLEY, M and ANDIAPPAN, P. Discrimination Against Pregnant Employees: An Analysis of Arbitration and Human Rights Tribunal Decisions in Canada. J Bus Ethics, 9(2), 143-149, F 90.

Recent arbitration and human rights boards of inquiry cases involving discrimination against pregnant employees are reviewed. A comparison is made between remedies available under each procedure. It is suggested that the human resource managers review their policies and procedures relevant to this issue to ensure that they do not have the effect or intent of discriminating against pregnant employees.

REBAGLIA, Alberta. Essere è percepire una struttura linguistica: Il pensiero di George Berkeley quale presupposto filosofico. Epistemologia, 12(1), 125-152, Ja-Je 89.

Albert Einstein often emphasized the analogy existing between the Berkeleyan *esse est percipi* and the antirealistic way of thinking of the "Copenhagen school," which, considering the quantistic theory complete, maintained that solely what is *observable* is *real*. It may be important to analyse this connection, in order to find those elements which can help us to give full consistency and autonomy to that antirealistic attitude, so as to give it a real philosophical meaning. The main reason of Berkeley's nearness to the "orthodox" interpretation of quantum mechanics may be found in his declaring that things in themselves not only are inexistent, but also meaningless. In this way even the Kantian claim to a noumenon as a limit concept with the function of separating human knowledge from divine creation becomes impossible. (edited)

REBOUL, Olivier. "The Figure and the Argument" in *From Metaphysics to Rhetoric*, MEYER, Michel (ed), 169-181. Norwell, Kluwer, 1989.

RECANATI, François. The Pragmatics of What is Said. Mind Lang, 4(4), 295-329, Wint 89.

Recent work in pragmatics has shown that the gap between the meaning of a sentence and 'what is said' (the proposition expressed) by uttering it is wider than was previously acknowledged. Besides the conversational implicatures, which are external to what is said, there are other nonconventional, pragmatic aspects of utterance meaning, which are constitutive of what is said. The issue discussed in this paper is that of the criteria which can be used to distinguish conversational implicatures from pragmatic constituents of what is said.

RECHNER, Paula L and DALTON, Dan R. On the Antecedents of Corporate Severance Agreements: An Empirical Assessment. J Bus Ethics, 8(6), 455-462, Je 89.

This study of major corporations ($n = 481$) provides an empirical assessment of the effects of several corporate governance variables (CEO duality, boards of director composition, officers and directors common stock holdings, institutional common stock holdings, number of majority owners) on the adoption of so-called severance agreements. A discriminant analysis indicates a significant multivariate function. Wilks lambda univariate analyses suggest that the percentage of common stock held by owners and directors and number of majority stock holders are the more robust discriminators.

REDDIFORD, Gordon. A Philosophical Education. Thinking, 8(2), 4-6, 1989.

A brief description of the foundation and development of the Cogito Society in Bristol/UK and the policy of its journal *Cogito*.

REDFERN, H B. Philosophical Aesthetics and the Education of Teachers. J Aes Educ, 22(2), 35-46, Sum 88.

REDFIELD, James M. Platonic Education. Thinking, 4(3-4), 30-37, 1982.

REDHEAD, M L G and DENBIGH, K G. Gibbs' Paradox and Non-Uniform Convergence. Synthese, 81(3), 283-312, D 89.

It is only when mixing two or more pure substances along a reversible path that the entropy of the mixing can be made physically manifest. It is not, in this case, a mere mathematical artifact. This mixing requires a process of successive stages. In any finite number of stages, the external manifestation of the entropy change, as a definite and measurable quantity of heat, is a *fully continuous* function of the relevant variables. It is only at an infinite and unattainable limit that a *non-uniform convergence* occurs. And this occurs when considered in terms of the number of stages together with a 'distinguishability parameter' appropriate to the particular device which is used to achieve reversibility. These considerations, which are of technological interest to chemical engineers, resolve a paradox derived in chemical theory called Gibbs' Paradox.

REDHEAD, Michael L G. "Nonfactorizability, Stochastic Causality, and Passion-at-a-Distance" in *Philosophical Consequences of Quantum Theory: Reflections on Bell's Theorem*, CUSHING, James T (ed), 145-153. Notre Dame, Univ Notre Dame Pr, 1989.

REDMON, Robert B. The Psychiatrist as Moral Advisor. Theor Med, 10(4), 331-337, D 89.

This paper is a critique of a paper by Robert Lipkin. Arguments for the following claims are put forward: (1) that what is 'essential' to the psychiatric relationship is what we want it to be for utilitarian reasons; (2) it would not be to our advantage to allow the medicalization of morality; (3) what we should expect from the psychiatrist is prudential advice, not moral advice, and that Lipkin has a confused view about the relationship between these two areas; and (4) we should not allow the psychiatrist to restrict individuals on moral grounds, but only on public safety grounds.

REDMOND, Walter. A Logic of Faith. Int J Phil Relig, 27(3), 165-180, Je 90.

REDNER, Harry. "Ethics in Unethical Times—Towards a Sociology of Ethics" in *The Institution of Philosophy: A Discipline in Crisis?*, COHEN, Avner (ed), 303-327. La Salle, Open Court, 1989.

Ethics has not developed in the same way as politics, economics and law, which are separate disciplines. The explanation for this is to be found in the historical development within modern society of autonomous spheres of politics, economics and law distinct from ethical norms. Ethics, too, has become specialized through a historical process of moralization, described in the work of Nietzsche, Weber, Elias and MacIntyre. In our century this process has been stultified by an inverse trend of de-moralization which has made ethical norms largely redundant. An attempt is made to overcome this crisis of morality by setting out the basis of a new ethics in the urgent problems facing humanity, the nuclear and ecological threats and the loss of individuality.

REDNER, Harry. "The Infernal Recurrence of the Same: Nietzsche and Foucault on Knowledge and Power" in *Knowledge and Politics*, DASCAL, Marcelo (ed), 291-315. Boulder, Westview Pr, 1988.

This article explores the relation between Foucault and Nietzsche by examining their attack of the idea of representation. Nietzsche countered the representational paradigm in epistemology and politics by means of his conception of the will to power. Foucault likewise resorted to a conception of power to oppose representation in all fields, and especially against the subject-object relation of epistemology. This article is critical of the emphasis on war and conflict in reality and discourse that results from this orientation, arguing that agreement at some level is essential for language and discourse to be possible.

REDNER, Harry. Representation in the Eighteenth Brumaire of Karl Marx. Manuscrito, 12(1), 7-37, Ap 89.

The paper aims to relate artistic, scientific and political representation in Marx focusing on *The Eighteenth Brumaire of Louis Bonaparte*. Section I begins with an exposition of dramatic representation by briefly illustrating the role of a few literary types, specifically Hamlet, in Marx's thought. It goes on with an account of the drama and metadrama underlying *The Eighteenth Brumaire*. Section II presents Marx's theory of class representation and relates it to his view of ideology as a system of representations. Marx's application of this theory to Louis Bonaparte and the 1848 Revolution is subjected to a thorough critique by reference to an analogous work of Max Weber, *Parliament and Government in a Reconstructed Germany*. What emerges in Section III from this confrontation is that Marx's work is more representatively real as art that it is as science.

RÉE, Jonathan and CHOMSKY, Noam and EDGLEY, Roy and OSBORNE, Peter and WILSON, Deirdre. Noam Chomsky: An Interview. Rad Phil, 53, 31-40, Autumn 89.

RÉE, Jonathan. Timely Meditations. Rad Phil, 55, 31-39, Sum 90.

REECE, William S. Why is the Bishops' Letter on the US Economy So Unconvincing? J Bus Ethics, 8(7), 553-560, Jl 89.

This paper evaluates the rhetoric of the US bishops' pastoral letter on the US economy from two perspectives. Is the letter convincing? Does it conform to the "conversational norms of civilization"? The paper argues that the bishops' letter fails by both standards because it ignores serious research on the US economy, it misstates important facts about the economy, and it sneers at professional economists. The paper concludes that the bishops' letter will not be convincing to well informed readers.

REED, Edward S. The Trapped Infinity: Cartesian Volition as Conceptual Nightmare. Phil Psych, 3(1), 101-121, 1990.

Descartes's theory of volition as expressed in his *Passions of the Soul* is analyzed and outlined. The focus is not on Descartes's proposed answers to questions about the nature and processes of volition, but on his way of formulating questions about the nature of volition. It is argued that the assumptions underlying Descartes's questions have become 'intellectual strait-jackets' for all who are interested in volition: neuroscientists, philosophers and psychologists. It is shown that Descartes's basic assumption—that volition causes change in the brain/mind, not in the world around us—has set in train a series of 'themata' that have dominated studies of the will, severely curtailing our understanding. It is then shown that these Cartesian themata are so limiting and confusing that a number of internally contradictory ideas have actually become mainstays of most theories of volition; in particular, the concepts of unconscious sensations and of involuntary volitions.

REEDER, Harry P. Hermeneutics and Apodicticity in Phenomenological Method. SW Phil Rev, 6(2), 43-69, Jl 90.

This article attempts to demonstrate that many of Husserl's critics do not fully appreciate either the hermeneutic nature of his phenomenological method or the full sense of his claim to have found a grounding for philosophy in "apodictic evidence." It is argued that (1) the "philosophy as a rigorous science" which Husserl thought phenomenology to be included linguistic and interpretative elements at its very core; and (2) Husserl established a new and defensible sense of "apodictic evidence," in part through a thoroughgoing critique of traditional concepts of such evidence.

REEDER, Harry P. Wittgenstein Never Was a Phenomenologist. J Brit Soc Phenomenol, 20(3), 257-276, O 89.

The article discusses recent arguments (by Paul Ricoeur, Nicholas Gier, Gerd Brand, Herbert Spiegelberg, Don Ihde, and Jaakko and Merrill Hintikka) that Wittgenstein, at some point in his career, was a phenomenologist. It is argued that (1) there is insufficient evidence for attributing such a view to Wittgenstein; (2) the claims made by these commentators are conflicting and sometimes contradictory; and (3) the decision concerning this issue must be based in careful comparison of the methodologies of Wittgenstein and of phenomenology.

REESE, William L. Morris Lazerowitz and Metaphilosophy. Metaphilosophy, 21(1-2), 28-43, Ja-Ap 90.

Defending Lazerowitz's interpretation of metaphilosophy as applied to standard philosophy, the article shows that Lazerowitz's proposal and standard philosophy share the same features. They are proposals "about" and "in" philosophy, and "in" the verbal idiom. The only philosophy in the ontological idiom is "philosophy of," that is, philosophy derived from and relating to one of the language games of the world. It is shown that there is support for the "philosophy of" interpretation in Wittgenstein's later writings, and that this interpretation is more viable than the alternative option that philosophy is to be reduced to ordinary language.

REESOR, Margaret E. *The Nature of Man in Early Stoic Philosophy*. New York, St Martin's Pr, 1989

This book presents a coherent account of Stoic epistemology and makes passages which are relevant available to readers who know little or no Greek. In the first chapter the nature of man is examined from several points of view, as a physical body, and as a metaphysical entity possessing various characteristics; in the second there is an analysis of 'the Stoic classes of Being'. The remaining chapters are an account of the Stoic theories of the mind: the presentation, the assent to the presentation, the criterion of truth, and the state of affairs signified by articulate sound.

REEVE, C D C. *Socrates in the Apology*: An Essay on Plato's *Apology of Socrates*. Indianapolis, Hackett, 1989

This book is a detailed interpretation of Plato's *Apology* and its historical context. It argues that Socrates' defense establishes his innocence of Meletus's charges. It develops a new account of Socrates' philosophical doctrines, and proposes novel solutions to the paradoxes which are central to them. It presents Socrates as a fundamentally nonironical figure who is above all just what he says he is: a philosopher servant of Apollo—a man whose religion is founded not in faith but in human wisdom, and whose wisdom is founded in an Apollonian recognition of the poverty of human wisdom in comparison to divine wisdom.

REEVES, M Francis. An Application of Bloom's Taxonomy to the Teaching of Business Ethics. J Bus Ethics, 9(7), 609-616, Jl 90.

Benjamin S Bloom and a large committee of educators did extensive research to develop a taxonomy of global educational goals and of ways to measure their achievement in the classroom. The result was a taxonomy of three domains: cognitive, affective, and motor skills. This paper examines the cognitive and affective domains and applies them to teaching business ethics. Each of the six levels of the cognitive domain is explained. A six-step case method model is used to illustrate how the six cognitive levels might be used and tested in the classroom. The five levels of the affective domain are also described. They are illustrated behaviorally in terms of a student's increasing interest, motivation and commitment to business ethics.

REGAN, Tom and SINGER, Peter. *Animal Rights and Human Obligations (Second Edition)*. Englewood Cliffs, Prentice-Hall, 1989

REGAN, Tom. The Thee Generation. J Soc Phil, 20(1-2), 31-33, Spr-Fall 89.

REGEHR, Marilyn G and CLIFTON, Robert K. Toward a Sound Perspective on Modern Physics: Capra's Popularization of Mysticism and Theological Approaches. Zygon, 25(1), 73-104, Mr 90.

Fritjof Capra's *The Tao of Physics*, one of several popularizations paralleling Eastern mysticism and modern physics, is critiqued, demonstrating that Capra gives little attention to the differing philosophies of physics he employs, utilizing whatever interpretation suits his purposes, without prior justification. The same critique is applied and similar conclusions drawn, about some recent attempts at relating theology and physics. In contrast, we propose the possibility of maintaining a cogent relationship between these disciplines by employing theological hypotheses to account for aspects of physics that are free from interpretive difficulties, such as the ability to create mathematical structures with extraordinary predictive success.

REGUERA, Eduardo Bello. The Theory of Democracy and the Ethics of Equality in the French Revolution (in Serbo-Croatian). Filozof Istraz, 30(3), 753-761, 1989.

L'approche à une théorie éthique comme fondement de la république démocratique, que l'A. propose, tourne autour de deux penseurs: Rousseau et Robespierre. Mais cet approche ne s'occupe pas du problème des influences. La théorie démocratique reçois son expression la plus précise—pendant la période de la Révolution française—dans la Constitution jacobine (1793). On peut concevoir son fondement éthique comme éthique de l'égalité, mais envisageant ce fondement dès trois points de vue: comme critique des privilèges de l'Ancien Régime, comme affirmation d'un autre grand principe de la conscience moderne, c'est-à-dire la liberté, et comme fondation d'une nouvelle légitimité juridique et politique.

REIDENBACH, R E and ROBIN, D P. Toward the Development of a Multidimensional Scale for Improving Evaluations of Business Ethics. J Bus Ethics, 9(8), 639-653, Ag 90.

This study represents an improvement in the ethics scales inventory published in a 1988 *Journal of Business Ethics* article. The article presents the distillation and validation process whereby the original 33-item inventory was reduced to eight items. These eight items comprise the following ethical dimensions: a moral equity dimension, a relativism dimension, and a contractualism dimension. The multidimensional ethics scale demonstrates significant predictive ability.

REIDENBACH, R Eric and ROBIN, Donald P. *Business Ethics: Where Profits Meet Value Systems*. Englewood Cliffs, Prentice-Hall, 1989

The purpose of this book is to provide the business person with a theoretically based but practical approach for developing an ethical and profitable organization. It recognizes the need for businesses to achieve and maintain profits and explains why ethical performance and profitability need not be incompatible. The book then presents its "parallel planning" approach in a way that simplifies application. The parallel planning process is an adaptation of strategic planning to the dual missions of ethics and profits. The authors use case histories throughout the book in order to illustrate their points.

REIDENBACH, R Eric and ROBIN, Donald P. Integrating Social Responsibility and Ethics into the Strategic Planning Process. Bus Prof Ethics J, 7(3-4), 29-46, Fall-Wint 88.

This article is adapted from a book by the same two authors, *Business Ethics: Where Profits Meet Value Systems* (Prentice-Hall, 1989). It recognizes the need for business to generate profits and efficiencies, as well as the need for ethics and social responsibility. A parallel planning approach is suggested to achieve these two objectives. Suggestions for implementing the resultant plans through the organizational culture, the concept of an ethical profile, and core values of an organization are also presented.

REIDHAAR-OLSON, Lisa. A New Proof of the Fixed-Point Theorem of Provability Logic. Notre Dame J Form Log, 31(1), 37-43, Wint 90.

In this paper we give a simple semantic proof of the fixed-point theorem of the modal system G (also known as GL, PRL, L, and K4W). This proof is modeled after a syntactic proof of Sambin's found in Sambin and Valentini, yet is simpler than his, due to our taking advantage of the Kripke semantics for G. Other semantic proofs of the theorem exist, e.g., in Gleit, and Goldfarb and Gleit; however, the advantages of this particular version are that it is less complicated and the fixed-point so obtained has the same general "appearance" as the original formula.

REILLY, Bernard J and KYJ, Myroslaw J. The Social Conscience of Business. Bus Prof Ethics J, 7(3-4), 81-101, Fall-Wint 88.

The issue of social ethics and its meaning become critical when space, time, and distances are narrowed by the expansion of technology, the potentials of indestructible chemicals and biologicals, the internationalization of product and financial markets, the multinational drug firm, and the marketing, communications, and information changes which deny the limitations of traditional markets. Therefore, ethical theory and practice begin with agreements on the categories of what is good and what is valuable, both for the individual and the society. This involves the development of categories of ethical values as they define relationships between corporations and their environments.

REIMAN, Jeffrey. The Death Penalty, Deterrence, and Horribleness: Reply to Michael Davis. Soc Theor Pract, 16(2), 261-272, Sum 90.

REIMAN, Jeffrey. *Justice and Modern Moral Philosophy*. New Haven, Yale Univ Pr, 1990

REIMAN, Jeffrey and VAN DEN HAAG, Ernest. On the Common Saying that it is Better that Ten Guilty Persons Escape than that One Innocent Suffer: Pro and Con. Soc Phil Pol, 7(2), 226-248, Spr 90.

REIMAN, Jeffrey. "Sartre's Annihilation of Morality" in *Inquiries into Values: The Inaugural Session of the International Society for Value Inquiry*, LEE, Sander H , 401-412. Lewiston, Mellen Pr, 1989.

REIMAN, Jeffrey. Why Worry about How Exploitation Is Defined? Reply to John Roemer. Soc Theor Pract, 16(1), 101-113, Spr 90.

REIMER, Bennett. *A Philosophy of Music Education (Second Edition)*. Englewood Cliffs, Prentice-Hall, 1988

REIN, Andrew. Stroud and Williams on Dreaming and Scepticism. Ratio, 3(1), 40-47, Je 90.

An argument of Williams's is elaborated in order to show (contra Stroud) that even if one accepts that in order to know that p one must know that one is not dreaming that p, empirical knowledge may still be possible.

REINER, Hans and SCHUHMANN, Karl. Ein Protokoll aus Husserls Logikseminar vom Winter 1925. Husserl Stud, 6(3), 199-204, 1989.

We began by tentatively defining logic as a science of meanings, distinguishing between meanings and their objects (references). We established that meanings exist concretely in psychic acts, thus allowing logic to be seen also as the science of thinking. After further consideration we concluded that logic is only concerned with true meanings, and is therefore a practical normative science. Its normative character, however, is limited to formal truths. In addition logic can also be defined as the science of objects taken in their most general sense. Indications were given how this general science of objects includes various mathematical disciplines.

REINGOLD, Eyal M and MERIKLE, Philip M. On the Inter-relatedness of Theory and Measurement in the Study of Unconscious Processes. Mind Lang, 5(1), 9-28, Spr 90.

In the present paper we identify the a priori assumptions underlying the dissociation paradigm employed by researchers on the unconscious. We argue that definitional chaos, and implicit assumptions that are rarely acknowledged, fuel the often futile controversy between 'believers' and 'nonbelievers' in the unconscious. We analyze the logical status of inferences based on the dissociation paradigm, and critique two major approaches to the measurement of consciousness. We then describe two alternative approaches which avoid the conceptual and methodological pitfalls of previous approaches, and thus have the potential to provide more conclusive evidence regarding the nature of conscious versus unconscious processes.

REISNER, Anne E and HAYS, Robert G. Media Ethics and Agriculture: Advertiser Demands Challenge Farm Press's Ethical Practices. Agr Human Values, 6(4), 40-46, Fall 89.

The agricultural communicator is a key link in transmitting information to farmers. If agricultural communicators' ethics are compromised, the resulting biases in news production could have serious detrimental effects on the quality of information conveyed to farmers. But, to date, agricultural communicators' perceptions of ethical problems they encounter at work has not been examined. This study looks at the dimensions of ethical concerns for topic area (agricultural) journalists as defined by practitioners. To determine these dimensions, we sent open-ended questionnaires to members of two professional agricultural journalist associations. Agricultural communicators overwhelmingly focus on one specific threat to objectivity—advertising pressure. Respondents indicated that agricultural journalists' responses to advertising pressure adversely affected the entire profession. The editors' and reporters' perceptions of advertising pressure clearly indicate that advertising abuses are a clear and present danger and one worthy of far more attention than it has previously received. (edited)

RELMAN, Arnold S. Publishing Biomedical Research: Roles and Responsibilities. Hastings Center Rep, 20(3), 23-27, My-Je 90.

REMBERT, Ron. "What is an Adventure?". Thinking, 4(1), 41-44, 1982.

REMER, Gary. Rhetoric and the Erasmian Defence of Religious Toleration. Hist Polit Thought, 10(3), 377-403, Autumn 89.

REMMEL, J B and NERODE, A. Complexity-Theoretic Algebra II: Boolean Algebras. Annals Pure Applied Log, 44(1-2), 71-99, O 89.

RENARDEL DE LAVALETTE, Gerald R. Interpolation in Fragments of Intuitionistic Propositional Logic. J Sym Log, 54(4), 1419-1430, D 89.

It is shown that all fragments of intuitionistic propositional logic based on a subset of the connectives conjunction, disjunction, implication and negation satisfy the interpolation property. Fragments containing bi-implication and/or double negation are briefly considered.

RENAUT, Alain and CATTANI, Mary Schnackenberg (trans) and FERRY, Luc. French Philosophy of the Sixties: An Essay on Antihumanism. Amherst, Univ of Mass Pr, 1990

The focus of this text is the philosophic interpretation of the French revolt in 1968. The interpretations of the French postmodernists of the revolt, and their attempt to find a nonmetaphysical form of humanism to explain the revolt are explicated. (staff)

RENAUT, Alain and PHILIP, Franklin (trans) and FERRY, Luc. Heidegger and Modernity. Chicago, Univ of Chicago Pr, 1990

The authors investigate the debate within French intellectualism regarding the relationship of Heidegger and Nazism. They consider the relations between Heidegger's phenomenology and his politics, and conclude that Heidegger's critique against modernity is flawed by ambiguities. (staff)

RENTSCH, Thomas. Martin Heideggers 100 Geburtstag: Profile der internationalen Diskussion. Phil Rundsch, 36(4), 257-290, 1989.

RESCHER, Nicholas. Moral Absolutes: An Essay on the Nature and Rationale of Morality. New York, Lang, 1989

RESCHER, Nicholas. A Useful Inheritance: Evolutionary Aspects of the Theory of Knowledge. Lanham, Rowman & Allanheld, 1989

RESNIK, Michael D. Immanent Truth. Mind, 99(395), 405-424, Jl 90.

The paper introduces the immanent conception of truth—a way of thinking about truth which leads one to rest with a truth predicate disquotationally defined for just one's own language. This conception contrasts with the usual correspondence and epistemic conceptions of truth, which transcend one's home language. For the purpose of formulating various versions of realism, the immanent conception is preferable to the correspondence and coherent conceptions. However, this conception may prove too narrow for general epistemology, methodology and philosophy of language.

RESNIK, Michael D. A Naturalized Epistemology for a Platonist Mathematical Ontology. Philosophica, 43(1), 7-29, 1989.

Beginning with an attack on the supposed ontic distinction between mathematical and physical objects, this paper proposes a naturalist account of the genesis of mathematical. It hypothesizes that our ancestors introduced mathematical objects as theoretical posits and brought them within our ken by postulating "bridge principles" connecting these objects to our inscribed computations and diagrams.

RESWEBER, Jean-Paul. Le Démenti de la vérité. Etudes, 371(5), 521-534, N 89.

REY TATO, J. El talante intelectual de la obra de Emmanuel Mounier. Pensamiento, 45(180), 477-484, O-D 89.

REY, Jean-Michel and STRONG, Tracy B (trans). "Commentary: Toward a New Logic—Singing the Sirens' Song" in Nietzsche's New Seas: Explorations in Philosophy, Aesthetics, and Politics, GILLESPIE, Michael Allen (ed), 75-96. Chicago, Univ of Chicago Pr, 1989.

Nietzsche's text represents a fundamental departure from all previous metaphysical thinking. By passing into the realm of fiction it produces a world for us which is precisely the world that "philosophy" wants to censure and control. Nietzsche's writing thus both gives us a world and makes us aware of our attempts to control it: it makes us aware that we are "commenting."

REYKOWSKI, Janusz. Is Socialism a Psychological Misunderstanding? Dialec Hum, 15(3-4), 205-221, Sum-Autumn 88.

It is gradually becoming clear that Poland is facing a great turning point. The economic reform of a few years ago, which many people vaguely associated with the process of improving whatever was there to improve, is now beginning to appear as the perspective of basic changes of the social and economic scenery in our country. The outlines of those changes are emerging and are creating, more and more irresistibly, the impression that the fundamental canon of principles which have determined our social and economic activities until now, has been challenged. There are indications, too, that we might diverge from the rules hitherto considered uninfringeable in politics as well. This situation raises many questions and doubts. I would like to deal with some of them here.

REYNOLDS, Noel B. Comment on Robert Summers on the Rule of Law. Ratio Juris, 1(3), 263-265, D 88.

REYNOLDS, Noel B. Grounding the Rule of Law. Ratio Juris, 2(1), 1-16, Mr 89.

Although the concept of Rule of Law has been revived and developed vigorously by mid-twentieth century conservative political theorists, contemporary legal positivists have not been impressed. The author reviews this confrontation, outlines the logic for a strong theory of Rule of Law, and surveys the leading attempts to provide compelling grounds for such a theory.

REYNOLDS, Noel B. Law as Convention. Ratio Juris, 2(1), 105-120, Mr 89.

The widely recognized impasse in legal theory, which requires an account of law as "both a social fact and a framework of reasons for action" has been most interestingly addressed in recent years by writers characterizing law as convention in the sense of a solution to a game theoretical "coordination problem." As critics have neutralized most of these proposals, the author advances an account of conventionalism, drawing on economic and sociological theory, which he claims makes the bridge between positivist and naturalist theories of law without compromising the basic insights of either. The result is a unified theory of law, politics and society.

REYNOLDS, Steven L. Imagining Oneself to be Another. Nous, 23(5), 615-633, D 89.

Philosophical thought experiments often ask us to imagine ourselves to be other people. Exactly what are we being asked to imagine? It has been argued that we do not imagine that a false identity statement is true, for (a) such statements are necessarily false, and hence cannot be imagined, and (b) they would not express our intuitive sense of what we imagine. I assume that such imagining is a kind of internal story telling, and so that the question as to what we imagine asks what is true in the fiction thus produced. I argue that in typical cases of such imagining, we merely imagine someone else in a first personal way.

REYNOLDS, William M. Reading Curriculum Theory: The Development of a New Hermeneutic. New York, Lang, 1989

This text is a study of curriculum theory texts of the 1980s. Focusing on three divisions within the theoretical traditions of the field—the conservative, the reconceptualist and the reproductionist—the book provides a hermeneutic reading of specific texts within each tradition. The book relies heavily upon the interpretation theory of Paul Ricoeur and discusses Ricoeur's theoretical works. The book reveals and demonstrates that the ultimate aim of interpretive reading or the hermeneutic process is enhanced self-understanding and understanding that understanding.

REZLER, André. "Esthétiques idéologiques, esthétiques et politiques" in Culture et Politique/Culture and Politics, CRANSTON, Maurice (ed), 110-119. Hawthorne, de Gruyter, 1988.

RHEINWALD, Rosemarie. Zur Frage der Vereinbarkeit von Freiheit und Determinismus. Z Phil Forsch, 44(2), 194-219, 1990.

The author defends a specific version of a conditional analysis of freedom in terms of counterfactuals and argues that freedom and responsibility are compatible with determinism. She tries to show that arguments of a certain type (similar to Ginet's and van Inwagen's arguments) against the compatibility thesis are not conclusive, given this conditional analysis of freedom. This analysis can be characterized as "cluster-of-conditionals analysis." It yields a rather vague notion of freedom but captures essential features of our intuitions about freedom and responsibility.

RHODEN, Nancy and ARRAS, John. *Ethical Issues in Modern Medicine (Third Edition)*. Mountain View, Mayfield, 1989

RICE, Daryl H. Plato on Force: Conflict Between his Psychology and Sociology and his Definition of Temperance in the *Republic*. Hist Polit Thought, 10(4), 565-576, Wint 89.

Plato's failure in *The Republic* to eliminate the coercive side of political power by wedding it with knowledge manifests itself in a dissonance between his political sociology and his definition of a temperate polis. This conflict is rooted in a more fundamental one between his psychology of the individual and his definition of a temperate soul. Possible alternatives for resolving these conflicts are explored, attending especially to recent interpretations of Plato's psychology by Julia Annas, George Klosko, Jon Moline, and Terry Penner. While these accounts are insightful in other respects, they do not aid in resolving the conflicts in question.

RICE, Daryl H. Whitehead and Existential Phenomenology: Is a Synthesis Possible? Phil Today, 33(2), 183-192, Sum 89.

A sizable body of literature calls for a synthesis of Whiteheadian process philosophy and the existential phenomenology of Sartre and Heidegger. However, although the two traditions agree on some points, they are fundamentally incompatible. Those proposing a synthesis see in it the possibility of integrating within a single scheme the viewpoint of natural science and the insights of existential fundamental ontology, but the denial of the possibility of such a smooth integration is at the very heart of the existential phenomenological position.

RICE, Lee C and BEAVERS, Anthony F. Doubt and Belief in the *Tractatus De Intellectus Emendatione*. Stud Spinozana, 4, 93-119, 1988.

We argue that Spinoza has a consistent account of the nature of doubt and belief in the *TIE*, and that this account, while not expounded explicitly in the *Ethics*, remains the consistent background for much of the development there. Finally, Spinoza's account of belief is defended against the cognitivist theory of propositional attitudes which is offered by thinkers such as Bennett and Braithwaite.

RICE, Lee C. Reflexive Ideas in Spinoza. J Hist Phil, 28(2), 201-211, Ap 90.

Many commentators see the account of reflexive ideas in Spinoza as an important component of his theory of mind, although there is less agreement as to the precise role which the account plays within the larger theory; and Bennett has recently called the doctrine's importance and coherence into question. I offer an interpretation which defends the doctrine's importance and consistency, and argue that this interpretation provides some rather satisfying results regarding the notion of consciousness in Spinoza.

RICE, Martin A. Turning Tricks with Convention T: Lessons Tarski Taught Me. SW Phil Rev, 6(1), 123-131, Ja 90.

I argue that Davidson's contention that a theory of meaning for a natural language just is a Tarski style truth theory for that language is patently absurd on three points: (1) non-standard truth theories using odd basis clauses in lieu of satisfaction by a sequence are quite easy to construct, although not as easy as Susan Haack thinks; (2) T sentences cannot function as translations of object language sentences into a meta-language; (3) if understanding a language consists in having a Tarski style truth theory for that language, then one must possess and understand infinitely many meta-languages—an impossibility.

RICHARD, Denis. Definability in Terms of the Successor Function and the Coprimeness Predicate in the Set of Arbitrary Integers. J Sym Log, 54(4), 1253-1287, D 89.

Using coding devices based on a theorem due to Zsigmondy, Birkhoff and Vandiver, we first define in terms of successor S and coprimeness predicate a full arithmetic over the set of powers of some fixed prime, then we define in the same terms a restriction of the exponentiation. Hence we prove the main result insuring that all arithmetical relations and functions over prime powers and their opposite are definable over Z in terms of S and the coprimeness predicate. Applications to definability over Z and N are stated as corollaries of the main theorem. (edited)

RICHARD, Jean. Le champ herméneutique de la révélation d'après Claude Geffré. Laval Theol Phil, 46(1), 17-30, F 90.

La tâche herméneutique de la théologie, telle que proposée plus spécialement par Claude Geffré, permet d'élargir le champ de la révélation selon l'espace et le temps, jusqu'à nous englober nous-mêmes aujourd'hui, qui vivons dans une situation historique et culturelle pourtant bien différente

de celle des premiers auditeurs du message chrétien. Mais cela n'est pas suffisant encore pour que la révélation du salut atteigne jusqu'aux confins du monde, puisque tous aujourd'hui ne se sentent pas ultimement, religieusement concernés par le message de Jésus-Christ. Il faudrait donc insister davantage sur le pôle universel qu'est le Verbe créateur et sur la médiation philosophique requise pour le penser dans toutes ses implications.

RICHARD, Mark. How I Say What You Think. Midwest Stud Phil, 14, 317-337, 1989.

A semantics for attitude verbs and 'that'-terms is given. The terms name fusions of linguistic items and Russellian referents; the verbs are treated as indexicals. The psychological objects of attitudes are taken to be the sort of things named by 'that'-terms. An ascription is true provided its 'that'-clause represents an object of attitude, with standards of representation varying contextually. The proposal is defended against various objections. Applications to various puzzle cases (e.g., Kripke's Paderewski case) are made; extensions of the proposal are discussed.

RICHARD, Mark. *Propositional Attitudes: An Essay on Thoughts and How We Ascribe Them*. New York, Cambridge Univ Pr, 1990

RICHARDS, David A J. The Strains of Virtue and Constitutionalism. Philosophia (Israel), 20(1-2), 115-125, Jl 90.

RICHARDS, Norvin. "Paternalism Toward Friends" in *Person to Person*, GRAHAM, George (ed), 235-244. Philadelphia, Temple Univ Pr, 1989.

It seems that a paternalistic measure can have a different moral status if its intended beneficiary is a friend than it would if it were directed toward someone else. A friend can be entitled to expect behavior which would be downright intrusive if directed toward a stranger, or, at best, supererogatory. The paper seeks to explain why, then argues that these variations in the morality of paternalism do not show that we have been wrong to believe morality requires impartiality.

RICHARDS, Robert J. Dutch Objections to Evolutionary Ethics. Biol Phil, 4(3), 331-343, Jl 89.

This article investigates the several logical and moral objections to an evolutionary ethics. The author considers these recent criticisms—especially the charge that an evolutionary ethics must commit the naturalistic fallacy—and shows them to be unavailing.

RICHARDSON, Henry S. Measurement, Pleasure, and Practical Science in Plato's *Protagoras*. J Hist Phil, 28(1), 7-32, Ja 90.

The practical "science of measurement" sketched at the end of Plato's *Protagoras* is not a form of maximizing hedonism. Its choice criteria are more complicated than interpreters have noticed, and can accommodate the case of incommensurable pleasures. Its role within the dialogue is fully explained by casting it as a metric prerequisite to choice rather than as a maximizing decision procedure; and attributing a commensurability claim needlessly heightens the clash with later dialogues. Since this science of measurement involves no commitment to commensurability, it cannot contribute to any argument for the rational necessity of commensurability.

RICHARDSON, John. Reply to Professor Robin Small's "Absolute Becoming and Absolute Necessity". Int Stud Phil, 21(2), 135-137, 1989.

RICHIR, Marc. On the Sublime in Politics (in Serbo-Croatian). Filozof Istraz, 30(3), 773-789, 1989.

Dans ce texte l'auteur traite le problème de rencontre entre phénoménologie et institution symbolique. D'après lui il n'y pas d'expérience concrète qui soit purement phénoménologique, car elle est toujours, d'une manière ou d'autre, à la rencontre du champ phénoménologique et du champ symbolique. Puis, il passe à la question du sublime en politique qui consiste en articulation du "moment" phénoménologique du sublime avec l'institution symbolique du socio-politique. A la fin il parle aussi de la démocratie comme du seul régime apte à poursuivre les oeuvres de la révolution, mais qui est précaire et fragile. Pourtant, devant cet abîme d'une "naturalisation" de l'humanité nous avons du moins la chance extraordinaire, qui est de la modernité, de pouvoir nous découvrir comme des hommes, conclut l'auteur.

RICHMAN, Fred. Intuitionism as Generalization. Phil Math, 5(1-2), 124-128, 1990.

Intuitionism, in its no-frills form of mathematics with intuitionistic logic, is a generalization of classical mathematics in much the same way as group theory is a generalization of Abelian group theory: intuitionists do not assume the law of excluded middle, group theorists do not assume the commutative law. As a result, intuitionistic theorems are valid in computational models of mathematics as well as the classical model.

RICHTER, Ewald. Heidegger These vom "Überspringen der Welt" in traditionellen Wahrheitstheorien und die Fortführung. Heidegger Stud, 5, 47-78, 1989.

This article interprets the overcoming of the "Überspringen der Welt" (omission of the world) as an important step in the development of the "Seinsfrage." As Heidegger showed in *Sein und Zeit*, the concepts of "subject" and "object" (which are remaining parts of the destroyed phenomenon of "being-in-the-world") lure on to misguided questions. A proposition should not be regarded as an active subjective achievement. Contrary to an assertion of E Tugendhat "being itself" appears even in a wrong proposition (although "verstellt"). The revelation of the "original" truth as "Unverborgenheit" (non-concealment) already indicates the vital point of Heidegger's later philosophy: the "Aufenthalt" (sojourn) of the human being in the "offenheit des Seins."

RICHTER, Leonhard. "Krugs Begriff einer philosophischen Propädeutik" in *Agora: Zu Ehren von Rudolph Berlinger*, BERLINGER, Rudolph (and other eds), 185-202. Amsterdam, Rodopi, 1988.

RICHTER, M M. Nonstandard Methods. Stud Log, 47(3), 181-191, S 88.

RICHTER, Melvin. Aristotle and the Classical Greek Concept of Despotism. Hist Euro Ideas, 12(2), 175-187, 1990.

RICKMAN, H P. A Philosophic Fairytale. Thinking, 5(4), 2-9, 1985.

RICKMAN, H P. Philosophy and Fiction. Metaphilosophy, 21(3), 253-261, Jl 90.

Philosophy is involved in fiction because novels depict characters reflecting on life. Furthermore philosophy is needed to solve the problem of how fiction, though not claiming to be literally true, can convince the reader that stories about individuals represent general truth. Verisimilitude is increased when the degree of knowledge supposedly displayed in a novel by an omniscient narrator, a participant observer, etc., matches epistemological presuppositions prevailing at the time. Furthermore, the inevitable selection which fiction makes of the material of experience is anticipated by the interpretations which naturally accompany that experience and are the very stuff of philosophy.

RICKMAN, H P. Science and Hermeneutics. Phil Soc Sci, 20(3), 295-316, S 90.

A methodology of the human studies needs to settle the conflict between the two long-established truth-seeking approaches. To be scientific, like physics, promises system, precision, and practical applicability but ignores the significant peculiarity of the subject matter: People talk. Hermeneutics, the methodology of interpretation, confronts the difficulties of understanding what people mean, but is suspected of lacking rigor. However, the two approaches are not exclusive alternatives. Sharing common procedures, such as classification and deduction, they also supplement each other: interpretation depends on factual evidence and scientific objectivity depends on reliable communication. Successful research needs to combine scientific study of facts with methodical interpretation of meaning.

RICOEUR, Paul. "Rhetoric-Poetics-Hermeneutics" in *From Metaphysics to Rhetoric*, MEYER, Michel (ed), 137-149. Norwell, Kluwer, 1989.

RICOEUR, Paul and IHDE, Don (ed). *The Conflict of Interpretations: Essays in Hermeneutics—Paul Ricoeur*. Evanston, Northwestern Univ Pr, 1988

RIEDEL, Herbert H J. Existentially Closed Algebras and Boolean Products. J Sym Log, 53(2), 571-596, Je 88.

RIEDEL, M. Vom epischen zum logischen sprechen: der spruch des Anaximander. Philosophia (Athens), 17-18, 191-219, 1987-88.

RIEDEL, Manfred. Naturhermeneutik und Ethik im Denken Heideggers. Heidegger Stud, 5, 153-172, 1989.

RIGHTER, William. Golden Rules and Golden Bowls. Phil Lit, 13(2), 262-281, O 89.

The relation of moral rules and narrative in *The Golden Bowl*: James's distinctive method uses the multiple focal lengths of narrative to explore the relationship between circumstantiality and general moral criteria. His vision of a beautiful form of existence, subjected to contingent terms, provides the novel's resolution. Yet in shaping it, James weaves patterns of decorum which subvert, for all the novel's preoccupation with moral choices, the very possibility of 'taking rules seriously'. No criterion is ultimately generalisable: the story becomes more intelligible than the 'explanation'. Incompatible concepts are absorbed by narrative into an understanding that pure argument could not accommodate.

RIGOBELLO, Armando. Ricerca ed affermazione. G Metaf, 11(1), 115-125, Ja-Ap 89.

RIGOL, Montserrat Negre. Fundamentación ontológica del sujeto en Kierkegaard. Anu Filosof, 21(1), 51-72, 1988.

RILEY, Jonathan. Rights to Liberty in Purely Private Matters: Part I. Econ Phil, 5(2), 121-166, O 89.

RILEY, Jonathan. Rights to Liberty in Purely Private Matters: Part II. Econ Phil, 6(1), 27-64, Ap 90.

RILEY, Jonathan. Utilitarian Ethics and Democratic Government. Ethics, 100(2), 335-348, Ja 90.

Utilitarian values are held to provide a normative foundation for democratic government. Democratic procedures are essentially purely ordinalist utilitarian procedures in which (loosely speaking) each citizen receives an equal opportunity to influence social decisions. Utilitarianism becomes democracy once we drop the fiction of an ideal impartial observer who costlessly operates the utilitarian calculus and assume instead that political institutions must be designed to mimic the utilitarian calculus in a world where utility information richer than purely ordinal utility information is too costly for society to retrieve. Ordinalist-utilitarians are shown to have good reason to prescribe simple majority rule in the case of direct democracy, and to prescribe a two-stage rule involving Hare's single transferable vote method of PR combined with majority voting by elected representatives in the case of representative democracy.

RINALDI, Giacomo. "The Identity of Thought and Being in Harris's Interpretation of Hegel's Logic" in *Dialectic and Contemporary Science*, GRIER, Philip T (ed), 69-88. Lanham, Univ Pr of America, 1989.

RINGEN, Jon. Response to Dietrich's "Computationalism". Soc Epistem, 4(2), 183-186, Ap-Je 90.

Teleological functions are presented as a type of function which will satisfy the constraints on Dietrich's computationalism, provide an account of how intelligence is exhibited by computational systems which lack the capacity to understand their own representations, and not require that the actions of intelligent systems are "willed" (freely or otherwise).

RINNE, H and SWINYARD, W R and KENG KAU, A. The Morality of Software Piracy: A Cross-Cultural Analysis. J Bus Ethics, 9(8), 655-664, Ag 90.

Software piracy is a damaging and important moral issue, which is widely believed to be unchecked in particular areas of the globe. This cross-cultural study examines differences in morality and behavior toward software piracy in Singapore versus the United States, and reviews the cultural histories of Asia versus the United States to explore why these differences occur. The paper is based upon pilot data collected in the US and Singapore, using a tradeoff analysis methodology and analysis. The data reveal some fascinating interactions between the level of ethical transgression and the rewards of consequences which they produce.

RINTALA, Janet A and THOMAS, Carolyn E. Injury as Alienation in Sport. J Phil Sport, 16, 44-58, 1989.

The purpose of the paper was to examine the effects of injury in sport related to potential alienation in sport. The parameters of isolation, powerlessness, anomie, and self/body alienation were explored. It was argued that the injured athlete becomes separated from and discarded by teammates and the sport world and that such injury may attenuate achievement of the unity of body and action possible before the injury. The doubt and vulnerability generated by injury were viewed as potentially negating optimal future potential as well as moving the body into object status incapable of the essential unity of body subject.

RIOJA, Ana. Einstein: el ideal de una ciencia sin sujeto. Rev Filosof (Spain), 2, 87-108, 1989.

Einstein's realistic interpretation of the quantum mechanics does not entail the ideal of a science without a subject. His epistemologic aprioristic position requires the intervention of a reason that would organise the given sensitive material so that it can be understood. The concept of "material object" in Einstein is that of a "creation" by the subject since he confers it a reality that cannot be reduced to the sensorial impressions. Thus his polemic with Bohr does not consist on the elimination of the subject but rather on the objectification of experience.

RIP, Arie. De oppervlakkigheid van de empirisch gewende wetenschapstheorie. Kennis Methode, 14(2), 216-221, 1990.

In a critical review of a collection of articles on recent historical and sociological perspectives in theory of science, a shared program is reconstructed. Historical situation (i.e., momentanism) and communal character of scientific knowledge are emphasized, and go with antifundamentalism, a penchant for (methodological) relativism, and symmetrical treatment of valid and invalid knowledge. While claiming to present recent developments in theory of science, the book thus forgets to address the central issue of the locus of reason in history.

RIPP, Zoltán. Georg Lukács and the Ideological Fronts 1946-1949 (in Hungarian). Magyar Filozof Szemle, 5, 564-603, 1989.

Nach 1945 hatten die Ideologen der Partei die Aufgabe die Theorie der "neuen Demokratie" (d.h. der "Volksdemokratie")—der deklarierten Richtlinie der Ungarischen Kommunistischen Partei entsprechend—auszuarbeiten, die Politik der Partei theoretisch zu untermauern. Die Mehrheit der kommunistischen Theoretiker war jedoch nicht fähig zu dieser, sehr bald zur Taktik degradierten Strategie eine wirklich fundamentale Theorie zu erarbeiten. Nur aus den Arbeiten von Georg Lukács können die Grundzüge einer politisch—philosophischen Theorie rekonstruiert werden, die den demokratischen und organischen Weg des Überganges zum organischen Weg des Überganges zum Sozialismus aufzeigten. (edited)

RIPSTEIN, Arthur. "Hobbes on World Government and the World Cup" in *Hobbes: War Among Nations*, AIRAKSINEN, Timo (ed), 112-129. Brookfield, Gower, 1989.

RISJORD, Mark. The Sensible Foundation for Mathematics: A Defense of Kant's View. Stud Hist Phil Sci, 21(1), 123-143, Mr 90.

RISSER, David T. Punishing Corporations: A Proposal. Bus Prof Ethics J, 8(3), 83-92, Fall 89.

RITCHIE, J Bonner. "Organizational Ethics: Paradox and Paradigm" in *Papers on the Ethics of Administration*, WRIGHT, N Dale (ed), 159-184. Albany, SUNY Pr, 1988.

RITCHIE, Karen. The Little Woman Meets Son of DSM-III. J Med Phil, 14(6), 695-708, D 89.

The author discusses conceptual problems in psychiatry, illustrated by a debate over inclusion of a new disorder, masochistic personality disorder, in DSM-III-R, the manual of psychiatric diagnoses. While the DSM committee has attempted to avoid assumptions about theory and values in an attempt to be scientific, this has proved impossible, as theory is an integral part of scientific observation and values are a prerequisite for any judgment. The foundation for psychiatry cannot be theory—it can only be patient need.

RIVADULLA, Andrés (trans) and ESSLER, Wilhelm. Filosofar abierto. Rev Filosof (Spain), 2, 155-168, 1989.

RIVERA DE VENTOSA, Enrique. Nota bibliográfica sobre cinco estudios agustinianos. Augustinus, 34(135-136), 389-394, Jl-D 89.

RIVERO, Francisco H. El estudio científico de la inteligencia: Acotaciones filosóficas. Anu Filosof, 22(2), 173-178, 1989.

RIVERSO, Emanuele. History as Metascience: A Vichian Cue to the Understanding of the Nature and Development of Sciences. New Vico Studies, 3, 49-59, 1985.

RIVIER, Dominique. Le physicien et ses principes. Rev Theol Phil, 122(1), 15-32, 1990.

Ayant précisé la distinction qu'il convient de faire en physique, entre les principes, les lois et les conditions aux limites, l'article analyse les changements de contenu et de forme subis ce dernier siècle par les principes du physicien en vue de fonder théories et modèles (principes d'invariance, principes cosmologiques). A la fois trame et nervures de ces modèles, les principes soulignent et soutiennent les frontières du savoir du physicien, d'où leur mobilité parfois surprenante.

RIX, Bo Andreassen. The Importance of Knowledge and Trust in the Definition of Death. Bioethics, 4(3), 232-236, Jl 90.

RIZVI, Fazal. Wittgenstein on Grammar and Analytic Philosophy of Education. Educ Phil Theor, 19(2), 33-46, 1987.

RIZZI, Lino. I presupposti assiologici del riconoscimento nello Hegel prejenese. Teoria, 9(1), 215-229, 1989.

ROBERT, René. Le "suaire" johannique: Réponse a quelques questions. Rev Thomiste, 89(4), 599-608, O-D 89.

ROBERTS, Craige. Modal Subordination and Pronominal Anaphora in Discourse. Ling Phil, 12(6), 683-721, D 89.

Modal subordination involves the apparent extension of the logical scope of natural language modal auxiliaries to include segments of discourse outside the sentence in which they occur; e.g., in "If I had a garden, I'd plant an apple tree. It would bear fruit in a few years." This presents problems for the analysis of the logical entailments of individual sentences in such contexts, and for theories of anaphora. This analysis preserves the assumption that operator scope is sentence-bound; apparent counterexamples involve the accommodation of a hypothetical common ground to restrict the domain of the modal in the subordinate sentence.

ROBERTS, Jean. Aristotle on Responsibility for Action and Character. Ancient Phil, 9 (1), 23-36, Spr 89.

ROBERTS, Jean. Political Animals in the *Nicomachean Ethics*. Phronesis, 34(2), 185-204, 1989.

ROBERTS, Richard. "Theological Rhetoric and Moral Passion in the Light of MacKinnon's 'Barth'" in *Christ, Ethics and Tragedy: Essays in Honour of Donald MacKinnon*, SURIN, Kenneth (ed), 1-14. New York, Cambridge Univ Pr, 1989.

Donald MacKinnon's early work is neglected despite his influence over many important British figures in the post-Second World War period. MacKinnon's two earliest books were excursions into a form of totalitarian theological dialecticism strongly influenced by Karl Barth and his Cambridge exponent E C Hoskyns. MacKinnon's explosive and uncompromising "theological rhetoric" failed to persuade its audience for complex reasons. Beneath the rhetoric lay an impulse towards a more measured exploration of the basis of moral agency. The later triumph of agonistic analysis should not be allowed to obscure a boldly un-English dialecticism that has not wholly lost its contemporary relevance.

ROBERTS, Robert C. Sense of Humor as a Christian Virtue. Faith Phil, 7(2), 177-192, Ap 90.

ROBERTSON, John A. Resolving Disputes Over Frozen Embryos. Hastings Center Rep, 19(6), 7-12, N-D 89.

This article argues that gamete providers "own" extracorporeal embryos and may choose transfer, discard, donation or research by advance directive in case of dispute or unavailability. If no prior agreement exists, disputes between the couple should be decided on the basis of relative burdens and benefits to the parties. On this analysis the *Davis* case should have been decided in favor of the husband.

ROBIN, D P and REIDENBACH, R E. Toward the Development of a Multidimensional Scale for Improving Evaluations of Business Ethics. J Bus Ethics, 9(8), 639-653, Ag 90.

This study represents an improvement in the ethics scales inventory published in a 1988 *Journal of Business Ethics* article. The article presents the distillation and validation process whereby the original 33-item inventory was reduced to eight items. These eight items comprise the following ethical dimensions: a moral equity dimension, a relativism dimension, and a contractualism dimension. The multidimensional ethics scale demonstrates significant predictive ability.

ROBIN, Donald P and REIDENBACH, R Eric. *Business Ethics: Where Profits Meet Value Systems*. Englewood Cliffs, Prentice-Hall, 1989

The purpose of this book is to provide the business person with a theoretically based but practical approach for developing an ethical and profitable organization. It recognizes the need for businesses to achieve and maintain profits and explains why ethical performance and profitability need not be incompatible. The book then presents its "parallel planning" approach in a way that simplifies application. The parallel planning process is an adaptation of strategic planning to the dual missions of ethics and profits. The authors use case histories throughout the book in order to illustrate their points.

ROBIN, Donald P and REIDENBACH, R Eric. Integrating Social Responsibility and Ethics into the Strategic Planning Process. Bus Prof Ethics J, 7(3-4), 29-46, Fall-Wint 88.

This article is adapted from a book by the same two authors, *Business Ethics: Where Profits Meet Value Systems* (Prentice-Hall, 1989). It recognizes the need for business to generate profits and efficiencies, as well as the need for ethics and social responsibility. A parallel planning approach is suggested to achieve these two objectives. Suggestions for implementing the resultant plans through the organizational culture, the concept of an ethical profile, and core values of an organization are also presented.

ROBINS, Michael H. "The Objectivity of Agent Relative Values" in *Inquiries into Values: The Inaugural Session of the International Society for Value Inquiry*, LEE, Sander H, 229-241. Lewiston, Mellen Pr, 1989.

In his recent book, *The View from Nowhere*, Thomas Nagel attempts to establish the objectivity of values as something that can be recognized stepping outside our subjective point of view. The force of his argument is that what makes the objects *values* is that such recognition is not simply cognitive but conative, i.e., carries "motivational content" for the agent. This ontology of values is also supposed to consist of two principal kinds: agent-neutral and agent-relative. The first carry motivation—supply the cognizing subject with reasons to act—*simpliciter*; the second carry motivation only from the point of view of the agent who has them. This paper shall show, first, that Nagel's conception of agent-relative values is inconsistent with his concept of value objectivity. In a word, either agent-relative values are not objective in his sense or are not values. Second, I will argue that agent-relative values concerning other agents can figure into an objective ontology when each of us relies on the intentions and commitments of other agents.

ROBINSON, Denis. Matter, Motion and Humean Supervenience. Austl J Phil, 67(4), 394-409, D 89.

ROBINSON, Howard. The Objects of Perceptual Experience—II. Aris Soc, SUPP 64, 151-166, 1990.

The paper is part of a symposium with Paul Snowdon. In the first half I discuss critically Snowdon's attack on the causal theory of perception and contest his claim that there is a clear and important distinction between analysis of the concept of perception and empirical facts about perception. In the second half I defend the argument from illusion as a means of supporting the causal theory.

ROBINSON, James V. The Tripartite Soul in the *Timaeus*. Phronesis, 35(1), 103-110, 1990.

Although the question of whether the soul in its true nature is simple or composite has been extensively debated, the position of the *Timaeus* on this issue is generally regarded as uncontroversial. Since we are explicitly told in this dialogue that *nous* is the only immortal part of the soul, scholars have assumed that *nous* alone will escape the cycle of rebirth. I challenge the accepted view by contending that the tripartite soul is everlasting (albeit not immortal) and that there is no escaping the cycle of rebirth.

ROBINSON, Jenefer. "Music as a Representational Art" in *What is Music?*, ALPERSON, Philip A , 165-192. New York, Haven, 1987.

I discuss three theories of pictorial representation: the resemblance theory, the reference of description theory (e g , Goodman), and the seeing-in theory (e.g., Wollheim). I claim that genuine pictorial representation requires both "description" and seeing-in. Music, however, although it can describe or characterize, does not involve hearing-in: we cannot hear an individual in a piece of music as we can see an individual in a picture. However, both pictures and pieces of music "describe" the world: that may be why music has been often thought to be representational.

ROBINSON, Jenefer and ROSS, Stephanie. Woman, Morality, and Fiction. Hypatia, 5(2), 76-90, Sum 90.

We apply Carol Gilligan's distinction between a "male" mode of moral reasoning, focussed on justice, and a "female" mode, focussed on caring, to the reading of literature. Martha Nussbaum suggests that certain novels are works of moral philosophy. We argue that what Nussbaum sees as the special ethical contribution of such novels is in fact training in the stereotypically female mode of moral concern. We show this kind of training is appropriate to *all* readers of these novels, not just to women. Finally, we explore what else is involved in distinctively *feminist* readings of traditional novels.

ROBINSON, Viviane and SWANTON, Christine and CROSTHWAITE, Jan. Treating Women as Sex-Objects. J Soc Phil, 20(3), 5-20, Wint 89.

ROBLES, José A. Berkeley y los *minima*. Analisis Filosof, 6(1), 1-12, My 86.

In this paper I argue against D Raynor's view that Berkeley's *minima* are extended. My claim is that exactly the opposite view is the one which is more congenial with Berkeley's general philosophical outlook, and is the one which he maintained in his works, including the *Philosophical Commentaries*. As another point I hold that there is a strong resemblance between Berkeley's position and Epicurus's on *minima*. It might be held that the atomist philosopher influenced Berkeley through Gassendi's translation of the former's 'Letter to Herodotus'.

ROBSON, John M. Mill in Parliament: The View from the Comic Papers. Utilitas, 2(1), 102-142, My 90.

ROBSON, John M (ed) and MILL, John Stuart. *Miscellaneous Writings (Collected Works of John Stuart Mill, Volume 31)*. Buffalo, Univ of Toronto Pr, 1989

ROBSON, John M. No Laughing Matter: John Stuart Mill's Establishment of Women's Suffrage as a Parliamentary Question. Utilitas, 2(1), 88-101, My 90.

The article is an analysis of the steps John Stuart Mill took to prevent, both inside the House of Commons and in the press, the ridicule that might so easily have greeted his amendment to the Reform Bill in 1867 to include women in the expanded suffrage. His success can be attributed to his reputation as a philosopher but perhaps more to the care he took to prepare the public mind, to avoid opportunities for levity, to present a carefully constructed, restricted argument and to have his supporters in their seats, briefed for debate.

ROBSON, John M (ed) and MILL, John Stuart and MOIR, Martin (ed) and MOIR, Zawahir (ed). *Writings on India (Collected Works of John Stuart Mill, Volume 30)*. Buffalo, Univ of Toronto Pr, 1990

ROCHE, John F. Building for Democracy: Organic Architecture in Relation to Progressive Education. Educ Theor, 40(3), 295-307, Sum 90.

Organic architecture, a term used by Louis Sullivan and Frank Lloyd Wright to denote an art where "form and function are one," had its basis in Romantic theory, as did many contemporary educational experiments. Friedrich Froebel was a key link: Sullivan titled his book urging reform of architectural instruction *Kindergarten Chats*, while Wright played as a child

with the Froebel "Gifts," creative toys that helped shape his aesthetics. Wright was also a very public supporter of progressive educators like Francis Parker, John Dewey, and Alexander Meikeljohn. Wright had a chance to put his ideas into action through his Taliesin Fellowship.

ROCHE, Mark W. "Plato and the Structures of Injustice" in *Inquiries into Values: The Inaugural Session of the International Society for Value Inquiry*, LEE, Sander H , 279-290. Lewiston, Mellen Pr, 1989.

ROCKMORE, Tom (ed) and MARGOLIS, Joseph (ed) and FARÍAS, Victor. *Heidegger and Nazism*. Philadelphia, Temple Univ Pr, 1989

This is the English translation of Victor Farias's *Heidegger et le Nazisme*. It is enlarged and extensively altered by the addition of new and replacement materials from the German edition. Also, substantive errors and errors in the Notes have been corrected. The editors provide a new introductory statement.

ROCKMORE, Tom. Epistemology as Hermeneutics: Antifoundationalist Relativism. Monist, 73(2), 115-133, Ap 90.

ROCKMORE, Tom. Foundationalism and Hegelian Logic. Owl Minerva, 21(1), 41-50, Fall 89.

ROCKMORE, Tom. *Habermas on Historical Materialism*. Bloomington, Indiana Univ Pr, 1989

ROCKMORE, Tom. Hegel and the Unity of Science Program. Hist Phil Quart, 6(4), 331-346, O 89.

ROCKMORE, Tom. "System and History: Harris on Hegel's Logic" in *Dialectic and Contemporary Science*, GRIER, Philip T (ed), 91-103. Lanham, Univ Pr of America, 1989.

ROCKMORE, Tom. Whitehead et Hegel: Réalisme, idéalisme et philosophie spéculative. Arch Phil, 53(2), 261-269, Ap-Je 90.

The relation between Hegel's and Whitehead's speculative views is more often mentioned than studied. The present discussion relies on the link between systematic thought and a reading of the history of philosophy to examine this relation.

RODENBURG, P H. Manufacturing a Cartesian Closed Category with Exactly Two Objects Out of a C-Monoid. Stud Log, 48(3), 279-283, S 89.

RODIS-LEWIS, Geneviève. Liberté et égalité chez Descartes. Arch Phil, 53(3), 421-430, Jl-S 90.

Equality of good sense or reason does not exclude inequality of minds. Between the beginning of the *Discourse* and the dedication of the *Principia* to Elisabeth Descartes has specified that understandings are unequal and that the judgment, even as speculative, is a matter of the will which is infinite in every man. Everyone who makes good use of it acquires his maximum of perfection: so freedom is the foundation of equality. Descartes addresses both sexes: the main thing is absence of prejudices. In 1692 Fr. Boschet jeers at the interest of the philosopher for women and inferiors. Descartes calls "brothers" the working man Ferrier and his servant Gillot who became professor of mathematics. Lastly, the "comédie" which began at Stockholm confirms that inequality is not opposed to generosity and love.

RODIS-LEWIS, Geneviève. Philosophes européens et confucianisme au tournant dex XVIIe siècles. Rev Phil Fr, 179(2), 145-162, Ap-Je 89.

RODRÍGUEZ HÖLKEMEYER, Patricia. El Paradigma de Sistemas: Posibilidades Para Una Práctica Social Emancipadora: Reevaluación Crítica (Primera Part). Rev Filosof (Costa Rica), 26, 77-87, D 88.

The author, from a systems-based perspective of social evolution, points in this article and in a second part that will be published in the next edition of *Revista Filosofia Universita*, to the blunder of the "cibernetic" approach, to the limitations of the probabilistic theory of information, to the obsolescence of the organism as a paradigmatic unit, to the role of the dialectical contradiction and to the importance of the primary life-world structures, in explaining self-organizing processes. She draws from the socio-biological concepts of "autopoiesis" a conception that breaks with the structural determinism of classical socialization theories, offering a perspective that revitalizes the individual and reassesses liberty.

RODRÍGUEZ, Juan Acosta. El aristotelismo de Juan de Secheville. Logos (Mexico), 17(51), 55-69, S-D 89.

The author presents the "De principiis naturae," by John of Secheville, as one of the first exponents on natural philosophy teaching in the middle of the thirteenth century. The work, written between 1260 and 1265, when ecclesiastical prohibitions of reading and commenting on Aristotle had become quite obsolete, shows a mentality strongly shaped by the Aristotelian dialectic Latinized first by Boethius and more recently by Gilbert of Poitiers. Among the "libri naturales" by Aristotle, the VII on metaphysics and the I and II on physics stand out quite remarkably. Master John continually refers to Averroes in the explanation and commentary.

RODRÍGUEZ, Ramón. Filosofía y conciencia histórica. Rev Filosof (Spain), 2, 5-29, 1989.

The purpose of the work is to examine the significance of the history of philosophy for the philosophical activity itself. The reference point is an analysis of the philosophical act which reveals its constitutive "indifference" to history. This result is then confronted both with Hegelian historicism and with contemporary hermeneutics, the most influential theories of historical consciousness. Two conclusions follow: (1) it is difficult to reconcile the Hegelian view of the past with the place of the past in the philosophical act; (2) it is impossible for hermeneutics to replace without loss the primary philosophical act.

RODRIGUEZ, Vincent. The Method of "Grounded Theory" in the Age-Old Debate about Induction. Epistemologia, 11(2), 211-234, Jl-D 88.

RODRÍGUEZ, Virgilio Ruiz. El deseo de ser. Rev Filosof (Mexico), 23(67), 63-70, Ja-Ap 90.

RODRIGUEZ-CONSUEGRA, Francisco A. Bertrand Russell 1895-1899: Una filosofía prelogicista de la geometría. Dialogos, 25(55), 71-123, Ja 90.

RODRÍGUEZ-CONSUEGRA, Francisco. The Origins of Russell's Theory of Descriptions. Russell, 9(2), 99-132, Wint 89-90.

I explain here Russell's way from the first paradoxes to the discovery that denotative functions can be derived from propositional functions. The main targets are (i) the theory of meaning of 1903 as trying to distinguish the logical and psychological notions; (ii) a great deal of unpublished work containing several attempts of incorporating the objectivity of Frege's semantics, and the need for distinguishing acquaintance and description to understand propositions; (iii) the theory of descriptions partially accepting Bradley's claim that proper names are disguised descriptions; (iv) a new methodological interpretation of the results, including an alternative view on its relationship with ordinary language.

RODZINSKA, Aleksandra (trans) and FRITZHAND, Marek. Is Marxism an Atheism? Dialec Hum, 16(2), 109-120, Spr 89.

RODZINSKA, Aleksandra (trans) and TANALSKI, Dionizy. John Paul II vis-à-vis Atheism and Materialism: Remarks on the Encyclical Dominum et vivificantem. Dialec Hum, 14(1), 99-108, Wint 87.

The encyclic "Domimum et vivificantem" underlines the problem of sin. The most important forms of this sin are "practical" materialism, theoretical materialism and atheism. Pope prefers ontological dualism—a theoretical basis for moral implications directed against non-Christians. The personalist trend disappears. The problem of sin has been interpreted in an extremely traditional way, without the social relations. It is impossible to solve the problem of justice only by means of faith of Christians alone, so we propose to join our efforts in common struggle against social sin and to set aside the accusations and moral discrimination caused by different world outlooks.

RODZINSKA, Aleksandra (trans) and NIZNIK, Józef. The Philosophical Implications of the Use of New Information Technologies: Introductory Reflections. Dialec Hum, 16(2), 187-193, Spr 89.

In very preliminary remarks, the author outlines some of the cognitive and epistemological effects of computerization and artificial intelligence projects. He argues that the new information technology leads to the redefinition of information and knowledge. It creates "epistemological compulsion" affecting human consciousness, the intellectual processes of man and the self-perception of man. This self-perception also has an impact on man's perception of nature. The paper has been designed as an introduction to a more comprehensive study.

RODZINSKA, Aleksandra (trans) and BIENIAK, Janusz. Remarks on the Dialogue Between Christians and Marxists. Dialec Hum, 15(3-4), 187-193, Sum-Autumn 88.

The paper was read at the Polish-Soviet philosophical conference (Warsaw, October 1987). It was made in connection with the author's activity in (existing 1986-1989) the Consultative Board attached to the Chairman of the Council of State. It should give arguments for introducing into the state an effective world outlook equality and tolerance. In detail, it was a polemic with an article of a Marxist philosopher Zdzislaw Cackowski, "Cultural Partnership—A Factor of Social Peace." In spite of that author an obstacle for cultural partnership is not religion but only all totalism and all inequality.

RODZINSKA, Aleksandra (trans) and MC GOVERN, Arthur F and PETROWICZ, Lech (trans). Response to Janusz's "Christianity and Marxism". Dialec Hum, 14(1), 89-92, Wint 87.

McGovern wrote "Is Atheism Essential to Marxism?" for the Journal of Ecumenical Studies (Summer, 1985). He argued that Marxist socialism need not be atheistic. Kuczynski responded in Dialectics and Humanism, arguing that McGovern effectively calls for Marxists to give up their atheism.

McGovern rejects that interpretation, and agrees that neither Christianity nor Marxism should seek dominance. He argues also that a humanistic materialism which stresses human initiative in transforming society, a humanism Kuczynski views as essential to Marxism, does not conflict with contemporary Christian views about change.

RODZINSKA, Aleksandra (trans) and KUCZYNSKI, Janusz and PETROWICZ, Lech (trans). Universalism as a Metaphilosophy of the New Peace Movement. Dialec Hum, 16(2), 61-78, Spr 89.

RODZINSKA, Aleksandra (trans) and KRAPIEC, Mieczyslaw A. The Human Dimension of Christian Culture—The Common Heritage of the Nations of Europe. Dialec Hum, 14(1), 5-23, Wint 87.

RODZINSKI, A. Aus den Überlegungen über die Moralsprachaspekte (in Polish). Stud Phil Christ, 25(1), 111-115, 1989.

Der Aufsatz, der den "Bemerkungen am Rande" Charakter hat, bietet und unterzeichnet die Grundübereinstimmung der Auffassungen vom Verfasser über das Thema des Rechtes zur Verbalverteidigund des Geheimnisses dar mit den Meinungen, die T Slipko in dem Aufsatz unter dem Titel: Prawda—klamstwo—nieprawda, "Chrzescijanin w swiecie" 1985 nr 11 (Wahrheit—Lüge—Unwahrheit, "Der Christ in der Welt") darstellt. Jede Lüge ist, Verfassers Meinung nach, nichtswürdig und als eine moralische Deviation der Verständigung mit jemandem unzulässig. Falle wenn die einzige Weise des erfolgreichen Bewahrens des moralisch nichtübermittelnden Wissens dem Aggressor die Angabe der nicht wahrheitsmässig Information ist, gibt es im Grunde genommen und tatsächlich keine Verständigung. Es kommt dort also keine Deviation dieser Art überhaupt vor.

ROE, Emery M. Nonsense, Fate, and Policy Analysis: The Case of Animal Rights and Experimentation. Agr Human Values, 6(4), 21-29, Fall 89.

Animal rights and experimentation have become the focus of a major controversy in the United States, with acute implications for animal-related research in the laboratories and veterinary schools of many American universities. To date, efforts to reduce fundamental disagreements between animal researchers and animal welfare groups or to redefine their differences in ways that satisfy all concerned have by and large not been successful. In such situations where it is not possible to identify a middle ground between conflicting positions, the best a policy analyst may be able to do is to accentuate the issue's manifest topsy-turviness and uncertainties. No one can afford or risk having an issue of such high uncertainty, inconsistency, and stakes defined in terms so stark that they feel compelled to choose between those who say they know that the future shall hold us accountable for our wholesale slaughter of animals and those who would blame us for the human deaths they say will surely follow when we do not allow that slaughter.

ROEPER, Peter and LEBLANC, Hugues. On Relativizing Kolmogorov's Absolute Probability Functions. Notre Dame J Form Log, 30(4), 485-512, Fall 89.

ROETZ, Heiner. Chinese Axial Age in the Light of Kohlberg's Developmental Logic of Moral Consciousness (in Serbo-Croatian). Filozof Istraz, 29(2), 473-487, 1989.

Kohlbergs "Entwicklungslogik des moralischen Bewusstseins", und die darin dargelegten 6 Stufen moralischen Räsonnements, erweist sich als sehr fruchtbar um die Ethik der chinesischen "Achsenzeit" (K Jaspers) im Geiste des ethischen Universalismus zu rekonstruieren. Vor dem Hintergrund der Ontogenese kann die Entwicklung der chinesischen Philosophie als Durchbruch zu einer "postkonventionellen" Perspektive in der Adoleszenzkrise der chinesischen Gesellschaft interpretiert werden. Von dieser Perspektive aus wird die konventionelle "Sittlichkeit" weder kritisch wiederhergestellt noch verworfen. Der radikale Taoismus, der sich auf der Stufe 4 1/2 befindet, hinterfragt dieser unter Rückgriff auf die nicht-entfremdete Rationalität des präkonventionellen Niveaus. Der Legalismus plädiert für eine Gesetz-und-Ordnung-"Moralität", die strikt an die Stufe 4 gebungen ist, sich jedoch auf der Orientierung on Strafe und Gehorsam der Stufe 1 gründet. Mo Di stellt den Utilitarismus der Sturfe 5 dar, während das konfuzianische "ren"-Konzept sich als Anwärter auf die universelle Moralität der Stufe 6 erweist.

ROGERS, G A J. "Hobbes's Hidden Influence" in Perspectives on Thomas Hobbes, ROGERS, G A J (ed), 189-205. New York, Clarendon/Oxford Pr, 1988.

Hobbes's Leviathan soon became notorious and therefore few, if any, openly admitted its influence on them. But did it, nevertheless, exercise such an influence? This paper argues that at least two important thinkers, Henry More and John Locke, were more indebted to Hobbes than they were prepared to acknowledge, especially in their understanding of the possibility of a demonstrative system of ethics.

ROGERS, G A J (ed) and RYAN, Alan (ed). *Perspectives on Thomas Hobbes*. New York, Clarendon/Oxford Pr, 1988

The papers in this collection provide views on central aspects of Hobbes's life and work, testifying to his enduring importance as a major philosopher, and help to unravel aspects of his intellectual autobiography. Hobbes is seen as a major figure not only in the English-speaking world but also by highly regarded scholars from France and Italy, whilst other contributors form an excellent mix between new and established Hobbes scholars, confirming the importance and depth of Hobbes's political theory and the wider thinking in which that political theory is set.

ROGERS, Joel and COHEN, Joshua. Reply to Beehler's "Autonomy and the Democratic Principle". Can J Phil, 19(4), 583-587, D 89.

ROGERSON, Kenneth F. Causal Hermits. Dialectica, 43(4), 387-396, 1989.

Michael Devitt, in a number of recent writings, maintains a particularly clear version of realism against antirealist criticisms. His strategy is to argue for a realist position quite apart from considerations of language and epistemology. He pushes hard for a causal theory of reference and a causally grounded version of correspondence truth as a way to explain the connection between language and a "real" world. In this paper the author will raise a problem for a causal theory of language. It is a polemical point against the realist who believes that a causal theory explains how we can refer to mind independent objects and fix determinant truth values about such things. The author hopes to show that a causal theory cannot be an adequate account of language for a realist. Quite simply, there are possible objects and states of affairs which a realist must seriously entertain in virtue of his metaphysics, but which he cannot accommodate within a causal theory of language. (edited)

ROGERSON, Kenneth F. The Inequality of Markets. Dialogue (Canada), 28(4), 553-567, 1989.

Ronald Dworkin attempts to defend free market economies on the grounds that market economies are consistent with the liberal ideal of treating persons equally with respect to their preferences for goods and careers. Following an analysis of Dworkin's ideal of equality, I argue that markets often fail to meet this ideal. The central problem for Dworkin's account is the fact that markets will favor popular preferences over unpopular ones owing to the efficiencies of mass producing and mass marketing. Accordingly, persons with unpopular preferences will need to pay much more to satisfy their preferences compared to persons whose preferences are widely shared.

ROGOGINSKI, Jacob. Forgetting Abdera (in Serbo-Croatian). Filozof Istraz, 30(3), 727-739, 1989.

L'auteur examine le *Conflit des facultés* de Kant, en ce qui concerne le progrès constant du genre humain, et la réfutation de l'hypothèse "abdéritiste" d'une éternelle stagnation. Ainsi, on parvient au signe d'histoire qui est, d'après Kant, "l'enthousiasme que des spectateurs désintéressés éprouvent pour la Révolution Française." Ce signe permet de prouver l'existence d'une tendance au progrès comme disposition constante dans l'histoire. Enfin, on conclut que "ce que signe réfléchit c'est l'Idée sublime d'une communauté universelle ordonnée leson les principes du droit, et la possibilité, à chacun offerte, d'y prendre part."

ROHATYN, Dennis. "The Devaluation of Value" in *Inquiries into Values: The Inaugural Session of the International Society for Value Inquiry*, LEE, Sander H , 115-117. Lewiston, Mellen Pr, 1989.

We examine Langdon Winner's claim that "values" are merely idle chatter, fit for after-dinner conversation. This is true because (if and only if) it's false. To condemn all values one must have some, just as to be a nihilist is to believe (for the moment) in one's unbelief. If we equate values with sheer human effort, hard work, or what we are compelled to sacrifice in order to make life bearable, then values will both cease to be meaningless and begin living up to their original Edenic promise.

ROHATYN, Dennis and NOLT, John Eric. *Schaum's Outline of Theory and Problems of Logic*. New York, McGraw-Hill, 1988

Intended to function either as a stand-alone textbook or supplement, this volume includes chapters on argument structure, argument evaluation, the propositional calculus, truth tables and refutation trees, categorical syllogisms, the predicate calculus, fallacies, induction, the probability calculus, and extensions of formal logic. Both formal and informal points of view are covered. It contains 524 solved problems.

ROHDEN, Valério. Ceticismo versus condições de verdade. Manuscrito, 11(2), 85-94, O 88.

I examine certain texts of the *Critique of Judgment*, with respect to the communicability of knowledge and judgment as a condition for their truth, as denied by the sceptic, and of *The Critique of Pure Reason*, concerning truth

conditions as a transcendental form of overcoming the difficulties directed by the sceptic against formal logic. I also observe that the negation of the transcendental perspective is specific to a gnoseological scepticism and that this affects the former's possible objectivity as well as its intersubjectivity.

ROHR, John A. "Reason of State as Political Morality: A Benign View" in *Papers on the Ethics of Administration*, WRIGHT, N Dale (ed), 185-223. Albany, SUNY Pr, 1988.

ROJAS, Jorge Ramos. Tiempo e Instante. Logos (Mexico), 17(51), 81-90, S-D 89.

Grace is an instant of encounter between epochs and eternity. Grace endows human being with eternity. Inbued with grace, human being accomplishes eternity, for he creates himself. The essence of mankind is theopoyetic, and also creator of eternity. Time is a symbolic expression of eternity, and history is the manifest of eternity. Mythology is the knowledge, to a subconscious level, of the symbolic expression systems, as pneumathology is the conscious knowledge.

ROLDÁN PANADERO, Concha. Das Vollkommenheitsprinzip bei Leibniz als Grund der Kontingenz. Stud Leibniz, 21(2), 188-195, 1989.

In Leibniz's work, anything is to be determined by safe principles. Logic order, ontology, metaphysics, ethics, even divine will, depend altogether from those. The principle of contradiction states the distinction between what is possible from the logical point of view and what is not. Moreover, Leibniz sees the principle of sufficient reason as the principle of existences. But the latter is not enough to explain the whole reality, and so the *principle of perfection* is needed, i.e., a consequence of the principle of reason which concretizes it. In my approach, the principle of perfection might be viewed as the root of contingence and, at the same time, as the foundation of freedom. In brief, it represents the cornerstone of the Leibnizian ethical cosmos.

ROLF, Eckard. How to Generalize Grice's Theory of Conversation. Manuscrito, 12(1), 55-69, Ap 89.

Grice's theory of conversation is designed for a kind of talk whose purpose is a maximally effective exchange of information. This specification is too narrow, if other kinds of talk are analyzed. As Grice himself has pointed out, his theory, therefore, needs to be generalized. This essay attempts to show how this could be done. Making use of concepts Searle has developed within his version of speech act theory, I call the conversational maxims established by Grice "assertive', and I argue that there are directive, commissive, expressive, and declarative maxims of conversation too. A pattern for generalization thus clearly emerges. Though the main value of Grice's theory lies in allowing for (a reconstruction of) interpretations of utterances, there still remains a whole set of utterances whose meaning this theory has not yet been able to grasp. Mentioning a few examples of such utterances, I try to show how their meaning(s) can be reconstructed, if conversational maxims other than Grice's are recognized. That the explanatory potential of Grice's theory can be raised by incorporating further maxims should be illustrated in this way.

ROLL-HANSEN, Nils. The Crucial Experiment of Wilhelm Johannsen. Biol Phil, 4(3), 303-329, Jl 89.

I call an experiment "crucial" when it makes possible a decisive choice between conflicting hypotheses. Johannsen's selection for size and weight within pure lines of beans played a central role in the controversy over continuity or discontinuity in hereditary change, often known as the biometrician-Mendelian controversy. The "crucial" effect of this experiment was not an instantaneous event, but an extended process of repeating similar experiments and discussing possible objections. The paper also argues that crucial experiments thus interpreted contradict certain ideas about the underdetermination of theories by facts and the theory-ladenness of facts which have been influential in recent history and sociology of science. (edited)

ROLLINS, Mark. *Mental Imagery: On the Limits of Cognitive Science*. New Haven, Yale Univ Pr, 1989

The purpose of the work is to consider recent research on mental imagery, and to assess arguments by philosophers and scientists regarding the possibility and nature of an acceptable theory of imagery in cognition. The larger concern is with mental representation as a theoretical construct and with explanation in cognitive science. The conclusion of the book is that no account of mental imagery is presently adequate. The framework for a new theory, more empirically and conceptually satisfactory, is developed. Its implications for representational theories generally are discussed in relation to work on perception and propositional attitudes.

ROLSTON III, Holmes. Environmental Justice. Between Species, 5(3), 147-153, Sum 89.

Peter S Wenz's *Environmental Justice* develops a theory of environmental ethics around distributive justice. Libertarian theory, laissez faire economics, efficiency theory, cost-benefit analysis, and Rawls's theory of justice are insufficient, even in combination. They count morally only subjective life. Among theories that count objective entities such as plants, species, and ecosystems, biocentrism cannot be consistently applied. Wenz places the personal moral agent at the center of widening concentric circles of weakening obligations. One problem is that the circles are both biographically and biologically determined. Another rises from using the category of justice to unify the theory.

ROLSTON III, Holmes. Treating Animals Naturally? Between Species, 5(3), 131-137, Sum 89.

Humans ought to treat animals naturally. The adverb "naturally" modifies both the human subject and the animal object. Humans ought to follow the nature in their human nature, a shared mammalian nature by which humans are omnivores and eat meat naturally in their ecology. By their distinctive nature humans are also cultural animals who emerge from nature with a "super-natural" conscience. When culture is superimposed on nature natural selection is relaxed and humans ought to treat humans humanely. By contrast wild animals remain in nature and ought to be treated naturally. This sets constraints on the treatment of domestic animals, an intermediate case.

ROMAN, Joël and MICHELMAN, Stephen (trans). Thinking Politics without a Philosophy of History: Arendt and Merleau-Ponty. Phil Soc Crit, 15(4), 403-422, 1989.

ROMÁN, Leopoldo and PARÉ, Robert. Monoidal Categories With Natural Numbers Object. Stud Log, 48(3), 361-376, S 89.

ROMANO, Carlin. "The Illegality of Philosophy" in The Institution of Philosophy: A Discipline in Crisis?, COHEN, Avner (ed), 199-216. La Salle, Open Court, 1989.

ROMANO, Daniel A. A Theorem on Cocongruence of Rings. Z Math Log, 36(1), 87-88, 1990.

RÖMER, Joachim. Risiko und Entscheidung aus ethischer Sicht. Deut Z Phil, 37(9), 862-866, 1989.

Engstens verbunden mit dem Risiko im technischen Schaffen ist die Entscheidung. Diese liegt im Spannungsfeld von Gut und Böse und bedarf folglich der weltanschaulichen und ethischen Fundierung. Mit der Risikoanalyse werden jene Faktoren erfasst, die auf den Verlauf der Aufgaben in Forschung und Entwicklung Einfluss haben. Diese Analyse ermöglicht zugleich, nichtgerechtfertigte Risiken auszugrenzen. Über die Risikobereitschaft der Subjekte entscheidet im Zusammenhang mit den moralischen, charakterlichen und Willensqualitäten vor allem der Grad der Interessenübereinstimmung.

RÖMPP, Georg. Der Andere als Zukunft und Gegenwart. Husserl Stud, 6(2), 129-154, 1989.

RÖMPP, Georg. Sich-Wissen als Argument: Zum Problem der Theoretizität des Selbstbewusstseins. Kantstudien, 80(3), 303-323, 1989.

RÖMPP, Georg. Truth and Interpersonality: An Inquiry into the Argumentative Structure of Heidegger's Being and Time. Int Phil Quart, 29(4), 429-447, D 89.

RONCAGLIA, Gino. Cum Deus Calculat—God's Evaluation of Possible Worlds and Logical Calculus. Topoi, 9(1), 83-90, Mr 90.

RONNEBERG, Heinz. Brauchen wir eine Kategorie Persönlichkeit? Deut Z Phil, 38(1), 69-72, 1990.

The present contribution is the concentrate of a section of a doctoral thesis not submitted. The author polemizes against the unrealistic thesis proposing that human individual development proceeded from the indetermined newly born child to a truly humanistic personality—a process essentially determined by societal conditions. The author argues that a realistic reflection calls for considering the stratified manifestation of the quality "human individuality," its quantitative expression being characterized by increase and decrease, by ascending and descending moments, by positive as well as negative aspects. (edited)

ROOCHNIK, David L. Can the Relativist Avoid Refuting Herself? Phil Lit, 14(1), 92-98, Ap 90.

This is a critique of Barbara Herrnstein Smith's Contingencies of Value. Smith argues that her book, which pivots on a defense of relativism, does not fall victim to the problem traditionally besetting relativism: self-refutation. I argue that she fails entirely to make her claim persuasive and that her failure is symptomatic of the weakness of relativism itself.

ROONEY, Ellen. Seductive Reasoning: Pluralism as the Problematic of Contemporary Literary Theory. Ithaca, Cornell Univ Pr, 1989

ROOT, Michael. Miracles and the Uniformity of Nature. Amer Phil Quart, 26(4), 333-342, O 89.

In Section X of An Inquiry Concerning Human Understanding, David Hume raises two questions about miracles and their relation to testimony. First, he asks whether it could even be reasonable to believe on the basis of testimony that nature does not fit the image of our science, and, second, he asks whether it could ever be reasonable to believe on the basis of testimony that nature is not uniform. Hume's answer to the first question is 'yes' and his answer to the second is 'no'. Hume thinks that a 'no' to the second question shows that belief in the Christian religion is less reasonable than a belief in modern science. However, Hume's 'no' seems to oppose his empiricism and his belief that there are no necessary truths about any matter of fact or experience. The point of this paper is to show that Hume can prove that there can be no testimony of such a quantity or quality to make it reasonable to believe that nature is not uniform and, as result, no testimony to make it reasonable to believe that God has ever caused a miracle.

ROOTHAAN, Angela and VAN ECK, Caroline. Anna Maria van Schurman's verhouding tot de wetenschap. Alg Ned Tijdschr Wijs, 82(3), 194-211, Jl 90.

Anna Maria van Schurman, the Dutch 17th century philosopher, theologian, poet and painter, expressed her views on the place of women in science, and on the relation between science and faith in two works, the Dissertatio de ingenii muliebris ad doctrinam... (1641), in which she argues that Christian women should have access to (university) education; secondly, her autobiography, the Eucleria (1673), in which she describes her choice to break off her scientific work and join the religious community of Jean de Labadie. Both works are analysed with respect to her attitude to philosophy and science and placed in their historical and intellectual context.

RORTY, Amelie Oksenberg. "Socrates and Sophia Perform the Philosophical Turn" in The Institution of Philosophy: A Discipline in Crisis?, COHEN, Avner (ed), 271-282. La Salle, Open Court, 1989.

RORTY, Richard. The Dangers of Over-Philosophication—Reply to Arcilla and Nicholson. Educ Theor, 40(1), 41-44, Wint 90.

RORTY, Richard. "Philosophy as Science, as Metaphor, and as Politics" in The Institution of Philosophy: A Discipline in Crisis?, COHEN, Avner (ed), 3-11. La Salle, Open Court, 1989.

RORTY, Richard. A Post-Philosophical Politics? An Interview by Danny Postel. Phil Soc Crit, 15(2), 199-204, 1989.

RORTY, Richard. "Science as Solidarity" in Dismantling Truth: Reality in the Post-Modern World, LAWSON, Hilary (ed), 6-22. New York, St Martin's Pr, 1989.

RORTY, Richard. Truth and Freedom: A Reply to Thomas McCarthy. Crit Inquiry, 16(3), 633-643, Spr 90.

Thomas McCarthy, like Jürgen Habermas, believes that "a moment of universal validity" is presupposed in any genuine communication situation. By contrast, I think we can make sense of communication and democratic politics without invoking the notion of universal validity, and can make do with the notion of freedom—where this is defined by reference to the actually existing institutions of contemporary democratic societies.

ROS, Arno. "Bedeutung", "Idee" und "Begriff": Zur Behandlung einiger bedeutungstheoretischer Paradoxien durch Leibniz. Stud Leibniz, 21(2), 133-154, 1989.

Common sense supposes that general terms, which are negative, nonreferring or contradictory, may be quite understandable, i.e., meaningful—just as "normal" general terms. But attempts to give a theoretical explanation of this fact very often came to the conclusion that this must be false. The article tries to show that Leibniz—thanks to his new understanding of ideas and notions—has been able to resolve a great part of meaning paradoxes, which are the consequences of that contradiction. The article includes a comparison of Leibniz's position with that of some other philosophers, especially that of Aristotle and Locke.

ROSALES, Alberto. Zur teleologischen Grundlage der transzendentalen Deduktion der Kategorien. Kantstudien, 80(4), 377-404, 1989.

This paper exposes (1) the role of the subjective deduction within the structure of the transcendental deduction; (2) Kant's interpretation of the subject as a teleological system; (3) this teleology as the ground of the logic structure of the subjective-objective deduction; and (4) in what sense is this deduction a priori knowledge of the subject, with a proper kind of truth.

ROSCA, I N. L'idée d'unité et d'autonomie des formes de la culture dans la conception de Titu Maiorescu. Phil Log, 32(3-4), 197-202, Jl-D 88.

ROSEN, Gideon. Modal Fictionalism. Mind, 99(395), 327-354, Jl 90.

This paper develops an ontologically innocent alternative to Lewis's modal realism. Statements of the form 'There is a world at which P' are read as elliptical for 'According to the hypothesis of a plurality of worlds, there is a world at which P', the latter being no more ontological loaded than

'According to Frege's theory, there is a set of all sets'. An analysis of modal discourse employing this fictionalist paraphrase is sketched—roughly: 'Possibly P' is true iff according to the hypothesis of a plurality of worlds, there is a world at which P—and compared with Lewis's realist construal of possible worlds talk.

ROSEN, Henryk and SWIDERSKA, Ewa (trans). The Concept of Alienation in Janusz Korczak's Works. Dialec Hum, 16(1), 135-147, Wint 89.

ROSEN, Menahem. Le problème du commencement dans la philosophie de Hegel. Can J Phil, 19(4), 551-574, D 89.

Hegel wants to build a System, in which every step is criticized. A linear mode of explanation cannot be accepted, for its beginning also must be checked! So is built a "circular" philosophy, where the beginning becomes a problem. Hegel solves it by proposing a "double mouvement" between the traditionally known two worlds: he opens his *Phenomenology* by the sensible, and his *Logic* by the intelligible. Now, is a philosophy "without presupposition" possible? In spite of the difficulties involved, a Hegelian solution can be found, if by "presupposition" we understand a proposition, necessary for building the System, and "deduced" inside the System.

ROSENBAUM, Alan S. Teaching "Ethics in America". Teach Phil, 12(4), 399-404, D 89.

In this article I describe how I adapted a modified version of "Ethics in America" for use in my second-year, ten-week "Morals and Rights" philosophy course. Also, I explain the basis for my satisfaction with the course's outcome for my class of 42 students, particularly owing to this pedagogical innovation. ("Ethics in America" is a newly-designed course and public television series produced by Columbia University's Seminars on Media and Society.)

ROSENBAUM, Alan S. The Use of Nazi Medical Experimentation Data: Memorial or Betrayal? Int J Applied Phil, 4(4), 59-67, Fall 89.

In this paper I address the issue whether (medical) scientific experimenters, researchers and editors of professional scientific journals today ought to use data which were obtained from unethical and illegal Nazi medical experiments. I deal with the two most obvious claims offered in support of using the data, viz., 'salvaging good from evil', and the 'greater social utility'. These claims are both rejected. My thesis is that these data should *not* be used except in three highly qualified instances.

ROSENBAUM, Stephen E. Epicurus on Pleasure and the Complete Life. Monist, 73(1), 21-41, Ja 90.

This article aims to provide part of the basis for understanding positively Epicurus's curious hedonism. Based on the hypothesis that there are much closer connections among Epicurean theses about pleasure, death, and desire than have yet been fully explicated, the article is a study of Epicurus's *Kuria Doxa* (Key Doctrine) 19, which entails that the length of a life is independent of how good that life is. The author interprets KD 19, and examines classical and contemporary objections to this "counterintuitive" thesis. Finally, the author shows that the plausibility of KD 19 depends on the obscure but significant Epicurean idea of complete living. The author contrasts Epicurus's view of the complete life with Aristotle's, and urges both that the Epicurean idea of complete living is plausible and that it is indispensable for appreciating Epicurean hedonism.

ROSENBAUM, Stephen E. The Symmetry Argument: Lucretius Against the Fear of Death. Phil Phenomenol Res, 50(2), 353-373, D 89.

An interpretation, discussion, and defense of the argument embodied in Lucretius's comments about the symmetry of prenatal and posthumous nonexistence. The author interprets the comments as an argument that it is not reasonable to fear death, and defends the argument against contemporary criticisms. The symmetry argument is shown to be a unique and important contribution to Epicurean thanatology, which sheds light on the sense in which Epicurus believed that it is not reasonable to fear one's death.

ROSENBAUM, Stuart E (ed) and BAIRD, Robert M (ed). *Euthanasia: The Moral Issues.* Buffalo, Prometheus, 1989

This work poses the moral dilemmas of euthanasia or mercy killing and provides a collection of essays that clarify the issues and present alternative views. Included is material by prominent thinkers such as Koop, Rachels, Sullivan, Fletcher, and Engelhardt. Also included are provocative essays by physicians recently appearing in the *Journal of the American Medical Association* and the *New England Journal of Medicine*. By analyzing the arguments of these essays, readers will be able to reach tentative conclusions, and become better equipped to make difficult decisions of their own concerning these matters.

ROSENBERG, Alan. "The Crisis of Knowledge and Understanding the Holocaust: Some Epistemological Remarks" in *Inquiries into Values: The Inaugural Session of the International Society for Value Inquiry,* LEE, Sander H , 539-547. Lewiston, Mellen Pr, 1989.

This paper states that Holocaust studies have reached a crisis with regard to understanding the meanings of the Holocaust for our time. The author suggests a number of reasons for this crisis, among the most important of which is the mystification of the event. Such concepts as the Holocaust's incomprehensibility, the idea that only survivors can achieve understanding, and the claim that the event is beyond language are explored. Also analyzed is the impact these concepts have on our coming to understand the significance of the Holocaust for the contemporary world.

ROSENBERG, Alexander. Intentionality, IntenSionality and Representation. Behaviorism, 17(2), 137-140, Fall 89.

A reply to Emmett (*Behaviorism* 17-2). I argue that intentionality requires representational content and so requires intensionality, contrary to Emmett's challenge against the arguments of "Intentional Psychology and Evolutionary Biology" (*Behaviorism* 14 (1987)).

ROSENBERG, Alexander. Normative Naturalism and the Role of Philosophy. Phil Sci, 57(1), 34-43, Mr 90.

The prescriptive force of methodological rules rests, I argue, on the acceptance of scientific theories; that of the most general methodological rules rests on theories in the philosophy of science, which differ from theories in the several sciences only in generality and abstraction. I illustrate these claims by reference to methodological disputes in social science and among philosophers of science. My conclusions substantiate those of Laudan except that I argue for the existence of transtheoretical goals common to all scientists and concrete enough actually to have bearing on methodology. And I argue that Laudan is committed to such goals himself, willy-nilly.

ROSENBERG, Jay F. "E M Adams and the Modern Mind" in *Mind, Value and Culture: Essays in Honor of E M Adams,* WEISSBORD, David (ed), 55-88. Atascadero, Ridgeview, 1989.

ROSENBERG, Jay F. Why the Theory of Knowledge Isn't the Same as Epistemology, and What It Might Be Instead. Phil Papers, 18(2), 161-168, S 89.

ROSENKRANTZ, Gary. Reference, Intentionality, and Nonexistent Entities. Phil Stud, 58(1-2), 165-171, Ja-F 90.

I shall begin with a brief summary of the central thesis of Chisholm's paper (with which I am in sympathy), and then discuss certain passages which I found ambiguous and raise some questions about Chisholm's account of our thought about things that do not exist.

ROSENOW, Eliyahu. Kierkegaard's Concept of Education (in Hebrew). Iyyun, 38(3-4), 209-227, Jl-O 89.

Kierkegaard's concept of education constitutes a reversal of traditional concepts of education. This reversal is due to his philosophy, which focuses on the existing individual and his way to himself. Kierkegaard therefore postulates self-education. However, for him self-education does not imply the process of acquisition of knowledge and promotion of intellectual ability, but rather the individual's process of becoming, i.e., the individual's way of realizing his subjectivity. Kierkegaard's concern is therefore the individual's inner personal certitude about his existential stand. (edited)

ROSENOW, Eliyahu. Nietzsche's Educational Dynamite. Educ Theor, 39(4), 309-316, Fall 89.

The concept of "self-overcoming" is Nietzsche's rendering of the traditional concept of self-domination. The analysis of Nietzsche's "revaluation" of this concept makes apparent that his idea of "overcoming the self" is an essential component of his conception of authenticity. Contemporary philosophy of education has adopted Nietzsche's notion of authenticity in a selective manner, omitting his idea of self-overcoming. The article concludes with a discussion of the educational aftermath of this partial adaptation of Nietzsche's philosophy.

ROSENTHAL, Abigail L (ed) and ROSENTHAL, Henry M. *The Consolations of Philosophy: Hobbes's Secret; Spinoza's Way.* Philadelphia, Temple Univ Pr, 1989

A theory of action, convergent with Spinoza's, is discerned in Hobbes, with the social contract imposing its *a priori* constraints on action in the public domain. In Spinoza, the social contract is further seen as a function of human individuation on the ontological level, with that individuation expressed in the world as "a career of resistance," and traced in the realms of private decision, the arts, and rites of passage. This meditative, two-part treatise eschews standard interpretations of Hobbes as reductionist-materialist or hypostatizer of seventeenth-century market relations, and of Spinoza as mystical pantheist or else proto-scientist.

ROSENTHAL, David M. "Philosophy and its History" in *The Institution of Philosophy: A Discipline in Crisis?,* COHEN, Avner (ed), 141-176. La Salle, Open Court, 1989.

ROSENTHAL, Henry M and ROSENTHAL, Abigail L (ed). *The*

Consolations of Philosophy: Hobbes's Secret; Spinoza's Way. Philadelphia, Temple Univ Pr, 1989

A theory of action, convergent with Spinoza's, is discerned in Hobbes, with the social contract imposing its *a priori* constraints on action in the public domain. In Spinoza, the social contract is further seen as a function of human individuation on the ontological level, with that individuation expressed in the world as "a career of resistance," and traced in the realms of private decision, the arts, and rites of passage. This meditative, two-part treatise eschews standard interpretations of Hobbes as reductionist-materialist or hypostatizer of seventeenth-century market relations, and of Spinoza as mystical pantheist or else proto-scientist.

ROSENTHAL, J W and MAGIDOR, M and RUBIN, M and SROUR, G. Some Highly Undecidable Lattices. Annals Pure Applied Log, 46(1), 41-63, Ja 90.

ROSENTHAL, Sandra B and BOURGEOIS, Patrick L. Heidegger and Peirce: Beyond "Realism or Idealism". SW Phil Rev, 4(1), 103-110, Ja 88.

In both the phenomenological ontology of Martin Heidegger and the pragmatism of Charles Peirce, the rejection of the Kantian phenomenal/noumenal distinction leads to a rejection of the alternatives of realism or idealism as well. In their respective denials of such an existential or ontological gap between appearance or phenomena and the ontologically real, they each establish a fundamental intentional unity between man and world which cannot be understood within the framework of realism or of idealism and which reveals deeply rooted affinities between the two positions.

ROSENTHAL, Sandra B. Peirce's Ultimate Logical Interpretant and Dynamical Object: A Pragmatic Perspective. Trans Peirce Soc, 26(2), 195-210, Spr 90.

This examination of the relation between the ultimate logical interpretant and the dynamical object proceeds by way of Peirce's understanding of the internal structure of the meanings through which we grasp a world of perceived objects. It explores the cumulative process by which the very structure of the ultimate logical interpretant in its relation to logical interpretants allows for the experience of the dynamical object, while the acquaintance with particular aspects of the dynamical object allows for the fuller development of the sign system incorporated within the ultimate logical interpretant.

ROSENTHAL, Sandra B and BOURGEOIS, Patrick L. The Philosophy of the Act and the Phenomenology of Perception: Mead and Merleau-Ponty. S J Phil, 28(1), 77-90, Spr 90.

Mead and Merleau-Ponty each portray the perceptual field as a field of spatially and temporally located, ontologically "thick" or resisting objects which are essentially related to the horizon of world, which allow for the very structure of the sensing which gives access to them, and whose manner of emergence undercuts the problematics of the subject-object split. This essay surveys this perceptual field as a focus for eliciting their more fundamental shared understanding of the dimensions of human activity which underlie its emergence.

ROSENTHAL, Sandra B. Pragmatism, Heidegger, and the Context of Naturalism. J Speculative Phil, 4(1), 1-12, 1990.

The explicit focus on the context of naturalism within pragmatic philosophy, combined with its interest in scientific method and the biological approach to the emergence of meanings, has been a key factor in the historical alienation of pragmatic philosophy and the thought of Martin Heidegger. This essay attempts to lay bare the three-fold sense of nature that is operative in pragmatic naturalism and that is supportive of, and finds its counterpart in, Heidegger's rejection of the "natural attitude."

ROSENTHAL, Sandra B and BOURGEOIS, Patrick L. Sensation, Perception and Immediacy: Mead and Merleau-Ponty. SW Phil Rev, 6(1), 105-111, Ja 90.

A focus on the relation between sensation and the perceptual object in the philosophies of G H Mead and Maurice Merleau-Ponty points toward their shared views of perception as non-reductionistic and holistic, as inextricably tied to the active role of the sensible body, and as involving a new understanding of the nature of immediacy within experience. This essay explores these shared views.

ROSIK, Seweryn. Gewissen als Eine Freiheitsnorm (in Polish). Stud Phil Christ, 25(1), 117-139, 1989.

In seiner Dissertation hebt der Autor eine fundamentale Tendenz des gegenwärtigen Menschens heraus, die man die Strömung zur Autonomie nennt und die mehrmals Extremformen annimmt. Unabhängig von der Gefährdung, die solche Tendenz mitbringt, ist aber die Freiheit eine fundamentale Eigenschaft der Menschenperson, als auch ihr Vorrecht und Gottesgabe (St. Paulus). Der Autor untersucht das Gewissensrecht auf

Freiheit der eigenen Überzeugung, d.h. das Recht auf Entscheidungsrisiko des Gutes und der Wahrheit, die man entdeckt hat, besonders dann, wenn man der Widerstand der befestigten Schemen des Denkens und Handels brechen muss. (edited)

ROSINSKI, F M. Das Verhältnis von Verbrecherinnen zu ihren Familien (in Polish). Stud Phil Christ, 25(1), 237-250, 1989.

In vorliegender Abhandlung wurde das Verhältnis von 200 Müttern, die wegen krimineller Vergehen längerfristige Freiheitsstrafen verbüssen (100 von ihnen das erste Mal, 100 mehrmalig) zu ihren Familien, besonders zu ihren minderjährigen Kindern, untersucht Die. statistische Auswertung ergab, dass die meisten Frauen ihren Elternpflichten nicht entsprechend nachkommen. Sehr oft begehen auch ihre Männer straffällige Taten, so dass die Frauen in ihnen keinen moralischen Rückhalt finden. (edited)

ROSINSKI, F M and LATAWIEC, A M. Die Verantwortung des Menschen für seine natürliche Umwelt (in Polish). Stud Phil Christ, 25(2), 121-137, 1989.

Im vorliegenden Artikel wurden 2 prinzipielle Verhaltenweisen: die sakrale und profane gegenüber der Umwelt hervorgehoben; beide haben eine sehr lange Tradition und ihre Befürworter berufen sich auf theologische und philosophische Argumente. Die Bedrohung der Umwelt bedeutet eine ernste Gefährdung der physischen und psychischen Integrität des Menschen; er muss sich dessen bewusst werden, dass er nicht nur Rechte gegenüber der Natur hat, aber auch moralische Pflichten, deren Begründung in vorliegender Arbeit erörtert wurde.

ROSMINI, Antonio and CLEARY, Denis (trans) and WATSON, Terence (trans). *Conscience*. Durham, Rosmini, 1989

ROSS, Don. Against Positing Central Systems in the Mind. Phil Sci, 57(2), 297-312, Je 90.

This paper is concerned with a recent argument of Jerry Fodor's to the effect that the frame problem in artificial intelligence is in principle insoluble. Fodor's argument is based on his contention that the mind is divided between encapsulated modular systems for information processing and 'central systems' for non-demonstrative inference. I argue that positing central systems is methodologically unsound, and in fact involves a muddle that bears a strong family resemblance to the basic error in dualism. I therefore conclude that Fodor's position on the frame problem should be rejected.

ROSS, James F. The Crash of Modal Metaphysics. Rev Metaph, 43(2), 251-279, D 89.

"Possible Worlds" metaphysics is bankrupt. This is a series of arguments to display that no "genuine semantics" for quantified modal logic is true. Even the formalizations themselves, understood extensionally, revise what we mean and commit us to realities we repudiate. Moreover, principles like "whatever is possible is necessarily possible," and "whatever is necessary is necessarily necessary," are demonstrably false. The merely possible, unrooted in the actual, cannot be brought within the range of reference. Whatever might have been, wholly other than what is ever actual, is logically inaccessible because it is without content.

ROSS, Judith Wilson. Commentary: Live Sperm, Dead Bodies. Hastings Center Rep, 20(1), 34, Ja-F 90.

ROSS, Murray and SELMAN, Mark. McClellan on Quine and Social Criticism. Proc Phil Educ, 45, 45-54, 1989.

In the Spring 1987 issue of *Educational Theory* James McClellan proposed a revived version of progressive education based on Quine's views of science. The authors take issue with the notion that Quine provides a necessary, or desirable, basis for a revived progressivism for two major reasons. The first of these involves the rather obscure position Quine takes with regard to normative statements, statements which, we argue, have an irreducible role in educational and political discourse. The second reason is that Quinian elimination of intentional terms is inconsistent with what Walzer argues have been the most common and effective forms of social criticism.

ROSS, Stephanie. Philosophy, Literature, and the Death of Art. Phil Papers, 18(1), 95-115, My 89.

I examine two arguments from Arthur Danto about the death of art and apply them to the case of literature. The first is a mimetic argument which claims that art will end when it perfectly reproduces reality; the second is a Hegelian argument which claims that art will end by turning into philosophy. While the first argument fails because it cannot accommodate all the arts, I claim that the second is also unsuccessful because art can philosophize while remaining art. I close by suggesting that literature may well die by being supplanted by a successor electronic art.

ROSS, Stephanie and ROBINSON, Jenefer. Woman, Morality, and Fiction. Hypatia, 5(2), 76-90, Sum 90.

We apply Carol Gilligan's distinction between a "male" mode of moral reasoning, focussed on justice, and a "female" mode, focussed on caring, to the reading of literature. Martha Nussbaum suggests that certain novels are works of moral philosophy. We argue that what Nussbaum sees as the special ethical contribution of such novels is in fact training in the stereotypically female mode of moral concern. We show this kind of training is appropriate to *all* readers of these novels, not just to women. Finally, we explore what else is involved in distinctively *feminist* readings of traditional novels.

ROSSER, Sue V. Re-Visioning Clinical Research—Gender and the Ethics of Experimental Design. Hypatia, 4(2), 125-139, Sum 89.

Since modern medicine is based substantially in clinical medical research, the flaws and ethical problems that arise in this research as it is conceived and practiced in the United States are likely to be reflected to some extent in current medicine and its practice. This paper explores some of the ways in which clinical research has suffered from an androcentric focus in its choice and definition of problems studied, approaches and methods used in design and interpretation of experiments, and theories and conclusions drawn from the research. Some examples of re-visioned research hint at solutions to the ethical dilemmas created by this biased focus; an increased number of feminists involved in clinical research may provide avenues for additional changes that would lead to improved health care for all.

ROSSETTI, Livio. La filosofia penale di Ippodamo e la cultura giuridica dei sofisti. Riv Int Filosof Diritto, 66(2), 315-335, Ap-Je 89.

Greek Sophists went well beyond the *nomos/phusis* antithesis and, especially in the field of penal law, contributed both a conceptual frame and whole sets of stock-arguments. Hippodamos (hardly a Pythagorean) ought to have argued for the distinction between offence and damage, with appropriate punishments for both. Antiphon argued that *nomos* allows unnatural and questionable facilities to defendants. Protagoras and Thucydides commented upon the aims of punishment. Several writers taught how to argue for one's own case when the trial is only based on circumstantial evidence (*logos amarturos*) and/or how to argue and counterargue by means of dilemmas.

ROSSETTI, Livio. The Rhetoric of Socrates. Phil Rhet, 22(4), 225-238, 1989.

My first contention is that one should analyse Socrates' conversational practices not only under such headings as Method, Irony, Maieutic, Dialectic, Dialogue, but also as a rhetorical strategy, of course different from the rhetorical strategies beloved by the Sophists, indeed highly innovative and possibly more powerful in comparison, and admittedly marked by different aims and means, but nevertheless rhetorical in character. I then try to qualify the Socratic rhetoric and its peculiar ambiguity, starting from the way Socrates "does things with words" in the items of dialogical interplay recorded by the Socratics.

ROSSIDES, Daniel. The Synthesis: A Sociopolitical Critique of the Liberal Professions. Soc Epistem, 4(2), 229-258, Ap-Je 90.

The author argues that the professions and disciplines are neither objective, nonpolitical, value-neutral, nor useful in solving social problems. The professions and disciplines are deficient because they are based on artificial subject matter, have splintered into incoherent subspecialties, and mistakenly assume the functionality of a society based on private property, science, professionalism, and markets. Improving the professions and disciplines is not a matter of better epistemology or education. Professional deficiencies stem from the problematic nature of society. If we want better thinking and policies, we must redesign the group structures (corporations, political parties, schools, etc.) that generate our science, professions, and policies.

ROSSOUW, G J. Is Atheism Essential to Marxism? (in Dutch). S Afr J Phil, 9(2), 110-115, My 90.

The question whether atheism is essential to Marxism is posed in this article against the backdrop of the relation between Christianity and Marxism. The answer to this question has important implications for any form of nonaggressive interaction between Christians and Marxists. The question is answered by making an analysis of Marx's and Engels's philosophy. The conclusion which is drawn from this analysis is that atheism is only essential to the Engelsian tradition in Marxism. It is not essential to the Marxian tradition in Marxism, whereas critique of religion is essential to this Marxian tradition.

ROSZAK, Theodore. The Folklore of Computers and the True Art of Thinking. Thinking, 7(3), 8-12, 1988.

ROTELLA, Oscar. Un desliz en la *Summa Logicae* de Guillermo de Ockham? Sapientia, 44(173), 221-224, Jl-S 89.

ROTENSTREICH, Nathan. Between Succession and Duration. Kantstudien, 81(2), 211-220, 1990.

There are in time two components or aspects. Succession connotes the very structure of time in which the linear aspect of sequence comes to the front. Duration points to that which is present in the sequential order of succession and continues, at least relatively, to go on against the background of succession. From the formal point of view there is primacy to succession.

ROTENSTREICH, Nathan. Can Expression Replace Reflection? Rev Metaph, 43(3), 607-618, Mr 90.

The article is a critical analysis of Richard Rorty's book *Contingency, Irony and Solidarity*. It attempts to see the book as presenting some norms for a modern culture by emphasizing the centrality of human expression as against reflection. The article analyzes the various concepts employed in the book—irony as a description of an attitude towards circumstances and solidarity as a description of interhuman relations. Because of the essence of these attitudes, the conclusion is that expression cannot be self-sufficient and has to be directed or overcome by reflection.

ROTENSTREICH, Nathan. Morality and Culture: A Note on Kant. Hist Phil Quart, 6(3), 303-316, Jl 89.

The article deals with the suggested affinity between culture and morality because culture, in spite of its connotation as being engaged in agriculture, is understood as shaping the personal character. Civilisation is understood as forming an external mode of behaviour in spite of its affinity with the notion of civility. Kant's various approaches to the two concepts are dealt with. Following the analysis of Kant's exposition comes Hegel's presentation which is not based on the duality of the two modes. The article winds up with a short analysis of the neo-Kantian positions commenting on the consequence of the comparative analysis that the concept of culture is far from being unequivocal.

ROTENSTREICH, Nathan. Reasons and Reason. J Value Inq, 24(3), 241-251, Jl 90.

The article analyzes the several frequent employments of the terms reason and reasons in general and in ethical discourse in particular. It points to the ambiguity pertaining to those employments, because reason is considered to be an overriding faculty or capacity while reasons are considered as arguments or grounds, both for discursive statements as well as for conducts and acts. In the latter sense reasons are, explicitly or not, synonymous with motives. Systematically speaking, it is essential to analyze the relation between these two connotations of the term reason or else to replace the term "reasons" with a different term.

ROTENSTREICH, Nathan. Self-Knowledge of the World. Schopenhauer Jahr, 70, 66-74, 1989.

The point of departure of the present analysis of Schopenhauer's system is his polemical rejection of Hegel's system. Since Hegel's system is based on the assumption that reality knows itself because the identity between it and reason, Schopenhauer rejects the position that the knowledge of the world is the knowledge of the world itself. A system is possible by presenting the structure of the world even when underlying that structure is the antirational factor or essence will. The systematic character of philosophy leads to the presentation of the relation between knowledge and ethics. Thus, the structure of the system as a system is independent of the quasi-presupposition that there is bound to be an identity between the object of knowledge and knowledge itself. (edited)

ROTH, John. "The Significance of Human Life after Auschwitz" in *Inquiries into Values: The Inaugural Session of the International Society for Value Inquiry*, LEE, Sander H , 549-556. Lewiston, Mellen Pr, 1989.

The immensity of the Holocaust becomes too impersonal and more inevitable than it really was if one overlooks the fact that individuals did make the decisions that destroyed millions. To drive home that lesson is one of the most important philosophical insights to derive from the Holocaust. By exploring realistically what people did or could have done in the midst of the destruction process, we can glimpse ways to redeem at least some fragments of the trust in the world that the Holocaust destroyed.

ROTH, Marie Louise. "Robert Musil: Utopie et Utopisme" in *Cultural Hermeneutics of Modern Art: Essays in Honor of Jan Aler*, DETHIER, Hubert (ed), 273-288. Amsterdam, Rodopi, 1989.

ROTH, Michael. The Wall and the Shield: K-K Reconsidered. Phil Stud, 59(2), 137-157, Je 90.

In this paper I argue, against Chisholm and Feldman, that given a fallibilist account of empirical propositional knowledge, the Gettier cases are simply irrelevant to the K-K thesis. In the first half of the paper I establish the metaphor of the "Wall" as a device to capture our fallibilistic intuitions. The oddball cases (i.e., the nonrelevant alternatives) are beyond the Wall which defines our epistemic landscape. Inside the Wall are all the contingencies which must be dealt with (the relevant alternatives). The way we deal with such contingencies is by "shielding" ourselves against their obtaining by gathering evidence. On the basis of the foregoing I conclude that the Gettier cases are all over the Wall and thus ignorable. Hence, for a knower who seeks to iterate her knowledge, the Gettier cases are not part of her epistemic concerns.

ROTH, Norman. "The Jews in Spain at the Time of Maimonides" in *Moses Maimonides and His Time*, ORMSBY, Eric L (ed), 1-20. Washington, Cath Univ Amer Pr, 1989.

ROTH, Robert J. Reply to Heyd's Reply to "Locke Is Not a Cartesian with Respect to Knowledge of our Own Existence". Int Phil Quart, 29(4), 469-472, D 89.

In reply to Heyd, I state the following. (1) I am *not* trying to make Locke into a Cartesian. (2) In *An Essay Concerning Human Understanding* (IV,ix,3), Locke states that, in our cognitive acts, "we are conscious to ourselves of our own being," not of our *idea* of our being. (3) Heyd claims that in Locke's theory of person (II,xxvii), he is clearly dealing with the *idea* of the person or self. But Heyd fails to note that there Locke is discussing the *nature* of the self, while in IV,ix,3 he is talking about the *existence* of the self.

ROTHBARD, Murray N. The End of the Secular Century. Free Inq, 9(4), 8-9, Fall 89.

Intellectuals have long held that the 20th century—a secular century—spelled the end of religious faith and the final triumph of secular modernity. The mighty upsurge of Christianity and Islam throughout the world in the last few decades makes it clear, however, that it is atheism, not God, that is dead, and that religion has resumed its dominant place in shaping the values and institutions of mankind. The sooner we all realize this, the better.

ROTHE, Barbara and STEININGER, H. Zur Diskussion um die Einheit und Vielfalt der Interessen im Sozialismus. Deut Z Phil, 37(9), 859-862, 1989.

The chances of a society to form his present time and his future are dependent of his capacity to recognize the own situation of interests and the fields of conflicts these interests. Today it is necessary to analyse the complex and the difference of the interests and to reply to the question: either economy either social politics. The authors are getting at these questions: the economical interests in a socialist society are inseparably connected with social interests of all peoples. The unity of the multifarious interests is only possible by way of unity of innovation, effective economy and social security.

ROTHENBERG, Paula. The Construction, Deconstruction, and Reconstruction of Difference. Hypatia, 5(1), 42-57, Spr 90.

The construction of difference is central to racism, sexism and other forms of oppression. This paper examines the similar and dissimilar ways in which race and gender have been constructed in the United States and analyzes the consequences of these differences in construction for the development of social policy and the growth and nature of movements for social change.

ROTHMAN, Cappy Miles. Commentary: Live Sperm, Dead Bodies. Hastings Center Rep, 20(1), 33-34, Ja-F 90.

ROTHSTEIN, Mark A. The Challenge of the New Genetics. Nat Forum, 69(4), 39-40, Fall 89.

ROTHSTEIN, Mark A. Medical Screening: AIDS, Rights, and Health Care Costs. Nat Forum, 69(4), 7-10, Fall 89.

ROTT, Hans. Conditionals and Theory Change: Revisions, Expansions, and Additions. Synthese, 81(1), 91-113, O 89.

This paper dwells upon formal models of changes of beliefs, or theories, which are expressed in languages containing a binary conditional connective. After defining the basic concept of a (nontrivial) belief revision model, I present a simple proof of Gärdenfors's (1986) triviality theorem. I claim that on a proper understanding of this theorem we must give up the thesis that consistent revisions ('additions') are to be equated with logical expansions. If negated or 'might' conditionals are interpreted on the basis of 'autoepistemic omniscience', or it autoepistemic modalities (Moore) are admitted, even more severe triviality results ensue. It is argued that additions cannot be philosophically construed as 'parasitic' (Levi) on expansions. In conclusion I outline some logical consequences of the fact that we must not expect 'monotonic' revisions in languages including conditionals.

ROTTSCHAEFER, William A and MARTINSEN, David. Really Taking Darwin Seriously: An Alternative to Michael Ruse's Darwinian Metaethics. Biol Phil, 5(2), 149-173, Ap 90.

Michael Ruse has proposed in his recent book *Taking Darwin Seriously* and elsewhere a new Darwinian ethics distinct from traditional evolutionary ethics, one that avoids the latter's inadequate accounts of the nature of morality and its failed attempts to provide a naturalistic justification of morality. Ruse argues for a sociobiologically based account of moral sentiments, and an evolutionarily based causal explanation of their function, rejecting the possibility of ultimate ethical justification. We find that Ruse's

proposal distorts, overextends and weakens both Darwinism and naturalism. So we propose an alternative Darwinian metaethics that both remedies the problems in Ruse's proposal and shows how a Darwinian naturalistic account of the moral good in terms of human fitness avoids the naturalistic fallacy and can provide genuine, even if limited, justifications for substantive ethical claims. Thus, we propose to really take Darwin seriously.

ROUNDS, William C and KASPER, Robert T. The Logic of Unification in Grammar. Ling Phil, 13(1), 35-58, F 90.

ROUSE, Fenella. Commentary: Prehospital DNR Orders. Hastings Center Rep, 19(6), 19, N-D 89.

ROUSE, Joseph. The Narrative Reconstruction of Science. Inquiry, 33(2), 179-196, Je 90.

In contrast to earlier accounts of the epistemic significance of narrative, it is argued that narrative is important in natural scientific knowledge. To recognize this, we must understand narrative not as a literary form in which knowledge is written, but as the temporal organization of the understanding of practical activity. Scientific research is a social practice, whereby researchers structure the narrative context in which past work is interpreted and significant possibilities for further work are projected. This narrative field displays a constant tension between a need for a coherent, shared understanding of the field and the incoherence threatened by divergent projects and interpretations. (edited)

ROUSSOPOULOS, George. Analytico-Referentiality and Legitimation in Modern Mathematics. Phil Math, 5(1-2), 3-22, 1990.

In this historico-philosophical essay we are concerned with the consecutive crises in the foundations of modern mathematics. We formulate the stages of the development of a dominant pattern of thought within mathematics (analytico-referentiality) and we play close attention to the form it takes in the foundations of mathematics (legitimation demand). In particular, we take the telescope as the paradigmatic metaphor of the emerging analytico-referential pattern in mathematics and we focus on the employment of the formal system as the vehicle of the legitimation demand.

ROUTLEY, Richard. "Philosophical and Linguistic Inroads: Multiply Intensional Relevant Logics" in *Directions in Relevant Logic*, NORMAN, Jean (ed), 269-304. Norwell, Kluwer, 1989.

ROUTLEY, Richard. "Semantics Unlimited I: A Relevant Synthesis of Implication with Higher Intensionality" in *Directions in Relevant Logic*, NORMAN, Jean (ed), 327-376. Norwell, Kluwer, 1989.

ROVANE, Carol. Branching Self-Consciousness. Phil Rev, 99(3), 355-395, Jl 90.

Parfit's thesis that persons could survive without identity is tenable only if first person modes of thought do not presuppose the identity of the subject. Armed with the pronoun "I*" subjects can form first person quasi-attitudes towards future and past selves with whom they are psychologically connected but not identical. When persons have foreknowledge of branching they can wield "I*" to direct quasi-intentions separately at distinct future selves. Such foreknowledge also makes possible attitudes of self-concern that extend to more than one future self. This approach to the first person reveals significant limitations on reductionism.

ROVENTA-FRUMUSANI, Daniela. Indirection et interaction conversationnelle. Phil Log, 32(3-4), 211-217, Jl-D 88.

ROVENTA-FRUMUSANI, Daniela. La relation de réfléchissement pensée/langage. Phil Log, 32(1-2), 89-94, Ja-Je 88.

ROVIRA, Rogelio. Kant ante la verdad como hija del tiempo. Rev Filosof (Spain), 1, 105-114, 1987-88.

ROWE, Christopher. "Philosophy, Love, and Madness" in *The Person and the Human Mind: Issues in Ancient and Modern Philosophy*, GILL, Christopher (ed), 227-246. New York, Clarendon/Oxford Pr, 1989.

The paper interprets the myth in Plato's *Phaedrus* through a critique of the radical reading proposed by Martha Nussbaum in *The Fragility of Goodness*. The myth suggests that we are ineluctably encumbered by irrational psychological elements which are not to be seen simply as the product of the temporary attachment of psyche to body; its moral is not (as proposed by Nussbaum) that we should value all aspects of the human psyche but rather that we should try to impose rational order on our 'bestial' aspects (especially the recalcitrant black horse).

ROWE, William L and WAINWRIGHT, William J. *Philosophy of Religion: Selected Readings (Second Edition)*. San Diego, Harcourt Brace Jov, 1989.

The aim of the volume is to introduce students to the philosophy of religion by acquainting them with the writings of some of the thinkers who have made substantial contributions in this area. This new edition expands the range of topics by including an entirely new chapter on death and immortality and a new subsection on the moral argument. There is also some new material on Wittgenstein and fideism, religious pluralism, and faith and the need for evidence. Almost every chapter has been changed by deletions or additons to update the selections and provide more material that is understandable to beginning students.

ROWE, William V. The Problem of Progress. Phil Reform, 55(1), 74-83, 1990.

ROWELL, Lewis. The Idea of Music in India and the Ancient West. Acta Phil Fennica, 43, 323-342, 1988.

ROWLANDS, Mark N J. Property Exemplification and Proliferation. Analysis, 49(4), 194-197, O 89.

ROWNEY, J I A and CAHOON, A R. Individual and Organizational Characteristics of Women in Managerial Leadership. J Bus Ethics, 9(4-5), 293-316, Ap-My 90.

Women are making a substantial impact on the employment market, both in terms of overall numbers as well as by appointment to male-dominated organizational roles. Research on women in leadership positions within organizations has concentrated on two main foci: firstly, the identification of relevant individual and organizational characteristics and secondly, on the impact of these variables on the women in management roles. This paper presents the findings from a series of studies in relation to these broad dimensions.

ROY, Dev K and WATNICK, Richard. Finite Condensations of Recursive Linear Orders. Stud Log, 47(4), 311-317, D 88.

The complexity of a Π_4 set of natural numbers is encoded into a linear order to show that the finite condensation of a recursive linear order can be Π_2-Π_1. A priority argument establishes the same result, and is extended to a complete classification of finite condensations iterated finitely many times.

ROY, Louis. Interpersonal Knowledge According to John Macmurray. Mod Theol, 5(4), 349-365, Jl 89.

To what extent does a philosophy based on interpersonal knowledge really differ from the kind of knowledge which obtains in social science? The article examines first Macmurray's distinction between personal and impersonal attitude, secondly his characterization of interpersonal reality, and thirdly his distinction between personal and impersonal reflection. The conclusion reached is that, although Macmurray rightly draws attention to the primacy of the interpersonal attitude over the scientific one, his epistemological shortcomings prevent him from sufficiently integrating the personal and functional sides of human relationships.

ROY, Subroto. *Philosophy of Economics: On the Scope of Reason in Economic Inquiry*. New York, Routledge, 1989

This may be the first work to have successfully bridged serious economics in the twentieth century with modern Anglo-American philosophy, in particular the work of Wittgenstein. The book raises some of the central philosophical questions facing modern economics, especially to do with the scope of objective reasoning in the making of evaluative judgments, the appropriate role of economic expertise, and the status of the concepts and theorems of mathematical economics. It is argued that careful description of the particular case in the light of general principles may be a starting point for analysis, even though there are no ultimate starting points. The work thus permits a sure and safe course to be found between scepticism and dogmatism for any project of economic inquiry. (edited)

ROYER, Ron. Science Begins with Everyday Thinking. Thinking, 7(2), 46-49, 1987.

Interest in science is defined as a search for causal relation. In preliterate children, ground rules for this search are themselves first set down. The essential form of Newton's methods is offered as a mature model of such a system of ground rules. Newton's method is compared to the essential form of the nature stories of Thornton W Burgess. This produces five premises by which children's nature literature may be evaluated as productive or counterproductive of later interest in and skill with science.

ROZOV, M A. The Mode of Existence of Mathematical Objects. Phil Math, 4(2), 105-111, 1989.

RUBEL, Maximilien and WALKER, R Scott (trans). The French Revolution and the Education of the Young Marx. Diogenes, 148, 1-27, Wint 89.

Marx the "communist" had to struggle throughout his career as man of science and as political militant in order to have his "bourgeois" claims triumph—the ideals proclaimed by the fundamental charter of liberal democracy, the Declaration of the Rights of Man and of the citizen. The historiography of the French Revolution profoundly marked his political theory. Political emancipation, while establishing legally the internal dichotomy—or 'alienation'—of modern man and the separation of modern society into classes, was the signal for a social movement dedicated to

human, and thus, total emancipation. Marx's political activity was a permanent struggle against Prussian absolutism, Russian Czarism and French Bonapartism.

RUBEN, David. "Realism in the Social Sciences" in *Dismantling Truth: Reality in the Post-Modern World*, LAWSON, Hilary (ed), 58-75. New York, St Martin's Pr, 1989.

One indication of whether a theory is to be construed realistically is the possibility of the theory being in error, mistaken, in certain ways. I compare physical theory, folk psychology, and social theory, and argue that social theory falls somewhere between incorrigibility and full corrigibility.

RUBEN, Peter. Schumpeters Theorie der Wirtschaftsentwicklung in philosophischer Sicht. Deut Z Phil, 38(4), 319-327, 1990.

RUBENSTEIN, Diane. The Mirror of Reproduction: Baudrillard and Reagan's America. Polit Theory, 17(4), 582-606, N 89.

RUBIDGE, Bradley. Descartes's *Meditations* and Devotional Meditations. J Hist Ideas, 51(1), 27-49, Ja-Mr 90.

RUBIN, M and MAGIDOR, M and ROSENTHAL, J W and SROUR, G. Some Highly Undecidable Lattices. Annals Pure Applied Log, 46(1), 41-63, Ja 90.

RUDDICK, Sara. *Maternal Thinking: Toward a Politics of Peace*. Boston, Beacon Pr, 1989

RUDEBUSCH, George. Aristotelian Predication, Augustine and the Trinity. Thomist, 53(4), 587-597, O 89.

Augustine wished to defend and make as intelligible as possible the Christian doctrine of the Trinity. I show how Augustine works with an Aristotelian model of predication, derives an incompleteness result within the standard forms of predication, and accepts, with some qualification, a nonstandard form of predication used by Aristotle for predicating primary substance of matter.

RUDEBUSCH, George. Does Plato Think False Speech is Speech? Nous, 24(4), 599-609, S 90.

There is an unsolved puzzle about Plato's *Theaetetus* and *Sophist* which has been too little noticed. The *Sophist* develops and accepts an account of false speech and belief as saying what is "other." But the *Theaetetus* rejects such accounts. The standard solution is that the *Sophist* is somehow meant to overcome or avoid the problems seen as overwhelming in the *Theaetetus*. I argue that such a solution fails.

RUDEBUSCH, George. Plato's Aporetic Style. S J Phil, 27(4), 539-547, Wint 89.

The Socratic, aporetic dialogues are meant to eliminate the conceit of wisdom in readers. There is a controversy as to whether, in addition, they are meant to elicit from the reader the understanding of a positive philosophical position. It has been argued that if Plato had been trying to present a positive doctrine, he would have chosen a more straightforward style than the aporetic dialogue. I show this argument to fail by finding a pedagogical reason for the aporetic dialogue.

RUDNICK, Abraham. Towards a Rationalization of Biological Psychiatry: A Study in Psychobiological Epistemology. J Med Phil, 15(1), 75-96, F 90.

Contemporary biological psychiatry is in a seemingly inchoate state. I assert that this state of biological psychiatry is due to its violation of an epistemological criterion of rationality, i.e., the relevance criterion; that is, contemporary biological psychiatry is irrational as it adopts a conception irrelevant to the psychobiological domain. This conception is mechanistic. The irrationality of biological psychiatry is manifest as the dominance of neurochemical explanations of psychopharmacological correlations, resulting in predictive sterility and, correspondingly, in the dominance of serendipity. I suggest a rationalization of biological psychiatry through a conception relevant to the psychobiological domain. This conception is hierarchical.

RUDOLPH, Günther and HERLITZIUS, Erwin. Thomas Muntzer— Humanist, Reformator, Revolutionär. Deut Z Phil, 37(12), 1057-1070, 1989.

A rough understanding of the German Peasant War even in terms of the earliest burgher reform (1517-1525) mainly preferred Thomas Müntzer's political doctrine. But his religious achievements are of initial account. God's speech is supposed to be the everlasting essence in the laymen's strive for social justice and equality. Faith has come alive as reason. Müntzer is one of those who fostered the Protestant movement self-reliantly; he abolished the Latin ritual even before Luther. Inquiries about the European Renaissance should take due notice of the different streams of early Bible humanism with its integrable publication and communication, affiliated to the rediscovery of ancient literature and art.

RUDY, John G. Wordsworth and the Zen Void. Thought, 65(257),

127-142, Je 90.

RUHNKA, John C and WELLER, Steven. The Ethical Implications of Corporate Records Management Practices and Some Suggested Ethical Values for Decisions. J Bus Ethics, 9(2), 81-92, F 90.

While the ethical implications of corporate actions have received increasing attention, one important area overlooked by both researchers and corporate codes of ethics is the significant ethical implications of corporate records management practices. This article discusses the operational and strategic purposes of modern corporate records management programs—including "scorched earth" programs which seek to reduce exposure to potential liability by eliminating documentary evidence from corporate files that could be used to establish culpability in future governmental investigations or in litigation by persons injured by corporate actions. As a first step toward developing relevant ethical guidelines and decision criteria for socially responsible records management practices, the ethical values of freedom of choice and avoidance of harm are applied to various corporate decisions as to (1) which information should be retained as records and for how long, (2) subsequent disclosure or nondisclosure of that information and to whom, and (3) decisions as to when information in corporate records may properly be destroyed.

RUMSEY, Jean P. Agency, Human Nature and Character in Kantian Theory. J Value Inq, 24(2), 109-121, Ap 90.

This paper examines problems in Kant's analysis of empirical character, specifically those arising for his autonomous agent in relation to gratitude and friendship. It is concluded that Kant's conception of human nature is inadequate as a basis for his moral theory, where the relevant deficiency is its failure to comprehend that humans are not only egoistic but social beings, with desires for both independence and connection, autonomy and affiliation.

RUNGGALDIER, Edmund. On the Scholastic or Aristotelian Roots of "Intentionality" in Brentano. Topoi, 8(2), 97-103, S 89.

The early Brentano identifies intentionality with "intentional inexistence," i.e., with a kind of indwelling of the intentional object in the mind. The latter concept cannot be grasped apart from its scholastic background and the Aristotelian-Thomistic doctrine of the multiple use of 'being' (to on legetai pollachos). The fact that Brentano abandoned the theory of the intentional inexistence in the course of time does not contradict the thesis that it is intentional inexistence and not the modern conception of reference or directedness to something other which comprises the essence of intentionality for the early Brentano.

RUNIA, D T. Dooyeweerd, Bos and the Grondmotief of Greek Culture. Phil Reform, 54(2), 160-175, 1989.

In Philosophia Reformata 51 (1986) 117-137, A P Bos criticized H Dooyeweerd's attempt to explain the development of Greek philosophy in terms of a religious 'grondmotief' involving a dialectical tension between form and matter. The present article continues the discussion, arguing that Bos's alternative in terms of a Titanic 'zin-perspectief' is insufficiently dialectical in character. It is suggested that the polarity between the divine and the random, such as is found in Plato's seminal dialogue, the Timaeus, might be helpful in understanding the religious roots of Greek philosophy.

RUNIA, David T. "Aristotle and Theophrastus Conjoined in the Writings of Cicero" in Cicero's Knowledge of the Peripatos, FORTENBAUGH, William W (ed), 23-38. New Brunswick, Transaction Books, 1989.

An analysis is given of the 16 passages in Cicero's rhetorical and philosophical works where the names of Aristotle and Theophrastus are mentioned together. Cicero joins them together so often (1) because of his great interest in philosophical successions, and (2) because he regards the encyclopedic research carried out in the early Peripatos as an example to follow in his own attempt to present philosophy to a Roman audience.

RUNIA, David T. Xenophanes on the Moon: A Doxographicum in Aëtius. Phronesis, 34(3), 245-269, 1989.

RUS, Vasile. Une conception unitaire, profondément scientifique sur la dynamique des étapes du processus (in Romanian). Rev Filosof (Romania), 36(1), 27-35, Ja-F 89.

RUSE, Michael. Philosophy of Biology Today. Albany, SUNY Pr, 1988

This is a short handbook introducing readers to the rapidly developing field of the philosophy of biology. Its chief virtue, other than brief guides to the major controversies, is a very comprehensive bibliography with over a thousand entries.

RUSE, Michael. "Sociobiology and Reductionism" in Reductionism and Systems Theory in the Life Sciences: Some Problems and Perspectives, HOYNINGEN-HUENE, Paul (ed), 45-83. Norwell, Kluwer, 1989.

RUSE, Michael. "The View from Somewhere: A Critical Defense of Evolutionary Epistemology" in Issues in Evolutionary Epistemology, HAHLWEG, Kai (ed), 185-228. Albany, SUNY Pr, 1989.

In this paper I argue that philosophers ought to take seriously evolutionary theory in their discussions of epistemology. I defend the evolutionary epistemologist against charges of scientism and conclude that some form of idealism better characterizes evolutionary epistemology than realism.

RÜSEN, Jörn. Rhetoric and Aesthetics of History. Hist Theor, 29(2), 190-204, My 90.

The article discusses the change of historiography from literature to science as it was realized in Ranke's works. It shows that scientific elements and rhetoric principles not exclude each other but build a new synthesis which is typical for the historicism of the 19th century. The specific aesthetic character of historiography signifies an internal theoretisation and rationalisation of historical thought which went along with the development of historical studies as academic discipline.

RUSSELL, Allan Melvin and GERHART, Mary. The Cognitive Effect of Metaphor. Listening, 25(2), 114-126, Spr 90.

RUSSELL, Bertrand. A Critical Exposition of the Philosophy of Leibniz. Wolfeboro, Longwood, 1989

RUSSELL, Bertrand and MARSH, Robert Charles (ed). Logic and Knowledge: Bertrand Russell, Essays 1901-1950. Winchester, Unwin Hyman, 1988

First published in 1956, Logic and Knowledge was an anticipation of the 28 volumes of the collected papers of Bertrand Russell now being prepared. It contains the text of 10 essays written by Russell between 1901-50, each of them a milestone in Russell's philosophical work. It has the advantage that the editor was in close communication with the author through the preparation of the text and that when required he provided correct readings of corrupt or ambiguous passages. The editor, then in residence in Cambridge, is now a retired member of the faculty of the University of Chicago.

RUSSELL, Bruce. "When Can What You Don't Know Hurt You?" in The Current State of the Coherence Theory, BENDER, John W (ed), 94-102. Norwell, Kluwer, 1989.

It looks as though certain Gettier cases that do not involve any false beliefs count against the view that knowledge is undefeated, justified true belief. To save the view one might require that both beliefs and assumptions be considered and argue that such Gettier cases involve false assumptions that do defeat the subject's belief. But modifying the view in that way will create problems in cases involving misleading, unpossessed evidence, for it seems that in such cases assumptions must be attributed to the subject that defeat his belief, and so destroy his knowledge, according to the modified account. The dilemmas cannot be avoided for knowledge is justified, non-accidentally held true belief and an accidentally held true belief may be justified but undefeated by any of the subject's beliefs while a non-accidentally held true belief may be justified but defeated by some misleading or remote piece of evidence. (edited)

RUSSELL, Christopher. Hintikka on Kant and Logic. Erkenntnis, 33(1), 23-38, Jl 90.

The role of intuition in Kant's theory of mathematics is similar to instantiation rules in first-order logic according to Jaakko Hintikka. This paper is a critical examination of Hintikka's interpretation and reconstruction of Kant's theory. It is argued that Kant's position is question-begging on this interpretation.

RUSSELL, Denise. Feminist Critique of Epistemology. Method Sci, 22(2), 87-103, 1989.

Theories of knowledge often focus on science as the area where the best, most or most useful knowledge resides. A key epistemological problem can be unearthed if we look at the dominant images of ideals of science. In very general terms, I take this problem to be concerned with the abstract logic of theory acceptance. I want to explore what this abstract logic is supposed to be, how it is linked with masculinity, and what is wrong with it from a feminist perspective. I will expose the propaganda that is used to attempt to invalidate these types of criticism and briefly mention some recent positive accounts which outline an ideal of science from a feminist perspective.

RUSSELL, John M. Beyond Our Species' Potentials: Charles Hartshorne on Humanism. Relig Hum, 24(3), 95-106, Sum 90.

Although Hartshorne presents a vigorous critique of humanism, his neoclassical theism shares some interesting, general affinities or tendencies with humanism. Hartshorne's agendas for both theism and humanism have classical supernaturalism as a common adversary. Each position criticizes supernaturalism for generally neglecting the so-called horizontal dimension of experience in favor of the transcendent or "vertical."

RUSSELL, Paul. A Hobbist Tory: Johnson on Hume. Hume Stud, 16(1),

75-79, Ap 90.

My concern in this paper is simply to draw the attention of Hume scholars to a largely neglected but nevertheless very interesting remark which Samuel Johnson passed about the Hobbist nature of Hume's political outlook. I point out that Johnson's remark may also be interpreted as an allusion to Hume's 'atheistic' or anti-Christian intentions, and, thus, reflects very deeply upon the general character of Hume's philosophy.

RUSSO, Francesco. Lungo i sentieri dell'essere: L'eredità di Heidegger a cento anni dalla nascita. Sapienza, 42(4), 407-413, O-D 89.

RUST, John. Delusions, Irrationality and Cognitive Science. Phil Psych, 3(1), 123-138, 1990.

Studies of irrationality in cognitive psychology have usually looked at areas where humans might be expected to be rational, yet appear not to be. In this paper the other extreme of human irrationality is examined: the delusion as it occurs in psychiatric illness. A parallel is suggested between the delusion as an aberration of cognition and some illusions which result from aberrations within optics. It is argued that, because delusions are found predominantly within certain limited areas of cognitive functioning, they may represent a form of mental aberration which may tell us something about the abstract properties of mind. Possible implications of this model for several areas of cognitive science are discussed.

RUTHERFORD, R B. The "Meditations" of Marcus Aurelius: A Study. New York, Clarendon/Oxford Pr, 1989

RUTHROF, Horst. Discourse and Metaphysics. Phil Today, 33(2), 130-143, Sum 89.

RYAN, Alan (ed) and ROGERS, G A J (ed). Perspectives on Thomas Hobbes. New York, Clarendon/Oxford Pr, 1988

The papers in this collection provide views on central aspects of Hobbes's life and work, testifying to his enduring importance as a major philosopher, and help to unravel aspects of his intellectual autobiography. Hobbes is seen as a major figure not only in the English-speaking world but also by highly regarded scholars from France and Italy, whilst other contributors form an excellent mix between new and established Hobbes scholars, confirming the importance and depth of Hobbes's political theory and the wider thinking in which that political theory is set.

RYAN, Alan. "Hobbes and Individualism" in Perspectives on Thomas Hobbes, ROGERS, G A J (ed), 81-105. New York, Clarendon/Oxford Pr, 1988.

The chapter argues that Hobbes was an individualist epistemologically, scientifically, morally, and in matters of religion. This meant that Hobbes's brand of "authoritarian liberalism" was solidly grounded in the thought that the natural diversity of mankind was valuable when harnessed to scientific debate, dangerous when it gave rise to political conflict, and either harmless or dangerous in matters of religion according to the good sense and political stability of the country in question.

RYAN, Cheyney. Life, Liberty and Exploitation. Rev Int Phil, 43(170), 390-408, 1989.

The contrast between the instrumental and expressive dimensions of thought and action has been a persistent theme of sociological theory, implicitly since its founding, explicitly since Weber. In this paper, I shall pursue some of its implications for political theory. I begin by considering how the contrast between the instrumental and the expressive emerges in the contrast between liberalism's two fundamental rights, the right to life and the right to liberty. I suggest how this contrast contributes to a conflict between those rights, hence a contradiction within liberal theory as a whole. I then consider how Hegel's dialectic of master and slave can be read as an attempt to resolve this contradiction. And, finally, I place Marx's concept of exploitation in the context of the various issues here raised.

RYAN, Mary Melville. Nature and Philosophy for Children. Thinking, 7(4), 12-15, 1988.

RYAN, Maura A. The Argument for Unlimited Procreative Liberty: A Feminist Critique. Hastings Center Rep, 20(4), 6-12, Jl-Ag 90.

This article explores from a feminist perspective the claim that the protection of procreative liberty for fertile individuals, extended to infertile individuals, implies a right to access to reproductive technology. It concludes that arguments for unlimited procreative liberty are problematic from the vantage point of feminist ethics in at least three areas: the implicit treatment of children as property; the use of contract models of the family; and a tendency to neglect moral concerns about the ways we reproduce in favor of desired ends.

RYDEN, Lars and WALLENSTEEN, Peter. The Talloires Network—A Constructive Move in a Destructive World. Phil Soc Act, 15(3-4), 75-85, Jl-D 89.

RYLE, G. Logical Atomism in Plato's Theaetetus. Phronesis, 35(1), 21-46, 1990.

SAATKAMP JR, Herman J. Hermes the Interpreter. Bull Santayana Soc, 3, 22-28, Fall 85.

A response to Paul Kuntz's "Santayana's Neo-Platonism" in which Santayana's spiritual pilgrimage is characterized as Neo-Platonic. In contrast, I hold that Santayana's decided view is naturalistic or materialistic and that any fundamental ties to Platonism or Neo-Platonism are better understood as biographical, indicating the development of Santayana's thought, and not as a final endorsement. Santayana's essay, "On Metaphysical Projection," indicates how Neo-Platonism is a projection, an imaginative fable launched from a material foundation.

SAATKAMP JR, Herman J. Santayana's Autobiography and the Development of his Philosophy. Bull Santayana Soc, 4, 18-27, Fall 86.

A discussion of the development of Santayana's thought based on previously unpublished material now incorporated in the critical edition of Santayana's autobiography, Persons and Places (MIT, 1986). There is an explication of Santayana's autobiographical account of his (1) materialism, (2) moral relativism, and (3) moral self-definition.

SABRE, Ru Michael. Peirce's Abductive Argument and the Enthymeme. Trans Peirce Soc, 26(3), 363-372, Sum 90.

SACCHI, Mario E. El Aristóteles de Hegel. Sapientia, 44(174), 305-308, O-D 89.

SACKS, Mark. The World We Found: The Limits of Ontological Talk. La Salle, Open Court, 1989

Philosophers, in the analytic tradition in particular, have largely left the debate between metaphysical realists and idealists unattended, not committing themselves beyond the confinement to internal or empirical realism. This outstanding metaphysical issue must be addressed if we are to answer the sceptic who questions whether the world is as we experience it to be. After discussions of Kant, Strawson, Putnam, Goodman, Carnap and others, an attempt is made to reveal an unnoticed incoherence pertaining to the ontological talk required equally by metaphysical realists, idealists and sceptics. Settling the outstanding issue leaves confinement to a reworked form of internalism stable.

SACKSTEDER, William. "Mutually Acceptable Glory: Rating among Nations in Hobbes" in The Causes of Quarrel: Essays on Peace, War, and Thomas Hobbes, CAWS, Peter (ed), 97-113. Boston, Beacon Pr, 1989.

That pursuit of reputation in the eyes of others which Hobbes calls "Glory" causes quarrel among nations admitting no higher power and remaining in a "posture of war" akin to the natural condition. International agreements and disputes proclaim reciprocal pretention to equal integrity and esteem. Hence professing mutual recognition of equality among national units is precondition without which viable intercourse is impossible. Only equal Glory is mutually acceptable to all nations. Admitting equality is advised by worldly-wise counsels of prudence; likewise acknowledging it is obliged by laws of nature commanding peace and those forms of equity which are its conditions.

SADURSKI, Wojciech. Natural and Social Lottery, and Concepts of the Self. Law Phil, 9(2), 157-175, My 90.

The article's aim is to reject the argument that the nullification of inequalities stemming from "natural" differences (as contrasted to social ones) violates individual selves. Two stages of this argument are identified and subsequently criticised: (1) that individual selves are constituted, among other things, by people's social positions, including products of their labour, (2) that differential social rewards for these labours are necessary ingredients of these social positions. It is argued that to say that a product of one's work is a part of one's self assumes what is in question—how much people should be allowed to keep of what they produce.

SAFAR, Z and HOGENOVA, A. On the Question of the Active Role of Reflection in Marxist-Leninist Epistemology (in Czechoslovakian). Filozof Cas, 37(6), 783-794, 1989.

This theoretical study sets itself the task of highlighting the intricate problems connected with the active role of reflection in the realm of human consciousness. The authors make use of several inspiring stimuli, drawn from their studies of phenomenological texts, which tend to develop and sometimes incorrectly overestimate the subjective aspect of the cognitive process. They single out several major aspects of the process of the reflection of objective and subjective reality, aspects that were critically analyzed for example by Kant. The authors also refer to the specific features of the processuality of reflections constituting themselves in various modes of psychological activities such as memories, phantasy or symbols. The article is primarily designed to serve in teaching the theory of reflection in Marxism-Leninism courses at universities. (edited)

SAFRANSKI, Rüdiger and OSERS, Ewald (trans). *Schopenhauer and the Wild Years of Philosophy*. Cambridge, Harvard Univ Pr, 1990

The author provides a detailed biography of Schopenhauer, examining his philosophy in relation to his predecessors and contemporaries. (staff)

SAGAL, Paul T and CLEVELAND, Timothy. Bold Hypotheses: The Bolder the Better? Ratio, 2(2), 109-121, D 89.

When scientists want an explanation of some puzzling or problematic event or phenomenon should they propose the boldest conceivable hypothesis? According to Popper's influential conjecture and refutation methodology they should, since such hypotheses are susceptible to more severe tests. This answer depends, however, on a certain notion of "boldness" or "measure of boldness" which leads to a dilemma. The solution is that there are two senses of "boldness," a *logical*, and a *psychological* sense, which go unrecognized and are confused or conflated in the Popperian account. What scientists want are hypotheses bold in the logical, but not in the psychological sense—hypotheses which, on the proposed account, will have both the virtues of boldness and conservatism. With this account, which will be elucidated in terms of subjective probability, one will see more clearly the kinds of reasoning which are involved when a hypothesis is proposed for testing. In fact, one will see that the reasoning involved in the context of discovery is not independent of reasoning in the context of justification.

SAGAL, Paul T. Coherence. Ideal Stud, 19(2), 121-130, My 89.

SAGAL, Paul T. Searle on Minds and Brains. Mod Sch, 66(4), 301-302, My 89.

SAGAL, Paul. Reflexive Consistency Proofs and Gödel's Second Theorem. Phil Math, 4(1), 58-60, 1989.

SAGARDOY, María A F. El bien en arquitectura. Anu Filosof, 20(2), 159-164, 1987.

SAGI, Avi and STATMAN, Daniel. What Could Be the Meaning of the Idea that Morality Depends on Religion? (in Hebrew). Iyyun, 38(2), 103-136, Ap 89.

The purpose of this paper is to ask whether the claim that God determines morality can be explained in a reasonable way. This claim has been the central thesis of divine command theories of morality, theories that have been the object of much criticism. We seek to argue that before any of the traditional objections to these theories can be considered, a fundamental issue must be faced, namely, that it is very difficult to give a reasonable and coherent account of the basic intuition underlying divine command theories of morality, the intuition that God makes it the case that some things are right while others are wrong. The article examines in detail the following interpretations of the relation between God and morality mentioned above: that God determines morality by an act of legislation; that God's command is the (only) justification for moral judgments; that God's command is the meaning of morality; that God's command is identical with morality. We show that each of these interpretations faces serious difficulties, which are a challenge to any philosopher who wishes to defend a divine command morality.

SAH, Hirendra Prasad. Methodological Realism: An Essential Requirement of Scientific Quest. Indian Phil Quart, SUPP 16(4), 14-20, O 89.

Relativism has emerged as a strong current in the contemporary philosophy of science. It is its merit to show that the naive realist view of science is not right. But it does not end up just here. Relativist authors often intend to argue in favour of some form of antirealism about science. The objective of this paper is to argue to the conclusion that antirealism can't furnish essential ground for scientific-quest because the methodology of science demands for a realistic presupposition.

SAHLIN, Nils-Eric. *The Philosophy of F P Ramsey*. New York, Cambridge Univ Pr, 1990

F P Ramsey (1903-1930) was a remarkably creative and subtle philosopher who made significant contributions to economics, logic, mathematics and philosophy. This book is a critical study of Ramsey's work, offering a thorough exposition and interpretation of his ideas, setting the ideas in their historical context and assessing their significance for contemporary research.

SAIN, Ildikó. Computer Science Temporal Logics Need their Clocks. Bull Sect Log, 18(4), 153-160, D 89.

SAIN, Ildikó. An Elementary Proof for Some Semantic Characterizations of Nondeterministic Floyd-Hoare Logic. Notre Dame J Form Log, 30(4), 563-573, Fall 89.

We give a relatively simple and direct proof for Csirmaz's characterization of Floyd-Hoare logic for nondeterministic programs. (This also yields a very simple proof for Leivant's characterization.) We also establish a direct connection between "relational traces" and "time-models" for nondeterministic programs.

SAIN, Ildikó. Is "Some-Other-Time" Sometimes Better Than "Sometime" for Proving Partial Correctness of Programs? Stud Log, 47(3), 279-301, S 88.

The main result of this paper belongs to the field of the *comparative study of program verification methods* as well as to the field called *nonstandard logics of programs*. We compare the program verifying powers of various well-known temporal logics of programs, one of which is the Intermittent Assertions Method, denoted as *Bur*. *Bur* is based on one of the simplest modal logics called *S5* or "sometime"-logic. We will see that the minor change in this "background" modal logic increases the program verifying power of *Bur*. The change can be described either technically as replacing the "reflexive version" of *S5* with an "irreflexive version," or intuitively as using the modality "some-other-time" instead of "sometime." Some insights into the nature of computational induction and its variants are also obtained.

SAINATI, Vittorio. Metafisica e teologia della parola. Teoria, 9(1), 3-16, 1989.

SAINSBURY, R M. "On Induction and Russell's Postulates" in *Rereading Russell: Essays on Bertrand Russell's Metaphysics and Epistemology*, SAVAGE, C Wade (ed), 200-219. Minneapolis, Univ of Minn Pr, 1989.

The article discusses Russell's views about induction in *Human Knowledge*, where he claims that contingent "postulates of scientific inference" have to be known a priori if there is to be any inductive knowledge. This is supposed to be possible in virtue of a low-key and non-conceptualist view of knowledge: "animal expectation." Russell's argument is conducted within an interesting version of foundationalism, which, I argue, is defensible, and so not what should be rejected to avoid the highly implausible conclusion. The source of this is, rather, Russell's unsuccessful, and often surreptitious, battle with the skeptic.

SAITO, Yuriko. Contemporary Aesthetic Issue: The Colorization Controversy. J Aes Educ, 23(2), 21-31, Sum 89.

SAKAMOTO, Tatsuya and RAPHAEL, D D. Anonymous Writings of David Hume. J Hist Phil, 28(2), 271-281, Ap 90.

This article publishes and discusses the text of a manuscript memorandum written by George Chalmers in 1788 which supports a recent conjecture by David Raynor that Hume was the author of an anonymous review of Adam Smith's *Theory of Moral Sentiments* in 1759. The memorandum also reports that Hume published and then retracted a pamphlet against Archibald Stewart, Lord Provost of Edinburgh when the Jacobites occupied the city in 1745. The authors show that the source of Chalmers's information was David Callander, a talented pupil of Adam Smith and a nephew of Hume's friend Michael Ramsay. (edited)

SAKELLARIADIS, Spyros and MACHAMER, Peter. "The Unity of Hobbes's Philosophy" in *Hobbes: War Among Nations*, AIRAKSINEN, Timo (ed), 15-34. Brookfield, Gower, 1989.

Critics have tended to view Hobbes in either of two ways: first, that Hobbes is simply wrong to think that natural philosophy is in the least way relevant to politics, or, second, that Hobbes, in principle, thinks he can, and, in fact, attempts to, reduce politics to physics. In this paper we show what truth there is to both these claims. We shall argue that neither is completely correct. Attempting to reconcile the insights behind these two positions will involve laying out the architectonic of Hobbes's philosophy and examining the interconnection of its various levels. In particular, we will show how Hobbes's version of a nominalistic theory of language acts to unify the various parts of his philosophy.

SALA, Giovanni B. Das Gesetz oder das Gute? II, Teil: Alleiniges Prinzip des sittlich guten Willens. Gregorianum, 71(2), 315-352, 1990.

SALA, Giovanni B. Das Gesetz oder das Gute? Zum Ursprung und Sinn des Formalismus in der Ethik Kants. Gregorianum, 71(1), 67-95, 1990.

SALAMUN, Kurt. The Ethos of Humanity in Karl Jaspers's Political Philosophy. Man World, 23(2), 225-230, Ap 90.

The crucial thesis of Jaspers's Existentialism is the idea that self-realisation as Existenz is possible only under two conditions: the experience of boundary situations and (or) of existential communication. Closely linked to the concepts of Existenz, boundary situation, existential communication, existential freedom, unconditioned decision, etc., is a set of moral attitudes which constitute an ethos of humanity in Jaspers's philosophy. The thesis of this article is that this ethos is basic not only for Jaspers's Existentialism but also for his political philosophy and philosophy of reason, which he created after World War II.

SALBU, Steven R. A Legal and Economic Analysis of Insider Trading: Establishing an Appropriate Sphere of Regulation. Bus Prof Ethics J, 8(2), 3-21, Sum 89.

SALLIS, John and BARET, Françoise (trans). Doublures. Rev Phil Fr, 180(2), 349-360, Ap-Je 90.

A reading of several texts by Jacques Derrida on Husserl and on Saussure. The reading is oriented to the figure of doubling.

SALLIS, John. Twisting Free: Being to an Extent Sensible. Res Phenomenol, 17, 1-22, 1987.

This paper shows that, despite the radicalness with which Heidegger's work twists free of the metaphysical opposition between intelligible and sensible, a certain reduction of the sensible continues to operate in *Being and Time*. By inhibiting this reduction and bringing the shining of the sensible fully into play, one would disrupt and transform the basic question of fundamental ontology.

SALMAN, Ton. Lukács, Adorno en de machteloze kritiek. Alg Ned Tijdschr Wijs, 81(4), 264-284, O 89.

This article attempts to reconstruct some of the aspects of the influence that Lukács's work exerted on Adorno's social philosophy. It focuses on Lukács's conceptualization of reification (Verdinglichung), and argues that Lukács's rather 'absolutistic' dialectical reasoning was of considerable importance to Adorno. On the one hand Adorno criticized Lukács's (and Hegel's) overambitious all-embracing dialectics. On the other hand Adorno was heavily indebted to Lukács's radical dialectical critique of Enlightment as the bearer of alienation. This two-sided effect of Lukács's heritage counts—in part—for the sometimes paradoxical and paralysing nature of Adorno's radical social critique.

SALMANN, Elmer. Conoscenza-sapienza-teologia oggi. Aquinas, 32(2), 301-322, My-Ag 89.

SALMON, Merrilee H. "Explanation in the Social Sciences" in *Scientific Explanation (Minnesota Studies in the Philosophy of Science, Volume XIII)*, KITCHER, Philip (ed), 384-409. Minneapolis, Univ of Minn Pr, 1989.

Despite protests of the critics of causal and nomological explanation in the social sciences, the best approximations to a satisfactory philosophical theory of explanation seem to embrace successful explanations in the social sciences as well as successful explanations in the physical sciences. None of the critics has demonstrated that the admitted differences between our social environment and our physical environment compel us to seek entirely different methods of understanding each.

SALMON, Merrilee H. *Introduction to Logic and Critical Thinking (Second Edition)*. San Diego, Harcourt Brace Jov, 1989

SALMON, Wesley C (ed) and KITCHER, Philip (ed). *Scientific Explanation (Minnesota Studies in the Philosophy of Science, Volume XIII)*. Minneapolis, Univ of Minn Pr, 1989

SALMON, Wesley C. "Four Decades of Scientific Explanation" in *Scientific Explanation (Minnesota Studies in the Philosophy of Science, Volume XIII)*, KITCHER, Philip (ed), 3-219. Minneapolis, Univ of Minn Pr, 1989.

SALMON, Wesley C. *Four Decades of Scientific Explanation*. Minneapolis, Univ of Minn Pr, 1989

SALOM, Roberto. Estrategia y Táctica: La Política Como Ciencia: Marx Y Engels. Rev Filosof (Costa Rica), 26, 89-96, D 88.

The present article analyzes the rise of a scientific conception about change, based on an objective analysis of social classes when capitalism was surging, as well as big industries and the proletariat as the guiding class in the process. We shall also analyze how the surging of Marxism created the possibility for the advancement of science, not only in the analysis of the material conditions of life but also of the forms of transition, that is, of all that concerns strategy and tactics.

SALTHE, Barbara M and SALTHE, Stanley N. Ecosystem Moral Considerability: A Reply to Cahen. Environ Ethics, 11(4), 355-361, Wint 89.

Appeals to science as a help in constructing policy on complex issues often assume that science has relatively clear-cut, univocal answers. That is not so today in the environmentally crucial fields of ecology and evolutionary biology. The social role of science has been as a source of information to be used in the prediction and domination of nature. Its perspectives are finely honed for such purposes. However, other more conscientious perspectives are now appearing within science, and we provide an example here in rebuttal to the claim that there is no warrant from within ecology for ecosystem moral considerability.

SALTHE, Stanley N and SALTHE, Barbara M. Ecosystem Moral Considerability: A Reply to Cahen. Environ Ethics, 11(4), 355-361, Wint 89.

Appeals to science as a help in constructing policy on complex issues often assume that science has relatively clear-cut, univocal answers. That is not so today in the environmentally crucial fields of ecology and evolutionary biology. The social role of science has been as a source of information to be used in the prediction and domination of nature. Its perspectives are finely honed for such purposes. However, other more conscientious perspectives are now appearing within science, and we provide an example here in rebuttal to the claim that there is no warrant from within ecology for ecosystem moral considerability.

SALVATI, Giuseppe M. Crisi ecologica e concezione cristiana di Dio. Sapienza, 43(2), 145-160, Ap-Je 90.

SALZANO, Francisco M. The Price of Silence: Commentary. Hastings Center Rep, 20(3), 34, My-Je 90.

The problem raised was whether a patient with Huntington disease, a genetic condition which causes irreversible mental and motor deterioration, has the right of hiding to her siblings and children that at middle age they may also develop the disease. Special problems related to the early diagnosis of a carrier status, and to the dialectical relationship of the right to know and the right not to know are discussed, taking into consideration the living conditions in Brazil

SAMONÀ, Leonardo. "Condurre tutte le metafore *ad absurdum*": Riflessioni filosofiche attorno alla poetica di Celan. G Metaf, 11(2), 273-291, My-Ag 89.

SAMONÀ, Leonardo. Concettualità del fondamento: Concetto e fondamento tra riflessione e speculazione. G Metaf, 10(3), 453-481, S-D 88.

SAMPEDRO, Ceferino. *El a priori histórico (la historia y sus hechos)*. Valencia, Soler, 1990

This book narrates and analyses the concept of objective historicism. The structure, influence, and newness of events are investigated, in addition to how events go through the transition to history. (staff)

SAMPSON, Geoffrey. Language Acquisition: Growth or Learning? Phil Papers, 18(3), 203-240, N 89.

Noam Chomsky has argued in numerous books and articles that human language acquisition is a genetically-controlled process akin to the growth of a bodily organ, rather than a case of "learning" as ordinarily understood. He has used many different strands of reasoning to support this claim, which has been widely accepted. This article systematically lists each argument used by Chomsky at various times, and shows that in every case the reasoning is fallacious. I conclude that we have no reason to dissent from the layman's assumption that language is a learned skill.

SAN MARTÍN, Javier. La fenomenología. Dialogo Filosof, 6(2), 213-240, My-Ag 90.

El presente trabajo aspira a centrar la discusión sobre la fenomenología en el estudio de su estructura y su función. Para elle en primer lugar y a caballo de los avances en la publicación de la obra de Husserl, se insiste en la dualidad presente en la fenomenología entre la estructura de sus conceptos y la función práctico-moral. En segundo lugar avanza la nueva perspectiva que ha asumido la clásica relación de la fenomenología y la psicología, que en la actualidad, profundizando la vieja relación con la filosofía analítica, abarca la relación de la fenomenología husserliana con la psicología cognitiva, a través de la interpetación fregeana de Husserl. Por último se trata de explorar, con el mismo objetivo de resaltar la función de la fenomenología, su relación a la historia, que es donde se ventila su intención y donde se diseña una filosofía de la historia que ha de operar como la filosofía fenomenológica de las ciencias humanas.

SANABRIA, José Rubén. Metafisica todavia? (cont). Rev Filosof (Mexico), 22(65), 189-206, My-Ag 89.

SANABRIA, José Rubén. Metafisica Todavia? (cont). Rev Filosof (Mexico), 23(67), 71-86, Ja-Ap 90.

El artículo hace ver que los llamados neopositivistas niegan la metafísica porque piensan que ella es proposiciones sin sentido, ya que no son verificables empíricamente. O porque son semánticamente insuficientes. Así desde los clásicos (M Schlick, R Carnap, F Waismann, etc.) hasta los últimos. Recientemente algunos neopositivistas aceptan cierta metafísica. Por ejemplo Ayer y especialmente K Popper para quien son metafísicos los enunciados y actitudes que no puden ser empíricamente falsados. Será verdad?

SANABRIA, José Rubén. Metafisica todavia? Heidegger y la metafisica (cont). Rev Filosof (Mexico), 22(66), 388-399, S-D 89.

Se trata de analizar si Heidegger negó la Metafísica o más bien de superarla por otra de acuerdo a las exigencias del pensamiento contemporáneo. El "primer" Heidegger acepta le Metafísica clásica, pero pronto la crítica porque se convirtió en onto-teología. Olvidó el ser y se dedicó al ente. El olvido del ser lleva la Metafísica a su fin. Este fin es otro comienzo. Es su superación. Este nueva Metafísica vuelve a lo religioso, al misterio. La poesía es la auténtica fundación del ser.

SÁNCHEZ MANZANO, M A. La expresión de la falsedad y del error en el vocabulario agustiniano de la mentira. Augustinus, 34(135-136), 267-279, Jl-D 89.

SÁNCHEZ NAVARRO, Luis. La noción de Dios en las "Confesiones". Augustinus, 34(135-136), 347-354, Jl-D 89.

SANCHEZ-ESTOP, Juan Dominguez. Des présages a l'entendement: Notes sur les présages, l'imagination et l'amour dans la lettre à P Balling. Stud Spinozana, 4, 57-74, 1988.

The letter to Peter Balling about the presages is among the most controversial texts in the history of Spinozism. The aim of this letter is to bring a friend (in despair because of his son's death) back to reason and philosophy. Spinoza exposes his view on a very delicate matter: the presages, that had been evocated by his friend in a previous letter. Trying to fit this favourite topic of superstition in his own system, our philosopher gives an explanation of it in which the very possibility of presages relating to another being (Balling's son in this case) is based upon the existence of one kind of imagination which is seen as completely independent from the body, and on the ontological union between individuals which results from love. (edited)

SANCHEZ-MAZAS, Miguel. Identification et analyse des classes d'équivalence de la logique modale par des invariants numériques. Log Anal, 30(120), 401-439, D 87.

SÁNCHEZ-MAZAS, Miguel. Une méthode arithmétique de décision pour le système modal S5. Theoria (Spain), 4(11), 491-513, F-My 89.

Il s'agit d'une méthode qui permet d'associer à chaque formule bien formée du système S5 de logique modale un nombre naturel invariant pour toutes les formules qui appartiennent à la même classe d'équivalence que la première. En particulier, étant donné que la méthode associe à toutes les tautologies du système le nombre 0 et à toutes les contradictions du système un certain nombre Φ, il suffit de calculer le nombre qui, en vertu des associations fondamentales, reste associé à n'importe quelle formule pour décider si cette dernière est tautologique, contradictoire ou contingente. La méthode décrite constitue donc une nouvelle méthode arithmétique de décision pour le système modal indiqué. (edited)

SANCHO, Jesús Conill. El enigma del animal fantastico: Bases para una antropologia y etica de la tecnica. Rev Filosof (Mexico), 23(67), 111-131, Ja-Ap 90.

SANCIPRIANO, Mario. Etica e realtà. Aquinas, 32(3), 513-524, S-D 89.

SANDBACKA, Carola. Understanding Other Cultures: Studies in the Philosophical Problems of Cross-Cultural Interpretation. Acta Phil Fennica, 42, 1-193, 1987.

The thesis deals with philosophical problems concerning the understanding of human practices and beliefs in societies very different from the investigator's own. It is not a study in anthropological method; on the contrary, its purpose is to show that the philosophical difficulties pertaining to the concept of understanding here are variations of difficulties within any attempt to understand human beliefs and behaviour. One of the work's main points is that an understanding of alien beliefs and customs is connected with the understanding of customs and beliefs not alien; and that this kind of study is, by its very nature, different from an investigation within natural science.

SANDERLIN, David. Faith and Ethical Reasoning in the Mystical Theology of St John of the Cross. Relig Stud, 25(3), 317-333, S 89.

SANDKÜHLER, Hans Jörg. In den Zeiten der Schwäche. Deut Z Phil, 38(4), 305-318, 1990.

SANDOZ, Ellis (ed) and VOEGELIN, Eric. *Autobiographical Reflections—Eric Voegelin*. Baton Rouge, Louisiana St Univ Pr, 1989

SANFORD, David H. *If "P", then "Q": Conditionals and the Foundations of Reasoning*. New York, Routledge, 1989

Part One is a history of theories of conditional sentences that covers the Stoics, medieval logic, and the modern period, including Frege, Russell, Wittgenstein, Ramsey, C I Lewis, Quine, Chisholm, Adams, D Lewis, and Stalnaker. Part Two criticizes several current theories. Rejecting attempts to define dependence by reference to conditionals, it refers to patterns of dependence to describe grounds for conditionals. The book accounts for objective dependence in terms of one-way conditionship. It also defends W E Johnson's theory of inference and entailment.

SANFORD, David H. The Truth about Neptune and the Seamlessness of Truth. Phil Stud, 58(1-2), 87-93, Ja-F 90.

This comment on Steven Boër's immediately preceding paper about object-dependent thoughts develops two examples: (1) a counterexample to the "axiom of the seamlessness of truth," namely, that there are no propositions, one true and one false, such that knowing the true one requires believing the false one; (2) a story about the first sighting of Neptune, by John Galle on September 23, 1846, that illustrates how one can understand Galle's remark "That is the planet whose position Leverrier calculated" without believing that there is something to which Galle refers.

SANGUINETI, Juan José. Il realismo nella filosofia della scienza contemporanea. Aquinas, 32(3), 525-541, S-D 89.

SANKEY, Howard. In Defence of Untranslatability. Austl J Phil, 68(1), 1-21, Mr 90.

This paper rebuts criticism of the idea of an untranslatable language which Putnam and Davidson have directed against the incommensurability thesis. It is argued that incommensurability involves at most limited untranslatability between the special languages of theories, and that translation between languages is not necessary for understanding. Davidson's attack on the scheme-content dualism is also criticized.

SANKOWSKI, E. Some Problems About One Liberal Conception of Autonomy. Austl J Phil, 67(3), 277-285, S 89.

SANKOWSKI, Edward. Blame, Fictional Characters, and Morality. J Aes Educ, 22(3), 49-61, Fall 88.

Studying moral attitudes of blame toward fictional characters yields interesting philosophical results. First, such blame is important in the experience and criticism of art, but easily misunderstood because of defective philosophy. Second, acknowledging that there is such blame compels our rejection or reformulation of some otherwise attractive ideas about blame. Third, study of such blame illuminates blaming attitudes toward real-life cases. In each of the three sections of this essay, one of the foregoing claims will be justified.

SANTAMBROGIO, Marco (ed) and ECO, Umberto (ed) and VIOLI, Patrizia (ed). *Meaning and Mental Representation*. Bloomington, Indiana Univ Pr, 1988

SANTAS, Gerasimos. Aristotle's Criticism of Plato's Form of the Good: Ethics Without Metaphysics? Phil Papers, 18(2), 137-160, S 89.

SANTONI, Ronald E. The Cynicism of Sartre's "Bad Faith". Int Phil Quart, 30(1), 3-15, Mr 90.

In his analysis of bad faith, Jean-Paul Sartre contends that bad faith consciousness is not cynical. I argue, here, against Sartre, that the lie which constitutes bad faith may be said to be cynical. Bad faith consciousness exploits the nature of faith, makes "knowing preparations" for its deceitful maneuvers and concepts, and in so doing manifests an indifference to truth. Further, though bad faith is a heavily qualified form of "lying to oneself," it shares—in a modified way—the pattern of "double denial" which Sartre places at the heart of the "ideal description" of his "cynical consciousness." Hence, it is cynical in Sartre's idiomatic sense.

SAPONTZIS, Steve F. Environmental Ethics and the Locus of Value. Between Species, 6(1), 8-9, Wint 90.

The author argues that values cannot exist without reference to the capacities of sentient beings and discusses objections to this thesis raised by realist environmental ethicists.

SAPONTZIS, Steve F. "Ethics, Subjective and Secular" in *Inquiries into Values: The Inaugural Session of the International Society for Value Inquiry*, LEE, Sander H, 243-252. Lewiston, Mellen Pr, 1989.

This paper discusses what does and does not follow, in the way of justification in ethics, from the following two propositions: the existence of values depends on the existence of valuers, and there is no valuer who values things for all times and places. Section I explicates the concept of a "valuer" and develops an affective theory of value. Section II develops a realistic case of argument about moral values to show that actual, rational limitations on arguments about moral values are compatible with the above propositions; hence, not all is permitted if ethics is subjective and secular.

SAPONTZIS, Steve F. Groundwork for a Subjective Theory of Ethics. Amer Phil Quart, 27(1), 27-38, Ja 90.

This paper develops a subjective theory of values and discusses the consequences of it for justification in ethics. This subjective conception of values is based on the following two propositions: the existence of valuers is a necessary condition for things having value, and there is no omniscient valuer whose evaluations establish "the true value" of everything.

SARANYANA, Josep-Ignasi. De la teología a la mística pasando por la filosofía: Sobre el itinerario intelectual de Avicena. Anu Filosof, 21(1), 85-95, 1988.

SARASON, Seymour B. The Lack of an Overarching Conception in

Psychology. J Mind Behav, 10(3), 263-279, Sum 89.

As a broad, sprawling field, American psychology has become increasingly molecular, making it inordinately difficult to discern or formulate an overarching conception that would counter the centrifugal forces that make psychology a conglomeration of interests for which there is no organizing center. To illustrate the lack of such a conception and its adverse consequences, the major works of two people who had such a conception but who have had no influence on psychology are discussed. One of them is John Dollard, who in the mid-thirties wrote *Criteria for the Life History*, which was nothing less than an indictment of the lack of such an overarching conception. The other is Alexis de Tocqueville, who wrote *Democracy in America*. How was this young Frenchman, who spent nine months in this country before the middle of the nineteenth century, able to write a book that explained so well the American character? What "psychology" permitted him to understand so much, to describe so clearly the individual *in* the larger picture? Dollard spelled out his conception, Tocqueville did not. An attempt is made to formulate Tocqueville's overarching conception.

SARAYDAR, Edward. The Inefficiency of Some Efficiency Comparisons: A Reply to Nye. Econ Phil, 6(1), 153-156, Ap 90.

SARIG, Gissi and FOLMAN, Shoshana. Intercultural Rhetorical Differences in Meaning Construction. Commun Cog, 23(1), 45-92, 1990.

Recent research seems to challenge Robert Kaplan's contrastive rhetoric hypothesis, a phenomenon which might have an effect on EFL written communication instruction. Three studies were set out to further test this hypothesis. We wanted to find out if and to what extent rhetorical structures preferred by native Hebrew speakers differ from those preferred by native English speakers when constructing meaning in reading and in writing in their native languages. Findings are presented and discussed in light of an oral to written diagnostic model developed for this study. On the basis of this analysis, the possible relationship between writing instructional norms or practices and intercultural rhetorical preferences are suggested. Implications for future research are drawn. (edited)

SARKAR, Sahotra. On Adaptation: A Reduction of the Kauffman-Levin Model to a Problem in Graph Theory and Its Consequences. Biol Phil, 5(2), 127-148, Ap 90.

It is shown that complex adaptations are best modelled as discrete processes represented on directed weighted graphs. Such a representation captures the idea that problems of adaptation in evolutionary biology are problems in a discrete space, something that the conventional representations using continuous adaptive landscapes do not. Further, this representation allows the utilization of well-known algorithms for the computation of several biologically interesting results such as the accessibility of one allele from another by a specified number of point mutations, the accessibility of alleles at a local maximum of fitness, the accessibility of the allele with the globally maximum fitness, etc. A reduction of a model due to Kauffman and Levin to such a representation is explicitly carried out and it is shown how this reduction clarifies the biological questions that are of interest.

SARKER, Sunil Kumar. The Concepts of Man and Nature in Marxism. Indian Phil Quart, 17(1), 49-61, Ja 90.

In Marxism, man is conceived of not quite materialistically. There is an insurmountable 'complexity threshold' between man and nature which are interdependent. The biological man becomes a species-being through 'communist labour' which is a pious but unrealistic concept. The concept of 'real man' or humane man remains unexplained, and points to the idealist and utopian trend in Marxism.

SARTORIUS, Rolf. "Positivism and the Foundations of Legal Authority" in *Issues in Contemporary Legal Philosophy: The Influence of H L A Hart*, GAVISON, Ruth (ed), 43-61. New York, Clarendon/Oxford Pr, 1987.

SARTWELL, Crispin. The Analytic Turn: An Institutional Account. Metaphilosophy, 20(3-4), 262-273, Jl-O 89.

This paper argues that the analytic turn in philosophy at the beginning of this century responded not only to intellectual pressures (e.g., the exhaustion of Hegelian idealism), but also to professional pressures in the academy (shrinking departments and lack of prestige).

SARTWELL, Crispin. Representation and Repetition. Phil Today, 33(3), 221-231, Fall 89.

This paper examines writings of Baudrillard, Peirce, and Kierkegaard to give an account of pictorial representation as repetition. Repetition in turn is treated as a play of resemblances. It concludes that representation is not a substitute for the actual, but a supplementation of it.

SARUP, Madan. *An Introductory Guide to Post-Structuralism and Postmodernism*. Athens, Univ of Georgia Pr, 1989

This text gives a clear exposition of the thought of Lacan, Derrida and

Foucault. The author explains the key concepts of poststructuralism and the way we think about the human subject, language, culture, philosophy, and politics. Reference is also made to the work of Lyotard and the questions raised by 'postmodernism'. The main concern of the book is the relationship between knowledge and power. It is shown that at the present time there are strong tendencies towards the fragmentary, the unstable, and the irrational. Against these tendencies, Sarup argues that the Enlightenment project is committed to education, rationality and progress, and that it has not failed.

SASAKI, Katsumi. The Simple Substitution Property of the Intermediate Propositional Logics. Bull Sect Log, 18(3), 94-99, O 89.

We study about the intermediate propositional logics obtained from the intuitionistic propositional logics by adding some axioms. We define the *simple substitution property* for a set of additional axioms. Hitherto have been known only three intermediate logics that have the additional axioms with the property, and in this paper, we add one more example, that is, we give new axioms with the property to the logic S_ω. Further, we decide which one among the axioms composed of one propositional variable has the property.

SASAKI, Ken-ichi. Naissance de l'auteur—Une Histoire de l'esthétique moderne autour de son alibi (in Japanese). Bigaku, 40(3), 1-11, Wint 89.

Il existe des témoignages d'une tendance individualiste avant 18e siècle (d'un Savonalora ou d'un R. de Piles). Pourtant, en montrant une curiosité de la manière des peintres, de Piles plaide le beau universel: ce rationalisme esthétique produit, à sa limite, l'illusionisme au seuil du 18e siècle. Ainsi l'esthétique des 17e et 18e siècles va du concept de beau à celui d'individualité en passant par l'illusionisme. (edited)

SASO, Michael. Derrida and the Decentered World of K'ou-Chuan: The Deconstruction of Taoist Semiotics. J Chin Phil, 17(1), 51-60, Mr 90.

SASSI, Maria Michela. Fra Platone e Lucrezio: prime linee di una storia degli studi di filosofia antica nell'ottocento italiano. Arch Stor Cult, 3, 165-199, 1990.

SASSO, Javier. Andrés Bello como filósofo. Rev Latin De Filosof, 15(2), 239-251, Jl 89.

In this book Arturo Ardao has gathered his various papers related to Andrés Bello's philosophical work, in order to mark out a global image of Bello's relation with philosophy. Ardao rebuilds the different stages of Bello's thought, and special attention is given not only to the main topics of *Philosophy of Understanding* but to others that not appear in it, as the problem of "logical grammar." In this commentary I describe Ardao's reconstruction and I discuss his interpretation of the two topics where Bello apparently stands closer to Berkeley (abstraction and matter), and in both cases an alternative interpretation is proposed.

SASSOWER, Raphael. Economics and Psychology: Estranged Bedfellows or Fellow Travellers? A Critical Synthesis. Soc Epistem, 3(4), 269-280, O-D 89.

The history of the relationship between psychology and economics is used to examine reductionism among the social sciences and the independence of particular fields of inquiry.

SASSOWER, Raphael and ORMISTON, Gayle L. *Narrative Experiments: The Discursive Authority of Science and Technology*. Minneapolis, Univ of Minn Pr, 1989

An examination of experimentation with certain prominent themes recurrent in the current literature of science and technology studies. Particular attention is given the "performative" function of language and the kinds of authority assigned and attributed to scientific and technological discourses. Using the notion that "use creates," the authority of selected "radical" philosophical perspectives—Feyerabend, Kuhn, Rorty—is questioned in terms of the "metaphysics" each utilizes and for what purposes. The final sections of the book are devoted to an analysis of the differences between discursive replacement and discursive displacement as each is used in certain scientific and philosophic contexts.

SASSOWER, Raphael. Scarcity and Setting the Boundaries of Political Economy. Soc Epistem, 4(1), 75-91, Ja-Mr 90.

Instead of assuming that the notion of scarcity is both empirically uncontestable and heuristically significant for anyone interested in social, political, and economic theory, this paper asks if it is impossible to conceive of political economy or social theory without using the notion of scarcity altogether.

SAUER, Werner. On the Kantian Background of Neopositivism. Topoi, 8(2), 111-119, S 89.

SAUNDERS, B A C and VAN BRAKEL, J. Moral and Political Implications of Pragmatism. J Value Inq, 23(4), 259-274, D 89.

SAUVÉ, Denis. Règles et langage privé chez Wittgenstein: deux interprétations. Philosophiques, 17(1), 45-70, 1990.

Whether Wittgenstein subscribes to a "community" or an "individualist" view of meaning and of rule following is a much debated question among students of the *Philosophical Investigations*. I will discuss this question by relating it to the issue concerning the correct interpretation of his well-known argument against the possibility of a private language. I will argue that, despite objections which have been raised by proponents of the "individualist" interpretation, a plausible reading of Wittgenstein's argument can be given within a "community" view of rule following.

SAVA, G. Vincenzo Lilla nella filosofia italiana dell' Ottocento. Il Protag, 6(9-10), 153-172, Je-D 86.

SAVAGE, C Wade (ed) and ANDERSON, C Anthony (ed). *Rereading Russell: Essays on Bertrand Russell's Metaphysics and Epistemology*. Minneapolis, Univ of Minn Pr, 1989

SAVAGE, C Wade. "Sense-Data in Russell's Theories of Knowledge" in *Rereading Russell: Essays on Bertrand Russell's Metaphysics and Epistemology*, SAVAGE, C Wade (ed), 138-168. Minneapolis, Univ of Minn Pr, 1989.

SAVAGE-RUMBAUGH, E S. Language as a Cause-Effect Communication System. Phil Psych, 3(1), 55-76, 1990.

Christopher Gauker has argued that a cause-effect analysis of the acquisition of communication skills in chimpanzees is adequate to describe the data reported in our work at the Language Research Center. I agree that the cause-effect approach to language function is the only viable method of analyzing language. Language must be studied as a process that functions to organize behavior between two or more individuals. However, the problem of language understanding is not addressed satisfactorily by the perspective offered by Gauker. Some more recent work, particularly with the pygmy chimpanzee 'Kanzi', is now beginning to explicate a cause-effect analysis of language comprehension. It is argued that in the young chimpanzee, as with children, language comprehension is the driving force underlying the language acquisition process. It is further argued that the transition from comprehension to production is made possible by the capacity for goal-directed observational imitation.

SAVILE, Anthony. "Beauty and Truth: The Apotheosis of an Idea" in *Analytic Aesthetics*, SHUSTERMAN, Richard (ed), 123-146. Cambridge, Blackwell, 1989.

SAVILE, Anthony. Narrative Theory: Ancient or Modern? Phil Papers, 18(1), 27-51, My 89.

SAVORELLI, Alessandro. Bruno 'Iulliano' nell'idealismo italiano dell'Ottocento (con un inedito di Bertrando Spaventa). G Crit Filosof Ital, 68(1), 45-77, Ja-Ap 89.

SAVORELLI, Alessandro. Pietro Siciliani o del virtuoso darwinismo. G Crit Filosof Ital, 68(2), 235-247, My-Ag 89.

SAXON, Charles S and ALLEN, Layman E and PAYTON, Sallyanne. Synthesizing Related Rules from Statutes and Cases for Legal Expert Systems. Ratio Juris, 3(2), 272-318, Jl 90.

Different legal expert systems may be incompatible with each other: a user in characterizing the same situation by answering the questions presented in a consultation can be led to contradictory inferences. Such systems can be "synthesized" to help users avoid such contradictions by alerting them that other relevant systems are available to be consulted as they are responding to questions. An example of potentially incompatible, related legal expert systems is presented here—ones for the New Jersey murder statute and the celebrated Quinlan case, along with one way of synthesizing them to avoid such incompatibility.

SAYER, Derek (ed). *Readings from Karl Marx*. New York, Routledge, 1989

SAYWARD, Charles and HUGLY, Philip. Can There Be a Proof That Some Unprovable Arithmetic Sentence Is True? Dialectica, 43(3), 289-292, 1989.

A common theme of logic texts is that the Gödel incompleteness result shows that some unprovable statement of arithmetic is true, or, at least, that determining whether arithmetic truth is axiomatizable is a logical or mathematical issue. Against this common theme we argue that the issue is a philosophical issue that has not been settled.

SAYWARD, Charles. Four Views of Arithmetic Truth. Phil Quart, 40(159), 155-168, Ap 90.

Four views of arithmetical truth are distinguished: the classical view, according to which each arithmetical sentence is true or false; the simple provability view, according to arithmetic truth is tied to derivability from axioms; the extended provability view, according to which the notion of proof is indefinite and extensible; the criterial view, suggested by Wittgenstein in the *Tractatus*. It is argued that the criterial view is the best of the four views.

SAYWARD, Charles and HUGLY, Philip. Tractatus 6.2-6.22. Phil Invest, 13(2), 126-136, Ap 90.

Implicit in Tractatus 6.2-6.22 are the ideas that the content of mathematical propositions consists in their use outside of mathematics, and that outside of mathematics these propositions function as rules, primarily rules of inference. These ideas are elaborated and defended.

SAZBÓN, José. La revisión antihistoricista de la Revolución Francesa. Cuad Filosof, 20(33), 3-29, O 89.

From the middle of the 1950s a development of critical studies on the history of the French Revolution has taken place, which tends to erode the notions established by the "orthodox" historiography, submitting alternative views and insisting, above all, on the inadequacy of the concept of "bourgeois revolution" to characterize the sense of the events that took place between 1789 and 1799. This work dwells on some aspects of what is agreed to call historical "revisionism" on the subject; also on the anti-historicist bias adopted by its allegations, and on the correspondence of the latter between some philosophic or social-scientific positions. In this sense, particular attention is devoted to the agreement between views of the English historian Alfred Cobban and the epistemologist Karl Popper, on the one hand, and that between the French historian François Furet and the anthropologist Lévi-Strauss, on the other.

SBISÀ, Marina. Semantica, Pragmatica, Atti linguistici: note in margine a una polemica. Teoria, 9(2), 161-171, 1989.

SCALONE, A. Decisione e origine: Appunti su Schmitt e Heidegger. Il Protag, 6(9-10), 173-178, Je-D 86.

SCALTSAS, Theodore. The Logic of the Dilemma of Participation and of the Third Man Argument. Apeiron, 22(4), 67-90, D 89.

In this paper I offer a detailed analysis of the Dilemma of Participation (*Parmenides*, 130e-131e), in which Plato considers the consequences of participation in the whole, and in a part of, a Form. This analysis explains, in contrast to existing interpretations of the argument, Plato's claim that participation in parts of a Form is incompatible with the *uniqueness* of the Form, and his modal claim that becoming equal by possessing part of the Equal is *absurd*. In the second part of the paper, I give the premises and logical steps of the Third Man Argument in the *Parmenides*, and show the premises to be committed to absurdity, even without the assumption that there is a unique Form per character F.

SCANLON, John. Dilthey on Psychology and Epistemology. Hist Phil Quart, 6(4), 347-355, O 89.

SCANLON, Thomas. Promises and Practices. Phil Pub Affairs, 19(3), 199-226, Sum 90.

Argues against the idea that the wrong involved in breaking a promise depends essentially on the existence of a social practice of promise making. An alternative account of this wrong is offered. This account employs ideas of expectation and reliance but attempts to broaden these ideas in such a way as to avoid familiar classes of counterexamples. The article concludes with a discussion of the contributions that social practices (while they are not essential) can make to the genesis of such obligations. The relation between promises and oaths is considered in an appendix.

SCANNONE, J C. Símbolo religioso, pensamiento especulativo y libertad. Stromata, 45(3-4), 315-320, Jl-D 89.

El artículo plantea un pensamiento especulativo que reflexione filosóficamente el sentido de "lo Santo" (y de "Dios") como se da en la experiencia religiosa. La *semántica* especulativa corresponderá verdaderamente a la religiosa, si también hay correspondencia *sintáctica* y *pragmática* entre ambos lenguajes. Tal es el caso del pensamiento y lenguaje *analógicos*. Su sintaxis (afirmación-negación-eminencia) corresponde—en el order del concepto—a la mediación simbólica, y su uso del concepto (pragmática) a la conversión del ídolo al símbolo. Así se piensa lo santo *como* santo.

SCARCELLA, Cosimo. Machiavelli, Tacito, Grozio: un nesso "ideale" tra libertinismo e previchismo. Filosofia, 41(2), 213-231, My-Ag 90.

SCARRE, Geoffrey. Demons, Demonologists and Descartes. Heythrop J, 31(1), 3-22, Ja 90.

The intellectual background to Descartes's evil deceiver speculation is examined in a study of medieval and early modern 'demonic epistemology'. It is argued that Descartes himself did not share the disappearing world-view within which the threat of a powerful *malin génie* could be taken seriously, but rather used the deceiver hypothesis as a methodological device for limbering up our critical faculties. Ironically, Descartes's restatement of the deceiver speculation gave it a new lease of life in the writings of modern epistemologists.

SCHACHAR, Yoram. "Comment: The Middle Way in the Philosophy of Punishment" in *Issues in Contemporary Legal Philosophy: The Influence of H L A Hart*, GAVISON, Ruth (ed), 238-244. New York, Clarendon/Oxford Pr, 1987.

SCHACHT, Richard. "Nietzsche" in *Ethics in the History of Western Philosophy*, CAVALIER, Robert J (ed), 271-305. New York, St Martin's Pr, 1988.

SCHADLER, F P and KARNS, J E. The Unethical Exploitation of Shareholders in Management Buyout Transactions. J Bus Ethics, 9(7), 595-602, Jl 90.

The accurate pricing of securities in the capital markets depends upon the markets being both efficient and fair. In management buyout transactions (MBOs), the price bid by inside managers enhances the efficient pricing of securities but raises a reasonable doubt about the fairness to existing shareholders. This study addresses this fairness question in MBOs and offers short-term and long-term legal alternatives which allow both the efficiency and fairness criteria to be met. In the short-term the case law established in the *Basic v. Levinson* decision for merger negotiation disclosures should be applied to MBO transactions. Over the longer horizon, legislative changes should be made to existing securities laws. Applying the investor protection principles of the 1933 and 1934 securities acts to MBO transactions will suppress the temptation of managers to extract shareholder wealth for their personal gain.

SCHAEFFER, John D. From Wit to Narration: Vico's Theory of Metaphor in Its Rhetorical Context. New Vico Studies, 2, 59-73, 1984.

SCHAEFFER, John D. *Sensus Communis* in Vico and Gadamer. New Vico Studies, 5, 117-130, 1987.

SCHALL, James V. Dwellers in an Unfortified City: Death and Political Philosophy. Gregorianum, 71(1), 115-139, 1990.

Formal political philosophy began with Plato's account of the death of Socrates at the hands of the Athenian state. Christ was also executed by an action of the Roman state. Politics, however, concerns man in this life, its ordering and its best ordering. The fact of death both signifies that there are things over which the state no longer has control and things that must not yield to its power. The relation of death to political philosophy brings up the question of the status of those things that are beyond politics and the way in which politics leads to questions that can no longer be adequately treated by politics. Philosophy was said to be a preparation for death. The meaning of politics then must be seen in the light of this higher relationship to philosophy.

SCHALL, James V. On Natural Law—Aristotle. Vera Lex, 7(1), 11-12,26, 1987.

Whether Aristotle held for a natural "law" or was merely a natural "right" theorist is a question of some importance and complexity. Natural law is said to require a theory of creation or revelation and hence something not found in Aristotle. On the other hand, Aristotle's understanding of nature, of stable essences which are not themselves self-caused, would at least leave his position open to a possible deepening that would not be contrary to his basic premises. The matter is of some importance in political philosophy and its understanding of modern natural right, which does not in principle presuppose anything but the human will. If there be a natural right which was contrary to this will, then what would be the origin of its claim? That is, the origin of its claim against modern natural right? The relation of natural law to natural right in this sense is of fundamental importance in political philosophy.

SCHALLER, Walter E. Are Virtues No More Than Dispositions to Obey Moral Rules? Philosophia (Israel), 20(1-2), 195-207, Jl 90.

Virtues are standardly understood as (1) essentially dispositions to perform certain actions and (2) having only instrumental value as motives to fulfill moral duties which can be fulfilled by persons lacking the virtue because the duties mandate only certain act-types. The argument of this article is that the duties of beneficence, gratitude and self-respect cannot be stated in terms of obligatory act-types because they cannot be fulfilled (except in deficient form) by persons lacking the appropriate virtue; they are, rather, duties to cultivate specific virtues which therefore cannot themselves be defined in terms of obligatory actions.

SCHALOW, F. Imagination, Totality, and Transcendence. Int Stud Phil, 22(1), 59-71, 1990.

This paper addresses the relationship between Heidegger's and Ricoeur's thought by focusing the different direction in which each develops the central issue of the imagination. A comparison is made between Ricoeur's quest to locate in the imagination a way of indirect access to the otherwise transcendent content of reason and Heidegger's more "violent" attempt to foster the overthrow of reason through a radicalized conception of the imagination as implying the disclosedness of Dasein as Being-in-the-world.

The paper concludes by weighing the positive contributions of each which, despite their important differences, point to a fuller appropriation of Kant's thought and an even more radical account of imagination.

SCHALOW, Frank. Heidegger, Kant and the 'Humanism' of Science. SW Phil Rev, 6(2), 71-78, Jl 90.

This paper attempts to show that Heidegger's earlier appropriation of Kant's notion of human finitude needs to be recast in light of the later critique of humanism developed in 1944. The key to this retrieval of Kantian thought lies in addressing the human essence in its affinity with the revelation of all beings, which is considered more originally in the Greek sense of nature as "self-emerging presence." The opportunity is then created to overcome further the subject-object dichotomy and to confront the challenges posed by science and technology.

SCHALOW, Frank. Religious Transcendence: Scheler's Forgotten Quest. Phil Theol, 4(4), 351-364, Sum 90.

This paper highlights Max Scheler's contribution to developing a 'phenomenological' account of religious transcendence in a way which remains unique among other proponents of that tradition of continental thought. It is argued that even in formulating his own concept of 'world-openness' (as precursor to Husserl's and Heidegger's view of the self's 'worldliness') Scheler continues to foster a vision of the human person's eternality and kinship with the Divine.

SCHALOW, Frank. Why Hegel? Heidegger and Speculative Philosophy. SW Phil Rev, 6(1), 29-35, Ja 90.

The purpose of this paper is to show that the latent source of Heidegger's interest in Hegel's speculative philosophy stems from the fact that Hegel's metaphysics leaves behind itself a "trace" of the modern tradition's dependence upon early Greek thought (in a way completely foreign to Kant) and thereby obliquely provides a clue to the forgetfulness of being. It is argued that even though Heidegger tends to align himself with Kant (in contrast to Hegel) in considering what remains unthought throughout the tradition Hegel alone suggests a way for unfolding the *historical dimension of the question of being*. The paper concludes that Heidegger's ability to appropriate speculative philosophy in a self-critical way hinges upon his establishing both the divergence and reciprocity between his own treatment of the pre-Socratics and Hegel's account of the same.

SCHANK, Roger and KASS, Alex. "Knowledge Representation in People and Machines" in *Meaning and Mental Representation*, ECO, Umberto (ed), 181-200. Bloomington, Indiana Univ Pr, 1988.

SCHAPER, Eva (ed) and VOSSENKUHL, Wilhelm (ed). *Reading Kant*. Cambridge, Blackwell, 1989

Twelve original essays by British, American and German scholars reassess the importance of Kant's arguments for contemporary philosophical debates. Topics covered include the nature and possibility of transcendental arguments, the prospect of a decisive refutation of scepticism, the role of space in our experience of the objective world, the nature of judgment, the identity of the subject and the tenability of transcendental idealism. Contributors are Eckart Forster, Graham Bird, Ross Harrison, Ralph Walker, Peter Bieri, Terry Greenwood, Paul Guyer, Rolf Peter Horstmann, Reinhard Brandt, Wilhelm Vossenkuhl, Gerd Buchdahl and Dieter Henrich.

SCHARF, David C. Quantum Measurement and the Program for the Unity of Science. Phil Sci, 56(4), 601-623, D 89.

It is quite extraordinary, philosophically speaking, that according to the orthodox interpretation: (a) quantum mechanics is a complete and comprehensive theory of microphysics, and yet (b) the role of measurement, in quantum mechanics, cannot be analyzed in terms of the collective effects of the microphysical particles making up the apparatus. It follows that, if the orthodox interpretation is correct, the measurement apparatus and its quantum physical effects cannot be accounted for microreductively. This is significant because it is widely believed that the relation between physical wholes and parts is microreductive. Indeed, many philosophers are persuaded of the inevitability of universal microreduction to the basic elements of microphysics. This is the viewpoint embodied in the program for the unity of science, espoused in recent years, most notably by Robert Causey (1977).

SCHARFF, Robert C. Mill's Misreading of Comte on 'Interior Observation'. J Hist Phil, 27(4), 559-572, O 89.

In *Auguste Comte and Positivism*, J S Mill defends introspection against Comte's alleged refutation of it. A careful reading of this defense reveals, however, that Mill misunderstands what Comte is attacking. Comte's villain is something he calls "l'observation intérieure"—a spurious metaphysical procedure deriving ultimately from Descartes, practiced by incurably prescientific thinkers like Cousin and Jouffroy, and leading inevitably to speculative doctrines about the Mind, or Self. Mill takes Comte instead to be attacking the empirical-psychological operation of first-person reporting of inner states. This article analyzes Mill's misreading in detail and suggests some reasons why, once the error is made, Comte in particular becomes Mill's enemy whenever he wants to defend the possibility of a scientific, introspection-based psychology.

SCHARFF, Robert C. Positivism, Philosophy of Science, and Self-Understanding in Comte and Mill. Amer Phil Quart, 26(4), 253-268, O 89.

This paper argues that as a philosopher of science, J S Mill is less reflective, i.e., less concerned with self-understanding, than Comte, and that as a result he fundamentally misreads Comte's pointed opposition to (1) developing a logic of scientific proof, (2) construing scientific laws in causal terms, and (3) searching for the laws of human mind psychologically instead of physiologically and sociologically. In each case, Comte's opposition makes sense only as part of his general effort to provide the positivist orientation itself with the sort of self-critical defense which Mill no longer takes seriously. It is suggested that precisely because Comte still thinks it is philosophy's task to offer such a defense—and all the more so because he conceives of this task in what we might now call a "quasi-hermeneutical" way—his positivism, though older than Mill's, has greater contemporary relevance.

SCHAUPP, Dietrich and LANE, Michael S. Ethics in Education: A Comparative Study. J Bus Ethics, 8(12), 943-949, D 89.

This study reports the results of a survey designed to assess the impact of education on the perceptions of ethical beliefs of students. The study examines the beliefs of students from selected colleges in an eastern university. The results indicate that beliefs which students perceive are required to succeed in the university differ among colleges. Business and economics students consistently perceive a greater need for unethical beliefs than students from other colleges.

SCHECHTMAN, Marya. Personhood and Personal Identity. J Phil, 87(2), 71-92, F 90.

Psychological continuity theorists of personal identity have defended their views from charges of circularity using "quasi" psychological states. I argue that these states are not and cannot be coherently specified, because the qualitative content of a psychological state cannot be specified without reference to facts about the identity of its subject. Once this fact is appreciated it becomes clear that it is impossible to give a noncircular psychological criterion of personal identity.

SCHEDLER, George. Does the Threat of AIDS Create Difficulties for Lord Devlin's Critics? J Soc Phil, 20(3), 33-45, Wint 89.

Although Devlin's critics have rightly attacked Devlin's legal moralism, they have overlooked his appeals to public harm, which are strengthened by the current risk of AIDS that attaches to homosexual intercourse. I refine and reconstruct Devlin's more plausible arguments and expose some difficulties with the views of Devlin's critics.

SCHEDLER, George. The Radical Feminist View of Motherhood: Epistemological Issues and Political Implications. Int J Applied Phil, 4(4), 25-34, Fall 89.

I argue that (1) it is unlikely that the radical feminist view of motherhood is an empirical view; (2) radical feminists must urge the government to use paternalistic measures to ensure that women do not choose motherhood; (3) it is difficult for radical feminists to avoid adopting a natural law view about women's nature (not unlike one on which male supremacists have relied to prevent women from pursuing careers outside the home).

SCHEDLER, George. Viewing Fetuses as Scarce Natural Resources. Phil Context, 19, 21-31, 1989.

If infants should not be killed, because there is a demand for them, then fetuses for which there is a demand should also afford some protection. This would be a special case of preserving natural resources rather than destroying them so others (pregnant women) can carry on their lives. Society can limit its demands to those pregnancies involving no trauma or danger to the woman. Society should also compensate her.

SCHEER, R K. What if Something Really Unheard-of Happened? Phil Invest, 13(2), 154-164, Ap 90.

SCHEER, Richard. Free Will. Phil Invest, 13(3), 197-212, Jl 90.

SCHEFFLER, Samuel. Deontology and the Agent: A Reply to Jonathan Bennett. Ethics, 100(1), 67-76, O 89.

SCHEIER, Claus-Artur. Contemporary Consciousness and Originary Thinking in a Nietzschean Joke. S J Phil, 27(4), 549-559, Wint 89.

The Nietzschean joke on Zola (KGA VI.3, p. 105, cf. V.2, p. 474) is developed into the differentiation between contemporary consciousness and originary thinking in Nietzsche's attitude to "Life." It is shown how Nietzsche's post-Zarathustrian shift from originary thinking to "metaphysics"

involuntarily prepares the way to ideology without itself falling victim to it.

SCHERER, Donald. "Ethics in America". Teach Phil, 12(4), 405-408, D 89.

SCHIBLI, H S. Apprehending Our Happiness: *Antilepsis* and the Middle Soul in Plotinus, *Ennead* I 4.10. Phronesis, 34(2), 205-219, 1989.

An examination of *Ennead* I.4.10, in conjunction with *Enneads* I.1.11.1-8 and I.1.7.9-18, shows that the cognitive capacity of apprehension is a function of the middle soul, that is, our ordinary state of consciousness. In this state we are able to experience the true happiness operating on the level of the higher soul, which continues whether we apprehend it or not. Our aim therefore should be to transcend the variable state of apprehension and to identify wholly with the higher, intellectual soul in order actually to *be* happiness. For this Plotinus demands the divestment of the ordinary self.

SCHICK JR, Theodore W. The Idealistic Implications of Bell's Theorem. Ideal Stud, 19(2), 131-140, My 89.

SCHIER, Flint. The Claims of Tragedy: An Essay in Moral Psychology and Aesthetics Theory. Phil Papers, 18(1), 7-26, My 89.

SCHILLER, Hans-Ernst. The Critique and Utopia of the Subject (in Serbo-Croatian). Filozof Istraz, 30(3), 851-863, 1989.

Der Verfasser geht von der These aus, dass die Französische Revolution die Inthronisierung des Subjekts, des sich selbst besimmenden Menschen ist. Dies Subjekt der Revolution und ihrer "Neuen Zeit" ist abstrakt, weil es von seinen historischen Bedingungen wie von den konkreten Inhalten seines Willens absieht. Die Allgemeinheit eines solchen Subjekts ist formell, seine heimatlichen Sphären sind Politik und Privatrecht. Die Marxsche Utopie des Subjekts ist durch zwei Momente bestimmt: das negative detrifft die Aufhebung verselbständigter Produktionsverhältnisse, das positive meint "reale Freiheit" als Aneignung der Produktivkräfte in der "Solidarität der freien Entwicklung Aller".

SCHILLER, Hans-Ernst. Zur sozialphilosophischen Bedeutung des Sprachbegriffs Wilhelm von Humboldts. Z Phil Forsch, 44(2), 253-272, 1990.

There are many close affinities between Humboldt and the Frankfurt School. For Marcuse, Humboldt's definition of language as "energeia" offers a paradigm for the critique of linguistic reification. Like Habermas, Humboldt claims that understanding is the telos of language; however, as opposed to Habermas, Humboldt neither reduces subjectivity to intersubjectivity, nor does he make a rigid distinction between labour and language. Finally, he anticipates Adorno's "utopia of knowledge," to which language is the model. Both Humboldt and Adorno use similar definitions of the dialectic between generality and individuality.

SCHIRALLI, Martin. Art and the Joycean Artist. J Aes Educ, 23(4), 37-50, Wint 89.

SCHIRN, Matthias. Frege on the Purpose and Fruitfulness of Definitions. Manuscrito, 13(1), 7-23, Ap 90.

In this paper I want to discuss some problems in Frege's theory of definition. I shall begin by characterizing his conception of definitions in *Begriffsschrift* of 1879. In the second part I shall deal with Frege's thesis about the systematic fruitfulness of "good" definitions in mathematics and logic, which he states in "Booles rechnende Logik und die Begriffsschrift" of 1880-81 and in *Die Grundlagen der Arithmetik* of 1884. In his mature period Frege abandoned this thesis. In the concluding and main part of the paper I shall investigate in detail the change of mind he had undergone concerning the purpose and value of definitions.

SCHIRN, Matthias. Frege's Objects of a Quine Special Kind. Erkenntnis, 32(1), 27-60, Ja 90.

SCHLANGER, Judith. La pensée et la nouveauté de pensée. Rev Metaph Morale, 94(2), 191-203, Ap-Je 89.

SCHLANGER, Judith. "Saying and Knowing" in *From Metaphysics to Rhetoric*, MEYER, Michel (ed), 89-94. Norwell, Kluwer, 1989.

SCHLEIFER, Michael and LEBUIS, Pierre and CARON, Anita. The Effect of the *Pixie* Program on Logical and Moral Reasoning. Thinking, 7(2), 12-16, 1987.

SCHLESINGER, George N. *New Perspectives on Old-Time Religion*. New York, Clarendon/Oxford Pr, 1988

SCHLESINGER, George N. Qualitative Identity and Uniformity. Nous, 24(4), 529-541, S 90.

SCHMERL, James H. Large Resplendent Models Generated by Indiscernibles. J Sym Log, 54(4), 1382-1388, D 89.

SCHMID, A Allan. *Property, Power, and Public Choice: An Inquiry into Law and Economics—Second Ed*. New York, Praeger, 1987

Market rules, whether competitive or not, are not naturally deterministic or matters of equilibrium, but issues for public choice, ethical debate, and persuasion. Each set of property rights has a derivative optimality and thus efficiency is no guide to choice of rights. Variables are identified to predict the substantive performance impact of institutional instrument, i.e., what engenders economic and political power. The inherent characteristics of goods constitute sources of human interdependence which are given order by rights. These include incompatible use, economies of scale, exclusion and information costs which interact with rights to produce a particular income distribution and economic growth.

SCHMIDT, Alfred. Physiologie und Transzendentalphilosophie bei Schopenhauer. Schopenhauer Jahr, 70, 43-53, 1989.

SCHMIDT, Dennis J. "Strangers in the Dark: On the Limitations of the Limits of *Praxis* in the Early Heidegger". S J Phil, SUPP(28), 43-49, 1989.

The author discusses the limitations of Heidegger's early conception of *praxis*, especially as it is developed in *Being and Time*, from the perspective of Heidegger's work during the 1930s. The argument is that a more radical sense of the possibility of human praxis is found during the work of the 1930s, and that texts of that period must be read as responding to the limitations of the early work on this question.

SCHMIDT, Dennis J. In Heidegger's Wake: Belonging to the Discourse of the "Turn". Heidegger Stud, 5, 201-211, 1989.

Concerned with the questions of tradition and language following Heidegger, more precisely, this piece is an attempt to ask how far thinking that takes its cue from Heidegger's work can be said to stand in a tradition and language inaugurated by Heidegger. Recent works, in English, French, and German, dealing with various themes are discussed in the context of those questions.

SCHMIDT, Hartwig. Fortschritt und Rückschritt. Deut Z Phil, 37(10-11), 1013-1022, 1989.

SCHMIDTZ, David. Charles Parsons on the Liar Paradox. Erkenntnis, 32(3), 419-422, My 90.

Although three-valued logics of the kind suggested by Charles Parsons block the inference of outright contradictions from Liar-type sentences, they still permit one to draw conclusions that are neither true nor false from true premises. With three-valued logics, then, standard rules of inference fail to preserve truth value.

SCHMIDTZ, David. Contractarianism without Foundations. Philosophia (Israel), 19(4), 461-469, D 89.

Michael Levin and others have turned to contractarianism in the hope that it would let them draw important conclusions about the scope of legitimate government without depending on controversial normative premises. I conclude that this is a false hope.

SCHMIT, Roger. Gebrauchssprache und Logik: Eine Philosophiehistorische Notiz zu Frege und Lotze. Hist Phil Log, 11(1), 5-17, 1990.

The connections that exist between the logical doctrines of G Frege and R H Lotze are, as shows their common treatment of natural language, deeper than is generally admitted. In particular, the logical criticism of language conceived by Frege is influenced in three points by Lotze. Firstly, Lotze postulates the strict separation of logic and natural language. Furthermore, the idea of logical simplicity plays an important role in his logic. Finally, he distinguishes objective thought from its tone.

SCHMITT, A. Das schöne: Gegenstand von Anschauung oder Erkenntnis? Philosophia (Athens), 17-18, 272-296, 1987-88.

In modern concepts the beautiful is primarily an object of the senses or of a mode of thinking (taste, common sense, etc.) in which thought is not (yet) separate from the senses. One important root of this concept is the 18th century differentiation between confused (sensible) ideas and the distinct ideas of mind, but this differentiation has its real origin in Plato. The article tries (1) to improve our understanding of Plato's thesis that only the mind has distinct cognition of the beautiful, and (2) to specify the process through which this Platonic concept has changed to the modern, purely aesthetic experience of the beautiful.

SCHMITT, Richard. Humanism and Socialism. Free Inq, 9(4), 16-19, Fall 89.

While Eastern Europeans reconsider the connections between socialism and humanism—the dedication to a rational and humane society—Westerners remain complacently convinced that capitalism is a guarantor of freedom. I raise a number of questions that require answers before that confidence can be shown to be justified.

SCHMITZ, Kenneth L. "Paradigms of Nature in Western Thought" in *Man and Nature: The Chinese Tradition and the Future*, TANG, Yi-Jie (ed), 33-54. Lanham, Univ Pr of America, 1989.

SCHMITZ, Manfred. Bibliographie der bis zum 8 Mai 1989 veröffentlichten Schriften Edmund Husserls. Husserl Stud, 6(3), 205-226, 1989.

SCHNECK, Stephen Frederick. Habits of the Head: Tocqueville's America and Jazz. Polit Theory, 17(4), 638-662, N 89.

The essay attempts an alternative interpretation of Tocqueville's *Democracy in America*. Drawing inspiration from Michel Foucault's poststructural attitude, the argument made is that Tocqueville's supposed structuralist recipe for viable democracy is a disguise. The America Tocqueville sees is an America Tocqueville creates.

SCHNEIDER, Hans Julius. Syntactic Metaphor: Frege, Wittgenstein and the Limits of a Theory of Meaning. Phil Invest, 13(2), 137-153, Ap 90.

The paper proposes an answer to Dummett's question, whether a *systematic* (Fregean) theory of meaning is possible in the framework of the later Wittgenstein. Wittgenstein's claim that it is only on the surface of grammar that 'expressing a proposition' is a uniform act seems to lead to the absurd consequence that we learn sentences not by learning how to use systematic procedures, but one by one. It is shown that by introducing the concept of a 'syntactic metaphor' and a level of 'abstract sense' (intermediate between Frege's levels of *sense* and *point*) Frege's and Wittgenstein's views can be combined.

SCHNEIDERMAN, Lawrence J. Exile and PVS. Hastings Center Rep, 20(3), 5, My-Je 90.

In prescribing treatments that prolong the lives of patients in a vegetative state, we are causing the *persistent* vegetative state (PVS), thus resurrecting the archaic practice of banishment. Permanently unconscious patients exist in a dehumanizing condition—enslaved to perpetual inertness, emotionless, helpless, unlike any other form of human existence, isolated from every human connection and communication—an exile that, whether perceived or not, is a terrible punishment, since it is void of context. If physicians find this view persuasive, then withdrawing life-supporting treatment from the patient in PVS becomes not merely ethically permissible, but an obligatory act of beneficence.

SCHOEMAN, Ferdinand. "Adolescent Confidentiality and Family Privacy" in *Person to Person*, GRAHAM, George (ed), 213-234. Philadelphia, Temple Univ Pr, 1989.

SCHOEN, Edward L. The Sensory Presentation of Divine Infinity. Faith Phil, 7(1), 3-18, Ja 90.

Reliable as well as unreliable indicators play a crucial role in various types of ordinary perceptual encounter. Since perceptual indicators may function perfectly well without any connection whatever to essences or essential natures, it is possible to find ways in which divine infinity may be perceptually encountered and even recognized as such in the course of ordinary human experience.

SCHOEN, Edward. Anthropomorphic Concepts of God. Relig Stud, 26(1), 123-139, Mr 90.

Traditionally, it has been claimed that religious anthropomorphism leads invariably to unseemly characterizations of the divine, that the radical difference between human beings and the divine renders such anthropomorphic language inappropriate and that anthropomorphic descriptions of the divine invariably spring from disreputable human motivations. Anthropomorphic language employed in computer science, however, suffers from no such defects. Thus, by scrutinizing this language, proper ways of attributing various human characteristics to radically nonhuman divinities can be specified.

SCHOLLMEIER, Paul and FEMENÍAS, María Luisa. Intuición práctica y ejemplo retórico. Cuad Filosof, 20(33), 41-48, O 89.

Assume that we have a faculty of theoretical intuition, through which we intuit theoretical principles, and a faculty of practical intuition, through which we intuit practical principles. Could we justify or verify our theoretical and practical intuitions in the same way? Despite recent attempts to do so, one would think not. For we assume that we have two different faculties grasping principles of different kinds. We would thus ask what method or technique we could use to justify or to verify our practical principles. Aristotle suggests that an art of discourse and an inductive technique might serve to justify practical intuitions about our ends. The art is rhetoric and the technique argument by example. After all, rhetoric is an art concerned with discourse of a practical kind, and example is an argument of an inductive sort.

SCHÖNBERGER, Rolf. Louis Lavelle: l'expérience de l'être comme acte. Arch Phil, 53(2), 271-280, Ap-Je 90.

According to Lavelle the concept of being is subordinated to the elementary experience of the self as "free agent," as being participation to reality which is not hindrance but experience of meaning. Such concept of being is understood both as fullness and univocal, which requires a study of the relation between logic of concept and concept of being.

SCHÖNING, Uwe. *Logic for Computer Scientists*. Cambridge, Birkhauser, 1989

This book introduces the notions and methods of formal logic from a computer science standpoint, covering propositional logic, predicate logic, and foundations of logic programming. It presents such modern applications and themes of current computer science research as resolution, automated deduction, and logic programming in a rigorous but readable way. The style and scope, rounded out by the inclusion of exercises and an up-to-date list of references, make this an appropriate textbook for an advanced undergraduate course in logic for computer scientists. (edited)

SCHÖNRICH, Gerhard. Innere Autonomie oder Zurechnungsfähigkeit? Z Phil Forsch, 44(2), 278-291, 1990.

The paper criticizes Tugendhat's approach to the concept of free will as a natural event and demonstrates that the concept of accountability presupposes a concept of autonomy. The concept of autonomy makes it possible to avoid some of the paradoxical consequences of Tugendhat's approach. The paper concentrates on two points: first, the question if the concept of consideration, which is presupposed by free will, can also be an object of free will, and secondly, the question, how should free will be conceived as a "self-relation"?

SCHONSHECK, Jonathan. "Constraints on *The Expanding Circle*: A Critique of Singer" in *Inquiries into Values: The Inaugural Session of the International Society for Value Inquiry*, LEE, Sander H , 695-707. Lewiston, Mellen Pr, 1989.

Peter Singer, in *The Expanding Circle*, endorses much of sociobiology. Singer believes that the selection pressures bearing on early hominids would favor groups whose individual members carried a genetic endowment predisposing them towards "sociability." And Singer claims that the "group" within which individuals are sociable has expanded; it now includes all humans, and some animals. I argue that Singer is mistaken about the consequences of kin and group selection, that selection pressures would favor "out-group enmity" as well as "in-group amity." The people of the earth are not members of a universal moral community, but of mutually suspicious and hostile groups.

SCHOPENHAUER, Arthur and HÜBSCHER, Arthur (ed) and PAYNE, E F J (trans). *Manuscript Remains, Volume IV: The Manuscript Books of 1830-1852 and Last Manuscripts*. New York, St Martin's Pr, 1990

SCHOPMAN, Joop. Is kennis belichaamd? Alg Ned Tijdschr Wijs, 82(2), 101-116, Ap 90.

The thesis is defended that developments within artificial intelligence (AI) have an impact on the philosophical reflection on the nature of knowledge. From a confrontation between standard AI and a new approach based on models of neural networks, it becomes evident that both incorporate a different concept of knowledge. A discussion is presented of efforts made by some philosophers to bridge the gap between the two positions. From this the conclusion is drawn that knowledge is *embodied*. A study of the exact nature of this embodiedness requires a serious cooperation between philosophers and cognitive scientists from other disciplinary backgrounds.

SCHOPP, Robert. Free Will as Psychological Capacity and the Justification of Consequences. Phil Forum, 21(3), 324-342, Spr 90.

This paper integrates familiar psychological and philosophical concepts in order to present a conception of free will as a set of psychological capacities that is consistent with current psychological theory and common moral intuitions. The author argues that this conception of free will provides the notion that we need and often intuitively apply in our moral and legal judgments.

SCHORE, Jean E and NELSON, Lawrence J and CLARK, H Westley and GOLDMAN, Robert L. Taking the Train to a World of Strangers: Health Care Marketing and Ethics. Hastings Center Rep, 19(5), 36-43, S-O 89.

SCHOTTLAENDER, Rudolf. Zu Spinozas Theorie des Glaubens. Stud Spinozana, 4, 227-242, 1988.

There is no place for a religious belief in Spinoza's philosophy. According to Spinoza, such belief could be accepted only for those who have not yet arrived at adequate knowledge. Religious belief is thus to be understood as an emotion which expresses 'a persuasion of that which is not recognizable'. This conviction is provided from the reality of what we believed by way of the will or willing against. But Spinoza's *Amor Dei intellectualis* cannot be the love of God out of such an emotion. The question remains, whether Spinoza's notion of God can be thought adequate to such a belief, if not pantheistically, yet perhaps immanentistically. (edited)

SCHOUWEY, Jacques. Philosophie et politique, un cas d'ambiguïté:

"l'affaire Heidegger". Frei Z Phil Theol, 36(3), 479-487, 1989.

What seemed to be, in a French-speaking context, a revelation about Heidegger's Nazi past is actually but a controversy regularly brought up. The debate aroused by Victor Farias's book, *Heidegger and Nazism* (1987), doesn't really tackle the question of Heidegger's thought, the thought of existence. This article tries to show that the thinker is not necessarily a politician but politics happens to recover the thought.

SCHRADER, David E. Background Rights and Judicial Decision. J Value Inq, 23(4), 285-297, D 89.

This paper argues for two theses about good judicial decision making. First, if a judge's decision making process is to avoid either arbitrariness or serious incompleteness, it must appeal to an understanding of those background rights which the judge takes to be embodied in the nation's constitution and body of laws. Second, in appealing to a conception of rights antecedent to the law, the judge is not assuming a fundamentally legislative role. Clearly some judges do, on occasion, arrogate a legislative function, but an appeal to the judge's conception of political morality does not necessarily involve such arrogation.

SCHRAG, Francis. Response to Bilow: Future Persons and the Justification of Education. Proc Phil Educ, 45, 331-334, 1989.

SCHRAG, Francis. Response to Feinberg's "Foundationalism and Recent Critiques of Education". Educ Theor, 40(2), 217, Spr 90.

SCHRAM, Stuart. *The Thought of Mao Tse-Tung*. New York, Cambridge Univ Pr, 1989

SCHREIER, Helmut. On Victor Guarda's "How Does the Child Benefit from 'Philosophy for Children'?". Thinking, 6(3), 31, 1986.

SCHRENK, Lawrence P. Proclus on Space as Light. Ancient Phil, 9 (1), 87-94, Spr 89.

SCHREYÖGG, Georg and STEINMANN, Horst. Corporate Morality Called in Question: The Case of Cabora Bassa. J Bus Ethics, 8(9), 677-685, S 89.

This article presents a case study of a big German enterprise (Siemens) facing a large wave of public critique and protest activities. The public was concerned about the political circumstances surrounding the construction of the Cabora Bassa hydroelectric dam in Mozambique in which Siemens was largely involved. This study reports the escalating protest against the firm over three years (1970-1972) and the firm's responses during that period. The analysis of the case focusses on the behaviour of the firm which is interpreted in the light of the business social responsibility doctrine. The article proposes that the firm experienced a legitimation crisis and responded by reorienting its philosophy of business.

SCHRIJVERS, Joke. Dialectics of a Dialogical Ideal: Studying Down, Studying Sideways and Studying Up. Kennis Methode, 13(4), 344-361, 1989.

SCHRÖDER, Richard. Kampf—Verhandlung—Dialog. Deut Z Phil, 38(4), 372-382, 1990.

Dieser Vortrag auf einer Veranstaltung des christlich-marxistischen Dialogs versucht, die Engführung der marxistischen Anthropologie aufzubrechen, die den Menschen bloss von seinen Bedürfnissen her versteht und in den permanenten Klassenkampf schickt. Sie vermag deshalb die Perspektive des Rechts und der Gerechtigkeit nicht zu erfassen. In Erläuterung der vier Sätze: (1) der Mensch ist das Gewohnheitswesen; (2) er ist das Bedürfniswesen; (3) er ist das Wesen, das anerkennen kann; (4) er kann der Wahrheit die Ehre geben soll gezeigt werden, dass das spezifisch menschliche Vermögen das Verhältnis zu seinen Bedürfnissen ist. Dies wird durch dieSätze 1, 3 und 4 erläutert, der in der Definition des Menschen als animal rationale das zweite Wort entspricht.

SCHROEDER, William R. Nietzsche's Synoptic and Utopian Vision. Int Stud Phil, 21(2), 15-20, 1989.

SCHROEDER-HEISTER, Peter and DOSEN, Kosta. Uniqueness, Definability and Interpolation. J Sym Log, 53(2), 554-570, Je 88.

Starting from a notion of a consequence relation which captures only the structural aspects of logic, we prove generalizations of Craig's interpolation lemma and Beth's definability theorem which are not restricted to the syntactic categories of nonlogical constants.

SCHUELER, George Frederick. *The Idea of a Reason for Acting: A Philosophical Argument*. Lewiston, Mellen Pr, 1989

The 'Humean' view of reasons for action is that if we are to claim that reasons can actually move us to *act* then we have to hold that they must involve some motivating factor, such as a desire or 'pro attitude'. This book examines a series of progressively more plausible defenses of this view, along with some of the intuitions that underlie them. All these defenses appear to fail for essentially the same reason, a failure at crucial points in the reasoning to clearly distinguish deliberation from explanation of the action.

SCHUERMAN, John R. Improving the Quality of Social Welfare Scholarship: Response to "Confirmational Response Bias". Sci Tech Human Values, 15(1), 56-61, Wint 90.

The article is a response to a study of the editorial practices of social work journals in which a fraudulent article was submitted to a number of journals to test the hypothesis of bias toward "positive" articles. The author discusses both the substance and the ethics of the study. It is concluded that the study fails to demonstrate the hypothesized bias and involves questionable research procedures.

SCHUHMANN, Karl and REINER, Hans. Ein Protokoll aus Husserls Logikseminar vom Winter 1925. Husserl Stud, 6(3), 199-204, 1989.

We began by tentatively defining logic as a science of meanings, distinguishing between meanings and their objects (references). We established that meanings exist concretely in psychic acts, thus allowing logic to be seen also as the science of thinking. After further consideration we concluded that logic is only concerned with true meanings, and is therefore a practical normative science. Its normative character, however, is limited to formal truths. In addition logic can also be defined as the science of objects taken in their most general sense. Indications were given how this general science of objects includes various mathematical disciplines.

SCHULHOFER, Stephen J. The Gender Question in Criminal Law. Soc Phil Pol, 7(2), 105-137, Spr 90.

SCHULTE, Joachim. "Stilfragen" in *Wittgenstein in Focus—Im Brennpunkt: Wittgenstein*, MC GUINNESS, Brian (ed), 143-156. Amsterdam, Rodopi, 1989.

Anhand eines Vergleichs mit den Stilbegriffen Spenglers und Goethes lassen sich in Wittgensteins Schriften wenigstens drei Bedeutungen des Wortes "Stil" auseinanderhalten: (1) Stil im Sinne einer individuellen, persönlichen Eigenart; (2) Stil im Sinnes des Geistes einer Kultur oder Epoche; (3) Stil im Sinne einer zeit-oder kulturtypischen Ausdrucksform, die zwar prägend, aber nicht zwingend verbindlich ist. Eine Erörterung des Stils in den Bedeutungen (2) und (3) zeigt, inwieweit dieser Begriff bei Wittgenstein "relativistisch"—d.h. kultur- und epochengebunden—aufgefasst wird.

SCHULZ, Walter. Acerca de la fundamentación de la ética. Rev Filosof (Argentina), 2(1), 21-27, My 87.

SCHUMACHER, John A. *Human Posture: The Nature of Inquiry*. Albany, SUNY Pr, 1989

In terms of the way we make places with our bodies we can explain how we think and feel. In the first of three parts, the terms of posture are developed through an account of our evolution that culminates in an analysis of Plato's and Aristotle's theories of vision. In the second part, a reinterpretation of physics from Newton to Einstein leads to a new theory of nervous system activity that reconnects us to each other and the world through our bodies. The third part extends the co-making of inquiry from the natural to the social sciences, including an analysis of the posture of our everyday lives.

SCHUMM, George F. Some Compactness Results for Modal Logic. Notre Dame J Form Log, 30(2), 285-290, Spr 89.

A modal logic L is said to be compact if every L-consistent set of formulas has a model on a frame for L. Some large classes of compact (noncompact) logics are identified, and it is shown that there are uncountably many compact (noncompact) logics.

SCHÜRMANN, Reiner. The Law of the One and the Law of Contraries in Parmenides. Grad Fac Phil J, 13(1), 3-20, 1988.

SCHURZ, Gerhard. Paradoxical Consequences of Balzer's and Gähde's Criteria of Theoreticity. Erkenntnis, 32(2), 161-214, Mr 90.

It is shown that the criteria of *T*-theoreticity proposed by Balzer and Gähde lead to strongly counterintuitive and in this sense 'paradoxical' results: most of the obviously empirical or at least nontheoretical terms come out as theoretical. The conclusion is drawn that the *T*-theoreticity of a term cannot possibly be 'proved' on the basis of the mathematical structure of theory *T* alone. Rather, an independent notion of pre-*T*-theoreticity and—more importantly—of empiricity is needed, i.e., "not empirical" and "not pre-*T*-theoretical" are necessary but not sufficient conditions for "*T*-theoretical." Finally it is asked whether the structuralist criterion of *T*-theoreticity complemented by such independent conditions would be a satisfactory answer to 'Putnam's challenge', and the answer again is negative. (edited)

SCHÜSSLER, Rudolf. Die Möglichkeit der Kooperation unter Egoisten: Neuere Ergebnisse spieltheoretischer Analysen. Z Phil Forsch, 44(2), 292-304, 1990.

The article discusses some new developments in the study of cooperation

among economic egoists. It directs attention to new results on cooperation in small and large groups, on solutions of the Hobbesian problem of order and the stability of free markets in a completely egoistic environment. These problems can be solved more easily by egoists than traditionally assumed in the social sciences.

SCHUSTER, Federico L. Negación intuicionista y divergencia lógica. Rev Filosof (Argentina), 3(2), 127-141, N 88.

Which are, actually, the relations between classical and nonclassical logics is something yet quite unknown. In this paper, we try to defend the thesis that intuitionistic logic is really a rival of classical logic. To do it we go through the works (as Kleene's or Gödel's) that intended to translate intuitionism into classical terms and we compare intuitionist logic with another nonclassical theory: von Wright's one. The main point of our argument settles on the meaning of negation. We try to show that intuitionistic negation is not a different connective from classical, in the sense that it doesn't exist incommensurability between them both.

SCHUURMAN, Henry. The Concept of a Strong Theodicy. Int J Phil Relig, 27(1-2), 63-85, Ap 90.

SCHWAN, Alexander. Heideggers "Beiträge zur Philosophie" und die Politik. Z Phil Forsch, 43(4), 593-617, O-D 89.

The article analyses Heidegger's "Beiträge zur Philosophie" with respect to the philosopher's attitude towards national socialism during the years 1936 to 1938. It comes to the result that he denies his attachment and activities for national socialism but in an ambivalent way, which did not mean an active resistance against its criminal policies but the resignation from any political commitment or practical activity at all.

SCHWARTZ, Dov. Human Knowledge and Divine Knowledge in Medieval Philosophy (in Hebrew). Iyyun, 39(2), 211-222, Ap 90.

This article examines two kinds of knowledge—human knowledge and divine knowledge—according to Avicenna, Maimonides, and Thomas Aquinas. Human knowledge is based on abstraction: the intellect abstracts the form out of the substance. God's knowledge, by contrast, is pure self-knowledge, the ideal forms of all beings existing in God's essence. Divine knowledge is, therefore, autonomous, while human knowledge is heteronomous. This view appears in medieval Jewish philosophy, especially in the writings of R Isaac Albalag and R Samuel Ibn Zarza. A close study of the fourteenth century Jewish thinker Ibn Zarza ends this survey.

SCHWARTZ, Joseph M. Arendt's Politics: The Elusive Search for Substance. Praxis Int, 9(1-2), 25-47, Ap-Jl 89.

SCHWARTZ, Robert John. Approximate Truth, Idealization, and Ontology. S J Phil, 28(3), 408-425, Fall 90.

SCHWARTZ, Stephen P. Intuitionism Versus Degrees of Truth. Analysis, 50(1), 43-47, Ja 90.

Putnam's intuitionist proposal for a logic of vague terms is defended. It is argued that both classical logic and the degrees of truth approach are committed to treating vague terms as having hidden precise borderlines. This is a crucial failing in a logic of vagueness. Intuitionism, because of the nature of intuitionist negation, avoids this failing.

SCHWARTZ, Stephen P. Vagueness and Incoherence: A Reply to Burns. Synthese, 80(3), 395-406, S 89.

Linda Burns in her article 'Vagueness and Coherence' (*Synthese* 68) claims to solve the sorites paradox. Her strategy consists in part in arguing that vague terms involve loose rather than strict tolerance principles. Only strict principles give rise to the sorites paradox. I argue that vague terms do indeed involve paradox-generating strict tolerance principles, although different ones from those Burns considers. The sorites paradox remains unsolved.

SCHWARZ, Georg. Response to Dietrich's "Computationalism". Soc Epistem, 4(2), 186-190, Ap-Je 90.

SCHWEIKER, William. From Cultural Synthesis to Communicative Action: The Kingdom of God and Ethical Theology. Mod Theol, 5(4), 367-387, Jl 89.

The purpose of this article is to trace a line of thought from Ernst Troeltsch's ethics and theory of culture to the work of Wolfhart Pannenberg and Trutz Rendtorff's *Ethics*. The contention of the essay is that Pannenberg and Rendtorff use paradigmatic acts to rethink Troeltsch's concern for moral good in a relativistic cultural situation. Pannenberg does so through the goal directed character of human action set within his eschatological understanding of the symbol of the Kingdom of God. Rendtorff, the article argues, shifts the discussion from individual action to the communicative shape of life as a giving and receiving of life. Based on this, Rendtorff is able to account for Troeltsch's concern with culture while articulating an ethical theory in conversation with discourse-ethics. The article concludes with criticisms of Pannenberg and Rendtorff that center on the need for a thick interpretation of human life beyond the possible formalism of their positions, a concern that expresses anew Troeltsch's insistence on the cultural context of life.

SCHWEITZER, Friederich. Forgetting about Auschwitz? Remembrance as a Difficult Task of Moral Education. J Moral Educ, 18(3), 163-173, O 89.

While Neo-Nazism is, in fact, only found in a small number of West German youths, and certain politicians would seem to prefer stepping 'out of the shadow of the Third Reich', it is argued that the question of how young Germans could or should relate to the Third Reich morally has in fact not been answered in any sufficient way. The author critically examines various approaches to the issue—from Adorno's classical statement on 'Education after Auschwitz' to the more recent attempts of using Auschwitz as a metaphor. Furthermore, it is suggested that the problem of 'Forgetting about Auschwitz' should also be understood in terms of the intergenerational processes involved. This in turn presupposes testing legal and moral concepts for their adequacy to the task of moral education. Finally, the issue of national identity is considered as the framework within which the educational problems have to be addressed.

SCHWEIZER-BJELIC, Shelley and BJELIC, Dusan I. 'God-Talk' and 'Tacit' Theo-Logic. Mod Theol, 6(4), 341-366, Jl 90.

SCILIRONI, Carlo. Per una storia dell'estetica nel Settecento: Le idee divulgate dal periodico "Il Caffè". Sapienza, 42(2), 195-201, Ap-Je 89.

SCOCCIA, Danny. Paternalism and Respect for Autonomy. Ethics, 100(2), 318-334, Ja 90.

SCOCCIA, Danny. Utilitarianism, Sociobiology, and the Limits of Benevolence. J Phil, 87(7), 329-345, Jl 90.

SCOFIELD, Giles. The Calculus of Consent. Hastings Center Rep, 20(1), 44-47, Ja-F 90.

SCOTT, Charles E (ed) and DALLERY, Arleen B (ed). *The Question of the Other: Essays in Contemporary Continental Philosophy*. Albany, SUNY Pr, 1989

SCOTT, Charles E. Heidegger and the Question of Ethics. Res Phenomenol, 18, 23-40, 1988.

SCOTT, David. Manichaean Responses to Zoroastrianism. Relig Stud, 25(4), 435-457, D 89.

SCOTT, P J and CROSSLEY, J N. Completeness Proofs for Propositional Logic with Polynomial-Time Connectives. Annals Pure Applied Log, 44(1-2), 39-52, O 89.

We introduce a conservative extension of propositional calculus which allows conjunctions and disjunctions of variable length. Consistency, completeness and decidability for both classical and intuitionistic systems are given provided some simple conditions on the formation of propositional letters are satisfied. We describe an application to PROLOG programming in the context of databases.

SCOTT, William G. "The Concentric Circles of Management Thought" in *Papers on the Ethics of Administration*, WRIGHT, N Dale (ed), 21-46. Albany, SUNY Pr, 1988.

SCOWCROFT, Philip. A New Model for Intuitionistic Analysis. Annals Pure Applied Log, 47(2), 145-165, My 90.

This paper presents, in classical mathematics, a model for a system of intuitionistic analysis including monotone bar induction, relativized dependent choice, Kripke's schema, and Brouwer's principle for numbers. The model resembles the topological model of J Moschovakis (*Compositio Math 26* (1973) 261-275), but uses a non-spatial complete Heyting algebra of truth values to achieve, more simply, consistency results first obtained by Krol (*Z Math Logik Grundlag Math 25* (1978) 427-436).

SCRIBANO, Emanuela. La prova a priori dell'esistenza di Dio nel Settecento inglese: da Cudworth a Hume. G Crit Filosof Ital, 68(2), 184-212, My-Ag 89.

SCRUTON, Roger. "Analytic Philosophy and the Meaning of Music" in *Analytic Aesthetics*, SHUSTERMAN, Richard (ed), 85-96. Cambridge, Blackwell, 1989.

Analytical philosophy delivers results about meaning in natural language: Can these be extended to music? Yes and no.

SCRUTON, Roger. "Musical Understanding and Musical Culture" in *What is Music?*, ALPERSON, Philip A , 349-358. New York, Haven, 1987.

The meaning of music is what we grasp when we understand it. Understanding involves response; correct understanding lies in the response that is made available by a musical culture. Musical culture is essentially a 'bourgeois' phenomenon—yet another virtue of the bourgeoisie.

SCUKA, Robert F. Resurrection: Critical Reflections on a Doctrine in Search of a Meaning. Mod Theol, 6(1), 77-95, O 89.

SEABRIGHT, Paul. Social Choice and Social Theories. Phil Pub Affairs, 18(4), 365-387, Fall 89.

This article examines recent contributions to social choice theory, arguing that since they examine the consistency of beliefs about the nature of the social good, they illuminate a number of issues of central concern to philosophers. It looks at attempts to relax the assumptions that lead to Arrow's impossibility result, at the literature generated by Sen's libertarian paradox, and at the integration of social choice with the theory of games.

SEARLE, John R. Consciousness, Unconsciousness, and Intentionality. Phil Topics, 17(1), 193-209, Spr 89.

SEARLE, John R. How Performatives Work. Ling Phil, 12(5), 535-558, O 89.

SECADA, J E K. Descartes on Time and Causality. Phil Rev, 99(1), 45-72, Ja 90.

This article claims that "Descartes had no views as to the continuity or discontinuity of time." It argues against both those that hold that Cartesian time is atomic and those that state it is continuous. The article examines the Aristotelian notion of continuity of Late Scholastic authors (Suárez, Toledo) and maintains that it is fundamentally not in conflict with Dedekin's mathematical account. Further, the article contends that Descartes's commentators have mistaken striking claims about causality for assertions about the structure of time. These causal views are discussed and compared with some found in the Scholastic tradition (Aquinas, Suárez).

SEDGWICK, Sally S. Can Kant's Ethics Survive the Feminist Critique? Pac Phil Quart, 71(1), 60-79, Mr 90.

Recent accounts of Kant's ethics have drawn attention to the fact that, on his view, emotion may play an important motivating role in the life of the moral agent, and empirical content may play an important role in guiding the application of the supreme moral law. The author argues that while such accounts successfully discredit some standard objections to Kant, they fail to put to rest that aspect of the feminist critique which urges that we think of emotion as a *constitutive* feature of moral agency.

SEDLEY, David. "Philosophical Allegiance in the Greco-Roman World" in *Philosophia Togata: Essays on Philosophy and Roman Society*, GRIFFIN, Miriam (ed), 97-119. New York, Clarendon/Oxford Pr, 1989.

From the fourth century BC to the end of antiquity, it is argued, philosophers observed a virtually religious commitment to the word of their school's founder. This reverence for biblical texts did not stifle originality, but it did largely determine the manner in which debates were conducted and new ideas presented. The rules of allegiance are amplified, and illustrated with the earliest surviving example—the Epicurean debate about rhetoric, recorded by Philodemus.

SEEBER, Federico Mihura. La certeza de la evolución (Reflexiones crítico-filosóficas). Sapientia, 44(173), 171-184, Jl-S 89.

SEEBOHM, Thomas M (ed) and GURWITSCH, Aron. Kants Theorie des Verstandes. Norwell, Kluwer, 1990

The volume presents: (1) "Kant's Transcendental Deduction in Leibnizian Perspective"—draft of a German book; (2) "The Concept of Consciousness in Kant and Husserl"—German essay published first Kant-Studien 1964; (3) "A Study of Kant's Conception of the Human Mind"—unpublished English outline of a research project; (4) "The Leibniz in Kant"—lecture, edited by L Embree. The unpublished material is taken from the Archives of the Center for Advanced Research in Phenomenology. Preface and an appendix deal with the general development of Gurwitsch's thoughts on Kant and his philosophy.

SEELIG, Wolfgang. "Schopenhauer und die Wirklichkeit" in *Schopenhauer: New Essays in Honor of His 200th Birthday*, VON DER LUFT, Eric (ed), 293-299. Lewiston, Mellen Pr, 1989.

SEESKIN, Kenneth. Jewish Philosophy in a Secular Age. Albany, SUNY Pr, 1990

SEGERBERG, Krister. Bringing It About. J Phil Log, 18(4), 327-347, N 89.

SEGERBERG, Krister. Notes on Conditional Logic. Stud Log, 48(2), 157-168, Je 89.

This paper consists of some lecture notes in which conditional logic is treated as an extension of modal logic. Completeness and filtration theorems are provided for some basis systems.

SEGERBERG, Krister. On the Question of Semantics in the Logic of Action: Some Remarks on Pörn's Logic of Action. Acta Phil Fennica, 38, 282-298, 1985.

Ingmar Pörn was one of the first to give a semantics for a logic of action. This paper is an effort to clarify some of the issues involved in Pörn's work.

SEGERBERG, Krister. Talking About Actions. Stud Log, 47(4), 347-352, D 88.

SEGERSTRALE, Ullica. The Murky Borderland Between Scientific Intuition and Fraud. Int J Applied Phil, 5(1), 11-20, Spr 90.

Scientists sometimes refer to 'intuition' as their guideline in distinguishing good science from bad. However, historically, intuition has led scientists both right and wrong, and occasionally to self-deception and fraud. Furthermore, interviews suggest that scientists may be more concerned that a result is *correct* than with *how* it was obtained. Science education also indirectly emphasizes the importance of being right rather than earnest. Pedagogically, there is a need for the explication of the meaning of 'good science', teaching of the history, sociology and psychology of science, and emphasis on process rather than product.

SEGERT, Astrid. Ökonomische Soziologie in Nowosibirst (Literaturbericht). Deut Z Phil, 37(10-11), 1029-1035, 1989.

SEGURA, Carmen. Verdad, juicio y reflexión según Tomás de Aquino. Anu Filosof, 21(1), 159-169, 1988.

SEGURA, Eugenio. Materialismo Presocrático. Rev Filosof (Costa Rica), 26, 103-108, D 88.

The Milesian philosophers explained change as transformation of the material principle. This was opposed by the Pythagoreans who, in their turn, were criticized. All this process led to the understanding of change in terms of strife between opposites and of thought as infinite indivisible identity. It also led to the explanation of movement as aggregation and disaggregation of identical or opposite elements which are infinite and indivisible.

SEIBOLD, J R. Intencionalidad, responsabilidad y solidaridad: Los nuevos ámbitos del compromiso ético. Stromata, 45(3-4), 309-313, Jl-D 89.

SEIDELMAN, William E. In Memoriam: Medicine's Confrontation with Evil. Hastings Center Rep, 19(6), 5-6, N-D 89.

SEIDMAN, Steven (ed) and HABERMAS, Jürgen. *Jürgen Habermas on Society and Politics: A Reader*. Boston, Beacon Pr, 1989

For more than three decades Habermas has attempted to supply foundations for a reconstructed critical social theory that provides a critical analysis of modernity. This anthology brings together in one volume his most important writings on society, the state and social theory.

SEIFFERT, Helmut. *Handlexikon zur Wissenschaftstheorie*. Munich, Ehrenwirth, 1989

SEIGEL, Jerrold. Avoiding the Subject: A Foucaultian Itinerary. J Hist Ideas, 51(2), 273-299, Ap-Je 90.

SEIGFRIED, Charlene Haddock. Poetic Invention and Scientific Observation: James's Model of "Sympathetic Concrete Observation". Trans Peirce Soc, 26(1), 115-130, Wint 90.

Scientific thinking differs from poetic thinking in that it abstracts partial aspects of phenomena, rather than comparing them globally. But both art and science require inventiveness and careful observation. I show how James transforms the positivist understanding of scientific observation by combining its notion of fidelity to objects in the natural world with observation as romantic vision. This model of sympathetic concrete observation brings together 'seeing' and 'seeing into', i.e., the scientific ideal of exactness and the poetic ideal of transfiguration, thereby disclosing the irreducible ambiguity at the heart of observation, whether scientific or poetic.

SEIGFRIED, Charlene Haddock. Weaving Chaos into Order: A Radically Pragmatic Aesthetic. Phil Lit, 14(1), 108-116, Ap 90.

Pragmatism's deconstructive side has been well captured by Richard Rorty, but not its corresponding reconstructive aspect. Just as the pragmatists take as their starting point the transactive constitution of self and world rather than language or free-floating interpretation, so they also do not end up in postmodernism or postrationalism, but in what can be called 'pragmatic rationalism'. Such rationalism organizes experience both aesthetically and practically. Experience, rather than language, is the central interpretive principle privileged by pragmatists.

SEIGFRIED, Hans. Nietzsche's Radical Experimentalism. Man World, 22(4), 485-501, D 89.

The literary complexity of Nietzsche's writings is by now largely familiar; it needs no further display. Instead, I try to reconstruct some of his ideas such that they amount to a sustained philosophical argument and promising project, namely, an attempt to understand—after the Kantian and Darwinian turns—the very possibility of the formation and continuation of infinite varieties of forms of life. I demonstrate that such a project could make good

sense only as a transcendental experiment in which the idea of a reality which is ready-made, immutable, and fixed "in itself" must not only be dismissed as something incomprehensible, but as something not in the least worth striving for, and replaced by the idea of synergetic processes (of self-organization) and what Nietzsche called art without an artist. Read as an empirical-historical narrative we would have to reject Nietzsche's account as a mere rhapsody and arrogant fantasy.

SEIGFRIED, Hans. Opposing Science with Art, Again? Nietzsche's Project According to Stack. Int Stud Phil, 21(2), 105-111, 1989.

Stack claims that Nietzsche uncritically accepted Lange's view that because of its nihilistic consequences we must balance and oppose scientific knowledge with art by superimposing on it some philosophico-religious ideal through creating a new counter-myth. I argue that Nietzsche radically rejected the idea that we must yearn for mythical access to some metaphysical meaning. Instead, he tried to demonstrate how we could succeed with what we do on purely aesthetic grounds, i.e., on the assumption that the sciences themselves are the forms of art through which we create the meaning we need in experimental transaction with nature.

SEKARAN, Uma. Frontiers and New Vistas in Women in Management Research. J Bus Ethics, 9(4-5), 247-255, Ap-My 90.

This paper addresses the theoretical and methodological issues in women in management research, as the field emerges out of its adulthood and steps into the age of maturity. The four fundamental issues addressed are (i) the need to conduct extensive research in this area; (ii) the need for synthesizing previous research findings and establishing a solid theory base on which further work can progress; (iii) the appropriate methodologies for generating further knowledge in the area; and (iv) future directions for research on women in management, taking both a "basic" and "applied" research perspective.

SEKIGUCHI, Hiroshi. Kunst und Geschichte bei Heidegger (in Japanese). Bigaku, 40(2), 50-61, Autumn 89.

Ein zur Geschichte bestimmtes Volk schafft, nach Heidegger, das "grosse" Kunstwerk dadurch, dass es sich sein Gewesenes aneignet, indem es sein Zukünftiges erkämpft. Durch das solcherweise geschaffene Werk kommt "das Seiende im Ganzen", d.h. Welt und Erde, "zu seinem Vor-schein". Dieses Geschehen ist gerade das, was Heidegger "die Geschichte selbst" nennt. Gleichzeitig mit diesem Zum-Vor-schein-kommen des Seienden im Ganzen stehen die Zeit und Geschichte anfänglich auf. Man meint gewöhnlich, dass eine Geschichte zuerst vorliege, und die Kunst nachträglich erst innerhalb des Ablaufs dieser Geschichte vorkomme. In Wahrheit verhält sich die Sache aber gerade umgekehrt. Indem das Kunstwerk in dem Dasein eines Volkes geschaffen wird, kann die Geschichte diese Volkes überhaupt erst anfangen. (edited)

SELBY, G Raymond. The Medical Dilemma. Ethics Med, 6(2), 30-31, Sum 90.

SELDIN, Jonathan P. Normalization and Excluded Middle, I. Stud Log, 48(2), 193-217, Je 89.

SELF, Donnie J and SKEEL, Joy D. An Analysis of Ethics Consultation in the Clinical Setting. Theor Med, 10(4), 289-299, D 89.

Only recently have ethicists been invited into the clinical setting to offer recommendations about patient care decisions. This paper discusses this new role for ethicists from the perspective of content and process issues. Among content issues are the usual ethical dilemmas such as the aggressiveness of treatment, questions about consent, and alternative treatment options. Among process issues are those that relate to communication with the patient. The formal ethics consult is discussed, the steps taken in such a consult, and whether there should be a fee charged. We conclude with an examination of the risks and benefits of formal ethics consults.

SELKIRK, John. The Incommensurability of Moral Argument. Eidos, 7(2), 175-182, D 88.

SELMAN, Mark and ROSS, Murray. McClellan on Quine and Social Criticism. Proc Phil Educ, 45, 45-54, 1989.

In the Spring 1987 issue of *Educational Theory* James McClellan proposed a revived version of progressive education based on Quine's views of science. The authors take issue with the notion that Quine provides a necessary, or desirable, basis for a revived progressivism for two major reasons. The first of these involves the rather obscure position Quine takes with regard to normative statements, statements which, we argue, have an irreducible role in educational and political discourse. The second reason is that Quinian elimination of intentional terms is inconsistent with what Walzer argues have been the most common and effective forms of social criticism.

SEN, Amartya. Justice: Means versus Freedoms. Phil Pub Affairs, 19(2),

111-121, Spr 90.

SENDEROWICZ, Yaron and DASCAL, Marcelo. Language and Thought in Kant's Theory of Knowledge (in Hebrew). Iyyun, 39(2), 151-175, Ap 90.

Why is there no theory of language in Kant's writings? We purport to show that a theory of language is a necessity for Kant's theory of knowledge. This is apparent, among other things, if one reflects on how 'empirical concepts' are possible on the basis of Kant's theory of judgment. The conclusion is that, while badly needed for Kant, a theory of language cannot be trivially supplied on the basis of his epistemology, for the very same arguments that show its need also show its impossibility within the Kantian framework.

SENOR, Thomas D. Incarnation and Timelessness. Faith Phil, 7(2), 149-164, Ap 90.

In this paper I present and defend two arguments which purport to show that the doctrines of timelessness and the Incarnation are incompatible. An argument similar to the first argument I consider is briefly discussed by Stump and Kretzmann in their paper "Eternity." I argue that their treatment of this type of objection is inadequate. The second argument I present is, as far as I know, original; it depends on a certain subtlety in the doctrine of the Incarnation, *viz.*, that the Son *took on* or *assumed* a human nature. It seems that there is no way to understand what it is for the Son to take on a human nature that doesn't entail his mutability; and mutability entails temporality. Thus, since Christ is said to take on a human nature, an orthodox Christology must maintain that the Son is temporal. I conclude by considering whether the Son's temporality entails the temporality of the Godhead.

SERAFINE, Mary Louise. What Music Is. J Aes Educ, 23(3), 31-37, Fall 89.

SERAFINI, Anthony. Callahan on Harming the Dead. J Phil Res, 15, 329-339, 1990.

In this paper I try to defend the notion that the dead can be harmed, in opposition to Callahan and in accord with some ideas of Feinberg. In agreement with Parfit, I argue that the existence of a person has degrees. I suggest that *properties* of a subject, such as "reputations" and claims, can persist after death, although the subject as such does not and that these can be harmed. A promise, e.g., can be frustrated merely by being ignored; in that sense a dead person can be wronged, and if wronged, s/he can be harmed.

SERAFINI, Anthony. *Ethics and Social Concern*. New York, Paragon House, 1989

The purpose of *Ethics and Social Concern* is to provide a collection of readings in medical ethics, business ethics and ethics in mass communications. Some of the distinguished contributors include David Thomasma, Daniel Callahan, H Tristram Engelhardt, Kenneth Goodpaster, Richard De George, Dan Brock, Anita Silvers, Sissela Bok, Tom Beauchamp, Ahura-Mazda, and others. The book is unique in that it features an extensive section on mass communications ethics as well as several readings on the *teaching* of ethics. The book is intended for courses in business, medical or journalistic ethics as well as for general introductory courses in applied ethics.

SERGOT, Marek and KOWALSKI, Robert. The Use of Logical Models in Legal Problem Solving. Ratio Juris, 3(2), 201-218, Jl 90.

The authors describe a logic programming approach to the representation of legislative texts. They consider the potential uses of simple systems which incorporate a single, fixed interpretation of a text. These include assisting in the routine administration of complex areas of the law. The authors also consider the possibility of constructing more complex systems which incorporate several, possibly conflicting interpretations. Such systems are needed for dealing with ambiguity and vagueness in the law. Moreover, they are more suitable than single interpretation systems for helping to test proposed legislation and for helping to give citizens advice.

SETTANNI, Harry. *Holism—A Philosophy for Today: Anticipating the Twenty First Century*. New York, Lang, 1990

The purpose of this work is to analyze the philosophic *foundations* of holism as these foundations exist in four fields: natural science, social science, religion and art (chapters 3, 4, 5, and 6) and then to analyze these foundations in evolution and literary romanticism (chapters 7, 8, 9, and 10). The foundations of holism, as defined on page 8, list three important features: (1) the interconnectedness of reality; (2) the interdependence of reality; (3) description of reality as linked by *Internal Relations*. The conclusion (Epilogue, page 155) is that man is vitally connected with others in the field of human relationships. For the twenty-first century, we must stop thinking of him as an isolated individual.

SETTE, Antonio M A and PEDROSA, Renato H L. A Representation Theorem for Languages with Generalized Quantifiers Through Back-and-Forth Methods. Stud Log, 47(4), 401-411, D 88.

We obtain in this paper a representation of the formulae of extensions of $L_{\omega\omega}$ by generalized quantifiers through functors between categories of first-order structures and partial isomorphisms. The main tool in the proofs is the back-and-forth technique. As a corollary we obtain the Caicedo's version of Fraïssé's theorem characterizing elementary equivalence for such languages. We also discuss informally some geometrical interpretations of our results.

SETTON, Mark. Tasan's "Practical Learning". Phil East West, 39(4), 377-392, O 89.

It was the feeling that Neo-Confucian orthodoxy had compromised the pristine Confucian spirit of practicality that galvanised its most outspoken critics during the late Choson dynasty. This article explores the work of the reform-minded Confucian philosopher Chong Yagyong (pen-name Tasan, 1762-1836) who gave critiques of orthodox Neo-Confucianism their most systematic expression by using the evidential methods of Ch'ing scholarship to undermine the conceptual framework of Chu Hsi's cosmology and ethics.

SEUREN, Pieter A M. Neue Entwicklungen im Wahrheitsbegriff. Stud Leibniz, 21(2), 155-173, 1989.

SEUREN, Pieter A M. Les paradoxes et le langage. Log Anal, 30(120), 365-383, D 87.

SEVERINO, Emanuele. *Il Giogo: Alle origini della ragione: Eschilo*. Milan, Adelphi, 1989

SEYMOUR, Michel. Référence et identité. Log Anal, 30(120), 353-363, D 87.

SHAGRIR, Oron. The Classical vs the PDP Model in Describing the Tic-Tac-Toe Game (in Hebrew). Iyyun, 38(3-4), 265-286, Jl-O 89.

The paper sets out to assess the two principal paradigms dominating today the field of cognitive science: the classical approach, which is based on the "computer metaphor," and the connectionist view founded on the "brain metaphor." The method suggested is a comparison of classical and PDP models describing identical cognitive phenomena. This method is presented here by a case study: playing the game of Tic-Tac-Toe. The comparison shows that the success of each model is focused on different aspects of the Tic-Tac-Toe game. The classical model can create and evaluate many future play-boards, but it cannot determine and evaluate in advance which are the better moves worth examining. The PDP model first converges to the better moves, but lacks the ability to check their potential later on. These findings give rise to wider questions, mainly, how do the advantages and limitations of a model reflect its paradigm's conception of cognitive phenomena.

SHAIDA, S A. Moral Scepticism. Indian Phil Quart, 16(3), 269-281, Jl 89.

The paper seeks to explain and briefly criticize some apparently cogent and popular grounds of moral scepticism which are (a) moral relativism in two forms which I characterize as the *general* theory and the *specific* theory of moral relativity; (b) subjectivism of different variety; (c) lack of a rational decision-making procedure in ethics; and (d) unanswerableness of the questions concerning ultimate values/obligations. It is emphasized that none of these convincingly support moral scepticism. It is concluded that its theoretical assumptions are weak and its practical consequences are morally damaging.

SHAKUN, Melvin F. Group Decision and Negotiation Support in Evolving, Nonshared Information Contexts. Theor Decis, 28(3), 275-288, My 90.

Based on evolutionary systems design (ESD), group decision and negotiation support in evolving, nonshared information contexts is discussed. A nonshared information context—one without full information sharing—is associated with what has been loosely called a 'noncooperative' context in the group decision and negotiation support systems (GDNSS) literature. Without full information sharing, we have a game with incomplete information that, in general, is evolving. The paper discusses how the GDNSS, MEDIATOR, supports evolution of the group problem representation—a process of consensus seeking (through information sharing, here partial) subject to problem adaptation and restructuring within which compromise is possible.

SHANAHAN, Timothy. Evolution, Phenotypic Selection, and the Units of Selection. Phil Sci, 57(2), 210-225, Je 90.

In recent years philosophers have attempted to clarify the units of selection controversy in evolutionary biology by offering conceptual analyses of the term 'unit of selection'. A common feature of many of these analyses is an emphasis on the claim that units of selection are entities exhibiting heritable variation in fitness. In this paper I argue that the demand that units of selection be characterized in terms of heritability is unnecessary, as well as undesirable, on historical, theoretical, and philosophical grounds. I propose a positive account of the proper referent of the term 'unit of selection', distinguishing between the processes of evolution and phenotypic selection. The main result of this analysis is greater clarity about the conceptual structure of evolutionary theory.

SHANAHAN, Timothy. Kant, *Naturphilosophie*, and Oersted's Discovery of Electromagnetism: A Reassessment. Stud Hist Phil Sci, 20(3), 287-305, S 89.

SHANER, David Edward. "The Japanese Experience of Nature" in *Nature in Asian Tradition of Thought: Essays in Environmental Philosophy*, CALLICOTT, J Baird (ed), 163-182. Albany, SUNY Pr, 1989.

SHANKER, George. The Constitutional Process and the Higher Law. Vera Lex, 7(2), 7-8,10, 1987.

Laws regarded as immoral by citizens in a democratic society, giving rise on their part to a desire to violate these laws, remain an enduring problem. May their actions be justified on grounds of conscience? A formulation of this problem is expressed through the particulars of an event in American history—the passage of the Fugitive Slave Law and affirmation of its constitutionality by the Supreme Court of the United States. The views of Ralph Waldo Emerson and Daniel Webster are examined.

SHANNON, Thomas A. *Surrogate Motherhood: The Ethics of Using Human Beings*. New York, Crossroads/Continuum, 1989

This book examines surrogate motherhood in the context of other uses of human bodies: wet-nursing, blood donation, human research and organ procurement. The book then examines the family, coercion and alienation to set an ethical background. Specific issues are then examined: the definition of motherhood, purposes of medicine, body as property, risks, the right to have children, compensation for the surrogate, the commodification of the child and surrogacy's impact on other family members. A review of national and international regulations is presented. The book concludes with an argument against surrogacy.

SHANON, Benny. Consciousness. J Mind Behav, 11(2), 137-151, Spr 90.

SHANON, Benny. What is Context? J Theor Soc Behav, 20(2), 157-166, Je 90.

The definition of the notion "context" is examined. It is pointed out that this notion can be defined neither in linguistic terms nor in terms of states of affairs in the external world, nor in ones pertaining to mental representations. The only viable option is to define context in terms of the interaction between the mind and the world. This appraisal has important ramifications for the nature of cognitive theory. The basic terms of such a theory should also be coined in a conceptual language which, in its very essence, brings together the internal and the external domains.

SHAOJUN, Weng. A Comparative Study of Natural Philosophy in Pre-Qin China and Ancient Greece. Chin Stud Phil, 21(2), 3-31, Wint 89-90.

This essay reflects on the differences between Chinese and Western philosophy from the perspective of their respective views of nature, and explores the inner factors of these differences. By comparing the religious atmosphere present during the formative periods of the different natural philosophies (in ancient China and in ancient Greece), this essay will attempt to reveal the reasons behind the different characteristics displayed by ancient China and ancient Greece in the transition from a religious consciousness to a natural philosophy. (edited)

SHAPARD, Leslie R. Group Rights. Pub Affairs Quart, 4(3), 299-308, Jl 90.

SHAPIRO, Gary (ed). *After the Future: Postmodern Times and Places*. Albany, SUNY Pr, 1989

This collection of nineteen original essays constitutes a many-sided exploration of postmodern thought and culture, including philosophy, architecture, painting, literature and literary theory.

SHAPIRO, Gary. "Derrida and the Question of Philosophy's History" in *History and Anti-History in Philosophy*, LAVINE, T Z (ed), 156-187. Norwell, Kluwer, 1989.

SHAPIRO, Gary. *Nietzschean Narratives*. Bloomington, Indiana Univ Pr, 1989

SHAPIRO, Kenneth Joel. The Death of the Animal: Ontological Vulnerability. Between Species, 5(4), 183-194, Fall 89.

SHAPIRO, Stewart. Second-order Logic, Foundations, and Rules. J Phil, 87(5), 234-261, My 90.

The purpose of this paper is to discuss the role of formal semantics in describing and codifying practice. The case study is the issue of second-order logic, with its various semantics. It is argued that the debate is likely to result in either a regress or a stand-off, with each side begging the central question of whether there is a clear and unequivocal understanding

of such locutions as "all properties" or "all subsets" of a fixed domain. The issue of second-order logic is related to the Wittgensteinian critique of rule-following. It is suggested that the insistence on standard semantics, despite the possibility of Skolemite reinterpretation (or misinterpretation), is closely analogous to the insistence that one is following a particular rule, despite the fact that no finite amount of behavior can rule out alternatives.

SHARP, Ann Margaret and LIPMAN, Matthew. Philosophy for Children: A Traditional Subject in a Novel Format. Thinking, 7(4), Supp 2-5, 1988.

An examination of alternative curricula for the teaching of thinking, and a closer look at Philosophy for Children. The article concludes with a set of claims regarding those achievements which are peculiar to Philosophy for Children.

SHARP, Ann Margaret and MAYS, Wolfe. Thinking Skill Programs: An Analysis. Thinking, 7(4), 2-11, 1988.

This paper deals with the attempt to develop thinking skills programmes to improve intellectual performance. It aims to give an account and an analysis of the principles on which they are based. Starting with Binet's mental orthopaedics it then considers the CORT system of de Bono, Feuerstein's Mediated Learning and Lipman's Philosophy for children. It compares these programmes and examines some of the criticisms levelled against them. It concludes that there seems some evidence that an adequate system of cognitive education will in some measure improve pupils' powers of judgment and also their motivation.

SHARPE, Kevin J. Relating the Physics and Religion of David Bohm. Zygon, 25(1), 105-122, Mr 90.

David Bohm's thinking has become widely publicized since the 1982 performance of a form of the Einstein-Podolsky-Rosen (EPR) experiment. Bohm's *holomovement* theory, in particular, tries to explain the nonlocality that the experiment supports. Moreover, his theories are close to his metaphysical and religious thinking. Fritjof Capra's writings try something similar: supporting a theory (the bootstrap theory) because it is close to his religious beliefs. Both Bohm and Capra appear to use their religious ideas in their physics. Religion, their source for physical hypotheses, provides the motivation to develop and uphold them.

SHARPLES, R W. More on Plato, *Meno* 82 c 2-3. Phronesis, 34(2), 220-226, 1989.

SHARPLIN, Arthur and PHELPS, Lonnie D. A Stakeholder Apologetic for Management. Bus Prof Ethics J, 8(2), 41-53, Sum 89.

Whom does management serve? The classical theory of the firm assumes that management acts to maximize shareholder wealth. From an agency theory perspective management is viewed as servant (agent) of a variety of constituents (principals). The shareholder may not be preeminent. Each group—communities, creditors, customers, employees, and shareholders—claims throughputs of value commensurate with its power to engage management as agent in its transactions with other stakeholders.

SHAVER, Robert. Rousseau and Recognition. Soc Theor Pract, 15(3), 261-283, Fall 89.

Rousseau criticizes civil society by showing how it leads to the problem of life in others, whereby people come to care most about how others represent them. I give an account of the problem and its causes, stressing the role of private property and divided labour. I also explain why life in others is a problem. I close by suggesting the significance of Rousseau's account, placing it in the context of Marx and the French moralists.

SHAW, Beverley. Sexual Discrimination and the Equal Opportunities Commission: Ought Schools to Eradicate Sex Stereotyping? J Phil Educ, 23(2), 295-302, Wint 89.

The paper challenges the view of the UK Equal Opportunities Commission, as expressed in its publication, *Do you provide equal opportunities?*, that "Primary school teachers need to take positive action to eradicate sex stereotyping...." It is argued that such stereotyping is irradicable; that schools do not have a mandate to eradicate sexual stereotyping seen as a widely accepted ideal of sexual difference; and, anyway, that providing equal opportunities does not require the total elimination of differences based upon sex.

SHAW, Brian J. Totality, Realism, and the Type: Lukács' Later Literary Criticism as Political Theory. Phil Forum, 21(4), 412-441, Sum 90.

Lukács's post-1930 literary criticism reveals a problematic continuity with the theory of totality articulated in *History and Class Consciousness* (1923). No longer the self-knowledge of a militant proletariat, totality emerges as the contemplative vision of great bourgeois novelists. Shorn of its earlier messianic overtones, the later criticism promises a more labile political theory whose possibilities have already been explored by theorists such as liberation theologians and socialist feminists. This same change, however, coupled with Lukács's failure to confront its metatheoretical consequences, severs theory and practice and threatens to reduce revolutionary activity to a subjective and strident moralizing.

SHAW, D. "After Chernobyl: The Ethics of Risk-Taking" in *Ethics and the Environmental Responsibility*, DOWER, Nigel (ed), 110-131. Aldershot, Avebury, 1989.

SHAW, Daniel. "Freedom and Indeterminism" in *Cause, Mind, and Reality: Essays Honoring C B Martin*, HEIL, John (ed), 17-31. Norwell, Kluwer, 1989.

SHAW, Daniel. "Popper, Natural Selection and Epiphenomenalism" in *Issues in Evolutionary Epistemology*, HAHLWEG, Kai (ed), 570-584. Albany, SUNY Pr, 1989.

SHAW, Daniel. Rorty and Nietzsche: Some Elective Affinities. Int Stud Phil, 21(2), 3-14, 1989.

The thesis of the article is that Richard Rorty has failed to sufficiently acknowledge Friedrich Nietzsche in his account of the intellectual precursors of postmodernism. It points out a number of striking similarities between central Nietzschean themes and the picture of philosophy (with a small "p") that emerges from *Philosophy and the Mirror of Nature* and *Consequences of Pragmatism*, without attempting to prove any direct influence. It concludes by urging Rorty to enlist Nietzsche as a powerful ally in the fight against Cartesianism.

SHAW, J L. 'Saturated' and 'Unsaturated': Frege and the Nyāya. Synthese, 80(3), 373-394, S 89.

The aim of this paper is to discuss why a predicate-expression alone is to be considered as unsaturated, and why a subject-expression is considered as saturated. In this context I would like to examine Frege's thesis that the subject of a thought is saturated while the predicate is unsaturated, and Strawson's defence of the view that a subject-expression carries the burden of a fact, while a predicate-expression has no such presupposition. The Nyāya philosophers of the classical Indian philosophy have also discussed these questions, but their answers are different from those of Frege and Strawson.

SHAW, Marvin C. The Moral Stance of Theism Without the Transcent God: Wieman and Heidegger. Process Stud, 18(3), 173-180, Fall 89.

The thesis is that both the American pragmatist and naturalist H N Wieman and the existentialist Heidegger, while rejecting the metaphysics of traditional theism, retain its moral posture; that is, both recommend openness to a source of fulfillment beyond human effort and calculation, but this attitude is not undertaken in relation to the transcendent God. This is demonstrated through a study of two phases of Wieman's thought, and some later writings of Heidegger.

SHAW, Roy. Democracy and Excellence. J Aes Educ, 22(3), 5-12, Fall 88.

SHEAFFER, Robert. Socialism is Incompatible with Humanism. Free Inq, 9(4), 19-20, Fall 89.

SHEARMUR, Jeremy. The Right to Subsistence in a "Lockean" State of Nature. S J Phil, 27(4), 561-568, Wint 89.

SHEEHAN, Colleen A. Madison's Party Press Essays. Interpretation, 17(3), 355-377, Spr 90.

SHEFFER, Susannah. The Apprenticeship Model: What We Can Learn from Gareth Matthews. Thinking, 8(3), 27-28, 1989.

SHEFFER, Susannah. Philosophy Outside of Schools. Thinking, 7(3), 19-20, 1988.

SHELAH, S and HRUSHOVSKI, E. A Dichotomy Theorem for Regular Types. Annals Pure Applied Log, 45(2), 157-169, D 89.

SHELAH, S and BUECHLER, S. On the Existence of Regular Types. Annals Pure Applied Log, 45(3), 277-308, D 89.

SHELAH, S and BALDWIN, J T. The Primal Framework I. Annals Pure Applied Log, 46(3), 235-264, Ap 90.

This paper begins a series developing a setting for abstract classification theory. The aim is to provide a common framework for first order stability theory and generalizations to, e.g., infinitary logic.

SHELAH, Saharon and MAKKAI, M. Categoricity of Theories in $L_{\kappa\omega}$ with κ a Compact Cardinal. Annals Pure Applied Log, 47(1), 41-97, Ap 90.

SHELAH, Saharon and BLASS, Andreas. Near Coherence of Filters III: A Simplified Consistency Proof. Notre Dame J Form Log, 30(4), 530-538, Fall 89.

In the model obtained from a model of the continuum hypothesis by iterating rational perfect set forcing $\aleph_2$ times with countable supports, every two nonprincipal ultrafilters on ω have a common image under a finite-to-one function.

SHELAH, Saharon and STEINHORN, Charles. The Nonaxiomatizability of $L(Q^2_{\aleph_1})$. By Finitely Many Schemata. Notre Dame J Form Log, 31(1), 1-13, Wint 90.

Under set-theoretic hypotheses, it is proved by Magidor and Malitz that logic with the Magidor-Malitz quantifier in the $\aleph_1$-interpretation is recursively axiomatizable. It is shown here, under no additional set-theoretic hypotheses, that this logic cannot be axiomatized by finitely many schemata.

SHELAH, Saharon. The Number of Pairwise Non-Elementarily-Embeddable Models. J Sym Log, 54(4), 1431-1455, D 89.

SHELAH, Saharon. Strong Negative Partition Above the Continuum. J Sym Log, 55(1), 21-31, Mr 90.

SHELEFF, Leon. "Comment: Autonomy, Toleration, and the Harm Principle" in *Issues in Contemporary Legal Philosophy: The Influence of H L A Hart*, GAVISON, Ruth (ed), 342-350. New York, Clarendon/Oxford Pr, 1987.

SHEN, Yeshayahu. Metaphors and the Symmetry/Asymmetry (in Hebrew). Iyyun, 38(3-4), 287-302, Jl-O 89.

A prominent theory within the study of metaphors (Ortony 1979) is introduced in the first section. Ortony maintains that the distinction between metaphorical and nonmetaphorical comparisons (both of the form "A is like B") is correlated with the symmetric/asymmetric distinction. According to this proposal metaphorical comparisons exhibit greater asymmetry than nonmetaphorical ones. The second section introduces a counter-argument to the above proposal, according to which there is no difference between metaphorical and nonmetaphorical comparisons with respect to the issue of salience imbalance. While rejecting the first premise the present paper holds that the second one is valid. In the third section I argue that this assumption can serve as the basis of a theory of symmetric and asymmetric (metaphorical and nonmetaphorical) comparisons. In the fourth section a cognitive account for the relative ease of processing the accepted order is proposed. This account centers of Rosch's idea of "Cognitive reference point" which, extended to the domain of comparison, can account for the ease of processing the "accepted order." (edited)

SHEPPARD, Alice. Suffrage Art and Feminism. Hypatia, 5(2), 122-136, Sum 90.

SHER, Gila. A Conception of Tarskian Logic. Pac Phil Quart, 70(4), 341-368, D 89.

Is the conception of logic that motivated the construction of modern semantics fully realized by the standard system of 1st-order logic? My answer is: No. Analysis of the conditions Tarski set on an adequate system of logic in view of its tasks reveals that the notion of logical term implicit in his account is much wider than commonly thought. In fact, it takes the full scope of generalized logics—logics in which higher-order mathematical terms in general play the role of logical terms—to carry out Tarski's project. The paper further investigates the consequences of this view of logic for the relation between mathematics and logic, logicism, and ontological commitment.

SHER, Gila. Ways of Branching Quantifiers. Ling Phil, 13(4), 393-422, Ag 90.

Tracing the historical development of the logico-linguistic theory of branching quantification since its inception in Henkin's work, the paper reopens the question of what the branching form is. Inspired by Barwise's work on branching generalized quantifiers in English, but unsatisfied with certain aspects of his account, I propose a new logico-philosophical analysis. This analysis reveals a whole family of branching structures, under which fall not only Henkin's and Barwise's quantifiers, but also other, both simpler and more complex, structures. Among the simple, first-order forms, are cumulative quantifications ("Four boys ate three apples"); "Most of my friends saw at least two of the same few Truffaut movies" illustrates one type of complex branching form.

SHERMAN, Rosalyn S. Is it Possible to Teach Socratically? Thinking, 6(4), 28-36, 1986.

SHEROVER, Charles M. *Time, Freedom, and the Common Good: An Essay in Public Philosophy*. Albany, SUNY Pr, 1989

This essay aims at systematic reconstruction of democratic theory by securing its foundation in the nature of human experience—always inherently involved in a politically organized social world whose temporal structure provides the ground of human freedom. As a consequence, it develops a theory of citizenship and of 'rights' that discloses a necessary continuity between governance and economic order. Disavowing liberalism's elitist atomism, the essay substitutes 'equalization' for egalitarianism, retrieves the tradition of classic republicanism, defends democratic capitalism, commends a progressive conservative outlook, and concludes by urging a pragmatic, rather than a utilitarian, method for evaluating social programs and proposals.

SHERRY, Patrick. "Modes of Representation and Likeness to God" in *Christ, Ethics and Tragedy: Essays in Honour of Donald MacKinnon*, SURIN, Kenneth (ed), 34-48. New York, Cambridge Univ Pr, 1989.

Donald MacKinnon often stresses how philosophers and theologians attempt to represent what transcends them whilst yet insisting on its transcendence. Following Nelson Goodman's *Languages of Art* I distinguish between representations and resemblances, and apply this distinction to MacKinnon's work: in particular, I contrast descriptions of God with likenesses of Him. I conclude by showing the relevance of the topic to the debate about theological realism.

SHERWIN, Susan. Feminist and Medical Ethics: Two Different Approaches to Contextual Ethics. Hypatia, 4(2), 57-72, Sum 89.

Feminist ethics and medical ethics are critical of contemporary moral theory in several similar respects. There is a shared sense of frustration with the level of abstraction and generality that characterizes traditional philosophic work in ethics and a common commitment to including contextual details and allowing room for the personal aspects of relationships in ethical analysis. This paper explores the ways in which context is appealed to in feminist and medical ethics, the sort of details that should be included in the recommended narrative approaches to ethical problems, and the difference it makes to our ethical deliberations if we add an explicitly feminist political analysis to our discussion of context. It is claimed that an analysis of gender is needed for feminist medical ethics and that this requires a certain degree of generality, i.e., a political understanding of context.

SHEVCHENKO, V N. On the Contemporary Theory of Socialism (The October Revolution and Perestroika). Dialec Hum, 15(3-4), 169-176, Sum-Autumn 88.

SHI-YING, Zhang. "The Development of the Principle of Subjectivity in Western Philosophy and of the Theory of Man in Chinese Philosophy" in *Man and Nature: The Chinese Tradition and the Future*, TANG, Yi-Jie (ed), 149-167. Lanham, Univ Pr of America, 1989.

The history of Chinese philosophy as compared with Western philosophy lacked a relatively systematic philosophy based on the principle of subjectivity. The impediment to the development of the principle of subjectivity came not from the theocracy of the next world as in the West, but rather from the monarchical power in this world, from the feudal ethical code and the hierarchical system. It is very important for the advancement of thinking and culture to overcome the elements which bar the growth and development of the subjectivity of the Chinese people. We should now make a greater effort to learn from the idea of placing emphasis on plurality and individuality as expressed in Western philosophy.

SHIBATA, Shingo. Considerations on Preparation of Societies for Life in Peace. Dialec Hum, 16(2), 79-86, Spr 89.

The significance of the UN documents "New Philosophy on Disarmament" (33/71/N, 1978) and "Declaration on the Preparation of Societies for Life in Peace" (33/73, 1978) is considered. These topics should be interpreted under the threat of nuclear and non-nuclear genocide in the nuclear age. In this context, the philosophical implications of "a new way of thinking," necessity of a new semantics, the expanded genres of "Hibakusha" (Atomic Bombed, Atomic Radiated and Atomic Threatened), the nuclear fuel cycle, the human rights declarations, and the role of anti-nuclear and anti-genocide culture and arts are discussed. Finally, a comprehensive and coordinated systematization of propositions is proposed.

SHIELL, Timothy C. Hartshorne on Humanism: A Comment. Relig Hum, 24(3), 107-112, Sum 90.

Russell offers an interesting glimpse of Hartshorne's objections to humanism that may profitably provoke humanists to reexamine their conception of and commitment to nonhuman parts of nature. The objections, however, ought not provoke humanists to abandon their view, for those objections—at least in their present form—appear shallow, question-begging, wrong-headed, or otherwise inadequate. Indeed, I might suggest that his complaints are more like attitudes than arguments capable of rational evaluation.

SHIMODA, M and KURATA, Reijiro. Some Combinatorial Principles Equivalent to Restrictions of Transfinite Induction Up to Γ_0. Annals Pure Applied Log, 44(1-2), 63-69, O 89.

SHIMONY, Abner. The Non-Existence of a Principle of Natural Selection. Biol Phil, 4(3), 255-273, Jl 89.

Each formulation of a proposed principle of natural selection is analyzable into a proposition about sources of fitness and one about consequences of fitness. The sources of fitness are local contingencies, and the consequences are essentially applications of probability theory. Hence there is no role and no need for a principle of natural selection, and any generalities holding in

the theory are derivative rather than fundamental.

SHIMONY, Abner. Reply to Sober's "Is the Theory of Natural Selection Unprincipled? Reply to Shimony". Biol Phil, 4(3), 281-286, Jl 89.

Sober is answered by making a clear distinction between a principle of a theory and a derivative proposition.

SHIMONY, Abner. "Search for a Worldview Which Can Accommodate Our Knowledge of Microphysics" in *Philosophical Consequences of Quantum Theory: Reflections on Bell's Theorem*, CUSHING, James T (ed), 25-37. Notre Dame, Univ Notre Dame Pr, 1989.

If scientific theories are interpreted realistically, and if the loopholes in the experimental disconfirmations of local hidden variables theories are regarded as insignificant, then metaphysical implications of quantum mechanics are unavoidable: objective indefiniteness, objective chance, objective probability, entanglement of many-particle states, and nonlocality. Because of open problems and anomalies, centering around the measurement problem, further modifications of our microphysics are probably required, and these will have further metaphysical implications.

SHINER, Roger A. The Divestiture Puzzle Dissolved. Analysis, 50(3), 205-210, Je 90.

The 'Divestiture Puzzle' as presented by Steven M Cahn purports to show divestiture can never be required by moral principle. To divest is to cause someone else to do wrong by holding shares. I criticize the putative causal connection. Seller's action does not conform to paradigms either of moral corruption or of coercing the will. The seller who rejects the puzzle for these reasons does assume a nonconsequentialist view of moral good, but that cannot be held to disqualify the reasons. The divestiture puzzle is therefore dissolved.

SHIOJI, Naoki and TANAKA, Kazuyuki. Fixed Point Theory in Weak Second-Order Arithmetic. Annals Pure Applied Log, 47(2), 167-188, My 90.

The purpose of this paper is to develop part of functional analysis concerned with fixed point theorems within a weak subsystem of second-order arithmetic WKL_0. The paper contributes to a broader program, Reverse Mathematics, whose ultimate goal is to answer the question: What set existence axioms are needed to prove the theorems of ordinary mathematics? Within the system WKL_0, Brouwer's fixed point theorem is proved and extended to its infinite dimensional analogue, from which the Cauchy-Peano theorem is obtained. The Markov-Kakutani theorem is also proved and applied to the Hahn-Banach theorem for separable Banach spaces.

SHIRLEY, Edward S. Putnam's Brains in a Vat and Bouwsma's Flowers. SW Phil Rev, 4(1), 121-126, Ja 88.

SHIRLEY, Edward S. Why the Problem of the Existence of the External Worlds is a Pseudo-Problem: A Revision of Putnam and Danto. SW Phil Rev, 6(1), 133-140, Ja 90.

SHIU, Godwin Y and TEOH, Hai Yap. Attitudes Towards Corporate Social Responsibility and Perceived Importance of Social Responsibility Information. J Bus Ethics, 9(1), 71-77, Ja 90.

This study addressed the questions of perceived importance of social responsibility information (SRI) characteristics in a decision context, as well as the attitudes of institutional investors toward social responsibility involvement. The results showed that SRI presently disclosed in company annual reports did not have any significant impact on institutional investors' decisions. However, if SRI were presented in quantified, financial form, and were focused on product improvement and fair business practices, such information would be perceived as more important for investment decisions. Attitudes toward corporate social responsibility also suggested that institutional investors were not totally opposed to company involvement in social activities.

SHLAPENTOKH, Vladimir. The Justification of Political Conformism: The Mythology of Soviet Intellectuals. Stud Soviet Tho, 39(2), 111-135, Mr 90.

SHOPE, Robert K. A Causal Theory of Intending. J Phil Res, 15, 361-394, 1990.

Having an intention can be analyzed in terms of certain causal powers possessed by an instance of one's having a thought of a certain state of affairs, where a certain preference is what causes those powers to be present. A suitable understanding of such a preference emerges from a discussion of Wayne A Davis's analysis of intending. However, Davis's emphasis on belief and desire rather than on instances of having a thought leads to difficulties for his analysis of intending. After supplementing my own analysis with a sufficient condition of intentional action, I defend my approach by relating it to D F Gustafson's *Intention and Agency*.

SHOPE, Robert K. Justification, Reliability and Knowledge. Philosophia

(Israel), 19(2-3), 133-154, O 89.

In the course of exposing some difficulties for Alvin I Goldman's recent accounts of justification and knowledge, especially in his book *Epistemology and Cognition*, I emphasize the need to discuss the relations between justification and rationality. This provides reason to suppose that reliability plays a less fundamental role in epistemology than Goldman proposes.

SHORT, David S. Confidentiality and Patient-Access to Records. Ethics Med, 4(2), 26-27, 1988.

Until November 1987, patients in the U.K. had no right to see their medical records. Since that date, they have had that right (with a few exceptions) in respect of computer-stored records. There is now pressure for this right to be extended to manual records. Starting with the principle that the paramount consideration must be the welfare of the patients, the author argues that it is not in their best interest for all the doctors' notes to be available to them.

SHPET, G. Theater as Art. Soviet Stud Phil, 28(3), 61-88, Wint 89-90.

SHRADER-FRECHETTE, K S. Idealized Laws, Antirealism, and Applied Science: A Case in Hydrogeology. Synthese, 81(3), 329-352, D 89.

When is a law too idealized to be usefully applied to a specific situation? To answer this question, this essay considers a law in hydrogeology called Darcy's Law, both as it is used in what is called the symmetric-cone model, and as it is used in equations to determine a well's groundwater velocity and hydraulic conductivity. After discussing Darcy's law and its applications, the essay concludes that this idealized law, as well as associated models and equations in hydrogeology, are not realistic in the sense required by the D-N account. They exhibit what McMullin calls mathematical idealization, construct idealization, empirical-causal idealization, and subjunctive-causal idealization. Yet this lack of realism in hydrogeology is problematic for reasons unrelated to the status of the D-N account. These idealizations are also problematic in applied situations. Their problems require developing two supplemental criteria, necessary for their productive application.

SHRADER-FRECHETTE, Kristin. Land Use Planning and Analytic Methods of Policy Analysis: Commentary on "The Expert and the Public". Bus Prof Ethics J, 6(2), 41-46, Sum 87.

Many scholars argue that analytic methods of policy analysis are of little help in resolving planning controversies characterized by conflicting interests. On the contrary, this essay argues that much can be said in favor of economic methods like benefit-cost analysis. They are the least objectionable methods of policy analysis available.

SHRAGE, Laurie. Feminist Film Aesthetics: A Contextual Approach. Hypatia, 5(2), 137-148, Sum 90.

This paper considers some problems with text-centered psychoanalytic and semiotic approaches to film that have dominated feminist film criticism, and develops an alternative contextual approach. I claim that a contextual approach should explore the interaction of film texts with viewers' culturally formed sensibilities and should attempt to render visible the plurality of meaning in art. I argue that the latter approach will allow us to see the virtues of some classical Hollywood films that the former approach has overlooked, and I demonstrate this thesis with an analysis of the film *Christopher Strong*.

SHU-HSIEN, Liu. On the Functional Unity of the "Book of Changes" (in Serbo-Croatian). Filozof Istraz, 29(2), 533-545, 1989.

SHUE, Henry. "Having It Both Ways: The Gradual Wrong in American Strategy" in *Nuclear Deterrence and Moral Restraint*, SHUE, Henry (ed), 13-49. New York, Cambridge Univ Pr, 1989.

SHUE, Henry (ed). *Nuclear Deterrence and Moral Restraint*. New York, Cambridge Univ Pr, 1989

SHUN, Kwong-loi. Mencius: The Mind-Inherence of Morality (in Serbo-Croatian). Filozof Istraz, 29(2), 517-521, 1989.

This paper discusses Mencius's views of how we come to know the truth of normative moral claims. It argues that for Mencius the mind has certain features that predispose us to morality. We arrive at morality by reflecting on these features. Such a view can be called "the mind-inheritance of morality." It implies a two-staged process of self-cultivation. First we reflect on certain spontaneous reactions of the mind. Then we behave in the ways indicated and acquire the appropriate feelings, thereby becoming virtuous. In this sense human nature (*hsing*) for Mencius means the tendency of human beings to develop in this moral direction; it is revealed by reflection on the activities of our mind. According to Chu Hsi, reflection on these spontaneous reactions reveals the perfect moral knowledge that we have all along, since *li* (pattern or principle) is already known to the mind. But whereas he agrees with Mencius that certain features of the mind provide the ultimate source of moral knowledge, he differs from him in his conception of those features. Mencius sees them based in certain spontaneous reactions, while Chu Hsi

regards them as based in a perfect moral knowledge that is partly but not totally obscured.

SHUN, Kwong-Loi. Moral Reasons in Confucian Ethics. J Chin Phil, 16(3-4), 317-343, D 89.

The paper discusses Mencius's conception of moral reasons, and relates that conception to those of other Confucians, including Hsün Tzu and Wang Yang-ming. It discusses two problems for these conceptions, and shows how these problems have a structure parallel to that of similar problems discussed in contemporary Anglo-American moral philosophy. That these are problems for different ethical traditions suggests that they are general problems concerning our understanding of our moral life. The paper ends with the suggestion that each of the two problems has to do with a tension generated by a certain direction of reflective thinking about our moral life.

SHUSTERMAN, Richard (ed). *Analytic Aesthetics*. Cambridge, Blackwell, 1989

This book collects ten new papers variously addressing the nature of the analytic approach, the history of its contribution to aesthetic understanding, its current and comparative value in treating particular issues in the arts, and the way it needs to be modified to improve aesthetic inquiry. The particular aesthetic uses it treats include expression, interpretation, beauty and truth, the aesthetic attitude, and aesthetic autonomy.

SHUSTERMAN, Richard. Beneath Interpretation: Against Hermeneutic Holism. Monist, 73(2), 181-204, Ap 90.

This paper argues that the popular position of hermeneutic universalism, which asserts (in Gadamer's words) that "all understanding is interpretation." This position gains much of its power through the rejection of any incorrigible, perspectiveless, "God's-eye" understanding of things. My paper argues that we can concede that all understanding is corrigible, perspectival, prejudiced, selective, and active while still allowing that understanding and interpretation can be profitably distinguished.

SHUSTERMAN, Richard. "Introduction: Analysing Analytic Aesthetics" in *Analytic Aesthetics*, SHUSTERMAN, Richard (ed), 1-19. Cambridge, Blackwell, 1989.

This paper assesses the nature, contribution, and continuing value of analytic aesthetics. It charts the development and different strains of analytic aesthetics and compares the analytic approach to rival approaches. Certain salient features of analytic aesthetics are treated in detail, e.g., its notion of analysis, its conception of meta-criticism, its privileging art over natural beauty, its comparative neglect of the issue of evaluation.

SHUSTERMAN, Richard. Why Dewey Now? J Aes Educ, 23(3), 60-67, Fall 89.

SICHEL, Betty A. Ethics of Caring and the Institutional Ethics Committee. Hypatia, 4(2), 45-56, Sum 89.

Institutional ethics committees (IECs) in health care facilities now create moral policy, provide moral education, and consult with physicians and other health care workers. After sketching reasons for the development of IECs, this paper first examines the predominant moral standards it is often assumed IECs are now using, these standards being neo-Kantian principles of justice and utilitarian principles of the greatest good. Then, it is argued that a feminine ethics of care, as posited by Carol Gilligan and Nel Noddings, is an unacknowledged basis for IEC discussions and decisions. Further, it is suggested that feminine ethics of care can and should provide underlying theoretical tools and standards for IECs.

SIDELLE, Alan. *Necessity, Essence, and Individuation: A Defense of Conventionalism*. Ithaca, Cornell Univ Pr, 1989

SIEG, Wilfried. Hilbert's Program Sixty Years Later. J Sym Log, 53(2), 338-348, Je 88.

This paper introduced the Symposium on Hilbert's Program at the Joint Meeting of the American Philosophical Association and the Association of Symbolic Logic in Washington, DC, in December of 1985. It traces the history of mathematical and philosophical developments related to Hilbert's Program. Taking into account significant recent results, critical questions of further philosophical and mathematical research are posed.

SIEGEL, Harvey. Is Translation Relevant to Educational Relevance? Proc Phil Educ, 45, 197-202, 1989.

SIEGEL, Harvey. Laudan's Normative Naturalism. Stud Hist Phil Sci, 21(2), 295-313, Je 90.

Unlike more standard non-normative naturalizations of epistemology and philosophy of science, Larry Laudan's naturalized philosophy of science explicitly maintains a normative dimension. This paper critically assesses Laudan's normative naturalism. After summarizing Laudan's position, the paper examines (1) Laudan's construal of methodological rules as 'instrumentalities' connecting methodological means and cognitive ends; (2)

Laudan's instrumental conception of scientific rationality; (3) Laudan's naturalistic account of the axiology of science; and (4) the extent to which a normative philosophy of science can be naturalized. It is concluded that Laudan's normative naturalism is as problematic as its non-normative naturalist cousins.

SIEGEL, Harvey. Philosophy of Science Naturalized? Some Problems with Giere's Naturalism. Stud Hist Phil Sci, 20(3), 365-375, S 89.

In a series of recent papers and book, Ronald N Giere argues for a naturalized philosophy of science. Giere contrasts his proposed approach with more traditional, non-natural approaches to philosophy of science, and so in effect argues for a reorientation of the discipline. In this paper I critically examine Giere's proposal for a naturalized philosophy of science. While sympathetic to a partially naturalized approach to science studies, I shall argue that naturalizing the philosophy of science in effect abandons philosophy of science's greatest task and promise: that of contributing to our understanding of the *epistemological* standing of science.

SIEGEL, Harvey. Why Be Rational? On Thinking Critically About Critical Thinking. Proc Phil Educ, 45, 392-401, 1989.

In this paper I review recent literature on the justification of rationality. I argue rationality can be justified in a noncircular, non-question-begging way.

SIEGEL, Steve. Grassroots Opposition to Animal Exploitation. Hastings Center Rep, 19(6), 39-41, N-D 89.

SIEVERS, K H. Chalmers on Unrepresentative Realism and Objectivism. Austl J Phil, 68(1), 89-102, Mr 90.

This article criticizes unrepresentative realism and objectivism, two positions defended by Alan Chalmers in the second edition of his book, *What Is This Thing Called Science?* It is argued unrepresentative realism is implausible and inconsistent with the theory-dependence of observations and his own account of perception. Against objectivism it is argued that we do not need to assume theories have independent existence to explain logical relations between sentences. Another criticism is that Chalmers does not tell us how our knowledge of logical relations between theories has anything to do with their supposed objective existence.

SIEVERT, Donald. Essential Truths and the Ontological Argument. SW Phil Rev, 6(1), 59-64, Ja 90.

Recent discussions by Curley, Rodis-Lewis and Grene focus on the structure of the *Meditations* and the occurrence in the fifth meditation of another theological proof. Authors wonder why there is another proof after the third meditation. I argue that (a) Descartes first presents his doctrine of essential truths in the fifth meditation and (b) the ontological argument depends on the doctrine of essential truths. It is no oversight, error, or embarrassment that the ontological argument is contiguous to a discussion of the essence of body. However, the uniqueness of the theological case may obscure its affinity with the other cases of essential truths.

SIGNORINI, Alberto. L'idea di creazione *ex nihilo* e la libertà nel pensiero di e Levinas. G Metaf, 11(2), 241-271, My-Ag 89.

SILLIMAN, Matt. The Closing of the Professorial Mind: A Meditation on Plato and Allan Bloom. Educ Theor, 40(1), 147-151, Wint 90.

The author takes issue with Allan Bloom's critique of higher education as discussed in Bloom's book *The Closing of the American Mind*. The author is particularly concerned with Bloom's reading and application of passages of Plato's *Republic* to concerns involving a proposed canon of authoritative literature to be used in education.

SILLS, Chip. Is Hegel's Logic a Speculative Tropology? Owl Minerva, 21(1), 21-40, Fall 89.

This paper argues that Hegel's insight into the *necessity* of image-based attempts to express truth underlies his account of the philosophical concept. The basic images, called tropes, are the first forms of truth. Hegel in effect connected the tropes of rhetoric—formal images—with the tropes of ancient skepticism—formal strategies for inducing doubt. This produced a unique genre of philosophical exposition whose originality has made Hegel notoriously hard to grasp. The movement from image-based thinking to properly conceptual thinking is itself "tropic," according to Hegel, and I suggest that we recognize certain specific coinages of Hegelian rhetoric (like "aufheben") as "speculative tropes."

SILVA CAMARENA, Juan Manuel. Dialogo sobre humanismo y existencialismo (cuarta y última parte). Rev Filosof (Mexico), 23(67), 87-110, Ja-Ap 90.

SILVA CAMARENA, Juan Manuel. Solamente un dios puede todavia salvarnos. Rev Filosof (Mexico), 22(66), 267-296, S-D 89.

SILVA CAMARENA, Juan Manuel. La superacion del analisis logico del lenguaje por medio de la metafisica. Rev Filosof (Mexico), 22(66),

354-374, S-D 89.

SILVA DE CHOUDENS, José R. Are There Corporeal Substances for Leibnitz? A Reaction to Stuart Brown. Dialogos, 25(55), 39-69, Ja 90.

SILVEIRA, L F B da. Charles Sanders Peirce: ciência enquanto semiótica. Trans/Form/Acao, 12, 71-83, 1989.

The diagram of sign when applied to the understanding of science gives place to an original correction correlation of abduction or retroduction, deduction and induction. The conjunction of abduction and deduction consists of a general form of logical possibility. Induction in its turn, establishes, in the long run, the ratio of frequency of the accomplishment of expected consequences of general representations in the universe of facts. As a formal construction, science as semiotics sustains itself even if it has as its object a universe of pure chance. Nevertheless, within Peirce's philosophical system, science retains its meaning only if it corresponds to the reality of Nature. The warrant of this statistically relevant correspondence would be the fact that human instinct belonged to the same stage of evolution as the whole universe.

SILVEIRA, Lígia Fraga. Descartes: um naturalista? Trans/Form/Acao, 12, 57-70, 1989.

The difficulties and solutions found by Descartes to solve the problem of the union of the substances are approached appealing to both his medical and moral conceptions put together.

SILVER, Lee M. New Reproductive Technologies in the Treatment of Human Infertility and Genetic Disease. Theor Med, 11(2), 103-110, Je 90.

In this paper I will discuss three areas in which advances in human reproductive technology could occur, their uses and abuses, and their effects on society. First is the potential to drastically increase the success rate and availability of in vitro fertilization and embryo freezing. Second is the ability to perform biopsies on embryos prior to the onset of pregnancy. Finally, I will consider the adding or altering of genes in embryos, commonly referred to as "genetic engineering." As new reproductive technologies pass from experimental models into the potential for medical utilization, I believe that it will be important for lawmakers everywhere to avoid the impulse to outlaw procedures that a society believes to be 'unnatural' at a first glance. Rather, I would hope that they can respond thoughtfully with legislation that serves two purposes—to protect the rights of couples to overcome infertility or to reduce the risk of genetic disease in their children-to-be, and more importantly, to protect children-to-be from the abuses that could result from some of the practices that I will discuss.

SILVER, Mitchell. The Morality of Refusing to Treat HIV-Positive Patients. J Applied Phil, 6(2), 149-157, O 89.

Do physicians and nurses have an obligation to treat patients who are HIV-positive? Although an initial review of the possible sources of such an obligation yields equivocal results, a closer examination reveals a clear obligation to treat. The current risk of job-caused HIV-infection is not sufficient to warrant a refusal to treat. This is so because there exist rationally justified, general social, as well as specific peer expectations, that helath care professionals treat HIV-positive patients. These expectations impose moral obligations on doctors and nurses. Moreover there is no sound libertarian argument entitling doctors and nurses to refuse to treat HIV-positive patients. A morally appropriate identification with his or her role would disincline a health care professional to refuse treatment to an HIV-positive patient. The likely source of such refusal is occupational alienation and an irrational reaction to AIDS symbolism.

SILVER, Ruth E. Controlling the Classroom Clamor: A Few Techniques to Facilitate Philosophical Discourse. Thinking, 5(1), 19-23, 1983.

SILVER, Ruth. A Good Day (for Philosophy) at Red Bank. Thinking, 6(2), 29-30, 1985.

SILVER, Ruth. Mind and Brain on Bergen Street. Thinking, 7(3), 18, 1988.

SILVERMAN, Allan. Color and Color-Perception in Aristotle's *De anima*. Ancient Phil, 9 (2), 271-292, Fall 89.

The paper aims to show that (1) colors, for Aristotle, are objective properties of material objects and that (2) the sense-faculty's taking on of the sensible form is a primitive and sui generis activity. To support these claims I offer a new interpretation of the actuality principle. I argue that a color is to be treated as a hylomorphic composite; its first actuality is identical with its essence; its second actuality, the form taken on in perception, is a necessary accident of its essence; and finally that the matter left behind in perception is the first actuality, the enmattered essence, itself.

SILVERMAN, Hugh J (ed). *Derrida and Deconstruction*. New York, Routledge, 1989

SILVERMAN, Hugh J. "Derrida, Heidegger, and the Time of the Line" in *Derrida and Deconstruction*, SILVERMAN, Hugh J (ed), 154-168. New York,

Routledge, 1989.

SILVERMAN, Hugh J (ed) and AYLESWORTH, Gary E (ed). *The Textual Sublime: Deconstruction and Its Differences.* Albany, SUNY Pr, 1990

This book addresses the question of deconstruction by asking what it is and by asking about its alternatives. To what extent does deconstruction derive from a philosophical stance, and to what extent does it depend upon a set of strategies, moves, and rhetorical practices that result in criticism? Special attention is given to the formulations offered by Jacques Derrida (in relation to Heidegger's philosophy) and by Paul de Man (in relation to Kant's theory of the sublime and its implications for criticism). And what, in deconstructive terms, does it mean to translate from one textual corpus into another? Is it a matter of different theories of translation or of different practices? And what of difference itself? Does not difference already invoke the possibility of deconstruction's "others"? Althusser, Adorno, and Deleuze are offered as exemplary cases. Includes extensive editors' introductory materials and a substantial bibliography.

SILVERN, Louise E. A Hermeneutic Account of Clinical Psychology: Strengths and Limits. Phil Psych, 3(1), 5-27, 1990.

There have been increasingly popular claims that hermeneutics provides an epistemology that is appropriate and sufficient for psychotherapy. The purpose of this paper is to evaluate and explain those claims. Hermeneutics proves to provide terms that legitimize aspects of clinical expertise that have been most ignored within the traditional empiricist epistemology; namely, hermeneutics articulates and provides standards for therapeutic interpretations about clients' idiosyncratic intentions and also for using clinical theories that defy empirical test. Nonetheless, hermeneutics also proves to be limited in its account of clinical knowledge. (edited)

SILVERS, Anita. Politics and the Production of Narrative Identities. Phil Lit, 14(1), 99-107, Ap 90.

I improve David Novitz's analogy between persons and art by recommending that the activity of establishing a personal identity be compared to narrative artwriting which establishes the character of works of art. Art historical scholarship offers many cases in which the creation of new works prompts artwriters to reverse characterizations of older works. The production of narrative identities for both art, and persons, should be understood as ontological, not, as Novitz insists, quintessentially political.

SILVERS, Anita. Why Philosophers Should Involve Themselves with Teaching Reasoning in the Schools. Thinking, 6(2), 25-26, 1985.

SILVERS, Stuart. "Coherence, Observation, and the Justification of Empirical Belief" in *The Current State of the Coherence Theory*, BENDER, John W (ed), 168-177. Norwell, Kluwer, 1989.

Coherence theories of justification for empirical knowledge and belief all confront the problem of getting empirical content somehow into the doxastic systems they characterize. On the one hand, the justification proceeds holistically in terms of the (proper) relations among the beliefs constituent of the system. On the other hand, empirical beliefs must satisfy conditions of (sensory) observation. In this paper, BonJour's (1985) coherence theory of knowledge is examined and found to lack arguments strong enough to make the appropriate connections between belief justification in virtue of (the degree of) coherence of the doxastic system and the required content for the system to have empirical content. It is also suggested that coherence theories of belief justification perhaps shouldn't bother with trying to connect what is conceptually disjoint.

SILVESTRE, Maria Luisa. *Nous*, the Concept of Ultimate Reality and Meaning in Anaxagoras. Ultim Real Mean, 12(4), 248-255, D 89.

SIMHONY, Avital. T H Green's Theory of the Morally Justified Society. Hist Polit Thought, 10(3), 481-498, Autumn 89.

The article seeks to show that a careful examination of the two central moral conceptions of Green's ethics—self-realization and the common good—elicits a coherent moral theory which culminates in a view of the morally justified society: the society which enables all (who are capable) to realize their capacities. That view of society is the focus of Green's societal morality, the basis of which is what I shall call two principles of justice: equal chance and nonexploitation. The morally justified society lies at the heart of Green's liberalism which cannot be fully appreciated without an adequate understanding of that kind of society.

SIMMEL, Georg. On the History of Philosophy. Thinking, 6(1), 42-45, 1985.

SIMMONS JR, Michael. Experience and Nature: Teacher as Story Teller. Proc Phil Educ, 45, 28-40, 1989.

SIMMONS, A John. Consent and Fairness in Planning Land Use. Bus Prof Ethics J, 6(2), 5-20, Sum 87.

The paper explores an analogy and its limits. The analogy is between the

moral positions of physicians and professional planners and is based on their similar needs to convey technical knowledge, on the uncertainty of risk assessment, and on the distrust and irrational fears of the "treatments" they prescribe. Both the physician and the planner must be centrally concerned with the informed consent of those with whom they deal, though in rather different ways. But the idea of fairness in the distribution of burdens must play a much more important role in the moral thinking of planners than in that of physicians.

SIMMONS, Keith. The Diagonal Argument and the Liar. J Phil Log, 19(3), 277-303, Ag 90.

SIMON, Caroline J. The Intuitionist Argument. S J Phil, 28(1), 91-114, Spr 90.

This article evaluates an argument for intuitionism, i.e., the view that the basic moral principles are irreducible moral, immediately apprehendable, objective truths. The structure of the argument reveals that intuitionism's proponents have seen it as the only alternative after alternatives (e.g., naturalism, noncognitivism, and error theories) have been shown to be unacceptable. The evaluation concludes that the soundness of the intuitionist argument rests on deep and important metaphysical issues, but that its strength is sufficient for intuitionism to be taken as a serious option concerning the status of ethics.

SIMON, Thomas W. Varieties of Ecological Dialectics. Environ Ethics, 12(3), 211-231, Fall 90.

A hierarchical ordering of approaches afflicts environmental thinking. An ethics of individualism unjustly overrides social/political philosophy in environmental debates. Dialectics helps correct this imbalance. In dialectical fashion, a synthesis emerges between conflicting approaches to dialectics and to nature from Marxism (Levins and Lewontin), anarchism (Bookchin), and Native Americanism (Black Elk). Conflicting (according to Marxists) and cooperative (according to anarchists) forces both operate in nature. Ethics (anarchist), political theory (Marxist), and spirituality (Native American) constitute the interconnected interpretative domains of a dialectically informed ecophilosophy. In a world painted too often in blacks and whites, ecological dialectics colors the picture a more realistic gray.

SIMON, Yves and NELSON, Ralph (trans). Knowledge of the Soul. Thomist, 54(2), 269-291, Ap 90.

The general disorder in the field of psychology prompted this study of the epistemological nature of psychology. It is important to make distinctions between different kinds of psychology, and to recognize their complementarity. Moral psychology is to be distinguished from applied psychology, a kind of technology. Theoretical psychology is divided into positive and philosophical. Though the author indicates the dangers implicit in applied psychology, he remains positive about it. He notes the unfortunate confusion between philosophical and positive psychology and argues for boundary maintenance. He ends with cautionary advice about the use and misuse of terminology in the field of psychology.

SIMONPIETRI MONEFELDT, Fannie A. El acceso del hombre a la realidad según Xavier Zubiri. Anu Filosof, 22(2), 113-130, 1989.

SIMONS, Margaret A. Sexism and the Philosophical Canon: On Reading Beauvoir's *The Second Sex*. J Hist Ideas, 51(3), 487-504, Jl-S 90.

SIMONS, Martin. The Rational Woman. Educ Phil Theor, 21(1), 36-46, 1989.

It has been claimed that female ways of understanding, different and broader than the masculine, have been stifled by male disciplines. This claim supports moves toward sex-segregated schooling. It is argued here that all human thought and feelings depend on common rational processes which both sexes demonstrably employ from the earliest moments of life. The potential for development of superior ways of thought and expression is open but new growth will spring from the same rational roots and cannot be exclusive: anything learnable by one human being, irrespective of sex, can and should be taught, to all.

SIMONS, Martin. Why Can't a Man Be More Like a Woman? (A Note on John Locke's Educational Thought). Educ Theor, 40(1), 135-145, Wint 90.

In some feminist writings on education it is claimed that boys have gained important advantages from schooling whereas girls have suffered by being excluded. A contrary historical point is argued here. Boys' schools from Renaissance times until at least the 19th century were often appallingly bad, cruel and brutalising. Locke recognised this. His recommendations for the education of boys were that they should be nurtured at home, as girls already were.

SIMONS, Peter. Combinators and Categorial Grammar. Notre Dame J Form Log, 30(2), 241-261, Spr 89.

From Ajdukiewicz onwards categorial grammar has failed to characterize adequately the twin roles of variable-binding operators and the variables they bind. Categorial grammars are, however, adequate for languages using combinators and dispensing with bound variables, but the combinators used hitherto have been insufficiently flexible to eliminate bound variables from languages which allow both higher-order quantification and multi-place functors, such as those of Lesniewski. This paper introduces seven multigrade combinators and shows how they can be used to eliminate bound variables from Lesniewskian languages, yielding logical languages as powerful as these but in perfect harmony with Ajdukiewicz's type of grammar. An alternative to multigrade combinators will also be considered and the significance of the result for the understanding of languages with more flexible category assignments is studied.

SIMPSON, Alan. Language, Literature, and Art. J Aes Educ, 22(2), 47-53, Sum 88.

SIMPSON, Evan. Conservatism, Radicalism and Democratic Practice. Praxis Int, 9(3), 273-286, O 89.

This paper enlists a form of moral conservatism in order to show how existing communicative practices might be extended to overcome the inhibiting effects of social structures upon institutional reform. Characteristics of the resulting consensual determination of social purposes suggest a moderation of differences about communicative competence between "conservatives" like Richard Rorty and radical reformers like Jurgen Habermas.

SIMPSON, Evan. *Good Lives and Moral Education*. New York, Lang, 1989

This book develops a "conservative" conception of morality and its implications for moral education. The argument stresses practices of living over rationalistic theories. At its center is an account of the education of the emotions, in which cultivating reflective imagination is more important than mastering universal principles. The central contrast is with Lawrence Kohlberg and his theory of moral development. The author sees extending democratic practices of discussion and argument as best answering the question how, lacking certain standards of judgment, we can decide between competing conceptions of human progress.

SIMPSON, Peter. Practical Knowing: Finnis and Aquinas. Mod Sch, 67(2), 111-122, Ja 90.

I argue that Finnis's account of practical knowing is false. It falls foul of dilemmas about the meaning of good, reasons for action, and truth. It is also not an accurate interpretation of Aquinas. Aquinas's own theory, when correctly stated, escapes all three dilemmas and makes far more sense. Finnis, however, may be right about the priority of good to nature in the order of knowing, if not about practical knowing as such.

SIMPSON, Stephen G. Partial Realizations of Hilbert's Program. J Sym Log, 53(2), 349-363, Je 88.

SIMPSON, Thomas M. John Stuart Mill, La falacia de composición y la naturaleza humana. Analisis Filosof, 7(2), 141-147, N 87.

SINDELAR, Dusan. The Horizon of Aesthetics (in Czechoslovakian). Estetika, 27(2), 65-80, 1990.

SINDELAR, Dusan. The Questions of Contemporary Aesthetics (in Czechoslovakian). Estetika, 26(4), 193-198, 1989.

SINGER, Beth J. Naturalism and Generality in Buchler and Santayana. Bull Santayana Soc, 3, 29-37, Fall 85.

Comparison of two widely different metaphysical systems in terms of three aspects of metaphysical generality: systematic generality, ontological generality, and genericness.

SINGER, Irving. Santayana's Philosophy of Love. Bull Santayana Soc, 5, 1-16, Fall 87.

This essay analyzes Santayana's philosophy of love in terms of his attempt to combine a type of twentieth-century Platonism with his own variety of metaphysical materialism. Examining works such as *Reason in Society* and *The Realm of Spirit*, the essay argues that Santayana's synthesis fails because it cannot properly explain the nature of idealization and the love of persons. Santayana's ideas about friendship are also studied. They are found to be more persuasive and defensible than his overall conception of love. A revised version of this essay appears in the third volume of Irving Singer's trilogy *The Nature of Love*.

SINGER, Linda. "Defusing the Canon: Feminist Rereading and Textual Politics" in *The Question of the Other: Essays in Contemporary Continental Philosophy*, DALLERY, Arleen B (ed), 103-116. Albany, SUNY Pr, 1989.

SINGER, Marcus G. Value Judgments and Normative Claims. Philosophy, 24, 145-172, 88 Supp.

SINGER, Peter and REGAN, Tom. *Animal Rights and Human Obligations*

(Second Edition). Englewood Cliffs, Prentice-Hall, 1989

SINGER, Peter (and others). The Ethical Assessment of Innovative Therapies: Liver Transplantation Using Living Donors. Theor Med, 11(2), 87-94, Je 90.

Liver transplantation is the treatment of choice for many forms of liver disease. Unfortunately, the scarcity of cadaveric donor livers limits the availability of this technique. To improve the availability of liver transplantation, surgeons have developed the capability of removing a portion of liver from a live donor and transplanting it into a recipient. A few liver transplants using living donors have been performed worldwide. Our purpose was to analyze the ethics of liver transplants using living donors and to propose guidelines for the procedure before it was introduced in the United States. We used a process of "research ethics consultation" that involves a collaboration between clinical investigators and clinical ethicists. We concluded that it was ethically appropriate to perform liver transplantation using living donors in a small series of patients on a trial basis, and we published our ethical guidelines in a medical journal before the procedure was introduced. We recommend this prospective, public approach for the introduction of other innovative therapies in medicine and surgery.

SINGER, Peter. To Do or Not to Do? Hastings Center Rep, 19(6), 42-44, N-D 89.

Is it justifiable to use illegal means to stop animal experimentation? This short essay is intended to stimulate thought about this question.

SINGH, Jang B and LAKHAN, V C. Business Ethics and the International Trade in Hazardous Wastes. J Bus Ethics, 8(11), 889-899, N 89.

The annual production of hazardous wastes, which was less than 10 million metric tonnes in the 1940s, is now in excess of 320 million metric tonnes. These wastes are, in the main, by-products of industrial processes that have contributed significantly to the economic development of many countries which, in turn, has led to lifestyles that also generate hazardous wastes. The phenomenal increase in the generation of hazardous wastes coupled with various barriers to local disposal has led to the thriving international trade in these environmentally hazardous substances. This paper examines the nature of the international trade in hazardous wastes and the ethical issues associated with such business activity.

SINGH, R Raj. Non-Violence, Gandhi and Our Times. Int J Applied Phil, 5(1), 35-41, Spr 90.

SINNOTT-ARMSTRONG, Walter and MOOR, James and FOGELIN, Robert. A Defence of Modus Tollens. Analysis, 50(1), 9-16, Ja 90.

Ernest Adams recently discussed an apparent counterexample to modus tollens: A asserts (1) If it rained, it didn't rain hard; B asserts (2) it rained hard; but it is paradoxical to conclude (3) it didn't rain. Adams avoids this paradox by claiming that (1) cannot be a material conditional, because A would not accept its contrapositive. We argue that (1) can be a material conditional; modus tollens is valid; Adams's contrapositive explanation fails; and no paradox arises, because it is illegitimate to draw conclusions from assertions when they can't both be true, and (1)-(2) can't both be true, given 'If it rained hard, it rained'.

SINNOTT-ARMSTRONG, Walter. *Moral Dilemmas*. Cambridge, Blackwell, 1988

Moral dilemmas are situations where moral requirements conflict but neither is overridden. The author uses moral residue (such as remorse) and a counterfactual definition of requirements to show that moral requirements conflict, and then uses symmetry and inexactness to show that some conflicts are unresolvable. The next step is to criticize the main arguments against and attempts to avoid moral dilemmas. Finally, the author shows that the possibility of moral dilemmas refutes both prescriptivism and an extreme form of moral realism, and also illuminates the purpose of moral theory and a variety of social and individual moral problems.

SINSHEIMER, Robert L. Whither the Genome Project? Hastings Center Rep, 20(4), 5, Jl-Ag 90.

The Human Genome Project, when successfully completed, will provide knowledge of the genetic basis of human existence. Possession of this knowledge will provide humanity with novel options. These will pose novel questions and require difficult, unprecedented decisions. Some of the likely issues, relating to privacy and to eugenics, are described and various possible points of view are discussed.

SINTONEN, Matti. "Explanation: In Search of the Rationale" in *Scientific Explanation (Minnesota Studies in the Philosophy of Science, Volume XIII)*, KITCHER, Philip (ed), 253-282. Minneapolis, Univ of Minn Pr, 1989.

The paper outlines a pragmatic notion in which scientific explanations are answers explanation-seeking questions. It argues that syntactic and semantic models work to the extent they can capture some pragmatic features of question-answer sequences. However, the logic of questions, even if coupled with pragmatic constraints derived from question-answer sequences, is too weak for an interesting notion of specifically scientific explanation. To this end we need a rich theory notion—the structuralist view—in which theory-laden contextual restrictions constrain potential answers. One virtue of the approach is that it can explicate explanatory unification.

SKALICKY, Carlo. Il dialogo cristiano-marxista a Budapest. Aquinas, 32(1), 73-106, Ja-Ap 89.

SKEEL, Joy D and SELF, Donnie J. An Analysis of Ethics Consultation in the Clinical Setting. Theor Med, 10(4), 289-299, D 89.

Only recently have ethicists been invited into the clinical setting to offer recommendations about patient care decisions. This paper discusses this new role for ethicists from the perspective of content and process issues. Among content issues are the usual ethical dilemmas such as the aggressiveness of treatment, questions about consent, and alternative treatment options. Among process issues are those that relate to communication with the patient. The formal ethics consult is discussed, the steps taken in such a consult, and whether there should be a fee charged. We conclude with an examination of the risks and benefits of formal ethics consults.

SKIDD, David R A. Corporate Responsibility: Morality Without Consciousness. Bus Prof Ethics J, 7(1), 75-89, Spr 88.

SKILLEN, Tony. Flew on Russell on Nozick: Uncharitable Interpretations of Justice and Unjust Views of Charity. J Applied Phil, 7(1), 87-89, Mr 90.

Flew agrees with Russell against Nozick that compulsory charity is legitimate. But Flew's way of distinguishing charity from justice makes this agreement puzzling. There are big problems for standard ways of distinguishing justice from charity, ways which reinforce norms of indifference.

SKINNER, S J and KELLEY, S W and FERRELL, O C. Ethical Behavior Among Marketing Researchers: An Assessment of Selected Demographic Characteristics. J Bus Ethics, 9(8), 681-688, Ag 90.

This study considers the relationship between perceptions of ethical behavior and the demographic characteristics of sex, age, education level, job title, and job tenure among a sample of marketing researchers. The findings of this study indicate that female marketing researchers, older marketing researchers, and marketing researchers holding their present job for ten years or more generally rate their behavior as more ethical.

SKOLIMOWSKI, Henryk. Is Ecology Transcending Both Marxism and Christianity? Dialec Hum, 14(1), 109-116, Wint 87.

Ecology can now be seen as a large philosophical metaphor helping us to rethink the whole structure of the cosmos. In the light of the ecological metaphor, we can clearly see the shortcomings of traditional Christianity and traditional Marxism. Each has conceived the universe too narrowly and elevated the human person too much. In order to survive, Christianity must incorporate the ecological perspective in its teaching, and the ecological perspective must incorporate traditonal spiritual values.

SKOLIMOWSKI, Henryk. Of Vision, Hope, and Courage. Bridges, 1(3-4), 85-92, Fall-Wint 89.

Hope is part of our ontological structure, an invisible scaffolding of our being. To understand the human condition is to understand the place of hope in it. In our crippled times particularly, the resurrection of hope is necessary for the resurrection of the human condition. We make a big mistake if we do not see that hope is our psychic oxygen. Hope is invisible, like oxygen, but equally important to our well-being.

SKORUPSKI, John. John Stuart Mill. New York, Routledge, 1989

SKUBIK, Daniel W. At the Intersection of Legality and Morality: Hartian Law as Natural Law. New York, Lang, 1990

SKURA, Tomasz. A New Criterion of Decidability for Intermediate Logics. Bull Sect Log, 19(1), 10-14, Mr 90.

The purpose of the work is to find a general criterion of decidability for propositional logics using simple algebraic methods. I prove that if a recursively axiomatizable logic has the recursive model property then it is decidable. There are logics without the finite model property that are decidable by this criterion. I also prove that if an intermediate logic has the r.m.p. then it has a recursive Lukasiewicz-style refutation formulation. (More general results of this kind were presented at the Logic Colloquium '90 in Helsinki.)

SKVORTSOV, D P. On Axiomatizability of Some Intermediate Predicate Logics (Summary). Rep Math Log, 22, 115-116, 1988.

SKYRMS, Brian. Correlated Equilibria and the Dynamics of Rational Deliberation. Erkenntnis, 31(2-3), 347-364, S 89.

Dynamic models of deliberation by expected utility maximizers are introduced. Under certain ideal conditions it is shown for a system of such deliberators playing a game that they are at a joint deliberational equilibrium iff they are at a game theoretic equilibrium. The dynamics of rational deliberation can produce correlations; the notion of a correlated equilibrium is used to characterize this phenomenon.

SKYRMS, Brian. Introduction to 'Three Theorems of Metaphysics'. Synthese, 81(2), 203-205, N 89.

SLAATTE, Howard A. *Religious Issues in Contemporary Philosophy*. Lanham, Univ Pr of America, 1988

A sequel to *Contemporary Philosophies of Religion* to sharpen issues of more current concern relative to the reference of religious matters to philosophy and popular discussion of the day. Begins with respect for the Absolute; deals with Kant's place for evil in man commonly overlooked by ethicists; moves into scientific problems relative to religious philosophy. Appeals to a balanced but not synthetic dialectics.

SLADE, Christina. Logic in the Classroom. Thinking, 8(2), 14-20, 1989.

SLADE, Christine. Logic in the International Elementary School. Thinking, 8(4), 12-19, 1990.

SLAGA, Szczepan W. What the Philosophy of Biology Is and Should Be (in Polish). Stud Phil Christ, 25(2), 155-175, 1989.

SLANEY, John. A General Logic. Austl J Phil, 68(1), 74-88, Mr 90.

This is a unified account of a range of logical systems including Anderson and Belnap's R, relatives of fuzzy logic, some modal logics and many weaker systems. It is designed to dispose of the claim that such systems are difficult, contrived and esoteric, assuming familiarity only with elementary logic in some such formulation as Lemmon's. Nonclassical logics as presented here have been introduced to students with no formal logical training beyond a standard one-semester first course.

SLATER, B H. Excluding the Middle. Critica, 20(60), 55-71, D 88.

SLATOR, Brian. Response to Dietrich's "Computationalism". Soc Epistem, 4(2), 190-193, Ap-Je 90.

The trouble with computationalism is pretty much the same as the trouble with evolution. Neither has much place in a feel-good "me" generation (and, after all, nearly every generation is one of those), and neither can be embraced by the human heart; at least not as gladly as other, competing theories can be. Dietrich's theory, computationalism, might never be accepted by the common citizen, and the "logical conclusions" will rankle against many. Dietrich will never make the cover of *People* magazine, at least not with this.

SLICER, Deborah. Teaching with a Different Ear: Teaching Ethics after Reading Carol Gilligan. J Value Inq, 24(1), 55-65, Ja 90.

Instructors of philosophic ethics show a bias toward Kohlberg's stage six, justice thinking, while giving little, if any, attention to an alternative model based on Carol Gilligan's ethic of care. I advocate attending to the "different" voice in the ethics classroom in order to provide students with the conceptual tools to evaluate the traditional model, to retrieve women philosophy students who might feel that philosophical ethics just does not "speak" to them, and to help women students take their own moral insights seriously in a culture which invalidates so many of their other insights and experiences.

SLOSS, Leon. "The Case for Deploying Strategic Defenses" in *Nuclear Deterrence and Moral Restraint*, SHUE, Henry (ed), 343-379. New York, Cambridge Univ Pr, 1989.

SLUGA, Hans. "Thinking as Writing" in *Wittgenstein in Focus—Im Brennpunkt: Wittgenstein*, MC GUINNESS, Brian (ed), 115-142. Amsterdam, Rodopi, 1989.

Following a suggestion made by Wittgenstein writing is treated as a manifestation of and model for thinking. An analysis of Wittgenstein's own writing as well as that of Plato, Kant, and Nietzsche reveals it as work carried out in multiple episodes of addition, deletion, and (re-)organization. Reflective writing of this kind is, in fact, a process of equilibration between local and global ideas which in philosophical work typically generates problems of coherence and closure. Nonreflective, immediate writing is not primary in philosophy, but characteristically presupposes a process of reflective rehearsal. The classical conception of thinking as an apprehension of thoughts derives from the mistaken idea of the primacy of immediate writing.

SMAJS, J and KOLARSKY, R. Philosophy and the Devastation of the Earth (in Czechoslovakian). Filozof Cas, 37(5), 617-623, 1989.

The article sets out to show in what sense the current ecological crisis grows up to be a truly philosophical problem. Basing their observations on contemporary data, the authors point to changes occurring in the relationship between culture and nature. They assert that the present-day ecological crisis does indeed constitute a philosophical problem in its own right, representing an impetus for reflecting on fundamental philosophical concepts, the subject of philosophy and its history. This reflection may, as it were, be of significance for efforts to tackle the current ecological crisis insofar as the philosophical concepts themselves tend to change into instruments for the formulation of objectives and insofar as they serve as a communication basis.

SMAJS, J. The Uniqueness and Value of Terrestrial Nature (in Czechoslovakian). Filozof Cas, 37(5), 644-654, 1989.

This study discusses the need of devising a new philosophical concept of nature and of rehabilitating its value. The author is critical of the still prevailing concept of nature as an abstract objective reality deprived of all qualities and values (save for the ability to exist in motion, space and time). The cornerstone of his arguments lies in a defence of the uniqueness of terrestrial nature, in an emphasis laid on its considerable evolutionary value, its appropriate uniqueness of evolutionary conditions and the amount of time gone by. (edited)

SMALL, Robin. Absolute Becoming and Absolute Necessity. Int Stud Phil, 21(2), 125-134, 1989.

Absolute becoming and absolute necessity play a crucial role in Nietzsche's thinking. He holds that these concepts are a valid characterisation of reality in general, but he also asserts that they are not usable in our attempts to gain knowledge of the world. In fact, our everyday thinking is constituted by a denial or negation of these absolute concepts. After analysing this complex process of denial in its several stages, I discuss the possibility of a process in the other direction: that is, leading to an affirmation which is also a participation in absolute becoming and absolute necessity.

SMALL, Robin. Nietzsche, Dühring, and Time. J Hist Phil, 28(2), 229-250, Ap 90.

Nietzsche was drawn to assert an infinity of past time, not only by his rejection of any notion of divine creation, but also by his own doctrine of eternal recurrence. In defending the adequacy of understanding a past infinity in terms of an infinite regress from the present moment, he attempted to rebut the opposing arguments of several contemporary philosophers—in particular, of Eugen Dühring. An analysis of their debate shows that neither writer states his case without making mistakes, and suggests that the real issue is an epistemological rather than a logical one.

SMART, B J. Understanding and Justifying Self-Defence. Int J Moral Soc Stud, 4(3), 231-244, Autumn 89.

Self-defence has often been justified by appealing to the aggressor's forfeiture of the right to life or to the principles of punishment. Neither appeal is acceptable, separately or conjointly. Self-defense, along with other-defence, can be justified only by considerations of the fair allocation of the rescue services available: the right to life is not forfeited by the aggressor, but the right to equal priority along with the victim is. Fault in causing the scarcity of rescue resources acts as a tiebreaker. A principle of restitution, applicable to rescue not involving aggression, can be extended to the aggressor and victim: aggressor must restore victim to the *status quo*.

SMART, J J C. "C B Martin, A Biographical Sketch" in *Cause, Mind, and Reality: Essays Honoring C B Martin*, HEIL, John (ed), 1-3. Norwell, Kluwer, 1989.

SMART, J J C. "Verificationism" in *Cause, Mind, and Reality: Essays Honoring C B Martin*, HEIL, John (ed), 261-270. Norwell, Kluwer, 1989.

SMART, Ninian. The Epistemology of Pluralism: the Basis of Liberal Philosophy. Phil Soc Act, 16(2), 5-14, Ap-Je 90.

SMEU, Grigore. Brâncusi et l'évolution de la perception (in Romanian). Rev Filosof (Romania), 36(2), 184-188, Mr-Ap 89.

SMILANSKY, Saul. Is Libertarian Free Will Worth Wanting? Phil Invest, 13(3), 273-276, Jl 90.

The question whether libertarian free will is 'worth wanting' was emphasized (and given a negative answer) by Dennett in his recent *Elbow Room*. I argue that this question is seriously ambiguous, and includes two different sorts of questions, which I attempt to elucidate. I then go on to argue that once the two questions are clearly perceived, the compatibilist case is hardly as strong. Even if libertarian free will is impossible (and is thus in one sense 'not worth wanting'), in another sense libertarian free will is 'worth wanting'.

SMILANSKY, Saul. Van Inwagen on the 'Obviousness' of Libertarian Moral Responsibility. Analysis, 50(1), 29-33, Ja 90.

The paper points out a crucial difficulty in Van Inwagen's *An Essay on Free Will*—his claim for the direct obviousness of the existence of libertarian moral responsibility. Van Inwagen's attempt to discredit the beliefs of the people who doubt the existence of libertarian moral responsibility is shown not to succeed. And since virtually all of Van Inwagen's case for the existence of libertarian free will depends on his case for the "obviousness" of libertarian moral responsibility, the failure of the latter undermines the former.

SMILEY, Marion. Paternalism and Democracy. J Value Inq, 23(4), 299-318, D 89.

The author argues that if liberals want to protect individuals from serious physical harm without treating them paternalistically, they will have to shift their attention away from the rationality of particular individuals to the relationships of domination and equality that characterize paternalism in practice.

SMILEY, Marion. Pragmatic Inquiry and Social Conflict: A Critical Reconstruction of Dewey's Model of Democracy. Praxis Int, 9(4), 365-380, Ja 90.

The essay has two major aims. One is to show that while Dewey is not able to generate new values out of scientific inquiry, he is able to generate such values out of a more purely political analysis of 20th century America. The other is to reconstruct Dewey's political analysis of 20th century America, along with his model of democracy, as the basis of a critical/political theory that is capable of moving beyond the status quo.

SMIT, P A. An Argumentation-Analysis of a Central Part of Lenin's Political Logic. Commun Cog, 22(3-4), 357-374, 1989.

With the help of a specific dialog-oriented method of argumentation-analysis, Lenin's polemics are critically scrutinized. The analysis shows that Lenin—in the role of evaluator of the arguments of his opponents—makes use of the following logical principles: (1) a logic of terms with two binary symmetric relations, in which the terms may be simple or relations; (2) a dichotomization of the field of discussion: on each subject of discussion there is only one right viewpoint, the rest is false. The political consequences of the use of these and other logical principles in Lenin's reasoning are discussed.

SMITH JR, Archie. Alien Gods in Black Experience. Process Stud, 18(4), 294-305, Wint 89.

The purpose of this essay is to bring three perspectives into dialogue around a single case study. The three perspectives are pastoral psychology, liberation and process theologies. The focus of the paper is on black people's experience of oppression. The question of an adequate description of oppression is raised. The Pauline term, "principalities and powers," is used to analyze the systemic nature of oppression. The underlying assumption is that oppression is a complex and socially constructed reality. It is also an integration of spiritual and material forces that circumscribe human existence. McClendon's three strands of ethics and the contributions of three black theologians are discussed.

SMITH, A D. Of Primary and Secondary Qualities. Phil Rev, 99(2), 221-254, Ap 90.

SMITH, C U M. "Evolution, Epistemology and Visual Science" in *Issues in Evolutionary Epistemology*, HAHLWEG, Kai (ed), 527-544. Albany, SUNY Pr, 1989.

It has frequently been argued that the dominant metaphor underlying contemporary epistemology is still that of mind as mirror. This metaphor has a very ancient lineage stretching back into antiquity but received classic expression in the Cartesian philosophy. It is argued that the mirror metaphor is based on what is now very obsolete neuroscience, and this chapter attempts to redress the balance by reviewing some of the findings of contemporary visual neuroscience and drawing out their epistemological implications.

SMITH, Dale E. Merleau-Ponty's Indirect Ontology. Dialogue (Canada), 27(4), 615-635, Wint 88.

SMITH, G W. Freedom and Virtue in Politics: Some Aspects of Character, Circumstances and Utility from Helvétius to J S Mill. Utilitas, 1(1), 112-134, My 89.

Investigated Mill's understanding of the doctrine of the social determination of character which he inherited from the French Enlightenment via Bentham and his father. Mill evolves a distinctive and original version of the theory and deploys it in the solution of two critical problems which he inherited as a utilitarian: (1) the collapse of the Helvetian theory of democracy in the face of Macaulay's attack on James Rice's essay *On Government*; (2) the challenge of Robert Owen's claim that we are necessarily creatures of circumstance and hence unfree. Mill attempts to reconcile liberty and civic virtue in a radically reconstructed theory of the social determination of character.

SMITH, George P. *Final Choices: Autonomy in Health Care Decisions.* Springfield, Thomas, 1989

This work analyzes the legal, medical and philosophical issues inherent in decision making at the end of life. It probes the strengths and weaknesses in present state laws and case decisions and calls for a change in the taxonomy of euthanasia. As such, the emphasis would be on recognition of a right of self-determination (and/or assisted suicide) and a de-emphasis of the state's asserted right to control personal issues of health maintenance under the parens patria powers.

SMITH, Holly M. Two-Tier Moral Codes. Soc Phil Pol, 7(1), 112-132, Autumn 89.

Moral codes have a practical function: guiding decision making. But an agent's false empirical beliefs can prevent her from using standard codes to make successful decisions. This paper examines the proposal to evade this problem by adopting a two-tier moral code, one in which the first tier presents the correct theoretical account of right and wrong, while the second tier provides associated, but distinct, rules to guide decision making. Traditional objections to two-tier codes are examined and found wanting, but new and more lethal difficulties are discovered.

SMITH, Huston and GRIFFIN, David Ray. *Primordial Truth and Postmodern Theology.* Albany, SUNY Pr, 1989

SMITH, James M. (ed) and BEAUCHAMP, Tom L (ed) and FEINBERG, Joel (ed). *Philosophy and the Human Condition (Second Edition).* Englewood Cliffs, Prentice-Hall, 1989

SMITH, Janet E. The *Munus* of Transmitting Human Life: A New Approach to *Humanae Vitae.* Thomist, 54(3), 385-427, Jl 90.

SMITH, Janet Farrell. "Russell on Indexicals and Scientific Knowledge" in *Rereading Russell: Essays on Bertrand Russell's Metaphysics and Epistemology*, SAVAGE, C Wade (ed), 119-137. Minneapolis, Univ of Minn Pr, 1989.

SMITH, John E. "Harris's Commentary on Hegel's Logic" in *Dialectic and Contemporary Science*, GRIER, Philip T (ed), 55-64. Lanham, Univ Pr of America, 1989.

SMITH, John K. *The Nature of Social and Educational Inquiry: Empiricism versus Interpretation.* Norwood, Ablex, 1989

SMITH, Joseph Wayne. Are There Really Perennial Philosophical Disputes? Indian Phil Quart, 17(1), 91-109, Ja 90.

SMITH, Joseph Wayne. The Logical Limits of Science. Epistemologia, 12(1), 153-160, Ja-Je 89.

SMITH, Kidder. Ch'eng I—The Pattern of Heaven-and-Earth (in Serbo-Croatian). Filozof Istraz, 29(2), 523-526, 1989.

Whereas Shun's article takes "the source of morality" as a question of "how do we arrive at knowledge of truth," this article instead inquires into Ch'eng I's view of "what makes something good." According to Ch'eng, the answer is li, the unitary pattern of heaven-and-earth, by virtue of which each thing attains its proper moral function. The student's task is to see the pattern as it exists in every situation he encounters and to act in accordance with it. Since his nature (hsing) is also this li, Ch'eng's system very deliberately conflates issues of human nature, morality and their source. In principle Chu Hsi agrees with all this. But because he is more pessimistic, systematic and comprehensive than Ch'eng, he foregrounds distinctions within the world such as the difficulties attending moral cultivation. It is therefore easier for his disciples to interpret "the pattern of heaven-and-earth" as "the principles of heaven-and-earth," as models and rules, constant and unchanging. Ch'eng I, however, insists that "The constant tao lies only in changing in accordance with the times."

SMITH, Laurence D. Models, Mechanisms, and Explanation in Behavior Theory: The Case of Hull Versus Spence. Behavior Phil, 18(1), 1-18, Spr-Sum 90.

The neobehaviorist Clark L Hull and his disciple Kenneth Spence shared in common many views on the nature of science and the role of theories in psychology. However, a telling exchange in their correspondence of the early 1940s reveals a disagreement over the nature of intervening variables in behavior theory. Spence urged Hull to abandon his interpretations of intervening variables in terms of physiological models in favor of positivistic, purely mathematical interpretations that conflicted with Hull's mechanistic explanatory aims and ontological commitment to materialism. This dispute is set against the background of similar disputes in physics, and the origins of Hull's and Spence's divergent views on theoretical explanation are described.

SMITH, M B E. Should Lawyers Listen to Philosophers about Legal Ethics? Law Phil, 9(1), 67-93, F 90.

In the recent spate of philosophers' writing on legal ethics, most contend that lawyers' professional role exposes them to great risk of moral wrongdoing; and some even conclude that the role's demands inevitably corrupt lawyers' characters. In assessing their arguments, I take up three questions: (1) whether philosophers' training and experience given them authority to scold lawyers; (2) whether anything substantive has emerged in the scolding that lawyers are morally bound to take to heart; and (3) whether lawyers ought to defer to philosophers' claims about moral principle. I return a negative answer to each.

SMITH, Nicholas D and BRICKHOUSE, Thomas C. A Matter of Life and Death in Socratic Philosophy. Ancient Phil, 9 (2), 155-165, Fall 89.

In this paper we argue that Socrates believes that everyone is better off dead. This belief, we argue, does not contradict either his famous profession of ignorance of what happens at death nor his conviction that certain lives are, and certain lives are not, worth living. Finally, we show why Socrates thinks that all human beings have reason to make themselves as good as possible while they are alive in spite of the fact that a better condition awaits them at death.

SMITH, Nicholas D and BRICKHOUSE, Thomas C. *Socrates on Trial.* Princeton, Princeton Univ Pr, 1989

This book attempts to provide an exhaustive historical and philosophical commentary on Plato's *Apology of Socrates*. Contrary to the received interpretation of the *Apology*, the authors argue that Plato's Socrates makes a sincere attempt to persuade the jury of his innocence.

SMITH, Nicholas D and MILLER JR, Fred D. *Thought Probes: Philosophy Through Science Fiction Literature (Second Edition).* Englewood Cliffs, Prentice-Hall, 1989

SMITH, Nicholas D and BRICKHOUSE, Thomas C. What Makes Socrates a Good Man? J Hist Phil, 28(2), 169-179, Ap 90.

This paper attempts to explain why Socrates is convinced that he is a good person even through he lacks the moral virtue he says he has spent his life seeking.

SMITH, P Christopher. The Ethical Dimension of Gadamer's Hermeneutical Theory. Res Phenomenol, 18, 75-91, 1988.

SMITH, Patricia G. Contemplating Failure: The Importance of Unconscious Omission. Phil Stud, 59(2), 159-176, Je 90.

The distinction between conscious and unconscious omission is significant, but generally overlooked, leaving an entire class—negligent omissions—with no adequate framework of analysis. In this paper I offer an analysis which can accommodate the distinction. Conscious omission can be represented by terms such as 'refrain'. Unconscious omission is entirely a matter of contextual framework, largely community standards, which I analyze as "reasonable expectations." Lastly, I consider some questions raised by the analysis.

SMITH, Patricia G. Recklessness, Omission, and Responsibility: Some Reflections on the Moral Significance of Causation. S J Phil, 27(4), 569-583, Wint 89.

Is causation decisive in assessing blameworthiness? No. Even if causation is relevant to ascribing responsibility, it does not follow that it is always decisive. Many factors are relevant, and some are more powerful than causation. I show that an important argument by Rachels is limited in its ability to assess the relevance of causation because of the presence of the powerful factors of intentional harm and special positive duty. So I use the context of recklessness, particularly reckless omissions. This context shows that failing to prevent harm, where culpable, is like recklessness or negligence, and not equivalent to intentional harm.

SMITH, Patricia. The Duty to Rescue and the Slippery Slope Problem. Soc Theor Pract, 16(1), 19-41, Spr 90.

The two questions addressed in this paper are (1) is there a universal positive duty to provide emergency aid which is appropriate to legal enforcement; (2) if so, can it be circumscribed by defining criteria sufficient to avoid a slippery slope to oppressive positive obligations? I argue that the answer is yes to both questions, and then spend the bulk of the paper formulating defining criteria. Finally, I argue that this duty holds even in the presence of others equally able to help.

SMITH, Peter. "Human Persons" in *The Person and the Human Mind: Issues in Ancient and Modern Philosophy*, GILL, Christopher (ed), 61-81. New York, Clarendon/Oxford Pr, 1989.

SMITH, Philip. Transient Natures at the Edges of Life: A Thomistic Exploration. Thomist, 54(2), 191-227, Ap 90.

SMITH, Plínio Junqueira. O ceticismo naturalista de David Hume. Manuscrito, 13(1), 69-86, Ap 90.

The interpretations usually held about Hume divide his works into two parts, one negative, one positive. The first would constitute his skepticism and the second, his naturalism. The only question that would remain to us is to examine how far he succeeded in reconciling these two parts. Our purpose is to show that this distinction between skepticism and naturalism is not present in the works of Hume. These have an argumentative unity, at the same time negative and positive. His solution to the problem of causality, the instinct of habit, is a skeptical and naturalist solution; and his moderated skepticism combines the radical, skeptical argument with the argument derived from the force of nature and avoids both sorts of dogmatism. To these stable, unitary doctrines we gave the name 'naturalist skepticism'.

SMITH, Quentin. Bruce Wilshire and the Dilemma of Nontheistic Existentialism. Phil Today, 33(4), 358-373, Wint 89.

It is argued that Wilshire's *Role Playing and Identity* suggests a dilemma about authentic existence that has not been appreciated by the German and French existentialists. The dilemma is that authentic existence requires a relation to God (as Marcel and Jaspers maintain) but that God cannot be known to exist (as Sartre and the early Heidegger maintain). The consequence is that authentic existence is impossible, *contra* the conclusions of the above-mentioned thinkers. In this paper, this dilemma is analyzed and a nontheistic solution is offered.

SMITH, Quentin. The Co-Reporting Theory of Tensed and Tenseless Sentences. Phil Quart, 40(159), 213-221, Ap 90.

The new tenseless theory of time, discussed by Smart, Mellor, Oaklander and Beer, holds that tensed utterances are untranslatable by tenseless utterances, but that tensed utterances nonetheless do not ascribe presentness, pastness or futurity. This paper examines Michelle Beer's unique version of the new tenseless theory and concludes her central argument is unsound. This paper argues that Beer's premises, along with certain semantic facts about tensed utterances, entail that these utterances not only report the earlier/simultaneity relations among events but also their properties of presentness, pastness or futurity.

SMITH, Quentin. A Natural Explanation of the Existence and Laws of Our Universe. Austl J Phil, 68(1), 22-43, Mr 90.

It is usually assumed that the only possible explanations of the existence and laws of our universe are theistic (that God created the universe for the sake of realizing goodness). This paper argues that this assumption is mistaken since a certain type of naturalistic explanation is also possible, viz., an inductive-statistical explanation whose premises state certain natural regularities. It is possible that the big bang singularity of our universe formed from a black hole in another unverse U1, such that a certain percentage of U1's black holes become big bang singularities of other universes. It is possible that U1's origin is in turn explained in terms of a black hole in another universe U2, U2 in terms of U3, and so on infinitely.

SMITH, Quentin. Temporal Indexicals. Erkenntnis, 32(1), 5-25, Ja 90.

The prevalent theory of temporal indexicals (words such as "now" and "yesterday") is the *direct reference* theory, espoused by Kaplan, Perry, Wettstein and others. I argue against this theory that temporal indexicals *both* refer directly to times and ascribe a temporal property or relation to the directly designated time. Further, I argue that the direct reference theory is incompatible with the relational theory of time (according to which times are sets of events) and entails the absolutist theory of time (according to which times are event-independent moments).

SMITH, Ralph A. The Changing Image of Art Education: Theoretical Antecedents of Discipline-Based Art Education. J Aes Educ, 21(2), 3-34, Sum 87.

SMITH, Richard and GRIFFITHS, Morwenna. Standing Alone: Dependence, Independence and Interdependence in the Practice of Education. J Phil Educ, 23(2), 283-293, Wint 89.

Independence—or autonomy—is usually seen as a desirable state of human beings, and, therefore, as a central aim of education. This paper explores the idea that the largely unreflective approval given to independence not only conceals a number of mutually incoherent concepts of independence, but also prevents us from understanding the nature of dependence. We argue that there is a need to reconceptualise both independence (and autonomy) and dependence and that this is an essential part of the educational project of enabling human beings to flourish.

SMITH, Timothy H. An Alternative View of Professionalization. Proc Phil Educ, 45, 119-124, 1989.

SMITH, Tony. Analytical Marxism and Marx's Systematic Dialectical Theory. Man World, 23(3), 321-343, Jl 90.

Marx's *Capital* can be read as a dialectical derivation of a set of socio-economic categories. Jon Elster, a leading analytical Marxist, has presented seven criticisms of this sort of theory. I answer each of these criticisms in detail, defending Marx's appropriation of Hegel's dialectical method. I also consider briefly the criticisms of dialectical method raised by John Roemer, another prominent analytical Marxist.

SMITH, Tony. The Debate Regarding Dialectical Logic in Marx's Economic Writings. Int Phil Quart, 30(3), 289-298, S 90.

In one reading of Marx's economic writings he presented a systematic ordering of economic categories following a dialectical method taken from Hegel's *Logic*. In another interpretation the stages of his theory present a logic of historical development. I argue that the latter reading cannot account for crucial parts of *Capital*. It is also the case that a systematic theory of economic categories is better able to attain three of Marx's central objectives: the overcoming of illusions, the assertion of theoretical claims of necessity, and the theoretical grounding of revolutionary politics.

SMOKLER, Howard. Are Theories of Rationality Empirically Testable? Synthese, 82(2), 297-306, F 90.

Since rationality is a normative ideal, it is difficult to see how a theory of rationality might be subjected to empirical evaluation. This paper explores various aspects of this problem in relation to the work of L J Cohen, Amos Tversky and Daviel Kahneman, Ellery Eells, Isaac Levi, and Henry Kyburg. Special consideration is given to its significance for testing systems of inductive logic.

SMOLENAARS, Anton J and VAN HEERDEN, Jaap. On Traits as Dispositions: An Alleged Truism. J Theor Soc Behav, 19(3), 297-309, S 89.

Traits are usually treated as dispositions. The notion of disposition, however, is not unproblematic. One problem is the demonstration that any given set of behaviour confirms what is meant by the dispositional term. Another is that not all dispositions require the same type of manifestation of behaviour. It is argued that in fact a disposition belongs to one of four categories according to the way it is empirically justified. It appears that traits belong exclusively to one category. From a theoretical point of view, dispositions lead to a need to spell out the intrinsic properties that they represent. Spelling out intrinsic properties is a normal way to enrich a theory and to increase its explanatory power. Although this seems a proper strategy for the development of a unifying trait theory, serious doubts are raised about whether traits can really be treated as dispositions. It is likely that the advancement of trait theory is best served by an abandonment of the assumption that traits are dispositional at all.

SMOOK, Roger. Logical and Extralogical Constants. Inform Log, 10(3), 195-198, Fall 88.

Some logicians propose to define logical consequence on the basis of a distinction between 'logical' and 'extralogical' constants. In the first and second parts of this paper I will criticize two recent examples of this approach due respectively to Rolf George and David Hitchcock. In the third part I will distinguish in my own way between logical and extralogical constants. The distinction, as understood by me, *presupposes* logical consequence hence cannot, on pain of vicious circularity, be appealed to in *defining* it. However the distinction can be enlisted without circularity in the definition of 'formal' logical consequence. My approach is motivated by the belief that for purposes of ordinary, everyday logic (what is usually called informal logic or critical thinking) there is no other useful or relevant way of drawing the distinction.

SMYTH, Richard. Peirce's Concept of Knowledge in 1868. Trans Peirce Soc, 26(3), 309-323, Sum 90.

SMYTH, Richard. "Voyage to Syracuse: Adams—Schiller—Emerson" in *Mind, Value and Culture: Essays in Honor of E M Adams*, WEISSBORD, David (ed), 89-113. Atascadero, Ridgeview, 1989.

SNOOK, Ivan. Contexts and Essences: Indoctrination Revisited. Educ Phil Theor, 21(1), 62-65, 1989.

The paper uses the indoctrination debate of fifteen years ago to reflect on the nature of philosophy of education. Replying to Neiman (*Educ. Phil. Theor.* 1988), who argued for a new contextualist approach to indoctrination, the writer argues that Neiman himself is sufficiently aware of context. The method of linguistic analysis criticised by Neiman has now been largely superseded in Australasia where it was never as influential as in Britain.

SNOW, Dale. The Role of the Unconscious in Schelling's System of Transcendental Idealism. Ideal Stud, 19(3), 231-250, S 89.

SNOWDON, P F. "On Formulating Materialism and Dualism" in *Cause, Mind, and Reality: Essays Honoring C B Martin*, HEIL, John (ed), 137-159. Norwell, Kluwer, 1989.

The issue is how to formulate materialism (and dualism). It is proposed that the fundamental claim of materialism is that physical states of affairs exhaustively constitute our psychological states. Constitution is clarified, compared with supervenience, and the proposal that the constitution claims are metaphysically necessary endorsed. Clarifications of the notion of the physical are also proposed, and some views of Stroud criticised. It emerges, given these resources, that there are basically *two* antidualist views, one reductive and the other not, between which we must choose. A formulation of dualism using the notion of constitution is also proposed.

SNOWDON, P F. "Persons, Animals, and Ourselves" in *The Person and the Human Mind: Issues in Ancient and Modern Philosophy*, GILL, Christopher (ed), 83-107. New York, Clarendon/Oxford Pr, 1989.

The question discussed is whether we are identical with animals. Most theories of personal identity, e.g., Lockean, Neo-Lockean and brain-centred theories, deny that we are. They give strong support to the denial by citing apparently possible cases where we survive outside the animal, e.g., brain-transplants. But arguments can be given for saying we *are* animals. This amounts to an antinomy. It is suggested that a theory be adopted according to which *we* are animals, without endorsing the thesis (suggested by Wiggins) that persons in general must be animals. Some implications of this are explored.

SNOWDON, Paul. The Objects of Perceptual Experience—I. Aris Soc, SUPP 64, 121-150, 1990.

The purpose is to analyse the concept of perceiving an object. The orthodox view is that it is to be analysed as requiring the object to cause an experience. It is argued that this is unsupported because it overlooks the possibility of a disjunctive theory of experience. That idea is clarified, and it is argued that the causal theory does not respect the manifest character of perception. An alternative analysis is proposed treating, e.g., seeing as a relation enabling a certain sort of demonstrative thought contact with the object to obtain.

SNOY, Bernard. Ethical Issues in International Lending. J Bus Ethics, 8(8), 635-639, Ag 89.

This article deals with the ethical issues faced by commercial banks, governments and international financial institutions in their international lending activities. Such issues include not only to whom and for what purpose such lending takes place but also the more delicate questions of the relations between sovereign lending and economic management, as well of lending to sovereign countries embroiled in situations of conflict. It leads to the ethical issues raised by the present international debt crisis: co-responsibility, burden-sharing, role of the international organisations. Finally, capital flight out of developing countries is studied as a special case.

SNYDER, Daniel T. Surplus Evil. Phil Quart, 40(158), 78-86, Ja 90.

Rowe's 1979 analysis of his fawn example assumes that preventable pointless evil is incompatible with God. But evil freely chosen can be preventable, pointless yet justifiably permitted. Rowe's reply to free-will theodicists implies that only evil not resulting from freedom is incompatible with God. Not so. Freedom requires that a range of real possibilities be open to one. An evil is surplus if there is no range R of real possibilities to which it belongs such that R's value outweighs its disvalue and the good which gives R value requires R. Many freely wrought evils are apparently surplus.

SNYDER, Douglas M. Complementarity and the Relation Between Psychological and Neurophysiological Phenomena. J Mind Behav, 11(2), 219-223, Spr 90.

SOARE, R I and AMBOS-SPIES, Klaus. The Recursively Enumerable Degrees have Infinitely Many One-Types. Annals Pure Applied Log, 44(1-2), 1-23, O 89.

SOBEL, Jordan Howard. Kent Bach on Good Arguments. Can J Phil, 19(3), 447-453, S 89.

Distinctions are drawn: An argument to show that some action is rational in a situation may be good in that (i) it does show that, (ii) doing the action would probably lead to a maximum payoff, or (iii) a disposition to such arguments in such situations would probably lead to maximum payoffs. It is observed that causal decision theorists claim their arguments are always good in the first two senses, but not possibly not always in the third. That good (ii) is consistent with not-good (iii) is related to ideas of D H Hodgson and David Gauthier.

SOBEL, Jordan Howard. Maximization, stability of Decision, and Actions in Accordance with Reason. Phil Sci, 57(1), 60-77, Mr 90.

Rational actions reflect beliefs and preferences in certain orderly ways. The problem of theory is to explain which beliefs and preferences are relevant to the rationality of particular actions, and exactly how they are relevant. One distinction of interest here is between an agent's beliefs and preferences *just before* an action's time, and his beliefs and preferences *at* its time. Theorists do not agree about the times of beliefs and desires that are relevant to the rationality of action. Another distinction is between actions that would, in one sense or another, *maximize* expected utilities given relevant beliefs and

desires, and actions, decisions for which would, in one sense or another, be *stable*. There is disagreement about the relevance of these things to the rationality of actions. Here, in the first part below, several possible positions on these issues are explained and compared. In the second part, I contrast perspectives on these issues, and comment on arguments that might be brought against the position I favor. In the third part, I restate and elaborate on this position.

SOBER, Elliott. Is the Theory of Natural Selection Unprincipled? A Reply to Shimony. Biol Phil, 4(3), 275-279, Jl 89.

Abner Shimony argues that the theory of natural selection, unlike the theory of heredity and variation, fails to contain a "first principle." I critically discuss Shimony's line of reasoning.

SOBER, Elliott. The Poverty of Pluralism: A Reply to Sterelny and Kitcher. J Phil, 87(3), 151-158, Mr 90.

Can all natural selection be represented as a competition between selfish genes? The thesis of *genic selectionism* says yes; Sterelny and Kitcher defend this idea, which stems from the work of George Williams and Richard Dawkins. I argue that genic selectionism, as they construe it, is either trivial or false. It *misrepresents* the biological issues that have been central to the units of selection problem.

SOBER, Elliott. What is Psychological Egoism? Behaviorism, 17(2), 89-102, Fall 89.

Egoism and altruism need not be characterized as *single factor* theories of motivation, according to which there is a single kind of preference (self-regarding or other-regarding) that moves people to action. Rather, each asserts a claim of *causal primacy*—a claim as to which sort of preference is the more powerful influence on behavior. This paper shows that this idea of causal primacy can be clarified in a standard scientific way. This formulation explains why many observed behaviors fail to discriminate between the hypothesis that the agent is altruistic and the hypotheses that the agent is egoistic. A distinction between altruistic motivation and altruistic action is then drawn, from which it follows that it is an open question how often altruists behave altruistically.

SOBLE, Alan (ed). *Eros, Agape and Philia: Readings in the Philosophy of Love*. New York, Paragon House, 1989

SOBOTKA, Milan. Two Theories of Ownership in German Classical Philosophy (in Czechoslovakian). Filozof Cas, 38(1-2), 188-201, 1990.

In this article the author compares Hegel's concept of ownership with Fichte's. The latter defines ownership as an "exclusive right to act and not to things," Hegel as "a person's external existence" or as "an outer sphere of the freedom of a person." According to Hegel, modern civil society is a society of owners who are equal as "persons," i.e., in general terms of their humanity. "What and how much I own" is, on the other hand, "legal fortuity." For his part, Fichte strove to constitute a system whereby each member would be guaranteed the right to pursue activities in the chosen branch and to adequate remuneration. There are signs, however, that the integration of the demand for freedom with that for equality tends to lead to a system of planned economy whose result is the individual's dependence on the plan. Having formulated his theory of ownership as an objectivization of the individual's will, Hegel actually bypassed these consequences. (edited)

SOBREVILLA, David. Las críticas de Leopoldo Zea a Augusto Salazar Bondy. Rev Latin De Filosof, 16(1), 25-45, Mr 90.

In his book, *La Filosofía Americana como Filosofía sin más* (1969) and in his lecture (1973) and later articles (1974), Leopoldo Zea has criticized the approach of *Existe una filosofía de nuestra América?* (1968) exposed by Augusto Salazar Bondi. In this paper those critiques are thoroughly examined. Many of them are considered to be incorrect, since Zea does not take into account the precise meaning given by Salazar to some key words, such as "originality" and "authenticity."

SÖDER, Hans-Peter. National Socialism in the History of Being? A Discussion of Some Aspects of the Recent "L'Affaire Heidegger". Phil Today, 33(2), 109-120, Sum 89.

Difficult about the Heidegger controversy are its hidden agendas. First, there is his own philosophical stance to National Socialism rooted in his theory of danger and elucidated through Hölderlin. Second there is the history of the Heidegger reception which shows how he figures into different discourses in the changing political landscape. Third, Heidegger is used to explain various "negative" aspects of German intellectual history. My paper highlights each strain and then asks if he has measured up to his own philosophy by looking at (1) more closely.

SODERBERG, William. "Do Living Will Statutes Embody a Claim Right or a Mere Privilege to Refuse Life-Prolonging Treatment?" in *Advance Directives in Medicine*, HACKLER, Chris (ed), 75-84. New York, Praeger, 1989.

Features of the right to refuse life-prolonging treatment granted in current state laws on living wills can best be accounted for by classifying the right as a mere privilege in some states and as close to a claim right in others. The right to refuse life-prolonging treatment is not regarded as a specification of the general right to refuse medical treatment by drafters of the current living-will laws.

SOFO, Frank. Revival of Reasoning in the Modern Age by Developing a Classroom Community of Inquiry Within College Students. Thinking, 6(3), 25-29, 1986.

SOFONEA, Liviu. The Areopagus of Values. Phil Log, 32(3-4), 271-279, Jl-D 88.

SOFONEA, Liviu and BENKÖ, Iosif. Die "platonische körper": Geometrische, physische, historische und epistemologische aspekte. Phil Log, 32(1-2), 63-73, Ja-Je 88.

SOGOLO, G S. Options in African Philosophy. Philosophy, 65(251), 39-52, Ja 90.

Practitioners of an emerging African philosophy are in a dilemma, torn between the demand for philosophical professionalism and the call for social relevance. The crisis has resulted in two major orientations, *professional philosophy* and *ethno-philosophy*. The first direction is assailed by analytic/technical handicap due mainly to lack of relevant supportive experience. At best, works along this option reduce to mere reformulation of familiar Western philosophical problems in African idiom, without offering any solution. The second option comprises unargued descriptive accounts of African world-views and therefore lacking in philosophical merit. A third option is proposed which (1) has social relevance because it is mounted on materials peculiar to African thought and (2) is philosophically tenable because it moves beyond the descriptive to the plane of analytic rigour.

SOKOLOWSKI, Robert. The Question of Being. Rev Metaph, 43(4), 707-716, Je 90.

The question of being is distinctive in not excluding anything from its scope. Deviations occur when one part of being (rest, matter, spirit, the actual, etc.) is taken as the whole. The dominant deviation now is to equate being with the scientifically objective, with the apparent taken as nonbeing. The correction to this would involve a better analysis of the being of appearance. One contribution toward this is proposed in the article: the study of mathematical mediation between matter and form. Examples are given from biology (with DNA codes as the mediation), economics and political life, and aesthetic structures.

SOLBAKKEN, Elisabeth (trans) and JÄHNIG, Dieter. On Schelling's Philosophy of Nature. Ideal Stud, 19(3), 222-230, S 89.

The author argues that Schelling's philosophy is best understood as a transformation within idealism. By turning his attention to nature, Schelling discovered a realm that is rationally ordered—but inexplicably so. Nature displays an after-the-fact ideality. Comprehended as self-production, nature is the proper home of free beings and not, as for Fichte, a barrier for them to overcome. Schelling's recognition of the autonomous structure of nature leads to the ethical imperative that is prominent in his middle period, that is, the imperative to sacrifice the narrow standpoint of the self in order to acknowledge and affirm otherness.

SOLL, Ivan. On Desire and its Discontents. Ratio, 2(2), 159-184, D 89.

This essay critically examines some arguments central to the traditional philosophical position, that the life in which the pursuit and satisfaction of desires occupies a central place is doomed to frustration and failure. Contrary to this, I maintain that a life in which desires are satisfied temporarily, only to recur again and again, is arguably better than one not beset by wants and desires. I consider two German philosophers of the 19th century, Hegel and Schopenhauer, who argued for the inevitable frustration of all desire, but from radically divergent conceptions of what constitutes the satisfaction of desire.

SOLOMON, Graham. Some Sources for Hume's Opening Remarks to *Treatise* I IV III. Hume Stud, 16(1), 57-66, Ap 90.

Hume remarks that "Several moralists have recommended it as an excellent method of becoming acquainted with our own hearts, and knowing our progress in virtue, to recollect our dreams in a morning, and examine them with the same rigour that we would our most serious and deliberate actions." I suggest that Hume is referring to John Byrom and Zeno of Citium.

SOLOMON, Graham. What Became of Russell's "Relation-Arithmetic"? Russell, 9(2), 168-173, Wint 89-90.

SOLOMON, Miriam. Apriority and Metajustification in BonJour's "Structure of Empirical Knowledge". Phil Phenomenol Res, 50(4), 767-777, Je 90.

BonJour argues that, despite current interest in externalist approaches, and despite difficulties with simple coherentist views, there are reasons to take

internalism, and his own more complex coherence view, seriously. On this view the need for an a priori metajustification of empirical knowledge arises. It is argued that there are difficulties with the metajustification that BonJour gives, which all stem from issues of apriority. This internal difficulty with BonJour's views serves to challenge the views about justification and knowledge that lead him to espouse the position. The paper concludes with a brief indication of the epistemological options remaining.

SOLOMON, Miriam. On Putnam's Argument for the Inconsistency of Relativism. S J Phil, 28(2), 213-220, Sum 90.

Since Plato's *Theaetetus*, it has been argued that relativism with regard to rationality is an incoherent or obviously flawed doctrine. In "Why Reason Can't be Naturalized," Putnam offers a new argument for the incoherence of relativism. This argument is examined and it is shown that it, as well as traditional arguments against relativism, fail. In conclusion, it is suggested that naturalized approaches to the debate over relativism will be more fruitful.

SOLOMON, Robert C. *Introducing Philosophy: A Text with Integrated Readings (Fourth Edition)*. San Diego, Harcourt Brace Jov, 1989

SOLOMON, Robert C. *Love: Emotion, Myth, and Metaphor*. Buffalo, Prometheus, 1990

This is the delayed paperback edition of the 1981 Doubleday book. It includes the entire original text "The Origins of Romantic Love," "What Do I Want When I Want You," "The Importance of Being Honest," "Beyond Sex and Gender," and "Towards a Theory of Love," together with a new preface and my "*Symposium* Revisited."

SOLOMON, Robert C. Nietzsche and Nehamas's Nietzsche. Int Stud Phil, 21(2), 55-61, 1989.

I have nothing but admiration for Alexander Nehamas's very original book on Nietzsche, and in particular his ingenious thesis concerning Nietzsche's "life as literature." I do question, however, the validity of the argument that Nietzsche becomes, through his works, his own creation, and I worry about the purely "aesthetic" quality of Nietzsche's moral philosophy. He was, after all, a philosopher whose goal was nothing less than to change history.

SOLOV'EV, V S. The Historical Tasks of Philosophy. Soviet Stud Phil, 28(3), 17-30, Wint 89-90.

SOLOVAY, Robert M. Injecting Inconsistencies Into Models of PA. Annals Pure Applied Log, 44(1-2), 101-132, O 89.

SOMERVILLE, James. Collingwood's Logic of Question and Answer. Monist, 72(4), 526-541, O 89.

Collingwood's mistaken identification, in *Speculum Mentis*, of questioning with supposal is based on their nonassertiveness. His later view that every statement is made in answer to a question, with its consequence that people can sometimes ask a question without being aware that they are, is shown to be gratuitous, brought about partly by his failure to distinguish questions from problems. His notion of a question being the right one to ask provides the bipolarity he holds is essential to thought; but whether a question is the right one to ask cannot be determined until it has been correctly answered.

SOMERVILLE, John. "Themes in Marxism" in *Reading Philosophy for the Twenty-First Century*, MC LEAN, George F (ed), 315-330. Lanham, Univ Pr of America, 1989.

SOMERVILLE, John. War, Omnicide and Sanity: The Lesson of the Cuban Missile Crisis. Dialec Hum, 16(2), 37-46, Spr 89.

SOMMERMEIER, Rolf (trans) and GUARDA, Victor. How Does the Child Benefit from "Philosophy for Children"? Thinking, 6(3), 30-31, 1986.

SOMMERMEIER, Rolf (trans) and CAMHY, Daniela G. How Does the Child Benefit from "Philosophy for Children"? Thinking, 6(3), 32, 1986.

SOMMERS, Christina Hoff. "Philosophers Against the Family" in *Person to Person*, GRAHAM, George (ed), 82-105. Philadelphia, Temple Univ Pr, 1989.

SOMMERS, Fred. Predication in the Logic of Terms. Notre Dame J Form Log, 31(1), 106-126, Wint 90.

SONDEREGGER, Erwin. "Denn das Sein oder Nichtsein ist kein Merkmal der Sache". Z Phil Forsch, 43(3), 489-508, Jl-S 89.

Aristotle opens *De Interpretatione* with some norms, which shall rule philosophical discourse. One of these norms—of greatest importance for the discourse about being—is the distinction between affirmation and meaning of a proposition. No verb, not even to be, will by itself state that really is, what it means. This new conception of the text is primarily grounded on observation of ordinary Greek speech: "a verb uttered just by itself" means the verb without the intention to affirm what it means, not the verb without a subject noun. Some glances at Plato and Kant (ontological argument) conclude the article.

SONGXING, Su and GUOZHENG, Lin. Integrative Thinking Is the Essential Characteristic of Creative Thinking. Chin Stud Phil, 21(2), 74-93, Wint 89-90.

At home and abroad, in recent theoretical studies concerning the nature of creative thought, the theory of divergent thinking has played an extremely important role. This essay proposes some disagreements with this traditional opinion; for we believe that it is integrative thinking that is the essence of creative thought. Our reason is this: Creative thought is realized through cognitive activity, and cognitive activity is always, continuously, in a process of combination. (edited)

SOO, Francis. China and Modernization: Past and Present. Stud Soviet Tho, 38(1), 3-54, Jl 89.

SOONTIENS, Frans. Biologie en Teleologie. Kennis Methode, 14(2), 166-182, 1990.

In this paper I argue that there is a fundamental misunderstanding about the concept of teleology (and chance) in Western thinking, as the consequence of a confusion of teleology with the 'argument of design'. The conclusions being reached are (1) teleology implies neither intentionality nor predictability as is often supposed by biologists; (2) teleology in evolution implies neither a *straightforward* progress to a *predetermined* goal, nor the exclusion of change; (3) the attempts of Ruse, Hull and Mayr to justify the scientific character of teleological explanation in biology are not adequate, because of their use of implicitly teleological concepts; (4) natural teleology is a requisite for an ecological ethics.

SOONTIËNS, Frans. Evolutie, teleologie en toeval. Alg Ned Tijdschr Wijs, 82(1), 1-14, Ja 90.

In this paper it is argued that there is a fundamental misunderstanding about the role of teleology and chance in evolutionary biology. This misunderstanding is the result of a historical development of the concept of teleology, in which the original Aristotelian concept was confused with a Christian, scholastic interpretation. This misunderstanding about the concept of teleology also results in a confusion about the concept of change and its role in evolution. The article ends with the question about the role of anthropomorphism in science. It seems that anthropomorphism is an unavoidable component of the explanation of nature.

SOPER, Kate. Feminism, Humanism and Postmodernism. Rad Phil, 55, 11-17, Sum 90.

SORELL, Tom. Hobbes's Persuasive Civil Science. Phil Quart, 40(160), 342-351, Jl 90.

Hobbes's argument for the inevitability of war in the state of nature rests on assumptions that would have struck his contemporaries, as well as later readers, as controversial. Despite that, he can be said to have a persuasive set of precepts for avoiding war—a persuasive civil science. The idea of a persuasive civil science seems unavailable to Hobbes in view of his tendency to exclude rhetoric from the sciences. But his concept of counsel may solve this problem.

SORELL, Tom. Hobbes's UnAristotelian Political Rhetoric. Phil Rhet, 23(2), 96-108, 1990.

Hobbes's departures from Aristotle's rhetoric may be understood in relation to two Aristotelian theses about the subject matter of rhetoric: (i) that rhetoric is the counterpart of dialectic; (ii) that rhetoric is an offshoot of ethical and political studies. Hobbes rejects Aristotle's grounds for distinguishing rhetoric from dialectic, and he has an interpretation of (ii) that is quite un-Aristotelian.

SORELL, Tom. "The Science in Hobbes's Politics" in *Perspectives on Thomas Hobbes*, ROGERS, G A J (ed), 67-80. New York, Clarendon/Oxford Pr, 1988.

Hobbes's civil science has less in common with scientific social studies than with certain applications of moral philosophy to rhetoric. It is not a science because of its connections to empirical psychology or physics.

SORENSEN, Roy A. Vagueness Implies Cognitivism. Amer Phil Quart, 27(1), 1-14, Ja 90.

My thesis is that all vague predicates are cognitive predicates. More precisely, there is a hidden inconsistency between the observation that a predicate is vague and the view that its predications are never true or false. Since noncognitivism is usually directed against predicates that are widely agreed to be vague, 'Vagueness implies cognitivism' should be bad news for most noncognitivists. For the sake of concreteness, the focus will be on ethical cognitivism but my comments apply equally well to cognitivism about aesthetics, politics, science, and indeed any field making essential use of vague predicates. Here's the basic argument: (1) If a predicate is vague, it has borderline cases. (2) If a predicate has borderline cases, it has clear cases. (3) Applying a predicate to a clear case yields a truth or a falsehood. (4) If a predicate sometimes yields a predication with a truth value, then it is

a cognitive predicate. (5) Therefore, all vague predicates are cognitive predicates.

SORENSON, John H. Ethics and Technology in Medicine: An Introduction. Theor Med, 11(2), 81-86, Je 90.

SORRENTINO, Sergio. Esperienza, rivelazione, simbolo: Discussione intorno alla ragione teologica. Sapienza, 43(2), 181-196, Ap-Je 90.

The article goes to a thoroughly critical review of the way by which the authors of *L'evidenza e la fede* (Milano 1988) suggest to overcome the separation philosophy and theology are undergoing in the context of Italian culture. From strictly philosophical standpoint are questioned these main points: (1) to think about critical explanation in terms of inference of the unconditioned; (2) to involve two different concepts of truth: as ultimate concern, and as "totality of conditions and of their *Grund*"; (3) to conceive theology like monolithic field, without granting any pluralism. The often occurring oxymoros of symbolic evidence denotes the aim we are referred to: to conceive faith like self-intelligible knowing; in the line of absolute truth, untenable for modern critical reason.

SOSA, Ernest. "Equilibrium in Coherence?" in *The Current State of the Coherence Theory*, BENDER, John W (ed), 242-250. Norwell, Kluwer, 1989.

The method of reflective equilibrium aims to maximize two factors in one's beliefs: harmonious coherence, and plausibility of content. Analytic philosophy has long paid deference to these factors, for instance in its ubiquitous use of the counterexample, which attacks a principle as *incoherent with the plausible* (by one's lights). A severe critique of this tradition has recently appeared, and it shall be my main objective here to assess its merits. An appendix shall apply our results to issues of moral relativism and rationality.

SOSA, Ernest. Surviving Matters. Nous, 24(2), 297-322, Ap 90.

The Paradox: Even though life L is optimal (in all dimensions), and even though if it were extended L would continue to be optimal, it does not follow that it is best to extend it, *even for the subject whose life L is*. What is the argument? Section II defends a certain view of the nature of persons and personal identity, and Section III then argues for the Paradox on that basis, and reflects on its philosophical implications and on the options it presents.

SOSA, Ernesto. Más allá del escepticismo, a nuestro leal saber y entender. Analisis Filosof, 8(2), 97-139, N 88.

This is a "state of the art" paper on some central issues of epistemology (commissioned by *Mind* for its series of such yearly papers). It focuses on (A) skepticism, and (B) theories of justification, and in each case focuses on work either published or widely discussed within the last five years. Part A discusses the work on skepticism of Robert Nozick, Barry Stroud, and P F Strawson. Part B discusses (1) reliabilism, and recent writings of Alvin Goldman; (2) coherentism, and recent writings of Keith Lehrer; (3) internalist foundationalism, and recent work by Roderick Chisholm, Earl Conee and Richard Feldman, and John Pollock; and (4) virtue perspectivism, and recent work by Alvin Plantinga and by the author.

SOSA, Ernesto and ZIRIÓN, Antonio (trans). Sobre la identidad, la existencia y la constitución de las personas y otros seres. Rev Latin De Filosof, 15(3), 259-292, N 89.

SOSA, Nicolás M. La conciencia ecológica como conciencia moral. Dialogo Filosof, 6(1), 40-51, Ja-Ap 90.

SOULEZ, Antonia. "Wittgenstein and Phenomenology or: Two Languages for One Wittgenstein" in *Wittgenstein in Focus—Im Brennpunkt: Wittgenstein*, MC GUINNESS, Brian (ed), 157-183. Amsterdam, Rodopi, 1989.

There is a Wittgensteinian use of "phenomenology" which is the grammar of the a priori possibility of facts, in contradistinction to a hermeneutical conception of language in the spirit of German phenomenology. Not only does Wittgenstein refer, as early as 1929, to such a "language" as opposed to a Husserlian "doctrine" of intuiting the phenomenal a priori, but he keeps using the term in a positive manner which does not allow us to declare that from the Tractatus to the early thirties Wittgenstein shifted from a kind of ineffabilist phenomenalism to physicalism. Rather the author of the *Philosophical Remarks* aims at freeing "phenomenology" from the earlier assumption of an atomistic basis providing a "primary language." Yet, Wittgenstein says in the same period that there is and there is not any confrontation with the given. Two ways of speaking about the connection between language and reality according to what is to be understood by "verifying" a sentence make Wittgenstein remain the same from one conception to the other.

SOULEZ, Philippe and BERGSON, Henri. La correspondance Bergson/Lévy-Bruhl—Lettres à L Lévy-Bruhl (1889-1932). Rev Phil Fr, 179(4), 481-492, O-D 89.

SOULEZ, Philippe. Généalogie ou archéologie de la psychanalyse? Rev Int Phil, 43(171), 571-577, 1989.

L'auteur critique le livre de Michel Henry *Généalogie de la psychanalyse* Paris 1985. Il lui reproche de ne pas distinguer la problématique de l'inconscient de celle de l'*inconscience*. Seule cette dernière notion concerne réellement la métaphysique de la représentation. L'inconscient de Bergson et celui de Freud n'ont pas la même fonction. Est inconscient ce qui échappe à toute introspection et ne revient que par *transfert*. Concernant la référence de Freud à Schopenhauer on ne peut pas négliger son aspect *stratégique*. Jung est un successeur plus authentique de Schopenhauer.

SOUQUE, Jean-Pascal. The Historical Epistemology of Gaston Bachelard and its Relevance to Science Education. Thinking, 6(4), 8-13, 1986.

SPAEMANN, Robert and ARMSTRONG, T J (trans). *Basic Moral Concepts*. New York, Routledge, 1989

The book is an introduction into ethical thinking dealing with the problems of the relativity of good and evil, justice and self-interest, responsibility, utilitarianism, and the role of the individual in society. It points out and discusses the philosophical importance of upbringing and education. Ethical relativism is criticized on the basis of the concept of the unconditional reflecting the tradition of ethical thinking from Plato and Aristotle to Kant and modern theories of value. The concluding chapter characterizes equanimity as the attitude to what we cannot change.

SPAEMANN, Robert. "Which Experiences Teach Us to Understand the World? Observations on the Paradigm of Whitehead's Cosmology" in *Whitehead's Metaphysics of Creativity*, RAPP, Friedrich (ed), 152-164. Albany, SUNY Pr, 1990.

SPANG, Kurt. Etica y estética en la literatura. Anu Filosof, 21(1), 171-181, 1988.

SPARIOSU, Mihai I. *Dionysus Reborn: Play and the Aesthetic Dimension in Modern Philosophical and Scientific Discourse*. Ithaca, Cornell Univ Pr, 1989

SPARSHOTT, Francis. "Aesthetics of Music: Limits and Grounds" in *What is Music?*, ALPERSON, Philip A , 33-98. New York, Haven, 1987.

This was meant as a general survey of topics to introduce a volume on the aesthetics of music. Leading themes include the following: (1) the cognitive, conative and affective aspects of music are so distinct as almost to generate three kinds of music rather than to constitute three aspects of a single practice; (2) every musical use of music material is music, but not every such use falls within the domain of art; (3) music making is sometimes more like communing with oneself or others than like composing and performing works for appreciation.

SPARSHOTT, Francis. Contexts of Dance. J Aes Educ, 24(1), 73-87, Spr 90.

The article discusses discursively what Hirsch's "cultural literary" requires literate Americans to know about dance. This includes the difference between artistic dance, social dance, and ethnic dance. The first requires an understanding of what art is and how concerts function; the second requires knowing who should do what when; the third calls for a schematized cultural map of the world. The article notes the degree of ignorance in this area found acceptable by Hirsch's colleagues, and ends by considering the relation between official education and what people need to know.

SPECHT, E K and ERICHSEN, N. "Die Empfindungen des Anderen: Ein Disput zwischen Cartesianer und Wittgensteinianer" in *Wittgenstein in Focus—Im Brennpunkt: Wittgenstein*, MC GUINNESS, Brian (ed), 305-334. Amsterdam, Rodopi, 1989.

Cartesianer und Wittgensteinianer diskutieren über die logischen Grundlagen der Empfindungssprache. Mit einem Gedankenexperiment suggeriert der Cartesianer die Notwendigkeit, "private Objekte" anzunehmen. Die Wittgensteinianer deckt die "grammatische Täuschung" auf, der der Cartesianer dabei unterliegt. Nun sucht dieser, seinen Ansatz zu retten, indem er die Empfindungen des anderen als "theoretische Entitäten" (etwa im Rahmen der Hirnphysiologie) konstruiert: Neucartesianismus. Bestimmte empirische Befunde könnten ihn dabei aber in das Dilemma bringen, entweder seine Theorie oder seine "natürliche Einstellung" zum anderen Menschen aufzugeben. Allerdings bleibt auch dem Wittgensteinianer ein ähnliches Dilemma letztlich nicht erspart.

SPECHT, Rainer. "Whitehead's Interpretation of Locke in *Process and Reality*" in *Whitehead's Metaphysics of Creativity*, RAPP, Friedrich (ed), 34-56. Albany, SUNY Pr, 1990.

SPECTOR, Horacio. Una nota sobre universalizabilidad. Analisis Filosof, 8(2), 161-170, N 88.

The author analyses Hare's different attempts to characterize and justify universalizability as a necessary feature of moral language. This task is conducted in three stages, each corresponding to a different conception of

universalizability advanced in Hare's works, called in this paper *generality*, *universality* and *subjunctivity* The author argues that the thesis of the generality of value-judgments and the thesis of the supervenience of value-terms are substantially different presentations of the same tenet. Although this tenet can be rendered plausible by appealing to the function of moral language, the author claims that Hare's arguments for justifying the universality and, especially, the subjunctivity of moral judgments are unsuccessful. This failure involves—the author contends—a victory for those skeptics who reject the possibility of finding "formal" features of moral language linked to substantive moral ideas, like impartiality.

SPEES, Emil Ray. *Higher Education: An Arena of Conflicting Philosophies*. New York, Lang, 1989

Higher education issues are more than just political. The way in which decisions are made is based on one's philosophy of what is needed or desired for our society. This is the case for the large state university, the private university, and the small liberal arts college. The interplay among the type of the institution; the roles of faculty, students, and administrators; federal and state regulations; and the curriculum determines the very nature of academic freedom. This interplay is educational, political, and philosophical.

SPELLMAN, Lynne. Specimens of Natural Kinds and the Apparent Inconsistency of *Metaphysics Zeta*. Ancient Phil, 9 (1), 49-65, Spr 89.

In this paper I argue that Aristotelian substances—that is, those entities which are supposed to be first in knowledge, definition and time—are specimens of natural kinds, where a specimen is distinguished from the sensible object with which it is numerically the same (but not identical) by virtue of having only those properties which are essential for membership in that kind.

SPENCER, Judith. Towards an Histrionic Aesthetics: Diderot's *Paradoxes* as Pre-Text for Romantic Irony. Man Nature, 7, 149-158, 1988.

SPICKARD, James V. Worldview, Beliefs and Society: Mary Douglas' Contribution to the Study of Human Ideas on Ultimate Reality and Meaning. Ultim Real Mean, 13(2), 109-121, Je 90.

Sociologists and theologians have long claimed that religious views of reality are perspectival: what one believes to be true depends on one's social location. Over the last two decades, anthropologist Mary Douglas has developed a theory that specifies the connection between such beliefs and social life. She argues that people's experiences in different kinds of institutions make different beliefs plausible, and that those beliefs reinforce the institutions in which they arise. Though beset by certain problems, Douglas's theory accounts for the patterns one finds cross-culturally in people's concepts of ultimate reality.

SPICKER, Stuart F and RATZAN, Richard M. *Ars Medicina et Conditio Humana* Edmund D Pellegrino, MD, on His 70th Birthday. J Med Phil, 15(3), 327-341, Je 90.

In his writings, Edmund Pellegrino analyzes four deficiencies in the humanity of those who fall ill: the loss of (1) freedom of action, (2) freedom to make rational choices, (3) freedom from the power of others, and (4) a sense of the integrity of the self. Since Pellegrino's analysis and commitment to virtue-based ethics preceded much of the attention later given by philosophers to the importance of the moral principle of *autonomy* (in contrast to *beneficence*) in patient care, it is helpful to trace the source of his commitment to virtue-based ethics and his account of freedom to Aristotle's analysis of the human soul, as an entelechy of an intact and healthy living organism that, unimpeded by illness, moves itself to act, to actualize its intellectual potential in the form of making rational choices, and to free itself from the power of others by remaining independent and without need of continuous assistance, while at the same time retaining the integrity of a unified self that can act, think, and choose for itself autonomously.

SPICKER, Stuart F. Overview of the Reports of the Ethics Committee of the American Fertility Society. J Med Phil, 14(5), 477-480, O 89.

SPIEGELBERG, Herbert. Response to Papers. J Brit Soc Phenomenol, 21(1), 80-81, Ja 90.

SPIERLING, Volker. El pesimismo de Schopenhauer: sobre la diferencia entre voluntad y cosa en sí. Rev Filosof (Spain), 2, 53-63, 1989.

SPIERS, Herbert R. AIDS and Civil Disobedience. Hastings Center Rep, 19(6), 34-35, N-D 89.

SPIKES, Michael. E D Hirsch's Misreading of Saul Kripke. Phil Lit, 14(1), 85-91, Ap 90.

E D Hirsch maintains in "Meaning and Significance Reinterpreted" that the theory of linguistic meaning he proposes in this essay is in essential respects consonant with Saul Kripke's notion of rigid designation and thus that Kripke's view might be used to confirm and reinforce that theory. I argue that Hirsch has misread Kripke. Kripke's position is not in accord with Hirsch's in the respects Hirsch believes; therefore, Kripke cannot be useful to Hirsch in the ways Hirsch thinks he can.

SPITZER, Alan B. John Dewey, the "Trial" of Leon Trotsky and the Search for Historical Truth. Hist Theor, 29(1), 16-37, F 90.

SPITZLEY, Thomas and CRAIG, Edward (trans). Davidson and Hare on Evaluations. Ratio, 3(1), 48-63, Je 90.

This paper has two parts. In the first I discuss Davidson's view of evaluations: what is the meaning and function of *prima facie*, 'all-things-considered' and 'sans phrase' judgments, and what is the role of his principle of continence? In the (shorter) second part I try to exploit Davidson's insights to elucidate the position of Hare: what is it to treat moral judgment as a *prima facie*, or as a critical moral judgment, and when *is* a moral judgment a critical moral judgment?

SPLITTER, Laurance J. Educational Reform Through Philosophy for Children. Thinking, 7(2), 32-39, 1987.

In the first part of the paper, I discuss factors which inhibit the growth of critical, reasoning and inquiry skills in the context of the familiar school and classroom environment. I then suggest as a way forward the transformation of classrooms into communities of inquiry. Finally, I examine the connection between thinking and inquiry on the one hand, and the discipline of philosophy on the other, arguing that the entire curriculum would be enriched by incorporating philosophy and its attendant subdisciplines (logic, epistemology, ethics, philosophy of science, etc.) into the daily fabric of school life.

SPLITTER, Laurance J. On Thinking for Yourself. Thinking, 6(3), 23-24, 1986.

Originally given as an address to a high school "speech night," my concern in this short paper is to urge school leavers to have the courage and the wherewithal to think for themselves, in the face of external pressures from the peer group, TV and fashion, society generally, the family, etc. Thinking for oneself means, among other things, weighing up relevant considerations objectively, challenging assumptions and assertions, and speaking up for what we believe—while being open to rational modification of our beliefs.

SPLITTER, Laurance J. Philosophy for Children: An Important Curriculum Innovation. Thinking, 5(4), 47-53, 1985.

In this paper I argue that Philosophy for Children can play a vital role in building the thinking and inquiry skills of primary school children, most of whom are both interested in and capable of thinking about philosophical ideas. I maintain that there is a connection between the failure to teach these skills and such problems as alienation and low self-esteem among students.

SPÖRK, Ingrid. Subject as the Intersect Between Semiotics and Symbol (in Serbo-Croatian). Filozof Istraz, 30(3), 1043-1052, 1989.

Julia Kristevas Subjektkonzept geht aus von der Lacan'schen "Umstürzung" des cartesianischen Subjekts, die er in seiner Freud-Lektüre deutlich macht. Das Subjekt ist dezentriert, d.h., es "ist" nicht dort, wo es denkt, es erfährt sich immer nur nachträglich, wird zum Ort eines Mangels. Die Einheit des Individuums, die das Kleinkind in einem ersten Blick in den Spiegel konstituiert, ist imaginär, immer schon über das Andere gebildet. Dem Spiegelstadium, das mit dem Spracherwerb (Fort-Da-Spiel) und ödipalen Konstellationen die Einsetzung des Symbolischen garantiert geht jedoch eine Phase voraus, die Kristeva in Zusammenhang mit den Arbeiten Melanie Kleins akzentuiert und als das Semiotische bezeichnet. Der semiotische Prozess liegt noch vor jeder Konstituierung eines Sems, ist Bahnung, Strukturierung, Spur, die semiotische Chora (Platon, Timaios) wird als kinetische Funktionalität im signifikanten Prozess verstanden, die der symbolischen Thesis entgegensteht und Signifikanz ermöglicht. Der Schnittpunkt von Semiotischem und Symbolischem ist der Ort des Subjekts, an dem es sich als Prozess konstituiert.

SPRIGGE, T L S. A J Ayer: An Appreciation. Utilitas, 2(1), 1-11, My 90.

This article is an appreciation of the philosophy of A J Ayer. Ayer played an important role in launching the new edition of the works of Jeremy Bentham and so this piece pays special attention to his stance on moral and social issues and to his place in the liberal empiricist tradition to which Bentham and Mill belonged. However, it also gives a general survey of the character of his philosophy as answering almost precisely to William James's conception of a tough-minded as opposed to tender-minded philosopher.

SPRIGGE, T L S. Personal and Impersonal Identity: A Reply to Oderberg. Mind, 98(392), 605-610, O 89.

The Hegelians claimed that genuine identity must be identity in difference. A=A is vacuous, and A=B is false, so a genuine identity truth must be of the form of AX=AY which implies a difference between its terms together with identity. This is usually thought superseded by Frege's treatment, but this only applies to identity truths of an 'ignorance removing' type, not those of

permanent interest strictly as identity truths. These latter are best understood, in a somewhat Hegelian way, as concerning universals, abstract or concrete. This position is defended here against D S Oderberg's criticism of Sprigge's earlier statement of it.

SPRIGGE, T L S. Utilitarianism and Respect for Human Life. Utilitas, 1(1), 1-21, My 89.

A common recent criticism of utilitarianism is that it does not imply the wrongness of taking human life in circumstances in which most people think it wicked. It is replied that human happiness cannot be great unless people feel about people in ways inseparable from a strong reluctance to kill them. If the importance for human life of such feelings is realized, utilitarianism will be seen not to have these consequences. Rather it explains why such killing is wrong on grounds in line with common moral thought. It may, however, help deal with cases widely considered problematic.

SPRIGGE, Timothy. Santayana and Panpsychism. Bull Santayana Soc, 2, 1-8, Fall 84.

George Santayana was an explicit opponent of panpsychism, for example, that advocated by Whitehead. However, an important place is played in his ontology by natural moments, certain ultimate events with a specially intensive unity in which essences are actualised all at once rather than in the more dispersed way in which larger units actualise them. It is difficult not to think that these are not conceived on the model of states of consciousness. If so, there is an unwitting hint of panpsychism in Santayana's system.

SPRINGBORG, Patricia. Arendt, Republicanism and Patriarchalism. Hist Polit Thought, 10(3), 499-523, Autumn 89.

Hannah Arendt represents the German branch of the "classical republican tradition," mythologizing the polis, its heroic and agonistic virtues, compared with monarchy and its mundane concerns. It is an achievement of this genre to claim for the great landed monarchies of Northern Europe the true legacy of Athens, while regimes of the near East, the original locale of city-republics, are "orientalized," or deemed "despotic." This mythology is seriously challenged by modern classical and Near Eastern scholarship. It is also open to challenge as denigrating the need-based structures of everyday life, which blur the lines between "public" and "private."

SROUR, G and MAGIDOR, M and ROSENTHAL, J W and RUBIN, M. Some Highly Undecidable Lattices. Annals Pure Applied Log, 46(1), 41-63, Ja 90.

SROUR, Gabriel. The Notion of Independence in Categories of Algebraic Structures, Part III: Equational Classes. Annals Pure Applied Log, 47(3), 269-294, Je 90.

STACK, George J. From Lange to Nietzsche: A Response to a Troika of Critics. Int Stud Phil, 21(2), 113-124, 1989.

This response to three critical commentaries on my book, *Lange and Nietzsche* (de Gruyter, 1983), deals with a defense of the value of tracing the influence of F A Lange's *History of Materialism* on Nietzsche and the impact that Lange's psychologistic, post-Kantian epistemology had on Nietzsche's skeptical phenomenalism (*contra* Breazeale). Wilcox's claim that Lange was sympathetic with Christianity is countered by indicating his interest in a post-Christian "new religion" and the elitist ideals of others he discusses. That eternal recurrence is meant cosmologically (Wilcox) is criticized by referring to texts expressing its subjective meaning. Seigfried's claim that Nietzsche's "artists' metaphysics" puts him in opposition to Lange is countered by indicating that it depended on Lange's "standpoint of the ideal" and *his* concern to find room for an aesthetic ideal in face of the "exact sciences."

STACK, George J. Riemann's Geometry and Eternal Recurrence as Cosmological Hypothesis: A Reply. Int Stud Phil, 21(2), 37-40, 1989.

In response to A Moles's argument that Nietzsche's theory of eternal recurrence is linked to Riemann's concept of space, it is contended that even though Moles is correct in seeing the influence of scientific theories (such as those of Mayer, Zöllner and Boscovich) on Nietzsche, Riemann's theory of curved space does not support eternal recurrence. Riemann's geometry was designed to be compatible with the empirical geometry of the earth's surface and refers to a material base. Moles may be right that the general idea of curved space played a role in Nietzsche's theory, but there is no direct relation between Riemann's geodesic theory and eternal recurrence.

STAHL, August. "Ein paar Seiten Schopenhauer"—überlegungen zu Rilkes Schopenhauer—Lektüre und deren Folgen (2 Teil). Schopenhauer Jahr, 70, 174-188, 1989.

STAHL, Gérold. Categorías aristotélicas y categorías intensionales. Theoria (Spain), 4(11), 461-469, F-My 89.

Did Aristotle, with his categories, classify only expressions or also something extralinguistic? In the second case his classification seems to be not exclusive, at least if the usual universes of discourse are considered.

However, if we use certain enlarged universes, which may have more than one individual for each individual of the usual universes, we may construct exclusive general classifications that approach the Aristotelian categories. The latter ones should then be considered second order classes that classify classes of (extralinguistic) individuals. If the individuals are taken from one of the indicated enlarged universes, we can obtain the exclusivity that we do not have for the usual universes.

STAICU, Constantin I. Fermat's Last Theorem, a General Dimensional Analysis Problem. Phil Log, 32(1-2), 163-170, Ja-Je 88.

STALEY, Kevin M. Thomas Aquinas and Contemporary Ethics of Virtue. Mod Sch, 66(4), 285-300, My 89.

STALLEY, R F. The Responsibility of Socrates. Polis, 6(1), 2-30, 1986.

In Plato's *Apology* Socrates appears to believe that no one willingly does wrong. This has been thought inconsistent with the belief that human beings are responsible for their acts. But Socrates evidently takes very seriously the idea that we are all responsible and may be called to account for what we do. We can make sense of Socrates' position only if we recognise that the knowledge that is virtue is not a techne. It is, rather, a matter of having a right conception of values. Vice results when or the conception of the good is distorted by appetites and desires.

STALNAKER, Robert. Mental Content and Linguistic Form. Phil Stud, 58(1-2), 129-146, Ja-F 90.

STALNAKER, Robert. On Grandy on Grice. J Phil, 86(10), 526-527, O 89.

STAMBAUGH, Joan. *Impermanence is Buddha-nature: Dōgen's Understanding of Temporality*. Honolulu, Univ of Hawaii Pr, 1990.

STAMMLER, Heinrich A. "Friedrich Nietzsche und Theodor Trajanov" in *Agora: Zu Ehren von Rudolph Berlinger*, BERLINGER, Rudolph (and other eds), 203-215. Amsterdam, Rodopi, 1988.

STAMPE, Dennis W. Desires as Reasons—Discussion Notes on Fred Dretske's "Explaining Behavior: Reasons in a World of Causes". Phil Phenomenol Res, 50(4), 787-793, Je 90.

STANCIULESCU, Traian Dinorel. La psychologie consonantiste et la créativité (in Romanian). Rev Filosof (Romania), 36(3), 286-293, My-Je 89.

STANCIULESCU, Traian-Dinorel. La hiérarchie des systèmes—à la frontière de l'intuition et de la certitude. Phil Log, 32(1-2), 59-61, Ja-Je 88.

STANDAERT, Nicolas. Science, Philosophy and Religion in the Seventeenth Century Encounter Between China and the West (in Serbo-Croatian). Filozof Istraz, 29(2), 449-465, 1989.

The relative success of Western sciences, introduced by the Jesuits in 17th century China, was partly due to the rediscovery of 'concrete studies' by the Chinese scholars. The notions 'investigation of things and fathoming principles' (gewu qiongli) from Chinese philosophy were central in this process. These expressions also form a key in the analysis of the evolution of the contacts between Jesuits and Chinese intellectuals at that time.

STANKEVICH, Vladimir (trans) and DUBROVSKY, David. *The Problem of the Ideal*. Chicago, Progress, 1988.

STANKIEWICZ, Mary Ann. Beauty in Design and Pictures: Idealism and Aesthetic Education. J Aes Educ, 21(4), 63-76, Wint 87.

This historical study documents specific links between Hegelian Idealism, William Torrey Harris, and American art education, via the work of Henry Turner Bailey, Massachusetts drawing supervisor. An analysis of Harris's aesthetics argues that Harris assimilated Hegelian aesthetic thought, then applied it to practical problems of education. As a popularizer of art in schooling, Bailey distorted Idealist belief, sometimes reversing or sentimentalizing it. This study illustrates how aesthetic theories may become part of taken-for-granted assumptions in art education.

STANLEY, Marjorie T. Ethical Perspectives on the Foreign Direct Investment Decision. J Bus Ethics, 9(1), 1-10, Ja 90.

This paper examines the foreign direct investment decision from an ethical perspective, and considers the moral agency involved in such decisions, with emphasis upon the corporate decision maker. Historical capital allocation models once regarded as both financially and ethically normative are shown to be deficient in today's environment. Work of modern western philosophical and theological ethicists is included in analyses of the applicability of selected ethical approaches or metaphors to multinational foreign direct investment decisions and the corporate manager's role and responsibility as corporate decision maker and moral agent. The ethical perspectives reviewed can serve as an aid to the individual manager's determination of what constitutes a responsible exercise of decision-making power.

STAPP, Henry P. "Quantum Nonlocality and the Description of Nature" in *Philosophical Consequences of Quantum Theory: Reflections on Bell's Theorem*, CUSHING, James T (ed), 154-174. Notre Dame, Univ Notre Dame Pr, 1989.

Various ontologies compatible with the predictions of quantum theory are described, and it is noted that all of them, whether deterministic or indeterministic, involve either (1) a branching of the full universe into separate parallel components only one of which can be perceived by anyone, or (2) faster-than-light influences. Attempts to prove that any ontology that reproduces the predictions of quantum theory must exhibit either this many-worlds feature or a failure of the no-faster-than-light condition are reviewed and further developed.

STARK, W Richard. A Logic for Distributed Processes. Z Math Log, 35(4), 311-320, 1989.

This paper was inspired by the problem of finding a procedure for (1) deciding whether or not a given function can be computed in a given synchronous bit-processing architecture, and if computable (2) constructing a program which will compute the function. We present a logic which brings these problems within the range of an automatic theorem prover. Given an architecture A, the decision procedure is expressed in language LDP_A (for Logic for Distributed Processes) by axioms which describe the notion of computation in the given architecture. A completeness theorem proves the LDP_A's axioms characterize computability in A.

STARRETT, Shari Neller. Nietzsche: Women and Relationships of Strength. SW Phil Rev, 6(1), 73-79, Ja 90.

STATEN, John C. *Conscience and the Reality of God: An Essay on the Experiential Foundations of Religious Knowledge*. Hawthorne, de Gruyter, 1989

The main thesis of this work is "that in 'conscience' we have a meaningful experiential locus for the knowledge of God." While delving into theological concerns pertaining to the reality of God and the meaning of God the author draws upon the insights of Bultmann, Ebeling and Heidegger. (staff)

STATMAN, Daniel and SAGI, Avi. What Could Be the Meaning of the Idea that Morality Depends on Religion? (in Hebrew). Iyyun, 38(2), 103-136, Ap 89.

The purpose of this paper is to ask whether the claim that God determines morality can be explained in a reasonable way. This claim has been the central thesis of divine command theories of morality, theories that have been the object of much criticism. We seek to argue that before any of the traditional objections to these theories can be considered, a fundamental issue must be faced, namely, that it is very difficult to give a reasonable and coherent account of the basic intuition underlying divine command theories of morality, the intuition that God makes it the case that some things are right while others are wrong. The article examines in detail the following interpretations of the relation between God and morality mentioned above: that God determines morality by an act of legislation; that God's command is the (only) justification for moral judgments; that God's command is the meaning of morality; that God's command is identical with morality. We show that each of these interpretations faces serious difficulties, which are a challenge to any philosopher who wishes to defend a divine command morality.

STAVI, Jonathan and NADEL, Mark. On Models of the Elementary Theory of {Z,+,1}. J Sym Log, 55(1), 1-20, Mr 90.

STEAD, Christopher. Augustine's Philosophy of Being. Philosophy, 25, 71-84, 89 Supp.

STEAD, Jean Garner and STEAD, W Edward and WORRELL, Dan L. An Integrative Model for Understanding and Managing Ethical Behavior in Business Organizations. J Bus Ethics, 9(3), 233-242, Mr 90.

Managing ethical behavior is one of the most pervasive and complex problems facing business organizations today. Employees' decisions to behave ethically or unethically are influenced by a myriad of individual and situational factors. Background, personality, decision history, managerial philosophy, and reinforcement are but a few of the factors which have been identified by researchers as determinants of employees' behavior when faced with ethical dilemmas. The literature related to ethical behavior is reviewed in this article, and a model for understanding ethical behavior in business organizations is proposed. It is concluded that managing ethics in business organizations requires that managers engage in a concentrated effort which involves espousing ethics, behaving ethically, developing screening mechanisms, providing ethical training, creating ethics units and reinforcing ethical behavior.

STEAD, W Edward and WORRELL, Dan L and STEAD, Jean Garner. An Integrative Model for Understanding and Managing Ethical Behavior in Business Organizations. J Bus Ethics, 9(3), 233-242, Mr 90.

Managing ethical behavior is one of the most pervasive and complex problems facing business organizations today. Employees' decisions to behave ethically or unethically are influenced by a myriad of individual and situational factors. Background, personality, decision history, managerial philosophy, and reinforcement are but a few of the factors which have been identified by researchers as determinants of employees' behavior when faced with ethical dilemmas. The literature related to ethical behavior is reviewed in this article, and a model for understanding ethical behavior in business organizations is proposed. It is concluded that managing ethics in business organizations requires that managers engage in a concentrated effort which involves espousing ethics, behaving ethically, developing screening mechanisms, providing ethical training, creating ethics units and reinforcing ethical behavior.

STECKER, Robert. The Boundaries of Art. Brit J Aes, 30(3), 266-272, Jl 90.

I suggest that recent attempts to define art fall into two classes: functionalist and relational. Typical of the former are attempts to define art in terms of aesthetic experience. Most prominent of the latter are institutional definitions. However, a more promising relational definition is a historical one recently proposed by J Levinson. After criticizing Levinson's proposal (and a similar one by N Carroll), I try to motivate a functional definition which avoids pitfalls of previous attempts in this class and captures the virtues of the historical approach.

STECKER, Robert. Lorand and Kant on Free and Dependent Beauty. Brit J Aes, 30(1), 71-74, Ja 90.

STEERE, Jane and DOWDALL, Terence. On Being Ethical in Unethical Places: The Dilemmas of South African Clinical Psychologists. Hastings Center Rep, 20(2), 11-15, Mr-Ap 90.

Practicing under the social and economic conditions created by apartheid, South African clinical psychologists face the task of questioning both the traditional values and the traditional social role of their profession. Dilemmas of trust, confidentiality, and professional competence highlight the limits of professional ethical codes.

STEGENGA, James A. Nuclearism and International Law. Pub Affairs Quart, 4(1), 69-80, Ja 90.

The paper first summarizes the provisions of the international law of armed conflict relevant for reaching a judgment about the legality of reliance upon nuclear weapons. Then it argues that almost any explosions of nuclear weapons would violate numerous of these provisions. Finally, deterrence threats are found to be illegal, criminally conspiratorial, and an effort is made to assign culpability.

STEGLICH, David. A God By Any Other Name.... Relig Stud, 26(1), 117-121, Mr 90.

In his book *Ethics Without God*, Kai Nielsen voices criticism of Christian thought and morality. In two of his major arguments, Nielsen contends that morality cannot be based on the Christian religion or similar theistic metaphysics and that if morality is based on God, or God's will, any 'moral decisions' are arbitrary and involve no reasoning on the part of the individual. By drawing upon the Ideal Observer Theory in ethics, I attempt to show that Nielsen's alternative 'moral decision-making' process collapses into the same ethical structure as Christian ethics and cannot present a less arbitrary system.

STEIN, Edith. La fenomenología de Husserl y la filosofía de Santo Tomás de Aquino. Dialogo Filosof, 6(2), 148-169, My-Ag 90.

La autora ensaya en este artículo una confrontación entre la filosofía de Sto. Tomás y la fenomenología de Edmundo Husserl. Ambos coinciden en considerar la filosofía como ciencia estricta que trata de obtener una imagen del mundo lo más universal y fundamentada posible. En esta tarea para Santo Tomás, la fe tiene un papel fundamentador (Filosofía teocéntrica), mientras que para Husserl el punto de partida es la conciencia pura transcendental (filosofía egocéntrica). Mientras que la fenomenología trata de establecerse como ciencia de escencias para una conciencia trascendental, para Tomás a las investigaciones de esencias deben añadirse los hechos de la experiencia natural y los que aporta la fe. Finalmente, el análisis de la cuestión de la "intuición" revela nuevas coincidencias y divergencias metodológicas entre los dos autores.

STEIN, Edward. God, the Demon, and the Status of Theodicies. Amer Phil Quart, 27(2), 163-167, Ap 90.

Consider an omnipotent, omniscient, all-evil creator of the universe and an argument against its existence based on the presence of good in the world. "Demonists" can respond to such arguments with "demonodicies," arguments that the demon's existence is compatible with the good in the world. Given that there is a demonodicy isomorphic to every theodicy, the theist, in addition to establishing the possibility and consistency of God's existence with the amount of evil in the world, must further establish the existence of a *good* supernatural being rather than an *evil* one. No current version of theism gives such an argument.

STEINBOCK, A J. Totalitarianism, Homogeneity of Power, Depth: Towards a Socio-Political Ontology. Tijdschr Filosof, 51(4), 621-648, D 89.

STEINBOCK, Anthony J. Whitehead's "Theory" of Propositions. Process Stud, 18(1), 19-29, Spr 89.

STEINDL, R and KAMARYT, J. On the Connection Between Ethology and Ecology (in Czechoslovakian). Filozof Cas, 37(5), 704-715, 1989.

Ethology closely connected with ecology and genetics, is currently one of the fastest growing biological disciplines. In terms of their theoretical content and their practical implications for industry, agriculture and medicine, these sciences influence the totality of contemporary cultural and civilization transformations. The close interconnection between ecology and ethology, which in the 19th century was perceived in biological classifications in more methodological terms, has nowadays come to the fore quite forcefully, also due to its contents and due to the urgent need of finding a practical solution to burning global problems, ecological crises and the necessity of grappling with a number of adverse civilization factors. (edited)

STEINER, Mark. The Autonomy of Mathematics. Iyyun, 39(1), 101-114, Ja 90.

STEINHART, Eric. Self-Recognition and Countermemory. Phil Today, 33(4), 302-317, Wint 89.

STEINHOFF, Gordon. Putnam on "Empirical Objects". Dialectica, 43(3), 231-248, 1989.

Putnam claims that the objects we experience are "mind-dependent" and "theory-dependent." He also writes that they are "constructed within our theories." It is difficult to say what he means by these claims. I conclude that, according to Putnam, "empirical objects" do not really exist. But I attempt to show the sense in which he can be considered a realist about these objects. Putnam has adopted an idealism which allows for the correctness of realist claims within appropriate contexts. I also discuss Putnam's solution to the problem of how we manage to refer to "empirical objects." I argue that this solution, and his views concerning the nature of objects, are faced with important difficulties.

STEINHORN, Charles and TOFFALORI, Carlo. The Boolean Spectrum of an o-Minimal Theory. Notre Dame J Form Log, 30(2), 197-206, Spr 89.

We show that the number of isomorphism types of Boolean algebras of definable subsets of countable models of an o-minimal theory is either 1 or $2^{\aleph_0}$. We also show that the number of such isomorphism types is 1 if and only if no countable model of the o-minimal theory contains an infinite discretely ordered interval.

STEINHORN, Charles and SHELAH, Saharon. The Nonaxiomatizability of L($Q^2_{\aleph_1}$) By Finitely Many Schemata. Notre Dame J Form Log, 31(1), 1-13, Wint 90.

Under set-theoretic hypotheses, it is proved by Magidor and Malitz that logic with the Magidor-Malitz quantifier in the $\aleph_1$-interpretation is recursively axiomatizable. It is shown here, under no additional set-theoretic hypotheses, that this logic cannot be axiomatized by finitely many schemata.

STEININGER, H and ROTHE, Barbara. Zur Diskussion um die Einheit und Vielfalt der Interessen im Sozialismus. Deut Z Phil, 37(9), 859-862, 1989.

The chances of a society to form his present time and his future are dependent of his capacity to recognize the own situation of interests and the fields of conflicts these interests. Today it is necessary to analyse the complex and the difference of the interests and to reply to the question: either economy either social politics. The authors are getting at these questions: the economical interests in a socialist society are inseparably connected with social interests of all peoples. The unity of the multifarious interests is only possible by way of unity of innovation, effective economy and social security.

STEINKE, Horst. Hintikka and Vico: An Update on Contemporary Logic. New Vico Studies, 3, 147-155, 1985.

STEINMANN, Horst and SCHREYÖGG, Georg. Corporate Morality Called in Question: The Case of Cabora Bassa. J Bus Ethics, 8(9), 677-685, S 89.

This article presents a case study of a big German enterprise (Siemens) facing a large wave of public critique and protest activities. The public was concerned about the political circumstances surrounding the construction of the Cabora Bassa hydroelectric dam in Mozambique in which Siemens was largely involved. This study reports the escalating protest against the firm over three years (1970-1972) and the firm's responses during that period. The analysis of the case focusses on the behaviour of the firm which is interpreted in the light of the business social responsibility doctrine. The article proposes that the firm experienced a legitimation crisis and responded by reorienting its philosophy of business.

STEINMETZ, Peter. "Beobachtungen zu Ciceros philosophischem Standpunkt" in *Cicero's Knowledge of the Peripatos*, FORTENBAUGH, William W (ed), 1-22. New Brunswick, Transaction Books, 1989.

Aus Selbstzeugnissen ergibt sich, dass Cicero in seiner Jugend zunächst im Anschluss an Philo sich zur akademischen Skepsis bekannt, dann unter dem Eirfluss des Antiochus den Schritt vom prinzipiellen zum methodischen Zweifel getan hat. Diese Haltung schimmert auch in den ersten grossen theoretischen Schriften durch (De oratore, De re publica, De legibus). Erst bei der referierenden/kritischen Darstellung der griechischen Philosophie in den Jahren 45/44 hat er sich wieder zu einer gemilderten Skepsis durchgerungen.

STELLINGWERFF, J. Verburg over Dooyeweerd. Phil Reform, 55(1), 84-93, 1990.

M E Verburg wrote a valuable book on the Christian philosopher Herman Dooyeweerd (1894-1977) In his critical study Stellingwerff estimates many new data and gives his insight on the influences of A Kuyper on the anthropology of Dooyeweerd. He also discusses the effect of M Heidegger on the concept of his theory of time. And he criticizes the neglect of the importance of D H Th Vollenhoven (1892-1978), co-philosopher and brother-in-law of Dooyeweerd. He also attracts attention to the early (1931) and fundamental critic of Dooyeweerd on the Berlin school of legal philosophy, that cleared the way for the national-socialistic state of Hitler.

STEMMER, Nathan. The Acquisition of the Ostensive Lexicon: A Reply to Professor Place. Behaviorism, 17(2), 147-149, Fall 89.

The paper discusses a number of arguments raised by Professor Place against empiricist theories of language acquisition. Reasons are given which suggest that the arguments are invalid.

STEMMER, Nathan. Empiricist Versus Prototype Theories of Language Acquisition. Mind Lang, 4(3), 201-221, Autumn 89.

Several cognitivist theories use the notion of prototypical concepts (or categories or representations) in order to account for the learning of the ostensive lexicon. In this paper, one of the most complete of these theories is examined, and it appears to be affected by various problems. None of these problems affects empiricist theories of language acquisition. Moreover, the latter theories have several additional advantages, not only over the particular prototype theory that is being examined but also over those that share its basic assumptions. This suggests that empiricist theories are superior to prototype theories.

STENECK, Nicholas H and HOLLANDER, Rachelle D. Science- and Engineering-Related Ethics and Value Studies: Characteristics of an Emerging Field of Research. Sci Tech Human Values, 15(1), 84-104, Wint 90.

The National Science Foundation began a program to support research and related educational projects about the ethical and value aspects of scientific and technological research, development and its applications in the mid-1970s. This article studies and characterizes 172 projects that have been supported. It reflects on the relationship between this area of study and the larger area of studies in science, technology and society. Arguing that the intellectual and institutional dimensions of this area of study are still unclear, the article ends with some recommendations for strengthening the progress that has been made.

STENECK, Nicholas H and HOSMER, LaRue Tone. Teaching Business Ethics: The Use of Films and Videotapes. J Bus Ethics, 8(12), 929-936, D 89.

Audio-visual material is extremely useful in the teaching of business ethics, yet no bibliography of the commercially available films and videotapes seems to be available. We have prepared a formal listing, complete with titles, descriptions, sources, prices and a brief evaluation, and have explained our selection and use of this material.

STENIUS, Erik. The So-Called Semantic Concept of Truth. Acta Phil Fennica, 38, 299-313, 1985.

STEPHENSON, Wendel. Fingarette and Johnson on Retributive Punishment. J Value Inq, 24(3), 227-233, Jl 90.

This paper brings out how an expanded version of Herbert Fingarette's retributivism escapes Oliver Johnson's critique of Fingarette's stated position. It argues that it escapes it by adding to the idea of law as requirement certain further ideas: the idea that lawbreakers in general are out to benefit by lawbreaking; that it is contrary to the making of law that people should benefit by breaking it; and that punishment is the only way to make lawbreaking detrimental to lawbreakers, in accordance with the intentions of lawbreakers.

STERBA, James P (ed) and CAVALIER, Robert J (ed) and GOUINLOCK, James (ed). *Ethics in the History of Western Philosophy*. New York, St Martin's Pr, 1988

This book presents the central ideas in the moral theory of major thinkers from Plato to Rawls. An acknowledged expert on the ethical theory of each philosopher characterises these ideas as they developed out of the historical context in which they were actually formulated. The cultural and intellectual conditions that generated each philosophy are set forth, and when pertinent, the personal experience of the philosopher as well. Accordingly the interested reader as well as the professional scholar will find in this book the actual intent and meaning of the greatest moral theories in the Western tradition.

STERBA, James P. *Contemporary Ethics: Selected Readings*. Englewood Cliffs, Prentice-Hall, 1989

STERBA, James P. "Toulmin to Rawls" in *Ethics in the History of Western Philosophy*, CAVALIER, Robert J (ed), 399-420. New York, St Martin's Pr, 1988.

STERELNY, Kim and KITCHER, Philip and WATERS, C Kenneth. The Illusory Riches of Sober's Monism. J Phil, 87(3), 158-161, Mr 90.

STERN, Cindy D. On Justification Conditional Models of Linguistic Competence. Mind, 99(395), 441-445, Jl 90.

In "What Dummett Says about Truth and Linguistic Competence," Kirkham rejects justification-conditional theories of meaning. He argues appeal to knowledge of truth conditions is needed to explain behavior manifesting ability to recognize logical consequence (ambiguous between truth-based and justification-based notions) in novel instances not entirely determined by form, like a congenitally blind person's asserting 'this is colored' is a logical consequence of 'this is red' without being told. I argue that whatever would enable one to recognize truth of the latter is sufficient for truth of the former would enable her to recognize that anything that justifies the latter justifies the former.

STERN, Josef. Logical Syntax as a Key to a Secret of the *Guide of the Perplexed* (in Hebrew). Iyyun, 38(2), 137-166, Ap 89.

In the first half of this essay the author discusses Maimonides' conception of logic, the philosophical study of language, against its Al-Farabian background. Maimonides' view, which is presented in its most explicit form in his early *Treatise on the Art of Logic*, is that logic is the study of the syntax of thought, the 'inner speech' underlying human 'external speech'. The second half of this essay examines Maimonides' discussion of divine attributes and names in Chapters I:50-63 of the *Guide*. (edited)

STERN, Joseph P. Ludwig Wittgenstein: Personality and Philosophy (in Czechoslovakian). Filozof Cas, 38(1-2), 147-161, 1990.

The author, who befriended L Wittgenstein at the time of his stay in Cambridge in World War II, presents the great philosopher's human portrait but also summarizes his basic ideas which culminated in his reflections at the time of the origin of his *Philosophische Untersuchungen*. He stresses the inner continuity of his intellectual development, thus opposing all those who would like to contrast an "Austrian" Wittgenstein with an "English" one. The author shows in what way the concept, presented in *Tractatus* from the year 1921, quite naturally flows into his later concept of "linguistic games." (edited)

STERN, Laurent. Factual Constraints on Interpreting. Monist, 73(2), 205-221, Ap 90.

Some contemporary writers no longer believe that interpretations discover the meaning of words and deeds. Meaning is a product of interpreting; interpretations are constructions. Due to this change, the standards for evaluating interpretations have been raised. Three constraints on interpreting are uncontroversial: (1) an interpretation must be considered applicable by a community concerned with what is interpreted; (2) interpretations are rejected, if contradicted by facts considered relevant; (3) interpretations are offered and accepted as the best available for a given purpose. Objections to an interpretation must be supported by a better construction or by evidence of a constraint's violation.

STERN, Laurent and FEHÉR, Márta. Philosophy in the United States (A Dialogue of Laurent Stern and Márta Fehér) (in Hungarian). Magyar Filozof Szemle, 4, 508-530, 1989.

STERN, Paul. On the Relation Between Rational Autonomy and Ethical Community: Hegel's Critique of Kantian Morality. Praxis Int, 9(3), 234-248, O 89.

STERN, Robert. Pippin on Hegel. Bull Hegel Soc Gt Brit, 19, 1-4, Spr-Sum 89.

This is a review of Robert Pippin's *Hegel's Idealism*, Cambridge University Press, Cambridge, 1989.

STERN-GILLET, Suzanne. Epicurus and Friendship. Dialogue (Canada), 28(2), 275-288, 1989.

STEUP, Matthias. "BonJour's Anti-Foundationalist Argument" in *The Current State of the Coherence Theory*, BENDER, John W (ed), 188-199. Norwell, Kluwer, 1989.

In *The Structure of Empirical Knowledge*, Laurence BonJour presents a refutation of foundationalism which rests on the presupposition that metajustification is a necessary condition of first level justification: a belief B is justified for a subject A only if A believes that B has a feature f such that most beliefs that have this feature are true. If this were correct, then there could not be any basic beliefs—beliefs that do not depend for their justification on other beliefs. Hence, foundationalism, affirming that knowledge rests on a foundation of basic beliefs, would be wrong. However, BonJour's presupposition is problematic because it makes skepticism inevitable. Furthermore, because of the specific way BonJour construes his conception of metajustification, he faces the same difficulty as do proponents of reliabilism: the problem of generality. In order to handle this problem, BonJour would have either to revise his account of metajustification or to countenance epistemic principles of foundational status, which would undermine the purity of his coherentist approach to the analysis of knowledge.

STEVENS, Bernard. Les deux sources de l'herméneutique. Rev Phil Louvain, 87(76), 504-515, Ag 89.

My article is a critical study of a recent book written by Georges Gusdorf, *Les origines de l'hermeneutique*. On the one hand I want to stress that Gusdorf's study is historically enlightening as to the exegetical (biblical) and philological (alexandrine) origin of hermeneutics. But on the other hand—compared to authors such as Gadamer or Ricoeur—it lacks methodological precision.

STEVENSON, Lois. Some Methodological Problems Associated with Researching Women Entrepreneurs. J Bus Ethics, 9(4-5), 439-446, Ap-My 90.

There is a need to feminize the research on entrepreneurs—to include the experiences of women in what we know to be true about entrepreneurs and the entrepreneurial process. This paper highlights some of the most significant methodological problems in researching women's entrepreneurial experience, problems which in the past, have prevented researchers from gaining an understanding of this experience, and which continues to stand in the way of developing female perspectives. Instead of using the existing "male-based" models, new approaches are called for in incorporating women's experiences into entrepreneurship theory. This paper outlines the state of research and suggests future directions for developing research on women as entrepreneurs.

STEWARD, Helen. Identity Statements and the Necessary A Posteriori. J Phil, 87(8), 385-398, Ag 90.

STEWART, Don. Democratic Sovereignty. Dialogue (Canada), 27(4), 579-589, Wint 88.

The paper argues that sovereignty should always be determined democratically by referendum. It claims that this right is fundamental to democracy and that, far from leading to the disintegration of multicultural states, it is the foundation of good government for *all* citizens of such states.

STEWART, Donald. Human Noises. J Speculative Phil, 3(4), 243-260, 1989.

The paper argues that both Rorty and Davidson mistake the nature of (literal) language in claiming that, speaking strictly, metaphor is a species of noise rather than meaning. It claims that consistency is neither a necessary nor sufficient condition of meaning at least if consistency is defined by what passes for literal language at any given period in the history of the language. On the positive side, it argues that the distinction between metaphorical and literal language is not a fundamental feature of language.

STEWART, M A. Berkeley's Introduction Draft. Berkeley News, 11, 10-19, 1989-90.

Bertil Belfrage has published an exemplary transcription of the draft introduction to Berkeley's *Principles*, but has misread evidence for its dating. Berkeley sought consistently, in the draft and later, to rebut Locke's thesis that general ideas are particular ideas used representatively, believing that representation entails copying. In the published text, contrary to Belfrage's account, Berkeley used the signification of ideas by words as an analogy to illumine a form of representation without copying which is distinctive to the use of lines in geometry; but the general ideas involved here are not the significations of general words. Belfrage's account of Berkeley's emotive theory of meaning also requires amendment.

STEWART, Philip D (trans) and MAMARDASHVILI, M K. The Problem of Consciousness and the Philosopher's Calling. Soviet Stud Phil, 29(1), 6-26, Sum 90.

STEWART, Robert Scott. Aristotle and Pleasure. Auslegung, 16(1),

97-108, Wint 90.

STEWART, Robert Scott. The Epistemological Function of Platonic Myth. Phil Rhet, 22(4), 260-280, 1989.

STICH, Stephen P. Building Belief: Some Queries about Representation, Indication, and Function. Phil Phenomenol Res, 50(4), 801-806, Je 90.

STICH, Stephen and RAMSEY, William. Connectionism and Three Levels of Nativism. Synthese, 82(2), 177-205, F 90.

Along with the increasing popularity of connectionist language models has come a number of provocative suggestions about the challenge these models present to Chomsky's arguments for nativism. The aim of this paper is to assess these claims. We begin by reconstructing Chomsky's "argument from the poverty of the stimulus" and arguing that it is best understood as three related arguments, with increasingly strong conclusions. Next, we provide a brief introduction to connectionism and give a quick survey of recent efforts to develop networks that model various aspects of human linguistic behavior. Finally, we explore the implications of this research for Chomsky's arguments. Our claim is that the relation between connectionism and Chomsky's views on innate knowledge is more complicated than many have assumed, and that even if these models enjoy considerable success the threat they pose for linguistic nativism is small.

STICKEL, George W. The Land as a Social Being: Ethical Implications From Societal Expectations. Agr Human Values, 7(1), 33-38, Wint 90.

The question to be answered is why do different cultures respond to the land differently? The question is born in the tension between Native American and the Anglo macroculture valuing of the land. Using the philosophy of George Herbert Mead, it is argued that the land is seen as a social being, in the same way that an individual sees another person. Mead's philosophy of the development of the individual begins with the relation of the developing self and a social other. That relationship defines acts acceptable within the society. As the individual grows, according to Mead, the social other becomes generalized to include objects of the environment, such as the land. The acts toward others now become acts toward the land. As the acts toward others have value within the society, so the acts toward the land take on the same values. (edited)

STIEGLER, Bernard. Mémoires gauches. Rev Phil Fr, 180(2), 361-394, Ap-Je 90.

STIEHLER, Gottfried. Ergebnisse und Probleme der Entwicklung des historischen Materialismus. Deut Z Phil, 37(10-11), 925-935, 1989.

Die Geschichtsphilosophie in der DDR hat Erfolge erzielt, aber manches bleibt noch zu leisten. Ergebnisse liegen unter anderem auf folgenden Gebieten vor: wissenschaftlich-technische Revolution, Individuum und Gesellschaft, Gesetz und Handeln, Produktivkräfte und Produktionsverhältnisse, Krieg und Frieden. Weitere Forschungsarbeiten sind notwendig bei der Begründung des Materialismus, der Verbindung von Materialismus und Dialektik und der kritischen Funktion der Philosophie.

STILE, Alessandro. Forme estetiche e possibilità utopica in Ernst Bloch. Arch Stor Cult, 1, 219-254, 1988.

STILL, Arthur and COSTALL, Alan. Gibson's Theory of Direct Perception and the Problem of Cultural Relativism. J Theor Soc Behav, 19(4), 433-441, D 89.

James Gibson's perceptual theory was directed against the dualisms of traditional psychology. His own work, however, seems to invoke a dichotomy between individual and socialized perception. It is argued that this unresolved dualism arose from his early concern with the problem of cultural relativism and the social stereotyping of perception. In his early work, he proposed a separate realm of 'literal perception', i.e., awareness that is essentially individual and pre-social. Despite radical developments in his later theory, he continued to return to this early solution of the problem of relativism when considering the influence of language on perception.

STOCK, Wolfgang G. Georg Klaus über Kybernetik und Information. Stud Soviet Tho, 38(3), 203-236, O 89.

Zwei Diskussionen werden in der DDR für die Klärung des Verhältnisses zwischen Kybernetik und marxistisch-leninistischer Philosophie relevant. (1) die Frage nach der Stellung der Information zur Grundfrage der Philosophie lässt G Klaus gegen Norbert Wiener und Gotthard Günther argumentieren. (2) die Frage nach der Stellung und des Allgemeinheitsgrades von Kybernetik und Philosophie führt zu Auseinandersetzungen mit Karl Steinbuch und Helmar Frank. Beide Diskussionen verweisen auf die Trennung von Philosophie und Informationsforschung und auf die praktische, technische Beherrschung und Anwendung der Informatik und Informationswissenschaft.

STOESZ, David. The Means of Analysis and the Future of Liberalism: A Response to Hariman. Soc Epistem, 3(3), 261-265, Jl-S 89.

Liberals must begin to control the means of analysis if they are to counter the conservative direction in public philosophy. To do so requires the recognition of pluralism in public policy, the centrality of an American philosophy to guide policy, a nonbureaucratic structure for policy analysis, and a postpositivist content of analysis. A radical pragmatism is the best candidate through which liberals can reassert their influence in domestic affairs.

STOHL, Johan. St Paul and Moral Responsibility. Free Inq, 10(2), 30-31, Spr 90.

In the 20th century, Saint Paul's theological and ethical "grid" continues to be the *normative filter* for the ideas and beliefs of evangelical and conservative Christians. This paper identifies specific ideas and beliefs from the Pauline legacy that challenge and undercut humanistic freedom and responsibility. Specifically the paper argues that *surrender* to the "indwelling" Christ brings about ego-displacement, leading to Sartrean "bad faith" and the abdication of moral ownership over one's own acts. The paper concludes by showing that much of the Pauline legacy is psychologically and morally irresponsible, and potentially dangerous to society.

STOKES, Geoff. "From Physics to Biology: Rationality in Popper's Conception" in *Issues in Evolutionary Epistemology*, HAHLWEG, Kai (ed), 488-509. Albany, SUNY Pr, 1989.

In Popper's early work, the epitome of rationality was a model of scientific method drawn from theoretical physics, and founded upon deductive logic. On Popper's criterion of demarcation, Darwinian evolutionary theory was unfalsifiable and thereby unscientific. Popper later adopts an evolutionary epistemology based on the natural process of evolution itself. Problem solving by trial and error becomes the model of rationality for both human and nonhuman organisms. Thus criteria for rational procedure are broader, and ethical considerations become important. By requiring natural scientists also to consider the consequences of their work, Popper indicates practical limits to the ruthless testing of bold conjectures.

STOKES, Michael. Some Pleasures of Plato, *Republic IX*. Polis, 9(1), 2-51, 1990.

The article analyses the three arguments concerning pleasure in *Republic* Book IX, establishing a closer than usual connection between them and the central Books and making other suggestions for contextual interpretation; the arguments thus gain in straightforwardness and respectability. The word commonly rendered 'intelligence' is referred to Plato's philosopher's whole intellectual achievement; by emendation false pleasures are eliminated from the first argument and pure pleasures from one awkward stretch of the second. This and the reinterpretation of a Greek 'particle' as adversative rather than progressive allow a more reasonable sequence of argument than some interpretations offer.

STOLL, Donald. Hegel and the Speech of Reconciliation. Ideal Stud, 19(2), 97-111, My 89.

STOLL, Donald. Kantian and Platonic Conceptions of Order. J Speculative Phil, 3(4), 231-242, 1989.

STOLTENBERG-HANSEN, V and TUCKER, J V. Complete Local Rings as Domains. J Sym Log, 53(2), 603-624, Je 88.

STOLTENBERG-HANSEN, Viggo and PALMGREN, Erik. Domain Interpretations of Martin-Löf's Partial Type Theory. Annals Pure Applied Log, 48(2), 135-196, Jl 90.

Partial type theory without universes is modelled in the category of effective Scott-Ershov domains, in order to give meaning to the iteration type (which makes the fixed point operator definable). We interpret families of types as continuously varying domains and elements of types as continuous functions. The intensional identity type is given a natural interpretation in terms of maximal common informational content. Finally an adequacy theorem is proved, stating that a term of partial type theory terminates (under lazy evaluation) if, and only if, its interpretation is not the least element of the domain.

STOMEO, A. Reale e complesso: osservazioni sul realismo scientifico e la storia della scienza. Il Protag, 6(9-10), 87-106, Je-D 86.

STONE, Harold (trans) and COHLER, Anne M (trans) and MILLER, Basia C (trans) and MONTESQUIEU, Charles. *The Spirit of the Laws: Charles Montesquieu*. New York, Cambridge Univ Pr, 1989.

STONE, Jim. Anselm's Proof. Phil Stud, 57(1), 79-94, S 89.

Anselm assumes that if God is possible, there is a possible being which is God. This is false. All Anselm can generate is a possible being that is God *if it is actual*. However, in *The Response*, Anselm maintains that for any x, if x is a mere possibility then, if x were actual, x would not exist necessarily. It follows that the being that is God if it is actual *is* actual. I argue that this

principle is false. God could not have been a mere possibility but a mere possibility could have been God.

STONE, Robert V and BOWMAN, Elizabeth A. "Dialectical Ethics: A First Look at Sartre's Unpublished Rome Lecture Notes" in *Inquiries into Values: The Inaugural Session of the International Society for Value Inquiry*, LEE, Sander H, 335-361. Lewiston, Mellen Pr, 1989.

STONE, Ronald H. Paul Tillich: On the Boundary between Protestantism et Marxism. Laval Theol Phil, 45(3), 393-404, O 89.

The essay traces the life-long internal dialogue between Protestantism and Marxism that shaped the thought of Paul Tillich. The paper moves from Tillich's World War I experiences of brokenness and turn to revolutionary socialism to his post-World War II rejection of the nuclear weapons of war. Even the early socialist writings of Paul Tillich were influenced by Max Weber. His major socialist work was directed against Nazism and for the mutual acceptance of socialism and religion. The understanding of humanity reflected both the convergence and divergence of Lutheran Protestantism and Marxism and they needed to learn from each other. With the dominance of Portestant categories over Marxist categories in his later work, he remained indebted to Marxist humanism and he developed insights into political ethics of enduring worth and refused to become captive to American cold-war ideology.

STORCKEN, A J A. Neutral, Stable and Pareto-Optimal Welfare Functions. Method Sci, 22(1), 23-41, 1989.

In the theory of social choice there have been various attempts to avoid the famous impossibility theorem of Arrow by relaxing the conditions in a more or less acceptable way. All these attempts yielded results with serious shortcomings. So we are still confronted with the search for 'good' relaxations to avoid Arrow's theorem. We claim that this search is far from easy and illustrate this by proving a new impossibility theorem, based on conditions which seem very acceptable.

STORHOLM, Gordon. Perceived Common Myths and Unethical Practices Among Direct Marketing Professionals. J Bus Ethics, 8(12), 975-979, D 89.

Two areas of continuing interest to direct marketing professionals are the perceived myths and unethical practices in the field. Documentation of specific cases and more abstract discussion of these two points of interest frequently appear in the direct marketing literature. Indeed, the Direct Marketing Association (DMA) has promulgated specific guidelines for ethical business practices within the industry. Up to this point, however, there has been no attempt at a systematic evaluation of the perceptions of professionals in the field. Such an evaluation of these two areas of practice would appear to beg the following questions: (1) What are the major common myths which abound in direct marketing as perceived by professionals who come into direct contact with the operations of direct marketing organizations? (2) Which of these so-called myths are most frequently mentioned? (3) What are the most commonly perceived unethical practices? (4) Which of these unethical practices are most frequently mentioned by direct marketing professionals? (5) To what extent do these perceived unethical practices coincide with the industry's own guidelines? (edited)

STOTT, Laurence J. *Essays in Philosophy and Education*. Lanham, Univ Pr of America, 1988

STRAMEL, James S. A New Verdict on the 'Jury Passage': *Theaetetus* 201A-C. Ancient Phil, 9 (1), 1-14, Spr 89.

This paper offers a new interpretation of the troublesome 'Jury Passage' where Socrates refutes the thesis that knowledge is true judgment. Plato's argument is that the juror does not know because he satisfies neither of two disjunctively necessary conditions for knowledge in this context: he was not an eyewitness and his only source of information—the litigant's persuasive testimony—cannot produce knowledge. It is shown that this interpretation reconciles Plato's use of both epistemic contrasts (teaching/persuasion and eyewitnessing/testimony), is intrinsically plausible and plausible in the mouths of the interlocutors, and is consistent with Plato's epistemology.

STRANZINGER, Rudolf. Neues zum Thema Gerechtigkeit? Conceptus, 23(59), 103-113, 1989.

This article is a critical review of three books (Jackson: *Matters of Justice*, 1986; Day: *Liberty and Justice*, 1987; and Höffe: *Politische Gerechtigkeit*, 1987) which all have not only the word "justice" in the title but also deal to a greater or lesser extent with Rawls's *A Theory of Justice*. Jackson's main objection against Rawls is that *Supererogations* are not dealt with (whereas Rawls asserts that his book includes the whole ethics). The other points are well known. Day's main critique is that we have justice as a *class of virtues* or as *one virtue out of a set of virtues*. Höffe's critical point is that Rawls and Nozick have *not given a real social contract theory*.

STRASSER, C. Rousseau, o el gobierno representativo. Rev Latin De Filosof,

16(1), 67-79, Mr 90.

STRASSER, Mark. Actual Versus Probable Utilitarianism. S J Phil, 27(4), 585-597, Wint 89.

Theorists who criticize actual consequence utilitarianism underappreciate the force of the actual consequence theorist's arguments and, further, fail to realize that many of the criticisms directed at actual consequence utilitarianism can also be directed at probable consequence utilitarianism and at many nonutilitarian systems. If indeed actual consequence utilitarianism offers an inappropriate method by which to assess the rightness and wrongness of actions, then probably consequence utilitarianism and various nonutilitarian systems suffer from the same defect and a much different kind of theory needs to be offered.

STRASSER, Mark. The Virtues of Utilitarianism. Philosophia (Israel), 20(1-2), 209-226, Jl 90.

STRAUSS, D F M. Certain Fundamental Problems and Trends of Thought in Mathematics. S Afr J Phil, 9(1), 28-42, F 90.

Both David Hilbert and Hermann Weyl—respectively representing the schools of axiomatic-formalism and intuitionism in 20th century mathematics—claim that the notion of infinity lies at the core of mathematics as such. Especially since Georg Cantor explored the mathematical use of the actual infinite in his set theory, the opposition between the potential and the actual infinite has turned out to be mathematically relevant and important. A brief survey is given of the way in which infinity functioned in Greek thought and through the history of philosophy and mathematics. In order to overcome the second foundational crisis of mathematics, Weierstrass, Cantor and Dedekind explicitly employed the actual infinite. Finally, a brief perspective is developed on the interrelations between the functional modes of number and space in order to account for the meaning of infinity in both of its primary forms—systematically preferably called the *successive* infinite and the *at once* infinite. (edited)

STRAUSS, Leo. Remarques sur *Le Livre de la connaissance* de Maïmonide. Rev Metaph Morale, 94(3), 293-308, Jl-S 89.

STRAWSON, P F. Conceptos y propiedades o Predicación y cópula. Critica, 20(59), 69-77, Ag 88.

STREMINGER, Gerhard. Religion a Threat to Morality: An Attempt to Throw Some New Light on Hume's Philosophy of Religion. Hume Stud, 15(2), 277-293, N 89.

STREMINGER, Gerhard. A Reply to Ellin's "Streminger: 'Religion a Threat to Morality'". Hume Stud, 15(2), 301-305, N 89.

STRIKE, Kenneth A. *Liberal Justice and the Marxist Critique of Education: A Study of Conflicting Research Programs*. New York, Routledge, 1989

STRIKER, Gisela. *Ataraxia*: Happiness as Tranquillity. Monist, 73(1), 97-110, Ja 90.

This article examines a conception of happiness that was popular in Hellenistic times. It argues that the term *ataraxia* probably derives from Democritus, and was used by Epicureans and Stoics to describe the psychological state of the happy person. Only the Pyrrhonists treated tranquillity as identical with happiness, and their example shows that a purely subjective conception of happiness may not be a good idea.

STRIKER, Gisela. "The Problem of the Criterion" in *Epistemology (Companions to Ancient Thought: 1)*, EVERSON, Stephen (ed), 143-160. New York, Cambridge Univ Pr, 1989.

STROHMEYER, Ingeborg and MITTELSTAEDT, Peter. Die kosmologischen Antinomien in der Kritik der reinen Vernunft und die moderne physikalische Kosmologie. Kantstudien, 81(2), 145-169, 1990.

STROLL, Avrum. What Water Is or Back to Thales. Midwest Stud Phil, 14, 258-274, 1989.

This paper challenges the Kripke/Putnam thesis that natural kinds are determined by their microstructure (chemical composition, DNA, etc.). Kripke/Putnam hold that water is identical with H_2O. But if water = H_2O, and ice = H_2O), and steam = H_2O, it follows that steam = ice which is nonsensical. What is true is that water *is composed* of H_2O, but that affirmation is not an identity statement. More generally, it is argued that one cannot determine what counts as a natural kind, such as water, without reference to the phenomenological properties of the kind (e.g., liquidity) and these cannot be inferred from the microcomposition of the kind.

STROLL, Avrum. "Wittgenstein's Nose" in *Wittgenstein in Focus—Im Brennpunkt: Wittgenstein*, MC GUINNESS, Brian (ed), 395-413. Amsterdam, Rodopi, 1989.

J J Gibson claims that one who is looking at Niagara Falls is seeing it directly, whereas one who is looking at a *picture* of Niagara Falls is seeing it indirectly or mediately. Gibson's cognitivist critics claim that all perception

is mediated and that "external objects" are never seen directly. Each side takes the debate to be a scientific issue. But following Wittgenstein's "nose" for detecting philosophical intrusions into what do not appear to be philosophical debates, the author shows how such elements play a decisive role in influencing the character of the argument. When the issue is seen from this perspective it can also be seen why both sides are mistaken in their claims.

STROMBERG, Roland N and CONKIN, Paul K. *Heritage and Challenge: The History and Theory of History*. Arlington Heights, Forum Pr, 1989

This book includes a history of historical writing by Roland Stormberg, and a series of essays on the critical philosophy of history by Paul Conkin. These essays (on definitions of history, the relation of history to the generalizing sciences, causation, objectivity, and the use of history) reflect a loosely pragmatic orientation. Conkin distinguishes historical inquiry from the social and physical sciences by differences in subject, form, and use, but not method. He defends a circumspect form of objectivity, one tied to rules or conventions, which he justifies largely by the human purposes they serve.

STRONG, Carson and ACKERMAN, Terrence F. *A Casebook of Medical Ethics*. New York, Oxford Univ Pr, 1989

STRONG, Robert A. "Winston Churchill and War in the Twentieth Century" in *Moral Reasoning and Statecraft: Essays Presented to Kenneth W Thompson*, DAVIS, Reed M (ed), 87-104. Lanham, Univ Pr of America, 1988.

The story of Winston Churchill's career as a soldier, journalist, politician, historian, and statesman is, in many ways, the story of the changing nature of warfare in this century. Churchill's responses to these changes were complicated and sometimes contradictory. He felt excitement during combat as a young man and revulsion at its aftermath. He advocated bold and brutal military ventures during war and moderate peace settlements when war was over. He promoted new technologies of destruction and doubted the ability of governments to control them. He supported rearmament in the 1930s and nuclear disarmament in the 1950s.

STRONG, Tracy B (ed) and GILLESPIE, Michael Allen (ed). *Nietzsche's New Seas: Explorations in Philosophy, Aesthetics, and Politics*. Chicago, Univ of Chicago Pr, 1989

STRONG, Tracy B (trans) and KOFMAN, Sarah. "Baubô: Theological Perversion and Fetishism" in *Nietzsche's New Seas: Explorations in Philosophy, Aesthetics, and Politics*, GILLESPIE, Michael Allen (ed), 175-202. Chicago, Univ of Chicago Pr, 1989.

Nietzsche is not only not a misogynist but in fact presents us with a profound new understanding of woman. Whereas perversion and degeneracy may seem attached to the feminine in Nietzsche's thought, Nietzsche also recognizes that seduction is the art of Dionysos. The affirmative woman, like Nietzsche's art itself, is profound in her superficiality and is a reflection of ascending life.

STRONG, Tracy B (trans) and REY, Jean-Michel. "Commentary: Toward a New Logic—Singing the Sirens' Song" in *Nietzsche's New Seas: Explorations in Philosophy, Aesthetics, and Politics*, GILLESPIE, Michael Allen (ed), 75-96. Chicago, Univ of Chicago Pr, 1989.

Nietzsche's text represents a fundamental departure from all previous metaphysical thinking. By passing into the realm of fiction it produces a world for us which is precisely the world that "philosophy" wants to censure and control. Nietzsche's writing thus both gives us a world and makes us aware of our attempts to control it: it makes us aware that we are "commenting."

STRONG, Tracy B. *The Idea of Political Theory: Reflections on the Self in Political Time and Place*. Notre Dame, Univ Notre Dame Pr, 1990

STRONG, Tracy B. "Nietzsche's Political Aesthetics" in *Nietzsche's New Seas: Explorations in Philosophy, Aesthetics, and Politics*, GILLESPIE, Michael Allen (ed), 153-174. Chicago, Univ of Chicago Pr, 1989.

Nietzsche is usually read as advocating a politics of domination. I argue that his politics is not concerned with facilitating and regulating the encounters of independent selves but with the question of what sorts of selves we could have. This is the basis of a politics of transfiguration, a politics of which Nietzsche paradoxically comes to despair in the last months of his life as he writes a series of explicitly political reflections and proclaims himself "ready to rule the world."

STRONG, V K and HOFFMAN, A N. There is Relevance in the Classroom: Analysis of Present Methods of Teaching Business Ethics. J Bus Ethics, 9(7), 603-607, Jl 90.

In 1988 the *Journal of Business Ethics* published a paper by David Mathison entitled "Business Ethics Cases and Decision Models: A Call for Relevancy in the Classroom." Mathison argued that the present methods of teaching business ethics may be inappropriate for MBA students. He believes that faculty are teaching at one decision-making level and that students are and will be functioning on another (lower) level. The purpose of this paper is to respond to Mathison's arguments and offer support for the present methods and materials used to teach Master level ethics classes. The support includes suggested class discussion ideas and assignments.

STROUD, Barry. "The Study of Human Nature and the Subjectivity of Value" in *The Tanner Lectures on Human Values, Volume X*, PETERSON, Grethe B (ed), 211-259. Salt Lake City, Univ of Utah Pr, 1989.

STROZIER, Robert M. *Saussure, Derrida, and the Metaphysics of Subjectivity*. Hawthorne, de Gruyter, 1988

This book is about the metaphysical status of the subject. It begins with an analysis of Saussure's methodology of metaphysics; it then moves to an analysis of Derrida's deconstructive methodology, both in general and as specifically focused on Saussure. (staff)

STRUB, Christian. Das Hässliche und die "Kritik der ästhetischen Urteilskraft". Kantstudien, 80(4), 416-446, 1989.

The validity of aesthetic judgments on the ugly is reconstructed analogous to that of judgments on the beautiful. This puts into a new perspective the range of Kant's analyses, the concept of "contention about taste" and the relation between the object and someone forming a pure judgment of taste.

STRUDLER, Alan. Response to Dietrich's "Computationalism". Soc Epistem, 4(2), 193-195, Ap-Je 90.

STRUEVER, Nancy S. Rhetoric and Philosophy in Vichian Inquiry. New Vico Studies, 3, 131-145, 1985.

STRUEVER, Nancy S. Vico, Foucault, and the Strategy of Intimate Investigation. New Vico Studies, 2, 41-57, 1984.

STRUMMIELLO, Giuseppina. La volontà di oblio: Per un'ermeneutica della morte. Ann Fac Lett Filosof, 31, 395-440, 1988.

STUART, J M. Obedience to Superior Orders. Int J Moral Soc Stud, 5(2), 155-174, Sum 90.

This article examines the development of the concept of individual legal accountability as it applies to the subordinate soldier in the relevant proceedings of military and international law in the twentieth century. It points out what the author considers to be the weaknesses of the defence of obedience to superior orders as it emerged from Leipzig, Nuremberg and subsequent trials and cases, compares these formulations with those of the national military law of four Western countries, and then proposes a possible solution to past inadequacies.

STUBBENS, Neil A. Naming God: Moses Maimonides and Thomas Aquinas. Thomist, 54(2), 229-267, Ap 90.

Moses Maimonides (1135-1204) and Thomas Aquinas (c. 1225-1274), two of the greatest theologians of the Jewish and Christian faiths, had much in common. Like other Christian writers, Aquinas made several criticisms of Maimonides' views on divine predication. In this article I will discuss these criticisms and evaluate them by means of a detailed exposition of Maimonides' position. I will then offer an account of Aquinas's justification of analogical predication and make some suggestions as to the role of causality in naming God.

STUBENBERG, Leopold. Divine Ideas: The Cure-All for Berkeley's Immaterialism? S J Phil, 28(2), 221-249, Sum 90.

STUCKI, Pierre-André. La compréhension en herméneutique: Un héritage de Bultmann. Laval Theol Phil, 46(1), 31-42, F 90.

Le "comprendre" joue un rôle de premier plan dans l'oeuvre de Bultmann. Nous lui consacrons le premier temps de notre réflexion, visant à montrer combien la "démythologisation" est tributaire de la phénoménologie de Husserl, plutôt que de Heidegger. Que devient alors la doctrine chrétienne? La dogmatique peut-elle se reconstituer en perspective herméneutique? La "compréhension de soi" bultmannienne est liée au message de la promesse. Celle-ci existe indéniablement dans le système de la communication; elle est le foyer de l'humanisme, dont l'homme moderne rencontre nécessairement la question, mais elle est, non moins certainement, impliquée par la vérité de la foi chrétienne.

STUHR, John J. *Classical American Philosophy: Essential Readings and Interpretative Essays*. New York, Oxford Univ Pr, 1987

STUHR, John J. On Re-Visioning Philosophy. Phil Today, 33(3), 264-274, Fall 89.

I argue for a radical redirection of the institutional practices of philosophy, and sketch some of the implications of this redirection. In doing so, I draw primarily on the pragmatist direction (especially James and Dewey)—but also on other philosophers (Nietzsche and Foucault), poets (Jeffers and

Williams), and other authors (Douglass and Merton). Specifically, I discuss possibilities for the institutional internalization of philosophical pluralism; the reconnection of institutional theory and practice; a new relation of philosophy to other disciplines; the restructuring of professionalism; and the relation of philosophy to public education and communication.

STUMP, David. Henri Poincaré's Philosophy of Science. Stud Hist Phil Sci, 20(3), 335-363, S 89.

STUMP, Eleonore S. Faith and Goodness. Philosophy, 25, 167-191, 89 Supp.

Current work in philosophy of religion on the subject of faith has tended to consider such issues as whether beliefs held on faith are rational or whether belief in God may be properly basic. Such work has been useful in drawing our attention to certain issues in the epistemology of religion, but it has also left unanswered some longstanding perplexities about faith. I look at Aquinas's account of the nature of faith in order to show a side of faith neglected in contemporary accounts. For these purposes, the most important thing about Aquinas's account is that it assigns the will a role in faith. This added element in Aquinas's account provides a resolution for some of the common puzzles about the notion of faith.

STUMP, Eleonore S and KRETZMANN, Norman. Theologically Unfashionable Philosophy. Faith Phil, 7(3), 329-340, Jl 90.

STUMP, Eleonore S. Visits to the Sepulcher and Biblical Exegesis. Faith Phil, 6(4), 353-377, O 89.

In this paper I juxtapose a representative sample of contemporary historical biblical scholarship, namely, Raymond Brown's well-regarded interpretation of the empty tomb stories in the Gospel of John, with an example of biblical exegesis drawn from a typical medieval play, *Visitatio Sepulchri*. The point of the comparison is to consider the presuppositions on which these differing approaches to the biblical texts are based. The naive inattention to history shown by the play shows the importance of the work of historically oriented biblical critics. On the other hand, reflection on the methodology of the play provides some reason for doubting that the methodology employed by Brown is acceptable in every case.

STURLESE, Loris. Filosofia e scienza della natura del "Lucidarius" medioaltotedesco. G Crit Filosof Ital, 68(2), 161-183, My-Ag 89.

STÜSSEL, Kerstin. "Wittgensteins Vorwort "im Januar 1945": Quellenkritik und Interpretation" in *Wittgenstein in Focus—Im Brennpunkt: Wittgenstein*, MC GUINNESS, Brian (ed), 207-226. Amsterdam, Rodopi, 1989.

Der "im Januar 1945" datierte Text darf nur dann als Vorwort der 1953 publizierten Fassung der "Philosophischen Untersuchungen" betrachtet werden, wenn nachzuweisen ist, dass Wittgenstein selbst diesen Text zum Vorwort der gedruckten Version bestimmt hat. Nimmt man dies versuchsweise an, so sollen die *Philosophischen Untersuchungen* dem Leser einen Gesamteindruck eines "Gedankengebiets" vermitteln, in dem die "Ergebnisse" verschiedener "Untersuchungen" versammelt sind. Die noch Gegenständen geordnete Zusammenfassung dieser Ergebnisse ist schwierig, weil die Gegenstände jeweils in verschiedenen Untersuchungen behandelt werden, und gleicht deshalb einer Reise "kreuz und quer". Da jedoch nicht die Zusammenfassung, sondern das Konglomerat der Untersuchungsergebnisse dokumentiert werden soll, muss der Leser wie aus einem "Album" einen Gesamteindruck des "Gedankengebiets" erschliessen und darf sich nicht auf die isolierte Betrachtung einzelner Textelemente beschränken.

STUY, Johan. Ecologische communicatie door disciplinering van de moraal. Tijdschr Stud Verlich Denken, 17(1-2), 153-174, 1989.

In his study 'Ökologische Kommunikation' Luhmann takes up a sceptical attitude towards ethics. This paper deals with the reconstruction of the theoretical foundations of this attitude. Some basic concepts of Luhmann's system theory point out the framework of his reflection on ecological problems: the difference of system and environment, autopoiesis and communication. The new social movements and the ethics of environment lack theory and foundation. The interactional function of ethics is central in every social system, but ethics itself cannot become a specific function system. Ethics always seem to be attached to the polemic side of the interpersonal condition and to the ambitions of the practical philosophy. A criterion of rationality in society that sufficiently takes account of the limits of function systems shows us how to think about ecological questions.

SUBER, Peter. A Case Study in *Ad Hominem* Arguments: Fichte's *Science of Knowledge*. Phil Rhet, 23(1), 12-42, 1990.

Fichte's narrative persona in the "Science of Knowledge" is obnoxious. I try to disentangle regrettable signs of immaturity and paranoia from justifiable *ad hominem* arguments. Many of Fichte's *ad hominen* attacks on metaphysical realists are justified by his metaphysics and epistemology. We cannot criticize an important class of these arguments unless we criticize his epistemology and metaphysics. They are not matters of "style" separable from "substance." I show this inseparability, and point out a few inconsistencies, but otherwise do not comment on Fichte's "substance."

SUBOTNIK, Rose Rosengard. "The Challenge of Contemporary Music" in *What is Music?*, ALPERSON, Philip A , 359-396. New York, Haven, 1987.

SUBRAHMANIAN, V S and BLAIR, Howard A. Paraconsistent Foundations for Logic Programming. J Non-Classical Log, 5(2), 45-73, N 88.

Paraconsistent logics are useful for reasoning about very large knowledge bases, which may contain inconsistencies. We present a notion of knowledge base defined by a set of formulae of a many-valued logic whose truth values form a complete lattice which may be inconsistent in the two-valued sense with inconsistency represented by the top of the truth-value lattice. We give a model theory for these knowledge bases and characterize models by an operator on structures. As a step toward computational efficiency a proof procedure based on AND/OR tree searching is given along with soundness and completeness results.

SUCHODOLSKI, Bogdan (and others). Discussion of Father Krapiec's Article "The Human Dimension of Christian Culture". Dialec Hum, 14(1), 24-34, Wint 87.

SUCHODOLSKI, Bogdan. Preparation for Life in Peace—Future Perspectives. Dialec Hum, 14(1), 159-166, Wint 87.

The author is persuaded that the life in peace needs an appropriated education of human being. Peace as utopian vision of happy life is also connected with some danger of egoism, passivity and consumptive way of life. It is necessary to inspire the sense and value of the life, individual and social one. But this life cannot be—at the same time—directed by combativeness and aggressivity. How to avoid two possible dangers—of passivity and aggressivity? egoism and heroism of struggles and devotion? The author analyses the role of culture, science and human community in the new program of education.

SUITS, Bernard. The Trick of the Disappearing Goal. J Phil Sport, 16, 1-12, 1989.

SULLIVAN, David. Frege on the Statement of Number. Phil Phenomenol Res, 50(3), 595-603, Mr 90.

Recent debate about the value of historical research into Frege's work has centered on the question of the determination of distinct sources for any of Frege's key doctrines. This paper provides a possible historical source for Frege's central doctrine on the content of the statement of number. The historical source is located in the work of Herbart, to which Frege makes direct reference in the *Grundlagen*. The connection between Frege and Herbart is further substantiated by other evidence, principally the remarks of Frege's contemporary, Husserl. It is suggested that Frege's intellectual milieu may have contributed substantially to the formulation of his doctrines, albeit within the context of Frege's development of quantification theory.

SULLIVAN, Michael. Pragmatism and Precedent: A Response to Dworkin. Trans Peirce Soc, 26(2), 225-248, Spr 90.

SUMARES, Manuel. Quando ser sujeito não é sujeitar-se. Rev Port Filosof, 45(2), 189-205, Ap-Je 89.

In the *Philosophical Investigations*, there is an intention which is concomitant with the wish to obtain full view of the functioning of language philosophizing; the problem in the *Tractatus* about seeing the world aright needs still to be rethought; a critique of correspondence theory and an analysis of the spontaneous relation of the subject with the rules that govern the functioning of language are necessary. However, the circular and reciprocal syntax which characterize philosophical discourse are still to be found in language-games; the subject inevitably defined as subjected. What I propose here is the possibility of considering the subject as essentially not subjected, i.e., as really autonomous in regards to logical and linguistical systems.

SUMBERG, Theodore A. Reading Vico Three Times. Interpretation, 17(3), 347-353, Spr 90.

SUMMERFIELD, Donna M. On Taking the Rabbit of Rule-Following out of the Hat of Representation: Response to 'The Reality of Rule-Following'. Mind, 99(395), 425-432, Jl 90.

I argue that those who want to answer Kripke's Wittgensteinian sceptic about rule-following on his own terms face a challenge: They must show either that the problem is not a very general problem about the possibility of representation, or they must take on that problem directly, and point to something that does not itself take on the status of a sign that may be interpreted in various ways. Philip Pettit fails to meet this challenge: either he presupposes what he needs to explain, or he fails to specify something that succeeds in determining a unique interpretation of the relevant sign.

SUMMERFIELD, Donna M.   *Philosophical Investigations* 201: A Wittgensteinian Reply to Kripke. J Hist Phil, 28(3), 417-438, Jl 90.

A reading of *Philosophical Investigations* 201 is offered according to which it articulates an *answer* to the rule-following paradox: If there is a skeptical paradox about the expression of a rule, there is a parallel skeptical paradox about the behavioral response to a rule. But the former paradox arises only so long as we assume, illegitimately, that the latter does not. In addition, the article articulates the problematic assumption that tempts us to formulate a paradox, presents Wittgenstein's solution to a legitimate remaining problem of representation, and shows how Wittgenstein escapes certain charges made successfully against Kripke's Wittgenstein.

SUMMERS, Robert S. The Ideal Socio-Legal Order: Its "Rule of Law" Dimension. Ratio Juris, 1(2), 154-161, Jl 88.

The author aims at defining the borderlines of the concept "rule of law." This has been often inflated to encompass several dimensions of an ideal legal order. The author on the contrary believes that the "rule of law" ought to be a "thin" ideal. As a matter of fact, when the "rule of law" signifies almost any dimension of an ideal legal order, it comes to stand for nothing essential in particular. Deflation is then advocated for the rehabilitation of the normative content of the "rule of law." This means that the "rule of law" should be defined as a concept covering only some well delimited dimensions of an ideal legal order.

SUMNER, L W. *The Moral Foundation of Rights*. New York, Oxford Univ Pr, 1989

This book aims to provide the moral foundations necessary for dispelling sceptical doubts about rights. Beginning with an analytical model of the nature of rights, it provides existence conditions for all varieties of conventional rights. Three moral/political theories are then examined as possible frameworks for justifying conventional rights, and natural rights and contractarianism are rejected in favor of a form of indirect consequentialism. The book's principal substantive conclusion is that consequentialists can, indeed must, take rights seriously.

SUNDBERG, Jacob. The Law of Nature, the Uppsala School and the *Ius Docendi* Affair. Vera Lex, 9(1), 3-7, 1989.

Purpose: to describe relationship between Law of Nature in human rights idea and Uppsala School of Scandinavian realism; and manifestations thereof in recent Stockholm affair concerning *ius docendi* of Professor of Jurisprudence, Dr. Jacob Sundberg. *Conclusions*: Uppsala school supporters could not destroy human rights teaching in Jurisprudence but may try again. *Merits*: When Uppsala school type 'social engineering' is central, legel thinking is made a manipulative technique, requiring 'sound' environment and no critique. In perspective of technique, human rights is only Natural Law superstition. Discussion of Uppsala school arguments in support of operation attempting the removal of Sundberg from teaching human rights perspective to his Jurisprudence classes. Attack derailed when legal scholars worldwide intervened.

SUNIC, Tomislav. History and Decadence: Spengler's Cultural Pessimism Today. Clio, 19(1), 51-62, Fall 89.

SUPERSON, Anita M. The Self-Interest Based Contractarian Response to the Why-Be-Moral Skeptic. S J Phil, 28(3), 427-447, Fall 90.

The paper analyzes yet another attempt to defeat skepticism about the rationality of acting morally, namely, that offered by self-interest based contractarians. The focus is on Gauthier's theory in *Morals by Agreement*. I aim to show the contractarian is committed to making what I call the dispositional move, but then is faced with the challenge of showing that the rationality of actions expressing the moral disposition depends on the rationality of that disposition. I examine Gauthier's arguments for the dependency thesis, and reject them in favor of the independency thesis offered by Parfit. Though neither view defeats skepticism, Gauthier's view is open to the charge that *no* moral acts are rational.

SUPPES, Patrick and ZANOTTI, Mario. Conditions on Upper and Lower Probabilities to Imply Probabilities. Erkenntnis, 31(2-3), 323-345, S 89.

In this paper we prove four theorems about the existence of a probability measure when a pair of upper and lower probability measures satisfy certain conditions. Essential to the proofs is the use of an approach we used in two earlier papers on qualitative probability. The approach is to move from a Boolean algebra of events to the semigroup of extended indicator functions generated by these events. This semigroup and others closely related to it are useful structures for studying various foundational questions in probability.

SUPPES, Patrick and CRANGLE, Colleen. Geometrical Semantics for Spatial Prepositions. Midwest Stud Phil, 14, 399-422, 1989.

The main aim of this article is to propose a classification of the kinds of geometry that underlie the basic meaning of various spatial prepositions. For example, the preposition *on* assumes an orientation of verticality that is missing from standard Euclidean geometry. On the other hand, the geometry underlying many uses of the preposition *in* is much weaker than Euclidean geometry, being mainly topological in character. We also consider prepositions that require assigning orientation to figures and shapes. Finally, some attention is given to space-time geometry as required for prepositions used in action sentences.

SUPPES, Patrick and CRANGLE, Colleen. Robots that Learn: A Test of Intelligence. Rev Int Phil, 44(172), 5-23, 1990.

Inattention to learning is characteristic of foundational discussions of artificial intelligence and of cognitive science in philosophy. The focus on intentionality has dominated much of the debate between philosophers and computer scientists about the nature of artificial intelligence. Detailed theories of learning provide a framework for a more adequate philosophical analysis of artificial intelligence or of intelligence in general. We attempt to provide one such analysis specifically aimed at tasks that robots need to master in order to claim any genuine learning ability. Finally, we present a detailed example of how we might expect a robot to learn through instruction by the use of ordinary language.

SURDU, Alexandru. Les mécanismes pentadiques de la tragédie antique (in Romanian). Rev Filosof (Romania), 36(2), 188-198, Mr-Ap 89.

SURGEY, John. Agriculture: A War on Nature? J Applied Phil, 6(2), 205-207, O 89.

Agriculture, in the ubiquitous debate concerning the environment, is often accused of being environmentally destructive as if farmers are waging a war on nature. The article discusses the role of aggression, competition and killing in agriculture and concludes that those warlike characteristics are a necessary part of agricultural practice. The article stresses, however, that agriculture is not literally a war on nature and points to a number of unwarlike characteristics that also belong to agriculture.

SURIN, Kenneth (ed). *Christ, Ethics and Tragedy: Essays in Honour of Donald MacKinnon*. New York, Cambridge Univ Pr, 1989.

SURIN, Kenneth. "Some Aspects of the 'Grammar' of 'Incarnation' and 'Kenosis'" in *Christ, Ethics and Tragedy: Essays in Honour of Donald MacKinnon*, SURIN, Kenneth (ed), 93-116. New York, Cambridge Univ Pr, 1989.

SURIN, Kenneth. Towards a "Materialist" Critique of "Religious Pluralism". Thomist, 53(4), 655-673, O 89.

SUSHINSKY, Mary Ann. Ideology and Epistemology: A Discussion of Mc Carney and Mills. Phil Forum, 21(4), 471-476, Sum 90.

SUTHERLAND, John W. Disciplining Qualitative Decision Exercises: Aspects of a Transempirical Protocol, I. Theor Decis, 28(1), 73-101, Ja 90.

This paper defines and defends certain procedural and instrumental initiatives taken to constitute a transempirical protocol. This protocol is intended to provide one avenue for extending the bounds of rationality to decision exercises where there are only limited opportunities for effecting objective or empirical discipline. That is, the practical purpose of the protocol's facilities is to help prevent decision exercises that must be conducted in the face of a signal sparsity of objective/empirical predicates from degenerating into an uncontrolled retreat from reason. The paper is divided into two essentially self-contained parts. Part I will try to establish the rationale for the transempirical protocol in light of the reach and limits of other decision-theoretic platforms, and briefly introduce the set of provisions it entails. Part II will then go through a technical elaboration of these provisions, suggesting how they might be brought towards operational significance.

SUTHERLAND, John W. Disciplining Qualitative Decision Exercises: Aspects of a Transempirical Protocol, II. Theor Decis, 29(2), 85-118, S 90.

SUTHERLAND, Stewart. Hope. Philosophy, 25, 193-206, 89 Supp.

SUTHREN HIRST, J G. The Place of Teaching Techniques in Samkara's Theology. J Indian Phil, 18(2), 113-150, Je 90.

This article is concerned with the way in which the language of the Upanishadic texts provides Samkara, the great Advaitin commentator, with a paradigm for religious language use. Scripture prescribes a range of methods which function within its interpretative framework of superimposition (adhyāsa) to show how the structures of this world give clues for their own dismantling. As part of this process, scripture sanctions formal argument. Scripturally-based religious language is seen as primarily directive, yet able to distinguish Brahman, the underlying reality, from the world of role and form, by a series of mutually constraining examples and predicates.

SUTTLE, Bruce. "Duties and Excusing Conditions" in *Inquiries into Values: The Inaugural Session of the International Society for Value Inquiry*, LEE, Sander H , 119-129. Lewiston, Mellen Pr, 1989.

Incorporated into most moral systems are two metaethical principles: that ought implies can and that there can be excusing conditions. While the first principle requires, for something to be one's duty, that one has the ability and opportunity to act dutifully, the second principle allows for one to be exempt from moral blame for not acting dutifully when certain conditions exist. I argue that these two principles employ inconsistent concepts of duty, such that while the principle of ought implies can treats one's ability and opportunity as duty-making conditions, the principle of excusing conditions treats one's ability and opportunity as responsibility-making conditions. The conflict comes from how the lack of ability and opportunity, relative to the principle of excusing conditions, does not alter the status of a duty, while relative to the principle of ought implies can, the lack of ability and opportunity does alter the status of a duty.

SUZUKI, Nobu-Yuki. An Algebraic Approach to Intuitionistic Modal Logics in Connection with Intermediate Predicate Logics. Stud Log, 48(2), 141-155, Je 89.

Modal counterparts of intermediate predicate logics will be studied by means of algebraic devise. Our main tool will be a construction of algebraic semantics for modal logics from algebraic frames for predicate logics. Uncountably many examples of modal counterparts of intermediate predicate logics will be given.

SUZUKI, Nobu-Yuki and ONO, Hiroakira. Relations Between Intuitionistic Modal Logics and Intermediate Predicate Logics. Rep Math Log, 22, 65-87, 1988.

Resemblance between modal operators and quantifiers has been often discussed. For example, modal operators of modal logic S5 behave just like quantifiers of the classical logic. So, it will be expected that the similar relation will hold between many pairs of an intuitionistic modal logic and an intermediate predicate logic. This paper treats the problem and proves some fundamental results on it. Among other things, countably many examples of pairs of logics are explicitly given, for which the above relation holds, by making use of the translation theorem proved early in the paper.

SVATON, Vladimir. Theory of Novel and Historical Poetics (in Czechoslovakian). Estetika, 27(1), 43-53, 1990.

SWAIN, Braja Kishore. Smarta-Varnasrama and the Law of Welfare. J Dharma, 14(3), 269-276, Jl-S 89.

"Society has its four-fold eternal divisions (intellectuals = brāhman, administrators = ksatrya, producers = vaisya, and labourers = sūdra) according to function. These are said as varna and their stage of function āsrama, where the being earns means according to his ability and utilises as per his necessity. Law thereof is framed primarily in family and for a century. This is smārtakāla. Within this, three generations continue consisting of father, son and grandson. It is suggested that abolition of divisions which is a slogan of the politicians is devoid of possibility insofar as society is concerned. This is a psychological division. Therefore, it is indispensable."

SWAIN, Marshall. "BonJour's Coherence Theory of Justification" in *The Current State of the Coherence Theory*, BENDER, John W (ed), 115-124. Norwell, Kluwer, 1989.

Some of the core arguments in *The Structure of Empirical Knowledge* are examined here and found inconclusive. BonJour's arguments against externalism fail against certain forms of externalism which are able to handle BonJour's alleged counterexamples. It also is argued that the "accessibility" requirement BonJour suggests is too stringent, and that BonJour's "metajustificatory" argument fails, because theoretical beliefs can satisfy coherence criteria and in the long run still not enjoy a high likelihood of truth. An example of this point is provided.

SWANGER, David. The Heart's Education: Why We Need Poetry. J Aes Educ, 23(2), 45-54, Sum 89.

The article examines Plato's "longstanding quarrel between philosophy and poetry" from the vantage of contemporary poetry, specifically, the author's own. Plato's poetics are found to be sound, although the implications of these poetics are contested: viz., we need poetry in education for precisely the reasons Plato would constrain poetry's power.

SWANTON, Christine. Robert Stevens on Offers. Austl J Phil, 67(4), 472-475, D 89.

SWANTON, Christine and ROBINSON, Viviane and CROSTHWAITE, Jan. Treating Women as Sex-Objects. J Soc Phil, 20(3), 5-20, Wint 89.

SWIDERSKA, Ewa (trans) and ROSEN, Henryk. The Concept of Alienation in Janusz Korczak's Works. Dialec Hum, 16(1), 135-147, Wint 89.

SWIDERSKI, E M (trans) and DAHM, Helmut. What Restoring Leninism Means. Stud Soviet Tho, 39(1), 55-76, F 90.

SWINBURNE, Richard. Arguments for the Existence of God. Philosophy,

24, 121-133, 88 Supp.

In an inductive argument data increase the probability of a hypothesis insofar as the hypothesis makes probable the data, the data are otherwise not likely to occur, and the hypothesis is simple. The cosmological argument from the existence of the universe, the teleological argument from its conformity to natural law, and other arguments from more detailed features of the universe each increase the probability that there is a God. I thus summarize in a simple form the main points of my book *The Existence of God*.

SWINBURNE, Richard. Could God Become Man? Philosophy, 25, 53-70, 89 Supp.

Christian orthodoxy has maintained that in Jesus Christ God became man, i.e., acquired a human nature, while remaining God. Given two not unreasonable restrictions on the understanding of "man," that claim is perfectly coherent. But if the New Testament is correct in claiming that in some sense Christ was ignorant, weak, and temptable, we have to suppose that Christ had a divided mind; or, in traditional terminology, that the two natures did not totally interpenetrate.

SWINBURNE, Richard. Tensed Facts. Amer Phil Quart, 27(2), 117-130, Ap 90.

I defend the A Theory of Time that there are tensed (and other indexical) facts, e.g., about what has happened, as well as tenseless facts, e.g., about what happened in the nineteenth century. I reject arguments of McTaggart and Grünbaum, but concentrate on Mellor's argument that tenseless truth-conditions can be given for the truth of every tensed sentence. My rebuttal of this argument depends on a distinction between the 'proposition' and the 'statement' expressed by a sentence. Statements have changeless truth-value, while propositions may change truth-value; but there is more to be known than knowledge of true statements can capture.

SWINDLER, J K. The Formal Distinction. SW Phil Rev, 4(1), 71-77, Ja 88.

Analysis of linguistic and ontological evidence suggested by Aristotle, Duns Scotus, and Frege leads to a distinction between universals, which are genuinely general, and properties, which are their particularized instances. Further distinction is drawn between instantiation of universals *in re* and *in intellectu*. Universals and properties are distinguished on grounds of degree of completeness. Universal instantiation and property possession are different relations, which implies that universals have properties.

SWINDLER, J K. MacIntyre's Republic. Thomist, 54(2), 343-354, Ap 90.

Contrary to his explicit aims, a careful reading of MacIntyre's *After Virtue*, Plato's *Republic*, and Aristotle's *Nichomachean Ethics* shows that MacIntyre's social theory is more Platonic than Aristotelian. Here it is shown that MacIntyre and Plato argue for and against the same crucial moral, social and political theses and that Plato has ready solutions to puzzles that MacIntyre acknowledges Aristotle cannot handle. Put in Platonic terms and context, MacIntyre's analysis of contemporary moral and social theory and the contemporary moral malaise gain in clarity and explanatory power.

SWINDLER, James K. Comments on Mark Brown's "Why Individual Identity Matters". SW Phil Rev, 6(2), 115-118, Jl 90.

Brown claims that isolation of the central nervous system accounts for the self's privacy, privileged access, self-concern, and concern for others. I argue that physicalism is unable to account for common cases of self-sacrifice and that it inherits traditional problems of identity for bodies. Moreover, since neurophysiological states are types, the approach cannot explain caring for the identity of any unique individual. The difference between self-interestedness and mattering to oneself is clear from the fact that many creatures act self-interestedly without consciousness, but one's own consciousness is precisely what's at stake in determining why one's identity matters to oneself.

SWINYARD, W R and RINNE, H and KENG KAU, A. The Morality of Software Piracy: A Cross-Cultural Analysis. J Bus Ethics, 9(8), 655-664, Ag 90.

Software piracy is a damaging and important moral issue, which is widely believed to be unchecked in particular areas of the globe. This cross-cultural study examines differences in morality and behavior toward software piracy in Singapore versus the United States, and reviews the cultural histories of Asia versus the United States to explore why these differences occur. The paper is based upon pilot data collected in the US and Singapore, using a tradeoff analysis methodology and analysis. The data reveal some fascinating interactions between the level of ethical transgression and the rewards of consequences which they produce.

SWISTAK, Piotr. Paradigms of Measurement. Theor Decis, 29(1), 1-17, Jl 90.

In this study some conceptual developments in the theory of measurement are reframed with the use of a model-theoretic interpretation. These paradigms (physical, extended physical and representational paradigm) which emerge in the process of reconceptualization are discussed. This discussion enables us to highlight a certain logic behind a series of developments in the theory of measurement and leads to a new, more general conceptualization.

SYCARA, Katia P. Persuasive Argumentation in Negotiation. Theor Decis, 28(3), 203-242, My 90.

This paper presents persuasive argumentation as a means of guiding the negotiation process to a settlement. Decision theoretic approaches construct prescriptive models of the negotiation process that make various assumptions about the behavior of the negotiation participants but do not model changes in behavior. On the other hand, models for decision support leave the actual decisions to human negotiators, again not modeling or automating the negotiating process. In contrast to both approaches, our work deals with automating the negotiating process. This paper focuses on modeling the process by which the beliefs and behavior of negotiators are changed via persuasive argumentation. We claim that persuasive argumentation lies at the heart of negotiation and embodies the dynamics of negotiation. We present a model of persuasive argumentation that integrates artificial intelligence and decision theoretic methods. The model has been implemented as part of the PERSUADER, a multi-agent computer program that operates in the domain of labor negotiations.

SYKES, John. Narrative Accounts of Biblical Authority: The Need for a Doctrine of Revelation. Mod Theol, 5(4), 327-342, Jl 89.

SYLVAN, Richard (ed) and NORMAN, Jean (ed). *Directions in Relevant Logic*. Norwell, Kluwer, 1989

SYLVAN, Richard and DA COSTA, Newton. Cause as an Implication. Stud Log, 47(4), 413-427, D 88.

An appropriately unprejudiced logical investigation of causation as a type of implication relation is undertaken. The implication delineated is bounded syntactically. The developing argument then leads to a very natural process analysis, which demonstrably captures the established syntactical features. Next relevantly-based semantics for the resulting logical theory are adduced, and requisite adequacy results delivered. At the end of the tour, further improvements are pointed out, and the attractive terrain beyond present developments is glimpsed.

SYLVAN, Richard and NORMAN, Jean. "Conclusion: Further Directions in Relevant Logics" in *Directions in Relevant Logic*, NORMAN, Jean (ed), 399-437. Norwell, Kluwer, 1989.

SYLVAN, Richard and NORMAN, Jean. "Introduction: Routes in Relevant Logic" in *Directions in Relevant Logic*, NORMAN, Jean (ed), 1-24. Norwell, Kluwer, 1989.

SYLVAN, Richard and URBAS, Igor. Prospects for Decent Relevant Factorisation Logics. J Non-Classical Log, 6(1), 63-79, My 89.

A family of logics in which prefixing and suffixing principles are replaced by weaker factorisation and summation principles is defined and investigated. It is shown that these logics fail to be relevant if idempotence and distribution principles are present unless simplification and addition are also removed.

SZABADOS, Béla. Embarrassment and Self-Esteem. J Phil Res, 15, 341-349, 1990.

Emotions are in as a philosophical topic. Yet the recent literature is bent on grand theorizing rather than attempting to explore particular emotions and their roles in our lives. In this paper, I aim to remedy this situation a little by exploring the emotion of embarrassment. First, I critically examine R C Solomon's conceptual sketch and try to distinguish "embarrassment" from "shame," "humiliation" and "being amused." Secondly, I argue that "private embarrassment" is a coherent and useful idea and social scientists and philosophers who dismiss it as unintelligible are mistaken. Thirdly, I discuss the question why is embarrassment (unlike other emotions) catching. Fourth, I make the heretical suggestion that doing philosophy is essentially embarrassing for Socratic interlocutors. Throughout the paper there is a discussion of possible links between embarrassment and loss of self-esteem.

SZABO, M E. Coherence in Cartesian Closed Categories and the Generality of Proofs. Stud Log, 48(3), 285-297, S 89.

SZABÓ, Tibor. The Moment of Ideology and the Human Factor in Lukác's Late Work (in Hungarian). Magyar Filozof Szemle, 5, 618-630, 1989.

Der Verfasser versucht zu beweisen, dass Lukács' *Ontologie* im doppelten Sinne ein Versuch zur Synthese ist. Einerseits innerhalb des Lebenswerks—zahlreiche, früher einmal schon (besonders im "Geschichte und Klassenbewusstsein") thematisierte und eigenartig gelöste Probleme wie die Dialektik der Natur, die Entfremdung, das Bewusstsein, die Praxis usw. werden hier vor einem neuen gesellschaftlichhistorischen Hintergrund wieder behandelt. Andererseits bedeutet das auch innerhalb des Marxismus des XX. Jahrhunderts einen Versuch zur Synthese, da Lukács sich zum Ziel setzt, die Theorie von Marx und Lenin wieder als ein einheitliches Ganzes—als Synthese eben—aufzufassen, im Gegensatz zu den zahlreichen Versuchen, die das Wesen der marxistischen Philosophie verzerren und ihre Einheit zersetzen wollen. (edited)

SZABÓ, Zoltán Z. János Hetényi—The Scientist, the Dilettante (in Hungarian). Magyar Filozof Szemle, 2-3, 183-204, 1989.

János Hetényi ist eine heute nur wenig bekannte Figur der Philosophie des neunzehnten Jahrhunderts. Seine philosophische Tätigkeit war mit den nationalen Zwecken der Reformepoche eng verbunden. Hetényi, seinem Vorbild, dem Politiker István Széchenyi ähnlich, hat den Grund der Probleme im Mangel an Selbstständigkeit gesehen. Er hat deshalb seine ganze Arbeit der Gestaltung eines sog. "selbstständigen und originellen" ungarischen philosophischen Systems gewidmet. Da sein Zweck mit den politischen Zwecken des Landes übereinstimmte, fand seine Tätigkeit eine positive Beurteilung. Seine Werke wurden der Reihe nach mit akademischen anerkannt, mit der Zeit wurde auch sein Name bekannt, endlich hat man ihn zum Mitglied der Akademie gewählt. So wurde er "Akademiker János Hetényi". (edited)

SZAKOLCZAI, Arpád and HORVÁTH, Ágnes. A Sweet and Sour Victory in Eastern Europe. Rad Phil, 55, 40-42, Sum 90.

SZAWARSKI, Zbigniew. Treatment and Non-Treatment of Defective Newborns. Bioethics, 4(2), 143-153, Ap 90.

SZCZEPANSKI, Jan and BYLINA, Maryna. Admonitions to Poland. Dialec Hum, 16(2), 87-91, Spr 89.

SZCZEPANSKI, Jan and PETROWICZ, Lech (trans). The Seventieth Anniversary of the October Revolution. Dialec Hum, 15(3-4), 93-98, Sum-Autumn 88.

SZCZEPANSKI, Jan and LECKI, Maciej (trans). Socialism and Atheism. Dialec Hum, 14(1), 43-47, Wint 87.

SZÉKELY, Laszlô. Motion and the Dialectical View of the World: On Two Soviet Interpretations of Zeno's Paradoxes. Stud Soviet Tho, 39(3-4), 241-255, Ap-My 90.

The purpose of the paper is to make the reader acquainted with two recent Soviet interpretations of Zeno's paradoxes. The official Soviet philosophy advances Zeno's motion-paradoxes to support the "contradiction-ontology" of dialectical materialism and to apply them as an argument to demonstrate that we need to restrict the logical law of noncontradiction. While this argument is refuted by Voishvilo's interpretation concretely, its invalidity follows indirectly from Janovskaja's concept, too. Voishvilo and Janovskaja's interpretations are relevant not only concerning the history of dialectical materialism but also with regard to the recent concepts of paraconsistent logics.

SZENDREI, Eric V. Bergson, Prigogine and the Rediscovery of Time. Process Stud, 18(3), 181-193, Fall 89.

My concern in this article is to challenge Prigogine's suggestions that Bergson's criticism of science is now obsolete, and that scientists are discovering time itself in their recognition of irreversibility in objective processes. I first show how Bergson's view of the limitations of science may be derived from his practical/speculative distinction (which I defend). I argue that temporal irreversibility is not only a physical impossibility, as Prigogine suggests, but a logical impossibility.

SZMATKA, Jacek. Reduction in the Social Sciences: The Future or Utopia? Phil Soc Sci, 19(4), 425-444, D 89.

Theoretical reduction or reductionism is strongly controversial among methodologists and philosophers. Its opponents consider it to be a method that is slowing down the development of science (Spinner 1973), while its adherents tend to treat current scientific discoveries as effects of the application of reduction. Adherents of theoretical reduction point to a group of biologists, often called mechanistic, who had a share in creating grounds for important discoveries in contemporary molecular biology. The controversies about this method are inflamed by reduction's victories as well as its defeats and disappointments.

SZOSTEK, Andrzej. L'homme en tant qu'autocréateur; fondements anthropologiques du rejet de l'encyclique (in Polish). Stud Phil Christ, 25(2), 43-63, 1989.

Dans le présent article on essaie det recontruire la philosophie de l'homme admise et développée par de nombreux théologues contemporains, philosophie sur laquelle est fondé le rejet des normes incluses dans l'encyclique Humanae Vitae. Selon l'auteur, l'idée principale de cette anthropologie est celle de l'homme en tant qu'autocréateur qui doit non pas déchiffrer à l'aide d'actes de la coscience les normes d'action en tant que données objectivement et au contenu bien défini, mais plutôt construire lui-même de telles normes grâce à sa liberté qui est essentielle crétive et qui ne peut être évaluée d'une façon adéquate du point de vue des normes morales générales. (edited)

SZWAST, Wieslaw. On the Generator Problem. Z Math Log, 36(1), 23-27, 1990.

A finite spectrum is the set of cardinalities of finite models of a first-order sentence. A Horn spectrum is a spectrum of a Horn sentence. The class of Horn spectra coincides with the class of multiplicatively closed spectra. The generator problem asks whether the generator of every Horn spectrum is again a spectrum. The generator of a multiplicatively closed set A is the smallest set whose multiplicative closure is A. It was shown in the paper that the relativized NEXPTIME=?Co-NEXPTIME question has a negative answer and the relativized generator problem has an affirmative answer for some oracle set.

SZYMANEK, Krzysztof. Classical Subtheories and Intuitionism. Bull Sect Log, 18(3), 112-115, O 89.

Let Taut be the set of all classical tautologies. Let $L(T)$ be, for a given classical theory T, the lattice of all subtheories of T. *Theorem 1*: If $T \neq$ Taut is a classical theory, then the content of $L(T)$ is equal to the set of all formulas provable in the intuitionistic calculus. *Theorem 2*: There exist three classical theories T_1, T_2, T_3 such that for every classical theory T: $L(T)$ is isomorphic to $L(T_1)$ or $L(T_2)$ or $L(T_3)$.

TABER, John A. The Mīmāmsā Theory of Self-Recognition. Phil East West, 40(1), 35-57, Ja 90.

The Pūrva Mīmāmsā school of Indian philosophy argued for the existence of a continuously existing, substantial self as follows: In the act of remembering, I who remember *recognize* myself as the subject of a past experience. I must therefore exist continuously and unchanged from the past to the present. This argument is distinguished from the Nyāya position and compared to the nearly identical view held by the Western philosophers Butler and Reid. Despite much lip-service paid to the latter recently, this argument has been neglected in the current discussion of personal identity.

TABER, John A. The Theory of the Sentence in Pūrva Mīmāmsā and Western Philosophy. J Indian Phil, 17(4), 407-430, D 89.

The Mīmāmsā school of Indian philosophy developed two distinct theories of the relation of the meaning of a sentence to the meanings of the words that comprise it, the *anviṭābhidhana* or "qualified designation" theory and the *abhihiṭānvaya* or "designated relation" theory. Both of these theories, I attempt to show, turn on the observation that the meanings of individual words change in different sentences. I go on to suggest that an appreciation of this fact can lead to a solution of the problem, first raised by Frege, of the change of meaning of terms in intensional contexts.

TAGHVA, Kazem. Model Completeness and Direct Power. Z Math Log, 36(1), 3-9, 1990.

TAGLIACOZZO, Giorgio. Toward a History of Recent Vico Scholarship in English, Part II: 1969-1973. New Vico Studies, 2, 1-40, 1984.

This article is the second in a series of five articles on Anglo-American Vico scholarship. It is particularly concerned with work which either began or gained importance between 1969 and 1973. (staff)

TAGLIACOZZO, Giorgio. Toward a History of Recent Vico Scholarship in English, Part IV: The Vico/Venezia Conference 1978, and Its Aftermath. New Vico Studies, 4, 1-24, 1986.

This article focuses on the Vico/Venezia conference which was held in Venice in 1978. It also examines the writing that resulted from the conference. This article is the fourth part of a five-part series and includes an index to the preceding three articles. (staff)

TAGLIACOZZO, Giorgio. Toward a History of Recent Vico Scholarship in English, Part V: After Vico/Venezia (1978-1987) and Appendix. New Vico Studies, 5, 1-56, 1987.

This final contribution to a series of five articles constitutes a bibliography of significant English language Vichian scholarship between the years 1978 and 1987. An index to the four earlier articles is included. (staff)

TAGLIACOZZO, Giorgio. Toward a History of Recent Vico Scholarship in English, Part III: 1974-1977. New Vico Studies, 3, 1-32, 1985.

In this, the third article in the series, the author deals with an acceleration in the amount of Vico research during the years of the mid-1970s. Important written works and conferences are discussed, and special attention is paid to the increasing interdisciplinary use of Vichian thought during this period. Included is an index to the first and second articles of the series. (staff)

TAGLIAPIETRA, Andrea. Metafora e concetto: sulla metafora dello specchio in Schelling e nel giovane Hegel. Filosofia, 40(2), 175-201, My-Ag 89.

TAIT, William. The Iterative Hierarchy of Sets. Iyyun, 39(1), 65-79, Ja 90.

TAKHO-GODI, A. Aleksei Fedorovich Losev. Soviet Stud Phil, 28(2), 30-44, Fall 89.

The purpose of the article is to survey the life of A F Losev (1893-1988), the last outstanding philosopher of the Russian "Silver Age," the author of important works in various fields of scientific research, written during the two main periods of his creative activity, 1920-1930 and 1950-1988. In spite of extremely hard circumstances he succeeded in reaching his goals. His life as a symbol of pan-unity still remains a kind of a riddle, which we are to puzzle over.

TALBOT, Theodore (trans) and BITTNER, Rüdiger. *What Reason Demands*. New York, Cambridge Univ Pr, 1980

This work is concerned with morality. Beginning with the question "Why should I be moral?" it moves on, in light of objections, to a fundamental query, "*Should* I be moral?" Resolving that we should not, on a vernacular conception, the author moves on to consideration of guides to action based upon morality-less rationality, arguing prudence and autonomy as proper guides. (staff)

TALBOTT, Thomas. The Doctrine of Everlasting Punishment. Faith Phil, 7(1), 19-42, Ja 90.

I argue that, although theism in general is consistent, many of the popular forms, specifically those that include the traditional doctrine of hell, are implicitly self-contradictory. After examining three varieties of theism, each of which involves, I contend, a logical impossibility of one kind or another, I conclude that nothing short of an explicit universalism—that is, nothing short of the view that God will eventually reconcile all persons to himself—is consistent with other doctrines essential to Christian theism.

TALIAFERRO, Charles and BEATY, Michael. God and Concept Empiricism. SW Phil Rev, 6(2), 97-105, Jl 90.

David Blumenfeld employs a version of concept empiricism to argue that there cannot be an omnipotent, omniscient being. We argue that Blumenfeld's defense of concept empiricism is inadequate and his argument fails.

TALIAFERRO, Charles. The Ideal Aesthetic Observer Revisited. Brit J Aes, 30(1), 1-13, Ja 90.

A normative theory of aesthetic judgments is defended against objections raised by John Hospers. An ideal observer aesthetics is developed similar to ideal observer ethics.

TALIAFERRO, Charles. The Possibility of God. Relig Stud, 25(2), 217-224, Je 89.

Defense of the thesis that the God of classical Christian theism suffers. Objections are raised against Richard Creel's impassibilism, according to which God is not subject to pain or suffering.

TALIAFERRO, Charles. The View from Above and Below. Heythrop J, 30(4), 385-402, O 89.

Defense of a unified framework in which to assess moral and nonmoral values with special attention given to the relationship between morality and aesthetics. Criticism of work on this topic by R M Adams, Thomas Nagel, Bernard Williams, and Susan Wolf.

TALIAFERRO, Charles. Why We Need Immortality. Mod Theol, 6(4), 367-377, Jl 90.

A case for the moral and religious desirability of belief in the afterlife. Objections are raised against Grace Jantzen's view that belief in the afterlife is not essential to Christianity.

TALLET, J A. *The Possible Universe*. Coral Gables, Publitex, 1990

This book explores a hypothetical philosophical synthesis based on the largest conceivable domain—the realm of the possible. Such a subject matter requires to be cast in the forms of logic. An excursion into logical analysis leads to an axiomatic system purporting to reflect a universal totality. This approach must deal with the paradoxes of infinity threatening self-contained entities. The synthesis is developed within an inferential class-propositional calculus that evades the paradoxical complications of undecidable formalisms and turns out to be more suitable for the problems of philosophy. Some special themes are treated in the light of this development, which comes to the conclusion that possibilities as such, even mutually contradictory contingencies, consistently coalesce as expressions of the possible universe.

TAMINIAUX, Jacques. "Voix" et "Phénomène" dans l'Ontologie fondamentale de Heidegger. Rev Phil Fr, 180(2), 395-408, Ap-Je 90.

TAMINIAUX, Jacques. Poiesis and Praxis in Fundamental Ontology. Res Phenomenol, 17, 137-169, 1987.

TAMINIAUX, Jacques. Sur l'héritage de Hobbes. Rev Theol Phil, 121(3), 259-271, 1989.

TAN, Yao-Hua. Een vergelijking van inductief-statistisch redeneren en default logica. Alg Ned Tijdschr Wijs, 82(2), 117-140, Ap 90.

Currently philosophy of science and the study of artificial intelligence are separate fields of research. We argue that both fields can benefit from each other. As an example of this mutual benefit we discuss the relation between inductive-statistical reasoning and default logic. One of the main issues in AI research is the study of reasoning with incomplete information. Default logic is especially developed to formalise this type of reasoning. It is shown that there are striking resemblances between inductive-statistical reasoning and default logic. A central theme in the logical positivist study of inductive-statistical reasoning such as Hempel's criterion of maximal specificity turns out to be equally important in the default logic. We also study to what extent the relevance of the results of logical positivism to AI research could contribute to a revival of logical positivism.

TANAKA, Kazuyuki and SHIOJI, Naoki. Fixed Point Theory in Weak Second-Order Arithmetic. Annals Pure Applied Log, 47(2), 167-188, My 90.

The purpose of this paper is to develop part of functional analysis concerned with fixed point theorems within a weak subsystem of second-order arithmetic WKL_0. The paper contributes to a broader program, Reverse Mathematics, whose ultimate goal is to answer the question: What set existence axioms are needed to prove the theorems of ordinary mathematics? Within the system WKL_0, Brouwer's fixed point theorem is proved and extended to its infinite dimensional analogue, from which the Cauchy-Peano theorem is obtained. The Markov-Kakutani theorem is also proved and applied to the Hahn-Banach theorem for separable Banach spaces.

TANALSKI, Dionizy and RODZINSKA, Aleksandra (trans). John Paul II vis-à-vis Atheism and Materialism: Remarks on the Encyclical *Dominum et vivificantem*. Dialec Hum, 14(1), 99-108, Wint 87.

The encyclic "Domimum et vivificantem" underlines the problem of sin. The most important forms of this sin are "practical" materialism, theoretical materialism and atheism. Pope prefers ontological dualism—a theoretical basis for moral implications directed against non-Christians. The personalist trend disappears. The problem of sin has been interpreted in an extremely traditional way, without the social relations. It is impossible to solve the problem of justice only by means of faith of Christians alone, so we propose to join our efforts in common struggle against social sin and to set aside the accusations and moral discrimination caused by different world outlooks.

TANG, Paul C L. Reply to Richard Bosley's "Virtues and Vices: East and West". J Chin Phil, 16(3-4), 411-417, D 89.

I make two major points in reply to Professor Bosley's paper. First, I argue that the dualism between science and ethics may not be as sharp as Bosley makes it out to be. Second, I argue that the East-West synthesis of Greek and Medieval theories of virtue on the one hand, and Confucian and neo-Confucian theories of virtue on the other hand, may not be possible because of the incommensurability of such East-West theories. Instead, I propose that a complementary model of such East-West theories might be more appropriate.

TANG, Paul C L. Die Unbestimmtheit von Theorien über die menschliche Natur im chinesischen Denken. Conceptus, 24(61), 27-34, 1990.

According to Confucius and Mencius, human nature is originally good. For Hsün Tzu, human nature is originally evil. Cua argues that the two theories can be rendered consistent. We present an alternative approach. We argue that many traditional philosophical theories have empirical import, and can be placed on a continuum with scientific theories. The theories of Mencius and Hsün Tzu can then be treated as underdetermined in Quine's sense. The consequences of this analysis are discussed. We then address the more fundamental question of human nature itself. Following the later Wittgenstein, we show how the problem can be dissolved. We conclude by suggesting that human nature can be treated as a kind of Kantian regulative principle.

TANG, Yi-Jie (ed) and ZHEN, Li (ed) and MC LEAN, George F (ed). *Man and Nature: The Chinese Tradition and the Future*. Lanham, Univ Pr of America, 1989

TÄNNSJÖ, Torbjörn. Methodological Individualism. Inquiry, 33(1), 69-80, Mr 90.

The doctrine of methodological individualism is clarified and different versions of it are distinguished. The main thesis of the article is that methodological individualism is either a false doctrine or else a doctrine compatible with functionalism, structuralism, and Marxism. Positively it is maintained that, for all we know, collective entities such as power structures may shape our beliefs and values; these beliefs and values may explain some of our actions and expectations. These actions and expectations, together with similar actions and expectations of other people, caused in a similar fashion, may in turn constitute social phenomena. This means that, for all we know, in our best explanations of some social phenomena we may well need to have recourse to collective entities.

TÄNNSJÖ, Torbjörn. Soft Determinism and How We Become Responsible for the Past. Phil Papers, 18(2), 189-201, S 89.

If soft determinism is true, i.e., if determinism is true and if we are sometimes 'free', in the sense relevant to morality, to act otherwise than we actually do, then the rightness or wrongness of our actions depends, not only on what happens in the future, after we have performed them, as compared to what would have happened in the future if we had not, but also on what went on before we performed them, as compared to what would have gone on before them, if we had not performed them.

TANSEY, Richard and HYMAN, Michael R. The Ethics of Psychoactive Ads. J Bus Ethics, 9(2), 105-114, F 90.

Many of today's ads work by arousing the viewer's emotions. Although emotion-arousing ads are widely used and are commonly thought to be effective, their careless use produces a side-effect: the *psychoactive ad*. A psychoactive ad is any emotion-arousing ad that can cause a meaningful, well-defined group of viewers to feel extremely anxious, to feel hostile toward others, or to feel a loss of self-esteem. We argue that, because some ill-conceived psychoactive ads can cause harm, ethical issues must arise during their production. Current pretesting methods cannot identify the potentially psychoactive ads; therefore, we offer some tentative guidelines for reducing the number of viewers harmed by psychoactive ads.

TARANCZEWSKI, Pawel. The Primacy of the Eye in Evaluating Colours and Colour Harmonies. Rep Phil, 13, 27-35, 1989.

TARASTI, Eero. On the Modalities and Narrativity in Music. Acta Phil Fennica, 43, 110-131, 1988.

TARNAY, Brúnó. Crisis of Values and Experience of Time (in Hungarian). Magyar Filozof Szemle, 2-3, 263-272, 1989.

TARSOLEA, Constantin. La problématique du progrès dans la philosophie rationnaliste roumaine de l'entre-deux-guerres (in Romanian). Rev Filosof (Romania), 36(1), 50-58, Ja-F 89.

TARTER, Sandro. Gesù e la morale (rilettura di un saggio di F Costa). Teoria, 9(1), 241-250, 1989.

TATTON, Susan. "John Locke, David Fordyce, and Jean-Jacques Rousseau: On Liberty" in *Early Modern Philosophy II*, TWEYMAN, Stanley (ed), 75-84. Delmar, Caravan Books, 1988.

Educational philosophy underwent a radical revision during the eighteenth century, as the severe discipline and restraint of the Scholastic method gave way to a liberal educational program. The Enlightenment period is often described as the age in which the child was liberated. Yet the liberty which the child was given was not a negative freedom, or lack of impediment; it was, rather, a controlled and formative liberty, which was bound by many strictures. The controlled freedom which provides the cornerstone of Enlightenment educational theories is traced in this paper through the writings of John Locke, David Fordyce and J J Rousseau.

TAUBMAN, Peter M. Achieving the Right Distance. Educ Theor, 40(1), 121-133, Wint 90.

TAYLOR, Angus. The Significance of Darwinian Theory for Marx and Engels. Phil Soc Sci, 19(4), 409-423, D 89.

Marx was no Social Darwinist, yet did perceive an important link between Darwinian theory and his own theory of history. He and Engels saw Darwinian theory (1) as a blow against idealist justifications of the social order, and (2) as providing, by its nonteleological approach to biological evolution, a parallel to their own view of social change. In the Marxian view the structural constraints inherent in society's interaction with nature regulate, but do not predetermine, the changes made from generation to generation by human agents in pursuit of their own goals. Like Darwinian theory, Marxian theory provides a mechanism for retrospectively understanding history.

TAYLOR, Bob Pepperman. John Dewey and Environmental Thought. Environ Ethics, 12(2), 175-184, Sum 90.

In response to Chaloupka's discussion of Dewey's "social aesthetics," I argue, first, that Chaloupka has failed to fully appreciate the democratic, political foundation of Dewey's aesthetic sensibility and, second, that his description of Dewey's naturalism is ambiguous and misleading. I conclude that Dewey does have things to say to environmental thinkers, but that his views regarding environmental issues are much less unique than Chaloupka suggests. His work stands more as a democratic challenge to environmentalists than as a guide for their thought.

TAYLOR, C C W. "Aristotle's Epistemology" in *Epistemology (Companions to Ancient Thought: 1)*, EVERSON, Stephen (ed), 116-142. New York, Cambridge Univ Pr, 1989.

The paper reviews Aristotle's classification of the kinds and methods of knowledge, following his conception of epistemology as concerned, not with justification, but with understanding what knowledge is and how it is attained. The various kinds of theoretical and practical knowledge are considered; while Aristotle considers both to conform to an axiomatic model, in which grasp of principles (*nous*) is founded on perceptual data, he does not give a clear account of the different kinds of *nous* or their relation to perception. Aristotle's account of perceptual knowledge is shown to fit awkwardly with its foundational role.

TAYLOR, Carol. Ethics in Health Care and Medical Technologies. Theor Med, 11(2), 111-124, Je 90.

In this paper a case is used to demonstrate how ethical analysis enables health care professionals, patients and family members to make treatment decisions which ensure that medical technologies are used in the overall best interests of the patient. The claim is made and defended that ethical analysis can secure four beneficial outcomes when medical technologies are employed: (1) not allowing any medical technologies to be employed until the appropriate decision makers are identified and consulted; (2) insisting that medical technologies be employed not merely to promote the medical interests of the patient but rather on the basis of their ability to contribute to the overall well-being of the patient; (3) challenging caregivers to reflect on the dynamic interplay between their conscious and unconscious values and consequent determinations of what is in the patient's best interests; and (4) providing a justification for selected interventions which makes possible rational dialogue between caregivers espousing different viewpoints about treatment options.

TAYLOR, G Stephen. Individual Privacy and Computer-Based Human Resource Information Systems. J Bus Ethics, 8(7), 569-576, Jl 89.

The proliferation of computers in the business realm may lead to ethical problems between individual and societal rights, and the organization's need to control costs. In an attempt to explore the causes of this potential conflict, this study examined the varying levels of sensitivity 223 respondents assigned to different types of information typically stored in computer-based human resource information systems. It was found that information most directly related to the job—pay rate, fringe benefits, educational history—was considered to be the most sensitive. Participants, however, were more concerned about certain types of individuals/groups accessing these systems than about the kinds of information contained in them. Implications of these findings are discussed.

TAYLOR, James E. Kelly on the Logic of Eternal Knowledge. Mod Sch, 67(2), 141-147, Ja 90.

In a recent article in *The Modern Schoolman* (Vol. LXVI, November 1988), Charles J Kelly argues that a natural rendering of propositions expressing God's eternal knowledge of future contingent events leads to a dilemma which is unacceptable to the classical theist. Kelly attempts to circumvent this difficulty by suggesting two alternative parsings of such propositions which, he argues, do not pose such a difficulty. In this paper, I argue first that the purported dilemma described by Kelly is not a genuine dilemma. Secondly, I argue that if the dilemma were genuine, Kelly's suggested solutions to it would fail.

TAYLOR, Mark C. *Tears*. Albany, SUNY Pr, 1990

TAYLOR, Michael. "Technicism, Education, and Living a Human Life" in *Inquiries into Values: The Inaugural Session of the International Society for Value Inquiry*, LEE, Sander H , 633-642. Lewiston, Mellen Pr, 1989.

Several writers have recently described the rise of what they call "technicisms" or "the technicist attitude" in educational contexts. I try to define the essential features involved in the technicist attitude as it occurs in educational thinking and practice and to specify some of the effects of this attitude on educational practices and values. I argue that when the technicist attitude becomes exclusive, some educational practices are threatened. Chief among these threatened practices are the disciplines known as "the humanities." I contend that while the subject matter and aims of the humanities often cannot meet the criterion embedded in technicism, such subject matter assists people in coping with or appreciating human life. My conclusion is that deprivation of such skills and resources as those provided by humanities education leaves people ill-prepared for coming to terms with some of the conditions that are inherent in the living of a human life.

TAYLOR, Paul. The Make-Up of Literature. Phil Papers, 18(1), 75-94, My 89.

This paper concerns the question of how the context of composing a literary work affects the nature and interpretation of the work. The discussion centers on cases of verbally identical works originating from different authors and concludes that such works are ontologically distinct and will invariably differ in respect of some of their literary qualities.

TAYLOR, Paul. New Trends in Literary Aesthetics: An Overview. Phil Papers, 18(1), 1-6, My 89.

TAYLOR, Paul and PITTS, Andrew M. A Note on Russell's Paradox in Locally Cartesian Closed Categories. Stud Log, 48(3), 377-387, S 89.

TAYLOR, Paul. Paintings and Identity. Brit J Aes, 29(4), 353-362, Autumn 89.

TAYLOR, Talbot J and HARRIS, Roy. Landmarks in Linguistic Thought: The Western Tradition from Socrates to Saussure. New York, Routledge, 1989

TEEPLE, G. The Doctoral Dissertation of Karl Marx. Hist Polit Thought, 11(1), 81-118, Spr 90.

Marx's doctoral dissertation remains one of the least examined and discussed of all his works. It is usually understood to belong to a 'philosophical', idealist, or Hegelian period with no lasting importance to his later writings. This detailed examination suggests otherwise. It is argued through textual analysis that there were two principal aims to the dissertation, namely, to find the source of concepts of essence in the real, sensuous world, and to establish that the nature of mind or human self-consciousness had a material, concrete basis which determined its existence. In making these arguments by means of a contrast between two materialists from antiquity, Marx established the starting point for his intellectual development, to wit, the basis of his notion of science and materialism that he employed and expanded in subsequent years.

TEICHMAN, Jenny. How to Define Terrorism. Philosophy, 64(250), 505-517, O 89.

Disagreement about terrorism due to fact that the word is used polemically. "Ordinary usage" definitions should be rejected. Terrorism originally meant government terror. Later it meant tyrannicide. Now it means violent rebellion involving acts like hostage-taking, attacks on neutrals. Terrorism best defined as a spectrum of three overlapping classes: state terrorism (reigns of terror); assassination of rulers or their agents; and "modern" terrorism, a species of nationalistic rebellion involving atrocities. Justification of acts of terror depends where in the spectrum they fall. Tyrannicide sometimes justified, atrocities never. No reason to suppose atrocity a specially effective method of warfare.

TEICHMANN, Roger. 'Actually'. Analysis, 50(1), 16-19, Ja 90.

The sentence "It is possible that everything which is actually red should have been shiny" (S), and sentences like it, are shown to be translatable as pieces of higher-order quantification with "Possibly" = there is no need for an "Actually" operator, pace Davies et al. The translation of S proceeds via the paraphrase "For some n, there are n things which are all red, and which alone are red, and it is possible they should all be shiny," which in turn receives logicist treatment.

TEICHMANN, Werner. Individualisierung als Emanzipationsprojekt? Deut Z Phil, 38(1), 78-82, 1990.

TEJERA, V (ed) and LAVINE, T Z (ed). History and Anti-History in Philosophy. Norwell, Kluwer, 1989

TEJERA, V. "Intellectual History as a Tool of Philosophy" in History and Anti-History in Philosophy, LAVINE, T Z (ed), 122-134. Norwell, Kluwer, 1989.

TEJERA, V. "Introduction: On the Nature of Philosophic Historiography" in History and Anti-History in Philosophy, LAVINE, T Z (ed), 1-18. Norwell, Kluwer, 1989.

TEJERA, V. "The Philosophical Historiography of J H Randall" in History and Anti-History in Philosophy, LAVINE, T Z (ed), 215-236. Norwell, Kluwer, 1989.

TEJERA, V. Spirituality in Santayana. Trans Peirce Soc, 25(4), 503-529, Fall 89.

TEKIPPE, Terry J. Lonergan's Analysis of Error: An Experiment. Gregorianum, 71(2), 353-374, 1990.

TELLER, Paul. A Modern Formal Logic Primer, Volume I and II. Englewood Cliffs, Prentice-Hall, 1989

A more fun less tears introduction to formal logic, through soundness and completeness. Includes independently usable Fitch style natural deduction and Jeffrey style trees, identity, function symbols, and definite descriptions. Volume I: Sentence Logic. Volume II: Predicate Logic and Metatheory.

TELLER, Paul. "Relativity, Relational Holism, and the Bell Inequalities" in Philosophical Consequences of Quantum Theory: Reflections on Bell's Theorem, CUSHING, James T (ed), 208-223. Notre Dame, Univ Notre Dame Pr, 1989.

TELLO, B D. Derecho natural. Sapientia, 44(173), 224-232, Jl-S 89.

TEN, C L. "Comment: Autonomy, Toleration, and the Harm Principle" in Issues in Contemporary Legal Philosophy: The Influence of H L A Hart, GAVISON, Ruth (ed), 334-341. New York, Clarendon/Oxford Pr, 1987.

TEN, C L. Moral Rights and Duties in Wicked Legal Systems. Utilitas, 1(1), 135-143, My 89.

TEN, C L. Positive Retributivism. Soc Phil Pol, 7(2), 194-208, Spr 90.

Retributivists and other non-consequentialists seek to justify the punishment of criminals without appealing to its deterrent effects. Two such theories of punishment are examined and rejected. The first claims that punishment restores a fair balance of benefits and burdens which the criminal's act upsets. But it is unclear how the balance can be restored by state punishment which does not confer additional benefits on the victims of crime. The second theory regards the penitential reform of offenders as the justifying aim of punishment. But the theory does not explain why punishment in the form of imprisonment is necessary for penitential reform, nor does it establish that this aim will in fact be achieved by such punishment. The paper concludes with a limited defense of general deterrence.

TEOH, Hai Yap and SHIU, Godwin Y. Attitudes Towards Corporate Social Responsibility and Perceived Importance of Social Responsibility Information. J Bus Ethics, 9(1), 71-77, Ja 90.

This study addressed the questions of perceived importance of social responsibility information (SRI) characteristics in a decision context, as well as the attitudes of institutional investors toward social responsibility involvement. The results showed that SRI presently disclosed in company annual reports did not have any significant impact on institutional investors' decisions. However, if SRI were presented in quantified, financial form, and were focused on product improvement and fair business practices, such information would be perceived as more important for investment decisions. Attitudes toward corporate social responsibility also suggested that institutional investors were not totally opposed to company involvement in social activities.

TERZIS, George N. Autonomy Without Indeterminism: A Reconstruction of Kant's Groundwork, Chapter Three. Mod Sch, 67(1), 1-13, N 89.

Kant's Groundwork, Chapter Three, attempts to derive the validity of the Moral Law from an account of the freedom of rational agency. How should we understand such freedom? My aim in this paper is to show that we can preserve the idea of autonomy Kant employs in defining freedom but without also having to accept his idea of indeterminism. Because of the problematic nature of the second of these two ideas, I believe Kant's derivation is strengthened by not having to presuppose its correctness.

TERZIS, George N. An Objection to Kantian Ethical Rationalism. Phil Stud, 57(3), 299-313, N 89.

By 'Kantian ethical rationalism' I understand a well-known philosophical position that attempts to derive moral requirements from a theory of rational agency that does not presuppose the correctness of any substantive moral considerations. Can such a position succeed in differentiating the norms of morality it defends from other reason-giving norms—e.g., those of prudence? I argue that considerations that allow the position to make this differentiation are ones to which it cannot legitimately appeal and that those to which it can so appeal are too weak to make it.

TESSIER, L J. Feminist Separatism—The Dynamics of Self-Creation. Process Stud, 18(2), 127-130, Sum 89.

A response to Nancy Howell's Whiteheadian analysis of feminist separatism, considering the role of separation and radical relatedness in the self-creation process.

TESSITORE, Aristide. Plato's Lysis: An Introduction to Philosophic Friendship. S J Phil, 28(1), 115-132, Spr 90.

This article takes issue with the practice of reading the Lysis as a less than successful prelude to Plato's mature teaching, especially in the Symposium. By taking my bearings from the dramatis personae, I argue for the literary and philosophical integrity of the dialogue as a whole. The Lysis is intended to "exhibit" a philosophic understanding of friendship. The inconclusive character of the discussion, although seemingly "ridiculous" from a conventional point of view, proves to be an essential part of Socratic-Platonic education to philosophic friendship.

TESSITORE, Fulvio. Per una storia della cultura. Arch Stor Cult, 1, 11-47, 1988.

THACHIL, Jose. Theology of Religions and Sacrifice. J Dharma, 14(4), 329-340, O-D 89.

The Vatican II prepared the ground for the meeting of the Christian Churches with non-Christian religions. To promote a better understanding among them, a comparative study of Vedic religion and Christianity on the point of sacrifice has been undertaken. In almost all religions sacrifice occupies the central place of importance, since it is the deepest and most common expression of man's relation to the Infinite. The conclusion reached is: in Vedic religion and Christianity the gift which one offers to God in sacrifice, is a symbol of the offering of one's own self.

THAGARD, Paul. Concepts and Conceptual Change. Synthese, 82(2), 255-274, F 90.

This paper argues that questions concerning the nature of concepts that are central in cognitive psychology are also important to epistemology and that there is more to conceptual change than mere belief revision. Understanding of epistemic change requires appreciation of the complex ways in which concepts are structured and organized and of how this organization can affect belief revision. Following a brief summary of the psychological functions of concepts and a discussion of some recent accounts of what concepts are, I propose a view of concepts as complex computational structures. This account suggests that conceptual change can come in varying degrees, with the most extreme consisting of fundamental conceptual reorganizations. These degrees of conceptual change are illustrated by the development of the concept of an acid.

THAGARD, Paul. The Conceptual Structure of the Chemical Revolution. Phil Sci, 57(2), 183-209, Je 90.

This paper investigates the revolutionary conceptual changes that took place when the phlogiston theory of Stahl was replaced by the oxygen theory of Lavoisier. Using techniques drawn from artificial intelligence, it represents the crucial stages in Lavoisier's conceptual development for 1772 to 1789. It then sketches a computational theory of conceptual change to account for Lavoisier's discovery of the oxygen theory and for the replacement of the phlogiston theory.

THAGARD, Paul. Connectionism and Epistemology: Goldman on Winner-Take-All Networks. Philosophia (Israel), 19(2-3), 189-196, O 89.

This paper examines Alvin Goldman's discussion of acceptance and uncertainty in chapter 15 of his book, *Epistemology and Cognition*. Goldman discusses how acceptance and rejection of beliefs might be understood in terms of "winner-take-all" connectionist networks. The paper answers some of the questions he raises in his epistemic evaluation of connectionist programs. The major tool for doing this is a connectionist model of explanatory coherence judgments (Thagard, *Behavioral and Brain Sciences*, 1989). Finally, there is a discussion of problems for Goldman's general epistemological project that arise if one adopts a different approach to connectionism based on distributed representations.

THAGARD, Paul. Philosophy and Machine Learning. Can J Phil, 20(2), 261-276, Je 90.

This article discusses the philosophical relevance of recent computational work on inductive inference being conducted in the rapidly growing branch of artificial intelligence called machine learning.

THAMM, Georg. Zu Hans Reiners Wertethik. Z Phil Forsch, 44(2), 305-309, 1990.

Ohne metaphysische Thesen aufzustellen, definiert Reiner "Wert" durch "erfreulichkeit", unterscheidet zwischen objektiven (absoluten und sozialen) und subjektiven Werten und leitet daraus Handlungsregeln ab. Thamm zeigt, dass aus Reiners Definition kein Unterschied zwischen absoluten und subjektiven Werten folgt und dass aus dem Unterschied zwischen sozialen und subjektiven Werten kein Vorzugskriterium abgeleitet werden kann. Daraus folgt: Die Theorie von den moralischen Werten kann nicht Fundament der Ethik sein.

THANDEKA. "I've Known Rivers": Black Theology's Response to Process Theology. Process Stud, 18(4), 282-293, Wint 89.

William R Jones, Theodore Walker and Henry James Young share a worldview which is not apparent. The purpose of this essay is to identify their common vision. This paper demonstrates that much of their vision cannot be interpreted by process categories. Their worldview has the integrity of the hard-edged hope of the oppressed. This worldview is not an adventure of ideas but rather the pathway of a people moving toward liberation. To the extent that process theologians understand this, they will be forced to acknowledge the partisan nature of their own metaphysical claims. This acknowledgement should bring forth a reevaluation of the implicit paternalism that allows process theologians to maintain a comfortable intellectual separation from the lived experiences of the oppressed. This paper accomplishes its task by analyzing the arguments of Jones, Walker and Young in support of their contention that process theology's current theodicy is inadequate.

THARP, Leslie. Myth and Mathematics: A Conceptualistic Philosophy of

Mathematics. Synthese, 81(2), 167-201, N 89.

THARP, Leslie. Three Theorems of Metaphysics. Synthese, 81(2), 207-214, N 89.

THEIS, R. Aspects et perspectives du problème de la limite dans la philosophie théorique de Kant. Tijdschr Filosof, 52(1), 62-89, Mr 90.

The article starts from the central stake of the problem of the limit in the *Critique of Pure Reason*. In a first step, the author analyses the articulation of this problem with sensibility, understanding and reason in mind. In a second step, the author questions himself about the anthropological signification of this theme. He thinks that two complementary existential categories can be released from the concept of the limit: that of finitude as well as that of desire. What is man? A finite being as well as a being of desire.

THEMUDO, Marina Ramos. Geometria em fragmentos: Forma e conteúdo no contexto wittgensteiniano. Rev Port Filosof, 45(2), 207-223, Ap-Je 89.

A single trace characterizes the texts, published by Wittgenstein, however much different they may be in style and context: the fragmentary quality of their discursivity, which surprisingly draws the Austrian thinker near to Heraclitus, the *Obscure*. Situated in a transitional epoch between modernity and what has been given in the context of Western civilization the designation of "post," the *Tractatus Logico-Philosophicus* and *Philosophische Untersuchungen* reveal an attractive, seductive ambiguity. Apparently in rupture with a tradition, they can be placed in the turning point of contemporary philosophy accentuating the theme of *difference*: critical of philosophy, they demonstrate the mutation occurring within the act and being of philosophizing. In the process of abandoning rational foundations, they reinvent the order of *logos*. (edited)

THÉRIAULT, J Yvon. La première crise de la raison. Rev Univ Ottawa, 57(4), 49-62, O-D 87.

THIBAUD, P. Nom propre et individuation chez Peirce. Dialectica, 43(4), 373-386, 1989.

This brief study is an attempt to show how Peirce's theory of individuation gives rise to the first modern analysis of the proper noun. Through a triple characterization—semantic (uniqueness of the referent), pragmatic (indexical nature of the reference) and semiotic (iconico-symbolic index)—of the proper noun, Peirce provides the first truly enlightening description of the conditions in which it becomes possible to designate individuals in language, which gives us a particularly suggestive example of what can be understood as universals of language.

THIBAUD, Pierre. Catégories et raison chez C S Peirce. Arch Phil, 52(4), 539-552, O-D 89.

Being ultimate conditions for the functioning of semiosis and therefore—according to Peirce—of thought, categories are here studied in themselves and in the relationship they have, in Peirce's works, with science and value.

THIELE, Leslie Paul. Nietzsche's Politics. Interpretation, 17(2), 275-290, Wint 89-90.

This article investigates Nietzsche's radical individualism and demonstrates how this antipolitical philosophy effectively was a spiritualization of politics. Like Plato's *Republic*, which stipulates that not the city—the soul writ large—but the soul of man itself must be the chief concern, Nietzsche's worlds employ a political vocabulary to describe the inner life of man. With the soul formulated as an agonistic political community, Nietzsche insists that the task of life is to create an internal order. This creation of spiritual unity is called style.

THIEME, Karl-Heinz. Schlüsseltechnologien—Herausforderung und Chance für moralischen Fortschritt. Deut Z Phil, 37(10-11), 945-955, 1989.

THISTLEWOOD, David. The MOMA and the ICA: A Common Philosophy of Modern Art. Brit J Aes, 29(4), 316-328, Autumn 89.

The paper argues for similarity in the inaugural exhibitions policies of Alfred Barr at the Museum of Modern Art, New York (est. 1929) and Herbert Read and Roland Penrose at the London Institute of Contemporary Arts (est. 1947). Both institutions featured contemporary and primitive art, and promoted 'biomorphic abstraction' as a goal for future aesthetic development. The ICA in effect vindicated MOMA policy. Paul Klee's painting, considered a prime exemplar of biomorphic abstraction, was interpreted at the ICA as offering insights into how complex emotional expression might be conveyed in simple organic constructions, thus identifying didactically the essence of contemporary art.

THOM, Paul. Young's Critique of Authenticity in Musical Performance. Brit J Aes, 30(3), 273-276, Jl 90.

A concept of authenticity as compliance with the work's explicit and implicit directives is applied to a recent 'authentic' performance of Berlioz's

Fantastic Symphony. The usefulness of such a concept is defended against J O Young's critique.

THOMAS, Carolyn E and RINTALA, Janet A. Injury as Alienation in Sport. J Phil Sport, 16, 44-58, 1989.

The purpose of the paper was to examine the effects of injury in sport related to potential alienation in sport. The parameters of isolation, powerlessness, anomie, and self/body alienation were explored. It was argued that the injured athlete becomes separated from and discarded by teammates and the sport world and that such injury may attenuate achievement of the unity of body and action possible before the injury. The doubt and vulnerability generated by injury were viewed as potentially negating optimal future potential as well as moving the body into object status incapable of the essential unity of body subject.

THOMAS, J L H. The Schoolman's Advocate: In Defence of the Academic Pursuit of Philosophy. Mind, 98(392), 483-506, O 89.

A fourfold defence of academic philosophy is undertaken. First, it is argued that the academic pursuit of philosophy is the necessary condition of the pursuit of philosophy in general, given five secondary features of philosophical activity, each implying a distinct, but related sense of 'academic'. Second, seven representative objections to academic philosophy, mainly by Germanic writers, are reproduced and assessed. Third, some of the merits and achievements of philosophy are presented and correctly ascribed to academic philosophers. Fourth, the current state of academic philosophy in Britain is described, its causes diagnosed, and seven suggestions offered to philosophers for ameliorating it.

THOMAS, John R. Reflections and Reservations Concerning Martin Buber's Dialogical Philosophy in Its Religious Dimension. Dialec Hum, 16(1), 183-189, Wint 89.

The question of the role and place of mystical religious experience in Buber's philosophy is explored. The importance of grounding in a particular historical setting in order for dialogue between man and God to occur is questioned, and whether Buber imposes limiting conditions on God's appearance to man and in the world.

THOMAS, Laurence. Doing Justice to Egoism. J Phil, 86(10), 551-552, O 89.

THOMAS, Laurence. "Friends and Lovers" in *Person to Person*, GRAHAM, George (ed), 182-198. Philadelphia, Temple Univ Pr, 1989.

THOMAS, Laurence. "Religion as Cultural Artifact" in *Mind, Value and Culture: Essays in Honor of E M Adams*, WEISSBORD, David (ed), 346-353. Atascadero, Ridgeview, 1989.

THOMAS, Laurence. Trust and Survival: Securing a Vision of the Good Society. J Soc Phil, 20(1-2), 34-41, Spr-Fall 89.

THOMAS, Max W. Misuse of Inference—OR—Why Sherlock Holmes is a Fake. Thinking, 8(4), 29-32, 1990.

Some critical thinking texts suggest that Conan Doyle's Sherlock Holmes is a paradigm for inference. I argue that this example is misleading because a proper inference must reach a specific conclusion to the exclusion of contrary possibilities.

THOMAS, R S D. Inquiry Into Meaning and Truth. Phil Math, 5(1-2), 73-87, 1990.

THOMASMA, David C. "Advance Directives and Health Care for the Elderly" in *Advance Directives in Medicine*, HACKLER, Chris (ed), 93-109. New York, Praeger, 1989.

The problem of caring for the elderly in light of social parsimony is addressed in this paper. Instead of viewing advance directives as a mechanism to detail preferences while dying a more expanded version is proposed. At retirement all persons might be required to institute an advance directive to cover all forms of care. This is but one component of a larger social system I call Eldercare that would help limit costs by encouraging choices regarding expensive treatment in the populace as a whole. Some problems a more enhanced model of advance directives might cause in a social system are also addressed at the end of the article.

THOMASMA, David C. Establishing the Moral Basis of Medicine: Edmund D Pellegrino's Philosophy of Medicine. J Med Phil, 15(3), 245-267, Je 90.

Edmund D Pellegrino's philosophy of medicine is explored in categories such as the motivation in constructing a philosophy of medicine, the method, the starting point of the doctor-patient relationship, negotiation about values in this relationship, the goal of the relationship, the moral basis of medicine, and additional concerns in the relationship (concerns such as gatekeeping, philosophical anthropology, axiology, philosophy of the body, and the general disjunction between science and morals). A critique of this philosophy is presented in the following areas: methodology, relation to ontology and sociology, the dynamic of individual and social concerns, and

the new social condition of medicine. Finally, some suggestions for the future revitalization of philosophy of medicine are made based on Pellegrino's ideas. The focus throughout is on the moral basis and moral consequences of the philosophy of medicine, and not on other important themes.

THOMASON, Richmond H (ed). *Philosophical Logic and Artificial Intelligence.* Norwell, Kluwer, 1989

In developing methods for modeling reasoning and intelligent behavior, workers in artificial intelligence have developed intellectual tools that are continuous with those already belonging to philosophy and logic, but that also incorporate many profound innovations that should be of value in philosophical pursuits. These deal with matters such as resource limited reasoning, perception, planning and plan recognition, reasoning about knowledge and belief, natural language understanding, knowledge representation and organizing common sense knowledge, uncertainty management, defeasible reasoning, reasoning about time and causality, explanation, and learning. Some of these topics are discussed in the volume to which this paper is an introduction.

THOMASSEN, Beroald. Schriftgemässe Philosophie als philosophische Laienmeditation? Phil Reform, 55(1), 1-15, 1990.

The essay of the contemporary Berlin philosopher Michael Theunissen ('O aiton lambanei. Der Gebetsblaube Jesu und die Zeitlichkeit des Christseins, in: *Jesus. Ort der Erfahrung Gottes*, Freiburg/Basel/Wien, 1976, 13-68) is interpreted as a contribution to a philosophy according to Scripture. The main points of discussion are the constitution of a philosophical communication with the biblical Jesus and the basic elements of the accomplishment of this communication.

THOMPKINS, E F. A Farewell to Forms of Life. Philosophy, 65(252), 181-197, Ap 90.

THOMPSON, Audrey. Friendship and Moral Character: Feminist Implications for Moral Education. Proc Phil Educ, 45, 61-75, 1989.

Current debates regarding the compatibility of an ethics of justice with an ethics of care have addressed such possibilities as combining the two theories, alternating between them, or identifying one or the other as derivative. This essay draws upon an analysis of friendship to argue that fully responsible moral character and conduct must resist circumscription within public or private spheres, and that the public/private dichotomy upon which theories of care and justice are predicated impoverishes our understanding of the conditions and consequences of moral action. While the alternative moral framework considered in the paper is necessarily somewhat speculative, it offers a challenge to existing approaches to moral education that neglect the relational, structural, and institutional dimensions of character and conduct.

THOMPSON, Henry O. "The Fear of the Lord is the Beginning of Wisdom" in *The Wisdom of Faith: Essays in Honor of Dr Sebastian Alexander Matczak*, THOMPSON, Henry O (ed), 101-126. Lanham, Univ Pr of America, 1989.

THOMPSON, Henry O (ed). *The Wisdom of Faith: Essays in Honor of Dr Sebastian Alexander Matczak.* Lanham, Univ Pr of America, 1989

THOMPSON, Janna. A Refutation of Environmental Ethics. Environ Ethics, 12(2), 147-160, Sum 90.

An environmental ethic holds that some entities in nature or in natural states of affairs are intrinsically valuable. I argue that proposals for an environmental ethic either fail to satisfy requirements which any ethical system must satisfy to be an ethic or they fail to give us reason to suppose that the values they promote are intrinsic values. If my arguments are correct, then environmental ethics is not properly ethics at all.

THOMPSON, Kirill O. Taoist Cultural Reality: The Harmony of Aesthetic Order. J Chin Phil, 17(2), 175-185, Je 90.

Taoist philosophers Lao Tzu and Chuang Tzu viewed society as a spontaneous anarchy of relative perspectives which reflected the underlying harmony of *Tao.* They considered genuine social harmony to be much the product of rulership's acquiescence in this basal harmony, and deemed discord as springing from the imposition of moral and legal codes and poverty as ensuing from undue official concern for wealth and power. Classical Taoist thinkers viewed society as a spontaneous mosaic of people's lives, its aesthetic order a composite of their relative perspectives. Rather than set forth general principles of reality and of conduct for all to live by, they therefore appealed to each person to open his mind to this fecund mosaic, offering a way to effect a greening of human life.

THOMPSON, Paul B. Agrarianism and the American Philosophical Tradition. Agr Human Values, 7(1), 3-8, Wint 90.

This article introduces a series of essays by other authors that discuss the links between agrarian values or experience and the more systematic writings of

Jefferson, Emerson, Dewey, Mead, and Wendell Berry. Background is provided by discussing the significance of Jefferson's comments on farming for philosophical ethics, and by summarizing a few key elements in Peirce's philosophy of science.

THOMPSON, Paul. Philosophy of Biology Under Attack: Stent Versus Rosenberg. Biol Phil, 4(3), 345-351, Jl 89.

THOMPSON, Paul. *The Structure of Biological Theories*. Albany, SUNY Pr, 1989

The central thesis of this book is that, in the context of biological theorizing, the semantic conception of the structure of scientific theories is logically, methodologically and heuristically richer than the standard conception according to which a theory is an axiomatic deductive structure partially interpreted by correspondence rules. A general exposition of each conception is offered followed in each case by an exposition, critical analysis, and comparison of evolutionary theory on each conception. The book concludes with discussions of the importance of theory structure to characterizations of the role of culture and cognition in evolutionary explanations of human behavior.

THOMSON, Anne. Emotional Origins of Morality—A Sketch. J Moral Educ, 18(3), 199-207, O 89.

This paper traces the origins of the development of our capacity to make critical moral judgments. It is suggested that such a capacity develops out of unlearnt tendencies to sympathy and resentment. In the first section, a cognitive view of the nature of emotion is presented—a view which stresses that, far from being irrational disturbances, emotions involve judgments as well as urges to act, and that these judgments are frequently correct assessments of a situation. Section II discusses one central feature of morality—the susceptibility of moral beings to remorse. Section III explores the nature of two particular emotions, sympathy and resentment, and suggests that remorse could develop out of primitive forms of these emotions, to which human beings are naturally subject. In the final section, a brief sketch is offered of the kind of process moral development must be if remorse does indeed develop from these primitive emotions.

THOMSON, James F. In Defense of '⊃'. J Phil, 87(2), 57-70, F 90.

THOMSON, Judith Jarvis. Morality and Bad Luck. Metaphilosophy, 20(3-4), 203-221, Jl-O 89.

THOMSON, Judith Jarvis. The No Good Reason Thesis. Soc Phil Pol, 7(1), 1-21, Autumn 89.

THORP, John. Aristotle's *Horror Vacui*. Can J Phil, 20(2), 149-166, Je 90.

Aristotle's resistance to the idea of empty space seems much stronger than the arguments he is able to produce to show that space is full. The present article inquires into this gap, and situates Aristotle's inability to conceive of the void in the fact that he lacked any other measure of *quantity of matter* than volume.

TIAN-MIN, Xu. China: Moral Puzzles. Hastings Center Rep, 20(2), 24-25, Mr-Ap 90.

TIAOGONG, Wu. Wang Yuyang's Natural Thought on Art. Chin Stud Phil, 21(3), 54-84, Spr 90.

TIBELL, Gunnar and GUSTAFSSON, Bengt. Critics of Science and Research Ethics in Sweden. Phil Soc Act, 15(3-4), 59-74, Jl-D 89.

TIBERG, Nils. Waste and Culture. Phil Soc Act, 15(3-4), 29-34, Jl-D 89.

TICHY, Pavel and ODDIE, Graham. Resplicing Properties in the Supervenience Base. Phil Stud, 58(3), 259-269, Mr 90.

John Bacon has recently argued that weak and strong supervenience are equivalent. He employs a novel closure principle: related classes of properties must be closed under 'resplicing'. This requirement is shown to render supervenience both too narrow and too wide. It rules out perfectly good supervenience bases, and permits counterintuitive relations of supervenience. If the approach is amended to rectify the former shortcoming the latter persists. This is because Bacon's strong and weak supervenience are both equivalent to old-style weak supervenience. This furnishes further arguments that weak supervenience is too weak to do the work required of it.

TIENSON, John L. About Competence. Phil Papers, 19(1), 19-36, Ap 90.

Chomsky used the word 'competence' for, among other things, what we might call a *cognitive system*: something *in* a cognizer that *produces* not previously present beliefs. Speakers surely have a system that produces knowledge of grammatical relations, etc., involved in understanding and producing novel speech. This knowledge is necessary for linguistic performance, but does not completely explain any linguistic performance. Thus a distinction must be made between competence and performance. There are many such cognitive systems, underlying not only language use,

but such diverse capacities as complex physical skills and the ability to make moral and aesthetic judgments. Thus, the importance of this notion of competence goes well beyond that of linguistic competence.

TIENSON, John L. Is This Any Way to be a Realist? Phil Psych, 3(1), 155-164, 1990.

Andy Clark argues that the reality and causal efficacy of the folk psychological attitudes do not require in-the-head correlates of the that-clauses by which they are attributed. The facts for which Fodor invokes a language of thought as empirical explanation—systematicity, for example—are, Clark argues, an *a priori* conceptual demand upon propositional attitude ascription, and hence not in need of empirical explanation. However, no such strategy can work. A priori demands imposed by our practices do not eliminate the need for empirical explanation of how these demands are satisfied by particular beings. And given the vast number of potential beliefs, and the interrelationships they exhibit, no one has the slightest idea how they might be explained except by in-the-head syntax.

TIENSON, John and HORGAN, Terence. Representations without Rules. Phil Topics, 17(1), 147-174, Spr 89.

We argue (1) that in order for a cognitive system to deal successfully with its environment (as organisms do), it needs syntactically structured mental representations that interact with each other in ways that depend upon their structure and content; and (2) that the relevant kind of processing is not describable by exceptionless rules statable over the representations themselves. Connectionism, we argue, appears to have the potential for showing how there can be cognitive processing that is structure sensitive and content sensitive without being rule governed.

TIERNEY, Brian. Origins of Natural Rights Language: Texts and Contexts, 1150-1250. Hist Polit Thought, 10(4), 615-646, Wint 89.

Modern histories of natural rights theories normally place the origin of such doctrines in the late medieval or early modern periods. Rights theories are commonly associated with the rise of nominalist philosophy or the beginning of a capitalist economy. This paper argues that the real origin is earlier, in the humanistic jurisprudence of the twelfth century. Medieval Decretists often defined *ius naturale* as a subjective force or power or faculty of the human person. From this they went on to develop theories of substantive natural rights.

TILES, J E. Our Perception of the External World. Philosophy, 24, 15-19, 88 Supp.

The problem of the external world is commonly motivated by distorting lessons which are learned from studying the physiology of perception. When the distortions are exposed, there is little to motivate the problem other than the questionable philosophic project of separating the 'given' in perception from the inferences we make about it. And one cannot secure the intelligibility of the problem of the external world from the standpoint of this questionable project unless one also makes highly disputable assumptions about what it is for the words, which we use to state the problem, to have a meaning.

TILES, Mary E. Method and the Authority of Science. Philosophy, 24, 31-51, 88 Supp.

Is it possible to say why we should give more credence to the pronouncements of scientists than of astrologers? By considering the respects in which Popper's affirmative response to this question is inadequate it is concluded that there is no single criterion which will distinguish between scientific and nonscientific ways of allowing observation to have a bearing on theoretical claims. It is suggested that the authority of science has a double grounding in manifest practical power on the one hand, and in the exercise of critical scrutiny at all levels of observation and theory on the other.

TILES, Mary E. *The Philosophy of Set Theory: An Historical Introduction to Cantor's Paradise*. Cambridge, Blackwell, 1989

This is an exploration of the status of transfinite set theory which takes the form of seeking a historical answer to the question "At what point does the classical finitism, derived from Aristotle, cease to be tenable?" The answer proposed is that it is with the acceptance of "pathological functions" as legitimate objects of mathematical study. After examining axiomatic set theory and the current status of Cantor's continuum hypothesis it is suggested that set theory should not be viewed as a foundation, but as a superstructure, an abstract recipient of all possible structure, which necessarily remains beyond complete mathematical determination.

TILGHMAN, B R. Literature, Philosophy and Nonsense. Brit J Aes, 30(3), 256-265, Jl 90.

Three of Marcel Aymé's short stories are described which appear to state philosophical theses about the notion of time. Taken as theses what he says is conceptual nonsense of the kind that Wittgenstein thinks infects philosophy. It is argued that his stories should not be taken as philosophy, but as conceptual jokes intended to illuminate some aspect of the human condition and are literary devices rather than philosophy. His commentators have been unable to appreciate this aspect of his work and to distinguish his nonsense from fantasy. Aymé's use of nonsense is compared with that of O K Bouwsma.

TILLEMANS, Tom J F. Forman and Semantic Aspects of Tibetan Buddhist Debate Logic. J Indian Phil, 17(3), 265-297, S 89.

TILLEMANS, Tom J F. On *Sapaksa*. J Indian Phil, 18(1), 53-79, Mr 90.

TILLEY, John. Moral Internalism and Moral Relativism. Method Sci, 23(2), 103-113, 1990.

TILLEY, Terrence W. God and the Silencing of Job. Mod Theol, 5(3), 257-270, Ap 89.

This article argues that the biblical book of Job portrays a god who tortures the first lamenting, then angry, Job into silence. The key verse portraying Job's submission, 42:6, is one of profound abjection. The often-alleged vindication of Job by God in the epilogue is shown to be no vindication at all. The text forces the serious reader to act: most interpreters join God in silencing the voice of the suffering one, rather than allowing the text to deconstruct their preconceived theodicies about how God and human suffering are related.

TILLEY, Terrence W. Incommensurability, Intratextuality, and Fideism. Mod Theol, 5(2), 87-111, Ja 89.

The 'New Yale' school of narrative theologians is often labeled 'fideist' for its characterizing religious discourse systems as incommensurable and intratextual. This article argues that Lindbeck's espousal of a pure intratextual semiotics to account for Christian discourse is incoherent and that Frei's dilemma of either intratextual reading of or extratextual interpretation of (and imposing alien meaning on) Scripture is avoidable. It sketches a 'dirty' intratextuality which recognizes the internal multiplicity of Christian discourses and avoids the relativist fideism of the 'New Yale' school without embracing the extravagant hermeneutics of the 'New Chicago' group (Tracy, Ricoeur).

TILLEY, Terrence W. Reformed Epistemology and Religious Fundamentalism: How Basic Are Our Basic Beliefs? Mod Theol, 6(3), 237-257, Ap 90.

This paper argues that epistemological reliablists such as A Plantinga and W Alston offer no help in discriminating justified from unjustified religious beliefs. It constructs a *reductio* argument to show that, on their accounts, fundamentalism is to be found as reliable as any other religious belief system. It suggests that the reliablists need to turn from their epistemological individualism to an analysis and evaluation of the concrete social discourse practices in which individuals' religious beliefs are formed if they are to provide a useful normative religious epistemology.

TILLIETTE, Xavier. Edith Stein et la philosophie chrétienne: A propos d'*Être fini et Être éternel*. Gregorianum, 71(1), 97-113, 1990.

TILLIETTE, Xavier. La filosofia cristiana di Edith Stein. Aquinas, 32(1), 131-137, Ja-Ap 89.

TILLIETTE, Xavier. La philosophie et l'absolu. Rev Phil Fr, 180(1), 79-87, Ja-Mr 90.

TINDER, Glenn. Community as Inquiry. Thinking, 7(3), 13-17, 1988.

TIRADO, Alvaro Rodriguez. El problema del realismo semántico y nuestro concepto de persona. Analisis Filosof, 7(2), 113-134, N 87.

This paper tries to show the compatibility of the subjective and objective viewpoints in our concept of a person. To this effect, it brings into play the Wittgensteinian conception of a human body, and it shows how to relate it with the most plausible view of realism in semantics.

TOBIN, Bernadette M. An Aristotelian Theory of Moral Development. J Phil Educ, 23(2), 195-211, Wint 89.

In this article, an Aristotelian theory of moral development is set out in four main parts: ideal outcome, preexisting condition, stages in development and varieties of moral failure. Ethical and developmental ideas employed in the theory come from Aristotle and from recent philosophical works which start from a virtues-based theory. One key idea is that cognitive, affective and conative aspects of development used to be identified at each point in such a theory.

TODISCO, Orlando. Ragione debole e metafisica: Spunti tra vecchia e nuova apologetica. Sapienza, 42(3), 309-317, Jl-S 89.

TOFFALORI, Carlo and STEINHORN, Charles. The Boolean Spectrum of an o-Minimal Theory. Notre Dame J Form Log, 30(2), 197-206, Spr 89.

We show that the number of isomorphism types of Boolean algebras of

definable subsets of countable models of an o-minimal theory is either 1 or $2^{\aleph_0}$. We also show that the number of such isomorphism types is 1 if and only if no countable model of the o-minimal theory contains an infinite discretely ordered interval.

TOGNONATO, Claudio. A proposito di Jean-Paul Sartre. Aquinas, 32(1), 153-163, Ja-Ap 89.

TOKARZ, Marek. Synonymy in Sentential Languages: A Pragmatic View. Stud Log, 47(2), 93-97, Je 88.

In this note two notions of meaning are considered and accordingly two versions of synonymy are defined, weaker and stronger ones. A new semantic device is introduced: a matrix is said to be *pragmatic* iff its algebra is in fact an algebra of meanings in the stronger sense. The new semantics is proved to be "universal enough" (Theorem 1), and it turns out to be in some sense a generalization of Wójcicki's referential semantics (Theorem 3).

TOLA, Fernando and DRAGONETTI, Carmen. La estructura de la mente según la escuela idealista budista (Yogachara). Pensamiento, 46(182), 129-147, Ap-Je 90.

Después de una somera información sobre las principales tendencias de la filosofía de la India, la escuela idealista budista y la teoría de las Tres Naturalezas, el artículo trata de la estructura de la mente en dicha escuela. La mente está formada por la conciencia-receptáculo, constituida por las impresiones subliminales dejadas por experiencias anteriores, y por la conciencia-función (conocimiento sensorial, mental y conciencia de "yo"), constituida a su vez por las impresiones subliminales hechas conscientes. Esta teoría explica la posición idealista extrema de la escuela. El artículo termina ocupándose de la teoría de la Mente Pura, que corona la concepción de la estructura de la mente propia de la filosofía budista idealista.

TOLA, Fernando and DRAGONETTI, Carmen. Some Remarks on Bhartrhari's Concept of Pratibhā. J Indian Phil, 18(2), 95-112, Je 90.

The word *pratibhā* is a very important one. It expresses some fundamental concepts. We start mentioning three of them, which have been analyzed in some valuable works. Other meanings, equally fundamental, will come to light when we study what Bhartrhari teaches about *pratibhā*. (edited)

TOLLIVER, Joseph Thomas. "The Saint Elizabethan World" in *The Current State of the Coherence Theory*, BENDER, John W (ed), 160-167. Norwell, Kluwer, 1989.

I take the following to be a platitude about knowledge: there would be no problem of knowledge if everything always had been, were, and always would be just as we believe it to be. A world where all beliefs are always true I call "an incorrigible world." One might hope that our best account of the nature of knowledge might explain why this platitude is platitudinous. If not, one would at least hope for the preferred account to be compatible with it. Unfortunately, coherence accounts of knowledge do not fulfill this hope, for they imply that there are some incorrigible worlds that are epistemically inaccessible. I consider the coherence analysis offered in *The Structure of Empirical Knowledge*, by Laurence BonJour, as a representative case. I end by suggesting that a solution to the problem is to abandon the presupposition present in many coherence theories that coherence properties are world-invariant. (edited)

TOMAN, Walter. Das Menschenbild in der Psychotherapie. Conceptus, 23(60), 23-36, 1989.

A view of man is being presented that is general and objective enough to be acceptable to psychotherapists of widely different schools. It is compatible with any view of man that a client may have. 37 German-speaking psychotherapists of 30 different forms or schools of psychotherapy have judged this view of man and used it as a common basis for their own respective contribution to a handbook of psychotherapy.

TOMASI, John. The Power Principle: "Inherent Defects" Reconsidered. Crim Just Ethics, 8(2), 56-60, Sum-Fall 89.

Is it possible to construct a theoretical argument against the *very idea* of centralized government? This paper examines one recent attempt to do so, by Randy Barnett in "Pursuing Justice in a Free Society: Part One—Power vs. Liberty" (4 *Crim Just Ethics*, 50-70, Summer/Fall 1985). Barnett's argument is rejected for its overemphasis on problems about human nature, and it is shown that any satisfactory pro-anarchy argument would need to take up problems about spontaneous order as well.

TOMBERLIN, James E. Deontic Paradox and Conditional Obligation. Phil Phenomenol Res, 50(1), 107-114, S 89.

TOMEK, V. The Individuum and the Context of Individual (in Czechoslovakian). Filozof Cas, 37(6), 812-826, 1989.

The concept of the individuum encompasses a dual accent of man's being since it points to the following: both the concrete historical context of determining "coordinates" of the individuum within the social process through which the individuum is determined as a social being and its irreplaceable uniqueness and autonomy which the individuum manifests and asserts in a concrete historical situation. Seen in this light, the individuum's autonomy is not a quality that originates by itself, out of itself or for itself. The autonomy of the individuum acquires its meaning only within the context of other individua. Only when set within the context of other individuals and through them does the irreplaceable agency of the individuum acquire its sense; it is in this particular connection that the individuum can reflect its meaning and value and project the scope and importance of its irreplaceable agency. Within the historical process and through its mediation the individuum is confirmed as an autonomous and simultaneously become a co-creator of the concrete historical context of individuals. (edited)

TOMINAGA, Nakamoto and PYE, Michael (trans). *Emerging from Meditation: Nakamoto Tominaga.* Honolulu, Univ of Hawaii Pr, 1990

TOMINAGA, Thomas T. Wittgenstein and Murdock on the 'Net' in a Taoist Framework. J Chin Phil, 17(2), 257-270, Je 90.

TOMLINSON, Hugh. "After Truth: Post-Modernism and the Rhetoric of Science" in *Dismantling Truth: Reality in the Post-Modern World*, LAWSON, Hilary (ed), 43-57. New York, St Martin's Pr, 1989.

TOMLINSON, Tom. Misunderstanding Death on a Respirator. Bioethics, 4(3), 253-264, Jl 90.

TOMM, Winnifred A. Sexuality, Rationality, and Spirituality. Zygon, 25(2), 219-238, Je 90.

Historical progress has largely been described in terms of the power to order social and ecological realities according to the interests of a few. Their concepts, images, and metaphors have transmitted knowledge (both explicit and tacit) that has come to be regarded as received wisdom. This kind of power, which has shaped (as well as described) history, has belonged primarily to men; whereas women's nature and, accordingly, their power have been defined primarily in terms of sexuality. Men's control of women's sexuality is therefore the source of the disqualification of women as free agents—that is, as significant participants in, say, scientific and religious meaning-giving processes. Thus morality requires reevaluation of our assumptions about human nature. Most importantly, it demands that female sexuality be considered within the context of rationality and spirituality.

TONG, Rosemarie. *Feminist Thought: A Comprehensive Introduction.* Boulder, Westview Pr, 1989

Feminism, like most broad-based philosophical perspectives, accommodates several species under its genus. No short list could be exhaustive, but many, although by no means all, feminist theorists are able to identify their approach as essentially liberal, Marxist, radical, psychoanalytic, socialist, existentialist, or postmodern. I understand each of these to be a partial and provisional answer to the "woman question(s)," providing a unique perspective with its own methodological strengths and weaknesses. In this book I analyze the way in which these partial and provisional answers intersect, joining together both to lament the ways in which women have been oppressed, repressed, and suppressed to celebrate the ways in which so many women have "beaten the system," taken charge of their own destinies, and encouraged each other to be happy as women.

TOPPER, David. Newton on the Number of Colours in the Spectrum. Stud Hist Phil Sci, 21(2), 269-279, Je 90.

In his *Opticks* (1704), Newton described the spectrum of light as divided into seven distinct colors. But his *Optical Lectures* of 1670-72 reveal that he initially saw only five colors (red, yellow, green, blue, and violet). Several hypotheses have been put forward to explain Newton's addition of orange and indigo, the most recent being that he drew upon the analogy between color and music. The argument in this paper qualifies that thesis, with the emphasis instead being upon aesthetic factors playing a key role in Newton's thinking.

TORGERSON, Jon N. Why I Teach Philosophy. Teach Phil, 13(1), 3-11, Mr 90.

TORMEY, Alan. Understanding Music: Remarks on the Relevance of Theory. Acta Phil Fennica, 43, 244-256, 1988.

TORNOS, Andrés. La filosofía del cristianismo y de la religión en Wittgenstein. Pensamiento, 46(181), 23-47, Ja-Mr 90.

Filosóficamente tiende Wittgenstein a considerar lo religioso "en el entero espacio lógico"; después del *Tractatus* cambia sustancialmente su concepción de dicho espacio. Inicialmente mantiene que no se puede hablar de lo religioso, pero en los "Diarios Filosóficos" y en la "conferencia sobre Etica" trata cuestiones religiosas importantes. En las "Conversaciones con Waismann" y en los "Comentarios a la Rama Dorada" se marca la

transición. Sobre la fe, el lenguaje de la fe, el acceso a la fe y la relación fe/salvación/conducta tratarán muchos pasajes de las "Observaciones" editadas por Von Wright.

TORTOLONE, Gian Michele. La trattazione dell'argomento ontologico nel carteggio Leibniz-Jaquelot (1702-1704). Filosofia, 41(1), 89-101, Ja-Ap 90.

TORTORA, Roberto and GERLA, Giangiacomo. Fuzzy Natural Deduction. Z Math Log, 36(1), 67-77, 1990.

Many systems of fuzzy logic have since been proposed as formal counterparts of approximate reasoning, obtained via suitable fuzzyfications of the ordinary Hilbert-type logical systems. Here we explore the possibility of introducing very general fuzzy analogues of the classical systems of natural deduction; in particular a consequence operator is defined and examined which associates to every fuzzy subset of assumptions the related fuzzy subset of consequences. This approach turns out to be an extension both of ordinary natural deduction and of the fuzzy logic as proposed by J Pavelka. Also, compactness and completeness are examined.

TOSEL, André. La critique marxienne de la religion. Arch Phil, 53(1), 31-47, Ja-Mr 90.

The Marxian critique has a twofold dimension: it is a hermeneutical theory of alienation and an analysis of ideological formations. The last religious form thematised by Marx is the economical religion itself, the capitalistic fetishism as issue of bourgeois christianism. The hermeneutics approach includes a metatheoretical dimension overdetermined by an absolute rationalism (an antinomiastic one) which compromises the finite rationalism inherent to Marxian analyses. Theses analyses are including together material production and symbolical production. Marx is investigating a production paradigm unifying the two forms of production. 'Science' itself is a specific symbolic production which reflects its genesis and its intricated being to imaginary and ideology.

TOTARO, Giuseppina. Un manoscritto inedito delle 'Adnotationes' al *Tractatus Theologico-Politicus* di Spinoza. Stud Spinozana, 5, 205-224, 1989.

In the Biblioteca Marucelliana in Florence, a copy of the first edition of Spinoza's *Tractatus theologico-politicus* is conserved which contains an unedited manuscript copy of the Latin redaction of the *Adnotationes*. This copy belongs to the same tradition as the Marchand manuscript at the University Library at Leiden, but it gives, as compared with the latter, significant variants. From the analysis of those different lectures and from the comparison with other sources, one can infer that the Florence copy and that of Marchand are independent copies of one and the same Latin manuscript which has not been handed down to us and which made use of the original Latin redaction by Spinoza himself as well as of the Saint Glain manuscript which has been lost as well.

TOURNIER, F. La fondation de la bioéthique: une perspective épistémologique. Philosophiques, 16(2), 257-291, Autumn 89.

In our view, the field of ethics is in jeopardy: the traditional approaches wanting to give an ontological foundation to ethics has led, on the contrary (by its constant failure to find them), to the victory of moral relativism; on the other hand, further support has been provided for relativism with the intervention of metaethics which defines ethics negatively in contrast to science (or descriptive sentences). Could there be another way to secure the foundation of ethics? In this paper, we try to see whether the perspective of the philosophy of science could not help us to choose rationally between moral rules and in this way to provide an indirect foundation for ethics and bioethics but nevertheless a foundation.

TOVEY, Barbara and KUHNS, Richard. Portia's Suitors. Phil Lit, 13(2), 325-331, O 89.

Suitors described in Act I, Scene ii of *The Merchant of Venice* are identified, and reasons given for the identifications. They are five of Shakespeare's important teachers and predecessors. Philosophical implications for the drama are stated.

TOWNSEND, Dabney. *Aesthetic Objects and Works of Art.* Wolfeboro, Longwood, 1989

Contemporary philosophy of the arts has tended to reject theory, but the need for an orderly philosophical understanding of the arts remains. This book proposes a radical shift from "aesthetic experience" as the focus for aesthetic theory to the aesthetic object itself. Two powerful tools are at hand: phenomenological description provides a neutral account of experience, and an analysis of reference gives an account of how objects can be in thought and language. The account of aesthetic phenomena which results from combining the two abandons the concept of a unique aesthetic experience and replaces it with a descriptive analysis of aesthetic objects and their relation to works of art.

TRÄGER, Franz. "Auf dem Weg zu Fichtes Urparadoxie" in *Agora: Zu Ehren von Rudolph Berlinger*, BERLINGER, Rudolph (and other eds), 217-230. Amsterdam, Rodopi, 1988.

TRAGESSER, Robert S. Sense Perceptual Intuition, Mathematical Existence, and Logical Imagination. Phil Math, 4(2), 154-194, 1989.

TRAPP, Rainer W. 'Utilitarianism Incorporating Justice'—A Decentralised Model of Ethical Decision Making. Erkenntnis, 32(3), 341-381, My 90.

Defying recent cognitivistic claims, the book argues for a *"semi-cognitivistic"* understanding of moral judgments. Its core presents (in full technical detail) a "decentralized" consequentialist all-purpose decision principle called UJ (= *"utilitarianism incorporating justice"*) designed to evade notorious criticism of both utilitarian and maximin conceptions of justice. UJ regards also "non-utility" information by weaving around the additive utility aggregation function some "parameters of justice" (including *claim/desert factors* and a measure of equality which favours more equal distributions of *deserved* utility levels). Subsequently numerous possible objections to UJ and its application in various contexts are discussed.

TRAVERS, Andrew. Shelf-Life Zero: A Classic Postmodernist Paper. Phil Soc Sci, 19(3), 291-320, S 89.

Exampling itself, an argument self-destructs in a paranoid attempt to write the event (Lyotard) of a narcissism-paranoia exchange said to be characteristic of postmodern structures of feeling. The semantic universe where this occurs is suggestively a Goffman-Baudrillard hermeneutic, and naturally the argument can have no value as a commodity.

TREBILCOT, Joyce. More Dyke Methods. Hypatia, 5(1), 140-144, Spr 90.

In response to a commentary by Jacquelyn N Zita on the essay "Dyke Methods," the three principles of that work—"I speak only for myself," "I do not try to get other wimmin to accept my beliefs in place of their own," and "There is no given"—are further clarified and developed.

TREFIL, James. *Reading the Mind of God: In Search of the Principle of Universality*. New York, Scribner's, 1989

TRELOAR, John L. Maimonides on Prophecy and Human Nature: A Problem in Philosophical Interpretation. Mod Sch, 67(1), 33-47, N 89.

Moses Maimonides' struggles with the philosophical problems surrounding prophecy can serve as a paradigm of inquiry for anyone who finds prophecy an important religious phenomenon. By examining Maimonides' theories of human unity, intellect and imagination, I show how prophecy relates to human cognitional experience and conclude that Maimonides is sensitive to both the philosophy of human nature and religious experience as he works out a theory of prophecy. Maimonides highlights that acceptance of prophecy as a legitimate phenomenon requires that our philosophical analysis meet certain systematic requirements such as a coordination with philosophy of human nature.

TRELOAR, John L. Pomponazzi's Critique of Aquinas' Arguments for the Immortality of the Soul. Thomist, 54(3), 453-470, Jl 90.

TREMBLAY, Robert. Analyse critique de quelques modèles sémiotiques de l'idéologie (prémière partie). Philosophiques, 17(1), 71-112, 1990.

This paper deals with the problem of analysing the question of ideology as a semiotic one. It shows the weakness of the main traditional developments on this issue. In this first part, the theories of Saussurian semioticians (Hjelmslev, Barthes and Greimas) are rejected, because of their conception of language and connotation. In the second part, we will analyse the sociosemiotic theories of Kristeva, Morris and Eco. In conclusion, we will show the relevance of a Peircean approach to this problematic.

TRENTMAN, J A. Richard Holdsworth and the Natural Law: An Early Linguistic Turn. Vera Lex, 8(2), 7-9, 1988.

TREY, George A. Modern Normativity and the Politics of Deregulation. Auslegung, 16(2), 137-147, Sum 90.

TRIANOSKY, Gregory W. On Cultivating Moral Character: Comments on "Moral Reasons in Confucian Ethics". J Chin Phil, 16(3-4), 345-354, D 89.

TRICAUD, François. "Hobbes's Conception of the State of Nature from 1640 to 1651: Evolution and Ambiguities" in *Perspectives on Thomas Hobbes*, ROGERS, G A J (ed), 107-123. New York, Clarendon/Oxford Pr, 1988.

Hobbes's conception of a state of nature is not so clear-cut and invariable as may appear. The question whether the phrase refers to an observable state or to a conceptual figment remains undecided, at least in *De Cive*. Two unexpected causes of the primordial war (the disagreement about what is reasonable, the existence of a natural right) are sometimes suggested. The role ascribed to vainglory hardly agrees with the 'utilitarian' motivation

theory. The stress laid on 'competition' in *Leviathan* hints at an explanation of the war quite different from that grounded on an inbred wickedness of men.

TRIENES, Rudie. Type Concept Revisited: A Survey of German Idealistic Morphology in the First Half of the Twentieth Century. Hist Phil Life Sci, 11(1), 23-42, 1989.

This article concerns a number of relatively important German zoologists and anatomists, who belonged to the group of idealistic morphologists, a group of scientists forming a counterpart to the experimental sciences on the European continent in the first half of the twentieth century. Idealistic morphology employed the type concept, i.e., the theoretical construct of an ideal form, which could be used as a unifying principle for ordering the multitude of actually existing forms. Given the logical primacy of the type concept, the idealistic morphologists constructed a number of kindred concepts, as, e.g., the concept of homology, finality and holism.

TRIFOGLI, Cecilia. Il luogo dell'ultima stera nei commenti tardo-antichi e medievali a "Physica" IV:5. G Crit Filosof Ital, 68(2), 144-160, My-Ag 89.

TRIGEAUD, Jean-Marc. *Humanisme de la liberté et philosophie de la justice, Tome II.* Bordeaux, Biere, 1990

"Nous avons été incité à délaisser le projet d'une exploration systématique de toutes les formes de positivisme, ce qui nous aurait conduit de la philosophie ou métaphysique du juste à une simple théorie du droit. Nous avons alors entrepris d'autres études et publications précisément axées sur la justice, notre dernier essai visant un thème que nous avons progressivement estimé décisif: la personne, distinguée de la nature de l'homme. Cette évolution et ces choix expliquent donc les limites assignées à ce livre comme le retard avec lequel il voit le jour."

TRILLAS, Enric and CASTRO, Juan Luis. Sobre preórdenes y operadores de consecuencias de Tarski. Theoria (Spain), 4(11), 419-425, F-My 89.

TRIPATHY, Laxman Kumar. Husserl and Heidegger on the Cartesian Legacy. Indian Phil Quart, SUPP 17(2), 35-47, Ap 90.

This essay attempts to show how the Cartesian insight becomes central in Husserlian and Heideggerian philosophy. For both, the basic validity of the Cartesian starting point is that it begins with the human subject. In Husserl this is seen in terms of the principle of consciousness and in Heidegger, in terms of the mode of being of the human subject. But for Husserl, that he misunderstands the nature of consciousness in its true essence, i.e., intentional. For Heidegger, Descartes misunderstands human being as a thinking substance.

TRIPLETT, Timm. Recent Work on Foundationalism. Amer Phil Quart, 27(2), 93-116, Ap 90.

This article presents a summary and categorization of recent work on epistemological foundationalism. There is a prominent view that foundationalism is no longer a viable theory. But this view ignores a good deal of recent work in the literature, some of which attempts to respond to standard criticisms of foundationalism by developing more modest versions of the theory. Other epistemologists continue to defend relatively strong, more traditional versions of foundationalism. A brief history of foundationalism is presented. Focussing on work published between 1975 and 1987, the article then categorizes the varieties of foundationalism and discusses the theories of Chisholm, Moser, Pollock and Foley in some detail.

TROOST, A. Praxeologie als wijsgerig thema. Phil Reform, 55(1), 48-73, 1990.

TROPER, Michel. Judges Taken Too Seriously: Professor Dworkin's Views on Jurisprudence. Ratio Juris, 1(2), 162-175, Jl 88.

The author analyses Ronald Dworkin's ideas about legal theory and legal philosophy, with particular regard to metatheoretical and methodological problems. He focuses on the questions of the function and the object of jurisprudence, and on those of the content and method of argumentation of jurisprudence. According to the author, Dworkin's theory is a normative theory, an ideology referred to the judicial practice. Although judges really make law, one can deny that they do. This strategy is the one judges traditionally employ when they say that they are merely applying the law-giver's intentions or fundamental principles that existed long before the case they have to decide. It is that discourse, not rights, that Dworkin takes seriously.

TROST, Klaus. "Entfremdung und Verfremdung in der russischen Literatur und Literaturtheorie" in *Agora: Zu Ehren von Rudolph Berlinger*, BERLINGER, Rudolph (and other eds), 355-385. Amsterdam, Rodopi, 1988.

TROTIGNON, P. Ontologie et sagesse. Rev Phil Fr, 179(3), 289-296, Jl-S 89.

TROTTER, R Clayton and DAY, Susan G and LOVE, Amy E. Bhopal, India and Union Carbide: The Second Tragedy. J Bus Ethics, 8(6), 439-454, Je

89.

The paper examines the legal, ethical, and public policy issues involved in the Union Carbide gas leak in India which caused the deaths of over 3000 people and injury to thousands of people. The paper begins with a historical perspective on the operating environment in Bhopal, the events surrounding the accident, then discusses an international situation audit examining internal strengths and weaknesses, and external opportunities and threats faced by Union Carbide at the time of the accident. There is a discussion of management of the various interests involved in international public relations and ethical issues. A review of the financial ratio analysis of the company prior and subsequent to the accident follows, then an examination of the second tragedy of Bhopal—the tragic failure of the international legal system to adequately and timely compensate victims of the accident. The paper concludes with recommendations towards public policy, as well as a call for congressional action regarding international safety of US-based multinational operations.

TRUNDLE, Robert. Religious Belief and Scientific Weltanschauungen. Laval Theol Phil, 45(3), 405 422, O 89.

The connection between social-political ideologies and recent challenges to Hebraic-Christian belief is clarified. It is argued *inter alia* that such challenges suppose controversial theories of truth and meaning, proper to science, which are surreptitiously applied to religious views of nature and human nature. When human nature and nature are assessed by ideologies in this manner, such ideologies appeal to or become scientific Weltanschauungen.

TRUOG, Robert D. Brain Death and the Anencephalic Newborns. Bioethics, 4(3), 199-215, Jl 90.

Should anencephalic newborns be considered brain dead? The recent successful transplants of hearts and kidneys from anencephalic newborns and the acute shortage of transplantable pediatric organs have made this question vitally important. We review selected medical aspects of anencephaly and outline the history of the use of anencephalics as organ sources. We then employ some of the arguments and justifications underlying the Uniform Determination of Death Act to claim that anencephaly is morally equivalent to brain death, i.e., the reasons for considering brain-dead patients to be dead also apply to anencephalics.

TSALIKIS, John and FRITZSCHE, David J. Business Ethics: A Literature Review with a Focus on Marketing Ethics. J Bus Ethics, 8(9), 695-743, S 89.

In recent years, the business ethics literature has exploded in both volume and importance. Because of the sheer volume and diversity of this literature, a review article was deemed necessary to provide focus and clarity to the area. The present paper reviews the literature on business ethics with a special focus in marketing ethics. The literature is divided into normative and empirical sections, with more emphasis given to the latter. Even though the majority of the articles deal with the American reality, most of the knowledge gained is easily transferable to other nations.

TSALIKIS, John and ORTIZ-BUONAFINA, M. Ethical Beliefs' Differences of Males and Females. J Bus Ethics, 9(6), 509-517, Je 90.

This study investigates the differences in ethical beliefs between males and females. 175 business students were presented with four scenarios and given the Reidenbach-Robin instrument measuring their ethical reactions to these scenarios. Contrary to previous research, the results indicate that the two groups have similar ethical beliefs, and they process ethical information similarly.

TSANG, Lap-Chuen. God, Morality, and Prudence: A Reply to Bernard Williams. Heythrop J, 30(4), 433-438, O 89.

Bernard Williams proposes a negative view of theistic morality in *Morality* (1972). Though flatly mistaken, the view has stood undisputed ever since. In his formulation Williams recapitulates two Kantian arguments against theistic morality. He argues that both the theist and the Kantian critic are mistaken because of unrealistic assumptions about the purity of moral motivations and then concludes that theistic morality is inherently incoherent. I shall contend that the Kantian arguments as Williams presents them are irrelevant because their conception of Christian theism is unrealistic and unhistorical and that Williams's own argument misconstrues the purity of moral motivations and related notions. (edited)

TSIPKO, A. Man Cannot Change His Nature. Soviet Stud Phil, 29(1), 27-54, Sum 90.

TSIRPANLIS, Constantine N. "Cyril Loukaris: A Protestant Patriarch or a Pioneer Orthodox Ecumenist?" in *The Wisdom of Faith: Essays in Honor of Dr Sebastian Alexander Matczak*, THOMPSON, Henry O (ed), 129-146. Lanham, Univ Pr of America, 1989.

TSOHATZIDIS, Savas L. Two Consequences of Hinting. Phil Rhet, 22(4), 288-293, 1989.

David Holdcroft has maintained that John Searle's claim to the effect that every illocutionary act performed inexplicitly can, in principle, be performed explicitly—a claim that is sometimes referred to as 'the principle of expressibility'—is incorrect. To date, Holdcroft's conclusion has been resisted by two philosophers, G J Warnock and Searle himself, on the grounds that there are good reasons *against* counting it as an illocutionary act, and therefore no reason to think that it represents a threat to the principle of expressibility. My purpose in this paper is twofold: first, to argue that neither Searle nor Warnock succeed in establishing their respective points; second, to argue that hinting creates a further problem for another component of Searle's philosophy of language, namely, for his account of proper names. (edited)

TUAN, Yi-Fu. *Morality and Imagination: Paradoxes of Progress*. Madison, Univ Wisconsin Pr, 1989

Morality and imagination, though both valued by Western society, appear to be at odds with each other: the moral person (the Tolstoyan peasant) lacks imagination and the imaginative person many lack the homely virtues. Not only moral-ethical systems (a type of edifice) but designed material environments (another type of edifice) are ambitious works of the imagination, the intent of which is to enhance the spiritual well-being of their inhabitants. Progress in the one does not, however, entail progress in the other: morality is too earthbound, whereas imagination is ever tempted into the realm of fantasy.

TUCK, Andrew P. *Comparative Philosophy and the Philosophy of Scholarship*. New York, Oxford Univ Pr, 1990

This is a study in cross-cultural hermeneutics. It specifically examines ways in which historically conditioned assumptions influence textual interpretation and philosophical understanding. The author looks at the Madhyamikakarika by Nājārjuna, which is an Indian Buddhist work, and the modern western philosophical interpretation of this text. (staff)

TUCK, Richard. "Hobbes and Descartes" in *Perspectives on Thomas Hobbes*, ROGERS, G A J (ed), . New York, Clarendon/Oxford Pr, 1988.

TUCKER, J V and STOLTENBERG-HANSEN, V. Complete Local Rings as Domains. J Sym Log, 53(2), 603-624, Je 88.

TUDOR, H (ed & trans) and DYSON, R W (ed & trans). Robertus Britannus, 'On the Best Form of Commonwealth': A Dialogue between Pierre du Chastel and Aymar Ranconet. Hist Polit Thought, 11(1), 37-58, Spr 90.

TUDOSESCU, Ion. Transformations dans la manière de penser de l'homme contemporain (in Romanian). Rev Filosof (Romania), 35(5), 445-450, S-O 88.

TULLOCH, Gail. Mill's Epistemology in Practice in his Liberal Feminism. Educ Phil Theor, 21(2), 32-39, 1989.

John Stuart Mill's utilitarianism needs no introduction; his liberal feminism does. It is the contention of this article that Mill's empiricist utilitarian epistemology was a significant factor in the development of his liberal feminism, and further, that the pressure his liberal feminism exerted crucially modified his utilitarianism. In the first part, Mill's epistemology is outlined and his methodological premises—liberal environmentalism and Associationist psychology—are related to the emphasis on education characteristic of enlightenment feminism. Links are also made with behaviourism. In the second part, the central arguments of Mill's liberal feminism are introduced as expressed most fully in *The Subjection of Women*. Of particular relevance are his arguments concerning nature and women since arguments for women's alleged nature have served, and continue to serve, as objections to sexual equality.

TUMULTY, Peter. Judging God By "Human" Standards: Reflections on William James' *Varieties of Religious Experience*. Faith Phil, 7(3), 316-328, Jl 90.

Contrary to religious fundamentalism, James insists on judging religion by human standards. Fundamentalists would object on two counts: (i) a truly religious person must be willing to sacrifice everything, even reason itself, on the alter of faith; and (ii) James reduces religion to a mere conventionalism by presuming to apply to it the very human standards religion itself must judge. The first response shows piety itself requires the autonomy of reason. The second shows James fully appreciates the critical role religion has played in our social evolution. However, this leads into a paradox, given our first argument, which is resolved if we accept at least the possibility, as James did, of a friendly relation between the divine and the human.

TUNDO, Laura (ed) and COLOMBO, Arrigo (ed). *Fourier: La Passione dell'Utopia*. Milan, Angeli, 1988

TUNG, Shih Ping. Algorithms for Sentences Over Integral Domains. Annals Pure Applied Log, 47(2), 189-197, My 90.

An arithmetic sentence φ is called an ∀∃ sentence if and only if φ is logically equivalent to a sentence of the form $\forall x \exists y \psi(x,y)$ where $\psi(x,y)$ is a formula containing no quantifiers and no other free variable except x and y. We prove that given an $\forall\exists$ sentence φ in conjunctive or disjunctive normal form there is a polynomial time algorithm to decide whether or not φ is true in every integral domain with characteristic 0. We then prove that there is an algorithm to decide whether or not an $\forall\exists$ sentence φ is true in every integral domain.

TUOMELA, Raimo. Are Reason-Explanations Explanations by Means of Structuring Causes? Phil Phenomenol Res, 50(4), 813-818, Je 90.

In his recent book *Explaining Behavior* Fred Dretske claims that all reason-explanations are explanations by means of structuring causes. The present paper argues by means of a counterexample that Dretske's claim is wrong at least if by 'reason-explanation' is meant what it normally means.

TUOMELA, Raimo. Methodological Individualism and Explanation. Phil Sci, 57(1), 133-140, Mr 90.

This critical note concerns Harold Kincaid's "Reduction, Explanation and Empiricism" (*Philosophy of Science*, December 1986). Kincaid criticizes methodological individualism on several grounds. The present note argues that Kincaid fails at least in his attempt to show that it is false that individualistic theory suffices to fully explain social phenomena. Kincaid's main reason for claiming that individualistic theory is insufficient is that it cannot adequately explain social kinds. The present note contends that an individualist can suitably reinterpret the social talk in question and so succeed in explaining social phenomena. In some cases his explanatory factors will presumably be direct counterparts to the holist's explanatory social kinds, whereas in some other cases they may not be—arguably need not be.

TUOMELA, Raimo. What are Goals and Joint Goals? Theor Decis, 28(1), 1-20, Ja 90.

The paper analyzes the notions of a goal and joint goal, with emphasis on intentionally held goals. Joint goals in the context of strategic interaction are classified and discussed.

TUORI, Kaarlo. Discourse Ethics and the Legitimacy of Law. Ratio Juris, 2(2), 125-143, Jl 89.

The reconstructive theory of the procedural legitimacy of modern law developed on the basis of the theory of discourse ethics has limited itself solely to the deontological, moral-normative aspects of the validity claims of legal norms and judgments. However, teleological and axiological aspects are also intertwined with legal validity claims and with the procedures in which legal norms and judgments are produced. The discursive-procedural concept of legitimacy seems to require as its support, instead of the theory of discourse ethics, a general theory of practical discourses or, more generally, of rational collective will-formation.

TURCHETTI, Giorgio. Forme simili, forme autosimilari. Epistemologia, 11(2), 299-304, Jl-D 88.

The genesis of forms is examined from the perspective of dynamical systems. The complexity of the structures arising in the biological and physical world at the macroscopic scale suggests that we are far from the well-ordered world of planetary motions where classical mechanics was first successful. Indeed now it is known that nonlinear processes can produce complex geometries and a rapid loss of the memory of initial conditions. Nevertheless the search of hidden symmetries of nonlinear nature can be a powerful tool to understand, classify and even generate a variety of forms: similarity and self-similarity are considered here. (edited)

TURCO, Giovanni. Miseria o valore della metafisica? Sapienza, 42(3), 349-360, Jl-S 89.

TURETZKY, Philip. Immanent Critique. Phil Today, 33(2), 144-158, Sum 89.

Acknowledging the phenomenological background in Foucault's thought, this paper uses some of Husserl's central concepts—epoché, constitution, and the distinction between material and formal universals—to unlock Foucault's procedures. The understanding achieved is then used to show how Foucault is able to counter the contention that Foucault's enterprise is conservative, and leaves everything where it is. Instead, Foucault offers a radical critique of forms of power based in a materially immanent critique rather than the formal immanent critique that Habermas recommends.

TURNER, D. Hypocrisy. Metaphilosophy, 21(3), 262-269, Jl 90.

This paper is an exploration of the formal nature of hypocrisy and of the proper place of hypocrisy in our moral thinking. A tentative analysis of hypocrisy is offered and defended, an analysis which deviates significantly from that presented by Eva Feder Kittay in her 1982 *Metaphilosophy* paper entitled "On Hypocrisy." It is then argued that not all hypocrisy is morally objectionable—that, indeed, some may be required.

TURNER, Dan. Rand Socialist? J Phil Res, 15, 351-359, 1990.

In an article for this journal Michael Goldman has argued, *inter alia*, that Ayn Rand's ethical views are, contrary to her own belief, inconsistent with capitalism. Despite the apparent perversity of such a claim, his argument has some plausibility. This paper is a response to Goldman's argument, a clarification of and among the relevant concepts, and a suggestion for an alternative—more plausible and interesting—interpretation of a relevant aspect of Rand's ethical position, viz., her views about how human beings ought to relate to each other.

TURNER, Dean and HAZELETT, Richard. *Benevolent Living: Tracing the Roots of Motivation to God*. Pasadena, Hope, 1990

This book attempts to define happiness, to distinguish between wise and unwise ways of pursuing it, and to determine what the conditions are that make it possible and enduring. Both empirically and creatively, the book examines every major aspect of the problem of happiness—the economics, politics, sociology, psychology, aesthetics and ethics of the sense of well-being and joy in being alive. The book not only talks of achieving a comprehensive philosophy of happiness but actually develops one that can be represented as solid and of distinct value in the face of sophisticated criticism.

TURNER, Joseph. Democratizing Science: A Humble Proposal. Sci Tech Human Values, 15(3), 336-359, Sum 90.

TURSMAN, Richard. Phanerochemistry and Semiotic. Trans Peirce Soc, 25(4), 453-468, Fall 89.

TWEYMAN, Stanley (ed) and CREERY, Walter E (ed). *Early Modern Philosophy II*. Delmar, Caravan Books, 1988

TYMOCZKO, Thomas. In Defense of Putnam's Brains. Phil Stud, 57(3), 281-297, N 89.

Putnam's argument that we are not brains in a vat is correct to this extent: if a causal or direct theory of reference is correct, then we are not brains in a vat. Many commentators have denied this connection, disturbed by the counterintuitive corollary that brains in a vat could give an analogous argument. This essay disarms that objection. It explains the referential shift that grounds Putnam's argument by comparing his account of the brains in a vat to the standard resolution of Skolem's Paradox in mathematical logic.

TYMOCZKO, Thomas. Mathematical Skepticism: Are We Brains in a Countable Vat? Philosophica, 43(1), 31-47, 1989.

Using a version of Skolem's Paradox, I attempt a mathematical analogue of empirical skepticism. Might we be brains in a countable vat? Several resolutions of the paradox are examined, before presenting an argument by Putnam which, if successful, simultaneously defeats mathematical and empirical skepticism. In conclusion, I turn to issues about realism and informal practice in set theory. I argue that what mathematicians say about what they do is an essential ingredient of mathematics. However, the realist bent of mathematical prose does not suffice to make set theory into a quasi-science. Instead it is better construed as a quasi-art.

TZAMALIKOS, P. Origen: The Source of Augustine's Theory of Time. Philosophia (Athens), 17-18, 396-418, 1987-88.

TZITZIS, S. Le droit à la jouissance, la jouissance des droits. Philosophia (Athens), 17-18, 419-450, 1987-88.

UHLIR, Zdenek. So Called Nonmusicality of Before Hussitic and Hussitic Reformation (in Czechoslovakian). Estetika, 26(3), 164-173, 1989.

ULANOWSKY, Carole and ALMOND, Brenda. HIV and Pregnancy. Hastings Center Rep, 20(2), 16-21, Mr-Ap 90.

Testing women of childbearing age for HIV infection and disclosure of HIV status should be examined from three interlocking perspectives—women's personal concerns, the interests of caregivers, and those of the community. In the absence of specific objections, testing for HIV infection should be considered a routine procedure in prenatal care.

ULLMANN-MARGALIT, Edna. Presumptive Norms and Norm Revision (in Hebrew). Iyyun, 39(2), 139-150, Ap 90.

ULRICH, Dolph. "The NonExistence of Finite Characteristic Matrices for Subsystems of R_1" in *Directions in Relevant Logic*, NORMAN, Jean (ed), 177-178. Norwell, Kluwer, 1989.

UNGUREANU, Manuela. L'analyse phénoménologique et la sémantique des mondes possibles (in Romanian). Rev Filosof (Romania), 36(2), 155-160, Mr-Ap 89.

UNNIA, Mario. Business Ethics in Italy: The State of the Art. J Bus Ethics, 9(7), 551-554, Jl 90.

Up until now, the work which has been done in Italy might be considered of a preparatory nature. In 1985 and in 1986, the association of Catholic businessmen produced two documents on the ethical implications of economic activity. But in those years, the world of big business had not yet realised how central the argument was becoming. The first significant signs of interest for business ethics appeared in 1987. In June, 1988, the first Italian National Conference on Business Ethics took place in Milan. The main outcome of that conference has been the constitution of the Italian Chapter of the European Network. There are, however, some very fundamental difficulties involved in the promotion of business ethics in Italy. As a self-conscious, self-aware nucleus of a sector of society, the Italian business community is a very recent, and rather minoritarian social phenomenon. (edited)

UNTERSEHER, Lutz. "Defending Europe: Toward a Stable Conventional Deterrent" in *Nuclear Deterrence and Moral Restraint*, SHUE, Henry (ed), 293-342. New York, Cambridge Univ Pr, 1989.

UNWIN, Nicholas. Can Emotivism Sustain a Social Ethic? Ratio, 3(1), 64-81, Je 90.

This article argues, against MacIntyre and others, that emotivist ethics, when properly construed, is quite capable of maintaining social cohesion. Indeed, it argues, further, that it is far better at sustaining a proper relationship between society and the individual than its more fashionable alternatives. The distinction between reporting and expressing an attitude is given a novel analysis in terms of language games, and it is thereby shown how the 'Frege problem' of unasserted contexts can be given a general solution.

URBAS, Igor. On the Positive Parts of the J-Systems of Arruda and Da Costa. Rep Math Log, 22, 27-38, 1988.

The systems J_1 to J_5 of Arruda and da Costa lack *modus ponens* but have fairly strong negation postulates which help to determine their positive parts. It is known that the theorems of the common positive subsystem are precisely those of positive intuitionistic logic (Bunder) and the positive theorems of J_3 are precisely those of classical logic (Arruda and da Costa). This paper completes the picture by showing that J_1 is a conservative extension of its positive subsystem while the positive theorems of J_2, J_4 and J_5 are, as with J_3, precisely those of classical logic.

URBAS, Igor. Paraconsistency and the C-Systems of DaCosta. Notre Dame J Form Log, 30(4), 583-597, Fall 89.

It is argued that, both in view of da Costa's conditions for paraconsistent systems and for independent reasons, the failure of the C-systems to enjoy the property of intersubstitutivity of provable equivalents constitutes a deficiency which it is reasonable to attempt to remedy. Two extensions of the C-systems are considered, and both are shown to collapse all but the base system C_ω into classical logic. The general result is established that there is no extension of the stronger C-systems which both enjoys the intersubstitutivity property and is weaker than classical logic. Methods of constructing alternative but related hierarchies for which this property might more successfully be secured are suggested.

URBAS, Igor. Paraconsistency. Stud Soviet Tho, 39(3-4), 343-354, Ap-My 90.

It is argued that the standard definition of paraconsistency as allowing non-trivial inconsistent theories is too weak in not guaranteeing non-triviality which is relative to primitive or definable connectives. Stronger definitions are proposed and it is shown that these lead naturally to the variable-sharing requirement of relevant logics.

URBAS, Igor and SYLVAN, Richard. Prospects for Decent Relevant Factorisation Logics. J Non-Classical Log, 6(1), 63-79, My 89.

A family of logics in which prefixing and suffixing principles are replaced by weaker factorisation and summation principles is defined and investigated. It is shown that these logics fail to be relevant if idempotence and distribution principles are present unless simplification and addition are also removed.

UREÑA, Enrique M. Modernidad y filosofía de la historia. Dialogo Filosof, 6(1), 33-39, Ja-Ap 90.

URMSON, J O. "The Methods of Aesthetics" in *Analytic Aesthetics*, SHUSTERMAN, Richard (ed), 20-31. Cambridge, Blackwell, 1989.

URMSON, John O. "The Analysts" in *Reading Philosophy for the Twenty-First Century*, MC LEAN, George F (ed), 265-286. Lanham, Univ Pr of America, 1989.

URQUHART, Alasdair. "What is Relevant Implication?" in *Directions in Relevant Logic*, NORMAN, Jean (ed), 167-174. Norwell, Kluwer, 1989.

This paper considers interpretations of relevant logics based on the propositions-as-types idea in the context of a version of the strict lambda-calculus with strict pairing. It argues that these interpretations lead to logics more natural than the original relevant logics of Ackermann, Anderson and Belnap.

USCATESCU, George. De nouvelles perspectives de la métaphysique (in Romanian). Rev Filosof (Romania), 36(3), 271-279, My-Je 89.

UTZ, Stephen G. The Authority of the Rules of Baseball: The Commissioner as Judge. J Phil Sport, 16, 89-99, 1989.

This article asks whether the contractually appointed decision makers of organized baseball have the authority to impose novel requirements on players and other team employees, violations of which are as such blameworthy, to be resented, and so forth. It is concluded that the nature of the organized sport could justify the arrogation of such authority and that similar authority may arise naturally within other collective enterprises. Further implications for the structure of law and morality are explored.

UUSITALO, Jyrki. The Recurring Postmodern: Notes on the Constitution of Musical Artworks. Acta Phil Fennica, 43, 257-277, 1988.

The conceptual content of the 'postmodern' is examined in the light of some basic intuitions of Joseph Margolis's theory of artworks as culturally produced and culturally emergent artefacts. The emphasis and the examples used center on the problem context of musical artworks in particular. The article proposes a definition of the postmodern where the latter is (1) understood as a way of being conscious about the significance of art as a form of value-producing human practice and (2) seen as the 'cognigenic' commentary of modernity and its underlying regularities.

UUSITALO, Liisa. Efficiency, Effectiveness and Legitimation: Criteria for the Evaluation of Norms. Ratio Juris, 2(2), 194-201, Jl 89.

The paper deals with the mutual interest of both economic and social theory in exploring a broader concept of the rational and in finding validity claims for rational discourse. Efficiency and effectiveness are discussed as possible validity criteria in evaluating norms in practical discussion. In addition to the problem of defining validity criteria for argumentation on norms and social choices, a major difficulty arises from the lack of a legitimate reflective centre in society which could integrate behaviour with norms and metapreferences. As ways of motivating cooperative, collective action, both norm commitment and self-interest should be appealed to.

UVILLER, H Richard. Client Taint: The Embarrassment of Rudolph Giuliani. Crim Just Ethics, 9(1), 3-10, Wint-Spr 90.

VACHON, Gérard. Freud-a-til vraiment renié le pouvoir thérapeutique de la psychanalyse? Dialogue (Canada), 28(4), 663-665, 1989.

Purpose: to show that Adolf Grünbaum, in *The Foundations of Psychoanalysis: A Philosophical Critique* (Berkeley, University of California Press, 1984), misinterpreted Freud's article of 1926, "Inhibitions, Symptoms and Anxiety." Grünbaum's interpretation is that Freud demoted psychoanalytic treatment from therapeutically indispensable to a mere expediter of otherwise expectable recoveries, thus abandoning what Grünbaum calls the "Necessary Condition Thesis." My text proves that this was not Freud's intention.

VAILATI, Ezio. Leibniz on Locke on Weakness of Will. J Hist Phil, 28(2), 213-228, Ap 90.

VAINA, Lucia M. "What" and "Where" in the Human Visual System: Two Hierarchies of Visual Modules. Synthese, 83(1), 49-91, Ap 90.

In this paper we focus on the modularity of visual functions in the human visual cortex, that is, the specific problems that the visual system must solve in order to achieve recognition of objects and visual space. The computational theory of early visual functions is briefly reviewed and is then used as a basis for suggesting computational constraints on the higher-level visual computations. The remainder of the paper presents neurological evidence for the existence of two visual systems in man, one specialized for spatial vision and the other for object vision. We show further clinical evidence for the computational hypothesis that these two systems consist of several visual modules, some of which can be isolated on the basis of specific visual deficits which occur after lesions to selected areas in the visually responsive brain. We will provide examples of visual modules which solve information processing tasks that are mediated by specific anatomic areas. We will show that the clinical data from behavioral studies of monkeys supports the distinction between two visual systems in monkeys, the 'what' system, involved in object vision, and the 'where' system, involved in spatial vision. (edited)

VAINA, Lucia M. Common Functional Pathways for Texture and Form Vision. Synthese, 83(1), 93-131, Ap 90.

A single case study of a patient, D.M., with a lesion in the region of the right occipito-temporal gyrus is presented. D.M. had well-preserved language and general cognitive abilities. Colour discrimination, contrast sensitivity, gross depth perception, spatial localization, and motion appreciation were within normal limits. On the evaluation of perceptual abilities, he failed to identify two-dimensional shapes from stereoscopic vision, motion, and texture although in all cases he was able to identify the rough area subtended by the shape. The hypothesis advanced here is that D.M.'s specific impairment occurs at a stage of visual processing at which details relating to a particular stimulus are assembled in proper local spatial relationships, although they are still not yet appreciated as parts of a shape. (edited)

VALDÉS, Margarita M. Dos teorías de la referencia en el *Cratilo*. Analisis Filosof, 7(2), 97-112, N 87.

A study of the two theories of reference advanced by Plato in the *Cratylus*, conventionalism and 'naturalism', and their relation with some recent proposals about the semantic nature of names. A comparison between conventionalism and the causal theory of names. 'Naturalism' and the description theory of names. Two different conceptions of language involved in conventionalism and 'naturalism'. Both Platonic theories are shown to represent two insights concerning language which seem to be both justified but difficult to reconcile.

VALDÉS, Margarita. Contingencia a priori. Critica, 20(59), 79-107, Ag 88.

The purpose of this article is to discuss Kripke's view concerning the possibility of knowing *a priori* certain contingent propositions. The first section formulates the problem within Kripke's semantic theory. The second section discusses Donnellan's interpretation of the problem and rejects his proposed solution. The third section revises G Evans's notion of a descriptive name, his distinction between proposition and cognitive content as well as his distinction between deeply contingent propositions and superficially contingent ones. In the last section an argument is offered to reject both Evans's proposed solution to the puzzle and Kripke's claim about the possibility of knowing *a priori* a contingent proposition.

VALLENTYNE, Peter. How to Combine Pareto Optimality with Liberty Considerations. Theor Decis, 27(3), 217-240, N 89.

I argue that the liberty condition of Sen's important impossibility of a Paretian liberal result is not a condition that liberals (or libertarians) would accept. The problem is that an appropriate liberty condition must be formulated in terms of consent—not in terms of preference. To formulate an adequate condition the framework needs to expand from collective choice rules (which only take information about preferences as input) to rights-based social choice rules (which also take as input information about which options have been consented to and which would violate someone's rights). I formulate a more adequate liberty condition based on the notion of consent that is acceptable to liberals, and then show that Pareto optimality is incompatible even with that condition. I then show how the liberty condition can be weakened in a plausible manner, and describe an interesting class of theories—rights-based Paretian theories—that satisfy the Pareto optimality requirement while being sensitive to liberty considerations.

VALLICELLA, William F. Reply to Zimmerman: Heidegger and the Problem of Being. Int Phil Quart, 30(2), 245-254, Je 90.

This is a ten-page reply to Michael E Zimmerman's "On Vallicella's Critique of Heidegger" (*Int Phil Quart*, 30(1), 75-100, Mar 90). In a series of articles I have elaborated the thesis that Heidegger's philosophy of Being either issues in an unacceptable form of idealism, or cannot make good on its claim to being phenomenological ontology. On this occasion I deepen my critique by way of responding to Zimmerman's meta-critique. The article divides into five sections: "How Not to Defend Heidegger"; "The Critique Restated"; "Zimmerman's Defense: Autodisclosure and Intrinsic Intelligibility"; "Autodisclosure as Non-Relational Appearing"; "Finitude, Transcendence and Hypostatization."

VALLONE, Gerard. Parrots Into Owls: The Metamorphosis of a Philosophy for Children Program. Thinking, 6(1), 34-40, 1985.

This is an account of the introduction of the "Philosophy for Children" program into the fourth grade gifted and talented program of the White Plains, New York school district.

VAN ASPEREN, Gertrud M. A Game-Theoretical Analysis of Ecological Problems (in Hungarian). Magyar Filozof Szemle, 2-3, 346-351, 1989.

VAN BENDEGEM, Jean Paul. Foundations of Mathematics or Mathematical Practice: Is One Forced To Choose? Philosophica, 43(1), 197-213, 1989.

This paper aims at bridging the gap between, on the one hand, foundational research in mathematics and, on the other hand, the more recent study of the actual practice of mathematics, as, e.g., in the sociology of mathematics. The basic idea is that both types of theories presuppose, implicitly or explicitly, a mathematical subject whose beliefs are supposed to correspond to the mathematical theory. Thus a continuum of mathematical subjects is obtained, ranging from the God-like foundational mathematician to the real mathematician in a social context.

VAN BENTHEM, Johan. Categorial Grammar and Type Theory. J Phil Log, 19(2), 115-168, My 90.

Categorial grammars in linguistics and type theories in mathematics share the same philosophical motivation and logical structure. The paper surveys the resulting analogies in the areas of model theory and proof theory (including issues of recognizing power). The basic perspective arising here is that of a categorial hierarchy of logics with few or no structural rules, with corresponding semantic fragments of the lambda calculus.

VAN BENTHEM, Johan. Kunstmatige intelligentie: Een voortzetting van de filosofie met andere middelen. Alg Ned Tijdschr Wijs, 82(2), 83-100, Ap 90.

There are striking analogies between current research in artificial intelligence and topics in traditional philosophy. This is not just a matter of broad shared concerns having to do with the mind-body problem, or the limits of cognition as such. It is also a fact of life in many specific areas of research, arising with such cognitive activities as problem solving, learning or reasoning under uncertainty. We survey a number of such specific interactions, involving both information structures and cognitive procedures over them—showing how contributions for the philosophical literature might be, and sometimes already have been, helpful to research in artificial intelligence. But also conversely, we suggest that certain attitudes from the latter field, and informatics generally, might affect philosophy itself. In particular, they might lead to a more 'process-oriented', rather than 'structure-oriented', conception of what constitutes a satisfactory solution to a philosophical problem.

VAN BRAKEL, J and JANSSENS, C J A M. Davidson's Omniscient Interpreter. Commun Cog, 23(1), 93-100, 1990.

In response to the skeptic's argument that a speaker and interpreter might understand one another on the basis of shared but erroneous beliefs, Davidson has provided an argument in which he asks us to imagine an interpreter who is omniscient. Davidson's omniscient interpreter also plays a role in his argument that the possibility of communication implies a form of realism. (edited)

VAN BRAKEL, J and SAUNDERS, B A C. Moral and Political Implications of Pragmatism. J Value Inq, 23(4), 259-274, D 89.

VAN BRAKEL, J and BRENNER-GOLOMB, N. Putnam on Davidson on Conceptual Schemes. Dialectica, 43(3), 263-269, 1989.

In *Dialectica* 41, 1987, Putnam claims to refute Davidson's objection to conceptual relativity by showing that knowledge of a *chosen* conceptual scheme (CS) is necessary for answering questions of existence, and thus, is a constraint on interpretation. Using his examples we defend Davidson's claim that their interpretation is a condition for attributing a CS to the speaker. We show that Putnam's discussion of the debate between Kant and Leibniz, or Carnap and the Polish Logician, displays all the characteristics of ascribing beliefs and a *language scheme* simultaneously, rather than choosing a CS and then considering which sentences are true.

VAN BUNGE, Wiep. On the Early Dutch Reception of the *Tractatus-Theologico Politicus*. Stud Spinozana, 5, 225-251, 1989.

In this article five Dutch refutations of Spinoza's TTP (1670) are considered, that appeared before the publication of the Opera Posthuma (1677). Calvinists, Cartesians, Arminians and Collegiants all suspected Spinoza of secretly being an atheist. His claims about biblical hermeneutics, the status of theology, and the possibilities for salvation of the masses were held to be spurious. What is more, early Dutch readers of the TTP felt that Spinoza had tried to cover up his naturalistic determinism by cunningly using 'double-talk'—a conclusion which shows a surprising similarity to much more recent research.

VAN BUNGE, Wiep. A Tragic Idealist: Jacob Ostens (1630-1678). Stud Spinozana, 4, 263-279, 1988.

In this paper the author presents his research on the Rotterdam Collegiant Jacob Ostens, who apart from being one of Spinoza's friends appears to have been a highly interesting apologist for religious tolerance and Christian reunification. Yet anonymously he fiercely attacked Calvinism. He was widely held to be a Socinian. Especially his views on predestination and the freedom of the will were derived from the Arminian Simon Episcopius. This makes it very unlikely that he was touched by Spinoza's philosophy like some other Collegiants were.

VAN BUREN, Edward J. The Young Heidegger: Rumor of a Hidden King (1919-1926). Phil Today, 33(2), 99-108, Sum 89.

A general account of Heidegger's early pre-*Being and Time* period (1919-1926) based on the recent publication of his lecture courses from the early twenties.

VAN BUREN, John. The Young Heidegger and Phenomenology. Man World, 23(3), 239-272, Jl 90.

This essay outlines Heidegger's critical appropriation of Husserl's phenomenology in his recently published lecture courses from the early

1920s.

VAN CAMP, Ingrid. Information Processing: From a Mechanistic to a Natural Systems Approach. Philosophica, 44(2), 119-133, 1989.

During the last decade connectionism attracted the enthusiasm of many AI-researchers. Yet there is doubt concerning the advantages of implementing the cognitive connectionist findings into cognitive psychology. The main problem is that the PDP-models use a mechanistic systems view to information processing, which doesn't coincide with the natural systems approach of cognitive psychology. In this paper we want to argue that connectionism is indeed compatible with the idea of an active information processor. Moreover we put forward the hypothesis that a mechanistic systems approach is a necessary preliminary phase in the evolution of all information processing models. We defend this hypothesis by applying the Overton-Reese analysis to the evolution of the different information processing models during the twentieth century. In this evolution we see a periodically reoccurring pendular movement between a mechanistic and a natural systems approach, giving way to a higher level theory applicable to human cognitive functioning.

VAN CLEVE, James. Supervenience and Closure. Phil Stud, 58(3), 225-238, Mr 90.

Recent investigations of the logic of supervenience have stipulated that the supervenience base, or set of "subvening" properties, be closed under various property-forming operations. For example, Kim has assumed that the base is closed under Boolean operations (disjunction, negation, etc.), and Bacon has assumed that the base is closed under an operation he calls "diagonalizing" or "resplicing." I argue here that it is generally reasonable to assume closure under disjunction and conjunction, but not always under negation or resplicing.

VAN DE WIELE, Jacques and ABRUSCI, V Michele and GIRARD, Jean-Yves. Some Uses of Dilators in Combinatorial Problems, II. J Sym Log, 55(1), 32-40, Mr 90.

We introduce sequences of ordinal numbers, called "increasing F-sequences" (where F is a dilator). By induction on dilators, we prove that every increasing F-sequence terminates. "Inverse Goodstein sequences" are particular increasing F-sequences: we show that the theorem "every inverse Goodstein sequence terminates" is not provable in the theory ID_1.

VAN DEN BELD, Antonie. *Non Posse Peccare*. Relig Stud, 25(4), 521-535, D 89.

Three arguments are presented against the view that man is not able not to sin *in via*, or, in other words, that the human person necessarily sins in this life. These same arguments seem to support the thesis that the human person has the ability not to sin, *in via* as well as *in gloria*, i.e., in eternal life. The arguments are based on considerations concerning human moral responsibility, the free will defence, and the nature of the divine/human relationship.

VAN DEN BERG, Hans and HOEKZEMA, Dick and RADDER, Hans. Accardi on Quantum Theory and the "Fifth Axiom" of Probability. Phil Sci, 57(1), 149-157, Mr 90.

In this paper we investigate Accardi's claim that the "quantum paradoxes" have their roots in probability theory and that, in particular, they can be evaded by giving up Bayes's rule, concerning the relation between composite and conditional probabilities. We reach the conclusion that, although it may be possible to give up Bayes's rule and define conditional probabilities differently, this contributes nothing to solving the philosophical problems which surround quantum mechanics.

VAN DEN DAELE, Wolfgang. El dilema argumentativo de la resistencia a las perspectivas técnicas de la biología moderna. Rev Filosof (Costa Rica), 26, 19-31, D 88.

Modern biotechnology makes human nature increasingly susceptible to technical analysis and reconstruction. The paper discusses social responses to this perspective with particular reference to debates in the Federal Republic of Germany. It gives reasons why efforts to abandon the application of the new technologies to humans are doomed to fail. Modern societies lack effective 'taboos' which exclude intervention into the human nature, individual rights imply access to modern technologies, and the legitimacy of public policies to prevent dangers does not include the option to halt processes of scientific and technological innovation.

VAN DEN DRIES, L. Dimension of Definable Sets, Algebraic Boundedness and Henselian Fields. Annals Pure Applied Log, 45(2), 189-209, D 89.

VAN DEN HAAG, Ernest and REIMAN, Jeffrey. On the Common Saying that it is Better that Ten Guilty Persons Escape than that One Innocent Suffer: Pro and Con. Soc Phil Pol, 7(2), 226-248, Spr 90.

VAN DEN WIJNGAARD, Marianne and HUYTS, Ini. Niet vrouw, niet man; wat dan? De rol van biomedische kennis bij de behandeling van pseudohermafrodieten. Kennis Methode, 13(4), 382-395, 1989.

Based on what knowledge and according to what images of masculinity and feminity treated physicians people born as intersex? Physicians used more traditional images of feminity and masculinity in the practice of construction of 'normal' women and men than fundamental researchers. Whilst the latter could afford to produce carefully balanced knowledge, in treatment, unambiguous criteria on which to base decisions remained highly desirable. Since there was (and is) a high degree of task-uncertainty in the field of medical practice, mechanisms to reduce the insecurity could be found. The simplification of results of fundamental research is an example of this.

VAN DER BURG, Wibren. The Myth of Civil Disobedience. Praxis Int, 9(3), 287-304, O 89.

This paper critiques the 'ruling' Rawlsian theory of civil disobedience. The theory is rejected because of its irrelevant and/or unsound assumption of a 'social contract'. Instead, an approach must be taken which does not assume one general political obligation. A more appropriate model is one which asserts the (possibility) and existence of various conditional reasons for obedience. Precisely these various reasons are critically analysed in this paper. In a final section this alternate approach is applied to disobedience performed by government officials and politicians.

VAN DER EIJK, P J. The 'Theology' of the Hippocratic Treatise On the Sacred Disease. Apeiron, 23(2), 87-119, Je 90.

The article deals with the statements, made by the author of MS, that "all diseases are divine and all are human," and aims at defining more accurately his position in religiosis. Diseases are divine in virtue of having a phusis, a regular pattern of origin and growth. However, this does not imply that the author rejects any form of divine intervention. He rather aims at marking off the boundaries between medicine and religion by showing that, whereas the gods are to be invoked for the purification of moral transgressions, diseases can be healed by normal dietetic measures.

VAN DER HOEVEN, J. Kant over Midden, Middel en Doel (I). Phil Reform, 54(2), 147-159, 1989.

Full title (in translation): "Kant on middle, means and end (with special notice of his view of culture)." Prepublication of a chapter in a book that will presumably be published with the title Middenfiguren (Figures of Mediation). This book deals with the significance and vicissitudes of the notions of "middle," "mediation" and "means" in Western thought and praxis. A summary of the conclusions reached will be given at the end of the second part of the article (to appear in June 1990).

VAN DER HOEVEN, J. Kant over midden, middel en doel II. Phil Reform, 55(1), 16-33, 1990.

VAN DER MEULEN, Barend and LEYDESDORFF, Loet. Effecten en gevolgen van wetenschapsbeleid voor de filosofiebeoefening aan de Nederlandse universiteiten. Alg Ned Tijdschr Wijs, 82(3), 173-193, Jl 90.

During the last five years, the Dutch Faculties of Philosophy went through a period of transition. First, in 1982, the national government introduced a new system of financing research at the universities. In 1983, a drastic reduction in the budget for philosophy was proposed. In 1987 a Visiting Committee reported on the weak and strong areas of Dutch philosophy and made proposals about a policy to strengthen Dutch philosophy. This study explores the possibilities of indicating the effects of the institutional reorganizations on the study of philosophy at the Faculties, using scientometric methods. Moreover at the end some remarks are made on possibilities for a functional policy.

VAN DER STEEN, Wim. Gedrag: wat zit er achter? Kennis Methode, 14(2), 230-236, 1990.

VAN DER VEKEN, Jan. "Creativity as Universal Activity" in Whitehead's Metaphysics of Creativity, RAPP, Friedrich (ed), 178-188. Albany, SUNY Pr, 1990.

VAN DER VEKEN, Jan. Merleau-Ponty on Ultimate Problems of Rationality. Ultim Real Mean, 12(3), 202-209, S 89.

VAN DER WEELE, Cor. Fundamenten, achtergronden of bondgenootschappen? Kennis Methode, 13(4), 396-403, 1989.

This article deals with relations between biology and worldviews, at the hand of two books: Michael Ruse's Taking Darwin Seriously and Mary Midgley's Evolution as a Religion. I argue that both these authors incorrectly describe the relationship between biology and worldviews as being essentially of one type, via the metaphysics they use (fundaments and frameworks respectively). With examples I show that, on the contrary, the relations are manifold and changing, which could be expressed by using human relations as metaphors.

VAN DER ZWEERDE, Evert. Recent Developments in Soviet Historiography of Philosophy. Stud Soviet Tho, 39(1), 1-53, F 90.

This paper examines the ways the perestrojka of Soviet philosophy affects historiography of philosophy, offering several examples. This quasi-independent discipline within the framework of Marxist-Leninist philosophy strongly tends to pure, ideologically neutral research, e.g., of "contemporary bourgeois" (= Western) philosophy. The theory of the history of philosophy developed to unite Marxist-Leninist philosophy and professional historiography of philosophy is stretched to its limits, but there are no signs of an alternative theory. The longed for but yet uncompleted establishment of a fully independent historiography is of utmost importance for the future development of philosophy in the USSR.

VAN DIJK, Teun A. "'Relevance' in Logic and Grammar" in *Directions in Relevant Logic*, NORMAN, Jean (ed), 25-57. Norwell, Kluwer, 1989.

Connectives in natural language must be analyzed in the framework of a formal text grammar, of which the semantic component is given in terms of a "text logic." Natural connectives (whether conjunctions, adverbs or other sentence or proposition linking devices) are to be accounted for in terms of conditionals of different strengths (enabling, making probable or making necessary, i.e., causing consequences). The same is true for the reverse relation (possible, probable or necessary conditions).

VAN ECK, Caroline and ROOTHAAN, Angela. Anna Maria van Schurman's verhouding tot de wetenschap. Alg Ned Tijdschr Wijs, 82(3), 194-211, Jl 90.

Anna Maria van Schurman, the Dutch 17th century philosopher, theologian, poet and painter, expressed her views on the place of women in science, and on the relation between science and faith in two works, the *Dissertatio de ingenii muliebris ad doctinam*... (1641), in which she argues that Christian women should have access to (university) education; secondly, her autobiography, the *Eucleria* (1673), in which she describes her choice to break off her scientific work and join the religious community of Jean de Labadie. Both works are analysed with respect to her attitude to philosophy and science and placed in their historical and intellectual context.

VAN EEMEREN, Frans H and GROOTENDORST, Rob. Speech Act Conditions as Tools for Reconstructing Argumentative Discourse. Argumentation, 3(4), 367-383, N 89.

According to the pragma-dialectical approach to argumentation, for analysing argumentative discourse, a normative reconstruction is required which encompasses four kinds of transformations. It is explained in this paper how speech act conditions can play a part in carrying out such a reconstruction. It is argued that integrating Searlean insights concerning speech acts with Gricean insights concerning conversational maxims can provide us with the necessary tools. For this, the standard theory of speech acts has to be amended in several respects and the conversational maxims have to be translated into speech act conditions. Making use of the rules for communication thus arrived at, and starting from the distribution of speech acts in a critical discussion as specified in the pragma-dialectical model, it is then demonstrated how indirect speech acts are to be transformed when reconstructing argumentative discourse.

VAN FRAASSEN, Bas C. "The Charybdis of Realism: Epistemological Implications of Bell's Inequality" in *Philosophical Consequences of Quantum Theory: Reflections on Bell's Theorem*, CUSHING, James T (ed), 97-113. Notre Dame, Univ Notre Dame Pr, 1989.

VAN FRAASSEN, Bas C. Laws and Symmetry. New York, Oxford Univ Pr, 1989

Metaphysicians speak of laws of nature in terms of necessity and universality; scientists do so in terms of symmetry and invariance. This book argues that no metaphysical account of laws can succeed. The author analyses and rejects the arguments that there are laws of nature, or that we must believe that there are. He argues that we should discard the idea of law as an inadequate clue to science. After exploring what this means for general epistemology, the book develops the empiricist view of science as a construction of models to represent the phenomena. Concepts of symmetry, transformation, and invariance illuminate the structure of such models. A central role is played in science by symmetry arguments, and it is shown how these function also in the philosophical analysis of probability. The advocated approach presupposes no realism about laws or necessities in nature.

VAN FRAASSEN, Bas. "Identity in Intensional Logic: Subjective Semantics" in *Meaning and Mental Representation*, ECO, Umberto (ed), 201-219. Bloomington, Indiana Univ Pr, 1988.

VAN GINNEKEN, Jaap. Het experiment als bron van artefacten. Kennis Methode, 13(4), 404-415, 1989.

VAN GULICK, Robert. What Difference Does Consciousness Make? Phil

Topics, 17(1), 211-230, Spr 89.

The functional role of phenomenal or qualitative states is examined. Various apriori arguments for the possibility of absent qualia are discussed and rejected. Further discussion focuses on empirical research regarding which mental processes in humans require phenomenal consciousness and how such dependencies might be explained by appeal to functional models of consciousness.

VAN HEERDEN, Jaap and SMOLENAARS, Anton J. On Traits as Dispositions: An Alleged Truism. J Theor Soc Behav, 19(3), 297-309, S 89.

Traits are usually treated as dispositions. The notion of disposition, however, is not unproblematic. One problem is the demonstration that any given set of behaviour confirms what is meant by the dispositional term. Another is that not all dispositions require the same type of manifestation of behaviour. It is argued that in fact a disposition belongs to one of four categories according to the way it is empirically justified. It appears that traits belong exclusively to one category. From a theoretical point of view, dispositions lead to a need to spell out the intrinsic properties that they represent. Spelling out intrinsic properties is a normal way to enrich a theory and to increase its explanatory power. Although this seems a proper strategy for the development of a unifying trait theory, serious doubts are raised about whether traits can really be treated as dispositions. It is likely that the advancement of trait theory is best served by an abandonment of the assumption that traits are dispositional at all.

VAN HUYSSTEEN, Wentzel. Evolution, Knowledge and Faith: Gerd Theissen and the Credibility of Theology. Mod Theol, 5(2), 145-159, Ja 89.

VAN INWAGEN, Peter. Four-Dimensional Objects. Nous, 24(2), 245-255, Ap 90.

It is argued that ordinary objects are three-dimensional and strictly persist through time. A consequence of this position is noted and accepted: that distinct regions of spacetime can be occupied by numerically the same three-dimensional object. Arguments for the incoherency of this consequence are considered and rejected. It is further argued that those who reject the position that ordinary objects are three-dimensional and strictly persist through time are committed to a counterpart-theoretic analysis of modal statements about individuals.

VAN KIRK, Carol A. Why Did Kant Bother About 'Nothing'? S J Phil, 28(1), 133-147, Spr 90.

This paper examines the "Table of Nothing" which Kant appended to the 'Transcendental Analytic' of the *Critique of Pure Reason*. The table is argued to highlight certain central theses of the First Critique and bears on Kant's notion of things in themselves.

VAN LAMBALGEN, Michiel. Algorithmic Information Theory. J Sym Log, 54(4), 1389-1400, D 89.

We present a critical discussion of the claim (most forcefully propounded by Chaitin) that algorithmic information theory sheds new light on Gödel's first incompleteness theorem.

VAN LUIJK, Henk J L. Recent Developments in European Business Ethics. J Bus Ethics, 9(7), 537-544, Jl 90.

In the first part of the paper, factual information is given about developments in European business ethics since it started on a more or less institutionalized basis, five or six years ago. In the second part some comments are presented on the meaning of the developments and the possible causes. Attention is given to resemblances and differences between American and European business ethics. In the short last part some suggestions are proposed about tasks business ethics will face in the next decade.

VAN LUIJK, Henk. Crucial Issues in Successful European Business. J Bus Ethics, 8(8), 579-582, Ag 89.

Time has come to put business ethics explicitly on the agenda of those who bear responsibility in the business world and of the scholars working in the field of business administration sciences. Reflection should bear on specific issues of concern, but also on processes of decision in business practices and on patterns of thought at work inside issues and processes. What the issues are, which processes and patterns need scrutiny, is to be decided upon in the course of the public normative debate in which ethicists, as experts of conceptual analysis and argumentation, and corporate executives, as experts in decision making, each take an equal and fair share, as people who are able and willing to proffer an argued personal standpoint in an open debate.

VAN MEEUWEN, Peter. Bemerkungen zu Ortega y Gassets Technikphilosophie. Tijdschr Stud Verlich Denken, 17(1-2), 57-62, 1989.

VAN NIEKERK, A A. Beyond the *Erklären-Verstehen* Dichotomy. S Afr J Phil, 8(3-4), 198-213, N 88.

In this article the methodological dualism represented by the traditional

(Diltheyan) dichotomy, between explanation and understanding as the distinct methods of the natural and human sciences, is challenged. The first part of the article contains a general outline of Dilthey's concept of understanding in order to trace its development from a psychologistic to a more objectivistic content. The second part is a discussion of two unacceptable suggestions as to how the dichotomy can be transcended. In the third part the author turns to an appraisal of Ricoeur's views, which entails restoration of the hermeneutical and scientific significance of textual interpretation for the reconciliation of the opposition between understanding and explanation. The last section is devoted to a critical appraisal of Ricoeur's efforts and to some suggestions as to how the deficiencies of his approach could be ameliorated. (edited)

VAN PEURSEN, C A. Discovery as the Context of Any Scientific Justification. Man World, 22(4), 471-484, D 89.

The quite divergent opinions on "contexts of discovery and justification" manifest, nevertheless, a similarity in their 'problematique'. (1) The "logic of the sciences" is often remote from scientific practice; it offers only a codification afterwards. (2) Although reality has become problematic, many philosophers acknowledge that scientific discoveries presuppose an interaction with such a reality. (3) Inquiry finds its context in biological and cultural conditions (Dewey). These three issues imply that (a) justification takes place within the wider context of culture and worldview; (b) justification functions in this restricted way as an indispensable 'fiat' afterwards within this wider context of discovery.

VAN PEURSEN, C A. Francis Bacon's "Ars Inveniendi". Tijdschr Filosof, 51(3), 486-516, S 89.

Bacon is not an empiricist. His critique concerns equally sense-experience and concept-formation. He uses the term "experience" in a wider sense, closely related to "wisdom." Bacon is not an inductionist. The falsification-principle is explicit in his philosophy. The new meaning of "induction" in Bacon implies that judgments are not mainly guided by the presence of phenomena but by their absence. Bacon is not the precursor of modern science as regards their contents. He has been, on this point, too much influenced by Renaissance natural magic. Bacon anticipates, however, modern sciences with regard to their method. The central issue of his philosophy is, according to his own words, the "ars inveniendi." In modern terminology: the context of discovery is the main objective of his new methodology.

VAN RIJEN, Jeroen. Some Misconceptions about Leibniz and the Calculi of 1679. Stud Leibniz, 21(2), 196-204, 1989.

In the April papers of 1679 Leibniz expounds an arithmetical model of the logic of categorical sentences. In later works one hardly finds any remaining trace of this project. This fact gave rise to the question why Leibniz abandoned his views of 1679. Several answers have been given. In this paper it is shown that all these answers are wrong and, moreover, that the question itself is pointless. It is argued that, although the arithmetical calculi are defective, Leibniz never abandoned them. Instead, he looked upon them as equivalent alternatives to his later deduction-theoretic representations of the same logic.

VAN STRAATEN, Zak. Models of Rationality. S Afr J Phil, 9(1), 18-23, F 90.

We do not at present have a unified general theory of rationality which can explain both the rationality of an action and the rationality of a set of beliefs. Various models of rationality are examined: Davidson's, game-theoretical rationality, prudence vs. subjectivism, a local vs. a global theory. It is argued that certain considerations show that only some of these will be part of a unified theory. The possibility of an asymmetry condition in the rationality of choice is also considered.

VAN TONGEREN, Paul. The Virtues of the Proprietor (Aristotle and Thomas Aquinas in Truth, Wealth and Poverty) (in Hungarian). Magyar Filozof Szemle, 2-3, 273-286, 1989.

VAN WENSVEEN SIKER, Louke. Christ and Business: A Typology for Christian Business Ethics. J Bus Ethics, 8(11), 883-888, N 89.

H Richard Niebuhr's typology of the relation between Christ and culture can function as a heuristic device to identify different approaches to Christian business ethics. Five types are outlined: Christ against Business, The Christ of Business, Christ above Business, Christ and Business in Paradox, and Christ the Transformer of Business. This typology may facilitate discussion on the relative adequacy of various theological assumptions about ethical change in business.

VAN WILLIGENBURG, Theo. Reaching Moral Conclusions on Purely Logical Grounds. Method Sci, 22(2), 104-121, 1989.

VAN WOUDENBERG, R. Scepticism, Certain Grounds and the Method of Reflexivity (in Dutch). Tijdschr Filosof, 52(2), 251-279, Je 90.

Some statements are called reflexive, for example, the statement: "This sentence consists of six words." The reflexivity lies in the fact that the statement refers to itself. Reflexivity in the sense of self-reference can be used systematically as a philosophical method. Usually the use of this method (as I explain in section I) leads to some form or other of scepticism. But in addition, and this is the point of the article, this method can be used as a means of finding certain grounds (foundations). This is argued in Sections II-IV by means of an analysis of the "transcendental pragmatics" of Karl-Otto Apel.

VAN WOUDENBERG, R. De transcendentale grondlegging van de ethiek van Karl-Otto Apel. Alg Ned Tijdschr Wijs, 82(1), 26-43, Ja 90.

In this article, a systematic description is given of K-O Apel's views on ethics. Firstly, the problem is discussed of the place of ethics in the modern world. The results of scientific thought require ethical reflection, but scientific thought itself appears to make such reflection impossible. Science *is*, and ethics *is not*, objective, recognised intersubjectively. Next, the human need for ethics and the way in which Apel wishes to provide ethics with a real foundation by way of 'transcendental-pragmatic reflection' is investigated. Finally, the problems which arise when applying an ethics of this kind are discussed.

VAN WYK, Robert N. When is Lying Morally Permissible? Casuistical Reflections on the Game Analogy, Self-Defense, Social Contract Ethics. J Value Inq, 24(2), 155-168, Ap 90.

One justification for lying and deception draws analogies between situations in which deception is justified and games such as poker. Another justification is similar to the justification for the use of force in self-defense. This paper discusses such justifications and reaches conclusions about when they are legitimate and when not. However, even when one has a "right" to deceive, one must still ask about the effect of deception on one's own character. The paper refers to various examples including some from "Is Business Bluffing Ethical?" by Albert Carr, a paper that appears in a number of business ethics and introduction to ethics anthologies.

VAN WYK, Robert. "Liberalism and Moral Education" in *Inquiries into Values: The Inaugural Session of the International Society for Value Inquiry*, LEE, Sander H , 643-656. Lewiston, Mellen Pr, 1989.

This paper discusses three versions of liberalism and their implications for moral education. The first is liberalism purely as a political doctrine of governmental neutrality. It is argued that value-neutral education, in particular value-neutral moral and value education is impossible and undesirable. The second is liberalism based on an ideal of the free and autonomous individual. But to believe that education should further such an ideal is to reject liberalism as neutralism. Once one does that there is no basis for claiming that publicly supported schools should only support the values of those citizens who are doctrinaire liberals. The third is a liberalism which fosters "good" self-determination and self-expression, where the criteria for goodness are those which have a broader base of support. I then set forth my views of what moral education should be in a democratic society, views which should be compatible with those of the third sort of liberals.

VANDAMME, Fernand. AI, as an Action Science, as an Utopia or as a Scapegoat. Rev Int Phil, 44(172), 118-130, 1990.

The functions and roles of AI are analysed. There are many myths related to it. However, once these are dissipated what is left has much of relevance. The point is made that one can better understand AI and its relative value if one considers it as an action science (cf. engineers, pedagogy, etc.) in the Piagetian sense, as opposed to a theoretical science.

VANDENBULCKE, J. Justification of Faith (in Dutch). Tijdschr Filosof, 52(1), 121-132, Mr 90.

In his article on *Religion and Truth* ("Religie en warrheid," *TvF* 51/1989, p. 407-426) Herman De Dijn separates dramatically the sphere of the religious from the truth into which we can have insight. On this basis, he essentially makes the justification of faith superfluous and almost inadmissible. In this reply, it has been shown that people have the fundamental possibility, also in the area of the religious, to distinguish between illusion and reality. If one wishes to be faithful to one's humanity, then a person *must* try to separate the religious truth from illusion, to discover where God truly announces himself in the interpersonal and social experience. This includes the possibility of some insight into the act of believing. In this article it has been indicated that there is a universality to religious reality that concerns the core of each human life. (edited)

VANDER WEEL, Richard L. A Note on Some Puzzling Phrases in Aquinas. New Scholas, 63(4), 510-513, Autumn 89.

VANHOOZER, Kevin J. *Biblical Narrative in the Philosophy of Paul Ricoeur: A Study in Hermeneutics and Theology*. New York, Cambridge Univ Pr, 1990

The author offers a creative interpretation of Ricoeur's hermeneutics by relating it to his earlier work in philosophical anthropology. He contends that Ricoeur's hermeneutics should be viewed in light of Kant's work on the creative imagination and Heidegger's work on human temporality. He then presents Ricoeur's recent narrative theory, arguing that it constitutes the high point of Ricoeur's philosophical anthropology and hermeneutics alike. In Part Two, the author considers the significance of Ricoeur's theory of narrative for Christian theology. He claims that Ricoeur's approach to the Gospels provides a surer hermeneutical foundation for a theology that remains primarily existential.

VÁRDY, Péter. Crisis and Programs of Identity (Notes to Debate Popular-Urban) (in Hungarian). Magyar Filozof Szemle, 2-3, 364-375, 1989.

VARNER, Gary E. Biological Functions and Biological Interests. S J Phil, 28(2), 251-270, Sum 90.

I defend the empirical claim that plants have needs, in some sense in which simple artifacts do not, and the normative claim that those needs qualify plants for direct moral consideration. Using the notion of a biological function we can specify, in a nonarbitrary way, what is and is not in the 'biological interests' of a plant, and we can say that plants have interests without implying that simple artifacts do. Certain inadequacies of the dominant mental state theory of individual welfare suggest that such 'biological interests' are morally genuine interests, which qualify their possessor for direct moral consideration.

VARNIER, Giuseppe. Tra intenzionalismo e antirelativismo: l'interpretazione di teorie filosofiche come traduzione. Teoria, 9(1), 159-185, 1989.

VASICEK, Milan. Aesthetic Valuing of Design (in Czechoslovakian). Estetika, 26(3), 174-189, 1989.

VASILIU, Emanuel. Sign and Knowledge. Phil Log, 32(3-4), 281-284, Jl-D 88.

VÁSQUEZ, Eduardo. Concepto y libertad. Dialogos, 25(55), 7-27, Ja 90.

VAUGHAN, Rachel. Searle's Narrow Content. Ratio, 2(2), 185-190, D 89.

Putnam claims that two *Doppelgänger* may be in type-identical mental states yet mean different things when uttering type-identical words because meanings are partly constituted by the 'external world'. Searle's internalist reply is that a speaker's concept determines what the word he uses refers to. I argue that if Searle's speakers are not *Doppelgänger* but one speaker in two possible worlds (the actual and counterfactual, where certain superficially identical objects differ in internal structure), his token-identical experience(s) have different intentional contents. Searle's attempt to provide an internalist solution to the problems raised by Putnam's Twin Earth seems to fail.

VAWTER, Dorothy E (ed) and HACKLER, Chris (ed) and MOSELEY, Ray (ed). *Advance Directives in Medicine*. New York, Praeger, 1989

VEATCH, Robert M. Bioethics Discovers the Bill of Rights. Nat Forum, 69(4), 11-13, Fall 89.

Traditional ethics of Western physicians traces its origins to the Hippocratic Oath and related documents. Many have not realized how different those ethical commitments are from the Judeo-Christian tradition and secular liberal political philosophy. The confrontation between the cultures can be traced to Nuremberg. Since then, especially since the 1960s, rights-based ethics in medicine have replaced those focusing patient-welfare. This has been manifest in claims to rights of confidentiality, consent and consent refusal, and other liberty rights. Bioethics will have to move beyond the Bill of Rights to a theory of justice to deal with entitlement rights claims to access to health care.

VEATCH, Robert M. Justice in Health Care: The Contribution of Edmund Pellegrino. J Med Phil, 15(3), 269-287, Je 90.

Edmund Pellegrino has pioneered work in medical ethics calling for a reconstruction of Hippocratic ethics. In particular, he has spoken of incorporating principles that concern justice and the common good. This article traces his commitment to the common good, concern for the poor, opposition to libertarianism, acknowledgement of the necessity of rationing, and reluctance to give clinicians social allocational tasks. It asks how Pellegrino relates distributive justice to the common good. Drawing on his theory relating autonomy to patient-centered beneficence (in which autonomy is one element of the good rather than a side constraint on the good), the author argues that Pellegrino appears to make justice one element of the common good rather than a distributional moral constraint on promoting the good. He suggests that Pellegrino stands in three

consequentialist or teleological moral traditions: professional physician ethics, Aristotelianism, and Catholic moral theology, but that there are the makings of a more independent, more egalitarian theory of justice in his writings.

VECCHIOTTI, Icilio. Sviluppo e senso delle annotazioni schopenhaueriane a Schelling (2 Teil). Schopenhauer Jahr, 70, 161-173, 1989.

VEDDER, Ben. The Latest Philosophical Anthropology of Max Scheler (in Dutch). Bijdragen, 4, 432-442, 1989.

From time to time, during the last years of his life, Max Scheler gave notice of the forthcoming publication of a complete survey of his theory of man. He promised to write an anthropology, but this work never appeared. In 1987 Manfred Frings edited the parts dealing with anthropology available in the posthumous publications of this philosopher, arranging them in accordance with the scheme of a proposed introduction by Max Scheler for his planned "anthropology." The fragments relate to the following subjects: (1) the history of human consciousness, (2) the theory of evolution, (3) human constitution, (4) the central position of man, (5) metaphysics of man, (6) aging and death. They do not, however, provide the complete theory of man which Scheler promised. (edited)

VEGAS, Serafín. Filosofía e historia de la filosofía en el pensamiento de Richard Rorty. Pensamiento, 46(182), 149-178, Ap-Je 90.

Día a día es creciente la atención que se está dedicando al provocativo programa metafilosófico de Richard Rorty y a sus aspiraciones de convertir el campo de lo epistemológico en un autónomo y autosuficiente diálogo solidario, ajeno a la investigación de la objetividad y de la verdad y conscientemente alejado de la tradición filosófica. A pesar del interés que puedan tener estas revolucionarias pretensiones, su viabilidad interna resulta, sin embargo, insostenible. Para demostrarlo, acaso la mejor estrategia sea poner de manifiesto cómo el engarce introducido por Rorty entre la filosofía y su historia se ve abocado a una contradictoria concepción, a la luz del modelo que de la "historia de la filosofía" ha elaborado el propio Richard Rorty.

VEJVODA, Ivan. Robespierre and Revolution (in Serbo-Croatian). Filozof Istraz, 30(3), 829-841, 1989.

Robespierres Bedeutung Für die Französische Revolution analysierend stellt der Autor fest, dass diese Revolution schon alle bedeutende Fragen der modernen politischen Verfassung aufstellt, so dass dementsprechend auch die Gestalt Robespierres zu betrachten ist. Sein Anteil am Fortschritt der Demokratie in moderner Zeit ist gross, obwohl dieser Fortschritt durch beträchtliche Widersprüche gekennzeichnet wurde.

VELARDE MAYOL, V. La teoría de los objetos en Alexius Meinong. Pensamiento, 45(180), 461-475, O-D 89.

Se comienza con una definición de la noción de objeto como el algo que es posible conocer, y se lo contrasta con el conocimiento del objeto imposible. Como la noción de objeto no es definible rigurosamente, se recurre a las vivencias que lo intencionan, que a su vez se utilizan para clasificar los objetos correspondientes en *objecta*, objetivos, dignitativos y desiderativos, de los que se hace una breve descripción. De esta cuatripartición se destaca la dependencia de los dos últimos respecto de los dos primeros, si bien cada uno de ellos es de índole distinta de los demás e irreducible.

VÉLEZ, Francisco Galán. La nocion de verdad en el ser y el tiempo (cont). Rev Filosof (Mexico), 22(66), 412-437, S-D 89.

This article is the first of two parts, about the Heideggerian notions of truth and scientific objectivity, which are exposed in *Sein und Zeit*. In this part the notions which bring support to the notion of truth are analyzed. The idea of understanding (*verstehen*) as spiral movement from a previous totality to this single being. The central idea of the sense is reviewed under this notion, as something that makes the movement possible from the whole to the part.

VÉLEZ, Francisco Galán. La nocion de verdad en el ser y el tiempo (cont). Rev Filosof (Mexico), 23(67), 1-27, Ja-Ap 90.

In this article, the second of two parts, the Heideggerians' notions of reality, truth and scientific objectivity are examined, as they appear in *Sein und Zeit*, paragraphs 43, 44 and 69. The phenomenological problem of the horizon is specially reviewed. The position of S.Z. pretend to escape the dilemma: idealism or realism, and the key is the notion of horizon and sense. But as we know, the main trouble with the reader of S.Z. is that the characterization of the last horizon of Being, is not precise, because of the unconcluded character of the book.

VELKLEY, Richard L. *Freedom and the End of Reason: On the Moral Foundation of Kant's Critical Philosophy*. Chicago, Univ of Chicago Pr, 1989

This study investigates the Rousseauian turn in Kant's thought which precedes and conditions the transcendental turn. It argues that Rousseau is crucial not only for the moral philosophy but for Kant's whole conception of reason, and that Rousseau instigates a "revolution in the end of reason." The study also offers a new account of the architectonic of Kant's thought, and of the role that the "end of reason" plays in it.

VELMANS, Max. Consciousness, Brain and the Physical World. Phil Psych, 3(1), 77-99, 1990.

Dualist and reductionist theories of mind disagree about whether or not consciousness can be reduced to a state of or function of the brain. They assume, however, that the contents of consciousness are separate from the external physical world as-perceived. According to the present paper this assumption has no foundation, either in everyday experience or in science. Drawing on evidence for perceptual 'projection' in both interoceptive and exteroceptive sense modalities, the case is made that the physical world as-perceived is a construct of perceptual processing and, therefore, part of the contents of consciousness—a finding which requires a reflexive rather than a dualist or reductionist model of how consciousness relates to the brain and the physical world. (edited)

VEMPENY, Alice. Reality—Realization through Self-Discipline. J Dharma, 14(2), 200-216, Ap-Je 89.

VENTIMIGLIA, Giovanni. La relazione trascendentale nella neoscolastica. Riv Filosof Neo-Scolas, 81(3), 416-465, Jl-S 89.

VENTURA, Antonino. Conoscenza e semantica. Riv Filosof Neo-Scolas, 81(2), 308-317, Ap-Je 89.

This work starts from the impossibility of excluding semantics in human knowledge and has as purpose the study of nature and of the forming of infinite knowledge. The conclusions show that limitless knowledge is intuitive and it implies a necessarily creative conscience. They have an exclusively gnosiological meaning but they are the result of arguments developed entirely within the limits of logic, which confirm the corresponding traditional arguments with fewer assumptions.

VENTURA, Antonino. La logica nella conoscenza. Riv Filosof Neo-Scolas, 81(1), 138-149, Ja-Mr 89.

The work starts from the different meanings, philosophically relevant, of the word "knowledge" in order to study the relations between knowledge and logic. The conclusions show the legitimacy of the logic both in the knowledge in itself and in the specific one, defining the constructive function of the logical criteria being presupposed in the different areas of knowledge. They outline the logic of knowing and explain that the constitution of differently reliable sciences comes out of the praxis and it is conditioned by reality. Finally some criteria for a logic of intentionality are given.

VERBEKE, G. "The Bible's First Sentence in Gregory of Nyssa's View" in *A Straight Path: Studies in Medieval Philosophy and Culture*, LINK-SALINGER, Ruth (ed), 230-243. Washington, Cath Univ Amer Pr, 1988.

The article deals with Gregory's interpretation of divine creation and arrives at the following conclusions: the words "in principio" do not refer to a preexisting matter, nor do they have a temporal meaning: the creative act is beyond time. All things were created simultaneously in an initial fullness. Creation is not a necessary process of emanation, but a free decision. Man is created in the image of God: as a consequence of a moral fault sexual life was introduced in view of procreation. As a particular privilege man is gifted with the power of free decision.

VERDU, Alfonso. "Die Problematik des Einen und Vielen in der geschichtlichen Entwicklung des buddhistischen Denkens" in *Agora: Zu Ehren von Rudolph Berlinger*, BERLINGER, Rudolph (and other eds), 231-262. Amsterdam, Rodopi, 1988.

VERENE, Donald Phillip. Eliade's Vichianism: The Regeneration of Time and the Terror of History. New Vico Studies, 4, 115-121, 1986.

The author discusses the senses in which Eliade's conception of history as cyclic and as mythic is similar to the view of history found in Vico's *New Science*.

VERENE, Donald Phillip. Imaginative Universals and Narrative Truth. New Vico Studies, 6, 1-19, 1988.

The article discusses the meaning of Vico's central concept in his *New Science*—imaginative universals (*universali fantastici*). It explores the logic of this conception of a first form of universals and the sense in which such universals lie at the base of human culture. It also shows how such a logic is transformed into a conception of narration that is the form of Vico's philosophy itself.

VERENE, Donald Phillip. Philosophical Laughter: Vichian Remarks on Umberto Eco's *The Name of the Rose*. New Vico Studies, 2, 75-81, 1984.

The paper discusses the sense in which Eco's *Name of the Rose* depends upon a conception of laughter as the basis of human knowledge in which

we must "make truth laugh." It connects this to the view of laughter in Vico.

VERENE, Donald Phillip. Vico's Influence on Cassirer. New Vico Studies, 3, 105-112, 1985.

This paper traces the references in Cassirer's works to Vico from Cassirer's earliest to his latest. It shows that Cassirer regarded Vico as the founder of the philosophy of the *Geisteswissenschaften*, and that Cassirer regarded Vico as the founder of the modern philosophy of mythology.

VERGES, S. Evolución de los derechos humanos en Spinoza y en Leibniz. Pensamiento, 45(180), 447-460, O-D 89.

Desde las ópticas distintas—aunque complementarias—de estos autores, el artículo pretende proyectar alguna luz sobre los derechos humanos, en su génesis *evolutiva* de la que ellos son mojones de no escasa importancia. Efectivamente, el tratamiento que ellos dispensan a estos derechos, sobre todo Leibniz—por más que respaldado por presupuestos ideológicos que le condicionan necesariamente—, representa un progreso nada irrelevante al respecto. Con todo, la valoración crítica, en su aspecto metodológico, sirve de clave de interpretación de sus logros y de sus deficiencias en este campo concreto.

VERHEY, Allen D. Talking of God—But with Whom? Hastings Center Rep, 20(4), Supp 21-24, Jl-Ag 90.

There are long and worthy traditions of theological reflection on medical ethics. By "selective retrieval" of these traditions theologians contributed to the "renaissance of medical ethics." Developments within the discipline, however, muted theological discourse. Renewed attention to theological traditions and candid "talk of God" in medical ethics are defended by attending to three different audiences for theological claims. Believing communities are the obvious audience for theologians; faithful decisions require religious integrity, not just impartial rationality. Doctors, nurses, and patients with a "natural piety" are a second audience. Finally, theological candor in the public discourse of pluralistic cultures is defended.

VERHOEVEN, C. The Dutch Words *besef* and *beseffen* (in Dutch). Tijdschr Filosof, 51(4), 601-620, D 89.

This essay is part of a study about constructivist intellectual elements in Dutch ordinary language words for thinking and speaking. It deals with the words 'besef' and 'beseffen' and their equivalents, approximately translated as to be aware, to have a notion, to realize or to understand. The main hypothesis is that in 'besef' and its equivalents always is spoken of a knowing 'that' about an important fact or situation, not about a knowing 'how' or 'why'. It is typical for the intellectual and moral preponderancy of the awareness or consciousness expressed by 'beseffen', that it contains no constructive elements stemming from an autonomous subject of thinking itself, and that nevertheless 'besef' refers to what is most evident or certain theoretically and obliging practically.

VERKERK, M J. Gödel, Escher, Bach and Dooyeweerd. Phil Reform, 54(2), 111-146, 1989.

In this article a critical study of the 'strong' AI is given by using Hofstadter's "Gödel, Escher, Bach" as a starting point. In the thought of Hofstadter about man an anthropological dualism is present, as well as a materialistic tendency. In view of the character and the history of metaphors, it is not probable that the computer metaphor will become an ultimate model. The computer metaphor is confronted with the reformational philosophy as developed by Herman Dooyeweerd. His anthropology gives a lot of attention to the diversity and unity of the human being.

VERMIJ, R H. Bernard Nieuwentijt and the Leibnizian Calculus. Stud Leibniz, 21(1), 69-86, 1989.

VERNANT, Jean Pierre. L'individuo nella città. Arch Stor Cult, 1, 137-149, 1988.

VERRI, A. Vico e Joyce attraverso Michelet. Il Protag, 6(9-10), 107-119, Je-D 86.

VERRONEN, Veli. *The Growth of Knowledge: An Inquiry into the Kuhnian Theory*. Jyvaskyla, Univ of Jyvaskyla, 1986

The present work is concerned with the paradigm theory of Thomas Kuhn, here given our own interpretation, in the course of which we consider the structure and nature of empirical theories and the development of science, taking also a stand on the question how growth and progress take place in empirical science. (edited)

VERRYCKEN, K. Apokatastasis en herhaling: Nietzsches eeuwigheidsbegrip. Tijdschr Filosof, 51(4), 649-668, D 89.

D'abord il faut insister sur l'évidence, trop souvent oubliée, que pour Nietzsche l'éternel retour constitue l'essence du temps: le retour, c'est maintenant qu'il s'accomplit; l'éternité, c'est à présent qu'elle exerce son empire. Or, on peut démontrer que cet aspect de l'éternel retour joue déjà un certain rôle dans *La naissance de la tragédie*: il représente en quelque sorte l'adaptation de la conception schopenhauerienne de l'éternité à la "métaphysique d'artist" du jeune Nietzsche. Par cette adaptation Nietzsche s'approche de la notion d'*apokatastasis*, non pas dans son sens répétitif usuel, mais dans le sens ontologique que lui ont donné parfois les néoplatoniciens tardifs: l'*apokatastasis* est le mode d'être de la réalité céleste, dont le mouvement circulaire est intermédiaire entre l'éternité statique du monde intelligible et le mouvement "linéaire" du monde sublunaire. En tant qu'*apokatastasis* l'éternel retour est l'identité de l'être et du devenir, de l'immobilité et du mouvement. (edited)

VERSTER, Ulrich. *Limits of Philosophy: (Limits of Reality?)*. Bedford, Dainichi, 1989

VERSTER, Ulrich. *Philosophical Problems (Consciousness, Reality and I)*. Bedford, Dainichi, 1990

The conventions and structures of the tradition and discourse of philosophy are investigated in terms of an original frame of reference. It is in terms of this original approach that the work treats with methodical disorientation, dislocating expectations of the concept of consciousness; of reality; of our selves, the self or "I's"; of experience; of meaning; of existence; and of many other issues and problems which are central to philosophizing.

VERSTER, Ulrich. *Philosophy—A Book*. Bedford, Dainichi, 1989

This is a book about understanding the traditions, structures, and methods of writing philosophy. (staff)

VERSTER, Ulrich. *Philosophy: A Manual and Workbook*. Bedford, Dainichi, 1989

VERSTER, Ulrich. *Relative Transcendentals: Conditions of Philosophy*. Bedford, Dainichi, 1989

VESEY, Godfrey. Responsibility and 'Free Will'. Philosophy, 24, 85-100, 88 Supp.

VETTERLING-BRAGGIN, Mary. A Note on the Legal Liberties of Children as Distinguished from Adults. Thinking, 4(3-4), 49-50, 1982.

VICEDO, Marga. T H Morgan, Neither an Epistemological Empiricist nor a "Methodological" Empiricist. Biol Phil, 5(3), 293-311, Jl 90.

T H Morgan (1866-1945), the founder of the *Drosophila* research group in genetics that established the chromosome theory of Mendelian inheritance, has been described as a radical empiricist in the historical literature. His empiricism, furthermore, is supposed to have prejudiced him against certain scientific conclusions. This paper aims to show two things: first, that the sense in which the term "empiricism" has been used by scholars is too weak to be illuminating. It is necessary to distinguish between empiricism as an epistemological position and the so-called "methodological" empiricism. Second, the author shows that T H Morgan was not an epistemological empiricist as this term is usually defined in philosophy. (edited)

VICKERS, John M. An Agenda for Subjectivism. Erkenntnis, 31(2-3), 397-416, S 89.

VICKERS, John M. Compactness in Finite Probabilistic Inference. J Phil Log, 19(3), 305-316, Ag 90.

This adds to the logic of probability quantifiers developed in *Chance and Structure* (Oxford, 1988). That work gives a semantics for inference involving embedded or reiterated rational-valued probabilities in standard first-order modles in a conservative extension of classical first order logic. Inconsistency in this system in demonstrably not compact. The present result shows that when only finite models are in question the system is axiomatizable and inconsistency is compact.

VICTOR, Bart and MC DONALD, Ross A. Towards the Integration of Individual and Moral Agencies. Bus Prof Ethics J, 7(3-4), 103-118, Fall-Wint 88.

VIDAM, Teodor. Quelques aspects psychiques de la conscience morale individuelle (in Romanian). Rev Filosof (Romania), 35(6), 563-570, N-D 88.

VIDANOVIC, Dorde. P F Strawson and the Social Context in Language (in Serbo-Croatian). Filozof Istraz, 30(3), 1003-1010, 1989.

In a recently published book (Potrc 1986), the author has tried to revitalize Strawson's communication-intention approach to semantics. The purpose of this paper is to examine critically such an approach and to show that a Strawsonian analysis of meaning is inadequate. Several counterarguments against a Strawsonian account are offered—some of them are based on Davidson's and Chomsky's proposals about language learnability and man's linguistic competence. Also, the problems of higher order intentions and intentional openness are examined. In the end, the question of demarcating semantics from pragmatics and the modularity of one and the other is brought up. It is argued that no satisfactory account of a socially based semantics can be produced within the framework proposed in Potrc 1986.

VIDEIRA, Antonio A P and PINHEIRO, Ulysses. A ética do poder na *História da sexualidade* de Michel Foucault. Manuscrito, 12(2), 35-48, O 89.

This article examines some concepts and hypotheses presented by Foucault in the first volume of his *Histoire de la sexualité—La volonté de savoir*—from the vantage point of the reformulation made in the second volume—*L'usage des plaisirs*. The study of this change is important to understand Foucault's work, since it reveals the transformation of one of his fundamental concepts: that of power. In *L'usage des plaisirs* Foucault separates the ethical sphere from that of power. The main question that guides our investigation is: what is the role of ethics in the context described in *La volonté de savoir*, in which power has a central place? Or: how does ethics (subjectivation) act in the dichotomy subject x object in the human sciences (which have the subject as its object)? Is it separated from power? With these questions we intend to emphasize the differences between the two first volumes of Foucault's *Histoire de la sexualité*.

VIDIELLA, Graciela. Sartre y la ética: De la mala fe a la conversión moral. Rev Filosof (Argentina), 4(2), 61-77, N 89.

This paper is concerned with the problem of giving a foundation to ethics in Sartrean philosophy. First, it outlines Sartre's ontology. Then, it tries to make consistent the description of human condition given by Sartre in his work *L'être et le néant* with his ethical remarks of his last philosophy, collected in *Cahiers pour una morale*. It concludes that there are several problems in Sartre's late concept of "moral conversion," which do not agree with his early existentialism.

VIEILLARD-BARON, Jean-Louis. Méditation malebranchiste sur le problème de l'illusion. Rev Phil Fr, 179(2), 193-208, Ap-Je 89.

VIGNA, Carmelo. Evidenza della fede? Riv Filosof Neo-Scolas, 81(3), 466-477, Jl-S 89.

Il saggio discute il libro *L'evidenza e la fede* (Milano 1988) che raccoglie i principali contributi teorici dei teologi della "Scuola" di Milano. Nel saggio, fondamentalmente, viene respinta con diverse argomentazioni la tesi—sostenuta nel libro—secondo cui alla fede cristiana appartiene anche l'evidenza. Di contro, si fa valere la tesi secondo cui alla fede religiosa si può solo attribuire una evidenza in senso lato, cioè quella che nasce da una certa convenienza con le esigenze della ragione nel suo uso pratico.

VIGNON, Jerome. Economic Constraints and Ethical Decisions in the Context of European Ventures. J Bus Ethics, 8(8), 663-666, Ag 89.

Relying on personal experience of political European venture during the last four years, this paper aims at illustrating the role of ethics in public policy making. Crucial importance of ethics is stressed upon at three different stages of the decision-making process: shaping a vision, devising strategy and choosing options in everyday life. Assuming that these stages could apply also to business management, the paper focusses finally on conditions for ethics' effectiveness: providing cohesion but no definite legitimacy, enforcing courage for taking risks in uncertainty but offering no insurance, it needs to be subject to mutual questioning.

VIGO, Alejandro G and JAUREGUI, Claudia. Algunas consideraciones sobre la Refutación del Idealismo. Rev Filosof (Argentina), 2(1), 29-41, My 87.

This paper deals with some assumptions of the *Refutation of Idealism*. First, it analyzes the function of inner sense in the consciousness of the own existence. Secondly, it points out that the permanent element required by the formal structure of inner sense may not be provided either by the 'I' nor by the pure forms of intuition, but only by the outer objects. Lastly, it emphasizes some aspects of the time-space relation presupposed in the proof.

VIGO, Alejandro G. El empleo del paradigma en Platón, *Politico* 277d-283a. Rev Filosof (Argentina), 1(1-2), 59-73, N 86.

In *Politicus* 277d-283a Plato gives account of a method that recurrently was made profitable in his philosophy and specially in the latter period: the recourse to paradigms. This paper deals with the meaning of such a method in connection with Plato's dialectic and ontology. This point brings useful consequences concerning Plato's conception about teaching and learning in philosophy. Lastly, it is pointed out the pertinence of this passage in dialog's context in according with M H Miller's views.

VILADESAU, Richard. The Trinity in Universal Revelation. Phil Theol, 4(4), 317-334, Sum 90.

Traditionally it has been presumed that the knowledge of God's triune nature could be derived only from positive Biblical revelation. However, the Second Vatican Council's teaching on the universal possibility of true salvific faith implies that supernatural revelation also occurs outside Christianity. Karl Rahner's explanation of the meaning of the Trinity as "concrete monotheism" raises the possibility of an implicit knowledge of God's self-revelation as "Word" and "Spirit" in the experience of grace and its formulation in the categories of the other world religions.

VILLANI, Arnaud. "Poststructuralist Alternatives to Deconstruction" in *The Textual Sublime: Deconstruction and Its Differences*, SILVERMAN, Hugh J (ed), 223-230. Albany, SUNY Pr, 1990.

VILLANI, Pasquale. Storia della cultura e storia sociale. Arch Stor Cult, 1, 49-79, 1988.

VILLANUEVA, Enrique. Realismo II: Donald Davidson. Analisis Filosof, 6(2), 115-124, N 86.

In this second paper on recent semantic realism I touch on Professor Donald Davidson's views. In the first part I summarize his notions of meaning and understanding; in the second the method of radical interpretation is introduced. Then a skeptical hypothesis is considered. Next causality is examined as a source of semantic realism to argue that Davidson is holding a nonphilosophical view which stands in need of philosophical argument if it is to answer the radical skeptic's doubts.

VINCENT, Andrew. Classical Liberalism and its Crisis of Identity. Hist Polit Thought, 11(1), 143-161, Spr 90.

Although many theorists have wanted to see a profound consistency in the classical liberal perspective, it is difficult to make out a case for it. Liberalism, as an ideological tradition, has slowly evolved from within and has been subject to a range of interpretations. Although these might be formal ideas which tend to provide some overall coherence, in the end they tell us very little. The crisis of liberalism is thus internal to the ideology itself. Liberals have found themselves committed to certain principles which could justify often quite contradictory social policies.

VINCENT, K Steven. Interpreting Georges Sorel: Defender of Virtue or Apostle of Violence? Hist Euro Ideas, 12(2), 239-257, 1990.

Following a review of the previous interpretive literature, this article suggests that the most convincing framework within which to situate Georges Sorel is a Left-wing French republican tradition, one which appealed to eighteenth century republican ideals like "virtue" (Montesquieu and Rousseau), but which reformulated these ideals in ways that made them more relevant to the socioeconomic changes associated with the growth of industry and technology. Sorel, following earlier French socialists like Saint-Simon and Proudhon, pushed this republican tradition in a nonpolitical direction, effectively arguing that "citizenship" should be based on labor, and that social regeneration could be achieved only through the ascendancy of the values associated with work, the patriarchal family, heroism, and virtuous self-denial.

VINEETH, V F. Dialogue and Theology of Religious Pluralism. J Dharma, 14(4), 376-396, O-D 89.

VINEY, Donald Wayne. Does Omniscience Imply Foreknowledge? Craig on Hartshorne. Process Stud, 18(1), 30-37, Spr 89.

Charles Hartshorne is known for the view that God is omniscient but does not have absolute foreknowledge. William Lane Craig has argued that there is nothing to commend Hartshorne's view, that there are positive arguments against it, and that absurd consequences follow from it. However, Craig misrepresents Hartshorne's view and, as a consequence, underestimates its strength. Once one is clear about the view that Hartshorne actually endorses, I argue, that there is something to commend Hartshorne's view, that the positive arguments against it are unsuccessful, and that, as far as Craig has shown, no absurd consequences follow from it.

VINK, A G. Philo's Final Conclusion in Hume's *Dialogues*. Relig Stud, 25(4), 489-499, D 89.

VINSON, Alain. Paramnésie et katamnèse. Arch Phil, 53(1), 3-29, Ja-Mr 90.

According to Bergson *memory of the present* is not at all active and makes him who experiences it take present perceptions as being simple repetition of a former perception. We describe this experience as eventually connected with an effort both of memory and of imagination through which we are able to discover what is always new in the present.

VIOLA, Francesco. Ermeneutica e diritto: Mutamenti nei paradigmi tradizionali della scienza giuridica. Riv Int Filosof Diritto, 66(2), 336-356, Ap-Je 89.

VIOLI, Patrizia (ed) and ECO, Umberto (ed) and SANTAMBROGIO, Marco (ed). *Meaning and Mental Representation*. Bloomington, Indiana Univ Pr, 1988

VIROLI, Maurizio. Republic and Politics in Machiavelli and Rousseau. Hist Polit Thought, 10(3), 405-420, Autumn 89.

VISSER, Albert. Peano's Smart Children: A Provability Logical Study of Systems with Built-In Consistency. Notre Dame J Form Log, 30(2), 161-196, Spr 89.

The systems studied in this article prove the same theorems (from the "extensional" point of view) as Peano Arithmetic, but are equipped with a self-correction procedure. These systems prove their own consistency and thus escape Gödel's second theorem. Here, the provability logics of these systems are studied. An application of the results obtained turns out to be the solution to a problem of Orey on relative interpretability.

VISSER, H. Flexibele begrippen in kennistheorie en kunstmatige intelligentie. Alg Ned Tijdschr Wijs, 82(2), 141-157, Ap 90.

A new proposal for a definition of 'commonsense knowledge' is used to illuminate the problem of the formalization of inexact commonsense notions. The hypothesis is defended that commonsense knowledge requires the use of *flexible* concepts for which formal counterparts can indeed be found. The connection between knowing and doing is emphasized by drawing attention to commonsense solutions of problems. The explication proposed takes into account that commonsense knowledge consists of both 'principles' and 'procedures'. References are given to constructive contributions by Pasch and Russell. Moreover Husserl's mereological theory is envisaged as a possible candidate for the formalization of flexible concepts.

VISSER, Henk. Adequate Representations of Condorcet Profiles. Method Sci, 22(1), 42-52, 1989.

VITALE, Vincenzo. La verità come inganno—L'Arte di Gorgia. Filosofia, 41(1), 3-12, Ja-Ap 90.

VITALI, Theodore R. Sport Hunting: Moral or Immoral? Environ Ethics, 12(1), 69-82, Spr 90.

Hunting for sport or pleasure is ethical because (1) it does not violate any animal's moral rights, (2) it has as its primary object the exercise of human skills, which is a sufficient good to compensate for the evil that results from it, namely, the death of the animal, and (3) it contributes to the ecological system by directly participating in the balancing process of life and death upon which the ecosystem thrives, thus indirectly benefiting the human community. As such, hunting is not only a natural good, but also a moral good.

VITELL, Scott J and DAVIS, Donald L. Ethical Beliefs of MIS Professionals: The Frequency and Opportunity for Unethical Behavior. J Bus Ethics, 9(1), 63-70, Ja 90.

The frequency and opportunity for unethical behavior by MIS professionals is examined empirically. In addition, the importance of top management's ethical stance, one's sense of social responsibility and the existence of codes of ethics in determining perceptions of the frequency and opportunity for unethical behavior are tested. Results indicate that MIS professionals are perceived as having the opportunity to engage in unethical practices, but that they seldom do so. Additionally, successful MIS professionals are perceived as ethical. Finally, while company codes of ethics were uncommon, top management was seen as supporting high ethical standards.

VITELL, Scott J and DAVIS, D L. The Relationship Between Ethics and Job Satisfaction: An Empirical Investigation. J Bus Ethics, 9(6), 489-494, Je 90.

The relationship between ethics and job satisfaction for MIS professionals is examined empirically. Five dimensions of job satisfaction are examined: (1) satisfaction with pay, (2) satisfaction with promotions, (3) satisfaction with co-workers, (4) satisfaction with supervisors, and (5) satisfaction with the work itself. These dimensions of satisfaction are compared to top management's ethical stance, one's overall sense of social responsibility and an ethical optimism scale (i.e., the degree of optimism that one has concerning the positive relationship between ethics and success in his/her company). Results indicate that MIS professionals are more satisfied with the various dimensions of their jobs when top management stresses ethical behavior and when they are optimistic about the relationship between ethics and success within their firms. The one exception to this is pay satisfaction which is unrelated to these constructs. One's sense of social responsibility is also relatively unrelated to job satisfaction.

VLASTOS, Gregory. Is the 'Socratic Fallacy' Socratic? Ancient Phil, 10(1), 1-16, Spr 90.

VOAKE, Ronald L. *Footsteps After Thought: Metaphorical Approaches from Within*. New York, Lang, 1989

This work explores the implications and extent of our creativity. It embodies a self-reflexive study of man's interaction with recurring metaphysical questions of human existence. Through this vehicle of the creative experience we explore the perhaps imaginary terrain of intuitive knowledge and its seemingly mystical element we experience as "inspiration." We examine how the varied and expressive "languages" of art may provide insight into metaphysical questions that have historically transcended our powers of logic and prosaic deliberation. The epistemological and ontological implications of such an approach are examined, as well as the affective dimension of artistic experience and its intricate relationship with belief. (edited)

VOEGELIN, Eric and SANDOZ, Ellis (ed). *Autobiographical Reflections—Eric Voegelin.* Baton Rouge, Louisiana St Univ Pr, 1989

VOGEL, Lise. Debating Difference: Feminism, Pregnancy, and the Workplace. Fem Stud, 16(1), 9-32, Spr 90.

This article considers the dilemma of reconciling gender equality with the demands of childbearing. Feminists disagree about which policy approach—the provision of substantive special benefits to pregnant workers, or adherence to a strict standard of equal treatment—would be more in the interests of women, men, and their families. Through an examination of a recent American court case, *Cal Fed* v. *Guerra*, the article places this contemporary controversy into broader historical and theoretical context. The author suggest a way to transcend the dichotomies that have haunted the debate without abandoning the strategic framework established by feminists in the 1960s and 1970s.

VOISVILO, E K. On the Development of Knowledge. Stud Soviet Tho, 39(3-4), 273-282, Ap-My 90.

VOLTOLINI, Alberto. Kripke e le intenzioni di riferimento. Teoria, 9(2), 87-112, 1989.

The two notions which Kripke adduces in support of his theory of singular reference—i.e., the notions of a general and a particular intention to refer—are here investigated in order to ascertain their conceptual legitimacy. As regards the first, everything stands good except for the fact whoever entertains it does not actually refer to anything at all. To entertain it is to make an "attributive" promise, that whereby one only *engages* to refer, by means of a certain name, to *whatever* one's mentors' referent under that name is. This is what "to refer parasitically to something" actually means. As for the second, it would be conceptually in order only on the assumption of a *coherent* realist paradigm of the relationship between the aboutness of a singular term and objecthood itself—an assumption which Kripke, in his description of how this alleged intention works, in the final analysis fails to make. Lastly, a brief sketch of singular reference is given, in which "to refer to something" may literally be seen as "to intend something," without this having to mean that referring to an object has to be supported by something like a particular intention to refer.

VON BILDERLING, Beatriz. Categorías puras y categorías esquematizadas. Rev Filosof (Argentina), 2(1), 67-79, My 87.

Once it has been made clear what must be understood as forms of judgment, pure categories, schematised categories and transcendental schemata, this article concerns itself primarily with the distinction between the pure concepts of understanding in the light of the relationship to time and transcendental time determinations. Finally, it examines the possibility of replacing the fourfold Kantian distinction with a more simple one according to which only logical forms and concept related to time would be maintained. This substitution bears in mind the presuppositions of the transcendental analytic on the one hand, and the Kantian system as whole on the other hand.

VON DER LUFT, Eric (ed). *Schopenhauer: New Essays in Honor of His 200th Birthday.* Lewiston, Mellen Pr, 1989

VON ECKARDT, Barbara. Some Remarks on Laudan's Theory of Scientific Rationality. J Phil Res, 15, 153-167, 1990.

When is it rational to pursue a research tradition? In *Progress and Its Problems*, Laudan suggests that if a research tradition RT has a higher rate of progress than any of its rivals, where the rate of progress of an RT is the problem solving effectiveness of its theories over time, then it is rational to pursue RT. In this paper I offer a number of criticisms of this suggestion, with special attention to the current controversy over the rational pursuability of cognitive science.

VON HERRMANN, Friedrich-Wilhelm. "The Flower of the Mouth": Hölderlin's Hint for Heidegger's Thinking of the Essence of Language. Res Phenomenol, 19, 27-42, 1989.

"The Flower of the Mouth" is Hölderlin's poetic word for the essence of language as experienced by him poetically. This word points for Heidegger to the four world regions which Hölderlin poetically experiences. Heidegger in thinking determines these regions as world's fourfold. One of these regions, namely earth, provides Heidegger with the possibility for determining the sounding character of language. While metaphysics interprets this character in terms of body (sensibility) as distinguished from mind, Heidegger determines in thinking this character of language as the earthbound emergence of the sounding from out of saying as letting appear of world.

VON HERRMANN, Friedrich-Wilhelm. "Kunstwerk und technisches

Produkt: *Erläuterungen zum Verhältnis von Kunst und Technik*" in *Cultural Hermeneutics of Modern Art: Essays in Honor of Jan Aler*, DETHIER, Hubert (ed), 13-37. Amsterdam, Rodopi, 1989.

It is the purpose of this essay to make an inquiry into the essential character of modern technology and technological products, as well as into the essential character of art and artwork. Having done this the essay proceeds to discuss the following three questions, which in 1973 Heidegger addressed to Jan Aler in an open letter: (1) the question regarding the relationship of artwork and technological products, (2) the question of the possibility of artwork in the consumer society, and (3) the question concerning the possibility of the disappearance of an authentic future.

VON PLATO, Jan. De Finetti's Earliest Works on the Foundations of Probability. Erkenntnis, 31(2-3), 263-282, S 89.

Bruno de Finetti's earliest works on the foundations of probability are reviewed. These include the notion of exchangeability and the theory of random processes with independent increments. The latter theory relates to de Finetti's ideas for a probabilistic science more generally. Different aspects of his work are united by his foundational programme for a theory of subjective probabilities.

VON SAVIGNY, Eike. Avowals in the "Philosophical Investigations": Expression, Reliability, Description. Nous, 24(4), 507-527, S 90.

In the *PI*, Wittgenstein construes psychological facts as patterns exhibited by 'weaves' which include a person's behaviour as well as its temporal and social surroundings. Avowals, in being linguistic elements of 'weaves', express psychological facts in a way that is normal with conspicuous elements of behavioural patterns. Speakers express psychological facts because avowals are semantically self-predicating. Avowals are reliable expressions of psychological facts, given normal human capacities of learning to behave in patterns; furthermore, avowals can supplement incomplete patterns and thus define them because articulated sentences add high amounts of complexity. Avowals can be descriptions in the way that stating one's impressions of x can be a description of x.

VON WRIGHT, Georg Henrik. Truth-Logics. Log Anal, 30(120), 311-334, D 87.

The concept of truth is treated as an operator *T* "it is true that" in analogy with the modal operators "it is necessary that," *etc.* In classical logic the operator is redundant ("it is true that p = p). In a logic which admits truth-value *gaps* or truth-value *overlaps* this is not the case. The differences between various types of logic: classical, intuitionist, paraconsistent, *etc.* can be systematically exhibited by changing the rules for the operator *T*.

VOORBRAAK, Frans. A Simplification of the Completeness Proofs for Guaspari and Solovay's R. Notre Dame J Form Log, 31(1), 44-63, Wint 90.

Alternative proofs for Guaspari and Solovay's completeness theorems for R are presented. R is an extension of the provability logic L and was developed in order to study the formal properties of the provability predicate of PA occurring in sentences that may contain connectives for witness comparison. (The primary example of sentences involving witness comparison is the Rosser sentence.) In this article the proof of the Kripke model completeness theorems employs tail models, as introduced by Visser, instead of the more usual *finite* Kripke models. The use of tail models makes it possible to derive arithmetical completeness from Kripke model completeness by *literally* embedding Kripke models into PA. Our arithmetical completeness theorem differs slightly from the one proved by Guaspari and Solovay, and it also forms a solution to the problem (advanced by Smorynski) of obtaining a completeness result with respect to a variety of orderings.

VOSS, Sarah. Depolarizing Mathematics and Religion. Phil Math, 5(1-2), 129-141, 1990.

Society today inherits a recent tradition rich in the polarization of mathematics and religion. For many, the two subjects appear to exist on opposite ends of a linear scale, and never the two shall meet! By altering a definition of religion drawn from theological literature to read "mathematics" instead of "religion," this study questions the validity of such separation and presents one way of investigating an alternative conception. The mathematical notion of the Moebius strip both illustrates the similarity between symbols used in the two fields and serves as a basic symbol of the depolarization process itself.

VOSS, Stephen H (trans) and DESCARTES, Rene. *The Passions of the Soul—Rene Descartes.* Indianapolis, Hackett, 1989

VOSSENKUHL, Wilhelm (ed) and SCHAPER, Eva (ed). *Reading Kant.* Cambridge, Blackwell, 1989

Twelve original essays by British, American and German scholars reassess the importance of Kant's arguments for contemporary philosophical debates. Topics covered include the nature and possibility of transcendental arguments, the prospect of a decisive refutation of scepticism, the role of space in our experience of the objective world, the nature of judgment, the identity of the subject and the tenability of transcendental idealism. Contributors are Eckart Forster, Graham Bird, Ross Harrison, Ralph Walker, Peter Bieri, Terry Greenwood, Paul Guyer, Rolf Peter Horstmann, Reinhard Brandt, Wilhelm Vossenkuhl, Gerd Buchdahl and Dieter Henrich.

VOSSENKUHL, Wilhelm. "Understanding Individuals" in *Reading Kant*, SCHAPER, Eva (ed), 196-214. Cambridge, Blackwell, 1989.

VROOM, Hendrik M. Do All Religious Traditions Worship the Same God? Relig Stud, 26(1), 73-90, Mr 90.

Arguments are analysed which affirm or deny that all religions worship the same God. Some authors base their view on their theology (Barth, Rahner); others defend it with reference to comparative religion (Smith), philosophy of religion (Hick) or philosophy (Copleston). The structure of the various arguments is analysed in order to see what kind of argument is decisive. A valid argument should consider all fields of study mentioned. After describing the method to reach a conclusion, an argument is elaborated. Do all religions worship the same God? Some do, but some do not.

VUCINICH, Alexander. *Darwin in Russian Thought*. Berkeley, Univ of Calif Pr, 1989

VUJADINOVIC, Dragica. Democratic Possibilities of French Revolution (in Serbo-Croatian). Filozof Istraz, 30(3), 879-888, 1989.

Die Autorin beginnt mit der Feststellung, die Französische Revolution soll mehrdimensional betrachtet werden, keineswegs einseitig oder reduzierend. Dementsprechend analysiert die Autorin drei Hauptprobleme: das demokratische Potential der Französischen Revolution, die Aktualität der jakobinischen (Erfahrung der zeitgenössischen Einparteisysteme) und die der liberal-demokratischen Erbschaft (Projekt des demokratischen Sozialismus).

VUJIC, Antum. Troubles with Popper (in Serbo-Croatian). Filozof Istraz, 29(2), 671-673, 1989.

In response to the critic of his book on Popper's philosophy (*Otvorena znanost i otvoreno drustvo*, Zagreb 1987), the author presents some factual and intentional misinterpretations of both Popper and himself, made by the critic D Polsek in *Filosofska istrazivanja*, No. 27 (4/1988).

WADE, Maurice and MC KENNA, Edward and ZANNONI, Diane. Rawls and the Minimum Demands of Justice. J Value Inq, 24(2), 85-108, Ap 90.

We demonstrate that by focusing on Rawls's view of the nature of the person and on his use of the Aristotelian Principle it is possible to counter many of the criticisms made against Rawls. In particular, we show why Rawls is correct in asserting that individuals in the original position will not use the principle of insufficient reason to assign probabilities to unknown states of nature, nor will they accept the principle of utility for the purposes of distributing primary goods. We then show, however, that the use of the Aristotelian Principle is more likely to lead to a distribution principle which guarantees minimum basic necessities than it is to lead to the difference principle.

WADHWANI-SHAH, Yashodhara. A New Plausible Exposition of Sānkhya-Kārikā-9. J Indian Phil, 17(3), 211-224, S 89.

The *Sānkhya-Kārikā* presents, in 72 couplets, the basic postulates of the dualistic Sānkhya system of Indian philosophy. Its verse 9 propounds the Sānkhya theory of causality, viz., that a product is always present in its cause in an unmanifest form, becoming manifest at the time of its so-called 'production'.

WADLEIGH, Julian. What is Conservatism? Humanist, 49(6), 20-26,42, N-D 89.

WAGNER DE CEW, Judith. Constitutional Privacy, Judicial Interpretation, and *Bowers versus Hardwick*. Soc Theor Pract, 15(3), 285-303, Fall 89.

I first examine versions of originalism, the approach to constitutional adjudication that accords binding authority to the text of the Constitution, to show it provides insufficient grounds for rejecting the legitimacy of constitutional privacy. I then strongly criticize *Bowers v. Hardwick*, in which the Supreme Court upheld Georgia's antisodomoy laws and refused to extend the scope of constitutional privacy. I briefly indicate, however, unexpected positive perspectives for the future of constitutional privacy protection.

WAGNER, Frank. Subgroups of Stable Groups. J Sym Log, 55(1), 151-156, Mr 90.

We define the notion of generic for an arbitrary subgroup *H* of a stable group, and show that *H* has a definable hull with the same generic properties. We then apply this to the theory of stable fields.

WAGNER, Günter P. "The Variance Allocation Hypothesis of Stasis" in *Reductionism and Systems Theory in the Life Sciences: Some Problems and*

Perspectives, HOYNINGEN-HUENE, Paul (ed), 161-185. Norwell, Kluwer, 1989.

WAGNER, Robert B. *Accountability in Education: A Philosophical Inquiry*. New York, Routledge, 1989

Individuals and institutions must frequently answer for the acts they have committed or for responsibilities they are expected to fulfill. The author presents a clear and penetrating analysis of the elements involved in accountability relationships and the conditions under which obligations of moral and legal accountability become valid and effective. The principles which evolve from this analysis are applied to the belief that student achievement can be improved by holding teachers more accountable for student performance. Chapters devoted to the issues of student and teacher accountability challenge this belief and several assumptions underlying the position of B F Skinner concerning human behavior.

WAINWRIGHT, William J and ROWE, William L. *Philosophy of Religion: Selected Readings (Second Edition)*. San Diego, Harcourt Brace Jov, 1989

The aim of the volume is to introduce students to the philosophy of religion by acquainting them with the writings of some of the thinkers who have made substantial contributions in this area. This new edition expands the range of topics by including an entirely new chapter on death and immortality and a new subsection on the moral argument. There is also some new material on Wittgenstein and fideism, religious pluralism, and faith and the need for evidence. Almost every chapter has been changed by deletions or additons to update the selections and provide more material that is understandable to beginning students.

WAINWRIGHT, William. Jonathan Edwards and the Sense of the Heart. Faith Phil, 7(1), 43-62, Ja 90.

This paper examines Edwards's attempt to make philosophical and theological sense of the regenerate person's new sense of the spiritual beauty of divine things. It is divided into six sections. The first two discuss the nature of the idea of spiritual beauty and Edwards's reasons for thinking that our apprehension of it is a kind of sensation or perception. The third explores the implications of Edwards's theory for the epistemic status of religious belief while the fourth and fifth examine his defense of the objectivity of the new "spiritual sense." The last section discusses the bearing of Edwards's remarks on current discussions.

WAITHE, Mary Ellen and OZAR, David T. The Ethics of Teaching Ethics. Hastings Center Rep, 20(4), 17-21, Jl-Ag 90.

WAKKER, Peter. A Graph-Theoretic Approach to Revealed Preference. Method Sci, 22(1), 53-66, 1989.

WAKKER, Peter. Under Stochastic Dominance Choquet-Expected Utility and Anticipated Utility Are Identical. Theor Decis, 29(2), 119-132, S 90.

The aim of this paper is to convince the reader that Choquet-expected utility, as initiated by Schmeidler (1982, 1989) for decision making under uncertainty, when formulated for decision making under risk naturally leads to anticipated utility, as initiated by Quiggin/Yaari. Thus the two generalizations of expected utility in fact are one.

WALD, Henri. Le talent. Phil Log, 32(1-2), 75-79, Ja-Je 88.

WALDRON, Jeremy. The Rule of Law in Contemporary Liberal Theory. Ratio Juris, 2(1), 79-96, Mr 89.

Existing accounts of the Rule of Law are inadequate and require fleshing out. The main value of the ideal of rule of law for liberal political theory lies in the notion of predictability, which is essential to individual autonomy. The author examines this connection and argues that conservative theories of rule of law claim too much. Liberal theory equates the rule of law with legality, which is only one of the elements necessary for a just social order.

WALICKI, Andrzej. The Rule of Law in the Russian Intellectual Tradition: Pre-Revolutionary Russia, the Soviet Union and Perestroika. Dialec Hum, 15(3-4), 19-26, Sum-Autumn 88.

WALKER JR, Theodore. Hartshorne's Neoclassical Theism and Black Theology. Process Stud, 18(4), 240-258, Wint 89.

WALKER, A D M. Character and Circumstance. Int J Moral Soc Stud, 5(1), 39-53, Spr 90.

I argue that the actions through which a person develops and exercises a particular virtue may have incidental features which cumulatively limit the extent to which he can acquire certain other virtues. I illustrate this possibility with Stuart Hampshire's version of the much discussed example of Sartre's pupil who had to choose between remaining at home to care for his mother and leaving home to join the Free French. Finally, I defend my argument against two objections: (i) that it would be possible for someone in circumstances like those of Sartre's pupil not to suffer harm to his character; and (ii) that my argument depends upon an unsatisfactory conception of the virtues.

WALKER, A D M. Obligations of Gratitude and Political Obligation. Phil Pub Affairs, 18(4), 359-364, Fall 89.

The paper defends the position outlined in "Political Obligation and the Argument from Gratitude" (*Philosophy and Public Affairs*, 17 No. 3) against George Klosko's objections (*Philosophy and Public Affairs*, 18 No. 4) that obligations of gratitude are not strong enough to provide the foundations of political obligation. I argue (1) that Klosko's case for the general weakness of obligations of gratitude rests on a confusion between the content and the stringency of an obligation, and (2) that he assumes too quickly that this general weakness must defeat any attempt to base political obligation on considerations of gratitude.

WALKER, A D M. Virtues and Character. Philosophy, 64(249), 349-362, JI 89.

Moral philosophers who, like Aristotle, give a prominent place to the virtues in their moral theories typically assume that as traits of character the virtues are mutually compatible. However, if the virtues require not merely action but action in the right spirit (i.e., from the appropriate motive and with the appropriate thoughts and feelings), and if the full development of a virtue involves its possession as a trait of character (i.e., as a firm and unshakable disposition), then, granted that certain pairs of virtues (e.g., justice and kindness) are very different in nature, it would seem that the person who has fully developed one of the pair can possess the other only to a limited extent. There are thus necessary incompatibilities between the virtues as traits of character. Aristotelians cannot evade the force of this argument by claiming that it depends on an unacceptable conception of the virtues.

WALKER, Arthur F. The Problem of Weakness of Will. Nous, 23(5), 653-676, D 89.

I survey discussions of akrasia over the last fifteen years, focusing on skeptical arguments that question the possibility of free, intentional akratic action done for a reason. I discuss arguments that akratic actions are not free, cannot be done for a reason, must involve extreme amounts of illogicality, or violate plausible principles of intentional action and desire. In conclusion, I offer a theory which explains how akratic actions can be done for reasons, a theory based on a distinction between two incommensurable types of reasons—"evaluative" and what I call "directive."

WALKER, Cheryl. Feminist Literary Criticism and the Author. Crit Inquiry, 16(3), 551-571, Spr 90.

The "death of the author" school of critical theory, deriving from French critics like Barthes, Foucault, and Derrida, presents problems for feminism that a number of recent feminist critics—Toril Moi, Nancy K Miller, Jan Montefiore—seem to overlook. A reexamination of the original "death of the author" essays shows that neither Barthes nor Foucault demanded a total erasure of all biographical and authorial reference. Feminist critics would do better to admit the validity of a reconceived sense of "author" along the lines suggested by third world and lesbian critics (Mohanty and Martin, e.g.) or poststructural Marxists like Cora Kaplan.

WALKER, J C. Democracy and Pragmatism in Curriculum Development. Educ Phil Theor, 19(2), 1-10, 1987.

According to orthodox democratic theory, the community in general has an interest in what is taught in schools. This implies some form of community control of education. Neither a centralised representative system, relying on hierarchical bureaucracy, nor a geographically decentralised system relying on extensive community participation, is satisfactory. In place of geographical decentralisation, we need functional decentralisation, and in place of centralisation we need compulsory coordination and negotiation between smaller representative bodies, if necessary achieved through arbitration. Levels and location of decision making should be determined pragmatically, depending on the nature of the problems and issues which the curriculum is designed to address.

WALKER, J C. Symbolic Orders and Discursive Practices. Educ Phil Theor, 21(1), 21,33-35, 1989.

In reply to an article by Bronwyn Davies (*Educ. Phil. Theor.* 21), dealing with the "male symbolic order," it is argued that "the analysis of discursive practices" is an inadequate method for depicting gender relations. Davies' quest for an alternative to the "male symbolic order"—the elimination of the male/female duality—is considered in the light of a physicalist and pragmatist theory of culture in which gender relations are shown to be more problematic, and more fluid, than Davies suggests.

WALKER, Margaret Urban. Augustine's Pretence: Another Reading of Wittgenstein's *Philosophical Investigations* 1. Phil Invest, 13(2), 99-109, Ap 90.

WALKER, Margaret Urban. Autonomy or Integrity: A Reply to Slote. Phil Papers, 18(3), 253-263, N 89.

WALKER, Margaret Urban. Further Notes on Feminist Ethics and Pluralism: A Reply to Lindgren. Hypatia, 5(1), 151-155, Spr 90.

In a comment on my paper, "Moral Understandings: Alternative Epistemology for a Feminist Ethics" (1989) Ralph Lindgren questions the wisdom of confrontational rhetoric in my paper and much feminist moral philosophy, and the consistency of this stance with pluralism about ethics. I defend both the rebellious rhetoric and the inclusivity of my own approach, but suggest that pluralism in moral philosophy is harder to define than Lindgren's comments suggest.

WALKER, Margaret Urban. Moral Understandings: Alternative "Epistemology" for a Feminist Ethics. Hypatia, 4(2), 15-28, Sum 89.

Work on representing women's voices in ethics has produced a vision of moral understanding profoundly subversive of the traditional philosophical conception of moral knowledge. I explicate this alternative moral "epistemology," identify how it challenges the prevailing views, and indicate some of its resources for a liberatory feminist critique of philosophical ethics.

WALKER, Pierre A (trans) and FOUCAULT, Michel. Photogenic Painting. Crit Texts, 6(3), 1-12, 1989.

WALKER, R Scott (trans) and POR, Peter. Fin de Siècle, End of the "Globe Style"? The Concept of Object in Contemporary Art. Diogenes, 147, 92-110, Fall 89.

The historical style—as it stood when at its peak between the "Lumières" and the turn towards modernism—is the form of creation and existence through which art undertakes the mission of ancient transcendent systems and transforms it into its own categories. The great filiation of the theories of historical style (Wölfflin, Riegl, Walzel) aims at conceptualizing the same ideal: an artistic synthesis—absolute, in terms of construction, relative, in terms of historical phenomenon—between *poiésis* and *techné*, idea and matter. The last blossoming of this artistical ideal was the "*fin de siècle*" period. The turn towards modern in art as well as in criticism happened through a radical break-away from this period and this ideal in general. It is precisely the eternal schism which was to be the creative principle behind, on the one side, the works of the *poiésis*, *eidos* (Eliot, Schönberg, Klee, etc.), and, on the other side, the works of the matter, and *techné* (lettrisme, repetitive music, Max Bill). Modern art and modern criticism are no longer conceived as creating a style.

WALKER, R Scott (trans) and RUBEL, Maximilien. The French Revolution and the Education of the Young Marx. Diogenes, 148, 1-27, Wint 89.

Marx the "communist" had to struggle throughout his career as man of science and as political militant in order to have his "bourgeois" claims triumph—the ideals proclaimed by the fundamental charter of liberal democracy, the Declaration of the Rights of Man and of the citizen. The historiography of the French Revolution profoundly marked his political theory. Political emancipation, while establishing legally the internal dichotomy—or 'alienation'—of modern man and the separation of modern society into classes, was the signal for a social movement dedicated to human, and thus, total emancipation. Marx's political activity was a permanent struggle against Prussian absolutism, Russian Czarism and French Bonapartism.

WALKER, Ralph C S. "Transcendental Arguments and Scepticism" in *Reading Kant*, SCHAPER, Eva (ed), 55-76. Cambridge, Blackwell, 1989.

There are certain premises and rules of inference which sceptics must accept as justified unless they put themselves beyond the reach of any argument. These yield transcendental arguments which refute the sceptic: but there is a sense in which scepticism remains standing, though as a position no one could hold. Confusion arises through unclarity over this, and through the failure to distinguish resoluble from irresoluble questions; it is exacerbated by the foggy idea of a conceptual scheme. Objections to the method can be seen to fail once this confusion is dissolved—a confusion which affected Kant himself.

WALKER, Ralph. Kant's Conception of Empirical Law—II. Aris Soc, SUPP 64, 243-258, 1990.

For Kant regulative principles function to provide assertibility conditions for statements of empirical law. The concepts of causality, etc., are *a priori*, but are applied to the phenomenal world with the aid of these principles. However what happens in that world depends on how things are in themselves. Transcendental idealism was meant to remove the problem of match between our *a priori* principles and the (phenomenal) world, but it can do so only for constitutive principles; with regulative principles a parallel problem remains, since our construction of the phenomenal world cannot ensure that empirical laws will continue to hold.

WALKER, Valerie. In Defense of a Different Taxonomy: A Reply to Owens. Phil Rev, 99(3), 425-431, JI 90.

Many philosophers urge that cognitive psychology should "narrow" the notion of content it uses to individuate mental states since the Twin Earth thought experiments demonstrate that content cannot supervene on current physical bodily states. Joseph Owens argues that this move to narrow content will not work, since narrow content is not a species of content. His claim rests on a dilemma concerning two ways to taxonomize behavior, neither of which can support a viable narrow content taxonomy. However, there is a third way to taxonomize behavior which Owens overlooks—one which does promote individuation by narrow yet genuinely contentful content.

WALLACE IV, Edwin R. Mind-Body and the Future of Psychiatry. J Med Phil, 15(1), 41-73, F 90.

Philosophical perspectives are deeply relevant to psychiatric theorization, investigation, and practice. There is no better instance of this than the perennially vexing mind-body problem. This essay eschews reductionist, dualist, and identity-theory attempts to resolve this problem, and offers an ontology—"monistic dual-aspect interactionism"—for the biopsychosocial model. The profound clinical, scientific, and moral consequences of positions on the mind-body relation are examined. I prescribe a radically biological cure for psychiatry's—and all medicine's—chronic dogmatism and fragmentation.

WALLACE, Mark I. Postmodern Biblicism: The Challenge of René Girard for Contemporary Theology. Mod Theol, 5(4), 309-325, Jl 89.

WALLACE, R Jay. How to Argue about Practical Reason. Mind, 99(395), 355-385, Jl 90.

This paper is a survey of recent work on practical reason, focussing on the question of the role of desire in the explanation of motivation and intentional action. The paper attempts to develop an improved account of what is at stake in debates between Humeans and Kantians (or rationalists) about practical reason; and it draws on this account, to argue that recent arguments for a broadly Humean position do not succeed.

WALLACE, William A. "Thomas Aquinas on Dialectics and Rhetoric" in *A Straight Path: Studies in Medieval Philosophy and Culture*, LINK-SALINGER, Ruth (ed), 244-254. Washington, Cath Univ Amer Pr, 1988.

WALLACE, William. Duhem and Koyré on Domingo de Soto. Synthese, 83(2), 239-260, My 90.

Galileo's view of science is indebted to the teaching of the Jesuit professors at the Collegio Romano, but Galileo's concept of mathematical physics also corresponds to that of Giovan Battista Benedetti. Lacking documentary evidence that would connect Benedetti directly with the Jesuits, or the Jesuits with Benedetti, I infer a common source: the 'Spanish connection', that is, Domingo de Soto. I then given indications that the fourteenth-century work at Oxford and Paris on *calculationes* was transmitted via Spain and Portugal to Rome and other centers where Jesuits had colleges, and figured in the rise of mathematical physics at the beginning of the seventeenth century. A result of these researches is their vindication of Duhem, as contrasted with Koyré, on the origins of modern mechanics.

WALLEN, Lincoln A. *Automated Deduction in Nonclassical Logics*. Cambridge, MIT Pr, 1990

WALLENIUS, J and KORHONEN, P. Supporting Individuals in Group-Decision Making. Theor Decis, 28(3), 313-329, My 90.

Pooling of different resources is typical among the member countries of the Council of Mutual Economic Assistance participating in joint large-scale construction projects. The problem faced by the members of the Council is to decide, how much of various resources each country should contribute to a construction project. In this paper we present a general approach to supporting individuals involved in such negotiations. We formulate the problem as a multiple criteria/multiple decision-maker model and use our approach to finding a compromise solution for the resource pooling problem within the Council of Mutual Economic Assistance. The approach is implemented on a computer, tested and illustrated using a prototypical example.

WALLENSTEEN, Peter and RYDEN, Lars. The Talloires Network—A Constructive Move in a Destructive World. Phil Soc Act, 15(3-4), 75-85, Jl-D 89.

WALLER, Bruce N. *Critical Thinking: Consider the Verdict*. Englewood Cliffs, Prentice-Hall, 1988

This is a critical thinking textbook that uses the courtroom and the jury room as sources for critical thinking exercises and as important and fascinating contexts for the development of critical thinking skills. It thoroughly covers the essential elements of learning to develop and critique arguments, and adds some special chapters—such as on evaluating expert testimony and eyewitness testimony—not usually covered in critical thinking texts. The book

examines critical thinking in many areas (including political argument, advertising, editorials, scientific disputes) but focuses on effective reasoning for conscientious jury members.

WALLER, Bruce N. From Hemlock to Lethal Injection: The Case for Self-Execution. Int J Applied Phil, 4(4), 53-58, Fall 89.

The contemporary movement to more "humane" methods of capital punishment (such as lethal injection) does nothing to alleviate and may well exacerbate the psychological torture of the executed. Self-execution would mitigate some of the worst features of capital punishment, and would help preserve the dignity of the condemned; and by focusing attention on the individuality and humanity of the condemned, it could ultimately promote abolition of capital punishment.

WALLER, Bruce N. Uneven Starts and Just Deserts. Analysis, 49(4), 209-213, O 89.

It has recently been claimed (by Dennett, Sher) that uneven starts in life do not eliminate differences in just deserts, since there is ample opportunity to overcome such initial disadvantages. However, unequal starts are in fact rarely balanced by subsequent events; instead, initial advantages and disadvantages are more likely to have a cumulative effect. It does not follow that there is never any way to overcome a bad start, but it does follow that claims of ultimate differences in just deserts are undermined by early events for which individuals are not morally responsible.

WALLHAUSSER, John. Schleiermacher's Critique of Ethical Reason: Toward a Systematic Ethics. J Relig Ethics, 17(2), 25-39, Fall 89.

Present in Schleiermacher's early *Outlines of a Critique of Previous Ethical Theories* are major themes regarding ethics which are developed more fully in his later writings. These themes include a division of ethical reflection into three parts: foundational principles (basic ontological and anthropological assumptions), ideas (the highest good, virtue, and duty), and concepts (ethics as systematic inquiry). The essay explores these three themes to explicate Schleiermacher's thought at the time of writing the *Critique* and to show its relation to the subsequent development of his ethics.

WALLIS, Charles. Response to Dietrich's "Computationalism". Soc Epistem, 4(2), 195-199, Ap-Je 90.

WALLS, Jerry L. Is Molinism as Bad as Calvinism? Faith Phil, 7(1), 85-98, Ja 90.

This paper compares the theories of providence and predistination in Molinism and Calvinism. My particular concern is with whether Molinism is beset with the same sort of disturbing moral implications which plague Calvinism. I conclude that Molinism is better off than Calvinism in this regard, but still fails to give us a satisfactory account of God's goodness and will to save all persons. I suggest an amended version of Molinism to repair this difficulty, according to which God gives all persons an optimal amount of grace and equal opportunity to respond to it.

WALSH, Harry. "The Place of Schopenhauer in the Philosophical Education of Leo Tolstoi" in *Schopenhauer: New Essays in Honor of His 200th Birthday*, VON DER LUFT, Eric (ed), 300-311. Lewiston, Mellen Pr, 1989.

WALSH, Sylvia I. The Subjective Thinker as Artist. Hist Euro Ideas, 12(1), 19-29, 1990.

WALSH, W H. "Hegel on Morality" in *Dialectic and Contemporary Science*, GRIER, Philip T (ed), 137-152. Lanham, Univ Pr of America, 1989.

WALTER, Edward. A Pragmatic Version of Natural Law. J Value Inq, 24(3), 213-225, Jl 90.

Natural law survives continual metaphysical and logical criticisms because legal systems seem chaotic and arbitrary without it. The difference between natural law philosophers and their opponents is that the former discerns ultimate human moral goals and the latter does not. By developing a pragmatic use of intuition, natural law hypothesizing is defended. The virtue of a pragmatic account of natural law is that it explains why particular historical social movements are approved and others are not.

WALTERS, Kenneth D. "Ethics and Responsibility" in *Papers on the Ethics of Administration*, WRIGHT, N Dale (ed), 24/1. Albany, SUNY Pr, 1988.

WALTERS, Kerry S. The Creator's Boundless Palace: William Bartram's Philosophy of Nature. Trans Peirce Soc, 25(3), 309-332, Sum 89.

WALTERS, Kerry S. Limited Paternalism and the Pontius Pilate Plight. J Bus Ethics, 8(12), 955-962, D 89.

Ebejer and Morden ("Paternalism in the Marketplace: Should a Salesman Be His Buyer's Keeper?," *Journal of Business Ethics 7*, 1988) propose 'limited paternalism' as a sufficient regulative condition for a professional ethic of sales. Although the principle is immediately appealing, its application can lead to a counterproductive ethical quandary I call the Pontius Pilate Plight. This quandary is the assumption that ethical agents' hands are clean in certain situations even if they have done something they condemn as immoral. Since limited paternalism can give rise to this queer conclusion in the salesperson/buyer relationship, the principle if suspect. It may be a necessary condition for ethical sales, but is not sufficient. This discussion concludes by suggesting two additional criteria which, when complemented by the limited paternalism principle, are jointly sufficient.

WALTERS, Kerry S. On World Views, Commitment and Critical Thinking. Inform Log, 11(2), 75-89, Spr 89.

WALTERS, Leroy (ed) and BEAUCHAMP, Tom L (ed). *Contemporary Issues in Bioethics (Third Edition)*. Belmont, Wadsworth, 1989

WALTERS, LeRoy (ed) and KAHN, Tamar Joy (ed). *Bibliography of Bioethics, Volume 15*. Washington, Kennedy Inst Ethics, 1989

WALTON, Doug. What Is Reasoning? What Is an Argument? J Phil, 87(8), 399-419, Ag 90.

WALTON, Douglas N. Courage, Relativism and Practical Reasoning. Philosophia (Israel), 20(1-2), 227-240, Jl 90.

This article discusses the elements of relativism to cultural norms, knowledge, or historical epochs, that seem to come in during any account of the virtue of courage in ethics. The problems discussed relate to what might be called casuistical concerns of evaluating a particular case that may be taken as a paradigm of courage or cowardice.

WALTON, Douglas N. *Informal Logic: A Handbook for Critical Argumentation*. New York, Cambridge Univ Pr, 1989

WALTON, Douglas N. Problems in the Use of Expert Opinion in Argumentation. Commun Cog, 22(3-4), 383-389, 1989.

WALTON, Roberto J. El tema principal de la fenomenología de Husserl. Rev Filosof (Argentina), 3(1), 53-73, My 88.

Husserl points out that the first breakthrough of the correlation between experience object and the manners of givenness around 1898 affected him "so deeply" that it dominated his subsequent life-work (Hua. VI, 169). This paper outlines the principle stages in the task of elaborating on this theme as well as the role played by human subjectivity. Finally, an attempt is made to show that Husserl has foreshadowed criticisms concerning the system of correlations between the world and world-consciousness.

WALZER, Michael. The Communitarian Critique of Liberalism. Polit Theory, 18(1), 6-23, F 90.

WALZER, Michael. A Critique of Philosophical Conversation. Phil Forum, 21(1-2), 182-196, Fall-Wint 89-90.

WAMBA-DIA-WAMBA, Ernest. The Crisis of Marxism and Some of Its Implications. Phil Soc Act, 16(1), 7-22, Ja-Mr 90.

WANG, Hao. Tharp and Conceptual Logic. Synthese, 81(2), 141-152, N 89.

WANG, Rui Shen. Die konfuzianischen Begriffe von Rechtlichkeit und Interesse und ihr Wert im Modernen China. Conceptus, 24(61), 43-49, 1990.

In respect of the question of righteousness and interests, there are three schools of thought in Chinese traditional philosophy: (1) Confucian school—the priority of its claim is righteousness; (2) Mohist school—it emphasizes interests; (3) Taoist school—as worshipper of nature it repels both the righteousness and interests, for their being artificial. Contemporary China is facing a reform drive and the commercialization of economy is the subject of our economic reform. On this background, how to estimate the Confucianist's concept of righteousness and interests is a problem deserving discussion.

WANG, Shiqiang. Inductive Rings and Fields. Annals Pure Applied Log, 44(1-2), 133-137, O 89.

By an inductive ring (or field) is meant a ring with unity (or a field) that satisfies Peano's induction scheme. In this article, some results on the inductivity or noninductivity of various rings and fields are recorded. Also, some possible applications of such rings and fields are briefly discussed, including applications to proofs of undefinability; to disprove quantifier elimination; and to get insights into some mathematical arguments. Besides, the author would like to add that it is also conceivable, for example, that the inductivity of the field of complex numbers may bring about some simplifications in the teaching of relevant topics.

WAPNER, Paul. What's Left: Marx, Foucault and Contemporary Problems of Social Change. Praxis Int, 9(1-2), 88-111, Ap-Jl 89.

A central dilemma for theorists of political change is the demise of grand political theory. Grand theory is the attempt to understand politics in an architectonic way; it tries to reveal the nature of human beings, society and history, and has faith in reason to discover these natures. Much

contemporary thought problematizes the project of developing grand theory. This article charts the demise of grand theory by presenting a Foucaultian critique of Marx. This includes an exposition of Marx's thought—especially his understanding of human nature, economic determinism and historical materialism—and an explication of Foucault's attack on these concepts and essentialist thought in general.

WARD, Andrew. The *Apology* and the *Crito*: A Misplaced Inconsistency. New Scholas, 63(4), 514-515, Autumn 89.

WARD, Andrew. Coherence and Warranted Theistic Belief. Int J Phil Relig, 28(1), 35-45, Ag 90.

WARD, Andrew. Mental Representations and Intentional Behavior. SW Phil Rev, 4(1), 95-101, Ja 88.

WARD, Andrew. Philosophical Functionalism. Behaviorism, 17(2), 155-158, Fall 89.

In his recent article "The Computational Model of the Mind and Philosophical Functionalism," Richard Double argues that there are some fairly forceful *a priori* arguments showing that philosophical functionalism cannot provide adequate explanations for phenomenal states, the nonphenomenal conscious states of common sense, and the theoretical states of cognitive psychology and linguistics. In this paper it is argued that none of Double's arguments are successful.

WARD, Andrew. Radical Interpretation and the Gunderson Game. Dialectica, 43(3), 271-280, 1989.

WARD, Andrew. Skepticism and Davidson's Omniscient Interpreter Argument. Critica, 21(61), 127-143, Ap 89.

WARD, Andrew. Talking Sense About Freedom. Phil Phenomenol Res, 50(4), 731-744, Je 90.

WARD, David. "Ethics and Reproductive Technologies" in *Inquiries into Values: The Inaugural Session of the International Society for Value Inquiry*, LEE, Sander H , 677-684. Lewiston, Mellen Pr, 1989.

WARD, Keith. God as Creator. Philosophy, 25, 99-118, 89 Supp.

WARD, Keith. Truth and the Diversity of Religions. Relig Stud, 26(1), 1-18, Mr 90.

A consideration of John Hick's 'Pluralist' hypothesis that all religions are salvific and state truths about 'the Real'. The hypothesis is rejected on the ground that the central concept of an unknowable 'Noumenon', appearing in radically different ways, is incoherent. It is shown that the concept of 'ineffability' is used in different ways; to make it refer to one reality commits the quantifier-shift fallacy. Some views of 'reality' must be false; nevertheless, 'soft pluralism' (that many traditions may contain resources conducive to salvation) is defensible.

WARD, Patrick J. "A Model of End-Directedness" in *Issues in Evolutionary Epistemology*, HAHLWEG, Kai (ed), 357-390. Albany, SUNY Pr, 1989.

WARNER, Richard. Reply to Baker and Grandy. J Phil, 86(10), 528-529, O 89.

WARNER, Stuart D. The Politics of the Book: The French Revolution and the Demise of Natural Rights Theory. Phil Theol, 4(3), 223-252, Spr 90.

The principal object of this essay is to elucidate some of the story of how a theory that was so entrenched in the minds of intellectuals, namely, natural rights theory, fell so out of favor. This is the story of how the terror, fear, and destruction that became part of the French Revolution was laid at the feet of natural rights theory by three powerful figures: Burke, Bentham, and Hegel. It was these three figures, more than any others, who were responsible for the demise of natural rights theory in the nineteenth century; and their respective criticisms of natural rights theory were made under the omnipresent shadow of, and in response to, the French Revolution.

WARNKE, Georgia. Rawls, Habermas, and Real Talk: A Reply to Walzer. Phil Forum, 21(1-2), 197-203, Fall-Wint 89-90.

WARNKE, Georgia. Social Interpretation and Political Theory: Walzer and His Critics. Phil Forum, 21(1-2), 204-226, Fall-Wint 89-90.

WARNOCK, G J. *J L Austin*. New York, Routledge, 1989

This book—a volume in the series 'The Arguments of the Philosophers'—offers a survey and critical appraisal of the principal themes in the works of the late Professor J L Austin, of Oxford.

WARREN, Karen J. The Power and the Promise of Ecological Feminism. Environ Ethics, 12(2), 125-146, Sum 90.

Ecological feminism is the position that there are important connections—historical, symbolic, theoretical—between the domination of women and the domination of nonhuman nature. I argue that because the conceptual connections between the dual dominations of women and nature are located in an oppressive patriarchal conceptual framework characterized by a logic of domination, (1) the logic of traditional feminism requires the expansion of feminism to include ecological feminism, and (2) ecological feminism provides a framework for developing a distinctively feminist environmental ethic. I conclude that any feminist theory and any environmental ethic which fails to take seriously the interconnected dominations of women and nature is simply inadequate.

WARREN, Mark. Liberal Constitutionalism as Ideology: Marx and Habermas. Polit Theory, 17(4), 511-534, N 89.

Strong democrats, Marxists, and neo-Marxists commonly see liberal constitutions as having ideological dimensions that undermine both individuality and democracy. These critiques highlight insensitivities to power in liberal regimes, but they can remain progressive only by incorporating liberal principles of protected individualism and discursively constituted public space. Marx's critique of liberalism presupposes the value of protected individualism. Habermas goes beyond Marx by relating protected individualism to protected public space, and by showing how liberal ideals of publicity have become increasingly ideological. A postliberal democracy should distinguish more carefully than either standard Marxism or contemporary liberal constitutionalism between social relations that support these two principles and those that undermine them.

WARREN, Mary Anne. The Abortion Struggle in America. Bioethics, 3(4), 320-332, O 89.

WARREN, Mary Anne. The Moral Significance of Birth. Hypatia, 4(3), 46-65, Fall 89.

Does birth make a difference to the moral rights of the fetus/infant? Should it make a difference to its legal rights? Most contemporary philosophers believe that birth cannot make a difference to moral rights. If this is true, then it becomes difficult to justify either a moral or a legal distinction between late abortion and infanticide. I argue that the view that birth is irrelevant to moral rights rests upon two highly questionable assumptions about the theoretical foundations of moral rights. If we reject these assumptions, then we are free to take account of the contrasting biological and social relationships that make even relatively late abortion morally different from infanticide.

WARREN, Virginia L. Feminist Directions in Medical Ethics. Hypatia, 4(2), 73-87, Sum 89.

I explore some new directions—suggested by feminism—for medical ethics and for philosophical ethics generally. Moral philosophers need to confront two issues. The first is *deciding which moral issues merit attention*. Questions which incorporate the perspectives of women need to be posed—e.g., about the unequal treatment of women in health care, about the roles of physician and nurse, and about relationship issues other than power struggles. "Crisis issues" currently dominate medical ethics, to the neglect of what I call "housekeeping issues." The second issue is *how philosophical moral debates are conducted*, especially how ulterior motives influence our beliefs and arguments. Both what we select—and neglect—to study as well as the "games" we play may be sending a message as loud as the words we do speak on ethics.

WASSERMANN, Gerhard D. 'Morality and Determinism': A Reply to Flew. Philosophy, 65(251), 99-101, Ja 90.

Flew's criticisms (*Philosophy* 64 (1989), 98-103) of the author's paper 'Morality and Determinism' (*Philosophy* 63 (1988), 211-230) are shown to be erroneous because of (1) Flew's disregard of the existence of extensive statistical (probabilistic) determinism in the natural sciences and (2) Flew's out-of-context quotations of parts of the author's sentences with resulting misrepresentations of the author's meanings. Additional serious errors by Flew are also rebutted.

WASZEK, Norbert. La réception du Saint-Simonisme dans l'école hégélienne: l'exemple d'Eduard Gans. Arch Phil, 52(4), 581-587, O-D 89.

Eduard Gans (1797-1839), Hegel's favourite and, perhaps, most gifted disciple, was the first among the Hegelians to look for a new answer to the pressing social problems of his age. In his search, Gans turned to the theories of the Saint-Simonians, especially to their idea of *association*. Gans accepts this slogan, but, by rejecting its collectivist connotations, interprets it in terms of proto-unionist demands. He thus strives towards a synthesis of Hegelianism and Saint-Simonism: a forward-looking reformulation of Hegel's 'corporate doctrine' (*Philosophy of Right*, sections 250-256).

WATERMAN, Alan S. Personal Expressiveness: Philosophical and Psychological Foundations. J Mind Behav, 11(1), 47-74, Wint 90.

Psychological and philosophical perspectives are employed in an exploration of the reasons particular individuals experience an activity as personally expressive while others may find the same activity neutral or even aversive. The relationships between personal expressiveness and intrinsic motivation, flow, and self-actualization are considered. The construct of personal expressiveness is shown to have its roots in eudaimonistic philosophy. Living in a manner consistent with one's daimon or "true self" gives rise to a cognitive-affective state labeled "eudaimonia" that is distinguishable from hedonic enjoyment. A personally expressive personality pattern is described integrating concepts from diverse theories including (a) a sense of personal identity, (b) self-actualization, (c) an internal locus of control, and (d) principled moral reasoning. A series of empirical investigations is proposed to test the theoretical concepts of personal expressiveness advanced.

WATEROUS, Frank B. From Salomon's House to the Land-Grant College: Practical Arts Education and the Utopian Vision of Progress. Educ Theor, 39(4), 359-372, Fall 89.

Emphasis on "practical arts" (e.g., applied science, agriculture, engineering, manufacturing, and business) and practical arts education has been an important theme in both utopian literature and American social development. The article explores this theme and its connections to the rise of the land-grant colleges in the United States. The author proposes that the land-grant colleges evolved at least in part as a response to the same desires expressed in literary utopias regarding the utilization of useful knowledge for human betterment, and as a further expression of the social utopianism evident in the development of the American republic.

WATERS, C Kenneth and KITCHER, Philip and STERELNY, Kim. The Illusory Riches of Sober's Monism. J Phil, 87(3), 158-161, Mr 90.

WATERS, C Kenneth. Rosenberg's Rebellion. Biol Phil, 5(2), 225-239, Ap 90.

Recent insights about biology have motivated revolutionary views concerning the nature of theories, functional explanation, and intertheoretic relations. The aim of this paper is to explain how Alexander Rosenberg's *The Structure of Biological Science* is counterrevolutionary. I argue that Rosenberg threatens to undermine the current trend by covertly reconciling the insights that gave rise to it with traditional postpositivism. The result is a global view of biological science which conflicts with much of what logical empiricists had to say about biology, but nevertheless tacitly presupposes their fundamental beliefs concerning the nature of science.

WATERS, James A and BIRD, Frederick. Attending to Ethics in Management. J Bus Ethics, 8(6), 493-497, Je 89.

Based on analysis of interviews with managers about the ethical questions they face in their work, a typology of morally questionable managerial acts is developed. The typology distinguishes acts committed against-the-firm (non-role and role-failure acts) from those committed on-behalf-of-the-firm (role-distortion and role-assertion acts) and draws attention to the different nature of the four types of acts. The argument is made that senior management attention is typically focused on the types of acts which are least problematical for most managers, and that the most troublesome types are relatively ignored.

WATKIN, Julia. Kierkegaard's View of Death. Hist Euro Ideas, 12(1), 65-78, 1990.

An analysis of Soren Kierkegaard's view of death in which it is shown that one's view of death is linked to one's total view of existence. Kierkegaard is seen to make an important distinction between views that presuppose only the world as we know it and views that presuppose in addition an actually transcendent world. The paper discusses Kierkegaard's analysis of the Hegelian world picture, various viewpoints belonging to the Greek world, Judaism, and finally different perspectives within Christianity. The conclusion argues that Kierkegaard gives death its proper significance, especially where the 20th century evasion of death is concerned.

WATKINS, John W N. *Hobbes's System of Ideas*. Brookfield, Gower, 1989

WATKINS, John. The Pragmatic Problem of Induction: Reply to Gower and Bamford. Analysis, 50(3), 210-212, Je 90.

WATNICK, Richard and ROY, Dev K. Finite Condensations of Recursive Linear Orders. Stud Log, 47(4), 311-317, D 88.

The complexity of a Π_4 set of natural numbers is encoded into a linear order to show that the finite condensation of a recursive linear order can be $\Pi_2 \cdot \Pi_1$. A priority argument establishes the same result, and is extended to a complete classification of finite condensations iterated finitely many times.

WATSON, A. Slaves Putting Themselves up for Sale. Int J Moral Soc Stud, 5(2), 175-178, Sum 90.

An ignored text of Justinian's *Digest*, 21.1.17.12, reveals that in Rome there were recognized places to which slaves could properly take themselves to set themselves up for sale even without the master's knowledge. No legal consequences would result from any arrangement by the slave unless the owner agreed to a sale. The procedure operated as a 'carrot' to keep the slave system running smoothly; and in one form or another is likely to have also existed elsewhere.

WATSON, Richard A. René Descartes n'est pas l'auteur de *La naissance de la paix*. Arch Phil, 53(3), 389-401, Jl-S 90.

The author discusses the following topics: (1) the ballet; (2) Descartes is not the author; (3) why it should be attributed to H Poirier; (4) the political meaning of the ballet; (5) conclusion; (6) note on Hélie Poirier. (edited)

WATSON, Stephen. Cancellations: Notes on Merleau-Ponty's Standing between Hegel and Husserl. Res Phenomenol, 17, 191-209, 1987.

WATSON, Terence (trans) and ROSMINI, Antonio and CLEARY, Denis (trans). *Conscience*. Durham, Rosmini, 1989

WATSON, W. "Hermeneutic Modes, Ancient and Modern" in *History and Anti-History in Philosophy*, LAVINE, T Z (ed), 135-155. Norwell, Kluwer, 1989.

All the uses of *hermeneia* and its cognates in Hellenic texts are examined. It is found that, contrary to Liddell and Scott and the general belief, these words never refer to *interpretation* (proceeding from text to meaning) but always to *expression* (proceeding from meaning to text). The different forms of expression in the ancient hermeneutics nevertheless correspond to the different forms of interpretation in the modern hermeneutics. Because of a printing error, only half the article appears in *History and Anti-History*; the complete article is available from the editors or the author.

WATT, David. Equiprobability. Log Anal, 30(120), 335-352, D 87.

Epistemic probability—i.e., probability relative to knowledge—is shown to be a common and indispensable concept. Many believe that entailment is the maximum epistemic probability, and entailed negation, the minimum probability. This belief is refuted, and simple alternative maxima and minima are given. Many believe that epistemic probabilities are numerical and satisfy the axioms of the calculus. But this is false: we prove that for some probabilities, the first is not greater than, equal to, or less than the second. When a certain kind of symmetry exists, then two probabilities are equal.

WATTENBERG, Frank. Nonstandard Analysis and Constructivism? Stud Log, 47(3), 303-309, S 88.

The purpose of this paper is to investigate some problems of using finite (or *finite) computational arguments and of the nonstandard notion of an infinitesimal. We will begin by looking at the canonical example illustrating the distinction between classical and constructive analysis, the Intermediate Value Theorem.

WATTERS, Wendell W. Moral Education: Homo Sapiens or Homo Religious? Free Inq, 10(1), 9-13, Wint 89-90.

WAXMAN, Wayne (trans) and LONGUENESSE, Béatrice. Actuality in Hegel's Logic. Grad Fac Phil J, 13(1), 115-124, 1988.

WAYNE, F Stanford. An Instrument to Measure Adherence to the Protestant Ethic and Contemporary Work Values. J Bus Ethics, 8(10), 793-804, O 89.

The problem of the current research is to develop an instrument that accurately measures individuals' adherence or nonadherence to both Protestant ethic and contemporary work values. The study confirms that the traditional Protestant ethic work values and the contemporary work values are different and the instrument used to measure the work values that individuals actually support is valid and reliable. Two scales were developed based on Protestant ethic work values and contemporary work values. A four-point Likert scale was used to indicate the extent of agreement or disagreement with statements written to represent Protestant ethic and contemporary work values. Face and content validities of the instrument were established by using two panels of experts—one consisted of authorities in the area of work values; the other consisted of editorial critics. Reliability of the instrument was confirmed by the Kuder-Richardson and test-retest methods. Four sets of work values emerged with significant discrimination among them.

WEARNE, Bruce C. *The Theory and Scholarship of Talcott Parsons to 1951: A Critical Commentary*. New York, Cambridge Univ Pr, 1990

Talcott Parsons's thought, as it developed from the early 1920s to 1951 when it reached its culmination in *The Social System*, is examined for its leading ideas and cumulative development. Parsons's theoretical orientation gained its momentum from the dogma that theory is a self-generating organism. This commitment has to be viewed as a religious point of departure which takes all of reality into view.

WEAVER, George. Classifying $\aleph_0$-Categorical Theories. Stud Log, 47(4), 327-345, D 88.

Among the complete $\aleph_0$-categorical theories with finite non-logical vocabularies, we distinguish three classes. The classification is obtained by looking at the number of bound variables needed to isolate complete types.

In class I theories, all types are isolated by quantifier free formulas; in class II theories, there is a least m, greater than zero, s.t. all types are isolated by formulas in no more than m bound variables: and in class III theories, for each m there is a type which cannot be isolated in m or fewer bound variables. Class II theories are further subclassified according to whether or not they can be extended to class I theories by the addition of finitely many new predicates. Alternative characterizations are given in terms of quantifier elimination and homogeneous models. It is shown that for each prime p, the theory of infinite Abelian groups all of whose elements are of order p is class I when formulated in functional constants, and class III when formulated in relational constants.

WEBB, Mark O. Natural Theology and the Concept of Perfection in Descartes, Spinoza and Leibniz. Relig Stud, 25(4), 459-475, D 89.

Descartes, Spinoza, and Leibniz, starting from what purports to be the same concept of God, and employing what they think is the same method, come to startlingly different conclusions about what may be inferred from that concept. The trouble comes from having no clear and defensible criterion for perfection. Similar difficulties plague their uses of the ontological argument.

WEBER, Andreas. "Hume and Gibbon: The Origin of Naturalistic Study of Religion" in *Early Modern Philosophy II*, TWEYMAN, Stanley (ed), 85-101. Delmar, Caravan Books, 1988.

WEBER, Bruce H (and others). Evolution in Thermodynamic Perspective: An Ecological Approach. Biol Phil, 4(4), 373-405, O 89.

Recognition that biological systems are stabilized far from equilibrium by self-organizing, informed, autocatalytic cycles and structures that dissipate unusable energy and matter has led to recent attempts to reformulate evolutionary theory. We hold that such insights are consistent with the broad development of the Darwinian tradition and with the concept of natural selection. This thermodynamic approach to evolution frees evolutionary theory from dependence on a crypto-Newtonian language more appropriate to closed equilibrial systems than to biological systems. It grounds biology nonreductively in physical law, and drives a conceptual wedge between functions of artifacts and functions of natural systems. This countenances legitimate use of teleology grounded in natural, teleomatic laws. (edited)

WEBER, Erik. Scientific Explanation, Necessity and Contingency. Philosophica, 44(2), 81-99, 1989.

The purpose of the paper is to discuss the relations between contemporary theories of scientific explanation and general "images of science" (i.e., more or less articulated views on the essential characteristics of scientific theories). More specifically, the results of studies in the domain of explanation are used to criticize a generally accepted image of science, viz., the idea that science is a system of natural (or social) laws that express relations of physical (or social) necessity between subsequent or simultaneous events.

WEBER, Frank. Nietzsche und George: Anmerkungen zu einem Buch von Heinz Raschel. Z Phil Forsch, 43(3), 528-533, Jl-S 89.

Raschel's analysis of Nietzsche's influence on Stefan George and his disciples does not cover the whole problem. It cannot be criticized that George had his own opinion of the philosopher. His impact on three academic studies on Nietzsche (by Bertram, Hildebrandt and E Gundolf) appears to be overvalued. As they are based on different approaches George's circle looks more independent than stated by Raschel. Since Raschel's study must be regarded as both biased and incomplete, this article refers to the recently published work by Frank Weber, *Die Bedeutung Nietzsches für Stefan George und seinen Kreis* (Bern/Frankfurt/Paris/New York, 1989).

WEBER, James. Measuring the Impact of Teaching Ethics to Future Managers: A Review, Assessment, and Recommendations. J Bus Ethics, 9(3), 183-190, Mr 90.

This paper takes a critical look at the empirical studies assessing the effectiveness of teaching courses in business and society and business ethics. It is generally found that students' ethical awareness or reasoning skills improve after taking the courses, yet this improvement appears to be short-lived. The generalizability of these findings is limited due to the lack of extensive empirical research and the inconsistencies in research design, empirical measures, and statistical analysis across studies. Thus, recommendations are presented and discussed for improving the generalizability and sophistication of future research efforts in this area.

WEBER, Leonard J and PURI, Vinod K. Limiting the Role of the Family in Discontinuation of Life Sustaining Treatment. J Med Human, 11(2), 91-98, Sum 90.

In matters of discontinuation of life-sustaining treatment, traditional role of the family to speak on behalf of the incompetent patient is questionable. We explore the reasons why physicians perceive patient autonomy to be transferrable to family members. Principle of patient autonomy may not suffice when futile treatment is demanded and may serve to erode the ethical integrity of medical profession. An enhanced role for bioethics committees is proposed when physicians propose to discontinue life-sustaining treatment against the wishes of the patient or their families.

WEBER NICHOLSEN, Shierry (trans) and HABERMAS, Jürgen and LENHARDT, Christian (trans). *Moral Consciousness and Communicative Action*. Cambridge, MIT Pr, 1990

WEBER-SCHÄFER, Peter. "Politics, a European Luxury?" in *Culture et Politique/Culture and Politics*, CRANSTON, Maurice (ed), 120-129. Hawthorne, de Gruyter, 1988.

WEDGWOOD, Ralph. Scepticism and Rational Belief. Phil Quart, 40(158), 45-64, Ja 90.

In this essay I aim to examine the relation between, on the one hand, a particular form of sceptical argument, and, on the other, a certain type of theory concerning the nature of knowledge and justified belief. I shall concentrate on this particular sceptical argument, and on this type of theory of justified belief, because they seem to me to be the most plausible. I shall not attempt here to discuss in detail their advantages over their rivals, although I hope to do so elsewhere. The sceptical argument that I shall consider can be used to argue for the impossibility of knowledge or justified belief on any subject whatsoever. We must therefore first consider what are the conditions for knowledge and justified belief; for it is these conditions that the sceptic maintains can so rarely be fulfilled.

WEDIN, M V. Aristotle on the Mechanics of Thought. Ancient Phil, 9 (1), 67-86, Spr 89.

The paper begins with a number of Aristotle's claims about thinking—for example, the sameness of mind and object of thought, the causal role of the object of thought in thinking, the identification of universals as objects of thought, and the autonomy of thought—and argues they are part of an account of, or are to be explained by, the mechanisms that underlie actual thinking. For the most part, these are lower level operations, ultimately involving images as representational devices. Productive and receptive minds are themselves construed as lower level systems required to explain how subjects can produce thoughts, autonomously, from a ready stock of concepts.

WEDIN, Michael V. Negation and Quantification in Aristotle. Hist Phil Log, 11(2), 131-150, 1990.

Two main claims are defended. The first is that negative categorical statements are not to be accorded existential import insofar as they figure in the square of opposition. Against Kneale and others, it is argued that Aristotle formulates his o statements, for example, precisely to avoid existential commitment. This frees Aristotle's square from a recent charge of inconsistency. The second claim is that the logic proper provides much thinner evidence than has been supposed for what appears to be the received view, that is, for the view that insofar as they occur in syllogistic negative categoricals have existential import. At most there is a single piece of evidence in favor of the view—a special case of echthesis or the setting out of a case in proof.

WEG, Eythan and RAPOPORT, Amnon. Effects of Fixed Costs in Two-Person Sequential Bargaining. Theor Decis, 28(1), 47-71, Ja 90.

Rubinstein (1982) considered the problem of dividing a given surplus between two players sequentially, and then proposed a model in which the two players alternately make and respond to each other's offers through time. He further characterized the perfect equilibrium outcomes, which depend on the players' time preferences and order of moves. Using both equal and unequal bargaining cost conditions and an unlimited number of rounds, two experiments were designed to compare the perfect equilibrium model to alternative models based on norms of fairness. We report analyses of final agreements, first offers, and number of bargaining rounds, which provide limited support to the perfect equilibrium model, and then conclude by recommending a shift in focus from model testing to specification of the conditions favoring one model over another.

WEI, Tan Tai. Bodily Continuity, Personal Identity and Life After Death. Sophia (Australia), 29(2), 33-39, Jl 90.

WEIDEMANN, Hermann. Aristotle on Inferences from Signs (*Rhetoric* I 2, 1357 b 1-25). Phronesis, 34(3), 343-351, 1989.

The article attempts to show (1) that the two sections 1357 b 14-17 and 1357 b 17-21 of Aristotle's *Rhetoric* are in the wrong order and should consequently be transposed, and (2) that arguments like "He has a fever, for he breathes fast" are treated differently in the *Rhetoric* on the one hand and in the *Analytics* on the other. Whereas in *Anal. Pr*. II 27 Aristotle treats argument of this kind as invalid inferences in the second syllogistic figure, he seems to treat them in *Rhet*. I 2 as valid but unsound first figure inferences

instead.

WEIDHAS, Roija. Zur Kognitionstheorie Humberto Maturanas. Deut Z Phil, 38(4), 363-371, 1990.

WEIER, Winfried. "Existenz zwischen Unbedingheit und Endlichkeit" in *Agora: Zu Ehren von Rudolph Berlinger*, BERLINGER, Rudolph (and other eds), 263-289. Amsterdam, Rodopi, 1988.

Wie kann die aufweisbare Unbedingtheit menschlicher Existenz zusammen bestehen mit der ebenfalls aufzeigbaren Endlichkeit des existentiellen Menschseins? Besagt doch Endlichkeit, dass ein Seiendes den Grund seines Seins nicht in sich selbst enthält, sondern aus anderem Ursprung empfängt, schliesst also Unbedingtheit gerade aus. Hieraus folgt, dass Existenz den Ursprung derselben zwar in sich, aber nicht aus sich hat, sondern *aus einem anderen Urgrund empfängt*. Was aber heisst das? Totale Seinsidentität unter beiden ist ausgeschlossen wegen der Heterogenität des endlichen und unendlichen Seins, partiale wegen der durchgängigen Seinseinheit beider. Bleibt nur, dass Existenz in ihrer Unbedingtheit nicht am *Sein*, sondern am *Sinn* des Unbedingten *teilhat*, d.h. diesen in ihrer Endlichkeit ausdrückt und realisiert. Entgegen immanentistischer und nihilistischer Existenzdeutung weist also das Phänomen menschlicher Existenz über sich selbst hinaus auf den Sinn der Transzendenz als der Bedingung seiner Möglichkeit. (edited)

WEIHER, Eckhard. "Zu Herkunft und Gebrauch der grammatischen Termini *Odusevlennyj* und *Neodusevlennyj* im Russischen" in *Agora: Zu Ehren von Rudolph Berlinger*, BERLINGER, Rudolph (and other eds), 387-413. Amsterdam, Rodopi, 1988.

WEIL, Carol J and JUENGST, Eric T. "Interpreting Proxy Directives" in *Advance Directives in Medicine*, HACKLER, Chris (ed), 21-37. New York, Praeger, 1989.

We criticize current standards for proxy decision making found in legal instructions to holders of durable powers of attorney for health care. We argue that the "explicit instructions" interpretation of the substituted judgment standard and the "medical indications" interpretation of the best interest standard should be supplemented with at least four other interpretations, which we call the "analogy test," the "worldwide test," the "special personal interests test" and the "reasonable person test."

WEIL, Vivian. How Can Philosophers Teach Professional Ethics? J Soc Phil, 20(1-2), 131-136, Spr-Fall 89.

Two problems are addressed: the shortage of well-trained teachers to teach ethics in professional education and the need for evidence about whether teaching professional ethics is effective and what works. An ethics-across-the-curriculum concept provides for teaching professional ethics to all students in professional training. Philosophers can bring their skills to bear by preparing faculty in professional education to include ethics in their courses. Given the number of alumni of ethics courses and the increase of research that is philosophical and empirical, it should now be feasible to devise research on the impact of classroom study of moral problems of professional life.

WEILER, Gershon. "Force and Fraud" in *Hobbes: War Among Nations*, AIRAKSINEN, Timo (ed), 99-111. Brookfield, Gower, 1989.

In the state of nature of Hobbes, force and fraud are the two skills necessary for survival. The purpose of this paper is to inquire whether it is possible to escape the burden of reliance on them in international relations, qua war and diplomacy, by establishing a world-order on analogy with territorial sovereignty. The answer is negative because nations, with their historically evolved identity, are not non-controversially like the natural individual. Thus wars remain one of the means through which groups establish themselves as players in the game of international politics.

WEIMER, Wolfgang. Die Gattungserinnerung: Ein Kehrichtfass und eine Rumpelkammer? Schopenhauer und die Geschichte (2 Teil). Schopenhauer Jahr, 70, 137-150, 1989.

WEINBERGER, Ota. The Role of Rules. Ratio Juris, 1(3), 224-240, D 88.

The author conceives rules as action-determining ideas. They are general and of hypothetical form, and they are of three semantic types: descriptive, technological, and normative rules. The most important categorisation of normative rules is the distinction between rules of behaviour and power-conferring rules. Both kinds of rules are necessary to establish institutions. Principles are a special kind of normative rules. The social existence of normative rules is connected with their institutionalisation as frames for action. The dynamics of rules is in principle based on two elements: on socially approved habit, and/or on authorised norm creation.

WEINGARTNER, Paul. Antinomies and Paradoxes and their Solutions. Stud Soviet Tho, 39(3-4), 313-331, Ap-My 90.

WEININGER, Otto and BURNS, S A M (trans). Metaphysics. J Phil Res, 15, 311-327, 1990.

This is a translation of a posthumous essay by the Viennese philosopher-psychologist, Otto Weininger (1880-1903). His main book, *Sex and Character*, was published in 1903 (English version, 1906). Many distinguished Viennese were deeply influenced by Weininger; among them was Ludwig Wittgenstein, who paid tribute to him even late in his life. In particular, he is known to have admired the present essay and its foray into "animal psychology." The investigation of the significance for human psychology of dogs and other animals is part of a larger scheme which Weininger sketches, to investigate the symbolism of all kinds of things. His ultimate goal is to reveal the relationship between the microcosm of the human consciousness and the macrocosm of the external universe. Hence the title, "Metaphysics."

WEINRYB, Elazar. Re-enactment in Retrospect. Monist, 72(4), 568-580, O 89.

According to Collingwood, historical understanding is achieved by the re-enactment of past thought in the historian's mind. Three commonly held interpretations of this doctrine are rejected and a purely counterfactual approach is suggested: re-enactment means the forming of counterfactuals, such as "If I were in Caesar's place, then I would have such and such reasons for crossing the Rubicon." But when justification of these counterfactuals comes into question, the attention is directed towards certain patterns of action explanation, and the counterfactual starting-point becomes redundant. The argument draws an analogy between re-enactment so interpreted and Hempel's counterfactually formulated criterion of adequacy for explanation.

WEINSTEIN, D. Equal Freedom, Rights and Utility in Spencer's Moral Philosophy. Hist Polit Thought, 11(1), 119-142, Spr 90.

WEINSTEIN, Mark. Critical Thinking and Moral Education. Thinking, 7(3), 42-49, 1988.

The recent interest in critical thinking has a deep philosophical and pedagogical affinity with moral education. This should not be looked at as supporting identification of the two concerns. Moral education is rooted in theoretical and pedagogical attitudes that are inconsistent with some of the fundamental assumptions of recent advocates of critical thinking. The paper outlines the main positions including values clarification and moral developmentalism and contrasts them with the critical thinking perspectives of Richard Paul and Matthew Lipman.

WEINSTEIN, Mark (ed) and BANU, Beatrice (ed). *The Fieldston Ethics Reader*. Lanham, Univ Pr of America, 1988

The Fieldston Reader introduces students to significant moral problems using critical thinking skills. Short pieces of classic and contemporary literature serve as vehicles for exploring ethical issues. All selections have been chosen for their appropriateness for secondary and junior college students as well as literary quality and relevance to issues confronting thoughtful adolescents.

WEINSTEIN, Mark and CANNON, Dale. Reasoning Skills: An Overview. Thinking, 6(1), 29-33, 1985.

The article attempts to develop a comprehensive conception of reasoning skills that explains the place of philosophical inquiry among the various kinds of reasoning and in the development of skill or competence in their practice. It defines philosophical reasoning as a matter of clarifying and improving the conceptual tools with which one thinks and reasons about other things. A novel taxonomy is developed which recognizes four dimensions of reasoning: formal, informal, interpersonal, and philosophical, and discusses representative examples of each dimension. The article goes on to explain the relation of this conception of philosophical reasoning to the traditional discipline of philosophy and to develop a case for recognizing an essentially moral component to human reasoning in terms of its interpersonal dimension.

WEINSTEIN, Scott and OSHERSON, Daniel N. On Advancing Simple Hypotheses. Phil Sci, 57(2), 266-277, Je 90.

We consider drawbacks to scientific methods that prefer simple hypotheses to complex ones that cover the same data. The discussion proceeds in the context of a precise model of scientific inquiry.

WEINSTEIN, Scott and GAIFMAN, Haim and OSHERSON, Daniel N. A Reason for Theoretical Terms. Erkenntnis, 32(2), 149-159, Mr 90.

The presence of nonobservational vocabulary is shown to be necessary for wide application of a conservative principle of theory revision.

WEINTRAUB, Ruth. Decision-Theoretic Epistemology. Synthese, 83(1), 159-177, Ap 90.

In this paper, I examine the possibility of accounting for the rationality of belief-formation by utilising decision-theoretic considerations. I consider the utilities to be used by such an approach, propose to employ verisimilitude as a measure of cognitive utility, and suggest a natural way of generalising any measure of verisimilitude defined on propositions to partial belief-systems, a generalisation which may enable us to incorporate Popper's insightful notion of verisimilitude within a Bayesian framework. I examine a dilemma generated by the decision-theoretic procedure and consider an adequacy condition (immodesty) designed to ameliorate one of its horns. Finally, I argue in a sceptical vein that no adequate verisimilitude measure can be used decision-theoretically.

WEIRICH, Paul. Conventions and Social Institutions. S J Phil, 27(4), 599-618, Wint 89.

According to one sense of convention, conventions are *practices* of a certain kind. According to another sense of convention, conventions are *rules* of a certain kind. I adopt David Lewis's definition of convention as a definition of convention in the practice sense. Then I define convention in the rule sense in terms of social institutions, which are in turn defined by generalizing some of H L A Hart's ideas about the law. Next I argue that the practice and rule senses of convention form a standard activity-product ambiguity. And I show that our account of convention answers certain questions raised by Margaret Gilbert.

WEISE, Peter and BRANDES, Wolfgang. A Synergetic View of Institutions. Theor Decis, 28(2), 173-187, Mr 90.

In this paper we attempt to demonstrate how, in the course of human cooperation, compulsions and forces come into existence which compel individuals into regularities of behavior. These behavioral regularities are labelled institutions; the approach selected is called synergetic, since it considers institutions to be the result of combined human actions. The compulsions and forces which emerge from human cooperation are generated by the individuals' dependencies, struggles for independence, and preferences. Whereas individuals act freely as subjects, they become objects under the compulsions and forces of compressed social interdependence.

WEISMANN, F J. La problemática de la libertad en San Agustín. Stromata, 45(3-4), 321-338, Jl-D 89.

This article is an analysis of the Augustinian approach: (I) a general presentation of "The Libero arbitrio" with the distinction between "liberum arbitrium" and "libertas"; (II) in the other "Dialogues"; and (III) in the "Confessions" with the shades of the theological freedom. The conclusion stresses the originality of this conception (with the Plotinian influence) as a clue for a hermeneutic of a complete freedom comprising the aspects of the whole human existence: his origin and final purpose.

WEISS, Harold. The Genealogy of Justice and the Justice of Genealogy. Phil Today, 33(1), 73-94, Spr 89.

The subtitle here is "Noam Chomsky and Edward Said vs. Michel Foucault and Paul Bové," being a critical comparison between two factions of the oppositional left with a similar political agenda, but a different theoretical defense thereof. Chomsky and Said share an essentially humanistic framework, while Foucault and Bové represent genealogical antihumanism. The latter is weighed for its possible benefits in critical and political struggles, though the possible incoherence of Foucauldian genealogy is targeted: Foucault subtly recapitulates elements of Enlightenment liberalism in his career-long rhetoric of "resistance," which seems incompatible with his theories of power, truth, and subjectivity.

WEISS, Raymond L. "On the Scope of Maimonides' *Logic*, Or, What Joseph Knew" in *A Straight Path: Studies in Medieval Philosophy and Culture*, LINK-SALINGER, Ruth (ed), 255-265. Washington, Cath Univ Amer Pr, 1988.

The author interprets Maimonides' *Treatise on the Art of Logic* as not simply a logical work in the narrow sense but as providing direction, more generally, for the art of rational discourse. Hence logic includes a discussion of the four causes, the distinction between potentiality and actuality, etc. The author also briefly explores the different kinds of argumentation used in the *Guide of the Perplexed*. Joseph ben Judah, the addressee of the *Guide*, had knowledge of logic; the significance of this for comprehending the *Guide* is underscored; the article attempts to prepare the ground for understanding the *Guide* in its own terms.

WEISS, Roslyn. The Hedonic Calculus in the *Protagoras* and the *Phaedo*. J Hist Phil, 27(4), 511-529, O 89.

Plato's *Protagoras* and *Phaedo* contain incompatible accounts of the relevance and value of a hedonic calculus with respect to the pursuit of virtue. It is argued that this incompatibility may be accounted for by the *Protagoras*' ironic identification of pleasure and the good, an identification entirely absent from the *Phaedo*. It is further argued that the Gosling-Taylor attempt to reconcile the two dialogues is misguided and unsuccessful.

WEISS, Roslyn. Hedonism in the *Protagoras* and the Sophist's Guarantee.

Ancient Phil, 10(1), 17-40, Spr 90.

It is argued that the hedonism in the *Protagoras* is not a Socratic view but is dictated by Socrates' larger project of reducing to absurdity the sophist's guarantee to improve those he teaches. On the (non-Socratic) assumption that pleasure is the good, moral conflict ceases, with the absurd result that a calculus of pleasure is all that is required for virtue. Consequently, the courageous man is he who knows the more pleasant (less fearful) alternative, the coward he who does not, while dispositionally and in terms of their goal they are indistinguishable from one another.

WEISS, Roslyn. A Rejoinder to Professors Gosling and Taylor. J Hist Phil, 28(1), 117-118, Ja 90.

It is claimed that the *Protagoras*'s hedonism is the radical view that pleasure represents the proper end of human existence—not the weaker view that the good life is also the most pleasant. *Contra* Gosling and Taylor it is argued that the *Protagoras*'s hedonism cannot be reconciled with the anti-hedonism of other dialogues, that what is at stake in all dialogues in which hedonism is discussed is whether or not pleasure qualifies as the correct standard for human choice, and that to this question the *Protagoras* alone responds in the affirmative.

WEISSBORD, David. "Categorial Analysis and the Logical Grammar of the Mind" in *Mind, Value and Culture: Essays in Honor of E M Adams*, WEISSBORD, David (ed), 131-146. Atascadero, Ridgeview, 1989.

This essay examines categorial analysis in the work of Professor E Maynard Adams. It explains (1) the foundations for a categorial realism and their relationship to logical grammar and ordinary discourse; (2) linguistic relativism; (3) Durkheim and historicity; and (4) a naturalistic versus a humanistic conception of the categories.

WEISSBORD, David. "Engaged Reflection: The Life and Work of E Maynard Adams" in *Mind, Value and Culture: Essays in Honor of E M Adams*, WEISSBORD, David (ed), 3-9. Atascadero, Ridgeview, 1989.

This essay is an introduction of *Mind, Value and Culture: Essays in Honor of E M Adams*. It gives a summary overview of Professor of Philosophy E Maynard Adams's work and life. It focuses on the tremendous impact his work has had in the areas of cultural criticism, metaphysics, epistemology, and ethics; and it highlights the moral impact his life has had on the cultural climate of the south in general and on issues of race relations in particular.

WEISSBORD, David (ed). *Mind, Value and Culture: Essays in Honor of E M Adams*. Atascadero, Ridgeview, 1989

This is a *Festschrift* that brings together sixteen philosophers, each of whom contributed an essay on some aspect of Professor of Philosophy E Maynard Adams's work. The book has five sections: "The Derangement of the Modern Western Mind"; "Categories, Categorial Analysis, and Value Realism"; "Meaning, the Mental, and the Language of Appearing"; "Ethics, Religion, and the Humanities" and "Rejoinder," a response to the essays by Professor Adams. The essays range in scope from an analysis of Adams's sweeping critique of modern culture to a detailed investigation of aspects of Adams's thought concerning philosophy of mind, philosophy of language, categorial analysis, and ethics.

WEISSMAN, David. *Hypothesis and the Spiral of Reflection*. Albany, SUNY Pr, 1989

WELCH, John R and PALOS, Ana María. Apuntes sobre el pensamiento matemático de Ramón Llull. Theoria (Spain), 4(11), 451-459, F-My 89.

WELCH, John R. Corporate Agency and Reduction. Phil Quart, 39(157), 409-424, O 89.

WELCHMAN, Jennifer. From Absolute Idealism to Instrumentalism: The Problem of Dewey's Early Philosophy. Trans Peirce Soc, 25(4), 407-419, Fall 89.

Of the British neo-Hegelians, Dewey's early idealism has been thought to be most deeply indebted to T H Green's work. I argue that stronger links exist between Dewey's idealism and the contemporary work of F H Bradley.

WELCHMAN, Jennifer. G E Moore and the Revolution in Ethics: A Reappraisal. Hist Phil Quart, 6(3), 317-329, Jl 89.

Moore's *Principia Ethica* has been credited with revolutionizing Anglo-American ethics in one or more of three ways: refuting idealist ethics; refuting naturalistic ethics; and/or transforming moral theorists' analytical methods. On the basis of a survey of philosophical responses to *Principia* (1903 through WW II), I argue that the book had none of the effects popularly attributed to it. I conclude that Moore's influence on Anglo-American ethics has been overrated.

WELLER, Steven and RUHNKA, John C. The Ethical Implications of Corporate Records Management Practices and Some Suggested Ethical Values for Decisions. J Bus Ethics, 9(2), 81-92, F 90.

While the ethical implications of corporate actions have received increasing attention, one important area overlooked by both researchers and corporate codes of ethics is the significant ethical implications of corporate records management practices. This article discusses the operational and strategic purposes of modern corporate records management programs—including "scorched earth" programs which seek to reduce exposure to potential liability by eliminating documentary evidence from corporate files that could be used to establish culpability in future governmental investigations or in litigation by persons injured by corporate actions. As a first step toward developing relevant ethical guidelines and decision criteria for socially responsible records management practices, the ethical values of freedom of choice and avoidance of harm are applied to various corporate decisions as to (1) which information should be retained as records and for how long, (2) subsequent disclosure or nondisclosure of that information and to whom, and (3) decisions as to when information in corporate records may properly be destroyed.

WELLMAN, Carl. Equal Opportunity. J Brit Soc Phenomenol, 21(1), 26-38, Ja 90.

This paper examines critically the attempts of Herbert Spiegelberg to ground our moral duty to equalize opportunity. It defines equal opportunity as sets of circumstances that are equally favorable for some kind of endeavor. It concludes that the human right to equal opportunity explains little because *its* grounds are equally obscure. When unequal opportunities have arisen from human action, remedial justice does ground a duty to equalize opportunity. Good fortune may occasionally constitute unjust enrichment and thereby ground this duty, but it is doubtful that natural unfairness ever does. Spiegelberg's hint centering on the I-am-me experience is worthy of further exploration.

WELLMER, Albrecht. Models of Freedom in the Modern World. Phil Forum, 21(1-2), 227-252, Fall-Wint 89-90.

WELLS, Donald A. In Defense of Innocents. J Soc Phil, 20(3), 59-63, Wint 89.

Military theorists have accused just war theorists of making just war impossible. Current just war theorists claim that military necessities obligate us to alter the criteria. Just war theory cannot afford to give up the class of "innocents." The US Army manual, *The Law of Land Warfare*, sanctioned the World War II policy of bombing civilian centers, while at the same time it claimed that we ought not to make deliberate bombing attacks on undefended places or innocents. To claim that every citizen of the enemy country is fair game makes just war theory bless whatever military leaders wish to do.

WELLS, Norman J. Objective Reality of Ideas in Descartes, Caterus, and Suárez. J Hist Phil, 28(1), 33-61, Ja 90.

WELSCH, Wolfgang. *Aisthesis: Grundzüge und Perspektiven der Aristotelischen Sinneslehre*. Stuttgart, Klett-Cotta, 1987

Aristotle presented the first comprehensive theory of perception. It has—also in its one-sidedness—remained exemplary for the tradition. The Aristotelian explication of *aisthesis* is emphatically "logical." This serves both the ennoblement and integrability of perception. From an ontological perspective, the sensible attains its perfection in human perception. n detailed analyses, all aspects of *aisthesis* in Aristotle's works are investigated. Among other things it is proved that Aristotle never argued for a "common sense."

WENDEL, Hans Jürgen. Evolutionäre Erkenntnistheorie und erkenntnistheoretischer Realismus. Z Phil Forsch, 44(1), 1-27, 1990.

WENDELL, Susan. Toward a Feminist Theory of Disability. Hypatia, 4(2), 104-124, Sum 89.

We need a feminist theory of disability, both because 16 percent of women are disabled, and because the oppression of disabled people is closely linked to the cultural oppression of the body. Disability is not a biological given; like gender, it is socially constructed from biological reality. Our culture idealizes the body and demands that we control it. Thus, although most people will be disabled at some time in their lives, the disabled are made "the other," who symbolize failure of control and the threat of pain, limitation, dependency, and death. If disabled people and their knowledge were fully integrated into society, everyone's relation to her/his real body would be liberated.

WENZ, Peter S. Concentric Circle Pluralism: A Response to Rolston. Between Species, 5(3), 155-157, Sum 89.

This is a reply to a review by Holmes Rolston III of my book *Environmental Justice* (SUNY, 1988). I argue that the concentric circle theory presented in my book can be used to explain why animals may be moved to avoid the destruction of a plant species, and why traditional Inuit may be permitted to kill animals who have a right to life. I maintain also that its pluralism should not be held against the concentric circle theory because, in practice, all of our ethical deliberations are pluralistic.

WENZ, Peter. "Democracy and Environmental Change" in *Ethics and the Environmental Responsibility*, DOWER, Nigel (ed), 91-109. Aldershot, Avebury, 1989.

This essay discusses the relationship between environmental change and institutions characteristic of western democracy, including voter participation, lobbying groups, legislatures, administrative agencies and the judiciary. The tension between majority rule and minority rights and the use of cost-benefit analysis are also discussed. The conclusion is reached that, given access to relevant information, people can employ the institutions of western democracies to act responsibly as citizens of the larger environmental whole.

WERBLAN, Andrzej. Changes in the Social Structures of the Central- and East-European Countries. Dialec Hum, 16(2), 121-138, Spr 89.

WERHANE, Patricia H. Corporate and Individual Moral Responsibility: A Reply to Jan Garrett. J Bus Ethics, 8(10), 821-822, O 89.

Jan Garrett's interpretation of Peter French's and my position leads him to the conclusion that "unredistributable corporate moral responsibility...seems to require the radical separability of moral responsibility and individual agency," is a position that neither French nor I hold. Rather, we have created another kind of entity, the corporation, which is also, at least secondarily, a moral agent. In other words, we have broadened the scope of moral responsibility, not reassigned it.

WERHANE, Patricia H. The Ethics of Insider Trading. J Bus Ethics, 8(11), 841-845, N 89.

Despite the fact that a number of economists and philosophers of late defend insider trading both as a viable and useful practice in a free market and as not immoral, I shall question the value of insider trading both from a moral and an economic point of view. I shall argue that insider trading both in its present illegal form and as a legalized market mechanism undermines the efficient and proper functioning of a free market, thereby bringing into question its own raison d'etre. It does so and is economically inefficient for the very reason that it is immoral. Thus this practice cannot be justified either from an economic or a moral point of view.

WERHANE, Patricia H. Mergers, Acquisitions and the Market for Corporate Control. Pub Affairs Quart, 4(1), 81-96, Ja 90.

While not bringing into question the value of the merger phenomenon, per se, I argue that in justifying merger activities through linking the theory of the market for corporate control with principal/agent theory sometimes produces inconsistent conclusions, because management does not, and indeed sometimes cannot, always represent the best interests of its shareholders either in a merger or in a leveraged buyout. I take issue with the claim that an efficient market is, in itself, an autonomous regulator of economic behavior. The essay concludes with some remedies for avoiding the questionable consequences of mergers that neither advocate overall regulation nor the abolishment of these activities.

WERHANE, Patricia H. The Role of Self-Interest in Adam Smith's *Wealth of Nations*. J Phil, 86(11), 669-680, N 89.

In this paper I argue that a proper reading of the *Wealth of Nations* in the context of Smith's arguments in the *Theory of Moral Sentiments* that human beings are motivated equally by selfish and social passions brings into question the allegedly central role of self-interest in economic affairs. Such an interpretation affects Smith's seminal notion of the invisible hand and thus his theory of a free market.

WERLEN, Benno. Die Situationsanalyse. Conceptus, 23(59), 49-65, 1989.

The claim that one may use the critical-rational methodology of the social sciences in regional geographical research faces several difficulties. On the one hand, the method of 'situational analysis' has never been fully expounded by Popper himself, so that it remains ambiguous in certain respects. The elucidation of this proposition in the philosophy of social science, which has hitherto been carried out predominantly in the English-speaking world, is accordingly controversial. On the other hand, empirical social research still takes its orientation from the scientific methodology of critical rationalism—social geographers concluding that the aim of their research should be to uncover 'spatial laws'. In this paper, an attempt is made to give a systematic account of Popper's ideas on the methodology of social sciences and to make them fruitful for practical empirical research. This implies a new orientation of regional geographical research, from an action-oriented spatial approach to a spatially-oriented science of action.

WERNHAM, James C S. James's Faith-Ladder. J Hist Phil, 28(1), 105-114, Ja 90.

WERTZ, S K. Reference in Anselm's Ontological Proof. Hist Phil Quart, 7(2), 143-157, Ap 90.

It has been claimed, e.g., by Hodges in *Logic*, that Anselm's ontological proof is fallacious because of referential failure. By using some medieval and contemporary theories of reference, I attempt to demonstrate that the proof's key terms possess "quasi-reference" or secondary reference. (Russell construed reference to be exclusively primary.) Strawson's theory is particularly helpful here in examining several interpretations of this celebrated argument. Traditionally the argument has been interpreted as a reductio. The reduction, I contend, is only a part of a larger analogical argument which has the painter illustration as the other half. The function of the painter illustration is to ward off charges of referential failure and to establish secondary reference.

WERTZ, S K. Why Is the Ontological Proof in Descartes' Fifth Meditation? SW Phil Rev, 6(2), 107-109, Jl 90.

This discussion is a reply to Donald Sievert's paper in the earlier issue of this journal on essential truths and the ontological argument in Descartes and his recent commentators. Sievert argues that the ontological proof is an instance of Descartes's account of essential truths. I argue for the converse of Sievert's thesis: that essential truths are dependent upon God and that Descartes is an irrationalist on this issue.

WESCOTT, Roger W. "Reunification and Rebuilding" in *The Wisdom of Faith: Essays in Honor of Dr Sebastian Alexander Matczak*, THOMPSON, Henry O (ed), 147-154. Lanham, Univ Pr of America, 1989.

The Unification Church resembles both the American Indian Ghost Dance and Melanesian Cargo Cults in asserting a pressing need to restore the harmony of God, Man, and Nature believed to have been lost as the result of some great misfortune. While most scriptural creeds, east and west, depict this misfortune as a moral or spiritual lapse, most preliterate myth depicts it as a global or cosmic physical disruption. Either way, however, it seems fair to characterize the prevalent religious mood of our species as one of nostalgia for a vanished order and yearning to regain that order.

WESSELS, Linda. "The Way the World Isn't: What the Bell Theorems Force Us to Give Up" in *Philosophical Consequences of Quantum Theory: Reflections on Bell's Theorem*, CUSHING, James T (ed), 80-96. Notre Dame, Univ Notre Dame Pr, 1989.

This article examines a set of assumptions that (1) are presupposed by classical physics and (2) jointly imply the Bell inequality, to determine which of these assumptions Bell's theorem forces us to abandon. Several plausible candidates are isolated. It is argued that giving up any one of these candidates will force a radical change in our physical world view—but clearly one must be given up.

WEST, Cornel. *The American Evasion of Philosophy: A Genealogy of Pragmatism*. Madison, Univ Wisconsin Pr, 1989

WEST, Judy F and NIXON, Judy C. The Ethics of Smoking Policies. J Bus Ethics, 8(6), 409-414, Je 89.

Smoking has long been declared a health hazard. In 1964, the US Surgeon General revealed that smoking was related to lung cancer. Subsequent reports linked smoking to numerous other health problems. Recent statements by the Surgeon General indicated smokers do have the right to decide to continue or quit; however, their choice to continue cannot interfere with the nonsmoker's right to breathe smoke-free air. The full impact of adverse health consequences of involuntary smoking may not be recognized yet. Smoke is now known to affect everyone who breathes it. Even when one doesn't smoke, the nonsmoker is susceptible to the ill effects because of inhaling smoke. Are smoking policies justified? Companies are disovering that smoking has a negative economic and ethical impact on business. Smoking has been linked to increased health care costs, reduced productivity, increased absenteeism, and lowered morale. (edited)

WESTMAN, Robert S. The Duhemian Historiographical Project. Synthese, 83(2), 261-272, My 90.

Duhem regarded the history of physical science as carrying a twofold lesson for the practicing physicist. First, history revealed the slow, groping, yet continuous development of physical theory toward a true description of the relations among natural entities. Second, history also unmasked false explanations and metaphysical beliefs that might seduce the unwary scientist into following an unfruitful line of research. This paper brings forth the central images underlying Duhem's historiographical project and uses the papers by S Menn and W A Wallace to ask what Duhem's enterprise actually meant in practice. I argue that the main question is the following: What is to count as the proper space of historical meaning and explanation? (edited)

WESTPHAL, Jonathan. Black. Mind, 98(392), 585-589, O 89.

WESTPHAL, Jonathan and CHERRY, Christopher. Is Life Absurd? Philosophy, 65(252), 199-203, Ap 90.

Nagel claims that we are like ants and that life, seen from an 'external' perspective, is absurd. We argue that the 'external' perspective is just another optional *internal* perspective, that life is not absurd, as demonstrated by art and faith, and that the metaphor of the ant is false, both to human beings and to ants. The lives of ants are filled with significance, for ants.

WESTPHAL, Jonathan. Leibniz and the Problem of Induction. Stud Leibniz, 21(2), 174-187, 1989.

WESTPHAL, Kenneth R. *Hegel's Epistemological Realism: A Study of the Aim and Method of Hegel's Phenomenology of Spirit*. Norwell, Kluwer, 1989

The author argues that Hegel's main aim in the *Phenomenology of Spirit* is to defend a social and historical account of empirical knowledge that is realist. He argues that Hegel's views are considered responses to skeptical problems posed by Sextus Empiricus—problems inadequately resolved not only by Descartes and Kant, but also by Carnap and Alston. Westphal reconstructs Hegel's criteria for the adequacy of philosophical theories of knowledge and analyzes Hegel's phenomenological method in detail. Hegel's "idealism" is shown to be a form of realist holism. The conclusion shows how Hegel's *Phenomenology* is unified by a complex argument for epistemological realism.

WESTRA, Laura. "Respect", "Dignity" and "Integrity": An Environmental Proposal for Ethics. Epistemologia, 12(1), 91-123, Ja-Je 89.

WESTRA, Laura. Terrorism, Self-Defense, and Whistleblowing. J Soc Phil, 20(3), 46-58, Wint 89.

Utilitarianism and contractarianism cannot support the terrorist's position (Narveson, 1988), whereas, I suggest, Kant's ethical doctrine permits us to view it from a different standpoint. In a society that condones and even extols many forms of violence (Annette Baier, 1988) and fighting for an issue which cannot be settled by the democratic process (Paul Gilbert, 1988), the "true" terrorist may see violence as the only alternative appropriate to defend his principles and integrity. I argue, however, that to be at all defensible, the violence should remain self-directed.

WESTRUM, Ron. Is Social Work Different? Comments on "Confirmational Response Bias". Sci Tech Human Values, 15(1), 62-64, Wint 90.

WETZEL, Linda. Dummett's Criteria for Singular Terms. Mind, 99(394), 239-254, Ap 90.

In *Frege: Philosophy of Language*, Michael Dummett proposes five criteria that are supposed to delimit formally the class of singular terms. I argue that Dummett's criteria, even as amended by Crispin Wright and Bob Hale, do not delimit the class of singular terms in English, that further refinements of the criteria probably will not help, and that in any event the criteria face other difficulties.

WEYEMBERGH, Maurice. La critique de l'utopie et de la technique chez J Ellul et H Jonas. Tijdschr Stud Verlich Denken, 17(1-2), 63-136, 1989.

This comparative study is divided into four sections: (1) Ellul's and Jonas's conception of technology; (2) their critique of utopian thinking (especially in its revolutionary form) as a completion and justification, on the level of consciousness, of the technological impulse and adventure; (3) the defence of a specific (nonuniversal) Christian morals by Ellul and of a morals of responsibility by Jonas as an answer to the challenge; (4) the question of the possible political translation and labeling of their thoughts.

WHALLEY, Michael J. The Practice of Philosophy in the Elementary School Classroom. Thinking, 5(3), 40-42, 1984.

WHALLEY, Michael. "Some Factors Influencing the Success of Philosophical Discussion in the Classroom. Thinking, 4(3-4), 2-5, 1982.

WHEATLEY, Margaret J. "The Motivating Power of Ethics in Times of Corporate Confusion" in *Papers on the Ethics of Administration*, WRIGHT, N Dale (ed), 139-157. Albany, SUNY Pr, 1988.

WHEELER, Arthur. "Donagan and Imaginary Cases" in *Inquiries into Values: The Inaugural Session of the International Society for Value Inquiry*, LEE, Sander H , 291-298. Lewiston, Mellen Pr, 1989.

In *The Theory of Morality* Alan Donagan defends traditional morality against the view that the size of possible evil consequences must be our guide to our actions. I argue that, in a way, Donagan incorporates much of that view into his own, he arguing that *Fiat justitia, ruat caelum* can only "be taken seriously if it is understood that nothing beyond tragedy will be a consequence of justice." Donagan treats some gory imaginary cases in a cavalier manner in his defense of traditional morality; I think this suggests that traditional morality is not as defensible against utilitarianism as he thinks.

WHEELER, David L. Toward a Process-Relational Christian Soteriology. Process Stud, 18(2), 102-113, Sum 89.

How might humanity experience ultimate reality as intimately related to us, as liberating us individually and corporately from disorder, and as

empowering our personal self-integration? With this question in mind, this work reexamines the images and concepts of Christian doctrinal tradition which—under the rubric of the "doctrine of the atonement"—have historically promoted this experience. The extended constructive essay which concludes the book makes extensive and foundational—though not uncritical—use of Whiteheadian process-relational thought to provide new ontological grounding to Christian images and concepts of atonement.

WHELAN, Ruth. Images de la Réforme chez Pierre Bayle ou l'histoire d'une déception. Rev Theol Phil, 122(1), 85-107, 1990.

L'interprétation proposée par Bayle de l'histoire de la Réforme soulève la question de ses propres convictions religieuses. Cette étude décrit l'évolution du regard que Bayle porte sur la Réforme et elle situe la formation de son jugement sur le protestantisme français dans le cadre des controverses qui secouèrent la communauté du Refuge aux Pays-Bas. A l'égard de la Réforme, l'idéalisme premier de Bayle semble avoir progressivement cédé le pas à la déception. Cependant sa désillusion n'est pas assimilable à de l'incroyance. Bayle paraît avoir voulu croire à la Réforme dans son image idéale, tout en critiquant son développement ultérieur.

WHEWELL, William and BUTTS, Robert E (ed). *Theory of Scientific Method—William Whewell*. Indianapolis, Hackett, 1989

The selections in this volume include William Whewell's seminal 19th-century studies of the logic of induction (with his critique of Mill's theory), arguments for his realist view that science discovers necessary truths about nature, and exercises in the epistemology and ontology of science. The book's arrangement sets forth a coherent statement of the historically important philosophy of science whose influence has never been greater: every one of Whewell's fundamental ideas about the philosophy of science is presented here. The introductory essay provides an overview of the main features of Whewell's theory of scientific method.

WHISENANT, James. Kierkegaard's Use of Lessing. Mod Theol, 6(3), 259-272, Ap 90.

WHISNER, William. Self-Deception, Human Emotion, and Moral Responsibility: Toward a Pluralistic Conceptual Scheme. J Theor Soc Behav, 19(4), 389-410, D 89.

The author develops a new conceptualization to account for the most frequent type of self-deception. He argues that recent accounts of self-deception, individually or collectively, do not provide criteria to identify this type. He specifies criteria for distinguishing self-deception attempts, successful self-deception attempts, and the state of self-deception that results from a successful attempt. The conceptualization is used to describe and explain how self-deception functions in the formation, maintenance, and termination of emotions. He criticizes the dominant psychological paradigm for understanding self-deception and self-esteem. He also suggests how his account is compatible with critical social theory and other social theoretical perspectives.

WHITE, Alan R. *The Language of Imagination*. Cambridge, Blackwell, 1990

First, in a survey of the history of philosophical theories it shows the traditional view, from Aristotle to Kant, as portraying imagining as imaging and/or as the having of images, and the twentieth century reaction, in Sartre, Ryle and Wittgenstein, though not rejecting imagery, as denying that images are mental pictures. Secondly, it examines the relations between the concept of imagination and various concepts, such as imaging, visualising, supposing, pretending, and remembering, with which it has been illegitimately linked or identified. It concludes with an analysis of imagination as the thinking of possibilities.

WHITE, Becky Cox. Overview of the OTA Report *Infertility: Medical and Social Choices*. J Med Phil, 14(5), 493-496, O 89.

The OTA Report, *Infertility: Medical and Social Choices*, is reviewed. The importance of significant educational components regarding demographics, causes, means of prevention, and methods for diagnosis and treatment of infertility is discussed. The major focus is on the absence of ethical, legal, and social consensus regarding appropriate uses of nontraditional methods of reproduction (in vitro fertilization, surrogate motherhood, etc.) to overcome infertility. Ethical and legal concerns are raised about use of the new reproductive technologies. It is suggested that much more information is required before consensus will be achieved and before policy can be legislated.

WHITE, F C. Love and Beauty in Plato's *Symposium*. J Hellen Stud, 109, 149-157, 1989.

WHITE, Gladys B. Ethical Analyses in the Development of Congressional Public Policy. J Med Phil, 14(5), 575-585, O 89.

A wide range of conflicting established moral viewpoints makes development of public policy related to infertility difficult. Where there are pluralities of viewpoints and no single established moral approach, uniform solutions are questionable. The Office of Technology Assessment (OTA) is a nonpartisan analytic support agency that serves the United States Congress by providing objective analyses of major public policy issues related to scientific and technological change. Because analysis of ethical issues is an important part of technology assessment, OTA included a thematic analysis of ethical issues in the report, *Infertility: Medical and Social Choices*. A consideration of whether infertility is a disease was an important conceptual starting point, and religious perspectives were reviewed as possible sources of moral and ethical insight.

WHITE, Michael J. Aristotle on 'Time' and 'A Time'. Apeiron, 22(3), 207-224, S 89.

WHITE, Morton. The Politics of Epistemology. Ethics, 100(1), 77-92, O 89.

WHITE, Morton. Pragmatism and the Revolt Against Formalism: Revising Some Doctrines of William James. Trans Peirce Soc, 26(1), 1-17, Wint 90.

WHITE, Nicholas P. Perceptual and Objective Properties in Plato. Apeiron, 22(4), 45-65, D 89.

WHITE, Nicholas P. Stoic Values. Monist, 73(1), 42-58, Ja 90.

WHITE, Richard. Love, Beauty, and Death in Venice. Phil Lit, 14(1), 53-64, Ap 90.

Thomas Mann's novella *Death in Venice* may be read as a sustained response to Plato, and every other philosophy which stresses the redemptive power of art or beauty. Moreover, a detailed discussion of this story allows us to consider the deeper question, "How can a work of literature comment effectively upon a work of philosophy?"

WHITE, Roger. "MacKinnon and the Parables" in *Christ, Ethics and Tragedy: Essays in Honour of Donald MacKinnon*, SURIN, Kenneth (ed), 49-70. New York, Cambridge Univ Pr, 1989.

WHITE, Roger. Political Theory as an Object of Discourse. Soc Theor Pract, 16(1), 85-100, Spr 90.

WHITE, Stephen K. Heidegger and the Difficulties of a Postmodern Ethics and Politics. Polit Theory, 18(1), 80-103, F 90.

WHITE, Stephen L. Transcendentalism and Its Discontents. Phil Topics, 17(1), 231-261, Spr 89.

WHITE, V Alan. How to *Mind* One's *Ethics*: A Reply to Van Inwagen. Analysis, 50(1), 33-35, Ja 90.

This paper replies to Peter van Inwagen's claim that two well-known compatibilist arguments (which he dubs the *Mind* and *Ethics* arguments) cannot both be sound. I argue that these arguments may easily be reconciled and that, in fact, they may be mutually necessary to form a composite concept of compatibilist free will.

WHITE, V Alan. The Single-Issue Introduction to Philosophy. Teach Phil, 13(1), 13-19, Mr 90.

This paper presents an alternative to more traditional approaches to teaching introductory philosophy in which the course focuses upon a "single issue" in great depth. A defense of the approach is offered along with an example of how I have taught such a course using the free will problem as the topic.

WHITE, W D. "Living Will Statutes: Good Public Policy?" in *Advance Directives in Medicine*, HACKLER, Chris (ed), 39-52. New York, Praeger, 1989.

Recent legislative activity giving legal underpinnings to so-called "living wills" is intended to foster rational decision making and patient autonomy in medicine. But such laws promise more, in the public imagination, than they are capable of delivering. There are a number of significant problems with "advance directives" in medicine, both on the conceptual or ideological level and on the pragmatic level of their implementation. Despite these problems, and the limited value of such laws, their passage nevertheless is probably good public policy. At the least, the legislative activity encourages a widespread discussion of the issues, and this is a public good. This essay examines some of the problems and limitations of living wills, and the potential value of such laws.

WHITEBOOK, Joel. Intersubjectivity and the Monadic Core of the Psyche: Habermas and Castoriadis on the Unconscious. Praxis Int, 9(4), 347-364, Ja 90.

WHITELEY, C H. McGinn on the Mind-Body Problem. Mind, 99(394), 289, Ap 90.

WHITTAKER, John H. Supernatural Acts and Supervenient Explanations. Sophia (Australia), 29(2), 17-32, Jl 90.

WHITTEMORE, Robert C. Santayana's Neglect of Hartshorne's

Alternative. Bull Santayana Soc, 4, 1-6, Fall 86.

WHYTE, J T. Success Semantics. Analysis, 50(3), 149-157, Je 90.

I develop and defend a thesis, first thought of by F P Ramsey, about the truth conditions of beliefs: namely, that a belief's truth condition is that which guarantees the fulfillment of any desire by the action which that belief and desire would combine to cause. Most importantly, I show how this thesis can explain the truth conditions of *all* beliefs, and not just those with explicitly instrumental contents. It can do this because all beliefs have instrumental implications: i.e., they all make you act in a certain way given other beliefs and desires.

WIANS, William. Aristotle, Demonstration, and Teaching. Ancient Phil, 9 (2), 245-253, Fall 89.

It is well known that the theory of science propounded in Aristotle's *Posterior Analytics* seems not to resemble the methodological practices of the treatises. Jonathan Barnes has put forward what has become perhaps the most influential recent attempt to resolve the tension. But what I call the Teaching Thesis—the view that the *APo* tells an instructor how to teach a finished discipline—faces at least two objections. First, it forces Barnes to regard virtually Aristotle's entire scientific corpus as preliminary reports. Second, demonstration is inherently incapable of teaching what a student most needs to learn.

WIATR, Jerzy J. Some Aspects of the Methodology of Comparative Research in Politics. Dialec Hum, 16(2), 149-157, Spr 89.

The paper is dedicated to Adam Schaff in connection with his 75th anniversary and discusses one aspect of his contribution, namely the promotion of comparative social science. Comparisons between countries of different social, economic and political orders are considered particularly fruitful. Different levels of comparative analysis and different methods (both quantitative and qualitative) are considered essential for successful cross-national analysis. Combining historical (diachronic) and synchronic comparisons are also of special interest. Polish-Austrian comparative studies are discussed to illustrate theoretical arguments.

WICCLAIR, Mark. Caring for Frail Elderly Parents: Past Parental Sacrifices and the Obligations of Adult Children. Soc Theor Pract, 16(2), 163-189, Sum 90.

Several objections to the view that parental sacrifices generate filial obligations are considered and rejected. It is argued that parental sacrifices can generate duties of gratitude and that the latter, in turn, provide the basis for filial obligations. However, it is concluded that due to the indeterminacy of duties of gratitude, (1) there are insufficient grounds for maintaining that adult children have a gratitude-based obligation to make the specific sacrifices that are often needed to provide adequate assistance to disabled elderly parents, and (2) a policy of placing the entire burden of caring for the frail elderly on their adult children cannot be justified by claiming that the latter owe assistance to parents out of gratitude.

WICHMAN, Alison and CARTER, Michele and MC CARTHY, Charles R. Regulating AIDS Research on Infants and Children: The Moral Task of Institutional Review Boards. Bridges, 2(1-2), 63-73, Spr-Sum 90.

Acquired Immunodeficiency Syndrome (AIDS) has created ethical dilemmas for research investigators as well as other healthcare professionals. One difficult problem facing research investigators and Institutional Review Boards (IRBs) (committees required to review and approve proposed research involving human subjects before the projects can be initiated) is to determine if, when, and under what circumstances it is permissible to conduct research involving children and infants infected with the AIDS virus as research subjects. The authors review existing Health and Human Services (HHS) regulations for the Protection of Human Subjects, present a prototypical case involving an infant infected with the AIDS virus, and conclude that the regulations provide a suitable framework for IRBs to consider the ethical problems facing pediatric AIDS research.

WICKS, Andrew C. Norman Bowie and Richard Rorty on Multinationals: Does Business Ethics Need 'Metaphysical Comfort?'. J Bus Ethics, 9(3), 191-200, Mr 90.

Norman Bowie wrote an article on the moral obligations of multinational corporations in 1987. This paper is a response to Bowie, but more importantly, it is designed to articulate the force and substance of the pragmatist philosophy developed by Richard Rorty. In his article, Bowie suggested that 'moral universalism' is the only credible method of doing business ethics across cultures. Bowie lumps Rorty into a 'bad guy' category without careful analysis of his philosophy and ascribes to him views which clearly do not fit. I attempt to provide both a more careful articulation of Rorty's views, and to use his pragmatism to illustrate an approach to business ethics which is more fruitful than Bowie's. (edited)

WIDER, Kathleen. Overtones of Solipsism in Thomas Nagel's "What is it

Like to Be a Bat?" and The View From Nowhere. Phil Phenomenol Res, 50(3), 481-499, Mr 90.

This paper examines the solipsistic strain present in Nagel's defense of the claim that a physicalist account of consciousness can provide only an incomplete analysis of mind because it cannot capture the subjective character of experience. I argue that given Nagel's use of the imagination in grounding our conception of how an experience is for another and given his view of the relationship between the mental and the physical, it follows that the true nature of an experience is *fully* comprehensible only to the experiencer herself. It is this consequence of his views that constitutes the solipsistic strain in his work.

WIDERKER, David. In Defense of Davidson's Identity Thesis Regarding Action Individuation. Dialectica, 43(3), 281-288, 1989.

WIDERKER, David. Troubles with Ockhamism. J Phil, 87(9), 462-480, S 90.

This paper examines the Ockhamistic response to the problem of reconciling divine foreknowledge and human freedom, based on the idea that we may have power over God's prior knowings of human free actions, since the latter are merely "soft" facts about the past, and not "hard" facts about the past. It is argued that the reasons offered by contemporary Ockhamists for so treating facts regarding God's foreknowledge of human free actions are either of doubtful relevance, or rest on assumptions that are mistaken. Moreover, it is shown that power over facts regarding God's foreknowledge of future contingent events gives an agent sometimes power over hard facts about the past, in which case the Ockhamist strategy of reconciling divine foreknowledge with human freedom collapses.

WIDERKER, David. Two Fallacious Objections to Adam's Soft/Hard Distinction. Phil Stud, 57(1), 103-107, S 89.

WIEGMANN, Hermann. Plato's Critique of the Poets and the Misunderstanding of his Epistemological Argumentation. Phil Rhet, 23(2), 109-124, 1990.

The so-called critique of the poets is in fact not a real critique of the poets at all, but has exclusively aimed at dividing domains of knowledge, and hence has an epistemological basis. When Plato, in the *Republic*, ranks art as at third remove from reality, a determinate kind of mimesis is intended, perhaps that of the portrait-artist, but the superior and real mimesis is that of Beauty, the representation designed with the help of the Muses.

WIEHL, Reiner (ed) and RAPP, Friedrich (ed). *Whitehead's Metaphysics of Creativity*. Albany, SUNY Pr, 1990.

The book contains twelve articles which were first presented at the International Whitehead Symposium held in Bad Homburg, West Germany, in October, 1983. The papers centre around the concept of creativity basic to Whitehead's novel system of categories which accords becoming priority over being. The book's four chapters treat Whitehead's place in the history of philosophy, the mutual dependence between the results obtained in empirical research and their metaphysical interpretation, the cosmological and the anthropological dimensions in Whitehead's philosophy and finally the relationship between the philosophical and the theological interpretations of creativity.

WIEHL, Reiner. "Whitehead's Cosmology of Feeling Between Ontology and Anthropology" in *Whitehead's Metaphysics of Creativity*, RAPP, Friedrich (ed), 127-151. Albany, SUNY Pr, 1990.

Whitehead's relativization of the opposition between creativity and rationality permits him to do justice to the intrinsic value of feelings, as modern metaphysics with its four-fold dualism cannot. By reducing the latter to the fundamental opposition between reality and possibility and by affirming the priority of the concrete over the abstract, Whitehead opens up a possibility for the surmounting of metaphysical dualism. While Whitehead's metaphysics of subjectivity shares with Hegel's the critique of the traditional ontology of substance, his reversal of the Hegelian priority of truth over the concrete life of the subject is crucial for the theory of feelings.

WIERSMA, Tjerk. Beter een verboden spiegelbeeld dan een onvruchtbare hybride: een repliek. Kennis Methode, 13(3), 337-340, 1989.

WIGGINS, Osborne. Herbert Spiegelberg's Ethics: Accident and Obligation. J Brit Soc Phenomenol, 21(1), 39-47, Ja 90.

WIGHT, Doris T. Metaphysics through Paradox in Eliot's *Four Quartets*. Phil Rhet, 23(1), 63-69, 1990.

WILCOX, John T. The Birth of Nietzsche Out of the Spirit of Lange. Int Stud Phil, 21(2), 81-89, 1989.

This is a favorable review essay on George Stack's book, *Lange and Nietzsche*. Stack shows heavy influence of Lange on Nietzsche, even on most distinctively Nietzschean themes. I focus on Christianity, necessity, reason, and the eternal return especially.

WILCOX, John T. *The Bitterness of Job: A Philosophical Reading*. Ann Arbor, Univ of Michigan Pr, 1989

Exposition of the book of Job's critique of the moral world order, based on recent biblical scholarship, aiming at the clarity of issues one expects in analytic philosophy and the depth one derives from Nietzschean concerns about no-saying. Some influence from Rawls and process theology. I argue that Job does curse God, as the Satan predicted (prologue), out of moral bitterness (defined here). I interpret the theophany's calls for intellectual humility, awareness of the limits of human power, and semi-Baalite appreciation of the amoral beauty of nature. The prologue and the epilogue yield to the theophany.

WILCOX, John T. Nature as Demonic in Thomson's Defense of Abortion. New Scholas, 63(4), 463-484, Autumn 89.

I show that most of the arguments in Judith Jarvis Thomson's famous "A Defense of Abortion" collapse unless we assume that nature is like a kidnapper, burglar, rapist or some other kind of rights violator, and that pregnancy is a violation of women's rights. Of course such a "demonic" conception of nature is implausible. But it expresses an anxiety of many women, and that fact may explain some of Thomson's huge success. Along the way I suggest other difficulties in her basic approach: its narrow ethical theory, its "weirdness," its neglect of blood ties, and its omission of fathers.

WILD, John. "The Existentialists" in *Reading Philosophy for the Twenty-First Century*, MC LEAN, George F (ed), 111-129. Lanham, Univ Pr of America, 1989.

WILENSKY, Sara Heller. "The *Guide* and the *Gate*: The Dialectical Influence of Maimonides on Isaac ibn Latif and Early Spanish Kabbalah" in *A Straight Path: Studies in Medieval Philosophy and Culture*, LINK-SALINGER, Ruth (ed), 266-278. Washington, Cath Univ Amer Pr, 1988.

WILES, Maurice. The Philosophy in Christianity: Arius and Athanasius. Philosophy, 25, 41-52, 89 Supp.

WILKERSON, T E. Hollis on Roles and Reason. Int J Moral Soc Stud, 5(1), 67-78, Spr 90.

In a recent book Martin Hollis argues that a complete account of rational choice must give a central place to the notion of a role, and that the 'sub-Humean' account in terms of the agent's desires and beliefs cannot make the right sort of provision for role playing. The author makes three main points. First, he argues that some of Hollis's material could be regarded as a development and enrichment of the sub-Humean view. Second, he claims that the adoption of a role cannot always be explained in sub-Humean terms, but expresses the discovery or acceptance of actions as worthy or desirable in themselves. Finally, he argues that Hollis's account of rational choice is inevitably incomplete, because it pays too little attention to irrational role playing, and to the reasons an agent might have for adopting a role.

WILKES, K V. Mind and Body. Philosophy, 24, 69-83, 88 Supp.

WILKES, K. "What is the Use of a Philosophy of Science for Scientists"? Filozof Cas, 37(4), 501-518, 1989.

Referring to the shortcomings of the philosophy of science, the author singles out some examples documenting that philosophical theses may mislead scientific progress, obstruct it or act irrelevantly towards it. In the given framework, the author clarifies the philosophical background to scientific pragmatism. He goes on to claim that the contemporary philosophy of science is characterized by tendencies towards a transition from the study of formal, axiomatized theories to a philosophy of experimental science. (edited)

WILKES, Kathy. "'External' Factors in the Development of Psychology in the West" in *Scientific Knowledge Socialized*, HRONSZKY, Imre (ed), 265-286. Norwell, Kluwer, 1989.

WILKINSON, Sue. The Impact of Feminist Research: Issues of Legitimacy. Phil Psych, 2(3), 261-269, 1989.

This paper examines issues of legitimacy surrounding feminist research in psychology, in relation to its current and future impact on the mainstream of the discipline. It argues that its relatively limited impact to date is due, in part, to the nature of feminist psychology, and, in part, to its interaction with the social institutions of psychology as a discipline. Further, the paper contends that the influence of the field may well remain relatively minor, however convincingly its potential benefits are argued, if it fails both to analyse and to utilize the social processes by which legitimacy is conferred.

WILKS, Yorick. Form and Content in Semantics. Synthese, 82(3), 329-351, Mr 90.

This paper continues a strain of intellectual complaint against the presumptions of certain kinds of formal semantics (the qualification is important) and their bad effects on those areas of artificial intelligence concerned with machine understanding of human language. After some discussion of the use of the term 'epistemology' in artificial intelligence, the paper takes as a case study the various positions held by McDermott on these issues and concludes, reluctantly, that, although he has reversed himself on the issue, there was no time at which he was right.

WILKS, Yorick. "Reference and Its Role in Computational Models of Mental Representations" in *Meaning and Mental Representation*, ECO, Umberto (ed), 221-236. Bloomington, Indiana Univ Pr, 1988.

WILL, Rosemarie. Rechtsstaalichkeit als Moment demokratischer politischer Machtausübung. Deut Z Phil, 37(9), 801-812, 1989.

WILLEMS, Eldert (ed) and DETHIER, Hubert (ed). *Cultural Hermeneutics of Modern Art: Essays in Honor of Jan Aler*. Amsterdam, Rodopi, 1989

WILLEMS, Eldert. "Aesthetic discursivity" in *Cultural Hermeneutics of Modern Art: Essays in Honor of Jan Aler*, DETHIER, Hubert (ed), 77-87. Amsterdam, Rodopi, 1989.

WILLEY, T E. "Schopenhauer, Modernism, and the Rejection of History" in *Schopenhauer: New Essays in Honor of His 200th Birthday*, VON DER LUFT, Eric (ed), 312-326. Lewiston, Mellen Pr, 1989.

In Schopenhauer's elaboration of Aristotle's famous relegation of history to a status inferior to poetry, he was out of step with Germany's post-Hegelian historical culture, but he articulated the later antihistorical spirit of modernism. Passing through Nietzsche, Ibsen and other prophets of modernist art, the Schopenhauerian suspicion of history has led to a pervasive rejection of historical consciousness by the artistic avant-garde in the twentieth century. But Schopenhauer's damnation of the historical was accompanied by some faint praise. This essay attempts to unravel his paradoxical treatment of history in *The World as Will and Idea*.

WILLIAMS, Bernard. Internal Reasons and the Obscurity of Blame. Logos (USA), 10, 1-11, 1989.

The article states again and defends the position advanced in an earlier piece, that (roughly) there are only internal reasons for action: that "A has a reason to φ" implies "A could reach the conclusion to φ by a sound deliberative route from the motivations s/he presently has." It is explained why this is a normative conception of a reason, and what counts as a sound deliberative route. The motivation for rejecting an external view (in particular, that moral and prudential considerations apply *a priori* to the question of what someone has a reason to do) is that it fails to make sense of the connections between normative and explanatory reasons. The account is extended to blame. Relative to an assumption that the *A ought to have φed* of "focused" blame is similar to the *A ought to φ* of advice, in implying a statement about A's reasons, the operation of such blame is explained in terms of the proleptic invocation of a reason: a reason which the agent will have in virtue of a disposition to want the respect of other people.

WILLIAMS, Bernard. Social Justice. J Soc Phil, 20(1-2), 68-73, Spr-Fall 89.

WILLIAMS, C J F. *What is Identity?*. New York, Clarendon/Oxford Pr, 1990

Wittgenstein's response to the Paradox of Identity was to deny that identity is a relation. This is accepted, but his further claim that we have no need of a sign for identity is not. The sign we need plays the same role as reflexive pronouns in converting two-place to one-place predicables. "Same" expresses the selfsame concept as "self." The sign we need gives appropriate expression to event-identity, to basic concepts of arithmetic, to the notion of correspondence as used in theories of truth, and helps to clarify uses of the first person pronoun.

WILLIAMS, Clifford. Teaching Virtues and Vices. Phil Today, 33(3), 195-203, Fall 89.

Virtues are rarely treated in introductory ethics courses; standard fare usually consists of ethical theory and contemporary social problems. These latter topics, however, do not "fit" our moral lives as closely as do the former, and studying them does not have as much effect on conduct as does studying virtues. For these reasons, it would be good to treat virtues in introductory ethics courses in addition to the standard topics.

WILLIAMS, Geraint. J S Mill and Political Violence. Utilitas, 1(1), 102-111, My 89.

The article examines the traditional view of J S Mill which sees him as the classic liberal who upholds reason and persuasion as the means of settling social conflicts and as the key instruments of progress. Through a study of his various writings on a number of revolutions and revolts throughout the world it argues against this orthodox view and concludes that Mill does indeed support the use of violence in politics but only if the cause is just, if peaceful means are impossible, and if conditions render success likely.

WILLIAMS, Howard. *Hegel, Heraclitus, and Marx's Dialectic*. New York, St Martin's Pr, 1989

Although the notion of the dialect is central to the writings of Hegel and Marx, the author of this book demonstrates that its origins can be traced back to Kant and the early Greek philosopher Heraclitus. He provides, using a wide variety of examples—in particular from Hegel's *The Science of Logic* and Marx's *Capital*—a clear account of how the dialectic method was received by the two philosophers. For Hegel, the dialectic is all-embracing, which implies that our concepts are interlinked and that through them the world is constructed; whereas for Marx, the dialectic allows us to reconstruct the world in thought, which implies that our concepts have to be interlinked to comprehend an ever-changing scene.

WILLIAMS, James G. On the Formalization of Semantic Conventions. J Sym Log, 55(1), 220-243, Mr 90.

This paper discusses six formalization techniques, of varying strengths, for extending a formal system based on traditional mathematical logic. The purpose of these formalization techniques is to simulate the introduction of new syntactic constructs, along with associated semantics for them. We show that certain techniques (among the six) subsume others. To illustrate sharpness, we also consider a selection of constructs and show which techniques can and cannot be used to introduce them. The six studied techniques were selected on the basis of actual practice in logic and computing. They do not form an exhaustive list.

WILLIAMS, Kevin. Dilemma of M Oakeshott: Oakeshott's Treatment of Equality of Opportunity in Education and His Political Philosophy. J Phil Educ, 23(2), 223-240, Wint 89.

The purpose of this article is to establish the relationship between Oakeshott's conception of education and his political philosophy. Although a political conservative, Oakeshott's conception of education is not elitist in nature as he believes that full educational opportunity should be open to everyone regardless of social class background. His theory of civil life, however, incorporates a definition of politics which is incapable of accommodating the kind of action required to realize the redistribution of resources necessary to promote genuine equality of educational opportunity. The political conservative cannot be a closet egalitarian and herein lies the dilemma of Michael Oakeshott.

WILLIAMS, Linda L. Merleau-Ponty's Tacit *Cogito*. Man World, 23(1), 101-111, Ja 90.

Bernard Williams has argued that Descartes cannot reach the conclusion of his Cogito argument given Descartes's methodological skepticism. This article summarizes and clarifies Merleau-Ponty's phenomenological analysis of the Cogito in his "cogito" chapter of *The Phenomenology of Perception*. Williams's objection to the Cartesian Cogito is avoided, one of the advantages of the phenomenological approach over the Cartesian method.

WILLIAMS, Meredith. Wittgenstein, Kant and the "Metaphysics of Experience". Kantstudien, 81(1), 69-88, 1990.

This paper is a critical examination of the Kantian interpretation of Wittgenstein's notion of "propositions that hold fast." The attempt to treat these certainties as synthetic a priori judgments, providing the limits of sense, is mistaken. Three conditions must be such in order to make sense of the idea of a substantive limit to intelligibility: (i) the thesis of a positive limit, (ii) the independence of the constituents of the boundary from what is conditioned by that boundary, and (iii) the thesis that there is a single explanation for the certainty that accrues to the boundary. The certainties of *On Certainty* meet none of these conditions.

WILLIAMS, Robert R. The Absolute, Community, and Time. Ideal Stud, 19(2), 141-153, My 89.

This article explores the development of Royce's thought in which the concept of the absolute knower (totum simul) is modified and transformed into a theory of interpretation and social ontology. The absolute is not simply abandoned in favor of an ontological theory of community, but is rather transformed into a social and historical conception. The unity of a community of interpretation is distinguished from the totum simul unity of an absolute knower. The latter is an abstraction from the former. This thesis is relevant to process theology and theodicy.

WILLIAMS, Rowan. "Trinity and Ontology" in *Christ, Ethics and Tragedy: Essays in Honour of Donald MacKinnon*, SURIN, Kenneth (ed), 71-92. New York, Cambridge Univ Pr, 1989.

WILLIAMSON, Colwyn. Following a Rule. Philosophy, 64(250), 487-504, O 89.

Peter Winch contends in *The Idea of a Social Science* that human behavior is invariably rule-governed, and he cites a number of examples apparently supporting this contention. But all his examples are distorted by his prior commitment to the theory they are supposed to illustrate; and this theory, it is argued, is purely metaphysical and incapable of yielding anything other than vacuous conclusions.

WILLIAMSON, Colwyn. Witchcraft and Winchcraft. Phil Soc Sci, 19(4), 445-460, D 89.

Peter Winch's *The Idea of a Social Science* represents a threat to the very possibility of social science. Central to the theory he advances is the idea that religion, like the other 'modes of social life' of which he speaks, has its own 'criteria of intelligibility'. In the grip of this *a priori* theory leads Winch to a thoroughly distorted understanding of the practices of witchcraft.

WILLIAMSON, Timothy. Two Incomplete Anti-Realist Modal Epistemic Logics. J Sym Log, 55(1), 297-314, Mr 90.

Anti-realist equations of truth with rational acceptability and the like are represented by (*): 'p iff possibly Ep', E an epistemic operator. Since Ep entails 'Possibly Ep', (*) has it entail p. KT* is an incomplete decidable conservative extension of the modal logic KT with only trivial or infinite models; KT4* and KTB* collapse modally. Non-trivial extensions of KT* do not permit false maximally specific propositions (an anti-realist objection to possible worlds?). They also do not permit E to be closed under &-elimination; possible interpretations of E are considered.

WILLM, J. Of Logical Education. Thinking, 4(1), 30-32, 1982.

WILLMS, Bernard. Leviathan and the Post-Modern. Hist Euro Ideas, 10(5), 569-576, 1989.

WILLMS, Bernard. "World-State or State-World: Hobbes and the Law of Nations" in *Hobbes: War Among Nations*, AIRAKSINEN, Timo (ed), 130-141. Brookfield, Gower, 1989.

WILLOUGHBY, Guy. Oscar Wilde and Poststructuralism. Phil Lit, 13(2), 316-324, O 89.

This article explores Oscar Wilde's aesthetics, explaining its relation to contemporary theory. Wilde's insistence on the relevance of aesthetics to life is traced, including his espousal of the subject's need to incorporate experience within a dynamic conception of the self. Wilde's achievement is compared with recent attacks on the integrity of the self, and his project is found suggestive because he grafts a reconciliatory poetics onto a relativist view of experience.

WILLOWEIT, Dietmar and WILLOWEIT, Hildegard. "Das Versprechen—problemgeschichtliche Aspekte eines rechtsphänomenologischen Paradigmas" in *Agora: Zu Ehren von Rudolph Berlinger*, BERLINGER, Rudolph (and other eds), 307-328. Amsterdam, Rodopi, 1988.

WILLOWEIT, Hildegard and WILLOWEIT, Dietmar. "Das Versprechen—problemgeschichtliche Aspekte eines rechtsphänomenologischen Paradigmas" in *Agora: Zu Ehren von Rudolph Berlinger*, BERLINGER, Rudolph (and other eds), 307-328. Amsterdam, Rodopi, 1988.

WILSON, Colin. *Existentially Speaking: Essays on the Philosophy of Literature*. San Bernardino, Borgo Pr, 1989

This collection of essays discusses literature and literary criticism from an existentialist perspective. A number of twentieth century thinkers are considered, including Sartre, Foucault, Camus, Husserl and others. (staff)

WILSON, David Sloan. Species of Thought: A Comment on Evolutionary Epistemology. Biol Phil, 5(1), 37-62, Ja 90.

The primary outcome of natural selection is adaptation to an environment. The primary concern of epistemology is the acquisition of knowledge. Evolutionary epistemology must therefore draw a fundamental connection between adaptation and knowledge. Existing frameworks in evolutionary epistemology do this in two ways: (a) by treating adaptation as a form of knowledge, and (b) by treating the ability to acquire knowledge as a biologically evolved adaptation. The author criticizes both frameworks for failing to appreciate that mental representations can motivate behaviors that are adaptive in the real world without themselves directly corresponding to the real world. He suggests a third framework in which mental representations are to reality as species are to ecosystems. This is a many-to-one relationship that predicts a diversity of adaptive representations in the minds of interacting people. (edited)

WILSON, Deirdre and CHOMSKY, Noam and EDGLEY, Roy and OSBORNE, Peter and RÉE, Jonathan. Noam Chomsky: An Interview. Rad Phil, 53, 31-40, Autumn 89.

WILSON, Fred. The Logic of Probabilities in Hume's Argument against Miracles. Hume Stud, 15(2), 255-275, N 89.

WILSON, John. Can One Promise to Love Another? Philosophy, 64(250), 557-563, O 89.

WILWERDING, Jonathan. Might. Midwest Stud Phil, 14, 357-371, 1989.

WIMMER, Reiner. Zur ethischen Problematik der Keimbahn-Gentherapie am Menschen. Z Phil Forsch, 44(1), 55-67, 1990.

It is argued that the *development* of gene-line therapy for human beings is absolutely immoral, because it violates the personality rights of those human embryos (as future persons if some of them survive as it is necessary for controlling the possible success of such experimentation) which have to be subjected to this procedure for developing the therapy without any possibility of consenting or dissenting. But next it is argued that the *application* of a successfully, although illegitimately, developed gene-line therapy is not unconditionally morally forbidden.

WINANCE, éleuthère. l'Être et le sensible: Edmund Husserl et Thomas D'Aquin. Rev Thomiste, 89(3), 357-404, Jl-S 89.

The purpose of the article is to give a tentative answer to the question: Is Husserl's turn from the realism of the *Logical Investigations* to the idealism of the *Cartesian Meditations* logically predictable? An analysis of the concepts of being, sensible, categorial intuition suggests that his realism was enigmatic. Being was not, as in the Aristotelian tradition, the very constituent of the sensible. The comments of Thomas on the chapter 15th of the *Posterior Analytics* II show us the intrinsic identity between the perceived and the understood, the sensible and the universal (being). Therefore, idealism was already "virtual" in the 6th Investigation. A descriptive account of the period between 1900 and 1907 (famous conferences: *The Idea of Phenomenology*) tries to explain why, according to Lowit (French translator) the virtual became "actual" so slowly and unexpectedly.

WINBLAD, Douglas G. Skepticism and Naturalized Epistemology. Philosophia (Israel), 19(2-3), 99-113, O 89.

This paper examines naturalized epistemology's prospects for dealing with Cartesian skepticism and the traditional problem of induction. It is argued that Quine's approach fails to satisfy the skeptic who does not already embrace some version of scientific method. In addition, it is argued that Goldman's reliabilism enables one to address these issues empirically only if one rejects the view that if we are capable of confirming an empirical hypothesis, we are also capable of disconfirming it. The article ends with a negative appraisal of the role relevant alternatives play in Goldman's account, particularly with regard to second order knowledge.

WINCH, Christopher. Reading and the Process of Reading. J Phil Educ, 23(2), 303-315, Wint 89.

A critique is offered of psycholinguistic accounts of how we learn to read, particularly the argument of F Smith and K Goodman. The positive argument is that what we call "reading" consists of a diverse family of activities which need to be learned in different ways.

WIND, James P. What Can Religion Offer Bioethics? Hastings Center Rep, 20(4), Supp 18-20, Jl-Ag 90.

WINKLER, Gunnar and HAHN, Toni. Soziale Sicherheit—Triebkraft ökonomischen Wachstums bei der Gestaltung der entwickelten sozialistischen Gesellschaft. Deut Z Phil, 38(1), 64-68, 1990.

Social security is an achievement of socialism. It depends on concrete individual experiences if it will become to a drive of economic growth. Especially young people are meaning, that there are restrictions of social security. In fact, this only exists if it is more than a system of social maintenance and rights. It has to include possibilities for responsible self-determination the quality of life. "From each according to his abilities" in work is required and also "to each according to his performance." It has to be guaranteed the "right of social inequality" following unequal achievement just as have to be excluded leveling equality and misuse of social rights.

WIPPEL, John F. "Thomas Aquinas and the Axiom 'What is Received is Received According to the Mode of the Receiver'" in *A Straight Path: Studies in Medieval Philosophy and Culture*, LINK-SALINGER, Ruth (ed), 279-289. Washington, Cath Univ Amer Pr, 1988.

WIPPEL, John F. Truth in Thomas Aquinas (I). Rev Metaph, 43(2), 295-326, D 89.

WIPPEL, John F. Truth in Thomas Aquinas, (II). Rev Metaph, 43(3), 543-567, Mr 90.

WISSING, Paula (trans) and HADOT, Pierre and DAVIDSON, Arnold (trans). Forms of Life and Forms of Discourse in Ancient Philosophy. Crit Inquiry, 16(3), 483-505, Spr 90.

Dans cette leçon inaugurale de la chaire d'Histoire de la pensée hellénistique et romaine, au Collège de France (Paris), l'auteur se propose de décrire la philosophie antique, non pas du point de vue de l'histoire des doctrines, mais comme un phénomène social et spirituel, comme une quête de la sagesse qui provoque une rupture entre le philosophe et le "quotidien".

Cette approche concrète du phénomène philosophique permet aussi d'aborder les oeuvres philosophiques de l'Antiquité avec une méthodologie nouvelle, notamment en considérant que leur structure et leur contenu sont étroitement liés à des conduites orales.

WITKOWSKI, Lech and PETROWICZ, Lech (trans). The Structure of Social Revolutions (Some Remarks and Hypotheses). Dialec Hum, 15(3-4), 117-127, Sum-Autumn 88.

WITT, Charlotte. Hylomorphism in Aristotle. Apeiron, 22(4), 141-158, D 89.

This paper addresses the question of the relationship between form and matter in an Aristotelian composite substance. The interpretation is based on two ideas. First, matter and form should be understood in terms of potentiality and actuality; second, potentiality and actuality should be understood adverbially, as ways of being. The bulk of the paper is devoted to spelling out what is meant by "ways of being" and how it is that actuality determines potentiality.

WITTBECKER, Alan E. Metaphysical Implications from Physics and Ecology. Environ Ethics, 12(3), 275-282, Fall 90.

I contrast metaphysical implications from physics and ecology and compare them through two concepts, the *field*, primary in physics and borrowed by ecology, and *wholeness*, postulated in ecology and borrowed by physics. I argue that several implications from physics are unacceptably reductive or erroneous and identify an old and a new ecology. Metaphysical implications from the old ecology are quite different from the new ecology, as well as from quantum or Newtonian physics.

WITTICH, Dieter. 40 Jahre Philosophie in der DDR. Deut Z Phil, 37(10-11), 990-1012, 1989.

WITTICH, Dietmar. Zur Problematik von Entwicklung und Fortschritt im soziologischen Werk Max Webers. Deut Z Phil, 38(1), 73-78, 1990.

WITZORECK, Kris. Mens en aarde: Het ecofilosofisch dilemma in het werk van Ludwig Klages. Tijdschr Stud Verlich Denken, 17(1-2), 9-55, 1989.

WOHL, Andrzej and GOLEBIOWSKI, Marek (trans). Whither the Way? Dialec Hum, 16(2), 139-147, Spr 89.

WOISHVILLO, E K. Philosophical-Methodological Aspects of Relevant Logic. Bull Sect Log, 18(4), 146-152, D 89.

WOJCIECHOWSKI, Jerzy A. "Evolution of the Knowledge of Knowledge" in *Issues in Evolutionary Epistemology*, HAHLWEG, Kai (ed), 294-312. Albany, SUNY Pr, 1989.

The paper discusses the incompleteness of our knowledge of knowledge in light of the author's theory of ecology of knowledge. The growing impact and practicalness of knowledge is analyzed in the context of the existential system of man (ESM) composed of humans, nature, knowledge construct and products. The ESM is a dynamic, growing system producing human evolution. Knowledge is a dynamic, evolving, systemic factor conditioned by and conditioning the three other elements of the ESM. It produces interdependence among humans leading to globalization of humanity.

WOJTYLAK, Piotr. Independent Axiomatizability of Sets of Sentences. Annals Pure Applied Log, 44(3), 259-299, O 89.

This expository paper deals with the problem if any set of sentences—in propositional or predicate logic—has or has not an independent axiomatization. There are relatively few subjects in logic which are so sensitive to the choice of language, the choice of the cardinality of sets, where the choice between classical and intuitionistic rules makes so much difference..

WOJTYLAK, Piotr. A Syntactical Characterization of Structural Completeness for Implicational Logics. Bull Sect Log, 19(1), 2-9, Mr 90.

The structurally complete extension of any pure implicational intermediate logic can be given as an extension of the logic with a certain family of schematically defined infinitary rules, the same rules are used for each logic. The cardinality of the family is continuum and in the case of the implicational fragment of intuitionistic logic the family cannot be reduced to a countable one.

WOKLER, Robert. "Our Illusory Chains: Rousseau's Images of Bondage and Freedom" in *Culture et Politique/Culture and Politics*, CRANSTON, Maurice (ed), 41-50. Hawthorne, de Gruyter, 1988.

WOLANDT, Gerd. "Kulturphilosophische Ästhetik: Ihr Verhältnis zur Geschichtlichkeit der Kunst" in *Cultural Hermeneutics of Modern Art: Essays in Honor of Jan Aler*, DETHIER, Hubert (ed), 89-102. Amsterdam, Rodopi, 1989.

WOLENSKI, Jan. Brentano's Criticism of the Correspondence Conception of Truth and Tarski's Semantic Theory. Topoi, 8(2), 105-110, S 89.

The paper confronts Brentano's criticism of the correspondence theory of

truth and Tarski's semantic conception. The author shows that Tarski's conception meets all of Brentano's objections. The special attention is devoted to the problem of circularity.

WOLENSKI, Jan. Deontic Logic and Consequence Operations. Acta Phil Fennica, 38, 314-326, 1985.

This paper presents the standard deontic logic via consequence operations. The main objective of the paper is to formulate the standard system of deontic logic based on the operator of prohibition as a deontic primitive. This is done with the help of so-called dual consequence operation.

WOLÉNSKI, Jan. *Logic and Philosophy in the Lvov-Warsaw School*. Norwell, Kluwer, 1989

WOLF, Dennie. Artistic Learning: What and Where Is It? J Aes Educ, 22(1), 143-155, Spr 88.

WOLF, Susan M. Nancy Beth Cruzan: In No Voice At All. Hastings Center Rep, 20(1), 38-41, Ja-F 90.

This article offers a feminist analysis of the right to refuse life-sustaining treatment. It focuses on the case of Nancy Beth Cruzan, the first right-to-die case to reach the US Supreme Court. The Court should reverse the Missouri court decision, which disregards Cruzan's prior statements and her family's reconstruction of her treatment preferences. The Missouri approach, also embraced by the courts of New York, pursues an exceedingly formalistic rights analysis that robs the patient of her voice, relationships, and body. That approach ignores the way people actually express their feelings about death, and so imprisons them on life-sustaining treatment.

WOLF-GAZO, Ernest. "Whitehead and Berkeley: On the True Nature of Sense Perception" in *Whitehead's Metaphysics of Creativity*, RAPP, Friedrich (ed), 21-33. Albany, SUNY Pr, 1990.

The article shows convincingly that it was Berkeley's critique of Newton's cosmology that got Whitehead seriously started in formulating his basic philosophical problem: the bifurcation of nature.

WOLFF, Kurt H. From Nothing to Sociology. Phil Soc Sci, 19(3), 321-339, S 89.

How can we justify doing anything other than work directly at averting an unprecedented possibility, humanity's doing what previously only nature or God could do: to destroy itself, life, and the earth? How in the face of this can we justify doing, for instance, sociology? But some sociology so grips us (as again other human activities and products can) that this question disappears. Otherwise very different examples of such sociology all vindicate the human subject, demonstrating their confidence and thus our hope in it.

WOLFF, Robert Paul. *About Philosophy (Fourth Edition)*. Englewood Cliffs, Prentice-Hall, 1989

WOLFF, Robert Paul. "Absolute Fruit and Abstract Labor" in *Knowledge and Politics*, DASCAL, Marcelo (ed), 171-187. Boulder, Westview Pr, 1988.

WOLFF, Robert Paul. Social Philosophy: The Agenda for the 'Nineties. J Soc Phil, 20(1-2), 4-17, Spr-Fall 89.

WOLNIEWICZ, Boguslaw. On Atomic Join-Semilattices. Bull Sect Log, 18(3), 105-111, O 89.

WOLTERSTORFF, Nicholas. Evidence, Entitled Belief, and the Gospels. Faith Phil, 6(4), 429-459, O 89.

In this paper I discuss the conditions under which a person is entitled to believe the gospels. And in particular, I have my eye on the Enlightenment thesis that one is not entitled to do so unless one has collected adequate evidence concerning the reliability of the writers and the content of what they said, and has adequately appraised this evidence. There is no way of answering our question, however, without asking it with respect to some interpretation of the gospels. Accordingly I explain and use Hans Frei's contention, that the gospels are identity narratives concerning Jesus of Nazareth.

WOLTERSTORFF, Nicholas. "Philosophy of Art After Analysis and Romanticism" in *Analytic Aesthetics*, SHUSTERMAN, Richard (ed), 32-58. Cambridge, Blackwell, 1989.

WOLTERSTORFF, Nicholas. "The Work of Making a Work of Music" in *What is Music?*, ALPERSON, Philip A , 101-129. New York, Haven, 1987.

WONG, David B. Universalism Versus Love with Distinctions: An Ancient Debate Revived. J Chin Phil, 16(3-4), 251-272, D 89.

WOOD, Allen W. The Emptiness of the Moral Will. Monist, 72(3), 454-483, Jl 89.

Hegel's most famous criticism of Kantian ethics is the "emptiness charge," the claim that Kant's moral principle is "empty of content." This is usually understood as an attack on the "universal law" formulation of Kant's principle of morality. This paper examines the sources of Hegel's charge in Hegel's Jena writings, where it was first expressed, and concludes that the charge is really a criticism of Kant's conception of the good will and the moral worth of actions, based on a rejection of Kantian moral psychology. Kant holds that an action has moral worth only if it is done from the motive of duty. On the basis of an alternative psychology of action, Hegel argues that a good will in Kant's sense would have to be one which acts from a principle which is empty of content. Hegel's basic criticism of Kant is not that the universal law formula is empty of content, but that if Kant begins with the conception of moral worth as acting from duty, then no contentful moral principle is available to him. The paper provides a discussion of the two philosophers' alternative moral psychologies, in order to clarify the real issues raised by the emptiness charge.

WOOD, David. Derrida and "Différance". Evanston, Northwestern Univ Pr, 1988

A collection of six essays by British and American philosophers focussed on Derrida's neologism: "differance," framed by an introductory letter by Derrida (to a Japanese friend) and a substantial interview at the end.

WOOD, David. Heidegger after Derrida. Res Phenomenol, 17, 103-116, 1987.

The trajectory of Derrida's reading of Heidegger makes his claim that Heidegger's thought is "the most...'powerful' defence of...the thought of presence" (Positions) less plausible. Heidegger's use of Eriegnis in Time and Being is so given by extension and dispersion that the thesis of his continuing attachment to the proper must be challenged. The great value of Derrida's reading is precisely that it opens up another reading of Heidegger—one from which the abyssal dimension of all thinking is never wholly absent.

WOOD, David. "The Possibility of Literary Deconstruction: A Reply to Donato" in The Textual Sublime: Deconstruction and Its Differences, SILVERMAN, Hugh J (ed), 53-59. Albany, SUNY Pr, 1990.

It has been argued (e.g., by Eugenio Donato) that literary deconstruction errs when it fails to grasp or to concern itself with the philosophical (especially Heideggerean) roots of Derrida's deconstruction. The importance of this indebtedness is indisputable. But the practice of literary deconstruction also rests on the possibility of recognizing, deploying, and elaborating certain formal schemata (e.g., the complex topologies of closure). Derrida's own readings must necessarily be open to formal description. And Donato's own lucid account of how any text is constituted by a destabilizing redoubling confirms this.

WOOD, Paul B. Thomas Reid's Critique of Joseph Priestley: Context and Chronology. Man Nature, 4, 29-45, 1985.

Drawing largely on his unpublished manuscripts, this paper first examines Thomas Reid's construction of a materialist canon in the period c. 1730 to 1770, and then explores his reaction during the 1770s and 1780s to Joseph Priestley's reformulation of the materialist system.

WOOD, Robert E. "The Phenomenologists" in Reading Philosophy for the Twenty-First Century, MC LEAN, George F (ed), 131-160. Lanham, Univ Pr of America, 1989.

WOODBRIDGE, Frederick J E. "The Son of Apollo": Themes of Plato. Woodbridge, Ox Bow Pr, 1989

This work is an unrevised reprint of a study which was originally published in 1919. The goal is to present an interpretation of the works of Plato as the work of an artist and not a metaphysician. The philosopher's Plato, the author suspects, is "more a product of biased tradition that of Athenian culture." This work attempts an interpretation which is intended to capture the spirit of that Athenian culture. (staff)

WOODBRIDGE, Frederick J E. Education and Philosophy. Thinking, 8(3), 2-9, 1989.

WOODRUFF, Paul. "Plato's Early Theory of Knowledge" in Epistemology (Companions to Ancient Thought: 1), EVERSON, Stephen (ed), 60-84. New York, Cambridge Univ Pr, 1989.

Plato's earlier epistemology concerns the special status of expert knowledge (techne), which Socrates disavows. Implicit in the earlier dialogues is a conception of ordinary, nonexpert knowledge which Socrates does not disavow. Elenchus is used negatively to refute claims to expert knowledge; in its positive role it aids in the discovery of ordinary knowledge. Discovery, not justification, is the positive legacy of the elenchus.

WOODS, John and HUDAK, Brent. By Parity of Reasoning. Inform Log, 11(3), 125-139, Fall 89.

We argue that arguments from analogy are a particular type of meta-argument, viz., arguments by parity of reasoning. Given this, we show that two arguments are analogous when they share a deep structure (which in the case of arguments from analogy amounts to logical form). Hence we

show that such arguments stand or fall together.

WOODS, John. "The Relevance of Relevant Logics" in Directions in Relevant Logic, NORMAN, Jean (ed), 77-86. Norwell, Kluwer, 1989.

Rivalries between classical and relevant logics frequently turn on the status of ex falso quodlibet, which asserts, in effect, that negation-inconsistency implies absolute consistency. The following things are proposed in the present work: (1) The contention is not resolvable in the intuitive pre-theory of entailment. (2) Since deductive rules for the entailment relation are not acceptable as rules of deductive inference, ex falso could be false of inference yet true of entailment. (3) Since relevant logic and classical logic are equally bad theories of inference, they contend only in the theory of entailment, where they are an open problem.

WOODWARD, James. "The Causal Mechanical Model of Explanation" in Scientific Explanation (Minnesota Studies in the Philosophy of Science, Volume XIII), KITCHER, Philip (ed), 357-383. Minneapolis, Univ of Minn Pr, 1989.

WOOLGAR, Steve. "The Ideology of Representation and the Role of the Agent" in Dismantling Truth. Reality in the Post-Modern World, LAWSON, Hilary (ed), 131-144. New York, St Martin's Pr, 1989.

Even virulent relativist-constructivist critiques of science do not dismantle truth per se, but merely substitute sociological, literary and philosophical truths for scientific truths. The more challenging task is to dismantle the ideology of representation, the assumption that reality exists antecedent to its signs. A critical assessment of the role of agency is key. We need to consider literary modes which encourage new sensitivity to representational authority. Since it is insufficient to argue this within existing conventions of representation, the paper finally (a) degenerates into an absurd attempt to effect a rhetorical shift, or (b) suggests some interesting opportunities for exploring alternative literary forms.

WÖRNER, Markus H. Eternity. Irish Phil J, 6(1), 3-26, 1989.

Contemporary interpretations of "eternity" in terms of sempiternity, omnitemporality or atemporality are flawed if they do not primarily refer to "possession of life" (Boethius) or "having one's being" (Aquinas) as systematic starting points.

WORRELL, Dan L and STEAD, W Edward and STEAD, Jean Garner. An Integrative Model for Understanding and Managing Ethical Behavior in Business Organizations. J Bus Ethics, 9(3), 233-242, Mr 90.

Managing ethical behavior is one of the most pervasive and complex problems facing business organizations today. Employees' decisions to behave ethically or unethically are influenced by a myriad of individual and situational factors. Background, personality, decision history, managerial philosophy, and reinforcement are but a few of the factors which have been identified by researchers as determinants of employees' behavior when faced with ethical dilemmas. The literature related to ethical behavior is reviewed in this article, and a model for understanding ethical behavior in business organizations is proposed. It is concluded that managing ethics in business organizations requires that managers engage in a concentrated effort which involves espousing ethics, behaving ethically, developing screening mechanisms, providing ethical training, creating ethics units and reinforcing ethical behavior.

WOZNICKI, Andrew N. Natural Sciences and Natural Philosophy of St Thomas Aquinas. Dialec Hum, 14(1), 219-231, Wint 87.

To resolve the conflicts which exist between sciences and philosophy, one must take into consideration the historical perspective of a given time. In this article the author examines the question of the codependency existing between natural philosophy and sciences in Thomas Aquinas in a twofold way, i.e., his attitude towards both the natural sciences and the philosophy of natural sciences. In this regard the author argues that, although St. Thomas did not always de facto distinguish between natural philosophy and sciences, nevertheless this distinction can be de jure justified in Aquinas's doctrine.

WREEN, Michael. The Asymmetry of Verification and Falsification. Sophia (Australia), 29(1), 42-55, Ap 90.

In a by-now famous—or maybe infamous—paper, "Theology and Verification," John Hick claims that some statements are verifiable but not falsifiable. One of his main claims is that (1) "God exists" is just such an asymmetrical statement, but he also thinks that (2) "I survive my bodily death," and (3) "Pi has three successive sevens in its decimal determination" are verifiable but not falsifiable. Focusing on (2) and (3), I argue that Hick is simply wrong about (2) and if he's right about (3), it's for utterly different reasons than the ones he has offered. (3), in fact, may be verifiable but not falsifiable, but it may well be falsifiable but not verifiable. Statements whose modal status is necessary are like that, I argue, since their status as verifiable (but not falsifiable) or falsifiable (but not verifiable) is a function of their actual truth value. If that's so, however, and if certain epistemic criteria have to be met in order to verify or falsify a necessary statement, then Hick's entire approach in respect to (1) is misdirected. His driving, then, even if flawless, is in the wrong direction.

WREEN, Michael. Jealousy. Nous, 23(5), 635-652, D 89.

Philosophical interest in the emotions has revived of late, with the focus being, in a number of cases, the proper analysis of particular emotions, and the approach taken decidedly more interdisciplinary than previous decades would have tolerated. A case in point is jealousy, the topic of this paper. What I'll be doing is focusing on the concept of jealousy and attempting to answer the question, What is jealousy? Three recent theories of the emotion will be exposed and subjected to criticism, but only in order to gather material for a positive theory of jealousy. After developing and defending that theory, its implications for the philosophy of mind and for ethics will be briefly explored.

WREEN, Michael. Light from Darkness, From Ignorance Knowledge. Dialectica, 43(4), 299-314, 1989.

This paper is a critical examination of *argumentum ad ignorantiam*, or arguing from ignorance. *Ad ignorantiam* is regarded as a fallacy, and certainly no route to knowledge, by most philosophers. However, case studies of *ad ignorantiam* are almost nonexistent, and theoretical discussions few in number. Thus this paper begins with a number of case studies. From them some morals are drawn. The morals concern the interpretation and evaluation of arguments in general and the nature and epistemic value of *ad ignorantiam* in particular. Two theoretical discussions of the argument-type are next considered, those of Richard Robinson and (in a jointly authored paper) John Woods and Douglas Walton. I conclude that there is no general fallacy of *ad ignorantiam*—no argument is fallacious just because it's an *ad ignorantiam*—and that sometimes no reason is good reason.

WREEN, Michael. Once Is Not Enough? Brit J Aes, 30(2), 149-158, Ap 90.

One of the things that Arthur Danto is known for is his claim that, as far as works of art are concerned, perceptual indistinguishability doesn't guarantee numerical distinctness. While not doubting that, I do doubt whether the case of Pierre Menard, a case that Danto brings up in support of his contention and lays heavy stress on, actually lends it any support. I expose Danto's argument, critique it, and go on to argue that there's positive reason for thinking that Pierre Menard didn't create a new *Quixote* at all. "His" *Quixote* is simply Cervantes'. Once is enough, as far as the tale of The Knight of Sorrowful Countenance is concerned.

WREN, Thomas. Principles and Moral Argumentation. J Chin Phil, 16(3-4), 309-315, D 89.

It is often assumed that a basic difference between Western and Chinese modes of moral reasoning is that Western moral discourse is a top-down, syllogistic sort of argumentation, as found in moral philosophy courses. I claim, on the contrary, that this is not an accurate or basic distinction, since in its practical use ("in vivo") the moral discourse of both cultures is a communal activity, in which reasons for action are presented, reconsidered and revised with the ultimate hope of securing not only cooperation but also mutual respect. The cultural differences in moral reasoning have to do with the methods whereby members of the respective cultures try to achieve this transcultural goal.

WRIGHT, Crispin. Misconstruals Made Manifest: A Response to Simon Blackburn. Midwest Stud Phil, 14, 48-67, 1989.

WRIGHT, Crispin. The Verification Principle: Another Puncture—Another Patch. Mind, 98(392), 611-622, O 89.

WRIGHT, Crispin. Wittgenstein's Later Philosophy of Mind: Sensation, Privacy, and Intention. J Phil, 86(11), 622-634, N 89.

WRIGHT, Edmond. Inspecting Images: A Reply to Smythies. Philosophy, 65(252), 225-228, Ap 90.

This is an answer to J R Smythies' comments (*Philosophy*, 1989) on my article 'Inspecting Images' (*Philosophy*, 1983). There are three points at issue. The first concerns the possibility of scientific account of subjective phenomena; I show that we are in agreement that this is possible. The second arose out of Smythies' misunderstanding over my views on Ryle's version of the Homunculus Objection; I agree with him that this is obsolete. The third concerned the equation of the self with the body-image; again I show that, with Smythies, I reject this.

WRIGHT, Edmond. New Representationalism. J Theor Soc Behav, 20(1), 65-92, Mr 90.

A detailed summary of new representationalist theory, bringing out criteria that distinguish it from sense-datum theory and answering the familiar objections against representational theories. The core of the article is an analysis of the intersubjective parameter of human perception, which is characterized by a systematic ambiguity of evolutionary value. J B Maund's and Virgil C Aldrich's distinction of sensory-field state (nonepistemic, but in principle scientifically describable) from perceived-entity state (epistemic) is shown to be an essential pillar of the theory. The article concludes by making plain the scope of the theory, and this is claimed to be one of its strengths.

WRIGHT, Kathleen. Comments on Michel Haar's Paper, "The Question of Human Freedom in the Later Heidegger". S J Phil, SUPP(28), 17-22, 1989.

After *Being and Time*, Heidegger claims that freedom is not a "property of man" but that man is the "possibility of [the] freedom" of Being. In my commentary on Haar's discussion of the absence of individual autonomy in this concept of freedom, I question the absence of *Miteinandersein*, of human solidarity, friendship, and love. I propose that the disappearance of these forms of shared freedom (versus freedom as someone's "property") is connected to Heidegger's rejection of Kantian liberalism in his 1930 lecture course, *On the Essence of Human Freedom*, and his consequent affirmation of National Socialism.

WRIGHT, Larry. *Practical Reasoning*. San Diego, Harcourt Brace Jov, 1989

WRIGHT, M R. "Presocratic Minds" in *The Person and the Human Mind: Issues in Ancient and Modern Philosophy*, GILL, Christopher (ed), 207-225. New York, Clarendon/Oxford Pr, 1989.

The essay aims to show that materialist theories of mind and its activities had their origins in the Presocratics. Firstly the external objects available for perception and thought are considered, then the complementary thinking subject, i.e., what it is in the individual which can respond. Thirdly there is the mutual reaction between object thought and thinking subject in which the ability to be aware of the outside world is dependent on physical make-up, both continually changing as a result of internal and external fluctuations; but some of the difficulties may be overcome by intellectual effort and perseverance.

WRIGHT, N Dale and MC KONKIE, Stanford S. "Introduction" in *Papers on the Ethics of Administration*, WRIGHT, N Dale (ed), 1-20. Albany, SUNY Pr, 1988.

WRIGHT, N Dale (ed). *Papers on the Ethics of Administration*. Albany, SUNY Pr, 1988

This is a collection of ten invited essays covering a wide range of topics from moral philosophy to applied ethics in administration. Interestingly, most all of the essays return to the familiar theme that organizational ethics is dependent on personal ethics. The essays describe a variety of ideas about how contemporary management can incorporate ideas like personal integrity, mutual trust, and true concern for others as the basis of organizational life. The authors are Norman E Bowie, F Neil Brady, David K Hart, David L Norton, J Bonner Ritchie, John A Rohr, William G Scott, Kenneth D Walters, and Margaret J Wheatley.

WRIGHT, Paul H. "The Essence of Personal Relationships and Their Value for the Individual" in *Person to Person*, GRAHAM, George (ed), 15-31. Philadelphia, Temple Univ Pr, 1989.

This chapter addresses two questions from the perspective of a socio-psychological theory: (1) What makes a human relationship personal? (2) Why are personal relationsips so highly valued? Relationships are held to be personal, as opposed to impersonal, to the degree that they involve nonobligatory interaction and a personalized interest and concern between the partners. They are valued because they are an important means of fulfilling a definable set of self-referent motives, i.e., they provide a sense of individuality, ego support, self-affirmation, utility, and security. Such rewardingness does not imply inevitably selfish motivation as "selfishness" is commonly defined.

WRIGHT, R M. The Origins of Political Theory. Polis, 7(2), 75-104, 1988.

The aim of the article is to show that the origins of political theory antedate Plato and Aristotle. A variety of early sources (including Homer, Hesiod, the elegists, Herodotus and some early Presocratics) provides evidence of reflection on key political concepts. These cover the criteria for authority, the origins and patterns of government, the claims of justice and mutual obligations, obedience to law versus anarchy, the role of tradition, nationalism, cooperation and consent, and the groundwork for the sophistic debate of law as convention in conflict with the natural rights of the stronger.

WROBLEWSKI, Jerzy and DASCAL, M. Transparency and Doubt: Understanding and Interpretation in Pragmatics and in Law. Theoria (Spain), 4(11), 427-450, F-My 89.

WRONA, Vera. Zum Philosophieverständnis bedeutender Persönlichkeiten der II. Internationale. Deut Z Phil, 37(10-11), 967-978, 1989.

Es werden theoretisch-methodische Fragestellungen aufgeworfen, die es besser ermöglichen sollen, das Verständnis der marxistischen Philosophie durch führende Theoretiker der II Internationale adäquat zu erfassen. Die Reihenfolge des Werdens einzelner Erkenntnisse im Marxismus wie ihres Umsetzens in politische Praxis geben kein methodisches Scheme ab, wonach philosophische Orientierungen bei einzelnen Persönlichkeiten "zurechtgestutzt" werden können. Verdeutlicht wird dieses Vorgehen u.a. an A Bebel, K Kautsky, G Plechanow, E Bernstein, F Mehring, R Luxemburg und K Liebknecht.

WUKETITS, Franz M (ed) and HOYNINGEN-HUENE, Paul (ed). *Reductionism and Systems Theory in the Life Sciences: Some Problems and Perspectives*. Norwell, Kluwer, 1989

WUKETITS, Franz M. "Organisms, Vital Forces, and Machines" in *Reductionism and Systems Theory in the Life Sciences: Some Problems and Perspectives*, HOYNINGEN-HUENE, Paul (ed), 3-28. Norwell, Kluwer, 1989.

WUNDERLICH, Gene. Agricultural Technology, Wealth, and Responsibility. J Agr Ethics, 3(1), 21-35, 1990.

Responsibility as a dual to human rights is presented as a moral alternative to extended, compex systems of animal and ecological rights. This simple idea of responsibility is then applied to four levels of agricultural technology: animal (nature) rights, conservation, organization of agriculture, and people versus planet relationships. The stewardship argument is freed from at least some of the complications of animal rights and ecology, but leaves responsibility with humans to do the right thing.

WURZER, Wilhelm S. "The Critical Difference: Adorno's Aesthetic Alternative" in *The Textual Sublime: Deconstruction and Its Differences*, SILVERMAN, Hugh J (ed), 213-221. Albany, SUNY Pr, 1990.

WYGANT, Steven A and JENSEN, Larry C. The Developmental Self-Valuing Theory: A Practical Approach for Business Ethics. J Bus Ethics, 9(3), 215-225, Mr 90.

Ethics in business has been an increasingly controversial and important topic of discussion over the last decade. Debate continues about whether ethics should be a part of business, but also includes how business can implement ethical theory in day-to-day operations. Most discussions focus on either traditional moral philosophy, which offers little of practical value for the business community, or psychological theories of moral reasoning, which have been shown to be flawed and incomplete. The theory presented here is called the Developmental Self-Valuing Theory, and adapts the general psychological theory of Albert Bandura for ethics in business. (edited)

WYLLER, Truls. Truth and Meaning in the Works of Tugendhat and Davidson (in Serbo-Croatian). Filozof Istraz, 30(3), 955-971, 1989.

In dem Aufsatz wird versucht, Ernst Tugendhats bisher wenig beachteten Neuansatz in der sprachanalytischen Philosophie durch eine Kontrastierung mit Donald Davidsons Theorien zu präsentieren. Diese beiden Autoren möchten, einen *semantischen Wahrheitsbegriff* aus sozial zugänglichen linguistischen und aussersprachlichen Faktoren gewinnen. Davidson betont, dass man nicht—wie in der empiristischen und idealistischen Tradition—die Bedeutung unserer Wörter unabhängig von ihrer Wirklichkeitsbezug in wahren Urteilen erfassen kann. Im Gegensatz sowohl zur traditionellen Philosophie wie zu Davidson gelingt indessen Tugendhat der Nachweis, dass der Bedeutungsgehalt eines Begriffes sich behaviouristisch in *Lern*situationen klären lässt, die Wirklichkeits*referenz* der Wortverwendung hingegen nicht: Letztere basiert auf Raumzeitpunkten und ist somit eher *intentionalen* als *kausalen* Charakters.

WYND, William R and MAGER, John. The Business and Society Course: Does It Change Student Attitudes? J Bus Ethics, 8(6), 487-491, Je 89.

The purpose of this research was to determine if there is a significant difference in the attitudes of students toward situations involving ethical decisions before and after taking a course in Business and Society. A simulated before and after design was used with Clark's personal business ethics and social responsibility scale serving as the measurement instrument. The result of the study indicated that the Business and Society class had no statistically significant impact on student attitudes.

WYSCHOGROD, Edith. "Derrida, Levinas and Violence" in *Derrida and Deconstruction*, SILVERMAN, Hugh J (ed), 182-200. New York, Routledge, 1989.

Levinas interprets violence in terms both of anonymous being, being imagined as prior to the emergence of existents, and of the forces of economy and polity that together comprise totality. Knowing as representation is in complicity with war but, as the concealment of being's violence, belongs to a different ontic framework. Derrida tracks down this concealment in his analyses of such "abstracts" as *differance*, dissemination and the logic of supplementarity. In so doing, he dissolves anonymous being and transcendence as described by Levinas into time-bound, intrahistorical

functions.

WYSCHOGROD, Edith. Interview with Emmanuel Levinas: December 31, 1982. Phil Theol, 4(2), 105-118, Wint 89.

This interview with Levinas was conducted and translated by Edith Wyschogrod. (edited)

WYSS, Dieter. La conciencia onírica: Observaciones sobre el problema del inconsciente. Rev Filosof (Costa Rica), 26, 3-8, D 88.

Dream life has been important in all times, although it is not until this century that it has been analyzed from a scientific standpoint. Nevertheless, many dream phenomena continue without explanation. In our dreams, we perceive ourselves free from our waking world. We are thus in liberty to create another world outside the time corresponding to our own existence. Any given rational explanation will comprise only part of these phenomena.

XENOS, Nicholas. *Scarcity and Modernity*. New York, Routledge, 1989

XICHENG, Yin. Soviet "New Political Thinking": Reflections on the Issues of Peace and War, War and Politics. Stud Soviet Tho, 38(1), 105-109, Jl 89.

Taking the basic principle of the "new political thinking" as the basis, this paper introduces and comments on the Soviet new concept concerning the issues of war and peace, war and politics: Nuclear war is no longer the continuation of politics, what follows nuclear war is not peace and revolution but the destruction of human civilization, it is the value of humankind that should be the only criterion for making options, and therefore, international relations should be completely democratized and humanized.

XUFANG, Zhan. Changes in the Attitude of Chinese Philosophical Circles Towards Pragmatism. Stud Soviet Tho, 38(1), 99-104, Jl 89.

XUNZI and KNOBLOCK, John (trans). *Xunzi: A Translation and Study of the Complete Works, Volume II—Books 7-16*. Stanford, Stanford Univ Pr, 1990

YABLO, Stephen. Truth, Definite Truth, and Paradox. J Phil, 86(10), 539-541, O 89.

YACK, Bernard. Natural Right and Aristotle's Understanding of Justice. Polit Theory, 18(2), 216-237, My 90.

This paper outlines and defends a reinterpretation of Aristotle's understanding of natural right and its relationship to justice. It argues that his claim in the *Nicomachean Ethics* about the existence of natural as well as conventional right does not commit him to the idea that there corresponds to every particular situation one inherently just state of affairs against which we should measure the justice of our actions and opinions. Aristotelian natural right refers to a *kind* of judgment about justice that develops naturally in political communities, rather than to a higher *standard* of justice.

YANDELL, Keith E. The Non-Epistemic Explanation of Religious Belief. Int J Phil Relig, 27(1-2), 87-120, Ap 90.

YAO, Jiehou. Die Kommunikation zwischen der Philosophie Chinas und Europas um die Wende zum 20 Jahrhundert. Conceptus, 24(61), 17-26, 1990.

Due to the unbalance of both social and philosophical development, the first direct communication between Chinese and western philosophy in the modern times shows complicated situation and implies profound sense. This communication has positive and passive duality, which can be found in four theoretical problems: evolutionism and dialectical thought of change and becoming; cosmology and outlook of nature exploring the relationship between mind and matter, human being and nature; theory of knowledge; philosophical understanding of human being. The conclusions drawn from the communication are four points: endogeny and national nature of philosophical tradition, necessity of mutual communication between different traditions; the principle of autonomy and reasonable selection in the communication; historical wholeness of mutual understanding; discriminative and analytical assimilation for promoting communication between the oriental and western philosophy.

YAPP, Brian. Some Reflections on Intelligence and the Nature—Nurture Issue. J Phil Educ, 23(2), 317-320, Wint 89.

YASUGI, Mariko. The Machinery of Consistency Proofs. Annals Pure Applied Log, 44(1-2), 139-152, O 89.

This survey tries to explicate the true aspect of the existing consistency proofs through reduction methods as an exact science. It analyses the machinery of the consistency proofs as follows. Its constituents are (c1) formalization of a formal system (S) to be studied, (c2) a proof-theoretical order structure (J), and (c3) a universe of 'mechanisms' (U). Its operations are (o1) the reduction of S by means of J and (o2) the accessibility proof for J by means of U. From this analysis, we proclaim that the major consequence of the machinery is the 'information extraction' from a formal proof by a mechanism in U.

YASUMOTO, Masahiro. Algebraic Extensions in Nonstandard Models and Hilbert's Irreducibility Theorem. J Sym Log, 53(2), 470-480, Je 88.

YEPES, Ricardo. El origen de la energeia en Aristóteles. Anu Filosof, 22(1), 93-109, 1989.

YETTER, David N. Quantales and (Noncommutative) Linear Logic. J Sym Log, 55(1), 41-64, Mr 90.

A semantics for a non-commutative version of J-Y Girard's linear logic in terms of Mulvey's models for the logic of quantum mechanics (quantales). A geometric proof theory in terms of drawings on surfaces labled by formulae is given, and Cut-elimination for the system is proved using geometrical rewrites.

YI-JIE, Tang. "On the Unity of Man and Heaven" in *Man and Nature: The Chinese Tradition and the Future*, TANG, Yi-Jie (ed), 13-24. Lanham, Univ Pr of America, 1989.

The relationship between man and heaven is the most fundamental issue in Chinese philosophy. The main traditional Chinese philosopher, whether Confucianist or Taoist, has taken as his main task to demonstrate or explain how heaven is integrated with man, and accordingly, how knowledge is integrated with practice, how feeling is integrated with scenery. These integrations tell us the way to be human, and to be in harmony with nature, society, other people, and oneself in both body and mind, inside and outside. From this point, we can say that Chinese philosophy is the philosophy of harmony.

YODER, John H and MOUW, Richard J. Evangelical Ethics and the Anabaptist-Reformed Dialogue. J Relig Ethics, 17(2), 121-137, Fall 89.

The recent resurgence of evangelical social action has been accompanied by some serious attention to issues in ethical thought. Evangelical scholars have been engaged in a search for ethical "roots," for traditions of theological-ethical discourse that can give shape to twentieth century ethical explorations. Of special interest to many in this regard are the longstanding tensions between Anabaptist and Reformed thought. In this essay we argue against the "received wisdom" that there is a strict polarity between these two perspectives. The ethical differences between the Reformed and Anabaptist communities are in fact "intra-family" ones that emerge out of some important commonalities. The exploration of these commonalities, we suggest, is crucial for the development of a healthier evangelical ethical perspective.

YOKOTA, Shin'ichi. Axiomatization of the First-Order Intermediate Logics of Bounded Kripkean Heights I. Z Math Log, 35(5), 415-421, 1989.

Let *n* be an arbitrarily fixed natural number. The author establishes finite axiomatization of the first-order intermediate logic determined by the class of all Kripke frames of height at most *n* with domains varying under the inclusion requirement, which logic had been known to be different from the first-order extension of its propositional counterpart (unless *n* is zero or one). Continued to Part 2 (to appear in the same journal).

YOKOTA, Shin-ichi. Some Modal Propositional Logics Containing CO:8. Rep Math Log, 22, 51-63, 1988.

The author researched S1, S0.9, and surrounding modal systems. His improvement on algebraic and frame semantics due to Shukla and to Cresswell with corrections to Routley and Montgomery's errors (cf. *NDJFL*, vols. 11, 13, 17, respectively) is reported. Shukla's "initial hope" is confirmed. As a basic system C0.8 is introduced. A new axiomatization of S1 is presented. As for the relation in a frame the notation in the author's old papers on (propositional and first-order) intuitionistic modal logics (*Commentarii Math Univ Sancti Pauli*, vols.34, 36) is employed.

YONAH, Yossi. The Rational Status of A-Moral Choices (in Hebrew). Iyyun, 39(2), 123-138, Ap 90.

What is the rational status of personal values which do not fall within the province of morality? This question will be addressed in this paper against the background of the instrumental conception of rationality. The instrumental conception purports to provide an account of human conduct which accomplishes both descriptive and normative tasks, using the same assumptions. That is, the instrumental conception purports to provide the criteria by which an action can be appraised as being either intelligible or unintelligible, and those by which it is appraised as being either rational or irrational. The purpose of this paper is to show why the instrumental conception cannot live up to its promise. (edited)

YOSHIOKA, Hiroshi. Adorno After Adorno (in Japanese). Bigaku, 40(2), 25-35, Autumn 89.

There is one (seemingly) serious question: Is any theory of art possible after Adorno? Seriousness comes from using Adorno as the name of basic conditions which our culture cannot escape. After Adorno "it goes without saying that nothing concerning art goes without saying" (the beginning sentence of "Aesthetic Theory"). This statement sound ambiguous, for on the

one hand it suggests an "anything goes" situation of postmodern culture, and on the other hand the fact that, this situation, ceasing to be privileged avantgardist experience, has become a matter of course. In order to read Adorno today, it is important to put stress on the latter aspect, and this enables us to go farther into considering the relationship between modernism and mass culture than Adorno himself did in terms of "Culture Industry." From that standpoint I hope we can reconsider postmodernism (along with its theoretical counterpart called poststructuralism) by stepping out of modernist fear of cultural contamination (A Huyssen), which many contemporary theories still fail to get rid of.

YOUNG, Ernlé W D. *Alpha and Omega: Ethics at the Frontiers of Life and Death*. Reading, Addison-Wesley, 1989

YOUNG, Henry James. Process Theology and Black Liberation: Testing the Whiteheadian Metaphysical Foundations. Process Stud, 18(4), 259-267, Wint 89.

YOUNG, Iris Marion (ed) and ALLEN, Jeffner (ed). *The Thinking Muse: Feminism and Modern French Philosophy*. Bloomington, Indiana Univ Pr, 1989

Marking a radical shift in the traditional philosophical separation between muse (female) and thinker (male), this book revises the scope and methods of philosophical reflection. These engaging essays by American feminists bring together feminist philosophy, existential phenomenology, and recent currents in French poststructuralist thought. The authors consider a broad range of modern French philosophers, including Camus, Cixous, Derrida, Foucault, Irigaray, Kristeva, Merleau-Ponty, Sartre, and Wittig. While finding gaps, biases, and silences in their writings, the authors show that the thinkers discussed provide fruitful modes of discourse, both for critique and for positive reflection. At the same time the essays illustrate the creation of feminist philosophical styles that give rise to positive accounts of women's experience. The editors provide an excellent introductory overview, making this an ideal book for courses in feminist theory and philosophy and modern French thought.

YOUNG, Robert. Equality of Opportunity. Pac Phil Quart, 70(3), 261-280, S 89.

I argue that any effective equalization of opportunities, in a substantive and not merely a formal sense, requires the equalization of life-changes. Only then can the *egalitarian* character of equality of opportunity be realised. The proposal is to make available to each a bundle or opportunities, supplemented where necessary with compensatory measures, to produce comparably desirable life-chances for all.

YOUNG, Robin Darling. Recent Interpretations of Early Christian Asceticism. Thomist, 54(1), 123-140, Ja 90.

YOUNGNER, Stuart J. "Advance Directives and the Denial of Death: Should the Conflict be Resolved?" in *Advance Directives in Medicine*, HACKLER, Chris (ed), 127-139. New York, Praeger, 1989.

YOUNGS, William H and HOWARD, George S. A Research Strategy for Studying Telic Human Behavior. J Mind Behav, 10(4), 393-411, Autumn 89.

Numerous writers have recently called for reform in psychological theorizing and research methodology designed to appreciate the teleological, active agent capacities of humans. This paper presents three studies that probe individual's abilities to volitionally control their eating behavior. These investigations suggest one way that researchers might consider the operation of telic powers in human action. Rather than seeing teleological explanations as rivals to the more traditional causal explanations favored in psychological research, this paper elaborates a position that sees human volition as a causal force embedded in (and influenced by) the traditional causal influences studied in psychological research. Finally, the theoretical and methodological refinements suggested here and elsewhere are seen against the backdrop of a philosophy of science that sees change as a more gradual, evolutionary process, rather than the Kuhnian, revolutionary process.

YOURGRAU, Palle. *Reflections on Kurt Gödel* by Hao Wang. Phil Phenomenol Res, 50(2), 391-408, D 89.

In *Reflections on Kurt Gödel*, Hao Wang has argued persuasively that Gödel should be taken seriously as a philosopher who has much to contribute to areas of contemporary philosophical concern. I discuss some of the central aspects of Gödel's philosophy, as Professor Wang presents it, and try to clarify, interrelate, and, in part, defend some of the less well known, as well as the less well appreciated, ideas and suggestions of Gödel's.

YOUZHENG, Li. Some Basic Problems in the Development of the Human Sciences in China Today. Stud Soviet Tho, 38(1), 77-98, Jl 89.

It outlines the structure of the Chinese humanities as a whole, especially philosophy, literature and history, pointing out its basic deficiencies and difficulties as well as recent progress caused by culture tensions, historical setbacks and quality of Chinese intellectuals. The paper also hints the intricate relationship between academic life, tradition, politics and ideology. For advancing and modernizing Chinese human sciences, the genuine situations and backgrounds should be understood at first.

YOVEL, Yirmiyahu. *Kant and the Philosophy of History*. Princeton, Princeton Univ Pr, 1989

YOXEN, Edward. The Limits of Public Participation in Science Revealed. Phil Soc Act, 15(3-4), 87-101, Jl-D 89.

YUNIS, Harvey. Rhetoric as Instruction: A Response to Vickers on Rhetoric in the *Laws*. Phil Rhet, 23(2), 125-135, 1990.

ZABALLOS, Juan Carlos. San Agustín y Unamuno. Augustinus, 34(135-136), 355-388, Jl-D 89.

ZABELL, Sandy L. The Rule of Succession. Erkenntnis, 31(2-3), 283-321, S 89.

ZABLUDOWSKI, Andrzej. On Synonymy and Ontic Modalities. Midwest Stud Phil, 14, 199-205, 1989.

ZAFRANY, Samy. On Analytic Filters and Prefilters. J Sym Log, 55(1), 315-322, Mr 90.

ZAGANO, Phyllis. Poetry as the Naming of the Gods. Phil Lit, 13(2), 340-349, O 89.

An analysis of the way in which poetry allows us to name reality and establish ourselves in relation to reality. If we are sure of our own existence as both fact and beyond our control, we can also assert (by naming) the existence of other realities we do not control, but which we can exist in the face of because of our ability to name. Exegesis of Martin Heidegger's "Hölderlin and the Essence of Poetry" and "What Are Poets For?" with reference to Wallace Stevens's "Sunday Morning."

ZAGLADIN, V V. Perestroika as a Continuation of the October Revolution. Dialec Hum, 15(3-4), 233-239, Sum-Autumn 88.

ZAGORIN, Perez. Hobbes on our Minds. J Hist Ideas, 51(2), 317-336, Ap-Je 90.

ZAGZEBSKI, Linda. Recent Work in the Philosophy of Religion. Phil Books, 31(1), 1-6, Ja 90.

ZAHN, M. Contemporary Trends in the Interpretation of Kant's Critical Philosophy. S Afr J Phil, 8(3-4), 129-147, N 88.

In this article the questions about the reason for the lively interest shown in our age for Kant's philosophy and the manifold way of its interpretation are raised. The latter finds its explanation, on one hand, in the manner in which the highly complex approach to the transcendental-critical enterprise represents itself systematically and conceptually. On the other, interpretation does not always reach Kant's high problem level. Again and again, this philosophy is subjected to perspectives which are totally foreign to it. This also holds true for the Kant interpretation that has made the greatest impact on the traditional Kant conception, that of German idealism. Subsequently it is demonstrated, by reference to five different types of Kant interpretation, that, already in Kant's lifetime, a great variety of controversial interpretations of the critical enterprise existed. From neo-Kantianism as the point of departure, the 'ontological Kant interpretation' of our century is discussed. Then, from the great number of contemporary Kant interpretations, six that are especially characteristic are selected for discussion, namely, those of Strawson, Popper, Heisenberg, Vollmer, Apel and Henrich.

ZAHN, Manfred. Hegel vor dem Forum der Wissenschaftslehre Fichtes: Reinhard Lauths Untersuchungen zum Frühidealismus. Kantstudien, 81(2), 221-231, 1990.

ZAKHARYASHCHEV, M V and CHAGROV, A V. On Halldén-Completeness of Intermediate and Modal Logics. Bull Sect Log, 19(1), 21-24, Mr 90.

ZALABARDO, José L. Rules, Communities and Judgements. Critica, 21(63), 33-58, D 89.

I endorse Kripke's (Wittgenstein's) conclusion that the standard of correct application required by the notion of rule-following can only be made sense of in terms of intersubjective agreement. This is not to be taken, as Kripke does, merely as providing assertibility conditions, but rather as a genuine account of what normativity consists in. As Blackburn has pointed out, this result entails that the notion of objective judgment is dependent, in a sense, on the shared inclinations of the members of the community. But since the sceptical paradox admits of no noncommunal solution, it has to be inclination-independence of the notion of objective judgment that has to be given up.

ZAMORA, Alvaro. El Flaubert de Sartre. Rev Filosof (Costa Rica), 26, 65-70, D 88.

We are considering here the conceptual way and method that Sartre uses to write *The Idiot of the Family*. Although this novel-essay is presented as a continuation of *Questions of Method*, we tried to determine the theoric articulation from earlier publications.

ZANARDI, William J. Consumer Responsibility from a Social Systems Perspective. Int J Applied Phil, 5(1), 57-66, Spr 90.

Are personal consumption of illegal drugs, an individual's purchase of pornographic materials, the shopper's casual selection of boycotted grapes morally blameworthy acts? Some have claimed, for instance, that recreational use of illegal drugs makes one an accomplice in murders occurring elsewhere in the economic cycle of drug production and exchange. Is this so? The paper reviews the difficulties in answering this question. Problems of probability and prediction block efforts to determine complicity or culpability. The paper concludes with a study of reasonable risk-taking and "risk-putting" as a way around the problems.

ZANARDI, William. Higher Education and the Crisis of Historicism. J Thought, 24(1-2), 75-93, Spr-Sum 89.

Why is it so difficult for faculty to achieve consensus on university requirements for liberally educated undergraduates? To this question I respond with reviews of the nineteenth-century crisis of historicism, later but similar crises in other disciplines, and their implications for educational theory and practice. I go on to suggest a curriculum design that incorporates cultural multiplicity and challenges faculty and students to reenact portions of the cultural journey from consensus to crisis. Finally, drawing on the work of Bernard Lonergan, I suggest how students might take the next step in that cultural journey.

ZANER, Richard M. Medicine and Dialogue. J Med Phil, 15(3), 303-325, Je 90.

Physicians have for some time been questioning the prevailing view of medicine as applied biology. It is urged that medicine needs to be reconceived so as to provide appropriate emphasis on the patient's experience and understanding of illness. After reviewing these arguments and the scientific paradigm underlying the received view in light of certain themes in medicine's history and of current thinking, Pellegrino's thesis is analyzed: medicine should be understood as an inherently moral enterprise, a form of praxis focused on "the healing relationship." Understanding the illness experience and the professed healer's "compassion" supports Pellegrino's view, and suggests that the healing relationship is perhaps best conceived as a form of dialogue.

ZANGWILL, Nick. Quasi-Quasi-Realism. Phil Phenomenol Res, 50(3), 583-594, Mr 90.

At first sight, Simon Blackburn seems to be right to emphasize that Humean 'projectivism' in morality is not or should not be associated with the 'subjectivist' view that moral judgments are beliefs about attitudes. The view that moral judgments express attitudes which we project onto the world is not a reductionist theory. This seems to remove various objections to projectivism, such as that it makes moral truth 'mind-dependent'. The author pursues the idea that the attempt to earn some form of mind-independence for a subjectivist can be at least as successful as the quasi-realist's attempt to earn it for projectivism. The aim is not so much to *succeed* in capturing mind-independence as to achieve *parity* of success with quasi-realism. (edited)

ZANNONI, Diane and MC KENNA, Edward and WADE, Maurice. Rawls and the Minimum Demands of Justice. J Value Inq, 24(2), 85-108, Ap 90.

We demonstrate that by focusing on Rawls's view of the nature of the person and on his use of the Aristotelian Principle it is possible to counter many of the criticisms made against Rawls. In particular, we show why Rawls is correct in asserting that individuals in the original position will not use the principle of insufficient reason to assign probabilities to unknown states of nature, nor will they accept the principle of utility for the purposes of distributing primary goods. We then show, however, that the use of the Aristotelian Principle is more likely to lead to a distribution principle which guarantees minimum basic necessities than it is to lead to the difference principle.

ZANOTTI, Mario and SUPPES, Patrick. Conditions on Upper and Lower Probabilities to Imply Probabilities. Erkenntnis, 31(2-3), 323-345, S 89.

In this paper we prove four theorems about the existence of a probability measure when a pair of upper and lower probability measures satisfy certain conditions. Essential to the proofs is the use of an approach we use in two earlier papers on qualitative probability. The approach is to move from a Boolean algebra of events to the semigroup of extended indicator functions generated by these events. This semigroup and others closely related to it are useful structures for studying various foundational questions in probability.

ZAPASNIK, Stanislaw and PETROWICZ, Lech (trans). Tolerance and the Question of Rationality. Dialec Hum, 14(1), 147-158, Wint 87.

Analysing the situation that has arisen in the humanities at the close of the 20th century, the philosopher cannot avoid the question of whether it is possible to create a philosophy that would be universal knowledge expressing the experience of people living in various areas of civilization. The continuing cultural differences and ideological contradictions make the answer to this question one of the most important moral imperatives. However, the philosopher cannot ignore the fact that the contemporary sciences dealing with culture have considerably undermined the trust in the form of reason that was shaped in Western culture over the past two hundred years. Today one finds it more difficult than ever before to free oneself from historical relativism. Nonetheless, the overcoming of historism is a necessity, since historism gives rise to skepticism, and the latter could only mean the destruction of Western culture. This fundamental question is at the root of the present essay. The aims of the essay are limited. It raises the question of whether the idea of tolerance could contribute to the creation of a new, constructive philosophical universalism.

ZAPPONE, Giuseppe. Heidegger e la sua intuizione di fondo. Sapienza, 42(2), 167-170, Ap-Je 89.

ZAWADZKI, Sylwester and PROTALINSKI, Grzegorz (trans). The Problem of Bureaucracy in a Socialist State. Dialec Hum, 16(2), 93-108, Spr 89.

ZAYTZEFF, Veronique (trans). Merleau-Ponty and Pseudo-Sartreanism. Int Stud Phil, 21(3), 3-47, 1989.

In *Adventures of the Dialectic*, Merleau-Ponty critiqued and found unsatisfactory Sartre's interpretation of the proletariat and of the Communist Party in *The Communists and Peace* (Les Communistes et la paix). Sartre never addressed the critique. Quoting extensively from Sartre's writings, Simone de Beauvoir seeks to demonstrate that Merleau-Ponty never understood Sartre's philosophy and utterly misinterpreted him and his ideas. This article by Simone de Beauvoir is one of her few technical philosophical essays. She seemingly departs from her ambivalent position toward Sartre's theory in her novels, and here, emphatically defends Sartre's theory of freedom.

ZEITZ, James V. Erich Przywara on Ultimate Reality and Meaning: *Deus Semper Major* 'God Ever Greater'. Ultim Real Mean, 12(3), 192-201, S 89.

Overall encyclopedic synthesis of Przywara's major insights and significance in research on ultimate reality and meaning. Gives a biographical sketch, his metaphysical method of "balance-in-tension," and examples of how he applies it to the cultural and religious situation of his day, and especially to the God question. As analogia entis, it is based on the scholastic *analogia entis*, as well as the (Augustinian) theological insight of God 'ever greater' in relation to all that is human. Also brings these ideas in relationship to Przywara's religious sources: his Jesuit (Ignatian) spirituality.

ZELECHOW, Bernard. *Fear and Trembling* and *Joyful Wisdom*—The Same Book; a Look at Metaphoric Communication. Hist Euro Ideas, 12(1), 93-104, 1990.

The purpose of this essay is to illuminate aspects of interpretive praxis. The essay explores the radically different rhetoric and metaphors (the language of God and the language of post-atheism) used by Nietzsche and Kierkegaard. The conclusion reached is that the existential communication about the human project is the same in *Fear and Trembling* and *Joyful Wisdom*.

ZELENY, J. Dialectical Contradiction and the Aristotelian Principle of Non-Contradiction (in Czechoslovakian). Filozof Cas, 37(4), 481-486, 1989.

The paper tries to clarify the relationship between "dialectical contradiction" and the Aristotelian principle of noncontradiction. No simple general answer can be given without carefully distinguishing different formulations of the Aristotelian principle in *Metaphysics*, Book 4, i.e., the formulation in terms of propositional logic, the ontological and the psychological formulations. Dialectical thinking complies with the principle of noncontradiction in its propositional-logical formulation. As to the ontological formulation, the answer is more complicated and depends on how we interpret this ontological statement of Aristotle.

ZELENY, Jindrich. On Dialectical Consistency. Stud Soviet Tho, 39(3-4), 199-203, Ap-My 90.

While the notions of consistency, inconsistency, and paraconsistency as used by paraconsistent logicians are defined on logical calculi only, dialectical consistency is a broader notion concerning the integration of manifold ways of acquisition and argumentation of true knowledge in its

development. The relationship between analytical and dialectical thinking within the dialectico-materialist type of rationality is one of the fundamental questions in this respect.

ZEMACH, Eddy M. Human Understanding. Synthese, 83(1), 31-48, Ap 90.

Contemporary thinkers either hold that meanings cannot be mental states, or that they are patterns of brain functions. But patterns of social, or brain, interactions cannot *be* that which we understand. Wittgenstein had another answer (not the one attributed to him by writers who ignore his work in psychology): understanding, he said, is seeing an item *as* embodying a type Q, thus constraining what items will be seen as "the same." Those who cannot see things under an aspect are meaning-blind. That idea is expanded in this article. Its ontology consists of types only: entities that recur in space, time, and possible worlds. Types (Socrates, Man, Red, On, etc.) overlap; Socrates = Bald at some index and not in another. The logic used is thus that of contingent identity. Now some possible worlds are mentally represented; the entities that occur in them are meanings. But such entities may also recur in the real world. Thus the entities we experience, the phenomena, which serve as our meanings, may be identical in the real world with real things. A correspondence theory of truth is thus developed: a sentence is true iff its meaning constitutes, in a specified way, a real situation.

ZEMACH, Eddy M. Not Good, Just Just. Amer Phil Quart, 26(4), 321-331, O 89.

Goodness is an empirically observable property; how much good and evil an action generates, i.e., what desires it satisfies, is a fact; thus the moral value of an action is a fact. But that fact cannot be known, because (1) the consequences of an action spread all over space and time and are incalculable; (2) desires too must be evaluated and modified by action. Thus it is impossible to evaluate actions morally. Instead of evaluating goodness, we evaluate justice. Justice is apparent harmony, a proportion between elements (service and remuneration, crime and punishment). It is an aesthetic and not a moral virtue. Aristotle flaunts the aesthetic nature of justice; Rawls covers it up. Rawls bases justice on agreement in the Original Position, but the grounds for accepting that position are aesthetic. Ethics, like science, seeks truth, but can only reach beauty.

ZEMACH, Eddy. Nesting: The Ontology of Interpretation. Monist, 73(2), 296-311, Ap 90.

An interpretation must say what the interpreted item says; so how can diverse interpretations be legitimate? How can repeatable artworks, that depend on others (performances) to exist, be objects? How can a ready-made artwork be identical with the thing of which it consists, and yet have a different value? Leibnizian Identity cannot handle these difficulties, but then it also fails to apply to all ordinary things. Instead, a new logic of identity, and ontology, is offered: An object b is NESTED in an object a iff every essential property (a property possessed by every occurrence) of a is an essential property of b. Nesting is not symmetrical: N(a,b) does not imply N(b,a).

ZEMACH, Eddy. "Wittgenstein on Meaning" in *Wittgenstein in Focus—Im Brennpunkt: Wittgenstein*, MC GUINNESS, Brian (ed), 415-435. Amsterdam, Rodopi, 1989.

Wittgenstein is usually taken to have held that the use of a term is not mentally constrained. That is utterly wrong. A use of language unconstrained by meaning is attributed by him to "meaning-blind" or "aspect-blind" creatures, not to us. We observe meaning when an aspect dawns on us; meaning is the impression (Eindruck) of a term as fitting something; hence, unlike pain, it cannot stand alone. That is a mentalistic theory of meaning: use is determined by images (Vorstellungen) that play semantic roles in virtue of their aesthetic properties. Although a term may be arbitrarily interpreted, aesthetic reasons determine which interpretation be seen as right for it.

ZEMAN, J. On the Critique of Energetism and Neoenergetism (in Czechoslovakian). Filozof Cas, 37(6), 761-772, 1989.

This article commences with a critical analysis of the philosophical views held by the chemist W Ostwald, who regarded energy as a universal substance which he intended to substitute for the term matter. The author goes on to trace the further development of energetism, particularly the opinions of F Auerbach, who contrasted entropy with the anti-enthropic-ectropic principle, conceiving of it, however, on a spiritualist basis. The author then points to the historical roots of spiritual neoenergetism which may be discerned in ancient Indian Shaivism and Vedanta, in the ancient Greek theory of the pneuma as well as in Taoism. The author concludes his study by analyzing the energoenthorpics of G N Alexayev as a concept standing in opposition to neoenergetism and based on the Marxist interpretation of energy, motion and matter and striving for a philosophical generalization of some universal concepts from physics and cybernetics. (edited)

ZENZINGER, Theodore S. The Resurgence of the Foole. Auslegung, 16(2), 191-208, Sum 90.

Hobbes's Foole has long been the bane of social contract theories. We argue that s/he remains so despite the best efforts of Hobbes, Gauthier and MacIntosh. After consideration of Gauthier's rejection of Hobbes, we examine Gauthier's argument for constrained maximization and the adoption of a disposition to be just. Following MacIntosh, we argue that individuals will not consider the adoption of this disposition rational, thus leaving Gauthier open to the Foole. MacIntosh suggests that the Foole can be defeated if individuals alter their preferences, yet their freedom to do so, we argue, undermines his response to the Foole.

ZEPPI, Stelio. Le origini dell'ateismo antico (II). G Metaf, 10(3), 421-438, S-D 88.

ZEPPI, Stelio. Le origini dell'ateismo antico (quarta parte). G Metaf, 11(2), 217-240, My-Ag 89.

ZEPPI, Stelio. Le origini dell'ateismo antico (terza parte). G Metaf, 11(1), 65-95, Ju-Ap 89.

ZHANG, Hwe Ik. Humanity in the World of Life. Zygon, 24(4), 447-456, D 89.

The position and role of humanity in the world of life is examined in the light of the ontological structure of life itself. This problem is approached by considering the possible units of life representing various modes of life phenomena. I argue that the only meaningful unit of life without interposing some special external conditions is "global life" framed in a star-planet system. Any other possible unit of life exhibited by various kinds of individuals is conditional in the sense that it would leave out an essential part as "co-life." The relationship between human being and the global life should be understood in this general scheme of individual and global life. It is emphasized, however, that human being occupies a unique position in global life in the sense that humanity can promote either a cancerous situation or a healthy higher-order enhancement of the global life.

ZHAOWU, He. The Concept of Natural Rights and the Cultural Tradition. Chin Stud Phil, 21(4), 3-33, Sum 90.

ZHEN, Li (ed) and TANG, Yi-Jie (ed) and MC LEAN, George F (ed). *Man and Nature: The Chinese Tradition and the Future.* Lanham, Univ Pr of America, 1989

ZHEN, Li. "Slave—Master—Friend, Philosophical Reflections Upon Man and Nature" in *Man and Nature: The Chinese Tradition and the Future*, TANG, Yi-Jie (ed), 113-127. Lanham, Univ Pr of America, 1989.

The relationship between man and nature is an everlasting theme of philosophical reflections of philosophers in the East and West. In antiquity, humans subordinated themselves to nature as "slave" to the master; from the early modern period as mankind's strength increased, they were unwilling to be slaves but sought to conquer nature and to be its "master"; in the contemporary world, human beings are recognising that man aand nature should be "friends" with each other. The harmonious relationship between man and nature is beneficial for the two parts.

ZHILIN, Li. The Differences Between Chinese and Western Concepts of Nature and the Trend Toward Their Convergence. Chin Stud Phil, 21(1), 20-49, Fall 89.

ZHIXIANG, Chen. On Splitting of a Recursive Set with Polynomial Time Minimal Pairs. Z Math Log, 35(5), 423-432, 1989.

Do there exist n recursive sets which split a set not in P such that any two of those sets form a minimal pair for the polynomial time many-one (Turing, strong Turing) reducibility? A positive answer is given to this problem when n is infinite, but a negative answer is given when n is finite and the set is splitted only with meets of it and sets in P. Another theorem is also established along the positive line when n is finite. Perhaps this theorem is optimal if our problem has negative answers when n is finite.

ZHMUD, Leonid J. "All is Number"? "Basic Doctrine" of Pythagoreanism Reconsidered. Phronesis, 34(3), 270-292, 1989.

ZIAREK, Krysztof. Semantics of Proximity: Language and the Other in the Philosophy of Emmanual Levinas. Res Phenomenol, 19, 213-247, 1989.

ZIELONKA, Wojciech. A Simple and General Method of Solving the Finite Axiomatizability Problems for Lambek's Syntactic Calculi. Stud Log, 48(1), 35-39, Mr 89.

In "Axiomatizability of Ajdukiewicz-Lambek calculus by means of cancellation schemes" (1981), I proved that the product-free fragment L of Lambek's syntactic calculus is not finitely axiomatizable if the only rule of inference admitted is Lambek's cut-rule. The proof (which is rather complicated and roundabout) was subsequently adapted by Kandulski to the non-associative variant NL of L. It turns out, however, that there exists an

extremely simple method of non-finite-axiomatizability proofs which works uniformly for different subsystems of L (in particular, for NL). We present it in this paper to the use of those who refer to the results of Kandulski and Zielonka. (edited)

ZILIAN, H G. *Klarheit und Methode: Felix Kaufmanns Wissenschaftstheorie.* Amsterdam, Rodopi, 1990

A presentation and critical discussion of Kaufmann's pioneering general theory of science as a theory of systematic problem solving, of his philosophy of the social sciences and his meta-theoretical contributions to various disciplines, such as sociology and (Austrian) economics. Kaufmann's work is discussed with reference to his intellectual mentors and companions—Kelsen, Husserl, Schuetz, Dewey, etc.—but also with an eye on recent developments in the philosophy of science, some of which can be found foreshadowed in Kaufmann's work to a hitherto unnoticed extent.

ZIMMERMAN, Michael E. The Limitations of Heidegger's Ontological Aestheticism. S J Phil, SUPP(28), 183-189, 1989.

In this essay, I argue that Heidegger—under the influence of Nietzsche and Jünger—tended to interpret the history of being as an aesthetic phenomenon, i.e., as the history of new modes of presencing brought forth by the work of art. I also argue that while John D Caputo is right for criticizing Heidegger's failure to appreciate the ethical dimension of history, Heidegger is not alone in Western history in emphasizing that there are "higher" concerns than those involving ordinary matters of justice and ethics. Still, such positions are dangerous.

ZIMMERMAN, Michael E. On Vallicella's Critique of Heidegger. Int Phil Quart, 30(1), 75-100, Mr 90.

William F Vallicella has argued that Heidegger's thought is deeply flawed by its tendency to reduce "being" to "truth," where being means the "presencing" of things and "truth" means the disclosure needed for such presencing. Insofar as this disclosure is constituted by human existence, Heidegger would seem to make "being" dependent on the contingent fact that humans exist. In this essay, I examine and evaluate critically Vallicella's arguments.

ZIMMERMAN, Michael E. Philosophy and Politics: The Case of Heidegger. Phil Today, 33(1), 3-20, Spr 89.

In this essay, I address three questions: the nature of Heidegger's involvement with National Socialism; whether there is an essential link between Heidegger's thought and his political decision to support Hitler; and allegations regarding anti-Semitism in his thought and politics.

ZIMMERMAN, Michael J. *An Essay on Moral Responsibility.* Lanham, Rowman & Allanheld, 1988

An analysis is proposed of the concept of moral responsibility and of its relations to freedom, control, luck, ignorance, negligence, attempts, omissions, compulsion, mental disorders, character, virtues and vices, desert, and punishment. Distinctions are drawn between various types of responsibility (including appraisability and liability, culpability and laudability, and direct and indirect responsibility) and also between responsibility and wrongdoing. With the use of these distinctions, the author calls into question much of our common practice of ascribing responsibility—praising, blaming, rewarding, and punishing.

ZIMMERMAN, Michael J. Where Did I Go Wrong? Phil Stud, 59(1), 55-77, My 90.

There are two main versions, actualism and possibilism, of the thesis that what one ought to do is the best that one can do. According to actualism, an agent S ought to do an act X if and only if what *would* happen if S did X is better than what *would* happen if S performed any alternative action. Possibilism replaces both instances of "would" in this formula with "could." In this paper, actualism is attacked and possibilism defended. Then an investigation is undertaken of what possibilism implies about just where it is that one goes wrong when one does go wrong.

ZIMMERMAN, R E. "Authenticity and Historicity: On the Dialectical Ethics of Sartre" in *Inquiries into Values: The Inaugural Session of the International Society for Value Inquiry*, LEE, Sander H , 413-426. Lewiston, Mellen Pr, 1989.

ZIMMERMANN, Jörg. Bach as a Paradigm in Aesthetic Discourse. Acta Phil Fennica, 43, 343-362, 1988.

ZIMMERMANN, Rolf. Equality, Political Order and Ethics: Hobbes and the Systematics of Democratic Rationality. Phil Soc Crit, 14(3-4), 339-358, 1988.

ZINGARI, Guido. Domanda e definizione nella filosofia di Heidegger: Motivi E riflessioni tratti da "Was ist das-die Philosophie?". Aquinas, 32(2), 323-336, My-Ag 89.

ZINKHAN, George M. MBAs' Changing Attitudes Toward Marketing

Dilemmas: 1981-1987. J Bus Ethics, 8(12), 963-974, D 89.

This study investigates the reactions of 561 MBA students to ethical marketing dilemmas. An analysis is conducted across time to determine how MBA students' attitudes about ethical marketing issues have been changing over the course of the 1980s. The findings show some support for the notion that MBA students in the late 1980s are somewhat less likely to use moral idealism when resolving an ethical dilemma and more likely to justify the decision in terms of its outcomes as compared with their counterparts at the start of the decade.

ZIRIÓN, Antonio (trans) and SOSA, Ernesto. Sobre la identidad, la existencia y la constitución de las personas y otros seres. Rev Latin De Filosof, 15(3), 259-292, N 89.

ZITA, Jacquelyn. Lesbian Angels and Other Matters. Hypatia, 5(1), 133-139, Spr 90.

In this commentary on Joyce Trebilcot's "Dyke Methods or Principles for the Discovery/Creation of the Withstanding," I discuss four areas of difficulty in Trebilcot's proposed methods: (1) an overly negative view of "the intention to persuade," (2) a tendency towards epistemological relativism and loss of cultural authorities, (3) a circularity in defining the proposed methods as dyke methods, and (4) a hint of repressive tolerance towards differences among lesbians by avoidance of painful confrontation involving those differences. Unlike Trebilcot, I make a distinction between the abuse of persuasion and the art of persuasion, reclaiming the latter as a caring and challenging strategy, rather than an invasion of adversarial heteropatriarchal tactics.

ZLOBIN, N S. Activity-Work-Culture (in Czechoslovakian). Filozof Cas, 37(4), 575-584, 1989.

This study's aim is to delineate the interrelationship between these three major philosophical categories, while trying to capture those parts of social reality which the given terms reflect. Activity is conceived here as man's social action performed by a subject of the cultural-historical process, a subject whose specific characteristic is an active, conscious and creative functioning in the objective world. This very operation—the production of the human world by man—constitutes the essence of culture, in which the social rootedness of the individual is manifested. Man's social nature is then scrutinized through the prism of cultural characteristics of work and in this connection the author formulates the necessary conditions which would guarantee to work its cultural functions (the surmounting of alienation) and which would position the cultural (active) content of work against the immediate labour process, thus transforming work into an action-filled manifestation of freedom and consequently into man's primary vital need.

ZNOJ, M. Marxism, the Ecological Crisis and a Master's Attitude to Nature (in Czechoslovakian). Filozof Cas, 37(5), 655-665, 1989.

The main purpose of this article is to single out problems whose clarification Marxist philosophy simply cannot afford to bypass as soon as it poses with utmost gravity the question as to the kind of challenge offered to human thinking by the threat of the ecological crisis. In the first part of his article the author explains the term ecological crisis, outlining the philosophical questions connected with the delineation of this concept; in the second part he gets down to discussing what he means under a master's attitude to nature. This analysis is carried out against the background of some ideas of Hegel and Kant. The underlying tenet of his master's approach appears to be the idea that nature has no sense in itself, that it is man himself who imparts to it such a meaning with his activities. Cartesianism is regarded as the first philosophical formulation of such an attitude. The author then studies the question as to what extent and in which particular shape is Marxism capable of thematizing the problems which are associated with that master's approach to nature.

ZNOJ, Milan (and others). Dispute over Democracy at the 17th International Philosophy Congress in Prague in 1934 (in Hungarian). Filozof Cas, 38(1-2), 87-98, 1990.

An international philosophy congress met in Prague in 1934 in a situation when Czechoslovakia had to stand up against mounting aggressiveness of German fascism. This particular gathering of philosophers in Prague was fairly symbolic, having its special significance, namely as a rallying call in defence against totalitarian ideology. The main purpose of this article is to recall that situation, clarify at least its underlying importance and outline some of the major answers the Prague congress gave to the challenges of its time. Seen in this light, the authors focused their attention on the proceedings in the following two sections of the congress: Crisis of Democracy and Philosophy in the Present Times. (edited)

ZOLO, Danilo. The Evolutionary Risks of Democracy. Praxis Int, 9(3), 220-233, O 89.

According to the author social transformations which on the threshold of the

third millennium come with the introduction of new technologies (telematic, robotic and multimedial ones) accelerate in a dramatic measure the evolutionary process of social differentiation and functional specialization. These transformations bring about a quick growth of the social environment's complexity. In highly differentiated and complex societies pluralism, party competition and electoral choice among competing political elites, which are the authentic pillars of the pluralist theory of democracy, prove to be ineffective. From all that derives the need for a 'reconstruction' of democratic theory.

ZOLO, Danilo. Reflexive Epistemology and Social Complexity: The Philosophical Legacy of Otto Neurath. Phil Soc Sci, 20(2), 149-169, Je 90.

According to the article, Neurath's reflexive epistemology—expressed by the metaphor of the ship in need of reconstruction on the open sea—represents a philosophical alternative to the classical and contemporary forms of scientific realism and ethical cognitivism, including Popper's falsificationism. Against Quine's reductive interpretation of Neurath's boat argument as the basis for a 'naturalized epistemology', the article maintains that the metaphor suggests the idea of an insuperable situation of linguistic and conceptual circularity. This prevents any attempt at self-foundation in scientific knowledge, as well as in ethics and politics, and rules out any 'constructive philosophy' aiming to break circularity in pursuit of some methodological beginning.

ZUBIRÍA, Martín (trans) and HEIDEGGER, Martin. Acerca de la pregunta por la determinante de la cosa del pensar. Rev Filosof (Mexico), 22(66), 320-331, S-D 89.

ZUBOFF, Arnold. One Self: The Logic of Experience. Inquiry, 33(1), 39-68, Mr 90.

Imagine that you and a duplicate of yourself are lying unconscious, next to each other, about to undergo a complete step-by-step exchange of bits of your bodies. It certainly seems that at no stage in this exchange of bits will you have thereby switched places with your duplicate. Yet it also seems that the end result, with all the bits exchanged, *will* be essentially that of the two of you having switched places. Where will you awaken? The author claims that one and the same person possesses both bodies, occupies both places and will experience both awakenings, just as a person whose brain has been bisected must at once experience both of the unconnected fields of awareness, even though each of these will falsely appear to him as the entirety of his experience. He also claims that the more usual apparent boundaries of persons are as illusory as those in brain bisection; personal identity remains unchanged through any variation or multiplication of body or mind. (edited)

ZUCKERMAN, Connie and COLLOPY, Bart and DUBLER, Nancy. The Ethics of Home Care: Autonomy and Accommodation. Hastings Center Rep, 20(2), Supp 1-16, Mr-Ap 90.

ZUCKERT, Catherine H. Martin Heidegger: His Philosophy and His Politics. Polit Theory, 18(1), 51-79, F 90.

The furor aroused by the publication of Farias's Heidegger et le Nazisme has once again raised the question: What was the connection, if any, between Heidegger's philosophy and his politics? The connection is to be found, I argue, in his concept of language. The explicitly poetic understanding of the "fatherland" he shared with Hoelderlin was not racist, but the political implications of his emphatically historical definition of "man" were no more egalitarian or liberal than was official Nazi dogma.

ZUNIGA, J A. "An Everyday Aesthetic Impulse: Dewey Revisited" in Inquiries into Values: The Inaugural Session of the International Society for Value Inquiry, LEE, Sander H , 585-592. Lewiston, Mellen Pr, 1989.

Using Dewey's comprehensive perspective on aesthetic experience as a point of departure, this paper posits the heuristic notion of an *aesthetic impulse*. In contrast to traditional aesthetics, the latter seeks recognition for a hitherto neglected phenomenon, namely, a potential for aesthetic creativity which is commonly (in various ways and situations) actualized in everyday human activity. Shifting away from the fine arts, many examples from daily life are handled by way of "proof." Such ideas as aesthetic *choice* and aesthetic *energy* emerge throughout the discussion. Gadamer is suggested as a source for later theoretical elaboration.

ZUORONG, He and QUANFU, Liu. A Systematic Exploration of the Marxist Theory of Human Nature. Chin Stud Phil, 21(2), 59-73, Wint 89-90.

ZÜRCHER, Joyce M. Contingencia y Analiticidad en Leibniz. Rev Filosof (Costa Rica), 26, 97-101, D 88.

This essay presents and solves a problem that appears in Leibniz's Discourse on Metaphysics and the Correspondence with Arnauld. Leibniz asserts that any true predicative proposition that names a substance—either individual or formal—is analytical; although individual substances are contingent beings and the propositions that refer to them are thus contingent. The solution consists in demonstrating that the contingency of an individual substance is due to its relation with the formal substance that it instantiates, and not to the relation held between the substances and its properties, which is a necessary relation in Leibniz's terms.

ZUSKA, Vlastimil. Husserl's Concept of Inner Temporal Consciousness and Aesthetics (in Czechoslovakian). Filozof Cas, 38(1-2), 99-106, 1990.

The author commences his study with a reference to the changed paradigms of time in physics and philosophy and to the fact that aesthetics has been lagging behind these changes, as corroborated by the notion of painting as "timeless" art. The initial hypothesis of this article is the finding that the temporal configuration of the phases of the reception process or the qualitative changes of internal temporal consciousness of the perceiving subject make up the constitutive component of the process of appropriation of a work of art. A proof of this assumption proceeds from Husserl's analysis of internal temporal consciousness, from his critique of the concept of "specious present." Simultaneously, it makes use of the notion of "neutral modification of consciousness" and conception of perception and temporal horizons for the vital transition into the sphere of aesthetic perception. (edited)

ZVESPER, John. The American Founders and Classical Political Thought. Hist Polit Thought, 10(4), 701-718, Wint 89.

ZWEERMAN, Theo. Spirituality in Modern Society (in Hungarian). Magyar Filozof Szemle, 2-3, 376-387, 1989.

ZYCINSKI, Joseph. A Return to Plato in the Philosophy of Substance. New Scholas, 63(4), 419-434, Autumn 89.

Guidance on the Use of the Book Review Index

The Book Review Index lists in alphabetical order the authors of books reviewed in philosophy journals. Each entry includes the author's name, the title of the book, the publisher, and the place and date of publication. Under each entry is listed the name of the reviewer, the journal in which the review appeared, along with the volume, pagination and date.

AARNIO, Aulis. *The Rational as Reasonable: A Treatise on Legal Justification*. Dordrecht, Reidel, 1987.
Wróblewski, Jerzy. *Ratio Juris* 1(3), 266-268 D 88

ABBS, Peter. *A Is for Aesthetics: Essays on Creative and Aesthetic Education*. Bristok, Falmer Pr, 1989.
Meeson, P. *Brit J Aes* 30(1), 85-86 Ja 90

ABEL, Donald C. *Freud on Instinct and Morality*. Albany, SUNY Pr, 1989.
Clegg, Jerry. *Can Phil Rev* 10(7), 259-261 Jl 90

ABELLAN, J L and others. *Existe una filosofía española?* Madrid, Fundación Fernando Rielo, 1988.
Rozalen Medina, José L. *Dialogo Filosof* 6(2), 263-268 My-Ag 90

ABELSON, Raziel. *Lawless Mind*. Philadelphia, Temple Univ Pr, 1988.
Williams, Clifford. *Can Phil Rev* 10(2), 45-47 F 90

ABHYANKAR, Vasudevsastri. *Advaitamoda: A Study of Advaita and Visistadvaita*. Delhi, Satguru, 1988.
Potter, Karl H. *Phil East West* 40(3), 405-406 Jl 90

ABOULAFIA, Mitchell. *The Mediating Self: Mead, Sartre, and Self-Determination*. New Haven, Yale Univ Pr, 1986.
Thompson, Tyler. *Ideal Stud* 19(3), 274-275 S 89

ABRAHAM, William J and HOLTZER, Steven W (eds). *The Rationality of Religious Belief: Essays in Honour of Basil Mitchell*. Oxford, Clarendon Pr, 1987.
Konyndyk, Kenneth. *Faith Phil* 7(3), 347-351 Jl 90

ACKERMAN, T F and GRABER, G C and REYNOLDS, C H and THOMASMA, D C (eds). *Clinical Medical Ethics: Exploration and Assessment*. Lanham, Univ Pr of America, 1987.
Yeo, Michael. *Teach Phil* 13(1), 60-63 Mr 90

ACKERMAN, Terence F and STRONG, Carson R. *A Casebook in Medical Ethics*. Oxford, Oxford Univ Pr, 1989.
Gillam, Lynn. *Bioethics* 4(3), 268-271 Jl 90

ACKERMANN, Robert John. *Wittgenstein's City*. Amherst, Univ of Massachusetts Pr, 1988.
Schiller, Britt-Marie. *J Hist Phil* 28(2), 310-311 Ap 90

ACZEL, Peter. *Non-well-founded sets*. Stanford, CSLI, 1988.
Hinnion, R. *Notre Dame J Form Log* 30(2), 308-312 Spr 89

ADAMS, Marilyn McCord. *William Ockham*, 2v. Notre Dame, Univ Notre Dame Pr, 1987.
Doyle, John P. *Mod Sch* 67(2), 150-153 Ja 90
Gelber, Hester G. *Faith Phil* 7(2), 246-252 Ap 90
Morris, Thomas V. *Int J Phil Relig* 27(3), 188-189 Je 90

ADAMS, Robert Merrihew. *The Virtue of Faith and Other Essays in Philosophical Theology*. New York, Oxford Univ Pr, 1987.
Mann, William E. *Phil Rev* 99(1), 135-138 Ja 90

ADORNO, A T. *Aesthetic Theory*, C Lenhardt (trans), Gretel Adorno and Rolf Tiedeman (eds). London, Routledge & Kegan Paul, 1984.
Ray, Larry. *Int Stud Phil* 22(1), 79-80 1990

ADORNO, Theodor W. *Kierkegaard: Construction of the Aesthetic*, Robert Hullot-Kentor (trans). Minneapolis, Univ of Minn Pr, 1989.
Martinez, Roy. *Can Phil Rev* 9(10), 391-393 O 89

AFANAS'EV, I N (ed). *There Is No Other Way*. Moscow, Progress, 1988.
Shevchenko, V N. *Soviet Stud Phil* 29(1), 70-85 Sum 90

AGACINSKI, Sylviane. *Aparté: Conceptions and Deaths of Soren Kierkegaard*, Kevin Newmark (trans). Tallahassee, Florida State Univ Pr, 1988.
Clark, Lorrie. *Phil Lit* 14(1), 191-193 Ap 90

AGASSI, Joseph. *Technology: Philosophical and Social Aspects*. Norwell, Reidel, 1986.
Davenport, Edward. *Phil Soc Sci* 20(1), 110-126 Mr 90

AGASSI, Joseph. *The Gentle Art of Philosophical Polemics*. LaSalle, Open Court, 1988.
Dale, A J. *Can Phil Rev* 10(3), 89-91 Mr 90

AGAZZI, Evandro (ed). *Probability in the Sciences*. Dordrecht, Kluwer, 1988.
de Swart, H C M. *Method Sci* 22(2), 122-123 1989

AHEARN, Edward. *Marx and Modern Fiction*. New Haven, Yale Univ Pr, 1989.
O'Neil, Mary Anne. *Phil Lit* 14(1), 209-210 Ap 90

AKHUNDOV, Murad. *Conceptions of Space and Time: Sources, Evolution, Directions*. Cambridge, MIT Pr, 1986.
Bradie, Michael. *Hist Phil Life Sci* 11(1), 186-189 1989

ALBANO, Maeve Edith. *Vico and Providence*. NY, Lang, 1986.
Munzel, Gisela Felicitas. *New Vico Studies* 5, 173-176 1987

ALBERT, Daniel A and others. *Reasoning in Medicine: An Introduction to Clinical Inference*. Baltimore, Johns Hopkins U Pr, 1988.
Lie, Reidar K. *Theor Med* 10(3), 269-270 S 89

ALBERT, Daniel and MUNSON, Ronald and RESNIK, Michael D. *Reasoning in Medicine: An Introduction to Clinical Inference*. Baltimore, Johns Hopkins U Pr, 1988.
Erde, Edmund L. *J Med Human* 10(2), 125-126 Fall-Wint 89

ALBERT, Hans. *Kritik der reinen Erkenntnislehre*. Tübingen, Mohr, 1987.
Pacho, Julian. *Z Phil Forsch* 44(2), 336-339 1990

ALBERTUS MAGNUS. *Physica: Libri 1-4*, Paulus Hossfeld (ed). Aschendorff, Monasteri Westfalorum, 1987.
Thijssen, J M M H. *Vivarium* 27(2), 159-161 N 89

ALBEVERIO, Sergio and others. *Nonstandard Methods in Stochastic Analysis and Mathematical Physics*. Orlando, Academic Pr, 1986.
Hoover, D N. *J Sym Log* 55(1), 362-363 Mr 90

ALBIAC, Gabriel. *La sinagoga vacia: Un estudio de las fuentes marranas del espinosismo*. Madrid, Hiperion, 1987.
Negri, Antonio. *Stud Spinozana* 4, 423-426 1988

ALEXANDER, Thomas M. *John Dewey's Theory of Art, Experience, and Nature: The Horizons of Feeling*. Albany, SUNY Pr, 1987.
Tejera, V. *Int Stud Phil* 22(1), 81 1990

ALLEN, Prudence. *The Concept of Woman: The Aristotelian Revolution 750 B.C.-A.D. 1250*. Montreal, Eden Pr, 1985.
Saxonhouse, Arlene. *Hist Euro Ideas* 12(2), 290-291 1990

ALLESCH, Christian G. *Geschichte der psychologischen Ästhetik*. Gottingen, Hogrefe, 1987.
Neumaier, Otto. *Conceptus* 23(59), 115-117 1989

ALLISON, Henry E. *Benedict de Spinoza: An Introduction*. New Haven, Yale Univ Pr, 1987.
Hardin, C L. *Phil Rev* 99(1), 114-116 Ja 90

ALMOND, Brenda and WILSON, Bryan (eds). *Values: A Symposium*. Atlantic Highlands, Humanities Pr, 1988.
Gowans, Christopher W. *Phil Books* 30(4), 232-233 O 89

ALONSO, José Manuel. *Introducción al principio antrópico*. Madrid, Encuentro, 1988.
Vegas, José M. *Dialogo Filosof* 5(3), 437-438 S-D 89

ALPERSON, Philip (ed). *What Is Music? An Introduction to the Philosophy of Music*. New York, Haven, 1987.
Berenson, Frances. *Brit J Aes* 29(4), 371-374 Autumn 89
Krausz, Michael. *Can Phil Rev* 10(2), 47-51 F 90

ALSTON, A J (trans). *The Method of the Vedanta: A Critical Account of the Advaita Tradition*. London, Kegan Paul, 1989.
Marathe, M P. *Indian Phil Quart* 16(4), 498-500 O 89

ANDERBERG, T and NILSTUN, T and PERSSON, I (eds). *Aesthetic Distinction: Essays Presented to Göran Hermerén on his 50th Birthday*. Lund, Lund Univ Pr, 1988.
Davies, Stephen. *Can Phil Rev* 9(9), 360-366 S 89

ANDERSON, C Anthony. *Handbook of Philosophical Logic, V2: Extensions of Classical Logic*. Dordrecht, Reidel, 1984.
Parsons, Charles. *J Sym Log* 55(2), 892-894 Je 90

ANDERSON, Douglas R. *Creativity and the Philosophy of C S Peirce*. Dordrecht, Nijhoff, 1987.
Esposito, Joseph L. *Trans Peirce Soc* 26(1), 153-156 Wint 90

ANGUS, Ian H. *George Grant's Platonic Rejoinder to Heidegger: Contemporary Political Philosophy and the Question of Technology*. Lewiston, Mellen Pr, 1987.
Burch, Robert. *Can Phil Rev* 9(9), 345-348 S 89

ANNAS, George J. *Judging Medicine*. Clifton, Humana Pr, 1988.
Kirby, Michael. *Bioethics* 3(4), 347-353 O 89

ANNAS, Julia (ed). *Oxford Studies in Ancient Philosophy, V3*. New York, Clarendon/Oxford Pr, 1985.
Tarrant, Harold. *Hist Euro Ideas* 12(1), 127-128 1990

ANNAS, Julia (ed). *Oxford Studies in Ancient Philosophy, V6*. Oxford, Clarendon Pr, 1988.
Hall, Pamela. *Rev Metaph* 43(3), 619-620 Mr 90

ANNAS, Julia and GRIMM, Robert (eds). *Oxford Studies in Ancient Philosophy, Supplementary Volume 1988*. New York, Oxford Univ Pr, 1989.

Upton, Thomas V. *Rev Metaph* 43(4), 849-850 Je 90

ANTONIETTI, Alessandro. *Cervello, mente, cultura*. Milan, Angeli, 1986.
Buzzoni, Marco. *Epistemologia* 12(1), 169-170 Ja-Je 89

APEL, K O. *Diskurs und Verantwortung*. Frankfurt am Main, Suhrkamp, 1988.
De Landázuri, Carlos O. *Anu Filosof* 22(1), 173-176 1989

APPELBAUM, P S and LIDZ, C W and MEISEL, A. *Informed Consent Legal Theory and Clinical Practice*. New York, Oxford Univ Pr, 1987.
Skene, Loane. *Bioethics* 3(4), 353-355 O 89

APPIAH, Anthony. *For Truth in Semantics*. Oxford, Blackwell, 1986.
Williamson, Timothy. *Ling Phil* 13(1), 129-135 F 90

AQUILA, Richard E. *Matter in Mind: A Study of Kant's Transcendental Deduction*. Bloomington, Indiana Univ Pr, 1989.
Dryer, D P. *Can Phil Rev* 10(3), 91-92 Mr 90
Kitcher, Patricia. *Rev Metaph* 43(4), 851-852 Je 90

ARAPURA, J G. *Hermeneutical Essays on Vedantic Topics*. Delhi, Motilal, 1986.
Timm, Jeffrey R. *Phil East West* 40(1), 107-108 Ja 90

ARBIB, Michael A and HESSE, Mary B. *The Construction of Reality*. New York, Cambridge Univ Pr, 1986.
Mercer, Mark. *Int Stud Phil* 22(1), 82 1990

ARENDS, J F M. *Die Einheit der Polis*. Leiden, Brill, 1988.
Wagner, Jochen. *Phil Rundsch* 37(1-2), 89-94 1990

ARIEW, Roger and GARBER, Daniel (eds & trans). *G W Leibniz: Philosophical Essays*. Indianapolis, Hackett, 1989.
Tlumak, Jeffrey. *Teach Phil* 12(3), 339-341 S 89

ARISTOTLE. *Politika, Tomislav Ladan (ed)*. Zagreb, Globus/SN Liber, 1988.
Culjak, Zvonimir. *Filozof Istraz* 30(3), 1053-1063 1989

ARMSTRONG, D M. *Universals: An Opinionated Introduction*. Boulder, Westview, 1989.
Goodman, Lenn and Westphal, Jonathan. *Mind* 99(395), 473-474 Jl 90
Teichmann, Roger. *Can Phil Rev* 10(7), 261-264 Jl 90

ARNASON, Johann P. *Praxis und Interpretation: Sozialphilosophische Studien*. Frankfurt, Suhrkamp, 1988.
Hackenesch, Christa. *Phil Rundsch* 36(4), 316-325 1989

ARONSON, Ronald. *Sartre's Second Critique*. Chicago, Univ of Chicago Pr, 1987.
Stack, George J. *J Hist Phil* 27(4), 634-638 O 89

ARRINGTON, Robert L. *Rationalism, Realism, and Relativism: Perspectives in Contemporary Moral Epistemology*. Ithaca, Cornell Univ Pr, 1989.
Johnson, Oliver A. *Can Phil Rev* 10(6), 217-219 Je 90
Paden, Roger. *Rev Metaph* 43(4), 852-853 Je 90

ARTHUR, C J. *Dialectics of Labour: Marx and His Relation to Hegel*. Oxford, Blackwell, 1986.
Thomas, Paul. *Hist Polit Thought* 10(4), 746-753 Wint 89

ARTIGAS, M. *Filosofía de la ciencia experimental*. Pamplona, EUNSA, 1989.
Vitoria, María Angeles. *Anu Filosof* 22(2), 181-184 1989

ASHCRAFT, Richard. *Revolutionary Politics and Locke's Two Treatises of Government*. Princeton, Princeton Univ Pr, 1986.
Schultz, David. *Int Stud Phil* 22(1), 83-84 1990

ASHLEY, Benedict. *Theologies of the Body: Humanist and Christian*. Braintree, Pope John XXIII Medical Moral Center, 1985.
May, William E. *Thomist* 54(1), 168-172 Ja 90

ATKINSON, Michael (ed & trans). *Plotinus: Ennead V.1. On the Three Principal Hypostases: A Commentary with Translation*. Oxford, Oxford Univ Pr, 1983.
Emilsson, Eyjólfur Kjalar. *Ancient Phil* 10(1), 146-149 Spr 90

ATTFIELD, Robin. *A Theory of Value and Obligation*. London, Croom Helm, 1987.
Feldman, Fred. *Nous* 24(4), 617-622 S 90

ATWELL, John E. *Ends and Principles in Kant's Moral Thought*. Dordrecht, Nijhoff, 1986.
Broadie, A. *Kantstudien* 81(1), 107-108 1990
Genova, A C. *Int Stud Phil* 22(1), 84-85 1990

AUBENQUE, Pierre (ed). *Études sur Parménide, 2v*. Paris, Vrin, 1987.
Kerferd, George. *Phronesis* 34(2), 227-231 1989
Pellegrin, Pierre. *Rev Phil Fr* 179(3), 352-356 Jl-S 89

AUBRY, C and others. *Figures de la philosophie québécoise*. Montreal,

UQAM, 1988.
Sahi, A Voho. *Philosophiques* 16(2), 347-358 Autumn 89

AUDARD, Catherine and DUPUY, Jean-Pierre and SÈVE, René (eds). *Individu et justice social: Autour de John Rawls*. Paris, Seuil, 1988.
Pestieau, Joseph. *Dialogue (Canada)* 28(3), 473-486 1989

AUNE, B. *Metaphysics: The Elements*. Minneapolis, Univ of Minnesota Pr, 1986.
Femenías, María Luisa. *Analisis Filosof* 7(1), 65-68 My 87

AUSTIN, David F (ed). *Philosophical Analysis: A Defense by Example*. Norwell, Kluwer, 1989.
Hart, W D. *Phil Books* 31(2), 92-93 Ap 90

AUSTIN, Scott. *Parmenides: Being, Bounds and Logic*. New Haven, Yale Univ Pr, 1986.
Ferguson, John. *Heythrop J* 31(1), 102-103 Ja 90

AUTRECOURT, Nicolaus von. *Briefe, R Imbach and D Perler (eds), D Perler (trans)*. Hamburg, Meiner, 1988.
Schönberger, Rolf. *Z Phil Forsch* 44(2), 328-331 1990

AVIS, Paul. *The Methods of Modern Theology*. London, Marshall Pickering, 1986.
Sedgwick, Peter H. *Mod Theol* 5(4), 391-392 Jl 89

AVRIMIDES, Anita. *Meaning and Mind: An Examination of a Gricean Account of Language*. Cambridge, MIT Pr, 1989.
Tiles, Mary. *Phil Books* 31(3), 160-161 Jl 90

AYOUB, Josiane. *Vers une redéfinition matérialiste du concept de culture*. Montréal, UQAM, 1987.
Ranger, Philippe. *Philosophiques* 16(2), 426-431 Autumn 89

AZAM, Gilbert. *El modernismo desde dentro*. Barcelona, Anthropos, 1989.
Heredia Soriano, Antonio. *Dialogo Filosof* 6(2), 268-271 My-Ag 90

BAARS, Bernard J. *The Cognitive Revolution in Psychology*. NY, Guilford Pr, 1986.
Pate, James L. *Phil Psych* 2(3), 315-324 1989

BABOLIN, Albino (ed). *Fede filosofica e filosofia della religione, V2*. Perugia, Benucci, 1989.
Rossi, Fabio. *Riv Filosof Neo-Scolas* 81(3), 496-499 Jl-S 89

BACH, Kent. *Thought and Reference*. NY, Oxford Univ Pr, 1988.
Luntley, Michael. *Phil Quart* 40(159), 266-270 Ap 90
Taschek, William W. *J Phil* 87(1), 38-45 Ja 90

BAILIN, Sharon. *Achieving Extraordinary Ends: An Essay on Creativity*. Boston, Kluwer, 1988.
Swanger, David. *J Aes Educ* 23(4), 118-119 Wint 89

BAIRD, Robert M and ROSENBAUM, Stuart E (eds). *The Philosophy of Punishment*. Buffalo, Prometheus, 1988.
Mullane, Harvey. *Teach Phil* 12(3), 324-327 S 89

BAKER, G P and HACKER, P M S. *Wittgenstein: Rules, Grammar and Necessity*. Oxford, Blackwell, 1985.
Harré, Rom. *Int Stud Phil* 21(3), 95-96 1989

BAKER, Gerald and CLARK, Len. *Explanation: An Introduction to the Philosophy of Science*. Mountain View, Mayfield, 1988.
Bradie, Michael. *Teach Phil* 12(3), 291-293 S 89

BAKER, Gordon. *Wittgenstein, Frege and the Vienna Circle*. Oxford, Blackwell, 1988.
Stern, David G. *Mind* 99(395), 479-482 Jl 90

BAKER, Lynne Rudder. *Saving Belief: A Critique of Physicalism*. Princeton, Princeton Univ Pr, 1987.
Avramides, Anita. *Dialogue (Canada)* 28(4), 693-694 1989
Lehman, Hugh. *Can Phil Rev* 10(6), 219-222 Je 90
Segal, Erwin M. *Phil Psych* 2(3), 347-350 1989
Welbourne, Michael. *Phil Books* 31(2), 103-105 Ap 90

BALDWIN, J T (ed). *Classification Theory, Proceedings of the U.S.-Israel Workshop on Model Theory in Mathematical Logic*. Berlin, Springer, 1987.
Goode, John B. *J Sym Log* 55(2), 878-881 Je 90

BALL, Terence. *Transforming Political Discourse: Political Theory and Critical Conceptual History*. Oxford, Blackwell, 1988.
McBeath, Graham B. *Rad Phil* 55, 55 Sum 90

BALZER, Wolfgang and MOULINES, C Ulises and SNEED, Joseph D. *An Architectonic for Science*. Dordrecht, Reidel, 1987.
Kroes, Peter. *Phil Sci* 57(2), 349-350 Je 90

BANERJEE, Nikunja Vihari. *Towards Perpetual Peace*. Delhi, Motilal, 1988.

Eastman, William. *Can Phil Rev* 9(11), 433-434 N 89

BARAZ, Michaél. *La Révolution Inespérée: Constantin Brunner*. Paris, Corti, 1986.
Harris, Errol E. *Stud Spinozana* 5, 427-432 1989

BARBER, Benjamin. *The Conquest of Politics: Liberal Philosophy in Democratic Times*. Princeton, Princeton Univ Pr, 1988.
Isaac, Jeffrey C. *Hist Polit Thought* 11(1), 168-173 Spr 90

BARNES, Annette. *On Interpretation: A Critical Analysis*. New York, Oxford Univ Pr, 1988.
Hancher, Michael. *Can Phil Rev* 10(3), 93-95 Mr 90

BARNES, Barry. *The Nature of Power*. Champaign, Univ of Illinois Pr, 1988.
Laycock, Henry. *Can Phil Rev* 9(10), 394-396 O 89

BARRY, Brian. *A Treatise of Social Justice, V1: Theories of Justice*. Berkeley, Univ of California Pr, 1989.
Pogge, Thomas W. *J Phil* 87(7), 375-384 Jl 90

BARRY, Brian. *Theories of Justice*. Berkeley, Univ of California Pr, 1989.
Kymlicka, Will. *Inquiry* 33(1), 99-119 Mr 90

BARTH, E M and KRABBE, E C W. *From Axiom to Dialogue: A Philosophical Study of Logics and Argumentation*. Hawthorne, de Gruyter, 1982.
Walton, Douglas N. *J Prag* 13(4), 634-637 Ag 89

BARUCH, Elaine Hoffman and D'AMADO JR, Amadeo F a n d SEAGER, Joni (eds). *Embryos, Ethics, and Women's Rights: Exploring the New Reproductive Technologies*. NY, Harrington Park Pr, 1988.
Holmes, Helen Bequaert. *Hypatia* 4(3), 150-159 Fall 89

BARWISE, Jon and ETCHEMENDY, John. *The Liar: An Essay on Truth and Circularity*. New York, Oxford Univ Pr, 1987.
Gupta, Anil. *Phil Sci* 56(4), 697-709 D 89

BARWISE, Jon. *The Situation in Logic*. Stanford, CSLI, 1989.
Urquhart, Alasdair. *Can Phil Rev* 10(3), 96-98 Mr 90

BASINGER, David and BASINGER, Randall. *Philosophy and Miracle: The Contemporary Debate*. Lewiston, Mellen Pr, 1987.
Burke, T E. *Mod Theol* 5(4), 392-393 Jl 89

BAUDOUIN, Jean. *Karl Popper*. Paris, PUF, 1989.
Largeault, Jean. *Rev Phil Fr* 179(4), 606-609 O-D 89

BAUM, Manfred. *Die Entstehung der Hegelschen Dialektik*. Bonn, Bouvier, 1986.
Angehrn, Emil. *Z Phil Forsch* 43(4), 702-705 O-D 89
Gérard, Gilbert. *Rev Phil Louvain* 88(77), 99-104 F 90

BAUMGARTH, William P and REGAN, Richard (eds). *Saint Thomas Aquinas: On Law, Morality and Politics*. Indianapolis, Hackett, 1988.
Lisska, Anthony J. *Teach Phil* 12(4), 429-431 D 89

BAUMGOLD, Deborah. *Hobbes's Political Theory*. Cambridge, Cambridge Univ Pr, 1988.
Lloyd, S A. *Ethics* 100(2), 421-422 Ja 90

BAYLES, Michael D. *Principles of Law: A Normative Analysis*. Dordrecht, Reidel, 1987.
Husak, Douglas N. *Law Phil* 8(3), 403-411 D 89

BAYNES, Kenneth and BOHMAN, James and MCCARTHY, Thomas (eds). *After Philosophy: End or Transformation?* Cambridge, MIT Pr, 1987.
Cascardi, Anthony J. *New Vico Studies* 5, 200-203 1987
Duvenage, Pieter. *S Afr J Phil* 9(1), 49-55 F 90
White, Hayden. *New Vico Studies* 6, 167-168 1988

BAZERMAN, Charles. *Shaping Written Knowledge: The Genre and Activity of the Experimental Article in Science*. Madison, Univ of Wisconsin Pr, 1988.
Gross, Alan G. *Stud Hist Phil Sci* 21(2), 341-349 Je 90

BEAUCHAMP, Tom and BOWIE, N (eds). *Ethical Theory and Business*. Englewood Cliffs, Prentice-Hall, 1988.
Hanly, Kenneth. *Can Phil Rev* 10(1), 1-2 Ja 90

BEAUCHAMP, Tom and CHILDRESS, James. *Principles of Biomedical Ethics, 3rd ed*. New York, Oxford Univ Pr, 1989.
Jonsen, Albert R. *Hastings Center Rep* 20(4), 32-34 Jl-Ag 90

BÉCARES, V (ed). *Apolonio Discolo: Sintaxis*. Madrid, Gredos, 1987.
Nubiola, Jaime. *Anu Filosof* 21(1), 185-187 1988

BECK, Heinrich. *Natürliche Theologie*. Munich, Anton Pustet, 1988.
Rath, Matthias. *Z Phil Forsch* 44(1), 165-169 1990

BECK, Lewis White (ed). *Kant: Selections*. New York, Macmillan, 1988.
Zweig, Arnulf. *Kantstudien* 81(2), 252-254 1990

BECKER, Lawrence C. *Reciprocity*. NY, Routledge & Kegan Paul, 1986.

Mohan, William J. *Int Stud Phil* 21(3), 97-98 1989

BEDAU, Hugo Adam. *Death is Different: Studies in the Morality, Law, and Politics of Capital Punishment*. Boston, Northeastern Univ Pr, 1987.
Davis, Michael. *Law Phil* 8(3), 412-419 D 89

BEIERWALTES, Werner. *Identità e differenza*. Milan, Vita e Pensiero, 1989.
Ivaldo, Marco. *Sapienza* 43(1), 71-75 Ja-Mr 90

BEILHARZ, Peter. *Trotsky, Trotskyism, and the Transition to Socialism*. Totowa, Barnes & Noble, 1987.
Anellis, Irving H. *Stud Soviet Tho* 38(4), 299-303 N 89

BEINER, Ronald. *Political Judgment*. Chicago, Univ of Chicago Pr, 1983.
Dallmayr, Fred R. *New Vico Studies* 6, 147-154 1988

BEISER, Frederick C. *The Fate of Reason: German Philosophy from Kant to Fichte*. Cambridge, Harvard Univ Pr, 1987.
Breazeale, Daniel. *Owl Minerva* 21(2), 190-197 Spr 90
Knodt, Eva M. *Phil Lit* 13(2), 422-424 O 89

BELFRAGE, Bertil (ed). *George Berkeley's Manuscript Introduction*. Oxford, Doxa, 1987.
Bracken, Harry M. *J Hist Phil* 28(3), 455-456 Jl 90

BELL, David. *Spinoza in Germany from 1670 to the Age of Goethe*. London, Univ of London, 1984.
Lichtigfeld, Adolph. *Int Stud Phil* 22(1), 85-86 1990

BELL, J L. *Toposes and Local Set Theories: An Introduction*. Oxford, Clarendon Pr, 1988.
McLarty, Colin. *Notre Dame J Form Log* 31(1), 150-161 Wint 90
Wraith, G C. *J Sym Log* 55(2), 886-887 Je 90

BELL, J S. *Speakable and Unspeakable in Quantum Mechanics*. New York, Cambridge Univ Pr, 1987.
Espinoza, M. *Arch Phil* 52(4), 665-667 O-D 89

BELL, Richard H (ed). *The Grammar of the Heart: New Essays in Moral Philosophy and Theology*. San Francisco, Harper & Row, 1988.
Ferreira, M Jamie. *Thomist* 54(3), 560-564 Jl 90

BENCIVENGA, Ermanno. *Kant's Copernican Revolution*. NY, Oxford Univ Pr, 1987.
Cooke, Vincent M. *Int Phil Quart* 30(1), 114-116 Mr 90
Robinson, Hoke. *J Hist Phil* 28(3), 458-460 Jl 90
Walker, Ralph C S. *Phil Rev* 99(3), 439-442 Jl 90

BENHABIB, Seyla and CORNELL, Drucilla (eds). *Feminism as a Critique*. Minneapolis, Univ of Minnesota Pr, 1989.
Rosen, Deborah M. *Can Phil Rev* 10(1), 3-5 Ja 90

BENHABIB, Seyla. *Critique, Norm, and Utopia: A Study of the Foundations of Critical Theory*. New York, Columbia Univ Pr, 1986.
Berman, Robert. *Owl Minerva* 21(1), 114-122 Fall 89

BENN, Stanley I. *A Theory of Freedom*. New York, Cambridge Univ Pr, 1988.
Baier, Kurt. *Ethics* 100(1), 93-107 O 89
Bellamy, Richard. *Hist Euro Ideas* 12(3), 420-422 1990
Gaus, Gerald. *Ethics* 100(1), 127-148 O 89
Gilbert, Paul. *Phil Books* 30(4), 226-228 O 89
Kleinig, John. *Ethics* 100(1), 108-115 O 89
Pettit, Philip. *Ethics* 100(1), 116-126 O 89

BENNETT, James T and DILORENZO, Thomas J. *Unfair Competition: The Profits of Nonprofits*. Lanham, Hamilton Pr, 1989.
Dienhart, John W. *J Bus Ethics* 9(1), 20,30,44 Ja 90

BENNETT, Jonathan. *Events and Their Names*. Oxford, Clarendon Pr, 1988.
Teichmann, Roger. *Mind* 99(394), 299-301 Ap 90
Wilkerson, T E. *Phil Books* 31(2), 99-101 Ap 90

BENTHAM, Jeremy. *First Principles Preparatory to Constitutional Code, Philip Schofield (ed)*. Oxford, Clarendon Pr, 1989.
Lively, J F. *Utilitas* 2(1), 150-151 My 90

BEORLEGUI, Carlos. *Lecturas de antropología filosófica*. Bilbao, Desclée de Brouwer, 1988.
Gutierrez Martinez, Alberto. *Theoria (Spain)* 4(11), 527-530 F-My 89
Ursua, Nicanor. *Theoria (Spain)* 4(11), 530-532 F-My 89

BERAN, Harry. *The Consent Theory of Political Obligation*. London, Croom Helm, 1987.
Rickard, Maurice. *Austl J Phil* 68(1), 121-124 Mr 90

BERKELEY, G. *Oeuvres II, G Brykman (ed)*. Paris, Pr Univ de France, 1987.
Clero, Jean-Pierre. *Rev Phil Fr* 179(2), 225-231 Ap-Je 89

BERMAN, David (ed). *George Berkeley: Essays and Replies*. Dublin, Irish

Academic Pr, 1985.
Wilkinson, Winston A. *Mod Sch* 67(1), 80-82 N 89

BERNAUER, James and RASMUSSEN, David (eds). *The Final Foucault.* Cambridge, MIT Pr, 1988.
Sawicki, Jana. *Teach Phil* 13(1), 66-69 Mr 90

BERNIER, Réjane. *Aux sources de la biologie, V2: Les théories de la génération après la Renaissance.* Frelighsburg, Orbis, 1986.
Asselin, Denis. *Dialogue (Canada)* 28(4), 689-692 1989

BERNSTEIN, John Andrew. *Nietzsche's Moral Philosophy.* Rutherford, Fairleigh Dickinson Univ Pr, 1987.
Jolley, Kelly Dean. *J Hist Phil* 28(3), 463-465 Jl 90

BERNSTEIN, Richard J. *Philosophical Profiles: Essays in a Pragmatic Mode.* Philadelphia, Univ of Pennsylvania Pr, 1986.
Hutton, Patrick H. *New Vico Studies* 4, 186-188 1986

BEROFSKY, Bernard. *Freedom from Necessity: The Metaphysical Basis of Responsibility.* London, Routledge & Kegan Paul, 1987.
Edwards, Jim. *Phil Books* 31(2), 105-107 Ap 90

BERRY, Thomas. *The Dream of the Earth.* San Francisco, Sierra Club Books, 1988.
Bratton, Susan Power. *Environ Ethics* 12(1), 87-89 Spr 90

BESNARD, Philippe. *An Introduction to Default Logic.* Berlin, Springer, 1989.
Gochet, Paul. *Rev Int Phil* 44(172), 145 1990

BEST, David. *Feeling and Reason in the Arts.* Winchester, Allen & Unwin, 1985.
Simpson, Alan. *J Aes Educ* 21(4), 155-158 Wint 87

BEUCHOT, Mauricio. *Ensayos marginales sobre Aristóteles.* México, UNAM, 1985.
Femenías, María Luisa. *Cuad Filosof* 20(33), 75-76 O 89

BEUCHOT, Mauricio. *Significado y discurso.* México, UNAM, 1988.
Stigol, Nora. *Analisis Filosof* 9(1), 96-98 My 89

BEWELL, Alan. *Wordsworth and the Enlightenment: Nature, Man, and Society in the Experimental Poetry.* New Haven, Yale Univ Pr, 1989.
Rudy, John G. *Thought* 65(257), 219-221 Je 90

BHASKAR, Roy. *Reclaiming Reality: A Critical Introduction to Contemporary Philosophy.* London, Verso, 1989.
Collier, Andrew. *Phil Books* 31(2), 93-94 Ap 90
Hayward, Tim. *Rad Phil* 55, 57 Sum 90

BIDNEY, Martin. *Blake and Goethe: Psychology, Ontology, Imagination.* Columbia, Univ of Missouri Pr, 1988.
Tonetto, Walter. *Phil Lit* 14(1), 198-199 Ap 90

BIGELOW, John. *The Reality of Numbers: A Physicalist's Philosophy of Mathematics.* Oxford, Clarendon Press, 1988.
Dale, A J. *Phil Books* 31(1), 61-62 Ja 90
Lewis, David. *Austl J Phil* 67(4), 487-489 D 89
Pollard, Stephen. *Rev Metaph* 43(4), 854 Je 90

BILIMORIA, Plurusottama and FENNER, Peter (eds). *Religions and Comparative Thought.* Delhi, Satguru, 1988.
Tiwari, Kapil N. *Austl J Phil* 67(3), 354-355 S 89

BILLECOQ, Alain. *Spinoza et les spectres: Un essai sur l'esprit philosophique.* Paris, Pr Univ de France, 1987.
Rice, Lee C. *Stud Spinozana* 4, 412-415 1988

BIRD, Graham. *William James.* New York, Routledge, 1986.
Hookway, Christopher. *Phil Rev* 98(4), 547-550 O 89

BIRNBACHER, Dieter. *Verantwortung für zukunftige Generationen.* Stuttgart, Reclam, 1988.
O'Hagan, Timothy. *Ratio* 2(2), 191-195 D 89

BIRNBAUM, Pierre. *States and Collective Action: The European Experience.* NY, Cambridge Univ Pr, 1988.
Levi, Margaret. *Polit Theory* 18(1), 174-176 F 90

BIRTEL, Frank T (ed). *Religion, Science, and Public Policy.* New York, Crossroad/Continuum, 1987.
Kaehler, Marian. *Zygon* 24(3), 385-388 S 89

BIXIO, Andrea. *Proprietà e appropriazione.* Milan, Giuffrè, 1988.
Jellamo, Anna. *Riv Int Filosof Diritto* 66(3), 539-541 Jl-S 89

BLACKMORE, John and HENTSCHEL, Klaus (eds). *Ernst Mach als Aussenseiter.* Vienna, Braumüller, 1985.
Holton, Gerald. *Method Sci* 22(2), 67-81 1989

BLACKWELL, Kenneth. *The Spinozistic Ethics of Bertrand Russell.* Winchester, Allen & Unwin, 1985.

DeDijn, Herman. *Int Stud Phil* 21(3), 99-101 1989
Den Uyl, Douglas J. *Stud Spinozana* 4, 434-439 1988

BLAGA, L. *Léon dogmatique.* Lausanne, Age d'Homme, 1988.
Tortolone, Gian Michele. *Filosofia* 40(2), 222-226 My-Ag 89

BLANK, Robert H. *Rationing Medicine.* New York, Columbia Univ Pr, 1988.
Breheny, James E. *Bioethics* 3(4), 361-362 O 89

BLOCH, Ernst. *Natural Law and Human Dignity*, Dennis J Schmidt (trans). Cambridge, MIT Pr, 1986.
Nenon, Tom. *Int Stud Phil* 22(1), 86-87 1990

BLOCH, Ernst. *The Principle of Hope, V1-3*, Neville Plaice and others (trans). Cambridge, Blackwell, 1986.
Boyne, Roy. *J Brit Soc Phenomenol* 20(3), 292-295 O 89

BLOOM, Allan. *The Closing of the American Mind.* NY, Simon & Schuster, 1987.
Littleford, Michael. *New Vico Studies* 6, 169-171 1988
Lynch, Tim. *Irish Phil J* 6(1), 178-181 1989
Wake, Susan Dawn. *Eidos* 8(1), 99-103 Je 89
Wolff, Robert Paul. *Irish Phil J* 6(1), 181-186 1989

BLUESTONE, Natalie Harris. *Women and the Ideal Society: Plato's "Republic" and Modern Myths of Gender.* Amherst, Univ of Massachusetts Pr, 1987.
Calvert, Brian. *Polis* 9(1), 85-97 1990
Canto, Monique. *Rev Phil Fr* 179(3), 358-362 Jl-S 89
Shute, Sara. *J Hist Phil* 28(2), 283-284 Ap 90

BLUMENBERG, Hans. *Höhlenausgänge.* Frankfurt am Main, Suhrkamp, 1989.
Bolz, Norbert. *Phil Rundsch* 37(1-2), 153-156 1990

BLUMSTEIN, James F and SLOAN, Frank A (eds). *Organ Transplantation Policy: Issues and Prospects.* Durham, Duke Univ Pr, 1989.
Edinger, Walter. *Med Human Rev* 4(2), 88-90 Jl 90

BLUNDELL, Mary Whitlock. *Helping Friends and Harming Enemies: A Study in Sophocles and Greek Ethics.* New York, Cambridge Univ Pr, 1989.
Teichman, Jenny. *Phil Lit* 14(1), 193-194 Ap 90

BOARDMAN, John and GRIFFIN, Jasper and MURRAY, Oswyn (eds). *Greece and the Hellenistic World: The Oxford History of the Classical World, V1.* Oxford, Oxford Univ Pr, 1988.
Dillon, John. *Hermathena* 147, 78-80 Wint 89

BODIFÉE, Gerard. *Ruimte voor vrijheid.* Kapellen, Pelckmans, 1988.
Burms, Arnold. *Tijdschr Filosof* 51(3), 528-533 S 89

BODNAR, Istvan M and MÁTÉ, Andras and POLOS, Laszlo (eds). *Intensional Logic, History of Philosophy, and Methodology.* Budapest, Kezirat, Gyanan, 1988.
Anderson, C Anthony. *Hist Phil Log* 11(2), 248-250 1990

BOËR, Steven E and LYCAN, William G. *Knowing Who.* Cambridge, MIT Pr, 1986.
Soames, Scott. *J Sym Log* 53(2), 657-659 Je 88

BOGDAN, Radu J (ed). *Roderick M Chisholm.* Dordrecht, Reidel, 1986.
Tomberlin, James E. *Nous* 24(2), 332-342 Ap 90

BÖHME, Gernot. *Philosophieren mit Kant.* Frankfurt am Main, Suhrkamp, 1986.
Reuber, Martin. *Phil Rundsch* 36(3), 248-251 1989

BOISVERT, Raymond D. *Dewey's Metaphysics.* New York, Fordham Univ Pr, 1988.
Marsoobian, Armen. *J Speculative Phil* 3(4), 282-289 1989
Stuhr, John J. *Trans Peirce Soc* 25(3), 361-369 Sum 89

BONGER, H. *Spinoza en Coornhert.* Leiden, Brill, 1989.
Henrard, Roger. *Stud Spinozana* 5, 450-452 1989

BONJOUR, Laurence. *The Structure of Empirical Knowledge.* Cambridge, Harvard Univ Pr, 1985.
Dretske, Fred. *Int Stud Phil* 21(3), 101-102 1989

BONOMI, Andrea. *Le immagini dei nomi.* Milan, Garzanti, 1987.
Penco, Carlo. *Epistemologia* 12(1), 167-169 Ja-Je 89

BOOTH, Wayne C. *The Company We Keep: An Ethics of Fiction.* Berkeley, Univ of Calif Pr, 1988.
Siebers, Tobin. *Phil Lit* 13(2), 375-376 O 89

BÖRGER, Egon. *Berechenbarkeit, Komplexität, Logic.* Brunswick, Vieweg, 1985.
Siefkes, Dirk. *J Sym Log* 54(4), 1490-1493 D 89

BÖRGER, Egon. *Berechenbarkeit, Komplexität, Logik, 2nd ed.* Brunswick,

Vieweg, 1986.
Siefkes, Dirk. *J Sym Log* 54(4), 1490-1493 D 89

BORRADORI, Giovanna (ed). *Recoding Metaphysics: The New Italian Philosophy*. Evanston, Northwestern Univ Pr, 1988.
Barbiero, Daniel. *Crit Texts* 7(1), 82-89 1990

BORUAH, Bijoy H. *Fiction and Emotion: A Study in Aesthetics and the Philosophy of Mind*. Oxford, Oxford Univ Pr, 1988.
Neill, Alex. *Brit J Aes* 30(1), 76-78 Ja 90
Solomon, Robert C. *Rev Metaph* 43(3), 620-621 Mr 90

BOSTOCK, David. *Plato's "Phaedo"*. Oxford, Clarendon/Oxford Pr, 1986.
Sharples, R W. *J Hellen Stud* 109, 224-225 1989

BOSTOCK, David. *Plato's "Theaetetus"*. Oxford, Clarendon Pr, 1988.
Benitez, E E. *Rev Metaph* 43(2), 385-387 D 89
Tiles, J E. *Phil Books* 30(4), 209-211 O 89

BOTWINICK, Aryeh. *Skepticism and Political Participation*. Philadelphia, Temple Univ Pr, 1990.
Gottfried, Paul. *Rev Metaph* 43(3), 621-622 Mr 90

BOUMA III, Hessel and others. *Christian Faith, Health, and Medical Practice*. Grand Rapids, Eerdmans, 1989.
Campbell, Courtney S. *Med Human Rev* 4(2), 93-98 Jl 90

BOURGEOIS, Patrick L and SCHALOW, Frank. *Traces of Understanding: A Profile of Heidegger's and Ricoeur's Hermeneutics*. Atlanta, Rodopi, 1990.
Seeburger, Frank. *SW Phil Rev* 6(2), 139-140 Jl 90

BOURNIQUE, Gladys. *La Philosophie de Josiah Royce*. Paris, Vrin, 1988.
Oppenheim, Frank M. *Trans Peirce Soc* 25(4), 557-563 Fall 89

BOUTOT, Alain. *Heidegger et Platon: le problème du nihilisme*. Paris, Pr Univ de France, 1987.
Destrée, Pierre. *Rev Phil Louvain* 87(76), 668-671 N 89

BOVÉ, Paul A. *Intellectuals in Power: A Genealogy of Critical Humanism*. New York, Columbia Univ Pr, 1986.
Edgar, Andrew. *Brit J Aes* 30(2), 196-198 Ap 90

BOWIE, Malcolm. *Freud, Proust, and Lacan: Theory as Fiction*. New York, Cambridge Univ Pr, 1987.
Brady, Patrick. *Phil Lit* 13(2), 391-393 O 89

BOWIE, Norman E (ed). *Equal Opportunity*. Boulder, Westview Pr, 1988.
Iwanicki, Jack. *Can Phil Rev* 10(5), 175-177 My 90
Sayers, Sean. *Phil Books* 31(3), 176-177 Jl 90
Young, Robert. *Austl J Phil* 67(3), 369 S 89

BOWLER, Peter J. *Evolution, The History of an Idea*. Berkeley, Univ of Calif Pr, 1984.
Sloep, Peter P. *Hist Phil Life Sci* 11(1), 156-158 1989

BOWLER, Peter J. *The Non-Darwinian Revolution: Reinterpeting a Historical Myth*. Baltimore, Johns Hopkins Univ Pr, 1988.
Mayr, Ernst. *Biol Phil* 5(1), 85-92 Ja 90

BOYD, K M (ed). *Report of a Working Party on the Teaching of Medical Ethics*. London, IME, 1987.
Komesaroff, Paul A. *Bioethics* 4(1), 66-77 Ja 90

BOYDSTON, Jo Ann (ed). *The Later Works of John Dewey, 1925-1953, V6: 1931-1932*. Carbondale, Southern Illinois Univ Pr, 1985.
Casey, David J. *Mod Sch* 66(4), 312-315 My 89

BOYDSTON, Jo Ann (ed). *The Later Works of John Dewey, 1925-1953, V7: 1932*. Carbondale, Southern Illinois Univ Pr, 1985.
Casey, David J. *Mod Sch* 66(4), 312-315 My 89

BRADSHAW, Leah. *Acting and Thinking: The Political Thought of Hannah Arendt*. Toronto, Univ of Toronto Pr, 1989.
Fuss, Peter. *Can Phil Rev* 9(12), 477-479 D 89

BRADY, F Neil. *Ethical Managing: Rules and Results*. New York, MacMillan, 1990.
Hanly, Ken. *Can Phil Rev* 10(3), 98-101 Mr 90

BRAGUE, Rémi. *Aristote et la question du monde*. Paris, Pr Univ de France, 1988.
Lachterman, David R. *Rev Metaph* 43(2), 387-390 D 89

BRAINE, David and LESSER, Harry (eds). *Ethics, Technology and Medicine*. Aldershot, Avebury, 1988.
Harris, John. *J Applied Phil* 6(2), 240-243 O 89

BRAINE, David. *The Reality of Time and the Existence of God: The Project of Proving God's Existence*. Oxford, Clarendon Pr, 1988.
Burrell, David. *Faith Phil* 7(3), 361-364 Jl 90

Clarke, W Norris. *Int Phil Quart* 30(1), 109-111 Mr 90

BRANCACCI, A. *Rhetorike philosophousa*. Napoli, Bibliopolis, 1986.
Spinelli, Emidio. *J Hist Phil* 27(4), 610-612 O 89

BRATMAN, Michael E. *Intention, Plans, and Practical Reason*. Cambridge, Harvard Univ Pr, 1987.
Adams, Frederick. *Ethics* 100(1), 198-199 O 89
Zimmerman, Michael. *Phil Phenomenol Res* 50(1), 189-197 S 89

BRAUNSTEIN, Jean-François. *Broussais et le Matérialisme*. Paris, Klincksieck, 1986.
Tsouyopoulos, Nelly. *Hist Phil Life Sci* 11(1), 83-88 1989

BRAYBROOKE, David. *Meeting Needs*. Princeton, Princeton Univ Pr, 1987.
Mitscherling, Jeff. *J Bus Ethics* 8(11), 846,872 N 89

BRAYBROOKE, David. *Philosophy of Social Science*. Englewood Cliffs, Prentice-Hall, 1986.
Levin, David Michael. *Phil Rev* 98(4), 566-569 O 89

BRECHER, Robert. *Anselm's Argument: The Logic of Divine Existence*. Brookfield, Gower, 1985.
Miller, Paul J W. *J Hist Phil* 27(4), 612-613 O 89

BRENNAN, Andrew. *Thinking about Nature: An Investigation of Nature, Value and Ecology*. New York, Routledge, 1988.
Attfield, Robin. *J Applied Phil* 6(2), 237-238 O 89

BRENNAN, Teresa (ed). *Between Feminism and Psychoanalysis*. New York, Routledge, 1989.
Ball, David. *Brit J Aes* 30(3), 293-294 Jl 90

BRENTANO, Franz. *Über Ernst Machs 'Erkenntnis und Irrtum'*, Roderick M Chisholm and Johann C Marek (eds). Atlanta, Rodopi, 1988.
George, Rolf. *Can Phil Rev* 10(6), 222-224 Je 90

BRETON, Stanislas. *Poétique du sensible*. Paris, Cerf, 1988.
Lendger, André. *Rev Thomiste* 90(2), 323-325 Ap-Je 90

BRICKNER, Philip W and others. *Long Term Health Care: Providing a Spectrum of Services to the Aged*. New York, Basic Books, 1987.
McCullough, Laurence B. *Hastings Center Rep* 19(5), 45-46 S-O 89

BRIEN, Kevin M. *Marx, Reason, and the Art of Freedom*. Philadelphia, Temple Univ Pr, 1987.
Isaac, Jeffrey C. *Phil Soc Sci* 20(3), 385-390 S 90
Murphy, John W. *Stud Soviet Tho* 38(4), 311-313 N 89

BRINK, David O. *Moral Realism and the Foundations of Ethics*. Cambridge, Cambridge Univ Pr, 1989.
Gay, Robert. *Mind* 99(395), 474-477 Jl 90
Killoran, John B. *Rev Metaph* 43(3), 622-624 Mr 90
Nelson, Mark T. *Phil Books* 31(3), 169-171 Jl 90

BRITISH MEDICAL ASSOC. *Philosophy & Practice of Medical Ethics*. London, BMA, 1988.
Kessel, R W I. *J Med Phil* 14(6), 709-710 D 89

BROAD, C D. *Ethics*, C Levy (ed). Dordrecht, Nijhoff, 1985.
Pontara, Giuliano. *Ideal Stud* 19(2), 181-182 My 89

BROADIE, Alexander. *Introduction to Medieval Logic*. NY, Clarendon Pr, 1987.
Clarke, P A. *Phil Quart* 40(159), 264-266 Ap 90
D'Ors, Angel. *Anu Filosof* 20(2), 194-199 1987
King, Peter. *Phil Rev* 99(2), 299-302 Ap 90

BROADIE, Alexander. *Notion and Object: Aspects of Late Medieval Epistemology*. Oxford, Clarendon Pr, 1989.
Ashworth, E J. *Hist Euro Ideas* 12(2), 309-310 1990
Fitzpatrick, F J. *Phil Books* 31(1), 18-21 Ja 90
Noone, Timothy B. *Rev Metaph* 43(2), 390-391 D 89

BRODSKY, Claudia J. *The Imposition of Form: Studies in Narrative Representation and Knowledge*. Princeton, Princeton Univ Pr, 1987.
Brown, Cornelia E. *Phil Lit* 13(2), 396-397 O 89

BRODY, Baruch A (ed). *Moral Theory and Moral Judgments in Medical Ethics*. Dordrecht, Kluwer, 1988.
Jonsen, Albert R. *Hastings Center Rep* 20(4), 32-34 Jl-Ag 90
Weising, Urban. *Theor Med* 11(1), 79-80 Mr 90

BRODY, Baruch A and ENGELHARDT JR, H Tristram (eds). *Bioethics: Readings and Cases*. Englewood Cliffs, Prentice-Hall, 1987.
Edinger, Walter and Skeel, Joy D. *J Med Human* 10(2), 118-120 Fall-Wint 89

BRODY, Baruch. *Life and Death Decision Making*. New York, Oxford Univ Pr, 1988.
Downie, R S. *Phil Books* 30(4), 234-235 O 89

BRONNER, Stephen Eric and KELLNER, Douglas (eds). *Passion and Rebellion: The Expressionist Heritage.* NY, Columbia Univ Pr, 1988.
Krukowski, Lucian. *Can Phil Rev* 9(9), 349-351 S 89

BROWN, David. *Continental Philosophy and Modern Theology.* Oxford, Blackwell, 1987.
Brinkman, B R. *Heythrop J* 31(3), 369-370 Jl 90
Macquarrie, John. *Int J Phil Relig* 28(1), 60-61 Ag 90

BROWN, Harold I. *Observation and Objectivity.* New York, Oxford Univ Pr, 1987.
Ackermann, Robert J. *Int Stud Phil* 22(1), 87-88 1990
Forge, John. *Austl J Phil* 67(3), 358-358 S 89
Schweitzer, Valerie. *Phil Soc Sci* 20(2), 257-259 Je 90

BROWN, Harold I. *Rationality.* NY, Routledge & K Paul, 1988.
Mullane, Harvey. *Teach Phil* 12(4), 435-438 D 89
Pisani, Assunta. *Sapienza* 43(1), 105-107 Ja-Mr 90

BROWN, Harvey R and HARRÉ, Rom (eds). *Philosophical Foundations of Quantum Field Theory.* Oxford, Clarendon Pr, 1988.
Van Bendegem, Jean Paul. *Philosophica* 44(2), 136-139 1989

BROWN, James Robert (ed). *Scientific Rationality: The Sociological Turn.* Dordrecht, Reidel, 1984.
Tibbetts, Paul. *Phil Sci* 57(1), 170-172 Mr 90

BROWN, Richard Harvey. *Society as Text: Essays on Rhetoric, Reason, and Reality.* Chicago, Univ of Chicago Pr, 1987.
Ward, J P. *Human Stud* 13(2), 187-191 Ap 90

BROWN, Robert. *Analyzing Love.* NY, Cambridge Univ Pr, 1987.
Brümmer, Vincent. *Relig Stud* 25(3), 407-408 S 89
Soble, Alan. *Phil Soc Sci* 19(4), 493-500 D 89

BROWN, Robert. *The Nature of Social Laws: Machiavelli to Mill.* Cambridge, Cambridge Univ Pr, 1984.
Haddock, Bruce A. *New Vico Studies* 4, 183-185 1986

BROWN, Stuart. *Leibniz.* Minneapolis, Univ of Minnesota Pr, 1985.
Bailhache, Patrice. *J Prag* 13(5), 787-790 O 89

BROWNING, Douglas. *Ontology and the Practical Arena.* University Park, Pennsylvania State Univ Pr, 1990.
Swindler, J K. *SW Phil Rev* 6(2), 125-130 Jl 90

BRUMBAUGH, Robert S. *Platonic Studies of Greek Philosophy.* Albany, SUNY Pr, 1989.
Hendley, Brian. *Rev Metaph* 43(2), 391-393 D 89

BRUN, Jean. *L'Europe philosophe, vingt-cinq siècles de pensée occidentale.* Paris, Stock, 1988.
Naert, Émilienne. *Rev Phil Louvain* 87(76), 666-667 N 89

BRUN, Jean. *Le néo-platonisme.* Paris, Pr Univ de France, 1988.
Lassègue, Monique. *Rev Phil Fr* 179(3), 362-364 Jl-S 89

BRUNDELL, Barry. *Pierre Gassendi: From Aristotelianism to a New Natural Philosophy.* Norwell, Reidel, 1987.
Blackwell, Richard J. *Mod Sch* 67(2), 149-150 Ja 90
Popkin, Richard H. *Can Phil Rev* 9(10), 396-403 O 89

BRUNER, Jerome. *Actual Minds, Possible Worlds.* Cambridge, Harvard Univ Pr, 1986.
Arnstine, Donald. *J Aes Educ* 23(4), 112-114 Wint 89
Giorgi, Amedeo. *New Vico Studies* 6, 171-173 1988

BRUNS, Gerald L. *Heidegger's Estrangements: Language, Truth and Poetry in the Later Writings.* New Haven, Yale Univ Pr, 1989.
Hodge, Joanna. *Rad Phil* 55, 58 Sum 90

BUBNER, R and others. *La filosofia oggi, tra ermeneutica e dialettica, E Berti (ed).* Rome, Studium, 1987.
Celano, Bruno. *G Metaf* 11(2), 322-324 My-Ag 89

BUBNER, Rüdiger. *Essays in Hermeneutics and Critical Theory, Eric Matthews (trans).* NY, Columbia Univ Pr, 1988.
Matustik, Martin J. *Auslegung* 16(1), 116-123 Wint 90

BUCHHOLZ, Rogene A. *Fundamental Concepts and Problems in Business Ethics.* Englewood Cliffs, Prentice-Hall, 1989.
Gilbert Jr, Daniel R. *J Bus Ethics* 9(6), 472,518 Je 90

BUCKLEY, Michael J. *At the Origins of Modern Atheism.* New Haven, Yale Univ Pr, 1987.
Peterson, Mark C E. *Int J Phil Relig* 28(1), 51-53 Ag 90

BUDD, Malcolm. *Music and the Emotions.* New York, Routledge, 1985.
Meynell, Hugo. *Heythrop J* 30(4), 485-486 O 89

BUJIC, Bojan (ed). *Music in European Thought, 1851-1912.* Cambridge, Cambridge Univ Pr, 1988.
Musgrave, Michael. *Brit J Aes* 30(2), 188-190 Ap 90

BULL, Robert and SEGERBERG, Krister. *Handbook of Philosophical Logic, V2: Extensions of Classical Logic.* Norwell, Reidel, 1984.
Kuhn, Steven T. *J Sym Log* 54(4), 1472-1477 D 89

BUNT, Harry C. *Mass Terms and Model-Theoretic Semantics.* New York, Cambridge Univ Pr, 1985.
Bricker, Phillip. *J Sym Log* 53(2), 653-656 Je 88

BURKE, Peter. *Vico.* NY, Oxford Univ Pr, 1985.
Palmer, Lucia M. *New Vico Studies* 4, 199-204 1986

BURLEIGH, Walter. *Von der Reinheit der Kunst der Logik.* Hamburg, Meiner, 1988.
Berger, H and Gombocz, W L. *Hist Phil Log* 11(2), 211-216 1990

BURNYEAT, Myles and others. *Notes on Eta and Theta of Aristotle's Metaphysics.* Oxford, Oxford Univ Pr, 1984.
Ide, Harry A. *Phil Rev* 99(2), 292-293 Ap 90

BURTCHAELL, James Tunstead. *The Giving and Taking of Life: Essays Ethical.* Notre Dame, Univ of Notre Dame Pr, 1989.
Kliever, Lonnie D. *Med Human Rev* 4(2), 66-68 Jl 90

BUSCH, Thomas W. *The Power of Consciousness and the Force of Circumstances in Sartre's Philosophy.* Bloomington, Indiana Univ Pr, 1990.
Stack, George J. *Rev Metaph* 43(4), 855-856 Je 90

BUTLER, Judith P. *Subjects of Desire: Hegelian Reflections in Twentieth Century France.* NY, Columbia Univ Pr, 1987.
Pippin, Robert B. *Phil Rev* 99(1), 129-131 Ja 90

BUTTS, Robert E (ed). *Kant's Philosophy of Physical Science.* Dordrecht, Reidel, 1986.
Mudroch, Vilem. *Kantstudien* 80(4), 477-480 1989

CADEVALL I SOLER, Magi. *La estructura de la teoría de la evolución.* Barcelona, Univ Autònoma de Barcelona, 1988.
Chamizo Domínguez, Pedro José. *Dialogo Filosof* 6(2), 256-258 My-Ag 90

CAHILL, Lisa Sowle. *Between the Sexes: Foundations for a Christian Ethics of Sexuality.* Philadelphia, Fortress Pr, 1985.
Suurmond, J-J. *Bijdragen* 2, 215-216 1990

CALLAHAN, Daniel. *Setting Limits: Medical Goals in an Aging Society.* New York, Simon & Schuster, 1987.
Bell, Nora K. *Hypatia* 4(2), 169-178 Sum 89
Churchill, Larry R. *Ethics* 100(1), 169-176 O 89

CALLAHAN, Joan C (ed). *Ethical Issues in Professional Life.* New York, Oxford Univ Pr, 1988.
Snider, Eric W. *Teach Phil* 12(3); 311-314 S 89

CALLAN, Eamonn. *Autonomy and Schooling.* Montreal, McGill-Queens U Pr, 1988.
Heslep, Robert D. *Educ Stud* 20(3), 233-246 Fall 89

CALVET DE MAGLAHÁES, Theresa. *Signe ou Symbole: Introduction à la théorie sémiotique de C S Peirce.* Louvain-la-nueve, Cabay, 1981.
De Tienne, A and Kloesel, C. *Trans Peirce Soc* 25(3), 341-355 Sum 89

CAMPBELL, Alastair V. *The Gospel of Anger.* London, SPCK, 1986.
Pattison, Stephen. *Mod Theol* 5(2), 186-187 Ja 89

CAMPBELL, Donald T. *Methodology and Epistemology for Social Science: Selected Papers.* Chicago, Univ of Chicago Pr, 1988.
Potvin, Raymond H. *Rev Metaph* 43(3), 624-625 Mr 90

CAMPBELL, Richmond and SOWDEN, Lanning (eds). *Paradoxes of Rationality and Cooperation.* Vancouver, Univ of Vancouver Pr, 1985.
Cargile, James. *Nous* 24(2), 352-357 Ap 90

CAMPBELL, Robert and COLLINSON, Diane. *Ending Lives.* Oxford, Blackwell, 1988.
Battin, Margaret P. *Bioethics* 4(2), 174-176 Ap 90

CAMPBELL, Tom. *Justice.* New York, Macmillan, 1988.
Hoag, Robert W. *Phil Books* 30(4), 247-248 O 89

CAMPBELL, Tom. *The Left and Rights: A Conceptual Analysis of Socialist Rights.* Boston, Routledge & Kegan Paul, 1983.
Tucker, D F B. *Crit Rev* 3(3-4), 554-567 Sum-Fall 89

CANFIELD, John V (ed). *The Philosophy of Wittgenstein, 15v.* New York, Garland, 1987.
Morris, William Edward. *Teach Phil* 12(3), 346-349 S 89

CAPALDI, Nicholas. *Out of Order: Affirmative Action and the Crisis of Doctrinaire Liberalism.* Buffalo, Prometheus, 1985.
Schultz, David. *Int Stud Phil* 22(1), 88-89 1990
Wortham, Anne. *Vera Lex* 9(1), 20-23 1989

CAPELLETTI, Angel J. *La idea de la libertad en el Renacimiento.* Caracas,

Alfadil, 1986.
Landa, Josu. *Rev Filosof (Mexico)* 23(67), 137-139 Ja-Ap 90

CAPLAN, Lional (ed). *Studies in Religious Fundamentalism*. New York, Macmillan, 1987.
Wilson, B R. *Relig Stud* 25(2), 250-252 Je 89

CAPRA, F. *The Turning Point*. Bern, Scherz, 1987.
Kamaryt, Jan. *Filozof Cas* 37(5), 743-752 1989

CAPUTO, John D. *Radical Hermeneutics: Repetition, Deconstruction and the Hermeneutic Project*. Bloomington, Indiana Univ Pr, 1987.
Lauder, Robert E. *Thomist* 53(4), 722-725 O 89

CARBONE JR, Peter F. *Value Theory and Education*. Melbourne, Krieger, 1987.
Heslep, Robert D. *Educ Stud* 20(3), 233-246 Fall 89

CARDONA, Carlos. *Metafísica del bien y del mal*. Pamplona, EUNSA, 1987.
Del Barco Collazos, José L. *Anu Filosof* 22(1), 176-179 1989
Vegas, José M. *Dialogo Filosof* 6(1), 105-107 Ja-Ap 90

CARE, Norman S. *On Sharing Fate*. Philadelphia, Temple Univ Pr, 1987.
Mulvaney, Robert J. *Behavior Phil* 18(1), 81-83 Spr-Sum 90

CARNOIS, Bernard. *The Coherence of Kant's Doctrine of Freedom*, David Booth (trans). Chicago, Univ of Chicago Pr, 1987.
Allison, Henry E. *Phil Rev* 99(1), 117-119 Ja 90

CARPENTER, James A. *Nature and Grace: Toward an Integral Perspective*. NY, Crossroad, 1988.
Galvin, John P. *Thomist* 54(1), 173-176 Ja 90

CARR, David. *Interpreting Husserl: Critical and Comparative Studies*. Dordrecht, Nijhoff, 1987.
Holmes, Richard. *Dialogue (Canada)* 28(3), 517-520 1989
Scanlon, John. *Husserl Stud* 7(1), 72-78 1990

CARR, David. *Time, Narrative, and History*. Bloomington, Indiana Univ Pr, 1986.
Kerby, Anthony. *Dialogue (Canada)* 27(4), 738-741 Wint 88
Medina, Angel. *Man World* 23(2), 231-237 Ap 90
Mudrovcic, María Inés. *Cuad Filosof* 20(33), 69-73 O 89
Rojcewicz, Richard. *Res Phenomenol* 18, 300-306 1988

CARRUTHERS, Peter. *Tractarian Semantics: Finding Sense in Wittgenstein's "Tractatus"*. Oxford, Blackwell, 1989.
Moore, A W. *Mind* 99(395), 482-485 Jl 90

CARTER, Alan. *The Philosophical Foundations of Property Rights*. Brighton, Harvester Wheatsheaf, 1989.
Menlowe, Michael A. *Phil Books* 31(1), 45-46 Ja 90

CARTWRIGHT, Nancy. *How the Laws of Physics Lie*. Oxford, Clarendon Pr, 1983.
Kyburg Jr, Henry E. *Nous* 24(1), 174-176 Mr 90

CARVALHO, Maria Cecília M de. *Paradigmas filosóficos da atualidade*. Campinas, Papirus, 1989.
Borges, Bento Itamar. *Educ Filosof* 4(7), 147-151 Jl-D 89

CASCARDI, Anthony J (ed). *Literature and the Question of Philosophy*. Baltimore, Johns Hopkins Univ Pr, 1988.
Seamon, Roger. *Can Phil Rev* 10(7), 264-268 Jl 90

CASEY, Edward S. *Remembering: A Phenomenological Study*. Bloomington, Indiana Univ Pr, 1987.
Krell, David Farrell. *Res Phenomenol* 19, 251-272 1989

CASTAÑEDA, Hector-Neri. *Sul metodo in filosofia*, Roberto Poli (ed). Trento, Luigi Reverdito, 1989.
Marletti, Carlo. *Teoria* 9(2), 177-178 1989

CASTAÑEDA, Hector-Neri. *Thinking, Language, and Experience*. Minneapolis, Univ of Minnesota Pr, 1989.
Hookway, Christopher. *Phil Books* 31(3), 161-163 Jl 90

CAUCHY, Venant (ed). *Philosophie et culture*, 5v. Montréal, Montmorency, 1988.
Boulad-Ayoub, Josiane. *Philosophiques* 16(2), 436-439 Autumn 89

CAVADI, A and GALANTINO, N and GUARNERI, E. *Alla ricerca dell'uomo*. Palermo, Augustinus, 1988.
Conigliaro, Francesco. *Sapienza* 42(2), 214-219 Ap-Je 89

CAVELL, Stanley. *Disowning Knowledge in Six Plays of Shakespeare*. Cambridge, Cambridge Univ Pr, 1987.
Bruns, Gerald L. *Crit Inquiry* 16(3), 612-632 Spr 90

CAVELL, Stanley. *In Quest of the Ordinary: Lines of Scepticism and Romanticism*. Chicago, Univ of Chicago Pr, 1988.

Gilbert, Paul. *Phil Books* 31(2), 95-96 Ap 90
Krajewski, Bruce. *Rev Metaph* 43(2), 393-394 D 89
Yousef, Nancy. *Crit Texts* 6(3), 30-40 1989

CAWS, Peter. *Structuralism: The Art of the Intelligible*. Atlantic Highlands, Humanities Pr, 1988.
Shapiro, Gary. *Teach Phil* 12(3), 327-329 S 89

CHAMPLIN, T S. *Reflexive Paradoxes*. London, Routledge & Kegan Paul, 1988.
Borst, Clive. *Phil Books* 31(1), 28-29 Ja 90
Grattan-Guinness, I. *Hist Phil Log* 11(2), 247-248 1990
Noonan, Harold W. *Philosophy* 64(250), 568-569 O 89

CHARLTON, William. *Philosophy and Christian Belief*. London, Sheed & Ward, 1988.
Morris, Thomas V. *Phil Books* 31(2), 120-124 Ap 90

CHARMÉ, Stuart L. *Meaning and Myth in the Study of Lives: A Sartrean Perspective*. Philadelphia, Univ of Penn Pr, 1984.
Josenas, Eliane. *Int Stud Phil* 21(3), 102-103 1989
Morris, Phyllis S. *J Brit Soc Phenomenol* 20(3), 295-298 O 89

CHARNIAK, Eugene and MCDERMOTT, Drew. *Introduction to Artificial Intelligence*. Reading, Addison-Wesley, 1986.
Shavit, Yaron. *J Prag* 13(4), 645-649 Ag 89

CHASE, Alston. *Playing God in Yellowstone: The Destruction of America's First National Park*. NY, Harcourt Brace Jovanovich, 1987.
Rolston III, Holmes. *Biol Phil* 5(2), 241-258 Ap 90

CHENEY, Lynne V. *50 Hours: A Core Curriculum for College Students*. Washington, NEH, 1989.
Myers, David. *Personalist Forum* 6(1), 93-97 Spr 90

CHERNIAK, Christopher. *Minimal Rationality*. Cambridge, MIT Pr, 1986.
Appiah, Anthony. *Phil Rev* 99(1), 121-123 Ja 90

CHINCHORE, Mangala R. *Dharmakirti's Theory of Hetu-Centricity of Anumāna*. Delhi, Motilal, 1989.
Marathe, M P. *Indian Phil Quart* 16(4), 492-497 O 89

CHISHOLM, Roderick M. *On Metaphysics*. Minneapolis, Univ of Minnesota Pr, 1989.
Knasas, John F X. *Rev Metaph* 43(4), 856-857 Je 90

CHO, Kah Kyung. *Bewusstsein und Natursein: Phänomenologischer West-Ost Diwan*. Freiburg, Alber, 1987.
Harries, Karsten. *Res Phenomenol* 19, 275-281 1989

CHOZA, J. *Manual de Antropología Filosófica*. Madrid, RIALP, 1988.
Fontán del Junco, Manuel. *Anu Filosof* 22(1), 182-187 1989

CHRISTENSEN, Darrel E. *Hegelian/Whiteheadian Perspectives*. Lanham, Univ Pr of America, 1989.
Lucas Jr, George R. *Can Phil Rev* 9(8), 305-306 Ag 89
Lucas Jr, George R. *Rev Metaph* 43(2), 394-395 D 89

CHRISTIAN, William A. *Doctrines of Religious Communities: A Philosophical Study*. New Haven, Yale Univ Pr, 1987.
D'Costa, Gavin. *Heythrop J* 31(3), 368-369 Jl 90

CHURCHLAND, Patricia. *Neurophilosophy: Toward a Unified Theory of the Mind/Brain*. Cambridge, MIT Press, 1988.
Akins, Kathleen A. *J Phil* 87(2), 93-102 F 90

CHURCHLAND, Paul M. *Matter and Consciousness*. Cambridge, MIT Pr, 1988.
Myin, Erik. *Philosophica* 45(1), 115-119 1990

CIAFARDONE, R. *la "Critica de lla ragione pura" nell'Aetas kantiana*. L'Aquila, Japadre, 1987.
Fernández Aguado, Javier. *Anu Filosof* 22(1), 180-182 1989

CIBA FOUNDATION. *Human Embryo Research: Yes or No?* London, Tavistock, 1986.
Mellor, Jane. *Ethics Med* 4(2), 30-31 1988

CIMINO, Guido. *la mente e il suo substratum*. Pisa, Domus Galilaeana, 1984.
Badano, Gigliola. *Epistemologia* 12(1), 173-177 Ja-Je 89

CLARK, Michael. *Jacques Lacan: An Annotated Bibliography*, 2v. New York, Garland, 1988.
Ver Eecke, Wilfried. *Rev Metaph* 43(4), 857-859 Je 90

CLARK, Peter and WRIGHT, Crispin (eds). *Mind, Psychoanalysis and Science*. Oxford, Blackwell, 1988.
Wilkes, Kathleen V. *Phil Quart* 40(159), 241-254 Ap 90

CLARK, Stephen R L. *The Mysteries of Religion*. Cambridge, Blackwell,

1986.
Sherry, Patrick. *Mod Theol* 6(1), 114-115 O 89

CLARKE JR, D S. *Practical Inferences*. Boston, Routledge & Kegan Paul, 1985.
Ullmann-Margalit, Edna. *Int Stud Phil* 21(3), 103-105 1989

CLARKE JR, D S. *Rational Acceptance and Purpose: An Outline of a Pragmatist Epistemology*. Totowa, Rowman & Littlefield, 1988.
Misak, Cheryl. *Can Phil Rev* 10(2), 52-54 F 90

CLARKE, D S. *Principles of Semiotic*. London, Routledge & Kegan Paul, 1978.
Uwajeh, M K C. *Commun Cog* 23(1), 111-116 1990

CLARKE, Desmond M. *Occult Powers and Hypotheses: Cartesian Natural Philosophy under Louis XIV*. Oxford, Clarendon Pr, 1989.
Jolley, Nicholas. *Phil Books* 31(3), 144-146 Jl 90
van Leeuwen, Evert. *Rev Metaph* 43(3), 625-627 Mr 90

CLAYTON, Philip. *Explanation from Physics to Theology*. New Haven, Yale Univ Pr, 1989.
King-Farlow, John. *Can Phil Rev* 9(11), 434-437 N 89

CLEARY, John J and SHARTIN, Daniel C (eds). *Proceedings of the Boston Area Colloquium in Ancient Philosophy, V4, 1988*. Lanham, Univ Pr of America, 1989.
Deslauriers, Marguerite. *Can Phil Rev* 10(2), 54-57 F 90
Glidden, David K. *Nous* 23(5), 711-712 D 89
Inwood, Brad. *Hermathena* 147, 75-77 Wint 89

COBY, Patrick. *Socrates and the Sophistic Enlightenment: A Commentary on Plato's "Protagoras"*. Lewisburg, Bucknell Univ Pr, 1987.
Morrisey, Will. *Interpretation* 17(2), 313-315 Wint 89-90

COCCHIARELLA, Nino B. *Logical Investigations of Predication Theory and the Problem of Universals*. Atlantic Highlands, Humanities Pr, 1986.
Williamson, Timothy. *Ling Phil* 13(2), 265-271 Ap 90

COCKS, Joan. *The Oppositional Imagination: Feminism, Critique and Political Theory*. London, Routledge, 1989.
Sandbacka, Carola. *Phil Invest* 13(2), 186-190 Ap 90
Tuxill, Cei. *J Applied Phil* 7(1), 113-114 Mr 90

CODE, Lorraine. *Epistemic Responsibility*. Hanover, Univ Pr of New England, 1987.
BonJour, Laurence. *Phil Rev* 99(1), 123-126 Ja 90
Thomson, Anne. *J Applied Phil* 7(1), 105-107 Mr 90

COFFEY, David. *Believer, Christian, Catholic: Three Essays in Fundamental Theology*. Sydney, Cath Inst of Sydney, 1986.
D'Costa, Gavin. *Mod Theol* 5(4), 395 Jl 89

COHEN, Arthur A. *Contemporary Jewish Religious Thought: Original Essays and Critical Concepts, Movements, and Beliefs*. NY, Scribner's, 1987.
Kluback, William. *Int J Phil Relig* 27(1-2), 125-127 Ap 90

COHEN, G A. *History, Labour, and Freedom: Themes from Marx*. Oxford, Oxford Univ Pr, 1988.
Little, Daniel. *Polit Theory* 18(2), 312-315 My 90
Shaw, William H. *Inquiry* 32(4), 437-453 D 89

COHEN, L Jonathan. *An Introduction to the Philosophy of Induction and Probability*. Oxford, Clarendon Pr, 1989.
Black, Robert. *Phil Books* 31(1), 57-59 Ja 90
Harriott, Howard H. *Hist Phil Log* 11(2), 254-259 1990
Milne, Peter. *Mind* 99(394), 313-315 Ap 90

COHEN, Richard (ed). *Face to Face with Levinas*. Albany, SUNY Pr, 1986.
McKimmy, Michael G. *Int Stud Phil* 22(1), 89-90 1990

COHEN, Sherrill and TAUB, Nadine (eds). *Reproductive Laws for the 1990s*. Clifton, Humana Pr, 1989.
Holmes, Helen Bequaert. *Hypatia* 4(3), 150-159 Fall 89

COHEN-SOLAL, Annie. *Sartre: A Life*, Anna Cancogni (trans). New York, Pantheon, 1987.
Henry, Patrick. *Phil Lit* 14(1), 117-141 Ap 90
Santoni, Ronald E. *J Brit Soc Phenomenol* 21(2), 185-188 My 90

COLAPIETRO, Vincent M. *Peirce's Approach to the Self: A Semiotic Perspective on Human Subjectivity*. Albany, SUNY PR, 1989.
Harrison, Stanley. *Int Phil Quart* 30(3), 359-366 S 90
Joswick, Hugh. *Trans Peirce Soc* 25(4), 549-557 Fall 89
Ochs, Peter. *J Speculative Phil* 4(2), 172-176 1990

COLEMAN, Earle J. *Varieties of Aesthetic Experience*. Lanham, Univ Pr of America, 1983.

Johnston, Marilyn. *J Aes Educ* 21(3), 125-126 Fall 87

COLES, Robert. *The Call of Stories: Teaching and the Moral Imagination*. Boston, Houghton Mifflin, 1989.
Poland, Helene Dwyer. *Teach Phil* 13(1), 75-76 Mr 90

COLISH, Marcia. *The Stoic Tradition from Antiquity to the Early Middle Ages*, 2v. Leiden, Brill, 1985.
Inwood, Brad. *Ancient Phil* 9 (2), 337-339 Fall 89

COLLINS, Arthur. *The Nature of Mental Things*. Notre Dame, Univ of Notre Dame Pr, 1987.
Brandom, Robert B. *Phil Rev* 99(1), 119-121 Ja 90

COLLINS, H M. *Changing Order*. London, Sage, 1985.
Rheinberger, Hans-Jörg. *Hist Phil Life Sci* 11(2), 388-390 1989

COLLINS, Hugh. *The Law of Contract*. London, Weidenfeld & Nicolson, 1986.
McLaughlin, Jeff. *Eidos* 8(1), 79-90 Je 89

COLOMBO, Giuseppe (ed). *L'evidenza e la fede*. Milan, Glossa, 1988.
Zen, Gianni. *Sapienza* 43(2), 212-214 Ap-Je 90

COMNINEL, George. *Rethinking the French Revolution: Marxism and the Revisionist Challenge*. London, Verso, 1987.
Judt, Tony R. *Hist Euro Ideas* 10(6), 732-734 1989

COMSTOCK, Gary (ed). *Is There a Moral Obligation to Save the Family Farm?* Ames, Iowa State Univ Pr, 1987.
Thompson, Paul B. *Agr Human Values* 6(4), 62-65 Fall 89

COMTE, Auguste. *Correspondance générale et Confessions, VII, 1853-1854*. Paris, Vrin, 1987.
Le Lannou, Jean-Michel. *Rev Phil Fr* 179(2), 238-240 Ap-Je 89

CONCHE, Marcel. *L'aléatoire*. Villers-sur-Mer, Mégare, 1989.
Vinson, Alain. *Rev Phil Fr* 180(2), 443-447 Ap-Je 90

CONCHE, Marcel. *Montaigne et la philosophie*. Villers-sur-mer, Mégare, 1987.
Bernhardt, Jean. *J Hist Phil* 27(4), 616-618 O 89

CONILL, Jesús. *El crepúsculo de la metafísica*. Barcelona, Anthropos, 1988.
Amengual, Gabriel. *Pensamiento* 45(180), 485-488 O-D 89

CONNELL, George. *To Be One Thing: Personal Unity in Kierkegaard's Thought*. Macon, Mercer Univ Pr, 1985.
Anderson, Thomas C. *Mod Sch* 67(1), 86-87 N 89

CONNER, Steven. *Postmodernist Culture: An Introduction to Theories of the Contemporary*. Oxford, Blackwell, 1989.
Parker, Noel. *Rad Phil* 55, 50-51 Sum 90

CONNOLLY, William E. *Appearance and Reality in Politics*. Cambridge, Cambridge Univ Pr, 1981.
Boesche, Roger. *Hist Euro Ideas* 10(6), 721-727 1989

CONNOLLY, William E. *Political Theory and Modernity*. NY, Blackwell, 1988.
Boesche, Roger. *Hist Euro Ideas* 10(6), 721-727 1989
Dallmayr, Fred. *Polit Theory* 18(1), 162-169 F 90

CONNOLLY, William E. *Politics and Ambiguity*. Madison, Univ of Wisconsin Pr, 1987.
Boesche, Roger. *Hist Euro Ideas* 10(6), 721-727 1989

CONWAY, Stephen (ed). *The Correspondence of Jeremy Bentham, V8, January 1809 to December 1816*. Oxford, Clarendon Pr, 1988.
Robson, John M. *Utilitas* 1(1), 153-156 My 89

COOPER, John Charles. *The Roots of the Radical Theology*. Lanham, Univ Pr of America, 1988.
Ryan, Herbert J. *Thought* 65(257), 203 Je 90

COOPER-WIELE, Jonathan Kearns. *The Totalizing Act: Key to Husserl's Early Philosophy*. Dordrecht, Kluwer, 1989.
Miller, J Philip. *Rev Metaph* 43(3), 627-628 Mr 90

COPLESTON, Frederick C. *Philosophy in Russia: From Herzen to Lenin and Berdyaev*. Notre Dame, Univ Notre Dame Pr, 1986.
Gavin, William J. *Stud Soviet Tho* 38(2), 183-186 Ag 89

CORDUA, Carla. *El mundo ético: Ensayos sobre la esfera del hombre en la filosofía de Hegel*. Barcelona, Anthropos, 1989.
Cruz Vergara, Eliseo. *Rev Latin De Filosof* 16(1), 119-126 Mr 90

CORETH, E and NEIDL, W M and PFLIGERSDORFFER, G (eds). *Christliche Philosophie im katholischen Denken des 19 und 20 Jahrhunderts, V2: Rückgriff auf scholastisches Erbe*. Graz, Styria, 1988.
Rosemann, Phillipp W. *Irish Phil J* 6(1), 170-178 1989

COSTA DE BEAUREGARD, Olivier. *Time, the Physical Magnitude*.

DANTE ALIGHIERI. *Monarchia*, Ruedi Imbach and Christoph Flüeler (eds & trans). Stuttgart, Reclam, 1989.
Bertelloni, Francisco. *Z Phil Forsch* 44(2), 323-328 1990

DANTO, Arthur C. *Connections to the World*. NY, Harper & Row, 1989.
Solomon, Robert C. *Teach Phil* 12(4), 1989 D 89

DANTO, Arthur C. *The Philosophical Disenfranchisement of Art*. NY, Columbia Univ Pr, 1986.
Carroll, Noël. *Hist Theor* 29(1), 111-124 F 90

DANTO, Arthur C. *The State of the Art*. NY, Prentice Hall, 1987.
Carroll, Noël. *Hist Theor* 29(1), 111-124 F 90
Devereaux, Mary. *Phil Lit* 14(1), 199-200 Ap 90

DANTO, Arthur C. *The Transfiguration of the Commonplace*. Cambridge, Harvard Univ Pr, 1981.
Carroll, Noël. *Hist Theor* 29(1), 111-124 F 90

DASENBROCK, Reed Way (ed). *Redrawing the Lines: Analytic Philosophy, Deconstruction, and Literary Theory*. Minneapolis, Univ of Minnesota Pr, 1989.
Flores, Ralph. *Phil Lit* 14(1), 196-197 Ap 90

DAUENHAUER, Bernard P. *The Politics of Hope*. New York, Routledge, 1986.
Boyne, Roy. *J Brit Soc Phenomenol* 20(3), 292-295 O 89
Lumsden, Charles J. *Biol Phil* 4(4), 495-502 O 89
Smook, Roger. *Zygon* 24(3), 377-379 S 89

DE BOLLA, Peter. *The Discourse of the Sublime: Readings in History, Aesthetics and the Subject*. Oxford, Blackwell, 1989.
Wilkinson, Robert. *Brit J Aes* 30(2), 181-183 Ap 90

DE GRAZIA, Sebastian. *Machiavelli in Hell*. Princeton, Princeton Univ Pr, 1989.
Kaufman-Osborn, Timothy V. *Phil Lit* 14(1), 205-207 Ap 90

DE LA TORRE, Bartholomew R. *Thomas Buckingham and the Contingency of Futures*. Notre Dame, Univ Notre Dame Pr, 1987.
Mulligan, Robert W. *Mod Sch* 66(4), 304-305 My 89

DE LIBERA, Alain (ed). *Ulrich of Strasbourg: De summo bono, Liber II, Tractatus 1-4*. Hamburg, Meiner, 1987.
Schenk, Richard. *Thomist* 54(3), 546-552 Jl 90

DE MAN, Paul. *Critical Writings, 1953-1978*, Lindsay Waters (ed). Minneapolis, Univ of Minnesota Pr, 1989.
Bernstein, J M. *Bull Hegel Soc Gt Brit* 18, 58-63 Autumn-Wint 88

DE MICHELIS, Cesare and PIZZAMIGLIO, Gilberto (eds). *Vico e Venezia*. Florence, Olschki, 1982.
Costa, Gustavo. *New Vico Studies* 2, 120-124 1984

DE NATALE, F and SEMERARI, G. *Skepsis: Studi husserliani*. Bari, Dedalo, 1989.
De Paoli, Marco. *Filosofia* 40(2), 226-232 My-Ag 89

DE PAOLO, Charles. *Coleridge's Philosophy of Social Reform*. New York, Lang, 1987.
Young, Art. *Clio* 18(4), 417-419 Sum 89

DE RIJK, L M. *Plato's Sophist*. Amsterdam, North-Holland, 1986.
Máté, András. *Tijdschr Filosof* 51(4), 696-702 D 89

DE RIJK, L M. *Some Earlier Parisian Tracts on Distinctiones Sophismatum*. Nijmegen, Ingenium, 1988.
D'Ors, Angel. *Anu Filosof* 22(1), 189-191 1989

DE ROSE, Maria. *Il pensiero della relazione: Gli scritti 1882-1888 di John Dewey*. Fasano, Schena, 1989.
Bottani, Livio. *Filosofia* 41(2), 244-246 My-Ag 90

DE SOUSA, Ronald. *The Rationality of Emotion*. Cambridge, MIT Pr, 1987.
Burns, Steven. *Dialogue (Canada)* 28(3), 499-507 1989
Lyons, William. *Phil Phenomenol Res* 50(3), 631-633 Mr 90
Walton, Douglas. *Phil Rhet* 22(4), 302-303 1989

DE VOGEL, C J. *Rethinking Plato and Platonism*. Leiden, Brill, 1986.
Rist, John M. *Ancient Phil* 10(1), 113-115 Spr 90

DEAN, William. *American Religious Empiricism*. Albany, SUNY Pr, 1986.
Shaw, Marvin C. *Zygon* 24(3), 382-385 S 89

DEANE, Seamus. *The French Revolution and Enlightenment in England: 1789-1832*. Cambridge, Harvard Univ Pr, 1988.
Philp, Mark. *Utilitas* 1(2), 310-313 N 89

DEAR, Peter. *Mersenne and the Learning of the Schools*. Ithaca, Cornell Univ Pr, 1988.
Garber, Daniel. *Stud Hist Phil Sci* 20(4), 531-539 D 89

Michael, Fred S and Michael, Emily. *Hist Euro Ideas* 12(1), 148-149 1990

DEARBORN, Mary V. *Love in the Promised Land*. New York, Free Pr, 1988.
Karier, Clarence J. *Educ Theor* 40(2), 255-265 Spr 90

DEATS JR, Paul and ROBB, Carol (eds). *The Boston Personalist Tradition*. Macon, Mercer Univ Pr, 1986.
Burrow Jr, Rufus. *Personalist Forum* 5(2), 137-144 Fall 89
Ferré, Frederick. *Ideal Stud* 19(3), 269-271 S 89
Neville, Robert. *Personalist Forum* 5(2), 145-147 Fall 89

DEGEORGE, Richard T. *The Nature and Limits of Authority*. Lawrence, Univ Pr of Kansas, 1985.
Adams, E M. *Int Stud Phil* 21(3), 106-108 1989

DELEUZE, Gilles. *Foucault*, Sean Hand (trans & ed). Minneapolis, Univ of Minnesota Pr, 1988.
Sawicki, Jana. *Teach Phil* 13(1), 66-69 Mr 90
Stack, George J. *Rev Metaph* 43(3), 629 Mr 90

DELGADO ANTOLIN, Salvador M. *El argumento anselmiano*. Sevilla, Univ de Sevilla, 1987.
Sanabria, José Rubén. *Rev Filosof (Mexico)* 22(65), 259-261 My-Ag 89

DEN OUDEN, Bernard and MOEN, Marcia (eds). *New Essays on Kant*. New York, Lang, 1987.
Vinci, Tom. *Can Phil Rev* 10(2), 57-60 F 90

DENNETT, Daniel C. *The Intentional Stance*. Cambridge, MIT Pr, 1987.
Hanna, Barbara. *Mind* 99(394), 291-297 Ap 90
Kitcher, Patricia. *Phil Rev* 99(1), 126-128 Ja 90
Shoemaker, Sydney. *J Phil* 87(4), 212-216 Ap 90
Zalta, Edward N. *Rev Metaph* 43(2), 397-400 D 89

DERRIDA, Jacques. *De l'esprit: Heidegger et la question*. Paris, Galilée, 1987.
Baptist, Gabriella. *Phil Rundsch* 36(4), 299-315 1989
Krell, David Farrell. *Res Phenomenol* 18, 205-230 1988

DERRIDA, Jacques. *Psyché: Inventions de l'autre*. Paris, Galilée, 1987.
Baptist, Gabriella. *Phil Rundsch* 36(4), 299-315 1989

DERRIDA, Jacques. *Vom Geist*. Frankfurt am Main, Suhrkamp, 1988.
Tichy, Matthias. *Z Phil Forsch* 44(2), 340-344 1990

DESAN, Wilfred. *Let the Future Come*. Washington, Georgetown Univ Pr, 1987.
Davis, John B. *Thomist* 54(3), 564-570 Jl 90
McBride, William L. *Man World* 23(1), 113-115 Ja 90

DESCOMBES, Vincent. *Objects of All Sorts: A Philosophical Grammar*. Baltimore, Johns Hopkins U Pr, 1986.
Leland, Dorothy. *Husserl Stud* 6(2), 186-192 1989

DESMOND, William. *Art and the Absolute: A Study of Hegel's Aesthetics*. Albany, SUNY Pr, 1986.
Luft, Eric. *Clio* 18(4), 409-415 Sum 89
Steinkraus, Warren E. *Int Stud Phil* 22(1), 94-95 1990

DESMOND, William. *Desire, Dialectic, and Otherness: An Essay on Origins*. New Haven, Yale Univ Pr, 1987.
Westphal, Merold. *Int J Phil Relig* 27(1-2), 127-128 Ap 90

DESPLAND, Michel. *The Education of Desire: Plato and the Philosophy of Religion*. Toronto, Univ of Toronto Pr, 1985.
Allis, James B. *Ancient Phil* 9(1), 121-125 Spr 89

DETMER, David. *Freedom As a Value: A Critique of the Ethical Theory of Jean-Paul Sartre*. La Salle, Open Court, 1988.
Ansell-Pearson, Keith. *Rad Phil* 54, 47 Spr 90

DEUTSCH, Morton. *Distributive Justice: A Social-Psychological Perspective*. New Haven, Yale Univ Pr, 1985.
Jackson, M W. *Int Stud Phil* 21(3), 108-109 1989

DEVITT, Michael and STERELNY, Kim. *Language and Reality: An Introduction to the Philosophy of Language*. Cambridge, MIT Pr, 1987.
Taylor, Kenneth A. *Phil Rev* 99(2), 260-263 Ap 90

DI GIOVANNI, George and HARRIS, H S (eds & trans). *Between Kant and Hegel: Texts in the Development of Post-Kantian Idealism*. Albany, SUNY Pr, 1985.
Lamb, David. *J Brit Soc Phenomenol* 21(2), 201-202 My 90
Sauer, Werner. *Kantstudien* 81(2), 256-260 1990

DI LUCA, Giovanni. *Critica della Religione in Spinoza*. L'Aquila, Japadre, 1982.
Rice, Lee C. *Stud Spinozana* 4, 419-422 1988

DIAMOND, Irene and QUINBY, Lee (eds). *Feminism and Foucault: Reflections on Resistance*. Boston, Northeastern Univ Pr, 1988.

Berns, Ute. *Rad Phil* 53, 43-44 Autumn 89

DICKIE, George. *Evaluating Art*. Philadelphia, Temple Univ Pr, 1988.
Wilson, Brendan. *Phil Books* 31(1), 53-55 Ja 90

DIETL, Paul Gerhard. *Die Rezeption der Hegelschen 'Rechtsphilosophie' in der Sowjetunion*. New York, Lang, 1988.
Idalovichi, Israel. *Hist Euro Ideas* 12(2), 271-275 1990

DIETZ, Mary. *Between the Human and the Divine: The Political Thought of Simone Weil*. Totowa, Rowman & Littlefield, 1988.
Elshtain, Jean Bethke. *Polit Theory* 18(3), 508-512 Ag 90

DIEUDONNÉ, J. *Pour l'honneur de l'esprit humain, les mathématiques aujourd'hui*. Paris, Hachette, 1987.
Largeault, Jean. *Rev Metaph Morale* 94(3), 419-421 Jl-S 89

DIFFEY, T J. *Tolstoy's "What is Art?"*. Wolfeboro, Croom Helm, 1985.
Simpson, Alan. *J Aes Educ* 22(2), 116-118 Sum 88

DILLON, J T. *Questioning and Teaching: A Manual of Practice*. New York, Teachers College Pr, 1988.
Senese, Guy B. *Educ Stud* 20(3), 279-282 Fall 89

DILLON, Martin C. *Merleau-Ponty's Ontology*. Bloomington, Indiana Univ Pr, 1988.
Johnson, Galen A. *Int Stud Phil* 22(1), 95-97 1990

DILMAN, Ilham. *Freud, Insight and Change*. Oxford, Blackwell, 1988.
Pitson, A E. *Phil Invest* 13(1), 69-73 Ja 90

DILMAN, Ilham. *Mind, Brain, and Behaviour: Discussions of B F Skinner and J R Searle*. New York, Routledge, 1988.
Howard, Deryl J. *Can Phil Rev* 9(7), 259-261 Jl 89

DILTHEY, Wilhelm. *Poetry and Experience: Selected Works, V5, R A Makkreel and F Rodi (eds)*. Princeton, Princeton Univ Pr, 1985.
Daniel, Stephen H. *New Vico Studies* 4, 175-178 1986

DINI, A. *Filosofia della Natura, Medicina, Religione: Lucantonio Porzio (1639-1734)*. Milan, Angeli, 1985.
Crispini, France. *Hist Phil Life Sci* 11(1), 143-145 1989

DINWIDDY, J R (ed). *The Correspondence of Jeremy Bentham, V7, January 1802 to December 1808*. Oxford, Clarendon Pr, 1988.
Cranston, Maurice. *Utilitas* 1(1), 151-153 My 89

DISSANAYAKE, Ellen. *What Is Art For?* Seattle, Univ of Washington Pr, 1988.
Stephenson, Susan. *Brit J Aes* 30(1), 86-87 Ja 90

DOBUZINSKIS, Laurent. *The Self-Organizing Polity: An Epistemological Analysis of Political Life*. Boulder, Westview Pr, 1987.
Rosenbaum, Alan S. *Phil Soc Sci* 20(2), 248-251 Je 90

DOFLEIN, Erich. *Gestalt und Stil in der Musik*. Bad Honnef, Schroder, 1987.
Wittek, Andreas. *Z Phil Forsch* 43(3), 570-573 Jl-S 89

DOMBROWSKI, Daniel A. *Hartshorne and the Metaphysics of Animal Rights*. Albany, SUNY Pr, 1988.
Cobb Jr, John B. *Environ Ethics* 11(4), 373-376 Wint 89

DONAGAN, Alan. *Choice: The Essential Element In Human Action*. New York, Routledge, 1987.
Bishop, John. *Austl J Phil* 67(3), 375-376 S 89

DONAGAN, Alan. *Spinoza*. Chicago, Univ of Chicago Pr, 1988.
Bagley, Paul J. *Rev Metaph* 43(2), 400-401 D 89
Sprigge, T L S. *Stud Spinozana* 5, 398-405 1989

DONEY, Willis (ed). *The Philosophy of Descartes, V1-4*. New York, Garland, 1987.
Cress, Donald A. *J Hist Phil* 28(3), 449-451 Jl 90

DONOVAN, Arthur and LAUDAN, Larry and LAUDAN, Rachel (eds). *Scrutinizing Science*. Dordrecht, Kluwer, 1988.
Curtis, Ron. *Phil Soc Sci* 20(3), 376-384 S 90

DOSSA, Shiraz. *The Public Realm and the Public Self: The Political Theory of Hannah Arendt*. Waterloo, Wilfrid Laurier Univ Pr, 1988.
Honig, Bonnie. *Polit Theory* 18(2), 320-323 My 90

DOWER, Nigel (ed). *Ethics and Environmental Responsibility*. Aldershot, Avebury, 1989.
Attfield, Robin. *Phil Books* 31(3), 172-173 Jl 90

DREIER, Horst. *Rechtslehre, Staatssoziologie und Demokratietheorie bei Hans Kelsen*. Baden-Baden, Nomos, 1986.
Paulson, Stanley L. *Ratio Juris* 1(3), 269-271 D 88

DRETSKE, Fred. *Explaining Behavior: Reasons in a World of Causes*. Cambridge, MIT Pr, 1988.
Clark, Andy. *Phil Quart* 40(158), 95-102 Ja 90

Jacobson, Anne Jaap. *Can Phil Rev* 9(8), 306-310 Ag 89
Smook, Roger. *Phil Books* 30(4), 228-229 O 89

DRETSKE, Fred. *Knowledge and the Flow of Information*. Cambridge, MIT Pr, 1981.
Teixeira, João de Fernandes. *Trans/Form/Acao* 12, 133-139 1989

DROIT, Roger-Pol. *L'oubli de l'Inde: Une amnésie philosophique*. Paris, PUF, 1989.
Labarrière, Pierre-Jean. *Arch Phil* 53(2), 283-285 Ap-Je 90

DRONKE, Peter (ed). *A History of Twelfth-Century Philosophy*. New York, Cambridge Univ Pr, 1988.
Perreiah, Alan R. *Hist Euro Ideas* 10(5), 621-624 1989

DRURY, Shadia B. *The Political Ideas of Leo Strauss*. New York, St Martin's Pr, 1988.
Craig, Leon H. *Can Phil Rev* 10(3), 104-109 Mr 90
Orwin, Clifford. *Polis* 9(1), 104-118 1990

DRYZEK, John S. *Rational Ecology: Environment and Political Economy*. Cambridge, Blackwell, 1987.
Sagoff, Mark. *Ethics* 100(1), 192-195 O 89

DUBIEL, Helmut. *Theory and Politics: Studies in the Development of Critical Theory, Benjamin Gregg (trans)*. Cambridge, MIT Pr, 1985.
Trey, George A. *Auslegung* 16(1), 129-132 Wint 90
White, Stephen K. *Int Stud Phil* 22(1), 97 1990

DUCHESNEAU, François. *Genèse de la théorie cellulaire*. Montréal, Bellarmin, 1987.
Gagnon, Maurice. *Philosophiques* 16(2), 395-404 Autumn 89

DUFF, R A. *Trials and Punishment*. NY, Cambridge Univ Pr, 1986.
Belliotti, Raymond A. *Int Stud Phil* 21(3), 109-110 1989

DUHOT, Jean-Joël. *La conception stoïcienne de la causalité*. Paris, Vrin, 1989.
Follon, Jacques. *Rev Phil Louvain* 88(77), 109-113 F 90

DUJARDIN, Philippe. *Le secret*. Lyon, Pr Univ de Lyon, 1987.
Beugnot, Barnard. *Dialogue (Canada)* 27(4), 734-738 Wint 88

DUMMETT, Michael. *Ursprünge der Analytischen Philosophie*. Frankfurt am Main, Suhrkamp, 1988.
Glock, Hans J. *Mind* 98(392), 646-649 O 89

DUMOULIN, Bertrand. *Analyse génétique de la "Métaphysique" d'Aristote*. Montréal, Bellarmin, 1986.
Dorion, Louis-André. *Dialogue (Canada)* 28(3), 520-524 1989

DUNNING, Stephen N. *Kierkegaard's Dialectic of Inwardness: A Structural Analysis of the Theory of Stages*. Princeton, Princeton Univ Pr, 1985.
Piety, Marilyn G. *Owl Minerva* 21(2), 205-208 Spr 90

DURCKHEIM, Karlfried Graf. *Hara: The Vital Centre of Man, Sylvia-Monica von Kospoth and Estelle R Healey (trans)*. London, Allen & Unwin, 1962.
Shaner, David Edward. *Phil East West* 40(1), 113-115 Ja 90

DURCKHEIM, Karlfried Graf. *The Way of Transformation*. London, Allen & Unwin, 1971.
Shaner, David Edward. *Phil East West* 40(1), 113-115 Ja 90

DURFEE, Harold A. *Foundational Reflections: Studies in Contemporary Philosophy*. Dordrecht, Nijhoff, 1987.
Martin, Dean M. *Int J Phil Relig* 27(1-2), 121-122 Ap 90

DWORKIN, Gerald. *The Theory and Practice of Autonomy*. Cambridge, Cambridge Univ Pr, 1988.
Mayo, Bernard. *Philosophy* 64(250), 571-572 O 89
Thomas, Laurence. *Phil Books* 31(1), 38-40 Ja 90

DWORKIN, Ronald. *A Matter of Principle*. Cambridge, Harvard Univ Pr, 1985.
Jabbari, David. *Hist Euro Ideas* 10(6), 729-730 1989
Luizzi, Vincent. *Vera Lex* 7(2), 23 1987

DWORKIN, Ronald. *Law's Empire*. Cambridge, Harvard Univ Pr, 1986.
Guastini, Riccardo. *Ratio Juris* 1(2), 176-180 Jl 88
Hallborg Jr, Robert B. *Int Stud Phil* 21(3), 110-112 1989
Padley, Anne. *Ratio Juris* 1(2), 181-186 Jl 88

DYCZKOWSKI, Mark S G. *The Doctrine of Vibration: An Analysis of the Doctrines and Practices of Kashmir Shaivism*. Albany, SUNY Pr, 1987.
Sharma, Arvind. *Phil East West* 40(1), 109-110 Ja 90

DYER, Allen R. *Ethics and Psychiatry: Toward Professional Definition*. Washington, American Psychiatric Pr, 1988.
Agich, George J. *Theor Med* 11(2), 167-168 Je 90

DZIEMIDOK, Bohdan and MCCORMICK, Peter (eds). *On the Aesthetics of Roman Ingarden: Interpretations and Assessments*. Norwell, Kluwer, 1988.
Stern, Laurent. *Can Phil Rev* 10(6), 225-228 Je 90

EASTHOPE, Antony. *British Post-Structuralism: Since 1968*. New York, Routledge, 1988.
Suchin, Peter. *Brit J Aes* 30(3), 294-296 Jl 90

ECHEVERRIA, Javier. *Análisis de la Identidad (Prolegómenos)*. Barcelona, Granica, 1987.
Nubiola, Jaime. *Anu Filosof* 21(2), 176-178 1988

ECO, Umberto. *Art and Beauty in the Middle Ages*, H Bredin (trans). New Haven, Yale Univ Pr, 1986.
Wood, Robert E. *Rev Metaph* 43(4), 859-863 Je 90

ECO, Umberto. *The Aesthetics of Thomas Aquinas*, H Bredin (trans). Cambridge, Harvard Univ Pr, 1988.
Wood, Robert E. *Rev Metaph* 43(4), 859-863 Je 90

EDEL, A and FLOWER, E and O'CONNOR, F W (eds). *Morality, Philosophy, and Practice*. Philadelphia, Temple Univ Pr, 1989.
Driver, Julia. *Teach Phil* 12(3), 283-285 S 89

EDEL, Abraham. *Interpreting Education: Science, Ideology and Value*. New Brunswick, Transaction, 1985.
Nicholson, Linda J. *Int Stud Phil* 22(1), 98 1990

EDELSON, Marshall. *Psychoanalysis: A Theory in Crisis*. Chicago, Univ of Chicago Pr, 1988.
Erwin, Edward. *Can Phil Rev* 10(4), 132-135 Ap 90

EDIE, James M. *Edmund Husserl's Phenomenology: A Critical Commentary*. Bloomington, Indiana Univ Pr, 1987.
Harvey, Charles. *Husserl Stud* 6(3), 235-242 1989
Willard, Dallas. *Phil Rev* 99(2), 303-305 Ap 90

EDWARDS, Rem B and GRABER, Glenn C (eds). *Bioethics*. San Diego, Harcourt Brace Jov, 1988.
Jones, Gary E. *Teach Phil* 12(3), 297-298 S 89

EIDELBERG, Paul. *Beyond the Secular Mind: A Judaic Response to the Problems of Modernity*. Westport, Greenwood Pr, 1989.
Yaffe, Martin D. *Can Phil Rev* 10(1), 11-13 Ja 90

EISENSTADT, Abraham S (ed). *Reconsidering Tocqueville's Democracy in America*. New Brunswick, Rutgers Univ Pr, 1988.
Lakoff, Sanford. *Utilitas* 2(1), 157-159 My 90

ELDER, George R (ed). *Buddhist Insight: Essays by Alex Wayman*. Delhi, Motilal, 1984.
Muller-Ortega, Paul E. *Phil East West* 40(2), 254-256 Ap 90

ELIAS, John L. *Moral Education: Secular and Religious*. Melbourne, Krieger, 1989.
Madigan, Tim. *Free Inq* 10(1), 58-59 Wint 89-90

ELSASSER, Walter M. *Reflections on a Theory of Organisms*. Montreal, Orbis, 1987.
Neumann, Joseph. *Philosophia (Israel)* 19(4), 493-498 D 89

ELSE, Gerald F. *Plato and Aristotle on Poetry*, Peter Burian (ed). Chapel Hill, Univ of North Carolina Pr, 1986.
Belfiore, Elizabeth. *Ancient Phil* 10(1), 138-140 Spr 90
Halliwell, S. *J Hellen Stud* 109, 232-233 1989

ELSTER, Jon and HYLLAND, Aanund (eds). *Foundations of Social Choice Theory*. New York, Cambridge Univ Pr, 1986.
Hammond, Peter J. *Ethics* 100(1), 190-191 O 89

ELSTER, Jon. *Le Laboureur et ses enfants*, A Gerschenfeld (trans). Paris, Minuit, 1986.
Imhoof, Stefan. *Rev Theol Phil* 121(3), 323-332 1989

EMILSSON, Eyjólfur Kjalar. *Plotinus on Sense-Perception: A Philosophical Study*. Cambridge, Cambridge Univ Pr, 1988.
Gaukroger, Stephen. *Austl J Phil* 68(1), 126-127 Mr 90
Gurtler, Gary M. *Int Phil Quart* 30(3), 379-382 S 90

ENGELHARDT JR, H Tristram. *The Foundations of Bioethics*. New York, Oxford Univ Pr, 1986.
Overall, Christine. *Hypatia* 4(2), 179-185 Sum 89

ENGELS, Frederick. *Karl Marx, Frederick Engels: Collected Works, V25*. New York, International, 1987.
Seddon, Fred. *Stud Soviet Tho* 39(2), 168-170 Mr 90

ENGLERT, Walter G. *Epicurus on the Swerve and Voluntary Action*. Atlanta, Scholars Pr, 1987.
Purinton, Jeffrey S. *J Hist Phil* 28(1), 123-125 Ja 90

ENSKAT, Rainer. *Wahrheit und Entdeckung*. Frankfurt am Main,

Klostermann, 1986.
Ferber, Rafael. *Z Phil Forsch* 43(4), 709-711 O-D 89

ERICSON, Edward L. *The Humanist Way: An Introduction to Ethical Humanist Religion*. New York, Continuum, 1988.
Olds, Mason. *Relig Hum* 24(3), 145-146 Sum 90

ESSLER, Wilhelm K and BRENDEL, Elke and MARTÍNEZ CRUZADO, Rosa F. *Grundzüge der Logik II: Klassen—Relationen—Zahlen*. Frankfurt, Klostermann, 1987.
Siegwart, Geo. *Erkenntnis* 32(2), 283-291 Mr 90

ETZIONI, Amitai. *The Moral Dimension: Toward a New Economics*. NY, Free Pr, 1988.
Rustin, Michael. *Rad Phil* 54, 43-44 Spr 90

EUBEN, J Peter (ed). *Greek Tragedy and Political Theory*. Berkeley, Univ of Calif Pr, 1986.
Smith, Nicholas D. *Ethics* 100(1), 187-188 O 89

EVANS, J D G. *Aristotle*. New York, St Martin's Pr, 1987.
Shields, Christopher. *Phil Rev* 99(3), 443-447 Jl 90

EVANS, Jonathan St B T. *Bias in Human Reasoning: Causes and Consequences*. London, Erlbaum, 1989.
Van Bendegem, Jean Paul. *Philosophica* 45(1), 121-122 1990

EVERNDEN, Neil. *The Natural Alien: Humankind and Environment*. Toronto, Univ of Toronto Pr, 1985.
Birch, Thomas H. *Environ Ethics* 12(3), 283-287 Fall 90

EWIN, R E. *Liberty, Community and Justice*. Totowa, Rowman & Littlefield, 1987.
Burnheim, John. *Austl J Phil* 67(3), 366-367 S 89

FABRIS, Matteo (ed). *L'Umanesimo di Sant'Agostino*. Bari, Levante, 1988.
Grosso, Giuseppe. *Filosofia* 40(2), 236-239 My-Ag 89

FADEN, Ruth R and BEAUCHAMP, Tom L. *A History and Theory of Informed Consent*. New York, Oxford Univ Pr, 1986.
Zimbelman, Joel. *J Med Human* 10(2), 138-139 Fall-Wint 89

FADINI, Ubaldo. *Il corpo imprevisto*. Milan, Angeli, 1988.
Fabris, Adriano. *Teoria* 9(1), 271-274 1989

FALCK, Colin. *Myth, Truth and Literature: Towards a True Post-Modernism*. Cambridge, Cambridge Univ Pr, 1989.
Eldridge, Richard. *Phil Lit* 14(1), 227-228 Ap 90
Warner, Martin. *Philosophy* 65(252), 237-239 Ap 90

FALLON, Timothy P and RILEY, Phillip B (eds). *Religion and Culture: Essays in Honour of Bernard Lonergan*. Albany, SUNY Pr, 1986.
Walmsley, Gerard. *Heythrop J* 31(1), 83-85 Ja 90

FARBER, Jerry. *A Field Guide to the Aesthetic Experience*. North Hollywood, Foreworks, 1982.
Johnston, Marilyn. *J Aes Educ* 21(3), 125-126 Fall 87

FARLEY, Frank H and NEPERUD, Ronald W (eds). *The Foundations of Aesthetics, Art, and Art Education*. New York, Praeger, 1988.
Larsen, Flemming M. *Educ Stud* 21(1), 59-64 Spr 90

FEFFER, Melvin. *Radical Constructionism*. New York, New York Univ Pr, 1988.
Levy, Donald. *Can Phil Rev* 9(7), 261-266 Jl 89

FEINBERG, Joel. *Harmless Wrongdoing: The Moral Limits of the Criminal Law, V4*. New York, Oxford Univ Pr, 1988.
Arneson, Richard J. *Ethics* 100(2), 368-385 Ja 90
Clark, Michael. *Phil Books* 30(4), 251-254 O 89

FEINSTEIN, Howard M. *Becoming William James*. Ithaca, Cornell Univ Pr, 1984.
Reck, Andrew J. *Int Stud Phil* 21(3), 112-113 1989

FEKETE, John (ed). *Life After Postmodernism: Essays on Value and Culture*. NY, St Martin's Pr, 1987.
Weinstein, Michael A. *Can Phil Rev* 9(10), 404-407 O 89

FELMAN, Shoshana. *Jacques Lacan and the Adventure of Insight*. Cambridge, Harvard Univ Pr, 1987.
Michelfelder, Diane. *Int Stud Phil* 22(1), 98-99 1990

FELSKI, Rita. *Beyond Feminist Aesthetics: Feminist Literature and Social Change*. London, Hutchinson Radius, 1989.
Battersby, Christine. *Rad Phil* 55, 46-47 Sum 90

FENN, Robert A. *James Mill's Political Thought*. New York, Garland, 1987.
Burns, J H. *Utilitas* 1(1), 156-162 My 89

FENNETAUX, Michel. *La psychanalyse, chemin des lumières?* Paris, Point

hors ligne, 1989.
Jacerme, Pierre. *Rev Phil Fr* 179(3), 343-347 Jl-S 89

FERGUSON, Ann. *Blood at the Root*. London, Pandora Pr, 1989.
Assiter, Alison. *Rad Phil* 55, 54 Sum 90

FERRARI, G R F. *Listening to the Cicadas: A Study of Plato's "Phaedrus"*. Cambridge, Cambridge Univ Pr, 1987.
Ferguson, John. *Heythrop J* 31(3), 374-375 Jl 90
Kerferd, G B. *J Hellen Stud* 109, 226-227 1989
Morgan, Michael L. *J Hist Phil* 28(1), 121-123 Ja 90
Price, A W. *Phil Rev* 99(3), 447-449 Jl 90

FERRARIS, M. *Storia dell'ermeneutica*. Milan, Bompiani, 1988.
Cislaghi, Alessandra. *Filosofia* 40(3), 424-426 S-D 89

FERRE, Frederick (ed). *Concepts of Nature and God: Resources for College and University Teaching*. Athens, Univ of Georgia, 1989.
Appleby, Peter C. *Teach Phil* 13(1), 72-74 Mr 90

FERRÉ, Frederick and MITCHAM, Carl (eds). *Research in Philosophy and Technology 9: Ethics and Technology*. Greenwich, JAI Pr, 1989.
Hickman, Larry. *Can Phil Rev* 10(4), 136-138 Ap 90

FERRÉ, Frederick. *Philosophy of Technology*. Englewood Cliffs, Prentice Hall, 1988.
Burch, Robert. *Can Phil Rev* 9(10), 407-410 O 89

FERREIRA, M Jamie. *Scepticism and Reasonable Doubt: The British Naturalist Tradition in Wilkins, Hume, Reid, and Newman*. NY, Clarendon Pr, 1987.
Schmitt, Frederick F. *Phil Rev* 99(2), 269-272 Ap 90

FERRETTI, G (ed). *La ratione e il male*. Genova, Marietti, 1988.
Priano, Giovanni Battista. *Riv Filosof Neo-Scolas* 81(3), 495-496 Jl-S 89

FERRY, Luc and RENAUT, Alain. *Heidegger et les Modernes*. Paris, Grasset, 1988.
Grondin, Jean. *Arch Phil* 52(4), 681-684 O-D 89

FERRY, Luc. *Philosophie politique, 3v*. Paris, Pr Univ de France, 1987.
Sosoe, Lukas K. *Z Phil Forsch* 43(3), 548-552 Jl-S 89

FETZER, J H (ed). *Probability and Causality*. Dordrecht, Reidel, 1988.
Arntzenius, Frank. *Phil Sci* 57(2), 338-340 Je 90

FICHTE, J G. *Essai d'une critique de toute révélation (1792-1793)*, J-C Goddard (ed & trans). Paris, Vrin, 1988.
École, Jean. *Rev Metaph Morale* 94(3), 425-427 Jl-S 89

FICHTE, Johann. *The Vocation of Man*, Peter Preuss (trans). Indianapolis, Hackett, 1987.
Cristi, Renato. *Dialogue (Canada)* 28(2), 344-345 1989

FINDLAY, J N. *Wittgenstein: A Critique*. New York, Routledge, 1984.
Bassols, Alejandro Tomasini. *Critica* 20(60), 145-149 D 88

FINE, Arthur. *The Shaky Game: Einstein, Realism and the Quantum Theory*. Chicago, Univ of Chicago Pr, 1986.
Healey, Richard. *Nous* 24(1), 177-180 Mr 90

FINGARETE, Herbert. *Heavy Drinking: The Myth of Alcoholism as a Disease*. Berkeley, Univ of California Pr, 1988.
Haskell, Robert E. *J Med Human* 11(2), 99-103 Sum 90

FINKEL, Norman J. *Insanity on Trial*. NY, Plenum Pr, 1989.
Cust, Kenneth F T. *Can Phil Rev* 9(9), 351-353 S 89

FINN, Louise M (ed & trans). *The Kulacudamani Tantra and the Vamakesvara Tantra*. Wiesbaden, Hassarassowitz, 1986.
Granoff, Phyllis. *J Indian Phil* 17(3), 309-325 S 89

FINOCCHIARO, Maurice A. *Gramsci and the History of Dialectical Thought*. Cambridge, Cambridge Univ Pr, 1989.
Plant, Sadie. *Rad Phil* 54, 48 Spr 90

FISCH, Max H. *Peirce, Semeiotic, and Pragmatism*, K L Ketner and C J W Kloesel (eds). Bloomington, Indiana Univ Pr, 1986.
Barnouw, Jeffrey. *New Vico Studies* 5, 187-191 1987

FISCHER, John Martin (ed). *Moral Responsibility*. Ithaca, Cornell Univ Pr, 1986.
Fitzpatrick, F J. *Heythrop J* 31(1), 110-112 Ja 90

FISCHER, Michael. *Stanley Cavell and Literary Skepticism*. Chicago, Univ of Chicago Pr, 1989.
Gould, Timothy. *Can Phil Rev* 10(1), 13-16 Ja 90
Neto, José R Maia. *Phil Lit* 14(1), 204-205 Ap 90

FISHER, Alec. *The Logic of Real Arguments*. New York, Cambridge Univ Pr, 1988.
Collinson, Diané. *Phil Books* 30(4), 219-220 O 89

FISHER, Sue. *In the Patient's Best Interest*. New Brunswick, Rutgers Univ Pr,

1986.
Dorsch, Ellen. *Hypatia* 4(2), 188-191 Sum 89

FISHKIN, James S. *Beyond Subjective Morality: Ethical Reasoning and Political Philosophy*. New Haven, Yale Univ Pr, 1984.
Schultz, David. *Int Stud Phil* 21(3), 113-114 1989

FITZPATRICK, F J. *Ethics in Nursing Practice: Basic Principles and their Application*. London, Linacre Centre, 1988.
Benjamin, Martin. *Phil Books* 31(3), 171-172 Jl 90
Harris, John. *J Applied Phil* 6(2), 240-243 O 89
Muschamp, David. *Bioethics* 4(1), 90-93 Ja 90

FLAGE, Daniel E. *Berkeley's Doctrine of Notions: A Reconstruction Based on His Theory of Meaning*. NY, St Martin's Pr, 1987.
Dancy, Jonathan. *Phil Rev* 99(1), 111-114 Ja 90
Flew, Antony. *J Hist Phil* 27(4), 622-624 O 89

FLASCH, Kurt. *Das philosophische Denken im Mittelalter von Augustin zu Machiavelli*. Stuttgart, Reklam, 1987.
McEvoy, James. *Irish Phil J* 6(1), 166-168 1989

FLATHMAN, Richard E. *Toward a Liberalism*. Ithaca, Cornell Univ Pr, 1989.
Wertheimer, Alan. *Polit Theory* 18(1), 180-184 F 90

FLEMING, Chet. *If We Can Keep a Severed Head Alive*. St Louis, Polinym Pr, 1987.
Belliotti, Raymond A. *Bioethics* 4(2), 167-168 Ap 90
Fleming, Chet. *Bioethics* 4(2), 162-166 Ap 90

FLETCHER, George P. *A Crime of Self-Defense: Bernhard Goetz and the Law on Trial*. NY, Free Pr, 1988.
Shiner, Roger A. *Can Phil Rev* 9(9), 353-358 S 89

FLEW, Antony (ed). *Readings in the Philosophical Problems of Parapsychology*. Buffalo, Prometheus, 1987.
Jordan, Jeff. *Teach Phil* 12(3), 296-297 S 89

FLEW, Antony and VESEY, Godfrey. *Agency and Necessity*. Cambridge, Blackwell, 1987.
Gustafson, Donald. *Teach Phil* 12(3), 285-287 S 89

FLEW, Antony. *David Hume: Philosopher of Moral Science*. Oxford, Blackwell, 1986.
Immerwahr, John. *Int Stud Phil* 22(1), 100 1990
Williams, Michael. *Phil Rev* 99(2), 294-296 Ap 90

FLEW, Antony. *Equality in Liberty and Justice*. London, Routledge, 1989.
Baxter, Brian. *Phil Books* 31(3), 179-180 Jl 90

FLOUCAT, Yves. *Vocation de l'homme et sagesse chrétienne*. Paris, Saint-Paul, 1989.
Hubert, Bernard. *Rev Thomiste* 90(2), 318-321 Ap-Je 90

FLYNN, Thomas R. *Sartre and Marxist Existentialism*. Chicago, Univ of Chicago Pr, 1984.
Anonymous. *Int Stud Phil* 22(1), 100-102 1990

FODOR, Jerry. *Psychosemantics: The Problem of Meaning in the Philosophy of Mind*. Cambridge, MIT Pr, 1987.
Egan, Frances. *Behavior Phil* 18(1), 59-61 Spr-Sum 90
Taylor, Kenneth. *Nous* 24(1), 181-184 Mr 90

FOGELIN, Robert. *Figuratively Speaking*. New Haven, Yale Univ Pr, 1988.
Lyas, Colin. *Phil Books* 31(3), 185-187 Jl 90

FOLEY, Richard. *The Theory of Epistemic Rationality*. Cambridge, Harvard Univ Pr, 1987.
Alston, William P. *Phil Phenomenol Res* 50(1), 135-147 S 89
Feldman, Richard. *Phil Phenomenol Res* 50(1), 149-158 S 89
Foley, Richard. *Phil Phenomenol Res* 50(1), 169-188 S 89
Kornblith, Hilary. *Phil Rev* 99(1), 131-134 Ja 90
Minto, W Richmond. *Eidos* 8(1), 105-110 Je 89
Moser, Paul K. *Nous* 24(1), 185-188 Mr 90
Swain, Marshall. *Phil Phenomenol Res* 50(1), 159-168 S 89

FONTINELL, Eugene. *Self, God, and Immortality: A Jamesian Investigation*. Philadelphia, Temple Univ Pr, 1986.
Moreland, J P. *Int Phil Quart* 29(4), 480-483 D 89

FORBES, Graeme. *Languages of Possibility*. Oxford, Blackwell, 1989.
Melia, Joseph. *Phil Quart* 40(159), 271-273 Ap 90
Pisani, Assunta. *Sapienza* 43(2), 219-221 Ap-Je 90

FORBES, Graeme. *The Metaphysics of Modality*. Oxford, Clarendon Pr, 1985.
Brown, Mark A. *Phil Phenomenol Res* 50(3), 615-619 Mr 90

FORD, Norman M. *When Did I Begin: Conception of the Human*

Individual in History, Philosophy and Science. New York, Cambridge Univ Pr, 1988.
Coughlan, Michael J. *Bioethics* 3(4), 333-341 O 89
Ford, Norman M. *Bioethics* 3(4), 342-346 O 89
Halliday, R J. *Hist Euro Ideas* 12(2), 308-309 1990

FORMAN, Frank. *The Metaphysics of Liberty.* Norwell, Kluwer, 1988.
Cust, Kenneth F T. *Can Phil Rev* 9(12), 479-480 D 89

FORMENT, Eudaldo. *Filosofía de Hispoanoamérica.* Barcelona, Univ de Barcelona, 1987.
Boburg, Felipe and Anguiano, David. *Rev Filosof (Mexico)* 22(65), 256-258 My-Ag 89

FORRESTER, James W. *Why You Should: The Pragmatics of Deontic Speech.* Hanover, Univ Pr of New England, 1989.
Morreall, John. *Can Phil Rev* 10(1), 16-19 Ja 90

FORSTER, Michael N. *Hegel and Skepticism.* Cambridge, Harvard Univ Pr, 1989.
Hanna, Robert. *Rev Metaph* 43(3), 630-631 Mr 90

FOSTER, John and ROBINSON, Howard (eds). *Essays on Berkeley: A Tercentennial Celebration.* New York, Clarendon/Oxford Pr, 1985.
Cummins, Phillip. *Ideal Stud* 19(2), 175-176 My 89
Dubois, Pierre. *Hist Euro Ideas* 10(5), 603-605 1989
Pitcher, George. *Int Stud Phil* 21(3), 114-116 1989

FOSTER, John. *A J Ayer.* New York, Routledge, 1985.
Fellows, Roger. *J Brit Soc Phenomenol* 20(3), 305-307 O 89

FOSTER, Susan Leigh. *Reading Dancing.* Berkeley, Univ of Calif Pr, 1986.
Snoeyenbos, Milton H. *J Aes Educ* 22(3), 118-120 Fall 88

FOTINIS, Athansios P. *The De Anima of Alexander of Aphrodisias: A Translation and Commentary.* Washington, Univ Pr of America, 1979.
Silverman, Allan. *Ancient Phil* 9 (2), 354-357 Fall 89

FOUCAULT, Michel. *Résumé des cours (1970-1982).* Paris, Julliard, 1989.
Paré, Jean-Rodrigue. *Laval Theol Phil* 46(1), 97-100 F 90

FOX, Christopher. *Locke and the Scriblerians: Identity and Consciousness in Early Eighteenth-Century Britain.* Berkeley, Univ of California Pr, 1988.
Pigden, Charles R. *Phil Lit* 14(1), 161-162 Ap 90
Southgate, B C. *Hist Euro Ideas* 12(2), 306-307 1990

FRANCHINI, Raffaello. *Eutanasia dei principi logici.* Naples, Loffredo, 1989.
Sorge, Valeria. *Sapienza* 43(1), 83-87 Ja-Mr 90

FRANK, D H. *The Arguments 'From the Sciences' in Aristotle's Peri Ideon.* NY, Lang, 1984.
Femenías, María Luisa. *Analisis Filosof* 8(1), 80-82 My 88

FRANKFURT, Harry G. *The Importance of What We Care About: Philosophical Essays.* New York, Cambridge Univ Pr, 1988.
Almond, Brenda. *Phil Books* 31(3), 173-174 Jl 90
Harriott, Howie H. *Int Phil Quart* 30(3), 371-373 S 90

FRANKLIN, Allan. *The Neglect of Experiment.* Cambridge, Cambridge Univ Pr, 1986.
French, Steven. *Nous* 24(4), 631-634 S 90

FREDE, Michael and PATZIG, Günther (eds & trans). *Aristoteles "Metaphysik Z".* Munich, Beck, 1988.
Schmitz, Hermann. *Phil Rundsch* 37(1-2), 95-109 1990

FREDE, Michael. *Essays in Ancient Philosophy.* Minneapolis, Univ of Minnesota Pr, 1987.
Madigan, Arthur. *Mod Sch* 67(2), 155-157 Ja 90
Sharples, R W. *Ancient Phil* 10(1), 123-127 Spr 90

FREGE, Gottlob. *Scritti postumi.* Naples, Bibliopolis, 1986.
Aimonetto, Italo. *Filosofia* 41(1), 117-120 Ja-Ap 90

FREMLIN, D H. *Consequences of Martin's Axiom.* New York, Cambridge Univ Pr, 1984.
Weiss, William. *J Sym Log* 53(2), 650-651 Je 88

FREUDENTHAL, Gad (ed). *Etudes sur Hélène Metzger.* Paris, Revue de philosophie, 1988.
Merllié, Dominique. *Rev Phil Fr* 179(4), 589-591 O-D 89

FRISBY, David. *Fragments of Modernity: Theories of Modernity in the Work of Simmel, Kracauer and Benjamin.* Cambridge, MIT Pr, 1986.
Schmidt, James. *Int Stud Phil* 22(1), 102-103 1990

FROLOV, Ivan. *Man-Science-Humanism: A New Synthesis.* Moscow, Progress, 1986.
Kurtz, Paul. *Free Inq* 10(2), 54-55 Spr 90

FRONDIZI, Risieri. *Ensayos filosóficos.* México, Fondo de Cultura Económica, 1986.
Kilgore, William J. *Rev Latin De Filosof* 16(1), 115-119 Mr 90

FROW, John. *Marxism and Literary History.* Oxford, Blackwell, 1986.
Trembath, Paul. *Phil Lit* 14(1), 178-179 Ap 90

FULLER, Robert C. *Americans and the Unconscious.* Oxford, Oxford Univ Pr, 1986.
Erwin, Edward. *Nous* 24(4), 635-639 S 90

FULLER, Steve. *Philosophy of Science and its Discontents.* Boulder, Westview Pr, 1989.
Roqué, Alicia Juarrero. *Rev Metaph* 43(4), 863-864 Je 90

FULLER, Steve. *Social Epistemology.* Bloomington, Indiana Univ Pr, 1988.
Ackermann, Robert. *Erkenntnis* 33(1), 131-135 Jl 90

FUNKE, Gerhard. *Phenomenology: Metaphysics or Method?*, David Parent (trans). Athens, Ohio Univ Pr, 1988.
Rée, Jonathan. *Rad Phil* 54, 37-38 Spr 90

FUNKENSTEIN, Amos. *Theology and the Scientific Imagination from the Middle Ages to the Seventeenth Century.* Princeton, Princeton Univ Pr, 1986.
Luft, Sandra Rudnik. *New Vico Studies* 6, 105-111 1988
Pérez-Ramos, A. *Stud Hist Phil Sci* 21(2), 323-339 Je 90

FURLEY, David. *Cosmic Problems: Essays on Greek and Roman Philosophy of Nature.* Cambridge, Cambridge Univ Pr, 1989.
Follon, Jacques. *Rev Phil Louvain* 88(77), 114-118 F 90

FURLEY, David. *The Greek Cosmologists, V1: The Formation of the Atomic Theory and its Earliest Critics.* Cambridge, Cambridge Univ Pr, 1987.
Mourelatos, Alexander P D. *Phil Rundsch* 37(1-2), 80-88 1990

FURTH, Montgomery. *Substance, Form and Psyche: An Aristotelian Metaphysics.* Cambridge, Cambridge Univ Pr, 1988.
Figal, Günter and Schütt, Hans-Peter. *Phil Rundsch* 37(1-2), 110-122 1990

FYNSK, Christopher. *Heidegger: Thought and Historicity.* Ithaca, Cornell Univ Pr, 1986.
White, Carol J. *Int Stud Phil* 22(1), 103-104 1990

GABBAY, D M and GUENTHER, F (eds). *Handbook of Philosophical Logic, V3: Alternatives to Classical Logic.* Norwell, Reidel, 1986.
Palladino, Dario. *Epistemologia* 11(2), 341-347 Jl-D 88

GABBAY, G and GUENTHNER, F (eds). *Handbook of Philosophical Logic, V4: Topics in the Philosophy of Language.* Dordrecht, Reidel, 1989.
Le Poidevin, Robin. *Phil Quart* 40(160), 395-397 Jl 90

GADAMER, Hans Georg. *Chi sono io, chi sei tu: Su Paul Celan*, Franco Camera (ed). Genoa, Marietti, 1989.
Bonola, Massimo. *Filosofia* 41(2), 248-252 My-Ag 90

GADAMER, Hans-Georg. *The Idea of the Good in Platonic-Aristotelian Philosophy*, P Christopher Smith (trans). New Haven, Yale Univ Pr, 1986.
Cleary, John J. *Int Stud Phil* 22(1), 104-105 1990
Ferguson, John. *Heythrop J* 31(1), 105-106 Ja 90

GAGE, Richard L (ed). *Choose Life: A Dialogue.* New York, Oxford Univ Pr, 1987.
Sen, Madhu. *Indian Phil Quart* 16(3), 357-364 Jl 89

GALATI, Jose Maria. *El poder y la justicia en el pensamiento platónico.* Buenos Aires, Club de Buenos Aires, 1987.
Boeri, Marcelo D. *Rev Filosof (Argentina)* 2(2), 179-182 N 87

GALISON, Peter. *How Experiments End.* Chicago, Univ of Chicago Press, 1987.
Hacking, Ian. *J Phil* 87(2), 103-106 F 90

GALL, Robert S. *Beyond Theism and Atheism: Heidegger's Significance for Religious Thinking.* Dordrecht, Nijhoff, 1987.
Bruzina, Ronald. *Int J Phil Relig* 27(3), 185-186 Je 90
Campbell, David M A. *Relig Stud* 26(1), 179-181 Mr 90

GALLIE, Roger D. *Thomas Reid and "The Way of Ideas".* Dordrecht, Kluwer, 1989.
Manns, James W. *Rev Metaph* 43(4), 864-866 Je 90

GALLOP, David. *Parmenides of Elea: Fragments.* Toronto, Univ of Toronto Pr, 1984.
Barker, Andrew. *Ancient Phil* 9 (2), 313-319 Fall 89

GALTON, Antony (ed). *Temporal Logics and Their Applications.* San Diego, Academic Pr, 1987.
Fariñas del Cerro, Luis. *J Sym Log* 55(1), 364-366 Mr 90

GAMM, Gerhard. *Wahrheit als Differenz.* Frankfurt am Main, Athenäum, 1986.
Kossler, Matthias. *Schopenhauer Jahr* 70, 233-235 1989

GAOS, José. *Del hombre*. México, UNAM, 1970.
Llano, Carlos. *Anu Filosof* 22(2), 187-192 1989

GARDEN, Rachel Wallace. *Modern Logic and Quantum Mechanics*. Bristol, Hilger, 1984.
Urquhart, Alasdair. *J Sym Log* 53(2), 648-649 Je 88

GARDINER, Patrick. *Kierkegaard*. New York, Oxford Univ Pr, 1988.
Donnelly, John. *Phil Books* 31(1), 24-26 Ja 90
Martinez, Roy. *Teach Phil* 12(3), 341-343 S 89
Whittaker, John. *Phil Invest* 13(2), 190-193 Ap 90

GARDNER, Howard. *The Mind's New Science: A History of the Cognitive Revolution*. New York, Basic Books, 1985.
Fagot-Largeault, A. *Hist Phil Life Sci* 11(1), 185-186 1989

GARFIELD, Jay L. *Belief in Psychology: A Study in the Ontology of Mind*. Cambridge, MIT Pr, 1988.
Fair, Frank. *Teach Phil* 12(3), 293-296 S 89

GARGANI, A G. *Sguardo e destino*. Bari, Laterza, 1988.
Dottori, Livio. *Filosofia* 40(2), 220-222 My-Ag 89

GARGANI, Aldo (ed). *Crisi della ragione: Nuovi modelli nel rapporto tra sapere e attività umane*. Turin, Einaudi, 1979.
Barbiero, Daniel. *Crit Texts* 7(1), 82-89 1990

GARRIDO, Manuel. *Lógica simbólica*. Madrid, Tecnos, 1983.
Palau, Gladys. *Analisis Filosof* 7(1), 61-63 My 87

GARVER, Eugene. *Machiavelli and the History of Prudence*. Madison, Univ of Wisconsin Pr, 1987.
Parel, A J. *J Hist Phil* 28(3), 445-447 Jl 90

GASCHÉ, Rodolphe. *The Tain of the Mirror: Derrida and the Philosophy of Reflection*. Cambridge, Harvard Univ Pr, 1989.
Jacobs, David. *Auslegung* 16(2), 219-223 Sum 90

GAUKROGER, Stephen. *Cartesian Logic: An Essay on Descartes's Conception of Inference*. Oxford, Clarendon Pr, 1989.
Buroker, Jill Vance. *Phil Books* 31(3), 143-144 Jl 90

GAUTHIER, David. *Morals by Agreement*. New York, Oxford Univ Pr, 1986.
Carson, Thomas L. *Int Stud Phil* 22(1), 106-108 1990
Schaber, Peter. *Z Phil Forsch* 44(1), 157-161 1990

GAUTHIER, Pierre. *Newman et Blondel: Tradition et ddveloppement du dogme*. Paris, Cerf, 1988.
Adam, Michel. *Rev Phil Fr* 179(2), 256-258 Ap-Je 89

GAVIN, William J (ed). *Context Over Foundation: Dewey and Marx*. Norwell, Reidel, 1988.
Safford, John L. *Can Phil Rev* 9(10), 411-412 O 89

GAVROGLU, K and GOUDAROULIS, Y and NICOLACOPOULOS, P (eds). *Imre Lakatos and Theories of Scientific Change*. Dordrecht, Kluwer, 1989.
Kindi, Vasso P. *Method Sci* 23(2), 114-116 1990

GAWLICK, Günter and KREIMENDAHL, Lothar. *Hume in der deutschen Aufklärung*. Stuttgart, Frommann, 1987.
Kuehn, Manfred. *J Hist Phil* 28(2), 301-304 Ap 90

GAZDAR, Gerald and others. *Generalized Phrase Structure Grammar*. Cambridge, Harvard Univ Pr, 1985.
Soames, Scott. *Phil Rev* 98(4), 556-566 O 89

GEACH, P T and SHAH, H J and JACKSON, A C. *Wittgenstein's Lectures on Philosophical Psychology 1946-47*. Chicago, Univ of Chicago Pr, 1988.
Gustafson, Donald. *Phil Psych* 2(3), 355-358 1989

GEHLHAAR, Sabine S. *Prophetie und Gesetz bei Jehudah Hallevi, Maimonides und Spinoza*. New York, Lang, 1987.
Levy, Ze'ev. *Stud Spinozana* 5, 419-426 1989

GELLNER, Ernest. *Plough, Sword and Book: The Structure of Human History*. Chicago, Univ of Chicago Pr, 1988.
McNeill, William H. *Hist Theor* 29(2), 234-240 My 90

GELLRICH, Michelle. *Tragedy and Theory: The Problem of Conflict Since Aristotle*. Princeton, Princeton Univ Pr, 1988.
Zanker, Graham. *Phil Lit* 14(1), 188-190 Ap 90

GENEQUAND, Charles. *Ibn Rushd's Metaphysics*. Leiden, Brill, 1986.
Macierowski, E M. *Ancient Phil* 9 (1), 144-147 Spr 89

GEORGE, Alexander (ed). *Reflections on Chomsky*. Oxford, Blackwell, 1989.
Smith, Amahl. *Mind Lang* 5(2), 174-185 Sum 90

GERASSI, John. *Jean-Paul Sartre: Hated Conscience of His Century, V1: Protestant or Protestor?* Chicago, Univ of Chicago Pr, 1989.
Gordon, Haim. *J Brit Soc Phenomenol* 21(2), 188-189 My 90

Henry, Patrick. *Phil Lit* 14(1), 117-141 Ap 90
Macey, David. *Rad Phil* 55, 59-60 Sum 90

GERGEN, Mary McCanney (ed). *Feminist Thought and the Structure of Knowledge*. New York, New York Univ Pr, 1988.
Code, Lorraine. *Can Phil Rev* 10(2), 60-63 F 90

GERIGK, Horst-Jürgen. *Unterwegs zur Interpretation Hinweise zu einer Theorie der Literatur in Auseinandersetzung mit Gadamers*. Hürtgenwald, Pressler, 1989.
Sullivan, Robert R. *Interpretation* 17(2), 305-308 Wint 89-90

GERSH, Stephen. *Middle Platonism and Neo-Platonism: The Latin Tradition, 2v*. Notre Dame, Univ of Notre Dame Pr, 1986.
Dillon, John. *Int Stud Phil* 22(1), 108 1990
Spade, Paul Vincent. *Nous* 24(2), 342-346 Ap 90

GERT, Bernard. *Morality: A New Justification of the Moral Rules*. NY, Oxford Univ Pr, 1988.
Hay, William H. *Ethics* 100(2), 411-412 Ja 90
Jecker, Nancy. *Rev Metaph* 43(3), 631-633 Mr 90

GERVAIS, Karen Grandstrand. *Redefining Death*. New Haven, Yale Univ Pr, 1988.
Beisheim, Peter H. *J Med Human* 10(2), 132-133 Fall-Wint 89

GHOSH, Ranjan K. *Concepts and Presuppositions in Aesthetics*. Delhi, Ajanta, 1987.
McAdoo, Nick. *Brit J Aes* 30(1), 84-85 Ja 90

GIBBINS, Peter. *Particles and Paradoxes: The Limits of Quantum Logic*. New York, Cambridge Univ Pr, 1987.
Dalla Chiara, Maria Luisa. *J Sym Log* 55(1), 354-355 Mr 90
Stairs, Allen. *Phil Sci* 56(4), 712-714 D 89

GILBERT, Margaret. *Social Facts*. London, Routledge, 1989.
Rosen, Michael. *Mind* 99(394), 308-310 Ap 90

GILDIN, Hilail (ed). *An Introduction to Political Philosophy: Ten Essays by Leo Strauss*. Detroit, Wayne State Univ Pr, 1989.
Morrisey, Will. *Interpretation* 17(3), 465-467 Spr 90

GILLESPIE, Michael Allen and STRONG, Tracy B (eds). *Nietzsche's New Seas: Explorations in Philosophy, Aesthetics, and Politics*. Chicago, Univ of Chicago Pr, 1988.
Divay, Gaby. *Phil Lit* 14(1), 224-225 Ap 90
Schrift, Alan D. *Can Phil Rev* 9(11), 437-439 N 89

GINSBERG, Matthew L. *Readings in Nonmonotonic Reasoning*. San Mateo, Morgan Kaufmann, 1989.
Nute, Donald. *Phil Psych* 2(3), 351-355 1989

GINSBERG, Robert (ed). *The Philosopher as Writer: The Eighteenth Century*. Selinsgrove, Susquehanna Univ Pr, 1987.
Perrett, Roy W. *Phil Lit* 13(2), 378-379 O 89

GIRARD, Jean-Yves. *Proof Theory and Logical Complexity, V1*. Naples, Bibliopolis, 1987.
Pfeiffer, Helmut. *J Sym Log* 54(4), 1493-1494 D 89

GIROUX, Henry A. *Schooling and the Struggle for Public Life: Critical Pedagogy in the Modern Age*. Minneapolis, Univ of Minnesota Pr, 1988.
Mandt, A J. *Personalist Forum* 6(1), 91-93 Spr 90

GIVONE, S. *Disincanto del mondo e pensiero tragico*. Milan, Saggiatore, 1988.
Panella, Giuseppe. *G Metaf* 11(2), 315-318 My-Ag 89

GLATZEL, Martin and MARTENS, Ekkehard (eds). *Philosophieren im Unterricht 5-10*. Munich, Urban & Schwarzenberg, 1982.
Rud, A G. *Thinking* 5(4), 67-68 1985

GLAZER, Nathan and LILLA, Mark (eds). *The Public Face of Architecture: Civic Culture and Public Spaces*. New York, Free Pr, 1987.
Levi, Albert William. *J Aes Educ* 22(3), 113-114 Fall 88

GLENDON, Mary Ann. *Abortion and Divorce in Western Law: American Failures, European Challenges*. Cambridge, Harvard Univ Pr, 1987.
Ver Eecke, Wilfried. *Rev Metaph* 43(4), 866-868 Je 90

GLOUBERMAN, M. *Descartes: The Probable and the Certain*. Amsterdam, Rodopi, 1986.
Carnes, Robert D. *Ideal Stud* 19(3), 275-276 S 89
Watson, Richard A. *J Hist Phil* 27(4), 618-620 O 89

GLOVER, Jonathan and others. *Fertility and the Family: The Glover Report on Reproductive Technologies to the European Commission*. London, Fourth Estate, 1989.
Warnock, Mary. *Bioethics* 4(2), 169-170 Ap 90

GLOVER, Jonathan. *Ethics of New Reproductive Technologies: The Glover Report to the European Commission*. DeKalb, Northern Illinois Univ Pr, 1989.

1986.
Doney, Willis. *Phil Rev* 98(4), 545-547 O 89
Kline, A David and Van Iten, R J. *Int Stud Phil* 21(3), 116-117 1989

GRAYLING, A C. *Wittgenstein*. New York, Oxford Univ Pr, 1988.
Bogen, James. *Teach Phil* 12(3), 344-345 S 89
Cooke, Vincent M. *Int Phil Quart* 30(2), 255-256 Je 90
Proudfoot, Michael. *Phil Books* 30(4), 215-216 O 89

GREELEY, Roger E (ed). *The Best of Humanism*. Buffalo, Prometheus Pr, 1988.
Brown, Todd R. *Personalist Forum* 5(2), 155-157 Fall 89

GREEN, Georgia M. *Pragmatics and Natural Language Understanding*. Hillsdale, Erlbaum, 1989.
Castelnovo, Walter. *Teoria* 9(2), 181-183 1989

GREEN, Leslie. *The Authority of the State*. Oxford, Oxford Univ Pr, 1988.
Flathman, Richard E. *Can Phil Rev* 9(10), 412-415 O 89
Johnson, Nevil. *Philosophy* 64(250), 566-567 O 89

GREEN, Lucy. *Music on Deaf Ears: Musical Meaning, Ideology, Education*. Manchester, Manchester Univ Pr, 1988.
Goehr, Lydia. *Brit J Aes* 30(2), 190-192 Ap 90

GREEN, Ronald M. *Religion and Moral Reason: A New Method for Comparative Study*. NY, Oxford Univ Pr, 1988.
Quinn, Philip L. *Ethics* 100(2), 418-419 Ja 90

GREEN-PEDERSEN, Niels Jorgan. *The Tradition of the Topics in the Middle Ages*. Munchen, Philosophia, 1984.
Lewis, Neil. *Ancient Phil* 9 (1), 147-150 Spr 89

GREENAWALT, Kent. *Conflicts of Law and Morality*. NY, Oxford Univ Pr, 1987.
Pincoffs, Edmund L. *Phil Rev* 99(3), 450-453 Jl 90
Smith, M B E. *Crim Just Ethics* 8(2), 60-70 Sum-Fall 89

GREENAWALT, Kent. *Religious Convictions and Political Choice*. NY, Oxford Univ Pr, 1988.
Audi, Robert. *Ethics* 100(2), 386-397 Ja 90
Hoekema, David A. *Crim Just Ethics* 8(2), 70-78 Sum-Fall 89

GRENE, Marjorie. *Descartes*. Minneapolis, Univ of Minnesota Pr, 1985.
Joy, Lynn S. *J Phil* 87(3), 161-165 Mr 90
Stohrer, Walter J. *Mod Sch* 67(1), 85-86 N 89

GRICE, Paul. *Studies in the Way of Words*. Cambridge, Harvard Univ Pr, 1989.
Over, D E. *Phil Quart* 40(160), 393-395 Jl 90
Rundle, Bede. *Phil Invest* 13(2), 167-180 Ap 90
Strawson, P F. *Synthese* 84(1), 153-161 Jl 90
White, Alan R. *Philosophy* 65(251), 111-113 Ja 90

GRIER, Philip T (ed). *Dialectic and Contemporary Science: Essays in Honor of Errol E Harris*. Lanham, Univ Pr of America, 1989.
Burbidge, John. *Can Phil Rev* 9(12), 486-487 D 89

GRIFFIN, David R (ed). *The Reenchantment of Science*. Albany, SUNY Pr, 1988.
Eastman, Timothy E. *Process Stud* 18(1), 69-75 Spr 89

GRIFFIN, David Ray. *God and Religion in the Postmodern World: Essays in Postmodern Theology*. Albany, SUNY Pr, 1989.
Dean, William. *Process Stud* 18(3), 208-212 Fall 89

GRIFFITHS, A Phillips (ed). *Contemporary French Philosophy*. Cambridge, Cambridge Univ Pr, 1987.
Bernstein, J M. *Phil Books* 31(2), 96-98 Ap 90

GRIFFITHS, Morwenna and **WHITFORD, Margaret (eds)**. *Feminist Perspectives in Philosophy*. New York, Macmillan, 1988.
Lennon, Kathleen. *J Applied Phil* 6(2), 238-240 O 89

GRIFFITHS, Paul. *On Being Mindless: Buddhist Meditation and the Mind-Body Problem*. LaSalle, Open Court, 1986.
Rajapakse, Vijitha. *Indian Phil Quart* 17(1), 111-117 Ja 90

GRIMALDI, N. *Introducción a la filosofía de la historia de Marx*. Madrid, Dossat, 1986.
García Marqués, Alfonso. *Anu Filosof* 20(1), 238-239 1987

GRIMALDI, Nicolas and **MARION, Jean-Luc (eds)**. *Le discours et sa méthode*. Paris, Pr Univ de France, 1987.
Cavaillé, Jean-Pierre. *Rev Phil Fr* 179(2), 214-218 Ap-Je 89

GRIMALDI, Nicolas. *Six études sur la volonté et la liberté chez Descartes*. Paris, Vrin, 1988.
Leduc-Fayette, D. *Rev Phil Fr* 179(2), 218-220 Ap-Je 89

GRIMALDI, W M A. *Aristotle, "Rhetoric II": A Commentary*. NY, Fordham Univ Pr, 1988.

Conley, Thomas. *Phil Rhet* 23(2), 141-147 1990

GRISWOLD JR, Charles L (ed). *Platonic Writings/Platonic Readings*. New York, Routledge, 1988.
Browne, Derek. *Phil Lit* 13(2), 405-406 O 89
Mitscherling, Jeff. *Can Phil Rev* 10(1), 22-24 Ja 90
Pehrson, Claude. *Rad Phil* 54, 42-43 Spr 90

GRISWOLD JR, Charles L. *Self-Knowledge in Plato's "Phaedrus"*. New Haven, Yale Univ Pr, 1986.
Ferguson, John. *Heythrop J* 31(1), 103-104 Ja 90
Hampton, Cynthia. *J Hist Phil* 27(4), 606-608 O 89

GROBSTEIN, Clifford (ed). *Science and the Unborn: Choosing Human Futures*. NY, Basic Books, 1988.
Dawson, Karen. *Bioethics* 4(2), 176-179 Ap 90

GROGIN, R C. *The Bergsonian Controversy in France, 1900-1914*. Calgary, Univ of Calgary Pr, 1988.
Goudge, Thomas A. *J Hist Phil* 28(2), 308-310 Ap 90

GRONDIN, Jean. *Kant et le problème de la philosophie: l'a priori*. Paris, Vrin, 1989.
Giroux, Laurent. *Laval Theol Phil* 46(2), 237-245 Je 90

GRONDIN, Jean. *Le tournant dans la pensée de Martin Heidegger*. Paris, Pr Univ de France, 1987.
Mattéi, Jean-François. *Dialogue (Canada)* 27(4), 675-685 Wint 88
Vigneault, Gilles. *Laval Theol Phil* 45(3), 447-449 O 89
Wurzer, William S. *Man World* 23(1), 116-119 Ja 90

GRONOW, Jukka. *On the Formation of Marxism*. Philadelphia, Coronet, 1986.
Albritton, Robert. *Phil Soc Sci* 19(3), 394-396 S 89

GROS ESPIELL, Héctor. *Estudios sobre Derechos Humanos, V2*. Madrid, Civitas, 1988.
Ruiz de Santiago, Jaime. *Rev Filosof (Mexico)* 23(67), 132-136 Ja-Ap 90

GROSSER, Günther (ed). *Wissenschaftlicher Sozialismus*. Berlin, Deutscher, 1988.
Möller, Bärbel. *Deut Z Phil* 37(10-11), 1050-1052 1989

GRUNWALD, Max. *Spinoza in Deutschland*. Aalen, Scientia, 1986.
Walther, Manfred. *Stud Spinozana* 5, 433-434 1989

GUARNERI, Enrico. *Karl Marx: Gli anni di apprendistato*. Palermo, Ila-Palma, 1986.
Cavadi, Augusto. *Sapienza* 43(1), 75-77 Ja-Mr 90

GUARNERI, Enrico. *Karl Marx: Le grandi polemiche*. Palermo, Ila-Palma, 1987.
Cavadi, Augusto. *Sapienza* 43(1), 75-77 Ja-Mr 90

GUEROULT, Martial. *Descartes' Philosophy Interpreted According to the Order of Reasons, II: The Soul and the Body*, Roger Ariew (trans). Minneapolis, Univ of Minnesota Pr, 1985.
Teske, Roland J. *Mod Sch* 67(1), 75-76 N 89

GUEROULT, Martial. *Histoire de l'histoire de la philosophie*. Paris, Aubier, 1988.
Boulad-Ayoub, Josiane. *Philosophiques* 16(2), 439-443 Autumn 89

GUERRERA, Francesca Brezzi (ed). *Hermes: dagli dei agli uomini*. Roma, Armando, 1989.
Moscone, Maurizio. *Aquinas* 32(2), 401-404 My-Ag 89

GUIBERT-SLEDZIEWSKI, Élisabeth and **VIELLARD-BARON, Jean-Louis (eds)**. *Penser le sujet aujourd'hui*. Paris, Méridiens Klincksieck, 1988.
Férréol, G. *Arch Phil* 53(1), 75-77 Ja-Mr 90

GUILLOUX, P. *El alma de San Agustin*. Madrid, Rialp, 1986.
Gándara, Inmaculada. *Anu Filosof* 20(1), 240-241 1987

GUINDON, André. *The Sexual Creators: An Ethical Proposal for Concerned Christians*. Lanham, Univ Pr of America, 1986.
Kelly, Kevin T. *Heythrop J* 30(4), 491-492 O 89

GUROIAN, Vigen. *Incarnate Love: Essays in Orthodox Ethics*. Notre Dame, Univ of Notre Dame Pr, 1987.
Kelly, Kevin T. *Heythrop J* 31(2), 223-224 Ap 90

GURTLER, Gary M. *Plotinus: The Experience of Unity*. New York, Lang, 1988.
Corrigan, Kevin. *Ancient Phil* 10(1), 143-145 Spr 90
Dillon, John. *Can Phil Rev* 10(7), 271-273 Jl 90

GUTHRIE, Kenneth Sylvan (trans). *Porphyry's Launching Points to the Realm of Mind*. Grand Rapids, Phanes Pr, 1988.
Novak, Joseph A. *Can Phil Rev* 10(1), 24-31 Ja 90

GUTHRIE, Kenneth Sylvan. *The Pythagorean Sourcebook and Library*.

Grand Rapids, Phanes Pr, 1987.
Novak, Joseph A. *Can Phil Rev* 10(1), 24-31 Ja 90

GUTMAN, Amy and THOMPSON, Dennis (eds). *Ethics and Politics: Cases and Comments.* Chicago, Nelson-Hall, 1984.
Fairchild, Paul. *Auslegung* 16(2), 227-230 Sum 90

GUTMANN, Amy. *Democratic Education.* Princeton, Princeton Univ Pr, 1987.
Jaggar, Alison M. *Phil Rev* 99(3), 468-472 Jl 90

GUYER, Paul. *Kant and the Claims of Knowledge.* New York, Cambridge Univ Pr, 1987.
Pippin, Robert B. *J Hist Phil* 28(1), 138-141 Ja 90
Waxman, Wayne. *Grad Fac Phil J* 13(1), 165-172 1988
Young, J Michael. *Kantstudien* 81(1), 99-101 1990

HAAKONSSEN, Knud (ed). *Traditions of Liberalism.* Sydney, Ctr Independent Stud, 1988.
Monro, D H. *Austl J Phil* 67(3), 351-352 S 89

HAAR, Michel. *Le chant de la terre.* Paris, Herne, 1987.
Lilly, Reginald. *J Hist Phil* 28(1), 149-151 Ja 90

HAARSCHER, G. *La raison du plus fort.* Bruxelles, Mardaga, 1988.
Bonvecchio, Claudio. *G Metaf* 11(1), 149-151 Ja-Ap 89

HABERMAS, Jürgen. *Logique des sciences sociales et autres essais.* Paris, Pr Univ de France, 1987.
Langlois, Luc. *Arch Phil* 52(4), 692-694 O-D 89

HABERMAS, Jürgen. *The Structural Transformation of the Public Sphere: An Inquiry into a Category of Bourgeois Society,* T Burger (trans). Cambridge, MIT Pr, 1989.
Allen, Barry. *Can Phil Rev* 10(6), 228-232 Je 90

HACKING, Ian. *Representing and Intervening: Introductory Topics in the Philosophy of Natural Science.* Cambridge, Cambridge Univ Pr, 1983.
Borges, Bento Itamar. *Educ Filosof* 2(3), 132-138 Jl-D 87

HACKLER, Chris and MOSELEY, Ray and VAWTER, Dorothy E (eds). *Advance Directives in Medicine.* NY, Praeger, 1989.
Glover, Jacqueline J. *Med Human Rev* 4(1), 24-26 Ja 90

HADDOCK, Bruce A. *Vico's Political Thought.* Swansea, Mortlake Pr, 1986.
Hutton, Patrick H. *New Vico Studies* 5, 176-179 1987

HADOT, Pierre (ed & trans). *Plotin: Traité 38.* Paris, Cerf, 1988.
Lassègue, Monique. *Rev Phil Fr* 179(3), 368-372 Jl-S 89

HAEFFNER, G. *Antropología Filosófica.* Barcelona, Herder, 1986.
Arregui, Jorge Vicente. *Anu Filosof* 20(1), 241-243 1987

HAHN, Lewis E and SCHILPP, Paul A (eds). *The Philosophy of W V Quine.* La Salle, Open Court, 1986.
Hattiangadi, J N. *Phil Soc Sci* 19(4), 461-481 D 89
Woods, John. *Can J Phil* 19(4), 617-659 D 89

HAHN, Robert. *Kant's Newtonian Revolution in Philosophy.* Carbondale, Southern Illinois Univ Pr, 1988.
Catudal, Jacques N. *Can Phil Rev* 9(7), 267-270 Jl 89

HALBERSTAM, Joshua (ed). *Virtues and Values: An Introduction to Ethics.* Englewood Cliffs, Prentice Hall, 1988.
Dixon, Nicholas. *Teach Phil* 13(1), 47-52 Mr 90

HALE, Bob. *Abstract Objects.* Cambridge, Blackwell, 1987.
Brown, James Robert. *Dialogue (Canada)* 27(4), 729-732 Wint 88

HALEY, Michael Cabot. *The Semeiosis of Poetic Metaphor.* Bloomington, Indiana Univ Pr, 1989.
Hookway, Christopher. *Trans Peirce Soc* 26(1), 156-163 Wint 90

HALLER, Rudolf. *Facta und Ficta: Studien zu Ästhetischen Grundlagenfragen.* Stuttgart, Reclam, 1985.
Münch, Dieter. *J Brit Soc Phenomenol* 21(2), 195-196 My 90

HALLER, Rudolf. *Questions on Wittgenstein.* London, Routledge & Kegan Paul, 1988.
Gomm, R M. *Phil Invest* 13(1), 65-69 Ja 90

HALLETT, Garth L. *Language and Truth.* New Haven, Yale Univ Pr, 1988.
Hudson, John. *Phil Books* 30(4), 220-222 O 89

HALLETT, Garth. *Reason and Right.* Notre Dame, Univ Notre Dame Pr, 1984.
Kelly, John. *Heythrop J* 30(4), 481-482 O 89

HALLIWELL, S. *Aristotle's Poetics.* London, Duckworth, 1986.
Bremer, J M. *J Hellen Stud* 109, 233-234 1989

HALPERN, Joseph Y. *Theoretical Aspects of Reasoning about Knowledge.* Los Altos, Morgan Kaufmann, 1986.

Rapaport, William J. *J Sym Log* 53(2), 660-670 Je 88

HAMLYN, D W. *Metaphysics.* Cambridge, Cambridge Univ Pr, 1984.
Villanueva, Enrique. *Rev Latin De Filosof* 15(3), 339-342 N 89

HAMOWY, Ronald. *The Scottish Enlightenment and the Theory of Spontaneous Order.* Carbondale, Southern Illinois Univ Pr, 1987.
Zachs, William. *J Hist Phil* 28(2), 304-305 Ap 90

HAMPSHIRE, Stuart. *Morality and Conflict.* Cambridge, Harvard Univ Pr, 1983.
Simon, Lawrence H. *New Vico Studies* 2, 131-135 1984

HAMPTON, Jean. *Hobbes and the Social Contract Tradition.* New York, Cambridge Univ Pr, 1986.
Edwards, Philip. *Educ Phil Theor* 21(1), 90-91 1989
Magri, Tito. *Hist Euro Ideas* 10(5), 597-601 1989
Russell, Paul. *J Hist Phil* 27(4), 620-622 O 89

HAMRICK, William S. *An Existential Phenomenology of Law: Maurice Merleau-Ponty.* Norwell, Nijhoff, 1987.
Marsh, James L. *Int Phil Quart* 30(3), 378-379 S 90
Paillard, Henri. *Can Phil Rev* 10(2), 64-66 F 90

HANFLING, Oswald. *The Quest for Meaning.* Cambridge, Blackwell, 1987.
Lyas, Colin. *Phil Invest* 12(4), 341-343 O 89

HANFLING, Oswald. *Wittgenstein's Later Philosophy.* London, Macmillan, 1989.
Leahy, M P T. *Phil Books* 31(3), 152-154 Jl 90

HANSEN, Frank-Peter. *Das älteste Systemprogramm des deutschen Idealismus.* Berlin, de Gruyter, 1989.
Depré, Olivier. *Rev Phil Louvain* 88(77), 79-98 F 90

HARDIN, C L. *Color for Philosophers: Unweaving the Rainbow.* Indianapolis, Hackett, 1988.
Schopman, Joop. *Commun Cog* 22(2), 229-230 1989
Smook, Roger. *Can Phil Rev* 10(6), 233-237 Je 90

HARDIN, Russell. *Morality Within the Limits of Reason.* Chicago, Univ of Chicago Pr, 1988.
Donner, Wendy. *Can Phil Rev* 10(3), 112-115 Mr 90
Ryan, Alan. *Polit Theory* 18(1), 176-180 F 90

HARDING, Sandra. *The Science Question in Feminism.* Ithaca, Cornell Univ Pr, 1986.
Safford, Betty. *Hypatia* 5(1), 181-182 Spr 90

HARE, Peter H (ed). *Doing Philosophy Historically.* Buffalo, Prometheus, 1989.
Dougherty, Jude. *Teach Phil* 12(4), 423-424 D 89
Kerby, Anthony. *Can Phil Rev* 10(3), 115-118 Mr 90
O'Hear, Anthony. *Phil Phenomenol Res* 50(3), 628-630 Mr 90

HARE, R M. *Essays in Ethical Theory.* Oxford, Clarendon Pr, 1989.
Charvet, John. *Philosophy* 65(252), 232-234 Ap 90

HARE, R M. *Essays in Political Morality.* Oxford, Clarendon Pr, 1989.
Charvet, John. *Philosophy* 65(252), 232-234 Ap 90

HARMAN, Gilbert. *Change in View: Principles of Reasoning.* Cambridge, MIT Pr, 1986.
Brueckner, Anthony L. *Metaphilosophy* 20(3-4), 356-370 Jl-O 89
Feldman, Richard. *Phil Rev* 98(4), 552-556 O 89

HARNEY, Maurita J. *Intentionality, Sense and the Mind.* Norwell, Kluwer, 1984.
Willard, Dallas. *J Brit Soc Phenomenol* 20(3), 299-301 O 89

HAROOTUNIAN, H D and MASAO, Miyoshi (eds). *Postmodernism in Japan.* Durham, Duke Univ Pr, 1988.
Odin, Steve. *Phil East West* 40(3), 381-387 Jl 90

HARPER, Douglas. *Working Knowledge: Skill and Community in a Small Shop.* Chicago, Univ of Chicago Pr, 1987.
Van Maanen, John. *Human Stud* 13(3), 275-284 Jl 90

HARRÉ, Rom. *Personal Being: A Theory for Individual Psychology.* Cambridge, Harvard Univ Pr, 1984.
March, Peter. *Eidos* 7(2), 245-247 D 88

HARRIS, Errol E. *The Reality of Time.* Albany, SUNY Pr, 1988.
Allan, George. *Hist Theor* 28(3), 348-356 O 89
Garcia, Pablo Sebastián. *Rev Filosof (Argentina)* 4(1), 49-54 My 89
Grier, Philip T. *J Speculative Phil* 4(2), 168-172 1990

HARRIS, John. *The Value of Life: An Introduction to Medical Ethics.* New York, Routledge, 1985.
Byrne, Peter. *Heythrop J* 30(4), 482-483 O 89

HARRIS, Leonard (ed). *The Philosophy of Alain Locke: Harlem Renaissance and Beyond*. Philadelphia, Temple Univ Pr, 1989.
Boxill, Bernard R. *Trans Peirce Soc* 26(3), 384-388 Sum 90

HARRIS, Paul (ed). *Civil Disobedience*. Lanham, Univ Pr of America, 1989.
Pocklington, T C. *Can Phil Rev* 10(3), 118-120 Mr 90

HARRIS, Zellig. *Language and Information*. New York, Columbia Univ Pr, 1988.
Warmbröd, Ken. *Can Phil Rev* 10(3), 121-123 Mr 90

HART, W D. *The Engines of the Soul*. New York, Cambridge Univ Pr, 1988.
Edwards, Jim. *Phil Quart* 39(157), 512-515 O 89
Vaughan, Rachel. *Hist Euro Ideas* 12(1), 151-153 1990

HARTLE, Ann. *Death and the Disinterested Spectator: An Inquiry into the Nature of Philosophy*. Albany, SUNY Pr, 1986.
Maschler, Chaninah. *Interpretation* 17(1), 152-161 Fall 89
Wyschogrod, Edith. *Int Stud Phil* 22(1), 110-111 1990

HARTLE, Anthony E. *Moral Issues in Military Decision Making*. Lawrence, Univ Pr of Kansas, 1989.
Acerra, Angelo T. *Rev Metaph* 43(3), 633-634 Mr 90

HARTMAN, Charles. *Han Yü and the T'ang Search for Unity*. Princeton, Princeton Univ Pr, 1986.
Chen, Jo-shui. *Phil East West* 40(3), 403-405 Jl 90

HARTSHORNE, Charles. *Wisdom as Moderation*. Albany, SUNY Pr, 1987.
Gordon, David. *Int Phil Quart* 30(1), 111-114 Mr 90

HASTEDT, Heiner. *Das Leib-Seele-Problem*. Frankfurt am Main, Suhrkamp, 1988.
Metzinger, Thomas. *Conceptus* 23(59), 118-121 1989

HATTIANGADI, J N. *How Is Language Possible? Philosophical Reflections on the Evolution of Language and Knowledge*. La Salle, Open Court, 1987.
D'Agostino, Fred. *Phil Soc Sci* 19(4), 507-509 D 89
Luce, Lila. *Mod Sch* 66(4), 308-311 My 89
Nicolson, Stewart. *Dialogue (Canada)* 28(3), 512-516 1989

HAUERWAS, Stanley. *Suffering Presence*. Notre Dame, Univ Notre Dame Pr, 1986.
Grugan, Arthur A. *Int Phil Quart* 29(4), 485-487 D 89

HAUGELAND, John. *Artificial Intelligence: The Very Idea*. Cambridge, MIT Pr, 1985.
Pohl, Ira. *J Sym Log* 53(2), 659-660 Je 88

HAVELOCK, Eric A. *The Muse Learns to Write*. New Haven, Yale Univ Pr, 1986.
Goldstein, Leon J. *Int Stud Phil* 22(1), 93-94 1990

HAWKING, Stephen W. *A Brief History of Time: From the Big Bang to Black Holes*. NY, Bantam, 1988.
Becker, Thomas. *Zygon* 24(4), 491-494 D 89

HAWKINS, Gordon and ZIMRING, Franklin E. *Pornography in a Free Society*. Cambridge, Cambridge Univ Pr, 1988.
Mendus, Susan. *J Applied Phil* 7(1), 110-111 Mr 90

HAWORTH, Lawrence. *Autonomy: An Essay in Philosophical Psychology and Ethics*. New Haven, Yale Univ Pr, 1986.
Kapur, Neera Badhwar. *Dialogue (Canada)* 28(3), 487-498 1989
Potter, Nelson. *Nous* 24(2), 357-359 Ap 90

HAYEK, F A. *The Fatal Conceit: The Errors of Socialism*. Chicago, Univ of Chicago Pr, 1989.
Miller, David. *Crit Rev* 3(2), 310-323 Spr 89
Yeager, Leland B. *Crit Rev* 3(2), 324-335 Spr 89

HAYES, Richard. *Dignaga on the Interpretation of Signs*. Norwell, Reidel, 1988.
Sinha, Debabrata. *Can Phil Rev* 9(8), 310-312 Ag 89

HEATH, M. *The Poetics of Greek Tragedy*. London, Duckworth, 1987.
Halliwell, Stephen. *J Hellen Stud* 109, 231 1989

HEBBLETHWAITE, Brian. *The Incarnation: Collected Essays in Christology*. Cambridge, Cambridge Univ Pr, 1987.
Morris, Thomas V. *Faith Phil* 7(3), 344-347 Jl 90

HEGEL, G W F. *Encyclopédie des Sciences Philosophiques, V3, Bernard Bourgeois (ed & trans)*. Paris, Vrin, 1988.
Kirscher, Gilbert. *Rev Phil Louvain* 87(76), 548-552 Ag 89

HEGEL, G W F. *Lectures on the Philosophy of Religion, Peter C Hodgson (ed), Robert F Brown and others (trans)*. Berkeley, Univ of California Pr, 1988.
Perkins, Robert L. *Clio* 18(4), 387-390 Sum 89

HEGEL, G W F. *The Philosophical Propaedeutic, Michael George and Andrew Vincent (eds), A V Miller (trans)*. NY, Blackwell, 1986.
Jurist, Elliot L. *Owl Minerva* 21(2), 203-205 Spr 90

HEGEL, G W F. *Vorlesungen über die Philosophie der Religion, 3v, Walter Jaeschke (ed)*. Hamburg, Meiner, 1985.
Wagner, Falk. *Phil Rundsch* 37(1-2), 44-59 1990

HEGEL, G W F. *Vorlesungsmanuskripte I (1816-1831), W Jaeschke (ed)*. Hamburg, Meiner, 1987.
De Vos, L. *Tijdschr Filosof* 51(3), 517-527 S 89

HEIDEGGER, Martin. *Hegel's Phenomenology of Spirit, Parvis Emad and Kenneth Maly (trans)*. Bloomington, Indiana Univ Pr, 1988.
Siemens, R L. *Can Phil Rev* 10(4), 138-141 Ap 90

HEIDEGGER, Martin. *History of the Concept of Time: Prolegomena, Theodore Kisiel (trans)*. Bloomington, Indiana Univ Pr, 1985.
Gorner, Paul. *J Brit Soc Phenomenol* 21(1), 86-91 Ja 90

HEIDEGGER, Martin. *Ormai solo un Dio ci può salvare, A Marini (ed)*. Parma, Guanda, 1987.
Penzo, Giorgio. *Riv Int Filosof Diritto* 66(3), 549-552 Jl-S 89

HEIDEGGER, Martin. *Zollikoner Seminare: Protokolle, Gespräche, Briefe, Medard Boss (ed)*. Frankfurt am Main, Klostermann, 1987.
Arlt, Gerhard. *Phil Rundsch* 36(4), 291-298 1989

HEIDEGGER, Martin. *Zur Bestimmung der Philosophie, Bernd Heimbüchel (ed)*. Frankfurt am Main, Klostermann, 1987.
Kovacs, George. *Res Phenomenol* 19, 304-311 1989

HEINEKAMP, Albert (ed). *Leibniz: Questions de Logique*. Stuttgart, Steiner, 1988.
Proust, Joëlle. *Arch Phil* 53(1), 78-83 Ja-Mr 90

HEINRICH, Richard. *Kants Erfahrungsraum*. Freiburg, Alber, 1986.
Sauer, Werner. *Kantstudien* 80(3), 357-359 1989

HEISE, Wolfgang. *Hölderlin: Schönheit und Geschichte*. Berlin, Aufbau, 1988.
Heininger, Jörg. *Deut Z Phil* 38(3), 298-300 1990

HEKMAN, S J. *Hermeneutics and the Sociology of Knowledge*. Oxford, Polity Pr, 1986.
Davey, Nicholas. *J Brit Soc Phenomenol* 21(2), 192-195 My 90

HELD, Virginia. *Rights and Goods: Justifying Social Action*. New York, Free Pr, 1984.
Schwarzenbach, Sibyl. *Metaphilosophy* 21(1-2), 162-178 Ja-Ap 90

HELLER, Agnes. *Beyond Justice*. New York, Blackwell, 1987.
Blanchette, Oliva. *Stud Soviet Tho* 39(2), 177-181 Mr 90

HELLER, Agnes. *General Ethics*. Oxford, Blackwell, 1988.
Adam, Michel. *Rev Phil Fr* 180(2), 467-469 Ap-Je 90

HELLER, Erich. *The Importance of Nietzsche: Ten Essays*. Chicago, Univ of Chicago Pr, 1988.
Watson, James R. *Can Phil Rev* 9(9), 358-360 S 89

HELM, Paul. *Eternal God: A Study of God without Time*. Oxford, Clarendon Pr, 1988.
Baird, Forrest E. *Phil Books* 31(1), 49-51 Ja 90
Garcia, Laura L. *Rev Metaph* 43(3), 634-636 Mr 90

HENDLEY, Brian P (ed). *Plato, Time and Education: Essays in Honor of Robert S Brumbaugh*. Albany, SUNY Pr, 1987.
Turnbull, Robert G. *Ancient Phil* 10(1), 127-130 Spr 90

HENKIN, Leon and MONK, J Donald and TARSKI, Alfred. *Cylindric Algebras, Part II*. Amsterdam, North-Holland, 1985.
Maddux, Roger D. *J Sym Log* 53(2), 651-653 Je 88

HENNESSY, Matthew. *Algebraic Theory of Processes*. Cambridge, MIT Pr, 1988.
Gunter, Carl A. *J Sym Log* 55(1), 366-368 Mr 90

HENNINGER, Mark G. *Relations: Medieval Theories 1250-1325*. New York, Oxford Univ Pr, 1989.
Santogrossi, Ansgar. *Rev Metaph* 43(4), 868-870 Je 90

HENNIS, Wilhelm. *Max Weber, Essays in Reconstruction, Keith Tribe (trans)*. Winchester, Allen & Unwin, 1988.
Scaff, Lawrence A. *Polit Theory* 17(4), 678-681 N 89

HENRICH, D and HORSTMANN, R-P (eds). *Hegels Philosophie des Rechts, Die Theorie der Rechtsformen und ihre Logik*. Stuttgart, Klett-Cotta, 1982.
Vollrath, Ernst. *Phil Rundsch* 37(1-2), 27-43 1990

HENRICH, Dieter (ed). *Hegels Wissenschaft der Logik: Formation und Rekonstruktion*. Stuttgart, Klett-Cotta, 1986.
Depré, Olivier. *Rev Phil Louvain* 87(76), 560-563 Ag 89

Houlgate, Stephen. *Owl Minerva* 21(2), 227-230 Spr 90
Westphal, Merold. *Heythrop J* 31(1), 106-107 Ja 90
White, Alan. *Owl Minerva* 21(1), 91-96 Fall 89

HÖVER, Gerhard. *Sittlich handeln im Medium der Zeit*. Würzburg, Echter, 1988.
Kissling, Christian. *Frei Z Phil Theol* 36(3), 500-503 1989

HOWARD, Dick. *From Marx to Kant*. Albany, SUNY Pr, 1985.
Küsters, Gerd-Walter. *Kantstudien* 81(1), 113-116 1990
Santamaria, U and Manville, A. *Phil Soc Sci* 19(3), 381-394 S 89

HOWIE, John (ed). *Ethical Principles and Practice*. Carbondale, Southern Illinois Univ Pr, 1987.
Vallentyne, Peter. *Can Phil Rev* 9(10), 416-417 O 89

HOWSON, Colin and URBACH, Peter. *Scientific Reasoning: The Bayesian Approach*. LaSalle, Open Court, 1989.
Dessì, P. *Hist Phil Log* 11(2), 259 1990
Gillies, Donald. *Ratio* 3(1), 82-98 Je 90

HUBBARD, B A F and KARNOFSKY, E S. *Plato's Protagoras: A Socratic Commentary*. Chicago, Univ of Chicago Pr, 1984.
Brumbaugh, Robert S. *Thinking* 5(4), 68 1985

HUDE, Henri. *"Philosophie européenne"*. Paris, Universitaires, 1990.
Humbrecht, Thierry-Dominique. *Rev Thomiste* 90(2), 315-318 Ap-Je 90

HUDSON, Deal W and MANCINI, Matthew J (eds). *Understanding Maritain: Philosopher and Friend*. Macon, Mercer Univ Pr, 1987.
Aeschliman, M D. *Thomist* 53(4), 727-731 O 89
Crosson, Frederick J. *Can Phil Rev* 9(7), 270-272 Jl 89

HUER, Jon. *Art, Beauty, and Pornography*. Buffalo, Prometheus, 1987.
Gracyk, Theodore A. *J Aes Educ* 22(2), 121-123 Sum 88

HUGHES, H Stuart. *Between Commitment and Disillusion*. Middletown, Wesleyan Univ Pr, 1987.
Roth, Michael S. *J Hist Ideas* 51(3), 505-515 Jl-S 90

HÜLSER, Karlheinz (ed). *Die Fragmente zur Dialektik der Stoiker*. Stuttgart, Frommann-Holzboog, 1987.
Ebert, Theodor. *Z Phil Forsch* 44(2), 331-336 1990

HUME, David. *Politische und ökonomische Essays*, Susanne Fischer (trans). Hamburg, pub unknown, 1988.
Streminger, Gerhard. *Conceptus* 23(59), 121-126 1989

HUME, David. *Sobre el suicidio y otros ensayos*. Madrid, Alianza, 1988.
López Sastre, Gerardo. *Rev Filosof (Spain)* 2, 187-190 1989

HUNDERT, Edward M. *Philosophy, Psychiatry and Neuroscience: Three Approaches to the Mind*. NY, Oxford Univ Pr, 1989.
Gillett, Grant. *Inquiry* 33(2), 231-244 Je 90
Stack, George J. *Rev Metaph* 43(3), 636-637 Mr 90

HUNNINGS, Gordon. *The World and Language in Wittgenstein's Philosophy*. Albany, SUNY Pr, 1988.
Churchill, John. *Thomist* 54(3), 554-558 Jl 90
Cooke, Vincent M. *Thought* 64(255), 419-420 D 89
Lewis, Andrew. *Phil Books* 31(1), 26-28 Ja 90

HUSSERL, Edmund. *Aufsätze und Vorträge (1911-1921)*, Thomas Nenon and Hans Rainer Sepp (eds). Dordrecht, Nijhoff, 1987.
Schuhmann, Karl. *Husserl Stud* 7(1), 68-71 1990

HUTCHESON, Francis. *Eine Untersuchung über den Ursprung unserer Ideen von Schönheit und Tugend*. Hamburg, Meiner, 1986.
Haakonssen, Knud. *J Hist Phil* 27(4), 626-628 O 89

HUTCHINSON, D S. *The Virtues of Aristotle*. New York, Routledge, 1986.
Novak, Joseph A. *Ancient Phil* 9 (2), 332-337 Fall 89
Young, Charles M. *Phoenix* 43(3), 280-281 Autumn 89

HYMAN, John. *The Imitation of Nature*. Oxford, Blackwell, 1989.
Woodfield, Richard. *Brit J Aes* 30(3), 280-282 Jl 90

IMHOF, Beat W. *Edith Steins Philosophische Entwicklung*. Cambridge, Birkhauser, 1987.
Schuhmann, Karl. *Husserl Stud* 6(1), 83-87 1989

INGRAM, Paul. *The Modern Buddhist-Christian Dialogue: Two Universalistic Religions in Transformation*. Lewiston, Mellen Pr, 1988.
Matthews, Robin. *Process Stud* 18(2), 131-137 Sum 89

INTELEX CORP. *Past Masters: Hobbes, Locke, Berkeley, Hume [software]*. Pittsboro, InteLex Corp, undated.
Blackburn, Simon. *Mind* 99(395), 489-491 Jl 90

INWOOD, Brad and GERSON, L P (trans). *Hellenistic Philosophy: Introductory Readings*. Indianapolis, Hackett, 1988.
Preuss, Peter. *Can Phil Rev* 9(9), 366-368 S 89

IOFRIDA, Manlio. *Forma e materia*. Pisa, ETS, 1988.
Fabris, Adriano. *Teoria* 9(1), 276-278 1989

IRWIN, Terence. *Aristotle's First Principles*. Oxford, Clarendon Pr, 1988.
Evans, J D G. *Hermathena* 147, 73-74 Wint 89
Hughes, Gerard J. *Heythrop J* 31(1), 67-70 Ja 90
Williams, C J F. *Phil Books* 31(3), 138-141 Jl 90

IRWIN, Terence. *Classical Thought: A History of Western Philosophy, V1*. Oxford, Oxford Univ Pr, 1989.
Dillon, John. *Hermathena* 147, 78-80 Wint 89
Gill, Christopher. *Phil Books* 31(3), 136-138 Jl 90
Modrak, D K W. *Rev Metaph* 43(2), 405-406 D 89
Panagiotou, Spiro. *Teach Phil* 13(1), 52-55 Mr 90

ISAAC, Jeffrey C. *Power and Marxist Theory: A Realist View*. Ithaca, Cornell Univ Pr, 1987.
Hudelson, Richard. *Phil Soc Sci* 20(3), 390-393 S 90

JACKSON, Frank. *Conditionals*. Cambridge, Blackwell, 1988.
Adams, Ernest W. *Phil Rev* 99(3), 433-435 Jl 90
Lance, Mark N. *Hist Phil Log* 11(1), 103-105 1990
Nute, Donald. *J Sym Log* 55(2), 891-892 Je 90
Papineau, David. *Phil Quart* 39(157), 493-498 O 89

JACKSON, J R de J. *Historical Criticism and the Meaning of Texts*. New York, Routledge, 1989.
McCarthy, John P. *Brit J Aes* 30(3), 289-290 Jl 90

JACOBELLI, J. *Croce Gentile: Dal sodalizio al dramma*. Milan, Rizzoli, 1989.
Cavallera, Hervé A. *Filosofia* 41(1), 126-127 Ja-Ap 90

JACQUES, Francis. *Différence et subjectivité*. Paris, Aubier-Montaigne, 1982.
Waldenfels, Bernhard. *Phil Rundsch* 36(3), 218-231 1989

JACQUES, Francis. *L'espace logique de l'interlocution*. Paris, Pr Univ de France, 1985.
Waldenfels, Bernhard. *Phil Rundsch* 36(3), 218-231 1989

JACQUES, Francis. *Über den Dialog*. Hawthorne, de Gruyter, 1986.
Waldenfels, Bernhard. *Phil Rundsch* 36(3), 218-231 1989

JAESCHKE, W. *Die Vernunft in der Religion*. Stuttgart, Frommann-Holzboog, 1986.
Samonà, Leonardo. *G Metaf* 11(2), 313-315 My-Ag 89

JAESCHKE, Walter. *Die Vernunft in der Religion*. Stuttgart, Frommann-Holzboog, 1986.
Schrödter, Hermann. *Z Phil Forsch* 44(1), 149-154 1990
Wagner, Falk. *Phil Rundsch* 37(1-2), 44-59 1990

JAKOBSON, Roman. *Language and Literature*, K Pomorska and S Rudy (eds). Cambridge, Harvard Univ Pr, 1987.
Carstairs, Andrew. *Phil Lit* 13(2), 387-388 O 89

JAMES, Susan. *The Content of Social Explanation*. Cambridge, Cambridge Univ Pr, 1985.
Fay, Brian. *Phil Soc Sci* 20(1), 131-135 Mr 90

JAMES, William. *Manuscript Essays and Notes*, Frederick H Burkhardt (ed). Cambridge, Harvard Univ Pr, 1988.
Bayley, James E. *Trans Peirce Soc* 25(3), 373-377 Sum 89
Kennett, Stephen A. *Auslegung* 16(1), 111-115 Wint 90

JAMES, William. *Manuscript Lectures*, Frederick H Burkhardt (ed). Cambridge, Harvard Univ Pr, 1988.
Anderson, Douglas R. *Trans Peirce Soc* 25(4), 565-570 Fall 89
Kennett, Stephen A. *Auslegung* 16(1), 111-115 Wint 90

JAMME, Christoph and SCHNEIDER, Helmut (eds). *Mythologie der Vernunft*. Frankfurt, Suhrkamp, 1984.
Depré, Olivier. *Rev Phil Louvain* 88(77), 79-98 F 90

JANAWAY, Christopher. *Self and World in Schopenhauer's Philosophy*. Oxford, Clarendon Pr, 1989.
Lewis, Peter. *Phil Books* 31(2), 80-82 Ap 90

JANICH, Peter. *Protophysics of Time*. Dordrecht, Reidel, 1985.
Sklar, Lawrence. *Int Stud Phil* 21(3), 121-122 1989

JASAY, Anthony de. *Social Contract, Free Ride: A Study of the Public Goods Problem*. Oxford, Clarendon Pr, 1989.
Crisp, Roger. *Phil Books* 31(2), 110-112 Ap 90
Cust, Kenneth F T. *Can Phil Rev* 10(4), 129-132 Ap 90
Schmidtz, David. *Int Phil Quart* 30(3), 369-370 S 90

JASAY, Anthony de. *The State*. NY, Blackwell, 1985.
Schultz, David. *Int Stud Phil* 21(3), 122-123 1989

JASPER, David (ed). *The Interpretation of Belief: Coleridge,*

Schleiermacher and Romanticism. Basingstoke, Macmillan, 1986.
Butler, Perry. *Heythrop J* 31(1), 108-109 Ja 90

JAY, Martin. *Fin-de-Siècle Socialism and Other Essays.* New York, Routledge, 1989.
Stirk, Peter M R. *Hist Polit Thought* 10(3), 553-557 Autumn 89

JEANROND, Werner G. *Text and Interpretation as Categories of Theological Thinking,* T J Wilson (trans). Dublin, Gill & Macmillan, 1987.
Biggar, Nigel. *Hermathena* 146, 81-86 Sum 89

JENA, Detlef. *Georgi Walentinowitsch Plechanow.* Berlin, Deutscher, 1989.
Hedeler, S and Mieth, E. *Deut Z Phil* 38(5), 494-495 1990

JENCKS, Charles. *Post-Modernism.* NY, Rizzoli, 1987.
Richardson, John Adkins. *J Aes Educ* 23(4), 114-116 Wint 89

JERMANN, Ch (ed). *Anspruch und Leistung von Hegels Rechtsphilosophie.* Stuttgart, Frommann-Holzboog, 1987.
Vollrath, Ernst. *Phil Rundsch* 37(1-2), 27-43 1990

JERMANN, Christoph. *Philosophie und Politik.* Stuttgart, Frommann-Holzboog, 1986.
Buchheim, Thomas. *Z Phil Forsch* 43(3), 552-556 Jl-S 89

JOFFE, Carole. *The Regulation of Sexuality: Experiences of Family Planning Workers.* Philadelphia, Temple Univ Pr, 1986.
Addelson, Kathryn Pyne. *Hypatia* 4(2), 191-197 Sum 89

JOHNSON, Harold J (ed). *The Medieval Tradition of Natural Law.* Kalamazoo, Medieval Institute, 1987.
Hundersmarck, Lawrence F. *Vera Lex* 9(2), 21-22 1989

JOHNSON, M. *Attribute-Value Logic and the Theory of Grammar.* Chicago, Univ of Chicago Pr, 1989.
Harris, R. *Hist Phil Log* 11(2), 252-253 1990

JOHNSON, Paul Owen. *The Critique of Thought: A Re-examination of Hegel's Science of Logic.* Brookfield, Gower, 1989.
Burbidge, John. *Can Phil Rev* 9(11), 440-441 N 89

JOHNSON, Peter. *Politics, Innocence, and the Limits of Goodness.* New York, Routledge, 1988.
George, David. *J Applied Phil* 6(2), 243-244 O 89
Hayward, T P. *Phil Books* 31(1), 46-47 Ja 90
Horton, John. *Utilitas* 1(2), 316-318 N 89
Hughes, Martin. *Philosophy* 64(249), 421-423 Jl 89
Marshall, S E. *Can Phil Rev* 10(5), 184-186 My 90

JOHNSON, Thomas M (trans). *Iamblichus: The Exhortation to Philosophy.* Grand Rapids, Phanes Pr, 1988.
Novak, Joseph A. *Can Phil Rev* 10(1), 24-31 Ja 90

JOHNSON-LAIRD, Philip N. *Modelli mentali.* Bologna, Mulino, 1988.
Napoli, Ernesto. *Teoria* 9(2), 145-160 1989

JOHNSTON, David. *The Rhetoric of "Leviathan": Thomas Hobbes and the Politics of Cultural Transformation.* Princeton, Princeton Univ Pr, 1986.
Costa, Margarita. *Analisis Filosof* 9(1), 93-96 My 89
Johnson, Paul J. *Hist Euro Ideas* 10(6), 730-732 1989
Mathie, William. *Interpretation* 17(1), 145-152 Fall 89

JOHNSTON, Mark D. *The Spiritual Logic of Ramon Llull.* NY, Oxford Univ Pr, 1987.
Vega Esquerra, Amador. *J Hist Phil* 28(1), 127-128 Ja 90

JOLIVET, Jean and RASHED, Roshdi (eds). *Etudes sur Avicenne.* Paris, Belles Lettres, 1984.
Brague, Rémi. *Rev Metaph Morale* 94(3), 415-417 Jl-S 89

JONAS, Hans. *The Imperative of Responsibility: In Search of an Ethics for the Technological Age.* Chicago, Univ of Chicago Pr, 1984.
Carvalho, John M. *Int Stud Phil* 22(1), 109 1990

JONES, Edwin. *Reading the Book of Nature: A Phenomenological Study of Creative Expression in Science and Painting.* Athens, Ohio Univ Pr, 1989.
Locke, Patricia M. *Rev Metaph* 43(3), 637-639 Mr 90

JONES, Howard. *The Epicurean Tradition.* New York, Routledge, Chapman & Hall, 1990.
Preuss, Peter. *Can Phil Rev* 10(7), 277-280 Jl 90

JONSEN, Albert R and TOULMIN, Stephen. *The Abuse of Casuistry: A History of Moral Reasoning.* Berkeley, Univ of California Pr, 1988.
Alonso, Alfred. *Rev Metaph* 43(3), 639-641 Mr 90
Arras, John D. *Hastings Center Rep* 20(4), 35-37 Jl-Ag 90
Cessario, Romanus. *Thomist* 54(1), 151-155 Ja 90

JOÓS, Ernest. *Poetic Truth and Transvaluation in Nietzsche's "Zarathustra".* New York, Lang, 1987.
Preuss, Peter. *Dialogue (Canada)* 27(4), 732-733 Wint 88

JOÓS, Ernst (ed). *Georg Lukács and His World: A Reassessment.* New York, Lang, 1987.
Miklós, Mesterházi. *Magyar Filozof Szemle* 5, 677-683 1989

JOÓS, Ernst. *Lukács's Last Autocriticism: The Ontology.* Atlantic Highlands, Humanities Pr, 1983.
Miklós, Mesterházi. *Magyar Filozof Szemle* 5, 677-683 1989

JORDAN, Bill. *The Common Good, Citizenship, Morality and Self-Interest.* Oxford, Blackwell, 1989.
Quinn, Michael. *Utilitas* 2(1), 144-149 My 90

JORDANOVA, Ludmilla. *Sexual Visions: Images of Gender in Science and Medicine between the Eighteenth and Twentieth Centuries.* Madison, Univ of Wisconsin Pr, 1989.
Cayleff, Susan E. *Med Human Rev* 4(2), 61-65 Jl 90

JOY, Lynn Sumida. *Gassendi the Atomist: Advocate of History in an Age of Science.* NY, Cambridge Univ Pr, 1987.
Kroll, Richard W F. *J Hist Phil* 28(2), 297-299 Ap 90
Popkin, Richard H. *Can Phil Rev* 9(10), 396-403 O 89

KAEHLER, Klaus Erich. *Leibniz' Position der Rationalität.* Freiburg, Alber, 1989.
Parkinson, G H R. *Stud Leibniz* 21(2), 209-211 1989

KAELIN, E F. *Heidegger's "Being and Time": A Reading for Readers.* Tallahassee, Florida St Univ Pr, 1988.
Prier, Raymond Adolph. *Phil Lit* 13(2), 406-408 O 89

KAIN, Philip J. *Marx and Ethics.* Oxford, Clarendon Pr, 1988.
Paskow, Alan. *Phil Books* 31(2), 84-86 Ap 90
Wallace, Gerry. *J Applied Phil* 7(1), 108-110 Mr 90

KAINZ, Howard P. *Ethics in Context: Towards the Definition and Differentiation of the Morally Good.* New York, Macmillan, 1988.
Holmes, Arthur. *Vera Lex* 9(1), 17-18 1989
O'Neill, Onora. *Phil Books* 30(4), 237-238 O 89

KAL, Victor. *On Intuition and Discursive Reasoning in Aristotle.* Leiden, Brill, 1988.
Martin, James T H. *Thomist* 54(1), 181-184 Ja 90

KALECHOFSKY, Robert. *The Persistence of Error: Essays in Developmental Epistemology.* Lanham, Univ Pr of America, 1987.
Greenwood, Robert L. *Can Phil Rev* 9(10), 418-420 O 89

KANE, Robert and PHILLIPS, Stephen H (eds). *Hartshorne, Process Philosophy, and Theology.* Albany, SUNY Pr, 1989.
Reck, Andrew J. *Can Phil Rev* 10(6), 237-240 Je 90

KANE, Rosalie A and KANE, Robert L. *Long-Term Care: Principles, Programs and Policies.* New York, Springer, 1987.
McCullough, Laurence B. *Hastings Center Rep* 19(5), 45-46 S-O 89

KASLER, Dirk. *Max Weber: An Introduction to His Life and Work.* Oxford, Polity Pr, 1988.
Ashcraft, Richard. *Hist Polit Thought* 10(3), 551-553 Autumn 89

KATZ, Jerrold J. *Cogitations.* Oxford, Oxford Univ Pr, 1988.
Nuchelmans, Gabriel. *Hist Phil Log* 11(1), 95-96 1990

KAULBACH, Friedrich. *Immanuel Kants 'Grundlegung zur Metaphysik der Sitten'.* Darmstadt, Wissenschaftliche Buchgesellschaft, 1988.
Wenzel, Uwe Justus. *Kantstudien* 80(4), 472-477 1989

KAVKA, Gregory S. *Hobbesian Moral and Political Theory.* Princeton, Princeton Univ Pr, 1986.
Cooper, Wesley. *Can J Phil* 19(3), 491-507 S 89
Costa, Margarita. *Rev Latin De Filosof* 15(3), 361-364 N 89

KAYE, Howard L. *The Social Meaning of Modern Biology—from Social Darwinism to Sociobiology.* New Haven, Yale Univ Pr, 1986.
Ehret, Charles F. *Zygon* 24(4), 489-490 D 89

KEARNEY, Richard. *Modern Movements in European Philosophy.* New York, St Martin's Pr, 1988.
Boyne, Roy. *J Brit Soc Phenomenol* 21(2), 198-200 My 90
Carvalho, John M. *Can Phil Rev* 9(8), 312-315 Ag 89
Caws, Peter. *Teach Phil* 12(3), 266-268 S 89

KEARNEY, Richard. *The Wake of Imagination: Toward a Postmodern Culture.* Minneapolis, Univ of Minnesota Pr, 1988.
Beisvert, Raymond D. *Personalist Forum* 5(2), 152-154 Fall 89
Moran, Dermot. *Irish Phil J* 6(2), 311-314 1989

KEE, Alistair and LONG, Eugene T (eds). *Being and Truth: Essays in Honour of John Macquarrie.* London, SCM Pr, 1986.
Langford, Thomas A. *Mod Theol* 6(3), 299-301 Ap 90

KEELEY, Michael. *A Social-Contract Theory of Organizations.* Notre Dame, Univ of Notre Dame Pr, 1988.

Charron, Donna Card. *Mod Sch* 67(1), 76-78 N 89

KEKES, John. *Moral Tradition and Individuality.* Princeton, Princeton Univ Pr, 1989.
Armour, Leslie. *Can Phil Rev* 10(4), 146-149 Ap 90
Mounce, H O. *Philosophy* 65(252), 234-236 Ap 90
Strasser, Mark. *Rev Metaph* 43(4), 870-871 Je 90

KEKES, John. *The Examined Life.* Lewisburg, Bucknell Univ Pr, 1988.
Butchvarov, Panayot. *Rev Metaph* 43(2), 406-408 D 89
Dent, N J H. *Can Phil Rev* 9(9), 369-371 S 89

KELLEY, David. *The Art of Reasoning.* New York, Norton, 1988.
Smook, Roger. *Teach Phil* 12(3), 288-290 S 89

KELLEY, Jane E and HANEN, Marsha. *Archaeology and the Methodology of Science.* Albuquerque, Univ of New Mexico Pr, 1988.
Levin, Michael. *Phil Soc Sci* 20(2), 252-255 Je 90

KELLEY, Theresa M. *Wordsworth's Revisionary Aesthetics.* New York, Cambridge Univ Pr, 1988.
Morse, David. *Brit J Aes* 29(4), 387-389 Autumn 89

KELLY, Christopher. *Rousseau's Exemplary Life: "The Confessions" as Political Philosophy.* Ithaca, Cornell Univ Pr, 1987.
Perkins, Jean A. *Phil Lit* 14(1), 176-178 Ap 90

KELSEN, H. *Die Illusion der Gerechtigkeit, Eine kritische Untersuchung der Sozialphilosophie Platons.* Wien, Manz, 1985.
Ferber, Rafael. *Z Phil Forsch* 43(3), 557-561 Jl-S 89

KELSEN, Hans. *Théorie pure du droit.* Neuchâtel, Baconnière, 1988.
Hartney, Michael. *Can Phil Rev* 9(11), 442-443 N 89
Sciacca, Fabrizio. *Riv Int Filosof Diritto* 66(3), 555-557 Jl-S 89

KEMAL, Salim. *Kant and Fine Art.* Oxford, Oxford Univ Pr, 1987.
Williams, Howard. *Kantstudien* 80(4), 481-482 1989

KENNEDY, Ian. *Treat Me Right: Essays in Medical Law and Ethics.* NY, Oxford Univ Pr, 1988.
Lamb, David. *Phil Books* 31(2), 65-69 Ap 90
Williams, Peter C. *Med Human Rev* 4(1), 65-68 Ja 90

KENNEDY, Leonard A (ed). *Thomistic Paper IV.* Houston, Center for Thomistic Studies, 1988.
Reichenbach, Bruce R. *Thomist* 54(2), 371-376 Ap 90

KENNY, Anthony. *Reason and Religion: Essays in Philosophical Theology.* Cambridge, Blackwell, 1987.
Davies, Brian. *Phil Invest* 12(4), 349-353 O 89
MacDonald, Scott. *Phil Rev* 99(1), 138-142 Ja 90
Quinn, Philip L. *Thomist* 53(4), 709-713 O 89
Tilley, Terrence W. *Mod Theol* 6(1), 115-116 O 89

KENNY, Anthony. *The Heritage of Wisdom: Essays in the History of Philosophy.* Oxford, Blackwell, 1987.
MacDonald, Scott. *Phil Rev* 99(1), 138-142 Ja 90

KERMAN, Joseph. *Contemplating Music.* Cambridge, Harvard Univ Pr, 1985.
Levinson, Jerrold. *J Aes Educ* 23(2), 113-117 Sum 89

KERR, Fergus. *Theology After Wittgenstein.* Oxford, Blackwell, 1986.
Edwards, James C. *Int J Phil Relig* 28(1), 59-60 Ag 90
Meynell, Hugo. *Heythrop J* 31(1), 80-81 Ja 90

KERRIGAN, William and BRADLEY, Gordon and BRADEN, Gordon. *The Idea of the Renaissance.* Baltimore, Johns Hopkins Univ Pr, 1989.
Foster, Edward E. *Phil Lit* 14(1), 202-204 Ap 90
Korg, Jacob. *Clio* 19(2), 184-187 Wint 90

KERSEY, Ethel M. *Women Philosophers: A Bio-critical Source Book.* Westport, Greenwood Pr, 1989.
Sherwin, Susan. *Can Phil Rev* 10(7), 280-282 Jl 90

KERSTEN, Fred. *Phenomenological Method: Theory and Practice.* Dordrecht, Kluwer, 1989.
Jones, Barry J. *J Brit Soc Phenomenol* 21(1), 96-99 Ja 90

KESLER, Charles R (ed). *Saving the Revolution.* New York, Free Pr, 1988.
Grasso, Kenneth L. *Thought* 64(255), 417-418 D 89

KILCULLEN, John. *Sincerity and Truth: Essays on Arnauld, Bayle and Toleration.* Oxford, Clarendon Pr, 1988.
Michael, Emily and Michael, Fred S. *Hist Euro Ideas* 12(1), 147-148 1990
Weinstein, Kenneth R. *Rev Metaph* 43(3), 641-642 Mr 90

KILMISTER, C W (ed). *Schrödinger: Centenary Celebration of a Polymath.* Cambridge, Cambridge Univ Pr, 1987.
Clifton, Robert K. *Phil Sci* 57(2), 342-343 Je 90

KIRJAVAINE, H and SAARINEN, R and TYÖRINOJA, R. *Faith, Will and Grammar.* Helsinki, Luther-Agricola Society, 1986.
White, Graham. *Mod Theol* 6(1), 111-112 O 89

KIRSCHER, Gilbert. *La philosophie d'Éric Weil.* Paris, Pr Univ de France, 1989.
Buée, Jean-Michel. *Rev Phil Louvain* 87(76), 657-662 N 89

KIRWAN, Christopher. *Augustine.* New York, Routledge, 1989.
Losoncy, Thomas A. *Can Phil Rev* 9(8), 315-318 Ag 89
Mann, William E. *Phil Books* 31(1), 15-18 Ja 90
Perreiah, Alan. *Teach Phil* 12(3), 337-339 S 89

KITCHENER, Richard F (ed). *The World View of Contemporary Physics: Does It Need a New Metaphysics?* Albany, SUNY Pr, 1988.
Sachs, Mendel. *Phil Soc Sci* 20(2), 233-247 Je 90

KITCHENER, Richard F. *Piaget's Theory of Knowledge: Genetic Epistemology and Scientific Reason.* New Haven, Yale Univ Pr, 1986.
Petersen, Arne Friemuth. *Phil Soc Sci* 20(2), 222-232 Je 90

KITCHING, Gavin. *Karl Marx and the Philosophy of Praxis.* New York, Routledge, 1988.
Fisk, Milton. *Clio* 18(4), 401-405 Sum 89
Wallace, Gerry. *J Applied Phil* 7(1), 108-110 Mr 90

KITTAY, Eva Feder and MEYERS, Diana T (eds). *Women and Moral Theory.* Totowa, Rowman & Littlefield, 1987.
Wagner, Shirley. *Hypatia* 4(2), 186-188 Sum 89

KIVY, Peter. *Osmin's Rage: Philosophical Reflections on Opera, Drama, and Text.* Princeton, Princeton Univ Pr, 1988.
Davies, Stephen. *Austl J Phil* 67(3), 373-375 S 89
Goehr, Lydia. *Can Phil Rev* 10(1), 31-34 Ja 90

KLEIN, Josef. *Die konklusiven Sprechhandlungen.* Tübingen, Niemeyer, 1987.
Kertész, András. *J Prag* 14(2), 340-345 Ap 90

KLIEVER, Lonnie D (ed). *Dax's Case: Essays in Medical Ethics and Human Meaning.* Dallas, Southern Methodist Univ Pr, 1989.
Burt, Robert A. *Med Human Rev* 4(1), 17-19 Ja 90

KLOESEL, Christian J W (ed). *Writings of Charles S Peirce: A Chronological Edition, V4.* Bloomington, Indiana Univ Pr, 1989.
Burch, Robert W. *Hist Phil Log* 11(2), 217-224 1990

KLOSKO, George. *The Development of Plato's Political Theory.* New York, Methuen, 1986.
Evans, J D G. *Phil Books* 30(4), 211-213 O 89
Ferguson, John. *Heythrop J* 30(4), 486-487 O 89
Williams, G L. *Polis* 6(1), 51-53 1986

KLUBACK, William. *The Idea of Humanity: Herman Cohen's Legacy to Philosophy and Theology.* Lanham, Univ Pr of America, 1987.
Gordon, Haim. *Int J Phil Relig* 26(3), 187-188 D 89

KLUBACK, William. *The Legacy of Hermann Cohen.* Atlanta, Scholars Pr, 1989.
Zac, Sylvain. *Arch Phil* 53(1), 87-89 Ja-Mr 90

KLUXEN, W (ed). *Tradition und Innovation: XIII Deutscher Kongress Für Philosophie.* Hamburg, Meiner, 1988.
Régnier, M. *Arch Phil* 52(4), 659-661 O-D 89

KNUUTILLA, S (ed). *Modern Modalities: Studies of the History of Modal Theories from Medieval Nominalism to Logical Positivism.* Dordrecht, Kluwer, 1988.
Kielkopf, Charles F. *Hist Phil Log* 11(1), 97-98 1990

KOBLER, John R. *Vatican II and Phenomenology: Reflections on the Life-World of the Church.* Dordrecht, Nijhoff, 1985.
Booth, Edward. *J Brit Soc Phenomenol* 21(2), 204-206 My 90

KOCKELMANS, Joseph J. *Heidegger on Art and Art Works.* Dordrecht, Nijhoff, 1985.
Harries, Karsten. *Int Stud Phil* 21(3), 126-127 1989

KOGAN, Barry S. *Averroes and the Metaphysics of Causation.* Albany, SUNY Pr, 1985.
Ivry, Alfred L. *Int Stud Phil* 21(3), 127-128 1989

KÖHN, Livia. *Seven Steps to the Tao: Sima Chengzhen's Zuowanglun.* Nettetal, Skyler, 1987.
Cahill, Suzanne. *Phil East West* 40(1), 105-107 Ja 90

KÖHNKE, Klaus Christian. *Entstehung und Aufstieg des Neukantianismus.* Frankfurt, Suhrkamp, 1986.
Holzhey, Helmut. *J Hist Phil* 28(1), 142-144 Ja 90

KOLAK, Daniel. *Wisdom without Answers: A Guide to the Experience of Philosophy.* Belmont, Wadsworth, 1989.

1986.
Lauer, Quentin. *Int Phil Quart* 30(2), 259-260 Je 90

LANDES, Joan B. *Women and the Public Sphere in the Age of the French Revolution*. Ithaca, Cornell Univ Pr, 1988.
Dietz, Mary G. *Polit Theory* 17(4), 692-696 N 89

LANDESMAN, Charles. *Color and Consciousness: An Essay in Metaphysics*. Philadelphia, Temple Univ Pr, 1989.
Pitson, Anthony E. *Phil Books* 31(3), 167-169 Jl 90
Smook, Roger. *Can Phil Rev* 10(6), 233-237 Je 90

LANDMAN, Fred. *Towards a Theory of Information: The Status of Partial Objects in Semantics*. Dordrecht, Foris, 1986.
Fenstad, Jens Erik and Langholm, Tore. *J Sym Log* 53(2), 656-657 Je 88

LANE, Gilles. *Pouvoir, justice et non-mépris*. Montréal, VLB, 1989.
Roy, Yves. *Philosophiques* 16(2), 405-407 Autumn 89

LANG, Candace D. *Irony/Humor: Critical Paradigms*. Baltimore, Johns Hopkins Univ Pr, 1988.
Millard, William B. *Crit Texts* 6(3), 58-66 1989

LANGER, Claudia. *Reform nach Prinzipien*. Stuttgart, Klett-Cotta, 1986.
Zenkert, Georg. *Phil Rundsch* 36(3), 251-255 1989

LANGFORD, Glenn. *Education, Persons and Society: A Philosophical Enquiry*. New York, Macmillan, 1985.
Sullivan, John. *Heythrop J* 30(4), 480-481 O 89

LANGFORD, Peter. *Modern Philosophies of Human Nature: Their Emergence from Christian Thought*. Norwell, Kluwer, 1986.
Hart, Kevin. *Austl J Phil* 67(3), 363-365 S 89

LANGLEY, Pat and SIMON, Herbert A and BRADSHAW, Gary L andZYTKOW, Jan M. *Scientific Discovery: Computational Explorations of the Creative Process*. Cambridge, MIT Pr, 1987.
Forster, Malcolm R. *Phil Sci* 57(2), 336-338 Je 90

LARMER, Robert A H. *Water into Wine? An Investigation of the Concept of Miracle*. Kingston, McGill-Queen's Univ Pr, 1988.
Basinger, David. *Faith Phil* 7(3), 369-371 Jl 90
Taliaferro, Charles. *Mod Theol* 6(4), 414-415 Jl 90

LARMORE, Charles E. *Patterns of Moral Complexity*. New York, Cambridge Univ Pr, 1987.
Anderson, Elizabeth S. *Phil Rev* 99(3), 472-474 Jl 90
Haworth, Lawrence. *Dialogue (Canada)* 27(4), 711-719 Wint 88
Lemos, Noah. *Int Stud Phil* 22(1), 119-120 1990

LARSEN, S U and HAGTVET, B and MYKLEBUST, J P (eds). *Who Were the Fascists? Social Roots of European Fascism*. Oslo, Universitetsforlaget, 1980.
Ofstad, Harald. *Inquiry* 32(4), 455-473 D 89

LARSON, Gerald James and BHATTACHARYA, Ram Shankar (eds). *Samkhya: A Dualist Tradition in Indian Philosophy*. Princeton, Princeton Univ Pr, 1987.
Parrott, Rodney J. *Phil East West* 40(3), 375-379 Jl 90

LASCAR, Daniel. *Stability in Model Theory*, J E Wallington (trans). New York, Wiley, 1987.
Pillay, Anand. *J Sym Log* 55(2), 881-883 Je 90

LATRAVERSE, François. *La pragmatique: histoire et critique*. Bruxelles, Mardaga, 1987.
Engel, Pascal. *Rev Phil Fr* 179(2), 262-264 Ap-Je 89
Laurier, Daniel. *Philosophiques* 16(2), 446-450 Autumn 89

LAUDAN, Larry. *La dynamique de la science*, Philip Miller (trans). Bruxelles, Mardaga, 1987.
Asselin, Denis. *Dialogue (Canada)* 28(3), 509-510 1989

LAUDAN, Rachel. *From Mineralogy to Geology: The Foundations of a Science, 1650-1830*. Chicago, Univ of Chicago Pr, 1987.
Frankel, Henry. *Phil Sci* 57(2), 340-342 Je 90

LE DOEUFF, Michèle. *The Philosophical Imaginary*, Colin Gordon (trans). London, Athlone Pr, 1989.
Tiles, Mary. *Rad Phil* 55, 43-44 Sum 90

LEAMAN, Oliver. *Averroes and His Philosophy*. Oxford, Clarendon Pr, 1988.
Druart, Thérèse-Anne. *Rev Metaph* 43(3), 642-643 Mr 90
Frank, Daniel H. *J Hist Phil* 28(3), 444-445 Jl 90

LEAR, Jonathan. *Aristotle: The Desire to Understand*. Cambridge, Cambridge Univ Pr, 1988.
Tarrant, Harold. *Hist Euro Ideas* 12(3), 425-427 1990

LECLERC, Ivor. *The Philosophy of Nature*. Washington, Cath Univ Pr, 1986.
Dombrowski, Daniel A. *Process Stud* 18(2), 139-140 Sum 89
Gabbey, Alan. *J Hist Phil* 27(4), 624-626 O 89

Sontag, Frederick. *Int Stud Phil* 21(3), 128-129 1989

LEE, Robert and MORGAN, Derek (eds). *Birthrights: Law and Ethics at the Beginnings of Life*. NY, Routledge Chapman & Hall, 1989.
Hoskins, Betty B. *J Med Human* 11(1), 57-59 Spr 90
Overall, Christine. *Can Phil Rev* 9(9), 371-373 S 89

LEE, Sang Hyun. *The Philosophical Theology of Jonathan Edwards*. Princeton, Princeton Univ Pr, 1988.
Hartshorne, Charles. *Trans Peirce Soc* 26(2), 249-252 Spr 90

LEE, V L. *Beyond Behaviorism*. Hillsdale, Erlbaum, 1988.
Leigland, Sam. *Behavior Phil* 18(1), 77-79 Spr-Sum 90

LEIBNIZ, G W. *Sämtliche Schriften und Briefe*. Berlin, Akademie, 1987.
Riley, Patrick. *Polit Theory* 17(4), 681-684 N 89

LEIDHOLD, Wolfgang. *Ethik und Politik bei Francis Hutcheson*. Freiburg, Alber, 1985.
Haakonssen, Knud. *J Hist Phil* 27(4), 626-628 O 89

LEISS, William. *C B Macpherson: Dilemmas of Liberalism and Socialism*. NY, St Martin's Pr, 1988.
Cooper, Barry. *Can Phil Rev* 9(9), 374-378 S 89

LEITES, Edmund (ed). *Conscience and Casuistry in Early Modern Europe*. Cambridge, Cambridge Univ Pr, 1988.
Moonan, Lawrence. *Phil Books* 31(1), 21-22 Ja 90

LEITH, Philip and INGRAM, Peter (eds). *The Jurisprudence of Orthodoxy: Queen's University Essays on H L A Hart*. New York, Routledge, 1988.
Duff, R A. *Phil Invest* 13(1), 85-90 Ja 90
Green, Leslie. *Phil Books* 30(4), 254-256 O 89

LEKAS, Padelis. *Marx on Classical Antiquity: Problems of Historical Methodology*. NY, St Martin's Pr, 1988.
Konstan, David. *Hist Theor* 29(1), 83-94 F 90

LEMKE, Christiane. *Persönlichkeit und Gesellschaft*. Opladen, Westdeutscher, 1980.
Teichmann, Werner. *Deut Z Phil* 37(10-11), 1044-1047 1989

LERER, Seth. *Boethius and Dialogue: Literary Method in the Consolation of Philosophy*. Princeton, Princeton Univ Pr, 1986.
Davis, Scott. *Ancient Phil* 9 (1), 133-137 Spr 89

LERMOND, Lucia. *The Form of Man: Human Essence in Spinoza's Ethic*. Leiden, Brill, 1988.
Cook, J Thomas. *Stud Spinozana* 4, 415-419 1988

LERNER, Laurence. *The Frontiers of Literature*. Cambridge, Blackwell, 1988.
Neill, Alex. *Brit J Aes* 29(4), 381-382 Autumn 89

LERNER, Ralph. *The Thinking Revolutionary: Principle and Practice in the New Republic*. Ithaca, Cornell Univ Pr, 1987.
Norton, Anne. *Polit Theory* 18(3), 496-499 Ag 90

LESLIE, John. *Universes*. London, Routledge, 1989.
Flew, Antony. *Phil Books* 31(3), 158-160 Jl 90

LETWIN, Oliver. *Ethics, Emotion and the Unity of the Self*. London, Croom Helm, 1988.
Lyon, Ardon. *Philosophy* 64(250), 569-571 O 89

LEVERING, Robert. *A Great Place to Work: What Makes Some Employers So Good*. New York, Random House, 1988.
Pfeiffer, Raymond S. *Teach Phil* 12(3), 315-317 S 89

LEVI, Margaret. *Of Rule and Revenue*. Berkeley, Univ of California Pr, 1988.
Stanton, Kimberly. *Ethics* 100(2), 430-432 Ja 90

LEVIN, David Michael. *The Body's Recollection of Being: Phenomenological Psychology and the Deconstruction of Nihilism*. London, Routledge & Kegan Paul, 1985.
Froman, Wayne. *Res Phenomenol* 18, 311-316 1988

LEVIN, Samuel R. *Metaphoric Worlds: Conceptions of a Romantic Nature*. New Haven, Yale Univ Pr, 1988.
Fischer, Michael. *Phil Lit* 14(1), 215-216 Ap 90

LEVINE, Andrew. *The End of the State*. New York, Verso, 1987.
Cunningham, Frank. *Can J Phil* 19(3), 467-475 S 89

LEVINE, Marvin. *Effective Problem Solving*. Englewood Cliffs, Prentice Hall, 1988.
Scherer, Donald. *Teach Phil* 12(3), 290-291 S 89

LEVINE, Michael P. *Hume and the Problem of Miracles: A Solution*. Norwell, Kluwer, 1988.
Penelhum, Terence. *Can Phil Rev* 9(12), 487-489 D 89

LEVINSON, Paul. *Mind at Large: Knowing in the Technological Age*.

Greenwich, JAI Pr, 1988.
Lambert, Kenneth A. *Hist Euro Ideas* 12(2), 307-308 1990

LEVINSON, Sanford. *Constitutional Faith*. Princeton, Princeton Univ Pr, 1988.
Nutting, Kurt. *Ethics* 100(1), 185-187 O 89

LIGHT, Stephen. *Shuzo Kuki and Jean-Paul Sartre*. Carbondale, Southern Illinois Univ Pr, 1987.
Edie, James M. *Nous* 24(1), 196-198 Mr 90

LIND, Peter. *Marcuse and Freedom*. NY, St Martin's Pr, 1985.
Murphy, Julien S. *Stud Soviet Tho* 38(4), 315-318 N 89

LINDBERG, David C and NUMBERS, Ronald L (eds). *God and Nature: Historical Essays on the Encounter between Christianity and Science*. Berkeley, Univ of California Pr, 1986.
Hilfstein, Erna. *Dialec Hum* 14(1), 275-276 Wint 87

LINGIS, Alphonso. *Deathbound Subjectivity*. Bloomington, Indiana Univ Pr, 1989.
Bryson, Ken A. *Can Phil Rev* 10(7), 283-285 Jl 90

LINK-SALINGER, Ruth (ed). *Of Scholars, Savants, and Their Texts: Studies in Philosophy and Religious Thought*. New York, Lang, 1989.
Buijs, Joseph A. *Can Phil Rev* 10(6), 240-243 Je 90

LITTLEFORD, Michael S. *Giambattista Vico, Post-Mechanical Thought, and Contemporary Psychology*. New York, Lang, 1988.
Buford, Thomas O. *Can Phil Rev* 9(7), 273-275 Jl 89

LIVELY, Jack and REEVE, Andrew (ed). *Modern Political Theory from Hobbes to Marx: Key Debates*. London, Routledge, 1988.
Quinn, M. *Phil Books* 31(2), 83-84 Ap 90

LIVINGSTON, James C. *Anatomy of the Sacred: An Introduction to Religion*. New York, Macmillan, 1989.
Chryssides, George D. *Teach Phil* 12(3), 332-334 S 89

LIVINGSTON, Paisley. *Literary Knowledge: Humanistic Inquiry and the Philosophy of Science*. Ithaca, Cornell Univ Pr, 1988.
Dumouchel, Paul. *Dialogue (Canada)* 28(2), 346-348 1989
Novitz, David. *Phil Lit* 14(1), 183-184 Ap 90

LLANO, Alejandro. *La nueva sensibilidad*. Madrid, Espasa Univ, 1989.
Ayala, Jorge M. *Dialogo Filosof* 5(3), 440-442 S-D 89

LLEWELLYN, John. *Beyond Metaphysics?: The Hermeneutic Circle in Contemporary Continental Philosophy*. Atlantic Highlands, Humanities Pr, 1985.
Bakan, Mildred. *Int Stud Phil* 21(3), 130-132 1989

LLEWELYN, John. *Derrida on the Threshold of Sense*. London, Macmillan, 1986.
Burke, Mark J. *Heythrop J* 31(1), 109-110 Ja 90
Harvey, Irene E. *J Brit Soc Phenomenol* 21(2), 191-192 My 90

LLOYD, Christopher. *Explanation in Social History*. Oxford, Blackwell, 1986.
Briggs, Asa. *Hist Theor* 29(1), 95-99 F 90

LLOYD, G E R. *Polarity and Analogy: Two Types of Argumentation in Early Greek Thought*. Bristol, Classical Pr, 1987.
King, Helen. *J Hellen Stud* 109, 225-226 1989

LLOYD, G E R. *The Revolutions of Wisdom: Studies in the Claims and Practice of Ancient Greek Science*. Berkeley, Univ of Calif Pr, 1987.
Dillon, John. *Amer J Philo* 110(3), 499-502 Fall 89

LLOYD, Genevieve. *The Man of Reason: "Male" and "Female" in Western Philosophy*. Minneapolis, Univ of Minnesota Pr, 1984.
McLean, Jeanne P. *Ancient Phil* 10(1), 154-157 Spr 90

LO, P C. *Treating Persons as Ends: An Essay on Kant's Moral Philosophy*. Lanham, Univ Pr of America, 1987.
Hill Jr, Thomas E. *Phil Rev* 99(2), 278-281 Ap 90
Van De Pitte, Frederick P. *Kantstudien* 81(1), 108-110 1990

LOCKWOOD, Alan L and HARRIS, David E. *Reasoning with Democratic Values: Ethical Problems in United States History, 2v*. New York, Teachers College Pr, 1985.
Leming, James S. *Thinking* 7(1), 21-22 1987

LOHR, Charles H. *Latin Aristotle Commentaries, V2: Renaissance Authors*. Florence, Olschki, 1988.
Flüeler, Christoph. *Frei Z Phil Theol* 36(3), 512-519 1989

LOLLI, Gabriele. *Capire una dimostrazione: Il ruolo della logica nella matematica*. Bologna, Mulino, 1988.
La Greca, Carla. *Sapienza* 43(2), 228-230 Ap-Je 90

LOMASKY, Loren E. *Persons, Rights, and the Moral Community*. New

York, Oxford Univ Pr, 1987.
Jecker, Nancy S. *Law Phil* 8(2), 279-285 Ag 89
Levine, Andrew. *Nous* 24(4), 627-631 S 90
Nickel, James W. *Mind* 98(392), 652-657 O 89
Paul, Jeffrey. *Phil Rev* 99(3), 455-460 Jl 90

LOMBA FUENTES, J. *El Oráculo de Narcisco*. Zaragoza, Univ Pr de Zaragoza, 1985.
Ayala, Jorge M. *Anu Filosof* 21(2), 180-183 1988

LOMBARD, Lawrence Brian. *Events: A Metaphysical Study*. London, Routledge & Kegan Paul, 1986.
Kuo, Lenore. *Nous* 24(2), 323-332 Ap 90

LOMBARDI, Louis G. *Moral Analysis: Foundations, Guides, and Applications*. Albany, SUNY Pr, 1988.
Johnson, Carla A H. *Teach Phil* 12(3), 309-311 S 89

LONG, A A and SEDLEY, D N. *The Hellenistic Philosophers, 2v*. Cambridge, Cambridge Univ Pr, 1987.
Brunschwig, Jacques. *Phoenix* 44(2), 186-189 Sum 90

LONG, A A. *Hellenistic Philosophy: Stoics, Epicureans, Sceptics, 2nd ed*. Berkeley, Univ of Calif Pr, 1986.
Dalzell, Alexander. *Ancient Phil* 9 (1), 131-132 Spr 89

LOPEZ JR, Donald S (ed). *Buddhist Hermeneutics*. Honolulu, Univ of Hawaii Pr, 1988.
Griffiths, Paul J. *Phil East West* 40(2), 258-262 Ap 90

LOPEZ, Pilar. *Introducción a Wittgenstein*. Barcelona, pub unknown, 1986.
Gaeta, Rodolfo. *Rev Latin De Filosof* 15(2), 253-255 Jl 89

LOSURDO, Domenico. *Hegel und das deutsche Erbe*. Köln, Pahl-Rugenstein, 1989.
Klenner, Hermann. *Deut Z Phil* 38(4), 391-393 1990

LOTT, Eric J. *Vision, Tradition, Interpretation: Theology, Religion, and the Study of Religion*. Berlin, Mouton, 1988.
Wattles, Jeffrey. *Phil East West* 40(1), 99-100 Ja 90

LOTZ, Johannès B. *Martin Heidegger et Thomas d'Aquin*. Paris, PUF, 1988.
Rioux, Bertrand. *Philosophiques* 16(2), 418-422 Autumn 89

LOTZE, Rudolf Hermann. *Logik, 2v, G Gabriel (ed)*. Hamburg, Meiner, 1989.
Frank, Hartwig and Pester, Reinhardt. *Deut Z Phil* 38(5), 491-493 1990
Schmit, R. *Hist Phil Log* 11(2), 235-238 1990

LOVIN, R W and REYNOLDS, F E (eds). *Cosmogony and Ethical Order: New Studies in Comparative Ethics*. Chicago, Univ of Chicago Pr, 1985.
Taber, Michael. *Phil East West* 39(4), 514-516 O 89

LUCAS JR, George R (ed). *Hegel and Whitehead: Contemporary Perspectives on Systematic Philosophy*. Albany, SUNY Pr, 1986.
Christensen, Darrel E. *Int Stud Phil* 21(3), 132-135 1989

LUCAS, H-CH and PÖGGELER, O (eds). *Hegels Rechtsphilosophie im Zusammenhang der europäischen Verfassungsgeschichte*. Stuttgart, Fromman-Holzboog, 1986.
Vollrath, Ernst. *Phil Rundsch* 37(1-2), 27-43 1990

LUCAS, Hans-Christian and PLANTY-BONJOUR, Guy (eds). *Logik und Geschichte in Hegels System*. Stuttgart, Frommann-Holzboog, 1989.
Depré, Olivier. *Rev Phil Louvain* 87(76), 563-565 Ag 89

LÜDEKING, Karlheinz. *Analytische Philosophie der Kunst*. Frankfurt am Main, Athenaeum, 1988.
Seel, Martin. *Phil Rundsch* 36(4), 337-340 1989

LUFT, Eric von der (ed & trans). *Hegel, Hinrichs, and Schleiermacher on Feeling and Reason in Religion: The Texts of their 1821-1822 Debate*. Lewiston, Mellen Pr, 1987.
Olson, Alan M. *Int J Phil Relig* 27(1-2), 123-125 Ap 90

LUKÁCS, Georg. *Demokratisierung heute und morgen, László Sziklai (ed)*. Budapest, Akadémiai Kiadó, 1985.
Tietz, Udo. *Deut Z Phil* 38(6), 589-591 1990

LUNGARZO, Carlos A. *Introducción a la teoria de la deducción*. Buenos Aires, Biblos, 1986.
Costa, Horacio Arló. *Rev Filosof (Argentina)* 1(1-2), 99-101 N 86

LUNTLEY, Michael. *Language, Logic, and Experience: The Case for Anti-Realism*. La Salle, Open Court, 1988.
Fales, Evan. *Can Phil Rev* 9(11), 448-451 N 89

LUPER-FOY, Stephen (ed). *Problems of International Justice*. Boulder, Westview Pr, 1988.
Dower, Nigel. *Phil Books* 31(2), 115-117 Ap 90
Nickel, James W. *Teach Phil* 12(4), 413-415 D 89

LYCAN, William G. *Consciousness.* Cambridge, MIT Pr, 1987.
DeVries, Willem A. *Phil Rev* 99(2), 263-266 Ap 90

LYCOS, Kimon. *Plato on Justice and Power: Reading Book I of Plato's "Republic".* Albany, SUNY Pr, 1987.
Browne, Derek. *Austl J Phil* 67(3), 352-354 S 89
Ferguson, John. *Heythrop J* 31(2), 228-229 Ap 90
Kerferd, G B. *Polis* 7(2), 134-139 1988
Sparshott, Francis. *Ancient Phil* 10(1), 120-123 Spr 90

LYOTARD, Jean-Francois and THÉBAUD, Jean-Loup. *Just Gaming.* Minneapolis, Univ of Minnesota Pr, 1985.
Murphy, John W. *Stud Soviet Tho* 39(2), 159-162 Mr 90

LYOTARD, Jean-François. *La diferencia.* Barcelona, Gedisa, 1988.
Murillo, Ildefonso. *Dialogo Filosof* 6(1), 107-109 Ja-Ap 90

MACDONALD, Graham and PETTIT, Philip. *Semantics and Social Science.* London, Routledge & Kegan Paul, 1981.
Simon, Lawrence H and Strikwerda, Robert A. *Nous* 23(5), 688-690 D 89

MACEY, David. *Lacan in Contexts.* London, Verso, 1988.
Lecercle, Jean-Jacques. *Rad Phil* 53, 41-42 Autumn 89

MACGREGOR, David. *The Communist Ideal in Hegel and Marx.* Toronto, Univ of Toronto Pr, 1984.
Duquette, David A. *Auslegung* 16(1), 123-129 Wint 90

MACHAN, Tibor R (ed). *Commerce and Morality.* Totowa, Rowman & Littlefield, 1988.
Brandon, Melvin J. *Ethics* 100(2), 432-434 Ja 90

MACHAN, Tibor R (ed). *The Main Debate: Communism Versus Capitalism.* New York, Random House, 1987.
Gordon, David. *Int Phil Quart* 30(3), 375-378 S 90

MACHAN, Tibor. *Individuals and Their Rights.* LaSalle, Open Court, 1989.
Warner, Stuart D. *Rev Metaph* 43(4), 873-875 Je 90

MACHIAVELLI. *Le Prince,* Gérald Allard (trans). Sainte-Foy, Griffon, 1984.
Ranger, Philippe. *Philosophiques* 16(2), 422-426 Autumn 89

MACHO, Thomas H. *Todesmetaphern.* Frankfurt am Main, Suhrkamp, 1987.
Villwock, Jörg. *Z Phil Forsch* 44(2), 344-349 1990

MACINTYRE, A. *Tras la virtud.* Barcelona, Crítica, 1987.
Serrano, Rafael. *Anu Filosof* 22(2), 193-195 1989

MACINTYRE, Alasdair. *After Virtue: A Study in Moral Theory,* 2nd ed. Notre Dame, Univ Notre Dame Pr, 1984.
Wallace, R Jay. *Hist Theor* 28(3), 326-348 O 89

MACINTYRE, Alasdair. *Whose Justice? Which Rationality?* Notre Dame, Univ of Notre Dame Pr, 1988.
Appel, Fredrick. *Phil Soc Sci* 20(1), 135-138 Mr 90
Barry, Brian. *Ethics* 100(1), 160-168 O 89
Brodsky, Garry M. *Can Phil Rev* 9(7), 276-279 Jl 89
Hartle, Ann. *J Hist Phil* 28(3), 470-473 Jl 90
Isaac, Jeffrey C. *Polit Theory* 17(4), 663-672 N 89
Matson, Wallace I. *Philosophy* 64(250), 564-566 O 89
Snider, Eric W. *Metaphilosophy* 20(3-4), 387-390 Jl-O 89
Wallace, R Jay. *Hist Theor* 28(3), 326-348 O 89
Wong, David. *Phil Books* 31(1), 7-14 Ja 90

MACKENZIE JR, Louis A. *Pascal's "Lettres Provinciales": The Motif and Practice of Fragmentation.* Birmingham, Summa, 1988.
Wetsel, David. *Phil Lit* 14(1), 221-222 Ap 90

MACKEY, James P (ed). *Religious Imagination.* Edinburgh, Edinburgh Univ Pr, 1986.
Wilson, Jonathan. *Mod Theol* 6(1), 116-118 O 89

MACKEY, Louis. *Points of View: Readings of Kierkegaard.* Tallahassee, Florida State Univ Pr, 1986.
Stack, George J. *Int Stud Phil* 22(1), 122-123 1990

MACKIE, J L. *Selected Papers, V1: Logic and Knowledge, V2: Persons and Values,* Joan Mackie and Penelope Mackie (eds). New York, Oxford Univ Pr, 1985.
Aune, Bruce. *Int Stud Phil* 22(1), 123-124 1990
Espinoza, M. *Arch Phil* 52(4), 686-688 O-D 89

MACKINNON, Catherine A. *Feminism Unmodified: Discourses on Life and Law.* Cambridge, Harvard Univ Pr, 1987.
Pateman, Carole. *Ethics* 100(2), 398-407 Ja 90

MACLANE, Saunders. *Mathematics: Form and Function.* New York, Springer, 1986.
Maddy, Penelope. *J Sym Log* 53(2), 643-645 Je 88

MACNAMARA, John. *A Border Dispute: The Place of Logic in Psychology.* Cambridge, MIT Pr, 1986.
O'Brien, David P. *Phil Sci* 57(2), 347-349 Je 90

MACNIVEN, Don. *Bradley's Moral Psychology.* Lewiston, Mellen Pr, 1987.
Lamb, David. *Phil Invest* 12(4), 353-357 O 89

MADELL, Geoffrey. *Mind and Materialism.* Edinburgh, Edinburgh Univ Pr, 1988.
Lesser, A H. *J Brit Soc Phenomenol* 21(1), 92-93 Ja 90

MADONNA, Luigi Cataldi. *La filosofia della probabilità nel pensiero moderno.* Rome, Cadmo, 1988.
Di Bella, Stefano. *Teoria* 9(2), 135-144 1989

MAGNI, Alberti. *Opera Omnia, Tomus IV Pars I: Physica, Libri 1-4.* Munster, Aschendorff, 1987.
Alarcón, Enrique. *Anu Filosof* 21(2), 173-175 1988

MAGRIS, A. *L'idea di destino nel pensiero antico,* 2v. Udine, Bianco, 1985.
Rossetti, Livio. *Anu Filosof* 20(1), 246-248 1987

MAH, Harold. *The End of Philosophy, the Origin of "Ideology": Karl Marx and the Young Hegelians.* Berkeley, Univ of California Pr, 1987.
Stepelevich, Lawrence S. *J Hist Phil* 28(2), 305-307 Ap 90

MAKER, William (ed). *Hegel on Economics and Freedom.* Macon, Mercer Univ Pr, 1987.
Dickey, Laurence. *Econ Phil* 6(1), 169-176 Ap 90

MALATESTA, Michele. *La lógica primaria.* Rome, LER, 1988.
Beuchot, Mauricio. *Rev Filosof (Mexico)* 22(65), 254-255 My-Ag 89

MALHERBE, Michel. *Thomas Hobbes ou L'Oeuvre de la Raison.* Paris, Vrin, 1984.
Schuhmann, Karl. *Hist Euro Ideas* 10(5), 595-597 1989

MANCINI, Sandro. *Sempre Di Nuovo/Merleau-Ponty e la dialettica dell'espressione.* Milan, Angeli, 1987.
Liggieri, Maria Carmela. *Aquinas* 32(1), 177-180 Ja-Ap 89

MANELI, Mieczyslaw. *Freedom and Tolerance.* NY, Octagon Books, 1984.
Zapasnik, Stanislaw. *Dialec Hum* 14(1), 295-298 Wint 87

MANGUM, John M (ed). *The New Faith-Science Debate: Probing Cosmology, Technology and Theology.* Minneapolis, Augsburg Fortress Pr, 1989.
Hefner, Philip. *Zygon* 24(4), 487-489 D 89

MANLYN, D W. *Metaphysics.* NY, Cambridge Univ Pr, 1985.
Femenías, María Luisa. *Analisis Filosof* 7(2), 149-151 N 87

MANSER, A and STOCK, G. *The Philosophy of F H Bradley.* Oxford, Clarendon Pr, 1986.
Bar-on, A Z. *Philosophia (Israel)* 19(4), 487-492 D 89

MARCH, James L. *Post-Cartesian Meditations: An Essay in Dialectical Phenomenology.* New York, Fordham Univ Pr, 1988.
Matustik, Martin J. *Method* 8(1), 94-105 Mr 90

MARCIL-LACOSTE, Louise and others. *Egalité et différence des sexes.* Montreal, ACFAS, 1986.
Poissant, Louise. *Dialogue (Canada)* 28(2), 338-344 1989

MARCUCCI, Silvestro. *Studi kantiani, I: Kant e la conoscenza scientifica.* Lucca, Pacini Fazzi, 1988.
Fabris, Adriano. *Teoria* 9(1), 260-263 1989

MARCUSE, Herbert. *Hegel's Ontology and the Theory of Historicity,* Seyla Benhabib (trans). Cambridge, MIT Pr, 1987.
Byrne, Laura. *Owl Minerva* 21(2), 197-203 Spr 90

MARENBON, John. *Later Medieval Philosophy (1150-1350): An Introduction.* London, Routledge & Kegan Paul, 1987.
Macierowski, E M. *Thomist* 54(1), 187-189 Ja 90
Maurer, Armand A. *J Hist Phil* 28(2), 288-289 Ap 90

MARGOLIS, Howard. *Patterns, Thinking, and Cognition: A Theory of Judgment.* Chicago, Univ of Chicago Pr, 1987.
Harman, Gilbert. *Ethics* 100(1), 200 O 89
Thagard, Paul. *Phil Psych* 3(1), 165-167 1990

MARGOLIS, Joseph. *Science Without Unity: Reconciling the Human and the Natural Sciences.* Oxford, Blackwell, 1987.
Collin, Finn. *Phil Phenomenol Res* 50(2), 425-428 D 89
Donovan, Rickard. *Int Phil Quart* 30(1), 122-125 Mr 90

MARGOLIS, Joseph. *Texts Without Reference: Reconciling Science and Narrative.* Oxford, Blackwell, 1989.
Donovan, Rickard. *Int Phil Quart* 30(1), 122-125 Mr 90

MARKIE, Peter J. *Descartes's Gambit.* Ithaca, Cornell Univ Pr, 1986.
Bolton, Martha Brandt. *Phil Rev* 99(2), 296-299 Ap 90

Hoffman, Paul. *Phil Phenomenol Res* 50(1), 199-205 S 89
Watson, Richard A. *Int Stud Phil* 22(1), 125 1990

MARKS, Joel (ed). *The Ways of Desire*. Chicago, Precedent, 1986.
Mele, Alfred. *Nous* 24(4), 611-613 S 90

MARSELLA, Anthony J and DEVOS, George and HSU, Francis L K (eds). *Culture and Self: Asian and Western Perspectives*. NY, Tavistock, 1985.
Obeyesekere, Gananath. *Phil East West* 40(2), 239-250 Ap 90

MARSH, James L. *Post-Cartesian Meditations: An Essay in Dialectical Phenomenology*. NY, Fordham Univ Pr, 1988.
Caputo, John D. *Int Phil Quart* 30(1), 101-107 Mr 90

MARSHALL, James D. *Positivism or Pragmatism: Philosophy of Education in New Zealand*. place unknown, NZARE, 1987.
Snook, Ivan. *Educ Phil Theor* 21(1), 83-87 1989

MARSHALL, James. *Why Go to School*. Palmerston North, Dunmore Pr, 1988.
Harris, Kevin. *Educ Phil Theor* 21(1), 82-83 1989

MARTI TUSQUETS, José Luis and MURCIA GRAU, Miguel. *Conceptos fundamentales de drogodependencias*. Barcelona, Herder, 1988.
Sobrino, M A. *Rev Filosof (Mexico)* 23(67), 139-141 Ja-Ap 90

MARTIN LOPEZ, E. *Fundamentos sociales de la felicidad individual*. Peru, Univ de Piura, 1986.
Gómez Cabranes, Leonor. *Anu Filosof* 21(1), 195-197 1988

MARTIN, Christopher. *The Philosophy of Thomas Aquinas: Introductory Readings*. New York, Routledge, 1988.
García-Huidobro, Joaquín. *Anu Filosof* 22(1), 191-193 1989

MARTIN, Michael. *The Legal Philosophy of H L A Hart: A Critical Appraisal*. Philadelphia, Temple Univ Pr, 1987.
DeCew, Judith Wagner. *Phil Rev* 99(2), 283-287 Ap 90

MARTIN, Mike W. *Everyday Morality: An Introduction to Applied Ethics*. Belmont, Wadsworth, 1989.
Turner, Dan. *Teach Phil* 12(3), 302-305 S 89

MARTIN, R M. *Mind, Modality, Meaning, and Method*. Albany, SUNY Pr, 1983.
Kaminsky, Jack. *Int Stud Phil* 21(3), 135-136 1989

MARTIN, Raymond. *The Past Within Us: An Empirical Approach to Philosophy of History*. Princeton, Princeton Univ Pr, 1989.
Dray, William H. *Clio* 19(2), 181-183 Wint 90

MARTIN, Rex. *Rawls and Rights*. Lawrence, Univ Pr of Kansas, 1985.
Rosenbaum, Alan S. *Phil Soc Sci* 19(4), 518-521 D 89

MARTIN, Robert M. *The Meaning of Language*. Cambridge, MIT Pr, 1987.
Hunter, J F M. *Dialogue (Canada)* 27(4), 741-744 Wint 88

MARTIN, Wallace. *Recent Theories of Narrative*. Ithaca, Cornell Univ Pr, 1986.
Farrell, Thomas B. *Phil Rhet* 22(4), 303-310 1989

MARTINETTI, Piero. *Spinoza*, Franco Alessio (ed). Naples, Bibliopolis, 1987.
Domínguez, Atilano. *Stud Spinozana* 5, 405-411 1989

MARX, Werner. *Is There a Measure on Earth? Foundations for a Nonmetaphysical Ethics*, T J Nenon and R Lilly (trans). Chicago, Univ of Chicago Pr, 1987.
Naus, John. *Mod Sch* 67(2), 159-161 Ja 90

MASI, Michael. *Boethian Number Theory: A Translation of the "De Institutione Arithmetica"*. Amsterdam, Rodopi, 1983.
Bowen, Alan C. *Ancient Phil* 9 (1), 137-143 Spr 89

MASON, J K. *Human Life and Medical Practice*. New York, Columbia Univ Pr, 1988.
Harrison, Christine. *Can Phil Rev* 9(8), 318-320 Ag 89

MASON, Jeff. *Philosophical Rhetoric: The Function of Indirection in Philosophical Writing*. London, Routledge, 1989.
Suber, Peter. *Phil Rhet* 23(2), 136-141 1990

MASTERS, Roger D. *The Nature of Politics*. New Haven, Yale Univ Pr, 1989.
Berry, Christopher J. *Hist Polit Thought* 11(1), 173-174 Spr 90

MATES, Benson. *The Philosophy of Leibniz: Metaphysics and Language*. NY, Oxford Univ Pr, 1986.
Cover, J A and Hartz, Glenn A. *Nous* 24(1), 169-174 Mr 90

MATHEWS, M Cash. *Strategic Intervention in Organizations: Resolving Ethical Dilemmas*. Newbury Park, Sage, 1988.
Perry, David L. *J Bus Ethics* 8(9), 686,744 S 89

MATILAL, Bimal Krishna and EVANS, Robert D (eds). *Buddhist Logic and Epistemology*. Norwell, Reidel, 1986.
Bastow, David. *Relig Stud* 25(2), 252-255 Je 89

MATTHEWS, Gareth B. *Dialogues with Children*. Cambridge, Harvard Univ Pr, 1984.
Benjamin, Martin. *Thinking* 6(1), 48-49 1985

MATTHEWS, Michael R (ed). *The Scientific Background to Modern Philosophy*. Indianapolis, Hackett, 1989.
Wilson, Catherine. *Can Phil Rev* 10(6), 243-244 Je 90

MATTICK JR, Paul. *Social Knowledge: An Essay on the Nature and Limits of Social Science*. Armonk, Sharp, 1989.
Murphy, John W. *Stud Soviet Tho* 39(2), 157-159 Mr 90

MAVRODES, George I. *Revelation in Religious Belief*. Philadelphia, Temple Univ Pr, 1988.
Levine, Michael P. *Int J Phil Relig* 27(3), 181-185 Je 90

MAXWELL, Nicholas. *From Knowledge to Wisdom: A Revolution in the Aims and Methods of Science*. Oxford, Blackwell, 1984.
Yates, Steven. *Metaphilosophy* 20(3-4), 371-386 Jl-O 89

MAY, Keith M. *Nietzsche and Modern Literature: Themes in Yeats, Rilke, Mann, and Lawrence*. New York, St Martin's Pr, 1988.
Winkler, Michael. *Phil Lit* 13(2), 382-384 O 89

MAY, Larry. *The Morality of Groups*. Notre Dame, Univ Notre Dame Pr, 1987.
Corlett, J Angelo. *J Bus Ethics* 8(10), 772,792,816 O 89
Graham, Gordon. *Phil Books* 30(4), 240-242 O 89
May, Larry. *Bus Prof Ethics J* 8(1), 83-88 Spr 89
Swindler, J K. *Nous* 24(3), 497-500 Je 90
Tam, Victor C K. *Bus Prof Ethics J* 8(1), 65-81 Spr 89

MAYNARD SMITH, John. *Le nuove frontiere della biologia*. Rome-Bari, Laterza, 1988.
Barucco, Armando. *Riv Int Filosof Diritto* 66(3), 558-559 Jl-S 89

MAYR, Ernst. *Toward a New Philosophy of Biology*. Cambridge, Harvard Univ Pr, 1988.
Shaner, David Edward and Hutchinson, Robert Darren. *Phil East West* 40(2), 264-266 Ap 90

MAZZARELLA, Eugenio. *Storia metafisica ontologia: Per una storia della metafisica tra Otto e Novecento*. Naples, Morano, 1987.
Reda, Clementina Gily. *Filosofia* 41(2), 246-248 My-Ag 90

MCCARTHY, Michael H. *The Crisis in Philosophy*. Albany, SUNY Pr, 1990.
Hodes, Greg. *Auslegung* 16(2), 223-227 Sum 90

MCCLENDON JR, James W. *Ethics*. Nashville, Abingdon Pr, 1986.
Adams, Robert Merrihew. *Faith Phil* 7(1), 117-123 Ja 90

MCCLOSKEY, Mary. *Kant's Aesthetics*. Albany, SUNY Pr, 1987.
Rogerson, Kenneth R. *Int Stud Phil* 22(1), 125-126 1990

MCCOOL, Gerald A. *From Unity to Pluralism: The Internal Evolution of Thomism*. New York, Fordham Univ Pr, 1989.
Hudson, Deal W. *Int Phil Quart* 30(3), 367-369 S 90

MCCORMICK, Peter J. *Fictions, Philosophies, and the Problems of Poetics*. Ithaca, Cornell Univ Pr, 1988.
Eldridge, Richard. *Phil Lit* 14(1), 207-208 Ap 90
Fischer, Michael. *Can Phil Rev* 10(2), 70-72 F 90
Pollard, D E B. *Brit J Aes* 30(2), 185-186 Ap 90
Sankowski, Edward. *J Aes Educ* 23(3), 111-113 Fall 89

MCCULLAGH, Peter. *The Foetus as Transplant Donor: Scientific, Social and Ethical Perspectives*. Chichester, Wiley, 1987.
Cameron, Nigel M de S. *Ethics Med* 4(2), 31-32 1988

MCCULLOCH, Gregory. *The Game of the Name, Introducing Logic, Language and Mind*. Oxford, Clarendon Pr, 1989.
Bell, David. *Phil Quart* 40(160), 388-392 Jl 90

MCCUMBER, John. *Poetic Interaction: Language, Freedom, Reason*. Chicago, Univ of Chicago Pr, 1989.
Ackerman, R D. *Phil Lit* 14(1), 219-220 Ap 90
Mitscherling, Jeff. *Can Phil Rev* 10(6), 245-247 Je 90

MCDONOUGH, Richard M. *The Argument of the 'Tractatus'*. Albany, SUNY Pr, 1986.
Stephens, Lynn. *Nous* 24(3), 492-494 Je 90

MCFAGUE, Sallie. *Models of God: Theology for an Ecological, Nuclear Age*. Philadelphia, Fortress Pr, 1987.
Runzo, Joseph. *Faith Phil* 7(3), 364-368 Jl 90

MCFALL, Lynne. *Happiness*. NY, Lang, 1989.

McDaniel, Jay B. *Process Stud* 18(3), 215-217 Fall 89

MURDOCH, Dugald. *Niels Bohr's Philosophy of Physics*. Cambridge, Cambridge Univ Pr, 1987.
Bub, Jeffrey. *Phil Sci* 57(2), 344-347 Je 90

MURDOCH, Iris. *Acastos: Two Platonic Dialogues*. NY, Viking Penguin, 1986.
Schuler, Jeanne A. *Int Phil Quart* 30(1), 118-119 Mr 90

MURDOCH, Iris. *Sartre: Romantic Rationalist*. London, Chatto & Windus, 1988.
Moulder, James. *S Afr J Phil* 9(1), 56 F 90

MURPHY, Jeffrie G and COLEMAN, Jules L. *Philosophy of Law*. Boulder, Westview Pr, 1989.
Dare, Tim. *Can Phil Rev* 10(5), 189-192 My 90

MURPHY, Jeffrie G and HAMPTON, Jean. *Forgiveness and Mercy*. Cambridge, Cambridge Univ Pr, 1989.
Edelman, John T. *Phil Invest* 13(2), 181-186 Ap 90
Rainbolt, George W. *Ethics* 100(2), 413-415 Ja 90
Telfer, Elizabeth. *Phil Books* 31(2), 108-109 Ap 90

MURPHY, John W. *Postmodern Social Analysis and Criticism*. Westpoint, Greenwood Pr, 1989.
Miles, Angela. *Can Phil Rev* 9(12), 490-492 D 89

MURRAY, Patrick. *Marx's Theory of Scientific Knowledge*. Atlantic Highlands, Humanities Pr, 1988.
Rehg, William. *Mod Sch* 66(4), 316-318 My 89

MYERS, Gerald E. *William James: His Life and Thought*. New Haven, Yale Univ Pr, 1986.
Daniel, Stephen H. *New Vico Studies* 6, 181-182 1988

NADLER, Steven M. *Arnauld and the Cartesian Philosophy of Ideas*. Princeton, Princeton Univ Pr, 1989.
Janowski, Zbigniew. *Rev Metaph* 43(3), 643-644 Mr 90

NAESS, Arne. *Ecology, Community and Lifestyle*, David Rothenberg (ed & trans). Cambridge, Cambridge Univ Pr, 1989.
Dobson, Andy. *Rad Phil* 54, 40-41 Spr 90

NAGEL, Thomas. *The View from Nowhere*. New York, Oxford Univ Pr, 1986.
Hahn, Carl. *Eidos* 8(1), 111-115 Je 89

NAGEL, Thomas. *Uno sguardo da nessun luogo*, A Besussi (trans). Milan, Saggiatore, 1988.
Tonino, Paolo. *Filosofia* 40(3), 421-423 S-D 89

NAGEL, Thomas. *What Does It All Mean?* Oxford, Oxford Univ Pr, 1987.
Benjamin, David and Scott, Jeremy. *Thinking* 7(4), 28-29 1988
Benjamin, Martin. *Thinking* 7(4), 26-28 1988

NÄGELE, Rainer (ed). *Benjamin's Ground: New Readings of Walter Benjamin*. Detroit, Wayne State Univ Pr, 1989.
Vieth, Lynne. *Phil Lit* 14(1), 166-167 Ap 90

NAISHTAT, Francisco S. *Lógica para computación*. Buenos Aires, Eudeba, 1986.
Lungarzo, Carlos A. *Rev Filosof (Argentina)* 2(1), 81-83 My 87

NAKAMURA, Hajime. *A Comparative History of Ideas*, 2nd ed. London, KPT, 1986.
Riepe, Dale. *Int Stud Phil* 21(3), 138-139 1989

NARVESON, Jan. *The Libertarian Idea*. Philadelphia, Temple Univ Pr, 1989.
Kelly, Paul J. *Phil Books* 31(1), 47-49 Ja 90
Mack, Eric. *Ethics* 100(2), 419-421 Ja 90

NASH, Roderick Frazier. *The Rights of Nature: A History of Environmental Ethics*. Madison, University of Wisconsin Press, 1989.
Hargrove, Eugene C. *Can Phil Rev* 9(11), 455-457 N 89
Loftin, Robert W. *Environ Ethics* 12(1), 83-85 Spr 90
Paden, Roger. *Agr Human Values* 7(1), 48-51 Wint 90

NASH, Ronald (ed). *Process Theology*. Grand Rapids, Baker Book, 1987.
Sessions, William Lad. *Faith Phil* 7(1), 123-127 Ja 90

NATANSON, Maurice. *Anonymity: A Study in the Philosophy of Alfred Schutz*. Bloomington, Indiana Univ Pr, 1986.
Langsdorf, Lenore. *Res Phenomenol* 18, 290-300 1988
Thomason, Burke C. *Human Stud* 13(1), 97-101 Ja 90

NATOLI, S. *Giovanni Gentile filosofo europeo*. Turin, Bollati Boringhieri, 1989.
Cavallera, Hervé A. *Filosofia* 41(1), 128-130 Ja-Ap 90

NEEL, Jasper. *Plato, Derrida and Writing*. Carbondale, Southern Illinois Univ Pr, 1988.
Lachterman, David R. *Phil Rhet* 22(4), 310-313 1989

NEGRE, M. *Poiesis y verdad en Giambattista Vico*. Sevilla, Univ de Sevilla, 1986.
Elósegui, María. *Anu Filosof* 21(2), 185-187 1988

NEHAMAS, Alexander and WOODRUFF, Paul (trans). *Plato's Symposium*. Indianapolis, Hackett, 1989.
Zembaty, Jame S. *Can Phil Rev* 10(1), 34-36 Ja 90

NELSON, John S and MEGILL, Allan and MCCLOSKEY, Donald N (eds). *The Rhetoric of the Human Sciences: Language and Argument in Scholarship and Public Affairs*. Madison, Univ of Wisconsin Pr, 1987.
Louch, Alfred R. *Hist Theor* 28(3), 357-366 O 89
McCloskey, Donald N. *J Hist Ideas* 51(1), 143-147 Ja-Mr 90
Munz, Peter. *J Hist Ideas* 51(1), 121-142 Ja-Mr 90
Redner, Harry. *Phil Soc Sci* 20(3), 408-412 S 90

NELSON, Paul. *Narrative and Morality: A Theological Inquiry*. University Park, Pennsylvania State Univ Pr, 1987.
Milbank, John. *Relig Stud* 25(3), 393-396 S 89

NELSON, R J. *The Logic of Mind*, 2nd ed. Boston, Reidel, 1989.
Grassl, Wolfgang. *Hist Phil Log* 11(2), 240-242 1990
Thomas, Stephen N. *Rev Metaph* 43(3), 644-646 Mr 90

NERSESSIAN, Nancy J (ed). *The Process of Science*. Dordrecht, Nijhoff, 1987.
Fuller, Steve. *Erkenntnis* 33(1), 121-129 Jl 90

NETHÖFEL, Wolfgang. *Moraltheologie nach dem Konzil*. Göttingen, Vandenhoeck & Ruprecht, 1987.
Hirschi, Hans. *Frei Z Phil Theol* 36(3), 503-506 1989

NEVILLE, Robert C (ed). *New Essays in Metaphysics*. Albany, SUNY Pr, 1987.
Colapietro, Vincent. *J Speculative Phil* 4(1), 97-104 1990

NEVILLE, Robert Cummings. *The Puritan Smile: A Look Toward Moral Reflection*. Albany, SUNY Pr, 1987.
Lucas Jr, George R. *Process Stud* 18(4), 306-311 Wint 89

NEWSOM, Robert. *A Likely Story: Probability and Play in Fiction*. New Brunswick, Rutgers Univ Pr, 1988.
Rodman, Jeffrey. *Brit J Aes* 30(3), 290-291 Jl 90

NIALL, R and MARTIN, D and BROWN, Stuart (eds & trans). *G W Leibniz: Discourse on Metaphysics and Related Writings*. Manchester, Manchester Univ Pr, 1988.
Tlumak, Jeffrey. *Teach Phil* 12(3), 339-341 S 89

NICHOLS, Mary P. *Socrates and the Political Community: An Ancient Debate*. Albany, SUNY Pr, 1987.
Allis, James B. *Ancient Phil* 9 (2), 323-326 Fall 89
Morrisey, Will. *Interpretation* 17(2), 317-319 Wint 89-90
Nichols, Mary P. *Polit Theory* 18(1), 154-158 F 90

NICKEL, James W. *Making Sense of Human Rights: Philosophical Reflections on the Universal Declaration of Human Rights*. Berkeley, Univ of California Pr, 1987.
Green, Leslie. *Phil Soc Sci* 19(4), 516-518 D 89

NIELSEN, Kai. *Marxism and the Moral Point of View: Morality, Ideology, and Historical Materialism*. Boulder, Westview Pr, 1989.
Brenkert, George G. *Can Phil Rev* 10(2), 73-75 F 90
Mew, Peter. *Phil Books* 31(2), 86-88 Ap 90
Ross, Steven. *Ethics* 100(2), 422-423 Ja 90
Sweet, Robert T. *Teach Phil* 12(3), 319-320 S 89

NIINILUOTO, Ilkka. *Truthlikeness*. Dordrecht, Reidel, 1987.
Adams, Ernest W. *Synthese* 84(1), 139-152 Jl 90

NILL, Michael. *Morality and Self-Interest in Protagoras, Antiphon and Democritus*. Leiden, Brill, 1985.
Kerferd, G B. *Polis* 7(2), 134-139 1988

NINO, Carlos S. *Introducción a la filosofía de la acción humana*. Buenos Aires, Eudeba, 1987.
Luna, Florencia. *Analisis Filosof* 7(2), 155-157 N 87

NITECKI, Matthew H (ed). *Evolutionary Progress*. Chicago, Univ of Chicago Pr, 1989.
Vicedo, Marga. *Can Phil Rev* 10(5), 192-195 My 90

NODDINGS, Nel. *Caring: A Feminine Approach to Ethics and Moral Education*. Berkeley, Univ of California Pr, 1984.
Card, Claudia. *Hypatia* 5(1), 101-108 Spr 90
Hoagland, Sarah Lucia. *Hypatia* 5(1), 109-114 Spr 90

Djossou, Joseph. *Laval Theol Phil* 46(2), 280-282 Je 90

OTTO, Herbert R and TUEDIO, James A. *Perspectives on Mind.* Norwell, Reidel, 1988.
Tieszen, Richard. *Husserl Stud* 6(2), 177-186 1989

OTTONELLO, Franco. *Luigi Scaravelli: La malattia dell'identità.* L'Aquila, Japadre, 1988.
Sorge, Valeria. *Sapienza* 43(1), 101-103 Ja-Mr 90

OTTONELLO, P P. *Struttura e forme del nichilismo europeo: Da Lutero a Kierkegaard.* L'Aquila-Roma, Japadre, 1988.
Colonnello, Pio. *Sapienza* 43(1), 99-101 Ja-Mr 90

OVERALL, Christine (ed). *The Future of Human Reproduction.* Toronto, Women's Pr, 1989.
Bonnicksen, Andrea L. *Med Human Rev* 4(2), 32-37 Jl 90

OVERALL, Christine. *Ethics and Human Reproduction.* Winchester, Allen & Unwin, 1987.
Yeo, Michael. *Dialogue (Canada)* 28(4), 655-661 1989

PACI, Enzo. *Il nulla e il problema dell'uomo*, Amedeo Vigorelli (ed). Milan, Bompiani, 1988.
Stella, Giuliana. *Riv Int Filosof Diritto* 66(3), 561-563 Jl-S 89

PACI, Enzo. *Il significato del Parmenide nella filosofia di Platone*, Carlo Sini (ed). Milan, Bompiani, 1988.
Stella, Giuliana. *Riv Int Filosof Diritto* 66(3), 561-563 Jl-S 89

PADRON, Hector Jorge. *Materia y materiales en Aristóteles.* Rosario, Fundacion Ross, 1987.
Bolzán, J E. *Sapientia* 44(173), 236-238 Jl-S 89

PAILIN, David A. *God and the Processes of Reality: Foundations of a Credible Theism.* London, Routledge & Kegan Paul, 1989.
Ford, Lewis S. *Process Stud* 18(2), 137-139 Sum 89
Shooman, A P. *Phil Books* 31(1), 51-53 Ja 90

PALMER, Anthony. *Concept and Object: The Unity of the Proposition in Logic and Psychology.* New York, Routledge, 1988.
Watts, Felicity A. *Phil Books* 30(4), 222-223 O 89

PALMER, Bernard (ed). *Medicine and the Bible.* Exeter, Paternoster Pr, 1986.
Vernon, David. *Ethics Med* 4(2), 30 1988

PALMER, Donald. *Looking at Philosophy: The Unbearable Heaviness of Philosophy Made Lighter.* Mountain View, Mayfield, 1988.
Rosen, Bernard. *Teach Phil* 12(3), 273-275 S 89

PANGLE, Thomas L (ed). *The Rebirth of Classical Rationalism: An Introduction to the Thought of Leo Strauss.* Chicago, Univ of Chicago Pr, 1989.
Morrisey, Will. *Interpretation* 17(3), 465-467 Spr 90

PANGLE, Thomas L. *The Spirit of Modern Republicanism: The Moral Vision of the American Founders and the Philosophy of Locke.* Chicago, Univ of Chicago Pr, 1988.
Ashcraft, Richard. *Polit Theory* 18(1), 159-162 F 90
Diggins, John Patrick. *Trans Peirce Soc* 25(3), 370-373 Sum 89
Zinman, M Richard. *Rev Metaph* 43(2), 409-413 D 89

PAPE, Helmut (ed). *Charles S Peirce: Naturordnung und Zeichenprozess, Schriften über Semiotik und Naturphilosophie*, B Kienzle (trans). Aachen, Alano, 1988.
Burch, Robert. *Trans Peirce Soc* 26(1), 147-152 Wint 90

PAPERT, Seymour. *Mindstorms.* New York, Basic Books, 1980.
Brown, Stephen I. *Thinking* 4(1), 50-53 1982

PAPROTTÉ, Wolf and DIRVEN, René (eds). *The Ubiquity of Metaphor.* Philadelphia, John Benjamins, 1985.
Thomas, Susan. *J Prag* 13(4), 615-621 Ag 89

PARFIT, Derek. *Reasons and Persons.* New York, Clarendon/Oxford Pr, 1984.
Adams, Robert Merrihew. *Phil Rev* 98(4), 439-484 O 89

PARKES, Graham (ed). *Heidegger and Asian Thought.* Honolulu, Univ of Hawaii Pr, 1987.
Maraldo, John C. *Phil East West* 40(1), 100-105 Ja 90

PARKINSON, G H R (ed). *An Encyclopaedia of Philosophy.* London, Routledge & Kegan Paul, 1988.
Hale, Bob. *Hist Phil Log* 11(1), 123-124 1990

PARODI, Massimo. *Il Conflitto dei Pensieri: Studio su Anselmo d'Aosta.* Bergamo, Lubrina, 1988.
Evans, G R. *Vivarium* 27(2), 153 N 89

PARRY, David M. *Hegel's Phenomenology of the "We".* NY, Lang, 1988.

Locke, Patricia M. *Rev Metaph* 43(2), 413-414 D 89

PAS, Julian F (comp). *A Select Bibliography on Taoism.* Stony Brook, Inst for Advanced Stud/World Religions, 1988.
Dragan, Raymond A. *Phil East West* 40(2), 262-263 Ap 90

PATEMAN, Carole. *The Sexual Contract.* Stanford, Stanford Univ Pr, 1988.
Hirschmann, Nancy J. *Polit Theory* 18(1), 170-174 F 90

PATEMAN, Trevor. *Language in Mind and Language in Society.* New York, Clarendon/Oxford Pr, 1987.
D'Agostino, Fred. *Phil Soc Sci* 19(3), 398-401 S 89

PATOCKA, Jan. *Le monde naturel et le mouvement de l'existence humaine*, Erika Abrams (trans). Norwell, Kluwer, 1988.
O'Connor, Dennis T. *Can Phil Rev* 9(11), 458-459 N 89

PATOCKA, Jan. *Philosophy and Selected Writings*, Erazim Kohák (trans). Chicago, Univ of Chicago Pr, 1989.
O'Connor, Dennis T. *Can Phil Rev* 10(6), 250-252 Je 90

PATTERSON, David. *Literature and Spirit: Essays on Bakhtin and His Contemporaries.* Lexington, Univ Pr Kentucky, 1988.
Emerson, Caryl. *Phil Lit* 13(2), 350-364 O 89

PAVKOVIC, Aleksandar (ed). *Contemporary Yugoslav Philosophy: The Analytic Approach.* Norwell, Kluwer, 1988.
Detlefsen, Michael. *Can Phil Rev* 9(12), 492-496 D 89

PAYER, Lynn. *Medicine and Culture: Varieties of Treatment in the United States, England, West Germany, and France.* New York, Holt, 1988.
Jecker, Nancy S. *Hastings Center Rep* 19(6), 46-47 N-D 89

PEACOCKE, A and GILLETT, G (eds). *Persons and Personality.* Cambridge, Blackwell, 1987.
Rudman, S. *Mod Theol* 5(4), 403-405 Jl 89

PEACOCKE, Arthur. *God and the New Biology.* London, Dent, 1986.
Knight, Christopher. *Mod Theol* 6(1), 118-119 O 89

PEARS, David. *The False Prison: A Study of the Development of Wittgenstein's Philosophy*, 2v. New York, Clarendon/Oxford Pr, 1988.
Glendinning, Simon. *Phil Books* 31(3), 156-158 Jl 90
Janik, Allan. *J Hist Phil* 28(3), 468-469 Jl 90
Mulhall, Stephen. *Phil Invest* 12(4), 327-340 O 89
Puhl, Klaus. *Phil Quart* 39(157), 503-509 O 89

PEARS, David. *The False Prison: A Study of the Development of Wittgenstein's Philosophy*, V2. New York, Oxford Univ Pr, 1988.
Stern, David. *Can Phil Rev* 10(2), 75-78 F 90

PEARS, David. *The False Prison: A Study of the Development of Wittgenstein's Philosophy*, V1. Oxford, Clarendon Pr, 1987.
Worthington, B A. *Hist Euro Ideas* 10(6), 740-741 1989

PECZENIK, Aleksander. *The Basis of Legal Justification.* Lund, pub unknown, 1983.
Stern, David S. *Vera Lex* 7(2), 24 1987

PELLEGRIN, Pierre. *Aristotle's Classification of Animals*, Anthony Preus (trans). Berkeley, Univ of Calif Pr, 1986.
Witt, Charlotte. *Phil Rev* 98(4), 543-544 O 89

PELLEGRINO, Edmund D and LANGAN, John P and HARVEY, John Collins (eds). *Catholic Perspectives on Medical Morals: Foundational Issues.* Dordrecht, Reidel, 1989.
Post, Stephen G. *J Med Human* 11(2), 103-104 Sum 90

PELLEGRINO, Edmund D and THOMASMA, David C. *For the Patient's Good: The Restoration of Beneficence in Health Care.* NY, Oxford Univ Pr, 1988.
VanDeVeer, Donald. *Ethics* 100(2), 434-436 Ja 90

PEÑA, Lorenzo. *Fundamentos de ontología dialéctica.* Madrid, Siglo XXI, 1987.
Luna, Florencia. *Analisis Filosof* 8(1), 82-85 My 88
Terzaga, Emilio. *Dialogo Filosof* 5(3), 431-433 S-D 89

PENELHUM, Terence. *Butler: The Arguments of the Philosophers*, Ted Honderich (ed). New York, Methuen, 1985.
MacKinnon, Barbara. *Mod Sch* 66(4), 318-321 My 89

PENNER, Terry. *The Ascent from Nominalism.* Dordrecht, Reidel, 1987.
Tweedale, Martin. *Can J Phil* 19(4), 685-703 D 89

PENZO, Giorgio (ed). *Karl Jaspers e la critica.* Brescia, Morcelliana, 1985.
Quintino, Raffaele. *Riv Filosof Neo-Scolas* 81(3), 510-513 Jl-S 89

PENZO, Giorgio. *Il superamento di Zarathustra.* Rome, Armando, 1987.
Moretti, Giampiero. *Riv Int Filosof Diritto* 66(3), 563-565 Jl-S 89

REESE, William L (ed). *The Best in the Literature of Philosophy and World Religions*. NY, Bowker, 1988.
Smart, Ninian. *Teach Phil* 12(4), 433-435 D 89

REEVE, C D C. *Philosopher-Kings: The Argument of Plato's "Republic"*. Princeton, Princeton Univ Pr, 1988.
Ferrari, G R F. *Amer J Philo* 111(1), 105-109 Spr 90
Kraut, Richard. *Polit Theory* 18(3), 492-496 Ag 90
Morgan, Michael L. *Rev Metaph* 43(2), 417-418 D 89
Rankin, David. *Phil Books* 31(2), 72-74 Ap 90

REGAN, Tom (ed). *G E Moore: The Early Essays*. Philadelphia, Temple Univ Pr, 1986.
Klemke, E D. *Int Stud Phil* 22(1), 131-132 1990

REGAN, Tom. *Animal Rights*. London, Routledge & Kegan Paul, 1988.
Dobson, Andy. *Rad Phil* 54, 40-41 Spr 90

REGAN, Tom. *Bloomsbury's Prophet: G E Moore and the Development of His Moral Philosophy*. Philadelphia, Temple Univ Pr, 1986.
Klemke, E D. *Int Stud Phil* 22(1), 131-132 1990

RELLA, Franco. *Asterischi*. Milan, Feltrinelli, 1989.
Bottani, Livio. *Filosofia* 41(1), 120-123 Ja-Ap 90

REMPEL, R A and BRINK, A and MORAN, M (eds). *The Collected Papers of Bertrand Russell, V12*. Winchester, Allen & Unwin, 1985.
Tully, R E. *Dialogue (Canada)* 27(4), 701-709 Wint 88

RENAUT, Alain. *Le système dur droit: Philosophie et droit dans la pensée de Fichte*. Paris, Pr Univ de France, 1986.
Cruz Cruz, Juan. *Anu Filosof* 21(2), 191-193 1988

RENTTO, Juha-Pekka. *Prudentia Iuris: The Art of the Good and the Just*. Turku, Turun Yliopisto, 1988.
Froelich, Gregory L. *Rev Metaph* 43(2), 418-420 D 89

RESCHER, Nicholas. *A Philosophical Inquiry into the Nature and the Rationale of Reason*. New York, Oxford Univ Pr, 1989.
Upton, Thomas V. *Rev Metaph* 43(4), 878-879 Je 90

RESCHER, Nicholas. *Moral Absolutes: An Essay on the Nature and Rationality of Morality*. NY, Lang, 1989.
Dougherty, Jude P. *Rev Metaph* 43(2), 420-421 D 89

RESCHER, Nicholas. *Rationality: A Philosophical Inquiry into the Nature and the Rationale of Reason*. Oxford, Clarendon Pr, 1988.
Haack, Susan. *Hist Phil Log* 11(1), 113-115 1990
Jewell, Robert D. *Phil Books* 31(1), 36-38 Ja 90

RESNIK, Michael D. *Choices: An Introduction to Decision Theory*. Minneapolis, Univ of Minnesota Pr, 1987.
Eells, Ellery. *Phil Rev* 99(2), 272-275 Ap 90

RICHARD, Marie-Dominique. *L'enseignement oral de Platon*. Paris, Cerf, 1986.
Marcos de Pinotti, Graciela E. *Rev Latin De Filosof* 15(3), 345-349 N 89

RICHARDS, Glyn. *Towards a Theology of Religions*. New York, Routledge, 1989.
Hick, John. *Relig Stud* 26(1), 175-177 Mr 90

RICHARDS, Robert J. *Darwin and the Emergence of Evolutionary Theories of Mind and Behavior*. Chicago, Univ of Chicago Pr, 1987.
Browning, Don. *Zygon* 24(3), 379-382 S 89
Ruse, Michael. *J Hist Phil* 28(1), 144-146 Ja 90

RICHARDSON, John. *Existential Epistemology: A Heideggerian Critique of the Cartesian Project*. New York, Clarendon/Oxford Pr, 1986.
Stevenson, Leslie. *Phil Phenomenol Res* 50(1), 210-213 S 89

RICKEN, Friedo. *Etica general*. Barcelona, Herder, 1987.
Ruiz Rodriguez, Virgilio. *Rev Filosof (Mexico)* 22(65), 248-253 My-Ag 89

RICKERT, Heinrich. *The Limits of Concept Formation in Natural Science, Guy Oakes (ed & trans)*. New York, Cambridge Univ Pr, 1986.
Rickman, H P. *Phil Soc Sci* 19(3), 401-404 S 89

RICKMAN, H P. *The Adventures of Reason: The Uses of Philosophy in Sociology*. Westport, Greenwood Pr, 1983.
Lucas, Hans-Christian. *Stud Spinozana* 5, 455-462 1989

RICOEUR, Paul. *Time and Narrative, V2*. Chicago, Univ of Chicago Pr, 1985.
Olafson, Frederick A. *Int Stud Phil* 21(3), 142-143 1989

RICONDA, G. *Invito al pensiero di Kant*. Milan, Mursia, 1987.
Fernández Aguado, Javier. *Anu Filosof* 22(1), 194-196 1989

RIFKIN, Jeremy. *Time Wars*. New York, Henry Holt, 1987.
Wu, Kuang-Ming. *Phil East West* 39(4), 516-520 O 89

RIGBY, Paul. *Original Sin in Augustine's "Confessions"*. Ottawa, Univ of
Ottawa Pr, 1987.
O'Connell, Robert J. *J Hist Phil* 28(1), 125-127 Ja 90

RIGBY, S H. *Marxism and History: A Critical Introduction*. Manchester, Manchester Univ Pr, 1987.
Isaac, Jeffrey C. *Phil Soc Sci* 19(4), 513-516 D 89

RIGOBELLO, Armando. *Autenticità nella differenza*. Rome, Studium, 1989.
Ivaldo, Marco. *Riv Filosof Neo-Scolas* 81(2), 324-326 Ap-Je 89

RILEY, Denise. *"Am I That Name?" Feminism and the Category of 'Women' in History*. Minneapolis, Univ of Minn Pr, 1989.
Grath, Pamela. *Teach Phil* 12(3), 270-273 S 89

RILEY, Jonathan. *Liberal Utilitarianism: Social Choice Theory and J S Mill's Philosophy*. Cambridge, Cambridge Univ Pr, 1988.
Weale, Albert. *Utilitas* 1(2), 306-307 N 89
Weinstein, D. *Polit Theory* 17(4), 684-688 N 89

RILEY, Patrick. *The General Will before Rousseau: The Transformation of the Divine into the Civic*. Princeton, Princeton Univ Pr, 1986.
Höpfl, H M. *Heythrop J* 31(1), 107-108 Ja 90

RIST, J M. *Platonism and its Christian Heritage*. London, Variorum, 1985.
Westerink, L G. *Phoenix* 43(4), 382-384 Wint 89

ROBERTS, David D. *Benedetto Croce and the Uses of Historicism*. Berkeley, Univ of California Pr, 1987.
Harris, H S. *J Hist Phil* 28(1), 148-149 Ja 90
Jacobitti, Edmund E. *New Vico Studies* 6, 113-127 1988

ROBERTS, Julian. *German Philosophy: An Introduction*. Atlantic Highlands, Humanities Pr, 1988.
Rethy, Robert. *Teach Phil* 12(3), 263-266 S 89

ROBINSON, T M. *Heraclitus: Fragments: A Text and Translation with a Commentary*. Toronto, Univ of Toronto Pr, 1987.
Osborne, Catherine. *Phil Rev* 99(1), 104-106 Ja 90

ROBINSON, William S. *Brains and People: An Essay on Mentality and Its Causal Conditions*. Philadelphia, Temple Univ Pr, 1988.
Seager, William. *Can Phil Rev* 10(6), 252-255 Je 90

ROCHBERG-HALTON, Eugene. *Meaning and Modernity: Social Theory in the Pragmatic Attitude*. Chicago, Univ of Chicago Pr, 1987.
Goehr, Lydia. *Human Stud* 13(2), 172-185 Ap 90

ROCKMORE, Tom (ed). *Lukács Today*. Norwell, Reidel, 1988.
Langlois, Luc. *Arch Phil* 52(4), 689-691 O-D 89

ROCKMORE, Tom. *Hegel's Circular Epistemology*. Bloomington, Indiana Univ Pr, 1986.
Labarriere, Pierre-Jean. *Rev Metaph Morale* 94(2), 277-279 Ap-Je 89
Rusch, Pierre. *Arch Phil* 53(1), 84-85 Ja-Mr 90
Smyth, P D. *Irish Phil J* 6(2), 303-311 1989

RODERICK, Rick. *Habermas and the Foundations of Critical Theory*. NY, St Martin's Pr, 1986.
Adelmann, Frederick J. *Stud Soviet Tho* 38(4), 307-309 N 89

RODI, Frithjof (ed). *Dilthey-Jahrbuch für Philosophie und Geschichte der Geistewissenschaften, V4*. Göttingen, Vandenhoeck & Ruprecht, 1987.
Owensby, Jacob. *Res Phenomenol* 19, 311-315 1989

ROGERS, G A J and RYAN, Alan (eds). *Perspectives on Thomas Hobbes*. Oxford, Clarendon Press, 1989.
Condren, Conal. *Hist Euro Ideas* 12(1), 156-157 1990
Somerville, James. *Phil Books* 31(2), 74-75 Ap 90

ROGERSON, Kenneth F. *Kant's Aesthetics: The Roles of Form and Expression*. Lanham, Univ Pr of America, 1986.
Kemal, Salim. *Kantstudien* 81(1), 110-113 1990

ROHRLICH, Fritz. *From Paradox to Reality: Our New Concepts of the Physical World*. Cambridge, Cambridge Univ Pr, 1987.
Ruys, P H M. *Method Sci* 22(2), 123-124 1989

ROLSTON III, Holmes. *Environmental Ethics: Duties to and Values in the Natural World*. Philadelphia, Temple Univ Pr, 1988.
Attfield, Robin. *Environ Ethics* 11(4), 363-368 Wint 89
Elliot, Robert. *Austl J Phil* 67(4), 493-494 D 89
Wenz, Peter S. *Ethics* 100(1), 195-197 O 89

ROLSTON III, Holmes. *Science and Religion: A Critical Survey*. New York, Random House, 1987.
Musser, Donald W. *Int J Phil Relig* 26(3), 185 D 89
Painter, John. *Austl J Phil* 67(3), 369-371 S 89

ROMANÒS, Konstantinos P. *Heimkehr*. Konigstein, Athenaum, 1988.
Kühn, Rolf. *Phil Rundsch* 36(3), 232-244 1989

ROPER, Jon. *Democracy and its Critics: Anglo-American Democratic Thought in the Nineteenth Century*. London, Unwin Hyman, 1989.
Arblaster, Anthony. *Utilitas* 2(1), 162-164 My 90

RORTY, Richard. *Contingency, Irony, and Solidarity*. Cambridge, Cambridge Univ Pr, 1989.
Flathman, Richard E. *Polit Theory* 18(2), 308-312 My 90
Lachterman, David R. *Clio* 18(4), 391-399 Sum 89
Ramazani, Jahan. *Crit Texts* 6(3), 40-47 1989
Stuhr, John J. *Personalist Forum* 5(2), 149-152 Fall 89

ROSE, Gilbert J. *Trauma and Mastery in Life and Art*. New Haven, Yale Univ Pr, 1987.
Spitz, Ellen Handler. *J Aes Educ* 22(3), 124-126 Fall 88

ROSEBURY, Brian. *Art and Desire: A Study in the Aesthetics of Fiction*. London, Macmillan, 1988.
Bredin, Hugh. *Brit J Aes* 30(1), 75-76 Ja 90

ROSENBAUM, Alan S. *Coercion and Autonomy: Philosophical Foundations, Issues, and Practices*. NY, Greenwood Pr, 1986.
Dobuzinskis, Laurent. *Phil Soc Sci* 19(4), 521-523 D 89

ROSENBERG, Alan and MYERS, Gerald E. *Echoes from the Holocaust: Philosophical Reflections on a Dark Time*. Philadelphia, Temple Univ Pr, 1988.
Pois, Robert A. *Hist Euro Ideas* 12(2), 277-281 1990

ROSENBERG, Alexander. *Philosophy of Social Science*. Oxford, Clarendon Pr, 1988.
Cole, Phillip. *Phil Books* 31(2), 119-120 Ap 90

ROSENBERG, Jay F. *The Thinking Self*. Philadelphia, Temple Univ Pr, 1986.
Marras, Ausonio. *Phil Phenomenol Res* 50(1), 214-216 S 89

ROSENBLUM, Nancy L. *Another Liberalism: Romanticism and the Reconstruction of Liberal Thought*. Cambridge, Harvard Univ Pr, 1987.
Vogel, Ursula. *Hist Polit Thought* 11(1), 165-168 Spr 90

ROSENTHAL, Bernice Glatzer (ed). *Nietzsche in Russia*. Princeton, Princeton Univ Pr, 1986.
Goodliffe, John. *Phil Lit* 13(2), 410-412 O 89

ROSENTHAL, David M. *Applied Ethics and Ethical Theory*. Salt Lake City, Univ of Utah Pr, 1988.
Singh, R Raj. *Eidos* 7(2), 221-231 D 88

ROSENTHAL, Henry M. *The Consolations of Philosophy: Hobbes's Secret; Spinoza's Way*, Abigail L Rosenthal (ed). Philadelphia, Temple Univ Pr, 1989.
Bagley, Paul J. *Rev Metaph* 43(4), 879-882 Je 90
Burstein, Harvey. *Interpretation* 17(3), 449-464 Spr 90
McCarthy, Jeremiah. *Can Phil Rev* 10(4), 155-157 Ap 90

ROSENTHAL, Sandra B. *Speculative Pragmatism*. Amherst, Univ of Mass Pr, 1986.
Colapietro, Vincent. *Int Phil Quart* 30(3), 373-375 S 90
Teske, Roland J. *Mod Sch* 66(4), 321-323 My 89

ROSKILL, Mark. *The Interpretation of Pictures*. Amherst, Univ of Mass Pr, 1989.
Mannings, David. *Brit J Aes* 30(3), 279-280 Jl 90

ROSS, D. *Teoría de las Ideas de Platón*. Madrid, Cátedra, 1986.
Del Barco, José Luis. *Anu Filosof* 20(1), 250-252 1987

ROTH, Michael S. *Knowing and History: Appropriations of Hegel in Twentieth-Century France*. Ithaca, Cornell Univ Pr, 1988.
Butler, Judith. *Hist Theor* 29(2), 248-258 My 90

ROTH, Paul. *Meaning and Method in the Social Sciences: A Case for Methodological Pluralism*. Ithaca, Cornell Univ Pr, 1987.
Fuller, Steve. *Phil Soc Sci* 20(1), 99-109 Mr 90

ROTHMAN, Barbara Katz. *The Tentative Pregnancy: Prenatal Diagnosis and the Future of Motherhood*. New York, Viking, 1986.
Addelson, Kathryn Pyne. *Hypatia* 4(2), 191-197 Sum 89

RÖTTGES, Heinz. *Dialektik und Skeptizismus*. Konigstein, Athenaum, 1987.
Depré, Olivier. *Rev Phil Louvain* 87(76), 556-559 Ag 89

ROUSE, Joseph. *Knowledge and Power: Toward a Political Philosophy of Science*. Ithaca, Cornell Univ Pr, 1987.
Ackermann, Robert. *Phil Rev* 99(3), 474-476 Jl 90

ROVIELLO, Anne-Marie. *Sens commun et modernité chez Hannah Arendt*. Brussels, Ousia, 1987.
Ponton, Lionel. *Laval Theol Phil* 45(3), 455-457 O 89

ROY, Yves. *Autorité politique et liberté*. Montréal, VLB, 1988.
Mercier, Benoit. *Philosophiques* 16(2), 407-410 Autumn 89

RUBIN, Ronald and YOUNG, Charles M. *Formal Logic: A Model of English*. Mountain View, Mayfield, 1989.
Nolt, John. *Teach Phil* 12(4), 424-426 D 89

RUE, Loyal D. *Amythia: Crisis in the Natural History of Western Culture*. Tuscaloosa, Univ of Alabama Pr, 1989.
Cupitt, Don. *Relig Stud* 26(1), 177-179 Mr 90

RUNDELL, John F. *Origins of Modernity: The Origins of Modern Social Theory from Kant to Hegel to Marx*. Madison, Univ of Wisconsin Pr, 1987.
Seddon, Fred. *Stud Soviet Tho* 39(2), 170-173 Mr 90

RUSE, Michael. *Homosexuality: A Philosophical Inquiry*. NY, Oxford Univ Pr, 1988.
Mc Carthy, Jeremiah. *Can Phil Rev* 9(10), 423-426 O 89

RUSE, Michael. *Taking Darwin Seriously: A Naturalistic Approach to Philosophy*. Oxford, Blackwell, 1986.
Brown, James Robert. *Can J Phil* 20(1), 129-145 Mr 90
Hull, Gerald. *Int Stud Phil* 21(3), 143-144 1989
Ridley, Mark. *Biol Phil* 4(3), 359-365 Jl 89

RUSSELL, Bertrand. *The Collected Papers of Bertrand Russell, V8: The Philosophy of Logical Atomism and Other Essays: 1914-19*. London, Allen & Unwin, 1986.
Linsky, Bernard. *Dialogue (Canada)* 28(4), 675-677 1989

RUSSELL, R J and STOEGER, W R and COYNE, G V (eds). *Physics, Philosophy and Theology: A Common Quest for Understanding*. Vatican, Vatican Observatory, 1988.
Byrne, Peter. *Relig Stud* 25(4), 542-543 D 89

RUSSMAN, Thomas A. *A Prospectus for the Triumph of Realism*. Macon, Mercer Univ Pr, 1987.
Greenwood, Robert L. *Int J Phil Relig* 26(3), 191-192 D 89
Haldane, John. *Heythrop J* 31(3), 372-374 Jl 90

RYAN, Alan. *Property*. Minnesota, Univ of Minn Pr, 1987.
Lemos, Ramon M. *Teach Phil* 12(3), 317-319 S 89

SACKS, Mark. *The World We Found: The Limits of Ontological Talk*. LaSalle, Open Court, 1989.
Robinson, William S. *Can Phil Rev* 10(4), 157-159 Ap 90

SAFRANSKI, Rüdiger. *Schopenhauer und Die wilden Jahre der Philosophie*. München, Hanser, 1987.
Baumann, Lutz. *Schopenhauer Jahr* 70, 239-242 1989
Maertz, Gregory. *Thought* 65(257), 215-217 Je 90

SAGOFF, Mark. *The Economy of the Earth: Philosophy, Law, and the Environment*. New York, Cambridge Univ Pr, 1988.
Anderson, Clifford. *Law Phil* 9(2), 217-221 My 90
Graham, George. *Teach Phil* 12(3), 299-301 S 89
Knowles, Dudley. *Phil Books* 30(4), 242-244 O 89

SAINSBURY, R M. *Paradoxes*. Cambridge, Cambridge Univ Pr, 1988.
Cargile, James. *Philosophy* 65(251), 106-111 Ja 90
Priest, Graham. *Hist Phil Log* 11(2), 245-247 1990

SALAMONE, Rosario. *Lingua e linguaggio nella filosofia di Giambattista Vico*. Rome, Ateneo, 1984.
Costa, Gustavo. *New Vico Studies* 4, 165-167 1986

SALAMUN, Kurt (ed). *Karl Popper und die Philosophie des Kritischen Rationalisus*. Atlanta, Rodopi, 1989.
Agassi, Joseph. *Can Phil Rev* 9(9), 378-381 S 89

SALLIS, John (ed). *Deconstruction and Philosophy: The Texts of Jacques Derrida*. Chicago, Univ of Chicago Pr, 1987.
Peterson, Richard T. *Mod Sch* 67(2), 166-168 Ja 90

SALLIS, John C and MONETA, Giuseppina and TAMINIAUX, Jacques. *The Collegium Phaenomenologicum, The First Ten Years*. Norwell, Nijhoff, 1989.
Bruzina, Ronald. *Can Phil Rev* 9(11), 468-472 N 89

SALLIS, John. *Spacings—Of Reason and Imagination—In Texts of Kant, Fichte, Hegel*. Chicago, Univ of Chicago Pr, 1987.
Sills, Chip. *Owl Minerva* 21(1), 122-124 Fall 89

SALMON, Wesley C. *Scientific Explanation and the Causal Structure of the World*. Princeton, Princeton Univ Pr, 1984.
Keita, Lansana. *Int Phil Quart* 30(2), 264-265 Je 90

SAMPFORD, Charles. *The Disorder of Law: A Critique of Legal Theory*. Boston, Blackwell, 1988.
Altman, Andrew. *Can Phil Rev* 10(5), 198-201 My 90

SÁNCHEZ MECA, D. *Martín Buber: Fundamento existencial*. Barcelona, Herder, 1988.
Elósegui Itxaso, María. *Anu Filosof* 20(1), 252-253 1987

SÁNCHEZ SORONDO, M. *Aristóteles y Hegel*. Buenos Aires, Herder, 1987.
Savagnone, Fiuseppe. *Sapienza* 42(4), 453-456 O-D 89

SANDERS, Andy F. *Michael Polanyi's Post-Critical Epistemology*. Amsterdam, Rodopi, 1988.
Gulick, W. *Can Phil Rev* 9(8), 330-333 Ag 89

SANGUINETI, J J. *Ciencia y modernidad*. Buenos Aires, Lohlé, 1988.
Vitoria, María Angeles. *Anu Filosof* 22(2), 208-211 1989

SANTAYANA, George. *The Sense of Beauty: Being the Outlines of Aesthetic Theory*, W G Holzberger and H J Saatkamp, Jr (eds). Cambridge, MIT Pr, 1988.
Arnett, Willard E. *Trans Peirce Soc* 25(4), 538-548 Fall 89
Price, Kingsley. *Brit J Aes* 30(3), 285-287 Jl 90

SANTINELLO, Giovanni (ed). *Storia delle storie generali della filosofia*, 2v. Padua, Antenore, 1988.
Harris, H S. *J Hist Ideas* 51(1), 115-120 Ja-Mr 90

SANTO TOMÁS, Juan de. *Compendio de lógica*, Mauricio Beuchot (trans). México, UNAM, 1986.
Herrera-Ibáñez, A. *Analisis Filosof* 7(2), 150-153 N 87

SANTURRI, Edmund N. *Perplexity in the Moral Life: Philosophical and Theological Considerations*. Charlottesville, Univ Pr of Virginia, 1987.
Quinn, Philip L. *Phil Rev* 99(1), 142-144 Ja 90
Turner, Philip. *Thomist* 54(1), 164-168 Ja 90

SAPONTZIS, S F. *Morals, Reasons, and Animals*. Philadelphia, Temple Univ Pr, 1987.
Frey, R G. *Ethics* 100(1), 191-192 O 89

SARTRE, Jean-Paul. *Mallarmé or the Poet of Nothingness*, Ernest Sturm (trans). University Park, Pennsylvania State Univ Pr, 1988.
Gordon, Haim. *J Brit Soc Phenomenol* 21(1), 95-96 Ja 90

SARUP, Madan. *An Introductory Guide to Post-Structuralism and Postmodernism*. London, Harvester-Wheatsheaf, 1988.
Parker, Noel. *Rad Phil* 55, 50-51 Sum 90

SASS, Hans-Martin and MASSEY, Robert U (eds). *Health Care Systems: Moral Conflicts in European and American Public Policy*. Dordrecht, Kluwer, 1988.
Jecker, Nancy S. *Hastings Center Rep* 19(6), 46-47 N-D 89
Smith, Chris Selby. *Bioethics* 4(1), 86-90 Ja 90

SASSO, Gennaro. *Per invigliare me stesso: I Taccuini di lavoro di Benedetto Croce*. Bologna, Mulino, 1989.
Cavallera, Hervé A. *Filosofia* 41(1), 123-126 Ja-Ap 90
Mangiagalli, Maurizio. *Riv Filosof Neo-Scolas* 81(3), 506-508 Jl-S 89

SASSOON, Anne Showstack. *Gramsci's Politics*. London, Hutchinson, 1987.
Court, A M. *S Afr J Phil* 9(1), 57-58 F 90

SATTLER, Rolf. *Biophilosophy: Analytic and Holistic Perspectives*. Berlin, Springer, 1986.
Szarski, Henryk. *Biol Phil* 5(1), 93-99 Ja 90

SAVAGE, C Wade and ANDERSON, C Anthony (eds). *Rereading Russell: Essays in Bertrand Russell's Metaphysics and Epistemology*. Minneapolis, Univ of Minnesota Pr, 1989.
Griffin, Nicholas. *Phil Books* 31(3), 151-152 Jl 90

SAVIGNY, Eike von. *The Social Foundations of Meaning*. Berlin, Springer, 1988.
Jaworski-Wieczorek, Malgorzata. *J Prag* 14(1), 171-177 F 90

SAVILE, Anthony. *Aesthetic Reconstructions: The Seminal Writings of Lessing, Kant and Schiller*. Oxford, Blackwell, 1987.
Genova, A C. *Kantstudien* 81(2), 254-256 1990
O'Hear, Anthony. *Phil Books* 31(1), 55-57 Ja 90
Schaper, Eva. *Brit J Aes* 30(1), 80-82 Ja 90

SAYER, Derek. *The Violence of Abstraction: The Analytic Foundations of Historical Materialism*. Oxford, Blackwell, 1987.
Murray, Patrick. *Phil Soc Sci* 20(1), 127-131 Mr 90

SCHALL, James V. *Reason, Revelation, and the Foundations of Political Philosophy*. Baton Rouge, Louisiana State Univ Pr, 1987.
Rehg, William R. *Mod Sch* 67(2), 161-163 Ja 90

SCHALOW, Frank. *Imagination and Existence: Heidegger's Retrieval of the Kantian Ethic*. Lanham, Univ Pr of America, 1986.
Dostal, Robert. *Int Stud Phil* 21(3), 144-145 1989

SCHARFSTEIN, Ben-Ami. *Of Birds, Beasts, and Other Artists: An Essay on the Universality of Art*. NY, New York Univ Pr, 1989.
Berleant, Arnold. *Can Phil Rev* 10(1), 37-39 Ja 90

SCHARLEMANN, Robert. *Inscriptions and Reflections: Essays in Philosophical Theology*. Charlottesville, Univ Pr of Virginia, 1989.
Harold, James. *Rev Metaph* 43(4), 882-883 Je 90

SCHECHNER, Richard. *Performance Theory*. New York, Routledge, 1988.
Whittock, Trevor. *Brit J Aes* 29(4), 378-379 Autumn 89

SCHEFFLER, S (ed). *Consequentialism and its Critics*. Oxford, Oxford Univ Pr, 1988.
Kelly, P J. *Utilitas* 1(1), 166-167 My 89

SCHEFFLER, Samuel. *The Rejection of Consequentialism*. New York, Oxford Univ Pr, 1982.
Schmidtz, David. *Nous* 24(4), 622-627 S 90

SCHELLING, F W J. *The Philosophy of Art*, Douglas W Stott (trans). Minneapolis, Univ of Minn Pr, 1989.
Lawrence, Joseph P. *Can Phil Rev* 10(5), 201-204 My 90

SCHIAVONE, Michele. *Psichiatria, Psicoanalisi, Sociologia*. Bologna, Pàtron, 1988.
Meo, Oscar. *Epistemologia* 11(2), 347-352 Jl-D 88

SCHIER, Flint. *Deeper into Pictures: An Essay on Pictorial Representation*. New York, Cambridge Univ Pr, 1986.
Raffman, Diana. *Phil Rev* 98(4), 576-578 O 89

SCHIFFER, Stephen and STEELE, Susan (eds). *Cognition and Representation*. Boulder, Westview Pr, 1988.
Bloom, Paul. *Mind Lang* 5(2), 166-173 Sum 90
Bogdan, Radu J. *Can Phil Rev* 10(1), 39-42 Ja 90

SCHIFFER, Stephen. *Remnants of Meaning*. Cambridge, MIT Pr, 1987.
Sidelle, Alan. *Phil Rev* 99(2), 255-260 Ap 90
Sterelny, Kim. *Mind* 98(392), 623-634 O 89

SCHILLEBEECKX, Edward. *Jesus in Our Western Culture: Mysticism, Ethics and Politics*. London, SCM Pr, 1987.
Jones, Gareth. *Mod Theol* 5(4), 393-394 Jl 89

SCHLAGEL, Richard H. *From Myth to the Modern Mind: A Study of the Origins and Growth of Scientific Thought*, V1. NY, Lang, 1985.
De Groot, Jean. *Ancient Phil* 9 (2), 319-321 Fall 89

SCHLEIERMACHER, F. *Kritische Gesamtausgabe*, V2. Hawthorne, de Gruyter, 1988.
Moretto, Giovanni. *G Metaf* 11(1), 147-148 Ja-Ap 89

SCHLEIERMACHER, F. *Kritische Gesemtausgabe*, V3. Hawthorne, de Gruyter, 1988.
Moretto, Giovanni. *G Metaf* 11(1), 144-146 Ja-Ap 89

SCHLESINGER, George N. *New Perspectives on Old-Time Religion*. New York, Oxford Univ Pr, 1988.
Morris, Thomas V. *Thomist* 54(2), 358-361 Ap 90

SCHLOSSER, Herta. *Marxistisch-Leninistische Theorie der Persönlichkeit*. Bonn, Bouvier, 1988.
Teichmann, Werner. *Deut Z Phil* 37(10-11), 1044-1047 1989

SCHLOSSER, Herta. *Wandel in der Marxistisch-Leninistischen Auffassung vom Menschen*. Bonn, Bouvier, 1988.
Teichmann, Werner. *Deut Z Phil* 37(10-11), 1044-1047 1989

SCHMIDT, Alfred. *Idee und Weltwille*. Wien, Hanser, 1988.
Kossler, Matthias. *Schopenhauer Jahr* 70, 242-246 1989

SCHMIDT, Dennis J. *The Ubiquity of the Finite: Hegel, Heidegger and the Entitlements of Philosophy*. Cambridge, MIT Pr, 1988.
Hodge, Joanna. *Bull Hegel Soc Gt Brit* 19, 42-49 Spr-Sum 89

SCHMIT, Roger. *Husserls Philosophie der Mathematik*. Bonn, Bouvier, 1981.
Tragesser, Robert. *J Sym Log* 53(2), 646-648 Je 88

SCHMITT, Charles and others (eds). *The Cambridge History of Renaissance Philosophy*. New York, Cambridge Univ Pr, 1988.
Colish, Marcia L. *J Hist Phil* 28(1), 128-130 Ja 90
Gaukroger, Stephen. *Austl J Phil* 67(3), 347-349 S 89

SCHMITZ, Hermann. *Der Ursprung des Gegenstandes: Von Parmenides bis Demokrit*. Bonn, Bouvier, 1988.
Figal, Günter and Schütt, Hans-Peter. *Phil Rundsch* 37(1-2), 110-122 1990

SCHMITZ, Hermann. *Die Ideenlehre des Aristoteles*, 2v. Bonn, Bouvier, 1985.
Figal, Günter and Schütt, Hans-Peter. *Phil Rundsch* 37(1-2), 110-122 1990

SCHNAUBELT, Joseph (ed). *Anselm Studies: An Occasional Journal*, V2. White Plains, Kraus, 1988.
Fidler, W Larch. *Thomist* 54(1), 184-186 Ja 90

SCHNEIDER, Jean and LEGER-ORINE, Monique (eds). *Frontiers and Space*

Cambridge Univ Pr, 1986.
Waluchow, W J. *Phil Soc Sci* 19(4), 501-505 D 89

SHAPIRO, Michael J. *The Politics of Representation*. Madison, Univ
Wisconsin Pr, 1988.
Levine, Sura and Parker, Andrew. *Polit Theory* 17(4), 696-701 N 89

SHEEHAN, Thomas. *Karl Rahner: The Philosophical Foundations*. Athens,
Ohio Univ Pr, 1987.
Dych, William V. *Int Phil Quart* 29(4), 487-489 D 89
Phan, Peter C. *Thomist* 54(3), 552-554 Jl 90

SHEPPARD, Anne. *Aesthetics: An Introduction to the Philosophy of Art*.
Oxford, Oxford Univ Pr, 1987.
Palmer, Anthony. *Philosophy* 65(251), 113-114 Ja 90

SHER, George. *Desert*. Princeton, Princeton Univ Pr, 1987.
Murphy, Jeffrie G. *Phil Rev* 99(2), 280-283 Ap 90

SHERMAN, Nancy. *The Fabric of Character*. Oxford, Clarendon Pr, 1989.
Dent, N J H. *Phil Books* 31(1), 14-15 Ja 90

SHKLAR, Judith N. *Ordinary Vices*. Cambridge, Harvard Univ Pr, 1984.
Benjamin, Martin. *Thinking* 7(1), 19-20 1987

SHOEMAKER, Sydney. *Identity, Cause, and Mind: Philosophical Essays*.
New York, Cambridge Univ Pr, 1984.
Jackson, Frank. *Phil Rev* 98(4), 550-552 O 89

SHOGAN, Debra. *Care and Moral Motivation*. Toronto, OISE Pr, 1988.
Noddings, Nel. *J Moral Educ* 18(3), 234-235 O 89

SHOWALTER, Elaine. *The Female Malady: Women, Madness and English
Culture, 1830-1980*. London, Virago Pr, 1987.
Fouché, Fidela. *S Afr J Phil* 9(1), 43-48 F 90

SHULMAN, George M. *Radicalism and Reverence: The Political Thought
of Gerrard Winstanley*. Berkeley, Univ of California Pr, 1989.
Hayes, Tom. *Clio* 19(2), 187-189 Wint 90

SHUSTERMAN, Richard (ed). *Analytic Aesthetics*. Oxford, Blackwell,
1989.
Barwell, Ismay. *Phil Lit* 14(1), 201-202 Ap 90
Hepburn, Ronald. *Phil Books* 31(3), 187-188 Jl 90
Humble, Paul. *Brit J Aes* 30(2), 175-176 Ap 90

SHUSTERMAN, Richard. *T S Eliot and the Philosophy of Criticism*. NY,
Columbia Univ Pr, 1988.
Jay, Gregory S. *Clio* 18(3), 315-319 Spr 89
Lamarque, Peter. *Brit J Aes* 29(4), 384-385 Autumn 89

SICHEL, Betty A. *Moral Education: Character, Community and Ideals*.
Philadelphia, Temple Univ Pr, 1988.
Losito, William F. *J Moral Educ* 18(3), 232-233 O 89

SIDOROV, I N. *Filisofia Deistviya v SSHA: Ot Emersona do D'yui*.
Leningrad, Leningrad Univ Pr, 1989.
Ryder, John. *Trans Peirce Soc* 26(2), 261-269 Spr 90

SIEBERS, Tobin. *The Ethics of Criticism*. Ithaca, Cornell Univ Pr, 1988.
Goodhart, Sandor. *Phil Lit* 14(1), 173-175 Ap 90

SIEBRAND, H J. *Spinoza and the Netherlanders: An Inquiry into the Early
Reception of His Philosophy of Religion*. Wolfeboro, Van Gorcum, 1988.
Schröder, Winfried. *Phil Rundsch* 36(4), 331-333 1989
Verbeek, Theo. *Stud Spinozana* 5, 442-449 1989

SIEGEL, Harvey. *Educating Reason: Rationality, Critical Thinking and
Education*. New York, Routledge, 1988.
Brown, Harold I. *Phil Soc Sci* 19(4), 509-512 D 89
Mackenzie, Jim. *Educ Phil Theor* 21(1), 87-90 1989
Madigan, Tim. *Free Inq* 10(1), 58-59 Wint 89-90
Weinstein, Mark. *Educ Stud* 20(4), 413-421 Wint 89

SILBURN, Lilian. *Kundalini: The Energy of the Depths, Jacques Gontier
(trans)*. Albany, SUNY Pr, 1988.
Kealey, Daniel A. *Phil East West* 40(3), 406-407 Jl 90

SILVERMAN, Hugh J (ed). *Philosophy and Non-Philosophy Since
Merleau-Ponty*. New York, Routledge, 1988.
Redding, Paul. *Phil Lit* 14(1), 190-191 Ap 90

SILVERMAN, Hugh J and WELTON, Donn (eds). *Postmodernism and
Continental Philosophy*. Albany, SUNY Pr, 1988.
Nye, Andrea. *Can Phil Rev* 10(5), 204-206 My 90

SILVERMAN, Hugh J. *Inscriptions: Between Phenomenology and
Structuralism*. New York, Routledge & K Paul, 1987.
Froman, Wayne. *Res Phenomenol* 19, 298-303 1989

SIMONS, Peter. *Parts: A Study in Ontology*. Oxford, Clarendon Pr, 1987.
Charpa, Ulrich. *Phil Rundsch* 36(4), 333-337 1989

Wolenski, Jan. *Rep Phil* 13, 93-96 1989

SIMPSON, David (ed). *The Origins of Modern Critical Thought: German
Aesthetic and Literary Criticism from Lessing to Hegel*. Cambridge,
Cambridge Univ Pr, 1988.
Leaman, Oliver. *Brit J Aes* 30(2), 183-184 Ap 90

SIMPSON, R L. *Essentials of Symbolic Logic*. London, Routledge & Kegan
Paul, 1988.
Mott, Peter. *Phil Books* 31(1), 33-34 Ja 90

SINGH, Karan and IKEDA, Daisaku. *Humanity at the Crossroads: An
Inter-Cultural Dialogue*. New York, Oxford Univ Pr, 1988.
Sen, Madhu. *Indian Phil Quart* 16(3), 357-364 Jl 89

SINNOTT-ARMSTRONG, Walter. *Moral Dilemmas*. Oxford, Blackwell,
1988.
Adam, Michel. *Rev Phil Fr* 180(2), 467-469 Ap-Je 90
McNaughton, David. *Phil Books* 30(4), 244-246 O 89

SIRAT, Colette. *A History of Jewish Philosophy in the Middle Ages*.
Cambridge, Cambridge Univ Pr, 1985.
Kellner, Manachem. *Int Stud Phil* 21(3), 149-150 1989

SKLAR, Lawrence. *Philosophy and Spacetime Physics*. Berkeley, Univ of
Calif Pr, 1985.
DiSalle, Robert. *Phil Sci* 56(4), 714-717 D 89

SLATER, B H. *Prolegomena to Formal Logic*. Brookfield, Gower, 1988.
Behboud, Ali. *Hist Phil Log* 11(1), 101-103 1990

SLOTE, Michael. *Beyond Optimizing: A Study of Rational Choice*.
Cambridge, Harvard Univ Pr, 1989.
Wolfram, Sybil. *Phil Books* 31(3), 174-176 Jl 90

SLOTERDIJK, Peter. *Critique of Cynical Reason, Michael Eldred (trans)*.
Minneapolis, Univ of Minn Pr, 1987.
Osborne, Peter. *Rad Phil* 55, 48-50 Sum 90
Westphal, Merold. *Int Phil Quart* 29(4), 479-480 D 89

SMART, J J C. *Our Place in the Universe*. Oxford, Blackwell, 1989.
Lucas, John. *Mind* 99(394), 315-316 Ap 90

SMELSER, Ronald. *Robert Ley: Hitler's Labour Front Leader*. Oxford, Berg,
1988.
Pois, Robert A. *Hist Euro Ideas* 12(2), 277-281 1990

SMETS, Philippe and others (eds). *Non Standard Logics for
Automated Reasoning*. London, Academic Pr, 1988.
Van Cleemput, Véronique. *Rev Int Phil* 44(172), 141-143 1990

SMITH, Barbara Herrnstein. *Contingencies of Value: Alternative
Perspectives for Critical Theory*. Cambridge, Harvard Univ Pr, 1988.
Cain, William E. *Phil Lit* 13(2), 376-378 O 89
Slote, Michael. *Rev Metaph* 43(3), 646-647 Mr 90

SMITH, Barry (ed). *Foundations of Gestalt Theory*. Munich, Philosophia,
1988.
Münch, Dieter. *Hist Phil Log* 11(2), 238-240 1990

SMITH, David Woodruff and MCINTYRE, Ronald. *Husserl and
Intentionality: A Study of Mind, Meaning and Language*. Dordrecht, Reidel,
1982.
Serrano de Haro, Agustín. *Rev Filosof (Spain)* 2, 169-177 1989

SMITH, Gary (ed). *On Walter Benjamin: Critical Essays and Recollections*.
Cambridge, MIT Pr, 1988.
Vieth, Lynne. *Phil Lit* 13(2), 390-391 O 89

SMITH, John H. *The Spirit and Its Letter: Traces of Rhetoric in Hegel's
Philosophy of "Bildung"*. Ithaca, Cornell Univ Pr, 1988.
Mason, Jeff. *Phil Lit* 14(1), 169-170 Ap 90
Verene, Donald Phillip. *Phil Rhet* 23(2), 147-150 1990

SMITH, Joseph Wayne. *Essays on Ultimate Questions*. Aldershot, Gower,
1988.
Malpas, J E. *Austl J Phil* 67(3), 361-363 S 89

SMITH, Joseph Wayne. *The Progress and Rationality of Philosophy as a
Cognitive Enterprise*. Aldershot, Gower, 1988.
Cole, David. *Teach Phil* 12(3), 268-270 S 89
Fox, John. *Austl J Phil* 67(4), 489-491 D 89

SMITH, K J M. *James Fitzjames Stephen, Portrait of a Victorian Rationalist*.
Cambridge, Cambridge Univ Pr, 1988.
Lewis, Andrew. *Utilitas* 2(1), 159-162 My 90

SMITH, Ralph A. *The Sense of Art: A Study in Aesthetic Education*. New
York, Routledge Chapman & Hall, 1989.
Brand, Peggy Zeglin. *Personalist Forum* 6(1), 89-91 Spr 90

SMITH, Rogers M. *Liberalism and American Constitutional Law*.

Cambridge, Harvard Univ Pr, 1985.
Harbour, William R. *Vera Lex* 7(2), 25 1987

SMITH, Steven B. *Hegel's Critique of Liberalism: Rights in Context*. Chicago, Univ of Chicago Pr, 1989.
Franco, Paul. *Ethics* 100(2), 424-426 Ja 90
Steinberger, Peter. *Polit Theory* 18(2), 318-320 My 90

SMITH, Steven G. *The Concept of the Spiritual: An Essay in First Philosophy*. Philadelphia, Temple Univ Pr, 1988.
Marres, René. *Rev Metaph* 43(3), 647-648 Mr 90

SOARE, Robert I. *Recursively Enumerable Sets and Degrees: A Study of Computable Functions and Computably Generated Sets*. Berlin, Springer, 1987.
Hermann, Eberhard and Downey, Rodney. *J Sym Log* 55(1), 356-357 Mr 90

SOBLE, Alan (ed). *Eros, Agape and Philia: Readings in the Philosophy of Love*. New York, Paragon, 1989.
Williams, Clifford. *Can Phil Rev* 10(6), 255-257 Je 90

SOBREVILLA, David. *Repensando la tradición occidental*. Lima, Amaru, 1986.
Cragnolini, Mónica Beatriz. *Rev Filosof (Argentina)* 3(1), 75-77 My 88
Moran, Julio César. *Rev Latin De Filosof* 15(3), 342-345 N 89

SOKOLOWSKI, Robert (ed). *Edmund Husserl and the Phenomenological Tradition: Essays in Phenomenology*. Washington, Cath Univ Pr, 1988.
Hart, James G. *Rev Metaph* 43(2), 423-425 D 89

SOKOLOWSKI, Robert. *Moral Action: A Phenomenological Study*. Bloomington, Indiana Univ Pr, 1985.
Weis, Gregory F. *Res Phenomenol* 18, 317-323 1988

SOLOMON, J Fisher. *Discourse and Reference in the Nuclear Age*. Norman, Univ of Oklahoma Pr, 1988.
Martin, Bill. *Auslegung* 16(2), 209-214 Sum 90

SOLOMON, Robert C. *Continental Philosophy Since 1750: The Rise and Fall of the Self*. New York, Oxford Univ Pr, 1988.
Breazeale, Daniel. *J Hist Phil* 28(3), 460-463 Jl 90
Wartenberg, Thomas E. *Teach Phil* 12(3), 261-262 S 89

SOLOMON, Yvette. *The Practice of Mathematics*. NY, Routledge & Kegan Paul, 1989.
Hamlyn, D W. *J Phil Educ* 23(2), 321-324 Wint 89

SOMMER, Manfred. *Husserl und der frühe Positivismus*. Frankfurt am Main, Klostermann, 1985.
Hart, James G. *Husserl Stud* 7(1), 59-67 1990

SOMMERS, Christina and SOMMERS, Fred (eds). *Vice and Virtue in Everyday Life: Introductory Readings in Ethics*, 2nd ed. San Diego, Harcourt Brace Jovanovich, 1989.
Dixon, Nicholas. *Teach Phil* 13(1), 47-52 Mr 90

SOPER, Philip. *A Theory of Law*. Cambridge, Harvard Univ Pr, 1984.
Kelly, Robert Q. *Vera Lex* 7(1), 23 1987

SORABJI, Richard (ed). *Philoponus and the Rejection of Aristotelian Science*. Ithaca, Cornell Univ Pr, 1987.
Blumenthal, H J. *J Hist Phil* 28(2), 284-286 Ap 90
Jordan, Mark D. *Phil Rev* 99(1), 107-109 Ja 90
Lang, Helen S. *Ancient Phil* 10(1), 149-153 Spr 90

SORELL, Tom. *Descartes*. Oxford, Oxford Univ Pr, 1987.
James, Peter J. *Hist Phil Life Sci* 11(2), 344-346 1989

SORELL, Tom. *Hobbes*. London, Routledge & Kegan Paul, 1986.
Bertman, Martin A. *Int Stud Phil* 22(1), 134-135 1990

SORENSEN, Roy A. *Blindspots*. Oxford, Clarendon Pr, 1988.
Humberstone, Lloyd. *Austl J Phil* 68(1), 119-120 Mr 90
Pagin, P. *Hist Phil Log* 11(2), 243-245 1990

SORENSEN, Villy. *Seneca: The Humanist at the Court of Nero*, W Glyn Jones (trans). Chicago, Univ of Chicago Pr, 1984.
Batinski, Emily E. *Ancient Phil* 9 (2), 351-353 Fall 89

SOROKIN, Pitirim A. *Social and Cultural Dynamics*. Boston, Porter Sargent, 1957.
Snauwaert, Dale T. *Educ Theor* 40(2), 231-235 Spr 90

SOSA, Ernest (ed). *Essays on the Philosophy of George Berkeley*. Norwell, Reidel, 1987.
MacKinnon, Barbara. *Mod Sch* 66(4), 305-306 My 89
McKim, Robert. *Berkeley News* 11, 28-32 1989-90

SOTO, M J. *Individuo y unidad: La sustancia individual según Leibniz*. Pamplona, EUNSA, 1988.
Ortíz, José M. *Anu Filosof* 21(2), 195-197 1988

SOULET, Marc Henry. *Le silence des intellectuels: Radioscopie de l'intellectuel québécois*. Montréal, Saint-Martin, 1987.
Ferland, Madeleine. *Philosophiques* 17(1), 143-149 1990

SOURIAU, Paul. *The Aesthetics of Movement*, Manon Souriau (ed & trans). Amherst, Univ of Mass Pr, 1984.
Snoeyenbos, Milton. *J Aes Educ* 21(3), 121-123 Fall 87

SOUTHWELL, Samuel B. *Kenneth Burke and Martin Heidegger: With a Note Against Deconstructionism*. Gainesville, Univ of Florida Pr, 1987.
McWhorter, Ladelle and Williams, David Cratis. *Phil Rhet* 23(1), 75-80 1990

SOWELL, Thomas. *Marxism, Philosophy and Economics*. New York, Morrow, 1985.
Colbert, James G. *Stud Soviet Tho* 38(3), 245-247 O 89

SPADE, Paul Vincent. *Lies, Language and Logic in the Late Middle Ages*. London, Variorum, 1988.
Bos, E P. *Hist Phil Log* 11(1), 93-95 1990

SPAEMANN, R. *Das Natürliche und das Vernünftige*. Munich, Piper, 1987.
Del Barco, José Luis. *Anu Filosof* 22(1), 196-200 1989

SPERBER, Dan and WILSON, Deirdre. *Relevance: Communication and Cognition*. Oxford, Blackwell, 1986.
Travis, Charles. *Can J Phil* 20(2), 277-304 Je 90

SPERLING, Susan. *Animal Liberators: Research and Morality*. Berkeley, Univ of California Pr, 1988.
Finsen, Susan M. *Teach Phil* 13(1), 63-65 Mr 90

SPICKER, Stuart F and BONDESON, William and ENGELHARDT JR, H Tristram. *The Contraceptive Ethos*. Norwell, Kluwer, 1987.
Meyer, Michael J. *J Med Human* 11(2), 104-107 Sum 90

SPINOZA, Baruch. *Korte verhandeling van God, de mensch en deszelvs welstand*, Filippo Mignini (ed & trans). L'Aquila, Japadre, 1986.
Steenbakkers, Piet. *Stud Spinozana* 4, 377-392 1988

SPINOZA, Baruch. *Opera V: Supplementa*, Norbert Altwicker (ed). Heidelberg, Winter, 1987.
Krämer, Felix. *Stud Spinozana* 4, 393-398 1988

SPITZ, Ellen Handler. *Art and Psyche: A Study in Psychoanalysis and Aesthetics*. New Haven, Yale Univ Pr, 1985.
Boettger, Suzaan. *J Aes Educ* 21(4), 164-165 Wint 87

SPRIGGE, T L S. *The Rational Foundations of Ethics*. New York, Routledge, 1988.
Wallace, R Jay. *Phil Quart* 39(157), 509-512 O 89

SPRIGGE, T L S. *The Significance of Spinoza's Determinism*. Leiden, Brill, 1989.
Den Uyl, Douglas J. *Stud Spinozana* 5, 411-412 1989

SPRINKER, Michael. *Imaginary Relations: Aesthetics and Ideology in the Theory of Historical Materialism*. London, Verso, 1987.
Taylor, Brian. *Brit J Aes* 30(2), 176-178 Ap 90

SPRINTZEN, David. *Camus: A Critical Examination*. Philadelphia, Temple Univ Pr, 1988.
Lauder, Robert E. *Can Phil Rev* 10(2), 83-87 F 90

SRUBAR, Ilja. *Kosmion*. Frankfurt am Main, Suhrkamp, 1988.
Vaitkus, Steven. *Phil Rundsch* 36(4), 326-330 1989

SRZEDNICKI, Jan T J (ed). *Stephan Körner—Philosophical Analysis and Reconstruction: Contributions to Philosophy*. Norwell, Nijhoff, 1987.
Butchvarov, Panayot. *Can Phil Rev* 9(9), 381-384 S 89

SRZEDNICKI, Jan. *The Democratic Perspective*. Norwell, Kluwer, 1987.
Ewin, R E. *Austl J Phil* 67(3), 367-368 S 89

STACK, George J. *On Kierkegaard: Philosophical Fragments*. Atlantic Highlands, Humanities Pr, 1976.
Thomas, J Heywood. *J Brit Soc Phenomenol* 21(2), 200-201 My 90

STALLEY, R F. *An Introduction to Plato's Laws*. Indianapolis, Hackett, 1983.
Pangle, Thomas L. *Ancient Phil* 9 (2), 321-323 Fall 89

STAMBOVSKY, Phillip. *The Depictive Image: Metaphor and Literary Experience*. Amherst, Univ of Massachusetts Pr, 1988.
Collinson, Diané. *Brit J Aes* 30(1), 91-92 Ja 90

STAROBINSKI, Jean. *Montaigne in Motion*. Chicago, Univ of Chicago Pr, 1986.
Levi, A H T. *Heythrop J* 30(4), 487-488 O 89

STARR, William C and TAYLOR, Richard C (eds). *Moral Philosophy: Historical and Contemporary Essays*. Milwaukee, Marquette Univ Pr, 1989.
Kremer, Elmar J. *Can Phil Rev* 10(5), 207-209 My 90

STEGMÜLLER, Wolfgang. *Die Entwicklung des neuen Strukturalismus seit*

1973. Berlin, Springer, 1986.
Leroux, Jean. *Dialogue (Canada)* 28(4), 677-682 1989

STEIN, Edith. *Essays on Woman*, L Gelber and Romaeus Leuven (eds), Freda Mary Oben (trans). Washington, ICS Publications, 1987.
Brady, Marian. *Thomist* 54(2), 379-383 Ap 90

STEINBERGER, Peter J. *Logic and Politics: Hegel's Philosophy of Right.* New Haven, Yale Univ Pr, 1988.
Franco, Paul. *Ethics* 100(2), 424-426 Ja 90
Goldstein, Leon J. *Int Stud Phil* 22(1), 91-93 1990
Stillman, Peter G. *Polit Theory* 17(4), 675-678 N 89

STEINER, Elizabeth. *Methodology of Theory Building.* Sydney, Educology Research Associates, 1988.
Gowin, D Bob. *Educ Stud* 21(1), 80-83 Spr 90

STEINER, George. *Real Presences.* Chicago, Univ of Chicago Pr, 1989.
Miller, Franklin G. *J Speculative Phil* 4(2), 176-180 1990

STERNBERG, Robert J and SMITH, Edward E (eds). *The Psychology of Human Thought.* NY, Cambridge Univ Pr, 1988.
Hughes, James M. *Phil Psych* 2(3), 345-347 1989

STERNFELD, Robert and ZYSKIND, Harold. *Meaning, Relation, and Existence in Plato's Parmenides: The Logic of Relational Realism.* New York, Lang, 1987.
Silverman, Allan. *Ancient Phil* 10(1), 131-135 Spr 90

STILLMAN, Peter G (ed). *Hegel's Philosophy of Spirit.* Albany, SUNY Pr, 1986.
Flay, Joseph C. *Int Stud Phil* 22(1), 135-137 1990

STOKES, Michael C. *Plato's Socratic Conversations: Drama and Dialectic in Three Dialogues.* Baltimore, Johns Hopkins U Pr, 1986.
Gooch, Paul W. *Phoenix* 43(3), 270-273 Autumn 89
Sharples, R W. *J Hellen Stud* 109, 224-225 1989

STONE, I F. *The Trial of Socrates.* Boston, Little Brown, 1988.
Boonin-Vail, David. *Crit Rev* 3(3-4), 579-588 Sum-Fall 89
Forde, Steven. *Ancient Phil* 10(1), 111-113 Spr 90
Sievers, Ken. *Rad Phil* 54, 35-37 Spr 90

STOTT, Laurence J. *Essays in Philosophy and Education.* Lanham, Univ Pr of America, 1988.
Stewart, Douglas. *Educ Stud* 20(4), 421-425 Wint 89

STOUT, Jeffrey. *Ethics after Babel: The Languages of Morals and their Discontents.* Boston, Beacon Pr, 1988.
Whitmore, Todd David. *Ethics* 100(1), 180-181 O 89

STOVE, D C. *The Rationality of Induction.* Oxford, Oxford Univ Pr, 1986.
Hawthorn, John. *Int Stud Phil* 22(1), 137-138 1990

STRAUSS, Leo. *The Rebirth of Classical Political Rationalism: Essays and Lectures.* Chicago, Univ of Chicago Pr, 1989.
Udoff, Alan. *Rev Metaph* 43(3), 648-650 Mr 90

STRAWSON, Galen. *Freedom and Belief.* Oxford, Oxford Univ Pr, 1986.
Double, Richard. *Behaviorism* 17(2), 177-179 Fall 89
Kane, Robert. *Int Phil Quart* 30(2), 260-262 Je 90

STRAWSON, P F. *Analyse et métaphysique.* Paris, Vrin, 1985.
Cassini, Alejandro. *Rev Filosof (Argentina)* 3(2), 165-169 N 88

STRAWSON, P F. *Scepticism and Naturalism: Some Varieties.* New York, Columbia Univ Pr, 1985.
Vander Veer, Garrett L. *Int Stud Phil* 22(1), 138-139 1990

STRIKE, K A and HALLER, E J and SOLTIS, J F. *The Ethics of School Administration.* New York, Teachers College Pr, 1988.
Heslep, Robert D. *Educ Stud* 20(3), 233-246 Fall 89

STRÖKER, Elisabeth. *Investigations in Philosophy of Space*, Algis Mickunas (trans). Athens, Ohio Univ Pr, 1987.
Drummond, John J. *Husserl Stud* 6(1), 73-78 1989

STRONG, Tracy B. *Friedrich Nietzsche and the Politics of Transfiguration.* Berkeley, Univ of California Pr, 1988.
Stelzmann, Rainulf A. *Thought* 65(257), 209-211 Je 90

STUMP, E. *Dialectic and its Place in the Development of Medieval Logic.* Ithaca, Cornell Univ Pr, 1989.
Perreiah, Alan R. *Hist Phil Log* 11(2), 232-234 1990

SUANCES MARCOS, Manuel. *Arthur Schopenhauer: Religión y Metafísica de la Voluntad.* Barcelona, Herder, 1989.
Sala, J F A. *Rev Filosof (Mexico)* 23(67), 141-143 Ja-Ap 90

SUCHOCKI, Marjorie Hewitt. *The End of Evil: Process Eschatology in Historical Context.* Albany, SUNY Pr, 1988.
Griffin, David Ray. *Process Stud* 18(1), 57-63 Spr 89

Suchocki, Marjorie Hewitt. *Process Stud* 18(1), 63-69 Spr 89

SULLIVAN, Roger J. *Immanuel Kant's Moral Theory.* Cambridge, Cambridge Univ Pr, 1989.
Gregor, Mary. *Rev Metaph* 43(3), 650-651 Mr 90
Pybus, Elizabeth. *Phil Books* 31(3), 149-150 Jl 90

SUMNER, L W. *The Moral Foundation of Rights.* New York, Clarendon/Oxford Pr, 1987.
Child, J W. *Phil Quart* 40(158), 112-116 Ja 90
Garner, Richard. *Teach Phil* 12(3), 305-309 S 89
Kelly, P J. *Utilitas* 1(2), 307-310 N 89
Martin, Rex. *Ethics* 100(2), 408-411 Ja 90

SUPPE, Frederick. *The Semantic Conception of Theories and Scientific Realism.* Urbana, Univ of Illinois Pr, 1989.
Schlagel, Richard H. *Rev Metaph* 43(4), 885-887 Je 90

SURIN, Kenneth. *Theology and the Problem of Evil.* Oxford, Blackwell, 1986.
Ward, Keith. *Heythrop J* 31(1), 79-80 Ja 90

SWARTZ, Norman. *The Concept of Physical Law.* New York, Cambridge Univ Pr, 1985.
Sklar, Lawrence. *J Phil* 87(8), 432-435 Ag 90

SWINBURNE, Richard (ed). *Miracles.* New York, Macmillan, 1989.
Beckwith, Francis J. *Teach Phil* 12(3), 335-337 S 89

SWINBURNE, Richard. *Responsibility and Atonement.* Oxford, Clarendon Pr, 1989.
Durrant, Michael. *Phil Books* 31(3), 190-192 Jl 90

SWINBURNE, Richard. *The Evolution of the Soul.* Oxford, Clarendon Pr, 1986.
Kitcher, Patricia. *Nous* 23(5), 708-710 D 89
Matthews, Gareth B. *Behaviorism* 17(2), 165-169 Fall 89

SZIKLAI, László (ed). *Lukács: Aktuell.* Budapest, Akadémiai Kiadó, 1989.
Tietz, Udo. *Deut Z Phil* 38(6), 589-591 1990

SZREDNICKI, J T J and STACHNIAK, Z (eds). *S Lesniewski's Lecture Notes on Logic.* Dordrecht, Kluwer, 1988.
Simons, P. *Hist Phil Log* 11(1), 107-110 1990

TAGLIACOZZO, Giorgio (ed). *Vico and Marx: Affinities and Contrasts.* Atlantic Highlands, Humanities Pr, 1983.
Lachterman, David. *New Vico Studies* 2, 114-118 1984

TAGORE, Rabindranath. *The Religion of Man.* London, Unwin, 1988.
van Bijlert, Victor A. *Phil East West* 40(3), 410-413 Jl 90

TALLIS, Raymond. *In Defence of Realism.* London, Arnold, 1988.
Robinson, Ian. *Phil Invest* 13(1), 74-79 Ja 90

TARCOV, Nathan. *Locke's Education for Liberty.* Chicago, Univ of Chicago Pr, 1989.
Herbert, Gary B. *Rev Metaph* 43(3), 651-652 Mr 90

TARRANT, H. *Scepticism or Platonism? The Philosophy of the Fourth Academy.* Cambridge, Cambridge Univ Pr, 1985.
Glucker, John. *J Hellen Stud* 109, 272-273 1989

TARSKI, Alfred and GIVANT, Steven. *A Formalization of Set Theory Without Variables.* Providence, American Mathematical Society, 1987.
Németi, István. *J Sym Log* 55(1), 350-352 Mr 90

TAYLOR, Barry (ed). *Michael Dummett: Contributions to Philosophy.* Norwell, Kluwer, 1987.
Bach, Kent. *Can Phil Rev* 10(4), 160-162 Ap 90
Johnson, Lawrence E. *Austl J Phil* 67(3), 355-358 S 89

TAYLOR, Charles. *Negative Frieheit? Zur Kritik des neuzeitlichen Individualismus.* Frankfurt, Suhrkamp, 1988.
Hackenesch, Christa. *Phil Rundsch* 36(4), 316-325 1989

TAYLOR, Donald S. *R G Collingwood: A Bibliography.* NY, Garland, 1988.
Connelly, James. *Brit J Aes* 30(1), 82-84 Ja 90

TAYLOR, Eugene. *William James on Exceptional Mental States, the 1896 Lowell Lectures.* NY, Scribner's, 1983.
Reck, Andrew J. *Int Stud Phil* 21(3), 150-151 1989

TAYLOR, Mark C. *Altarity.* Chicago, Univ of Chicago Pr, 1987.
Gray, Susan. *Eidos* 7(2), 233-238 D 88
Wirzer, Wilhelm S. *Can Phil Rev* 9(7), 290-293 Jl 89

TAYLOR, Paul W. *Respect for Nature: A Theory of Environmental Ethics.* Princeton, Princeton Univ Pr, 1986.
Caro, T M. *Biol Phil* 4(3), 353-357 Jl 89

TAYLOR, Rodney L and WATSON, Jean (eds). *They Shall Not Hurt:*

Human Suffering and Human Caring. Boulder, Colorado Associated Univ Pr, 1989.
Vaux, Kenneth and Smith, Corey. *Med Human Rev* 4(2), 85-87 Jl 90

TAYLOR, Rodney L. *The Confucian Tradition of Contemplation: Okada Takehiko and the Tradition of Quiet-Sitting.* Columbia, Univ of South Carolina Pr, 1988.
Berthrong, John. *Phil East West* 40(3), 413-415 Jl 90

TEICHMAN, Jenny. *Pacifism and the Just War: A Study in Applied Philosophy.* Cambridge, Blackwell, 1986.
Rule, Paul. *Austl J Phil* 67(3), 365-366 S 89

TEICHMAN, Jenny. *Philosophy and the Mind.* Oxford, Blackwell, 1988.
Macrae, Kristina. *Austl J Phil* 68(1), 124-126 Mr 90

TEJERA, V. *Nietzsche and Greek Thought.* Dordrecht, Nijhoff, 1987.
Garelick, Herbert. *Mod Sch* 67(2), 153-155 Ja 90

TEJERA, V. *Plato's Dialogues One by One: A Structural Interpretation.* New York, Irvington, 1984.
Havelock, Eric A. *Int Stud Phil* 22(1), 139-140 1990
Malcolm, John. *Ancient Phil* 10(1), 135-137 Spr 90

TELOH, Henry. *Socratic Education in Plato's Early Dialogues.* Notre Dame, Univ of Notre Dame Pr, 1986.
Smith, Nicholas D. *Ancient Phil* 10(1), 105-111 Spr 90

TENNANT, Neil. *Anti-Realism and Logic: Truth as Eternal.* New York, Oxford Univ Pr, 1987.
Hart, W D. *J Sym Log* 54(4), 1485-1486 D 89
Weir, Alan. *Can Phil Rev* 9(7), 293-296 Jl 89

TERAN, Oscar. *En busca de la ideología argentina.* Buenos Aires, Catálogos, 1986.
Amuchástegui, Rodrigo Hugo. *Rev Filosof (Argentina)* 2(1), 83-87 My 87

TERTULIAN, Nicolas. *Georges Lukács: Étapes de sa pensée esthétique.* Paris, Sycomore, 1980.
Rockmore, Tom. *Stud Soviet Tho* 38(2), 190-192 Ag 89

TESTART, Jacques. *L'Oeuf Transparent.* Paris, Flammarion, 1986.
Moulin, Anne Marie. *J Med Phil* 14(5), 587-591 O 89

THAGARD, Paul. *Computational Philosophy of Science.* Cambridge, MIT Pr, 1989.
Ross, Don. *Can Phil Rev* 10(7), 285-288 Jl 90

THEUNISSEN, Michael. *The Other, Studies in the Social Ontology of Husserl, Heidegger, Sartre, and Buber.* Cambridge, MIT Pr, 1986.
Lichtigfeld, Adolph. *Int Stud Phil* 22(1), 140-141 1990

THÉVENOT, Xavier. *La Bioéthique: Début et fin de vie.* Paris, Centurion, 1989.
de Wachter, Maurice A M. *Med Human Rev* 4(2), 91-92 Jl 90

THIEBAUT, Carlos. *Cabe Aristóteles.* Madrid, Visor, 1988.
Casimiro Elena, César. *Dialogo Filosof* 6(1), 123-125 Ja-Ap 90

THOMAS, Geoffrey. *The Moral Philosophy of T H Green.* New York, Clarendon/Oxford Pr, 1987.
Nicholson, Peter P. *Utilitas* 1(1), 163-166 My 89
Stock, Guy. *Phil Quart* 39(157), 518-520 O 89

THOMAS, John E and **WALUCHOW, Wilfred J.** *Well and Good: Case Studies in Biomedical Ethics.* Peterborough, Broadview Pr, 1987.
Komesaroff, Paul A. *Bioethics* 4(1), 66-77 Ja 90

THOMAS, Laurence. *Living Morally: A Psychology of Moral Character.* Philadelphia, Temple Univ Pr, 1989.
Clarke, Stanley G. *Can Phil Rev* 10(7), 288-291 Jl 90

THOMAS, Louis-Vincent and others. *Réincarnation, immortalité, résurrection.* Bruxelles, Univ Saint-Louis, 1988.
Couture, André. *Laval Theol Phil* 46(1), 111-113 F 90

THOMPSON, Ann and **WILCOX, Helen (eds).** *Teaching Women: Feminism and English Studies.* Manchester, Manchester Univ Pr, 1989.
Prior, Patricia. *Rad Phil* 55, 56-57 Sum 90

THOMPSON, Paul. *The Structure of Biological Theories.* Albany, SUNY Pr, 1989.
Collier, John. *Can Phil Rev* 10(4), 163-165 Ap 90

THOMSON, Garrett. *Needs.* New York, Routledge, 1987.
Keshen, Richard. *Ethics* 100(1), 179-180 O 89
Wellman, Carl. *Phil Phenomenol Res* 50(2), 428-430 D 89

THOMSON, Judith Jarvis. *Rights, Restitution and Risk: Essays in Moral Theory.* Cambridge, Harvard Univ Pr, 1986.
Hallborg Jr, Robert B. *Int Stud Phil* 22(1), 141-142 1990

THORNTON, James E and **WINKLER, Earl R (eds).** *Ethics and Aging: the*

Right to Live, the Right to Die. Vancouver, Univ of British Columbia Pr, 1988.
Sax, Sidney. *Bioethics* 4(3), 265-267 Jl 90
Waymack, Mark H. *Can Phil Rev* 9(8), 336-338 Ag 89

TILES, J E. *Dewey.* New York, Routledge, 1988.
Grossman, Morris. *Can Phil Rev* 9(7), 296-299 Jl 89
Sleeper, R W. *Trans Peirce Soc* 26(2), 252-261 Spr 90
Welchman, Jennifer. *J Hist Phil* 28(3), 465-466 Jl 90

TILES, Mary. *Bachelard: Science and Objectivity.* Cambridge, Cambridge Univ Pr, 1984.
Gutting, Gary. *Phil Sci* 57(2), 343-344 Je 90

TILES, Mary. *The Philosophy of Set Theory: An Historical Introduction to Cantor's Paradise.* Oxford, Blackwell, 1989.
Potter, M D. *Phil Books* 31(1), 63 Ja 90

TILLIETTE, Xavier. *L'Absolu et la philosophie: Essais sur Schelling.* Paris, Pr Univ de France, 1987.
Depré, Olivier. *Rev Phil Louvain* 87(76), 569-572 Ag 89

TILLIETTE, Xavier. *Schelling im Spiegel seiner Zeitgenossen.* Milan, Mursia, 1988.
Vetö, M. *Arch Phil* 52(4), 676-677 O-D 89

TLABA, Gabriel Masooane. *Politics and Freedom: Human Will and Action in the Thought of Hannah Arendt.* Lanham, Univ Pr of America, 1987.
Daniel, Mano. *Eidos* 7(2), 239-244 D 88

TODD, D D (ed). *The Philosophical Orations of Thomas Reid.* Carbondale, Southern Illinois Univ Pr, 1989.
Stewart-Robertson, Charles. *Can Phil Rev* 9(8), 338-341 Ag 89

TODOROV, Tzvetan. *Literature and Its Theorists,* Catherine Porter (trans). New York, Routledge, 1988.
Dutton, Richard. *Brit J Aes* 29(4), 382-384 Autumn 89

TODOROV, Tzvetan. *Nous et les autres: La réflexion française sur la diversité humaine.* Paris, Seuil, 1989.
Knee, Philip. *Laval Theol Phil* 46(1), 100-103 F 90

TOMASINI BASSOLS, Alejandro. *Los atomismos lógicos de Russell y Wittgenstein.* México, UNAM, 1986.
Cabanchik, Samuel M. *Rev Latin De Filosof* 15(3), 335-336 N 89

TOMBERLIN, J E (ed). *Agent, Language, and the Structure of the World: Essays Presented to Hector-Neri Castañeda, With his Replies.* Indianapolis, Hackett, 1983.
Kapitan, Tomis. *Rev Latin De Filosof* 16(1), 87-107 Mr 90

TOMBERLIN, James E (ed). *Hector-Neri Castañeda.* Boston, Reidel, 1986.
Kapitan, Tomis. *Nous* 24(3), 473-486 Je 90

TONELLI, Giorgio. *Da Leibniz a Kant.* Napoli, Prismi, 1987.
Tognini, Giorgio. *Teoria* 9(1), 257-260 1989

TONELLI, Giorgio. *La pensée philosophique de Maupertius.* NY, Olms, 1987.
Tognini, Giorgio. *Teoria* 9(1), 257-260 1989

TONELLI, Giorgio. *La pensée philosophique de Maupertuis: Son milieu et ses sources.* Hildesheim, Olms, 1987.
Arana, Juan. *Rev Latin De Filosof* 16(1), 108-113 Mr 90

TONG, Rosemarie. *Feminist Thought: A Comprehensive Introduction.* Boulder, Westview Pr, 1989.
Ginsberg, Ruth. *Teach Phil* 12(4), 409-411 D 89

TOOLEY, Michael. *Abortion and Infanticide.* Oxford, Oxford Univ Pr, 1983.
Wreen, Michael. *Nous* 23(5), 690-696 D 89

TOOLEY, Michael. *Causation: A Realist Approach.* Oxford, Clarendon Pr, 1987.
Brown, Bryson. *Hist Phil Log* 11(1), 110-113 1990
Fales, Evan. *Phil Phenomenol Res* 50(3), 605-610 Mr 90

TOSEL, André. *Kant Révolutionnaire.* Paris, Pr Univ de France, 1988.
Ponton, Lionel. *Laval Theol Phil* 45(3), 450-453 O 89

TOULMIN, Stephen. *The Return to Cosmology.* Berkeley, Univ of California Pr, 1982.
Palmer, L M. *New Vico Studies* 2, 135-138 1984

TRAGESSER, Robert S. *Husserl and Realism in Logic and Mathematics.* Cambridge, Cambridge Univ Pr, 1984.
McIntyre, Ronald. *Phil Phenomenol Res* 50(3), 624-628 Mr 90

TRAVIS, Charles. *The Uses of Sense: Wittgenstein's Philosophy of Language.* Oxford, Clarendon Pr, 1989.
McGinn, Marie. *Phil Books* 31(2), 88-89 Ap 90

Rundle, Bede. *Mind* 99(395), 485-487 Jl 90

TRAWEEK, Sharon. *Beam Times and Life Times, The World of High Energy Physicists*. Cambridge, Harvard Univ Pr, 1988.
Latour, Bruno. *Stud Hist Phil Sci* 21(1), 145-171 Mr 90

TRÍAS, Eugenio. *La aventura filosófica*. Madrid, Mondadori, 1988.
Murillo, Ildefonso. *Dialogo Filosof* 5(3), 439-440 S-D 89

TRIGEAUD, Jean-Marc. *Humanisme de la liberté et philosophie de la justice, V1*. Bordeaux, Biere, 1985.
Tusa, Carlo. *Riv Int Filosof Diritto* 66(3), 569-571 Jl-S 89

TUCK, Richard. *Hobbes*. Oxford, Oxford Univ Pr, 1989.
Morgan, Michael L. *Rev Metaph* 43(3), 652-654 Mr 90

TUGWELL, Simon (ed & trans). *Albert and Thomas: Selected Writings*. New York, Paulist Pr, 1988.
Woods, Richard. *Thomist* 54(3), 541-545 Jl 90

TULLY, James (ed). *Meaning and Context: Quentin Skinner and His Critics*. Princeton, Princeton Univ Pr, 1988.
Morgan, Michael L. *Rev Metaph* 43(2), 425-426 D 89
Shapiro, Ian. *Can Phil Rev* 10(7), 291-294 Jl 90

TUOMELA, Raimo. *Science, Action and Reality*. Dordrecht, Reidel, 1985.
Fernández Beites, Pilar. *Rev Filosof (Spain)* 2, 179-181 1989

TURK, Christopher. *Coleridge and Mill: A Study of Influence*. Brookfield, Gower, 1988.
Mendus, Susan. *Utilitas* 1(2), 314-315 N 89
Morrow, John. *Hist Polit Thought* 10(4), 753-754 Wint 89

TURNER, William B. *Nothing and Non-Existence: The Transcendence of Science*. New York, Philosophical Lib, 1986.
Taft, Richard. *Mod Sch* 66(4), 325-327 My 89

TURSMAN, Richard. *Peirce's Theory of Scientific Discovery: A System of Logic Conceived as Semiotic*. Bloomington, Indiana Univ Pr, 1987.
Sullivan, Patrick. *J Hist Phil* 28(2), 307-308 Ap 90

TYE, Michael. *The Metaphysics of Mind*. Cambridge, Cambridge Univ Pr, 1989.
Brewer, Bill. *Mind* 99(394), 310-313 Ap 90
Hart, W D. *Phil Quart* 40(159), 255-257 Ap 90

TYMOCZKO, Thomas (ed). *New Directions in the Philosophy of Mathematics*. Boston, Birkhauser, 1986.
Hale, Susan C. *Hist Phil Log* 11(1), 117-119 1990

UCHIDA, Hiroshi. *Marx's Grundrisse and Hegel's Logic*. London, Routledge & Kegan Paul, 1988.
Arthur, Chris. *Rad Phil* 53, 45 Autumn 89

ULLMAN-MARGALIT, E (ed). *Science in Reflection*. Norwell, Reidel, 1988.
Fuhrmann, André. *Hist Euro Ideas* 10(5), 625-627 1989

UMEN, Samuel. *Images of Man: Essays on Philosophy and Religion*. NY, Philosophical Library, 1985.
Clift, Wallace B. *Mod Sch* 67(1), 84-85 N 89

URBACH, Peter. *Francis Bacon's Philosophy of Science: An Account and A Reappraisal*. La Salle, Open Court, 1987.
Walton, Craig. *J Hist Phil* 28(2), 289-293 Ap 90

URBANAS, Alban. *La notion d'accident chez Aristote: Logique et métaphysique*. Montreal, Bellarmin, 1988.
Matthews, Gareth B. *Ancient Phil* 10(1), 141-143 Spr 90

URMSON, J O. *Aristotle's Ethics*. Oxford, Blackwell, 1988.
Swanton, Christine. *Austl J Phil* 68(1), 127-128 Mr 90

USPENSKY, V A. *Gödel's Incompleteness Theorem, Neal Koblitz (trans)*. Moscow, Mir Publishers, 1987.
Boolos, George. *J Sym Log* 55(2), 889-891 Je 90

VALLE, L (ed). *Verità e interpretazione*. Alessandria, dell'Orso, 1988.
Bottani, Livio. *Filosofia* 40(3), 429-433 S-D 89

VAN BALEN, Petrus. *De verbetering der gedachten*. Baarn, Ambo, 1988.
Roothaan, A C M. *Stud Spinozana* 5, 413-416 1989

VAN BENTHEM, Johan. *A Manual of Intensional Logic, 2nd ed*. Stanford, CSLI, 1988.
Bull, R A. *J Sym Log* 54(4), 1489 D 89

VAN BENTHEM, Johan. *A Manual of Intensional Logic*. Stanford, CSLI, 1985.
Bull, R A. *J Sym Log* 54(4), 1489 D 89

VAN BENTHEM, Johan. *Modal logic and Classical logic*. Naples, Bibliopolis, 1985.
Padilla Galvez, Jesús. *Theoria (Spain)* 4(11), 539-542 F-My 89

VAN DEN HOBEN, M J. *Petrus van Balen en Spinoza over de verbetering van het verstand*. Leiden, Brill, 1988.
Roothaan, A C M. *Stud Spinozana* 5, 413-416 1989

VAN DER LEEUW, Karel and MOSTERT, Pieter. *Philosophieren Lehren*. Delft, Eburon, 1988.
Alexander, John V I. *Teach Phil* 13(1), 76-81 Mr 90
Van der Leeuw, Karel and Mostert, Pieter. *Teach Phil* 13(1), 81-85 Mr 90

VAN DER LINDEN, Harry. *Kantian Ethics and Socialism*. Indianapolis, Hackett, 1988.
McMurtry, John. *Can Phil Rev* 9(10), 426-428 O 89
Wood, Allen. *Ideal Stud* 19(3), 271-273 S 89

VAN DER SANDT, Rob. *Context and Presupposition*. Beckenham, Croom Helm, 1988.
Dolitsky, Marlene. *J Prag* 14(2), 345-348 Ap 90

VAN DER STEEN, W J and THUNG, P J. *Faces of Medicine*. Norwell, Kluwer, 1988.
Hoffmaster, Barry. *Can Phil Rev* 9(8), 341-344 Ag 89

VAN EEMEREN, Frans H and others (eds). *Argumentation: Across the Lines of Discipline, Proceedings of the Conference on Argumentation 1986*. Dordrecht, Foris, 1987.
Cooper, Martha. *Phil Rhet* 23(1), 70-75 1990

VAN EEMEREN, Frans H and others (eds). *Argumentation: Analysis and Practices, Proceedings of the Conference on Argumentation 1986*. Dordrecht, Foris, 1987.
Cooper, Martha. *Phil Rhet* 23(1), 70-75 1990

VAN EEMEREN, Frans H and others (eds). *Argumentation: Perspectives and Approaches, Proceedings of the Conference on Argumentation 1986*. Dordrecht, Foris, 1987.
Cooper, Martha. *Phil Rhet* 23(1), 70-75 1990

VANCE, Eugene. *From Topic to Tale: Logic and Narrativity in the Middle Ages*. Minneapolis, Univ of Minnesota Pr, 1987.
Brault, Gerard J. *Phil Lit* 14(1), 187-188 Ap 90

VATTIMO, Gianni (ed). *Filosofia '87*. Bari, Laterza, 1988.
Bottani, Livio. *Filosofia* 40(2), 232-235 My-Ag 89

VATTIMO, Gianni. *The End of Modernity: Nihilism and Hermeneutics in Postmodern Culture, Jon R Snyder (trans)*. Baltimore, Johns Hopkins Univ Pr, 1988.
Gaukroger, Stephen. *Phil Lit* 14(1), 195-196 Ap 90

VEATCH, Robert M (ed). *Cross Cultural Perspectives in Medical Ethics: Readings*. Boston, Jones & Bartlett, 1989.
Bilimoria, Purusottama. *Bioethics* 4(2), 171-173 Ap 90

VEATCH, Robert M (ed). *Medical Ethics*. Boston, Jones & Bartlett, 1989.
Gillam, Lynn. *Bioethics* 4(3), 268-271 Jl 90

VEATCH, Robert M. *Death, Dying, and the Biological Revolution: Our Last Quest for Responsibility*. New Haven, Yale Univ Pr, 1989.
Jones, David H. *Rev Metaph* 43(2), 426-428 D 89

VELARDE, Julián. *Historia de la lógica*. Oviedo, Univ de Oviedo, 1989.
Vega, Luis. *Theoria (Spain)* 4(11), 517-525 F-My 89

VENDLER, Zeno. *The Matter of Minds*. Oxford, Oxford Univ Pr, 1984.
Balowitz, Victor. *Int Stud Phil* 22(1), 142-143 1990

VERENE, Donald Phillip (ed). *Vico and Joyce*. Albany, SUNY Pr, 1987.
Bishop, John. *New Vico Studies* 6, 133-142 1988
Schaeffer, John D. *New Vico Studies* 6, 129-132 1988

VERENE, Donald Phillip. *Hegel's Recollection: A Study of Images in the "Phenomenology of Spirit"*. Albany, SUNY Pr, 1985.
Vater, Michael G. *Mod Sch* 67(1), 73-75 N 89

VERRI, A. *Vico e Herder nella Francia della Restaurazione*. Ravenna, Longo, 1984.
Quarta, Cosimo. *Il Protag* 6(9-10), 213-217 Je-D 86

VERRI, Antonio. *Presenza di Vico: Confronti e paralleli*. Lecce, Milella, 1986.
Colonnello, Pio. *Sapienza* 43(1), 96-99 Ja-Mr 90

VESEY, G (ed). *Philosophers, Ancient and Modern*. NY, Cambridge Univ Pr, 1989.
Mackenzie, P T. *Can Phil Rev* 9(10), 428-431 O 89

VICKERS, Brian (ed). *Rhetoric Revalued: Papers from the International Society for the History of Rhetoric*. Binghamton, Center for Medieval Studies, 1982.
Shapiro, Gary. *New Vico Studies* 5, 195-198 1987

VICKERS, Brian. *In Defence of Rhetoric*. New York, Clarendon/Oxford Pr,

Wood, Robert E. *Mod Sch* 66(4), 327-328 My 89

YARCE, Jorge (ed). *Filosofia de la Communicación*. Pamplona, Univ Navarra, 1986.
Cadó, Valdemar. *Laval Theol Phil* 45(3), 461-463 O 89

YOLTON, John W. *Locke: An Introduction*. Oxford, Blackwell, 1985.
Morris, William Edward. *Teach Phil* 13(1), 57-60 Mr 90

YOUNG, J Z. *I filosofi e il cervello*. Turin, Bollati Boringhieri, 1988.
Di Mieri, Fernando. *Sapienza* 42(2), 229-231 Ap-Je 89

YOUNG, J Z. *Philosophy and the Brain*. Oxford, Oxford Univ Pr, 1987.
Gillett, Grant. *Phil Sci* 57(1), 172-173 Mr 90

YOUNG, Julian. *Willing and Unwilling: A Study in the Philosophy of Arthur Schopenhauer*. Dordrecht, Nijhoff, 1987.
Hough, Ronald. *J Hist Phil* 27(4), 632-634 O 89

YOVEL, Yirmiyahu. *Spinoza and Other Heretics*. Princeton, Princeton Univ Pr, 1989.
Janowski, Zbigniew. *Rev Metaph* 43(4), 888-889 Je 90
Kurtz, Paul. *Free Inq* 10(3), 55 Sum 90

YSAAC, Walter L (ed). *The Third World and Bernard Lonergan*. Manila, Lonergan Centre, 1986.
De Neeve, Eileen. *Method* 8(1), 89-93 Mr 90

ZAHAR, Elie. *Einstein's Revolution*. La Salle, Open Court, 1989.
Shanks, Niall. *Can Phil Rev* 10(1), 42-44 Ja 90

ZALTA, Edward N. *Intensional Logic and the Metaphysics of Intensionality*. Cambridge, MIT Pr, 1988.
Champlin, T S. *Hist Phil Log* 11(1), 100-101 1990

ZANER, Richard M (ed). *Death: Beyond Whole-Brain Criteria*. Dordrecht, Kluwer, 1988.
Geis, Robert. *Rev Metaph* 43(3), 656-657 Mr 90

ZAPATA, René. *La philosophie russe et soviétique*. Paris, Pr Univ de France, 1988.
Boulad-Ayoub, Josiane. *Philosophiques* 16(2), 443-445 Autumn 89

ZARKA, Yves-Charles. *La Décision Métaphysique de Hobbes*. Paris, Vrin, 1987.
Thierry, Yves. *Hist Euro Ideas* 10(5), 602-603 1989

ZEYL, Donald J (trans). *Plato: Gorgias*. Indianapolis, Hackett, 1985.
DeFilippo, Joseph G. *Ancient Phil* 10(1), 116-119 Spr 90

ZIFF, Paul. *Epistemic Analysis*. Dordrecht, Reidel, 1984.
Kaminsky, Jack. *Int Stud Phil* 22(1), 153-154 1990

ZIMMERMAN, Michael J. *An Essay on Moral Responsibility*. Totowa, Rowman & Littlefield, 1988.
Pfeiffer, Raymond S. *Can Phil Rev* 9(12), 505-507 D 89

ZIMMERMANN, Albert and KOPP, Clemens (eds). *Thomas von Aquin: Werk und Wirkung im Licht neurer Forschung*. New York, de Gruyter, 1988.
Schenk, Richard. *Thomist* 54(2), 376-379 Ap 90

ZIMMERN, Alice (trans). *Porphyry's Letter to His Wife Marcella*. Grand Rapids, Phanes Pr, 1986.
Novak, Joseph A. *Can Phil Rev* 10(1), 24-31 Ja 90

ZUBIRI, Xavier. *Estructura dinámica de la realidad*. Madrid, Alianza, 1989.
Murillo, Ildefonso. *Dialogo Filosof* 6(2), 271-273 My-Ag 90

ZUCKERT, Catherine H (ed). *Understanding the Political Spirit: Philosophical Investigations from Socrates to Nietzsche*. New Haven, Yale Univ Pr, 1988.
Morrisey, Will. *Interpretation* 17(2), 309-312 Wint 89-90

ZUM BRUNN, Emilie. *St Augustine: Being and Nothingness*, Ruth Namad (trans). New York, Paragon, 1988.
Burns, J Patout. *Int J Phil Relig* 27(3), 190-192 Je 90
Teske, Roland J. *Mod Sch* 66(4), 303-304 My 89

ZUMBACH, Clark. *The Transcendent Science: Kant's Conception of Biological Methodology*. The Hague, Nijhoff, 1984.
Gregor, Mary. *Int Stud Phil* 22(1), 154 1990

ZWIEBACH, Burton. *The Common Life: Ambiguity, Agreement, and the Structure of Morals*. Philadelphia, Temple Univ Pr, 1988.
Gibbons, Michael T. *Polit Theory* 18(2), 323-326 My 90